PHILIP'S

STREE[T ATLAS]

London

www.philips-maps.co.uk

First published 2000 by

Philip's, a division of
Octopus Publishing Group Ltd
www.octopusbooks.co.uk
2–4 Heron Quays
London E14 4JP
An Hachette Livre UK Company

Third edition 2007
First impression 2007
LONCB

ISBN-10 0-540-09036-0 paperback
ISBN-10 0-540-09035-2 spiral

ISBN-13 978-0-540-09036-5 paperback
ISBN-13 978-0-540-09035-8 spiral

Printed and bound in Spain by Cayfosa-Quebecor.

Contents

II Our Top 10 tips to avoid parking penalties
V Mobile speed camera sites
VI **Key to map pages**
VIII Administrative and Postcode boundaries
X **Route planning**

XXVIII **Key to map symbols**
1 **Street maps**

228 **Keys to enlarged map pages and symbols**
229 **Enlarged street maps**

271 **Index**
428 **List of numbered locations**

444 Hospitals
445 Places of interest
446 Shopping, theatres, cinemas
448 Central London buses
450 Local rail and London Underground

Digital Data

The exceptionally high-quality mapping found in this atlas is available as digital data in TIFF format, which is easily convertible to other bitmapped (raster) image formats.

The index is also available in digital form as a standard database table. It contains all the details found in the printed index together with the National Grid reference for the map square in which each entry is named.

For further information and to discuss your requirements, please contact james.mann@philips-maps.co.uk

Our Top 10 Tips to avoid parking penalties

David Willis / Alamy

When it comes to parking, London's streets are mean and its traffic regulators keen. Lucky motorists might find a marked bay, or at night a patch of single line, but that could just be the start of the problem. It's all too easy to pick the wrong space or the wrong time of day.

Getting a ticket for over-staying, or using a suspended bay or a resident's only space, is invariably expensive and sometimes the pain doesn't end there. What's the worst that can happen? Well, the car could be clamped or towed away. But in either case it's excruciatingly costly and time-consuming to retrieve the vehicle, especially after 10pm, when London black cab prices go through the roof.

Why has parking become so hazardous? The whole process used to be much less complex, and far easier to understand. The hours of parking control were fairly standard right across the capital, and enforcement was also uniform, with traffic wardens attached to the police service. Then came the Road Traffic Act 1991, which took responsibility away from the police and into the hands of local authorities.

The post-code lottery

Since 1994 parking in London has been run by the borough councils. Most choose to employ private contractors to operate the parking penalty service. In common with all other companies, these outfits are in pursuit of profit – and they haven't been disappointed. Parking fines are big business in London these days.

Latest figures show that more than five million parking penalties were levied on motorists in 2005/6 (see table). In bald terms, that's nearly one for every person living in Greater London. These penalties produced an income for the boroughs of some £279 million in a year. Once the operators have taken their slice, the money goes into the coffers of London's 33 boroughs as well as Transport for London, which has recently stepped up its enforcement activities, especially on red routes.

There is huge variation among the 32 boroughs, with central London by far the riskiest place to park. Westminster held the 2005 record for issuing the greatest number of fines, even though its total of 715,085 was about 100,000 less than the previous year. The fewest parking fines were given in the City of London.

There is one piece of good news. A third fewer cars were clamped than in 2004/5 – nearly 50,000 fewer. But there was a sharp 18% increase in cars removed to pounds. To acknowledge this grim statistic, Philip's London street atlases are now the first to locate Car Pounds on the maps using this symbol:

The figures also reveal the trendsetters among the boroughs:

Camden for the most cars clamped.

Parking fines 2005/6

	Borough	fines
1	**Westminster**	715085
2	**Camden**	448085
3	**Kensington and Chelsea**	294932
4	**Lambeth**	255066
5	**Wandsworth**	245475
6	**Ealing**	212656
7	**Islington**	210685
8	**Newham**	188465
9	**Barnet**	168681
10	**Hammersmith and Fulham**	165196
11	**Hackney**	140966
12	**Waltham Forest**	140216
13	**Southwark**	135045
14	**Haringey**	134551
15	**Brent**	133561
16	**Enfield**	100087
17	**Redbridge**	95966
18	**Hounslow**	92764
19	**Croydon**	86534
20	**Harrow**	83303
21	**Tower Hamlets**	72858
22	**Richmond upon Thames**	72526
23	**Bromley**	69538
24	**Bexley**	65739
25	**Kingston upon Thames**	63980
26	**Lewisham**	63250
27	**Hillingdon**	61211
28	**Merton**	56860
29	**Sutton**	48965
30	**Greenwich**	48892
31	**Barking and Dagenham**	42416
32	**Havering**	40141
33	**City of London**	37478
34	**Transport for London**	304305
		5,095,478

Westminster for the most cars removed to pounds.

The boroughs where the number of tickets issued grew the fastest were: Ealing (+55%), Enfield (+47%) and Hackney (+46%)

The boroughs who saw the biggest falls were: Greenwich (-21%), Richmond (-25%) and Islington (-26%)

The sheer number of different authorities shelling out penalties can make the London street parking issue seem baffling. Arrangements in Richmond

Top 10 Tips

1 Check borough boundaries. One common pitfall for London's drivers is to pump cash into a meter belonging to one borough while being parked in another. This is especially problematic around the London museums. Numerous visitors perfectly willing to pay the charge have fed money into a meter belonging to the Royal Borough of Kensington and Chelsea when they have inadvertently parked in a bay operated by Westminster council. The signage, campaigners claim, is inadequate – so beware.

2 Keep plenty of loose change if you intend to use parking meters. If a parking attendant happens along while you have toddled off to find the correct coinage you have no defence against a ticket.

3 If you've been caught fair and square, pay the ticket within 14 days to take advantage of the cash discount scheme. Prompt settlement usually means coughing up just half the full amount.

4 Assume nothing. Just because you are often permitted to park on single yellow lines after 6.30 doesn't mean it is always so. There are an increasing number of parking places reserved for 'residents only' and these are frequently governed by a 10pm rule. Moreover some zones are 24 hour no parking areas. Look for signs to indicate what rules apply to the parking space before moving into it. Don't forget that some parking areas are watched by cameras that can capture your licence plate, so don't imagine you are safe to contravene regulations on the basis that parking attendants will have ended their shift. If you have received a penalty charge notice in an area where the signs outlining the regulations on parking are obscured by trees or even missing then you may have grounds for appeal. Take photographs as evidence before embarking on the appeals process.

5 If you return to your vehicle while a parking attendant is in the process of writing the ticket don't hesitate to drive off if you can do so without endangering anyone. Parking offences are not criminal offences, so you are not leaving the scene of a crime. The relevant legislation makes it clear that the completed ticket must be either given to the driver or attached to the vehicle. If not, the ticket is invalid.

6 There are loopholes in parking regulations to capitalise upon. A ticket is invalid if the parking attendant is not wearing full uniform, including a hat, or if his identification number is not clearly visible. There might be discrepancies in the ticket regarding the timings or your vehicle. Sometimes the markings on the road are awry or the position of the meter is misleading. If the parking attendant is present request that he makes a note of your objections as this may assist in any pending appeals process.

7 Don't be afraid to appeal against a penalty that in your view has been wrongly issued. The number of appeals is surprisingly small (fewer than 1%) and yet more than 60% are successful. It generally costs nothing to appeal so what have you got to lose? At first glance the process is daunting but stick with it if you feel you have been unfairly targeted with a ticket. Whatever you do, don't ignore it! See 'How to appeal' on the following page.

8 When cars are clamped or towed retrieve the vehicle fast – within 24 hours if possible. This is an expensive business because drivers must pay the penalty charge notice as well as a fee to release the vehicle. If it's not recovered promptly expect a daily charge for 'storage' on top. Afterwards, study the timings on the ticket. Most councils permit a 15 or 20 minute grace period after a parking ticket has run out before clamping or towing. Anything less than that is grounds for appeal. Remember, if you return to your vehicle before the clamp is locked or before the wheels are raised from the ground if it is being towed then the penalty charge notice is invalid.

9 Look out for cashless parking zones. Some are already on trial in central London. Drivers can ring a database to establish an arrival time. Then the clock starts running until the driver calls again to signal departure. The amount due is automatically debited from the driver's account. There's no doubt that new technology will play its part on the parking scene in the over-crowded capital. And it's sensible recognition at last that drivers may have many talents but are not as yet blessed with the foresight to know the precise moment that they will return to their vehicles.

10 Don't forget the other offences. London drivers not only have to be careful about parking. There's the congestion charge to consider as well as fines for using bus lanes illegally and other moving traffic fines orchestrated by local authorities. Congestion charge boundaries, bus lanes, red lights and yellow box junctions are generally monitored by enforcement cameras and evidence is extremely difficult to dispute.

Dominic Burke / Alamy

Parking on a suspended bay will almost certainly result in your car being towed to the borough pound.

may be substantially different to those in Redbridge. Charges and hours of operation for meters and ticket machines vary hugely, sometimes even on opposite sides of the same street. So there's 'stranger danger' not only for those from outside London, or suburbanites driving into central London, but even for Inner Londoners crossing borough borders.

But that isn't what most alarms the average motorist. There's a widely held belief that wardens have quotas to fill, and can get bonuses for over-achieving. Examples of predatory behaviour are

legendary. Favourite times for ticketing are the first and last 10 minutes of the controlled period, when wardens are often seen out in large numbers. There have been reports of tickets being issued to removal vans during house moves, to security company vans when rogue burglar alarms are clanging, and to numerous traders unloading goods for their shops – sometimes in the middle of the night.

In short, it is not only motorists who have broken parking regulations that are being fined, but also the unwary and the downright unlucky - in the right place, at the right time but with a wrong-minded attendant in the vicinity.

Some of the villains have been weeded out. Certain boroughs are ensuring those patrolling the streets have undergone a re-education process that will cast them as a friend to the motorist rather than a foe. It's not in your best interest to assume the whole system is unfair and take out your frustrations upon the parking attendant who just might have ticketed you legitimately.

However, the activities of a few parking regulators deserve close scrutiny. Clampers in particular have earned themselves a cowboy image that is finally arousing the interest of the legislators. A House of Commons Transport Committee Report has urged that operators should 'consider restricting clamping to persistent offenders and unregistered vehicles'. There's even talk in the document that towing a car may be incompatible with our human rights. That's perhaps why the number of cars being clamped in the capital has gone down by some 50,000.

Of course, there are always reasons to justify a harsh parking regime. It keeps London traffic on the move, making journey times more predictable and curtailing traffic mayhem. That's the official line – which never mentions just how valuable the income generated by parking penalties is to the enforcers. Further, authorities don't talk about targets in relation to parking fines, rather 'baseline performance indicators'.

So if you are going to park in London, especially in the centre, beware, be aware – and know your rights. If you do get fined and you think you have a case, be prepared to appeal. Fewer than 1% of motorists did appeal in 2004/5 (do we detect money-raising by inertia?), but over 60% of those appeals were allowed. Remember, if you do not get a response to your appeal within 56 days, your appeal is automatically allowed.

How to appeal

■ Begin with a letter sent by recorded delivery within 14 days. That generally means the clock will stop on the prompt payment discount scheme and it will still be available if the initial appeal is unsuccessful – although some councils claim the reduced amount isn't open to those who embark on this route. Keep copies of the correspondence and any supporting evidence you send with it. Always quote the Penalty Charge Notice number. If you hear nothing for more than 56 days then the council is deemed out of time and the ticket should be cancelled.

■ Do not pay any part of the fine if you are intending to appeal. Once payment is received by the authority the case is closed.

■ If your appeal is turned down don't accept a letter couched in general terms. Write back to ask about the specifics of your case. The council will either stand by the notice and issue a Notice of Rejection or allow the appeal.

■ If the authority endorses the ticket its next step is to issue a Notice to Owner and that should happen within six months. According to the Road Traffic Act of 1991 the owner is liable for violations linked to his vehicle. Disturbingly, it is only at this stage that many motorists discover they are being pursued for a parking offence. If you are the sole driver of a vehicle that hasn't been stolen the ticket has clearly not been either attached to the vehicle or handed to you, the driver, as the law demands. Respond within 28 days filing the relevant information. This is known as Formal Representation. (If you do not answer in the specified time the council may well up the fine and send in the bailiffs to recover the amount.)

■ If this petition is rejected by the local authority then it's time to take the case to the Parking and Traffic Appeals Service. You can select a postal or personal adjudication. Internet advice favours face time with the adjudicator as local councils are known to frequently cave in at the prospect of putting evidence before an official tribunal on the grounds of cost, although there's no guarantee of this happening. The adjudicator's decision is final as there is no recourse to law.

Helpful information

The Knowledge A telephone advisory service run by off-duty London taxi drivers. They will help with problems including parking and directions. The number is 0906 265 6565 (premium rate) or try *www.theknowledge.com*

Transport for London (TfL) Responsible for 360 miles of roads, 4,600 traffic lights and London's red routes. It is also a fine-issuing authority. Contact Tfl on 0207 2221234 or *www.tfl.gov.uk.*

www.ticketbusters.co.uk is a website devoted to assisting London motorists, offering tailored advice on parking ticket appeals.

www.parkingticket.co.uk also offers support for London drivers.

Dominic Burke / Alamy

Clamping rates are falling but you are still at risk – especially in Camden and Westminster.

Mobile speed camera sites

This table lists the sites where the local safety camera partnership may enforce speed limits through the use of mobile cameras or detectors. These are usually set up on the roadside or a bridge spanning the road and operated by a police or civilian enforcement officer.

Barking & Dagenham

A13
Alfreds Way IG11
Alfreds Way IG12
Ripple Rd IG11
Ripple Rd RM9

A406
Barking Relief Rd IG11

A1153
Porters Avenue RM8

B178
Ballards Rd RM10

Barnet

A5
Hendon Broadway NW9

A406
North Circular Rd N3

Unclassified
Oakleigh Rd South N11

Bexley

A20
Sidcup Rd SE9

Unclassified
Abbey Rd DA17
Bellegrove Rd DA16
Erith Rd DA17
Farady Avenue DA14
King Harolds Way DA17
Lower Rd DA17
Penhill Rd DA5
Pickford Lane DA7
Well Hall Rd SE9
Woolwich Rd DA17

Brent

A5
Edgware Rd NW2

A406
North Circular Rd NW2
North Circular Rd NW10

A4006
Kenton Rd HA3

Unclassified
Crest Rd NW2
Fryent Way, Kingsbury NW9
Hillside NW10
Kingsbury Rd NW9
Watford Rd, Wembley HA0
Watford Rd, Sudbury HA0
Woodcock Hill HA3

Bromley

A20
Sidcup By-Pass DA14

A213
Croydon Rd SE20

A222
Bromley Rd BR2
Bromley Rd BR3

Unclassified
Beckenham Rd BR3
Burnt Ash Lane BR1
Crystal Palace Park Rd SE26
Elmers End Rd BR3
Main Rd TN16
Sevenoaks Way BR5
Wickham Way BR3

Camden

A501
Euston Rd NW1

Chadwell

M11
Chadwell IG8

City of Westminster

A40
Westway W2

Unclassified
Great Western Rd W11
Millbank SW1
Vauxhall Bridge Rd SW1

Croydon

A22
Godstone Rd CR8

A215
Beulah Hill SE19

A217
Garratt Lane SW18

Unclassified
Brigstock Rd CR7
Coulsdon Rd, Coulsdon CR5
Long Lane, Addiscombe CR0
Portnalls Rd, Coulsdon CR5
Thornton Rd CR0

Ealing

A40
Perivale UB6
Western Avenue UB5
Western Avenue UB6

Unclassified
Greenford Rd, Greenford UB6
Greenford Rd, Southall UB1
Horn Lane W3
Lady Margaret Rd UB1
Ruislip Rd UB5
Uxbridge Rd UB2

Egham

M25
Egham TW20

Elmbridge

M25
Byfleet KT14

Enfield

A10
Great Cambridge Rd N18

A110
Enfield Rd EN2

Unclassified
Fore Street N9

Forest Hill

Unclassified
Stanstead Rd SE23

Greenwich

A20
Sidcup Rd SE9

Unclassified
Beresford Street SE18
Court Rd SE9
Creek Rd SE10
Glenesk Rd SE9
Rochester Way SE3
Rochester Way SE9
Woolwich Church Street SE18

Hackney

A10
Stamford Hill N16

Unclassified
Clapton Common E5
Seven Sisters Rd N4
Upper Clapton Rd E5

Hammersmith & Fulham

A40
Westway W2
Westway W12

A219
Scrubs Lane W12

Unclassified
Fulham Palace Rd SW6
Uxbridge Rd W12

Haringey

A503
Seven Sisters Rd N15

Unclassified
Belmont Rd N15
Bounds Green Rd N11
Seven Sisters Rd N4
White Hart Lane N22

Harrow

Unclassified
Alexandra Avenue HA2
Harrow View HA3
Honeypot Lane NW9
Porlock Avenue HA2
Uxbridge Rd, Harrow Weald HA3
Watford Rd HA1

Havering

Unclassified
Brentwood Rd, Romford RM1
Chase Cross Rd RM5
Eastern Avenue RM14
Eastern Avenue East RM14
Hall Lane RM14
Ingrebourne Gardens, Upminster RM14
Ockenden Rd RM14
Parkstone Avenue, Hornchurch RM11
Wingletye Lane RM11

Hillingdon

M25
Colnbrook SL3
West Drayton UB7

A40
Western Avenue, Ruislip UB10

A312
Hayes UB3

Unclassified
Church Hill, Harefield UB9
Cowley Rd, Uxbridge UB8
Cowley High Rd UB8
Joel Street, Northwood Hills HA6
Kingshill Avenue, Hayes UB4
Park Rd UB8
Stockley Rd UB7
Uxbridge Rd, Hayes UB4

Hounslow

A4
Great West Rd, Brentford TW8
Great West Rd, Hounslow TW7
Great West Rd, Hounslow W4

A315
High Street TW8

Unclassified
Castle Way, Hanworth TW13
Great West Rd TW5
Harlington Rd West TW14
Hatton Rd, Bedfont TW14

Islington

Unclassified
Holloway Rd N19
Seven Sisters Rd N4
Upper Street N1

Kensington & Chelsea

Unclassified
Barlby Rd W10
Chelsea Embankment SW3
Chesterton Rd W10
Holland Park Avenue W11
Holland Villas Rd W14
Kensington Park Rd W11
Kensington Rd SW7
Ladbroke Grove W11
Latimer Rd W10
Royal Hospital Rd SW3
Sloane Street SW1
St Helens Gardens W10

Kingston upon Thames

A3
Kingston By-Pass SW20

A240
Kingston Rd KT4

Unclassified
Manor Drive North KT3
Richmond Rd KT2

Lambeth

Unclassified
Atkins Rd SW12
Brixton Hill SW2
Brixton Rd SW9
Clapham Rd SW9
Herne Hill Rd SE24
Kennington Park Rd SE11
Kings Avenue SW4
Streatham High Rd SW16

Lewisham

A21
Bromley Rd BR1

Unclassified
Brockley Rd SE4
Brockley Rd SE23
Bromley Rd SE6
Brownhill Rd SE6
Burnt Ash Hill SE12
Lee High Rd SE12
Lewisham Way SE4
Westwood Hill SE26

Merton

A298
Bushey Rd SW20

Unclassified
Central Rd SM4
High Street, Colliers Wood SW19
Hillcross Avenue SM4
London Rd CR4
Martin Way SM4
Martin Way SW20
Ridgway Place SW19
West Barnes Lane SW20

Newham

A13
Alfreds Way IG11

A124
Barking Rd E6

A1020
Royal Albert Dock Way E6
Royal Docks Rd E6

Unclassified
Barking Rd E13
Romford Rd E7

Redbridge

A406
Southend Rd IG8

Unclassified
Manford Way, Hainault IG7
Woodford Avenue IG8
Woodford Rd E18

Richmond upon Thames

A205
Upper Richmond Rd West SW14

Unclassified
Kew Rd TW9
Sixth Cross Rd TW2
Uxbridge Rd TW12

Ruislip

Unclassified
Field End Rd HA4

Runnymeade

M25
Runnymede TW20

Southwark

Unclassified
Albany Rd SE5
Alleyn Park SE21
Brenchley Gardens SE15
Camberwell New Rd SE5
Denmark Hill SE5
Kennington Park Rd SE11
Linden Grove SE15
Old Kent Rd SE1
Old Kent Rd SE14
Old Kent Rd SE17
Peckham Rye SE15
Salter Rd SE16
Southwark Pk Rd SE16
Sunray Avenue SE24

Spelthorne

M25
Staines TW18

Sutton

A232
Cheam Rd SM1

B272
Foresters Drive SM6

B278
Green Lane SM4

B279
Tudor Drive SM4

Unclassified
Malden Rd SM3
Middleton Rd SM5
Beddington Lane CR0
Cheam Common Rd KT4

Tower Hamlets

A102
Homerton High Street E9

Unclassified
Bow Rd E3
Cambridge Heath Rd E2
Manchester Rd E14
Mile End Rd E1
Upper Clapton Rd E5
Westferry Rd E14

Waltham Forest

Unclassified
Chingford Rd E4
Chingford Rd E17
Hoe Street E17
Larkshall Rd E4

Wandsworth

A3
Kingston Rd SW15

A214
Trinity Rd SW18

A3220
Latchmere Rd SW11

Unclassified
Battersea Park Rd SW11
Garratt Lane SW18
Upper Richmond Rd SW15

Windsor & Maidenhead

M25
Wraysbury TW19

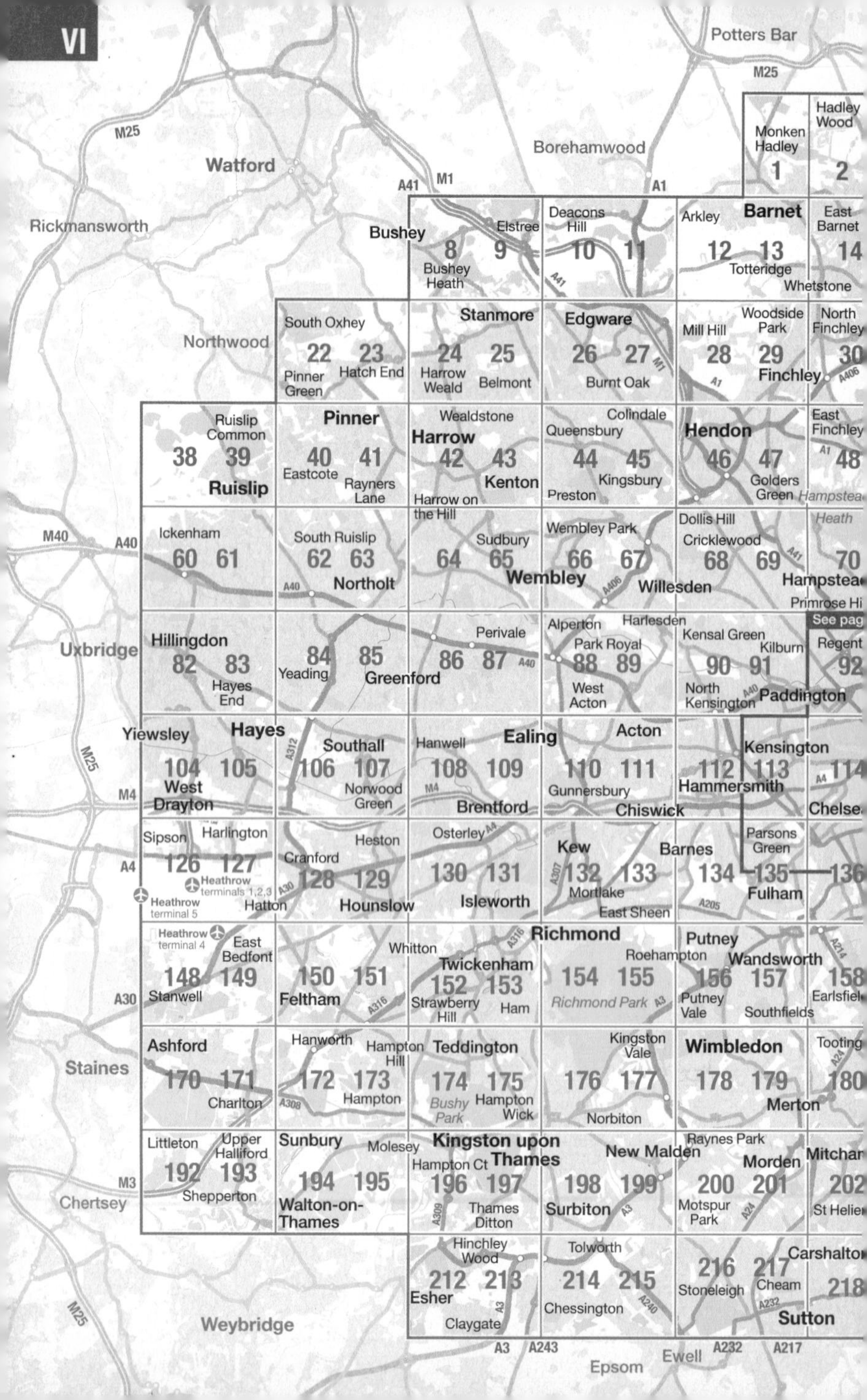

Potters Bar
M25
Monken Hadley 1
Hadley Wood 2
Borehamwood
Watford
M25
M1
A41
A1
Rickmansworth
Bushey 8 9 Elstree
Bushey Heath
Deacons Hill 10 11
A41
Arkley 12 13 Barnet
Totteridge
East Barnet 14
Whetstone
Northwood
South Oxhey 22 23 Hatch End
Pinner Green
Stanmore 24 25
Harrow Weald
Belmont
Edgware 26 27
Burnt Oak
M1
Mill Hill 28
Woodside Park 29
Finchley
A1
North Finchley 30
A406
Ruislip Common 38 39
Ruislip
Pinner 40 41
Eastcote
Rayners Lane
Wealdstone
Harrow 42 43
Kenton
Harrow on the Hill
Colindale
Queensbury 44 45
Kingsbury
Preston
Hendon 46 47
Golders Green
East Finchley
A1 48
Hampstead Heath
M40
A40
Ickenham 60 61
South Ruislip 62 63
Northolt
A40
Sudbury 64 65
Wembley
Wembley Park 66 67
A406
Willesden
Dollis Hill
Cricklewood 68 69
A41
70
Hampstead
Primrose Hill
Uxbridge
Hillingdon 82 83
Hayes End
Yeading 84 85
Greenford
Perivale 86 87
A40
Alperton
Harlesden
Park Royal 88 89
West Acton
Kensal Green
Kilburn
90 91
North Kensington
A40
Paddington
See page
Regent's 92
Yiewsley
Hayes
M25
104 105
West Drayton
M4
A312
Southall 106 107
Norwood Green
Hanwell 108 109
M4
Brentford
Ealing
Acton
110 111
Gunnersbury
Chiswick
112 113
Kensington
Hammersmith
A4 114
Chelsea
Sipson
Harlington
A4
126 127
Heathrow terminals 1,2,3
Heathrow terminal 5
Hatton
A30
Cranford 128 129
Heston
Hounslow
Osterley A4
130 131
Isleworth
Kew
A307
132 133
Mortlake
East Sheen
Barnes
134
A205
Parsons Green
135 136
Fulham
Heathrow terminal 4
East Bedfont
148 149
Stanwell
A30
150 151
Feltham
A316
Whitton
A316
Twickenham
152 153
Strawberry Hill
Ham
Richmond
154 155
Richmond Park
A3
Roehampton
Putney
156 157
Putney Vale
Wandsworth
Southfields
A214
158
Earlsfield
Ashford
Staines
170 171
Charlton
Hanworth
172 173
A308
Hampton Hill
Hampton
Teddington
174 175
Bushy Park
Hampton Wick
Kingston Vale
176 177
Norbiton
Wimbledon
178 179
Merton
Tooting
A24
180
Littleton
Upper Halliford
192 193
Shepperton
M3
Chertsey
Sunbury
194 195
Walton-on-Thames
Molesey
Kingston upon Thames
Hampton Ct
196 197
A309
Thames Ditton
New Malden
198 199
Surbiton
A3
Raynes Park
Morden
200 201
Motspur Park
A24
Mitcham
202
St Helier
Hinchley Wood
212 213
Esher
A3
Claygate
Tolworth
214 215
Chessington
A240
216 217
Stoneleigh
Cheam
Carshalton
218
A232
Sutton
M25
Weybridge
A3
A243
Epsom
Ewell
A232
A217

Key to map pages

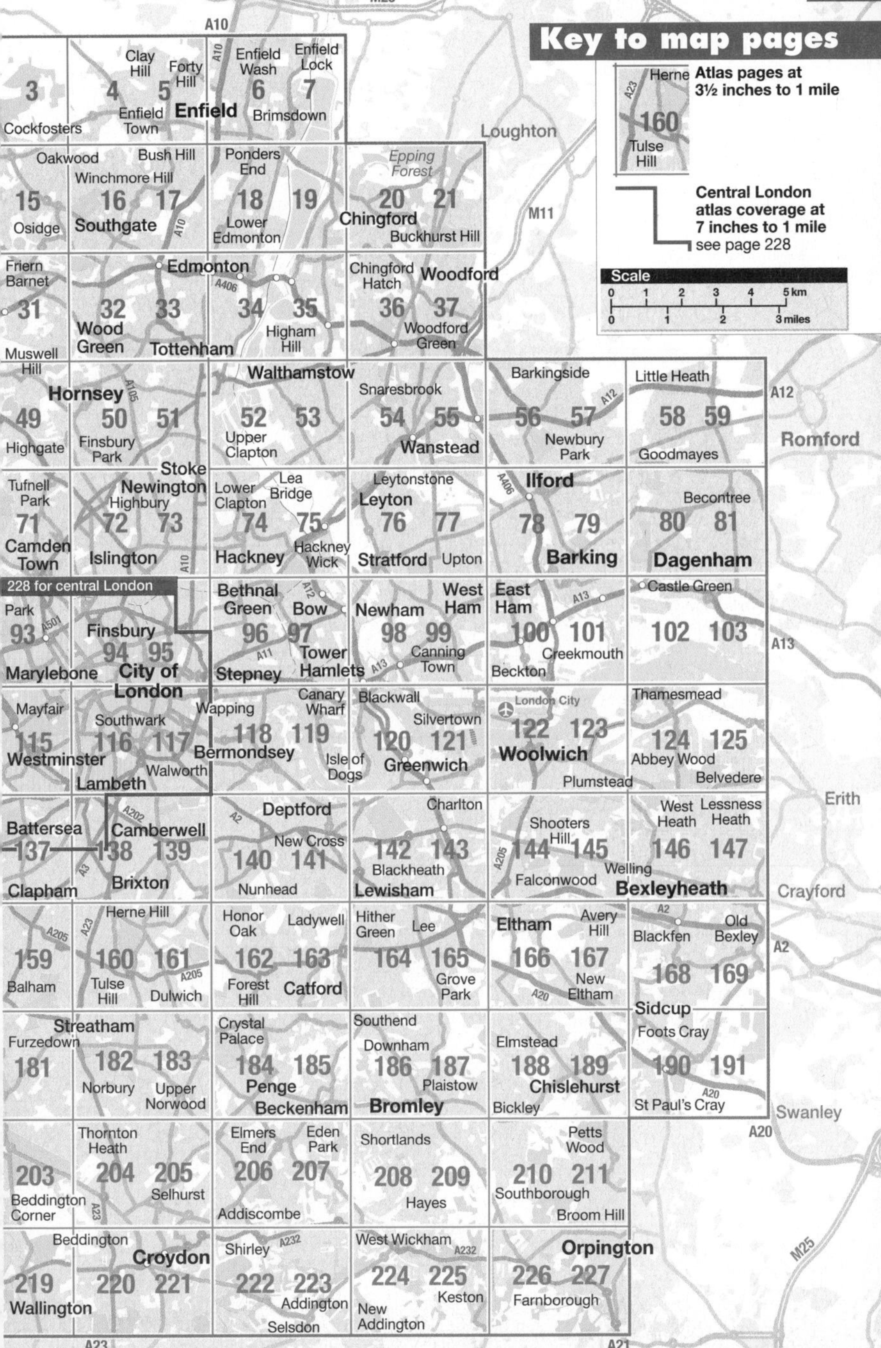

1 Hammersmith and Fulham
2 Royal Borough of Kensington and Chelsea
3 County of the City of London

Major administrative and Postcode boundaries

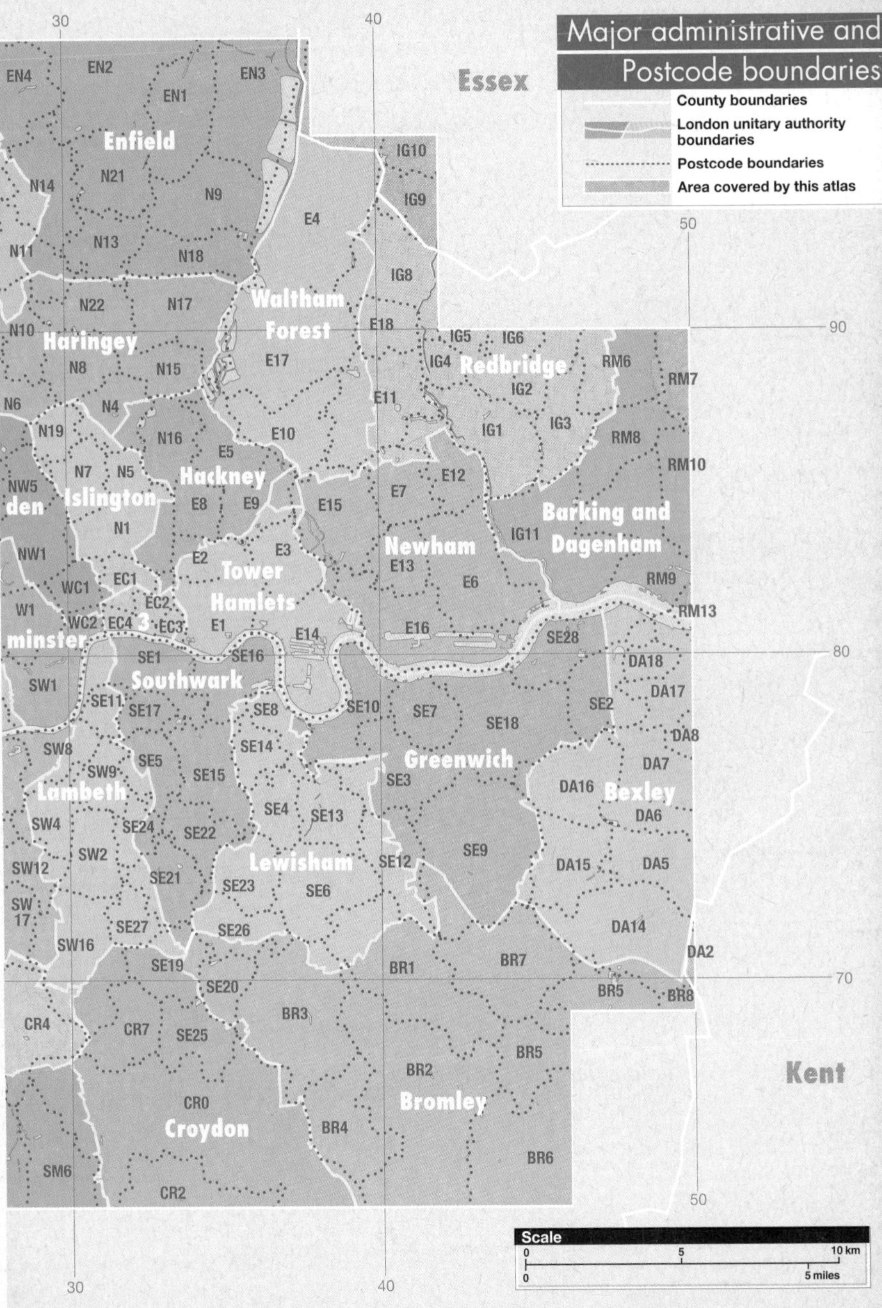

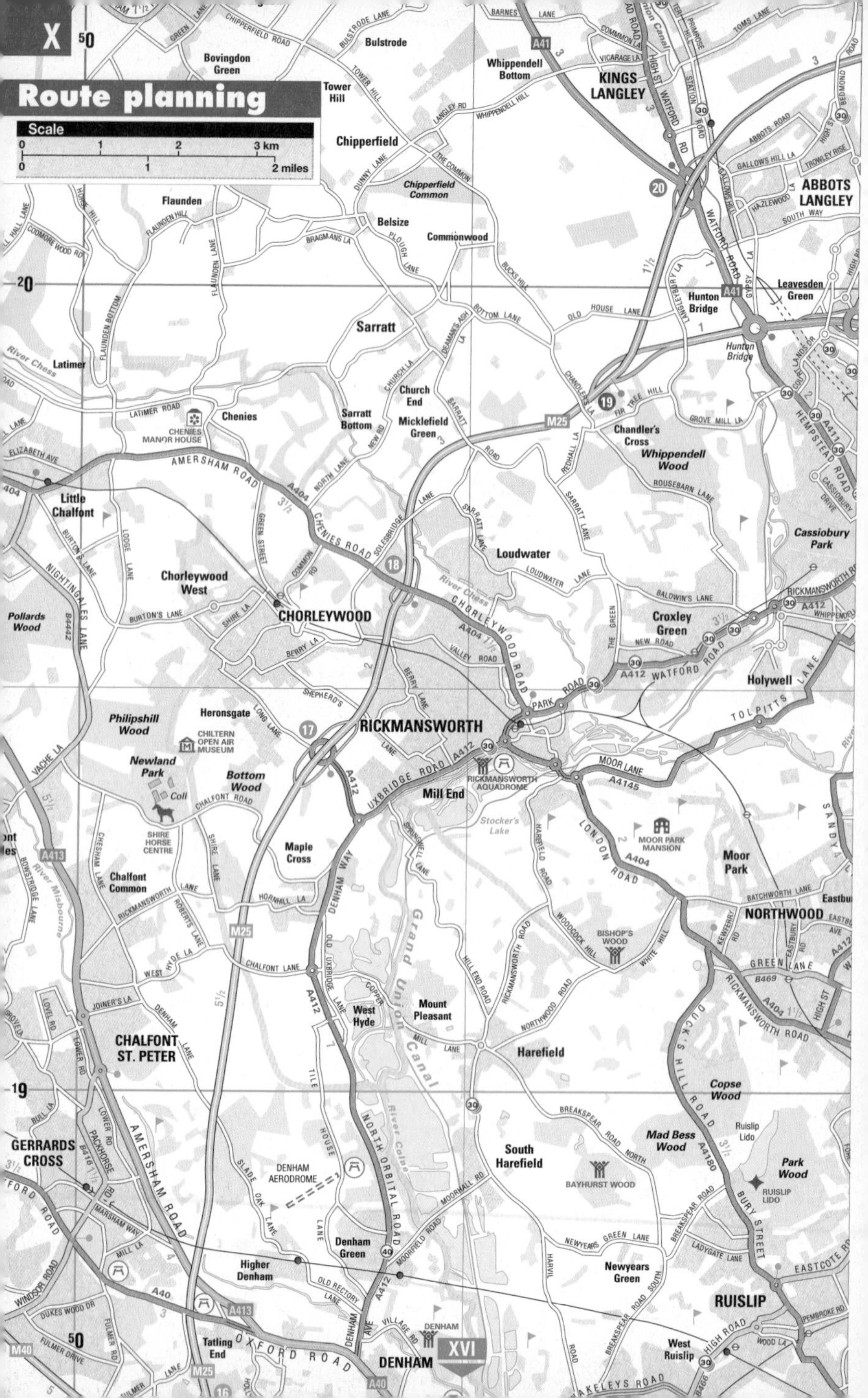
X
Route planning
Scale
0
1
2
3 km
0
1
2 miles
Bovingdon Green
Bulstrode
Tower Hill
Chipperfield
Chipperfield Common
Whippendell Bottom
KINGS LANGLEY
ABBOTS LANGLEY
Flaunden
Belsize
Commonwood
Leavesden Green
Hunton Bridge
Sarratt
Latimer
River Chess
Church End
Sarratt Bottom
Micklefield Green
Chenies
CHENIES MANOR HOUSE
Chandler's Cross
Whippendell Wood
Little Chalfont
Chorleywood West
CHORLEYWOOD
Loudwater
Cassiobury Park
Croxley Green
Pollards Wood
Holywell
Philipshill Wood
Heronsgate
CHILTERN OPEN AIR MUSEUM
RICKMANSWORTH
Newland Park
Coll
Bottom Wood
Mill End
RICKMANSWORTH AQUADROME
Stocker's Lake
SHIRE HORSE CENTRE
Maple Cross
MOOR PARK MANSION
Moor Park
Chalfont Common
NORTHWOOD
BISHOP'S WOOD
Grand Union Canal
West Hyde
Mount Pleasant
Harefield
CHALFONT ST. PETER
Copse Wood
GERRARDS CROSS
Mad Bess Wood
Ruislip Lido
Park Wood
DENHAM AERODROME
South Harefield
BAYHURST WOOD
RUISLIP LIDO
River Colne
Denham Green
Higher Denham
Newyears Green
RUISLIP
DENHAM
Tatling End
West Ruislip
XVI
AMERSHAM ROAD
CHENIES ROAD
CHORLEYWOOD ROAD
UXBRIDGE ROAD
LONDON ROAD
MOOR LANE
NORTH ORBITAL ROAD
OXFORD ROAD
RICKMANSWORTH ROAD
WATFORD ROAD
HEMPSTEAD ROAD
M25
A41
A404
A412
A413
A40
A4145
B4442
A4180
B469
M40
20
19
50
17
18
16

South Mimms
Mimmshall Brook
SOUTH MIMMS SERVICES
M25
A1(M)
MUTTON LANE
BILLY LOWS LA
THE CAUSEWAY
NORTHAW RD WEST
B156
COOPERS LANE ROAD
POTTERS BAR
Shenley
Ridge
Dancers Hill
Bentley Heath
DANCERS HILL ROAD
BARNET ROAD
A1000
STAG HILL
WAGON ROAD
Hadley Wood
Enfield Chase
FERNY HILL
BEECH HILL
Well End
TROTTERS BOTTOM
ST. ALBANS ROAD
A1081
BARNET BY-PASS
ELSTREE WAY
Film Studios
Rowley Green
Monken Hadley
Monken Hadley Common
Hadley
TRENT
COCKFOSTERS ROAD
A111
Cockfosters
New Barnet
BARNET
Arkley
WOOD ST
Underhill
UNDERHILL
GREAT NORTH ROAD
EAST BARNET
CAT HILL
BRAMLEY ROAD
Stirling Corner
Barnet Gate
Deacons Hill
Scratchwood
LONDON GATEWAY SERVICES
M1
BARNET WAY
HENDON WOOD LA
B552
Totteridge
TOTTERIDGE LANE
A5109
Oak Hill Park
Whetstone
OSIDGE LA
Osidge
OAKLEIGH RD NORTH
FRIERN BARNET LANE
Apex Corner
A41
WATFORD WAY
THE RIDGEWAY
Woodside Park
Arnos Grove
EDGWARE
Mill Hill Circus
Mill Hill
Mill Hill East
West Finchley
North Finchley
FRIERN BARNET
A406
Colney Hatch
COPTHALL STADIUM
Fiveways Corner
Church End
FINCHLEY
Grahame Park
Burnt Oak
RAF MUSEUM
Coldfall Wood
Alexandra Palace
HENDON
CHURCH FARM MUSEUM
Henley's Corner
NORTH CIRCULAR ROAD
Muswell Hill
Fortis Green
Kingsbury
Colindale
East Finchley
LYTTELTON ROAD
Highgate Wood
Queen's Wood
Temple Fortune
Hampstead Garden Suburb
ARCHWAY RD
Crouch End
West Hendon
Brent Cross Shopping Centre
Brent Cross
Golders Green
Barn Hill
Brent Reservoir (Welsh Harp)
Staples Corner
HAMPSTEAD HEATH
KENWOOD HOUSE
Highgate
Hampstead Heath
Highgate Ponds
Parliament Hill
Wembley Park
Neasden Circle
Neasden
Dollis Hill
Child's Hill
Golders Hill Park
Dartmouth Park
Gospel Oak
HAMPSTEAD
KEATS HOUSE
FENTON HOUSE
Gladstone Park
Cricklewood
Tufnell Park
GRANGE MUSEUM
WEMBLEY ARENA
WEMBLEY STADIUM
WILLESDEN
Belsize Park
Archway

IX
XVIII

XIII
Cattlegate
Bury Green
CHESHUNT
WALTHAM ABBEY
Wood Green
Waltham Cross
Holdbrook
M25
Crews Hill
Whitewebbs Park
CAPEL MANOR
Freezy Water
Clay Hill
FORTY HALL
Forty Hill
Enfield Wash
Enfield Lock
High Beach
Gordon Hill
Enfield Highway
Sewardstone
QUEEN ELIZABETH STADIUM
Brimsdown
ENFIELD
World's End
King George's Reservoir
Ponders End
Sewardstonebury
Grange Park
Bush Hill Park
Chingford Green
SOUTHGATE
Grovelands Park
Winchmore Hill
William Girling Reservoir
CHINGFORD
PICKETT'S LOCK
Friday Hill
Lower Edmonton
Palmers Green
Great Cambridge Junction
Pymmes Park
Cooks Ferry
Woodford Wells
Broomfield Park
Chingford Hatch
Angel Edmonton
Hall Lane
EDMONTON
Higham's Park
Bowes Park
Clockhouse Junction
NEW RIVER STADIUM
Hale End
Banbury Reservoir
WALTHAMSTOW STADIUM
Woodford Green
WOOD GREEN
BRUCE CASTLE MUSEUM
WHITE HART LANE
Crooked Billet
Higham Hill
Waterworks Corner
Noel Park
TOTTENHAM
Bruce Grove
Reservoirs
West Green
Tottenham Hale
WALTHAMSTOW
Snaresbrook
Seven Sisters
VESTRY HOUSE MUSEUM
HORNSEY
Harringay
South Tottenham
Stroud Green
WANS
Finsbury Park
Stamford Hill
Upper Clapton
Green Man Interchange
Leytonstone
STOKE NEWINGTON
Clapton
Lea Bridge
Hackney Marsh
LEYTON
EMIRATES STADIUM
Shacklewell
Nags Head
Highbury
XIX
Clapton Park
Lea Interchange
Temple Mills
Canonbury
Forest Gate
XIV

XIV
Claverhambury
Almes Green
Cobbins Brook
EPPING
Coopersale
Coopersale Street
Gaynes Park
Bell Common
Ivy Chimneys
Copthall Green
Upshire
ALTHAM ABBEY
Fiddlers Hamlet
Mount End
Wood Green
M25
M11
Wakearms Rdbt
Theydon Garnon
Hobbs Cross
Theydon Mount
Theydon Bois
Debden Green
High Beach
Epping Forest
STAPLEFORD AERODROME
Abridge
Debden
LOUGHTON
Sewardstonebury
River Roding
Nature Reserve
CHINGFORD
Lambourne End
Friday Hill
Buckhurst Hill
Chigwell Row
HAINULT FOREST
CHIGWELL
Woodford Wells
WOODFORD
Grange Hill
Woodford Bridge
Hainault
Woodford Green
Fairlop
Collier Row
Charlie Browns Rdbt
Clayhall
Fulwell Cross
FAIRLOP WATERS
Marks Gate
Snaresbrook
Barkingside
Little Heath
Redbridge
Newbury Park
Gants Hill
Seven Kings Park
Chadwell Heath
Moby Dick
Redbridge Rdbt
WANSTEAD
Green Man Interchange
Valentines Park
Seven Kings
Wanstead Park
Cranbrook
Goodmayes
Leytonstone
XX
Wanstead Flats
REDBRIDGE MUSEUM

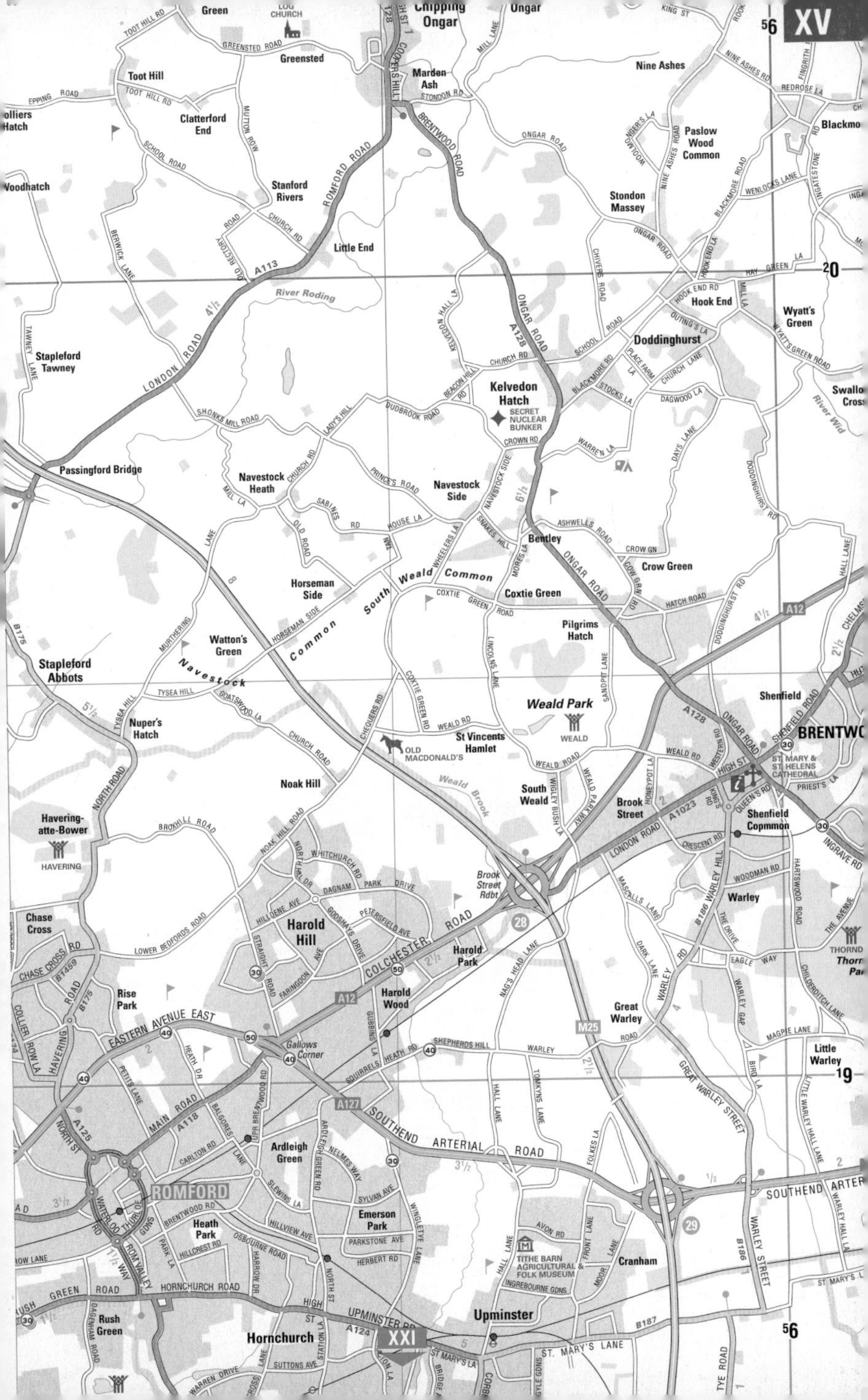
Chipping Ongar
Greensted
Toot Hill
Marden Ash
Nine Ashes
Clatterford End
Paslow Wood Common
Blackmore
Woodhatch
Stanford Rivers
Stondon Massey
Little End
River Roding
Hook End
Wyatt's Green
Stapleford Tawney
Doddinghurst
Kelvedon Hatch
SECRET NUCLEAR BUNKER
Passingford Bridge
Navestock Heath
Navestock Side
Bentley
Crow Green
Horseman Side
South Weald Common
Coxtie Green
Pilgrims Hatch
Watton's Green
Navestock
Stapleford Abbots
Weald Park
WEALD
Shenfield
BRENTWOOD
Nuper's Hatch
St Vincents Hamlet
OLD MACDONALD'S
ST. MARY & ST. HELENS CATHEDRAL
Noak Hill
South Weald
Brook Street
Shenfield Common
Havering-atte-Bower
HAVERING
Brook Street Rdbt
Warley
Chase Cross
Harold Hill
Harold Park
Rise Park
Harold Wood
Great Warley
Gallows Corner
Little Warley
Ardleigh Green
ROMFORD
Emerson Park
Heath Park
Cranham
TITHE BARN AGRICULTURAL & FOLK MUSEUM
Rush Green
Upminster
Hornchurch
XXI
A113
A128
A12
A1023
M25
A127
A118
A125
A124
B175
B1459
B186
B187
SOUTHEND ARTERIAL ROAD
COLCHESTER ROAD
EASTERN AVENUE EAST
LONDON ROAD
ONGAR ROAD
ROMFORD ROAD
BRENTWOOD ROAD
20
19
56

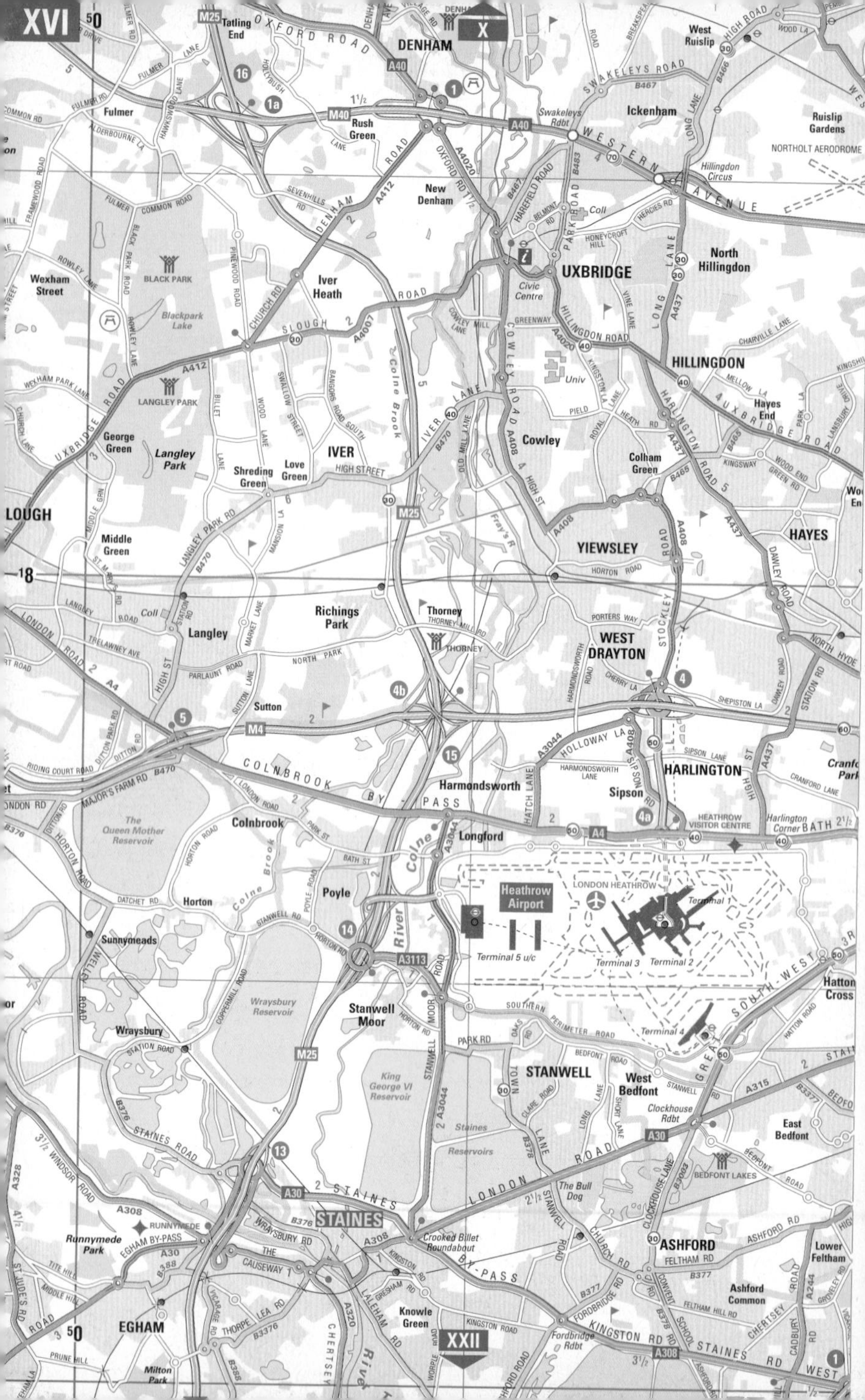
DENHAM
Tatling End
Fulmer
Rush Green
New Denham
Ickenham
West Ruislip
Ruislip Gardens
NORTHOLT AERODROME
Hillingdon Circus
UXBRIDGE
North Hillingdon
Wexham Street
BLACK PARK
Blackpark Lake
Iver Heath
Civic Centre
HILLINGDON
LANGLEY PARK
Hayes End
George Green
Langley Park
Cowley
IVER
Shreding Green
Love Green
Colham Green
SLOUGH
Middle Green
YIEWSLEY
HAYES
Richings Park
Thorney
Langley
WEST DRAYTON
Sutton
Harmondsworth
HARLINGTON
Sipson
Colnbrook
Longford
The Queen Mother Reservoir
Horton
Poyle
Heathrow Airport
LONDON HEATHROW
Terminal 1
Terminal 2
Terminal 3
Terminal 4
Terminal 5 u/c
Sunnymeads
Wraysbury Reservoir
Stanwell Moor
Hatton Cross
Wraysbury
King George VI Reservoir
STANWELL
West Bedfont
Clockhouse Rdbt
East Bedfont
Staines Reservoirs
BEDFONT LAKES
The Bull Dog
STAINES
RUNNYMEDE
Runnymede Park
Crooked Billet Roundabout
ASHFORD
Lower Feltham
Ashford Common
EGHAM
Knowle Green
XXII
Fordbridge Rdbt
Milton Park
HEATHROW VISITOR CENTRE
Harlington Corner
OXFORD ROAD
WESTERN AVENUE
UXBRIDGE ROAD
COLNBROOK BY-PASS
LONDON ROAD
STAINES BY-PASS
KINGSTON RD
M25
M40
M4
A40
A4
A30
A308

NORTHOLT
GREENFORD
WEMBLEY
EALING
ACTON
SOUTHALL
HANWELL
HESTON
BRENTFORD
CHISWICK
HOUNSLOW
ISLEWORTH
RICHMOND
TWICKENHAM
FELTHAM
HANWORTH
TEDDINGTON
KINGSTON UPON THAMES
South Ruislip
South Harrow
Sudbury
North Wembley
Wembley Park
Perivale
Alperton
Stonebridge
Park Royal
Yeading
Hayes Town
Dormer's Wells
Drayton Green
West Ealing
West Acton
South Acton
Norwood Green
Osterley Park
Gunnersbury Park
Northfields
Kew
North Hyde
Hounslow West
Hounslow Heath
Woodlands
Whitton
St Margarets
Petersham
Ham
Richmond Park
Richmond Hill
North Sheen
East Sheen
Mortlake
Old Deer Park
Syon Park
Hanworth Park
Western Avenue
Great West Road
River Thames
Grand Union Canal
XI
XXIII
XVIII
52
18

XVIII
XII
XXIV
XVII
18
52
Gladstone Park
Cricklewood
WILLESDEN
Stonebridge Park
Stonebridge
Harlesden
Brondesbury
Kilburn
West Hampstead
Belsize Park
Swiss Cottage
Kentish Town
CAMDEN TOWN
Primrose Hill
JEWISH MUSEUM
LONDON ZOO
Regents Park
St John's Wood
Maida Vale
Kensal Rise
Park Royal
Old Oak Common
Grand Union Canal
Wormwood Scrubs Park
LINFORD CHRISTIE STADIUM
West Acton
Gipsy Corner
East Acton
ACTON
Savoy Circus
White City
LOFTUS ROAD
Notting Hill
Westbourne Park
MUSEUM OF BRANDS
PADDINGTON
Bayswater
Marylebone
Marylebone Flyover
MADAME TUSSAUD'S
MARYLEBONE
Euston
St Pancras
Hyde Park
Kensington Gardens
KENSINGTON PALACE
Mayfair
ROYAL ACADEMY
NATIONAL GALLERY
Green Park
St James's Palace
BUCKINGHAM PALACE
St James's Park
APSLEY HOUSE
Hyde Park Corner
Knightsbridge
ROYAL ALBERT HALL
NATURAL HISTORY
Holland Park
Sheperd's Bush
South Acton
Bedford Park
HAMMERSMITH
Olympia
CHELSEA
Victoria
Pimlico
NATIONAL ARMY MUSEUM
RANELAGH GDNS
Chiswick Rdbt
CHISWICK
CHISWICK HOUSE
Hogarth Rdbt
Hammersmith Br
Hammersmith Broadway
THE QUEEN'S CLUB
Earl's Court
STAMFORD BRIDGE
Parsons Green
Chelsea Br
Albert Br
CHILDREN'S ZOO
Battersea Park
Battersea Br
Kew Bridge
Public Record Office
Grove Park
Barnes Br
WETLANDS CENTRE
River Thames
FULHAM
BARNES
CRAVEN COTTAGE
Chiswick Br
North Sheen
Mortlake
Chalkers Corner
Manor Circus
Putney Br
Hurlingham Park
WESTLAND HELIPORT
Clapham Junction
BATTERSEA
CLAPHAM
Wandsworth Br
Wandsworth Gyratory
Clapham Common
East Sheen
Red Rover
PUTNEY
WANDSWORTH
RICHMOND
Roehampton
Putney Heath
West Hill
Wandsworth Common
Balham
Grange Mills
Tibbet's Corner
Richmond Park
Roads in Richmond Park open in daylight hours only
Southfields
Earlsfield
Upper Tooting
Tooting Bec Common
Putney Vale
Robin Hood
Wimbledon Park
WIMBLEDON L.T.A.
TENNIS MUSEUM
WIMBLEDON STADIUM
Tooting Bec
Kingston Vale
Wimbledon Common
WIMBLEDON
Tooting
Furzedown
Crooked Billet
Collier's Wood
Coombe
Coombe Lane
KINGSTON UPON THAMES
Norbiton
NEW MALDEN
Morden Hall Park
MITCHAM
Bushey Mead
Raynes

XIX
54
XIII
XX
XXV
18
17
ISLINGTON
SHOREDITCH
FINSBURY
HACKNEY
STRATFORD
BETHNAL GREEN
BOW
POPLAR
WEST HAM
Highbury
Canonbury
Dalston
Clapton Park
Forest Gate
Upton
Victoria Park
Old Ford
Plaistow
Holborn
Spitalfields
Stepney
Aldgate
Wapping
Limehouse
Canary Wharf
Canning Town
Blackwall
Blackwall Tunnel
North Greenwich
Rotherhithe
BERMONDSEY
ISLE OF DOGS
Millwall
LAMBETH
Elephant & Castle
Walworth
Kennington
DEPTFORD
GREENWICH
Peckham
New Cross
CAMBERWELL
Camberwell Green
BLACKHEATH
BRIXTON
East Dulwich
Nunhead
Brockley
LEWISHAM
Hither Green
Honor Oak
Ladywell
Lee
Brockwell Park
Dulwich Park
CATFORD
Forest Hill
Tulse Hill
West Dulwich
Dulwich
STREATHAM
Bellingham
Bell Green
PENGE
Downham
Norwood
Streatham Common
Beckenham Place Park
Plaistow
Norbury
Anerley
BECKENHAM
Elmers End
River Thames
Surrey Quays
Rotherhithe Tunnel
Westminster Br
Waterloo
London Bridge
Tower Br
Houses of Parliament
Imperial War Museum
Millennium Dome
Crystal Palace National Sports Centre
Horniman Museum
Picture Gallery
National Maritime Museum
Greenwich Park
Greenwich Observatory
Livesey Museum
Gas Museum
House Mill Distillery
Excel Centre
Royal Victoria
Cutty Sark
The New Den
The Oval
Law Courts
Guildhall
Globe Theatre & Exhibition
Tate Modern
Design Mus
Brunel Engine House Museum
Tower of London
Hay's Galleria
London Eye
Catford Gyratory
Temple Mills
Hackney Wick
Lea Interchange

XIV
ILFORD
Ilford Interchange
REDBRIDGE MUSEUM
Loxford
Little Ilford
Manor Park
Forest Gate
Wanstead Flats
Goodmayes
Becontree
Fair Cross
Mayesbrook Park
BARKING
Castle Green
Ripple Road
Heathway
Plashet
Upton
West Ham Park
Upton Park
WEST HAM
BOLEYN GD (UPTON PARK)
Barking Flyover
Wallend
EAST HAM
EASTBURY MANOR HOUSE
Movers Lane
Plaistow
Beckton Alps
Beckton
Barking Creek
Creekmouth
River Thames
Prince Regent
Canning Town
Custom House
Blackwall
Blackwall Tunnel
EXCEL CENTRE
Royal Victoria Dock
Royal Albert Dock
CITY AIRPORT
King George V Dock
MILLENNIUM DOME
North Greenwich
Silvertown
Thames Barrier
North Woolwich
OLD STATION RAILWAY MUSEUM
Woolwich Ferry
THAMES BARRIER VISITOR CENTRE
WOOLWICH
THE VALLEY
Thamesmead
CROSSNESS PUMPING STATION
Abbey Wood
Plumstead
Belvedere
XIX
GREENWICH
Greenwich Park
Charlton
Woolwich Common
Bostall Woods
West Heath
Lessness Heath
East Wickham
Sun in the Sands Rdbt
Shooters Hill
Kidbrooke
Eltham Common
Oxleas Wood
Welling
Bexleyheath
BLACKHEATH
Kidbrooke Intc
Blackheath Park
Falconwood
Danson Park
THE RED HOUSE
Danson Interchange
BEXLEY
LEWISHAM
Hither Green
Yorkshire Grey
ELTHAM
Avery Hill
Blackfen
Lee
Cliftons Rdbt
ELTHAM PALACE
Old Bexley
New Eltham
Mottingham
Longlands
SIDCUP
North Cray
Grove Park
Downham
Elmstead Wood
Elmstead
Foots Cray
Plaistow
Sundridge Park
Chislehurst Common
XXVI
CHISLEHURST
Frognal Corner
Scadbury Park Nature Reserve
Crinall's Corner
Ruxley
Upper Ruxley
18
54

XV
Upminster
Hornchurch
Rush Green
Eastbrookend
Elm Park
Corbets Tey
Hacton
North Ockenden
River Ingrebourne
Hornchurch
South Hornchurch
Dagenham
Rainham Hall (N.T.)
Rainham
Belhus Woods
South Ockendon
Grangewater
Belhus Park
Wennington
North Stifford
Aveley
Wennington Marshes
High Speed 1 (Channel Tunnel Rail Link)
Thurrock Services
Aveley Marshes
Mar Dyke
Chafford Hundred
Lakeside Shopping Centre
Erith
Purfleet
West Thurrock
South Stifford
North End
Crayford Marshes
Dartford Marshes
Dartford Crossing
West Thurrock Marshes
Grays
Northumberland Heath
Dartford Tunnel
Barnehurst
Slade Green
River Darent
Queen Elizabeth II Bridge
River Thames
Swanscombe Marshes
Crayford
Temple Hill
Greenhithe
Barnes Cray
Stone
Stone Lodge Farm Park
Hall Place
Dartford
Swanscombe
Coldblow
Bluewater Shopping Centre
Fleet-Downs
Swanscombe Park
Maypole
Darenth Wood
Bean
Hook Green
Wilmington
Joyden's Wood
Darenth
Lane End
Lords Wood
Betsham
Beacon Wood
Hawley
Southfleet
St. John's Jerusalem (N.T.)
Hextable
Clement Street
Green St Green
Sutton-at-
XXVII

XVI
EGHAM
Knowle Green
Milton Park
Stroude
Callow Hill
Virginia Water
Thorpe
THORPE PARK
Laleham
Littleton
Queen Mary Reservoir
Charlton
Shepperton Green
Upper Halliford
Shepperton
Lower Halliford
CHERTSEY
CHERTSEY MUSEUM
Lyne
Chertsey Common
Addlestonemoor
Woburn Park
WEYBRIDGE
ELMBRIDGE MUSEUM
Oatlands Park
ADDLESTONE
Ottershaw
Row Town
New Haw
BROOKLANDS MUSEUM
St George's Hill
FAIROAKS AERODROME
Woodham
Brooklands
Whiteley Village
Anningsley Park
Dartnell Park
Horsell Common
Sheerwater
West Byfleet
Byfleet
COBHAM BUS MUSEUM
Silver Mere
Pain's Hill
Cheapside
Horsell
Foxwarren Park
Pyrford
Wisley
Maybury
Pyrford Green
Wisley Common
Bolder Mere
Telegraph Hill
R.H.S. GARDEN WISLEY
WOKING
Elm Corner
Hook Heath
Ripley Green
Martyr's Green
Bridge End
Westfield
Old Woking
Ripley
Ockham Park
Church End
Ockham
Mayford
Cartbridge
Send
Send Marsh
Hungry Hill
Sutton Green
River Thames
M25
M3
A3
A320
A317
A318
A319
A245
A308
A244
A3050
A247
A3046
B3376
B388
B389
B377
B376
B3366
B375
B387
B386
B3121
B385
B373
B372
B374
B366
B382
B367
B380
B2215
B368
B2039
B378
THORPE BY-PASS
RIPLEY BY-PASS
PORTSMOUTH ROAD
WOODHAM LANE
GUILDFORD ROAD
ST GEORGE'S AVE
BYFLEET ROAD
CHERTSEY LANE
STAINES ROAD
KINGSTON RD
SHEPPERTON RD
LALEHAM RD
CHERTSEY RD
WEYBRIDGE RD
HIGH ST
CHOBHAM ROAD
VICTORIA WAY
OLD WOKING ROAD
SEND ROAD
SEND MARSH RD
NEWARK LANE
OCKHAM ROAD NORTH
River Wey
Broad Water
17
16
50

XXIII
XVII
XXIV
TEDDINGTON
Hampton
Bushy Park
Hampton Wick
Kingston Br
Norbiton
NEW MALDEN
SUNBURY
KEMPTON PARK
Molesey Reservoirs
Bessborough Res
Knight Res
River Thames
Hampton Ct Br
HAMPTON COURT PALACE
Hampton Court Park
County Hall
Univ
SURBITON
East Molesey
Queen Elizabeth II Reservoir
Island Barn Reservoir
Thames Ditton
Berrylands
WALTON-ON-THAMES
Fieldcommon
River Ember
Coll
Rydens
SANDOWN PARK
Hinchley Wood
Long Ditton
Tolworth
Littleworth Common
Govt Offices
Hook Interchange
ESHER
HERSHAM
CHESSINGTON
HORTON
West End Common
River Mole
CLAREMONT LANDSCAPE GARDEN
CLAYGATE
Arbrook Common
West Ewell
Esher Common
CHESSINGTON WORLD OF ADVENTURES
Oxshott
Heath
Malden Rushett
Fairmile
Prince's Coverts
Cobham
Oxshott
Stoke Wood
Epsom Common
EPSOM
The Forest
Little Heath
Cobham Park
Stoke D'Abernon
Pachesham Park
Wood Field
Woodcote
Downside
Lower Ashstead
Langley Vale
Leatherhead Common
Ashstead
LEATHERHEAD
Banks Common
Great Bookham Common
Little Bookham Common
Fetcham
Tyrell's Wood
Effingham Common
Leatherhead Downs
Nower Wood
Little Bookham
BROCKETTS FARM PARK
Givons Grove
Headley
Great Bookham
Fetcham Downs
Mickleham Downs
A316
A308
A3050
A309
A307
A3
A240
A244
A317
A243
A245
A24
A246
B2430
B2122
M25
17
16
52

XVIII
NEW MALDEN
Raynes Park
Bushey Mead
MORDEN
Morden Hall Park
MITCHAM
Mitcham Common
Berrylands
West Barnes
Morden Park
Motspur Park
Lower Morden
Rosehill
St Helier
Beddington Corner
Old Malden
Tolworth
Hackbridge
Beddington Park
Worcester Park
North Cheam
CARSHALTON
Stoneleigh
WALLINGTON
SUTTON
Nonsuch Park
West Ewell
Ewell
Organ Crossroads
CHEAM
Belmont
Carshalton on the Hill
South Beddington
East Ewell
Little Woodcote
Oaks Park
XXIII
EPSOM
North Looe
Woodmansterne
Clock House
16
Nork
BANSTEAD
Woodcote
Coulsdon
Great Burgh
Park Downs
Chipstead
Langley Vale
Burgh Heath
Banstead Wood
Walton Downs
Kingswood
Hooley
Tadworth
Walton on the Hill
Nower Wood
Headley
Banstead Heath
Lower Kingswood
Walton Heath
Headley Heath
52
Mogador
Margery
Gatton
Merstham
Buckland Hills
A3
A24
A217
A232
A240
A2043
A2022
A23
M25
A237
A297
A239
A298
A238
B2032
B2219
B2220
B2221
B2217
B2230
B278
B279
B284
B280
B290
B291
B2033

BECKENHAM
Anerley
South Norwood
Elmers End
Eden Park
Shortlands
Park Langley
THORNTON HEATH
Selhurst
Woodside
Upper Elmers End
West Wickham
Hayes
Shirley Oaks
CROYDON
ADDISCOMBE
Shirley
Spring Park
Coney Hall
BEDDINGTON
Waddon
Upper Shirley
Coombe Park
Spring Park
Addington
Nash
South Croydon
Roundshaw
New Addington
Selsdon
Russell Hill
Purley
Sanderstead
Selsdon Wood
Kings Wood
Farleigh
Fickleshole
Kenley
Hamsey Green
Chelsham
Kenley Common
Whyteleafe
Warlingham
Old Coulsdon
Woldingham Garden Village
Woldingham
Botley Hill
Chaldon
CATERHAM
Winders Hill
Gravelly Hill
Warwick Wold
OXTED

XIX
XXVI

XX
XXV
CHISLEHURST
BROMLEY
ORPINGTON
Chislehurst Common
Sundridge Park
Elmstead
Foots Cray
Frognal Corner
Scadbury Park Nature Reserve
Critnall's Corner
Ruxley
Upper Ruxley
Widmore
Bickley
Shortlands
St Paul's Cray
Hockenden
Petts Wood
Poverest
St Mary Cray
Kevingtown
Broom Hill
Southborough
Bromley Common
Hayes
Keston Mark
Crofton
Locksbottom
Goddington
Coney Hall
Keston
The Fantail
Farnborough
Chelsfield
Maypole
Nash
Green Street Green
High Elms
Cuckoo Wood
Pratt's Bottom
Leaves Green
Downe
Down House (Charles Darwin Museum)
Hazelwood
Halstead
Biggin Hill Aerodrome
Luxted
Newyears Wood
Fickleshole
Single Street
Cudham
Knockholt Pound
Berry's Green
Knockholt
Letts Green
Biggin Hill
Horns Green
Chevening
South Street
Tatsfield Green
Tatsfield
Botley Hill
Hill Park
Force Green
River Darent
Sundridge
Titsey
Brasted
Quebec House (N.T.)
Farley Common
Titsey Wood
Clacket Lane Services
Westerham
Chislehurst Caves
Jubilee
M25
A21
A20
A222
A232
A233
A208
A223
A224
A25
B264
B265
B228
B251
B2158
B258
B2024
B2211

XXVII
XXI
17
Hextable
Clement Street
Sutton-at-Hone
South Darenth
Green St Green
Pinden
Longfield
Swanley Village
Swanley
Horton Kirby
Farningham Wood
Hartley Green
Farningham
Crockenhill
Horton Wood
Eynsford Castle
Eynsford
Fawkham Green
Bird of Prey Centre
Lullingstone Roman Villa
Lullingstone Castle
Beechen Wood
Maplescombe
Brands Hatch
Ash
High Castle Wood
West Kingsdown
Timberden Bottom
Knatts Valley
Shoreham
Romney Street
Magpie Bottom
Woodlands
Twitton
Otford
Crowdleham
Kemsing
Heaverham
Wrotham
Dunton Green
Longford
Greatness
Seal
Styants Bottom
Oldbury
Ightham
Chipstead
Riverhead
Wildernesse
Seal Chart
Godden Green
Stone Street
Ightham Common
SEVENOAKS
Kippington
Knole (N.T.)
Lower Bitchet
Bitchet Green
Ivy Hatch
Yopps Green
Fawke Common
Knole Park
M25
M20
M26
A20
A225
A224
A25
A227
B2019
B258
B260
B2173
River Darent
Dartford Road
Main Road
London Road
Maidstone Rd
Sevenoaks Road
Ightham By-Pass
Pilgrims Way
Seal Rd
High St
Otford Rd
London Rd
Bradbourne Vale Rd
St John's Hill
Tonbridge Road
St John's Jerusalem (N.T.)

Key to map symbols

Roads

- **Motorway with junction number** (22a)
- **Primary route** – single, dual carriageway
- **A road** – single, dual carriageway
- **B road** – single, dual carriageway
- **Through-route** – single, dual carriageway
- **Minor road** – single, dual carriageway
- **Road under construction**
- **Rural track, private road or narrow road in urban area**
- **Path, bridleway, byway open to all traffic, road used as public path**
- **Tunnel, covered road**
- **Speed camera** – single, multiple (30)
- **Congestion Charge Zone boundary** Roads within the zone are outlined in green
- **Gate or obstruction, car pound**
- **Parking, park and ride** (P, P&R)
- **Road junction name** (Crooked Billet)
- **Pedestrianised, restricted access area**

Public transport

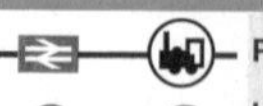

- **Railway station, private rail station**
- **London Underground station, Docklands Light Railway station**
- **Tramway or miniature railway**
- **Bus or coach station, tram stop**

Scale

3½ inches to 1 mile 1:18103

0 220yds 440yds 660yds ½ mile

0 250m 500m 750m 1km

Emergency services

- **Ambulance, police, fire station**
- **Hospital, accident and emergency entrance** (H)

General features

- **Market, public amenity site**
- **Sports stadium**
- **Information centre, post office** (i, PO)
- **Roman, non-Roman antiquity** (VILLA, *House*)
- **House number, spot height** – metres (100, .304)
- **Christian place of worship**
- **Mosque, synagogue**
- **Other place of worship**
- **Houses, important buildings**
- **Woods, parkland/common**
- **Adjoining page number** (123)

Leisure facilities

- **Camp site, caravan site**
- **Golf course, picnic site, view point**

Boundaries

- **Postcode boundaries** (NW6)
- **County and unitary authority boundaries** (Westminster)

Water features

- **Water name**
- **Tidal water**
- **River or canal** – minor, major
- **Stream**
- **Water**

Abbreviations

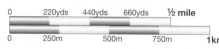

Acad	Academy
Allot Gdns	Allotments
Bndstd	Bandstand
Btcl	Botanical
Bwg Gn	Bowling
Cemy	Cemetery
Ctr	Centre
C Ctr	Civic Centre
CH	Club House
Ctry Pk	Country Park
Coll	College
Ct	Court
Crem	Crematorium
Crkt	Cricket
Ent	Enterprise
Ex H	Exhibition Hall
Fball	Football
Gdns	Gardens
Glf C	Golf Course
Glf Crs	Golf Course
Drv Rng	Golf Driving Range
Gn	Green
Gd	Ground
Hort	Horticultural
Ind Est	Industrial Estate
Inst	Institute
Int	Interchange
Ct	Law Court
L Ctr	Leisure Centre
LC	Level Crossing
Liby	Library
Mkt	Market
Meml	Memorial
Mon	Monument
Mus	Museum
Nat Res	Nature Reserve
Obsy	Observatory
Pav	Pavilion
Pk	Park
Pl Fld	Playing Field
Pal	Royal Palace
PH	Public House
Recn Gd	Recreation Ground
Resr	Reservoir
Ret Pk	Retail Park
Sch	School
Sh Ctr	Shopping Centre
Sp	Sports
Stad	Stadium
Sw Pool	Swimming Pool
Tenn Cts	Tennis
TH	Town Hall
Trad Est	Trading Estate
Univ	University
YH	Youth Hostel

A1000 Potters Bar
A
B
C
D
Wrotham Park
Home Farm
Cockshot Hill
Ganwick Farm
WAGON RD
Lower Kitt's End Farm
KITT'S END RD
Kitt's End
Kitt's End Farm
BARNET RD
A1000
Bartram's Quash
Hertfordshire
Enfield
Pl Fld
Hadley Wood
GREENACRE CL
BEAUMONT PL
HADLEY HIGHSTONE
Hertfordshire
Barnet
EN4
Barnet
Enfield
Old Fold Manor
LANGLEY ROW
TAYLOR'S LA
OLD FOLD CL
FOLD LA
MILL CNR
Tenn Cts
Monken Hadley CE Prim Sch
St Martha's Senior Sch
CAMLET WAY
HATHERLEIGH CL
PAGITTS GR
BROADGATES AVE
PARKGATE AVE
PARKGATE CRES
BOUNDARY CL
EN5
Hadley Green
Convent
DURY RD
Bournwell Hill
Monken Hadley Common
Allot Gdns
ST ALBANS RD
SYDNEY CHAPMAN WAY
HADLEY GREEN RD
HADLEY GN W
Monken Hadley
HADLEY GN
SUNSET VIEW
Cemy
HADLEY WOOD RD
Priddeon's Hill
HADLEY GR
GLADSMUIR RD
WROTHAM RD
FALKLAND RD
PULLER RD
CHRIST CHURCH LA
LIVINGSTONE CT
FIRE STATION AL
London Loop
BAKERS HILL
THE SPINNEY
HADLEY HTS
THE CRESCENT
The Tudor
Tudor Sp Gd
TA Ctr
A1081
Barnet Mkt
GROVE CT
BELGRAVIA CL
HADLEY RIDGE
WYBURN AVE
EAST VIEW
Hadley
King George's Field
LATIMER RD
SHAKESPEARE CT
LOWNDES CT
HADLEYVALE CT
CLIFFORD RD
VINCENT CL
Allot Gdns
TUDOR RD
CH
Tenn Cts
SEBRIGHT RD
ALSTON RD
LUCAN RD
STRAFFORD RD
CARNARVON RD
Liby
CHIPPING CL
BRUCE RD
BATH PL
HYDE CL
HURST RISE
JULIAN CL
NORFOLK RD
SANDFORD CT
RONALD CT
HADLEY RD
ORCHARD CT
SLADE CT
Allot Gdns
PENRAY
WENTWORTH
SALISBURY RD
STAPYLTON RD
The Spires
GREAT NORTH RD
High Barnet
SOUTH CL
MOON LA
MOXON ST
BOSWORTH RD
CATHERINE CT
DENBY CT
WOODVILLE RD
Cromer Road Sch
THE DRIVE
THE AVENUE
THORNTON RD
HART LO
UNION ST
Sch
PO
GILLINGS CT
TAPSTER ST
VICTORS WAY
Barnet Trad Est
Pl Fld
Tenn Cts
MEADWAY CL
BURNSIDE CL
MARK'S CL
PEARSON CL
POTTER'S RD
SHERIDAN LO
Pl Flds
CROMER RD
SHAFTESBURY AVE
BOLEYN WAY
WOOD ST
A411
HIGH ST
PARK RD
QUEEN ELIZABETH CT
GORDON WAY
Queen Elizabeth's Sch
MEADWAY
MARTINS MOUNT
EN5
CRABTREE CT
HEXHAM RD
HADRIAN CT
HUGHENDON
BARNARD LO
CATTLEY CL
Mus
Barnet Coll
MANOR CL
ELM RD
KINGSMEAD
HILLARY RISE
KING EDWARD RD
BARON CT
SHELDON CT
BULWER RD
BULWER GDNS
MASEFIELD CT
HASTINGS
SUTHERLAND CL
SCHOLARS CL
Bwg Gns
ORCHARD RD
VICTORIA LA
LAWN MANS
High Barnet
POTTER'S LA
PROSPECT RD
LEAF HO
WARWICK RD
VALE CT
LEICESTER RD
PLANTAGENET RD
DUNCAN CL
LEECROFT RD
PINECROFT CR
MANORSIDE
HILLSIDE GDNS
Chipping Barnet
AVENUE MANS
HILLSIDE MANS
A1000
BARNET HILL
BRACKENWOOD LO
WINDERMERE HO
MERTON CT
BARNES CT
RODINGS ROW
WILLOW DR
MANOR RD
Tenn Cts
NEWLYN RD
FITZJOHN AVE
NORMANDY AVE
BEDFORD AVE
HILTON AVE
WOODFALL AVE
VALE DR
Sch
RAVENSCROFT COTTS
ESMOND CT
ABBOTTS RD
THE HIGHLANDS
Highlands Gdns
HIGHWOOD CT
HIGHLANDS RD
HOMESTEAD CT
STATION RD
MOWBRAY RD
ASHLEY CT
COLGATE CT
TELFORD CT
A110
ELLESMERE GR
ELTON AVE
MARSTON
13
UNDERHILL CT
COLLINGWOOD
SOMERSET RD
NORTH LO
THE THOMAS WATSON COTTAGE HOMES
Allot Gdns
BARNET
POTTERIES
BROOK PL
WESTCOMBE DR
FAIRFIELD
New Barnet
Lyonsdown Sch
RICHMOND
BARRIE
Hertfordshire STREET ATLAS
A1081 Hatfield (A1(M)), M25
A411 Borehamwood, A1

Hertfordshire STREET ATLAS
A111 Potters Bar, M25
A
B
C
D
Cockshot Hill
Ganwick Farm
Spoilbank Wood
Slopers Pond Farm
Salmon's Brook
STAGG HILL A111
WAGON RD
WAGGON RD
Hertfordshire
Enfield
Bartram's Quash
Pl Fld
Hadley Wood Prim Sch
Hadley Wood
Tenn Cts
CLAREMONT RD
COURTLEIGH AVE
DUCHY RD
HELENA CL
SANDRIDGE CL
Monken Mead Brook
KINGWELL RD
West Lodge Park (Hotel)
LANCASTER AVE
GABLE LO
BARTRAMS LA
PO
Hadley Wood
CRESCENT W
CRESCENT E
ALDERWOOD MEWS
ST RONANS CL
PARKLANDS CL
OLD ORCHARD CL
FERNY HILL
BEECH HILL
Great Broadgates Hill
CORBAR CL
WALMAR CL
WOOD RIDE
CH
EN4
MUSGRAVE CL
BEECH HILL AVE
BURWOOD PL
CAMLET WAY
BROADGATES AV
PARKGATE AVE
PARKGATE CRES
NEWMAN'S WAY
GREENBROOK AVE
COVERT WAY
Fernyhill Wood
Hadley Wood
Green Brook
Monken Hadley Common
Nature Reserve
Sewits Hill
Newman's Hill
GREENOAK PL
DORMERS LO
KINGSDALE CT
COOMBEHURST CL
COCKFOSTERS RD
Enfield
Barnet
Wr Twr
BAKERS HILL
THE SPINNEY
HADLEY HTS
The Tudor
HADLEY WOOD RD
Beech Hill Lake
London Loop
Tudor Sp Gd
East Barnet Sch
Tenn Cts
Livingstone Prim Sch
BOURNWELL CL
SOVEREIGN MEWS
FAIRGREEN
FAIRGREEN CT
FAIRGREEN E
HADLEYVALE CT
CLIFFORD RD
CH
Tenn Cts
Pav
HERTFORD CL
WESTBROOK SQ
HERTFORD RD
WESTBROOK CRES
WESTBROOK CL
ARMSTRONG CRES
ARUNDEL RD
SOMERCOATES CL
NORTHFIELD RD
LINTHORPE RD
THE GRANGE
GAMES RD
HADLEY RD
ORCHARD CT
Allot Gdns
GALDANA AVE
BOLEYN WAY
MORREL CL
CASTLEWOOD RD
BARING RD
FORDHAM CL
GROVE RD
LUDGROVE HALL
Pl Flds
LICHFIELD CL
OAKHAM CL
WEST FARM CT
VERWOOD DR
Bwg Gn
Cromer Road Sch
LAWTON RD
FORDHAM RD
LUDGROVE CT
MOUNT PAR
OSBORNE CL
CHERITON CL
GATCOMBE WAY
THE PADDOCKS
CHALK LA
EN5
POTTER'S RD
SHERIDAN LO
Pl Flds
CROMER RD
SHAFTESBURY AVE
LEE CL
ARTESIAN GR
MIDDLETON CT
Tenn Cts
ST JAMES CL
Victoria Recn Gd
APPLETREE GDNS
KENLEY CL
EDGEWORTH RD
PO
ROSEFIELD CL
LANGFORD RD
WILTON RD
Pav
Sp Gd
CRABTREE CT
HEXHAM RD
HADRIAN CT
HUGHENDON
BARNARD LO
BULWER GDNS
HASTINGS CL
MASEFIELD CT
STOCKTON CL
Bwg Gn
Pymme's Brook
PYMMES BROOK DR
PENDALL CL
PENSILVER CL
The Abbey Art Ctr
HAMILTON RD
HAMILTON CL
BEVAN RD
LANGFORD CRES
CHRIST CHURCH LO
BULWER RD
PLANTAGENET RD
LYTTON RD
NEWBURY HO
ALBERT RD
GLYN AVE
ALEXANDER CL
VICTORIA RD
PARK RD
SILVERCLIFFE GDNS
HERONS RISE
Trent CE Prim Sch
CHURCH WAY
VALE CT
LEICESTER RD
MERTON CT
BARNES CT
DUNCAN CL
FALCON CT
A110
STATION APP
APPROACH RD
EAST BARNET RD
MULBERRY CL
MARGARET CT
MARGARET RD
CHICHESTER CT
HILL CT
BOTANY CL
WALDEN HO
DIANNE WAY
ELY HO
ROLFE CL
IBSLEY WAY
CARSON RD
MOUNT PLEASANT
Cockfosters
EVELYN RD
NORRYS RD
NORRYS CL
STATION RD
NOWBRAY RD
ASHLEY CT
SOMERSET RD
NORTH
TEWKESBURY CL
VICTORIA AVE
VICTORIA CL
CRESCENT RD
MOUNT RD
HIGH TREES
ECCLESTON CL
BELL AVE
HEDDON CT
ASHURST RD
HEDDON COURT AVE
New Barnet
Lyonsdown Sch
RICHMOND RD
WALTON CT
LYONSDOWN RD
CLARENCE CL
New Barnet
EDWARD
HENRY RD
BRUNSWICK
BROWNLOW
LANCASTER
ST WILFRID'S CL
ST WILFRID'S RD
CRESCENT RISE
ADDINGTON CL
PILGRIM'S RISE
KEELY CL
Pleasure Gd
Allot Gdns
BARRIE CT
EASTBURY CT
YORK
Tenn
99
98
97
96
6
5
4
3
2
1
26
27
14
30

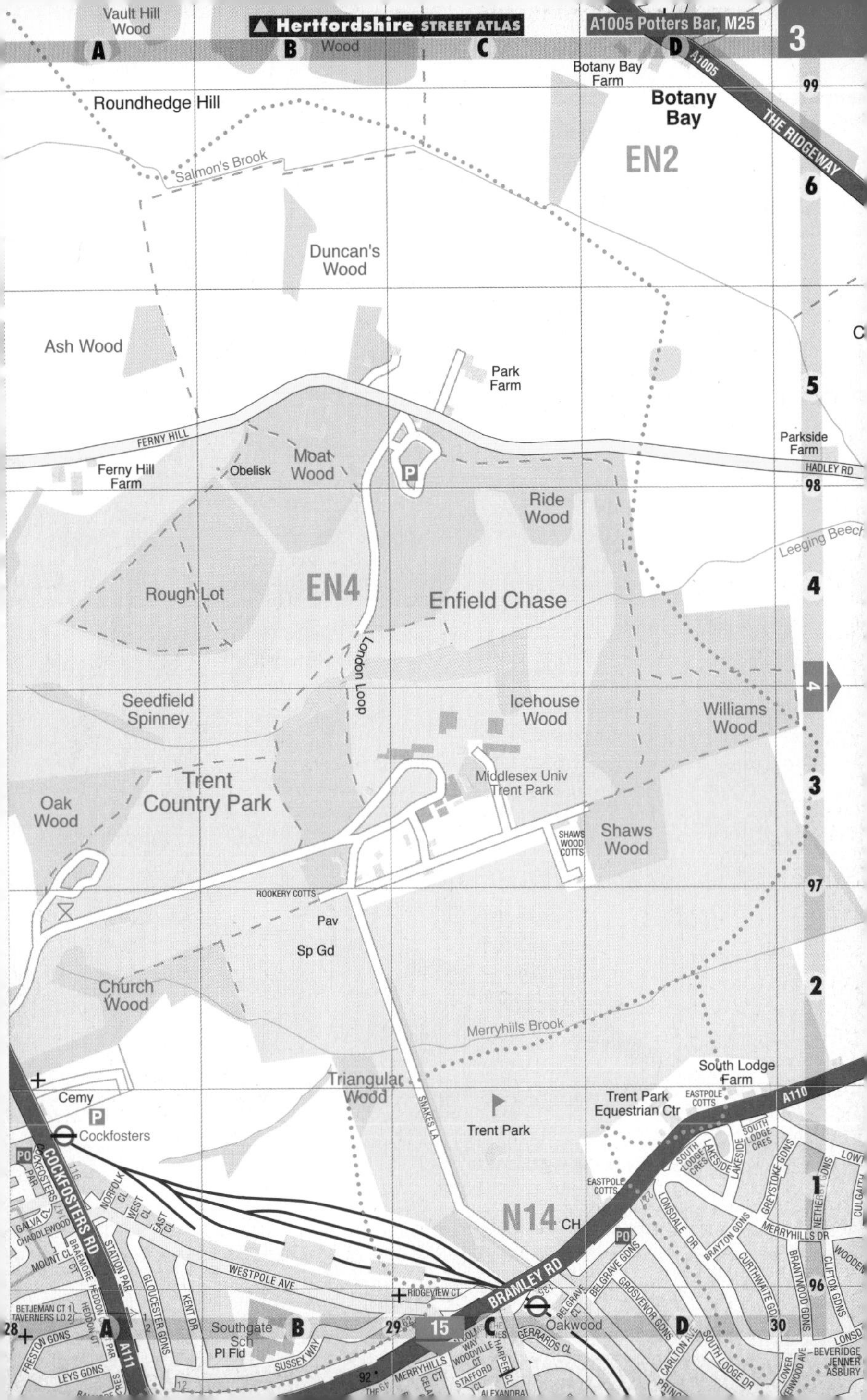
Vault Hill Wood
A
B
C
D
Wood
A1005
THE RIDGEWAY
Botany Bay Farm
Botany Bay
99
Roundhedge Hill
Salmon's Brook
EN2
6
Duncan's Wood
Ash Wood
Park Farm
5
FERNY HILL
Parkside Farm
HADLEY RD
Ferny Hill Farm
Obelisk
Moat Wood
P
98
Ride Wood
Leeging Beech
Rough Lot
EN4
Enfield Chase
4
London Loop
4
Seedfield Spinney
Icehouse Wood
Williams Wood
Middlesex Univ Trent Park
3
Trent Country Park
Oak Wood
SHAWS WOOD COTTS
Shaws Wood
ROOKERY COTTS
97
Pav
Sp Gd
Church Wood
2
Merryhills Brook
South Lodge Farm
Triangular Wood
Cemy
Trent Park Equestrian Ctr
EASTPOLE COTTS
A110
SNAKES LA
Trent Park
Cockfosters
PO
COCKFOSTERS RD
COCKFOSTERS PAR
NORFOLK CL
WEST CL
EAST CL
SOUTH LODGE CRES
LAKESIDE
SOUTH LODGE CRES
GREYSTOKE GDNS
NETHERCOURT GDNS
LOW...
1
EASTPOLE COTTS
GALVA CL
CHADDLEWOOD
MOUNT CL
BRAEMORE CT
STATION PAR
N14
CH
LONSDALE DR
MERRYHILLS DR
PO
BELGRAVE GDNS
BRAYTON GDNS
CURTHWAITE GDNS
BRANTWOOD GDNS
CLIFTON GDNS
WESTPOLE AVE
BRAMLEY RD
GROSVENOR GDNS
96
BETJEMAN CT
TAVERNERS LO
HEDDON CT
GLOUCESTER GDNS
KENT DR
RIDGEVIEW CT
BELGRAVE CT
28
A
Southgate Sch
B
29
15
C
Oakwood
D
30
FRESTON GDNS
Pl Fld
SUSSEX WAY
GERRARDS CL
CARLTON AVE
SOUTH LODGE DR
LOWER ...WOOD AVE
BEVERIDGE
JENNER
ASBURY
LEYS GDNS
A111
92
MERRYHILLS CL
WOODVILLE CT
STAFFORD CL
HARPER CL
ALEXANDRA

4
Hertfordshire STREET ATLAS
A
B
C
D
King's Oak Plain
St John's CE Prim Sch
THEOBALDS PARK RD
STRAYFIELD RD
ROSSENDALE CL
Nursery
PH
Queenswood Farm
The Red House
Rectory Farm
THE RIDGEWAY
A1005
99
6
5
4
3
2
1
98
97
96
Turkey Brook
The Kings Oak (Private)
EN2
London Loop
Cuckolds Hill
Hotel
HIGHRIDGE PL
KINGFISHER CT
ROUNDHEDGE WAY
WILLIAM COVELL CL
SPRING COURT RD
OAK AVE
MOUNT VIEW
HOLYWELL LO
HIGH OAKS
ARAGON CL
Chase Farm
Allot Gdns
Cemy
Parkside Farm
HADLEY RD
RIDGE CREST
HARFIELD CL
HUNTERS WAY
ALBUHERA CL
SHOOTERS RD
COMREDDY CL
LAVENDER HILL
LAVENDER GDNS
RENDLESHAM
Leeging Beech Gutter
Vicarage Farm
FARORNA WLK
FARMLANDS
JAYCROFT
HARDY WAY
ACORN CL
HARRIS CL
LEE VIEW
HEDGE HILL
Gordon Hill
FAIRVIEW RD
HANSART WAY
DRAPERS RD
Cts
Hog Hill
WOODRIDGE CL
AVALON CL
JOHN GOOCH DR
PADSTOW RD
HOLTWHITE'S HILL
WOODSIDE CT
BANKSIDE CL
CHASEWOOD AVE
HEATHER DR
Williams Wood
AMESBURY CT 1
CAPSTAN RIDE 2
KINGS CHASE VIEW 3
CROFTON WAY
LANSDOWNE HO
DUNRAVEN DR
INGLEBOROUGH
VALLEY FIELDS CRES
CAVELL DR
AUDLEY RD
SORBUS CT
ROWANTREE RD
MCADAM DR
WELLESLEY PARK MEWS
PERRY MEAD
BYCULLAH RD
ROBSON CL
COPPERWOOD LO
BYRON CT
RIDDELL LO
North London Nuffield
THE GROVE
HAVENHURST RISE
VULCAN GATE
UPLANDS PARK RD
STOCKBRIDGE HO
CANFORD CL
ROWANWOOD MEWS
HOLLY TREE LO
HERMITAGE CL
CHASE RIDINGS
ENGLEFIELD CL
MILNE CT
CULLODEN RD
CEDARWOOD HO
PARK WAY
WINDMILL GDNS
SLADES GDNS
THE GLADE
POSTERN GN
RIDGEMOUNT GDNS
COLONELS WLK
TEMPLE GR
PINEWOOD CT
BYCULLAH AVE
THE OAKS
OAKDENE HO
BYCULLAH CT
GLEBE AVE
BERKELEY LO
TRENTWOOD SIDE
GRAFTON RD
ELMER CL
Allot Gdns
SLADES HILL
FIONA CT
HIGH DENE
TAUNTON DR
SLADES CL
SLADES RISE
HUNTING GATE CL
WINDMILL HILL
A110
PO
LINKSIDE GDNS
LINKSIDE CL
LINKS SIDE
BINCOTE RD
FOXMEAD CL
Liby
ENFIELD RD
30
COTSWOLD WAY
WINSMOOR CT 1
THORPE CT 2
WANSBECK CT 3
THE OLD SCHOOL HO 4
BARRYDENE CT 5
SALMONS BROOK HO 6
THORNBURY LO 7
OLD PARK VIEW
MILLERS GREEN CL
HIGH ACRE
OLD PARK RD
CALSHOT WAY
HELEN CLARE CT
WYNDCROFT CL
WAVERLEY RD
BADGERS
CRESCENT RD
South Lodge Farm
EASTPOLE COTTS
World's End
Merryhills Prim Sch
COTSWOLD GN
GLENBROOK N
GLENBROOK S
Salmon's Brook
CH
THE HASELWOOD DR
COPPICE
THE GLEN
OLD PARK RD S
GLADBECK
Enfield
MOUNTFORD HO 1
CLAREMONT HTS 2
ELMWOOD HO 3
LAKESIDE
SOUTH LODGE CRES
GREYSTOKE GDNS
NETHERBY GDNS
LOWTHER DR
CORBY CRES
CULGAITH GDNS
BEWCASTLE GDNS
LONSDALE DR N
CHILTERN DENE
Boxer's Lake
Highlands Sch
LONSDALE DR
N21
BRAYTON GDNS
MERRYHILLS DR
CURTHWAITE GDNS
BRANTWOOD GDNS
CLIFTON GDNS
WOODEND GDNS
SILVERDALE
ROUNDHILL DR
RUSHEY HILL
LINDAL CRES
Grange Park Prim Sch
CHADWICK AVE
WORLD'S END LA
1 ADAM LO
2 SUTTON HO
6 AVON HO
7 SYLVAN HO
8 ASPEN HO
9 PITCAIRNE CT
10 GILLIES CT
BARNABAS CT
TARNBANK
CORFIELD RD
SIMPSON CL
BUCHANAN CL
HANSEN DR
FLEMING
TRESILIAN AVE
MACLEOD RD
UPLANDS WAY
Allot Gdns
16
31
BEVERIDGE CT 1
JENNER CT 2
ASBURY CT 3
SEACOLE LO
TREVES CL
ANDERSON CL
FLOREY SQ
DONOVAN PL
SOUTH LODGE DR

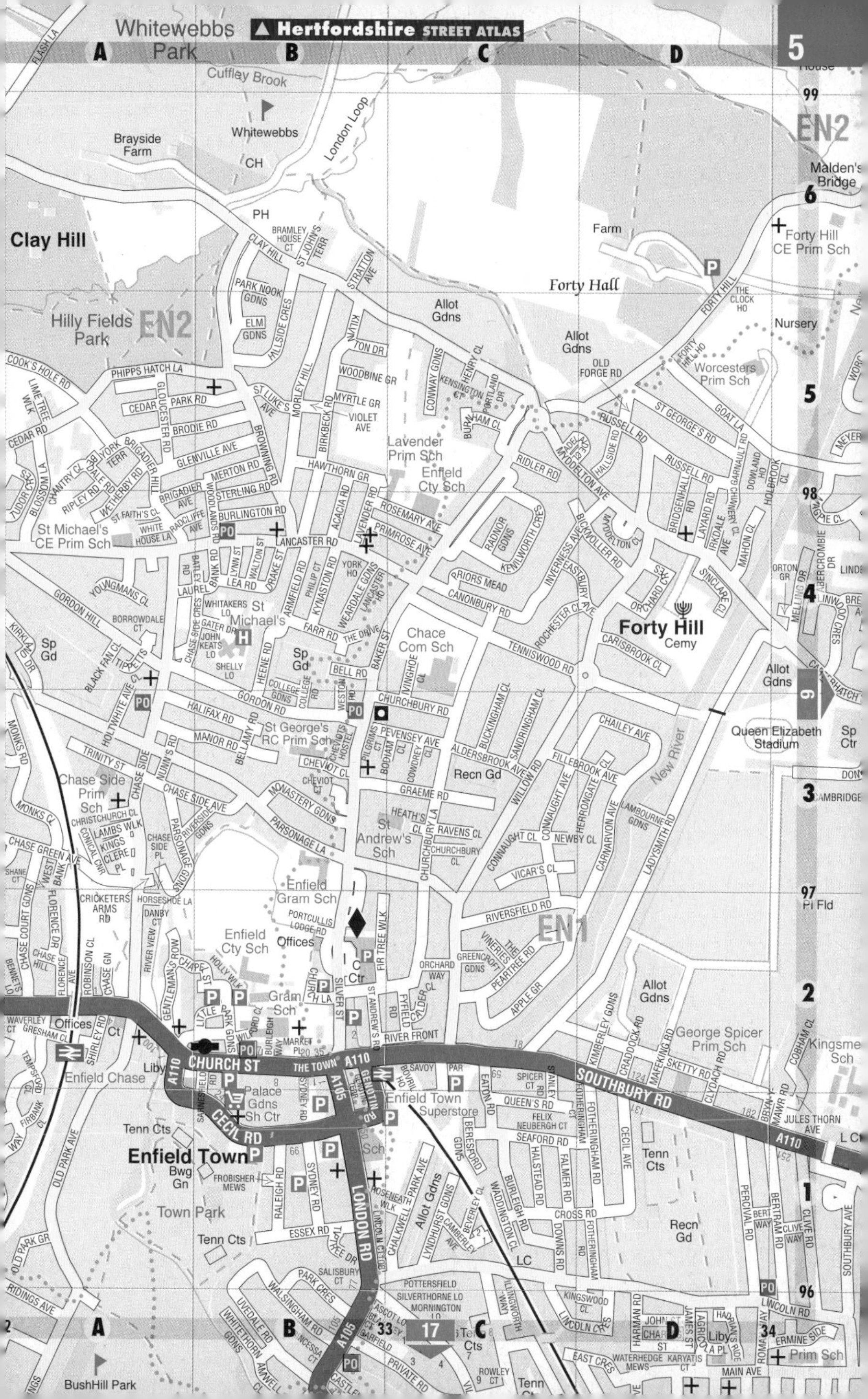
Whitewebbs Park
Cuffley Brook
Whitewebbs
Brayside Farm
London Loop
Clay Hill
Hilly Fields Park
EN2
Forty Hall
Allot Gdns
Farm
Forty Hill CE Prim Sch
Malden's Bridge
Nursery
Worcesters Prim Sch
Lavender Prim Sch
Enfield Cty Sch
St Michael's CE Prim Sch
St Michael's
Chase Side Prim Sch
Chace Com Sch
St George's RC Prim Sch
St Andrew's Sch
Forty Hill Cemy
Queen Elizabeth Stadium
Enfield Gram Sch
Enfield Cty Sch
Offices
Recn Gd
New River
EN1
George Spicer Prim Sch
Kingsmead Sch
Enfield Chase
Enfield Town
Enfield Town Superstore
Palace Gdns Sh Ctr
Town Park
Tenn Cts
Bush Hill Park
CHURCH ST
SOUTHBURY RD
LONDON RD
CECIL RD
A110
A105
A
B
C
D
17
33
34

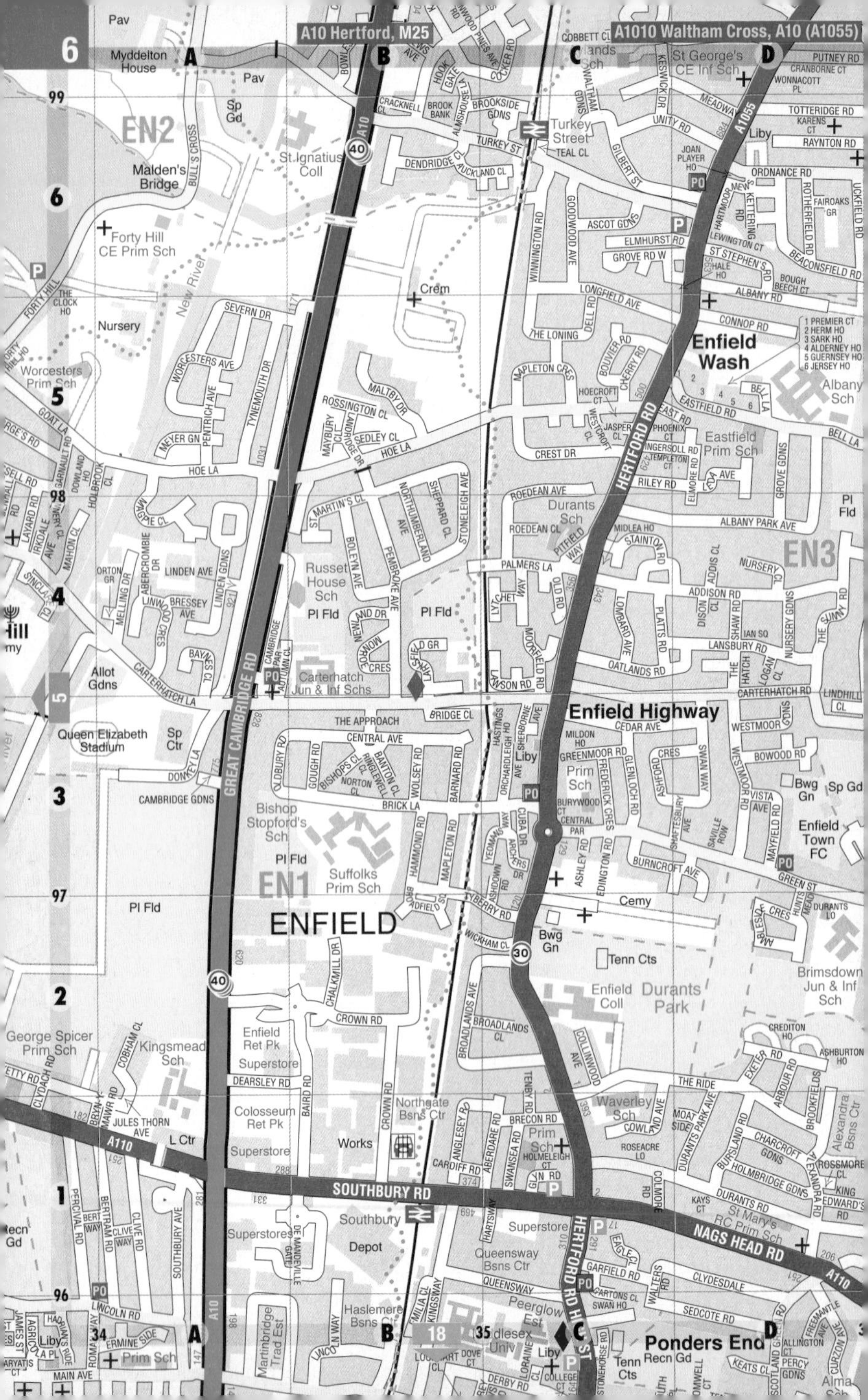
A10 Hertford, M25
A1010 Waltham Cross, A10 (A1055)
EN2
EN1
EN3
ENFIELD
Enfield Wash
Enfield Highway
Ponders End
GREAT CAMBRIDGE RD
HERTFORD RD
SOUTHBURY RD
NAGS HEAD RD
HOE LA
CARTERHATCH LA
Turkey Street
Southbury
Forty Hill CE Prim Sch
Malden's Bridge
Myddelton House
St Ignatius Coll
Crem
Russet House Sch
Carterhatch Jun & Inf Schs
Durants Sch
Eastfield Prim Sch
Queen Elizabeth Stadium
Bishop Stopford's Sch
Suffolks Prim Sch
Enfield Coll
Durants Park
Enfield Town FC
Brimsdown Jun & Inf Sch
Kingsmead Sch
George Spicer Prim Sch
Enfield Ret Pk
Colosseum Ret Pk
Northgate Bsns Ctr
Waverley Sch
Queensway Bsns Ctr
Haslemere Bsns Est
Martinbridge Trad Est
Peerglow Est
Middlesex Univ
St Mary's RC Prim Sch
Alexandra Sch
Albany Sch
18
34
35

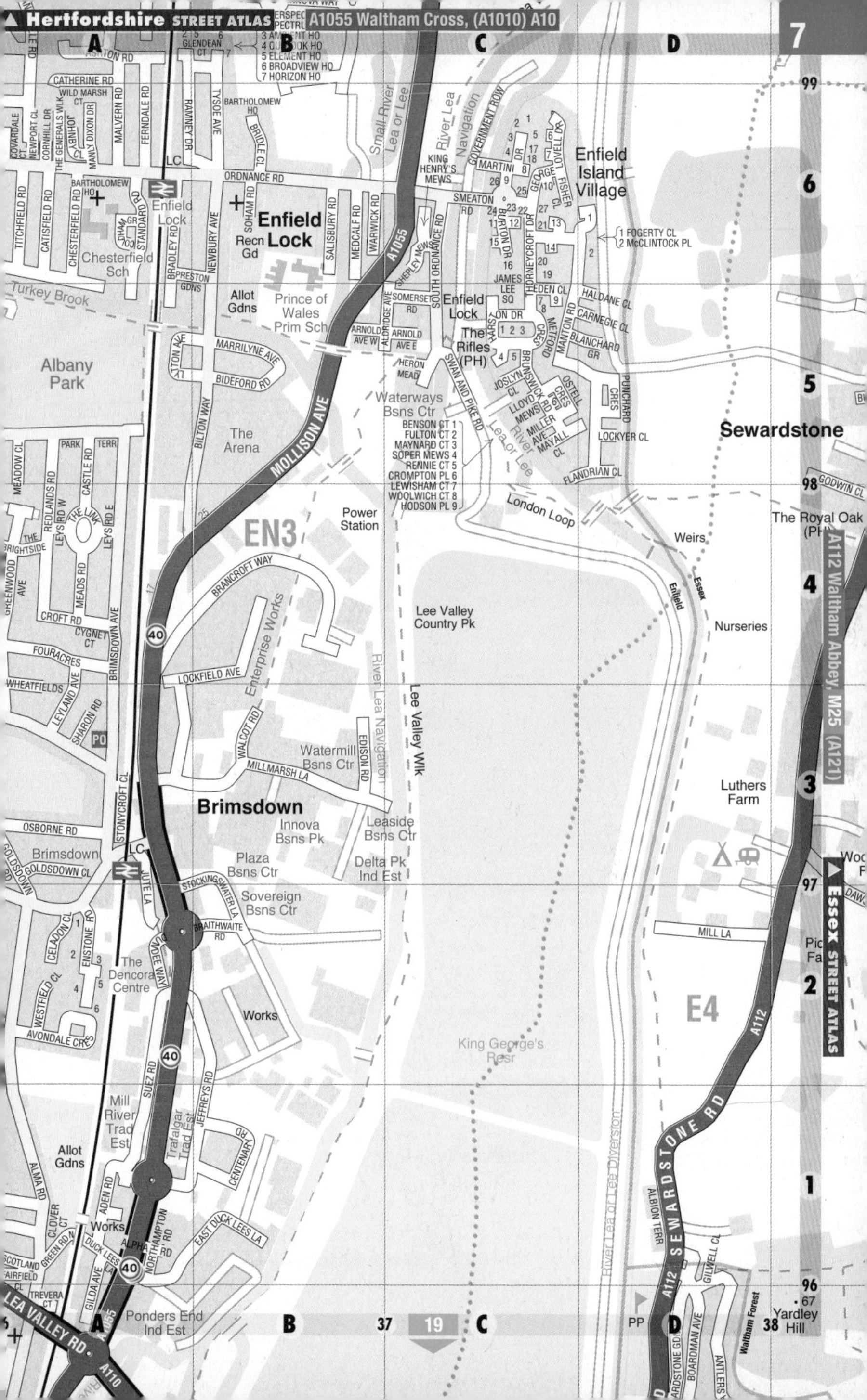
Enfield Lock
Enfield Island Village
Albany Park
The Arena
EN3
Power Station
Lee Valley Country Pk
Sewardstone
Brimsdown
Innova Bsns Pk
Plaza Bsns Ctr
Sovereign Bsns Ctr
Watermill Bsns Ctr
Leaside Bsns Ctr
Delta Pk Ind Est
The Dencora Centre
Mill River Trad Est
Ponders End Ind Est
Trafalgar Trad Est
Chesterfield Sch
Prince of Wales Prim Sch
Waterways Bsns Ctr
The Rifles (PH)
The Royal Oak (PH)
King George's Resr
River Lea or Lee Diversion
Lee Valley Wlk
River Lea Navigation
Small River Lea or Lee
London Loop
Nurseries
Luthers Farm
Weirs
E4
MOLLISON AVE
SEWARDSTONE RD
LEA VALLEY RD
A112 Waltham Abbey, M25 (A121)
▲ Essex STREET ATLAS
1 FOGERTY CL
2 McCLINTOCK PL
BENSON CT 1
FULTON CT 2
MAYNARD CT 3
SOPER MEWS 4
RENNIE CT 5
CROMPTON PL 6
LEWISHAM CT 7
WOOLWICH CT 8
HODSON PL 9
3 AMBIENT HO
5 ELEMENT HO
6 BROADVIEW HO
7 HORIZON HO
Yardley Hill

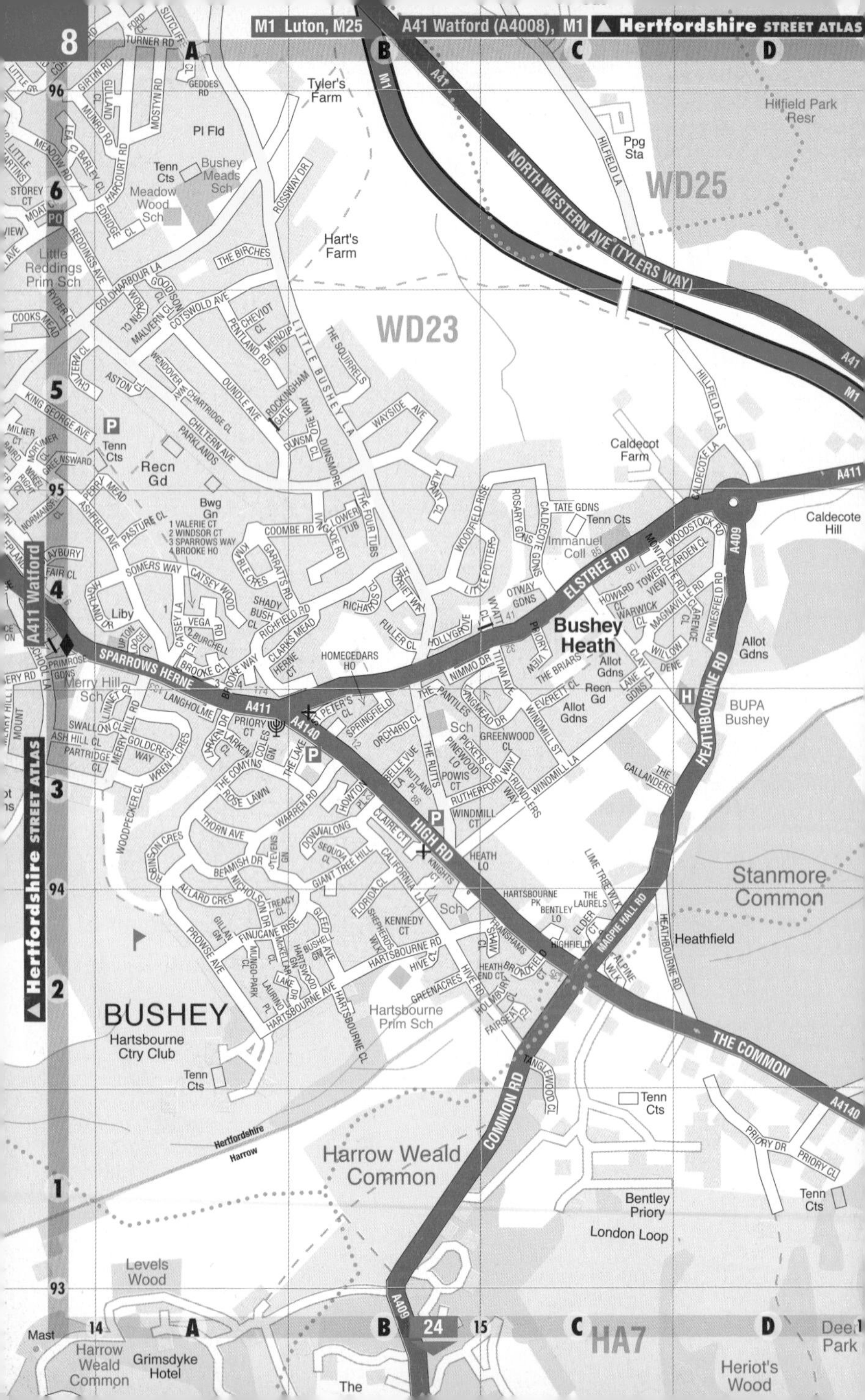
A
B
C
D
96
6
5
95
4
3
94
2
1
93
Tyler's Farm
Hilfield Park Resr
Ppg Sta
WD25
NORTH WESTERN AVE (TYLERS WAY)
Pl Fld
Bushey Meads Sch
Meadow Wood Sch
Tenn Cts
Little Reddings Prim Sch
Hart's Farm
WD23
LITTLE BUSHEY LA
Caldecot Farm
A411
Caldecote Hill
Recn Gd
Bwg Gn
1 VALERIE CT
2 WINDSOR CT
3 SPARROWS WAY
4 BROOKE HO
Immanuel Coll
Bushey Heath
ELSTREE RD
SPARROWS HERNE
Merry Hill Sch
Liby
Allot Gdns
BUPA Bushey
HEATHBOURNE RD
HIGH RD
A4140
Stanmore Common
Heathfield
BUSHEY
Hartsbourne Ctry Club
Hartsbourne Prim Sch
THE COMMON
COMMON RD
Harrow Weald Common
Bentley Priory
London Loop
Levels Wood
A409
A411 Watford
Hertfordshire STREET ATLAS

A
B
C
D
Home Farm
Allot Gdns
96
Aldenham Ctry Pk
LISTER COTTS
Laboratory
DAGGER LA
Aldenham Resr
Sailing Club
Pav
ALDENHAM RD
A5183
B5378
ALLUM
ELSTREE HILL N
6
ROMELAND CT
THE BARTONS
St Nicholas CE Prim Sch
Elstree
Sp Gd
Tenn Cts
WD6
LANDS' END
WATFORD RD
HIGH ST
NEW RD
YEW TREE CT
OAK TREE CT
GEORGES MEAD
5
SCHUBERT RD
PO
A411
PH
ELSTREE RD
Lismirrane Ind Pk
FOX CL
BRITTEN CL
RODGERS CL
DELIUS CL
WEBBER CL
SULLIVAN WAY
BEETHOVEN RD
DYLAN CL
ELGAR CL
COATES RD
BEEHIVE
WEST VIEW GDNS
SUMMER GR
VALENTINE CT
FORTUNE LA
MAY GDNS
Tenn Cts
95
The
Edgwarebury House Farm
ELSTREE HILL S
NORTH WESTERN AVE (WATFORD BY-PASS)
CENTENNIAL AVE
Centennial Pk
Centennial Ct
4
WD23
Hertfordshire
Harrow
10
Brockleyhill Farm
A5
4
Hertfordshire
Barnet
M1
3
London Loop
Sp Gd
Brockley Grange
Tenn Cts
BROCKLEY HILL HO
94
HA8
Annandale
NUTT GR
A41 EDGWARE WAY (WATFORD BY-PASS)
Works
HA7
SIR HENRY FLOYD CT
Royal National Orthopaedic
H
Grove Farm
Pear Wood Cottages
2
Wood Farm
Pear Wood
BROCKLEY HILL
THE LIMES
Limes House
WARREN LA
WOOD LA
Crkt Gd
CH
Brockley Hill
Barnet
Harrow
LANCASTER HO
Pav
Tenn Cts
Cloisters Wood
Springbok House
Tenn Cts
SPRINGFIELD CL
PARK LA
HILLTOP WAY
LITTLE COMMON
BROOMFIELD HO 1
FALLOWFIELD CT 2
HILL HO 3
WELLINGTON HO 4
STANMORE HILL
DENNIS LA
Stanmore Hall
FALLOWFIELD
AYLMER CL
30
GRANTHAM CL
NEWLANDS CL
PIPERS GREEN LA
HAMLYN CL
1
JULIUS CAESAR WAY
AUGUSTUS CL
CLAUDIUS CL
BROCKLEY AV
93
A5
FAUNA CL
CHEVALIER CL
BERRY HILL
PARTRIDGE CL
REES DR
A4140
AYLMER DR
HERIOTS CL
PINE CL
OLD FORGE CL
SPRING LAKE
St Johns
DENNIS LA
GREENGLASS
GLANLEAM RD
A
B
17
25
C
D
18

Elstree
Allum La
B5378
A5183
Elstree Hill
Cemy
London Loop
St Nicholas CE Prim Sch
Elstree
Barnet La
A411
Deacons Hill
WD6
Elstree Tunnel
Woodcock Hill
Tenn Cts
Abbotsbury
The Leys
Edgwarebury House Farm
Penniwells Farm
Edgwarebury Ctry Club
Hertfordshire
Barnet
NW7
M1
Edgwarebury Farm
Bury Farm
Edgware Bury
DUNBLANE CL 1
KINROSS CL 2
MOIDART CT 3
MALLAIG CT 4
OBAN CT 5
ARRAN CT 6
TORRIDON CT 7
ROSS CT 8
Edgwarebury La
Clay La
Cemy
Pl Fld
Pav
Broadfields Prim Sch
A41 Edgware Way (Watford By-Pass)
HA8
Edgwarebury Park
Tenn Cts
Edgwarebury
HA7
PARKLANDS PL 6
COMPASS CL 7
Spur Rd
A410
A5
1 WARE CT
2 WAKEMAN HO
3 ABINGDON CT
4 CHICHELE HO
5 HAVILLAND CT
Edgware Way (Watford By-Pass)
Acad
Sch

9
26
18
19
50

BOREHAMWOOD
WD6
EN5
NW7
Barnet Gate
EDGWARE
BARNET LA
BARNET RD
BARNET BY-PASS
BARNET WAY (BARNET BY-PASS)
Stirling Cnr
Scratch Wood
Scratchwood Open Space
Nature Trail
Thistle Wood
Moat Mount Open Space
Mill Hill
Hemmings Wood
Nut Wood
Stoney Wood Lake
London Gateway Service Area
Motel
Rowley Bank Nurseries
Arkley
Rowley Lodge
Memorial Sp Ctr
Hyver Hall
Hyver Farm
Barnet Gate Wood
Mote End Farm
Mill Hill Cty High Sch
Highwood House
Highwood Hill
HIGHWOOD HILL
MARSH LA
ON WOOD LA
Saffron Green Prim Sch
Fairway Prim Sch
Northway Sch
Stoneyfields Park
London Loop
Dean's Brook
1 WILLOW GN
2 HUNTER WLK
3 CLYDESDALE PATH
4 DALES PATH
5 SADDLERS PATH
Tenn Cts
Stirling Ind Ctr
Stirling Ret Pk
Furze Hill
Windmill (dis)
Apex Cnr
EDGWAREWAY (WATFORD BY-PASS)
NORTHWAY CIR
St Joseph's Coll Mill Hill
Lawrence Green
Allot Gdns
A411
B552
A5109
A41
A1
M1
96
95
94
93
6
5
4
3
2
1
A
B
C
D
12
27
21
22

A411 High Barnet
Arkley
Arkley
BARNET RD
A411
ROWLEY GREEN RD
Rowley Lodge
Wr Twr
Allot Gdns
EN5
Whitings Hill
Whitings Hill Prim Sch
Cemy
Ducks Island
Recn Gd
Cottage Farm
Pl Fld
Sp Gd
Dollis Brook
London Loop
Brent Lodge Farm
N20
HENDON WOOD LA
Fairlight Cottage
Sp Gd
Pav
TOTTERIDGE PK
Abattoir
Tenn Cts
TOTTERIDGE COMMON
A5109
Oak Lodge
Totteridge Common
Ellern Mead Farm
Fairlawn
HIGHWOOD HILL
Highwood Hill
B552 HIGHWOOD HILL
Holecombe Dale
NW7
Folly Farm
Belmont Mill Hill Jun Sch
Pl Fld
Tenn Cts
Sp Fld
Pav
Sp Gd
Lawrence Green
St Joseph's Coll Mill Hill
St Paul's
Burtonhole Farm
1 WEARDALE CT
2 ELVASTON CT
3 DEBENHAM CT

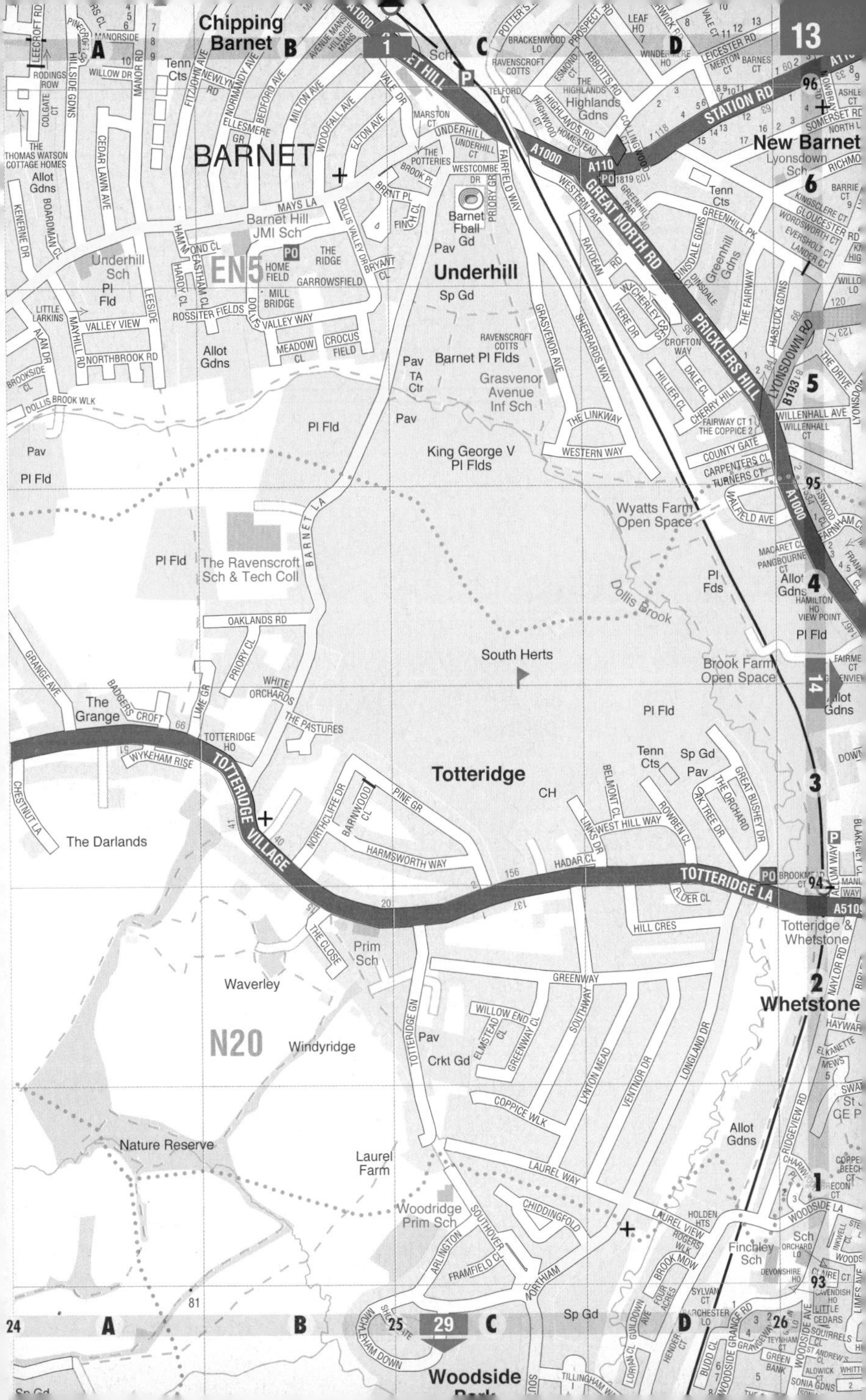

Chipping Barnet
BARNET
EN5
Underhill
New Barnet
Barnet Hill JMI Sch
Underhill Sch
Barnet Fball Gd
King George V Pl Flds
Barnet Pl Flds
Gravesnor Avenue Inf Sch
Wyatts Farm Open Space
Dollis Brook
South Herts
Brook Farm Open Space
The Ravenscroft Sch & Tech Coll
Totteridge
TOTTERIDGE LA
TOTTERIDGE VILLAGE
The Grange
The Darlands
Waverley
N20
Windyridge
Nature Reserve
Laurel Farm
Woodridge Prim Sch
Totteridge & Whetstone
Whetstone
Finchley Sch
Woodside Park
GREAT NORTH RD
PRICKLERS HILL
STATION RD
Highlands Gdns
Greenhill Gdns

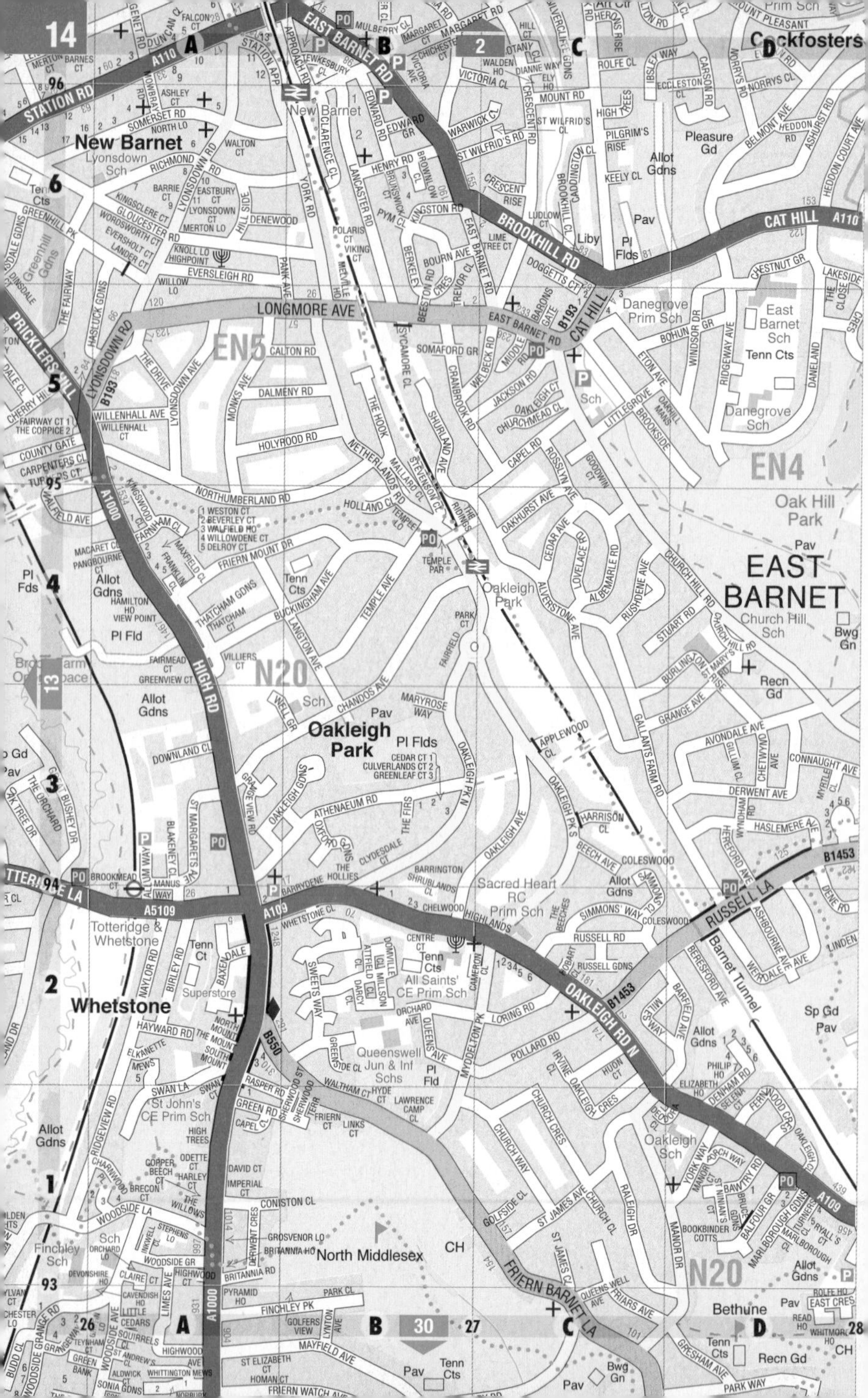

14
A
B
C
D
2
Cockfosters
New Barnet
EAST BARNET RD
STATION RD
A110
STATION APP
APPROACH RD
MULBERRY CL
MARGARET CT
MARGARET RD
TEWKESBURY CL
CHICHESTER CT
VICTORIA AVE
VICTORIA CL
BOTANY CL
WALDEN HO
DIANNE WAY
ELY HO
SILVERCLIFFE GDNS
HERONS RISE
ROLFE CL
IBSLEY WAY
CARSON RD
ECCLESTON CL
NORRYS RD
NORRYS CL
MOUNT PLEASANT
BELMONT AVE
HEDDON RD
ASHURST RD
HEDDON COURT AVE
MERTON CT
BARNES CT
ASHLEY CT
MOWBRAY RD
DUNCAN CL
FALCON CT
GENET RD
SOMERSET RD
NORTH LO
WALTON CT
Lyonsdown Sch
RICHMOND RD
LYONSDOWN RD
YORK RD
CLARENCE CL
EDWARD RD
EDWARD GR
HENRY RD
BROWNLOW RD
LANCASTER RD
BRUNSWICK CT
PYM CL
KINGSTON RD
MOUNT RD
CRESCENT RD
ST WILFRID'S CL
ST WILFRID'S RD
WARWICK CL
HIGH TREES
PILGRIM'S RISE
CADDINGTON CL
KEELY CL
Pleasure Gd
Allot Gdns
Pav
CRESCENT RISE
BROOKHILL CL
LUDLOW CT
Liby
Pl Flds
BROOKHILL RD
CAT HILL
A110
Tenn Cts
6
GREENHILL PK
Greenhill Gdns
KINGSCLERE CT
GLOUCESTER RD
WORDSWORTH CT
EVERSHOLT CT
LANDER CT
BARRIE CT
EASTBURY CT
LYONSDOWN CT
MERTON LO
HILL SIDE
DENEWOOD
KNOLL LO
HIGHPOINT
EVERSLEIGH RD
WILLOW LO
POLARIS CT
VIKING CT
BERKELEY CRES
BOURN AVE
BEESTON RD
TREVOR CL
LIME TREE CT
EAST BARNET RD
DOGGETTS CT
BARONS GATE
CHESTNUT GR
LAKESIDE
THE CLOSE
THE FAIRWAY
HASLUCK GDNS
PARK AVE
MELVILLE HO
LONGMORE AVE
EAST BARNET RD
B193
CAT HILL
Danegrove Prim Sch
BOHUN GR
WINDSOR DR
RIDGEWAY AVE
East Barnet Sch
Tenn Cts
DANELAND
PRICKLERS HILL
LYONSDOWN RD
EN5
CALTON RD
SYCAMORE CL
SOMAFORD GR
WELBECK RD
MIDDLE RD
PO
JACKSON RD
OAKLEIGH CT
CHURCHMEAD CL
Sch
LITTLEGROVE
ETON AVE
OAKHILL MANS
BROOKSIDE
Danegrove Sch
5
CHERRY HILL
FAIRWAY CT
THE COPPICE
WILLENHALL AVE
WILLENHALL CT
THE DRIVE
LYONSDOWN AVE
MONKS AVE
DALMENY RD
HOLYROOD RD
THE HOOK
SHURLAND AVE
CRANBROOK RD
CAPEL RD
ROSSLYN AVE
GOODWIN CT
EN4
COUNTY GATE
CARPENTERS CL
95
NORTHUMBERLAND RD
NETHERLANDS RD
MALLARD CL
STEVENSON CL
THE RIDINGS
OAKHURST AVE
CEDAR AVE
LOVELACE RD
Oak Hill Park
WALFIELD AVE
A1000
KINGSWOOD CL
FARNHAM CL
1 WESTON CT
2 BEVERLEY CT
3 WALFIELD HO
4 WILLOWDENE CT
5 DELROY CT
HOLLAND CL
TEMPLE LO
TEMPLE PAR
MAXFIELD CL
FRIERN MOUNT DR
FRANKLIN CL
MACARET CL
PANGBOURNE CT
Allot Gdns
Pl Fds
4
Tenn Cts
BUCKINGHAM AVE
Oakleigh Park
ALBEMARLE RD
RUSHDENE AVE
ALVERSTONE AVE
CHURCH HILL RD
EAST BARNET
Pav
Church Hill Sch
STUART RD
Bwg Gn
HAMILTON HO
VIEW POINT
Pl Fld
THATCHAM GDNS
THATCHAM CT
LANGTON AVE
TEMPLE AVE
PARK CT
FAIRFIELD CL
CHURCH HILL RD
ST MARY'S RISE
BURLINGTON RISE
Recn Gd
13
FAIRMEAD CT
GREENVIEW CT
VILLIERS CT
N20
HIGH RD
Allot Gdns
WELL GR
Sch
CHANDOS AVE
MARYROSE WAY
Pav
Oakleigh Park
Pl Flds
GRANGE AVE
GALLANTS FARM RD
AVONDALE AVE
GILLUM CL
CHETWYND AVE
CONNAUGHT AVE
APPLEWOOD CL
DOWNLAND CL
CEDAR CT 1
CULVERLANDS CT 2
GREENLEAF CT 3
OAKLEIGH PK N
DERWENT AVE
MYRTLE CL
3
THE ORCHARD
GREAT BUSHEY DR
OAK TREE DR
GRANGE VIEW RD
OAKLEIGH GDNS
ATHENAEUM RD
THE FIRS
OXFORD GDNS
CLYDESDALE CT
OAKLEIGH AVE
OAKLEIGH PK S
HARRISON CL
WYNDHAM RD
HEREFORD AVE
HASLEMERE AVE
ST MARGARETS AVE
BLAKENEY CL
ALLUM WAY
PO
THE HOLLIES
BARRINGTON
SHRUBLANDS CL
BEECH AVE
COLESWOOD
B1453
94
TOTTERIDGE LA
BROOKMEAD CT
MANUS WAY
A5109
BARRYDENE
A109
CHELWOOD
HIGHLANDS
Sacred Heart RC Prim Sch
Allot Gdns
SIMMONS' WAY
SIMMONS' CL
RUSSELL LA
DENE RD
Totteridge & Whetstone
WHETSTONE CL
CENTRE CT
Tenn Cts
CAMERON CL
THE BEECHES
COLESWOOD
RUSSELL RD
RUSSELL GDNS
HOBART CL
ASHBOURNE AVE
WEIRDALE AVE
LINDEN
2
Tenn Ct
BAXENDALE
NAYLOR RD
BIRLEY RD
Superstore
SWEETS WAY
ATTFIELD CL
DOMVILLE CL
MILLSON CL
DARCY CL
All Saints' CE Prim Sch
OAKLEIGH RD N
B1453
BERESFORD AVE
Barnet Tunnel
Whetstone
HAYWARD RD
NORTH MOUNT
THE MOUNT
SOUTH MOUNT
B550
ORCHARD AVE
QUEENS AVE
MYDDELTON PK
LORING RD
MILES WAY
BARFIELD AVE
Sp Gd
Pav
ELKANETTE MEWS
POLLARD RD
IRVINE CL
OAKLEIGH CRES
HUON CT
Allot Gdns
PHILIP HO
ELIZABETH HO
DENHAM RD
SELENA
FERNWOOD CRES
SWAN LA
St John's CE Prim Sch
GREENSIDE CL
Queenswell Jun & Inf Schs
Pl Fld
RASPER RD
GREEN RD
CAPEL CT
SHERWOOD ST
SHERWOOD TERR
WALTHAM CT
HYDE CT
LAWRENCE CAMP CL
FRIERN CT
LINKS CT
CHURCH CRES
CHURCH WAY
DEODORA CL
Oakleigh Sch
OAKLEIGH PK
Allot Gdns
RIDGEVIEW RD
HIGH TREES
ODETTE CT
COPPER BEECH CT
HARLEY CT
DAVID CT
IMPERIAL CT
1
CHARNWOOD PL
BRECON CT
THE WILLOWS
CONISTON CL
GOLFSIDE CL
ST JAMES AVE
CHURCH CL
RALEIGH DR
YORK WAY
MANOR CT
BEECH WAY
ST NINIAN'S CT
BAWTRY RD
BRUCE GDNS
BALFOUR GR
MARLBOROUGH GDNS
TURNERS CL
RYALL'S CT
MARLBOROUGH CL
PO
A109
WOODSIDE LA
INKWELL CL
STEPHENS CT
Sch
Finchley Sch
ORCHARD
GROSVENOR LO
BRITANNIA HO
DERWENT CRES
North Middlesex
CH
MANOR DR
BOOKBINDER COTTS
Allot Gdns
93
DEVONSHIRE HO
CLAIRE CT
WOODSIDE GR
HIGHWOOD CT
BRITANNIA RD
FRIERN BARNET LA
ST JAMES CL
QUEENS WELL AVE
FRIARS AVE
N20
PYRAMID HO
FINCHLEY PK
PARK CL
CAVENDISH HO
LITTLE CEDARS
LIMES AVE
Bethune
Pav
ROLFE HO
EAST CRES
26
GOLFERS VIEW
LYNTON AVE
B
30
27
C
D
28
READ HO
WHITMORE HO
CH
WOODSIDE GRANGE RD
GRANGEWAY
WOODSIDE AVE
SQUIRRELS
ST ANDREW'S CL
HIGHWOOD AVE
MAYFIELD AVE
GRESHAM AVE
Tenn Cts
Recn Gd
BUDD CL
GREEN BANK
ALDWICK CT
WHITTINGTON MEWS
ST ELIZABETH CT
HOMAN CT
Pav
Tenn Cts
Bwg Gn
Pav
SONIA GDNS
FRIERN WATCH AVE
PARK WAY

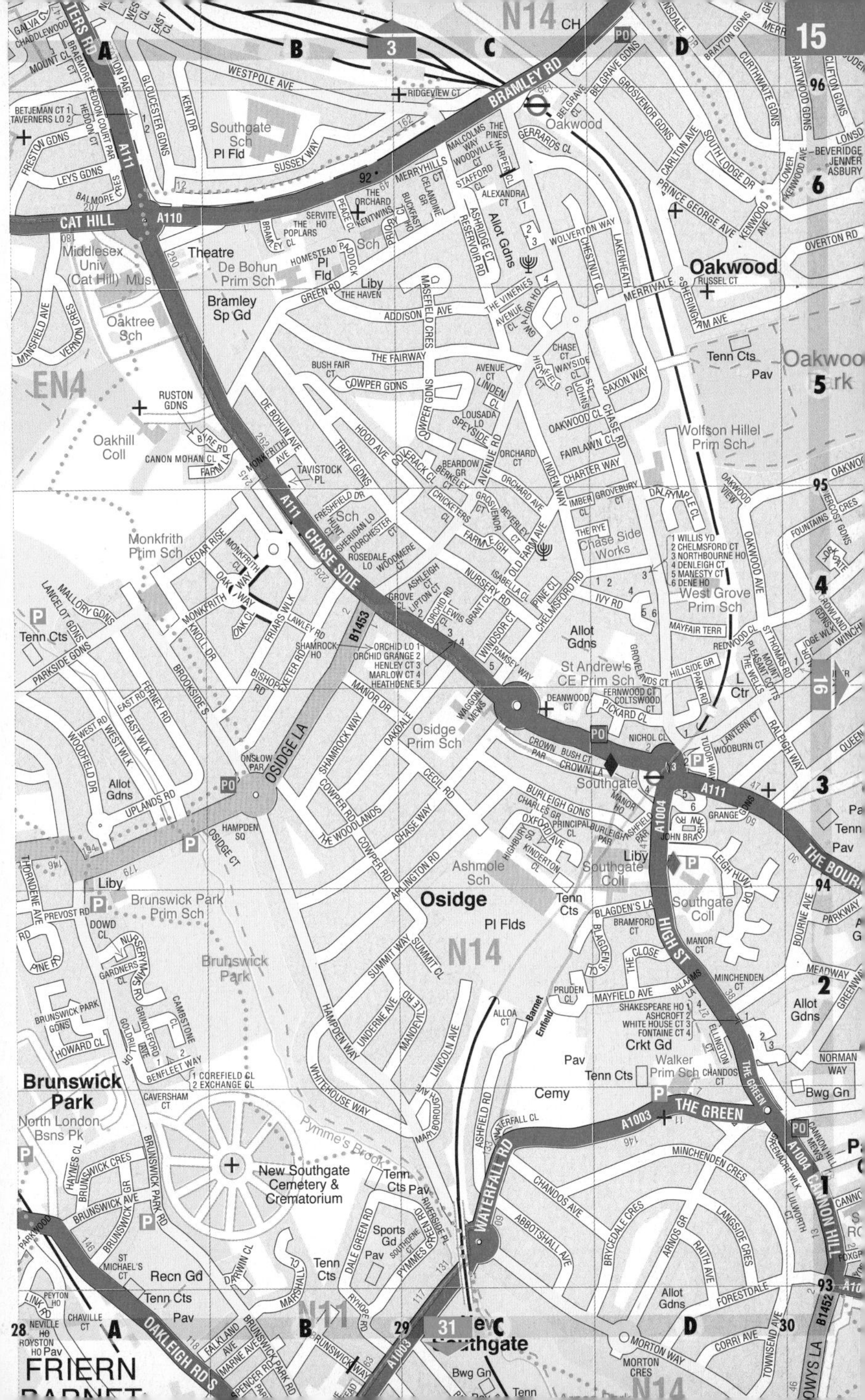
A
B
C
D
3
N14
Bramley Rd
Westpole Ave
Ridgeview Ct
Southgate Sch
Pl Fld
Sussex Way
Gloucester Gdns
Kent Dr
Cat Hill
A110
A111
Middlesex Univ (Cat Hill)
Theatre
De Bohun Prim Sch
Bramley Sp Gd
Oaktree Sch
EN4
Oakhill Coll
Ruston Gdns
Canon Mohan Cl
Farm La
Monkfrith Prim Sch
Monkfrith Way
Cedar Rise
Oak Way
Friars Wlk
Mallory Gdns
Lancelot Gdns
Tenn Cts
Parkside Gdns
Brookside S
Allot Gdns
Uplands Rd
Osidge La
B1453
Hampden Sq
Osidge Ct
Liby
Brunswick Park Prim Sch
Brunswick Park
Brunswick Park
North London Bsns Pk
New Southgate Cemetery & Crematorium
Pymme's Brook
Recn Gd
Tenn Cts
Pav
Oakleigh Rd S
Friern Barnet
N11
28
29
31
New Southgate
30
Chase Side
Osidge Prim Sch
Osidge
Pl Flds
N14
Ashmole Sch
Southgate Coll
Southgate
High St
A1004
A1003
The Green
Crkt Gd
Cemy
Walker Prim Sch
Waterfall Rd
Minchenden Cres
Allot Gdns
Morton Way
Bourne Ave
Cannon Hill
Oakwood
Oakwood
Merrivale
Oakwood Park
Tenn Cts
Pav
Wolfson Hillel Prim Sch
West Grove Prim Sch
St Andrew's CE Prim Sch
Chase Side Works
L Ctr
16
Allot Gdns
Prince George Ave
Carlton Ave
Grosvenor Gdns
Belgrave Gdns
Brayton Gdns
Curthwaite Gdns
Lonsdale
Overton Rd
Saxon Way
Chase Rd
Linden Way
Avenue Rd
Addison Ave
The Fairway
Cowper Gdns
Hood Ave
Trent Gdns
Ivy Rd
Oakwood Ave
Fountains Cres
Mayfair Terr
Raleigh Way
Burleigh Gdns
Cecil Rd
Arlington Rd
Summit Way
Hampden Way
Whitehouse Way
Lincoln Ave
Chandos Ave
Abbotshall Ave
Brycedale Cres
Langside Cres
Forestdale
Corri Ave
Townsend Ave
B1452
1 Willis Yd
2 Chelmsford Ct
3 Northbourne Ho
4 Denleigh Ct
5 Manesty Ct
6 Dene Ho
1 Orchid Lo
2 Orchid Grange
3 Henley Ct
4 Marlow Ct
5 Heathdene
1 Shakespeare Ho
2 Ashcroft
3 White House Ct
4 Fontaine Ct
1 Corefield Cl
2 Exchange Cl
92
93
94
95
96
1
2
3
4
5
6

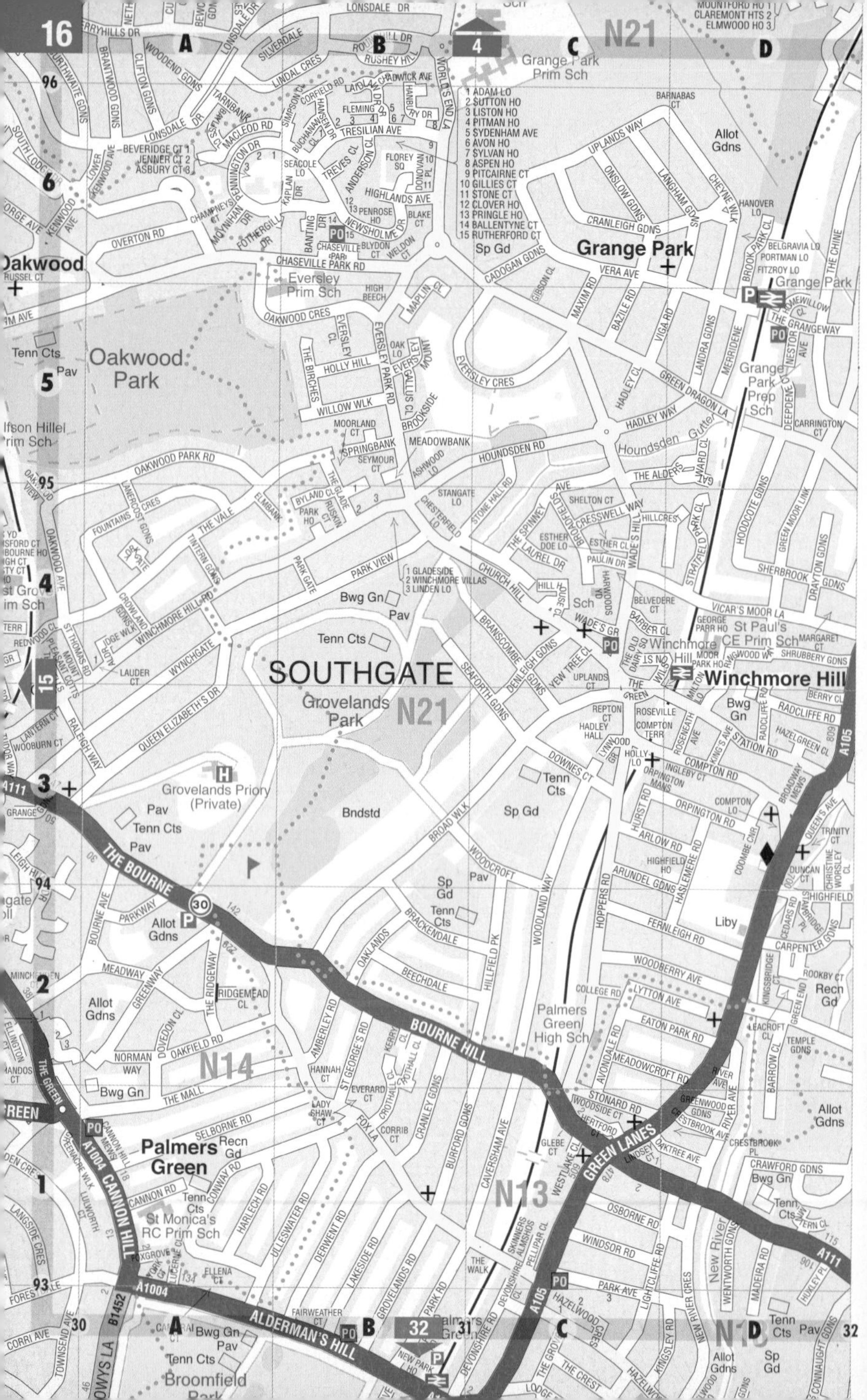
16
A
B
C
D
4
N21
Grange Park Prim Sch
LONSDALE DR
SILVERDALE
RUSHEY HILL
WORLDS END LA
LINDAL CRES
CHADWICK AVE
WOODEND GDNS
BRANTWOOD GDNS
CLIFTON GDNS
96
TARNBANK
CORFIELD RD
HANSEN DR
FLEMING DR
HANBURY DR
TRESILIAN AVE
MACLEOD RD
LONSDALE DR
SIMPSON CL
BUCHANAN CL
BEVERIDGE CT 1
JENNER CT 2
ASBURY CT 3
PENNINGTON DR
SEACOLE LO
TREVES CL
ANDERSON CL
FLOREY SQ
DONOVAN PL
KAPLAN DR
HIGHLANDS AVE
PENROSE HO
BLAKE CT
NEWSHOLME DR
BANTING DR
CHASEVILLE PAR
BLYDON CT
WELDON CT
CHAMPNEYS CT
MOYNIHAN DR
FOTHERGILL DR
OVERTON RD
KENWOOD AVE
LOWER KENWOOD AVE
SOUTH LODGE DR
6
1 ADAM LO
2 SUTTON HO
3 LISTON HO
4 PITMAN HO
5 SYDENHAM AVE
6 AVON HO
7 SYLVAN HO
8 ASPEN HO
9 PITCAIRNE CT
10 GILLIES CT
11 STONE CT
12 CLOVER HO
13 PRINGLE HO
14 BALLENTYNE CT
15 RUTHERFORD CT
Sp Gd
BARNABAS CT
UPLANDS WAY
ONSLOW GDNS
LANGHAM GDNS
CHEYNE WLK
Allot Gdns
CRANLEIGH GDNS
HANOVER LO
Grange Park
BROOK PARK CL
BELGRAVIA LO
PORTMAN LO
FITZROY LO
THE CHINE
Oakwood
RUSSEL CT
CHASEVILLE PARK RD
Eversley Prim Sch
HIGH BEECH
OAKWOOD CRES
CADOGAN GDNS
GIBSON CL
MAXIM RD
VERA AVE
BAZILE RD
VIGA RD
Grange Park
HOMEWILLOW CL
THE GRANGEWAY
MAPLIN CL
EVERSLEY CL
THE BIRCHES
HOLLY HILL
EVERSLEY PARK RD
OAK LO
EVERSLEY MOUNT
GALLUS CL
EVERSLEY CRES
LANDRA GDNS
MERRIDENE
NESTOR AVE
Grange Park Prep Sch
Tenn Cts
Oakwood Park
5
Pav
WILLOW WLK
BROOKSIDE
HADLEY CL
GREEN DRAGON LA
DEEPDENE CT
HADLEY WAY
CARRINGTON CT
MOORLAND CT
SPRINGBANK
SEYMOUR CT
MEADOWBANK
ASHWOOD LO
HOUNDSDEN RD
Houndsden Gutter
THE ALDERS
WARD CL
95
OAKWOOD PARK RD
THE GLADE
BYLAND CL
PARK HO
RUSKIN CT
ELMBANK
STANGATE LO
CHESTERFIELD LO
STONE HALL RD
SHELTON CT
CRESSWELL WAY
HILLCREST
STRAFIELD PARK CL
HOODCOTE GDNS
GREEN MOOR LINK
LANERCOST GDNS
FOUNTAINS CRES
THE VALE
OAKWOOD AVE
TINTERN GDNS
YORK GATE
THE SPINNEY
BROADFIELDS AVE
ESTHER DOE LO
ESTHER CL
LAUREL DR
PAULIN DR
WADE'S HILL
DRAYTON GDNS
4
PARK GATE
PARK VIEW
1 GLADESIDE
2 WINCHMORE VILLAS
3 LINDEN LO
CHURCH HILL
HILL HOUSE CL
HARWOODS YD
SHERBROOK GDNS
CROWLAND GDNS
WINCHMORE HILL RD
Bwg Gn
Pav
Sch
BELVEDERE CT
VICAR'S MOOR LA
REDWOOD CL
ST THOMAS RD
MOUNT PLEASANT COTTS
ALDRIDGE WLK
BRANSCOMBE
WADE'S GR
BARBER CL
GEORGE PARR HO
St Paul's CE Prim Sch
MARGARET CT
Tenn Cts
THE OLD DAIRY SQ
Winchmore Hill
MOOR PARK HO
WOOD WAY
SHRUBBERY GDNS
LAUDER CT
WYNCHGATE
SOUTHGATE
DENLEIGH GDNS
YEW TREE CL
WILSON ST
15
QUEEN ELIZABETH'S DR
SEAFORTH GDNS
UPLANDS CT
THE GREEN
MILTON LO
Winchmore Hill
BERRY CL
Grovelands Park
N21
REPTON CT
HADLEY HALL
ROSEVILLE
COMPTON TERR
ROSENEATH AVE
KING'S AVE
Bwg Gn
RADCLIFFE RD
LANTERN CT
WOOBURN CT
RALEIGH WAY
LYNWOOD GR
HOLLY LO
STATION RD
HAZELGREEN CL
A105
DOWNES CT
INGLEBY CT
COMPTON RD
3
A111
Grovelands Priory (Private)
Tenn Cts
ORPINGTON MANS
BROADWAY MEWS
GRANGE
Pav
Tenn Cts
Pav
Bndstd
Sp Gd
HURST RD
ORPINGTON RD
COMPTON LO
QUEEN'S AVE
TRINITY CT
BROAD WLK
ARLOW RD
COOMBE CNR
DUNCAN CT
CHRISTINE WORSLEY CL
THE BOURNE
94
HIGHFIELD HO
HASLEMERE RD
ARUNDEL GDNS
WOODCROFT
Pav
Sp Gd
HIGHFIELD
30
BOURNE AVE
PARKWAY
Allot Gdns
Tenn Cts
WOODLAND WAY
HOPPERS RD
Liby
CEDARS RD
BRIDGE
BRACKENDALE
FERNLEIGH RD
CARPENTER GDNS
HILLFIELD PK
THE RIDGEWAY
OAKLANDS
BEECHDALE
WOODBERRY AVE
ROOKBY CT
MEADWAY
GREENWAY
RIDGEMEAD CL
COLLEGE RD
LYTTON AVE
KINGSBRIDGE CT
GREEN END
Recn Gd
2
Allot Gdns
AMBERLEY RD
Palmers Green High Sch
EATON PARK RD
LEACROFT CL
DOVEDON CL
OAKFIELD RD
BOURNE HILL
AVONDALE RD
TEMPLE GDNS
MEADOWCROFT RD
BARROW CL
NORMAN WAY
N14
HANNAH CT
ST GEORGE'S RD
KERRY CT
CROTHALL CL
RIVER AVE
Bwg Gn
THE MALL
EVERARD CT
STONARD RD
WOODSIDE CT
GREENWOOD GDNS
Allot Gdns
THE GREEN
GREEN
LADY SHAW CT
FOX LA
HERTFORD CT
CRESTBROOK AVE
CRESTBROOK PL
SELBORNE RD
CORRIB CT
GRANLEY GDNS
BURFORD GDNS
CAVERSHAM AVE
GLEBE CT
GREEN LANES
OAKTREE AVE
LINDSEY CT
Recn Gd
CRAWFORD GDNS
Palmers Green
CONWAY RD
WESTLAKE CL
Bwg Gn
1
CANNON HILL
A1004
CANNON MEWS
PENNACRE WLK
LULWORTH CT
HARLECH RD
ULLESWATER RD
DERWENT RD
N13
OSBORNE RD
Tenn Cts
CANNON RD
Tenn Cts
St Monica's RC Prim Sch
LAKESIDE RD
GROVELANDS RD
SKINNERS ALMSHOUSES
PELLIPAR CL
WINDSOR RD
A111
LANGSIDE CRES
FOXGROVE
YORK GA
LUCERNE CT
ELLENA CT
THE WALK
New River
WENTWORTH GDNS
MADEIRA RD
HUXLEY PL
93
FORESTDALE
A1004
PARK RD
DEVONSHIRE GDNS
PO
LIGHTCLIFFE RD
PARK AVE
HAZELWOOD CRES
B1452
ALDERMAN'S HILL
FAIRWEATHER CT
DEVONSHIRE RD
A105
CORRI AVE
TOWNSEND AVE
30
A
Bwg Gn
Pav
Tenn Cts
Broomfield Park
B
32
31
NEW PARK HO
Palmers Green
C
THE GROVE
THE CREST
KINGSLEY RD
NEW RIVER CRES
N13
D
Tenn Cts
Pav
32
Allot Gdns
Sp Gd
CONNAUGHT GDNS

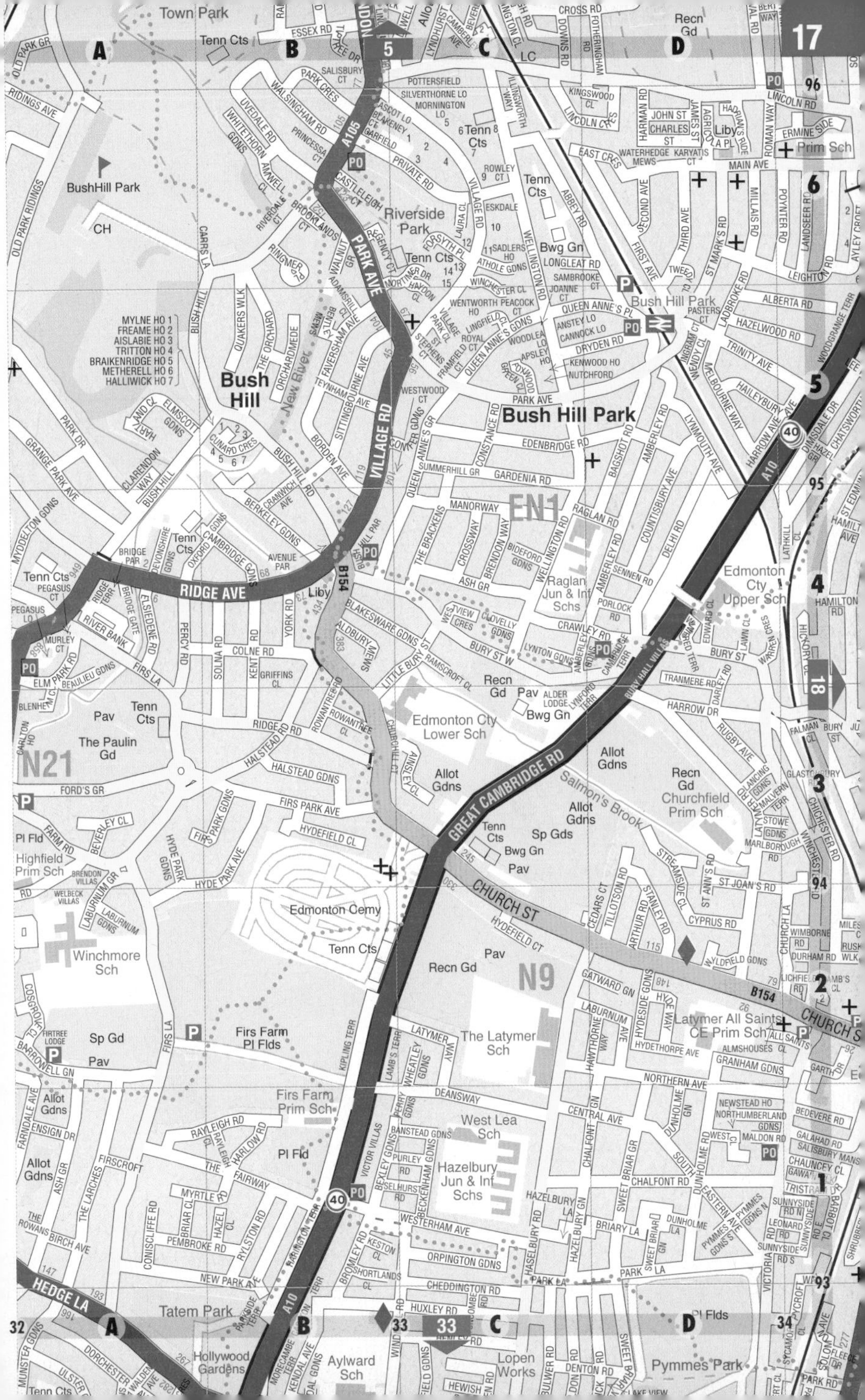

Town Park
Bush Hill Park
Bush Hill
Riverside Park
Bush Hill Park
EN1
N21
N9
The Paulin Gd
Edmonton Cty Lower Sch
Edmonton Cty Upper Sch
Raglan Jun & Inf Schs
Churchfield Prim Sch
Edmonton Cemy
Winchmore Sch
Firs Farm Pl Flds
Firs Farm Prim Sch
The Latymer Sch
West Lea Sch
Hazelbury Jun & Inf Schs
Latymer All Saints CE Prim Sch
Highfield Prim Sch
Tatem Park
Hollywood Gardens
Aylward Sch
Lopen Works
Pymmes Park
RIDGE AVE
VILLAGE RD
PARK AVE
GREAT CAMBRIDGE RD
CHURCH ST
HEDGE LA
Salmon's Brook
New River

5
18
33

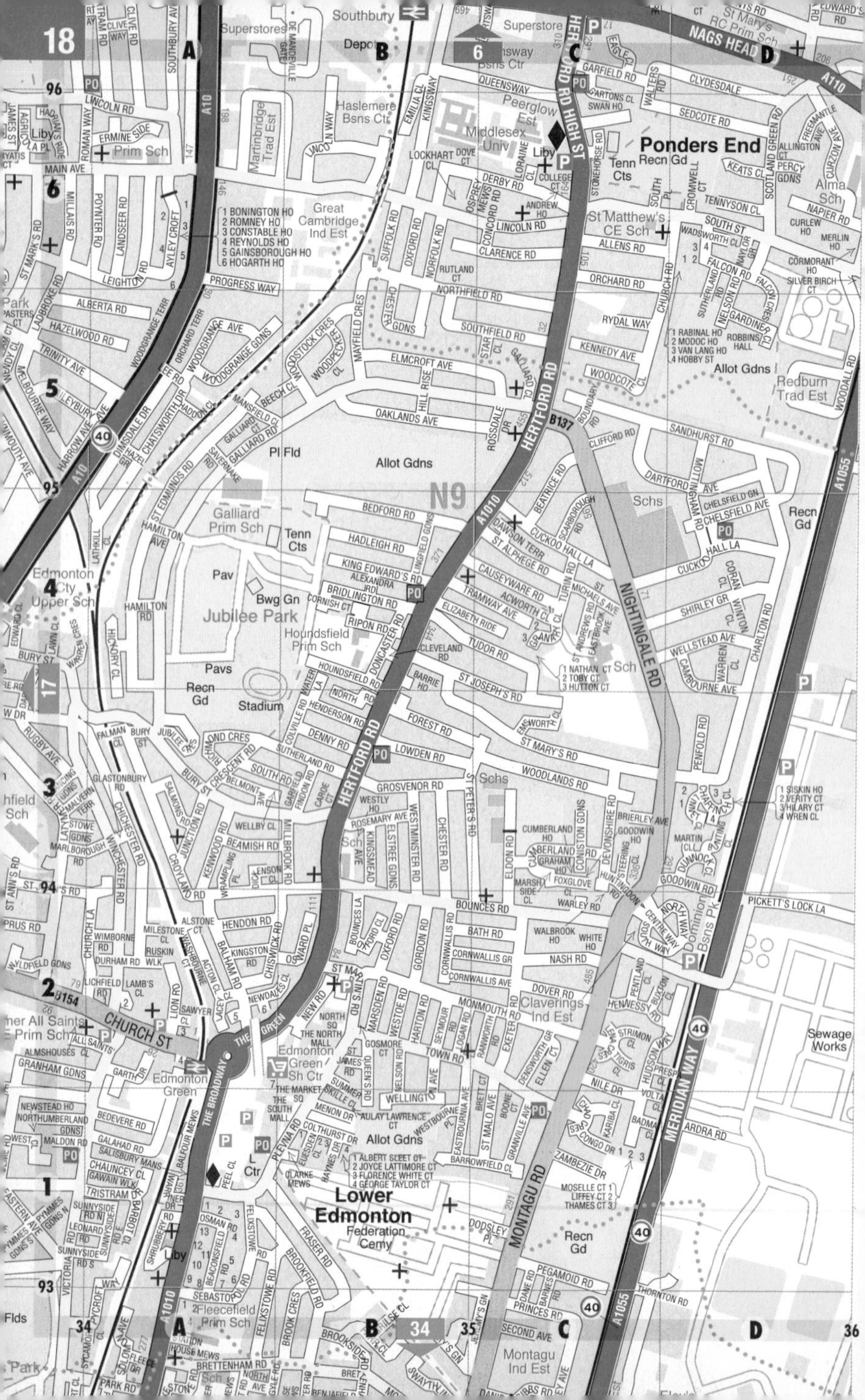
Southbury
Superstores
DE MANDEVILLE GATE
Depot
Superstore
Queensway Bsns Ctr
NAGS HEAD RD
St Mary's RC Prim Sch
A110
CLIVE RD
CLIVE WAY
SOUTHBURY AV
LINCOLN RD
HADRIAN'S RIDE
AGRICOLA PL
Liby
ERMINE SIDE
Prim Sch
ROMAN WAY
MAIN AVE
A10
Martinbridge Trad Est
Haslemere Bsns Ctr
LINCOLN WAY
EMILIA CL
KINGSWAY
QUEENSWAY
HERTFORD RD HIGH ST
GARFIELD RD
EAGLE CL
CLYDESDALE
CARTONS CL
SWAN HO
WALTERS RD
SEDCOTE RD
Peerglow Est
Middlesex Univ
Ponders End
Recn Gd
Tenn Cts
FREEMANTLE AVE
CURZON AVE
ALLINGTON CT
PERCY GDNS
KEATS CL
Alma Sch
LOCKHART CL
DOVE CT
DERBY RD
COLLEGE CT
STONEHORSE RD
SOUTH PL
CROMWELL CT
TENNYSON CL
SCOTLAND GREEN RD
NAPIER RD
CURLEW HO
MERLIN HO
MILLAIS RD
POYNTER RD
LANDSEER RD
AYLEY CROFT
1 BONINGTON HO
2 ROMNEY HO
3 CONSTABLE HO
4 REYNOLDS HO
5 GAINSBOROUGH HO
6 HOGARTH HO
Great Cambridge Ind Est
SUFFOLK RD
OXFORD RD
NORFOLK RD
OSPREY MEWS
CONCORD RD
LORAINE CL
ANDREW HO
LINCOLN RD
St Matthew's CE Sch
SOUTH ST
WADSWORTH CL
CLARENCE RD
ALLENS RD
FALCON RD
NAYLOR GR
CORMORANT HO
SILVER BIRCH CT
ST MARK'S RD
LEIGHTON RD
PROGRESS WAY
RUTLAND CT
ORCHARD RD
CHURCH ST
SUTHERLAND CL
NELSON RD
FALCON CRES
NORTHFIELD RD
Park
PASTERS CT
LADBROKE RD
ALBERTA RD
HAZELWOOD RD
WOODGRANGE TERR
ORCHARD TERR
WOODGRANGE AVE
WOODGRANGE GDNS
WOODSTOCK CRES
WOODPECKER CL
MAYFIELD CRES
CHESTER GDNS
SOUTHFIELD RD
RYDAL WAY
GARDINER CL
1 RABINAL HO
2 MODOC HO
3 VAN LANG HO
4 HOBBY ST
ROBBINS HALL
TRINITY AVE
ELMCROFT AVE
STAR CL
GALLIARD CL
KENNEDY AVE
Allot Gdns
Redburn Trad Est
WOODALL RD
MELBOURNE WAY
TILEYBURY AVE
HARROW AVE
DIMSDALE DR
CHATSWORTH DR
HADDON CL
MANSFIELD CL
BEECH CL
HILL RISE
WOODCOTE CL
BOUNDARY RD
OAKLANDS AVE
ROSSDALE DR
HERTFORD RD
B137
CLIFFORD RD
SANDHURST RD
GALLIARD CL
GALLIARD RD
SAVERNAKE
Pl Fld
Allot Gdns
BEATRICE RD
DARTFORD AVE
WILLOUGHBY RD
CHELSFIELD GN
CHELSFIELD AVE
Recn Gd
ST EDMUNDS RD
HAZEL GR
N9
A1010
SCARBOROUGH RD
Schs
A1055
Galliard Prim Sch
Tenn Cts
BEDFORD RD
HADLEIGH RD
LINGFIELD GDNS
DAWSON TERR
CUCKOO HALL LA
ST ALPHEGE RD
LATHKILL CL
HAMILTON AVE
Edmonton Cty Upper Sch
Pav
KING EDWARD'S RD
ALEXANDRA RD
CAUSEYWARE RD
TURIN RD
ST MICHAELS AVE
NIGHTINGALE RD
CORAN CL
WINTON CL
BRIDLINGTON RD
CORNISH CT
TRAMWAY AVE
ACWORTH CL
SHIRLEY GR
CHARLTON RD
Bwg Gn
Jubilee Park
HAMILTON RD
ELIZABETH RIDE
GRANARY CL
ST ANDREWS RD
EASTBROOK AVE
RIPON RD
Houndsfield Prim Sch
DONCASTER RD
CLEVELAND RD
TUDOR RD
Sch
WELLSTEAD AVE
BURY ST
LAWN CL
WARREN CRES
HICKORY CL
WATER LA
HOUNDSFIELD RD
BARRIE HO
1 NATHAN CT
2 TOBY CT
3 HUTTON CT
WARREN CL
CAMBOURNE AVE
Pavs
Recn Gd
Stadium
COLVILLE RD
NORTH RD
ST JOSEPH'S RD
HENDERSON RD
FOREST RD
EMSWORTH CL
PENFOLD RD
RUGBY AVE
FALMAN CL
BURY ST
JUBILEE CRES
RICHMOND CRES
DENNY RD
LOWDEN RD
ST MARY'S RD
SUTHERLAND RD
WOODLANDS RD
CRESCENT RD
GLASTONBURY RD
SOUTH RD
BELMONT AVE
GARFIELD RD
FINDON RD
CAROE CT
GROSVENOR RD
ST PETER'S RD
Schs
BRIERLEY AVE
1 SISKIN HO
2 VERITY CT
3 HILARY CT
4 WREN CL
CHAFFINCH CL
MALVERN TERR
STOWE GDNS
MARLBOROUGH RD
CHICHESTER RD
WINCHESTER RD
SALMONS RD
JUNCTION RD
WELLBY CL
WESTLY HO
ROSEMARY AVE
KINGSMEAD
ELSTREE GDNS
WESTMINSTER RD
CHESTER RD
CUMBERLAND HO
CONISTON GDNS
DEVONSHIRE RD
GOODWIN HO
BEAMISH RD
MILLBROOK RD
ELDON RD
CUMBERLAND GRAHAM HO
STEERING
MARTIN CL
DUNNOCK CL
BUNTING CL
CROYLAND RD
KENWOOD RD
WRAMPLING PL
DICKENSON CL
Sch
MARSH SIDE CL
FOXGLOVE CL
HUNTINGDON RD
GOODWIN RD
ST ANN'S RD
CHURCH LA
BOUNCES RD
WARLEY RD
PICKETT'S LOCK LA
WIMBORNE RD
MILESTONE CT
ALSTONE CT
HENDON RD
BATH RD
WALBROOK HO
WHITE HO
NORTH WAY
CENTRE WAY
SOUTH WAY
Dominion Bsns Pk
DURHAM RD
RUSKIN WLK
KINGSTON RD
WARD PL
BOUNCES LA
FORD CL
OXFORD RD
GORDON RD
CORNWALLIS RD
CORNWALLIS GR
CORNWALLIS AVE
NASH RD
WYLDFIELD GDNS
LICHFIELD RD
LAMB'S CL
LION RD
BALHAM RD
CHISWICK RD
ST MARTIN'S RD
DOVER RD
PENTLAND CL
BUXTON CL
B154
CHURCH ST
SAWYER CL
LACEY CL
NEWDALES CL
NEW RD
MARSDEN RD
WESTOE RD
HARTON RD
MONMOUTH RD
Claverings Ind Est
HENNESSY RD
All Saints Prim Sch
ALL SAINTS CL
THE GREEN
NORTH SQ
THE NORTH MALL
SEYMOUR RD
LOGAN RD
RANWORTH RD
EXETER RD
STRIMON CL
HUDSON WAY
Sewage Works
ALMSHOUSES
GRANHAM GDNS
THE BROADWAY
Edmonton Green Sh Ctr
GOSMORE CT
ST JAMES RD
QUEEN'S RD
TOWN RD
DENSWORTH GR
ELLEN CT
TIGRIS CL
MERIDIAN WAY
Edmonton Green
GARTH RD
THE MARKET SQ
SUMMERSKILLE CL
NELSON RD
DYSON AVE
BRETT CT
NILE DR
VOLTA
NEWSTEAD HO
NORTHUMBERLAND GDNS
BEDEVERE RD
BALFOUR MEWS
THE SOUTH MALL
MENON DR
WELLINGTON
CHAD CRES
KARIBA CL
PRESPA
WEST CL
MALDON RD
GALAHAD RD
SALISBURY MANS
COLTHURST DR
AULAY LAWRENCE CT
WESTBOURNE
EASTBOURNIA AVE
ST MALO AVE
BOONE CT
GRANVILLE AVE
BADMA CL
ARDRA RD
CHAUNCEY CL
GAWAIN WLK
TRISTRAM DR
PLEVNA RD
EUSDEN CL
HAYNES DR
Allot Gdns
CONGO DR
ZAMBEZIE DR
PEEL CL
L Ctr
1 ALBERT SLEET CT
2 JOYCE LATTIMORE CT
3 FLORENCE WHITE CT
4 GEORGE TAYLOR CT
BARROWFIELD CL
MONTAGU RD
EASTERN AVE
PYMMES GDNS N
PYMMES GDNS S
SUNNYSIDE RD N
SUNNYSIDE RD E
SUNNYSIDE RD S
BARBOT CL
CLARKE MEWS
Lower Edmonton
MOSELLE CT
LIFFEY CT
THAMES CT
LEONARD RD
OSMAN RD
FELIXSTOWE RD
FRASER RD
Federation Cemy
DODSLEY PL
Recn Gd
VICTORIA RD
SHRUBBERY RD
Liby
BEACONSFIELD RD
BROOKFIELD RD
PEGAMOID RD
DANE RD
BARNES RD
THORNTON RD
YCROFT WAY
SEBASTOPOL RD
Fleecefield Prim Sch
BROOK CRES
PRINCES RD
Flds
SYCAMORE CL
FLEECE DR
STATION HOUSE MEWS
BRETTENHAM RD
BROOKSIDE CL
SECOND AVE
Montagu Ind Est
JEREMY'S GN
Park
PARK RD
FELIXSTOWE RD
Sch
BENJAFIELD CL

6
17
34

A
B
7
C
D
Works
Ponders End Ind Est
LEA VALLEY RD
A1055
A110
40
Ponders End
WHARF RD
Valleylink Est
Riverside Est
Works
MORSON RD
EN3
LEA VALLEY RD
River Lea or Lee
Lee Valley Wlk
Lee Valley L Ctr
Lee Valley Leisure
N9
William Girling Resr
Pickett's Lock
River Lee Navigation
River Lea or Lee Diversion
LEE PARK WAY
SEWARDSTONE RD
A112
PP
SEWARDSTONE GDNS
BOARDMAN AVE
ANTLERS HILL
GILWELL CL
Waltham Forest
DEERLEAP GR
YARDLEY CL
YARDLEY LA
Yardley Hill
96
6
Yardley Prim Sch
HAWKWOOD CRES
HAWKDENE
EPPING GLADE
Allot Gdns
EPPING WAY
5
CHELWOOD CL
ALBANY CT 1
RIVERSIDE CT 2
AMESBURY DR
DRYSDALE AVE
MARK AVE
MARGARET AVE
REDWOOD GDNS
DELLS CL
SOUTH AVE
95
MARKFIELD GDNS
HARFORD CL
Chingford Green
BAYTREE HO 3
STONEHILL CT 4
WINGROVE HO
LAUREL GDNS
HARFORD RD
HOMEBUSH HO
HOLLY DR
4
MERRYHILL CL
MAIDA WAY
KINGS HEAD HILL
MAIDA AVE
Enterprise
LOW HALL CL
COLLEGE GDNS
20
Pl Fld
A1037
MANSFIELD HILL
SEYMOUR RD
SUNSET AVE
COLLEGE GDNS
E4
MOUNT ECHO DR
3
ECHO CL
MEADOW CL
MOUNT ECHO AVE
Chingford Foundation Sch
NEVIN DR
THE RIDGEWAY
Mansfield Pk
VALLEY SIDE
VALLEY SIDE PAR
94
BELLE STAINES PLEASAUNCE
SILVERTHORN GDNS
B169
MULBERRY CL
Ridgeway Park
EATONS MEAD
LAWRENCE HILL
LAMBOURNE GDNS
2
PEEL CL
DOVE HOUSE GDNS
LANSDOWNE RD
DENNER RD
RETINGHAM WAY
WALMER CL
MARESBY HO
HERIOT AVE
WELLINGTON AVE
Wellington Prim Sch
HEATHCOTE GR
LEADALE AVE
CHINGFORD AVE
WALTHAM WAY
BRINDWOOD RD
MORELAND WAY
MISTRAL CT 1
MAGNOLIA LODGE 2
PHOENIX CT 3
ALDBOROUGH CT 4
CELANDINE CT 5
INGREBOURNE CT 6
OLD CHURCH RD
MAYHEW CL
RAMPTON CL
RECTORY CL
PRIORY CL
Cemy
GUNNER
PRIORY AVE
1
CHERRYDOWN CL
MIDDLETON CL
MIDDLETON AVE
CHERRYDOWN AVE
WINTER'S CT
MORRIS CT
FLAXEN RD
ALPHA RD
SALISBURY
HURST AVE
CHURCHILL TERR
MOUNT AVE
Allot Gdns
FLAXEN CL
HAROLD RD
GROVE RD
SUFFIELD RD
ST JOHN'S RD
CHIVERS RD
HURST CL
TEMPLETON AVE
93
THE RIDGES
Larkswood Prim Sch
BROOK CRES
BROOK GDNS
36
A
B
37
35
C
PO
D
38
NEW RD
A1009
MARMION AVE
Liby
MAYA ANGELOU CT
A1009
HALL LA
DORCHESTER

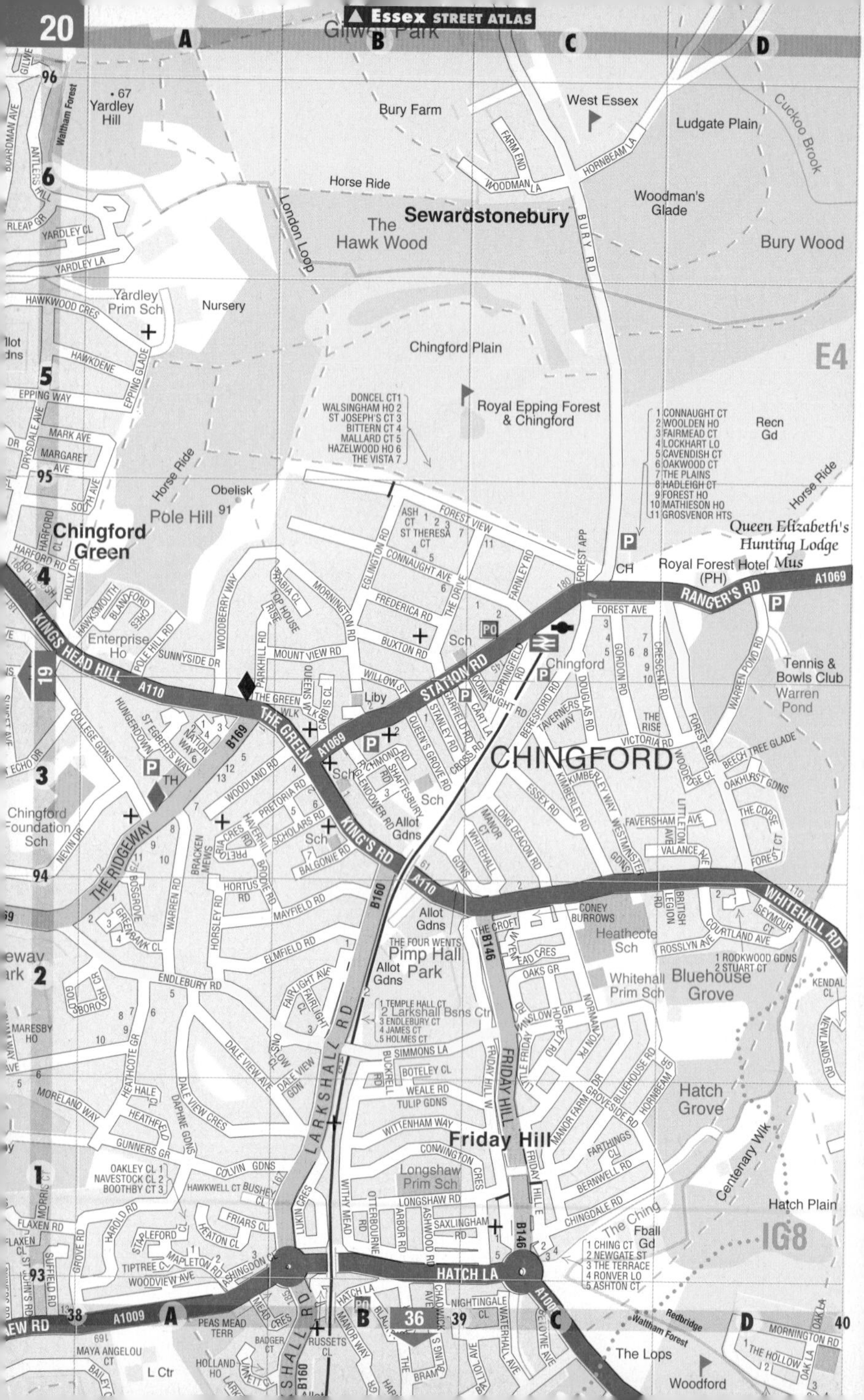

Gilwell Park
Yardley Hill
Bury Farm
West Essex
Ludgate Plain
Cuckoo Brook
Horse Ride
Sewardstonebury
Woodman's Glade
The Hawk Wood
Bury Wood
London Loop
Yardley Prim Sch
Nursery
Chingford Plain
Royal Epping Forest & Chingford
DONCEL CT 1
WALSINGHAM HO 2
ST JOSEPH'S CT 3
BITTERN CT 4
MALLARD CT 5
HAZELWOOD HO 6
THE VISTA 7
1 CONNAUGHT CT
2 WOOLDEN HO
3 FAIRMEAD CT
4 LOCKHART LO
5 CAVENDISH CT
6 OAKWOOD CT
7 THE PLAINS
8 HADLEIGH CT
9 FOREST HO
10 MATHIESON HO
11 GROSVENOR HTS
Recn Gd
Obelisk
Pole Hill
Chingford Green
Queen Elizabeth's Hunting Lodge Mus
Royal Forest Hotel (PH)
RANGER'S RD
A1069
Enterprise Ho
KINGS HEAD HILL
A110
STATION RD
THE GREEN
Chingford
Tennis & Bowls Club
Warren Pond
CHINGFORD
Chingford Foundation Sch
THE RIDGEWAY
KING'S RD
WHITEHALL RD
Allot Gdns
THE FOUR WENTS
Pimp Hall Park
Heathcote Sch
Whitehall Prim Sch
Bluehouse Grove
1 ROOKWOOD GDNS
2 STUART CT
1 TEMPLE HALL CT
2 Larkshall Bsns Ctr
3 ENDLEBURY CT
4 JAMES CT
5 HOLMES CT
LARKSHALL RD
FRIDAY HILL
Friday Hill
Hatch Grove
Centenary Wlk
Longshaw Prim Sch
OAKLEY CL 1
NAVESTOCK CL 2
BOOTHBY CT 3
Hatch Plain
The Ching
Fball Gd
1 CHING CT
2 NEWGATE ST
3 THE TERRACE
4 RONVER LO
5 ASHTON CT
IG8
E4
HATCH LA
A1009
The Lops
Woodford
Redbridge
Waltham Forest
MAYA ANGELOU CT
L Ctr

19
36

A
B
C
D
Long Hills
Centenary Wlk
Epping Forest
Mon
PALMER'S BRIDGE
The Warren
WARREN HILL
Magpie Hill
Connaught Water
IG10
69 Warren Hill
A1069
EPPING NEW RD
RANGER'S RD
The Ching
MANOR RD
Holmehurst
HIGH RD
A121
A104
LOUGHTON
Oaklands Sch
THE WILLOWS
NEWNHAM HO
NEWNHAM CL
SUMMERFIELD RD
SPRING GR
HILLCREST RD
THE CRESCENT
THE AVENUE
CRESCENT VIEW
ALGERS RD
ALGERS CL
ALBION HILL
ALBION PK
HIGH VIEW CL
NURSERY RD
NORTHFIELD
WESTFIELD
LONGFIELD
SOUTHERNHAY
UPPER PK
CLOVERLEYS
PARK HILL
HIGH GABLES
HIGH SILVER
CONNAUGHT AVE
OLLARD'S GR
GRANGE CT
NAFFENTON RISE
FAIRMEADSIDE
POLLARDS CL
A121 Loughton, M11 (A1168)
STATION RD
DEPOT COTTS
THE SIDINGS 1
LUKINSTONE CL 2
SEYMOUR CL 3
TEWKESBURY
The Warren Wood (PH)
Oak Hall
Waltham Forest
Epping Forest
TRINITY TERR
Powell's Forest
AVENUE GATE
SWAN LA
TREETOPS VIEW
KINGS PL
HARVEST LA
RICHMOND PK
FALLOW FIELDS
THE CHASE
MEWS
WOODCOTE
THE FOUNTAINS
REGENT'S PL
PONDFIELD END
THE STABLES
GUY'S RETREAT
THE DRIVE
NORTH END
ROEBUCK HTS
POWELL RD
ROEBUCK LA
LITTLE PLUCKETT'S WAY
STRADBROKE GR
THE RISE
RODING VIEW
LOUGHTON WAY
RIVER RD
ROUS RD
DENE RD
HURST RD
MAPLE LO
THE MEADWAY
PALACE GDNS
DALEFIELD
AMBERLEY RD
SCOTLAND RD
WESTBURY RD
RUSSELL RD
ORMONDE RISE
WAIKATO LO
LUCTONS AVE
GREENHILL
FOREST SIDE
GLADSTONE RD
ST JOHN'S CT
HAWSTEAD
ARDMORE LA
ARDMORE PL
QUEENSBURY
Sch
St John's CE Prim Sch
IG9
Essex STREET ATLAS
THAXTED RD
RACKMORE RD
FELSTEAD RD
KIRBY CL
TYLERS CL
Whitehall Plain
HERON CL
STARLING CL
ALBANY VIEW
FERNSIDE
ELIZABETH CT
THE CEDARS
BROOK RD
ICENI CT
CHURCH RD
BOLEYN CT
CHEQUERS
TRENT RD
HILL'S RD
OSBORNE RD
ST JAMES GATE
THE GREEN
GLENMEAD
PALMERSTON RD
B170
RODING LA
DEVON CL
THE RETREAT CVN SITE
FAIRLANDS AVE
FOREST HTS
PARK SIDE
STAG LA
WESTBURY LA
The Daiglen Sch
ANDREWS CL
QUEEN'S RD
LANGFORDS
BACK LA
KING'S AVE
VICTORIA RD
Buckhurst Hill
YEW CL
BEATRICE CT
ALFRED RD
ALBERT TERR
THE WINDSORS
LOWER QUEEN'S RD
Buckh Cty Pr
Allot Gdns
TILNEY DR 1
TILNEY RD 2
TILNEY CT 3
HURSTCOMBE 4
TUTTLEBEE LA
OAKLAND PL
The Birkbeck
CHANDOS CL
DUCHESS GR
THE DRUMMONDS
KNIGHTON LA
WIMBORNE CL
WOODSIDE
PRINCES RD
PRINCES WAY
MONARCH PL
KINGS PL
GEORGE CT
BRIAR CL
ELGAR CL
CEDAR CL
ALBERT RD
CASCADE
Liby
TRITON CT
HEMPSTEAD CL
WHITEHALL LA
BANCROFT AVE
BRANCEPETH GDNS
ALMONDS AVE
BENTLEY WAY
1 HEPWORTH HO
2 WHITEHALL LO
Reeds Forest
REDWOOD CL
BEECH LA
LINGROVE GDNS
KNIGHTON GN
Holly House
Buckhurst Hill
ELM CL
LIME CL
MAPLE CL
BIRCH CL
WILLOW CL
HOLLY CL
CHESTNUT CL
CASCADE CL
OAK RISE
HORNBEAM CL
HAWTHORNS
Bancrofts Sch
FOREST RD
BELGRAVE TERR
CHILTERN WAY
A110
THE DELL
DELL CL
WOODLAND CL
WOODLAND WAY
IG8
Knighton Wood
Lord's Bushes
MONKHAMS LA
Essex
Redbridge
FOREST EDGE
BUCKHURST WAY
WALNUT WAY
CHESTNUT AVE
HORNBEAM RD
SQUIRREL'S LA
Sp Gd
Allot Gdns
Woodford Wells
BURLINGTON PL
THE GLADE
FOREST CL
BROADFIELD WAY
FIELD CL
FARM CL
FARM WAY
Roding Valley
STATION WAY
1 STATION APP
2 STATION PAR
Woodford
WOODSIDE RD
FOREST WAY
MONTROSE MEWS
St Antony's Sch
ALDEBURGH PL
KNIGHTON DR
DENEHURST GDNS
DALE GDNS
Wells Sch
BELMONT CL
MONKHAM'S LA
BERESFORD DR
CHERRY TREE RISE
Sewage

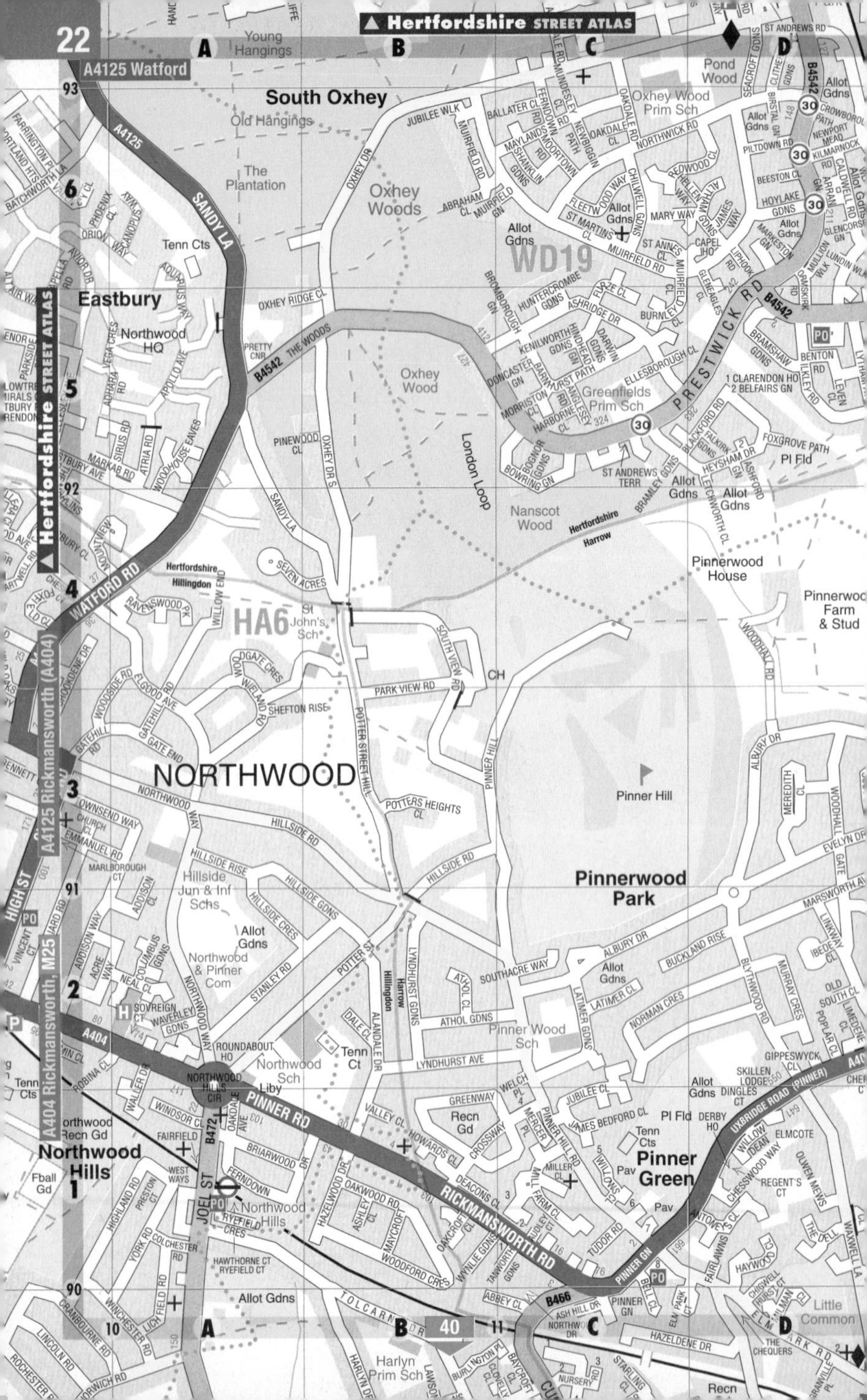
A4125 Watford
South Oxhey
Oxhey Woods
Eastbury
Northwood HQ
WD19
HA6
NORTHWOOD
Pinner Hill
Pinnerwood Park
Pinner Green
Northwood Hills
Pinnerwood House
Pinnerwood Farm & Stud
London Loop
Oxhey Wood
Nanscot Wood
Greenfields Prim Sch
Oxhey Wood Prim Sch
Pinner Wood Sch
Northwood Sch
Hillside Jun & Inf Schs
Northwood & Pinner Com
Harlyn Prim Sch
PRESTWICK RD
PINNER RD
RICKMANSWORTH RD
WATFORD RD
SANDY LA
A4125 Rickmansworth (A404)
A404 Rickmansworth, M25
Hertfordshire
Harrow
Hillingdon

40

A
B
C
D
Mutton Wood
Levels Wood
93
BELLINGDON
Carpenders Park Cemy
London Loop
Valley View Farm
COMPTON PL
ST GEORGE'S DR
HARROW WAY
ROMILLY DR
OULTON WAY
B4542
A4008
Mast
Harrow Weald Common
Grimsdyke Hotel
6
ASS HOUSE LA
Weald Wood
OLD REDDING
Woodhall Prim Sch
LITTLE OXHEY LA
WD19
Burnt Oak Farm
CH
Grims Dyke
HA3
Stony Wood
Hertfordshire
Harrow
Oxheylane Farm
CHERRY HILLS
Pl Fld
Sir James Altham Pool
OXHEY LA
5
WHITE CRAIG CL
SADDLERS CL
ROYSTON PARK RD
92
NEWLAND CL
Saddlers Mead
MEADWAY CL
HIGHBANKS RD
SYLVIA AVE
DERWENT AVE
LYNDON AVE
Grimsdyke Fst & Mid Sch
WITNEY CL
OAKLEIGH RD
KENNEDY CL
ARGENT HO
THE AVENUE
ROYSTON GR
LANGWORTHY
Pav
CLONARD WAY
WEALDWOOD GDNS
SEQUOIA PK
ROWLANDS AVE
PINEWOOD CL
4
ASHCROFT
Tenn Cts
OAKMEADE
HAZELCROFT
PINEWOOD AVE
OXHEY LA
Athletics Tk
THORNTON GR
WALPOLE CL
CEDAR DR
COLBURN AVE
HILLVIEW RD
HILLVIEW CL
THORNDYKE CT
MARDON
RANDOLPH CT
LIMETREE CT
FURHAM FIELD
THE LAWNS
A4008
24
HA5
Pl Fld
Hatch End
STAPLEFIELD CL
FERNDOWN CL
GRIMSDYKE RD
WESTFIELD PK
ELM
HATCH
BRAESIDE CL
RIDGEWAY CT
MILNE FIELD
168
SHERINGTON AVE
106
A410
ARTHUR CHICHELEY
BROADMEAD CL
WESSEX DR
LANGLAND DR
ALBURY DR
HALLAM GDNS
WOODRIDINGS CL
LEEWAY CL
OAKDENE CL
UXBRIDGE ROAD (HATCH END)
DOVE PK
BEETON CL
GABLE CL
Hatch End
Superstore
BONIFACE WLK
UFFORD RD
UFFORD CL
BONIFACE GDNS
TILLOTSON RD
3
CHICHELEY GDNS
LANGTON
WHITTLESEA CL
LYTTON RD
FELDEN CL
LONSDALE CL
ALTHAM RD
THE BROADWAY
PO
CORNWALL RD
HELSTON CL
ANSELM RD
ILDEA CL
PARK VIEW
Pl Flds
Pav
WINSTON CT
Hatch End High Sch
91
TOOKE CL
TOWERS RD
DEVONSHIRE RD
WELLINGTON RD
WELLINGTON AVE
LITTLECOTE PL
1 DEVONSHIRE CT
2 AVON MEWS
3 BENEDICT CT
4 TRURO HO
MULLION CL
WEST CHANTRY
CHANTRY RD
HEADSTONE LA
WHITTLESEA PATH
COURTENAY AVE
Shaftesbury Sch
St Teresa's Sch
ST BA
2
A410
A404
SEYMOUR CL
NUGENTS CT
NUGENT'S PK
CAVAN PL
BAYFORD LODGE
WOODRIDINGS AVE
Pl Fld
Pav
Rugby Gd
Sp Gd
Pav
CHANTRY PL
UXBRIDGE ROAD (PINNER)
ST THOMAS CT
ST THOMAS' DR
OLD HALL DR
OLD HALL CL
HOLLY GR
40
BRIANTS CL
River Pinn
JUXON CL
THEOBALD CRES
BANCROFT GDNS
AUGUSTINE RD
Headstone Lane
PARKFIELD HO
SECKER CRES
WOODHALL AVE
LITTLE ORCHARD CL
BARROW POINT LA
BURHILL GR
LITTLE MOSS LA
GEORGE V AVE
RANDON CL
BROADFIELDS
FERNLEIGH CT
BARMOR CL
LAURA TEMS CL
PARKFIELD AVE
OAKHILL AVE
BARROWDENE CL
MOSS CL
Pinner Park Farm
Model Rly
HA2
Pav
1
FULBECK WAY
VERWOOD RD
PARKFIELD CRES
OAKHILL AVE
MOSS LA
Tenn Cts
Bwg Gn
Sp Gd
BARROW POINT AVE
PAINE'S LA
Pav
Allot Gdns
Pl Fld
ALMOND WAY
WILLOW CT
PINNER PARK
EAST END WAY
BLOOMSBURY CT
Pinner Park Schs
90
AVENUE RD
LOVE LA
Cemy
A404
MELBOURNE
HOLMWOOD CL
PARKFIELD GDNS
LEIGHTON AVE
CHISWICK CT
GREYSTOKE AVE
MANOR PARK DR
AINSDALE
BIRKDALE AVE
Open Air Theatre
Nower Hill
EASTGLADE
ANGLES
Tenn Cts
13
41
14

A
B
8
C
D
Bentley Priory
London Loop
Levels Wood
93
Mast
Harrow Weald Common
Grimsdyke Hotel
6
Weald Wood
OLD REDDING
A409
HA7
Heriot's Wood
The Kiln
Priory House
PH
Harrow Weald Common
PORTMAN HALL
Tenn Cts
BROOKSHILL DR
HA3
Stony Wood
Copse Farm
Lower Priory Farm
Tenn Cts
Bentley Wood High Sch
5
Hillside
BROOKSHILL AVE
CLAMP HILL
BROOKSHILL
KEMBLE HO
FLECKER CL
BRIDGES RD
AMBERDENE 1
CORONET HO 2
CYGNET HO 3
KIPLING PL 4
SINCLAIR HO 5
FERN HO 6
BROOKSHILL GATE
SITWELL GR
MASEFIELD AVE
BROCKHURST CL
NEWBOLT RD
92
Allot Gdns
HARROW WEALD PK
Harrow Coll (Harrow Weald Campus)
Tenn Cts
Harrow Weald Cemy
ACACIA CL
30
WARBURTON CL
LAKELAND CL
TEMPLARS DR
WEST DR
FORTNUMS ACRE
CAIRN WAY
HOLME WAY
HEATHER WAY
4
The Bannister Sp Ctr
BELLFIELD AVE
PARK DR
Pl Fld
ALL SAINTS MEWS
COPPINS
LAVENDER GDNS
CHARLWOOD
WINSTON CL
Athletics Tk
CARRINGTON SQ
WEST DRIVE GDNS
GILLIAN HO
CHERRY HILL
LAWRIE CT
BERWICK
GORDON AVE
23
BIRCH PK
ROSS CL
130
UXBRIDGE RD (HARROW WEALD)
FONTWELL CL
KELVIN CRES
RICHMOND GDNS
KINGSTON PL
HUTTON WLK
WOOD
STAMFORD CL
ELMS RD
WILSMERE DR
A410
ARTILLERY PL
HUTTON GDNS
MEPHAM CRES
KYNASTON CL
MONRO GDNS
WYNCHGATE
WHITE GATE GDNS
TREVOR CL
3
BONIFACE WLK
UFFORD CL
CHICHELEY RD
CHICHELEY GDNS
MEPHAM GDNS
HUTTON LA
BOXTREE RD
PARKVIEW CT
DROMEY GDNS
KENTON LA
TILLOTSON RD
LANGTON RD
Kingsley High Sch
BELSIZE RD
SILVER CL
Tenn Cts
Recn Gd
Bwg Gn
Pav
TWICKENHAM GDNS
LORRAINE PK
COLLEGE CL
Weald Fst & Mid Schs
DRUMMOND DR
WHITTLESEA CL
STAFFORD RD
BELMONT LO
BLACKWELL CL
AZURE APPARTMENTS
HIGH VIEW CT
LEONARD CT
TALLACK CL
WHISPERWOOD CL
ROBIN HOOD DR
KINGFISHER CL
91
Hatch End High Sch
WHITTLESEA RD
BOXTREE LA
COLMER PL
HITHERWELL DR
ELM TERR
ALMA ROW
Tenn Cts
BARNVIEW LO
COLLEGE RD
HOLLYBUSH CL
WEALD RISE
CHESTNUT DR
WOODPECKER CL
RUSSELL MEAD
Cedars Fst & Mid Schs
Harrow Weald
MARICAS AVE
HIGH RD
PO
PARK CL
Shaftesbury Sch
St Teresa's Sch
GREER RD
WEIGHTON RD
PARK CRES
THE AVENUE
2
PO
COURTENAY AVE
ST BARNABAS CT
LONG ELMES
MEAD CL
BASLOW CL
ASTALL CL
ORCHID CT
HAREWOOD CT
COLLEGE AVE
JUNIPER CT
WILLOW CT
COLLEGE HILL RD
HEADSTONE LA
CHANTRY PL
JUXON CL
THEOBALD CRES
BANCROFT GDNS
CARMELITE CL
STOX MEAD
STANHOPE AVE
DERBY AVE
SEFTON AVE
MAISON ALFORT
PARK RISE
THE MEADOW WAY
THE BYE WAY
ADDERLEY RD
CONNAUGHT RD
Headstone Lane
AUGUSTINE RD
SECKER CRES
CARMELITE WLK
CLEWER CRES
WINDSOR RD
HAMPDEN RD
ENDERLEY RD
DURRANT CT
RISINGHOLME CL
THE GREEN WAY
THE CROSS WAY
CHURCH LA
DRYDEN RD
BROADFIELDS
FERNLEIGH CT
BARMOR CL
BANCROFT RD
WEALD LA
BARCHESTER CL
FARMSTEAD RD
QUEENS TERR
NEWTON RD
RISINGHOLME RD
ANNETTE CL
Allot Gdns
HARKETT CT
FISHER RD
Pav
LAURA CL
TEMSFORD CL
PARKFIELD AVE
COURTENAY GDNS
CARMELITE WAY
CYPRESS RD
BRINSLEY RD
BENGARTH DR
NICOLA CL
WHITEFRIARS DR
Coll
Sch
SPENCER RD
THE MIDDLE WAY
HIBBERT RD
Belmont Fst & Mid Sch
HA2
1
Sp Gd
FULBECK WAY
PARKFIELD CRES
CARMELITE RD
SARITA CL
TOORACK RD
HARROW
THE BROADWAY
HARKETT CL
BYRON RD
LEIGHTON RD
ATHELSTONE RD
WARHAM RD
VERWOOD RD
WICKHAM RD
MARTHORNE CRES
MINSTREL CT
CLAREMONT RD
ALMOND WAY
WILLOW CT
THE CLOSE
TUDOR GDNS
TUDOR RD
BRUCE RD
HIGH ST
DAUPHINE CT
MONTROSE RD
ABERDEEN RD
LORNE RD
LOCKET RD
PINNER PARK AVE
THE RISE
HARROW VIEW
PINNER PARK GDNS
LYNN CL
Whitefriars Trad Est
Sch
WHITEFRIARS AVE
LADYSMITH RD
TALBOT
90
Pinner Park Schs
HOLMWOOD
BARRATT WAY
Pl Fld
GRAHAM RD
CARDINAL WAY
STIRLING RD
ARCHERY
14
A
Sp Gd
B
42
15
C
D
SHERATON LO
THOMSON RD
GREENLEAF
GRANT RD
AVONDALE
PARKFIELD GDNS
Pav
Open Air Theatre
Tenn Cts
Tenn Cts
Bwg Gns
WELLINGTON RD
HAVELOCK RD
WOLSELEY RD
A409
GEORGE
LOMOND CT
CANNING RD
CUMBERLAND CT
GORDON RD
CECIL RD

A
B
9
C
D
STANMORE HILL
Stanmore Hall
DENNIS LA
JULIUS CAESAR WAY
CLAUDIUS CL
AUGUSTUS CL
FAUNA CL
CHEVALIER CL
BERRY HILL
BROCKLEYSIDE
REENGLASS RD
PARTRIDGE
A5
93
FALLOWFIELD
AYLMER CL
AYLWARDS RISE
AYLMER DR
HERIOTS CL
PINE CL
A4140
HALL FARM CL
OLD FORGE CL
SPRING LAKE
ADELAIDE CL
St Johns Sch
GREEN LANE COTTS
Sch
EMBRY CL
EMBRY WAY
CULVER LANDS
STANMORE LO
HILL CL
EATON CL
HEWETT CL
TANGATE GDNS
Recn Gd
Bwg Gn
Pav
LABURNUM CT
KNIGHTS RD
OAKMEAD CT
VALENCIA RD
WARREN FIELDS
ARRAN DR
RUSPER CL
WHITE HO
KERRY AVE
KERRY CT
GLANLEAM RD
LONDON RD
A410
6
Stanmore
SNARESBROOK DR
COURT DR
TINTAGEL DR
MORECAMBE GDNS
BROCKLEY CL
WESTBERE CT
WESTBERE DR
PANGBOURNE DR
DOVERCOURT
HERONSLEA DR
DALKEITH GR
5
Aylward Schs
ATKINSON
Tenn Cts
North Lo Collegiate
92
Tenn Cts
QUEENS M
WEYMOUTH
SUSSEX
YORK
SURREY
BEDFORD
DOVER
DURHAM
HAMPSHIRE
SUFFOLK
DUDLEY
HEREFORD
RUTLAND
KENT
NORFOLK
GRAHAM
4
Canons Park
Allot Gdns
26
BEN HALE CL
WOODSIDE CL
GREEN LA
HALSBURY CL
PYNNACLES CL
ALBERT HO
WINDSOR HO
STEWART HO
CHERCHEFELL MEWS
T Cts
RAY CL
RAY GDNS
Liby
GREYFELL CL
DENNIS GDNS
OAK LODGE CL
BELMONT
COPLEY
THE BROADWAY
CHURCH RD A410
PO
P
GLEBE CT
GLEBE RD
CLAIRE GDNS
BEAUCHAMP CT
ALBEMARLE PK
DENE GDNS
BEECH TREE CL
MERRION AVE
CRAIGWEIL DR
SANDYMOUNT AVE
CHARLBURY AVE
CRAIGWEIL CL
OLDFIELD CL
WINSCOMBE WAY
HOLLAND WLK
HOLLAND CL
BOWLES CT
LINDEN CT
OLD LODGE WAY
DEARNE CT
RIVERINE LO
STANMORE
THE CHANTRIES
BENTLEY WAY
WHITE ORCHARDS
UXBRIDGE RD
GLANVILLE MEWS
LADY ALESFORD AVE
RECTORY LA
WOLSTENHOLME
TUDOR WELL CL
RECTORY CL
MANOR HOUSE EST
ELM PK
HAIG RD
INGRAM CL
BYWORTH HO
YORK CL
MALCOLM CT
LEMON
NELSON RD
MERRYFIELD GDNS
ELIZABETH GDNS
ORFORD CT
DU CROS DR
PETERS CL
DOUGLAS CL
WILLIAM DR
GLYN CT
CHAMBERS WALK
ELLIOTT RD
SHERBOURNE PL
CAROLINE CT
EMBRY DR
BOYLE AVE
CARR CL
CHERRY TREE WAY
Stanmore Coll
BEATTY RD
MARSH LA
TALMAN GR
HA8
THE CHASE
DOWDING PL
CONWAY CL
GOODHALL CL
POND HO
CHANDOS CT
CASTLEREAGH HO
ROBB RD
TRENCHARD CL
BERNAYS CL
NARESBY FOLD
THE RIDGEWAY
VERSTON WAY
WYCHWOOD AVE
WYCHWOOD CL
HOWBERRY RD
CHEYNEYS AVE
KENNETH GDNS
SALMOND CL
Temple Pond
TEMPLE MEAD CL
OAKLAWN CT
SEPTEMBER WAY
WATER GDNS
LEAVESDEN RD
CAPUCHIN CL
GORDON AVE
ROSEDALE CL
LAURIMEL CL
LINDETH CL
SAVERNAKE CT
OLD CHURCH LA
BARN CRES
LANSDOWNE RD
WILDCROFT GDNS
HOWBERRY CL
CLOYSTER WOOD
SALISBURY HO
LINKS VIEW CL
WEYMOUTH WLK
GEORGIAN CL
WENTWORTH PL
GREENACRES DR
GLENEAGLES
COLMAN CT
KENILWORTH HO
CH
OVERTON RD
COURTENS MEWS
ALCUIN CT
CRANMER CL
GREEN VERGES
CORNBURY RD
LONGCROFTE RD
BARTHOLOMEW RD
WATERSFIELD WAY
DONNEFIELD AVE
CANONS PARK CL
HA7
Stanmore
THE QUADRANGLE
ABERDEEN COTTS
GOLF CL
TRACY CT
BELMONT LA
ABERCORN RD
Whitchurch Schs
STATION PAR
3
B461
Belmont
105
ACORN CL
OAK TREE CL
Sp Gd
Stanburn Schs
AMBER HO
BRAMBLE CL
BRICK LA
HONISTER GDNS
HONISTER CL
WEMBOROUGH RD
HOMEMEAD
91
MAYCHURCH CL
Tenn Cts
Pav
PARR RD
Honeypot Bsns Ct
GARLAND RD
Allot Gdns
VERNON CT
HONISTER PL
BELLAMY CT
VERNON DR
FLORISTON GDNS
FLORISTON CL
COLEDALE DR
GYLES PK
BROMEFIELD
BUSH GR
ST EDMUNDS DR
BELLAMY DR
ST ANDREWS DR
KYNANCE GDNS
BRAITHWAITE GDNS
LYON MEADE
PICKETT CROFT
2
WIGTON GDNS
HERMITAGE WAY
BEVERLEY GDNS
FELBRIDGE AVE
WESTON DR
Belmont
CURZON AVE
KENTON LA
MOUNTBEL RD
BELMONT CIRC
VENTNOR AVE
YORK AVE
WETHERAL DR
CROWSHOTT AVE
THISTLECROFT GDNS
BURNELL GDNS
LAMORNA GR
LADYCROFT WLK
ANMERSH GR
PEARESWOOD GDNS
Works
DALSTON GDNS
ALDRIDGE AVE
STATION PAR
WARWICK PAR
Sch
CLIFTON AVE
ST ANDREWS CL
Centenary Park
BROADCROFT AVE
HONEYPOT LA
GODDARD CT
DOBBIN CL
HA3
KENTON LA
GRANGE AVE
UPPINGHAM AVE
DERWENT CRES
Park High Sch
CARISBROOKE CL
PORTLAND CRES
FAIRWAYS
COLLINS AVE
1
BORROWDALE AVE
GRASMERE GDNS
CROSS RD
KENMORE AVE
ELGIN AVE
KINGSHILL DR
TENBY AVE
ASHLEY CT
ROCKLANDS DR
Sp Gd
CULVER GR
Bwg Gn
Tenn Cts
LANGLAND CRES
ELIZABETH HO
BALMORAL
RADCLIFFE RD
IVANHOE DR
JERSEY AVE
QUEENS CT
HILIARY GDNS
MORLEY CRES E
MORLEY CRES W
CHARMIAN AVE
Pl Fld
QUEENS AVE
Priestmead Schs
90
A4140
PEMBROKE AVE
Recn Gd
17
43
CLYDESDALE AVE
PORTLAND CRES
18
BELMONT RD
IRVINE AVE
HARTFORD AVE
FORMBY AVE
STREATFIELD RD
BOOTHMAN HO
QUEENSBURY CIRC PAR
MOORHOUSE RD
Allot
Schs

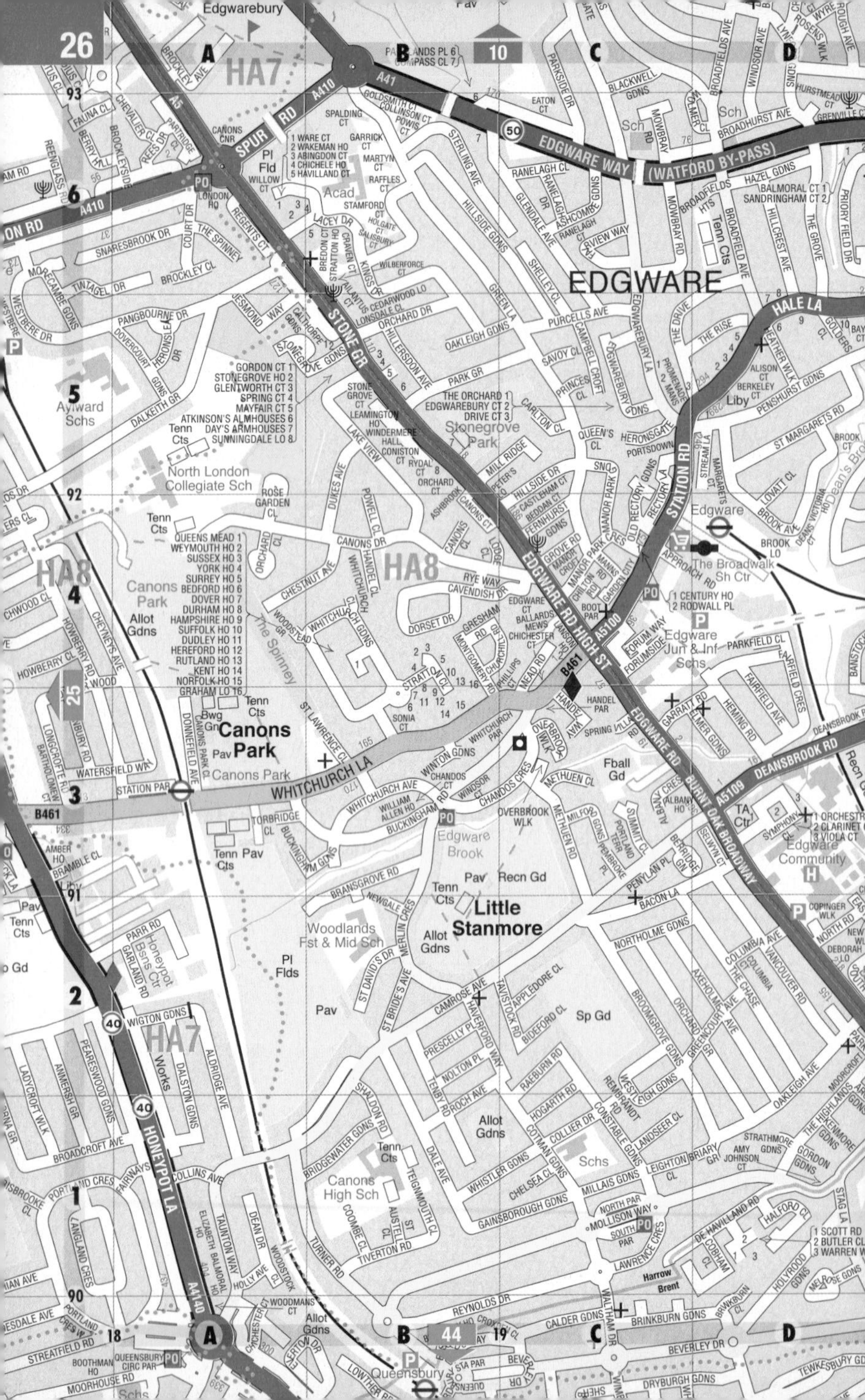

Edgwarebury
HA7
EDGWARE WAY (WATFORD BY-PASS)
EDGWARE
STONE GR
HALE LA
STATION RD
HA8
Stonegrove Park
North London Collegiate Sch
Canons Park
Aylward Schs
EDGWARE RD HIGH ST
WHITCHURCH LA
The Broadwalk Sh Ctr
Edgware Jun & Inf Schs
DEANSBROOK RD
BURNT OAK BROADWAY
Edgware Community
Little Stanmore
Woodlands Fst & Mid Sch
Canons High Sch
HONEYPOT LA
Queensbury

Mill Hill
NW7
NW4
NW9
HENDON
Arrandene Open Space
The Ridgeway
Hammers La
Daws La
Watford Way
Great North Way (Barnet By-Pass)
Bittacy Hill
Sanders La
Pursley Rd
Wise La
Page St
Ashley La
Holders Hill Rd
Millspit Hill
St Paul's CE Prim Sch
Mill Hill Sch
Goodwyn Sch
St Vincent's RC Sch
Mount Sch
Mill Hill Cemy
Copthall Sch
Dollis Jun & Inf Schs
Chase Lodge Pl Flds
Barnet Copthall Sp Ctr
Hendon Stadium
Swimming Baths
Hendon Cemy & Crem
Hasmonean High Sch (Girls)
Five Ways Cnr
RAF Mus
Battle of Britain Museum
Police HQ
Barnet Coll (Grahame Pk Ctr)
St James' RC High Sch
Sunnyhill Park
Bittacy Park
Oakfields
Burtonhole Farm
Folly Farm
Drivers Hill
Featherstone Hill
Mill Hill Park
School Park
Holders Hill
Pentavia Ret Pk
Mill Hill Ind Est
Univ of London Obsy
St Joseph's Coll Mill Hill Missionaries
Lawrence Green

12
46

A
B
C
D
13
Woodridge Prim Sch
CHIDDINGFOLD
LAUREL VIEW
HOLDEN HTS
Finchley Sch
ARLINGTON
SOUTHOVER
FRAMFIELD CL
NORTHIAM
SHORTGATE
MICHLEHAM DOWN
Sp Gd
BROOK MDW
FOUR ACRES
GUILDOWN AVE
SYLVAN CT
BARCHESTER LO
HENDERSON CT
WOODSIDE GRANGE RD
GRANGEWAY
TEYNHAM CT
GREEN BANK
BUDD CL
LORIAN CL
DEVONSHIRE HO
93
CLAIRE CT
CAVENDISH HO
LITTLE CEDARS
SQUIRRELS
ST ANDREW'S
WOODSIDE AVE
LIMES AVE
HIGHWOOD
WHITTINGTON
6
SONIA CT
CLIVEDEN CL
1 FREDERICK'S
2 THEOBALDS AVE
AVENUE RD
ARDEN GRANGE
EMERALD CT
CHOLMELEY CT
WOODSIDE PARK RD
CLARENDON HO
LODGE LA
ALBERT ST
Sch
PERCY RD
GAINSBOROUGH RD
NETHERFIELD RD
5
HUGHES CL
COLERIDGE RD
DERBY AVE
Woodside Park
N12
Tenn Cts
Bwg Gn
Folly Brook
TILLINGHAM WAY
TWINEHAM GN
RIVERSIDE HO
HOLDEN RD
Woodside Park
Sch
THE OAKS
DORIE MEWS
HOPTREE CL
HOLDEN AVE
DOWNING CT
FINCHLEY LO
THE GABLES
PYCOMBE CNR
SCAYNES LINK
CHANCTONBURY WAY
BROOKDENE
VICARAGE CT
THE GARTH
HOLMDENE
HOLDEN RD
GARDEN CT
RODMELL SLOPE
CISSBURY RING N
SINGLETON SCARP
LULLINGTON GARTH
BARHAM CT
FRITH MANOR COTTS
Allot Gdns
OFFHAM SLOPE
WOLSTONBURY
SUSSEX RING
ARGYLE RD
WORCESTER CT
AVONDALE AVE
GAINSBOROUGH CT
AVON CT
SPRINGFIELD CL
Frith Manor Prim Sch
FOLKINGTON CNR
CISSBURY RING S
SADDLESCOMBE WAY
POYNINGS WAY
STEYNINGS WAY
WALMINGTON FOLD
Tenn Ct
WESTBURY RD
COURT HOUSE RD
NETHER ST
FOLEY CT
BIRKBECK RD
VIVIAN CT
QUEENSGATE CT
ALBANY CT
HUTTON GR
ALEXANDRA GR
BARCLAY CT
DALE GR
PUGET CT
92
KNIGHTSWOOD HO
READING WAY
HOLMES AVE
APPROACH LA
ROSS AVE
GAWTHORNE AVE
HENRY DARLOT DR
ROBERTS RD
LIDBURY RD
KENNY RD
PAGE CL
KELLY RD
DREW AVE
TWINN RD
WARREN WAY
WILLIAMSON WAY
Inglis Barracks
BURTONHOLE LA
81
LINKSIDE
ELLE CT
THE CREST
WESTLEIGH CT
HILLCOURT AVE
MOSSBOROUGH CL
MOSS HALL CT
THYRA GR
GREENLAWNS
Superstore
VINE LO
4
CHRISTCHURCH
Finchley
Allot Gdns
CHESTERFIELD RD
WESTBURY GR
NETHERCOURT AVE
COURT HOUSE GDNS
THE LAURELS
FURSBY AVE
WESTLINTON CL
NW7
FRITH LA
CH
Nether Court
Tenn Cts
Pavs
BRENT WAY
MAPLE CT
SALIX CT
WEST AVE
HAMILTON WAY
PENSTEMON CL
Moss Hall Schs
NORTHUMBERLAND HO
PAMELA CT
THE LANTERNS
MOSS HALL GR
MOSS HALL CRES
WOODBERRY WAY
GLOWHILL CT
NEWBURN CT
PO
West Finchley
ESSEX PK
FINCHLEY CT
HARTLEY HO
DOUGLAS BADER HO
30
Mill Hill East
Bittacy Bsns Ctr
Superstore
Dollis Brook
OAKDENE PK
LANSDOWNE RD
FINCHLEY WAY
CEDAR CT
THE DRIVE
CHIVINS CT
CARLTON CT
HOWCROFT CRES
WENTWORTH CL
BROWNLOW RD
BALLARDS LA
THE FOUNTAINS
SOLAR CT
GRANVILLE RD
ETCHINGHAM CT
ST MARY'S CT
BITTACY CT
CRANBOURNE CT
LANGSTONE WAY
NEW RD
ROCKLANDS
GORDON RD
GROSVENOR RD
CHESTNUT ROW
NETHER CL
WENTWORTH AVE
GRUNEISEN RD
MARWOOD CT
WENTWORTH PK
ROSSANNE HO
SEYMOUR RD
NIGEL CT
Bwg Gn
Bwg Gn
3
FINCHLEY
VINEYARD AVE
DOLLISCROFT
B552
ABERCORN CL
MALLOW MEAD
ABERCORN RD
RUTH CT
BROOK CL
Allot Gdns
EVERSLEIGH RD
EVERSLEIGH CT
ELM PARK RD
SELLERS HALL CL
CORNWALL AVE
ADAMS CL
CLAVERLEY VILLAS
ST PAUL'S WAY
THE RIDGEWAY
Pavs
Tenn Cts
ETCHINGHAM PARK RD
PARK CRES
BARRYMORE
QUEEN'S AVE
B1462
DOLLIS RD
LINKS VIEW
THYME CT
REGEL CT
PO
HORNFIELD PAR
THORNFIELD CT
MILL CT
THORNFIELD AVE
Sch
Pl Fld
Allot Gdns
BOSE CL
Pav
CRESCENT RD
DOLLIS CT
CRESCENT RISE
NETHER ST
B1462
THE GROVE
GROVE AVE
FALKLAND AVE
MILLERS YD
WILLOW WAY
PARKSIDE
MARLEX LO
Victoria Park
91
WOODLANDS AVE
POPES DR
SHAKESPEARE RD
ALAN LO
ALBERT PL
STANTON
CLAVERLEY GR
PRINCES AVE
DORSET MEWS
REDBOURNE HO
REDBOURNE AVE
PREMIER LO
DUKES AVE
VINES AVE
OAKFIELD CT
PARK VIEW RD
PARK AVE
Manorside Sch
2
HOLDERS HILL PAR
HOLDERS HILL RD
HAWTHORN MEWS
OAKDALE CL
PARAGON CT
FORELAND CT
CLAREMONT PK
LYNDHURST GDNS
DOLLIS PK
LAXMI CT
BRUNSWICK HO
CLIFTON AVE
DOLLIS MEWS
N3
HERVEY CL
BERKELEY CT
OAKFIELD RD
LONG LA
SQUIRES LA
QUEENS
AVONDALE RD
Tenn Cts
GRASS PK
GRENVILLE CL
KINGSWOOD PK
THE LINTONS
DOLLIS AVE
CHURCH CRES
VICTORIA AVE
PEWTERERS CT
Ct
Finchley Central
STATION CL
CLAIGMAR GDNS
CADOGAN GDNS
STRATHMORE GDNS
VINEYARD GR
LAKESIDE
MONTPELIER RD
CROMWELL RD
ABINGDON
QUEENSWOOD PK
HENDON AVE
PRIORY CL
RECTORY CL
Liby
COLLEGE CL
A598
A5000
ARCADIA AVE
WOOTTON GR
STATION RD
DOUGLAS CT
NURSERY AVE
RATHGAR CL
Schs
REGENCY HO
ROCHESTER CT
VILLAGE RD
CYPRUS GDNS
PRESTON PK
SAMUEL LO
BLAKE LO
ST MARY'S AVE
HENDON LA
GRAVEL HILL
SPENCER CL
THE AVENUE
GLENHILL CL
LICHFIELD GR
SYLVAN AVE
Pav
Church End
Allot Gdns
MADDISON CL
THE MEAD
FREELAND PK
1 COLERNE CT
2 CUMBERLAND GDNS
CYPRUS AVE
GOLDA CL
ST MICHAEL'S CL
TEMPLE CL
BISWORTH RD
BISWORTH LO
EMBASSY LO
DERBY AVE
ELLERTON LO
Sp Gd
Tenn Cts
SPRING PL
MANOR VIEW
DUDLEY RD
ROSEMARY AVE
PRIMROSE CL
1
Windsor Open Space
WINDSOR RD
WINDSOR CT
A504
PO
EAST END RD
Pav
Bwg Gn
Sp Gd
BRIARFIELD AVE
MANOR COTTS AVE
MANOR COTTS
CHAMPION
CRANMER CT
PAUL CT
Coll
GRENACRES
CROWN LO
SALISBURY CT
ARUNDEL LO
NORTH CRES
CYPRUS RD
COLOSSEUM CT
STANHOPE CT
STANHOPE AVE
EASTGATE CT
CAVENDISH AVE
TEMPLARS CRES
HOLMWOOD GDNS
WINDERMERE AVE
PAVILION MEWS
Sch
Mus
Middlesex Cty Crkt Sch
TANGLE TREE CL
A406
BRIAR CL
RICHMOND RD
Fld
90
HOLDERS HILL GDNS
WICKLIFFE AVE
CHARLTON CT
STAFFORDSHIRE HO
ELIZABETHAN
HELEN CT
VOYSEY CL
SALISBURY AVE
ARDEN RD
SURREY CL
MOUNTFIELD RD
LUKES CT
St Theresa's RC Prim Sch
EAST END RD
CRANBOURNE CT
BENEDICT
26
25
47
50
WAVERLEY GR
FITZALAN RD
IVOR CT
ALLANDALE
MAYFLOWER LO
HOLLY PARK GDNS
ORCHARD
AMBERDEN AVE
BASING WAY
MOAT CRES
THE CRESCENT
REMEMBRANCE AVE
CYPRESS AVE
Crem
EAST END RD
N3
HENDON LA
PARK RD

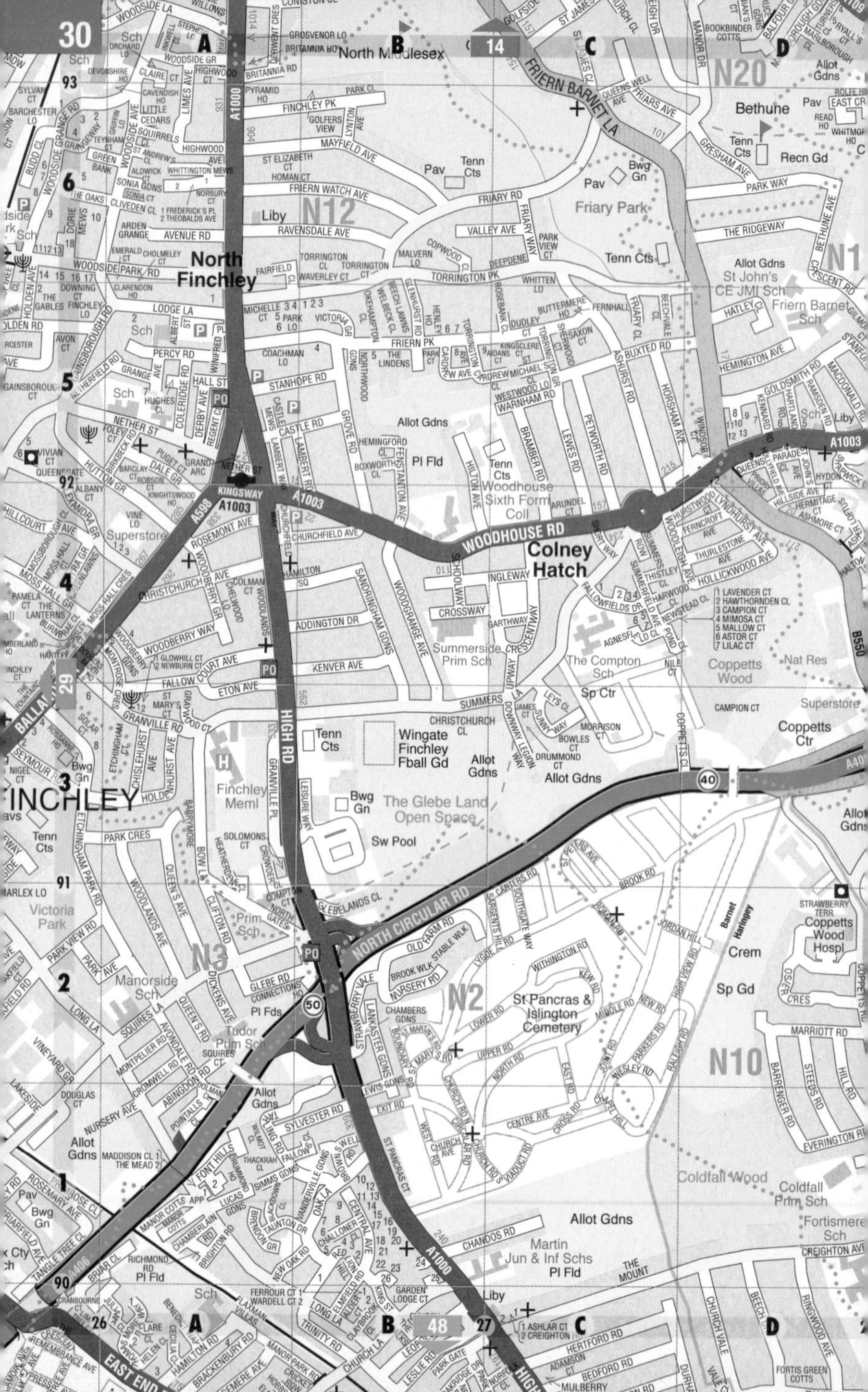
North Middlesex
N20
Bethune
N12
North Finchley
Friary Park
Colney Hatch
Woodhouse Sixth Form Coll
Summerside Prim Sch
The Compton Sch
Coppetts Wood
Coppetts Ctr
Wingate Finchley Fball Gd
Finchley Meml
The Glebe Land Open Space
FINCHLEY
Victoria Park
N3
Manorside Sch
Tudor Prim Sch
N2
St Pancras & Islington Cemetery
Coppetts Wood Hospl
N10
Coldfall Wood
Coldfall Prim Sch
Fortismere Sch
Martin Jun & Inf Schs
NORTH CIRCULAR RD
WOODHOUSE RD
HIGH RD
FRIERN BARNET LA
A1000
A1003
A598
A406
14
29
48

New Southgate
FRIERN BARNET
N11
N14
N13
N22
N10
N8
OAKLEIGH RD S
BOWES RD
STATION RD
TELFORD RD (NORTH CIRCULAR RD)
PINKHAM WAY NORTH CIRCULAR RD
FRIERN BARNET RD
COLNEY HATCH LA
ALEXANDRA PARK RD
ALBERT RD
DURNSFORD RD
BOUNDS GREEN RD
WILMER WAY
POWYS LA
BROWNLOW RD
MUSWELL HILL BDWY
Betstyle Circus
Arnos Park
Arnos Grove
Friern Bridge Ret Pk
Bounds Green Ind Est
Hollickwood Park
Muswell Hill
Alexandra Park Sch
Rhodes Avenue Prim Sch
Alexandra Palace
The Lake
Alexandra Park
Bounds Green
Colney Hatch
Wood Green Tunnel
Superstore
Broomfield Sch
Bowes Prim Sch
St Martin of Porres RC Prim Sch
Hollickwood Prim Sch
Our Lady of Muswell RC Prim Sch
Blanche Nevile Sch
Fortismere Sch (South Wing)
Coppetts Wood Prim Sch
Norfolk House Sch
1 CROMWELL HO
2 SYDNEY HO
3 CLEEVE CT
4 QUEENSLAND CT
5 NEALE CT
6 BRISBANE CT
7 MELBOURNE CT
8 SLADE CT
9 CONSTANCE CT
1 CARADOC EVANS CL
2 ROBERTS HO
3 LORNE HO
4 SELLSBY CT
5 NORTHERN STAR HO
1 BELMONT CT
2 EDWARDS DR
3 BADEN CT
4 ST GABRIELS CT
5 MADISON APARTMENTS
1 AVENUE MANS
2 CAVERSHAM LO
15
49
32

16
50
31
A
B
C
D
93
6
5
92
4
3
91
2
1
90
30
31
N13
N22
N8
Broomfield Park
Bowes Park
WOOD GREEN
Noel Park
Palmers Green
ALDERMAN'S HILL
A1004
POWYS LA
B1452
WILMER WAY
BOWES RD (NORTH CIRCULAR RD)
A406
NORTH CIRCULAR RD
HIGH RD
A109
BOUNDS GREEN RD
B106
BROWNLOW RD
LORDSHIP LA
A105
STATION RD
B138
MAYES RD
PARK AVE
WESTBURY AVE
A1080
Clockhouse Junction
St Annes Catholic High Sch for Girls (Upper)
Broomfield Sch
Bowes Prim Sch
Tottenhall Inf Sch
St Michael-at-Bowes CE Jun Sch
Woodside Park
St Thomas More Sch
Earlham Prim Sch
White Hart Lane Sec Sch
New River Sp & Recn Ctr
St George Ind Est
Hazelwood Jun & Inf Schs
Alexandra Palace
Alexandra Prim Sch
Wood Green Common
Nightingale Gardens
Avenue Gdns
Noel Park Prim Sch
Olympia Ind Est
Pymme's Brook
New River
Allot Gdns
Sp Gd
Tenn Cts
Bwg Gn
Pl Fld
Pav
Liby
Bndstd
Shop City
Rec Gd

EDMONTON
TOTTENHAM
Tatem Park
Hollywood Gardens
Aylward Sch
Lopen Works
Pymmes Park
Pl Flds
Great Cambridge Junction
STERLING WAY (NORTH CIRCULAR RD)
North Middlesex University
Oakthorpe Prim Sch
Wilbury Prim Sch
Landmark Commerical Ctr
Langhedge Lane Ind Est
Frontier Works
Devonshire Hill Prim Sch
Middlesex Univ
Peacock Ind Est
White Hart Lane
Tottenham Hotspur Fball Club
Tottenham Cemy
The Moselle
N17
Risley Avenue Sch
Bruce Castle Park
Bruce Castle Mus
THE ROUNDWAY
Tower Gardens
LORDSHIP LA
HIGH RD
BRUCE GR
Broadwater Farm Prim Sch
William C Harvey Sch
Moselle Sch
Lordship Recn Gd
Open Air Theatre
DOWNHILLS WAY
Bruce Grove
Bruce Grove Prim Sch
Silver Ind Est
Enfield
Haringey
17
34
51
A
B
C
D
A10
A406
A1010
A1080
A109
B155
A111

34
A
B
C
D
Edmonton
Federation
18
Recn Gd
40
93
Pl Flds
6
EDMONTON
5
92
4
3
91
2
1
90
TOTTENHAM
A1010
FORE ST
HIGH RD
A406
A1055
B137
A109
A10
ANGEL ROAD (NORTH CIRCULAR ROAD)
CONDUIT LA
MERIDIAN WAY
WATERMEAD WAY
BLACKHORSE LA
B179
LEESIDE RD
Angel Edmonton
Kenninghall
Cooks Ferry
ADVENT WAY
ARGON RD
Fleecefield Prim Sch
STATION HOUSE MEWS
BRETTENHAM RD
SEBASTOPOL RD
FELIXSTOWE RD
BROOKFIELD RD
FRASER RD
BROOK CRES
BROOKSIDE
PEGAMOID RD
THORNTON RD
PRINCES RD
SECOND AVE
Montagu Ind Est
JEREMY'S GN
SWAYTHLING CL
MONTAGU GDNS
MONTAGU CRES
CAMERON CL
DANIEL CL
GIBBS RD
STACEY AVE
BECKET RD
FIRST AVE
RAYS AVE
RAYS RD
Eley's Est
NOBEL RD
KYNOCH RD
ELEY RD
N18
Tenn Cts
Recn Gd
Bwg Gn
LYNDHURST RD
MORLEY AVE
FAIRFIELD RD
ABERDEEN RD
CAVENDISH RD
DERBY RD
NEW PARK EST
Angel Rd Works
Angel Road
BANKSIA RD
Ravenside Ret Pk
HAWLEY RD
Stonehill Bsns Pk
Superstore
GLOVER DR
WHITEHURST DR 1
GREYSWOOD AVE 2
SILVERMERE DR
Lea Valley Trad Est
ANTHONY WAY
Kingsway Est
Edmonton Wharf
TOWPATH RD
RAYNHAM RD
Raynham Prim Sch
Pl Fld
UPTON RD
YORKSHIRE GDNS
LADYSMITH RD
ALSTON RD
Upper Edmonton
STOCKTON RD
LEYBURN RD
MIDDLEHAM RD
CLAREMONT ST
ALPHA RD
WILLOUGHBY LA
Elm Lea Trad Est
BRANTWOOD RD
Triumph Trad Est
Royal London Est
Hotspur Ind Est
Lake Bsns Ctr
Sp Gd
Sp Ctr
Bwg Gns
Nrthmbrlnd Park Ind Est
Leeside Trad Est
Leeside Ind Est
Mowlem Trad Est
Leeside Works
Canal Bridge
N17
CONISTON RD
BURLEIGH CT
NORTHUMBERLAND PK
SCOTSWOOD WLK
Coll
Sch
Northumberland Pk Sp Ctr
Tottenham Hotspur Fball Club
PAXTON RD
PARK LA
Northumberland Park
Unicorn Works
Recn Gd
MARIGOLD RD
Allot Gdns
Tottenham Marshes
MARSH LA
ARGYLE RD
ASPLINS RD
FOYLE RD
MANOR RD
LANSDOWNE RD
Depot
River Lee Navigation
River Lea or Lee Diversion
Lee Flood Relief Channel
Coleraine Park Prim Sch
GLENDISH RD
HALEFIELD RD
POYNTON RD
ROSEBERY AVE
SHERRINGHAM AVE
SEYMOUR AVE
THACKERAY AVE
DOWSETT RD
CAREW RD
MAFEKING RD
BULLER RD
HOLCOMBE RD
Rosebery Ind Pk
Pymmes Brook
Haringey
Waltham Forest
Lockwood Reservoir
Allot Gdns
Lea Valley Technopark
Down Lane Park
Millmead Ind Ctr
52
35
Lockwood Ind Pk
Tenn Cts
Silver Ind Est
Bruce Grove
NORFOLK RD
WORCESTER RD
WOOLSTON CL
LOCKWOOD WAY
GLOUCESTER RD
CLARENCE RD
UPLANDS AVE
Uplands Bsns Pk
PRIESTLEY WAY
Forest Trad Est
Higham Lodge Bsns Ctr
33

35
A
B
C
D
19
93
92
91
90
6
5
4
3
2
1
36
37
38
53
N18
E4
HALL LA
A1009
A1037
A112
A406
A503
B179
River Lea or Lee Diversion
Enfield
Waltham Forest
MIDDLETON CL
MARMION CL
MARMION APP
MARMION AVE
HURST CL
CHURCHILL TERR
ALPHA RD
SALISBURY
MOUNT AVE
TEMPLETON AVE
THE RIDGES
Larkswood Prim Sch
WINTER'S CT
FLAXEN RD
FLAXEN CL
Allot Gdns
ST JOHN'S RD
CHIVERS RD
SUFFIELD RD
GROVE RD
TIPTREE CL
WOODVIEW
WINDSOR RD
BROOK CRES
BROOK GDNS
NEW RD
MAYA ANGELOU CT
L Ctr
Liby
RUSSELL RD
WAVERLEY AVE
BEVERLEY CT
HALL GDNS
YORK HO
CHASE GDNS
DORCHESTER GDNS
ALBERT AVE
ALBERT CRES
PEACH CT
ORCHARD CL
BEECH HO
TUFTON RD
NORMANSHIRE DR
LARKSWOOD RD
Larkswood Pl Fld
Larks
LOWER HALL LA
MANDEVILLE CT
HOLLYWOOD RD
Chingford Ind Ctr
CORK TREE WAY
Chase Lane Jun & Inf Schs
FRANKLAND RD
KINGSWOOD CT
NORTON CL
LIBRO CT
PARK VIEW HO
KINGSLEY GDNS
War Meml Recn Gd
SOPER CL
HAMPTON RD
NORBURY RD
CHINGFORD MOUNT RD
GENEVER CL
FINCH GDNS
THE LAWNS
ACORN CL
OAKFIELD
B Gn
AINSLIE WOOD GDNS
BOURNE GDNS
UNDERWOOD RD
PALACE VIEW RD
VILLAGE CL
LARKSHALL CT
GREENWOOD DR
ROPERS AVE
BURNHAM RD
YORK RD
GARDEN CT
PEWSEY CL
WARWICK RD
TITLEY CL
AINSLIE WOOD RD
Ainslie Wood Prim Sch
Ainslie Wood
MORLEY CT
SINCLAIR RD
BURLEY CL
BROAD OAK CL
ROYSTON AVE
ROLLS PARK RD
WOODSIDE GDNS
Rolls Sp Gd
RIVERLEIGH CT
Hall Lane
SHADBOLT AVE
WESTWARD RD
ROLLS PARK AVE
CRANSTON GDNS
1 OAK CT
2 BIRCH CT
3 POPLAR CT
4 HAWTHORNE CT
5 FERN CT
6 ELM CT
7 SPARROW CT
MAPLE AVE
LILAC CL
HAZEL WAY
CABINET WAY
LABURNUM CL
SILVER BIRCH AVE
HARDY RD
ASHLEY RD
BATEMAN RD
Allot Gdns
FRANCES RD
EDWARD AVE
CONINGSBY GDNS
LENA KENNEDY CL
HARBET RD
Cork Tree Ret Pk
Hastingwood Trad Est
ARNETT SQ
HEATHER RD
ROWAN AVE
LEONARD RD
MAY RD
LOCKWOOD PL
FIELD CL
GEORGE RD
BURNSIDE AVE
L Ctr
PIGEON CT
ST NICHOLAS CT
HIGHAM STATION AVE
TUDOR RD
BEAUFORT CL
THURLOW CL
LONG LEYS
Sch
HIGHAM HO
OSPREY HO
Superstore
LIME GR
ADAM RD
KEATLEY GN
CHING WAY
IRIS WAY
GREENHAM CL
TRINITY WAY
JUSTIN RD
MORRISON AVE
ROWDEN PARADE
ROWDEN PARK GDNS
MARLBOROUGH RD
BELLAMY RD
APPLEBY
WALTHAMSTOW AVE
Avenue Ind Est
The Ching
Salisbury Hall Pl Flds
SALISBURY HALL GDNS
NELSON RD
HELWYS CT
SELWYN
CAVENDISH
CHINGFORD RD
ROWDEN RD
Allot Gdns
MINERVA RD
LOXHAM RD
RUSHCROFT RD
Rush Croft Sch
ROEBUCK CT
Highams Park
(NORTH CIRCULAR RD)
50
FOLLY LA
Superstore
Banbury Resr
Walthamstow Stad
Wadham Lodge Sp Gd
PEACOCK CL
Hale End Sp Gd
Sports Ctr
Sp Gd
EMPRESS PAR
EMPRESS AVE
GROVE PARK AVE
1 GREENSHANK CL
2 CORMORANT CL
Pl Fld
WADHAM AVE
WALTHAM PARK WAY
GOODRIDGE HO
BANBURY RD
GREBE CL
OSPREY CL
STOW CRES
Crooked Billet
SWIFT CL
COGAN AVE
SWAN CL
DURBAN RD
Walthamstow Acad
WALTHAM PK
WADHAM RD
NORTH CIRCULAR RD
ASCHAM END
CHENEY ROW
William Morris Sch
KIMBERLEY RD
Kimberley Ind Est
CECIL RD
CECIL HO
VALOGNES AVE
AMBER AVE
FOLLY LA
MCENTEE AVE
BILLET RD
George White Sp Gd
KNEBWORTH AVE
KNEBWORTH HO
Chapel End Jun Sch
CHESHIRE CL
Wadham Lodge Sp Gd
FRIARS CT
MONOUX GR
DOUGLAS AVE
SHAW SQ
GUILDSWAY
LYNE CRES
WIGTON RD
ARDLEIGH RD
MANSEL GR
LEWIS AVE
ROBERTS RD
BERESFORD RD
KITCHENER RD
1 KINGS FARM
2 CHAPEL END HO
3 HIGHCROFT POINT
4 HYH HO
GARNER RD
BRIDGE END
FAIR VIEW CL
Sch
Higham Hill
MILLFIELD AVE
BOSWORTH CL
WILLIAMS AVE
KEITH RD
PENRHYN AVE
PENRHYN GR
BRETTENHAM AVE
Bwg Gn
WALTHAM CT
Bwg Gn
Recn Gd
Sch
CARLTON RD
LONGLANDS CT
KELMSCOTT CL
NORTH COUNTESS RD
RUSHBROOK CRES
BRETTENHAM RD
LAVEHHAM HO
CAZENOVE RD
HEAVITREE CT
Chapel End Inf Sch
BROOKSCROFT RD
QUEENSWOOD
HECHAM CL
Tenn Cts
MANOR RD
MANOR CL
MOUNT PLEASANT RD
RODNEY PL
WARWICK RD
HERON CL
THORPE CRES
PENNANT TERR
FLEEMING CL
Aveling Park Sch
AVELING PARK RD
MARTEN RD
DRAYTON RD
STURGE AVE
NORTHBANK RD
WOODEND RD
FULBOURNE RD
MAYFIELD RD
OAKFIELD RD
WINDSOR AVE
Liby
PRIORS CROFT
QUEENSLAND CL
PHOENIX CL
ELPHINSTONE RD
FLEEMING RD
CARR RD
Lloyd Park
LIVINGSTONE CL
EVESHAM AVE
Sir George Monoux Sixth Form Coll
WARBURTON TERR
THORPE RD
ST JOHN'S RD
VICTORIA RD
Walthamstow Bsns Ctr
Allot Gdns
CUMBERLAND RD
CLAREMONT RD
RENFREW HO
SHANKLIN HO
ABBOTS HO
UPSHIRE HO 1
VERMONT HO 2
WASHINGTON HO 3
TUSCANY HO 4
SHERWOOD CL
XAVIER HO
PRIORY CT
LINDEN HO
LISBON
Bwg Gn
Chestnut Sp Gd
LOWTHER RD
CHURCH RD
HIGHAM HILL RD
BRAMLEY CL
HAMILTON RD
COLVILLE RD
Allot Gdns
CAPRI HO
DARNDALE CL
DEVON HO
EASTLEIGH RD
KNROSS TERR
CHESTER MEWS
CHANDOS AVE
Waltham Forest Coll
SPRUCE HILLS RD
CLIFF
ORD RD
KINGSLEY
ST ANDREWS RD
OATLAND RISE
DILWYN CT
HILLFIELD
FAIRFIELD RD
BALMORAL HO
EVERGLADE HO
BEDFORD RD
DUDLEY RD
BROMLEY RD
Allot Gdns
LOWTON LO
GREEN POND RD
ADELAIDE HO
WINNS AVE
BADLIS RD
WINNS TERR
Bwg Gn
Gall
WALTHAMSTOW
STIRLING RD
Sch
HIGHAM PL
BROOK CT
PROND RD CL
BEMSTEAD RD
MERSEY RD
DIANA RD
TH
KENILWORTH AVE
FARNAN AVE
SUTHERLAND RD
HIGHAM ST
CHAMBERLAIN PL
NORTH COUNTESS RD
WILLIAM MORRIS CL
MILES AVE
FOREST RD
The Bell
Ct
C Ctr
PARKSTONE
Thorpe Coombe
Coll

A
B
C
D
IG8
E4
E17
20
35
54
HATCH LA
NEW RD
A1009
Chingford Hatch
LARKSHALL RD
B160
B146
Larks Wood
Larkswood Pl Fld
L Ctr
Allot Gdns
Jubilee Sp Gd
The Lops
Woodford
The Highams Park
Boating Lake
Highams Park
Hale End
Rolls Sp Gd
Bwg Gns
Wks
Schs
Sch
Liby
PO
LC
Ainslie Wood
Ainslie Wood Prim Sch
Woodford Cty High Sch
Rugby Fball Gd
St Aubyn's Sch
Hotel
Wadham Lodge Sp Gd
Sports Ctr
Rushcroft Sch
WINCHESTER RD
NORTH CIRCULAR RD
SOUTHEND ROAD
WOODFORD NEW RD
A104
A503
A406
FOREST RD
FULBOURNE RD
CHINGFORD LA
HIGH ROAD WOODFORD GN
Thorpe Hall Prim Sch
Whitefield Sch
Waterworks Cnr
Hyland House Sch
Upper Walthamstow
Gilbert's Slade
Woodside Schs
Thorpe Coombe
Tenn Cts
Bwg Gn
Monoux Coll
Waltham Forest Coll
Walthamstow Bsns Ctr
Redbridge
Waltham Forest
1 CHING CT
2 NEWGATE ST
3 THE TERRACE
4 RONVER LO
5 ASHTON CT
1 THE ALBANY
2 HATCHWOODS
3 HOBART CT
4 AURORA CT
5 HIGHWOOD
1 OAK CT
2 BIRCH CT
3 POPLAR CT
4 HAWTHORNE CT
5 FERN CT
6 ELM CT
7 SPARROW CT
1 FUCHSIA CT
2 CAMELIA CT
3 AZALEA CT
4 PEONY CT
5 MATSON CT
1 BEECH FARM COTTS
2 SWALLOW CT
3 LESTER HO
4 MONTSERRAT AVE
1 HEMPSTEAD RD
2 DENNIS CT
1 KING FARM
2 CHAPEL END HO
3 HIGHCROFT POINT
4 HYH HO

Woodford Wells
Knighton Wood
Roding Valley
IG9
IG8
WOODFORD
Woodford Green
South Woodford
E18
Ray Park
Ray Lodge Prim Sch
Woodbridge High Sch
Churchfields Jun & Inf Schs
Queen Mary & Westfield Coll (Halls of Residence)
Oakdale Jun Sch
Woodford Green Prep Sch
Avon House Sch
Trinity RC High Sch (Lower)
Woodford Trad Est
Charlie Browns Rdbt
HIGH ROAD WOODFORD GN
BROADMEAD RD
CHIGWELL RD
SOUTHEND RD
SNAKES LA EAST
SNAKES LA WEST
M11 Stansted Airport, M25
A113 Chigwell, M11 (A1168)
Essex STREET ATLAS
River Roding
Commerce Est
Allot Gdns
Sp Gd
Pl Fld

21
55

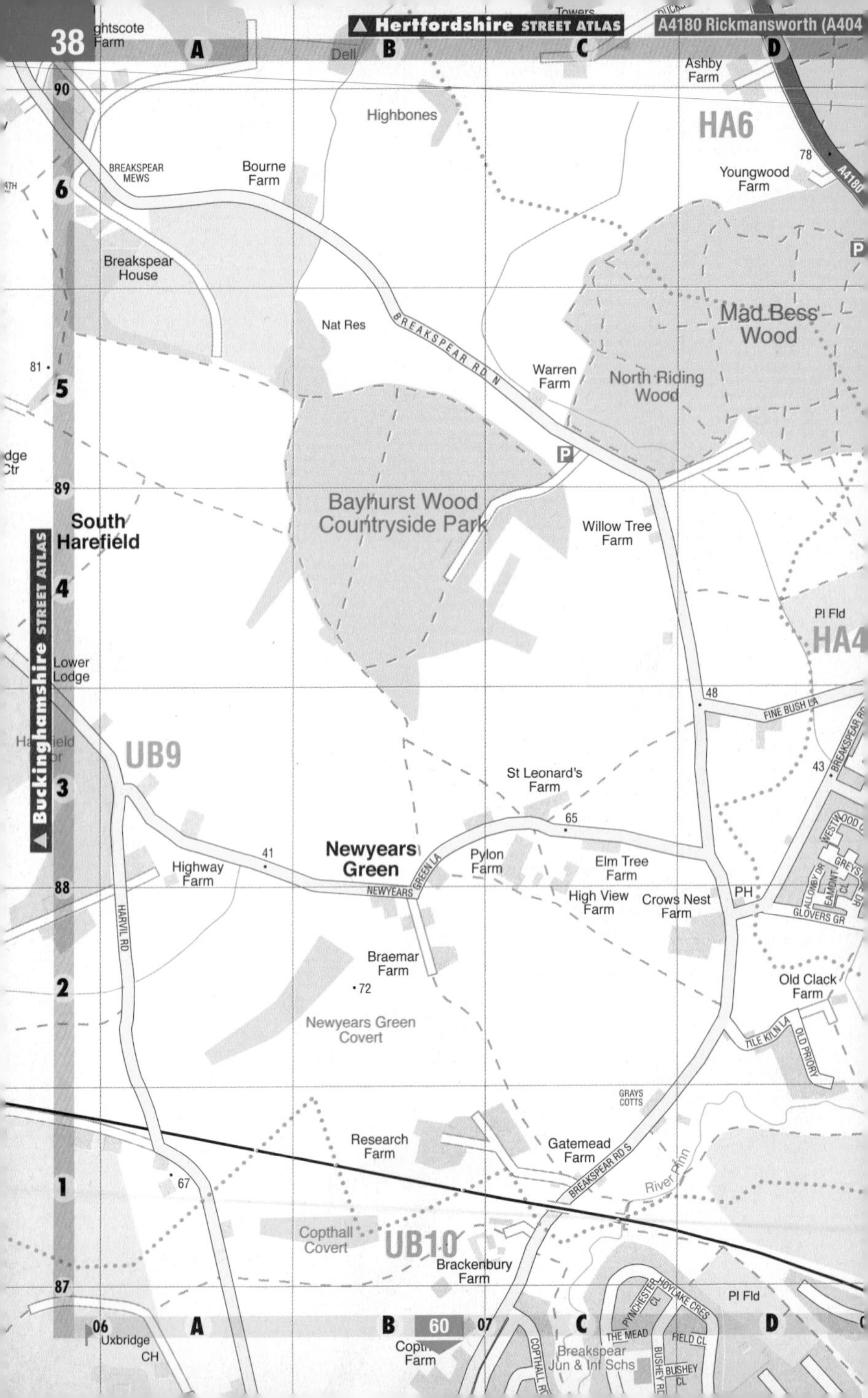
A
B
C
D
90
6
5
89
4
3
88
2
1
87
Dell
Ashby Farm
Highbones
HA6
78
A4180
Youngwood Farm
BREAKSPEAR MEWS
Bourne Farm
Breakspear House
Mad Bess Wood
Nat Res
BREAKSPEAR RD N
81
Warren Farm
North Riding Wood
Bayhurst Wood Countryside Park
South Harefield
Willow Tree Farm
Pl Fld
HA4
Lower Lodge
48
FINE BUSH LA
UB9
St Leonard's Farm
43
BREAKSPEAR RD
65
Newyears Green
41
Highway Farm
Pylon Farm
Elm Tree Farm
GREEN LA
NEWYEARS
High View Farm
Crows Nest Farm
PH
GLOVERS GR
ALLONBY DR
EAMONT CL
HARVIL RD
Braemar Farm
72
Old Clack Farm
Newyears Green Covert
TILE KILN LA
OLD PRIORY
GRAYS COTTS
Research Farm
Gatemead Farm
BREAKSPEAR RD S
67
River Pinn
Copthall Covert
UB10
Brackenbury Farm
Pl Fld
PYNCHESTER CL
HOYLAKE CRES
THE MEAD
FIELD CL
06
07
Uxbridge CH
Breakspear Jun & Inf Schs
COPTHALL RD
BUSHEY RD
BUSHEY CL

60

A
B
C
D
Haste Hill
Nat Res
Copse Wood
HA6
LC
Poor's Field
Haste Hill
BRAMLEY CL 1
HEATHERFOLD WAY 2
THEODORA WAY 3
St Vincent's
CRANBOURNE RD
LINCOLN RD
ROCHESTER RD
NORWICH RD
WINCHESTER RD
LICHFIELD RD
B472
Haydon Sch
Tenn Cts
BEATRICE CL 1
SILVESTER HO 2
FERNLY CL 3
SEYMOUR HO 4
ASPEN GR
WILTSHIRE LA
LIME CL
LYNEHAM WLK
WYLCHIN CL
EVERETT CL
ORCHARD RISE
Recn Gd
DUCKS HILL RD
Young Wood
Nurseries
CHIPPENHAM CL
MALMESBURY CL
FAIRACRE
SALISBURY RD
SOMERFORD
Ruislip Lido Railway
Ruislip Lido
HA5
Park Wood
LAKESIDE CL
RESERVOIR RD
ABERCORN GR
DELL FARM RD
WITHY LA
CONISTON GDNS
MAYBANK GDNS
FORE ST
Grangewood Sch
Ruislip Common
Fball Gd
Crem
GRANGEWOOD CL
Coteford Jun Sch
WOOD RISE
COTEFORD CL
BRICKETT CL
STANDALE GR
ST CATHERINES RD
WOODSIDE CL
LABURNUM GR
DORMYWOOD
LOVATT DR
40
RIVER CL
ELMBRIDGE DR
ARMSTRONG CL
ELMBRIDGE CL
BURY AVE
HOWLETTS LA
BOSTON GR
OLD HOWLETTS LA
PLOUGH FARM CL
KESWICK GDNS
ST EDMUNDS AVE
BROADWOOD AVE
Pl Flds
ST CATHERINES FARM CT
ARLINGTON DR
FLEET CL
WELL WAY
THAMES DR
ISIS CL
STANFORD CL
WAYBORNE GR
WYE CL
Bwg Gn
MARLBOROUGH AVE
COPPICE CL
BURY ST
SHERWOOD AVE
PARK AVE
Pav
MEADOW CL
YEOMANS ACRE
EVELYN AVE
MAYFLOWER CL
LADYGATE LA
ST MARGARETS RD
Allot Gdns
MEADWAY GDNS
MEAD WAY
HA4
KINGS COLLEGE RD
OAKFIELD CL
EASTCOTE RD
HALE END RD
HUME WAY
Whiteheath Jun & Inf Sch
WHITEHEATH AVE
FAIRFIELD AVE
GLENFIELD CRES
VICARAGE CL
LARCHMONT
PINN WAY
ST MARTIN'S APP
BROOK CL
BROOK DR
COURTLANDS CL
FAIRACRES
HIGHGROVE WAY
WESTBURY CL
B466
RUISLIP
GRASMERE AVE
ELLESMERE CL
ROUNDWOOD CL
DEBORAH CRES
BLAYDON CL
MOAT DR
WARRENDER WAY
RAVENSCOURT CL
ARDLEY CL
King's Gdns
Pl Fld
Bishop Winnington-Ingram CE Sch
Liby
Manor Farm
Bwg Gn
Pav
A4180
Pl Fld
Warrender Prim Sch
THE RIDGEWAY
WOODVILLE GDNS
HEATHFIELD RISE
WESTCOTE RISE
SOUTHCOTE RISE
BARRINGERS CT
NEATS ACRE
SHARPS LA
BELL VIEW MANOR
Church Field Gdns
T Cts
NORTH DR
Bishop Ramsey CE Sch (Annexe)
GLENALLA RD
LARNE RD
OLD HATCH MANOR
HAWTREY
River Pinn
GLENHURST AVE
ORCHARD CL
GLEBE CT
THE OAKS
1 ROSEDENE CT
2 THE THOMAS MORE BLDG
MIDCROFT
MANOR WAY
WEST HATCH MANOR
PRIORY CL
WINDMILL HILL
WESTHOLME GDNS
WALLIS HO
Allot Gdns
FIELD WAY
FIELD CL
COTTAGE CL
MANOR RD
DEAN HO
KING EDWARD'S RD
HIGH ST
SOUTH DR
CROFT GDNS
MANOR CL
WINDMILL WAY
GREEN WLK
WEST WAY
CROWN HO
EAST WAY
PARK WAY
Ruislip Manor
HILL RISE
WALLIS HO
SHARPS LA
CHURCH AVE
MONARCH'S WAY
KINGS GRANGE
CROFT CT
CLACK LA
HILL LA
FIVEWAYS
POPLARS CL
REGENCY DR
PRINCESS LA
GHEYNE CT
BRICKWALL LA
PEMBROKE RD
PARK WAY CT
LINDEN CL
FAIRFIELD CT
SOVEREIGN CL
KINGSEND
KINGS LO
STATION APP
LYON CT
Recn Gd
Ruislip
HARWELL CL
CHERRY TREE HO
GLADSTONE CT
KINGSEND CT
Ruislip
WILLOW GR
SHENLEY AVE
Ruislip Manor
WEST RUISLIP CT 1
BEAUFORT RD 2
ICKENHAM RD
SEAFORD CL
WOOD LA
ROSEBURY VALE
SUNNINGDALE AVE
Drv Rng
CH
CORDINGLEY RD
09
61
10
Pav
THE GREENWAY
BUCKLAND CT
ICKENHAM CL
BARNWOOD CL
LYSANDER RD
CHICHESTER AVE
SHERLEYS CT 1
MASTERS CT 2
Sp Gd
GARDEN CL
CRANLEY DR
GROSVENOR VALE
EVERSLEY CRES
POND GN
Allot Gdns
West Ruislip
West Ruislip
LYMINGTON DR
HERON CT
KESTREL CT
FALCON CT
HAMBLE CL
WHITSTABLE CL
88
87
89
90
1
2
3
4
5
6

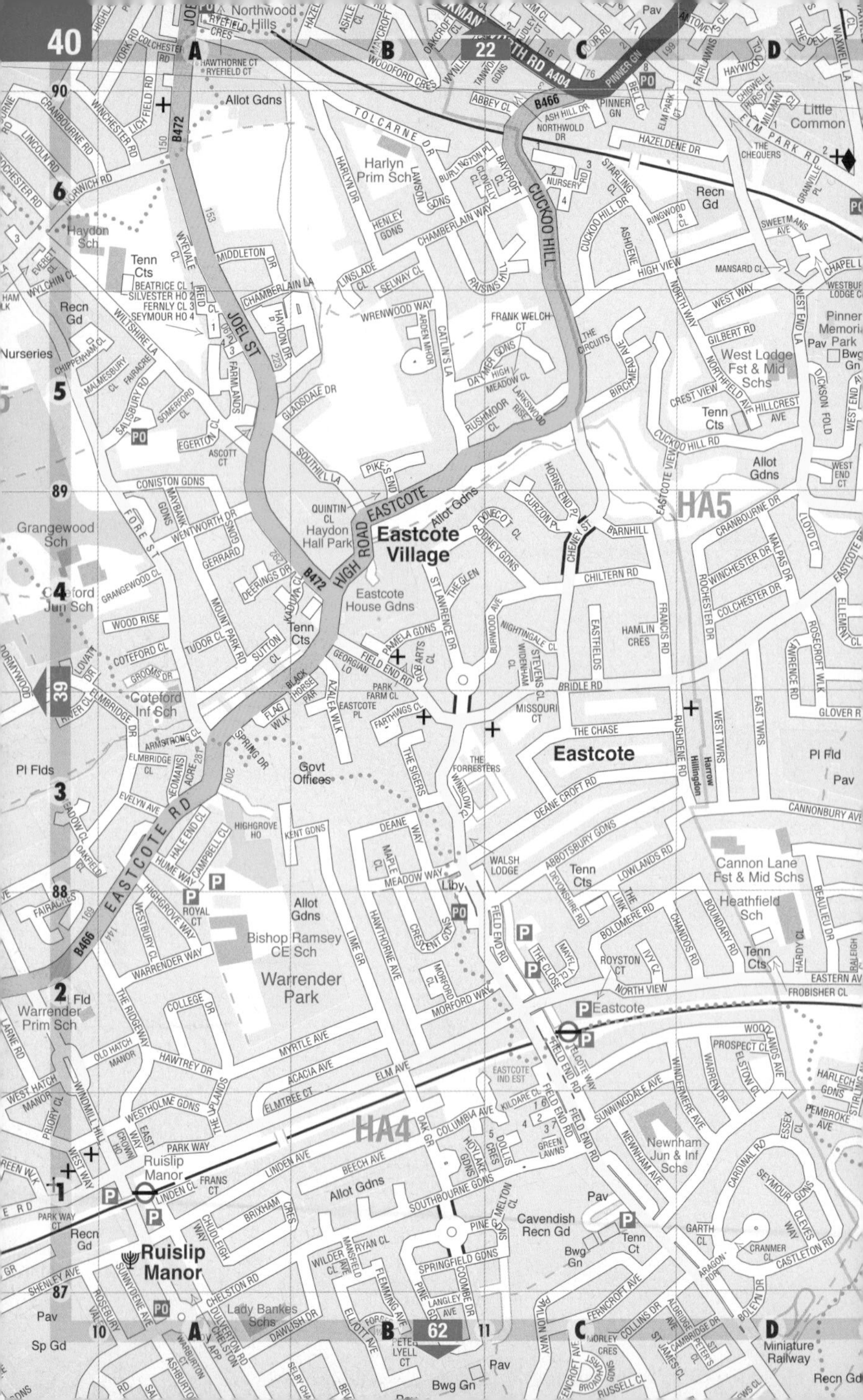
Northwood Hills
22
Little Common
Harlyn Prim Sch
Haydon Sch
Recn Gd
Nurseries
Eastcote Village
Eastcote House Gdns
Haydon Hall Park
Grangewood Sch
Coteford Jun Sch
Coteford Inf Sch
Govt Offices
Eastcote
HA5
West Lodge Fst & Mid Schs
Pinner Memorial Park
Cannon Lane Fst & Mid Schs
Heathfield Sch
Bishop Ramsey CE Sch
Warrender Park
Warrender Prim Sch
HA4
Ruislip Manor
Newnham Jun & Inf Schs
Cavendish Recn Gd
Lady Bankes Schs
Miniature Railway
JOEL ST
HIGH ROAD EASTCOTE
EASTCOTE RD
CUCKOO HILL
FIELD END RD
39
62

A
B
C
D
23
63
42
90
89
88
87
6
5
4
3
2
1
PINNER
Nower Hill
Headstone
North Harrow
Rayners Lane
HA5
HA2
A404
A4090
GEORGE V AVE
IMPERIAL DR
ALEXANDRA AVE
A404 PINNER RD
OAKHILL AVE
PAINES LA
MOSS LA
BARROW POINT AVE
EAST END WAY
LOVE LA
AVENUE RD
LEIGHTON AVE
Cemy
BLOOMSBURY CT
CHISWICK CT
EASTGLADE
BEECHENGROVE
TERRILANDS
BRIDGE ST
HIGH ST
GRANGE CT
PINNER HO
BARTERS WLK
STATION APP
CHURCH LA
SHELBOURNE CL
GRANGE GDNS
WAKEHAMS HILL
THE SQUIRRELS
ANGLESMEDE WAY
ANGLESMEDE CRES
GREYSTOKE AVE
AINSDALE CRES
BIRK DALE AVE
MELBOURNE AVE
MANOR PARK DR
GREENFIELD WAY
HOLM DENE AVE
ELMCROFT CRES
HILLVIEW GDNS
HEADSTONE LA
PARKFIELD GDNS
HOLMWOOD CL
WILLOW CT
Pinner Park Schs
Bwg Gn
Tenn Cts
Pav
Allot Gdns
Pl Fld
Open Air Theatre
Headstone Manor
Harrow Mus & Her Ctr
Headstone Manor Recn Gd
Pavs
Pinner
WEST END AVE
SCHOOL LA
WEALL CT
Liby
CECIL PK
NOWER CT
NOWER HILL
MAYFIELD DR
CAPEL GDNS
THE CHASE
COPPERFIELD WAY
FIRE BRIGADE COTTS
Nower Hill High Sch
PINNER CT
PINNER RD
PRIORY WAY
MANOR WAY
HAZELWOOD CL
SOUTHFIELD PK
PARKSIDE WAY
WOODBERRY AVE
KINGSWAY CRES
WENTWORTH WAY
ASHRIDGE GDNS
HOLWELL PL
MARSH RD
MEADOW RD
PENWOOD CT
MELROSE RD
KINGSLEY RD
CHESSINGTON CT
THRUSH GN
SOUTH WAY
WOODLANDS
BETJEMAN CL
OSBOURNE CT
YEW TREE CL
MARSH POINT
Sch
BIRCHES CL
EASTCOTE RD
GROVE AVE
PINNER GR
GROVE RD
MOUNT DR
THE RIDGEWAY
NORTHUMBERLAND RD
CAMBRIDGE RD
BROADWALK
HOOKING GN
CHAUCER HO
CANTERBURY RD
STATION RD
KINGSFIELD AVE
ALLERFORD CT
ALLINGTON RD
Pinner Village Gardens
VALE CROFT
CANNON LA
HEREFORD GDNS
LYNCROFT AVE
MOORCROFT WAY
COMPTON RISE
LINCOLN CL
LINCOLN RD
CUMBERLAND RD
GLOUCESTER RD
WESTMORLAND RD
DURHAM RD
APSLEY CL
CANTERBURY RD
HOLSWORTH CL
HIGHFIELD AVE
LADBROOK CL
WHITTINGTON WAY
North Harrow
CHURCHILL CT
NORFOLK RD
SURREY RD
CORNWALL RD
ST URSULA GR
HILL RD
DAWLISH DR
TEWKESBURY AVE
TREVONE GDNS
ST MICHAEL'S CRES
SUFFOLK RD
CHESTER DR
LANCASTER RD
COLLAPIT CL 1
LABURNUM CT 2
ACACIA CT 3
ARGYLE RD
BLENHEIM RD
MARLOW CT
BLADON GDNS
NORTH AVE
DEWSBURY CL
CHURCH AVE
THE GARDENS
RAYNERS LA
LANKERS DR
NORWOOD DR
CHURCH DR
HAWTHORN DR
PARKTHORNE DR
PARKTHORNE CL
ELM DR
ELM CL
GROSVENOR AVE
SANDHURST AVE
BEAUMONT AVE
DORCHESTER AVE
Vaughan Sch
West Harrow
CANNONBURY AVE
CHESTNUT DR
LULWORTH DR
WIMBORNE DR
DURLEY AVE
BRUNSWICK CL
THE GREENWAY
HILLCROFT AVE
Longfield Fst & Mid Schs
IMPERIAL CL
DUKES AVE
FARM AVE
THE RIDGEWAY
ALFRISTON AVE
ROMNEY DR
SOUTHBOURNE CL
DOWNS AVE
WEST AVE
CENTRAL AVE
THE AVENUE
THE CROFT
THE CLOSE
PARK DR
IMPERIAL CT
Recn Gd
THE DRIVE
RODNEY CL
HAMLANDS DR
EASTERN AVE
POSTMASTERS LODGE
THE GLEN
VILLAGE WAY
VILLAGE WAY E
VICARAGE WAY
MONARCHS CT
ELM GR
BEECHCROFT AVE
ROMNEY CL
FERNBROOK DR
WILSON GDNS
West Harrow Recn Gd
EXCHANGE WLK
EDINBURGH CL
CARLISLE CL
STIRLING AVE
TRESCOE GDNS
NEWLYN GDNS
SOUTH CL
Rayners Lane
THE RETREAT
OAKINGTON AVE
ULLSWATER CT
TWYFORD RD
WHITMORE
RAYNTON CL
HIGH WORPLE
WORPLE CL
WORPLE WAY
1 STOCKTON HO
2 MACMILLAN CT
STRONGBRIDGE CL
WELBECK RD
FURNESS RD
CHATSWORTH GDNS
TINTERN WAY
Whitmore High Sch
KELVIN CT
SPINNELLS RD
Sp Gd
FAIRVIEW CRES
Roxbourne Park
Yeading Brook
WAVERLEY RD
TORBAY RD
WARDEN AVE
BERRITON RD
RAYNERS LA
KARMA WAY
UNION TERR
PROVIDENCE AVE
GOLDSMITH CL
Grange Schs
ABERCORN CRES
SOUTHDOWN CRES
SHAFTESBURY CIRC
YEADING AVE
OVESDON AVE
PERWELL AVE
CHICHESTER CT
OXLEAY RD
CAPTHORNE AVE
CLITHEROE AVE
Tenn Cts
AUSTEN RD
SCOTT CRES
EASTWAY CRES
HILLSIDE CRES
EXETER RD
DRAKE RD
LUCAS AVE
Fball Gd
UNITY TERR
DRINKWATER RD
SWIFT CL
CONCORD TERR
LODGE PARK CL
FRANKLINS MEWS
Roxbourne Fst & Mid Schs
TORBAY
NEWQUAY CRES
Allot Gdns
Newton Farm Fst & Mid Sch
Newton Farm Ecology Pk
PRIEST PARK AVE
MARYATT AVE
FENTIMAN WAY
ARCHES
13
14
30
40

A
B
C
D
24
90
6
5
89
4
41
3
88
2
1
87
14
15
64
HA2
HA3
HA1
Pinner Park Schs
ALMOND WAY
WILLOW CT
PINNER PARK AVE
THE CLOSE
PINNER PARK GDNS
THE RISE
TUDOR GDNS
WICKHAM RD
Whitefriars Trad Est
TUDOR RD
BARRATT WAY
Pl Fld
Tudor Ent Pk
BRUCE RD
LADYSMITH RD
HIGH ST
MINSTREL CT
CLAREMONT RD
DAUPHINE CT
MONTROSE RD
ABERDEEN RD
LORNE RD
LOCKET RD
WARHAM RD
TALBOT RD
ARCHERY CL
AVONDALE RD
RONART ST
BYRON RD
STUART RD
LOMOND CT
GRANT RD
CHRISTIE HO
CANNING RD
THOMSON RD
STIRLING RD
GREENLEAF RD
Wealdstone
PEEL RD
Bwg Gn
Sw Pool
L Ctr
PALMERSTON RD
OXFORD RD
Palmerston Ctr
MASONS AVE
CHRISTCHURCH AVE
FORWARD DR
HERGA RD
MOON HO
Ind Est
GEORGE GANGE WAY
A409
SHERATON LO
CARDINAL WAY
WOLSELEY RD
WELLINGTON RD
GRAHAM RD
HAVELOCK RD
GORDON RD
CECIL RD
HAILSHAM DR
SUNSET HO
GLADSTONE WAY
ELLEN WEBB DR
WARWICK CT
Waverley Ind Pk
Ct
Works
Sp Gd
Pav
Bwg Gns
Open Air Theatre
Tenn Cts
Headstone Manor
DOWNING CL
WOOSTER MEWS
FAIRFIELD DR
VICTOR RD
EDWARD RD
SIDNEY RD
ATHERTON PL
Harrow Mus & Her Ctr
Headstone Manor Recn Gd
Pavs
ALBERT RD
CUMBERLAND CT 1
BANNISTER HO 2
POPPY CT 3
KARMAN CT 4
AMBASSADOR HO 5
CHURCH PAR 6
CENTURY HO 7
REGENCY LO 8
1 CLARENDON HO
2 BEVERLEY CT
HEADSTONE DR
GLOUCESTER CT
HEREFORD CT
DANES GATE
WORCESTER CT
EARLS CRES
PRINCES DR
DUKES AVE
Harrow & Wealdstone
THE BRIDGE
SANDRIDGE CL
CHURCHILL PL
BARONS MEAD
KINGS WAY
QUEENS WLK
MARLBOROUGH HILL
DALTRY HO
Liby
C Ctr
RAILWAY APP
HEADSTONE GDNS
HARROW VIEW
Allot Gdns
Headstone
BROOK DR
WALTON CL
WALTON RD
VIEW CL
HARLEY CT
HARLEY RD
HARLEY CRES
MOAT DR
PARKSIDE WAY
WOODBERRY AVE
HILLFIELD CL
CHURCHFIELD CL
KINGSWAY CRES
BOLTON RD
THE BOLTONS
HAMPDEN CT
HIDE RD
LONGLEY RD
CROSS RD
WALTON DR
RANMOOR GDNS
RANMOOR CL
MARLBOROUGH CT
BADMINTON CL
RUSLAND HTS
RUSLAND PARK RD
Sch
TORVER RD
SPARKBRIDGE RD
MILTON RD
POETS WAY
BLAWITH RD
FROGNAL AVE
ROSSLYN CRES
Phoenix Ind Est
STATION RD
KINGSFIELD AVE
ALLERFORD CT
ALLINGTON RD
PINNER VIEW
CUNNINGHAM PK
BUCKINGHAM RD
RUGBY RD
RADNOR AVE
LOWICK RD
BETHECAR RD
COLTON RD
NIBTHWAITE RD
HIGH MEAD
ISOBEL HO
WATKINS HO
WOODLANDS RD
ELMGROVE RD
CRYSTAL WAY
Greenhill
Super store
DOMINION PAR
HAMILTON RD
RADNOR RD
ST SAVIOURS CT
WARRINGTON RD
Sp Gd
CUMBERLAND RD
T Cts
WESTMORLAND RD
DURHAM RD
APSLEY CL
ALTHORPE RD
BERESFORD RD
LEYS CL 1
CHILTERN CT 2
MILES LO 3
HOLLY LO 4
CUNNINGHAM CT 5
EVELYN HO
SALISBURY RD
BALFOUR RD
Quainton Hall Sch
HINDES RD
GAINSBOROUGH LODGE
CANTERBURY RD
HOLSWORTH CL
CHANDOS RD
GRAFTON RD
Recn Gd
MIDSUMMER CT
Norbury Sch
WELLDON CT
FAIRHOLME RD
WELLESLEY RD
CENTRAL PAR
SOVEREIGN PL
GLENWOOD CL
CATHERINE PL
DUFFIELD CL
COURTFIELD AVE
SUSSEX RD
NORFOLK RD
SURREY RD
SOMERSET RD
CORNWALL RD
Bwg Gn
A4005
A404
PINNER RD
MARLOW CT
BEDFORD RD
RUTLAND RD
OXFORD RD
DEVONSHIRE RD
HARROW
Cemy
ROXBOROUGH RD
HEADSTONE RD
OAKLEY RD
ST KILDA'S RD
SPRINGFIELD RD
WELLDON CRES
ANGEL RD
FENHILL RD
BYRON CT
MANOR PAR
MANOR CT
BONNERSFIELD LA
KENSINGTON HTS
CHESTER CT
NORTHWICK PARK RD
TEMPSFORD CT
HANBURY CT
BRANDRETH CT
ELMER CT
DORSET RD
NORTH AVE
BLADON GDNS
St Georges Sh & L Ctr
GREENHILL WAY
CLARENDON RD
ST ANN'S RD
HAVELOCK PL
VICTORIA CL
ST JOHN'S RD
LYON RD
SHEEPCOTE RD
GROSVENOR AVE
SANDHURST AVE
BEAUMONT AVE
DORCHESTER AVE
THE GARDENS
Vaughan Sch
MAYBURY CT
SHERIDAN CT
NEPTUNE RD
KYMBERLEY RD
JUNCTION RD
St Ann's Ctr
GAYTON RD
ASHBURNHAM AVE
ASHBURNHAM GDNS
B458
COLLEGE RD
Harrow-on-the-Hill
WILLIAM CAREY WAY
BADGERS CL
FORSYTH CT
BOUVERIE RD
VAUGHAN RD
West Harrow
North Harrow
Allot Gdns
BUTLER AVE
HALE LO
APPIN CT
WHITEHALL RD
LOWLANDS RD
Recn Gd
Harrow Coll
KENTON AVE
KENTON RD
TYBURN LA
GROVE HILL RD
WILSON GDNS
HEATH RD
BUTLER RD
BOWEN RD
SPRINGWAY
FORD CL
ANTHONY CT
WARNER HO
HOBART CT
LORNE CT
LANSDOWNE RD
SHERIDAN PL
A312
SUMNER RD
COLBECK RD
MERIVALE RD
MARSHALL CL
HAWKINS CL
LASCELLES AVE
ROXBOROUGH AVE
MAXTED PK
PICKWICK
The Grove Open Space
1 JARDINE HO
2 HILLBOROUGH CT
3 DRUMMOND CT
4 LITTLE CT
5 CHESTNUT CT
Pl Flds
West Harrow Recn Gd
West Harrow
DRURY RD
LANCE RD
TREVE AVE
WOOD CL
CHARLES CRES
POOL RD
FARNBOROUGH CL
ANDREWS CL
RETLAS CT
SHEPPARD'S CT
LYCHGATE MANOR
BRACONHYRST
COPPERFIELDS
St Anselm's RC Prim Sch
WHITMORE RD
Tenn Cts
Whitmore High Sch
PORLOCK AVE
FURNESS RD
WORDSWORTH CT 1
CHARLES CRES 2
KINGSFIELD RD 3
BURRELL CT 4
HANOVER CT 5
KINGSFIELD CT 6
BESSBOROUGH RD
TRAFALGAR TERR
NELSON RD
YEW WLK
MEADOW VIEW
CHURCH HILL
THE GARLANDS
GARLANDS LA
FOOTBALL LA
Capital Ring
Harrow Sch
PETERBOROUGH RD
KELVIN CT
FERRING CL
MERTON RD
SHAFTESBURY CIRC
SHAFTESBURY AVE
GREVILLE HO
PAVILION LO
WEST ST
WELLINGTON TERR
VICTORIA TERR
CROWN ST
Running Tk
Grange Schs
ABERCORN CRES
SOUTHDOWN CRES
HILLSIDE CRES
FIELDERS CL
THE CRESCENT
DUDLEY GDNS
JOLLYS LA
The John Lyon Sch
LEIGH CT
KING HENRY MEWS
BYRON HILL RD
WALDRON RD
1 CROWN CT
2 CHILTERN HO
Harrow on the Hill
MIDDLE RD
RIVERSTONE CL
A312 LOWER RD
WHITWELL PL
CLONMELL RD
HAMSON
WEST HILL
GRANGE FARM CL
WESLEY CL
FRANKLINS MEWS
LODGE CL
PARK CL
THE ARCHES
CONCORD TERR
OSMOND CL
WALDRON'S YD
ASHBOURNE AVE
BRIGADE CL
ROXETH HILL
COTTAGE CL
HARROW PK
KENNETT HO
Bowden House

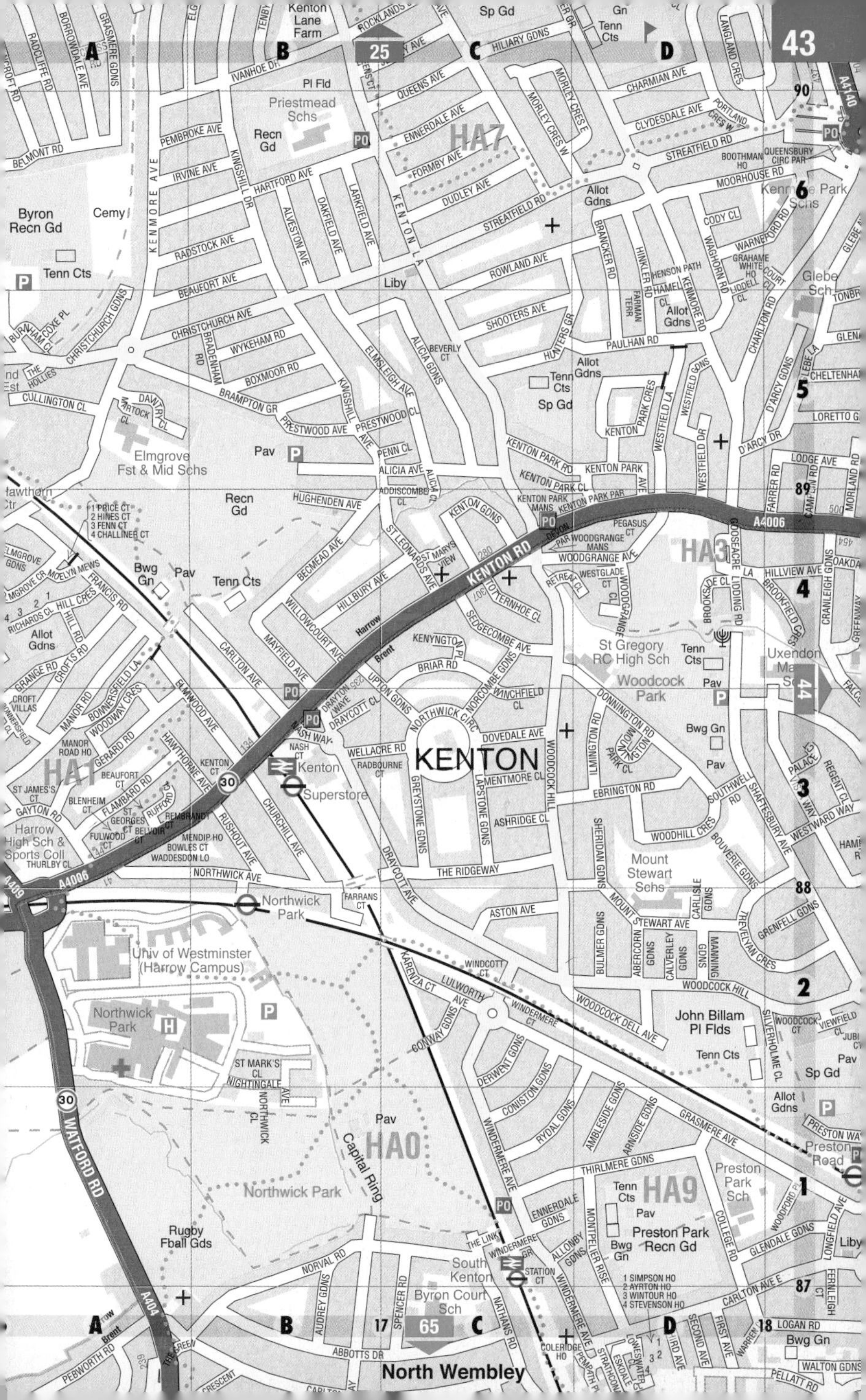
43
A
B
C
D
25
65
KENTON
North Wembley
HA7
HA3
HA1
HA0
HA9
KENTON RD
A4006
WATFORD RD
A404
Northwick Park
Kenton
South Kenton
Preston Road
Univ of Westminster (Harrow Campus)
St Gregory RC High Sch
Woodcock Park
Mount Stewart Schs
Preston Park Recn Gd
Byron Recn Gd
Elmgrove Fst & Mid Schs
Priestmead Schs
Capital Ring
Byron Court Sch
John Billam Pl Flds
44

44
A
B
26
C
D
90
89
88
87
6
5
4
3
2
1
HA8
HA3
NW9
A4140
A4006
HONEYPOT LA
KINGSBURY RD
FRYENT WAY
Queensbury
Kingsbury
Preston
Preston Road
Kenmore Park Schs
Glebe Sch
Recn Gd
St Bernadette's RC Prim Sch
Superstore
Bowman Trad Est
Eton Grove Open Space
Roe Green Schs
Kingsbury High Sch (Upper Sch)
Roe Green Park
Annexe
Claremont High Sch
Uxendon Manor Sch
JFS Sch
Michael Sobell Sinai Sch
Kingsbury Green Prim Sch
Fryent Country Park
Capital Ring
Barn Hill Open Space
Barn Hill
• 86
John Billam Pl Flds
Preston Park Sch
Allot Gdns
Tenn Cts
Bwg Gn
Pav
Sp Gd
Games Ct
Pl Fd
Liby
TA Ctr
1 TUDOR HO
2 STUART HO
3 WINDSOR HO
REYNOLDS DR
BEVERLEY DR
WALTHAM DR
WINCHESTER AVE
PRINCES AVE
KENTON RD
WESTMORELAND RD
PRESTON HILL
PRESTON RD
UXENDON CRES
CARLTON AVE E
ELMSTEAD AVE
WEST HILL
UXENDON HILL
WENTWORTH HILL
WYKEHAM HILL
FORTY AVE
43
66
18
19

A
B
C
D
27
67
HENDON
Police HQ
Museum
Colindale
Colindale
Central Pub Health Lab
British Liby (Newspaper Liby)
Recn Gd
Peel Ctr (Met Pol Training Estab)
Sp Gd
AERODROME RD
COTTENHAM DR
PEEL DR
DENMARK HILL DR
ROWAN DR
JOHNSON CT 1
WILSHAW CL 2
COLMORE CT 3
CHANCELLOR
BELVEDERE
KINGFISHER WLK
COLINDALE AVE
EDGWARE RD THE HYDE
A5
Barnet
Harrow
CARLISLE RD
HOLMSTALL AVE
BIRCHWOOD CT
OAKLEIGH
SOUTHBOURNE
GREENWAY GDNS
PORTMAN GDNS
THE GREENWAY
Tenn Cts
Colindale Bsns Pk
Capitol Ind Pk
CAPITOL WAY
Superstore
Oriental City
PLAZA WK
Athletic Gd
Pav
ANNESLEY AVE
CRANESBILL CL
STONECROP CL
SHOELANDS CT
SILK HO
PENN CT
AJAX CT
AJAX AVE
CHEQUERS CL
RANKIN CL
SHEAVESHILL AVE
Allot Gdns
Silk Stream
CHALFONT CT
MARLOW CT
COLINDEEP LA
A5150
1 SATIN CT
2 BROCADE CT
Technology Pk
THE CHESTNUTS
HANOVER CT
ROSS CT
BARNABY CT
CECIL RD
ST ALPHAGE CT
PARK PAR
Beis Yaakov Prim Sch
Superstore
MANOR WAY
BEAULIEU CL
COURT WAY
ORCHARD GATE
COLIN PARK RD
SHEAVESHILL CT
COLIN PAR
SHEAVESHILL AVE
POOLSFORD RD
THE LONING
CLOVELLY AVE
LYNTON AVE
Pl Fld
Colindale Prim Sch
Rushgrove Park
Tenn Cts
RUSHGROVE AVE
COLIN GDNS
COLIN CRES
COLIN DEEP BRIDGE
NEW WAY RD
COLIN CT
WOODFIELD AVE
HILLFIELD AVE
CROSSWAY
ST MATTHIAS CL
VERNON HO
SILKFIELD RD
RUSHGROVE CT
SCOTSWELL DR
ROOKERY CL
ROOKERY WAY
GENEVA CT
Connaught Bsns Ctr
The Hyde Ind Est
The Hyde
COLIN DR
DEERFIELD CL
Superstores
HYDE ESTATE RD
Garrick Ind Ctr
Superstore
SILK BRIDGE
GARRICK RD
RUSSELL RD
WILBERFORCE RD
Hendon Sch
EDGEWORTH CL
Malcolm Pa
MALCOLM CRES
ASH HO
STAG LA
WESTFIELD CL
GROVE PK
ST GEORGE'S AVE
ROSE GLEN
EVELYN AVE
ROE END
ROE LA
EDGBURY CT
GOLDSMITH LA
Schs
GROVE CRES
Liby
Kingsbury High Sch (Lwr Sch)
KENWOOD CT
HARTGROVE CT
HINDHURST CT
ELMWOOD CRES
HAY LA
HAYDON CL
HAYDON CT
CHERRY TREE CT
PARK VIEW CT
Tenn Cts
STUBBS CL
BACON LA
FAIRFIELDS CRES
FAIRFIELDS CL
HILLSIDE
THE RETREAT
HAYLAND CL
PEAR CL
SUNNY VIEW
MOUNT VIEW RD
RIDGE CL
LARKWAY CL
THE RIDGEWAY
WATLING GATE
SUMMIT CL
WAKEMANS HILL AVE
HIGHCROFT
STANCROFT
FOREST GATE
YARLEY PAR
MEADOW WAY
HILL VIEW GDNS
SUMMIT AVE
SPRINGFIELD MOUNT
RYDAL GDNS
LODORE GDNS
ENNERDALE DR
DERWENT AVE
CRUMMOCK GDNS
ROE GN
HIGHFIELD AVE
HIGHFIELD CL
MOUNTAIRE CT
SHIRLEY CT
BUCK LA
ROCHESTER CT
THE GROVE
ASH TREE DELL
OAK TREE DELL
HIGH MEADOW CRES
UPHILL DR
MEAD CT
BOWATER CL
A4006
CONISTON GDNS
Oliver Goldsmith Prim Sch
SPRINGFIELD GDNS
MARDALE DR
SPRING GDNS
KINGSBURY RD
OLD KENTON LA
SUNNINGDALE GDNS
FERNDENE
STANMUIR LO
PIPERS GN
CHARLOTTE PL
WOODLAND CL
GREEN CT
B454
Ind Est
BARNINGHAM WAY
Kingsbury Trad Est
JUBILEE CL
NW9
TALGARTH WLK
DERWENT RISE
HYDE CRES
The Hyde Sch
REETS FARM CL
GOLDSMITH AVE
FRYENT FIELDS
LAMPETER CL
NORTHGATE DR
SNOWDON DR
RUTHIN CL
AMROTH GN
AMMANFORD GN
FRYENT GR
COLWYN GN
CALDICOTE GN
FRYENT CRES
GADSBURY CL
Ct
Superstores
Tenn Cts
Pav
Bwg Gn
LEWGARS AVE
St Robert Southwell RC Prim Sch
SLOUGH LA
BRIARWOOD CL
BAIRD CL
BOYCROFT AVE
CAMPBELL CT
STEWART CL
BURGESS AVE
Tenn Cts
Pav
Recn Gd
CARTER CL
BARONS CT
Kingsbury
ELTHORNE WAY
Allot Gdns
Silver Jubilee Park
TOWNSEND LA
1 CAMBRIAN GN
2 CAMARTHEN GN
3 CORRIS GN
4 BRECON GN
5 BEAUMARIS GN
6 PENDRAGON WLK
7 WELSHSIDE
8 TINTERN PATH
9 BALA GN
10 WELSHSIDE WLK
Pav
West Hendon Pl Flds
RAMSEY CL
MARSH DR
BORTHWICK RD 1
RAVENSTONE RD 2
MARRIOTTS CL
WENDOVER LO
West Hendon
York Park
FRANKLIN HO
HERBERT RD
A504
YORK PAR
PERRYFIELD WAY
WEST HENDON BROADWAY
TYRREL WAY
WARNER CL
ROSEMEAD
ESMAR CRES
SEELIG AVE
STUART AVE
WOOLMEAD AVE
DEHAR CRES
VERULAM CT
Riding Sch
TUNWORTH CL
THE ELMS
HAWTHORNE GR
ELTHORNE CT
ELTHORNE RD
HYDE CT
SUNNYMEAD RD
Prim Sch
SALMON ST
BUSH GR
LABURNUM GR
HOLLY GR
MAPLE GR
SYCAMORE GR
LYNE CT
MEADOWBANK RD
PARK RD
Kingsbury Town Fball Gd
TOWNSEND CT
REEVES AVE
ELVIN CT
CHURCH LA
QUEENSBURY RD
KINGSMEAD AVE
WOOD CL
PERTH AVE
WINSTON AVE
KINLOCH DR
RANNOCK AVE
BLAIR AVE
HILLWAY
Allot Gdns
COOL OAK LA
Tenn Cts
Pav
Bwg Gn
MALLARD WAY
MALLARD CT
ALINGTON CRES
MERLEY CT
CHURCH CL
WOOD LA
Allot Gdns
DORS CL
DOREEN AVE
FAIRFIELDS AVE
GLENWOOD AVE
Woodfield Park
Barnet
Brent
LAVENDER AVE
LANGDON DR
ROSSDALE DR
GLENWOOD GR
HOLDEN AVE
DIMSDALE DR
CHURCH DR
Welsh Harp Fld Ctr
Woodfield Sch
Sp Gd
Pav
Capital Ring
London Group Bsns Pk
HILL DR
DUNSTER DR
Welsh Harp
KINGSMERE PK
DEANSCROFT AVE
ST ANDREWS RD
WELLS DR
LEITH CL
Allot Gdns
Brent Resr
MAPLE LO
Sailing Club
Sp Gd
A406
The Harp Bs Ctr
Welling Park
APSLEY WAY
Phoenix Pk
SHEPHERD FIELD
A4140
SALMON ST
CHERRYLANDS CL
QUEENS WLK
St Nicholas Sch
TUDOR CL
TUDOR GDNS
THE MOUNT
OLD CHURCH LA
BIRCHEN CL
OLD ST ANDREWS MANS
RIVERVIEW
Neasden Recn Gd
BALLARDS
1
2
3
4
5
6
87
88
89
90
46
21
22

A
B
C
D
28
68
45
HENDON
The Hyde
NW4
Sunny Hill Park
AERODROME RD
Sp Gd
PEEL DR
DENMARK HILL DR
ROWAN DR
The Bridges
BUCKINGHAM CT
JOHNSON CT 1
WILSHAW CL 2
COLMORE CT 3
CLARENDON GDNS
SOUTHFIELDS
CANBERRA CL
HENLEY CT
M1
A41
WATFORD WAY
A5150
COLIN DEEP BRIDGE
SELBORNE GDNS
GROVE GDNS
HENDALE AVE
GREYHOUND HILL
SUNNY HILL
ST MARY'S CRES
HATCHCROFT
Sunnyfields Prim Sch
Sports Pitch
Allot Gdns
Church Farm Ho Mus
Middlesex Univ
DANIEL ALMSHOUSE
CHURCH END
CHURCH TERR
Liby
TH
ST JOSEPHS GR
St Joseph's RC Schs
THE BURROUGHS
EGERTON GDNS
BRAMPTON CT
CHAPEL WLK
BRAMPTON GR
RAFFLES HO
Tenn Cts
QUADRANT CL
PROTHERO GDNS
St Mary's & St John's CE Prim Sch
Hendon Central
WYKEHAM CT
WYKEHAM RD
QUEEN'S RD
B551
CENTRAL CIR
Pav
Tenn Cts
Hendon Park
PARK HTS
ST ANN'S CT
NURSERY WLK CT
HENDON LO
CLARICE CT
SUNNINGFIELDS RD
GARDENS RD
ROWSLEY AVE
DOWNAGE
SHERWOOD RD
MEADOW DR
CHRISTOPHER CT
ASHLEY LA
The Garden
Sch
EDINBURGH HO 1
MARKHAM CT 2
DOWNHURST CT
CHESHUNT HO
THURLBY CROFT
PEMBROKE HALL
FLORENCE ST
SUNNY PL
CHURCH RD
SUTTON PAR
FINCHLEY LA
PARSON ST
B552
A502
LODGE RD
RAVENSHURST
JOHN'S AVE
SOMERSET RD
BABINGTON RD
WROUGHTON TERR
USHER HALL
Coll
PO
DERBY HO
HANBURY CL
HADDON CT
GLEBE CRES
LAWFIELD CL
BURNHAM CT
FIRST AVE
SECOND AVE
BLENHEIM CT
OYH Prim Sch
VICTORIA RD
ALEXANDRA RD
ALBERT RD
NORA GDNS
HILLVIEW GDNS
BOYNE AVE
WHITEWAYS
Sch
Schs
CAROL CL
STRATFORD RD
SENTINEL HO
SENTINEL SQ
BELL CT
BELL LA
VINCENT CT
GREEN WLK
LANGHAM CT
GREEN LA
CHESHIR HO
FOSTER CT
UPPER FOSTERS
LOWER FOSTERS
NEW BRENT ST
NORTH ST
COWLEY PL
EATON RD
HERIOT RD
RALEIGH CL
SYDNEY GR
BEATRICE CT
HENDON PARK MANS
COLLINGWOOD CT
WATER BROOK LA
BRENT ST
CREST CT
THE CREST
GOLDERS RISE
THE APPROACH
Hendon Sch
AMBASSADOR CT
WEST AVE
HOLMFIELD AVE
BRENTWOOD CT
HOLMDALE GDNS
CENTURY HO
HIGHBUSH CT
DANESCROFT
DANESCROFT AVE
WOODBURN CL
BRENT GN
GOODYERS GDNS
ELM PK GDNS
BETHEL CT
ELMS AVE
ELM CL
HAMPSHIRE CT
PARK VIEW GDNS
SHIREHALL LA
SHIREHALL PK
SHIREHALL CL
SHIREHALL GDNS
MAYFIELD GDNS
HASLEMERE AVE
A502
A406
BRENTMEAD PL
SINCLAIR GR
WESTERN AVE
HEATHFIELD GDNS
Brent Cross
OAKFIELD CT
BRENTFIELD GDNS
WOODVILLE GDNS
GREAT NORTH WAY (BARNET BY-PASS)
A1
HOLDERS HILL
HOLDERS HILL AVE
OCTOBER PL
ROBIN LA
WESTCHESTER DR
WEST CHESTER DR
HENDON HALL CT
ORMONDE CT
TENTERDEN CL
TENTERDEN GDNS
TENTERDEN DR
CEDARS CL
BOLTMORE CL
FINCHLEY BRIDGE
CHATTERIS CT
GARRICK WAY
BRINSDALE RD
MILLS GR
WESTHORPE GDNS
CORRIGAN CL
A504
GROVE HO
EDGEWORTH CRES
EDGEWORTH AVE
EDGEWORTH CL
ADMIRAL CT
VAUGHAN AVE
FABER GDNS
WOODWARD AVE
TALBOT CRES
Malcolm Park
MALCOLM CRES
MALCOLM CT
STATION RD
HIGH MOUNT
SPENCER HO
NEELD CRES
RUNDELL CRES
ALDERTON CRES
ALDERTON WAY
PARADE MANS
VIVIAN AVE
Coll
Tenn Cts
FOSCOTE RD
CRESPIGNY RD
ALLINGTON RD
KENNYLAND CT
GRAHAM LO
GRAHAM RD
AUDLEY RD
SEVINGTON RD
CHEYNE WLK
BEAUFORT GDNS
DENEHURST GDNS
BRENT CROSS GDNS 1
COOPER RD 2
CLIVE LO 3
RENTERS AVE
HALEY RD
HENDON WAY
BRENT CROSS FLYOVER
SPALDING RD
MONTAGU RD
DARTMOUTH RD
BERTRAM RD
Barnet Coll
ALGERNON RD
VICARAGE RD
MOUNT RD
ELLIOT RD
FAIRFIELD AVE
PARK RD
DANIEL PL
ST DAVID'S PL
Recn Gd
Pl Fld
Parkfield Prim Sch
STURGESS AVE
RIVERSIDE
LAYFIELD CRES
LAYFIELD RD
LAYFIELD CL
BRENT PARK RD
River Brent
Brent Cross Sh Ctr
PRINCE CHARLES DR
STADIUM RD E
ETHERIDGE RD
TEMPELHOF AVE
NORTH CIRCULAR RD
TILLING RD
Brent Cross Interchange
Superstores
Mapledown Sch
Whitefield Sch
Sports Ctr
TOPAZ WLK
MARBLE DR
PEARL CL
JADE CL
AMBER GR
WALLCOTE AVE
PRAYLE GR
Allot Gdns
A41
DYSON CT
ANDERSON CT
WHITEFIELD AVE
RAWLINSON CT 1
WHYCHCOTE POINT 2
CLARE POINT 3
NORDEN POINT
ROSA FREEDMAN CTR
CLAREMONT WAY
CLAREMONT RD
Claremont Way Ind Est
BRENT TERR
CLITTERHOUSE RD
CLITTERHOUSE CRES
Clitterhouse Pl Flds
Hendon Fball Gd
Claremont Prim Sch
COTSWOLD GDNS
Brent Sidings
Staples Corner (East)
Staples Corner Ret Pk
Staples Corner (West)
Staples Corner Bsns Pk
Superstores
GERON WAY
Oxgate Ctr
The Edge Bsns Ctr
Humber
Atlas Bsns Ctr
EYHURST CL
KELCEDA CL
OXGATE GDNS
STREAKES FIELD RD
WATERLOO RD
DELTA CT
COLES GREEN CT
OXGATE CT
The Harp Bsns Ctr
Wellington Park
Apsley Ctr
APSLEY WAY
Phoenix Pk
A406
A5
EDGWARE ROAD
London Group Bsns Pk
JVC Bsns Pk
Aquarius Bsns Pk
PRIESTLEY WAY
THE LINK
Barnet
Brent
ADRIAN AVE
BRENT PARK RD
VERULAM CT
WOOLMEAD AVE
SEELIG AVE
STUART AVE
DEHAR CRES
ESMAR CRES
WARNER CL
ROSEMEAD
TYRREL WAY
FRANKLIN HO
York Park
WEST HENDON BROADWAY
BRENT VIEW RD
PO
YORK PAR
PERRYFIELD WAY
HERBERT RD
A5
Hendon Sch
SILK BRIDGE
GARRICK RD
RUSSELL RD
WILBERFORCE RD
MARSH DR
COLIN CRES
COLIN GDNS
SCOTSWELL DR
COLIN DR
LINCOLN CT
BAVDENE MEWS
BURROUGHS GDNS
CHURCH END
PRINCE OF WALES CL
FULLER ST
NURSERY WLK
GARRICK PK
CLAYDON HO
ASHLEY CT
MANOR HALL DR
SUNNINGFIELDS CRES
SUNNY HILL CT
HENDALE AVE
NEWARK WAY
SHERROCK GDNS
HANDOWNE CL
RICKARD CL
ENDERSLEIGH GDNS
BARTON CL
COLINDEEP GDNS
RICHMOND GDNS
BRENTFIELD GDNS

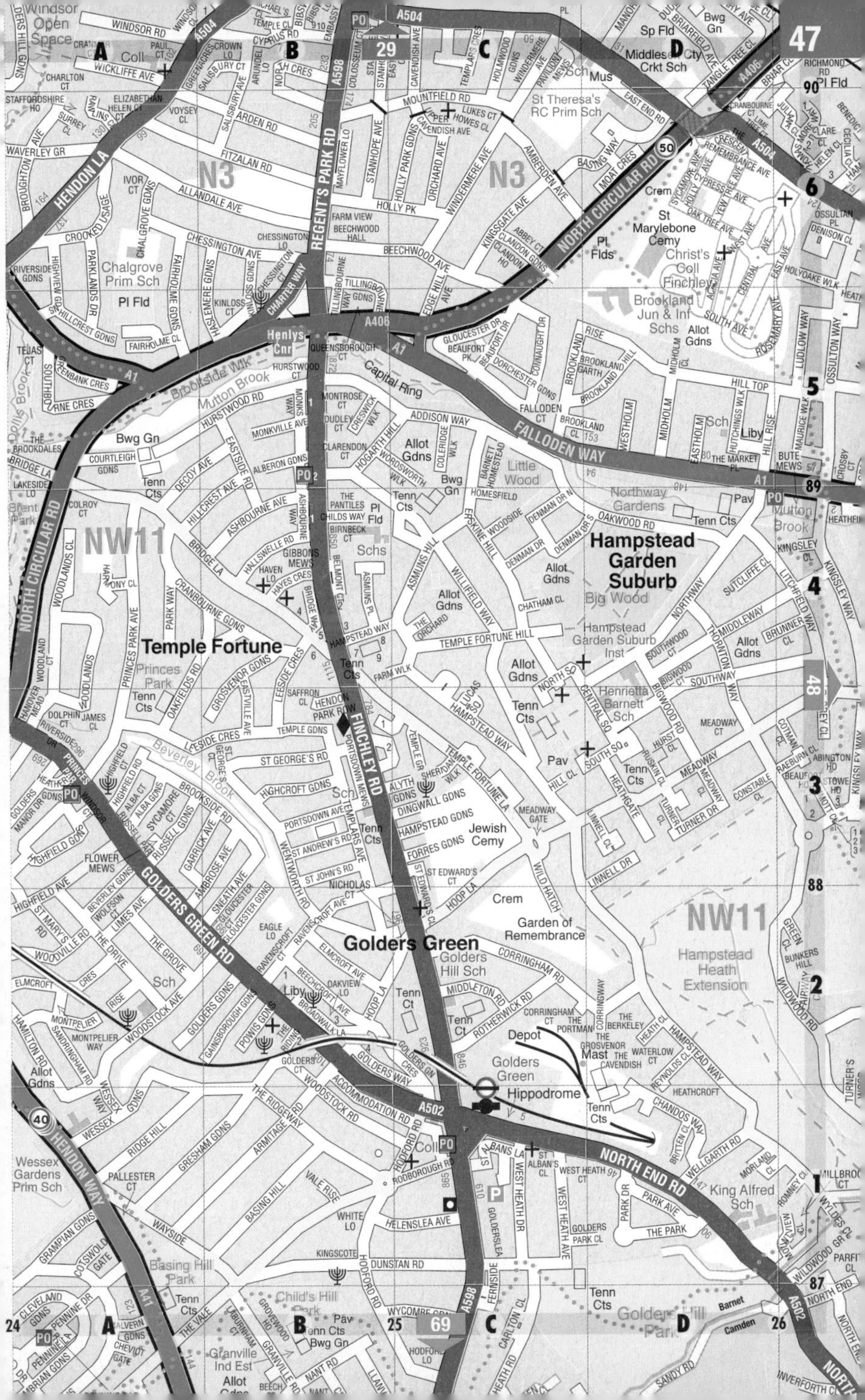
A
B
C
D
29
A504
N3
NW11
Temple Fortune
Hampstead Garden Suburb
Golders Green
Hampstead Heath Extension
Regent's Park Rd
Finchley Rd
North Circular Rd
Hendon La
Hendon Way
Golders Green Rd
North End Rd
Falloden Way
Henlys Cnr
A406
A1
A598
A502
A41
Capital Ring
Mutton Brook
Brookside Wlk
Beverley Brook
St Marylebone Cemy
Christ's Coll Finchley
Brookland Jun & Inf Schs
Chalgrove Prim Sch
St Theresa's RC Prim Sch
Middlesex Cty Crkt Sch
Little Wood
Big Wood
Northway Gardens
Hampstead Garden Suburb Inst
Henrietta Barnett Sch
Jewish Cemy
Crem
Garden of Remembrance
Golders Hill Sch
Golders Green Hippodrome
Depot
Mast
King Alfred Sch
Wessex Gardens Prim Sch
Basing Hill Park
Child's Hill Park
Golders Hill Park
Granville Ind Est
Princes Park
Windsor Open Space
Allot Gdns
Tenn Cts
Pl Fld
Bwg Gn
48
88
89
87
90
24
25
26
69
1
2
3
4
5
6
Barnet
Camden

48
A
B
C
D
30
Allot Gdns
Fortismere Sch
Martin Jun & Inf Schs
Pl Fld
THE MOUNT
CREIGHTON AVE
CHURCH VALE
BEECH DR
RINGWOOD AVE
MANOR COTTS
CHAMPLAIN
BRENDON GR
TAUNTON DR
CHALLONER
CENTRAL AVE
BRIGHTON RD
A406
90
BRIAR CL
RICHMOND RD
Pl Fld
Sch
NEW OAK RD
FERROUR CT
WARDELL CT
LONG LA
ELMFIELD RD
KING ST
GARDEN LODGE CT
CHURCH CT
THE WALKS
A1000
Liby
1 ASHLAR CT
2 CREIGHTON HO
HERTFORD RD
ADAMSON CT
BEDFORD RD
MULBERRY CT
HUNTINGDON RD
LEICESTER RD
LEICESTER MEWS
LINCOLN RD
VICEROY PAR
DURHAM RD
VALE CL
FORTIS GREEN COTTS
TWYFORD AVE
THE COPSE
LYNTON GRANGE
PRIORY GRANGE
DENMARK TERR
WESTSIDE
CHESSING CT
FORTIS GN
A504
FORTIS GREEN AVE
ANNINGTON RD
KEYNES CL
LAURADALE
FLAXMAN VILLAS
BENEDICT WAY
HAMILTON RD
BRACKENBURY RD
SEDGEMERE AVE
MANOR PARK RD
CRICKET ROW
HOBBS GN
ELM GDNS
TRINITY RD
CHURCH LA
LEOPOLD RD
LESLIE RD
PARK GATE
OAKRIDGE DR
NEW ASH CL
PARK RD
NORFOLK CL
HIGH RD
6
CRESCENT
REMEMBRANCE AVE
CYPRESS
YEW
OAK TREE AVE
A504
PO
OSSULTAN PL
DENISON CL
EAST END RD
NEALE CL
PARK FARM CL
HAMPSTEAD HTS
TRINITY AVE
ELMHURST AVE
TALBOT AVE
Holy Trinity CE Prim Sch
EAGANS CL
CHAPEL CT
KITCHENER RD
BERESFORD RD
MARKET PL
PO
VICEROY CL
HOLYOAKE WLK
CENTRAL AVE
EAST AVE
SOUTH AVE
Allot Gdns
ROSEMARY AVE
HEATH VIEW
HEATH VIEW CL
Tenn Ct
PULHAM AVE
ELMHURST CRES
OAKVIEW GDNS
STANLEY RD
PROSPECT
ASHBURNHAM CL
DEANERY CL
EVERDALE CT
CHALICE CT
STOKES CT
DIPLOMA AVE
DIPLOMA CT
THE CAUSEWAY
GREAT NORTH RD
FAIRLAWN AVE
PARK HALL RD
SUMMERLEE AVE
SPRINGCROFT AVE
WESTERN RD
BEECHWOOD AVE
BEVERLEY CL
EASTERN RD
FRANCIS RD
ALEXANDRA MEWS
LUDLOW WAY
OSSULTON WAY
MAYA RD
THE LEYS
Oak Lodge Sch
ABBOTS GDNS
CEDAR DR
P
East Finchley
BARONSMERE RD
INGRAM RD
SUMMERLEE GDNS
SOUTHERN RD
BUCKDEN CL
5
TOP
HOWARD WLK
Sch
HUTCHINGS WLK
HILL RISE
MAURICE WLK
Liby
BUTE MEWS
THE MARKET PL
CROSBY CT
GREENHALGH WLK
BLANDFORD CL
BRIM HILL
East Finchley
GURNEY DR
CORNWOOD CL
WIDECOMBE CT
WIDECOMBE WAY
TOTNES WLK
DEVON RISE
HARFORD WLK
DEANSWAY
EDMUNDS WLK
BROMPTON GR
CHERRY TREE RD
SHAKESPEARE GDNS
GREENFIELD DR
Allot Gdns
Tenn Cts
Fortis Green
Cherry Tree Wood
Tenn Cts
A1
89
Pav
PO
Mutton Brook
Tenn Cts
HEATHFIELDE
LYTTELTON CT
BROWNLOW CT
MONARCH CT
LYTTELTON RD
40
VIVIAN WAY
BELVEDERE CT
THE BISHOPS AVE
BISHOPS CT
WELLINGTON PL
Allot Gdns
THE DRIVE
FORDINGTON RD
WOODSIDE AVE
KINGSLEY CL
Pav
Tenn Cts
Bwg Gn
Kerem Sch
DEACONS RISE
N2
BANCROFT AVE
HIGH GATE EDGE
CHERRY TREE HILL
LINKSVIEW
LANCHESTER RD
4
MIDDLEWAY
LITCHFIELD WAY
KINGSLEY WAY
Lyttelton Plg Flds
NOBLEFIELD HTS
THE CHESTNUTS
MANSFIELD HTS
DORAN MANOR
MANOR
AYLMER PAR
SUSSEX GATE
SUSSEX GDNS
Tenn Cts Depot
BRUNNER CL
Allot Gdns
47
LINDEN LEA
NORRICE LEA
CHURCH MOUNT
AYLMER RD
40
Pl Fld
Pav
WHITTINGTON CT
A1000
A1
MILTON CL
ROWAN WLK
LYTTON CL
Allot Gdns
AYLMER CT
HIGH SHELDON
TOYNE WAY
BAKER'S LA
B519
MEADWAY CT
COTMAN CL
GREY CL
HOLNE CHASE
CHALTON DR
Annemount Sch
WINNINGTON CL
Barnet
Haringey
KENWOOD RD
GASKELL RD
NORTH HILL AVE
HERON'S LEA
Highgate Prim Sch
3
RAEBURN CL
ABINGTON HO
BEAUFORT HO
STOWE HO
KINGSLEY WAY
SPENCER DR
CARLYLE CL
BISHOPS GR
BYRON DR
WHITE LODGE CL
STOREY RD
YEATMAN RD
Allot Gdns
EMMOTT CL
NEVILLE DR
1 CARPENTER HO
2 KINGSLEY HO
3 COSWAY HO
Highgate CH
SHELDON AVE
Highgate Private
H
VIEW RD
88
NW11
WINNINGTON RD
ARDEN COURT GDNS
DENEWOOD RD
WILLOWDENE
APOLLO HO
BROADLANDS LO
Hampstead Heath Extension
GREEN CL
BUNKERS HILL
Hampstead
CANONS CL
COURTENAY AVE
STORMONT RD
Tenn Cts
BROADLANDS
Tenn Cts
Sp Ctr
2
WILDWOOD RD
FAIRWAY CL
WIGRAM AVE
COMPTON AVE
BISHOPSWOOD RD
Highgate Sch
Sp Gd
CH
HAMPSTEAD LA
Pav
Haringey
Turner's Wood
TURNER'S WOOD
PARK FLATS
B519
Camden
SPANIARDS CL
KENWOOD CL
P
H
Athlone House
WILDWOOD RISE
Kenwood House
SPANIARDS END
The Spaniards Inn (PH)
Millfield La
ORLAND CL
MILLBROOK CT
1
King Alfred Sch
ROMNEY CL
WYLDES CL
MOUNT TYNDAL
Open Air Stage
Tenn Cts
Bwg Gn
Allot Gdns
FITZROY PK
THE HEXAGON
HIGHFIELDS GR
FITZROY CL
WILDWOOD GR
PARFITT CL
Sandy Heath
COLUMBAS DR
Ken Wood
N6
87
Barnet
Camden
NORTH END
A502
North End
NORTH END AVE
SPANIARDS RD
B519
Mast
Tenn Cts
115
26
A
B
70
27
C
D
28
Hampstead Heath
INVERFORTH CL
MERTON LA

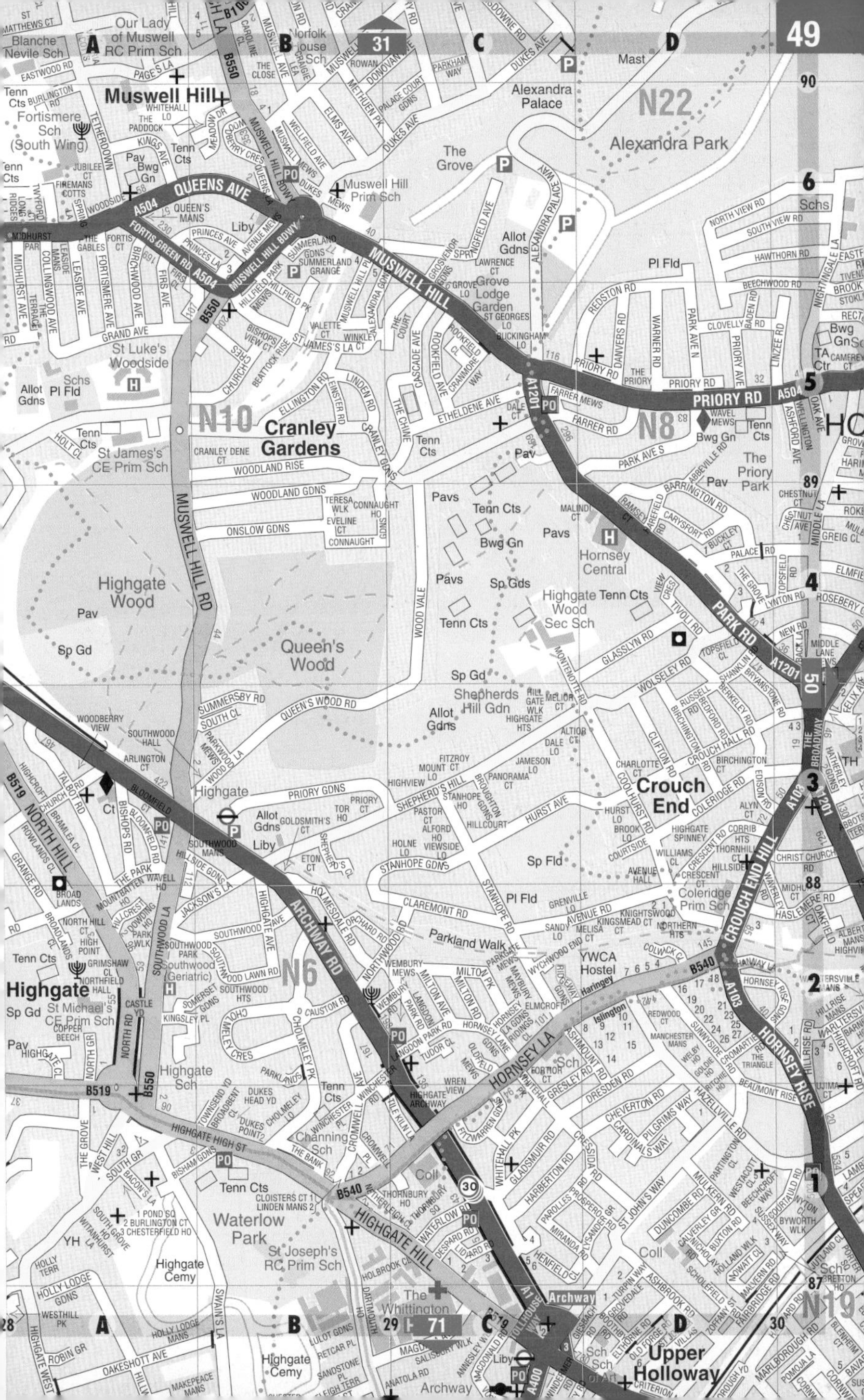
Muswell Hill
Alexandra Palace
Alexandra Park
N22
N10
N8
N6
N19
Cranley Gardens
Highgate Wood
Queen's Wood
Crouch End
Highgate
Upper Holloway
Archway
Waterlow Park
Highgate Cemy
The Priory Park
Hornsey Central
Highgate Wood Sec Sch
Shepherds Hill Gdn
Parkland Walk
St Luke's Woodside
St James's CE Prim Sch
Muswell Hill Prim Sch
Coleridge Prim Sch
St Michael's CE Prim Sch
Channing Sch
Highgate Sch
St Joseph's RC Prim Sch
The Whittington
Our Lady of Muswell RC Prim Sch
Fortismere Sch (South Wing)
Blanche Nevile Sch
Southwood (Geriatric)
YWCA Hostel
MUSWELL HILL RD
ARCHWAY RD
PARK RD
PRIORY RD
QUEENS AVE
MUSWELL HILL
HORNSEY LA
CROUCH END HILL
HORNSEY RISE
HIGHGATE HILL
HIGHGATE HIGH ST
NORTH HILL
31
50
71
30

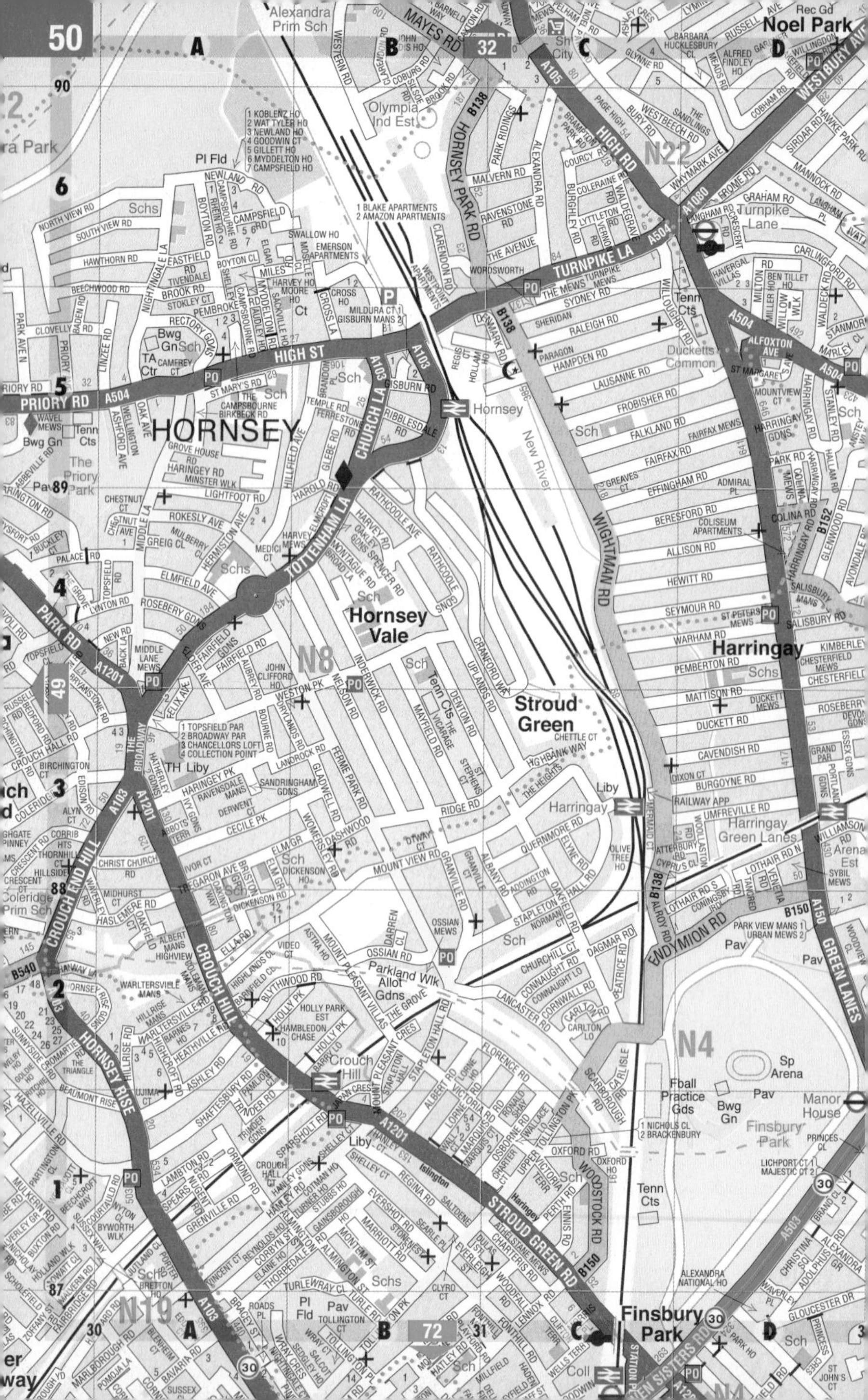

A
B
C
D
32
72
49
Noel Park
HORNSEY
Hornsey Vale
Stroud Green
Harringay
Finsbury Park
Manor House
N22
N8
N4
N19
Turnpike Lane
Hornsey
Harringay
Harringay Green Lanes
Crouch Hill
New River
Olympia Ind Est
The Priory Park
Ducketts Common
Parkland Wlk
Allot Gdns
Fball Practice Gds
Sp Arena
Alexandra Prim Sch
Coleridge Prim Sch
Sh City
HIGH ST
PRIORY RD
TURNPIKE LA
HIGH RD
WESTBURY AVE
GREEN LANES
HORNSEY PARK RD
TOTTENHAM LA
CHURCH LA
PARK RD
CROUCH END HILL
CROUCH HILL
HORNSEY RISE
STROUD GREEN RD
WIGHTMAN RD
ENDYMION RD
MAYES RD
WESTERN RD
ALEXANDRA RD
RIDGE RD
MOUNT VIEW RD
OSSIAN RD
FERME PARK RD
HARRINGAY RD
A504
A105
A103
A1201
A1080
A503
A150
B138
B150
B152
B540
1 KOBLENZ HO
2 WAT TYLER HO
3 NEWLAND HO
4 GOODWIN CT
5 GILLETT HO
6 MYDDELTON HO
7 CAMPSFIELD HO
1 BLAKE APARTMENTS
2 AMAZON APARTMENTS
1 TOPSFIELD PAR
2 BROADWAY PAR
3 CHANCELLORS LOFT
4 COLLECTION POINT
1 NICHOLS CL
2 BRACKENBURY
PARK VIEW MANS 1
URBAN MEWS 2
LICHPORT CT 1
MAJESTIC CT 2
90
89
88
87
6
5
4
3
2
1
30
31

A
B
C
D
33
TOTTENHAM
Recn Gd
N17
Open Air Theatre
The Moselle
Bruce Grove
Bruce Grove Prim Sch
6 Tottenham Hale
West Green
Downhills Park
Downhills Recn Gd
PHILIP LA
WEST GREEN RD
N15
Seven Sisters
BROAD LA
MONUMENT WAY
HIGH RD
5
4
3
2
1
South Tottenham
52
89
90
88
87
Chestnuts Recn Gd
St Ann's General
ST ANN'S RD
Superstore
Arena Bsns Ctr
Crusader Ind Est
N4
N16
SEVEN SISTERS RD
AMHURST PK
Stamford Hill
STAMFORD HILL
East Resr
West Resr
Capital Ring
Stamford Hill
MANOR RD
LORDSHIP PK
Abney Park Cemy
STOKE NEWINGTON
Stoke Newington
73
32
A1080
B155
A504
B153
B152
A503
A1055
A10
A107
A105
B105

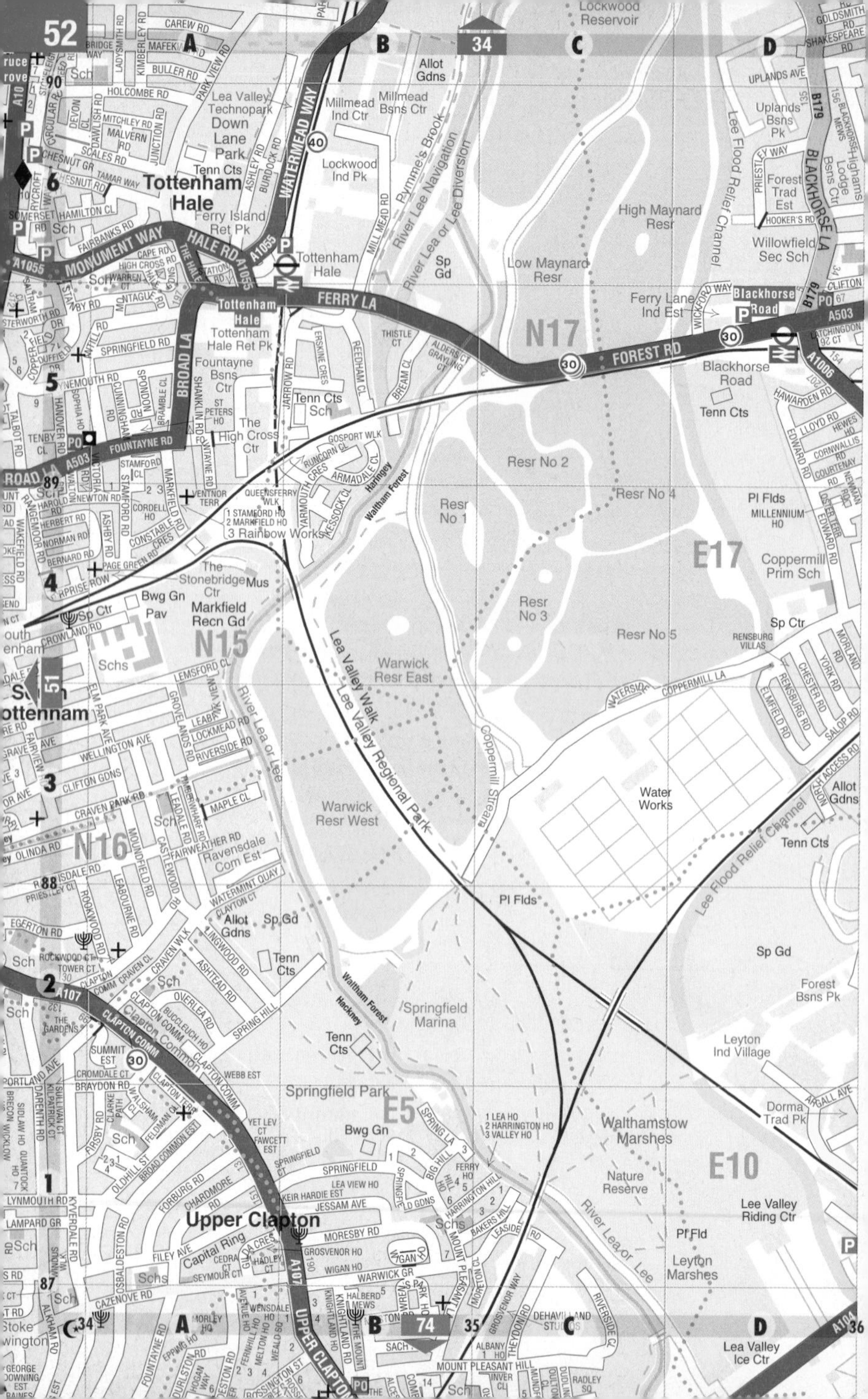
52
A
B
C
D
34
Lockwood Reservoir
Allot Gdns
Millmead Ind Ctr
Millmead Bsns Ctr
Lea Valley Technopark
Down Lane Park
Tottenham Hale
Ferry Island Ret Pk
Tenn Cts
Lockwood Ind Pk
WATERMEAD WAY
Rymme's Brook
River Lee Navigation
River Lea or Lee Diversion
High Maynard Resr
Low Maynard Resr
Lee Flood Relief Channel
Uplands Bsns Pk
Forest Trad Est
Higham's Lodge Bsns Ctr
Willowfield Sec Sch
BLACKHORSE LA
Ferry Lane Ind Est
Blackhorse Road
N17
FOREST RD
FERRY LA
MONUMENT WAY
HALE RD
Tottenham Hale Ret Pk
Fountayne Bsns Ctr
The High Cross Ctr
BROAD LA
FOUNTAYNE RD
Tenn Cts Sch
Sp Gd
Resr No 1
Resr No 2
Resr No 3
Resr No 4
Resr No 5
Pl Flds
E17
Coppermill Prim Sch
Sp Ctr
COPPERMILL LA
Water Works
Coppermill Stream
3 Rainbow Works
The Stonebridge Ctr
Mus
Markfield Recn Gd
Bwg Gn
Pav
N15
Schs
South Tottenham
51
Lea Valley Walk
Lee Valley Regional Park
Warwick Resr East
Warwick Resr West
River Lea or Lee
N16
Ravensdale Com Est
Allot Gdns
Tenn Cts
Tenn Cts
Springfield Marina
Springfield Park
E5
Clapton Common
Walthamstow Marshes
Nature Reserve
Leyton Marshes
Pl Fld
E10
Lee Valley Riding Ctr
Sp Gd
Forest Bsns Pk
Leyton Ind Village
Dorma Trad Pk
Upper Clapton
Capital Ring
Lea Valley Ice Ctr
Stoke Newington
74
35
36
A104
A107
A503
A1055
A10
B179
A1006
90
89
88
87
6
5
4
3
2
1

WALTHAMSTOW
E17
E10
Chestnut Sp Gd
Waltham Forest Coll
Allot Gdns
Forest Rd
Hoe St
Lea Bridge Rd
Markhouse Rd
High Rd
Church Rd
High Road Leyton
Chingford Rd
Blackhorse Rd
St James Street
Walthamstow Central
Walthamstow Queens Road
Queens Road Cemy
South Grove Prim Sch
Kelmscott L Ctr
Kelmscott Sch
St Saviour's CE Prim Sch
Barn Croft Prim Sch
Leyton Link Est
Roxwell Trad Pk
Cromwell Est
Eastgate Bsns Pk
Period Wks
Sybourn Inf Sch Annexe
The Lammas Sch
Willow Brook Prim Sch
Lea Park Trad Est
St Joseph's RC Inf Sch
Fairways Bsns Pk
George Mitchell Sch
Vestry Ho (Mus)
The Holy Family RC Coll
Thorpe Coombe
Leyton Green Rd
35
75
54

36
A
B
C
D
FOREST RD
A503
Upper
Walthamstow
Allot Gdns
Liby
Woodside
Sch
Thorpe
Coombe
Coll
Sch
CORBETT RD
WOODLANDS RD
WAVERLEY RD
AVON RD
HILLSIDE GDNS
Tenn
Cts
Bwg
Gn
BROADWALK
CHEYNE AVE
E18
Sp Gd
Snaresbrook
Gilbert's
Slade
WOODFORD NEW RD
A104
B160
UPPER WALTHAMSTOW RD
Nature
Reserve
E17
Wood
Street
GREENWAY AVE
Pav
Sp Gd
Forest
Sch
OAKHURST GDNS
SNARESBROOK RD
Eagle Pond
WOOD ST
Warwick
Sch for
Boys
The
Holy
Family
RC Coll
MARLOWE RD
VALLENTIN RD
CHURCH HILL RD
PROSPECT HILL
MAYNARD RD
BARCLAY RD
Schs
WHIPPS CROSS
TA
Ctr
A114
Hollow Pond
WHIPPS CROSS RD
Ct
Redbridge
Waltham Forest
Centenary Walk
E11
HOLLYBUSH HILL
A1199
LEA BRIDGE RD
CARNARVON RD
LIVERPOOL RD
Leyton
Sixth Form
Coll
Whipps Cross
Connaught
Day
Barclay
Sch
Leytonstone
Bsns & Spec
Sch
E10
Belmont
Pk Sch
LEYTON GREEN RD
B159
A112
HIGH RD
SANDRINGHAM RD
Gwyn Jones
Prim Sch
Tenn
Cts
Abbotts
Park
GAINSBOROUGH RD
A106
Super
store
Green Man
Int
A12
A113
Leyton
Midland
Road
Norlington
Sch for Boys
George
Mitchell
Sch
Sp
Gd
Leytonstone
Liby
George
Tomlinson
Prim Sch
Leytonstone
Davies Lane
Prim Sch
Leytonstone
High Road
Wanstead
Flats
Dawlish
Prim Sch
Newport
Sch
Noor Ul Islam
Prim Sch
FRANCIS RD
HIGH ROAD LEYTON
76
1
2
3
4
5
6
53
89
88
87
90

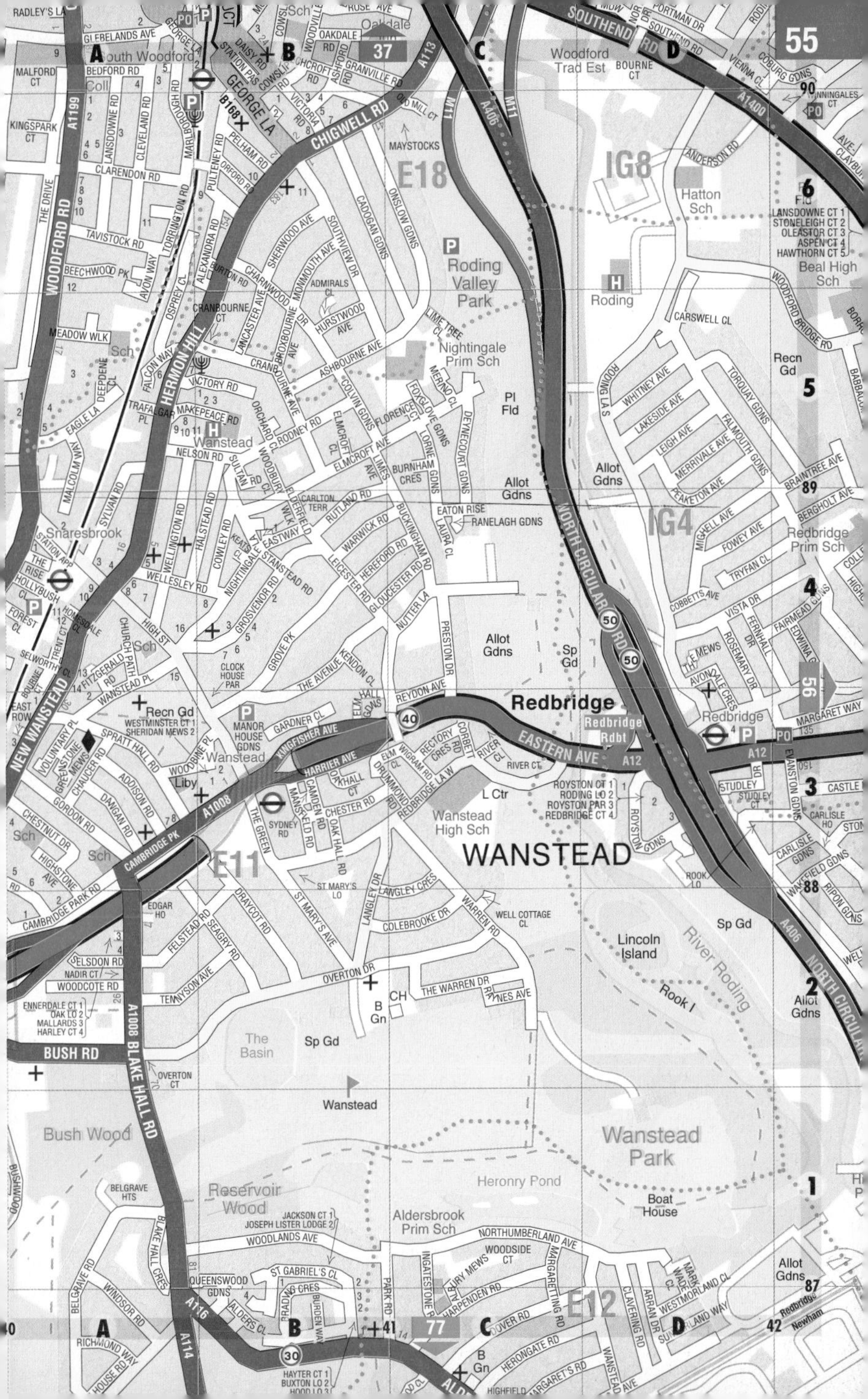
A
B
C
D
37
E18
IG8
IG4
E11
E12
WANSTEAD
Redbridge
South Woodford
Woodford Trad Est
Roding Valley Park
Nightingale Prim Sch
Hatton Sch
Beal High Sch
Roding
Snaresbrook
Wanstead
Wanstead High Sch
Redbridge Prim Sch
Redbridge Rdbt
Lincoln Island
River Roding
Rook I
Wanstead Park
Heronry Pond
Boat House
The Basin
Bush Wood
Reservoir Wood
Aldersbrook Prim Sch
Recn Gd
Allot Gdns
Sp Gd
Pl Fld
L Ctr
Liby
SOUTHEND RD
A1400
A113
CHIGWELL RD
GEORGE LA
B168
M11
A406
NORTH CIRCULAR RD
EASTERN AVE
A12
A1199
WOODFORD RD
HERMON HILL
NEW WANSTEAD
HIGH ST
CAMBRIDGE PK
A1008
BLAKE HALL RD
BUSH RD
A116
A114
WOODLANDS AVE
NORTHUMBERLAND AVE
WOODFORD BRIDGE RD
KINGFISHER AVE
HARRIER AVE
REYDON AVE
OVERTON DR
THE WARREN DR
WARREN RD
COLEBROOKE DR
ST MARY'S AVE
DRAYCOT RD
TENNYSON AVE
GROVE PK
THE AVENUE
NUTTER LA
PRESTON DR
LEICESTER RD
BUCKINGHAM RD
CHARNWOOD DR
ASHBOURNE AVE
ELMCROFT AVE
FLORENCE CT
DEYNECOURT GDNS
RODING LA S
WHITNEY AVE
LAKESIDE AVE
LEIGH AVE
MERRIVALE AVE
TORQUAY GDNS
FALMOUTH GDNS
FOWEY AVE
TRYFAN CL
COBBETTS AVE
VISTA DR
ROSEMARY DR
FERNHALL DR
STUDLEY DR
EVANSTON GDNS
CARLISLE GDNS
WAKEFIELD GDNS
MARGARET WAY
CASTLE
ROYSTON GDNS
MAYSTOCKS
6
5
4
3
2
1
90
89
88
87
56
50
40
30
77
42
41
Redbridge
Newham

56
Essex STREET ATLAS
A
B
C
D
CLAYHALL AVE
STRADBROKE GR
WINNINGALES CT
PEEL DR
BRINKWORTH RD
MARLBOROUGH DR
MARLANDS RD
GAYFERE RD
CHADACRE AVE
MELLOWS RD
DYMCHURCH CL
TIVERTON AVE
LESSINGHAM AVE
RUSHDEN GDNS
TAPTREE CRES
SANDPIPER TERR
BEAMINSTER GDNS
MOSSFORD CT
1 PUFFIN TERR
2 OYSTER CATCHER TERR
HATFIELD CL 1
LOOE GDNS 2
CHERRY CT 3
LICHEN CT 4
Cemy
ANDERSON RD
Hatton Sch
CLAYBURY BROADWAY
HEATHERLEY DR
STONELEIGH RD
HERENT DR
LORD AVE
Schs
WERNETH HALL RD
LONGWOOD PAR
OAKLEAFE GDNS
MAPLELEAFE GDNS
GREENLEAFE DR
Pl Fld
LANSDOWNE CT 1
STONELEIGH CT 2
OLEASTOR CT 3
ASPEN CT 4
HAWTHORN CT 5
ORIEL GDNS
ABBOTSWOOD GDNS
MONKSWOOD GDNS
WRAY AVE
EVESHAM WAY
DELLWOOD GDNS
LONGWOOD GDNS
GAYSHAM HALL
Sp Gd
Beal High Sch
IG5
EARLSWOOD GDNS
GLENTHORNE GDNS
WOODVILLE GDNS
CARSWELL CL
WOODFORD BRIDGE RD
BORROWDALE
LODGE HILL
PARK VIEW GDNS
LORD GDNS
Clayhall Park
ROSEDENE GDNS
THORPEDALE GDNS
BEATTYVILLE GDNS
GEORGEVILLE GDNS
HAIGVILLE GDNS
GEARIESVILLE GDNS
BRANDVILLE GDNS
Recn Gd
BABBACOMBE GDNS
WIDECOMBE GDNS
CONISTON GDNS
DERWENT GDNS
QUEENBOROUGH GDNS
NORTHWOOD GDNS
SUNNYMEDE DR
TORQUAY GDNS
FALMOUTH GDNS
MERRIVALE AVE
WOODFORD AVE
B Gn
1 HEDGELEY
2 QUEENS GATE
HIGHWOOD GDNS
BEECHWOOD GDNS
LITTLE GEARIES
SOUTHWOOD GDNS
A123
KESWICK GDNS
BRANTWOOD GDNS
GRASMERE GDNS
AMBLESIDE GDNS
COLLINWOOD GDNS
HEDGEWOOD GDNS
BRONTE CL
BRAINTREE AVE
BERGHOLT AVE
Prep Sch
GOSFORD GDNS
B192
GLENWOOD GDNS
KENWOOD GDNS
SWALLOW CT
BUTE RD
LOUDOUN AVE
Redbridge Prim Sch
COLLEGE GDNS
GRANGEWAY GDNS
RIDGEWAY GDNS
SOMERSBY GDNS
GANTSHILL CRES
Schs
Sch
SHORE CL
CHALFORD CT
FOWEY AVE
MICHELL AVE
TRYFAN CL
HIGHCLIFFE GDNS
FAIRMEAD GDNS
EDWINA GDNS
LIMEWOOD CT
ROLL GDNS
SHERE RD
WAREMEAD RD
ICKNIELD DR
VISTA DR
FERNHALL DR
ROSEMARY DR
REDBRIDGE LA E
WINDERMERE GDNS
DANEHURST GDNS
INGLEHURST GDNS
CROMBIE CL
WYCOMBE RD
SEVEN WAYS PAR
GAYSHAM AVE
GLENHAM DR
MARTLEY DR
AVERY GDNS
RADNOR CRES
SUSSEX CL
A1400
ETHELBERT GDNS
WAYSIDE MEWS
Liby
HEADLEY APP
PARHAM DR
ASHURST DR
THE MEWS
AVON
55
Redbridge
MARGARET WAY
ELLESMERE GDNS
EASTERN AVE
BEEHIVE LA
Gants Hill
OTLEY DR
OTLEY APP
HEADLEY DR
A12
BEEHIVE CT
Coll
CLARENCE AVE
PAINFIELD MEWS
THE CRESCENT
FRINTON MEWS
LONSDALE CRES
SOUTH VIEW CRES
LYNTON CRES
ALBEMARLE GDNS
ALBEMARLE APP
EVANSTON GDNS
CASTLE DR
CASTLEVIEW GDNS
HILLVIEW CRES
DEVONPORT GDNS
BLENHEIM AVE
BRAMLEY CRES
CARLISLE HO
STONEHALL AVE
PRESTON GDNS
ST HELEN'S RD
Gants Hill
Valentines High Sch (Upper)
Pl Fld
Min Glf Crs
IG2
MIDDLETON GDNS
MIDDLEFIELD GDNS
CARLISLE GDNS
WAKEFIELD GDNS
RIPON GDNS
WANSTEAD LA
Sp Gd
ST EDMUND'S RD
FAIRHOLME RD
MORNINGTON AVE
CRANBROOK RD
1 BRAMLEY HO
2 CHARLOTTE CT
3 VI & JOHN RUBENS HO
4 ABRAHAM COHEN CT
PERTH RD
WORCESTER GDNS
HEREFORD GDNS
IG1
CRANBROOK RISE
ELY GDNS
Bwg Gn
1 GLOUCESTER CT
2 LINCOLN CT
3 PAVILION RD
Sp Gd
River Roding
WELLS GDNS
GLOUCESTER GDNS
PETERBOROUGH GDNS
ST GEORGE'S RD
MISTLEY THORN
TILLOTSON RD
EMERSON RD
Valentines Park
A406
NORTH CIRCULAR RD
LINCOLN GDNS
ST ANDREW'S RD
CANTERBURY AVE
THE DRIVE
WILSON RD
BETHELL AVE
THE SQUARE
Allot Gdns
TRURO GDNS
CHELMSFORD GDNS
VAUGHAN GDNS
COWLEY RD
HOLCOMBE RD
QUEBEC RD
Pav
CHICHESTER GDNS
ROCHESTER GDNS
WHITFIELD CT
CLARENDON GDNS
Bwg Gn
Crkt Gd
EXETER GDNS
RANELAGH GDNS
ARLINGTON GDNS
REDCLIFFE GDNS
Cranbrook
WANSTEAD PARK RD
HIGHLANDS GDNS
LENNOX GDNS
STANHOPE GDNS
SACKVILLE GDNS
CAVENDISH GDNS
BEAUFORT GDNS
The Lake
Bwg Gn
Highlands Prim Sch
SEYMOUR GDNS
KENSINGTON GDNS
ENDSLEIGH GDNS
VALENTINES RD
INGLEBY RD
MELBOURNE RD
COVENTRY RD
WARWICK GDNS
CH
BELGRAVE RD
DE VERE GDNS
RUTLAND AVE
MAYFAIR AVE
GREENWAY CT
PARK AVE
BATHURST RD
AIRLIE GDNS
WELLESLEY RD
Allot Gdns
EMPRESS AVE
Park Sch
GRANVILLE RD
ADELAIDE RD
Redbridge
Newham
42
43
BELGRAVE
78
Coll
MANSFIELD RD
MORLAND RD
Sch
Ilford
WANSTEAD PARK
MARKET
WESTBURY RD
ARGYLE RD
BEAL RD
HERON CT
BALFOUR RD
HAINAULT ST

Fairlop Waters Ctry Pk
Fairlop Plain
Ilford Jewish Prim Sch
Sch of Riding
Barkingside
Aldborough Hall Farm
Aldborough Hatch
Aldborough House Farm
Fullwood Prim Sch
Superstore
Oaks Park High Sch
William Torbitt Prim Sch
Newbury Park
Seven Kings Park
Farnham Green Prim Sch
Seven Kings High Sch
Downshall Prim Sch
Westwood Rec Gd
Seven Kings
St Aidan's RC Sch
Canon Palmer RC Sch
Christchurch Prim Sch
Redbridge Ent Ctr
EASTERN AVE
HIGH RD
IG1
IG2
IG3
IG6

58
79
46

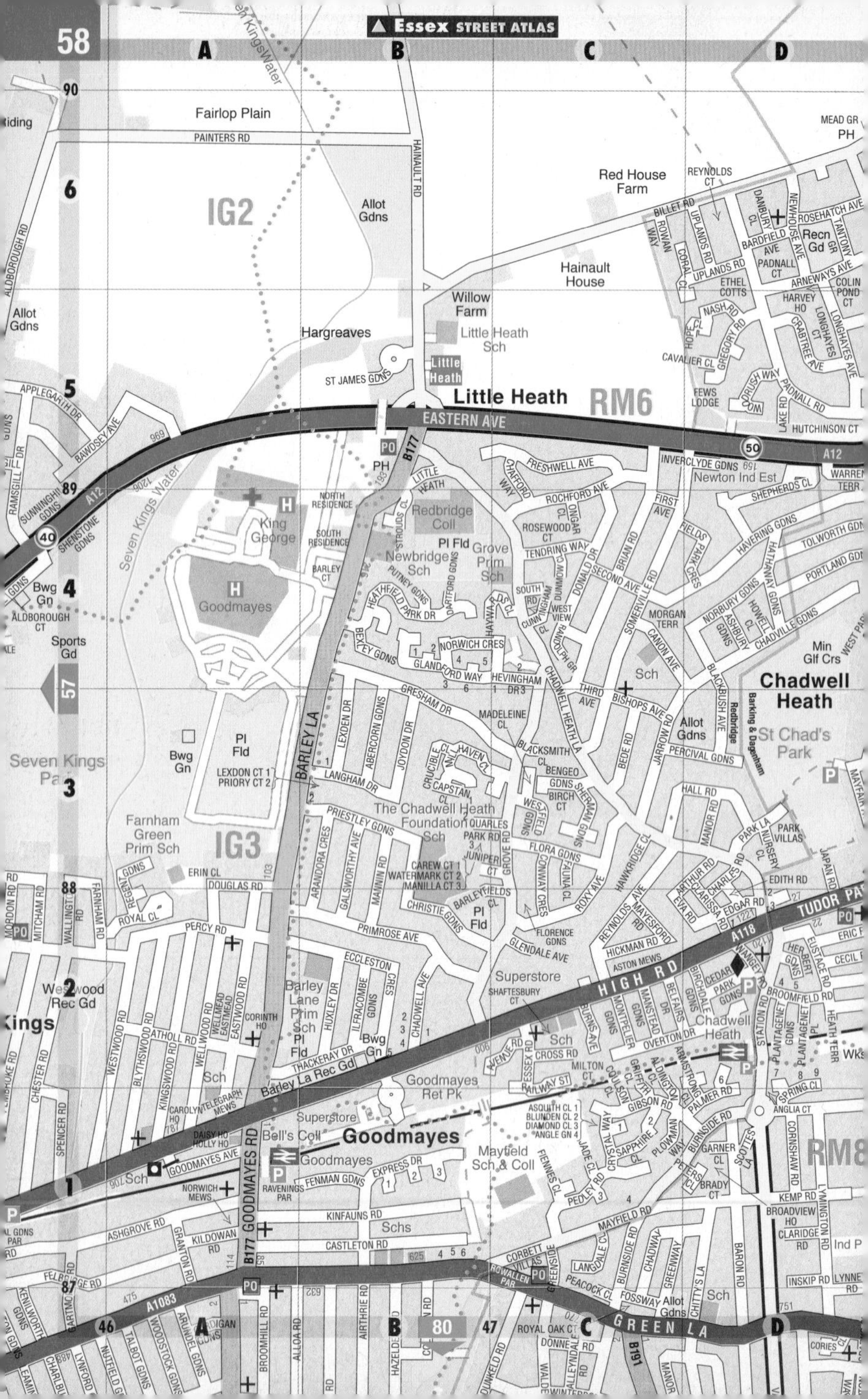
A
B
C
D
Fairlop Plain
PAINTERS RD
HAINAULT RD
IG2
Allot Gdns
Red House Farm
Hainault House
Willow Farm
Little Heath Sch
Hargreaves
ST JAMES GDNS
Little Heath
RM6
EASTERN AVE
A12
Seven Kings Water
King George
Goodmayes
Redbridge Coll
Newbridge Sch
Grove Prim Sch
BARLEY LA
Chadwell Heath
St Chad's Park
The Chadwell Heath Foundation Sch
IG3
Farnham Green Prim Sch
Seven Kings Park
Westwood Rec Gd
HIGH RD
TUDOR PA
Superstore
Barley Lane Prim Sch
Goodmayes Ret Pk
Goodmayes
Mayfield Sch & Coll
GOODMAYES RD
Bell's Coll
KINFAUNS RD
CASTLETON RD
A1083
GREEN LA
RM8
80
57
50
46
47
40

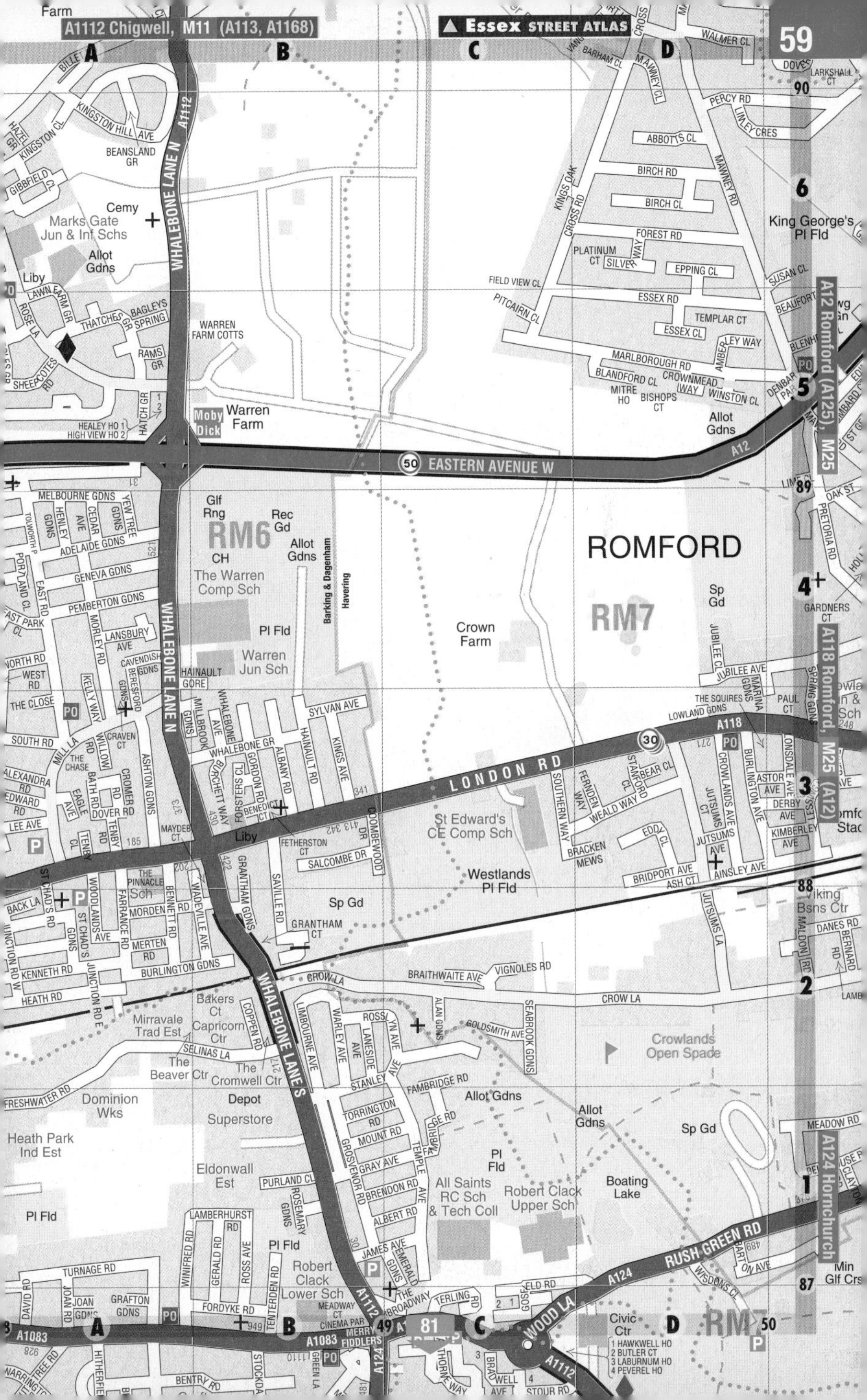
ROMFORD
RM6
RM7
WHALEBONE LANE N
EASTERN AVENUE W
LONDON RD
WHALEBONE LANE S
RUSH GREEN RD
CROW LA
Marks Gate Jun & Inf Schs
Warren Farm
The Warren Comp Sch
Warren Jun Sch
Crown Farm
St Edward's CE Comp Sch
Westlands Pl Fld
Crowlands Open Space
All Saints RC Sch & Tech Coll
Robert Clack Upper Sch
Robert Clack Lower Sch
Boating Lake
Heath Park Ind Est
Dominion Wks
Eldonwall Est
Mirravale Trad Est
Capricorn Ctr
The Beaver Ctr
The Cromwell Ctr
Viking Bsns Ctr
King George's Pl Fld
Civic Ctr
A12 Romford (A125), M25
A118 Romford, M25 (A12)
A124 Hornchurch

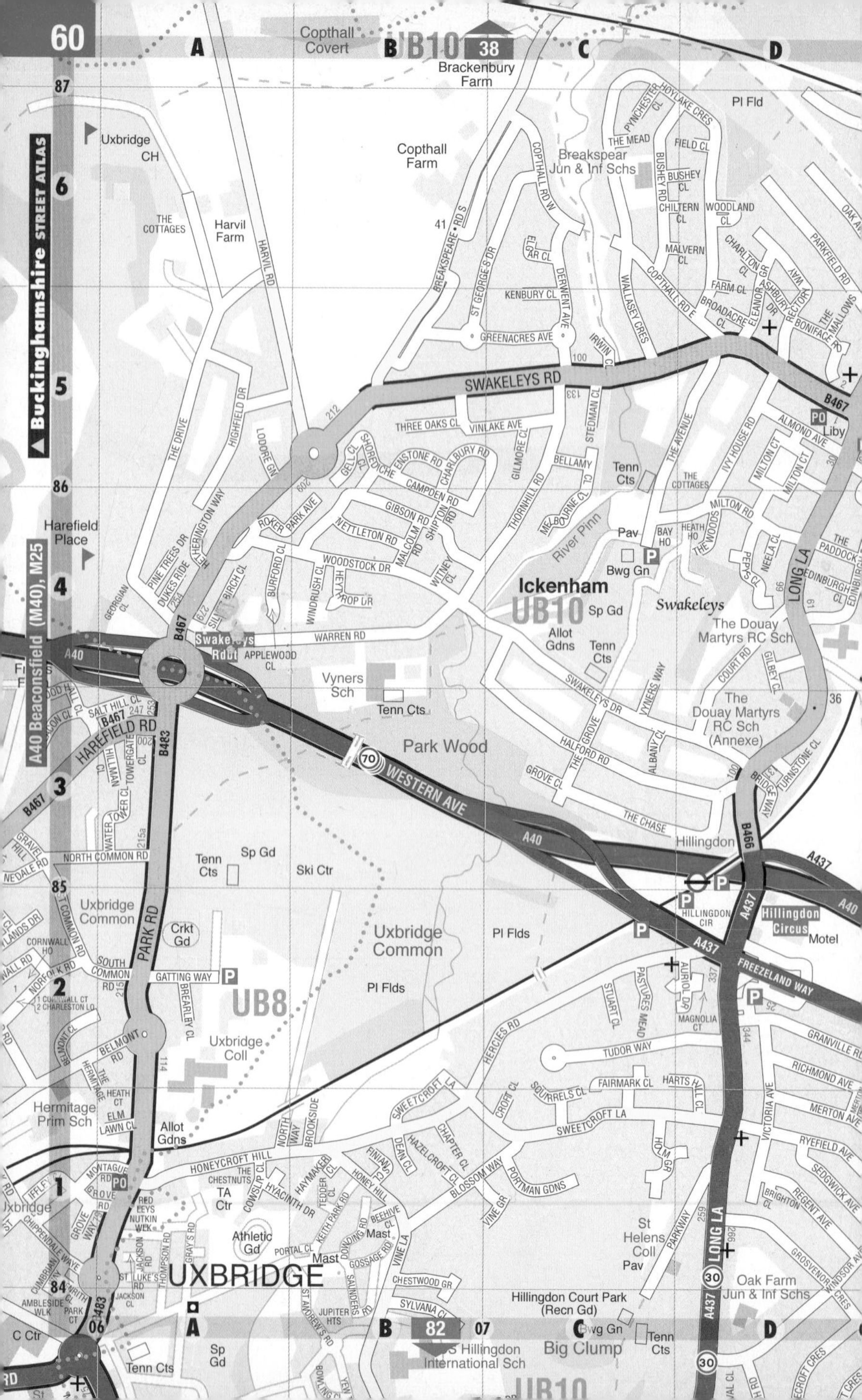
Copthall Covert
UB10
38
Brackenbury Farm
Uxbridge CH
Copthall Farm
Breakspear Jun & Inf Schs
Pl Fld
THE COTTAGES
Harvil Farm
HARVIL RD
Buckinghamshire STREET ATLAS
SWAKELEYS RD
B467
Harefield Place
A40 Beaconsfield (M40), M25
Ickenham
UB10
Swakeleys
The Douay Martyrs RC Sch
Swakeleys Rdbt
Vyners Sch
Tenn Cts
Park Wood
WESTERN AVE
A40
Hillingdon
HARFIELD RD
Uxbridge Common
Ski Ctr
Pl Flds
Hillingdon Circus
Motel
FREEZELAND WAY
A437
PARK RD
B483
UB8
Uxbridge Coll
Hermitage Prim Sch
Allot Gdns
HONEYCROFT HILL
TA Ctr
Athletic Gd
UXBRIDGE
St Helens Coll
Oak Farm Jun & Inf Schs
LONG LA
Hillingdon Court Park (Recn Gd)
Big Clump
82
Hillingdon International Sch
A
B
C
D
1
2
3
4
5
6
84
85
86
87
06
07

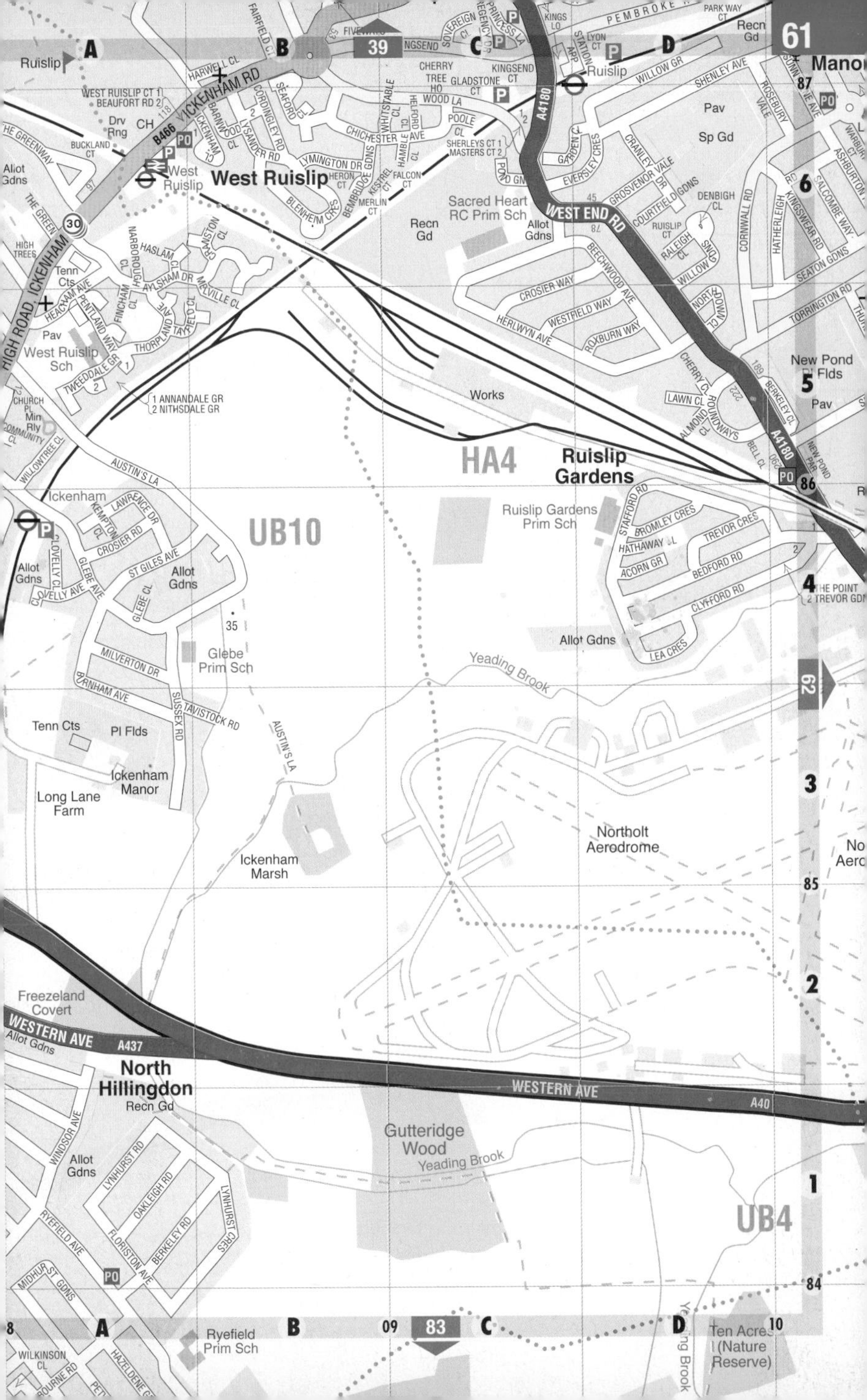
West Ruislip
Ruislip
Ruislip Gardens
HA4
UB10
UB4
North Hillingdon
Northolt Aerodrome
Ickenham Marsh
Ickenham Manor
Long Lane Farm
Freezeland Covert
Gutteridge Wood
Yeading Brook
WESTERN AVE
A40
A437
A4180
WEST END RD
ICKENHAM RD
B466
HIGH ROAD, ICKENHAM
Sacred Heart RC Prim Sch
Ruislip Gardens Prim Sch
Glebe Prim Sch
West Ruislip Sch
Ryefield Prim Sch
Ten Acres (Nature Reserve)
New Pond Pl Flds
Works
Allot Gdns
Recn Gd
AUSTIN'S LA
39
62
83

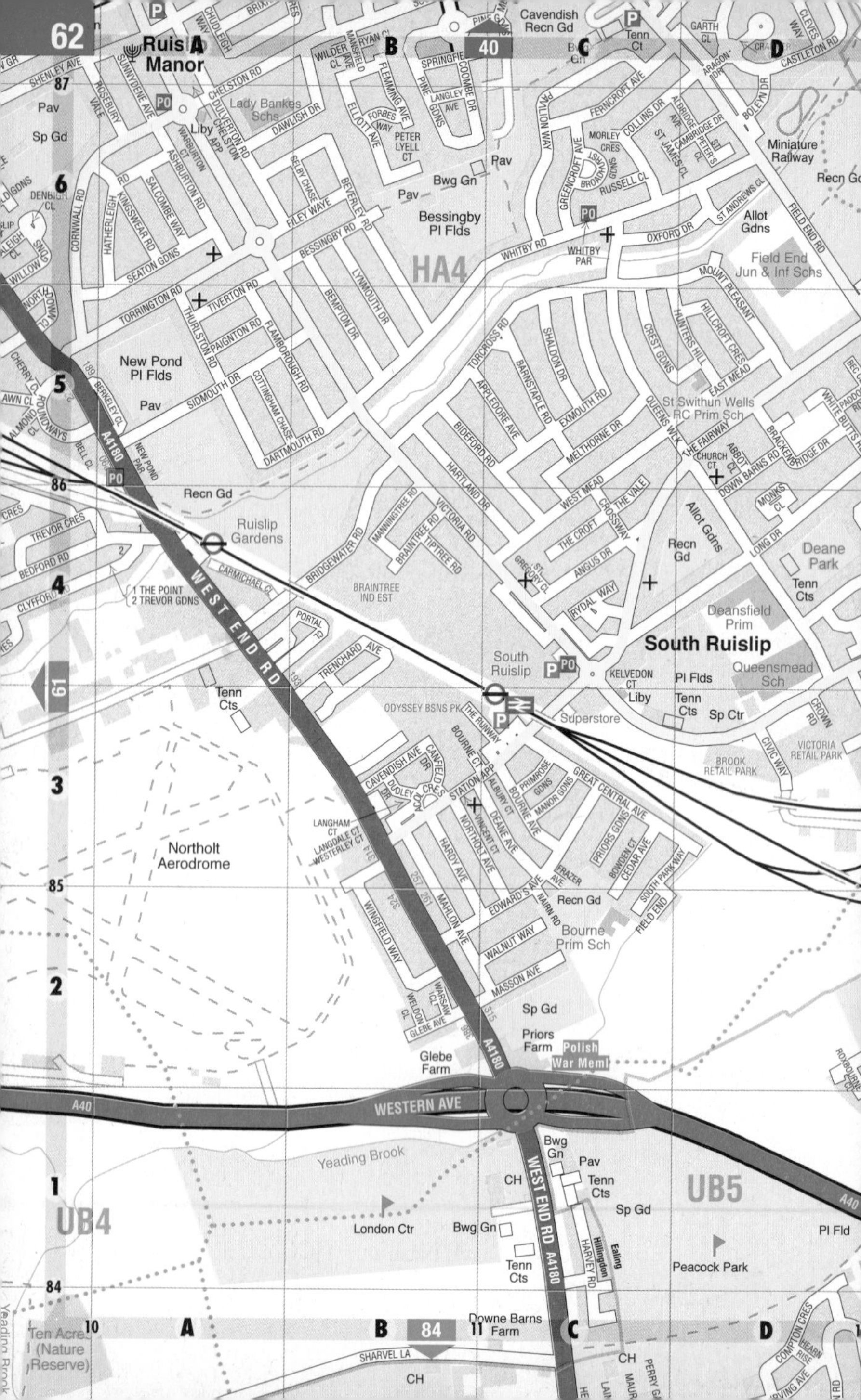
Ruislip Manor
Cavendish Recn Gd
Lady Bankes Schs
Miniature Railway
Bessingby Pl Flds
HA4
Field End Jun & Inf Schs
New Pond Pl Flds
St Swithun Wells RC Prim Sch
Ruislip Gardens
Braintree Ind Est
Deane Park
Deansfield Prim
South Ruislip
Queensmead Sch
Odyssey Bsns Pk
Superstore
Victoria Retail Park
Brook Retail Park
Northolt Aerodrome
Bourne Prim Sch
Priors Farm
Polish War Meml
Glebe Farm
Western Ave
West End Rd
A4180
A40
Yeading Brook
UB4
UB5
London Ctr
Peacock Park
Downe Barns Farm
Ten Acres (Nature Reserve)
Sharvel La
Hillingdon
Ealing

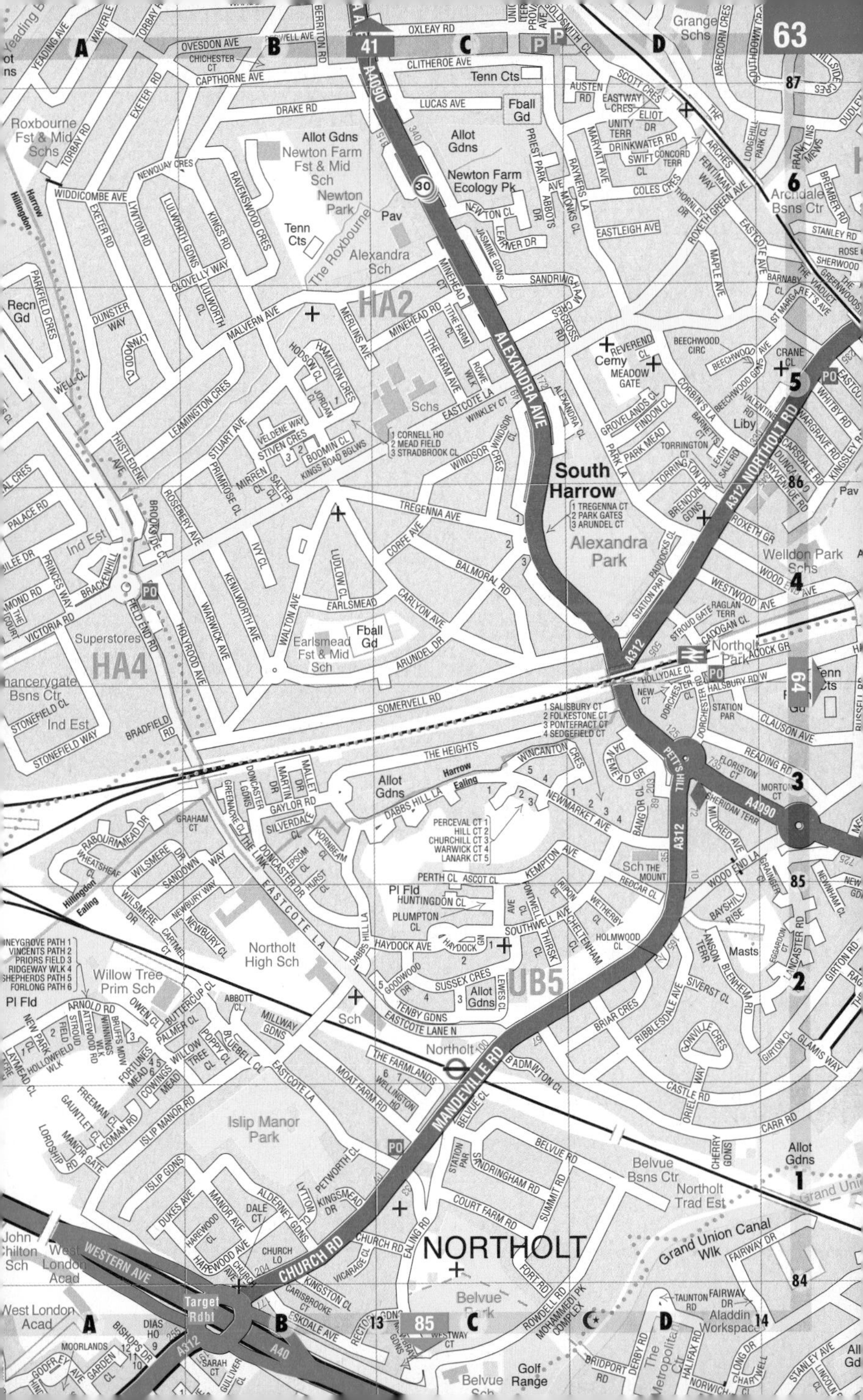
HA2
HA4
UB5
South Harrow
NORTHOLT
Alexandra Park
Islip Manor Park
Northolt High Sch
Willow Tree Prim Sch
Roxbourne Fst & Mid Schs
Newton Farm Fst & Mid Sch
Alexandra Sch
Earlsmead Fst & Mid Sch
Welldon Park Schs
Newton Farm Ecology Pk
Grand Union Canal Wlk
Belvue Bsns Ctr
Northolt Trad Est
Aladdin Workspace
West London Acad
John Chilton Sch
Target Rdbt
WESTERN AVE
CHURCH RD
MANDEVILLE RD
ALEXANDRA AVE
NORTHOLT RD
EASTCOTE LA
A4090
A312
A40
41
64
85

A
B
C
D
42
1 CROWN CT
2 CHILTERN HO
Harrow on the Hill
Running Tk
Tenn Cts
Pav
The John Lyon Sch
PAVILION LO
SHAFTESBURY AVE
SOUTHDOWN CRES
HILLSIDE CRES
DUDLEY GDNS
JOLLYS LA
FIELDERS
THE CRESCENT
RIVERSTONE CL
MIDDLE RD
CHARTWELL PL
CLONMEL CL
BYRON HILL RD
KING HENRY MEWS
WALDRON
HIGH ST
B458
A312
A4005
DUDLEY RD
WESLEY CL
GRANGE FARM CL
OSMOND CL
LODGEHILL PARK CL
FRANKLINS MEWS
HA2
Roxeth
Archdale Bsns Ctr
Superstore
BREMBER RD
STANLEY RD
PITT RD
ROSE CT
SHERWOOD RD
THE GREENWOODS
THE VIADUCT
BARNABY CL
ST MARGARET'S AVE
EASTCOTE AVE
MAPLE AVE
ROXETH GREEN AVE
THORNLEY DR
THE ARCHES
CONCORD TERR
HAMSON CT
BRICKFIELDS CT
GLASFRYN CT
ASHBOURNE AVE
WALDRON'S YD
ROXETH HILL
WEST HILL
Sch
T Cts
Cts
COTTAGE CL
ELMFIELD CL
GEORGIAN WAY
ABBOTTS CT
GRANGE RD
BRIGADE CL
HORNBUCKLE CL
COWEN AVE
ATHENA CL 1
BRICKFIELDS 2
WEST HILL HALL 3
THE MOAT LODGE 4
EDWARD CT 5
CHYNGTON CT 6
BLAKE HO 7
KEATS HO 8
LANGTON HO 9
SYCAMORE LODGE 10
MOUNT PARK AVE
THE MOUNT
T Cts
St Dominic's Coll(RC)
HARROW PK
KENNETT HO
LONDON RD
THE WOODLANDS
Bowden House (Private)
JULIAN HILL
RAMA CT
T Cts
HERGA CT
WENDELA CT
GOODEN CT
HIGHLAWN HALL
FIRCROFT GDNS
PENAIR LODGE
ROWSHAM CT
The Clementine Churchill
SUDBURY HILL
CHASEWOOD PK
GRANTCHESTER CL
HERITAGE VIEW
St George's RC Prim Sch
A4127
30
Allot Gdns
THORNCROFT
BROOKE AVE
ASHNEAL GDNS
INGLEBY DR
MOUNT PARK RD
BERMUDA HO
PENKETH DR
South Harrow
PARKFIELD RD
EASTCOTE RD
WHITBY RD
WARGRAVE RD
SCARSDALE RD
KINGSLEY RD
DUNCAN HO
WYVENHOE RD
A312 NORTHOLT RD
BEECHWOOD CIRC
BEECHWOOD AVE
BEECHWOOD GDNS
CRANE CL
CORBIN'S LA
BARNETTS
TORRINGTON CT
VALENTINE
Liby
SACKVILLE CL
ARDEN CL
Orley Farm Sch
HA1
Pl Fld
HARROW FIELDS GDNS
Tenn Cts
Capital Ring
Sp Gds
LANFRANC CT
ASHTON CT
ASSISI CT
ST FRANCIS LODGE
SUDBURY HILL CL
MONTAGUE FELL
THOMAS A BECKET
SOUTH HILL AVE
OAKMEAD
Toll Gates
Allot Gdns
Bwg Gn
Pav
Roxeth Recn Gd
Tenn Cts
ORLEY FARM RD
HILL CL
RUNNELFIELD
Tenn Ct
SOUTH VALE
GREVILLE CT
NEW RD
HUSSAIN CL
KIDMORE CL
SADDLERS MEWS
PRIORY CL
THE BOLDONS
A4005
Sudbury Hill Pl Flds
Tenn Cts
Allot Gdns
1 HUTTON CL
2 BRASHER CL
3 HEMERY RD
4 TESSA SANDERSON WAY
5 HAMMOND CL
ROXETH GR
BRENDON GDNS
Welldon Park Schs
Allot Gdns
Harrow
Ealing
WOOD END AVE
WOOD END RD
UB5
ROSS CL
TYRELL CL
SOUTH HILL GR
Sudbury Hill Harrow
HARTINGTON CL
CAVENDISH AVE
Sudbury Hill
TOWER BRIDGE MEWS
ROSEBANK AVE
FERNBANK AVE
RAGLAN TERR
STROUD GATE
CADOGAN CL
Northolt Park
ACOCK GR
63
HALSBURY RD E
CASSANDRA CL
Recn Gd
Tenn Cts
Recn Gd
RUSSELL RD
KILLOWEN AVE
CLAUSON AVE
Tenn Cts
Bwg Gn
BANNISTER CL
Ealing Northern Sp Ctr
THOMAS HEWLETT HO 1
JEM PATERSON CT 2
GREENBANKS 3
LYDIA LODGE 4
WALTON CROFT 5
HORSENDEN AVE
HIGHFIELD AVE
HORSENDEN CRES
RIDDING LA
ALLEN CT
GAINSBORO GDNS
UB6
ROSEHILL GDNS
NORTHOLT GDNS
MORDEN GDNS
NORTHWOOD GDNS
FLORISTON CL
READING RD
MORTON CT
WOOD END GDNS
WOOD END WAY
MARY PETERS DR
BEDSER DR
LILIAN BOARD WAY
RAMSEY CL
CHAPPELL GOOD CL
LARWOOD CL
HENDREN CL
MATTHEWS RD
DIMMOCK DR
Schs
Pl Fld
VERNON RISE
A4090
MERTON AVE
KEBLE CL
PILGRIMS CL
SHERIDAN TERR
MILDRED AVE
PETT'S HILL
A312
Liby
WHITTON AVE W
CARLTON CL
NEWNHAM GDNS
NEWNHAM CL
ORCHARD CL
OLDFIELDS CIR
QUANTOCK CT
GREENFORD RD
A4127
ENNISMORE AVE
SHERWOOD AVE
MELVILLE AVE
Allot Gdns
Allot Gdns
CAMBRIDGE AVE
BOURNE VIEW
DREW GDNS
OLDFIELD CL
MALDEN AVE
WADHAM GDNS
HADDEN WAY
RUGBY AVE
OLDFIELD LANE N
HORSENDEN LA N
LINDEN CRES
HAVERSHAM CT
SHEPPARD'S CT
ROBIN HOOD WAY
Tenn Cts
Bwg Gn
The Ballot Box (PH)
BAYSHILL RISE
GRAINGER CL
EGGARDON CT
LANCASTER RD
Masts
ANSON TERR
SIVERST CL
BUCHEM RD
GIRTON RD
THE FAIRWAY
RAGLAN WAY
WORCESTER GDNS
CURREY RD
CLARE RD
ROTHESAY AVE
WILLIAM PERKIN CT
OLDFIELD RD
BERKELEY AVE
BURWELL AVE
Horsenden Prim Sch
ELTON AVE
GONVILLE CRES
GIRTON CL
GLAMIS WAY
CASTLE RD
ORIEL WAY
CARR RD
Pl Fld
Allot Gdns
CHERRY GDNS
Grand Union Canal Paddington Branch
AURIOL DR
Grand Union Canal Walk
Recn Gd
HORSENDEN LANE N
Northolt Trad Est
Grand Union Canal Wlk
FAIRWAY DR
STATION APP
ALLINGTON CL
HILL RISE
BELLE VUE
Greenford
OLDFIELD LANE N
ROCKWARE AVE
Rockware Bsns Ctr
GREEN PARK WAY
Sears Ret Pk
TAUNTON RD
FAIRWAY DR
Aladdin Workspace
86
A4127
HALIFAX RD
LONG DR
CHARTWELL
STANLEY AVE
Allot Gdns
BIRKBECK AVE
BIRKBECK WAY
HILLBECK WAY
STATION VIEW
PEACE CL
UNEEDA DR
LEXHAM CT
Perivale
87
86
85
84
6
5
4
3
2
1

A
B
43
C
D
North Wembley
South Kenton
Byron Court Sch
Preston Park Rec Gd
Wembley Commercial Ctr
East Lane Bsns Pk
Wembley High Tech Coll
HA0
Vale Farm Sp Gd
Sp Arena
Vale Farm Sp Ctr
Sudbury
Sudbury Prim Sch
Butler's Gn
Sudbury & Harrow Road
Barham Park
Old Court (Mus & Liby)
Maybank Open Space
Sudbury Town
WEMBLEY
Barham Prim Sch
Horsenden Hill
Horsenden Farm
UB6
Grand Union Canal Paddington Branch
Grand Union Canal Walk
Alperton Cemy
Alperton Lower Sch
Alperton
King Edw VII Pa
WATFORD RD
HARROW RD
EAST LA
WHITTON AVE E
BRIDGEWATER RD
EALING RD
SUDBURY COURT DR
A404
A4088
A4127
A4005
A4090
A4089
87
66

66
A
Preston
B
44
C
D
87
6
5
86
4
3
85
2
1
84
18
88
19
65
A4140
A4088
A4089
A479
A404
A4005
A406
B4557
CARLTON AVE E
LOGAN RD
Bwg Gn
WALTON GDNS
PELLATT RD
Sp Gd
Gec Est
AYLANDS CL
ORCHID CT
PRESTON RD
Tenn Cts
Sp Gd
Preston Manor High Sch
ASHLEY GDNS
KEYSHAM CT
HOLLYCROFT AVE
PERRIN GRANGE
FORTY AVE
CENTURY HO 1
TAVERNERS CT 2
ESSENCE CT
WESSEX CT
SOUTH GDNS
BOWLING GREEN CT
PARGRAVES CT
RICHMOND CT
FORTY CL
BROOK AVE
HARRIS CT
CARRINGTON LO
OAKINGTON AVE
GABRIELLE CL
HIGHFIELD AVE
TALISMAN WAY
MARSH HALL
THE MARTINS
CROWN WLK
ELLIOT CL
St Christopher's Sch
WAYSIDE CT
ELMSIDE RD
KINGSWOOD RD
Wembley Park
BRIDGE RD
Tenn Cts
Sp Gd
Bwg Gn
Pav
GRAND PAR
FORTY LA
LINEAR VIEW
Superstore
BOWATER RD 1
WALTON AVE 2
BOYLE HO 3
CURIE HO 4
CHALKHILL RD
WINDSOR CRES
THE BOBBY MOORE BRIDGE
DANES CT
EMPIRE CT
NORTH END RD
Chalkhill Prim Sch
Stadium Bsns Ctr
Wembley Park Bsns Ctr
WATKIN RD
FULTON RD
Olympic Ret Pk
The Junction Wembley Ret Pk
FIFTH WAY
Wembley Stadium Ind Est
Metro Trad Ctr
Wembley Stadium Ind Est
Stadium Ret Pk
Wembley Park
Palace of Ind
HA9
IMPERIAL CT
ENGINEERS WAY
Wembley Arena
LAKESIDE WAY
Wembley
Cannon Trad Est
The Mirage Ctr
Towers Bsns Pk
Conference Centre
STADIUM WAY
Hotel
Exhibition Halls
ROYAL ROUTE
Wembley Stadium
SOUTH WAY
Pop In Bsns Ctr
Adams Bridge Bsns Ctr
Wembley Stadium
PARK VIEW
Sherrans Farm Open Space
Oakington Manor Sch
OAKINGTON MANOR DR
TUDOR COURT N
TUDOR COURT S
VIVIAN AVE
T Cts
CHIPPENHAM AVE
BRENT WAY
WEMBLEY WAY
CHALFONT AVE
WYLD WAY
VICTORIA AVE
GEORGIAN CT
BABINGTON RISE
ELSLEY CT
Tokyngton
STONEBRIDGE WAY
Allot Gdns
GRITTLETON AVE
Liby
Recn Gd
MONKS PARK GDNS
HARROW RD
30
Allot Gdns
WIGGINTON AVE
BOVINGDON AVE
TOKYNGTON AVE
ALDBURY AVE
SYLVIA GDNS
DEREK AVE
POINT PL
Stonebridge Park
ARGENTA WAY
PENDOLINO WAY
Stonebridge Park
BRENTFIELD
BRIDGE PK
50
WEMBLEY PARK DR
HOMEFIRS HO
BALMORAL CT
MORELLO CT
BEECHCROFT GDNS
PADFIELD CT
EMPIRE PAR
THE GABLES
RAGLAN CT
PARK CHASE
ASHWOOD CT
HILLCROFT CRES
MANOR DR
RAGLAN CT
ADA LEWIS HO
ALEXANDRA CT
EMPIRE WAY
HILLSIDE AVE
ROSKILD CT
HIGH ST
PARK PL
DAGMAR AVE
LINDEN AVE
CROWN HO
MOSTYN AVE
CORINIUM CT
LEA GDNS
DENNIS AVE
WEMBLEY HILL RD
PARK LA
PARK CT
JUNIPER CL
ECCLESTONE PL
Wembley Stadium
1 CRESSWELL HO
2 LOXLEY HO
3 KIRK HO
4 BELL HO
HIRST CRES
COURTENAY RD
OSRAM RD
TOWER LA
MAIN DR
QUAD RD
TILLING WAY
BELL LA
WESTLAKE RD
MAGNET RD
LUMEN RD
EDISON DR
CHAMBERLAYNE AVE
ST AUGUSTINE'S AVE
BLENHEIM GDNS
THE BROADWAY
CASTLETON GDNS
Wembley Prim Sch
Sch
QUEENSCOURT
THE DENE
KINGSWAY
WEMBLEY HILL RD
King Edward VII Park
Tenn Cts
Park Lane Sch
Tenn Cts
KESWICK GDNS
Bwg Gn
PRINCES CT
ST JOHN'S RD
PEMBROKE RD
HUTCHINSON TERR
LOCKER WLK
LAMBERT WLK
WINTHROP WLK
EVERARD WAY
CLARENDON GDNS
ROSSLYN CRES
CASTLETON AVE
MEADOW WAY
THE GLEN
LLANOVER RD
FELPHAM CT
GREENS CT
ST JOHN'S CL
ACACIA AVE
ELM RD
ECCLESTONE MEWS
HIGH RD
ROSEMEAD AVE
BEATRICE AVE
LONSDALE AVE
WALROND AVE
CECIL AVE
Copland Sch
St Joseph's RC Schs
BRENT HO
ELIZABETH HO
CHATSWORTH AVE
WAVERLEY AVE
VIVIAN GDNS
GRAND AVE
NEELD CT
NEELD CRES
Allpt Gdns
Pl Flds
STANLEY RD
JESMOND AVE
JESMOND CT
BERKHAMSTED AVE
NORTHCHURCH RD
GADDESDEN AVE
NETTLEDEN AVE
TRINGE AVE
CORSHAM HO
VICTORIA CT
ST MICHAEL'S AVE
Elsley Prim Sch
LANTERNS CT
ROSECROFT WLK
THURLOW GDNS
ELSPETH RD
TURTON RD
Colls
1 2 Mkt
A404
CURTIS
Wembley Central
LONDON RD
STATION GR
COPLAND RD
UNION RD
PARK RD
Liby
RICHFIELD CT
TALBOT RD
CHASE CT
NAPIER RD
RANELAGH RD
LINCOLN RD
WEMBLEY
SCARLE RD
SWINDERBY RD
VORA HO
THURLBY RD
NORTON RD
EAGLE RD
BOWRONS AVE
BRAEMAR AVE
HA0
EALING RD
THE CLOSE
CHRISTCHURCH GN
CHRISTCHURCH AVE
DOUGLAS AVE
WESTBURY AVE
WESTBURY RD
HAYNES CL
CLAYTON AVE
LYON PARK AVE
BRIDGEWAY
HILLFIELD AVE
VALLEY GDNS
Allot Gdns
HIGHMEAD CRES
KATHLEEN AVE
VICTOR GR
DOROTHY AVE
NEWTON RD
EGERTON RD
LOMOND CL
LYON ROWLEY CL
STANLEY AVE
Alperton Com Sch
HURST LO
WOODSTOCK RD
VINCENT RD
Lyon Park Jun & Inf Schs
Pl Flds
LYON PARK AVE
MARQUIS CL
HEATHER PARK PAR
THE GRANGE
HEATHER PARK DR
KENMERE GDNS
LABURNHAM CL
HIGHCROFT AVE
CRAIGMUIR PK
MOUNT PLEASANT
STANLEY HO
RUSSELL CT
ANNE CARVER LO
LIGHTLEY CL
MOUNT PLEASANT
BELMONT AVE
STANLEY PARK RD
ST JAMES' GDNS
WYATT CT
ORCHARD CL
Allot Gdns
Alperton Lower Sch
Alperton
WOODSIDE CL
WOODSIDE AVE
CLIFTON WAY
SUNLEIGH RD
Abbey Manufacturing Est
Liby
Liberty Ctr
BERESFORD AVE
Northfield Ind Est
WYCOMBE RD
ATLIP RD
CARLYON
PILGRIMS WAY
WINTON CL
BARN HILL
MIDHOLM
BARN RISE
WICKLIFFE GDNS
BARN WAY
EAST HILL
THE CROSSWAYS
EVERSLEY AVE
GRENDON GDNS
NEWLAND CT
CORRINGHAM RD
MAYFIELDS
MAYFIELDS CL
LAWNS CT
HILLVIEW
MASON CT
BASING HILL
CHARLTON RD
THE AVENUE
ELMSTEAD AVE
ELMSTEAD CT
CARLTON AVE E
PRINCESS AVE
CARLTON PAR
LONGFIELD AVE
FERNLEIGH CT
WARREN CL
FIRST AVE
SECOND AVE
KINGS CT
KINGS DR
CAMEL CT
GREENHILL WAY
THE PADDOCKS
ADAMS CL
TH
FARNBOROUGH CL
PEACE GR
HAVENWOOD
SPRING CRES
ROOK CL
DUGOLLY AVE
ANTON PL
RAWLINGS CRES
SECOND WAY
FIRST WAY
THIRD WAY
CAREY WAY

67
Welsh Harp
45
A
B
C
D
Brent Resr
Sailing Club
Allot Gdns
Sp Gd
The Harp Bsns Ctr
Wellington Park Est
Phoenix Pk
St Nicholas Sch
Gower Ho Sch
Neasden Recn Gd
Pav
SALMON ST
A4140
B454
BLACKBIRD HILL
NEASDEN LA
A406
A4088
DUNSTER DR
DEANSCROFT AVE
QUEENS WLK
CHERRYLANDS CL
TUDOR GDNS
OLD CHURCH LA
BIRCHEN GR
HARP ISLAND CL
REVIEW RD
DAWPOOL RD
HEATHER RD
WARREN RD
SELSDON RD
LINKS RD
Braintcroft Prim Sch
John Kelly Tech Colls
RANDALL AVE
VINCENT GDNS
Allot Gdns
Dollis Hill Est
5
6
Wykeham Prim Sch
Sports Gd
Tenn Cts
Pl Fld
St Margaret Clitherow RC Prim Sch
Wembley Stadium Ind Est
Hallmark Trad Ctr
Neasden Depot
Neasden
GREAT CENTRAL WAY
Neasden Junction
NORTH CIRCULAR RD
DUDDEN HILL LA
NEASDEN LA
B453
Northview Prim Sch
Falcon Pk Ind Est
Dudden Hill
4
3
Gladst
89
Dollis Hill
DRURY WAY
Drury Way Ind Est
Vernon House Sch
Superstore
Central Bsns Ctr
Brent Trad Est
Coll of NW London (Willesden Ctr)
Church End
Pav
Bwg Gn
River Brent
Tokyngton Recn Gd
Mitchell Brook Prim Sch
Gibbons Recn Gd
The Swaminarayan Sch
Mandir
Brentfield Prim Sch
Canal Feeder
Power Sta
St Mary's CE Prim Sch
Cemy
Games Ct
Allot Gdns
HIGH RD
CHURCH RD
A407
Superstore
Brent New Ent Ctr
Cobbold Ind Est
Trojan Ind Est
Sapcote Trad Ctr
2
NW10
WILLESDEN
Leopold Prim Sch
Willesden New Cemy
Brahma Kumaris World Spiritual Univ
Willesden Jew Cemy
1
Newfield Prim Sch
Summer Theatre
Roundwood Park
Bwg Gn
Allot Gdns
Harlesden
Stonebridge
Our Lady of Lourdes RC Sch
Recn Gd
HILLSIDE
A404
CRAVEN PK
84
85
86
87
22
21
89
A
B
C
D

Staples Corner (West)
46
Staples Corner Bsns Pk
The Harp Bsns Ctr
Wellington Park Est
The Apsley Ctr
Phoenix Pk
Atlas Bsns Ctr
Oxgate Ctr
Ind Est
The Edge Bsns Ctr
Humber Trad Est
Millennium Bsns Ctr
Superstores
Brent Sidings
Hendon Fball Gd
Claremont Prim Sch
Clitterhouse Pl Flds
EDGWARE RD
Our Lady of Grace RC Inf Sch
NW2
Donoghue Bsns Pk
John Kelly Tech Colls
Allot Gdns
Dollis Hill Est
Dollis Hill
Pl Fld
Games Ct
Gladstone Park
Tenn Cts
Bwg Gn
Mora Prim Sch
Cricklewood
CRICKLEWOOD BROADWAY
Broadway Ret Pk
Superstore
Liby
Dudden Hill
Gladstone Park Sch
Anson Prim Sch
CHICHELE RD
DUDDEN HILL LA
Coll NW London (Willesden Ctr)
Sapcote Trad Ctr
Chapmans Park Ind Est
HIGH RD
WALM LA
Willesden Green
WILLESDEN LA
Liby & Mus
Super store
Schs
Sch
Coll
NW10
WILLESDEN
Willesden New Cemy
Brahma Kumaris World Spiritual Univ
Willesden Jewish Cemy
The Willesden Com
Summer Theatre
Roundwood Park
Allot Gdns
Newfield Prim Sch
Crkt Gd
Pav
Queens Park Com Sch
Maloree Jun & Inf Sch
Capital City Acad
Willesden Sp Ctr
Brondesbury Park
Harlesden
90
A B C D
1 2 3 4 5 6

69
47
A
B
C
D
Child's Hill
West Hampstead
NW2
NW3
NW6
HAMPSTEAD
South Hampstead
Brondesbury
Kilburn
West Heath
Golders Hill Park
Hampstead Cemy
Fortune Green
FINCHLEY RD
CRICKLEWOOD LA
HENDON WAY
SHOOT-UP HILL
WILLESDEN LA
WEST END LA
FORTUNE GREEN RD
NORTH END WAY
70
91

Sandy Heath
North End
Hampstead Heath
Ken Wood
Parliament Hill
Highgate Ponds
West Heath
East Heath
Vale of Health
Hampstead Ponds
NW3
N6
Hampstead
Rosslyn Hill
Haverstock Hill
Fleet Rd
Royal Free
Maitland Park
Belsize Tunnel
Belsize New Tunnel
Fitzjohn's Ave
Finchley Rd
HAMPSTEAD
NW6
South Hampstead
Swiss Cottage
Adelaide Rd
Primrose Hill
Primrose Hill Tunnels
Avenue Rd
Belsize Rd
Abbey Rd

Waterlow Park
Highgate Cemy
Highgate Cemy
Brookfield Prim Sch
Dartmouth Park
Upper Holloway
Archway
The Whittington
Whittington Park
Yerbury Prim Sch
Tufnell Park Hall
Tufnell Park
Tufnell Park Prim Sch
Holloway Sch
Gospel Oak
Parliament Hill Sch
William Ellis Sch
La Saint Union RC Sec Sch
Acland Burghley Sch
City Farm
Carlton Prim Sch
Kentish Town
Kentish Town West
The Camden Sch for Girls
Roundhouse Theatre
CAMDEN TOWN
Superstore
Camden Mkt
JUNCTION RD
HOLLOWAY RD
FORTESS RD
KENTISH TOWN RD
CAMDEN RD
BRECKNOCK RD
HIGHGATE RD
CHALK FARM RD
DARTMOUTH PARK HILL
ROYAL COLLEGE
YORK WAY
N6
N19
N7
NW5
NW1
N1
A
B
C
D
1
2
3
4
5
6
49
72
231
93
231
84
85
86
87
30
29

A
B
C
D
50
N19
N4
N7
N5
N1
Finsbury Park
SEVEN SISTERS RD
STATION PL
ROCK ST
BLACKSTOCK RD
STROUD GREEN RD
HORNSEY RD
HOLLOWAY RD
TOLLINGTON PK
TOLLINGTON RD
TOLLINGTON WAY
MORAY RD
FONTHILL RD
ISLEDON RD
PARKSIDE CRES
GILLESPIE RD
Gillespie Park
Arsenal
Highbury
HIGHBURY PK
HIGHBURY HILL
DRAYTON PK
Emirates (Arsenal FC)
QUEENSLAND RD
Drayton Park
Holloway Road
Nags Head
CAMDEN RD
PARKHURST RD
TUFNELL PARK RD
MERCERS RD
MARGERY FRY CT
HM Prison
Lower Holloway
HILLMARTON RD
CALEDONIAN RD
Caledonian Road
Caledonian Park
Hall of Residence
MARKET RD
BREWERY RD
Fball Gd
Acorn Production Ctr
Barnsbury
Caledonian Road & Barnsbury
Copenhagen Junction
YORK WAY
CAMDEN PARK RD
Paradise Park
SHERINGHAM RD
ISLINGTON
LIVERPOOL RD
Highbury Fields
Highbury Pool
Highbury & Islington
Highbury Corner
HIGHBURY STATION RD
UPPER STREET
CANONBURY RD
CANONBURY
ESSEX RD
BARNSBURY PK
BARNSBURY SQ
THORNHILL RD
Liby
Sch
Univ
Coll
Colls
PO
233
94
234
30
31
84
85
86
87
A1
A1200
A1201
A103
A503
A5200
A5203
B515
B150

73
A
B
C
D
51
74
235
95
87
6
5
4
3
2
1
86
85
84
33
34
STOKE NEWINGTON
Abney Park Cemy
Stoke Newington
Clissold Park
Shacklewell
Canonbury
Kingsland
De Beauvoir Town
Dalston
Dalston Kingsland
Dalston Jct
Essex Road
Rectory Road
Frogmore Ind Est
Aberdeen Ctr
The Petchey Acad
Ridley
Tenn Cts
Bwg Gn
Capital Ring
N4
N16
N5
N1
E8
MANOR RD
LORDSHIP PK
BROWNSWOOD RD
GREEN LANES
STOKE NEWINGTON CHURCH ST
STOKE NEWINGTON HIGH ST
KINGSLAND HIGH ST
KINGSLAND RD
RECTORY RD
ALBION RD
NEWINGTON GREEN RD
ST PAUL'S RD
BALLS POND RD
ESSEX RD
SOUTHGATE RD
QUEENSBRIDGE RD
EVERING RD
MANSE RD
STOKE NEWINGTON COMM
SHACKLEWELL LA
MILDMAY PK
MILDMAY GR N
MILDMAY GR S
CLISSOLD CRES
HIGHBURY NEW PK
HIGHBURY QUADRANT
NORTHCHURCH RD
DOWNHAM RD
BALMES RD
DE BEAUVOIR CRES
A105
A10
A1199
A104
A1207
A1200
B105
B104
B111
B102
B108

Upper Clapton
A
B
52
C
D
Lee Valley Riding Ctr
Pl Fld
Leyton Marshes
River Lea or Lee
Capital Ring
Stoke Newington
CAZENOVE RD
UPPER CLAPTON RD
A107
DEHAVILLAND STUDIOS
Lea Valley Ice Ctr
MOUNT PLEASANT HILL
NORTHWOLD RD
B111
SOUTHWOLD RD
Clapton
Recn Gd
LEA BRIDGE RD
A104
N16
RECTORY RD
E5
Nature Reserve
Lea Valley Wlk
Lea Bridge
Mandeville Prim Sch
Rectory Road
KENNINGHALL RD
Shacklewell
DOWNS RD
Hackney Downs
Mossbourne Com Acad
CRICKETFIELD RD
LOWER CLAPTON RD
Lower Clapton
Clapton Park
The Petchey Acad
Homerton University
PEMBURY RD
A104
DALSTON LA
AMHURST RD
Hackney Downs
Sutton House
Prim Sch
HOMERTON HIGH ST
A106
Homerton
MORNING LA
Hackney Central
Superstore
Digby Bsns Ctr
WICK RD
GRAHAM RD
A1207
B113
Dalston
E8
HACKNEY
CASSLAND RD
A102
Homerton
MARE ST
QUEENSBRIDGE RD
B108
London Fields
E9
Well Street Common
WELL ST
VICTORIA PARK RD
Pl Flds
96
Royal Gate
34
35
84
85
86
87

53
E10
Running Track
Orient Way
Waltham Forest
Hackney
Leyton Orient Fball Gd
Church Rd
High Road Leyton
Ruckholt Rd
New Spitalfields Market
Market Pavilion
E5
Hackney Marsh
Recn Gds
Lea Valley Wlk
River Lee Navigation Hackney Cut
River Lea or Lee
Homerton Rd
Eastway
Lee Valley Sp Ctr
Temple Mills
E9
East Cross Route
Hackney Wick
Hackney Stadium
E15
Cycle Circuit
Chapman Rd
Wick Rd
White Post La
Carpenter's Rd
Waterworks River
City Mill River
Victoria Park
Stratford Marsh
Hertford Union Canal
Leyton Mills
Gainsborough Prim Sch
Kingsmead Prim Sch
76
97

54
LEYTON
Leytonstone
STRATFORD
Stratford New Town
E10
E11
E7
E15
St Patrick's RC Cemy
West Ham Cemy
Wanstead Flats
Stratford International
Stratford Marsh
HIGH ROAD LEYTON
GROVE GREEN RD
LEYTON RD
ROMFORD RD
CARPENTER'S RD
HARROW RD
CATHALL RD
FRANCIS RD
WARREN RD
GREAT EASTERN RD
MAJOR RD
VICARAGE LA
BROADWAY
WEST HAM LA
PORTWAY
98
39

Aldersbrook Prim Sch
55
E12
Aldersbrook
Wanstead Flats
E7
Centenary Walk
Manor Park
The Manor Park Cemy & Crem
City of London Cem
Crem
Forest Gate
Woodgrange Park
Woodgrange Park Cemy
Plashet
Plashet Jewish Cemy
Upton
Upton Park
West Ham Park
William Davies Sch
Monega Sch
Plashet Park
East Ham Meml
Aldersbrook Rd
Centre Rd
Woodford Rd
Woodgrange Rd
Romford Rd
Forest Dr
Station Rd
Green St
Katherine Rd
Plashet Gr
Plashet Rd
Upton La
Redbridge Horse Ride
78
99

A
B
56
C
D
Allot Gdns
Redbridge
Newham
Ilford
City of London Cemy
Crem
Manor Park
Alders Brook
ILFORD
IG1
The Exchange
Ilford Interchange
ILFORD HILL
WANSTEAD PARK RD
COURTLAND AVE
MAYFAIR AVE
BELGRAVE RD
SELBORNE RD
MANSFIELD RD
ARGYLE RD
BEAL RD
YORK RD
Maytime Sch
A406
A118
A123
A116
A117
FOREST DR
STATION RD
ROMFORD RD
RABBITS RD
FOREST VIEW RD
CARLYLE RD
Liby & Mus
Prim Sch
LITTLE ILFORD LA
B165
NORTH CIRCULAR RD
ILFORD LA
Little Ilford Park
Little Ilford
E12
Avenue Prim Sch
HIGH ST N
Plashet
Plashet Jewish Cemy
Essex Prim Sch
BROWNING RD
Kensington Prim Sch
EAST AVE
East Ham
E6
Plashet Park
East Ham Meml
Plashet Sch
PLASHET GR
Uphall Prim Sch
IG11
Riverside Works
Pacific Wharf
River Roding
Superstore
Sports Gd
Barking Flyover
A124
LONDON RD
ABBEY RD
Recn Gd
100
RON LEIGHTON WAY
Park

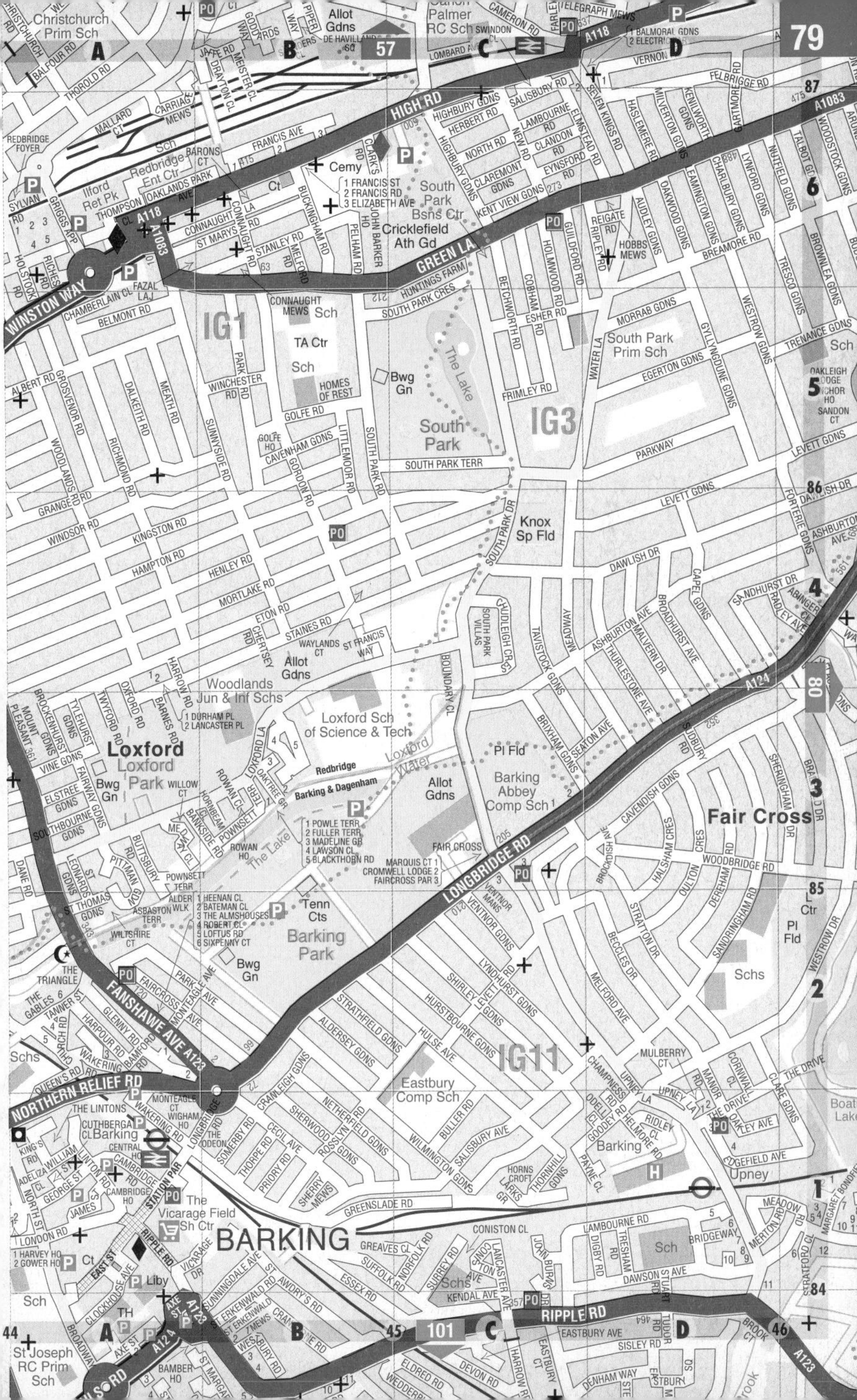
Christchurch Prim Sch
Allot Gdns
Canon Palmer RC Sch
CAMERON RD
TELEGRAPH MEWS
57
A118
1 BALMORAL GDNS
2 ELECTRIC
A
B
C
D
BALFOUR RD
THOROLD RD
JAFFE RD
MEISTER CL
DRAYTON CL
LOMBARD AVE
SALISBURY RD
SEVEN KINGS RD
VERNON
FELBRIGGE RD
GARTMORE RD
87
A1083
HIGH RD
HIGHBURY GDNS
HERBERT RD
NORTH RD
LAMBOURNE GDNS
NEW RD
CLANDON RD
ELMSTEAD RD
HASLEMERE RD
MILVERTON GDNS
KENILWORTH GDNS
WOODSTOCK GDNS
TALBOT GDNS
MALLARD CT
CARRIAGE MEWS
FRANCIS AVE
REDBRIDGE FOYER
Redbridge Ent Ctr
BARONS CT
OAKLANDS PARK AVE
Ilford Ret Pk
Cemy
1 FRANCIS ST
2 FRANCIS RD
3 ELIZABETH AVE
South Park Bsns Ctr
CLAREMONT GDNS
EYNSFORD RD
KENT VIEW GDNS
6
SYLVAN RD
GRIGGS APP
THOMPSON CL
CONNAUGHT LA
CONNAUGHT RD
ST MARYS RD
STANLEY RD
MELFORD RD
BUCKINGHAM RD
JOHN BARKER HO
PELHAM RD
Cricklefield Ath Gd
GREEN LA
HUNTINGS FARM
SOUTH PARK CRES
REIGATE RD
RIPLEY RD
HOBBS MEWS
HOLMWOOD RD
GUILDFORD RD
AUDLEY GDNS
OAKWOOD GDNS
LEAMINGTON GDNS
CHARLBURY GDNS
LYNFORD GDNS
NUTFIELD GDNS
BREAMORE RD
BROWNLEA GDNS
TRESCO GDNS
HOLSTOCK RD
WINSTON WAY
CHAMBERLAIN CL
FAZAL LAJ
BELMONT RD
CONNAUGHT MEWS
Sch
IG1
TA Ctr
BETCHWORTH RD
COBHAM RD
ESHER RD
MORRAB GDNS
South Park Prim Sch
WESTROW GDNS
TRENANCE GDNS
The Lake
WATER LA
EGERTON GDNS
GYLLYNGDUNE GDNS
OAKLEIGH LODGE
ANCHOR HO
SANDON CT
5
ALBERT RD
GROSVENOR RD
DALKEITH RD
MEATH RD
WINCHESTER RD
PARK RD
HOMES OF REST
Bwg Gn
FRIMLEY RD
IG3
WOODLANDS RD
RICHMOND RD
SUNNYSIDE RD
GOLFE RD
GOLFE HO
CAVENHAM GDNS
LITTLEMOOR RD
SOUTH PARK RD
South Park
SOUTH PARK TERR
PARKWAY
LEVETT GDNS
GORDON RD
GRANGE RD
WINDSOR RD
KINGSTON RD
HAMPTON RD
HENLEY RD
MORTLAKE RD
ETON RD
STAINES RD
CHERTSEY RD
WAYLANDS CT
ST FRANCIS WAY
SOUTH PARK DR
Knox Sp Fld
DAWLISH DR
86
FORTERIE GDNS
ASHBURTON AVE
SANDHURST DR
ABINGER CL
RADLEY AVE
CAPEL GDNS
BROADHURST AVE
MALVERN DR
THURLESTONE AVE
TAVISTOCK GDNS
MEADWAY
CHUDLEIGH CRES
SOUTH PARK VILLAS
BOUNDARY CL
4
Allot Gdns
HARROW RD
Woodlands Jun & Inf Schs
1 DURHAM PL
2 LANCASTER PL
BARNES RD
OXFORD RD
TWYFORD RD
TYLEHURST GDNS
BROCKENHURST GDNS
MOUNT PLEASANT
Loxford Sch of Science & Tech
Loxford Water
A124
80
BRIXHAM GDNS
SEATON AVE
SUDBURY RD
Loxford
Loxford Park
VINE GDNS
ELSTREE GDNS
FAIRWAY GDNS
SOUTHBOURNE GDNS
Bwg Gn
WILLOW CT
LOXFORD LA
ROWAN CL
OAKTREE GR
Redbridge
Barking & Dagenham
Allot Gdns
Pl Fld
Barking Abbey Comp Sch
CAVENDISH GDNS
SHERINGHAM DR
3
Fair Cross
HORNBEAM CL
BANKSIDE RD
POWNSETT TERR
ROWAN HO
The Lake
1 POWLE TERR
2 FULLER TERR
3 MADELINE GR
4 LAWSON CL
5 BLACKTHORN RD
FAIR CROSS
MARQUIS CT 1
CROMWELL LODGE 2
FAIRCROSS PAR 3
LONGBRIDGE RD
BROCKDISH AVE
HALSHAM CRES
OULTON CRES
DEREHAM RD
WOODBRIDGE RD
DANE RD
LEONARDS GDNS
PITTMAN GDNS
BUTTSBURY RD
ST THOMAS GDNS
ASBASTON TERR
ALDER WLK
1 HEENAN CL
2 BATEMAN CL
3 THE ALMSHOUSES
4 ROBERT CL
5 LOFTUS RD
6 SIXPENNY CT
Tenn Cts
Barking Park
VENTNOR MANS
VENTNOR GDNS
STRATTON DR
BECCLES DR
SANDRINGHAM RD
85
L Ctr
Pl Fld
WESTROW DR
WILTSHIRE CT
THE TRIANGLE
THE GABLES
TANNER ST
FAIRCROSS AVE
PARK AVE
Bwg Gn
LYNDHURST GDNS
SHIRLEY GDNS
LEVETT GDNS
HURSTBOURNE GDNS
MELFORD AVE
Schs
2
FANSHAWE AVE
A123
GLENNY RD
HARPOUR RD
BAMFORD RD
MONTEAGLE AVE
STRATHFIELD GDNS
ALDERSEY GDNS
HULSE AVE
IG11
CHURCH RD
WAKERING RD
QUEEN'S RD
NORTHERN RELIEF RD
LONGBRIDGE RD
CRANLEIGH GDNS
SHERWOOD GDNS
NETHERFIELD GDNS
Eastbury Comp Sch
BULLER RD
MULBERRY CT
CHAMPNESS RD
UPNEY LA
THE DRIVE
CLARE GDNS
CORNWALL CL
MANOR RD
THE LINTONS
CUTHBERGA CL
MONTEAGLE CT
WIGHAM HO
WAKERING HO
Barking
CENTRAL HO
THE ODEON
SOMERBY RD
THORPE RD
CECIL AVE
ROSSLYN RD
WILMINGTON GDNS
SALISBURY AVE
ODELL CL
GOODEY RD
HELMORE RD
RIDLEY CL
Barking
OAKLEY AVE
EDGEFIELD AVE
Upney
Boating Lake
KING'S RD
WILLIAM ST
ADELIZA
LINTON RD
GEORGE ST
NORTH ST
CAMBRIDGE RD
CAMBRIDGE HO
STATION PAR
JAMES
PRIORY RD
SHERRY MEWS
HORNS CROFT
LARKS GR
THORNHILL GDNS
PAYNE CL
H
1
The Vicarage Field Sh Ctr
GREENSLADE RD
MEADOW RD
MERTON RD
MARGARET BONDFIELD
LONDON RD
1 HARVEY HO
2 GOWER HO
Ct
RIPPLE RD
EAST ST
VICARAGE DR
BARKING
CONISTON CL
LAMBOURNE RD
DIGBY RD
TRESHAM RD
JOHN BURNS DR
Sch
BRIDGEWAY
STRATFORD CL
84
Sch
CLOCKHOUSE AVE
Liby
SUNNINGDALE AVE
ST ERKENWALD RD
ST AWDRY'S RD
GREAVES CL
SUFFOLK RD
NORFOLK RD
ESSEX RD
SURREY RD
CONISTON AVE
LANCASTER AVE
Schs
KENDAL AVE
DAWSON AVE
STUART RD
RIPPLE RD
TUDOR RD
EASTBURY AVE
SISLEY RD
BROOK CT
46
A123
TH
AXE ST
ST ERKENWALD MEWS
45
101
44
St Joseph RC Prim Sch
BROADWAY
A124
BAMBER HO
WESTBURY RD
ELDRED RD
DEVON RD
HARROW RD
EASTBURY CT
DENHAM WAY
WEDDERBURN

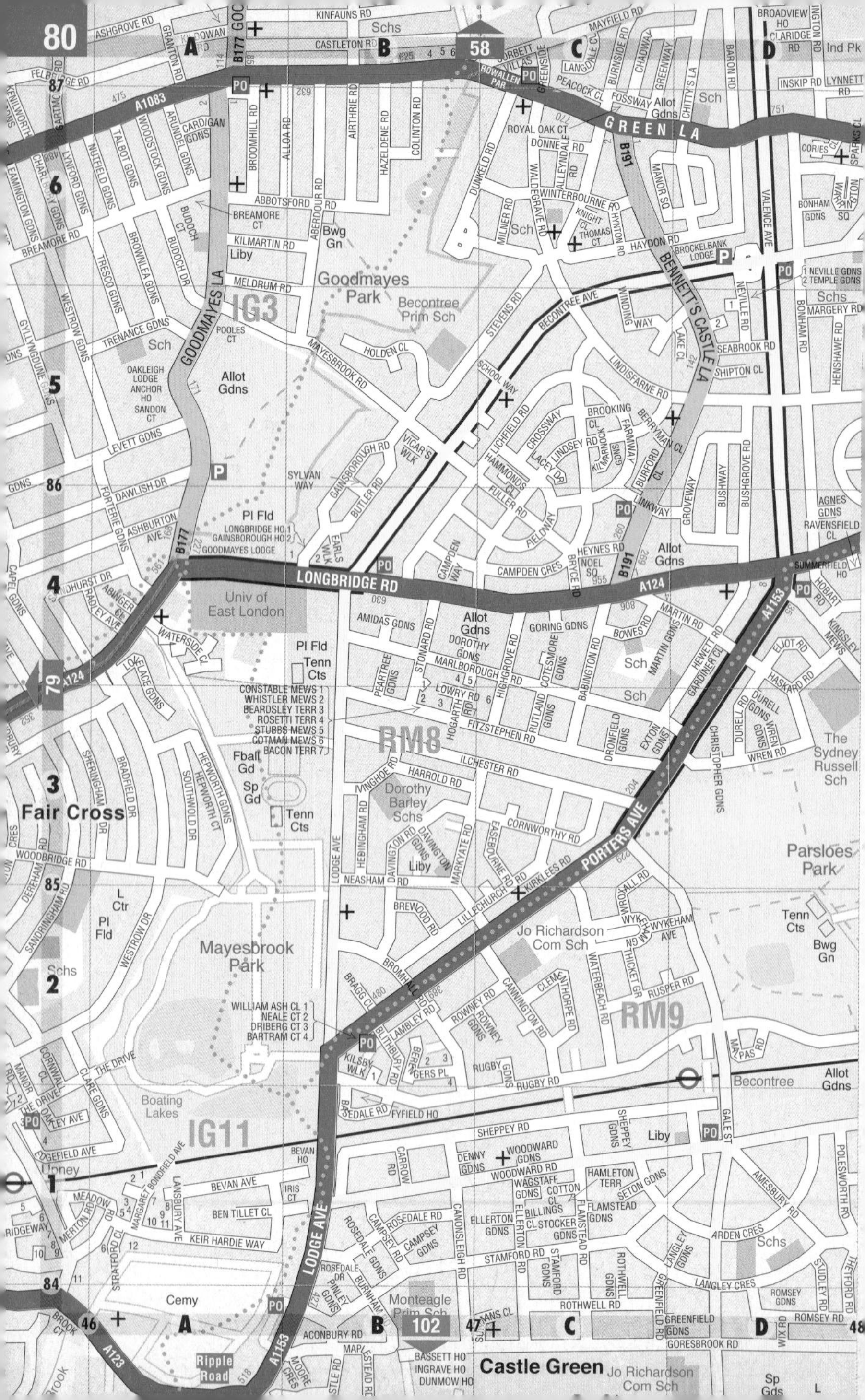
58
79
102
Fair Cross
Goodmayes Park
Mayesbrook Park
Parsloes Park
Castle Green
IG3
RM8
RM9
IG11
LONGBRIDGE RD
GREEN LA
GOODMAYES LA
BENNETT'S CASTLE LA
PORTERS AVE
LODGE AVE
BECONTREE AVE
Becontree
Upney
Univ of East London
Dorothy Barley Schs
Jo Richardson Com Sch
Becontree Prim Sch
Monteagle Prim Sch
The Sydney Russell Sch
Boating Lakes
Ripple Road

81
59
103
Becontree
DAGENHAM
RM7
RM8
RM9
RM10
Central Park
Valence Park
Goresbrook Park
Old Dagenham Park
Dagenham Heathway
Dagenham East
Dagenham & Redbridge Fball Gd
Valence House Mus
Becontree Day
Grafton Jun & Inf Schs
Five Elms Prim Sch
Trinity Sch
Hunters Hall Prim Sch
Godwin Prim Sch
Thomas Arnold Prim Sch
Dagenham Park Com Sch
Robert Clack Lower Sch
Heathway Ind Est
Sterling Ind Est
Midas Bsns Ctr
Civic Ctr
WOOD LA
RAINHAM RD N
RAINHAM RD S
HEATHWAY
RUSH GREEN RD
BALLARDS RD
A1112 Dagenham East
ESSEX STREET ATLAS

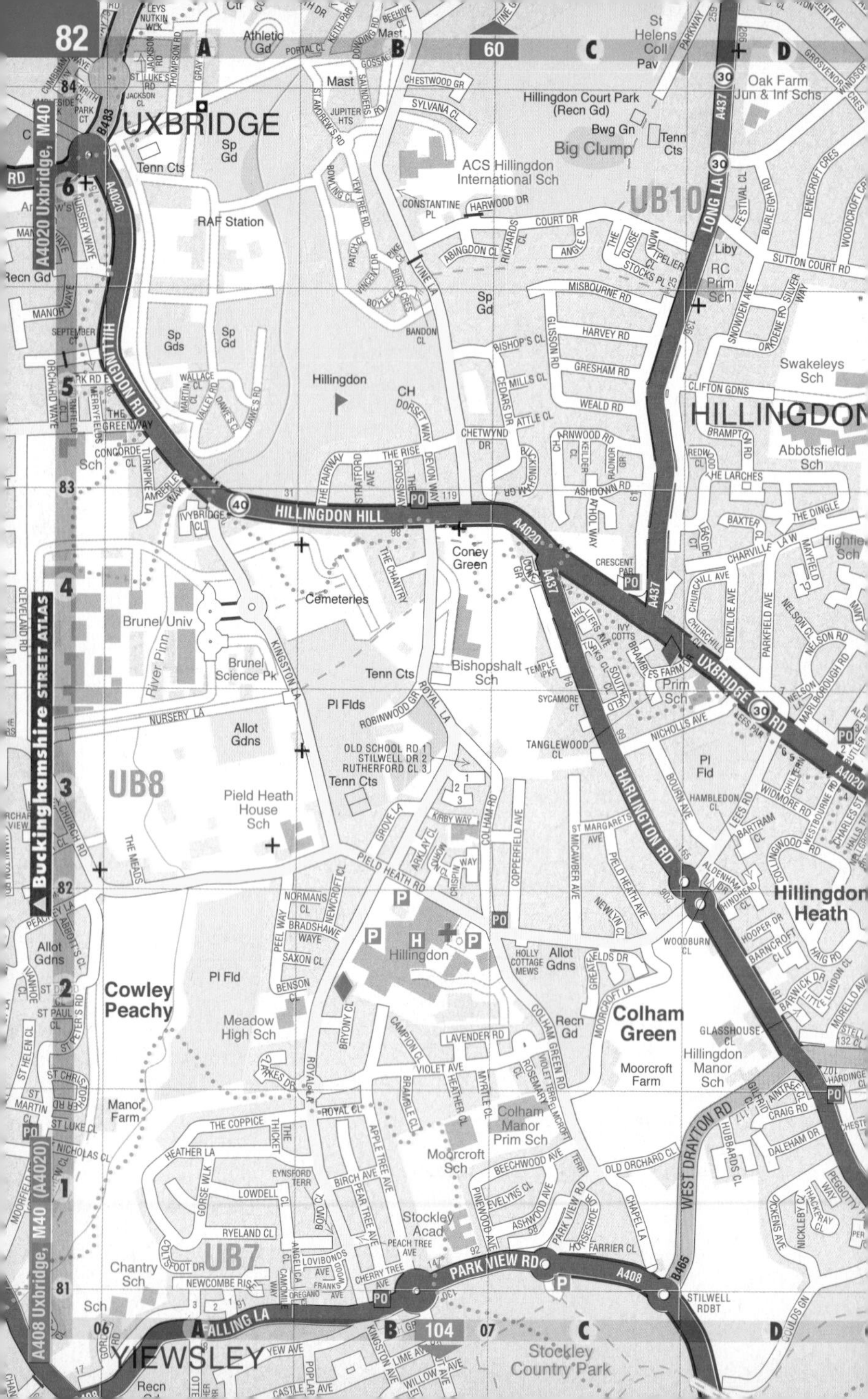
UXBRIDGE
HILLINGDON
Hillingdon Heath
Colham Green
Cowley Peachy
YIEWSLEY
UB8
UB10
UB7
HILLINGDON HILL
HILLINGDON RD
HARLINGTON RD
UXBRIDGE RD
LONG LA
PARK VIEW RD
FALLING LA
WEST DRAYTON RD
PIELD HEATH RD
Brunel Univ
Brunel Science Pk
Cemeteries
Coney Green
Bishopshalt Sch
ACS Hillingdon International Sch
Hillingdon Court Park (Recn Gd)
Big Clump
RAF Station
Meadow High Sch
Moorcroft Sch
Stockley Acad
Colham Manor Prim Sch
Hillingdon Manor Sch
Swakeleys Sch
Abbotsfield Sch
Stockley Country Park
Pield Heath House Sch
A4020 Uxbridge, M40
A408 Uxbridge, M40 (A4020)
Buckinghamshire STREET ATLAS
60
104

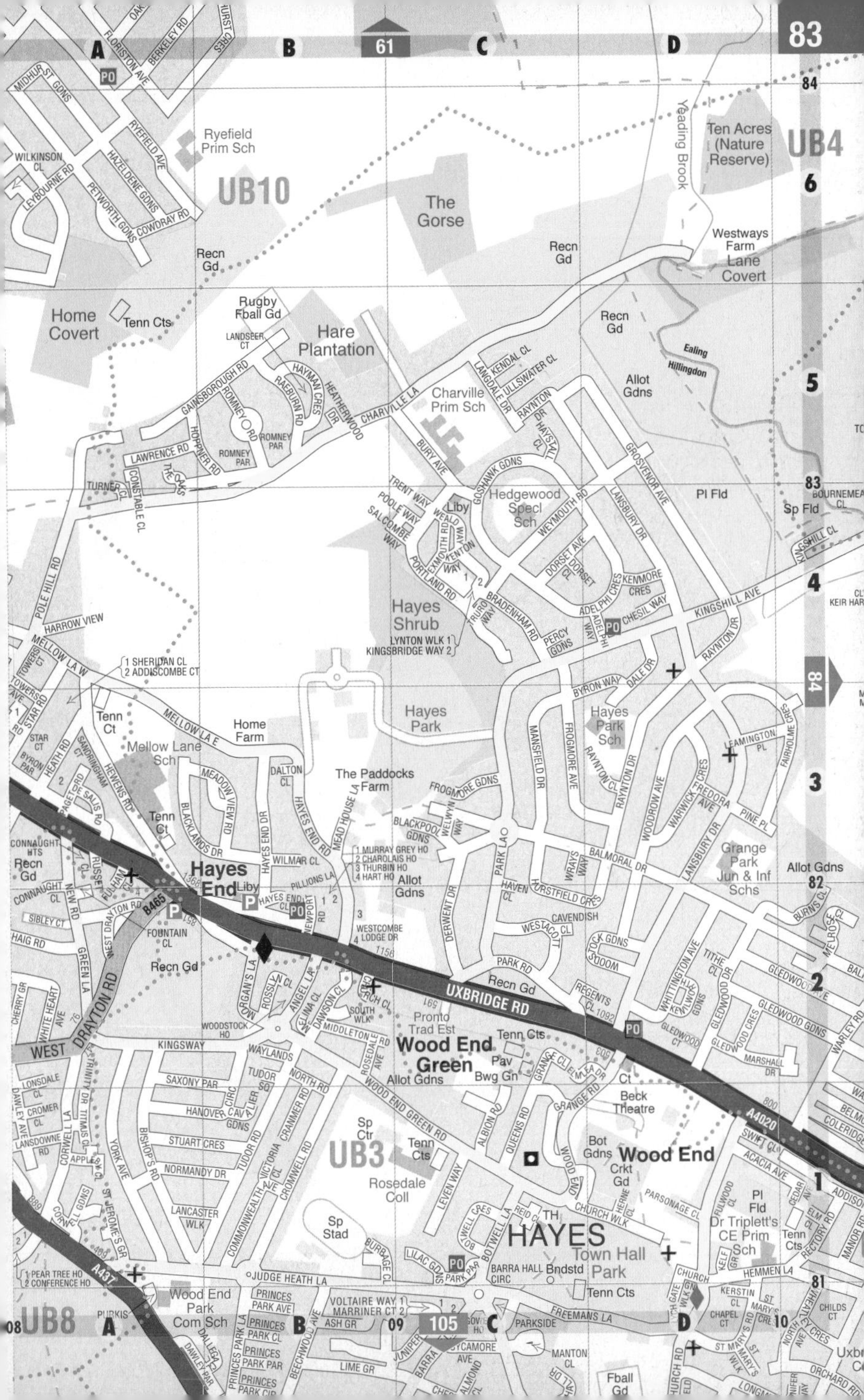
A
B
61
C
D
84
UB4
Ten Acres (Nature Reserve)
Yeading Brook
Ryefield Prim Sch
UB10
The Gorse
Recn Gd
Westways Farm
Lane Covert
Home Covert
Tenn Cts
Rugby Fball Gd
Hare Plantation
Ealing
Hillingdon
Allot Gdns
Charville Prim Sch
CHARVILLE LA
Hedgewood Specl Sch
Liby
Pl Fld
Sp Fld
Hayes Shrub
LYNTON WLK 1
KINGSBRIDGE WAY 2
1 SHERIDAN CL
2 ADDISCOMBE CT
Hayes Park
Hayes Park Sch
Home Farm
Mellow Lane Sch
Tenn Ct
The Paddocks Farm
1 MURRAY GREY HO
2 CHAROLAIS HO
3 THURBIN HO
4 HART HO
Allot Gdns
Grange Park Jun & Inf Schs
Hayes End
UXBRIDGE RD
Pronto Trad Est
Wood End Green
Beck Theatre
Wood End
UB3
Rosedale Coll
Sp Stad
HAYES
Town Hall Park
Dr Triplett's CE Prim Sch
1 PEAR TREE HO
2 CONFERENCE HO
VOLTAIRE WAY 1
MARRINER CT 2
UB8
Wood End Park Com Sch
105
A4020
A437
B465
WEST DRAYTON RD
JUDGE HEATH LA
FREEMANS LA
HEMMEN LA
6
5
4
3
2
1
83
82
81
08
09
10

UB4
UB5
UB3
Ten Acres (Nature Reserve)
Westways Farm
Lane Covert
West London Shooting Grounds
Downe Barns Farm
SHARVEL LA
WEST END RD
RUISLIP RD
Lime Tree Park
St Raphael's RC Prim Sch
Downe Manor Prim Sch
Belmore Prim Sch
Brookside Prim Sch
Viking Prim Sch
Yeading
White Hart Rdbt
KINGSHILL AVE
OWEN RD
THE PARKWAY
Yeading Brook
Yeading Jun & Inf Schs
Warren Park
Grange Park Jun & Inf Schs
Allot Gdns
Pl Fld
Vehicle Testing Sta & Driving Test Ctr
Grand Union Canal Walk
UXBRIDGE RD
A4020
A312
A4180
B455
Dr Triplett's CE Prim Sch
Uxbridge Coll
Lombardy Ret Pk
OSSIE GARVIN RDBT
Liby
Peacock Park

62
83
106

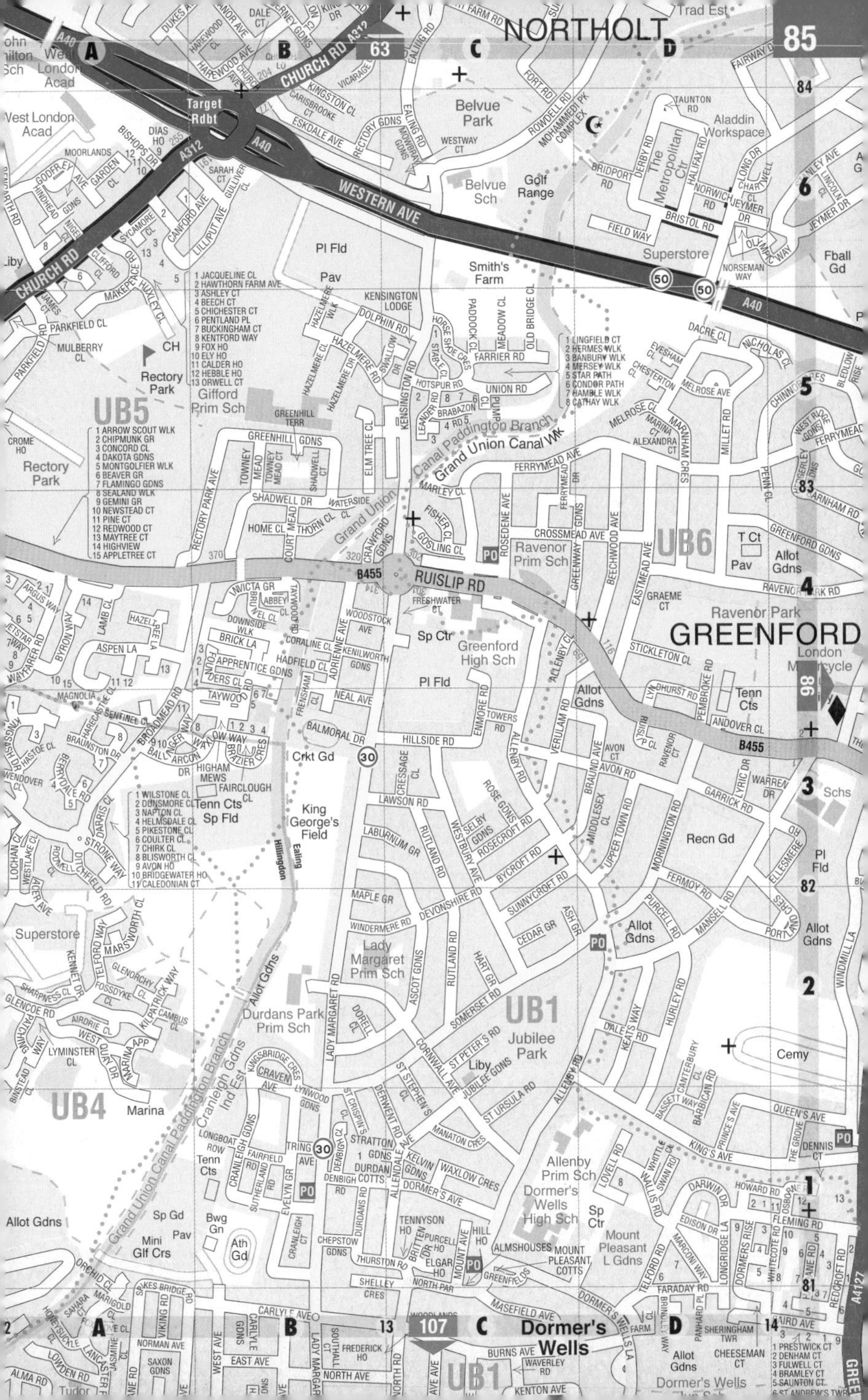
A
B
C
D
63
84
6
5
4
3
2
1
83
82
81
98
Target Rdbt
CHURCH RD
WESTERN AVE
A40
A312
Belvue Park
Belvue Sch
Golf Range
Smith's Farm
Superstore
Aladdin Workspace
The Metropolitan Ctr
UB5
UB6
UB1
UB4
Rectory Park
Gifford Prim Sch
West London Acad
Grand Union Canal Paddington Branch
Grand Union Canal Wk
RUISLIP RD
B455
Ravenor Prim Sch
GREENFORD
Ravenor Park
Greenford High Sch
King George's Field
Lady Margaret Prim Sch
Durdans Park Prim Sch
Jubilee Park
Allenby Prim Sch
Dormer's Wells High Sch
Mount Pleasant L Gdns
Cemy
Recn Gd
Marina
Dormer's Wells
107
A4127

Greenford
GREENFORD
Perivale Park
Grand Union Canal Walk
Perival Wood
Oldfield Recn Gd
Western Ave
Greenford Rdbt
Greenford Rd
Ruislip Rd East
Rockware Bsns Ctr
Sears Ret Pk
Selborne Prim Sch
South Greenford
Ravenor Park
London Motorcycle Mus
Litten Nature Reserve
Edward Betham CE Prim Sch
Coston Prim Sch
Oldfield Prim Sch
Brentside High Sch
Brentside Prim Sch
The Cardinal Wiseman RC Sch
Mayfield Prim Sch
Andre Malraux Sch
Hobbayne Prim Sch
Drayton Manor High Sch
Castle Bar Park
Drayton Green
Gurnell Swimming Pool
Brent Valley
River Brent
Capital Ring
Aladdin Workspace
UB6
W7
A40
A4127
B455
B452
64
85
108

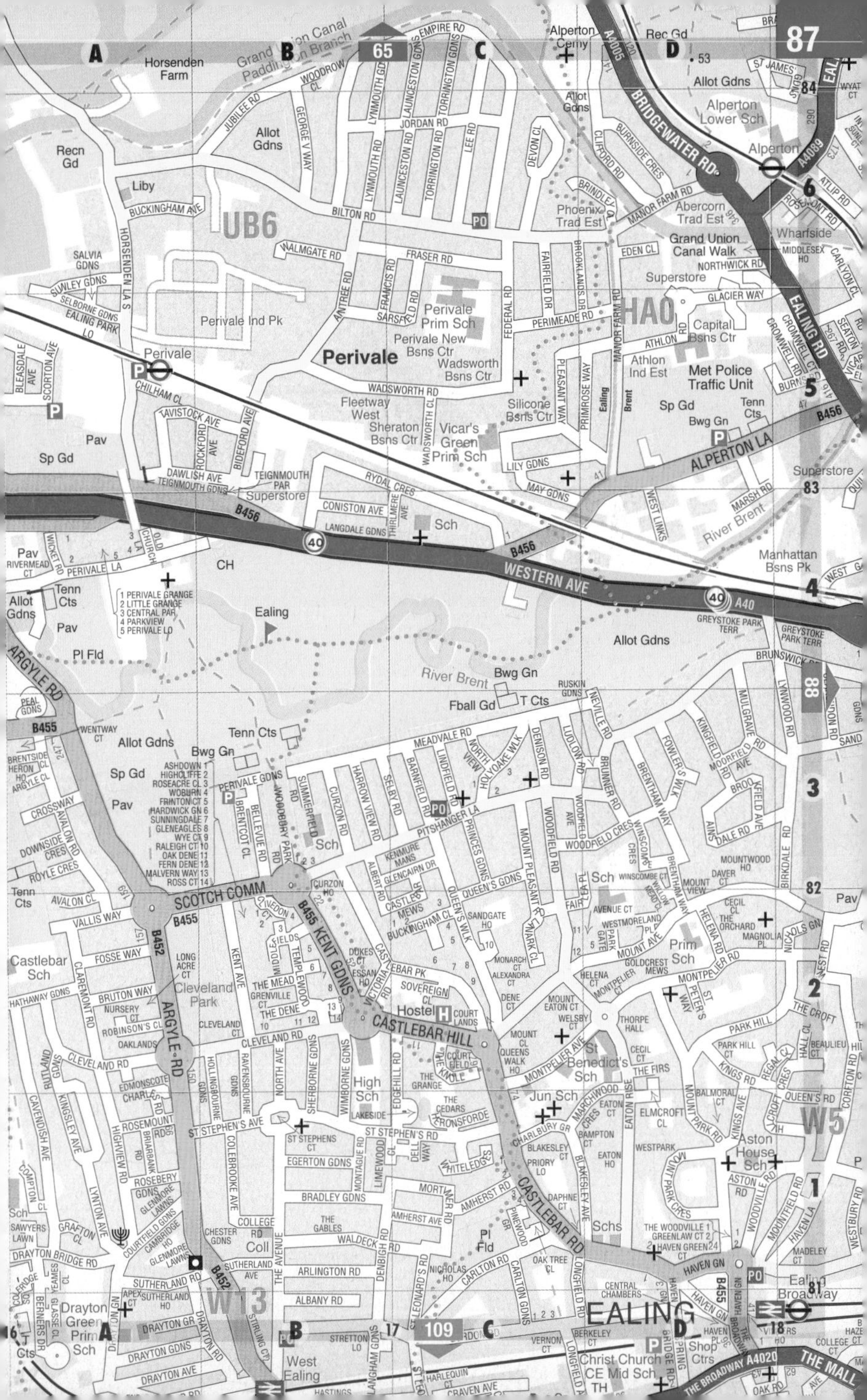

Perivale
UB6
HA0
W13
W5
EALING
Ealing Broadway
Alperton
Western Ave
Scotch Comm
Castlebar Hill
Castlebar Rd
Argyle Rd
Kent Gdns
Pitshanger La
Perivale La
Alperton La
Bridgewater Rd
Ealing Rd
Manor Farm Rd
Horsenden La S
The Broadway
The Mall
River Brent
Grand Union Canal Walk
Perivale Ind Pk
Cleveland Park
65
109
88

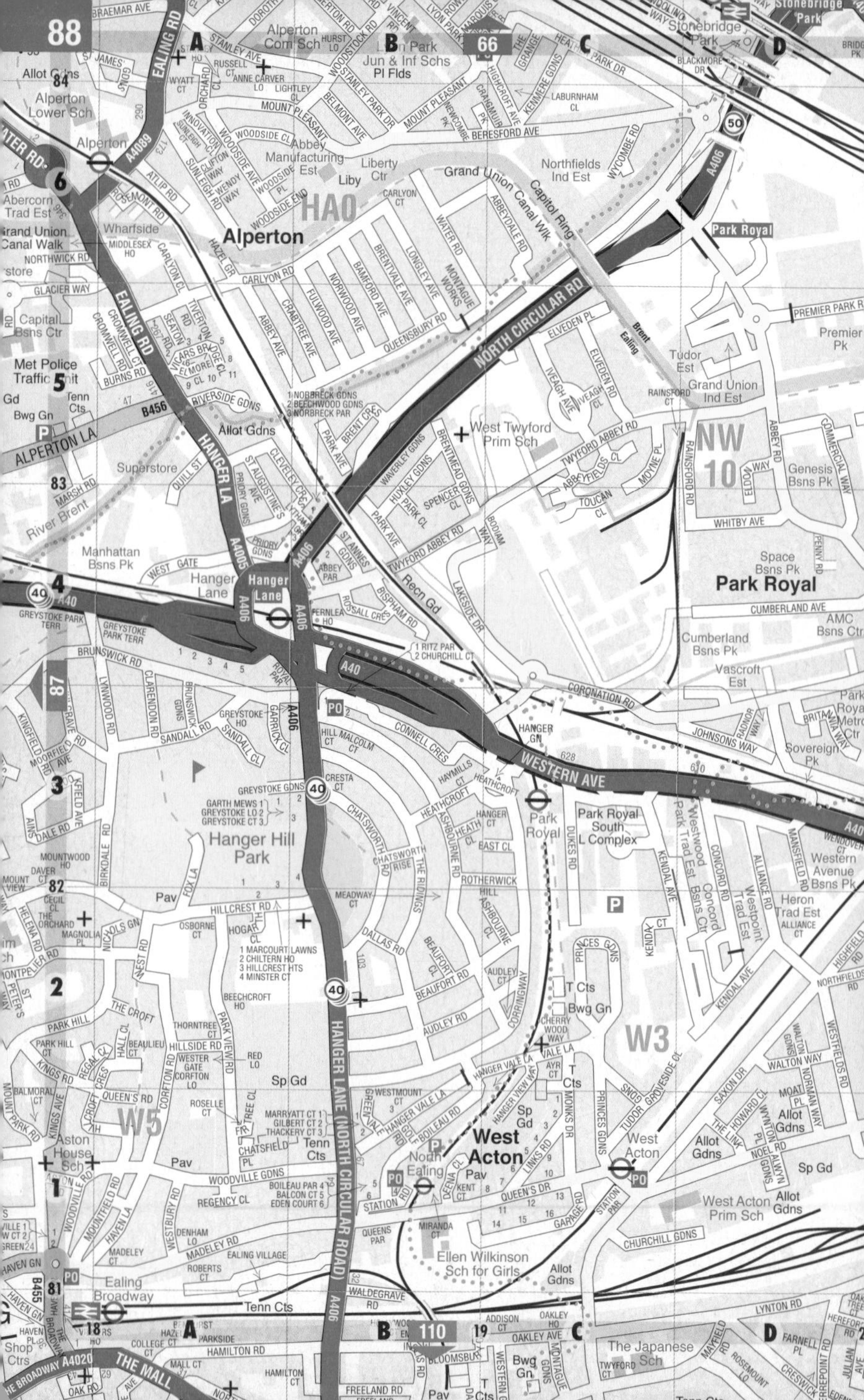
88
66
87
110
A
B
C
D
1
2
3
4
5
6
Alperton
Alperton Com Sch
Alperton Lower Sch
Allot Gdns
Lyon Park Jun & Inf Schs
Pl Flds
Stonebridge Park
Abbey Manufacturing Est
Liberty Ctr
Liby
Northfields Ind Est
Grand Union Canal Wlk
Capitol Ring
HA0
Abercorn Trad Est
Grand Union Canal Walk
Wharfside
Capital Bsns Ctr
Met Police Traffic Unit
Tenn Cts
Bwg Gn
Superstore
River Brent
Manhattan Bsns Pk
Hanger Lane
Park Royal
NW 10
Tudor Est
Grand Union Ind Est
Premier Pk
West Twyford Prim Sch
Genesis Bsns Pk
Space Bsns Pk
Cumberland Bsns Pk
AMC Bsns Ctr
Vascroft Est
Park Royal Metro Ctr
Sovereign Pk
Recn Gd
Hanger Hill Park
Park Royal South L Complex
Westwood Park Trad Est
Concord Bsns Ctr
Westpoint Trad Est
Western Avenue Bsns Pk
Heron Trad Est
W3
W5
West Acton
North Ealing
West Acton Prim Sch
Ellen Wilkinson Sch for Girls
Aston House Sch
Ealing Broadway
The Japanese Sch
Sp Gd
Pav
EALING RD
HANGER LA
HANGER LANE (NORTH CIRCULAR ROAD)
NORTH CIRCULAR RD
WESTERN AVE
ALPERTON LA
A40
A406
A4005
A4089
B456
B455
A4020
THE MALL
THE BROADWAY
CORONATION RD
CUMBERLAND AVE
TWYFORD ABBEY RD
HEATHER PARK DR
BERESFORD AVE
MOUNT PLEASANT
CARLYON RD
QUEENSBURY RD
BRUNSWICK RD
HILLCREST RD
AUDLEY RD
MADELEY RD
WOODVILLE GDNS
QUEEN'S DR
CHURCHILL GDNS
OAKLEY AVE
HAMILTON RD
LYNTON RD
WALTON WAY
WHITBY AVE
JOHNSONS WAY
PREMIER PARK RD
STATION RD
WALDEGRAVE RD

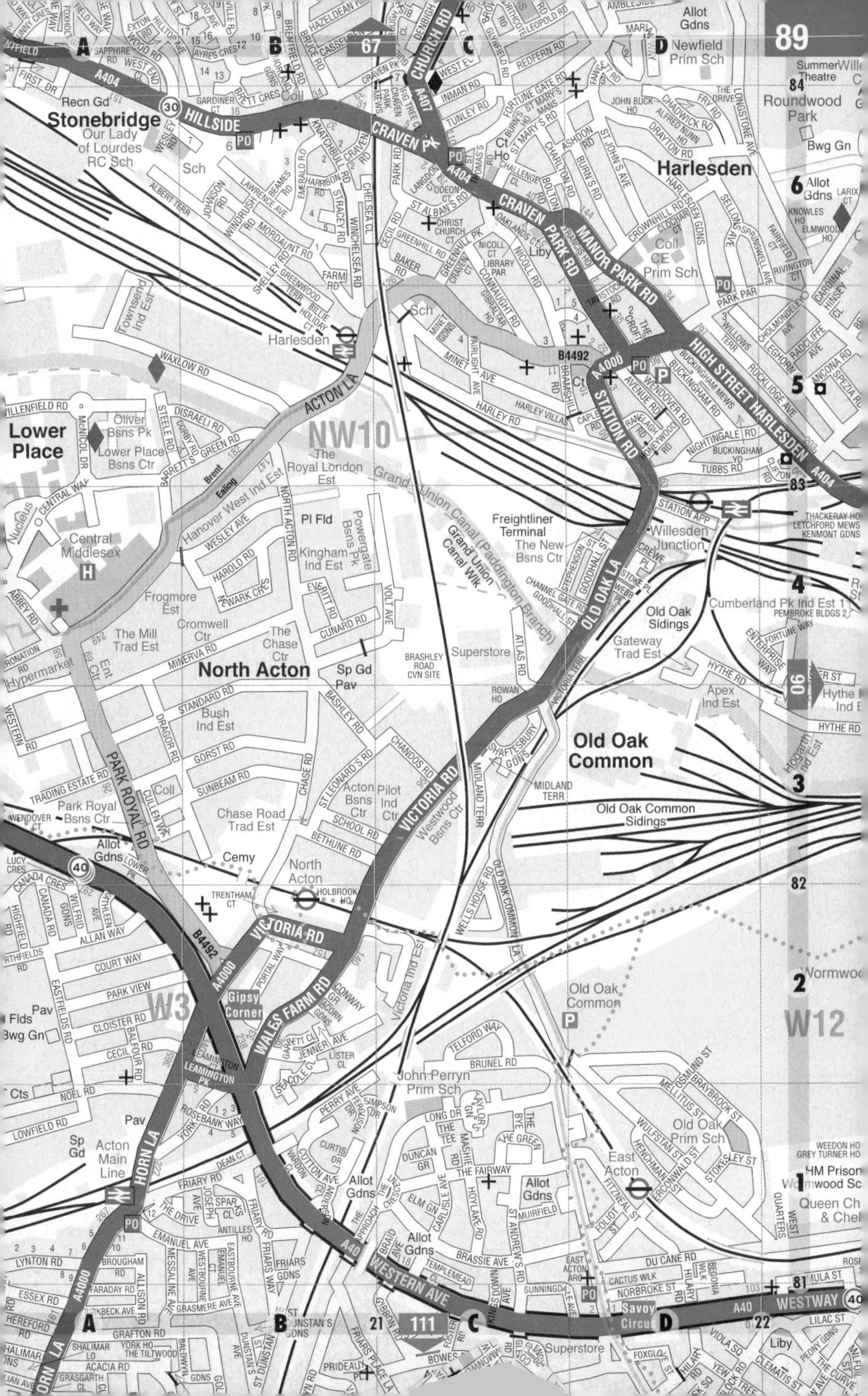
Stonebridge
Harlesden
Lower Place
NW10
North Acton
Old Oak Common
W3
W12
Grand Union Canal (Paddington Branch)
Willesden Junction
Freightliner Terminal
Old Oak Common Sidings
Central Middlesex
Roundwood Park
Gipsy Corner
Savoy Circus
East Acton
North Acton
Acton Main Line
Western Ave
Westway
High Street Harlesden
Victoria Rd
Old Oak La
Park Royal Rd
Horn La

Harlesden
Willesden Green
Brondesbury Park
Kensal Rise
Kensal Green
College Park
W10
Kensal Green Cemy (All Souls)
Grand Union Canal (Paddington Branch)
Grand Union Canal Wlk
Wormwood Scrubs Park
W12
The Linford Christie Stadium
HM Prison Wormwood Scrubs
Queen Charlottes & Chelsea
Hammersmith
North Kensington
Little Wormwood Scrubs (Recn Gd)
Mitre Bridge Ind Pk
Willesden Junction
Hythe Road Ind Est
Rutland Studios
Cumberland Pk Ind Est
Roundwood Park
Cardinal Hinsley RC High Sch (Boys)
Capital City Acad
Willesden Sp Ctr
Queens Park Com Sch
Burlington Danes Sch
Wood Lane High Sch
White City
Latimer Road
Westway
High Street Harlesden
Harrow Rd
Scrubs La
Wood La
NW6

68
89
112

A
B
C
D
69
Kilburn
NW6
Paddington Cemy
Salusbury Prim Sch
Queen's Park
Brondesbury Park
WILLESDEN LA
KILBURN HIGH RD
BRONDESBURY RD
BRONDESBURY VILLAS
HARVIST RD
KILBURN LA
Premier Corner
Kilburn High Road
ABBEY RD
BELSIZE RD
NW8
229
83
84
B507
B509
Kilburn Park
St Mary's Sch
CARLTON VALE
KILBURN PARK RD
Paddington Recn Gd
Maida Vale
MAIDA VALE
West Kilburn
WALTERTON RD
SHIRLAND RD
W9
Westbourne Green
92
HARROW RD
Kensal Town
Grand Union Canal
Paddington Com
Westbourne Park
GREAT WESTERN RD
WESTWAY (ELEVATED RD)
LADBROKE GR
Portobello Rd
Instituto Espanol
W10
A404
A40
236
Royal Oak
PORCHESTER RD
WESTBOURNE PARK VILLAS
W2
CHEPSTOW RD
WESTBOURNE PARK RD
WESTBOURNE GR
BISHOP'S BRIDGE
Dominican Republic
Ladbroke Grove
W11
KENSINGTON PARK RD
QUEENSWAY
Bayswater
244
113
245
25
26
81
82
1
2
3
4
5
6

92
NW6
Hampstead
A
B
C
D
70
230
Primrose Hill Tunnels
St Paul's
NW3
Primrose Hill
Barrow Hill
NW8
St John's Barracks
St John's Wood
Marlborough Day
St John & Elizabeth
The Wellington
St John's Wood
Lord's (MCC & Middlesex Cty Crkt Gd)
Crkt Mus
Winfield House
London Central Mosque
NW1
Boating Lake
The Holme
London Business Sch
Maida Vale
W9
Lisson Grove
Marylebone
Baker Street
Charter Nightingale
Edgware Road
Little Venice
Warwick Avenue
St Mary's Gardens Coll
PADDINGTON
Paddington Basin
St Mary's
Marylebone Flyover
Paddington
Royal Oak
Dominican Republic
W2
Bayswater
Marble Arch
Speakers' Corner
114
237
229
91
236
FINCHLEY RD
WELLINGTON RD
ABBEY RD
MAIDA VALE
AVENUE RD
PRINCE ALBERT RD
(Regent's Canal)
Grand Union Canal
PARK RD
ST JOHN'S WOOD ROAD
GROVE END RD
LISSON GR
HARROW RD
WESTWAY (ELEVATED) HARROW RD (UNDER)
A40 MARYLEBONE FLYOVER
MARYLEBONE RD
GLOUCESTER PL
BAKER ST
EDGWARE RD
PRAED ST
SUSSEX GDNS
BISHOP'S BRIDGE RD
EASTBOURNE TERR
CLIFTON GDNS
QUEENSWAY
NORTH CARRIAGE DR
NORTH RIDE
Victoria Gate

93
Camden Town
Regent's Park
NW1
London Zoo
Somers Town
Euston
Fitzrovia
Bloomsbury
Marylebone
Soho
Oxford Circus
Tottenham Court Road
Goodge Street
Warren Street
Great Portland Street
Mornington Crescent
Bond Street
British Mus
University of London
Queen Mary's Gardens
Open Air Theatre
Royal Acad of Music
Royal Coll of Physicians
Euston Underpass
Britannia Junc
Camden Mkt
Cumberland Gate
St Pancras
Somers Town
N1
W1
231
232
238
239
115
94

A
B
C
D
72
233
234
240
116
241
93
84
83
82
81
6
5
4
3
2
1
N1
EC1
WC1
WC2
ISLINGTON
Pentonville
FINSBURY
St Pancras
King's Cross
Somers Town
Bloomsbury
St Giles
Gray's Inn
Holborn
Clerkenwell
Camden Pas
Angel
Barnard Park
The British Liby
British Mus
St Pancras International
King's Cross (Thameslink)
Russell Square
Farringdon
Chancery Lane
Covent Garden
Leicester Square
Temple
Blackfriars
Smithfield Mkt
Chapel Mkt
Leather Lane
Lincoln's Inn Fields
Royal Courts of Justice
Somerset House
City Thameslink
Family Records Ctr
Eastman Dental
Coram's Fields
University of London
Russell Square Garden
Bsns Design Ctr
City Univ
Depot
St Barts
YORK WAY
CALEDONIAN RD
COPENHAGEN ST
LIVERPOOL RD
UPPER ST
ESSEX RD
PENTONVILLE RD
KING'S CROSS RD
GRAY'S INN RD
ROSEBERY AVE
FARRINGDON RD
GOSWELL RD
ST JOHN ST
CLERKENWELL RD
THEOBALD'S RD
HOLBORN
HIGH HOLBORN
NEW OXFORD ST
KINGSWAY
SOUTHAMPTON ROW
GUILFORD ST
HUNTER ST
JUDD ST
PANCRAS RD
MIDLAND RD
CHANCERY LA
FETTER LA
FLEET ST
ALDWYCH
STRAND
VICTORIA EMBANKMENT
HOLBORN VIADUCT
NEW BRIDGE ST
FARRINGDON ST
CHARING CROSS RD
SHAFTESBURY AVE
BLOOMSBURY ST
LONG ACRE
DRURY LA
WHARFDALE RD
RICHMOND AVE
CARNEGIE ST
WHITE LION ST
CHARTERHOUSE ST
SKINNER ST
PERCIVAL ST

SHOREDITCH
Hoxton
Haggerston
Haggerston Park
Shoreditch Park
St Luke's
Barbican
Barbican Arts & Con Ctr
Broadgate
Spitalfields
Old Spitalfields
Whitechapel
Aldgate
Brick Lane
Columbia Rd
Petticoat Lane
Guildhall
Mansion House
Cannon Street
Monument
Tower Hill
Tower Gateway
Fenchurch Street
Liverpool Street
Moorgate
Bank
Old Street
Aldgate East
Tower 42
Swiss Re Bldg
Lloyds Bldg
Grand Union Canal
(Regent's Canal)
Kingsland Basin
City Road Basin
CITY OF LONDON
St Paul's Cath
E8
E2
E1
EC2
EC3
EC4
NEW NORTH RD
KINGSLAND RD
HACKNEY RD
CITY RD
OLD ST
GREAT EASTERN ST
SHOREDITCH HIGH ST
BETHNAL GREEN RD
COMMERCIAL ST
BISHOPSGATE
LONDON WALL
ALDERSGATE ST
UPPER THAMES ST
QUEENSBRIDGE RD
COLUMBIA RD
CHISWELL ST
BUNHILL ROW
PITFIELD ST
EAST RD
WHITECHAPEL HIGH ST
MINORIES
BRICK LA
HOUNDSDITCH
GRACECHURCH ST
A
B
C
D
1
2
3
4
5
6
73
235
96
243
242
117

A
B
C
D
74
HACKNEY
South Hackney
E8
E9
E2
E1
Haggerston
Haggerston Park
Cambridge Heath
BETHNAL GREEN
Bethnal Green
STEPNEY
Spitalfields
Shadwell
Ratcliff
Globe Town
Meath Gardens
Royal Gate East
Royal Gate West
Gore Gate
Crown Gate West
The Royal London (Mile End)
Morpeth Sec Sch
Anchor Ret Pk
Stepney Green
Swanlea Sec Sch
Weavers Fields
Allen Gdns
Osmani Sch
Royal London
Watney
Columbia Rd
Fball Gd
Works
Super store
Superstore
VICTORIA PARK RD
WELL ST
MIDDLETON RD
ALBION DR
SHRUBLAND RD
BROWNLOW RD
REGENT'S ROW
WHISTON RD
DOVE ROW
Regent's Canal
BISHOP'S WAY
SEWARDSTONE RD
OLD FORD RD
ROMAN RD
HACKNEY RD
QUEENSBRIDGE RD
OLD BETHNAL GREEN RD
GOSSET ST
BETHNAL GREEN RD
CAMBRIDGE HEATH RD
CHESHIRE ST
DUNBRIDGE ST
THREE COLTS LA
BRICK LA
VALLANCE RD
WHITECHAPEL RD
WHITECHAPEL HIGH ST
MILE END RD
GLOBE RD
STEPNEY GN
COMMERCIAL RD
NEW RD
CANNON STREET RD
CABLE ST
THE HIGHWAY
LEMAN ST
ROYAL MINT ST
95
243
118
1
2
3
4
5
6

A
B
C
D
75
Victoria Park
Victoria Fntn
Gunmakers Gate
Old Ford
BOW
Mile End Park
Mile End
Univ of London
Stratford Marsh
The Marshgate Ctr
Pudding Mill Lane
St Clement's Wharf
Iceland Wharf
Swan Wharf
Crown Wharf
Vulcan Wharf
Grove Hall Park
Bow Church
Bow Road
Bromley
Bow Common
Devons Road
Tower Hamlets Cemy
The Royal London (St Clements)
E3
Gas Works
TOWER HAMLETS
East London Stadium
Hackney Coll
Langdon Park
Bartlett Park
POPLAR
Limehouse
Limehouse Basin
Brickfield Gardens
EAST INDIA DOCK RD
EAST CROSS ROUTE
BLACKWALL TUNNEL NORTHERN APPROACH
BOW RD
GROVE RD
BURDETT RD
DEVONS RD
ST PAUL'S WAY
FAIRFIELD RD
Hertford Union Canal
Regent's Canal
River Lea or Lee
Lea Valley Wlk
98
119
Westferry

76
Stratford Marsh
Newham Coll (Stratford Campus)
WEST HAM LA
VICARAGE LA
PORTWAY
HIGH ST
Stratford Workshops
Channelsea River
Depot
NEW PLAISTOW RD
PLAISTOW RD
Plaistow
Vanguard Trad Ctr
Marsh Gate Bsns Ctr
Axis Bsns Ctr
Vulcan Wharf
E15
Mill Meads
Abbey Creek
Channelsea Bsns Ctr
Ranelagh Prim Sch
CORPORATION ST
Meeson's Wharf
BOW BRIDGE
Three Mills Green
Prescott Channel
Allot Gdns
West Ham
Memorial Recn Gd
East London Cemy
Cycleway
Tredegar Wharf
THREE MILLS STUDIOS
CROWS RD
Superstore
Gas Works
NEWHAM
MANOR RD
Bromley-by-Bow
97
BLACKWALL TUNNEL NORTHERN APPROACH
Bow Locks
TWELVETREES CRES
Mus
Twelvetrees Bsns Pk
E16
Eastlea Com Sch
Star Prim Sch
Recn Gd
Hackney Coll
Barratt Ind Pk
Lea Valley Wlk
Data Point Bsns Ctr
Gemini Bsns Ctr
Pylon Trad Est
STEPHENSON ST
Star Park
St Leonard's Wharf
Islay Wharf
South Bromley
Devon Wharf
River Lea or Lee
Bow Creek
Blackwall Trad Est
Langdon Park
ABBOTT RD
Gas Works
Canning Town
Bow Creek Mills
EAST INDIA DOCK RD
LOWER LEA CROSSING
120
East India Dock Basin
Hercules Wharf
Orchard Wharf
East India
Blackwall
Poplar
COTTON ST
Canning Town

99
Upton
BOLEYN RD
STUKELEY RD
77
PLASHET GR
Bndst
Tenn Cts
NEVILLE RD
PLASHET RD
E7
E15
UPTON CROSS
A114
B165
B167
B109
STOPFORD RD
ELIZABETH RD
VICTORIA AVE
84
OUTRAM RD
MALVERN RD
STAMFORD RD
Upton Park
Queen's Mkt
Liby
GREEN ST
Upton Park
Priory Park
Cleves Prim Sch
6
OAKFIELD RD
WAKEFIELD ST
KATHERINE RD
WEST HAM
TERRACE RD
HAROLD RD
ROCHESTER AVE
WAGHORN RD
TUDOR RD
Sch
Boleyn Gd (West Ham Utd FC)
PELLY RD
QUEEN'S RD W
Lister Com Sch
Allot Gdns
Plaistow Prim Sch
JUNCTION RD
A124
30
KIMBERLEY AVE
LADYSMITH AVE
Prim Sch
5
HIGH ST
SOUTHERN RD
Plaistow
H
CASTLE ST
THE BROADWAY
Curwen Prim Sch
Liby
Pl Fld
EDINBURGH CT
CENTRAL PARK RD
B167
CHELTENHAM GDNS
83
GREENGATE ST
A112
JEDBURGH RD
JACOBS HO
COTSWOLD GDNS
MONTPELIER GDNS
HENNIKER GDNS
E6
HALDANE RD
CHESTERTON TERR
HOWARD'S RD
Recn Gd
Plaistow
BURKE LODGE
BALAAM ST
B116
E13
DONGOLA RD
KHARTOUM RD
TUNMARSH LA
HUMBERSTONE RD
FRINTON RD
LICHFIELD RD
DENBIGH RD
4
Brampton Prim Sch
BARKING RD
ST ANDREW'S RD
PRINCE REGENT LA
CROFTON RD
WIGSTON RD
WANLIP RD
Newham General
Roman Road Prim Sch
100
LONSDALE AVE
LONSDALE CL
L Ctr
LAWRENCE HALL
1 LARCH CL
2 BELGRAVE CT
Cumberland Sch
Brampton Manor Sch
Newham Sixth Form Coll
APPLEWOOD DR
1 NEWPORT AVE
2 JONES RD
Newham Ctr for Mental Health
3
STOKES RD
ELKINGTON RD
JENKINS RD
Tollgate Prim Sch
Stadium
A13
50
PALMER RD
MAYBURY RD
82
East Ham Ind Est
HOLBORN RD
BROCK RD
SELBY RD
CHADWIN RD
CHALK RD
L Ctr
Games Ct
Pav
Horse Ride
KILDARE RD
RAVENSCROFT RD
NEWHAM WAY
Prince Regent
GOLDCREST CL
TOLLGATE RD
2
Canning Town
Tenn Cts
Rosetta Prim Sch
Recn Gd
Liby
COLMAN RD
E16
1 PEACOCK WLK
2 RUSTIC WLK
MORTLAKE RD
VARLEY RD
DEVONSHIRE RD
Scott Wilkie Prim Sch
King George V Park
Becton District Park
HIGH HEADS RD 1
BROADGATE RD 2
Hallsville Prim Sch
CHURCHILL RD
KING GEORGE AVE
Will Thorne Pav
1
Recn Gd
BOREHAM AVE
COOLFIN RD
Custom House
Com Sch
Calverton Prim Sch
RICHARD HOUSE DR
81
Allot Gdns
Allot Gdns
VICTORIA DOCK RD
A
B
C
D
Custom House for ExCeL
41
121
42
CONNAUGHT RD
A112
A1020
Royal Victoria
SEAGULL LA
Hotel
1 WOOD ST
2 BETTS RD
3 CHAUNTLER CL
4 SANDSTONE LA
Prince Regent
DOCKSIDE RD
Royal Albert

EAST HAM
Wallend
Beckton
Cyprus
Central Park
East Ham Jewish Cemy
Brampton Prim Sch
Brampton Park
Roman Road Prim Sch
Flanders Pl Fld
Gooseley's Pl Flds
Beckton Triangle Ret Pk
Gateway Ret Pk
Beckton Alps
Alpine Bsns Ctr
Beckton Ret Pk
North Beckton Prim Sch
East Beckton Dist Ctr
Kingsford Com Sch
New Becton Park
Winsor Prim Sch
Gallions Prim Sch
Gallions Reach
Beckton Park
Royal Albert
Univ of East London
East Ham Ind Est
Becton District Park
The Will Thorne Pav
Calverton Prim Sch
Langdon Sch
Barking Flyover
NORTH CIRCULAR RD
ROYAL DOCKS RD
BARKING RD
HIGH ST S
NEWHAM WAY
WOOLWICH MANOR WAY
ROYAL ALBERT WAY
RANCLIFFE RD
RON LEIGHTON WAY
Horse Ride
E6
IG11
78
99
122

BARKING
79
A
B
C
D
RIPPLE RD
ST PAULS RD
A124
A123
Gascoigne Prim Sch
Greatfields Park
Movers Lane (Flyover)
ALFRED'S WAY (EAST HAM AND BARKING BY-PASS)
A13
IG11
Cuckold's Haven
New England Est
Barking Ind Pk
Wayside Commercial Est
Lyon Bsns Pk
Kingsbridge Ind Est
Thames View Inf Sch
Thames View Jun Sch
Barking Bsns Ctr
Katella Trad Est
Cromwell Trad Ctr
River Road Bsns Pk
Creekmouth Ind Pk
THAMES RD
RIVER RD
LONG REACH RD
Sewage Works
Barking Creek
Creekmouth
Trafalgar Bsns Ctr
Anglian Ind Est
Balmoral Trad Est
Buzzard Creek Ind Est
River Roding
Barking Barrier
Horse End
Superstore
Gallions Reach Shp Pk
E6
Depot
ARMADA WAY
Jetty
Pier
Margaret or Tripcock Ness
Mast
102
123
45
46
81
82
83
84
1
2
3
4
5
6
Thamesmead Sh Ctr

Castle Green
RM9
IG11
Cemy
Ripple Road
Monteagle Prim Sch
Jo Richardson Com Sch
Rec Gd
Liby
Sp Gds
L Ctr
Barking Ind Pk
Works
Alfred's Way Ind Est
The Invicta Ctr
Wayside Commercial Est
Davenport Ctr
Rippleside Commercial Est
Portland Commercial Est
Maybells Commercial Est
Freightliner Terminal
Thames View Inf Sch
Thames View Jun Sch
Pl Fld
Barking Bsns Ctr
Riverside Ind Est
Bankside Pk
City Farm & Eco Pk
Allot Gdns
Buzzard Creek Ind Est
Anglian Ind Est
Balmoral Trad Est
Pier
Barking or False Point
Barking Reach
River Thames
Cross Ness
Castilion Prim Sch
Crossway Lake Nature Reserve
Green Chain Wlk
Ppg Sta
Linton Mead Prim Sch
Bishop John Robinson Prim Sch
Thamesmead Sh Ctr
RIPPLE RD
ALFRED'S WAY (EAST HAM AND BARKING BY-PASS)
LODGE AVE
RIVER RD
CENTRAL WAY

80
101
124

DAGENHAM
Goresbrook Park
Old Dagenham Park
Arnold Prim Sch
Broad Street
Dagenham Park Com Sch
RM10
RM9
IG11
Allot Gdns
Sch
PO
Heathway
RIPPLE RD
A1306
A1240
B178
NEW RD
Superstore
Merrielands Ret Pk
Marsh Green Prim Sch
Motor Works
Dagenham Dock
LC
Channel Tunnel Rail Link
A13
Dagenham Breach
Thames Gateway Pk
Horse Shoe Corner
Power Sta
Ind Est
Works
Jetties
Jetty
River Thames
Beam River
Halfway Reach
Barking & Dagenham
Bexley
Havering
Drv Rng
Crossness Pumping Station
SE28
SE2
RM13
Riverside
CHEQUERS LA
CHOATS MANOR WAY
BREACH LA
HINDMANS WAY
KENT AVE
THAMES AVE
FIESTA DR
THUNDERER RD
BALLARDS RD
OVAL RD N
OVAL RD S
BEAM AVE
THIRD AVE
SECOND AVE
FIRST AVE
CENTRE RD
CROSBY RD
EAST ENTRANCE
SIERRA DR
LINK RD
SCHOOL RD
ORCHARD RD
PEARLSTONES CT
ARNOLD RD
RON TODD CL
DIGBY GDNS
LOWER BROAD ST
MORLAND RD
CAUSTON SQ
MORGAN CL
GORESBROOK RD
TRESWELL RD
STARMANS CL
DAGENHAM AVE
VINCENT RD
ELSTOW GDNS
ELSTOW RD
SHAW AVE
RATTONS TERR
LYTHAM CL
CHART HILLS CL
SUNNINGDALE CL
A1306 Rainham
A13 Stanford-le-Hope, M25 Tilbury (A1089)
Essex STREET ATLAS
81
125
A
B
C
D
84
6
5
83
4
3
82
2
1
81
49
50

82
YIEWSLEY
Stockley Country Park
WEST DRAYTON
R A F Station
West Drayton
Grand Union Canal
Grand Union Canal Wlk
STOCKLEY RD
Heathrow Express Tunnel
Harmondsworth
Holiday Inn
UB7
UB11
UB3
A408 Uxbridge, M40 (A4020)
Buckinghamshire STREET ATLAS
M4 Slough, M25
126
Heathrow
HOLLOWAY LA
SIPSON RD
HARMONDSWORTH RD
FALLING LA
PARK VIEW RD
STILWELL RDBT
Cherry Lane Prim Sch
West Drayton Prim Sch
Longmead Prim Sch
The Closes (Recn Gd)
Horton Road Ind Est
Paynes Farm

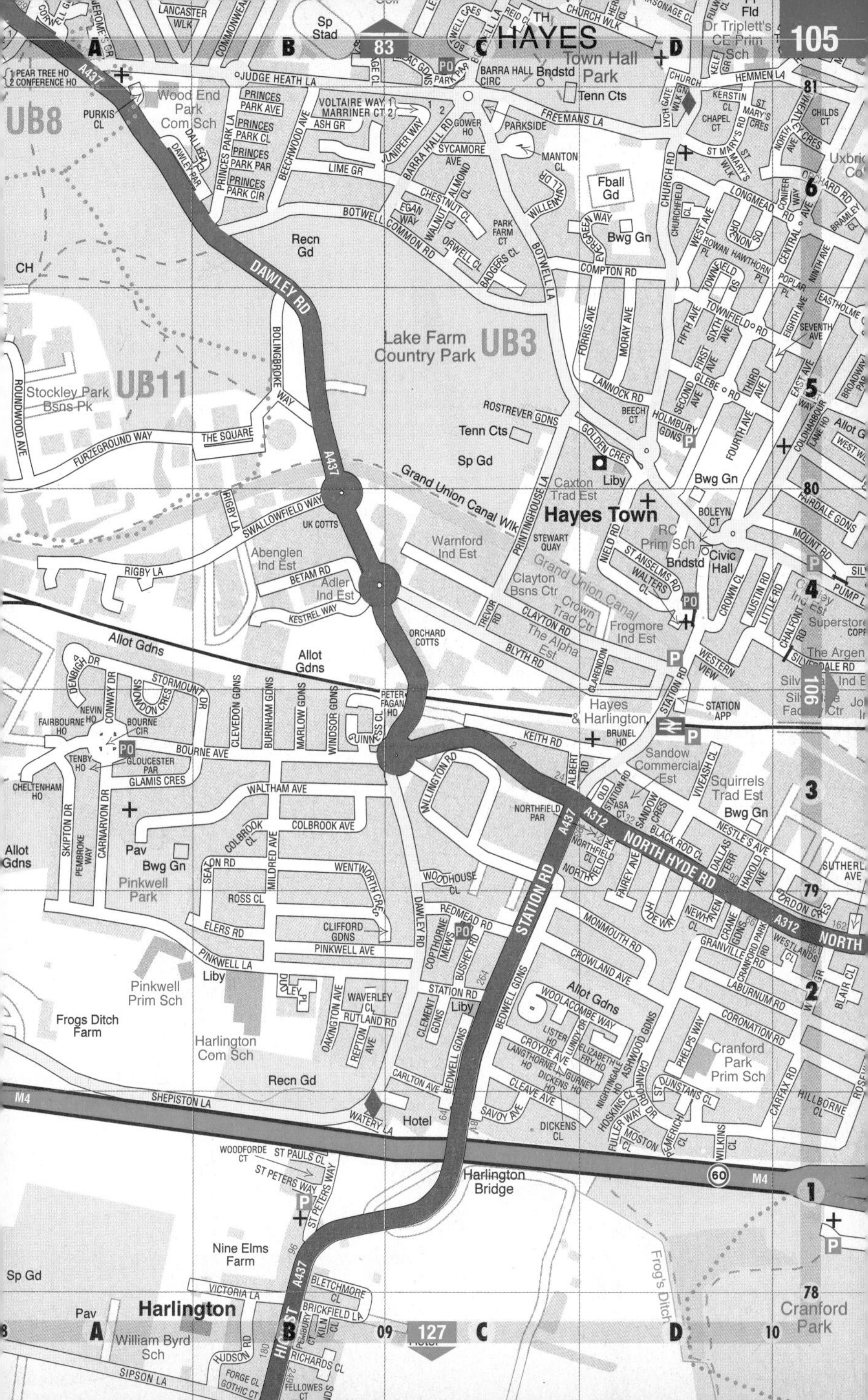
HAYES
Town Hall Park
Hayes Town
Lake Farm Country Park
UB3
UB8
UB11
Stockley Park Bsns Pk
Harlington
Harlington Bridge
Cranford Park
Nine Elms Farm
Frogs Ditch Farm
Pinkwell Park
Pinkwell Prim Sch
Harlington Com Sch
William Byrd Sch
Cranford Park Prim Sch
Wood End Park Com Sch
Dr Triplett's CE Prim Sch
RC Prim Sch
Civic Hall
Hayes & Harlington
Grand Union Canal
Grand Union Canal Wlk
Warnford Ind Est
Abenglen Ind Est
Adler Ind Est
Clayton Bsns Ctr
Crown Trad Ctr
The Alpha Est
Frogmore Ind Est
Caxton Trad Est
Sandow Commercial Est
Squirrels Trad Est
DAWLEY RD
NORTH HYDE RD
STATION RD
A437
A312
M4
83
127
106
A
B
C
D
09
10
81
80
79
78
1
2
3
4
5
6

UXBRIDGE RD
A4020
84
A312
Lombardy Ret Pk
Superstore
Uxbridge Coll
OSSIE GARVIN RDBT
Elystan Bsns Ctr
Hexagon Bsns Ctr
Metro Ctr
Hayes Bridge Ret Pk
Hayes Town
Minet Jun & Inf Schs
Minet Country Park
Allot Gdns
Sp Gd
Bsns Pk
Brook Ind Est
Swallowbrook Bsns Ctr
Guru Nanak Sikh Prim & Sec Schs
Blair Peach Prim Sch
1 GLENISTER HO
2 FITZGERALD HO
3 WELLINGS HO
UB3
UB4
UB1
Yeading Brook
Grand Union Canal Paddington Branch
Grand Union Canal Wlk
Chailey Ind Est
Provident Ind Est
Regent Bsns Ctr
The Argent Ctr
Peter James Bsns Ctr
Halls Bsns Ctr
Silverdale Ind Est
Silverdale Factory Ctr
Johnson's Ind Est
Civic Hall
105
Balfour Bsns Ctr
Brent Park Ind Est
International Trad Est
THE PARKWAY
NORTH HYDE RD
Bulls Bridge Ind Est
Superstore
Featherstone Prim Sch
Grand Union Canal
Western International Market
THE MARKET CTR
UB2
Cranford Park Prim Sch
River Crane
TW5
M4
Tenn Cts
The Heston Ctr
The Spitfire Est
Airlinks Ind Est
Airlinks
Lower Park Farm
Heston Motorway Service Area
Cranford Park
128

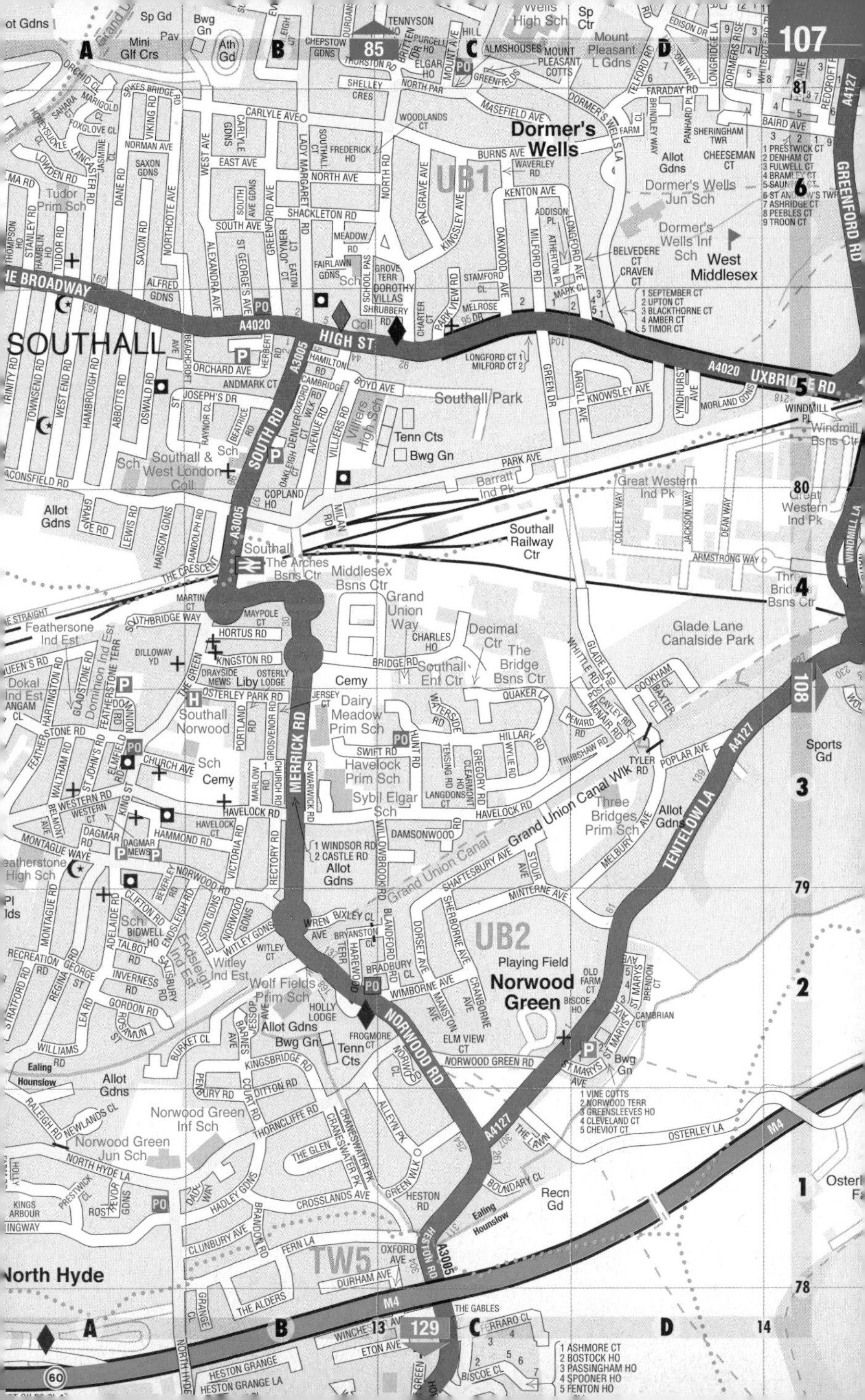
SOUTHALL
Dormer's Wells
UB1
UB2
TW5
Norwood Green
North Hyde
Southall Park
West Middlesex
HIGH ST
UXBRIDGE RD
SOUTH RD
MERRICK RD
NORWOOD RD
TENTELOW LA
GREENFORD RD
Grand Union Canal
Glade Lane Canalside Park
Great Western Ind Pk
Southall Railway Ctr
85
108
129

Brent Valley
86
Hobbayne Prim Sch
Drayton Green
Drayton Manor High Sch
ELMWOOD GDNS
GROVE AVE
HAWTHORNE MEWS
FLEMING RD
WHITECOTE RD
HALDANE RD
REDCROFT RD
BAIRD AVE
SHERINGHAM TWR
CHEESEMAN CT
1 PRESTWICK CT
2 DENHAM CT
3 FULWELL CT
4 BRAMLEY CT
5 SAUNTON CT
6 ST ANDREW'S TWR
7 ASHRIDGE CT
8 PEEBLES CT
9 TROON CT
GREENFORD RD
A4127
Sp Gd
CH
West Middlesex
Churchfields Recn Gd
Bwg Gn
MADGE HILL
CHURCH RD
CUCKOO LA
APRIL CL
DRAYTON BRIDGE RD
COWPER RD
SHAKESPEARE RD
MILTON RD
ALLINGHAM CL
TENNYSON RD
1 SHERIDAN CT
2 KIPLING CT
Hanwell
YORK AVE
UB1
1 ALDERSON PL
2 IRON BRIDGE CL
3 ALEXANDER CL
A4020 UXBRIDGE RD
WINDMILL PL
Windmill Bsns Ctr
Triangle Ctr
BRENTVALE AVE
BLACKMORE AVE
Allot Gdns
River Brent
HALLIDAY SQ
WEST PARK RD
Ealing
Great Western Ind Pk
ARMSTRONG WAY
Three Bridges Bsns Ctr
Grand Union Canal Wlk
1 WATER LILY CL
2 COMER CRES
3 TULIP CL
WINDMILL BRIDGE
Glade Lane Canalside Park
107
UB2
WOLSEY CL
Sports Gd
Sp Ctr
Capital Ring
LOWER BOSTON RD
A4001 BOSTON RD
A3002
City of Westminster Cemy
1THORNWELL CT
2 ST MARK'S CT
3 DU BURSTOW TERR
4 CHURCHFIELD RD
5 MALLARD CL
6 QUEENS TERR COTTS
Waterside Trad Ctr
W7
Elthorne Park
Elthorne Park High Sch
Boston Bsns Pk
River Brent Bsns Pk
Pl Fld
The Aviary
River Brent
Grand Union Canal
WINDMILL LA
Osterley Lock
TENTELOW LA
Trumper's Wood
OSTERLEY LA
M4
Hare & Hounds (PH)
Osterley Park Farm
TW7
Osterley Park
Osterley Park House
Bwg Gn
Tenn Cts
Sp Gd
Wyke Green
B454 SYON LA
130

87
A
B
C
D
W13
EALING
West Ealing
Drayton Green Prim Sch
West Ealing Bsns Ctr
West Prim Sch
Christ Church CE Mid Sch
Shop Ctrs
Ealing Broadway
THE BROADWAY A4020
THE MALL
NEW BROADWAY
UXBRIDGE RD
BROADWAY
A4020
B452
B455
Mus & Art Gall
Ealing Studios
Walpole Park
Lammas Park
Thames Valley Univ
YMCA
Allot Gdns
Bwg Gn
Tenn Cts
South Ealing
Northfields
Liby
Fielding Prim Sch
NORTHFIELD AVE
ST MARY'S RD
SOUTH EALING RD
LITTLE EALING LA
B4491
BOSTON RD
BOSTON MANOR RD
WINDMILL RD
EALING RD
Northfields Recn Gd
Depot
South Ealing Cemy
Phoenix Trad Pk
W5
Boston Manor
Boston Manor Pl Flds
Boston Manor Park
Gunnersbury RC Sch
Reynard Mills Trad Est
Grand Union Canal Wlk
Grand Union Canal
Ealing Road Trad Est
Brook La Bns Ctr
Griffin Park Fball Gd
M4 (ELEVATED)
M4
A4
A3002
TW7
TW8
BRENTFORD
B Sky B HQ
131
110
80
79
78
1
2
3
4
5
6

Ealing Broadway
Ealing Common
W5
W3
W4
TW8
Gunnersbury Park
Gunnersbury Park Mus
Gunnersbury
Chiswick Pk
South Acton
Acton Town
Twyford CE High Sch
The Japanese Sch
Acton High Sch
North Korea
South Ealing Cemy
Gunnersbury Cemy
International Sch of London
Lionel Road Prim Sch
Kew Bridge
Brentford Fountain L Ctr
Strand on the Green
Brentford Ait
Kew Pier
UXBRIDGE RD
GUNNERSBURY AVENUE
NORTH CIRCULAR ROAD
GUNNERSBURY LA
POPE'S LA
GREAT WEST RD (UNDER)
M4 (ELEVATED)
CHISWICK HIGH RD
WELLESLEY RD A3000
EALING RD
THE MALL
HIGH ST
88
109
132

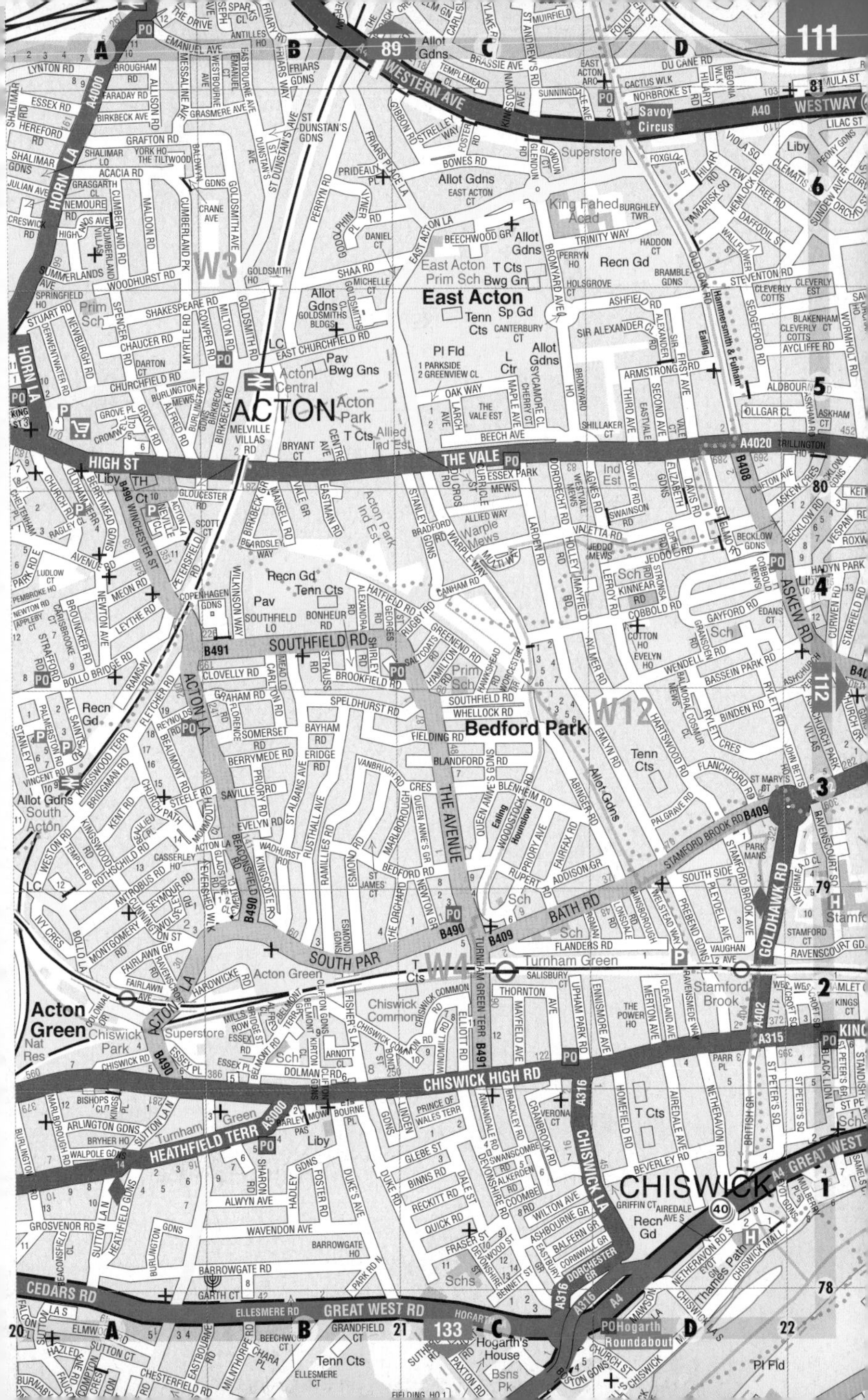
A
B
C
D
89
WESTERN AVE
A40
WESTWAY
Savoy Circus
81
EAST ACTON ARC
DU CANE RD
CACTUS WLK
NORBROKE ST
BRASSIE AVE
TEMPLEMEAD CL
ST ANDREW'S RD
KINGS DOWN AVE
HORN LA
A4000
EMANUEL AVE
LYNTON RD
BROUGHAM RD
FARADAY RD
ESSEX RD
BIRKBECK AVE
HEREFORD RD
GRAFTON RD
SHALIMAR GDNS
ACACIA RD
JULIAN AVE
GRASGARTH CL
NEMOURE RD
CRESWICK RD
SUMMERLANDS AVE
WOODHURST RD
SPRINGFIELD AVE
STUART RD
SHAKESPEARE RD
CHAUCER RD
DARTON CT
CHURCHFIELD RD
GOLDSMITH AVE
CUMBERLAND PK
MALDON RD
CRANE AVE
W3
FRIARS GDNS
ST DUNSTAN'S GDNS
ST DUNSTAN'S AVE
PERRYN RD
PRIDEAUX PL
FRIARS PLACE LA
GIBBON RD
STRELLEY WAY
BOWES RD
Allot Gdns
EAST ACTON CT
EAST ACTON LA
BEECHWOOD GR
DANIEL CT
SHAA RD
MICHELLE CT
GOLDSMITHS BLDGS
EAST CHURCHFIELD RD
East Acton Prim Sch
T Cts
Bwg Gn
East Acton
Tenn Cts
Sp Gd
CANTERBURY CT
Pl Fld
L Ctr
1 PARKSIDE
2 GREENVIEW CL
OAK WAY
THE VALE EST
BEECH AVE
Superstore
King Fahed Acad
BURGHLEY TWR
TRINITY WAY
HADDON CT
Recn Gd
PERRYN HO
HOLSGROVE CT
BROMYARD AVE
ASHFIELD RD
SIR ALEXANDER CL
ARMSTRONG RD
SHILLAKER CT
OLD OAK RD
Hammersmith & Fulham
Ealing
BRAMBLE GDNS
STEVENTON RD
CLEVERLY COTTS
CLEVERLY EST
BLAKENHAM CT
AYCLIFFE RD
SEDGEFORD RD
ALDBOURNE RD
OLLGAR CL
ASKHAM CT
WORMHOLT RD
VIOLA SQ
YEW TREE RD
HEMLOCK RD
TAMARISK SQ
DAFFODIL ST
WALLFLOWER ST
FOXGLOVE ST
CLEMATIS ST
Liby
LILAC ST
PEONY GDNS
SUNDEW AVE
ORCHID ST
5
6
ACTON
Acton Central
LC
Pav
Bwg Gns
Acton Park
T Cts
Allied Ind Est
MELVILLE VILLAS RD
BRYANT CT
HIGH ST
THE VALE
A4020
B408
TRILLINGTON HO
ESSEX PARK MEWS
DU CROS RD
CURRICLE ST
GROVE PL
CROMWELL
BURLINGTON MEWS
BIRKBECK CT
ALFRED RD
KING ST
TH
GLOUCESTER RD
SCOTT CT
B490
WINCHESTER ST
PETERSFIELD RD
ACTON LA
CHURCH RD
OLDHAM TERR
BERRYMEAD GDNS
RAGLEY CL
AVENUE RD
BIRKBECK GR
MANSELL RD
VALE GR
EASTMAN RD
Acton Park Ind Est
STANLEY GDNS
BRADFORD RD
ALLIED WAY
Warple Mews
WARPLE WAY
DORDRECHT RD
WESTVALE MEWS
AGNES RD
Ind Est
SWAINSON RD
COWLEY RD
ELIZABETH GDNS
DAVIS RD
VALETTA RD
JEDDO MEWS
JEDDO RD
BECKLOW GDNS
BECKLOW RD
COBBOLD MEWS
ASKEW CRES
CLIFTON AVE
80
ASKEW RD
HADYN PARK
VESPAN RD
CURWEN RD
STARFIELD RD
4
BEARDSLEY WAY
WILKINSON WAY
Recn Gd
Tenn Cts
COPENHAGEN GDNS
SOUTHFIELD LO
BONHEUR RD
HATFIELD RD
ALEXANDRA RD
GEORGES RD
RUGBY RD
CANHAM RD
LUDLOW CT
PEMBROKE HO
NEWTON RD
APPLEBY CT
STRAFFORD RD
BROUNCKER RD
CARISBROOKE
NEWTON AVE
MEON RD
LEYTHE RD
BOLLO BRIDGE RD
RAMSAY RD
FLETCHER RD
B491
SOUTHFIELD RD
CLOVELLY RD
CARLTON RD
MEAD LO
STRAUSS RD
SHIRLEY RD
BROOKFIELD RD
SALTCOATS RD
GREENEND RD
HAMILTON RD
Prim Sch
HAWKSHEAD RD
WORCESTER GDNS
SOUTHFIELD RD
WHELLOCK RD
SPELDHURST RD
GRAHAM RD
FLORENCE RD
REYNOLDS RD
BEAUMONT RD
SOMERSET RD
BERRYMEDE RD
BAYHAM RD
ERIDGE RD
FIELDING RD
Bedford Park
BLANDFORD RD
W12
Tenn Cts
COBBOLD RD
KINNEAR RD
STRONSA RD
LEFROY RD
MAYFIELD RD
HOLLEY RD
COTTON HO
EVELYN HO
AYLMER RD
EMLYN RD
HARTSWOOD RD
WENDELL RD
BASSEIN PARK RD
GAYFORD RD
GRANSDEN RD
EDANS CT
BALMORAL MEWS
COSMUR CL
BINDEN RD
RYLETT CRES
RYLETT RD
ASHCHURCH GR
ASHCHURCH VILLAS
JOHN BETTS
112
FLANCHFORD RD
ST MARY'S CT
3
Allot Gdns
Recn Gd
ALL SAINTS RD
PALMERSTON RD
STANLEY RD
VINCENT RD
KINGSWOOD TERR
BRIDGMAN RD
CHURCH PATH
STEELE RD
SAVILLE RD
PRIORY RD
EVELYN RD
KENT RD
KINGSWOOD RD
Allot Gdns
South Acton
WESTON RD
TEMPLE RD
ROTHSCHILD RD
BEAULIEU PL
MONMOUTH CT
ST ALBANS AVE
RUSTHALL AVE
RAMILLIES RD
WADHURST RD
KINGSCOTE RD
BEACONSFIELD RD
GLADSTONE RD
CASSERLEY HO
ANTROBUS RD
SEYMOUR RD
CUNNINGTON ST
WOLSEY
EVERSHED WLK
VANBRUGH RD
MARLBOROUGH CRES
QUEEN ANNE'S GR
QUEEN ANNE'S GDNS
ESMOND RD
ST JAMES' CT
BEDFORD RD
NEWTON GR
THE ORCHARD
THE AVENUE
BLENHEIM RD
WOODSTOCK RD
Ealing
Hounslow
PRIORY AVE
ABINGER RD
RUPERT RD
FAIRFAX RD
ADDISON GR
Allot Gdns
PALGRAVE RD
STAMFORD BROOK RD
B409
PARK MANS
SOUTH SIDE
PLEYDELL AVE
STAMFORD BROOK AVE
GOLDHAWK RD
WERMEAD CL
79
Stamford
MONTGOMERY RD
IVY CRES
BOLLO LA
LC
FAIRLAWN GR
FAIRLAWN AVE
RAVENSCROFT RD
SOUTH PAR
Acton Green
HARDWICKE RD
ESMOND GDNS
B490
B409
BATH RD
Sch
FLANDERS RD
GAINSBOROUGH RD
WELSTEAD WAY
PREBEND GDNS
VAUGHAN AVE
STAMFORD CT
RAVENSCOURT GD
W4
Turnham Green
T Cts
SALISBURY CT
Stamford Brook
THORNTON AVE
UPHAM PARK RD
ENNISMORE AVE
THE POWER HO
MERTON AVE
CLEVELAND AVE
RAVENSMEDE WAY
A402
2
KINGS CT
Acton Green
Nat Res
Chiswick Park
Superstore
COLONIAL DR
MILLS ROW
BRIDGE ST
ESSEX PL
BELMONT RD
BELMONT TERR
CLIFTON GDNS
KIRTON CL
ARNOTT CL
Chiswick Common
CHISWICK COMMON RD
FISHER'S LA
ELLIOTT RD
WINDMILL RD
TURNHAM GREEN TERR
MAYFIELD AVE
A315
CHISWICK WR RD
DOLMAN RD
CHISWICK HIGH RD
BISHOPS CL
ARLINGTON GDNS
BRYHER HO
WALPOLE GDNS
Turnham Green
HEATHFIELD TERR
A3000
BARLEY MOW PAS
BOURNE PL
Liby
PRINCE OF WALES TERR
GLEBE ST
BINNS RD
RECKITT RD
QUICK RD
DALE ST
FRASER ST
DEVONSHIRE RD
SWANSCOMBE RD
ALKERDEN RD
COOMBE RD
WILTON AVE
ASHBOURNE GR
BALFERN GR
CORNWALL GR
VERONA CT
A316
CHISWICK LA
HOMEFIELD RD
T Cts
AIREDALE AVE
NETHERAVON RD
BEVERLEY RD
PARR PL
BRITISH GR
ST PETER'S SQ
ST PETER'S GR
BLACK LION LA
CHISWICK
1
A4
GREAT WEST
40
GRIFFIN CT
AIREDALE AVE S
Recn Gd
NETHERAVON RD S
EYOT GN
Thames Path
CHISWICK MALL
MULBERRY PL
MARLBOROUGH RD
BURLINGTON RD
SUTTON LA N
HEATHFIELD GDNS
GROSVENOR RD
BEACONSFIELD CL
SHARON RD
ALWYN AVE
HADLEY GDNS
FOSTER RD
DUKE'S AVE
DUKE RD
WAVENDON AVE
BARROWGATE HO
BARROWGATE RD
GARTH CT
PARK RD N
BENNETT ST
DORCHESTER GR
Schs
78
CEDARS RD
ELLESMERE RD
GREAT WEST RD
HOGARTH
Hogarth Roundabout
MAWSON LA
CHISWICK LA S
20
21
22
133
FALCON
ELMWOOD
HAZLEDENE RD
SUTTON CT
BURNABY
COMPTON
CHESTERFIELD RD
EASTBOURNE
MILNTHORPE RD
CHARA PL
BEECHWOOD CT
GRANDFIELD CT
Tenn Cts
ELLESMERE CT
SUTHERLAND
PAXTON RD
Hogarth's House
Bsns Pk
CHURCH ST
CHISWICK
BOSTON GDNS
Pl Fld
FIELDING HO

Queen Charlottes & Chelsea
WESTWAY
White City
Shepherd's Bush
Wormholt Park
UXBRIDGE RD
GOLDHAWK RD
HAMMERSMITH
Brook Green
KING ST
GREAT WEST RD
Hammersmith Flyover
River Thames
Thames Path
W12
W6
W14
W11
BBC Television Ctr
Westfield Ctr (Under Construction)
Shepherd's Bush Common
Ravenscourt Park
HAMMERSMITH BRIDGE
FULHAM PALACE RD
SHEPHERD'S BUSH RD
WOOD LA
WEST CROSS ROUTE
Charing Cross
St Paul's Sch

90
111
134

Notting Hill
KENSINGTON
Holland Park
West Kensington
Earl's Court
West Brompton
Kensington Palace
Olympia Ex Ctr
Earl's Court Ex Ctr
The Queen's Club
Bayswater
High Street Kensington
Kensington Olympia
HOLLAND PARK AVE
NOTTING HILL GATE
KENSINGTON HIGH ST
KENSINGTON CHURCH ST
HAMMERSMITH RD
CROMWELL RD
WEST CROMWELL RD
TALGARTH RD
OLD BROMPTON RD
NORTH END RD
EARL'S COURT RD
WARWICK RD
HOLLAND RD
LADBROKE GR
KENSINGTON PARK RD
PEMBRIDGE VILLAS
QUEENSWAY

Bayswater
Kensington Gardens
Hyde Park
The Serpentine
The Long Water
Round Pond
Knightsbridge
Brompton
South Kensington
CHELSEA
W2
W8
SW7
SW3
SW10
Marble Arch
Speakers' Corner
BAYSWATER RD
KENSINGTON RD
KNIGHTSBRIDGE
CROMWELL RD
BROMPTON RD
OLD BROMPTON RD
FULHAM RD
KING'S RD
SLOANE ST
GLOUCESTER RD
QUEENSWAY
Natural History Mus
Science Mus
Victoria & Albert Mus
Royal Albert Hall
Albert Meml
Brompton Oratory
Royal Marsden
Royal Brompton
Saatchi Gal
Duke of York's HQ
Burton's Court
Serpentine Gall
The Lido
Diana Princess of Wales Memorial Fountain
Diana Princess of Wales Memorial Walk
Ranger's Lodge
Serpentine Lodge
New Lodge
Temple Lodge
Serpentine Bridge
Holocaust Memorial
The Dell
Edinburgh Gate
Alexandra Gate
Queen's Gate
Palace Gate
Lancaster Gate
Victoria Gate
Marlborough Gate
246
92
247
256
136
257
113
A
B
C
D
1
2
3
4
5
6

MARYLEBONE
248
93
249
A
B
C
D
OXFORD ST
PORTMAN ST
ORCHARD ST
DUKE ST
Mus
Coll
Govt Offices
NEW BOND ST
CONDUIT ST
REGENT ST A4201
CARNABY ST
Berwick St
WARDOUR ST
OLD COMPTON ST
CAMBRIDGE CIR
CHARING CROSS RD
SHAFTESBURY AVE
GERRARD ST
CRANBOURN ST
LISLE ST
Leicester Square
NORTH ROW
GREEN ST
LEES PL
UPPER BROOK ST
GROSVENOR ST
Grosvenor Sq Gardens
BROOK'S MEWS
GROSVENOR HILL
BRUTON ST
CLIFFORD ST
SAVILE ROW
OLD BURLINGTON ST
BURLINGTON VIGO ST
GLASSHOUSE ST
Piccadilly Circus
PICCADILLY CIR
A4201
Eros
HAYMARKET
National Gallery
ORANGE ST
WILLIAM IV ST
Mayfair
MOUNT ST
SOUTH AUDLEY ST
Liby
Sch
PARK LA
40
REEVES MEWS
ADAM'S ROW
BERKELEY SQ
HAY HILL
DOVER ST
ALBEMARLE ST
OLD BOND ST
Royal Academy of Arts
JERMYN ST
CHARLES II ST
B327
PALL MALL E
TRAFALGAR
Nelson's Mon
Charing Cross
COCKSPUR ST
PICCADILLY
A4
ST JAMES'S ST
St James
PALL MALL
CARLTON HOUSE TERR
Admiralty Arch
Art Galls
Govt Offices
Horse Guards Parade
WHITEHALL
5
6
CHESTERFIELD HILL
CHARLES ST
CLARGES ST
HALF MOON ST
BOLTON ST
STRATTON ST
CURZON ST
SHEPHERD ST
HERTFORD ST
WHITE HORSE ST
Green Park
Diana Princess of Wales Memorial Walk
Bndstd
LOVER'S WALK
BROAD WLK
A4202
Hyde Park Corner
QUEEN'S WLK
Mus
St James's Palace
Clarence House
MARLBOROUGH RD
STABLE YD RD
THE MALL (CLOSED TO TRAFFIC ON SUNDAYS)
SW1
Duck Island
Diana Princess of Wales Memorial Walk
St James's Park Lake
HORSE GUARDS RD
DOWNING ST
Govt Offices
80
KING CHARLES ST
Cabinet War Rooms & Churchill Mus
A3214
PARLIAMENT ST
4
Horse Ride
CONSTITUTION HILL (CLOSED TO TRAFFIC ON SUNDAYS)
Queen Victoria Meml
St James's Park
GREAT GEORGE ST
Buckingham Palace Gardens
WESTMINSTER
BIRDCAGE WLK
Guildhall
PARLIAMENT SQ
A302
116
Buckingham Palace
Queens Gall
Wellington Barracks
Mus
Govt Offices
Meth Hall
TOTHILL ST
BUCKINGHAM GATE
B323
PETTY FRANCE
BROADWAY
St James's Park
New Scotland Yard
THE SANCTUARY
Westminster Abbey
The Royal Mews
A3217
A3214
CAXTON ST
Govt Offices
VICTORIA ST
GREAT SMITH ST
B326
ABBEY ORCHARD ST
GREAT COLLEGE ST
3
GREAT PETER ST
WILTON CRES
B310
GROSVENOR CRES
A302
GROSVENOR PL
BELGRAVE SQ
Tenn Ct
HALKIN ST
CHAPEL ST
UPPER BELGRAVE ST
LR GROSVENOR PL
BRESSENDEN PL
GROSVENOR GDNS
Victoria
A3215
BUCKINGHAM PALACE RD
A302
A202
WILTON RD
HOWICK PL
ASHLEY PL
Cath
Schs
CARLISLE PL
MORPETH TERR
ROCHESTER ROW
B324
GREYCOAT PL
HORSEFERRY RD
MARSHAM ST
Govt Offices
79
B323
B319
WEST HALKIN ST
LOWNDES ST
EATON SQ
A3213
ECCLESTON ST
ELIZABETH ST
CHESTER SQ
EBURY ST
Victoria
Passport Off
FRANCIS ST
VINCENT SQ
Tenn Cts
Pl Fld
PAGE ST
Govt Offices
THORNEY ST
2
CADOGAN LA
CLIVEDEN PL
SLOANE SQ
Sloane Square
Belgravia
Victoria Coach
Liby
Govt Offices
VAUXHALL BRIDGE RD
B324
BELGRAVE RD
WARWICK WAY
JOHN ISLIP ST
Tate Britain
B326
ATTERBURY ST
MILLBANK
PIMLICO RD
B313
B324
EBURY BRIDGE RD
Sch
CHURTON ST
TACHBROOK ST
Pimlico
Liby
BESSBOROUGH ST
A3213
BESSBOROUGH GDNS
A3212
A202
1
LOWER SLOANE ST
A3214
B302
Chelsea Barracks
City of Westminster
Kensington & Chelsea
CHELSEA BRIDGE RD
Royal Hospital (Army Pensioners)
Pimlico
LUPUS ST
Pimlico Sch
CHICHESTER ST
ST GEORGE'S SQ
AYLESFORD ST
30
VAUXHALL BRIDGE
Wharves
78
Ranelagh Gardens (Site of Chelsea Flower Show)
Lister
Dock
Tenn Cts
CHURCHILL GARDENS RD
DOLPHIN SQ
CLAVERTON ST
A3212
28
A
258
B
29
137
C
259
D
30
CHELSEA EMBANKMENT
CHELSEA BRIDGE
GROSVENOR BRIDGE
GROSVENOR RD
Wharves
Tenn Ct
Wharf
A3205
River Thames
City of Westminster
Wandsworth
Battersea
New Covent Garden

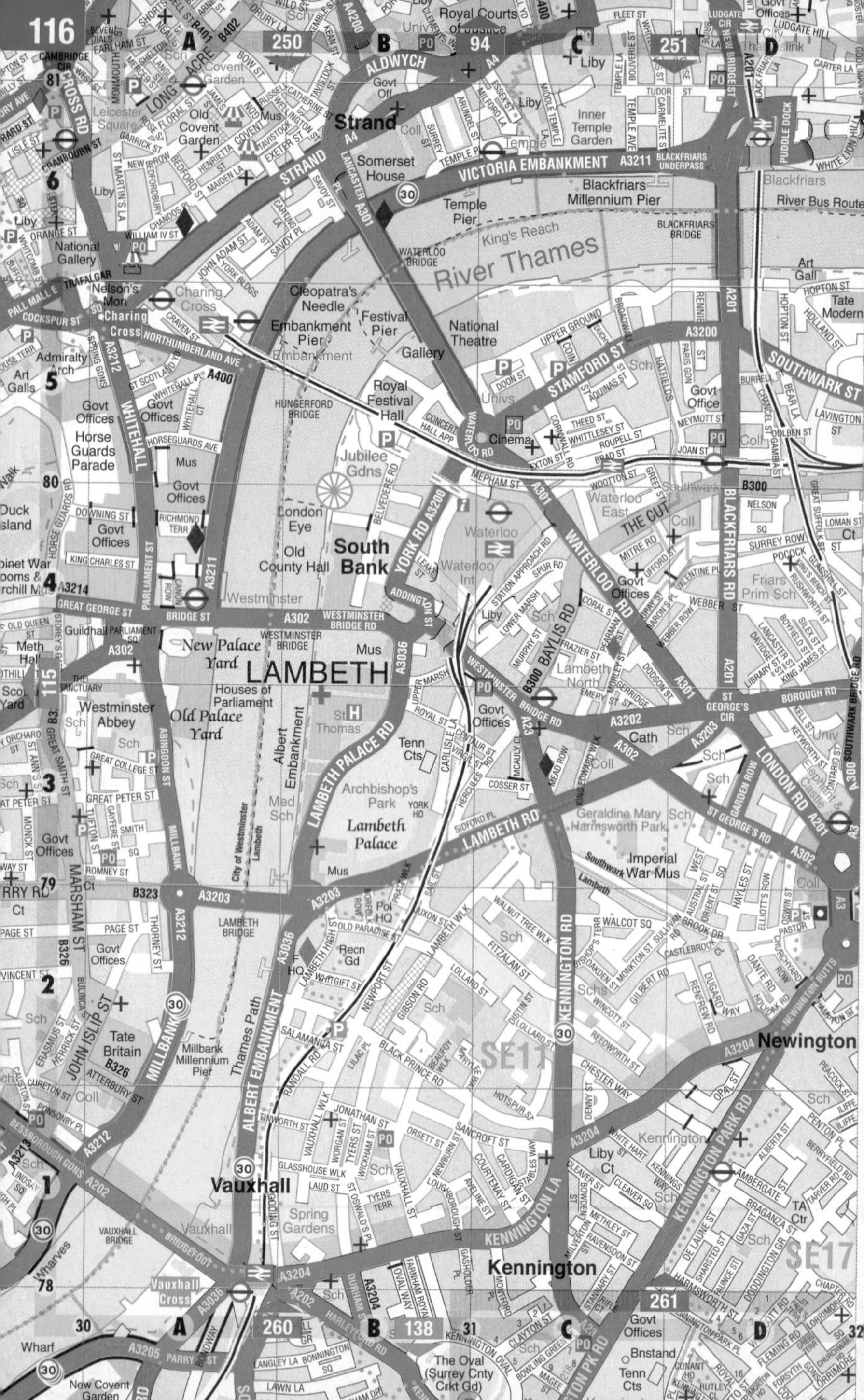
Strand
Aldwych
Victoria Embankment
River Thames
Blackfriars Millennium Pier
National Gallery
Charing Cross
Westminster
Westminster Abbey
Houses of Parliament
LAMBETH
South Bank
London Eye
Waterloo
Lambeth Palace
Imperial War Mus
Tate Britain
Vauxhall
Kennington
Newington
The Oval (Surrey Cnty Crkt Gd)
SE11
SE17

Whitechapel
A
B
C
D
252
95
EC4
EC3
CITY OF LONDON
St Paul's Cath
Mansion House
Cannon Street
Bank
Lloyds Bldg
Swiss Re Bldg
Aldgate
Fenchurch Street
Tower Hill
Tower Gateway
Monument
EASTCHEAP
UPPER THAMES ST
LOWER THAMES ST
BYWARD ST
TOWER HILL
ROYAL MINT ST
EAST SMITHFIELD
MINORIES
CHEAPSIDE
CORNHILL
LEADENHALL ST
FENCHURCH ST
GREAT TOWER ST
ARTHUR ST
MONUMENT ST
QUEEN VICTORIA ST
CANNON ST
MILLENNIUM FOOTBRIDGE
Bankside Pier
BANKSIDE
The Globe Theatre
SOUTHWARK BRIDGE
SOUTHWARK BRIDGE RD
Swan Lane Pier
City of London
Southwark
LONDON BRIDGE
Custom House
Thames Path
The Tower
Tower Millennium Pier
Traitors Gate
TOWER BRIDGE
The London Dungeon
London Bridge City Pier
London Bridge
TOOLEY ST
City Hall
Upper Pool
St Katharine Docks
East Dock
St Katharine's Pier
Tower Hamlets
Butler's Wharf Pier
Tower Bridge Wharf
Jetty
SHAD THAMES
253
80
E1
SOUTHWARK ST
Borough
Cath
Guy's
THOMAS ST
UNION ST
The Borough
BOROUGH HIGH ST
MARSHALSEA RD
Liby
Govt Offices
LONG LA
BERMONDSEY ST
Bermondsey Leather Mkt
CRUCIFIX LA
DRUID ST
TOWER BRIDGE RD
BERMONDSEY
Sterling Sta
BERMONDSEY WALL W
JAMAICA RD
ABBEY ST
118
4
5
6
GREAT DOVER ST
Fball Gd
Crown Cts
SE1
HARPER RD
Caledonian Market
GRANGE RD
SE16
3
Elephant & Castle
NEW KENT RD
Bricklayers Arms
Elephant & Castle
DEACON WAY
HEYGATE ST
RODNEY RD
MANDELA WAY
DUNTON RD
OLD KENT RD
Superstore
ROLLS RD
263
2
79
1
78
WALWORTH RD
Walworth
EAST ST
PORTLAND ST
BAGSHOT ST
262
139
33
34
Cobourg Prim Sch
Burgess Park
Pl Fld
TRAFALGAR AV
Surrey Wharf
John Ruskin
ALBANY RD

96
Shadwell
CABLE ST
THE HIGHWAY
Ratcliff
Free Trade Wharf
St George in the East
Tobacco Dock Sh Vill
Shadwell New Basin
London Docks
Shadwell Old Basin
Shadwell Entrance
E1
East Dock
St Katharine Docks
253
St Katharine Pier
Metropolitan Wharf
New Crane Wharf
Lower Pool
Wapping
Thames Path
Surrey Entrance
Tower Bridge Wharf
Butler's Wharf Pier
Wapping Pier Head
Wapping Old Stairs
King Henry's Wharves
Wapping Pier
River Thames
Upper Pool
River Bus Route
Sterling Wharf Stairs
Cherry Garden Pier
BERMONDSEY
Rotherhithe
JAMAICA RD
117
SE16
Canada Water
King George's Field
Surrey Quays Sh Ctr
Mulberry Bsns Ctr
Albion Channel
Tower Bridge Bsns Complex
Tower Bridge Bsns Sq
St Joseph's RC Prim Sch
Southwark Park
Sports Complex
SOUTHWARK PARK RD
RAYMOUTH RD
LOWER RD
263
SE1
Paterson Park
Admiral Hyson Ind Est
Bermondsey Trad Est
South Bermondsey
ROTHERHITHE NEW RD
ROLLS RD
CATLIN ST
The New Den (Millwall FC)
Orion Bsns Ctr
British Wharf Ind Est
Works
OLD KENT RD
Wevco Wharf
Excelsior Ind Est
140
Canal Bridge
Cantium Ret Pk
Sandgate Trad Est
Kent Pk Ind Est
Elizabeth Ind Est
1 HYNDMAN ST
2 MURDOCK ST
3 SKENFRITH HO
4 SARNESFIELD HO

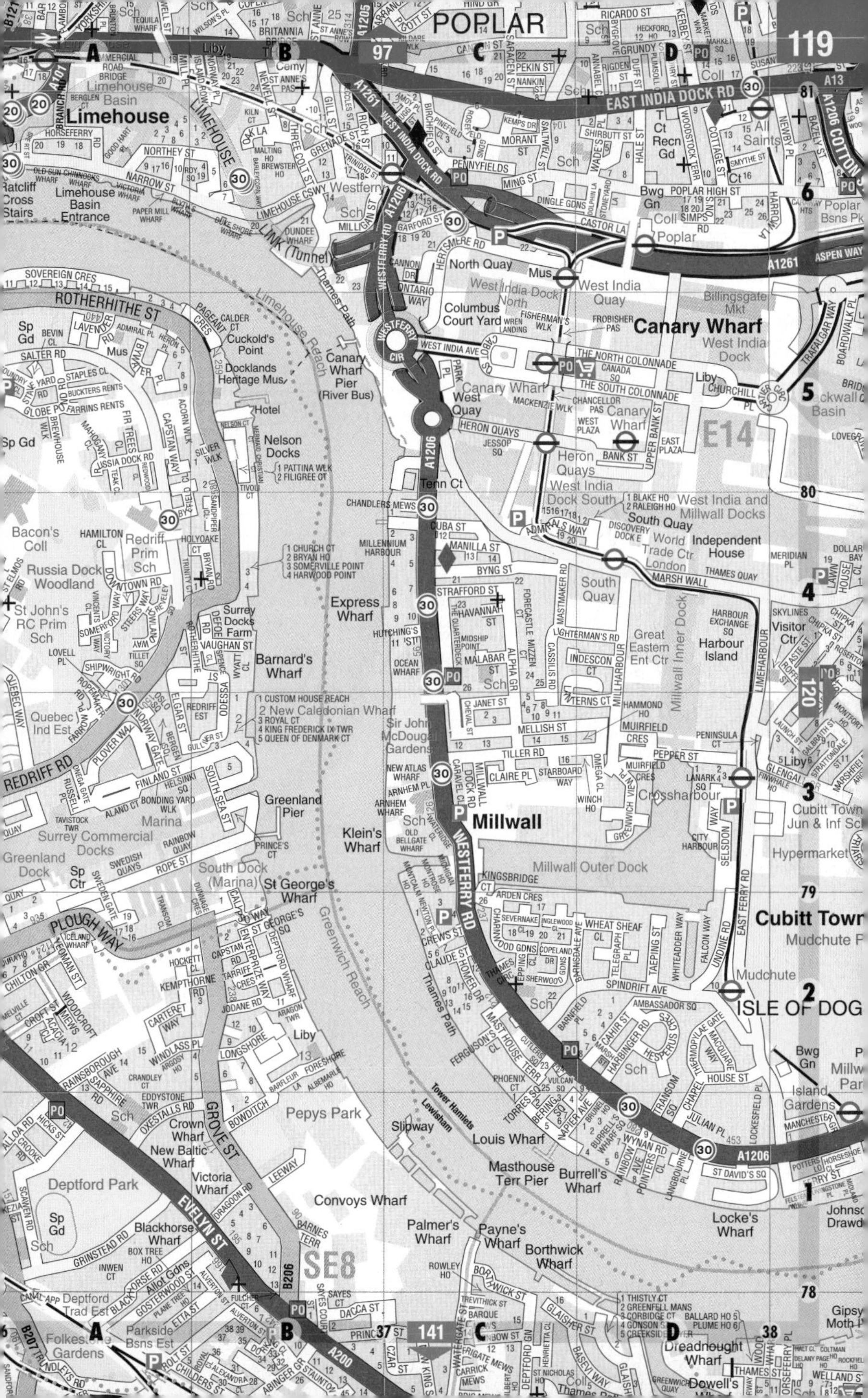
119
POPLAR
97
141
A
B
C
D
1
2
3
4
5
6
78
79
80
81
Limehouse
Limehouse Basin
Limehouse Basin Entrance
Ratcliff Cross Stairs
EAST INDIA DOCK RD
WEST INDIA DOCK RD
POPLAR HIGH ST
Canary Wharf
West India Quay
North Quay
West India Dock North
Columbus Court Yard
Canary Wharf Pier (River Bus)
Westferry
WESTFERRY CIR
Billingsgate Mkt
West India Dock
THE NORTH COLONNADE
THE SOUTH COLONNADE
Heron Quays
West India Dock South
West India and Millwall Docks
South Quay
Independent House
MARSH WALL
E14
Millwall Inner Dock
Harbour Island
Great Eastern Ent Ctr
Crossharbour
Millwall
Millwall Outer Dock
WESTFERRY RD
Mudchute
ISLE OF DOG
Cubitt Town
Mudchute P
Island Gardens
Locke's Wharf
Burrell's Wharf
Masthouse Terr Pier
Louis Wharf
Slipway
Greenwich Reach
Limehouse Reach
Thames Path
Tower Hamlets
Lewisham
ROTHERHITHE ST
Cuckold's Point
Docklands Heritage Mus
Nelson Docks
Surrey Docks Farm
Barnard's Wharf
Russia Dock Woodland
Bacon's Coll
Redriff Prim Sch
St John's RC Prim Sch
Quebec Ind Est
REDRIFF RD
Surrey Commercial Docks
Greenland Dock
Greenland Pier
South Dock (Marina)
St George's Wharf
PLOUGH WAY
GROVE ST
EVELYN ST
Pepys Park
Deptford Park
Convoys Wharf
Crown Wharf
New Baltic Wharf
Victoria Wharf
Blackhorse Wharf
Palmer's Wharf
Payne's Wharf
Borthwick Wharf
SE8
Deptford Trad Est
Folkestone Gardens
Parkside Bsns Est
Dreadnought Wharf
Dowell's
Express Wharf
Klein's Wharf
Sir John McDougal Gardens
Hypermarket
Cubitt Town Jun & Inf Sch
A1206
A1261
A13
A200
B206
120

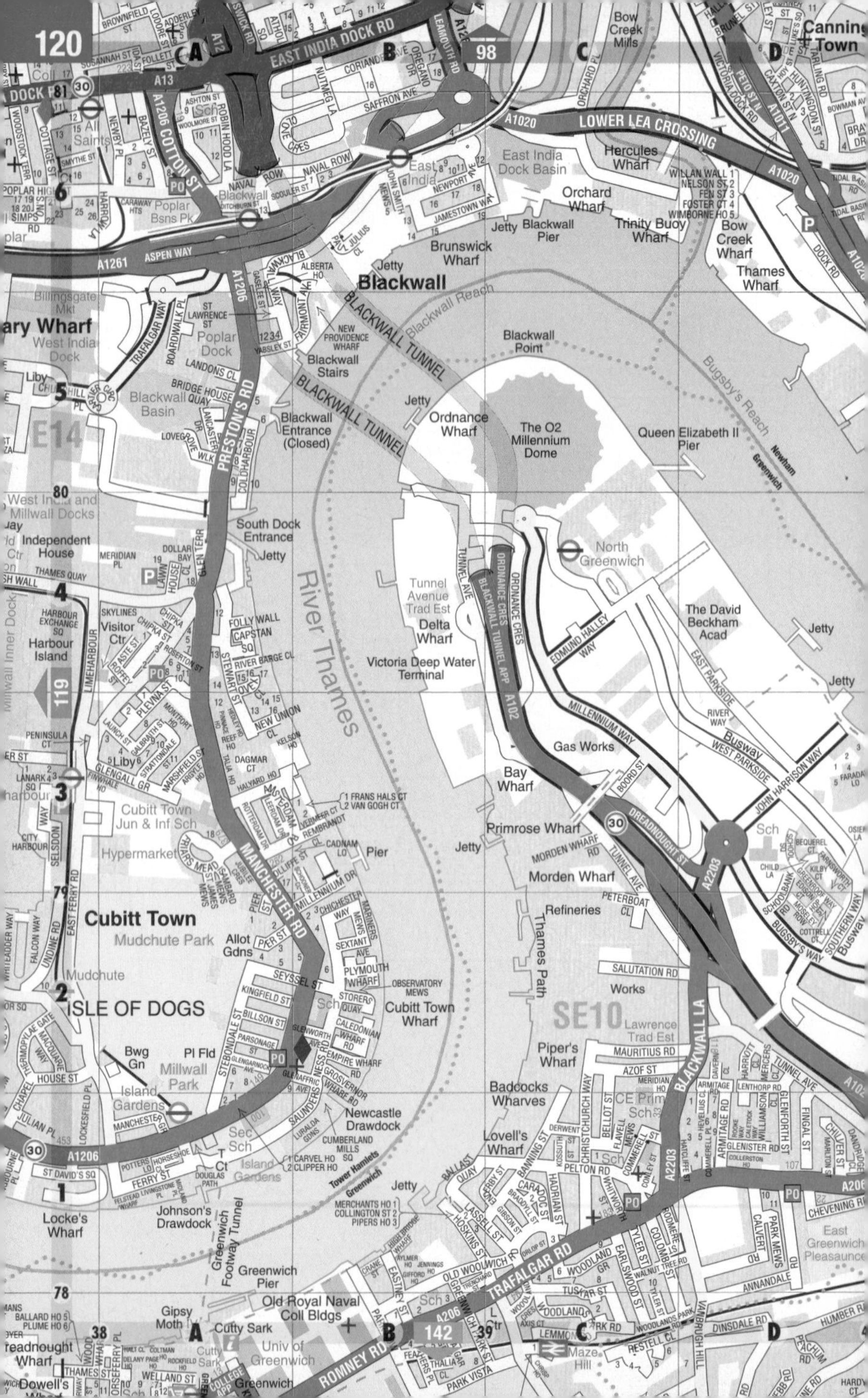

120
A
B
C
D
98
EAST INDIA DOCK RD
A13
A12
Canning Town
Bow Creek Mills
LOWER LEA CROSSING
A1020
A1011
Hercules Wharf
East India Dock Basin
East India
Orchard Wharf
Trinity Buoy Wharf
Bow Creek Wharf
Thames Wharf
Blackwall Pier
Brunswick Wharf
Blackwall
All Saints
COTTON ST
A1206
Poplar Bsns Pk
Blackwall
NAVAL ROW
ASPEN WAY
A1261
Billingsgate Mkt
ary Wharf
West India Dock
Poplar Dock
PRESTON'S RD
Blackwall Basin
Blackwall Stairs
BLACKWALL TUNNEL
Blackwall Entrance (Closed)
Blackwall Reach
Blackwall Point
Ordnance Wharf
The O2 Millennium Dome
Queen Elizabeth II Pier
Bugsby's Reach
Newham
Greenwich
E14
West India and Millwall Docks
Independent House
South Dock Entrance
River Thames
Tunnel Avenue Trad Est
Delta Wharf
Victoria Deep Water Terminal
North Greenwich
The David Beckham Acad
EDMUND HALLEY WAY
MILLENNIUM WAY
Gas Works
Busway
WEST PARKSIDE
JOHN HARRISON WAY
Bay Wharf
Primrose Wharf
A102
DREADNOUGHT ST
A2203
Harbour Island
Visitor Ctr
Millwall Inner Dock
119
Liby
Cubitt Town Jun & Inf Sch
Hypermarket
MANCHESTER RD
Morden Wharf
Refineries
Thames Path
Cubitt Town
Mudchute Park
Allot Gdns
Mudchute
ISLE OF DOGS
Cubitt Town Wharf
SE10
Lawrence Trad Est
Piper's Wharf
BLACKWALL LA
Bwg Gn
Pl Fld
Millwall Park
Island Gardens
Newcastle Drawdock
Badcocks Wharves
Lovell's Wharf
CE Prim Sch
A1206
Locke's Wharf
Johnson's Drawdock
Greenwich Footway Tunnel
Tower Hamlets
Greenwich
Greenwich Pier
TRAFALGAR RD
East Greenwich Pleasaunce
Old Royal Naval Coll Bldgs
Gipsy Moth
Cutty Sark
Univ of Greenwich
142
ROMNEY RD
A206
Maze Hill
Greenwich

Custom House
Silvertown
GREENWICH
New Charlton
Charlton
River Thames
Royal Victoria Dock
E16
SE7
SE10
SE3
ExCeL Ex Ctr
The Thames Barrier
Thames Barrier Visitor Ctr
Thames Barrier Park
Woolwich Reach
Bugsby's Reach
Maryon Park
Maryon Wilson Park
The Valley (Charlton Athletic FC)
NORTH WOOLWICH RD
WOOLWICH RD
CONNAUGHT RD
CONNAUGHT BRIDGE
CHARLTON PARK RD
London City Airport
99
122
143

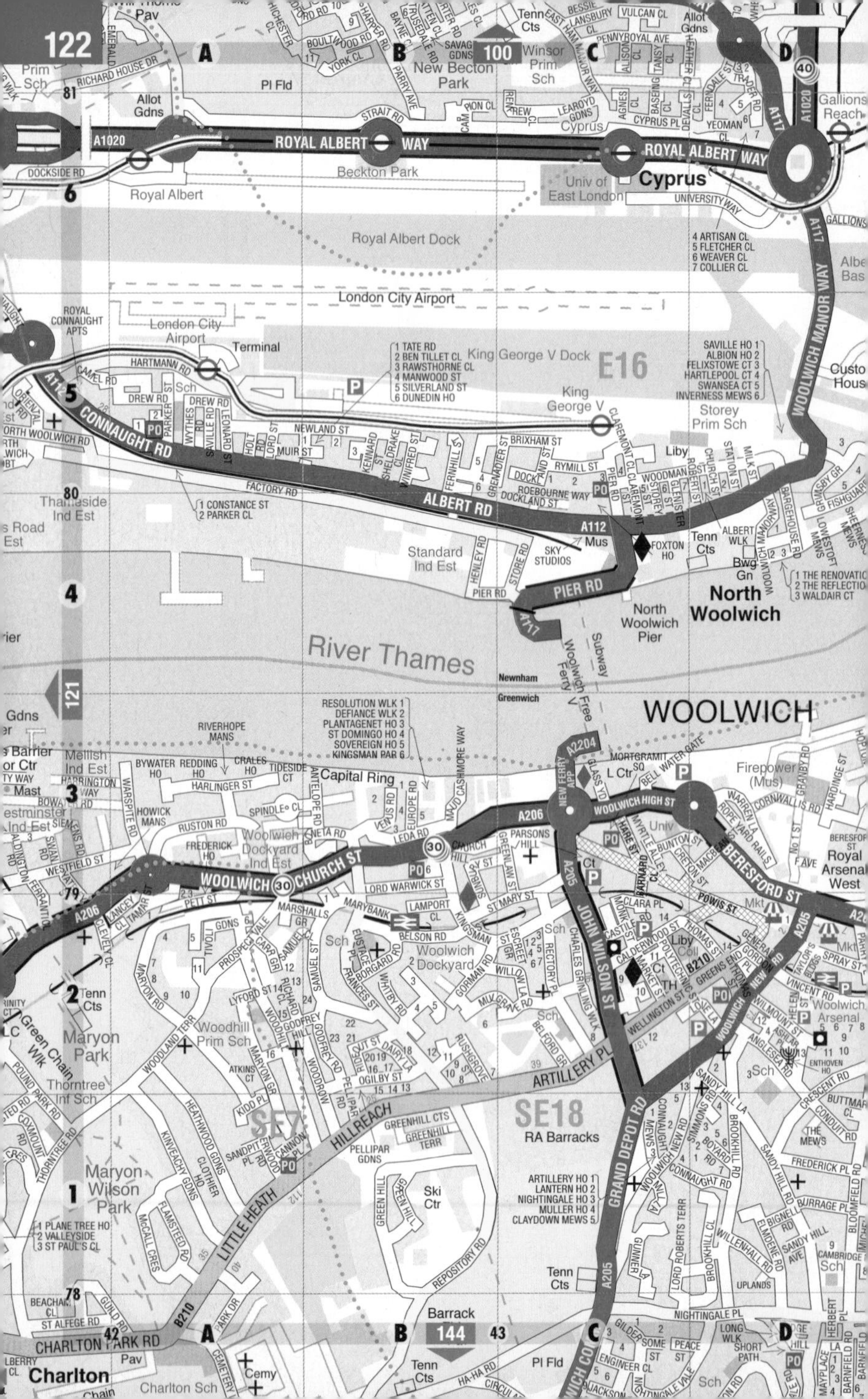

Royal Albert Way
Beckton Park
Royal Albert
Cyprus
Univ of East London
Royal Albert Dock
London City Airport
King George V Dock
E16
King George V
Connaught Rd
Albert Rd
Woolwich Manor Way
Pier Rd
North Woolwich
North Woolwich Pier
River Thames
Woolwich Free Ferry
Subway
WOOLWICH
Woolwich Church St
Woolwich High St
Beresford St
John Wilson St
Grand Depot Rd
Artillery Pl
Hillreach
Little Heath
Woolwich Dockyard
Maryon Park
Maryon Wilson Park
SE7
SE18
RA Barracks
Royal Arsenal West
Woolwich Arsenal
Firepower (Mus)
Charlton Park Rd
Charlton
Thameside Ind Est
Standard Ind Est
Woolwich Dockyard Ind Est
Capital Ring
Ski Ctr
Barrack
100
121
144

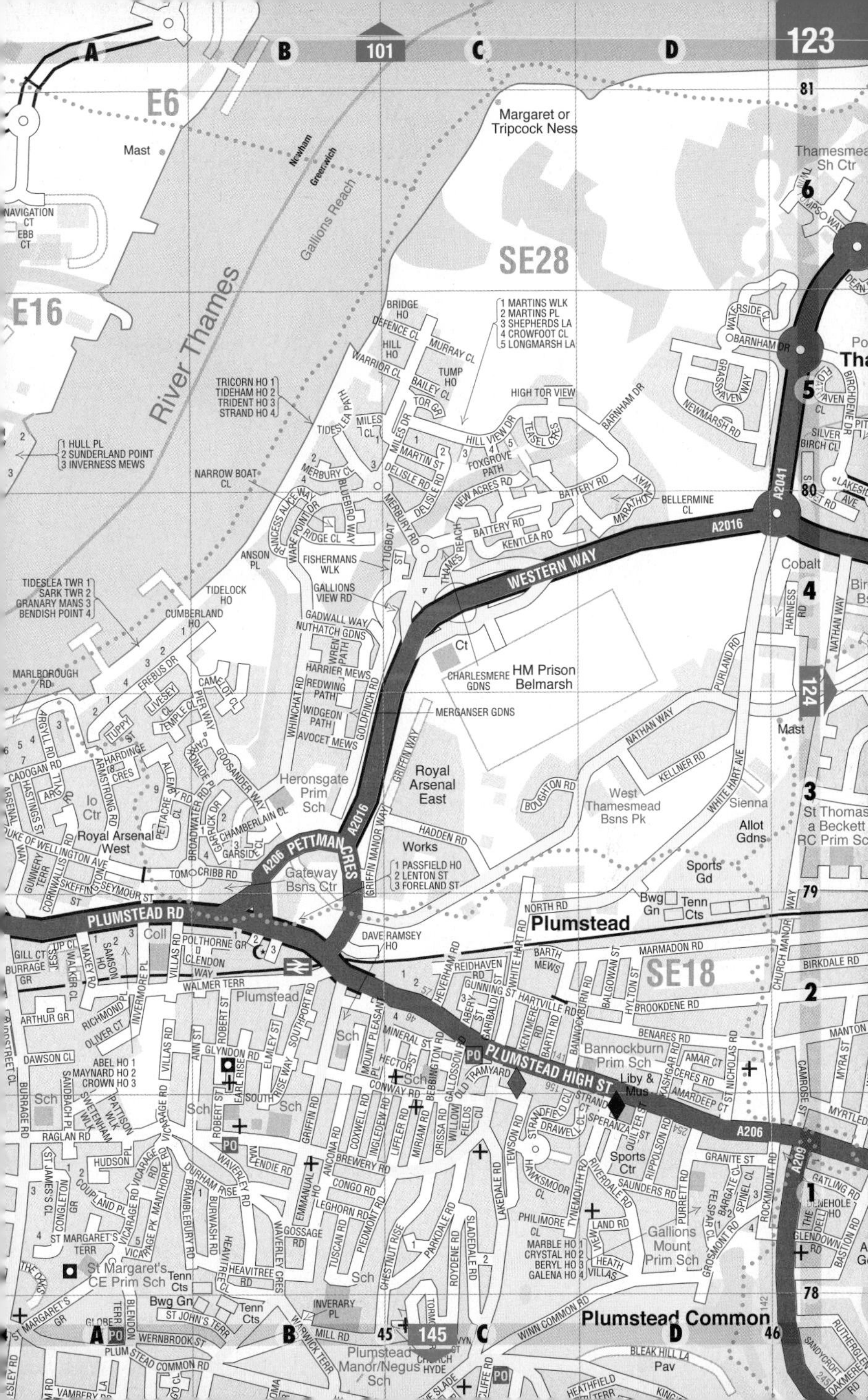

A
B
101
C
D
E6
E16
SE28
SE18
River Thames
Gallions Reach
Margaret or Tripcock Ness
Thamesmead Sh Ctr
HM Prison Belmarsh
Royal Arsenal East
Royal Arsenal West
West Thamesmead Bsns Pk
Plumstead
Plumstead Common
PLUMSTEAD RD
PLUMSTEAD HIGH ST
WESTERN WAY
PETTMAN CRES
124
145

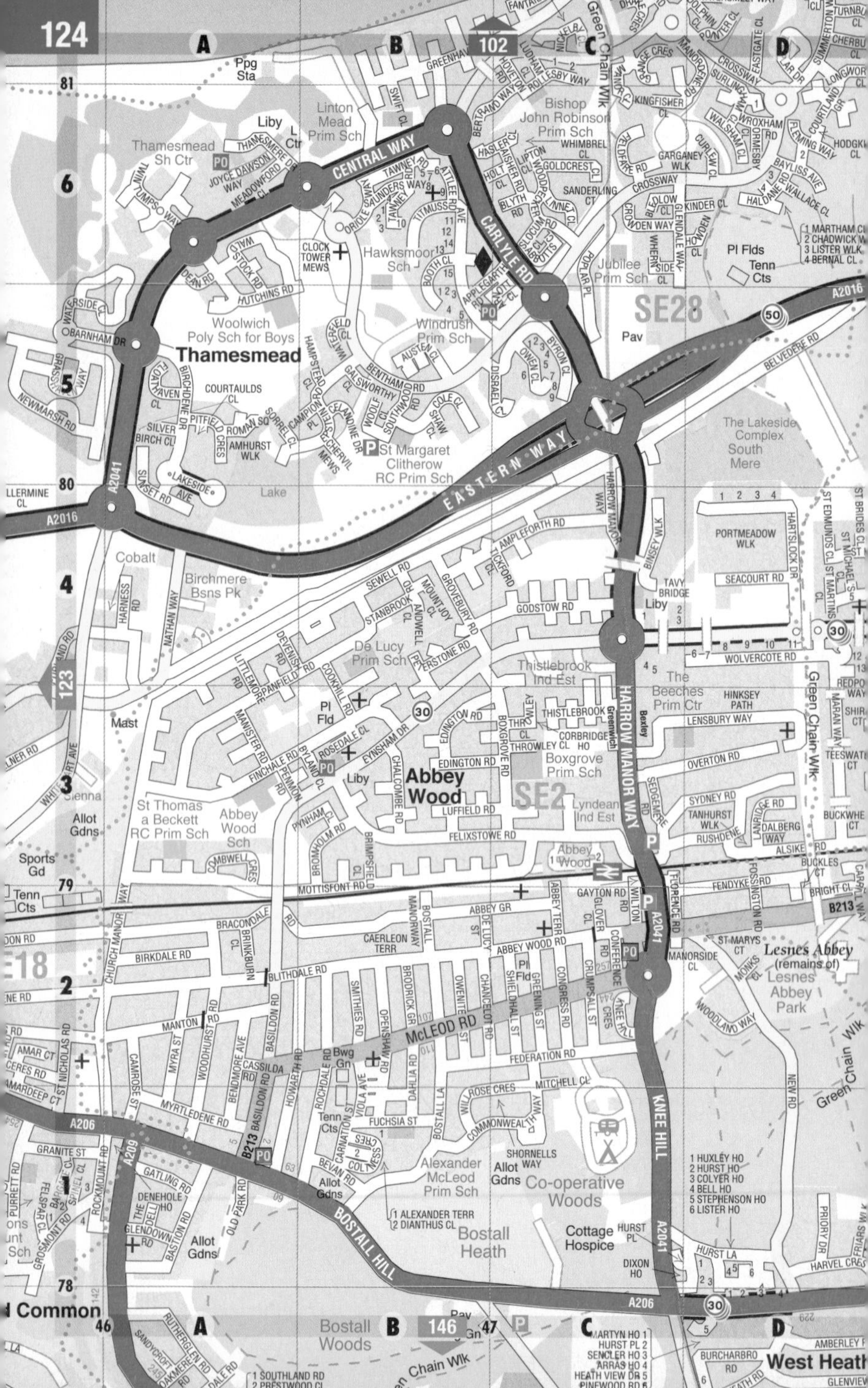
A
B
C
D
102
Thamesmead
Thamesmead Sh Ctr
Woolwich Poly Sch for Boys
Linton Mead Prim Sch
Bishop John Robinson Prim Sch
Hawksmoor Sch
Windrush Prim Sch
St Margaret Clitherow RC Prim Sch
Jubilee Prim Sch
SE28
CENTRAL WAY
CARLYLE RD
EASTERN WAY
A2016
A2041
HARROW MANOR WAY
The Lakeside Complex South Mere
Birchmere Bsns Pk
Cobalt
De Lucy Prim Sch
Thistlebrook Ind Est
The Beeches Prim Ctr
Abbey Wood
SE2
Boxgrove Prim Sch
Lyndean Ind Est
St Thomas a Beckett RC Prim Sch
Abbey Wood Sch
SE18
McLEOD RD
Lesnes Abbey (remains of)
Lesnes Abbey Park
Alexander McLeod Prim Sch
Co-operative Woods
Bostall Heath
Cottage Hospice
BOSTALL HILL
KNEE HILL
A206
A209
B213
Green Chain Wlk
Bostall Woods
West Heath
146
123
81
80
79
78
6
5
4
3
2
1
46
47

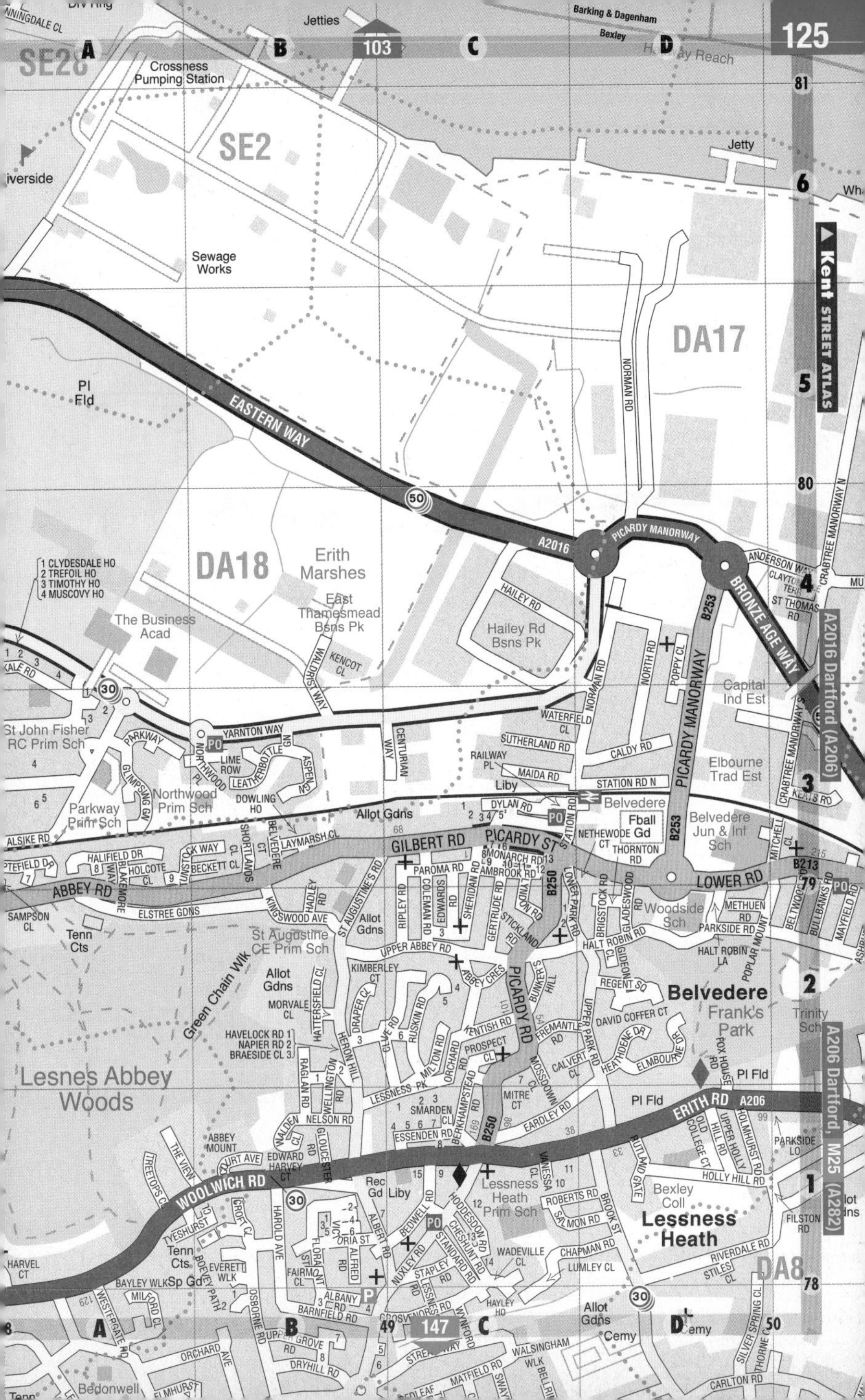
SE28
SE2
DA17
DA18
DA8
Jetties
Crossness Pumping Station
Sewage Works
Jetty
Barking & Dagenham
Bexley
Halfway Reach
Riverside
Pl Fld
EASTERN WAY
A2016
PICARDY MANORWAY
BRONZE AGE WAY
NORMAN RD
Erith Marshes
East Thamesmead Bsns Pk
Hailey Rd Bsns Pk
The Business Acad
Capital Ind Est
Elbourne Trad Est
1 CLYDESDALE HO
2 TREFOIL HO
3 TIMOTHY HO
4 MUSCOVY HO
St John Fisher RC Prim Sch
Parkway Prim Sch
Northwood Prim Sch
YARNTON WAY
Belvedere
Fball Gd
Belvedere Jun & Inf Sch
GILBERT RD
PICARDY ST
LOWER RD
ABBEY RD
Woodside Sch
St Augustine CE Prim Sch
Allot Gdns
Green Chain Wlk
Lesnes Abbey Woods
Belvedere
Frank's Park
Trinity Sch
ERITH RD
A206
WOOLWICH RD
Lessness Heath Prim Sch
Bexley Coll
Lessness Heath
Cemy
A2016 Dartford (A206)
A206 Dartford, M25 (A282)
Kent STREET ATLAS
103
147

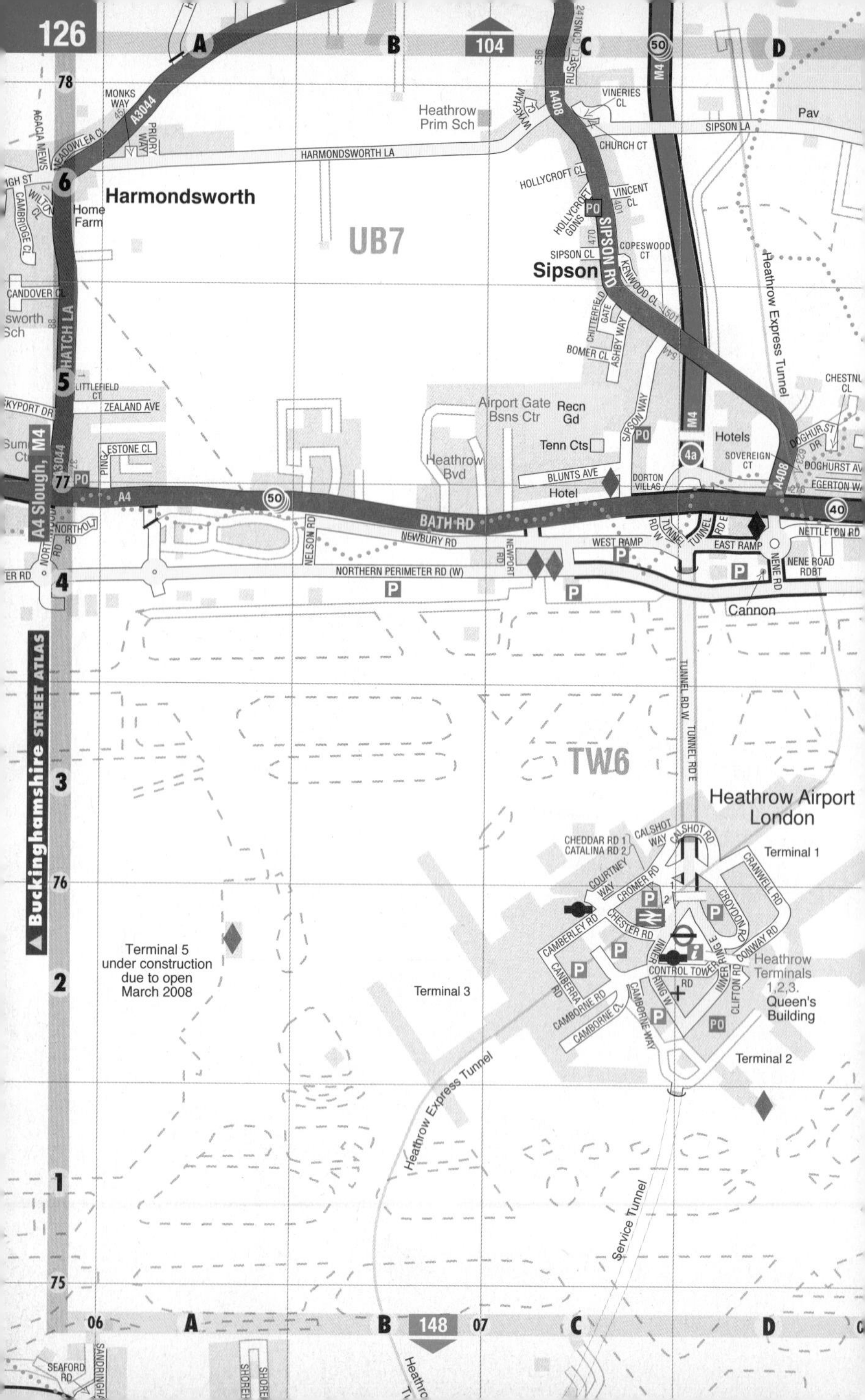

104
Harmondsworth
UB7
Sipson
Heathrow Prim Sch
HARMONDSWORTH LA
SIPSON LA
SIPSON RD
A3044
A408
M4
HATCH LA
Airport Gate Bsns Ctr
Recn Gd
Tenn Cts
Heathrow Bvd
Hotels
Hotel
BATH RD
A4
NEWBURY RD
NORTHERN PERIMETER RD (W)
WEST RAMP
EAST RAMP
NENE ROAD RDBT
Cannon
Heathrow Express Tunnel
TW6
Heathrow Airport London
Terminal 1
Terminal 2
Terminal 3
Terminal 5 under construction due to open March 2008
Heathrow Terminals 1,2,3. Queen's Building
CONTROL TOWER RD
TUNNEL RD W
TUNNEL RD E
Service Tunnel
A4 Slough, M4
Buckinghamshire STREET ATLAS
148

Nine Elms Farm
105
Harlington
William Byrd Sch
Hotel
Gravel Pits
Cranford Park
UB3
CRANFORD LA
The White House
Poultry Farm
HIGH STREET HARLINGTON
HIGH ST
SIPSON LA
BATH RD
Harlington Cnr
Hotels
World Bsns Ctr
Visitor Ctr
NORTHERN PERIMETER RD
The White Hart (PH)
TW6
ENFIELD ROAD RDBT
EASTERN PERIMETER RD
Eastern Bsns Pk
EASTCHURCH ROAD RDBT
VANGUARD WAY
HATTON CROSS RDBT
Hatton Cross
GREAT SOUTH-WEST RD
SOUTHERN PERIMETER RD
Hatton
Radius Pk
128
London Loop
Playground
Tenn Cts
Fball Gd
Cemy
149

Cranford
UB3
TW5
TW6
TW4
TW14
Cranford Park
Hounslow West
North Feltham
Heston Motorway Service Area
Heston Phoenix Distribution Pk
Parkway Trad Est
Lower Park Farm
Cranford Com Coll
The Queen's Head (PH)
Rectory Farm
The Cedars Prim Sch
Avenue Park
The White Hart (PH)
Waggoners Rdbt
Henleys Rdbt
Cranford Jun & Inf Schs
The Haslemere & Heathrow Est
Cranebank
River Crane
London Loop
Heathrow Causeway Est
Heathrow International Trad Est
Wallbrook Bsns Ctr
Sun Life Trad Est
Beavers Com Prim Sch
Prologis Pk
Beavers Lane Camp
Lawrence Est
Maple Gr Bsns Ctr
Tamian Ind Est
North Feltham Trad Est
River Gdns Bsns Ctr
Freehold Ind Ctr
Fairway Est
Central Pk Est
Haslemere Ind Est
Dockwell's Ind Est
Radius Pk
Hotel
Airlinks Ind Est
The Spitfire Est
THE PARKWAY
BATH RD
GREAT SOUTH-WEST RD
CAUSEWAY
EASTERN PERIMETER RD
A4
A30
A312
A3006
M4
106
127
150
A
B
C
D
1
2
3
4
5
6
75
76
77
78
10
11

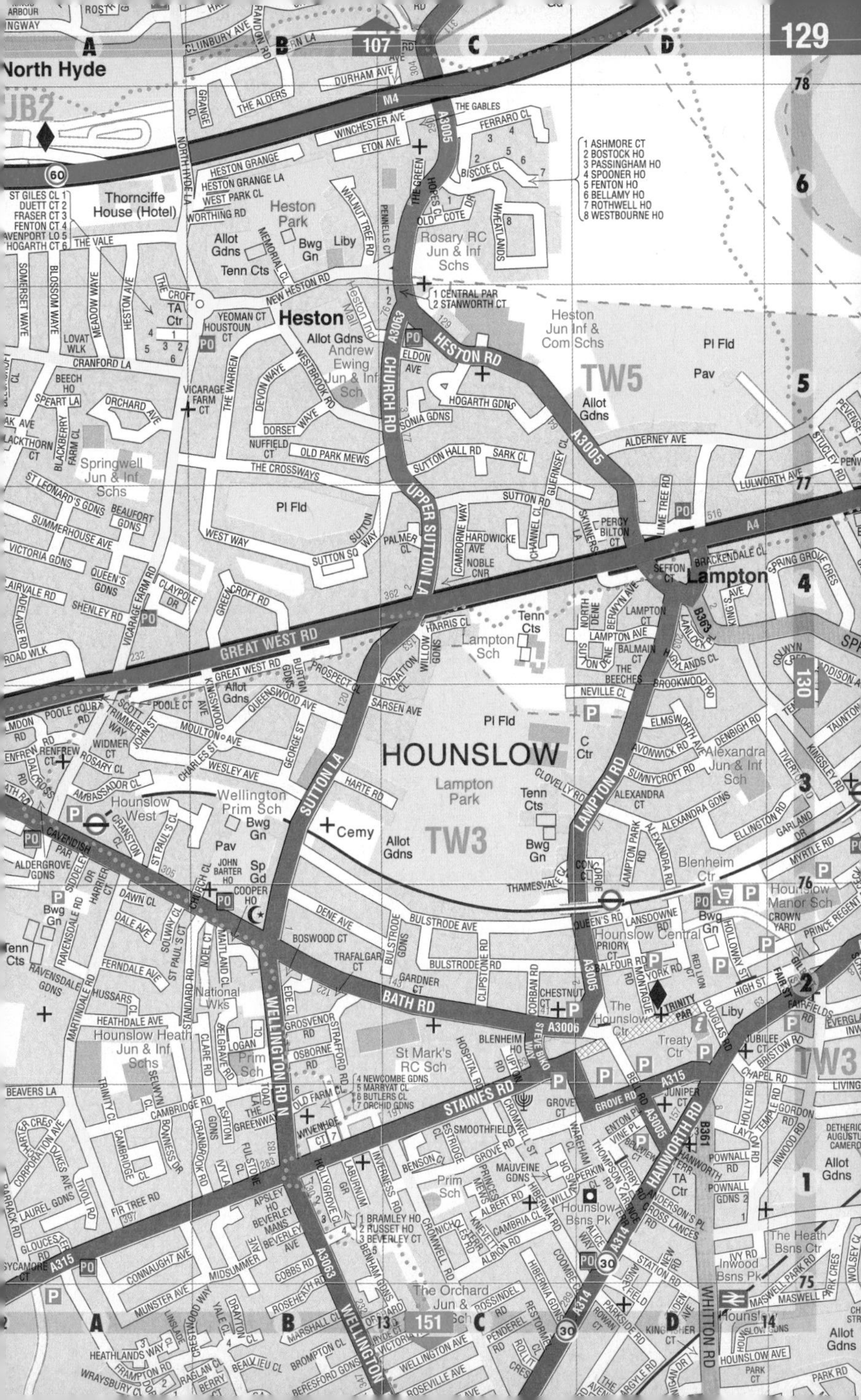
North Hyde
Heston
HOUNSLOW
Lampton
TW5
TW3
M4
A3005
A3063
A4
A315
A3006
A314
B363
B361
GREAT WEST RD
HESTON RD
CHURCH RD
UPPER SUTTON LA
SUTTON LA
LAMPTON RD
BATH RD
STAINES RD
WELLINGTON RD N
HANWORTH RD
WHITTON RD
Heston Park
Lampton Park
Hounslow West
Hounslow Central
Thorncliffe House (Hotel)
107
130
151

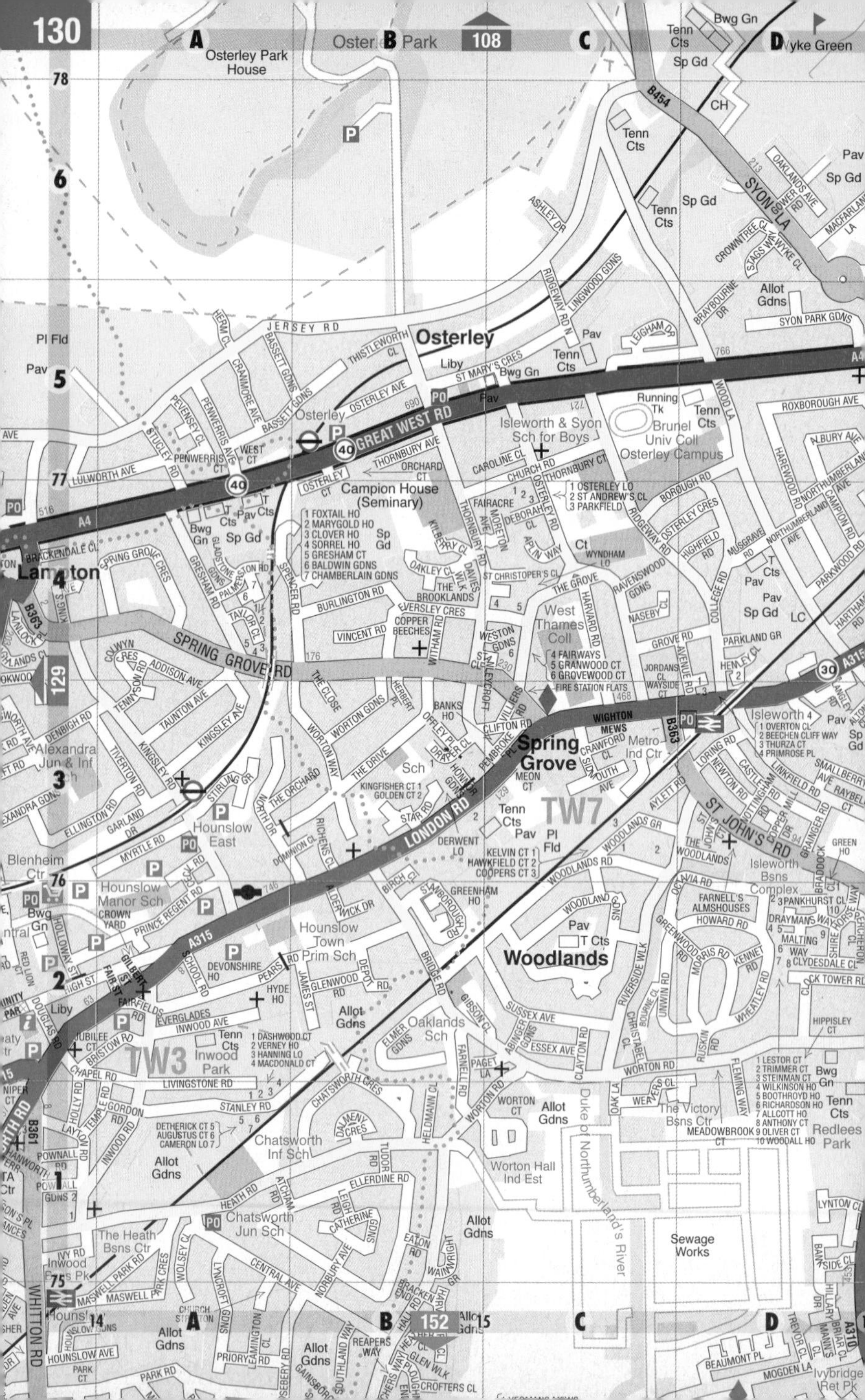

Osterley Park
108
Osterley Park House
Wyke Green
Osterley
GREAT WEST RD
Lampton
SPRING GROVE RD
Spring Grove
LONDON RD
TW7
Hounslow East
Woodlands
Isleworth
ST JOHN'S RD
SYON LA
TW3
Inwood Park
Brunel Univ Coll Osterley Campus
Campion House (Seminary)
West Thames Coll
Isleworth & Syon Sch for Boys
Hounslow Manor Sch
Hounslow Town Prim Sch
Oaklands Sch
Chatsworth Inf Sch
Chatsworth Jun Sch
Worton Hall Ind Est
Sewage Works
Duke of Northumberland's River
The Victory Bsns Ctr
Redlees Park
Isleworth Bsns Complex
The Heath Bsns Ctr
WHITTON RD
152
129

BRENTFORD
B Sky B HQ
Centaurs Bsns Pk
West Cross Ctr
Allot Gdns
River Brent
Grand Union Canal
Great West Ho
Brentside Executive Ctr
Great West Trad Est
TW8
GREAT WEST RD
BOSTON MANOR RD
Brentford
Brentford Sch for Girls
Griffin Park Fball Gd
EALING RD
HIGH ST
Brentford Bsns Ctr
Marina
Brentwaters Bsns Pk
Brentford End
London Butterfly House
Syon Park
Syon House & Gdns
LONDON RD
Syon Lane Pl Fld
The Green Sch (Girls)
Cemy
West Middlesex Univ
River Thames
Thames Path
Queen Charlotte's Cottage
King's Steps Gate
Royal Mid-Surrey
Old Deer Park
Kew Observatory
Isleworth Ait
TW7
ISLEWORTH
TW9
Richmond Healthcare Hamlet
Richmond Athletic Gd
Richmond Adult Com Coll
Old Deer Park Recn Gd
TW1
Richmond Lock
TWICKENHAM RD
RICHMOND
Richmond Green
Richmond Circus
TWICKENHAM RD
RICHMOND RD
SOUTH ST
132
109
153

110
A
B
C
D
6
5
4
3
2
1
77
76
75
131
154
BRENTFORD
Kew Bridge
KEW BRIDGE RD
HIGH ST
EALING RD
B455
A315
Brentford Ait
Lots Ait
Thames Path
Strand on the Green
STRAND-ON-THE-GREEN
Kew Pier
Kew Green
Kew
Kew Palace
Royal Botanic Gardens
Palm House
Arboretum
Temperate House
Pagoda
Herbarium Liby
Kew Green Prep Sch
Griffin Park F'ball Gd
Marina
The National Archives
Kew Ret Pk
Marlborough Trad Est
KEW RD
A307
A205
B353
MORTLAKE RD
SANDYCOMBE RD
KEW GARDENS RD
Kew Gardens
North Sheen
TW9
North Sheen Cemy (Fulham)
Hammersmith New Cemy
Chalkers Cnr
LOWER RICHMOND RD
A3003
CLIFFORD AVE
Manor Circus
Sandycombe Ctr
LOWER MORTLAKE RD
A316
Richmond Circus
Old Deer Park
Richmond Healthcare Hamlet
Richmond Athletic Gd
Christ Church
Superstores
North Sheen
Holy Trinity CE Prim Sch
MANOR RD
SHEEN RD
A305
RICHMOND
Richmond
THE QUADRANT
GEORGE ST
PARADISE RD
RED LION ST
B322
Pl Fld
1 ARUNDEL HO
2 MARLBOROUGH HO
3 BUCKINGHAM HO
4 OSBOURNE HO
5 YORK HO
6 SANDRINGHAM HO
7 KENT HO
8 NORFOLK HO
9 RUNNYMEDE HO
10 CARISBROOKE HO

133
111
155
134
A
B
C
D
1
2
3
4
5
6
GROSVENOR RD
WAVENDON AVE
QUICK RD
BARROWGATE RD
FRASER ST
DEVONSHIRE ST
ASHBOURNE GR
BALFERN GR
CORNWALL GR
DORCHESTER GR
AIREDALE AVE S
Recn Gd
NETHERAVON RD S
Thames Path
CHISWICK MALL
St Pa
CEDARS RD
GARTH CT
ELLESMERE RD
GREAT WEST RD
HOGARTH LA
A4
A316
Hogarth Roundabout
Schs
PARK RD
BENNETT ST
ELMWOOD RD
HAZLEDENE RD
SUTTON CT
GRANDFIELD CT
BEECHWOOD CT
CHARA PL
MILNTHORPE RD
EASTBOURNE RD
Tenn Cts
ELLESMERE CT
SUTHERLAND RD
SHORT RD
PAXTON RD
Hogarth's House
Bsns Pk
MAWSON LA
CHISWICK LA S
CHURCH ST
BOSTON
CHESTERFIELD RD
CHATSWORTH RD
SUTTON COURT RD
FAUCONBERG RD
COMPTON CRES
FLORENCE GDNS
NIGHTINGALE CL
ST THOMAS RD
1 MONTGOMERY CT
2 FAUCONBERG CT
3 EGERTON HO
4 BOURNE CT
5 CHISWICK PLAZA
6 SUTTON COURT MANS
FIELDING HO 1
GARRICK HO 2
HAMILTON HO 3
CHISWICK SQ 4
PAGE'S YD 5
Chiswick House
LANGHAM PL
DARTMOUTH PL
OLD CHISWICK YD
CORNEY RD
POWELL'S WLK
PUMPING STATION RD
BEDFORD CL
LATTIMER PL
CORNEY REACH WAY
CHISWICK WHARF
Corney Reach
1 OSIER MEWS
2 MALTHOUSE DR
3 RUSSELL CL
4 GWYNNE CL
WINDERMERE CT
FERRY LA
B350
Pl Fld
The Swedish Sch
HOWSMAN RD
EVERDON RD
1 GRASMERE CT
2 QUEENSMERE CT
VERDUN RD
KENTWODE GN
STAVELEY RD
Pav
LAWFORD RD
GROVE PARK MEWS
GROVE PARK BRIDGE
FITZROY CRES
CROFTON AVE
GRANTHAM RD
WHITTINGHAM CT
EDENSOR RD
MOLDOVA
EDENSOR GDNS
Chiswick Pier
The Harrodian Sch
Tenn Cts
Sp Gd
GROVE PARK GDNS
GROVE PARK RD
STATION APPR
BURLINGTON LA
Chiswick Com Sch
ALEXANDRA GDNS
Sch
PROMENADE APPROACH RD
1 MEADOW PL
2 THAMES CRES
3 WILLOW CT
4 OAST LD
5 MALTINGS LO
6 CHESTERMAN CT
7 NICHOLAS CT
8 CLAREMONT GR
ANSTICE CL
Bwg Gn
BELGRAVE RD
ATHERTON RD
GALATA RD
ULLSW
KINNAIRD AVE
Chiswick
SPENCER RD
RUSSELL KERR CL
WAR MEMORIAL HOMES
WILMINGTON AVE
Allot Gdns
Pav
Tenn Cts
Bwg Gn
Allot Gdns
Riverside Recn Gd
LONSDALE RD
DEVONSHIRE GDNS
CONISTON CL
BOLTON RD
MARAIS
KELVIN CT
STATION GDNS
1 HUNTINGDON GDNS
2 BURLINGTON CT
3 QUINTIN CT
4 WINDRUSH CL
5 THE LINDENS
Cemy
RIVERSIDE DR
CONISTON CL
Recn Gd
SUFFOLK RD
Grove Park
HARTINGTON RD
ST ANDREWS CT
CAVENDISH RD
Tenn Cts
W4
STAVELEY GDNS
Sp Gd
Tenn Cts
Civil Service Sp Gd
Tenn Cts
Thames Path
WALNUT TREE CL
DIANA HO
Pav
Tenn Cts
Bwg Gn
Pav
LOWTHER RD
PARKE RD
BERKELEY RD
WALSINGHAM LODGE
FERRY RD
CUMBERLAND RD
The Quintin Hogg Meml Gd
THAMES VILLAGE
CHISWICK QUAY
Pav
GREAT CHERTSEY RD
Allot Gdns
Pav
Bwg Gn
Bnstnd
THE PROMENADE
CHARLOTTE RD
GERARD RD
WESTMORELAND RD
ELLERTON RD
Tenn Cts
Stadium
IBIS LA
Riverside Lands School Pl Flds
Riverside L Ctr
BARNES
THE HERMITAGE
NASSAU RD
MELVILLE RD
KITSON RD
GRANGE RD
KING EDWARD MEWS
Sp Gd
River Thames
Tenn Cts
LYRIC RD
ST ANNS RD
Bwg Gn
JULIAN CT
Sch
CHURCH RD
A3003
Duke's Meadows
B350
SWAN PL
BARNES HIGH ST
BRACKEN
CHISWICK BRIDGE
Allot Gdns
Tenn Cts
Drv Rng
Sp Gd
Pav
TERRACE GDNS
LIFFORDS PL
STANTON RD
ESSEX CT
B349 STATION RD
THE CRESCENT
HILLERSDON AVE
GLEBE RD
MEREDYTH
CLIFFORD AVE
Pav
Tenn Cts
BARNES BRIDGE
LIMES AVE
GROVE RD
ELLISON RD
CLEVELAND RD
CAMBRIDGE RD
BEVERLEY CL
CEDARS RD
CARDIGAN
THAMES BANK
VARSITY ROW
REID CT
PARLIAMENT MEWS
Bwg Gn
Allot Gdns
TIDEWAY YD 1
TIDEWAY WHARF 2
THE BROADWAY 3
RIVER HO 4
ELM BANK MANS 5
MALTINGS CL 6
MALTHOUSE PAS 7
1 WATNEY COTTS
2 LANGDON PL
3 ROSEMARY LA
4 WALDECK TERR
5 ROSEMARY GDNS
6 HUNTINGDON CT
7 ST LEONARDS CT
8 MODEL COTTS
Hounslow
Richmond upon Thames
THE TERRACE
Barnes Bridge
ELM BANK GDNS
CLEVELAND GDNS
BROOKWOOD AVE
WILLOW AVE
B349
COMBE HO
WILLIAMS LA
SHIP LA
BULLS ALLEY
DUKES CT
ASHLEIGH HO 1
RIPLEY HO 2
CHARLES ST
THORNE ST
SHERIDAN PL
BEVERLEY RD
ORCHARD CL
SCARTH RD
Barn Com
Sp Gd
Mortlake
WATNEY RD
CH
LADY ELIZABETH HO
CROMWELL PL
MORTLAKE HIGH ST
VINEYARD PATH
VICTORIA RD
MULLINS PATH
FITZGERALD RD
RIPLEY GDNS
AVONDALE RD
ASHLEIGH RD
COWLEY RD
SECOND AVE
FIRST AVE
LIMES FIELD RD
ARCHWAY ST
CROSS ST
WESTFIELDS AVE
WESTFIELDS
Recn Gd
BROOK GDNS
BEVERLEY GDNS
Bwg Gn
Pavs
LCs
STATION RD
WALDECK RD
ALDER RD
WRIGHTS WLK
WORPLE ST
Sch
RAILWAY SIDE
WHITE HART LA
SW13
B351
HANSON CL
Mortlake
LC
THE RETREAT 1
BUXTON RD 2
BROOK CT 3
TUDOR GDNS 4
NORTH WORPLE WAY
SOUTH WORPLE WAY
PRIORY GDNS
THE ELMS
VINE RD
EASTBOURNE GDNS
BEXHILL RD
PALMERS RD
ST LEONARDS RD
LITTLE ST LEONARDS
MOORE CL
HOWGATE RD
OAKLANDS RD
GLENDOWER RD
ALEXANDRA RD
Cemy
Barnes
SOUTH WORPLE AVE
ELEANOR GR
ROSSLYN AVE
WOODLANDS RD
THE BYEWAY
VERNON RD
CHURCH AVE
PRINCE'S RD
LODGE AVE
GOSPATRIC HOME RD
FITZGERALD AVE
TREEN AVE
WESTWOOD GDNS
WESTWOOD RD
Barnes Common
LEONARDS RD
BEECHCROFT RD
ELM RD
EARL RD
CONNAUGHT AVE
LEINSTER AVE
MILTON RD
THORNTON RD
PORTMAN AVE
PAYNESFIELD AVE
LEWIN RD
KING'S RD
QUEEN'S RD
AVENUE GDNS
NOR GDNS
GROSVENOR AVE
SUTHERLAND GDNS
PRIESTS BRIDGE
THE WILLOUGHBYS
LEICONFIELD RD
1 LOUISA HO
2 ESME HO
3 SARAH HO
Red Rover
A306
B306
Liby
1 PENRHYN CRES
2 CEDAR CT
Milestone Green
UPPER RICHMOND RD
A205
MITCHELL CT
ARABELLA DR
LUDOVICK WLK
Paddock Sch
Rosslyn Park
Pav
DUNGARVAN AVE
LANGSIDE AVE
UPPER RICHMOND RD W
LARCHES AVE
SW14
WALLORTON GDNS
GORDON AVE
SHOTTFIELD AVE
Sch
BURKE CL
WOKING CL
Tenn Cts
COVAL PAS
COLSTON RD
East Sheen
MUIRDOWN AVE
PARKFIELD AVE
Shene Sch
ROCKINGHAM CL
PRIORY LA
ELLENBOROUGH
REDCROFT GDNS
GRAND PAR
SHEEN GATE GDNS
SHEEN LA
SHREWSBURY AVE
GILPIN AVE
1 SHEENGATE MANS
2 PARKWAY HO
Tenn Cts
CH
Roehampton Sports Club
ROEHAMPE
PALMERSTON RD
FIRS AVE
RICHMOND PARK RD
PARK AVE
HERTFORD AVE
DOWDESWELL CL
PRIORY CT
OBSERVATORY RD
PERCIVAL RD
WELLSIDE GDNS
B351
PALEWELL PK
EAST SHEEN AVE
PARK DR
SUNBURY AVE
Allot Gdns
The Priory
SW15
FAIRACRES
CROMWELL HO
ELDO GDNS
WELL LA
WAYSIDE
VICARAGE GDNS
Sp Gd
Tenn Cts
A306
CHRISTCHURCH RD
YORK AVE
VICARAGE RD
VICARAGE DR
ENMORE CT
STONEHILL CL
ENMORE GDNS
PALEWELL COMMON DR
Allot Gdns
Tenn Cts
CH
Roehampton
Roehampton Univ. (Southlands Coll)
SHEEN WOOD
THE MALL
HOOD AVE
STONEHILL RD
SHEEN
PRIORY LA
Sacr

River Thames
Richmond upon Thames
Thames Path
Tenn Cts
St Paul's Sch
Pl Flds
LONSDALE RD
The Swedish Sch
HAMMERSMITH BRIDGE
112
W6
King Henry's Reach
Charing Cross
FULHAM PALACE RD
CASTELNAU
London Wetland Centre
London Wetland Visitor Ctr
QUEEN ELIZABETH WLK
Lowther Prim Sch
Recn Gd
BARNES
CHURCH RD
133
SW6
Blakes Wharves
Eternit Wharf
Stevenage Wharves
Craven Cottage (Fulham FC)
FULHAM
Barn Elms Pl Flds
Running Tk
Barn Elms Schs Sp Ctr
Beverley Brook
Putney Lower Common
Old Barnes Cemy
SW13
MILL HILL RD
ROCKS LA
Barnes Common
LOWER RICHMOND RD
QUEEN'S RIDE
UPPER RICHMOND RD
SW15
Roehampton
Rosslyn Park
Roehampton Sports Club
Roehampton Univ (Southlands Coll)
156
PUTNEY
Lion House Sch
Hotham Prim Sch
All Saints CE Prim Sch

135
113
265
136
157
West Brompton
Brompton Cemy
Walham Green
Stamford Bridge (Chelsea F'ball Club)
Fulham Broadway
Parsons Green
Eel Brook Common
Queen's Club
Normand Park
SW6
SW15
South Park
Hurlingham Park
Hurlingham House
Hurlingham & Chelsea Sec Sch
Chelsea Coll of Art & Design
Hurlingham Wharf
Wandsworth Bridge
River Thames
Hammersmith & Fulham
Wandsworth
Putney Bridge
Putney Pier
Sands End
Fulham Wharf
Imperial Wharf
Gas Works
Wandsworth Town
Wandsworth Gyratory
East Putney
Brandlehow Park
Wandsworth Park
Samuel Lewis Trust Dwellings
LILLIE RD
DAWES RD
FULHAM RD
NORTH END RD
KING'S RD
NEW KING'S RD
FULHAM BROADWAY
HARWOOD RD
WANDSWORTH BRIDGE RD
FULHAM PALACE RD
FULHAM HIGH ST
PUTNEY BRIDGE RD
PUTNEY BRIDGE APP
HURLINGHAM RD
FINBOROUGH RD
REDCLIFFE GDNS
GUNTER GR
SWANDON WAY
ARMOURY WAY
UPPER RICHMOND RD

SW10
A
B
114
C
D
CHELSEA
FULHAM RD
FINBOROUGH RD
REDCLIFFE GDNS
Chelsea & Westminster
KING'S RD
OLD CHURCH ST
BEAUFORT ST
OAKLEY ST
ROYAL HOSPITAL RD
CHELSEA EMB
Thames Path
Cadogan Pier
Chelsea Reach
ALBERT BRIDGE (SUSPENSION)
Terrace Wlk
THE PARADE
Kensington & Chelsea
Wandsworth
BATTERSEA BRIDGE
Bridge Wharf
Ransome's Dock
Fountain Lake
CARRIAGE DRIVE N
CHEYNE WLK
EDITH GR
GUNTER GR
CREMORNE RD
Old Ferry Wharf
Chelsea Wharf
Cremorne Wharf
River Thames
BATTERSEA BRIDGE RD
ALBERT BRIDGE RD
Festival Pleasure Gardens
CENTRAL AVE
SW11
BATTERSEA
Gas Works
Chelsea Creek
CHELSEA HARBOUR
WESTBRIDGE RD
Hammersmith & Fulham
Wandsworth
VICARAGE CRES
SURREY LA
PRINCE OF WALES DR
Imperial Wharf
Chelsea Harbour Pier
266
267
135
BATTERSEA PARK RD
Regent Wharf
LOMBARD RD
BATTERSEA HIGH ST
1 GREENSWARD HO
2 CHAPLOW CL
3 ARCADIAN HO
4 POTTERS RD
York Road Bsns Ctr
Heliport
The Heliport Est
Battersea Reach
WANDSWORTH BRIDGE RD
YORK RD
LATCHMERE RD
Falcon Park
FALCON RD
Christ Church CE Prim Sch
Sands End
Fulham Wharf
Charterhouse Works
Sherwood Wharf
1 SALTBURN HO
2 BRIDLINGTON HO
3 LERWICK HO
4 FILEY HO
5 DUNGENESS HO
6 DORIS EMMERTON CT
7 BALTIMORE HO
8 COMODORE HO
THE VILLAGE 1
BATTERSEA HTS 2
WANDSWORTH BRIDGE
Gargoyle Wharf
Clapham Junction
ST JOHN'S HILL
BATTERSEA RISE
ELSPETH RD
LAVENDER HILL
BARNARD MEWS 1
CARRINGTON CT 2
ABYSSINIA CL 3
CLAPHAM JUNCTION EST
SWANDON WAY
EAST HILL
NORTH SIDE WANDSWORTH COMMON
158
Spencer Park
Belleville Prim Sch

Royal Hospital Army Pensioners
Ranelagh Gardens (Site of Chelsea Flower Show)
Lister
Dock
Tenn Cts
Pimlico Sch
CHICHESTER ST
CHURCHILL GARDENS RD
GROSVENOR ROAD
A3212
Wharves
Wharf
CHELSEA BRIDGE
GROSVENOR BRIDGE
Thames Path
River Thames
City of Westminster
Wandsworth
Battersea Wharf
Jetty
A3216
QUEENSTOWN RD
Tideway Ind Est
NINE ELMS LA
A3205
New Covent Garden Flower Mkt
South Bank Bsns Ctr
CARRIAGE DRIVE N
Athletic Gd
Children's Zoo
Battersea Power Station (disused)
Nine Elms
John Milton Prim Sch
SW8
POST OFFICE WAY
PONTON RD
CRINGLE ST
KIRTLING ST
WANDSWORTH RD
Battersea Dogs Home
Boating Lake
Battersea Park
QUEEN'S CIR
SLEAFORD ST
SAVONA ST
ASCALON ST
Ind Est
New Covent Garden Fruit & Vegetable Market
CARRIAGE DR S
PRINCE OF WALES DR
BATTERSEA PARK RD
Queenstown Road
Bsns Ctr
THESSALY RD
CORUNNA RD
PATMORE ST
STEWART'S RD
LINFORD ST
Coll
Univ
A3036
Larkhall Park
Sir James Barrie Prim Sch
268
269
138
Wandsworth Road
SW4
B224
SILVERTHORNE RD
Parkfield Ind Est
Heathbrook Park
PORTSLADE RD
ALBION AVE
UNION GR
LARKHALL RISE
CLAPHAM MANOR ST
Clapham High Street
Clapham North
CLAPHAM HIGH ST
CLAPHAM
CEDARS RD
LAVENDER HILL
NORTH ST
OLD TOWN
B303
CLAPHAM COMMON NORTH SIDE
LONG RD
A3
Clapham Common
A24
CLAPHAM PARK RD
A2217
BEDFORD RD
B221
1 ST SAVIOURS
2 LYNCOTT CRES
3 SALCOMBE GDNS
4 BARKER MEWS
5 WOODLANDS
6 OKEOVER MANOR
Clapham Common
Windmill on the Common (PH)
159
Lambeth Coll
Lambeth Acad
Ellerslie Ind Est
Recn Gd
Bndstd
Mount Pond
A205
A
B
C
D
1
2
3
4
5
6

Vauxhall
VAUXHALL BRIDGE
Spring Gardens
KENNINGTON LA
116
Kennington
261
SE17
Vauxhall Cross
A3204
A3036
A202
A203
HARLEYFORD RD
SE11
Govt Offices
Bnstnd
Tenn Cts
KENNINGTON PK RD
Wharf
A3205
PARRY ST
BONDWAY
The Oval
KENNINGTON OVAL
New Covent Garden Flower Mkt
Vauxhall Park
Kennington Park
Fball Gd
Kennington Oval
South Bank Bsns Ctr
Bwg Gn
Kennington Park
CAMBERWELL NEW RD
WYVIL RD
RITA RD
FENTIMAN RD
COTTINGHAM RD
PRIMA RD
HANWORTH HO
WANDSWORTH RD
SOUTH LAMBETH RD
HEYFORD AVE
DORSET RD
RICHBORNE TERR
OVAL PL
HANDFORTH RD
CRANMER RD
270
CREWDSON RD
Liby
WILCOX RD
DAVIDSON GDNS
MEADOW PL
SOUTH ISLAND PL
MOWLL ST
VASSALL RD
THORNCROFT ST
WILKINSON ST
THORNE RD
ALDEBERT TERR
CALDWELL ST
SW8
CLAPHAM RD
LIBERTY ST
MORAT ST
BRIXTON RD
MANSION CL
HAMPSON WAY
PORTLAND GR
LANSDOWNE WAY
HILLYARD ST
NORMANDY RD
South Lambeth
Larkhall Park
BINFIELD RD
Stockwell Park Sch
GROVEWAY
Allot Gdns
Mostyn Gdns
MOSTYN RD
FOUNTAIN
Myatt's Fields Pk
Stockwell
137
SW4
STUDLEY RD
LORN RD
INGLETON ST
SW9
PARADISE RD
YMCA
STOCKWELL RD
ROBSART ST
Prim Sch
AYTOUN PL
WYNNE RD
BRIXTON
VILLA RD
ANGELL RD
Loughborough Junc
Coll
Allot Gdns
Stockwell
Lambeth
Clapham North
Clapham High Street
STOCKWELL PARK WLK
CANTERBURY CRES
BRIXTON STATION RD
PULROSS RD
COLDHARBOUR LA
Brixton
ATLANTIC RD
A2217
BEDFORD RD
SW4
SANDMERE RD
ELECTRIC AVE
Liby
ACRE LA
Works
MERVAN RD
LOUGHBOROUGH PK
SHAKESPEARE RD
MILKWOOD RD
Ellerslie Ind Est
Bsns Ctr
Ret Pk
EFFRA RD
A204
160
B223
RAILTON RD
A
B
C
D
1
2
3
4
5
6
75
76
77
78
30

262
117
263
CAMBERWELL
SE15
SE5
Burgess Park
Burgess Ind Pk
CAMBERWELL RD
CAMBERWELL CHURCH ST
PECKHAM RD
ALBANY RD
SOUTHAMPTON WAY
TRAFALGAR AVE
PECKHAM HILL ST
OLD KENT RD
DENMARK HILL
COLDHARBOUR LA
CHAMPION PK
GROVE LA
DOG KENNEL HILL
GROVE VALE
EAST DULWICH GR
HERNE HILL
WILLOWBROOK RD
COMMERCIAL WAY
ST GEORGE'S WAY
The Maudsley
King's College
Denmark Hill
The Weston Ed Ctr
Coldharbour Ind Est
Camberwell Trad Est
Camberwell Green
Ruskin Park
William Booth Meml Trng Coll
Lucas Gdns
St Giles
Coll of Arts
The Acad at Peckham
Peckham Rye
Print Village Ind Est
Bellendon Rd Bsns Ctr
Cobourg Prim Sch
Gloucester Prim Sch
John Ruskin Sch
St Saviour's Sch
Bessemer Grange Prim Sch
The Charter Sch
East Dulwich
Dulwich
Goose Green
Herne Hill
140
161
East Du

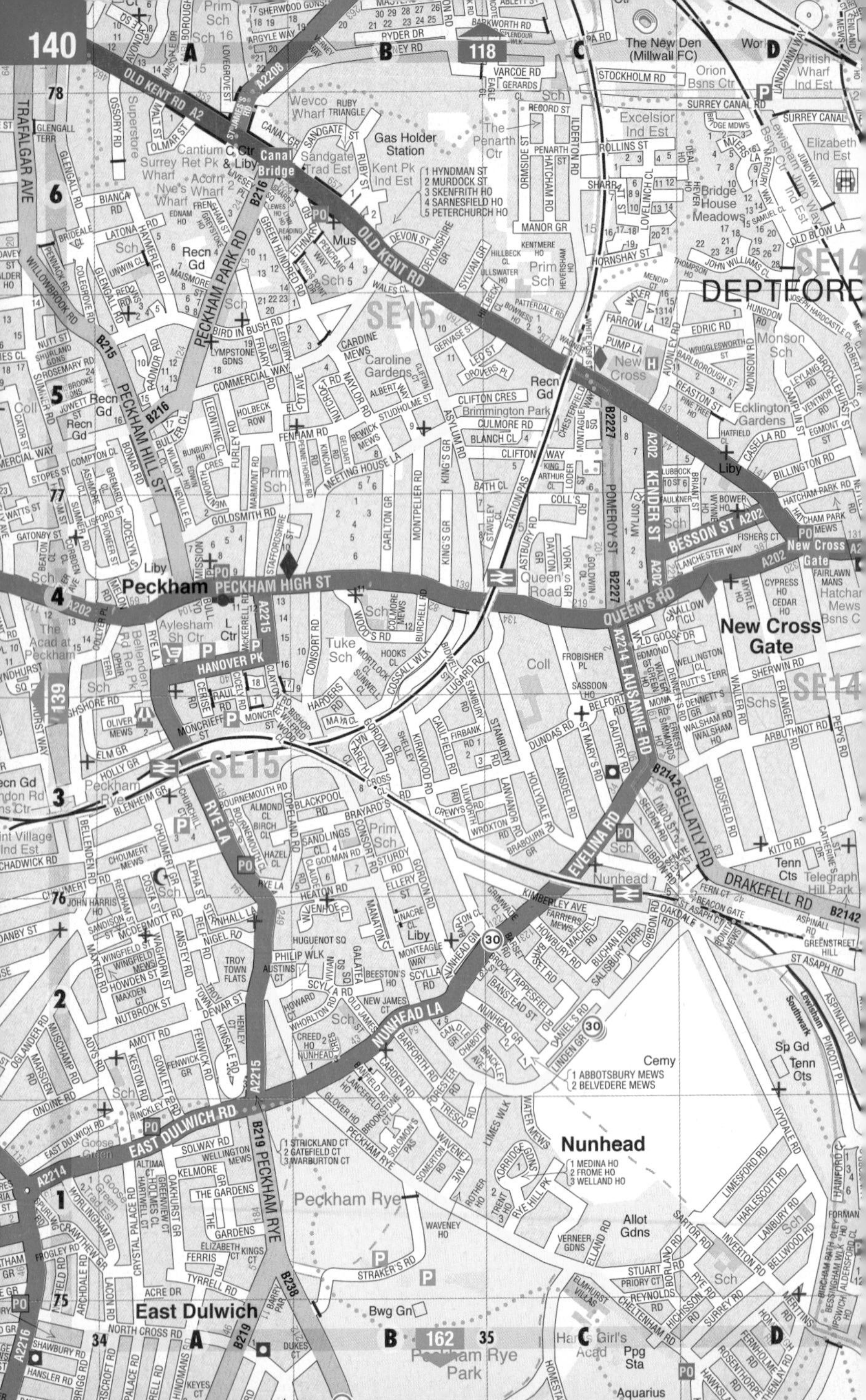

118
The New Den (Millwall FC)
OLD KENT RD A2
A2208
Canal Bridge
Wevco Wharf
RUBY TRIANGLE
Gas Holder Station
Sandgate Trad Est
Kent Pk Ind Est
1 HYNDMAN ST
2 MURDOCK ST
3 SKENFRITH HO
4 SARNESFIELD HO
5 PETERCHURCH HO
The Penarth Ctr
Orion Bsns Ctr
STOCKHOLM RD
SURREY CANAL RD
Excelsior Ind Est
Elizabeth Ind Est
Bridge House Meadows
Lewisham Bsns Ctr
Juno Way Ind Est
DEPTFORD
SE14
SE15
Cantium Ret Pk
Surrey Ret Pk
Nye's Wharf
Acorn Wharf
TRAFALGAR AVE
PECKHAM PARK RD
PECKHAM HILL ST
B215
B216
Caroline Gardens
Brimmington Park
New Cross
Ecklington Gardens
Monson Sch
Peckham
PECKHAM HIGH ST
A202
A2215
HANOVER PK
Aylesham Sh Ctr
Bellenden Rd Ret Pk
The Acad at Peckham
QUEEN'S RD
Queen's Road
B2227
KENDER ST
BESSON ST A202
New Cross Gate
A2214 LAUSANNE RD
139
Peckham Rye
RYE LA
Tuke Sch
Coll
B2142 GELLATLY RD
DRAKEFELL RD B2142
EVELINA RD
Nunhead
Telegraph Hill Park
Tenn Cts
Troy Town Flats
NUNHEAD LA
Cemy
1 ABBOTSBURY MEWS
2 BELVEDERE MEWS
Nunhead
1 MEDINA HO
2 FROME HO
3 WELLAND HO
Allot Gdns
Sp Gd
EAST DULWICH RD
A2214
B219 PECKHAM RYE
1 STRICKLAND CT
2 GATEFIELD CT
3 WARBURTON CT
Peckham Rye
Goose Green
Goose Green Trad Est
B238
East Dulwich
Bwg Gn
162
Peckham Rye Park
Harris Girl's Acad
Ppg Sta
Aquarius
A2216
78
77
76
75
34
35
A B C D
6 5 4 3 2 1

River Thames
SE8
119
New Cross
St Johns
SE14
SE4
SE10
SE13
Brockley
Hilly Fields Park
Deptford
Greenwich
Fordham Park
Ladywell Cemy
Brockley Cemy
163
142

A
B
C
D
120
78
Greenwich Footway Tunnel
Greenwich Pier
Gipsy Moth IV
Old Royal Naval Coll Bldgs
Cutty Sark
Univ of Greenwich
Dreadnought Wharf
THAMES ST
WELLAND ST
HORSEFERRY PL
6
CREEK RD
A200
ROMNEY RD
A206
TRAFALGAR RD
PARK ROW
KING WILLIAM WLK
NELSON RD
COLLEGE APP
GREENWICH CHURCH ST
Greenwich
OLD WOOLWICH RD
WOODLANDS PARK RD
LEMMON RD
Maze Hill
RESTELL CL
VANBRUGH HILL
DINSDALE RD
GREENWICH
PARK VISTA
BARDSLEY LA
Recn Gd
ROAN ST
DEVONPORT HO
The Queen's House
Maze Hill House Gate
National Maritime Mus
St Mary's Gate
One Tree Hill
Maze Hill Gate
MAZE HILL
National Fan Mus
HIGHMORE RD
WESTCOMBE PARK RD
The John Roan Sch
SE10
Flamsteed House
Meridian Building
The Royal Observatory
Tea House
GREAT CROSS AVE
Bndstd
Vanbrugh Park Gate
Blackheath
VANBRUGH PK
THE AVENUE
STRAIGHTSMOUTH
Greenwich Ind Est
5
GREENWICH HIGH RD
GREENWICH SOUTH ST
A2211
B209
ROYAL HILL
South Building
Greenwich Park
The Wilderness (Deer Park)
BLACKHEATH AVE
BOWER AVE
CROOMS HILL
Croomshill Gate
HYDE VALE
ASHBURNHAM GR
77
WELLINGTON GR
Resr
CHARLTON WAY
Ranger's House (The Wernher Collection)
Chesterfield Wlk
Blackheath Gate
Blackheath The Point
GENERAL WOLFE RD
CADE RD
B209
4
A2
BLACKHEATH HILL
30
B210
SHOOTERS HILL RD
SE3
PRINCE CHARLES RD
PRINCE OF WALES RD
B212
DARTMOUTH HILL
DARTMOUTH ROW
LONG POND RD
Whitfield's Mound
Blackheath
GOFFERS RD
DUKE HUMPHREY RD
TALBOT PL
Blackheath Vale
141
LEWISHAM RD
HARE AND BILLET RD
MOUNTS POND RD
MONTPELIER ROW
SOUTH ROW
PARAGON PL
3
Elverson Road
BLACKHEATH RISE
LEWISHAM HILL
ELIOT HILL
ELIOT PL
ELIOT VALE
TRANQUIL VALE
ROYAL PAR
Works
Superstore Lewisham
76
THURSTON RD
THE MEADWAY
BAIZDON RD
WEMYSS RD
BLACKHEATH GR
GRANVILLE PK
ST JOSEPH'S VALE
Blackheath
BENNETT PK
CRESSWELL PK
PLOUGH BRIDGE
LOAMPIT VALE
Loampit Vale
Sixth Form Coll
Pl Fld
Acad
THE GLEBE
LAWN TERR
B220
SPANGATE
MEADOWBANK
2
CRESSINGHAM RD
BOYNE RD
CATERHAM RD
BELMONT HILL
Blackheath RC Prim Sch
LEE TERR
A21
LEWISHAM HIGH ST
A20
MOLESWORTH ST
Lewisham Ctr
DACRE PK
LEE PK
LEE RD
PRIORY PK
Kid Brook
SE13
1
Depot
LEWISHAM
LEE HIGH RD
WILLOWCROFT
Allot Gdns
Prim Sch
SE12
SLAITHWAITE RD
Liby
75
Lee Green
A2212
38
DERMODY RD
B
164
39
C
D
Tenn Cts
Manor House Gardens
A
Allot Gdns
LEWISHAM HIGH ST
Leis Ctr
River
Tenn Cts

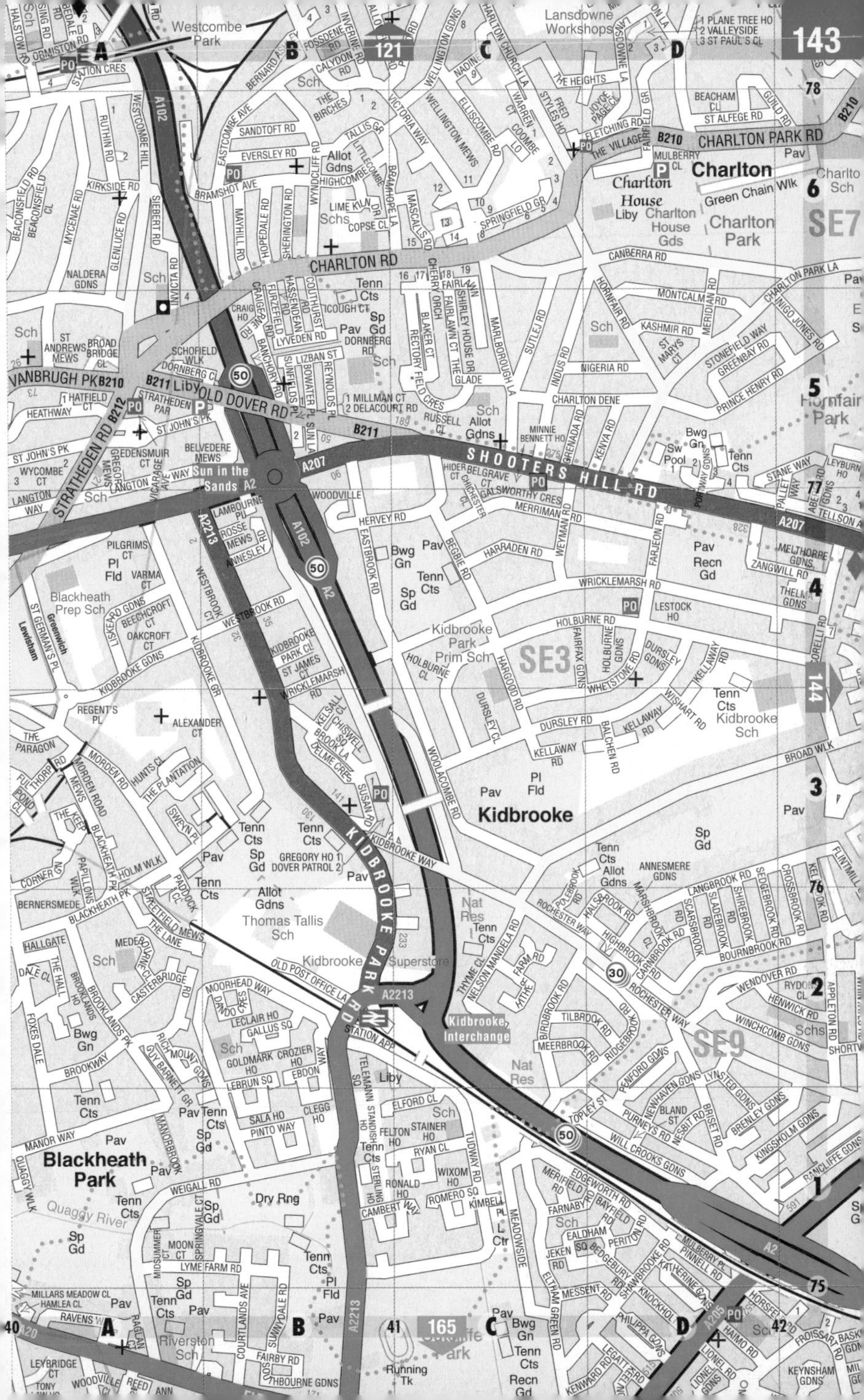
Westcombe Park
Lansdowne Workshops
Charlton
Charlton House
Charlton House Gds
Charlton Park
SE7
Hornfair Park
SHOOTERS HILL RD
CHARLTON RD
CHARLTON PARK RD
OLD DOVER RD
VANBRUGH PK
STRATHEDEN RD
Sun in the Sands
Blackheath Prep Sch
SE3
Kidbrooke Park Prim Sch
Kidbrooke
Kidbrooke Sch
KIDBROOKE PARK RD
Thomas Tallis Sch
Kidbrooke Superstore
Kidbrooke Interchange
SE9
Blackheath Park
Quaggy River
Riverston Sch
Running Tk
121
144
165
A
B
C
D
1
2
3
4
5
6

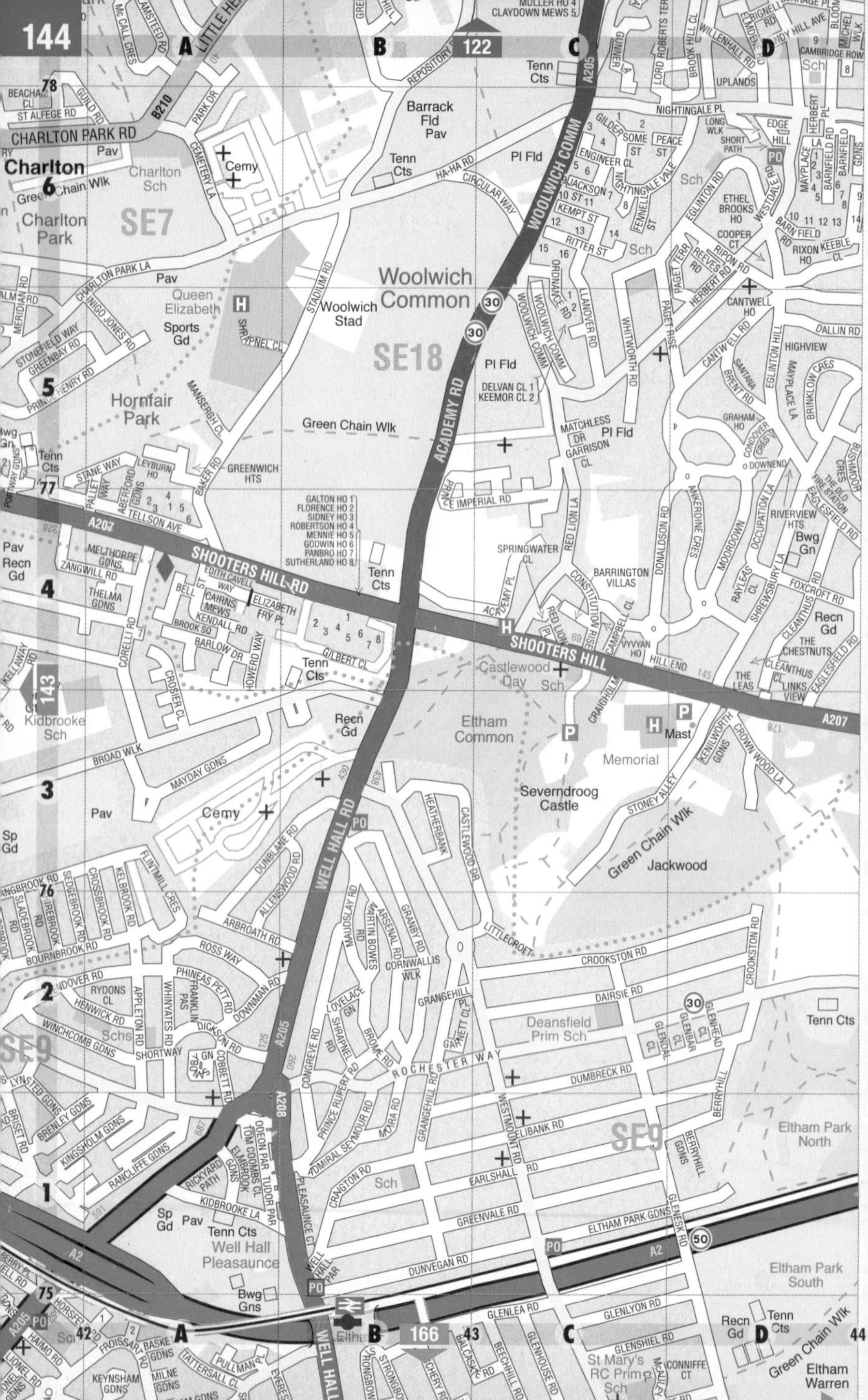

Charlton
SE7
SE18
SE9
Woolwich Common
Charlton Park
Hornfair Park
Eltham Common
Severndroog Castle
Jackwood
Eltham Park North
Eltham Park South
Eltham Warren
Well Hall Pleasaunce
CHARLTON PARK RD
WOOLWICH COMM
ACADEMY RD
SHOOTERS HILL RD
SHOOTERS HILL
WELL HALL RD
ROCHESTER WAY
Green Chain Wlk
122
143
166

123
Plumstead Common
Plumstead Manor/Negus Sch
St Margaret's CE Prim Sch
Rockliffe Manor Prim Sch
The William Barefoot Garden
SE18
Shrewsbury Park
Green Chain Wlk
Willow Dene Sch
Shooters Hill
Woodlands Farm
DOVER RD
DA16
BELLEGROVE RD
East Wickham Schs
East Wickham Open Space
146
Oxleas Wood Nature Reserve
Eastcote Prim Sch
Falconwood Field
SE9
Falconwood
Bishop Ridley CE Prim Sch
EAST ROCHESTER WAY
Crown Woods Sch
167
DA15
A2
A207
A209

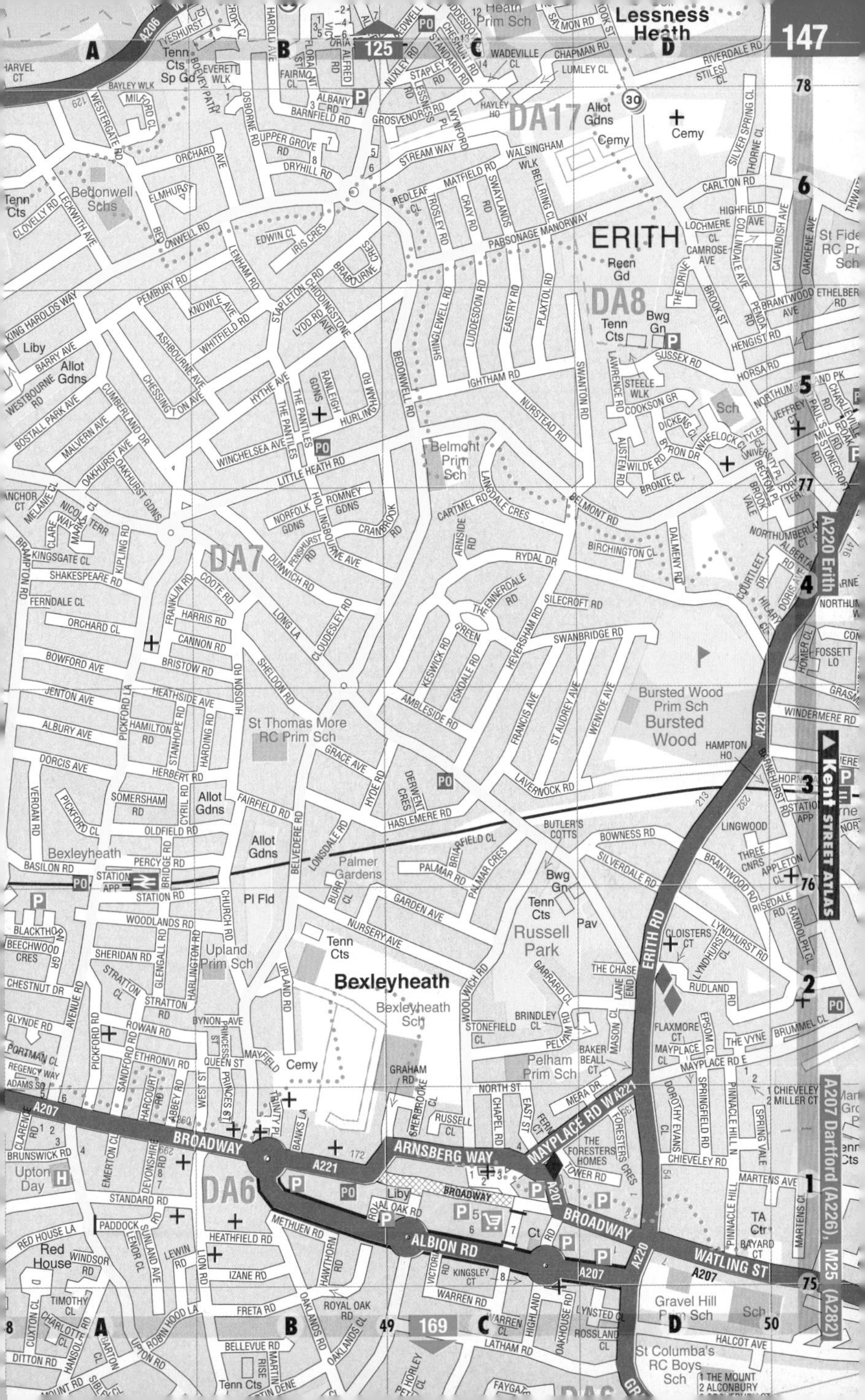
147
Lessness Heath
Heath Prim Sch
125
169
A
B
C
D
78
77
76
75
6
5
4
3
2
1
49
50
A206
A207
A220
A221
A220 Erith
Kent STREET ATLAS
A207 Dartford (A226), M25 (A282)
DA17
DA8
DA7
DA6
ERITH
Bexleyheath
Tenn Cts Sp Gd
Bedonwell Schs
Allot Gdns
Cemy
Recn Gd
Tenn Cts
Bwg Gn
Belmont Prim Sch
St Thomas More RC Prim Sch
Bursted Wood Prim Sch
Bursted Wood
Hampton Ho
Lingwood
Three Cnrs
Palmer Gardens
Pl Fld
Upland Prim Sch
Bexleyheath Sch
Russell Park
Pav
Pelham Prim Sch
The Foresters Homes
Liby
Upton Day
Red House
TA Ctr
Gravel Hill Prim Sch
St Columba's RC Boys Sch
St Fidelis RC Prim Sch
Station App
Tyeshurst Cl
Harvel Ct
Bayley Wlk
Milford Cl
Westergate Rd
Everett Wlk
Osborne Rd
Harold Ave
Fairmont Cl
Albany Rd
Barnfield Rd
Alfred Rd
Nuxley Rd
Lessness Rd
Standard Rd
Cheshunt Rd
Wadeville Cl
Chapman Rd
Lumley Cl
Riverdale Rd
Stiles Cl
Grosvenor Rd
Hayley Ho
Upper Grove Rd
Dryhill Rd
Stream Way
Walsingham Wlk
Orchard Ave
Elmhurst
Bedonwell Rd
Leckwith Ave
Clovelly Rd
Edwin Cl
Iris Cres
Redleaf Cl
Matfield Rd
Trosley Rd
Cray Rd
Swaylands Rd
Bellring Cl
Parsonage Manorway
Silver Spring Cl
Thorne Cl
Carlton Rd
Highfield Ave
Lochmere Cl
Collindale Ave
Camrose Ave
Cavendish Ave
Oakdene Ave
The Drive
Brook St
Brantwood Ave
Penda Rd
Hengist Rd
Horsa Rd
Lenham Rd
Pembury Rd
Knowle Ave
Whitfield Rd
Ashbourne Ave
Stapleton Rd
Chiddingstone Ave
Lydd Rd
Brabourne Cres
Shinglewell Rd
Luddesdon Rd
Eastry Rd
Plaxtol Rd
Swanton Rd
King Harolds Way
Barry Ave
Westbourne Rd
Bostall Park Ave
Cumberland Dr
Malvern Ave
Oakhurst Ave
Oakhurst Gdns
Chessington Ave
Hythe Ave
The Pantiles
Raleigh Gdns
Hurlingham Rd
Bedonwell Rd
Ightham Rd
Nurstead Rd
Sussex Rd
Lawrence Rd
Steele Wlk
Cookson Gr
Dickens Cl
Austen Rd
Wilde Rd
Byron Dr
Bronte Cl
Wheelock Cl
Tyler Cl
University Pl
Becton Pl
Brook Vale
Jeffrey Cl
Mill Rd
Stonecroft
York Ter
Northumberland Pk
Northumberland Cl
Alberta Rd
Courtleet Dr
Hilary Cl
Doris Ave
Winchelsea Ave
Little Heath Rd
Hollingbourne Ave
Romney Gdns
Norfolk Gdns
Cranbrook Rd
Penshurst Rd
Dunwich Rd
Langdale Cres
Cartmel Rd
Arnside Rd
Belmont Rd
Birchington Cl
Dalmeny Rd
Rydal Dr
Ennerdale Rd
The Green
Silecroft Rd
Swanbridge Rd
Keswick Rd
Eskdale Rd
Heversham Rd
Ambleside Rd
Francis Ave
St Audrey Ave
Wenvoe Ave
Lavernock Rd
Anchor Ct
Melanie Cl
Nicola Terr
Clare Way
Kipling Rd
Kingsgate Cl
Shakespeare Rd
Brampton Rd
Ferndale Cl
Orchard Cl
Coote Rd
Franklin Rd
Harris Rd
Cannon Rd
Bristow Rd
Bowford Ave
Jenton Ave
Albury Ave
Dorcis Ave
Heathside Ave
Pickford La
Hamilton Rd
Stanhope Rd
Harding Rd
Hudson Rd
Long La
Cloudesley Rd
Sheldon Rd
Herbert Rd
Somersham Rd
Cyril Rd
Pickford Cl
Veroan Rd
Oldfield Rd
Fairfield Rd
Grace Ave
Hyde Rd
Derwent Cres
Haslemere Rd
Belvedere Rd
Lonsdale Rd
Briarfield Cl
Palmar Rd
Palmar Cres
Butler's Cotts
Bowness Rd
Silverdale Rd
Brantwood Rd
Hornbeam Rd
Barnehurst Rd
Appleton Cl
Risedale Rd
Randolph Cl
Basilon Rd
Percy Rd
Bridge Rd
Station Rd
Church Rd
Burr Cl
Garden Ave
Nursery Ave
Blackthorn
Beechwood Cres
Woodlands Rd
Sheridan Rd
Glengall Rd
Harlington Rd
Chestnut Dr
Stratton Cl
Stratton Rd
Avenue Rd
Upland Rd
Erith Rd
Cloisters Ct
Lyndhurst Cl
Lyndhurst Rd
Rudland Rd
The Chase
Lane End
Garrard Cl
Woolwich Rd
Brindley Cl
Stonefield Cl
Pelham Rd
Mason Cl
Baker Beall Ct
Flaxmore Ct
Epsom Cl
Mayplace Cl
The Vyne
Brummel Cl
Mayplace Rd E
Mayplace Rd W
Glynde Rd
Portman Cl
Regency Way
Adams Sq
Pickford Rd
Rowan Rd
Bynon Ave
Sandford Rd
Ethronvi Rd
Queen St
Princes St
Mayfield
West St
Abbey Rd
Harcourt Rd
Trinity Pl
Banks La
Graham Rd
Sherbrooke Cl
Russell Cl
North St
Chapel Rd
East St
Fern Ct
Mera Dr
Foresters Cres
Dorothy Evans Cl
Springfield Rd
Pinnacle Hill N
Spring Vale
Chieveley Rd
Chieveley Ct
Miller Ct
Martens Ave
Martens Cl
Pinnacle Hill
Bayard Ct
Clarence Rd
Brunswick Rd
Emerton Cl
Devonshire Rd
Broadway
Arnsberg Way
Tower Rd
Standard Rd
Red House La
Paddock
Sunland Ave
Lenior Cl
Lewin Rd
Lion Rd
Heathfield Rd
Methuen Rd
Royal Oak Rd
Albion Rd
Victoria Rd
Kingsley Ct
Warren Rd
Warren Cl
Highland Rd
Oakhouse Rd
Lynsted Cl
Rossland Cl
Watling St
Halcot Ave
Windsor Rd
Izane Rd
Timothy Cl
Charlotte Cl
Cuxton Cl
Hansol Rd
Barton Cl
Ditton Rd
Robin Hood La
Upton Rd
Freta Rd
Hawthorn Rd
Oaklands Rd
Oaklands Cl
Bellevue Rd
Martin Rise
Latham Rd
Horley Cl
Faygate
Mount Rd
Sibley Cl
Tenn Cts
1 The Mount
2 Alconbury

148
A
B
126
C
D
Service Tunnel
75
Heathrow Express Tunnel
Cargo Terminal
Terminal 4
PO
SEAFORD RD
SANDRINGHAM RD
SHOREHAM RD (W)
SHOREHAM RD (E)
6
LINDSAY CL
HENDON WAY
Bwg Gn
Pav
STANWELL MOOR
RIVERSIDE PL
RIVERSIDE RD
SHORT RD
SOUTHAMPTON RD
STIRLING RD
STANSTED RD
SEALAND RD
TW6
TUNNEL LINK RD
SOUTHERN PERIMETER RD
CALLIS FARM CL
DE HAVILLAND WAY
WESTLAND CL
BRISTOL CL
LANCASTER CL
WHITLEY CL
DUTCH BARN CL
5
Surrey
CLEVELAND PK
NORTHUMBERLAND CL
BEDFONT RD
Court Farm Ind Est
Blackburn Trad Est
FULWOOD CT
CLAY LA
BROOK CL
Hillingdon
CRANE RD
BEACON RDBT
BEACON RD
SANCTUARY RD
Longford River
SCYLLA RD
SCYLLA CRES
Hounslow
STANWELL RD
FALCON DR
Sch
74
EVEREST RD
WELLINGTON CT
COMET RD
CORSAIR CL
CORSAIR RD
BRITANNIA WAY
HANNIBAL RD
CLARE RD
Stanwell Fields CE Prim Sch
TW19
The Camgate Ctr
Broadview Est
WARDS COTTS
West Bedfont
ANSON CT
CORDELIA RD
CORDELIA GDNS
FROBISHER CRES
FROBISHER GDNS
CAMBRIA GDNS
Recn Gd
1 LANCASTER CT
2 TENSING CT
3 HILLARY CT
4 LIVINGSTONE CT
5 CHICHESTER CT
4
Liby
HADRIAN WAY
DOVE CT
EDDYSTONE WLK
CANOPUS WAY
CRANFORD CL
HADRIAN CL
ELSINORE AVE
HUNTLEY CL
Pav
Fball Gd
PARK MEWS
CRANFORD AVE
THE HEATHERS
TRIDENT HO
HERON CT
VISCOUNT RD
CALEDONIA RD
HILLINGDON AVE
OSBORNE AVE
THE NIGHTINGALES
ENSIGN WAY
ENSIGN CL
EXPLORER AVE
RAVENSBOURNE AVE
LONG LA
MILTON GDNS
CHESTERTON DR
MASEFIELD RD
NUTHATCH CL
SHORT LA
Sp Gd
CLYDE RD
LONGFORD WAY
LONGFORD AVE
LABURNUM WAY
GENESIS CL
Hounslow
Surrey
Surrey STREET ATLAS
3
Stanwell
MULBERRY AVE
HOLYWELL WAY
MARQUIS CT
GWENDOLEN HO
PUCCINIA CT
WHEAT HO
HAMMONDS HO
KINGSWAY
SCOTS CL
VIOLA AVE
VERONICA CT
YEOMAN DR
VICTORY CL
Sp Gd
STAINES RD
A30
B3003
Westgate Est
WINDERMERE CL
QUEEN MARY CL
LANG HO
BARLEY CT
GREENAWAY TERR
ASHDALE CL
73
B378
Superstore
Staines Resrs
WILLOWBROOK RD
Cemy
ELLIES MEWS
ALBAIN CRES
Ashford
MAPLE GDNS
LONDON RD
AMANDA CT
BARRY TERR
LONDON RD
HARROW RD
ASCOT RD
2
TOWN LA
LUD LO
ST DAVIDS CT
EDWARD WAY
ORCHARD WAY
DESFORD WAY
The Bull Dog
A30
PO
LODGE WAY
ASHWELL CT
SEATON DR
SILCHESTER CT
Pl Fld
A30 Staines (A308), M25
KENILWORTH RD
STANWELL RD
GORDON RD
WYVERN CT
The Ashford Tech Coll
CLOCKHOUSE LA
RUXBURY CT
CUMBERLAND RD
ASHFORD CRES
Bridge Farm
1
AVONDALE RD
DORSET RD
PORTLAND RD
SALCOMBE RD
THETFORD RD
HENGROVE CRES
GLENALMOND HO
HEATHFIELD CT
St David's Sch
TW15
CHURCH RD
ANGLESEY CL
HAVEN RD
72
Clarendon Sch
Ashford
STATION RD
STATION CRES
REEDSFIELD CL
REEDSFIELD RD
THE YEWS
SANDRINGHAM DR
06
A
B
170
07
VILLAGE WAY
GLEN AVE
C
PARKLAND GR
PARKLAND RD
CLIFFORD GR
B3003
30
GRAYS LA
WENTWORTH CL
D
Chattern Hill
Recn Gd
TUDOR CL
CONNAUGHT AVE
LANCASTER RD
STATION APP
FREDERICK HO
B378
Spelthorne Coll
MEADWAY
Recn Gd
QUEENS WLK
WEST CL
GWENDOLINE CT
Pl Fld
Allot

Hatton
Radius Pk
TW6
TW14
TW13
TW15
East Bedfont
Lower Feltham
Bedfont Lakes Country Park
Heathrow Terminal 4
Hotel
Playground
Cemy
Masts
Superstore
Marjory Kinnon Sch
Bedfont Jun & Inf Schs
Allot Gdns
Recn Gd
Duke of Northumberland's River
Longford Com Sch
Southville Jun & Inf Schs
Fairholme Prim Sch
Edward Pauling Prim Sch
Vineyard Nurseries
Grosvenor Park
HM Young Offender Institution & Remand Ctr
Bedfont Ind Pk
Bedfont Ind Pk N
Ashford Ind Est
Mereside Pk
STAINES RD
GREAT SOUTH-WEST RD
BEDFONT LA
BEDFONT RD
ASHFORD RD
KENDAL CL 1
APPLEBY GDNS 2
DERWENT CL 3
MISSENDEN CL 4
BUTTERMERE CL 5
AMBER CT 1
RUSSET CT 2
GARNET CT 3
OCHRE CT 1
SIENNA CT 2
VERMILLION CT 3
FUSCIA CT 4
INDIGO CT 5
VIRIDIAN CT 6
TOPAZ CT 7
THE HERMITAGE 8
SPRING CNR 9
QUEENS PARK GDNS 10
1 SHETLAND RD
2 TERMINAL FOUR RDBT
Clockhouse Rdbt

127
150
171

North Feltham
North Feltham Trad Est
Haslemere Ind Est
Mercury Ctr
Superstore
Griffin Ctr
Willow Ho
Duke of Northumberland's River
Dockwell's Ind Est
Freehold Ind Ctr
Fairway Est
Tamian Ind Est
River Gdns Bsns Ctr
Maple Gr Bsns Ctr
Central Pk Est
STAINES RD
FAGG'S RD
HARLINGTON RD W
HARLINGTON RD E
HOUNSLOW RD
BEDFONT LA
NEW RD
HANWORTH RD
UXBRIDGE RD
HIGH ST
Hounslow Heath
London Loop
Sparrow Farm Schs
TW14
Feltham Arena
1 FRANK TOWELL CT
2 BRASSEY CL
3 EASTLEIGH WAY
4 ORCHARD RD
5 PEACH RD
6 ALMOND CL
7 HAZEL GR
8 HUNTER HO
9 HAWTHORN RD
10 TILLEY RD
11 PLUM CL
12 ARCHER CT
13 MAGNOLIA CT
14 LEMON GR
15 BELVEDERE HO
16 QUINCE HO
17 CAMELLIA HO
1 BERGENIA HO
2 AZALEA HO
3 HAMLYN HO
Feltham
The Centre
Victoria Jun Sch
1 BROOKLYN CT
2 DEVONSHIRE CT
Feltham Com Sch
Grosvenor Park
FELTHAM
Feltham Bsns Complex
1 PARKFIELD PAR
2 ROCHESTER PAR
3 THE VINEYARDS
4 CHERVIL CL
Feltham Corporate Ctr
Felthambrook Ind Est
Hanworth Park House
Hanworth Park
TW13
Lower Feltham
Hanworth
1 BLAKEWOOD CL
2 SHAKESPEARE WAY
128
149
172

129
152
173
Hounslow Heath
Nature Reserve
TW4
TW2
TW13
London Loop
The Heathland Sch
The Orchard Jun & Inf Sch
Hounslow Bsns Pk
Inwood Bsns Pk
Hounslow
Millfarm Bsns Pk
Hounslow
Richmond upon Thames
River Crane
Crem
Cemy
Recn Gd
Nursery
Heathfield Jun & Inf Schs
Bishop Perrin CE Prim Sch
St Edmund's RC Prim Sch
Whitton Sch
Crane Park Prim Sch
Hampton Farm Ind Est
Hanworth Trad Est
The Lion Ctr
Apex Ret Pk
Links Ind Est
Oriel Prim Sch
Hospital Bridge Rdbt
Crane Park
Fulwell Park
CH Twickenham
Drv Rng
Apex Cnr
HANWORTH RD
WELLINGTON RD S
NELSON RD
HOSPITAL BRIDGE RD
GREAT CHERTSEY RD
TWICKENHAM RD
STAINES RD
HAMPTON RD W
HOUNSLOW RD
WHITTON RD
A3063
A314
A315
A316
A305
A312
B358
B361
SHERIDAN CT 1
PICKWICK CL 2
HEATHLANDS CT 3
BRAMLEY WAY 4
ALLIANCE CL 5
BODICEA MEWS 1
SHELBURNE DR 2
FOUR SQUARE CT 3
SLADE HO 1
JAMIESON HO 2
ATHERLEY WAY 1
DUNLEARY CL 2
DANIEL CL 3
1 MALLARD CL
2 BRUNEL WLK
3 BRACKEN CL
4 HEATHER WLK
CORFE CL 1
CARISBROOKE CL 2
1 TOWFIELD CT
2 NORMAN HO
3 RIVER CRANE WAY
1 WHITELY CT
2 BUTTS COTTS
1 EDWIN STRAY HO
2 CRANE HO
3 GLEBE HO
4 CHERTSEY HO
5 WHITELEYS HO
6 BUTTS HO
7 GLEBE COTTS
A B C D
13 14
72 73 74 75
1 2 3 4 5 6

152
A
B
C
D
130
Chatsworth Jun Sch
The Heath Bsns Ctr
Inwood Bsns Pk
Sewage Works
Duke of Northumberland's River
WHITTON RD
MASWELL PARK RD
MASWELL PK
Hounslow
HOUNSLOW GDNS
HOUNSLOW AVE
PARK CT
PARK RD
WOLSEY DR
PARK CRES
LYNCROFT GDNS
CENTRAL AVE
CHURCH STRETTON RD
LEAMINGTON CL
PRIORY RD
ROSEBERY RD
NORBURY AVE
CATHERINE GDNS
EATON RD
WAINWRIGHT GR
BRACKEN END
HALL RD
HARVESTERS CL
SOUTHLAND WAY
REAPERS WAY
THATCHERS WAY
HEATHER CL
GLEN WLK
PLOUGHMANS END
CROFTERS CL
GAINSBOROUGH GDNS
CONSTABLE GDNS
MUNNINGS GDNS
Allot Gdns
ARNOLD CRES
1 YEOMANS MEWS
2 REGENCY MEWS
BEAUMONT PL
MOGDEN LA
TREVOR CL
HILLARY DR
MANNS CL
BRIAR CL
BANKSIDE CL
LYNTON CL
A310
Ivybridge Ret Pk
Superstore
EASEDALE HO
SUMMERWOOD RD
1 THIRLMERE HO
2 HAWESWATER HO
3 WINDERMERE HO
Ivybridge Prim Sch
VARSITY DR
Twickenham Trad Ctr
BUTTERFIELD CL
RUGBY RD
SHIRLEY DR
SHIRLEY CL
MILLWOOD RD
PARK CL
DEAN RD
SANDRA CL
MARZENA CT
COLONIAL AVE
Hounslow
Richmond upon Thames
WHITTON DENE
WHITTON MANOR RD
AMBERSIDE CL
KNELLER GDNS
CONSORT MEWS
QUEENSBRIDGE PK
HARLEQUIN CL
Pav
Museum of Rugby
Twickenham Rugby Football Union Ground
Pl Fld
CEDAR AVE
OLD MANOR DR
Bnstand
Tenn Cts
Royal Military Sch of Music (Kneller Hall)
Sp Gd
DUKE OF CAMBRIDGE CL
B361
RYDAL GDNS
RUNNYMEDE RD
DERWENT RD
CONISTON RD
KESWICK RD
HOUNSLOW RD
VICARAGE RD
BRAMLEY CL
PROSPECT CRES
SHIRE MEWS
NELSON RD
SEATON RD
SEATON CL
KNELLER RD
1 SULLIVAN HO
2 PURCELL HO
3 HANDEL HO
4 ELGAR HO
Chase Bridge Prim Sch
WHITTON RD
TAYBEN AVE
CHUDLEIGH RD
PALMERSTON RD
MARLOW CRES
GLEBE SIDE
Whitton Road Rdbt
ERNCROFT WAY
RUSSELL RD
CHUDLEIGH RD
ST VINCENT RD
WARREN RD
SOUTH LO
SALLIESFIELD
CHASE GDNS
KENDREY GDNS
TALMA GDNS
HEATHFIELD N
HEATHFIELD S
MILTON LO
COURT WAY
GRIMWOOD RD
LATHAM CL
NELSON RD
ASHDALE CL
WILLOWDENE CL
PALGRAVE HO
CRANE WAY
Whitton
Liby
THE RIDGE
MILNER DR
HALL FARM DR
GODFREY AVE
ALTON GDNS
Richmond upon Thames Coll
EGERTON RD
ASHDALE WAY
HIGH ST
CYPRESS AVE
OAKLANDS
HAZEL CL
TRANMERE RD
MELROSE AVE
MAYFAIR AVE
OAKLANDS DR
BRITANNIA LA
CONSTANCE RD
SHORT WAY
REDWAY DR
TWICKENHAM
LANGHORN DR
CHALLENGE CT
CRANEFORD WAY
CRANEMEAD CT
CRANEFORD CL
CARLING CT 1
WHITEHEAD CT 2
SWANSTON CT 3
Tenn Cts
HEATHAM PK
Stoop Memorial Gd (Rugby Gd)
Pl Fld
Allot Gdns
River Crane
SIMBA CT 1
LANSDOWNE CL 2
STATION RD
SHERLAND RD
CHERTSEY RD
ROSEBINE AVE
GLADSTONE AVE
DENEHURST GDNS
ROSECROFT GDNS
BRIDGE WAY
Whitton
MONTROSE AVE
151
JUBILEE AVE
BLANDFORD AVE
FAIRFIELD AVE
PAULINE CRES
PERCY WAY
STRATHEARN AVE
RYECROFT AVE
Perrin Sch
PARK CRES
POST LA
COLLEGE CL
Kneller Gardens
BARNEBY CL
ROWNTREE RD
FORMAN CT
Coll
NORCUTT RD
WARWICK RD
HAMILTON RD
TALBOT RD
ALBERT RD
STATEN GDNS
GROVE AVE
TUDOR GDNS
CLIFDEN RD
COPTHALL GDNS
DEVON AVE
DORSET WAY
WILTSHIRE GDNS
GLOUCESTER RD
PERCY RD
Tenn Cts
MEADWAY
MEREWAY RD
GOULD RD
CRANE RD
EDWIN RD
MARSH FARM RD
LION RD
LAUREL AVE
LION AVE
STABLE MEWS
HOLLY RD
HEREFORD GDNS
MELBOURNE CT
ANDOVER RD
GRAVEL RD
MAY RD
KNIGHT'S PL
ALBION RD
KNOWLE RD
HEATH RD
ROSS HO
Whitton Sch
ROSS RD
SELKIRK RD
LINCOLN AVE
CAMPBELL CL
CHURCHVIEW RD
WALSINGHAM HO
BRINSWORTH CL
Mereway Ind
COLNE RD
HUNTING GATE MEWS
CAMAC RD
BRIAR RD
THE GREEN
SAVILLE RD
BRADLEY HO
RADNOR RD
TENNYSON AVE
MICHELL HO
Liby
A316
MORECROFT
CRANEBROOK
BELMONT RD
ELMSLEIGH HO
WILKINSON HO
CHERRY TREE HO
SECOND CROSS RD
CHESTNUT
FIRST CROSS RD
Twickenham Green
SYCAMORE HO
A311 THE GREEN
POPES GR
TRINITY CT
HEATHLANDS
HEATH GDNS
HOLLIES
RADNOR GDNS
CROSS DEEP GDNS
Games Ct
Sp Gd
River Crane
Crane Park
TW2
MANOR CT
MURRAY CT
MANOR RD
GREYSTONES
SELBY CT
ABBEY CT
MELBURY HO
GOTHIC RD
ELMSLEIGH RD
THIRD CROSS RD
LOUISA CT
CHILVERS CL
VICARAGE RD
GRANGE AVE
UPPER GROTTO RD
GROTTO RD
CEASORS CT
TW1
POPE'S GR
ABBOTSMEDE CL
HOLMES RD
MILL RD
FULWELL PARK AVE
AUGUSTA RD
LISBON AVE
OSBOURNE HO
RUTLAND RD
WOODBINE CL
FOURTH CROSS RD
TRAFALGAR RD
Inf & Jun Schs
KENILWORTH CT
BOX CNR
WALPOLE CT
GRACE CT
CORTAYNE CT
WALPOLE RD
POPE'S AVE
MANOR HO
ALEXANDER CL
ORFORD GDNS
BONSER RD
RIVER VIEW GDNS
CROSS DEEP
BRIDGE RD
MANOEL RD
PORTUGAL GDNS
NORWOOD CL
APPLEBY CL
FIFTH CROSS RD
BEDFORD RD
DENMARK RD
HAMPTON RD
CARPENTERS CT
SPENCER RD
JORDANS MEWS
Strawberry Hill
WALDEGRAVE GDNS
A309
CHILLINGWORTH GDNS
WARWICK LO
STAINES RD
A305
Waldegrave Sch
Tenn Cts
AUDLEY CT
PRESTON CL
WELLESLEY CRES
WELLESLEY RD
THURNBY CT
TOWER RD
DOWNSIDE
FORTESCUE AVE
TURNER AVE
TWINING AVE
FIELDING AVE
BRUNSWICK CL
SHAFTESBURY WAY
MILTON CT
CH
COURT CLOSE AVE
30
SIXTH CROSS RD
CLARENDON CRES
WELLESLEY CT 1
WENTWORTH CT 2
BERKLEY CL 3
ROYMOUNT CT 4
RUTLAND CT 5
1 STANGATE MANS
Strawberry Hill
Pl Fld
MULBERRY CT
STRAWBERRY HILL RD
Fulwell Park
Allot Gdns
B358
GROVE RD
QUEEN ANNES CL
STANLEY RD
GOLF SIDE
St James's RC Prim Sch
Strawberry Hill
NATALIE MEWS
SOUTH RD
STRAWBERRY HILL CL
St Mary's Coll
Garden Ctr
Superstore
Tenn Cts
WALDEGRAVE RD
14
174
15
WELLINGTON GDNS
STRATHMORE RD
Stanley Inf & Jun Schs
SOUTHFIELD GDNS
WALDEGRAVE PK
1 CUSACK CL
2 BRIDGE CL
Fulwell
CH
WILCOX RD
Cemy

153
RICHMOND
131
Richmond Lock
175
154
TW1
TW7
TW10
A
B
C
D
1
2
3
4
5
6
St Margarets
Cambridge Park
Ham
Twickenham
Marble Hill Park
Marble Hill House
River Thames
River Crane
Eel Pie Island
Ham House
Richmond Green
Richmond Landing Stage
St Helena Pier
Orleans House Gallery
Orleans Park Sch
St Mary's CE Prim Sch
York House
The German Sch
The Russell Sch
Strathmore Sch
Grey Court Sch
St Catherine's Sch
St James Ind Sch for Boys
Thames Path
Ferry P
Sp Gd
Pl Fld
Allot Gdns
Tenn Cts
Bwg Gn
Moor Mead Gd
St Margarets Rdbt
London Road Rdbt
TWICKENHAM BRIDGE
TWICKENHAM RD
THE AVENUE
CHERTSEY RD
ST MARGARET'S RD
RICHMOND RD
RICHMOND BRIDGE
CROWN RD
PETERSHAM RD
HILL RISE
RICHMOND HILL
GEORGE ST
HILL ST
KING ST
YORK ST
LONDON RD
CROSS DEEP
STRAWBERRY VALE
HAM ST
SANDY LA
RIVER LA
HAM COMM
MEADLANDS DR
BUCKINGHAM RD
ASHBURNHAM RD
WOODVILLE RD
RIVERSIDE
RIVERSIDE DR
A305
A307
A310
A316
A3004
A3004
B321
B352
Sudbrook P
Richmond
Meadlands Prim Sch
Teddington
Cassel

RICHMOND
132
SHEEN RD
A305
SHEEN RD
PARADISE RD
GEORGE ST
RED LION ST
HILL ST
A307
WORPLE WAY
ALBANY RD
HYDE RD
PRINCES RD
HOUBLON RD
ALBERT RD
B322
CHURCH RD
WINTER BOX WLK
PELDON CT
FLOYER CL
QUEENS CRES
SPRING GROVE RD
CHARMOUTH CT
AUDLEY RD
KINGS RD
King's House Sch
DENBIGH GDNS
MARCHMONT RD
COURTLANDS
Pl Fld
Allot Gdns
Christ's Sch
Cemy
1 ARUNDEL HO
2 MARLBOROUGH HO
3 BUCKINGHAM HO
4 OSBOURNE HO
5 YORK HO
6 SANDRINGHAM HO
7 KENT HO
8 NORFOLK HO
9 RUNNYMEDE HO
10 CARISBROOKE HO
11 GLOUCESTER HO
KINGS RIDE GATE
SHEEN COMMON DR
ORCHARD RISE
BERWYN RD
East Sheen Common
Fball Gd
Tenn
Bwg Gn
LONGFIELD DR
MONROE DR
UPLANDS CL
WEST TEMPLE SHEEN
COVAL LA
ALBANY CL
DERBY RD
Richmond Hill
Richmond Landing Stage
PETERSHAM RD
B321
RICHMOND HILL
FRIARS STILE RD
B353
QUEEN'S RD
CHESTER AVE
QUEEN'S RISE
PARK RD
MARLBOROUGH RD
GREVILLE RD
LOWER GROVE RD
PYRLAND RD
PARK HILL
MANNING PL
GROVE RD
KINGSMEAD
KING GEORGE SQ
CAMBRIAN RD
HOBART PL
SAYER'S WLK
STAFFORD PL
The Vineyard Sch
Richmond Coll
ROSEMONT RD
CARDIGAN RD
MONTAGUE RD
ONSLOW AVE
ONSLOW RD
CHISLEHURST RD
ROYSTON RD
MOUNT ARARAT RD
THE VINEYARD
GROSVENOR RD
HALFORD RD
LANCASTER PK
ELLERKER GDNS
HILL RISE
HOWSONS TERR
ROBINS CT
PARK HO
HAVERSHAM CL
NIGHTINGALE LA
Star & Garter Home
STAR AND GARTER HILL
RICHMOND GATE
SAWYER'S HILL
The Bog
Horse Ride
Bog Lodge
Saw Pit Plantation
TW10
Capital Ring
Sidmouth Wood
PETERSHAM RD
Petersham
RUTLAND DR
FORGE LA
MEADOW CL
CEDAR HTS
ASHFIELD CL
BUTE AVE
SUDBROOK LA
DICKENS CL
The German Sch
The Russell Sch
SANDPITS RD
PETERSHAM CL
HENLOW PL
CLIFFE RD
Pembroke Lodge
QUEEN'S RD
Petersham Park
Pen Ponds
Sudbrook Park
CH
Richmond
Pond Plantation
Pond Slade
Hamcross Plantation
B352
HAM GATE AVE
176
Ham Gate
Ham
Cemy
Isabella Plantation
1 CAMBRIDGE PARK CT
2 MEADOWSIDE
153

SW15
SW14
TW10
KT2
Roehampton
Richmond Park
Palewell Common
Palewell Fields
Adam's Pond
East Sheen Gate
Roehampton Gate
Polo Field
Horse Ride
The Royal Ballet Sch (White Lodge)
Deer Park
Pen Ponds
Spankers Hill Wood
Beverley Brook
Robin Hood Gate
Kingston Vale
Kingston Univ Roehampton Vale Campus
Chohole Gate
Superstore
War Meml
Old House
Roehampton Univ (Froebel Coll)
Roehampton Univ (Digby Stuart Coll)
Roehampton Univ (Southlands Coll)
Ibstock Place Sch
South Thames Coll
The Huntercombe Roehampton
Roehampton Sports Club
The Priory
SHEEN LA
ROEHAMPTON LA
ROEHAMPTON VALE
KINGSTON VALE
PRIORY LA
CLARENCE LA
DANEBURY AVE
ALLENFORD HO 1
SWAYTHLING HO 2
TATCHBURY HO 3
PENWOOD HO 4
BRAMLEY HO 5
SHALDEN HO 6
DUNBRIDGE HO 7
DENMEAD HO 8
CHARCOT HO 9
PORTSWOOD PL 10
BROCKBRIDGE HO 11
HURSTBOURNE HO 12
FINCHDEAN HO 1
HOLMSLEY HO 2
OVERTON HO 3
REDENHAM HO 4
MOUNT ANGELUS RD 5
1 MARTINDALE
2 SPENCER GDNS
FLORENCE TERR 1
EBOR COTTS 2
133
156
177

Roehampton
Allot Gdns
Putney Park Sch
134
PUTNEY
Tenn Ct
Roehampton Univ (Southlands Coll)
Sacred Heart RC Prim Sch
Roehampton Univ (Digby Stuart Coll)
Tenn Cts
Roehampton Univ (Froebel Coll)
Pl Fld
Queen Mary's Univ
SW15
Pav
South Thames Coll
Schs
Allot Gdns
Granard Prim Sch
Elliott Sch
Tenn Ct
Tenn Cts
1 ANDREW HO
2 HARTLEY HO
3 PEMBROKE HO
4 REED HO
5 CLINE HO
6 DOUGLAS HO
7 HAMILTON HO
Putney Heath
Putney Heath
Roehampton CE Prim Sch
Liby
Univ
The Huntercombe Roehampton
Tibbet's Corner
WILDCROFT MANOR
King's Mere
Putney Heath
Roehampton Lane
Jerry's Hill
Chohole Gate
Crem
Superstore
Cemy
Putney Vale
Queen's Mere
CH
Wimbledon Windmill Mus
SW19
Hall Sch Wimbledon
Allot Gdns
War Meml
London Scottish
Parkside (private)
Wimbledon Common
155
178
ROEHAMPTON LA
KINGSTON RD
ROEHAMPTON VALE
WIMBLEDON PARK SIDE
PARKSIDE
PUTNEY HILL
TIBBET'S RIDE
WEST HILL
PUTNEY HEATH
WESTLEIGH AVE
CHARTFIELD AVE
HAZLEWELL RD
PUTNEY PARK LA
DOVER HOUSE RD
CRESTWAY
HIGHDOWN RD
PARKMEAD
WESTMEAD
TELEGRAPH RD
WILDCROFT RD
PORTSMOUTH RD
Horse Ride
Wandsworth
Merton
Richmond upon Thames
SEDGEWICK HO 1
GODDARD HO 2
PLOWMAN HO 3
HEATHVIEW CT 4
A B C D
75 6 5 74 4 3 73 2 1 72
22 23

WANDSWORTH
West Hill
Southfields
Wimbledon Park
Wandsworth Gyratory
WANDSWORTH HIGH ST
MERTON RD
DURNSFORD RD
GARRATT LA
WEST HILL
UPPER RICHMOND RD
BUCKHOLD RD
A217 ARMOURY WAY
East Putney
Putney
Royal Hospl
King George's Park
Southside Sh Ctr
The All England Lawn Tennis & Croquet Club
Wimbledon Lawn Tennis Mus
Wimbledon Park Lake
Athletics Gd
Wimbledon Stadium
Earlsfield
SW15
SW18
SW19
135
158
179

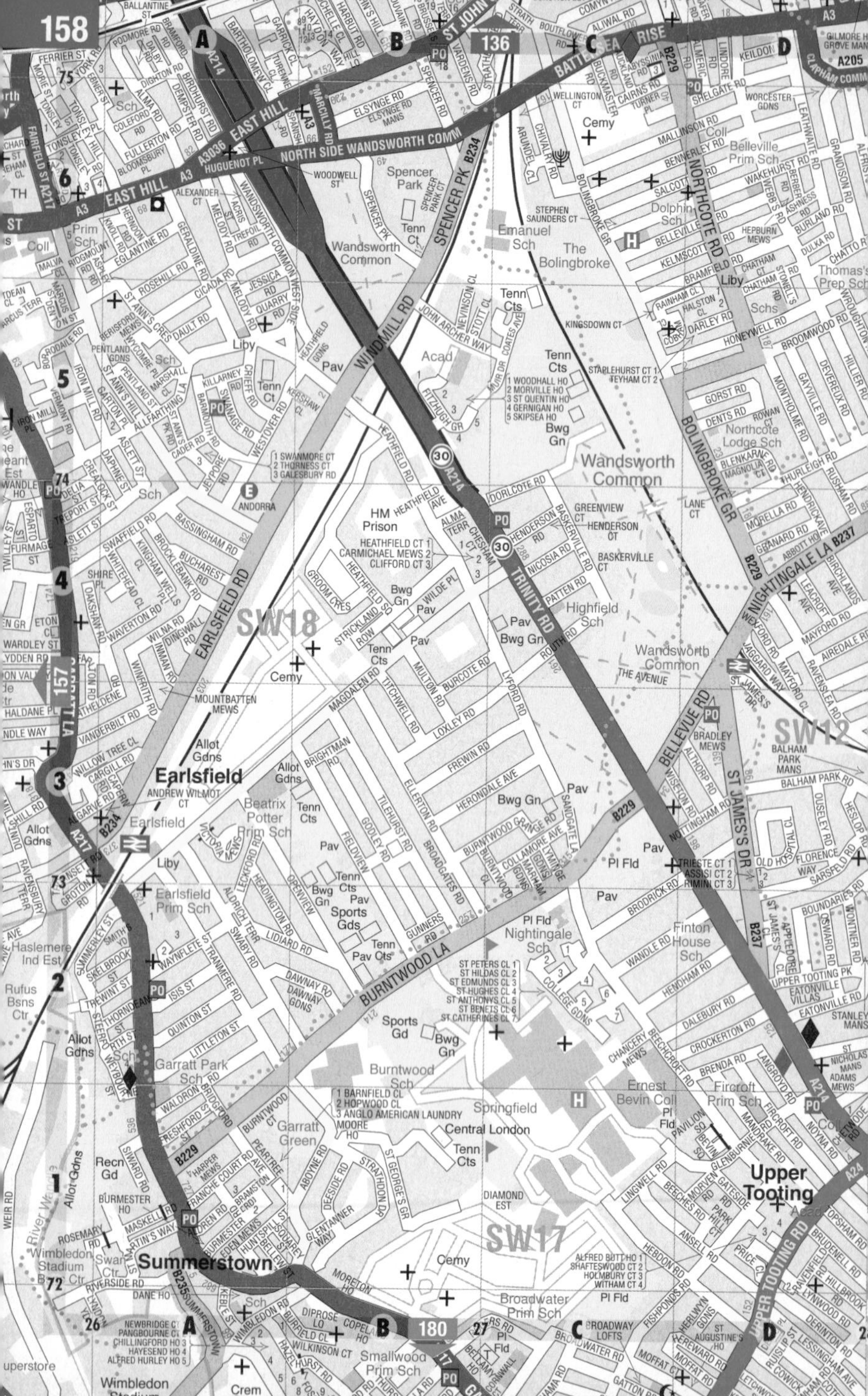
A
B
C
D
136
157
180
1
2
3
4
5
6
72
73
74
75
26
27
SW18
SW17
SW12
Earlsfield
Summerstown
Upper Tooting
Wandsworth Common
Spencer Park
HM Prison
The Bolingbroke
Emanuel Sch
Springfield
Central London
Ernest Bevin Coll
Burntwood Sch
Garratt Green
Garratt Park Sch
Earlsfield Prim Sch
Beatrix Potter Prim Sch
Nightingale Sch
Finton House Sch
Fircroft Prim Sch
Broadwater Prim Sch
Smallwood Prim Sch
Highfield Sch
Belleville Prim Sch
Dolphin Sch
Northcote Lodge Sch
Thomas's Prep Sch
Wimbledon Stadium
Haslemere Ind Est
Rufus Bsns Ctr
Swan Ctr
River Wandle
Allot Gdns
Recn Gd
Cemy
Crem
Liby
Acad
Tenn Cts
Bwg Gn
Pav
Sports Gds
Pl Fld
DIAMOND EST
ANDORRA
EAST HILL
NORTH SIDE WANDSWORTH COMM
BATTERSEA RISE
ST JOHN'S HILL
WANDSWORTH COMMON WEST SIDE
SPENCER PK
WINDMILL RD
TRINITY RD
EARLSFIELD RD
GARRATT LA
BURNTWOOD LA
NIGHTINGALE LA
BELLEVUE RD
BOLINGBROKE GR
NORTHCOTE RD
ST JAMES'S DR
UPPER TOOTING RD
MAGDALEN RD
HEATHFIELD RD
FAIRFIELD ST A217
A3
A214
A217
A24
A205
B229
B234
B235
B237
A3036

138
182
159
A
B
C
D
1
2
3
4
5
6
SW2
SE24
SE27
W16
Streatham Hill
Tulse Hill
Brockwell Park
HM Prison
ACRE LA
BRIXTON HILL
STREATHAM HILL
STREATHAM PL
CHRISTCHURCH RD
TULSE HILL
NORWOOD RD
DULWICH RD
EFFRA RD
KINGS AVE
THORNTON AVE
STREATHAM HIGH RD

Herne Hill
East Dulwich
SE22
SE24
SE21
SE27
Dulwich Village
Dulwich College
Dulwich Park
Belair Park
Knight's Hill
West Dulwich
West Norwood
Dulwich
Dulwich & Sydenham
Sydenham Hill
Dulwich Wood
HALF MOON LA
VILLAGE WAY
EAST DULWICH GR
LORDSHIP LA
CROXTED RD
DULWICH COMM
SOUTH CROXTED RD
COLLEGE RD
BARRY RD
HERNE HILL
THURLOW PARK RD
139
183
162

East Dulwich
Peckham Rye Park
Honor Oak
SE22
SE23
SE26
Camberwell Old Cemetery
Camberwell New Cemy
One Tree Hill (Recn Gd)
Honor Oak Park
Brenchley Gardens
Harris Girl's Acad
Horniman Mus
Horniman Sch
Forest Hill
Dulwich & Sydenham
Dulwich Wood
Sydenham Hill Wood (Nat Res)
Sydenham High Sch
Sydenham Wells Park
Forest Hill Sec Sch
Eliot Bank Prim Sch
Fairlawn Prim Sch
Malham Road Ind Est
Dulwich Bsns Ctr
Forest Hill Ind Est
Forest Hill Bsns Ctr
Willow Bsns Pk
Mayow Pk
FOREST HILL RD
LONDON RD
DARTMOUTH RD
HONOR OAK PK
WALDRAM PARK RD
PERRY VALE
BARRY RD
SYDENHAM HILL
WELLS PARK RD
DENHAM KIRKDALE
The Grove
140
161
184
A
B
C
D
1
2
3
4
5
6

A
B
C
D
141
Brockley
Brockley Cemy
Ladywell Cemy
Brockley Prim Sch
Crofton Park
SE4
Ladywell
SE13
Lewisham
Lewisham Park
Ladywell Arena
Ladywell Fields
Greyhound Stadium
Crofton L Ctr
Crofton Sch
Guy's Hospital Athletic Gd
Stillness Jun & Inf Schs
Holbeach Prim Sch
Catford
Catford Bridge
St Dunstan's Coll
Catford Gyratory
Rushey Green Prim Sch
Forest Hill
SE23
Rathfern Prim Sch
Kilmorie Prim Sch
CATFORD
SE6
Athelney Prim Sch
Bellingham
Bromley Road Ret Pk
Bellingham Trad Est
Greenvale Sch
Adamsrill Prim Sch
SE26
Bell Green
Superstore
Elfrida Sch
Pool River
Ravensbourne River
BROCKLEY RD
STONDON PK
BROCKLEY RISE
STANSTEAD RD
CATFORD RD
CATFORD HILL
PERRY HILL
PERRY RISE
BELL GN
STANTON WAY
RUSHEY GN
BROMLEY RD
LEWISHAM HIGH ST
LADYWELL RD
ADELAIDE AVE
PLASSY RD
A21
A205
A212
A2218
B218
B236
B238
B227
164
185
1
2
3
4
5
6
72
73
74
37
38

LEWISHAM
LEE HIGH RD
142
A
B
C
D
SLAITHWAITE RD
THE GLASSHOUSE
MORLEY RD
WRIGHT CL
HOLLY LODGE
TRINITY CL
COLLEGE PARK
WISTERIA RD
WATERSIDE
WEARDALE RD
MERIDIAN CT
ABERNETHY RD
LOCHABER RD
HAMLET CL
OLD RD
BANKWELL RD
AISLIBIE RD
LENHAM RD
SIMS WLK
MEADOWCOURT RD
OSBORN TERR
B212
Lee Green
ELTHAM RD
A20
A2212
BURNT ASH RD
LEEGATE
LADYWELL RD
B236
Ladywell
LEWISHAM HIGH ST
LONGBRIDGE WAY
COURTHILL RD
MORLEY CT
WHITBURN RD
Leis Ctr
COLFE & HATCHCLIFFE'S GLEBE
LEGGE ST
ROMBOROUGH GDNS
ROMBOROUGH WAY
CAMPSHILL RD
CAMPSHILL PL
Allot Gdns
GUYSCLIFF RD
ST MAURITIUS HO
BENDEN HO
MONUMENT GDNS
CANADA GDNS
KEMPS GDNS
CHIDDINGSTONE
THORNFORD RD
RYECROFT RD
COURTHILL RD
HOLLY HEDGE TERR
DERMODY RD
DERMODY GDNS
PASCOE RD
Manor Park
Quaggy River
NORTHBROOK RD
CORDWELL RD
WOLFRAM CL
KELLERTON RD
CHALCROFT RD
THORNWOOD RD
MANOR PK
MANOR LA
Liby
Tenn Cts
Manor House Gardens
LAMPMEAD RD
BRIGHTFIELD RD
HEDGLEY MEWS
HEDGLEY ST
ST PETER'S CT
THE MET APPTS
TAUNTON RD
BARNSTAPLE HO
GLASTONBURY HO
WIMBORNE CL
EFFINGHAM RD
MERRIDALE
Brindishe Prim Sch
RC Inf Sch
HANDEN RD
WANTAGE RD
MICHELDEVER RD
SE12
SOUTHBROOK RD
SOUTHBROOK MEWS
CARSTON CL
SE13
MERBURY CL
KNOWLES HILL CRES
BRAMLEY CT
ENNERSDALE RD
NIGHTINGALE GR
ARLINGTON CL
HOLM HURST
HOLLYDENE
ST SWITHUN'S RD
MOUNTFIELD CT
LEAHURST RD
STAPLEHURST RD
LONGHURST RD
LEAMINGTON VILLAS
HEREFORD GDNS
GUARDIAN CT
MAYTHORNE COTTS
FERNBROOK RD
FERNBROOK CRES
Lee Manor Sch
Hither Green
Hither Green
CANTERBURY
Lewisham Park
KEMSLEY
MALLING
BREDGAR
HARVARD RD
FORDYCE RD
LITTLEWOOD
RADFORD RD
LEWISHAM PK
PLUMMER CT
CROFT CT
MOUNT PLEASANT RD
ALDWORTH GR
ROXLEY
LANIER RD
THEODORE RD
THEODORE CT
BEACON RD
ARDMERE RD
BRIGHTSIDE RD
Prim Sch
GEORGE LA
LARA CL
SPRINGRICE RD
HITHER GREEN LA
MALLET RD
ELTHRUDA RD
BLAGDON RD
THACKERAY'S ALMSHOUSES
Lewisham
DAVENPORT RD
SYCAMORE GR
OAKLEY DR
HIGHFIELD CL
KINGSWOOD CT
CATALPA CT
DESVIGNES DR
ROSSE GDNS
DUNCRIEVIE RD
SPRINGBANK RD
WELLMEADOW RD
Chiltonian Ind Est
SYCAMORE CT
MAURICE HO
HOLME LACEY RD
DALLINGER RD
MILBOROUGH CRES
Lee
RC Jun Sch
KIMBOLTON CL
ROSENTHAL RD
ROSENTHAL HO
Bwg Gn
LULLINGSTONE LA
OAKWOOD CL
GREENWICH HO
FARLEY RD
FARLEY MEWS
Mountsfield Park
HOSPITAL WAY
HEATHER CL
FIRTREE HO
WOODLANDS ST
BENIN ST
BLASHFORD ST
LANAIN CT
NEWSTEAD RD
MANOR LA
PARKCROFT RD
LANNE
COMPTON MEWS
STONEYCROFT CL
BIRCH GR
MARTIN CT
WILDWOOD CL
Allot Gdns
HONLEY RD
CUDHAM ST
FAIRFIELDS
RINGSTEAD RD
RINGSTEAD BLDGS
CARSWELL RD
Pl Fld
MELBOURNE MEWS
STAINTON RD
MOUNTFIELD CL
THE WOODLANDS
ATHLONE CT
HILLCREST CT
A21
A205
ST MILDREDS RD
RAYFORD AVE
HELDER GR
KENDALE RD
LINCHMERE RD
PLASSY RD
OCTAVIA HO
REDFERN RD
BRITTON CL
BROWNHILL RD
ELMER RD
FLEET TERR
SPORTSBANK ST
ARNGASK RD
FORDEL RD
GLENFARG RD
SANDHURST MKT
SANDHURST RD
KILLEARN RD
BRAIDWOOD RD
TORRIDON RD
ARDGOWAN RD
MINARD RD
BROADFIELD RD
WELLMEADOW RD
FURTHER GREEN RD
Sandhurst Jun & Inf Schs
Allot Gdns
WAITE DAVIES RD
SUMMERFIELD ST
RIVERVIEW RD
BOWNESS RD
JUTLAND RD
ALLENFIELD RD
163
ENGLEHEART RD
HARRIS LO
SANGLEY RD
WINDSOR MEWS
CULVERLEY RD
Allot Gdns
SHORNDEAN ST
ST FILLANS RD
Holy Cross RC Prim Sch
Rushey Green Prim Sch
1 CAVENDISH CT
2 STANNARD CT
SOUTH PARK CRES
PASTURE RD
SEDGEWAY
CUMBERLAND PL
ASHMORE CT
BURLEIGH WLK
PENERLEY RD
BARGERY RD
SAMBRUCK MEWS
INCHMERY RD
THORNSBEACH RD
PENBERTH RD
MUIRKIRK RD
DOWANHILL RD
VERDANT LA
HAFTON RD
ABBOTSHALL RD
BALLOCH RD
BIRKHALL RD
ARDFILLAN RD
Pl Fld
Pav
MERCHISTON RD
ARDOCH RD
SE6
Allot Gdns
Cemy
ARRAN RD
NEWQUAY RD
MUNCIES MEWS
CRANTOCK RD
PENDERRY RISE
Torridon Jun & Inf Schs
HAZELBANK RD
Allot Gdns
Downham Ent Ctr
Crem
CALLANDER RD
Bwg Gn
Pav
GREENSIDE CL
WENTLAND CL
WENTLAND RD
MORDRED RD
BAUDWIN RD
CASTILLON RD
WINGROVE RD
EVANS RD
CRUTCHLEY RD
MELIOT RD
ECTOR RD
PELINORE RD
PERSANT RD
BOUNDFIELD RD
DANEBY RD
HOLLY CT
Pav
Pl Fld
Tenn Cts
BELLINGHAM RD
BATTERSBY RD
LONGHILL RD
SCARLET RD
HEXAL RD
GILTON RD
WATERS RD
Forster Park Prim Sch
KNIGHT'S CT
JENNIFER RD
Catford High Sch
Forster Park
BROMLEY RD
WOODHAM RD
PASSFIELDS
DANESWOOD AVE
1 NEWNHAM HO
2 WHITCHURCH HO
CARSTAIRS RD
ARKINDALE RD
BOSBURY RD
CONSBOROUGH CRES
WHITEFOOT TERR
LINCOMBE RD
BIDEFORD RD
ILFRACOMBE RD
CRANMORE RD
LENTMEAD RD
WOODBANK RD
NORTHOVER
ROUNDTABLE RD
BR1
UNDERSHAW RD
SHAW RD
SHAW PATH
SHROFFOLD RD
LEEDS CT
ORFORD RD
WHITEFOOT LA
FORSTER HO
ORCHARD CT
Pav
Pl Fld
Green Chain Wlk
NUBIA WAY
Bonus Pastor RC Sch
FALKLAND HO
A
St John Baptist CE Prim Sch
COTTON HILL
B
186
39
C
New Woodlands Sch
D
GITTENS CL
LAMEROCK RD
TRISTRAM RD
CAMLAN RD
CAPSTONE RD
MOORSIDE RD
CHURCHDOWN
Southend
BEACHBOROUGH RD
BROCKMAN RISE
SOUTHVIEW RD
OAKSHADE RD
DOWNDERRY RD
Downderry Prim Sch
RAVENSCAR RD
Allot Gdns
ALLERFORD RD
WATERBANK RD
WATERMEAD RD
NAYLAND HO
FARMSTEAD RD
A2218
A21
ALLERFORD CT
TREWSBURY HO
BRADSTOCK HO
HUNSTER HO
75
74
73
72
6
5
4
3
2
1
38

Sutcliffe Park
ELTHAM RD
ELTHAM HILL
WESTHORNE AVE
Eltham Green
Yorkshire Grey
Eltham Green Specialist Sports Coll
Cliftons Roundabout
Moatbridge Sch
Colfe's Sch
Riverston Sch
Horn Park
Mottingham Farm
Hadlow Coll
Hadlow Coll Nature Reserve
Eltham Coll Jun Sch
Eltham Coll
SE12
SE9
Mottingham
Grove Park
BARING RD
CHINBROOK RD
GROVE PARK RD
SIDCUP RD
Green Chain Wk
Quaggy River
Haberdashers' Aske's Knights Acad
BR1
143
187
166
A2212
A2213
A210
A205
A20
B226
A2
Lewisham
Greenwich
Bromley

A
B
C
D
144
Well Hall Pleasaunce
Tenn Cts
Bwg Gns
ELTHAM PARK GDNS
GREENVALE RD
DUNVEGAN
A2
50
Eltham Park South
Recn Gd
Tenn Cts
Green Chain Wlk
Eltham Warren
CH
Eltham
WELL HALL RD
GLENLEA RD
GLENLYON RD
GLENSHIEL RD
St Mary's RC Prim Sch
CONNIFFE CT
GLENURE RD
MCAULEY CL
ELDERSLIE RD
LABURNHAM PL
HAMLET HO
GREENHOLM RD
BALCASKIE RD
BEECHHILL RD
GLENHOUSE RD
ARCHERY RD
STRONGBOW RD
STRONGBOW CRES
ELSTOW CL
ELSTOW RD
GOUROCK RD
FRIARS MEWS
FIFTEENPENNY FIELDS
DOBELL RD
ORANGERY LA
BLUNTS RD
Liby
Sch
ELTHAM
A208
1 WEATHERSFIELD CT
2 PHILPOT PATH
ELTHAM HIGH ST
A210
ELTHAM HILL
A205
HORSFIELD RD
HAIMO RD
LIONEL RD
FROISSART RD
BASKET GDNS
TATTERSALL CL
PULLMAN PL
EVEREST RD
KEYNSHAM GDNS
MILNE GDNS
BLOXAM GDNS
KEYNSHAM RD
JOHN RD
LILBURNE RD
LILBURNE GDNS
CARNECKIE GDNS
SHERARD RD
LASSA RD
SOWERBY CL
PRINCE JOHN RD
VANDYKE CROSS
YOLANDE GDNS
Tenn Cts
Recn Gd
Eltham Hill Tech Coll for Girls
QUEENSCROFT RD
Moatbridge Sch
BEACH CT
CEDAR CT
GROVE MARKET PL
RUSKIN CT
WYTHFIELD RD
KING'S ORCH
ELIZABETH TERR
PASSEY PL
PHILIPOT ALMSHO
ST MARY'S PL
POUND PL
MESSETER PL
WOODINGTON CL
MARLOWE GDNS
PIPPENHALL
A211
WYTHENS WLK
SOUTHEND CRES
SOUTHEND CL
OAKWAYS
BUTTERFLY LA
Bwg Gn
Pav
Sp Gd
Nursery
TRINITY CT
WENSLEY CL
WOLSEY CT
NORTH PK
PALACE CT
CHAUNDRYE CL
COURT YD
MOAT CT
TILT YARD APP
GREENACRES
DARWIN CT
ELMSLIE CT
LADYSMITH RD
HALONS RD
ENSLIN RD
Allot Gdns
KINGSGROUND
KING JOHN'S WLK
Green Chain Wlk
Eltham Palace
Tenn Cts
CH
Bwg Gn
SOUTHEND HO
INCA DR
Pavs
Tenn Cts
GLASBROOK RD
CUFF CRES
THE VISTA
MIDDLE PARK AVE
NEWMARKET GN
Pl Fld
King John's Wlk
COURT RD
Royal Blackheath
STARBUCK CL
CLARE CNR
FOOTSCRAY RD
B263
Green Chain Wlk
Allot Gdns
165
WOODMERE
TARNWOOD PK
The Tarn
Mottingham
BRITTAIN CT
SHRUBSALL CL
SIDCUP RD
A20
40
STATION APP
1 POPE STREET CT
2 MOTTINGHAM CT
3 PICKWICK CT
4 ROYAL CT
SE9
Allot Gdns
CAMBRIDGE GN
CASTLEFORD AVE
IVOR GR
Bwg Gn
Tenn Cts
HAINAULT ST
BLANMERLE RD
KIPPINGTON DR
MOTTINGHAM GDNS
WEST HALLOWES
LAYZELL WLK
SIDCUP RD
LUXFIELD RD
PRIORY LEAS
HINTON CL
CROSSMEAD
Tenn Cts
Fairy Hill
LAWN
BROAD WLK
New Eltham
COLLEGE VIEW
HIGHCOMBE CL
EVELYN CT
WEST PK
SYCAMORE CL
Liby
HARTSMEAD RD
DOWNLEYS CL
LEYSDOWN RD
MINISTRY WAY
BILL HAMLING CL
L Ctr
Sp Gd
Green Lane Bsns Pk
PARKVIEW RD
EDITH POND CT
Allot Gdns
Sp Gd
St Olaves Prep Sch
SOUTHWOOD RD
DEVONSHIRE RD
B226
PORCUPINE CL
BOWMEAD
MARGARET GARDNER DR
BIRBETTS RD
CHAPEL FARM RD
Greenacres Prim Sch & Language Impairment Unit
Games Cts
Coldharbour Sp Ctr
BROOKS CL
Altash Gardens
ALTASH WAY
GREEN LA
Fiveways
SOUTHWOOD HO
COLYER CL
LARCHWOOD RD
CADWALLON RD
GROVE PARK RD
THE CROSSWAY
TEIGN MEWS
DORSET RD
PORTLAND RD
SILVERDALE DR
CLARENCE RD
LULWORTH RD
ELMHURST RD
AVONDALE RD
LAVIDGE RD
THE UNDERWOOD
WITHERSTON WAY
CHARLDANE RD
FELHAMPTON RD
Tenn Cts
Pav
Sp Gd
MODEL FARM CL
ALBERT RD
SHOTTERY CL
GEFFREY'S CT
BELVOIR CL
BLANCHARD CL
MOTTINGHAM RD
WYNFORD WAY
WOODCROFT
1 THE LINK
2 THE MOUND
3 COLDHARBOUR CREST
4 JAMES NEWMAN CT
Allot Gdns
MONTBELLE RD
CHANCTONBURY WAY
SENNEN WLK
NUNNINGTON CL
Recn Gd
GREENFIELD CT
COURT FARM RD
HAVEN CL
BROMHEDGE
LITTLEMEDE
LITTLE MEDE
PARTRIDGE GN
BAREFOOT DR
LEAS DALE
BADGERS CROFT
THE COURSE
CROUCH CROFT
COLEMANS HEATH
Pav
HIGH POINT
DOMONIC DR
Pl Fld
GARDENERS CL
Allot Gdns
WIDECOMBE RD
THURSLEY RD
RAVENSCROFT CRES
Sch
KINGSLEY WOOD DR
MOTTINGHAM RD
SPEKEHILL
SOUTHOLD RISE
LONGCROFT
SANDLING RISE
Liby
WILLIAM BAREFOOT DR
GREAT HARRY DR
Tenn Cts
Allot Gdns
DUNKERY RD
BEACONSFIELD RD
BUCKLER GDNS
RAVENSWORTH RD
A208
HARTING RD
Sch
HASSOP WLK
KERSEY GDNS
HORNING CL
FRAMLINGHAM CRES
TENTERDEN CL
SMARDEN GR
ORPENHAM RD
188
BIDDENDEN WAY
SWITHLAND GDNS
JASON WLK
BEANSHAW
BEAUMANOR GDNS
MILVERTON WAY
ADDERLEY GDNS
SHALLONS RD
DOMONIC DR
BROWNSPRING DR
Sch
30
DUDDINGTON CL
CASTLETON RD
KIMMERIDGE RD
CALCOTT WLK
B263
42
43
72
73
74
1
2
3
4
5
6
75
Lewisham
Bromley
Greenwich
Bromley

A
B
C
D
145
168
189
Cemy
Crown Woods Sch
EAST ROCHESTER WAY
A2
SUTHERLAND AVE
DA15
SE9
BR7
BEXLEY RD
BLACKFEN RD
A210
Avery Hill
Avery Hill Park
Univ of Greenwich Avery Hill Campus Mansion Site
Univ of Greenwich Avery Hill Campus Southwood Site
DARLAND HO 1
WOOTTON HO 2
WAYFIELD LINK 3
TEYNHAM HO 4
OSPRINGE CT 5
TRINITY MEWS 6
AVERY HILL RD
B2214
Our Lady of the Rosary RC Prim Sch
Hollyoak Wood Park
Willersley Park
Burnt Oak Jun Sch
HALFWAY ST
Sparrow's Farm L Ctr
Green Chain Wlk
New Eltham
Dulverton Prim Sch
King George's Field
LONGLANDS CT 1
THE FIRS 2
SANDALWOOD HO 3
BUCKTHORN HO 4
MOAT CT 5
Sidcup
Longlands Prim Sch
West Lodge Sch
SIDCUP RD
A20
SIDCUP BY PASS RD
MAIN RD
A211
Longlands
Mulligan's
STATION RD
A222

BEXLEY
146
A
B
C
D
Danson House
Danson Park
Bexley Gram Sch
Tenn Cts
Pl Fld
DA16
DA6
The Lake
Allot Gdns
EAST ROCHESTER WAY
BLACKFEN RD
Danson Intc
DANSON RD
Blackfen
Blackfen Sch for Girls
Sherwood Park Prim Sch
DANSON UNDERPASS 1
KESTLAKE RD 2
Penhill Park
DA5
PENHILL RD
BLENDON RD
Hollyoak Wood Park
Willersley Park
DA15
Marlborough Park
River Shuttle
Sidcup
Chatsworth Inf Sch
Hurstmere Sch for Boys
Recn Gd
Hurst Prim Sch
Rose Bruford Coll
Lamorbey Park
Holy Trinity Lamorbey CE Prim Sch
Burnt Oak Jun Sch
Chislehurst & Sidcup Gram Sch
HURST RD
Cemy
Albany Park
Abbeyhill Park
STATION RD
Birkbeck Prim Sch
Waring Park
West Lodge Sch
DA14
Cleeve Park Sch
North Gray Wood
Foots Cray Place
HIGH ST
167
190

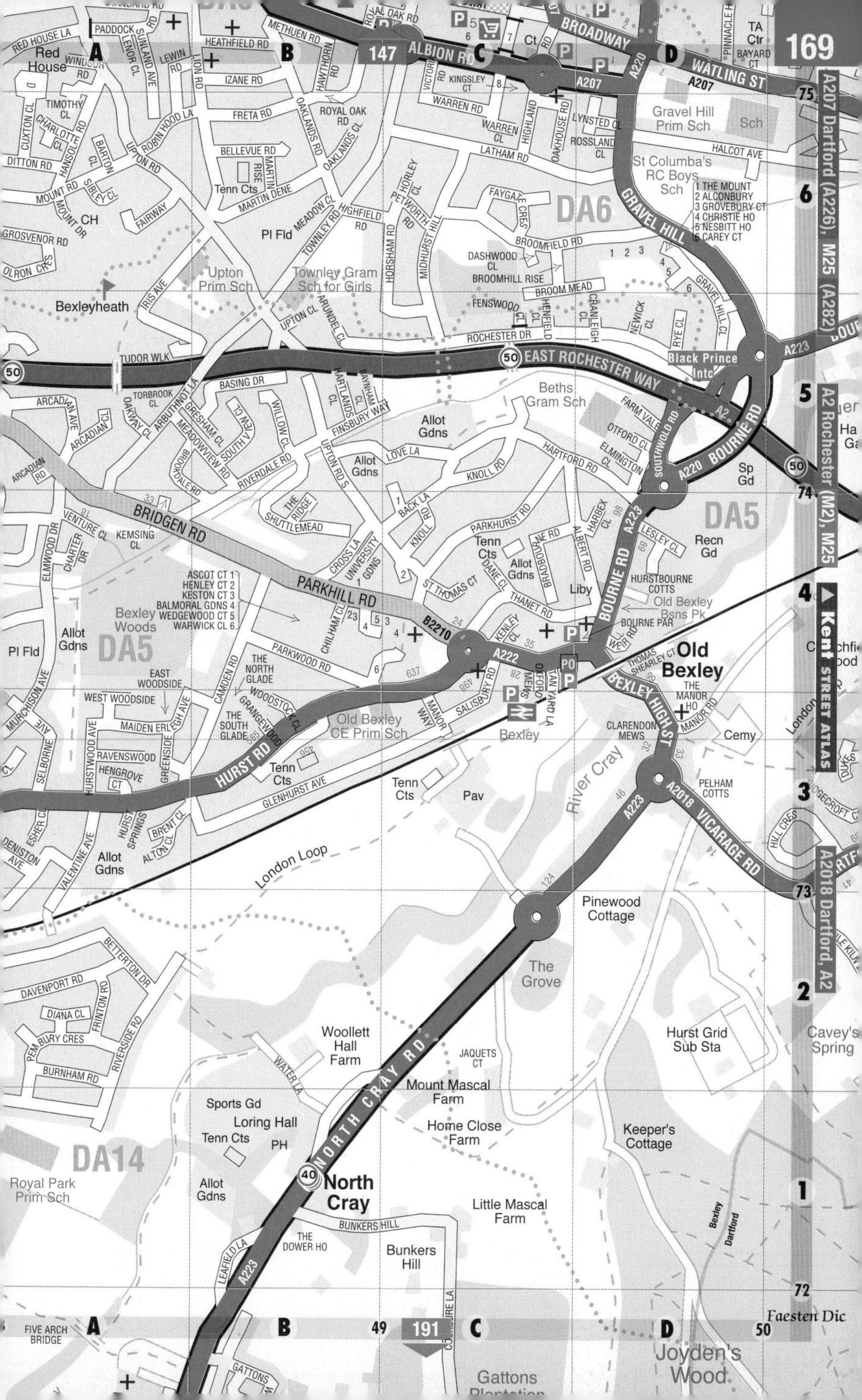
Red House
Bexleyheath
DA6
DA5
DA14
Old Bexley
North Cray
Joyden's Wood
Broadway
Watling St
A207
Gravel Hill
East Rochester Way
A2
Bourne Rd
A220
A223
Bridgen Rd
Parkhill Rd
B2210
A222
Hurst Rd
Bexley High St
A2018
Vicarage Rd
North Cray Rd
River Cray
London Loop
Upton Prim Sch
Townley Gram Sch for Girls
Beths Gram Sch
Gravel Hill Prim Sch
St Columba's RC Boys Sch
Old Bexley CE Prim Sch
Royal Park Prim Sch
Bexley Woods
Black Prince Intc
Bexley
Pinewood Cottage
The Grove
Woollett Hall Farm
Mount Mascal Farm
Home Close Farm
Little Mascal Farm
Loring Hall
Hurst Grid Sub Sta
Keeper's Cottage
Bunkers Hill
Gattons Plantation
Cavey's Spring
Faesten Dic
A207 Dartford (A226), M25 (A282)
A2 Rochester (M2), M25
Kent STREET ATLAS
A2018 Dartford, A2
147
191
49
50
75
74
73
72
1 THE MOUNT
2 ALCONBURY
3 GROVEBURY CT
4 CHRISTIE HO
5 NESBITT HO
6 CAREY CT
ASCOT CT 1
HENLEY CT 2
KESTON CT 3
BALMORAL GDNS 4
WEDGEWOOD CT 5
WARWICK CL 6

148
St David's Sch
Clarendon Sch
Spelthorne Coll
Liby
Ashford
Chattern Hill
Recn Gd
Allot Gdns
Pav
T Cts
Tenn Cts
Pl Fld
Sp Ctr
St Michael RC Prim Sch
The Echelford Prim Sch
Ashford Manor
CH
ASHFORD
TW15
Fordbridge Roundabout
STAINES BY-PASS
KINGSTON RD
Staines Reservoirs Aqueduct
School Road
Bwg Gn
Works
River Ash
TW18
Gravel Pit
Queen Mary Resr
TW17
CHURCH RD
FORDBRIDGE RD
CONVENT RD
SCHOOL RD
CLOCKHOUSE LA
ASHFORD RD
A308 Staines, M25 (A30)
VAUGHAN ALMSHOS 1
BEAUFORT HO 2
MORGAN CT 3
ASHTREE CT 4
WORCESTER CT 5
ASTLEHAM RD 1
ASTLEHAM WAY 2
192
STUDIOS RD
Surrey STREET ATLAS

149
193
172
A
B
C
D
TW13
TW15
TW16
Lower Feltham
Felthamhill
Ashford Common
Sunbury Common
Littleton Common
Charlton
Bedfont Ind Pk N
Court One
Bedfont Ind Pk
Ashford Ind Est
Mereside Pk
ASHFORD RD
FELTHAM RD
CHERTSEY RD
CADBURY RD
WINDMILL RD
STAINES RD W
FELTHAM HILL RD
Ashford Bsns Complex
Allot Gdns
Sp Gd
Spelthorne Inf & Jun Schs
Meadhurst Sports Club
Hounslow
Surrey
Kenyngton Manor Prim Sch
Feltham Hill Brook
Recn Gd
The Shears
Spelthorne Sports Club
Wks
Action Ct
West Surrey Est
Windmill Bsns Village
Superstore
Sunbury Int Bsns Ctr
The Dolphin Est
Water Works
Springfield Prim Sch
Sunbury Cross
Sunbury
Upper Halliford
The Bishop Wand CE Sch
Hawkedale Inf Sch
Sports Gd
Cemy
Works
M3
A244
A308
B377

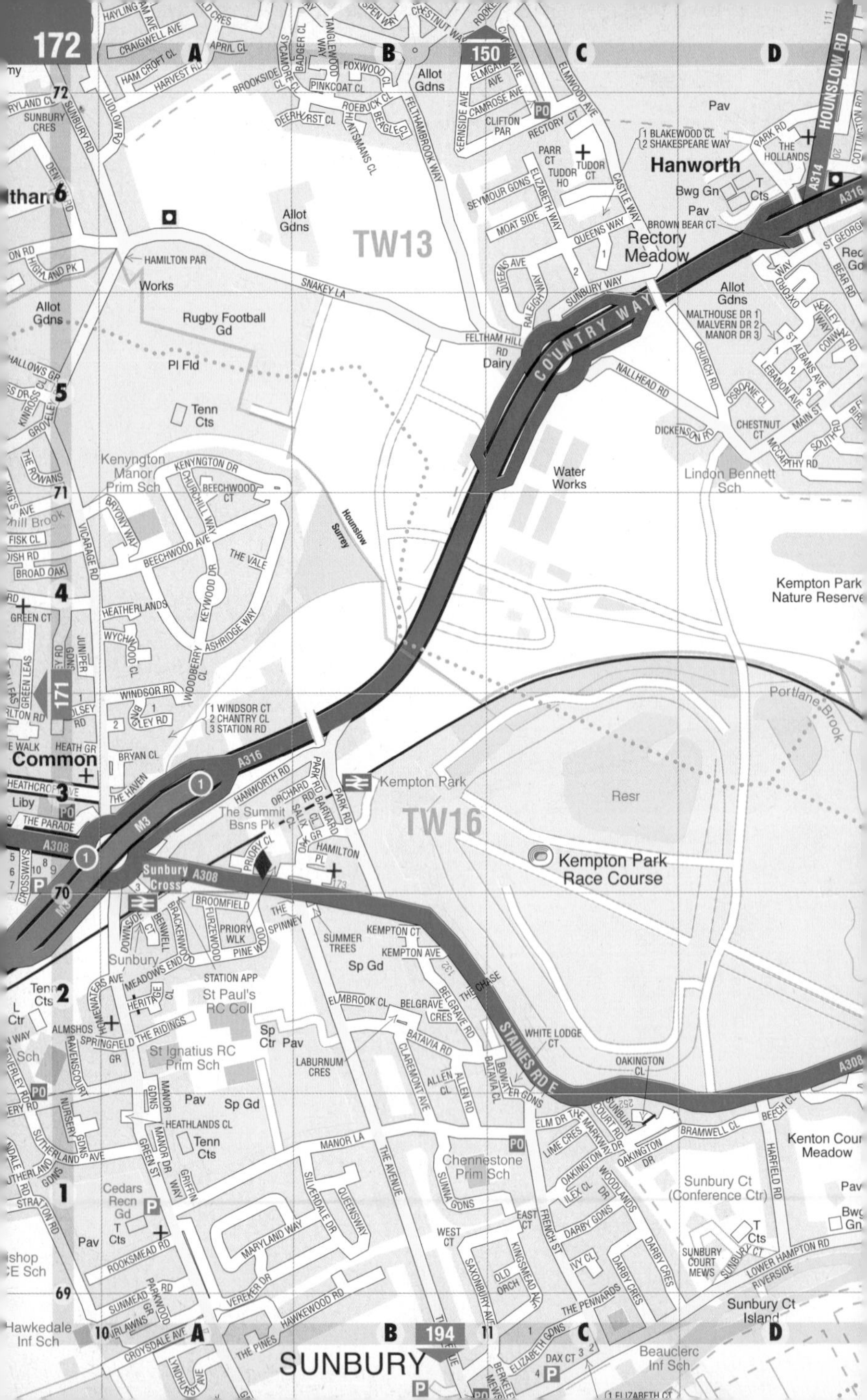
A
B
C
D
150
TW13
TW16
Hanworth
Rectory Meadow
Allot Gdns
Rugby Football Gd
Pl Fld
Works
Tenn Cts
Kenyngton Manor Prim Sch
Water Works
Lindon Bennett Sch
Kempton Park Nature Reserve
Portlane Brook
Resr
Kempton Park
Kempton Park Race Course
The Summit Bsns Pk
Sunbury Cross
St Paul's RC Coll
St Ignatius RC Prim Sch
Chennestone Prim Sch
Sunbury Ct (Conference Ctr)
Kenton Court Meadow
Sunbury Ct Island
Cedars Recn Gd
Hawkedale Inf Sch
Beauclerc Inf Sch
Common
SUNBURY
COUNTRY WAY
STAINES RD E
HOUNSLOW RD
SNAKEY LA
FELTHAM HILL RD
A316
A308
A314
M3
171
173
194

Twickenham
Apex Cnr
Hampton Hill
Fulwell Park
Hampton
TW12
TW16
UXBRIDGE RD
UPPER SUNBURY RD
THAMES ST
LOWER HAMPTON RD
LOWER SUNBURY RD
River Thames
Platt's Eyot
Longford River
London Loop
Thames Path
Hampton Com Coll
Lady Eleanor Holles Sch (Junior Girls)
Lady Eleanor Holles Sch (Senior Girls)
Hampton Sch
Carlisle Park
Carlisle Inf Sch
Denmead Sch
Castle Bsns Village
Kingsway Bsns Pk
Oldfield House Unit (Clarendon Sch)
St Mary's
Hatherop Road Recn Gd
Hydes Field
Stain Hill Resrs
Sunnyside Resr
Water Wks
Hurst Park Prim Sch
Forge Lane Sch
Oriel Prim Sch
Apex Ret Pk
Links Ind Est
Richmond upon Thames
Hounslow
151
174
195

152
173
196
Strawberry Hill
Fulwell Park
Fulwell
Hampton Hill
TW2
TW1
TW11
TW12
KT8
Bushy Park
National Physical Laboratory
Canal Plantation
Round Plantation
Willow Plantation
Woodland Gdn
Deer Park
Broom Clumps
Diana Fountain
Bushy House
Bartons Cottage
Hampton Court House
Hampton Court Green
Hurst Park
Garrick's Ait
Taggs Island
River Thames
Longford River
London Loop
Teddington Memorial
St Mary's Coll
Stanley Inf & Jun Schs
St James's RC Prim Sch
WELLINGTON RD
HIGH ST
PARK RD
HAMPTON RD
BROAD ST
FULWELL RD
STANLEY RD
CHURCH RD
WALDEGRAVE RD
QUEEN'S RD
THAMES ST
HAMPTON COURT RD
HURST RD
CHURCH ST
SOUTH RD
1 Hampton Hill Bsns Pk
2 EDWARD CL
3 RADCLIFF MEWS
4 GORDON CT
5 DEERHURST CRES
6 PARK VIEW HO
7 PARK GATE CT
1 THE CEDARS
2 WHITE HERON MEWS
3 QUEEN'S HO
4 THE LINK
5 BRAGG RD
6 ADMIRALTY RD
1 CUSACK CL
2 BRIDGE CL
BERKLEY CL 3
ROYMOUNT CT 4
RUTLAND CT 5
ROYAL MEWS 1
ROTARY CT 2
PALACE GATE 3

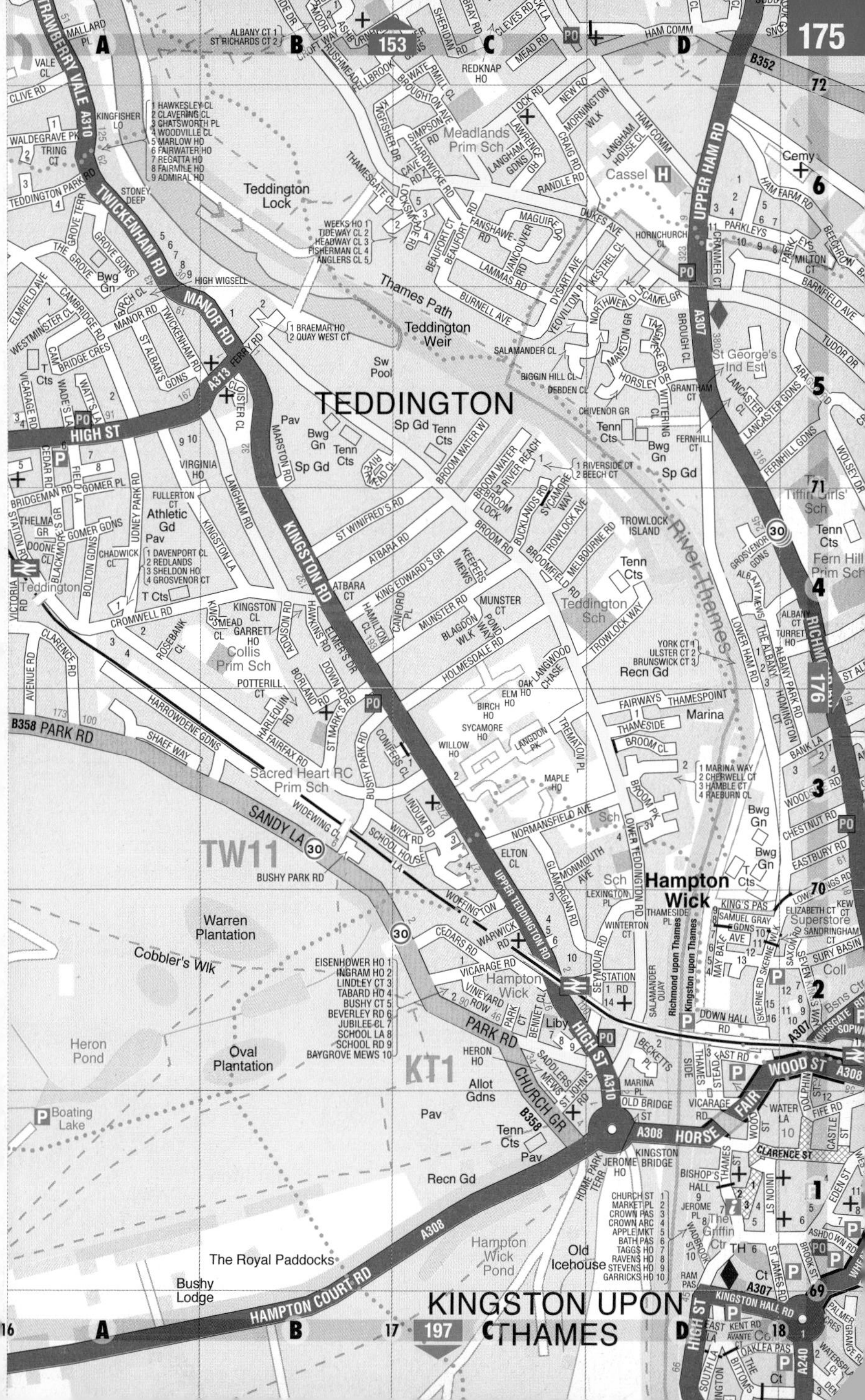
TEDDINGTON
Teddington Lock
Teddington Weir
Thames Path
River Thames
Hampton Wick
KINGSTON UPON THAMES
TW11
KT1
Warren Plantation
Cobbler's Wlk
Heron Pond
Oval Plantation
Boating Lake
The Royal Paddocks
Bushy Lodge
Old Icehouse
Hampton Wick Pond
Recn Gd
Allot Gdns
Meadlands Prim Sch
Cassel
Collis Prim Sch
Sacred Heart RC Prim Sch
Teddington Sch
Tiffin Girls' Sch
Fern Hill Prim Sch
St George's Ind Est
Trowlock Island
Marina
Superstore
Kingston Bridge
Old Bridge
TWICKENHAM RD
MANOR RD
HIGH ST
KINGSTON RD
UPPER TEDDINGTON RD
PARK RD
SANDY LA
HAMPTON COURT RD
UPPER HAM RD
RICHMOND RD
HORSE FAIR
WOOD ST
CHURCH GR
LOWER TEDDINGTON RD
LOWER HAM RD
STRAWBERRY VALE
FERRY RD
BROOM RD
BUSHY PARK RD
A310
A313
A308
A307
B358
B352
153
176
197
Richmond upon Thames
Kingston upon Thames

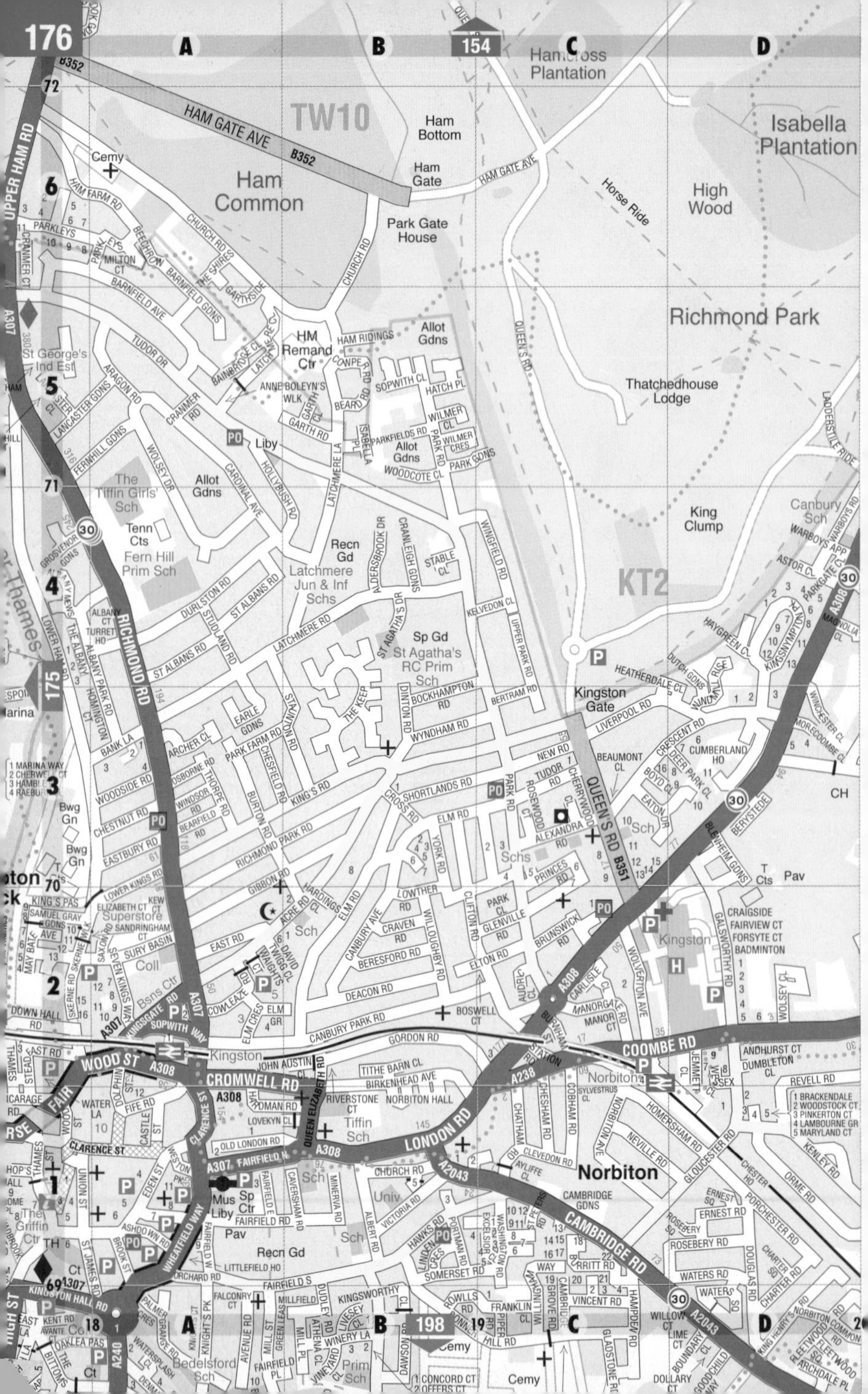
A
B
C
D
154
198
175
TW10
KT2
Ham Common
Ham Bottom
Ham Gate
Hamcross Plantation
Isabella Plantation
High Wood
Park Gate House
Richmond Park
Thatchedhouse Lodge
King Clump
Kingston Gate
HAM GATE AVE
B352
Horse Ride
QUEEN'S RD
UPPER HAM RD
RICHMOND RD
CHURCH RD
HM Remand Ctr
Allot Gdns
St George's Ind Est
The Tiffin Girls' Sch
Tenn Cts
Fern Hill Prim Sch
Recn Gd
Latchmere Jun & Inf Schs
Sp Gd
St Agatha's RC Prim Sch
LATCHMERE RD
KING'S RD
RICHMOND PARK RD
CANBURY PARK RD
GORDON RD
COOMBE RD
CROMWELL RD
LONDON RD
CAMBRIDGE RD
QUEEN ELIZABETH RD
CLARENCE ST
WOOD ST
FAIRFIELD N
Kingston
Norbiton
Canbury Sch
Tiffin Sch
Univ
Mus Liby
Sp Ctr
Pav
Bedelsford Sch
Cemy
Superstore
Coll
Bsns Ctr
1 MARINA WAY
2 CHERWELL CT
3 HAMBLE
4 RAEBURN
1 BRACKENDALE
2 WOODSTOCK CT
3 PINKERTON CT
4 LAMBOURNE GR
5 MARYLAND CT
CRAIGSIDE
FAIRVIEW CT
FORSYTE CT
BADMINTON
A307
A308
A238
A2043
A240
B351

KT2
A
B
155
C
D
Robin Hood
War Meml
Wandsworth
FUSION CT
A308 KINGSTON VALE
Kingston Vale
ROBINWOOD PL
MARY ADELAIDE CL
DERWENT AVE
ROBIN HOOD LA
VALE CRES
A3
Pl Fld
SW15
SW1
Horse Ride
WOODVIEW CL
GRASMERE AVE
ULLSWATER CL
ULLSWATER CRES
CEDAR CL
KINGSTON HILL PL
WINDERMERE RD
ROBIN HOOD LA
Richmond upon Thames
Kingston upon Thames
Sch
Kingston Univ
Coombehurst (Kingston University)
BOWNESS CRES
RYDAL GDNS
ROBIN HOOD WAY
KINGSTON BY PASS
Pav
Horse Ride
Tenn Cts
Merton
Kingston upon Thames
COOMBE PL
RANDOLPH CL
COOMBE WOOD RD
COOMBE PK
KESWICK AVE
Allot Gdns
KINGSTON HILL
CORSCOMBE CL
COOMBE RIDINGS
PAGET PL
Pl Fld
SW19
Allot Gdns
Mill Corner
Warren House
KT2
Coombe Hill
FAIRLAWN CL
COTSWOLD CL
THE WATERGARDENS
WARREN PK
WARREN RD
SW20
178
Coombe Wood
HIGH COOMBE PL
WARREN CUTTING
THE LEIGH
GOLF CLUB DR
CH
GREENWOOD PK
Pl Fld
Tenn Cts
ELLERTON
RENFREW RD
STOKE RD
GEORGE RD
COOMBE NEVILLE
EDGECOOMBE CL
COOMBE END
COOMBE HILL RD
BEVERLEY LA
COOMBE HILL GLADE
HENLEY DR
Nat Res
PRESTON RD
Holy Cross Prep Sch
GATEHOUSE CL
THE DRIVE
Schs
Coombe
MOOR PARK GDNS
DEVEY CL
WARBANK LA
HOOD RD
LORD CHANCELLOR WLK
BALLARD CL
COOMBE LA WEST
B283
FITZGEORGE AVE
OAKCOMBE CL
COOMBE BANK
WONFORD CL
New Victoria
A3
BEVERLEY AVE
HOLLAND AVE
MELVILLE AVE
BURDETT AVE
SOUTHWOOD AVE
WARREN RISE
COOMBE HOUSE CHASE
NEVILLE AVE
THE FAIRWAY
THE CHESTERS
Coombe Lane
COOMBE LANE FLYOVER 1
BEVERLEY CT 2
BEVERLEY WAY
KINGSTON BY PASS
Kingston upon Thames
Merton
COTTENHAM PARK RD
A238
BROOK GDNS
COOMBE RISE
ORCHARD RISE
WEST RD
CROWN RD
Coombe Hill Jun & Inf Schs
TRAPS LA
THE MOAT
BURGHLEY AVE
WEST COOMBE AVE
Pl Flds
A238
ALBION RD
BEECHCROFT AVE
HIGH DR
BRANKSOME WAY
WOODLANDS AVE
MATLOCK WAY
CROMFORD WAY
SOAMES WLK
BUXTON DR
CARDINAL CRES
DICKERAGE RD
ARUNDEL RD
Coombe Girls Sch
DARLEY DR
BAKEWELL WAY
BADGERS WLK
KT3
Coombe Brook
Malden
ELY CL
OVERDALE AVE
OAK RD
LANGLEY GR
CH
GOLF SIDE CL
Tenn Cts
Sp Gd
CH
Allot Gdns
OLIVER RD
CLARENCE AVE
ASH CL
CARLTON RD
BURBERRY CL
SELBORNE RD
DELL WLK
LINKSIDE
CAMBRIDGE AVE
ABOYNE RD
1 PERTH CL
2 HUNTLEY WAY
THE TRIANGLE
PO
MUYBRIDGE RD
MYRTLE GR
THE CLOSE
THE CRESCENT
LABURNUM GR
Allot Gdns
BARTON GN
WOODSIDE RD
ROWAN CL
Allot Gdns
MIDDLETON RD
THE GREEN
LONG WLK
BEACONSFIELD RD
POPLAR GDNS
LAWN CL
FORSYTH CT
ORCHARD AVE
ROSEBERRY AVE
DICKERAGE HILL
ASHCOMBE SQ
SALISBURY RD
SYCAMORE GR
EDGAR CT
COOMBE RD
HOPPINGWOOD AVE
69
WARWICK RD
A
B
199
C
D
22
MOUNT PLEASANT RD
Bwg Gn
Sch
LIME GR
ST MARY CT
LINCOLN HO
ALRIC AVE
Corpus Christi RC Prim Sch
BEECH GR
ELM RD
MOUNT RD
POPLAR GR
VANFAME CT
PHOENIX HO
Beverley Park
CRAMER CT
DICKERAGE LA
LINCOLN RD
ROSEMONT RD
STAFFORD RD
CHESTNUT GR
CHESTNUT GROVE CT
Beverley
72
6
5
71
4
3
70
2
1
21
Gra

A
B
C
D
156
Wimbledon Common
SW15
SW19
SW20
London Scottish
Gravelly Hill
Wimbledon Common
Caesar's Camp
Royal Wimbledon
Crooked Billet
Cannizaro Park
Copse Hill
Cottenham Park
Raynes Park
Bushey Mead
The Buddhapadipa Temple
The Study Prep Sch
King's Coll Sch
Wimbledon Common Prep Sch
Wimbledon Coll
The Norwegian Sch
Ursuline High Sch
Hall Sch
Hollymount Sch
St Matthew's CE Prim Sch
Horse Ride
Sunset Rd
Camp Rd
The Causeway
Cannizaro Rd
Parkside
High St
West Side Comm
Woodhayes Rd
Cottenham Park Rd
Coombe La
Durham Rd
Worple Rd
Kingston Rd
Bushey Rd
Copse Hill
Beverley Way
Kingston By Pass
St Barnes La
177
200
Kingston upon Thames

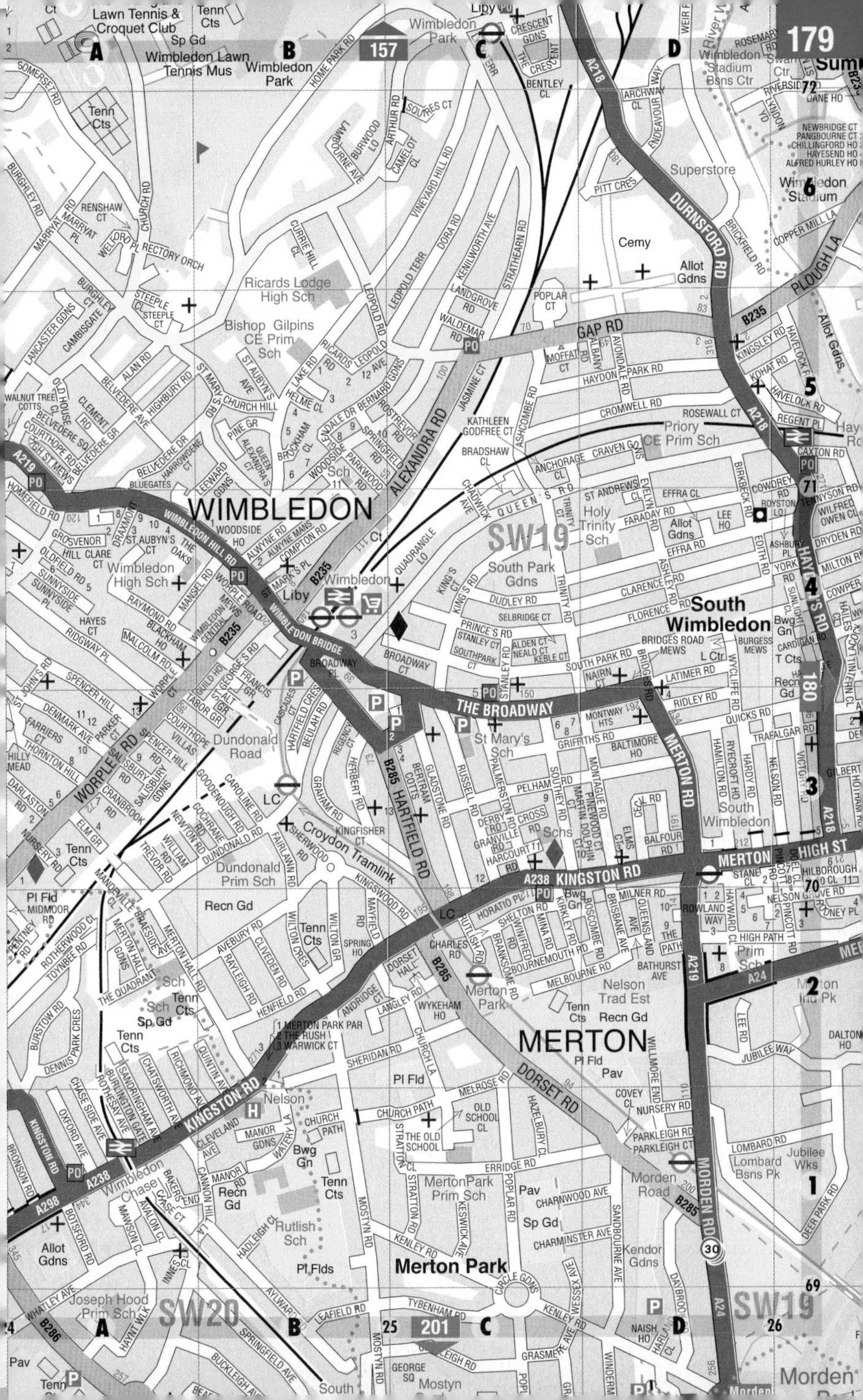

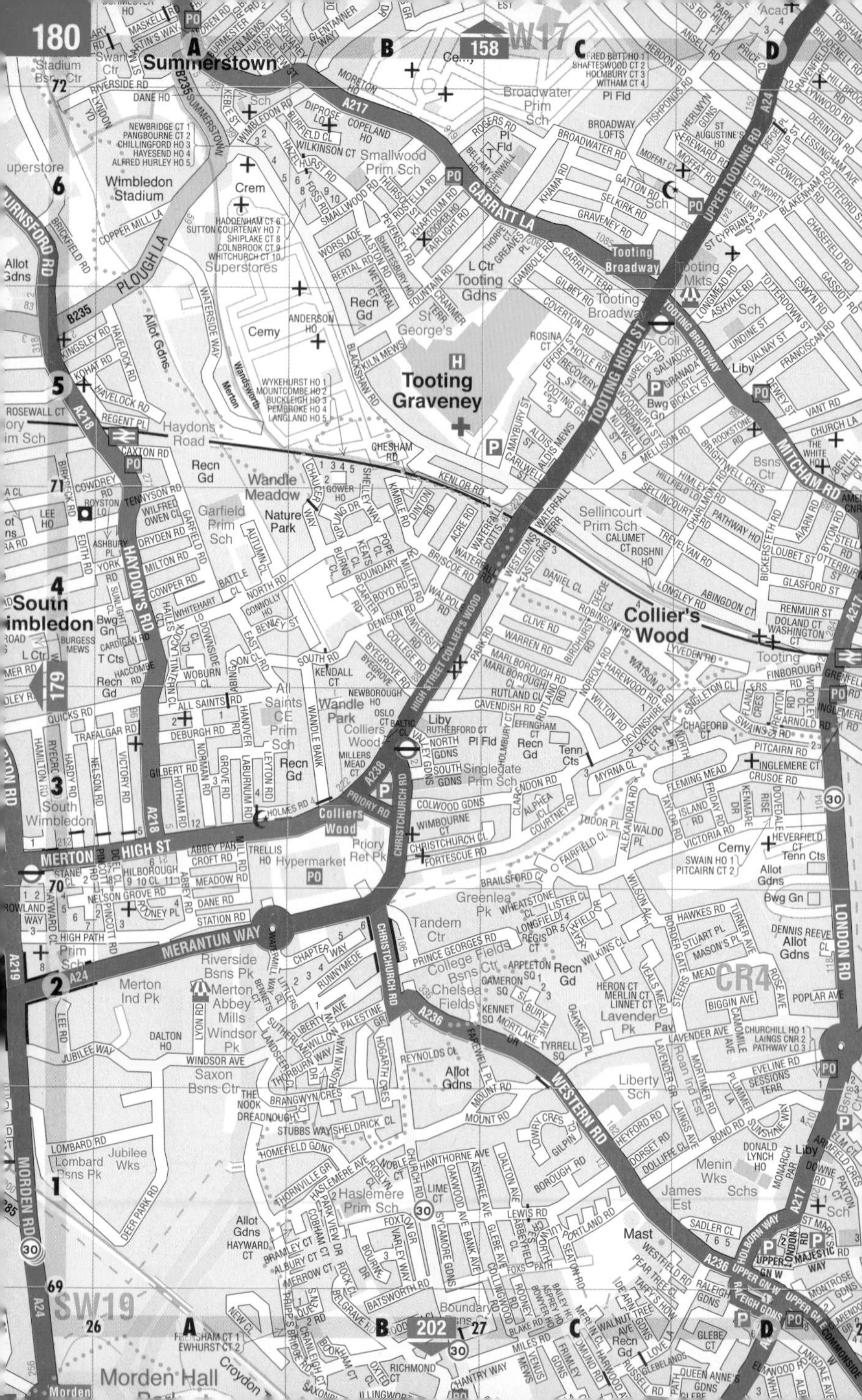
A
B
C
D
158
SW17
Summerstown
Stadium Bsns Ctr
Swan Ctr
Wimbledon Stadium
Crem
Smallwood Prim Sch
Broadwater Prim Sch
Pl Fld
GARRATT LA
A217
A24
A218
B235
PLOUGH LA
SUMMERSTOWN
WIMBLEDON RD
BROADWATER RD
UPPER TOOTING RD
Tooting Broadway
Tooting Mkts
Tooting Gdns
St George's
Tooting Graveney
Cemy
Superstores
Allot Gdns
Haydons Road
Recn Gd
Wandle Meadow Nature Park
Garfield Prim Sch
TOOTING HIGH ST
HIGH STREET COLLIER'S WOOD
Sellincourt Prim Sch
Collier's Wood
MITCHAM RD
South Wimbledon
HAYDON'S RD
All Saints CE Prim Sch
Wandle Park
Colliers Wood
Liby
Singlegate Prim Sch
Tenn Cts
Priory Ret Pk
Hypermarket
MERTON HIGH ST
MERANTUN WAY
Riverside Bsns Pk
Tandem Ctr
College Fields Bsns Ctr
Chelsea Fields
Merton Ind Pk
Merton Abbey Mills
Windsor Pk
Saxon Bsns Ctr
Greenlea Pk
Lavender Pk
Liberty Sch
Roan Ind Est
CHRISTCHURCH RD
WESTERN RD
LONDON RD
CR4
Cemy
Allot Gdns
Bwg Gn
Jubilee Wks
Lombard Bsns Pk
MORDEN RD
Haslemere Prim Sch
Menin Wks
James Est
Schs
Mast
Boundary Bsns
SW19
202
179
Morden Hall
Croydon
Morden
1
2
3
4
5
6
69
70
71
72
26
27
30

159
Tooting Bec Common
A
B
C
D
Streatham Park
Tooting Bec Lido
TOOTING BEC RD
Horse Ride
FISHERS CL 1
SAXONCROFT HO 2
WELLINGTON MEWS 3
GARRAD'S RD
WOODBOURNE AV
Tenn Cts
TARRINGTON CL
BECMEAD AVE
NUNEHAM
PRENTIS RD
PINKERTON PL
STEEP HILL
ASTORIA
A23
Lib
PINFOLD
SHRUBBERY
A214
B242
B241
A214
ELMBOURNE RD
MONTANA RD
ROMBERG RD
AVOCA RD
TOPSHAM RD
BRUDENELL RD
HILLBROOK RD
TREHERN CT
BARRINGER SQ
1 BRUCE LAWNS
2 BRUCE HALL MEWS
FRANCISCAN RD
GROOMFIELD CL
MACMILLAN WAY
MOLYNEUX DR
LISLE CL
DOULTON DR
GEARING CL
MASSINGBERD WAY
HENTY WALK
MANTILLA RD
MORING RD
LUCIEN RD
DERINTON RD
LESSINGHAM AVE
COTEFORD ST
COWICK RD
OKEBURN RD
CHURCH LA
ELDERFIELD PL
ELIZABETH CT
Furzedown
SW17
OLDFIELD HO
CROSSLEIGH CT
Athletics Gd
WEST DR
RAMBLER CL
MULBERRY CL
NORTH DR
COLSON WAY
Bwg Gn
PRINGLE GDNS
ULLATHORNE RD
SHEPLEY CT
TOOTING BEC GDNS
THE ALDERS
Capital Ring
RIGGINDALE RD
THIRLMERE RD
FERNWOOD AVE
THE GLEBE
TOOTING BEC GDNS
AMBLESIDE AVE
A216
RYDAL RD
CAMPBELL
GLENELDON MEWS
BOURNEVALE RD
ASHLAKE RD
STANTHORPE
BRAY CT
FURZEDOWN RD
CLAIRVIEW RD
BROOKVIEW RD
WOODNOOK RD
PARKLANDS RD
HESTER CT
NUGENT CT
BUSBY HO
BOYCE HO
ABBOTSLEIGH RD
ALDRINGTON RD
GRIERSON HO
SHENSTONE HO
WHINFELL CL
Sch
KEENS CL
BABINGTON RD
TYRONE CT
GLENEAGLE MEWS
STATION APP
STREATHAM
STANEDGE CT
Streatham
BIRCHWOOD RD
DALESIDE RD
GRACEDALE RD
FURZEDOWN DR
COLWYN CL
THRALE RD
FAYLAND AVE
FIR TREE CL
SWALLOW GDNS
GLENEAGLE RD
FAIRMILE AVE
Tenn Cts
CHILLERTON RD
RAMSDALE RD
MANSARD BEECHES
GORSE RISE
CROWBOROUGH RD
RECTORY LA
CHURCH LA
ST BENEDICT'S CL
CARLISLE WAY
HAWTHORN CRES
SOUTHVIEW CL
CHERTSEY ST
GASSIOT RD
ABBEY DR
MITCHAM LA
CONAL CT 1
LYNN CT 2
BABINGTON CT 3
CLIVE CT 4
SHACKLETON LO 5
CHURCHILL LO 6
PANKHURST HO 7
CONYER'S RD
Ice Rink
HIGH RD
ELLORA RD
HAMBRO RD
FERRERS RD
NATAL RD
MONICA CT
LEWIN RD
LEWIN CT
Bwg Gns
Graveney Sch
Inst
SPALDING RD
LONGSTONE RD
NIMROD RD
MOYSER RD
RIBBLESDALE RD
PENDLE RD
PRETORIA RD
PENWORTHAM RD
RACKHAM MEWS
WESTCOTE RD
BLEGBOROUGH RD
PENRITH ST
CUNLIFFE ST
MASTERS CL
BRUNSWICK MEWS
POTTER'S LA
SOMERVILLE CT
BARROW RD
B272
WESTWELL RD
IDLECOMBE RD
SALTERFORD RD
FRESHWATER RD
FRESHWATER CL
WELHAM RD
Sch
BECLANDS RD
SOUTHCROFT RD
KNAPTON MEWS
LINKS WAY
Links Sch
FERNTHORPE RD
DAHOMEY RD
CORSEHILL ST
Eardley Sch
EARDLEY RD
GREYSWOOD ST
EDENCOURT RD
CREDENHILL ST
LEVERSON ST
ESTREHAM RD
PATHFIELD RD
ROTHERHILL AVE
GREYHOUND LA
Superstore
Immanuel Sch
182
A217
ASCOT RD
BOSCOMBE RD
CROMER RD
DEAL RD
EASTBOURNE RD
FRINTON RD
GUNTON RD
HAILSHAM RD
SEELY RD
IPSWICH RD
JERSEY RD
SWAIN CL
VECTIS GDNS
VECTIS RD
LINKS RD
STANLEY GDNS
SIRDAR RD
Wandsworth
Merton
EASTWOOD ST
KETTERING ST
FALLSBROOK RD
BESLEY ST
EDGINGTON RD
ABERFOYLE RD
Liby
CARNFORTH RD
RURAL WAY
RUSTIC AVE
THE BUNGALOWS
BROOKSIDE CT
ANVIL CL
MANTLET CL
BROADVIEW RD
Streatham Common
BUCKLEIGH RD
KEMPSHOTT RD
PRESCOTT
TANKERVILLE RD
FARNINGHAM CT
BRUCE RD
HEATON RD
TYNEMOUTH RD
THIRSK RD
STANLEY RD
MILTON RD
EDENVALE RD
EDENVALE CL
WOODLAND WAY
ASHBOURNE RD
RIDGE RD
MASKANI WLK 1
SUMMERENE CL 2
Allot Gdns
BATES CRES
DONNYBROOK RD
CANMORE GDNS
BENCROFT RD
ABERCAIRN RD
Streatham Vale
WOODGATE DR
WILMINGTON CT
ELLISON RD
GUILDERSFIELD
ST BARNABAS RD
ST BARNABAS HO
GORRINGE PARK AVE
CAITHNESS RD
PARK AVE MEWS
PARK AVE
MELROSE AVE
GARDEN AVE
ELMHURST AVE
BEECHOLME AVE
HILL RD
Merton
Lambeth
STREATHAM VALE
GRAYSCROFT RD
Allot Gdns
BRIDGEWOOD RD
GLENISTER PARK RD
DRAKEWOOD RD
NETTLEWOOD RD
BODIAM RD
HAWKHURST RD
SHERWOOD AVE
RAMA CL
70
CARLINGFORD GDNS
FIGGE'S RD
ST JAMES' RD
CR4
FRAMFIELD RD
MANSHIP RD
UCKFIELD GR
Figge's Marsh
STREATHAM RD
FARMHOUSE RD
LARBERT RD
MEADFOOT RD
GRANTON RD
BRAESIDE RD
Sch
CHURCHMORE RD
HELMSDALE RD
Allot Gdns
FIELDEND RD
GREENOCK RD
STOCKPORT RD
RUNNYMEDE CRES
WOODMANSTERNE RD
Lambeth
LACROSSE WAY
2
Mitcham Ind est
Beecholme Prim Sch
LONGLANDS CT
THE DRIFTWAY
LONESOME WAY
Pav
Bwg Gn
BENNETTS CL
BRIGGS CL
ALLEN CL
LEONARD RD
GREYHOUND TERR
MARIAN RD
LILIAN RD
JUNIPER GDNS
RENSHAW CNR
A216
Sch
BEAULIEU CL
TUDOR HO
SPRING GR
SUMMERHILL WAY
ELMFIELD AVE
Tenn Cts
HASTY CL
PEARSON WAY
EDGEHILL RD
Streatham Vale
T Cts
WOODSIDE WAY
OAKLEIGH WAY
EBENEZER WLK
VERONICA GDNS
ROWAN CRES
B272
HASSOCKS RD
Woodmansterne Prim Sch
Pl Fld
Sp Gd
Norbury Manor Prim Sch
PROCTOR CL
GRAHAM AVE
GRAHAM RD
FERNLEA RD
EVE CT
STEPNEY WAY
FIRS CL
BIRCH WLK
BOLSTEAD RD
LIMETREE PL
MAPLE CL
WARMINSTER WAY
ELDERTREE WAY
ELDERTREE PL
MEOPHAM RD
Caplan Est
ROWAN CL
STIRLING CL
BYARDS CROFT
OXTOBY WAY
CHILMARK RD
Stanford Prim Sch
Pav
WINDERMERE RD
Sp Gd
TURLE RD
ORMEROD GDNS
GUYATT GDNS
FOWLER RD
PRIESTLEY RD
ROPER WAY
GROVE RD
Lonesome Prim Sch
St Mark's CE Acad
WOODSTOCK WAY
OAK ROW
SW16
LONGTHORNTON RD
LYMINGTON CL
BURLEY CL
BROCKENHURST WAY
STANFORD RD
BENETT GDNS
ISHAM RD
CAREW RD
Allot Gdns
EASTFIELDS RD
RIALTO RD
Recn Gd
HOLLAND CL
THRUPP CL
Tenn Cts
Recn Gd
ROWAN RD
CHURCH WLK
MIDDLE RD
DARCY RD
TISBURY RD
1
LANSDELL RD
TONSTALL RD
LEATHER CL
LABURNUM RD
LC
Crem
ST OLAVE'S WLK
STANFORD WAY
MIDDLE WAY
BECKWAY RD
LYNDHURST AVE
Recn Gd
BEDFONT CL
ST MARK'S RD
PEMBROKE AVE
BARNARD RD
ACACIA RD
HAMMOND AVE
MOORE CL
POTTER CL
PAIN'S CL
CLAY AVE
Cemy
AVENUE RD
Allot Gdns
NORTHBOROUGH
CHALKLEY CL
BAKER LA
HILARY AVE
WORCESTER CL
STAINBANK RD
KINGSMEAD AVE
ROSEMEAD AVE
SUNNYMEAD AVE
69
NORBURY AVE
NORBURY RISE
NORBURY CROSS
MITCHAM
Tenn Cts
Pl Fld
NORTHBOROUGH RD
THE GABLES
Sp Gd
203
Pl Fld
30
Harris Acad
GROVE RD
KINGS RD
MAYTREE CT
SPENCER RD
Prim Sch
HALLOWELL CL
COMMONSIDE EAST
Pl Fld
JESMOND CL
TAMWORTH LA
CROSSWAYS RD
HOYLAKE GDNS
Pav
William Morris
Recn Gd
3
4
5
6
71
72
29

A
B
C
D
160
SE27
STREATHAM
Streatham
STREATHAM HIGH RD
STREATHAM COMMON N
CROWN LA
Capital Ring
St Andrews RC Prim Sch
Streatham Common
Horse Ride
STREATHAM COMMON S
1 ELPHINSTONE CT
2 RIDLEY CT
3 BLADON CT
4 COMMONSIDE CT
5 SANDERS HO
6 BYBON CL
7 HAMBLY MANS
8 ST JOHNS HO
Sunnyhill Prim Sch
St Julian's Prim Sch
Bishop Thomas Grant RC Sec Sch
Crown Lane Prim Sch
St Joseph's RC Coll
Norwood Grove
Superstore
Immanuel Sch
Ice Rink
Streatham Common
Streatham Vale
GREYHOUND LA
181
SW16
Norbury Park
Norbury Manor Bsns & Enterprise Coll for Girls
Norbury
Norbury Manor Prim Sch
Stanford Prim Sch
Kensington Avenue Prim Sch
Norbury Trad Est
St James The Great RC Prim Sch
GREEN LA
LONDON RD
A23
A214
A215
B272
B273
Lambeth
Croydon
204
Harris Acad
SW16

183
West Norwood
Crem
Elm Wood Prim Sch
Park Hall Road Trad Est
161
SOUTH CROXTED RD
A2199
Kingsdale Sec Sch
Sydenham Hill
Low Cross Wood La
TRITTON RD
CARNAC ST
MOUNT PLEASANT
DURBAN RD
ST CLOUD RD
ST LOUIS RD
ST GOTHARD RD
AUCKLAND HILL
WEST NORWOOD HIGH ST B232
Allot Gdns
WINDSOR GR
WINDSOR CL
BALMORAL CT
CLYTHA CT
GIPSY RD
ROMMANY RD
Hamilton Rd Ind Est
ST SAVIOUR'S COLL
DULWICH WOOD PK
A2199
COLLEGE RD
HITHERWOOD DR
HITHERWOOD CT
LYALL AVE
Liby
ROCK HILL
CHESTNUT PL
WOODSYRE
GREAT BROWNINGS
DOME HILL PK
TALISMAN SQ
VIGILANT CL
HIGH LEVEL DR
THE GRADIENT
HILLCREST
FOUNTAIN DR
HOGARTH CT
WAVEL PL
1 SHAMROCK HO
2 CAMBRIA HO
3 TARQUIN HO
4 PEMBERTON
5 LONGHEDGE
6 GUNNELL CL
Kingswood Prim Sch
ANTIGUA WLK
CLAYLANDS CT
ELDER RD B232
NORWOOD PARK RD
EYLEWOOD RD
FINCH AVE
1 LEVEHURST HO
2 HALLANE HO
3 PONDFIELD HO
4 WHITTAM HO
5 ELDERWOOD PL
Games Ct
Norwood Park
Lambeth
Croydon
Gipsy Hill
GIPSY HILL
SAINSBURY RD
ST KITTS TERR
SALTER'S HILL
MONTSERRAT CL
BERRIDGE RD
BRISTOW RD
WHITELEY RD
ALEXANDRA DR
KNOLL CT
LOWOOD CT
CRYSTAL DRAKE CT
FARQUHAR RD
CRYSTAL PALACE PAR
A212
Mast
Crystal Palace Park
Crystal Palace
Capital Ring
Southwark
Bromley
ROWN DALE
WYCHWOOD WAY 1
LAMBETH PROSPECT 2
ROMANY PROSPECT 3
ESSEX CT 4
ILKLEY CL 5
MOUNT RD 6
Norwood
St Joseph's RC Jun & Inf Schs
Norwood New Town
CENTRAL HILL
A214 WESTOW HILL
1 NIGHTINGALE CT
2 MOLLIE DAVIS CT
3 TELFORD CL
4 BRUNEL CL
Mus
ANERLEY HILL
CRYSTAL PALACE STATION
LEDRINGTON RD
184
GROSVENOR CT
PATTERSON RD
HIGHLANDS CT
WOODLAND HILL
WOODLAND CL
CAMDEN HILL RD
VICARS OAK RD
OAKWOOD DR
BEAUMONT RD
WEDGWOOD WAY
RYEFIELD RD
PYTCHLEY CRES
HERMITAGE RD
HERMITAGE GDNS
FOUNDERS GDNS
Pav
Rockmount Prim Sch
CHEVENING RD
EVERSLEY RD
Recn Gd
Tenn Cts
Upper Norwood
SE19
BEDWARDINE RD
COXWELL RD
NESBITT SQ
ROSETTA CT
SILVERTON LO
CHURCH RD
BEULAH HILL
Downsview Prim Sch
DOWNSVIEW GDNS
THE WOODLANDS
GLENHURST RISE
Pl Fld
1 SOUTH VIEW CT
2 WHITEOAK HO
Tenn Cts
Westwood Language Coll
ELIZABETH WAY
MATILDA CL
ELLERY RD
ESKMONT RIDGE
COLLEGE GN
WAKEFIELD GDNS
FITZROY GDNS
HOMELANDS DR
HAMLYN GDNS
EFFRA CT
Pl Fld
FOX HILL
REYNARD DR
Allot Gdns
MOWBRAY RD
Harris City Tech Coll
Lewis Sp & L Ctr
SE19
WESTWOOD AVE
WADDINGTON WAY
SPURGEON RD
SPURGEON AVE
DALE PARK RD
Allot Gdns
David Livingstone Prim Sch
UPPER BEULAH HILL
All Saint's Schs
CRANBROOK HO 1
RAVENSROOST 2
WINDSOR CT 3
BLENHEIM CT 4
SCORESDALE 5
SOUTHHOLME CL
AUCKLAND RISE
AUCKLAND RD
KITLEY GDNS
SYLVAN RD
CANTLEY GDNS
1 ROLAND CT
2 CARLTON CT
3 ENDERLEY HO
4 MOWBRAY CT
5 CLOVELLY GDNS
Allot Gdns
Orch
Mast TV Sta
1 EVEREST CT
2 BRAE CT
3 WILKINSON GDNS
4 BEAULIEU HTS
Cypress Inf Sch
CYPRESS LO
Cypress Jun Sch
Pav
Pl Fld
Tenn Cts
Bwg Gn
South Norwood Lake
1 WETHERBY CT
2 THE BIRCHES
3 HARDING CT
4 FRANCES CT
St Cyprian's Prim Sch
NORTHWOOD RD
PENRITH RD
WESTBROOK RD
PEPPERCORN CL
BEAUCHAMP RD
TEMPLETON CL
HILLTOP CT
GRANGE RD
A212
A215
DORRINGTON CT
Spurgeon's Coll
WHARNCLIFFE GDNS
FALKLAND PARK AVE
SOUTH NORWOOD HILL
HOWDEN RD
WOODVALE AVE
ROCHESTER CT
AVENUE GDNS
CR7
LAKEMAN CT
MERSHAM RD
LIVINGSTONE RD
ANNSWORTHY CRES
Beulah Schs
PARCHMORE RD
Grangewood Park
Pav
Bwg Gn
Tenn Cts
Tenn Cts
33
205
34
A
B
C
D
6
5
4
3
2
1
72
71
70
69

162
Upper Sydenham
Sydenham Wells Park
SE26
Sydenham
Crystal Palace
Crystal Palace National Sports Ctr
Crystal Palace Park
Penge East
PENGE
Penge West
SE20
Anerley
SE19
Betts Park
South Norwood Lake
Orchard School Sp Ctr
Anerley Prim Sch
Malcolm Prim Sch
Royston Prim Sch
Alexandra Jun Sch
Forest Hill Sec Sch
Mayow Park
Avenue Road
Birkbeck
Elmers End
Churchfields Prim Sch
Croydon Tramlink
WESTWOOD HILL
CRYSTAL PALACE PARK RD
ANERLEY HILL
ANERLEY RD
CROYDON RD
HIGH ST
NEWLANDS PK
SYDENHAM RD
KIRKDALE
COLLEGE RD
CRYSTAL PALACE PAR
PENGE RD
ELMERS END RD
PARISH LA
GREEN LA
183
206
A B C D

163
Bell Green
Lower Sydenham
SE26
SE6
Bellingham
New Beckenham
Beckenham Junction
BR3
BECKENHAM
Kelsey Park
Beckenham Hill
Beckenham Place
186
207
SYDENHAM RD
SOUTHEND LA
BECKENHAM HILL RD
SOUTHEND RD
BECKENHAM RD
RECTORY RD
HIGH ST
MANOR RD
BROMLEY RD
WICKHAM RD
STANTON WAY
BELL GN
KENT HOUSE RD
KANGLEY BRIDGE RD
WORSLEY BRIDGE RD
COPERS COPE RD
BRACKLEY RD
PARK RD
QUEENS RD
THE AVENUE
ALBEMARLE RD
CROMWELL RD
CLOCK HOUSE RD
CROYDON RD
BECKENHAM PLACE PK
FOXGROVE RD
Lewisham
Bromley
A2218
A212
A2015
A234
A222
B227
B230

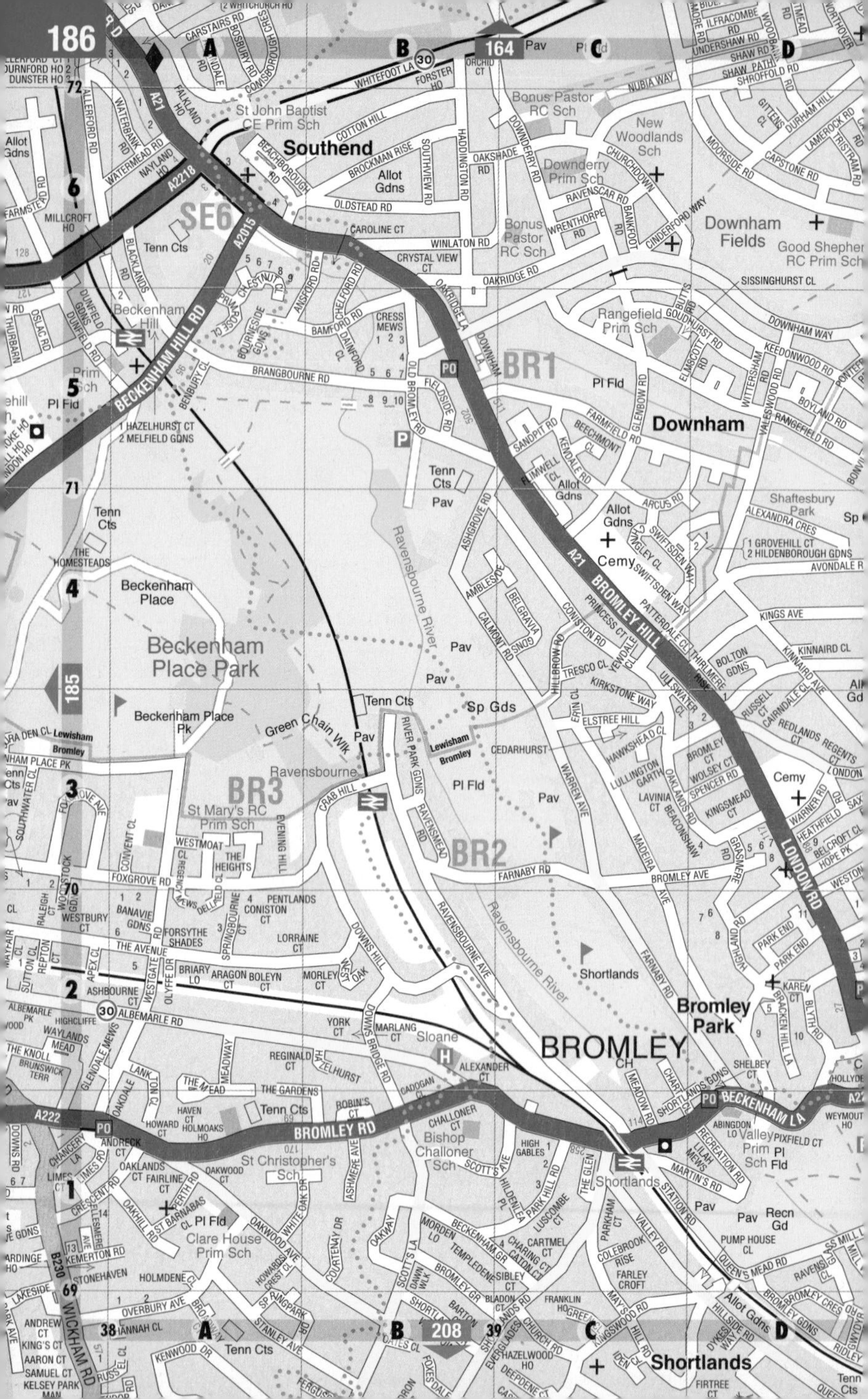

Southend
SE6
Beckenham Hill
BR1
Downham
Downham Fields
Beckenham Place Park
BR3
BR2
BROMLEY
Bromley Park
Shortlands
Ravensbourne
Sloane
BECKENHAM HILL RD
BROMLEY HILL
LONDON RD
BROMLEY RD
BECKENHAM LA
WICKHAM RD
Ravensbourne River
Green Chain Wlk
Bonus Pastor RC Sch
St John Baptist CE Prim Sch
New Woodlands Sch
Downderry Prim Sch
Rangefield Prim Sch
Good Shepherd RC Prim Sch
St Mary's RC Prim Sch
Bishop Challoner Sch
St Christopher's Sch
Clare House Prim Sch
Valley Prim Sch
Shaftesbury Park
Lewisham
Bromley

164
185
208

A
B
C
D
165
SE12
SE9
BR1
BR7
BR1
188
209
BROMLEY
Sundridge
Plaistow
Elmstead
Sundridge Park
Sundridge Park Mansion
Garden Wood
High Grove
Marvels Wood
Elmstead Wood
Elmstead Woods
Rockpit Wood
Castlecombe Prim Sch
Green Chain Wlk
Grove Park
Haberdashers' Aske's Knights Acad
Launcelot Prim Sch
Plaistow Green
Bromley North
Bromley South
Bromley C Ctr
Holy Trinity Coll Prep Sch
Scotts Park Prim Sch
Breaside Prep Sch
Bickley Prim Sch
Ashgrove Sch
The Glades Sh Ctr
The Pavilion L Ctr
Queens Gdns
Church House Gdns
Waldo Ind Est 1
Bromley Ind Ctr 2
BARING RD
A2212
BURNT ASH LA
COLLEGE RD
A222
WIDMORE RD
BICKLEY RD
B264
B265
PAGE HEATH LA
A21 KENTISH WAY
TWEEDY RD
HIGH ST
NEW STREET HILL
LEAMINGTON AVE
PORTLAND RD
ROCHESTER AVE
NIGHTINGALE LA
1 WOODBURY GDNS
2 ABBEY LO
1 LAVISHAM HO
2 MEDE HO
3 WELLS HO
4 BURNT ASH HTS
5 LLOYD HO
6 SUNDRIDGE HO
7 MILLER CL
1 CHARLES DARWIN HO
2 LINDEN HO
3 LANGTRY HO
4 LEWIS KING HO
5 ANDREW WELLS HO
6 THE GABLES
7 GRAHAM CT
8 RICHMOND CT
9 ABINGDON HO
CLEVEDEN HO 1
LAMBOURN HO 2
BOUGHTON HO 3
ARBURY HO 4
1 PAT DREW HO
2 ORCHARD GN
72
71
70
69
6
5
4
3
2
1
42
41

A
B
C
D
166
210
187
SE9
BR7
Elmstead
Chislehurst West
Widmore
Bickley
Marvels Wood
Elmstead Wood
Elmstead Woods
Rockpit Wood
Castlecombe Prim Sch
Green Chain Wlk
Ravensbourne Coll
Babington House Sch
Red Hill Prim Sch
Bullers Wood Sch
Camden Park
Chislehurst
Caves
Bickley Park Sch
WHITE HORSE HILL
RED HILL
CHISLEHURST HIGH ST
GREEN LA
BICKLEY RD
BICKLEY PARK RD
CHISLEHURST RD
OLD HILL
SUMMER HILL
BROMLEY RD
PAGE HEATH LA
STATION APP
ELMSTEAD LA
YESTER RD
SOUTHILL RD
LOWER CAMDEN
CAMDEN PARK RD

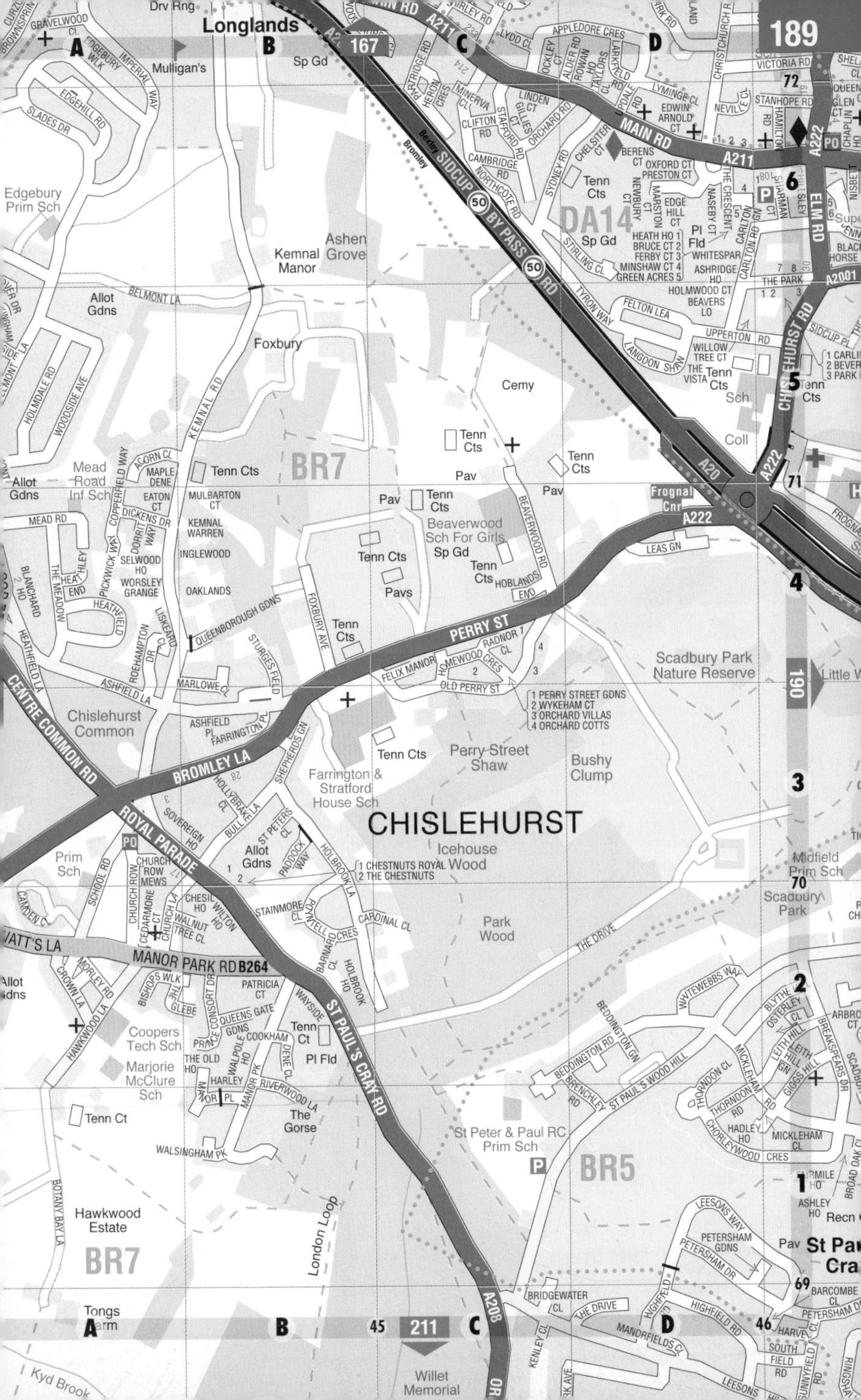

Longlands
Mulligan's
Sp Gd
167
A211
A20
Edgebury Prim Sch
Kemnal Manor
Ashen Grove
Allot Gdns
BELMONT LA
Foxbury
KEMNAL RD
BR7
Tenn Cts
Cemy
Pav
Mead Road Inf Sch
Beaverwood Sch For Girls
BEAVERWOOD RD
SIDCUP BY PASS RD
MAIN RD
DA14
Sp Gd
Pl Fld
Frognal Cnr
A222
LEAS GN
PERRY ST
Scadbury Park Nature Reserve
190
CENTRE COMMON RD
Chislehurst Common
BROMLEY LA
ROYAL PARADE
Farrington & Stratford House Sch
Perry Street Shaw
Bushy Clump
CHISLEHURST
Icehouse Wood
Park Wood
1 PERRY STREET GDNS
2 WYKEHAM CT
3 ORCHARD VILLAS
4 ORCHARD COTTS
1 CHESTNUTS ROYAL
2 THE CHESTNUTS
Midfield Prim Sch
Scadbury Park
THE DRIVE
MANOR PARK RD B264
ST PAUL'S CRAY RD
Coopers Tech Sch
Marjorie McClure Sch
The Gorse
St Peter & Paul RC Prim Sch
BR5
Hawkwood Estate
BR7
London Loop
A208
Tongs Farm
211
Willet Memorial
Kyd Brook
St Paul's Cray

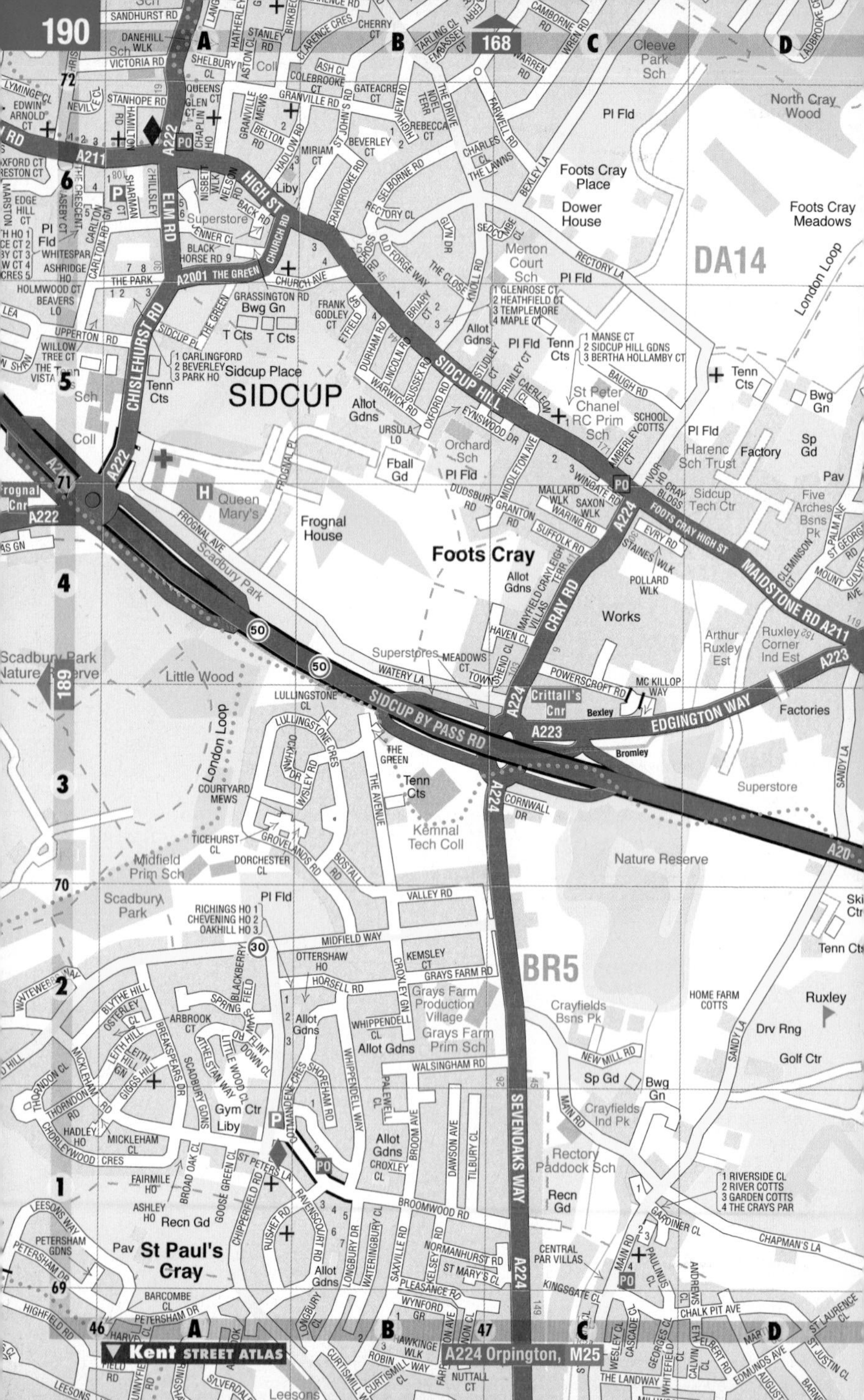

168
SIDCUP
Foots Cray
St Paul's Cray
DA14
BR5
Foots Cray Place
Dower House
Foots Cray Meadows
North Cray Wood
Cleeve Park Sch
Merton Court Sch
Sidcup Place
Queen Mary's
Frognal House
Scadbury Park
Scadbury Park Nature Reserve
Little Wood
London Loop
Nature Reserve
Kemnal Tech Coll
Midfield Prim Sch
Grays Farm Production Village
Grays Farm Prim Sch
Crayfields Bsns Pk
Crayfields Ind Pk
Rectory Paddock Sch
St Peter Chanel RC Prim Sch
Harenc Sch Trust
Sidcup Tech Ctr
Five Arches Bsns Pk
Arthur Ruxley Est
Ruxley Corner Ind Est
Ruxley
Golf Ctr
Crittall's Cnr
Frognal Cnr
Bexley
Bromley
SIDCUP HILL
SIDCUP BY PASS RD
SEVENOAKS WAY
EDGINGTON WAY
MAIDSTONE RD A211
FOOTS CRAY HIGH ST
CRAY RD
HIGH ST
ELM RD
CHISLEHURST RD
A2001 THE GREEN
A222
A224
A223
A211
A20
A224 Orpington, M25
Kent STREET ATLAS

A
B
C
D
169
Bunkers Hill
BUNKERS HILL
THE TOWER HO
Farm
LEAFIELD LA
A223
72
Faesten Dic
FIVE ARCH BRIDGE
Joyden's Wood
Home Wood
Gattons Plantation
GATTONS WAY
COCKSURE LA
6
River Cray
GROVE
PARSONAGE LA
THE SPINNEY
THE
ST JAMES WAY
NORTH CRAY RD
Manor Farm
HIGH BEECHES
5
DA14
ELLENBOROUGH RD
BURDETT CL
BEDENS RD
1 THURSLAND RD
2 FOWLER CL
3 CHANTRY CL
40
CALVERT CL
HONEYDEN RD
CORNELL CL
71
NORTH CRAY RD
BARTON RD
Chalk Wood
STONEHILL WOODS PK
4
Kent STREET ATLAS
WHITNEY WLK
B2173
Ruxley Cnr
CH
Upper Ruxley Farm
Ruxley Wood
Ruxley
Church
Ruxley Manor Nursery
1 VICTOR MILLS COTTS
2 THE CAMP SITE
Stoneh Farm
3
Upper Ruxley
OLD MAIDSTONE RD
MAIDSTONE RD
Bexley
Bromley
Timbertops Farm
Mast
VICTORIA BGLWS
70
B2173
2
Upper Hockden
LONDON
COOKHAM RD
CH
BR5
BR8
Burnt House Farm
A20
A20 Swanley (B2173), M20, M25
Cray Valley
KIDDENS
1
Barnfield Bank
HOCKENDEN LA
CHAPMANS END
CHAPMAN'S LA
CHAPMAN'S LA
69
Hockenden
49
50
Kent STREET ATLAS
Pauls Cray Hill Park
Hockenden House

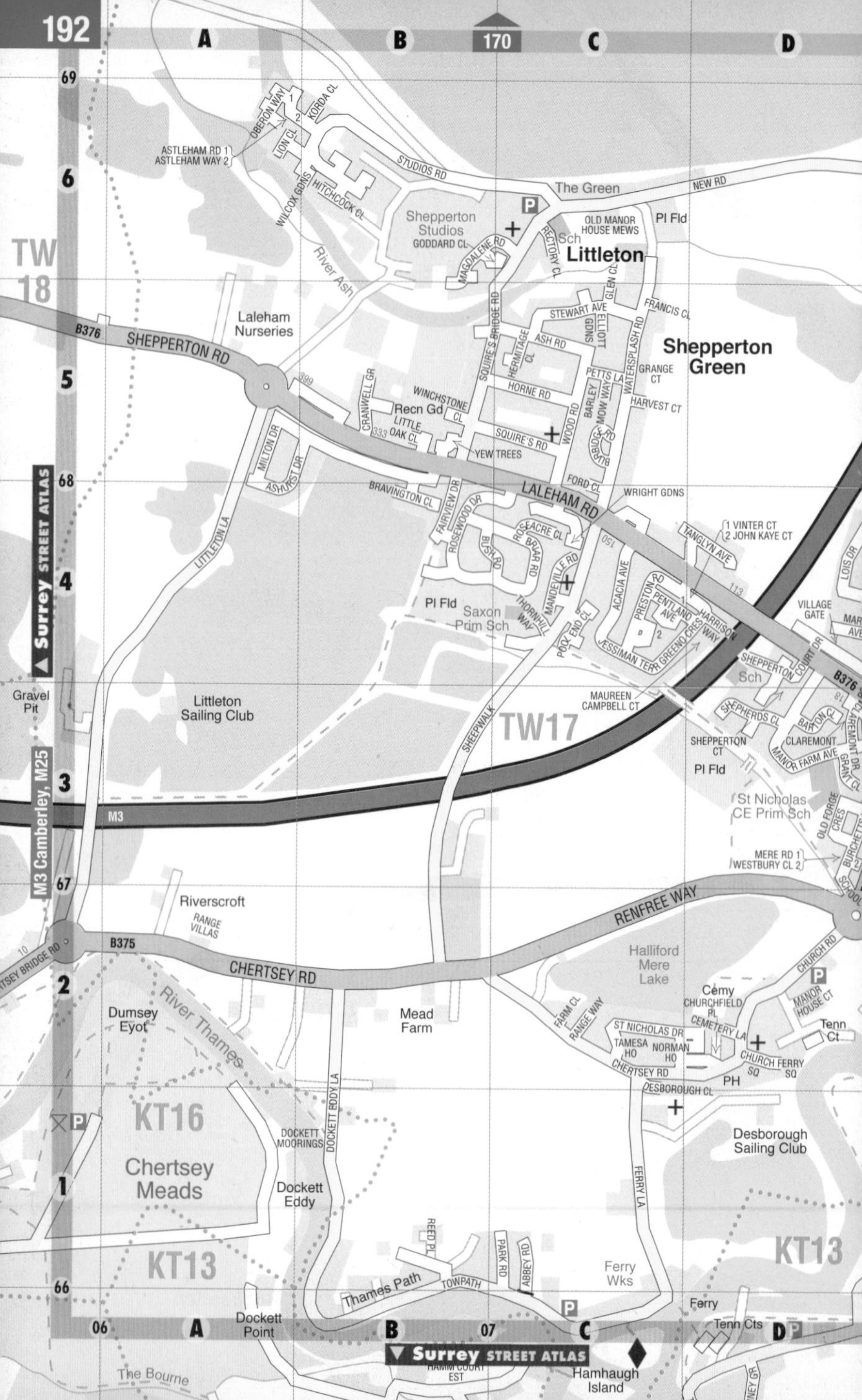

A
B
170
C
D
69
6
TW 18
5
68
4
3
67
2
1
66
OBERON WAY
KORDA CL
LION CL
ASTLEHAM RD 1
ASTLEHAM WAY 2
STUDIOS RD
WILCOX GDNS
HITCHCOCK CL
The Green
NEW RD
Shepperton Studios
GODDARD CL
MAGDALENE RD
RECTORY CL
OLD MANOR HOUSE MEWS
Pl Fld
Sch
Littleton
River Ash
GLEN CL
FRANCIS CL
STEWART AVE
ELLIOTT GDNS
WATERSPLASH RD
Shepperton Green
Laleham Nurseries
B376
SHEPPERTON RD
SQUIRE'S BRIDGE RD
HERMITAGE CL
ASH RD
GRANGE CT
PETTS LA
HORNE RD
BARLEY MOW WAY
HARVEST CT
399
CRANWELL GR
WINCHSTONE CL
Recn Gd
LITTLE OAK CL
333
SQUIRE'S RD
WOOD RD
BURBIDGE RD
YEW TREES
MILTON DR
ASHURST DR
BRAVINGTON CL
FORD CL
LALEHAM RD
WRIGHT GDNS
FAIRVIEW DR
ROSEWOOD DR
ROSE ACRE CL
BUSH RD
BRIAR RD
MANDEVILLE RD
150
ACACIA AVE
1 VINTER CT
2 JOHN KAYE CT
TANGLYN AVE
LOIS DR
LITTLETON LA
Pl Fld
Saxon Prim Sch
THORNHILL WAY
POOL END CL
PRESTON RD
PENTLAND AVE
HARRISON WAY
JESSIMAN TERR
GREENO CRES
113
VILLAGE GATE
MAR AVE
SHEPPERTON COURT DR
Sch
B376
Gravel Pit
Littleton Sailing Club
SHEEPWALK
TW17
MAUREEN CAMPBELL CT
SHEPHERDS CL
BARTON CL
CLAREMONT DR
CLAREMONT
MANOR FARM AVE
GRANT CL
SHEPPERTON CT
Pl Fld
Surrey STREET ATLAS
M3 Camberley, M25
M3
St Nicholas CE Prim Sch
OLD FORGE CRES
BURCHETTS
MERE RD 1
WESTBURY CL 2
SCHOOL
Riverscroft
RANGE VILLAS
RENFREE WAY
CHERTSEY BRIDGE RD
B375
CHERTSEY RD
Halliford Mere Lake
CHURCH RD
Dumsey Eyot
River Thames
Mead Farm
Cemy
CHURCHFIELD PL
MANOR HOUSE CT
FARM CL
RANGE WAY
ST NICHOLAS DR
CEMETERY LA
Tenn Ct
TAMESA HO
NORMAN HO
CHURCH FERRY SQ
CHERTSEY RD
DESBOROUGH CL
PH
KT16
DOCKETT MOORINGS
DOCKETT EDDY LA
Desborough Sailing Club
Chertsey Meads
Dockett Eddy
FERRY LA
REED PL
PARK RD
ABBEY RD
KT13
KT13
Ferry Wks
Thames Path
TOWPATH
Ferry
06
Dockett Point
07
Tenn Cts
Surrey STREET ATLAS
HAMM COURT EST
Hamhaugh Island
The Bourne

Charlton
171
The Bishop Wand CE Sch
Hawkedale Inf Sch
Recn Gd
Sports Gd
Pl Fld
Grange Farm Est
Hazelwood
CH
Allot Gdns
Cemy
TW16
Sunbury
Recn Gd
Upper Halliford
Vicarage Farm
TW17
River Ash
Nursery
Rodd Est
Shepperton Bsns Pk
Longwood Bsns Pk
Campasps Bsns Pk
Shepperton
Watersplash Farm
194
Lower Halliford
Tenn Cts
Thamesmead Sec Sch
Shepperton
Liby
Recn Gd
Allot Gdns
Marina
Halliford Sch
Gravel Pit
Bishop Duppas Park
Bwg Gn
Las Palmas Est
Pl Fld
Desborough Island
Thames Path
Pav
River Thames
Thames Meadow
Works
Engine River
Desborough Channel
KT12
KT13
Ashley Park
The Heart
UPPER HALLIFORD RD
GASTON BRIDGE RD
WALTON BRIDGE RD
GREEN LA
RUSSELL RD
WALTON LA
CHARLTON LA
HALLIFORD RD
FORDBRIDGE RD
NEW ZEALAND AVE
OATLANDS DR
CHURCH ST
BRIDGE ST
HEPWORTH WAY
M3
A244
B3366
B375
B376
A3050
B365

SUNBURY
The Walled Garden
River Thames
Thames Path
Sunbury Lock
Sunbury Ct Island
Apps Court Farm
Knight Resr
Rivernook Farm
Bramble Hill Farm
Wheatley's Ait
Leisure Ctr
Fball Gd
KT12
Thamesfield Farm
TW16
Queen Elizabeth Storage Resr
WALTON-ON-THAMES
TERRACE RD
HURST RD
WALTON RD
CHURCH ST
NEW ZEALAND AVE
HERSHAM RD
Ashley Park
A244 Esher
Surrey STREET ATLAS
172
193
A
B
C
D
69
6
5
68
4
3
67
2
1
66

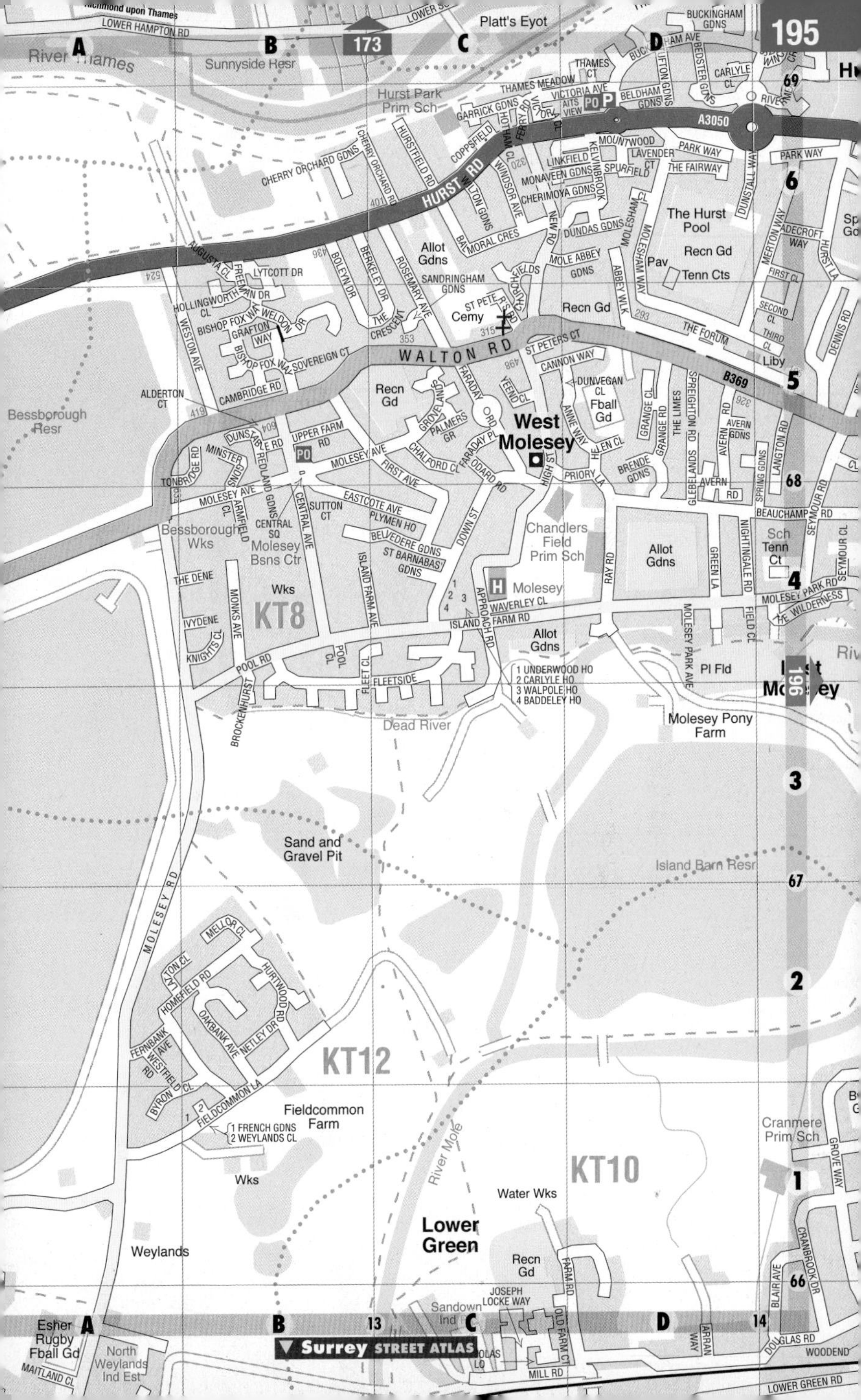

Richmond upon Thames
LOWER HAMPTON RD
173
Platt's Eyot
River Thames
Sunnyside Resr
Hurst Park Prim Sch
HURST RD
WALTON RD
West Molesey
Bessborough Resr
Bessborough Wks
Molesey Bsns Ctr
KT8
Chandlers Field Prim Sch
Molesey
The Hurst Pool
Recn Gd
Allot Gdns
Cemy
Dead River
Molesey Pony Farm
Sand and Gravel Pit
Island Barn Resr
MOLESEY RD
KT12
Fieldcommon Farm
River Mole
KT10
Water Wks
Lower Green
Weylands
Sandown Ind
Cranmere Prim Sch
Esher Rugby Fball Gd
North Weylands Ind Est
MILL RD
LOWER GREEN RD
1 UNDERWOOD HO
2 CARLYLE HO
3 WALPOLE HO
4 BADDELEY HO
1 FRENCH GDNS
2 WEYLANDS CL
A3050
B369
196

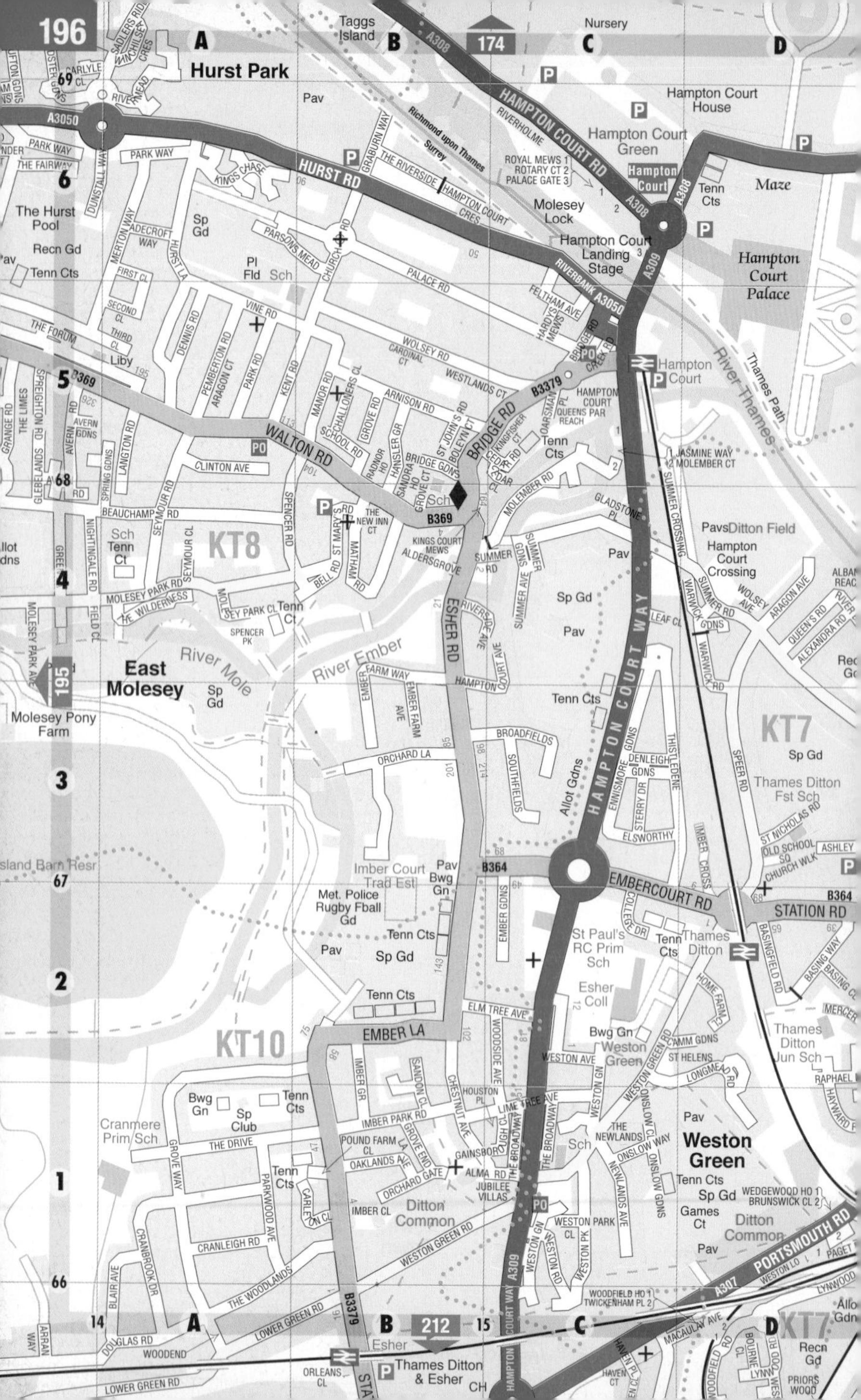

Hurst Park
East Molesey
Hampton Court Palace
Hampton Court Green
Weston Green
River Thames
River Mole
River Ember
KT8
KT7
KT10
HAMPTON COURT WAY
HURST RD
WALTON RD
ESHER RD
BRIDGE RD
EMBERCOURT RD
STATION RD
PORTSMOUTH RD
EMBER LA
Thames Ditton
Esher
Ditton Common
Hampton Court Crossing
Molesey Lock
Taggs Island
Thames Ditton & Esher

174
195
212

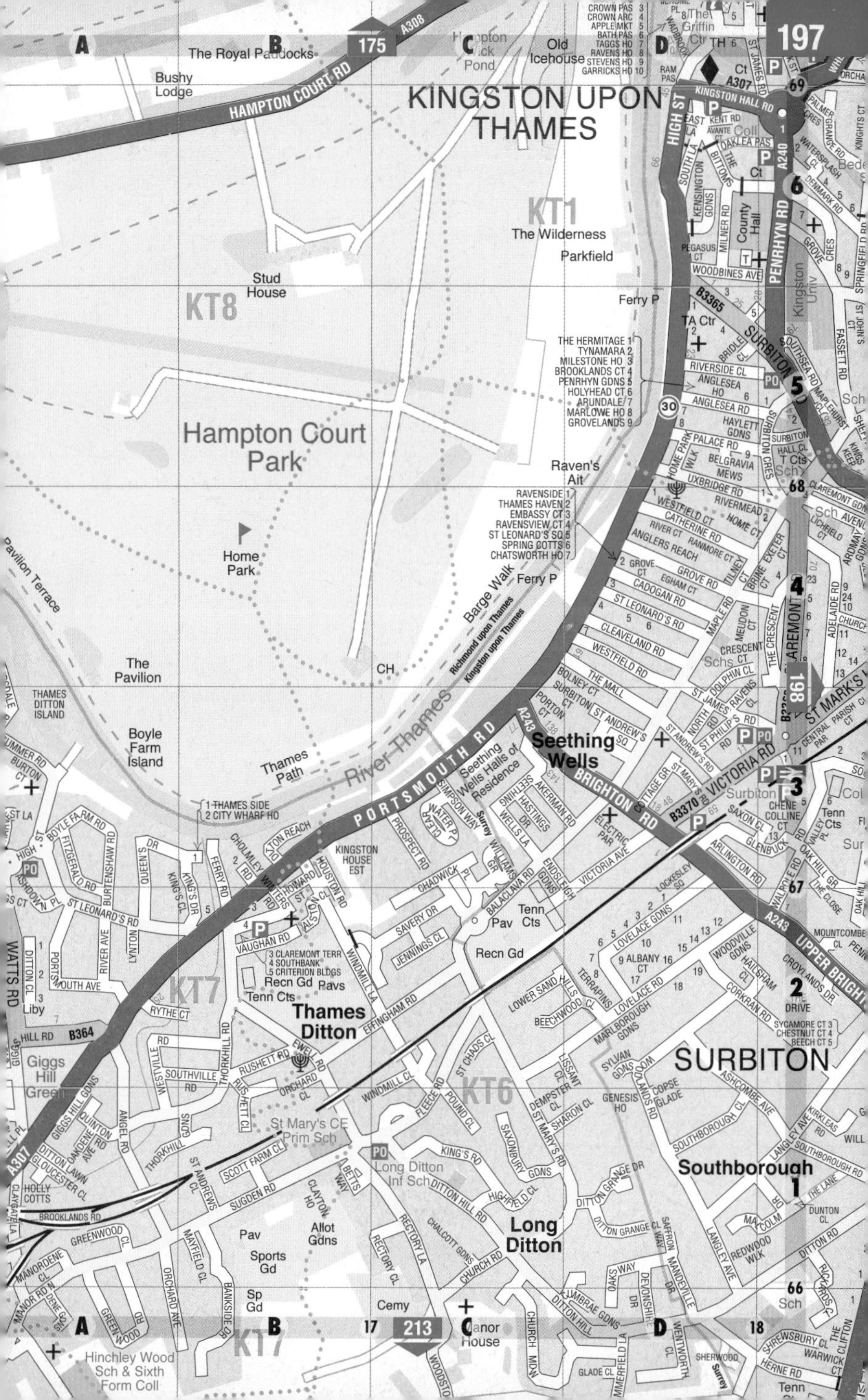

KINGSTON UPON THAMES
Hampton Court Park
Home Park
The Royal Paddocks
Bushy Lodge
HAMPTON COURT RD
Stud House
KT8
KT1
KT6
KT7
The Wilderness
Parkfield
Old Icehouse
The Pavilion
Pavilion Terrace
Thames Ditton Island
Boyle Farm Island
Thames Path
River Thames
Barge Walk
Raven's Ait
PORTSMOUTH RD
Seething Wells
Seething Wells Halls of Residence
BRIGHTON RD
VICTORIA RD
UPPER BRIGHTON RD
HIGH ST
PENRHYN RD
County Hall
Kingston Univ
Thames Ditton
Giggs Hill Green
SURBITON
Southborough
Long Ditton
Manor House
Hinchley Wood Sch & Sixth Form Coll
St Mary's CE Prim Sch
Long Ditton Inf Sch
Allot Gdns
Sports Gd
Recn Gd
Tenn Cts
Cemy
175
213
198
A307
A308
A243
A240
B3365
B3370
B364
CROWN PAS 3
CROWN ARC 4
APPLE MKT 5
BATH PAS 6
TAGGS HO 7
RAVENS HO 8
STEVENS HO 9
GARRICKS HO 10
THE HERMITAGE 1
TYNAMARA 2
MILESTONE HO 3
BROOKLANDS CT 4
PENRHYN GDNS 5
HOLYHEAD CT 6
ARUNDALE 7
MARLOWE HO 8
GROVELANDS 9
RAVENSIDE 1
THAMES HAVEN 2
EMBASSY CT 3
RAVENSVIEW CT 4
ST LEONARD'S SQ 5
SPRING COTTS 6
CHATSWORTH HO 7
1 THAMES SIDE
2 CITY WHARF HO
3 CLAREMONT TERR
4 SOUTHBANK
5 CRITERION BLDGS
SYCAMORE CT 3
CHESTNUT CT 4
BEECH CT 5

198
176
214
197
A
B
C
D
1
2
3
4
5
6
KT1
KT5
KT6
SURBITON
Southborough
Berrylands
Surbiton
Tolworth
HIGH ST
KINGSTON HALL RD
PENRHYN RD
A240
SURBITON RD
B3365
SURBITON HILL RD
B3370
ST MARK'S HILL
CLAREMONT RD
B3363
VICTORIA RD
UPPER BRIGHTON RD
A243
KINGSDOWNE RD
A3210
EWELL RD
HOOK RD
DITTON RD
B3364
CAMBRIDGE RD
A2043
TOLWORTH BROADWAY
WARREN DR N
LOWER MARSH LA
Thames Down Link
London Loop
Sewage Works
Kingstonians FC
Kingsmill Bsns Pk
Fairfield Ind Est
County Hall
Kingston Univ
Bedelsford Sch
The Hollyfield Sch
Christ Church CE Prim Sch
Dysart Sch
Tolworth Jun & Inf Schs
Recn Gd
Cemy
Crem
Allot Gdns
Nat Res
SURBITON HILL PK
THE RIDGE
THE RIDINGS
THE ROYSTONS
THE BYEWAYS
CHILTERN DR
PEMBROKE AVE
THE CREST
PINE WLK
PINE GDNS
KINGS DR
QUEENS DR
ALEXANDRA DR
AVENUE S
COURTLANDS RD
MANOR DR
VILLIERS AVE
CRANES PARK AVE
LINGFIELD AVE
GROVE LA
ALFRED RD
PORTLAND RD
BERRYLANDS RD
RAEBURN AVE
ELGAR AVE
NORTON AVE
MORESBY AVE
BERESFORD AVE
GRAND AVE
CROYLANDS DR
ASHCOMBE AVE
LANGLEY AVE
MALVERN RD
COTTERILL RD
ELLERTON RD
DOUGLAS RD
WORTHINGTON RD
RAVENSCAR RD
KINGSMEAD AVE
PRINCES AVE
OAKLEIGH AVE
1 TWYFORD PAR
2 THE BROADWAY
3 TUDOR HO
4 RUTLAND HO
5 DRAYCOT RD
1 RUSSELL CT
2 THOMAS POOLEY CT
SYCAMORE CT 3
CHESTNUT CT 4
BEECH CT 5
1 CONCORD CT
2 OFFERS CT
3 WITTS HO
TADLOW 1
STAPLEFORD CL 2
FOXTON 3
CHILDERLY 4

177
A
B
C
D
Allot Gdns
69
MUYBRIDGE RD
MIDLETON RD
ASHCOMBE SQ
LONG WLK
THE CRESCENT
THE GREEN
THE CLOSE
MYRTLE GR
LABURNUM
BEACONSFIELD RD
SALISBURY RD
POPLAR GDNS
POPLAR GR
SYCAMORE GR
EDGAR CT
ROWAN CL
Bwg Gn
Sch
COOMBE RD
DELL WLK
LINKSIDE
FORSYTH CT
CAMBRIDGE AVE
HOPPINGWOOD AVE
ORCHARD AVE
ROSEBERY AVE
ALRIC AVE
MOUNT PLEASANT RD
Corpus Christi RC Prim Sch
BEECH GR
ELM RD
MOUNT RD
LIME GR
ST MARY'S CT
CONCORD HO
CHESTNUT GR
CHESTNUT GROVE CT
STAFFORD RD
WARWICK RD
DICKERAGE LA
DICKERAGE HILL
LINCOLN RD
ROSEMONT RD
Superstores
AVENUE TERR
ST JOHNS RD
FAIRMEAD CL
ACACIA GR
LINDEN GR
CHARTER CT
ST GEORGE'S SQ
MAPLE CT
JACARANDA CL
FAIRACRE
New Malden
PHOENIX HO
VANFAME CT
Beverley Park
Beverley Brook
Kingston upon Thames
Merton
APSLEY RD
CHELTENHAM
WELLINGTON CRES
NORTHCOTE RD
HIGHCLERE RD
KINGSCOTE RD
MELROSE GDNS
HOLMWOOD CT
LC
Kingspark Bsns Ctr
LEIGH CL
Ind Est
STRATFORD CT
DORCHESTER MEWS
STATION AVE
DUKES AVE
BURBANK
PRINCES
HILLBROW
ST ANDREW'S CT
MALDEN HILL
MALDEN HILL GDNS
THE MOUNT
PARK VIEW
Blagdon House
GRAFTON RD
TREGARON GDNS
AVENUE RD
RABY RD
KT3
HIGH ST
HOWARD RD
KINGS AVE
COOMBE GDNS
ALVERSTONE RD
EGMONT RD
EGERTON RD
ONSLOW RD
Shannon Commercial Ctr
KINGSTON RD
GEORGIA RD
SPRINGFIELD PL
BERESFORD RD
DUNBAR RD
WILLOW RD
VIRGINIA CL
ALBANY RD
PENRITH RD
MONTEM RD
CAMBRIDGE RD
CLEVELAND RD
CONNAUGHT RD
SUSSEX RD
SUSSEX PL
SUSSEX CL
BLAGDON RD
NEW MALDEN
Schs
BEVERLEY RD
COCKS CRES
Shannon Cnr
B282
NEVADA CL 1
OREGON CL 2
LOCKWOOD CT 3
WINDRUSH 4
POTTERS GR
FRANKS AVE
SOUTH PARK GR
SOUTH LA
NEWBOROUGH GN
GRAYHAM RD
GRAYHAM CRES
WAITELANDS HO
PARK RD
PARK CT
CADOGAN CT
Liby
BERKELEY LO
GLOSTER RD
A2043
B283
BURLINGTON RD
WALTON AVE
Shannon Cnr Ret Pk
Recn Gd
HIGHBURY CL
FOUNTAIN CT
GOODING CL
BARNSBURY CL
RUSHEY CL
ALBEMARLE GDNS
ETON AVE
SANDAL RD
CADMER CL
Sch
GILPIN HO
RODNEY RD
RODNEY CL
OXLEIGH CL
BALGOWAN CL
PRESBURG RD
RUSHMAN VILLAS
CAVENDISH RD
VINCENT HO
QUEEN'S RD
GEORGE RD
ALBERT RD
68
50
MALDEN RD
GREEN LA
HAWKHURST WAY
GROVELAND WAY
WESTBURY RD
RANELAGH PL
SPINNEY CL
MALDEN RD
CROMWELL AVE
TADWORTH AVE
HADDON CL
CHATSWORTH GDNS
A3
SHELLEY CT
COBHAM AVE
STANLEY AVE
Allot Gdns
SELWYN RD
Sch
THE CROFT
WELBECK CL
ST JAMES' CL
WOODFIELD GDNS
KIRRANE CL
COLLEGE GDNS
4
Coombe Boys' Sch
WINDSOR LO
COTSFORD AVE
LYNTON RD
MARIA THERESA CL
The Study Sch
COOMBEFIELD CL
Malden
T Cts
Pavs
ALLAN CL
NELSON RD
THETFORD CT
THETFORD RD
OAKFIELD CL
BLAKES LA
THE GRANGE
WINDSOR AVE
BAZALGETTE CL
BAZALGETTE GDNS
BODLEY RD
BODLEY CL
SAVILE CL
WOODFIELD HO
Hogsmill River
T Cts
KINGSTON BY PASS
MALDEN WAY
WICKHAM CL
SOMERSET CL
TCts
GAYTON CT
WILTON GR
SPEIRS CL
200
Sp Gd
London Loop & Thames Down Link
KNIGHTWOOD CRES
FIR GR
BLAKES AVE
Tenn Cts
ELMBRIDGE AVE
MEADOW HILL
FIELD PL
MALDEN PK
BRAMSHAW RISE
OXFORD CRES
BARNFIELD
CANFORD GDNS
FRITHAM CL
KINGSWOOD CL
VOEWOOD CL
WEMBOROUGH
OVER DR
HORNBEAM
3
Bwg Gn
AMBERWOOD RISE
PARKSIDE CRES
Allot Gdns
MINSTEAD WAY
ALDRIDGE RISE
WAVERLEY CRES
BROADLANDS WAY
PURBECK AVE
HOLLINGTON CRES
CHILMARK GDNS
ANCASTER CRES
Grand Avenue Prim Sch
ROMNEY RD
TURNER RD
LANDSEER RD
MILLAIS RD
LAWRENCE AVE
HOLMSLEY CL
LYNDHURST DR
PORTLAND AVE
67
ELGAR AVE
PERAK CT
GAINSBOROUGH RD
VAN DYCK AVE
REYNOLDS RD
KNELLER RD
SOUTH LA
GLEBE GDNS
GREENLAW GDNS
Pav
T Cts
Manor Pk
Allot Gdns
LAWRENCE AVE
ELM CL
MALDEN RD
6 TREVELYAN CT
7 MARLFIELD CT
8 RYEHILL CT
9 COLUMBIA CT
Bwg Gn
2
Sp Gd
Richard Challoner Sch
MANOR DR N
Sch
SHEEPHOUSE WAY
NEWHOUSE CL
COLUMBIA AVE
ASHDOWN CT
BURFORD RD
BROADMEAD AVE
WOODSIDE CL
SOUTHWOOD DR
ARMESTON
Malden Manor
STROUDES CL
B284
IDMISTON RD
IDMISTON SQ
COLLINGWOOD AVE
OAKDENE DR
LUMLEY HO
MELDONE
BROCKENHURST AVE
Old Malden
THE GLEBE
MALDEN GREEN AVE
MAYFAIR AVE
CLINTON HO
WITTEN HO
OPAL HO
Liby
DOWNFIELD HO
TOPAZ HO
PERCY GDNS
AGATE HO
ONYX HO
CHURCH RD
YEW TREE HO
HOW LA
AVONDALE AVE
FULLBROOKS AVE
FOREST SIDE
GRENVILLE CL
RALEIGH DR
Allot Gdns
JASPER HO
GARNET HO
MANOR FARM CL
NEW TREE
PERRY HOW
MANOR WAY
ELMDENE
WARREN DR S
Malden CE Prim Sch
MANOR CL
KT4
THE HOLLANDS
KEBLE CL
DOWNFIELD
A2043
MALDEN RD
1
BARNSBURY LA
MEADWAY
FIRDENE
KNOLLMEAD
VICARAGE CL
THE MANOR DR
Pl Fld
PADDOCK CL
LEYFIELD
LADY HAY
ORCHARD CL
66
HAZELBANK
ALPINE AVE
TAMESIS GDNS
Allot Gdns
KT5
215
HIGHDOWN
BADGERS COPSE
22
SQUIRRELS GN
RUSHMERE CT
Pl Fld
Sp Gd
Pav
Tenn Cts
Knollmead Prim Sch
BARROW HILL
THE DENNINGTONS
CLEVELAND GDNS
CLEVELAND RD
DENE CL
THE AVENUE
AVON CL
ROYAL CL
DAPHNE
SERVITE HO
Mobile Home

Raynes Park
Bushey Mead
SW20
West Barnes
Motspur Park
KT3
SM4
KT4
NEW MALDEN
Cannon Hill Common
Cannon Hill
Beverley Park
Blagdon House
Coombe Boys' Sch
Athletic Gd
Morden Cemy
Merton & Sutton Joint Cemy
Green Lane Prim Sch
St John Fisher RC Prim Sch
Worcester Park
Manor Pk
BEVERLEY WAY KINGSTON BY-PASS
MALDEN WAY
BURLINGTON RD
WEST BARNES LA
GRAND DR
BUSHEY RD
MALDEN RD
CENTRAL RD
TUDOR DR
178
199
216

A
B
C
D
179
Merton Park
SW20
SW19
SM4
SM3
SM1
Rutlish Sch
Pl Flds
Sp Gd
Kendor Gdns
Joseph Hood Prim Sch
Allot Gdns
Tenn Cts
Recn Gd
South Merton
Mostyn Gardens
Tenn Cts
Poplar Prim Sch
George Sq
Morden
Morden Hall
Morden Hall Park
Liby
Crown Par
Martin Way
Crown La
Aberconway Rd
Morden Hall Rd
London Rd
Morden Ct Par
Pl Fld
Hillcross Prim Sch
Allot Gdns
Pav
Tenn Cts
Depot
Morden South
St Ann's Sch
Abbotsbury Prim Sch
Morden Park Sch Sports Ctr
Merton Coll
Central Rd
Hatfield Prim Sch
Morden Park
Recn Gd
Bwg Gn
Tenn Cts
MORDEN
St Helier
Haig Homes
Trenchard Ct
Green La
Lower Morden La
Cardinal Ave
Tudor Dr
Epsom Rd
Lower Morden
Elizabeth Ct
The Woodstock
Stonecot Hill
Sutton Common Rd
Allot Gdns
Recn Gd
Bwg Gn
Abbey Prim Sch
Glenthorne High Sch
Reigate Ave
Rose Hill
Rosehill
Rosehill Park East
Festival Ct 1
Gallica Ct 2
Harkness Ct 3
Cleeve Way 4
Wheatcroft Ct 5
Damask Ct 6
1 Thompson Cl
2 Anderson Cl
1 Arlington Cl
2 Oakwood Gdns
3 Highfields
Brookfield Prim Sch
Liby
Cemy
Allot Gdns
Kimpton Trade & Bsns Ctr
Kimpton Park Way
Fball Gd
Bwg Gn
Recn Gd
Pav
St Helier Ave
Rosehill Park W
A24
A239
A297
A217
B286
B278
B279
B2230
217
202
25
26
66
67
68
69
1
2
3
4
5
6

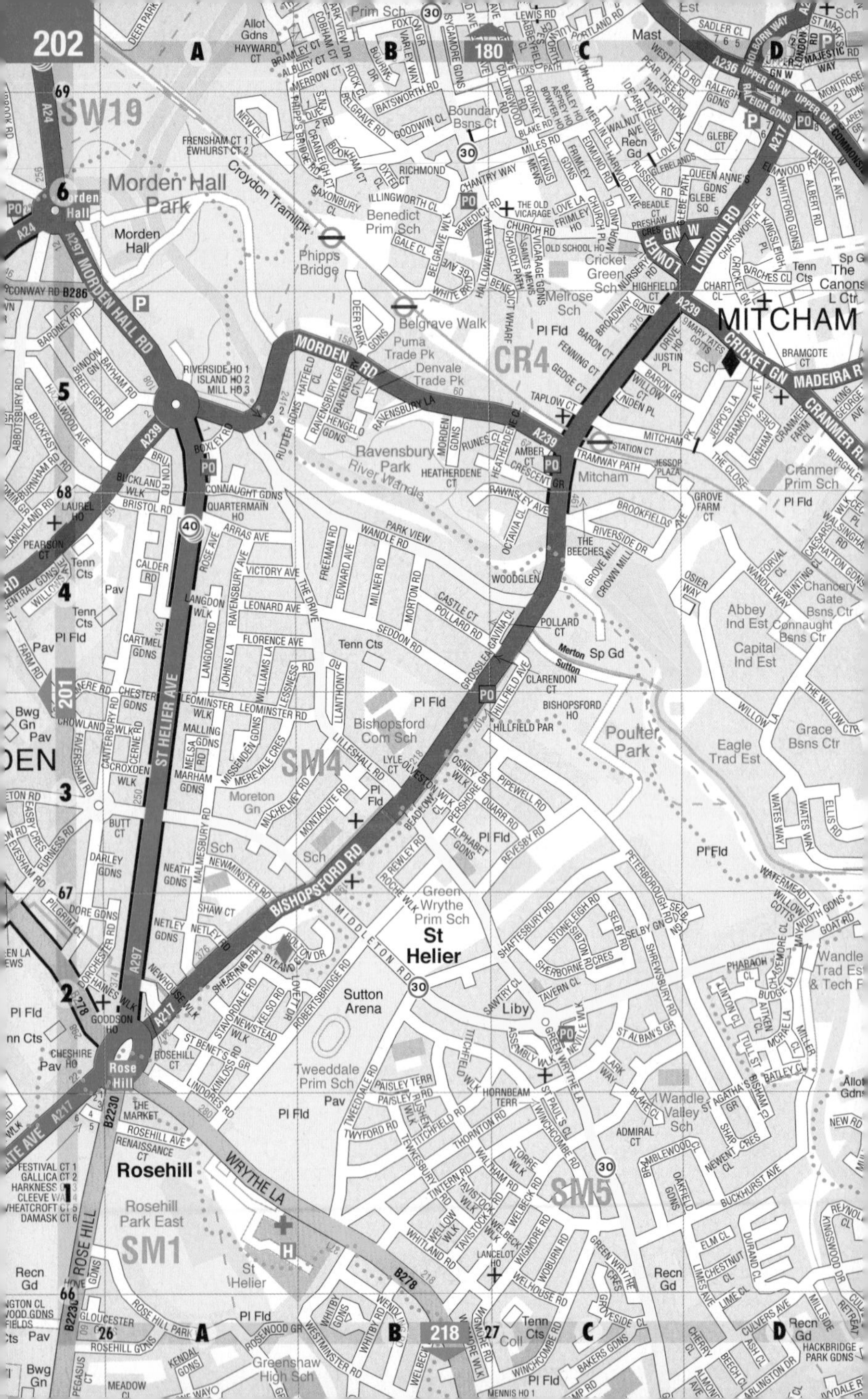
202
A
B
C
D
180
SW19
Morden Hall Park
Morden Hall
Croydon Tramlink
Phipps Bridge
Belgrave Walk
Benedict Prim Sch
Boundary Bsns Ct
Cricket Green Sch
Melrose Sch
MITCHAM
CR4
MORDEN RD
Puma Trade Pk
Denvale Trade Pk
Ravensbury Park
River Wandle
Mitcham
Cranmer Prim Sch
MORDEN HALL RD
ST HELIER AVE
BISHOPSFORD RD
LONDON RD
CRICKET GN
MADEIRA RD
CRANMER RD
UPPER GN W
UPPER GN E
LOWER GN W
Abbey Ind Est
Chancery Gate Bsns Ctr
Connaught Bsns Ctr
Capital Ind Est
Poulter Park
Eagle Trad Est
Grace Bsns Ctr
Bishopsford Com Sch
SM4
Moreton Gn
Green Wrythe Prim Sch
St Helier
Sutton Arena
Tweeddale Prim Sch
Wandle Valley Sch
Wandle Trad Est & Tech Pk
SM5
Rosehill
Rosehill Park East
SM1
St Helier
WRYTHE LA
ROSE HILL
Greenshaw High Sch
201
218
DEN
Merton
Sutton
Sp Gd
Pl Fld
Tenn Cts
Liby
Coll
Recn Gd
Bwg Gn
Pav
Mast
1
2
3
4
5
6
26
27
66
67
68
69

MITCHAM
CR4
CR0
SM6
Mitcham Common
Mitcham Junction
Beddington Corner
Hackbridge
Beddington Sewage Treatment Works
Beddington Farm
Beddington Lane
Brookmead Ind Est
Windmill Trad Est
Mill House
The Sherwood Sch
Garden Prim Sch
William Morris Prim Sch
Harris Acad
The Tramsheds Ind Est
Prologis Pk
Valley Point Ind Est
Pioneer Ind Pk
Mill Green Bsns Pk
Felnex Trad Est
Soho Mills
Croydon Tramlink
CROYDON RD
COMMONSIDE EAST
CARSHALTON RD
LONDON RD
WINDMILL RD
MANOR RD
BEDDINGTON LA
MILE RD
COOMBER WAY
WATNEYS RD
SHERWOOD PARK RD
NORTHBOROUGH RD
COMMONSIDE W
CRANMER RD
RED HOUSE RD
ROCHFORD WAY
THERAPIA LA
GREENLAND WAY
JESSOPS WAY
BROOKMEAD RD
ELBERON AVE
181
204
219
29
30
66
67
68
69

A
B
C
D
182
203
220
SW16
CR4
CR7
CR0
Harris Acad
William Morris Prim Sch
Recn Gd
Liby
Norbury Court Rd
Northborough Rd
Beatrice Ave
Pollards Hill N
Pollards Hill E
Pollards Hill W
Pollards Hill S
Pollards Cres
Cranbourne Cl
Recreation Way
Forrest Gdns
Highdaun Dr
Tall Trees
Wharfedale Gdns
Lonsdale Gdns
Headcorn Rd
Galpin's Rd
Mayfield Cres
Mayfield Rd
Silverleigh Rd
London Rd
A23
A235
A236
A213
B266
B272
Winterbourne Jun & Inf Schs
Winterbourne Rd
Stratford Rd
Richmond Rd
Langdale Rd
Lyndhurst Rd
Malvern Rd
Colliers Water La
Brigstock Rd
Queen's Ct
Thornton Row
Raymead Ave
Thornton Heath Pond
Thornton Rd
Gonville Prim Sch
Gonville Rd
Limpsfield Ave
Trafford Rd
Trafford Villas
Bwg Gn
Allot Gdns
Pl Fld
Sp Gd
Fball Gd
Crem
Cemy
Pav
1 Powell Terr
2 Peralte Terr
3 Buckingham Rd
4 Buckingham Ct
5 Lincoln Ct
6 Sussex Ct
7 Lincoln Rd
Commonside E
Northumberland Gdns
Westmorland Way
Southampton Gdns
The Archbishop Lanfranc Sch
Peall Rd Ind Est
Thornton Rd Ind Est
Aurelia Gdns
Aurelia Rd
Shamrock Rd
Ash Tree Villas
The Courtyard
Croydon Ho
Flint Ct
Peall Rd
Thornton Ave
Lavender Rd
Songhurst Cl
Brading Rd
Rosecourt Rd
Cecil Rd
Tankerton Terr
Beddington Terr
Lombard Rdbt
Rochford Way
Saffron Cl
Therapia La
Therapia Lane
Alfriston Ave
Stonecroft Way
Westcombe Ave
Ringwood Ave
Dacre Rd
Rosedene Ave
Ockley Rd
The Tramsheds Ind Est
Coomber Way
Endeavour Way
Prologis Pk
Valley Point Ind Est
Beddington Cross
Stirling Way
Brazil Cl
Franklin Way
Kelvin Gdns
Maxwell Cl
Wimshurst Cl
Beddington Farm Rd
Pioneers Ind Pk
Beddington Trad Est
Bath House Rd
Pylon Way
Ind Est
Croydon Tramlink
Ampere Way
Newman Rd
Chesterman Way
Volta Way
Faraday Way
Galvani Way
Waddon Marsh Way
Daniell Way
Superstore
Purley Way
Purley Way Cres
Drake Rd
Lombard Bsns Pk
Mitcham Rd
Thornton Heath
Mayday University
Broad Green
Mayday Rd
Sharland Cl
Crossland Rd
Colchester Villas
Cheltenham Villas
Canterbury Rd
Midhurst Ave
Greenside Rd
Fairholme Rd
Pemdevon Rd
Brockwell Ct
Sutherland Rd
Wentworth Rd
Priory Rd
Onslow Rd
Chapman Rd
Thomson Cres
Kingsley Rd
Euston Rd
Sumner Rd
Sumner Rd S
Bute Rd
Grafton Rd
Leighton Gdns
Leighton St
Albion St
Handcroft Rd
Elmwood Schs
Elmwood Rd
Frederick Gdns
Micklefield Ct
Robinson Ct
The Interchange
Broad Green Ave
Kelling Gdns
Dartmouth Ho
Wellington Rd
Zodiac Ct
Cavendish Rd
Chatfield Rd
Montague Rd
Nelson Rd
Parson's Mead
Renown
TA Ctr
The Pilton Est
Factory La
Waddon Marsh
Trafalgar Way
Martin Cres
Enterprise Cl
Miller Rd
Gurney Cres
Allen Rd
Effingham Rd
Fairmead Rd
Beddington Farm Rd
Marlowe Way
Peterwood Pk
Westfield Rd 1
Lower Church St 2
Bourne St 3
Theobald Rd
Beddington

CR7
SE25
CR0
South Norwood
Selhurst
Thornton Heath
Norwood Junction
West Croydon
East Croydon
GRANGE RD
WHITEHORSE RD
SOUTH NORWOOD HILL
SELHURST RD
NORTHCOTE RD
WINDMILL RD
ST JAMES'S RD
LOWER ADDISCOMBE RD
MORLAND RD
HIGH ST
WHITEHORSE LA
CHERRY ORCHARD RD
WELLESLEY RD
PARCHMORE RD
Selhurst Park (Crystal Palace Fball Club)
Croydon Coll
Selhurst Performing Arts & Tech Sch
Heavers Farm Prim Sch
Davidson Prim Sch
Broadmead Jun & Inf Schs
Ecclesbourne Jun & Inf Schs
Bensham Manor Sch
St Chad's Sch
Woodside Jun & Inf Sch
Oval Prim Sch
St Mary's Jun & Inf Schs
Whitgift Ctr
Centrale Ctr
Croydon Tramlink
Roman Ind Est
Tait Rd Ind Est
Hampton Road Ind Pk
Grangewood Park
South Norwood Allot Gdns
Cemy
Recn Gd
Tenn Cts
Bwg Gn
Liby
Selhurst Works
183
206
221
A
B
C
D
1
2
3
4
5
6

A
B
C
D
184
222
205
1
2
3
4
5
6
Elmers End
South Norwood
Country Park
SE25
BR3
CR0
Woodside
Addiscombe
Shirley
Birkbeck
Harrington
Road
Elmers
End
Norwood
Junction
Arena
Blackhorse
Lane
Woodside
Croydon Tramlink
Sports
Arena
Ryelands
Prim Sch
Golf Ctr
Long Lane
Wood
Nat
Res
Ashburton
Learning Village
Shirley Oaks
Ashburton
Park
Monks
Orchard
Sch
Churchfield
Prim Sch
Crem
Cemy
Superstore
Croydon Road
Ind Est
Chaffinch
Bsns Pk
PENGE RD
A213
HIGH ST
A215
MANOR RD
PORTLAND RD
SPRING LA
LONG LA
A222
ELMERS END RD
A214
LOWER ADDISCOMBE RD
SHIRLEY RD
WOODSIDE GN
B243
ADDISCOMBE RD
A232
WARWICK RD
HARRINGTON RD
ALBERT RD
TENNYSON RD
ENMORE RD
STROUD GREEN WAY
PRIMROSE LA
ASHBURTON AVE
BYWOOD AVE
WOODMERE AVE
SHIRLEY AVE
SHIRLEY OAKS RD

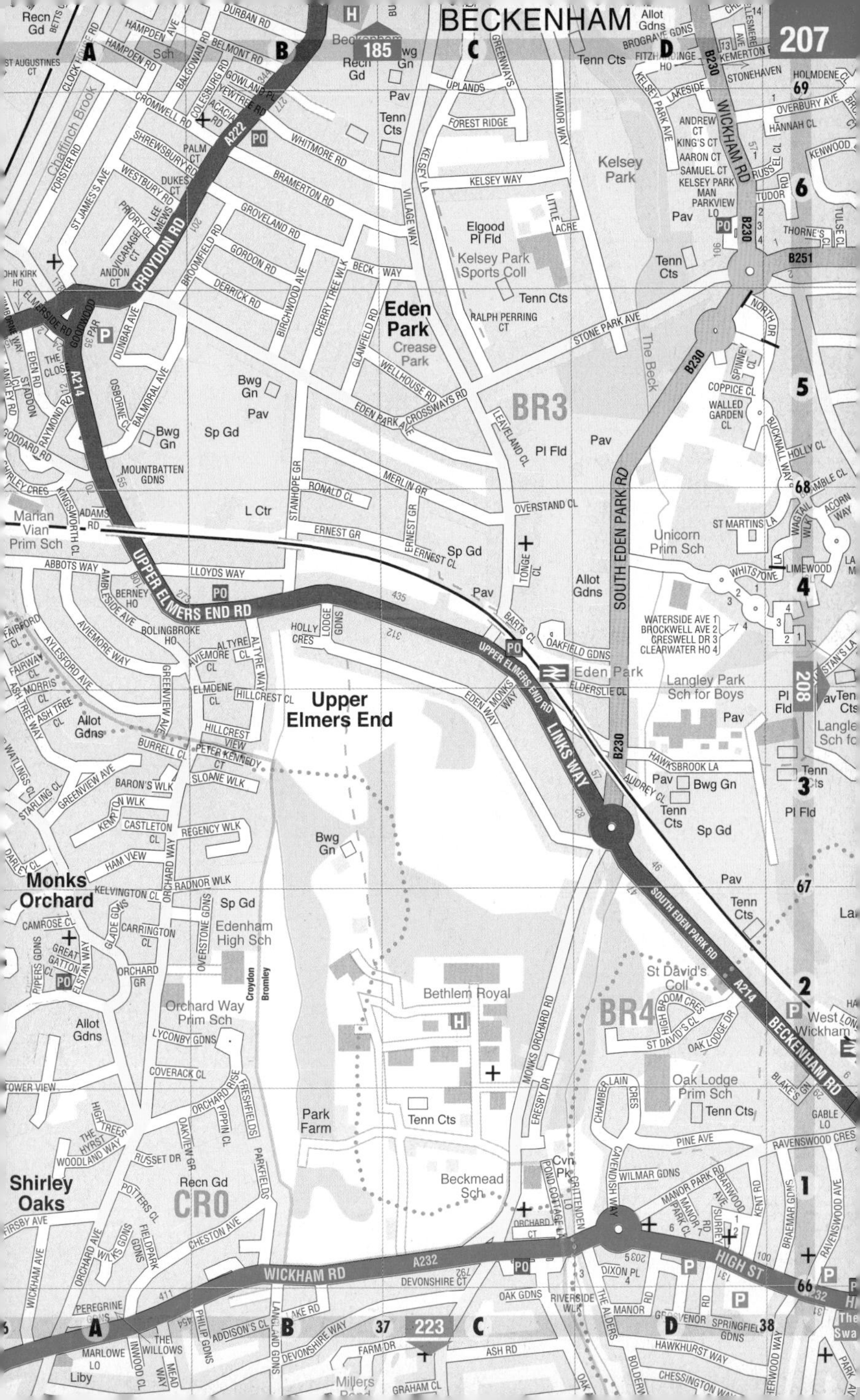
BECKENHAM
Upper Elmers End
Eden Park
Monks Orchard
Shirley Oaks
BR3
BR4
CR0
185
208
223
A
B
C
D
1
2
3
4
5
6
CROYDON RD
UPPER ELMERS END RD
LINKS WAY
SOUTH EDEN PARK RD
WICKHAM RD
BECKENHAM RD
HIGH ST
Kelsey Park
Bethlem Royal
Edenham High Sch
Orchard Way Prim Sch
Unicorn Prim Sch
Langley Park Sch for Boys
Oak Lodge Prim Sch
Kelsey Park Sports Coll
St David's Coll
Beckmead Sch
Eden Park
West Wickham

Shortlands
BR2
BR3
BR4
Park Langley
Langley Park
Pickhurst Green
West Wickham
Cupola Wood
Highfield Jun & Inf Schs
Langley Park Sch for Girls
Pickhurst Jun Sch
Pickhurst Inf Sch
Hawes Down Schs
Oak Lodge Prim Sch
Clare House Prim Sch
HAYES LA
PICKHURST LA
WESTMORELAND RD
WICKHAM RD
BECKENHAM RD
STATION RD
HIGH ST
HAWES LA
WICKHAM WAY
BARNFIELD WOOD RD
THE AVENUE
WICKHAM CHASE
LANGLEY WAY
THE DRIVE
PICKHURST RISE
RED LODGE RD
HAYES CHASE
THE CRESCENT
WEST WAY
GOODHART WAY
BUSHEY WAY
OVERHILL WAY
WOODMERE WAY
BRABOURNE RISE
STYLES WAY
WHITECROFT WAY
MALMAINS WAY
ELWILL WAY
HAYES WAY
WHITECROFT CL
KINGSWOOD AVE
ROMANHURST AVE
SOUTH HILL RD
TOOTSWOOD RD
ST MARY'S AVE
HAWKSBROOK LA
MOUNTHURST RD
HAYES HILL
HEPBURN GDNS
LINKS RD
THE MEAD
RAVENSWOOD CRES
RAVENSWOOD AVE
186
207
224

BROMLEY
BR1
BR2
Bromley South
Masons Hill
Kentish Way
Hayes Rd
Hayes La
Hayes St
Bromley Common
Page Heath La
Westmoreland Rd
Homesdale Rd
Norman Park
Fisher's Wood
Scrogginhill Wood
Brook Wood
Mazzards Wood
Rookery Lake
Ravens Bourne
Hayes Street Farm
Oakley House
Hayes
Bromley Common
The Ravensbourne Sch
Raglan Prim Sch
Bickley Prim Sch
Hayes Prim Sch
Bromley Coll of F & H Ed
Bromley Fball Gd
Athletics Tk
Chartwell Bsns Ctr
Waldo Ind Est 1
Bromley Ind Ctr 2
Old Rectory Gdns
Allot Gdns
Pl Fld
Pav
P&R
A21
A233
B265
B2212
B228
B251
187
210
225
41
42
69
66
A
B
C
D
1
2
3
4
5
6

Bickley
Bickley Park Sch
Bickley
BICKLEY PARK RD
A222
PAGE HEATH LA
B265
HAWTHORNE RD
OLDFIELD RD
SOUTHBOROUGH RD
BR1
Bromley High Sch
Jubilee Park Country Park
Thornet Wood
BR5
St James RC Prim Sch
SOUTHBOROUGH LA
Southborough Prim Sch
BR2
Southborough
Bromley Common
Parkfield Recn Gd
Bishop Justus CE Sch
Princes Plain Prim Sch
Prince's Plain
BROMLEY COMMON
A21
A233
London Loop
Sparrow Wood
Crofton Heath
Scrubs Farm
Oakley House
Knowlehill Wood
Knowl Wood
1 ST HILARY'S CT
2 PERCY TERR
3 PARKLAND MEAD
4 ST DAVID'S CT
1 PEMBURY HO
2 KINGSMEAD COTTS
188
209
226
42
43
A
B
C
D
69
68
67
66
6
5
4
3
2
1

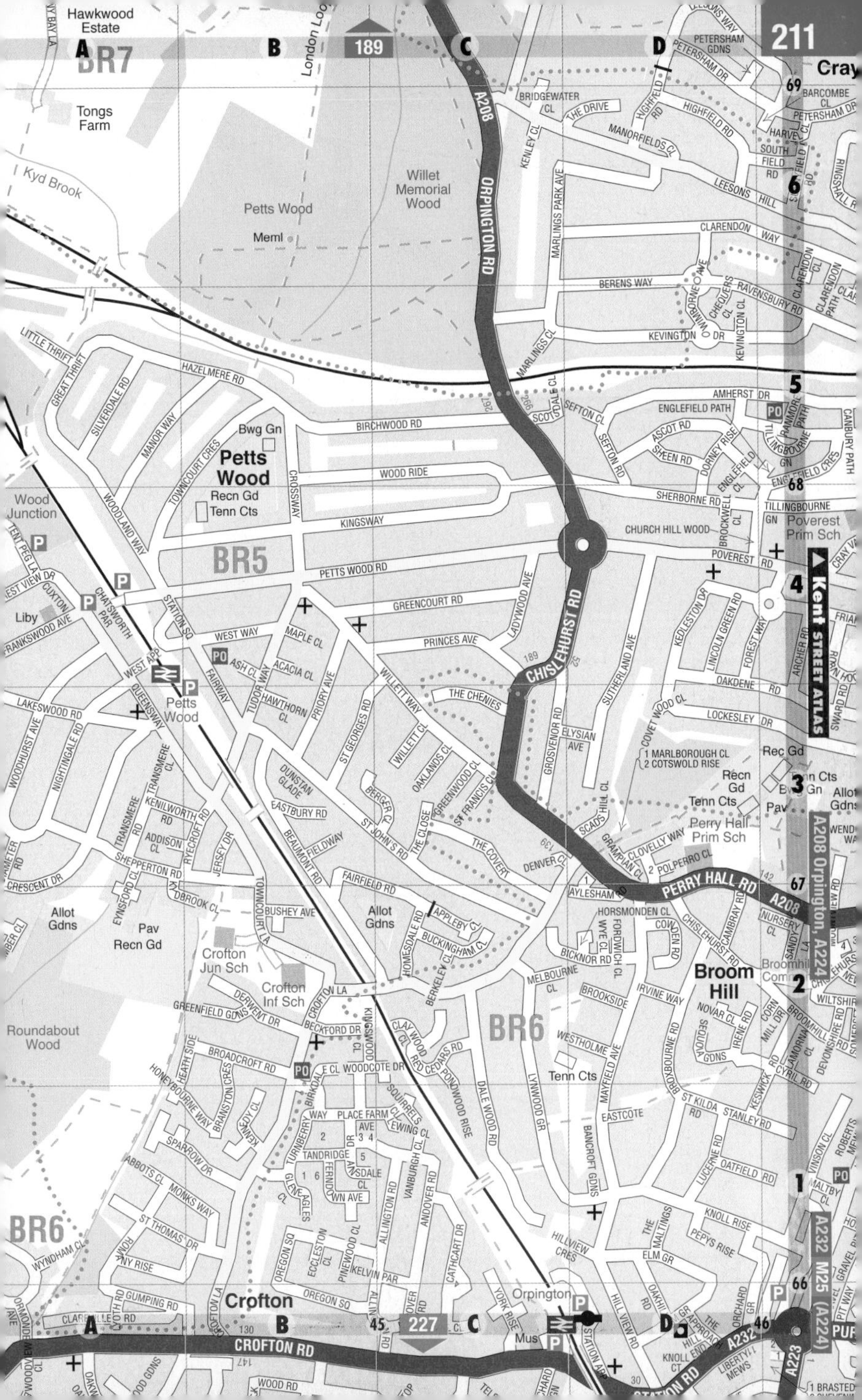
Hawkwood Estate
BR7
189
Tongs Farm
Kyd Brook
Petts Wood
Meml
Willet Memorial Wood
ORPINGTON RD
A208
Cray
BR5
BR6
Petts Wood
Wood Junction
Liby
Recn Gd
Tenn Cts
Bwg Gn
HAZELMERE RD
BIRCHWOOD RD
WOOD RIDE
KINGSWAY
PETTS WOOD RD
GREENCOURT RD
PRINCES AVE
CHISLEHURST RD
SHERBORNE RD
CHURCH HILL WOOD
POVEREST RD
Poverest Prim Sch
Kent STREET ATLAS
PERRY HALL RD
Perry Hall Prim Sch
Broom Hill
Allot Gdns
Pav
Recn Gd
Crofton Jun Sch
Crofton Inf Sch
Roundabout Wood
Crofton
CROFTON RD
227
Orpington
Mus
STATION RD
A232 M25 (A224)
A208 Orpington, A224
A223
Tenn Cts
Rec Gd

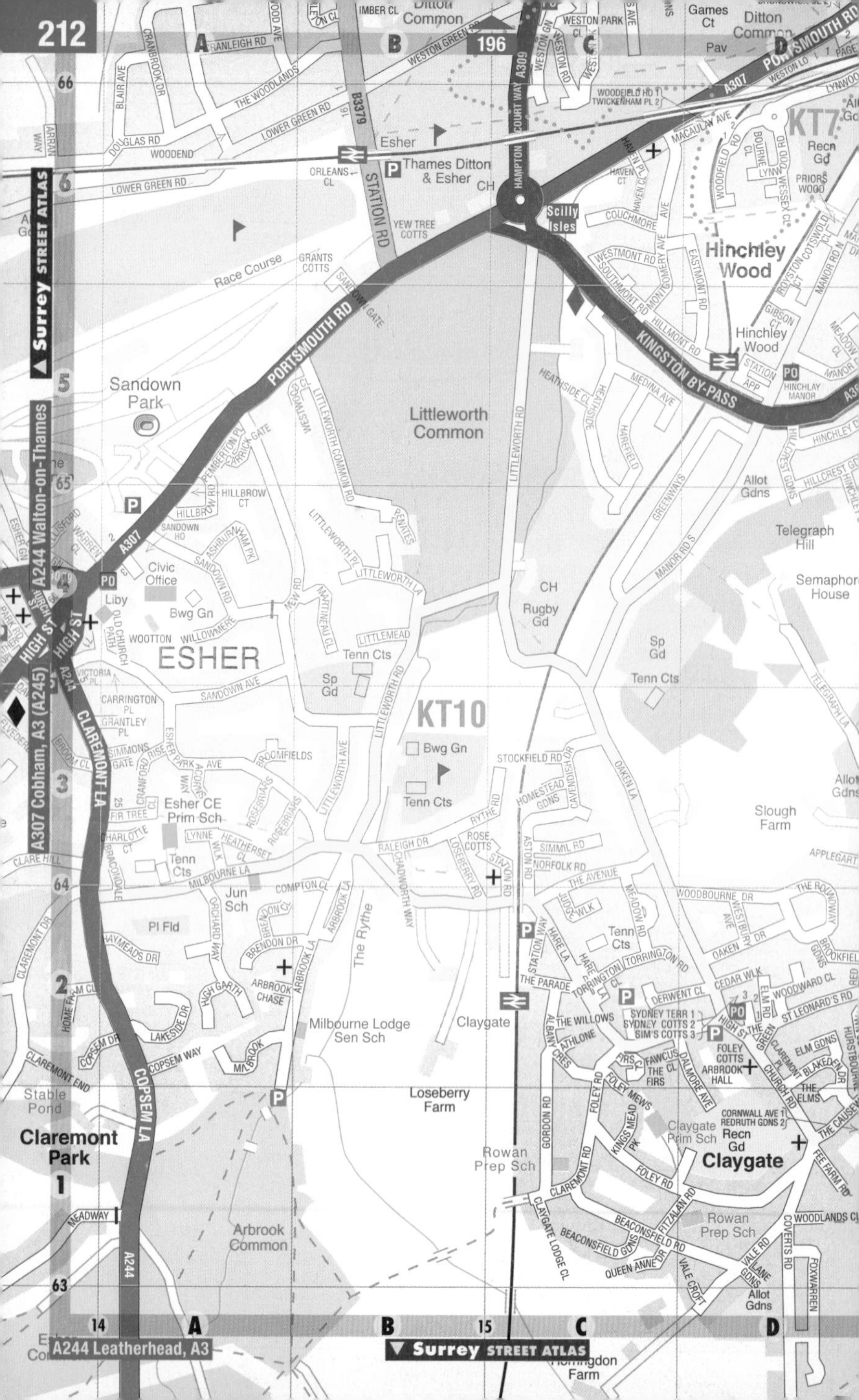
196
A
B
C
D
66
6
5
65
4
3
64
2
1
63
14
15
Surrey STREET ATLAS
A244 Walton-on-Thames
A307 Cobham, A3 (A245)
A244 Leatherhead, A3
Surrey STREET ATLAS
Ditton Common
IMBER CL
Games Ct
Pav
WESTON PARK
CRANLEIGH RD
WESTON GREEN RD
PORTSMOUTH RD
A307
A309
THE WOODLANDS
LOWER GREEN RD
DOUGLAS RD
WOODEND
BLAIR AVE
CRANBROOK DR
ARRAN WAY
B3379
Esher
Thames Ditton & Esher
CH
ORLEANS CL
STATION RD
HAMPTON COURT WAY
LOWER GREEN RD
WOODFIELD HO 1
TWICKENHAM PL 2
MACAULAY AVE
HAVEN RD
HAVEN PL
HAVEN CT
KT7
Recn Gd
PRIORS WOOD
WOODFIELD RD
BOURNE LYNN
WESSEX CL
Scilly Isles
YEW TREE COTTS
GRANTS COTTS
Race Course
COUCHMORE AVE
WESTMONT RD
SOUTHMONT RD
MONTGOMERY AVE
EASTMONT RD
HILLMONT RD
Hinchley Wood
ROYSTON CT
COTSWOLD CL
MANOR RD N
GIBSON CT
KINGSTON BY-PASS
STATION APP
PO
HINCHLAY MANOR
SANDOWN GATE
Sandown Park
Littleworth Common
LITTLEWORTH RD
HEATHSIDE CL
HEATHSIDE
MEDINA AVE
HAREFIELD
HINCHLEY DR
HILLCREST GDNS
HILLCREST GDNS
Allot Gdns
GREENWAYS
MANOR RD S
Telegraph Hill
Semaphore House
CARRICK GATE
PEMBERTON PL
HILLBROW RD
HILLBROW CT
SANDOWN HO
ASHBURNHAM PK
SANDOWN RD
LITTLEWORTH COMMON RD
WESTON CL
LITTLEWORTH PL
LITTLEWORTH LA
PENATES
Civic Office
Liby
Bwg Gn
WOOTTON
WILLOWMERE
OLD CHURCH PATH
NEW RD
MARTINEAU CL
LITTLEMEAD
CH
Rugby Gd
ESHER
HIGH ST
Tenn Cts
Sp Gd
Sp Gd
Tenn Cts
VICTORIA PL
CARRINGTON PL
GRANTLEY PL
SANDOWN AVE
KT10
TELEGRAPH LA
CLAREMONT LA
SIMMONS GATE
ESHER PARK AVE
BROOMFIELDS
LITTLEWORTH AVE
Bwg Gn
STOCKFIELD RD
CAVENDISH DR
OAKEN LA
Allot Gdns
HOMESTEAD GDNS
CRANFORD CL
ACORNS WAY
Esher CE Prim Sch
ROSEBRIARS
Tenn Cts
RYTHE RD
Slough Farm
FIR TREE
CHARLOTTE CT
LYNNE WLK
HEATHERSET CL
RALEIGH DR
ROSE COTTS
SIMMIL RD
APPLEGARTH
CLARE HILL
BRACONDALE
Tenn Cts
MILBOURNE LA
Jun Sch
COMPTON CL
CHADWORTH WAY
LOSEBERRY RD
STATION RD
ASTON RD
NORFOLK RD
THE AVENUE
MEADOW RD
WOODBOURNE DR
THE ROUNDWAY
WESTBURY AVE
CLAREMONT DR
Pl Fld
ORCHARD WAY
BRENDON CL
ARBROOK LA
The Rythe
JUDGE WLK
Tenn Cts
OAKEN DR
BROOKFIELD GDNS
HAYMEADS DR
BRENDON DR
STATION WAY
HARE LA
TORRINGTON RD
TORRINGTON CL
CEDAR WLK
WOODWARD CL
HOME FARM CL
HIGH GARTH
ARBROOK CHASE
THE PARADE
DERWENT CL
ELM RD
ST LEONARD'S RD
LAKESIDE DR
Milbourne Lodge Sen Sch
Claygate
THE WILLOWS
SYDNEY TERR 1
SYDNEY COTTS 2
SIM'S COTTS 3
HIGH ST
THE GREEN
COPSEM DR
COPSEM WAY
MILBROOK
ALBANY CRES
ATHLONE
FIRS CL
FAWCUS CL
THE FIRS
DALMORE AVE
FOLEY COTTS
ARBROOK HALL
CLAREMONT RD
CHURCH RD
ELM GDNS
BLAKEDEN DR
HURSTBOURNE
THE ELMS
CLAREMONT END
Stable Pond
COPSEM LA
Loseberry Farm
GORDON RD
FOLEY RD
FOLEY MEWS
KINGS MEAD PK
Claygate Prim Sch
CORNWALL AVE 1
REDRUTH GDNS 2
Recn Gd
THE CAUSEWAY
Claremont Park
Rowan Prep Sch
CLAREMONT RD
FOLEY RD
Claygate
FEE FARM RD
MEADWAY
CLAYGATE LODGE CL
FITZALAN RD
Rowan Prep Sch
WOODLANDS CL
Arbrook Common
BEACONSFIELD GDNS
BEACONSFIELD RD
QUEEN ANNE DR
VALE CROFT
VALE RD
LANE GDNS
COVERTS RD
FOXWARREN
A244
Allot Gdns
Horringdon Farm

Long Ditton
197
KT7
KT6
KT10
KT9
Hinchley Wood Sch & Sixth Form Coll
Hinchley Wood Prim Sch
Hill Park Nurseries
Ditton Hill Nurseries
Manor House
Cemy
KINGSTON BY-PASS
A309
A3
A243
HOOK RD
LEATHERHEAD RD
The Waffrons
Surbiton
Manor Farm
Elm Farm
Lower Wood
Barwell
Lovelace Prim Sch
St Philip's Sch
Ellingham Prim Sch
Chessington South
Com Coll
Barwell Bsns Pk
Chessington
214
Claygate Common
A3 Guildford, M25
Surrey STREET ATLAS
A243 Leatherhead, M25

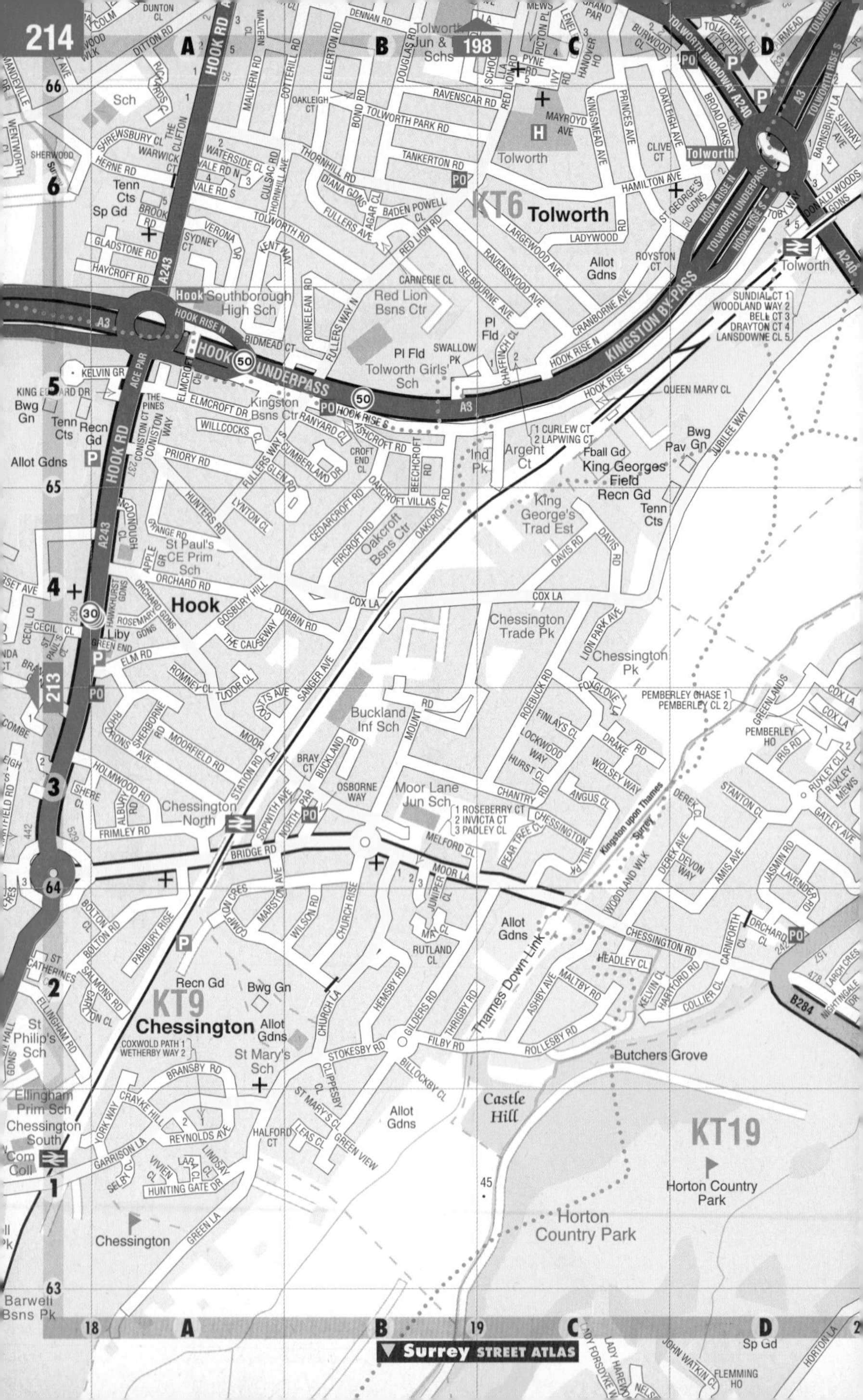
198
Tolworth
Tolworth Jun & Schs
KT6
Hook
Southborough High Sch
Red Lion Bsns Ctr
Tolworth Girls' Sch
Kingston Bsns Ctr
King Georges Field
Recn Gd
King George's Trad Est
Oakcroft Bsns Ctr
St Paul's CE Prim Sch
Chessington Trade Pk
Chessington Pk
Buckland Inf Sch
Moor Lane Jun Sch
Chessington North
KT9
Chessington
St Mary's Sch
Castle Hill
Butchers Grove
KT19
Horton Country Park
Ellingham Prim Sch
Chessington South
St Philip's Sch
Barwell Bsns Pk
HOOK UNDERPASS
KINGSTON BY-PASS
TOLWORTH UNDERPASS
Thames Down Link
213
18
19
63
64
65
66
Surrey STREET ATLAS

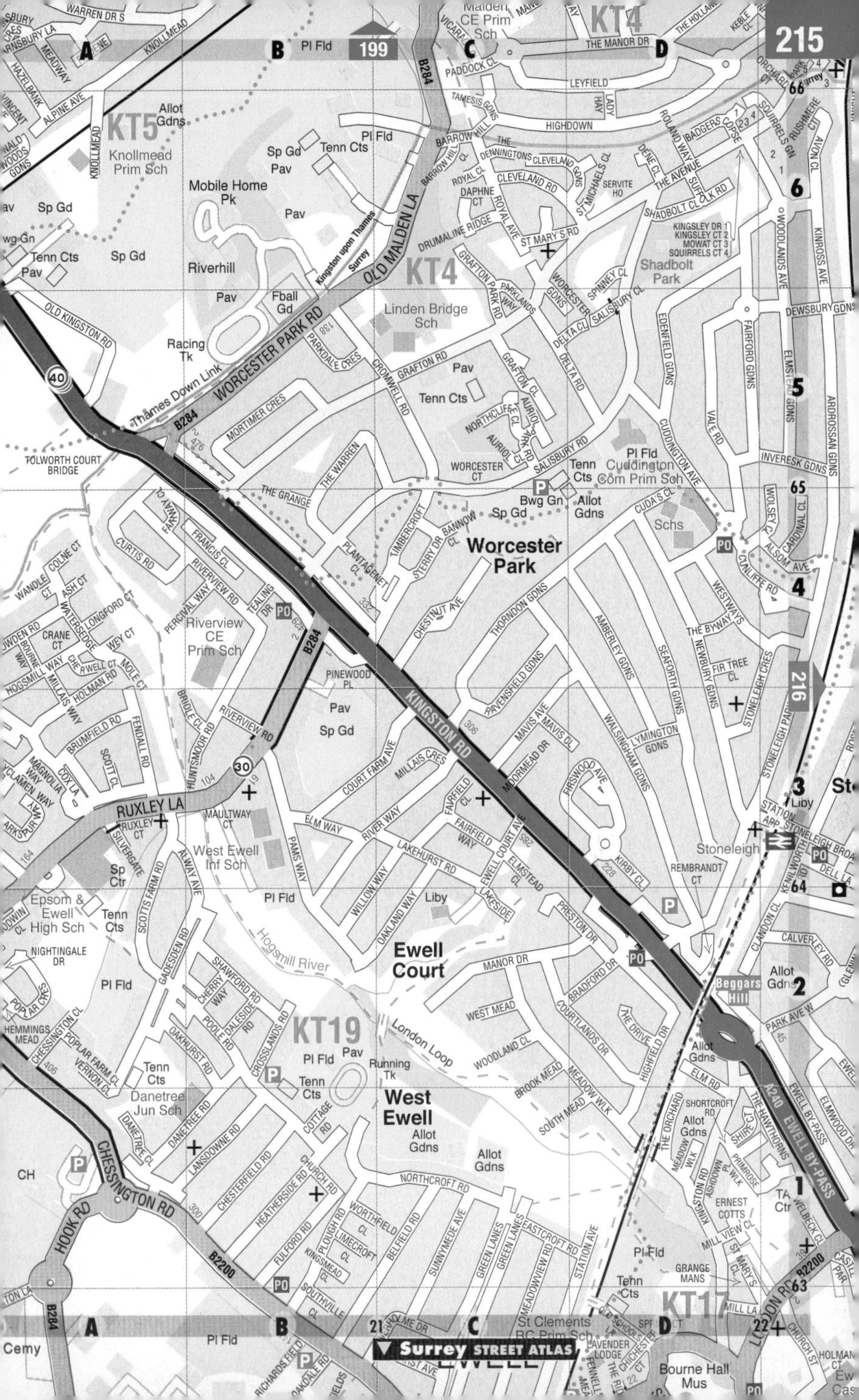

200
A
B
C
D
6
5
4
3
2
1
66
65
64
63
22
23
215
Worcester Park
North Cheam
KT4
Stoneleigh
Nonsuch Park
SM3
SM2
KT17
CENTRAL RD
CHEAM COMMON RD
LONDON RD
MALDEN RD
EWELL BY-PASS
A2043
A24
A240
A232
B2200
Organ Crossroads
Nonsuch Prim Sch
Nonsuch High Sch for Girls
Cheam Park
Harefield Bridge
Recn Gd
Superstore
Nursery
St Cecilia's RC Prim Sch
Stoneleigh Broadway
Ewell Castle
Bourne Hall Mus
A24 Epsom
Surrey STREET ATLAS
A232 Epsom (A24

SM3
SM1
SM2
Cheam
Belmont
Sutton
Cheam Village
Oldfields Trad Est
Westbourne Prim Sch
Cheam Park Farm Inf Sch
Cheam Park Farm Jun Sch
Cheam High Sch
Cheam Fields Prim Sch
Kimpton Trade & Bsns Ctr
Kimpton Link Bsns Ctr
Brookfield Prim Sch
Homefield Prep Sch
Glaisdale Sch
West Sutton
Sutton Common
Manor Park
A217 OLDFIELDS RD
ST DUNSTAN'S HILL
CHEAM RD
SUTTON COMMON RD
ANGEL HILL
HIGH ST
ST NICHOLAS WAY
THROWLEY WAY
BRIGHTON RD
BELMONT RISE
MALDEN RD
STATION WAY
BURDON LA
ROSE HILL
A217 Banstead, M25
Surrey STREET ATLAS
201
218

SM1
A
B
C
D
202
217
St Helier
Park East
Recn Gd
Pl Fld
Greenshaw High Sch
Allot Gdns
Benhilton
Royston Park
Tenn Cts
Coll
Muschamp Prim Sch
The Wrythe
Aultone Yd Ind Est
Chantry Ct
Carshalton High Sch for Girls
Recn & Sp Gd
CARSHALTON
Carshalton
Carshalton Coll
Honeywood Heritage Ctr
Jun Sch
Schs
Manor Park
Superstore
SUTTON
Sutton
War Memorial
SM5
SM2
Carshalton Beeches
Stanley Park Jun & Inf Schs
Barrow Hedges Prim Sch
ROSE HILL PARK W
ROSEHILL GDNS
ANGEL HILL
AULTONE WAY
WESTMINSTER RD
WIGMORE RD
WRYTHE LA
GREEN WRYTHE LA
NIGHTINGALE RD
ERSKINE RD
ST ANDREW'S CT
BENHILL RD
BENHILL AVE
WESTMEAD RD
SHIRLEY AVE
NORTH ST
WEST ST
POUND ST
CARSHALTON RD
THROWLEY WAY
BRIGHTON RD
CAVENDISH RD
DOWNSIDE RD
WAVERLEY WAY
PARK HILL
BEECHES AVE
WOODMANSTERNE RD
BANSTEAD RD
KINGS AVE
CROSSWAYS
THE GALLOP
HILL RD
GORDON RD
STANLEY PARK RD
B278
B2230
B277
B271
A232

203
A
B
C
D
Hackbridge
Felnex Trad Est
Beddington Park
River Wandle
Wallington Cty Gram Sch
Westcroft Sports Ctr
Wallington Green
Bandonhill
SM6
SM5
Carshalton Park
WALLINGTON
South Beddington
Carshalton on the Hill
Stanley Park High Sch
Bandon Hill Prim Sch
Foresters Prim Sch
Mellows Park
Beddington Park Prim Sch
Carew Manor Sch
Sherwood Park Sch
Holy Trinity Sch
Inf Sch
Cemy
LONDON RD
MANOR RD
WOODCOTE RD
CROYDON RD
ACRE LA
HIGH ST
STAFFORD RD
STANLEY PARK RD
RUSKIN RD
PARK LA
BOUNDARY RD
SANDY LANE S
FORESTERS DR
BEDDINGTON LA
220
A237 Coulsdon, A23
Surrey STREET ATLAS

204
219
Beddington Trad Est
Ind Est
Beddington
Peterwood Pk
Progress Bsns Pk
Commerce Pk
The Orion Ctr
Anchor Bsns Pk
ZK Park
Allot Gdns
Mill Lane Trad Est
Superstore
Beddington Park Prim Sch
Link Prim Sch
Link Sec Sch
Waddon Marsh
Croydon Tramlink
Wandle Park
Wandle Pk
Waddon
Fiveways
Playing Field
Red Gates Sch
Waddon Inf Sch
Duppas Jun Sch
St Andrew's High Sch
Recn Gd
Supermarket
Stafford Cross Bsns Pk
Spitfire Bsns Pk
Silver Wing Ind Est
Wilson's Sch
Mellows Park
Bandon Hill Prim Sch
St Elphege's RC Jun & Inf Schs
Croydon Airport Ind Est
Connaught Bsns Ctr
Swift Ctr
Hotel
The Colonnades
Purley Way Pl Fld
St Giles Sch
Haling Manor High Sch
Roundshaw
Amy Johnson Prim Sch
Roundshaw Park
Foresters Prim Sch
Haling Manor High Sch (Pampisford Wing)
CR0
CR2
SM6
PURLEY WAY
CROYDON RD
DUPPAS HILL RD
DENNING AVE
STAFFORD RD
BEDDINGTON LA
PLOUGH LA
ROMAN WAY
OLD TOWN
FORESTERS DR
1 WINDSOR GDNS
2 KINGSTON GDNS
3 PETERSHAM TERR
4 OLD FORD HO
5 WANDLE LO
6 WANDLE CT
7 BEACON PL
8 CAMDEN HO
9 MARLOW HO
10 CAVERSHAM HO
WESTFIELD RD 1
LOWER CHURCH ST 2
BOURNE ST 3
RAMSEY CT 4
LATIMER RD 1
CROMWELL HO 2
1 CENTRAL PAR
2 STAFFORD CT
DOWNES HO 1
ARNOLD HO 2
HILLSIDE HO 3
ELIS DAVID ALMSHOUSES 4
MORRIS CT 5
KEELING CT 6
MESSER CT 7
MELROSE TUDOR 1
PARK CT 2
HASLEMERE CL 3
ABINGER CT 4
1 PENNY ROYAL
2 HILLIARD CT
FAYGATE CT 1
PENSHURST CT 2
HARTFIELD CT 3

221
A
B
C
D
205
CROYDON
Wellesley Road
East Croydon
Whitgift Ctr
Centrale Ctr
Drummond Ctr
George St
Church Street
Lebanon Road
Sandilands
Fairfield Halls
Coll
Liby
TH
Park Hill
Park Hill Inf & Jun Schs
Twr
Tenn Cts
CR0
CE High Sch
Lloyd Park
Coombe Park
Vanguard Way
Croydon Tramlink
Allot Gdns
Howard Prim Sch
South Croydon
Whitgift Sch
Haling Park
Croham Hurst Sch
Prim Sch
Selsdon Road Ind Est
Two Bridges Ind Est
Capital Bsns Ctr
South Croydon
CR2
Croham Hurst
Breakneck Hill
144
CH
Sp Gd
Pav
Pl Fld
Bwg Gn
Recn Gd
Sanderstead
A235 Purley, A23
Surrey STREET ATLAS
222
WELLESLEY RD
A212
A232
A222
B243
B274
B275
B269
A235
A236
ADDISCOMBE RD
LYNDEN HYRST
CHEPSTOW RD
FAIRFIELD RD
BARCLAY RD
PARK LA
COOMBE RD
LOWER COOMBE ST
ST PETER'S RD
SOUTH PARK HILL RD
PARK HILL RD
SOUTH END
SOUTHBRIDGE RD
BRIGHTON RD
SELSDON RD
UPPER SELSDON RD
WARHAM RD
CROHAM RD
MANOR WAY
HAREWOOD RD
RAYLEIGH RISE
HURST WAY
SANDERSTEAD RD
MAYFIELD RD
ESSENDEN RD
BRAMBLEDOWN RD
BEECHWOOD RD
SANDHURST WAY
LYTCHGATE CL
HIGH BEECH
CROHAM MANOR RD
WINCHELSEA RISE
BANKSIDE
COLLEGE RD
GEORGE ST
PARK ST
HIGH ST
KATHARINE ST
MINT WLK
HAZLEDEAN RD
ALTYRE RD
ADDISCOMBE GR
CEDAR RD
CHERRY ORCHARD RD
LANSDOWNE RD
DINGWALL RD
SYDENHAM RD
BEDFORD PK
ST MICHAEL'S RD
POPLAR WLK
STATION RD
NORTH END
CROWN HILL
SURREY ST
MIDDLE ST
BEECH HOUSE RD
WOODSTOCK RD
MULGRAVE RD
EDEN RD
CHATSWORTH RD
LE CHATEAU
TEMPLE RD
HEATHFIELD GDNS
ABERDEEN RD
DEAN RD
DEANFIELD GDNS
HURST RD
THORNBURY CT
WENDERHOLME
MUGGERIDGE CL
ST PETER'S ST
SUSSEX RD
BIRCHEND CL
MORETON RD
DORNTON RD
DOVETON RD
NORMANTON RD
WARD CL
HOLLYCROFT CL
BROADEAVES CL
SPENCER RD
CRANBROOK CT
CAMPDEN RD
CROHAM PARK AVE
CASTLEMAINE AVE
BALLATER RD
MELVILLE AVE
PILGRIM'S WAY
BENCHFIELD
BINFIELD RD
BLOSSOM CL
LLOYD PARK AVE
LARCOMBE CL
COOMBE AVE
RUTLAND GDNS
WITHERBY CL
DITTONCROFT CL
BEECH COPSE
BIRDHURST RISE
BIRDHURST RD
BIRDHURST GDNS
SPRINGWOOD CT
AUTUMN LO
ROSAMUND CL
LYNNE CT
STANHOPE RD
WATER TOWER HILL
SHERIDAN CT
STEEP HILL
SPINDLEWOOD GDNS
HOLMLEA CT
GARLANDS CT
WREN CT
COPPING CL
TIPTON DR
CAROLINE CL
BROWNLOW RD
HUNTERS WAY
CHICHELE GDNS
WEAVER CL
SUDBURY GDNS
LANGTON WAY
SELBORNE RD
WALDEGROVE
RANMORE AVE
DEEPDENE AVE
COVERDALE GDNS
LYNDHURST CL
DANECOURT GDNS
HARLAND AVE
WOODCROFT
MARESFIELD
ST ARVANS CL
TIDENHAM GDNS
CHICHESTER RD
CHILTERN CL
THANESCROFT GDNS
WILLOW MOUNT
PARK HILL RISE
DEANS CL
GARDEN CT
ROWAN GDNS
RADCLIFFE RD
DIGBY PL
HARDING CL
MULBERRY LA
HAVELOCK RD
CREED CT
OUTRAM RD
ELGIN RD
CLYDE RD
WAVELL CT
CANNING RD
ADDISCOMBE COURT RD
ROWLAND CT
TUNSTALL RD
HERON RD
LEBANON RD
CHISHOLM RD
BISENDEN RD
BRICKWOOD RD
BLAKE RD
COLSON RD
BILLINTON HILL
PARK HILL CT
MAYBOURNE GRANGE
TURNPIKE LINK
LEAPY WAY
ASHBURTON GDNS
NORTHAMPTON RD
JUNCTION RD
UPLAND RD
DROVERS RD
RUSKIN PAR
YE MARKET
WILSON CL
BAINES CL
WHITGIFT AVE
WHITGIFT HO
HALING RD
HELDER ST
JARVIS RD
NEWARK RD
MANSFIELD RD
CRUNDEN RD
ORIANA CT
NAPIER RD
ROLLESTON RD
CHAMBERS PL
KENSINGTON TERR
PURLEY RD
WYCHE GR
CHURCHILL RD
DARMAINE CL
BLENHEIM PARK RD
BLENHEIM CRES
HALING GR
MARLBOROUGH RD
AVONDALE RD
AVON PATH
TIRLEMONT RD
OAKFIELD CT
MALATIA
NICOLA CL
ROSS CT
LIME TREE CT
PELTON CT
KESTREL CT
SYLVAN CT
GREENDALE CT
GIBSON HO
CANTERBURY CT
HARLEQUIN CT
FELBRIDGE CT
OUTWOOD CT
SUNNIHOLME CT
NOTTINGHAM RD
QUEEN'S CT
BARTLETT ST
ARUNDEL RD
LEDBURY RD
ELMHURST CT
PARKER RD
SPICES YD
TANFIELD RD
BRAFFERTON RD
KEEN'S RD
DERING PL
DERING RD
BARHAM RD
WEST ST
QUEEN ST
MASON'S AVE
THANET PL
MEADOW STILE
FRIENDS' RD
ARTHUR CT
FAIRFIELD PATH
ALDEN CT
ELIZABETH CT
THE AVENUE
PAGEANT WLK
COTELANDS
CRUSOE RD
ST BERNARDS
ALPINE CL
MERLIN CL
MINSTER DR
SELSDON AVE
SUSSEX RD
WHITMEAD CL
ROCKHAMPTON CL
LISMORE RD
ELM CL
CROHAM CL
HURST VIEW RD
REGENTS CL
CARLTON AVE
CARLTON RD
CROHAM MOUNT
WEST HILL
SANDHURST CL
TRINITY CL
ELMFIELD WAY
FEWHURST AVE
WISBOROUGH RD
BARNFIELD RD
MANOR GDNS
NORMANTON CT
CLEVEDEN CT
NORTHUMBERLAND CT
ATHERTON HO
WIMBOURNE CT
HURSTBOURNE PRIORS
BRETHERTON CT
SYCAMORE CL
WELLS CL
HARESTONE CT
SONNING
COLLEGE
FURZE CT
WALCOT
33
34
63
64
65
66

Coombe Park
Lloyd Park
Coombe Farm
Oaks Farm
Shirley Park
Addington Hills
CR0
Trinity Sch
Windmill (dis)
Coloma Convent Girls' Sch
Shirley High Sch
Upper Shirley
Royal Russell Sch
Coombe Lane
Heathfield
Bramley Bank
Nat Res
London Loop
Vanguard Way
Croydon Tramlink
Croham Hurst
Littleheath Woods
Selsdon High Sch
Selsdon
CR2
ADDISCOMBE RD
SHIRLEY RD
WICKHAM RD
COOMBE RD
COOMBE LA
OAKS RD
SHIRLEY HILLS RD
BALLARDS WAY
BALLARDS FARM RD
CROHAM VALLEY RD
FARLEY RD
SUNKEN RD
Sandilands
Pl Fld
Tenn Cts
Pav
Sp Gd
Hotel
Abbots Green
Surrey STREET ATLAS

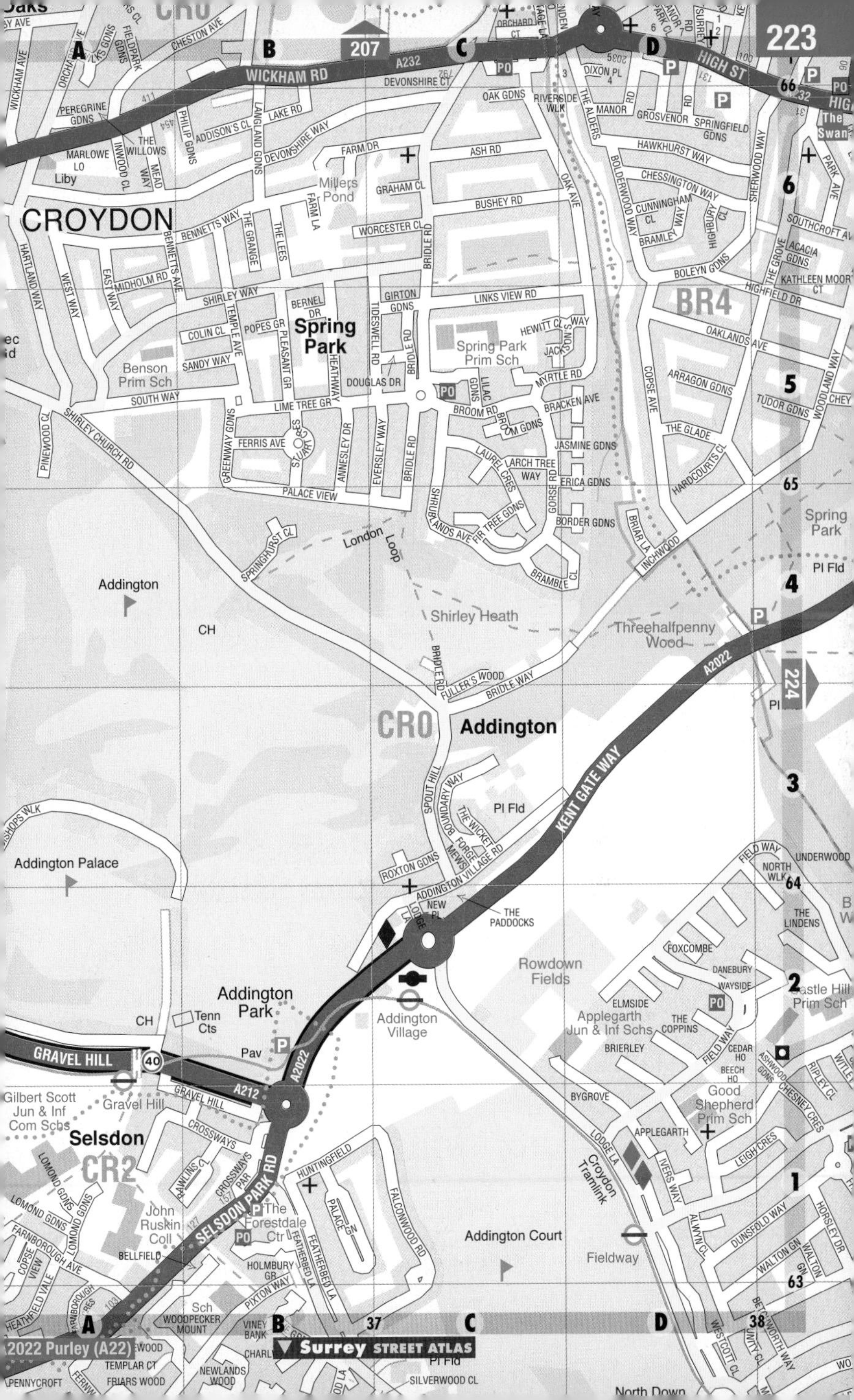

207
WICKHAM RD
A232
DEVONSHIRE CT
HIGH ST
CROYDON
Spring Park
Spring Park Prim Sch
Benson Prim Sch
Millers Pond
BR4
London Loop
Shirley Heath
Threehalfpenny Wood
Addington
CR0
KENT GATE WAY
A2022
224
Addington Palace
Addington Park
Addington Village
Rowdown Fields
Applegarth Jun & Inf Schs
Good Shepherd Prim Sch
Castle Hill Prim Sch
Croydon Tramlink
Addington Court
Fieldway
GRAVEL HILL
A212
Gilbert Scott Jun & Inf Com Schs
Gravel Hill
Selsdon
CR2
SELSDON PARK RD
John Ruskin Coll
The Forestdale Ctr
A2022 Purley (A22)
Surrey STREET ATLAS

208
A
B
C
D
HIGH ST
A232
A214
PO
The Swan
Liby
LINKS RD
THE MEAD
HAYES HILL
HEPBURN GDNS
SAVILLE ROW
Fld
Hawes Down Schs
CROFT AVE
OAK GR
ASH GR
BRAEMAR
RAVENSWOOD
SPRINGFIELD GDNS
GROSVENOR
SHERWOOD WAY
CHATSWORTH LO
WICKHAM COURT RD
GLEBE WAY
WICKHAM CRES
ROSE WLK
LINDEN LEAS
MARTINS CL
Glebe Sch
Allot Gdns
PHOENIX CL
HAWES LA
HIGH MEAD
MOUNT CT
KESWICK RD
WINDERMERE RD
Pl Fld
RYDAL DR
HEYDON CT
West Wickham
SILVER LA
30
PARK AVE
SOUTHCROFT AVE
ACACIA GDNS
THE GROVE
HIGHBURY CL
BOLEYN GDNS
KATHLEEN MOORE CT
HIGHFIELD DR
ABERDARE CL
Pl Fld
Tenn Cts
Bwg Gn
Sp Gd
Pav
ATKINS DR
PALMER CL
BENCURTIS PK
SEABROOK DR
LITTLE CT
ADDINGTON RD
LENNARD CL
LENNARD AVE
CONEY HILL RD
ABBOTSBURY RD
WESTLAND DR
SANDILAND CRES
HOLLAND WAY
HOLLAND CL
BOURNE WAY
PRICKLEY WOOD
MARWELL CL
Tenn Cts
Pav
BR4
OAKLANDS AVE
STAMBOURNE WAY
CORKSCREW HILL
COURTFIELD RISE
Coney Hall Rdbt
GLEBE WAY
PRIORY LO
DUKES WAY
CROYDON RD
A232
ROSSLYN CL
FARM CL
West Wickham Common
Coney Hall
ARRAGON GDNS
TUDOR GDNS
WOODLAND WAY
CHEYNE PARK DR
WOOD LODGE LA
A2022
CROYDON RD
SOUTH WLK
CONEY HALL PAR
CHURCH DR
KINGSWAY
COLIN CL
THE GLADE
HARDCOURTS CL
PP
Pav
Sparrows Den Sp Gd
Tenn Cts
Bwg Gn
Pav
PRINCES WAY
QUEENSWAY
Spring Park
ADDINGTON RD
BR4
Wickham Court
Wickham Court Sch
All Saints RC Sch
Coney Hall Recn Gd
SYLVAN WAY
CHESTNUT AVE
HAWTHORN DR
BIRCH TREE AVE
CHERRY TREE WLK
LIME TREE WLK
Pl Fld
Halfpenny Wood
223
Pl Fld
Fox Hill
Wickham Court Farm
LAYHAMS RD
Well Wood
3
FIELD WAY
UNDERWOOD
NORTH WLK
64
THE LINDENS
Birch Wood
OAK BANK
Bromley
Croydon
FOXCOMBE
DANEBURY
WAYSIDE
2
CR0
Castle Hill Prim Sch
THE COPPINS
DUNLEY DR
MERROW WAY
PIRBRIGHT CRES
CLAYGATE CRES
ALFORD GN
Castlehill Ruffs
CEDAR HO
BEECH HO
ASHWOOD GDNS
RIPLEY CL
ABINGER CL
WITLEY CRES
BURFORD WAY
Good Shepherd Prim Sch
CHESNEY CRES
HEADLEY DR
BROCKHAM CRES
MICKLEHAM WAY
NETLEY CL
LEIGH CRES
LOMAS CL
FRIMLEY CL
FRIMLEY CRES
THURSLEY CRES
FRENSHAM DR
129
Bradmanshill Wood
BR2
1
Mast
Allot Gdns
DUNSFOLD WAY
HORSLEY DR
GOLDCREST WAY
Mast
ALWYN CL
WALTON GN
CASTLE HILL AVE
Wolsey Jun & Inf Schs
New Addington
63
TILFORD AVE
PP
38
39
KING HENRY'S DR
WESTCOTT CL
BETCHWORTH WAY
WOLSEY CRES

209
Keston Mark
Keston
Nash
Hayes Common
Baston Manor
Hayes Court
Hast Hill House
Rouse Farm
Fuller's Wood
James's Wood
Milchden
Keston Court
Keston Common
Colyers Wood
Barnet Wood
Simpson's Cott
Ravens Wood Sch
Keston CE Prim Sch
Wickham Common Prim Sch
Baston Sch
Hayes Sch
The Priory
Ravensbourne Bsns Ctr
ROMAN MAUSOLEUM
Windmill
London Loop
Ravens Bourne
BR4
BR2
CROYDON RD
BASTON RD
HEATHFIELD RD
WESTERHAM RD
OAKLEY RD
FIVE ELMS RD
WEST COMMON RD
BASTON MANOR RD
GATES GREEN RD
JACKASS LA
NASH LA
NORTH POLE LA
FOX LA
HERITAGE HILL
LEAFY GR
FISHPONDS RD
BARNET WOOD RD
CHURCH RD
RECTORY RD
BLACKNESS LA
ORCHARD PL
DOWNE RD
LONGDON WOOD
BEECHWOOD DR
BROCKDENE DR
HASSOCK WOOD
COMMONSIDE
OAKFIELD LA
LAKES RD
KESTON AVE
GREYS PARK CL
REGENTS DR
WINDMILL DR
STOUR CL
KESTON GDNS
HEATHFIELD CL
THE DRIFT
THE AVENUE
QUIET NOOK
PHOENIX DR
THANET DR
THE DALE
RUSHLEY CL
MARK CL
SWIRES SHAW
COLLIERS SHAW
POULTERS WOOD
ROLINSDEN WAY
CEDAR CL
CHEYNE CL
OAKLEY DR
ROSS RD
DOVES CL
GRAVEL RD
WEALD CL
THE LIMES
THE COURTYARD
ROBINS GR
HARTFIELD CRES
HARTFIELD RD
HARVEST BANK RD
RODNEY GDNS
LAWRENCE RD
WARREN RD
RIDGEWAY
STATION HILL
STATION APP
HAYES GDN
THE KNOLL
FORGE CL
HOPTON CT
GLEBE HOUSE DR
BURWOOD AVE
GROVE CL
HAYES CL
REDGATE DR
PRESTONS RD
1 LARKFIELD CL
2 WENTWORTH CL
3 HAWTHORNDENE CL
4 HAWTHORNDENE RD
5 WARREN WOOD CL
B251
B265
A232
A233
A233 Biggin Hill
226
Kent STREET ATLAS

210
Keston Mark
Sp Gd
Pav
Pl Fld
Ravens Wood Sch
Allot Gdns
OAKLEY RD
A233
A21
HASTINGS RD
PO
40
WEALD CL
CHERRY ORCHARD RD
JACKSON RD
COPTHORNE AVE
KNOWLE RD
DAERWOOD CL
JACKSON RD
BRADFORD CL
RIBSTON CL
LOWER GRAVEL RD
RANDOLPH RD
Knowlehill Wood
Knowl Wood
BR2
CROSS RD
DOVES CL
GRAVEL RD
BARNET DR
BEVERLEY RD
THE LIMES Recn Gd
Allot Gdns
Hollydale Recn Gd
KEMBLE DR
OAKLEY DR
CEDAR CL
CEDAR CRES
CHEYNE CL
LAKESIDE DR
ROWAN WLK
HOLLYDALE DR
FARNBOROUGH COMM
A232
CROYDON RD
Keston Mark
EBURY CL
KESTON PARK CL
RUSHLEY CL
MARK CL
LONGDON WOOD
FOREST DR
FOREST RIDGE
PINE GLADE
BEECH DELL
HOLWOOD PARK AVE
The Fantail
THE DRIFT
THE AVENUE
PHOENIX DR
THANET DR
THE DALE
BEECHWOOD DR
BROCKDENE DR
HASSOCK WOOD
ROLAND DEN WAY
POULTERS WOOD
225
WESTERHAM RD
London Loop
Tenn Cts
Lake Wood
Ninhams Wood
Caesar's Camp
THE COURTYARD
Holwood
Tenn Cts
Broom Bank
The Larches
SHIRE LA
Lower Hook Farm
North End Farm
London Loop
BOGEY LA
NORTH END LA
FARTHING ST
Holwood Farm
Farthing Street
DOWNE RD
NEW ROAD HILL
THE PADDOCK
RECTORY RD
A233 Biggin Hill
Kent STREET ATLAS
BIRCH MEAD
ST ANTHONY'S CT
JASMINE CL
FAIRBANK AVE
ROSE DALE
LIME GR
WISTARIA CL
POPLAR AVE
DRAYTON AVE
LANSDOWNE AVE
WOOD WAY
HAZEL GR
SUNNYDALE
LARCH DENE
NUFFIELD WAY
BURLINGTON CL
HENSON CL
PERCIVAL RD
GLYNDEBOURNE PK
RED OAK CL
MADA RD
PARK AVE
MERESIDE
MERE CL
MUNNERY WAY
CROFTON RD
LANGDALE CL
WINDERMERE CL
GRASMERE AVE
GRASMERE RD
GRASMERE GDNS
THE GLEN
MEADOW WAY
ELM WLK
PO
STARTS CL
Locksbottom
Tenn Cts
Recn Gd
Pav
Allot Gdns
Darrick Wood Sch
Darrick Wood Inf Sch
Darrick Wood Jun Sch
PRINCESS PAR
PALLANT WAY
FIR DENE
Princess Royal University
WILLOW WLK
BARKWAY DR
WELLBROOK RD
DENNARD WAY
SCOTNEY CL
HILDA VALE RD
LANTERN CL
WINTON RD
CLAREMONT CL
VALE CL
HILDA VALE CL
STARTS HILL RD
BASSETTS WAY
BASSETTS CL
ROYAL CL
ASHTREE CL
ACORN WAY
ARDEN GR
ROMSEY CL
LYNDHURST CL
PADDOCK
PINECREST GDNS
STARTS HILL
NINHAMS WOOD
WOLDS DR
THE BIRCHES
FARNBOROUGH COMMON
PRUDENCE LA 1
SANDRINGHAM LO 2
BALMORAL LO 3
SUMMERLANDS LO 4
FLEETWOOD CT 5
TUGMUTTON CL 1
HARLANDS GR 2
B2158
ELGAL CL 1
LIMES ROW 2
ORCHARD RD
STRAWBERRY FIELDS
BR6
A21
A B C D
42 43
66 65 64 63
6 5 4 3 2 1

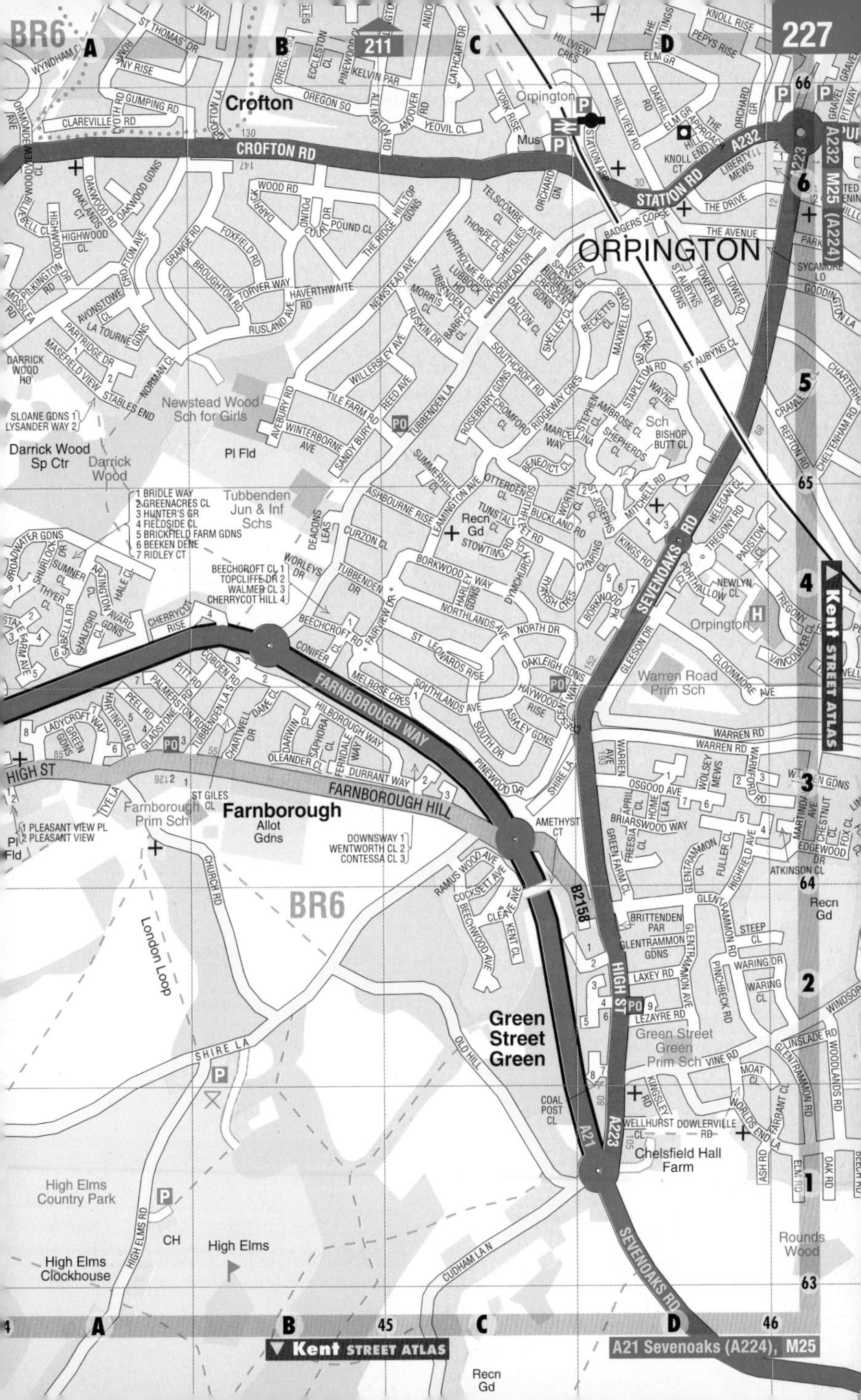

Kent STREET ATLAS

Key to enlarged map pages

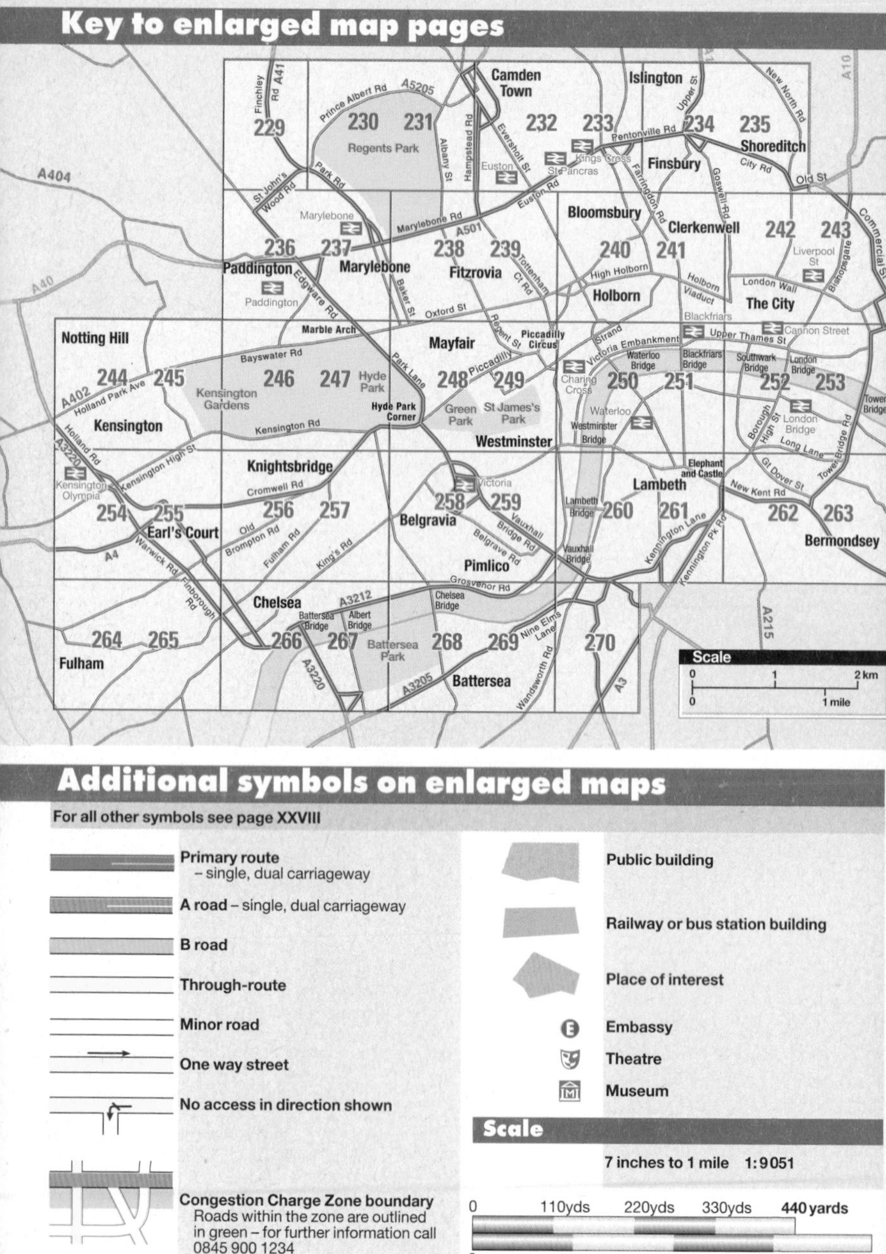

Additional symbols on enlarged maps

For all other symbols see page XXVIII

Primary route
– single, dual carriageway

A road – single, dual carriageway

B road

Through-route

Minor road

One way street

No access in direction shown

Congestion Charge Zone boundary
Roads within the zone are outlined in green – for further information call 0845 900 1234

Public building

Railway or bus station building

Place of interest

Embassy

Theatre

Museum

Scale

7 inches to 1 mile 1:9051

0 110yds 220yds 330yds 440 yards

0 125m 250m 325m 500 met

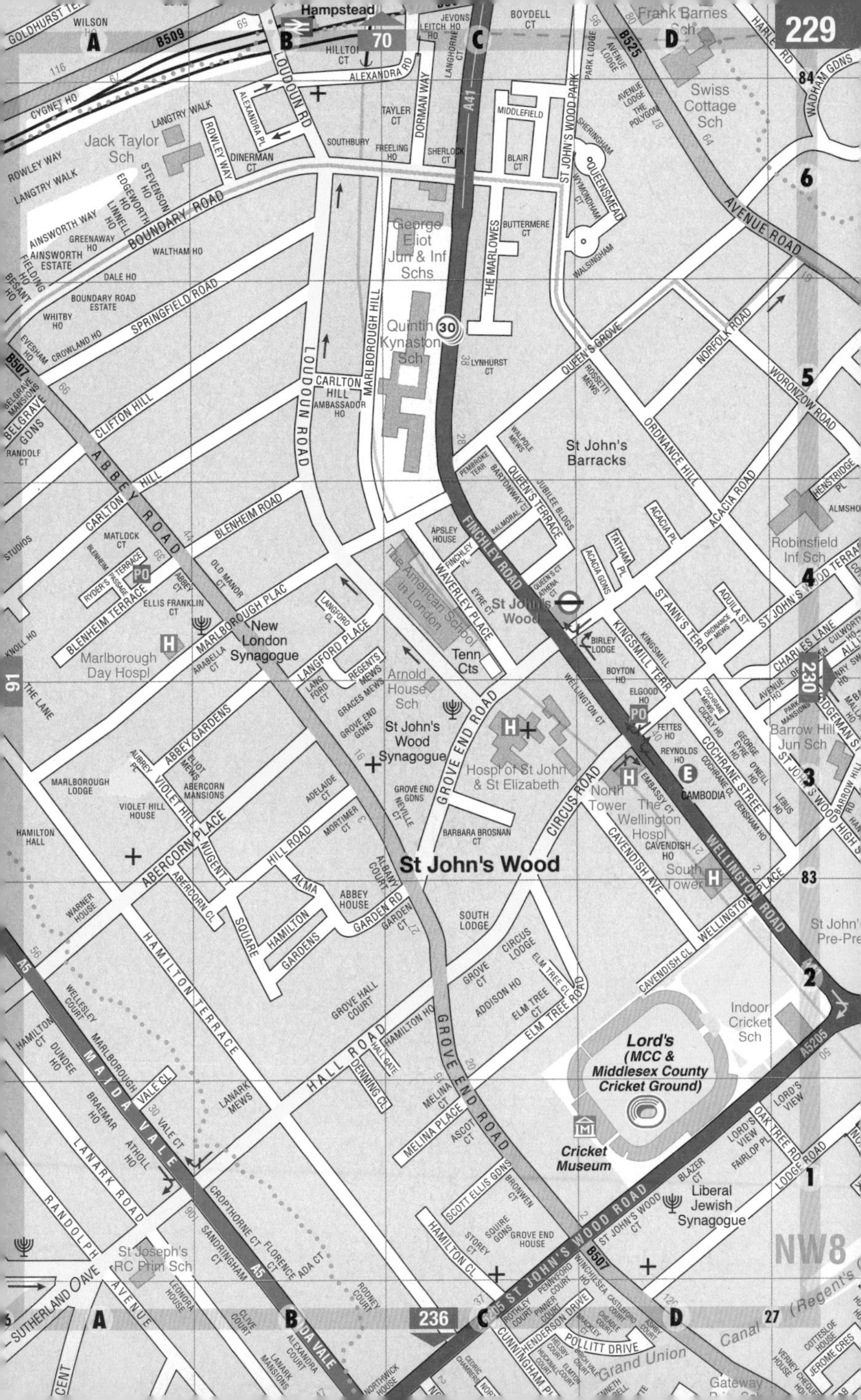
229
Hampstead
70
A
B
C
D
B509
B525
A41
B507
A5
A5205
Jack Taylor Sch
Swiss Cottage Sch
Frank Barnes Sch
George Eliot Jun & Inf Schs
Quintin Kynaston Sch
St John's Barracks
Robinsfield Inf Sch
New London Synagogue
Marlborough Day Hospl
Arnold House Sch
St John's Wood Synagogue
The American School in London
Tenn Cts
St John's Wood
Hospl of St John & St Elizabeth
North Tower
The Wellington Hospl
South Tower
CAMBODIA
Barrow Hill Jun Sch
St John's Pre-Prep
Indoor Cricket Sch
Lord's (MCC & Middlesex County Cricket Ground)
Cricket Museum
Liberal Jewish Synagogue
St Joseph's RC Prim Sch
NW8
Grand Union Canal (Regent's
BOUNDARY ROAD
SPRINGFIELD ROAD
LOUDOUN ROAD
MARLBOROUGH HILL
ALEXANDRA RD
DORMAN WAY
ROWLEY WAY
LANGTRY WALK
AINSWORTH WAY
CLIFTON HILL
CARLTON HILL
ABBEY ROAD
BLENHEIM ROAD
BLENHEIM TERRACE
MARLBOROUGH PLACE
LANGFORD PLACE
WAVERLEY PLACE
FINCHLEY ROAD
QUEEN'S GROVE
QUEEN'S TERRACE
NORFOLK ROAD
AVENUE ROAD
WORONZOW ROAD
ORDNANCE HILL
ACACIA ROAD
ST JOHN'S WOOD PARK
QUEENSMEAD
THE MARLOWES
ST ANN'S TERR
KINGSMILL TERR
WELLINGTON ROAD
WELLINGTON PLACE
COCHRANE STREET
CIRCUS ROAD
CAVENDISH AVE
GROVE END ROAD
ABBEY GARDENS
ABERCORN PLACE
HILL ROAD
ALMA SQUARE
HAMILTON GARDENS
GARDEN RD
HAMILTON TERRACE
HALL ROAD
ELM TREE ROAD
MELINA PLACE
SCOTT ELLIS GDNS
ST JOHN'S WOOD ROAD
LODGE ROAD
OAK TREE RD
MAIDA VALE
LANARK ROAD
RANDOLPH AVENUE
SUTHERLAND AVE
CROPTHORNE CT
POLLITT DRIVE
HENDERSON DRIVE
CUNNINGHAM PL
ST JOHN'S WOOD TERRACE
CHARLES LANE
91
230
236
6
5
4
3
2
1
84
83
27

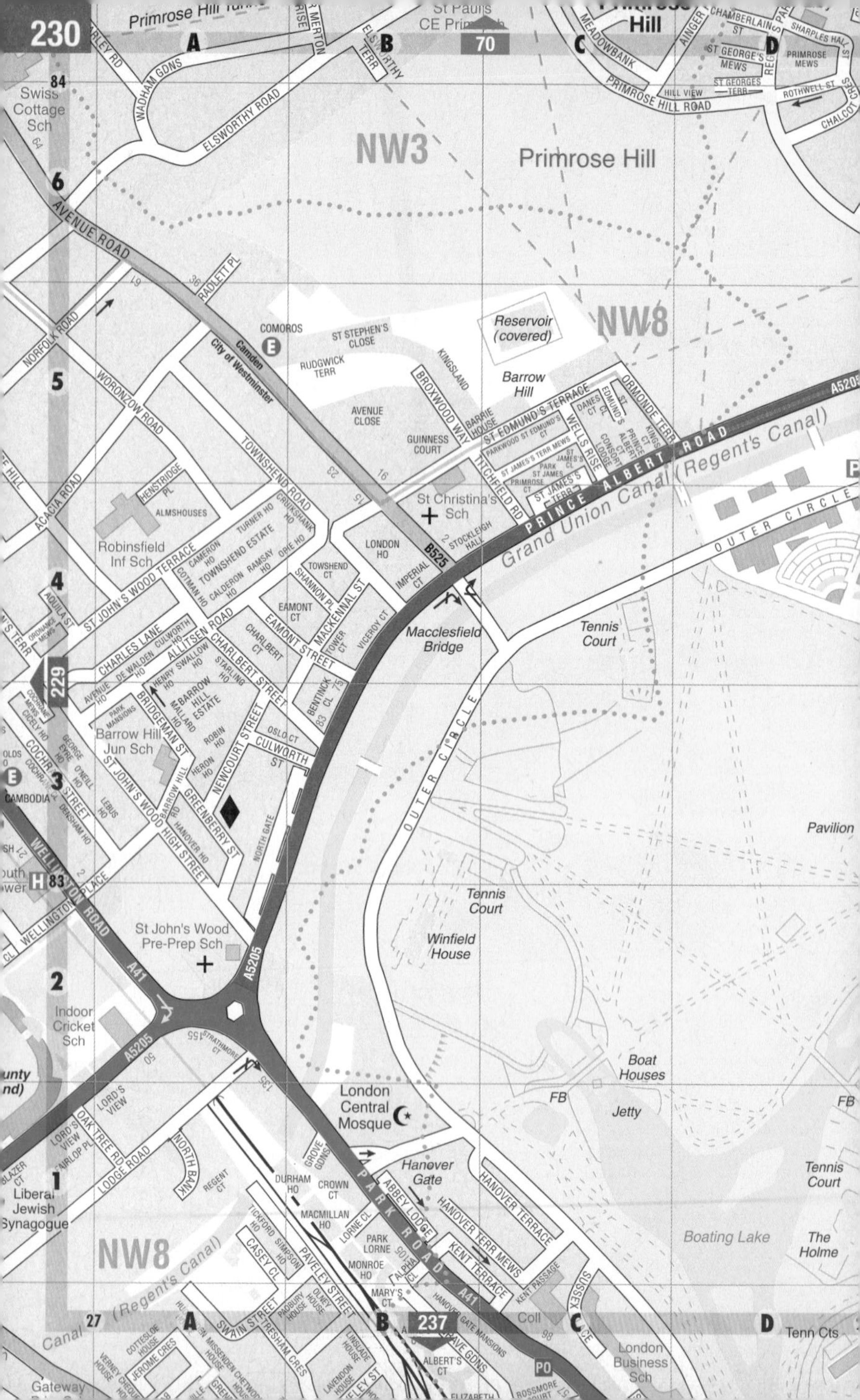
NW3
Primrose Hill
NW8
Reservoir (covered)
Barrow Hill
AVENUE ROAD
ELSWORTHY ROAD
WADHAM GDNS
NORFOLK ROAD
WORONZOW ROAD
TOWNSHEND ROAD
ACACIA ROAD
ST JOHN'S WOOD TERRACE
CHARLES LANE
ALLITSEN ROAD
CHARLBERT STREET
EAMONT STREET
MACKENNAL ST
NEWCOURT STREET
CULWORTH ST
ST JOHN'S WOOD HIGH STREET
WELLINGTON ROAD
WELLINGTON PLACE
PRINCE ALBERT ROAD
Grand Union Canal (Regent's Canal)
OUTER CIRCLE
PARK ROAD
ST EDMUND'S TERRACE
BROXWOOD WAY
KINGSLAND
ST STEPHEN'S CLOSE
RUDGWICK TERR
AVENUE CLOSE
GUINNESS COURT
TOWNSHEND ESTATE
BARROW HILL ESTATE
Robinsfield Inf Sch
Barrow Hill Jun Sch
St Christina's Sch
St John's Wood Pre-Prep Sch
Macclesfield Bridge
Tennis Court
Winfield House
Pavilion
Boat Houses
Jetty
Boating Lake
The Holme
London Central Mosque
Hanover Gate
HANOVER TERRACE
KENT TERRACE
SUSSEX PLACE
Liberal Jewish Synagogue
Indoor Cricket Sch
LODGE ROAD
NORTH BANK
London Business Sch
Swiss Cottage Sch
Primrose Hill
PRIMROSE HILL ROAD
Camden
City of Westminster
COMOROS
CAMBODIA
A5205
A41
B525
229
237
70
NW8
Canal (Regent's Canal)

A
B
C
D
71
238
232
Primrose Hill
Utopia Village
Primrose Hill Sch
London Zoo
Regent's Park
Queen Mary's Gardens
Open Air Theatre
Refreshment Room
Stones
Broad Walk
Cumberland Gate
Camden
City of Westminster
Camden Mkt
Camden Town
Hawley Inf Sch
The Cavendish Sch
Britannia Junc
The Jewish Mus
North Bridge House Senior Sch
Gloucester Gate Bridge
St Katharine's Precinct
Regent's Park Barracks
NW1
Christ Church Sch
Allot Gdns
St George's Cathedral
Liby
Netley Prim Sch
Westminster Kingsway Coll
Royal College of Physicians
New Lodge
Tenn Cts
Pav
Regent's Park Road
Regal Lane
Gloucester Avenue
Gloucester Crescent
Oval Road
Regent's Park Terr
Jamestown Rd
Inverness Street
Parkway
Delancey Street
Arlington Road
Albert Street
Camden High St
Kentish Town Rd
Camden Rd
Mornington Street
Mornington Terrace
Mornington Crescent
Park Village East
Park Village West
Albany Street
Outer Circle
Inner Circle
Cumberland Terrace
Cumberland Terrace Mews
Chester Terrace
Chester Road
Chester Gt
Chester Cl N
Chester Cl S
Cambridge Terr
Cambridge Gate
Robert Street
Stanhope Street
Augustus Street
Granby Terr
Cumberland Market
Clarence Gardens
Longford St
Munster Sq
Princess Road
Chalcot Road
Fitzroy Road
Edis Street
Egbert St
Manley St
Calvert St
Kingstown St
Albert Terr
Albert Terr Mews
St Mark's Cres
Gloucester Gate Mews
Gloucester Gt
Greenland Rd
Greenland Pl
Pratt Mews
Miller St
Carlow St
A5205
A503
A4201
A400
A502

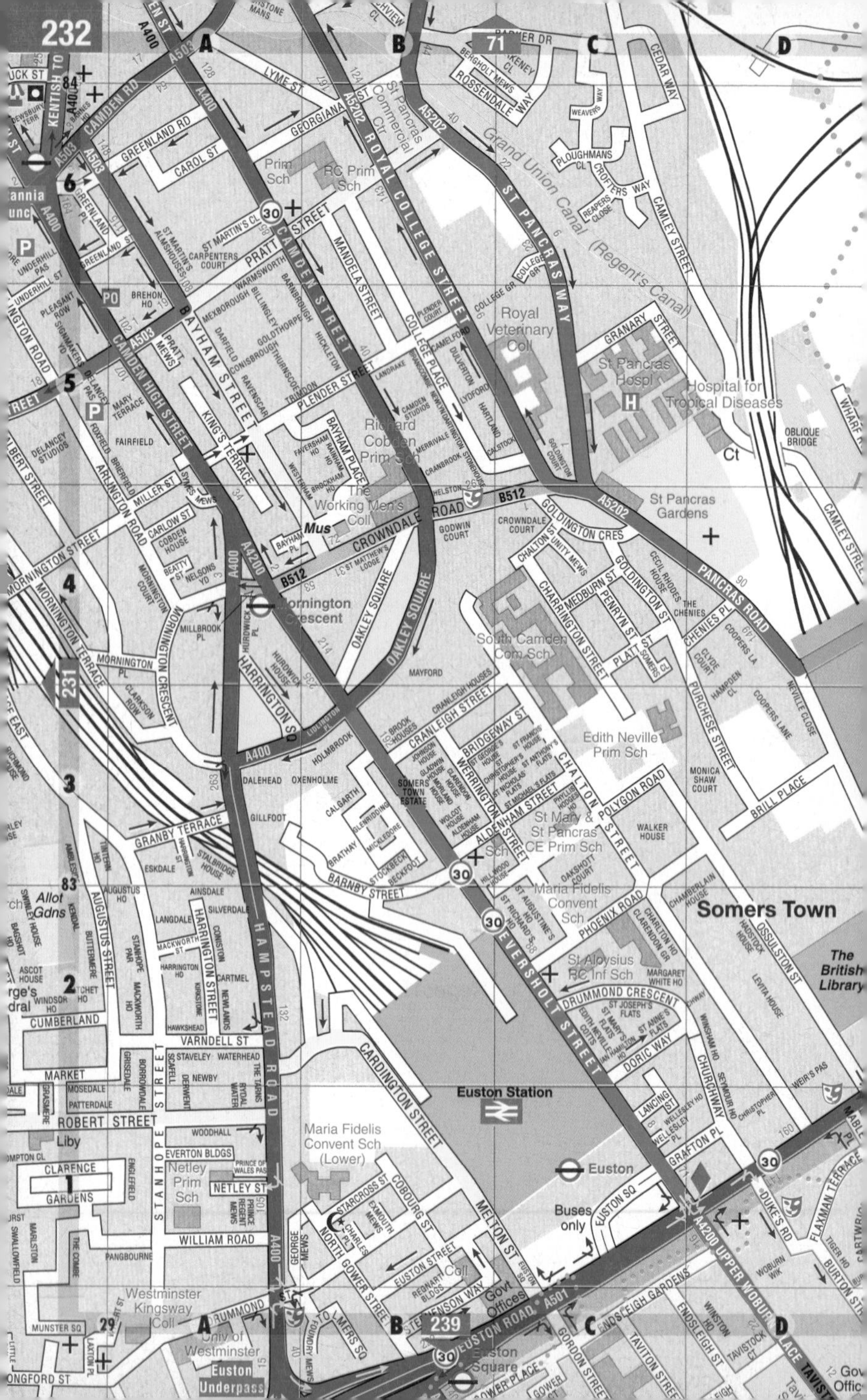
71
A
B
C
D
Camden Rd
Camden Street
Royal College Street
St Pancras Way
Grand Union Canal (Regent's Canal)
Pratt Street
Georgiana St
Greenland Rd
Carol St
Lyme St
Bayham Street
Camden High Street
Plender Street
Royal Veterinary Coll
St Pancras Hospl
Hospital for Tropical Diseases
Granary Street
Camley Street
Crowndale Road
Richard Cobden Prim Sch
The Working Men's Coll
Mornington Crescent
Oakley Square
Goldington Cres
St Pancras Gardens
Pancras Road
South Camden Com Sch
Edith Neville Prim Sch
Mornington Street
Mornington Terrace
Arlington Road
Harrington Sq
Somers Town Estate
Cranleigh Street
Chalton Street
Polygon Road
Brill Place
Eversholt Street
Somers Town
The British Library
Granby Terrace
Hampstead Road
Augustus Street
Harrington Street
Varndell St
Robert Street
Stanhope Street
William Road
Cardington Street
Euston Station
Euston
Euston Sq
Buses only
Maria Fidelis Convent Sch (Lower)
Drummond Crescent
Doric Way
Churchway
Ossulston St
Phoenix Road
St Aloysius RC Inf Sch
Euston Road
Upper Woburn Place
Duke's Rd
Flaxman Terrace
Endsleigh Gardens
Gordon Street
Melton St
Cobourg St
North Gower Street
Euston Street
Westminster Kingsway Coll
Univ of Westminster
Euston Underpass
Euston Square
Netley Prim Sch
Clarence Gardens
Cumberland Market
Munster Sq
Longford St
231
239
Oblique Bridge
Camley Street

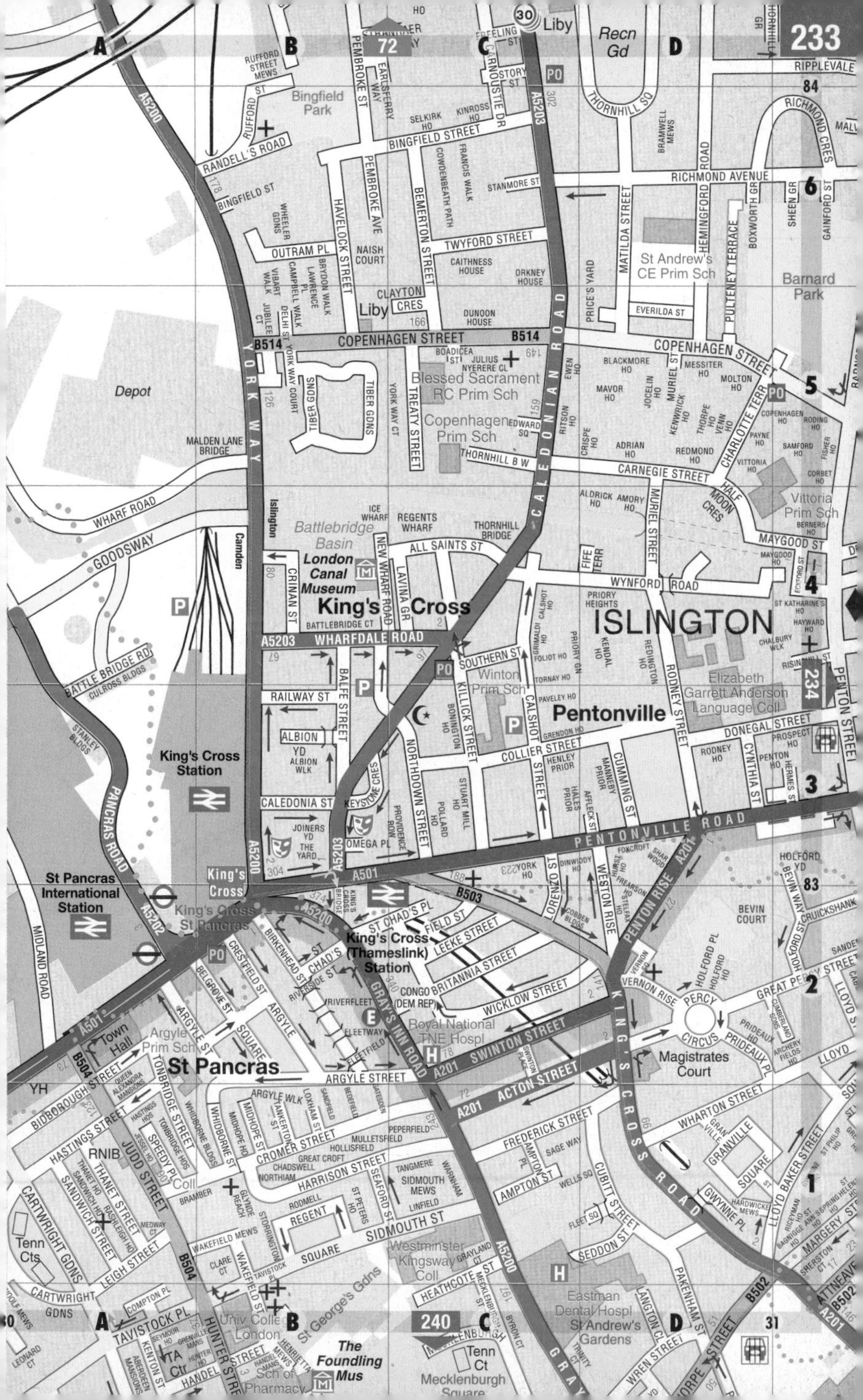

ISLINGTON
King's Cross
Pentonville
St Pancras
King's Cross Station
St Pancras International Station
King's Cross (Thameslink) Station
London Canal Museum
Battlebridge Basin
Depot
Bingfield Park
Barnard Park
Recn Gd
St Andrew's CE Prim Sch
Blessed Sacrament RC Prim Sch
Copenhagen Prim Sch
Vittoria Prim Sch
Winton Prim Sch
Elizabeth Garrett Anderson Language Coll
Royal National TNE Hospl
Magistrates Court
Westminster Kingsway Coll
Eastman Dental Hospl
St Andrew's Gardens
The Foundling Mus
Univ College London
Sch of Pharmacy
Argyle Prim Sch
Town Hall
YORK WAY
CALEDONIAN ROAD
COPENHAGEN STREET
PENTONVILLE ROAD
GRAY'S INN ROAD
KING'S CROSS ROAD
PANCRAS ROAD
WHARFDALE ROAD
SWINTON STREET
ACTON STREET
ARGYLE STREET
JUDD STREET
WHARF ROAD
GOODSWAY
RICHMOND AVENUE
CARNEGIE STREET
WYNFORD ROAD
MIDLAND ROAD

72
234
240

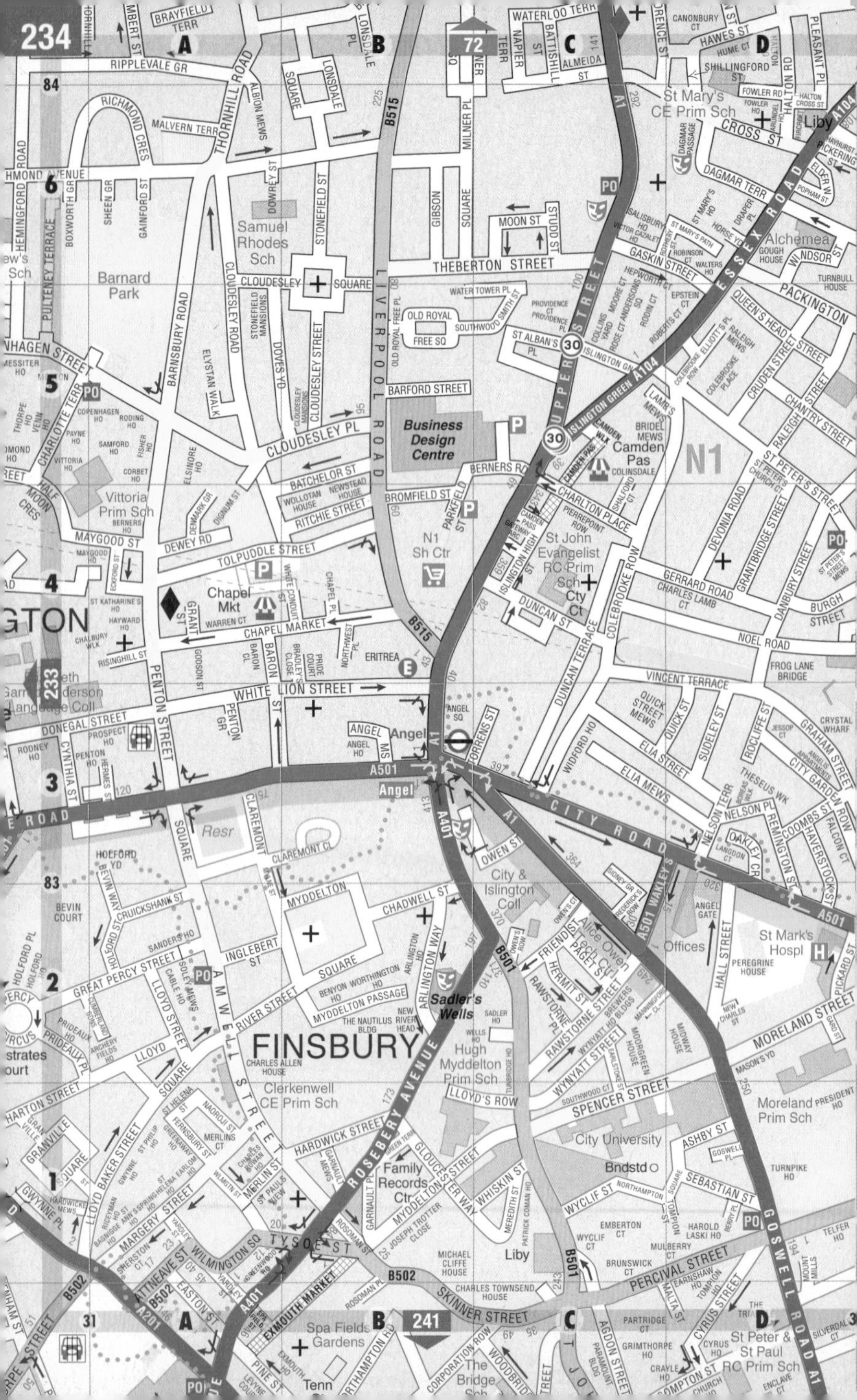

234
72
241
233
A
B
C
D
1
2
3
4
5
6
84
83
31
N1
FINSBURY
Barnard Park
Samuel Rhodes Sch
Vittoria Prim Sch
Chapel Mkt
Business Design Centre
N1 Sh Ctr
Camden Pas
St John Evangelist RC Prim Sch
St Mary's CE Prim Sch
Alchemea
Liby
Angel
Resr
City & Islington Coll
Alice Owen Tech Ctr
Sadler's Wells
Hugh Myddelton Prim Sch
Clerkenwell CE Prim Sch
Family Records Ctr
City University
Bndstd
Offices
St Mark's Hospl
Moreland Prim Sch
Spa Fields Gardens
St Peter & St Paul RC Prim Sch
Elizabeth Garrett Anderson Language Coll
RIPPLEVALE GR
RICHMOND CRES
RICHMOND AVENUE
MALVERN TERR
THORNHILL ROAD
BARNSBURY ROAD
CLOUDESLEY ROAD
CLOUDESLEY SQUARE
CLOUDESLEY PL
CLOUDESLEY STREET
STONEFIELD ST
LONSDALE SQUARE
LIVERPOOL ROAD
B515
THEBERTON STREET
MOON ST
STUDD ST
GIBSON SQUARE
MILNER SQUARE
OLD ROYAL FREE SQ
BARFORD STREET
BERNERS RD
BROMFIELD ST
PARKFIELD ST
UPPER STREET
A1
ISLINGTON GREEN
A104
ESSEX ROAD
ISLINGTON HIGH ST
CAMDEN PAS
CHARLTON PLACE
COLEBROOKE ROW
DUNCAN TERRACE
DUNCAN ST
GERRARD ROAD
NOEL ROAD
VINCENT TERRACE
DEVONIA ROAD
GRANTBRIDGE STREET
DANBURY STREET
BURGH STREET
PACKINGTON
QUEEN'S HEAD STREET
CRUDEN STREET
CHANTRY STREET
RALEIGH STREET
ST PETER'S STREET
DAGMAR TERR
CROSS ST
GASKIN STREET
COPENHAGEN STREET
CHARLOTTE TERR
PULTENEY TERRACE
MAYGOOD ST
TOLPUDDLE STREET
CHAPEL MARKET
WHITE LION STREET
PENTON STREET
DONEGAL STREET
CYNTHIA ST
PENTONVILLE ROAD
A501
CITY ROAD
ELIA STREET
ELIA MEWS
QUICK ST
SUDELEY ST
GRAHAM STREET
CITY GARDEN ROW
NELSON TERR
NELSON PL
REMINGTON ST
WAKLEY ST
HALL STREET
MORELAND STREET
GOSWELL ROAD
A401
ST JOHN STREET
B501
OWEN ST
MYDDELTON SQUARE
CHADWELL ST
INGLEBERT ST
CLAREMONT CL
AMWELL STREET
RIVER STREET
LLOYD SQUARE
LLOYD STREET
GREAT PERCY STREET
PERCY CIRCUS
ROSEBERY AVENUE
ARLINGTON WAY
MYDDELTON PASSAGE
RAWSTORNE STREET
WYNYATT STREET
SPENCER STREET
LLOYD'S ROW
HARDWICK STREET
LLOYD BAKER STREET
MARGERY STREET
GRANVILLE SQUARE
WHARTON STREET
GWYNNE PL
WILMINGTON SQ
TYSOE ST
EXMOUTH MARKET
B502
SKINNER STREET
PERCIVAL STREET
SEBASTIAN ST
ASHBY ST
NORTHAMPTON SQUARE
WYCLIF ST
CYRUS STREET
CORPORATION ROW
WOODBRIDGE ST
A201
PO

SHOREDITCH
Shoreditch Park
NEW NORTH ROAD
CITY ROAD
OLD STREET
EAST ROAD
Regent's Canal
Grand Union Canal
City Road Basin
Wenlock Basin
Old Street
Moorfields Eye Hospl
Whitmore Prim Sch
Rotherfield Prim Sch
Rosemary Gardens
Canonbury Bsns Ctr
City & Islington Coll
Thomas Fairchild Com Sch
Crusoe House Sch
Hanover Prim Sch
St John the Baptist CE Prim Sch
St Luke's CE Prim Sch
Central Foundation Sch
The Brewery Ind Est
City Central Est
Islington
Hackney
73
84
95
83
242
33

A
B
C
D
229
246
Jewish Synagogue
St Joseph's RC Prim Sch
DERDALE ROAD
SUTHERLAND AVE
RANDOLPH AVENUE
WARRINGTON CRESCENT
RANDOLPH CRESCENT
W9
MAIDA VALE
A5
CLIFTON ROAD
B413
CLIFTON GARDENS
CLARENDON GDNS
RANDOLPH MEWS
RANDOLPH ROAD
MAIDA AVENUE
BLOMFIELD ROAD
WARWICK AVENUE
Warwick Avenue
FORMOSA STREET
CLIFTON VILLAS
BRISTOL GDNS
BRISTOL MEWS
WARWICK PLACE
Grand Union Canal Wlk
DELAMERE TERRACE
WARWICK CRESCENT
Little Venice
HOWLEY PLACE
PARK PLACE VILLAS
ST MARY'S TERR
JOHN AIRD COURT
Paddington Green Prim Sch
St Mary's Gardens
City of Westminster Coll
CROMPTON STREET
HALL PLACE
ADPAR STREET
CHURCH STREET
NEWCASTLE PL
HARROW ROAD
A404
A40
WESTWAY (ELEVATED) HARROW RD (UNDER)
A5205 ST JOHN'S WOOD RD
B507
ABERDEEN PLACE
LYONS PLACE
CUNNINGHAM PL
NORTHWICK TERR
POLLITT DRIVE
Grand Union Canal
Gateway Prim Sch
CAPLAND STREET
FISHERTON STREET
ORCHARDSON STREET
FRAMPTON STREET
LUTON STREET
HATTON ST
BOSCOBEL ST
VENABLES ST
PENFOLD STREET
PADDINGTON
W2
RANELAGH BRIDGE
WESTBOURNE BRIDGE
SHELDON SQ
BISHOP'S ROAD BRIDGE
A4206
DUDLEY HOUSE
HERMITAGE ST
Paddington Acad
NORTH WHARF ROAD
Paddington Basin
HARBET ROAD
Alexander Fleming Laboratory Mus
SOUTH WHARF ROAD
St Mary's Hosp
Medical Sch
Paddington (Hammersmith & City)
Heathrow Express Terminal Paddington Station
A4205
EASTBOURNE TERRACE
BISHOP'S BRIDGE ROAD
ORSETT TERRACE
WESTBOURNE TERRACE
GLOUCESTER TERRACE
PORCHESTER SQUARE
WINSLAND STREET
PRAED STREET
NORFOLK PLACE
NORFOLK SQUARE
LONDON ST
Hilton London Paddington Hotel
Paddington
SPRING ST
B410
CONDUIT MEWS
SUSSEX GARDENS
SUSSEX PLACE
A4209
CLEVELAND SQUARE
CLEVELAND GDNS
CHILWORTH STREET
CHILWORTH MEWS
GLOUCESTER MEWS
CRAVEN ROAD
CRAVEN HILL
Halfield Jun & Inf Schs
LEINSTER GARDENS
QUEEN'S GARDENS
Bayswater
INVERNESS TERRACE
BATHURST MEWS
WESTBOURNE CRES
HYDE PARK
STANHOPE TERRACE
1
2
3
4
5
6
26
81
82
91

NW8
A
B
C
D
230
Boating Lake
The Holme
(Regent's Canal)
Tenn Cts
NW1
Regent's College
London Business Sch
Sussex Place
Sussex Pl
Clarence Gate
Outer Circle
Sherlock Holmes Mus
Royal Coll of Ophthalmologists
Cornwall Terrace
Allsop Place
York Terrace
Baker Street
Marylebone Road
University of Westminster
Rossmore Road
Lisson Grove
Alfie's Antq Mkt
Sylvia Young Theatre Sch
St Edward's RC Prim Sch
Marylebone Station
Marylebone
Govt Offices
The Charter Nightingale Hospl
The Landmark Hotel
The Western Eye Hospl
Samaritan Hospl for Women
Westminster Acad
Edgware Rd (Bakerloo)
Edgware Road
Marylebone Flyover
Chapel St
Edgware Road
Old Marylebone Road
Courts
Crawford Street
Montagu Place
Gloucester Place
Baker Street
George Street
Seymour Place
Bryanston Square
Montagu Square
Portman Towers
Courtauld Inst of Art
Portman Square
W1
W2
Sussex Gardens
Hyde Park Crescent
Norfolk Crescent
Oxford Square
Connaught Street
Connaught Square
Upper Berkeley Street
Western Marble Arch Synagogue
West London Synagogue
Seymour Street
Bryanston Street
Cumberland Hotel
Marble Arch
Tyburn Tree (site of)
Connaught Place
Hyde Park Square
Hyde Park Street
Cumberland Gate
Sri Lanka
247
1
2
3
4
5
6

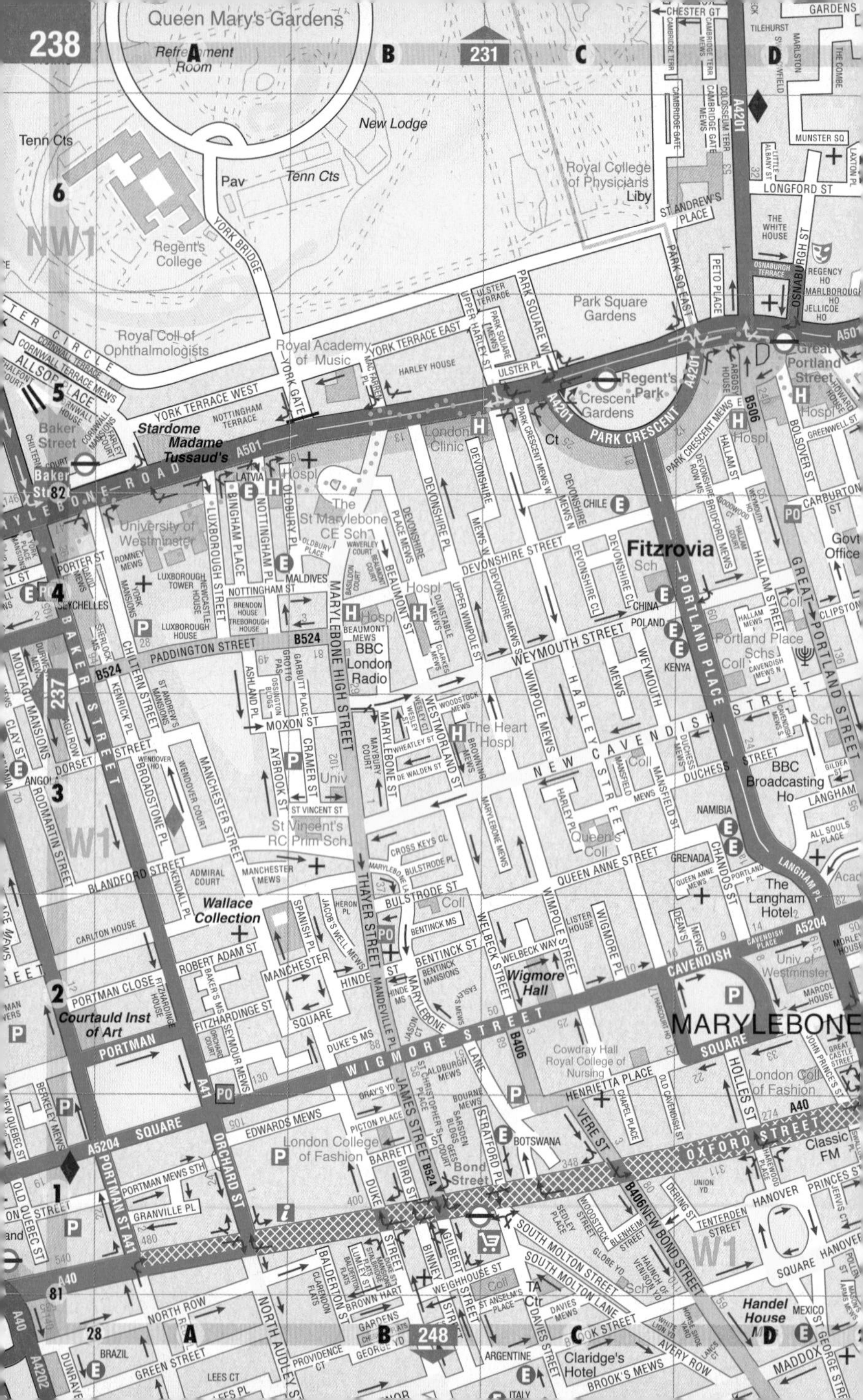
238
A
B
C
D
231
248
1
2
3
4
5
6
NW1
W1
Queen Mary's Gardens
Refreshment Room
New Lodge
Tenn Cts
Pav
Regent's College
York Bridge
Royal College of Physicians
Liby
St Andrew's Place
Chester Gt
Cambridge Terr
Cambridge Terr Mews
Cambridge Gate
Cambridge Gate Mews
Colosseum Terr
A4201
Gardens
Tilehurst
Marlston
The Combe
Munster Sq
Laxton Pl
Little Albany St
Longford St
The White House
Osnaburgh Terrace
Osnaburgh St
Regency Ho
Marlborough Ho
Jellicoe Ho
Peto Place
Park Sq East
Park Square Gardens
Park Square W
Park Square Mews
Ulster Terrace
Upper Harley St
Ulster Pl
York Terrace East
York Terrace West
Harley House
Royal Academy of Music
York Gate
Nottingham Terrace
Royal Coll of Ophthalmologists
Outer Circle
Cornwall Terrace
Cornwall Terrace Mews
Allsop Place
Chalfont Court
Cornwall Mansions
Farley Court
Baker Street
Chiltern Court
Stardome
Madame Tussaud's
A501
Marylebone Road
Regent's Park
Crescent Gardens
Park Crescent
Park Crescent Mews W
Park Crescent Mews E
Great Portland Street
Argosy House
B506
Howard House
Bolsover St
Greenwell St
Carburton St
Govt Office
Clipstone
London Clinic
Hospl
Devonshire Mews W
Devonshire Mews N
Devonshire Pl
Devonshire Place Mews
Devonshire Street
Devonshire Cl
Chile
Fitzrovia
Sch
Portland Place
Bridford Mews
Hallam St
Hallam Mews
Weymouth Mews
Goodwood Ct
Hallam Ct
Latvia
Oldbury Pl
Oldbury Place
Nottingham Pl
Bingham Place
Luxborough Street
University of Westminster
The St Marylebone CE Sch
Waverley Court
Beaumont Court
Basildon Court
Beaumont St
Dunstable Mews
Upper Wimpole St
Maldives
Nottingham St
Brendon House
Treborough House
Luxborough Tower
Luxborough House
Newcastle House
York Mansions
Romney Mews
Porter St
Seychelles
Sherlock Ms
Durweston Mews
Montagu Mansions
Baker Street
Paddington Street
B524
Chiltern Street
Kenrick Pl
St Andrew's Mansions
Ashland Pl
Grotto Pas
Garbutt Place
Marylebone High Street
Beaumont Mews
BBC London Radio
Clarkes Mews
Weymouth Street
China
Poland
Kenya
Wimpole Mews
Harley Street
Weymouth
Mews
Portland Place Schs
Coll
Cavendish Mews N
New Cavendish Street
Moxon St
Aybrook St
Cramer St
Univ
Maybury Court
Wesley St
Wheatley St
Westmorland St
Woodstock Mews
Browning Mews
The Heart Hospl
De Walden St
Marylebone St
Mansfield Mews
Mansfield St
Duchess Mews
Duchess
BBC Broadcasting Ho
Langham
Gildea St
Clay St
Dorset Street
Angola
Rodmartin Street
Broadstone Pl
Wendover Ho
Wendover Court
Manchester Street
St Vincent St
St Vincent's RC Prim Sch
Cross Keys Cl
Marylebone La
Bulstrode Pl
Bulstrode St
Marylebone Mews
Harley Pl
Queen's Coll
Queen Anne Street
Namibia
Grenada
Chandos St
Queen Anne Mews
Portland Pl
The Langham Hotel
Langham Pl
All Souls Place
Blandford Street
Kendall Pl
Admiral Court
Manchester Mews
Wallace Collection
Spanish Pl
Jacob's Well Mews
Heron Pl
Thayer Street
Bentinck Ms
Bentinck St
Bentinck Mansions
Welbeck Street
Welbeck Way
Lister House
Wimpole Street
Wigmore Pl
Wigmore Hall
Dean's Mews
Cavendish Place
A5204
Univ of Westminster
Carlton House
Robert Adam St
Baker's Ms
Manchester Square
Hinde St
Hinde Ms
Mandeville Pl
Easley's Mews
Cavendish Square
Marcol House
Marylebone
Portman Close
Fitzhardinge House
Fitzhardinge St
Seymour Mews
Orchard Court
Courtauld Inst of Art
Portman Square
Duke's Ms
Jason Ct
Marylebone Lane
B406
Wigmore Street
Cowdray Hall Royal College of Nursing
Harcourt Ho
Square
Holles St
John Prince's St
Great Castle St
London Coll of Fashion
A41
PO
Berkeley Mews
Edwards Mews
Gray's Yd
St Christopher's Place
Aldburgh Mews
Bourne Mews
Sarsden Bldgs
Stratford Pl
Henrietta Place
Chapel Place
Old Cavendish St
Vere St
Oxford Street
A40
Classic FM
New Quebec St
Picton Place
London College of Fashion
Barrett St
Bird St
James Street
Gees Court
Bond Street
Botswana
Union Yd
Harewood Place
Dering St
Old Quebec St
Portman Mews Sth
Granville Pl
Portman St
Orchard St
Duke Street
Binney St
Gilbert St
Tenterden Street
Hanover Square
Princes St
Jervis Ct
Sedley Place
Woodstock Street
Blenheim Street
New Bond Street
B406
South Molton Street
South Molton Lane
Globe Yd
Haunch of Venison Yd
Weighhouse St
St Anselm's Place
TA Ctr
Davies Mews
Davies Street
Brook Street
Avery Row
Claridge's Hotel
Brook's Mews
Handel House
Mexico
St George Street
Maddox
Balderton St
Clarendon Flats
Lumley Flats
Brown Hart Gardens
George Yd
North Row
North Audley St
Green Street
Providence Ct
Lees Ct
Lees Pl
Argentine
Italy
Brazil
Dunraven
A4202
Horse Shoe Yard
White Lion Yd
Lancs Ct

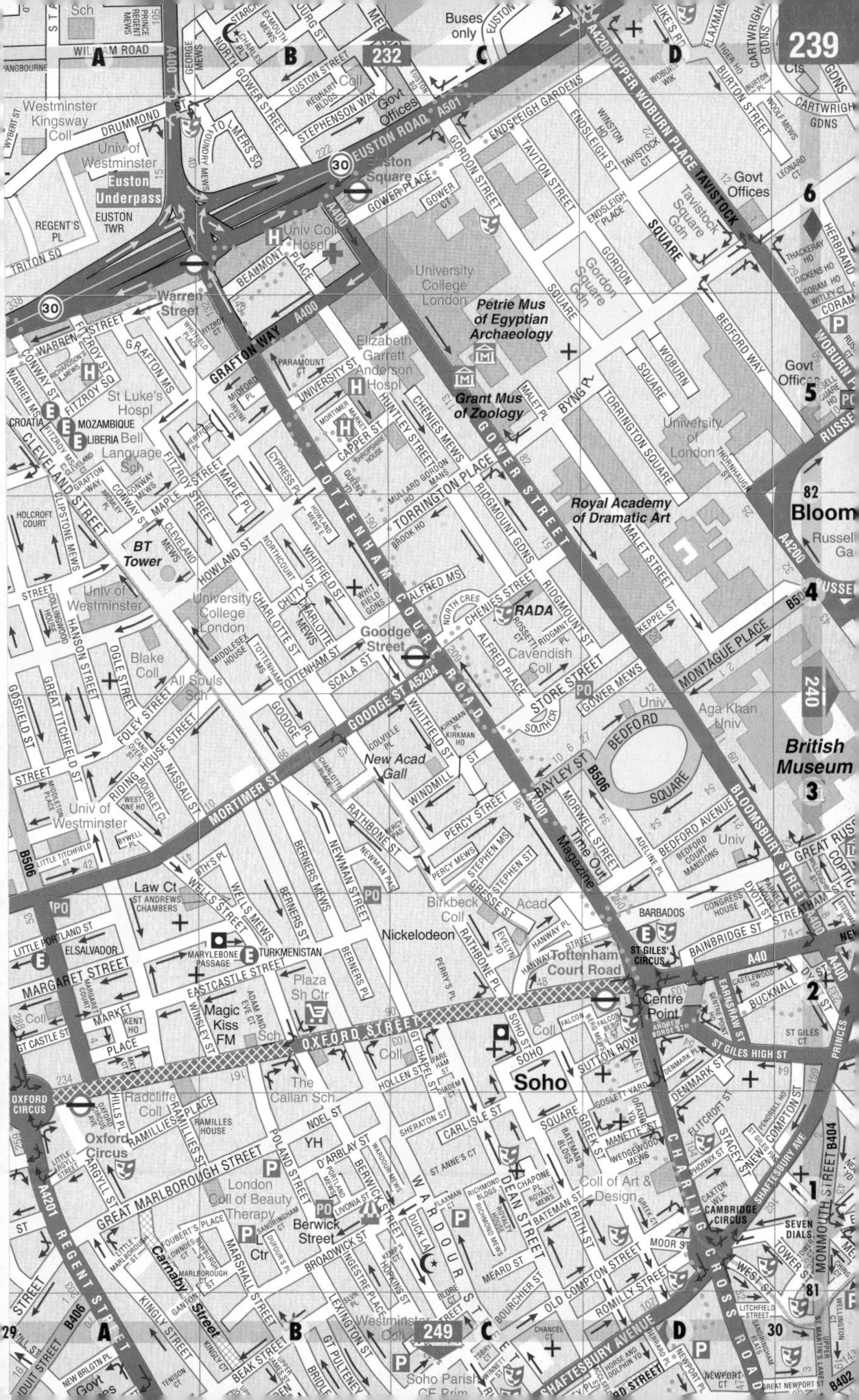
232
249
240
Buses only
Westminster Kingsway Coll
Univ of Westminster
Euston Underpass
EUSTON TWR
REGENT'S PL
TRITON SQ
WILLIAM ROAD
DRUMMOND ST
EUSTON ROAD
A501
Euston Square
Warren Street
Govt Offices
EUSTON STREET
STEPHENSON WAY
GOWER STREET
GOWER PLACE
Univ Coll Hospl
BEAUMONT PLACE
University College London
Petrie Mus of Egyptian Archaeology
Grant Mus of Zoology
Elizabeth Garrett Anderson Hospl
GORDON STREET
ENDSLEIGH GARDENS
ENDSLEIGH ST
ENDSLEIGH PLACE
TAVITON STREET
Gordon Square Gdn
Tavistock Square Gdn
TAVISTOCK SQUARE
UPPER WOBURN PLACE
A4200
BEDFORD WAY
WOBURN SQUARE
TORRINGTON SQUARE
University of London
Royal Academy of Dramatic Art
MALET STREET
MALET PL
BYNG PL
GRAFTON WAY
WARREN STREET
FITZROY SQ
St Luke's Hospl
CROATIA
MOZAMBIQUE
LIBERIA
Bell Language Sch
CLEVELAND STREET
CONWAY ST
FITZROY STREET
MAPLE ST
BT Tower
HOWLAND ST
TOTTENHAM COURT ROAD
CHENIES MEWS
HUNTLEY STREET
TORRINGTON PLACE
RIDGMOUNT GDNS
GOWER STREET
CHENIES STREET
RADA
ALFRED PLACE
Cavendish Coll
STORE STREET
GOWER MEWS
KEPPEL ST
MONTAGUE PLACE
Goodge Street
GOODGE ST
A5204
CHARLOTTE ST
WHITFIELD ST
University College London
Univ of Westminster
Blake Coll
All Souls Sch
NEW CAVENDISH STREET
GREAT TITCHFIELD ST
HANSON STREET
FOLEY STREET
RIDING HOUSE STREET
NASSAU ST
MORTIMER ST
New Acad Gall
RATHBONE ST
PERCY STREET
BEDFORD SQUARE
BAYLEY ST
B506
MORWELL STREET
Time Out Magazine
BEDFORD AVENUE
Aga Khan Univ
BLOOMSBURY STREET
British Museum
Bloomsbury
Russell
GREAT RUSSELL
Law Ct
WELLS STREET
BERNERS ST
NEWMAN STREET
Birkbeck Coll
Nickelodeon
Tottenham Court Road
ST GILES' CIRCUS
Centre Point
BAINBRIDGE ST
BUCKNALL
ST GILES HIGH ST
BARBADOS
TURKMENISTAN
MARGARET STREET
EASTCASTLE STREET
Plaza Sh Ctr
Magic Kiss FM
OXFORD STREET
Oxford Circus
OXFORD CIRCUS
The Callan Sch
Radcliffe Coll
Soho
SOHO SQUARE
SUTTON ROW
CHARING CROSS ROAD
DENMARK ST
FLITCROFT ST
NEW COMPTON ST
SHAFTESBURY AVE
CAMBRIDGE CIRCUS
SEVEN DIALS
MONMOUTH STREET
B404
GREAT MARLBOROUGH STREET
London Coll of Beauty Therapy
Carnaby Street
REGENT STREET
A4201
POLAND STREET
BERWICK STREET
Berwick Street
WARDOUR STREET
DEAN STREET
FRITH ST
GREEK ST
Coll of Art & Design
OLD COMPTON STREET
ROMILLY STREET
SHAFTESBURY AVENUE
BROADWICK ST
MARSHALL STREET
KINGLY STREET
Westminster Coll
Soho Parish CE Prim
A B C D
1 2 3 4 5 6

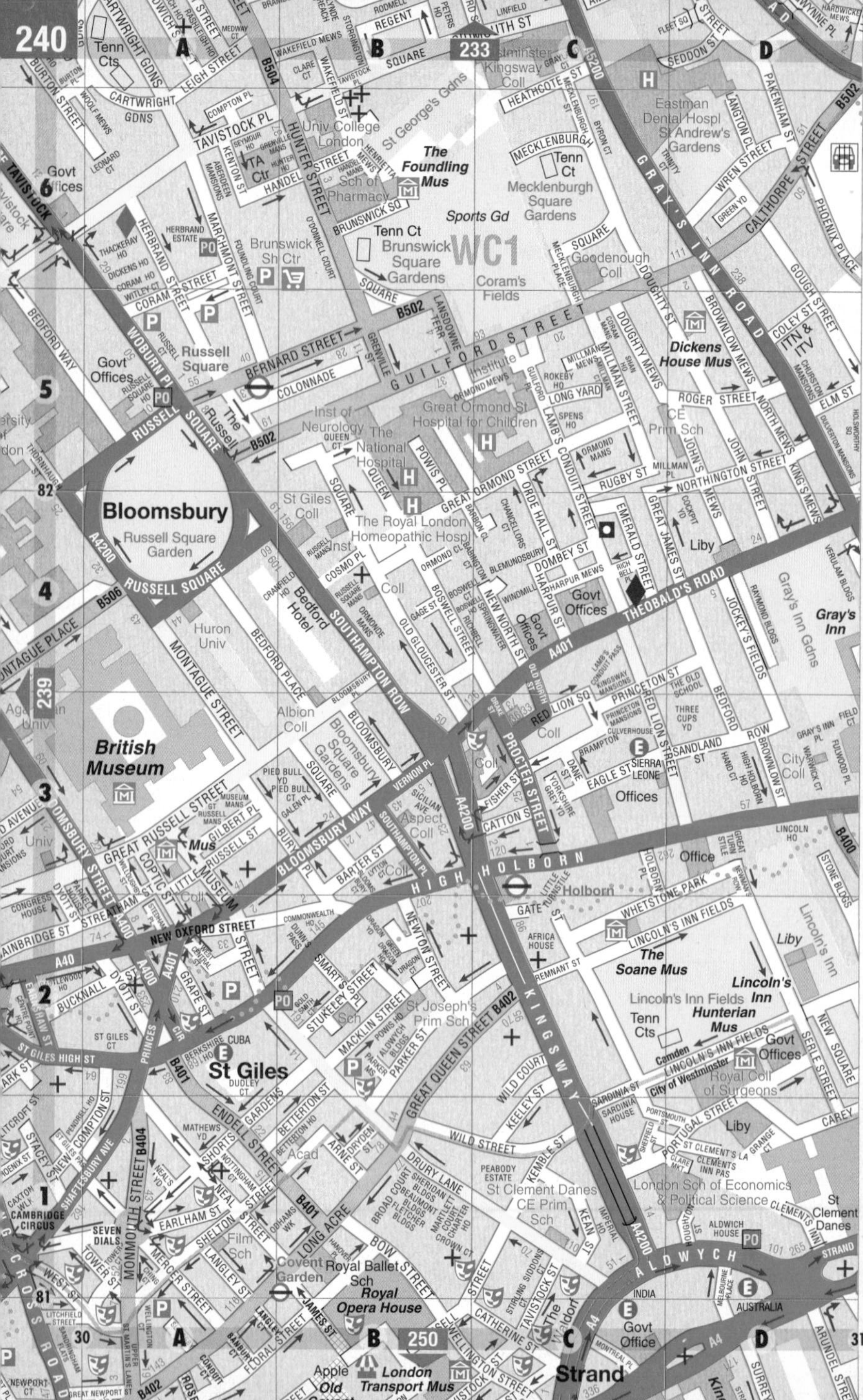
233
Tenn Cts
Cartwright Gdns
Tavistock Pl
Hunter Street
Univ College London
St George's Gdns
The Foundling Mus
Sch of Pharmacy
Brunswick Sq
Tenn Ct
Brunswick Square Gardens
Brunswick Sh Ctr
Kingsway Coll
Heathcote St
Mecklenburgh Square Gardens
Sports Gd
WC1
Coram's Fields
Goodenough Coll
Gray's Inn Road
Eastman Dental Hospl
St Andrew's Gardens
Calthorpe Street
Phoenix Place
Gough Street
Govt Offices
Tavistock Square
Woburn Pl
Bedford Way
Russell Square
Bernard Street
Guilford Street
Great Ormond St Hospital for Children
Inst of Neurology
The National Hospital
Dickens House Mus
Doughty St
John Street
Roger Street
Northington Street
ITN & ITV
Bloomsbury
Russell Square Garden
St Giles Coll
The Royal London Homeopathic Hospl
Great Ormond Street
Lamb's Conduit Street
Theobald's Road
Gray's Inn Gdns
Gray's Inn
Montague Place
Montague Street
Bedford Place
Bedford Hotel
Southampton Row
Huron Univ
British Museum
239
Bloomsbury Square Gardens
Albion Coll
Red Lion Sq
Procter Street
Red Lion Street
Sierra Leone Offices
City Coll
Great Russell Street
Bloomsbury Way
Aspect Coll
High Holborn
Holborn
Lincoln's Inn Fields
The Soane Mus
Lincoln's Inn
Hunterian Mus
Royal Coll of Surgeons
New Oxford Street
St Giles High St
St Giles
Shaftesbury Ave
Kingsway
Great Queen Street
St Joseph's Prim Sch
Drury Lane
Long Acre
St Clement Danes CE Prim Sch
London Sch of Economics & Political Science
Aldwych
St Clement Danes
Cambridge Circus
Seven Dials
Monmouth Street
Neal Street
Endell Street
Film Sch
Covent Garden
Royal Ballet Sch
Royal Opera House
Bow Street
250
London Transport Mus
The Waldorf
Strand
Govt Office
India
Australia
Charing Cross Road
30
31
81
82

241
234
242
251
A
B
C
D
1
2
3
4
5
6
EC1
EC4
Clerkenwell
Holborn
Mt. Pleasant Mail Sorting Office
Spa Fields Gardens
House of Detention
The Bridge Sch
Farringdon
Barbican
Smithfield Market
Central Criminal Court (Old Bailey)
St Bartholomew's Hospl
Barts & The London Sch of Medicine & Dentistry
Mus of St John
Central Sch of Ballet
The London Inst Coll
St Alban's CE Prim Sch
Chancery Lane
Holborn Circus
Gresham Coll
St Andrew
St Sepulchre
City Thameslink
Ludgate Circus
St Bride
St Paul's Cathedral
Stock Exchange
Dr Johnson's House Mus
King's Coll Liby
Royal Courts of Justice
Temple Bar
St Dunstan-in-the-West
Inner Temple
Middle Temple
Blackfriars
St Botolph without Aldersgate
St Peter & St Paul RC Prim Sch
Dallington Sch
Govt Offices
St Martin
St Andrew
Coll of Arms
Leather Lane
Clerkenwell Road
Farringdon Road
Rosebery Avenue
Goswell Road A1
Charterhouse Street
Holborn Viaduct
Newgate Street
Fleet Street
Farringdon Street
New Bridge Street
Chancery Lane
Fetter Lane
New Fetter Lane
Hatton Garden
St John Street
Skinner Street
Percival Street
Exmouth Market
Tysoe St
Holborn
Ludgate Hill
Aldersgate Street
Cowcross Street
Greville Street
St Cross Street
Warner Street
Great Sutton Street
Old Street
Shoe Lane
St Bride St
Tudor Street
Carter Lane
Queen Victoria Street

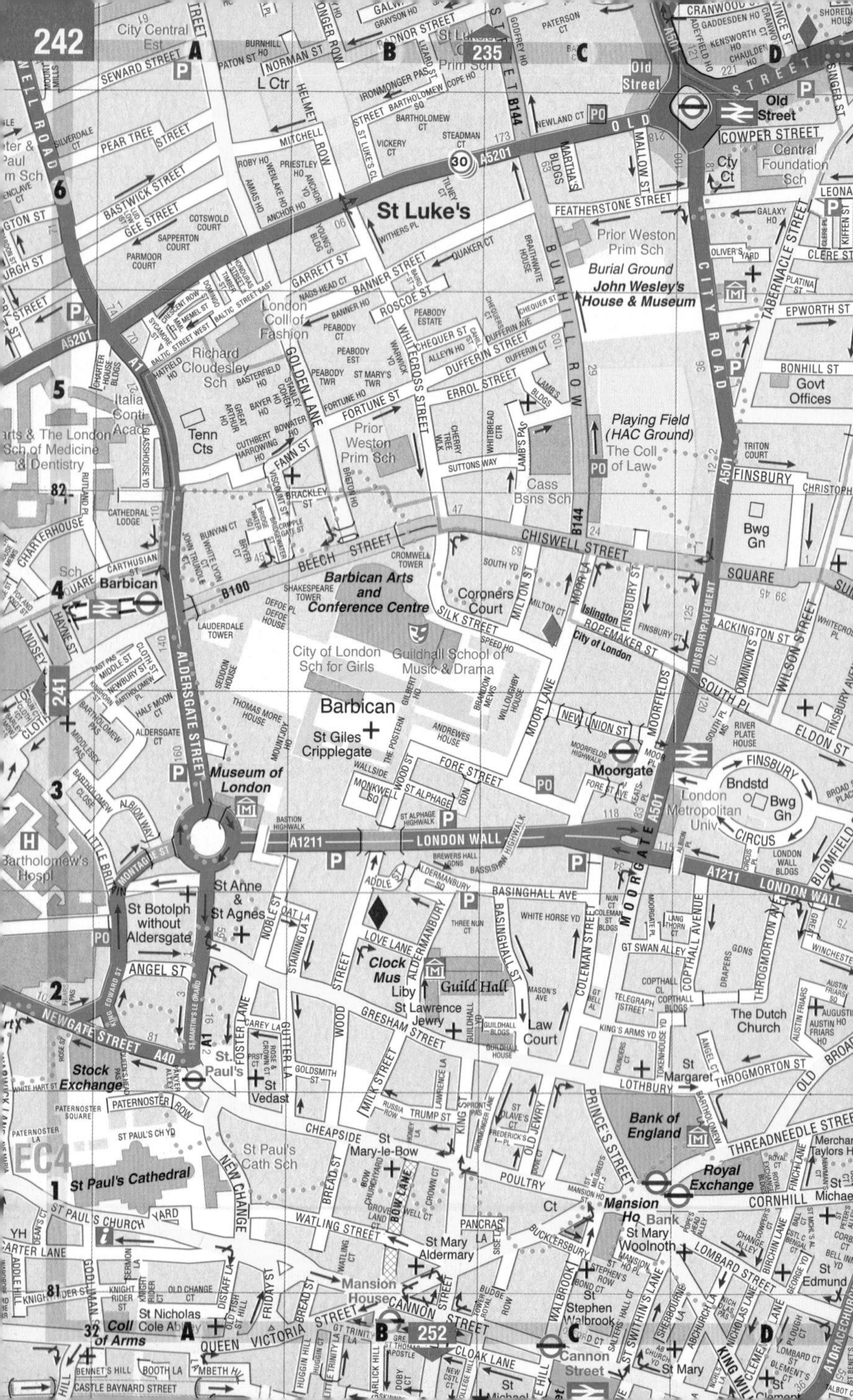
City Central Est
A
B
C
D
235
Old Street
St Luke's
Seward Street
Paton St
Norman St
Radnor Street
Ironmonger Row
Ironmonger Pas
Helmet Row
Mitchell Street
Pear Tree Street
Bastwick Street
Gee Street
Old Street
A5201
Bunhill Row
City Road
Featherstone Street
Prior Weston Prim Sch
Burial Ground
John Wesley's House & Museum
Tabernacle Street
Epworth St
Bonhill St
Govt Offices
Cowper Street
Central Foundation Sch
Whitecross Street
Golden Lane
Banner Street
Garrett St
Roscoe St
Chequer St
Dufferin Street
Errol Street
Fortune St
London Coll of Fashion
Richard Cloudesley Sch
Tenn Cts
Peabody Estate
Playing Field (HAC Ground)
The Coll of Law
Cass Bsns Sch
Finsbury
Bwg Gn
Chiswell Street
Beech Street
B100
Barbican
Barbican Arts and Conference Centre
Coroners Court
Silk Street
Ropemaker St
Finsbury Pavement
Square
City of London Sch for Girls
Guildhall School of Music & Drama
Barbican
St Giles Cripplegate
Aldersgate Street
Museum of London
Moor Lane
New Union St
Moorfields
Moorgate
Finsbury Circus
London Metropolitan Univ
London Wall
A1211
Fore Street
Wood St
St Alphage
Bassishaw Highwalk
Blomfield St
Charterhouse Square
Carthusian St
Long La
Lindsey St
Middle St
Half Moon Ct
Albion Way
Little Britain
Montague St
Bartholomew's Hospl
St Botolph without Aldersgate
St Anne & St Agnes
Noble St
Love Lane
Aldermanbury
Basinghall Ave
Basinghall St
Coleman Street
Clock Mus
Liby
Guild Hall
St Lawrence Jewry
Gresham Street
Law Court
Copthall Avenue
Throgmorton Ave
Throgmorton St
The Dutch Church
Angel St
King Edward St
Newgate Street
A40
Stock Exchange
St. Paul's
Foster Lane
Gutter La
St Vedast
Milk Street
Paternoster Row
Cheapside
New Change
St Paul's Cath Sch
St Mary-le-Bow
Poultry
Prince's Street
Lothbury
St Margaret
Bank of England
Threadneedle Street
Royal Exchange
Cornhill
Mansion Ho
Bank
St Mary Woolnoth
Lombard Street
St Edmund
EC4
St Paul's Cathedral
St Paul's Church Yard
Carter Lane
Watling Street
Bread St
Bow Lane
St Mary Aldermary
Bucklersbury
Walbrook
St Stephen Walbrook
Mansion House
Cannon Street
Queen Victoria Street
St Nicholas Cole Abbey
Coll of Arms
252
Cloak Lane
Cannon Street
St Swithin's Lane
Abchurch La
King William St
Nicholas Lane
Clements Lane
Castle Baynard Street
Bennet's Hill

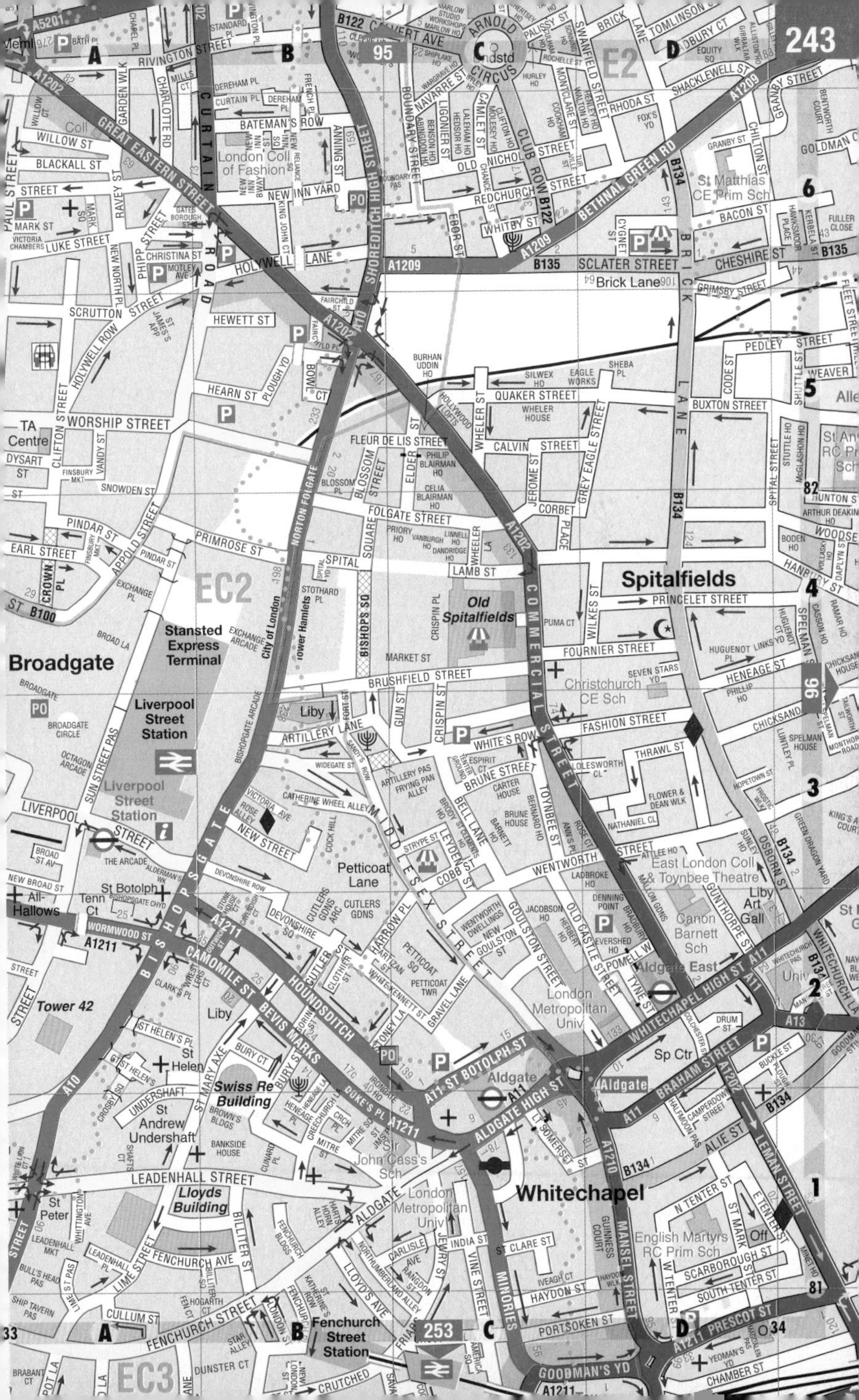

A
B
C
D
E2
EC2
EC3
Arnold Circus
Rivington Street
Curtain Road
Great Eastern Street
Calvert Ave
Shoreditch High Street
Boundary Street
Club Row
Swanfield Street
Brick Lane
Tomlinson Cl
Shacklewell St
Granby Street
Bethnal Green Rd
Rhoda St
Redchurch Street
Old Nichol Street
Sclater Street
Cheshire St
Bacon St
Brick Lane
Holywell Lane
Hewett St
Scrutton Street
Holywell Row
Clifton Street
Worship Street
Hearn St
Plough Yd
Bateman's Row
New Inn Yard
London Coll of Fashion
Willow St
Blackall St
Luke Street
Mark St
Paul Street
Christina St
Phipp Street
Quaker Street
Wheler Street
Calvin Street
Fleur de Lis Street
Blossom Street
Elder St
Folgate Street
Norton Folgate
Jerome St
Grey Eagle Street
Corbet Place
Pedley Street
Buxton Street
Weaver St
Spital Street
Hanbury St
Princelet Street
Fournier Street
Spitalfields
Old Spitalfields
Commercial Street
Lamb St
Crispin Pl
Wilkes St
Brushfield Street
Fashion Street
Christchurch CE Sch
Heneage St
Chicksand St
Thrawl St
Flower & Dean Wlk
Wentworth Street
East London Coll & Toynbee Theatre
Osborn St
Canon Barnett Sch
Gunthorpe St
Whitechapel High St
Aldgate East
Primrose St
Pindar St
Appold Street
Earl Street
Exchange Pl
Broadgate
Broadgate Circle
Stansted Express Terminal
Liverpool Street Station
Liverpool Street
Sun Street Pas
Bishopsgate
Artillery Lane
Middlesex Street
Petticoat Lane
Petticoat Sq
New Street
Devonshire Sq
Cutlers Gdns
Houndsditch
Bevis Marks
Camomile St
Wormwood St
All-Hallows
St Botolph
Tower 42
St Helen's Pl
St Mary Axe
Swiss Re Building
St Andrew Undershaft
Leadenhall Street
Lloyds Building
Fenchurch Ave
Fenchurch Street
Fenchurch Street Station
Lime Street
Billiter St
Aldgate
Aldgate High St
Duke's Pl
St Botolph St
Sir John Cass's Sch
London Metropolitan Univ
Minories
Vine Street
Jewry St
Goulston Street
Old Castle Street
Whitechapel
Mansell Street
Leman Street
Alie St
Braham Street
Goodman's Yd
Portsoken St
Haydon St
Prescot St
Chamber St
English Martyrs RC Prim Sch
Scarborough St
South Tenter St
Crutched
Dunster Ct
Cullum St
Petticoat Twr
Gravel Lane
Toynbee St
Bell Lane
Brune Street
Leyden St
Cobb St
Harrow Pl
Stoney La
A1202
A10
A1209
A1211
A11
A1210
A13
B134
B135
B122
B100
95
96
253
1
2
3
4
5
6

Notting Hill
W11
W8
W14
Holland Park
Ladbroke Square Gardens
Avondale Park
Holland Park Tennis Ground
The Orangery Gallery
Kensington Sp Ctr
Grenfell Tower
Holland Park Sch
The Cardinal Vaughan Memorial Sch
Ripples Montessori Sch
Norland Place Sch
St Clement & St James CE Prim Sch
Avondale Park Prim Sch
Colville Prim Sch
Holland Park Avenue
Ladbroke Grove
Kensington Park Road
Portobello Road
Westbourne Grove
Clarendon Road
Portland Road
Lansdowne Crescent
Ladbroke Gdns
Lansdowne Walk
Ladbroke Road
Holland Park Mews
Abbotsbury Road
Addison Road
Holland Villas Road
Addison Crescent
Holland Rd
Holland Park Gdns
Royal Crescent
St James's Gdns
Queensdale Road
Walmer Road
Pottery Lane
Princedale Road
Norland Square
Campden Hill Road
Aubrey Road
Aubrey Walk
Holland Wlk
Ilchester Place
Oakwood Court
Elsham Road
Russell Gdns Mews
Blenheim Crescent
Elgin Crescent
Arundel Gardens
Rosmead Rd
Lansdowne Rise
St John's Gdns
Ladbroke Square
Ladbroke Walk
Ladbroke Terr
Wilsham Street
Penzance Place
Mary Place
Bomore Road
Avondale Park Road
Sirdar Road
St Ann's Rd
Upper Addison Gdns
Lower Addison Gdns
Woodsford Square
Ukraine
Algeria
Uzbekistan
Cameroon
Greece
Iraq
A402
A3220
B450
B415
91
254
112
Tenn Ct
Tenn Cts
YH
A
B
C
D
1
2
3
4
5
6

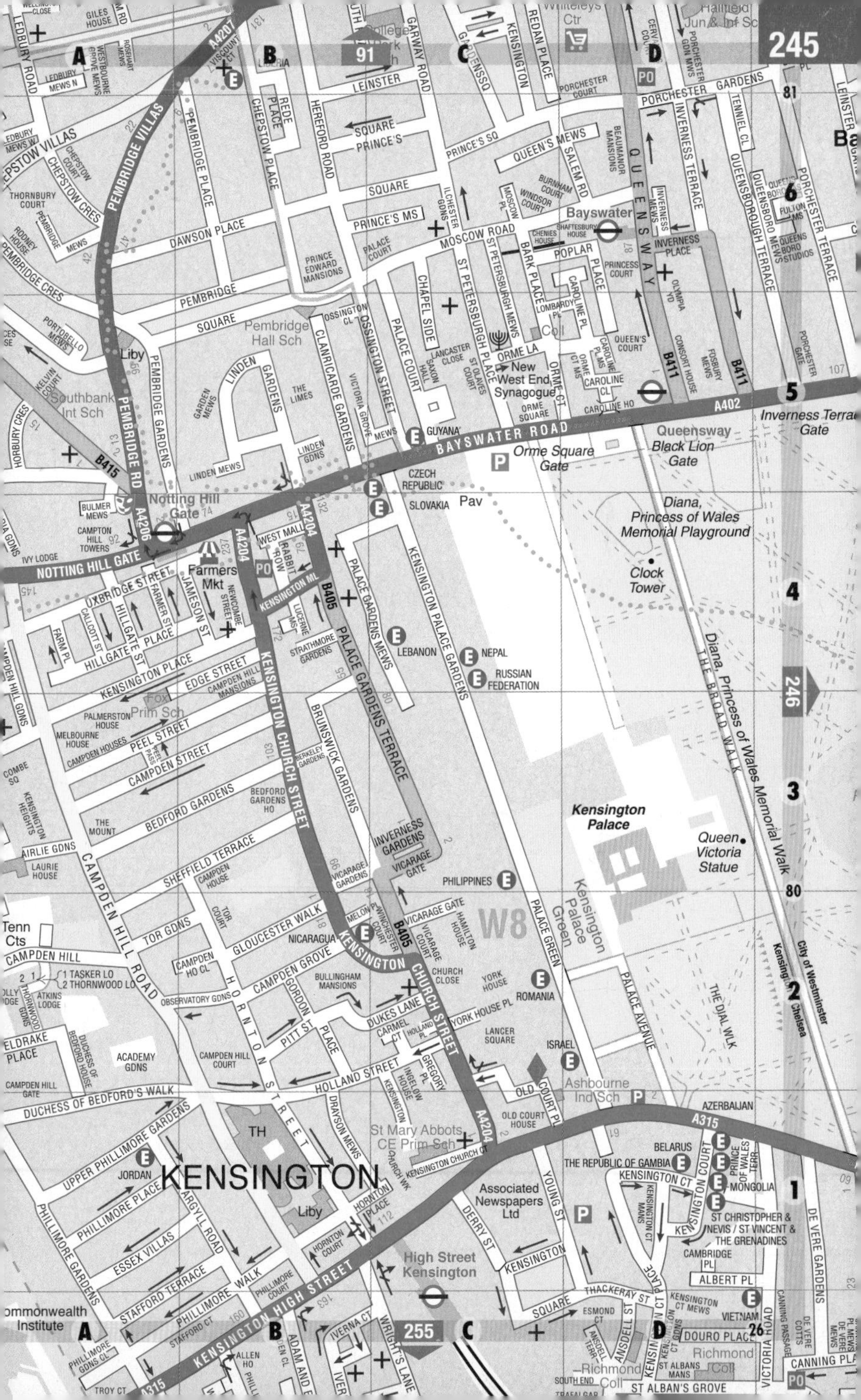

245
A
B
C
D
91
255
246
1
2
3
4
5
6
KENSINGTON
W8
BAYSWATER ROAD
A402
NOTTING HILL GATE
KENSINGTON HIGH STREET
A315
KENSINGTON CHURCH STREET
A4204
PEMBRIDGE VILLAS
A4207
PEMBRIDGE RD
A4206
B415
B405
B411
QUEENSWAY
LEDBURY ROAD
GILES HOUSE
LEDBURY MEWS N
WESTBOURNE GROVE MEWS
ROSEHART MEWS
VISCOUNT CT
LIBERIA
CHEPSTOW PLACE
REDE PLACE
HEREFORD ROAD
GARWAY ROAD
LEINSTER
SQUARE
PRINCE'S
PRINCE'S MS
PRINCE'S SQ
KENSINGTON GDNS SQ
REDAN PLACE
Whiteleys Ctr
PORCHESTER COURT
PORCHESTER GARDENS
PORCHESTER GDN MEWS
PORCHESTER TERRACE
PORCHESTER GATE
INVERNESS TERRACE
INVERNESS MEWS
INVERNESS PLACE
TENNIEL CL
QUEENSBOROUGH TERRACE
QUEENSBORO MEWS
QUEENS BORO STUDIOS
FULTON MS
LEINSTER
QUEEN'S MEWS
SALEM RD
BEAUMANOR MANSIONS
BURNHAM COURT
WINDSOR COURT
MOSCOW PL
MOSCOW ROAD
ILCHESTER GDNS
Bayswater
CHENIES HOUSE
SHAFTESBURY HOUSE
BARK PLACE
POPLAR PLACE
PRINCESS COURT
OLYMPIA YD
CAROLINE PL
LOMBARDY PL
Coll
QUEEN'S COURT
CAROLINE PL MS
CAROLINE CL
CAROLINE HO
CONSORT HOUSE
FOSBURY MEWS
ST PETERSBURGH PLACE
ST PETERSBURGH MEWS
CHAPEL SIDE
PALACE COURT
ORME LA
ORME CT
ORME CT MS
ORME SQUARE
New West End Synagogue
LANCASTER CLOSE
SAXON HALL
ST OLAVES COURT
PRINCE EDWARD MANSIONS
OSSINGTON CL
OSSINGTON STREET
CLANRICARDE GARDENS
VICTORIA GROVE MEWS
GUYANA
CHEPSTOW VILLAS
CHEPSTOW COURT
CHEPSTOW CRES
THORNBURY COURT
PEMBRIDGE MEWS
RODNEY HOUSE
PEMBRIDGE CRES
PEMBRIDGE PLACE
DAWSON PLACE
PEMBRIDGE SQUARE
Pembridge Hall Sch
PORTOBELLO MEWS
Liby
KELVIN COURT
Southbank Int Sch
HORBURY CRES
PEMBRIDGE GARDENS
LINDEN GARDENS
GARDEN MEWS
THE LIMES
LINDEN GDNS
LINDEN MEWS
Notting Hill Gate
BULMER MEWS
CAMPTON HILL TOWERS
IVY LODGE
WEST MALL
RABBIT ROW
KENSINGTON ML
PO
Farmers Mkt
UXBRIDGE STREET
JAMESON ST
NEWCOMBE STREET
FARMER ST
HILLGATE ST
HILLGATE PLACE
CALLCOTT ST
FARM PL
KENSINGTON PLACE
EDGE STREET
CAMPDEN HILL MANSIONS
Fox Prim Sch
PALMERSTON HOUSE
MELBOURNE HOUSE
CAMPDEN HOUSES
PEEL STREET
PEEL PASS
CAMPDEN STREET
BEDFORD GARDENS
BEDFORD GARDENS HO
THE MOUNT
SHEFFIELD TERRACE
CAMPDEN HOUSE
AIRLIE GDNS
LAURIE HOUSE
CAMPDEN HILL ROAD
KENSINGTON HEIGHTS
COMBE SQ
CAMPDEN HILL GDNS
Tenn Cts
CAMPDEN HILL
1 TASKER LO
2 THORNWOOD LO
ATKINS LODGE
THORNWOOD GDNS
TOR GDNS
TOR COURT
CAMPDEN HO CL
OBSERVATORY GDNS
GLOUCESTER WALK
CAMPDEN GROVE
HORNTON STREET
NICARAGUA
GORDON PLACE
BULLINGHAM MANSIONS
DUKES LANE
PITT ST
CARMEL CT
HOLLAND PL
CAMPDEN HILL COURT
HOLLAND STREET
ACADEMY GDNS
DUCHESS OF BEDFORD HOUSE
SHELDRAKE PLACE
CAMPDEN HILL GATE
DUCHESS OF BEDFORD'S WALK
TH
UPPER PHILLIMORE GARDENS
JORDAN
PHILLIMORE PLACE
PHILLIMORE GARDENS
ARGYLL ROAD
ESSEX VILLAS
STAFFORD TERRACE
PHILLIMORE WALK
PHILLIMORE COURT
STAFFORD CT
Commonwealth Institute
PHILLIMORE GDNS CL
TROY CT
ALLEN HO
HORNTON COURT
HORNTON PLACE
DRAYSON MEWS
INGLEW HOUSE
KENSINGTON CHURCH CT
CHURCH WK
St Mary Abbots CE Prim Sch
GREGORY PL
High Street Kensington
IVERNA CT
WRIGHT'S LANE
ADAM AND EVE
STRATHMORE GARDENS
LUCERNE MS
PALACE GARDENS MEWS
PALACE GARDENS TERRACE
BRUNSWICK GARDENS
BERKELEY GARDENS
INVERNESS GARDENS
VICARAGE GATE
VICARAGE GARDENS
MELON PL
WINCHESTER COURT
VICARAGE COURT
HAMILTON HOUSE
CHURCH CLOSE
YORK HOUSE
YORK HOUSE PL
LANCER SQUARE
ROMANIA
ISRAEL
OLD COURT PL
OLD COURT HOUSE
Ashbourne Ind Sch
LEBANON
NEPAL
RUSSIAN FEDERATION
CZECH REPUBLIC
SLOVAKIA
PHILIPPINES
KENSINGTON PALACE GARDENS
PALACE GREEN
Kensington Palace Green
Kensington Palace
PALACE AVENUE
Pav
Orme Square Gate
Queensway
Black Lion Gate
Inverness Terrace Gate
Diana, Princess of Wales Memorial Playground
Clock Tower
THE BROAD WALK
Diana, Princess of Wales Memorial Walk
Queen Victoria Statue
THE DIAL WLK
City of Westminster
Kensington & Chelsea
AZERBAIJAN
BELARUS
THE REPUBLIC OF GAMBIA
KENSINGTON CT
KENSINGTON COURT
KENSINGTON CT MANS
PRINCE OF WALES TERR
MONGOLIA
ST CHRISTOPHER & NEVIS / ST VINCENT & THE GRENADINES
CAMBRIDGE PL
ALBERT PL
KENSINGTON CT MEWS
VIETNAM
Associated Newspapers Ltd
DERRY ST
YOUNG ST
KENSINGTON SQUARE
THACKERAY ST
ESMOND CT
ANSDELL ST
ANSDELL TERR
KENSINGTON CT PLACE
KENSINGTON CT GDNS
DOURO PLACE
ST ALBANS MANS
Richmond Coll
ST ALBAN'S GROVE
SOUTH END
VICTORIA ROAD
CANNING PASSAGE
CANNING PLACE
DE VERE GARDENS
DE VERE COTTS
DE VERE MEWS

Bayswater
Kensington Gardens
Round Pond
The Long Water
W2
SW7
Bayswater Road
Kensington Road
Lancaster Terr
Leinster Terr
Queensborough Terrace
Porchester Terrace
Inverness Terrace
Craven Hill
Westbourne Street
Sussex Gdns
Hyde Park Gate
Palace Gate
Prince Consort Road
Royal Lancaster Hotel
Lancaster Gate
Marlborough Gate
Westbourne Gate
Inverness Terrace Gate
Queensway
Black Lion Gate
Diana, Princess of Wales Memorial Playground
Diana, Princess of Wales Memorial Walk
St Agnes' Well
The Fountains
Bayard's Watering Place (site of)
Bayswater Road Mkt
Speke's Monument
Peter Pan Statue
Physical Engery Statue
Temple Lodge
Serpentine Bridge
Queen Victoria Statue
Bandstand
Serpentine Gallery
Diana, Princess of Wales Memorial Fountain
The Flower Walk
Albert Memorial
Coalbrookdale Gate
Alexandra Gate
Palace Gate
Queen's Gate
Royal Coll of Art
Royal Albert Hall
Royal Geographical Society
Royal Coll of Organists
Royal College of Science
Royal College of Music
Polish Inst & Sikorski Museum
Richmond Coll
Kensington & Chelsea
City of Westminster
236
245
256

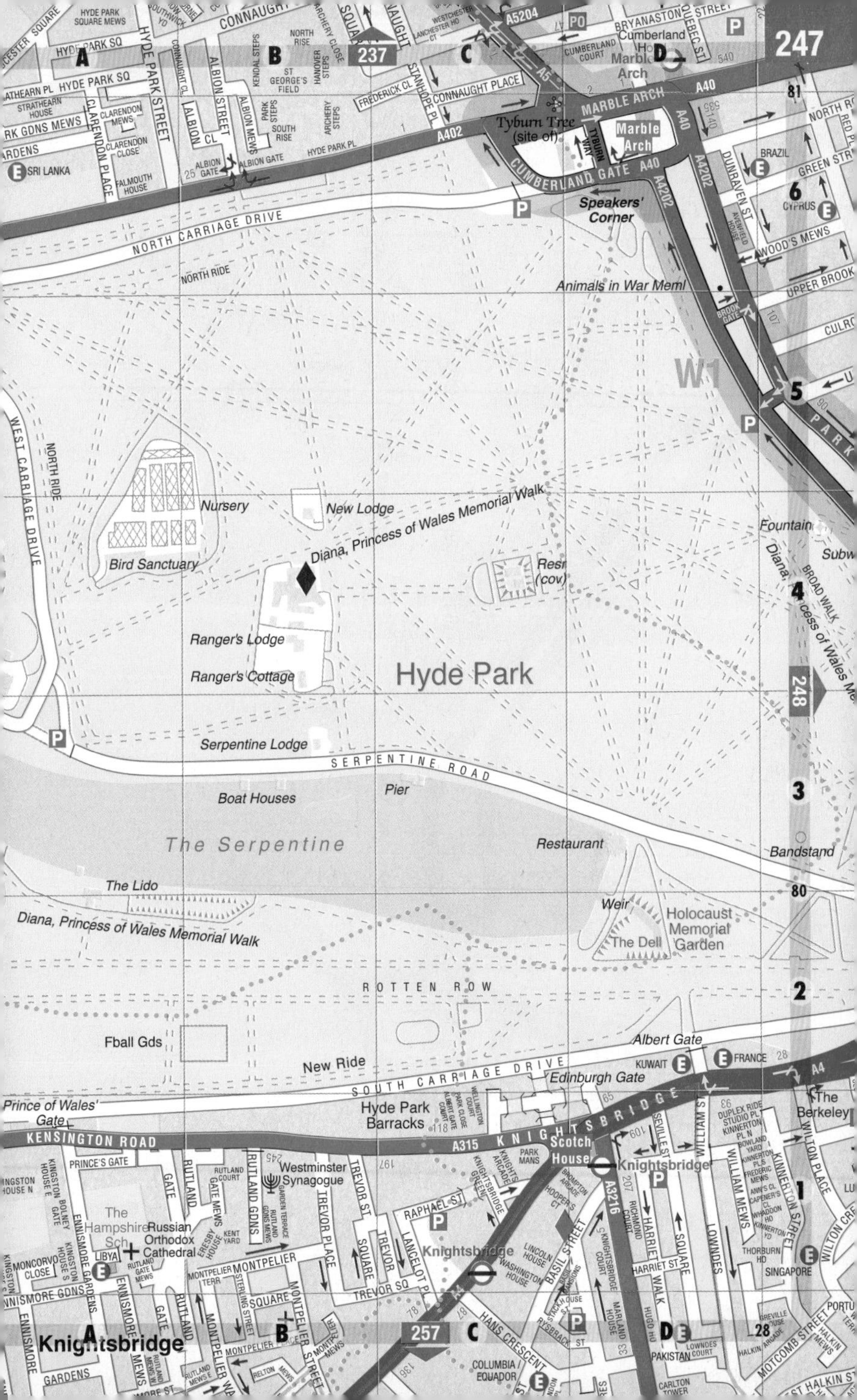

247
237
248
257
A
B
C
D
Hyde Park
The Serpentine
Marble Arch
Tyburn Tree (site of)
Cumberland Gate
Speakers' Corner
North Carriage Drive
North Ride
West Carriage Drive
Animals in War Meml
W1
Nursery
Bird Sanctuary
New Lodge
Diana, Princess of Wales Memorial Walk
Resr (cov)
Ranger's Lodge
Ranger's Cottage
Serpentine Lodge
Serpentine Road
Boat Houses
Pier
Restaurant
Bandstand
The Lido
Weir
The Dell
Holocaust Memorial Garden
Rotten Row
Fball Gds
New Ride
South Carriage Drive
Albert Gate
Edinburgh Gate
Hyde Park Barracks
Prince of Wales' Gate
Kensington Road
Knightsbridge
Scotch House
Westminster Synagogue
Russian Orthodox Cathedral
The Hampshire Sch
The Berkeley
Fountain
Broad Walk
Connaught Place
Hyde Park Square
Hyde Park Street
Albion Street
Clarendon Place
Sri Lanka
Brazil
Cyprus
Kuwait
France
Libya
Singapore
Pakistan
Columbia / Equador
Park Lane
Hans Crescent
Basil Street
Montpelier Square
Trevor Place
Ennismore Gardens
Lowndes Square
Wilton Place
Kinnerton Street
William Mews
Motcomb Street

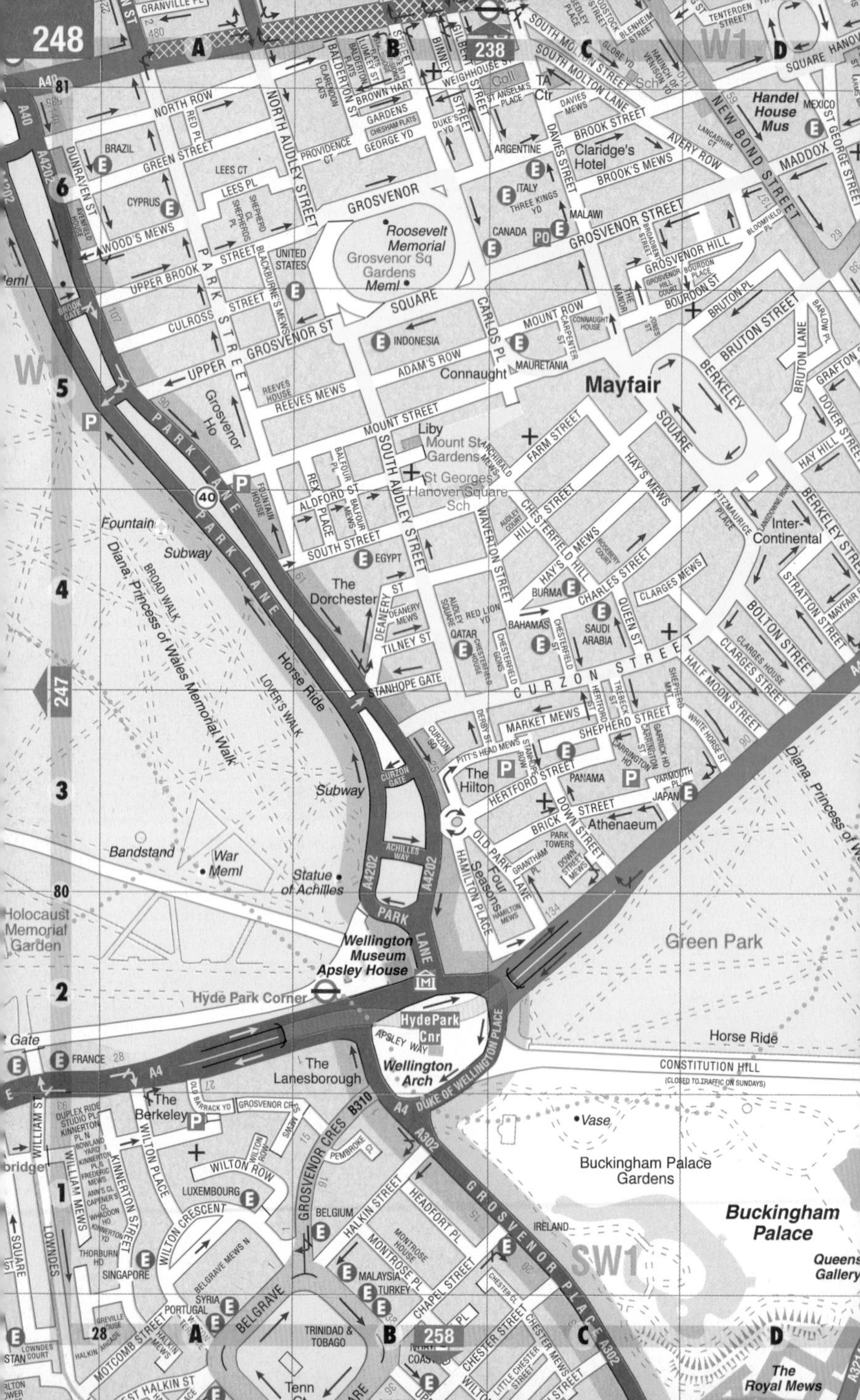

248
238
258
247
A
B
C
D
W1
SW1
1
2
3
4
5
6
28
80
81
Granville Pl
North Row
Green Street
Brazil
Cyprus
Dunraven St
Wood's Mews
Upper Brook Street
Culross Street
Brook Gate
Upper Grosvenor St
Park Street
North Audley Street
Lees Ct
Lees Pl
Shepherds Pl
Blackburne's Mews
United States
Providence Ct
George Yd
Gardens
Brown Hart
Balderton St
Lumley St
Clarendon Flats
Binney St
Gilbert Street
Weighhouse St
Duke's Yd
St Anselm's Place
Argentine
Italy
Three Kings Yd
Canada
Malawi
PO
Grosvenor
Grosvenor Street
Roosevelt Memorial
Grosvenor Sq Gardens
Meml
Square
Indonesia
Adam's Row
Carlos Pl
Mount Row
Carpenter St
Connaught House
Mauretania
Connaught
Reeves Mews
Reeves House
Grosvenor Ho
Mount Street
Liby
Mount St Gardens
St Georges Hanover Square Sch
Archibald Mews
South Audley Street
Balfour Pl
Rex Place
Aldford St
Balfour Mews
South Street
Fountain House
Egypt
The Dorchester
Deanery St
Deanery Mews
Tilney St
Stanhope Gate
Audley Square
Red Lion Yd
Qatar
Chesterfield House
Chesterfield Gdns
Waverton Street
Hill Street
Chesterfield Hill
Audley Court
Hay's Mews
Farm Street
Mayfair
Burma
Bahamas
Chesterfield St
Charles Street
Saudi Arabia
Queen St
Clarges Mews
Curzon Street
Hertford St
Trebeck St
Shepherd Mkt
Market Mews
Shepherd Street
Derby St
Curzon Sq
Pitt's Head Mews
Stanhope Row
Carrington St
Carrington Ho
Garrick Ho
White Horse St
Half Moon Street
Clarges Street
Clarges House
Bolton Street
Stratton Street
Mayfair Pl
Berkeley Street
Inter-Continental
Fitzmaurice Place
Lansdowne Row
Berkeley Square
Bruton Lane
Bruton Street
Bruton Pl
Barlow Pl
Grafton St
Dover Street
Hay Hill
The Hilton
Hertford Street
Panama
Yarmouth Pl
Japan
Brick Street
Down Street
Athenaeum
Park Towers
Grantham Pl
Down Street Mews
Old Park Lane
Four Seasons
Hamilton Place
Hamilton Mews
South Molton Street
South Molton Lane
Davies Mews
Davies Street
Brook Street
Claridge's Hotel
Brook's Mews
Avery Row
Lancashire Ct
New Bond Street
Handel House Mus
Mexico
St George Street
Maddox
Tenterden Street
Hanover Square
Blenheim Street
Globe Yd
Haunch of Venison Yd
Sch
TA Ctr
Coll
Sedley Place
Woodstock Street
Broadbent Street
Grosvenor Hill
Grosvenor Hill Court
Bourdon Place
Bourdon St
The Manor
Jones St
Bloomfield Pl
Park Lane
Horse Ride
Fountain
Subway
Diana, Princess of Wales Memorial Walk
Broad Walk
Lover's Walk
Bandstand
War Meml
Statue of Achilles
Curzon Gate
Achilles Way
A4202
Park Lane
Holocaust Memorial Garden
Wellington Museum
Apsley House
Hyde Park Corner
Hyde Park Cnr
Apsley Way
Wellington Arch
Duke of Wellington Place
Green Park
Horse Ride
Constitution Hill
(Closed to traffic on Sundays)
Vase
Buckingham Palace Gardens
Buckingham Palace
Queens Gallery
The Royal Mews
Gate
France
A4
The Lanesborough
The Berkeley
Old Barrack Yd
Grosvenor Cres Mews
Grosvenor Cres
B310
Pembroke Cl
Wilton Row
Wilton Place
Luxembourg
Wilton Crescent
Belgium
Halkin Street
Headfort Pl
Montrose House
Montrose Pl
Malaysia
Turkey
Chapel Street
Ireland
Grosvenor Place
A302
Chester Cl
Chester Street
Chester Mews
Little Chester Street
Belgrave
Trinidad & Tobago
Syria
Portugal
Singapore
Thorburn Ho
Kinnerton Street
Kinnerton Yd
Whaddon Ho
Capener's Cl
Ann's Cl
Frederic Mews
Bowland Yard
Studio Pl
Duplex Ride
William Mews
William St
Lowndes Square
Motcomb Street
Halkin Mews
Halkin Arcade
Greville House
Lowndes Court
Halkin St
A40
A4202
A321

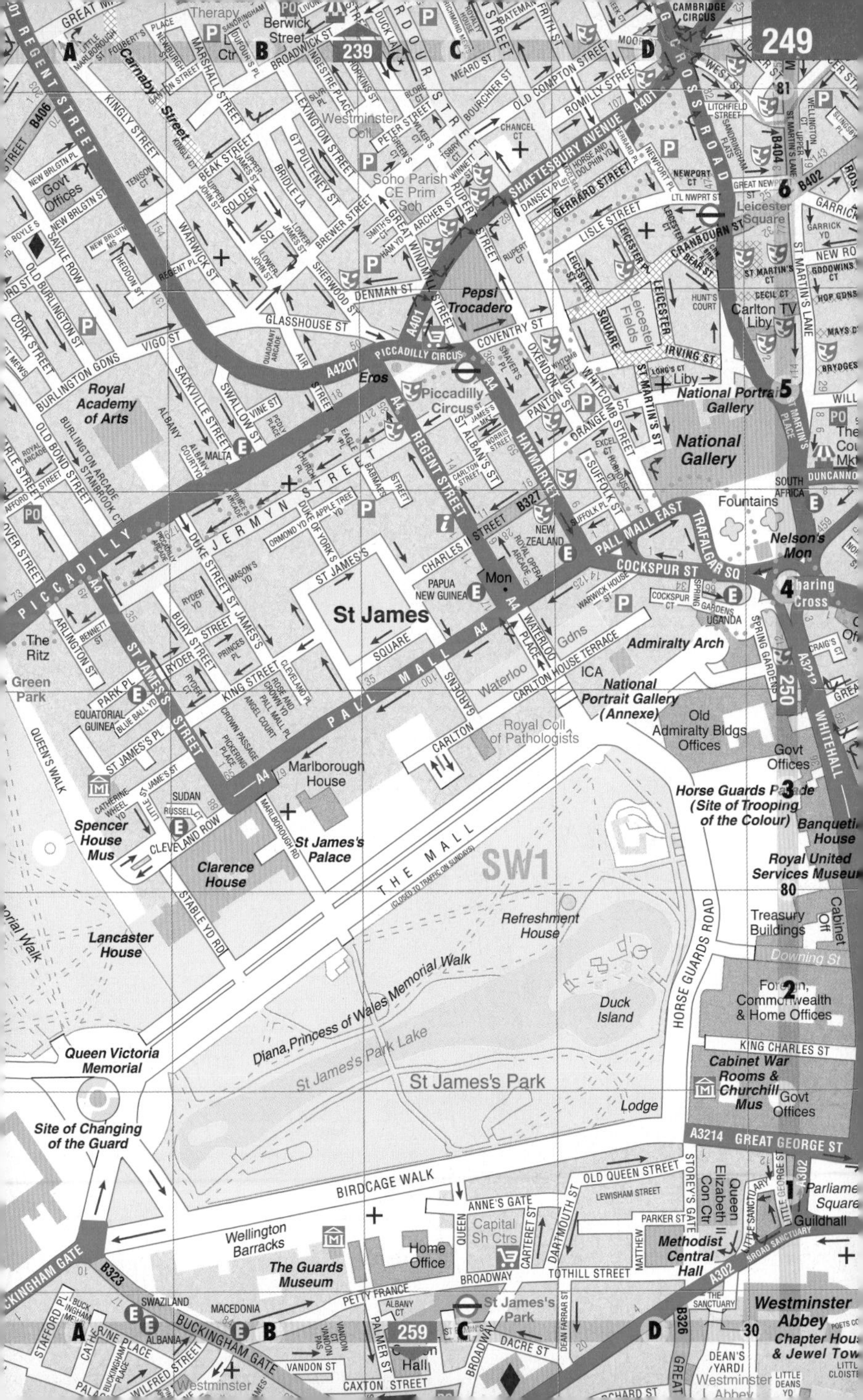
249
239
250
259
A
B
C
D
1
2
3
4
5
6
REGENT STREET
Carnaby Street
KINGLY STREET
MARSHALL STREET
BROADWICK ST
Berwick Street
Therapy
LEXINGTON STREET
Westminster Coll
GT PULTENEY ST
BRIDLE LA
PETER STREET
Soho Parish CE Prim Sch
BREWER STREET
GREAT WINDMILL STREET
ARCHER ST
RUPERT STREET
SHAFTESBURY AVENUE
A401
OLD COMPTON STREET
ROMILLY STREET
MEARD ST
BOURCHIER ST
CHANCEL CT
FRITH ST
BATEMAN
MOOR
CAMBRIDGE CIRCUS
CHARING CROSS ROAD
WEST ST
LITCHFIELD STREET
NEWPORT CT
NEWPORT PL
GERRARD STREET
GERRARD PL
DANSEY PL
HORSE AND DOLPHIN YD
LISLE STREET
LEICESTER CT
LEICESTER PL
LEICESTER ST
Leicester Fields
LEICESTER SQUARE
Leicester Square
CRANBOURN ST
BEAR ST
IRVING ST
HUNT'S COURT
Carlton TV Liby
ST MARTIN'S LANE
ST MARTIN'S CT
CECIL CT
GARRICK YD
NEW ROW
GOODWINS CT
HOP GDNS
MAYS CT
BRYDGES
B404
B402
Govt Offices
NEW BRLGTN PL
NEW BRLGTN ST
BOYLE S
SAVILE ROW
OLD BURLINGTON ST
CORK STREET
BURLINGTON GDNS
Royal Academy of Arts
OLD BOND STREET
BURLINGTON ARCADE
ALBANY
SACKVILLE STREET
SWALLOW ST
VINE ST
AIR STREET
VIGO ST
GLASSHOUSE ST
SHERWOOD ST
DENMAN ST
WARWICK ST
GOLDEN SQ
BEAK STREET
HEDDON ST
REGENT PL
A4201
PICCADILLY CIRCUS
Eros
Piccadilly Circus
Pepsi Trocadero
COVENTRY ST
OXENDON ST
WHITCOMB ST
PANTON ST
ORANGE ST
HAYMARKET
A4
ST ALBAN'S ST
NORRIS STREET
CARLTON STREET
SUFFOLK ST
St Martin's Liby
National Portrait Gallery
National Gallery
ST MARTIN'S PL
ST MARTIN'S ST
The Courtyard Mkt
DUNCANNON
SOUTH AFRICA
Fountains
Nelson's Mon
Charing Cross
TRAFALGAR SQ
PALL MALL EAST
COCKSPUR ST
SPRING GARDENS
UGANDA
WARWICK HOUSE ST
NEW ZEALAND
B327
CHARLES II STREET
ROYAL OPERA ARCADE
PAPUA NEW GUINEA
Mon
JERMYN STREET
PICCADILLY
MALTA
EAGLE PL
CHURCH PL
BABMAES STREET
DUKE OF YORK ST
APPLE TREE YD
ORMOND YD
ST JAMES'S SQUARE
St James
DUKE STREET ST JAMES'S
MASON'S YD
RYDER YD
BURY STREET
RYDER STREET
PRINCES PL
KING STREET
ROSE AND CROWN YD
PALL MALL PL
ANGEL COURT
CROWN PASSAGE
PICKERING PLACE
CLEVELAND PL
ST JAMES'S STREET
ARLINGTON ST
BENNETT ST
The Ritz
Green Park
PARK PL
BLUE BALL YD
EQUATORIAL GUINEA
ST JAMES'S PL
QUEEN'S WALK
CATHERINE WHEEL YD
LITTLE ST JAMES'S ST
SUDAN
RUSSELL CT
CLEVELAND ROW
Spencer House Mus
PALL MALL
Marlborough House
MARLBOROUGH RD
St James's Palace
Clarence House
STABLE YD RD
Lancaster House
WATERLOO PLACE
Waterloo Gdns
CARLTON HOUSE TERRACE
CARLTON GARDENS
Royal Coll of Pathologists
ICA
National Portrait Gallery (Annexe)
Admiralty Arch
Old Admiralty Bldgs Offices
Govt Offices
Horse Guards Parade (Site of Trooping of the Colour)
Banqueting House
Royal United Services Museum
Treasury Buildings
Cabinet Off
WHITEHALL
CRAIG'S CT
Downing St
Foreign, Commonwealth & Home Offices
KING CHARLES ST
Cabinet War Rooms & Churchill Mus
Govt Offices
A3214
GREAT GEORGE ST
THE MALL
(CLOSED TO TRAFFIC ON SUNDAYS)
SW1
Refreshment House
Duck Island
HORSE GUARDS ROAD
Diana, Princess of Wales Memorial Walk
St James's Park Lake
St James's Park
Lodge
Queen Victoria Memorial
Site of Changing of the Guard
BIRDCAGE WALK
Wellington Barracks
The Guards Museum
OLD QUEEN STREET
LEWISHAM STREET
DARTMOUTH ST
ANNE'S GATE
QUEEN
Capital Sh Ctrs
CARTERET ST
Home Office
PARKER ST
MATTHEW
Methodist Central Hall
STOREY'S GATE
Queen Elizabeth II Con Ctr
LITTLE SANCTUARY
LITTLE GEORGE ST
A302
Parliament Square
Guildhall
BROAD SANCTUARY
TOTHILL STREET
BROADWAY
PETTY FRANCE
St James's Park
DACRE ST
DEAN FARRAR ST
THE SANCTUARY
Westminster Abbey
Chapter House & Jewel Tower
DEAN'S YARD
B326
BUCKINGHAM GATE
B323
SWAZILAND
MACEDONIA
ALBANIA
ALBANY CT
PALMER ST
VANDON ST
VANDON CT
CAXTON STREET
Caxton Hall
STAFFORD PL
CATHERINE PLACE
BUCKINGHAM PLACE
WILFRED STREET
PALACE
Westminster

240
A
B
C
D
SEVEN DIALS
EARLHAM ST
SHELTON ST
MONMOUTH ST
MERCER STREET
LANGLEY ST
Film Sch
LONG ACRE
Covent Garden
Royal Ballet Sch
BOW STREET
Royal Opera House
JAMES ST
FLORAL STREET
RUSSELL ST
WELLINGTON ST
CATHERINE ST
TAVISTOCK ST
The Waldorf
ALDWYCH
ALDWICH HOUSE
INDIA
AUSTRALIA
Govt Office
MONTREAL PL
MELBOURNE PLACE
A4
A4200
Strand
King's College
SURREY STREET
STRAND LANE
WC2
TEMPLE PL
Courtauld Inst of Art
Somerset House
A301
LANCASTER PLACE
30
Templ Pier
Thames Police Station
River Bus Route
WATERLOO BRIDGE
Savoy Pier
WEST ST
81
A401
CHARING CROSS ROAD
LITCHFIELD STREET
SANDRINGHAM FLATS
TOWER ST
AB404
UPPER ST MARTIN'S LANE
WELLINGTON CT
SLINGSBY PL
ROSE ST
CONDUIT CT
BANBURY CT
LANGLEY CT
B402
GREAT NEWPORT ST
NEWPORT CT
NEWPORT PL
6
LTL NWPT ST
Leicester Square
LEICESTER CT
CRANBOURN ST
BEAR ST
LEICESTER ST
HUNT'S COURT
CECIL CT
ST MARTIN'S CT
ST MARTIN'S LANE
GARRICK ST
GARRICK YD
NEW ROW
GOODWINS CT
HOP GDNS
BEDFORDBURY
MAYS CT
BRYDGES PL
DAVEY'S CT
BEDFORD CT
Channel 5
Apple
Old Covent Garden
KING STREET
INIGO PL
HENRIETTA ST
BEDFORD STREET
SUSSEX MANSIONS
MAIDEN LANE
SOUTHAMPTON ST
COVENT GDN
Jubilee
London Transport Mus
EXETER ST
BURLEIGH ST
HARLEQUIN CT
STRAND
SAVOY ROW
SAVOY STREET
SAVOY STEPS
SAVOY WAY
SAVOY HILL
Office
The Savoy
CARTING LANE
SAVOY PLACE
BULL INN CT
LUMLEY CT
TURNER HO
EXCHANGE CT
CHANDOS PLACE
AGAR ST
ZIMBABWE
IVYBRIDGE LA
ADAM ST
ADELPHI TERR
JOHN ADAM STREET
ROBERT ST
LWR ROBERT ST
YORK BLDGS
DURHAM HO ST
GEORGE CT
YORK PL
BUCKINGHAM ST
VILLIERS ST
WATERGATE WALK
Victoria Embankment Gardens
VICTORIA EMBANKMENT
Cleopatra's Needle
Carlton TV
Liby
IRVING ST
LONG'S CT
ST MARTIN'S ST
5
National Portrait Gallery
National Gallery
WILLIAM IV ST
ADELAIDE ST
The Courtyard Mkt
ST MARTIN'S PLACE
DUNCANNON ST
SOUTH AFRICA
Fountains
Nelson's Mon
Charing Cross
Charing Cross Station
Embankment
Bndstd
TRAFALGAR SQ
COCKSPUR ST
COCKSPUR CT
SPRING GARDENS
UGANDA
4
Admiralty Arch
NORTHUMBERLAND AVE
NORTHUMBERLAND ST
CORNER HOUSE
CRAVEN STREET
CRAVEN PAS
HUNGERFORD LA
EMBANKMENT PL
THE ARCHES
A400
Embankment Pier
City of Westminster
Lambeth
Festival Pier (South Bank)
Riverside Wlk
National Film Theatre
Queen Elizabeth Hall & Purcell Room
Hayward Gallery
Royal Festival Hall
GOLDEN JUBILEE FOOTBRIDGES
Govt Offices
CRAIG'S CT
NIGERIA
GREAT SCOTLAND YD
SCOTLAND PLACE
WHITEHALL PLACE
A3212
WHITEHALL
249
Old Admiralty Bldgs Offices
Horse Guards Parade (Site of Trooping of the Colour)
3
WHITEHALL CT
Thames Path
HUNGERFORD BRIDGE
South Bank
CONCERT HALL APPROACH
BELVEDERE ROAD
SUTTON WLK
Shell Ctr
HORSE GUARDS AVE
Banqueting House
Royal United Services Museum
WHITEHALL GDNS
Whitehall Stairs
80
HORSE GUARDS ROAD
Treasury Buildings
Cabinet Off
Downing St
London Eye
Jubilee Gdns
Waterloo Millennium Pier
A3200
CHICHELEY ST
RICHMOND TERR
2
Foreign, Commonwealth & Home Offices
Cenotaph
PARLIAMENT ST
KING CHARLES ST
DERBY GATE
CANON ROW
Premier League Hall of Fame
Old County Hall
YORK ROAD
LEAKE ST
Waterl Internati
Cabinet War Rooms & Churchill Mus
River Bus Route
Westminster Pier
Westminster
A3211
London Aquarium
ADDINGTON ST
A3214 GREAT GEORGE ST
BRIDGE STREET
A302 WESTMINSTER BR RD
A23
WESTMINSTER BRIDGE
STOREY'S GATE
PARKER ST
1
Queen Elizabeth II Con Ctr
LITTLE SANCTUARY
LITTLE GEORGE ST
A302
Parliament Square
Guildhall
ST MARGARET ST
New Palace Yard
Big Ben
Florence Nightingale Museum
Methodist Central Hall
BROAD SANCTUARY
THE SANCTUARY
Westminster Abbey Chapter House & Jewel Tower
Old Palace Yard
Houses of Parliament
260
LAMBETH
A3036
UPPER MARSH
CANTERBURY HOUSE
ROYAL STREET
STANGATE
B326
DEAN'S YARD
LITTLE CLOISTERS
LITTLE DEANS YD
St Thomas' Hospl

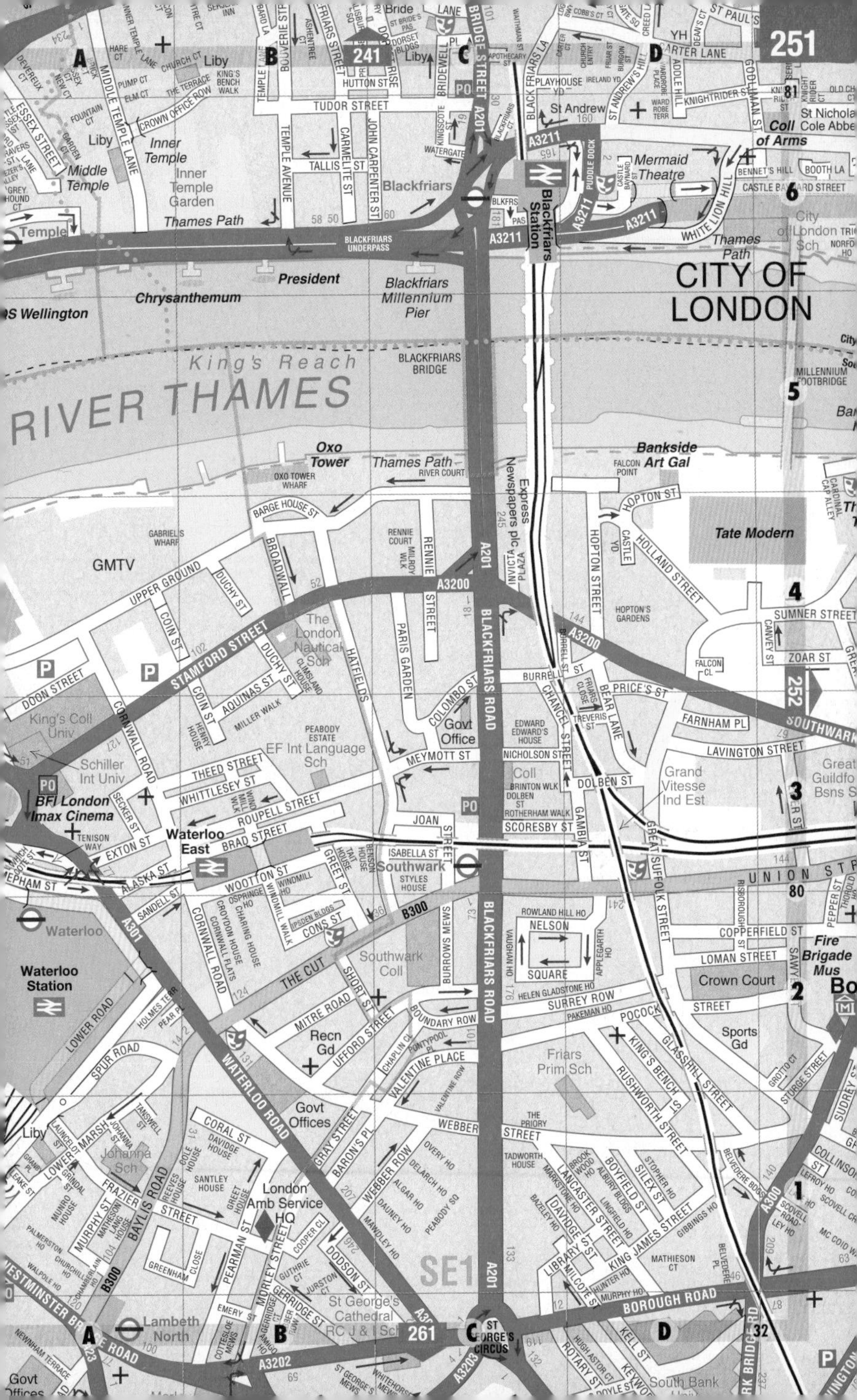
RIVER THAMES
King's Reach
CITY OF LONDON
Blackfriars Station
Blackfriars Millennium Pier
BLACKFRIARS BRIDGE
Inner Temple
Middle Temple
Inner Temple Garden
Thames Path
President
Chrysanthemum
Oxo Tower
Bankside Art Gal
Tate Modern
GMTV
Mermaid Theatre
Coll of Arms
MILLENNIUM FOOTBRIDGE
BLACKFRIARS ROAD
STAMFORD STREET
UPPER GROUND
UNION STREET
THE CUT
WATERLOO ROAD
BOROUGH ROAD
Waterloo Station
Waterloo East
Southwark
Lambeth North
BFI London Imax Cinema
King's Coll Univ
Schiller Int Univ
EF Int Language Sch
Southwark Coll
Crown Court
Fire Brigade Mus
St George's Cathedral RC J & I Sch
London Amb Service HQ
Friars Prim Sch
Govt Offices
SE1
ST GEORGE'S CIRCUS
241
252
261
A
B
C
D
1
2
3
4
5
6

242
A
B
C
D
81
6
5
4
3
80
2
1
32
WATLING STREET
Mansion House
CANNON STREET
QUEEN VICTORIA STREET
St Nicholas Cole Abbey
Coll of Arms
KNIGHTRIDER ST
OLD CHANGE CT
DISTAFF LA
FRIDAY ST
BREAD ST
GODLIMAN ST
ADDLE HILL
BENNET'S HILL
BOOTH LA
LAMBETH HILL
CASTLE BAYNARD STREET
WHITE LION HILL
Thames Path
City of London Sch
TRIG LA
HIGH TIMBER ST
NORFOLK HO
STEW LANE
QUEEN'S QUAY
QUEENHITHE
UPPER THAMES STREET
A300
QUEEN ST PL
GARLICK HILL
HUGGIN HILL
LITTLE TRINITY LA
St James
COLLEGE STREET
CLOAK LANE
St Michael
DOWGATE HILL
Cannon Street
Cannon Street Station
WALBROOK
St Stephen Walbrook
St Mary Woolnoth
LOMBARD STREET
ABCHURCH LA
St Mary
NICHOLAS LANE
KING WILLIAM STREET
CLEMENT'S LANE
St Clement
St Edmund
BUSH LANE
SUFFOLK LANE
LAURENCE POUNTNEY HILL
MARTIN LANE
ARTHUR ST
The Monument
FISH ST H
A3211
A10
COUSIN LANE
ALLHALLOWS LA
ANGEL PASS
SWAN LANE
St Magnus the Martyr
30
CITY OF LONDON
Queenhithe Stairs
Southwark Bridge Stairs
City of London
Southwark
MILLENNIUM FOOTBRIDGE
Bankside Pier
SOUTHWARK BRIDGE
Princess Elizabeth
River Bus Route
Swan Lane Pier
LONDON BRIDGE
BANKSIDE
The Globe Theatre
Tate Modern
NEW GLOBE WLK
BEAR GDNS
ROSE ALLEY
The Financial Times Ltd
Shakespeare's Globe Theatre (site of)
PARK STREET
Bear Gardens Mus
EMERSON ST
Winchester Palace
The Golden Hinde
CLINK ST
Vinopolis
Thames Path
Old London Bridge (site of)
SUMNER STREET
CANVEY ST
ZOAR ST
GREAT GUILDFORD STREET
SUMNER BLDGS
CONGO (HON CONSUL)
ANCHOR TERRACE
OLD THEATRE CT
PORTER ST
PERKINS SQUARE
GATEHOUSE SQ
SOUTHWARK BRIDGE ROAD
BANK END
Riverside Workshops
PARK STREET
MAIDEN LANE
LUCY BROWN HO
WINCHESTER SQ
WINCHESTER WLK
STONEY STREET
CATHEDRAL ST
Southwark Cathedral
MONTAGUE CL
Borough
London Bridge
TOOLEY ST
DUKE ST HILL
A200
A3
RAILWAY APPROACH
LONDON BR ST
London Bridge Station
FALCON
251
FARNHAM PL
SOUTHWARK STREET
LAVINGTON STREET
PEABODY ESTATE
Hotels
Bramah Mus
THRALE ST
REDCROSS WAY
A3200
BOROUGH HIGH STREET
ST THOMAS STREET
Grand Vitesse Ind Est
Great Guildford Bsns Sq
EWER ST
KEPPEL ROW
WARDENS GR
AMERICA ST
CROWNE HO
FLATIRON SQ
OMEARA ST
TRIANGLE CT
Coll
KING'S HEAD YD
Guy's Hospl Sch
CALVERT'S BUILDINGS
ST MARGARET'S COURT
MAIDSTONE BLDGS
TALBOT YD
QUEEN'S HEAD YD
KENTISH BLDGS
Guy's Hospl
UNION STREET
B300
FLATIRON YD
REDCROSS WAY
AYRES STREET
Cathedral Sch of St Saviour & St Mary Overie Prim Sch
St Joseph's RC Prim Sch
GREAT MAZE POND
RISBOROUGH ST
PEPPER ST
COPPERFIELD ST
LOMAN STREET
SAWYER ST
Crown Court
Fire Brigade Mus
The Borough
DOYCE ST
QUILP ST
A3201
MARSHALSEA ROAD
LITTLE DORRIT CT
BABINGTON HOUSE
Little Dorrit Park
NEWCOMEN STREET
MERMAID CT
CHAPEL CT
TENNIS STREET
Liby
ANGEL PL
Govt Offices
City Banking Co
SNOWSFIELDS
Sports Gd
GLASSHILL STREET
ILFRACOMBE FLATS
MINT ST
TRUNDLE ST
WELLER ST
DOUGLAS BUILDINGS
GAITSKELL WAY
LANT STREET
SUDREY ST
BITTERN ST
TOULMIN ST
PICKWICK STREET
Charles Dickens Prim Sch
Borough
CROSBY ROW
PORLOCK ST
Beormund Prim Sch
KIPLING STREET
GUY STREET
WESTON STREET
LOCKYER ST
SE1
A2
A2198
SILVESTER ST
GREAT SUFFOLK STREET
COLLINSON
STONES END ST
TRINITY ST
SWAN STREET
COLE STREET
HORSEMONGERS MEWS
NEBRASKA STREET
STERRY ST
PILGRIMAGE STREET
HANKEY PLACE
LONG LANE
A3202
A300
Tabard Gardens
KING'S PL
TRIO PLACE
City Ct
GLOBE ST
GREAT DOVER STREET
TABARD STREET
MANCIPLE STREET
STAPLE STREET
B240
NEWINGTON CAUSEWAY
Inner London & Southwark Crown Cts
GLOUCESTER CT
TRINITY STREET
MERRICK SQUARE
BECKET ST
Fball Gd
BOROUGH ROAD
262

A
B
C
D
243
EC3
FENCHURCH AV
FENCHURCH STREET
Fenchurch Street Station
MINORIES
MANSEL STREET
PRESCOT ST
ROYAL MINT ST
St Margaret Pattens
GREAT TOWER STREET
St Olave's
PEPYS STREET
Tower Hill
London Wall
Tower Gateway
LOWER THAMES ST
BYWARD ST
TOWER HILL A3211
Trinity Sq Gdns
All-Hallows
Custom House
St Peter ad Vincula
Royal Fusiliers Mus
The Tower
The Royal Armouries
St John's Chapel
EAST SMITHFIELD
E1
West Dock
East Dock
St Katharine Docks
Ivory House
ST KATHARINE'S WAY
TOWER BR APPROACH A100
RIVER THAMES
Pontoon
Tower Stairs
Tower Millennium Pier
Traitors Gate
Thames Path
London Bridge City Pier
River Bus Route
HMS Belfast
TOWER BRIDGE
Upper Pool
Jetty
St Katharine's Pier
Dock Entrance
West India Dock Pier 4km
London City Airport 11km
Greenwich Pier 5km
Horselydown Old Stairs
Butler's Wharf Pier
Hay's Galleria
Crown Court
Britain at War Experience
The Scoop
City Hall
London Bridge City Park
Unicorn
Lambeth Tertiary Coll (Tower Bridge Centre)
TOOLEY STREET
A200
TOWER BRIDGE RD
SHAD THAMES
Wharves
Design Museum
Glass House
CRUCIFIX LANE
Snowsfields Prim Sch
Leathermarket Com Park
Leathermarket Gdns
The Fashion & Design Museum
BERMONDSEY STREET
LEATHERMARKET ST
Tower Bridge Prim Sch
BERMONDSEY
JAMAICA ROAD
DRUID STREET
MILLSTREAM RD
St Joseph's RC Jun & Inf
Tenn Cts
Caledonian Market
ABBEY STREET
263
118
1
2
3
4
5
6
80
81

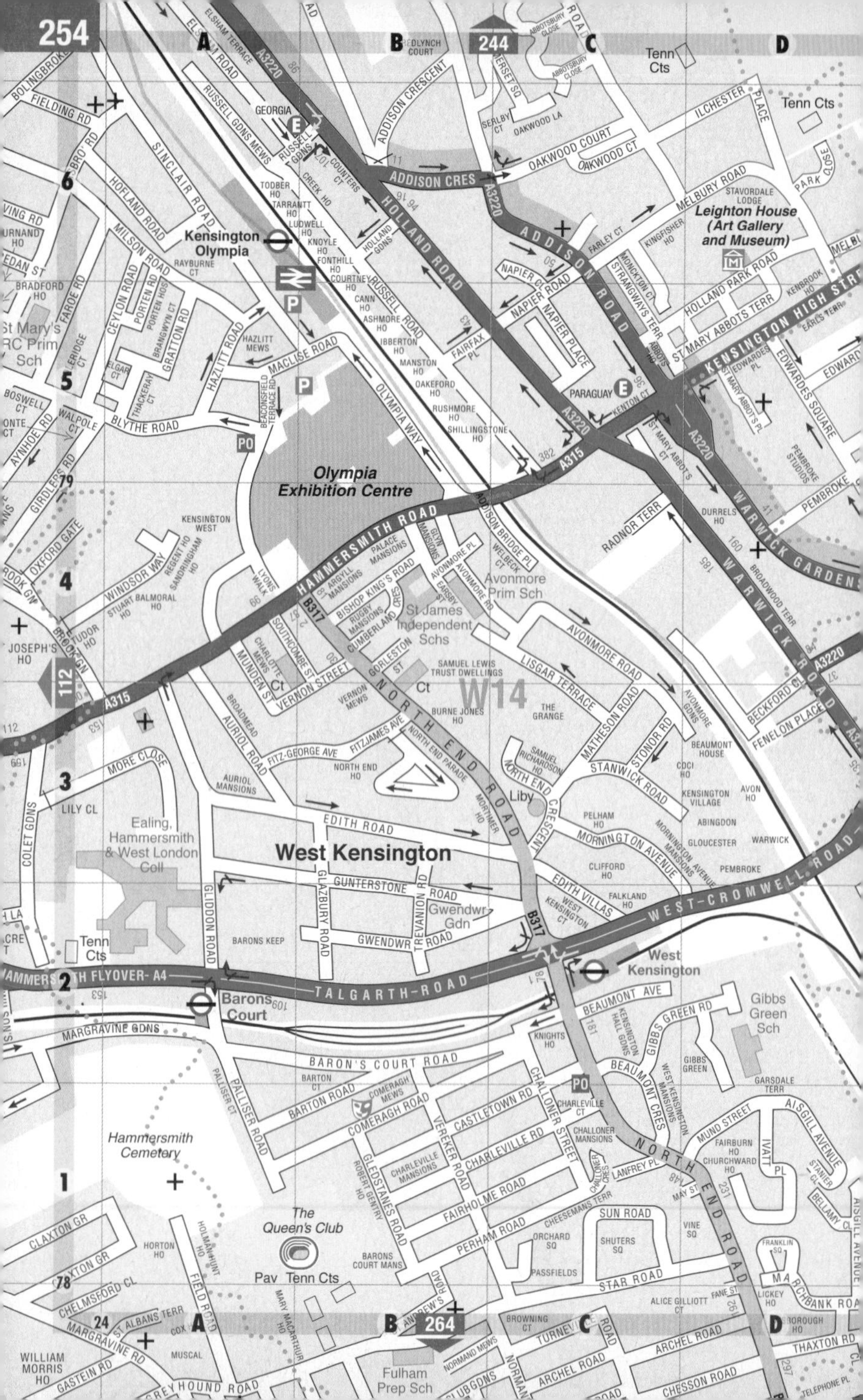

Kensington Olympia
Olympia Exhibition Centre
Leighton House (Art Gallery and Museum)
West Kensington
W14
Hammersmith Cemetery
The Queen's Club
Ealing, Hammersmith & West London Coll
HAMMERSMITH ROAD
HOLLAND ROAD
ADDISON ROAD
NORTH END ROAD
TALGARTH ROAD
WEST CROMWELL ROAD
WARWICK ROAD
KENSINGTON HIGH STREET

244
112
264

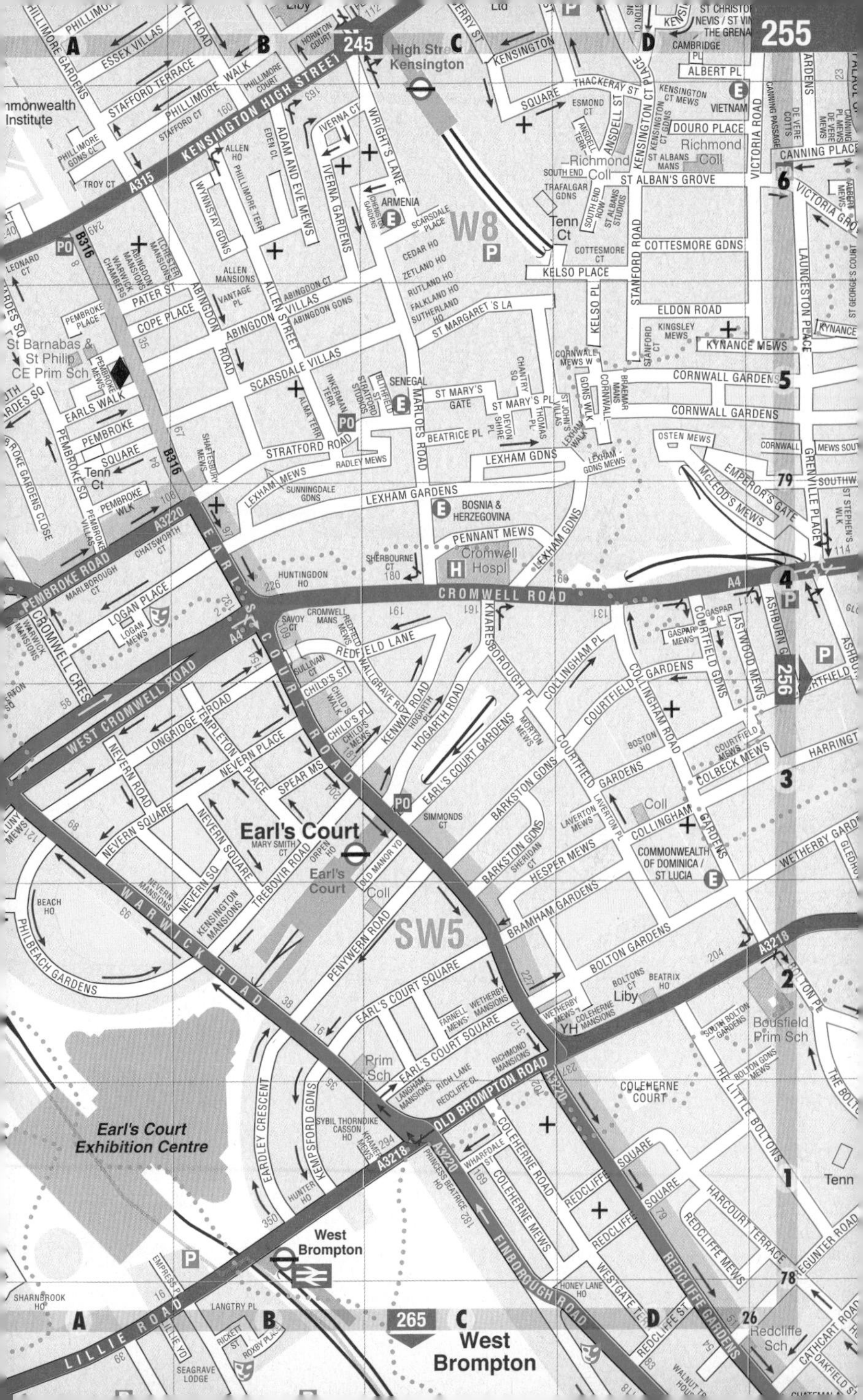
A
B
C
D
245
High Street Kensington
Commonwealth Institute
PHILLIMORE GARDENS
ESSEX VILLAS
STAFFORD TERRACE
PHILLIMORE WALK
KENSINGTON HIGH STREET
A315
HORNTON COURT
PHILLIMORE COURT
ADAM AND EVE MEWS
WRIGHT'S LANE
IVERNA CT
IVERNA GARDENS
KENSINGTON SQUARE
THACKERAY ST
ESMOND CT
ANSDELL ST
KENSINGTON CT PLACE
CAMBRIDGE PL
ALBERT PL
KENSINGTON CT MEWS
VIETNAM
DOURO PLACE
Richmond Coll
VICTORIA ROAD
CANNING PASSAGE
DE VERE COTTS
CANNING PLACE
ST ALBANS MANS
SOUTH END
ST ALBAN'S GROVE
TRAFALGAR GDNS
SOUTH END ROW
ST ALBANS STUDIOS
Tenn Ct
W8
COTTESMORE CT
COTTESMORE GDNS
KELSO PLACE
KELSO PL
STANFORD ROAD
ELDON ROAD
KINGSLEY MEWS
KYNANCE MEWS
KYNANCE PL
LAUNCESTON PLACE
VICTORIA GROVE
ARMENIA
SCARSDALE PLACE
CEDAR HO
ZETLAND HO
RUTLAND HO
FALKLAND HO
SUTHERLAND HO
ST MARGARET'S LA
TROY CT
ALLEN HO
PHILLIMORE TERR
WYNNSTAY GDNS
B316
ABINGDON MANSIONS
WARWICK CHAMBERS
ALLEN MANSIONS
PATER ST
VANTAGE PL
ABINGDON CT
ABINGDON VILLAS
ABINGDON GDNS
ALLEN STREET
ABINGDON ROAD
PEMBROKE PLACE
COPE PLACE
St Barnabas & St Philip CE Prim Sch
SCARSDALE VILLAS
EARLS WALK
PEMBROKE SQ
PEMBROKE SQUARE
PEMBROKE GARDENS CLOSE
PEMBROKE VILLAS
PEMBROKE WLK
INKERMAN TERR
ALMA TERR
STRATFORD STUDIOS
SENEGAL
MARLOES ROAD
ST MARY'S GATE
ST MARY'S PL
CHANTRY SQ
CORNWALL MEWS W
CORNWALL GDNS WLK
CORNWALL GARDENS
BRAEMAR MANS
ST JOHN'S VILLAS
LEXHAM WALK
BEATRICE PL
DEVONSHIRE PL
THOMAS PL
STRATFORD ROAD
RADLEY MEWS
LEXHAM MEWS
LEXHAM GDNS
LEXHAM GARDENS
LEXHAM GDNS MEWS
SUNNINGDALE GDNS
OSTEN MEWS
EMPEROR'S GATE
McLEOD'S MEWS
GRENVILLE PLACE
ST STEPHEN'S WLK
BOSNIA & HERZEGOVINA
PENNANT MEWS
Cromwell Hospl
SHERBOURNE CT
HUNTINGDON HO
CHATSWORTH CT
PEMBROKE ROAD
A3220
EARL'S COURT ROAD
CROMWELL ROAD
A4
MARLBOROUGH CT
LOGAN PLACE
LOGAN MEWS
CROMWELL CRES
WARWICK MANSIONS
WEST CROMWELL ROAD
SAVOY CT
CROMWELL MANS
REDFIELD LANE
SULLIVAN CT
CHILD'S ST
CHILD'S WALK
CHILD'S PL
CHILD'S MEWS
WALLGRAVE RD
KENWAY ROAD
HOGARTH PL
HOGARTH ROAD
KNARESBOROUGH PL
EARL'S COURT GARDENS
MORTON MEWS
COLLINGHAM PL
COLLINGHAM GARDENS
COLLINGHAM ROAD
COURTFIELD GARDENS
COURTFIELD GDNS
GASPAR CL
GASPAR MEWS
ASTWOOD MEWS
ASHBURN G
256
BOSTON HO
COURTFIELD MEWS
COLBECK MEWS
HARRINGTON
LONGRIDGE ROAD
TEMPLETON PLACE
NEVERN PLACE
NEVERN ROAD
SPEAR MS
PO
SIMMONDS CT
BARKSTON GDNS
LAVERTON MEWS
LAVERTON PL
Coll
COLLINGHAM GARDENS
Earl's Court
MARY SMITH CT
NEVERN SQUARE
TREBOVIR ROAD
ORPEN HO
OLD MANOR YD
HESPER MEWS
SHERIDAN CT
COMMONWEALTH OF DOMINICA / ST LUCIA
WETHERBY GARDENS
NEVERN MANSIONS
NEVERN SQ
KENSINGTON MANSIONS
BEACH HO
WARWICK ROAD
PENYWERN ROAD
SW5
BRAMHAM GARDENS
BOLTON GARDENS
A3218
PHILBEACH GARDENS
EARL'S COURT SQUARE
WETHERBY MANSIONS
FARNELL MEWS
BOLTONS CT
BEATRIX HO
Liby
WETHERBY MEWS
COLEHERNE MANSIONS
YH
SOUTH BOLTON GARDENS
Bousfield Prim Sch
BOLTON GDNS MEWS
THE LITTLE BOLTONS
Prim Sch
LANGHAM MANSIONS
RICH LANE
REDCLIFFE CL
RICHMOND MANSIONS
OLD BROMPTON ROAD
COLEHERNE COURT
Earl's Court Exhibition Centre
EARDLEY CRESCENT
KEMPSFORD GDNS
SYBIL THORNDIKE CASSON HO
KRAMER MEWS
HUNTER HO
PRINCESS BEATRICE HO
WHARFDALE ST
COLEHERNE ROAD
COLEHERNE MEWS
REDCLIFFE SQUARE
HARCOURT TERRACE
REDCLIFFE MEWS
Tenn
West Brompton
FINBOROUGH ROAD
HONEY LANE HO
WESTGATE TER
REDCLIFFE GARDENS
REDCLIFFE ST
SHARNBROOK HO
EMPRESS PL
LANGTRY PL
LILLIE ROAD
RICKETT ST
ROXBY PLACE
SEAGRAVE LODGE
265
WALNUT TR HOUS
Redcliffe Sch
CATHCART ROAD
OAKFIELD ST
1
2
3
4
5
6

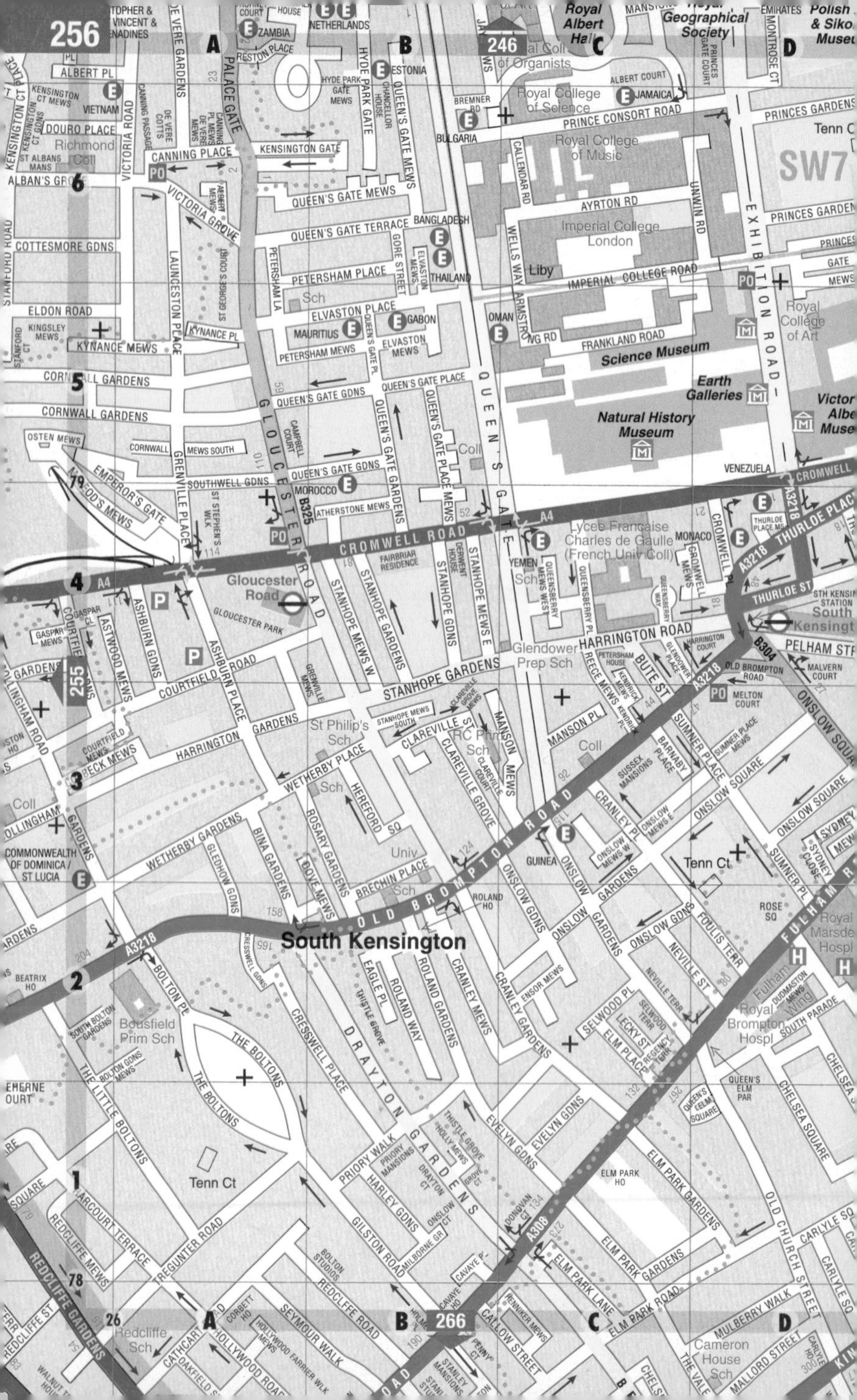
Royal Albert Hall
Royal Geographical Society
Royal College of Organists
Royal College of Science
Royal College of Music
Imperial College London
Science Museum
Earth Galleries
Natural History Museum
SW7
Royal College of Art
Lycee Francaise Charles de Gaulle (French Univ Coll)
Gloucester Road
South Kensington
Glendower Prep Sch
St Philip's Sch
Bousfield Prim Sch
Redcliffe Sch
Cameron House Sch
Royal Brompton Hospl
Royal Marsden Hospl
CROMWELL ROAD
OLD BROMPTON ROAD
GLOUCESTER ROAD
QUEEN'S GATE
EXHIBITION ROAD
PRINCE CONSORT ROAD
FULHAM ROAD
DRAYTON GARDENS
THE BOLTONS
REDCLIFFE GARDENS
246
255
266

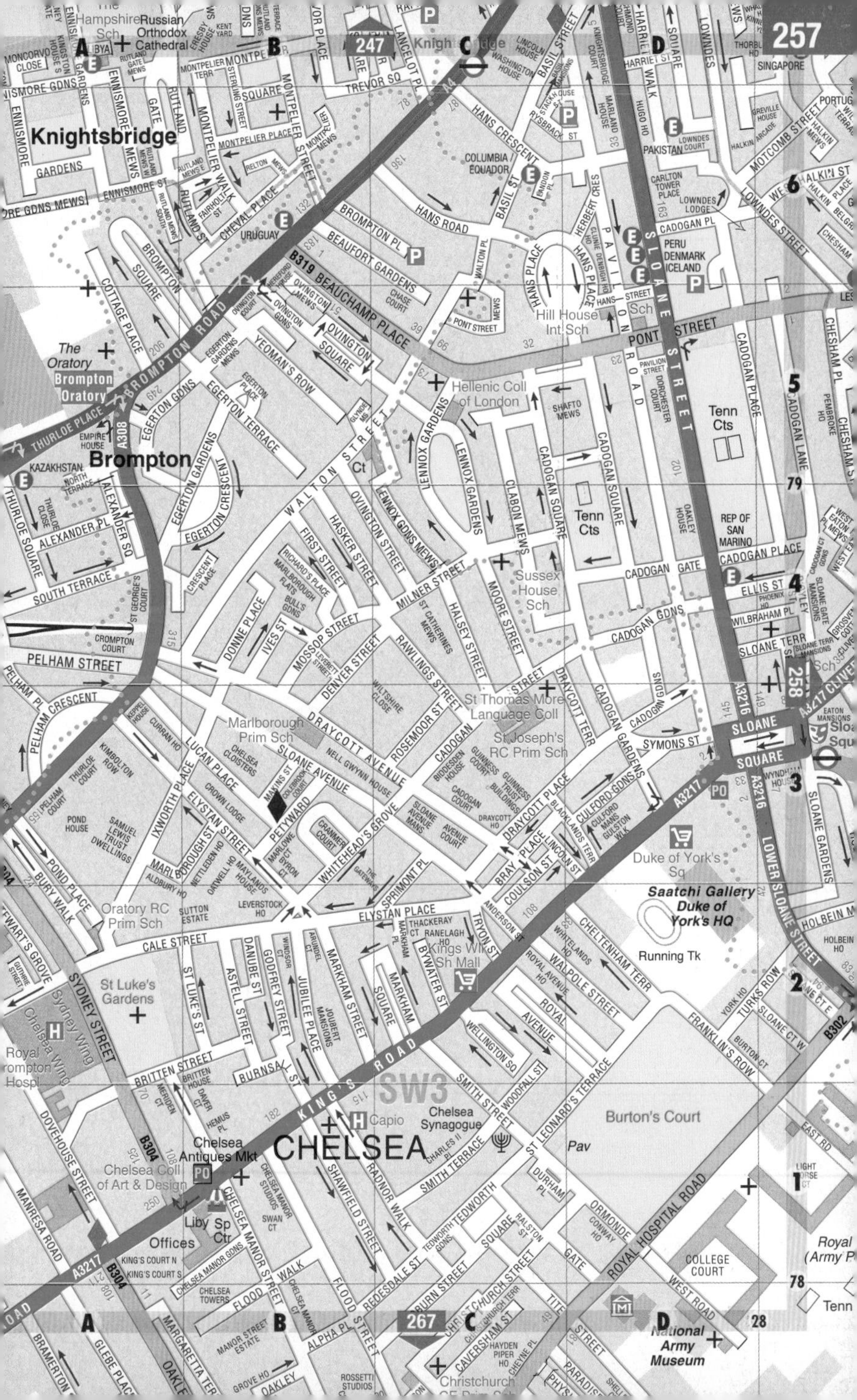
Knightsbridge
Brompton
CHELSEA
SW3
BROMPTON ROAD
KING'S ROAD
SLOANE STREET
SLOANE SQUARE
LOWER SLOANE STREET
PONT STREET
BEAUCHAMP PLACE
WALTON STREET
DRAYCOTT AVENUE
SLOANE AVENUE
FULHAM ROAD
SYDNEY STREET
ROYAL HOSPITAL ROAD
CADOGAN SQUARE
CADOGAN PLACE
HANS PLACE
HANS CRESCENT
HANS ROAD
PELHAM STREET
CALE STREET
ELYSTAN PLACE
The Oratory
Brompton Oratory
Russian Orthodox Cathedral
Hill House Int Sch
Hellenic Coll of London
Sussex House Sch
St Thomas More Language Coll
St Joseph's RC Prim Sch
Marlborough Prim Sch
Oratory RC Prim Sch
Duke of York's Sq
Saatchi Gallery Duke of York's HQ
Running Tk
Burton's Court
St Luke's Gardens
Royal Brompton Hospl
Chelsea Wing
Sydney Wing
Kings Wlk Sh Mall
Chelsea Synagogue
Capio
Chelsea Antiques Mkt
Chelsea Coll of Art & Design
Liby
Sp Ctr
Offices
National Army Museum
Christchurch
247
258
267

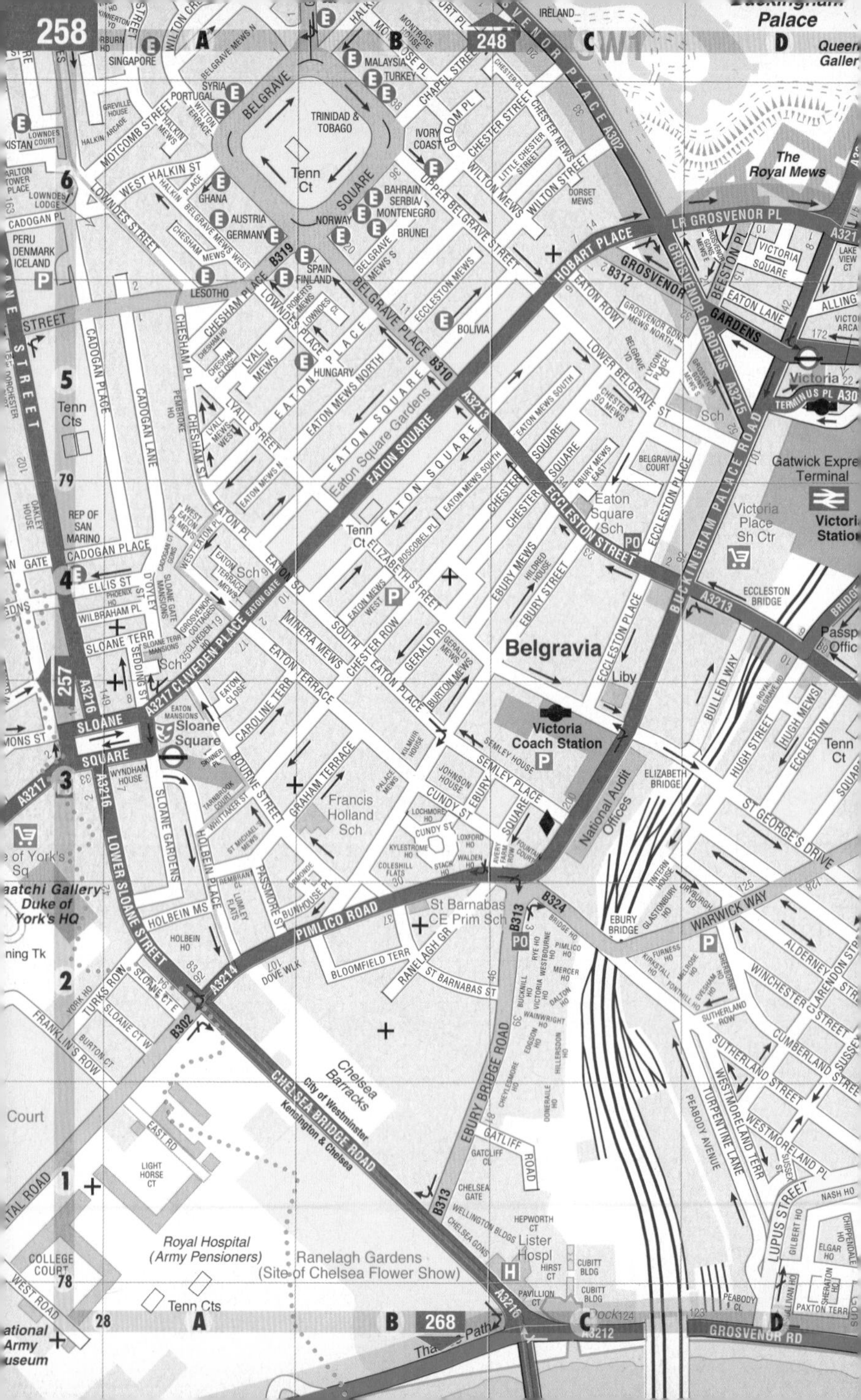
248
268
257
Buckingham Palace
Queen's Gallery
The Royal Mews
SW1
Belgravia
Victoria Coach Station
Victoria Station
Gatwick Express Terminal
Victoria Place Sh Ctr
Eaton Square Gardens
Sloane Square
Francis Holland Sch
St Barnabas CE Prim Sch
Chelsea Barracks
City of Westminster
Kensington & Chelsea
Royal Hospital (Army Pensioners)
Ranelagh Gardens (Site of Chelsea Flower Show)
Lister Hospl
National Audit Offices
Saatchi Gallery
Duke of York's HQ
National Army Museum
BELGRAVE SQUARE
EATON SQUARE
EATON PLACE
CHESTER SQUARE
ECCLESTON STREET
BUCKINGHAM PALACE ROAD
GROSVENOR GARDENS
GROSVENOR PLACE
HOBART PLACE
LOWER BELGRAVE ST
ELIZABETH STREET
EBURY STREET
CLIVEDEN PLACE
SLOANE SQUARE
LOWER SLOANE STREET
PIMLICO ROAD
CHELSEA BRIDGE ROAD
EBURY BRIDGE ROAD
GROSVENOR RD
WARWICK WAY
ST GEORGE'S DRIVE
LUPUS STREET
SLOANE STREET
CADOGAN PLACE
LOWNDES STREET
MOTCOMB STREET
WEST HALKIN ST
UPPER BELGRAVE STREET
BELGRAVE PLACE
CHESTER STREET
WILTON STREET
LR GROSVENOR PL

Wellington Barracks
The Guards Museum
249
Home Office
Capital Sh Ctrs
Methodist Central Hall
Westminster Abbey
Chapter House & Jewel Tower
St James's Park
Caxton Hall
New Scotland Yard
SW1
Westminster City Sch
Westminster City Hall
Westminster Coll
Westminster Cathedral
WESTMINSTER
Victoria Street
Buckingham Gate
Petty France
Broadway
Tothill Street
Great Smith Street
Horseferry Road
Vauxhall Bridge Road
Belgrave Road
Rochester Row
Vincent Square
Marsham Street
Millbank
The Grey Coat Hosp Sch
RHS (Lawrence Hall & Conf Ctr)
Channel 4 TV Corp
Govt Offices
Coroner's Court
St John's Gdns
RHS (Lindley Hall)
Tenn Cts
Pl Fld
Pav
The Gordon Hospl
Tate Britain
Chelsea Coll of Art & Design
Fairley House Sch
Pimlico
Westminster Cath RC Prim Sch
Pimlico Sch
Churchill Gardens Prim Sch
St Gabriel's CE Prim Sch
Dolphin Square
St George's Square Gdns
Lupus Street
Grosvenor Road
Thames Path
Wharves
Westminster Boating Base
Churchill Gardens Road
St George's Drive
Warwick Way
Bessborough Gdns
Ponsonby Place
Atterbury St
John Islip St
260
269
City of Westminster
Wandsworth
Lambeth

LAMBETH
Westminster Abbey
Chapter House & Jewel Tower
Old Palace Yard
Houses of Parliament
Victoria Tower
The Victoria Tower Gardens
St Thomas' Hospl
St Thomas's Hospital Medical School
Albert Embankment
Lambeth Palace
Mus of Garden History
Lambeth Pier
LAMBETH PALACE ROAD
Archbishop's Park
Westminster Abbey Choir Sch
Westminster Sch
GREAT COLLEGE STREET
GREAT PETER STREET
GREAT SMITH STREET
ABINGDON STREET
MILLBANK
St Johns Concert Hall
SMITH SQ
Govt Offices
ROMNEY ST
LAMBETH BRIDGE
MARSHAM STREET
St John's Gdns
PAGE STREET
THORNEY STREET
Offices
Fire Brigade Pier
Fire Brigade HQ
Police HQ
LAMBETH HIGH STREET
Recn Gd
Millbank Tower
RIVER THAMES
Thames Path
ALBERT EMBANKMENT
Millbank Millennium Pier
Tate Britain
JOHN ISLIP STREET
ATTERBURY ST
Chelsea Coll of Art & Design
PONSONBY PLACE
BESSBOROUGH GDNS
VAUXHALL BRIDGE
SALAMANCA STREET
Pedlers Park
BLACK PRINCE ROAD
JONATHAN STREET
TINWORTH ST
VAUXHALL WALK
GLASSHOUSE WALK
Gunhouse Stairs (site of)
Vauxhall
Vauxhall City Farm
Spring Gardens
Vauxhall Prim Sch
LAMBETH WALK
KENNINGTON LANE
Vauxhall Cross
Lilian Baylis Tech Sch
St Anne's RC Prim Sch
Westminster Bsns Sq
St Mark's CE Prim Sch
HARLEYFORD ROAD
DURHAM ST A3204
City of Westminster
Lambeth
Wandsworth

250
259
270

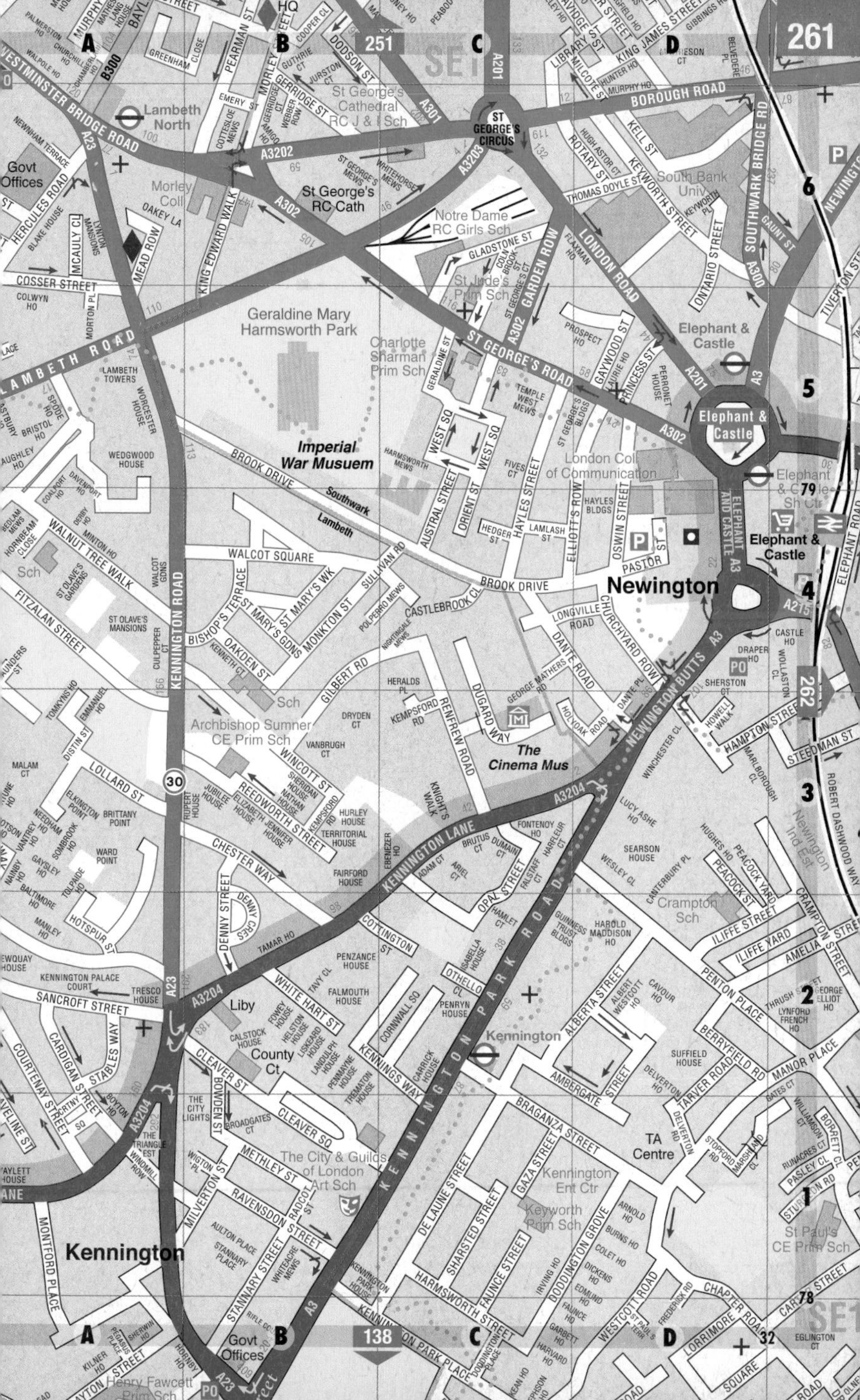

261
251
262
138
Lambeth North
St George's Circus
St George's Cathedral
St George's RC Cath
Geraldine Mary Harmsworth Park
Imperial War Museum
Elephant & Castle
Newington
The Cinema Mus
Kennington
WESTMINSTER BRIDGE ROAD
LAMBETH ROAD
BOROUGH ROAD
ST GEORGE'S ROAD
LONDON ROAD
KENNINGTON ROAD
KENNINGTON LANE
KENNINGTON PARK ROAD
NEWINGTON BUTTS
BROOK DRIVE

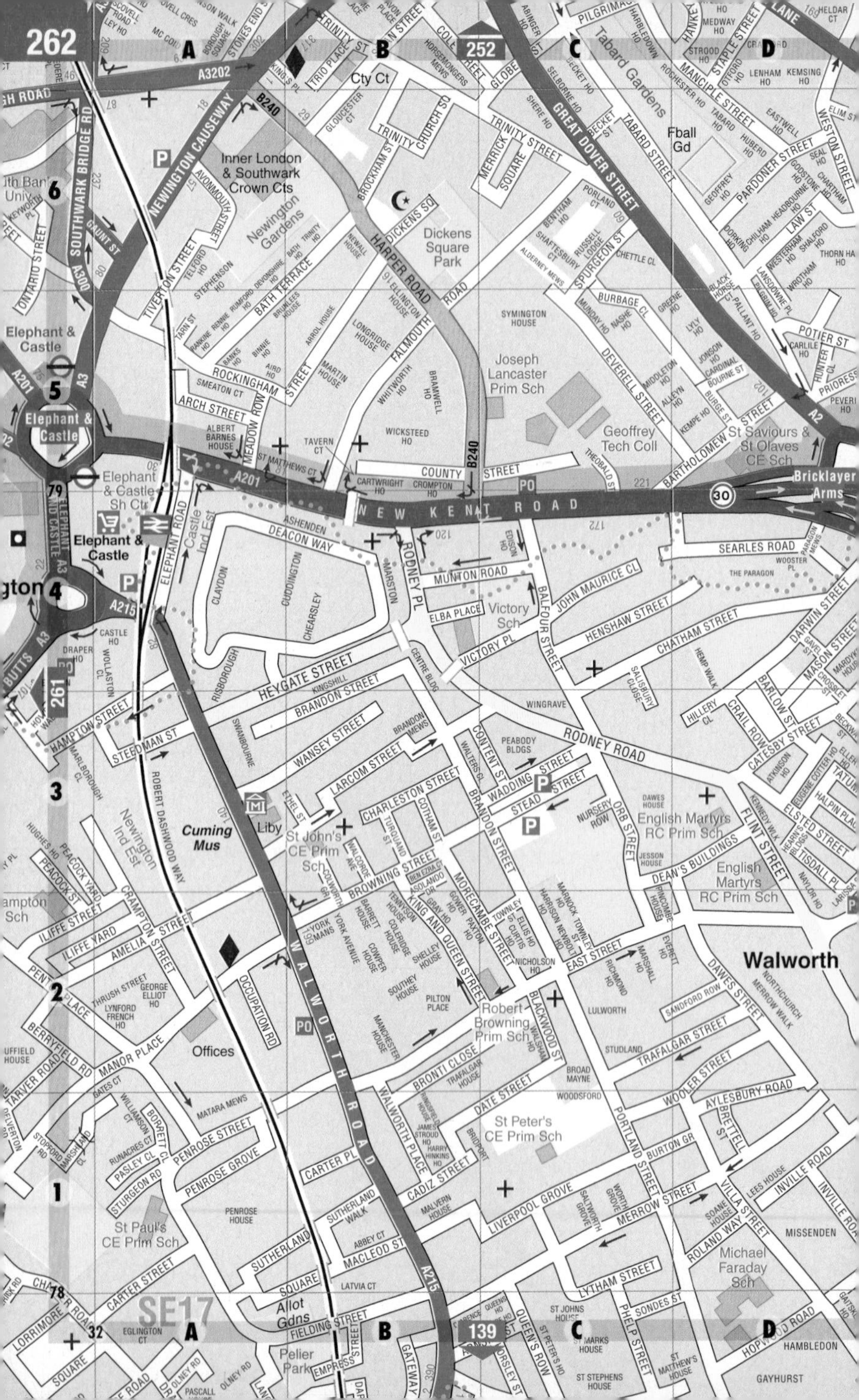

A
B
C
D
252
Tabard Gardens
Fball Gd
Inner London & Southwark Crown Cts
Newington Gardens
Dickens Square Park
Joseph Lancaster Prim Sch
Geoffrey Tech Coll
St Saviours & St Olaves CE Sch
Bricklayer Arms
Elephant & Castle
Elephant & Castle Sh Ctr
Castle Ind Est
NEW KENT ROAD
NEWINGTON CAUSEWAY
GREAT DOVER STREET
HARPER ROAD
WALWORTH ROAD
RODNEY ROAD
Victory Sch
Cuming Mus
Liby
St John's CE Prim Sch
Newington Ind Est
English Martyrs RC Prim Sch
Walworth
Robert Browning Prim Sch
St Peter's CE Prim Sch
Offices
St Paul's CE Prim Sch
Michael Faraday Sch
Allot Gdns
Pelier Park
SE17
139
261

253
A
B
C
D
Caledonian Market
BERMONDSEY SQ
TOWER BRIDGE ROAD
ABBEY STREET
A2198
B202
A2205
A2206
Southwark Coll (Grange Centre)
GRANGE ROAD
Grange Prim Sch
GRANGE WALK
GRANGE YARD
SPA ROAD
Liby
Bermondsey Spa Gdns
Alscot Rd Ind Est
Boutcher CE Prim Sch
Aylwin Girls Sch
ENID STREET
TA Ctr
Voyager Bsns
NECKINGER ESTATE
A100
TOWERGATE
PAGE'S WALK
MANDELA WAY
WILLOW WALK
DUNTON ROAD
B203
LYNTON ROAD
FORT ROAD
118
ROLLS ROAD
B204
OLD KENT ROAD
A2
Superstore
Amazonas
Surrey Square Jun & Inf Schs
SE17
Surrey Square Park
Walworth Sch
Burgess Park
SE5
SE 15
ALBANY ROAD
B214
TRAFALGAR AVENUE
B215
COBOURG ROAD
Cobourg Jun & Inf Sch
Tenn Cts
Pl Fld
LONCROFT ROAD
WAITE STREET
GLENGALL TERR
139
34
78
79
1
2
3
4
5
6

The Queen's Club
Pav
Tenn Cts
A
B
C
D
254
134
135
W6
SW6
FULHAM
HORTON HO
FIELD ROAD
BARONS COURT MANS
FAIRHOLME
CHEESEMANS
SUN ROAD
ORCHARD SQ
SHUTERS SQ
VINE SQ
PASSFIELDS
STAR ROAD
MARCHBANK ROAD
LICKEY HO
DESBOROUGH HO
THAXTON RD
TELEPHONE PL
B317
A3218
A3219
A219
A304
CHELMSFORD CL
MARGRAVINE RD
ST ALBANS TERR
COX HO
MUSCAL
WILLIAM MORRIS HO
STEIN RD
GREYHOUND ROAD
SPENCER MEWS
TASSO ROAD
KINNOUL ROAD
MUSARD ROAD
MARY MACARTHUR HO
ST ANDREW'S ROAD
Fulham Prep Sch
NORMAND MEWS
QUEEN'S CLUB GDNS
QUEEN'S CLUB GARDENS
BROWNING CT
TURNEVILLE ROAD
ALICE GILLIOTT CT
FANE ST
ARCHEL ROAD
CHESSON ROAD
NORMAND ROAD
BRAMBER ROAD
MULGRAVE RD
Normand Croft Com Sch
Normand Park
Bwg Gn
Liby
P
OAKLEY WLK
ADENEY CL
CRAMMOND CL
ABBEY GARDENS
WENTWORTH CT
PAYNES WLK
LAMPETER SQ
LAUNDRY RD
HUMBOLT ROAD
TASSO YD
DISBROWE ROAD
MOYLAN ROAD
St Augustine's RC Prim Sch
LILLIE ROAD MANS
LILLIE ROAD
BRECON ROAD
LINTAINE CL
ANCILL CL
CREFELD CL
CAROLINE WLK
BAYONNE RD
PURCELL CRES
TWYNHOLM MANS
TILTON ST
St John Lillie Prim Sch
DELAFORD STREET
BEAUFORT MEWS
GEORGE'S SQUARE
PEABODY ESTATE
CHESTNUT CT
CHESTNUT ALLEY
CLEM ATTLEE PAR
CHUTER EDE HO
STAFFORD CRIPPS HO
JIM GRIFFITHS HO
TOM WILLIAMS HO
HUGH GAITSKELL CL
ELLEN WILKINSON HO
MANNY HINWELL HO
MARGARET HERBISON HO
BARBARA CASTLE CL
HAROLD WILSON HO
COOMER PL
CROWTHER CL
HUGH DALTON AVE
HERBERT MORRISON HO
CLEM ATTLEE CT
FRANK BESWICK HO
FRANK SOSKICE HO
JOHN WHEATLEY HO
JOHN STRACHEY HO
DOUGLAS JOHNSTONE HO
MARGARET INGRAM CL
LEN FREEMAN PL
KENNETH YOUNGER HO
BUCKLER'S ALLEY
HALDANE ROAD
RYLSTON ROAD
JOHN SMITH AVE
GEORGE LINDGREN HO
EDITH SUMMERSKILL HO
NYE BEVAN HO
ST THOMAS'S WAY
TOURNAY ROAD
EPIRUS ROAD
Recn Ground
CHALDON ROAD
WILLIAMS CL
PELLANT ROAD
MENDORA ROAD
PROTHERO ROAD
ROCQUE CLYDE FLATS
MATON HO
ESTCOURT ROAD
HARTOPP POINT
CHASEMORE HO
DONNELLY CT
LANNOY POINT
BEDFORD PAS
STRODE ROAD
ROYAL PAR
Fulham Cross Sec Sch
St Thomas of Canterbury RC Prim Sch
MIRABEL ROAD
FABIAN ROAD
HARTISMERE ROAD
SHORROLDS ROAD
PALACE MEWS
HANNELL ROAD
DAWES ROAD
PO
AINTREE STREET
MUNSTER ROAD
ROSALINE ROAD
ROSALINE TERR
SHERBROOKE TERR
SHERBROOKE ROAD
VARNA ROAD
LETTERSTONE RD
SALISBURY MEWS
PARKVILLE ROAD
HOMESTEAD ROAD
GOATER'S ALLEY
GIRONDE ROAD
MABLETHORPE ROAD
ROWALLAN ROAD
ALLESTREE ROAD
ORBAIN ROAD
ST OLAF'S ROAD
ROSAVILLE ROAD
BROOKVILLE ROAD
MARVILLE ROAD
FILMER ROAD
BLOOM PARK RD
WHEATSHEAF TERR
BURNTHWAITE ROAD
LANCASTER CT
Cemetery
THE QUADRANGLE
BRONSART ROAD
KILMAINE ROAD
ST PETER'S TERR
REPORTON RD
KINGWOOD ROAD
WYFOLD ROAD
ATALANTA ST
BRANKSEA ST
MARRYAT SQ
THE CODA CTR
Henry Compton Sec Sch
FERNHURST RD
MUNSTER RESIDENCES
BISHOPS RD
KELVEDON RD
DARLAN ROAD
ARUNDEL MANSIONS
Kensington Prep Sch
CRAVEN LODGE
ROBERT OWEN HOUSE
CHILDERLEY ST
DANEHURST ST
CONNAUGHT MANS
St John's CE Prim Sch
FLORENCE MANS
HAZELWOOD MANSIONS
QUENINGTON MANSIONS
CHESILTON RD
RADIPOLE RD
LILYVILLE RD
WINCHENDON RD
CLONMEL RD
Al-Muntada Islamic Sch
EPPLE RD
FINLAY ST
LAMBROOK TERR
SIDBURY ST
WARDO AVE
GOWAN AVE
ROSTREVOR MANS
PENHURST MANS
AVONDALE MANS
DEEPDENE MANS
FILMER HO
FILMER MEWS
SWIFT ST
ROSTREVOR RD
FELDEN ST
ROSTREVOR MEWS
FULHAM RD
PURSERS CROSS RD
ST MAUR RD
WHITTINGSTALL RD
WHITTINGSTALL MANSIONS
BEACONSFIELD WLK
FULHAM PALACE RD
ELLERBY ST
THE COURTYARD
VERA RD
KIMBELL GDNS
PARK MANSIONS
COLEHILL LA
HORDER RD
BURNFOOT AVE
MIMOSA ST
CROOKHAM RD
DANCER RD
LETTICE ST
DONERAILE ST
EDGARLEY TERR
FIRTH GDNS
ELY COURT FLATS
WOODLAWN RD
RINGMER AVE
WALDEMAR AVENUE MANSIONS
COLEHILL GDNS
HESTERCOMBE AVE
DURRELL RD
WILSTON CT
CLARIDGE CT
WILLIAM BANFIELD HO
ARTHUR HENDERSON HOUSE
HEATHMAN'S RD
CLONCURRY ST
BISHOP'S PARK RD
BISHOP'S MANSIONS
BISHOP'S AVE
LALOR ST
WALDEMAR AVE
OXBERRY AVE
DORNCLIFFE RD
ETHEL RANKIN CT
FULHAM PARK
MUNSTER CT
MUSTOW PL
PLATO PL
ST DIONIS RD
GUION RD
DORIA
EDENHURST / DISCOMBE
LAUREL

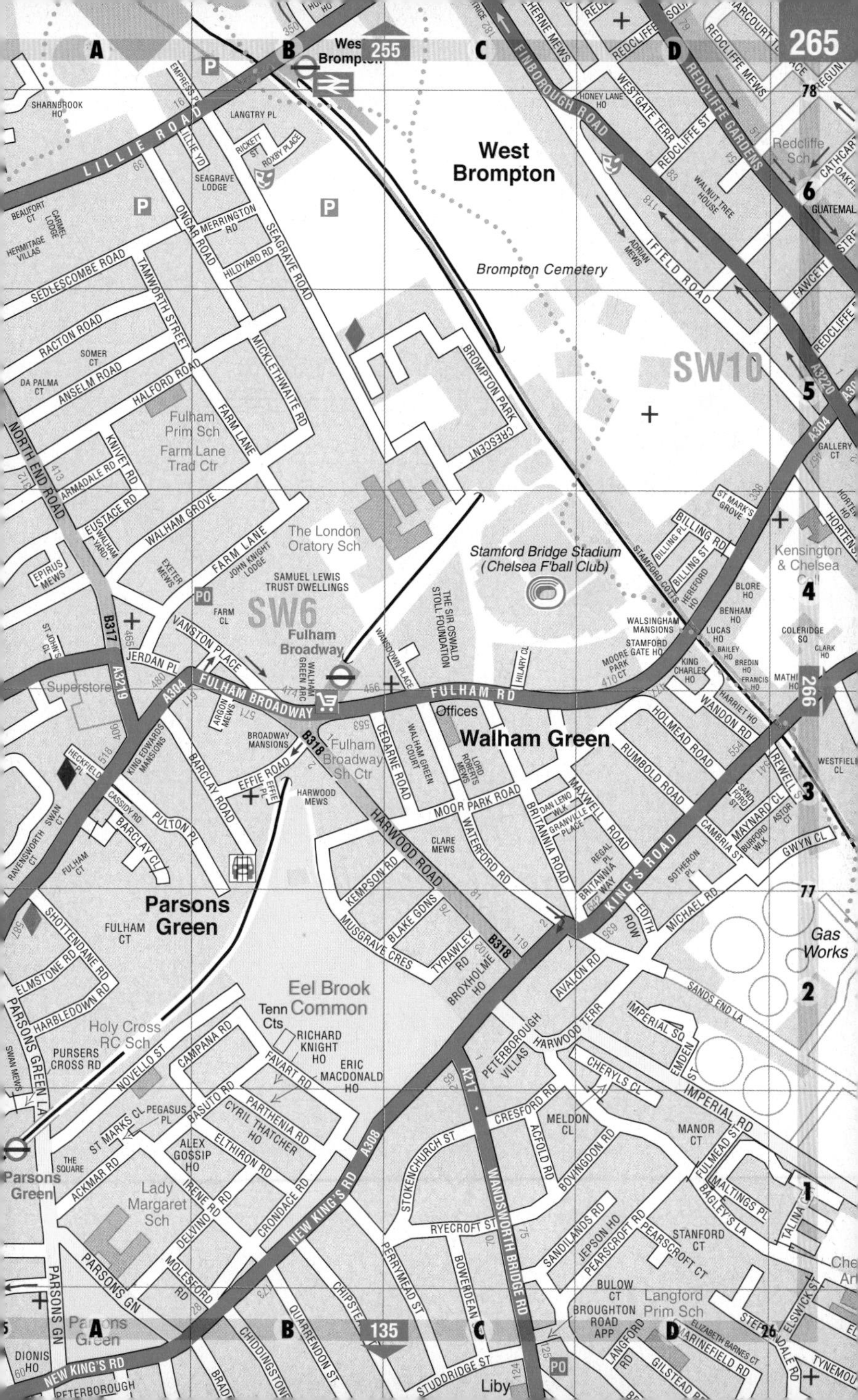
West Brompton
Brompton Cemetery
SW10
SW6
Stamford Bridge Stadium
(Chelsea F'ball Club)
Fulham Broadway
Walham Green
Parsons Green
Eel Brook Common
Gas Works
LILLIE ROAD
FULHAM BROADWAY
FULHAM RD
KING'S ROAD
NEW KING'S RD
WANDSWORTH BRIDGE RD
NORTH END ROAD
SEAGRAVE ROAD
FINBOROUGH ROAD
REDCLIFFE GARDENS
IFIELD ROAD
HARWOOD ROAD
IMPERIAL RD
PARSONS GREEN LA
The London Oratory Sch
Fulham Prim Sch
Farm Lane Trad Ctr
Holy Cross RC Sch
Lady Margaret Sch
Langford Prim Sch
Kensington & Chelsea Coll
Fulham Broadway Sh Ctr
Redcliffe Sch
255
266
135

A
B
C
D
256
136
265
6
5
4
3
2
1
78
77
26
SW10
TREGUNTER ROAD
GILSTON ROAD
ONSLOW CT
MILBORNE GR
BOLTON STUDIOS
REDCLIFFE ROAD
REDCLIFFE GARDENS
ELM PARK GARDENS
ELM PARK LANE
ELM PARK ROAD
CARLYLE SQ
MULBERRY WALK
MALLORD STREET
THE VALE
Cameron House Sch
Redcliffe Sch
CATHCART ROAD
HOLLYWOOD ROAD
SEYMOUR WALK
OAKFIELD ST
GUATEMALA STREET
CLIFTON GATE
Servite RC Prim Sch
FAWCETT
REDCLIFFE PL
FULHAM ROAD
NIGHTINGALE PL
NETHERTON GROVE
Chelsea & Westminster Hospl
CALLOW STREET
HENNIKER MEWS
STANLEY MANSIONS
STANLEY STUDIOS
WINTERTON PL
ELM PARK MANSIONS
THE SANDHILLS
PARK WALK
LIMERSTON STREET
CAMERA PL
CHELSEA PK GDNS
BEAUFORT
THE PORTICOS
Park Walk Prim Sch
GERTRUDE STREET
SHALCOMB ST
HOBURY ST
LAMONT ROAD
LANGTON STREET
KING'S ROAD
MILMAN'S STREET
ANN LANE
RILEY ST
BOWLING GREEN HO
BRUNEL HO
Lindsey House
CHEYNE WALK
A3220
A308
A304
A3217
A3212
GUNTER GROVE
FERNSHAW ROAD
EDITH TERRACE
EDITH GROVE
SLAIDBURN STREET
GALLERY CT
HORTENSIA ROAD
COLLEGE PL
HUDSON HO
Kensington & Chelsea Coll
COLERIDGE SQ
WORLD'S END PL
Ashburnham Com Sch
BLANTYRE STREET
BERENGER WLK
DARTREY WALK
WHISTLER WLK
ASHBURNHAM ROAD
CREMORNE ROAD
CONINGHAM CT
CORNWALL MANSIONS
ASHBURTON MANSIONS
TETCOTT RD
THORNDIKE CL
Westfield Park
WESTFIELD CL
LOTS ROAD
POOLES LANE
UVERDALE ROAD
UPCERNE ROAD
BURNABY STREET
TADEMA ROAD
STADIUM STREET
Thames Path
Cremorne Gdns
Old Ferry Wharf
Chelsea Wharf
Cremorne Wharf
Heatherley Sch of Fine Art
RIVER THAMES
Kensington & Chelsea
Hammersmith & Fulham
Wandsworth
Gas Works
SANDS END LA
IMPERIAL RD
CHELSEA HARBOUR DR
THE QUADRANGLE
THAMES AVE
ADMIRAL SQ
KING'S QUAY
THAMES QUAY
Chelsea Harbour Design Ctr
HARBOUR AVE
Imperial Wharf
THE BOULEVARD
THE BELVEDERE
CHELSEA CRES
Chelsea Harbour Pier
Fulham Bsns Exchange
Chelsea Coll of Art & Design
TOWNMEAD RD
TYNEMOUTH ST
ELSWICK ST
BAGLEY'S LA
TALINA CTR
THORNEY CRES
WHISTLERS AVENUE
BATTERSEA CHURCH RD
CREWKERNE CT
EXFORD CT
SELWORTHY HO
SPARKFORD HO
SUNBURY LA
OLD SWAN WHARF
VICARAGE WLK
VALIANT HO
THE RIVERAINS
VICARAGE CRES
BATTERSEA SQ
COTSWOLD MEWS
Royal Academy of Dance
Thomas's London Day Schs
BATTERSEA HIGH ST
GRANFIELD ST
B305
GROVESIDE CT
Tenn Cts
Fred Wells Gdns
ORVILLE RD
MORGAN CT
WINDSOR CT
Regent

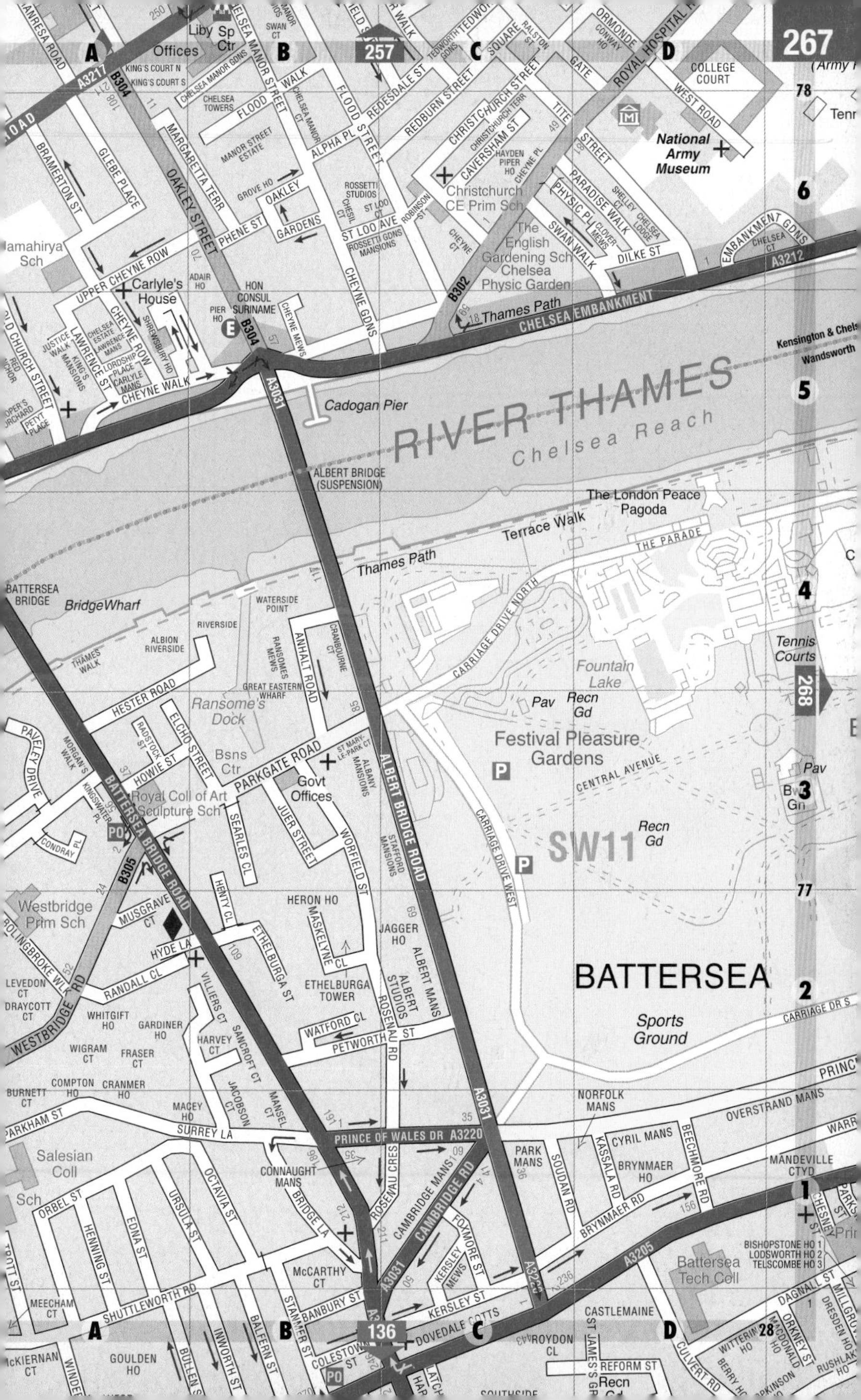
RIVER THAMES
Chelsea Reach
BATTERSEA
SW11
Festival Pleasure Gardens
National Army Museum
Carlyle's House
Chelsea Physic Garden
The English Gardening Sch
Christchurch CE Prim Sch
Cadogan Pier
ALBERT BRIDGE (SUSPENSION)
BATTERSEA BRIDGE
The London Peace Pagoda
Terrace Walk
Thames Path
Bridge Wharf
Ransome's Dock
Bsns Ctr
Govt Offices
Royal Coll of Art Sculpture Sch
Westbridge Prim Sch
Salesian Coll
Battersea Tech Coll
Fountain Lake
Sports Ground
Tennis Courts
CHELSEA EMBANKMENT
ALBERT BRIDGE ROAD
BATTERSEA BRIDGE ROAD
PRINCE OF WALES DR A3220
CARRIAGE DRIVE NORTH
CARRIAGE DRIVE WEST
CENTRAL AVENUE
ROYAL HOSPITAL RD
OAKLEY STREET
CHEYNE WALK
PARKGATE ROAD
HESTER ROAD
SURREY LA
CAMBRIDGE RD
WESTBRIDGE RD
SHUTTLEWORTH RD
BRYNMAER RD
Kensington & Chelsea
Wandsworth
257
268
136

Royal Hospital (Army Pensioners)
Ranelagh Gardens (Site of Chelsea Flower Show)
Tenn Cts
Thames Path
GROSVENOR RD
CHELSEA BRIDGE
GROSVENOR BRIDGE
Battersea Wharf
Kensington & Chelsea
Wandsworth
CARRIAGE DRIVE NORTH
QUEENSTOWN ROAD
Battersea Power Station (disused)
Children's Zoo
Tennis Courts
Millennium Arena (Sports Arena)
Recn Gd
War Meml
CARRIAGE DRIVE EAST
CENTRAL AVENUE
Battersea Park
Boating Lake
Bwg Gn
Battersea Dogs Home
QUEEN'S CIRCUS
Battersea Park
PRINCE OF WALES DR
Cloisters Bsns Ctr
Newton Prep Sch
St Mary's RC Prim Sch
Queenstown Road
Abbey Bsns Ctr
Westminster Kingsway Coll
BATTERSEA PARK RD
CARRIAGE DR S
Battersea Tech Coll
Liby
Prim Sch
QUEENSTOWN MEWS
QUEENSTOWN RD
Stewart's Lane
Broughton Street Arches Ind Area

258
267
137

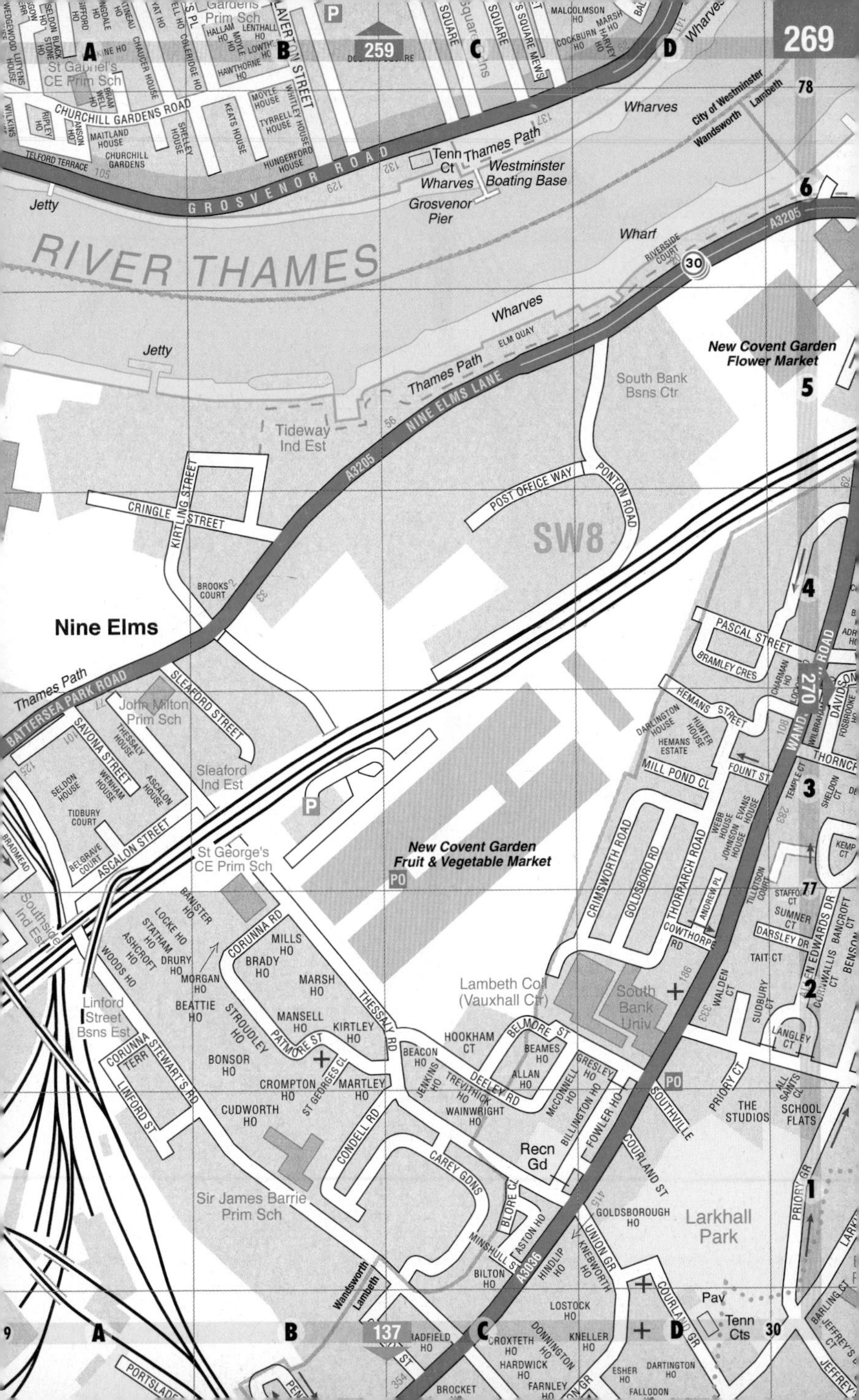

RIVER THAMES
Nine Elms
SW8
GROSVENOR ROAD
NINE ELMS LANE
BATTERSEA PARK ROAD
Thames Path
Wharves
Jetty
Grosvenor Pier
Westminster Boating Base
Tenn Ct
Tideway Ind Est
South Bank Bsns Ctr
New Covent Garden Flower Market
New Covent Garden Fruit & Vegetable Market
Sleaford Ind Est
John Milton Prim Sch
St George's CE Prim Sch
Sir James Barrie Prim Sch
Lambeth Coll (Vauxhall Ctr)
South Bank Univ
Linford Street Bsns Est
Southside Ind Est
Larkhall Park
Recn Gd
CHURCHILL GARDENS ROAD
CRINGLE STREET
KIRTLING STREET
SLEAFORD STREET
SAVONA STREET
ASCALON STREET
POST OFFICE WAY
PONTON ROAD
PASCAL STREET
BRAMLEY CRES
HEMANS STREET
MILL POND CL
CRIMSWORTH ROAD
GOLDSBORO RD
THORPARCH ROAD
COWTHORPE RD
FOUNT ST
WANDSWORTH ROAD
CORUNNA RD
THESSALY RD
PATMORE ST
CONDELL RD
CAREY GDNS
DEELEY RD
BELMORE ST
COURLAND ST
UNION GR
PRIORY GR
PRIORY CT
SOUTHVILLE
A3205
A3036
City of Westminster
Lambeth
Wandsworth

259
137
270

Vauxhall Cross
Vauxhall
260
St George Wharf
Thames Path
New Covent Garden Flower Market
Vauxhall Park
The Oval (Surrey County Cricket Ground)
Lilian Baylis Tech Sch
St Anne's RC Prim Sch
Westminster Bsns Sq
St Mark's CE Prim Sch
Harleyford Road
Kennington Oval
Wandsworth Road
South Lambeth Road
Wyvil Road
Wyvil Prim Sch
Fentiman Road
Meadow Road
Rita Road
Cottingham Rd
Claylands Road
Trigon Road
Dorset Road
Richborne Terrace
Oval Place
Wilkinson Street
Albert Square
Aldebert Terrace
Thorne Road
Herbert Morrison Prim Sch
St Stephen's CE Prim Sch
Clapham Road
Caldwell Street
Reay Prim Sch
Durand Prim Sch
Lansdowne Way
Lansdowne Gdns
Larkhall La
South Lambeth
Stockwell
Stockwell Park Sch
Allen Edwards Prim Sch
Larkhall Park
SW8
SW9
SW4
269
138

Index

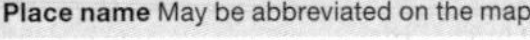

Place name May be abbreviated on the map → **Church Rd** 6 Beckenham BR2......**53** C6 **228** C6

Location number Present when a number indicates the place's position in a crowded area of mapping

Locality, town or village Shown when more than one place has the same name

Postcode district District for the indexed place

Standard-scale reference Page number and grid reference for the standard-scale mapping on pages 1–227

Large-scale reference Page number and grid reference for the large-scale central London mapping on pages 229–270, underlined in red

Cities, towns and villages are listed in **CAPITAL LETTERS** **Public and commercial buildings** are highlighted in magenta
Places of interest are highlighted in blue with a star★

Abbreviations used in the index

Acad	**Academy**	Comm	**Common**	Gd	**Ground**	L	**Leisure**	Prom	**Promenade**
App	**Approach**	Cott	**Cottage**	Gdn	**Garden**	La	**Lane**	Rd	**Road**
Arc	**Arcade**	Cres	**Crescent**	Gn	**Green**	Liby	**Library**	Recn	**Recreation**
Ave	**Avenue**	Cswy	**Causeway**	Gr	**Grove**	Mdw	**Meadow**	Ret	**Retail**
Bglw	**Bungalow**	Ct	**Court**	H	**Hall**	Meml	**Memorial**	Sh	**Shopping**
Bldg	**Building**	Ctr	**Centre**	Ho	**House**	Mkt	**Market**	Sq	**Square**
Bsns, Bus	**Business**	Ctry	**Country**	Hospl	**Hospital**	Mus	**Museum**	St	**Street**
Bvd	**Boulevard**	Cty	**County**	HQ	**Headquarters**	Orch	**Orchard**	Sta	**Station**
Cath	**Cathedral**	Dr	**Drive**	Hts	**Heights**	Pal	**Palace**	Terr	**Terrace**
Cir	**Circus**	Dro	**Drove**	Ind	**Industrial**	Par	**Parade**	TH	**Town Hall**
Cl	**Close**	Ed	**Education**	Inst	**Institute**	Pas	**Passage**	Univ	**University**
Cnr	**Corner**	Emb	**Embankment**	Int	**International**	Pk	**Park**	Wk, Wlk	**Walk**
Coll	**College**	Est	**Estate**	Intc	**Interchange**	Pl	**Place**	Wr	**Water**
Com	**Community**	Ex	**Exhibition**	Junc	**Junction**	Prec	**Precinct**	Yd	**Yard**

Index of towns, villages, streets, hospitals, industrial estates, railway stations, schools, shopping centres, universities and places of interest

A

Aaron Ct BR3 . . . . **207** D6
Aaron Hill Rd E6 . . . . . **100** C2
Abady Ho SW1 . . . . . . **259** D4
Abberley Mews 9 SW8 . . . . **137** B2
Abberton IG8 . . . . **37** C5
Abbess Cl
  11 Newham E6 . . . . . **100** A2
  Streatham SW2 . . . . . **160** D3
Abbeville Mews 3 SW4 . . . . **137** D1
Abbeville Rd
  Clapham Pk SW4 . . . . **159** C6
  Hornsey N8 . . . . **49** D5
Abbey Ave HA0 . . . . **88** A5
Abbey Bsns Ctr SW8 . . . . **137** B4 **268** D2
Abbey Cl Hayes UB3 . . **106** B5
  Northolt UB5 . . . . **85** B4
  Pinner HA5 . . . . **40** C6
Abbey Cres DA17 . . . . **125** C2
Abbey Ct
  6 Bedford Pk W12 . . . . **111** C3
  Camberwell SE17 . . . **262** B1
  Church End N3 . . . . **47** C6
  5 Edgware HA8 . . . . . . **26** D5
  Hampton TW12 . . . . . **173** C3
  St John's Wood NW8 **229** A4
  Twickenham TW2 . . . . . **152** B2
Abbeydale Rd HA0 . . . . **88** C6
Abbey Dr SW17 . . . . . . **181** A5
Abbeyfield Cl CR4 . . . . **180** C1
Abbeyfield Rd SE16 . . **118** C2
Abbeyfields Cl NW10 . . **88** C5
Abbey Gdns
  10 Bermondsey SE16 . . . . **118** A2
  Chislehurst BR7 . . . . . **188** C2
  St John's Wood NW8 . . . . **92** A5 **229** B3
  West Kensington W6 . . . . . . **135** A6 **264** A5
Abbey Gr SE2 . . . . **124** B2
Abbeyhill Rd DA15 . . . **168** C2
Abbey Ho
  Newham E15 . . . . **98** C5
  St John's Wood NW8. **229** B2
Abbey Ind Est CR4 . . **202** D4
Abbey La
  Beckenham BR3 . . . . **185** C3
  Mill Meads E15 . . . . **98** B5
Abbey Lane Commercial Est 1 E15 . . . . **98** C5
Abbey Lo
  Bromley SE12 . . . . **187** B6
  1 Ealing W5 . . . . **109** C6
  Lisson Gr NW8 . . . . . **230** B1
Abbey Manufacturing Est HA0 . . . . **88** B6
Abbey Mews
  Brentford TW7 . . . . **131** B4
  Walthamstow E17 . . . . . **53** C4
Abbey Mount DA17 . . . **125** B1
Abbey Orchard Street Est SW1 . . . . **259** D6
Abbey Orchard St SW1 . . . . **115** D3 **259** D6
Abbey Par NW10 . . . . . . **88** B4
Abbey Park Ind Est IG11 . . . . **101** A6
Abbey Par SW19 . . . . . **180** A3
Abbey Pk BR3 . . . . **185** C3
Abbey Prim Sch SM4 . . . . **201** C2
Abbey Rd
  Barking IG11 . . . . **100** D6
  Bexley DA7 . . . . **147** A1
  Croydon CR0 . . . . **220** D5
  Enfield EN1 . . . . **17** C6
  Erith DA17 . . . . **125** A3
  Ilford IG2 . . . . **57** B4
  Lower Halliford TW17 . . . . **192** C1
  Merton SW19 . . . . . . **180** A2
Abbey Rd Motorist Ctr 4 NW6 . . . . **91** D6
Abbey Rd
  Newham E15 . . . . **98** C5
  St John's Wood NW8 . . . . . . **92** A5 **229** A4
  Wembley NW10 . . . . **88** D5
Abbey St
  Bermondsey SE1 . . . . . . **117** D3 **263** C6
  Newham E13 . . . . **99** A3
Abbey Terr SE2 . . . . . . **124** C2
Abbey Trad Est SE26 . . . . **185** B5
Abbey View NW7 . . . . . . **11** D1
Abbey Wlk KT8 . . . . . . **195** D5
ABBEY WOOD **124** B3
Abbey Wood Rd SE2 . . . . **124** C2
Abbey Wood Sch SE2 . . . . **124** A3
Abbey Wood Sta SE2 . . . . **124** C3
Abbot Cl HA4 . . . . **62** D5
Abbot Ct SW8 . . . . . . **270** A3
Abbot Ho 14 E14 . . . . . **119** D6
Abbotsbury Cl
  Kensington W14 . . . . . **113** B4 **244** C1
  Mill Meads E15 . . . . **98** A5
Abbotsbury Gdns HA5 . . . . **40** C3
Abbotsbury Ho W14. **244** B2
Abbotsbury Mews SE15 . . . . **140** C2
Abbotsbury Prim Sch SM4 . . . . **201** D4
Abbotsbury Rd
  Coney Hall BR2, BR4 . . . . **224** D6
  Kensington W14 . . . . . **113** B4 **244** C1
  Morden SM4 . . . . **201** D5
Abbots Cl BR5 . . . . **211** A1
Abbots Ct SE25 . . . . . . **205** C6
Abbots Dr HA2 . . . . **63** C6
Abbotsfield Sch UB10 . . . . **82** D5
Abbotsford Ave N15 . . . **51** A5
Abbotsford Gdns IG8 . . . . **37** A3
Abbotsford Rd IG3 . . . . **80** B6
Abbots Gdns N2 . . . . . . **48** B5
Abbots Gn CR0, CR2 . . **222** D2
Abbots Green CR2 . . . **222** D2
Abbotshade Rd 15 SE16 . . . . **118** D5
Abbotshall Ave N14 . . . **15** C1
Abbotshall Rd SE6 . . . **164** B2
Abbots Ho
  Kensington W14 . . . . **254** C5
  Pimlico SW1 . . . . **259** C1
  Walthamstow E17 . . . . . **35** B1
Abbots La SE1 . . . . **117** C5 **253** B3
Abbotsleigh Cl SM2 . . **217** D1
Abbotsleigh Rd SW16 . . . . **181** C5
Abbotsmede Cl TW1 . . . . **152** D2
Abbots Pk SW2 . . . . . . **160** C3
Abbot's Pl NW6 . . . . **91** D6
Abbots Rd
  Burnt Oak HA8 . . . . **27** B3
  Cheam SM3 . . . . **217** A4
  Newham E6 . . . . **99** D6
Abbots Terr N8 . . . . **50** A3
Abbot St E8 . . . . **73** D2
Abbotstone Ho 4 E5 . . **74** A6
Abbotstone Rd SW15 . . . . **134** C2
Abbotsview Ct NW7 . . . **12** A1
Abbots Way BR3 . . . . . **207** A4
Abbotswell Rd SE4 . . . **163** B6
Abbotswood Cl 7 DA17 . . . . **125** A3
Abbotswood Gdns IG5 . . . . **56** B6
Abbotswood Rd
  London SE22 . . . . **139** C1
  Streatham SW16 . . . . **159** D1
Abbotswood Way UB3 . . . . **106** B5
Abbott Ave SW20 . . . . **178** D2
Abbott Cl
  Hampton TW12 . . . . . **173** A4
  Northolt UB5 . . . . **63** B2
Abbott Ho SW12 . . . . . **158** D4
Abbott Rd E14 . . . . **98** B1
Abbotts Cl
  Canonbury N1 . . . . **73** A2
  Romford RM7 . . . . **59** D6
  Woolwich SE28 . . . . . **124** C6
Abbotts Cres
  Chingford E4 . . . . **36** B6
  Enfield EN2 . . . . **4** D3
Abbotts Ct HA2 . . . . **64** B6
Abbotts Dr HA0 . . . . **65** B6
Abbotts Park Rd E10 . . **54** A2
Abbotts Rd Barnet EN5 . . **1** D1
  Mitcham CR4 . . . . **203** C5
  Southall UB1 . . . . **107** A5
Abbotts Wharf 4 E14 . . . . **97** C1
Abbott's Wlk DA7 . . . . **146** D5
Abchurch La EC2, EC4 . . . . **117** B6 **252** D6
Abchurch Yd EC4 . . . . **252** C6
Abdale Rd W12 . . . . . . **112** B5
Abel Ho
  7 Kennington SE11 . . . . **138** C6
  Woolwich SE18 . . . . . **123** A2
Abenglen Ind Est UB3 . . . . **105** B4
Aberavon Rd E3 . . . . . . **97** A4
Abercairn Rd SW16 . . **181** C3
Aberconway Rd SM4 . . . . **201** D5
Abercorn Cl
  Finchley NW7 . . . . **29** A3
  St John's Wood NW8 . . . . . . **92** A4 **229** A2
Abercorn Cres HA2 . . . **41** D1
Abercorn Gdns
  Harrow HA3 . . . . **43** D2
  Ilford RM6 . . . . **58** B3
Abercorn Gr HA4 . . . . . **39** B5

Abercorn Mans NW8 229 B3
Abercorn Mews 10 TW10 132 B1
Abercorn Pl NW8 92 A5 229 A3
Abercorn Rd
Finchley NW7 29 A3
Stanmore HA7 25 C3
Abercorn Trad Est HA0 87 D6
Abercorn Way SE1 118 A1
Abercrombie Dr EN1 6 A4
Abercrombie Ho 1 W12 112 B6
Abercrombie St SW11 136 C3
Aberdale Ct 22 SE16 118 D4
Aberdare Cl BR4 224 A6
Aberdare Gdns
Finchley NW7 28 D3
South Hampstead NW6 69 D1
Aberdare Rd EN3 6 C1
Aberdeen Cotts HA7 25 C3
Aberdeen Ct
Canonbury N5 73 A3
Paddington W2 236 C5
Aberdeen Ctr N5 73 A3
Aberdeen La N5 73 A3
Aberdeen Mans WC1 240 A6
Aberdeen Par N18 34 B5
Aberdeen Pk N5 73 A3
Aberdeen Pl NW8 92 B3 236 C6
Aberdeen Rd
Canonbury N5 73 A4
Croydon CR0 221 B4
Dudden Hill NW10 67 D3
Edmonton N18 34 B5
Harrow HA3 24 D1
Aberdeen Terr SE3 142 B3
Aberdour Rd IG3 80 B6
Aberdour St SE1 117 C2 263 A4
Aberfeldy Ho SE5 138 D5
Aberfeldy St E14 98 A1
Aberford Gdns SE18 144 A4
Aberfoyle Rd SW16 181 D4
Abergeldie Rd SE12 165 B5
Abernethy Rd SE13 142 C1
Abersham Rd E8 73 D3
Abery St SE18 123 C2
Ability Plaza 8 E8 73 D1
Ability Twrs EC1 235 A2
Abingdon Cl
Fulham SE1 263 D2
Hillingdon UB10 82 B6
Kentish Town NW1 71 D2
Wimbledon SW19 180 A4
Abingdon Ct
Earl's Ct W8 255 B5
Edgware HA8 26 A6
Upper Tooting SW17 180 D4
Abingdon Gdns W8 255 B5
Abingdon Ho
Bromley BR1 187 B3
Spitalfields E2 243 C6
Abingdon Lo
2 Barnet EN5 1 A1
Bromley BR2 186 D1
Abingdon Mans W8 255 A6
Abingdon Rd
Finchley N3 30 A1
Kensington W8 113 C3 255 B5
Thornton Heath SW16 182 A2
Abingdon St SW1 116 A3 260 A6
Abingdon Villas W8 113 C3 255 B5
Abingdon W14 254 D3
Abinger Cl
Barking IG11 80 A4
Bickley BR1 210 A6
New Addington CR0 224 A2
Wallington SM6 220 A3
Abinger Ct
3 Ealing W5 109 C6
Thornton Heath CR0 204 D2
Wallington SM6 220 A3
Abinger Gdns TW7 130 C2
Abinger Gr SE8 141 B6
Abinger Ho
Borough The SE1 252 C1
2 Kingston u T KT2 176 D3
Abinger Mews W9 91 C3
Abinger Rd W4 111 C3
Abington Ho NW11 48 A3
Ablett St SE16 118 C1
Abney Gdns 5 N16 73 D6
Abney Park Cemetery* N16 73 C6
Abney Park Ct N16 73 D6
Aborfield 6 NW5 71 C3
Aboyne Dr SW20 178 A1
Aboyne Rd
Neasden NW10 67 C5
Wandsworth SW17 158 B1
Abraham Cl WD19 22 B6
Abraham Cohen Ct IG1 56 C3
Abraham Fisher Ho 2 E12 78 C3
Abridge Way IG11 102 B5
Abyssinia Cl SW11 136 C1
Abyssinia Rd SW11 136 C1
Acacia Ave
Brentford TW8 131 B5
East Finchley N2 47 D6
Hayes UB3 83 D1
Littleton TW17 192 C4
Ruislip HA4 40 B2
Tottenham N17 33 B3
Wembley HA9 66 A3
Yiewsley UB7 104 B6
Acacia Bsns Ctr 1 E11 76 C5
Acacia Cl
Penge SE20 184 A1
Petts Wood BR5 211 B4
Rotherhithe SE8 119 A2
Stanmore HA7 24 C4
Acacia Ct Harrow HA1 41 D3
5 West Norwood SW16 182 C5
Acacia Dr SM3 201 C1
Acacia Gdns
St John's Wood NW8 229 D4
West Wickham BR4 224 A6
Acacia Gr
Dulwich SE21 161 B2
Kingston u T KT3 199 C6
Acacia Ho
Brockley SE4 141 B1
1 New Malden KT3 199 C5
Stoke Newington N16 73 B6
Wood Green N22 32 C2
Acacia Lo 6 N3 29 B1
Acacia Pl NW8 92 B5 229 D4
Acacia Rd Acton W3 111 A6
Beckenham BR3 207 B6
Enfield EN2 5 B4
Hampton TW12 173 C4
Leyton E11 76 C6
Mitcham CR4 181 B1
St John's Wood NW8 92 B5 229 D4
Thornton Heath SW16 182 A2
Walthamstow E17 53 A3
Wood Green N22 32 C2
Acacias Lo EN4 14 B6
Acacias The EN4 14 B6
Acacia Way DA15 167 D3
Acacia Wlk SW10 266 B3
Acad at Peckham The SE15 139 D4
Academy Ct 13 E2 96 C4
Academy Gdns
Croydon CR0 205 D1
Kensington W8 245 A2
Northolt UB5 84 D5
Academy Pl SE18 144 C4
Academy Rd SE18 144 B5
Academy Sch The NW3 70 B4
Academy The 2 N19 49 C1
Acad of Live & Recorded Arts The SW18 158 B5
Acanthus Dr SE1 118 A1
Acanthus Rd SW11 137 A2
Accadia Ct NW9 67 A6
Accommodation Rd NW11 47 B1
Ace Par KT9 214 A5
Acer Ave UB4 85 A2
Acer Ct
2 Cricklewood NW2 68 D4
3 Enfield EN3 7 A2
Acers BR7 188 A3
Acfold Rd SW6 265 C1
Achilles Cl SE1 118 A1
Achilles Ho 16 E2 96 B5
Achilles Rd NW6 69 C3
Achilles St SE14 141 A5
Achilles Way W1 248 B3
Acklam Rd W10 91 B2
Acklington Dr NW9 27 C2
Ackmar Rd SW6 135 C4 265 A1
Ackroyd Dr E3 97 C2
Ackroyd Rd SE23 163 A4
Acland Burghley Sch NW5 71 B4
Acland Cl SE18 145 B5
Acland Cres SE5 139 B2
Acland Ho SW9 138 B3
Acland Rd NW2 68 B2
Acock Gr UB5 64 A4
Acol Cres HA4 62 B3
Acol Ct 3 NW6 69 C1
Acol Rd NW6 69 D1
Aconbury Rd RM9 102 B6
Acorn Cl Chingford E4 35 D5
Chislehurst BR7 189 A5
Enfield EN2 4 D4
1 Hampton TW12 173 D4
Stanmore HA7 25 B3
Acorn Ct 5 Bow E3 97 C5
Hampton TW12 173 B5
Ilford IG2 57 C4
Upton Pk E6 78 A1
Wood Green N11 31 D4
Acorn Gdns
North Acton W3 89 B2
South Norwood SE19 183 D2
Acorn Gr
Harlington UB3 127 D5
Ruislip HA4 61 D4
Acorn Par 7 SE15 140 B5
Acorn Production Ctr N7 72 A1
Acorns The 21 SW19 156 D3
Acorns Way KT10 212 A3
Acorn Way
Beckenham BR3 208 A4
Forest Hill SE23 162 D1
Orpington BR6 226 D4
Acorn Wharf SE15 140 A6
Acorn Wlk SE16 119 A5
Acqua Ho TW9 132 D5
Acre Dr SE22 140 A1
Acrefield Ho 4 NW4 46 D5
Acre La Brixton SW2 138 B1
Wallington SM5 219 A4
Acre Path UB5 63 A2
Acre Rd
Dagenham RM10 81 D1
Kingston u T KT2 176 B2
Mitcham SW19 180 B4
Acre Way HA6 22 A2
Acris St SW18 158 A6
ACS Hillingdon International Sch UB10 82 B6
Action Ct TW15 171 A2
ACTON 111 B5
Acton Bsns Ctr NW10 89 B3
Acton Central Ind Est 4 W3 110 D5
Acton Central Sta W3 111 B5
Acton Cl N9 18 A2
ACTON GREEN 111 A2
Acton High Sch W3 110 C4
Acton Hill Mews W3 110 D5
Acton Ho
5 Acton W3 89 A1
10 Haggerston E8 95 D6
Acton Hospl W3 110 C4
Acton La
Acton Green W4 111 A2
Acton W3 111 A4
Harlesden NW10 89 B5
Acton Main Line Sta W3 89 A1
Acton Mews E8 95 D6
Acton Park Ind Est W3 111 B4
Acton St WC1 94 B4 233 C1
Acton Town Sta W3 110 C4
Acton Vale Ind Pk W3 111 D5
Acuba Ho SW18 157 D3
Acuba Rd SW18 157 D2
Acworth Cl N9 18 C4
Acworth Ho 1 SE18 144 D6
Ada Ct Islington N1 235 A5
St John's Wood W9 92 A4 229 B1
Ada Gdns
Plaistow E15 98 D6
South Bromley E14 98 B1
Ada Ho 23 E2 96 A6
Adair Cl SE25 206 B6
Adair Ho SW3 267 B6
Adair Rd W10 91 A3
Adair Twr 7 W10 91 A3
Ada Kennedy Ct 6 SE10 142 A5
Ada Lewis Ho HA9 66 B4
Adam Cl SE6 185 C6
Adam Ct
Newington SE11 261 C3
15 Sutton SM1 218 A4
Adam & Eve Ct W1 239 B2
Adam & Eve Mews W8 113 C3 255 B6
Adamfields NW3 70 B1
Adam Lo N21 16 B6
Adam Rd E4 35 B4
Adams Bridge Bsns Ctr HA9 66 D3
Adams Cl Finchley N3 29 C3
Surbiton KT5 198 B3
Wembley Pk NW9 66 D6
Adams Ct E17 53 A3
Adams Gardens Est 5 SE16 118 C4
Adams Ho
3 South Bromley E14 98 B1
3 Streatham SW16 181 C5
Adams Mews
Upper Tooting SW17 158 D2
Wood Green N22 32 B3
Adamson Ct N2 48 C6
Adamson Rd
Hampstead NW3 70 B1
Newham E16 99 A1
Adamson Way BR3 208 A4
Adams Pl N7 72 B3
Adams Qtr TW8 131 C6
Adams Rd
Beckenham BR3 207 A4
Tottenham N17 33 B1
Adamsrill Cl EN1 17 B5
Adamsrill Prim Sch SE26 163 A1
Adamsrill Rd SE26 185 A6
Adam's Row W1 115 A6 248 B5
Adams Sq DA6 147 A2
Adam St WC2 116 A6 250 B5
Adams Way CR0 206 A3
Adams Wlk 11 KT1 176 A1
Adam Wlk SW6 134 C5
Ada Pl E2 96 A6
Ada Rd
Camberwell SE5 139 C5
Wembley HA0, HA9 65 D5
Adare Ctr The SW16 160 A1
Adare Wlk SW16, SW2 160 B2
Ada St E8 96 B6
Adcot Wlk 6 BR6 227 D4
Adderley Gdns SE9 188 C6
Adderley Gr SW11 159 A6
Adderley Rd HA3 24 D2
Adderley St E14 98 A1
Addey Ho SE8 141 B5
Addey & Stanhope Sch SE14 141 C4
ADDINGTON 223 C3
Addington Ct 7 SW14 133 B2
Addington Dr N12 30 B4
Addington Gr SE26 185 A6
Addington Ho 13 SW9 138 B3
Addington Rd Bow E3 97 C4
Newham E16 98 C3
Stroud Green N4 50 C3
Thornton Heath CR0 204 C1
West Wickham BR4 224 C6
West Wickham BR4, CR0 224 B4
Addington Sq SE5 139 B5
Addington St SE1 116 B4 250 D1
Addington Village Rd CR0 223 C3
Addington Village Sta CR0 223 C2
Addis Cl EN3 6 D4
ADDISCOMBE 206 A1
Addiscombe Ave CR0 206 A2
Addiscombe Cl HA3 43 C4
Addiscombe Court Rd CR0 221 C6
Addiscombe Ct UB10 83 A3
Addiscombe Rd CR0 222 B6
Addiscombe Sta CR0 206 A1
Addis Ho 18 E1 96 C2
Addison Ave
Hounslow TW3 130 A4
Notting Hill W11 113 A5 244 A3
Southgate N14 15 C5
Addison Bridge Pl W14 113 B2 254 C4
Addison Cl
Northwood HA6 22 A2
Addison Cl *continued*
Orpington BR5 211 A3
Addison Cres W14 113 A3 254 B6
Addison Ct
3 Belmont SM2 217 D1
Ealing W5 110 C6
Twickenham TW1 153 A3
Addison Dr SE12 165 B6
Addison Gdns
Hammersmith W14 112 D3
Kingston u T KT5 198 B5
Addison Gr W4 111 C3
Addison Ho NW8 92 B4 229 C2
Addison Park Mans 12 W14 112 D4
Addison Pl
Notting Hill W11 113 A5 244 A3
Southall UB1 107 C6
Addison Prim Sch W14 112 D3
Addison Rd
Bromley BR2 209 D4
Croydon SE25 206 A5
Enfield EN3 6 D4
Kensington W14 113 B3 254 C6
Teddington TW11 175 B4
Walthamstow E17 54 A4
Wanstead E11 55 A3
Addison's Cl CR0 223 B6
Addison Way
Hampstead Garden Suburb NW11 47 C5
Hayes UB3 84 A1
Northwood HA6 22 A2
Addle Hill EC4 241 D1
Addle St EC2 242 B3
Addlestone Ho 4 W10 90 C2
Addy Ho SE16 118 C2
Adecroft Way KT8 196 A6
Adela Ave KT3 200 B5
Adela Ho 9 W6 112 C1
Adelaide Ave SE4 141 C1
Adelaide Cl
Brixton SW9 138 C1
Enfield EN1 5 C5
Stanmore HA7 25 A6
Adelaide Ct
15 Beckenham BR3 185 C3
Hackney E5 75 A3
Hanwell W7 108 D4
St John's Wood NW8 229 B3
Adelaide Gdns RM6 59 A4
Adelaide Gr W12 112 A5
Adelaide Ho E17 53 B6
Adelaide Rd
Ashford TW15 170 A6
Chislehurst BR7 188 D5
Ealing W13 109 A4
Heston TW5 129 A4
Ilford IG1 78 D6
Kingston u T KT6 198 A4
Leyton E10 76 A5
Primrose Hill NW3 70 C1
Richmond TW9 132 B1
Southall UB2 107 A2
Teddington TW11 174 D4
2 Wandsworth SW18 157 C6
Adelaide St WC2 250 A5
Adelaide Terr TW8 109 D1
Adela St W10 91 A3
Adelina Gr E1 96 C2
Adelina Mews SW12 159 D3
Adeline Pl WC1 93 D2 239 D3
Adelphi Cres UB4 83 D4
Adelphi Ct
10 Finchley N2 30 B1
20 Rotherhithe SE16 118 D4
Adelphi Terr WC2 250 B5
Adelphi Way UB4 83 D4
Adeney Cl W6 134 D6
Aden Gr N16 73 B4
Aden Ho 15 E1 96 D2
Aden Lo N16 73 B4
Adenmore Rd SE6 163 C4
Aden Rd Enfield EN3 7 A1
Ilford IG1 57 A2
Adeyfield Ho EC1 235 D1
Adhara Rd HA6 22 A5
Adie Rd W6 112 C3
Adine Rd E13 99 B3
Adisham Ho 4 E5 74 B3
Adler Ind Est UB3 105 B4
Adler St E1 96 A1
Adley St E5 75 A3
Adlington Cl N18 33 C5
Admaston Rd SE18 145 A6
Admiral Ct
Barking IG11 102 C5
Carshalton SM5 202 C1
Chelsea SW10 136 A4 266 B2
Hendon NW4 46 A4
Marylebone W1 238 A3
Admiral Ho TW11 175 A6
Admiral Hyson Ind Est SE16 118 B1
Admiral Mews W10 90 D3
Admiral Pl
Harringay N8 50 D5
Rotherhithe SE16 119 A5
Admirals Cl E18 55 B5
Admirals Ct
Bermondsey SE1 253 C3
3 Newham E6 100 D1
32 Putney SW19 156 D3
Admiral Seymour Rd SE9 144 B1
Admirals Gate SE10 141 D4
Admiral Sq SW10 136 A4 266 B2
Admiral St SE8 141 C4
Admirals Way E14 119 C4
Admiral's Wlk NW3 70 A5
Admiralty Arch* SW1 249 D4
Admiralty Cl 1 SE8 141 C4
Admiralty Rd TW11 174 D4
Admiralty Way TW11 174 D4
Admiral Wlk W9 91 C2
Adolf St SE6 185 D6
Adolphus Rd N4 50 D1
Adolphus St SE8 141 B5
Adomar Rd RM8 81 A5
Adpar St W2 92 B2 236 C4
Adrian Ave NW2 46 B1
Adrian Bolt Ho 2 E2 96 B4
Adrian Cl EN5 12 D5
Adrian Ho
Islington N1 233 D5
South Lambeth SW8 270 A4
Stratford E15 76 B1
Adrian Mews SW10 265 D6
Adriatic Bldg 18 E14 119 A6
Adriatic Ho 18 E1 96 D3
Adrienne Ave UB1 85 B4
Adron Ho 18 SE16 118 C2
Adstock Ho 5 N1 72 D1
ADT Coll SW15 157 B6
Advance Rd SE27 183 A6
Advent Ct IG8 36 D5
Adventurers Ct 17 E14 120 B6
Advent Way N18 34 D5
Adyar Ct 7 SW19 179 A3
Adys Lawn NW2 68 B2
Adys Rd SE15 139 D2
Aegean Apts 7 E16 121 A6
Aegon Ho 3 E14 119 D3
Aerodrome Rd NW4, NW9 45 D6
Aerodrome Way TW5 128 C6
Aeroville NW9 27 C1
Affleck St N1 233 D3
Afghan Rd SW11 136 C3
Africa Ho WC2 240 C2
Afsil Ho EC1 241 B3
Aga Khan Univ WC1 239 D3
Agamemnon Rd NW6 69 B3
Agar Cl KT6 214 B6
Agar Gr NW1 71 D1
Agar Ho 6 KT1 198 A6
Agar Pl NW1 71 C1
Agar St WC2 250 B5
Agate Cl E16 99 D1
Agate Ho
New Malden KT4 199 C1
12 Penge SE26 184 B5
Agate Rd W6 112 C3
Agatha Cl E1 118 C5
Agaton Rd SE9 167 A2
Agave Rd NW2 68 C4
Agdon St EC1 94 D3 241 C6
Agincourt E11 54 D3
Agincourt Rd NW3 70 D4
Agnes Ave IG1 78 D4
Agnes Cl E6 122 C6
Agnes Ct 11 SW18 136 B1
Agnesfield Cl N12 30 C4
Agnes Gdns RM8 80 D4
Agnes Ho 18 W11 112 D6
Agnes Rd W3 111 D4
Agnes St E14 97 B1
Agnew Rd SE23 162 D4
Agricola Pl EN1 17 D6
Aidan Cl RM8 81 A4
Aidans Ct N12 30 C5
Aigburth Mans 5 SW9 138 C5
Ailantus Ct HA8 26 B5

Aileen Wlk E15 76 D1
Ailsa Ave TW1 153 B6
Ailsa Rd TW1 153 B6
Ailsa St E14 98 A2
Ainger Rd NW3 70 D1
Ainsdale Cl BR6 211 B1
Ainsdale Cres HA5 41 C6
Ainsdale Dr SE1 118 A1
Ainsdale NW1 232 A2
Ainsdale Rd W5 87 D3
Ainsley Ave RM7 59 D3
Ainsley Cl N9 17 C3
Ainsley St E2 96 B4
Ainslie Ct 2 HA0 88 A5
Ainslie Ho 1 E4 35 C5
Ainslie Wlk 8 SW12 159 B4
Ainslie Wood Cres E4 35 D5
Ainslie Wood Gdns E4 35 D5
Ainslie Wood Prim Sch E4 35 D5
Ainslie Wood Rd E4 35 D5
Ainsty St 20 SE16 118 C4
Ainsworth Cl
Camberwell SE5 139 C3
Dollis Hill NW2 68 A5
Ainsworth Est NW8 92 A6 229 A6
Ainsworth Ho NW8 91 D6
Ainsworth Rd
Croydon CR0 220 D6
Hackney E9 74 C1
Ainsworth Way NW8 92 A6 229 A6
Aintree Ave E6 100 A6
Aintree Cl UB8 82 D2
Aintree Ho SE26 184 B4
Aintree Rd UB6 87 B5
Aintree St SW6 135 A5 264 B4
Airborne Ho 10 SM6 219 B4
Aird Ct TW12 173 D2
Aird Ho SE1 262 A5
Airdrie Cl
Barnsbury N1 72 B1
Hayes UB4 85 A2
Airedale Ave W4 111 D1
Airedale Ave S W4 111 D1
Airedale Rd
Balham SW12 158 D4
Ealing W5 109 D3
Airlie Gdns Ilford IG1 56 D1
Kensington W8 113 C5 245 A3
Airlinks Ind Est TW5 106 C1
Air Park Way TW13 150 B2
Airport Gate Bsns Ctr UB7 126 C5
Airport Ho CR0 220 C2
Airport Rdbt E16 121 D5
Air St W1 249 B5
Airthrie Rd IG3 80 B6
Aisgill Ave SW5 113 B1 254 D1
Aisher Rd SE28 124 C6
Aislabie Ho N21 17 B5
Aislibie Rd SE12 142 C1
Aiten Pl W6 112 A2
Aithan Ho 15 E14 97 B1
Aitken Cl
Carshalton CR4 202 D2
Hackney E8 96 A6
Aitken Rd Barnet EN5 12 C6
Catford SE6 163 D2
Aits View KT8 195 D6
Ajax Ave NW9 45 C6
Ajax Ct NW9 45 C6
Ajax Ho 15 E2 96 B5
Ajax Rd NW6 69 C3
Akabusi Cl SE25 206 A3
Akbar Ho 7 E14 119 D2
Akehurst St SW15 156 A4
Akenside Ct 3 NW3 70 B3
Akenside Rd NW3 70 B3
Akerman Rd
Brixton SW9 138 D4
Kingston u T KT6 197 C3
Akintaro Ho 7 SE8 141 B6
Akiva Sch N3 29 D1
Alabama St SE18 145 C5
Alacross Rd W5 109 D4
Aladdin Workspace UB6 85 D6
Alamaro Lo 5 SE10 120 D3
Alandale Dr HA5 22 B2
Aland Ct SE16 119 A3
Alander Mews E17 54 A5
Alan Dr EN5 13 A5
Alan Gdns RM7 59 C2
Alan Hocken Way E15 98 C5
Alan Lo N3 29 C2
Alan Preece Ct NW6 68 D1
Alan Rd SW19 179 A5
Alanthus Cl SE12 165 A5
Alaska Bldg 12 SE13 141 D4
Alaska St SE1 251 A3
Alastor Ho 10 E14 120 A3
Alba Cl UB4 84 D3
Albacore Cres SE13 163 D5
Alba Gdns NW11 47 A3
Alban Cres TW15 148 A2
Alba Mews SW18, SW19 157 C2
Alban Ho
Hampstead NW3 70 A2
New Cross SE14 141 B4
Albans Cl SW16 160 A1
Albany Cl Bushey WD23 8 B5
Ickenham UB10 60 C3
Mortlake SW14 132 D1
Sidcup DA5 168 D4
West Green N15 51 A5
Albany Coll Hendry Ho NW4 46 B4
Albany Coll NW4 46 C4
Albany Cres
Claygate KT10 212 C2
Edgware HA8 26 C3
Albany Ct
Ashford TW15 171 B4
Cheam SM1 217 B4
Chingford E4 19 D5
College Pk NW10 90 B4
Finchley N12 29 D4
Grahame Pk HA8 27 B2
Kingston u T KT2 176 A4
NW8 229 C3
Richmond TW10 153 B1
Surbiton KT6 197 D2
Walthamstow E10 53 C2
Westminster SW1 259 C6
8 Whitechapel E1 96 A1
Albany Ctyd W1 249 B5
Albany Ho
6 Brentford TW8 132 A6
Edgware HA8 26 C3
Upper Clapton E5 74 C6
Albany Mans SW11 267 B3
Albany Mews
Camberwell SE5 139 A6
Islington N1 72 C1
Kingston u T KT2 175 D4
Plaistow BR1 187 A4
Sutton SM1 217 D3
Albany Par 4 TW8 132 A6
Albany Park Ave EN3 6 D4
Albany Park Rd KT2 176 A4
Albany Park Sta DA14 168 D2
Albany Pas 12 TW10 154 A6
Albany Pl TW8 131 D6
Albany Rd
Brentford TW8 131 D6
Camberwell SE5 139 C6
Chislehurst BR7 188 D5
Dagenham RM6 59 B3
Ealing W13 109 B6
Enfield EN3 6 D5
Erith DA17 147 B6
Leyton E10 53 C2
Manor Pk E12 77 D4
New Malden KT3 199 B5
Richmond TW10 154 A6
Sidcup DA5 168 C4
Stroud Green N4 50 C3
Upper Edmonton N18 34 C5
Walthamstow E17 53 A3
Wimbledon SW19 179 D5
Albany Reach KT7 196 D4
Albany Sch EN3 6 D5
Albany St NW1 93 B4 231 D2
Albany Terr 6 TW10 154 B6
Albany The
Kingston u T KT2 175 D4
Woodford IG8 36 D6
Albany View IG9 21 A3
Albany W1 249 A5
Albany Wlk N15 50 D5
Alba Pl W11 91 B1
Albatross Cl E6 100 B3
Albatross 31 NW9 27 D1
Albatross St SE18 145 C5
Albemarle App IG2 56 D3
Albemarle Ave TW2 151 B3
Albemarle Gdns
Ilford IG2 56 D3
New Malden KT3 199 B5
Albemarle Ho
2 Brixton SW9 138 C2
Rotherhithe SE8 119 B2
Albemarle Lo SE26 185 A5
Albemarle Mans NW3 69 D4
Albemarle Pk
Beckenham BR3 185 D2
Stanmore HA7 25 C5
Albemarle Prim Sch SW19 157 A2
Albemarle SW19 156 D2
Albemarle Rd
Beckenham BR2, BR3 186 A2
East Barnet EN4 14 C4
Albemarle St W1 115 C6 249 A5
Albemarle Way EC1 241 C5
Alberon Gdns NW11 47 B5
Alberta Ave SM1 217 B3
Alberta Ct 1 TW10 154 B6
Alberta Ho
Blackwall E14 120 A5
Hayes UB4 84 B4
Alberta Rd EN1 18 A5
Alberta St SE17 116 D1 261 D2
Albert Ave
Chingford E4 35 C6
South Lambeth SW8 270 C3
Albert Barnes Ho SE1 262 A5
Albert Bigg Point E15 98 A6
Albert Bridge Rd SW11 136 D5 267 C3
Albert Carr Gdns SW16 182 A5
Albert Cl
11 Hackney E9 96 B6
Wood Green N22 31 D2
Albert Cotts 2 E1 96 A2
Albert Cres E4 35 C6
Albert Ct
Knightsbridge SW7 246 C1
9 Putney SW19 157 A3
Albert Dr SW19 157 A3
Albert Emb SE1 116 A2 260 B3
Albert Gate Ct SW1 247 C1
Albert Gdns E1 96 D1
Albert Gray Ho SW10 266 C4
Albert Gr SW20 178 D2
Albert Hall Mans SW7 114 B4 246 C1
Albert Ho
Stanmore HA7 25 B5
5 Wanstead E18 55 B6
2 Woolwich SE28 123 A3
Albert Mans
Battersea SW11 267 C2
Hornsey N8 50 A2
Albert Meml* SW7 114 B4 246 C1
Albert Mews W8 256 A6
Albert Palace Mans SW11 268 B2
Albert Pl Finchley N3 29 C2
Kensington W8 113 D4 245 D1
Albert Rd
Ashford TW15 170 B5
Bromley Comm BR2 209 D4
Buckhurst Hill IG9 21 D2
Chislehurst SE9 166 A1
Croydon SE25 206 B5
Dagenham RM8 59 C1
Ealing W5 87 B3
East Barnet EN4 2 A1
Erith DA17 125 B1
Finsbury Pk N4 50 B2
Hampton TW12 174 A5
Harrow HA2 42 A6
Hayes UB3 105 C3
Hendon NW4 46 D5
Hounslow TW3 129 C1
Ilford IG1 79 A5
Kilburn NW6 91 B5
Kingston u T KT1 176 B1
Leyton E10 54 A1
Mill Hill NW7 27 D5
Mitcham CR4 202 D6
Newham E16 122 B4
New Malden KT3 199 D5
Penge SE20 184 D4
Richmond TW10 154 B6
Sidcup DA5 169 D4
Southall UB2 106 D3
South Tottenham N15 51 C3
Sutton SM1 218 B3
Teddington TW11 174 D4
Twickenham TW1 152 D3
Walthamstow E17 53 C4
4 Wanstead E18 55 B6
Wood Green N22 31 C2
Yiewsley UB7 104 A5
Albert's Ct NW1 237 B6
Albert Sleet Ct N9 18 B1
Albert Sq Leyton E15 76 C3
Albert Sq *continued*
South Lambeth SW8 138 B5 270 C3
Albert Starr Ho 7 SE8 118 D2
Albert St
Camden Town NW1 93 B6 231 D5
North Finchley N12 30 A5
Albert Studios SW11 267 C2
Albert Terr
Buckhurst Hill IG9 21 D2
Camden Town NW1 93 A6 231 A5
Albert Terr Mews NW1 231 A5
Albert Terr NW10 89 A6
Albert Victoria Ho N22 32 C2
Albert Way SE15 140 B5
Albert Westcott Ho SE17 261 D2
Albert Whicher Ho 3 E17 54 A5
Albert Wlk E16 122 D4
Albion Ave
Clapham SW8 137 D3
Muswell Hill N10 31 A2
Albion Cl W2 247 B6
Albion Coll WC1 94 A2 240 B3
Albion Ct
7 Hammersmith W6 112 B2
Sutton SM2 218 B1
2 Woolwich SE7 122 A2
Albion Dr E8 74 A1
Albion Est SE16 118 C4
Albion Gate W2 247 B6
Albion Gdns 1 W6 112 B2
Albion Gr N16 73 C4
Albion Hill IG10 21 D6
Albion Ho
17 Deptford SE8 141 C5
EC1 241 C4
Newham E16 122 D5
Albion Mews
Bayswater W2 114 C6 247 B6
6 Hammersmith W6 112 B2
Islington N1 234 A6
Albion Pk IG10 21 D6
Albion Pl
Broadgate EC2 242 D3
Clerkenwell EC1 241 C4
Hammersmith W6 112 B2
South Norwood SE25 206 A6
Albion Prim Sch SE16 118 C4
Albion Rd
Bexley DA6 147 C1
Dagenham RM10 81 B3
Hayes UB3 83 C1
Hounslow TW3 129 C1
Kingston u T KT2 177 A2
Stoke Newington N16 73 B4
Sutton SM2 218 B1
Tottenham N17 34 A1
Twickenham TW2 152 C3
Walthamstow E17 54 A6
Albion Riverside SW11 267 A4
Albion Sq E8 73 D1
Albion St
Bayswater W2 114 C6 247 B6
Rotherhithe SE16 118 C4
Thornton Heath CR0 204 D1
Albion Terr
Hackney E8 73 D1
Sewardstone E4 7 D1
Albion Villas Rd SE23, SE26 162 C1
Albion Way
Barbican EC1 242 A3
Lewisham SE13 142 A1
Wembley HA9 66 C5
Albion Wlk N1 233 B3
Albion Works Studios 14 E8 74 A3
Albion Yd N1 233 B3
Albon Ho SW18 157 D5
Albrighton Rd SE5, SE22 139 C2
Albuhera Cl EN2 4 C4
Albury Ave
Bexleyheath DA7 147 A3
Hounslow TW7 130 D5
Albury Bldgs SE1 251 D1
Albury Cl TW12 173 D4
Albury Ct
4 Croydon CR0 221 A4
Deptford SE8 141 C6
Mitcham CR4 180 B1
6 Northolt UB5 84 C4
Albury Ct *continued*
Ruislip HA4 62 C3
Sutton SM1 218 A4
Albury Dr HA5 22 D3
Albury Lo 7 SW2 160 B4
Albury Mews E12 77 C6
Albury Rd KT9 214 A3
Albury St SE8 141 C6
Albyfield BR1 210 B6
Albyn Rd SE8 141 C4
Alcester Cres E5 74 B6
Alcester Ct 4 SM6 219 B4
Alcester Rd SM6 219 B4
Alchemea Coll of Audio Engineering N1 94 D6 234 D6
Alcock Cl SM6 219 D1
Alcock Rd TW5 128 D5
Alconbury DA6 169 D6
Alconbury Rd E5 74 A6
Alcorn Cl SM3 217 C6
Alcott Cl W7 86 D2
Aldborough Ct
Chingford E4 19 D1
Ilford IG2 57 D4
ALDBOROUGH HATCH 57 C5
Aldborough Rd IG2 57 D6
Aldborough Rd N IG2 57 D4
Aldborough Rd S IG3 57 C2
Aldbourne Rd W12 112 A5
Aldbridge St SE17 117 C1 263 B2
Aldburgh Mews W1 238 B2
Aldbury Ave HA9 66 D1
Aldbury Ho SW3 257 A3
Aldbury Mews N9 17 B4
Aldebert Terr SW8 138 B5 270 C3
Aldeburgh Cl 16 E5 74 B6
Aldeburgh Pl
Greenwich SE10 121 A2
Woodford IG8 37 A6
Aldeburgh St SE10 121 A1
Alden Ave E15 98 D4
Alden Ct
South Croydon CR0 221 C5
Wimbledon SW19 179 C4
Aldenham Ctry Pk WD6 9 B6
Aldenham Dr UB8 82 D3
Aldenham Ho NW1 232 B3
Aldenham Rd WD6 9 C6
Aldenham St NW1 93 D5 232 C3
Alden Ho E8 96 B6
Aldensley Rd W6 112 B3
Alderbrook Prim Sch SW12 159 B4
Alderbrook Rd SW12 159 B5
Alderbury Rd SW13 134 A6
Alder Ct
East Finchley N2 48 B6
3 West Norwood SW16 182 C5
Alder Gr NW2 68 B6
Aldergrove Gdns TW4 129 A3
Aldergrove Ho 3 E5 74 A6
Alder Ho
Camberwell SE15 139 D6
1 Maitland Pk NW3 70 D2
St Johns SE4 141 C2
Alderley Ho 36 SW8 137 D3
Alder Lodge N9 17 C3
Alder Lo SW6 134 D4
Alderman Ave IG11 102 A4
Aldermanbury EC2 95 A1 242 B2
Aldermanbury Sq EC2 242 B3
Alderman Ct 13 N11 30 D5
Alderman Judge Mall 6 KT1 176 A1
Alderman's Hill N13 32 B6
Alderman's Wlk EC2 243 A3
Aldermary Rd BR1 187 A2
Aldermead 2 TW3 129 D1
Alder Mews 12 N19 71 C6
Aldermoor Rd SE6 163 B1
Alderney Ave TW5 129 D5
Alderney Gdns UB5 63 B1
Alderney Ho
20 Canonbury N1 73 A2
Enfield EN3 6 D5
Alderney Mews SE1 262 C6
Alderney Rd E1 96 D3
Alderney St SW1 115 B1 258 D2
Alder Rd
Mortlake SW14 133 B2
Sidcup DA14 167 D1
Alders Ave IG8 36 C4
ALDERSBROOK 77 C6
Aldersbrook Ave EN1 5 C3
Aldersbrook Dr KT2 176 B4
Aldersbrook La E12 78 B5
Aldersbrook Prim Sch E12 77 C6
Aldersbrook Rd E11, E12 77 C6
Alders Cl Ealing W5 109 D3
Edgware HA8 27 A5
Wanstead E11 77 B6
Alders Ct N17 52 B5
Aldersey Gdns IG11 79 B2
Aldersford Cl SE4 140 D1
Aldersgate Ct EC1 242 A3
Aldersgate St EC1 95 A2 242 A3
Aldersgrove Ave SE9, SE12 165 D1
Aldersgrove KT8 196 B4
Aldershot Rd NW6 91 B6
Aldersmead Ave CR0 206 D3
Aldersmead Rd BR3 185 A3
Alderson Pl UB2 108 A5
Alderson St W10 91 A3
Alders Rd HA8 27 A5
Alders The
Feltham TW13 173 A6
Heston TW5 129 B6
Southgate N21 16 C5
Streatham SW16 181 C6
West Wickham BR4 223 D6
Alderton Cl NW10 67 B5
Alderton Cres NW4 46 B4
Alderton Ct KT8 195 B5
Alderton 9 KT2 176 D2
Alderton Rd
Croydon CR0 206 A2
Herne Hill SE24 139 A2
Alderton Way NW4 46 B4
Alderville Rd SW6 135 B3
Alderwick Ct N7 72 B2
Alderwick Dr TW3 130 B2
Alder Wlk IG11 79 A2
Alderwood Mews EN4 2 A5
Alderwood Prim Sch SE9 167 C5
Alderwood Rd SE9 167 B5
Aldford St W1 115 A5 248 B4
Aldgate East Sta E1 95 D1 243 D2
Aldgate EC3 95 C1 243 B1
Aldgate High St EC3 95 D1 243 C1
Aldgate Sta EC3 95 D1 243 C1
Aldham Hall 1 E11 55 A3
Aldham Ho SE4 141 B4
Aldine Ct W12 112 C5
Aldine St W12 112 C4
Aldington Cl RM8 58 C1
Aldington Ct 1 E8 74 A1
Aldington Rd SE18 121 D3
Aldis Mews
3 Holdbrook EN3 7 C6
Upper Tooting SW17 180 C5
Aldis St SW17 180 C5
Aldred Rd NW6 69 C3
Aldren Rd SW17 158 A1
Aldriche Way E4 36 A4
Aldrich Gdns SM3 217 B5
Aldrich Terr SW18 158 A2
Aldrick Ho N1 233 D4
Aldridge Ave
Edgware HA8 10 D1
Holdbrook EN3 7 C5
Ruislip HA4 62 D6
Stanmore HA7 26 A2
Aldridge Ct W11 91 B2
Aldridge Rd Villas W11 91 B2
Aldridge Rise KT3 199 C3
Aldridge Wlk N14 16 A4
Aldrington Rd SW16 181 C6
Aldsworth Cl W9 91 D3
Aldwich Ho WC2 240 D1
Aldwick Cl SE9 167 B1
Aldwick Ct N12 30 A6
Aldwick Rd CR0 220 B4
Aldworth Gr SE13 164 A5
Aldworth Rd E15 76 C1
Aldwych Ave IG6 57 A5
Aldwych Bldgs WC2 240 B2
Aldwych WC2 94 B1 240 D1
Aldwyn Ho SW8 270 A3
Alers Rd DA6 168 D6
Alesia Cl N22 32 A3
Alestan Beck Rd E16 99 D1
Alexa Ct 4 SM2 217 C2
Alexander Ave NW10 68 B1

Alexander Cl
Barnet EN4 ... 2 B1
Hayes BR2 ... 209 A1
Sidcup DA15 ... 167 C5
Southall UB2 ... 108 A5
Twickenham TW2 ... 152 D2
Alexander Ct
Beckenham BR3 ... 186 B2
Greenwich SE3 ... 143 B3
Stanmore HA7 ... 44 B6
14 Surbiton KT6 ... 197 D2
Wandsworth SW18 ... 158 A6
Alexander Evans Mews SE23 ... 162 D2
Alexander Fleming Laboratory Mus* W2 ... 236 D2
Alexander Ho
8 Kingston u T KT2 ... 176 A2
15 Millwall E14 ... 119 C3
16 Sutton SM2 ... 218 A2
Alexander Lo SM1 ... 217 B3
Alexander McLeod Prim Sch SE2 ... 124 B1
Alexander Mews 2 W2 ... 91 D1
Alexander Pl SW7 ... 257 A4
Alexander Rd
Bexley DA7 ... 146 D3
Chislehurst BR7 ... 188 D5
Upper Holloway N19 ... 72 A6
Alexander Sq SW3 ... 114 C2 257 A4
Alexander St W2 ... 91 C1
Alexander Terr SE2 ... 124 B1
Alexandra Ave
Battersea SW11 ... 268 A1
Harrow HA2 ... 63 C5
Southall UB1 ... 107 B6
Sutton SM1 ... 217 C5
Wood Green N22 ... 31 D2
Alexandra Bsns Ctr EN3 ... 6 D1
Alexandra Cl
Ashford TW15 ... 171 B3
Deptford SE8 ... 141 B6
Harrow HA2 ... 63 D5
Alexandra Cotts
New Cross SE14 ... 141 B4
Penge SE20 ... 184 D4
Alexandra Cres BR1 ... 186 D4
Alexandra Ct
Ashford TW15 ... 171 B4
Ealing W5 ... 87 C2
Greenford UB6 ... 85 D5
Hounslow TW3 ... 129 D3
Paddington W9 ... 236 B6
4 Shacklewell N16 ... 73 D4
5 Shepherd's Bush W12 ... 112 A4
Southgate N14 ... 15 C6
Wembley HA9 ... 66 B4
Alexandra Dr
Surbiton KT5 ... 198 C2
West Norwood SE19 ... 183 C5
Alexandra Gdns
Chiswick W4 ... 133 C5
Cranley Gdns N10 ... 49 B5
Hounslow TW3 ... 129 D3
Wallington SM5 ... 219 A1
Alexandra Gr
Finchley N12 ... 29 D4
Finsbury Pk N4 ... 50 D1
Alexandra Ho 13 W6 ... 112 C1
Alexandra Inf Sch
Kingston u T KT2 ... 176 C3
Penge BR3 ... 184 D3
Alexandra Jun & Inf Sch TW3 ... 129 D3
Alexandra Jun Sch SE26 ... 184 D4
Alexandra Mans
Chelsea SW3 ... 266 C5
Cricklewood NW2 ... 68 D3
6 Hampstead NW6 ... 69 C3
9 Shepherd's Bush W12 ... 112 C5
Alexandra Mews N2 ... 48 D6
Alexandra National Ho N4 ... 72 D6
Alexandra Palace Sta N22 ... 32 A1
Alexandra Palace Way N10 ... 49 C6
Alexandra Pal* N22 ... 31 D1
Alexandra Park Rd N10, N22 ... 31 D2
Alexandra Park Sch N11 ... 31 C2
Alexandra Pl
Croydon CR0 ... 205 C1
Alexandra Pl *continued*
South Norwood SE25 ... 205 B4
St John's Wood NW8 ... 92 A6 229 B6
Alexandra Prim Sch N22 ... 32 B1
Alexandra Rd
Acton W4 ... 111 B4
Ashford TW15 ... 171 C4
10 Brentford TW8 ... 131 D6
Croydon CR0 ... 205 C2
Dagenham RM6 ... 59 A3
Edmonton N9 ... 18 B4
Enfield EN3 ... 6 D1
Hampstead NW8 ... 70 B1
Hendon NW4 ... 46 D5
Hornsey N8, N22 ... 50 C6
Hounslow TW3 ... 129 D3
Kingston u T KT2 ... 176 C3
Leyton E10 ... 76 A5
Mitcham SW19 ... 180 C3
Mortlake SW14 ... 133 B2
Muswell Hill N10 ... 31 B3
Penge SE26 ... 184 D4
Richmond TW9 ... 132 B3
Thames Ditton KT7 ... 196 D4
Tottenham N15 ... 51 B4
Twickenham TW1 ... 153 C5
Wallend E6 ... 100 C4
Walthamstow E17 ... 53 B2
Wanstead E18 ... 55 B6
Wimbledon SW19 ... 179 C5
Alexandra Sch HA2 ... 63 C6
Alexandra Sq SM4 ... 201 C4
Alexandra St
5 Deptford SE14 ... 141 A5
Newham E16 ... 99 A2
Alexandra Wlk 8 SE19 ... 183 C5
Alexandria Rd W13 ... 109 B6
Alex Gossip Ho SW6 ... 265 A1
Alexis St SE16 ... 118 A2
Alfearn Rd E5 ... 74 C4
Alford Ct
18 Belmont SM2 ... 217 D1
Shoreditch N1 ... 235 B3
Alford Gn CR0 ... 224 B2
Alford Ho
Crouch End N6 ... 49 C3
6 Woolwich SE18 ... 144 D6
Alford Pl N1 ... 235 B3
Alfoxton Ave N8, N15 ... 50 D5
Alfreda Ct SW11 ... 268 C1
Alfreda St SW11 ... 137 B4 268 C1
Alfred Butt Ho SW17 ... 158 D1
Alfred Cl W4 ... 111 B2
Alfred Findley Ho N22 ... 32 D1
Alfred Gdns UB1 ... 107 A6
Alfred Ho E9 ... 75 A3
Alfred Hurley Ho SW17 ... 180 A6
Alfred Mews W1, WC1 ... 239 C4
Alfred Nunn Ho NW10 ... 89 D6
Alfred Pl WC1 . 93 D2 239 C4
Alfred Prior Ho 7 E12 ... 78 C4
Alfred Rd Acton W3 ... 111 A5
Buckhurst Hill IG9 ... 21 D2
Croydon SE25 ... 206 A4
Erith DA17 ... 125 B1
Feltham TW13 ... 150 C2
Kingston u T KT1 ... 198 B6
Leyton E15 ... 76 D3
Paddington W2 ... 91 C2
Sutton SM1 ... 218 A3
Alfred Salter Ho SE1 ... 263 D3
Alfred Salter Prim Sch SE16 ... 118 D4
Alfred's Gdns IG11 ... 101 C5
Alfred St E3 ... 97 B4
Alfred's Way (East Ham & Barking By-Pass) IG11 ... 101 B5
Alfred's Way Ind Est IG11 ... 102 A6
Alfred Villas 9 E17 ... 54 A5
Alfreton Cl SW19 ... 156 D1
Alfriston Ave
Harrow HA2 ... 41 C2
Thornton Heath CR0 ... 204 A2
Alfriston Cl KT5 ... 198 B3
Alfriston Rd SW11 ... 158 D6
Alfriston KT5 ... 198 B3
Algar Cl
Isleworth TW7 ... 131 A2
Stanmore HA7 ... 24 D5
Algar Ct TW12 ... 173 D2
Algar Ho SE1 ... 251 C1
Algar Rd TW7 ... 131 A2
Algarve Rd SW18 ... 157 D3
Algernon Rd
Hendon NW4 ... 46 A3
Kilburn NW6 ... 91 C6
Lewisham SE13 ... 141 D1
Algers Cl IG10 ... 21 D6
Algers Rd IG10 ... 21 D6
Alghers Mead IG10 ... 21 D6
Algiers Rd SE13 ... 141 C1
Alguin Ct HA7 ... 25 C3
Alibon Gdns RM10 ... 81 C3
Alibon Rd RM10 ... 81 C3
Alice Cl 13 EN5 ... 2 A1
Alice Ct 10 N3 ... 29 C2
Alice Gilliott Ct W14 ... 264 D6
Alice La E3 ... 97 B6
Alice Mews 3 TW11 ... 174 D5
Alice Owen Tech Ctr EC1 ... 234 C2
Alice Shepherd Ho 12 E14 ... 120 A4
Alice St SE1 ... 117 C3 263 A5
Alice Thompson Cl SE12 ... 165 C2
Alice Walker Cl 8 SE24 ... 138 D1
Alice Way TW3 ... 129 D1
Alicia Ave HA3 ... 43 C5
Alicia Cl HA3 ... 43 C5
Alicia Gdns HA3 ... 43 C5
Alicia Ho DA16 ... 146 B4
Alie St E1 ... 95 D1 243 D1
Alington Cres NW9 ... 45 A1
Alison Cl
Croydon CR0 ... 206 D1
Newham E6 ... 100 C1
Alison Ct HA8 ... 26 D5
Aliwal Rd SW11 ... 136 C1
Alkerden Rd W4 ... 111 C1
Alkham Rd N16 ... 73 D6
Allam Ho W11 ... 244 A6
Allan Barclay Cl N15 ... 51 D3
Allanbridge N16 ... 51 C2
Allan Cl KT3 ... 199 B4
Allandale Ave N3 ... 47 B6
Allan Ho SW8 ... 269 C2
Allanson Ct E10 ... 75 C6
Allan Way W3 ... 89 A2
Allard Cres WD23 ... 8 A2
Allard Gdns SW4 ... 159 D6
Allardyce St SW4, SW9 ... 138 B1
Allbrook Cl TW11 ... 174 C5
Allbrook Ho 4 SW15 ... 156 A4
Allcot Cl TW14 ... 149 D3
Allcott Ho TW7 ... 130 D2
Allcroft Rd NW5 ... 71 A2
Allder Way CR2 ... 220 D1
Allenby Cl UB6 ... 85 C4
Allenby Prim Sch UB1 ... 85 C1
Allenby Rd
Forest Hill SE23 ... 163 A1
Southall UB1 ... 85 C3
Woolwich SE28 ... 123 A3
Allen Cl
Streatham CR4 ... 181 C2
Sunbury TW16 ... 172 B2
Allen Ct
Greenford UB6 ... 64 D3
Walthamstow E17 ... 53 C3
Allendale Ave UB1 ... 85 C1
Allendale Cl
Camberwell SE5 ... 139 B4
Forest Hill SE26 ... 184 D5
Allendale Rd UB6 ... 65 B2
Allen Edwards Dr SW8 ... 138 A4 270 A2
Allen Edwards Prim Sch SW4 ... 138 A4 270 A1
Allenford Ho SW15 ... 155 D5
All England Lawn Tennis & Croquet Club The SW19 ... 157 A1
Allen Ho W8 ... 255 B6
Allen Mans W8 ... 255 B6
Allen Rd Old Ford E3 ... 97 B5
Penge BR3 ... 184 D1
Stoke Newington N16 ... 73 C4
Sunbury TW16 ... 172 B1
Thornton Heath CR0 ... 204 C1
Allensbury Pl
7 Camden Town NW1 ... 71 D1
Camden Town NW1 ... 72 A1
Allens Rd EN3 ... 18 C6
Allen St W8 ... 113 C3 255 B5
Allenswood 12 SW19 ... 157 A3
Allenswood Rd SE9 ... 144 B3
Allerdale Ho 7 N4 ... 51 B2
Allerford Ct
Catford SE6 ... 163 D1
Harrow HA2 ... 42 A4
Allerford Rd SE6 ... 185 D6
Allerton Ct
5 Hendon NW4 ... 28 D1
North Cheam SM3 ... 216 D6
Allerton Ho
4 Merton SW19 ... 180 A3
Shoreditch N1 ... 235 D3
Allerton Rd N16 ... 73 A6
Allerton St N1 ... 235 D2
Allerton Wlk 11 N7 ... 72 B6
Allestree Rd SW6 ... 135 A5 264 A3
Alleyn Cres SE21 ... 161 B2
Alleyndale Rd RM8 ... 80 C6
Alleyn Ho
Bermondsey SE1 ... 262 C5
St Luke's EC1 ... 242 B5
Alleyn Pk
Dulwich SE21 ... 161 C1
Southall UB2 ... 107 C1
Alleyn Rd SE21 ... 161 C1
Alleyn's Sch SE22 ... 161 C6
Allfarthing La SW18 ... 158 A5
Allfarthing Prim Sch SW18 ... 158 A5
Allgood Cl SM4 ... 200 D3
Allgood St 10 E2 ... 95 D5
Allhallows La EC4 ... 252 C5
Allhallows Rd E6 ... 100 A1
All Hallows Rd N17 ... 33 C2
Alliance Cl
Twickenham TW4 ... 151 B6
Wembley HA0 ... 65 D4
Alliance Ct Acton W3 ... 88 D2
Ashford TW15 ... 171 A6
Alliance Rd Acton W3 ... 88 D3
East Wickham SE18 ... 146 A5
1 Newham E16 ... 99 C2
Allied Ind Est W3 ... 111 C5
Allied Way W3 ... 111 C4
Allingham Cl W7 ... 108 D6
Allingham Ct NW3 ... 70 C3
Allingham Mews N1 ... 235 A4
Allingham St N1 ... 95 A5 235 A4
Allington Ave
Tottenham N17 ... 33 C4
Upper Halliford TW17 ... 193 C6
Allington Cl
Greenford UB6 ... 64 A1
3 Wimbledon SW19 ... 178 D5
Allington Ct
6 Clapham SW8 ... 137 C3
Croydon CR0 ... 206 C3
Enfield EN3 ... 18 D6
Allington Rd
Harrow HA2 ... 42 A4
Hendon NW4 ... 46 B3
Kensal Rise W10 ... 91 A5
Orpington BR6 ... 211 C1
Allington St SW1 ... 258 D5
Allison Cl SE10 ... 142 A4
Allison Gr SE21 ... 161 C3
Allison Rd Acton W3 ... 111 A6
Harringay N8 ... 50 D4
Alliston Ho 27 E2 ... 95 D4
Allitsen Rd NW8 ... 92 C5 230 A4
All Nations Ho 10 E8 ... 74 B1
Allnutt Way SW4 ... 159 D6
Alloa Ct N14 ... 15 C2
Alloa Rd IG3 ... 80 A6
Allom Ct 11 SW4 ... 138 A3
Allonby Dr HA4 ... 38 D2
Allonby Gdns HA9 ... 43 C1
Allonby Ho E14 ... 97 A2
Alloway Rd E3 ... 97 A4
Allport Ho SE5 ... 139 B2
Allport Mews 44 E1 ... 96 C3
All Saints' Benhilton CE Prim Sch SM1 ... 217 D5
All Saint's CE Jun Sch SE19 ... 183 C2
All Saints' CE Prim Sch
Blackheath Vale SE3 ... 142 C3
Child's Hill NW2 ... 69 B5
East Barnet N20 ... 14 B2
All Saints CE Prim Sch
Merton SW19 ... 180 A3
Putney SW15 ... 134 C2
All Saints' CE Prim Sch SM5 ... 219 A3
All Saints Church 9 N19 ... 71 D5
All Saints' Cl N9 ... 18 A2
All Saints Ct
Heston TW5 ... 128 D4
Lower Clapton E5 ... 74 C4
10 Shadwell E1 ... 118 C6
All Saints Dr SE3 ... 142 D3
All Saints Ho 2 W11 ... 91 B2
All Saint's Inf Sch SE19 ... 183 C2
All Saints Mews HA3 ... 24 C4
All Saints Pas SW18 ... 157 C6
All Saints RC Sch BR4 ... 224 B4
All Saints RC Sch & Tech Coll RM8 ... 59 C1
All Saints' Rd W3 ... 111 A3
All Saints Rd
Merton SW19 ... 180 A3
Notting Hill W11 ... 91 B1
Sutton SM1 ... 218 A5
All Saints Sta E14 ... 119 D6
All Saints St N1 ... 94 B5 233 C4
All Saints Twr 19 E10 ... 53 D2
Allsop Pl NW1 ... 92 D3 237 D5
All Souls' Ave NW10 ... 90 B6
All Souls CE Prim Sch W1 ... 93 C2 239 A4
All Souls Pl W1 ... 238 D3
Allum La WD6 ... 10 A6
Allum Way N20 ... 14 A3
Allwood Cl SE26 ... 184 D6
Alma Ave E4 ... 36 A3
Alma Birk Ho 1 NW6 ... 69 B1
Almack Rd E5 ... 74 C4
Alma Cl N10 ... 31 B2
Alma Cres SM1 ... 217 A3
Alma Gr SE1 . 117 D2 263 D3
Alma Ho
7 Brentford TW8 ... 132 A6
2 Edmonton N9 ... 34 A6
Alma Pl
College Pk NW10 ... 90 B4
Penge SE19 ... 183 D3
Thornton Heath CR7 ... 204 C4
Alma Prim Sch
Bermondsey SE16 ... 118 A2
Enfield EN3 ... 18 D6
Alma Rd
Carshalton SM5 ... 218 C3
Enfield EN3 ... 7 A1
Muswell Hill N10 ... 31 B3
Sidcup DA14 ... 168 A1
Southall UB1 ... 107 A6
Thames Ditton KT10, KT7 ... 196 C1
Wandsworth SW18 ... 158 A6
Alma Row HA3 ... 24 B2
Alma Sq NW8 ... 92 A4 229 B2
Alma St
Camden Town NW5 ... 71 B2
Stratford New Town E15 ... 76 B2
Alma Terr
Earl's Ct W8 ... 255 B5
Wandsworth SW18 ... 158 B4
Almeida St 10 N1 ... 72 D1
Almeric Rd SW11 ... 136 D1
Almer Rd SW20 ... 178 A3
Almington St N4 ... 50 B1
Almond Ave
Carshalton SM5 ... 218 D6
Ealing W5 ... 110 A3
Uxbridge UB10 ... 60 D5
West Drayton UB7 ... 104 C3
Almond Cl
Bromley BR2 ... 210 C2
Charlton TW17 ... 171 A1
Feltham TW14 ... 150 A3
Hayes UB3 ... 105 C6
Peckham SE15 ... 140 A3
Ruislip HA4 ... 61 D5
Almond Gr TW8 ... 131 B5
Almond Ho SE4 ... 141 B3
Almond Rd
Bermondsey SE16 ... 118 B2
Tottenham N17 ... 34 A3
Almonds Ave IG9 ... 21 A2
Almond Way
Bromley BR2 ... 210 C2
Harrow HA2 ... 24 A1
Mitcham CR4 ... 203 D5
Almorah Rd
De Beauvoir Town N1 ... 73 B1
Heston TW5 ... 128 D4
Almshouse La EN1 ... 6 B6
Almshouses
Edmonton N9 ... 17 D2
Leyton E10 ... 75 D6
Southall UB1 ... 85 C1
Sunbury TW16 ... 171 D2
Almshouses The IG11 ... 79 A2
Al-Muntada Islamic Sch SW6 ... 135 B4 264 D2
Alnmouth Ct 10 UB1 ... 86 A1
Al-Noor Muslim Prim Sch IG3 ... 58 B1
Alnwick Gr SM4 ... 201 D5
Alnwick Rd
Eltham SE12 ... 165
Newham E16 ... 99
Alnwick 8 N17 ... 34
Alonso Ho 4 DA17 ... 125
ALPERTON ... 88
Alperton Com Sch HA0 ... 66
Alperton La UB6 ... 87
Alperton Lower Sch HA0 ... 87
Alperton Sta HA0 ... 88
Alperton St W10 ... 91
Alphabet Gdns SM5 ... 202
Alphabet Sq E3 ... 97
Alpha Bsns Ctr E17 ... 53
Alpha Cl NW8 .. 92 C4 230
Alpha Ct 6 NW5 ... 71
Alpha Est The UB3 ... 105
Alpha Gr E14 ... 119
Alpha Ho
19 Brixton SW4 ... 138
Kilburn NW6 ... 91
Lisson Gr NW8 ... 237
Alpha Pl
Chelsea SW3 ... 136 C6 267
Kilburn NW6 ... 91 C
Alpha Rd Chingford E4 .. 19 D
Croydon CR0 ... 205 C
Edmonton N18 ... 34 A
Enfield EN3 ... 7 A
Hillingdon UB10 ... 82 D
New Cross SE14 ... 141 B
Surbiton KT5 ... 198 B
Teddington TW12 ... 174 B
Alpha St SE15 ... 140 A
Alphea Cl SW19 ... 180 C
Alpine Ave KT5 ... 215 A
Alpine Bsns Ctr E6 ... 100 C
Alpine Cl CR0 ... 221 C
Alpine Copse BR1 ... 188 C
Alpine Ct SE12 ... 142 D
Alpine Gr 37 E9 ... 74 C
Alpine Rd
Deptford SE16 ... 118 D
Leyton E10 ... 75 D
Walton-on-T KT12 ... 194 A
Alpine View SM5 ... 218 C
Alpine Way E6 ... 100 C
Alpine Wlk HA7 ... 8 C
Alric Ave
Kingston u T KT3 ... 199 D
Willesden NW10 ... 67 B
Alroy Rd N4 ... 50 C
Alsace Rd SE17 ... 117 C1 263 A
Al Sadiq & Al Zahra Schs NW6 ... 91 A
Alscot Rd SE1 ... 117 D3 263 D
Alscot Road Ind Est SE1 ... 263 D
Alscot Way SE1 ... 263 C
Alsike Rd DA18 ... 125 A3
Alsom Ave KT19, KT4 ... 216 A
Alston Cl KT7 ... 197 B2
Alston Ct 2 EN5 ... 1 A2
Alstone Ct N9 ... 18 A2
Alston Rd
Edmonton N18 ... 34 B5
High Barnet EN5 ... 1 A2
Upper Tooting SW17 ... 180 B6
Altair Cl N17 ... 33 D4
Altair Ct N1 ... 73 B2
Altash Way SE9 ... 166 C2
Altenburg Ave W13 ... 109 B3
Altenburg Gdns SW11 ... 136 D1
Alt Gr SW19 ... 179 B3
Altham Gdns WD19 ... 22 D6
Altham Rd HA5 ... 23 A3
Althea St SW6 ... 135 D2
Althorne Gdns E18 ... 54 D5
Althorne Way RM10 ... 81 C6
Althorp Cl EN5 ... 12 A4
Althorpe Mews SW11 ... 266 D1
Althorpe Rd HA1 ... 42 A4
Althorp Rd SW17 ... 158 D3
Altima Ct SE22 ... 140 A1
Altior Ct N6 ... 49 C3
Altmore Ave E6 ... 100 B6
Altmore Inf Sch E6 ... 100 B6
Alton Ave HA7 ... 24 D3
Alton Cl
Isleworth TW7 ... 130 D3
Sidcup DA5 ... 169 A3
Alton Ct 18 BR3 ... 185 C3
Alton Gdns
Beckenham BR3 ... 185 C3
Twickenham TW2 ... 152 B4
Alton Ho 3 E3 ... 97 D4
Alton Rd
Croydon CR0 ... 220 C5

Alton Rd *continued*
Richmond TW10,
TW9 132 A1
Roehampton SW15 156 A3
Tottenham N17 51 B6
Alton St E14 97 D2
Altyre Cl BR3 207 B4
Altyre Rd CR0 221 B6
Altyre Way BR3 207 B4
Alum Ct KT5 198 B3
Alumni Ct SE1 253 D2
Alvanley Ct NW3 69 D3
Alvanley Gdns NW6 69 D3
Alvanley Ho 14 SW9 138 C4
Alvernia Lo SM1 217 D5
Alverstone Ave
East Barnet EN4 14 C4
Wimbledon SW18,
SW19 157 C2
Alverstone Gdns
SE9 167 A3
Alverstone Ho 11
SE11 138 C6
Alverstone Rd
Little Ilford E12 78 C4
New Malden KT3 199 D5
Wembley HA9 44 B1
Willesden NW2 68 C1
Alverston Gdns
SE25 205 C4
Alverton St SE8 141 B6
Alveston Ave HA3 43 B6
Alveston Sq 5 E18 37 A1
Alvey St SE17 263 A2
Alvia Gdns SM1 218 A4
Alvington Cres E8 73 D3
Alway Ave KT19 215 B3
Alwen Cotts CR0 222 D4
Alwold Cres SE12 165 C5
Alwyn Ave W4 111 B1
Alwyn Cl
Borehamwood
WD6 10 B5
New Addington CR0 223 D1
Alwyne La N1 72 D1
Alwyne Mans SW19 179 B4
Alwyne Pl N1 73 A1
Alwyne Rd
Canonbury N1 73 A1
Ealing W7 108 C6
Wimbledon SW19 179 B4
Alwyne Sq N1 73 A2
Alwyne Villas N1 72 D1
Alwyn Gdns Acton W3 88 D1
Hendon NW9 46 A5
Alyn Ct N8 49 D3
Alyth Gdns NW11 47 C3
Alzette Ho 11 E2 96 D5
Amalgamated Dr
TW8 131 B6
Amanda Ct
Ashford TW15 148 B2
Chingford E4 36 C4
Aman Dalvi Ho
SW18 157 A4
Amar Ct SE18 123 D2
Amardeep Ct SE18 123 D1
Amazon Apartments
N8 50 B6
Amazonas
SE1 117 C2 263 B3
Amazon St E1 96 B1
Ambassador Cl
TW3 129 A3
Ambassador Ct
9 Hampstead
NW6 69 C3
Hendon NW4 46 D4
Ambassador Gdns
E6 100 B2
Ambassador Ho
Harrow HA3 42 C6
St John's Wood NW8 229 B5
Ambassador Sq
E14 119 D2
Amber Ave E17 35 A2
Amber Ct
Feltham TW13 149 C1
Islington N7 72 C2
Mitcham CR4 202 C5
Southall UB1 107 D5
Amberden Ave N3 47 C6
Amberdene HA7 24 D4
Ambergate St
SE17 116 D1 261 D2
Amber Gr NW2 46 D1
Amber Ho HA7 25 D3
Amberley Cl
2 Orpington
BR6 227 D3
Pinner HA5 41 B6
Amberley Ct
2 Brixton SW9 138 D2
Sidcup DA14 190 C5
Sutton SM2 218 A1
Amberley Gdns
Enfield EN1 17 C4
Amberley Gdns *continued*
Worcester Pk KT19 215 D4
Amberley Gr
Croydon CR0 205 D2
Penge SE26 184 B5
Amberley Ho
8 Barnet EN5 1 D1
7 Ealing W7 108 C5
Amberley Rd
Buckhurst Hill IG9 21 C3
Enfield EN1 17 D5
Palmers Green N13 16 B2
Walthamstow E10 53 D2
Westbourne Green
W9 91 C2
West Heath SE2 146 D6
Amberley Way
Heston TW4 150 C6
Morden SM4 201 B2
Romford RM7 59 D5
Uxbridge UB10 82 A5
Amberside Cl TW2 152 B5
Amber Wharf 29 E2 95 D6
Amberwood Cl SM6 220 A3
Amberwood Rise
KT3 199 C3
Amblecote Cl SE12 165 B1
Amblecote Mdws
SE12 165 B1
Amblecote Rd SE12 165 B1
Ambler Prim Sch N4 72 D6
Ambler Rd N4 72 D5
Ambleside Ave
Beckenham BR3 207 A4
Streatham SW16 181 D6
Walton-on-T KT12 194 C1
Ambleside BR1 186 B4
Ambleside Cl
Lower Clapton E9 74 C3
5 Tottenham N17 51 D6
Walthamstow E10 53 D2
Ambleside Cres EN3 6 D2
Ambleside Dr TW14 149 D3
Ambleside Gdns
Redbridge IG4 56 A4
Streatham SW16 181 D5
Sutton SM2 218 A2
Wembley HA9 43 D1
Ambleside Ho HA8 27 A5
Ambleside Point 1
SE15 140 C5
Ambleside 13 SW19 157 A3
Ambleside Rd
Bexleyheath DA7 147 C3
Willesden NW10 67 D1
Ambleside NW1 231 D3
Ambrook Ct SM1 218 B3
Ambrook Rd DA17 125 C3
Ambrosden Ave
SW1 115 C3 259 B5
Ambrose Ave NW11 47 B3
Ambrose Cl
6 Newham E6 100 B2
Orpington BR6 227 D5
Ambrose Ho 9 E14 97 C2
Ambrose Mews 2
SW11 136 D3
Ambrose St SE16 118 B2
Ambrose Wlk E3 97 C5
AMC Bsns Ctr NW10 88 D4
Amelia Cl W3 110 D4
Amelia Ho 5 W6 112 C1
Amelia St
SE17 117 A1 262 A2
Amen Cnr
Holborn EC4 241 D1
Streatham SW17 181 A4
Amen Ct EC4 94 D1 241 D1
Amenity Way SM4 200 C2
American
Intercontinental Univ
W1 93 A2 238 B3
American Sch in
London The
NW8 92 B5 229 C4
American Univ in
London The N7 72 B5
America Sq EC3 253 C6
America St SE1 252 A3
Ameriand Rd SW18 157 B5
Amersham Ave N18 33 B4
Amersham Gr SE14 141 B5
Amersham Rd
New Cross SE14 141 B4
Thornton Heath CR0 205 B3
Amersham Vale SE14,
SE8 141 B5
Amery Gdns NW10 90 B6
Amery Ho SE17 263 B2
Amery Rd HA1 65 A6
Amesbury Ave SW2 160 B2
Amesbury Cl KT4 200 C1
Amesbury Ct EN2 4 C3
Amesbury Dr E4 19 D5
Amesbury Rd
Bromley BR1 209 D6
Dagenham RM9 80 D1
Amesbury Rd *continued*
Feltham TW13 150 D2
Amesbury Twr 4
SW8 137 C3
Ames Cotts 12 E3 97 A2
Ames Ho 10 E2 96 D5
Amethyst Ct 1 EN3 7 A2
Amethyst Cl N11 31 D3
Amethyst Ct BR6 227 C3
Amethyst Rd E15 76 B4
Amherst Ave W13 87 C1
Amherst Dr BR5 211 D5
Amherst Gdns 2
W13 87 C1
Amherst Rd W13 87 C1
Amhurst Ct N4 51 B2
Amhurst Gdns TW7 131 A3
Amhurst Par N16 51 D2
Amhurst Pk N4, N16 51 C2
Amhurst Rd E8, N16 74 A4
Amhurst Terr E8 74 A4
Amhurst Wlk SE28 124 A5
Amias Ho EC1 242 A6
Amidas Gdns RM8 80 B4
Amiel St 15 E1 96 C3
Amies St SW11 136 D2
Amigo Ho SE1 261 B6
Amina Way SE16 118 A3
Amis Ave KT19 214 D3
Amity Gr SW20 178 C2
Amity Rd E15 76 D1
Ammanford Gn NW9 45 C3
Ammonite Ho 3 E15 76 D1
Amner Rd SW11 159 A5
Amora 8 HA7 25 C6
Amor Rd W6 112 C3
Amory Ho N1 233 D4
Amott Rd SE15 140 A2
Amoy Pl E14 119 C6
Ampere Way CR0 204 B1
Ampleforth Rd SE2 124 C4
Ampton Pl WC1 233 C1
Ampton St
WC1 94 B4 233 C1
Amroth Cl SE23 162 B3
Amroth Gn NW9 45 C3
Amstel Ct 12 SE15 139 D5
Amsterdam Rd E14 120 A3
Amundsen Ct 7
E14 119 C1
Amundsen Ho 6
NW10 67 B1
Amwell Cl EN2 17 B6
Amwell St
EC1 94 C4 234 A2
Amyand Cotts 12
TW1 153 B5
Amyand Park Gdns 2
TW1 153 B4
Amyand Park Rd
TW1 153 B4
Amy Cl SM6 220 A1
Amy Johnson Ct HA8 26 D1
Amy Johnson Prim Sch
SM6 220 A1
Amyruth Rd SE4 163 C6
Amy Warne Cl E6 100 A3
Anarth Ct KT13 193 C1
Anatola Rd N19 71 C6
Ancaster Cres KT3 200 A3
Ancaster Mews
CR0 206 D6
Ancaster Rd BR3 206 D6
Ancaster St SE18 145 C5
Anchorage Cl SW19 179 C5
Anchorage Point 1
E14 119 C4
Anchorage Point Ind Est
SE7 121 C3
Anchor Bsns Pk CR0,
SM6 220 A5
Anchor Cl IG11 102 B4
Anchor Ct
Bexley DA7 147 A4
5 Enfield EN1 17 C6
Anchor Ho Ilford IG3 80 A5
Newham E16 99 C1
Anchor & Hope La
SE7 121 C2
Anchor Ho EC1 242 A6
Anchor Mews SW12 159 B5
Anchor Ret Pk E1 96 C3
Anchor St SE16 118 B2
Anchor Terr SE1 252 B4
Anchor Yd EC1 242 B6
Ancill Cl W6 135 A6 264 A5
Ancona Rd
Plumstead SE18 123 B1
Willesden Green
NW10 90 A5
Andace Pk BR1 187 C2
Andalus Rd SW9 138 A2
Andaman Ho 3 E1 97 A2
Ander Cl HA0 65 D4
Andersens Wharf 9
E14 97 B1
Anderson Cl
Morden SM3 201 C1
North Acton W3 89 B1
Southgate N21 16 B6
Anderson Ct NW2 46 C2
Anderson Dr TW15 171 A6
Anderson Ho
1 Barking IG11 101 B5
10 Blackwall E14 120 A6
Upper Tooting SW17 180 B5
Anderson Rd
Homerton E9 74 D2
Redbridge IG8 55 D6
Anderson's Pl TW3 129 D1
Andersons Sq N1 234 C5
Anderson St SW3 257 C2
Anderson Way
Erith DA17 125 D4
Erith DA17 125 D4
Anderton Cl SE5 139 B2
Anderton Ct N22 31 D1
Andhurst Ct KT2 176 D2
Andmark Ct UB1 107 B5
Andon Ct BR3 207 A6
Andorra Ct BR1 187 C2
Andover Ave E16 99 D1
Andover Cl
East Bedfont
TW14 149 D3
Greenford UB6 85 D3
Andover Ho 5 N7 72 B6
Andover Pl NW6 91 D5
Andover Rd
Finsbury Pk N7 72 B6
Orpington BR6 211 C1
Twickenham TW2 152 B3
Andoversford Ct 2
SE15 139 C6
Andrecht Terr CR4 203 D5
Andreck Ct BR3 186 A1
Andre Malraux Sch
W7 86 C2
Andre St E8 74 A3
Andrew Borde St
WC2 239 D2
Andrew Ct
Beckenham BR3 207 D6
2 Forest Hill SE23 162 D2
Andrewes Ct 2 W7 108 C5
Andrewes Gdns E6 100 A1
Andrewes Ho
Barbican EC2 242 B3
Sutton SM1 217 C4
Andrew Ewing Jun & Inf
Sch TW5 129 B5
Andrew Ho
Enfield EN3 18 C6
New Cross SE4 141 B3
Putney SW15 156 A6
Andrew Logan's Glass
Ho* SE1 253 A2
Andrew Marvell Ho 12
N16 73 C4
Andrew Pl SW8 269 D2
Andrew Reed Ho
SW18 157 A4
Andrews Cl
Buckhurst Hill IG9 21 C2
Harrow HA1 42 B2
North Cheam KT4 216 D6
Sidcup BR5 190 D1
Andrews Crosse
WC2 241 A1
Andrew's Rd E8 96 B6
Andrew St E14 98 A1
Andrews Wharf 14
E8 96 B6
Andrews Wlk SE17 138 D6
Andrew Wells Ho
BR1 187 B3
Andrew Wilmot Ct
SW18 158 A3
Andridge Ct SW19 179 B2
Andringham Lo 4
BR1 187 B2
Andrula Ct N22 32 D2
Andwell Cl SE2 124 B4
ANERLEY 184 B2
Anerley Ct SE20 184 B3
Anerley Gr SE19 183 D3
Anerley Hill SE19 183 D4
Anerley Park Rd
SE20 184 B3
Anerley Pk SE20 184 B3
Anerley Rd SE20 184 B2
Anerley Sta SE20 184 B2
Anerley Station Rd
SE20 184 B2
Anerley Vale SE19 184 A3
Aneurin Bevan Ct
NW2 68 B6
Aneurin Bevan Ho
N11 31 D3
Anfield Cl SW12 159 C4
Angela Ct 2 SE23 162 C3
Angela Davis Ind Est 20
SW9 138 D1
Angel Cl N18 34 A6
Angel Corner Par 6
N18 34 A6
Angel Ct
Broadgate EC2 242 D2
St James SW1 249 B3
5 Willesden NW2 68 A2
Angel EC1 94 D5 234 D3
Angel Edmonton
N18 34 A5
Angelfield TW3 151 D6
Angel Gate EC1 234 D2
Angel Hill Dr SM1 217 D5
Angel Hill SM1 217 D5
Angel Ho N1 234 B3
Angelica Cl UB7 82 B1
Angelica Dr E6 100 C2
Angelica Gdns CR0 206 D1
Angelina Ho 2
SE15 140 A4
Angelis Appartments
N1 234 D3
Angel La Hayes UB3 83 B2
Stratford E15 76 B2
Angell Park Gdns 4
SW9 138 C2
Angell Rd SW9 138 D2
Angel Mews
Finsbury N1 234 B3
Putney SW15 156 A4
Stepney E1 118 B6
Angel Pas
EC4 117 B6 252 C5
Angel Pl
Borough The SE1 252 C2
1 Edmonton N18 34 A5
Angel Rd HA1 42 C3
Angel Rd (North
Circular Rd) N18 34 B5
Angel Rd KT7 197 A1
Angel Rd Works N18 34 C5
Angel Road Sta N18 34 C5
Angel Sq N1 234 B3
Angel Sta EC1 94 C5 234 B3
Angel St EC1 95 A1 242 A2
Angel Wlk W6 112 C2
Angerstein Bsns Pk
SE10 121 A2
Angerstein La SE3 142 D4
Anglebury 5 W2 91 C1
Angle Cl UB10 82 C6
Angle Gn RM8 58 C1
Anglers Cl TW10 175 C6
Anglers La NW5 71 B2
Anglers Reach KT6 197 D4
Anglesea Ave 4
SE18 122 D2
Anglesea Ho KT1 197 D5
Anglesea Mews 12
SE18 122 D2
Anglesea Rd
Kingston u T KT1 197 D5
Woolwich SE18 122 D2
Anglesey Cl TW15 148 C1
Anglesey Court Rd
SM5 219 A2
Anglesey Ct W7 86 D3
Anglesey Gdns SM5 219 A2
Anglesey Ho 13 E14 97 C1
Anglesey Rd
Enfield EN3 6 B1
South Oxhey WD19 22 C5
Anglesmede Cres
HA5 41 C6
Anglesmede Way
HA5 41 C6
Angles Rd SW16 182 A6
Anglia Cl N17 34 B3
Anglia Ct RM8 58 D1
Anglia Ho 13 E14 97 A1
Anglian Ind Est
IG11 101 D2
Anglian Rd E11 76 B5
Anglia Wlk E6 100 C6
Anglo American
Laundry SW17 158 A1
Anglo Rd 16 E3 97 B5
Angrave Ct 4 E8 95 D6
Angrave Pas 5 E8 95 D6
Angus Cl KT9 214 C3
Angus Dr HA4 62 C4
Angus Gdns NW9 27 B2
Angus Ho 12 SW12 159 D4
Angus Rd E13 99 C4
Angus St SE14 141 A5
Anhalt Rd
SW11 136 C5 267 B4
Animals in War Meml*
W1 247 D6
Ankerdine Cres
SE18 144 D4
Anlaby Rd TW11 174 C5
Anley Rd W14 112 D4
Anmersh Gr HA7 25 D2
Annabel Cl E14 97 D1
Anna Cl E8 95 D6
Annadale N22 32 B5
Annandale Gr UB10 61 A5
Annandale Rd
Chiswick W4 111 C1
Croydon CR0 222 A6
Greenwich SE10 120 D1
Sidcup DA15 167 D4
Anna Neagle Cl 2
E7 77 A4
Anne Boleyn's Wlk
Belmont SM3 217 A1
Kingston u T KT2 176 A5
Anne Compton Mews
SE12 164 D4
Anne Goodman Ho 3
E1 96 C1
Anne Kerr Ct 18
SW15 156 D5
Annemount Sch N2 48 B3
Anne's Ct NW8 237 B6
Annesley Ave NW9 45 B6
Annesley Cl NW10 67 C5
Annesley Dr CR0 223 B5
Annesley Ho
31 Brixton SW9 138 C4
15 Kennington SW9 138 C5
Annesley Rd SE3 143 B4
Annesley Wlk N19 71 C6
Annesmere Gdns
SE3 143 D2
Anne St E13 99 A3
Annett Cl TW17 193 C5
Annette Cl HA3 24 C1
Annette Cres 16 N1 73 A1
Annette Ct N7 72 B5
Annette Rd N7 72 B4
Annette White Lo 20
N2 30 B1
Annett Rd KT12 194 A2
Anne Way KT8 195 D5
Annie Besant Cl E3 97 B6
Annie Taylor Ho 2
E12 78 C4
Anning St E2 243 B6
Annington Rd N2 48 D6
Annis Rd E9 75 A2
Ann La
SW10 136 B6 266 C5
Ann Moss Way
SE16 118 C3
Ann Parkes Ct TW5 128 D3
Ann's Cl SW1 248 A1
Ann's Pl E1 243 C3
Ann Stroud Ct SE12 165 A6
Ann St SE18 123 B2
Annsworthy Ave
CR7 205 B6
Annsworthy Cres
CR7 183 B1
Annunciation RC Inf
Sch The HA8 27 B2
Annunciation RC Jun
Sch The HA8 27 B4
Ansar Gdns E17 53 B4
Ansdell Rd SE15 140 C3
Ansdell St
W8 113 D3 255 D6
Ansdell Terr
W8 113 D3 255 D6
Ansell Gr SM5 203 A1
Ansell Ho E1 96 C2
Ansell Rd SW17 158 D1
Anselm Cl CR0 221 D5
Anselm Rd
Hatch End HA5 23 B3
West Brompton
SW6 135 C6 265 A5
Ansford Rd BR1, SE6 186 B6
Ansleigh Pl W11 112 D6
Anson Ct TW19 148 A4
Anson Ho
Pimlico SW1 269 A6
6 Tower Hamlets E1 97 A3
Anson 30 NW9 27 D1
Anson Pl SE28 123 B4
Anson Prim Sch
NW2 68 D3
Anson Rd
Cricklewood NW2 68 C3
Tufnell Pk N7 71 D4
Anson Terr UB5 63 D2
Anstey Ct 6 W3 110 D4
Anstey Ho 7 E9 96 C6
Anstey Lo EN1 17 C5
Anstey Rd SE15 140 A2
Anstey Wlk N15 51 A5
Anstice Cl W4 133 C5
Anstridge Rd SE9 167 B5
Antelope Rd SE18 122 B3
Antenor Ho 11 E2 96 B5
Anthony Cl NW7 27 C6
Anthony Cope Ct
N1 235 D2
Anthony Ct
Harrow HA1 42 B2

Anthony Ct *continued*
Isleworth TW7 130 D2
Anthony Ho NW8 237 A5
Anthony Kendal Ho 4 E5 74 B5
Anthony Rd
Croydon SE25 206 A3
East Wickham DA16 146 A4
Greenford UB6 86 C4
Anthony St E1 96 B1
Antigua Wlk SE19 183 B5
Antilles Bay 19 E14 120 A4
Antilles Ho W3 89 B1
Antill Rd Mile End E3 97 A4
Tottenham Hale N15 52 A5
Antill Terr 5 E1 96 D1
Antlers Hill E4 19 D6
Anton Cres SM1 217 C5
Antoneys Cl HA5 22 D1
Antonine Hts SE1 253 A1
Anton Pl HA9 66 D5
Anton St E8 74 A3
Antony Ho
4 Deptford SE14 140 D5
2 Rotherhithe SE16 118 C2
Antrim Gr NW3 70 D2
Antrim Ho SW11 137 A2
Antrim Mans NW3 70 D2
Antrim Rd NW3 70 D2
Antrobus Cl SM1 217 B3
Antrobus Rd W4 111 A3
Anvil Cl SW16 181 C3
Anvil Ho 10 N9 18 A1
Anvil Rd TW16 194 A6
Anworth Cl IG8 37 B4
Apex Cl BR3 185 D2
Apex Cnr
Edgware NW7 27 B6
Twickenham TW13 151 B1
Apex Ct W13 87 A1
Apex Ind Est NW10 89 D3
Apex Lo 10 EN5 14 A6
Apex Ret Pk TW13 151 B1
Aphrodite Ct 11 E14 119 C2
Aplin Ct 4 SM1 217 D2
Aplin Way TW7 130 C4
Apollo Ave
Bromley BR1 187 B2
Loughton HA6 22 A5
Apollo Bldg 2 E14 119 C2
Apollo Ho
Chelsea SW10 266 C5
32 Hackney E2 96 B5
Highgate N6 48 D2
Apollo Ind Bsns Ctr 29 SE8 140 D6
Apollo Pl
Chelsea SW10 266 C4
6 Leyton E11 76 C5
Apollo Studios 18 NW5 71 D3
Apollo Way 1 SE18 123 B3
Apostle Way CR7 182 D1
Apothecary St EC4 241 C1
Appach Rd SW2 160 C5
Appin Ct HA1 42 C2
Appleby Cl
Chingford E4 36 A4
Hayes UB3, UB8 83 A1
Orpington BR5 211 C2
Twickenham TW2 152 B2
West Green N15 51 B4
Appleby Ct W3 111 A4
Appleby Gdns TW14 149 D3
Appleby Rd
Hackney E8 74 A1
Newham E16 99 A1
Appleby St E2 95 D5
Appledore Ave HA4 62 C5
Appledore Cl
Bromley BR2 209 A4
Edgware HA8 26 C2
Upper Tooting SW12, SW17 158 D2
Appledore Cres DA14 167 D1
Appledore Way NW7 28 D3
Appleford Ho 6 W10 91 A3
Appleford 8 NW5 71 C3
Appleford Rd W10 91 A3
Apple Garth TW8 109 D2
Applegarth KT10 212 D3
Applegarth Dr IG2 57 D5
Applegarth Ho
Borough The SE1 251 D2
9 Camberwell SE15 140 A5
Applegarth Inf Sch CR0 223 D2
Applegarth Jun Sch CR0 223 D2
Applegarth CR0 223 D1
Applegarth Rd
Hammersmith W14 112 D3
Woolwich SE28 124 C6
Apple Gr
Chessington KT9 214 A4
Enfield EN1 5 C2
Apple Lo HA0 65 C5
Apple Mkt KT1 175 D1
Apple Mkt WC2 250 B6
Apple Rd E11 76 C5
Appleshaw Ho 4 SE5 139 C2
Appleton Ct 30 E8 74 B3
Appleton Gdns KT3 200 A3
Appleton Rd SE9 144 A2
Appleton Sq CR4 180 C2
Apple Tree Ave UB7 82 B1
Appletree Cl 5 SE20 184 B2
Appletree Ct
Lewisham SE13 142 B1
Northolt UB5 85 A4
Appletree Gdns EN4 2 C1
Apple Tree Yd SW1 249 B4
Applewood Cl
Dollis Hill NW2 68 B5
Ickenham UB10 60 A4
Oakleigh Pk N20 14 C3
Applewood Dr E13 99 B3
Appold St EC2 95 C2 243 A4
Apollo Ct 7 SW9 138 C4
Apprentice Gdns UB5 85 B4
Apprentice Way 5 E5 74 B4
Approach Cl N16 73 C4
Approach La NW7 29 A5
Approach Rd
Ashford TW15 171 A4
Bethnal Green E2 96 C5
East Molesey KT8 195 C4
Edgware HA8 26 C4
Merton SW20 178 C1
New Barnet EN4, EN5 2 B1
Approach The
Acton W3 89 B1
Enfield EN1 6 B3
Hendon NW4 46 D4
Orpington BR6 227 D6
Aprey Gdns NW4 46 C5
April Cl Ealing W7 108 C6
Feltham TW13 150 A1
Orpington BR6 227 D3
April Ct 20 E2 96 A5
April Glen SE23 162 D1
April St E8 73 D4
Apsley Cl HA2 42 A4
Apsley Ctr The NW2 68 A6
Apsley Ct SM2 218 A2
Apsley Ho Enfield EN1 17 C5
Hounslow TW4 129 B1
Stepney E1 96 C2
St John's Wood NW8 229 C4
Apsley Rd
Croydon SE25 206 B5
Kingston u T KT3 199 A6
Apsley Way
Dollis Hill NW2 68 A6
Mayfair W1 248 B2
Aquarius Bsns Pk NW2 46 A1
Aquarius TW1 153 B3
Aquarius Way HA6 22 A6
Aquila St NW8 92 B5 229 D4
Aquinas St SE1 116 C5 251 B3
Arabella Ct NW8 229 B4
Arabella Dr SW15 133 C1
Arabia Cl E4 20 B4
Arabian Ho 3 E1 97 A3
Arabin Rd SE4 141 B1
Aragon Ave KT7 196 D4
Aragon Cl
Ashford TW16 171 D3
Bromley BR2 210 B1
Enfield EN2 4 B5
Aragon Ct
Beckenham BR3 186 A2
East Molesey KT8 196 A5
Aragon Dr HA4 40 D1
Aragon Pl SM4 201 A2
Aragon Prim Sch SM4 200 D2
Aragon Rd
Kingston u T KT2 176 A5
West Barnes SM4 201 A2
Aragon Twr SE8 119 B2
Arakan Ho 4 N16 73 B4
Aral Ho 14 E1 96 D3
Arandora Cres RM6 58 B2
Aranya Ct 3 E17 35 A1
Arapiles Ho 6 E14 98 B1
Arbery Rd E3 97 A5
Arbon Ct N1 235 B5
Arbor Cl BR3 185 D1
Arbor Ct N16 73 B6
Arborfield Cl SW2 160 B3
Arborfield Ho 7 E14 119 C6
Arbor Rd E4 20 B1
Arbour Ho 3 E1 96 D1
Arbour Rd EN3 6 D2
Arbour Sq E1 96 D1
Arbroath Rd SE9 144 A2
Arbrook Chase KT10 212 A2
Arbrook Ct
Chessington KT9 213 D3
St Paul's Cray BR5 190 A2
Arbrook Hall KT10 212 D2
Arbrook La KT10 212 B2
Arbury Ho BR1 188 A3
Arbury Terr 3 SE26 162 B1
Arbuthnot La DA5 169 A5
Arbuthnot Rd SE14 140 D3
Arbutus St E8 95 D6
Arcade Ho 7 NW11 47 B4
Arcade The
Broadgate EC2 243 A3
2 Eltham SE9 166 C5
1 Tufnell Pk N7 72 A4
Walthamstow E17 53 C5
Arcadia Ave N3 29 C2
Arcadia Centre The W5 109 D6
Arcadia Cl SM5 219 A4
Arcadian Ave DA5 169 A5
Arcadian Cl DA5 169 A5
Arcadian Gdns N22 32 C3
Arcadian Ho SW6 136 A3
Arcadian Pl SW18 157 B4
Arcadian Rd DA5 169 A5
Arcadia St E14 97 C1
Archangel St SE16 118 D4
Archbishop Coggan Ho SE13 142 B1
Archbishop Lanfranc Sch The CR0 204 A3
Archbishop Michael Ramsey Tech Coll SE5 138 D5
Archbishop's Pl 1 SW2 160 B4
Archbishop Sumner CE Prim Sch SE11 116 C2 261 B3
Archbishop Tenison's CE High Sch CR0 221 D5
Archbishop Tenison's Sch SE11 138 B6 270 D5
Archdale Bsns Ctr HA2 64 A6
Archdale Ct W12 112 B5
Archdale Ho SE1 263 A6
Archdale Pl KT3 198 D6
Archdale Rd SE22 139 D1
Archdeacon Cambridge's CE Prim Sch TW2 152 C2
Archel Rd W14 135 B6 264 C6
Archer Cl KT2 176 A3
Archer Ct TW13 150 A3
Archer Ho
1 Battersea SW11 136 B3
Ealing W13 109 B5
24 Hoxton N1 95 C6
1 New Cross SE14 141 A4
Notting Hill W11 244 D6
Archer Mews TW12 174 A4
Archer Rd SE25 206 B5
Archers Ct 3 CR2 221 A3
Archers Dr EN3 6 C3
Archers Lo 22 SE16 118 A1
Archer Sq SE14 141 A6
Archer St W1 249 C6
Archer Terr UB7 104 A6
Archery Cl
Harrow HA3 42 D6
Paddington W2 237 B1
Archery Fields Ho WC1 234 A2
Archery Rd SE9 166 B6
Archery Stps W2 247 B6
Arches Bsns Ctr The UB2 107 B4
Arches The
Harrow HA2 63 D6
Strand WC2 250 B4
Archgate Bsns Ctr 1 N12 30 A5
Archibald Mews W1 248 C5
Archibald Rd N7 71 D4
Archibald St E3 97 C4
Archie Cl UB7 104 C4
Archie St SE1 253 B1
Arch St SE1 117 A3 262 A5
Archway Bsns Ctr 5 N19 71 D5
Archway Cl
North Kensington W10 90 D2
2 Upper Holloway N19 71 C6
Wallington SM6 220 A5
Wimbledon SW19 179 D6
Archway Hts 5 N19 49 C1
Archway N19 71 C6
Archway Mews SW15 135 A1
Archway Rd N6 49 B2
Archway Sta N19 71 C6
Archway St SW13, SW14 133 C2
Arcola St E8 73 D3
Arcon Dr UB5 85 A3
Arctic St NW5 71 B3
Arcus Rd BR1 186 C4
Ardbeg Rd SE24 161 B6
Arden Cl
Bushey Heath WD23 8 D4
Erith SE28 102 D1
Harrow HA1 64 B5
Arden Court Gdns N2 48 B3
Arden Cres
Dagenham RM9 80 D1
Millwall E14 119 C2
Arden Grange N12 30 A6
Arden Gr BR6 226 D4
Arden Ho
21 Hoxton N1 95 C5
29 Stockwell SW9 138 A3
Vauxhall SE11 260 C3
Arden Mews E17 53 D4
Arden Mhor HA5 40 B5
Arden 17 SW19 156 D3
Arden Rd
Ealing W13 109 C6
Finchley N3 47 B6
Ardent Cl SE25 205 C6
Ardent Ho 30 E3 97 A5
Ardfern Ave SW16 204 C6
Ardfillan Rd SE6 164 B2
Ardgowan Rd SE6 164 C3
Ardilaun Rd N5 73 A4
Ardingly Cl CR0 222 D5
Ardleigh Gdns SM3 201 C2
Ardleigh Ho 5 IG11 101 A6
Ardleigh Rd
Kingsland N1 73 C2
Walthamstow E17 35 B2
Ardleigh Terr E17 35 B2
Ardley Cl
Forest Hill SE6 163 A1
Neasden NW10 67 C5
Ruislip HA4 39 A2
Ardlui Rd SE27 161 A2
Ardmay Gdns KT6 198 A4
Ardmere Rd SE13 164 B5
Ardmore La IG9 21 B4
Ardmore Pl IG9 21 B4
Ardoch Rd SE6 164 B2
Ardra Rd N9 18 D1
Ardrossan Gdns KT4 216 A5
Ardshiel Cl SW15 134 D2
Ardwell Ave IG6 57 A4
Ardwell Rd SW2 160 A2
Ardwick Rd NW2 69 C4
Arena Bsns Ctr N4 51 A3
Arena Est N4 50 D3
Arena Sta SE25 206 C4
Arena The EN3 7 B5
Ares Ct 16 E14 119 C2
Arethusa Ho 8 E14 119 D2
Argali Ho 3 DA18 125 A3
Argall Ave E10 52 D1
Argall Way E10 53 A1
Argenta Way NW10 66 D1
Argent Ctr The UB3 106 A4
Argent Ct KT6 214 C5
Argent Ho HA5 23 B4
Argo Bsns Ctr 7 NW6 91 C4
Argon Mews SW6 265 B3
Argon Rd N18 34 D5
Argos Ct 5 SW9 138 C4
Argos Ho 8 E2 96 B5
Argosy Ho
Fitzrovia W1 238 D5
Rotherhithe SE8 119 A2
Argus Way UB5 85 A4
Argyle Cl W13 87 A3
Argyle Ho
Cubitt Town E14 120 A3
Richmond TW10 153 C2
Sutton SM2 218 A2
Teddington TW11 174 C5
Argyle Mans 4 NW2 68 D4
Argyle Pl W6 112 B2
Argyle Prim Sch WC1 94 A4 233 A2
Argyle Rd Ealing W13 87 A2
Edmonton N18 34 A6
Harrow HA2 41 D3
Hounslow TW3 151 D6
Ilford IG1 78 C6
Leyton E15 76 C4
Newham E16 99 B1
Stepney E1 96 D3
Tottenham N17 34 A2
Woodside Pk N12 29 C5
Argyle Sq WC1 94 A4 233 B2
Argyle St WC1 94 A4 233 B2
Argyle Way SE16 118 A1
Argyle Wlk WC1 233 B1
Argyll Ave UB1 107 D5
Argyll Cl SW9 138 B2
Argyll Ct 15 SW2 160 A4
Argyll Gdns HA8 26 D2
Argyll Mans
Chelsea SW3 266 D6
West Kensington W14 254 B4
Argyll Rd
Kensington W8 113 C4 245 B1
Woolwich SE18 123 A3
Argyll St W1 93 C1 239 A1
Aria Ct IG2 57 A3
Arica Ho SE16 118 B3
Arica Rd SE4 141 A2
Ariel Ct
5 Belvedere DA17 125 C1
5 Hammersmith W12 112 A3
Newington SE11 261 C3
Ariel Rd NW6 69 C2
Ariel Way
Hounslow TW4 128 B2
Shepherd's Bush W12 112 C5
Aristotle Rd SW4 137 D2
Arizona Bldg 10 SE13 141 D4
Arkansas Ho 21 N19 49 D2
Ark Ct N16 73 D6
Arkell Gr SW16 182 D3
Arkindale Rd SE6 164 A1
Arklay Cl UB8 82 B3
ARKLEY 12 A6
Arkley Cres E17 53 B4
Arkley Dr EN5 12 B6
Arkley Pk EN5 11 B5
Arkley Rd E17 53 B4
Arklow Ho SE17 139 B6
Arklow Mews 4 KT6 214 A6
Arklow Rd SE14 141 B6
Arklow Road Trad Est SE14 141 B6
Arkwright Ho 23 SW2 160 A4
Arkwright Mans NW3 70 A3
Arkwright Rd NW3 70 A3
Arlesey Cl SW15 157 A6
Arlesford Rd SW9 138 A2
Arless Ho 8 HA1 42 D4
Arlidge Ho EC1 241 B4
Arlingford Rd SW2 160 C5
Arlington Ave N1 95 A6 235 B5
Arlington Cl
Lewisham SE13 164 B6
Sidcup DA15 167 C4
Sutton SM1 217 C6
Twickenham TW1 153 C5
Arlington Ct
13 Acton W3 110 D5
Highgate N6 49 A3
4 Twickenham TW1 153 C5
Arlington Dr
Carshalton SM5 218 D6
Ruislip HA4 39 B3
Arlington Gdns
Acton Green W4 111 A1
Ilford IG1 56 C1
Arlington Gn NW7 28 D3
Arlington Ho
3 Deptford SE8 141 B6
Finsbury EC1 234 B2
1 Shepherd's Bush W12 112 B5
Arlington Lo SW2 138 B1
Arlington N12 13 C1
Arlington Park Mans 1 W4 111 A1
Arlington Pl 7 SE10 142 A5
Arlington Rd
Ashford TW15 170 B5
Camden Town NW1 93 B6 231 D5
Ealing W13 87 B1
Arlington Rd *continued*
Osidge N14 15 C3
Richmond TW10 153 D2
Surbiton KT6 197 D3
Teddington TW11 174 D6
Twickenham TW1 153 C5
Woodford IG8 37 B3
Arlington Sq N1 95 A6 235 B5
Arlington St SW1 115 C5 249 A4
Arlington Way EC1 94 C4 234 B2
Arliss Way UB5 84 C6
Arlow Rd N21 16 C3
Armada Ct 11 SE8 141 C6
Armadale Cl N17 52 B5
Armadale Rd
Feltham TW14 150 A6
West Brompton SW6 265 A5
Armada St 10 SE8 141 C6
Armada Way E6 101 B1
Armagh Rd E3 97 B6
Armeston KT3 199 B2
Armfield Cl KT8 195 B4
Armfield Cotts 3 SW19 180 D1
Armfield Cres CR4 180 D1
Armfield Rd EN2 5 B4
Arminger Rd W12 112 B5
Armistice Gdns SE25 206 A6
Armitage Ho NW1 92 C2 237 B4
Armitage Rd
Golders Green NW11 47 B1
Greenwich SE10 120 D1
Armour Cl N7 72 B2
Armoury Ho E3 97 A6
Armoury Rd SE8 141 D3
Armoury Way SW18 157 C6
Armsby Ho 17 E1 96 C2
Armstead Wlk RM10 81 C1
Armstrong Ave IG8 36 C4
Armstrong Cl
Bickley BR1 210 A6
Dagenham RM8 58 D2
Newham E6 100 B1
Pinner HA5 40 A3
Walton-on-T KT12 194 A3
Armstrong Cres EN4 2 B2
Armstrong Ho 8 SW15 156 D5
Armstrong Rd
East Acton W3 111 D5
Feltham TW13 173 A5
Knightsbridge SW7 256 C5
Woolwich SE18 123 A3
Armstrong Way UB2 107 D4
Armytage Rd TW5 128 D5
Arnal Cres SW18 157 A4
Arncliffe Cl N11 31 A4
Arncliffe NW6 91 D6
Arncroft Ct IG11 102 B4
Arndale Wlk 6 SW18 157 D6
Arndell Ho 16 SM1 218 A4
Arne Gr BR6 227 D5
Arne Ho SE11 260 C2
Arne St WC2 94 A1 240 B1
Arnett Sq E4 35 B4
Arneways Ave RM6 58 D6
Arneway St SW1 259 D5
Arne Wlk SE3 142 D1
Arnewood Cl SW15 156 A3
Arney's La CR4 203 A3
Arngask Rd SE6 164 B4
Arnhem Pl E14 119 C3
Arnhem Way 3 SE22 161 C6
Arnhem Wharf E14 119 C3
Arnhem Wharf Prim Sch E14 119 C3
Arnison Rd KT8 196 B5
Arnold Ave E EN3 7 C5
Arnold Ave W EN3 7 B5
Arnold Cir E2 95 D4
Arnold Cl HA3 44 B2
Arnold Cres TW7 152 B6
Arnold Ct E18 36 D2
Arnold Dr KT9 213 D2
Arnold Est SE1 253 D1
Arnold Gdns N13 32 D5
Arnold Ho
Croydon CR0 220 D4
Newington SE17 261 D1
9 Stoke Newington N16 73 C5
Arnold House Sch NW8 92 B5 229 C3
Arnold Rd Bow E3 97 C4
Dagenham RM10 81 C1
Mitcham SW17 180 D3
Northolt UB5 63 A2
Tottenham N15 51 D6

s Gr N14 15 D1
s Grove Ct 4
31 C5
s Grove Sta N11 31 C6
s Rd N11 31 C6
: Ho 27 SE5 139 A5
t Cl
n Green W4 111 B2
esmead SE28 124 C5
ld Ave SE5 139 B1
erg Way DA6,
147 C1
de Gdns HA9 43 D1
de Ho 2 SE17 139 B6
de Rd DA7 147 C4
de St SE17 139 A6
f St SE6 185 D6
l's Rd SW16 182 D4
ene Rd SW2 160 B5
Rd 8 TW1 153 D5
on Gdns
atham SW16 182 A3
t Wickham BR4 223 D5
on Rd
ham E6 99 D6
wickenham
V1 153 A3
dsworth SW18 157 C3
Cl SM6 219 C4
Ct Edgware HA8 10 D2
Hendon NW9 27 D1
sden NW10 67 B5
dene Ho 3
190 B1
Dr
more HA7 25 C6
stead E12 77 D6
Ho
Canary Wharf
4 120 A5
e Newington N16 51 D1
Mews W5 110 B5
Rd SE6 164 A2
Wlk N1 73 A1
Ave SM4 202 A4
Ho SE2 146 D6
Ho SE1 262 B5
Rd BR3 206 D6
ve Ct 6 E5 74 B4
/ Ho 23 N1 95 C6
v Rd E3 97 D4
v Scout Wlk
85 A4
vsmith Ho SE11 260 C2
al Rd SE9 144 B2
al Sta N5 72 C5
al Way SE18 123 A3
Ho 26 E1 96 C1
is Ct 14 E14 119 C2
is Pl SW18 157 B4
berry Rd SW20,
9 178 D2
ian Cl NW10 67 B1
ian Gr EN5 2 A1
ian Rd W2 91 C1
ian Wlk 4 E11 76 C5
gworth St E15 98 C6
r Ct
ersea SW11 268 B1
North Kensington
10 90 D1
lington W2 91 D1
h Croydon CR0 221 B5
r Deakin Ho 1
96 A2
rdon Rd SE4 163 C6
r Gr SE18 123 A2
r Henderson Ho
rouch End N19 49 D2
ulham SW6 135 B3
r Newton Ho 20
136 B2
r Rd
enham RM6 58 D3
onton N9 17 D2
ingston u T KT2 176 C3
er Holloway N7 72 B4
ham E6 100 B5
Barnes KT3 200 B4
bledon SW19 179 C6
r Ruxley Est
190 D4
r St
117 B6 252 D6
r Wade Ho 7
95 D4
Walls Ho 3
78 C5
oke Hill 8 E1 118 B6
oke Mews 5
139 B4
oke Pl SE5 139 B4
ery Cl IG2 57 A3
ery Ho Bow E3 97 A6
minster SW1 259 C5
wich SE18 122 C1

Artillery La
Broadgate
E1 95 C2 243 B3
North Kensington
W12 90 A1
Artillery Pas E1 243 B3
Artillery Pl
Harrow Weald HA3 24 A3
Westminster SW1 259 C5
Woolwich SE18 122 C2
Artillery Row SW1 259 C5
Artington Cl BR6 227 A4
Artisan Cl E16 122 D6
Artisan Ct E8 74 A2
Artisan Mews 9
NW10 90 D4
Artisan Quarter 10
NW10 90 D4
Artizan St E1 243 B2
Arton Wilson Ho 12
SW15 156 A6
Arts Educational Sch
The W4 111 C2
Arundale KT1 197 D5
Arundel Ave SM4 201 B5
Arundel Bldgs SE1 263 B5
Arundel Cl
Croydon CR0 220 D5
Hampton TW12 173 D5
Leyton E15 76 C4
Sidcup DA5 169 B5
Wandsworth SW11 158 C6
Arundel Ct
Barnes SW13 134 B6
4 Beckenham BR2 186 C1
2 Bexley DA6 147 A1
Chelsea SW3 257 B2
Colney Hatch N12 30 C4
3 Croydon CR0 220 D5
Harrow HA2 63 C4
Putney SW15 156 D6
Tottenham N17 34 A2
Arundel Dr
Borehamwood
WD6 11 A6
Harrow HA2 63 C4
Woodford IG8 37 A3
Arundel Gdns
Burnt Oak HA8 27 B3
Ilford IG3 80 A6
Notting Hill
W11 113 B6 244 C6
Southgate N21 16 C3
Arundel Gr N16 73 C3
Arundel Ho
Croydon CR0 221 B3
Islington N1 94 D6 234 D6
Richmond TW10 154 C6
3 South Acton W3 110 D4
Arundel Lo
Church End N3 29 B1
9 Upper Holloway
N19 72 A6
Arundel Mans
Barnes SW13 134 B6
Fulham SW6 264 D2
Arundel Pl N1, N7 72 C2
Arundel Rd
Belmont SM2 217 B1
Cockfosters EN4 2 C2
Hounslow TW4 128 C2
Kingston u T KT1 177 A1
Thornton Heath CR0 205 B3
Arundel Sq N7 72 C2
Arundel St
WC2 116 B6 250 D6
Arundel Terr SW13 134 B6
Arun Ho 5 KT2 175 D2
Arvon Rd N5 72 C3
Asa Ct UB3 105 D3
Asaph Ho SE14 141 B4
Asbaston Terr IG11 79 A2
Asbury Ct N21 16 A6
Ascalon Ct 16 SW2 160 B4
Ascalon Ho SW8 269 A3
Ascalon St
SW8 137 C5 269 A3
Ascham Dr E4 35 C3
Ascham End E17 35 A2
Ascham St NW5 71 C3
Aschurch Rd CR0 205 D2
Ascot Cl
Borehamwood
WD6 10 C6
Northolt UB5 63 C3
Ascot Ct
8 Brixton SW4 138 A1
Bromley BR1 188 A1
Old Bexley DA5 169 B4
St John's Wood NW8 229 C1
Ascot Gdns Enfield EN3 6 C6
Southall UB1 85 C2
Ascot Ho
6 Acton Green
W4 111 A1
1 Paddington W9 91 C2
Penge SE26 184 B4

Ascot Ho *continued*
Regent's Pk NW1 231 D2
Ascot Lo Enfield EN1 17 B6
Paddington NW6 91 D5
Ascot Par 9 SW4 138 A1
Ascot Pl 12 HA7 25 C5
Ascot Rd
East Bedfont
TW14 148 D2
Edmonton N18 34 A6
Newham E6 100 B4
Orpington BR5 211 D5
Streatham SW17 181 A4
Tottenham N15 51 B4
Ascott Ave W5 110 A4
Ascott Ct HA5 40 A5
Ashbourne Ave
East Barnet N20 14 D2
Erith DA7 147 A5
Harrow HA2 64 B6
Temple Fortune
NW11 47 B4
Wanstead E18 55 B5
Ashbourne Cl
Ealing W5 88 C2
18 Woodside Pk N12 29 D6
Ashbourne Ct
Beckenham BR3 186 A2
Clapton Pk E5 75 A4
13 Woodside Pk N12 29 D6
Ashbourne Gr
Chiswick W4 111 C1
East Dulwich SE22 139 D1
Edgware NW7 27 B5
Ashbourne Ind Sch
W8 113 D4 245 C1
Ashbourne Lo 2
N13 32 C6
Ashbourne Par 2
NW11 47 B5
Ashbourne Rd
Ealing W5 88 B3
Mitcham CR4 181 A3
Ashbourne Rise
BR6 227 C4
Ashbourne Terr 1
SW19 179 C3
Ashbourne Way
NW11 47 B4
Ashbridge Ct 3 W6 112 B3
Ashbridge Rd E11 54 D2
Ashbridge St
NW8 92 C3 237 A5
Ashbrook HA8 26 B4
Ashbrook Rd
Dagenham RM10 81 D5
Upper Holloway N19 71 D6
Ashburn Ct BR1 187 A3
Ashburn Gdns SW7 256 A4
Ashburnham Ave
HA1 42 D3
Ashburnham Cl N2 48 B5
Ashburnham Com Sch
SW10 266 C4
Ashburnham Gdns
HA1 42 D3
Ashburnham Gr
SE10 141 D5
Ashburnham Pk
KT10 212 A4
Ashburnham Pl
SE10 141 D5
Ashburnham Rd
Chelsea
SW10 136 A5 266 B3
Kensal Rise NW10 90 C5
Richmond TW10 153 B1
Ashburnham Retreat 4
SE10 141 D5
Ashburnham Twr
SW10 266 C4
Ashburn Pl
SW7 114 A2 256 A3
Ashburton Ave
Croydon CR0 206 B1
Ilford IG3 79 D4
Ashburton Cl CR0 206 A1
Ashburton Ct 1 HA5 40 D6
Ashburton Gdns
CR0 222 A6
Ashburton Ho
Enfield EN3 6 D2
2 Wallington SM6 219 D3
Ashburton Jun & Inf
Sch CR0 206 B3
Ashburton Learning
Village CR9 206 B2
Ashburton Mans
SW10 266 B4
Ashburton Rd
Croydon CR0 222 A6
Newham E16 99 A1
Ruislip HA4 62 A6
Ashburton Terr 2
E13 99 A5
Ashbury Dr UB10 60 D5
Ashbury Gdns RM6 58 D4

Ashbury Pl SW19 180 A4
Ashbury Rd SW11 137 A2
Ashby Ave KT19,
KT9 214 C2
Ashby Ct NW8 236 D6
Ashby Grange 7
SM6 219 C2
Ashby Gr N1 73 A1
Ashby Ho
6 Brixton SW9 138 D3
17 Islington N1 73 A1
3 Northolt UB5 85 B3
14 Surbiton KT6 198 A3
Ashby Mews
10 Clapham Pk
SW2 160 A6
New Cross SE4 141 B3
Ashby Rd
New Cross SE4 141 B3
South Tottenham N15 52 A4
Ashby St EC1 94 D4 234 D1
Ashby Way UB7 126 C5
Ashby Wlk CR0 205 A3
Ashchurch Ct 2
W12 112 A3
Ashchurch Gr W12 112 A3
Ashchurch Park Villas
W12 112 A3
Ashchurch Terr
W12 112 A3
Ash Cl
Carshalton SM5 218 D6
Edgware HA8 27 A6
Kingston u T KT3 177 B1
Penge SE20 184 C1
Petts Wood BR5 211 B4
Sidcup DA14 168 B1
Stanmore HA7 25 A4
Ashcombe Ave KT6 197 D2
Ashcombe Ct 4
SW15 157 A6
Ashcombe Gdns HA8 26 C6
Ashcombe Ho 39 E3 97 D4
Ashcombe Pk NW2 67 C5
Ashcombe Rd
Wallington SM5 219 A2
Wimbledon SW19 179 C5
Ashcombe Sq KT3 199 A6
Ashcombe St SW6 135 D3
Ashcroft Ave DA15 168 A5
Ashcroft Cres DA15 168 A5
Ashcroft Ct
5 Eltham SE9 166 C5
Wembley HA0 65 A4
3 Whetstone N20 14 B2
Ashcroft HA5 23 C4
Ashcroft Ho SW8 269 A2
Ashcroft N14 15 D2
Ashcroft Rd Bow E3 97 A4
Chessington KT9 214 B5
Ashcroft Sq 8 W6 112 C2
Ash Ct Chingford E4 20 B4
Clapham SW11 159 A6
Lee SE12 165 A4
Marylebone W1 237 C2
Romford RM7 59 D3
6 Rotherhithe
SE16 119 A5
Upper Holloway N19 71 C6
West Ewell KT19 215 A4
2 West Norwood
SW16 182 C5
9 Wimbledon
SW19 179 A3
Woodford E18 37 C2
Ashdale Cl
Stanwell TW19 148 A2
Twickenham TW2 152 A4
Ashdale Gr HA7 24 D4
Ashdale Ho N4 51 B2
Ashdale Rd SE12 165 B3
Ashdale Way TW2 151 D4
Ashdene Cl TW15 171 A3
Ashdene
6 Deptford SE15 140 B5
Pinner HA5 40 C6
Ashdon Cl IG8 37 B4
Ashdon Rd NW10 89 D6
Ashdown Cl 13 BR3 185 D1
Ashdown Cres NW5 71 A3
Ashdown Ct
Dulwich SE22 162 A3
Ilford IG1 78 D2
New Malden KT4 199 D2
Sutton SM2 218 A2
Ashdown W13 87 B2
Ashdowne Ct N17 34 A2
Ashdown Ho 7 E5 74 A6
Ashdown Pl
Ewell KT17 215 D1
Thames Ditton KT7 197 A2
Ashdown SW15 156 D6
Ashdown Rd
Enfield EN3 6 C3
Hillingdon UB10 82 C5
Kingston u T KT1 176 A1

Ashdown Way
SW17 159 A2
Ashdown Wlk 20
E14 119 C2
Ashe Ho 9 TW1 153 D5
Ashenden Rd E5 75 A3
Ashenden SE17 262 B4
Ashen Gr SW19 157 C2
Ashen E6 100 C1
Ashentree Ct EC4 241 B1
Asher Loftus Way
N11 30 D4
Asher Way E1 118 A6
Ashfield Ave
Bushey WD23 8 A4
Feltham TW13 150 B3
Ashfield Cl
Beckenham BR3 185 C3
Richmond TW10 154 A3
Ashfield Ct SW9 138 A3
Ashfield Ho 5 N5 73 A3
Ashfield La BR7 189 A3
Ashfield Par N14 15 D3
Ashfield Pl BR7 189 B3
Ashfield Rd
East Acton W3 111 D5
New Southgate N14 15 C1
Tottenham N4 51 A3
Ashfield St E1 96 C2
Ashfield Yd 21 E1 96 C2
ASHFORD 170 B4
Ashford Ave
Ashford TW15 170 D4
Hayes UB4 84 D1
Hornsey N8 50 A5
Ashford Bsns Complex
TW15 171 A6
Ashford CE Prim Sch
TW15 170 D4
Ashford Cl
Ashford TW15 170 A6
Walthamstow E17 53 B3
ASHFORD COMMON
171 B4
Ashford Cres EN3 6 C3
Ashford Ct
Cricklewood NW2 68 D4
Edgware HA8 10 D1
Ashford Gn WD19 22 D5
Ashford Ho
14 Brixton SW9 138 D1
11 Deptford SE8 141 B6
Ashford Hospl
TW15 148 A2
Ashford Ind Est
TW15 171 A6
Ashford Mews N17 34 A2
Ashford Rd
Cricklewood NW2 68 D4
Feltham TW13,
TW15 171 B6
Littleton TW15,
TW17 171 A3
Staines TW18 170 A4
Wallend E6 78 C1
Woodford E18 37 B1
Ashford St N1 95 C4
Ash Gr
Cricklewood NW2 69 A4
Ealing W5 110 A3
East Bedfont TW14 149 C3
Edmonton N13 17 A1
Enfield EN1 17 C4
Hackney E8 96 B6
Hayes UB3 105 B6
Heston TW5 128 D5
Ashgrove Ct 2 W9 91 C2
Ashgrove Ho SW1 259 D2
Ashgrove SE12 165 A3
Ashgrove Rd
Ashford TW15 171 B5
Catford BR1 186 B4
Ashgrove Sch BR1 187 B1
Ash Gr Penge SE20 184 C1
Southall UB1 85 C2
Wembley HA0 65 A4
West Wickham BR4 208 A1
Yiewsley UB7 104 B6
Ash Hill Dr HA5 40 C6
Ash Ho
3 Canary Wharf
E14 120 A4
Fulham SE1 263 D3
Kenton NW9 45 A6
Lewisham SE12 165 A3
2 Teddington
TW11 175 C3
Ashingdon Cl E4 20 A1
Ashington Ho 18 E1 96 B3
Ashington 1 NW5 71 B2
Ashington Rd SW6 135 B3
Ashlake Rd SW16 182 A6
Ashland Pl W1 238 A4
Ashlar Ct N2 48 C6
Ashlar Pl SE18 122 D2
Ashleigh Commercial
Est SE7 121 D3

Ashleigh Ct
Ealing W5 109 D2
Osidge N14 15 C4
Penge SE26 184 B4
Ashleigh Gdns SM1 217 D6
Ashleigh Ho
Mortlake SW14 133 C2
1 Streatham SW16 182 B6
Ashleigh Point 8
SE26 162 D1
Ashleigh Rd
Mortlake SW14 133 C2
Penge SE20 206 B6
Ashley Ave SM4 201 C4
Ashley CE Prim Sch
KT12 194 A1
Ashley Cl
Hendon NW4 28 C1
Oatlands Pk KT12,
KT13 193 D1
Pinner Green HA5 22 B1
Ashley Cres
Clapham SW11 137 A2
Wood Green N22 32 C1
Ashley Ct
Hampstead NW3 69 D3
Hendon NW4 28 C1
19 Kingsland N16 73 C3
New Barnet EN5 14 A6
Northolt UB5 85 A6
Stanmore HA7 25 B1
Yiewsley UB7 104 A5
Ashley Dr
Borehamwood
WD6 11 B6
Hounslow TW7 130 C6
Twickenham TW2 151 D3
Ashley Gdns
Edmonton N13 33 A6
Orpington BR6 227 C3
Richmond TW10 153 D2
Wembley HA9 66 A6
Ashley Ho BR5 190 A1
Ashley La
Croydon CR0 220 D4
Edgware NW7 28 D3
Hendon NW4 28 C1
Ashley Park Ave
KT12 193 D1
Ashley Park Cres
KT12 194 A1
Ashley Pl
Walton-on-T
KT12 194 A1
Westminster
SW1 115 C3 259 A5
Ashley Rd
Chingford E4 35 C4
Enfield EN3 6 C3
Hampton TW12 173 C2
Hornsey N19 50 A2
Richmond TW9 132 A2
Thames Ditton KT7 196 D3
Thornton Heath CR7 204 B5
Tottenham Hale N17 52 A6
Upton E7 77 C1
Walton-on-T KT12 194 A1
Wimbledon SW19 179 D4
Ashleys Alley N15 51 A5
Ashley Wlk NW7 28 D3
Ashling Ho 2 N17 33 D1
Ashling Rd CR0 206 A1
Ashlin Rd E15 76 B4
Ash Lo
2 Ashford TW16 171 D3
Fulham SW6 134 D4
Ashlone Rd SW15 134 D2
Ashlyns Way KT9 213 D2
Ashmead Bsns Ctr 2
E16 98 B3
Ashmead Gate BR1 187 C2
Ashmead Ho E9 75 A3
Ashmead Prim Sch
SE8 141 C3
Ashmead Rd
East Bedfont
TW14 150 A3
St Johns SE8 141 C3
Ashmead 4 N14 15 C6
Ashmere Ave BR3 186 B1
Ashmere Cl SM3 216 D3
Ashmere Gr 11 SW2,
SW4 138 A1
Ashmere Ho 10
SW2 138 A1
Ashmill Ct CR0 205 A3
Ashmill St
NW8 92 C2 237 A4
Ashmole Prim Sch
SW8 138 B6 270 D5
Ashmole Sch N14 15 C3
Ashmole St
SW8 138 B6 270 D5
Ashmoor Lo NW7 27 B4

Ashmore Cl SE15 139 D5
Ashmore Ct
Catford SE6 164 C3
Colney Hatch N11 30 D4
Heston TW5 129 C6
Ashmore Gr DA16 145 C2
Ashmore Ho W14 254 B5
Ashmore NW1 71 D1
Ashmore Rd W9 91 B4
Ashmount Prim Sch
N19 49 C2
Ashmount Rd
Crouch End N19 49 D2
South Tottenham N15 51 D4
Ashmount Terr W5 109 D2
Ashneal Gdns HA1 64 B5
Ashness Gdns UB6 65 B2
Ashness Rd SW11 158 D6
Ashpark Ho 4 E14 97 B1
Ash Rd Cheam SM3 201 B1
Croydon CR0 223 C6
Littleton TW17 192 C5
Orpington BR6 227 D1
Plashet E15 76 D3
Ashridge Cl HA3 43 C3
Ashridge Cres SE18 145 A5
Ashridge Ct
Southall UB1 108 A6
Southgate N14 15 C6
Ashridge Dr WD19 22 C5
Ashridge Gdns
Bowes Pk N13 32 A5
Pinner HA5 41 A5
Ashridge Ho DA14 189 D6
Ashridge Way
Ashford TW16 172 A4
Merton SM4 201 B5
Ash Row BR2 210 C3
Ashtead Ct 15
SW19 156 D3
Ashtead Rd E5 52 A2
Ash Tech Coll The
TW15 148 A1
Ashton Cl SM1 217 C4
Ashton Ct
1 Beckenham
BR3 185 B2
Chingford E4 20 C1
Harrow HA1 64 D5
Ashton Gdns
Dagenham RM6 59 A3
Hounslow TW4 129 B1
Ashton Ho
13 Kennington
SW9 138 C5
Roehampton SW15 156 B4
Ashton Rd E15 76 B3
Ashton St E14 120 A6
Ashtree Ave CR4 180 B1
Ash Tree Cl CR0 207 A3
Ashtree Cl BR6 226 D4
Ash Tree Cl 1 KT6 198 A1
Ashtree Ct TW15 170 D5
Ash Tree Dell NW9 45 B4
Ash Tree Villas CR0 204 B3
Ash Tree Way CR0 207 A3
Ashurst Cl SE20 184 B2
Ashurst Dr
Ilford IG2, IG6 57 A4
Littleton TW17 192 A4
Ashurst Lo 4 N5 72 D3
Ashurst Rd
Cockfosters EN4 14 D6
Colney Hatch N12 30 C5
Ashurst Wlk CR0 222 B6
Ashvale Rd SW17 180 D5
Ashview Cl TW15 170 A5
Ashview Gdns
TW15 170 A5
Ashville Rd E11 76 B6
Ashwater Rd SE12 165 A3
Ashway Ctr 5 KT2 176 A2
Ashwell Cl 8 E6 100 A1
Ashwell Ct TW15 148 A2
Ashwin St E8 73 D2
Ash Wlk HA0 65 C4
Ashwood Ave UB8 82 C1
Ashwood Ct HA9 66 B4
Ashwood Gdns
Hayes UB3 105 D2
New Addington CR0 224 A2
Ashwood Ho 10 NW4 46 C5
Ashwood Lo
9 New Barnet
EN5 13 D6
Southgate N21 16 B5
Ashwood Pk 6
SM2 217 C1
Ashwood Rd E4 20 B1
Ashworth Cl SE5 139 B3
Ashworth Mans W9 91 D4
Ashworth Rd W9 91 D4
Aske Ho 2 N1 95 C4
Asker Ho N7 72 A4
Askern Cl DA6 146 D1
Aske St N1 95 C4
Askew Cres W12 112 A4
Askew Mans 14
W12 112 A4
Askew Rd W12 112 A4
Askham Ct W12 112 A5
Askham Lo 5 SE12 165 A4
Askham Rd W12 112 A5
Askill Dr SW15 157 A6
Asland Rd E15 98 B6
Aslett St SW18 158 A4
Asmara Rd NW2 69 A3
Asmuns Hill NW11 47 C4
Asmuns Pl NW11 47 B4
Asolando Dr SE17 262 B3
Aspect Coll
WC1 94 A2 240 B3
Aspect Ho 7 E14 120 A4
Aspects SM1 217 D3
Aspen Cl Ealing W5 110 B4
13 Upper Holloway
N19 71 C6
Yiewsley UB7 104 B5
Aspen Copse BR1 188 B1
Aspen Ct 10 Acton W3 89 A1
12 Hackney E8 74 A3
Redbridge IG5 56 A6
Richmond TW9 132 C5
Aspen Dr HA0 65 A5
Aspen Gdns
Ashford TW15 171 A5
2 Hammersmith
W6 112 B1
Mitcham CR4 203 A4
Aspen Gn DA18 125 B3
Aspen Gr HA5 39 D6
Aspen Ho
8 Deptford SE15 140 C6
4 Maitland Pk NW3 70 D2
Richmond TW9 132 C5
2 Sidcup DA15 168 A1
Southgate N21 16 B6
Aspen La UB5 85 A4
Aspenlea Rd W6 134 D6
Aspen Lo 1 SW19 179 B4
Aspen Way
Canary Wharf
E14 120 A6
Feltham TW13 150 B1
Aspern Gr NW3 70 C3
Aspinall Ho SW12 160 A3
Aspinall Rd SE4 140 D2
Aspinden Rd SE16 118 B2
Aspire Bld 10 SW15 157 B6
Aspley Rd SW18 157 D6
Asplins Rd N17 34 B2
Asprey Ho CR4 202 C6
Asquith Cl RM8 58 C1
Assam SE1 253 D3
Assam St E1 96 A1
Assata Mews N1 72 D2
Assembly Pas E1 96 C2
Assembly Wlk SM5 202 C2
Assheton-Bennett Ho
16 KT6 198 A4
Ass House La HA3 23 D6
Assisi Ct
Upper Tooting
SW12 158 D3
Wembley HA0 64 D5
Astall Cl HA3 24 C2
Astbury Bsns Pk 6
SE15 140 C4
Astbury Ho SE11 261 A5
Astbury Rd SE15 140 C4
Astell St
SW3 114 C1 257 B2
Aster Ct 3 HA8 27 A6
Aster Ho 3 SE13 142 A3
Aste St E14 120 A4
Astey's Row 1 N1 73 A1
Asthall Gdns IG6 57 A5
Astins Ho 4 E17 53 D5
Astleham Rd TW17 192 A6
Astleham Way
TW17 192 A6
Astle St SW11 137 A3
Astley Ave NW2 68 C3
Astley Ho Fulham SE1 263 D2
39 Paddington W2 91 C2
8 West Norwood
SE27 183 A6
Aston Ave HA3 43 C2
Aston Cl Bushey WD23 8 A5
Sidcup DA14 168 A1
Aston Ct
Stoke Newington
N4 73 A6
3 Wimbledon
SW19 178 C3
10 Woodford IG8 37 A4
Aston Gn TW5 128 C3
Aston Ho
Notting Hill W11 244 D6
South Lambeth SW8 269 C1
Aston House Sch W5 87 D1
Aston Mews RM6 58 C2
Aston Pl SW16 182 D4
Aston Rd
Claygate KT10 212 C3
Ealing W5 87 D1
Merton SW20 178 C1
Aston St E14 97 A2
Astonville St SW18 157 C3
Astor Ave RM7 59 D3
Astor Cl KT2 176 D4
Astor Ct
Colney Hatch N12 30 C4
Newham E16 99 C1
Walham Green SW6 266 A3
Astoria Mans 18
SW16 160 A1
Astoria Par SW16 160 A1
Astoria Wlk SW9 138 C2
Astra Ct W13 109 A5
Astra Ho 4 Bow E3 97 B4
Hornsey N4 50 B2
Astrid Ho TW13 150 C2
Astrop Mews W6 112 C3
Astrop Terr W6 112 C4
Astwood Mews SW7 256 A4
Asylum Rd SE15 140 B5
Atalanta St
SW6 134 D5 264 A3
Atbara Ct TW11 175 B4
Atbara Rd TW11 175 B4
Atcham Rd TW3 130 A1
Atcost Rd IG11 102 A2
Atheldene Rd SW18 158 A3
Athelney Prim Sch
SE6 163 C1
Athelney St SE6 163 C1
Athelstan Ct E6 100 C5
Athelstane Gr E3 97 B5
Athelstane Mews N4 50 C1
Athelstan Gdns 8
NW6 69 A1
Athelstan Ho
Hackney Wick E9 75 B3
Kingston u T KT1 198 B5
Stoke Newington N16 73 C4
Athelstan House Sch
TW12 173 C2
Athelstan Rd KT1 198 B5
Athelstan Way BR5 190 A2
Athelstone Rd HA3 24 B1
Athena Cl
Harrow HA2 64 C6
Kingston u T KT1 198 B6
Athena Ct
Bermondsey SE1 253 A1
St John's Wood NW8 229 C4
Athenaeum Pl 3
N10 49 B6
Athenaeum Rd N20 14 B3
Athenia Ho 7 E14 98 B1
Athenlay Rd SE15 162 D6
Athenoeum Ct N5 73 A4
Athens Gdns W9 91 C3
Atherden Rd E5 74 C4
Atherfield Ct SW18 157 D5
Atherfold Rd SW9 138 A2
Atherley Way TW4 151 B4
Atherstone Ct W2 91 D2
Atherstone Mews
SW7 114 A2 256 B4
Atherton Dr SW19 178 D6
Atherton Ho CR2 221 C2
Atherton Hts HA0 65 C2
Atherton Mews E7 77 A2
Atherton Pl
Harrow HA2 42 B6
Southall UB1 107 C6
Atherton Rd
Barnes SW13 134 A5
Stratford E7 76 D2
Atherton St SW11 136 C3
Athlone KT10 212 C2
Athlone Cl 24 E5 74 B3
Athlone Ct
Lewisham SE6 164 B4
Upper Walthamstow
E17 54 B6
Athlone Ho
16 Camden Town
NW5 71 A2
9 Stepney E1 96 C1
Athlone House N6 48 D1
Athlone Rd SW2 160 C4
Athlone St NW5 71 A2
Athlon Ind Est HA0 87 D5
Athlon Rd HA0 87 D5
Athol Cl HA5 22 B2
Athol Ct 15 N4 72 B6
Athole Gdns EN1 17 C6
Athole Terr CR7 183 A1
Athol Gdns HA5 22 B2
Atholl Ho W9 229 A1
Atholl Rd IG3 58 A2
Athol Sq E14 98 A1
Athol Way UB10 82 C4
Atkins Ct
13 Old Ford E3 97 B6
Atkins Ct *continued*
Woolwich SE7 122 A2
Atkins Dr BR4 224 B6
Atkins Lo W8 245 A2
Atkinson Ct 3 E10 53 D2
Atkinson Ho
11 Battersea
SW11 137 A3
Battersea SW11 268 A1
15 Hackney E2 96 A5
Newham E13 98 D3
Walworth SE17 262 D3
Atkinson Rd E16 99 C2
Atkinson's Almhouses
HA8 26 B5
Atkins Rd
Streatham SW4,
SW12 159 D4
Walthamstow E10 53 D3
Atlanta Bldg 8
SE13 141 D4
Atlanta Ct CR7 205 A6
Atlantic Ct 19 E14 120 B6
Atlantic Ho
5 Putney SW15 157 B6
4 Tower Hamlets E1 97 A2
Atlantic Rd SW2, SW9,
SE24 138 C1
Atlantis Cl IG11 102 B4
Atlas Bsns Ctr NW2 68 B6
Atlas Gdns SE7 121 C2
Atlas Mews
Dalston E8 73 D2
Islington N7 72 B2
Atlas Rd
Friern Barnet N11 31 A4
Newham E13 99 A5
North Acton NW10 89 C4
Wembley HA9 67 A4
Atley Rd E3 97 C6
Atlip Rd HA0 88 A6
Atney Rd SW15 135 A1
Atria Rd HA6 22 A5
Atrium 9 IG9 21 D2
Atterbury Rd N4 50 D3
Atterbury St
SW1 116 A2 260 A3
Attewood Ave NW10 67 C5
Attewood Rd UB5 63 A2
Attfield Cl N20 14 B2
Attilburgh Ho SE1 263 C6
Attleborough Ct 4
SE21 162 B2
Attle Cl UB10 82 C5
Attlee Cl Hayes UB4 84 B4
Thornton Heath CR7 205 A4
Attlee Ct UB4 84 B4
Attlee Ho E1 243 D3
Attlee Rd Hayes UB4 84 B4
Thamesmead SE28 124 B6
Attlee Terr 3 E17 53 D5
Attneave St WC1 234 A1
Atwater Cl SW2 160 C3
Atwell Cl E10 53 D3
Atwell Pl KT7 197 A1
Atwell Rd 6 SE15 140 A3
Atwood Ave TW9 132 C3
Atwood Ho SE21 161 C1
Atwood Rd W6 112 B2
Aubert Ct N5 72 D4
Aubert Pk N5 72 D4
Aubert Rd N5 72 D4
Aubrey Beardsley Ho
SW1 259 B3
Aubrey Mans NW1 237 A4
Aubrey Moore Point
E15 98 A5
Aubrey Pl NW8 229 A3
Aubrey Rd
Hornsey N8 50 A4
Kensington
W14 113 B5 244 D3
Walthamstow E17 53 D6
Aubrey Wlk
W14 113 B5 244 D3
Auburn Cl SE14 141 A5
Aubyn Hill SE27 183 B6
Aubyn Sq SW15 156 A6
Auckland Cl
Enfield EN1 6 B6
South Norwood
SE19 183 D2
Auckland Ct UB4 84 C3
Auckland Gdns
SE19 183 D2
Auckland Hill SE27 183 A6
Auckland Ho 11
W12 112 B6
Auckland Rd
Clapham SW11 136 C1
Ilford IG1 57 A2
Kingston u T KT1 198 B5
Leyton E10 75 D5
South Norwood
SE19 183 D2
Auckland Rise SE19 183 C2
Auckland St SE11 260 C1
Audax 29 NW9 27 D1
Auden Dr WD6 10 C6
Auden Pl NW1 231 A6
Audley Cl
8 Clapham
SW11 137 A2
Muswell Hill N10 31 B3
Audley Ct Ealing W5 88 C2
Mayfair W1 248 C4
Northolt UB5 84 C4
Pinner Green HA5 22 C1
Snaresbrook E11, E18 54 D5
Surbiton KT5 198 B3
Twickenham TW2 152 B1
Audley Dr 3 E16 121 B5
Audley Gdns IG3 79 D6
Audley Ho N8 50 A5
Audley Pl SM2 217 D1
Audley Rd Ealing W5 88 B2
Enfield EN2 4 D3
Hendon NW4 46 B3
Richmond TW10 154 B6
Audley Sq W1 248 B4
Audrey Cl BR3 207 D3
Audrey Gdns HA0 65 B6
Audrey Ho EC1 241 B3
Audrey Rd IG1 78 D5
Audrey St E2 96 A5
Audric Cl KT2 176 C2
Augurs La 3 E13 99 B4
Augusta Cl KT8 195 B6
Augusta Ct NW4 28 C1
Augusta Rd TW2 152 A2
Augusta St E14 97 D1
Augustine Ho
Broadgate EC2 242 D2
New Cross SE4 141 B4
Augustine Rd
Hammersmith
W14 112 D3
Harrow Weald HA3 24 A2
Augustines Ct E9 74 C3
Augustus Cl
Brentford TW8 131 D5
Hammersmith W12 112 B3
Stanmore HA7 9 D1
Augustus Ct
Feltham TW13 173 B6
Isleworth TW3 130 A1
8 Putney SW19 157 A3
South Norwood
SE19 183 C3
Streatham SW16 159 D2
Augustus Ho NW1 232 A2
Augustus Rd SW19 157 A3
Augustus St
NW1 93 B4 231 D2
Aulay Lawrence Ct
N9 18 B1
Aultone Way
Carshalton SM5 218 D5
Sutton SM1 218 A6
Aultone Yd Ind Est
SM5 218 D5
Aulton Pl SE11 261 B1
Aura Ho 3 TW9 132 D4
Aurelia Gdns CR0 204 B3
Aurelia Rd CR0 204 B3
Auriga Mews N1 73 B3
Auriol Cl KT4 215 C5
Auriol Dr
Greenford UB6 64 B1
Hillingdon UB10 60 D2
Auriol Jun Sch
KT19 215 D4
Auriol Mans W14 254 A3
Auriol Park Rd KT4 215 C5
Auriol Rd
W14 113 A2 254 A3
Aurora Bldg 4 E14 120 A5
Aurora Ct IG8 36 D6
Aurora Ho E14 97 D1
Austell Gdns NW7 11 C1
Austell Hts NW7 11 C1
Austen Cl SE28 124 B5
Austen Ho 5 NW6 91 C4
Austen Rd Erith DA8 147 D5
Harrow HA2 63 D6
Austin Ave BR1, BR2 210 A4
Austin Cl
Forest Hill SE23 163 B4
Twickenham TW1 153 C6
Austin Ct
9 Enfield EN1 17 C6
9 Newham E6 99 C6
Austin Friars EC2 242 D2
Austin Friars Ho
EC2 242 D2
Austin Friars Sq
EC2 242 D2
Austin Ho
6 Brixton SW2 160 B6
19 Kingston u T KT6 198 A4
1 New Cross SE14 141 B5
Austin Rd
Battersea
SW11 137 A4 268 A1
Austin Rd *continued*
Hayes UB3 1
Austins Ct SE15
Austin's La UB10
Austin St E2
Austral Cl DA15 1
Australia Rd W12 1
Austral St
SE11 116 D2 2
Austyn Gdns KT5 1
Autumn Cl Enfield EN1
Wimbledon SW19 1
Autumn Gr BR1
Autumn Lo CR2 2
Autumn Rise 9 W4
Autumn St E3
Avalon BR7
Avalon Cl Ealing W13
Enfield EN2
Merton SW20 1
Avalon Ct CR0 2
Avalon Rd Ealing W13
Parsons Green
SW6 135 D4 2
Avante Ct KT1 1
Avard Gdns BR6 2
Avarn Rd SW17 1
Avebury Ct N1 2
Avebury Rd
Leytonstone E11
Merton SW19 1
Orpington BR6 2
Avebury St N1 2
Aveley Ct 15 E5
Aveley Mans 1 IG11
Aveline St
SE11 116 C1 2
Aveling Ho 12 N19
Aveling Park Rd E17
Aveling Park Sch
E17
Ave Maria La EC4 2
Avenell Mans N5
Avenell Rd N5
Avenfield Ho W1 2
Avening Rd SW18
Avening Terr SW18
Avenons Rd E13
Avenue Cl
Cranford TW5 1
Primrose Hill
NW8 92 C6 2
Southgate N14
Avenue Cres
Cranford TW5
South Acton W3
Avenue Ct
Chelsea SW3 2
Cricklewood NW2
Ealing W5
Penge SE20
Redbridge IG5
Southgate N14
Avenue Elmers KT6
Avenue Gate IG10
Avenue Gdns
Cranford TW5
Mortlake SW14 1
South Acton W3 1
South Norwood
SE25 1
Teddington TW11 1
Avenue Hall N6
Avenue Ho
St John's Wood
NW8 2
Upper Clapton N16
Willesden Green
NW10
Avenue Ind Est E4
Avenue Lo 12 NW8
Avenue Mans
Barnet EN5
Clapham SW11
Hampstead NW3
Muswell Hill N10
Willesden NW2
Avenue Mews N10
Avenue Park Rd SE21,
SE27
Avenue Par
Southgate N21
Sunbury TW16
Avenue Prim Sch
E12
Avenue Rd
Bexley DA6, DA7
Brentford TW8
Crouch End N6
Feltham TW13
Forest Gate E7
Hampton TW12
Harlesden NW10
Hounslow TW7
Ilford RM6
Kingston u T KT1
Mitcham SW16

ue Rd *continued*
Malden KT3 199 C5
h Finchley N12 30 A6
ge BR3, SE20 184 D2
er HA5 41 A6
rose Hill
W8 92 C6 230 A6
th Acton W3 110 D4
hall UB1 107 B5
hgate N14 15 C5
h Norwood
25 184 A1
lington TW11 175 A4
enham N15 51 B4
ington SM6 219 C1
nbledon SW20 178 B1
odford IG8 37 C4
ue Road Sta
184 D1
ue Sch The
5 69 A1
ue S KT5 198 C2
ue Terr
rd IG2 57 C3
ston u T KT3 199 A6
ue The
net EN5 1 A2
kenham BR3 186 A2
ford Pk W4 111 C3
mley BR1 209 D6
ndesbury Pk NW6 91 A6
Buckhurst Hill IG9 21 C2
ngford E4 36 B5
pham SW4 159 A6
gate KT10 212 C3
nford TW5 128 A4
ng W13 87 B1
chley N3 29 C1
ern Barnet N11 31 B5
enwich SE10 142 B5
mpton TW12 173 B4
row HA3 24 D2
ch End HA5 23 B4
nsey N8 50 C6
unslow TW3 151 D6
eworth TW1 153 B6
ston Mark BR2 225 D5
ghton IG10 21 D5
swell Hill N10 31 C1
New Malden KT4 200 A1
ington BR6 227 D6
ner HA5 41 B3
hmond TW9 132 B3
cup DA5 168 D4
uth Croydon CR0 221 C5
neleigh KT17,
M3 216 C1
Paul's Cray BR5 190 B3
nbury TW16 172 B1
biton KT5 198 B3
tenham N17 33 C1
bridge UB10 60 D5
llington SM5 219 A1
ndsworth SW18,
W12 158 C4
nstead E11 55 B4
mbley HA9 44 B1
st Wickham BR4 208 C2
rcester Pk KT4 215 D6
il Gr SW16 182 D4
ill St W6 134 D6
n Gdns KT8 195 D5
n Rd KT8 195 D5
y Ct [1] SE20 184 B3
y Farm Row
1 258 C3
y Gdns IG2 56 B4
RY HILL 167 B5
y Hill Coll (Mile
d Annexe) E3 97 B3
y Hill Rd SE9 167 B3
y Row
115 B6 248 D6
ry Cl E16 98 D2
more Cl BR3 207 B4
more Way BR3 207 A4
non Rd SE4 140 D2
gdor Ct [10] W3 111 A5
gton Ct SE1 263 B3
gton Gr SE20 184 C3
n Cres NW7,
9 28 A2
Sq E1 96 D1
a Rd SW17 181 A6
et Cl SE1 118 A1
et Mews SE28 123 B3
Cl Hayes UB4 84 C3
ton SM1 218 A4
rcester Pk KT4 216 A6
Ct [1] Acton W3 89 A1
Chingford E4 20 A3
enford UB6 85 D3
th Finchley N12 29 D5
Putney SW15 157 A6
mbley HA0 65 A4
dale Ave
net EN4 14 D3

Avondale Ave *continued*
Finchley N12 29 D5
Hinchley Wood KT10 213 A5
Neasden NW2 67 C5
New Malden KT4 199 D1
Avondale Cres
Enfield EN3 7 A2
Redbridge IG4 55 D4
Avondale Ct
Canning Town E16 98 C2
Leytonstone E11 54 C1
[9] Sutton SM2 218 A1
Woodford E18 37 B2
Avondale Dr UB3 106 B5
Avondale Gdns
TW4 151 B6
Avondale Ho
[11] Bermondsey
SE1 118 A1
[6] Mortlake SW14 133 B2
Avondale Mans SW6 264 C2
Avondale Park Gdns
W11 113 A6 244 A5
Avondale Park Prim Sch
W11 113 A6 244 A5
Avondale Park Rd
W11 113 A6 244 A6
Avondale Pavement [7]
SE1 118 A1
Avondale Rd
Bexley DA16 146 C3
Bromley BR1 186 D4
Chislehurst SE9 166 A2
Finchley N3 30 A2
Harringay N15 50 D4
Harrow HA3 42 D6
Mortlake SW14 133 B2
Newham E16 98 C2
South Croydon CR2 221 A2
Southgate N13 16 C2
Walthamstow E17 53 C2
Wimbledon SW19 179 D5
Avondale Rise SE15 139 D2
Avondale Sq SE1 118 A1
Avondale N22 32 A3
Avonfield Ct E17 54 B6
Avon Ho
[2] Islington N1 72 C1
[7] Kingston u T KT2 175 D2
Northolt UB5 85 A3
Southgate N21 16 B6
[14] Stoke Newington
N16 73 B4
Avon House Sch IG8 37 A6
Avon Ho W14 254 D3
Avonhurst Ho NW6 69 A1
Avonley Rd SE14 140 C5
Avon Mews HA5 23 B2
Avonmore Gdns
W14 254 D3
Avonmore Pl W14 254 B4
Avonmore Prim Sch
W14 113 A2 254 B4
Avonmore Rd
W14 113 B2 254 C4
Avonmouth St SE1 262 A6
Avon Path CR0 221 A1
Avon Pl SE1 252 B1
Avon Rd
Ashford TW16 171 D3
Greenford UB6 85 D3
St Johns SE4 141 C2
Upper Walthamstow
E17 54 B6
Avonstowe Cl BR6 227 A5
Avon Way E18 55 A6
Avonwick Rd TW3 129 D3
Avril Way E4 36 A5
Avriol Ho W12 112 B5
Avro Ct E9 75 A3
Avro Way SM6 220 A1
Awlfield Ave N17 33 B2
Awliscombe Rd
DA16 145 D3
Axeholm Ave HA8 26 D2
Axe St IG11 101 A6
Axford Ho SW2 160 D3
Axiom Apartments [5]
BR2 209 B5
Axis Bsns Ctr E15 97 D6
Axis Ct
[7] Bermondsey
SE16 118 A4
Greenwich SE10 142 C6
Axminster Cres
DA16 146 C4
Axminster Rd N7 72 B5
Axon Pl [5] IG1 79 A6
Aybrook St
W1 93 A2 238 A3
Aycliffe Cl BR1 210 B5
Aycliffe Rd W12 112 A5
Ayerst Ct [1] E10 54 A2
Aylands Cl HA9 66 A6
Aylesbury Cl E7 76 D2
Aylesbury Ct SM1 218 A5

Aylesbury Ho [13]
SE15 140 A6
Aylesbury Rd
Bromley BR2 209 A6
Walworth
SE17 117 B1 262 D1
Aylesbury St
Clerkenwell
EC1 94 D3 241 C5
Neasden NW10 67 B5
Ayles Ct UB4 84 B4
Aylesford Ave BR3 207 A4
Aylesford Ho SE1 252 D1
Aylesford St
SW1 115 D1 259 C1
Aylesham Cl NW7 28 A3
Aylesham Rd BR6 211 D2
Aylesham Sh Ctr
SE15 140 A4
Ayles Rd UB4 84 B4
Aylestone Ave NW6 90 D6
Aylestone Ct [10] HA0 66 A2
Aylett Rd
Croydon SE25 206 B5
Isleworth TW7 130 C3
Ayley Croft EN1 18 A6
Ayliffe Cl KT1 176 C1
Aylmer Cl HA7 25 A6
Aylmer Ct N2 48 D4
Aylmer Dr HA7 25 A6
Aylmer Ho SE10 120 B1
Aylmer Par N2 48 D4
Aylmer Rd
Acton W12 111 D4
Dagenham RM8 81 A5
East Finchley N2 48 C4
Leytonstone E11 54 D1
Ayloffe Rd RM9 81 B2
Aylsham Dr UB10 61 A6
Aylton Est [28] SE16 118 C4
Aylward Fst & Mid Schs
HA7 25 D5
Aylward Rd
Forest Hill SE23 162 D2
Merton SW20 201 B6
Aylward Sch N18 33 B6
Aylwards Rise HA7 25 A6
Aylward St E1 96 D1
Aylwin Est SE1 263 B6
Aylwin Girls Sch
SE1 117 D2 263 D4
Aynhoe Mans W14 112 D2
Aynhoe Rd W14 112 D3
Ayr Ct W3 88 C2
Ayres Cl E13 99 A4
Ayres Cres NW10 67 B1
Ayres St SE1 117 A4 252 B2
Ayrsome Rd N16 73 C5
Ayrton Gould Ho [9]
E2 96 D4
Ayrton Ho HA9 65 D6
Ayrton Rd
SW7 114 B3 256 C6
Aysgarth Ct SM1 217 D5
Aysgarth Rd SE21 161 C4
Ayshford Ho E1 96 B4
Ayston Ho [19] SE8 118 D2
Aytoun Ct [17] SW9 138 B3
Aytoun Pl SW9 138 B3
Aytoun Rd SW9 138 B3
Azalea Cl Ealing W7 108 D5
Ilford IG1 78 D3
Azalea Ct
Chingford IG8 36 C3
Ealing W7 108 D5
Azalea Ho
Feltham TW13 150 B3
New Cross SE14 141 B5
Azalea Wlk HA5 40 B3
Azania Mews NW5 71 B2
Azenby Rd SE15 139 D3
Azhar Acad E7 77 A2
Azof St SE10 120 C2
Azov Ho [10] E1 97 A3
Aztec Ct [8] N16 73 C2
Azure Appartments
HA3 24 B3
Azure Ct TW13 149 D1
Azure Ho [28] E2 96 A4

B

Baalbec Rd N5 72 D3
Babbacombe Cl
KT9 213 D3
Babbacombe Gdns
IG4 56 A5
Babbacombe Rd
BR1 187 A2
Baber Bridge Par
TW14 150 C5
Baber Dr TW14 150 C5
Babington Ct
Bloomsbury WC1 240 B4
Streatham SW16 181 D5
Babington Ho SE1 252 B2

Babington House Sch
BR7 188 B4
Babington Rd
Dagenham RM8 80 C4
Hendon NW4 46 B5
Streatham SW16 181 D5
Babington Rise HA9 66 C2
Babmaes St SW1 249 C5
Bacchus Wlk [12] N1 95 C5
Bache's St N1 95 B4 235 D1
Back Church La E1 96 A1
Back Hill EC1 241 B5
Backhouse Pl SE1 263 B3
Back La
Brentford TW8 131 D6
Buckhurst Hill IG9 21 D2
Burnt Oak HA8 27 A2
Dagenham RM6 59 A2
Hampstead NW3 70 A4
Hornsey N8 50 A4
Richmond TW10 153 C2
Sidcup DA5 169 C4
Backley Gdns SE25 206 A3
Back Rd Sidcup DA14 190 A6
Teddington TW11 174 C3
Bacon Gr
SE1 117 D3 263 C5
Bacon La
Edgware HA8 26 C2
Queensbury NW9 44 D5
Bacon's Coll SE16 119 A4
Bacon's La N6 49 A1
Bacon St E2 95 D3 243 D6
Bacon Terr RM8 80 B3
Bacton NW5 71 A3
Bacton St E2 96 C4
Baddeley Cl [11] EN3 7 C6
Baddeley Ho
East Molesey KT8 195 C4
Vauxhall SE11 260 D2
Baddow Cl
Dagenham RM10 103 C6
Woodford IG8 37 D4
Baddow Wlk N1 235 A6
Baden Ct N11 31 D3
Baden Pl SE1 252 C2
Baden Powell Cl
Dagenham RM9 103 A6
Surbiton KT6 214 B6
Baden Powell Ho [11]
DA17 125 C3
Baden Powell Sch
E5 74 B5
Baden Rd Hornsey N8 49 D5
Ilford IG1 78 D3
Badger Cl
Feltham TW13 150 B1
Hounslow TW4 128 C2
Ilford IG2 57 A2
Badger Ct
Chingford E4 36 B6
Dollis Hill NW2 68 C5
Badgers Cl
Ashford TW15 170 B5
Enfield EN2 4 D2
Harrow HA1 42 B3
Hayes UB3 105 C6
Badgers Copse
Orpington BR6 227 D6
Worcester Pk KT4 215 D6
Badgers Croft
Barnet N20 13 A3
Chislehurst SE9 166 C1
Badgers Hole CR0 222 D4
Badgers Wlk KT3 177 C1
Badlis Rd E17 53 C6
Badma Cl N9 18 C1
Badminton Cl
Harrow HA1 42 C5
Northolt UB5 63 C2
Badminton Ct [9] N4 51 A2
Badminton Ho SE22 139 C1
Badminton KT2 176 D2
Badminton Mews [9]
E16 121 A5
Badminton Rd
SW12 159 A5
Badric Ct SW11 136 B3
Badsworth Rd [3]
SE5 139 A4
Bagley Cl UB7 104 A4
Bagley's La
SW6 135 D4 265 D1
Bagleys Spring RM6 59 A5
Bagnigge Ho WC1 234 A1
Bagshot Ho NW1 231 D2
Bagshot Rd EN1 17 D5
Bagshot St
SE17 117 C1 263 B1
Baildon [27] E2 96 C5
Baildon St SE8 141 B5
Bailey Cl Chingford E4 36 A6
Wood Green N11 31 D3
Woolwich SE28 123 C5
Bailey Cres KT9 213 D1
Bailey Ct
[4] Chingford E4 36 B5

Bailey Ct *continued*
[9] Shepherd's Bush
W12 112 A4
Bailey Ho
Mitcham CR4 202 C6
[11] Penge SE26 184 B5
Walham Green
SW10 265 D4
Bailey Mews
Brixton SW2 160 C6
Chiswick W4 132 D6
Bailey Pl SE26 184 D4
Bainbridge cl KT2 176 A5
Bainbridge Rd RM9 81 B4
Bainbridge St WC1 239 D2
Baines Cl CR2 221 B3
Bain Ho [23] SW9 138 A3
Baird Ave UB1 108 A6
Baird Cl
Kingsbury NW9 45 A3
Walthamstow E10 53 C1
Baird Gdns SE19 183 C6
Baird Ho
[12] Belvedere
DA17 125 C3
[29] Shepherd's Bush
W12 112 B6
Baird Rd EN1 6 B1
Baird St EC1 242 B6
Bairny Wood App
IG8 37 B4
Baizdon Rd SE3 142 C3
Baker Beall Ct DA7 147 D2
Baker Ct E11 76 B5
Baker Ho
[12] Bromley E3 97 D4
Ealing W7 108 D5
Baker La CR4 203 A6
Baker Rd
Harlesden NW10 89 C6
Kidbrooke SE18 144 A4
Bakers' Almshouses
E10 53 D3
Bakers Ave E17 53 D3
Bakers Ct RM8 59 B2
Bakers Ct SE25 205 C6
Bakers End SW20 179 A1
Bakers Field N7 72 A4
Bakers Gdns SM5 218 C6
Bakers Hall Ct EC3 253 B5
Bakers Hill Barnet EN5 1 D3
Upper Clapton E5 52 C1
Bakers Ho W5 109 D5
Baker's La N6 48 D3
Bakers Mews [9]
BR6 227 D2
Baker's Mews W1 238 A2
Bakers Pas [22] NW3 70 A4
Bakers Rents [13] E2 95 D4
Bakers Row E15 98 C5
Baker's Row
EC1 94 C3 241 A5
Baker St Enfield EN1 5 B4
Marylebone
W1 92 D2 237 D4
Baker Street Sta
NW1 92 D3 237 D5
Baker Street
W1 92 D2 237 D4
Baker's Yd EC1 241 A5
Bakery Cl SW9 270 D3
Bakery Mews KT6 198 C1
Bakewell Way KT3 177 C1
Balaam Ho SM1 217 C4
Balaams La N14 15 D2
Balaam St E13 99 B4
Balaclava Rd
Bermondsey
SE1 117 D2 263 D3
Kingston u T KT6 197 C2
Bala Gn NW9 45 C3
Balcaskie Rd SE9 166 B6
Balchen Rd SE3 143 D3
Balchier Rd SE22 162 B5
Balcombe Cl DA6 146 D1
Balcombe Ho
Lisson Gr NW1 237 C6
[3] Streatham SW2 160 B3
Balcombe St
NW1 92 D3 237 C5
Balcon Ct W5 88 B1
Balcorne St E9 74 C1
Balder Rise SE12 165 B2
Balderton Flats W1 238 B1
Balderton St
W1 93 A1 238 B1
Baldewyne Ct N17 34 A2
Baldock Ho [31] SE5 139 A3
Baldock St E3 97 D5
Baldrey Ho [1] SE10 120 D1
Baldry Gdns SW16 182 B4
Baldwin Cres SE5 139 A4
Baldwin Gdns TW3 130 A4
Baldwin Ho
[15] Streatham
SW2 160 C3
Wallend E12 78 C1

Baldwin's Gdns
EC1 94 C2 241 A4
Baldwin St EC1 235 C1
Baldwin Terr
N1 95 A5 235 A4
Baldwyn Gdns W3 111 B6
Balearic Apts [3]
E16 121 A6
Bale Rd E1 97 A2
Bales Coll W10 90 D4
Balfern Gr W4 111 C1
Balfern St SW11 136 C3
Balfe St N1 94 A5 233 B3
Balfour Ave W7 108 D5
Balfour Bsns Ctr
UB2 106 D3
Balfour Gr N20 14 D1
Balfour Ho W10 90 D2
Balfour Mews
Edmonton N9 18 A1
Mayfair W1 248 B4
Balfour Pl
Mayfair W1 248 B5
Putney SW15 134 B1
Balfour Rd
Bromley Comm
BR2 209 D4
Croydon SE25 206 A5
Ealing W13 109 B4
Harrow HA1 42 B4
Highbury N5 73 A4
Hounslow TW3 129 D2
Ilford IG1 57 A1
Merton SW19 179 D3
North Acton W3 89 A2
Southall UB2 106 D3
Wallington SM5 218 D1
Balfour St
SE17 117 B2 262 C4
Balfron Twr [4] E14 98 A1
Balgonie Rd E4 20 B3
Balgowan Cl KT3 199 C5
Balgowan Prim Sch
BR3 185 A1
Balgowan Rd BR3 185 B1
Balgowan St SE18 123 D2
BALHAM 159 A3
Balham Gr SW12 159 A4
Balham High Rd SW12,
SW17 159 A3
Balham Hill SW12 159 B5
Balham New Rd
SW12 159 B4
Balham Park Mans
SW12 158 D3
Balham Park Rd SW12,
SW17 159 A3
Balham Rd N9 18 A2
Balham Sta SW12 159 B3
Balham Station Rd
SW12 159 B3
Balin Ho SE1 252 C2
Balkan Wlk E1 118 B6
Balladier Wlk E14 97 D2
Ballamore Rd BR1 165 A1
Ballance Rd E9 75 A2
Ballantine St SW18 136 A1
Ballantrae Ho NW2 69 B4
Ballard Cl KT2 177 B3
Ballard Ho SE10 141 D6
Ballards Cl RM10 103 D6
Ballards Farm Rd CR0,
CR2 222 A2
Ballards La N3 29 D3
Ballards Mews HA8 26 C4
Ballards Rd
Dagenham RM10 103 D6
Dollis Hill NW2 68 A6
Ballards Rise CR2 222 A2
Ballards Way CR0,
CR2 222 B2
Ballast Quay SE10 120 B1
Ballater Cl WD19 22 C6
Ballater Rd
Brixton SW2,
SW4 138 A1
South Croydon CR2 221 D3
Ball Ct EC3 242 D1
Ballentyne Ct N21 16 B6
Ballina St SE23 162 D4
Ballin Ct [14] E14 120 A4
Ballingdon Rd
SW11 159 A5
Ballinger Point [18]
E3 97 D4
Ballinger Way UB5 85 A3
Balliol Ave E4 36 C6
Balliol Ho [11] SW15 156 D5
Balliol Rd
Bexley DA16 146 B3
North Kensington
W10 90 D1
Tottenham N17 33 C2
Balloch Rd SE6 164 B2

Ballogie Ave NW10....67 C4
Ballow Cl 15 SE5.....139 C5
Ball's Pond Pl 3 N1 ..73 B2
Ball's Pond Rd N1 ....73 C2
Balmain Cl W5 ......109 D5
Balmain Ct TW3 .....129 D4
Balman Ho 3 SE16 ..118 D2
Balmer Rd E3 ....97 B5
Balmes Rd
N1..........95 B6 235 D6
Balmoral Ave
Beckenham BR3 .... 207 A5
Friern Barnet N11.....31 B5
Balmoral Cl 1
SW15.............156 D5
Balmoral Cres KT8...195 C6
Balmoral Ct
18 Belmont SM2.... 217 C1
Ealing W5 ....87 D1
Edgware HA8.........26 D6
Grove Pk SE12........187 B6
North Cheam KT4 ....216 B6
21 Rotherhithe
SE16............ 118 D5
St John's Wood NW8 229 C4
Wembley HA9 ....66 B5
West Norwood SE27 . 183 A6
Balmoral Dr
Borehamwood
WD6................11 B6
Hayes UB4............83 D3
Southall UB1 ....85 B3
Balmoral Gdns
Ealing W13 .... 109 A3
Ilford IG3 ....57 D1
Old Bexley DA5 ......169 B4
Balmoral Gr N7.......72 B2
Balmoral Ho
2 Isle Of Dogs
E14............. 119 D3
Stanmore HA7........26 A1
Stoke Newington N4 ...51 A1
Walthamstow E17.....35 B1
West Kensington
W14............ 254 A4
Balmoral Lo BR6......226 C4
Balmoral Mews
W12...............111 D3
Balmoral Rd
Forest Gate E7 ....77 C3
Harrow HA2 ....63 C4
Kingston u T KT1.....198 B5
Leyton E10..........75 D6
North Cheam KT4 ....216 B6
Willesden NW2.......68 B2
Balmoral Trad Est
IG11.............. 101 D2
Balmore Cl E14.......98 A1
Balmore Cres EN4 ....15 A6
Balmore St N19........71 B6
Balmuir Gdns SW15..134 C1
Balnacraig Ave
NW10...............67 C4
Balniel Gate SW1 ... 259 D2
Balsam Ho 9 E14....119 D6
Baltic Apts 5 E16....121 A6
Baltic Cl SW19.......180 B3
Baltic Ho 7 SE5 .....139 A3
Baltic St E
EC1 ....95 A3 242 A5
Baltic St W
EC1 ....95 A3 242 A5
Baltimore Ho
Clapham SW18 ..... 136 A1
Kennington SE11.... 261 A2
Merton SW19 ...... 179 D3
Baltimore Pl DA16 ...145 D3
Balvaird Pl SW1 .... 259 D1
Balvernie Gr SW18...157 C4
Bamber Ho IG11.....101 A6
Bamber Rd 5 SE15 ..139 D4
Bamborough Gdns 12
W12...............112 C4
Bamburgh 9 N17.....34 B3
Bamford Ave HA0 .....88 B5
Bamford Ct E15.......75 D3
Bamford Rd
Barking IG11.........79 A2
Catford BR1.........186 B5
Bampfylde Cl SM6 ....219 C5
Bampton Ct W5........87 D1
Bampton Dr NW7 .....28 A3
Bampton Rd SE23.....162 D1
Banavie Gdns BR3 ...186 A2
Banbury Cl EN2........4 D4
Banbury Ct
11 Belmont SM2 .... 217 C1
Ealing W13 .... 109 A3
Strand WC2........ 250 A6
Banbury Ho 5 E9.....74 D1
Banbury Rd
Higham Hill E17.......35 A3
Homerton E9.........74 D1
Banbury St 3
SW11..............136 C3
Banbury Wlk UB5 .....85 C5
Banchory Rd SE3 ....143 B5
Bancroft Ave
East Finchley N2 ......48 C4
Woodford IG9 ....21 A2
Bancroft Cl TW15 ....170 C5
Bancroft Ct
Northolt UB5 ....84 C6
South Lambeth SW8 . 270 A2
Bancroft Gdns
Harrow Weald HA3 ....24 A2
Orpington BR6...... 211 D1
Bancroft Ho 11 E1 ....96 C3
Bancroft Rd
Bethnal Green E1 .....96 D3
Harrow Weald HA3 ....24 A1
Bancrofts Sch IG8.....21 A1
Bandon Cl UB10 ......82 B5
BANDONHILL 219 D3
Bandon Hill Prim Sch
SM6.............. 219 D2
Bandon Rise SM6 ....219 D3
Banff Ho 1 NW3.......70 C2
Banfield Rd SE15 .....140 B2
Banfor Ct SM6 ....219 C3
Bangabandhu Prim Sch
E2...................96 C4
Bangalore St SW15 ..134 D2
Bangor Cl UB5........63 D3
Banim St W6 ....112 B2
Banister Ho
Hackney E9 ....74 D3
Nine Elms SW8 ..... 269 B2
9 West Kilburn W10 ..91 A4
Banister Rd W10......90 D4
Bank Ave CR4........180 B1
Bank Bldgs 13
SW16..............181 C5
Bank Ct SW11 ...... 268 C2
Bank End SE1 ...... 252 B4
Bankfoot Rd BR1.....186 C6
Bankhurst Rd SE6....163 B4
Bank La
Kingston u T KT2.... 176 A3
Roehampton SW15 .. 155 C6
Bank Mews SM1 .....218 A2
Bank of England*
EC2 ....95 B1 242 C1
Bank of England Mus*
EC2 ....95 B1 242 C1
Bank Par N11.........31 B5
Banks Ho
Isleworth TW7...... 130 C3
Newington SE1 ..... 262 A5
Banksia Rd N18.......34 D5
Bankside Art Gal*
SE1 .... 116 D6 251 D5
Bankside Ave
1 Lewisham
SE13............ 142 A2
Northolt UB5 ....84 A5
Bankside
Borough The
SE1...... 117 A6 252 A5
Borough The SE1.... 252 B4
Bankside Cl
Carshalton SM5..... 218 C2
Isleworth TW7....... 130 D1
Bankside Dr KT7......213 B6
Bankside EN2 ....4 D4
Bankside Ho EC3 .... 243 B1
Bankside Pier
SE1........ 117 A6 252 A5
Bankside Pk IG11 .. 102 A4
Bankside Rd IG1.......79 B3
Bankside
Southall UB1 .... 106 D5
South Croydon CR2 .. 221 D2
Bankside Way 6
SE19...............183 C4
Banks La DA6.........147 B1
Bank Sta EC3. 95 B1 242 D1
Bank St E14 ....119 D5
Banks Way E12 ....78 C4
Bank The N6..........49 B1
Bankton Rd SW2......138 C1
Bankwell Rd SE13....142 C1
Banner Ct 5 SE16 ...118 C2
Banner Ho EC1 ..... 242 B5
Bannerman Ho SW8 270 C5
Banner St
EC1 ....95 A3 242 B6
Banning Ho 4
SW19...............156 D3
Banning St SE10.....120 C1
Bannister Cl
Greenford UB6 ....64 B3
Streatham SW2..... 160 C3
Bannister Ho
28 Deptford SE14 ... 140 D6
Harrow HA3 ....42 C6
Bannister Sports Ctr
The HA3.............24 A4
Bannockburn Prim Sch
SE18.............. 123 D2
Bannockburn Rd
SE18.............123 D2
Bannow Cl KT19 .....215 C4
Banqueting Ho*
SW1............. 250 A3
Banstead Ct
Stoke Newington
N4 ....51 A1
Walthamstow E10.....53 D1
Banstead Gdns N9....17 C1
Banstead Rd SM5....218 C1
Banstead St SE15 ...140 C2
Banstead Way SM6...220 A3
Banstock Rd HA8 .....26 D4
Banting Dr N21........16 B6
Banting Ho 6 NW2 ...68 A5
Bantock Ct 1 N20 ....14 D2
Bantock Ho 8 W10 ...91 A4
Banton Cl EN1.........6 B3
Bantry Ho 18 E1 ......96 D3
Bantry St SE5.........139 B5
Banville Ho SW8.... 270 D3
Banwell Rd DA5 .....168 D5
Banyan Ho 8 NW3....69 D2
Banyard Rd SE16......118 B3
Baptist Gdns NW5 ....71 A2
Barandon Wlk 6
W11...............112 D6
Barbanel Ho 20 E1....96 C3
Barbara Brosnan Ct
NW8.............. 229 C3
Barbara Castle Cl
SW6.............. 264 D5
Barbara Cl TW17.....192 D4
Barbara Hucklesbury Cl
N22 ....32 D1
Barbara Martin Ho 1
N11 ....31 C5
Barbara Rudolph Ct 5
N19 ....50 A2
Barbara Ward Ct 3
E11.................76 C6
Barbauld Rd N16 .....73 C5
Barber Beaumont Ho 21
E1...................96 D4
Barber Cl N21 ....16 C4
Barberry Ct E15 ......76 C2
Barbers Alley 1 E13 ..99 B4
Barbers Rd E15.......97 D5
BARBICAN 95 A2
Barbican Arts & Con
Ctr* EC2.....95 A2 242 B4
Barbican*
EC2 ....95 A2 242 B3
Barbican Rd UB1 .....85 D1
Barbican Sta
EC1 .... 95 A2 242 A4
Barb Mews W6 ....112 C3
Barbon Cl WC1 ..... 240 C4
Barbot Cl N9 ....18 A1
Barbrook Ho E9 ......74 C2
Barchard St SW18....157 D6
Barchester Cl W7....108 D5
Barchester Lo N12....29 D6
Barchester Rd HA3.... 24 B1
Barchester St E14.....97 D2
Barclay Cl
SW6........135 C5 265 A3
Barclay Ct N12........30 A5
Barclay Ho 21 E9......74 C1
Barclay Oval IG8......37 A6
Barclay Prim Sch
E10..................54 B3
Barclay Rd
Edmonton N18........33 B4
Leyton E11...........54 D1
Newham E13..........99 C3
Parsons Green
SW6..... 135 C5 265 B3
South Croydon CR0 ...221 B5
Walthamstow E17......54 A4
Barcombe Ave SW2 ..160 B2
Barcom Trad Est 1
CR0 .... 204 A2
Bardell Ho 17 SE1.....118 A4
Barden St SE18 ......145 C5
Bardfield Ave RM6 ....58 D6
Bardney Rd SM4 .....201 D5
Bardolph Rd
Richmond TW9........132 B2
Tufnell Pk N7.........72 A4
Bard Rd W10 ....112 D6
Bardsey Pl 41 E1......96 C3
Bardsey Wlk 5 N1.....73 A2
Bardsley Cl CR0......221 D5
Bardsley Ho 6
SE10...............142 A6
Bardsley La SE10.....142 A6
Barents Ho 10 E1 .....96 D3
Barfett St W10........91 B3
Barfield Ave N20......14 D2
Barfield Rd
Bromley BR1,
BR7............. 210 C6
Leytonstone E11 ......54 D1
Barfleur La SE8......119 B2
Barford Cl NW4.......28 A2
Barford Ho 23 E3 .....97 B5
Barford St N1 . 94 C6 234 B5
Barforth Rd SE15 ....140 B2
Barfreston Way
SE20...............184 B2
Bargate Cl
New Malden KT3.... 200 A2
Plumstead Comm
SE18............ 123 D1
Bargehouse Rd E16 ..122 D4
Barge House St SE1. 251 B4
Barge La 10 E3 ....97 B6
Bargery Rd SE6......163 D3
Bargrove Cl 8
SE20...............184 A3
Bargrove Cres SE6...163 B2
Barham Cl
Chislehurst BR7..... 188 D5
Keston Mark BR2 .... 210 A1
Wembley HA0 ....65 C2
Barham Ct
8 Croydon CR2 .... 221 A4
Keston Mark BR2 .... 210 A1
Wembley HA0 ....65 C2
Woodside Pk N12 .....29 B5
Barham Ho SE17..... 263 B2
Barham Prim Sch
HA0 ....65 C2
Barham Rd
Chislehurst BR7..... 188 D5
Croydon CR2 .... 221 A3
Wimbledon SW20 ... 178 A3
Baring Cl SE12.......165 A2
Baring Ct N1 .... 235 C5
Baring Ho 15 E14 .....97 C1
Baring Prim Sch
SE12............ 165 A4
Baring Rd Barnet EN4 ... 2 B2
Croydon CR0 .... 206 A1
Grove Pk SE12...... 165 A2
Baring St N1 .. 95 B6 235 C5
Barker Cl
Kingston u T KT3.... 198 D5
Richmond TW9...... 132 D3
Barker Dr NW1 ....71 D1
Barker Ho
Dulwich SE21....... 161 C1
3 Harringay N15.....50 D5
Walthamstow E17.....53 B2
Walworth SE17 ..... 263 A3
Barker Mews SW4 ...137 B1
Barker St SW10..... 266 A6
Barker Wlk SW16 ....159 D1
Barkham Rd N17......33 C3
BARKING 79 B1
Barking Abbey Comp
Sch (Sports &
Humanities Coll))
IG11.................79 C3
Barking Abbey Sch
(Sports & Humanities
Coll) IG11 ....79 D2
Barking Bsns Ctr
IG11............. 102 A4
Barking Flyover
IG11................78 D1
Barking Hospl IG11...79 D1
Barking Ind Pk
IG11............. 102 A6
Barking Rd
East Ham E6 ....100 B6
Plaistow E13.........99 B4
BARKINGSIDE 57 A6
Barkingside Sta IG6 ..57 B6
Barking Sta IG11.....79 A1
Bark Pl W2...113 D6 245 C6
Barkston Gdns
SW5........113 D2 255 C3
Barkway Cl BR6......226 C4
Barkway Ct N4 ....73 A6
Barkwith Ho 27
SE14...............140 D6
Barkworth Rd SE16 ..118 C1
Barlborough St
SE14...............140 D5
Barlby Gdns W10 .....90 D3
Barlby Prim Sch
W10.................90 D3
Barlby Rd W10.......90 D2
Barley Cl WD23 ....8 A6
Barleycorn Way
E14...............119 B6
Barley Ct Ilford IG3 ....58 B4
Stanwell TW19 ..... 148 A3
Barleyfields Cl RM6 ...58 C2
Barley La IG3.........58 B3
Barley Lane Prim Sch
RM6.................58 B2
Barley Mow Pas
Chiswick W4 ....111 B1
Clerkenwell EC1 .... 241 D3
Barley Mow Way
TW17...............192 C5
Barley Shotts Bsns Pk
W10.................91 B2
Barling Ct 1 SW4....138 A3
Barling 6 NW1........71 B1
Barlings Ho 2 SE4...140 D1
Barloch Ho 14
SW11..............137 A3
Barlow Cl SM6.......220 A1
Barlow Dr SE18......144 A4
Barlow Ho
14 Bermondsey
SE16..............118 B2
Notting Hill W11 .... 244 A6
Shoreditch N1 ...... 235 C2
Barlow Pl W1....... 248 D5
Barlow Rd Acton W3 . 110 D5
Brondesbury NW6.....69 B2
Hampton TW12 ..... 173 C3
Barlow St
SE17........117 B2 262 D3
Barmeston Rd SE6 ...163 D2
Barmor Cl HA2 ....23 D1
Barmouth Ave UB6....86 D5
Barmouth Ho 6 N7 ...72 B6
Barmouth Rd
Croydon CR0 .... 222 D6
Wandsworth SW18 .. 158 A5
Barnabas Ct N21......16 D6
Barnabas Ho EC1 ... 235 A1
Barnabas Lo SW8 ... 270 B2
Barnabas Rd E9 ......74 D3
Barnaby Cl HA2.......64 A6
Barnaby Ct NW9 ......45 C6
Barnaby Pl SW7 .... 256 C3
Barnard Cl
Chislehurst BR7......189 B2
Sunbury TW16.......172 B3
Wallington SM6...... 219 D1
Woolwich SE18 ..... 122 C3
Barnard Ct SW16 ....160 B1
Barnard Gdns
Hayes UB4...........84 B3
West Barnes KT3 ... 200 A5
Barnard Gr E15.......76 D1
Barnard Hill N10.......31 B2
Barnard Ho 17 E2.....96 B4
Barnard Lo
New Barnet EN5 ....2 A1
10 Paddington W9.....91 C2
Barnard Mews
SW11..............136 C1
Barnardo Dr IG6......57 A5
Barnardo Gdns 1
E1.................118 D6
Barnardo St E1.......96 D1
Barnard Rd
Clapham SW11 ..... 136 C1
Enfield EN1 ....6 B3
Mitcham CR4....... 181 A1
Barnard's Inn EC4... 241 B2
Barnbrough NW1 ... 232 A5
Barnby Sq 1 E15 .....98 C6
Barnby St
Somers Town
NW1.......93 C4 232 B2
2 West Ham E15.....98 C6
Barn Cl
Ashford TW15 ...... 170 D5
19 Kentish Town
NW5................71 D3
Northolt UB5 ....84 C5
Barn Cres HA7.......25 C4
Barncroft Cl UB8.....82 D2
Barn Croft Prim Sch
E17..................53 A3
Barneby Cl TW2 .....152 C3
Barnehurst Rd DA7 ..147 D3
Barnersbury Ho N7 ...72 A4
BARNES 133 D4
Barnes Ave
Barnes SW13 ...... 134 A5
Southall UB2 ....107 B2
Barnes Bridge Sta
SW13............ 133 C3
Barnes Cl E12 ....77 D4
Barnes Common*
SW13............ 134 A2
Barnes Ct Barnet EN5 ...1 D1
Islington N1 ....72 C1
3 Newham E16 ......99 C2
South Norwood CR7 . 205 A6
Woodford IG8........37 D5
Wood Green N22......32 A3
Barnes End KT3......200 A4
Barnes High St
SW13..............133 D3
Barnes Ho
8 Barking IG11.....101 B6
14 Bethnal Green E2...96 C5
Camden Town NW1.. 231 D6
26 Deptford SE14 ... 140 D6
Hornsey N19..........50 A2
Barnes Hospl SW14. 133 C2
Barnes Prim Sch
SW13............ 133 D2
Barnes Qtr 6 TW8 ...131 C5
Barnes Rd
Edmonton N18........34 C6
Ilford IG1 ....79 A3
Barnes Sta SW13 ... 134 A2
Barnes St E14 ....97 A1
Barnes Terr SE8......
Barnes Wallis Ct
HA9.................
BARNET.............
Barnet By-Pass WD6..
Barnet Coll EN5 ......
Barnet Coll (Grahame
Park Ctr) NW9......
Barnet Coll (Montagu
Rd) NW4...........
Barnet Dr BR2.......2
BARNET GATE ....
Barnet Gate La EN5 ...
Barnet Gr E2 ....
Barnet Hill EN5 ....
Barnet Hill JMI Sch
EN5 ....
Barnet Ho 35 SE5 1
Barnet La
Barnet EN5, N20 ......
Borehamwood WD6....
Barnet Mus* EN5 .....
Barnet Rd Barnet EN5..
Edgware EN5.........
Barnett Ho E1 2
Barnett Homestead
NW11................
Barnet Trad Est EN5 ..
Barnetts Ct HA2 ......
Barnett St 18 E1 ......
Barnet Way (Barnet By
Pass) EN5, NW7,
WD6................
Barnet Wood Rd
BR2 2
Barney Cl SE7 1
Barnfield Ave
Croydon CR0 2
Kingston u T KT2..... 1
Mitcham CR4........2
Barnfield Cl
London N4...........
Wandsworth SW17 .. 1
Barnfield Gdns
Kingston u T KT2 1
Shooters Hill SE18... 1
Barn Field NW3.......
Barnfield KT3.........1
Barnfield Pl E14 1
Barnfield Prim Sch
HA8 ....
Barnfield Rd
Burnt Oak HA8 ....
Ealing W5 ....
Erith DA17...........1
Shooters Hill SE18... 1
Barnfield Wood Cl
BR3 2
Barnfield Wood Rd
BR3 2
Barnham Dr SE28....1
Barnham Rd UB6 .....
Barnham St SE1 2
Barnhill Ave BR2.....2
Barnhill Com High Sch
UB4 ....
Barnhill Ct UB4.......
Barnhill La UB4.......
Barnhill HA5.........
Barnhill Rd
Hayes UB4..........
Wembley HA9 ....
Barn Hill HA9.........
Barnhurst Path
WD19...............
Barningham Way
NW9................
Barnlea Cl TW13.....1
Barnmead Ct RM9 ....
Barnmead Gdns RM9..
Barnmead Rd
Dagenham RM9.......
Penge BR3......... 1
Barn Rise HA9........
BARNSBURY ....
Barnsbury Cl KT3 1
Barnsbury Cres KT5..1
Barnsbury Gr N7......
Barnsbury Ho 12
SW4.................1
Barnsbury La KT5....1
Barnsbury Pk N1 .....
Barnsbury Rd
N1 ....94 C6 2
Barnsbury Sq N1 .....
Barnsbury St N1......
Barnsbury Terr N1 ....
Barnscroft SW20.....2
Barnsdale Ave E14....1
Barnsdale Rd W9 .....
Barnsley St E1........
Barnstaple Ho SE12..1
Barnstaple La SE13 ..1
Barnstaple Rd HA4....
Barn St N16 ....
Barnston Wlk N1 ... 2
Barnview Lo HA3 ....

ay HA9 66 C6
ell Ho 1 SE5 139 C4
ell Rd SW2 160 C6
ood Cl
N20 13 B3
HA4 61 B6
ourne Green
91 D3
Cl
Barnet N11 31 B5
on N1 234 A4
Ct Barnet EN5 1 D1
m CR4 202 C5
ss Rd 5 E2 95 D4
t Gr N17 34 A2
t Rd N17 34 A2
Gdns IG6 57 A6
Gr CR4 202 C5
Ho 6 SW19 180 B2
Rd RM8 58 D1
14 BR3 185 D1
Court Mans
254 B1
s Court Rd
113 A1 254 B2
Court Sta
113 A1 254 A2
Ct Ilford IG1 79 B6
bury NW9 45 B3
gton SM6 219 D5
field Rd TW1 153 B5
Gate
Barnet EN4 14 C5
uth Acton W4 111 A3
s Keep
113 A1 254 A2
Lo 9 E14 120 A2
Mead HA1 42 C5
mead Rd
134 A4
mede W5 110 B4
mere Ct 9
1 A1
mere Rd N2 48 C5
s Pl
116 C4 251 B1
The TW1 153 B5
St N1 94 C5 234 A4
s Wlk CR0 207 A3
Wlk E16 98 D2
Mews SE8 141 C6
k Rd TW4 129 A1
ell Ho 15
112 D3
Hall Cir UB3 83 C1
Hall Rd UB3 105 C6
s Cl 7 EN3 7 C6
Ave N22 32 B1
Ho 15 N1 72 D1
Ind Pk
E3 98 A3
all UB1 107 C5
Way HA3 42 B6
acon SE23 162 C4
ger Rd N10 30 D1
Ho NW6 91 C6
Ct 2 NW10 89 C5
Rd E17 54 A5
's Green Rd
89 B5
's Gr N16 73 C3
St W1 93 A1 238 B1
Rd SW2 160 A2
Ct EN5 14 A6
dale SE14 141 A3
Ho Acton W3 111 A4
water W2 246 B5
nton N9 18 B4
ose Hill NW8 230 B5
oke Newington
73 C5
Gdns Pier
121 D3
Point Rd
121 C4
gers Ct HA4 39 B2
ger Sq SW17 181 A6
gton Cl NW5 71 A3
gton Ct
ton W3 110 D4
sh Town NW5 71 A3
swell Hill N10 31 B1
uth Lambeth
9 138 A3
gton N20 14 B3
gton Prim Sch
146 D3
gton Rd
DA7 146 D3
n SW9 138 D2
n SM3 201 C1
sey N8 49 D4
Ilford E12 78 C2
gton Villas
144 C4
gton Wlk 9
183 C4

Barrow Ave SM5 218 D1
Barrow Cl N21 16 D2
Barrow Ct 6 SE6 164 D3
Barrowdene Cl HA5 23 A1
Barrowell Gn N21 17 A2
Barrowfield Cl N9 18 C1
Barrowgate Ho W4 111 B1
Barrowgate Rd W4 111 B1
Barrow Hedges Cl
SM5 218 C1
Barrow Hedges Prim Sch SM5 218 C1
Barrow Hedges Way
SM5 218 C1
Barrow Hill Cl KT4 215 C6
Barrow Hill Est
NW8 92 C5 230 A3
Barrow Hill Jun Sch
NW8 92 C5 230 A3
Barrow Hill Rd NW8 230 A3
Barrow Hill KT4 215 C6
Barrow Point Ave
HA5 23 A1
Barrow Point La HA5 23 A1
Barrow Rd
Croydon CR0 220 C3
Streatham SW16 181 D4
Barrow Wlk TW8 109 C1
Barrs Rd NW10 67 B1
Barry Ave Erith DA7 147 A5
South Tottenham N15 51 D3
Barry Cl BR6 227 C5
Barry Ct SW4 159 C5
Barrydene Ct EN2 4 D2
Barrydene N20 14 B2
Barry Ho 4 SE16 118 B1
Barry Lo N4 50 B2
Barrymore N12 30 A3
Barry Par SE22 140 A1
Barry Rd
London SE22 162 A6
Newham E6 100 A1
Willesden NW10 67 A1
Barry Terr TW15 148 B2
Barset Rd SE15 140 C2
Barsons Cl SE20 184 C3
Barston Rd SE27 161 A1
Barstow Cres SW2 160 B3
Bartell Ho SW2 160 C5
Barter St WC1 94 A2 240 B3
Barters Wlk HA5 41 A6
Barth Mews SE18 123 C2
Bartholomew Cl
Barbican EC1 242 A3
Wandsworth SW18 136 A1
Bartholomew Ct
16 Blackwall E14 120 B6
Edgware HA8 25 D3
St Luke's EC1 242 B6
Bartholomew Ho
22 Camberwell
SE5 139 A3
Enfield EN3 7 A6
Bartholomew La
EC2 242 D1
Bartholomew Pas
EC1 241 D3
Bartholomew Pl
EC1 242 A3
Bartholomew Rd
NW5 71 C2
Bartholomew Sq
18 Bethnal Green
E1 96 B3
St Luke's EC1 242 B6
Bartholomew St
SE1 117 B3 262 D5
Bartholomew Villas
NW5 71 C2
Barth Rd SE18 123 C2
Bartle Ave E6 100 A5
Bartle Rd W11 91 A1
Bartlett Cl E14 97 C1
Bartlett Ct EC4 241 B2
Bartletts Cotts 4 EN5 1 A2
Bartletts Ho 10 RM10 81 D2
Bartlett St CR2 221 B3
Bartok Ho W11 244 C5
Barton Ave RM7 59 D1
Barton Cl
Bexley DA6 169 A6
Hackney E9 74 C3
Hendon NW4 46 A5
2 Newham E6 100 B1
Peckham SE15 140 B2
Shepperton TW17 192 D3
Barton Ct
Beckenham BR2 208 B6
10 South Lambeth
SW4 138 A3
3 Sutton SM1 217 D2
West Kensington
W14 254 B2
Barton Gn KT3 177 B1
Barton Ho
8 Bromley E3 97 D4
Islington N1 72 D1

Barton Ho *continued*
Sands End SW6 135 D2
Barton Mdws IG6 57 A5
Barton Rd
Sidcup DA14 191 A4
West Kensington
W14 113 A1 254 B1
Bartons The WD6 9 D5
Barton St SW1 260 A6
Bartonway NW8 229 C4
Bartram Cl UB8 82 D3
Bartram Ct RM9 80 B2
Bartram Rd SE4 163 A5
Bartrams La EN4 2 A5
Bartrip St E9 75 B2
Barts Cl BR3 207 C4
Barts & The London Sch of Medicine & Dentistry
EC1 94 D3 241 D5
Barville Cl SE4 141 A1
Barwell Bsns Pk
KT9 213 D1
Barwell Ho 7 E2 96 A3
Barwell La KT9 213 C1
Barwick Dr UB8 82 D2
Barwick Ho 7 W3 111 A4
Barwick Rd E7 77 B4
Barwood Ave BR4 207 D1
Bascome St 13 SW2 160 C5
Basden Gr TW13 151 C2
Base Apartments 8
N1 73 A1
Basedale Rd RM9 80 B1
Baseing Cl E6 122 C6
Baseline Business Studios 18 W11 112 D6
Basevi Way SE8 141 D6
Bashley Rd NW10 89 B3
Basil Ave E6 100 A4
Basil Ct 11 EN5 2 A1
Basildene Rd TW4,
TW5 128 D2
Basildon Ct W1 238 B4
Basildon Rd SE2 124 A1
Basil Gdns
Croydon CR0 206 D1
West Norwood SE27 183 A5
Basil Ho
South Lambeth
SW8 270 A4
22 Whitechapel E1 96 A1
Basil Mans SW1 247 C1
Basilon Rd DA7 147 A3
Basil Spence Ho N22 32 B2
Basil St
Knightsbridge
SW1 114 D4 247 C1
Knightsbridge SW1,
SW3 114 D3 257 C6
Basin App 20 E14 97 A1
Basing Cl KT7 196 D2
Basing Ct 13 SE15 139 D4
Basingdon Way SE5 139 B1
Basing Dr DA5 169 B5
Basingfield Rd KT7 196 D2
Basinghall Ave
EC2 95 B1 242 C2
Basinghall St
EC2 95 B1 242 C2
Basing Hill
London NW11 47 B1
Wembley HA9 44 C1
Basing Ho
7 Barking IG11 101 B6
Catford SE6 185 C6
Basing House Yd 22
E2 95 C4
Basing Pl E2 95 C4
Basing St W11 91 B1
Basing Way
London N3 47 D6
Thames Ditton KT7 196 D2
Basire St N1 95 A6 235 B6
Baskerville Ct
South Norwood
SE25 205 C4
Wandsworth SW18 158 C4
Baskerville Gdns
NW10 67 C4
Baskerville Rd
SW18 158 C4
Basket Gdns SE9 166 A6
Basle Ho 3 E15 76 C3
Baslow Cl HA3 24 B2
Baslow Wlk E5 74 D4
Basnett Rd 9 SW11 137 A2
Basque Ct 21 SE16 118 D4
Bassano St SE22 161 D6
Bassant Rd SE18 145 D6
Bassein Park Rd
W12 111 D4
Bassett Gdns TW7 130 A5
Bassett Ho RM9 102 B6
Bassett Rd W10 90 D1
Bassetts Cl BR6 226 D4
Bassett St NW5 71 A2

Bassetts Way BR6 226 D4
Bassett Way UB1 85 D1
Bassingbourn Ho 3
N1 72 D1
Bassingham Rd
Wandsworth
SW18 158 A4
Wembley HA0 65 D2
Bassishaw Highwalk
EC2 242 C3
Basswood Cl 5
SE15 140 B2
Bastable Ave IG11 102 A5
Basterfield Ho EC1 242 A5
Bastion Highwalk
EC2 242 A3
Bastion Rd SE18,
SE2 124 A1
Baston Manor Rd BR2,
BR4 225 B4
Baston Rd BR2 225 B5
Baston Sch BR2 225 B6
Bastwick St
EC1 95 A3 242 A6
Basuto Rd
SW6 135 C4 265 B1
Batavia Cl TW16 172 C2
Batavia Ho 1 SE14 141 A5
Batavia Mews 3
SE14 141 A5
Batavia Rd
Deptford SE14 141 A5
Sunbury TW16 172 B2
Batchelor St
N1 94 C6 234 B5
Bateman Cl IG11 79 A2
Bateman Ho 8
SE17 138 D6
Bateman Rd E4 35 C4
Bateman's Bldgs
W1 239 C1
Bateman's Row
EC2 95 C3 243 B6
Bateman St
W1 93 D1 239 C1
Bates Cres
Croydon CR0 220 C3
Streatham SW16 181 C3
Bateson St 3 SE18 123 C2
Bate St 10 E14 119 B6
Bath Cl SE15 140 B5
Bath Ct Finsbury EC1 235 C1
3 Forest Hill SE26 162 A1
Holborn EC1 241 A5
Bathgate Ho 8
SW9 138 D4
Bathgate Rd SW19 156 D1
Bath Gr E2 96 A5
Bath Ho
Bethnal Green E2 96 A3
Borough The SE1 262 B6
Bath House Rd CR0 204 A1
Bath Pas KT1 175 D1
Bath Pl Barnet EN5 1 B2
14 Hammersmith
W6 112 C1
11 Shoreditch EC2 95 C4
Bath Rd Acton W4 111 C2
Cranford TW3, TW4,
TW5 128 C4
Dagenham RM6 59 A3
Harlington TW6, UB7,
TW5 127 B4
Harmondsworth TW6,
UB7 126 B4
Lower Edmonton N9 18 C2
Upton E7 77 D2
Baths Rd BR1, BR2 209 D5
Bath St EC1 95 B4 235 C1
Bath Terr
SE1 117 A3 262 A6
Bathurst Ave SW19 179 D2
Bathurst Gdns NW10 90 B5
Bathurst Ho 2 W12 112 B6
Bathurst Mews
W2 114 B6 246 D6
Bathurst Rd IG1 56 D1
Bathurst St W2 246 D6
Bathway 11 SE18 122 C2
Batley Cl CR4 202 D2
Batley Pl 3 N16 73 D5
Batley Rd Enfield EN2 5 B4
Shacklewell N16 73 D5
Batman Cl W12 112 B5
Batoum Gdns W6 112 C3
Batson Ho 29 E1 96 A1
Batson St W12 112 A4
Batsworth Rd CR4 202 B6
Battenburg Wlk 10
SE19 183 C5
Batten Cl E6 100 B1
Batten Ho
7 London SW4 159 C6
8 Walthamstow E17 53 D6
10 West Kilburn W10 91 A4
Batten St SW11 136 C2
Battersby Rd SE6 164 B1

BATTERSEA 136 D4
Battersea Bridge Rd
SW11 136 C5 267 A3
Battersea Bsns Ctr
SW11 137 A2
Battersea Church Rd
SW11 136 B4 266 D2
Battersea Dogs Home
SW8 137 B5 268 D3
Battersea High St
SW11 136 B3
Battersea Hts SW11 136 D2
Battersea Park*
SW11 137 A5 268 A3
Battersea Park Rd SW11,
SW8 267 D1
Battersea Park Sta
SW8 137 B5 268 C3
Battersea Power Station(dis)
SW8 137 B6 268 D6
Battersea Rise
SW11 136 C1
Battersea Sq SW11 266 D1
Battery Rd SE28 123 C4
Battishill St 9 N1 72 D1
Battlebridge Ct
NW1 233 B4
Battle Bridge La
SE1 117 C5 253 A3
Battle Bridge Rd
NW1 94 A5 233 A4
Battle Cl SW19 180 A4
Battledean Rd N5 72 D3
Battle Ho 8 SE15 140 A6
Battle House Mews 7
EN5 2 A1
Battle of Britain Mus*
NW9 27 D1
Batty St E1 96 A1
Baty Ho SW2 160 B3
Baudwin Rd SE6 164 C2
Baugh Rd DA14 190 C5
Baulk The SW18 157 C4
Bavant Rd SW16 182 B1
Bavaria Rd N19 72 A6
Bavdene Mews NW4 46 B5
Bavent Rd SE5 139 A3
Bawdale Rd SE22 161 D6
Bawdsey Ave IG2 57 D5
Bawtree Rd SE14 141 A5
Bawtry Rd N20 14 D1
Baxendale N20 14 A2
Baxendale St E2 96 A4
Baxter Cl
Bromley BR1 210 D6
Hillingdon UB10 82 D4
Southall UB2 107 D3
Baxter Ho 11 E3 97 D4
Baxter Rd
Edmonton N18 34 B6
Ilford IG1 78 D3
Islington N1 73 B2
Newham E16 99 C1
Bayard Ct DA7 147 D1
Baycliffe Ho 8 E9 74 D2
Baycroft Cl HA5 40 C6
Bay Ct Ealing W5 110 A3
7 Stepney E1 96 D3
Baydon Ct BR2 208 D6
Bayer Ho EC1 242 A5
Bayes Ct NW3 70 D1
Bayeux Ho 10 SE7 143 C6
Bayfield Ho 3 SE4 140 D1
Bayfield Rd SE9 143 D1
Bayford Lodge HA5 23 B2
Bayford Rd NW10 90 D4
Bayford St Ind Ctr 4
E8 74 B1
Bayford St 5 E8 74 B1
Baygrove Mews
KT1 175 C2
Bayham Pl
NW1 93 C6 232 B5
Bayham Rd
Acton W4 111 B3
Ealing W13 109 B5
Morden SM4 202 A5
Bayham St
NW1 93 C6 232 A5
Bay Ho UB10 60 C4
Bayhurst Ho N4 51 A2
Bayhurst Wood Countryside Park
UB9 38 B4
Bayleaf Cl TW12 174 B5
Bayley St WC1 239 C3
Bayley Wlk SE2 125 A1
Baylis Mews TW1 153 A4
Baylis Rd
SE1 116 C4 251 A1
Bayliss Ave SE28 124 D6
Bayliss Cl
4 Southall UB1 85 D1
Southgate N21 16 A6
Bayne Cl E6 100 B1
Baynes Cl EN1 6 A4

Baynes Mews 2
NW3 70 B2
Baynes St NW1 71 C1
Baynham Cl DA5 169 B5
Bayon Ho 27 N19 49 D2
Bayonne Rd W6 264 A5
Bays Cl SE26 184 C5
Bays Ct HA8 26 D5
Bayshill Rise UB5 63 D2
Bayston Rd N16 73 D5
BAYSWATER 114 A6
Bayswater Rd
W2 114 B6 246 C5
Bayswater Sta
W2 113 D6 245 D6
Bayton Ct 2 E8 74 A1
Baytree Cl
Bromley BR1 187 D2
Sidcup DA15 167 D3
Baytree Ho E4 19 D4
Baytree Rd SW2 138 B1
Bazalgette Cl KT3 199 B4
Bazalgette Gdns
KT3 199 B4
Bazalgette Ho NW8 236 D6
Bazeley Ho SE1 251 C1
Bazely St E14 120 A6
Bazile Rd N21 16 C5
BBC Television Ctr
W12 112 C5
Beacham Cl SE7 143 D6
Beachborough Rd
BR1 186 A6
Beachcroft Ave UB1 107 B5
Beachcroft Rd E11 76 C5
Beach Ct SE9 166 A5
Beach Gr TW13 151 C2
Beach Ho SW5 255 A2
Beachy Rd E3 75 C1
Beaconfield Terrace Rd
W14 254 A5
Beacon Gate SE14 140 D2
Beacon Gr SM5 219 A4
Beacon Hill N7 72 A3
Beacon Ho
11 Camberwell
SE5 139 C5
7 Isle Of Dogs E14 119 D1
10 Penge SE26 184 B5
South Lambeth SW8 269 C2
Beacon House Sch
W5 110 B5
Beacon Pl CR0 220 A5
Beacon Rdbt TW6 148 C5
Beacon Rd
Harlington TW19,
TW6 148 C5
Hither Green SE13 164 B5
Beacons Cl 10 E6 100 A2
Beaconsfield Cl
Acton Green W4 111 A1
Friern Barnet N11 31 A5
Greenwich SE3 143 A6
Beaconsfield Ct N11 31 A5
Beaconsfield Gdns
KT10 212 C1
Beaconsfield Par 1
SE9 188 A6
Beaconsfield Prim Sch
UB2 107 A5
Beaconsfield Rd
Acton W4 111 B3
Bromley BR1 209 D6
Claygate KT10 212 C1
Ealing W5 109 D4
Edmonton N9 18 A1
Elmstead SE9 188 A6
Enfield EN3 6 D6
Friern Barnet N11 31 A6
Greenwich SE3 143 A5
Hayes UB4 106 C5
Kingston u T KT3 177 B1
Leyton E10 76 A5
Newham E16 98 D3
Southall UB1 107 A5
South Tottenham N15 51 C5
Surbiton KT5 198 B2
Thornton Heath CR0 205 B3
Twickenham TW1 153 B5
Walthamstow E17 53 B3
Walworth
SE17 117 C1 263 A1
Willesden NW10 67 D2
Beaconsfield Wlk
SW6 135 B4 264 D1
Beaconshaw BR1 186 C3
Beacontree Ave E17 36 B1
Beacontree Rd E11 54 D2
Beadle Ct CR4 202 C6
Beadlow Cl SM4 202 B3
Beadman Pl SE27 182 D6
Beadman St SE27 182 D6
Beadnell Rd SE23 162 D3

Beadon Rd
Bromley BR2 209 A4
Hammersmith W6 112 C2
Beaford Gr SW20 201 B6
Beagle Cl TW13 172 B6
Beak St W1 115 C6 249 B6
Beal Cl DA16 146 A4
Beale Cl N13 32 D5
Beale Ho 7 SW9 138 B3
Beale Pl E3 97 B5
Beale Rd E3 97 B6
Beal High Sch IG5 56 A5
Beal Rd IG1 78 C6
Beam Ave RM10 103 D6
Beames Ho SW8 269 C2
Beames Rd NW10 89 B6
Beaminster Ct N15 51 B4
Beaminster Gdns IG6 56 D6
Beaminster Ho SW8 270 C4
Beamish Dr WD23 8 A3
Beamish Ho 7 SE16 118 C2
Beamish Rd N9 18 A3
Beanacre Cl E9 75 B2
Bean Rd DA6 146 D1
Beanshaw SE9 188 C6
Beansland Gr RM6 59 A6
Bear Alley EC4 241 C2
Bear Cl RM7 59 D3
Bear Croft Ho 6 SW6 135 B3
Beardell St SE19 183 D4
Beardow Gr N14 15 C5
Beard Rd KT2 176 B5
Beardsfield E13 99 A5
Beards Hill Cl TW12 173 C2
Beard's Hill TW12 173 C2
Beardsley Terr RM8 80 B3
Beardsley Way W3 111 B4
Beard's Rd TW15, TW16 171 C4
Bearfield Rd KT2 176 A3
Bear Gardens Mus* SE1 117 A5 252 A4
Bear Gdns SE1 117 A5 252 A4
Bear La SE1 116 D5 251 D3
Bear Rd TW13 172 D6
Bearstead Rise SE4 163 B6
Bearsted Terr 7 BR3 185 C2
Bear St WC2 249 D6
Beasley's Ait La TW16, TW17 193 D3
Beasley's Ait TW17 193 D3
Beaton Cl SE15 139 D4
Beatrice Ave
Thornton Heath SW16 182 B1
Wembley HA9 66 A3
Beatrice Cl
Newham E13 99 A3
Pinner HA5 40 A5
Beatrice Ct
Buckhurst Hill IG9 21 D2
Hendon NW4 46 C4
Beatrice Ho
1 Brixton SW2 160 B6
Forest Hill SE6 163 C2
4 Hammersmith W6 112 C1
2 Stepney E1 96 D2
Beatrice Lo 3 N12 30 A4
Beatrice Pl W8 255 C5
Beatrice Rd
Bermondsey SE1 118 A2
Edmonton N9 18 C4
Finsbury Pk N4 50 C2
2 Richmond TW10 154 B6
Southall UB1 107 B5
Walthamstow E17 53 C4
Beatrice Tate Sch E2 96 B4
Beatrice Webb Ho 4 E3 97 A5
Beatrix Ho SW5 255 D2
Beatrix Potter Prim Sch SW18 158 A3
Beatson Wlk 23 SE16 118 D5
Beattie Cl TW14 149 D3
Beattie Ho SW8 269 B2
Beattock Rise N10 49 B5
Beatty Ho 16 E14 119 C4
Beatty Rd
Stanmore HA7 25 C4
Stoke Newington N16 73 C4
Beatty St NW1 232 A4
Beattyville Gdns IG6 56 D5
Beauchamp Cl 17 W4 111 A3
Beauchamp Ct HA7 25 C5
Beauchamp Pl SW3 114 C3 257 B5
Beauchamp Rd
Clapham SW11 136 D1
East Molesey KT8 196 A4
South Norwood SE19 183 B2
Sutton SM1 217 C4
Twickenham TW1 153 A4
Upton E7 77 B1
Beauchamp St EC1 241 A3
Beauchamp Terr SW15 134 B2
Beauclerc Inf Sch TW16 194 C6
Beauclerc Rd W6 112 B3
Beauclere Ho 1 SM2 218 A1
Beauclerk Cl TW13 150 B3
Beauclerk Ho 10 SW16 160 A1
Beaudesert Mews UB7 104 A4
Beaufort Ave HA3 43 B6
Beaufort Cl
Chingford E4 35 D4
Ealing W5 88 B2
Putney SW19 156 B4
Beaufort Ct
Friern Barnet N11 31 B5
Harrow HA3 43 A3
3 New Barnet EN5 14 A6
Richmond TW10 175 C6
West Brompton SW6 265 A6
Beaufort Dr NW11 47 C5
Beaufort Gdns
Hendon NW4 46 C3
Heston TW5 129 A4
Ilford IG1 56 C1
Knightsbridge SW3 114 C3 257 B6
South Norwood SW16 182 B3
Beaufort Ho
Ashford TW15 170 D5
Battersea SW11 136 C3
Chelsea SW3 266 D5
Hampstead Garden Suburb NW11 48 A3
20 Millwall E14 119 C4
Pimlico SW1 259 C1
8 South Tottenham N15 51 D5
1 Wimbledon SW20 178 D2
Beaufort Mans SW3 266 D5
Beaufort Mews SW6 264 D6
Beaufort E6 100 C2
Beaufort Pk NW11 47 C5
Beaufort Rd
Ealing W5 88 B2
Kingston u T KT1, KT5, KT6 198 A5
Richmond TW10 175 C6
Ruislip HA4 61 B6
Twickenham TW1 153 C4
Beaufort St SW3 136 B6 266 C6
Beaufort Way KT17 216 A1
Beaufoy Ho
South Lambeth SW8 270 C4
3 West Norwood SE27 160 D1
Beaufoy Rd
11 London SW8 137 B2
Tottenham N17 33 C3
Beaufoy Wlk SE11 116 B2 260 D3
Beaulieu Ave
Forest Hill SE26 184 B6
1 Newham E16 121 B5
Beaulieu Cl
Camberwell SE5 139 B2
Colindale NW9 45 C5
Hounslow TW4 151 B6
Mitcham CR4 181 A2
14 Twickenham TW1 153 D5
Beaulieu Ct W5 88 A2
Beaulieu Dr HA5 40 D2
Beaulieu Gdns N21 17 A4
Beaulieu Ho 6 NW4 28 D1
Beaulieu Hts CR7 183 C2
Beaulieu Pl W4 111 A3
Beaumanor Gdns SE9 188 C6
Beaumanor Mans W2 245 D6
Beaumaris 5 N11 32 A4
Beaumaris Dr IG8 37 D3
Beaumaris Gn NW9 45 C3
Beaumaris Twr 2 W3 110 D4
Beaumont Ave
Harrow HA2 41 D3
Richmond TW9 132 B2
Wembley HA0 65 C4
Beaumont Ave *continued*
West Kensington W14 113 B1 254 C2
Beaumont Bldgs WC2 240 B1
Beaumont Cl KT2 176 C3
Beaumont Cres W14 113 B1 254 C1
Beaumont Ct
10 Acton Green W4 111 A1
18 Hendon NW9 27 D1
Lower Clapton E5 74 B5
Marylebone W1 238 B4
7 Mile End E1 97 A4
6 Mitcham CR4 181 A1
Wembley HA0 65 C3
17 Wimbledon SW19 178 D3
Beaumont Dr
Ashford TW15 171 B5
New Malden KT4 200 B2
Beaumont Gdns NW3 69 C5
Beaumont Gr E1 96 D3
Beaumont Ho
12 Leyton E10 53 D2
1 Streatham SW2 160 A3
West Kensington W14 254 D3
Wimbledon SW19 157 C1
Beaumont Lo E8 74 A2
Beaumont Pl
Barnet EN5 1 B4
Fitzrovia NW1, WC1, W1 93 C3 239 B6
Isleworth TW7 152 D6
Beaumont SW15 157 A6
Beaumont Rd
Leyton E10 53 D2
Newham E13 99 B4
Orpington BR5 211 B3
Putney SW15, SW19 157 A4
South Acton W4 111 A3
South Norwood SE19 183 A4
Beaumont Rise N19 49 D1
Beaumont Sch The E10 53 D1
Beaumont Sq E1 96 D2
Beaumont St W1 238 B4
Beaumont Terr 1 SE13 164 C4
Beaumont Wlk NW3 70 D1
Beauvais Terr UB5 84 D4
Beauvale 6 NW1 71 A1
Beauval Rd SE22 161 D5
Beaverbank Rd SE9 167 B3
Beaver Cl
Hampton TW12 173 D2
9 Penge SE20 184 A3
West Barnes SM4 200 C2
Beaver Ctr The RM8 59 A2
Beaver Gr UB5 85 A4
Beavers Com Prim Sch TW4 128 C2
Beavers Cres TW4 128 D1
Beavers La TW4 128 C2
Beavers Lo DA14 189 D5
Beaverwood Rd BR7 189 C4
Beaverwood Sch for Girls BR7 189 C4
Beavis Ho N16 73 C5
Beavor La W6 112 A1
Bebbington Rd SE18 123 C2
Beblets Cl 4 BR6 227 D3
Beccles Dr IG11 79 D2
Beccles St E14 119 B6
Bec Cl HA4 62 D5
Bechervaise Ct 2 E10 53 D1
Beck Cl SE13 141 D4
Beck Ct BR3 206 D6
BECKENHAM 185 C1
Beckenham Bsns Ctr BR3 185 A4
Beckenham Ct BR3 185 C2
Beckenham Gdns N9 17 C1
Beckenham Gr BR2 186 B1
Beckenham Hill Rd BR3, SE6 186 A5
Beckenham Hill Sta SE6 186 A5
Beckenham Hospl BR3 185 B1
Beckenham Junction Sta BR3 185 C2
Beckenham La BR1, BR2 186 D1
Beckenham Place Pk BR3 185 D3
Beckenham Rd BR3 185 A2
Beckenham Rd Sta BR3 185 A2
Beckenham Rd BR3, BR4 208 A2
Beckers The N16 74 A4
Becket Ave E6 100 C4
Becket Cl
Croydon SE25 206 A3
2 Merton SW19 179 D2
Becket Fold 10 HA1 42 D4
Becket Ho SE1 252 C1
Becket Rd N18 34 C6
Becket St SE1 262 C6
Beckett Cl
Abbey Wood DA17 125 B3
Streatham SW16 159 D2
Willesden NW10 67 C2
Beckett Ho
28 London SW9 138 A3
15 Stepney E1 96 C2
Becketts Cl
Feltham TW14 150 B5
Orpington BR6 227 D5
Becketts Pl KT1 175 D2
Beckett Wlk BR3 185 A4
Beckfoot NW1 232 B3
Beckford Cl W14 254 D3
Beckford Dr BR5 211 B2
Beckford Ho 18 N16 73 C3
Beckford Prim Sch NW6 69 B3
Beckford Rd CR0 205 D3
Beckham Ho SE11 260 D3
Beck Ho
4 Edmonton N18 34 A5
Stoke Newington N16 73 C5
Beckington 18 NW5 71 A2
Beck La BR3 206 D6
Beckley Ho E3 97 B3
Becklow Gdns
Chiswick W12 111 D4
1 Shepherd's Bush W12 112 A4
Becklow Mews 7 W12 112 A4
Becklow Rd W12 112 A4
Beckmead Sch BR3 207 C1
Beck Rd E8 96 B6
Beck River Pk 10 BR3 185 C2
Becks Rd DA14 168 A1
BECKTON 100 D2
Beckton Alps E6 100 C3
Beckton Alps Ski Ctr E6 100 C3
Beckton Park Sta E6 122 B6
Beckton Rd E16 98 D2
Beckton Ret Pk E6 100 C2
Beckton Sta E6 100 C2
Beckton Triangle Ret Pk E6 100 D3
Beck Way BR3 207 B6
Beckway Rd SW16 181 D1
Beckway St SE17 117 C2 263 A3
Beckwith Ho 22 E2 96 B5
Beckwith Rd SE24 161 B6
Beclands Rd SW17 181 A4
Becmead Ave
Harrow HA3 43 B4
Streatham SW16 181 D6
Becondale Rd SE19 183 C5
BECONTREE 81 A4
Becontree Ave RM8 80 C5
Becontree Day Hospl RM8 81 A6
Becontree Prim Sch RM8 80 B5
Becontree Sta RM9 80 D2
Bective Pl SW15 135 B1
Bective Rd
Forest Gate E7 77 A4
Putney SW15 135 B1
Becton Pl DA8 147 D5
Bedale Rd EN2 5 A5
Bedale St SE1 252 C3
Beddan Ct HA8 26 C4
BEDDINGTON 220 A6
BEDDINGTON CORNER 203 A2
Beddington Cross CR0 204 A2
Beddington Farm Rd CR0 204 A1
Beddington Gdns SM5, SM6 219 A2
Beddington Gn BR5 189 D2
Beddington Gr SM6 219 D3
Beddington Inf Sch SM6 219 C4
Beddington Lane Sta CR0 203 C3
Beddington La
Wallington CR0 203 D2
Wallington CR0 220 A6
Beddington Manor SM2 218 B2
Beddington Park Cotts SM6 219 D5
Beddington Park Prim Sch CR0 219 D5
Beddington Rd
Ilford IG3 57 D2
St Paul's Cray BR5 189 D2
Beddington Terr CR0 204 B2
Beddington Trad Est CR0 204 A1
Bede Cl HA5 22 D2
Bedefield WC1 233 B1
Bede Ho
London SE14 141 B4
5 Putney SW15 156 D5
Bedelsford Sch KT1 198 A6
Bedens Rd DA14 191 A5
Bede Rd RM6 58 C3
Bedevere Rd N9 18 A1
Bedfont Cl
East Bedfont TW14 149 A5
Mitcham CR4 181 A1
Bedfont Green Cl TW14 149 A3
Bedfont Ind Pk TW15 149 B1
Bedfont Ind Pk N TW15 149 A1
Bedfont Jun & Inf Schs TW14 149 C5
Bedfont La TW14, TW13 149 D4
Bedfont Lakes Ctry Pk TW14 149 A2
Bedfont Rd
East Bedfont TW13, TW14 149 B2
Stanwell TW19 148 B5
Bedford Ave
Barnet EN5 13 B6
Bloomsbury WC1 93 D2 239 D3
Hayes UB4 84 B1
Bedfordbury WC2 116 A6 250 A5
Bedford Cl
Chiswick W4 133 D6
Muswell Hill N10 31 A3
Bedford Cnr 3 W4 111 C2
Bedford Court Mans WC1 239 D3
Bedford Ct
6 Richmond TW9 132 B1
South Norwood SE19 183 D2
St James WC2 250 A5
Wembley HA0 65 D4
Bedford Gardens Ho W8 245 B3
Bedford Gdns W8 113 C5 245 B3
Bedford Hill SW12 159 B2
Bedford Ho
2 Acton W4 111 C2
Edgware HA8 26 B3
7 Stockwell SW4 138 A1
Bedford Mews SE6 163 D2
BEDFORD PARK 111 C3
Bedford Park Cnr 5 W4 111 C2
Bedford Park Mans 4 W4 111 B2
Bedford Pas SW6 264 B4
Bedford Pk CR0 205 A1
Bedford Pl
Bloomsbury WC1 94 A2 240 A4
Croydon CR0 205 B1
Bedford Rd
Acton W4 111 C3
Barking E6 100 C6
Crouch End N8 49 D3
Ealing W13 109 B6
East Finchley N2 48 C6
Edgware NW7 11 C1
Edmonton N9 18 B4
Harrow HA1 42 A3
Ilford IG1 78 D5
North Cheam KT4 216 C6
Ruislip HA4 61 D4
Sidcup DA15 167 C1
South Tottenham N15 51 C5
Stockwell SW2, SW4 138 A1
Twickenham TW2 152 B1
Walthamstow E17 53 C6
Woodford E18 37 A1
Wood Green N22 32 A1
Bedford Row WC1 94 B2 240 D3
Bedford Sq WC1 93 D2 239 D3
Bedford St WC2 116 A6 250 B5
Bedford Terr SM2
Bedford Villas 3 SM5
Bedford Way WC1 93 D3
Bedgebury Gdns SW19
Bedgebury Rd SE9
Bedivere Rd BR1
Bedlam Mews SE11
Bedlow Cl NW8
Bedlow Way CR0
Bedonwell Inf Sch DA17
Bedonwell Jun Sch DA17
Bedonwell Rd
Bexley DA17
Erith DA7
Bedser Cl
Kennington SE11
South Norwood CR7
Bedser Ct 7 SW4
Bedser Dr UB6
Bedster Gdns KT8
Bedwardine Rd SE19
Bedwell Ct 4 RM6
Bedwell Gdns UB3
Bedwell Ho 18 SW9
Bedwell Rd
Belvedere DA17
Tottenham N17
Beeby Rd E16
Beech Ave Acton W3
Brentford TW8
4 Chigwell IG9
East Barnet N20
Ruislip HA4
Sidcup DA15
Beech Cl
Ashford TW15
Carshalton SM5
Deptford SE8
Enfield N9
Putney SW15
Sunbury TW16
West Drayton UB7
Wimbledon SW19
Beech Copse
Bickley BR1
South Croydon CR2
Beechcroft Ave
Golders Green NW11
Harrow HA2
Kingston u T KT1, KT3
Beechcroft BR7
Beechcroft Cl
Heston TW5
Orpington BR6
Streatham SW16
Beechcroft Ct
3 Golders Green NW11
Greenwich SE3
Beech Croft Ct N5
Beechcroft Ct 8 N12
Beechcroft Gdns HA9
Beechcroft Ho W5
Beechcroft 3 KT2
Beechcroft Lo 6 SM2
Beechcroft Mans SW16
Beechcroft Rd
Chessington KT9
Mortlake SW14
Orpington BR6
Upper Tooting SW17
Woodford E18
Beechcroft Way N19
Beech Ct
Beckenham BR3
3 Buckhurst Hill IG9
Child's Hill NW2
Hayes UB3
6 Ilford E12
Marylebone W1
Northolt UB5
43 Notting Hill W2
7 Rotherhithe SE16
Surbiton KT6
Teddington TW11
Walthamstow E17
4 West Norwood SW16
Beechdale Rd SW2
Beechdale N21
Beech Dell BR2, BR6
Beechdene 4 SE15
Beech Dr N2

en Cliff Way
... 130 D3
engrove HA5 ... 41 B6
en Pl SE23 ... 162 C2
es Ave SM5 ... 218 C1
es Cl SE20 ... 184 C2
es Ct BR1 ... 187 A4
es Prim Ctr The
... 124 C3
es Rd
m SM3 ... 201 A1
r Tooting
/17 ... 158 D1
es The
g W7 ... 108 D4
Barnet N20 ... 14 C2
Ham E12 ... 78 B1
slow TW3 ... 129 D4
am CR4 ... 202 C4
pper Holloway
9 ... 50 A1
ey Ho 30 E1 ... 118 B5
Farm Cotts
... 36 B3
field Cotts 5
... 187 C1
field Ct 7
... 221 A4
field Rd
ley BR1 ... 187 C1
st Hill SE6 ... 163 B3
ingay N4 ... 51 A3
Gdns
enham RM10 ... 81 D1
g W5 ... 110 A3
Gr
ston u T KT3 ... 199 B6
ham CR4 ... 203 D5
Hall Cres E4 ... 36 B3
Hall Rd E4 ... 36 B3
Hill Ave EN4 ... 2 B4
Hill EN4 ... 2 C5
hill Rd SE9 ... 166 C6
Ho
gford E4 ... 35 C6
es UB4 ... 84 D2
on TW5 ... 129 A5
Maitland Pk NW3 ... 70 D2
Addington CR0 ... 223 D2
Rotherhithe
E16 ... 118 C4
Sidcup DA15 ... 168 A1
Stoke Newington
16 ... 73 B6
h House Rd
... 221 B5
h Ho 12 SM6 ... 219 C2
h La IG9 ... 21 B2
h Lawns N12 ... 30 B5
hmont Cl BR1 ... 186 C5
hmore Gdns
... 216 D6
hmore Rd
1 ... 136 D4 267 D1
hmount Ave W7 ... 86 C2
holme Ave
... 181 B2
holme Est E5 ... 74 B5
holme 15 N12 ... 29 D6
holme Prim Sch
... 181 B2
h Rd
es Pk N11 ... 32 A4
Bedfont TW14 ... 149 C4
nton Heath
W16 ... 204 B6
hrow KT2 ... 176 A6
h St EC2 ... 95 A2 242 B4
h Tree Cl
gton N1 ... 72 C1
more HA7 ... 25 C5
h Tree Glade
... 20 D3
h Tree Pl SM1 ... 217 D3
hvale Cl N12 ... 30 C5
hway DA5 ... 168 D5
h Way
kenham TW2 ... 151 C1
esden NW10 ... 67 B1
h Wlk NW7 ... 27 C4
hwood Ave
ford TW16 ... 172 A4
Finchley N3 ... 47 C6
enford UB6 ... 85 D4
row HA2 ... 63 D5
es UB3 ... 105 B6
ngdon UB8 ... 82 C1
ington BR6 ... 227 C2
mond TW9 ... 132 C4
slip HA4 ... 61 D6
rnton Heath CR7 ... 204 D5
hwood Circ
... 63 D5
hwood Cl
ware NW7 ... 27 C5
is Green N2 ... 48 D5
biton KT6 ... 197 D2

Beechwood Cres
DA7 ... 147 A2
Beechwood Ct
Ashford TW16 ... 172 A5
Carshalton SM5 ... 218 D4
Cheam SM1 ... 217 C3
Chiswick W4 ... 133 B6
Stamford Hill N16 ... 51 C2
Sutton SM2 ... 218 B2
Beechwood Dr
Keston BR2 ... 225 D4
Woodford IG8 ... 36 D5
Beechwood Gdns
Ealing NW10 ... 88 B4
Harrow HA2 ... 63 D5
Ilford IG5 ... 56 C5
Beechwood Gr W3 ... 111 C6
Beechwood Hall N3 ... 47 B6
Beechwood Ho 23
E2 ... 96 A5
Beechwood Mews 2
N9 ... 18 A2
Beechwood Pk E18 ... 55 A6
Beechwood Rd
Dalston E8 ... 73 D2
London N8 ... 50 A5
South Croydon CR2 ... 221 C1
Beechwood Rise
BR7 ... 188 D6
Beechwoods Ct 5
SE19 ... 183 D5
Beechworth Cl NW3 ... 69 C6
Beecroft La SE4 ... 163 A6
Beecroft Mews SE4 ... 163 A6
Beecroft Rd SE4 ... 163 A6
Beehive Cl Dalston E8 ... 73 D1
Elstree WD6 ... 9 D5
Hillingdon UB10 ... 60 B1
Beehive Ct IG1 ... 56 B3
Beehive La IG1 ... 56 B3
Beehive Pl SW9 ... 138 C2
Beehive Prep Sch
IG4 ... 56 B4
Beeken Dene BR6 ... 227 A4
Beeleigh Rd SM4 ... 201 D5
Beemans Row 1
SW18 ... 158 A2
Beeston Cl
5 Dalston E8 ... 74 A3
South Oxhey WD19 ... 22 D6
Beeston Pl SW1 ... 258 D6
Beeston Rd EN4 ... 14 B5
Beeston's Ho SE15 ... 140 B2
Beeston Way TW14 ... 150 C5
Beethoven Rd WD6 ... 9 D5
Beethoven St W10 ... 91 A4
Beeton Cl HA5 ... 23 C3
Begbie Ho SW9 ... 138 B3
Begbie Rd SE3 ... 143 C4
Beggars Hill KT17 ... 215 D2
Beggar's Roost La
SM1 ... 217 C2
Begonia Cl E6 ... 100 B3
Begonia Pl 1 TW12 ... 173 C4
Begonia Wlk W12 ... 89 D1
Beira St SW12 ... 159 B4
Beis Chinuch Lebonos
Girls Sch N4 ... 51 A2
Beis Rochel d'Satmar
Girls Sch N16 ... 51 C2
Beis Soroh Schneirer
(Sch) NW4 ... 46 A3
Beis Yaakov Prim Sch
NW9 ... 45 B6
Bekesbourne St 17
E14 ... 97 A1
Belcroft Cl BR1 ... 186 D3
Beldanes Lo NW10 ... 68 A1
Beldham Gdns KT8 ... 195 D6
Belenoyd Ct SW16 ... 160 B1
Belfairs Dr RM6 ... 58 C2
Belfairs Gn WD19 ... 22 D5
Belfast Rd
Croydon SE25 ... 206 B5
Stoke Newington N16 ... 73 D6
Belfield Rd KT19 ... 215 C1
Belfont Wlk N7 ... 72 A4
Belford Gr SE18 ... 122 C2
Belford Ho 7 E8 ... 95 D6
Belfort Rd SE15 ... 140 C3
Belfry Cl 33 SE16 ... 118 B1
Belgrade Ho N16 ... 73 C4
Belgrade Rd
Hampton TW12 ... 173 D2
Stoke Newington N16 ... 73 C4
Belgrave Cl
1 Acton W3 ... 111 A4
Burnt Oak NW7 ... 27 B5
Southgate N14 ... 15 C6
Belgrave Cres
TW16 ... 172 B2
Belgrave Ct
8 Acton Green
W4 ... 111 A1
Charlton SE3 ... 143 C5
22 Limehouse E14 ... 119 B6
Newham E13 ... 99 C3

Belgrave Ct *continued*
Nine Elms SW8 ... 269 A3
Belgrave Gdns
Kilburn NW8 ... 91 D6
Southgate N14 ... 3 D1
1 Stanmore HA7 ... 25 C5
St John's Wood NW8 ... 229 A5
Belgrave Ho SW9 ... 138 C5
Belgrave Hts E11 ... 55 A1
Belgrave Mans NW8 ... 229 A5
Belgrave Market IG1 ... 78 C6
Belgrave Mews N
SW1 ... 248 A1
Belgrave Mews S
SW1 ... 115 A3 258 B6
Belgrave Mews W
SW1 ... 258 A6
Belgrave Pl
SW1 ... 115 A3 258 B5
Belgrave Rd
Barnes SW13 ... 133 D5
Hounslow TW4 ... 129 B2
Leyton E10 ... 54 A1
Mitcham CR4 ... 202 B6
Newham E13 ... 99 C3
Redbridge IG1 ... 56 B1
South Norwood
SE25 ... 205 D5
Sunbury TW16 ... 172 B2
Walthamstow E17 ... 53 C3
Wanstead E11 ... 55 A1
Westminster
SW1 ... 115 C2 259 A3
Belgrave Sq
SW1 ... 115 A3 258 A6
Belgrave St E1 ... 96 D1
Belgrave Terr IG8 ... 21 A1
Belgrave Wlk CR4 ... 202 B6
Belgrave Wlk Sta
CR4 ... 202 B5
Belgrave Yd SW1 ... 258 C5
BELGRAVIA ... 115 B2
Belgravia Cl EN5 ... 1 B2
Belgravia Ct SW1 ... 258 C5
Belgravia Gdns BR1 ... 186 C4
Belgravia Ho
11 London SW4 ... 159 D5
1 Teddington
TW11 ... 175 C3
Belgravia Lo N21 ... 16 D6
Belgravia Mews
KT1 ... 197 D5
Belgrove St WC1 ... 233 B2
Belham Wlk 13 SE5 ... 139 B4
Belinda Rd 8 SW9 ... 138 D2
Belitha Villas N1 ... 72 C1
Bel La TW13 ... 151 B1
Bellamy Cl
Edgware HA8 ... 11 A1
13 Millwall E14 ... 119 C4
Uxbridge UB10 ... 60 C5
West Kensington
SW5 ... 254 D1
Bellamy Ct HA7 ... 25 B2
Bellamy Dr HA7 ... 25 B2
Bellamy Ho
Harrow HA3 ... 44 A2
Heston TW5 ... 129 C6
Upper Tooting SW17 ... 180 B6
Bellamy Rd
Chingford E4 ... 35 D4
Enfield EN2 ... 5 B3
Bellamy's Ct 16
SE16 ... 118 D5
Bellamy St SW12 ... 159 B4
Bellasis Ave SW2 ... 160 A2
Bell Ave UB7 ... 104 B3
Bellclose Rd UB7 ... 104 A4
Bell Cl Pinner HA5 ... 40 C6
Ruislip HA4 ... 61 D5
Bell Ct Hendon NW4 ... 46 C5
Ladywell SE13 ... 163 C6
Tolworth KT5 ... 214 D6
Bell Dr SW18 ... 157 A4
Bellefields Rd SW9 ... 138 B2
Bellegrove Cl DA16 ... 145 D3
Bellegrove Par
DA16 ... 145 D2
Bellegrove Rd DA16 ... 145 D3
Bellenden Prim Sch
SE15 ... 140 A3
Bellenden Rd SE15 ... 139 D3
Bellenden Rd Ret Pk
SE15 ... 140 A4
Bellendon Road Bsns
Ctr SE15 ... 139 D3
Bellerbys Coll SE8 ... 141 C6
Bellermine Cl SE28 ... 123 D4
**Belle Staines
Pleasaunce** E4 ... 19 C2
Belleville Prim Sch
SW11 ... 158 D6
Belleville Rd SW11 ... 158 D6
Belle Vue Gdns
SW9 ... 138 A3
Belle Vue UB6 ... 86 B6
Belle Vue La WD23 ... 8 B3

Bellevue Mews N11 ... 31 A5
Bellevue Pk CR7 ... 205 A5
Bellevue Pl E1 ... 96 C3
Bellevue Rd
Barnes SW13 ... 134 A3
Bexley DA6 ... 169 B6
Belle Vue Rd E17 ... 36 B1
Bellevue Rd
Ealing W13 ... 87 B3
Friern Barnet N11 ... 31 A5
Belle Vue Rd 8 NW4 ... 46 C5
Bellevue Rd
Kingston u T KT1 ... 198 A6
Upper Tooting
SW17 ... 158 D3
Bellew St SW17 ... 158 A1
Bellfield Ave HA3 ... 24 B4
Bellfield CR0 ... 223 B1
Bell Flats 4 NW2 ... 68 A2
Bellflower Cl 2 E6 ... 100 A2
Bellflower Ct SE13 ... 141 D1
Bellgate Mews NW5 ... 71 B5
Bell Gn SE26 ... 185 B6
Bellgrave Lo 9 W4 ... 110 D1
BELL GREEN ... 163 B1
Bell Green La SE26 ... 185 B6
Bell Ho
6 Dagenham
RM10 ... 81 D2
Greenwich SE10 ... 142 A6
15 Streatham SW2 ... 160 C4
Wembley HA9 ... 66 A5
West Heath SE2 ... 124 D1
Bellina Mews NW5 ... 71 C4
Bell Ind Est 2 W4 ... 111 A2
BELLINGHAM ... 185 C5
Bellingham Ct IG11 ... 102 B4
Bellingham Gn SE6 ... 163 C1
Bellingham Rd SE6 ... 164 A1
Bellingham Sta SE6 ... 163 D1
Bellingham 10 N17 ... 34 B3
Bellingham Trad Est
SE6 ... 163 D2
Bell Inn Yd EC3 ... 242 D1
Bell La Enfield EN3 ... 6 D5
Hendon NW4 ... 46 D5
Bell Lane Prim Sch
NW4 ... 46 D5
Bell La E16 ... 121 A5
Bell Language Sch
W1 ... 93 C3 239 A5
Bell La
Spitalfields
E1 ... 95 D2 243 C3
Twickenham TW1 ... 153 A3
Wembley HA9 ... 65 D6
Bellmaker Ct 13 E3 ... 97 C2
Bell Mdw SE19 ... 183 C6
Bell Moor NW3 ... 70 A5
Bellmore Ct 5 CR0 ... 205 D1
Bello Cl SE24, SW2 ... 160 D3
Bellot Gdns 1 SE10 ... 120 C1
Bellot St SE10 ... 120 C1
Bell Rd
East Molesey KT8 ... 196 B4
Enfield EN1 ... 5 B4
Hounslow TW3 ... 129 D1
Bellring Cl DA17 ... 147 C6
Bell's Coll IG3 ... 58 A1
Bells Hill EN5 ... 12 D6
Bell St
Kidbrooke SE18 ... 144 A4
Paddington
NW1 ... 92 C2 237 A4
Bell The E17 ... 53 C6
Bell View BR3 ... 185 B3
Bellview Ct TW3 ... 129 D1
Bell View Manor
HA4 ... 39 C2
Bell Water Gate
SE18 ... 122 C3
Bell Wharf La EC4 ... 252 B6
Bellwood Rd SE15 ... 140 D1
Bell Yard Mews SE1 ... 253 B1
Bell Yd WC2 ... 94 C1 241 A1
BELMONT ... 25 B2
Belmont Ave
Bowes Pk N13 ... 32 B5
Cockfosters EN4 ... 14 D6
Edmonton N9 ... 18 A3
Falconwood DA16 ... 145 C2
Southall UB2 ... 107 A3
Tottenham N17 ... 51 A6
Wembley HA0 ... 88 B6
West Barnes KT3 ... 200 A5
Belmont Circ HA3 ... 25 B2
Belmont Cl
Chingford E4 ... 36 B5
Clapham SW4 ... 137 C2
Cockfosters EN4 ... 2 D1
Totteridge N20 ... 13 D3
Uxbridge UB8 ... 60 A2
Woodford IG8 ... 37 B6
Belmont Ct
Highbury N5 ... 73 A4
6 Stamford Hill N16 ... 51 C1

Belmont Ct *continued*
Temple Fortune
NW11 ... 47 B4
1 Whetstone N20 ... 14 A1
Wood Green N11 ... 31 D3
Belmont Fst & Mid Schs
HA3 ... 24 D1
Belmont Gr
Chiswick W4 ... 111 B2
Lewisham SE13 ... 142 B2
Belmont Hall Ct
SE13 ... 142 B2
Belmont Hill SE13 ... 142 B2
Belmont Jun & Inf Schs
N22 ... 51 A6
Belmont La
Chislehurst BR7 ... 189 A5
Stanmore HA7 ... 25 C3
Belmont Lo
Harrow HA3 ... 24 B3
Stanmore HA7 ... 25 C6
Belmont Mews
SW19 ... 156 D2
Belmont Mill Hill Jun
Sch NW7 ... 12 A1
Belmont Par BR7 ... 189 A5
Belmont Park Cl
SE13 ... 142 C1
Belmont Park Rd
E10 ... 53 D3
Belmont Par 2
NW11 ... 47 B4
Belmont Pk SE13 ... 142 C1
Belmont Pk Sch E10 ... 54 A3
Belmont Prim Sch
Chiswick W4 ... 111 B2
Erith DA8 ... 147 C5
Belmont Rd
Beckenham BR3 ... 185 B1
Chislehurst BR7 ... 188 D5
Clapham SW4 ... 137 C2
Croydon SE25 ... 206 B4
Erith DA8 ... 147 D4
Harrow HA3 ... 43 A6
Ilford IG1 ... 79 A5
London W4 ... 111 B2
Twickenham TW2 ... 152 B2
Uxbridge UB8 ... 60 A2
Wallington SM6 ... 219 C3
West Green N15, N17 ... 51 A5
Belmont Rise SM1,
SM2 ... 217 B1
Belmont St NW1 ... 71 A1
Belmont Terr W4 ... 111 B2
Belmor WD6 ... 10 C5
Belmore Ave UB4 ... 84 A1
Belmore Ho N7 ... 71 D3
Belmore La N7 ... 71 D3
Belmore Prim Sch
UB4 ... 84 B4
Belmore St
SW8 ... 137 D4 269 C2
Beloe Cl SW15 ... 134 A1
Belper Ct 11 E5 ... 74 D4
Belsham St E9 ... 74 C2
Belsize Ave
Bowes Pk N13 ... 32 B4
Ealing W13 ... 109 B3
Maitland Pk NW3 ... 70 C3
Belsize Court Garages
1 NW3 ... 70 B3
Belsize Cres NW3 ... 70 B2
Belsize Ct NW3 ... 70 B3
Belsize Gdns SM1 ... 217 D4
Belsize Gr NW3 ... 70 C2
Belsize La NW3 ... 70 B3
Belsize Mews NW3 ... 70 B2
Belsize Park Gdns
NW3 ... 70 C2
Belsize Park Mews 1
NW3 ... 70 B2
Belsize Park Sta
NW3 ... 70 C3
Belsize Pk NW3 ... 70 B2
Belsize Pl NW3 ... 70 B3
Belsize Rd
Harrow HA3 ... 24 B3
Kilburn NW6 ... 91 D6
Belsize Sq NW3 ... 70 B2
Belsize Terr NW3 ... 70 B2
Belson Rd SE18 ... 122 B2
Beltane Dr SW19 ... 156 D1
Belthorn Cres
SW12 ... 159 C4
Belton Rd Leyton E11 ... 76 C4
Sidcup DA14 ... 190 A6
Tottenham N17 ... 51 C6
Upton E7 ... 77 B1
Willesden NW2 ... 68 A2
Belton Way E3 ... 97 C2
Beltran Rd SW6 ... 135 D3
BELVEDERE ... 125 D2
Belvedere Ave
SW19 ... 179 A5
Belvedere Bldgs
SE1 ... 251 D1
Belvedere Cl TW11 ... 174 C5

Belvedere Ct
Abbey Wood
DA17 ... 125 B3
Brondesbury NW2 ... 68 D2
7 Clapham Pk SW4 ... 159 D5
East Finchley N2 ... 48 B4
8 Kingston u T KT2 ... 176 C3
Putney SW15 ... 134 C1
33 Shoreditch N1 ... 95 C6
Southall UB1 ... 107 D6
Southgate N21 ... 16 C4
Belvedere Dr SW19 ... 179 A5
Belvedere Gdns
KT8 ... 195 C4
Belvedere Gr SW19 ... 179 A5
Belvedere Ho TW14 ... 150 A3
Belvedere Htss NW8 ... 237 A6
Belvedere Jun & Inf Sch
DA17 ... 125 D3
Belvedere Mews
Greenwich SE3 ... 143 B5
Nunhead SE15 ... 140 C2
Belvedere Pl
Brixton SW2 ... 138 B1
Lambeth SE1 ... 251 D1
Belvedere Rd
Bexleyheath DA7 ... 147 B3
Erith SE2, SE28 ... 124 D5
Hanwell W7 ... 108 D3
Lambeth
SE1 ... 116 B5 250 D3
Penge SE19 ... 183 D3
Walthamstow E10 ... 53 A1
Belvedere Sq SW19 ... 179 A5
Belvedere Sta DA17 ... 125 D3
Belvedere Strand
NW9 ... 27 D1
Belvedere The
SW10 ... 266 B1
Belvedere Way HA3 ... 44 A3
Belvoir Cl SE9 ... 166 A1
Belvoir Ct HA3 ... 43 A3
Belvoir Lo SE22 ... 162 A4
Belvoir Rd SE22 ... 162 A4
Belvue Bsns Ctr UB5 ... 63 D1
Belvue Cl UB5 ... 63 C1
Belvue Rd UB5 ... 63 C1
Belvue Sch UB5 ... 85 C6
Bembridge Cl NW6 ... 69 A1
Bembridge Gdns
HA4 ... 61 B6
Bembridge Ho
9 Deptford SE8 ... 119 B2
Wandsworth SW18 ... 157 D5
Bemersyde Point 6
E13 ... 99 B4
Bemerton St
N1 ... 94 B6 233 C6
Bemish Rd SW15 ... 134 D2
Bempton Dr HA4 ... 62 B5
Bemsted Rd E17 ... 53 B6
Benabo Ct 6 E8 ... 74 A3
Benares Rd SE18,
SE2 ... 123 D2
Benbow Ct W6 ... 112 B3
Benbow Ho 12 SE8 ... 141 C6
Benbow Rd W6 ... 112 B3
Benbow St SE8 ... 141 C6
Benbury Cl BR1 ... 186 A5
Bence Ho 13 SE8 ... 119 A2
Bench Field CR2 ... 221 D3
Bencroft Rd SW16 ... 181 C3
Bencurtis Pk BR4 ... 224 B6
Bendall Mews NW1 ... 237 B4
Bendemeer Rd
SW15 ... 134 D2
Benden Ho SE13 ... 164 A6
Bendish Point SE28 ... 123 A4
Bendish Rd E6 ... 78 A1
Bendmore Ave SE2 ... 124 A2
Bendon Valley
SW18 ... 157 D4
Benedict Cl
9 Erith DA17 ... 125 A3
Orpington BR6 ... 227 C5
Benedict Ct
Dagenham RM9 ... 59 B3
Pinner HA5 ... 23 B2
Benedict Dr TW14 ... 149 B4
Benedict House Prep
Sch DA15 ... 168 A1
Benedict Prim Sch
CR4 ... 202 B6
Benedict Rd
London SW9 ... 138 B2
Mitcham CR4 ... 202 B6
Benedict Way N2 ... 48 A6
Benedict Wharf
CR4 ... 202 C6
Benenden Gn BR2 ... 209 A4
Benenden Ho SE17 ... 263 B2
Benett Gdns SW16 ... 182 A1
Beney Ct BR3 ... 185 C1
Ben Ezra Ct SE17 ... 262 B3

Benfleet Cl SM1 218 A5
Benfleet Ct 6 E8 95 D6
Benfleet Way N11 15 A2
Bengal Ct EC3 242 D1
Bengal Ho E1 96 D2
Bengal Rd IG1 78 D5
Bengarth Dr HA3 24 B1
Bengarth Rd UB5 85 A6
Bengeo Gdns RM6 58 C3
Bengeworth Rd
Camberwell SE5 139 A2
Harrow HA1 65 A5
Ben Hale Cl HA7 25 B5
Benham Cl
1 Battersea SW11 136 B2
Chessington KT9 213 C2
Benham Gdns TW3, TW4 151 B6
Benham Ho SW10 265 D4
Benham Rd W7 86 C2
Benham's Pl 11 NW3 70 A4
Benhill Ave SM1 218 A4
Benhill Rd
London SE5 139 B4
Sutton SM1 218 B4
Benhill Wood Rd SM1 218 A4
BENHILTON 218 A5
Benhilton Ct SM1 218 A5
Benhilton Gdns SM1 217 D5
Benhurst Ct
Ealing W5 110 A6
12 Penge SE20 184 B2
West Norwood SW16 182 C5
Benhurst La SW16 182 C5
Benington Ct N4 73 A6
Benin St SE13 164 B4
Benjafield Cl N18 34 B6
Benjamin Cl E8 96 A6
Benjamin Ct
4 Ealing W7 108 C5
4 Erith DA17 147 B6
Littleton TW15 171 A3
Benjamin Ho 12 W3 110 D5
Benjamin Mews SW12 159 C4
Benjamin St EC1 241 C4
Ben Jonson Ct 30 N1 95 C5
Ben Jonson Prim Sch E1 97 A3
Ben Jonson Rd E1 97 A2
Benledi Rd E14 98 B1
Bennelong Cl W12 90 B1
Bennerley Rd SW11 158 D6
Bennet Cl KT1 175 C2
Bennets Ct SW19 180 A2
Bennetsfield Rd UB11 104 D5
Bennet's Hill EC4 251 D6
Bennets Lo EN2 5 A2
Bennett Cl
Twickenham TW4 151 A6
Welling DA16 146 A3
Bennett Ct
Hampstead NW6 69 D2
Lower Holloway N7 72 B5
7 South Acton W3 110 D4
Bennett Gr SE13 141 D4
Bennett Ho
2 Streatham SW4 159 D4
Westminster SW1 259 D4
Bennett Pk SE3 142 D2
Bennett Rd
Brixton SW9 138 C3
Dagenham RM6 59 A2
Newham E13 99 C3
Bennetts Ave
Croydon CR0 223 A6
Greenford UB6 86 C6
Bennett's Castle La RM8 80 D5
Bennetts Cl
Mitcham CR4, SW16 181 B2
Tottenham N17 33 D4
Bennetts Copse BR7 188 A4
Bennett St
Chiswick W4 111 C1
St James SW1 249 A4
Bennetts Way CR0 223 B6
Bennett's Yd SW1 259 D5
Benn Ho
Bethnal Green E2 96 A4
7 Greenwich SE7 121 C1
Benningholme Rd HA8 27 C4
Bennington Rd
Chingford IG8 36 C3
Bennington Rd *continued*
Tottenham N17 33 C2
Benn St E9 75 A2
Benns Wlk 8 TW9 132 A1
Bensbury Cl SW15 156 C4
Bensham Cl CR7 205 A5
Bensham Gr CR7 183 A1
Bensham La CR0, CR7 204 D3
Bensham Manor Rd CR7 205 A5
Bensham Manor Sch CR7 205 A4
Bensington Ct TW14 149 B5
Bensley Cl 7 N11 30 D5
Ben Smith Way 21 SE16 118 A3
Benson Ave E13, E6 99 D5
Benson Cl
Hillingdon UB8 82 A2
Hounslow TW3 129 C1
Benson Ct
Holdbrook EN3 7 C5
South Lambeth SW8 270 A2
1 Tufnell Pk N19 71 C4
Benson Ho
Lambeth SE1 251 B3
1 Richmond TW10 153 C1
Shoreditch E2 243 C6
Benson Prim sch CR0 223 A5
Benson Quay E1 118 C6
Benson Rd
Croydon CR0 220 C5
Forest Hill SE23 162 C3
Bentall Sh Ctr The 10 KT1 176 A1
Bentfield Gdns SE9 165 D1
Benthal Ct N16 74 A5
Benthal Prim Sch N16 74 A5
Benthal Rd N16 74 A5
Bentham Ct 11 N1 73 A1
Bentham Ho SE1 262 C6
Bentham Rd
Homerton E9 74 D2
Woolwich SE28 124 B5
Bentham Wlk NW10 67 A3
Ben Tillet Cl E16 122 B5
Ben Tillet Ho N15 50 D6
Bentinck Cl NW8 230 B3
Bentinck Ho
4 Richmond TW10 153 C1
4 Shepherd's Bush W12 112 B6
Bentinck Mans W1 238 B2
Bentinck Mews W1 238 B2
Bentinck Rd UB7 104 A5
Bentinck St W1 93 A1 238 B2
Bentley Cl SW19 157 C1
Bentley Ct SE13 142 A1
Bentley Dr IG2 57 A3
Bentley Ho
6 Bow E3 97 C3
4 Camberwell SE5 139 C4
Bentley Lo WD23 8 C2
Bentley Mews EN1 17 B5
Bentley Rd N1 73 C2
Bentley Way
Stanmore HA7 25 A5
Woodford IG8 21 A1
Bentley Wood High Sch HA7 24 D5
Benton Rd
Ilford IG1, IG2 57 B1
South Oxhey WD19 22 D5
Benton's La SE27 183 A6
Benton's Rise SE27 183 B5
Bentry Cl RM8 81 A6
Bentry Rd RM8 81 B6
Bentworth Ct 1 E2 96 A3
Bentworth Prim Sch W12 90 B1
Bentworth Rd W12 90 B1
Benwell Ct TW16 172 A2
Benwell Rd N7 72 C3
Benwick Cl SE16 118 B2
Benwick Ct SE20 184 C2
Benwood Ct SM1 218 A5
Benworth St E3 97 B4
Benyon Ho EC1 234 B2
Benyon Rd N1 95 B6 235 D6
Benyon Wharf 31 E8 95 C6
Beormund Prim Sch SE1 117 B4 252 D1
Bequerel Ct SE10 120 D3
Berberis Ct IG1 78 D2
Berberis Ho 17 E3 97 C2
Berberis Wlk UB7 104 A2
Berber Pl 2 E14 119 C6
Berber Rd SW11 158 D6
Berberry Cl 5 HA8 27 A6
Bercta Rd SE9 167 A2
Berebinder Ho 21 E3 97 B5
Berengers Pl RM9 80 B2
Berenger Twr SW10 266 C4
Berenger Wlk SW10 266 C4
Berens Ct DA14 189 D6
Berens Rd NW10 90 D4
Berens Way BR5, BR7 211 D6
Beresford Ave
Ealing W7 86 C2
Friern Barnet N20 14 D2
Tolworth KT5 199 A2
Twickenham TW1 153 C5
Wembley HA0 88 C6
Beresford Ct
Homerton E9 75 A3
11 Twickenham TW1 153 C5
Beresford Dr
Bickley BR1 210 A6
Woodford IG8 37 C6
Beresford Gdns
Dagenham RM6 59 A4
Enfield EN1 5 C1
Hounslow TW4 151 B6
Beresford Ho
Dulwich SE21 161 C1
15 Stockwell SW4 138 A1
Beresford Lo N4 73 B3
Beresford Rd
Belmont SM2 217 B1
Canonbury N5 73 B3
Chingford E4 20 C3
East Finchley N2 48 C6
Harringay N8 50 D4
Harrow HA1 42 B4
Kingston u T KT2 176 B2
New Malden KT3 199 A5
Southall UB1 106 D5
Walthamstow E17 35 D2
Beresford Square Mkt SE18 122 D2
Beresford Sq 1 SE18 122 D2
Beresford St SE18 122 D3
Beresford Terr 3 N5 73 A3
Bere St E1 118 D6
Berestede Rd 4 W6 111 D1
Bergen Ho 1 SE5 139 A3
Bergenia Ho TW13 150 B3
Bergen Sq SE16 119 A3
Berger Cl BR5 211 C3
Berger Prim Sch E9 74 D2
Berger Rd E9 74 D2
Berghem Mews W14 112 D3
Bergholt Ave IG4 56 A4
Bergholt Cres N16 51 C2
Bergholt Mews 4 NW1 71 D1
Berglen Ct E14 119 A6
Berica Ct IG6 57 A6
Bering Sq E14 119 C1
Bering Wlk E16 99 D1
Berisford Mews SW18 158 A5
Berkeley Ave
Cranford TW4 128 A3
Erith DA16 146 D4
Northolt UB6 64 C2
Berkeley Cl
Borehamwood WD6 10 C6
Broom Hill BR5 211 C2
2 Kingston u T KT2 176 A3
Ruislip HA4 62 A5
Berkeley Cres EN4 14 B6
Berkeley Ct
Ealing W5 109 C6
Edgware HA8 26 D5
Finchley N3 29 D2
1 Golders Green NW11 47 B2
Marylebone NW1 237 D5
Southgate N14 15 C5
Wallington SM6 219 C4
Willesden NW10 67 C4
Berkeley Dr KT8 195 C6
Berkeley Gdns
Claygate KT10 213 A2
Kensington W8 245 B3
Southgate N21 17 B4
Walton-on-T KT12 193 D2
Berkeley Ho
17 Bow E3 97 C4
11 Brentford TW8 131 D6
8 Deptford SE8 119 B1
Berkeley Lo
Enfield EN2 4 C2
New Malden KT3 199 C5
Berkeley Mews
Marylebone W1 237 D1
Sunbury TW16 194 C6
Berkeley Pl SW19 178 D4
Berkeley Prim Sch TW5 128 D5
Berkeley Rd
Barnes SW13 134 A4
Crouch End N8 49 D3
Hillingdon UB10 61 A1
Manor Pk E12 78 A3
Queensbury NW9 44 C4
Stamford Hill N15 51 B3
Berkeley Sq W1 115 B6 248 D5
Berkeleys The SE25 206 A5
Berkeley St W1 115 B5 248 D4
Berkeley The NW11 47 D2
Berkeley Waye TW5 128 D5
Berkeley Wlk 1 N7 72 B6
Berkhampstead Rd DA17 125 C1
Berkhamsted Ave HA9 66 C2
Berkley Cl TW2 152 C1
Berkley Ct 8 TW1 153 A4
Berkley Gr NW1 71 A1
Berkley Rd NW1 70 D1
Berkshire Ct 1 W7 86 D3
Berkshire Gdns
Bowes Pk N13 32 C4
Upper Edmonton N18 34 B5
Berkshire Ho
Catford SE6 185 C6
St Giles WC2 240 A2
Berkshire Rd E9 75 B2
Berkshire Way CR4 204 A5
Bermans Way NW10 67 D4
BERMONDSEY 118 A4
Bermondsey Leather Mkt SE1 253 A1
Bermondsey Mkt* SE1 117 C3 263 B6
Bermondsey Sq SE1 263 B6
Bermondsey St SE1 117 C4 253 A1
Bermondsey Trad Est SE16 118 C1
Bermondsey Wall E SE16 118 B4
Bermondsey Wall W SE1, SE16 118 A4
Bermuda Ho HA1 64 B5
Bernal Cl SE28 124 D6
Bernard Angell Ho 4 SE10 142 B6
Bernard Ashley Dr SE7 121 B1
Bernard Ave W13 109 B3
Bernard Cassidy St 2 E16 98 D2
Bernard Gdns SW19 179 B5
Bernard Ho E1 243 C3
Bernard Rd
South Tottenham N15 51 D4
Wallington SM5, SM6 219 B4
Bernard Shaw Ct 5 NW1 71 C1
Bernard Shaw Ho 2 NW10 89 B6
Bernard St WC1 94 A3 240 B5
Bernays Cl HA7 25 C4
Bernay's Gr SW9 138 B1
Bernel Dr CR0 223 B5
Berne Rd CR7 205 A4
Berners Dr W13 109 A6
Berners Ho N1 234 A4
Bernersmede SE3 143 A2
Berners Mews W1 93 C2 239 B3
Berners Pl W1 239 B2
Berners Rd
Islington N1 234 C5
Wood Green N22 32 C1
Berners St W1 93 C1 239 B2
Berner Terr 27 E1 96 A1
Berney Ho BR3 207 A4
Berney Rd CR0 205 B2
Bernhard Baron Ho 23 E1 96 A1
Bernhardt Cres NW8 237 A6
Bernhart Cl HA8 27 A3
Bernie Grant Ho 40 E9 74 C1
Bernwell Rd E4 20 C1
Bernwood Ho 6 N4 51 B2
Berridge Gn HA8 26 C3
Berridge Mews NW6 69 C3
Berridge Rd SE19 183 C5
Berriman Rd N7 72 B5
Berrite Works UB7 104 C4
Berriton Rd HA2 41 B1
Berrybank Cl 4 E4 20 A2
Berry Cl
Dagenham RM10 81 C3
Southgate N21 16 D3
Berry Cotts 2 E14 97 A1
Berry Ct TW4 151 B6
Berrydale Rd UB4 85 A3
Berryfield Cl BR1 188 A1
Berry Field Cl 8 E17 53 D5
Berryfield Rd SE17 116 D1 261 D2
Berryhill Gdns SE9 144 D1
Berryhill SE9 144 D1
Berry Hill HA7 25 D6
Berry Ho
10 Battersea SW11 136 D3
25 Bethnal Green E1 96 B3
BERRYLANDS 198 C3
Berrylands Ct 16 SM2 217 D1
Berrylands Rd KT5 198 B3
Berrylands Sta KT5 198 D5
Berrylands
Surbiton KT5 198 C3
West Barnes SW20 200 C5
Berry La SE21 183 B6
Berryman Cl RM8 80 C5
Berryman's La SE26 184 D6
Berrymead Gdns W3 111 A4
Berrymede Inf Sch W3 110 D4
Berrymede Jun Sch W3 110 D4
Berrymede Rd W4 111 B3
Berry Pl EC1 234 D1
Berry St EC1 241 D5
Berry Way W5 110 A3
Bertal Rd SW17 180 B6
Bertha Hollamby Ct DA14 190 C5
Bertha James Ct BR2 209 B5
Bertha Neubergh Ho 1 SE5 139 A4
Berthan Gdns E17 54 B4
Berthon St SE8 141 C6
Bertie Rd
Penge SE26 184 D4
Willesden NW10 68 A2
Bertram Cotts SW19 179 C3
Bertram Rd Enfield EN1 6 A1
Hendon NW4 46 A3
Kingston u T KT2 176 C3
Bertram St N19 71 B6
Bertrand Ho 11 SW16 160 A1
Bertrand St SE13 141 D2
Bertrand Way SE28 124 C6
Bert Rd CR7 205 A4
Bert Reilly Ho 1 SE18 123 B1
Bertrum House Sch SW17 159 A2
Bert Way EN1 5 D1
Berwick Ave UB4 106 D6
Berwick Cl
Harrow HA7 24 D4
Twickenham TW2 151 C3
Berwick Cres DA15 167 C5
Berwick Ct 8 BR3 185 C2
Berwick Gdns SM1 218 A5
Berwick Ho 10 N2 30 B1
Berwick Rd
Newham E16 99 C1
Tottenham N22 32 D2
Welling DA16 146 B4
Berwick St W1 93 C1 239 B1
Berwyn Ave TW3 129 D4
Berwyn Ho 3 N16 51 D1
Berwyn Rd
Mortlake SW14, TW10 132 D1
Streatham SE24 160 D3
Beryl Ave E6 100 A2
Beryl Harding Ho 3 SW19 178 D3
Beryl Ho SE18 123 D1
Beryl Rd W6 112 D1
Berystede KT2 176 D3
Besant Cl NW2 69 A5
Besant Ct
Canonbury N1 73 B3
15 Thamesmead SE28 124 B6
Besant Ho NW8 229 A5
Besant Pl SE22 139 D1
Besant Rd NW2 69 A4
Besant Way NW10 67 A3
Besant Wlk N7 72 B6
Besford Ho 26 E2 96 A5
Besley St SW16 181 C4
Bessant Dr TW9 132 D4
Bessborough Gdns SW1 115 D1 259 D2
Bessborough Pl SW1 115 D1
Bessborough Rd
Harrow HA1
Roehampton SW15
Bessborough St SW1 115 D1
Bessborough Wks KT8
Bessemer Ct 7 NW1
Bessemer Grange Pri Sch SE5
Bessemer Park Ind Es 3 SE24
Bessemer Rd SE5
Bessie Lansbury Cl E6
Bessingby Rd HA4
Bessingham Wlk SE4
Besson St SE14
Bessy St E2
Bestwood St SE8
Beswick Mews 1 NW6
Betam Rd UB3
Beta Pl 20 SW4
Betchworth Cl SM1
Betchworth Ho 8 N7
Betchworth Rd IG3
Betham Rd UB6
Bethany Ct 8 DA6
Bethany Waye TW14
Bethecar Rd HA1
Bethel Cl NW4
Bethell Ave Ilford IG1
Newham E13, E16
Bethel Lo N11
Bethel Rd DA16
Bethersden Cl BR3
Bethersden Ho SE17
Bethesda Ct 5 SE20
Beth Jacob Gram Sch NW4
Bethlehem Ho 13 E14
Bethlem Royal Hospl BR3
BETHNAL GREEN
Bethnal Green Rd
Bethnal Green E2
Shoreditch E1, E2 95 D3
Bethnal Green Sta
Bethnal Green E1
Bethnal Green E2
Bethnal Green Tech Coll E2
Beths Gram Sch DA5
Bethune Ave N11
Bethune Rd
North Acton NW10
Stamford Hill N16
Bethwin Rd SE5
Betjeman Cl HA5
Betjeman Ct EN4
Betony Cl CR0
Betoyne Ave E4
Betsham Ho SE1
Betspath Ho 6 N11
Betstyle Circus N11
Betstyle Ho 2 N10
Betstyle Rd N11
Betterton Dr DA14
Betterton Ho WC2
Betterton St WC2 94 A1
Bettons Pk E15
Bettridge Rd SW6
Betts Cl BR3
Betts Ho E1
Betts Mews E17
Betts Rd E16
Betts St E1
Betts Way
Long Ditton KT6
Penge SE20
Bettswood Ct 15 SE20
Betty Brooks Ho E11
Betty Layward Prim Sc N16
Betty May Gray Ho 2 E14
Beulah Ave CR7
Beulah Cl HA8
Beulah Cres CR7
Beulah Gr CR0
Beulah Hill SE19
Beulah Inf Sch CR7
Beulah Jun Sch CR7

h Rd
on SW19 ... 179 B3
h Norwood CR7 . 205 A6
on SM1 ... 217 C4
hamstow E17 ... 53 D4
eigh Ct E17 ... 54 B4
Ave IG11 ... 80 A1
Ct
don CR0 ... 220 C3
wickenham
V1 ... 153 D5
Ho IG11 ... 80 B1
Rd
fosters EN4 ... 2 D1
nstead Comm
2 ... 124 B1
n St N1 ... 95 A6 235 B5
Callender Cl 4
... 137 B2
nden St
... 95 B4 235 D2
rcote Wlk 1
7 ... 147 B6
ridge Ct
thgate N21 ... 16 A6
Thamesmead
28 ... 124 B6
ridge Rd 1
0 ... 67 C1
rley Ave
nslow TW4 ... 129 B1
cup DA15 ... 167 D4
nbledon SW20 ... 177 D2
rley Cl
nes SW13 ... 134 A3
ssington KT9 ... 213 C4
monton N21 ... 17 A3
eld EN1 ... 5 C1
Wandsworth
W11 ... 136 B1
rley Cotts
15 ... 155 C1
rley Cres IG8 ... 37 B2
rley Ct
Acton Green
V4 ... 111 A1
Acton W12 ... 111 C4
ckley SE4 ... 141 B2
Cheam SM2 ... 217 C2
ngford Hatch E4 ... 35 B6
tis Green N2 ... 48 D5
rrow HA2 ... 42 B6
unslow TW4 ... 129 B1
ngton N5 ... 72 D2
tholt UB5 ... 84 C5
leigh Pk N20 ... 14 A4
wood N14 ... 15 C4
cup DA14 ... 190 B6
mbledon SW20 ... 177 D2
rley Dr HA8 ... 44 C6
rley Gdns
nes SW13 ... 133 D2
ndon NW11 ... 47 A2
New Malden KT4 . 200 A1
nmore HA7 ... 25 A2
mbley HA9 ... 44 C1
rley Ho 5 BR1 ... 186 B5
rley Hyrst 10
) ... 221 D6
rley La KT2 ... 177 C3
rley Lo 6
10 ... 154 A6
rley Mans TW4 ... 129 B1
rley Path 9
13 ... 133 D3
rley Rd
rnes SW13 ... 133 D2
ngford E4 ... 36 B4
swick W4 ... 111 D1
genham RM9 ... 81 A4
ston Mark BR2 ... 226 A6
tcham CR4 ... 203 D5
wham E6 ... 99 D4
rth Cheam KT4 ... 216 C6
nge SE20 ... 184 B1
islip HA4 ... 62 B6
uthall UB2 ... 107 A3
nbury TW16 ... 171 D2
ddington KT1 ... 175 C2
est Barnes KT3 ... 200 A5
rley DA14 ... 190 A5
erley Trad Est
4 ... 200 D2
erley Way (Kingston
Pass) KT3,
/20 ... 200 A6
erley Way KT3, SW20,
2 ... 177 D2
erly Ct HA3 ... 43 C5
ersbrook Rd N19 ... 71 D5
erstone Rd
ndon SW2 ... 160 B6
ornton Heath CR7 . 204 D5
erston Mews
/1 ... 237 C3
ill Allen Cl
/17 ... 180 D5
Bevill Cl SE25 ... 206 A6
Bevin Cl SE16 ... 119 A5
Bevin Ct WC1 ... 233 D2
Bevington Prim Sch
W10 ... 91 A2
Bevington Rd
Beckenham BR3 ... 185 D1
Kensal Town W10 ... 91 A2
Bevington St SE16 ... 118 A4
Bevin Ho
35 Bethnal Green
E2 ... 96 C4
8 Bow E3 ... 97 C4
Bevin Rd UB4 ... 84 B4
Bevin Sq SW17 ... 158 D1
Bevin Way WC1 ... 234 A2
Bevis Marks
EC3 ... 95 C1 243 B2
Bewcastle Gdns EN2 ... 4 A1
Bew Ct SE21 ... 162 A4
Bewdley Ho N4 ... 51 A2
Bewdley St N1 ... 72 C1
Bewick Mews SE15 ... 140 B5
Bewick St SW8 ... 137 B3
Bewley Ct SW2 ... 160 B5
Bewley Ho 7 E1 ... 118 B6
Bewley St
Stepney E1 ... 118 B6
Wimbledon SW19 ... 180 A4
Bewlys Rd SE27 ... 182 D5
Bexhill Cl TW13 ... 151 A2
Bexhill Rd
Catford SE4 ... 163 B5
Mortlake SW14 ... 133 A2
Wood Green N11 ... 31 D5
Bexhill Wlk 6 E15 ... 98 C6
BEXLEY ... 146 B1
Bexley Coll (Erith Rd
Campus) DA17 ... 125 D1
Bexley Gdns
Edmonton N9 ... 17 B1
Ilford RM6 ... 58 B4
Bexley Gram Sch
DA16 ... 146 B1
BEXLEYHEATH ... 147 B2
Bexleyheath Sch
DA8 ... 147 C2
Bexleyheath Sta
DA7 ... 147 A3
Bexley High St DA5 ... 169 D3
Bexley Ho SE4 ... 141 A1
Bexley La DA14 ... 168 C1
Bexley Rd SE9 ... 167 A6
Bexley Sta DA5 ... 169 C3
Beynon Rd SM5 ... 218 D3
BFI London Imax
Cinema
SE1 ... 116 C5 251 A3
Bglws The SM6 ... 219 B3
Bianca Rd SE1, SE15 ... 140 A6
Bibsworth Lo N3 ... 29 B1
Bibsworth Rd N3 ... 29 B1
Bicester Rd TW9 ... 132 D2
Bickenhall Mans
W1 ... 237 D4
Bickenhall St
W1 ... 92 D2 237 D4
Bickersteth Rd
SW17 ... 180 D4
Bickerton Rd N19 ... 71 C6
BICKLEY ... 188 B1
Bickley Cres BR1 ... 210 A5
Bickley Ct
10 Merton SW19 ... 179 C3
1 Stanmore HA7 ... 25 C6
Bickley Park Rd BR1,
BR7 ... 210 B6
Bickley Park Sch
BR1 ... 210 A6
Bickley Prim Sch
BR1 ... 209 C6
Bickley Rd
Bromley BR1 ... 187 D1
Leyton E10 ... 53 D2
Bickley Sta BR1 ... 210 A6
Bickley St SW17 ... 180 D5
Bicknell Ho 34 E1 ... 96 A1
Bicknell Rd SE5 ... 139 A2
Bicknoller Rd EN1 ... 5 D4
Bicknor Ho 2 E5 ... 74 B3
Bicknor Rd BR6 ... 211 D2
Bidborough Cl 3
BR2 ... 208 D4
Bidborough St N1,
WC1 ... 94 A4 233 A1
Biddenden Way
SE9 ... 188 C6
Biddenham Ho 18
SE16 ... 118 D2
Bidder St E16 ... 98 C2
Biddesden Ho SW3 . 257 C3
Biddestone Rd N7 ... 72 B4
Biddulph Ho 22
SE18 ... 122 B2
Biddulph Mans W9 ... 91 D4
Biddulph Rd W9 ... 91 D4
Bideford Ave UB6 ... 87 B5
Bideford Cl
Edgware HA8 ... 26 C2
Twickenham TW13 ... 151 B1
Bideford Gdns EN1 ... 17 C4
Bideford Rd
Catford BR1 ... 164 D1
East Wickham DA16 ... 146 B5
Enfield EN3 ... 7 B5
Ruislip HA4 ... 62 B5
Bidmead Ct KT6 ... 214 A5
Bidwell Gdns N11 ... 31 C3
Bidwell Ho
Southall UB2 ... 107 A2
3 Willesden NW2 ... 68 A5
Bidwell St SE15 ... 140 B4
Big Ben* SW1 ... 250 B1
Bigbury Cl N17 ... 33 C3
Biggerstaff Rd E15 ... 98 A6
Biggerstaff St N4 ... 72 C6
Biggin Ave CR4 ... 180 D2
Biggin Hill Cl KT2 ... 175 C5
Biggin Hill SE19 ... 182 D3
Biggin Way SE19 ... 183 A3
Bigginwood Rd
SW16 ... 182 D2
Bigg's Row SW15 ... 134 D2
Big Hill E5 ... 52 B1
Bigland Green Prim Sch
E1 ... 96 B1
Bigland St E1 ... 96 B1
Bignell Rd SE18 ... 122 D1
Bignold Rd E7 ... 77 A4
Bigwood Ct NW11 ... 47 D4
Bigwood Rd NW11 ... 47 D3
Biko Ho 1 NW10 ... 67 B1
Bilberry Ho 18 E3 ... 97 C2
Bilberry Manor
SM2 ... 218 A1
Billet Rd Ilford RM6 ... 58 C6
Walthamstow E17 ... 35 B2
Billets Hart Cl W7 ... 108 C4
Bill Hamling Cl SE9 ... 166 B2
Billie Holiday Ct
NW10 ... 89 B5
Billingford Cl SE4 ... 140 D1
Billing Ho 7 E1 ... 96 D1
Billingley NW1 ... 232 A5
Billing Pl
SW10 ... 135 D5 265 D4
Billing Rd
SW10 ... 135 D5 265 D4
Billings Cl RM9 ... 80 C1
Billingsgate Mkt
E14 ... 119 D5
Billing St
SW10 ... 135 D5 265 D4
Billington Ho SW8 ... 269 D1
Billington Rd SE14 ... 140 D5
Billinton Hill CR0 ... 221 B6
Billiter Sq EC3 ... 243 B1
Billiter St EC3 . 95 C1 243 B1
Bill Nicholson Way
N17 ... 33 D3
Billockby Cl KT9 ... 214 B2
Billsley Ct SE25 ... 205 C5
Billson St E14 ... 120 A2
Bilsby Gr SE9 ... 187 D6
Bilton Ho SW8 ... 269 C1
Bilton Rd UB6 ... 87 B6
Bilton Twrs W1 ... 237 D1
Bilton Way Enfield EN3 . 7 B5
Hayes UB3 ... 106 B4
Bina Gdns
SW5 ... 114 A2 256 A3
Binbrook Ho 13 W10 ... 90 C2
Bincote Rd EN2 ... 4 B2
Binden Rd W12 ... 111 D3
Bindon Gn SM4 ... 201 D5
Binfield Ct SE5 ... 139 A3
Binfield Rd
London
SW4 ... 138 A4 270 B1
South Croydon CR2 . 221 D3
Bingfield St
N1 ... 94 B6 233 C6
Bingham Cnr CR0 ... 206 A1
Bingham Pl
W1 ... 93 A2 238 A4
Bingham Point 11
SE18 ... 122 D2
Bingham Rd CR0 ... 206 B1
Bingham St N1 ... 73 B2
Bingley Rd
Ashford TW16 ... 172 A3
Newham E16 ... 99 C1
Southall UB6 ... 86 A2
Binley Ho SW15 ... 155 D5
Binney St W1 . 93 A1 238 B1
Binnie Ct SE10 ... 141 D5
Binnie Ho SE1 ... 262 A5
Binns Rd W4 ... 111 C1
Binns Terr 3 W4 ... 111 C1
Binsey Wlk 1 SE2 ... 124 C4
Binstead Cl UB4 ... 85 A2
Binstead Ho SW18 ... 157 D5
Binyon Cres HA7 ... 24 D5
Binyon Ho 8 N16 ... 73 C4
Birbeck Ho 4 N19 ... 49 D1
Birbetts Rd SE9 ... 166 B2
Bircham Path SE4 ... 140 D1
Birchanger Rd SE25 ... 206 A4
Birch Ave
Edmonton N13 ... 17 A1
Hillingdon UB7 ... 82 B1
Birch Cl
Brentford TW8 ... 131 B5
Buckhurst Hill IG9 ... 21 D1
Hounslow TW3 ... 130 B3
Newham E16 ... 98 C2
Peckham SE15 ... 140 A3
Romford RM7 ... 59 D6
Teddington TW11 ... 175 A5
Upper Holloway N19 ... 71 C6
Birch Cres UB10 ... 82 B6
Birch Ct Chingford E4 ... 35 D4
Forest Gate E7 ... 76 D4
Ilford RM6 ... 58 C3
Sutton SM1 ... 218 A4
9 Wallington SM6 ... 219 B4
7 Woodside Pk N12 ... 29 D6
Birchdale Gdns RM6 ... 58 D2
Birchdale Rd E7 ... 77 C3
Birchdene Dr SE28 ... 124 A5
Birchdown Ho 32 E3 ... 97 D4
Birchen Cl NW9 ... 67 B6
Birchend Cl CR2 ... 221 B2
Birchen Gr NW9 ... 67 B6
Birches Cl
Mitcham CR4 ... 202 D6
Pinner HA5 ... 41 A4
Birches The
2 Beckenham
BR2 ... 208 D5
Bushey WD23 ... 8 A6
Camberwell SE5 ... 139 C3
Greenwich SE7 ... 143 B6
Manor Pk E12 ... 78 A4
Orpington BR6 ... 226 C4
Southgate N21 ... 16 B5
South Norwood
SE25 ... 183 D1
Twickenham TW4 ... 151 B4
Birchfield Ho 3
E14 ... 119 C6
Birchfield St E14 ... 119 C6
Birch Gn NW9 ... 27 C3
Birch Gr Acton W3 ... 110 C6
Bexley DA16 ... 146 A1
Lewisham SE12 ... 164 D4
Leyton E11 ... 76 C5
Birchgrove Ho TW9 ... 132 D5
Birch Gr TW17 ... 171 C1
Birch Hill CR0 ... 222 D3
Birch Ho
New Cross Gate
SE14 ... 141 B4
Teddington TW11 ... 175 C3
8 Tulse Hill SW2 ... 160 C5
Birchington Cl DA7 ... 147 D4
Birchington Ct
Crouch End N8 ... 49 D3
2 Kilburn NW6 ... 91 D6
Birchington Ho 1
E5 ... 74 B3
Birchington Rd
Crouch End N8 ... 49 D3
Kilburn NW6 ... 91 C6
Surbiton KT5 ... 198 B2
Birchin La EC3 ... 242 D1
Birchlands Ave
SW12 ... 158 D4
Birchmead Ave HA5 ... 40 C5
Birch Mead BR2,
BR6 ... 226 C6
Birchmere Bsns Pk
SE2 ... 124 A4
Birchmere Lo 13
SE16 ... 118 B1
Birchmere Row
SE3 ... 142 D3
Birchmore Wlk N5 ... 73 A5
Birch Pk HA3 ... 24 A3
Birch Rd
Feltham TW13 ... 172 D5
Romford RM7 ... 59 D6
Birch Row BR2 ... 210 C3
Birch Tree Ave BR4 ... 224 D4
Birch Tree Ho 16
SE7 ... 143 C6
Birch Tree Way CR0 ... 222 B6
Birch Vale Ct NW8 ... 236 D6
Birchway UB3 ... 106 A5
Birch Wlk CR4 ... 181 B2
Birchwood Ave
Beckenham BR3 ... 207 B5
Hackbridge SM5,
SM6 ... 219 B5
Muswell Hill N10 ... 49 A6
Sidcup DA14 ... 168 C1
Birchwood Cl SM4 ... 201 D5
Birchwood Ct
Burnt Oak HA8 ... 27 A1
Edmonton N13 ... 32 D5
Birchwood Dr NW3 ... 69 D5
Birchwood Gr
TW12 ... 173 C4
Birchwood Rd
Orpington BR5 ... 211 C5
Streatham SW17 ... 181 B5
Birdbrook Rd SE3 ... 143 C2
Birdcage Wlk
SW1 ... 115 D4 249 C1
Bird Coll DA14 ... 168 A1
Birdham Cl BR1 ... 210 A4
Birdhurst Ave CR2 ... 221 B4
Birdhurst Ct SM6 ... 219 C1
Birdhurst Gdns CR2 ... 221 B4
Birdhurst Rd
London SW18 ... 158 A6
Mitcham SW19 ... 180 C4
South Croydon CR2 . 221 C3
Birdhurst Rise CR2 ... 221 C3
Bird In Bush Rd
SE15 ... 140 A5
Bird-in-Hand La
BR1 ... 187 D1
Bird-In-Hand Pas
SE23 ... 162 C2
Bird In Hand Yd 24
NW3 ... 70 A4
Birdsall Ho 5 SE5 ... 139 C2
Birdsfield La 12 E3 ... 97 B6
Bird St W1 ... 238 B1
Bird Wlk TW2 ... 151 B3
Birdwood Cl TW11 ... 174 C6
Birkbeck Ave
Acton W3 ... 111 A6
Greenford UB6 ... 86 A6
Birkbeck Coll
W1 ... 93 D1 239 C2
Birkbeck Ct W3 ... 111 B5
Birkbeck Gdns IG8 ... 21 A2
Birkbeck Gr W3 ... 111 B4
Birkbeck Hill SE21 ... 160 D3
Birkbeck Mews 5
E8 ... 73 D3
Birkbeck Pl SE21 ... 161 A2
Birkbeck Prim Sch
DA14 ... 168 B1
Birkbeck Rd
Acton W3 ... 111 B5
Dalston E8 ... 73 D3
Ealing W5 ... 109 C2
Edgware NW7 ... 27 D5
Enfield EN2 ... 5 B5
Hornsey N8 ... 50 A5
Ilford IG2 ... 57 B4
North Finchley N12 ... 30 A5
Penge BR3 ... 184 D1
Sidcup DA14 ... 168 A1
Tottenham N17 ... 33 D2
Wimbledon SW19 ... 179 D4
Birkbeck Sta SE20 ... 206 C6
Birkbeck St E2 ... 96 B4
Birkbeck Way UB6 ... 86 B6
Birkdale Ave HA5 ... 41 C6
Birkdale Cl
30 Bermondsey
SE16 ... 118 B1
Crofton BR6 ... 211 B2
Erith SE28 ... 102 D1
Birkdale Ct 3 UB1 ... 86 A1
Birkdale Gdns CR0 ... 222 D4
Birkdale Rd
Abbey Wood SE2 ... 124 B2
Ealing W5 ... 88 A3
Birkenhead Ave
KT2 ... 176 B2
Birkenhead Ho 11
N7 ... 72 C3
Birkenhead St
WC1 ... 94 A4 233 B2
Birkhall Rd SE6 ... 164 B2
Birkwood Cl SW12 ... 159 D4
Birley Lo NW8 ... 229 D4
Birley Rd N20 ... 14 A2
Birley St SW11 ... 137 A3
Birnam Rd N4 ... 72 B6
Birnbeck Ct NW11 ... 47 B4
Birnham Ho TW1 ... 153 C4
Birrell Ho 9 SW9 ... 138 B3
Birse Cres NW10 ... 67 C4
Birstal Gn WD19 ... 22 D6
Birstall Rd N15 ... 51 C4
Birtwhistle Ho 5 E3 ... 97 B6
Biscay Ho 11 E1 ... 96 D3
Biscay Rd W6 ... 112 D1
Biscoe Cl TW5 ... 129 C6
Biscoe Ho UB2 ... 107 D2
Biscoe Way SE13 ... 142 B2
Biscott Ho 3 E3 ... 97 D3
Bisenden Rd CR0 ... 221 C6
Bisham Cl CR4 ... 202 D1
Bisham Gdns N6 ... 49 A1
Bishop Butt Cl BR6 ... 227 D5
Bishop Challoner
Collegiate Sch E1 ... 96 C1
Bishop Challoner Sch
BR2 ... 186 B1
Bishop Ct 20 SW2 ... 160 C5
Bishop Douglass RC
High Sch N2 ... 48 A6
Bishop Duppa's
Almshouses 7
TW10 ... 154 A6
Bishop Duppas Pk
TW17 ... 193 C2
Bishop Fox Way
KT8 ... 195 B5
Bishop Gilpins CE Prim
Sch SW19 ... 179 B5
Bishop John Robinson
CE Prim Sch
SE28 ... 124 C6
Bishop Justus CE Sch
BR2 ... 210 A2
Bishop Ken Rd HA3 ... 24 D2
Bishop King's Rd
W14 ... 113 A2 254 B4
Bishop Perrin CE Prim
Sch TW2 ... 151 D3
Bishop Ramsey CE Sch
(Annexe) HA4 ... 39 D2
Bishop Ramsey CE Sch
HA4 ... 40 A2
Bishop Rd N14 ... 15 B4
Bishop Ridley CE Prim
Sch DA16 ... 145 C1
Bishops Ave
Borehamwood
WD6 ... 10 B6
Bromley BR1 ... 209 C6
Bishop's Ave SW6 ... 135 A3
Bishops Ave
Ilford RM6 ... 58 C3
Newham E13 ... 99 B6
Bishops Ave The N2 ... 48 B3
Bishopsbourne Ho
BR1 ... 187 B3
Bishop's Bridge Rd
W2 ... 92 A1 236 A2
Bishops Cl
Acton Green W4 ... 111 A1
Barnet EN5 ... 12 D5
Bishop's Cl N19 ... 71 C5
Bishops Cl EN1 ... 6 B3
Bishop's Cl UB10 ... 82 C5
Bishops Cl
New Eltham SE9 ... 167 A2
Richmond TW10 ... 153 D1
Sutton SM1 ... 217 C5
Bishop's Cl E17 ... 53 D5
Bishopscourt 8
CR0 ... 221 D6
Bishops Ct
1 Ashford TW16 ... 171 D3
13 Bayswater W2 ... 91 D1
East Finchley N2 ... 48 C5
Bishop's Ct
Holborn EC4 ... 241 C2
Holborn WC2 ... 241 A2
Bishops Ct
Richmond TW9 ... 132 A2
Romford RM7 ... 59 D5
Wembley HA0 ... 65 B4
Bishopsdale Ho 8
NW6 ... 91 C6
Bishops Dr
East Bedfont
TW14 ... 149 B5
Northolt UB5 ... 85 A6
Bishopsford Com Sch
SM4 ... 202 B3
Bishopsford Ho
SM4 ... 202 C3
Bishopsford Rd
SM4 ... 202 B3
Bishopsgate Arc E1 . 243 B3
Bishopsgate
Churchyard EC2 ... 243 A2
Bishopsgate
EC2 ... 95 C1 243 A2
Bishops Gn BR1 ... 187 C2
Bishops Gr
East Finchley N2 ... 48 C3
Feltham TW12 ... 173 B6
Bishop's Hall KT1 ... 175 D1
Bishopshalt Sch UB8 . 82 B4
Bishops Hill KT12 ... 194 A2
Bishops Ho SW8 ... 270 B3
Bishop's Mans SW6 . 134 D3
Bishops Mead SE5 ... 139 A5
Bishop's Park Rd
SW6 ... 134 D3
Bishops Park Rd
SW16 ... 182 A2
Bishop's Pl SM1 ... 218 A3
Bishops Rd
SW6 ... 135 B4 264 C2
Bishop's Rd
Hanwell W7 ... 108 C4
Hayes UB3 ... 83 A1
Bishops Rd N6 ... 49 A3
Bishop's Rd CR0 ... 204 D2

Bishops Sq E1 243 B4
Bishop's Terr SE11 116 C2 261 B4
Bishopsthorpe Rd SE26 184 D6
Bishop St N1 95 A6 235 A6
Bishopstone Ho [4] SW11 137 A3
Bishop Stopford's Sch EN1 6 B3
Bishops View Ct N10 49 B5
Bishop's Way E2 96 C5
Bishops Wlk
Chislehurst BR7 189 A2
South Croydon CR0, CR9 223 A3
Bishopswood Rd N6 48 D2
Bishop Thomas Grant RC Sec Sch SW16 182 B5
Bishop Wand CE Sch The TW16 171 D1
Bishop Way NW10 67 C1
Bishop Wilfred Wood Cl SE15 140 A3
Bishop Wilfred Wood Ct [3] E13 99 C5
Bishop Winnington-Ingram CE Prim Sch HA4 39 B2
Bisley Cl KT4 200 C1
Bisley Ho SW19 156 D2
Bispham Rd NW10 88 B4
Bissextile Ho SE13 141 D3
Bisson Rd E15 98 A5
Bisterne Ave E17 54 B6
Bittacy Bsns Ctr NW7 29 A3
Bittacy Cl NW7 28 D4
Bittacy Ct NW7 29 A3
Bittacy Hill NW7 28 D4
Bittacy Park Ave NW7 28 D5
Bittacy Rd NW7 28 D4
Bittacy Rise NW7 28 D4
Bittern Cl UB4 84 D2
Bittern Ct
Chingford E4 20 B4
[7] Deptford SE8 141 C6
Hendon NW9 27 C1
Bittern Ho SE1 252 A1
Bittern St SE1 252 A1
Bittoms The KT1 197 D6
Bixley Cl UB2 107 B2
Blackall St EC2 243 A6
Blackberry Cl TW17 193 C5
Blackberry Farm Cl TW5 129 A5
Blackberry Field BR5 190 A2
Blackbird Ct NW9 67 B5
Blackbird Hill NW9 67 B5
Blackborne Rd RM10 81 D2
Black Boy La N15 51 A4
Blackbrook La BR1, BR2 210 C5
Blackburn Ct [21] SW2 160 C5
Blackburne's Mews W1 248 A5
Blackburn [28] NW9 27 D1
Blackburn Rd NW6 69 D2
Blackburn Trad Est TW19 148 B5
Blackburn Way TW4 151 A6
Blackbush Ave RM6 58 D4
Blackbush Cl SM2 217 D1
Blackcap Ct NW9 27 C1
Blackdown Cl N2 30 A1
Blackdown Ho E8 74 A4
Blackett St SW15 134 D2
Black Fan Cl EN2 5 A4
BLACKFEN 168 A5
Blackfen Par DA15 168 A5
Blackfen Rd DA15 168 B5
Blackfen Sch for Girls DA15 168 B5
Blackford Rd WD19 22 D5
Blackfriars Bridge EC4 251 C5
Blackfriars Ct EC4 251 C6
Black Friars La EC4 94 D1 241 C1
Blackfriars Pas EC4 251 C6
Blackfriars Pier EC4 251 C6
Blackfriars Rd SE1 116 D5 251 C3
Blackfriars Sta EC4 116 D6 251 C6
Blackfriars Underpass EC4 116 C6 251 B6
Blackham Ho SW19 179 A4
BLACKHEATH 142 C2
Blackheath Ave SE3 142 C5
Blackheath Bluecoat CE Sec Sch SE3 143 B5
Blackheath Bsns Est SE10 142 A4
Blackheath Gr SE3 142 D3
Blackheath High Sch
Blackheath SE3 142 D3
Greenwich SE3 143 A5
Blackheath Hill SE10 142 A4
Blackheath Hospl SE3 142 C2
Blackheath* SE3 142 C4
BLACKHEATH PARK 143 A1
Blackheath Pk SE3 143 A2
Blackheath Prep Sch SE3 143 A4
Blackheath Rd SE10 141 D4
Blackheath Rise SE13 142 A3
Blackheath Sta SE3 142 D2
BLACKHEATH VALE 142 D3
Blackheath Vale SE3 142 C3
Blackheath Village SE3 142 D3
Black Horse Ct SE1 262 D6
Blackhorse La
Croydon CR0 206 A2
Higham Hill E17 34 D1
Blackhorse La Sta CR0 206 A2
Blackhorse Mews E17 52 D6
Black Horse Par HA5 40 B4
Blackhorse Rd SE8 141 A6
Black Horse Rd DA14 190 A6
Blackhorse Rd E17 53 A5
Blackhorse Road Sta E17 52 D5
Blackhorse Road E17 52 D5
Blacklands Dr UB4 83 A3
Blacklands Rd SE6 186 A6
Blacklands Terr SW3 257 D3
Black Lion La W6 112 A2
Black Lion Mews [4] W6 112 A2
Blackmore Ave UB1 108 B5
Blackmore Dr NW10 66 D1
Blackmore Ho
Forest Hill SE23 163 B3
Islington N1 233 D5
[2] Wandsworth SW18 157 D6
Blackmore's Gr TW11 175 A4
Blackmore Twr [1] W3 111 A3
Blackness La BR2 225 D1
Blackpool Gdns UB4 83 C3
Blackpool Rd SE15 140 B3
Black Prince Intc DA6 169 D5
Black Prince Rd SE1, SE11 116 B2 260 D3
Black Rod Cl UB3 105 D3
Black Roof Ho [9] SE5 138 D4
Blackshaw Rd SW17 180 B5
Blacksmith Cl RM6 58 C3
Blacksmiths Ho [7] E17 53 C5
Black's Rd W6 112 C2
Blackstock Ho [2] N5 72 D5
Blackstock Mews N4 72 D5
Blackstock Rd N4, N5 72 D6
Blackstone Ho
Dulwich SE21 161 C1
Pimlico SW1 259 A1
Blackstone Rd NW2 68 C4
Black Swan Yd SE1 253 A2
Blackthorn Ave UB7 104 C3
Blackthorn Ct
[20] Camberwell SE15 139 D5
Heston TW5 129 A5
[4] Leyton E15 76 B4
[6] West Norwood SW16 182 C5
Blackthorne Ave CR0 206 C1
Blackthorne Ct
[2] Littleton TW15 171 A3
Southall UB1 107 D5
Blackthorne Dr E4 36 B6
Blackthorn Gr DA7 147 A2
Blackthorn Rd IG1 79 B3
Blackthorn St E3 97 C3
Blacktree Mews [11] SW9 138 C2
BLACKWALL 120 B6
Blackwall Sta E14 120 A6
Blackwall Trad Est E14 98 B2
Blackwall Tunnel App SE10 120 C4
Blackwall Tunnel E14, SE10 120 B5
Blackwall Tunnel Northern Approach E14, E3 98 A3
Blackwall Way E14 120 A6
Blackwater Cl E7 76 D4
Blackwater Ho NW8 236 D4
Blackwater St SE22 161 D6
Blackwell Cl
[10] Clapton Pk E5 74 D4
Harrow HA3 24 B3
Blackwell Gdns HA8 10 C1
Blackwell Ho [3] SW4 159 D5
Blackwood Ho [11] E1 96 B3
Blackwood St SE17 117 B1 262 C2
Blade Ho TW1 153 D5
Blade Mews SW15 135 B1
Bladen Ho [4] E1 96 D1
Blades Ct
[4] Hammersmith W6 112 B1
Putney SW15 135 B1
Blades Ho [12] SE11 138 C6
Blades Lo [10] SW2 160 C5
Bladindon Dr DA5 168 D4
Bladon Ct
Beckenham BR2 208 C6
Streatham SW16 182 A4
Bladon Gdns HA2 41 D3
Blagden's Cl N14 15 D2
Blagden's La N14 15 D2
Blagdon Ct W7 108 C6
Blagdon Rd
London SE13 163 D5
New Malden KT3 199 D5
Blagdon Wlk TW11 175 C4
Blagrove Rd [1] W10 91 B2
Blair Ave London NW9 45 C2
Thames Ditton KT10 212 A6
Blair Cl
Avery Hill DA15 167 C6
Canonbury N1 73 A2
Hayes UB3 106 A2
Blair Ct
Beckenham BR3 185 D2
[8] Carshalton SM5 218 D5
[7] Catford SE6 164 D3
St John's Wood NW8 229 C6
Blairderry Rd SW2 160 A2
Blairgowrie Ct [13] E14 98 B1
Blair Ho SW9 138 B3
Blair Peach Prim Sch UB1 106 D5
Blair St E14 98 B1
Blake Apartments N8 50 B6
Blake Ave IG11 101 D6
Blake Cl
Bexley DA16 145 C4
Carshalton SM5 202 C1
Blake Coll W1 93 C2 239 A4
Blake Ct
[8] Bermondsey SE16 118 B1
[9] Clapham SW8 137 C3
Croydon CR2 220 D3
Kilburn NW6 91 C4
Southgate N21 16 B6
Blakeden Dr KT10 212 D2
Blake Gdns SW6 135 D4 265 C2
Blake Hall Cres E11 55 A1
Blakehall Rd SM5 218 D2
Blake Hall Rd E11 55 A2
Blake Ho
[6] Beckenham BR3 185 D4
[2] Deptford SE8 141 C6
Harrow HA1 64 C6
Isle Of Dogs E14 119 D4
[1] Kentish Town N19 71 D3
Lambeth SE1 261 A6
[14] Stoke Newington N16 73 C4
Blake Lo N3 29 B1
Blake Mews [15] TW9 132 C4
Blakemore Rd
Streatham SW16 160 A1
Thornton Heath CR7 204 B4
Blakemore Way DA17 125 A3
Blakeney Ave BR3 185 B2
Blakeney Cl
[5] Camden Town NW1 71 D1
[4] Dalston E8 74 A3
Whetstone N20 14 A3
Blakeney Ct EN2 17 B6
Blakeney Rd BR3 185 B2
Blakenham Ct W12 112 A5
Blakenham Rd SW17 180 D6
Blaker Ct SE7 143 C5
Blake Rd
Croydon CR0 221 C6
Mitcham CR4 202 C6
Newham E16 98 D3
Wood Green N11 31 C3
Blaker Rd E15 98 A6
Blakes Ave KT3 199 D3
Blakes Cl W10 90 C2
Blake's Gn BR4 208 A1
Blakes La KT3 199 D4
Blakesley Ave W5 87 C1
Blakesley Ct W5 87 C1
Blakesley Ho [4] E12 78 C5
Blake's Rd SE15 139 C5
Blakes Terr KT3 200 A4
Blakesware Gdns N9 17 B4
Blakewood Cl TW13 172 C6
Blakewood Ct [5] SE20 184 B3
Blanca Ho [16] N1 95 C5
Blanchard Cl SE9 166 A1
Blanchard Gr EN3 7 D5
Blanchard Ho
Chislehurst BR7 189 A4
[7] Twickenham TW1 153 D5
Blanchard Way E8 74 A2
Blanch Cl SE15 140 C5
Blanchedowne SE5 139 B1
Blanche Nevile Sch N10 31 A1
Blanche St E16 98 D3
Blanchland Rd SM4 201 D4
Blandfield Rd SW12 159 A4
Blandford Ave
[2] Beckenham BR3 185 A1
Twickenham TW2 151 D3
Blandford Cl
London N2 48 A5
Romford RM7 59 D5
Wallington CR0 220 A5
Blandford Cres E4 20 A4
Blandford Ct
Brondesbury Pk NW6 69 A1
[6] De Beauvoir Town N1 73 C1
Blandford Ho SW8 270 C4
Blandford Rd
Acton W4 111 C3
Ealing W5 109 D4
Penge BR3 184 D1
Southall UB2 107 C2
Teddington TW11 174 C5
Blandford Sq NW1 237 B5
Blandford St W1 93 A2 238 A3
Blandford Waye UB4 84 C1
Bland Ho SE11 260 D2
Bland St SE9 143 D1
Blaney Cres E6 100 D4
Blanmerle Rd SE9 166 D3
Blann Cl SE9 165 D5
Blantyre St SW10 136 B5 266 C4
Blantyre Twr SW10 266 C4
Blantyre Wlk SW10 136 B5 266 C4
Blashford NW3 70 D1
Blashford St SE13 164 B4
Blasker Wlk [8] E14 119 D1
Blatchford Ct KT12 194 A1
Blatchford Ho [8] RM10 81 C5
Blawith Rd HA1 42 D5
Blaxland Ho [12] W12 112 B6
Blaydon Cl HA4 39 C2
Blaydon Ct [4] UB5 63 C2
Blaydon Wlk N17 34 B3
Blazer Ct NW8 229 D1
Bleak Hill La SE18 145 D6
Blean Gr SE20 184 C3
Bleasdale Ave UB6 87 A5
Blechynden Ho [17] W10 90 D1
Blechynden St W10 112 D6
Bledlow Cl SE28 124 C6
Bledlow Rise UB6 86 A5
Bleeding Heart Yd EC1 241 B3
Blegborough Rd SW16 181 C4
Blemundsbury WC1 240 C4
Blendon Dr DA5 168 D5
Blendon Path [9] BR1 186 D3
Blendon Rd DA5 168 D5
Blendon Terr SE18 145 A6
Blendworth Point [4] SW15 156 B3
Blenheim Ave IG2 56 C3
Blenheim Bsns Ctr CR4 180 D1
Blenheim Centre [7] SE20 184 D3
Blenheim Cl
Edmonton N21 17 A3
Eltham SE12 165 B3
Greenford UB6 86 B5
Wallington SM6 219 C1
West Barnes SW20 200 C6
Blenheim Cres
Notting Hill W11 91 A1
Notting Hill W11 244 B6
Ruislip HA4 61 B6
South Croydon CR2 221 A1
Blenheim Ct
Barnsbury N7 72 A2
Beckenham BR2 208 D5
[5] Hampton TW12 173 C2
Harrow HA3 43 A3
Hendon NW4 46 D5
Longlands DA14 167 B1
Blenheim Ctr TW3 129 D2
Blenheim Ct
Richmond TW9 132 B2
[17] Rotherhithe SE16 118 D5
South Norwood SE19 183 C2
Sutton SM2 218 A2
Upper Holloway N19 72 A6
Woodford IG8 37 B3
Blenheim Dr DA16 145 D4
Blenheim Gdns
Clapham Pk SW2 160 B5
Dollis Hill NW2 68 C3
Kingston u T KT2 176 D3
Wallington SM6 219 C1
Wembley HA9 66 A5
Blenheim Gr SE15 140 A3
Blenheim Ho
[6] Edmonton N9 18 A1
Hounslow TW3 129 C2
[8] Woolwich SE18 123 A3
Blenheim Par [2] UB10 82 D3
Blenheim Park Rd CR2 221 A1
Blenheim Pas NW8 229 A4
Blenheim Pl TW11 174 D5
Blenheim [26] SW19 156 D3
Blenheim Rd
Acton W4 111 C3
Bromley BR1, BR2 210 A5
Harrow HA2 41 D3
Leyton E15 76 C4
Newham E6 99 D4
Northolt UB5 63 D2
Penge SE20 184 C3
Sidcup DA15 168 C3
St John's Wood NW8 92 A5 229 B4
Sutton SM1 217 D5
Walthamstow E17 53 A6
West Barnes SW20 200 C6
Blenheim Rise N15 51 D5
Blenheim St W1 238 C1
Blenheim Terr NW8 92 A5 229 A4
Blenheim Way TW7 131 A4
Blenkarne Rd SW11 158 D5
Bleriot [27] NW9 27 D1
Bleriot Rd TW5 128 C5
Blessbury Rd HA8 27 A2
Blessed Dominic RC Sch NW9 27 D1
Blessed Sacrament RC Prim Sch N1 94 B6 233 C5
Blessington Cl SE13 142 B2
Blessington Rd SE13 142 B1
Blessing Way IG11 102 C5
Bletchingley Cl CR7 204 D5
Bletchington Ct [2] DA17 125 C2
Bletchley Ct N1 235 C3
Bletchley St N1 95 A5 235 B3
Bletchmore Cl UB3 105 B1
Bletsoe Wlk N1 235 B4
Blewbury Ho [3] SE2 124 C4
Blick Ho [1] SE16 118 C3
Bligh Ho [4] SE27 183 A6
Blincoe Cl SW19 156 D2
Blissett St SE10 142 A4
Blissland Ct [5] N12 30 A4
Bliss Mews [14] W10 91 A4
Blisworth Cl UB4 85 A3
Blisworth Ho [12] E2
Blithbury Rd RM9
Blithdale Rd SE2 1
Blithfield St W8 2
Blockley Rd HA0
Bloemfontein Ave W12 1
Bloemfontein Rd W12 1
Blomfield Ct
Battersea SW11 2
Paddington W9 2
Blomfield Ho [4] E14 1
Blomfield Mans [3] W12 1
Blomfield Rd W9 92 A2 2
Blomfield St EC2 95 B2 2
Blomfield Villas W9 2
Blomville Rd RM8
Blondel St SW11 1
Blondin Ave W5 1
Blondin St E3
Bloomburg St SW1 2
Bloomfield Cres IG2
Bloomfield Ct N6
Bloomfield Ho [10] E1
Bloomfield Pl W1 2
Bloomfield Rd
Bromley Comm BR2 20
Highgate N6
Kingston u T KT1 1
Woolwich SE18 1
Bloomfield Terr SW1 115 A1 2
Bloom Gr SE27 1
Bloomhall Rd SE19 1
Bloom Park Rd SW6 2
BLOOMSBURY
Bloomsbury Cl
Ealing W5 1
Edgware NW7
Bloomsbury Ct
Cranford TW5 1
Leytonstone E11
Pinner HA5
St Giles WC1 2
Bloomsbury Ho [10] SW4 1
Bloomsbury Pl
London SW18 1
St Giles WC1 2
Bloomsbury Sq WC1 94 A2 2
Bloomsbury St WC1 93 D2 2
Bloomsbury Way WC1 94 A2 2
Blore Cl SW8 2
Blore Ct W1 2
Blore Ho SW10 2
Blossom Cl
Dagenham RM9 10
Ealing W5 11
South Croydon CR2 22
Blossom La EN2
Blossom Pl E1 2
Blossom St E1 95 C3 2
Blossom Waye TW5 12
Blossom Way
Hillingdon UB10 6
West Drayton UB7 10
Blount St E14 9
Bloxam Gdns SE9 16
Bloxhall Rd E10 5
Bloxham Cres TW12 17
Bloxworth Cl SM6 21
Blucher Rd SE5 13
Blue Anchor Alley [4] TW9 13
Blue Anchor La SE16 11
Blue Anchor Yd E1 11
Blue Ball Yd SW1 2
Bluebell Ave E12 7
Bluebell Cl
Forest Hill SE26 18
Hackbridge SM6 20
[10] Hackney E9 9
Northolt UB5 6
Orpington BR6 22
Bluebell Ct [4] N12 1
Bluebell Way IG1 7
Blueberry Cl IG8 3
Blueberry Ct
Edgware HA8 2
[3] Enfield EN2
Bluebird La RM10 8
Bluebird Way SE28 12
Bluefield Cl TW12 17
Blue Gate Fields Jun & Inf Schs E1 11
Bluegate Mews E1 11

es
igh KT17 216 A1
don SW19 179 A5
use Rd E4 20 C1
n Pl SE1 263 A6
int Ct 2 HA1 42 D4
nt Apartments
2 159 B4
h The TW7 131 A2
l Cl E8 74 A4
l Rd HA8 27 C3
l St N7 72 A2
n Cl RM8 58 C1
d CR0 221 B3
Ave UB7 126 C5
Rd SE9 166 C6
Rd E5 74 D4
Ct N21 16 B6
itt Town
120 B2
nham TW1 152 D5
Cl SE23 163 B4
Hill SE6 163 B4
Hill La SE6 163 B3
Hill BR5 190 A2
Ho 8 SE11 138 C6
Mews 2
112 D3
ndale Ho 34
96 A5
Rd
113 A3 254 A5
St E2 96 B4
wood Pl 4
182 B6
Vale SE6 163 B3
wood 5 SM1 218 B3
d
ey BR1 186 D2
UB3 105 C4
amstow E17 53 B2
wich SE28 124 C6
Wharf E14 119 A6
wood Rd IG3 58 A2
ood Pk 10
186 D2
ood Rd
n N4 50 A2
HA5 22 D2
Jerusalem Sch
51 B2
s Mews 3
70 B4
ea St N1 233 C5
nan Ave E4 19 D6
nan Cl EN5 13 A6
walk Pl E14 120 A5
ound 25 NW9 27 D1
y Ho SE17 263 A3
nah Wlk 21
138 C3
ouse Ctr The
90 D3
ouse Wlk 24
139 D5
ifter Way 19
119 A2
nker Cl 1 E13 99 A4
n Cl SW4 137 C2
Moore Bridge
HA9 66 C5
arley Way 11
138 C1
hompson Ct
66 D5
ampton Rd
176 B3
ng St E8 96 B6
cott Cl SW19 157 A2
ngton Gdns
110 C4
ngton Ho 2
140 C4
ney Ho 10 SE5 139 C4
n Ho 4 E1 96 A2
m Cl EN1 5 C3
m Ct
enham BR2 208 D5
n SM1 218 B4
m Rd SW16 181 D3
m Way NW10 88 B4
ea Mews TW4 151 C5
gton Ct 2
112 D4
y Cl KT3 199 C4
y Manor Way
160 C4
y Rd KT3 199 C4
in Cl HA2 63 B5
in Gr SM4 201 D4
in 26 NW9 27 D1
in St SW18 157 C3
ant Gdns
0 200 B6
ey Rd E5, E8 74 B3
g Way UB2 106 B3

Boevey Path DA17 125 B1
Bogart Ct 13 E14 119 C6
Bognor Gdns WD19 22 C5
Bognor Rd DA16 146 D4
Bohemia Pl 1 E8 74 B2
Bohn Rd E1 97 A2
Bohun Gr EN4 14 D5
Boileau Par W5 88 B1
Boileau Rd
Barnes SW13 134 B6
Ealing W5 88 B1
Boilerhouse SE1 253 C3
Boisseau Ho 31 E1 96 C2
Bolden St SE8 141 D3
Boldero Pl NW8 237 A5
Bolderwood Way
BR4 223 D6
Boldmere Rd HA5 40 C2
Boleyn Ave EN1 6 B4
Boleyn Ct
Beckenham BR3 186 A2
Buckhurst Hill IG9 21 B3
East Molesey KT8 196 B5
Hayes UB3 105 D4
Walthamstow E17 53 C5
Boleyn Dr
East Molesey KT8 195 B6
Ruislip HA4 62 D6
Boleyn Gdns BR4 223 D6
Boleyn Ground(Upton Park) (West Ham Utd FC) E13, E6 99 D5
Boleyn Rd
Newham E6 99 D5
Stoke Newington N16 73 C3
Upton E7 77 B1
Boleyn Way EN5 2 A2
Bolina Rd SE16 118 C1
Bolingbroke Gr
SW11 158 D5
Bolingbroke Ho
Beckenham BR3 207 A4
Catford BR3 185 D5
Bolingbroke Hospl The
SW11 158 C6
Bolingbroke Rd
W14 112 D3
Bolingbroke Way UB3, UB11 105 B5
Bolingbroke Wlk
SW11 136 C4 267 A2
Bollo Bridge Rd
W3 111 A4
Bollo Ct 2 W3 111 A3
Bollo La W3 110 D3
Bolney Ct KT6 197 D4
Bolney Gate SW7 247 A1
Bolney St
SW8 138 B5 270 C3
Bolsover St
W1 93 B3 238 D5
Bolstead Rd CR4 181 B2
Bolster Gr N22 31 D2
Bolt Ct EC4 241 B1
Boltmore Cl NW4 46 D6
Bolton Cl
Chessington KT9 214 A2
Penge SE20 184 A1
Bolton Cres SE5 138 D5
Bolton Ct SW11 268 B1
Bolton Dr SM4 202 B2
Bolton Gdns
Bromley BR1 186 D4
Kensal Rise NW10 90 D5
Bolton Gdns Mews
SW10 256 A2
Bolton Gdns
South Kensington
SW5 113 D1 255 D2
Teddington TW11 175 A4
Bolton Ho 4 SE10 120 C1
Bolton Pl SW5 256 A2
Bolton Rd
Chessington KT9 214 A2
Chiswick W4 133 A5
Edmonton N18 33 D5
Harlesden NW10 89 C6
Harrow HA1 42 B5
Kilburn NW8 91 D6
Stratford E15 76 D2
Boltons Ct SW5 255 D2
Bolton's La TW6,
UB7 127 A5
Boltons The
Harrow HA1 42 A5
South Kensington
SW10 114 A1 256 A2
6 Stratford E15 76 D2
Wembley HA0 64 D4
Woodford IG8 37 A6
Bolton Studios
SW10 256 B1
Bolton St
W1 115 B5 248 D4
Bolton Wlk N7 72 B6
Bombay Ct 8 SE16 118 C4

Bombay St SE16 118 B2
Bomer Cl UB7 126 C5
Bomore Rd
W11 113 A6 244 A6
Bonar Pl BR7 188 A3
Bonar Rd SE15 140 A5
Bonchester Cl BR7 188 C3
Bonchurch Cl SM2 217 D1
Bonchurch Rd
Ealing W13 109 B5
Kensal Town W10 91 A2
Bond Cl UB7 82 B1
Bond Ct EC4 242 C1
Bondfield Ave UB4 84 A4
Bondfield Rd 4 E6 100 B2
Bond Gdns SM6 219 C4
Bond Ho 4 NW6 91 B5
Bonding Yard Wlk
SE16 119 A3
Bond Prim Sch CR4 180 D1
Bond Rd
Mitcham CR4 180 D1
Surbiton KT6 214 B6
Bond St Chiswick W4 111 B2
Ealing W5 109 D6
Bond Street Sta
W1 93 A1 238 B1
Bond St E15 76 C3
Bondway
SW8 138 A6 270 B6
Boneta Rd SE18 122 B3
Bonfield Rd SE13 142 A1
Bonham Gdns RM8 80 D6
Bonham Ho W11 244 C4
Bonham Rd
Brixton SW2 160 B6
Dagenham RM8 80 D5
Bonheur Rd W4 111 B4
Bonhill St
EC2 95 B3 242 D5
Boniface Gdns HA3 23 D3
Boniface Rd UB10 60 D5
Boniface Wlk HA3 23 D3
Bonington Ho
Enfield EN1 18 A6
Pentonville N1 233 C3
Bonita Mews SE15 140 D2
Bonne Marche Terr
Mews 18 SE27 183 C6
Bonner Hill Rd KT1 198 C6
Bonner Ho 3 SW15 156 A6
Bonner Prim Sch E2 96 C4
Bonner Rd E2 96 C5
Bonnersfield Cl HA1 43 A3
Bonnersfield La
Greenhill HA1 42 D3
Kenton HA1, HA3 43 A3
Bonner St E2 96 C5
Bonneville Gdns
SW4 159 C5
Bonneville Prim Sch
SW4 159 C5
Bonnington Ct 14
UB5 84 D5
Bonnington Ho 9
SM2 217 D2
Bonnington Sq
SW8 138 B6 270 C6
Bonnington Twr
BR2 210 A3
Bonny St NW1 71 C1
Bonser Rd TW1 152 D2
Bonsor Ho SW8 269 B2
Bonsor St SE5 139 C5
Bonthron Ho SW15 134 C3
Bonus Pastor RC Sch
BR1 186 C6
Bonville Gdns 17
NW4 46 A5
Bonville Rd BR1 186 D5
Bookbinder Cotts
N20 14 D1
Booker Cl 11 E3 97 B2
Booker Rd 5 N18 34 A5
Bookham Ct CR4 202 B6
Boone Ct N9 18 C1
Boones Rd SE13 142 C1
Boone St SE13 142 C1
Boord St SE10 120 C3
Boothby Ct E4 20 A1
Boothby Ho 2
SW16 181 C5
Boothby Rd N19 71 D6
Booth Cl
10 Hackney E9 96 B6
Thamesmead SE28 124 B6
Booth Ho
9 Brentford
TW8 131 C5
2 Streatham SW2 160 C4
Booth La EC4 252 A6
Boothman Ho HA3 43 D6
Booth Rd
Croydon CR0 220 D6
Hendon NW9 27 C1
Boothroyd Ho TW7 130 D2
Booth's Pl W1 239 B3

Boot Par HA8 26 C4
Boot St N1 95 C4
Bordars Rd W7 86 D2
Bordars Wlk W7 86 C2
Bordeaux Ho 1 E15 76 C3
Borden Ave EN1 17 B5
Border Cres SE26 184 B5
Border Gate CR4 180 D2
Border Gdns CR0 223 D4
Border Rd SE26 184 B5
Bordesley Rd SM4 201 D5
Bordeston Ct 11
TW8 131 C5
Bordley Ct 4 N20 14 D2
Bordon Wlk 5
SW15 156 A4
Boreas Wlk N1 234 D3
Boreham Ave E16 99 A1
Boreham Cl E11 54 A1
Boreham Rd N22 33 A1
BOREHAMWOOD 11 A5
Boreman Ho 11
SE10 142 A6
Borgard Rd SE18 122 B2
Borkwood Pk BR6 227 D4
Borkwood Way BR6 227 C4
Borland Rd
London SE15 140 C1
Teddington TW11 175 B3
Borneo St SW15 134 C2
Borough High St
SE1 117 B5 252 C4
Borough Hill CR0 220 D5
Borough Mkt* SE1 252 C3
Borough Rd
Hounslow TW7 130 D4
7 Kingston u T KT2 176 C3
Lambeth
SE1 116 D3 261 D6
Mitcham CR4 180 C1
Borough Sq SE1 252 A1
Borough Sta
SE1 117 A4 252 B1
BOROUGH THE 117 A4
Borrett Cl
SE17 117 A1 262 A1
Borrodaile Rd
SW18 157 D5
Borrowdale Ave HA3 25 A1
Borrowdale Cl IG4 56 A5
Borrowdale Ct EN2 5 A4
Borrowdale NW1 232 A1
Borthwick Mews E15 76 C4
Borthwick Rd
Leyton E15 76 C4
London NW9 45 D3
Borthwick St SE8 119 C1
Borwick Ave E17 53 B6
Bosbury Rd SE6 164 A1
Boscastle Rd NW5 71 B5
Boscobel Cl BR1 188 B1
Boscobel Ho 4 E8 74 B2
Boscobel Pl SW1 258 B4
Boscobel St
NW8 92 B3 236 D5
Boscombe Ave E10 54 B2
Boscombe Circus
NW9 27 B1
Boscombe Cl E5 75 A3
Boscombe Gdns
SW16 182 A4
Boscombe Ho CR0 205 B1
Boscombe Rd
Merton SW19 179 D2
North Cheam KT4 200 D1
Shepherd's Bush
W12 112 A4
Streatham SW17 181 A4
Bose Cl N3 29 A2
Bosgrove E4 20 A2
Boss Ho SE1 253 C2
Boss St SE1 253 C2
Bostall Hill SE2 124 B1
Bostall La SE2 124 B1
Bostall Manorway
SE2 124 B2
Bostall Park Ave
DA7 147 A5
Bostall Rd BR5 190 B3
Bostock Ho TW5 129 C6
Boston Bsns Pk W7 108 C3
Boston Ct
South Norwood
SE25 205 D5
Sutton SM2 218 A1
Boston Gdns
Brentford TW8 109 B2
Chiswick W4 133 C6
Boston Gr HA4 39 A3
Boston Ho
24 Camberwell
SE5 139 A3
Earl's Ct SW5 255 D3
Lisson Gr NW1 237 C6
Boston Lo W13 109 C1
Boston Manor Ho
TW8 109 B1

Boston Manor Rd
TW8 109 B1
Boston Manor Sta
TW8 109 A2
Boston Park Rd
TW8 109 C1
Boston Par W7 109 A2
Boston Pl
NW1 92 D3 237 C5
Boston Rd
Burnt Oak HA8 27 A3
Ealing W7 109 A3
Newham E6 100 A4
Thornton Heath CR0 204 C3
Bostonthorpe Rd
W7 108 C4
Boston Vale W7 109 A2
Bosun Cl 22 E14 119 C4
Boswell Ct
Bloomsbury WC1 240 B4
9 Hammersmith
W14 112 D3
Kingston u T KT2 176 C2
Boswell Ho
Bloomsbury WC1 240 B4
Bromley Comm BR2 209 D4
5 Streatham SW16 181 C5
Boswell Rd CR7 205 A5
Boswell St
WC1 94 A2 240 B4
Boswood Ct TW4 129 B2
Bosworth Cl E17 35 B2
Bosworth Ho 4 W10 91 A3
Bosworth Rd
Barnet EN5 1 C2
Dagenham RM10 81 C5
Kensal Town W10 91 A3
Wood Green N11 31 D4
Botany Bay La BR7 189 A1
Botany Cl EN4 2 C1
Boteley Cl E4 20 B2
Botham Cl 6 HA8 27 A3
Botha Rd E13 99 C2
Bothwell Cl E16 98 D2
Bothwell St 4 W6 134 D6
Botolph Alley EC3 253 A6
Botolph La EC3 253 A6
Botsford Rd SW20 179 A1
Bott's Mews W2 91 C1
Botwell Common Rd
UB3 105 C6
Botwell Cres UB3 83 C1
Botwell House RC Prim
Sch UB3 105 D4
Botwell La UB3 105 C6
Boucher Cl TW11 174 D5
Bouchier Ho 6 N2 30 B1
Bough Beech Ct EN3 6 D6
Boughton Ave BR2 208 D2
Boughton Ho
Borough The SE1 252 C2
Bromley BR1 188 A3
Boughton Rd SE28 123 C3
Boulcott St E1 96 D1
Boulevard The
Chelsea SW6 266 B1
4 Upper Tooting
SW17 159 A2
Boullen Ct SM1 218 A4
Boulogne Ho SE1 263 C6
Boulogne Rd CR0 205 A3
Boulter Ho 4 SE14 140 C4
Boulters Ct HA0 65 A4
Boulton Ho TW8 110 A1
Boulton Rd RM8 81 B6
Boultwood Rd E6 100 B1
Bounces La N9 18 B2
Bounces Rd N9 18 C2
Boundaries Mans 3
SW12 159 A3
Boundaries Rd
Feltham TW13 150 C3
Upper Tooting
SW12 159 A3
Boundary Ave E17 53 B2
Boundary Bsns Ct
CR4 202 B6
Boundary Cl
Barnet EN5 1 B4
Ilford IG3 79 C4
Kingston u T KT1 198 D6
Penge SE20 184 A1
Southall UB2 107 C1
Boundary Ct
3 Edmonton N18 33 D4
9 New Southgate
N11 31 B6
Boundary Ho
Balham SW12 159 B3
1 Camberwell SE5 139 A5
Edgware HA8 44 B6
Isleworth TW1 153 B6
15 Notting Hill W11 112 D5
Boundary La
Camberwell SE17 139 A6
Newham E13, E6 99 D3
Boundary Pas E2 243 C6

Boundary Rd
Avery Hill DA15 167 C6
Barking IG11 101 A5
London N2 30 B2
Mitcham SW19 180 B4
Newham E13 99 D4
Pinner HA5 40 D2
Ponders End N9 18 C5
St John's Wood
NW8 92 A6 229 B6
Tottenham N22 33 A1
Wallington SM5,
SM6 219 A1
Walthamstow E17 53 C3
Boundary Road Est
NW8 92 A6 229 A5
Boundary Row SE1 251 C2
Boundary St
E2 95 D3 243 C6
Boundary Way CR0 223 C3
Boundfield Rd SE6 164 C2
Bounds Green Ct
N11 31 D4
Bounds Green Ind Est
N11 31 C4
Bounds Green Jun & Inf
Schs N11 32 A3
Bounds Green Rd
London N11 31 D4
Wood Green N22 32 A3
Bounds Green Sta
N11 31 D3
Bourbon Ho 9 SE6 186 A6
Bourchier St W1 249 C6
Bourdillon Ct 2
SE9 166 A2
Bourdon Pl W1 248 D6
Bourdon Rd SE20 184 C1
Bourdon St
W1 115 B6 248 D5
Bourke Cl
London SW4 160 A5
Willesden NW10 67 C2
Bourlet Cl W1 239 A3
Bourn Ave
Hillingdon UB8 82 C3
New Barnet EN4 14 B6
West Green N15 51 B5
Bournbrook Rd SE3,
SE9 143 D2
Bourne Ave
Hayes UB3 105 B3
Palmers Green N14 16 A2
Ruislip HA4 62 C3
Bourne Cir UB3 105 A3
Bourne Cl
Hinchley Wood
KT7 212 D6
Isleworth TW7 130 C2
Bourne Ct
Chiswick W4 133 A6
Ruislip HA4 62 B3
Wanstead E11 55 A4
Woodford IG8 37 D1
Bourne Dr CR4 180 B1
Bourne Gdns E4 35 D6
Bourne Hill N13 16 B2
Bourne Ho
4 Ashford TW15 170 C5
3 Buckhurst Hill IG9 21 D1
5 Clapham SW4 137 C1
1 Dollis Hill NW2 68 A5
Bourne Mans N13 32 C5
Bournemead Ave
UB5 84 A5
Bournemead Cl UB5 84 A4
Bournemead Way
UB5 84 B5
Bourne Mews W1 238 B1
Bournemouth Cl
SE15 140 A3
Bournemouth Ct 6
SM1 218 A3
Bournemouth Rd
London SE15 140 A3
Merton SW19 179 C2
Bourne Par DA5 169 D4
Bourne Pl W4 111 B1
Bourne Prim Sch
HA4 62 C2
Bourne Rd
Bexley DA5 169 D5
Bromley BR2 209 D5
Hornsey N8 50 A3
Leyton E7, E11 76 D5
Bournes Ho 4 N15 51 C3
Bourneside Cres 6
N14 15 D3
Bourneside Gdns
SE6 186 A5
Bourneside 5 N14 15 D3
Bourne St
Belgravia
SW1 115 A2 258 A3

Bourne St *continued*
Croydon CR0 ... 220 D6
Bourne Terr W2 ... 91 D2
Bourne The N14 ... 16 A3
Bourne Vale BR2 ... 209 A2
Bournevale Rd SW16 ... 182 A6
Bourne View UB6 ... 64 D3
Bourne Way
Cheam SM1 ... 217 B3
Coney Hall BR2, BR4 ... 224 D6
West Ewell KT19 ... 215 A4
Bournewood Rd SE18 ... 146 A5
Bournville Rd SE6 ... 163 C4
Bournwell Cl EN4 ... 2 D3
Bourton Cl UB3 ... 106 A5
Bousfield Prim Sch SW10 ... 114 A1 256 A2
Bousfield Rd SE14 ... 140 D3
Boutcher CE Prim Sch SE1 ... 117 D2 263 C4
Boutflower Rd SW11 ... 136 C1
Bouverie Ct 4 SW16 ... 182 A5
Bouverie Gdns HA3 ... 43 D3
Bouverie Mews N16 ... 73 C6
Bouverie Pl W2 ... 236 D2
Bouverie Rd
Harrow HA1 ... 42 A3
Stoke Newington N16 ... 73 C6
Bouverie St EC4 ... 94 C1 241 B1
Bouvier Rd EN3 ... 6 C5
Boveney Rd SE23 ... 162 D4
Bovill Rd SE23 ... 162 D4
Bovingdon Ave HA9 ... 66 C2
Bovingdon Cl 4 N19 ... 71 C6
Bovingdon La NW9 ... 27 C2
Bovingdon Rd SW6 ... 135 D4 265 D1
Bovril Ho EN1 ... 5 C2
BOW ... 97 B5
Bowater Cl
Clapham Pk SW2 ... 160 A5
Kingsbury NW9 ... 45 B4
Bowater Gdns TW16 ... 172 C2
Bowater Ho EC1 ... 242 B5
Bowater Pl SE3 ... 143 B5
Bowater Rd
Greenwich SE18 ... 121 D3
Wembley HA9 ... 66 D5
Bow Brook The 20 E2 ... 96 D5
Bow Church Sta E3 ... 97 C4
BOW COMMON ... 97 D2
Bow Common La E3 ... 97 B3
Bowden Cl TW14 ... 149 C3
Bowden Ct HA4 ... 62 C3
Bowden Ho 20 E3 ... 97 D4
Bowden House Hospl (Private) HA1 ... 64 C6
Bowden St SE11 ... 116 C1 261 B1
Bowditch SE8 ... 119 B1
Bowdon Rd E17 ... 53 C2
Bowen Ct 2 N5 ... 72 D4
Bowen Dr SE21 ... 161 C1
Bowen Rd HA1 ... 42 A2
Bowen St E14 ... 97 D1
Bower Ave SE3 ... 142 C5
Bower Cl UB5 ... 84 C5
Bowerdean St SW6 ... 135 D3
Bower Ho SE14 ... 140 D4
Bowerman Ave SE14 ... 141 A6
Bowerman Ct 1 N19 ... 71 D6
Bowers Ho 5 IG11 ... 78 D1
Bower St E1 ... 96 D1
Bowers Wlk 1 E6 ... 100 B1
Bowery Ct 16 RM10 ... 81 D2
Bowes Cl DA15 ... 168 B5
Bowes Ho N13 ... 32 B5
Bowes-Lyon Hall 13 E16 ... 121 A5
Bowes Lyon Ho 2 TW10 ... 153 C1
BOWES PARK ... 32 A4
Bowes Park Sta N22 ... 32 A3
Bowes Prim Sch N11 ... 31 D5
Bowes Rd Acton W3 ... 111 C6
Dagenham RM8 ... 80 C4
New Southgate N11 ... 31 C5
Bowes Rd (North Circular Rd) N13 ... 32 A5
Bowes Rd KT12 ... 194 B1
Bowfell Rd W6 ... 134 C6
Bowford Ave DA7 ... 147 A4
Bowhill Cl SW9 ... 138 C5
Bow Ho 1 E3 ... 97 C4
Bowie Cl SW4 ... 159 D4
Bow Ind Pk E15 ... 75 C1
Bow La
Barbican EC2, EC4 ... 95 A1 242 B1
Finchley N12 ... 30 A3
Bowland Ho N4 ... 51 A2
Bowland Rd
London SW4 ... 137 D1
Woodford IG8 ... 37 C4
Bowland Yd SW1 ... 247 D1
Bowl Ct EC2 ... 243 B5
Bowles Ct
Finchley N12 ... 30 C3
Harrow HA3 ... 43 A3
Bowles Rd 1 SE1 ... 140 A6
Bowley Cl SE19 ... 183 D4
Bowley Ho 6 SE16 ... 118 A3
Bowley La SE19 ... 183 D5
Bowling Cl UB10 ... 82 B6
Bowling Green Cl SW19 ... 156 B4
Bowling Green Ct HA9 ... 66 B6
Bowling Green Ho SW10 ... 266 C4
Bowling Green La EC1 ... 94 C3 241 B6
Bowling Green Pl SE1 ... 252 C2
Bowling Green Row 1 SE18 ... 122 B2
Bowling Green St SE11 ... 138 C6
Bowling Green Wlk N1 ... 95 C4
Bowls Cl HA7 ... 25 B5
Bowman Ave E16 ... 120 D6
Bowman Homes W5 ... 109 D4
Bowman Mews
St George in t East E1 ... 118 A6
Wandsworth SW18 ... 157 B3
Bowmans Cl W13 ... 109 B5
Bowmans Lea SE23 ... 162 C4
Bowman's Meadow SM6 ... 219 B5
Bowman's Mews N7 ... 72 A5
Bowman's Pl N7 ... 72 A5
Bowman Trad Est NW9 ... 44 C5
Bowmar Lo 13 EN5 ... 1 D1
Bowmead SE9 ... 166 B2
Bowmore Wlk NW1 ... 71 D1
Bowness Cl 5 E8 ... 73 D2
Bowness Cres KT2, SW15 ... 177 C5
Bowness Dr TW4 ... 129 A1
Bowness Ho SE15 ... 140 C5
Bowness Rd
Catford SE6 ... 163 D4
Erith DA7 ... 147 D3
Bowood Rd
Clapham SW11 ... 159 A6
Enfield EN3 ... 6 D3
Bow Rd E3 ... 97 C4
Bowring Gn WD19 ... 22 C5
Bow Road Sta E3 ... 97 C4
Bowrons Ave HA0 ... 65 D1
Bowry Ho 14 E14 ... 97 B2
Bow Sch E3 ... 97 C4
Bowsley Ct TW13 ... 150 A2
Bowsprit Point 1 E14 ... 119 C3
Bowstead Ct SW11 ... 266 D1
Bow St
St Giles WC2 ... 94 A1 240 B1
Stratford E15 ... 76 C3
Bow Triangle Bsns Ctr 17 E3 ... 97 C3
Bowyer Cl E6 ... 100 B2
Bowyer Ct 4 E4 ... 20 A3
Bowyer Ho
Mitcham CR4 ... 202 C6
27 Shoreditch N1 ... 95 C6
Wandsworth SW18 ... 157 D5
Bowyer Pl SE5 ... 139 A5
Bowyer St 15 SE5 ... 139 A5
Boxall Rd SE21 ... 161 C5
Box Cnr TW2 ... 152 C2
Box Elder Cl HA8 ... 27 A5
Boxgrove Prim Sch SE2 ... 124 C3
Boxgrove Rd SE2 ... 124 C3
Box La IG11 ... 102 C5
Boxley Ho 3 E5 ... 74 B3
Boxley Rd SM4 ... 202 A5
Boxley St E16 ... 121 B5
Boxmoor Ho
16 Hackney E2 ... 96 A6
9 Shepherd's Bush W11 ... 112 D5
Boxmoor Rd HA3 ... 43 B5
Boxoll Rd RM9 ... 81 B5
Boxshall Ho 7 SE18 ... 144 D6
Box Tree Ho SE8 ... 119 A1
Boxtree La HA3 ... 24 B3
Boxtree Rd HA3 ... 24 B3
Boxwood Cl UB7 ... 104 B4
Boxworth Cl N12 ... 30 B5
Boxworth Gr N1 ... 94 B6 233 D6
Boyard Rd SE18 ... 122 D1
Boyce Ho
Streatham SW16 ... 181 C5
1 West Kilburn W10 ... 91 B4
Boyce Way E13 ... 99 A3
Boycroft Ave NW9 ... 45 A3
Boyd Ave UB1 ... 107 B5
Boyd Cl KT2 ... 176 C3
Boyd Ct SW15 ... 156 C5
Boydell Ct NW8 ... 70 B1
Boyden Ho 8 E17 ... 54 A6
Boyd Rd SW19 ... 180 B4
Boyd St E1 ... 96 A1
Boyfield St SE1 ... 116 D4 251 D1
Boyland Rd BR1 ... 186 D5
Boyle Ave HA7 ... 25 A4
Boyle Cl UB10 ... 82 B5
Boyle Farm Rd KT7 ... 197 A3
Boyle Ho
13 Belvedere DA17 ... 125 C3
Wembley HA9 ... 66 D5
Boyle St W1 ... 249 A6
Boyne Ave NW4 ... 46 D5
Boyne Ct NW10 ... 68 A1
Boyne Ho 10 E5 ... 74 B6
Boyne Rd
Dagenham RM10 ... 81 C5
Lewisham SE13 ... 142 B2
Boyne Terr Mews W11 ... 113 B5 244 C4
Boyson Rd 10 SE17 ... 139 B6
Boyton Cl London N8 ... 50 A6
Stepney E1 ... 96 D3
Boyton Ho
Kennington SE11 ... 261 A1
St John's Wood NW8 ... 229 D4
Boyton Rd N8 ... 50 A6
Brabant Ct EC3 ... 253 A6
Brabant Rd N22 ... 32 B1
Brabazon Ave SM6 ... 220 A1
Brabazon Rd
Heston TW5 ... 128 D5
Northolt UB5 ... 85 C5
Brabazon St E14 ... 97 D2
Brabner Ho 3 E2 ... 96 A4
Brabourne Cl 7 SE19 ... 183 C5
Brabourne Cres DA7 ... 147 B6
Brabourne Hts NW7 ... 11 C1
Brabourne Rise BR3 ... 208 B4
Brabourn Gr SE15 ... 140 C3
Brabrook Ct SM6 ... 219 B3
Brabstone Ho 2 UB6 ... 86 D5
Bracer Ho 1 N1 ... 95 C5
Bracewell Ave UB6 ... 65 A2
Bracewell Rd W10 ... 90 C2
Bracewood Gdns CR0 ... 221 D5
Bracey Mews 1 N4 ... 72 A6
Bracey St N4 ... 72 A6
Bracken Ave
Balham SW12 ... 159 A4
Croydon CR0 ... 223 C5
Brackenbridge Dr HA4 ... 62 D5
Brackenbury Gdns W6 ... 112 B3
Brackenbury N4 ... 50 B1
Brackenbury Prim Sch W6 ... 112 B3
Brackenbury Rd
East Finchley N2 ... 48 A6
Hammersmith W6 ... 112 B3
Bracken Cl
Ashford TW16 ... 171 D4
Newham E6 ... 100 B2
Twickenham TW4 ... 151 C4
Brackendale Cl TW5 ... 129 D4
Brackendale Ct 2 BR3 ... 185 C3
Brackendale
Kingston u T KT1 ... 176 D1
Southgate N21 ... 16 B2
Bracken End TW7 ... 152 B6
Brackenfield Cl E5 ... 74 B5
Bracken Gdns SW13 ... 134 A3
Bracken Hill Cl 5 BR1 ... 186 D2
Bracken Hill La BR1 ... 186 D2
Brackenhill HA4 ... 63 A4
Bracken Ho 16 E3 ... 97 C2
Bracken Mews
Chingford E4 ... 20 A3
Bracken Mews *continued*
Romford RM7 ... 59 D3
Brackens BR3 ... 185 C3
Brackens The EN1 ... 17 C4
Bracken The E4 ... 20 A2
Brackenwood Lo EN5 ... 1 C1
Brackenwood TW16 ... 172 A2
Brackley Ave SE15 ... 140 C2
Brackley Cl SM6 ... 220 A1
Brackley Ct NW8 ... 236 D6
Brackley Rd
Beckenham BR3 ... 185 C3
Chiswick W4 ... 111 C1
Brackley Sq IG8 ... 37 D3
Brackley St EC1 ... 242 B4
Brackley Terr 6 W4 ... 111 C1
Bracklyn Ct N1 ... 235 C4
Bracklyn St N1 ... 235 C4
Bracknell Cl N22 ... 32 C2
Bracknell Gate NW3 ... 69 D3
Bracknell Gdns NW3 ... 69 D4
Bracknell Way NW3 ... 69 D4
Bracondale KT10 ... 212 A3
Bracondale Rd SE2 ... 124 A2
Braconhyrst HA1 ... 42 C2
Bradbeer Ho 24 E2 ... 96 C4
Bradbourne Ct 11 SM2 ... 217 D2
Bradbourne Rd DA5 ... 169 C4
Bradbourne St SW6 ... 135 C3
Bradbury Cl UB2 ... 107 B2
Bradbury Ct
4 Barnet EN5 ... 1 D1
2 Greenwich SE3 ... 143 A5
Merton SW20 ... 178 C1
Bradbury Ho E1 ... 243 D2
Bradbury St 28 N16 ... 73 C3
Bradby Ho NW8 ... 91 D5
Braddock Cl TW7 ... 130 D3
Braddon Rd TW9 ... 132 B2
Braddyll St SE10 ... 120 C1
Bradenham Ave DA16 ... 146 A1
Bradenham Cl SE17 ... 139 B6
Bradenham Rd
Harrow HA3 ... 43 B5
Hayes UB4 ... 83 C4
Bradenham 11 SE17 ... 139 B6
Braden St W9 ... 91 D3
Bradfield Ct 14 NW1 ... 71 B1
Bradfield Dr IG11 ... 80 A3
Bradfield Ho 15 SW8 ... 137 D3
Bradfield Rd
Newham E16 ... 121 B4
Ruislip HA4 ... 63 A3
Bradford Cl
Bromley BR2 ... 210 B1
Forest Hill SE26 ... 184 B6
Tottenham N17 ... 33 D4
Bradford Dr KT19 ... 215 D2
Bradford Ho 4 W14 ... 112 D3
Bradford Rd
Acton W3 ... 111 C4
Ilford IG1 ... 57 C1
Bradgate Rd SE6 ... 163 D5
Brading Cres E11 ... 77 B6
Brading Rd
Streatham SW2 ... 160 B4
Thornton Heath CR0 ... 204 B3
Brading Terr W12 ... 112 A3
Bradiston Rd W9 ... 91 B4
Bradley Cl N7 ... 72 B2
Bradley Ct CR0 ... 220 C4
Bradley Gdns W13 ... 87 B1
Bradley Ho
Bermondsey SE16 ... 118 B2
1 Bromley E3 ... 97 D4
Twickenham TW1 ... 152 D3
Woodford IG8 ... 37 A3
Bradley Mews SW12 ... 158 D3
Bradley Rd Enfield EN3 ... 7 A6
South Norwood SE19 ... 183 A4
Wood Green N22 ... 32 B1
Bradley's Cl N1 ... 234 B4
Bradley Stone Rd E6 ... 100 B2
Bradlord Ho SE21 ... 161 C1
Bradman Row 7 HA8 ... 27 A3
Bradmead SW8 ... 137 C5 269 A3
Bradmore Ct 2 EN3 ... 7 A2
Bradmore Park Rd W6 ... 112 B2
Bradon 24 NW9 ... 27 D1
Bradshaw Cl SW19 ... 179 C4
Bradshaw Dr NW7 ... 28 D3
Bradshawe Waye UB8 ... 82 B2
Bradshaws Cl SE25 ... 206 A6
Bradsole Ho 13 BR3 ... 185 C3
Bradstock Ho E9 ... 75 A1
Bradstock Rd
Homerton E9 ... 74 D2
Stoneleigh KT17 ... 216 B3
Brad St SE1 ... 116 C5 251 B3
Bradwell Ave RM10 ... 81 C6
Bradwell Cl E18 ... 54 D5
Bradwell Ho
8 Kilburn NW6 ... 91 D6
9 Walthamstow E17 ... 53 D6
Bradwell Mews 5 N18 ... 34 A6
Brady Ct RM8 ... 58 D1
Brady Dr BR1 ... 210 C6
Brady Ho
London SW4 ... 159 D6
South Lambeth SW8 ... 269 B2
Bradymead E6 ... 100 D1
Brady St E1 ... 96 B3
Braeburn Ct 1 EN4 ... 2 C1
Brae Ct
2 Kingston u T KT2 ... 176 C2
South Norwood SE25 ... 183 C2
Braefoot Ct SW15 ... 156 D6
Braemar Ave
Thornton Heath CR7 ... 204 D6
Welsh Harp NW10 ... 67 B6
Wembley HA0 ... 66 A1
Wimbledon SW18, SW19 ... 157 C2
Wood Green N22 ... 32 A2
Braemar Ct
4 Brentford TW8 ... 131 D6
5 Catford SE6 ... 164 D3
Braemar Gdns
Hendon NW9 ... 27 B2
Longlands DA15 ... 167 B1
West Wickham BR4 ... 208 A1
Braemar Ho
Richmond TW11 ... 175 B5
St John's Wood W9 ... 229 A1
Braemar Mans W8 ... 255 D5
Braemar SW15 ... 156 D5
Braemar Rd
Brentford TW8 ... 131 D6
Newham E13 ... 98 D3
North Cheam KT4 ... 216 B5
South Tottenham N15 ... 51 C4
Braemore Ct EN4 ... 3 A1
Braeside Ave SW19 ... 179 A2
Braeside BR3 ... 185 D5
Braeside Cl HA5 ... 23 C3
Braeside Rd SW16 ... 181 C3
Braeside Sch
Buckhurst Hill IG9 ... 21 B3
Buckhurst Hill IG9 ... 21 C2
Braes St N1 ... 72 D1
Braesyde Cl DA17 ... 125 B2
Brafferton Rd CR0 ... 221 A4
Braganza St SE17 ... 116 D1 261 C1
Bragg Cl RM8 ... 80 B2
Bragg Rd TW11 ... 174 D4
Braham Ho SE11 ... 260 D1
Braham St E1 ... 243 D2
Brahma Kumaris World Spiritual Univ NW10 ... 68 A1
Braid Ave W3 ... 89 C1
Braid Cl TW13 ... 151 B2
Braid Ho SE10 ... 142 A4
Braidwood Ho 2 CR7 ... 204 D5
Braidwood Rd SE6 ... 164 B3
Braidwood St SE1 ... 117 C5 253 A3
Braikenridge Ho N21 ... 17 B5
Brailsford Cl SW19 ... 180 C3
Brailsford Rd SW2 ... 160 C5
Braintcroft Prim Sch NW2 ... 67 D5
Brainton Ave TW14 ... 150 C4
Braintree Ave IG4 ... 56 A5
Braintree Ho 6 E1 ... 96 C3
Braintree Ind Est HA4 ... 62 B4
Braintree Rd
Dagenham RM10 ... 81 C5
Ruislip HA4 ... 62 B4
Braintree St E2 ... 96 C4
Braithwaite Ave RM7 ... 59 C2
Braithwaite Gdns HA7 ... 25 C2
Braithwaite Ho EC1 ... 242 C6
Braithwaite Rd EN3 ... 7 B2
Braithwaite Twr W2 ... 236 C4
Brake Shear Ho 1 EN5 ... 1 B2
Bramah Gn SW9 ... 138 C4
Bramah Mus of Tea & Coffee* SE1 ... 252 B3
Bramalea Cl N6 ... 49 A3
Bramall Cl E15 ... 76 D3
Bramall Ct N7
Bramber Ct TW8
Bramber Ho 9 KT2
Bramber Rd
Colney Hatch N12
Fulham W14 ... 135 B6
Bramber WC1
Bramble Acres Cl SM2
Bramblebury Rd SE18
Bramble Cl
Beckenham BR3
Croydon CR0
Hillingdon UB8
South Tottenham N15
Stanmore HA7
Upper Halliford TW17
Brambledown Cl BR2, BR4
Brambledown 8 N4
Brambledown Rd
South Croydon CR2
Wallington SM5, SM6
Bramble Gdns W12
Bramble Ho 16 E3
Bramble La TW12
Brambles Cl TW7, TW8
Brambles Farm Dr UB10
Brambles The
West Drayton UB7
8 Wimbledon SW19
Bramblewood Cl SM5
Brambling Ct
25 Deptford SE8
South Norwood SE25
Bramblings The E4
Bramcote Ave CR4
Bramcote Ct CR4
Bramcote Gr SE16
Bramcote Rd SW15
Bramdean Cres SE12
Bramdean Gdns SE12
Bramerton NW6
Bramerton Rd BR3
Bramerton St SW3 ... 136 C6
Bramfield Ct N4
Bramfield Rd SW11
Bramford Ct N14
Bramford Rd SW18
Bramham Gdns
Chessington KT9
South Kensington SW5 ... 113 D1
Bramham Ho SE22
Bramhope La SE7
Bramlands Cl SW11
Bramley Ave TW17
Bramley Cl
Croydon CR2
East Barnet N14
Hayes UB3
Higham Hill E17
Orpington BR6
Pinner HA5
Twickenham TW2
Woodford IG8
Bramley Cres
Ilford IG2
Nine Elms SW8 ... 137 D5
Bramley Ct
2 Barnet EN4
9 Chingford E4
Dollis Hill NW2
Feltham TW14
Hither Green SE13
Mitcham CR4
Southall UB1
Wallington SM6
Welling DA16
Bramley Gdns WD19
Bramley Hill CR2
Bramley Ho
Hounslow TW3
Ilford IG2
1 Kingston u T KT2
19 North Kensington W10
Roehampton SW15
Bramley House Ct EN2
Bramleyhyrst CR2
Bramley Lo HA0

ey Rd
W5 ... 109 C3
Kensington
0 ... 90 D1
gate N14 ... 15 C6
n SM1 ... 218 B3
ey Way
slow TW4 ... 151 B6
Wickham BR4 ... 223 D6
oton Cl 14 E5 ... 74 B6
oton Coll NW4 ... 46 C5
oton Ct NW4 ... 46 B5
oton Gr
w HA3 ... 43 B5
on NW4 ... 46 C5
bley HA9 ... 44 C1
oton La 6 NW4 ... 46 C5
oton Lo DA7 ... 146 D5
oton Manor Sch
... 99 D3
oton Park Rd
... 50 C6
oton Prim Sch
y DA7 ... 146 D3
am E6 ... 100 A4
pton Rd
yheath DA7 ... 147 A4
don CR0 ... 205 D3
ngay N15 ... 51 A4
gdon UB10 ... 82 D5
am E6 ... 99 D4
nsbury NW9 ... 44 C5
pton WC1 ... 240 C3
shaw Gdns
9 ... 22 D5
shaw Rd E9 ... 74 D2
shaw Rise KT3 ... 199 C3
shill Gdns NW5 ... 71 B5
shill Rd NW10 ... 89 D5
shot Ave SE7 ... 143 B6
shott Ct 3
... 198 A3
shurst NW8 ... 91 D6
ston Rd
esden NW10 ... 90 A5
dsworth SW17 ... 158 A1
well Cl TW16 ... 172 D1
well Ho
ugh The SE1 ... 262 B5
sea SW1 ... 269 A6
well Mews N1 ... 233 D6
caster Dr NW7 ... 28 A3
caster Ho
Globe Town E1 ... 96 D4
ngton N5 ... 72 D3
caster Rd
d E12 ... 78 B4
bury Pk IG2 ... 57 C3
atham SW16 ... 160 A1
cepeth Gdns
... 21 A2
ch Hill NW3 ... 70 A5
ch Ho 13 SM1 ... 218 A4
ch Pl N1 ... 95 B6 235 D6
ch Rd E14 ... 119 A6
ch St SE15 ... 139 C5
cker Rd HA3 ... 43 D6
croft Way EN3 ... 7 B4
dan Ho 11 HA1 ... 42 D4
d Cl N4 ... 50 D1
den Lo 13 W4 ... 111 A1
dlehow Rd
5 ... 135 B1
don Ho BR3 ... 185 D5
don Mews
bican EC2 ... 242 C4
worth SE17 ... 262 B3
don Pl N8 ... 50 B5
don Rd
nsbury N7 ... 72 A1
thall UB2 ... 107 B1
on SM1 ... 217 D4
thamstow E17 ... 54 A6
don St
7 ... 117 A2 262 B3
dram Rd SE13 ... 142 C1
drams Wharf
5 ... 118 C4
dreth Ct HA1 ... 42 D3
dreth Rd
ham E6 ... 100 B1
er Tooting SW17 ... 159 B2
dries The SM6 ... 219 D5
d St SE10 ... 142 A5
dville Gdns IG6 ... 56 D5
dville Rd UB7 ... 104 A4
dy Way SM2 ... 217 C1
gbourne Rd
... 186 A5
gton Rd SE11 ... 260 D1
gwyn Cres
9 ... 180 B1
gwyn Ct W14 ... 254 A5
ham Ho 1
... 122 D1
ksea St
5 ... 135 A5 264 A3

Branksome Ave N18 ... 33 D5
Branksome Cl
Teddington TW11 ... 174 B6
Walton-on-T KT12 ... 194 D1
Branksome Ct 6 N2 ... 48 A6
Branksome Ho SW8 ... 270 C4
Branksome Rd
London SW2 ... 160 A6
Merton SW19 ... 179 C2
Branksome Way
Harrow HA3 ... 44 B3
Kingston u T KT3 ... 177 B2
Bransby Ct 4 N16 ... 73 C4
Bransby Rd KT9 ... 214 A2
Branscombe Ct
BR2 ... 208 C4
Branscombe Gdns
N21 ... 16 C4
Branscombe NW1 ... 232 B5
Branscombe St
SE13 ... 141 D2
Bransdale Cl NW6 ... 91 C6
Bransgrove Rd HA8 ... 26 B3
Branston Cres BR5 ... 211 B1
Branstone Ct 9
TW9 ... 132 B4
Branstone Rd TW9 ... 132 B4
Branston Ho N7 ... 72 C3
Brants Wlk W7 ... 86 C3
Brantwood Ave
Erith DA8 ... 147 D5
Isleworth TW7 ... 131 A1
Brantwood Cl E17 ... 53 D6
Brantwood Gdns
Enfield EN2 ... 16 A6
Redbridge IG4 ... 56 A5
Brantwood Ho 9
SE5 ... 139 A5
Brantwood Rd
Erith DA7 ... 147 D3
Herne Hill SE24 ... 161 A6
Tottenham N17 ... 34 A4
Brasenose Dr SW13 ... 134 C6
Brasher Cl UB6 ... 64 B3
Brashley Road Cvn Site
NW10 ... 89 C4
Brassett Point 3
E15 ... 98 C6
Brassey Cl TW14 ... 150 A3
Brassey Ho
1 Millwall E14 ... 119 D2
Walton-on-T KT12 ... 194 A1
Brassey Rd NW6 ... 69 B2
Brassey Sq SW11 ... 137 A2
Brassie Ave W3 ... 89 C1
Brass Talley Alley 31
SE16 ... 118 D4
Brasted Cl
Bexley DA6 ... 168 D6
Forest Hill SE26 ... 184 C6
Brasted Lo 11 BR3 ... 185 C3
Brathay NW1 ... 232 B3
Brathway Rd SW18 ... 157 C4
Bratley St 11 E1 ... 96 A3
Bratten Ct CR0 ... 205 B3
Braund Ave UB6 ... 85 D3
Braundton Ave
DA15 ... 167 D3
Braunston Dr UB4 ... 85 A3
Braunston Ho TW8 ... 131 C6
Bravington Cl TW17 ... 192 B4
Bravington Pl W9 ... 91 B3
Bravington Rd W9 ... 91 B4
Brawne Ho 12 SE17 ... 138 D6
Braxfield Rd SE4 ... 141 B1
Braxted Pk SW16 ... 182 B4
Brayard's Rd SE15 ... 140 B3
Braybourne Dr
TW7 ... 130 D5
Braybrooke Gdns
SE19 ... 183 C3
Braybrook St W12 ... 89 D1
Brayburne Ave SW4 ... 137 C3
Braycourt Ave KT12 ... 194 C2
Bray Cres SE16 ... 118 D4
Bray Ct
Chessington KT9 ... 214 B3
Streatham SW16 ... 182 A5
Braydon Rd N16 ... 52 A1
Bray Dr E16 ... 120 D6
Brayfield Terr N1 ... 72 C1
Brayford Sq 12 E1 ... 96 C1
Bray NW3 ... 70 C1
Bray Pl SW3 ... 114 D2 257 C3
Bray Rd NW7 ... 28 D4
Brayton Gdns EN2 ... 3 D1
Braywick Ct 9 KT2 ... 176 C3
Braywood Rd SE9 ... 145 B1
Brazier Cres UB5 ... 85 B3
Brazil Cl CR0 ... 204 A2
Breach La RM9 ... 103 C4
Bread St EC2, EC4 ... 242 B1
Breakspeare SE21 ... 161 D1
Breakspear Jun & Inf
Schs UB10 ... 60 C6
Breakspear Rd N
UB9 ... 38 B5

Breakspear Rd HA4,
UB9 ... 38 D3
Breakspear Rd S UB9,
UB10 ... 38 C1
Breakspears Dr
BR5 ... 190 A2
Breakspears Mews
SE4 ... 141 C3
Breakspears Rd
SE4 ... 141 C2
Breakwell Ct 16 W10 ... 91 A3
Bream Cl N17 ... 52 B5
Bream Gdns E6 ... 100 C4
Breamore Cl SW15 ... 156 A3
Breamore Ct IG3 ... 80 A6
Breamore Ho 21
SE15 ... 140 A5
Breamore Rd IG3 ... 79 D6
Bream's Bldgs
EC4 ... 94 C1 241 A2
Bream St E3 ... 75 C1
Breamwater Gdns
TW10 ... 153 B1
Brearley Cl
Burnt Oak HA8 ... 27 A3
Uxbridge UB8 ... 60 A2
Breaside Prep Sch
BR1 ... 187 D2
Breasley Cl SW15 ... 134 B1
Brechin Pl
SW7 ... 114 A2 256 B3
Brecknock Prim Sch
N7 ... 71 D2
Brecknock Rd N19 ... 71 D3
Breckonmead BR1 ... 187 C1
Brecon Cl
Mitcham CR4 ... 204 A6
North Cheam KT4 ... 216 C6
Brecon Ct
7 Eltham SE9 ... 166 C5
Whetstone N12 ... 14 A1
Brecon Gn NW9 ... 45 C3
Brecon Ho
Stamford Hill N16 ... 51 D1
Wandsworth SW18 ... 157 C4
Brecon Rd Enfield EN3 ... 6 C1
Fulham W6 ... 135 A6 264 B5
Brede Cl E6 ... 100 C4
Bredel Ho 1 E14 ... 97 C2
Bredgar SE13 ... 163 D6
Bredgar Rd N19 ... 71 C6
Bredhurst Cl SE20 ... 184 C4
Bredinghurst SE22 ... 162 A4
Bredinghurst Sch
SE15 ... 140 D1
Bredin Ho SW10 ... 265 D4
Bredo Ho IG11 ... 102 B4
Bredon Ct HA8 ... 26 B6
Bredon Rd CR0 ... 205 D2
Breer St SW6 ... 135 D2
Breezer's Ct 22 E1 ... 118 A6
Breezer's Hill E1 ... 118 A6
Brehon Ho NW1 ... 232 A5
Brember Rd HA2 ... 64 A6
Bremer Mews E17 ... 53 D5
Bremner Rd SW7 ... 256 B6
Brenchley Cl
Chislehurst BR7 ... 188 C2
Hayes BR2 ... 208 D3
Brenchley Gdns SE15,
SE22, SE23 ... 162 D5
Brenchley Rd BR5 ... 189 D1
Bren Ct 27 EN3 ... 7 C6
Brenda Rd SW17 ... 158 D2
Brende Gdns KT8 ... 195 D5
Brendon Ave NW10 ... 67 C4
Brendon Cl
Esher KT10 ... 212 A2
Harlington UB7 ... 127 A5
Brendon Ct
3 London N20 ... 14 C2
Southall UB2 ... 107 D2
Brendon Dr KT10 ... 212 A2
Brendon Gdns
Harrow HA2 ... 63 D4
Ilford IG2 ... 57 C4
Brendon Gr N2 ... 30 A1
Brendon Ho
Marylebone W1 ... 238 A4
Sutton SM2 ... 218 A2
Brendon Rd
Dagenham RM8 ... 59 C1
New Eltham SE9 ... 167 B2
Brendon St
W1 ... 92 C1 237 B2
Brendon Villas N21 ... 17 A3
Brendon Way EN1 ... 17 C4
Brenley Cl CR4 ... 203 A6
Brenley Gdns SE9 ... 143 D1
Brenley Ho SE1 ... 252 C2
Brennands Ct 10 N19 ... 71 C5
Brent Adult Comm
Education Service
Coll NW10 ... 89 B6
Brent Cl DA5 ... 169 A3
Brentcot Cl W13 ... 87 B3
Brent Cres NW10 ... 88 B5

Brent Cross Flyover NW2,
NW4 ... 46 D2
Brent Cross Gdns
NW4 ... 46 D3
Brent Cross
Interchange NW2,
NW4 ... 46 D2
Brent Cross Sh Ctr
NW4 ... 46 C2
Brent Cross Sta
NW11 ... 46 D2
Brent Ct
5 Acton W12 ... 111 C3
Ealing W7 ... 108 B6
Hendon NW11 ... 46 D2
Brentfield Cl NW10 ... 67 B2
Brentfield Gdns
NW2 ... 46 D2
Brentfield Ho 7
NW10 ... 67 B1
Brentfield Prim Sch
NW10 ... 67 B2
Brentfield Rd NW10 ... 67 B2
Brentfield NW10 ... 66 D1
BRENTFORD ... 131 B6
Brentford Bsns Ctr
TW8 ... 131 C5
Brentford Cl UB4 ... 84 D3
BRENTFORD END ... 131 C4
Brentford Fountain L
Ctr W4 ... 110 C1
Brentford Ho 6
TW1 ... 153 B4
Brentford Sch for Girls
TW8 ... 131 D6
Brentford Sta TW8 ... 131 C6
Brent Gn NW4 ... 46 D4
Brentham Way W5 ... 87 D3
Brent Ho
3 Catford BR1 ... 186 B5
16 Hackney E9 ... 74 C2
Brenthouse Rd E9 ... 74 C2
Brent Ho HA9 ... 66 B3
Brenthurst Rd NW10 ... 67 D2
Brent Knoll Sch
SE26 ... 162 D1
Brent Lea TW8 ... 131 C5
Brent Mans NW4 ... 46 C4
Brentmead Cl W7 ... 108 C6
Brentmead Gdns
NW10 ... 88 B5
Brentmead Pl NW11 ... 46 D3
Brent Mus* NW10 ... 68 B2
Brent New Ent Ctr
NW10 ... 67 D2
Brenton Ct E9 ... 75 A3
Brenton St E14 ... 97 A1
Brent Park Ind Est
UB2 ... 106 C3
Brent Park Rd NW4 ... 46 B2
Brent Pl EN5 ... 13 B6
Brent Rd
Brentford TW8 ... 131 C6
Newham E16 ... 99 A2
Southall UB2 ... 106 C3
Woolwich SE18 ... 144 D5
Brentside TW8 ... 131 C6
Brentside Cl W13 ... 87 A3
Brentside Executive Ctr
TW8 ... 131 B6
Brentside High Sch
W7 ... 86 C3
Brentside Prim Sch
W7 ... 86 C3
Brent St NW4 ... 46 C4
Brent Trad Est NW10 ... 67 C3
Brentvale Ave
Southall UB1 ... 108 B5
Wembley HA0 ... 88 B6
Brent View Rd NW9 ... 46 A2
Brentwaters Bsns Pk
TW8 ... 131 C5
Brent Way
Brentford TW8 ... 131 D5
Finchley N3 ... 29 C4
Wembley HA9 ... 66 D2
Brentwick Gdns
TW8 ... 110 A2
Brentwood Cl SE9 ... 167 A3
Brentwood Ho 2
SE18 ... 143 D5
Brentwood Lo NW4 ... 46 D4
Brereton Ho 4
SW2 ... 160 C4
Brereton Rd N17 ... 33 D3
Bressenden Pl
SW1 ... 115 C3 259 A6
Bressey Ave EN1 ... 6 A4
Bressey Gr E18 ... 36 D1
Bretherton Ct CR2 ... 221 C2
Breton Ho
Bermondsey SE1 ... 263 C6
St Luke's EC2 ... 242 B5
Brett Cl
15 Northolt UB5 ... 84 D4
Stoke Newington N16 ... 73 C6
Brett Cres NW10 ... 89 B6

Brett Ct N9 ... 18 C2
Brettell St SE17 ... 262 D1
Brettenham Ave E17 ... 35 C2
Brettenham Prim Sch
N18 ... 34 A6
Brettenham Rd
Edmonton N18 ... 34 A6
Walthamstow E17 ... 35 C2
Brett Ho 1 SW15 ... 156 D4
Brett House Cl 2
SW15 ... 156 D4
Brettinghurst 8
SE1 ... 118 A1
Bretton Ho N19 ... 50 A1
Brett Pas 28 E8 ... 74 B3
Brett Rd Barnet EN5 ... 12 C6
Hackney E8 ... 74 B3
Brewers Bldgs EC1 ... 234 C2
Brewers Ct W2 ... 236 A2
Brewer's Gn SW1 ... 259 C6
Brewers Hall Gdns
EC2 ... 242 B3
Brewers La 11 TW9 ... 153 D6
Brewer St
W1 ... 115 C6 249 B6
Brewery Cl HA0 ... 65 A4
Brewery Ind Est The
N1 ... 235 B3
Brewery Mews Bsns Ctr
1 TW7 ... 131 A2
Brewery Rd
Islington N7 ... 72 A2
Keston Mark BR2 ... 210 A1
Plumstead SE18 ... 123 B1
Brewery Sq
Bermondsey SE1 ... 253 C3
Clerkenwell EC1 ... 241 D6
Brewhouse La
Putney SW15 ... 135 A2
Wapping E1 ... 118 B5
Brewhouse Rd 3
SE18 ... 122 B2
Brewhouse Wlk
SE16 ... 119 A5
Brewhouse Yd EC1 ... 241 C6
Brewood Rd RM8 ... 80 B2
Brewster Gdns W10 ... 90 C2
Brewster Ho
Bermondsey SE1 ... 263 D4
Poplar E14 ... 119 B6
Brewster Rd E10 ... 53 D1
Brian Ct N10 ... 31 B2
Brian Rd RM6 ... 58 C4
Briant Ho SE1 ... 260 D5
Briants Cl HA5 ... 23 B1
Briant St SE14 ... 140 D5
Briar Ave SW16 ... 182 B3
Briarbank Rd W13 ... 87 A1
Briar Cl
Buckhurst Hill IG9 ... 21 D2
Edmonton N13 ... 17 A1
Finchley N2 ... 30 A1
Hampton TW12 ... 173 B5
Isleworth TW7 ... 152 D6
Briar Cres UB5 ... 63 D2
Briar Ct 7 Bow E3 ... 97 C5
Cheam SM3 ... 216 C4
Dalston E8 ... 73 D1
Hampton TW12 ... 173 D5
Leytonstone E11 ... 54 B2
Briardale HA8 ... 27 B6
Briardale Gdns NW3 ... 69 C5
Briardale Ho 12 N16 ... 51 C1
Briardale SW19 ... 157 B3
Briarfield Ave N3 ... 29 D1
Briarfield Cl DA7 ... 147 C3
Briar Gdns BR2 ... 208 D1
Briaris Cl 11 N17 ... 34 B3
Briar La CR0 ... 223 D4
Briar Lo E18 ... 37 C2
Briar Rd
Cricklewood NW2 ... 68 C4
Harrow HA3 ... 43 C4
Littleton TW17 ... 192 C4
Thornton Heath
SW16 ... 204 B6
Twickenham TW2 ... 152 C3
Briars The WD23 ... 8 C4
Briarswood Way
BR6 ... 227 D3
Briar The 11 SM1 ... 218 A4
Briarview Ct E4 ... 36 B4
Briar Way UB7 ... 104 C4
Briar Wlk
Burnt Oak HA8 ... 27 A3
Putney SW15 ... 134 B1
West Kilburn W10 ... 91 A3
Briarwood Cl
Feltham TW13 ... 149 C1
Kingsbury NW9 ... 45 A3
Briarwood Ct 5
KT4 ... 200 A1
Briarwood Dr HA6 ... 22 A1
Briarwood Rd
London SW4 ... 159 D6
Stoneleigh KT17 ... 216 A2
Briary Cl NW3 ... 70 C1

Briary Ct
10 Canning Town
E16 ... 98 D1
Sidcup DA14 ... 190 B5
Briary Gdns BR1 ... 187 B5
Briary Gr HA8 ... 26 D1
Briary La N9 ... 17 D1
Briary Lo BR3 ... 186 A2
Brickbarn Cl SW10 ... 266 B4
Brick Ct EC4 ... 241 A1
Brickett Cl HA4 ... 39 A4
Brick Farm Cl TW9 ... 132 D4
Brickfield Cl TW8 ... 131 C5
Brickfield Cotts
SE18 ... 145 D6
Brickfield Farm Gdns
BR6 ... 227 A4
Brickfield La
Edgware EN5 ... 11 D5
Harlington UB3 ... 127 B6
Brickfield Rd
South Norwood CR7,
SW16 ... 182 D2
Wimbledon SW19 ... 179 D6
Brickfields HA2 ... 64 B6
Brickfields Way
UB7 ... 104 B3
Brick La Enfield EN1 ... 6 B3
Northolt UB5 ... 85 B4
Shoreditch E2 ... 95 D4
Spitalfields
E1 ... 95 D3 243 D5
Stanmore HA7 ... 25 D3
Bricklayers Arms
SE1 ... 262 D5
Brick St W1 ... 115 B5 248 C3
Brickwall La HA4 ... 39 D1
Brickwood Cl SE26 ... 162 B1
Brickwood Rd CR0 ... 221 C6
Brickworth Ho 28
SW9 ... 138 C4
Brideale Cl SE15 ... 139 D6
Bride Ct EC4 ... 241 C1
Bride La EC4 ... 94 D1 241 C1
Bridel Mews N1 ... 234 C5
Bride St N7 ... 72 B2
Bridewain St SE1 ... 263 C6
Bridewell Pl
Holborn EC4 ... 241 C1
20 Wapping E1 ... 118 B5
Bridford Mews W1 ... 238 D4
Bridge App NW3 ... 71 A1
Bridge Ave Ealing W7 ... 86 B2
Hammersmith W6 ... 112 C1
Bridge Avenue Mans 1
W6 ... 112 C1
Bridge Bsns Ctr The
UB2 ... 107 C4
Bridge Cl Enfield EN1 ... 6 B3
13 North Kensington
W10 ... 90 D1
Teddington TW11 ... 174 D6
Walton-on-T KT12 ... 193 D1
Bridge Ct
9 Blackwall E14 ... 120 B6
Leyton E10 ... 53 B2
2 Walton-on-T
KT12 ... 193 D1
7 Willesden NW10 ... 67 C1
Bridge Dr N13 ... 32 B6
Bridge End E17 ... 36 A2
Bridge Field Ho 7
W2 ... 91 D1
Bridgefield Rd SM1 ... 217 C2
Bridgefoot
SE1 ... 116 A1 260 B1
Bridge Gate N21 ... 17 A4
Bridge Gdns
Canonbury N16 ... 73 B4
East Molesey KT8 ... 196 B5
Littleton TW15 ... 171 A3
Bridge Ho
Brockley SE4 ... 141 B1
1 Camden Town
NW1 ... 71 A1
Ealing TW8 ... 109 A2
Homerton E9 ... 74 D3
Bridge Ho S TW8 ... 109 A2
Bridge House Quay
E14 ... 120 A5
Bridge Ho SE28 ... 123 C5
Bridge La
SW11 ... 136 C4 267 B1
Bridgeland Rd E16 ... 121 A6
Bridgelands Cl BR3 ... 185 B3
Bridge La NW11 ... 47 B4
Bridgeman Ho 19 E9 ... 74 C1
Bridgeman Rd
Islington N1 ... 72 B1
Teddington TW11 ... 175 A4
Bridgeman St
NW8 ... 92 C5 230 A3

Bridge Meadows SE14 140 D6
Bridgend Rd SW18 136 A1
Bridgenhall Rd EN1 5 D4
Bridgen Ho 9 E1 96 B1
Bridgen Rd DA5 169 A4
Bridge Par
- 7 Croydon CR0 220 D5
- Edmonton N21 17 A4

Bridge Pk
- 7 London SW18 157 C6
- Wembley NW10 66 D1

Bridge Pl
- Belgravia SW1 115 B2 258 D4
- Croydon CR0 205 B1

Bridgepoint Lofts 2 E7 77 C1
Bridgeport Pl 4 E1 118 A5
Bridge Rd
- Beckenham BR3 185 B3
- Bexleyheath DA7 147 A3
- Chessington KT9 214 A3
- East Ham E6 78 B1
- East Molesey KT8 196 C5
- Isleworth TW3, TW7 130 B2
- Southall UB2 107 C4
- Stratford Marsh E15 98 B6
- Sutton SM2 217 D2
- Twickenham TW1 153 B5
- Wallington SM6 219 C3
- Walthamstow E17 53 B2
- Wembley HA9 66 C5
- Willesden NW10 67 C2
- Wood Green N22 32 A2

Bridge Row CR0 205 B1
Bridge Sch The
- Clerkenwell EC1 94 D3 241 C6
- Shoreditch N1 95 A6 235 B6

Bridges Ct SW11 136 B3
Bridges Ho 15 SE5 139 B5
Bridges La CR0 220 A4
Bridges Rd
- Stanmore HA7 24 D5
- Wimbledon SW19 179 D4

Bridges Road Mews SW19 179 D4
Bridge St W4 111 B2
Bridges The NW4 46 A6
Bridge St Pinner HA5 41 A6
- Richmond TW10 153 D6
- Walton-on-T KT12 193 D2
- Westminster SW1 116 A4 250 B1

Bridge Terr E15 76 B1
Bridge The HA3 42 D5
Bridgetown Cl 5 SE19 183 C5
Bridgeview 2 W6 112 C1
Bridgewater Cl BR7 211 C6
Bridgewater Ct HA0 65 C2
Bridgewater Gdns HA8 26 B1
Bridgewater Ho UB5 85 A3
Bridgewater Rd
- Ruislip HA4 62 B4
- Stratford Marsh E15 98 A6
- Wembley HA0 65 C1

Bridgewater Sq EC2 242 A4
Bridgewater St EC2 242 A4
Bridgeway IG11 79 D1
Bridge Way NW11 47 B4
Bridgeway St NW1 93 C5 232 B3
Bridge Way
- Twickenham TW2 152 A4
- Uxbridge UB10 60 D3

Bridgeway HA0 66 B1
Bridge Wharf 18 E2 96 D5
Bridge Wharf Rd TW7 131 B2
Bridgewood Cl SE20 184 B3
Bridgewood Rd
- North Cheam KT17, KT4 216 A4
- Streatham SW16 181 D3

Bridge Yd SE1 252 D4
Bridgford St SW17, SW18 158 A1
Bridgman Rd W4 111 A3
Bridgnorth Ho 10 SE15 140 A6
Bridgwater Ho W2 236 A2
Bridle Cl Enfield EN3 7 B6
- Kingston u T KT1 197 D5
- Sunbury TW16 194 A6
- West Ewell KT19 215 B3

Bridle La
- Marylebone W1 115 C6 249 B6

Bridle La *continued*
- Twickenham TW1 153 B5

Bridle Path The IG8 36 C3
Bridle Path CR0 220 A5
Bridlepath Way TW14 149 C3
Bridle Rd
- Addington CR0 223 C4
- Claygate KT10 213 B2
- Croydon CR0 223 C6
- Pinner HA5 40 C4

Bridle Way
- Addington CR0 223 C3
- Orpington BR6 227 A4

Bridle Way The SM6 219 C3
Bridlington Ho SW18 136 A1
Bridlington Rd N9 18 B4
Bridport Ave RM7 59 D3
Bridport Ho
- 6 Edmonton N18 34 A5
- Shoreditch N1 235 D5

Bridport Pl N1 95 B6 235 D5
Bridport Rd
- Edmonton N18 33 D5
- Greenford UB6 85 D6
- Thornton Heath CR7 204 D6

Bridport SE17 262 B1
Bridstow Pl W2 91 C1
Brief St SE5 138 D4
Brierfield NW1 232 A5
Brierley Ave N9 18 C3
Brierley Cl SE25 206 A5
Brierley Ct W7 108 C6
Brierley CR0 223 D2
Brierley Rd
- Leyton E11 76 B4
- Upper Tooting SW12 159 C2

Brierly Gdns E2 96 C5
Brigade Cl HA2 64 B6
Brigade St SE3 142 D3
Brigadier Ave EN2 5 A4
Brigadier Hill EN2 5 A5
Briggeford Cl 5 E5 74 A6
Briggs Cl CR4 181 B2
Briggs Ho 20 E2 95 D4
Bright Cl DA17 124 D2
Bright Ct 8 SE28 124 C5
Brightfield Rd SE12 164 D6
Brightling Rd SE4 163 B5
Brightlingsea Pl 5 E14 119 B6
Brightman Rd SW18 158 B3
Brighton Ave E17 53 B4
Brighton Bldgs SE1 263 A5
Brighton Cl UB10 60 D1
Brighton Ct SW15 157 B5
Brighton Dr 3 UB5 63 C2
Brighton Gr SE14 141 A4
Brighton Ho 7 SE5 139 B4
Brighton Rd
- Belmont SM2 217 D1
- Finchley N2 30 A1
- South Croydon CR2 221 B2
- Stoke Newington N16 73 C4
- Surbiton KT6 197 D3
- Sutton SM2 218 A1
- Wallend E6 100 C4

Brighton Terr SW9 138 B1
Brightside Rd SE13 164 B5
Brightside The EN3 7 A4
Bright St E14 97 D2
Brightwell Cl CR0 204 C1
Brightwell Cres SW17 180 D5
Brightwell Ct N7 72 B3
Brightwells 1 SW6 135 D3
Brig Mews SE8 141 C6
Brigstock Ho SE5 139 A3
Brigstock Par 1 CR7 204 C4
Brigstock Rd
- Belvedere DA17 125 D2
- Thornton Heath CR7 204 D4

Brill Ho NW10 67 B5
Brill Pl NW1 93 D5 232 D3
Brim Hill N2 48 B5
Brimpsfield Cl SE2 124 B3
BRIMSDOWN 7 B3
Brimsdown Ave EN3 7 A4
Brimsdown Ho E3 98 A3
Brimsdown Jun & Inf Sch EN3 6 D2
Brimsdown Sta EN3 7 A3
Brimstone Ho 4 E15 76 C1
Brindishe Prim Sch SE12 164 D6
Brindle Gate DA15 167 C3
Brindley Cl
- Bexleyheath DA7 147 D2
- Wembley HA0 87 D6

Brindley Ho
- Carshalton SM1 218 C3
- 37 Notting Hill W2 91 C2

Brindley Ho *continued*
- 22 Streatham SW12 160 A4

Brindley St SE14 141 B4
Brindley Way
- Bromley BR1 187 B5
- Southall UB1 107 D6

Brindwood Rd E4 19 C1
Brine Ct KT6 197 D4
Brine Ho 11 E3 97 A5
Brinkburn Cl
- Abbey Wood SE2 124 A2
- Edgware HA8 44 D6

Brinkburn Gdns HA8 44 C6
Brinkley 18 KT1 176 C1
Brinkley Rd KT4 216 B6
Brinklow Cres SE18 144 D5
Brinklow Ho W2 91 D2
Brinkworth Rd IG5 56 A6
Brinkworth Way E9 75 B2
Brinsdale Rd NW4 46 D6
Brinsley Ho 17 E1 96 C1
Brinsley Rd HA3 24 B1
Brinsley St 35 E1 96 B1
Brinsworth Cl TW2 152 B2
Brinton Wlk SE1 251 C3
Brion Pl E14 98 A2
Brisbane Ave SW19 179 D2
Brisbane Ct N10 31 B3
Brisbane Ho 3 W12 112 B6
Brisbane Rd
- Ealing W13 109 A4
- Ilford IG1 57 A1
- Leyton E10 75 D6

Brisbane St SE5 139 B5
Briscoe Cl E11 76 D6
Briscoe Rd SW19 180 B4
Briset Rd SE9 143 D1
Briset St EC1 94 D3 241 C5
Briset Way N7 72 B6
Bristol Cl
- Stanwell TW19 148 A5
- Wallington SM6 220 A1

Bristol Ct 11 TW19 148 A5
Bristol Gdns
- Putney SW15 156 C4
- Westbourne Green W9 91 D3

Bristol Ho
- 1 Barking IG11 80 A1
- SE11 261 A5

Bristol Mews W9 91 D3
Bristol Park Rd 1 E17 53 A5
Bristol Rd
- Greenford UB6 85 D6
- Morden SM4 202 A4
- Upton E7 77 D2

Briston Gr N8 50 A3
Briston Mews NW7 28 A3
Bristowe Cl 24 SW2 160 C5
Bristow Rd
- Bexleyheath DA7 147 A4
- Hounslow TW3 130 A2
- Wallington CR0 220 A4
- West Norwood SE19 183 C5

Britain at War Experience* SE1 253 A3
Britannia Building N1 235 C2
Britannia Cl
- London SW4 137 D1
- Northolt UB5 84 D4

Britannia Gate 11 E16 121 A5
Britannia Ho N20 14 A1
Britannia Junc NW1 231 D6
Britannia La TW2 152 A4
Britannia Rd
- Ilford IG1 78 D5
- 23 Millwall E14 119 C2
- Surbiton KT5 198 B2
- Walham Green SW6 135 D5 265 C3
- Whetstone N12 14 A1

Britannia Row N1 95 A6 235 A6
Britannia St WC1 94 B4 233 C2
Britannia Village Prim Sch E16 121 B5
Britannia Way NW10 88 D3
Britannia Wlk N1 235 C2
British Coll of Osteopathic Medicine NW3 70 A2
British Gr W4 111 D1
British Grove Pas 2 W4 111 D1
British Grove S 3 W4 111 D1
British Home & Hospl for Incurables SE27 182 D5
British Legion Rd E4 20 D2
British Library (Newspaper Library) NW9 45 C6
British Library The* WC1 93 D4 232 D2
British Mus* WC1 94 A2 240 A3
British St E3 97 B4
British Wharf Ind Est SE14 140 D6
Britley Ho 16 E14 97 B1
Brittain Ct SE9 166 A3
Brittain Rd RM8 81 B5
Brittany Ho SW15 134 C1
Brittany Point SE11 261 A3
Britten Cl Elstree WD6 9 D5
- Golders Green NW11 47 D1

Brittenden Cl 1 BR6 227 D2
Brittenden Par BR6 227 D2
Britten Dr UB1 85 C1
Britten Ho SW3 257 B2
Britten St SW3 114 C1 257 A2
Britton Cl SE6 164 B4
Britton St EC1 94 D3 241 C5
Brixham Cres HA4 40 A1
Brixham Gdns IG3 79 C3
Brixham Rd DA16 146 D4
Brixham St E16 122 C5
BRIXTON 138 C2
Brixton Day Coll SW9 138 A2
Brixton Hill Ct 5 SW2 160 B6
Brixton Hill SW2 160 B5
Brixton Hill Pl SW2 160 A4
Brixton Mkt SW9 138 C1
Brixton Oval 7 SW2 138 C1
Brixton Rd SW9 138 C4
Brixton Sta SW9 138 C1
Brixton Station Rd SW9 138 C2
Brixton Water La SW2 160 B6
Broadacre Cl UB10 60 D5
Broadbent Cl N6 49 B1
Broadbent St W1 248 C6
Broadberry Ct N18 34 B5
Broadbridge Cl SE3 143 A5
Broad Common Est N16 52 A1
Broadcoombe CR2 222 D1
Broadcroft Ave HA7 25 D1
Broadcroft Rd BR5 211 B2
Broad Ct WC2 240 B1
Broadeaves Cl CR2 221 C3
Broadfield Cl
- Croydon CR0 220 B6
- Dollis Hill NW2 68 C5

Broadfield Ct
- Bushey WD23 8 C2
- Edgware HA8 10 D1

Broadfield La NW1 72 A1
Broadfield NW6 69 D2
Broadfield Rd SE6 164 C3
Broadfields Ave
- Edgware HA8 10 D1
- Southgate N21 16 C4

Broadfields HA2 23 D1
Broadfields Hts HA8 26 D6
Broadfields Prim Sch HA8 10 C2
Broadfield Sq EN1 6 B3
Broadfields KT8 196 C3
Broadfields Way NW10 67 D3
Broadfield Way IG9 21 C1
Broadford Ho 12 E1 97 A3
BROADGATE 95 C2
Broadgate Circ EC2 95 C2 243 A3
Broadgate EC2 95 C2 243 A4
Broadgate Rd E16 99 D1
Broadgates Ave EN4 1 D4
Broadgates Ct SE11 261 B1
Broadgates Rd SW18 158 B3
BROAD GREEN 204 D3
Broad Green Ave CR0 204 D2
Broadhead Strand NW9 27 D2
Broadheath Dr BR7 188 B5
Broadhinton Rd SW4 137 C2
Broadhurst Ave
- Edgware HA8 26 D6
- Ilford IG3 79 D4

Broadhurst Cl
- Hampstead NW6 70 A2
- 9 Richmond TW10 154 B6

Broadhurst Gdns
- Hampstead NW6 69 D2

Broadhurst Gdns *continued*
- Ruislip HA4 62 C6

Broadhurst Mans NW6 69 D2
Broad La
- Broadgate EC2 243 A4
- Hampton TW12 173 C4
- Hornsey Vale N8 50 B4

Broadlands Ave
- Enfield EN3 6 B2
- Shepperton TW17 193 A3
- Streatham SW16 160 A2

Broadlands Cl
- Enfield EN3 6 C2
- Highgate N6 49 A2
- Streatham SW16 160 A2

Broadlands Ct TW9 132 C5
Broadlands
- Feltham TW13 151 C1
- Highgate N6 49 A2

Broadlands Lo N6 48 D2
Broadlands Mans 2 SW16 160 A2
Broadlands Rd
- Grove Pk BR1 187 B6
- Highgate N6 48 D2

Broadlands Way KT3 199 D3
Broad La
- South Tottenham N15 51 D5
- South Tottenham N15 52 A5

Broadlawns Ct HA3 24 D2
Broad Lawn SE9 166 C3
Broadley St NW8 92 C2 237 A4
Broadley Terr NW1 92 C3 237 B5
Broadmayne SE17 262 C2
Broadmead Ave KT4 200 A2
Broadmead SE6 163 C1
Broadmead Cl
- Hampton TW12 173 C4
- Pinner HA5 23 A3

Broadmead Ct 6 IG8 37 A4
Broadmead TW12 173 C4
Broadmead Inf Sch CR0 205 B2
Broadmead Jun Sch CR0 205 B3
Broadmead Rd
- Northolt UB5 85 A3
- Woodford IG8 37 B3

Broadmead W14 254 A3
Broad Oak TW16 171 D4
Broad Oak Cl
- Chingford E4 35 C5
- St Paul's Cray BR5 190 A1

Broadoak Ct 8 SW9 138 C2
Broadoak Ho 11 NW6 91 D6
Broadoaks BR7 188 D4
Broad Oaks KT6 214 D6
Broadoaks Way BR2 208 D4
Broad Oak IG8 37 B5
Broad St Ave EC2 243 A3
Broad Sanctuary SW1 250 A1
Broad St RM10 81 C1
Broadstone Ho SW8 270 C3
Broadstone Pl W1 238 A3
Broad Street Health Ctr RM10 103 C6
Broad Street Pl EC2 242 D3
Broad St TW11 174 D4
Broadview Est TW19 148 C4
Broadview Ho RM8 58 D1
Broadview NW9 44 C3
Broadview Rd SW16 181 D3
Broadwalk HA2 41 D4
Broadwalk Ho SW7 246 A1
Broadwalk La NW11 47 B2
Broadwalk Sh Ctr The HA8 26 D4
Broadwalk E18 54 D6
Broadwall SE1 116 C5 251 B4
Broadwater Farm Prim Sch N17 33 B1
Broadwater Gdns BR6 227 A4
Broadwater Prim Sch SW17 180 C6
Broadwater Rd
- Plumstead SE18 123 B3
- Tottenham N17 33 C1
- Upper Tooting SW17 180 C6

Broadway Arc 3 W6 112 C2
Broadway Ave
- Thornton Heath CR0 2
- Twickenham TW1 1

Broadway
- Barking IG11 1
- Bexley DA6 1
- Bexleyheath DA6 1

Broadway Bldgs 5 W7 1
Broadway Cl IG8
Broadway Ct BR3 2
Broadway Ctr The 6 W6 1
Broadway Ct SW19 1
Broadway Gdns
- Mitcham CR4 2
- Woodford IG8

Broadway W7 1
Broadway Ho 2 E8 1
Broadway Ho 5 SW19 1
Broadway Lofts SW17 1
Broadway Mans SW6 2
Broadway Market E8
Broadway Market Mew
- 21 E8

Broadway Mews
- Bowes Pk N13
- Southgate N21
- Stamford Hill E5

Broadway Par
- Chingford E4
- Hayes UB3 1
- Hornsey N8
- West Drayton UB7 1

Broadway Pl SW19 1
Broadway Ret Pk NW2
Broadway Sh Ctr 5 DA6 1
Broadway E15
Broadway The
- Barnes SW13 1
- Cheam SM3 2
- Chingford E4
- Dagenham RM8
- Ealing W5 1
- Edgware NW7
- Edmonton N9
- Friern Barnet N11
- Greenford UB6
- Harrow HA3
- Hornsey N8
- Merton SW19 1
- Newham E13
- Pinner HA5
- South Acton W3 1
- Southall UB1 1
- 2 Southgate N14
- Stanmore HA7
- Sutton SM1 2
- Thames Ditton KT10 1
- Tolworth KT6 1
- Wallington SM6 2
- Wembley HA9
- Woodford IG8
- Wood Green N22

Broadway
- West Ealing W13 1
- Westminster SW1 115 D3 2

Broadway Wlk 4 E14 1
Broadwell Ct TW5 1
Broadwick St W1 93 C1 2
Broad Wlk
- Eltham SE3, SE18 1
- Heston TW5 1
- Mayfair W1 115 A5 2
- Regent's Pk NW1 93 A5 2
- Richmond TW9 1
- Southgate N21

Broad Wlk The W8 113 D5 2
Broadwood Ave HA4
Broadwood Terr W14 2
Broad Yd EC1 2
Brocade Ct NW9
Brocas Cl NW3
Brockbridge Ho SW15 1
Brockdene Dr BR2 2
Brockdish Ave IG11 2
Brockelbank Lo RM8
Brockenhurst Ave KT4 1
Brockenhurst KT8 1
Brockenhurst Gdns
- Edgware NW7 2
- Ilford IG1

nhurst Mews 9
....34 A6
nhurst Rd
....206 B2
nhurst Way
....181 D1
t Ho 16 SW8...137 D3
am Cl SW19...179 B5
am Cres CR0..224 B1
am Ct
mont SM2....217 D1
uth Croydon
....221 A3
am Dr
IG2....57 A4
ham SW2....160 B4
am Ho
en Town
....232 B5
eatham SW2...160 B4
am St SE1...262 B6
urst Cl HA7....24 D4
urst Ho N4....51 B2
l Cres SE4....141 A1
ebank Ho 7
....122 C5
ebank Rd
wich SE7....121 B2
sworth SW18..158 A4
ebank Road Ind
E7....121 A2
ehurst St
....140 D5
esby Rd SE25..206 B5
KLEY....141 B1
ey Ave HA7....10 A1
ey Cl HA7....26 A6
ey Cross Bsns Ctr
....141 A2
ey Cross SE4...141 B2
ey Gdns SE4...141 B3
ey Gr SE4....163 B6
ey Hall Rd
....163 A6
ey Hill Ho HA7...9 C3
ey Hill HA7, HA8..9 D2
ey Ho SE17...263 A2
ey Mews SE4..163 A6
ey Pk SE23....163 A4
ey Prim Sch
....163 B6
ey Rd SE4....163 B6
ey Rise SE23...163 A4
eyside HA7....26 A6
ley Sta SE4...141 A2
ey View SE23..163 A4
ey Way SE4...163 A6
nan Rise BR1..186 B6
ner Ho 5 E1..118 B6
Pl E3....97 D3
Rd E13....99 B2
s Dr SM3....217 A5
shot Cl 11
....131 D6
St SE15....140 C2
way Cl E11....76 C6
weir 28 E2....96 C5
well Ave BR3...207 D4
well Cl BR5....211 D4
well Ct
ondon SW2....160 C6
nton Heath CR0.204 D2
well Ho SE11..270 D6
well Park Gdns
....160 D4
well Park Row
....160 C5
well Park*
....160 D5
worth 8 KT2..176 D2
rick Ho SE21...161 C1
Rd N16....73 C5
ck Ho 12 E3....97 B5
e Ct E10....54 B1
e Ho
ondsey SE1....263 D2
allington SM6...219 B4
e Rd
gford E4....20 A2
ld EN2....5 A5
e St
....117 D1 263 D2
ove La E1....118 D6
ick Gr SE2....124 B2
ick Rd SW17...158 C2
Ho E1....243 C3
ave Gdns BR3..185 D1
n Wharf EC4..252 A6
sley St E3....97 B4
Wlk
ney E8....95 D6
ackney E8....96 A6
er Rd SE5....139 C2
orough Gn
9....22 C5
efield HA7....25 C2
ehead St 8 E1..96 C1

Bromell's Rd SW4....137 C1
Brome Rd SE9....144 B2
Bromfelde Rd SW4...137 D3
Bromfield Ct 20
SE16....118 A3
Bromfield St N1....234 B4
Bromhall Rd RM8....80 B2
Bromhedge SE9....166 B1
Bromholm Rd SE2...124 B3
Bromleigh Ct 1 SE21,
SE22....162 B2
Bromleigh Ho SE1..263 C6
BROMLEY E3....97 D4
BR1....186 C2
Bromley Ave BR1....186 C3
Bromley-by-Bow Sta
E3....98 A4
Bromley Coll BR1....187 A2
Bromley Coll of F & H
Ed BR2....209 D3
Bromley Comm
BR2....209 D4
BROMLEY
COMMON....210 A3
Bromley Cres
Beckenham BR2....208 D6
Ruislip HA4....61 D4
Bromley Ct BR1....186 D3
Bromley Gdns BR2...208 D6
Bromley Gr BR2....186 B1
Bromley Hall Rd E14..98 A2
Bromley High Sch
BR1....210 C5
Bromley High St E3...97 D4
Bromley Hill BR1....186 C4
Bromley Ho 5 BR1...187 A2
Bromley Ind Ctr
BR1....209 D6
Bromley La BR7....189 B3
Bromley Lo 2 W3....89 A1
Bromley Manor Mans 3
BR1....209 A6
Bromley North Sta
BR1....187 A2
BROMLEY PARK....186 D2
Bromley Pk 11 BR1...186 D2
Bromley Pl W1....239 A4
Bromley Rd
Beckenham BR3....185 D2
Bromley BR2, BR3....186 B1
Catford SE6....163 D1
Chislehurst BR7....188 D2
Edmonton N18....17 B1
Leyton E10....53 D3
Tottenham N17....34 A2
Walthamstow E17....53 C6
Bromley Road Inf Sch
BR3....185 D2
Bromley Road Ret Pk
SE6....163 D2
Bromley South Sta
BR2....209 A6
Bromley St E1....96 D1
BROMPTON....114 B3
Brompton Arc SW1....247 D1
Brompton Cl
Hounslow TW4....151 B6
Penge SE20....184 A1
Brompton Ct 4 HA7..25 C6
Brompton Gr N2....48 C5
Brompton Ho 3 N9...34 A6
Brompton Oratory
SW3....114 C3 257 A5
Brompton Park Cres
SW6....135 D6 265 C5
Brompton Pl
SW3....114 C3 257 B6
Brompton Rd
SW3....114 C3 257 A5
Brompton Sq
SW3....114 C3 257 A6
Bromstone Ho 19
SW9....138 C4
Bromwich Ave N6....71 A6
Bromwich Ho 3
TW10....154 A5
Bromyard Ave W3....111 C6
Bromyard Ho
Acton W3....111 C5
3 Peckham SE15....140 B5
Bron Ct NW6....91 C6
BRONDESBURY....69 A2
Brondesbury Coll for
Boys NW6....69 A1
Brondesbury Ct NW2..68 D2
Brondesbury Mews 11
NW6....69 C1
BRONDESBURY PARK
....90 D6
Brondesbury Park Sta
NW6....91 A6
Brondesbury Pk
NW2....68 D1
Brondesbury Rd
NW6....91 C5
Brondesbury Sta
NW6....69 B1

Brondesbury Villas
NW6....91 C5
Bronhill Terr N17....34 A2
Bronsart Rd
SW6....135 A5 264 A3
Bronson Rd SW20....179 A1
Bronte Cl Erith DA8...147 D5
1 Forest Gate E7....77 A4
Ilford IG2....56 C5
Bronte Ct 8 W14....112 D3
Bronte Ho
Kilburn NW6....91 C4
6 Stoke Newington
N16....73 C3
Bronti Cl
SE17....117 A1 262 B2
Bronwen Ct NW8....229 C1
Bronze Age Way
DA17....125 D4
Bronze St SE8....141 C5
Brook Ave
Dagenham RM10....81 D1
Edgware HA8....26 D4
Wembley HA9....66 C5
Brookbank Ave W7...86 B2
Brook Bank EN1....6 B6
Brookbank Rd SE13..141 D2
Brook Cl Acton W3....110 C5
Finchley N12....29 A3
Ruislip HA4....39 C2
Stanwell TW19....148 B4
Upper Tooting
SW17....159 A2
West Barnes SW20...200 B6
Brook Com Prim Sch
E8....74 A3
Brook Cres
Chingford E4....35 D6
Edmonton N9....34 B6
Brook Ct
Barking IG11....101 D6
Beckenham BR3....185 B2
5 Brentford TW8...131 D6
Cheam SM3....216 C4
Edgware HA8....26 D5
2 Leyton E11....76 C5
Mortlake SW14....133 C2
Stratford New Town
E15....76 A3
Walthamstow E17....53 A6
Brookdale N11....31 C6
Brookdale Rd
Catford SE6....163 D4
Lewisham SE6....163 D5
Sidcup DA5....169 A5
Walthamstow E17....53 C6
Brookdales The NW4..47 A5
Brookdene N12....29 D6
Brookdene Rd SE18,
SE2....123 D2
Brook Dr Harrow HA1..42 A5
Newington
SE11....116 D2 261 C4
Ruislip HA4....39 C2
Brooke Ave HA2....64 A5
Brooke Cl WD23....8 A4
Brooke Ct
Kilburn W10....91 A5
7 Kingston u T KT2..175 D6
Brooke Ho
Bushey WD23....8 A4
4 New Cross Gate
SE14....141 A4
Brookehowse Rd
SE6....163 D1
Brookend Rd DA15....167 C3
Brooke Rd
Shacklewell E5,
N16....74 A5
Walthamstow E17....54 A5
Brookes Ct EC1....241 A4
Brooke's Mkt EC1....241 B4
Brooke St
EC1....94 C2 241 A3
Brooke Way WD23....8 A4
Brookfield Ave
Carshalton SM1,
SM5....218 C5
Ealing W5....87 D3
Mill Hill NW7....28 B4
Walthamstow E17....54 A5
Brookfield Cl NW7....28 B4
Brookfield Cres
Harrow HA3....44 A4
Mill Hill NW7....28 B4
Brookfield Ct
Greenford UB6....86 A4
1 London N12....29 D6
Brookfield
Dartmouth Pk N6....71 A5
1 Finsbury Pk N4....72 C6
Brookfield Gdns
KT10....212 D2
Brookfield Ho 23 E2...96 B5
Brookfield House Sch
IG8....36 C4
Brookfield Path IG8...36 C4

Brookfield Pk NW5....71 B5
Brookfield Prim Sch
Cheam SM3....201 A1
Dartmouth Pk N19....71 B6
Brookfield Rd
Acton W4....111 B4
Edmonton N9....18 B1
Homerton E9....75 A2
Brookfields Ave
CR4....202 C4
Brookfields EN3....6 D1
Brookgate N16....73 B6
Brook Gate
W1....114 D6 247 D5
Brook Gdns
Barnes SW13....133 D2
Chingford E4....35 D6
Kingston u T KT2....177 A2
Brook Gn W6....112 D2
BROOK GREEN....112 D2
Brook Green Flats 11
W14....112 D3
Brookhill Cl
East Barnet EN4....14 C6
Woolwich SE18....122 D1
Brookhill Ct 2 EN4...14 C5
Brookhill Rd
East Barnet EN4....14 C6
Woolwich SE18....122 D1
Brook Ho
3 Clapham Pk
SW4....159 C6
Ealing W3....110 C4
3 Edmonton N9....18 A1
4 Hammersmith
W6....112 C2
Marylebone WC1....239 C4
Brook Hos NW1....232 B3
Brook Ho 4 TW1....153 A4
Brookhouse Gdns E4..36 C6
Brook House Sixth
Form Coll E5....74 B5
Brook Ind Est UB4..106 C5
Brooking Cl RM8....80 C5
Brooking Rd E7....77 A3
Brook La Bexley DA5..168 D5
Greenwich SE3....143 B3
Brook La N 3 TW8...131 D6
Brookland Cl NW11...47 C5
Brookland Garth
NW11....47 D5
Brookland Hill NW11..47 D5
Brookland Jun & Inf
Schs NW11....47 D5
Brookland Rise
NW11....47 C5
Brooklands Ave
New Eltham DA15....167 B2
Wandsworth SW18..157 D2
Brooklands Cl
TW16....171 C2
Brooklands Court
Apartments 3
NW6....69 B1
Brooklands Ct
10 Clapham SW8...137 C3
Enfield N21....17 B6
Kingston u T KT1....197 D5
2 London NW6....69 B1
2 Mitcham CR4....180 B1
Brooklands Dr UB6...87 D6
Brooklands Ho SE3..143 A2
Brooklands Pk SE3...143 A2
Brooklands Pl
TW12....173 D5
Brooklands Prim Sch
SE3....143 A2
Brooklands Rd KT7..197 A1
Brooklands The
TW7....130 B4
Brook Lane Bns Ctr
TW8....109 D1
Brook La BR1....187 A4
Brooklea Cl NW9....27 C2
Brook Lo
Crouch End N8....49 D3
Edgware HA8....26 D4
Hendon NW4....46 D4
Brooklyn Ave SE25...206 B5
Brooklyn Cl SM5....218 C6
Brooklyn Ct
Feltham TW13....150 B2
Shepherd's Bush
W12....112 C5
Brooklyn Gr SE25....206 B5
Brooklyn SE20....184 A3
Brooklyn Rd
Bromley BR2....210 A4
Croydon SE25....206 B5
Brookmarsh Ind Est
SE10....141 D5
Brook Mdw N12....13 D1
Brookmead Ave BR1,
BR2....210 B4
Brookmead Ct N20....14 A2
Brookmead Ind Est
CR4....203 C3

Brook Meadow Cl
IG8....36 C4
Brookmead Rd CR0..203 C3
Brook Mead KT19....215 C2
Brook Mews N
W2....114 A6 246 B6
Brookmill Rd SE8....141 C4
Brook Park Cl N21....16 D6
Brook Pl EN5....13 C6
Brook Rd
Buckhurst Hill IG9....21 A3
Dollis Hill NW2....68 A6
Finchley N12....30 C3
Hornsey N8....50 A5
Ilford IG2....57 C3
Brook Rd S TW8....131 D6
Brook Rd
South Norwood
CR7....205 A5
Surbiton KT6....214 A6
Twickenham TW1....153 A5
Wood Green N22....50 B6
Brook Ret Pk HA4....62 D3
Brooks Ave E6....100 B3
Brooksbank Ho 7
E9....74 C2
Brooksbank St 9 E9..74 C2
Brooksby Ho 9 N1....72 C1
Brooksby Mews N1...72 C1
Brooksby St N1....72 C1
Brooksby's Wlk E9...74 D3
Brooks Cl SE9....166 C2
Brookscroft Rd E17...35 D2
Brookscroft E17....53 D6
Brooks Ct
3 London SW4....138 A3
Nine Elms SW8....269 B4
Brookshill Ave HA3...24 C5
Brookshill Dr HA3....24 B5
Brookshill Gate HA3..24 B5
Brookshill HA3....24 B5
Brooks Ho 6 SW2...160 C3
Brookside BR6....211 D2
Brookside Cl
Barnet EN5....13 A5
Feltham TW13....150 A1
Harrow HA3....43 D4
South Harrow HA2,
HA4....63 A4
Brookside Cres 1
KT4....200 A1
Brookside Ct SW16..181 C3
Brookside EN4....14 C5
Brookside Gdns EN1...6 C6
Brookside UB10....60 B1
Brookside Ho N17....33 C1
Brookside Prim Sch
UB4....84 C4
Brookside Rd
Edmonton N9....34 B6
Hayes UB4....106 C6
Temple Fortune
NW11....47 B3
Upper Holloway N19...71 C6
Brookside S EN4....15 A4
Brookside
Southgate N21....16 B5
Wallington SM5....219 A3
Brookside Way CR0..206 D3
Brooks La W4....132 C6
Brook's Mans 5 IG3...58 B1
Brook's Mews
W1....115 B6 248 C6
Brook's Par 6 IG3....58 B1
Brook Sq SE18....144 A4
Brooks Rd W4....110 C1
Brook's Rd E13....99 A6
Brook St
Bayswater
W2....114 B6 246 D6
Erith DA8....147 D5
Kingston u T KT1....176 A1
Mayfair W1. 115 B6 248 C6
Brookstone Ct SE15..140 B1
Brook St 7 N17....33 D1
Brooksville Ave NW6..91 A6
Brook Vale DA8....147 D4
Brookview Ct 11 EN1..17 C6
Brookview Rd
SW16....181 C5
Brookville Rd
SW6....135 B5 264 C3
Brookway SE3....143 A2
Brook Wlk
Burnt Oak HA8....27 B4
Finchley N2....30 B2
Brookwood Ave
SW13....133 D3
Brookwood Cl BR2...208 D5
Brookwood Ho SE1 . 251 D1
Brookwood Rd
Hounslow TW3....129 D4
Wandsworth SW18..157 C3
Broom Ave BR5....190 B1
Broom Cl
Bromley Comm
BR2....210 A3

Broom Cl *continued*
Teddington KT1,
TW11....175 D3
Broomcroft Ave UB5..84 C4
Broome Ct 3 TW9...132 C4
Broome Ho 7 E5....74 B3
Broome Rd TW12....173 B2
Broome Way SE5....139 B5
Broom Farm SW6....135 C3
Broomfield Ave N13...32 B5
Broomfield 7 NW1...71 A1
Broomfield Cotts
N13....32 A5
Broomfield Ct N13....32 A5
Broomfield Ho
Stanmore HA7....9 A1
4 St Paul's Cray
BR5....190 B1
Broomfield House Sch
TW9....132 B4
Broomfield Ho SE17. 263 A3
Broomfield La N13....32 B6
Broomfield Pl W13...109 B5
Broomfield Rd
Beckenham BR3....207 B6
Bexley DA6....169 C6
Bowes Pk N13....32 A5
Dagenham RM6....58 D2
Ealing W13....109 B5
Richmond TW9....132 B4
Surbiton KT5....198 B1
Teddington TW11....175 C4
Broomfield Sch N14..31 D5
Broomfields KT10....212 A3
Broomfield St E14....97 D2
Broomfield
Sunbury TW16....172 A2
Walthamstow E17....53 B2
Broom Gdns CR0....223 C5
Broomgrove Gdns
HA8....26 C2
Broomgrove Rd
SW9....138 B3
BROOM HILL....211 D2
Broomhill Ct 2 IG8...37 A4
Broomhill Rd
Broom Hill BR6....211 D2
Ilford IG3....80 A6
Wandsworth SW18..157 C6
Woodford IG8....37 A4
Broomhill Rise DA6..169 C6
Broomhill Wlk IG8....36 D3
Broomhouse La
SW6....135 C2
Broomhouse Rd
SW6....135 C3
Broomleigh BR1....187 A2
Broomloan La SM1..217 C6
Broom Lock TW11....175 C4
Broom Mead DA6....169 C6
Broom Pk KT1....175 D3
Broom Rd
Croydon CR0....223 C5
Teddington TW11....175 C4
Broomsleigh Bsns Pk
SE26....185 B5
Broomsleigh St NW6..69 B3
Broom Water TW11..175 C5
Broom Water W
TW11....175 C5
Broomwood Cl CR0..206 D4
Broomwood Hall Sch
SW12....159 A4
Broomwood Rd
London SW11....159 A6
St Paul's Cray BR5...190 B1
Broseley Gr SE26....185 A5
Broster Gdns SE25...205 D6
Brougham Rd
Acton W3....89 A1
Hackney E8....96 A6
Brougham St SW11..136 D3
Brough Cl
Kingston u T KT2....175 D5
South Lambeth SW8 . 270 B3
Broughton Ave
London N3....47 A6
Richmond TW10....175 C6
Broughton Ct W13...109 B6
Broughton Dr 19
SW9....138 D1
Broughton Gdns N6...49 C3
Broughton Ho 10
SW19....179 A3
Broughton Rd
Ealing W13....109 B6
Orpington BR6....227 B6
Sands End SW6....135 D3
Thornton Heath CR7 . 204 C3
Broughton Road App 2
SW6....135 D3
Broughton St SW8....137 B3
Brouncker Rd W3....111 A4
Browells La TW13....150 B2

Brown Bear Ct TW13 172 D6
Brown Cl SM6 220 A1
Browne Ho
13 Deptford SE8 141 C5
9 Penge SE26 184 B5
Brownfield St E14 98 A1
Brownflete Ho SE4 141 A1
Browngraves Rd UB7 127 A5
Brown Hart Gdns W1 248 B6
Brownhill Rd SE6 164 A4
Browning Ave
Carshalton SM1 218 C4
Ealing W7 86 D1
North Cheam KT4 200 B1
Browning Cl
Bexley DA16 145 C4
Feltham TW12 173 B6
Paddington W9 236 B5
Walthamstow E17 54 A5
Browning Ct W14 264 C6
Browning Ho
2 London SE14 141 A4
7 Shepherd's Bush W12 90 C1
10 Stoke Newington N16 73 C4
Browning Mews W1 238 B3
Browning Rd
Enfield EN2 5 B5
Leytonstone E11 54 D2
Plashet E12 78 B2
Browning St SE17 117 A2 262 B3
Browning Way TW5 128 D4
Brownlea Gdns IG3 80 A6
Brownlow Cl EN4 14 B6
Brownlow Ct
2 Bowes Pk N11 32 A4
Hampstead Garden Suburb N2 48 A4
Brownlow Ho 10 SE16 118 A4
Brownlow Lo 1 N11 32 A4
Brownlow Mews WC1 94 B3 240 D5
Brownlow Rd
Bowes Pk N11 32 A4
6 Ealing W13 109 A5
Finchley N3 29 D3
3 Forest Gate E7 77 A4
Hackney E8 96 A6
South Croydon CR0 221 D4
Willesden NW10 67 C1
Brownlow St WC1 94 B2 240 D3
Brownrigg Rd TW15 170 C6
Brown's Bldgs EC3 243 B1
Brownsea Wlk NW7 28 D4
Brownspring Dr SE9 166 D1
Brown's Rd
Surbiton KT5, KT6 198 B2
Walthamstow E17 53 C6
Brown St W1 92 D1 237 C2
Brownswell Rd N2 30 B1
Brownswood Rd N4 73 A6
Broxash Rd SW11 159 A5
Broxbourne Ave E18 55 B5
Broxbourne Ho 1 E3 97 D3
Broxbourne Rd
Broom Hill BR6 211 D2
Wanstead E7 77 A5
Broxholme Ho SW6 265 C2
Broxholm Rd SE27, SW16 160 C1
Broxted Rd SE6 163 B2
Broxwood Way NW8 92 C6 230 B5
Bruce Ave TW17 193 A3
Bruce Castle Ct N17 33 C2
Bruce Castle Mus* N17 33 C2
Bruce Castle Rd N17 33 D2
Bruce Cl
North Kensington W10 90 D2
Welling DA16 146 B4
Bruce Ct DA15 189 D6
Bruce Gdns N20 14 D1
Bruce Glasier Ho 13 N19 49 D2
Bruce Grove Prim Sch N17 33 D1
Bruce Grove Sta N17 33 D1
Bruce Grove N17 33 D1
Bruce Gr N17 33 D1
Bruce Hall Mews SW17 181 A6
Bruce Ho
4 Clapham Pk SW4 159 D5
5 Greenhill HA1 42 D4
North Kensington W10 90 D2
Preston HA3 44 A2
Putney SW15 156 B6
Bruce Lawns SW17 181 A6
Bruce Rd Barnet EN5 1 A2
Bromley E3 97 D4
Harrow HA3 24 C1
Mitcham CR4 181 A3
South Norwood SE25 205 B5
Willesden NW10 67 B1
Bruckner St W10 91 B4
Brudenell Rd SW17 181 A6
Bruffs Meadow UB5 63 A2
Bruges Pl 10 NW1 71 C1
Brumfield Rd KT19 215 A3
Brune Ho E1 243 C3
Brunel Cl
Cranford TW5 128 B5
Northolt UB5 85 B4
Penge SE19 183 D4
Brunel Ct 8 SW13 133 D3
Brunel Engine House Rotherhithe* SE16 118 C4
Brunel Est W2 91 C2
Brunel Ho
Chelsea SW10 266 D4
4 Gospel Oak NW5 71 B4
Hayes UB3 105 D3
Millwall E14 119 D1
New Cross SE8 141 B5
25 Streatham SW2 160 A4
Brunel Mews NW10 90 D4
Brunel Pl 7 UB1 85 D1
Brunel Rd Acton W3 89 C2
Walthamstow E17 53 A3
Wapping SE16 118 C5
Brunel Science Pk UB8 82 A4
Brunel St E16 98 D1
Brunel Univ Coll Osterley Campus TW7 130 D5
Brunel Univ UB8 82 A4
Brunel Wlk
South Tottenham N15 51 C5
Twickenham TW4 151 C4
Brune St E1 95 D2 243 C3
Brunlees Ho SE1 262 B5
Brunner Cl NW11 48 A4
Brunner Ho 6 SE6 186 A6
Brunner Rd
Ealing W5 87 D3
Walthamstow E17 53 B4
Bruno Ct 5 E8 74 A2
Bruno Pl NW9 67 A6
Brunswick Ave N11 15 A1
Brunswick Cl
Bexley DA6 146 D1
Pinner HA5 41 A3
Thames Ditton KT7 196 D1
Twickenham TW2 152 B1
Brunswick Cres N11 15 A1
Brunswick Ct
Bermondsey SE1 117 C4 253 B2
Finsbury EC1 234 C1
Kingston u T KT2 175 D4
New Barnet EN4 14 B6
2 Penge SE19 184 A3
Westminster SW1 259 D3
2 Wimbledon SW19 179 A3
Brunswick Gdns
Ealing W5 88 A3
Kensington W8 113 C5 245 B3
Brunswick Gr N11 15 A1
Brunswick Ho
Church End N3 29 B2
4 Haggerston E2 95 D5
Lisson Gr NW1 237 C6
Brunswick Lo 6 E4 20 A2
Brunswick Manor SM1 218 A4
Brunswick Mews
Marylebone W1 237 D2
Streatham SW16 181 D4
BRUNSWICK PARK 15 A1
Brunswick Park Gdns N11 15 A2
Brunswick Park Prim Sch
Brunswick Pk N14 15 A2
Camberwell SE5 139 B5
Brunswick Park Rd N11 15 A1
Brunswick Pk SE5 139 C4
Brunswick Pl
Penge SE19 184 A3
Shoreditch N1 95 B4 235 D1
Brunswick Quay SE16 118 D3
Brunswick Rd
Bexley DA6 147 A1
Ealing W5 88 A4
Holdbrook EN3 7 C5
Kingston u T KT2 176 C2
Leyton E10 54 A1
Poplar E14 98 A1
South Tottenham N15 51 C4
South Tottenham N15 51 C5
Sutton SM1 217 D4
Brunswick Sh Ctr WC1 94 A3 240 B6
Brunswick Sq
St Pancras WC1 94 A3 240 B6
Tottenham N17 33 D4
Brunswick St E17 54 A4
Brunswick Terr BR3 185 D2
Brunswick Villas 2 SE5 139 C4
Brunswick Way N11 31 B6
Brunton Pl E14 97 A1
Brushfield St E1 95 D2 243 C4
Brushwood Lo 1 DA17 125 C2
Brussels Ct N18 33 C5
Brussels Rd SW11 136 B1
Bruton Cl BR7 188 B3
Bruton La W1 115 B6 248 D5
Bruton Pl W1 115 B6 248 D5
Bruton Rd SM4 202 A5
Bruton St W1 115 B6 248 D5
Bruton Way W13 87 A2
Brutus Ct SE11 261 C3
Bryan Ave NW10 68 B1
Bryan Cl TW16 172 A3
Bryan Ct W1 237 C2
Bryan Ho SE16 119 B4
Bryan Rd SE16 119 B4
Bryanston Ave TW2 151 D3
Bryanston Cl UB2 107 B2
Bryanston Ct W1 237 C2
Bryanstone Ct SM1 218 A5
Bryanstone Rd N8 49 D4
Bryanston Ho 12 SE15 139 D4
Bryanston Mans W1 237 C4
Bryanston Mews E W1 237 C3
Bryanston Mews W W1 92 D1 237 C2
Bryanston Pl W1 92 D2 237 C3
Bryanston Sq W1 92 D1 237 C2
Bryanston St W1 92 D1 237 D1
Bryant Cl EN5 13 B6
Bryant Ct Acton W3 111 B5
Haggerston E2 95 D5
Bryant Rd UB5 84 C4
Bryant St E15 76 C1
Bryantwood Rd N5, N7 72 C3
Brycedale Cres N14 15 D1
Bryce Ho 25 SE14 140 D6
Bryce Rd RM8 80 C4
Brydale Ho 2 SE16 118 D2
Bryden Cl SE26 185 A5
Brydges Pl WC2 250 A5
Brydges Rd E15 76 B3
Brydon Wlk N1 233 B6
Bryer Ct EC2 242 A4
Bryett Rd N7 72 A5
Bryher Ho W4 111 A1
Brymay Cl E3 97 C5
Brymon Ct W1 237 D3
Brynmaer Ho SW11 267 D1
Brynmaer Rd SW11 136 D4 267 D1
Bryn-y-Mawr Rd EN1 5 D1
Bryony Cl UB8 82 B2
Bryony Rd W12 112 A6
Bryony Way TW16 172 A4
B Sky B Hq TW7 131 A6
BT Telecom Twr* W1 93 C2 239 A4
Buccleuch Ho E5 52 A2
Buchanan Cl N21 16 B6
Buchanan Ct 16 SE16 118 D2
Buchanan Gdns NW10 90 B5
Buchanan Ho
Dulwich SE21 161 C1
Wandsworth SW18 157 C4
Buchan Ho W3 110 D4
Buchan Rd SE15 140 C2
Bucharest Rd SW18 158 A4
Buckden Cl
Fortis Green N2 48 D5
Lee SE12 165 A5
Buckfast Ct W13 109 A6
Buckfast Ho N14 15 C6
Buckfast Rd SM4 201 D5
Buckfast St E2 96 A4
Buck Hill Wlk W2 114 B6 246 D5
Buckhold Rd SW18 157 C5
Buckhurst Ave CR4, SM5 202 D1
Buckhurst Ct 7 IG9 21 D2
BUCKHURST HILL 21 C2
Buckhurst Hill Ho 3 IG9 21 B2
Buckhurst Hill Sta IG9 21 D2
Buckhurst Ho 15 N7 71 D3
Buckhurst St E1 96 B3
Buckhurst Way IG9 21 D1
Buckingham Ave
East Molesey KT8 173 D1
Falconwood DA16 145 C1
Feltham TW14 150 B5
Oakleigh Pk N20 14 B4
South Norwood CR7 182 C2
Wembley UB6 87 A6
Buckingham Cl
Broom Hill BR5 211 C2
Ealing W5 87 C2
Enfield EN1 5 C3
Hampton TW12 173 B5
Buckingham College Sch HA1 42 C4
Buckingham Ct
2 Ealing W7 86 D3
Hendon NW4 46 A6
Mitcham CR4 204 A4
Northolt UB5 85 A6
Wembley HA0 65 C2
Buckingham Dr BR7 189 A5
Buckingham Gate SW1 115 C3 259 B6
Buckingham Gdns
East Molesey KT8 173 D1
Edgware HA8 26 B3
South Norwood CR7 182 C1
Buckingham Gr UB10 82 C5
Buckingham Ho
1 Acton W3 88 C1
Finsbury Pk N4 51 A1
Richmond TW10 154 C6
Buckingham La SE23 163 A4
Buckingham Lo N10 49 C5
Buckingham Mans NW6 69 D3
Buckingham Mews
Harlesden NW10 89 D5
7 Kingsland N1 73 C2
Westminster SW1 259 A6
Buckingham Palace Rd SW1 115 B2 258 D4
Buckingham Pal* SW1 115 C4 249 A1
Buckingham Par 19 HA7 25 C5
Buckingham Pl SW1 259 A6
Buckingham Prim Sch TW12 173 B5
Buckingham Rd
Edgware HA8 26 B3
Hampton TW12, TW13 173 B5
Harlesden NW10 89 D5
Harrow HA1 42 B4
Ilford IG1 79 B6
Kingsland N1 73 C2
Kingston u T KT1 198 B5
Leyton E10 75 D5
Mitcham CR4 204 A4
Richmond TW10 153 D2
Stratford E15 76 D3
Wanstead E11 55 C4
Woodford E18 36 D2
Wood Green N22 32 A2
Buckingham St WC2 250 B5
Buckingham Way SM6 219 C1
Buckingham Yd NW10 89 D5
Buck La NW9 45 B4
Buckland Cl NW7 28 A6
Buckland Cres NW3 70 B2
Buckland Ct
6 Shoreditch N1 95 C5
Uxbridge UB10 61 A6
Buckland Ho 3 N1 72 C1
Buckland Inf Sch KT9 214 B3
Buckland Rd
Chessington KT9 214 B3
Leyton E10 76 A6
Orpington BR6 227 C4
Buckland Rise HA5 22 D2
Bucklands Rd TW11 175 C4
Buckland St N1 95 B5 235 D3
Buckland Way KT4 200 C1
Buckland Wlk
2 Acton W3 111 A4
Morden SM4 202 A5
Buckle Ct HA8 27 A3
Buckleigh Ave SW20 201 B6
Buckleigh Ho SW17 180 B5
Buckleigh Rd SW16 182 A3
Buckleigh Way SE19 183 D3
Buckler Gdns SE9 166 B1
Buckler's Alley SW6 264 D4
Bucklersbury EC2, EC4 242 C1
Bucklers' Way SM5 218 D5
Buckles Ct DA17 124 D2
Buckle St
15 Whitechapel E1 96 A1
Whitechapel E1 243 D2
Buckley Cl SE23 162 B4
Buckley Ct
5 Brondesbury NW6 69 B1
London N8 49 D4
Buckley Ho W3 110 C5
Buckley Rd NW6 69 B1
Buckmaster Cl 1 SW9 138 C2
Buckmaster Ho 1 N7 72 B4
Buckmaster Rd SW11 136 C1
Bucknall St WC1 240 A2
Bucknall Way BR3 208 A5
Bucknell Cl SW2 138 B1
Buckner Rd SW2 138 B1
Buckrell Rd E4 20 B2
Buckridge Bldg EC1 241 A4
Buckshead Ho 19 W2 91 C2
Buck St NW1 71 B1
Buckstone Cl SE23 162 C5
Buckstone Rd N18 34 A5
Buckters Rents SE16 119 A5
Buckthorne Rd SE4 163 A6
Buckthorn Ho DA15 167 D1
Buckwheat Ct DA18 124 D3
Budd Cl N12 29 D6
Buddings Circ HA9 67 A5
Bude Cl E17 53 B4
Budge La CR4 202 D2
Budge Row EC4 242 C1
Budge's Wlk W2 114 A5 246 B4
Budleigh Cres DA16 146 C4
Budleigh Ho 19 SE15 140 A5
Budoch Ct IG3 80 A6
Budoch Dr IG3 80 A6
Buer Rd SW6 135 A3
Bugsby's Way SE10 120 D2
Buick Ho 4 E3 97 C3
Building 36 7 SE18 123 A3
Building 47 6 SE18 123 A3
Building 48 5 SE18 123 A3
Building 49 4 SE18 123 A3
Building 50 3 SE18 123 A3
Bulbarrow NW8 91 D6
Bulganak Rd CR7 205 A5
Bulinca St SW1 115 D2 259 D3
Bullace Row SE5 139 B4
Bull Alley DA16 146 B2
Bullard Rd TW11 174 D4
Bullards Pl 13 E2 96 D4
Bull Dog The (Juct) TW15 148 A2
Bulleid Way SW1 115 B2 258 D3
Bullen Ho 13 E1 96 B3
Bullen St SW11 136 C3
Buller Cl SE15 140 A5
Buller Rd
Barking IG11 79 C1
Kensal Green NW10 90 D4
South Norwood CR7 205 B6
Tottenham N17 34 A1
Wood Green N22 32 C1
Bullers Cl DA14 191 A5
Bullers Wood Dr BR7 188 B3
Bullers Wood Sch BR7 188 A2
Bullescroft Rd HA8 10 D1
Bullfinch Ct 4 SE21 161 B2
Bullingham Mans W8
Bull Inn Ct WC2
Bullivant St 9 E14
Bull La
Chislehurst BR7
Dagenham RM10
Edmonton N18
Bull Rd E15
Bullrush Cl
Carshalton SM5
Thornton Heath CR0
Bulls Alley SW14
Bulls Bridge Ind Est UB2
Bulls Bridge Rd UB2
Bullsbrook Rd UB4
Bull's Cross EN1, EN2
Bull's Gdns SW3
Bulls Head Pas EC3
Bull Yd SE15
Bulmer Gdns HA3
Bulmer Mews W11 113 C5
Bulow Ct 3 SW6
Bulstrode Ave TW3
Bulstrode Gdns TW3
Bulstrode Pl W1
Bulstrode Rd TW3
Bulstrode St W1 93 A1
Bulwer Court Rd E11
Bulwer Ct E11
Bulwer Gdns EN5
Bulwer Rd
Edmonton N18
Leytonstone E11
New Barnet EN5
Bulwer St W12
Bunbury Ho SE15
Bunces La IG8
Bungalow Rd SE25
Bungalows The
Leyton E10
Mitcham SW16
Bunhill Row EC1 95 B3
Bunhouse Pl SW1
Bunker's Hill DA17
Bunkers Hill
London NW11
North Cray DA14
Bunning Ho N7
Bunning Way N7
Bunn's La NW7
Bunsen Ho 2 E3
Bunsen St 3 E3
Buntingbridge Rd IG2
Bunting Cl London N9
Mitcham CR4
Bunting Ct NW9
Bunton St SE18
Bunyan Ct EC2
Bunyan Rd E17
Buonaparte Mews SW1
BUPA Bushey Hospl WD23
Burbage Cl
Bermondsey SE1 117 B3
Hayes UB3
Burbage Ho
16 Deptford SE14
Shoreditch N1
Burbage Rd SE21, SE24
Burbage Sch N1
Burbank KT3
Burberry Cl KT3
Burberry Ct 8 N3
Burbidge Rd TW17
Burbridge Way N17
Burcham St E14
Burcharbro Rd SE2
Burchell Ct WD23
Burchell Ho SE11
Burchell Rd
Leyton E10
London SE15
Burcher Gale Gr 5 SE15
Burchetts Way TW17
Burchett Way RM6
Burcote Rd SW18
Burden Cl TW8
Burden Ho SW8
Burdenshott Ave TW10
Burden Way E11
Burder Cl N1
Burder Rd N1
Burdett Ave SW20

dett Cl
Ealing W7 108 D5
dcup DA14 191 A5
dett Coutts &
wnshend CE Prim
h SW1 115 D2 259 D3
dett Mews 4 W2 91 D1
dett Rd
chmond TW9 132 B2
ornton Heath CR0 205 B3
wer Hamlets E3 97 B2
detts Rd RM9 103 B6
dock Cl CR0 206 D1
dock Rd N17 52 A6
don Ct 3 E8 74 A2
don La SM2 217 A1
e Ct 17 EN5 13 D6
field Cl SW17 180 B6
ford Cl
genham RM8 80 C5
enham UB10 60 A4
ord IG6 57 A5
ford Ct SE8 141 C6
ford Gdns N13 16 B1
ford Ho
Brentford
TW8 110 A1
South Lambeth
SW9 138 B3
ford Rd
entford TW8 110 A1
omley BR1 210 A5
rest Hill SE6 163 B2
wham E6 100 A4
w Malden KT4 200 A2
Stratford Marsh
E15 98 B6
tton SM1 217 C6
ford Way CR0 224 A2
ford Wlk SW6 265 D3
gate Ct 9 SW9 138 C2
ges Gr SW13 134 B5
ges Rd E6 78 B1
gess Ave NW9 45 B3
gess Cl 4 TW13 173 A6
gess Ct
London N20 14 D2
Southall UB1 85 D1
allend E12 78 C1
gess Hill NW2 69 C4
gess Ho 3 SE5 139 A5
gess Ind Pk SE5 139 B5
gess Mews
/19 179 D4
gess Park Mans
V6 69 C4
gess Rd
tton E15 76 C4
tton SM1 217 D4
gess St E14 97 C2
ge St SE1 262 D5
ghill Rd SE26 185 A6
ghley Ave
rehamwood
WD6 11 A6
ngston u T KT3 177 B2
ghley Ct SW19 179 A5
ghley Hall Cl
/19 157 A3
ghley Ho SW19 157 A1
ghley Pl CR4 202 D5
ghley Rd
mden Town NW5 71 B4
ytonstone E11 54 C1
ndon N8 50 C6
mbledon SW19 179 A6
ghley Twr W3 111 D6
gh St N1 94 D5 234 D4
gon St EC4 241 D1
gos Cl CR0 220 C2
gos Gr SE10 141 D4
goyne Rd
hford TW16 171 D4
xton SW9 138 B2
rringay N4 50 D3
uth Norwood
SE25 205 D5
ham Cl SE20 184 C3
han Uddin Ho
243 C5
ill Gr HA5 23 A1
ton Ho 9 SW15 156 B3
ke Cl SW15 133 C1
ke Ho 1 SW11 136 B1
ke Lodge E13 99 B4
ke St E16 98 D2
ket Cl UB2 107 B2
land Rd SW11 158 D6
eigh Ave
xley DA15 167 D6
ckbridge SM6 219 B5
eigh Ct N17 34 A4
eigh Gdns
hford TW15 171 A5
dge N14 15 C3
eigh Ho
eam SM3 201 A1

Burleigh Ho *continued*
Chelsea SW3 266 D5
North Kensington
W10 90 D2
Burleigh Lo 3
SW19 179 D3
Burleigh Par N14 15 D3
Burleigh Pl SW15 156 D6
Burleigh Rd
Cheam SM3 201 A1
Enfield EN1 5 C1
Hillingdon UB10 82 D6
Burleigh St WC2 250 C6
Burleigh Way EN2 5 B2
Burleigh Wlk SE6 164 A3
Burley Cl Chingford E4 35 C5
Mitcham SW16 181 D1
Burley Ho E1 96 D1
Burley Rd E16 99 C2
Burlington Apartments
SE20 184 B3
Burlington Arc W1 249 A5
Burlington Ave
Richmond TW9 132 C4
Romford RM7 59 D3
Burlington Cl
East Bedfont
TW14 149 B4
5 Newham E6 100 A1
Orpington BR6 226 D6
Paddington W9 91 C3
Pinner HA5 40 B6
Burlington Ct
Chiswick W4 133 A5
Highgate N6 49 A1
Burlington Danes Sch
W12 90 B1
Burlington Gate
SW20 179 A1
Burlington Gdns
Acton Green W4 111 A1
Acton W3 111 A5
Dagenham RM6 59 A2
Fulham SW6 135 A3
Marylebone
W1 115 C6 249 A5
Burlington Ho NW3 70 B3
Burlington Inf Sch
KT3 199 D5
Burlington Jun Sch
KT3 199 D5
Burlington La W4 133 B5
Burlington Lo BR7 188 B3
Burlington Mews
Acton W3 111 A5
2 Putney SW15 157 B6
Burlington Park Ho 6
HA7 25 C6
Burlington Pl
Fulham SW6 135 A3
Woodford IG8 21 A1
Burlington Rd
Acton Green W4 111 A1
Enfield EN2 5 B4
Fulham SW6 135 A3
Hounslow TW7 130 B4
Muswell Hill N10 49 A6
New Malden KT3 199 D5
South Norwood CR7 183 B1
Tottenham N17 34 A2
Burlington Rise EN4 14 D4
Burma Rd N16 73 B4
Burmarsh Ct SE20 184 C2
Burmarsh 6 NW5 71 A2
Burma Terr 11 SE19 183 C5
Burmester Ho
SW17 158 A1
Burmester Rd
SW17 158 A1
Burnaby Cres W4 133 A6
Burnaby Ct 31 SE16 118 A4
Burnaby Gdns W4 132 D6
Burnaby St
SW10 136 A5 266 B3
Burnand Ho 3
W14 112 D3
Burnbrae Cl N12 29 D4
Burnbury Rd SW12 159 C3
Burncroft Ave EN3 6 C3
Burndell Way UB4 84 D2
Burne Jones Ho
W14 254 B3
Burnell Ave
Richmond TW10 175 C5
Welling DA16 146 A3
Burnell Gdns HA7 25 D1
Burnell Ho 18 SW2 160 C3
Burnell Rd SM1 217 D4
Burnell Wlk SE1 263 D2
Burnels Ave E6 100 C4
Burness Cl N7 72 B2
Burne St NW1 237 A4
Burnett Cl E9 74 C3
Burnett Ct SW11 267 A1
Burnett Ho 6 SE13 142 A3
Burney Ave KT5 198 B4
Burney Ho 4 SW16 181 C5

Burney St SE10 142 A5
Burnfoot Ave
SW6 135 A4 264 B1
Burnham Ave UB10 61 A4
Burnham Cl
Bermondsey SE1 263 D3
Enfield EN1 5 C5
Harrow HA3 43 A5
Hendon NW7 28 A3
Burnham Cres E11 55 C5
Burnham Ct
Bayswater W2 245 D6
Hendon NW4 46 C5
15 Stanmore HA7 25 C5
Burnham Dr KT4 216 D6
Burnham Est 8 E2 96 C4
Burnham Gdns
Cranford TW4 128 B4
Croydon CR0 205 D2
Hayes UB3 105 B3
Burnham NW3 70 C1
Burnham Rd
Chingford Hatch E4 35 B5
Dagenham RM9 102 B6
Morden SM4 201 D5
Sidcup DA14 169 A2
Burnham St
Bethnal Green E2 96 C4
Kingston u T KT2 176 C2
Burnham Way
Ealing W13 109 B3
Penge SE26 185 B5
Burnhill Ho EC1 235 A1
Burnhill Rd BR3 185 C1
Burnley Cl WD19 22 C5
Burnley Rd
London SW9 138 B3
Willesden NW10 68 A3
Burnsall St
SW3 114 C1 257 B2
Burns Ave
Blackfen DA15 168 B5
Feltham TW14 150 A5
Ilford RM6 58 C2
Southall UB1 107 C6
Burns Cl
Bexley DA16 145 D4
Hayes UB4 84 A2
Mitcham SW17 180 B4
Walthamstow E17 54 A5
Burns Ct
Tottenham N17 34 B3
Wallington SM6 219 B1
Burns Ho
18 Bethnal Green
E2 96 C4
Bexley DA16 146 C4
1 Islington N7 72 B2
Kennington SE17 261 D1
Burn's Ho NW10 89 C6
Burns Ho 11 N16 73 C4
Burnside Ave E4 35 B4
Burnside Cl Barnet EN5 1 C2
Rotherhithe SE16 118 D5
Twickenham TW1 153 A5
Burnside Cres HA0 87 D6
Burnside Ct 1 SM6 219 A5
Burnside Rd RM8 58 D1
Burns Rd
Battersea SW11 136 D3
Ealing W13 109 B4
Burn's Rd NW10 89 D6
Burns Rd HA0 88 A5
Burns Way TW5 128 D4
Burnt Ash Hill
Lee SE12 164 D5
Lewisham SE12 165 A3
Burnt Ash Hts BR1 187 B5
Burnt Ash La BR1,
SE12 187 B5
Burnt Ash Prim Sch
BR1 187 A5
Burnt Ash Rd SE12 164 D6
Burnthwaite Rd
SW6 135 B5 264 D3
BURNT OAK 27 B3
Burnt Oak Broadway
HA8 26 D2
Burnt Oak Fields
HA8 27 A2
Burnt Oak Jun Sch
DA15 168 A3
Burnt Oak La DA15 168 B3
Burnt Oak Sta HA8 27 A2
Burntwood Cl SW18 158 C3
Burntwood Ct
SW17 158 A1
Burntwood Grange Rd
SW18 158 C3
Burntwood La
SW17 158 B2
Burntwood Sch
SW17 158 B2
Burntwood View 6
SE19 183 D5
Buross St E1 96 B1
Burpham Cl UB4 84 D2

Burrage Ct 17 SE16 118 D2
Burrage Gr SE18 123 A2
Burrage Pl SE18 122 D1
Burrage Rd SE18 123 A1
Burrard Ho 11 E2 96 C5
Burrard Rd
Newham E16 99 B1
West Hampstead
NW6 69 C4
Burr Cl
Bexleyheath DA7 147 B2
St George in t East
E1 118 A5
Burrell Cl
Croydon CR0 207 A3
Edgware HA8 10 D2
Burrell Ct HA1 42 B2
Burrell Ho 4 TW1 153 B4
Burrell Row BR3 185 C1
Burrells 9 BR3 185 D1
Burrell St
SE1 116 D5 251 C4
Burrell's Wharf Sq
E14 119 D1
Burrell Twrs E10 53 C2
Burrhill Ct SE16 118 D3
Burritt Rd KT1 176 C1
Burrmead Ct NW2 67 D5
Burroughs Gdns
NW4 46 B5
Burroughs The NW4 46 B5
Burrow Ho 10 SW9 138 B3
Burrow Rd SE22 139 C1
Burrows Mews SE1 251 C2
Burrows Rd NW10 90 C4
Burrow Wlk SE21 161 A4
Burr Rd SW18 157 C4
Bursar St SE1 253 A3
Bursdon Cl DA15 167 D2
Bursland Rd EN3 6 D1
Burslem St E1 96 A1
Bursted Wood Prim Sch
DA7 147 D3
Burstock Rd SW15 135 A1
Burston Rd SW15 156 D6
Burstow Rd SW20 179 A2
Burtenshaw Rd KT7 197 A3
Burtley Cl N4 51 A1
Burton Bank N1 73 B1
Burton Cl
Chessington KT9 213 D1
South Norwood CR7 205 B6
Burton Ct
Chelsea SW3 257 D2
10 Friern Barnet N11 30 D5
Thames Ditton KT7 197 A3
Burton Dr EN3 7 C6
Burton Gdns TW5 129 B4
Burton Gr SE17 262 C1
Burton Ho
8 Bermondsey
SE16 118 B4
Brixton SE5 138 D4
Burtonhole Cl NW7 28 D6
Burtonhole La
Finchley NW7 29 A6
Mill Hill NW7 28 D6
Burton Ho SE26 184 B5
Burton La 3 SW9 138 C3
Burton Lo 6 SW15 157 B6
Burton Mews SW1 258 B3
Burton Pl WC1 232 D1
Burton Rd
7 Brixton SW9 138 C3
Brixton SW9 138 D3
Brondesbury NW6 69 B1
Kingston u T KT2 176 A3
Wanstead E18 55 B6
Burtons Ct E15 76 B1
Burtons Rd TW12 174 A6
Burton St
WC1 93 D3 239 D6
Burtonwood Ho N4 51 B2
Burt Rd E16 121 C5
Burtt Ho 6 N1 95 C4
Burtwell La SE21,
SE27 183 B6
Burvill Ct SW20 178 C2
Burwash Ho SE1 252 D1
Burwash Rd SE18 123 B1
Burwell Ave UB6 64 C2
Burwell Cl 27 E1 96 B1
Burwell 2 KT1 176 C1
Burwell Rd E10 53 A1
Burwell Wlk 14 E3 97 C3
Burwood Ave
Hayes BR2 225 B6
Pinner HA5 40 C4
Burwood Cl KT6 198 C1
Burwood Ct SE23 162 C4
Burwood Ho 11
SW9 138 D1
Burwood Lo SW19 179 B6
Burwood Pl Barnet EN4 2 A4
Paddington W2 237 B2
Bury Ave Hayes UB4 83 C5
Ruislip HA4 39 A3

Bury Cl SE16 118 D5
Bury Ct EC3 243 B2
Buryfield Ct 23 SE8 118 D2
Bury Gr SM4 201 D4
Bury Hall Villas N9 17 D4
Bury Pl WC1 94 A2 240 B3
Bury Rd Chingford E4 20 C6
Dagenham RM10 81 D3
Hornsey N22 50 C6
Bury St W N9 17 C4
Buryside Cl IG2 57 D5
Bury St Edmonton N9 18 A3
Ruislip HA4 39 B3
St James
SW1 115 C5 249 B4
Whitechapel
EC3 95 C1 243 B2
Bury Wlk
SW3 114 C1 257 A2
Burywood Ct EN3 6 C3
Busbridge Ho 24 E14 97 C2
Busby Ho SW16 181 C6
Busby Mews 5 NW1 71 D2
Busby Pl NW5 71 D2
Busch Cl TW7 131 B4
Busch Cnr TW7 131 B4
Bushbaby Cl SE1 263 A5
Bushberry Rd E9 75 A2
Bush Cl IG2 57 B4
Bush Cotts 12 SW18 157 C6
Bush Ct London N14 15 C3
7 Shepherd's Bush
W12 112 D4
Bushell Cl SW2 160 B2
Bushell Gn WD23 8 B2
Bushell Ho 3 SE27 183 A6
Bushell Way BR7 188 C5
BUSHEY 8 A2
Bushey Ave
Crofton BR5 211 B2
Snaresbrook E18 54 D6
Bushey Cl
Chingford E4 20 A1
Ickenham UB10 60 C6
Bushey Ct SW20 178 B1
Bushey Down SW12 159 B2
Bushey Hall SE5 139 D4
BUSHEY HEATH 8 C4
Bushey Heath Prim Sch
WD23 8 B3
Bushey Hill Rd SE5 139 D4
Bushey Ho SE12 165 C1
Bushey La SM1 217 C4
Bushey Lees DA15 167 D5
BUSHEY MEAD 200 D6
Bushey Meads Sch
WD23 8 A6
Bushey Rd
Croydon CR0 223 C6
Hayes UB3 105 C2
Ickenham UB10 60 C6
Newham E13 99 C5
South Tottenham N15 51 C3
Sutton SM1 217 C4
West Barnes SW20 178 D1
Bushey Way BR3 208 B4
Bush Fair Ct N14 15 B5
Bushfield Cl HA8 10 D2
Bushfield Cres HA8 10 D2
Bushfield Ho N5 73 A3
Bush Gr NW9 45 A2
Bushgrove Rd RM8 80 D5
Bush Gr HA7 25 D2
BUSH HILL 17 B5
Bush Hill N21 17 A5
Bush Hill Par EN1 17 B4
BUSH HILL PARK 17 C5
Bush Hill Park Prim Sch
EN1 18 A6
Bush Hill Park Sta
EN1 17 D5
Bush Hill Rd
Enfield N21 17 B5
Harrow HA3 44 B3
Bush Ind Est NW10 89 B3
Bush La EC4 117 B6 252 C6
Bushmead Cl 7 N15 51 D5
Bushmoor Cres
SE18 144 D5
Bushnell Rd SW17 159 B1
Bush Rd
Bermondsey SE8 118 D2
Hackney E8 96 B6
Littleton TW17 192 B4
Richmond TW9 132 B6
Wanstead E11 55 A2
Woodford IG9 37 D6
Bushway RM8 80 D5
Bushwood Dr
SE1 117 D2 263 D3
Bushwood Rd TW9 132 C6
Bushwood E11 55 A1
Bushy Ct KT1 175 C2
Bushy Park Gdns
TW12 174 B5
Bushy Park Rd
TW11 175 B3

Bushy Rd TW11 174 D3
Business Acad Bexley
The DA18 125 A4
Business Design Ctr*
N1 94 C6 234 B5
Buspace Studios 3
W10 91 A3
Butcher Row E1 96 D1
Butchers Rd E16 99 A1
Bute Ave TW10 154 A2
Bute Ct SM6 219 C3
Bute Gardens W
SM6 219 C3
Bute Gdns
Hammersmith
W6 112 D2
Wallington SM6 219 C3
Bute House Prep Sch
W6 112 D2
Bute Mews NW11 48 A4
Bute Rd Ilford IG6 56 D4
Thornton Heath CR0 204 C1
Wallington SM6 219 C4
Bute St SW7 114 B2 256 C4
Bute Wlk 18 N1 73 B2
Butfield Ho 6 E9 74 C2
Butler Ave HA1 42 B2
Butler Cl HA8 26 D1
Butler Ct
Dagenham RM8 81 C6
Wembley HA0 65 A4
Butler Ho
32 Bethnal Green
E2 96 C4
5 Brixton SW9 138 D4
11 Poplar E14 97 B1
Butler Pl SW1 259 C6
Butler Rd
Dagenham RM8 80 B4
Harrow HA1 42 A2
Willesden NW10 67 D1
Butlers Cl TW3 129 B1
Butlers & Colonial
Wharf SE1 253 D2
Butler's Cotts DA7 147 C3
Butler St
33 Bethnal Green
E2 96 C4
Hillingdon UB10 82 D3
Butler's Wharf W
SE1 253 C3
Butley Ct 8 E3 97 A5
Butt Ct SM4 202 A3
Buttercup Cl UB5 63 B2
Butterfield Cl
1 Bermondsey
SE16 118 B4
Tottenham N17 33 A4
Twickenham TW1 152 D5
Butterfield Ho 4 EN2 4 D3
Butterfields E17 54 A4
Butterfield Sq 10
E6 100 B1
Butterfly Ct E6 100 B4
Butterfly La SE9 166 D5
Butterfly Wlk 2
SE5 139 B4
Butter Hill SM5,
SM6 219 A4
Butteridges Cl RM9 103 B6
Buttermere Cl
Bermondsey SE1 263 C3
East Bedfont TW14 149 D3
Leyton E11 76 B4
West Barnes SM4 200 D3
Buttermere Ct NW8 229 C6
Buttermere Dr
SW15 157 A6
Buttermere Ho
London N12 30 C5
13 Tower Hamlets E3 97 B4
Buttermere NW1 231 D2
Buttermere Wlk 9
E8 73 D2
Butterwick W6 112 C2
Butterworth Ct
SW16 160 A1
Butterworth Gdns
IG8 37 A5
Buttesland St
N1 95 B4 235 D2
Buttfield Cl RM10 81 D2
Buttmarsh Cl SE18 122 D1
Buttsbury Rd IG1 79 A3
Butts Cotts TW13 151 B1
Butts Cres TW13 151 C1
Butts Ho TW13 151 C1
Butts Piece UB5 84 B5
Butts Rd BR1 186 C5
Butts The TW8 131 D6
Buxhall Cres E9 75 B2
Buxlow Prep Sch
HA9 66 A5

Buxted Rd
Camberwell SE22 ... 139 C1
Colney Hatch N12 .....30 C5
Dalston E8...........73 D1
Buxton Cl London N9...18 C2
Woodford IG8........37 D4
Buxton Cres SM3 ....217 A4
Buxton Ct
1 Leyton E11........54 D2
Shoreditch N1 ...... 235 B2
Buxton Dr
Kingston u T KT3......177 B1
Leytonstone E11 ......54 C5
Buxton Gdns W3.....110 D6
Buxton Ho
Leytonstone E11 ......54 C5
3 London SW11......136 B1
Buxton Lo E11........77 B6
Buxton Mews SW4...137 D3
Buxton Rd
Chingford E4 ....20 B4
Ilford IG2 ....57 C3
Mortlake SW14 ..... 133 C2
Newham E6........ 100 A4
Stratford E15.........76 C3
Thornton Heath CR7 . 204 D4
Upper Holloway N19...49 D1
Walthamstow E17.......53 A5
Willesden NW2 ....68 B2
Buxton St E1 ..95 D3 243 D5
Buzzard Creek Ind Est
IG11.............. 102 A2
Byam Shaw Sch of Art
N19...............71 D6
Byam St SW6........136 A3
Byards Croft SW16...181 D2
Byards Ct SE16 ......118 D3
Byas Ho 6 E3 ....97 B4
Byatt Wlk TW12.......173 A4
Bychurch End 11
TW11.............174 D5
Bycroft Rd UB1 ....85 C3
Bycroft St SE20 ......184 D3
Bycullah Ave EN2 ......4 D3
Bycullah Ct EN2 ....4 D2
Bycullah Rd EN2 ....4 D3
Byefield Cl SE16 ......119 A4
Byegrove Ct SW19 ...180 B4
Byegrove Rd SW19...180 B4
Byelands Cl 12
SE16..............118 D5
Bye The W3 ....89 C1
Byeways The KT5 ....198 D4
Bye Ways TW2.........151 D1
Bye Way The HA3 .....24 D2
Byeway The SW14....133 A2
Byfeld Gdns SW13 ...134 A4
Byfield Ct KT3 ....200 A5
Byfield Rd TW7 ....131 A2
Byford Cl E15.........76 C1
Bygrove CR0.........223 D1
Bygrove Prim Sch
E14................97 D1
Bygrove St E14 ....97 D1
Byland Cl
Abbey Wood SE2 .....124 B3
Carshalton SM4......202 B2
Southgate N21.........16 B4
Byne Rd
Carshalton SM5..... 218 C6
Forest Hill SE26..... 184 C5
Bynes Rd CR2.........221 B1
Byng Pl WC1 ..93 D3 239 C5
Byng St E14 ....119 C4
Bynon Ave DA7 ......147 B2
Byre Rd N14...........15 B5
Byrne Ho 11 SW2 ....160 B6
Byrne Rd SW12 ......159 B2
Byron Ave
Borehamwood
WD6..............10 C6
Cranford TW4 ....128 B3
Byron Ave E SM1.....218 B4
Byron Ave
Plashet E12..........78 A2
Queensbury NW9 .....44 D6
Sutton SM1 ....218 B4
West Barnes KT3 .... 200 A4
Woodford E18........36 D1
Byron Cl
Feltham TW12.......173 B6
Forest Hill SE26..... 185 A6
Hackney E8..........96 A6
Streatham SW16..... 182 A4
Thamesmead SE28 .. 124 C5
Walton-on-T KT12 ... 195 A1
Byron Court Prim Sch
HA0 ....65 C6
Byron Ct
Chelsea SW3....... 257 B3
Dulwich SE21....... 162 A3
Ealing W7 .... 109 A2
Enfield EN2 ....4 D3
3 Hampstead NW6...70 A1

Byron Ct *continued*
Harrow HA1 ....42 C3
4 New Barnet EN5 ....2 A1
Paddington W9 ....91 C3
1 Richmond TW10.. 175 D6
South Norwood CR7 . 183 A1
St Pancras WC1...... 240 C6
11 Wanstead E11 .....55 A5
Woodford E18 ....37 B2
Byron Dr
East Finchley N2 ......48 B3
Erith DA8.......... 147 D5
Byron Gdns SM1.....218 B4
Byron Hill Rd HA1,
HA2 ....64 C6
Byron Ho 5 BR3....185 D4
Byron Mews
Hampstead NW3......70 C4
2 Maida Vale W9.....91 C3
Byron Par UB10.......83 A3
Byron Rd
Dollis Hill NW2 ....68 B6
Ealing W5 ....110 B5
Edgware NW7.........28 A5
Harrow HA1 ....42 C3
Leyton E10...........53 D1
Walthamstow E17 .....53 C6
Wealdstone HA3 ....24 D1
Wembley HA0 ....65 C5
Byron St E14 ....98 A1
Byron Way
Hayes UB4............83 D3
Northolt UB5 ....85 A4
West Drayton UB7....104 B2
Bysouth Cl N15 ....51 B5
Bythorn St SW9......138 B1
Byton Rd SW17 ......180 D4
Byward Ave TW14.....150 C5
Byward St
EC3 ....117 C6 253 B5
Bywater Ho SE18 ....122 A3
Bywater Pl SE16 .....119 A5
Bywater St
SW3........114 D1 257 C2
Byway The KT19 .....215 D4
Bywell Pl W1........ 239 A3
Bywood Ave CR0.....206 D3
Bywood Terr CR0.....206 C3
Byworth Ho HA7 ......25 C4
Byworth Wlk N19 .....50 A1

C

Cabbell St
NW1.........92 C2 237 A3
Cabinet Off SW1.... 250 A2
Cabinet War Rooms &
Churchill Mus*
SW1....... 115 D4 249 D2
Cabinet Way E4........35 B4
Cable Ho WC1 ...... 234 A2
Cable Pl SE10........142 A4
Cable St E1..........118 B6
Cabot Ct SE16 ....118 D3
Cabot Sq E14 ....119 C5
Cabot Way 3 E6......99 D6
Cabul Rd SW11 ......136 C3
Cactus Cl SE5.......139 C3
Cactus Wlk W12 ....89 D1
Cadbury Cl
Ashford TW16 ...... 171 C3
Isleworth TW7...... 131 A4
Cadbury Rd TW16....171 C4
Cadbury Way 1
SE16...............118 A2
Caddington Cl EN4....14 C6
Caddington Rd NW2 ..69 A5
Caddis Cl HA7 ....24 D3
Cadell Cl E2..........95 D5
Cadell Ho 12 E2.......95 D5
Cade Rd SE10.........142 B4
Cader Rd SW18 ......158 A5
Cadet Dr
SE1....... 117 D1 263 D2
Cade Tyler Ho 10
SE10...............142 A4
Cadiz St
SE17........117 A1 262 B1
Cadley Terr SE23 .....162 C2
Cadman Cl SW9 .....138 D5
Cadmer Cl KT3 ......199 C5
Cadmore Ho 4 N1....72 D1
Cadmus Cl 9 SW4 ...137 D2
Cadmus Ct 6 SW9...138 C4
Cadnam Lo E14.......120 B3
Cadnam Point 15
SW15..............156 B3
Cadogan Cl
Beckenham BR3 .....186 B1
Hackney Wick E9......75 B1
Harrow HA2 ....63 D4
Teddington TW11.... 174 C5
Cadogan Ct SW3.... 257 C3
Cadogan Ct Gdns
SW1............... 258 A4

Cadogan Ct
New Malden KT3.... 199 C5
Sutton SM2 .... 217 D2
Cadogan Gate
SW1....... 114 D2 257 D4
Cadogan Gdns
Chelsea
SW3 .....114 D2 257 D3
Finchley N3 ....29 D2
Southgate N21........16 C6
Wanstead E18.........55 B6
Cadogan Ho SW3 ... 266 D5
Cadogan La
SW1.........115 A3 258 A5
Cadogan Pl
SW1....... 114 D3 257 D5
Cadogan Rd
Kingston u T KT6.... 197 D4
Woolwich SE18 ..... 123 A3
Cadogan Sq
SW1....... 114 D3 257 D5
Cadogan St
SW3..........114 D2 257 C3
Cadogan Terr E9......75 B1
Cadoxton Ave 3
N15 ....51 D3
Cadwallon Rd SE9 ....167 A2
Caedmon Rd N7 ......72 B4
Caerleon Cl
Claygate KT10.......213 B1
Sidcup DA14 .... 190 C5
Caerleon Terr SE2....124 B2
Caernafon Ho HA7 ....25 A5
Caernarvon Cl CR4....204 A6
Caernarvon Ct 3
KT5 ....198 B4
Caernarvon Ho W2 . 236 A2
Caesar Ct 25 E2.......96 D5
Caesar's Way TW17 ..193 B3
Caesars Wlk CR4.....202 D4
Cahill St EC1 .... 242 B5
Cahir St E14.........119 D2
Cain Ct 2 W5 ....87 C2
Caine Ho W3 ....110 D4
Cain's La TW14 ......149 C6
Caird St W10 ....91 B4
Cairn Ave W5.........109 D5
Cairndale Cl BR1......186 D3
Cairnfield Ave NW2 ...67 D5
Cairnfield Ct NW2 ....67 C5
Cairngorm Cl 3
TW11...............175 A5
Cairn Ho 3 SW19....180 C3
Cairns Ho 3 N7 ......72 B4
Cairns Mews SE18 ....144 A4
Cairns Rd SW11......158 C6
Cairn Way HA7 ....24 D4
Cairo New Rd CR0 ...220 D6
Cairo Rd E17 ....53 C5
Caister Ho N7 ....72 B2
Caistor Ho
10 Balham SW12 ....159 B4
5 West Ham E15......98 D6
Caistor Mews SW12..159 B4
Caistor Park Rd E15...98 D6
Caistor Rd SW12......159 B4
Caithness Gdns
DA15 ....167 D5
Caithness Ho N1.... 233 C6
Caithness Rd
Hammersmith
W14 .... 112 D3
Mitcham CR4........181 B3
Calabria Rd N5 ....72 D3
Calais Gate SE5......138 D4
Calais St SE5 ....138 D4
Calbourne Rd SW12..159 A4
Calcott Wlk SE9 .....187 D6
Calcraft Ho 10 E2 .....96 C5
Caldbeck Ave KT4....200 B1
Caldecot Ct SE5 .....139 A3
Caldecote Gdns WD23.. 8 C4
Caldecote 3 KT1 .....176 C1
Caldecote La WD23 ....8 D5
Caldecot Rd SE5......139 A3
Caldecott Way E5......74 D5
Calder Ave UB6 ....86 D5
Calder Cl EN1 ....5 C2
Calder Ct SE16.......119 B5
Calder Gdns HA8 .....44 C6
Calder Ho UB5.........85 A6
Calderon Ho NW8.... 230 A4
Calderon Pl 20 W10...90 C2
Calderon Rd E11......76 B5
Calder Rd SM4........202 A4
Caldervale Rd SW4 ..159 D6
Calderwood St
SE18...............122 C2
Caldew Ct NW7.......28 A3
Caldew St SE5 ....139 B5
Caldicote Gn NW9 ....45 C3
Caldon Ho 2 UB5.....85 B3
Caldwell Rd WD19 ....22 D6
Caldwell St
SW9.......138 B5 270 D3
Caldy Rd DA17........125 D3
Caldy Wlk 19 N1 ......73 A2

Caleb St SE1........ 252 B2
Caledonia Ct
Barking IG11....... 102 C5
Hendon NW4.........28 C1
Caledonia Ho 15 E14 ..97 A1
Caledonian Cl 1 IG3...58 B1
Caledonian Ct UB5...85 A3
Caledonian Market
SE1.........117 C3 263 B6
Caledonian Rd
Islington
N1 ....94 B6 233 C5
Lower Holloway N7....72 B2
Caledonian Road &
Barnsbury Sta N7...72 B1
Caledonian Road Sta
N7 ....72 B2
Caledonian Sq 6
NW1...............71 D2
Caledonian Wharf Rd
E14...............120 B2
Caledonia Rd TW19 ..148 A3
Caledonia St N1 .... 233 B3
Caledon Rd
East Ham E6 ....78 B1
Hackbridge SM5,
SM6 .... 219 A4
Cale St SW3 ..114 C1 257 A2
Caletock Way SE10...120 D1
Calgarth NW1 ...... 232 B3
Calgary Ct 30 SE16...118 C4
Caliban Twr 9 N1.....95 C5
Calico Ho 4 SW11...136 A2
Calico Row 5
SW11..............136 A2
Calidore Cl SW2 .....160 B5
California Bldg 2
SE13...............141 D4
California La WD23 .... 8 B3
California Rd KT3.....199 A6
Callaby Terr 11 N1 ....73 B2
Callaghan Cl SE13 ...142 C1
Callahan Cotts 8 E1...96 C2
Callander Rd SE6 ....164 A2
Callanders The WD23 .. 8 C3
Callan Sch The
W1.........93 C1 239 B2
Callard Ave N13 ....32 D6
Callcott Ct NW6 ......69 B1
Callcott Rd NW6......69 B1
Callcott St W8...... 245 A4
Callendar Rd SW7 .. 256 C6
Callingham Cl 13 E14 .97 B2
Callingham Ho 1
SW4...............138 A2
Callis Farm Cl
TW19..............148 A5
Callis Rd E17 ....53 B3
Callonfield 3 E17 .....53 A5
Callow St
SW3........136 B6 266 C6
Calmington Rd SE5 .139 C6
Calmont Rd BR1 ......186 C4
Calonne Rd SW19....178 D6
Calshot Ho N1...... 233 C4
Calshot Rd TW6 .....126 D3
Calshot St N1.. 94 B5 233 C3
Calshot Way
Enfield EN2 ....4 D2
Harlington TW6...... 126 C3
Calstock Ho SE11 ... 261 B2
Calstock NW1 ...... 232 C5
Calthorpe Gdns
Edgware HA8.........26 B5
Sutton SM1 .... 218 A5
Calthorpe St
WC1.........94 B3 240 D6
Calton Ave SE21 .....161 C5
Calton Rd EN5 ....14 B5
Calumet Ct SW17 ....180 C4
Calver Ct E17 ....54 B6
Calverley Cl BR3.....185 D4
Calverley Cres RM10 ..81 C6
Calverley Gdns HA3 ...43 D2
Calverley Gr N19......49 D1
Calverley Rd KT17....216 A2
Calver 13 NW5........71 B4
Calvert Ave E2........95 D4
Calvert Cl
Belvedere DA17 .... 125 D2
Sidcup DA14 .... 191 A4
Calvert Ct
1 London N19 ....49 C1
5 Richmond TW9....132 B1
Calvert Ho 9 W12 ...112 B6
Calverton Prim Sch
E16.................99 D1
Calverton Rd E6 .....100 C6
Calverton SE5 ....139 C6
Calvert Rd SE10......120 D1
Calvert's Bldgs SE1 . 252 C3
Calvert St
NW1.........93 A6 231 A6
Calvin St E1 ...95 D3 243 C5
Calydon Rd SE7.......121 B1
Calypso Cres 6
SE15...............139 D5

Calypso Way SE8,
SE16..............119 B2
Camac Rd TW2 ......152 B3
Camarthen Gn NW9...45 C3
Cambalt Ho 3
SW15..............156 D6
Cambalt Rd SW15....156 D6
Cambay Ho 7 E1 .....97 A3
Cambell Jun & Inf Schs
RM9................80 D1
Camber Ho 4 SE15 ..140 C6
Camberley Ave
Enfield EN1 ....5 C1
Wimbledon SW20 ....178 B1
Camberley Cl SM3 ...216 D5
Camberley Ct 15
SM2...............217 D1
Camberley Ho NW1 . 231 D3
Camberley Rd TW6 ..126 C2
Cambert Way SE9...143 B1
CAMBERWELL 139 A4
Camberwell Bsns Ctr
SE5................139 B5
Camberwell Church St
SE5................139 B4
Camberwell Coll of
Arts
Camberwell SE5 .... 139 C4
Camberwell SE15 ... 139 D5
Camberwell Glebe
SE5................139 C4
Camberwell Gn SE5..139 B4
Camberwell Green
SE5................139 A4
Camberwell Gr SE5 ..139 C3
Camberwell New Rd
SW9................138 D5
Camberwell Rd SE5..139 A5
Camberwell Station Rd
SE5................139 A4
Camberwell Trad Est
SE5............... 139 A4
Cambeys Rd RM10 ....81 D3
Cambisgate SW19 ...179 A5
Camborne Ave W13..109 C4
Camborne Cl TW6 ...126 C2
Camborne Rd
Belmont SM2....... 217 D1
Bexley DA16 .... 145 D3
Croydon CR0 .... 206 A2
Harmondsworth
TW6 .... 126 C2
Sidcup DA14 .... 168 C1
Wandsworth SW18 .. 157 C4
West Barnes SM4 ... 200 D4
Camborne Way
Harlington TW6..... 126 C2
Heston TW5........ 129 C4
Cambourne Ave N9 ...18 D4
Cambourne Mews 6
W11................91 A1
Cambrai Ct N13.......32 A6
Cambray Rd
Broom Hill BR6 ..... 211 D2
Streatham SW12..... 159 C3
Cambria 6 BR3......185 D1
Cambria Cl
Hounslow TW3 ..... 129 C1
Sidcup DA15 .... 167 C3
Cambria Ct TW14 ....150 B4
Cambria Gdns
TW19..............148 A4
Cambria Ho
Forest Hill SE26.... 184 A6
14 Limehouse E14.....97 A1
Cambria Lo 3
SW15..............157 B6
Cambrian Ave IG2 ....57 C4
Cambrian Cl SE27....160 D1
Cambrian Ct UB2 ....107 D2
Cambrian Gn NW9 ....45 C4
Cambrian Rd
Leyton E10...........53 C1
Richmond TW10......154 B5
Cambria Rd SE5 .....139 A2
Cambria St
SW6....... 135 D5 265 D3
Cambridge Ave
Falconwood DA16 ... 145 D1
Greenford UB6 ....64 D3
Kilburn NW6 ....91 C5
Kingston u T KT3,
SW20............ 177 D1
Cambridge Barracks Rd
11 SE18.............122 B2
Cambridge Cir
WC2..........93 D1 239 D1
Cambridge Cl
Hounslow TW4 ..... 129 A1
Walthamstow E17.....53 B3
Willesden NW10 ......67 A5
Wimbledon SW20 ....178 B2
Wood Green N22......32 C2
Cambridge Cotts
TW9...............132 C6

Cambridge Cres
20 Bethnal Green
E2..................96
Teddington TW11.... 175
Cambridge Ct
4 Barnet EN5 1
26 Bethnal Green E2...96
7 Hammersmith
W6............. 112
2 Kilburn NW6 91
Marylebone W2..... 237
Stamford Hill N16 51
Wembley HA0 65
Wimbledon SW20 178
Cambridge Dr
Lee SE12.......... 165
Ruislip HA4 62
Cambridge Gate Mews
NW1............. 238
Cambridge Gate
NW1............. 238
Cambridge Gdns
Enfield EN1 6
Kilburn NW6 91
Kingston u T KT1 176
Muswell Hill N10......31
North Kensington
W10................91
Southgate N21........17
Tottenham N17 33
Cambridge Gn SE9...166
Cambridge Gr W6 ...112
Cambridge Grove Rd
13 Kingston u T
KT1.............. 176
Kingston u T KT1 198
Cambridge Gr SE20 ..184
Cambridge Heath Rd E1,
E2..................96
Cambridge Heath Sta
E2..................96
Cambridge Ho
Barking IG11.........79
Ealing W13 87
Fulham SW6 135
2 Teddington
TW11........... 175
8 Woolwich SE18 ...122
Cambridge Mans
SW11.............. 267
Cambridge Par EN1.... 6
CAMBRIDGE PARK
...................153
Cambridge Park Ct
TW1...............153
Cambridge Park Rd
E11..................55
Cambridge Pas 9
E9..................74
Cambridge Pk
Twickenham TW1.... 153
Wanstead E11 55
Cambridge Pl W8... 245
Cambridge Rd
Barking IG11.........79
Barnes SW13 133
Battersea
SW11 .... 136 D4 267
Carshalton SM5..... 218
3 Chingford E4 20
East Molesey KT8 195
Hampton TW12 173
Hanwell W7......... 108
Harrow HA2 41
Hounslow TW4 129
Ilford IG3 57
Kilburn NW6 91
Kilburn NW6 91
Kingston u T KT1 176
Leytonstone E11 54
Littleton TW15...... 171
Mitcham CR4....... 203
New Malden KT3.... 199
Cambridge Rd N
W4.................110
Cambridge Rd
Penge SE20.........206
Plaistow BR1........ 187
Richmond TW9....... 132
Sidcup DA14 189
Cambridge Rd S 3
W4.................110
Cambridge Rd
Southall UB1 107
Teddington TW11.... 175
Twickenham TW1.... 153
Walton-on-T KT12 194
Wimbledon SW20 178
Cambridge Row
SE18...............122
Cambridge Sch W6..112
Cambridge Sq
W2..........92 C1 237
Cambridge St
SW1.........115 C1 259
Cambridge Terr N9 ...17

bridge Terr Mews
1 ... 231 D1
bridge Terr
1 ... 231 C1
bstone Cl N11 ... 15 A2
bus Cl UB4 ... 85 A2
bus Rd E16 ... 99 A2
Ct 2 SE15 ... 139 D6
dale Rd SE18 ... 145 D5
den Ave
tham TW13 ... 150 C3
res UB4 ... 106 D6
den Cl BR7 ... 189 A2
den Coll of English
1 ... 71 A1
den Ct 9 DA17 ... 125 C1
den Gdns
nden Town NW1 ... 71 B1
ton SM1 ... 217 D3
rnton Heath CR7 ... 204 D6
den Gr BR7 ... 188 D4
den High St
1 ... 93 C6 232 A5
den Hill Rd
9 ... 183 C4
den Ho
Deptford SE8 ... 119 B1
llington CR6 ... 220 A5
denhurst St E14 ... 97 A1
den Jun Sch
5 ... 218 D4
den Lock Pl
1 ... 71 B1
den Mews NW1 ... 71 D2
den Mkt*
1 ... 93 B6 231 D6
den Park Rd
nden Town
W1 ... 71 D2
islehurst West
R7 ... 188 C3
den Pas
... 94 D6 234 C5
den Rd
nden Town
W1 ... 93 B6 231 D6
rshalton SM5 ... 218 D4
Bexley DA5 ... 169 B4
tton SM1 ... 217 D3
lthamstow E17 ... 53 B3
nstead E11 ... 55 B3
den Road Sta
1 ... 71 C1
den Row SE3 ... 142 C3
den Sch for Girls
e NW5 ... 71 C2
den Sq NW1 ... 71 D2
den St
1 ... 93 C6 232 B5
den Studios
1 ... 232 B5
den Terr 17
1 ... 71 D2
DEN TOWN ... 71 B1
den Town Sta
1 ... 93 B6 231 D6
den Way
slehurst West
R7 ... 188 C3
rnton Heath CR7 ... 204 D6
den Wlk N1 ... 234 C5
eford Ct 20
12 ... 160 A4
elford Ct 15
1 ... 91 A1
elford Ho SE1 ... 260 B1
elford NW1 ... 232 B5
elford Wlk 13
1 ... 91 A1
el Gr KT2 ... 175 D5
elia Ct IG8 ... 36 C4
ellia Ct 20 BR3 ... 185 C3
ellia Ho
tham TW13 ... 150 A3
w Cross SE8 ... 141 B5
ellia Pl TW2 ... 151 D4
ellia St SW8 ... 270 A3
elot Cl
mstead SE18 ... 123 B4
mbledon SW19 ... 179 C6
elot Ho 15 NW1 ... 71 D2
elot Prim Sch
15 ... 140 B6
el Rd E16 ... 121 D5
era Pl SW10 ... 266 C6
eret Ct 6 W11 ... 112 D4
eron Cl
t Barnet N20 ... 14 C2
monton N18 ... 34 B5
eron Ct 3
19 ... 157 A3
eron Ho
Bromley BR1 ... 186 D2
nberwell SE5 ... 139 A5
John's Wood NW8 ... 230 A4
eron House Sch
10 ... 266 D6

Cameron Lo TW3 ... 130 A1
Cameron Pl SW16 ... 160 C2
Cameron Rd
Bromley BR2 ... 209 A4
Forest Hill SE6 ... 163 B2
Ilford IG3 ... 57 C1
Thornton Heath CR0 ... 204 D3
Cameron Sq CR4 ... 180 C2
Camerton Cl 8 E8 ... 73 D2
Camfrey Ct N8 ... 50 A5
Camgate Ctr The
TW19 ... 148 B4
Camilla Cl TW16 ... 171 D4
Camilla Ct 12 SM2 ... 217 C1
Camilla Rd SE16 ... 118 B2
Camille Cl SE25 ... 206 A6
Camlan Rd BR1 ... 186 D6
Camlet St E2 ... 243 C6
Camlet Way EN4 ... 1 D4
Camley St
NW1 ... 93 D5 232 D4
Camm Gdns
5 Kingston u T
KT1 ... 176 B1
Thames Ditton KT7 ... 196 D2
Camm 23 NW9 ... 27 D1
Camomile Ave CR4 ... 180 D2
Camomile St
EC3 ... 95 C1 243 B2
Camomile Way UB7 ... 82 A1
Campaign Ct W9 ... 91 B3
Campana Rd
SW6 ... 135 C4 265 B2
Campasps Bsns Pk
TW16 ... 193 D4
Campbell Ave IG6 ... 57 A5
Campbell Cl
Ruislip HA4 ... 40 A3
Shooters Hill SE18 ... 144 C4
Streatham SW16 ... 181 D6
Twickenham TW2 ... 152 B3
Campbell Croft HA8 ... 26 C5
Campbell Ct
Dulwich SE21 ... 162 A3
Ealing W7 ... 108 C6
Kingsbury NW9 ... 45 A3
South Kensington
SW7 ... 256 A5
Tottenham N17 ... 33 D2
Campbell Gordon Way
NW2 ... 68 B4
Campbell Ho
Paddington W2 ... 236 C5
Pimlico SW1 ... 259 A1
30 Shepherd's Bush
W12 ... 112 B6
6 Wallington SM6 ... 219 B4
Campbell Rd Bow E3 ... 97 C4
Ealing W7 ... 108 C6
Newham E6 ... 100 A6
Stratford E15 ... 76 D4
Thornton Heath CR0 ... 204 D3
Tottenham N17 ... 34 A2
Twickenham TW2 ... 152 B2
Walthamstow E17 ... 53 B5
Campbell Wlk N1 ... 233 B6
Campdale Rd N7 ... 71 D5
Campden Cres
Dagenham RM8 ... 80 C4
Wembley HA0 ... 65 B5
Campden Gr
W8 ... 113 C4 245 B2
Campden Hill Ct W8 ... 245 B2
Campden Hill Gate
W8 ... 245 A2
Campden Hill Gdns
W8 ... 245 A4
Campden Hill Mans
W8 ... 245 B4
Campden Hill Pl
W14 ... 244 D4
Campden Hill Rd
W8 ... 113 C4 245 A2
Campden Hill Sq
W14 ... 113 B5 244 D4
Campden Hill
W8 ... 113 C4 245 A2
Campden Ho 4 NW6 ... 70 B1
Campden Hos W8 ... 245 A3
Campden House Cl
W8 ... 245 B2
Campden Rd
Ickenham UB10 ... 60 B4
South Croydon CR2 ... 221 C3
Campden St
W8 ... 113 C5 245 A3
Campden Way RM8 ... 80 B4
Campe Ho 1 N10 ... 31 A3
Campen Cl SW19 ... 157 A2
Camperdown St E1 ... 243 D1
Campfield Rd SE9 ... 165 D4
Campion Cl
Harrow HA3 ... 44 B3
Hillingdon UB8 ... 82 B2
Newham E6 ... 122 B6
South Croydon CR2 ... 221 C4

Campion Ct
London N12 ... 30 C4
10 Wembley HA0 ... 88 A5
Campion Gdns IG8 ... 37 A5
Campion Ho 15 N16 ... 73 C3
Campion House
(Seminary) TW7 ... 130 B4
Campion Pl SE28 ... 124 B5
Campion Rd
Hounslow TW7 ... 130 D4
Putney SW15 ... 156 C6
Campion Terr NW2 ... 68 D5
Campion Way HA8 ... 27 A6
Camplin Rd HA3 ... 44 A4
Camplin St SE14 ... 140 D5
Camp Rd SW19 ... 178 C5
Campsbourne Ho 3
N8 ... 50 A5
Campsbourne Jun & Inf
Schs N8 ... 50 A6
Campsbourne Rd
Hornsey N8 ... 50 A5
Hornsey N8 ... 50 A6
Campsbourne The
N8 ... 50 A5
Campsey Gdns RM9 ... 80 B1
Campsey Rd RM9 ... 80 B1
Campsfield Ho N8 ... 50 A6
Campsfield Rd N8 ... 50 A6
Campshill Pl SE13 ... 164 A6
Campshill Rd SE13 ... 164 A6
Camp Site The BR8 ... 191 C3
Campton Hill Twrs
W8 ... 245 A4
Campus Rd E17 ... 53 B3
Camp View SW19 ... 178 B5
Cam Rd E15 ... 98 B6
Camrose Ave
Edgware HA8 ... 26 B2
Erith DA8 ... 147 D6
Feltham TW13 ... 172 C6
Camrose Cl
Croydon CR0 ... 207 A2
Morden SM4 ... 201 C5
Camrose St SE2 ... 124 A2
Camsey Ho 8 SW2 ... 160 B6
Canada Ave N18 ... 33 A4
Canada Cres W3 ... 89 A3
Canada Gdns SE13 ... 164 A6
Canada Rd W3 ... 89 A2
Canada Sq E14 ... 119 D5
Canada St SE16 ... 118 D4
Canada Water Sta
SE16 ... 118 D3
Canada Way W12 ... 112 B6
Canadian Ave SE6 ... 163 D3
Canal App SE8 ... 141 A6
Canal Bldg N1 ... 235 A4
Canal Bridge SE15 ... 140 A6
Canal Bvd 7 NW1 ... 71 D2
Canal Cl Mile End E1 ... 97 A3
North Kensington
W10 ... 90 D3
Canal Gr SE15 ... 140 B6
Canal Head Public Sq
1 SE15 ... 140 A4
Canal Path 22 E2 ... 95 D6
Canalside Studios 29
N1 ... 95 C6
Canal St SE5 ... 139 B6
Canal Way W10 ... 90 D3
Canal Wlk
Croydon CR0 ... 205 D3
Forest Hill SE26 ... 184 C5
Shoreditch
N1 ... 95 B6 235 D6
CANARY WHARF ... 119 D5
Canary Wharf*
E14 ... 119 D5
Canary Wharf Pier
(River Bus) E14 ... 119 B5
Canary Wharf Sta
E14 ... 119 D5
Canary Wharf Sta (DLR)
E14 ... 119 C5
Canberra Cl NW4 ... 46 A6
Canberra Dr UB4 ... 84 C4
Canberra Ho 7 HA4 ... 40 C1
Canberra Prim Sch
W12 ... 112 B6
Canberra Rd
Charlton SE7 ... 143 D6
Ealing W13 ... 109 A5
Erith DA7 ... 146 D6
Harlington TW6 ... 126 C2
Newham E6 ... 100 B6
Canbury Ave KT2 ... 176 B2
Canbury Bsns Pk 3
KT2 ... 176 A2
Canbury Ct 3 KT2 ... 176 A3
Canbury Mews
SE26 ... 162 A1
Canbury Park Rd
KT2 ... 176 B2
Canbury Sch KT2 ... 176 D4
Cancell Rd SW9 ... 138 C4
Candahar Rd SW11 ... 136 C3

Candida Ct 9 NW1 ... 71 B1
Candishe Ho SE1 ... 253 C2
Candle Gr SE15 ... 140 B2
Candlelight Ct 5
E15 ... 76 D2
Candlemakers 25
SW11 ... 136 B2
Candler Mews TW1 ... 153 A4
Candler St N15 ... 51 B3
Candover St W1 ... 239 A3
Candy St E3 ... 97 B6
Caney Mews NW2 ... 68 D6
Canfield Dr HA4 ... 62 B3
Canfield Gdns NW6 ... 69 D1
Canfield Ho N15 ... 51 C3
Canfield Pl NW6 ... 70 A2
Canford Ave UB5 ... 85 A6
Canford Cl EN2 ... 4 C3
Canford Gdns KT3 ... 199 C3
Canford Pl TW11 ... 175 C4
Canford Rd SW11 ... 159 A6
Canham Rd
Acton W3 ... 111 C4
South Norwood
SE25 ... 205 C6
Canmore Gdns
SW16 ... 181 C3
Cann Hall Prim Sch
E11 ... 76 D5
Cann Hall Rd E11 ... 76 D4
Cann Ho W14 ... 254 B5
Canning Cres N22 ... 32 B2
Canning Cross SE5 ... 139 C3
Canning Ct N22 ... 32 B2
Canning Ho 23 W12 ... 112 B6
Canning Pas
W8 ... 114 A3 256 A6
Canning Pl Mews
W8 ... 256 A6
Canning Pl
W8 ... 114 A3 256 A6
Canning Rd
Croydon CR0 ... 221 D6
Harrow HA3 ... 42 D6
Highbury N5 ... 72 D5
Walthamstow E17 ... 53 A6
West Ham E15 ... 98 C5
Cannington 14 NW5 ... 71 A2
Cannington Rd RM9 ... 80 C2
CANNING TOWN ... 99 B2
Canning Town E16 ... 98 C1
Canning Town Sta
E16 ... 98 C1
Cannizaro Rd SW19 ... 178 D5
Cannock Ho N4 ... 51 B2
Cannock Lo EN1 ... 17 C5
Cannonbury Ave
HA5 ... 40 D3
Cannon Cl
Hampton TW12 ... 173 D4
West Barnes SW20 ... 200 C6
Cannon Dr 21 E14 ... 119 C6
Cannon Hill La SM4,
SW20 ... 201 A5
Cannon Hill Mews
N14 ... 16 A1
Cannon Hill
Palmers Green
N14 ... 16 A1
West Hampstead
NW6 ... 69 C3
Cannon Ho
Lambeth SE11 ... 260 D3
Penge SE26 ... 184 B4
Cannon La NW3 ... 70 B5
Cannon Lane Fst & Mid
Schs HA5 ... 40 D3
Cannon La HA5 ... 41 A3
Cannon Pl
Hampstead NW3 ... 70 B5
Woolwich SE7 ... 122 A1
Cannon Rd
Erith DA7 ... 147 B4
Palmers Green N14 ... 16 A1
Cannon St
EC4 ... 117 A6 252 B6
Cannon Street Rd E1 ... 96 B1
Cannon Street Sta
EC4 ... 117 B6 252 C6
Cannon Trad Est
HA9 ... 66 D4
Cannon Way KT8 ... 195 D5
Cannon (W End of
General Roy's Base
Line)* TW6 ... 126 D4
Cannon Wharf Bsns Ctr
12 SE8 ... 119 A2
Canon Ave RM6 ... 58 C4
Canon Barnett Prim Sch
E1 ... 95 D1 243 D2
Canon Beck Rd
SE16 ... 118 C4
Canonbie Rd SE23 ... 162 C4
CANONBURY ... 73 A2
Canonbury Bsns Ctr
N1 ... 235 B6
Canonbury Cres N1 ... 73 A1

Canonbury Ct 21 N1 ... 72 D1
Canonbury Gr N1 ... 73 A1
Canonbury Hts 6 N1 ... 73 B2
Canonbury La N1 ... 72 D1
Canonbury Pk N N1 ... 73 A2
Canonbury Pk S N1 ... 73 A2
Canonbury Pl N1 ... 72 D2
Canonbury Prim Sch
N1 ... 72 D2
Canonbury Rd
Enfield EN1 ... 5 C4
Islington N1 ... 72 D1
Canonbury Sq N1 ... 72 D1
Canonbury Sta N1,
N5 ... 73 A3
Canonbury St N1 ... 73 A1
Canonbury Villas N1 ... 72 D1
Canon Mohan Cl N14 ... 15 B5
Canon Murnane Rd
SE1 ... 263 C5
Canon Palmer RC Sch
IG3 ... 57 C1
Canon Rd BR1 ... 209 D6
Canon Row
SW1 ... 116 A4 250 A1
Canons Cl
East Finchley N2 ... 48 B2
Edgware HA8 ... 26 B4
Canons Cnr HA8 ... 26 A6
Canons Ct
Edgware HA8 ... 26 B4
Leyton E15 ... 76 C4
Canons Dr HA8 ... 26 B4
Canons High Sch
HA8 ... 26 B1
Canons L Ctr The
CR4 ... 202 D5
Canonsleigh Rd RM9 ... 80 B1
CANONS PARK ... 26 A3
Canons Park Cl HA8 ... 26 A3
Canons Park Sta
HA8 ... 26 A3
Canon St N1 ... 95 A6 235 A5
Canon's Wlk CR0 ... 222 D5
Canopus Way
Northwood HA6 ... 22 A6
Stanwell TW19 ... 148 A4
Canrobert St E2 ... 96 B4
Cantelowes Ho EN5 ... 12 D6
Cantelowes Rd NW1 ... 71 D2
Canterbury Ave
Redbridge IG1 ... 56 A2
Sidcup DA15 ... 168 C2
Canterbury Cl
Beckenham BR3 ... 185 D2
16 Camberwell SE5 ... 139 A3
7 Newham E6 ... 100 B1
North Cheam KT4 ... 216 D6
Southall UB6 ... 85 D2
Canterbury Cres
SW9 ... 138 C2
Canterbury Ct
Acton W3 ... 111 C5
4 Ashford TW15 ... 170 B6
Eltham SE12 ... 165 B1
15 Hendon NW9 ... 27 D1
Kilburn NW6 ... 91 C5
South Croydon CR2 ... 221 A1
Thornton Heath CR0 ... 204 C2
Canterbury Gr SE27,
SW16 ... 160 C1
Canterbury Hall
KT4 ... 200 B2
Canterbury Ho
2 Barking IG11 ... 80 A1
6 Bromley E3 ... 97 D4
Lambeth SE1 ... 260 D6
Canterbury Ind Pk 15
SE15 ... 140 C6
Canterbury SE13 ... 164 A6
Canterbury Mans
NW6 ... 69 D2
Canterbury Pl SE17 ... 261 D3
Canterbury Rd
Feltham TW13 ... 151 A2
Harrow HA1, HA2 ... 42 A4
Kilburn NW6 ... 91 C5
Leyton E10 ... 54 A3
Morden SM4 ... 202 A3
Thornton Heath CR0 ... 204 C2
Canterbury Terr
NW6 ... 91 C5
Cantium Ret Pk
SE1 ... 140 A6
Cantley Gdns
Ilford IG2 ... 57 A3
South Norwood
SE19 ... 183 D2
Cantley Rd W7 ... 109 A3
Canton St E14 ... 97 C1
Cantrell Rd E3 ... 97 C3
Cantwell Ho SE18 ... 144 D5
Cantwell Rd SE18 ... 144 D5
Canute Ct SW16 ... 160 C1
Canute Gdns SE16 ... 118 D2
Canute Ho 1 TW8 ... 131 C5
Canvey St SE1 ... 252 A4

Cape Cl IG11 ... 78 D1
Cape Henry Ct 15
E14 ... 120 B6
Capel Ave SM6 ... 220 B3
Capel Cl
Keston Mark BR2 ... 210 A1
Whetstone N20 ... 14 A1
Capel Ct SE20 ... 184 C2
Capel Gdns Ilford IG3 ... 79 D4
Pinner HA5 ... 41 B5
Capel Ho
17 Hackney E9 ... 74 C1
South Oxhey WD19 ... 22 D6
Capella Ho 1 SE7 ... 143 B6
Capel Lo
5 Richmond
TW9 ... 132 B4
12 Streatham SW2 ... 160 B4
Capel Point E7 ... 77 B4
Capel Rd
East Barnet EN4 ... 14 C5
Forest Gate E7, E12 ... 77 C4
Capel KT5 ... 198 B2
Capener's Cl SW1 ... 248 A1
Cape Rd N17 ... 52 A6
Capern Rd SW18 ... 158 A3
Cape Yd 6 E1 ... 118 A5
Capio Nightingale Hospl
SW3 ... 257 B1
Capital Bsns Ctr
South Croydon
CR0 ... 221 B1
Wembley HA0 ... 87 D5
Capital City Acad
NW10 ... 90 B6
Capital East Apts 8
E16 ... 121 A6
Capital Ind Est
Belvedere DA17 ... 125 D3
Mitcham CR4 ... 202 D4
Capital Interchange
Way TW8 ... 110 C1
Capital Sh Ctrs SW1 ... 249 C1
Capital Wharf 15
E1 ... 118 A5
Capitol Ind Pk NW9 ... 45 A6
Capitol Way NW9 ... 45 A6
Capland Ho NW8 ... 236 D6
Capland St
NW8 ... 92 B3 236 D6
Caplan Est CR4 ... 181 C2
Caple Ho SW10 ... 266 B4
Caple Rd NW10 ... 89 D5
Capper St
WC1 ... 93 C3 239 B5
Caprea Cl UB4 ... 84 D2
Capricorn Ctr RM8 ... 59 B2
Capri Ho E17 ... 35 B1
Capri Rd CR0 ... 205 D2
Capstan Cl RM6 ... 58 B3
Capstan Ho 6 E14 ... 120 A2
Capstan Rd SE8 ... 119 B2
Capstan Ride EN2 ... 4 C3
Capstan Sq E14 ... 120 A4
Capstan Way SE16 ... 119 A5
Capstone Rd BR1 ... 186 D6
Capthorne Ave HA2 ... 41 B1
Capuchin Cl HA7 ... 25 B4
Capulet Mews 1
E16 ... 121 A5
Capworth St E10 ... 53 D2
Caradoc Cl W2 ... 91 C1
Caradoc Evans Cl
N11 ... 31 B5
Caradoc St SE10 ... 120 C1
Caradon Cl 4 E11 ... 76 C6
Caradon Ct 7 TW1 ... 153 C5
Caradon Way N15 ... 51 B5
Cara Ho 10 N1 ... 72 C1
Caranday Villas 5
W11 ... 112 D5
Caravel Cl E14 ... 119 C3
Caravelle Gdns 1
UB5 ... 84 D4
Caravel Mews 14
SE8 ... 141 C6
Caraway Cl E13 ... 99 B2
Caraway Hts E14 ... 120 A6
Caraway Pl SM6 ... 219 B5
Carberry Rd 12
SE19 ... 183 C4
Carbery Ave W3 ... 110 B4
Carbis Cl E4 ... 20 B3
Carbis Rd E14 ... 97 B1
Carbroke Ho 9 E9 ... 96 C6
Carburton St
W1 ... 93 B3 238 D5
Cardale St 1 E14 ... 120 A3
Cardamom Ct 1 E12 ... 78 C4
Carden Rd SE15 ... 140 B2
Cardiff Ho 9 SE15 ... 140 A6
Cardiff Rd Ealing W7 ... 109 A3
Enfield EN3 ... 6 B1
Cardiff St SE18 ... 145 C5

Cardigan Ct 3 W7 ... 86 D3
Cardigan Gdns IG3 ... 80 A6
Cardigan Rd
Barnes SW13 ... 134 A3
Bow E3 ... 97 B5
Richmond TW10 ... 154 A5
Wimbledon SW19 ... 180 A4
Cardigan St
SE11 ... 116 C1 261 A2
Cardigan Wlk 10 N1 ... 73 A1
Cardinal Ave
Kingston u T KT2 ... 176 A4
West Barnes SM4 ... 201 A3
Cardinal Bourne St
SE1 ... 262 D5
Cardinal Cap Alley
SE1 ... 252 A5
Cardinal Cl
Burnt Oak HA8 ... 27 B3
Chislehurst BR7 ... 189 B2
West Barnes SM4 ... 201 A3
Worcester Pk KT19, KT4 ... 216 A4
Cardinal Cres KT3 ... 177 A1
Cardinal Ct KT8 ... 196 B5
Cardinal Dr KT12 ... 194 D1
Cardinal Hinsley Cl
NW10 ... 90 A5
Cardinal Hinsley RC High Sch (Boys)
NW10 ... 90 A6
Cardinal Pl SW15 ... 134 D1
Cardinal Pole RC Sch
London E9 ... 74 D1
London E9 ... 75 A3
Cardinal Rd
Feltham TW13 ... 150 B3
Ruislip HA4 ... 40 D1
Cardinal Road Inf Sch
TW13 ... 150 B3
Cardinals Way N19 ... 49 D1
Cardinal's Wlk
Ashford TW16 ... 171 C4
Hampton TW12 ... 174 A3
Cardinal Vaughan Meml Sch The W14 ... 244 A2
Cardinal Way HA3 ... 42 C6
Cardinal Wiseman RC Sch The UB6 ... 86 A2
Cardinal Wlk SW1 ... 259 A5
Cardine Mews SE15 ... 140 B5
Cardington Sq TW4 ... 128 D1
Cardington St
NW1 ... 93 C4 232 B1
Cardozo Rd N7 ... 72 A3
Cardrew Ave N12 ... 30 B5
Cardrew Cl N12 ... 30 B5
Cardrew Ct 8 N12 ... 30 B5
Cardross St W6 ... 112 B3
Cardwell Prim Sch
SE18 ... 122 B2
Cardwell Rd 3 N7 ... 72 A4
Career Ct 11 SE16 ... 118 D4
Carew Cl N7 ... 72 B6
Carew Ct
15 Deptford SE14 ... 140 D6
Ilford RM6 ... 58 B3
Carew Ho
West Norwood SW16 ... 160 C1
23 Woolwich SE18 ... 122 B2
Carew Manor Sch
SM6 ... 219 D5
Carew Rd
Ashford TW15 ... 171 A4
Ealing W13 ... 109 C4
Mitcham CR4 ... 181 A1
Thornton Heath CR7 . 204 D5
Tottenham N17 ... 34 A1
Wallington SM6 ... 219 C2
Carew St SE5 ... 139 A3
Carey Ct Bexley DA6 ... 169 D6
20 Camberwell SE5 ... 139 A5
Carey Gdns
SW8 ... 137 D4 269 C1
Carey Ho E5 ... 74 B5
Carey La EC2 ... 242 A2
Carey Pl SW1 ... 259 C3
Carey Rd RM9 ... 81 A4
Carey St WC2 .. 94 B1 240 D1
Carey Way HA9 ... 66 D4
Carfax Pl SW4 ... 137 D1
Carfax Rd UB3 ... 106 A2
Carfree Cl 5 N1 ... 72 C1
Cargill Rd SW18 ... 158 A3
Cargreen Pl SE25 ... 205 D5
Cargreen Rd SE25 ... 205 D5
Cargrey Ho 9 HA7 ... 25 C5
Carholme Rd SE23 ... 163 B3
Carillon Ct W5 ... 109 D6
Carinthia Ct 5 SE8 ... 119 A2
Carisbrook Cl EN1 ... 5 D4
Carisbrooke Ave
DA5 ... 168 D3
Carisbrooke Cl
Stanmore HA7 ... 25 D1
Twickenham TW4 ... 151 A4
Carisbrooke Ct
Acton W3 ... 111 A4
Belmont SM2 ... 217 B1
Northolt UB5 ... 85 B6
1 Streatham SW16 ... 160 B1
Carisbrooke Gdns
SE15 ... 139 D5
Carisbrooke Ho
10 Kingston u T KT2 ... 176 A2
Richmond TW10 ... 154 C6
Carisbrooke Rd
Bromley BR2 ... 209 C5
Mitcham CR4 ... 204 A5
Walthamstow E17 ... 53 A4
Carisbrook 2 N10 ... 31 B1
Carleton Ave SM6 ... 219 D1
Carleton Cl KT10 ... 196 B1
Carleton Gdns N19 ... 71 C3
Carleton Ho 4 N8 ... 50 A4
Carleton Rd N7 ... 71 D4
Carley Ct 6 N12 ... 30 B5
Carlile Cl E3 ... 97 B5
Carlile Ho SE1 ... 262 D5
Carlina Gdns IG8 ... 37 B5
Carling Ct TW1 ... 152 D4
Carlingford Gdns
CR4 ... 181 A3
Carlingford Rd
Hampstead NW3 ... 70 B4
London N15 ... 50 D6
West Barnes SM4 ... 200 D3
Carlingford DA14 ... 190 A5
Carlisle Ave
Acton W3 ... 89 C1
Whitechapel EC3 ... 243 C1
Carlisle Cl
Kingston u T KT2 ... 176 C2
Pinner HA5 ... 41 A2
Carlisle Gdns
Harrow HA3 ... 43 D2
Redbridge IG1 ... 56 A3
Carlisle Ho
6 Dartmouth Pk NW5 ... 71 C5
Redbridge IG1 ... 56 A3
Carlisle Inf Sch
TW12 ... 173 D4
Carlisle La
SE1 ... 116 B3 260 D6
Carlisle Lo 1 N3 ... 29 B1
Carlisle Pl
London N11 ... 31 B6
Westminster SW1 ... 115 C3 259 A5
Carlisle Rd
Cheam SM1 ... 217 B2
Finsbury Pk N4 ... 50 C2
Hampton TW12 ... 173 D3
Hendon NW9 ... 45 A6
Kilburn NW6 ... 91 A6
Leyton E10 ... 53 C1
Carlisle St
W1 ... 93 D1 239 C1
Carlisle Way SW17 ... 181 A5
Carlisle Wlk 6 E8 ... 73 D2
Carlos Pl
W1 ... 115 B6 248 C5
Carlow St NW1 ... 232 A4
Carlson Ct SW15 ... 135 B1
Carlton Ave E HA9 ... 65 D6
Carlton Ave
Feltham TW14 ... 150 C5
Harrow HA3 ... 43 B4
Hayes UB3 ... 105 C2
South Croydon CR2 ... 221 C1
Southgate N14 ... 15 D6
Carlton Ave W HA0 ... 65 B6
Carlton Cl
Chessington KT9 ... 213 D2
Child's Hill NW3 ... 69 C6
Edgware HA8 ... 26 C5
Northolt UB5 ... 64 A3
Carlton Cres SM3 ... 217 A4
Carlton Ct
Brixton SW9 ... 138 D4
Ealing W7 ... 108 D4
Finchley N3 ... 29 C3
Ilford IG6 ... 57 B6
Kilburn NW6 ... 91 D5
11 Penge SE20 ... 184 B2
South Norwood SE19 ... 183 D2
8 Willesden NW2 ... 68 C2
Carlton Dr Ilford IG6 ... 57 B6
Putney SW15 ... 157 A6
Carlton Gdns
Ealing W5 ... 109 C6
St James SW1 ... 115 D5 249 C3
Carlton Gn DA14 ... 189 D6
Carlton Gr SE15 ... 140 B4
Carlton Hill
NW8 ... 92 A5 229 A4
Carlton Ho
Cheam SM1 ... 217 B2
Edmonton N21 ... 17 A3
Feltham TW14 ... 149 D5
Hounslow TW4 ... 151 C5
8 Kilburn NW6 ... 91 B5
Kilburn NW6 ... 91 C5
Marylebone W1 ... 237 D2
Carlton House Terr
SW1 ... 115 D5 249 D4
Carlton Lo N4 ... 50 C2
Carlton Mans
Brixton SW9 ... 138 C1
Cricklewood NW2 ... 68 D3
Kensington W14 ... 244 B2
Maida Vale W9 ... 91 D4
7 South Hampstead NW6 ... 69 C1
Stamford Hill N16 ... 51 D1
Carlton Park Ave
SW20 ... 178 D1
Carlton Par HA9 ... 44 A1
Carlton Prim Sch
NW5 ... 71 A3
Carlton Rd Acton W4 ... 111 B4
Ashford TW16 ... 171 D3
Ealing W5 ... 87 C1
Erith DA8 ... 147 D6
Finsbury Pk N4 ... 50 C2
Friern Barnet N11 ... 31 A5
Higham Hill E17 ... 35 A2
Kingston u T KT3 ... 177 C1
Leytonstone E11 ... 54 D1
Manor Pk E12 ... 77 D4
Mortlake SW14 ... 133 A1
Sidcup DA14 ... 189 D6
South Croydon CR2 ... 221 B1
Walton-on-T KT12 ... 194 B2
Welling DA16 ... 146 B2
Carlton Sq E1 ... 96 D3
Carltons The 5
SW15 ... 157 A6
Carlton St SW1 ... 249 C5
Carlton Terr
Edmonton N18 ... 33 B6
Forest Hill SE26 ... 162 C1
Upton E7 ... 77 C1
Wanstead E11 ... 55 B4
Carlton Tower Pl
SW1 ... 257 D6
Carlton Twrs SM5 ... 218 D5
Carlton Vale Inf Sch
NW6 ... 91 B4
Carlton Vale NW6 ... 91 C5
Carlwell St SW17 ... 180 C5
Carlyle Ave
Bromley BR1 ... 209 D6
Southall UB1 ... 107 B6
Carlyle Cl
East Molesey KT8 ... 173 D1
Hampstead Garden Suburb N2 ... 48 A3
Carlyle Gdns UB1 ... 107 B6
Carlyle Ho
4 Camberwell SE5 ... 139 A5
Chelsea SW3 ... 266 D6
Ealing W5 ... 109 D2
East Molesey KT8 ... 195 C4
12 Stoke Newington N16 ... 73 C5
Carlyle Lo 6 EN5 ... 14 A6
Carlyle Mans SW3 ... 267 A5
Carlyle Mews 24 E1 ... 96 D3
Carlyle Pl SW15 ... 134 D1
Carlyle Rd
Croydon CR0 ... 222 A6
Ealing W5 ... 109 C2
Manor Pk E12 ... 78 A4
1 Stonebridge NW10 ... 89 B6
Woolwich SE28 ... 124 C6
Carlyle's Ho* SW3 ... 267 A5
Carlyle Sq
SW3 ... 114 B1 256 D1
Carlyon Ave HA2 ... 63 C4
Carlyon Cl HA0 ... 88 A6
Carlyon Ct HA0 ... 88 B6
Carlyon Mans 1
HA0 ... 88 A5
Carlyon Rd
Hayes UB4 ... 84 C2
Wembley HA0 ... 88 A6
Carlys Cl BR3 ... 184 D1
Carmalt Gdns SW15 ... 134 C1
Carmarthen Ct 4
W7 ... 86 D3
Carmarthen Ho 8
SW15 ... 156 C4
Carmarthen Pl SE1 ... 253 A2
Carmel Ct
Kensington W8 ... 245 C2
Wembley Pk HA9 ... 66 D6
Carmelite Cl HA3 ... 24 A2
Carmelite Rd HA3 ... 24 A1
Carmelite St
EC4 ... 116 C6 251 B6
Carmelite Way HA3 ... 24 A1
Carmelite Wlk HA3 ... 24 A2
Carmel Lo SW6 ... 265 A6
Carmen St E14 ... 97 D1
Carmichael Cl
9 London SW11 ... 136 B2
Ruislip HA4 ... 62 A4
Carmichael Ct 5
SW13 ... 133 D3
Carmichael Ho
17 Dulwich SE21 ... 183 C6
6 Poplar E14 ... 120 A6
Carmichael Mews
SW18 ... 158 B4
Carmichael Rd
SE25 ... 206 A5
Carminia Rd SW17 ... 159 B2
Carnaby St*
W1 ... 93 C1 239 A1
Carnac St SE21, SE27 ... 161 B1
Carna Ct TW9 ... 132 A2
Carnanton Rd E17 ... 36 B2
Carnarvon Ave EN1 ... 5 D3
Carnarvon Dr UB3 ... 105 A3
Carnarvon Rd
Barnet EN5 ... 1 A2
Leyton E10 ... 54 A4
Stratford E15 ... 76 D2
Woodford E18 ... 36 D2
Carnation St SE2 ... 124 B1
Carnbrook Rd SE3 ... 143 D2
Carnecke Gdns SE9 ... 166 A6
Carnegie Cl
Holdbrook EN3 ... 7 D5
Surbiton KT6 ... 214 B6
Carnegie Ho NW3 ... 70 B5
Carnegie Pl SW19 ... 156 D1
Carnegie St
N1 ... 94 B6 233 D5
Carnforth Cl KT19 ... 214 D2
Carnforth Rd SW16 ... 181 D3
Carnicot Ho 9
SE15 ... 140 B4
Carnoustie Cl SE28 ... 102 D1
Carnoustie Dr N1 ... 72 B1
Carnwath Ho SW6 ... 135 D2
Carnwath Rd SW6 ... 135 D2
Caroe Ct N9 ... 18 B3
Carol Cl NW4 ... 46 D5
Carole Ho 13 SE20 ... 184 B2
Carolina Cl E15 ... 76 C3
Carolina Rd CR7 ... 183 A2
Caroline Cl
Bayswater W2 ... 245 D5
Hounslow TW7 ... 130 C5
Muswell Hill N10 ... 31 B1
South Croydon CR0 ... 221 C4
Streatham SW16 ... 160 B1
Caroline Ct
Ashford TW15 ... 170 D4
Catford SE6 ... 186 B6
Stanmore HA7 ... 25 A4
17 Surbiton KT6 ... 197 D2
23 Woodside Pk N12 ... 29 D6
Caroline Gdns E2 ... 95 C4
Caroline Ho
Bayswater W2 ... 245 D5
20 Hammersmith W6 ... 112 C1
Caroline Martyn Ho 8
N19 ... 49 D2
Caroline Pl
Bayswater W2 ... 245 D5
Clapham SW11 ... 137 A3
Harlington UB3 ... 127 C5
Caroline Pl Mews
W2 ... 245 D5
Caroline Rd SW19 ... 179 B3
Caroline St E1 ... 96 D1
Caroline Terr
SW1 ... 115 A2 258 A3
Caroline Wlk W6 ... 264 A5
Carol St NW1 ... 93 C6 232 A6
Carolyn Ho IG3 ... 58 A1
Caronia Ct 4 SE16 ... 119 A2
Carpenter Gdns N21 ... 16 D2
Carpenter Ho
London NW11 ... 48 A3
11 Tower Hamlets E14 ... 97 C2
5 Tufnell Pk N19 ... 71 D4
Carpenters Bsns Pk
E15 ... 75 D1
Carpenters Cl EN5 ... 13 D5
Carpenters Ct
Camden Town NW1 ... 232 A6
5 Dagenham RM10 ... 81 D2
Twickenham TW2 ... 152 C2
Carpenter's Pl SW4 ... 137 D1
Carpenters Prim Sch
E15 ... 98 A6
Carpenter's Rd E15 ... 75 D1
Carpenter St W1 ... 248 C5
Carradale Ho 2 E14 ... 98 A1
Carrara Cl 18 SW9 ... 138 D1
Carrara Wharf SW6 ... 135 A2
Carr Cl HA7 ... 25 A4
Carr Gr SE18 ... 122 A2
Carriage Dr E
SW11 ... 137 A5 268 B4
Carriage Drive E
SW11 ... 137 A5 268 B4
Carriage Drive N SW11, SW8 ... 137 A6 268 B5
Carriage Dr N
Battersea SW8, SW11 ... 136 D5 267 C4
Battersea SW8, SW11 ... 137 A6 268 B5
Carriage Dr S
SW11 ... 137 A4 268 A2
Carriage Dr W
SW11 ... 136 D5 267 C3
Carriage Mews IG1 ... 79 A6
Carriage Pl 14
SW16 ... 181 C5
Carrick Cl TW7 ... 131 A2
Carrick Gate KT10 ... 212 A5
Carrick Gdns N17 ... 33 C3
Carrick Ho
Islington N7 ... 72 B2
Kennington SE11 ... 261 C2
Carrick Mews SE8 ... 141 C6
Carrill Way DA17 ... 124 D3
Carrington Ave
Borehamwood WD6 ... 10 D6
Hounslow TW3 ... 151 D6
Carrington Cl
Barnet EN5 ... 12 A6
Borehamwood WD6 ... 11 A6
Croydon CR0 ... 207 A2
Carrington Ct
London SW11 ... 136 C1
3 New Malden KT3 ... 199 C5
Southgate N21 ... 16 D5
Carrington Gdns 4
E7 ... 77 A4
Carrington Ho
Mayfair W1 ... 248 C3
7 Merton SW19 ... 179 C3
Carrington Lo
3 Richmond TW10 ... 154 A6
Wembley HA9 ... 66 B5
Carrington Pl KT10 ... 212 A4
Carrington Rd
TW10 ... 132 C1
Carrington Sq HA3 ... 24 A3
Carrington St W1 ... 248 C3
Carrol Cl NW5 ... 71 B4
Carroll Cl E15 ... 76 D3
Carroll Ct Acton W3 ... 110 D3
4 Shacklewell E5 ... 74 A5
Carroll Ho W2 ... 246 C6
Carronade Pl SE18 ... 123 B3
Carron Cl E14 ... 97 D1
Carroun Rd
SW8 ... 138 B5 270 C4
Carroway La UB6 ... 86 B4
Carrow Rd RM9 ... 80 B1
Carr Rd Northolt UB5 ... 64 A1
Walthamstow E17 ... 35 C1
Carrs La N21 ... 17 B6
Carr St 5 E14 ... 97 A1
CARSHALTON ... 218 C4
Carshalton, Beddington & Wallington War Meml Hospl SM5 ... 218 D2
Carshalton Beeches Sta
SM5 ... 218 D2
Carshalton Boys Sports Coll SM5 ... 218 C6
Carshalton Coll
SM5 ... 218 D5
Carshalton Gr SM1 ... 218 B3
Carshalton High Sch for Girls SM5 ... 218 C5
CARSHALTON ON THE HILL ... 219 B1
Carshalton Park Rd
SM5 ... 218 D3
Carshalton Pl SM5 ... 219 A3
Carshalton Rd
Mitcham CR4 ... 203 A4
Sutton SM1, SM5 ... 218 B3
Carshalton Sta SM5 ... 218 D4
Carslake Rd SW15 ... 156 C5
Carson Rd
Cockfosters EN4 ... 2 D1
Dulwich SE21 ... 161 B2
Newham E16 ... 99 A2
Carstairs Rd SE6 ... 164 A1
Carston Cl SE12 ... 164 D6
Carswell Cl IG4 ... 55 D5
Carswell Rd SE6 ... 164 A4
Carter Cl Kenton NW9 ... 45 B3
Wallington SM6 ... 219 D1
Carter Ct EC4 ... 241 D1
Carteret Ho 8 W12 ... 112 B6
Carteret St SW1 ... 249 C1
Carteret Way SE8 ... 119 A2
Carterhatch Jun & Inf Schs EN1 ... 6
Carterhatch La EN1 ... 6
Carterhatch Rd EN3 ... 6
Carter Ho
11 London SW2 ... 160
Spitalfields E1 ... 243
Carter La EC4 ... 94 D1 241
Carter Pl
SE17 ... 117 A1 262
Carter Rd
Mitcham SW19 ... 180
Newham E13 ... 99
Carters Cl
10 Kentish Town NW5 ... 71
North Cheam KT4 ... 200
Carters Hill Cl SE9 ... 165
Carters La SE23 ... 163
Carters Rd N2 ... 50
Carter St
SE17 ... 117 A1 262
Carter's Yd SW18 ... 157
Carthew Rd W6 ... 112
Carthew Villas W6 ... 112
Carthusian St EC1 ... 242
Cartier Circ E14 ... 120
Carting La
WC2 ... 116 A6 250
Cart La E4 ... 20
Cartmel Cl N17 ... 34
Cartmel Ct
Beckenham BR2 ... 186
Northolt UB5 ... 63
Cartmel Gdns SM4 ... 202
Cartmel NW1 ... 232
Cartmel Rd DA7 ... 147
Carton Ho
4 Bermondsey SE16 ... 118
2 Dollis Hill NW2 ... 68
12 Shepherd's Bush W11 ... 112
Cartoon Mus The*
WC1 ... 94 A2 240
Cartwright Gdns
WC1 ... 94 A4 233
Cartwright Ho SE1 ... 262
Cartwright Rd RM9 ... 81
Cartwright St
E1 ... 117 D6 253
Cartwright Way
SW13 ... 134
Carvel Ho E14 ... 120
Carver Cl 15 W4 ... 111
Carver Rd SE24 ... 161
Carville Cres TW8 ... 110
Caryl Ho 6 SW19 ... 156
Cary Rd E11 ... 76
Carysfort Rd
Canonbury N16 ... 73
London N8 ... 49
Casby Ho 7 SE16 ... 118
Cascade Ave N10 ... 49
Cascade Cl IG9 ... 21
Cascade Rd IG9 ... 21
Cascadia Ho 22 KT1 ... 176
Casella Rd SE14 ... 140
Casewick Rd SE27 ... 182
Casey Cl NW8 ... 92 C4 230
Casimir Rd E5 ... 74
Casino Ave SE24 ... 161
Caspian Ho 10 E1 ... 96
Caspian St SE5 ... 139
Caspian Wlk E16 ... 99
Cassandra Cl UB5 ... 64
Cassandra Ct 7
NW2 ... 68
Cass Bsns Sch
EC1 ... 95 B3 242
Casselden Rd NW10 ... 67
Cassel Hospl TW10 ... 175
Cassell Ho 21 SW9 ... 138
Casserley Ho W4 ... 111
Cass Ho 23 E9 ... 74
Cassidy Rd SW6 ... 265
Cassilda Rd SE2 ... 124
Cassilis Rd
Millwall E14 ... 119
Twickenham TW1 ... 153
Cassinghurst SE24 ... 161
Cassiobury Ave
TW14 ... 149
Cassiobury Rd E17 ... 53
Cassland Rd
Homerton E9 ... 74
South Norwood CR7 ... 205
Casslee Rd SE6 ... 163
Cassocks Sq TW17 ... 193
Casson Ho 18 E1 ... 96
Casson St E1 ... 96
Castalia Sq 6 E14 ... 120
Castellain Mans W9 ... 91
Castellain Rd W9 ... 91
Castellane Cl HA7 ... 24
Castell Ho 11 SE8 ... 141
Castello Ave SW15 ... 156

stelnau SW13 134 B5
stelnau Gdns
W13 134 B6
stelnau Mans
W13 134 B6
stelnau Row
W13 134 B6
sterbridge
ilburn NW6 91 D6
1 Notting Hill W11 91 C1
sterbridge Rd
3 143 A2
sterton St E8 74 B2
stile Rd SE18 122 C2
stilion Prim Sch
28 102 C1
stillon Rd SE6 164 C2
stlands Rd SE6 163 B2
stleacre W2 237 A1
stle Ave
hingford E4 36 B5
ewsley UB7 104 B6
stlebar Ct 5 W5 87 C2
stlebar Hill W5 87 C2
stlebar Mews W5 87 C2
stle Bar Park Sta
7 86 D2
stlebar Pk W5 87 B2
stlebar Rd W5 87 C1
stlebar Sch W13 87 A2
stle Baynard St
C4 117 A6 252 A6
stlebrook Cl
E11 116 D2 261 C4
stle Bsns Village
W12 173 D2
stle Cl
2 Acton W3 111 A4
shford TW16 171 C3
eckenham BR2 208 C6
omerton E9 75 A3
outh Acton W3 110 D4
Vimbledon SW19 156 D1
stlecombe Dr
W19 156 D4
stlecombe Prim Sch
E9 188 A5
stlecombe Rd
E9 188 A6
stle Ct
elmont SM2 217 C2
ity of London EC3 242 D1
agenham RM9 103 A6
orest Hill SE26 185 A6
orden SM4 202 B4
stleden Ho NW6 70 B1
stledine Rd SE20 184 B3
stle Dr IG4 56 A3
stleford Ave SE9 166 D3
stleford Cl N17 33 D4
stleford Ct NW8 236 D6
stlefrank Ho 20
95 C4
stlegate TW9 132 B2
STLE GREEN 102 C6
stleham Ct HA8 26 C4
stlehaven Rd NW1 71 B1
stle Hill Ave CR0 224 A1
stle Hill Prim Sch
R0 224 A2
stle Ho
7 Belmont SM2 217 C1
1 Chingford E4 36 B5
ewington SE1 262 A4
outh Lambeth SW8 270 B4
stle Hts RM9 102 B6
stle Ind Est SE17 262 A4
stle La
W1 115 C3 259 A6
stleleigh Ct EN2 17 B6
stlemaine Ave
R2 221 D3
stlemaine 8
W11 136 D3
stlemaine St 2 E1 96 B2
stle Mead SE5 139 A5
stle Mews
amden Town NW1 71 B2
orth Finchley N12 30 A5
stle Par KT17 216 A1
stle Pl
1 Acton W4 111 C2
amden Town NW1 71 B2
stle Point 4 E13 99 C5
stle Rd
amden Town NW1 71 B2
agenham RM9 102 B6
nfield EN3 7 A5
leworth TW7 130 D3
orth Finchley N12 30 B5
ortholt UB5 63 D1
outhall UB2 107 B3
stlereagh Ho HA7 25 B4
stlereagh St W1 237 C2
stle St
ngston u T KT2 176 A1
ewham E6 99 C5

Castleton Ave HA9 66 A4
Castleton Cl CR0 207 A3
Castleton Ct KT5 198 B4
Castleton Gdns HA9 66 A5
Castleton Ho 3
E14 120 A2
Castleton Rd
Chingford E17 36 B1
Ilford IG3 58 B1
Mitcham CR4 203 D5
Mottingham SE12,
SE9 187 D6
Ruislip HA4 40 D1
Castletown Rd
W14 113 A1 254 B1
Castleview Cl N4 73 A6
Castleview Gdns IG1 56 B3
Castle Way
Feltham TW13 172 C6
Wimbledon SW19 156 D1
Castle Wlk TW16 194 C6
Castlewood Day Hospl
SE18 144 C4
Castlewood Dr SE9 144 B3
Castlewood Ho WC1 239 D2
Castlewood Rd
Barnet EN4 2 B2
Stamford Hill N16 52 A3
Castle Yd Highgate N6 49 A2
Lambeth SE1 251 D4
18 Richmond TW10 153 D6
Castor La E14 119 D6
Catalina Rd TW6 126 C2
Catalpa Ct SE13 164 B5
Caterham Rd SE13 142 B2
Catesby Ho 25 E9 74 C1
Catesby St
SE17 117 B2 262 D3
CATFORD 163 C3
Catford Br SE6 163 C4
Catford Bridge Sta
SE6 163 C4
Catford Broadway
SE6 163 D4
Catford Gyratory
SE6 163 D4
Catford High Sch
SE6 164 A1
Catford Hill SE6 163 C3
Catford Rd SE6 163 C4
Catford Sh Ctr SE6 163 D4
Catford Sta SE6 163 C4
Cathall Rd E11 76 B5
Cathay Ho SE16 118 B4
Cathay St 12 SE16 118 B4
Cathay Wlk UB5 85 C5
Cathcart Dr BR6 211 C1
Cathcart Hill N19 71 C5
Cathcart Rd
SW10 136 A6 266 A6
Cathcart St NW5 71 B2
Cathedral Ct EC4 241 D1
Cathedral Lo EC1 242 A4
Cathedral Sch of St
Saviour & St Mary
Overie Prim Sch
SE1 117 A4 252 B2
Cathedral St
SE1 117 B5 252 C4
Cathedral Wlk SW1 259 A6
Catherall Rd N5, N16 73 A5
Catherine Baird Ct 12
SW12 159 B4
Catherine Ct
Barnet EN5 1 D2
1 Ilford IG2 57 A3
2 Southgate N14 15 C6
3 Wimbledon
SW19 179 B5
Catherine Dr
Ashford TW16 171 D4
Richmond TW9 132 A1
Catherine Gdns
TW3 130 B1
Catherine Godfrey Ho
RM9 103 B6
Catherine Griffiths Ct
EC1 241 B6
Catherine Gr SE10 141 D4
Catherine Ho
Isleworth TW7 131 B4
16 Shoreditch N1 95 C6
Catherine Lo E18 37 C2
Catherine Pl
Harrow HA1 42 D4
Westminster
SW1 115 C3 259 A6
Catherine Rd
Enfield EN3 7 A6
Kingston u T KT6 197 D4
Catherine St
WC2 116 B6 250 C6
Catherine Wheel Alley
E1 243 B3
Catherine Wheel Rd
TW8 131 D5

Catherine Wheel Yd
SW1 249 A3
Catherwood Ct N1 235 C3
Cat Hill EN4 14 D6
Cathles Rd SW12 159 B5
Cathnor Rd W12 112 B4
Catisfield Rd EN3 7 A6
Catlin Cres TW17 193 B4
Catling Cl SE23 162 D1
Catlin's La HA5 40 B5
Catlin St SE16 118 B1
Catman Ho N4 50 B1
Caton Ct BR2 186 C1
Cato Rd SW4 137 D1
Cator La BR3 185 B2
Cator Park Sch BR3 185 A3
Cator Rd
Penge SE20,
SE26 184 D5
Wallington SM5 218 D3
Cator St
Camberwell SE15 139 D5
Camberwell SE15 139 D6
Cato St W1 92 C1 237 B2
Catsey La WD23 8 A4
Catsey Wood WD23 8 A4
Catterick Cl N11 31 A4
Cattistock Rd SE9 188 B5
Cattley Cl EN5 1 A1
Catton St WC1 240 C3
Caughley Ho SE11 261 A5
Caulfield Ct 11 NW1 71 C1
Caulfield Rd
East Ham E6 78 B1
London SE15 140 B3
Causeway TW14,
TW4 128 B1
Causeway The
Carshalton SM5 219 A6
Chessington KT9 214 A4
Claygate KT10 212 D1
East Finchley N2 48 C5
Teddington TW11 174 D4
Wandsworth SW18 157 D6
Wimbledon SW19 178 C5
Causeyware Rd N9 18 C4
Causton Cotts 3
E14 97 A1
Causton Ho SE5 139 A5
Causton Rd N6 49 B2
Causton Sq RM10 81 C1
Causton St
SW1 115 D1 259 D2
Cautley Ave SW4 159 C6
Cavalier Cl RM6 58 D5
Cavalier Gdns UB3 83 B1
Cavalier Ho W5 109 C6
Cavalry Cres TW4 128 D1
Cavalry Gdns SW15 157 B6
Cavan Pl HA5 23 B2
Cavaye Ho SW10 266 B6
Cavaye Pl SW10 256 B1
Cavell Ct 5 N19 71 C6
Cavell Dr EN2 4 C3
Cavell Ho 8 N1 95 C6
Cavell Rd N17 33 B3
Cavell St E1 96 B2
Cavendish Ave
Ealing W13 87 A1
Falconwood DA16 145 D2
Finchley N3 29 C1
Harrow HA1 64 C4
Ruislip HA4 62 B3
Sidcup DA15 168 A4
St John's Wood
NW8 92 B5 229 D3
West Barnes KT3 200 B5
Woodford IG8 37 B3
Cavendish Cl
Ashford TW16 171 D4
Brondesbury NW6 69 B2
Edmonton N18 34 B5
Hayes UB4 83 C2
3 Putney SW15 157 A6
St John's Wood
NW8 92 B4 229 D2
Cavendish Coll
WC1 93 D2 239 C4
Cavendish Cres WD6 10 C6
Cavendish Ct
Ashford TW16 171 D4
Catford SE6 163 D3
5 Chingford E4 20 C4
Wallington SM6 219 B2
Wembley HA0 65 D3
Whitechapel EC2 243 B2
Cavendish Dr
Claygate KT10 212 C3
Edgware HA8 26 B4
Leytonstone E11 54 B1
Cavendish Gdns
Barking IG11 79 D3
Clapham Pk SW4 159 C5
Dagenham RM6 59 A4
Ilford IG1 56 C1
Cavendish Ho
London N12 30 A6

Cavendish Ho *continued*
5 Muswell Hill N10 31 A3
3 Richmond TW10 153 C1
South Lambeth SW8 270 A2
St John's Wood NW8 229 D3
Twickenham TW1 153 A5
Cavendish Mans
2 Clapham Pk
SW12 159 C5
Hackney E5 74 C3
Holborn EC1 241 A5
8 West Hampstead
NW6 69 C3
Cavendish Mews N
W1 238 D4
Cavendish Mews S
W1 238 D3
Cavendish Par
Balham SW12 159 B5
Hounslow TW4 129 A3
Cavendish Pl
Balham SW4 159 B5
Bromley BR1 210 B6
Brondesbury NW2 68 D2
Marylebone W1 238 D2
Cavendish Prim Sch
W4 133 C5
Cavendish Rd
Ashford TW16 171 D4
Brondesbury NW6 69 B1
Chingford E4 36 A4
Chiswick W4 133 A4
Clapham Pk SW12 159 C5
Edmonton N18 34 B5
Harringay N4 50 D3
Mitcham SW19 180 C3
New Malden KT3 199 D5
Sutton SM2 218 A1
Thornton Heath CR0 204 D1
Cavendish Sch The
NW1 93 B6 231 D6
Cavendish Sq
W1 93 B1 238 D2
Cavendish St
N1 95 B5 235 C3
Cavendish Terr
Feltham TW13 150 A2
11 Tower Hamlets E3 97 B4
Cavendish The NW11 47 D2
Cavendish Way BR4 207 D1
Cavenham Gdns IG1 79 B5
Cave Rd Newham E13 99 B4
Richmond TW10 175 C6
Caverleigh Way
KT4 200 B2
Caversham Ave
Cheam SM3 217 A6
Palmers Green N13 16 C1
Caversham Ct N11 15 A1
Caversham Ho
8 Kingston u T
KT1 176 A1
7 Peckham SE15 140 A6
Wallington CR0 220 A5
West Green N15 51 A5
Caversham Lo N10 31 C1
Caversham Rd
Kentish Town NW5 71 C2
Kingston u T KT1 176 B1
West Green N15 51 A5
Caversham St
SW3 136 D6 267 C6
Caverswall St W12 90 C1
Caveside Cl BR7 188 C2
Cavour Ho SE17 261 D2
Cawdor Cres W7 109 A2
Cawnpore St SE19 183 C5
Cawston Ct 8 BR1 186 D3
Caxton Gr E3 97 C4
Caxton Hall* SW1 259 C6
Caxton Rd
Shepherd's Bush
W12 112 D4
Southall UB2 106 D3
Wimbledon SW19 180 A5
Wood Green N22 32 B1
Caxton St N E16 98 D1
Caxton St
SW1 115 D3 259 C6
Caxton Trad Est
UB3 105 C5
Caxton Wlk WC2 239 D1
Cayford Ho 1 NW3 70 D3
Caygill Cl BR2 208 D5
Cayley Cl SM6 220 A1
Cayley Prim Sch E14 97 A1
Cayley Rd UB2 107 D3
Cayton Pl EC1 235 C1
Cayton Rd UB6 86 C5
Cayton St EC1 235 C1
Cazenove Mans 1
N16 74 A6
Cazenove Rd
Stoke Newington
N16 74 A6
Walthamstow E17 35 C2
Cearns Ho E6 99 D6

Ceasors Ct TW1 152 D2
Cecil Ave
Barking IG11 79 B1
Enfield EN1 5 D1
Wembley HA9 66 B3
Cecil Cl
Chessington KT9 213 D4
Ealing W5 87 D2
Littleton TW15 171 A3
Cecil Ct
Chelsea SW10 266 A6
12 Croydon CR0 221 D6
Ealing W5 87 D2
South Hampstead
NW6 69 D1
St James WC2 250 A5
Cecile Pk N8 50 A3
Cecil Ho E17 35 C2
Cecilia Cl N2 48 A6
Cecilia Rd E8 74 A3
Cecil Lo KT9 213 D4
Cecil Mans 2
SW17 159 A2
Cecil Pk HA5 41 A5
Cecil Pl CR4 202 D4
Cecil Rd Acton W3 89 A2
Ashford TW15 171 A4
Cheam SM1, SM2 217 B2
Colindale NW9 45 C6
Dagenham RM6 58 D2
Enfield EN2 5 B1
Harlesden NW10 89 C6
Harrow HA3 42 C6
Hounslow TW3 130 A3
Ilford IG1 78 D4
Leyton E11 76 C5
Merton SW19 179 D3
Muswell Hill N10 31 B1
Newham E13 99 A6
Osidge N14 15 C3
Thornton Heath CR0 204 B3
Walthamstow E17 35 C2
Cecil Rhodes Ho
NW1 232 C4
Cecil Rosen Ct HA0 65 B5
Cecil Way BR2 209 A1
Cedar Ave
Dagenham RM6 59 A4
East Barnet EN4 14 C4
Enfield EN3 6 C3
Hayes UB3 84 A1
Ruislip HA4 62 C3
Sidcup DA15 168 A4
Twickenham TW2 152 A5
Yiewsley UB7 104 B6
Cedar Cl
Buckhurst Hill IG9 21 D2
East Molesey KT8 196 C5
Keston Mark BR2 226 A5
Kingston u T KT2 177 B6
Old Ford E3 97 B6
Wallington SM5 218 D2
West Norwood SE21 161 A2
Cedar Copse BR1 188 B1
Cedar Cres BR2 226 A5
Cedarcroft Rd KT9 214 B4
Cedar Ct
7 Brentford
TW8 131 D6
19 Charlton SE7 143 C6
Edgware HA8 11 A1
Eltham SE9 166 A5
Finchley N3 29 C3
Islington N1 73 A1
Marylebone W1 237 B2
Mortlake SW14 133 A1
1 Muswell Hill N10 31 B1
5 New Southgate
N11 31 C5
Oakleigh Pk N20 14 B3
Stoneleigh KT17 216 A1
3 Sutton SM2 218 A2
6 Wanstead E11 55 B4
Wembley HA0 65 B4
Wimbledon SW19 156 D1
5 Woodford E18 37 A2
Cedar Dr London N2 48 C5
Pinner HA5 23 C4
Cedar Gdns SM2 218 A2
Cedar Grange 10
EN1 17 C6
Cedar Gr Ealing W5 110 A3
Sidcup DA5 168 D5
Southall UB1 85 C2
Cedar Ho
Ashford TW16 171 D3
5 Cubitt Town E14 120 A4
Hayes UB4 84 C3
Kensington W8 255 C6
New Addington CR0 223 D2
New Cross Gate
SE14 140 D4
5 Richmond TW9 132 D4
16 Rotherhithe
SE16 118 D4
Wood Green N22 32 C2
Cedar Hts TW10 154 A3

Cedarhurst BR1 186 C3
Cedarhurst Dr SE9 165 C6
Cedar Lawn Ave EN5 13 A6
Cedar Lo
Brondesbury NW2 69 B2
Fulham SW6 134 D4
Cedarmore Ct BR7 189 A2
Cedar Mount SE9 165 D3
Cedarne Rd
SW6 135 D5 265 C3
Cedar Park Gdns
RM6 58 D2
Cedar Park Rd EN2 5 A5
Cedar Pl 3 SE7 121 C1
Cedar Rd
Bromley BR1 187 C1
Cranford TW5 128 C3
Cricklewood NW2 68 C4
Croydon CR0 221 C6
East Bedfont TW14 149 B3
East Molesey KT8 196 C5
Enfield EN2 5 A5
Sutton SM2 218 A2
Teddington TW11 175 A5
Tottenham N17 33 D2
Cedar Rise N14 15 A4
Cedars Ave
Mitcham CR4 203 A6
Walthamstow E17 53 C4
Cedars Cl
Hendon NW4 46 D6
Lewisham SE13 142 B2
Cedars Ct
Edmonton N9 17 D2
Putney SW15 156 A5
Cedars Dr UB10 82 C5
Cedars Fst & Mid Schs
HA3 24 A2
Cedars Ho
21 London SW2 138 B1
15 Walthamstow E17 53 D6
5 West Norwood
SW27 182 D5
Cedars Mews SW4 137 B1
Cedars Prim Sch The
TW5 128 A5
Cedars Rd
Barnes SW13 134 A3
Beckenham BR3 185 B1
Clapham SW4 137 B1
4 Lower Edmonton
N9 18 A2
Morden SM4 201 C5
Stratford E15 76 C2
Teddington KT8 175 C2
Wallington CR0 220 A4
Winchmore Hill N21 16 D2
Cedars The
Buckhurst Hill IG9 21 A3
Ealing W13 87 C1
Hackney E9 74 D1
4 Kingston u T KT2 176 D2
Teddington TW11 174 D4
Wallington SM6 219 C4
Cedar Terr
9 Dagenham RM8 58 D2
Richmond TW9 132 A1
Cedar Tree Gr SE27 182 D5
Cedarville Gdns
SW16 182 B4
Cedar Way
Ashford TW16 171 C3
Camden Town
NW1 93 D6 232 C6
Cedar Wlk KT10 212 D2
Cedarwood BR3 185 B3
Cedarwood Ho EN2 4 D3
Cedarwood Lo HA8 26 B5
Cedra Ct N16 52 A1
Cedric Chambers
NW8 236 C6
Cedric Rd SE9 167 A1
Celadon Cl EN3 7 A2
Celandine Cl E3, E14 97 C2
Celandine Ct E4 19 D1
Celandine Dr
Dalston E8 73 D1
Woolwich SE28 124 B5
Celandine Gr N14 15 C6
Celandine Way E15 98 C4
Celbridge Mews W2 91 D1
Celestial Gdns SE13 142 B1
Celia Blairman Ho
E1 243 C4
Celia Ct 7 TW9 132 B4
Celia Ho 10 N1 95 C5
Celia Rd N19 71 C4
Celtic Ave BR2 208 C6
Celtic St E14 97 D2
Cemetery La
Lower Halliford
TW17 192 D2
Woolwich SE7 144 A6

Cemetery Rd
East Wickham SE2 146 B5
Forest Gate E7 76 D4
Tottenham N17 33 C3
Cenacle Cl NW3 69 C5
Cenotaph* SW1 250 A2
Centaur Ct 3 TW8 110 A1
Centaurs Bsns Pk TW7 131 A6
Centaur St SE1 116 B3 260 D6
Centenary Rd EN3 7 B1
Centennial Ave WD6 9 C4
Centennial Ct WD6 9 C4
Centennial Pk HA7, WD6 9 C4
Central Ave
Battersea SW11 136 D5 267 D3
East Finchley N2 47 D6
East Molesey KT8 195 B4
Edmonton N9 17 D1
Enfield EN1 6 B3
Finchley N2 30 B1
Hayes UB3 106 A6
Isleworth TW3, TW7 130 A1
Leyton E11 76 B6
Pinner HA5 41 B2
Wallington SM6 220 A3
Welling DA16 146 A3
Central Bsns Ctr NW10 67 C3
Central Chambers W5 109 D6
Central Cir NW4 46 B4
Central Criminal Court (Old Bailey)* EC4 94 D1 241 D2
Central Ct 2 SE18 122 D2
Centrale Ctr CR0 221 A6
Central Foundation Boys' Sch EC2 95 B3 242 D6
Central Foundation Lower Girls Sch The E3 97 A4
Central Foundation Upper Girls Sch The E3 97 B4
Central Gdns SM4 201 D4
Central Hill SE19 183 B4
Central Ho
Barking IG11 79 A1
Mill Meads E15 98 A5
Central Mans
8 London NW4 46 B4
1 Streatham SW16 182 A6
Central Middlesex Hospl NW10 89 A4
Central Par
Croydon CR0 220 C4
Ealing UB6 87 A4
Enfield EN3 6 C3
Feltham TW14 150 C4
Harrow HA1 42 D4
Heston TW5 129 C5
Ilford IG2 57 B3
Central Park Ave RM10 81 D5
Central Park Prim Sch E6 99 D5
Central Park Rd E6 99 D5
Central Par
Penge SE20 184 D3
South Acton W3 110 D4
2 Streatham SW16 182 A6
Surbiton KT6 198 A3
Central Par Villas BR5 190 C1
Central Par 8 E17 53 C5
Central Pk Est TW4 128 D1
Central Public Health Laboratories NW9 45 C6
Central Rd
Morden SM4 201 D4
Wembley HA0 65 B3
Worcester Pk KT4 216 A6
Central St Martins Coll EC1 94 C3 241 B5
Central St Martins Coll of Art & Design (The London Inst) WC1 94 B2 240 C3
Central St Martin's Coll of Art & Design W1 93 D1 239 D1
Central Sch of Ballet EC1 94 C3 241 B5
Central Sch of Speech & Drama The NW3 70 B1
Central Sq
East Molesey KT8 195 B5

Central Sq *continued*
Hampstead Garden Suburb NW11 47 D3
4 Wembley HA9 66 A3
Central St EC1 95 A4 235 A1
Central Terr BR3 206 D6
Central Way
Feltham TW14 150 B6
Lower Place NW10 89 A4
Sutton SM5 218 C1
Thamesmead SE28 124 B6
Centre Ave
Acton W3 111 B5
Finchley N2 30 C1
Centre Bldg SE17 262 B4
Centre Common Rd BR7 189 A3
Centre Court Sh Ctr 3 SW19 179 B4
Centre Ct N20 14 B2
Centre Dr E7 77 C4
Centre Hts 5 NW3 70 B1
Centre Point Ho WC2 239 D2
Centre Point 3 SE1 118 A1
Centre Rd
Dagenham RM10 103 D5
Wanstead E7, E11 77 A6
Centre St E2 96 B5
Centre The TW13 150 B3
Centreway 4 IG1 79 A6
Centre Way N9 18 D2
Centro Ct E11 54 C1
Centurian Way DA18 125 C3
Centurion Bldg SW8 268 C5
Centurion Cl N7 72 B1
Centurion Ct
Hackbridge SM6 219 B6
7 Woolwich SE18 122 B2
Centurion La E3 97 B5
Centurion Lodge 2 RM10 81 D2
Century Cl NW4 46 D4
Century Ho
Edgware HA8 26 C3
Harrow HA3 42 C6
Lewisham SE13 141 D3
Wembley HA9 66 B6
Century Rd E17 53 A6
Century Yd SE23 162 C2
Cephas Ave E1 96 C3
Cephas Ho 9 E1 96 C3
Cephas St E1 96 C3
Ceres Ct 12 KT1 176 A1
Ceres Rd SE18 123 D2
Cerise Rd SE15 140 A4
Cerne Cl UB4 106 C6
Cerne Rd SM4 202 A3
Cerney Mews W2 246 C6
Cervantes Ct 12 W2 91 D1
Cester St E2 96 A6
Ceylon Rd
6 Hammersmith W14 112 D3
Kensington W14 254 A5
Chabot Dr SE15 140 B2
Chace Com Sch EN1 5 C4
Chadacre Ave IG5 56 B6
Chadacre Ct E15 99 A6
Chadacre Ho 10 SW9 138 D1
Chadacre Rd KT17 216 B3
Chadbourn St E14 97 D2
Chadbury Ct NW7 28 A2
Chad Cres N9 18 C1
Chadd Dr BR1 210 A6
Chadd Gn E13 99 A6
Chaddlewood EN4 3 A1
Chadston Ho 17 N1 72 D1
Chadswell WC1 233 B1
Chadview Ct 2 RM6 58 D2
Chadville Gdns RM6 58 D4
Chadway RM8 58 C1
Chadwell Ave RM6 58 B2
CHADWELL HEATH 58 D4
Chadwell Heath Foundation Sch The RM6 58 B3
Chadwell Heath Hospl RM6 58 B4
Chadwell Heath Ind Pk RM8 58 D1
Chadwell Heath La RM6 58 C3
Chadwell Heath Sta RM6 58 D2
Chadwell Prim Sch RM6 58 C2
Chadwell St EC1 94 C4 234 B2
Chadwick Ave
Chingford E4 36 B6
Enfield N21 4 B1
Wimbledon SW19 179 C4

Chadwick Cl
12 Ealing W7 86 D2
Roehampton SW15 155 D4
Teddington TW11 175 A4
Chadwick Ct 4 SE28 124 B5
Chadwick Pl KT6 197 C3
Chadwick Rd
Harlesden NW10 89 D6
Ilford IG1 78 D5
Leytonstone E11 54 D3
Peckham SE15 139 D3
Chadwick St SW1 115 D3 259 C5
Chadwick Way SE28 124 D6
Chadwin Rd E13 99 B2
Chadworth Ho
Finsbury EC1 235 A1
Finsbury Pk N4 51 A1
Chadworth Way KT10 212 B3
Chaffey Ho 6 SE7 121 C1
Chaffinch Ave CR0 206 D3
Chaffinch Bsns Pk CR0 206 D5
Chaffinch Cl
Croydon CR0 206 D3
Edmonton N9 18 D3
Tolworth KT6 214 C5
Chaffinch Rd BR3 185 A2
Chafford Way RM6 58 C5
Chagford Ct SW19 180 C3
Chagford Ho
38 Bromley E3 97 D4
Marylebone NW1 237 C5
Chagford St NW1 92 D3 237 D5
Chailey Ave EN1 5 D3
Chailey Cl TW5 128 D4
Chailey Ind Est UB3 106 A4
Chailey St E5 74 C5
Chalbury Ho 8 SW9 138 B1
Chalbury Wlk N1 234 A4
Chalcombe Rd SE2 124 B3
Chalcot Cl SM2 217 C1
Chalcot Cres NW1 92 D6 230 D6
Chalcot Gdns NW3 70 D2
Chalcot Mews SW16 160 A1
Chalcot Rd NW1 93 A6 231 A6
Chalcot Sch NW1 71 B1
Chalcot Sq NW1 71 A1
Chalcott Gdns KT6 197 C1
Chalcroft Rd SE13 164 C6
Chaldon Rd SW6 135 A5 264 B4
Chale Rd SW2 160 A5
Chalfont Ave HA9 66 D2
Chalfont Ct
3 Belvedere DA17 125 C1
12 Harrow HA1 42 D3
Hendon NW9 45 D6
Marylebone NW1 237 D5
Chalfont Gn N9 17 C1
Chalfont Ho
2 Bermondsey SE16 118 B3
Willesden NW10 67 B5
Chalfont Rd
Edmonton N9 17 D1
Hayes UB3 106 A4
South Norwood SE25 205 D6
Chalfont Way W13 109 B3
Chalfont Wlk 5 HA5 22 C1
Chalford Cl KT8 195 C5
Chalford Ct Ilford IG2 56 D4
15 Putney SW15 156 D5
Surbiton KT6 198 B2
Chalford 7 NW3 70 A2
Chalford Rd SE21 183 B6
Chalford Wlk IG8 37 D3
Chalgrove Ave SM4 201 C4
Chalgrove Gdns N3 47 A6
Chalgrove Prim Sch N3 47 A6
Chalgrove Rd
Sutton SM2 218 B1
Tottenham N17 34 B2
Chalice Cl SM6 219 D2
Chalice Ct N2 48 C5
Chalkenden Cl SE20 184 B3
Chalkers Cnr TW9 132 D2
Chalk Farm Rd NW1 71 A1
Chalk Farm Sta NW3 71 A1
Chalkhill Prim Sch HA9 66 D5
Chalk Hill Rd W6 112 D2
Chalkhill Rd HA9 67 A5
Chalk La EN4 2 D1
Chalklands HA9 67 A5
Chalkley Cl CR4 181 A1
Chalkmill Dr EN1 6 B2

Chalk Pit Ave BR5 190 C1
Chalk Pit Way SM1 218 A3
Chalk Rd E13 99 C2
Chalkstone Cl DA16 146 A4
Chalkwell Ho 10 E1 96 D1
Chalkwell Park Ave EN1 5 C1
Challenge Cl NW10 89 C6
Challenge Ct TW2 152 C4
Challenge Rd TW15 149 B1
Challenger Ho 7 E14 119 A6
Challice Way SW2 160 B3
Challiner Ct HA1 43 A4
Challin St 1 SE20 184 C2
Challis Rd TW8 109 D1
Challoner Cl N2 30 B1
Challoner Cres W14 254 C1
Challoner Ct BR2 186 B1
Challoner Mans W14 254 C1
Challoners Cl KT8 196 B5
Challoner St W14 113 B1 254 C1
Chalmers Ho
13 London SW11 136 A2
Walthamstow E17 53 D4
Chalmers Rd TW15 170 D5
Chalmers Rd E TW15 171 A5
Chalmers Way TW14 150 B6
Chalmer's Wlk 14 SE17 138 D6
Chalner Ho SW2 160 C3
Chaloner Ct SE1 252 C2
Chalsey Lodge SE4 141 B1
Chalsey Rd SE4 141 B1
Chalton Dr N2 48 B3
Chalton St NW1 93 D5 232 C3
Chamberlain Cl
Ilford IG1 79 A5
Plumstead SE18 123 B3
Chamberlain Cotts SE5 139 B4
Chamberlain Cres BR4 207 D1
Chamberlain Gdns TW3 130 A4
Chamberlain Ho 6 E1 118 C6
Chamberlain La HA5 40 A5
Chamberlain Pl E17 53 A6
Chamberlain Rd
Ealing W13 109 A4
Finchley N2 30 A1
Chamberlain St 7 NW1 70 D1
Chamberlain Way
Pinner HA5 40 B6
Surbiton KT6 198 A2
Chamberlain Wlk 5 TW13 173 A6
Chamberlayne Ave HA9 66 A6
Chamberlayne Mans 3 NW10 90 D4
Chamberlayne Rd NW10 90 C6
Chambers Gdns N2 30 B2
Chambers Ho 2 SW16 181 C6
Chambers La NW10 68 C1
Chambers Pl CR2 221 B1
Chambers Rd N7 72 A4
Chambers St SE16 118 A4
Chamber St E1 117 D6 253 D6
Chambers Walk HA7 25 B5
Chambon Pl 7 W6 112 A2
Chambord Ho 24 E2 95 D4
Chambord St E2 95 D4
Chamomile Ct E17 53 C3
Champa Cl N17 33 D1
Champion Cres SE26 185 A6
Champion Gr SE5 139 B2
Champion Hill SE5 139 B2
Champion Pk SE5 139 B3
Champion Rd SE26 185 A6
Champlain Ho 26 W12 112 B6
Champness Cl 9 SE27 183 B6
Champness Rd IG11 79 D1
Champneys Cl SM2 217 B1
Champneys Ct N21 16 A6
Chancel Ct W1 249 C6
Chancellor Gr SE21 161 A1
Chancellor Ho
South Kensington SW7 256 B6
29 Wapping E1 118 B5
Chancellor Pas E14 119 C5
Chancellor Pl NW9 27 D1
Chancellors' Ct WC1 240 C4

Chancellors Loft N8 50 A3
Chancellor's Rd W6 112 C1
Chancellors St W6 112 C1
Chancellors Wharf 21 W6 112 C1
Chancelot Rd SE2 124 B2
Chancel St SE1 116 D5 251 C3
Chancery Bldgs 14 E1 118 C6
Chancery Gate Bsns Ctr CR4 202 D4
Chancerygate Bsns Ctr HA4 63 A3
Chancery Ho WC2 241 A3
Chancery La
Beckenham BR3 185 D1
Holborn EC4 94 C1 241 A2
Chancery Lane Sta WC1 94 C2 241 A3
Chancery Mews SW17 158 C2
Chance St E2 243 C6
Chanctonbury Cl SE9 166 D1
Chanctonbury Gdns SM2 217 D1
Chanctonbury Way N12 29 C6
Chanderia Ct 5 CR0 221 A5
Chand Ho 7 N12 30 A5
Chandler Ave E16 99 A2
Chandler Cl TW12 173 C2
Chandler Ct
Feltham TW14 150 A5
Thornton Heath CR7 204 D4
2 Tolworth KT5 198 D1
8 Wallington SM6 219 B2
Chandlers Cl TW14 149 D4
Chandlers Field Prim Sch KT8 195 C4
Chandlers Mews E14 119 C4
Chandler St E1 118 B5
Chandlers Way 11 SE24 160 C4
Chandler Way SE15 139 D5
Chandlery Ho 26 E1 96 A1
Chandon Lo SM2 218 A1
Chandos Ave
Ealing W5 109 D2
New Southgate N14 15 C1
Oakleigh Pk N20 14 B3
Walthamstow E17 35 C1
Chandos Bsns Ctr 11 SM6 219 C2
Chandos Cl IG9 21 B2
Chandos Cres HA8 26 C3
Chandos Ct
Edgware HA8 26 B3
Palmers Green N14 15 D2
Stanmore HA7 25 B4
Chandos Pl WC2 116 A6 250 A5
Chandos Rd
Cricklewood NW2 68 C3
Finchley N2 30 C1
Harrow HA1 42 A4
Old Oak Comm NW10 89 C3
Pinner HA5 40 D2
Stratford New Town E15 76 B3
Tottenham N17 33 C1
Chandos St W1 93 B2 238 D3
Chandos Way NW11 47 D1
Change Alley EC3 242 D1
Channel Cl TW5 129 C4
Channel Gate Rd NW10 89 C4
Channel Ho E14 97 A2
Channelsea Bsns Ctr E15 98 B5
Channelsea Rd E15 98 B6
Channing Sch N6 49 B1
Channon Ct 3 KT6 198 A4
Chantrey Rd SW9 138 B2
Chantries The HA7 25 A5
Chantry Cl
2 Abbey Wood SE2 124 C3
Edgware NW7 11 D4
Enfield EN2 5 A5
Harrow HA3 44 B4
Sidcup DA14 191 A5
Sunbury TW16 172 A3
West Kilburn W9 91 B3
Chantry Cres NW10 67 D2
Chantry Ct SM5 218 C5
Chantry Ct SW6 135 A2
Chantry La BR2 209 D4
Chantry Pl HA3 23 D2
Chantry Rd
Chessington KT9 214 C3
Harrow HA3 23 D2
Chantry Sch UB7 104 A6

Chantry Sq W8 113 D3 255
Chantry St N1 94 D6 234
Chantry The
3 Chingford E4 20
Hillingdon UB8 82
Chantry Way CR4 202
Chant Sq E15 76
Chant St E15 76
Chapel Cl NW10 67
Chapel Ct
Borough The SE1 252
East Finchley N2 48
Hayes UB3 105
Chapel End Ho E17 35
Chapel End Inf Sch E17 35
Chapel End Jun Sch E17 35
Chapel Farm Rd SE9 166
Chapel Hill N2 30
Chapel House St E14 119
Chapel La
5 Dagenham RM6 58
Hillingdon UB8 82
Pinner HA5 40
Chapel Market N1 94 C5 234
Chapel Mill Rd KT1 198
Chapel Pl
Islington N1 234
Marylebone W1 238
12 Shoreditch EC2 95
Tottenham N17 33
Chapel Rd
Bexleyheath DA7 147
Ealing W13 109
Hounslow TW3 129
Ilford IG1 78
Twickenham TW1 153
West Norwood SE27 182
Chapel Side W2 113 D6 245
Chapel St Enfield EN2 5
Paddington NW1 92 C2 237
Westminster SW1 115 A4 248
Chapel View CR2 222
Chapel Wlk NW4 46
Chapleton Ho SW2 160
Chaplin Cl
Lambeth SE1 251
Wembley HA0 65
Chaplin Cres TW16 171
Chaplin Ho
6 London SW9 138
Sidcup DA14 190
Chaplin Rd
Dagenham RM9 81
3 Tottenham N17 51
Wembley HA0 65
West Ham E15 98
Willesden NW2 68
Chaplow Cl SW6 136
Chapman Cl UB7 104
Chapman Cres HA3 44
Chapman Gn N22 32
Chapman Ho
26 Stepney E1 96
2 West Norwood SE27 160
Chapman Rd
Belvedere DA17 125
Hackney Wick E9 75
Thornton Heath CR0 204
Chapmans End BR5 191
Chapman's La BR5 190
Chapmans Park Ind Est NW10 67
Chapman Sq SW19 156
Chapman St E1 118
Chapone Pl W1 239
Chapter Cl
Hillingdon UB10 60
16 South Acton W4 111
Chapter House & Jewel Twr* SW1 260
Chapter Rd
Kennington SE17 116 D1 261
Willesden NW2 68
Chapter St SW1 259
Chapter Way
Hampton TW12 173
Mitcham SW19 180
Chara Pl W4 133
Charcot Ho SW15 155
Charcroft Ct 11 W14 112
Charcroft Gdns EN3 6
Chard Ho 7 N7 72
Chardin Ho 30 SW9 138

'din Rd 11 W4 111 C2
'dmore Rd N16 52 A1
'dwell Cl E6 100 B1
'ecroft Way
2 112 D4
'field Ct W9 91 D3
'ford Rd E16 99 A2
'geable La E13 99 A3
'geable St E16 98 D3
'grove Cl 24
6 118 D4
'ring Cl BR6 227 D4
ring Cross Hospl
112 D1
'ring Cross Rd
2 93 D1 239 D1
ring Cross Sta
2 116 A5 250 B4
'ring Cross
1 116 A5 250 A4
'ring Ct BR2 186 C1
'ring Ho SE1 251 B2
'riot Cl 3 E3 97 C6
'lbert Ct NW8 230 A4
'lbert St
8 92 C5 230 A4
'lbury Ave HA7 25 D5
'lbury Gdns IG3 79 D6
'lbury Gr W5 87 C1
'lbury Ho 1 E12 78 C5
'lbury Rd UB10 60 B5
'ldane Rd SE9 166 D1
'lecote Gr SE26 162 B1
'lecote Rd RM8 81 A5
'lemont Rd E6 100 C4
rles Allen Ho
234 A2
rles Auffray Ho 30
96 C2
rles Babbage Cl
9 213 C1
rles Barry Cl
4 137 C2
rles Bradlaugh Ho
N17 34 B3
rles Burton Ct
75 A4
rles Cl DA14 190 B6
rles Cobb Gdns
0 220 C3
rles Coveney Rd 4
15 139 D4
rles Cres HA1 42 B2
rles Ct 5 TW11 174 C5
rles Darwin Ho
, Bethnal Green
E2 96 B4
omley BR1 187 B3
rles Dickens Ct
25 206 A5
rles Dickens Ho 1
96 B4
rles Dickens Prim
ch SE1 117 A4 252 A1
rles Edward Brooke
ch (Dennen Site)
5 138 D4
rles Edward Brooke
ch SW9 138 D4
rlesfield SE12 165 C1
rles Flemwell Mews
E16 121 A5
rles Goddard Ho 3
0 65 D3
rles Grinling Wlk
18 122 C2
rles Gr N14 15 C3
rles Haller St 25
2 160 C4
rles Harrod Ct
13 134 C6
rles Hobson Ho 4
10 67 C1
rles Hocking Ho 8
111 A4
rles Ho
uthall UB2 107 C4
Tottenham N17 33 D3
rles II Pl
3 114 D1 257 C1
rles II St
1 115 D5 249 C4
rles Lamb Ct N1 234 D4
rles Lamb Prim Sch
95 A6 235 A6
rles La
8 92 C5 230 A4
rles Lesser KT9 213 D3
rles Mackenzie Ho
SE16 118 A2
rlesmere Gdns
28 123 C4
rles Mills Ct
16 182 A4
rles Pl NW1 232 B1
rles Rd
genham RM6 58 D3

Charles Rd *continued*
Ealing W13 87 A1
Merton SW19 179 C2
Upton E7 77 C1
Charles Rowan Ho
WC1 234 A1
Charles Sevright Dr
NW7 28 D5
Charles Sq
N1 95 B4 235 D1
Charles Staunton Ho 3
SE27 183 B6
Charles St
Barnes SW13 133 C3
Croydon CR0 221 A5
Enfield EN1 17 D6
Hillingdon UB10 82 D3
Hounslow TW3 129 B3
Mayfair W1 115 B5 248 C4
Newham E16 121 C5
Charleston Cl TW13 150 A1
Charleston St SE17 262 B3
Charles Townsend Ho
EC1 241 C6
Charles Utton Ct E8 74 A4
Charles Whincup Rd 2
E16 121 B5
Charlesworth Ho 6
E14 97 C1
Charleville Cir SE26 184 A5
Charleville Ct SW5 254 C1
Charleville Mans
W14 254 B1
Charleville Mews
TW7 131 B1
Charleville Rd
W14 113 B1 254 C1
Charlie Browns Rdbt
E18 37 C1
Charlmont Rd
SW17 180 D4
Charlotte Cl DA6 169 A6
Charlotte Ct
Crouch End N8 49 D3
Esher KT10 212 A3
10 Hammersmith
W6 112 A2
Ilford IG2 56 C3
11 Wembley HA0 66 A2
Charlotte Despard Ave
SW11 137 A4 268 B1
Charlotte Ho 12 W6 112 C1
Charlotte Mews
Marylebone W1 239 B4
North Kensington
W10 90 D1
West Kensington
W14 254 A4
Charlotte Par SE23 163 A2
Charlotte Park Ave
BR1 210 A6
Charlotte Pl
Kenton NW9 45 A4
Marylebone W1 239 B3
Westminster SW1 259 A3
Charlotte Rd
Barnes SW13 133 D4
Dagenham RM10 81 D2
Shoreditch
EC2 95 C3 243 A6
Wallington SM6 219 C2
Charlotte Row SW4 137 C2
Charlotte Sharman Prim
Sch SE11 116 D3 261 C5
Charlotte Sq 5
TW10 154 B5
Charlotte St
W1 93 C2 239 B4
Charlotte Terr
N1 94 B6 233 D5
CHARLTON 143 D6
171 B1
Charlton Church La
SE7 121 C1
Charlton Cl UB10 60 D6
Charlton Cres IG11 101 D5
Charlton Ct
Finchley N3 29 A1
28 Hackney E2 95 D6
17 Kentish Town N7 71 D3
Newham E6 100 B4
Charlton Dene SE7 143 D5
Charlton Gate Bsns Pk
SE7 121 C2
Charlton Ho
5 Brentford
TW8 132 A6
Charlton TW17 171 A1
Somers Town NW1 232 C2
Charlton King's Rd
NW5 71 D3
Charlton La
Greenwich SE7 121 D1
Upper Halliford
TW17 193 B5
Upper Halliford
TW17 193 C5

Charlton Lo 1 NW11 47 B3
Charlton Manor Prim
Sch SE7 143 D5
Charlton Park La
SE7 144 A6
Charlton Park Rd
SE7 143 D6
Charlton Pl
N1 94 D5 234 C4
Charlton Rd
Charlton TW17 171 A1
Edmonton N9 18 D4
Greenwich SE3, SE7 143 B6
Harlesden NW10 89 C6
Harrow HA3 43 D5
Wembley HA9 44 B1
Charlton Sch SE7 144 A6
Charlton Way SE10,
SE3 142 C4
Charlwood Cl HA3 24 C4
Charlwood Ho
Richmond TW9 132 D5
1 Streatham SW2 160 B3
Westminster SW1 259 C3
Charlwood Pl
SW1 115 C2 259 B3
Charlwood Rd
SW15 134 D1
Charlwood St
SW1 115 C1 259 B2
Charlwood Terr 5
SW15 134 D1
Charman Ho
18 London SW2 160 C5
South Lambeth SW8 270 A4
Charmian Ave HA7 25 D1
Charmian Ho 19 N1 95 C5
Charminster Ave
SW19 179 D1
Charminster Ct 3
KT6 197 D2
Charminster Rd
Mottingham SE12,
SE9 187 D6
North Cheam KT4 200 D1
Charmouth Ct
TW10 154 B6
Charmouth Ho SW8 270 C4
Charmouth Rd
DA16 146 C4
Charnock Ho 22
W12 112 B6
Charnock Rd E5 74 B5
Charnwood Ave
SW19 179 D1
Charnwood Cl KT3 199 C5
Charnwood Dr E18 55 B5
Charnwood Gdns
E14 119 C2
Charnwood Ho 9 E5 74 B6
Charnwood Pl N20 14 A1
Charnwood Rd
Hillingdon UB10 82 C5
South Norwood
SE25 205 B5
Charnwood St E5 74 B6
Charolais Ho UB4 83 B2
Charrington Ho 42
E1 96 C3
Charrington Rd 2
CR0 221 A6
Charrington St
NW1 93 D5 232 C4
Charsley Rd SE6 163 D2
Chart Cl
Bromley BR2 186 C2
Croydon CR0 206 C3
Mitcham CR4 202 D5
Charter Ave IG2 57 B2
Charter Bldgs 14
SE10 141 D4
Charter Cres TW4 129 A1
Charter Ct
Finsbury Pk N4 50 C1
Kingston u T KT3 199 C6
Marylebone W1 237 B3
Southall UB1 107 C5
Wood Green N22 31 D2
Charter Dr DA5 169 A4
Charterhouse Ave
HA0 65 C3
Charterhouse Bldgs
EC1 242 A5
Charterhouse Mews
EC1 241 D4
Charterhouse Rd E8 74 A3
Charterhouse Sq
EC1 94 D2 241 D4
Charterhouse Square
Sch EC1 94 D2 241 D4
Charterhouse St
EC1 241 C3
Charterhouse Works
SW18 136 A1
Charter Ho WC2 240 B1

Charteris Rd
Finsbury Pk N4 50 C1
Kilburn NW6 91 B6
Woodford IG8 37 B4
Charter Nightingale
Hospl The
NW1 92 C2 237 B4
Charter Rd KT1 198 D6
Charter Rd The IG8 36 D4
Charter Sch The
SE24 161 B6
Charters Cl SE19 183 C5
Charter Sq KT1 176 D1
Charter Way
London NW3 47 B5
Southgate N14 15 D5
Chartes Ho SE1 263 B6
Chartfield Ave
SW15 156 C6
Chartfield Sch
SW15 156 B6
Chartfield Sq SW15 156 D6
Chartham Ct 12
SW9 138 C2
Chartham Gr SE27 160 D1
Chartham Ho SE1 262 D6
Chartham Rd SE25 206 B6
Chart Hills Cl SE28 103 A1
Chart Ho 7 SW19 180 D1
Chart House The 5
E14 119 D1
Chartley Ave
Harrow HA7 24 D4
Neasden NW2 67 C5
Charton Cl 5 DA17 147 B6
Chartres Ct UB6 86 B5
Chartridge Cl
Barnet EN5 12 A6
Bushey WD23 8 A5
Chartridge Ct 6 HA7 25 C5
Chartridge SE17 139 B6
Chart St N1 95 B4 235 D2
Chartwell Bsns Ctr
BR1 209 D6
Chartwell Cl
2 Croydon CR0 205 B1
Greenford UB6 85 D6
Sidcup SE9 167 B2
Chartwell Ct
10 Barnet EN5 1 A1
Dollis Hill NW2 68 A5
2 Woodford IG8 37 A3
Chartwell Dr BR6 227 B3
Chartwell Gdns
SM3 217 A4
Chartwell Lo 5
BR3 185 C3
Chartwell Pl
Cheam SM3 217 B4
Harrow HA2 64 B6
Chartwell 25 SW19 156 D3
Chartwell Way 3
SE20 184 B2
Charville Ct 8 HA1 42 D3
Charville La UB4 83 C5
Charville La W UB10 82 D4
Charville Prim Sch
UB4 83 C5
Charwood SW16 182 C6
Chase Bridge Prim Sch
TW2 152 C5
Chase Court Gdns
EN2 5 A2
Chase Ct
Chelsea SW3 257 C5
Isleworth TW7 131 A3
Merton SW20 179 A1
Chase Ctr The NW10 89 B4
Chase Ct
Southgate N14 15 C5
Wembley HA0 65 D2
Chase Farm Hospl
EN2 4 C5
Chasefield Rd
SW17 180 D6
Chase Gdns
Chingford E4 35 C6
Twickenham TW2 152 B4
Chase Gn EN2 5 A2
Chase Green Ave EN2 5 A3
Chase Hill EN2 5 A2
Chase La IG6 57 B4
Chase Lane Inf Sch
E4 35 B6
Chase Lane Jun Sch
E4 35 B6
Chaseley Ct
Gunnersbury W4 110 D1
Oatlands Pk KT13 193 C1
Chaseley St E14 97 A1
Chasemore Cl CR4 202 D2
Chasemore Gdns
CR0 220 C3
Chasemore Ho SW6 264 B4
Chase Rd
North Acton NW10 89 B3
Southgate N14 15 D5

Chase Ridings EN2 4 C3
Chase Road Trad Est
NW10 89 B3
Chase Side Ave
Enfield EN2 5 A3
Merton SW20 179 A1
Chase Side Cres EN2 5 A4
Chase Side
East Barnet N14 15 B4
Enfield EN2 5 A3
Chase Side Pl EN2 5 A3
Chase Side Prim Sch
EN2 5 A3
Chase Side Works
N14 15 D4
Chase The
Bromley BR1 209 B6
Clapham SW4 137 B2
Dagenham RM6 59 A3
Eastcote HA5 40 C3
Edgware HA8 26 D2
Erith DA7 147 D2
Ickenham UB10 60 C3
Loughton IG10 21 D4
Manor Pk E12 77 D4
Pinner HA5 41 B5
South Norwood
SW16 182 C3
Stanmore HA7 25 A4
Sunbury TW16 172 B2
Wallington CR0,
SM6 220 B3
Chaseville Park Rd
N21 16 B6
Chaseville Par N21 16 B6
Chase Way N14 15 C3
Chasewood Ave EN2 4 D3
Chasewood Ct 4
NW7 27 B5
Chasewood Pk HA1 64 C5
Chateau The 4
SM5 218 D5
Chatelain Ho NW7 28 C6
Chater Ho 6 E2 96 D4
Chatfield Rd
London SW11 136 A2
Thornton Heath CR0 204 D1
Chatham Ave BR2 209 A2
Chatham Cl
Cheam SM3 201 B2
Hampstead Garden
Suburb NW11 47 C4
Chatham Ct SW11 158 D6
Chatham Ho
7 London SE5 139 C3
6 Wallington SM6 219 B3
21 Woolwich SE18 122 B2
Chatham Pl E9 74 C2
Chatham Rd
Clapham SW11 158 D6
Kingston u T KT1,
KT2 176 C1
Walthamstow E17 53 A6
1 Woodford E18 36 D1
Chatham St
SE17 117 B2 262 D4
Chatsfield Pl W5 88 A1
Chatsworth Ave
Grove Pk BR1 187 B6
Hendon NW4 28 C1
Merton SW20 179 A1
Sidcup DA15 168 A3
Wembley HA9 66 B3
Chatsworth Cl
Coney Hall BR2,
BR4 224 D6
Hendon NW4 28 C1
Chatsworth Cres TW3,
TW7 130 B2
Chatsworth Ct
Brondesbury NW2 68 D2
Clapton Pk E5 74 D4
Earl's Ct W8 255 A4
5 Stanmore HA7 25 C5
Thornton Heath
SW16 204 B6
Chatsworth Dr EN1 18 A5
Chatsworth Est E5 74 D4
Chatsworth Gdns
Acton W3 110 D5
Harrow HA2 41 D1
New Malden KT3 199 D4
Chatsworth Ho
2 Bromley BR2 209 A5
Kingston u T KT6 197 D4
Chatsworth Inf Sch
Isleworth TW3 130 A1
Sidcup DA15 168 A3
Chatsworth Jun Sch
TW3 130 A1
Chatsworth Lo
1 Chiswick W4 111 B1
West Wickham BR4 224 A6
Chatsworth Par
BR5 211 A4
Chatsworth Pl
Mitcham CR4 202 D6

Chatsworth Pl *continued*
Teddington TW11 175 A6
Chatsworth Rd
Brondesbury NW2 68 D2
Cheam SM3 217 A4
Chiswick W4 133 A6
Clapton Pk E5 74 D4
Ealing W5 88 B3
Hayes UB4 84 B3
South Croydon CR0 221 B5
Stratford E15 76 D3
Chatsworth Rise W5 88 B3
Chatsworth Way
SE27 161 A1
Chattenden Ho 8
N4 51 B2
Chatteris Ct NW4 46 D6
CHATTERN HILL 170 D6
Chattern Hill TW15 170 D6
Chattern Rd TW15 171 A6
Chatterton Ct TW9 132 B3
Chatterton Rd
Bromley Comm
BR2 209 D4
Highbury N4 72 D5
Chatton Ct 5 NW9 46 A5
Chatto Rd SW11 158 D6
Chaucer Ave
Cranford TW4 128 B3
Hayes UB4 84 A2
Richmond TW9 132 C3
Chaucer Cl N11 31 D5
Chaucer Ct
14 New Barnet
EN5 13 D6
17 Stoke Newington
N16 73 C4
Chaucer Dr
SE1 117 D2 263 D3
Chaucer Gdns SM1 217 C5
Chaucer Gn CR0 206 C2
Chaucer Ho
Harrow HA2 41 D4
Pimlico SW1 259 A1
Sutton SM1 217 C5
2 West Norwood
SE27 183 A6
Chaucer Rd
Acton W3 111 A5
Ashford TW15 170 B6
Bexley DA16 145 D4
Chingford E17 36 A1
Herne Hill SE24 160 D6
Sidcup DA15 168 C3
Sutton SM1 217 C4
Upton E7 77 A2
Wanstead E11 55 A3
Chaucer Way SW17 180 B5
Chaulden Ho EC1 235 D1
Chauncey Cl N9 18 A1
Chaundrye Cl SE9 166 B5
Chauntler Cl E16 121 B6
Chaville Ct N11 31 A6
Cheadle Ct NW8 236 D6
Cheadle Ho 17 E14 97 B1
CHEAM 217 B3
Cheam Common Inf Sch
KT4 216 B6
Cheam Common Jun
Sch KT4 216 B6
Cheam Common Rd
KT4 216 C5
Cheam Court Flats 1
SM3 217 A2
Cheam Fields Prim Sch
SM3 217 A3
Cheam High Sch
SM3 217 A4
Cheam Mans SM3 217 A1
Cheam Park Farm Inf
Sch SM3 217 A5
Cheam Park Farm Jun
Sch SM3 217 A5
Cheam Park Way
SM3 217 A2
Cheam Rd
Belmont SM2,
SM3 216 D1
Cheam SM1 217 C2
Cheam Sta SM2 217 A1
Cheam St 6 SE15 140 B2
Cheam Village SM3 217 A2
Cheapside
Barbican
EC2 95 A1 242 B1
Edmonton N13 33 A6
Chearsley SE17 262 B4
Cheddar Cl 1 N11 31 A4
Cheddar Rd TW6 126 C3
Cheddar Waye UB4 84 B1
Cheddington Ho 9
E2 96 A6
Cheddington Rd N18 33 C6
Chedworth Cl E16 98 D1

Chedworth Ho
London N15 ... 51 B5
2 Stoke Newington E5 ... 74 A6
Cheeseman Cl TW12 ... 173 A4
Cheeseman Ct UB1 ... 107 D6
Cheesemans Terr W14 ... 254 C1
Cheffrey Ct TW15 ... 170 D4
Cheldon Ave NW7 ... 28 D3
Chelford Rd BR1 ... 186 B5
Chelmer Cres IG11 ... 102 B5
Chelmer Ct E18 ... 37 B2
Chelmer Rd E9 ... 74 D3
Chelmsford Cl
Fulham W6 ... 134 D6
Newham E6 ... 100 B1
Chelmsford Ct N14 ... 15 D4
Chelmsford Gdns IG1 ... 56 B2
Chelmsford Ho 5 N7 ... 72 B4
Chelmsford Rd
Leytonstone E11 ... 54 B1
London N14 ... 15 C4
Walthamstow E17 ... 53 C3
Woodford E18 ... 36 D2
Chelmsford Sq NW10 ... 90 C6
CHELSEA ... 114 C1
Chelsea Barracks* SW1 ... 115 A1 258 B1
Chelsea Bridge Rd SW1 ... 115 A1 258 B1
Chelsea Bridge SW1 ... 137 B6 268 C6
Chelsea Cl
Edgware HA8 ... 26 C1
Hampton TW12 ... 174 A5
New Malden KT4 ... 200 A2
Chelsea Cloisters SW3 ... 257 B3
Chelsea Cl NW10 ... 89 B6
Chelsea Coll of Art & Design
Chelsea SW3 ... 114 C1 257 A1
Pimlico SW1 ... 116 A1 260 A2
Chelsea Cres
Brondesbury NW2 ... 69 B2
Chelsea SW10 ... 266 B1
Chelsea Ct
Chelsea SW3 ... 268 A6
8 Chingford E4 ... 20 A3
Sutton SM2 ... 217 D2
Chelsea Emb SW3 ... 136 D6 267 C5
Chelsea Est SW3 ... 267 A5
Chelsea Farm Ho SW10 ... 266 D5
Chelsea Fields SW19 ... 180 B2
Chelsea Gate SW1 ... 258 B1
Chelsea Gdns
Cheam SM3 ... 217 A4
Chelsea SW1 ... 258 B1
Ealing W13 ... 86 D2
Chelsea Harbour Design Ctr SW10 ... 266 B2
Chelsea Harbour Dr SW10 ... 136 A4 266 B2
Chelsea Harbour Pier SW10 ... 266 C1
Chelsea Lo SW3 ... 267 D6
Chelsea Manor Ct SW3 ... 267 B6
Chelsea Manor Gdns SW3 ... 257 B1
Chelsea Manor St SW3 ... 114 C1 257 B1
Chelsea Manor Studios SW3 ... 257 B1
Chelsea Park Gdns SW3 ... 136 B6 266 C6
Chelsea Physic Gdn* SW1 ... 267 C6
Chelsea Reach Twr SW10 ... 266 C4
Chelsea Sq SW3 ... 114 B1 256 D1
Chelsea Twrs SW3 ... 267 B6
Chelsea & Westminster Hospl SW10 ... 136 A6 266 B5
Chelsfield Ave N9 ... 18 D4
Chelsfield Gdns SE26 ... 162 C1
Chelsfield Gn N9 ... 18 D4
Chelsfield Ho SE17 ... 263 A3
Chelsfield Point 3 E9 ... 74 D1
Chelsham Ho 1 SW4 ... 137 D2
Chelsham Rd
London SW4 ... 137 D2
South Croydon CR2 ... 221 B2
Chelsiter Ct DA14 ... 189 D6
Chelston App HA4 ... 62 A6
Chelston Ct 2 E11 ... 55 B4
Chelston Rd HA4 ... 40 A1
Chelsworth Dr SE18 ... 145 B6
Cheltenham Ave 10 TW1 ... 153 A4
Cheltenham Cl
Kingston u T KT3 ... 199 A6
Northolt UB5 ... 63 D2
Cheltenham Ct 8 HA7 ... 25 C5
Cheltenham Gdns E6 ... 100 A5
Cheltenham Ho UB3 ... 105 A3
Cheltenham Pl
10 Acton W3 ... 110 D5
Acton W3 ... 111 A4
Harrow HA3 ... 44 A5
1 South Acton W3 ... 110 D4
Cheltenham Rd
Leyton E10 ... 54 A3
London SE15 ... 162 C6
Cheltenham Terr SW3 ... 114 D1 257 D2
Cheltenham Villas CR7 ... 204 C3
Chelverton Ct SW15 ... 134 D1
Chelverton Rd SW15 ... 134 D1
Chelwood Cl E4 ... 19 D5
Chelwood Ct
Battersea SW11 ... 266 D2
9 South Croydon CR2 ... 221 A3
Chelwood Gdns TW9 ... 132 C3
Chelwood NW5 ... 71 A3
Chelwood Ho W2 ... 236 D1
Chelwood Lo N12 ... 30 A4
Chelwood N20 ... 14 B2
Chenappa Cl E13 ... 99 A4
Chenduit Way HA7 ... 24 D5
Chene Colline Ct KT6 ... 198 A3
Cheney Ct SE23 ... 162 D3
Cheney Row E17 ... 35 B2
Cheneys Rd E11 ... 76 C5
Cheney St HA5 ... 40 C4
Chenies Ho W2 ... 245 C6
Chenies Mews WC1 ... 239 C5
Chenies Pl NW1 ... 232 D4
Chenies St WC1 ... 93 D2 239 C4
Chenies The
Orpington BR6 ... 211 C3
Somers Town NW1 ... 232 D4
Cheniston Gdns W8 ... 255 C6
Chennestone Prim Sch TW16 ... 172 B1
Chepstow Cl SW15 ... 157 A6
Chepstow Cres
Ilford IG3 ... 57 C3
Notting Hill W11 ... 113 C6 245 A6
Chepstow Ct W11 ... 245 A6
Chepstow Gdns UB1 ... 85 B1
Chepstow Pl W2 ... 113 C6 245 B6
Chepstow Rd
Croydon CR0 ... 221 D6
Ealing W7 ... 109 A3
Paddington W2 ... 91 C1
Chepstow Rise CR0 ... 221 C5
Chepstow Villas W11 ... 113 C6 245 A6
Chequers IG9 ... 21 B3
Chequers Cl
London NW9 ... 45 C6
Orpington BR5 ... 211 D5
Chequers Ct
7 Croydon CR0 ... 205 D1
St Luke's EC1 ... 242 C5
Chequers Ho NW8 ... 237 A6
Chequers La RM9 ... 103 C5
Chequers Par
Dagenham RM9 ... 103 C6
Edmonton N13 ... 33 A5
Chequer St EC1 ... 95 A3 242 B5
Chequers The HA5 ... 40 D6
Chequers Way N13 ... 32 D5
Cherbury Cl SE28 ... 102 D1
Cherbury Ct N1 ... 235 D3
Cherbury St N1 ... 95 B5 235 D3
Cherchefells Mews HA7 ... 25 B5
Cherimoya Gdns KT8 ... 195 D6
Cherington Rd W7 ... 108 D5
Cheriton Ave BR2 ... 209 A4
Cheriton Cl
Cockfosters EN4 ... 2 D1
10 Ealing W5 ... 87 C2
Cheriton Ct
4 Lee SE12 ... 165 A4
South Norwood SE25 ... 205 C4
Walton-on-T KT12 ... 194 C1
Cheriton Dr SE18 ... 145 B6
Cheriton Ho 9 E5 ... 74 B3
Cheriton Sq SW17 ... 159 A2
Cherry Ave UB1 ... 106 D5
Cherry Blossom Cl N13 ... 32 D5
Cherry Cl
Carshalton SM5 ... 218 D6
Ealing W5 ... 109 D3
Merton SM4 ... 201 A5
Ruislip HA4 ... 61 D5
7 Streatham SW2 ... 160 C4
Walthamstow E17 ... 53 D4
Cherrycot Hill BR6 ... 227 B4
Cherrycot Rise BR6 ... 227 A4
Cherry Cres TW8 ... 131 B5
Cherry Croft Gdns 3 HA5 ... 23 B3
Cherry Ct Acton W3 ... 111 C5
Hackbridge CR4 ... 203 A1
Ilford IG6 ... 56 D6
Pinner HA5 ... 22 D2
5 Rotherhithe SE16 ... 119 A5
Sidcup DA14 ... 168 B1
Cherrydeal Ct E11 ... 54 B2
Cherrydown Ave E4 ... 19 C1
Cherrydown Cl E4 ... 19 C1
Cherrydown Rd DA14 ... 168 D2
Cherry Garden Ho 7 SE16 ... 118 B4
Cherry Garden Sch SE16 ... 118 A2
Cherry Garden St SE16 ... 118 B4
Cherry Garth TW8 ... 109 D1
Cherry Gdns
Dagenham RM9 ... 81 B3
Northolt UB5 ... 63 D1
Cherry Gr
Hayes UB3 ... 106 B5
Hillingdon UB8 ... 83 A2
Cherry Hill Gdns CR0 ... 220 B4
Cherry Hill EN5 ... 13 D5
Cherry Hills WD19 ... 23 A5
Cherry Hill HA3 ... 24 C4
Cherrylands Cl NW9 ... 67 A6
Cherry Lane Prim Sch UB7 ... 104 B2
Cherry Laurel Wlk SW2 ... 160 B5
Cherry La UB7 ... 104 C2
Cherry Orchard Gdns
7 Croydon CR0 ... 205 B1
East Molesey KT8 ... 195 B6
5 South Croydon CR0 ... 221 B6
Cherry Orchard Prim Sch SE7 ... 143 C5
Cherry Orchard Rd
Croydon CR0 ... 205 C1
East Molesey KT8 ... 195 C6
Keston Mark BR2 ... 226 A6
Cherry Orch
Charlton SE7 ... 143 C6
West Drayton UB7 ... 104 A4
Cherry Rd EN3 ... 6 C5
Cherry Tree Ave UB7 ... 82 B1
Cherry Tree Cl
11 Hackney E9 ... 96 C6
Wembley HA0 ... 65 A4
Cherry Tree Ct
1 Camden Town NW1 ... 71 C1
17 Charlton SE7 ... 143 C6
Kingsbury NW9 ... 45 A5
11 Peckham SE15 ... 140 B4
3 Woodford E18 ... 36 D1
Cherry Tree Dr SW16 ... 160 A1
Cherry Tree Hill N6 ... 48 D4
Cherry Tree Ho SE14 ... 141 B3
Cherrytree Ho 8 W10 ... 90 D4
Cherry Tree Ho
Ruislip HA4 ... 39 C1
Twickenham TW2 ... 152 B2
Wood Green N22 ... 32 A3
Cherry Tree Rd
London N2 ... 48 D5
Stratford E15 ... 76 C3
Cherry Tree Rise IG9 ... 37 D6
Cherry Trees Sch The E3 ... 97 C4
Cherry Tree Terr SE1 ... 253 B2
Cherry Tree Way HA7 ... 25 B4
Cherry Tree Wlk
Beckenham BR3 ... 207 B5
Coney Hall BR4 ... 224 D4
St Luke's EC1 ... 242 B5
Cherry Way
Upper Halliford TW17 ... 193 C5
West Ewell KT19 ... 215 B2
Cherry Wlk BR2 ... 209 A1
Cherrywood Cl
Bow E3 ... 97 A4
Kingston u T KT2 ... 176 C3
Cherrywood Ct 1 TW11 ... 175 A5
Cherrywood Dr SW15 ... 156 D6
Cherrywood La SM4, SW20 ... 201 A5
Cherry Wood Way W5 ... 88 C2
Chertsey Ct SW14 ... 132 D2
Chertsey Dr SM3 ... 217 A6
Chertsey Ho
Feltham TW13 ... 151 C1
37 Shoreditch E2 ... 95 D4
Chertsey Rd
Ashford TW15, TW16 ... 171 B4
Feltham TW13, TW16 ... 171 C6
Ilford IG1 ... 79 B4
Leyton E11 ... 76 B6
Lower Halliford TW17 ... 192 C2
Shepperton TW17 ... 192 A2
Twickenham TW2 ... 152 B4
Chertsey St SW17 ... 181 A5
Chervil Cl TW13 ... 150 A1
Chervil Mews SE28 ... 124 B5
Cherwell Ct
Teddington KT1 ... 175 D3
West Ewell KT19 ... 215 A4
Cherwell Ho NW8 ... 236 D5
Cherwell Way HA4 ... 39 A3
Cheryls Cl SW6 ... 135 D4 265 D2
Cheseman St SE26 ... 162 B1
Chesfield Rd KT2 ... 176 A3
Chesham Ave BR2, BR5 ... 210 D3
Chesham Cl SW1 ... 258 A5
Chesham Cres SE20 ... 184 C2
Chesham Ct SW18 ... 158 B4
Chesham Flats W1 ... 248 B6
Chesham Ho SW1 ... 258 A5
Chesham Mews SW1 ... 258 A6
Chesham Pl SW1 ... 115 A3 258 A5
Chesham Rd
Kingston u T KT1, KT2 ... 176 C1
Mitcham SW19 ... 180 B4
Penge SE20 ... 184 C2
Chesham St
Westminster SW1 ... 115 A3 258 A5
Willesden NW10 ... 67 B5
Chesham Terr W13 ... 109 B4
Cheshire Cl
Chingford E17 ... 35 D2
Mitcham CR4, SW16 ... 204 A6
Cheshire Gdns KT9 ... 213 D2
Cheshire Ho SM4 ... 201 D2
Cheshire Rd N22 ... 32 B4
Cheshire St E2 ... 95 D3 243 D6
Cheshir Ho NW4 ... 46 C5
Chesholm Rd N16 ... 73 C5
Cheshunt Ho
Hendon NW4 ... 46 C6
9 Kilburn NW6 ... 91 D6
Cheshunt Rd
Belvedere DA17 ... 125 C1
Upton E7 ... 77 B2
Chesil Ct
17 Bethnal Green E2 ... 96 C5
Chelsea SW3 ... 267 B6
Chesil Ho BR7 ... 189 B2
Chesilton Rd SW6 ... 135 B4 264 C2
Chesil Way UB4 ... 83 D4
Chesley Gdns E6 ... 100 A4
Chesney Cres CR0 ... 224 A1
Chesney Ct W9 ... 91 C3
Chesney Ho SE13 ... 142 B1
Chesney St SW11 ... 268 A1
Chesnut Gr N17 ... 51 D6
Chesnut Rd N17 ... 51 D6
Chessell Cl CR7 ... 204 D5
Chessholme Ct TW16 ... 171 C3
Chessholme Rd TW15 ... 171 A4
Chessing Ct N2 ... 48 D6
CHESSINGTON ... 214 A2
Chessington Ave
Church End N3 ... 47 B6
Erith DA7 ... 147 A5
Chessington Cl KT19 ... 215 A2
Chessington Com Coll KT9 ... 213 D1
Chessington Ct
London N3 ... 47 B6
Pinner HA5 ... 41 B5
Chessington Hall Gdns KT9 ... 213 D1
Chessington Hill Pk KT9 ... 214 C3
Chessington Ho 19 SW8 ... 137 D3
Chessington Lo N3 ... 47 B6
Chessington Mans
Leyton E10 ... 53 C2
Leytonstone E11 ... 54 C2
Chessington North Sta KT9 ... 214 A3
Chessington Par KT9 ... 213 D3
Chessington Pk KT9 ... 214 C4
Chessington Rd KT19 ... 215 B1
Chessington South Sta KT9 ... 213 D1
Chessington Trade Pk KT9 ... 214 C4
Chessington Way BR4 ... 223 D6
Chesson Rd W14 ... 135 B6 264 D6
Chessum Ho E8 ... 74 A2
Chesswood Way HA5 ... 22 D1
Chestbrook Ct 12 EN1 ... 17 C6
Chester Ave
Richmond TW10 ... 154 B5
Twickenham TW2 ... 151 B3
Chester Cl
Ashford TW15 ... 171 B5
Barnes SW13 ... 134 B2
Hayes UB8 ... 82 D1
Knightsbridge SW1 ... 248 C1
Chester Close N NW1 ... 231 D2
Chester Close S NW1 ... 231 D1
Chester Cl
1 Richmond TW10 ... 154 B5
Sutton SM1 ... 217 C6
Chester Cres E8 ... 73 D3
Chester Ct
2 Acton W3 ... 88 C1
Bermondsey SE8 ... 118 D1
4 Camberwell SE5 ... 139 B5
Gospel Oak NW5 ... 71 A4
Harrow HA1 ... 42 D3
Regent's Pk NW1 ... 231 D1
Chester Dr HA2 ... 41 C3
Chesterfield Ct
Ashford TW15 ... 170 A6
Kingston u T KT6 ... 198 A4
Lewisham SE13 ... 142 A2
Chesterfield Dr KT10 ... 213 A6
Chesterfield Flats EN5 ... 12 D6
Chesterfield Gdns
Greenwich SE10 ... 142 B5
Harringay N4 ... 50 D4
Mayfair W1 ... 248 C4
Chesterfield Gr SE22 ... 161 D6
Chesterfield Hill W1 ... 115 B5 248 C4
Chesterfield Ho
Highgate N6 ... 49 A1
Mayfair W1 ... 248 B4
6 Streatham SW16 ... 181 C5
Chesterfield Lo N21 ... 16 B4
Chesterfield Mews
Ashford TW15 ... 170 A6
Harringay N4 ... 50 D4
Chesterfield Rd
Ashford TW15 ... 170 A5
Barnet EN5 ... 12 D6
Chiswick W4 ... 133 A6
Enfield EN3 ... 7 A6
Finchley N3 ... 29 C4
Leyton E10 ... 54 A3
West Ewell KT19 ... 215 B1
Chesterfield Sch EN3 ... 7 A6
Chesterfield St W1 ... 248 C4
Chesterfield Way
Hayes UB3 ... 106 A4
Chesterfield Way *continued*
Peckham SE15 ... 140
Chesterford Gdns NW3 ... 69
Chesterford Ho SE18 ... 143
Chesterford Rd E12 ... 78
Chester Gate NW1 ... 231
Chester Gdns
Ealing W13 ... 87
Enfield EN3 ... 18
Morden SM4 ... 202
Chester Ho
5 Barnet EN5 ... 1
Dartmouth Pk N19 ... 71
1 Deptford SE8 ... 141
Kingston u T KT1 ... 176
Chesterman Ct W4 ... 133
Chester Mews
Belgravia SW1 ... 258
Walthamstow E17 ... 35
Chester Pl NW1 ... 231
Chester Rd
Avery Hill DA15 ... 167
Dartmouth Pk N19 ... 71
Edmonton N9 ... 18
Harlington TW6 ... 126
Hounslow TW4 ... 128
Ilford IG3 ... 57
Newham E16 ... 98
Regent's Pk NW1 ... 93 B4 231
Tottenham N17 ... 51
Upton E7 ... 77
Walthamstow E17 ... 52
Wanstead E11 ... 55
Wimbledon SW19, SW20 ... 178
Chester Row SW1 ... 115 A2 258
Chester Sq Mews SW1 ... 258
Chester Sq SW1 ... 115 B2 258
Chester St E2 ... 96
Chesters The KT3 ... 177
Chester St SW1 ... 115 A3 258
Chester Terr NW1 ... 93 B4 231
Chesterton Cl
Greenford UB6 ... 85
Wandsworth SW18 ... 157
Chesterton Ct W3 ... 110
Chesterton Dr TW19 ... 148
Chesterton Ho
21 Battersea SW11 ... 136
3 Kensal Town W10 ... 91
3 Sutton SM1 ... 218
Chesterton Prim Sch SW11 ... 137 A4 268
Chesterton Rd
Kensal Town W10 ... 91
Newham E13 ... 99
Chesterton Sq W8 ... 255
Chesterton Terr
6 Kingston u T KT1 ... 176
Newham E13 ... 99
Chester Way SE11 ... 116 C2 261
Chesthunte Rd N17 ... 33
Chestnut Alley SW6 ... 264
Chestnut Ave
Brentford TW8 ... 109
Buckhurst Hill IG9 ... 21
Coney Hall BR4 ... 224
Edgware HA8 ... 26
Forest Gate E7 ... 77
Hampton TW12 ... 173
Hornsey N8 ... 50
Kingston u T KT8, KT11 ... 174
11 Mortlake SW14 ... 133
Chestnut Ave N E17 ... 54
Chestnut Ave S E17 ... 54
Chestnut Ave
Thames Ditton KT10 ... 196
Wembley HA0 ... 65
Worcester Pk KT19 ... 215
Yiewsley UB7 ... 104
Chestnut Cl
Buckhurst Hill IG9 ... 21
Carshalton SM5 ... 202
Catford SE6 ... 186
Chattern Hill TW15 ... 170
Harlington UB7 ... 126
Hayes UB3 ... 105
New Cross Gate SE14 ... 141
Sidcup DA15 ... 168
Southgate N14 ... 15

stnut Cl *continued*
Stoke Newington
N16 ... 73 B6
nbury Comm
TW16 ... 171 D4
est Norwood
SW16 ... 182 C6
stnut Ct
eckenham BR3 ... 185 C3
Cheam SM2 ... 217 C2
Croydon CR0 ... 221 A4
ltham TW13 ... 172 D5
arrow HA1 ... 42 C2
ornsey N8 ... 50 A4
ounslow TW3 ... 129 C2
ngston u T KT3 ... 199 C6
urbiton KT6 ... 198 A2
embley HA0 ... 65 B3
est Brompton SW6 264 D6
stnut Dr
exley DA7 ... 147 A2
arrow HA3 ... 24 D2
nner HA5 ... 41 A3
anstead E11 ... 55 A3
estnut Gr
ockfosters EN4 ... 14 D6
aling W5 ... 109 D3
sleworth TW7 ... 131 A1
ingston u T KT3 ... 199 B6
itcham CR4 ... 203 D5
estnut Grove Sch
W12 ... 159 A3
estnut Gr
enge SE20 ... 184 C3
outh Croydon CR2 ... 222 B1
pper Tooting
SW12 ... 159 A3
Vembley HA0 ... 65 B3
estnut Ho
Acton W4 ... 111 C2
rockley SE4 ... 141 B2
7 Maitland Pk NW3 ... 70 D2
West Norwood SE27 ... 161 A1
estnut La N20 ... 13 A3
estnut Pl SE19 ... 183 D6
estnut Rd
shford TW15 ... 170 D6
Kingston u T KT2 ... 176 A3
Twickenham TW2 ... 152 C2
West Barnes SW20 ... 178 D1
West Norwood SE21,
SE27 ... 161 A1
estnut Rise SE18 ... 123 C1
estnut Row N3 ... 29 C3
estnuts Ct 3 E17 ... 54 A6
estnuts Prim Sch
N15 ... 51 A4
estnuts Royal
BR7 ... 189 B3
estnuts The
Chislehurst BR7 ... 189 B3
Colindale NW9 ... 45 C6
East Finchley N2 ... 48 D4
7 Erith DA17 ... 125 B1
1 Highbury N5 ... 72 D4
Penge BR3 ... 206 D6
8 Pinner HA5 ... 23 B3
Shooters Hill SE18 ... 144 D4
Uxbridge UB10 ... 60 A1
Walton-on-T KT12 ... 194 B1
estnut Way TW13 ... 150 B1
estnut Wlk
Upper Halliford
TW17 ... 193 C5
Woodford IG8 ... 37 A5
heston Ave CR0 ... 207 B1
estwood Gr UB10 ... 60 B1
ettle Cl SE1 ... 262 C6
ettle Ct N8 ... 50 C3
etwode Ho NW8 ... 237 A6
etwode Rd SW17 ... 158 D1
hetwood Wlk 13
E6 ... 100 A2
etwynd Ave EN4 ... 14 D3
etwynd Dr UB10 ... 82 B5
hetwynd Rd NW5 ... 71 B5
eval Ct SW15 ... 134 B1
hevalier Cl HA7 ... 26 A6
heval Pl
SW7 ... 114 C3 257 B6
heval St E14 ... 119 C3
hevender BR7 ... 188 D3
heveney Wlk 2
BR2 ... 209 A6
hevening Ho BR5 ... 190 A2
hevening Rd
Cubitt Town SE10 ... 120 D1
Kilburn NW6 ... 91 A6
South Norwood
SE19 ... 183 B4
hevenings The
DA14 ... 168 C1
heverell Ho 25 E2 ... 96 A5
heverton Rd N19 ... 49 D1
hevet St E9 ... 75 A3
hevington NW2 ... 69 B2

Cheviot Cl
Bushey WD23 ... 8 A5
Enfield EN1 ... 5 B3
Harlington UB3 ... 127 B5
Cheviot Ct
16 Deptford SE14 ... 140 C5
Enfield EN2 ... 5 B3
Southall UB2 ... 107 D2
Cheviot Gate NW2 ... 69 A6
Cheviot Gdns
Cricklewood NW2 ... 69 A6
West Norwood
SE27 ... 182 D6
Cheviot Ho N16 ... 51 D1
Cheviot Rd SE27 ... 182 D5
Cheviots Hostel EN1 ... 5 B3
Cheviot 4 N17 ... 34 B3
Cheviot Way IG2 ... 57 C5
Chevron Cl E16 ... 99 A1
Chevy Rd UB2 ... 108 A4
Chewton Rd E17 ... 53 A5
Cheylesmore Ho
SW1 ... 258 C2
Cheyne Ave
Snaresbrook E18 ... 54 D6
Twickenham TW2 ... 151 B3
Cheyne Cl
6 Hendon NW4 ... 46 B4
Keston Mark BR2 ... 226 A5
Cheyne Ct
Chelsea SW3 ... 267 C6
1 Croydon CR0 ... 221 D6
Ruislip HA4 ... 39 C1
4 Wallington SM6 ... 219 B2
Cheyne Gdns
SW3 ... 136 C6 267 B5
Cheyne Hill KT5 ... 198 B5
Cheyne Mews
SW3 ... 136 C6 267 B5
Cheyne Park Dr
BR4 ... 224 A5
Cheyne Path W7 ... 86 D1
Cheyne Pl SW3 ... 267 C6
Cheyne Rd TW15 ... 171 B4
Cheyne Row
SW3 ... 136 C6 267 A5
Cheyne Wlk
Chelsea
SW10 ... 136 B5 266 C4
Croydon CR0 ... 222 A6
Hendon NW4 ... 46 C3
Southgate N21 ... 16 D6
Cheyney Ho 2 E9 ... 74 D2
Cheyneys Ave HA8 ... 25 D4
Chichele Gdns CR0 ... 221 C4
Chichele Ho HA8 ... 26 B6
Chichele Mans NW2 ... 68 D3
Chichele Rd NW2 ... 68 D3
Chicheley Gdns HA3 ... 24 A3
Chicheley Rd HA3 ... 24 A3
Chicheley St SE1 ... 250 D2
Chichester Ave HA4 ... 61 B6
Chichester Cl
Hampton TW12 ... 173 B4
Kidbrooke SE3 ... 143 C4
Newham E6 ... 100 A1
Chichester Ct
Barnet EN4 ... 2 B1
2 Camden Town
NW1 ... 71 C1
Edgware HA8 ... 26 C4
Harrow HA2 ... 41 B1
Northolt UB5 ... 85 A6
3 Sidcup DA5 ... 169 C4
Stanmore HA7 ... 44 A6
Stanwell TW19 ... 148 A3
Chichester Gdns IG1 ... 56 B2
Chichester Ho
Kilburn NW6 ... 91 C5
2 Kingston u T KT2 ... 176 D2
Chichester Mews
SE27 ... 182 C6
Chichester Rd
Bayswater W2 ... 91 D2
Edmonton N9 ... 18 A3
Kilburn NW6 ... 91 C5
Leyton E11 ... 76 C5
South Croydon CR0 ... 221 C5
Chichester Rents
WC2 ... 241 A2
Chichester St
SW1 ... 115 C1 259 B1
Chichester Way
Cubitt Town E14 ... 120 B2
Feltham TW14 ... 150 C4
Chicksand Ho 14 E1 ... 96 A2
Chicksand St
E1 ... 95 D2 243 D3
Chicksand Street E1 ... 96 A2
Chiddingfold N12 ... 13 C1
Chiddingstone Ave
DA7 ... 147 B5
Chiddingstone
SE13 ... 164 A6
Chiddingstone St
SW6 ... 135 C3
Chieveley Par DA7 ... 147 D2

Chieveley Rd DA7 ... 147 D1
Chignell Pl 7 W13 ... 109 A5
Chigwell Ct 1 E9 ... 75 A2
Chigwell Hill E1 ... 118 B6
Chigwell Hurst Ct
HA5 ... 40 D6
Chigwell Rd
Wanstead E18 ... 55 B6
Woodford IG8 ... 37 D3
Chiham Ho 5 SE15 ... 140 C6
Chilchester Ct 3
BR3 ... 207 D6
Chilcombe Ho 6
SW15 ... 156 A4
Chilcot Cl 13 E14 ... 97 D1
Chilcott Cl HA0 ... 65 C4
Child Ct E11 ... 54 B2
Childebert Rd SW17 ... 159 B2
Childeric Prim Sch
SE14 ... 141 A5
Childeric Rd SE14 ... 141 A5
Childerley St
SW6 ... 135 A4 264 A2
Childerly KT1 ... 198 C6
Childers St SE8 ... 141 B6
Child La SE10 ... 120 D3
Childs Ct UB3 ... 106 A6
CHILD'S HILL ... 69 C6
Child's Hill Prim Sch
NW2 ... 69 A5
Childs La 11 SE19 ... 183 C4
Child's Mews SW5 ... 255 B3
Child's Pl SW5 ... 255 B3
Child's St SW5 ... 255 B3
Childs Way NW11 ... 47 B4
Child's Wlk SW5 ... 255 B3
Chilham Cl
Old Bexley DA5 ... 169 B4
Wembley UB6 ... 87 A5
Chilham Ct 13 SW9 ... 138 C2
Chilham Ho SE1 ... 262 D6
Chilham Rd SE9 ... 188 A6
Chilham Way BR2 ... 209 A2
Chillerton Rd SW17 ... 181 B5
Chillingford Ho
SW17 ... 180 A6
Chillington Dr
SW11 ... 136 B1
Chillingworth Gdns
TW1 ... 152 D1
Chillingworth Rd N7 ... 72 C3
Chilmark Gdns KT3 ... 200 A3
Chilmark Rd SW16 ... 181 D2
Chiltern Ave
Bushey WD23 ... 8 A5
Twickenham TW2 ... 151 C3
Chiltern Cl Bus WD23 ... 8 A5
Ickenham UB10 ... 60 C6
North Cheam KT4 ... 216 C6
South Croydon CR0 ... 221 C5
Chiltern Ct
15 Deptford SE14 ... 140 C5
6 East Barnet N20 ... 14 C2
11 Eltham SE9 ... 166 C5
Harrow HA1 ... 42 B4
Hillingdon UB8 ... 82 D3
Marylebone NW1 ... 237 D5
Muswell Hill N10 ... 31 A1
1 New Barnet EN5 ... 14 A6
Chiltern Dene EN2 ... 4 B1
Chiltern Dr KT5 ... 198 D4
Chiltern Gdns
Beckenham BR2 ... 208 D5
Cricklewood NW2 ... 68 D5
Chiltern Ho
Camberwell SE17 ... 139 B6
Ealing W5 ... 88 A2
5 Edmonton N9 ... 18 A1
Harrow HA1 ... 42 C1
4 Kensal Town W10 ... 91 A2
5 Stamford Hill N16 ... 51 D1
Chiltern Rd Bow E3 ... 97 C3
Ilford IG2 ... 57 C4
Pinner HA5 ... 40 C4
Chilterns The BR1 ... 187 B1
Chiltern St
W1 ... 93 A2 238 A4
Chiltern Way IG8 ... 21 A1
Chilthorne Cl SE6 ... 163 B4
Chilton Ave W5 ... 109 D2
Chilton Gr SE8 ... 119 A2
Chiltonian Ind Est
SE12 ... 164 D5
Chilton Rd
Edgware HA8 ... 26 C4
Richmond TW9 ... 132 C2
Chilton St E2 ... 95 D3 243 D6
Chiltons The 1 E18 ... 37 A1
Chilvers Cl TW2 ... 152 C2
Chilver St SE10 ... 120 D1
Chilwell Gdns WD19 ... 22 C6
Chilworth Ct 8
SW19 ... 156 D3
Chilworth Gdns
SM1 ... 218 A5
Chilworth Mews
W2 ... 92 B1 236 C1

Chilworth St
W2 ... 92 A1 236 B1
Chimes Ave N13 ... 32 D6
Chimney Ct 23 E1 ... 118 B5
Chimneys Ct 2
SW19 ... 178 C3
China Ct 1 E1 ... 118 B5
China Hall Mews 16
SE16 ... 118 C3
China Mews 17
SW2 ... 160 B4
Chinbrook Cres
SE12 ... 165 B1
Chinbrook Rd SE12 ... 165 B1
Chinchilla Dr TW4 ... 128 C3
Chindit Ho 11 N16 ... 73 B4
Chine The
London N10 ... 49 C5
Southgate N21 ... 16 D6
Wembley HA0 ... 65 B3
Ching Ct Chingford E4 ... 20 C1
St Giles WC2 ... 240 A1
Chingdale Rd E4 ... 20 C1
CHINGFORD ... 20 C3
Chingford Ave E4 ... 19 D2
Chingford CE Inf Sch
E4 ... 20 B3
Chingford CE Jun Sch
E4 ... 20 B3
Chingford Foundation
Sch E4 ... 19 D3
CHINGFORD GREEN ... 20 A4
Chingford Hall Com
Prim Sch E4 ... 35 B4
CHINGFORD HATCH ... 36 B6
Chingford Hospl E4 ... 20 A1
Chingford Ind Ctr E4 ... 35 A5
Chingford La IG8 ... 36 D5
Chingford Mount Rd
E4 ... 35 C5
Chingford Rd
Highams Pk E4 ... 35 C3
Walthamstow E17 ... 35 D1
Chingford Sta E4 ... 20 C4
Chingley Cl BR1 ... 186 C4
Ching Way E4 ... 35 B4
Chinnery Cl EN1 ... 5 D4
Chinnocks Wharf
E14 ... 119 A6
Chinnor Cres UB6 ... 86 A5
Chipka St E14 ... 120 A4
Chipley St SE14 ... 141 A6
Chipmunk Gr UB5 ... 85 A4
Chippendale Ho
SW1 ... 258 D1
Chippendale St E5 ... 74 D5
Chippenham Ave
HA9 ... 66 D3
Chippenham Cl HA5 ... 39 D5
Chippenham Gdns
NW6 ... 91 C4
Chippenham 4 KT1 ... 176 B1
Chippenham Mews
W9 ... 91 C3
Chippenham Rd W9 ... 91 C3
Chipperfield Rd
BR5 ... 190 A1
CHIPPING BARNET ... 1 B1
Chipping Cl EN5 ... 1 A2
Chipstead Ave CR7 ... 204 D5
Chipstead Cl SE19 ... 183 D3
Chipstead Gdns NW2 ... 68 B6
Chipstead Ho 4
SW2 ... 160 A3
Chipstead St SW6 ... 135 C3
Chip St SW4 ... 137 D1
Chirk Cl UB4 ... 85 A3
Chirk Ct SE4 ... 141 B3
Chisenhale Prim Sch
E3 ... 97 A5
Chisenhale Rd E3 ... 97 A5
Chisholm Ct 1 W6 ... 112 A1
Chisholm Rd
Croydon CR0 ... 221 C6
13 Richmond TW10 ... 154 B5
Chisledon Wlk E9 ... 75 B2
CHISLEHURST ... 189 C3
Chislehurst Ave N12 ... 30 A3
Chislehurst High St
BR7 ... 188 D4
Chislehurst Rd
Bromley BR1,
BR7 ... 188 A2
Broom Hill BR6 ... 211 D2
Orpington BR5, BR6,
BR7 ... 211 C4
Richmond TW10 ... 154 A6
Sidcup DA14 ... 190 A5
Chislehurst St Nicholas
CE Prim Sch BR7 ... 189 A3
Chislehurst & Sidcup
Gram Sch DA15 ... 168 B2
Chislehurst Sta BR7 188 C1
CHISLEHURST WEST
... 188 C4
Chislet Cl BR3 ... 185 C3
Chislet 5 NW5 ... 71 A2

Chisley Rd 5 N15 ... 51 C3
Chiswell Sq SE3 ... 143 B3
Chiswell St
Barbican
EC1 ... 95 B2 242 C4
Camberwell SE5 ... 139 B5
CHISWICK ... 111 D1
Chiswick & Bedford
Park Prep Sch
W4 ... 111 C2
Chiswick Cl CR0 ... 220 B5
Chiswick Common Rd
W4 ... 111 B2
Chiswick Com Sch
W4 ... 133 B5
Chiswick Ct HA5 ... 41 B6
Chiswick Green Studios
1 W4 ... 111 A2
Chiswick High Rd
W4 ... 111 C2
Chiswick High Road
(North Circular Rd)
W4 ... 110 C1
Chiswick Ho* W4 ... 133 B6
Chiswick La W4 ... 111 C1
Chiswick La S W4 ... 133 D6
Chiswick Mall W4 ... 111 D1
Chiswick Maternity
Hospl W4 ... 111 D1
Chiswick Park Sta
W4 ... 111 A2
Chiswick Pier W4 ... 133 D5
Chiswick Pk W4 ... 110 D2
Chiswick Plaza W4 ... 133 A6
Chiswick Quay W4 ... 133 A4
Chiswick Rd W4 ... 111 A2
Chiswick Rdbt W4 ... 110 C1
Chiswick Rd N9 ... 18 A2
Chiswick Sq W4 ... 133 C6
Chiswick Sta W4 ... 133 A5
Chiswick Staithe
W4 ... 133 A4
Chiswick Terr 6
W4 ... 111 A2
Chiswick Village
W4 ... 132 D6
Chiswick Wharf W4 ... 133 D6
Chitterfield Gate
UB7 ... 126 C5
Chitty's La RM8 ... 80 D6
Chitty St W1 ... 93 C2 239 B4
Chivalry Rd SW11 ... 158 C6
Chivelston 27 SW19 ... 156 D3
Chivenor Gr KT2 ... 175 D5
Chivers Rd E4 ... 35 D6
Chivins Ct N3 ... 29 C3
Choats Manor Way
RM9 ... 103 B4
Choats Rd IG11 ... 102 D4
Chobham Gdns
SW19 ... 156 D2
Chobham Rd E15 ... 76 B3
Cholmeley Cres N6 ... 49 B2
Cholmeley Ct N12 ... 30 A6
Cholmeley Lo N6 ... 49 B1
Cholmeley Pk N6 ... 49 B2
Cholmley Gdns NW6 ... 69 C3
Cholmley Rd KT7 ... 197 B3
Cholmondeley Ave
NW10 ... 90 A5
Cholmondeley Wlk
TW9 ... 153 C6
Chopin's Ct 13 E1 ... 118 B5
Chopwell Cl E15 ... 76 B1
Chorleywood Cres
BR5 ... 190 A1
Choumert Gr SE15 ... 140 A3
Choumert Mews
SE15 ... 140 A3
Choumert Rd SE15 ... 139 D3
Choumert Sq 4
SE15 ... 140 A3
Chow Sq 2 E8 ... 73 D3
Chrisp Ho SE10 ... 142 C6
Chrisp St E14 ... 97 D1
Christabel Cl TW7 ... 130 C2
Christchurch Ave
Brondesbury Pk
NW6 ... 69 A1
Finchley N12 ... 30 A4
Harrow HA3 ... 42 D5
Harrow HA3 ... 43 A5
5 Teddington
TW11 ... 175 A5
Wembley HA0 ... 66 A2
Christ Church Bentinck
CE Prim Sch
NW1 ... 92 C2 237 B4
Christ Church CE Mid
Sch W5 ... 109 D6
Christ Church CE
Prim Sch
Battersea SW11 ... 136 C2
Brondesbury NW6 ... 69 B1
Camberwell SW9 ... 138 C4
Cubitt Town SE10 ... 120 C1

Christ Church CE Prim
Sch *continued*
Forest Hill SE23 ... 162 D2
Shooters Hill SE18 ... 144 C4
Surbiton KT5 ... 198 C3
Christchurch CE Prim
Sch SW3 ... 136 D6 267 C6
Christchurch CE Sch
E1 ... 95 D2 243 D3
Christchurch Cl
Enfield EN2 ... 5 A3
Finchley N12 ... 30 B3
Mitcham SW19 ... 180 B3
Christ Church Ct
1 Brondesbury Pk
NW6 ... 69 A1
Harlesden NW10 ... 89 C6
Christchurch Ct UB4 ... 84 C3
Christchurch Gdns
HA3 ... 43 A5
Christchurch Gn HA0 ... 66 A2
Christchurch Hill
NW3 ... 70 B4
Christchurch Ho 2
SW2 ... 160 A3
Christ Church La EN5 ... 1 A3
Christchurch Lo EN4 ... 2 D1
Christ Church New
Malden CE Prim Sch
KT3 ... 199 C6
Christchurch Pas
NW3 ... 70 A5
Christchurch Pk
SM2 ... 218 A1
Christ Church Prim Sch,
Hampstead NW3 ... 70 B5
Christchurch Prim Sch
IG1 ... 57 A1
Christ Church Rd
1 Beckenham
BR3 ... 185 C1
Hornsey N8 ... 50 A3
Christchurch Rd
Ilford IG1 ... 57 A1
Mitcham SW19 ... 180 B3
Mortlake SW14 ... 155 A6
Sidcup DA15 ... 167 D1
Streatham SW2 ... 160 C3
Christ Church Rd
KT5 ... 198 B3
Christ Church TW9 ... 132 A2
Christ Church Sch
NW1 ... 93 B4 231 D2
Christchurch Sq 2
E9 ... 96 C6
Christ Church
Streatham CE Prim
Sch SW2 ... 160 B3
Christchurch St
SW3 ... 136 D6 267 C6
Christchurch Terr
SW3 ... 267 C6
Christchurch Way
SE10 ... 120 C1
Christian Ct SE16 ... 119 B5
Christian Fields
SW16 ... 182 C3
Christian St E1 ... 96 A1
Christie Ct
Maitland Pk NW3 ... 70 C3
2 Upper Holloway
N19 ... 72 A6
Christie Dr SE25 ... 206 A4
Christie Gdns RM6 ... 58 B2
Christie Ho
Bexley DA6 ... 169 D6
2 Cubitt Town
SE10 ... 120 D1
Harrow HA3 ... 42 D6
4 West Wickham
BR4 ... 207 D1
Christie Rd E9 ... 75 A2
Christina Sq N4 ... 50 D1
Christina St EC2 ... 243 A6
Christine Worsley Cl
N21 ... 16 D3
Christopher Ave
W7 ... 109 A3
Christopher Boone's
Almshouses SE13 ... 142 B1
Christopher Cl
Bexley DA15 ... 167 D6
Rotherhithe SE16 ... 118 D4
Christopher Ct
Ashford TW15 ... 170 A5
12 Barnet EN5 ... 1 D1
6 Croydon CR0 ... 206 A1
Hendon NW4 ... 28 C1
23 Surbiton KT6 ... 198 A4
Sutton SM1 ... 217 C3
Christopher France Ho
6 E1 ... 97 A4
Christopher Gdns
RM9 ... 80 D3

Christopher Hatton Prim Sch EC1 94 C3 241 A5
Christopher Lo 2 N6 49 D2
Christopher Pl NW1 232 D1
Christopher Rd UB2 106 B2
Christopher St EC2 95 B3 242 D5
Christ's Coll Finchley NW11 47 D6
Christ's Coll Upper Sch N3 29 B1
Christ's Sch TW10 154 C6
Christ the King RC Fst Sch TW19 148 A5
Christ the King RC Prim Sch N4 72 B6
Christ the King Sixth Form Coll SE13 142 B2
Chryssell Rd SW9 138 C5
Chubworthy St 5 SE14 141 A6
Chudleigh Cres IG3 79 C4
Chudleigh Gdns SM1 218 A5
Chudleigh Rd
 Hampstead NW6 68 D1
 London SE4 163 C6
 Twickenham TW1, TW2 152 D4
Chudleigh 1 DA14 190 B6
Chudleigh St E1 96 D1
Chudleigh Way HA4 40 A1
Chulsa Rd SE26 184 B5
Chumleigh Gdns SE5 139 C6
Chumleigh St SE5 139 C6
Chumleigh Wlk KT5 198 B5
Church App SE21 161 B1
Church Ave
 Beckenham BR3 185 C2
 Camden Town NW1 71 B2
 Chingford E4 36 B4
 Finchley N2 30 B2
 Mortlake SW14 133 B2
 Northolt UB5 63 B1
 Pinner HA5 41 B3
 Ruislip HA4 39 B1
 Sidcup DA14 190 B5
 Southall UB2 107 A3
Churchbank E17 53 C5
Churchbury Cl EN1 5 C3
Churchbury La EN1 5 C3
Churchbury Rd
 Eltham SE9 165 D4
 Enfield EN1 5 C3
Church Cl
 Edgware HA8 27 A5
 Friern Barnet N20 14 C1
 Hayes UB4 83 B2
 Hounslow TW4 129 B3
 Kensington W8 245 C2
 West Drayton UB7 104 A3
Church Cres
 Church End N3 29 B2
 Cranley Gdns N10 49 B5
 Friern Barnet N20 14 C1
 Hackney E9 74 D1
Churchcroft Cl SW12 159 A4
Church Ct
 East Finchley N2 48 B6
 Forest Hill SE26 185 A5
 Harmondsworth UB7 126 C6
 Holborn EC4 241 B1
 16 Richmond TW10 153 D6
 Rotherhithe SE16 119 B4
 Ruislip HA4 62 D5
 5 West Norwood SE27 182 D6
Churchdale Ct 1 W4 110 D1
Churchdown BR1 186 C6
Church Dr
 Coney Hall BR4 224 C5
 Harrow HA2 41 C3
 Welsh Harp NW9 45 B1
Church Elm La RM10 81 C2
CHURCH END N3 29 C1
 NW10 67 D3
Church End
 Hendon NW4 46 B6
 Walthamstow E17 53 D5
Church Entry EC4 241 D1
Church Estate Almshouses 8 TW9 132 B1
Church Farm House Mus* NW4 46 B6
Church Farm La SM3 217 A2
Churchfield Ave N12 30 B4
Churchfield Cl
 Harrow HA2 42 A5
 Hayes UB3 105 D6
Churchfield Ho W2 236 C5
Churchfield Mans 5 SW6 135 B3
Churchfield Pl TW17 192 D2
Churchfield Prim Sch N9 17 D3
Churchfield Rd
 Acton W3 111 A5
 Ealing W13 109 C5
 Hanwell W7 108 C4
 Walton-on-T KT12 194 A1
 Welling DA16 146 A2
Churchfields Ave TW13 151 C1
Churchfields
 East Molesey KT8 195 C6
 Greenwich SE10 142 A6
Churchfields Jun & Inf Sch E18 37 A2
Churchfields Prim Sch BR3 206 D6
Churchfields Rd BR3 185 A1
Churchfields E18 37 A2
Churchfield Way N12 30 A4
Church Garth 4 N19 71 D6
Church Gate SW6 135 A2
Church Gdns
 Ealing W5 109 D4
 Wembley HA0 65 A4
Church Gn
 4 Brixton SW9 138 C3
 Hayes UB3 83 D1
Church Gr
 London SE13 163 D6
 Teddington KT1 175 C1
Churchhill Gardens Prim Sch SW1 115 C1 259 B1
Church Hill HA1 42 C1
Church Hill Rd
 Cheam SM1, SM3 217 A4
 East Barnet EN4 14 D4
 Kingston u T KT6 198 A4
 Walthamstow E17 53 D5
Church Hill Sch EN4 14 D4
Church Hill
 Southgate N21 16 C4
 Wallington SM5 218 D3
 Walthamstow E17 53 D5
 Wimbledon SW19 179 B5
Church Hill Wood BR5 211 D4
Church Hill SE18 122 B3
Church Ho EC1 241 D6
Church Hyde SE18 145 C6
Churchill Ave
 Harrow HA3 43 B3
 Hillingdon UB10 82 D4
Churchill Cl
 East Bedfont TW14 149 D3
 Hillingdon UB10 82 D4
Churchill Ct
 Ealing W5 88 B3
 Edmonton N9 17 B3
 4 Farnborough BR6 227 A3
 Finsbury Pk N4 50 C2
 Harrow HA2 41 D4
 7 Ilford IG1 78 D5
 Northolt UB5 63 C3
 Peckham SE15 140 A3
 Willesden NW2 68 B3
 9 Woolwich SE18 122 B2
Churchill Gdns
 Acton W3 88 C1
 Pimlico SW1 137 C6 269 A6
Churchill Gdns Rd SW1 137 C6 269 A6
Churchill Ho
 Brentford TW8 109 C1
 Mitcham CR4 180 D2
Churchill Lodge IG6 57 A5
Churchill Lo
 Streatham SW16 181 D5
 Woodford IG8 36 D4
Churchill Mews IG8 36 D4
Churchill Pl
 Canary Wharf E14 119 D5
 Harrow HA1 42 C5
Churchill Rd
 Edgware HA8 26 C4
 Gospel Oak NW5 71 B4
 Newham E16 99 C1
 South Croydon CR2 221 A1
 Willesden NW2 68 B2
Churchill Terr E4 19 C1
Churchill Way
 Ashford TW16 172 A4
Churchill Way *continued*
 Bromley BR1 187 A1
Churchill Wlk E9 74 C3
Church La
 Chessington KT9 214 B2
 Chislehurst BR7 189 A2
 Dagenham RM10 81 D1
 Ealing W5 109 D4
 East Finchley N2 48 B6
 Edmonton N9 18 A2
 Enfield EN1 5 B2
 Harrow HA3 24 D2
 Hornsey N8 50 B5
 Keston Mark BR2 210 A1
 Kingsbury NW9 45 B2
 Leytonstone E11 54 C1
 Merton SW19 179 C2
 Pinner HA5 41 B6
 Teddington TW11 174 D5
 Thames Ditton KT7 197 A3
 Tottenham N17 33 C2
 Twickenham TW1 153 A3
 Upper Tooting SW17 181 A5
 Wallington SM6 219 D5
 Walthamstow E17 53 D5
Churchley Rd SE26 184 B6
Churchley Villas SE26 184 B6
Church Lo UB5 63 B1
Church Manor Way SE18, SE2 124 A2
Church Mdw KT6 213 C6
Churchmead Cl EN4 14 C5
Church Mead Inf Sch E10 53 C1
Churchmead Rd NW10 68 A2
Church Mead SE5 139 A5
Churchmore Rd SW16 181 D2
Church Mount N2 48 B4
Church Paddock Ct SM6 219 D5
Church Par
 5 Ashford TW15 170 B6
 Harrow HA3 42 C6
Church Path
 Merton SW19 179 C1
 Mitcham CR4 202 C6
 South Acton W4 111 A3
 Walthamstow E17 53 D5
 Wanstead E11 55 A4
Church Pl Ealing W5 109 D4
 Mitcham CR4 202 C6
 St James SW1 249 B5
 Uxbridge UB10 61 A5
Church Rd Acton W3 111 A4
 Ashford TW15 170 B6
 Barking IG11 79 A2
 Barnes SW13 134 A4
 Beckenham BR2 208 C6
 Bexleyheath DA7 147 B2
 Bromley BR1, BR2 187 A1
 Buckhurst Hill IG9 21 B3
 24 Canonbury N1 73 A2
 Cheam SM3 217 A2
 Claygate KT10 212 D1
 Cranford TW5 128 B6
 Croydon CR0 221 A5
 Ealing W7 108 C6
 East Molesey KT8 196 B6
 Enfield EN3 18 C6
 Farnborough BR6 227 B3
 Feltham TW13 172 D5
 Hayes UB3 105 D6
 Hendon NW4 46 C5
 Heston TW5 129 C5
 Higham Hill E17 35 A1
 Highgate N6 49 A3
 Hillingdon UB8 82 A3
 Hounslow TW7 130 C5
 Ilford IG2 57 C3
 Keston BR2 225 D1
 Kingston u T KT1 176 B1
 Leyton E10 75 C6
 Long Ditton KT6 197 C1
 Lower Halliford TW17 192 D2
 Manor Pk E12 78 A3
 Mitcham CR4 202 C6
 Mitcham CR4, SW19 180 B1
 New Malden KT4 199 C1
Church Rd N N2 30 B2
Church Rd
 Northolt UB5 85 A6
 Richmond TW10 176 A6
 Richmond TW10, TW9 154 A6
 Sidcup DA14 190 A6
Church Rd S N2 30 B2
Church Rd
 Southall UB2 107 B3
 South Norwood SE19 183 C3
 Stanmore HA7 25 B5
 Teddington TW11 174 D5
Church Rd *continued*
 Tottenham N17 33 D3
 Wallington SM6 219 D5
 Welling DA16 146 B3
 West Drayton UB7 104 A3
 West Ewell KT19 215 B1
 Willesden NW10 67 C1
 Wimbledon SW19 179 A6
Church Rise
 Chessington KT9 214 B2
 Forest Hill SE23 162 D2
Church Row
 Chislehurst BR7 189 A2
 Hampstead NW3 70 A4
Church Row Mews BR7 189 A3
Church St N E15 98 C6
Church St Sta CR0 221 A6
Church Sq TW17 192 D2
Church St
 Chiswick W4 133 D6
 Croydon CR0 220 D6
 Croydon CR0 221 A6
 Dagenham RM10 81 D2
 Edmonton N9 17 C2
 Enfield EN2 5 B2
 Hampton TW12 174 A2
 Isleworth TW7 131 B3
 Kingston u T KT1 175 D1
 Lisson Gr NW8 92 C3 237 A5
 Newham E16 122 D5
Church Street Est NW8 236 D5
Church Stretton Rd TW3 152 A6
Church St
 Sunbury TW16 194 B6
 Twickenham TW1 153 A3
Church Studios 10 NW1 71 D2
Church St
 Walton-on-T KT12 194 A2
 West Ham E15 98 D6
Church Terr
 Hendon NW4 46 B6
 Lewisham SE13 142 C2
 21 Richmond TW10 153 D6
Church Vale
 Forest Hill SE23 162 D2
 Muswell Hill N2 48 D6
Churchview Rd TW2 152 B2
Church Villa TW16 194 B6
Churchward Ho
 Camberwell SE17 138 D6
 West Kensington SW5 254 D1
Church Way
 Cockfosters EN4 2 D1
 Friern Barnet N20 14 C1
Churchway NW1 232 D2
Church Wlk
 Barnes SW13 134 A4
 Brentford TW8 131 C6
 Canonbury N16 73 B4
 Child's Hill NW2 69 B5
 Dartmouth Pk N6 71 A5
 Hayes UB3 83 D1
 Mitcham SW16 181 C1
 15 Richmond TW10 153 D6
 Thames Ditton KT7 196 D3
 Walton-on-T KT12 194 A1
 Welsh Harp NW9 67 B6
 West Barnes SW20 200 C6
Churchwood Gdns IG8 37 A6
Churchyard Row SE11 116 D2 261 D4
Churnfield 2 N4 72 C6
Churston Ave E13 99 B6
Churston Cl 10 SW2 160 C3
Churston Dr SM4 201 A4
Churston Gdns N11 31 C4
Churston Mans WC1 240 D5
Churton Pl
 Brentford W4 132 D6
 Pimlico SW1 259 B3
Churton St SW1 115 C2 259 B3
Chute Ho 17 SW9 138 C3
Chuter Ede Ho SW6 264 D5
Chyngton Cl DA15 167 D1
Chyngton Ct HA1 64 C6
Cibber Rd SE23 162 D2
Cicada Rd SW18 158 A6
Cicely Ho NW8 229 D3
Cicely Rd SE15 140 A4
Cinderford Way BR1 186 C6
Cinema Mus The* SE11 261 C3
Cinema Par RM8 81 B6
Cinnabar Wharf Central 17 E1 118 A5
Cinnabar Wharf East 16 E1 118 A5
Cinnabar Wharf West 18 E1 118 A5
Cinnamon Cl
 8 Camberwell SE15 139 D5
 Thornton Heath CR0 204 A2
Cinnamon Row 3 SW11 136 A2
Cinnamon St E1 118 B5
Cinnamon Wharf SE1 253 D2
Cinque Cotts SW19 178 C4
Cintra Ct SE19 183 D4
Cintra Pk SE19 183 D3
Circle Ct HA0 65 D4
Circle Gdns SW19 179 C1
Circle Ho 14 E14 98 B1
Circle The
 Bermondsey SE1 253 D2
 Burnt Oak NW7 27 B4
 Neasden NW2 67 C5
Circuits The HA5 40 C5
Circular Rd
 London N2 30 B2
 Tottenham N17 51 D6
Circular Way SE18 144 C6
Circus Lo NW8 229 C2
Circus Mews W1 237 C4
Circus Pl EC2 242 D3
Circus Rd NW8 92 B5 229 C3
Circus St SE10 142 A5
Cirencester St W2 91 D2
Cirrus Cl 4 SM6 220 A1
Cirrus 17 NW9 27 D1
Cissbury Ho 6 SE26 162 A1
Cissbury Rd N15 51 B4
Cissbury Ring N N12 29 C5
Cissbury Ring S N12 29 B5
Citadel Pl SE11 260 C2
Citizen Ho N7 72 C4
Citizen Rd N7 72 C4
Citron Terr 4 SE15 140 B2
Citrus Ho 14 SE8 119 B1
City Banking Coll SE1 117 B4 252 D2
City Bsns Ctr 33 SE16 118 C4
City Central Est EC1 235 A1
City Coll N1 235 C2
City Coll of London The WC1 240 D3
City Forum EC1 95 A4 235 A2
City Garden Row N1 94 D5 234 D3
City Gate E1 96 C3
City & Guilds of London Art Sch The SE11 116 C1 261 B1
City Harbour E14 119 D3
City & Islington 6th Form Coll EC1 94 D4 234 C2
City & Islington Coll
 Finsbury Pk N4 72 D6
 Lower Holloway N7 72 A4
 Lower Holloway N7 72 B4
 Shoreditch EC1 95 A4 235 B1
 Shoreditch N1 95 B6 235 C6
City Lights The SE11 261 B1
CITY OF LONDON 117 A6
City of London Sch EC4 117 A6 252 A6
City of London Sch for Girls EC2 95 A2 242 B4
City of Westminster Coll, Maida Vale Ctr W9 91 D4
City of Westminster Coll
 Paddington NW1 92 C2 237 B4
 Paddington W2 92 B2 236 C4
City of Westminster Coll, Queens Park Ctr W9 91 C4
City Prospect 5 SE19 183 C4
City Rd EC1 95 A4 235 B2
City Thameslink Sta EC4 94 D1 241 C1
City University EC1 94 D4 234 C1
City View 3 IG1 79 A6
City Wharf Ho KT7 197 B3
City Wlk SE1 253 A1
Civic Way Ilford IG6 57 A5
 Ruislip HA4 62 D3
Civil Service Coll SW1 115 C2 259
Clabon Mews SW1 114 D2 257
Clack St SE16 118
Clacton Rd
 Newham E6 99
 Tottenham N17 33
 Walthamstow E17 53
Claigmar Gdns N3 29
Claire Ct
 Brondesbury NW2 69
 Bushey WD23 8
 4 Pinner HA5 23
 Whetstone N12 14
Claire Gdns HA7 25
Claire Pl E14 119
Clairvale Rd TW5 129
Clairview Rd SW16 181
Clairville Gdns W7 108
Clairville Point 12 SE23 162
Clamp Hill HA7 24
Clancarty Rd SW6 135
Clandon Cl
 South Acton W3 110
 Stoneleigh KT17 216
Clandon Ct
 Plaistow BR1 187
 Sutton SM2 218
Clandon Gdns N3 47
Clandon Ho
 East Finchley N3 47
 12 Kingston u T KT2 176
Clandon Rd IG3 79
Clandon St SE8 141
Clanfield Ho 12 SW15 156
Clanricarde Gdns W2 113 C6 245
CLAPHAM 137
Clapham Common* SW4 137
Clapham Common North Side SW4 137
Clapham Common South Side SW4 159
Clapham Common Sta SW4 137
Clapham Common West Side
 Clapham SW4, SW11 136
 Clapham SW11 159
Clapham Computer & Secretarial Coll SW11 158
Clapham Court Terr 2 SW4 160
Clapham Cres SW4 137
Clapham Ct 3 SW4 160
Clapham High St SW4 137
Clapham High Street Sta SW4 137
Clapham Junction Est SW11 136
Clapham Junction Sta SW11 136
Clapham Manor Ct 1 SW4 137
Clapham Manor Prim Sch SW4 137
Clapham Manor St SW4 137
Clapham Mans SW4 159
Clapham North Bsns Ctr 10 SW4 137
Clapham North Sta SW4 138
CLAPHAM PARK 159
Clapham Park Rd SW4 137
Clapham Park Terr 4 SW2 160
Clapham Rd SW9 138 B5 270
Clapham South Sta SW4 159
Claps Gate La E6 100
Clapton Comm E5 52
Clapton Girls Tec Coll E5 74
CLAPTON PARK 74
Clapton Pas E5 74
Clapton Sq E5 74
Clapton Sta E5 74
Clapton Terr E5 52
Clapton Way E5 74
Clara Grant Ho 10 E14 119
Clara Grant Prim Sch The E3 97
Clara Pl SE18 122

are Cl
Borehamwood
WD6 ... 10 B5
East Finchley N2 ... 48 A6
are Cnr SE9 ... 166 D4
are Ct
Chislehurst BR7 ... 188 B2
St Pancras WC1 ... 233 B1
Wimbledon SW19 ... 179 A4
aredale Ct SM2 ... 218 A1
aredale Ho 3 E2 ... 96 B5
aredale St E2 ... 96 A5
lare Gdns
Barking IG11 ... 80 A1
Forest Gate E7 ... 77 A4
Notting Hill W11 ... 91 A1
lare Ho
Bermondsey SE1 ... 263 D2
4 Burnt Oak HA8 ... 27 A1
5 Ealing W7 ... 108 D5
6 Old Ford E3 ... 97 B6
lare House Prim Sch
BR3 ... 186 A1
lare La N1 ... 73 A1
lare Lawn Ave
SW14 ... 155 B6
lare Mews SW6 ... 265 C3
lare Mkt WC2 ... 240 D1
laremont Ave
Harrow HA3 ... 44 A4
Sunbury TW16 ... 172 B2
West Barnes KT3 ... 200 B4
laremont Cl
Finsbury
N1 ... 94 C5 234 B3
Newham E16 ... 122 C5
Orpington BR6 ... 226 C4
4 Streatham SW2 ... 160 B3
laremont Ct 1 W9 ... 91 B5
laremont Dr TW17 ... 192 D3
laremont Gdns
Ilford IG3 ... 79 C6
Kingston u T KT6 ... 198 A4
laremont Gr
Chiswick W4 ... 133 C5
Woodford IG8 ... 37 C4
laremont High Sch
HA3 ... 44 A4
laremont Ho 15
SM2 ... 217 C1
laremont Hts EN2 ... 4 D1
laremont La KT10 ... 212 A3
laremont Lo 12
SW19 ... 178 D3
laremont Pk N3 ... 29 A2
laremont Pl KT10 ... 212 D2
laremont Prim Sch
NW2 ... 68 D6
laremont 1 SW15 ... 157 A6
laremont Rd
Bromley BR1 ... 210 B5
Claygate KT10 ... 212 C1
Croydon CR0 ... 206 A1
Ealing W13 ... 87 A2
Forest Gate E7 ... 77 C3
Hadley Wood EN4 ... 2 B6
Harrow HA3 ... 24 C1
Hendon NW2 ... 68 D6
Higham Hill E17 ... 35 A1
Highgate N6 ... 49 C2
Kingston u T KT6 ... 198 A4
Leyton E7 ... 76 B5
Teddington TW11 ... 174 D6
Twickenham TW1 ... 153 C5
West Kilburn W9 ... 91 B5
Claremont TW17 ... 192 D3
Claremont Sq
N1 ... 94 C5 234 A3
Claremont St
Edmonton N18 ... 34 A4
Greenwich SE10 ... 141 D6
Newham E16 ... 122 C4
Claremont Terr KT7 ... 197 B2
Claremont Way NW2 ... 46 C1
Claremont Way Ind Est
NW2 ... 46 C1
Clarence Ave
Bromley BR1,
BR2 ... 210 A5
Clapham Pk SW4 ... 159 D5
Ilford IG2 ... 56 C3
Kingston u T KT3 ... 177 B1
Clarence Cl
Bushey WD23 ... 8 D4
New Barnet EN4 ... 14 B6
Clarence Cres
Clapham Pk SW4 ... 159 D5
Sidcup DA14 ... 168 B1
Clarence Ct
Edgware NW7 ... 27 D5
10 Hammersmith
W6 ... 112 B2
5 North Finchley
N12 ... 30 B5
Clarence Gate Gdns
NW1 ... 237 D5
Clarence Gate NW1 ... 237 D6
Clarence Gdns
NW1 ... 93 B4 231 D1
Clarence Ho SE17 ... 139 A6
Clarence Ho*
SW1 ... 115 C5 249 B3
Clarence La SW15 ... 155 D5
Clarence Mews
Balham SW12 ... 159 B4
Hackney E5 ... 74 B3
1 Rotherhithe
SE16 ... 118 D5
Clarence Pl 25 E5 ... 74 B3
Clarence Rd
Bexley DA6 ... 147 A1
Brentford W4 ... 110 C1
Bromley BR1, BR2 ... 210 A6
Brondesbury NW6 ... 69 B1
Chislehurst SE9 ... 166 A2
Enfield EN3 ... 18 C6
Harringay N15 ... 51 A4
Higham Hill E17 ... 34 D1
Lower Clapton E5 ... 74 B4
Manor Pk E12 ... 77 D3
Newham E16 ... 98 C3
Richmond TW9 ... 132 C4
Sidcup DA14 ... 168 B1
Sutton SM1 ... 217 D3
Teddington TW11 ... 175 A4
Thornton Heath CR0 ... 205 B2
Wallington SM6 ... 219 B3
Wimbledon SW19 ... 179 D4
Wood Green N22 ... 32 A3
Clarence St
Kingston u T KT1,
KT2 ... 176 A1
5 Richmond TW9 ... 132 A1
Southall UB2 ... 106 D3
Clarence Terr
Hounslow TW3 ... 129 D1
Lisson Gr NW1 ... 237 D6
Clarence Way NW1 ... 71 B1
Clarence Wlk 9
SW4 ... 138 A3
Clarendon Cl
Bayswater W2 ... 247 A6
38 Hackney E9 ... 74 C1
Clarendon Cres
TW2 ... 152 B1
Clarendon Cross
W11 ... 244 B5
Clarendon Ct
London NW11 ... 47 B5
Mitcham SM4 ... 202 C4
Paddington W9 ... 236 B6
1 Richmond TW9 ... 132 C4
Willesden NW2 ... 68 C1
Clarendon Dr SW15 ... 134 C1
Clarendon Flats W1 ... 238 B1
Clarendon Gdns
Hendon NW4 ... 46 B6
Paddington
W9 ... 92 A3 236 B5
Redbridge IG1 ... 56 B2
Wembley HA9 ... 66 A4
Clarendon Gr
Mitcham CR4 ... 202 D6
Somers Town NW1 ... 232 C2
Clarendon Ho
Harrow HA2 ... 42 B6
North Finchley N12 ... 30 A5
Somers Town NW1 ... 232 B3
South Oxhey WD19 ... 22 D5
Clarendon Mews
Bayswater W2 ... 247 A6
Old Bexley DA5 ... 169 D3
Clarendon Pl
W2 ... 114 C6 247 A6
Clarendon Prim Sch
TW15 ... 170 B6
Clarendon Rd
Ashford TW15 ... 170 B6
Croydon CR0 ... 220 D6
Ealing W5 ... 88 A3
Edmonton N18 ... 34 A5
Harrow HA1 ... 42 C3
Hayes UB3 ... 105 D4
Hornsey N8 ... 50 B6
Leytonstone E11 ... 54 B1
Mitcham SW19 ... 180 C3
Notting Hill
W11 ... 113 A6 244 B5
Wallington SM6 ... 219 C2
Walthamstow E17 ... 53 D3
Wanstead E18 ... 55 A6
West Green N15 ... 51 A5
Wood Green N22 ... 32 B1
Clarendon Rise
SE13 ... 142 A1
Clarendon Sch
TW12 ... 173 D4
Clarendon St
SW1 ... 115 B1 258 D2
Clarendon Terr W9 ... 236 B6
Clarendon Way
Enfield N21 ... 17 A5
Orpington BR5, BR7 ... 211 D6
Clarendon Wlk 11
W11 ... 91 A1
Clarens St SE6 ... 163 B2
Clare Pl SW15 ... 155 D4
Clare Point NW2 ... 46 D1
Clare Rd
Hounslow TW4 ... 129 B2
Leytonstone E11 ... 54 B3
New Cross Gate
SE14 ... 141 B4
Northolt UB6 ... 64 B2
Stanwell TW19 ... 148 A4
Willesden NW10 ... 68 A1
Clare St E2 ... 96 B5
Claret Gdns SE25 ... 205 C5
Clareville Ct SW7 ... 256 B3
Clareville Grove Mews
SW7 ... 256 B3
Clareville Gr
SW7 ... 114 A2 256 B3
Clareville Rd BR5 ... 227 A6
Clareville St
SW7 ... 114 A2 256 B3
Clare Way DA7 ... 147 A4
Clarewood Ct W1 ... 237 C3
Clarewood Wlk
SW9 ... 138 C1
Clarges Ho W1 ... 248 D4
Clarges Mews
W1 ... 115 B5 248 C4
Clarges St
W1 ... 115 B5 248 D4
Clariat Ct W3 ... 110 C4
Claribel Rd SW9 ... 138 D3
Clarice Ct NW4 ... 46 B6
Claridge Ct SW6 ... 264 C1
Claridge Rd RM8 ... 58 D1
Clarinet Ct HA8 ... 26 D3
Clarissa Ho 7 E14 ... 97 D1
Clarissa Rd RM6 ... 58 D2
Clarissa St E8 ... 95 D6
Clark Ct 17 NW10 ... 67 B1
Clarke Ho
2 London SW4 ... 137 C2
5 Richmond TW10 ... 153 C1
Clarke Mans 9 IG11 ... 79 D1
Clarke Mews N9 ... 18 B1
Clarke Path N16 ... 52 A1
Clarke's Ave KT4,
SM3 ... 216 D6
Clarkes Dr UB8 ... 82 A2
Clarkes Mews W1 ... 238 B4
Clark Ho SW10 ... 266 A4
Clark Lawrence Ct 11
SW11 ... 136 B2
Clarks Mead WD23 ... 8 B4
Clarkson Rd E16 ... 98 D1
Clarkson Row NW1 ... 232 A3
Clarkson St E2 ... 96 B4
Clarksons The IG11 ... 101 A5
Clark's Pl EC2 ... 243 A2
Clark's Rd IG1 ... 79 B6
Clark St E1 ... 96 C2
Clark Way TW5 ... 128 D5
Classic Mans 33 E9 ... 74 C1
Classinghall Ho 14
SW15 ... 156 D5
Classon Cl UB7 ... 104 A4
Claude Rd Leyton E10 ... 54 A1
London SE15 ... 140 B3
Newham E13 ... 99 B6
Claude St E14 ... 119 C2
Claudia Jones Way
SW2 ... 160 A5
Claudia Pl SW19 ... 157 A3
Claudius Cl HA7 ... 9 D1
Claughton Rd E13 ... 99 C5
Clauson Ave UB5 ... 64 A3
Clavell St 8 SE10 ... 142 A6
Claverdale Rd SW2 ... 160 C4
Clavering Ave SW13 ... 134 B6
Clavering Cl TW1 ... 175 A6
Clavering Ho SE13 ... 142 B1
Clavering Rd E12 ... 77 D6
Claverings Ind Est
N9 ... 18 C2
Claverley Gr N3 ... 29 D2
Claverley Villas N3 ... 29 D3
Claverton St
SW1 ... 115 C1 259 B1
Clave St E1 ... 118 C5
Claxton Gr
W6 ... 112 D1 254 A1
Clay Ave CR4 ... 181 B1
Claybank Gr SE13 ... 141 D2
Claybee Ct N22 ... 32 B5
Claybourne Mews 2
SE19 ... 183 D3
Claybridge Rd SE12 ... 187 C6
Claybrook Cl N2 ... 48 B6
Claybrook Rd W6 ... 134 D6
Claybury Broadway
IG5 ... 56 A6
Clay Ct E17 ... 54 B6
Claydon Dr CR0 ... 220 A4
Claydon Ho NW4 ... 28 D1
Claydon SE17 ... 262 A4
Claydown Mews
SE18 ... 122 C1
Clayfarm Rd SE9 ... 167 A2
CLAYGATE ... 212 D1
Claygate Cres CR0 ... 224 B2
Claygate Ct SM1 ... 218 A5
Claygate La
Hinchley Wood
KT10 ... 213 A6
Thames Ditton KT7 ... 197 A1
Claygate Lodge Cl
KT10 ... 212 C1
Claygate Prim Sch
KT10 ... 212 C1
Claygate Rd W13 ... 109 B3
Claygate Sta KT10 ... 212 C2
CLAYHALL ... 56 B6
Clayhall Ct 20 E3 ... 97 B5
CLAY HILL ... 5 A6
Clayhill Cres SE12,
SE9 ... 187 D6
Clay Hill EN2 ... 5 B6
Clay La WD23 ... 8 C4
Claylands Ct SE19 ... 183 B5
Claylands Pl SW8 ... 138 C5
Claylands Rd
SW8 ... 138 B6 270 D5
Clay La TW19 ... 148 B4
Claymill Ho 2 SE18 ... 123 A1
Claymore Cl SM3,
SM4 ... 201 C2
Claymore Ct 4 E17 ... 35 A2
Claypole Ct E17 ... 53 C4
Claypole Dr TW5 ... 129 A4
Claypole Rd E15 ... 98 A5
Clayponds Ave TW8 ... 110 A2
Clayponds Gdns
W5 ... 109 D2
Clayponds Hospl & Day
Treatment Ctr
TW8 ... 110 A2
Clayponds La TW8 ... 110 A1
Clays Ct N16 ... 51 D1
Clays La E15 ... 75 D3
Clays Lane Cl E15 ... 75 D3
Clays Lane Cvn Site
E15 ... 76 A3
Clay St W1 ... 92 D2 237 D3
Clayton Ave HA0 ... 66 A1
Clayton Bsns Ctr
UB3 ... 105 C4
Clayton Cl 3 E6 ... 100 B1
Clayton Cres
Brentford TW8 ... 109 D1
Islington N1 ... 233 C5
Clayton Ct
1 Higham Hill E17 ... 35 A1
Stamford Hill N16 ... 52 A2
Clayton Field NW9 ... 27 C2
Clayton Ho
22 Hackney E9 ... 74 C1
Long Ditton KT7 ... 197 B1
Clayton Mews SE10 ... 142 B4
Clayton 22 NW9 ... 27 D1
Clayton Rd
Chessington KT10,
KT9 ... 213 D4
Hayes UB3 ... 105 C4
Isleworth TW7 ... 130 C2
Peckham SE15 ... 140 A4
Clayton St SE11 ... 138 C6
Clayton Terr UB4 ... 84 D2
Claytonville Terr
DA17 ... 125 D4
Clay Wood Cl BR6 ... 211 C2
Clayworth Cl DA15 ... 168 B5
Cleanthus Cl SE18 ... 144 D4
Cleanthus Rd SE18 ... 144 D4
Clearbrook Way 13
E1 ... 96 C1
Clearmont Ho UB2 ... 107 C3
Clear Water Ho 9
TW10 ... 154 A6
Clearwater Ho BR3 ... 207 D4
Clearwater Pl KT6 ... 197 C3
Clearwater Terr 4
W11 ... 112 D4
Clearwell Dr W9 ... 91 D3
Cleave Ave
Hayes UB3 ... 105 C2
Orpington BR6 ... 227 C2
Cleaveland Rd KT6 ... 197 D4
Cleaverholme Cl
SE25 ... 206 B3
Cleaver Ho 6 NW3 ... 70 D1
Cleaver Sq
SE11 ... 116 C1 261 B1
Cleaver St
SE11 ... 116 C1 261 B2
Cleave's Almshos 1
KT2 ... 176 A1
Cleeve Ct
East Bedfont
TW14 ... 149 C3
Muswell Hill N10 ... 31 B3
Cleeve Hill SE23 ... 162 B3
Cleeve Ho 15 E2 ... 95 C4
Cleeve Park Gdns
DA14 ... 168 B2
Cleeve Park Sch
DA14 ... 168 C1
Cleeve Way
Cheam SM1 ... 201 D1
Roehampton SW15 ... 155 D4
Cleeve Workshops 14
E2 ... 95 C4
Clegg Ho SE3 ... 143 B1
Clegg St Newham E13 ... 99 A5
16 Wapping E1 ... 118 B5
Cleland Ho 19 E2 ... 96 C5
Clematis Gdns IG8 ... 37 A5
Clematis St W12 ... 112 A6
Clem Atlee Par SW6 ... 264 D5
Clem Attlee Ct
SW6 ... 135 B6 264 D5
Clemence St E14 ... 97 B2
Clement Attlee Ho
NW10 ... 67 D1
Clement Ave SW4 ... 137 D1
Clement Cl
Acton W4 ... 111 B2
Hampstead NW6 ... 68 C1
Clement Danes Ho 2
W12 ... 90 B1
Clement Gdns UB3 ... 105 C2
Clement Ho
14 Deptford SE8 ... 119 A2
17 North Kensington
W10 ... 90 C2
Clementhorpe Rd
RM9 ... 80 C2
Clementina Rd E10 ... 53 B1
Clementine Churchill
Hospl The HA1 ... 64 D5
Clementine Cl W13 ... 109 B4
Clementine Wlk 4
IG8 ... 37 A3
Clement Rd
Penge BR3 ... 184 D1
Wimbledon SW19 ... 179 A5
Clements Ave 1
E16 ... 121 A6
Clements Cl 10 N12 ... 29 D6
Clements Ct
Hounslow TW4 ... 128 D1
5 Ilford IG1 ... 78 D5
Clements Ho N17 ... 34 A2
Clements Inn Pas
WC2 ... 240 D1
Clements Inn
WC2 ... 94 B1 240 D1
Clement's La EC2,
EC4 ... 117 B6 252 D6
Clements La IG1 ... 78 D5
Clements Pl TW8 ... 109 D1
Clements Rd
East Ham E6 ... 78 B1
Ilford IG1 ... 78 D5
Clement's Rd SE16 ... 118 B3
Cleminson Ct DA14 ... 190 D4
Clemson Ho 9 E8 ... 95 D6
Clendon Way SE18 ... 123 B2
Clennam St SE1 ... 252 B2
Clensham Ct SM3 ... 217 C6
Clensham La SM1 ... 217 C6
Clenston Mews W1 ... 237 C2
Clent Ho 4 N16 ... 51 D1
Cleopatra's Needle*
WC2 ... 116 B6 250 C5
Clephane Rd 13 N1 ... 73 A2
Clephane Rd N N1 ... 73 A2
Clephane Rd S N1 ... 73 B2
Clere Pl EC2 ... 242 D6
Clere St EC2 ... 95 B3 242 D6
Clerics Wlk TW17 ... 193 B3
CLERKENWELL ... 94 D3
Clerkenwell Cl
EC1 ... 94 C3 241 B5
Clerkenwell Gn
EC1 ... 94 D3 241 C5
Clerkenwell Parochial
CE Prim Sch
EC1 ... 94 C4 234 A1
Clerkenwell Rd
EC1 ... 94 D3 241 C5
Clermont Rd E9 ... 96 C6
Cleveden Ct CR2 ... 221 C3
Cleveden Ho BR1 ... 188 A3
Clevedon Ct
Battersea SW11 ... 267 A2
Dulwich SE21 ... 161 B1
Clevedon Gdns
Cranford TW5 ... 128 B4
Hayes UB3 ... 105 B3
Clevedon Ho 4
SM1 ... 218 A4
Clevedon Mans NW5 ... 71 A4
Clevedon Rd
Kingston u T KT1 ... 176 C1
Penge SE20 ... 184 D2
Twickenham TW1 ... 153 D5
Cleve Ho NW6 ... 69 D1
Cleveland Ave
Chiswick W4 ... 111 D2
Cleveland Ave *continued*
Hampton TW12 ... 173 B3
Merton SW20 ... 179 B1
Cleveland Cres WD6 ... 11 A6
Cleveland Ct
Ealing W13 ... 87 B2
Marylebone W1 ... 239 B5
Southall UB2 ... 107 D2
Cleveland Gdns
Barnes SW13 ... 133 D3
Harringay N4, N15 ... 51 A4
Hendon NW2 ... 68 D6
Paddington
W2 ... 92 A1 236 A1
Worcester Pk KT4 ... 215 D6
Cleveland Gr 39 E1 ... 96 C3
Cleveland Ho 7 N2 ... 30 B1
Cleveland Inf Sch
IG1 ... 78 D5
Cleveland Jun Sch
IG1 ... 78 D5
Cleveland Mans
8 Brixton SW9 ... 138 C5
4 Brondesbury NW6 ... 69 B1
Paddington W9 ... 91 C3
Cleveland Mews W1 ... 239 A4
Cleveland Park Ave
E17 ... 53 C5
Cleveland Park Cres
E17 ... 53 C5
Cleveland Pk TW19 ... 148 A5
Cleveland Pl SW1 ... 249 B4
Cleveland Rd
Barnes SW13 ... 133 D3
Bexley DA16 ... 145 D3
Ealing W13 ... 87 B2
Edmonton N9 ... 18 B4
Ilford IG1 ... 78 D5
Isleworth TW7 ... 131 A1
Islington N1 ... 73 B1
New Malden KT3 ... 199 C5
14 South Acton W4 ... 111 A3
Wanstead E18 ... 55 A6
Worcester Pk KT4 ... 215 C6
Cleveland Rise SM4 ... 200 D2
Cleveland Row
SW1 ... 115 C5 249 B3
Cleveland Sq
W2 ... 92 A1 236 A1
Cleveland St
W1 ... 93 C3 239 A5
Cleveland Terr
W2 ... 92 A1 236 B2
Cleveland Way E1 ... 96 C3
Cleveley Cres W5 ... 88 B5
Cleveleys Rd E5 ... 74 B5
Clevely Cl SE7 ... 121 D2
Clevendon Cl N16 ... 73 D5
Cleve Rd
Sidcup DA14 ... 168 D1
South Hampstead
NW6 ... 69 D1
Cleverly Cotts W12 ... 111 D5
Cleverly Est W12 ... 112 A6
Cleves Ct KT6 ... 198 A3
Cleves Prim Sch E6 ... 99 D6
Cleves Rd Newham E6 ... 99 D5
Richmond TW10 ... 153 C1
Cleves Way
Ashford TW16 ... 171 D4
Hampton TW12 ... 173 B3
Ruislip HA4 ... 40 D1
Clewer Cres HA3 ... 24 B2
Clewer Ct 2 E10 ... 53 C1
Clewer Ho 6 SE2 ... 124 D4
Cley Ho SE4 ... 140 D1
Clichy Ho 32 E1 ... 96 C2
Clifden Centre
(Richmond Adult &
Com Coll) TW1 ... 152 D3
Clifden Ho 6 TW8 ... 131 D6
Clifden Mews E5 ... 74 D3
Clifden Rd
Brentford TW8 ... 131 D6
Homerton E5 ... 74 D3
Twickenham TW1 ... 152 D3
Cliff Ct 14 NW1 ... 71 D2
Cliffe Ho 4 SE10 ... 120 D1
Cliffe Rd CR2 ... 221 B3
Cliffe Wlk 2 SM1 ... 218 A3
Clifford Ave
Elmstead BR7 ... 188 B4
Mortlake SW14 ... 133 A3
Mortlake SW14,
TW9 ... 132 D2
Wallington SM6 ... 219 C4
Clifford Cl UB5 ... 85 A6
Clifford Ct
Bayswater W2 ... 91 D2
Wandsworth SW18 ... 158 B4
Willesden NW10 ... 67 C4
Clifford Dr SW9 ... 138 D1
Clifford Gdns
Hayes UB3 ... 105 B2

Clifford Gdns *continued*
Kensal Green NW10 90 C5
Clifford Gr TW15 170 C6
Clifford Haigh Ho SW6 134 D5
Clifford Ho
[2] Beckenham BR3 185 D4
West Kensington W14 254 C3
Clifford Lo [5] N3 29 B1
Clifford Rd Barnet EN5 1 D2
Chingford E17 36 A1
Croydon SE25 206 A5
Hounslow TW4 128 D2
Newham E16 98 D3
Ponders End N9 18 C5
Richmond TW10 153 D2
Wembley HA0 87 D6
Clifford's Inn Pas EC4 241 A1
Clifford St W1 115 C6 249 A5
Clifford Way NW10 67 D4
Cliff Rd NW1 71 D2
Cliff Road Studios [13] NW1 71 D2
Cliffsend Ho [23] SW9 138 C4
Cliff Terr SE8 141 C3
Cliffview Rd SE13 141 C2
Cliff Villas NW1 71 D2
Cliff Wlk E16 98 D2
Clifton Ave
Church End N3 29 B2
Feltham TW13 150 C1
Shepherd's Bush W12 111 D5
Stanmore HA7 25 B1
Walthamstow E17 52 D6
Wembley HA9 66 B2
Clifton Cl [8] BR6 227 A3
Clifton Cres SE15 140 B5
Clifton Ct
[1] Beckenham BR3 185 D2
Finsbury Pk N4 72 C6
Paddington NW8 236 C6
Peckham SE15 140 B5
Putney SW15 156 D6
South Norwood SE25 205 C4
[9] Stanwell TW19 148 A5
Surbiton KT5 198 B2
[3] Woodford IG8 37 A4
Clifton Gate SW10 266 A6
Clifton Gdns
Chiswick W4 111 B2
Enfield EN2 16 A6
Hillingdon UB10 82 D5
Paddington W9 92 A3 236 A5
South Tottenham N15 51 D3
[2] Temple Fortune NW11 47 B3
Clifton Gr E8 74 A2
Clifton Hill NW8 92 A6 229 A5
Clifton Ho Leyton E11 76 C6
Shoreditch E2 243 C6
Clifton Mans [4] SW9 138 C1
Clifton Mews SE25 205 C5
Clifton Par TW13 172 C6
Clifton Park Ave SW20 178 C1
Clifton Pl
Paddington W2 236 D1
Rotherhithe SE16 118 C4
Clifton Prim Sch UB2 107 A2
Clifton Rd
Bexley DA16 146 C2
Crouch End N8 49 D3
Finchley N3 30 A2
Greenford UB6 86 B3
Harlesden NW10 90 A5
Harlington TW6 126 D2
Harrow HA3 44 B4
Ilford IG2 57 B3
Isleworth TW7 130 C3
Kingston u T KT2 176 B2
Newham E16 98 C2
Paddington W9 92 A3 236 B6
Sidcup DA14 189 C6
Southall UB2 107 A2
South Norwood SE25 205 C5
Teddington TW11 174 C6
Upton E7 77 D2
Wallington SM6 219 B3
Wimbledon SW19 178 D4
Wood Green N22 31 C2
Clifton Rise SE14 141 A5
Cliftons Roundabout SE9, SE12 165 C5
Clifton St EC2 95 C3 243 A5
Clifton Terr N4 72 C6
Clifton The KT6 214 A6
Clifton Villas W9 92 A2 236 A4
Cliftonville Ct SE12 165 A3
Clifton Way
Peckham SE15 140 C5
Wembley HA0 88 A6
Climsland Ho SE1 251 B4
Clinch Ct [11] E16 99 A2
Cline Ho SW15 156 A6
Cline Rd N11 31 C4
Clinger Ct N1 95 C6
Clink St SE1 117 B5 252 C4
Clinton Ave
Bexley DA16 146 A1
East Molesey KT8 196 A5
Clinton Ho
New Malden KT3 199 B1
[6] Surbiton KT6 197 D2
Clinton Rd Bow E3 97 A4
Forest Gate E7 77 A4
West Green N15 51 B5
Clipper Appts [12] SE10 142 A6
Clipper Cl [3] SE16 118 D4
Clipper Ho E14 120 A1
Clipper Way SE13 142 A1
Clippesby Cl KT9 214 B2
Clipstone Ho [10] SW15 156 A6
Clipstone Mews W1 239 A4
Clipstone Rd TW3 129 C2
Clipstone St W1 93 C2 239 A4
Clissold Cl N2 48 D6
Clissold Cres N16 73 B4
Clissold Ct N4 73 A6
Clissold Ho [4] N16 73 B6
Clissold Rd N16 73 B5
Clitheroe Ave HA2 41 C1
Clitheroe Rd SW9 138 A3
Clitherow Ave W7 109 A3
Clitherow Rd TW8 109 C1
Clitterhouse Cres NW2 46 C1
Clitterhouse Rd NW2 46 C1
Clive Ave N18 34 A4
Clive Ct
Paddington W9 236 B6
Streatham SW16 181 D5
Tolworth KT6 214 C6
Cliveden Cl N12 30 A6
Cliveden Ho SW1 258 A4
Cliveden Pl
Belgravia SW1 115 A2 258 A4
Shepperton TW17 193 A3
Cliveden Rd SW19 179 B2
Clivedon Ct
Ealing W13 87 B2
[6] New Barnet EN5 2 A1
Clivedon Rd E4 36 C5
Clive Ho
[18] Clapham SW8 137 D3
[3] Croydon CR0 205 D1
Greenwich SE10 142 A6
Clive Lloyd Ho N15 51 A4
Clive Lo NW4 46 D3
Clive Rd
Belvedere DA17 125 C2
Enfield EN1 6 A1
Feltham TW14 150 A5
Mitcham SW19 180 C4
Teddington TW1 175 A6
West Norwood SE21, SE27 161 B1
Clivesdale Dr UB3 106 B5
Clive Way EN1 6 A1
Cloak La EC4 117 B6 252 C6
Clochar Ct NW10 89 D6
Clock Ct [2] E11 55 B5
Clock Ho N16 51 D2
Clock Ho The EN2 5 D6
Clockhouse Ave IG11 101 A6
Clockhouse Cl SW19 156 C2
Clock House Ct [1] BR3 185 A1
Clockhouse Junc N13 32 C5
Clockhouse La TW14, TW15 148 D2
Clockhouse Mans N13 32 C5
Clockhouse Par N13 32 C5
Clock House Par E11 55 B3
Clockhouse Pl SW15 157 A5
Clock House Rd BR3 185 A1
Clockhouse Rdbt TW14 149 A3
Clock House Sta BR3 185 A2
Clockhouse The SW19 156 C1
Clock Ho E17 54 B5
Clock Mus* EC2 95 A1 242 B2
Clock Tower Mews N1 235 B5
Clocktower Mews [6] W7 108 C5
Clock Tower Mews SE28 124 B6
Clock Tower Pl N7 72 A2
Clock Tower Rd TW7 130 D2
Cloister Cl TW11 175 B5
Cloister Gdns
Croydon SE25 206 B3
Edgware HA8 27 A5
Cloister Rd Acton W3 89 A2
Child's Hill NW2 69 B6
Cloisters Ave BR1, BR2 210 B4
Cloisters Ct
Erith DA7 147 D2
Highgate N6 49 B1
Cloisters Ho [8] SW19 179 C3
Cloisters The [22] SW9 138 C4
Clonard Way HA5 23 C4
Clonbrock Rd N16 73 C4
Cloncurry St SW6 134 D3
Clone Ct [4] W12 111 C3
Clone The [5] KT2 176 D3
Clonmel Cl HA2 42 B1
Clonmell Rd N17 51 B6
Clonmel Rd
Fulham SW6 135 B4 264 D2
Teddington TW11 174 B6
Clonmore St SW18 157 B3
Cloonmore Ave BR6 227 D4
Clorane Gdns NW3 69 C5
Close The
Beckenham BR3 207 A5
Cheam SM3 201 B2
Chingford E4 36 A3
Cockfosters EN4 14 D6
Croydon SE25 206 A3
Dagenham RM6 59 A3
Eastcote HA5 40 C2
Harrow HA2 24 A1
Hillingdon UB10 82 C6
Hounslow TW7 130 B3
Ilford IG2 57 C3
Kingston u T KT3 177 A1
Lewisham SE3 142 B3
Mitcham CR4 202 D5
Mortlake TW9 132 D2
Muswell Hill N10 31 B1
[1] Old Bexley DA5 169 C4
Palmers Green N14 15 D2
Petts Wood BR5 211 C3
Rayners La HA5 41 B2
Sidcup DA14 190 B5
Surbiton KT6 198 A3
Totteridge N20 13 B2
Wembley HA0 66 A2
Wembley Pk HA9 67 A5
Cloth Ct EC1 241 D3
Cloth Fair EC1 94 D2 241 D3
Clothier Ho SE7 122 A1
Clothier St EC3 243 B2
Cloth St EC1 95 A2 242 A4
Clothworkers Rd SE18 145 B5
Cloudesdale Rd SW17 159 B2
Cloudesley Mans N1 234 B5
Cloudesley Pl N1 94 C6 234 B5
Cloudesley Rd
Erith DA7 147 B4
Islington N1 94 C6 234 A5
Cloudesley Sq N1 94 C6 234 B6
Cloudesley St N1 94 C6 234 B5
Clouston Cl SM6 220 A3
Clova Rd E7 77 A3
Clove Cres E14 120 B6
Clovelly Ave
London NW9 45 D5
Uxbridge UB10 61 A4
Clovelly Cl
Pinner HA5 40 C6
Uxbridge UB10 61 A4
Clovelly Ct NW2 68 C3
Clovelly Gdns
Enfield EN1 17 C4
Clovelly Gdns *continued*
South Norwood SE19 183 D2
Clovelly Ho W2 236 A2
Clovelly Rd
Acton W4 111 B4
Ealing W5 109 C4
Erith DA7 147 A6
Hornsey N8 49 D5
Hounslow TW3 129 C3
Clovelly Way
Harrow HA2 63 B6
Orpington BR6 211 D3
Stepney E1 96 C1
Clover Cl E11 76 B6
Clover Ct Enfield EN3 7 A1
Sutton SM2 217 D2
Cloverdale Gdns DA15 167 D5
Clover Ho
Hounslow TW3 130 A4
Southgate N21 16 B6
Cloverleys IG10 21 D6
Clover Mews SW3 267 D6
Clover Way SM6 203 A1
Clove St [9] E13 99 A3
Clowders Rd SE6 163 B1
Clowes Ho [3] SW4 138 A1
Clowser Cl [4] SM1 218 A3
Cloysters Gn E1 118 A5
Cloyster Wood HA8 25 D4
Club Gardens Rd BR2 209 A2
Club Row E2 95 D3 243 C6
Clumps The TW15 171 B6
Clunbury Ave UB2 107 B1
Clunbury St N1 235 D3
Clunie Ho SW1 257 D6
Cluny Mews SW5 255 A3
Cluny Pl SE1 117 C3 263 A6
Cluse Ct N1 235 A4
Clutton St E14 97 D2
Clydach Rd EN1 5 D1
Clyde Cir N15 51 C5
Clyde Ct NW1 232 D4
Clyde Flats SW6 264 C4
Clyde Ho [9] KT2 175 D2
Clyde Pl E10 53 D2
Clyde Rd
Croydon CR0 221 D6
South Tottenham N15 51 C5
Stanwell TW19 148 A3
Sutton SM1 217 C3
Wallington SM6 219 C2
Wood Green N22 31 D2
Clydesdale Ave HA7 43 D6
Clydesdale Cl
Borehamwood WD6 11 B6
Isleworth TW7 130 D2
Clydesdale Ct N20 14 B3
Clydesdale EN3 6 D1
Clydesdale Gdns TW10 132 D1
Clydesdale Ho
Abbey Wood DA18 125 A4
[4] Notting Hill W11 91 B1
Clydesdale Path WD6 11 B6
Clydesdale Rd W11 91 B1
Clyde St SE8 141 B6
Clyde Terr SE23 162 C2
Clyde Vale SE23 162 C2
Clyde Works [10] SM6 219 C2
Clyfford Rd HA4 61 D4
Clymping Dene TW14 150 B4
Clynes Ho
[6] Dagenham RM10 81 C5
[3] Globe Town E2 96 D4
Hayes UB4 84 A4
Clyro Ct N4 50 B1
Clyston St SW8 137 C3
Clytha Ct SE27 183 A6
Coach & Horses Yd W1 249 A6
Coach House La
Highbury N5 72 D4
Wimbledon SW19 156 D1
Coach House Mews SE23 162 D5
Coach House Yd [5] NW3 70 B4
Coach Ho NW10 67 A1
Coachmaker Mews [5] SW9 138 A2
Coachman Lo N12 30 A5
Coalbrook Mans [3] SW12 159 B3
Coaldale Wlk SE21 161 A4
Coalecroft Rd SW15 156 C6
Coalport Ho SE11 261 A4
Coal Post Cl BR6 227 D2
Coatbridge Ho [8] N1 72 B1
Coates Ave SW18 158 C5
Coates Cl CR7 205 A6
Coates Ct NW3 70 C3
Coates Hill Rd BR1 188 C1
Coates Rd WD6 9 D4
Coate St E2 96 A5
Coates Wlk TW8 110 A1
Cobalt SE2 124 A4
Cobalt Cl CR0 206 D5
Cobb Cl WD6 11 A6
Cobbett Rd
Kidbrooke SE9 144 A2
Twickenham TW2 151 C3
Cobbetts Ave IG4 55 D4
Cobbett St SW8 138 B5 270 D3
Cobble La N1 72 D1
Cobble Mews N4, N5 73 A5
Cobbler's Wlk TW11 174 D3
Cobblestone Pl CR0 205 A1
Cobbold Ct SW1 259 C4
Cobbold Ind Est NW10 67 D2
Cobbold Mews W12 111 D4
Cobbold Rd
Bedford Pk W12 111 D4
Leyton E11 76 D5
Willesden NW10 67 D2
Cobb's Hall [1] SW6 134 D6
Cobbs Rd TW4 129 B1
Cobb St E1 243 C3
Cobden Bldgs WC1 233 C2
Cobden Ct
Bromley BR2 209 C5
[9] Thamesmead SE28 124 C5
Cobden Ho
[11] Bethnal Green E2 96 A4
Regent's Pk NW1 232 A4
Cobden Mews SE26 184 B5
Cobden Rd
Croydon SE25 206 A4
Leyton E11 76 C6
Orpington BR6 227 B4
Cobham Ave KT3 200 A4
Cobham Cl
[2] Blackfen DA15 168 B5
Bromley BR2 210 A2
Clapham SW11 158 C5
Edgware HA8 26 D1
Enfield EN1 6 A2
Wallington SM6 220 A2
Cobham Ct CR4 180 B1
Cobham Ho IG11 101 A6
Cobham Mews [3] NW1 71 D1
Cobham [21] NW9 27 D1
Cobham Pl DA6 168 D6
Cobham Rd
Chingford E17 36 A2
Harringay N22 50 D6
Heston TW5 128 C5
Ilford IG3 79 C5
Kingston u T KT1, KT2 176 C1
Cobland Rd SE12 187 C6
Coborn Mews [9] E3 97 B4
Coborn Rd E3 97 B4
Coborn St E3 97 B4
Cobourg Prim Sch SE5 139 D6
Cobourg Rd SE5 139 D6
Cobourg St NW1 93 C4 232 B1
Coburg Cl SW1 259 B4
Coburg Cres SW2 160 C3
Coburg Dwellings [11] E1 118 C6
Coburg Gdns IG5 37 D1
Coburg Rd N22 32 B1
Cochrane Cl NW8 229 D3
Cochrane Ct [3] E10 53 C1
Cochrane Ho [15] E14 119 C4
Cochrane Mews NW8 92 B5 229 D3
Cochrane Rd SW19 179 B3
Cochrane St NW8 92 B5 229 D3
Coci Ho W14 254 D3
Cockburn Ho SW1 259 D1
Cockerell Rd E17 53 A3
COCKFOSTERS 2 D1
Cockfosters Par EN4 3 A1
Cockfosters Rd EN4 2 D3
Cockfosters Sta EN4 3 A1
Cock Hill E1 243 B3
Cock La EC1 94 D2 241 D3
Cockpit Yd WC1 240 D4
Cocks Cres KT3 199 D5
Cocksett Ave BR6 227 C2
Cockspur Ct SW1 249 D4
Cockspur St SW1 115 D5 249
Cocksure La DA14 191
Coda Ctr The SW6 135 A4 264
Code St E1 95 D3 243
Codicote Ho [22] SE8 118
Codicote Terr N4 73
Codling Cl [13] E1 118
Codling Way HA0 65
Codrington Ct [3] SE16 119
Codrington Hill SE23 163
Codrington Ho [7] E1 96
Codrington Mews W11 91
Cody Cl Harrow HA3 43
Wallington SM6 219
Cody Rd E16 98
Coe Ave SE25 206
Coe's Alley EN5 1
Coffey St SE8 141
Cogan Ave E17 35
Cohen Ho NW7 28
Cohen Lo E5 75
Coin St SE1 116 C5 251
Coity Rd NW5 71
Cokers La SE21 161
Coke St E1 96
Colab Ct N22 32
Colas Mews [7] NW6 91
Colbeck Mews SW5 113 D2 255
Colbeck Rd HA1 42
Colberg Pl N16 51
Colbert [1] SE5 139
Colborne Ct [8] SW19 179
Colborne Ho [8] E14 119
Colborne Way KT4 216
Colbrook Ave UB3 105
Colbrook Cl UB3 105
Colburn Ave HA5 23
Colburn Way SM1 218
Colby Rd
Walton-on-T KT12 194
West Norwood SE19 183
Colchester Ave E12 78
Colchester Dr HA5 40
Colchester Ho [17] SW8 137
Colchester Rd
Burnt Oak HA8 27
Leyton E10 54
Pinner HA6 22
Walthamstow E17 53
Colchester St E1 243
Colchester Villas CR7 204
Coldbath Sq EC1 241
Coldbath St SE13 141
Cold Blow La SE14 140
Coldershaw Rd W13 109
Coldfall Ave N10 31
Coldfall Prim Sch N10 30
Coldham Ct N22 32
Coldham Gr EN3 7 A
Coldharbour Crest SE9 166 C
Coldharbour E14 120 A
Coldharbour Ind Est SE5 139 A
Coldharbour La
Brixton SW9 138
Bushey WD23 8 A
Hayes UB3 106 A
Coldharbour Lane Ho UB3 106 A
Coldharbour Pl SE5 139 B
Coldharbour Rd CR0 220 C
Coldharbour Sports Ctr SE9 166 C
Coldharbour Way CR0 220 C
Coldstream Gdns SW18 157 B
Colebeck Mews N1 72 D
Colebert Ave E1 96 C
Colebert Ho [21] E1 96 C
Colebrook Cl
Edgware NW7 28 D
Putney SW19 156 D
Colebrook Ct SW3 257 B
Colebrooke Ave W13 87 B
Colebrooke Ct DA14 190 B
Colebrooke Dr E11 55 C
Colebrooke Pl N1 234 D
Colebrooke Row
Islington N1 94 D5 234 C
Islington N1 234 D

olebrook Ho 1 E14...97 D1
olebrook Rd SW16...182 A2
olebrook Rise BR2...186 C1
olebrook Way N11...31 B5
oleby Path 21 SE5...139 B5
olechurch Ho 9
SE1...118 A1
ole Cl SE28...124 B5
ole Court Lo 9
TW1...153 A4
oledale Dr HA7...25 C2
olefax Bldg 12 E1...96 A1
oleford Rd SW18...158 A6
ole Gdns TW5...128 A5
olegrave Prim Sch
E15...76 B3
olegrave Rd E15...76 B3
olegrove Rd SE15...139 D6
oleherne Ct
SW10...113 D1 255 D1
oleherne Mans
SW5...255 D2
oleherne Mews
SW10...113 D1 255 C1
oleherne Rd
SW10...113 D1 255 C1
olehill Gdns SW6...264 A1
olehill La
SW6...135 A4 264 B1
ole Ho SE1...251 B1
oleman Cl SE25...184 A1
oleman Ct SW18...157 C4
oleman Fields
N1...95 A6 235 B6
oleman Mans N19...50 A2
oleman Rd
Belvedere DA17...125 C2
Camberwell SE5...139 C5
Dagenham RM9...81 A2
olemans Heath
SE9...166 D1
oleman St
EC2...95 B1 242 C2
oleman Street Bldgs
EC2...242 C2
olenso Dr NW7...28 A3
olenso Rd Ilford IG2...57 C2
Lower Clapton E5...74 C4
ole Park Gdns
TW1...153 A5
ole Park Rd TW1...153 A5
ole Park View 2
TW1...153 A5
olepits Wood Rd
SE9...167 B6
oleraine Park Prim
Sch N17...34 B2
oleraine Rd
Greenwich SE3...142 D6
Hornsey N8, N22...50 C6
ole Rd TW1...153 A5
oleridge Ave
Carshalton SM1...218 C4
Plashet E12...78 A2
oleridge Cl SW8...137 B3
oleridge Ct
Hammersmith
W14...112 D3
15 New Barnet EN5...13 D6
2 Richmond TW10...175 D6
Coleridge Gdns NW6...70 A1
Coleridge Ho
Pimlico SW1...259 B1
Walworth SE17...262 B2
Wembley HA9...65 D6
Coleridge Prim Sch
N8...49 D2
Coleridge Rd
Ashford TW15...170 B6
Crouch End N8...49 D3
Croydon CR0...206 C2
Finsbury Pk N4, N7...72 C6
North Finchley N12...30 A5
Walthamstow E17...53 B5
Coleridge Sq
Chelsea SW10...266 A4
Ealing W13...87 A1
Coleridge Way
Borehamwood
WD6...10 C6
Hayes UB4...84 A1
West Drayton UB7...104 B2
Coleridge Wlk NW11...47 C5
Colerne Ct NW4...29 A1
Colesburg Rd BR3...185 B1
Coles Cres HA2...63 D6
Coles Ct SW11...266 D1
Coles Gn WD23...8 A3
Coles Green Ct NW2...68 A6
Coles Green Rd NW2...68 B6
Coleshill Flats SW1...258 B3
Coleshill Rd TW11...174 C4
Colestown St 4
SW11...136 C3
Cole St SE1...117 A4 252 B1
Coleswood N20...14 C3
Colesworth Ho 1
HA8...27 A1
Colet Cl N13...32 D4
Colet Gdns W14...112 D2
Colet Ho SE17...261 D1
Colette Ct 5 SE16...118 D4
Coley St WC1...94 B3 240 D5
Colfe & Hatchcliffe's
Glebe SE13...163 D6
Colfe Rd SE23...163 A3
Colfe's Sch SE12...165 A5
Colgate Ct EN5...13 A6
Colgate Ho SE13...141 D3
Colgate Pl 10 EN3...7 C6
Colham Ave UB7...104 A5
COLHAM GREEN...82 C2
Colham Green Rd
UB8...82 C2
Colham Manor Prim
Sch UB8...82 C1
Colham Rd UB8...82 B3
Colina Mews N8, N15...50 D5
Colina Rd N8, N15...50 D4
Colin Blanchard Ho
SE4...141 C3
Colin Cl
Colindale NW9...45 C5
Coney Hall BR4...224 D5
Croydon CR0...223 B5
Colin Cres NW9...45 D5
Colin Ct
Forest Hill SE6...163 B4
Hendon NW9...45 D5
Streatham SW16...159 D2
COLINDALE...45 C6
Colindale Ave NW9...45 C6
Colindale Bsns Pk
NW9...45 A6
Colindale Hospl
NW9...45 C6
Colindale Prim Sch
NW9...45 D5
Colindale Sta NW9...45 C6
Colindeep Gdns
NW4...46 A5
Colindeep La NW9,
NW4...45 D5
Colin Dr NW9...45 D4
Colinette Rd SW15...134 C1
Colin Gdns NW9...45 D5
Colin Park Rd NW9...45 C5
Colin Par NW9...45 C5
Colin Pond Ct RM6...58 D6
Colin Rd NW10...68 A2
Colinsdale N1...234 C5
Colinton Rd IG3...80 B6
Colin Winter Ho 45
E1...96 C3
Coliseum Apartments
N8...50 D4
Coliston Pas SW18...157 C4
Coliston Rd SW18...157 C4
Collamore Ave
SW18...158 C3
Collapit Cl HA1...41 D3
Collard Pl NW1...71 B1
Collard's Almshouses 1
E17...54 A4
Collcutt Lo SW4...138 A1
Collection Point N8...50 A3
College App SE10...142 A6
College Ave HA3...24 C2
College Cl
Edmonton N18...33 D5
Hackney E5...74 C3
Harrow HA3...24 C3
Twickenham TW2...152 B3
College Cres NW3...70 B2
College Cross N1...72 C1
College Ct
Chelsea
SW3...114 D1 257 D1
Croydon CR0...222 A6
Ealing W5...110 A6
Enfield EN3...18 C6
3 Hammersmith
W6...112 C1
Hampstead NW3...70 B2
College Dr
Ruislip HA4...40 A2
Thames Ditton KT7...196 C2
College Fields Bsns Ctr
SW19...180 B2
College Gdns
Chingford E4...20 A3
Dulwich SE21...161 C3
Edmonton N18...34 A5
Enfield EN2...5 B4
New Malden KT3...199 D4
Redbridge IG4...56 A4
Upper Tooting
SW17...158 C2
College Gn SE19...183 C3
College Green Ct
SW9...138 D2
College Gr NW1...232 C6
College Hill EC4...252 B6
College Hill Rd HA3...24 C3
College La NW5...71 B4
College Mews 5
SW18...157 D6
COLLEGE PARK...90 B4
College Park Cl
SE13...142 B1
College Park Rd N17...33 D4
College Park Sch
W2...91 D1
College Pl
Camden Town
NW1...93 C6 232 B5
Chelsea SW10...266 A4
Walthamstow E17...54 C5
College Pt 3 E15...76 D2
College Rdbt 1
KT1...198 A6
College Rd
Dulwich SE19,
SE21...161 C2
Ealing W13...87 B1
Enfield EN2...5 B3
Harrow HA1...42 C3
Harrow Weald HA3...24 C2
Hounslow TW7...130 D4
Kensal Green NW10...90 C5
Mitcham SW19...180 B4
Plaistow BR1...187 A3
South Croydon CR0...221 B6
Southgate N21...16 C2
Tottenham N17...33 D4
Walthamstow E17...54 A4
Wembley HA9...43 D1
College St
EC4...117 A6 252 B6
College Terr Bow E3...97 B4
Church End N3...29 B1
College View SE9...165 D3
College Way
Ashford TW15...170 B6
Hayes UB3...106 A6
College Wlk 10 KT1...198 A6
Collent Ho 12 E9...74 C2
Collent St E9...74 C2
Collerston Ho SE10...120 D1
Colless Rd N15...51 D4
Collette Ct SE25...205 C4
Collette Ho N16...51 D1
Collett Ho SE13...141 D2
Collett Rd SE16...118 A3
Collett Way UB2...107 D4
Colley Ho 12 N7...71 D3
Collier Cl
Newham E16...122 D6
West Ewell KT19...214 D2
Collier Dr HA8...26 C1
Colliers Shaw BR2...225 D3
Collier St N1...94 B5 233 C3
Colliers Water La
CR7...204 C4
COLLIER'S WOOD...180 C4
Colliers Wood
SW19...180 B3
Collier's Wood Sta
SW19...180 B3
Collindale Ave
Erith DA8...147 D6
Sidcup DA15...168 A3
Collingbourne Rd
W12...112 B5
Collingham Gdns
SW5...113 D2 255 D3
Collingham Pl
SW5...113 D2 255 D4
Collingham Rd
SW5...113 D2 255 D3
Collingham Sixth Form
Coll SW5...113 D2 255 D3
Collings Cl N22...32 B4
Collington Ho 2
SE7...143 B6
Collington St SE10...120 B1
Collingtree Rd SE26...184 C6
Collingwood Ave
London N10...49 A5
Tolworth KT5...199 A1
Collingwood Cl
2 Penge SE20...184 B2
Twickenham TW2,
TW4...151 C4
Collingwood Ct
London NW4...46 C4
New Barnet EN5...13 D6
Sutton SM1...217 C4
Collingwood Ho
27 Bethnal Green
E1...96 B3
Marylebone W1...239 A4
Collingwood Rd
Hillingdon UB8...82 D3
Mitcham CR4...202 C6
South Tottenham N15...51 C5
Sutton SM1...217 C4
Collingwood Sch
SM6...219 B3
Collingwood St E1...96 B3
Collins Ave HA7...26 A1
Collins Ct Dalston E8...74 A2
3 Loughton IG10...21 D6
Collins Dr HA4...62 C6
Collins Ho
8 Barking IG11...78 D1
6 Cubitt Town
SE10...120 D1
4 Poplar E14...120 A6
Collinson Ct
Borough The SE1...252 A1
Edgware HA8...26 B6
Collinson Ho 14
SE15...140 A5
Collinson St SE1...252 A1
Collinson Wlk SE1...252 A1
Collins Rd N5, N16...73 A4
Collins Sq SE3...142 D3
Collins St SE3...142 C3
Collins Yd N1...234 C5
Collinwood Ave EN3...6 C2
Collinwood Gdns
IG5...56 C5
Collison Pl N16...51 C1
Collis Prim Sch
TW11...175 B4
Coll of Arms*
EC4...117 A6 252 A6
Coll of Central London
The EC2...243 A6
Coll of Law The
EC1...95 B3 242 C5
Coll of North East
London The N15...51 D5
Coll of NW London
NW6...91 C6
Coll of NW London
(Willesden Centre)
NW10...67 D3
Coll of Optometrists
The SW1...250 A4
Coll Sharp Ct 42 E2...95 D4
Coll's Rd SE15...140 C4
Collyer Ave CR0...220 A4
Collyer Pl SE15...140 A4
Collyer Rd CR0...220 A4
Colman Ct
London N12...30 A4
Stanmore HA7...25 B4
Colman Rd E16...99 C2
Colmans Wharf 5
E14...97 D2
Colmar Cl 3 E1...96 D3
Colmer Pl HA3...24 B3
Colmer Rd SW16...182 A3
Colmore Ct NW4...46 A6
Colmore Mews
SE15...140 B4
Colmore Rd EN3...6 C1
Colnbrook Ct SW17...180 B6
Colnbrook St SE1...261 C6
Colne Ct Ealing W7...86 B1
West Ewell KT19...215 A4
Colne Ho
Barking IG11...78 D2
Paddington NW8...236 D5
Colne Rd
Clapton Pk E5...75 A4
Southgate N21...17 B4
Twickenham TW1,
TW2...152 C3
Colne St E13...99 A4
COLNEY HATCH...30 C4
Colney Hatch La N10...31 A3
Colney Hatch N10...31 A3
Cologne Rd SW11...136 B1
Coloma Convent Girls
Sch CR0...222 D5
Colombo Rd IG1...57 A2
Colombo St SE1...251 C3
Colomb St SE10...120 C1
Colonades The 4
SE5...139 B4
Colonels Wlk EN2...4 D2
Colonial Ave TW2...152 A5
Colonial Dr W4...111 A2
Colonial Rd TW14...149 C4
Colonnade Ho SE3...142 D3
Colonnades The
Croydon CR0...220 C2
6 Hackney E8...74 B2
Colonnade The 12
SE8...119 B2
Colonnade WC1...240 B5
Colorado Bldg 9
SE13...141 D4
Colosseum Ct N3...29 B1
Colosseum Ret Pk
EN1...6 A1
Colosseum Terr
NW1...238 D6
Colour Ho SE1...253 B1
Colroy Ct NW4...47 A4
Colson Rd CR0...221 C6
Colson Way SW16...181 C6
Colstead Ho 22 E1...96 B1
Colsterworth Rd N15...51 D5
Colston Ave SM1,
SM5...218 C4
Colston Ct SM5...218 D4
Colston Rd
Mortlake SW14...133 A1
Upton E7...77 D2
Colthurst Cres N4...73 A6
Colthurst Dr N9...18 B1
Coltman Ho SE10...142 A6
Coltman St E14...97 A2
Colt Mews 5 EN3...7 C6
Coltness Cres SE2...124 B1
Colton Gdns N17...51 A6
Colton Rd HA1...42 C4
Coltsfoot Dr UB7...82 A1
Coltswood Ct N14...15 D3
Colts Yd E11...54 D2
Columba Ho SE14...141 B4
Columbas Dr NW3...48 B1
Columbia Ave
Edgware HA8...26 D2
New Malden KT4...199 D2
Ruislip HA4...40 B1
Columbia Ct
Edgware HA8...26 D2
New Malden KT3...199 D2
Columbia Ho 18 E3...97 C4
Columbia Point 7
SE16...118 C3
Columbia Prim Sch
E2...95 D4
Columbia Rd
9 Hackney E2...96 A5
Newham E13...98 D3
Shoreditch E2...95 D4
Columbia Road Mkt
E2...95 D4
Columbine Ave
Croydon CR2...220 D1
Newham E6...100 A2
Columbus Gdns HA6...22 A2
Colveiw Ct SE9...165 D3
Colverson Ho 14 E1...96 C2
Colvestone Cres E8...73 D3
Colvestone Prim Sch
E8...73 D3
Colville Gdns W11...91 B1
Colville Ho
32 Bethnal Green
E2...96 C5
Notting Hill W11...91 B1
Colville Mews W11...91 B1
Colville Pl W1...239 B3
Colville Prim Sch
W11...91 B1
Colville Rd
Edmonton N9...18 B3
Higham Hill E17...35 A1
Leyton E11...76 A5
Notting Hill W11...91 B1
South Acton W3...110 D3
Colville Sq W11...91 B1
Colville Terr W11...91 B1
Colvin Cl SE26...184 C5
Colvin Gdns
Chingford E4...20 A1
Wanstead E11...55 B5
Colvin Rd
Thornton Heath
CR7...204 C4
Upton Pk E6...78 A1
Colwall Gdns IG8...37 A5
Colwall Ho 18 SW9...138 B3
Colwell Rd SE22...161 D6
Colwick Cl N6...49 D2
Colwith Rd W6...134 C6
Colwood Gdns
SW19...180 B3
Colworth Gr SE17...262 B3
Colworth Rd
Croydon CR0...206 A1
Leytonstone E11...54 C2
Colwyn Ave UB6...86 D5
Colwyn Cl SW16...181 C5
Colwyn Cres TW3...130 A4
Colwyn Gn NW9...45 C3
Colwyn Ho SE1...261 A5
Colwyn Rd NW2...68 B5
Colyer Cl SE9...166 D2
Colyer Ho SE2...124 D1
Colyton Cl
Erith DA16...146 D4
Wembley HA0...65 C2
Colyton La 14 SW16...182 C5
Colyton Rd SE22...162 B6
Colyton Way N18...34 A5
Combe Ave SE3...142 D5
Combedale Rd
SE10...121 A1
Combe Ho
Mortlake SW14...133 A3
20 Paddington W2...91 C2
Combe Lane Sta
CR0...222 C3
Combemartin Rd
SW18...157 A3
Combe Mews 4
SE3...142 D5
Comber Cl NW2...68 B6
Comber Grove Prim Sch
SE5...139 A5
Comber Gr SE5...139 A5
Comber Ho SE5...139 A5
Combermere Rd
London SW9...138 B2
Morden SM4...201 D4
Comberton 10 KT1...176 C1
Comberton Rd E5...74 B6
Combeside SE18...145 D5
Combes Rd RM9...81 B1
Combe The NW1...231 D1
Combwell Cres SE2...124 A3
Com Coll Hackney The
E8...96 B6
Comely Bank Rd E17...54 A4
Comeragh Mews
W14...254 B1
Comeragh Rd
W14...113 A1 254 B1
Comer Cres UB2...108 A4
Comerford Rd SE4...141 B1
Comer Ho 10 EN5...2 A1
Comet Cl E12...77 D4
Comet Pl SE8...141 C5
Comet St SE8...141 C5
Comins Ho SW4...159 C6
Commerce Est E18...37 C1
Commerce Pk CR0...220 B6
Commerce Rd
Brentford TW8...131 C5
Wood Green N22...32 B2
Commerce Way
CR0...220 B6
Commercial Rd
Edmonton N18...33 C4
Stepney E1...96 C1
Whitechapel E1...96 A1
Commercial St
E1...95 D2 243 C4
Commercial Way
Peckham SE15...140 A5
Wembley NW10...88 D5
Commerell Pl SE10...120 D1
Commerell St SE10...120 C1
Commodity Quay E1...253 D5
Commodore Ct SE8...141 C4
Commodore Ho 7
E14...120 A6
Commodore St E1...97 A3
Commondale SW15...134 C2
Common La KT10...213 A1
Common Rd
Barnes SW13...134 A2
Claygate KT10...213 A1
Stanmore HA7...8 C1
Commonside BR2...225 C4
Commonside Ct
SW16...182 A4
Commonside E CR4...203 B6
Commonside W
CR4...203 A6
Common The
Ealing W5...110 A5
Southall UB2...106 D2
Stanmore HA7...8 D2
1 Stratford E15...76 D2
Common View
SW15...134 C2
Commonwealth Ave
Hayes UB3...83 B1
21 Shepherd's Bush
W12...112 B6
25 Shepherd's Bush
W12...112 B6
Commonwealth Ho
WC1...240 B2
Commonwealth Rd
N17...34 A3
Commonwealth Way
SE2...124 C1
Community Cl
Cranford TW5...128 B4
Uxbridge UB10...61 A5
Community Rd
Greenford UB6...86 A6
Stratford New Town
E15...76 B3
Comodore Ho
SW18...136 A1
Como Rd SE23...163 A2
Compania Bldg 12
E1...118 D6
Compass Cl
Edgware HA8...26 B6
Littleton TW15...171 A3
Compass Ct SE1...253 C3
Compass Hill TW10...153 D5
Compass Ho
Bayswater W2...91 D1
London SE8...141 D3

Compass Point 10 E14 119 C6
Compayne Gdns NW6 69 D1
Compton Ave
Islington N1 72 D2
London N6 48 C2
Newham E6 99 D5
Wembley HA0 65 C4
Compton Cl
5 Burnt Oak HA8 27 A3
Camberwell SE15 139 D5
Cricklewood NW11 63 D6
Ealing W13 87 A1
Esher KT10 212 B3
Regent's Pk NW1 231 D1
Compton Cres
Chessington KT9 214 A2
Chiswick W4 133 A6
Northolt UB5 84 D6
Tottenham N17 33 A3
Compton Ct
London N12 30 A2
Sutton SM1 218 A4
9 West Norwood SE19 183 C5
Compton Ho SW11 267 A2
Compton Lo N21 16 D3
Compton Pas EC1 241 D6
Compton Pl
Bloomsbury WC1 240 A6
South Oxhey WD19 23 A6
Compton Rd
Croydon CR0 206 B1
Hayes UB3 105 D6
Islington N1 72 D2
Kensal Green NW10 90 D4
Southgate N21 16 D3
Wimbledon SW19 179 B4
Compton Rise HA5 41 B4
Compton Sch The N12 30 C4
Compton St EC1 94 D3 241 D6
Compton Terr
Islington N1 72 D2
Southgate N21 16 C3
Comreddy Cl EN2 4 D4
Comus Ho SE17 263 A3
Comus Pl SE17 117 C2 263 A3
Comyn Rd SW11 136 C1
Comyns Cl E16 98 D2
Comyns Rd RM9 81 C1
Comyns The WD23 8 A3
Conal Ct SW16 181 D5
Conant Ho SE11 138 D6
Conant Mews 1 E1 118 A6
Concanon Rd SW2, SW4 138 B1
Concert Hall App SE1 116 B5 250 D3
Concord Bsns Ctr W3 88 D2
Concord Cl UB5 85 A4
Concord Ct KT1 198 B6
Concorde Cl
Hounslow TW3 129 D3
Uxbridge UB10 82 A5
Concorde Dr E6 100 B2
Concorde Way SE16 118 D2
Concord Ho
Kingston u T KT3 199 C6
5 Tottenham N17 33 D3
Concordia Wharf 10 E14 120 A5
Concord Rd
Acton W3 88 D3
Enfield EN3 18 C6
Concord Terr HA2 63 D6
Concourse The
32 Edgware NW9 27 D2
7 Edmonton N9 18 A2
Condell Rd SW8 137 C4 269 B1
Conder St E14 97 A1
Condor Path UB5 85 C5
Condover Cres SE18 144 D5
Condray Pl SW11 267 A3
Conduit Ct WC2 250 A6
Conduit Ho SE10 142 B4
Conduit La
London N18 34 C5
South Croydon CR0 222 A3
Conduit Mews W2 92 B1 236 C1
Conduit Pas W2 236 C1
Conduit Pl W2 236 C1
Conduit Rd SE18 122 D1
Conduit St W1 115 C6 249 A6
Conduit Way NW10 67 A1
Conewood St N5 72 D5
Coney Acre SE21 161 A3
Coney Burrows E4 20 C2
Coney Gr UB8 82 C4
Coneygrove Path UB5 63 A2
CONEY HALL 224 D5
Coney Hall Par BR4 224 C5
Coney Hall Rdbt BR4 224 C5
Coney Hill Rd BR4 224 D6
Coney Way SW8 270 D5
Conference Cl 3 E4 20 A2
Conference Ho UB8 83 A1
Conference Rd SE2 124 C2
Congers Ho SE8 141 C5
Congleton Gr SE18 123 A1
Congo Dr N9 18 C1
Congo Rd SE18 123 B1
Congress Ho WC1 239 D2
Congress Rd SE2 124 C2
Congreve Ho 10 N16 73 C3
Congreve Rd SE9 144 B2
Congreve St SE17 117 C2 263 A3
Congreve Wlk 6 E16 99 D2
Conical Cnr EN2 5 A3
Conifer Cl BR6 227 B4
Conifer Ct
Ashford TW15 170 B5
Hendon NW4 28 C1
Ilford IG1 78 D2
23 Putney SW19 156 D3
Sutton SM2 218 B2
Conifer Gdns
Enfield EN1 17 C5
Streatham SW16 160 B1
Sutton SM1 217 D6
Conifer Ho SE4 141 B1
Conifers Cl TW11 175 C3
Conifer Way
Hayes UB3 106 A6
Wembley HA0 65 C5
Coniger Rd SW6 135 C3
Coningham Ct SW10 266 B4
Coningham Mews W12 112 A5
Coningham Rd W12 112 B4
Coningsby Ave NW9 27 C1
Coningsby Cotts W5 109 D4
Coningsby Ct 4 CR4 181 A1
Coningsby Gdns E4 35 D4
Coningsby Rd
Ealing W5 109 D4
Harringay N4 50 D2
Conington Rd SE13 142 A3
Conisbee Ct 3 N14 15 C6
Conisborough Cres SE6 164 A1
Conisbrough NW1 232 A5
Coniscliffe Cl BR7 188 C2
Coniscliffe Rd N13 17 A1
Coniston Ave
Barking IG11 79 C1
Ealing UB6 87 B4
Falconwood DA16 145 C2
Coniston Cl
Barking IG11 79 C1
Barnes SW13 133 D5
Chiswick W4 133 A5
West Barnes SM4 200 D3
Whetstone N20 14 A1
Coniston Ct
Beckenham BR3 186 A2
Chessington KT9 214 A5
Edgware HA8 26 B5
4 Finchley NW7 29 A3
Marylebone W2 237 B1
Penge SE26 184 B4
6 Rotherhithe SE16 118 D4
3 Wallington SM6 219 B4
Conistone Way N7 72 A1
Coniston Gdns
Edmonton N9 18 C3
Kingsbury NW9 45 B4
Pinner HA5 40 A5
Redbridge IG4 56 A5
Sutton SM2 218 B2
Wembley HA9 43 C1
Coniston Ho
14 Bow E3 97 B4
18 Camberwell SE5 139 A5
Coniston NW1 232 A2
Coniston Rd
Catford BR1 186 C4
Croydon CR0 206 A2
Muswell Hill N10 31 B1
Tottenham N17 34 A4
Twickenham TW2 151 D5
Coniston Way KT9 214 A5
Coniston Wlk E9 74 C3
Conlan St W10 91 A3
Conley Rd NW10 67 C2
Conley St SE10 120 C1
Connaught Ave
Ashford TW15 170 A6
Barnet EN4 14 D3
Chingford E4 20 B4
Enfield EN1 5 C3
Hounslow TW4 129 A1
Mortlake SW14 133 A1
Connaught Bridge E16 121 D6
Connaught Bsns Ctr
London NW9 45 D4
Mitcham CR4 202 D4
Wallington CR0 220 B2
Connaught Cl
Carshalton SM1 218 B6
Enfield EN1 5 C3
Hillingdon UB8 83 A3
Lea Bridge E10 75 A6
Marylebone W2 237 B1
Connaught Ct
1 Chingford E4 20 C4
9 Walthamstow E17 53 D5
Connaught Day Hospl E11 54 C3
Connaught Dr NW11 47 C5
Connaught Gdns
Cranley Gdns N10 49 B4
Edmonton N13 32 D6
Morden SM4 202 A5
Connaught Grange N13 32 D6
Connaught Ho
College Pk NW10 90 B4
London N10 49 B4
Mayfair W1 248 C5
Connaught Hts UB10 83 A3
Connaught La IG1 79 B6
Connaught Lo N4 50 C2
Connaught Mans
Battersea SW11 267 B1
3 Brixton SW9 138 C1
15 Canonbury N16 73 B4
Fulham SW6 264 A2
Connaught Mews
Ilford IG1 79 B6
Woolwich SE18 122 C1
Connaught Pl W2 237 C1
Connaught Rd
Barnet EN5 12 D5
Carshalton SM1 218 B6
Chingford E4 20 C3
Ealing W13 109 B6
Finsbury Pk N4 50 C2
Harlesden NW10 89 C5
Harrow HA3 24 D2
Ilford IG1 79 B6
Leytonstone E11 54 B1
Newham E16 121 D5
New Malden KT3 199 C5
5 Richmond TW10 154 B6
Teddington TW11, TW12 174 B5
Walthamstow E17 53 C4
Woolwich SE18 122 D1
Connaught Sch for Girls (Annexe) E11 76 C6
Connaught Sch for Girls E11 54 C1
Connaught Sq W2 92 D1 237 C1
Connaught St W2 92 C1 237 B1
Connaught Way N13 32 D6
Connaught Works E3 97 A6
Connections Ho N2 30 B2
Connell Cres W5 88 B3
Connell Ct 6 SE14 140 D6
Connell Ho 6 SM6 219 C2
Connemara Cl WD6 11 B5
Conniffe Ct SE9 166 D6
Connington Cres E4 20 B1
Connington 5 KT1 176 C1
Connolly Ho SW19 180 A4
Connoly Ct NW2 68 B5
Connop Rd EN3 6 D5
Connor Cl E11 54 C2
Connor Ct SW11 268 C1
Connor Rd RM9 81 B4
Connor St E9 96 D6
Conolly Rd W7 108 C5
Conrad Dr KT4 200 D1
Conrad Ho
8 Limehouse E16 119 A6
South Lambeth SW8 270 A4
12 Stoke Newington N16 73 C3
Conrad Twr W3 110 D3
Conroy Ct 6 DA14 190 A6
Conservatory Ct SE19 183 C3
Consfield Ave KT3 200 A4
Consort Ho
Bayswater W2 245 D5
Edgware NW7 27 D5
Consort Lo NW8 230 C5
Consort Mews TW7 152 B6
Consort Rd SE15 140 B3
Cons St SE1 251 B2
Constable Ave E16 121 B5
Constable Cl
12 Friern Barnet N11 30 D5
Hampstead Garden Suburb NW11 47 D3
Hayes UB4 83 A5
Constable Cres N15 52 A4
Constable Ct 11 SE16 118 B1
Constable Gdns
Edgware HA8 26 C1
Isleworth TW7 152 B6
Constable Ho
Enfield EN1 18 A6
25 Millwall E14 119 C4
13 Northolt UB5 84 D5
Primrose Hill NW3 70 D1
Constable Mews RM8 80 B4
Constable Wlk SE21 161 C1
Constance Cres BR2 208 D1
Constance Ct N10 31 B3
Constance Rd
Enfield EN1 17 C5
Sutton SM1 218 A4
Thornton Heath CR0 204 D2
Twickenham TW2 151 D4
Constance St E16 122 A5
Constant Ho 26 E14 119 D6
Constantine Ho SW2 160 D3
Constantine Pl UB10 82 B6
Constantine Rd NW3 70 C4
Constitution Hill SW1, W1 115 B4 248 D2
Constitution Rise SE18 144 C4
Consul Ho 5 E3 97 C3
Content St SE17 117 B2 262 C3
Contessa Cl BR6 227 C3
Control Tower Rd TW6 126 D2
Convair Wlk 11 UB5 84 D4
Convent Cl BR3 186 A3
Convent Gdns
Ealing W5 109 C2
Notting Hill W11 91 B1
Convent Hill SE19 183 A4
Convent Lo TW15 170 D5
Convent of Jesus & Mary Language Coll NW10 89 D6
Convent of Jesus & Mary RC Inf Sch NW2 68 C2
Convent Rd TW15 170 D5
Convent Way UB2 106 D2
Conway Cl HA7 25 A4
Conway Cres
Dagenham RM6 58 C3
Greenford UB6 86 C5
Conway Dr
Ashford TW15 171 A4
Hayes UB3 105 A3
Sutton SM2 217 D2
Conway Gdns
Enfield EN2 5 C5
Mitcham CR4 204 A5
Wembley HA9 43 C2
Conway Gr W3 89 B2
Conway Ho
Chelsea SW3 257 D1
5 Millwall E14 119 D2
6 Streatham SW2 160 A3
Conway Mews W1 239 A5
Conway Prim Sch SE18 123 C2
Conway Rd
Dollis Hill NW2 68 C6
Feltham TW13 172 D5
Harlington TW6 126 D2
Harringay N15 51 A4
Palmers Green N14 16 A1
Plumstead SE18 123 C2
Twickenham TW4 151 C4
Wimbledon SW20 178 C2
Conway St W1 93 C3 239 A5
Conway Wlk TW12 173 B4
Conybeare NW3 70 C1
Conyers Cl IG8 36 C4
Conyer's Rd SW16 181 D5
Conyer St 21 E3 97 A5
Cooden Cl BR1 187 B3
Cookes Cl E11 76 D6
Cookes La SM3 217 A2
Cooke St 3 IG11 101 A6
Cookham Cl UB2 107 D4
Cookham Cres SE16 118 D4
Cookham Dene Cl BR7 189 B2
Cookham Ho E2 243 C6
Cookham Rd BR8, DA14 191 C2
Cookhill Rd SE2 124 B3
Cooks Ferry N18 34 D5
Cook's Hole Rd EN2 5 A5
Cookson Gr DA8 147 D5
Cook's Rd
Camberwell SE17 138 D6
Stratford Marsh E15 97 D5
Coolfin Rd E16 99 B1
Coolgardie Ave E4 36 B5
Coolgardie Rd TW15 171 A5
Coolhurst Rd N8 49 D3
Cool Oak La NW9 45 D2
Coomassie Rd W9 91 B3
COOMBE 177 B3
Coombe Ave CR0 221 C4
Coombe Bank KT2, KT3 177 C2
Coombe Boys' Sch KT3 200 A4
Coombe Cl
Edgware HA8 26 B1
Hounslow TW3 129 C1
Coombe Cnr N21 16 D3
Coombe Cres TW12 173 A3
Coombe Ct 2 BR3 185 B2
Coombe Dr HA4 40 B1
Coombe End KT2 177 B3
Coombefield Cl KT3 199 C4
Coombe Gdns
New Malden KT3 199 D5
Wimbledon SW20 178 A2
Coombe Girls Sch KT3 177 B1
Coombe Hill Glade KT2 177 C3
Coombe Hill Inf Sch KT2 177 B2
Coombe Hill Jun Sch KT2 177 B2
Coombe Hill Rd KT2 177 C3
Coombe Ho 13 N7 71 D3
Coombe House Chase KT3 177 B2
Coombehurst Cl EN4 2 D3
Coombehurst (Kingston University) KT2 177 A5
Coombe Lane Flyover SW20 177 D2
Coombe La CR0 222 B3
Coombe La W KT2 177 B2
Coombe Lea BR1 210 A6
Coombe Lo SE7 143 C6
Coombe Neville KT2 177 B3
Coombe Pk KT2 177 B5
Coombe Pl KT2 177 A5
Coombe Rd
Bushey WD23 8 B4
Chiswick W4 111 C1
Ealing W13 109 B3
Forest Hill SE26 184 B6
Hampton TW12 173 B4
New Malden KT3 199 C6
Norbiton KT2 176 C2
South Croydon CR0, CR2 221 C4
Willesden NW10 67 B5
Wood Green N22 32 C2
Coomber Ho SW6 135 D2
Coombe Ridings KT2 177 A5
Coombe Rise KT2 177 A2
Coomber Way CR0 203 D3
Coombes Rd RM9 103 B6
Coombe Wlk SM1 217 D5
Coombewood Dr RM6 59 B3
Coombe Wood Rd KT2 177 A5
Coombs St N1 234 D3
Coomer Mews SW6 264 D5
Coomer Pl SW6 135 B6 264 D5
Cooms Wlk HA8 27 A2
Cooperage Cl 5 N17 33 D4
Cooperage The SE1 253 C3
Cooper Ave E17 35 A2
Cooper Cl SE1 251 B1
Cooper Cres SM5 218 D5
Cooper Ct
Shooters Hill SE18 144 D6
Stratford New Town E15 76 A3
Cooper Ho
Hounslow TW4 129 B2
Paddington NW8 236 C5
Upper Tooting SW17 180 B6
Cooper Ho *continued*
7 West Norwood SE27 18
Cooper Rd
Croydon CR0, CR9 22
Hendon NW4 46
Willesden NW10 68
Coopersale Cl 3 IG8 37
Coopersale Rd E9 74
Coopers Cl
Bethnal Green E1 96
Dagenham RM10 81
Coopers Ct
9 Acton W3 111
4 Friern Barnet N20 14
Isleworth TW7 130
Tower Hamlets E3 97
Coopers La SE12 165
Cooper's La E10 54
Cooper's Lane Prim Sch SE12 165
Coopers La NW1 232
Coopers Lo SE1 253
Coopers Mews BR3 185
Cooper's Rd SE1 117 D1 263
Cooper's Row EC3 117 D6 253
Cooper St 10 E16 98
Coopers Tech Sch BR7 189
Coopers Yd N1 72
Cooper's Yd SE19 183
Coote Gdns RM8 81
Coote Rd
Dagenham RM8 81
Erith DA7 147
Cope Ho EC1 235
Copeland Dr E14 119
Copeland Ho
Lambeth SE11 260
Upper Tooting SW17 180
Copeland Rd
London SE15 140
Walthamstow E17 53
Copelands BR3 185
Copeman Cl SE26 184
Copenhagen Gdns W4 111
Copenhagen Ho N1 234
Copenhagen Pl E14 97
Copenhagen Prim Sch N1 94 B6 233
Copenhagen St N1 94 B6 233
Cope Pl W8 113 C3 255
Copers Cope Rd BR3 185
Cope St SE16 118
Copeswood Ct UB7 126
Copford Wlk N1 235
Copgate Path SW16 182
Copinger Wlk HA8 26
Copland Ave HA0 65
Copland Cl HA0 65
Copland Com Sch & Tech Ctr HA9 66
Copland Ho UB1 107
Copland Mews 8 HA0 66
Copland Rd HA0 66
Copleston Rd SE15 139
Copley Cl
15 Camberwell SE17 138
Ealing W7 86
Copley Dene BR1 187
Copley Pk SW16 182
Copley Rd HA7 25
Coppard Gdns KT9 213
Coppedhall 2 SE21 161
Coppelia Rd SE3 142
Coppen Rd RM8 59
Copperas St SE8 141
Copperbeech Cl NW3 70
Copper Beech Ct N20 14
Copper Beeches TW7 130
Copper Beech N6 49
Copper Cl
Penge SE19 183
Tottenham N17 34
Copperdale Rd UB3 106
Copperfield Ave UB8 82
Copperfield Ct
Blackheath SE3 142
Ilford IG6 57
Copperfield Dr N15 51
Copperfield Ho 12 SE1 118
Copperfield Mews N18 33

opperfield Rd
Stepney E3 97 A2
Thamesmead SE28 102 C1
opperfields 5
BR3 186 A2
opperfields Ct W3 110 C4
opperfields HA1 42 C2
opperfield St
SE1 117 A4 252 A2
opperfield Way
Chislehurst BR7 189 A4
Pinner HA5 41 B5
oppergate Cl BR1 187 B2
oppermead Cl NW2 68 C5
opper Mews 19
W4 111 A3
opper Mill Dr
TW7 130 D3
oppermill La E17 52 D4
opper Mill La
SW17 180 A6
oppermill Prim Sch
E17 52 D4
opper Row SE1 253 C3
opperwood Lo EN2 4 D3
oppetts Cl N12 30 D3
oppetts Ctr N12 30 D3
oppetts Rd N10 30 D2
oppetts Wood Hospl
N10 30 D2
oppetts Wood Prim
Sch N10 31 A2
Coppice Cl
Beckenham BR3 207 D5
Harrow HA7 24 D4
Ruislip HA4 39 B3
West Barnes SW20 200 C6
Coppice Dr SW15 156 B5
Coppice The
Ashford TW15 170 D4
Enfield EN2 4 D1
Hillingdon UB7 82 A1
New Barnet EN5 13 D5
Coppice Way E18 54 D6
Coppice Wlk N20 13 C1
Coppies Gr N11 31 B6
Copping Cl CR0 221 C4
Coppin Ho SW2 160 D3
Coppins The
2 Ilford RM6 58 B2
New Addington CR0 223 D2
Stanmore HA3 24 C4
Coppock Cl SW11 136 C3
Coppsfield KT8 195 C6
Copse Ave BR4 223 D5
Copse Cl SE7 143 B6
Copse Ct SW15 157 A6
Copse Glade KT6 197 D1
COPSE HILL 178 B3
Copse Hill
Belmont SM2 217 D1
Wimbledon SW20 178 B3
Copsem Dr KT10 212 A2
Copsem La KT10 212 A1
Copsem Way KT10 212 A2
Copse The
Chingford E4 20 D3
Muswell Hill N2 48 D6
Copse View CR2 223 A1
Copsewood Cl
DA15 167 C5
Coptefield Dr DA17 125 A3
Copthall Ave
EC2 95 B1 242 D2
Copthall Bldgs EC2 242 D2
Copthall Cl EC2 242 C2
Copthall Dr NW7 28 A4
Copthall Gdns
Hendon NW7 28 A3
Twickenham TW1 152 D3
Copthall Rd E UB10 60 C5
Copthall Rd W UB10 60 C6
Copthall Sch NW7 28 B3
Copthall Sports Ctr
NW4 28 B2
Copthorne Ave
Bromley BR2 226 B6
Streatham SW12 159 D4
Copthorne Chase 3
TW15 170 B6
Copthorne Cl TW17 193 A3
Copthorne Ct SM1 218 A5
Copthorne Mews
UB3 105 C2
Coptic St
WC1 94 A2 240 A3
Copton Cl E3 97 C2
Copwood Cl N12 30 B6
Coral Apts 6 E16 121 A6
Coral Cl RM6 58 C6
Coral Ho 5 E1 97 A3
Coraline Cl UB1 85 B4
Coralline Wlk 4
SE2 124 C4
Coral Row 14 SW11 136 A2
Coral St SE1 116 C4 251 B1
Coram Ho
Bloomsbury WC1 240 A6
9 Chiswick W4 111 C1
Coram Mans WC1 240 C5
Coram St
WC1 94 A3 240 A5
Coran Cl N9 18 D4
Corban Rd TW3 129 C2
Corbar Cl EN4 2 B4
Corbden Cl SE15 139 D4
Corbet Cl CR4, SM6 219 A6
Corbet Ct EC3 242 D1
Corbet Ho N1 234 A5
Corbet Pl E1 95 D2 243 C4
Corbett Ct SE26 185 B6
Corbett Gr N22 32 A3
Corbett Ho SW10 266 A6
Corbett Rd
Walthamstow E17 54 A6
Wanstead E11 55 C3
Corbett's La SE16 118 C2
Corbetts Pas 8
SE16 118 C2
Corbett Villas RM8 58 C1
Corbicum E11 54 C2
Corbidge Ct SE8 141 D6
Corbiere Ct SW19 178 D4
Corbiere Ho 5 N1 95 C6
Corbin Ho 7 E3 97 D4
Corbin's La HA2 63 D5
Corbridge Cres E2 96 B5
Corbridge Ho SE2 124 C3
Corbridge 5 N17 34 B3
Corby Cres EN2 4 A1
Corbylands Rd
DA15 167 C3
Corbyn St N4, N19 50 A1
Corby Rd NW10 89 B5
Corby Way E3 97 C3
Cordelia Cl SE24 138 D1
Cordelia Gdns
TW19 148 A4
Cordelia Ho 26 N1 95 C5
Cordelia Rd TW19 148 A4
Cordelia St E14 97 D1
Cordell Ho N15 51 D4
Cordingley Rd HA4 61 B6
Cording St E14 97 D2
Cordwainers Ct 18
E9 74 C1
Cordwainers Wlk 9
E13 99 A5
Cordwain Ho 7 N18 34 A5
Cordwell Rd SE13 164 C6
Corefield Cl N11 15 A2
Corelli Rd SE3 144 A4
Corfe Ave HA2 63 C4
Corfe Cl Hayes UB4 84 C1
Twickenham TW4 151 A3
Corfe Ho SW8 270 C4
Corfe Lodge 15
SE21 161 B2
Corfe Twr 6 W3 111 A4
Corfield Rd N21 16 B6
Corfield St E2 96 B4
Corfton Lo W5 88 A2
Corfton Rd W5 88 A2
Coriander Ave E14 98 B1
Coriander Ct SE1 253 D2
Cories Cl RM8 80 D6
Corigan Ct 6 E11 76 C6
Corinium Cl HA9 66 B4
Corinne Rd N19 71 C4
Corinth Ho IG3 58 A2
Cork St Mews W1 249 A5
Corkscrew Hill BR4 224 B5
Cork Sq E1 118 B5
Cork St W1 115 C6 249 A5
Cork Tree Ho 3
SW27 182 D5
Cork Tree Ret Pk
N18 35 A4
Cork Tree Way E4 35 A5
Corlett St NW1 237 A4
Cormont Rd SE5 138 D4
Cormorant Cl E17 35 A3
Cormorant Ct
36 Deptford SE8 141 B6
13 Dulwich SE21 161 B2
Cormorant Ho EN3 18 D6
Cormorant Pl SM1 217 B3
Cormorant Rd E7 76 D3
Cornbury Ho 5 SE8 141 B6
Cornbury Rd HA8 25 D3
Cornel Ho 4 DA15 168 A1
Cornelia Dr UB4 84 C3
Cornelia St N7 72 B2
Cornelion Cotts 1
SM6 219 B3
Cornelius Ct 4 N12 30 A5
Cornell Bldg 9 E1 96 A1
Cornell Cl DA14 191 A4
Cornell Ct 4 EN3 7 A2
Cornell Ho HA2 63 B5
Corner Fielde SW2 160 B3
Corner Gn SE3 143 A3
Corner House St
WC2 250 A4
Corner Mead NW9 27 D2
Cornerside TW15 171 A3
Cornerstone Ct 13
E1 96 A3
Cornerways
Harrow HA1 65 A5
Putney SW15 134 A1
Corney Rd W4 133 C6
Corney Reach Way
W4 133 C5
Cornflower La CR0 206 D1
Cornflower Terr
SE22 162 B5
Cornford Cl BR2 209 A4
Cornford Gr SW12 159 B2
Cornhill Dr EN3 7 A6
Cornhill EC3 95 B1 242 D1
Cornick Ho 7 SE16 118 B3
Cornish Ct N9 18 B4
Cornish Gr SE20 184 B2
Cornish Ho
Brentford TW8 110 B1
7 Camberwell
SE17 138 D6
Cornmill La SE13 142 A2
Cornmow Dr NW10 68 A3
Cornshaw Rd RM8 58 D1
Cornthwaite Rd E5 74 C5
Cornwall Ave
Bethnal Green E2 96 C4
Claygate KT10 212 D1
Falconwood DA16 145 D2
Finchley N3 29 C3
Southall UB1 85 C2
Wood Green N22 32 A2
Cornwall Cl IG11 79 D2
Cornwall Cres W11 91 A1
Cornwall Ct
5 Ealing W7 86 D3
5 Pinner HA5 23 B3
Upper Tooting
SW17 180 C6
Cornwall Dr BR5 190 C3
Cornwall Flats SE1 251 B2
Cornwall Gdns
Kensington
SW7 113 D3 255 D5
Willesden NW10 68 B2
Cornwall Gdns Wlk
SW7 255 D5
Cornwall Gr W4 111 C1
Cornwall Ho
Marylebone NW1 237 D5
3 Putney SW15 156 C4
Cornwallis Ave
London N9 18 C2
New Eltham SE9 167 B2
Cornwallis Ct SW8 270 A2
Cornwallis Gr N9 18 C2
Cornwallis Ho 24
W12 112 B6
Cornwallis Rd
Dagenham RM9 81 A4
Edmonton N9 18 B2
Upper Holloway N19 72 A6
Walthamstow E17 52 D5
Woolwich SE18 122 D3
Woolwich SE18 123 A3
Cornwallis Sq N19 72 A6
Cornwallis Wlk SE9 144 B2
Cornwall Mans
Chelsea SW10 266 B4
Marylebone NW1 237 D5
Cornwall Mews S
SW7 256 A5
Cornwall Mews W
SW7 255 D5
Cornwall Rd
Belmont SM2 217 B1
Croydon CR0 220 D6
Edmonton N18 34 A5
Finsbury Pk N4 50 C2
Harrow HA1 42 A3
Lambeth
SE1 116 C4 251 B2
Pinner HA5 23 B3
Ruislip HA4 61 D6
Twickenham TW1 153 A3
West Green N15 51 B4
Cornwall Sq SE11 261 C2
Cornwall St 4 E1 118 B6
Cornwall Terrace Mews
NW1 237 D5
Cornwall Terr NW1 237 D5
Corn Way E11 76 C5
Cornwood Cl N2 48 B5
Cornwood Dr E1 96 C1
Cornworthy Rd RM8 80 C3
Corona Rd SE12 165 A4
Coronation Ave 1
N16 73 D4
Coronation Cl
Bexley DA5 168 D5
Ilford IG6 57 A5
Coronation Ct
19 North Kensington
W10 90 C2
Stratford E15 76 D2
Coronation Rd
Acton NW10 88 C3
Hayes UB3 105 D2
Newham E13 99 C4
Coronet Ho HA7 24 D4
Coronet Par 9 HA0 66 A2
Coronet St N1 95 C4
Corporation Ave
TW4 129 A1
Corporation Row
EC1 241 B6
Corporation St
Lower Holloway N7 72 A3
West Ham E15 98 D5
Corpus Christi RC
Prim Sch
Brixton SW2 160 B6
Kingston u T KT3 199 A6
Corrance Rd SW2,
SW4 138 A1
Corri Ave N14 31 D6
Corrib Ct N13 16 B1
Corrib Dr SM1 218 C3
Corrib Hts N8 49 D3
Corrigan Cl NW4 46 C6
Corringham Ct NW11 47 C2
Corringham Ho 11
E1 96 D1
Corringham Rd
London NW11 47 C2
Wembley HA9 66 C6
Corringway Ealing W5 88 C2
Golders Green NW11 47 D2
Corris Gn NW9 45 C3
Corry Dr SW9 138 D1
Corry Ho 2 E14 119 D6
Corsair Cl TW19 148 A4
Corsair Rd TW19 148 A4
Corscombe Cl KT2 177 A5
Corsehill St SW16 181 C4
Corsell Ho 5 TW8 131 C5
Corsham Ho HA9 66 C2
Corsham St
N1 95 B4 235 D1
Corsica St N5 72 D2
Corsley Way E9 75 B2
Cortayne Ct TW2 152 C2
Cortayne Rd SW6 135 B3
Cortis Rd SW15 156 B5
Cortis Terr SW15 156 B5
Corunna Rd
SW8 137 C4 269 B2
Corunna Terr SW8 269 A2
Corvette Sq 5 SE10 142 B6
Corwell Gdns UB8 83 A1
Corwell La UB8 83 A1
Coryton Path W9 91 B3
Cosbycote Ave
SE24 161 A6
Cosdach Ave SM6 219 D1
Cosedge Cres CR0,
CR9 220 D3
Cosgrove Cl
Edmonton N21 17 A2
Hayes UB4 84 D3
Cosgrove Ho 11 E2 96 A6
Cosmo Pl WC1 240 B4
Cosmur Cl W12 111 D3
Cossall Wlk SE15 140 B4
Cossar Mews 10
SW2 160 C6
Cosser St
SE1 116 C3 261 A6
Costa St SE15 140 A3
Coston Prim Sch
UB6 86 A4
Costons Ave UB6 86 B4
Costons La UB6 86 B4
Coston Wlk 4 SE4 140 D1
Cosway Ho NW11 48 A3
Cosway Mans NW1 237 B4
Cosway St
NW1 92 C2 237 B4
Cotall St E14 97 C2
Coteford Cl HA5 40 A4
Coteford Inf Sch
HA5 40 A3
Coteford Jun Sch
HA5 39 D4
Coteford St SW17 181 A6
Cotelands CR0 221 C5
Cotesbach Rd E5 74 C5
Cotes Ho NW8 237 A5
Cotesmore Gdns
RM8 80 C4
Cotford Rd CR7 205 A5
Cotham St SE17 262 B3
Cotherstone Rd
SW2 160 B3
Cotleigh Ave DA5 168 D2
Cotleigh Rd NW6 69 C1
Cotman Cl
London NW11 48 A3
Cotman Cl *continued*
Putney SW15 156 D6
Cotman Ct BR3 185 B2
Cotmandene Cres
BR5 190 A1
Cotman Gdns HA8 26 C1
Cotman Ho
5 Northolt UB5 84 D5
St John's Wood NW8 230 A4
Cotman Mews RM8 80 C3
Cotmans Cl UB3 106 A5
Coton Rd DA16 146 A2
Cotrill Gdns E8 74 B2
Cotsford Ave KT3 199 B4
Cotswold Ave WD23 8 A5
Cotswold Cl
Hinchley Wood
KT10 212 D6
Kingston u T KT2 177 A4
Cotswold Ct
London N11 31 A6
St Luke's EC1 242 A6
3 Wembley UB6 86 D5
Cotswold Gate NW2 47 A1
Cotswold Gdns
Hendon NW2 68 D6
Ilford IG2 57 B2
Newham E6 99 D5
Cotswold Gn EN2 4 B1
Cotswold Ho N16 51 D1
Cotswold Mews
SW11 266 D1
Cotswold Rd TW12 173 C4
Cotswold Rise BR6 211 D3
Cotswold St SE27 182 D6
Cotswold Way
Enfield EN2 4 B2
North Cheam KT4 216 C6
Cottage Ave BR2 210 A1
Cottage Cl
Harrow HA2 64 C6
Ruislip HA4 39 B1
Cottage Field Cl
DA14 168 C3
Cottage Gn SE5 139 B5
Cottage Gr
London SW9 138 A2
Surbiton KT6 197 D3
Cottage Pl
SW3 114 C3 257 A5
Cottage Rd KT19 215 B1
Cottage St E14 119 D6
Cottages The
Ickenham UB10 60 A6
Lambeth SE1 260 C5
Uxbridge UB10 60 D5
Cottage Wlk 2 N16 73 D5
Cottenham Dr
London NW9 45 D6
Wimbledon SW20 178 B3
Cottenham Ho 5
N19 72 A6
COTTENHAM PARK
178 B2
Cottenham Park Rd
SW20 178 C3
Cottenham Par
SW20 178 B1
Cottenham Pl SW20 178 B3
Cottenham Rd E17 53 B5
Cotterill Rd KT6 198 B1
Cottesbrook St 9
SE14 141 A5
Cottesloe Ho NW8 237 A6
Cottesloe Mews SE1 261 B6
Cottesmore Ct W8 255 D6
Cottesmore Gdns
W8 113 D3 255 D6
Cottimore Ave KT12 194 B1
Cottimore Cres
KT12 194 B2
Cottimore La KT12 194 B2
Cottimore Terr
KT12 194 B2
Cottingham Chase
HA4 62 A5
Cottingham Rd
Penge SE20 184 D3
South Lambeth
SW8 138 B5 270 D4
Cottington Rd
TW13 172 D6
Cottington St SE11 261 C2
Cotton Ave W3 89 B1
Cotton Cl
Dagenham RM9 80 C1
12 Leyton E11 76 C6
Cottongrass Cl 1
CR0 206 D1
Cotton Hill BR1 186 B6
Cotton Ho
Bedford Pk W12 111 D4
18 Streatham SW12 160 A4
Cotton Row SW11 136 B2
Cotton's Gdns E2 95 C4
Cottons La SE1 252 D4
Cotton St E14 120 A6
Cottrell Ct SE10 120 D2
Cotts Cl 13 W7 86 D2
Couchman Ho 8
SW4 159 C5
Couchmore Ave
KT10 212 C6
Coulgate St SE4 141 A2
Coulsdon Ct 4 N8 49 D4
Coulsdon Ho 5
SW2 160 A3
Coulson Cl RM8 58 C1
Coulson St
SW3 114 D1 257 C2
Coulter Cl UB4 85 A3
Coulter Rd W6 112 B3
Coulthurst Ct SW16 182 A3
Coults Cres NW5 71 A5
Councillor St SE5 139 A5
Counters Ct W14 254 B6
Counter St SE1 253 A3
Countess Rd NW5 71 C3
Countisbury Ave EN1 17 D4
Countisbury Ho
SE26 162 A1
Country Way TW13,
TW16 172 C5
County Gate
Longlands SE9 167 A1
New Barnet EN5 13 D5
County Gr SE5 139 A4
County Ho
22 Herne Hill
SE24 138 D1
9 South Lambeth
SW9 138 C4
County Par TW8 131 D5
County Rd
Newham E6 100 D2
South Norwood CR7 182 D1
County St
SE1 117 A3 262 B5
Coupland Pl SE18 123 A1
Courcy Rd N8, N22 50 C6
Courier Ho 17 SW2 160 C4
Courland Gr SW8 137 D3
Courland St
SW8 137 D4 269 D1
Course The SE9 166 C1
Courtauld Ho 12 E2 96 A5
Courtauld Inst of
Art*
Marylebone W1 237 D2
Strand WC2 250 C6
Courtauld Rd N19 50 A1
Courtaulds Cl SE28 124 A5
Court Ave DA17 125 B1
Court Cl HA3 44 A6
Court Close Ave TW13,
TW2 151 D1
Court Cl
Twickenham TW13,
TW2 151 D1
Wallington SM6 219 D1
Court Cres KT9 213 D2
Court Downs Rd
BR3 185 D1
Court Dr
Carshalton SM1 218 C4
Edgware HA7 26 A6
Hillingdon UB10 82 C6
Wallington CR0 220 B4
Courtenay Ave
Harrow HA3 24 A2
Highgate N6 48 C2
Courtenay Dr BR3 186 B1
Courtenay Gdns HA3 24 A1
Courtenay Mews E17 53 A4
Courtenay Pl E17 53 A4
Courtenay Rd
Leyton E11 76 D5
North Cheam KT4,
SM3 216 C5
Penge BR3, SE20 184 D4
Walthamstow E17 52 D5
Courtenay Rd HA9 65 D5
Courtenay Sq SE11 261 A1
Courtenay St
SE11 116 C1 261 A2
Courtens Mews HA7 25 C3
Court Farm Ave
KT19 215 B3
Court Farm Ind Est
TW19 148 B5
Court Farm Rd
Chislehurst SE9 166 A1
Northolt UB5 63 C1
Courtfield Ave HA1 42 D4
Courtfield Cres HA1 42 D4
Courtfield W13 87 C2
Courtfield Gdns
Ealing W13 87 A1
Ruislip HA4 61 D6
South Kensington
SW5 113 D2 255 D3

Courtfield Ho EC1 241 A4
Courtfield Mews
SW7 255 D3
Courtfield Rd
Ashford TW15 170 D4
South Kensington
SW7 114 A2 256 A3
Courtfield Rise BR4 224 B5
Courtgate Cl NW7 27 D4
Court Gdns N7 72 C2
Courthill Rd SE13 142 A1
Courthope Ho
14 Rotherhithe
SE16 118 C3
South Lambeth SW8 270 A3
Courthope Rd
Gospel Oak NW3 70 D4
Greenford UB6 86 B5
Wimbledon SW19 179 A5
Courthope Villas
SW19 179 A3
Court House Gdns
N3 29 C4
Court House Rd N12 29 D4
Court La SE21 161 D4
Courtland Ave
Chingford E4 20 D2
Edgware NW7 11 C1
Redbridge IG1 78 B6
South Norwood
SW16 182 B3
Courtland Gr SE28 124 D6
Courtland Rd E6 100 A6
Courtlands Ave
Hampton TW12 173 B4
Hayes BR2 208 D1
Lee SE12 165 B6
Richmond TW9 132 D3
Courtlands
11 Beckenham
BR3 185 D1
8 Belmont SM2 217 D1
Courtland Sch NW7 11 C2
Courtlands Cl HA4 39 D2
Courtlands Dr KT19 215 D2
Courtlands W5 87 C2
Courtlands Rd KT5 198 C2
Courtlands
Richmond TW10 154 C6
5 Upper Clapton E5 52 B1
Walton-on-T KT12 194 A2
Court Lane Gdns
SE21 161 C4
Courtleet Dr DA8 147 D4
Courtleigh Ave EN4 2 B5
Courtleigh Gdns
NW11 47 A5
Courtleigh 6 NW11 47 B4
Court Lo 11 DA17 125 C1
Courtman Rd N17 33 A3
Court Mans 8 W6 112 A2
Courtmead Cl SE24 161 A5
Court Mead UB5 85 B4
Courtnell St W2 91 C1
Courtney Cl SE19 183 C4
Courtney Cres SM5 218 D1
Courtney Ct N7 72 C3
Courtney Ho
1 Hendon NW4 46 C5
Kensington W14 254 B6
Courtney Pl CR0 220 C5
Courtney Rd
Croydon CR0 220 C5
Islington N7 72 C3
Mitcham SW19 180 C3
Courtney Twrs IG2 57 B3
Courtney Way TW6 126 C2
Court One TW15 149 A1
Court Par HA0 65 B5
Courtrai Rd SE23 163 A5
Court Rd Eltham SE9 166 B4
Southall UB2 107 B1
South Norwood
SE25 205 D6
Uxbridge UB10 60 D4
Court Royal SW15 157 A6
Courtside
Crouch End N8 49 D3
Forest Hill SE23 162 C1
Court St
Bromley BR1 187 A1
3 Stepney E1 96 B2
Court The London N10 49 C5
Ruislip HA4 63 A4
Court Three TW15 149 A1
Court Two TW15 149 A1
Courtville Ho 12 W10 91 A4
Court Way Acton W3 89 A2
Colindale NW9 45 C5
Ilford IG6 57 A6
Twickenham TW1,
TW2 152 D4
Courtway IG8 37 C5
Courtyard Apartments
TW11 174 B5
Courtyard Mews
BR5 190 A3
Courtyard The
Fulham
SW6 135 A4 264 A1
Islington N1 72 B1
Keston BR2 226 A2
Thornton Heath CR0 204 B3
13 Wandsworth
SW18 136 B1
Court Yd SE9 166 B5
Cousin La
EC4 117 B6 252 C5
Cousins Cl 2 UB7 104 A6
Cousins Ct 2 NW9 46 A5
Couthurst Rd SE3 143 B5
Coutts Ave KT9 214 A3
Couzens Ho 8 E3 97 B2
Coval Gdns SW14 132 D1
Coval La SW14 132 D1
Coval Pas SW14 133 A1
Coval Rd SW14 133 A1
Covardale Ct EN3 7 A6
Covelees Wall E6 100 C1
Covell Ct 16 SE8 141 C5
Covent Garden Sta
WC2 94 A1 240 B1
Covent Gdn*
WC2 116 A6 250 B6
Coventry Cl
Kilburn NW6 91 C6
9 Newham E6 100 B1
Coventry Rd
Bethnal Green E1 96 B3
Croydon SE25 206 A5
Ilford IG1 56 D1
Coventry St W1 249 C5
Coverack Cl
Croydon CR0 207 A2
Southgate N14 15 C5
Coverdale Cl HA7 25 B5
Coverdale Gdns
CR0 221 D5
Coverdale Rd
Brondesbury NW2 69 A2
Friern Barnet N11 31 A4
Hammersmith W12 112 B4
Hampstead NW6 68 D1
Coverdales The
IG11 101 B5
Coverham Ho 5
SE4 140 D1
Coverley Cl E1 96 A2
Coverley Point SE11 260 C3
Coverton Rd SW17 180 C5
Coverts Rd KT10 212 D1
Covert The BR6 211 C3
Covert Way EN4 2 A3
Covet Wood Cl BR5 211 D3
Covey Cl SW19 179 D1
Covington Gdns
SW16 182 D3
Covington Way
South Norwood
SW16 182 C3
South Norwood
SW16 182 D3
Cowan Cl E6 100 A2
Cowan Ct 14 NW10 67 B1
Cowan Lo 6 IG8 37 C4
Cowbridge La IG11 78 D1
Cowbridge Rd HA3 44 B5
Cowcross St
EC1 94 D2 241 C4
Cowdenbeath Path
N1 233 C6
Cowden Rd BR6 211 D2
Cowden St SE6 185 C6
Cowdray Hall Royal Coll
of Nursing
W1 93 B1 238 C2
Cowdray Ho 22
SE22 139 C2
Cowdray Rd UB10 83 A6
Cowdrey Cl EN1 5 C3
Cowdrey Rd SW19 180 A5
Cowdry Rd E9 75 B2
Cowell Lo E4 36 D5
Cowen Ave HA2 64 B6
Cowen Ho 4 SE18 144 D6
Cowgate Rd UB6 86 B4
Cowick Rd SW17 180 D6
Cowings Mead UB5 63 A2
Cowland Ave EN3 6 C1
Cow Leaze E6 100 C1
Cowleaze Rd KT2 176 A2
Cowley Ct 8 E18 37 A1
Cowley La E11 76 C5
COWLEY PEACHY 82 A2
Cowley Pl NW4 46 C4
Cowley Rd
Brixton SW9 138 C4
East Acton W3 111 D5
16 Kennington SW9 138 C5
Mortlake SW14 133 C2
Cowley Rd *continued*
Redbridge IG1 56 B2
Wanstead E11 55 B4
Cowley St SW1 260 A5
Cowling Cl W11 244 A4
Cowper Ave
Sutton SM1 218 B4
Upton Pk E6 78 A1
Cowper Cl
Bexley DA16 168 A6
Bromley BR2 209 D5
Cowper Gdns
Southgate N14 15 C5
Wallington SM6 219 C2
Cowper Ho
Pimlico SW1 259 D1
Walworth SE17 262 B2
Cowper Rd
Acton W3 111 B5
6 Belvedere DA17 125 C2
Bromley BR2 209 D5
Ealing W7 108 D6
East Barnet N14 15 B3
Edmonton N18 34 A5
Kingston u T KT2 176 B5
Stoke Newington N16 73 C4
Wimbledon SW19 180 A4
Cowper's Ct EC3 242 D1
Cowper St EC1,
EC2 95 B3 242 D6
Cowper Terr W10 90 D2
Cowslip Cl UB10 60 A1
Cowslip Rd E18 37 B1
Cowthorpe Rd SW8 269 D2
Cox Ct 3 EN4 2 C1
Coxe Pl HA3 43 A5
Cox Ho W6 264 A6
Cox La
Chessington KT9 214 B4
West Ewell KT19 215 A3
Coxmount Rd SE7 121 D1
Coxs Ave TW17 193 C6
Coxson Way SE1 253 C1
Coxwell Rd
Plumstead SE18 123 B1
South Norwood
SE19 183 C3
Coxwold Path KT9 214 A1
Coysh Ct 8 SW15 157 A6
Crabbs Croft Cl 7
BR6 227 A3
Crab Hill BR3 186 B3
Crabtree Ave
Dagenham RM6 58 D5
Wembley HA0 88 B5
Crabtree Cl E2 95 D5
Crabtree Ct Barnet EN5 1 D1
Temple Mills E15 75 D3
Crabtree Hall SW6 134 C5
Crabtree La SW6 134 D5
Cracknell Cl EN1 6 B6
Craddock Rd EN1 5 D2
Craddock St NW5 71 A2
Cradley Rd SE9 167 B3
Cragie Ho SE1 263 D3
Craig Dr UB8 82 D1
Craigen Ave CR0 206 B1
Craigerne Rd SE3 143 B5
Craig Gdns E18 36 D1
Craig Ho Ealing W13 109 B6
Greenwich SE3 143 B5
Craigholm SE18 144 C4
Craigie Lea N10 31 B1
Craigleith SW15 156 D5
Craigmuir Pk HA0 88 B6
Craignair Rd SW2 160 C4
Craignish Ave SW16 182 B1
Craig Park Rd N18 34 B6
Craig Rd TW10 175 C6
Craig's Ct SW1 250 A4
Craigside KT2 176 D2
Craigton Rd SE9 144 B1
Craigweil Cl HA7 25 D5
Craigweil Dr HA7 25 D5
Craigwell Ave
TW13 150 A1
Craik Ct NW6 91 B5
Crail Row
SE17 117 B2 262 D3
Crales Ho SE18 122 A3
Cramer Ct KT3 199 A6
Cramer St W1 93 A2 238 B3
Cramhurst Ho 3
SM1 218 B3
Crammond Cl W6 264 A5
Cramond Ct TW14 149 C3
Cramonde Ct DA16 146 A3
Crampton Rd SE20 184 C4
Crampton Sch
SE17 116 D1 261 D2
Crampton St
SE17 117 A1 262 A2
Cranberry Cl 2 UB5 84 D5
Cranberry La E16 98 C3
Cranborne Ave
Southall UB2 107 C2
Tolworth KT6, KT9 214 C5
Cranborne Rd IG11 101 B6
Cranborne Waye
Hayes UB4 84 B1
Hayes UB4 106 C6
Cranbourn Alley
WC2 249 D6
Cranbourne Cl
SW16 204 A6
Cranbourne Ct
East Finchley N2 47 D6
2 Edgware HA8 26 D5
Finchley NW7 29 A3
SW11 267 B4
Walton-on-T KT12 194 B2
Wanstead E18 55 B5
Cranbourne Dr HA5 40 D4
Cranbourne Gdns
Ilford IG6 57 A6
Temple Fortune
NW11 47 B4
Cranbourne Rd
Leyton E15 76 A4
London N10 31 B1
Manor Pk E12 78 A3
Northwood HA6 39 D6
Cranbourn Ho 6
SE16 118 B4
Cranbourn Pas 5
SE16 118 B4
Cranbourn St
WC2 115 D6 249 D6
CRANBROOK 56 C1
Cranbrook Cl BR2 209 A3
Cranbrook Coll (Boys)
IG1 78 C6
Cranbrook Ct
8 Brentford
TW8 131 D6
South Croydon CR2 221 C3
Cranbrook Dr
Thames Ditton
KT10 196 A1
Twickenham TW2 151 D3
Cranbrook Ho
5 Hackney E5 74 B3
South Norwood
SE19 183 B2
Cranbrook La N11 31 B6
Cranbrook Mews
E17 53 B4
Cranbrook NW1 232 B5
Cranbrook Pk N22 32 C2
Cranbrook Rd
Chiswick W4 111 C1
Erith DA7 147 B4
Hounslow TW4 129 B1
Ilford IG1, IG2 56 C3
New Barnet EN4 14 B5
South Norwood CR7 183 A1
St Johns SE8 141 C4
Wimbledon SW19 179 A3
Cranbrook Rise IG1 56 B2
Cranbrook St E2 96 D5
Cranbury Rd SW6 135 D3
Crandale Ho 8 E5 74 B3
Crandley Ct SE8 119 A2
Crane Ave Acton W3 111 A6
Isleworth TW7 153 A6
Cranebank TW4 128 B2
Cranebank Mews
TW1 131 A1
Cranebrook TW2 152 A2
Crane Cl
Dagenham RM10 81 C2
Harrow HA2 64 A5
Crane Ct
7 Acton W12 111 C4
Holborn EC4 241 B1
West Ewell KT19 215 A4
Craneford Cl TW2 152 D4
Craneford Way
TW2 152 D4
Crane Gdns UB3 105 D2
Crane Gr N7 72 C2
Crane Ho 24 Bow E3 97 A5
9 Catford BR1 186 B5
Feltham TW13 151 C1
10 Peckham SE15 139 D4
Crane Lodge Rd
TW5 128 B6
Crane Mead Ct
TW1 152 D4
Crane Mead SE16 118 D2
Crane Park Prim Sch
TW13 151 B2
Crane Park Rd TW2 151 D2
Crane Rd
Stanwell TW19 148 C5
Twickenham TW2 152 C3
Cranesbill Cl NW9 45 B6
Cranes Dr KT5 198 B5
Cranes Park Ave KT5,
KT6 198 B5
Cranes Park Cres
KT5 198 B5
Cranes Pk KT5, KT6 198 A4
Crane St
Greenwich SE10 120 B1
6 Peckham SE15 139 D4
Craneswater TW6 127 D5
Craneswater Pk
UB2 107 B1
Cranes Way WD6 11 A6
Crane Way TW2 152 A4
Cranfield Ct
Marylebone NW1 237 B3
2 Woodford IG8 37 A6
Cranfield Dr NW9 27 C3
Cranfield Ho WC1 240 B4
Cranfield Rd SE4 141 B2
CRANFORD 128 C4
Cranford Ave
Bowes Pk N13 32 A5
Stanwell TW19 148 B4
Cranford Cl
Stanwell TW19 148 A4
Wimbledon SW20 178 B3
Cranford Com Coll
TW5 128 B6
Cranford Cotts 8
E1 118 D6
Cranford Ct SM1 218 A4
Cranford Dr UB3 105 D2
Cranford Jun & Inf Schs
TW4 128 B3
Cranford La
Harlington TW6 127 D4
Harlington UB3 127 C5
Hatton TW6 127 D2
Heston TW5 128 C5
Cranford Lo SW19 156 D2
Cranford Park Prim Sch
UB3 105 D2
Cranford Park Rd
UB3 105 D2
Cranford Rise KT10 212 A3
Cranford St E1 118 D6
Cranford Way N8 50 C4
Cranhurst Rd NW2 68 C3
Cranleigh Cl
Bexley DA5 169 D5
Penge SE20 184 B1
Cranleigh Ct
1 Barnet EN5 1 D1
Mitcham CR4 202 B6
Richmond TW9 132 C2
Southall UB1 85 B1
4 Stamford Hill N16 51 C1
Cranleigh Gardens Ind
Est UB1 85 B2
Cranleigh Gdns
Barking IG11 79 B2
Harrow HA3 44 A4
Kingston u T KT2 176 B4
Southall UB1 85 B1
Southgate N21 16 C6
South Norwood
SE25 205 C6
Sutton SM1 217 D6
Cranleigh Hos NW1 232 B3
Cranleigh Ho SW20 178 B1
Cranleigh Mews
SW11 136 D3
Cranleigh Rd
Feltham TW13 171 D6
Harringay N15 51 A4
Merton SW19 201 C6
Thames Ditton KT10 196 A1
Cranleigh St
NW1 93 C5 232 B3
Cranleigh W11 244 C4
Cranley Dene Ct N10 49 B5
Cranley Dr Ilford IG2 57 A2
Ruislip HA4 61 D6
CRANLEY GARDENS
49 B5
Cranley Gdns
London N10 49 B5
Palmers Green N13 16 B1
South Kensington
SW7 114 B1 256 C2
Wallington SM6 219 C1
Cranley Mews
SW7 114 A1 256 B2
Cranley Par 2 SE9 188 A6
Cranley Pl
SW7 114 B2 256 C3
Cranley Rd Ilford IG2 57 A2
Newham E13 99 B2
Cranmer Ave W13 109 B3
Cranmer Cl
Ruislip HA4 40 D1
Stanmore HA7 25 C3
West Barnes SM4 200 D3
Cranmer Ct
Chelsea SW3 257 B3
Church End N3 29 A1
Hampton TW12 173 D5
Kingston u T KT2 175 D6
Cranmere Prim Sch
KT10 196 A1
Cranmer Farm Cl
CR4 202 D5
Cranmer Ho SW11 267
Cranmer Prim Sch
CR4 202
Cranmer Rd
Brixton SW9 138
Croydon CR0 221
Edgware HA8 10
Forest Gate E7 77
Hampton TW12 173
Hayes UB3 83
Kingston u T KT2 176
Mitcham CR4 202
Cranmer Terr SW17 180
Cranmore Ave TW7 130
Cranmore Rd
Catford BR1 164
Elmstead BR7 188
Cranmore Way N10 49
Cranston Cl
Hounslow TW3,
TW4 129
Uxbridge UB10 61
Cranston Ct 6 N20 14
Cranston Gdns E4 35
Cranston Rd SE23 163
Cranswick Rd SE16 118
Crantock Rd SE6 164
Cranwell Cl E3 97 D
Cranwell Ct
Croydon CR0 222 D
6 Hendon NW9 27 D
Cranwell Gr TW17 192
Cranwell Rd TW6 126
Cranwich Ave N21 17
Cranwich Rd N16 51 C
Cranwood Ct EC1 235 D
Cranwood St
EC1 95 B4 235 D
Cranworth Cres 7
E4 20 B
Cranworth Gdns
SW9 138 C
Cranworth Ho 6 N7 72 B
Craster Rd SW2 160 B
Craston Ho 2 SE5 139 C
Crathie Rd SE12 165 B
Crathorne Ho N2 30 B
Cravan Ave TW13 150 A
Craven Ave
Ealing W5 109 C
Southall UB1 85 B
Craven Cl Hayes UB4 84 A
Stamford Hill N16 52 A
Craven Cottage (Fulham
FC) SW6 134 D
Craven Ct
Dagenham RM6 59 A
Edgware HA8 26 B
Harlesden NW10 89 C
Southall UB1 107 D
Craven Gdns
Barking IG11 101 C
Ilford IG6 57 B
Wimbledon SW19 179 D
Craven Hill Gdns
W2 114 A6 246 A
Craven Hill Mews
W2 246 B
Craven Hill
W2 114 A6 246 B
Craven Ho
Ealing W5 109 C6
16 Finchley N2 30 B
2 Mortlake SW14 133 B2
Craven Lo
Bayswater W2 246 B
Fulham SW6 134 D4
Craven Mews 6
SW11 137 A2
Craven Park Mews
NW10 89 C6
Craven Park Rd
Harlesden NW10 89 C6
South Tottenham N15 52 A3
Craven Pas WC2 250 A4
Craven Pk NW10 89 C6
Craven Rd
Croydon CR0 206 B1
Ealing W5 109 C6
Kingston u T KT2 176 B2
Paddington
W2 92 A1 236 B1
Stonebridge NW10 89 B6
Craven St
WC2 116 A5 250 A4
Craven Terr
W2 114 A6 246 B6
Craven Wlk E5, N16 52 A2
Crawford Ave HA0 65 D3
Crawford Bldgs
NW1 237 B3
Crawford Cl TW7 130 C3
Crawford Ct SE18 146 A6
Crawford Gdns
Edmonton N13 16 D1
Northolt UB5 85 B4
Crawford Mews W1 237 C3

ford Pas EC1... 241 B5
ford Place
ellings NW1... 237 B3
ford Pl
... 92 C2 237 B3
ford Point 4
... 98 D1
ford Prim Sch
... 139 A4
ford Rd SE5... 139 A3
ford St
ylebone
1... 92 D2 237 C3
Willesden NW10... 67 B1
ley Rd
eld EN1... 17 D4
on E10... 53 D1
enham N22... 33 A1
shay Ct SW9... 138 C4
shay Ho 13 N16... 73 B4
thew Gr SE22... 139 D1
Bldgs DA14... 190 C4
brooke Rd
4... 190 B6
bury End SE9... 167 A2
fields Bsns Pk
... 190 C2
fields Ind Pk
... 190 C1
ford Cl E6... 100 A1
ford Ho
mondsey SE1... 252 D1
Lower Holloway
7... 72 A4
ford Rd N7... 72 A4
ke Hill KT9... 214 A1
e Ho EC1... 241 D6
eigh Terr
4... 190 C4
onne Cl TW16... 171 C2
Rd Erith DA17... 147 C6
cup DA14... 190 C4
Par The BR5... 190 C1
lock Gr IG8... 36 D5
lock St SW18... 157 D5
sy Est SE1... 263 A5
or St SE22... 162 A5
enhall Dr BR2... 210 B1
enhill Ho 2
5... 140 B5
enhill St SW16... 181 C4
iton Hill NW6... 69 D3
iton Ho EN3... 6 D2
iton Rd
ndesbury Pk
W10... 90 D6
wham E16... 99 A1
iton Way KT10... 213 A3
on Rd
mondsey SE16... 118 B1
wham E13... 99 C5
church La EC3... 243 B1
church Pl EC3... 243 B1
d Ct 5 E1... 97 A4
d Ho SE15... 140 B2
d La EC4... 241 D1
k Ho W14... 254 B6
EKMOUTH... 101 D2
kmouth Ind Pk
... 101 D3
k Rd
king IG11... 101 D4
t Molesey KT8... 196 C5
eenwich SE10,
E8... 141 D6
k Road Ind Est
... 141 D6
kside Foyer
... 141 D6
ekside SE8... 141 D5
k The TW16... 194 A4
land Gr SE6... 163 B3
eld Cl
... 135 A6 264 A5
field Rd W3,
... 110 C6
ghton Ave
don N2, N10... 30 D1
wham E6... 99 D5
ghton Cl W12... 112 B6
ghton Ho N2... 48 C6
ghton Rd
ing W5... 109 D3
nsal Rise NW6... 90 D5
tenham N17... 33 C3
ner Bsns Ctr 8
... 95 D5
ner Ho 9 SE8... 141 C5
ner St E2... 95 D5
norne Rd
10... 136 B5 266 C4
n Ct 3 SW9... 138 C4
cent Arc 1
0... 142 A6
cent Court Bsns Ctr
E16... 98 B3

Crescent Ct
Clapham Pk SW4... 159 D6
Crouch End N8... 49 D3
Kingston u T KT6... 197 D4
14 Sidcup DA15... 168 A1
Crescent Dr BR5... 211 A3
Crescent EC3... 253 C6
Crescent E EN4... 2 A5
Crescent Gdns
Ruislip HA4... 40 B2
Wimbledon SW19... 157 C1
Crescent Gr
London SW4... 137 C1
Mitcham CR4... 202 C5
Crescent Ho
London SE13... 141 D3
5 Wimbledon
SW20... 178 D2
Crescent La SW4... 159 D6
Crescent Mans
Islington N5... 72 D3
Notting Hill W11... 244 B6
Crescent Par UB10... 82 C4
Crescent Pl SW3... 257 B4
Crescent Rd
Beckenham BR3... 185 D1
Chingford E4... 20 C4
Church End N3... 29 B2
Crouch End N8... 49 D3
Dagenham RM10... 81 D5
East Barnet EN4... 14 C6
Edmonton N9... 18 A3
Enfield EN2... 4 D1
Friern Barnet N11... 30 D6
Harringay N15... 50 D6
Kingston u T KT2... 176 D3
Leyton E10... 75 D6
Plaistow BR1... 187 A3
Shepperton TW17... 193 A4
Sidcup DA15... 167 D1
Upton Pk E6... 99 C6
West Ham E13... 99 A6
Wimbledon SW20... 178 D2
Woodford E18... 37 C2
Wood Green N22... 31 D2
Woolwich SE18... 122 D2
Crescent Rise
East Barnet EN4... 14 C6
3 Finchley N3... 29 C2
Wood Green N22... 31 D2
Crescent Row EC1... 242 A5
Crescent Stables
SW15... 157 A6
Crescent St N1... 72 B1
Crescent The
Acton W3... 89 C1
Ashford TW15... 170 B5
Barnes SW13... 134 A3
Barnet EN5... 1 D3
Beckenham BR3... 185 C2
Bexley DA5... 168 C4
Coombe KT3... 177 A1
Dollis Hill NW2... 68 B5
East Finchley N2... 47 D6
East Molesey KT8... 195 C5
Friern Barnet N11... 31 A6
Harlington UB7... 127 B5
Harrow HA2... 42 A1
Ilford IG2... 56 C3
Loughton IG10... 21 D5
Lower Halliford
TW17... 193 D2
Sidcup DA14... 189 D6
Southall UB1... 107 A4
Surbiton KT6... 198 A4
Sutton SM1... 218 B3
Thornton Heath CR0... 205 B3
Walthamstow E17... 53 A4
Wembley HA0... 65 B6
West Wickham BR4... 208 C3
Wimbledon SW19... 157 C1
Crescent View IG10... 21 D6
Crescentway N12... 30 C4
Crescent Way
London SE4... 141 C2
Orpington BR6... 227 C3
South Norwood
SW16... 182 C3
Crescent W EN4... 2 A5
Crescent Wood Rd SE21,
SE26... 162 A1
Cresford Rd
SW6... 135 D4 265 C1
Crespigny Rd NW4... 46 B3
Cressage Cl UB1... 85 C3
Cressage Ho 9
TW8... 132 A6
Cressall Ho 14 E14... 119 C3
Cresset Ho 8 E9... 74 C2
Cresset Rd E9... 74 C2
Cresset St SW4... 137 D2
Cressfield Cl NW5... 71 A3
Cressida Rd N19... 49 D1
Cressingham Ct 1
DA17... 125 C3
Cressingham Gr
SM1... 218 A4

Cressingham Rd
Burnt Oak HA8... 27 B3
Lewisham SE13... 142 A2
Cressington Cl 4
N16... 73 C3
Cress Mews BR1... 186 B5
Cresswell Gdns SW5 256 A2
Cresswell Ho HA9... 66 A5
Cresswell Pk SE3... 142 D2
Cresswell Pl
SW10... 114 A1 256 B2
Cresswell Rd
Croydon SE25... 206 A5
Feltham TW13... 173 A6
Twickenham TW1... 153 D5
Cresswell Way N21... 16 C4
Cressy Ct
Hammersmith W6... 112 B3
6 Stepney E1... 96 C2
Cressy Ho SW13... 134 B2
Cressy Hos 7 E1... 96 C2
Cressy Pl E1... 96 C2
Cressy Rd NW3... 70 D4
Cresta Ct W5... 88 B3
Cresta Ho 7 Bow E3... 97 C3
Hampstead NW6... 70 B1
Crestbrook Ave N13... 16 D1
Crestbrook Pl N13... 16 D1
Crest Ct NW4... 46 C4
Crest Dr EN3... 6 C5
Crestfield St N1,
WC1... 233 B2
Crest Gdns HA4... 62 C5
Crest Ho 3 TW15... 170 C5
Creston Way KT4... 200 D1
Crest Rd
Dollis Hill NW2... 68 A6
Hayes BR2... 208 D2
South Croydon CR2... 222 B1
Crest The
Edmonton N13... 32 C6
Finchley N12... 29 D4
Hendon NW4... 46 C4
Surbiton KT5... 198 C4
10 West Norwood
SW27... 182 D5
Crest View Dr BR5... 211 A4
Crestview NW5... 71 B5
Crest View HA5... 40 D5
Crestway SW15... 156 B5
Crestwood Way
TW4... 151 A6
Creswell Dr BR3... 207 D4
Creswick Ct W3... 110 D6
Creswick Rd W3... 110 D6
Creswick Wlk
7 Bow E3... 97 C4
Temple Fortune
NW11... 47 B5
Creton St SE18... 122 C3
Crewdson Rd SW9... 138 C5
Crewe Pl NW10... 89 D4
Crewkerne Ct SW11. 266 D2
Crews St E14... 119 C2
Crewys Rd
Child's Hill NW2... 69 B6
London SE15... 140 B3
Crichton Ave SM6... 219 D4
Crichton Rd SM5... 218 D1
Crichton St SW8... 137 C3
Cricket Ct E6... 100 B4
Cricketers Arms Rd
EN2... 5 A3
Cricketers Cl
Chessington KT9... 213 D4
Oakwood N14... 15 C4
Cricketers Mews 4
SW18... 157 D6
Cricketers Terr
SM5... 218 C5
Cricketers Wlk
SE26... 184 C5
Cricketfield Rd E5... 74 B4
Cricket Gn CR4... 202 D5
Cricket Green Sch
CR4... 202 C6
Cricket Ground Rd
BR7... 188 D2
Cricket La BR3... 185 A4
Cricket Row N2... 48 B6
Cricklade Ave SW2... 160 B2
CRICKLEWOOD... 68 D4
Cricklewood Broadway
NW2... 68 D4
Cricklewood La NW2... 69 B5
Cricklewood Sta
NW2... 68 D4
Cridland St E15... 98 D6
Crieff Ct 3 TW11... 175 C3
Crieff Rd SW18... 158 A5
Criffel Ave SW2... 159 D3
Crimscott St
SE1... 117 C3 263 B5
Crimsworth Rd
SW8... 137 D5 269 D3
Crinan St N1... 94 A5 233 B4

Cringle St
SW8... 137 C5 269 A4
Cripplegate St EC1... 242 B4
Cripps Gn UB4... 84 B3
Crispe Ho
4 Barking IG11... 101 B5
Islington N1... 233 D5
Crispen Rd TW13... 173 A6
Crispian Cl NW10... 67 C4
Crispin Cl SM6... 220 A6
Crispin Cres SM6... 219 D6
Crispin Ct SE17... 263 A3
Crispin Pl E1... 243 C4
Crispin Rd HA8... 27 A4
Crispin St E1... 95 D2 243 C3
Crispin Way UB8... 82 B3
Crisp Rd W6... 112 C1
Cristowe Rd SW6... 135 B3
Criterion Bldgs KT7... 197 B2
Criterion Mews N19... 71 D6
Crittall's Cnr DA14... 190 C3
Crittenden Lo BR4... 207 C1
Crockerton Rd
SW17... 158 D2
Crockham Way SE9... 188 C6
Crocus Cl CR0... 206 D1
Crocus Field EN5... 13 B5
Croft Ave BR4... 208 A1
Croft Cl Edgware NW7... 11 C1
Elmstead BR7... 188 B5
Erith DA17... 125 B1
Harlington UB7... 127 A5
Hillingdon UB10... 60 C1
Croft Ct London SE13... 164 A5
Ruislip HA4... 39 D1
Croftdown Rd NW5... 71 B5
Croft End Cl KT9... 214 B5
Crofters Cl TW7... 152 B6
Crofters Ct 9 SE8... 119 A2
Crofters Way
NW1... 93 D6 232 C6
Croft Gdns
Ealing W7... 109 A4
Ruislip HA4... 39 D1
Croft Ho
Putney SW15... 157 A5
11 West Kilburn W10... 91 A4
Croft Lodge Cl IG8... 37 B4
Croft Mews 3 N12... 14 A1
CROFTON... 227 B6
Crofton Ave
Chiswick W4... 133 B5
Orpington BR6... 227 A6
Sidcup DA5... 168 D4
Crofton Gate Way
SE4... 163 A6
Crofton Gr E4... 36 B6
Crofton Inf Sch BR5... 211 B2
Crofton Jun Sch
BR5... 211 B2
Crofton La BR5, BR6... 211 B2
Crofton L Ctr SE4... 163 C5
Crofton Park Rd
SE4... 163 B5
Crofton Park Sta
SE4... 163 A6
Crofton Rd
Camberwell SE5... 139 C3
Locksbottom BR6... 226 C5
Newham E13... 99 B3
Crofton Roman Villa*
BR6... 227 C6
Crofton Sch SE4... 163 C5
Crofton Terr
Homerton E5... 75 A3
Richmond TW9... 132 B1
Crofton Way
Enfield EN2... 4 C3
New Barnet EN5... 13 D5
Croft Rd
Carshalton SM1... 218 C3
Enfield EN3... 7 A4
Merton SW19... 180 A3
Plaistow BR1... 187 A4
South Norwood
SW16... 182 C3
Crofts Ho 21 E2... 96 A5
Croftside The 3
SE25... 206 A6
Crofts La N22... 32 C3
Crofts Rd HA1... 43 A4
Crofts St E1... 118 A6
Crofts The TW17... 193 C5
Croft St SE8... 119 A2
Croft The Barnet EN5... 1 A1
Chingford E4... 20 C2
Ealing W5... 88 A2
Edgware HA8... 26 D3
Harlesden NW10... 89 D5
Heston TW5... 129 A5
New Malden KT3... 199 C4
Pinner HA5... 41 B2
Ruislip HA4... 62 C4
Wembley HA0... 65 C3
Croft Villas HA1... 43 A3
Croft Way
Richmond TW10... 153 B1

Croft Way *continued*
Sidcup DA15... 167 C1
Crogsland Rd NW1... 71 A1
Croham Cl CR2... 221 C1
Croham Hurst Sch
CR2... 221 D3
Croham Manor Rd
CR2... 221 C2
Croham Mount CR2... 221 C1
Croham Park Ave
CR2... 221 D3
Croham Rd CR2... 221 C3
Croham Valley Rd
CR2... 222 B1
Croindene Rd SW16... 182 A2
Crokesley Ho 2 HA8... 27 A1
Cromartie Rd N19... 49 D2
Cromarty Ct 7 BR1... 187 C1
Cromarty Ho 8 E1... 97 A2
Cromarty Rd HA8... 10 D2
Cromberdale Ct N17... 34 A2
Crombie Cl IG4... 56 B4
Crombie Mews 5
SW11... 136 C3
Crombie Rd DA15... 167 B3
Cromdale Ct N16... 51 D2
Crome Ho UB5... 85 A5
Cromer Cl UB8... 83 A1
Cromer Ct
Streatham SW16... 160 A1
Wandsworth SW18... 157 B5
Crome Rd NW10... 67 C2
Cromer Mans 6
SM1... 217 D3
Cromer Pl 5 BR6... 211 B1
Cromer Rd Barnet EN5... 2 A2
Croydon SE25... 206 B6
Dagenham RM6... 59 A3
Harlington TW6... 126 C3
Leyton E10... 54 B2
Streatham SW17... 181 A4
Tottenham N17... 34 A1
Woodford IG8... 37 A6
Cromer Road Prim Sch
EN5... 2 A2
Cromer St
WC1... 94 A4 233 B1
Cromer Terr
Dalston E8... 74 A3
3 Ilford RM6... 58 B4
Cromer Villas Rd
SW18... 157 B5
Cromford Cl BR6... 227 C5
Cromford Path 1 E5... 74 D4
Cromford Rd SW18... 157 C6
Cromford Way KT3... 177 B2
Cromlix Cl BR7... 188 D1
Crompton Ct SW3... 257 A4
Crompton Ho
Borough The SE1... 262 B5
Paddington W2... 236 C5
South Lambeth SW8... 269 B1
Crompton Pl EN3... 7 C5
Crompton St
W2... 92 B3 236 C5
Cromwell Ave
Bromley BR2... 209 B5
Hammersmith W6... 112 B2
Highgate N6... 49 B1
New Malden KT3... 199 D4
Cromwell Cl
Acton W3... 111 A5
Bromley BR2... 209 B5
East Finchley N2... 48 B5
2 Gunnersbury W4... 110 D1
Walton-on-T KT12... 194 B1
Cromwell Cres
SW5... 113 C2 255 A4
Cromwell Ct
Enfield EN3... 18 D6
15 Kingston u T KT2... 176 C3
Cromwell Ctr
Barking IG11... 102 A4
North Acton NW10... 89 B4
Cromwell Ctr The
RM8... 59 B2
Cromwell Ct HA0... 88 A5
Cromwell Est E10... 53 A1
Cromwell Gdns
SW7... 114 B3 256 D5
Cromwell Gr W6... 112 C3
Cromwell Ho
Battersea SW11... 268 B1
2 Croydon CR0... 220 D5
Muswell Hill N10... 31 B3
Putney SW15... 134 A1
Cromwell Hospl
SW5... 113 D2 255 C4
Cromwell Lo
Barking IG11... 79 C3
40 Bethnal Green E1... 96 C3
Cromwell Mans
SW5... 255 B4
Cromwell Mews
SW7... 256 D4
Cromwell Pl
5 Acton W3... 111 A5

Cromwell Pl *continued*
Highgate N6... 49 B1
Mortlake SW14... 133 A2
South Kensington
SW7... 114 B2 256 D4
Cromwell Rd
Beckenham BR3... 207 A6
Brixton SW9... 138 D4
Feltham TW13... 150 B3
Finchley N3... 30 A2
Hayes UB3... 83 B1
Hounslow TW3... 129 C1
Kingston u T KT2... 176 A2
Muswell Hill N10... 31 A3
South Kensington
SW7... 256 B4
Teddington TW11... 175 A4
Thornton Heath CR0... 205 B2
Upton E7... 77 C1
Walthamstow E17... 54 A4
Walton-on-T KT12... 194 B1
Wembley HA0... 88 A5
Wimbledon SW19... 179 D5
Worcester Pk KT4... 215 C5
Cromwell St TW3... 129 C1
Cromwell Trad Ctr
IG11... 101 C4
Cromwell Twr EC2... 242 B4
Crondace Rd
SW6... 135 C4 265 B1
Crondall Ct 7 N1... 95 C5
Crondall Ho SW15... 156 A3
Crondall Pl 15 N1... 95 C5
Crondall St N1... 95 C5
Crone Ct 5 NW6... 91 B5
Cronin St SE15... 139 D5
CROOKED BILLET... 178 C4
Crooked Billet
Chingford E4... 35 C3
Wimbledon SW19... 178 C4
Crooked Billet Yd 18
E2... 95 C4
Crooked Usage N3... 47 A6
Crooke Rd SE8... 119 A1
Crookham Rd
SW6... 135 B4 264 C1
Crook Log DA6... 146 D1
Crook Log L Ctr
DA7... 146 D2
Crook Log Prim Sch
DA6... 146 D1
Crookston Rd SE9... 144 C2
Croombs Rd E16... 99 C2
Croom's Hill Gr
SE10... 142 A5
Croom's Hill SE10... 142 B5
Cropley Ct N1... 235 C4
Cropley St N1... 95 B5 235 C4
Croppath Rd RM10... 81 C4
Cropthorne Ct W9... 229 B1
Crosbie Ho 20 E17... 53 D6
Crosbie 10 NW9... 27 D1
Crosby Cl TW13... 173 A6
Crosby Ct
Borough The SE1... 252 C2
East Finchley N2... 48 A5
7 New Southgate
N11... 31 B6
Crosby Ho
18 Cubitt Town
E14... 120 A3
Forest Gate E7... 77 A2
Crosby Rd
Dagenham RM10... 103 D6
Upton E7... 77 A2
Crosby Row
SE1... 117 B4 252 C2
Crosby Sq EC3... 243 A2
Crosby Wlk
3 Dalston E8... 73 D2
Streatham SE24... 160 C4
Crosfield Ct 3 W10... 90 D1
Crosfield Ho W11... 244 A5
Crosier Cl SE3... 144 A3
Crosier Rd UB10... 61 A4
Crosier Way HA4... 61 C5
Crosland Pl 5
SW11... 137 A2
Crossbow Ho
Ealing W13... 109 B5
15 Shoreditch N1... 95 C6
Crossbrook Rd SE3... 144 A2
Cross Cl SE15... 140 B3
Cross Ct London SE5... 139 B2
11 Thamesmead
SE28... 124 B6
Cross Deep Gdns
TW1... 152 D2
Cross Deep TW1... 153 A2
Crossfield Rd
Hampstead NW3... 70 B2
London N17... 51 A6
Crossfield St SE8... 141 C5
Crossford St SW9... 138 B3

Crossgate
Edgware HA8 10 C1
Wembley UB6 65 B2
Crossharbour Sta
E14 119 D3
Cross Ho N8 50 B5
Cross Keys Cl
5 Edmonton N9 18 A2
Marylebone W1 238 B3
Cross La
City of London EC3 253 A5
Hornsey N8 50 B5
Cross Lances Rd
TW3 129 D1
Crossland Rd CR7 204 D3
Crosslands Ave
Ealing W5 110 B5
Southall UB2 107 B1
Crosslands Rd KT19 215 B2
Cross La DA5 169 B4
Crossleigh Ct
3 New Cross
SE14 141 B5
Streatham SW16 181 B6
Crosslet St SE17 262 D4
Crosslet Vale SE10 141 D4
Crossley St N7 72 C2
Crossman Hos 19
SW12 160 A4
Crossmead Ave UB6 85 C4
Crossmead SE9 166 B3
Crossmount Ho 13
SE5 139 A5
Crossness Rd IG11 101 D4
Cross Rd Belmont HA3 25 A1
Camberwell SE5 139 C3
Chingford E4 20 C3
Croydon CR0 205 B1
Enfield EN1 5 C1
Feltham TW13 173 A6
Finchley N2 30 C1
Friern Barnet N11 31 B5
Harrow HA1 42 B4
Ilford RM6 58 C2
Keston Mark BR2 226 A6
Kingston u T KT2 176 B3
Merton SW19 179 C3
Romford RM7 59 C6
Sidcup DA14 190 B6
South Harrow HA2 63 D5
Sutton SM1 218 B3
Wood Green N22 32 C3
Cross St
2 Edmonton N18 34 A5
Hampton TW12 174 A5
Islington N1 94 D6 234 D6
Mortlake SW13 133 C2
Crossthwaite Ave SE5,
SE24 139 B1
Crosstrees Ho 7
E14 119 C3
Crosswall
EC3 117 D6 253 C6
Crossway Ct SE4 141 A3
Crossway
Dagenham RM8 80 C5
Ealing W13 87 A3
Enfield EN1 17 C4
Finchley N12 30 B4
Hayes UB3 106 A5
Hendon NW9 45 D5
Kingsland E8, N16 73 C3
Crossway Par N22 32 D3
Crossway
Petts Wood BR5 211 B4
Pinner HA5 22 B1
Ruislip HA4 62 C4
Crossways Acad
SE4 141 A3
Crossways TW16 171 D3
Crossways Par CR2 223 B1
Crossways Rd
Beckenham BR3 207 C5
Mitcham CR4 203 B6
Crossways
South Croydon
CR2 223 B1
Sutton SM2 218 B1
Crossways The
Heston TW5 129 B5
Wembley HA9 66 C6
Crossway SE28 102 D1
Crossway The SE9 165 D2
Cross Way The HA3 24 C1
Crossway The
Hillingdon UB10 82 B5
Tottenham N22 32 D3
Crossway
West Barnes KT3,
SW20 200 C5
Woodford IG8 37 C6
Crosswell Cl TW17 171 A1
Croston St E8 96 A6
Crothall Cl N13 16 B1
Crouch Ave IG11 102 B5
Crouch Cl BR3 185 C4
Crouch Croft SE9 166 C1
CROUCH END 49 D3
Crouch End Hill N8 49 D2
Crouch Hall Ct N19 50 A1
Crouch Hall Rd N8 49 D3
Crouch Hill N4, N8,
N19 50 A2
Crouch Hill Sta N4 50 B2
Crouchmans Cl SE21,
SE26 162 A1
Crouch Rd NW10 67 B1
Crowborough Ct
W13 109 C6
Crowborough Path
WD19 22 D6
Crowborough Rd
SW17 181 A5
Crowden Way SE28 124 C6
Crowder Cl N12 30 A3
Crowder St E1 118 B6
Crowfield Ho N5 73 A4
Crowfoot Cl
Hackney Wick E9 75 B3
Woolwich SE28 123 C5
Crowhurst Cl SW9 138 C3
Crowhurst Ct N17 34 B2
Crowhurst Ho 21
SW9 138 B3
Crowhurst SE25 206 A6
Crowland Ave UB3 105 D2
Crowland Gdns N14 16 A4
Crowland Ho NW8 229 A5
Crowland Prim Sch
N15 52 A4
Crowland Rd
South Norwood
CR7 205 B5
South Tottenham N15 51 D4
Crowlands Ave RM7 59 D3
Crowland Terr N1 73 B1
Crowland Wlk SM4 202 A3
Crow La RM7, RM8 59 D2
Crowley Cres CR0 220 C3
Crowline Wlk 1 N1 73 A2
Crowmarsh Gdns
SE23 162 C4
Crown Arc KT1 175 D1
Crown Bldgs 4 E4 20 B3
Crownbourne Ct
SM1 217 D4
Crown Cl Bow E3 97 C6
Edgware NW7 11 D2
Hampstead NW6 69 D2
Hayes UB3 105 D4
Crown Close Bsns Ctr
12 E3 97 C6
Crown Cl
Walton-on-T
KT12 194 C2
Wood Green N22 32 C2
Crown Ct
Bromley BR1 209 D4
City of London EC4 242 B1
Harrow HA2 42 C1
Lee SE12 165 B5
11 Muswell Hill N10 31 A3
4 Putney SW15 134 D1
St Giles WC2 240 B1
St John's Wood NW8 230 B1
3 Twickenham
TW1 153 B4
Crowndale Ct NW1 232 C4
Crowndale Rd
NW1 93 C5 232 B4
Crown Dale SE19 183 A5
Crowne Ho SE1 252 B3
Crownfield Ave IG2 57 C4
Crownfield Rd E15 76 B4
Crowngate Ho 33 E3 97 B5
Crown Hill CR0 221 A5
Crownhill Rd NW10 89 D6
Crown Ho Ruislip HA4 40 A1
Wembley HA9 66 B3
Woolwich SE18 123 A2
Crown La
Bromley Comm
BR2 209 D4
Chislehurst BR7 189 A2
Merton SM4 201 C6
Crown Lane Gdns
SE27 182 C5
Crown Lane Prim Sch
SE27 182 D5
Crown Lane Spur
BR2 209 D3
Crown La Osidge N14 15 C3
South Norwood SE19,
SW16 182 C5
Crownleigh Ct SW2 160 C6
Crown Lo
Chelsea SW3 257 B3
Finchley N3 29 B1
Crownmead Way
RM7 59 D5
Crown Mews
2 Newham E13 99 C6
9 Stepney E1 96 D2
Crown Mill CR4 202 C4
Crown Office Row
EC4 251 A6
Crown Par
London N14 15 C3
Morden SM4 201 D5
Crown Pas
Kingston u T KT1 175 D1
St James SW1 249 B3
Crown Pl
Broadgate EC2 243 A4
Kentish Town NW5 71 B2
Crown Point Par
SE19 182 D4
Crown Rd Enfield EN1 6 B2
Ilford IG6 57 B5
Kingston u T KT3 177 A2
Morden SM4 201 D5
Muswell Hill N10 31 A3
Ruislip HA4 62 D3
Sutton SM1 217 D4
Twickenham TW1 153 B5
Crown Reach SW1 259 D1
Crown St Acton W3 110 D5
Camberwell SE5 139 A5
Dagenham RM10 81 D2
Harrow HA2 42 C1
Crownstone Ct 1
SW2 160 C6
Crownstone Rd
SW2 160 C6
Crown Terr TW9 132 B1
Crown Trad Ctr
UB3 105 C4
Crowntree Cl TW7 130 D6
Crown Way UB7 104 B5
Crown Wlk HA9 66 B5
Crown Wood La
SE18 144 D3
Crown Woods Sch
SE9 167 A6
Crown Woods Way
SE9 167 B6
Crown Yard TW3 130 A2
Crowshott Ave HA7 25 D2
Crows Rd
Barking IG11 78 D2
Mill Meads E15 98 B4
Crowther Ave TW8 110 A2
Crowther Cl
SW6 135 B6 264 D5
Crowther Rd SE25 206 A5
Crowthorne Cl
SW18 157 B3
Crowthorne Rd W10 90 D1
Croxall Ho KT12 194 C3
Croxden Cl HA8 44 C6
Croxden Wlk SM4 202 A3
Croxford Gdns N22 32 D3
Croxley Cl BR5 190 B1
Croxley Gn BR5 190 B2
Croxley Rd W9 91 B4
Croxted Cl SE21 161 A4
Croxted Rd SE21,
SE24 161 B3
Croxteth Ho 11
SW8 137 D3
Croxton 17 KT1 176 C1
Croyde Ave
Greenford UB6 86 A4
Hayes UB3 105 C2
Croyde Cl DA15 167 B4
Croyden Ct HA0 65 D2
CROYDON 221 B5
Croydon Airport Ind Est
CR0 220 B2
Croydon Coll Annexe
CR0 205 B1
Croydon Coll (Selhurst
Tertiary Ctr) SE25 205 B4
Croydon Coll CR0 221 B6
Croydon Flyover The
CR0 221 A5
Croydon Gr CR0 204 D1
Croydon Ho
Lambeth SE1 251 B2
Thornton Heath CR0 204 B3
Croydon Rd
Bandonhill CR0, SM5,
SM6 219 C5
Beckenham BR3 207 A6
Coney Hall BR2, BR4 224 D5
Harlington TW6 126 D2
Croydon Rd Ind Est
BR3 206 D5
Croydon Rd
Keston Mark BR2, BR4,
BR6 225 C5
Mitcham CR0, CR4 203 C4
Newham E13 98 D3
Penge SE20 184 C2
Waddon CR0 220 B4
Croydon N17 33 B1
Croydon Valley Trade
Pk 2 CR0 204 A2
Croyland Rd N9 18 A3
Croylands Dr KT6 198 A2
Croysdale Ave
TW16 194 A6
Crozier Ho
Blackheath Pk
SE3 143 B2
South Lambeth SW8 270 C3
Crozier Terr E9 74 D3
Crucible Cl RM6 58 B3
Crucifix La
SE1 117 C4 253 A2
Cruden Ho 15 Bow E3 97 B5
11 Camberwell
SE17 138 D6
Cruden St N1 94 D6 234 D5
Cruickshank St WC1 234 A2
Cruikshank Ho NW8 230 B4
Cruikshank Rd E15 76 C3
Crummock Gdns
NW9 45 C4
Crumpsall St SE2 124 C2
Crundale Ave NW9 44 C4
Crunden Rd CR2 221 B1
Crusader Gdns CR0 221 C5
Crusader Ho EC1 241 C5
Crusader Ind Est N4 51 A3
Crusoe Ct E11 76 D5
Crusoe House Sch
N1 95 B4 235 C2
Crusoe Mews N16 73 B6
Crusoe Rd CR4 180 D3
Crutched Friars
EC3 117 C6 253 B6
Crutchfield La KT12 194 B1
Crutchley Rd SE6 164 C2
Crystal Ct SE19 183 D5
Crystal Ctr The 1
HA1 42 D4
Crystal Ho SE18 123 D1
CRYSTAL PALACE 184 A5
Crystal Palace Mus*
SE19 183 D4
Crystal Palace National
Sports Ctr SE20 184 A4
Crystal Palace Par
SE19 183 D5
Crystal Palace Park Rd
SE26 184 B5
Crystal Palace Rd
SE22 162 A6
Crystal Palace Sta
SE19 184 A4
**Crystal Palace Station
Rd** SE19 184 A4
Crystal Terr SE19 183 B4
Crystal View Ct BR1 186 B6
Crystal Way
Dagenham RM8 58 C1
Harrow HA1 42 D4
Crystal Wharf N1 234 D3
Cuba Dr EN3 6 C3
Cuba St E14 119 C4
Cubitt Bldg SW1 258 C1
Cubitt Ho 4 SW4 159 C5
Cubitt Sq UB2 108 A5
Cubitt St WC1 94 B4 233 D1
Cubitt Terr SW4 137 C2
CUBITT TOWN 120 A2
Cubitt Town Jun & Inf
Sch E14 120 A3
Cuckoo Ave W7 86 C3
Cuckoo Dene W7 86 B2
Cuckoo Hall La N9 18 D4
Cuckoo Hall Prim Sch
N9 18 C4
Cuckoo Hill Dr HA5 40 C6
Cuckoo Hill HA5 40 C6
Cuckoo Hill Rd HA5 40 D5
Cuckoo La W7 108 C6
Cuda's Cl KT19 215 D4
Cuddington Ave KT19,
KT4 215 D5
Cuddington Com Prim
Sch KT4 215 D5
Cuddington SE17 262 B4
Cudham La N BR6 227 C1
Cudham St SE6 164 A4
Cudworth Ho SW8 269 B1
Cudworth St E1 96 B3
Cuff Cres SE9 165 D5
Cuffley Ho 3 W10 90 C2
Cuff Point 12 E2 95 D4
Culand Ho SE17 263 A3
Culford Gdns
SW3 114 D2 257 D3
Culford Gr N1 73 C2
Culford Mans SW3 257 D3
Culford Mews N1 73 C2
Culford Rd
Kingsland N1 73 C2
Shoreditch N1 95 C6
Culgaith Gdns EN2 4 A1
Culham Ho
21 Paddington W2 91 C2
Culham Ho *continued*
33 Shoreditch E2 95 D4
Cullen Ho W9 91 B5
Cullen Way NW10 89 A3
Culling Rd SE16 118 C3
Cullington Cl HA3 43 A5
Cullingworth Rd
NW10 68 B3
Culloden Cl 21 SE16 118 A1
Culloden Prim Sch
E14 98 A1
Culloden Rd EN2 4 D3
Cullum St EC3 253 A6
Culmington Mans
W13 109 C6
Culmington Par
W13 109 C6
Culmington Rd
Ealing W13, W5 109 C5
South Croydon CR2 221 A1
Culmore Rd SE15 140 C5
Culmstock Rd
SW11 159 A6
Culpepper Cl N18 34 B5
Culpepper Ct SE11 261 A4
Culross Bldgs NW1 233 A4
Culross Cl N15 51 A5
Culross St
W1 115 A6 248 A5
Culsac Rd KT6 214 A6
Culver Ct SW18 157 D5
Culverden Rd SW12 159 C2
Culver Gr HA7 25 C1
Culverhouse Gdns
SW16 160 B1
Culverhouse WC1 240 C3
Culverin Ct 1 N7 72 B3
Culverlands Cl HA7 25 B6
Culverlands Ct N20 14 B3
Culverley Rd SE6 164 A3
Culvers Ave SM5 218 D6
Culvers House Prim Sch
CR4 203 A1
Culvers Retreat
SM5 218 D6
Culverstone Cl BR2 208 D4
Culvers Way SM5 218 D6
Culvert Ct SW11 137 A3
Culverton Ct 8
DA14 190 A6
Culvert Pl SW11 137 A3
Culvert Rd
London SW11 136 D3
South Tottenham N15 51 C4
Culworth Ho NW8 230 A4
Culworth St NW8 230 A3
Cumber Ho SW18 157 C3
Cumberland Ave
Falconwood DA16 145 D1
Wembley NW10 88 D4
Cumberland Bsns Pk
NW10 88 D4
Cumberland Cl
Dalston E8 73 D2
2 Twickenham
TW1 153 B5
8 Wimbledon
SW20 178 D3
Cumberland Cres
W14 254 B4
Cumberland Ct
4 Croydon CR0 205 B1
7 Finchley N3 29 B1
Harrow HA1 42 C6
Marylebone W1 237 D1
Woodford IG8 37 B3
Cumberland Dr
Chessington KT9 214 B5
Erith DA7 147 A5
Hinchley Wood KT10 213 A6
Cumberland Gate
W1 114 D6 247 D6
Cumberland Gdns
Church End NW4 29 A1
Finsbury WC1 234 A2
Cumberland Ho
Edmonton N9 18 C3
Kingston u T KT2 176 D3
Paddington W9 236 A5
1 Putney SW15 156 C4
Woolwich SE28 123 B4
Cumberland Mans
Marylebone W1 237 C2
7 West Hampstead
NW6 69 C3
Cumberland Market
NW1 93 B4 231 D2
Cumberland Mills Sq
E14 120 B1
Cumberland Park Ind
Est NW10 90 A4
Cumberland Pk W3 111 A6
Cumberland Pl
Catford SE6 164 D3
Regent's Pk NW1 231 C2
Sunbury TW16 194 A5
Cumberland Rd
Acton W3
Ashford TW15
Barnes SW13
Beckenham BR2
Croydon SE25
Edmonton N9
Hanwell W7
Harrow HA1
Higham Hill E17
Manor Pk E12
Newham E13
Richmond TW9
Stanmore HA7, HA8
Wood Green N22
Cumberland Sch E13
Cumberland St
SW1 115 B1
**Cumberland Terrace
Mews** NW1
Cumberland Terr
NW1
Cumberland Villas
W3
Cumberland Wharf 12
SE16
Cumberlow Ave
SE25
Cumbernauld Gdns
TW16
Cumberton Rd N17
Cumbrae Gdns KT6
Cumbrian Gdns NW2
Cuming Mus* SE17
Cumming St N1
Cumnor Cl 23 SW9
Cumnor Gdns KT17
Cumnor Rd SM2
Cunard Cres N21
Cunard Pl EC3
Cunard Rd NW10
Cunard Wlk 3
SE16
Cundy Rd E16
Cundy St
SW1 115 A2
Cunliffe Rd KT19
Cunliffe St SW16
Cunningham Cl
Dagenham RM6
West Wickham BR4
Cunningham Ct
Harrow HA1
Paddington W2
Cunningham Ho 16
SE5
Cunningham Pk HA1
Cunningham Pl
NW8 92 B3
Cunningham Rd N15
Cunnington St W4
Cupar Rd SW11
Cupola Cl BR1
Cureton St
SW1 115 D2
Curie Gdns NW9
Curie Ho 1 HA9
Curlew Cl SE28
Curlew Ct KT6
Curlew Ho
Brockley SE4
Enfield EN3
7 Peckham SE15
Curlew St
SE1 117 D4
Curlew Way UB4
Curness St SE13
Curnick's La SE27
Curran Ave
Bexley DA15
Hackbridge SM6
Curran Ho SW3
Currey Rd UB6
Curricle St W3
Currie Hill Cl SW19
Currie Ho 13 SW12
Curry Rise NW7
Cursitor St
EC4 94 C1
Curtain Pl EC2
Curtain Rd
EC2 95 C3
Curthwaite Gdns
EN2
Curtis Dr W3
Curtis Field Rd
SW16
Curtis Ho
7 London N11
Walworth SE17
Curtis La HA0
Curtis Rd
Twickenham TW4
West Ewell KT19
Curtis St
SE1 117 D2

tis Way
rmondsey SE1 263 C4
Thamesmead
SE28 124 B6
lington Ho 3
8 27 A1
e Bldg The SE4 163 B6
e The
ling W5 109 D4
epherd's Bush
W12 112 A6
wen Ave E7 77 B4
wen & New Acad
ll* W1 239 C3
wen Prim Sch
3 99 A5
wen Rd W12 112 A4
zon Ave
field EN3 18 D6
anmore HA7 25 A2
zon Cl BR6 227 B4
zon Cres
rking IG11 101 D4
llesden NW10 67 C1
zon Ct SE9 167 A1
zon Gate W1 248 B3
zon Ho W5 87 B3
zon Pl HA5 40 C4
zon Rd Ealing W5 87 B3
uswell Hill N10 31 B1
ornton Heath CR7 204 C3
zon Sq W1 248 B3
zon St
1 115 B5 248 C4
ack Cl TW1 174 D6
stance Ho N1 235 C3
stance St N1 235 C2
STOM HOUSE 121 C6
stom House
3 117 C6 253 A5
stom House for
xCeL Sta E16 121 B6
stom House Reach
16 119 B3
bush Ho N7 71 D3
combe Rd SE5 139 A3
hberga Cl IG11 79 A1
hbert Gdns
25 205 C6
hbert Harrowing Ho
1 242 A5
hbert Ho W2 236 C4
hbert Rd
oydon CR0 220 D6
Edmonton N18 34 A6
althamstow E17 54 A6
hbert St W2 236 C5
hill Wlk 3 SE5 139 B4
lers Gdns Arc
2 243 B2
lers Gdns EC2 243 B2
lers Sq E14 119 C2
ler St EC2 243 B2
The SE1 116 C4 251 B2
ty Sark Ho 10
4 119 D2
tty Sark Ret
evelopment
10 142 A6
ty Sark* SE10 142 A6
tty Sark Sta SE10 142 A6
ton BR5 211 A4
ton Cl DA6 169 A6
ton Ho SE17 263 B2
lamen Cl 4
W12 173 C4
lamen Way
19 215 A3
lops Mews 12
4 119 C2
gnet Ave TW14 150 D4
gnet Cl NW10 67 B3
gnet Ct EN3 7 A4
gnet Ho
arrow HA7 24 D4
John's Wood NW8 229 A6
gnet House N 18
4 97 D1
gnet House S 19
4 97 D1
gnet St E1 243 D6
gnets The TW13 173 A6
gnet Way UB4 84 D2
gnus Bsns Ctr
W10 67 D2
mbeline Ct 6 HA1 42 D3
na Ct 5 E11 55 A3
nthia St N1 233 D3
ntra Pl 8 E8 74 B1
press Ave
ndon N2 47 D6
vickenham TW2 152 A4
press Cl 9 E5 74 A6
press Ct
eam SM1 217 C2
Leyton E11 76 B4

Cypress Ct *continued*
7 West Norwood
SW16 182 C5
Cypress Gdns SE4 163 A6
Cypress Ho SE14 140 D4
Cypress Inf Sch
SE25 183 C1
Cypress Jun Sch
SE25 183 C1
Cypress Lo SE25 183 C1
Cypress Pl W1 239 B5
Cypress Rd
Harrow HA3 24 B1
South Norwood
SE25 183 C1
Cypress Tree Cl
DA15 167 D3
CYPRUS 122 C6
Cyprus Ave N3 29 A1
Cyprus Cl N4 50 C3
Cyprus Ct 9 N3 29 B1
Cyprus Gdns N3 29 A1
Cyprus Ho 10 N3 29 B1
Cyprus Pl
23 Bethnal Green
E2 96 C5
Newham E6 122 C6
Cyprus Rd
Church End N3 29 B1
Edmonton N9 17 D2
Cyprus Sta E6 122 C6
Cyprus St E2 96 C5
Cyrena Rd SE22 161 D6
Cyril Jackson Prim Sch
(North Bldg) E14 119 B6
Cyril Jackson Prim Sch
(South Bldg) E14 119 B6
Cyril Lo 2 DA14 190 A6
Cyril Mans SW11 267 D1
Cyril Rd DA7 147 A3
Cyril Smith Ho N13 32 B5
Cyril Thatcher Ho
SW6 265 B1
Cyrus Ho EC1 241 D6
Cyrus St EC1 94 D3 241 D6
Czar St SE8 141 C6

D

Dabbs Hill La UB5 63 C3
Dabb's La EC1 241 B5
Dabin Cres SE10 142 A4
Dacca St SE8 141 B6
Dace Rd E3 97 C6
Dacre Cl UB6 85 D5
Dacre Gdns
Borehamwood
WD6 11 B6
Lewisham SE13 142 C1
Dacre Ho SW3 266 D5
Dacre Pk SE13 142 C1
Dacre Pl SE13 142 C2
Dacre Rd
Leytonstone E11 54 D1
Newham E13 99 B6
Thornton Heath CR0 204 A2
Dacres Rd SE23 162 D1
Dacre St
SW1 115 D3 259 C6
Dade Way UB2 107 B1
Daerwood Cl BR2 210 B1
Daffodil Cl CR0 206 D1
Daffodil Gdns IG1 78 D3
Daffodil Pl 7 TW12 173 C4
Daffodil St W12 111 D6
Dafforne Rd SW17 159 A1
DAGENHAM 81 D1
Dagenham Ave
Dagenham RM9 81 B1
Dagenham RM9 103 A6
Dagenham Dock Sta
RM9 103 B5
Dagenham East Sta
RM10 81 D3
Dagenham Heathway
Sta RM9 81 B2
Dagenham Park Com
Sch RM10 103 D6
Dagenham Rd
Dagenham RM10 81 D4
London E10 53 B1
Dagger La WD23 9 A6
Dagmar Ave HA9 66 B4
Dagmar Ct
Cubitt Town E14 120 A3
South Tottenham N15 51 B5
Dagmar Gdns NW10 90 D5
Dagmar Mews UB2 107 A3
Dagmar Pas N1 234 D6
Dagmar Rd
Camberwell SE5 139 C4
Finsbury Pk N4 50 C2
4 Kingston u T KT2 176 C3
Southall UB2 107 A3
South Norwood
SE25 205 C4

Dagmar Rd *continued*
West Green N15 51 B5
Wood Green N22 31 D2
Dagmar Terr
N1 94 D6 234 D6
Dagnall Pk SE25 205 C4
Dagnall Rd SE25 205 C4
Dagnall St
SW11 137 A4 268 A1
Dagnan Rd SW12 159 C4
Dagobert Ho 27 E1 96 C2
Dagonet Gdns BR1 165 A1
Dagonet Rd BR1 165 A1
Dahlia Gdns
Ilford IG1 78 D2
Mitcham CR4 203 D5
Dahlia Rd SE2 124 B2
Dahomey Rd SW16 181 C4
Daiglen Sch The IG9 21 C2
Daimler Ho 8 E3 97 C3
Daimler Way SM6 220 A1
Daines Cl E12 78 B5
Dainford Cl BR1 186 B5
Dainton Cl 1 BR1 187 B2
Dainton Ho 22 W2 91 C2
Daintry Cl HA3 43 A5
Daintry Way E9 75 B2
Dairsie Ct 3 BR1 187 C1
Dairsie Rd SE9 144 C2
Dairy Cl Bromley BR1 187 B3
South Norwood CR7 183 A1
Willesden NW10 90 A6
Dairy La SE18 122 B2
Dairyman Cl NW2 69 A5
Dairy Meadow Prim Sch
UB2 107 B3
Daisy Cl CR0 206 D1
Daisy Dormer Ct 11
SW9 138 B1
Daisy Ho IG3 58 A1
Daisy La SW6 135 C2
Daisy Rd Newham E16 98 C3
Woodford E18 37 B1
Dakin Pl 9 E1 97 A2
Dakota bldg 6
SE13 141 D4
Dakota Cl SM6 220 B1
Dakota Gdns
Newham E6 100 A3
Northolt UB5 85 A4
Dalberg Rd SW2 160 C6
Dalberg Way SE2 124 D3
Dalby Ho 6 SW9 138 B1
Dalby Rd SW18 136 A1
Dalbys Cres N17 33 C4
Dalby St NW5 71 B2
Dalcross Rd TW4,
TW5 129 A3
Dale Ave
Edgware HA8 26 B1
Hounslow TW4 129 A2
Dalebury Rd SW17 158 D2
Dale Cl
Blackheath Pk
SE3 143 A2
New Barnet EN5 13 D5
Pinner HA5 22 B2
Dale Croft N4 73 A5
Dale Ct
Cranley Gdns N8 49 C5
3 Kingston u T KT2 176 B3
Northolt UB5 63 B1
Wembley HA0 65 D4
Woodford E18 37 A1
Dale Dr UB4 83 D4
Dalefield IG9 21 D3
Dale Gdns IG8 37 B6
Dale Green Rd N11 15 B1
Dale Gr N12 30 A5
Dalehaed NW1 232 A3
Daleham Dr UB8 82 D1
Daleham Gdns NW3 70 B2
Daleham Mews NW3 70 B2
Dale Ho London SE4 141 A1
St John's Wood NW8 229 A6
Dale Lo N6 49 C3
Dalemain Ho 5
SW8 137 D3
Dalemain Mews 12
E16 121 A5
Dale Park Ave SM5 218 D6
Dale Park Rd SE19 183 B2
Dale Rd
Ashford TW16 171 D3
Camberwell SE17 138 D6
Cheam SM1 217 B4
Gospel Oak NW5 71 A3
Southall UB6 85 D2
Walton-on-T KT12 193 D2
Dale Row W11 91 A1
Daleside Rd
Streatham SW17 181 B5
West Ewell KT19 215 B2
Dales Path WD6 11 B6
Dales Rd WD6 11 B6
Dale St W4 111 C1
Dale The BR2 225 D4

Dale View Ave E4 20 A2
Dale View Cres E4 20 A1
Dale View Gdns E4 20 B1
Daleview Rd N15 51 C3
Dalewood Gdns
KT4 216 B6
Dale Wood Rd BR6 211 C1
Daley Ho 6 W12 90 B1
Daley St E9 74 D2
Daley Thompson Way
7 SW8 137 B2
Dalgarno Gdns W10 90 C2
Dalgarno Way W10 90 C3
Daling Way E3 97 A5
Dalkeith Ct SW1 259 D3
Dalkeith Gr HA7 26 A5
Dalkeith Ho 6 SW9 138 D4
Dalkeith Rd
Ilford IG1 79 A5
West Norwood SE21 161 A4
Dallas Ct SM3 217 A2
Dallas Rd
Cheam SM3 217 A2
Ealing W5 88 B2
Forest Hill SE26 162 B1
Hendon NW4 46 A2
Dallas Terr UB3 105 D3
Dallega Cl UB3 105 B6
Dallinger Rd SE12 164 D5
Dalling Rd W6 112 B2
Dallington Sch
EC1 94 D3 241 D6
Dallington St
EC1 94 D3 241 D6
Dallin Rd
Bexley DA6 146 D1
Woolwich SE18 144 D5
Dalmain Prim Sch
SE23 163 A3
Dalmain Rd SE23 162 D3
Dalmally Pas CR0 205 D2
Dalmally Passage
CR0 205 D3
Dalmally Rd CR0 206 A2
Dalmeny Avenue Est 3
N7 71 D4
Dalmeny Ave
Thornton Heath
SW16 182 C1
Tufnell Pk N7 71 D4
Dalmeny Cl HA0 65 C2
Dalmeny Cres TW3 130 B1
Dalmeny Ct 4 SW4 138 A3
Dalmeny Rd
Erith DA8 147 D4
New Barnet EN5 14 A5
North Cheam KT4 216 B5
Tufnell Pk N7 71 D4
Wallington SM5 219 A1
Dalmeyer Rd NW10 67 D2
Dalmore Ave KT10 212 D2
Dalmore Rd SE21 161 A2
Dalrymple Cl N14 15 D4
Dalrymple Rd SE4 141 A1
DALSTON 74 A2
Dalston Gdns HA7 26 A1
Dalston Jct E8 73 D2
Dalston Kingsland Sta
E8 73 D3
Dalston La E8 74 A3
Dalton Ave CR4 180 C1
Dalton Cl Hayes UB4 83 B3
Orpington BR6 227 C5
Dalton Ho
7 Balham SW12 159 B4
10 Bow E3 97 A5
18 Deptford SE14 140 D6
Merton SW19 180 A2
Stanmore HA7 25 B5
Dalton St SE27 160 D1
Daltry Ho HA1 42 D5
Dalwood St SE5 139 C4
Daly Ct E15 76 A3
Daly Dr BR1 210 C6
Dalyell Rd SW9 138 B2
Damascene Wlk
SE21 161 A3
Damask Cres E16 98 C3
Damask Ct SM1 201 D1
Damer Ho 9 TW10 154 B5
Damer Terr SW10 266 B3
Dames Rd E7 77 A5
Dame St N1 95 A5 235 A4
Damien Ct 12 E1 96 B1
Damien St E1 96 B1
Damon Cl DA14 168 B1
Damon Ct DA14 168 B1
Damon Ho 2 N12 30 B5
Damory Ho 1 SE16 118 C2
Damson Dr UB3 106 A6
Damsonwood Rd
UB2 107 C3
Danbrook Rd SW16 182 A3
Dan Bryant Ho 5
SW12 159 C4
Danbury Cl RM6 58 D6

Danbury Mans 3
IG11 78 D1
Danbury Mews SM5,
SM6 219 B4
Danbury St
N1 94 D5 234 D4
Danbury Way IG8 37 C4
Danby Ct EN2 5 A2
Danby Ho
23 Hackney E9 74 C1
3 West Kilburn W10 91 B4
Danby St SE15 139 D2
Dancastle Ct 7 N3 29 C2
Dancer Rd
Fulham
SW6 135 B4 264 C1
Richmond TW9 132 C2
Dando Cres SE3 143 B2
Dandridge Cl SE10 120 D1
Dandridge Ho E1 243 C4
Danebury Ave
SW15 155 D5
Danebury
New Addington
CR0 223 D2
18 North Kensington
W10 90 C2
Daneby Rd SE6 164 A2
Dane Cl
Farnborough BR6 227 B3
Sidcup DA5 169 C4
Danecourt Gdns
CR0 221 D5
Danecroft Rd SE24 161 B6
Daneglen Ct 18 HA7 25 C5
Danegrove Prim Sch
EN4 14 C5
Danegrove Sch EN4 14 D5
Danehill Wlk DA14 168 A1
Dane Ho
15 London SE5 139 A3
Upper Tooting
SW17 180 A6
Danehurst TW8 131 C5
Danehurst Gdns IG4 56 B4
Danehurst St
SW6 135 A4 264 A2
Daneland EN4 14 D5
Danemead Gr UB5 63 D3
Danemere St SW15 134 C2
Dane Pl E3 97 B5
Dane Rd
Ashford TW15 171 B4
Ealing W13 109 C5
Ilford IG1 79 A3
Lower Edmonton N18 18 C1
Merton SW19 180 A2
Southall UB1 107 A6
Danesbury Rd
TW13 150 B3
Danescombe SE12 165 A3
Danescourt Cres
SM1 218 A6
Danescroft Ave NW4 46 D4
Danescroft Gdns
NW4 46 D4
Danescroft
Hendon NW4 46 D4
3 North Finchley
N12 30 A5
Danes Ct
Primrose Hill NW8 230 C5
Wembley HA9 66 D5
Danesdale Rd E9 75 A2
Danesfield SE5 139 C6
Danes Gate HA1 42 C6
Danes Ho 10 W10 90 C2
Dane St WC1 240 C3
Daneswood Ave
SE6 164 A1
Danethorpe Rd HA0 65 D2
Danetree Cl KT19 215 A1
Danetree Jun Sch
KT19 215 A1
Danetree Rd KT19 215 A1
Danette Gdns RM8 81 B6
Daneville Rd SE5 139 B4
Danford Ho 9 N11 31 C5
Dangan Rd E11 55 A3
Daniel Almshouse
NW4 46 B5
Daniel Bolt Cl E14 97 D2
Daniel Cl London N18 34 C6
Twickenham TW4 151 B4
Upper Tooting
SW17 180 C4
Daniel Ct Acton W3 111 C6
3 Beckenham BR3 185 C3
7 Edgware HA8 26 D5
10 Hendon NW9 27 C2
Daniel Gdns SE15 139 D5
Daniel Ho 1 HA5 22 C1
Daniell Ho N1 235 D4
Daniell Way CR0 204 B1
Daniel Pl NW4 46 B2
Daniel Rd W5 110 B6
Daniel's Rd SE15 140 C2

Dan Leno Wlk SW6 265 C3
Dansey Pl W1 249 C6
Dansington Rd
DA16 146 A1
Danson Cres DA16 146 B2
Danson House*
DA6 146 C1
Danson Intc DA5 168 C5
Danson La DA16 146 B1
Danson Mead DA16 146 C2
Danson Prim Sch
DA16 146 A1
Danson Rd DA5 168 D6
Danson Underpass
DA5 168 C5
Dante Pl SE11 261 D3
Dante Rd
SE11 116 D2 261 C4
Danube Ct 13 SE15 139 D5
Danube St
SW3 114 C1 257 B2
Danvers Ho 35 E1 96 A1
Danvers Rd N8 49 D5
Danvers St
SW3 136 B6 266 D5
Da Palma Ct SW6 265 A5
Daphne Ct Ealing W5 87 C1
Wembley HA0 65 D3
Worcester Pk KT4 215 C6
Daphne Gdns E4 20 A1
Daphne Ho N22 32 C2
Daphne St SW18 158 A5
Daplyn St 6 E1 96 A2
D'arblay St
W1 93 C1 239 B1
Darby Cres TW16 172 C1
Darby Gdns TW16 172 C1
Darcy Ave SM6 219 C4
Darcy Cl N20 14 B2
D'arcy Dr HA3 43 D5
D'arcy Gdns
Dagenham RM9 103 B6
Harrow HA3 44 A5
Darcy Ho E8 96 B6
D'arcy Pl BR2 209 A5
D'arcy Rd SM3 216 D4
Darcy Rd
Isleworth TW7 131 A4
Thornton Heath
SW16 182 A1
Dare Ct 2 E10 54 A2
Dare Gdns RM8 81 A5
Darell Prim Sch
TW9 132 C2
Darell Rd TW9 132 C2
Daren Ct N7 72 A4
Darent Ho
4 Catford BR1 186 B5
Lisson Gr NW8 236 D4
Darenth Rd
Stamford Hill N16 51 D1
Welling DA16 146 A4
Darfield NW1 232 A5
Darfield Rd SE4 163 B6
Darfield Way W10 90 D1
Darfur St SW15 134 D2
Dargate Cl SE19 183 D3
Darien Ho
17 London SW11 136 B2
11 Stepney E1 96 D2
Darien Rd SW11 136 B2
Daring Ho 23 E3 97 A5
Darland Ho SE9 167 B5
Darlands Dr EN5 12 D6
Darlan Rd
SW6 135 B5 264 D3
Darlaston Rd SW19 179 A3
Darley Cl CR0 207 A3
Darley Dr KT3 177 B1
Darley Gdns SM4 201 D3
Darley Ho SE11 260 C1
Darley Rd
Clapham SW11 158 D5
Edmonton N9 17 D3
Darling Ho 12 TW1 153 D5
Darling Rd SE4 141 C2
Darling Row E1 96 B3
Darlington Ct 8
SE6 164 D3
Darlington Ho
South Lambeth
SW8 269 D3
2 Surbiton KT6 197 D2
Darlington Rd SE27 182 D5
Darmaine Cl CR2 221 A1
Darnall Ho 4 SE10 142 A4
Darnay Ho 5 SE16 118 A3
Darndale Cl E17 35 B1
Darnell Ho 9 SE10 142 A5
Darnley Ho 7 E14 97 A1
Darnley Rd
Hackney E9 74 C2
Woodford IG8 37 B2

Darnley Terr 12
W11 ... 112 D5
Darrell Ct BR2 ... 208 C6
Darrell Rd SE22 ... 162 A6
Darren Cl N4 ... 50 B2
Darrick Wood Ho
BR6 ... 227 A5
Darrick Wood Inf Sch
BR6 ... 226 D5
Darrick Wood Jun Sch
BR6 ... 226 D4
Darrick Wood Rd
BR6 ... 227 B6
Darrick Wood Sch
BR6 ... 226 D5
Darrick Wood Sports
Ctr BR6 ... 227 A5
Darris Cl UB4 ... 85 A3
Darsley Dr
SW8 ... 138 A4 270 A2
Dartford Ave N9 ... 18 D5
Dartford Gdns RM6 ... 58 B4
Dartford Ho SE1 ... 263 D4
Dartford St SE17 ... 139 A6
Dartington Ho
Bayswater W2 ... 91 D2
7 London SW8 ... 137 D3
Dartington NW1 ... 232 B5
Dartle Ct 23 SE16 ... 118 A4
Dartmoor Wlk 18
E14 ... 119 C2
Dartmouth Cl W11 ... 91 C1
Dartmouth Ct SE10 ... 142 A4
Dartmouth Gr SE10 ... 142 A4
Dartmouth Hill
SE10 ... 142 A4
Dartmouth Ho
Dartmouth Pk N19 ... 71 B6
11 Kingston u T KT2 ... 176 A2
Lewisham SE10 ... 142 A3
Thornton Heath CR0 ... 204 D2
DARTMOUTH PARK ... 71 B5
Dartmouth Park Ave
NW5 ... 71 B5
Dartmouth Park Hill
N19 ... 71 B6
Dartmouth Park Rd
NW5 ... 71 B5
Dartmouth Pl
Chiswick W4 ... 133 C6
Forest Hill SE23 ... 162 C2
Dartmouth Rd
Brondesbury NW2 ... 68 D2
Forest Hill SE23,
SE26 ... 162 C1
Hayes BR2 ... 209 A2
Hendon NW4 ... 46 A3
Ruislip HA4 ... 62 A5
Dartmouth Row
SE10 ... 142 A4
Dartmouth St
SW1 ... 115 D4 249 D1
Dartmouth Terr
SE10 ... 142 B4
Dartnell Rd CR0 ... 205 D2
Darton Ct W3 ... 111 A5
Dartrey Twr SW10 ... 266 C4
Dartrey Wlk
SW10 ... 136 A5 266 B4
Dart St W10 ... 91 B4
Darville Rd N16 ... 73 D5
Darwell Cl E6 ... 100 C5
Darwen Pl E2 ... 96 B6
Darwin Cl
Farnborough BR6 ... 227 B3
New Southgate N11 ... 15 B1
Darwin Ct
Eltham SE9 ... 166 C5
Newham E13 ... 99 B4
Primrose Hill NW1 ... 231 B6
Darwin Dr UB1 ... 85 D1
Darwin Gdns WD19 ... 22 C5
Darwin Ho
8 London SE13 ... 142 A3
2 Wembley HA9 ... 67 A5
Darwin Rd
Ealing W5 ... 109 C2
Falconwood DA16 ... 145 D2
Tottenham N22 ... 32 D1
Darwin St
SE17 ... 117 B2 262 D4
Daryngton Dr UB6 ... 86 C5
Daryngton Ho SW8 ... 270 A3
Dashwood Cl DA6 ... 169 C6
Dashwood Ct TW3 ... 130 A1
Dashwood Ho SE21 ... 161 D1
Dashwood Rd N8 ... 50 B3
Dassett Rd SE27 ... 182 D5
Data Point Bsns Ctr
E16 ... 98 B3
Datchelor Pl 14 SE5 ... 139 B4
Datchet Ho NW1 ... 231 D2
Datchet Rd SE6 ... 163 B2
Datchett Ho 40 E2 ... 95 D4
Datchwood Ct N4 ... 73 A5
Datchworth Ct 7
EN1 ... 17 C6
Datchworth Ho 8
N1 ... 72 D1
Date St SE17 .. 117 B1 262 C1
Daubeney Gdns N17 ... 33 A3
Daubeney Pl TW12 ... 173 D1
Daubeney Prim Sch
E5 ... 75 A4
Daubeney Rd
Clapton Pk E5 ... 75 A4
Tottenham N17 ... 33 A3
Daubeney Twr 2
SE8 ... 119 B1
Dault Rd SW18 ... 158 A5
Dauney Ho SE1 ... 251 C1
Dauphine Ct HA3 ... 24 C1
Dave Adams Ho 8
E3 ... 97 B5
Davenant Ho 20 E1 ... 96 A2
Davenant Rd
Croydon CR0,
CR9 ... 220 D4
Upper Holloway N19 ... 71 D6
Davenant St E1 ... 96 A2
Davenport Cl TW11 ... 175 A4
Davenport Ctr IG11 ... 102 B5
Davenport Ho SE11 ... 261 A5
Davenport Lo TW3 ... 129 A5
Davenport Mews 6
W12 ... 112 B5
Davenport Rd
London SE6 ... 164 A5
Sidcup DA14 ... 169 A2
Daventer Dr HA7 ... 24 D3
Daventry Ave E17 ... 53 C3
Daventry St
NW1 ... 92 C2 237 A4
Dave Porter Hts
SW19 ... 157 A4
Dave Ramsey Ho
SE18 ... 123 B2
Daver Ct
Chelsea SW3 ... 257 B1
Ealing W5 ... 87 D3
Davern Cl SE10 ... 120 D2
Davey Cl
Bowes Pk N13 ... 32 B5
Islington N7 ... 72 B2
Davey Ho HA9 ... 67 A6
Davey Rd E9 ... 75 C1
Davey's Ct WC2 ... 250 A6
Davey St SE15 ... 139 D6
David Ave UB6 ... 86 C5
David Beckham Acad
The SE10 ... 120 D4
David Cl UB3 ... 127 C5
David Coffer Ct
DA17 ... 125 D2
David Ct N20 ... 14 A1
David Devine Ho 7
E8 ... 74 A3
David Game Coll
SW7 ... 256 C3
Davidge Ho SE1 ... 251 B1
Davidge St
SE1 ... 116 D4 251 D1
David Henry Waring Ct
TW14 ... 149 A3
David Hewitt Ho 2
E3 ... 97 D2
David Ho
8 Putney SW15 ... 156 A6
South Lambeth SW8 ... 270 A4
South Norwood
SE25 ... 206 A6
David Lee Point 4
E15 ... 98 C6
David Livingstone Prim
Sch CR7 ... 183 A2
David Mews W1 ... 237 D4
David Rd RM8 ... 81 A6
Davidson Gdns
SW8 ... 138 A5 270 A4
Davidson Ho 7 N19 ... 71 C4
Davidson Lo CR0 ... 205 C2
Davidson Prim Sch
CR0 ... 205 D2
Davidson Rd CR0 ... 205 D3
Davidson Terrs E7 ... 77 B3
David's Rd SE23 ... 162 C3
David St E15 ... 76 B3
David Twigg Cl KT2 ... 176 A2
Davies Cl CR0 ... 206 A3
Davies Laing & Dick
Coll W1 ... 93 A1 238 B2
Davies La E11 ... 76 D6
Davies Lane Prim Sch
E11 ... 76 D6
Davies Mews W1 ... 248 C6
Davies St
W1 ... 115 B6 248 C6
Davies Walk TW7 ... 130 B4
Davina Ho
Brondesbury NW2 ... 69 B2
14 Hackney E5 ... 74 B3
Da Vinci Ct 12 SE16 ... 118 B1
Davington Ct 19
SM2 ... 217 C1
Davington Gdns RM8 ... 80 B3
Davington Rd RM8 ... 80 B3
Davis Ct 1 N20 ... 14 B2
Davis Ho 35 W12 ... 112 B6
Davis Rd
Bedford Pk W3 ... 111 D4
Chessington KT9 ... 214 C4
Davis Sch The E10 ... 53 D1
Davis St E13 ... 99 B5
Davisville Rd W12 ... 112 A4
Davmor Ct TW8 ... 109 C1
Dawes Ave TW7 ... 131 A1
Dawe's Cl UB10 ... 82 A5
Dawes Ho SE17 ... 262 C3
Dawes Rd
SW6 ... 135 B5 264 C4
Dawe's Rd UB10 ... 82 A5
Dawes St
SE17 ... 117 B1 262 D2
Dawley Ave UB8 ... 83 A1
Dawley Par UB3 ... 105 A6
Dawley Rd
Harlington UB3 ... 105 C2
Hayes UB3 ... 105 B6
Dawlish Ave
Bowes Pk N13 ... 32 A5
Wandsworth SW18 ... 157 D2
Wembley UB6 ... 87 A5
Dawlish Dr Ilford IG3 ... 79 D4
Pinner HA5 ... 41 A3
Ruislip HA4 ... 62 B6
Dawlish Prim Sch
E10 ... 54 A1
Dawlish Rd
Brondesbury NW2 ... 68 D2
Leyton E10 ... 76 A6
Tottenham Hale N17 ... 52 A6
Dawnay Gdns SW18 ... 158 B2
Dawnay Rd SW17,
SW18 ... 158 B2
Dawn Cl TW4 ... 129 A2
Dawn Cres E15 ... 98 B6
Dawn Wlk BR2 ... 186 B1
Dawpool Rd NW2 ... 67 D6
Daws La NW7 ... 28 A5
Dawson Ave
Barking IG11 ... 79 D1
St Paul's Cray BR5 ... 190 B1
Dawson Cl Hayes UB3 ... 83 B2
Woolwich SE18 ... 123 A2
Dawson Gdns 10
IG11 ... 79 D1
Dawson Ho
23 Bethnal Green
E2 ... 96 C4
5 Camberwell SE5 ... 139 C4
Dawson Pl
W2 ... 113 C6 245 B6
Dawson Rd
Cricklewood NW2 ... 68 C4
Kingston u T KT1 ... 198 B6
Dawson St E2 ... 95 D5
Dawson Terr N9 ... 18 C4
Dax Ct TW16 ... 194 C6
Daybrook Rd SW19 ... 201 D6
Day Ho 2 SE5 ... 139 A5
Daylesford Ave
SW15 ... 134 A1
Daymer Gdns HA5 ... 40 C5
Daynor Ho 4 NW6 ... 91 C6
Day's Armhouses
HA8 ... 26 B5
Daysbrook Rd SW2 ... 160 B3
Days La DA15 ... 167 C4
Days Lane Prim Sch
DA15 ... 167 D5
Daytone Ho SW20 ... 178 D2
Dayton Gr SE15 ... 140 C4
Deaconess Ct 5 N15 ... 51 D5
Deacon Ho SE11 ... 260 D3
Deacon Mews N1 ... 73 B1
Deacon Rd
Kingston u T KT2 ... 176 B2
Willesden NW2 ... 68 A2
Deacons Cl HA5 ... 22 B1
DEACONS HILL ... 10 C5
Deacon's Hill Rd
WD6 ... 10 C6
Deacons Hts WD6 ... 10 C5
Deacons Leas BR6 ... 227 B4
Deacons Rise N2 ... 48 B4
Deacons Wlk TW12 ... 173 C6
Deacon Way
SE17 ... 117 A2 262 B4
Deal Ct
13 Hendon NW9 ... 27 D1
7 Southall UB1 ... 86 A1
Deal Ho
Deptford SE15 ... 140 D6
Walworth SE17 ... 263 B2
Deal Porters Way
SE16 ... 118 D3
Deal Rd SW17 ... 181 A4
Deal St E1 ... 96 A2
Dealtry Rd SW15 ... 134 C1
Deal Wlk 3 SW9 ... 138 C5
Dean Bradley St
SW1 ... 260 A5
Dean Cl Hackney E9 ... 74 C3
Hillingdon UB10 ... 60 B1
Rotherhithe SE16 ... 118 D5
Dean Coll of London
N7 ... 72 B5
Deancross St E1 ... 96 C1
Dean Ct Acton W3 ... 89 B1
Ealing W13 ... 109 B5
10 Kingston u T KT2 ... 176 C3
South Lambeth SW8 ... 270 A3
Wembley HA0 ... 65 B5
Dean Dr HA7 ... 26 A1
Deane Ave HA4 ... 62 C3
Deane Croft Rd HA5 ... 40 C3
Deanery Cl N2 ... 48 C5
Deanery Mews W1 ... 248 B4
Deanery Rd E15 ... 76 C2
Deanery St
W1 ... 115 A5 248 B4
Deanesfield Prim
HA4 ... 62 D4
Deane Way HA4 ... 40 B3
Dean Farrar St SW1 ... 259 D6
Deanfield Gdns CR0 ... 221 B4
Dean Gdns E17 ... 54 B5
Deanhill Ct 2
SW14 ... 132 D1
Deanhill Rd SW14 ... 132 D1
Dean Ho London N4 ... 51 A2
New Cross SE14 ... 141 B5
Ruislip HA4 ... 39 B1
Stamford Hill N16 ... 51 D1
18 Stepney E1 ... 96 C1
Dean Rd
Croydon CR0 ... 221 B4
Hampton TW12 ... 173 C5
Hounslow TW3 ... 151 D6
Thamesmead SE28 ... 124 A6
Willesden NW2 ... 68 C2
Dean Ryle St SW1 ... 260 A4
Dean's Bldgs
SE17 ... 117 B2 262 D3
Deansbrook Cl HA8 ... 27 A3
Deansbrook Jun & Inf
Schs NW7 ... 27 A4
Deansbrook Rd
Burnt Oak HA8 ... 27 B4
Edgware HA8 ... 26 D3
Deans Cl
Burnt Oak HA8 ... 27 A4
Chiswick W4 ... 132 D6
South Croydon CR0 ... 221 D5
Deanscroft Ave NW9 ... 45 A1
Dean's Ct EC4 ... 241 D1
Deans Ct HA8 ... 26 D4
Deans Dr N13 ... 32 D4
Dean's Dr HA8 ... 27 B5
Deansfield Prim Sch
Eltham SE9 ... 144 C2
Ruislip HA4 ... 62 D4
Deans Gate Cl SE23 ... 162 D1
Deanshanger Ho 21
SE8 ... 118 D2
Dean's La HA8 ... 27 A4
Dean's Mews W1 ... 238 D2
Dean's Rd W7 ... 108 D4
Deans Rd SM1 ... 217 D5
Dean Stanley St
SW1 ... 260 A5
Dean St
Forest Gate E7 ... 77 A3
Soho W1 ... 93 D1 239 C1
Deansway
East Finchley N2 ... 48 B5
Edmonton N9 ... 17 C1
Deans Way HA8 ... 27 A5
Deanswood N11 ... 31 D4
Dean's Yd SW1 ... 259 D6
Dean Trench St
SW1 ... 260 A5
Dean Way UB2 ... 107 D4
Dean Wlk HA8 ... 27 B3
Deanwood Ct N14 ... 15 C3
Dearmer Ho 6
SW2 ... 160 C4
Dearne Cl HA7 ... 25 A5
De'arn Gdns CR4 ... 202 C6
Dearsley Rd EN1 ... 6 A2
Deason St E15 ... 98 A6
Deauville Ct
14 London SW4 ... 159 C5
4 Rotherhithe
SE16 ... 118 D4
Deauville Mans 13
SW4 ... 159 C5
De Barowe Mews 1
N5 ... 72 D3
Debdale Ho 20 E2 ... 96 A6
Debden Cl
7 Edgware NW9 ... 27 C2
Kingston u T KT2 ... 175 D5
Woodford IG8 ... 37 D3
Debden N17 ... 33 B1
De Beauvoir Cres N1 ... 95 C6
De Beauvoir Ct N1 ... 73 B1
De Beauvoir Pl 5
N1 ... 73 C2
De Beauvoir Prim Sch
N1 ... 73 C2
De Beauvoir Rd N1 ... 73 C1
De Beauvoir Sq N1 ... 73 C1
DE BEAUVOIR TOWN
... 73 C1
Debenham Ct
Barnet EN5 ... 12 C6
Hackney E8 ... 96 A6
Debham Ct NW2 ... 68 C5
Debnams Rd SE16 ... 118 C2
De Bohun Ave N14 ... 15 B5
De Bohun Prim Sch
N14 ... 15 B6
Deborah Cl TW7 ... 130 C4
Deborah Cres HA4 ... 39 B2
Deborah Ct 7 E18 ... 55 B6
Deborah Lo HA8 ... 26 D2
De Broome Rd
TW13 ... 150 C3
De Burgh Ho 10
SW19 ... 180 A3
Deburgh Rd SW19 ... 180 A3
Debussy 9 NW9 ... 27 D1
Decimal Ctr UB2 ... 107 C4
Decima St
SE1 ... 117 C3 263 A6
Decimus Cl CR7 ... 205 B5
Deck Cl SE16 ... 118 D5
Decoy Ave NW11 ... 47 A5
De Crespigny Pk
SE5 ... 139 B3
Dedham Ho 1 SE6 ... 186 A6
Dee Ct W7 ... 86 B1
Deeley Rd
SW8 ... 137 D4 269 C2
Deena Cl W3 ... 88 B1
Deepdale Ave BR2 ... 208 D5
Deepdale Cl N11 ... 31 A4
Deepdale Highbury N4 ... 72 D5
Wimbledon SW19 ... 178 D6
Deepdene Ave CR0 ... 221 D5
Deepdene Cl E11 ... 55 A5
Deepdene Ct
Beckenham BR2 ... 208 C6
Southgate N21 ... 16 D5
Deepdene Gdns
SW2 ... 160 B4
Deepdene Ho N16 ... 51 B1
Deepdene N12 ... 30 C6
Deepdene Lo 5
SW2 ... 160 B4
Deepdene Mans
SW6 ... 264 C2
Deepdene Point 9
SE26 ... 162 D1
Deepdene Rd
London SE5, SE24 ... 139 B1
Welling DA16 ... 146 A2
Deepwell Cl TW7 ... 131 A4
Deepwood La UB6 ... 86 B4
Deerbrook Rd SE24,
SW2 ... 160 D3
Deerdale Rd SE24 ... 139 A1
Dee Rd TW9 ... 132 B1
Deerfield Cl NW9 ... 45 D4
Deerhurst Cl TW13 ... 172 B6
Deerhurst Cres
TW12 ... 174 A5
Deerhurst Ct CR0 ... 204 D1
Deerhurst Ho 6
SE15 ... 140 A6
Deerhurst 7 KT2 ... 176 D2
Deerhurst Rd
Brondesbury NW2 ... 68 D2
Streatham SW16 ... 182 B5
Deerhurst 5 SW16 ... 182 A5
Deerings Ct 2 N20 ... 14 B2
Deerings Dr HA5 ... 40 A4
Deerleap Gr E4 ... 19 D6
Deer Lo SW6 ... 135 A2
Deer Park Cl KT2 ... 176 D3
Deer Park Gdns
CR4 ... 202 B5
Deer Park Rd SW19 ... 180 A1
Deer Park Way BR4 ... 224 D6
Deesdale Ct CR2 ... 221 B4
Deeside Rd SW17 ... 158 B1
Dee St E14 ... 98 A1
Defence Cl SE28 ... 123 C5
Defiance Wlk SE18 ... 122 B3
Defiant 18 NW9 ... 27 D1
Defiant Way SM6 ... 220 A1
Defoe Ave TW9 ... 132 C5
Defoe Cl SW17 ... 180 C4
Defoe Ho
Barbican EC2 ... 242 A4
5 Stoke Newington
N16 ... 73 C5
Defoe Pl
Barbican EC2 ... 242 A4
Upper Tooting
SW17 ... 180 D6
Defoe Rd
Rotherhithe SE16 ... 1
Stoke Newington N16 ..
De Frene Rd SE26 ... 1
De Gama Pl 3 E14 ... 1
Degema Rd BR7 ... 1
Dehar Cres NW9 ...
De Haviland Dr 8
SE18 ... 1
Dehavilland Cl UB5 ...
De Havilland Rd
Edgware HA8 ...
Heston TW5 ... 1
De Havilland Sq IG1 ..
Dehavilland Studios
E5 ...
De Havilland Way
TW19 ... 1
Dekker Ho 19 SE5 ... 1
Dekker Rd SE21 ... 1
Delacourt Rd SE3 ... 1
Delafield Ho 25 E1 ...
Delafield Rd SE7 ... 1
Delaford Rd SE16 ... 1
Delaford St
SW6 ... 135 A6 2
Delamare Cres CR0 .. 2
Delamere Gdns NW7 ..
Delamere Ho 4 N4 ...
Delamere Rd
Ealing W5 ... 1
Hayes UB4 ... 1
Wimbledon SW20 ... 1
Delamere St W2 ... 2
Delamere Terr W2 ...
Delancey Pas NW1 ... 2
Delancey St
NW1 ... 93 B6 2
Delancey Studios
NW1 ... 2
Delany Ho SE10 ... 1
Delarch Ho SE1 ... 2
De Laune St
SE17 ... 116 D1 2
Delaware Rd W9 ...
Delawyk Cres SE24 ... 1
Delcombe Ave KT4 ... 2
Delft Ho 8 KT2 ... 1
Delft Way 2 SE22 ... 1
Delhi Rd EN1 ...
Delhi St N1 ... 94 A6 2
Delia St SW18 ... 1
Delisle Rd SE28 ... 1
Delius Cl WD6 ...
Delius Gr E15 ...
Dellafield N4 ...
Della Path E5 ...
Dellbow Rd TW14 ... 1
Dell Cl
Stratford Marsh
E15 ...
Wallington SM6 ... 2
Woodford IG8 ...
Dellfield Cl BR3 ... 1
Dell La KT17 ... 2
Dellors Cl EN5 ...
Dellow Cl IG2 ...
Dellow Ho 6 E1 ... 1
Dellow St E1 ... 1
Dell Rd Enfield EN3 ...
Stoneleigh KT17 ... 2
West Drayton UB7 ... 1
Dells Cl Chingford E4 ...
Teddington TW11 ... 1
Dell's Mews SW1 ... 2
Dell The
Brentford TW8 ... 1
Feltham TW14 ... 1
Pinner HA5 ...
Plumstead Comm
SE2 ... 1
South Norwood
SE19 ... 1
Wembley HA0 ...
Woodford IG8 ...
Dell Way W13 ...
Dell Wlk KT3 ...
Dellwood Gdns IG5 ...
Delme Cres SE3 ... 1
Delmey Cl CR0 ... 2
Deloraine Ho SE8 ... 1
Deloraine St SE8 ... 1
Delorme St W6 ... 1
Delphian Ct 5
SW16 ... 1
Delroy Ct N20 ...
Delta Bldg 7 E14 ...
Delta Cl KT4 ... 2
Delta Ct NW2 ...
Delta Gr UB5 ...
Delta Ho N1 ... 2
Delta Pk Ind Est EN3 ...
Delta Pk SW18 ... 1
Delta Point 5 E2 ...
Delta Rd KT4 ... 2
Delta St 4 E2 ...

cy Prim Sch
.........124 B4
cy St SE2 ......124 B2
n Cl SE18 ......144 C5
rton Ho SE17 .. 261 D2
rton Rd SE17 .. 261 D1
ho Rd
........135 C4 265 B1
andeville Gate
...... 6 B1
esne Rd SM6 ....219 D4
eta Cl HA9 ....67 A5
ontfort Ct 1
6.............160 A1
ontfort Rd
6.............160 A2
organ Rd SW6 ..135 D2
oster Cl KT6......197 C1
oster Rd SW18 ..158 A6
erry Dr DA14 ...168 B1
igh Cl
am SM1.........217 B3
stead BR7 ....188 B4
ing Hill
11..... 113 B6 244 D6
slip HA4 ....61 D6
thall UB1 ....85 B1
esden NW10 ......67 C1
igh Ct
Ealing W7..........86 D2
wham E6..........99 D4
igh Dr UB3 .....105 A4
igh Gdns
10..............154 B6
igh Ho
ghtsbridge
W1............ 257 D6
Notting Hill W11 ...91 B1
ing Hill W11 .... 244 D6
igh Mews SW1. 259 A3
igh Pl
........115 C1 259 A2
igh Rd
ng W13 ....87 B1
unslow TW3 ..... 129 D3
wham E6..........99 D4
ting Hill
W11 .... 113 B6 244 D6
thall UB1 ....85 B1
igh St
........115 C1 259 B2
igh Terr
.........113 B6 244 D6
ridge Rd BR1,
..............188 B1
bury Ho 48 E3.....97 D4
by Ct Barnet EN5.....1 D2
abeth SE11 .... 260 D4
ce Ho 15 E2.......96 A4
chworth Ho 14
9...............138 C3
Cl BR2, BR3 ......208 B6
cliffe 2 TW15 ...170 C5
cora Centre The
...............7 A2
dridge Cl EN1...... 6 B6
e Ave
ckfen DA15.......168 B4
unslow TW3 ......129 B2
e Cl Brockley SE4..141 A1
yes BR2.......... 208 D1
rcester Pk KT4... 215 D6
ecroft Cres UB10..82 D6
e Ct Ealing W5 .....87 C2
nwell W7........ 108 D4
e Gdns
chley Wood
T7............. 213 A6
nmore HA7.........25 C5
ehole Ho SE18 ...124 A1
e Ho N14 ....15 D4
ehurst Gdns
on W3.......... 110 D5
ndon NW4.........46 C3
mond TW10..... 132 C1
ckenham TW2.....152 B4
odford IG8 ....37 B6
e Mans 1 NW6 ...69 C2
e Rd
khurst Hill IG9.....21 D3
ern Barnet N11.....14 D2
esmead SE24 ....161 A6
e The Ealing W13 ...87 B2
t Molesey KT12,
T8..............195 B4
th Croydon CR0... 222 D4
mbley HA9 ....66 A4
ewood Ho 6
1...............218 A4
ewood EN5 ....14 A6
ewood Rd N6......48 D2
gie Wlk N1 ..... 235 A6
ham Cl DA16.....146 C2
ham Cres CR4 ..202 D5
ham Ct
est Hill SE26......162 B1
thall UB1....... 108 A6

Denham Dr IG2.......57 A3
Denham Ho 32 W12..112 B6
Denham Lo W5.........88 A1
Denham Rd
Feltham TW14 ...... 150 C4
Friern Barnet N20.....14 D1
Denham St SE10.....121 A1
Denham Way IG11...101 D6
Denholme Rd W9.......91 B4
Deniel Lo TW9.......153 C6
Denise Ct HA0.........65 C4
Denison Cl N2.........48 A6
Denison Rd Ealing W5..87 C3
Feltham TW13 ...... 171 D6
Mitcham SW19 ......180 B4
Deniston Ave DA5....169 A3
Denland Ho SW8..... 270 D3
Denleigh Ct N14 ......15 D4
Denleigh Gdns
Southgate N21.........16 C4
Thames Ditton KT7 .. 196 C3
Denman Dr
Ashford TW15 ...... 170 D4
Claygate KT10...... 213 A3
Hampstead Garden
Suburb NW11.........47 C4
Denman Dr N NW11...47 C4
Denman Dr S NW11...47 C4
Denman Ho N16 ......73 C6
Denman Rd SE15 ....139 D3
Denman St W1 ..... 249 C5
Denmark Ave SW19..179 A3
Denmark Ct SM4.....201 C4
Denmark Gdns SM5..218 D5
Denmark Gr N1...... 234 A4
Denmark Hill Dr
NW9.................46 A6
Denmark Hill SE5....139 B3
Denmark Hill Sta
SE5.................139 B3
Denmark Ho 9 SE7..122 A2
Denmark Mans 14
SE5.................139 A3
Denmark Pl
2 Bromley E3.........97 C4
Soho WC2 .... 239 D2
Denmark Rd
Bromley BR1........187 B2
Camberwell SE5 .... 139 A3
Carshalton SM5..... 218 D5
Croydon SE25 ....206 B4
Ealing W13 ....109 B6
Hornsey N8 ....50 C5
Kilburn NW6 ....91 B5
Kingston u T KT1.... 198 A6
Twickenham TW2.....152 B1
Wimbledon SW19 ... 178 D4
Denmark St
8 Leyton E11........76 C5
Newham E13.........99 B2
Soho WC2 .... 239 D2
Tottenham N17 ....34 B3
Denmark Terr NW2.....48 D6
Denmead Ho SW15 ..155 D5
Denmead Rd CR0 ....204 D1
Denmead Sch
TW12.............. 173 D3
Denmead Upper Sch
TW12.............. 173 D3
Denmore Ct SM6......219 B3
Dennan Rd KT6.......198 B1
Dennard Way BR6....226 C4
Denner Rd E4 ....19 C2
Denne Terr E8 ....95 D6
Dennett Rd CR0......204 C2
Dennett's Gr SE14 ...140 D3
Dennett's Rd SE14 ...140 C4
Denning Ave CR0 ....220 C3
Denning Cl
Hampton TW12 ......173 B5
St John's Wood
NW8.......92 A4 229 B1
Denning Point E1.... 243 D2
Denning Rd NW3 ......70 B4
Dennington Cl 17 E5 ..74 B6
Dennington Park
Mansions 12 NW6 ...69 C3
Dennington Park Rd
NW6...................69 C2
Denningtons The
KT4 ....215 C6
Dennis Ave HA9.......66 B3
Dennis Cl TW15.......171 B3
Dennis Ct
Chingford E17 ....36 B1
Greenford UB6 ....86 A1
Lewisham SE10...... 142 A4
Dennis Gdns HA7 .....25 C5
Dennis Ho 4 Bow E3 ..97 B5
Sutton SM1 .... 217 C4
Dennis La HA7.........25 B6
Dennison Point E15....76 A1
Dennis Park Cres
SW20..................179 A2
Dennis Par 1 N14 ....15 D3
Dennis Rd KT8.........196 A5

Dennis Reeve Cl
CR4 ....180 D2
Dennis Way SW4......137 D2
Denny Cl 15 E6 ......100 A2
Denny Cres SE11...... 261 B2
Denny Gdns RM9 .....80 B1
Denny Rd N9 ....18 B3
Denny St
SE11..........116 C1 261 B2
Den Rd BR2 ....208 B6
Densham Ho NW8 .. 229 D3
Densham Rd E15 .....98 C6
Densole Cl BR3 ......185 A2
Denstone Ho 5
SE15.................140 A6
Densworth Gr N9 .....18 C2
Dent Ho SE17....... 263 A3
Denton Cl EN5.........12 C6
Denton Ct BR2.......210 C2
Denton Ho N1 ....72 D1
Denton NW1...........71 A2
Denton Rd
Bexley DA16 .... 146 C5
Edmonton N18........33 C6
Hornsey N8 ....50 B3
Twickenham TW1..... 153 D5
Denton St SW18 .....157 D5
Denton Way E5 ......74 D5
Dents Rd SW11 ......158 D5
Denvale Trade Pk
CR4 ....202 B5
Denver Cl BR6 ....211 C3
Denver Ct UB1.......107 B5
Denver Rd N16 ....51 C2
Denwood SE23 ....162 D1
Denyer Ho 1 NW5 ....71 B4
Denyer St
SW3........114 C2 257 B4
Denys Bldg EC1...... 241 A4
Denziloe Ave UB10....82 D4
Denzil Rd NW10 ......67 D3
Deodar Rd SW15.....135 A1
Deodora Cl N20.......14 D1
Depot App NW2 ......68 D4
Depot Rd
Isleworth TW3,
TW7 ....130 B2
Shepherd's Bush
W12 .... 112 C6
Depot St SE5 ....139 B6
DEPTFORD 140 D6
Deptford Bridge
SE8.................141 C4
Deptford Bridge Sta
SE8................. 141 C4
Deptford Broadway SE8,
SE14................141 C4
Deptford Church St
SE8..................141 C5
Deptford Ferry Rd 24
E14...................119 C2
Deptford Gn SE8.....141 C6
Deptford Green Sch
(Annex) SE14 ..... 141 A5
Deptford Green Sch
SE14.................141 B5
Deptford High St
SE8..................141 C5
Deptford Park Prim Sch
SE8................. 119 A1
Deptford Sta SE8 ... 141 C5
Deptford Trad Est
SE8................. 141 A6
Deptford Wharf
SE8...................119 B2
Dept of Transport &
Environment SW1 259 D5
De Quincey Mews 3
E16...................121 A5
De Quincey Rd N17 ...33 B2
Derby Ave
Harrow HA3 ....24 B2
North Finchley N12.....30 A5
Romford RM7 ....59 D3
Derby Ct
8 Clapton Pk E5......74 D4
Woodford E18 ....36 D2
Derby Gate SW1 .... 250 A2
Derby Hill Cres
SE23..................162 C2
Derby Hill SE23 .....162 C2
Derby Ho
Hendon NW4.........46 C6
Lambeth SE11 ...... 261 A4
Pinner HA5 ....22 D1
4 Wallington SM6 ...219 B3
Derby Lo N3............29 B1
Derby Rd
Cheam SM1, SM2 ....217 B2
Edmonton N18.........34 C5
Enfield EN3 ....18 C6
Greenford UB6 ....85 D6
Hounslow TW3 ...... 129 D1
Merton SW19 .... 179 C3
Mortlake SW14 ...... 132 D1
South Hackney E9 .....96 D6
Surbiton KT5, KT6 ... 198 C1

Derby Rd *continued*
Thornton Heath CR0 . 204 D1
Upton E7 ....77 D1
Woodford E18 ....36 D2
Derbyshire St E2 .....96 A4
Derby St W1........ 248 B3
Dereham Ho 7
SE4..................140 D1
Dereham Pl EC2 .... 243 B6
Dereham Rd IG11 .....79 D3
Derek Ave
Chessington
KT19............ 214 D3
Wallington SM6......219 B4
Wembley HA9 ....66 D1
Derek Cl KT19 ....214 D3
Derek Walcott Cl
SE24................160 D6
Dericote St E8........ 96 B6
Deri Dene Cl 2
TW19.................148 A5
Derifall Cl E6 ....100 B2
Dering Pl CR0 ....221 A4
Dering Rd CR0.......221 A4
Dering St W1....... 238 D1
Derinton Rd SW17 ...181 A6
Derley Rd UB2 ....106 D3
Dermody Gdns
SE13.................164 B6
Dermody Rd SE13.....164 B6
Deronda Rd SE24,
SW2..................160 D3
Deroy Cl SM5 ....218 D2
Derrick Gdns SE7 ....121 C2
Derrick Ho 13 SW2...160 C3
Derrick Rd BR3 ......207 B5
Derrycombe Ho 18
W2...................91 C2
Derry Rd CR0, SM6 ...220 A5
Derry St W8 ..113 D4 245 C1
Dersingham Ave E12..78 C4
Dersingham Inf Sch
E12...................78 C3
Dersingham Rd NW2..69 A5
Derwent Ave
Barnet EN4 ....14 D3
Burnt Oak NW7.......27 B4
Edmonton N18.........33 B5
Hyde The NW9.........45 C4
Kingston u T SW15 .. 177 C6
Pinner HA5 ....23 A4
Uxbridge UB10 ....60 C5
Derwent Cl
Claygate KT10...... 212 D2
East Bedfont TW14 .. 149 D3
Derwent Cres
Bexleyheath DA7..... 147 C3
Stanmore HA7........25 C1
Whetstone N20 ....14 A1
Derwent Ct
2 Hammersmith
W6............ 112 A2
Hornsey N8 ....50 A3
8 Rotherhithe
SE16.............. 118 D4
Derwent Dr
Crofton BR5..........211 B2
Hayes UB4............83 C2
Derwent Gdns
Redbridge IG4........56 A5
Wembley HA9 ....43 C2
Derwent Gr SE22.....139 D1
Derwent Ho
Penge SE20...........184 B1
South Kensington
SW7 .... 256 B4
Tower Hamlets E3......97 B3
Derwent Lo
Hounslow TW7 ......130 B3
North Cheam KT4 ....216 B6
Derwent NW1 ...... 232 A1
Derwent Rd
Ealing W5 .... 109 C3
Palmers Green N13.....16 B1
Penge SE20...........184 B1
Southall UB1 ....85 B1
Twickenham TW2..... 151 D5
West Barnes SM4 ... 200 D3
Derwent Rise NW9 ....45 C3
Derwent St SE10......120 C1
Derwentwater Mans 2
W3...................111 A5
Derwentwater Prim Sch
W3................ 111 A5
Derwentwater Rd
W3...................111 A5
Derwent Wlk SM6.....219 B1
Derwent Yd W5.......109 C3
De Salis Rd UB10 .....83 A3
Desborough Cl
Bayswater W2.........91 D2
Lower Halliford
TW17 .... 192 C2
Desborough Ct
SE25................206 B5
Desborough Ho
W14.............. 264 D6

Desenfans Rd SE21 ..161 C5
Deseret Ho 6 CR4 ...202 D6
Desford Rd E16........98 C3
Desford Way TW15....148 B2
Desmond Ho 4 EN4 ..14 C5
Desmond St SE14.....141 A6
Desmond Tutu Dr
SE23.................163 A3
Despard Ho SW2.....160 C2
Despard Rd N19 ......49 C1
Dessouter 19 NW9 ....27 D1
Desvignes Dr SE13...164 B5
Dethick Ct TW3......130 A1
Dethick Ct E3 ....97 A6
Detling Ho SE17 .... 263 A3
Detling Rd BR1 ......187 A5
Detmold Rd E5 ....74 C6
Devalls Cl E6 ....122 C6
Devana End SM5......218 D5
Devas Rd SW20.......178 C2
Devas St E3 ....97 D3
Devema Cl BR7 ....188 C2
Devenay Rd E15 ......76 D1
Devenish Rd SE2......124 A4
Deventer Cres 8
SE22.................161 C6
Deveraux Cl BR3.....208 A4
De Vere Cotts W8 ... 256 A6
De Vere Ct 1 E5 .....74 B5
De Vere Gdns
Kensington
W8...... 114 A4 246 A1
Redbridge IG1.........56 B1
Deverell St
SE1.......... 117 B3 262 C5
De Vere Mews W8 .. 256 A6
Devereux Ct WC2 .. 241 A1
Devereux Ho 7
SW15.................156 A6
Devereux La SW13....134 B5
Devereux Rd SW11...158 D5
Deverill Ct SE20 .....184 C2
Devey Cl KT2 ....177 B5
Devitt Ho 5 E14.....119 D6
Devizes St N1 ...... 235 D5
Devon Ave TW2.......152 A3
Devon Cl Chigwell IG9 ..21 B2
Tottenham N17 ....51 D6
Wembley UB6 ....87 C6
Devoncroft Gdns
TW1.................153 A4
Devon Ct
3 Acton W3..........88 C1
2 Ealing W7.........86 D2
Hampton TW12 ..... 173 C3
Devon Gdns N4.......50 D3
Devon Ho
9 Penge SE20 ....184 B3
Walthamstow E17 .....35 B1
6 Wanstead E11 .....55 A4
Devonhurst Pl 4
W4...................111 B1
Devonia Gdns N18 ....33 A4
Devonia Rd
N1 ....94 D5 234 D4
Devon Mans SE1.... 253 B2
Devon Par HA3 ....43 C4
Devonport Gdns IG1 ..56 B3
Devonport Ho
Greenwich SE10 .... 142 A6
23 Paddington W2......91 C2
Devonport Rd W12...112 B4
Devonport St E1.......96 D1
Devonport W2....... 237 A2
Devon Rd IG11 ....101 C6
Devon Rise N2........ 48 B5
Devonshire Ave
SM2...................218 A1
Devonshire Cl
Edmonton N13.........32 C6
Leyton E15.............76 C4
Marylebone W1 ..... 238 C4
Devonshire Cres
NW7...................28 D3
Devonshire Ct
14 Balham SW12 ....159 B4
Croydon CR0 .... 207 C1
Feltham TW13 ....150 B2
Pinner HA5 ....23 B2
6 Richmond TW9.....132 B4
Tottenham N17 ....33 A4
Devonshire Dr
London SE10 .... 141 D4
Long Ditton KT6..... 213 D6
Devonshire Gdns
Chiswick W4 .... 133 A5
Edmonton N21.........17 A4
Tottenham N17 ....33 A4
Devonshire Gr SE15..140 B6
Devonshire Hall 15
E9.....................74 C2
Devonshire Hill La
N17 ....33 A4
Devonshire Hill Prim
Sch N17.............33 B4
Devonshire Ho
Brondesbury NW6.....69 B2

Devonshire Ho *continued*
Hounslow TW3 ..... 130 A2
Newington SE1 ..... 262 A6
Paddington W2 ..... 236 D4
2 Putney SW15.... 156 C4
Devonshire Hospl
W1.........93 A2 238 B4
Devonshire Ho 10
SM2.................218 A1
Devonshire House Prep
Sch NW3 ....70 B3
Devonshire House Sch
NW3..................70 A3
Devonshire Ho
Westminster SW1... 259 D2
Whetstone N12 ....14 A1
Devonshire Mews 2
W4....................111 C1
Devonshire Mews N
W1................. 238 C4
Devonshire Mews S
W1................. 238 C4
Devonshire Mews W
W1................. 238 B4
Devonshire Place Mews
W1................ 238 B4
Devonshire Pl
Child's Hill NW2 ......69 C5
Kensington W8 ..... 255 C5
Marylebone
W1........93 A2 238 B4
Devonshire Prim Sch
SM2 .... 218 A1
Devonshire Rd
Bexley DA6 .... 147 A1
Chislehurst SE9...... 166 A2
Chiswick W4 .... 111 C1
Ealing W5 .... 109 C3
Eastcote HA5.........40 C2
Edmonton N9...........18 C3
Feltham TW13 ...... 173 A6
Forest Hill SE23..... 162 C4
Hackbridge SM5,
SM6 .... 219 A4
Harrow HA1 ....42 B3
Hatch End HA5 ....23 B2
Ilford IG2 ....57 C2
Mill Hill NW7..........28 D3
Mitcham SW19 ..... 180 C3
Newham E16...........99 B1
Palmers Green N13.....32 C6
Southall UB1 ....85 C2
Sutton SM2 .... 218 A1
Thornton Heath CR0 ..205 B2
Tottenham N17 ....33 A4
Walthamstow E17 .....53 C3
Devonshire Row
EC2 .... 243 B3
Devonshire Row Mews
W1................. 238 D5
Devonshire Sq
Bromley BR2.........209 B5
Whitechapel
EC2........95 C1 243 B2
Devonshire St
Chiswick W4 .... 111 C1
Marylebone
W1.........93 B2 238 C4
Devonshire Terr
W2..........92 A1 236 B1
Devonshire Way
Croydon CR0, CR9....223 B6
Hayes UB4............84 B1
Devons Rd E3 ....97 D3
Devons Road Sta E3..97 D3
Devon St SE15 ....140 B6
Devon Way KT9.......213 C3
Devon Waye TW5 ....129 B5
Devon Way
Ewell KT19.......... 214 D3
Hillingdon UB10.......82 B5
De Walden Ho NW8 . 230 A4
De Walden St W1... 238 B3
Dewar Ho 2 SW17...180 C5
Dewar St SE15........140 A2
Dewberry Gdns E6...100 A2
Dewberry St E14......98 A2
Dewey Rd
Dagenham RM10......81 D2
Islington N1 . 94 C5 234 A4
Dewey St SW17.......180 D5
Dewhurst Rd W14 ....112 D3
Dewlands Ct 7 NW4..28 D1
Dewsbury Cl HA5 ....41 A3
Dewsbury Ct 5 W4...111 A2
Dewsbury Gdns
KT4 ....216 A5
Dewsbury Rd NW10 ...68 A3
Dewsbury Terr NW1. 231 D6
Dexter Ho 2 DA18...125 A3
Dexter Rd EN5.........12 D5
Deyncourt Rd N17 ....33 A2
Deynecourt Gdns
E11....................55 C5

D'eynsford Rd SE5 ... 139 B4
Dhonau Ho SE16 .... 263 D4
Diadem Ct W1 ...... 239 C2
Dial Wlk The
W8 .... 113 D4 245 D2
Diameter Rd BR5 ..... 211 A3
Diamond Cl RM8 ..... 58 C1
Diamond Ct 8 W7 ... 108 C5
Diamond Est SW17 ... 158 C1
Diamond Ho 22 E3 .... 97 A5
Diamond Rd HA4 ..... 63 A4
Diamond St
18 London NW10 ..... 67 B1
SE15 ..... 139 C5
Diamond Terr SE10 ... 142 A4
Diana Cl
27 Deptford SE8 ..... 141 B6
Sidcup DA14 ..... 169 A2
Woodford E18 ..... 37 B2
Diana Ct SM5 ..... 219 A1
Diana Gdns KT6 ..... 214 B6
Diana Ho
Barnes SW13 ..... 133 D4
4 Brixton SW2 ..... 160 B6
Diana, Princess of Wales Mml Wlk
W2 ..... 114 A5 246 A3
Diana Rd E17 ..... 53 B6
Dianne Ct SE12 ..... 165 A3
Dianne Way EN4 ..... 2 C1
Dianthus Cl SE2 ..... 124 B1
Dias Ho UB5 ..... 85 A6
Dibden Ho 8 SE5 ..... 139 C5
Dibden St N1 .. 95 A6 235 A6
Dibdin Cl SM1 ..... 217 C5
Dibdin Ho W9 ..... 91 D5
Dibdin Rd SM1 ..... 217 C6
Dicey Ave NW2 ..... 68 C4
Dickens Ave
Finchley N3 ..... 30 A2
Hayes UB8 ..... 82 D1
Dickens Cl Erith DA8 .. 147 D5
Hayes UB3 ..... 105 C2
Richmond TW10 ..... 154 A2
Dickens Ct
Clerkenwell EC1 ..... 241 C5
10 Wanstead E11 ..... 55 A5
Wembley HA0 ..... 65 C5
Dickens Dr BR7 ..... 189 A4
Dickens Ho
Bloomsbury WC1 ..... 240 A6
3 Erith DA17 ..... 125 B1
Hayes UB3 ..... 105 C2
Kennington SE17 ..... 261 D1
Kilburn NW6 ..... 91 C4
Paddington NW8 ..... 236 D6
Dickens House Mus*
WC1 ..... 94 B3 240 D5
Dickens La N18 ..... 33 C5
Dickenson Cl N9 ..... 18 A3
Dickenson Ho N8 ..... 50 B3
Dickenson Rd
Feltham TW13 ..... 172 D5
Hornsey N8 ..... 50 A2
Dickenson's La
SE25 ..... 206 A3
Dickenson's Pl
SE25 ..... 206 A3
Dickens Rd E6 ..... 99 D5
Dickens Sq
SE1 ..... 117 A3 262 B6
Dickens St SW8 ..... 137 B3
Dickenswood Cl
SE19 ..... 182 D3
Dickerage Hill
Kingston u T KT3 ..... 177 A1
Kingston u T KT3 ..... 199 A6
Dickerage La KT3 ..... 199 A6
Dickerage Rd KT1, KT2,
KT3 ..... 177 A1
Dickinson Ho 18 E2 ..... 96 A4
Dicksee Ho NW8 ..... 236 C5
Dick Shepherd Ct 17
SW2 ..... 160 C5
Dickson Fold HA5 ..... 40 D5
Dickson Ho
3 Charlton SE18 ..... 144 A4
4 Stepney E1 ..... 96 B1
Dickson Rd SE9 ..... 144 A2
Dick Turpin Way
TW14 ..... 127 D1
Didbin Ho N7 ..... 72 B6
Didsbury Cl E6 ..... 100 B6
Digby Bsns Ctr E9 ..... 74 D2
Digby Cres N4 ..... 73 A6
Digby Gdns RM10 ..... 103 C6
Digby Mans W6 ..... 112 C1
Digby Pl CR0 ..... 221 D5
Digby Rd
Barking IG11 ..... 79 D1
Homerton E9 ..... 74 D2
Digby St E2 ..... 96 C4
Diggon St E1 ..... 96 D2
Dighton Ct SE17 ..... 139 A6
Dighton Rd SW18 ..... 136 A1
Dignum St N1 ..... 234 A4
Digswell St N7 ..... 72 C2
Dilhorne Cl SE12 ..... 165 B1
Dilke St
SW3 ..... 136 D6 267 D6
Dilloway Yd UB2 ..... 107 A4
Dillwyn Cl SE26 ..... 185 A6
Dilston Cl 1 UB5 ..... 84 C4
Dilston Gr SE16 ..... 118 C2
Dilton Gdns SW15 ..... 156 B3
Dilwyn Ct E17 ..... 35 A1
Dimes Pl 9 W6 ..... 112 B2
Dimmock Dr UB6 ..... 64 B3
Dimond Cl E7 ..... 77 A4
Dimsdale Dr
Enfield EN1 ..... 18 A5
Welsh Harp NW9 ..... 45 A1
Dimsdale Wlk 4 E13 .. 99 A5
Dimson Cres E3 ..... 97 C4
Dinerman Ct NW8 ..... 229 B6
Dingle Cl EN5 ..... 11 D5
Dingle Ct 16 HA7 ..... 25 C5
Dingle Gdns E14 ..... 119 C6
Dingle Rd TW15 ..... 170 D5
Dingles Ct HA5 ..... 22 D1
Dingle The UB10 ..... 82 D4
Dingley La SW16 ..... 159 D2
Dingley Pl
EC1 ..... 95 A4 235 B1
Dingley Rd
EC1 ..... 95 A4 235 A1
Dingwall Ave CR0 ..... 221 A6
Dingwall Gdns NW11 .. 47 C3
Dingwall Rd
South Croydon
CR0 ..... 221 B6
Wandsworth SW18 ..... 158 A4
Dinmont Ho 27 E2 ..... 96 A5
Dinmont St 1 E2 ..... 96 B5
Dinmore Ho 6 E9 ..... 96 C6
Dinnington Ho 17 E1 .. 96 B3
Dinorben SM6 ..... 219 C1
Dinsdale Ct EN5 ..... 13 D6
Dinsdale Gdns
New Barnet EN5 ..... 13 D6
South Norwood
SE25 ..... 205 C4
Dinsdale Rd SE3 ..... 142 D6
Dinsmore Rd SW12 ..... 159 B4
Dinton Ho NW8 ..... 237 A6
Dinton Rd
Kingston u T KT2 ..... 176 B3
Mitcham SW19 ..... 180 B4
Dinwiddy Ho N1 ..... 233 C3
Dionis Ho SW6 ..... 135 C3
Diploma Ave N2 ..... 48 C5
Diploma Ct N2 ..... 48 C5
Diprose Lo SW17 ..... 180 B6
Dirleton Rd E15 ..... 98 D6
Disbrowe Rd
W6 ..... 135 A6 264 B5
Discovery Bsns Pk 13
SE16 ..... 118 A3
Discovery Dock E
E14 ..... 119 D4
Discovery Ho 1
E14 ..... 120 A6
Dishforth La NW9 ..... 27 C2
Disley Ct 2 UB1 ..... 85 D1
Disney Pl SE1 ..... 252 B2
Disney St SE1 ..... 252 B2
Dison Cl EN3 ..... 6 D4
Disraeli Cl
1 Acton W4 ..... 111 B2
Thamesmead SE28 ..... 124 C5
Disraeli Gdns SW15 ..... 135 B1
Disraeli Rd
Acton NW10 ..... 89 B5
Ealing W5 ..... 109 D5
Putney SW15 ..... 135 A1
Upton E7 ..... 77 A2
Diss St E2 ..... 95 D4
Distaff La EC4 ..... 252 A6
Distillery La W6 ..... 112 C1
Distillery Rd W6 ..... 112 C1
Distillery Wlk 14
TW8 ..... 132 A6
Distin Ct 3 SM1 ..... 217 D3
Distin St
SE11 ..... 116 C2 261 A3
District Rd HA0 ..... 65 B3
Ditchburn St E14 ..... 120 A6
Ditchfield Rd UB4 ..... 85 A3
Ditchley Ct W7 ..... 86 D2
Dittisham Rd SE9 ..... 188 A6
Ditton Cl KT7 ..... 197 A2
Dittoncroft Cl CR0 ..... 221 C4
Ditton Grange Cl
KT6 ..... 197 D1
Ditton Grange Dr
KT6 ..... 197 D1
Ditton Hill KT6 ..... 213 D6
Ditton Hill Rd KT6 ..... 197 C1
Ditton Ho 10 E5 ..... 74 B3
Ditton Lawn KT7 ..... 197 A1
Ditton Pl 6 SE20 ..... 184 B2
Ditton Rd
Bexley DA6 ..... 169 A6
Southall UB2 ..... 107 B1
Surbiton KT6 ..... 198 B1
Ditton Reach KT7 ..... 197 B3
Divis Way SW15 ..... 156 B5
Dixon Clark Ct N1 ..... 72 D2
Dixon Cl 4 E6 ..... 100 B1
Dixon Ct N4 ..... 50 C3
Dixon Ho
20 North Kensington
NW10 ..... 90 D1
West Heath SE2 ..... 124 C1
Dixon Pl BR4 ..... 207 D1
Dixon Rd
London SE14 ..... 141 A4
South Norwood
SE25 ..... 205 D6
Dixon's Alley 10
SE16 ..... 118 B4
Dobbin Cl HA3 ..... 25 A1
Dobell Rd SE9 ..... 166 B6
Dobree Ave NW10 ..... 68 B1
Dobson Cl NW6 ..... 70 B1
Dobson Ho 18 SE14 .. 140 D6
Doby Ct EC4 ..... 252 B6
Dockers Tanner Rd 26
E14 ..... 119 C2
Dockett Eddy La KT16,
TW17 ..... 192 B1
Dockett Moorings
KT16 ..... 192 B1
Dockhead
SE1 ..... 117 D4 253 D1
Dockhead Wharf
SE1 ..... 253 D2
Dock Hill Ave SE16 ..... 118 D4
Docklands Ct 20 E14 .. 97 B1
Docklands Heritage
Mus* SE16 ..... 119 B5
Dockland St E16 ..... 122 C5
Dockley Rd SE16 ..... 118 A3
Dockley Road Ind Est 11
SE16 ..... 118 A3
Dock Offices 12
SE16 ..... 118 C3
Dock Rd
Brentford TW8 ..... 131 D5
Canning Town E16 ..... 120 D6
Dockside Rd E16 ..... 121 D6
Dock St E1 ..... 118 A6
Dockwell Cl TW14 ..... 128 A1
Dockwell's Ind Est
TW14 ..... 150 B6
Doctor Johnson Ho 2
SW16 ..... 181 D6
Doctors Cl SE26 ..... 184 C5
Doctor Spurstowe
Almshouses 9 E8 ... 74 B2
Docura Ho N7 ..... 72 B6
Docwras Bldgs N1 ..... 73 C2
Dodbrooke Rd
SE27 ..... 160 D1
Dodd Ho 18 SE16 ..... 118 B2
Doddington Gr
SE17 ..... 116 D1 261 D1
Doddington Pl 4
SE17 ..... 138 D6
Dodsley Pl N9 ..... 18 C1
Dodson St
SE1 ..... 116 C4 251 B1
Dod St E14 ..... 97 C1
Doebury Wlk SE18 ..... 146 A6
Doel Cl SW19 ..... 180 A3
Doggett Rd SE6 ..... 163 C4
Doggetts Ct EN4 ..... 14 C6
Doghurst Ave UB3 ..... 126 D5
Doghurst Dr UB7 ..... 126 D5
Dog Kennel Hill
SE22 ..... 139 C2
Dog Kennel Hill Sch
SE22 ..... 139 C2
Dog La NW10 ..... 67 C4
Dogrose Ct 14 NW9 ..... 46 A5
Doherty Rd E13 ..... 99 A3
Dokal Ind Est UB2 ..... 107 A4
Doland Ct SW17 ..... 180 D4
Dolben Ct SW1 ..... 259 D3
Dolben St
SE1 ..... 116 D5 251 D3
Dolby Rd SW6 ..... 135 B3
Doleman Ho 19
SE10 ..... 141 D4
Dolland Ho SE11 ..... 260 D1
Dolland St SE11 ..... 260 D1
Dollar Bay E14 ..... 120 A4
Dollary Ct KT3 ..... 198 D6
Dolliffe Cl CR4 ..... 180 D1
Dollis Ave N3 ..... 29 B2
Dollis Brook Wlk
EN5 ..... 13 A5
Dollis Cres HA4 ..... 40 C1
Dolliscroft NW7 ..... 29 A3
Dollis Ct N3 ..... 29 B2
DOLLIS HILL 68 B5
Dollis Hill Ave NW2 ..... 68 B5
Dollis Hill Est NW2 ..... 68 A5
Dollis Hill La NW2 ..... 68 A5
Dollis Hill Sta NW2 ..... 68 A3
Dollis Hts NW2 ..... 68 B5
Dollis Jun & Inf Schs
NW7 ..... 28 C3
Dollis Mews N3 ..... 29 C2
Dollis Pk N3 ..... 29 B2
Dollis Rd N3, NW7 ..... 29 B3
Dollis Valley Dr EN5 ..... 13 B6
Dollis Valley Way
EN5 ..... 13 B5
Dolman Cl N3 ..... 30 A1
Dolman Rd W4 ..... 111 B2
Dolman St SW4 ..... 138 B1
Dolphin Cl
Kingston u T KT6 ..... 197 D4
2 Rotherhithe
SE16 ..... 118 D4
Thamesmead SE28 ..... 102 D1
Dolphin Ct
London NW11 ..... 47 A3
Merton SW19 ..... 179 C3
Tufnell Pk N7 ..... 71 D4
2 Wallington SM6 ..... 219 B2
Dolphin Est The
TW16 ..... 171 B2
Dolphin La E14 ..... 119 D6
Dolphin Rd TW16 ..... 171 C2
Dolphin Rd N TW16 ..... 171 C2
Dolphin Rd UB5 ..... 85 B5
Dolphin Rd S TW16 ..... 171 C2
Dolphin Rd W
TW16 ..... 171 C2
Dolphin Sch SW11 ..... 158 D6
Dolphin Sq
SW1 ..... 115 C1 259 B1
Dolphin St KT2 ..... 176 A2
Dolphin Twr 21 SE8 ..... 141 B6
Dombey Ho
18 Bermondsey
SE1 ..... 118 A4
4 Shepherd's Bush
W11 ..... 112 D5
Dombey St WC1 ..... 240 C4
Dome Hill Pk SE26 ..... 183 D6
Domelton Ho SW18 ..... 157 D5
Domett Cl SE5 ..... 139 B1
Domfe Pl E5 ..... 74 C4
Domingo St EC1 ..... 242 A5
Dominica Cl 6 E6 ..... 99 D5
Dominion Bsns Pk
N9 ..... 18 D2
Dominion Cl TW3 ..... 130 B3
Dominion Ind Est
UB2 ..... 107 A4
Dominion Par HA1 ..... 42 D4
Dominion Rd
Croydon CR0 ..... 205 D2
Southall UB2 ..... 107 A3
Dominion St
EC2 ..... 95 B2 242 D4
Dominion Wks RM8 ..... 59 A1
Domonic Dr SE9 ..... 166 D1
Domville Cl N20 ..... 14 B2
Donaghue Cotts 11
E14 ..... 97 A2
Donald Dr RM6 ..... 58 C4
Donald Lynch Ho
CR4 ..... 180 D1
Donald Rd
Newham E13 ..... 99 B6
Thornton Heath CR0 ..... 204 B2
Donaldson Rd
Kilburn NW6 ..... 91 B6
Shooters Hill SE18 ..... 144 C4
Donald Woods Gdns
KT5 ..... 215 A6
Doncaster Dr UB5 ..... 63 B3
Doncaster Gdns
London N4 ..... 51 A3
Northolt UB5 ..... 63 B3
Doncaster Gn WD19 ..... 22 C5
Doncaster Rd N9 ..... 18 B4
Doncel Ct E4 ..... 20 B4
Donegal Ho 2 E1 ..... 96 C3
Donegal St
N1 ..... 94 B5 233 D3
Doneraile Ho SW1 ..... 258 C1
Doneraile St SW6 ..... 134 D4
Dongola Rd
Newham E13 ..... 99 B4
Tottenham N17 ..... 51 C6
Tower Hamlets E1 ..... 97 A2
Dongola Rd W 5
E13 ..... 99 B4
Don Gratton Ho 23
E1 ..... 96 A2
Donington Ave IG6 ..... 57 A4
Donkey Alley SE22 ..... 162 A5
Donkey La EN1 ..... 6 A3
Donkin Ho 15 SE16 ..... 118 B2
Donne Ct SE24 ..... 161 A5
Donnefield Ave HA8 ..... 26 A3
Donne Ho
18 Canonbury N16 ..... 73 B4
14 Deptford SE14 ..... 140 D6
11 Poplar E14 ..... 97 C1
Donnelly Ct SW6 ..... 264 B4
Donne Pl
Chelsea
SW3 ..... 114 C2 257 B4
Mitcham CR4 ..... 203 B5
Donne Rd RM8 ..... 80 C6
Donnington Ct
11 Camden Town
NW1 ..... 71 B1
Willesden NW10 ..... 68 B1
Donnington Ho 12
SW8 ..... 137 D3
Donnington Prim Sch
NW10 ..... 90 B6
Donnington Rd
Harrow HA3 ..... 43 D3
Willesden Green
NW10 ..... 90 B6
Worcester Pk KT4 ..... 216 A6
Donnybrook Rd
SW16 ..... 181 D3
Donoghue Bsns Pk
NW2 ..... 68 D5
Donovan Ave N10 ..... 31 C1
Donovan Ct SW7 ..... 256 C1
Donovan Ho 4 E1 ..... 118 C6
Donovan Pl N21 ..... 16 B6
Don Phelan Cl SE5 ..... 139 B4
Doone Cl TW11 ..... 175 A4
Doon St SE1 .. 116 C5 251 A4
Doradus Ct 20
SW19 ..... 156 D3
Dora Ho
11 Shepherd's Bush
W11 ..... 112 D6
1 Tower Hamlets
E14 ..... 97 B1
Doral Way SM5 ..... 218 D3
Doran Ct E6 ..... 100 B5
Dorando Cl W12 ..... 112 B6
Doran Gr SE18 ..... 145 C5
Doran Manor N2 ..... 48 D4
Doran Wlk
Stratford E15 ..... 76 A1
Stratford Marsh E15 ..... 98 A6
Dora Rd SW19 ..... 179 C6
Dora St E14 ..... 97 B1
Dora Way SW9 ..... 138 C3
Dorcas Ct 9 SW18 ..... 136 B1
Dorchester Ave
Edmonton N13 ..... 33 A6
Harrow HA2 ..... 42 A3
Sidcup DA5 ..... 168 D4
Dorchester Cl
Northolt UB5 ..... 63 D3
St Paul's Cray BR5 ..... 190 B3
Dorchester Ct
Cricklewood NW2 ..... 68 D5
1 De Beauvoir Town
N1 ..... 73 C1
East Barnet N14 ..... 15 B4
Herne Hill SE24 ..... 161 A6
Knightsbridge SW1 ..... 257 D5
1 Muswell Hill N10 ..... 49 B6
5 Streatham SW16 ..... 160 A2
2 Woodford E18 ..... 36 D2
Dorchester Dr
Feltham TW14 ..... 149 C5
Herne Hill SE24 ..... 161 A6
Dorchester Gdns
Chingford E4 ..... 35 C6
East Finchley NW11 ..... 47 C5
Dorchester Gr W4 ..... 111 D1
Dorchester Ho
Richmond TW9 ..... 132 D5
Wallington SM5 ..... 218 D3
Dorchester Mews
New Malden KT3 ..... 199 B5
Twickenham TW1 ..... 153 C5
Dorchester Prim Sch
KT4 ..... 200 C1
Dorchester Rd
Cheam SM4 ..... 202 A2
North Cheam KT4 ..... 200 C1
Northolt UB5 ..... 63 D3
Dorchester Waye
Hayes UB4 ..... 84 B1
Hayes UB4 ..... 84 C1
Dorchester Way HA3 ..... 44 B3
Dorcis Ave DA7 ..... 147 A3
Dordrecht Rd W3 ..... 111 C5
Dore Ave E12 ..... 78 C3
Doreen Ave NW9 ..... 45 B1
Doreen Capstan Ho 5
E11 ..... 76 C5
Dore Gdns SM4 ..... 201 D2
Dorell Cl UB1 ..... 85 B2
Dorey Ho 7 TW8 ..... 131 C5
Doria Rd SW6 ..... 135 B3
Doric Ho 7 E2 ..... 96 D5
Doric Way
NW1 ..... 93 D4 232 C2
Dorie Mews N12 ..... 29 D6
Dorien Rd SW20 ..... 178 D1
Doris Emmerton Ct
SW18 ..... 136 A1
Doris Rd
Ashford TW15 ......
Upton E7 ....
Dorking Cl
Deptford SE8 ....
North Cheam KT4 ...
Dorking Ct N17 .....
Dorking Ho SE1 .....
Dorland Ct SW15 ...
Dorlcote Rd SW18 ..
Dorleston Ct N1 ....
Dorly Cl TW17 ......
Dorman Pl 6 N9 ...
Dorman Way
NW8 .... 92 B6
Dorman Wlk NW10 ..
Dorma Trad Pk E10 ..
Dormay St SW18 .....
Dormer Cl Barnet EN5
Stratford E15 ....
Dormer's Ave UB1 ...
Dormers Lo EN4 .....
Dormers Rise UB1 ...
DORMER'S WELLS .
Dormer's Wells High
Sch UB1 ....
Dormers Wells Ho
UB4 ....
Dormer's Wells Inf S
UB1 ....
Dormer's Wells Jun
UB1 ....
Dormer's Wells La
UB1 ....
Dormstone Ho SE17.
Dormywood HA4 .....
Dornberg Cl SE3 ....
Dornberg Rd SE3 ....
Dorncliffe Rd SW6 ...
Dorney Ct SW6 ......
Dorney NW3 ....
Dorney Rise BR5 .....
Dorney Way TW4 ....
Dornfell St NW6 .....
Dornoch Ho 26 E3 ...
Dornton Rd
South Croydon
CR2 ....
Upper Tooting SW12,
SW17 ....
Dorothy Ave HA0 .....
Dorothy Barley Schs
RM8 ....
Dorothy Charrington
1 SE22 ....
Dorothy Evans Cl
DA7 ....
Dorothy Gdns RM8 ...
Dorothy Pettingel Ho
SM1 ....
Dorothy Rd SW11 ....
Dorothy Villas UB1 ...
Dorrien Wlk SW16 ...
Dorrington Ct SE25 ..
Dorrington Point 20
E3 ....
Dorrington St EC1 ..
Dorrington Way
BR3 ....
Dorrit Ho 2 W11 ....
Dorrit Mews N18 ....
Dorrit St SE1 ....
Dorrit Way BR7 ......
Dorryn Ct SE26 ......
Dors Cl NW9 ....
Dorset Ave
Falconwood DA16 ...
Hayes UB4 ....
Southall UB2 ....
Dorset Bldgs EC4 ...
Dorset Cl Hayes UB4 ..
Marylebone NW1 ....
Dorset Ct
3 Ealing W7 ....
3 London N1 ....
4 Northolt UB5 .....
Dorset Dr HA8 ....
Dorset Gdns SW16 ...
Dorset Hall SW19 ....
Dorset Ho 1 SE20 ...
Dorset Mans 2 W6 ..
Dorset Mews
Belgravia SW1 ......
Finchley N3 ....
Dorset Pl E15 ....
Dorset Rd
Ashford TW15 ......
Chislehurst SE9 .....
Ealing W5 ....
Harrow HA1 ....
Merton SW19 ......
Mitcham CR4 ....
Penge BR3 ....
South Lambeth
SW8 ..... 138 B5
Upton E7 ....
West Green N15 .....

set Rd *continued*
ood Green N22......32 A2
set Rise
4 ....94 D1 241 C1
set Road Inf Sch
9...............166 A2
set Sq
V1........92 D3 237 C5
set St W1..92 D2 237 D3
set Waye TW5....129 B5
set Way
lingdon UB10.......82 B5
ickenham TW2.......152 B3
ton Cl 6 SE15....139 C5
ton Villas UB7....126 C4
ville Cres W6 ....112 B3
ville Rd SE12.......165 A6
hill Rd SE18.......145 A5
ai Gr TW12.......174 A2
ay Martyrs RC Sch
nnexe) The
310..............60 D3
ay Martyrs RC Sch
ne UB10..........60 D4
ghty Ct 11 E1 ....118 B5
ghty Mews
C1.........94 B3 240 C5
ghty St
C1.........94 B3 240 C5
uglas Ave
althamstow E17.....35 C2
embley HA0........66 A1
est Barnes KT3 ....200 B5
uglas Bader Ho
3..................29 D4
uglas Bldgs SE1..252 B2
uglas Cl
anmore HA7........25 A5
allington SM6.....220 A2
uglas Cres UB4.....84 D3
uglas Ct London N3..29 D1
4 South Hampstead
NW6...............69 C1
4 Upper Tooting
SW17...........180 C4
uglas Dr CR0.......223 C5
uglas Gracey Ho
W18...............157 A4
uglas Ho
sleworth TW1.......153 B6
utney SW15.......156 A5
estminster SW1....259 C3
uglas Johnstone Ho
W6...............264 C5
uglas Mews NW2....69 A5
uglas 20 NW9.......27 D1
uglas Path E14....120 A1
uglas Rd
hingford E4.........20 C3
ounslow TW3 .....129 D2
ford IG3...........58 A3
slington N1 ....73 A1
lburn NW6 ....91 B6
ngston u T KT1....176 D1
4 Newham E16 ......99 A2
uglas Rd N N1.....73 A2
uglas Rd S N1......73 A2
uglas Rd
anwell TW19 .....148 A5
urbiton KT6........198 B1
hames Ditton KT10 . 212 A6
elling DA16........146 B4
ood Green N22......32 C2
uglas Robinson Ct
W16...............182 A3
uglas Sq SM4 .....201 C3
uglas St
W1.......115 D2 259 C3
uglas Terr E17 .....35 B2
uglas Waite Ho
W6................69 D1
uglas Way SE8 ....141 B5
ulton Ho SE11.....260 D4
ulton Mews 4
W6................69 D2
unesforth Gdns
W18...............157 D3
uro Pl
8........113 D3 255 D6
uro St E3...........97 C5
uthwaite Sq 12
1..................118 A5
ve App E6 ....100 A2
ve Cl Hendon NW7...27 D3
ortholt UB5........84 D3
allington SM6......220 B1
vecot Cl HA5.......40 C4
vecote Gdns 8
W14...............133 B2
ve Ct
ty of London EC2 .. 242 C1
nfield EN3 ....18 B6
anwell TW19 .....148 A4
vedale Ave HA3 ....43 C3
vedale Cl DA16 ....146 A3
vedale Cotts 6
W11...............136 D3

Dovedale Ho N16 .....51 B2
Dovedale Rd SE22 ....162 B5
Dovedale Rise CR4 ...180 D3
Dovedon Cl N14 ......16 A2
Dove House Gdns E4..19 C2
Dovehouse Mead
IG11................101 B5
Dovehouse St
SW3.........114 C1 257 A1
Dove Mews
SW7.........114 A1 256 B2
Dove Pk HA5 ....23 C3
Dover Cl NW2 ....68 D6
Dovercourt Ave
CR7..................204 C5
Dovercourt Gdns
HA7..................26 A5
Dovercourt La SM1 ..218 A5
Dovercourt Rd
SE22.................161 D5
Dover Ct
Clerkenwell EC1 .... 241 C6
17 Greenwich SE10.. 141 D4
Sutton SM1 ....218 B4
Dove Rd N1 ....73 B2
Doverfield Rd SW2...160 A4
Dover Flats SE1..... 263 B3
Dover Gdns SM5 .....218 D5
Dover Ho
7 Beckenham
BR3............ 185 C3
Brixton SE5 .... 138 D4
11 Deptford SE15 ... 140 C6
Edgware HA8.........26 B3
14 Penge SE20 ......184 B2
Dover House Rd
SW15...............156 B6
Doveridge Gdns N13..32 D6
Dover Mans 16
SW9................138 C2
Dove Row E2 ....96 A6
Dover Park Dr
SW15...............156 B5
Dover Patrol SE3 ....143 C3
Dover Rd
Dagenham RM6.......59 A3
Lower Edmonton N9 ...18 C2
South Norwood
SE19...............183 B4
Wanstead E12........77 C6
Woolwich SE18 ..... 145 A3
Dover St W1..115 C5 249 A4
Dover Terr TW9......132 C3
Dover Yd W1 .... 249 A4
Doves Cl BR2 ....226 A6
Doves Yd N1...94 C6 234 A5
Dovet Ct SW8........ 270 C2
Doveton Ho 7 E1.....96 C3
Doveton Rd CR2 .....221 B3
Doveton St 8 E1 .....96 C3
Dove Wlk SW1...... 258 A2
Dovey Lo 4 N1.......72 C1
Dowanhill Rd SE6.....164 B3
Dowd Cl N11 ....15 A2
Dowdeny Cl 12 NW5...71 C3
Dowdeswell Cl
SW15...............133 C1
Dowding Ho N6.......49 A2
Dowding Pl HA7 ......25 A4
Dowding Rd UB10.....60 B1
Dowe Ho SE3.........142 C2
Dowell Ho SE21.......161 D1
Dower Ho The
DA14................169 B1
Dowes Ho 13 SW16...160 A1
Dowgate Hill EC4 ... 252 C6
Dowland Ho EN1.......5 D5
Dowland St W10.......91 A4
Dowlas St SE5 ....139 C5
Dowlen Ct 14 E14 ....119 C4
Dowler Ct 2 KT2 ....176 B2
Dowler Ho 32 E1.......96 A1
Dowlerville Rd BR6 ..227 D2
Dowling Ho DA17 ....125 B3
Dowman Cl 2
SW19................179 D3
Downage NW4.........46 C6
Downalong WD23.......8 B3
Down Barns Rd HA4...62 D5
Downbarton Ho 11
SW9................138 C4
Downbury Mews 13
SW18...............157 C6
Down Cl UB5 ....84 B5
Downderry Prim Sch
BR1 ....186 C6
Downderry Rd BR1...186 C6
Downe Cl DA16 ......146 C5
Downe Ho 9 SE7 ....143 C6
Downe Manor Prim Sch
UB5 ....84 B4
Downend Ct 1
SE15................139 C6
Downend SE18 ......144 D5
Downe Rd CR4........180 D1
Downer's Cotts
SW4.................137 C1

Downes Cl TW1......153 B5
Downes Ct N21 ....16 C3
Downes Ho CR0 .....220 D4
Downey Ho 6 E1.....96 D3
Downfield Cl W9 .....91 D3
Downfield Ho KT3 ...199 B1
Downfield KT4.......200 A1
Down Hall Rd KT2....175 D2
DOWNHAM 186 C5
Downham Ct 1 N1 ...73 B1
Downham Ent Ctr
SE6.................164 D2
Downham La BR1.....186 B5
Downham Rd N1.......73 B1
Downham Way BR1 ..186 C6
Downhills Ave N17....51 B6
Downhills Park Rd
N17 ....51 A6
Downhills Prim Sch
N15 ....51 B5
Downhills Way N17 ...33 A1
Downhurst Ave NW7 ..27 B5
Downhurst Ct NW4 ...46 C6
Downing Cl HA2 ......42 A6
Downing Ct N12 ......29 D5
Downing Dr UB6.......86 C6
Downing Ho
9 Merton SW19.... 179 C3
2 North Kensington
W10.................90 D1
4 Putney SW15..... 156 A6
Downing Rd RM9 .....81 B1
Downings E6 ....100 C1
Downing St*
SW1......... 116 A4 250 A2
Downland Cl N20 ....14 A3
Downland Ct E11 .....76 C6
Downleys Cl SE9.....166 B2
Downman Rd SE9....144 A2
Down Pl W6..........112 B1
Down Rd TW11 ....175 B4
Down St Mews W1.. 248 C3
Downs Ave
Elmstead BR7 ....188 B5
Pinner HA5 ....41 B2
Downs Bridge Rd
BR3 ....186 B2
Downs Ct
16 Hackney E8 ....74 B3
13 Wimbledon
SW19 ....178 D3
Downsell Prim Sch
E15.................76 B4
Downsell Rd E15......76 B4
Downsfield Rd E17....53 A3
Downshall Ave IG3....57 C3
Downshall Ct IG3.....57 C3
Downshall Prim Sch
IG3..................57 C2
Downs Hill BR2, BR3..186 B2
Downshire Hill NW3 ..70 B4
Downside Cl SW19...180 A4
Downside Cres
Ealing W13 ....87 A3
Maitland Pk NW3 .....70 C3
Downside 2 SW15...157 A6
Downside Rd SM2 ...218 C2
Downside
Sunbury TW16...... 172 A2
Twickenham TW1.... 152 D1
Downside Wlk UB5.... 85 B4
Downs La 2 E5.......74 B4
Downs Park Rd E5,
E8....................74 A3
Downs Rd
Beckenham BR3 .... 185 D1
Enfield EN1 ....5 C1
Shacklewell E5, N16 ...74 A4
South Norwood CR7 . 183 A2
Down St KT8 ....195 C4
Downs The SW19,
SW20................178 D3
Down St W1 ..115 B5 248 C3
Downsview Gdns
SE19................183 A3
Downs View TW7 ....131 A4
Downs View Lo 9
KT6 ....198 A3
Downsview Prim Sch
SE19................183 A3
Downsview Rd
SE19................183 A3
Downsview Sch E5 ...74 B4
Downsway BR6 ......227 C3
Downton Ave SW2 ...160 B2
Downtown Rd SE16 ..119 A4
Downway N12 ....30 C3
Down Way UB5 ....84 B4
Dowrey St N1....... 234 A6
Dowsett Rd N17 ......34 A1
Dowson Cl SE5 ......139 B1
Dowson Ct SE13 .....142 B2
Dowson Ho 8 E1 .....96 D1
Doyce St SE1 .... 252 A2
Doyle Gdns NW10.....90 B6
Doyle Ho W3 ....110 D4
Doyle Rd SE25 ....206 A5

D'Oyley St SW1..... 258 A4
Doynton St N19.......71 B6
Draco St SE17 ....139 A6
Dragon Ct WC2 ..... 240 B2
Dragonfly Cl E13......99 B4
Dragon Rd SE15 .....139 C6
Dragon Yd WC1 ..... 240 B2
Dragoon Rd SE8 .....119 B1
Dragor Rd NW10.......89 A3
Drake Cl 30 SE16.....118 D4
Drake Cres SE28 .....102 C1
Drake Croft N16 ......73 B6
Drake Ct
Dulwich SE19....... 183 D5
5 Hammersmith
W12 ....112 B4
Kingston u T KT5 .....198 B5
Drakefell Rd SE4,
SE14................140 D2
Drakefield Rd
SW17...............159 A1
Drake Hall 13 E16....121 B5
Drake Ho
2 Limehouse
E14............. 119 A6
20 Stepney E1........96 C2
Drakeley Ct N5 ....72 D4
Drake Mews BR2.....209 C5
Drake Rd
Brockley SE4....... 141 C2
Chessington KT9..... 214 C3
Harrow HA2 ....63 B6
Mitcham CR4........ 203 A3
Thornton Heath CR0 ..204 B2
Drakes Ct SE23 .....162 C3
Drakes Ctyd NW6 .....69 B1
Drake St Enfield EN2 .... 5 B4
Holborn WC1....... 240 C3
Drakes Wlk E6.......100 B6
Drakewood Rd
SW16................181 D3
Draper Cl
Belvedere DA17 ......125 B2
Hounslow TW7 ......130 B3
Draper Ct BR1 ......210 A5
Draper Ho SE1...... 261 D4
Draper Pl N1 .... 234 D6
Drapers Almshouses 5
E3...................97 C4
Draper's Cottage Homes
NW7.................28 A6
Drapers Gdns EC2 .. 242 D2
Drapers Rd Enfield EN2.. 4 D4
Leyton E15...........76 B4
Tottenham N17 ....51 D6
Drappers Way 8
SE16................118 A2
Draven Cl BR2 ......208 D2
Drawell Cl SE18......123 C1
Drax Ave SW20 ......178 A3
Draxmont SW19 .....179 A4
Draycot Rd
Tolworth KT6....... 198 C1
Wanstead E11........55 B2
Draycott Ave
Chelsea
SW3..... 114 C2 257 B3
Harrow HA3 ....43 C3
Draycott Cl
Camberwell SE5 .....139 B5
Cricklewood NW2 .....68 D5
Harrow HA3 ....43 B3
Draycott Ct SW11... 267 A2
Draycott Ho SW3 ... 257 C3
Draycott Pl
SW3........114 D2 257 C3
Draycott Terr
SW3........ 114 D2 257 D3
Drayford Cl W9 ....91 B3
Dray Gdns SW2 ......160 B6
Draymans Ct 4
SW9................138 B2
Draymans Way
TW7................130 D2
Drayside Mews UB2..107 B4
Drayson Mews
W8..........113 C4 245 B1
Drayton Ave
Ealing W13 .... 109 A6
Orpington BR6...... 210 D1
Drayton Bridge Rd
Ealing W7, W13..... 108 D6
Ealing W13 ....87 A1
Drayton Cl
Hounslow TW4 ......151 B6
Ilford IG1 ....57 B1
Drayton Ct
South Kensington
SW10............ 256 B1
Tolworth KT5....... 214 D6
West Drayton UB7....104 B2
Drayton Gdns
Ealing W13 .... 109 A6
Southgate N21........16 D4
South Kensington
SW10.... 114 A1 256 B1
West Drayton UB7... 104 A4

Drayton Gn W13.....109 A6
Drayton Gr W13 .....109 A6
Drayton Green Prim Sch
W13............. 109 A6
Drayton Green Rd
W13................109 B6
Drayton Green Sta
W7..................86 D1
Drayton Ho
14 Camberwell
SE5...............139 B5
Leytonstone E11 ......54 B1
Drayton Lo E17 ....35 D1
Drayton Manor High
Sch W7...............86 D1
Drayton Park Mews 12
N5 ....72 C3
Drayton Park Prim Sch
N5 ....72 C3
Drayton Park Sta N5..72 C3
Drayton Pk N5, N7.....72 C4
Drayton Rd
Croydon CR0 .... 220 D6
Ealing W13 ....109 B6
Harlesden NW10......89 D6
Leytonstone E11 ......54 B1
Tottenham N17 ....33 C1
Drayton Waye HA3.... 43 B3
Dreadnought Cl
SW19...............180 B1
Dreadnought St
SE10................120 C3
Drenon Sq UB3 ......105 D6
Dresden Cl NW6 ......69 D2
Dresden Ho
5 Clapham
SW11........... 137 A3
Lambeth SE11...... 260 D4
Dresden Rd N19 ......49 D1
Dressington Ave
SE4.................163 C5
Drew Ave NW7........29 A4
Drewery Ct SE3......142 C2
Drewett Ho 31 E1.....96 A1
Drew Gdns UB6.......64 D2
Drew Ho 12 SW16 ....160 A1
Drew Prim Sch E16. 122 A5
Drew Rd E16 ....122 A5
Drewstead La
SW16...............159 D2
Drewstead Rd
SW16...............159 D2
Driberg Ct RM9.......80 B2
Driffield Ct 4 NW9 ...27 C2
Driffield Rd E3 ....97 A5
Drift The BR2 ....225 D5
Driftway Ho 19 E3.....97 B5
Driftway The CR4 .....181 A2
Drinkwater Ho 11
SE5.................139 B5
Drinkwater Rd HA2 ...63 D6
Drive Ct HA8 ....26 C5
Drive Ho CR4 ....202 C5
Drive Mans SW6 .....135 A3
Drive The Acton W3....89 A1
Ashford TW15 ....171 B3
Barking IG11.........79 D1
Barking IG11.........80 A2
Barnet EN5 ....1 A2
Beckenham BR3 .... 185 C2
Bexley DA5 .... 168 D4
Buckhurst Hill IG9.....21 C4
Chingford E4 ....20 B4
Chislehurst BR7...... 189 D2
Edgware HA8.........26 C5
Enfield EN2 ....5 B4
Erith DA8........... 147 D6
Feltham TW14 .... 150 C4
Finchley N3 ....29 C3
Fortis Green N6.......48 D4
Harlesden NW10......89 D6
Harrow HA2 ....41 C2
Hendon NW11.........47 A2
Hounslow TW3,
TW7 ....130 B3
Ickenham UB10.......60 A5
Islington N7 ....72 B2
Kingston u T KT2 .... 177 A3
Morden SM4 ....202 B4
New Barnet EN5 ......14 A5
Orpington BR6...... 227 D6
Redbridge IG1........56 B2
Sidcup DA14 ....190 B6
South Norwood CR7 ..205 B5
St Paul's Cray BR7 .. 211 D6
Surbiton KT6 .... 198 A2
Thames Ditton KT10 . 196 A1
Walthamstow E17 .....53 D6
Wanstead E18.........55 A6
Wembley Pk HA9.......67 A6
West Ewell KT19..... 215 D2
West Wickham BR4 ...208 B2
Wimbledon SW19,
SW20............. 178 C3
Wood Green N11......31 D4
Dr Johnson Ave
SW17...............159 B1

Dr Johnson's House
Mus* EC4........... 241 B1
Droitwich Cl SE26.....162 A1
Dromey Gdns HA3 ....24 D3
Dromore Rd SW15 ...157 A5
Dronfield Gdns RM8 ..80 C3
Dron Ho E1...........96 C2
Droop St W10 ....91 A3
Drovers Ct
3 Kingston u T
KT1............. 176 A1
Lewisham SE13..... 142 A2
Drovers Pl SE15......140 B5
Drovers Rd CR2......221 B3
Dr Triplett's CE Prim
Sch UB3..............83 D1
Druce Rd SE21.......161 C5
Druid St SE1..117 D4 253 C1
Druids Way BR2 .....208 B5
Drumaline Ridge
KT4 ....215 C6
Drummer Lo N7 ......72 B5
Drummond Castle Ct
E7....................76 D4
Drummond Cres
NW1.........93 D4 232 C2
Drummond Ct
Finchley N12 ....30 C3
Harrow HA1 ....42 C2
Drummond Ctr CR0. 221 A6
Drummond Dr HA7 ...24 D3
Drummond Gate
SW1............. 259 D2
Drummond Ho
13 Bethnal Green
E2..................96 A5
Finchley N2 ....30 A1
Drummond Rd
Bermondsey SE16....118 B3
Croydon CR0 .... 221 A6
Wanstead E11........55 C3
Drummonds Pl
TW9................132 A1
Drummonds The IG9..21 B2
Drummond St
NW1.........93 C3 239 A6
Drum St E1......... 243 D2
Drury Cres CR0 ......220 C6
Drury Ho SW8 .... 269 A2
Drury La WC2.. 94 A1 240 B1
Drury Rd HA1.........42 A2
Drury Way Ind Est
NW10................67 B3
Drury Way NW10......67 B3
Dryad St SW15.......134 D2
Dryburgh Gdns NW9 ..44 C6
Dryburgh Ho SW1... 258 D2
Dryburgh Mans
SW15...............134 C2
Dryburgh Rd SW15....134 C2
Dryden Ave W7.......86 D1
Dryden Bldg 10 E1 ....96 A1
Dryden Ct
Lambeth SE11...... 261 B3
11 Richmond TW10.. 175 D6
Dryden Ho
Bromley Comm
BR2............ 209 D4
6 Camberwell SE5.. 139 C4
16 Stoke Newington
N16.............73 C5
Dryden Rd
Bexley DA16 .... 145 D4
Enfield EN1 ....17 D5
Harrow HA3 ....24 D2
Wimbledon SW19 ... 180 A4
Dryden St WC2 ..... 240 B1
Dryer Ct 21 EN3........7 C6
Dryfield Cl NW10 .....67 A2
Dryfield Rd HA8 ......27 A4
Dryfield Wlk 1 SE8 ..141 C6
Dryhill Rd DA17......147 B6
Dryland Ave 5 BR6 ..227 D4
Drylands Rd N8........50 A3
Drysdale Ave E4 ......19 D5
Drysdale Flats 3 E8 ..73 D3
Drysdale Ho 19 E2 ....95 C4
Drysdale Pl N1 ....95 C4
Drysdale St N1 ....95 C4
Dublin Ave E8 ....96 A6
Du Burstow Terr
W7.................108 C4
Ducal St 25 E2.......95 D4
Ducane Cl 6 W12 ....90 C1
Du Cane Ct SW12 ....159 A3
Du Cane Rd W12......90 A1
Ducavel Ho SW2......160 B3
Duchess Cl
London N11..........31 B5
Sutton SM1 .... 218 A4
Duchess Gr IG9.......21 B2
Duchess Mews W1.. 238 D3
Duchess of Bedford Ho
W8............. 245 A2

Duchess of Bedford's Wlk W8 ... 113 C4 245 A1
Duchess St W1 ... 93 B2 238 D3
Duchy Rd EN4 ... 2 B5
Duchy St SE1 ... 116 C5 251 B4
Ducie Ho
8 Charlton SE7 ... 143 C6
2 Putney SW15 ... 156 C6
Ducie St SW4 ... 138 B1
Duckett Mews N4 ... 50 D3
Duckett Rd N4 ... 50 D3
Duckett St E1 ... 97 A2
Duck La W1 ... 239 C1
Duck Lees La EN3 ... 7 A1
Ducks Hill Rd HA4, HA6 ... 39 A5
DUCKS ISLAND ... 12 D5
Duck's Wlk TW1 ... 153 C6
Du Cros Dr HA7 ... 25 D4
Du Cros Rd W3 ... 111 C5
DUDDEN HILL ... 68 A3
Dudden Hill La NW10 ... 67 D3
Duddington Cl SE9 ... 187 D6
Dudley Ave HA3 ... 43 C6
Dudley Ct
Colney Hatch N12 ... 30 C5
Marylebone W1 ... 237 C1
St Giles WC2 ... 240 A2
Temple Fortune NW11 ... 47 B5
14 Wanstead E11 ... 55 A4
Wembley HA0 ... 65 D3
Dudley Dr Ruislip HA4 ... 62 B3
West Barnes SM4 ... 201 A2
Dudley Gdns
Ealing W13 ... 109 B4
Harrow HA2 ... 42 B1
Dudley Ho
13 Brixton SW9 ... 138 C3
Edgware HA8 ... 26 B3
Paddington W2 ... 236 C3
Dudley Mews 14 SW2 ... 160 C5
Dudley Pl UB3 ... 105 B2
Dudley Rd
Ashford TW15 ... 170 B6
East Bedfont TW14 ... 149 B3
Finchley N3 ... 29 D1
Harrow HA2 ... 64 A6
Ilford IG1 ... 78 D4
Kilburn NW6 ... 91 B5
Kingston u T KT1 ... 198 B6
Richmond TW9 ... 132 B3
Southall UB2 ... 106 D3
Walthamstow E17 ... 35 C1
Walton-on-T KT12 ... 194 A2
Wimbledon SW19 ... 179 C4
Dudley St W2 ... 236 C3
Dudlington Rd E5 ... 74 C6
Dudmaston Mews SW3 ... 256 D2
Dudsbury Rd DA14 ... 190 B4
Dudset La TW5 ... 128 A4
Duett Ct TW3 ... 129 A5
Duffell Ho SE11 ... 260 D1
Dufferin Ave EC1 ... 242 C5
Dufferin Ct EC1 ... 242 C5
Dufferin St EC1 ... 95 A3 242 B5
Duffield Cl HA1 ... 42 D4
Duffield Dr N15 ... 51 D5
Duffield Ho N4 ... 51 A2
Duff St E14 ... 97 D1
Dufour's Pl W1 ... 239 B1
Dugard Way SE11 ... 116 D2 261 C3
Dugdale Ho 10 N7 ... 71 D3
Duggan Dr BR7 ... 188 A4
Dugolly Ave HA9 ... 66 D5
Duke Gdns IG6 ... 57 B5
Duke Humphrey Rd SE3 ... 142 C3
Duke Of Cambridge Cl TW2 ... 152 B5
Duke Of Edinburgh Rd SM1 ... 218 B6
Duke Of Wellington Ave SE18 ... 123 A3
Duke of Wellington Pl SW1, W1 ... 248 B2
Duke of York's Sq SW3 ... 114 D2 257 D3
Duke of York St SW1 ... 249 B4
Duke Rd
Chiswick W4 ... 111 B1
Ilford IG6 ... 57 B5
Duke St Hill SE1 ... 252 D4
Duke St St James's SW1 ... 115 C5 249 B4
Dukes Ave
Edgware HA8 ... 26 B5
Finchley N3 ... 29 D2
Hornsey N10 ... 49 C6
Hounslow TW4 ... 129 A1
Kingston u T KT3 ... 199 D6
Duke's Ave W4 ... 111 B1
Dukes Ave
Northolt UB5 ... 63 A1
Rayners La HA2, HA5 ... 41 B3
Richmond KT2, TW10 ... 175 D6
Wealdstone HA1 ... 42 C5
Dukes Cl
Ashford TW15 ... 171 A6
Hampton TW12 ... 173 B5
Dukes Ct Barking E6 ... 100 C6
Beckenham BR3 ... 207 A6
Dulwich SE22 ... 162 A3
Ealing W13 ... 87 B2
East Dulwich SE22 ... 162 B6
Lewisham SE13 ... 142 A3
Mortlake SW14 ... 133 B3
Dukes Gate 4 W4 ... 111 A2
Dukes Green Ave TW14 ... 150 A6
Dukes Head Yd N6 ... 49 B1
Duke Shore Wharf E14 ... 119 B6
Duke's Ho SW1 ... 259 D4
Dukes La W8 ... 113 D4 245 C2
Dukes Mews N10 ... 49 B6
Duke's Mews W1 ... 238 B2
Duke's Pl EC3 ... 95 C1 243 B1
Dukes Point N6 ... 49 B1
Dukes Rd Acton W3 ... 88 C3
Barking E6 ... 100 C6
Duke's Rd WC1 ... 93 D4 232 D1
Dukes Ride UB10 ... 60 A4
Dukesthorpe Rd SE26 ... 184 D6
Duke St W1 ... 93 A1 238 B1
Duke Street Mans W1 ... 238 B1
Duke St
Richmond TW10, TW9 ... 153 D6
Sutton SM1 ... 218 B4
Dukes Way BR4 ... 224 C5
Duke's Yd W1 ... 248 B6
Dulas St N4 ... 50 B1
Dulford St W11 ... 113 A6 244 A6
Dulka Rd SW11 ... 158 D6
Dulverton Ct 12 KT6 ... 198 A4
Dulverton Mans WC1 ... 240 D5
Dulverton NW1 ... 232 B5
Dulverton Prim Sch SE9 ... 167 B2
Dulverton Rd
New Eltham SE9 ... 167 B2
Ruislip HA4 ... 62 A6
DULWICH ... 161 C1
Dulwich Bsns Ctr SE23 ... 162 D3
Dulwich Coll SE21 ... 161 C2
Dulwich Coll Picture Gall* SE21 ... 161 C4
Dulwich Coll Prep Sch SE21 ... 161 C1
Dulwich Comm SE21 ... 161 C3
Dulwich Ct SE22 ... 162 B3
Dulwich Hamlet Jun Sch SE21 ... 161 B5
Dulwich Hospl SE22 ... 139 C1
Dulwich Lawn Cl SE22 ... 161 D6
Dulwich Mead SE24 ... 161 A5
Dulwich Mews
1 East Dulwich SE22 ... 139 D1
East Dulwich SE22 ... 161 D6
Dulwich Oaks The SE21 ... 161 D1
Dulwich Rd SE24 ... 160 D5
DULWICH VILLAGE ... 161 C4
Dulwich Village CE Inf Sch SE21 ... 161 C5
Dulwich Village SE21 ... 161 C5
Dulwich Wood Ave SE19 ... 183 C5
Dulwich Wood Pk SE19 ... 183 C6
Dumain Ct SE11 ... 261 C3
Du Maurier Ho 2 NW3 ... 70 D3
Dumbarton Ct 16 SW2 ... 160 A4
Dumbarton Rd SW2 ... 160 A5
Dumbleton Cl KT2 ... 176 D2
Dumbreck Rd SE9 ... 144 C2
Dumont Rd N16 ... 73 C5
Dumphreys Ho 5 SW4 ... 159 D4
Dumpton Pl NW1 ... 71 A1
Dunally Pk TW17 ... 193 B2
Dunbar Ave
Beckenham BR3 ... 207 A5
Dagenham RM10 ... 81 C5
Thornton Heath SW16 ... 182 C1
Dunbar Cl UB4 ... 84 A2
Dunbar Ct
3 London N12 ... 29 D6
Sutton SM1 ... 218 B3
Walton-on-T KT12 ... 194 C1
Dunbar Gdns RM10 ... 81 D3
Dunbar Rd
New Malden KT3 ... 199 A5
Tottenham N22 ... 32 D2
Upton E7 ... 77 A2
Dunbar St SE27 ... 161 A1
Dunbar Wharf 20 E14 ... 119 B6
Dunblane Cl HA8 ... 10 D2
Dunblane Rd SE9 ... 144 A3
Dunboe Pl TW17 ... 193 A2
Dunboyne Rd NW3 ... 70 D3
Dunbridge Ho SW15 ... 155 D5
Dunbridge St
Bethnal Green E2 ...
Bethnal Green E2 ... 96 B3
Duncan Cl EN5 ... 2 A1
Duncan Ct
5 London N12 ... 29 D5
3 Poplar E14 ... 98 A2
Southgate N21 ... 16 D3
Duncan Gr W3 ... 89 C1
Duncan Ho
Harrow HA2 ... 64 A5
3 Primrose Hill NW3 ... 70 D1
Duncannon Ho SW1 ... 259 D1
Duncannon St WC2 ... 250 A5
Duncan Rd
Hackney E8 ... 96 B6
Richmond TW9 ... 132 A1
Duncan St N1 ... 94 D5 234 C4
Duncan Terr N1 ... 94 D5 234 C4
Dunch St 33 E1 ... 96 B1
Dunchurch Ho RM10 ... 81 C1
Duncombe Hill SE23 ... 163 A4
Duncombe Ho 7 SW19 ... 156 D3
Duncombe Prim Sch N19 ... 50 A1
Duncombe Rd N19 ... 49 D1
Duncrievie Rd SE13 ... 164 B5
Duncroft SE18 ... 145 C5
Dundalk Ho 2 E1 ... 96 C1
Dundalk Rd SE4 ... 141 A2
Dundas Gdns KT8 ... 195 D6
Dundas Ho 12 E2 ... 96 C5
Dundas Mews 4 EN3 ... 7 C6
Dundas Rd SE15 ... 140 C3
Dundee Ct 38 E1 ... 118 B5
Dundee Ho W9 ... 229 A2
Dundee Rd
Croydon SE25 ... 206 B4
Newham E13 ... 99 B5
Dundee St E1 ... 118 B5
Dundee Way EN3 ... 7 A2
Dundee Wharf E14 ... 119 B6
Dundela Gdns KT17, KT4 ... 216 B4
Dundonald Cl 6 E6 ... 100 A1
Dundonald Prim Sch SW19 ... 179 B3
Dundonald Rd
Brondesbury Pk NW10 ... 90 D6
Merton SW19 ... 179 B3
Dundonald Road Sta SW19 ... 179 B3
Dundry Ho 8 SE26 ... 162 A1
Duneaves HA1 ... 64 C5
Dunedin Ho E16 ... 122 B5
Dunedin Rd
Ilford IG1 ... 57 A1
Leyton E10 ... 75 D5
Dunedin Way UB4 ... 84 C3
Dunelm Gr SE27 ... 161 A1
Dunelm St E1 ... 96 D1
Dunfield Gdns SE6 ... 185 D5
Dunfield Rd SE6 ... 185 D5
Dunford Ct 9 HA5 ... 23 B3
Dunford Rd N7 ... 72 B4
Dungarvan Ave SW15 ... 134 A1
Dungeness Ho SW18 ... 136 A1
Dunheved Cl CR7 ... 204 C3
Dunheved Ct 2 CR7 ... 204 C3
Dunheved Rd N CR7 ... 204 C3
Dunheved Rd S CR7 ... 204 C3
Dunheved Rd W CR7 ... 204 C3
Dunhill Point 12 SW15 ... 156 B3
Dunholme Gn N9 ... 17 D1
Dunholme La N9 ... 17 D1
Dunholme Rd N9 ... 17 D1
Dunkeld Ho 15 E14 ... 98 B1
Dunkeld Rd
Dagenham RM8 ... 80 C6
South Norwood SE25 ... 205 B5
Dunkery Rd SE9 ... 166 A1
Dunkirk St 12 SE27 ... 183 A6
Dunlace Rd E5 ... 74 D4
Dunleary Cl TW4 ... 151 B4
Dunley Dr CR0 ... 224 A2
Dunlin Ct 12 SE21 ... 161 B2
Dunlin Ho 13 SE16 ... 118 D2
Dunloe Ave N17 ... 51 B6
Dunloe Ct 7 E2 ... 95 D5
Dunloe St E2 ... 95 D5
Dunlop Pl SE16 ... 117 D3 263 D5
Dunmore Point 15 E2 ... 95 D4
Dunmore Rd
Kilburn NW6 ... 91 A6
Wimbledon SW20 ... 178 D2
Dunmow Cl
Dagenham RM6 ... 58 C4
3 Feltham TW13 ... 173 A6
Dunmow Ho
Dagenham RM9 ... 102 B6
Vauxhall SE11 ... 260 D2
Dunmow Rd E15 ... 76 B4
Dunmow Wlk N1 ... 235 A6
Dunnage Cres SE16 ... 119 A2
Dunne Mews 11 NW5 ... 71 C3
Dunnet Ho 27 E3 ... 97 B5
Dunnico Ho SE17 ... 263 A2
Dunn Mead NW9 ... 27 D3
Dunnock Cl N9 ... 18 D3
Dunnock Ct 11 SE21 ... 161 B2
Dunnock Rd E6 ... 100 A1
Dunn's Pas WC1 ... 240 B2
Dunn St E8 ... 73 D3
Dunollie Pl NW5 ... 71 C3
Dunollie Rd NW5 ... 71 C3
Dunoon Gdns SE23 ... 162 D4
Dunoon Ho N1 ... 233 C5
Dunoon Rd SE23 ... 162 C4
Dunraven Dr EN2 ... 4 C3
Dunraven Ho 12 TW9 ... 132 B4
Dunraven Rd W12 ... 112 A5
Dunraven Sch SW16 ... 160 B1
Dunraven St W1 ... 114 D6 247 D6
Dunrobin Ct NW3 ... 69 D3
Dunsany Rd W14 ... 112 D3
Dunsfold Ct 14 SM2 ... 217 D1
Dunsfold Ho
10 Kingston u T KT2 ... 176 D4
4 Streatham SW2 ... 160 B4
Dunsfold Way CR0 ... 223 D1
Dunsford Way SW15 ... 156 B5
Dunsmore Cl
Bushey WD23 ... 8 B5
Hayes UB4 ... 85 A3
Dunsmore Rd KT12 ... 194 B3
Dunsmore Way WD23 ... 8 B5
Dunsmure Rd N16 ... 51 C1
Dunstable Ct 3 SE3 ... 143 A5
Dunstable Mews W1 ... 238 B4
Dunstable Rd
East Molesey KT8 ... 195 B5
Richmond TW10, TW9 ... 132 A1
Dunstall Ho 9 SE15 ... 140 A4
Dunstall Rd SW19, SW20 ... 178 C4
Dunstall Way KT8 ... 195 D6
Dunstall Welling Est DA16 ... 146 B3
Dunstan Cl 2 N2 ... 48 A6
Dunstan Glade BR5 ... 211 B3
Dunstan Ho SE4 ... 141 B3
Dunstan Hos 5 E1 ... 96 C2
Dunstan Rd NW11 ... 47 C1
Dunstan's Gr SE22 ... 162 B5
Dunstan's Rd SE22 ... 162 A5
Dunster Ave SM4 ... 200 D1
Dunster Ct EC3 ... 253 B6
Dunster Dr NW9 ... 45 A1
Dunster Gdns NW6 ... 69 B1
Dunster Ho SE6 ... 163 D1
Dunsterville Way SE1 ... 252 D1
Dunster Way
Carshalton CR4 ... 203 A1
Harrow HA2 ... 63 A5
Dunston Rd
Clapham SW11 ... 137 A3
Hackney E8 ... 95 D6
Dunston St E8 ... 95 D6
Dunton Cl KT6 ... 198 A1
Dunton Ct 5 SE26 ... 162 B2
Dunton Ho 14 SW16 ... 160 A1
Dunton Rd
Bermondsey SE1 ... 117 D2 263 C3
Leyton E10 ... 53 D2
Duntshill Rd SW18 ... 157 D3
Dunvegan Cl KT8 ... 195 D5
Dunvegan Rd SE9 ... 144 B1
Dunwich Ct 2 RM6 ... 58 B4
Dunwich Rd DA7 ... 147 B4
Dunworth Mews W11 ... 91 B1
Duplex Ride SW1 ... 247 D1
Dupont Rd SW20 ... 178 D1
Duppas Ave CR0 ... 220 D4
Duppas Cl TW17 ... 193 B4
Duppas Ct CR0 ... 220 D5
Duppas Hill La CR0 ... 220 D4
Duppas Hill Rd CR0 ... 220 D4
Duppas Hill Terr CR0 ... 220 D5
Duppas Jun Sch CR0 ... 220 D3
Duppas Rd CR0 ... 220 D5
Dupree Rd SE7 ... 121 B1
Dura Den Cl BR3 ... 185 D3
Durand Cl SM5 ... 202 D1
Durand Gdns SW9 ... 138 B4 270 D1
Durand Prim Sch SW9 ... 138 B4 270 D2
Durand Way NW10 ... 67 A1
Durants Lo EN3 ... 6 D2
Durants Park Ave EN3 ... 6 D1
Durants Rd EN3 ... 6 D1
Durants Sch EN3 ... 6 C4
Durant St E2 ... 96 A4
Durban Ct E7 ... 77 D1
Durban Ho 28 W12 ... 112 B6
Durban Rd
Beckenham BR3 ... 185 B1
Ilford IG2 ... 57 C1
Newham E15 ... 98 C4
Tottenham N17 ... 33 D4
Walthamstow E17 ... 35 B2
West Norwood SE27 ... 183 B6
Durbin Ho 13 N9 ... 18 A1
Durbin Rd KT9 ... 214 B4
Durdan Cotts UB5 ... 85 B1
Durdans Ho 3 NW1 ... 71 C1
Durdans Park Prim Sch UB1 ... 85 B2
Durdans Rd UB1 ... 85 B1
Durell Gdns RM9 ... 80 D3
Durell Rd RM9 ... 80 D3
Durfey Pl SE5 ... 139 B5
Durford Cres SW15 ... 156 B3
Durham Ave
Beckenham BR2 ... 208 D5
Hounslow TW5 ... 107 B1
Woodford IG8 ... 37 D5
Durham Cl SW20 ... 178 B1
Durham Ct
2 Barnet EN5 ... 1 B2
Brockley SE4 ... 141 C2
4 Kilburn NW6 ... 91 C5
Teddington TW11 ... 174 C6
Durham Hill BR1 ... 186 D6
Durham Ho
3 Barking IG11 ... 80 A1
7 Dartmouth Pk NW5 ... 71 C5
Edgware HA8 ... 26 B3
Lisson Gr NW8 ... 230 B1
Durham House St WC2 ... 250 B5
Durham Pl
Chelsea SW3 ... 257 C1
Ilford IG1 ... 79 A4
Durham Rd
Beckenham BR2 ... 208 D6
Ealing W5 ... 109 D3
Edmonton N9 ... 18 A2
Feltham TW14 ... 150 C4
Harrow HA1 ... 41 D4
Lower Holloway N4, N7 ... 72 B6
Manor Pk E12 ... 77 D4
Muswell Hill N2 ... 48 D6
Newham E16 ... 98 C3
Sidcup DA14 ... 190 B5
Wimbledon SW20 ... 178 B2
Durham Rise SE18 ... 123 B1
Durham Row E1 ... 97 A2
Durham St SE11 ... 138 B6 27
Durham Terr W2 ... 9
Durham Wharf Dr TW8 ... 13
Durley Ave HA5 ... 4
Durley Rd N16 ... 5
Durlock Ho 16 SW9 ... 13
Durlston Rd
Kingston u T KT2 ... 17
Stoke Newington E5 ... 7
Durnford Ho SE6 ... 16
Durnford St
4 Greenwich SE10 ... 14
South Tottenham N15 ... 5
Durning Rd SE19 ... 18
Durnsford Ave SW18, SW19 ... 15
Durnsford Ct 5 EN3 ...
Durnsford Rd
London N11 ... 3
Wimbledon SW18, SW19 ... 15
Durnston Ct 2 SM1 ... 21
Durrant Ct HA3 ... 2
Durrant Way BR6 ... 22
Durrell Rd SW6 ... 26
Durrell Way TW17 ... 19
Durrels Ho W14 ... 25
Durrington Ave SW20 ... 17
Durrington Park Rd SW20 ... 17
Durrington Rd E5 ... 7
Durrington Twr 3 SW8 ... 13
Durrisdeer Ho NW2 ... 6
Dursley Cl SE3 ... 14
Dursley Gdns SE3 ... 14
Dursley Rd SE3 ... 14
Durston House Middleton's Sch W5 ... 8
Durston House Prep Sch W5 ... 8
Durston NW5 ... 7
Durward St E1 ... 9
Durweston Mews W1 ... 23
Durweston St W1 ... 23
Dury Rd EN5 ...
Dutch Gdns KT2 ... 17
Dutch Yd SW18 ... 15
Dutton Ho SW2 ... 16
Dutton St SE10 ... 14
Duxberry Cl BR2 ... 21
Duxford Ho 10 SE2 ... 12
Duxford 21 KT1 ... 17
Dwight Ct SW6 ... 13
Dycer Ho 10 E9 ... 7
Dye House La E3 ... 9
Dyer Ho
Hampton TW12 ... 17
New Cross SE4 ... 14
Dyer's Bldgs EC1 ... 24
Dyers Hall Rd
Leyton E11 ... 7
Leytonstone E11 ... 5
Dyer's La SW15 ... 13
Dykes Ct 11 SW2 ... 16
Dykes Way BR2 ... 20
Dylan Cl WD6 ...
Dylan Rd
Belvedere DA17 ... 12
2 Brixton SE24 ... 13
Dylways SE5 ... 13
Dymchurch Cl
Ilford IG5 ... 5
Orpington BR6 ... 22
Dymchurch Ho 12 E5 ... 7
Dymes Path SW19 ... 15
Dymock St SW6 ... 13
Dyneley Rd SE12 ... 16
Dyne Rd NW6 ... 6
Dynevor Rd
Richmond TW10 ... 15
Shacklewell N16 ... 7
Dynham Rd NW6 ... 6
Dyott St Soho WC1 ... 23
St Giles WC1, WC2 ... 94 A1 24
Dysart Ave KT2, TW10 ... 17
Dysart Sch KT6 ... 19
Dysart St EC2 ... 95 C3 24
Dyson Ct London NW2 ... 4
Wembley HA0 ... 6
Dyson Ho 3 SE10 ... 12
Dyson Rd
Leytonstone E11 ... 5
Stratford E15 ... 7
Dyson's Rd N18 ... 3

Rd N4 ... 51 A2
ns Cl N2 ... 48 B6
e Ave RM6 ... 59 A3
e Cl
mondsey
E16 ... 118 C1
ield EN3 ... 6 C1
llington SM6 ... 220 A2
e Ct
Dulwich SE21 ... 161 B2
nonton N18 ... 33 D4
born EC1 ... 241 C4
Wanstead E11 ... 55 A5
e Dr NW9 ... 27 C1
le Dwellings EC1 235 B2
e Hill SE19 ... 183 B4
e Ho
Bethnal Green
1 ... 96 B3
sbury Pk N7 ... 72 B5
le House Sch
4 ... 180 D1
le Hts 10 SW11 ... 136 C2
e La E11 ... 55 A5
e Lo
ytonstone E11 ... 54 D5
ndon NW11 ... 47 B2
le Mans N16 ... 73 D3
le Mews N1 ... 73 C2
le Pl
uth Kensington
SW7 ... 114 A1 256 B2
James SW1 ... 249 B5
le Rd
tton TW6 ... 127 D2
embley HA0 ... 65 D1
lesfield Rd SE18 .. 144 D4
le Star Ho SM1 ... 217 D4
le St WC1 .. 94 B2 240 C3
le Terr IG8 ... 37 B3
le Trad Est CR4 .. 202 D3
le Wharf Rd
... 95 A5 235 B4
le Wharf SE1 ... 253 C3
le Works E1 ... 243 D5
ling Cl E3 ... 97 C4
com Ct W5 ... 110 B5
dham Prim Sch
9 ... 143 C1
dham Sq SE9 ... 143 C1
LING ... 109 D6
ing Broadway Ctr
5 ... 109 D6
ing Broadway Sta
5 ... 109 D6
ing Coll W13 ... 87 B1
ing Coll of Higher Ed
5 ... 109 D5
ing Common W5 .. 110 B6
ing Common Sta
5 ... 110 B5
ing Court Man
5 ... 109 D4
ing Gateway W5 .. 109 C6
ing Gn W5 ... 109 D5
ing, Hammersmith &
est London Coll
14 ... 113 A1 254 A2
ing Hospl UB1,
B2 ... 108 B4
ing Park Gdns
5 ... 109 C2
ing Park Lo UB6 ... 87 A5
ing Park Mans
5 ... 109 D3
ing Rd
rentford TW8 ... 109 D2
ortholt UB5 ... 63 C1
embley HA0 ... 66 A1
ing Road Trad Est
W8 ... 109 D1
ing Tertiary Coll
3 ... 110 D5
ing Village W5 ... 88 A1
ing & West London
oll W5 ... 109 D5
mann Casey Ho 34
W9 ... 138 C4
mont Cl HA4 ... 38 D2
mont Ct NW8 ... 230 B4
mont St
W8 ... 92 C5 230 B4
rdley Cres
W5 ... 113 C1 255 B1
rdley Point 9
E18 ... 122 D2
rdley Rd
elvedere DA17 ... 125 C1
treatham SW16 ... 181 C4
rdley Sch SW16 .. 181 C4
rl Cl N11 ... 31 B5
rldom Rd SW15 ... 134 C1
rle Gdns KT2 ... 176 A3
rle Ho SW1 ... 259 D3

Earlham Gr
Forest Gate E7 ... 77 A3
Wood Green N22 ... 32 B3
Earlham Prim Sch
Stratford E7 ... 76 D3
Wood Green N22 ... 32 C3
Earlham St
WC2 ... 94 A1 240 A1
Earl Ho NW1 ... 237 B5
Earlom Ho WC1 ... 234 A1
Earl Rd SW14 ... 133 A1
Earl Rise SE18 ... 123 B2
EARL'S COURT ... 113 C1
Earl's Court Ex Ctr*
SW5 ... 113 C1 255 A1
Earl's Court Gdns
SW5 ... 113 D2 255 C3
Earl's Court Rd SW5,
W8 ... 113 C2 255 B4
Earl's Court Sq
SW5 ... 113 D1 255 C2
Earl's Court Sta
SW5 ... 113 C2 255 B3
Earls Cres HA1 ... 42 C5
Earlsdown Ho 6
IG11 ... 101 B5
Earlsferry Way N1 ... 72 A1
EARLSFIELD ... 158 A3
Earlsfield Ho 16
KT2 ... 175 D2
Earlsfield Prim Sch
SW18 ... 158 A2
Earlsfield Rd SW18 ... 158 A4
Earlsfield Sta SW18. 158 A3
Earlshall Rd SE9 ... 144 C1
Earlsmead Fst & Mid
Sch HA2 ... 63 B4
Earlsmead HA2 ... 63 B4
Earlsmead Prim Sch
N15 ... 51 D5
Earlsmead Rd
Kensal Green
NW10 ... 90 C4
South Tottenham N15 .. 51 D4
Earl St EC2 ... 95 C2 243 A4
Earls Terr W8 ... 254 D5
Earlsthorpe Mews 3
SW12 ... 159 A5
Earlsthorpe Rd
SE26 ... 184 D6
Earlstoke St EC1 ... 234 C2
Earlston Gr E9 ... 96 B6
Earls Wlk
Dagenham RM8 ... 80 B4
Kensington
W8 ... 113 C3 255 A5
Earlswood Ave CR7 .. 204 C4
Earlswood Cl 10
SE10 ... 120 C1
Earlswood Gdns IG5 .. 56 C6
Earlswood Ho 2
SW2 ... 160 B3
Earlswood St SE10 ... 120 C1
Early Mews NW1 ... 231 D6
Earnshaw Ho EC1 ... 234 D1
Earnshaw St WC1,
WC2 ... 239 D2
Earsby St W14 ... 254 B4
Earth Galleries*
SW7 ... 114 B3 256 D5
Easby Cres SM4 ... 201 D3
Easebourne Rd RM8 .. 80 C3
Easedale Ho TW7 ... 152 D6
Eashing Point 5
SW15 ... 156 B3
Easleys Mews W1 ... 238 B2
East 10 Ent Pk E10 ... 53 A1
EAST ACTON ... 111 C5
East Acton Arc W3 ... 89 D1
East Acton Ct W3 ... 111 C6
East Acton La W3 ... 111 C6
East Acton Prim Sch
W3 ... 111 C6
East Acton Sta W12 .. 89 D1
East Arbour St E1 ... 96 D1
East Ave
Croydon CR0 ... 220 B3
East Finchley NW2 ... 48 A6
Hayes UB3 ... 106 A5
Plashet E12 ... 78 A1
Southall UB1 ... 107 B6
Walthamstow E17 ... 53 D5
East Bank N16 ... 51 C2
Eastbank Rd TW12 ... 174 A5
EAST BARNET ... 14 D4
East Barnet Rd EN4 ... 2 B1
East Barnet Sch
Barnet EN4 ... 2 B2
East Barnet EN4 ... 14 D5
East Beckton District
Ctr E6 ... 100 B2
EAST BEDFONT ... 149 C3
East Block 5 E1 ... 118 D6
Eastbourne Ave W3 ... 89 B1
Eastbourne Gdns
SW14 ... 133 A2

Eastbourne Mews
W2 ... 92 A1 236 B2
Eastbourne Rd
Brentford TW8 ... 109 D1
Chiswick W4 ... 133 A6
Feltham TW13 ... 150 D2
South Tottenham N15 .. 51 C3
Streatham SW17 ... 181 A4
Wallend E6 ... 100 C4
West Ham E15 ... 98 C6
Eastbourne Terr
W2 ... 92 A1 236 B2
Eastbournia Ave N9 ... 18 B1
Eastbrook Ave N9 ... 18 C4
Eastbrook Rd SE3 ... 143 B4
EASTBURY ... 22 A5
Eastbury Ave
Barking IG11 ... 101 C6
Enfield EN1 ... 5 D4
Mo Pk HA6 ... 22 A5
Eastbury Comp Sch
IG11 ... 79 C2
Eastbury Ct
Barking IG11 ... 101 C6
New Barnet EN5 ... 14 A6
Eastbury Gr W4 ... 111 C1
Eastbury Inf Sch
IG11 ... 79 D1
Eastbury Rd
Kingston u T KT2 ... 176 A3
Newham E6 ... 100 C3
Orpington BR5 ... 211 B3
Eastbury Sq IG11 ... 101 D6
Eastbury Terr E1 ... 96 D3
Eastcastle St
W1 ... 93 C1 239 B2
Eastcheap
EC3 ... 117 C6 253 A6
East Churchfield Rd
W3 ... 111 B5
Eastchurch Rd TW6 .. 127 C2
Eastchurch Road Rdbt
TW6 ... 127 C3
East Cl Cockfosters EN4 .. 3 A1
Ealing W5 ... 88 C3
Greenford UB6 ... 86 A5
Eastcombe Ave SE7 .. 143 B6
EASTCOTE ... 40 C3
Eastcote Ave
East Molesey KT8 ... 195 C4
Harrow HA2 ... 64 A6
Wembley UB6 ... 65 A3
Eastcote BR6 ... 211 D1
Eastcote Ind Est HA4 .40 C2
Eastcote La HA2 ... 63 C5
Eastcote La N UB5 ... 63 C2
Eastcote La UB5 ... 63 B2
Eastcote Pl HA5 ... 40 B3
Eastcote Prim Sch
DA16 ... 145 B2
Eastcote Rd
Bexley DA16 ... 145 B3
Harrow HA2 ... 64 A5
Pinner HA5 ... 40 D4
Ruislip HA4 ... 40 A3
Eastcote Sta HA5 ... 40 C2
Eastcote St SW9 ... 138 B3
Eastcote View HA5 ... 40 C5
EASTCOTE VILLAGE .. 40 B4
Eastcourt Ind Sch
IG3 ... 58 A1
East Cres Enfield EN1 ... 17 D6
Friern Barnet N11 ... 30 D6
Eastcroft Rd KT19 ... 215 C1
East Cross Ctr E15 ... 75 C2
East Cross Route
Bow E3 ... 97 C6
Hackney Wick E9 ... 75 B3
East Croydon Sta
CR0 ... 221 B6
East Ct
Sunbury TW16 ... 172 C1
Wembley HA0 ... 65 C6
Eastdown Ho E8 ... 74 A4
Eastdown Pk SE13 ... 142 B1
East Duck Lees La
EN3 ... 7 B1
EAST DULWICH ... 162 A6
East Dulwich Gr
SE22 ... 161 C6
East Dulwich Rd SE15,
SE22 ... 140 A1
East Dulwich Sta
SE22 ... 139 C1
East End Rd
East Finchley N2,
N3 ... 48 A6
Finchley N3 ... 29 C1
East End Way HA5 ... 41 A6
East Entrance
RM10 ... 103 D5
Eastern Ave
Gants Hill IG1, IG2,
IG4 ... 56 C3
Newbury Pk IG2 ... 57 B3
Eastern Avenue W
RM7 ... 59 C5

Eastern Ave
Pinner HA5 ... 40 D2
Wanstead E11 ... 55 C3
Eastern Bsns Pk
TW16 ... 127 D3
Eastern Perimeter Rd
TW14 ... 127 D3
Eastern Quay 15
E16 ... 121 B5
Eastern Rd
Brockley SE4 ... 141 C1
Fortis Green N2 ... 48 D5
Newham E13 ... 99 B5
Walthamstow E17 ... 54 A4
Wood Green N22 ... 32 A2
Easternville Gdns
IG2 ... 57 A3
Eastern Way SE28 ... 124 B4
East Ferry Rd E14 ... 119 D2
Eastfield Gdns RM10 .. 81 C4
Eastfield Prim Sch
EN3 ... 6 D5
Eastfield Rd
Dagenham RM9 ... 81 B4
Dagenham RM10 ... 81 C4
Enfield EN3 ... 6 D5
Hornsey N8 ... 50 A6
Walthamstow E17 ... 53 C5
Eastfields Ave
SW18 ... 135 C1
Eastfields HA5 ... 40 C4
Eastfields Rd
Acton W3 ... 89 A2
Mitcham CR4 ... 181 A1
Eastfield St E14 ... 97 A2
EAST FINCHLEY ... 48 B5
East Finchley Sta N2 .48 C5
Eastgate Bsns Pk
E10 ... 53 A1
Eastgate Cl SE28 ... 102 D1
Eastgate Ct N3 ... 29 C1
East Gdns SW17 ... 180 C4
Eastglade HA5 ... 41 B6
EAST HAM ... 100 A5
Eastham Cl EN5 ... 13 B6
East Ham Ind Est
E6 ... 100 A2
East Ham Manor Way
E6 ... 100 C1
East Ham Meml Hospl
E7 ... 77 D1
East Ham Sta E6 ... 78 A1
East Harding St EC4 .. 241 B2
East Heath Rd NW3 ... 70 B5
East Hill
London SW18 ... 158 A6
Wembley HA9 ... 44 C1
Eastholme UB3 ... 106 A5
Eastholm NW11 ... 47 D5
East India Bldgs 9
E14 ... 119 C6
East India Ct 7
SE16 ... 118 C4
East India Dock Basin*
E14 ... 120 C6
East India Dock Rd
E14 ... 119 D6
East India Dock Road
Tunnel 18 E14 ... 98 B1
East India Sta E14 ... 120 B6
East India Way CR0 .. 205 D1
East La
5 Bermondsey
SE16 ... 118 A4
Bermondsey SE16 ... 118 A4
Eastlake Ho NW8 ... 236 D5
Eastlake Rd SE5 ... 139 A3
East La KT1 ... 197 D6
Eastland Ct 2 BR1 ... 187 C1
Eastlands Cres
SE21 ... 161 D5
East Lane Bsns Pk
HA9 ... 65 D5
East La HA0, HA9 ... 65 D5
Eastlea Com Sch E16 .98 C3
Eastlea Mews E16 ... 98 C3
Eastleigh Ave HA2 ... 63 D6
Eastleigh Cl
Belmont SM2 ... 217 D1
Neasden NW2 ... 67 C5
Eastleigh Rd E17 ... 35 B1
Eastleigh Way
TW14 ... 150 A3
Eastleigh Wlk 9
SW15 ... 156 A4
East London Coll
E11 ... 76 C6
East London Coll &
Toynbee Theatre
E1 ... 95 D2 243 D3
East London Stad E3 .97 B2
Eastman Dental Hospl
WC1 ... 94 B3 240 C6
Eastman Ho 7
SW4 ... 159 C5
Eastman Rd W3 ... 111 B4

East Mascalls 15
SE7 ... 143 C6
Eastmead Ave UB6 ... 85 D4
Eastmead Cl BR1 ... 188 A1
Eastmead IG3 ... 58 A2
East Mead HA4 ... 62 D5
Eastmearn Rd SE21,
SE27 ... 161 A2
EAST MOLESEY ... 196 A4
Eastmont Rd KT10 ... 212 D6
Eastmoor Pl SE7 ... 121 D3
Eastmoor St SE7 ... 121 D3
East Mount St E1 ... 96 B2
Eastney Rd CR0 ... 204 D1
Eastney St SE10 ... 120 B1
Eastnor Rd SE9 ... 167 A3
Easton Ho 4 SE27 ... 160 D1
Easton St WC1 ... 241 A6
East Park Cl RM6 ... 59 A4
East Parkside SE10 .. 120 D4
East Pas EC1 ... 242 A4
East Plaza E14 ... 119 D5
East Pl SE27 ... 183 A6
East Point 4 SE1 ... 118 A1
Eastpole Cotts N14 ... 3 D1
East Poultry Ave
EC1 ... 241 C3
East Putney Sta
SW15 ... 157 A6
East Ramp TW6 ... 126 D4
East Rd Burnt Oak HA8 .. 27 A2
Chelsea
SW1 ... 115 A1 258 A1
Dagenham RM6 ... 59 A4
East Barnet EN4 ... 15 A3
East Bedfont TW14 ... 149 B4
Enfield EN3 ... 6 C5
Finchley N2 ... 30 C2
Kingston u T KT2 ... 176 A2
Newham E15 ... 99 A6
Shoreditch
N1 ... 95 B4 235 D2
Welling DA16 ... 146 B3
West Drayton UB7 ... 104 C2
Wimbledon SW19 ... 180 A4
East Rochester Way DA5,
DA15, SE9 ... 168 C5
East Row
Kensal Town W10 ... 91 A3
Wanstead E11 ... 55 A3
Eastry Ave BR2 ... 208 D3
Eastry Ho SW8 ... 270 A3
Eastry Rd DA8 ... 147 C5
EAST SHEEN ... 133 B1
East Sheen Ave
SW14 ... 133 B1
East Sheen Prim Sch
SW14 ... 133 C1
Eastside Rd NW11 ... 47 B5
East Smithfield
E1 ... 117 D6 253 D5
East St Barking IG11 ... 79 A1
Bexleyheath DA7 ... 147 C1
Brentford TW8 ... 131 C5
Bromley BR1 ... 187 A1
Walworth
SE17 ... 117 B1 262 C2
East Surrey Gr
SE15 ... 139 D5
East Tenter St
E1 ... 95 D1 243 D1
East Terr DA15 ... 167 C3
East Thamesmead Bsns
Pk DA18 ... 125 B4
East Towers HA5 ... 40 D3
Eastvale W3 ... 111 D5
Eastview Ave SE18 ... 145 C5
East View Barnet EN5 ... 1 B2
Chingford E4 ... 36 A5
Hampstead NW3 ... 70 B6
East View Ho 13 N2 ... 30 B1
Eastville Ave NW11 ... 47 B3
Eastway Cres HA2 ... 63 D6
East Way CR0 ... 223 A5
Eastway BR2 ... 209 A2
East Way UB3 ... 106 A5
Eastway SM4, SW20 ... 201 A5
East Way HA4 ... 40 A1
Eastway
South Hackney E3,
E9 ... 97 A6
Temple Mills E9, E10 ... 75 C4
Wallington SM6 ... 219 C4
Wanstead E11 ... 55 B4
Eastwell Cl BR3 ... 185 A2
Eastwell Ho SE1 ... 262 D6
Eastwick Ct 2
SW19 ... 156 D3
EAST WICKHAM ... 146 A5
East Wickham Inf Sch
DA16 ... 145 D4
East Wickham Jun Sch
DA16 ... 146 A4
East Wlk
East Barnet EN4 ... 15 A3
Hayes UB3 ... 106 A5

Eastwood Cl
2 Islington N7 ... 72 C3
7 Tottenham N17 ... 34 B3
Woodford E18 ... 37 A1
Eastwood Rd
Ilford IG3 ... 58 A2
Muswell Hill N10 ... 31 A1
West Drayton UB7 ... 104 C4
Woodford E18 ... 37 A1
East Woodside DA5 .. 169 A3
Eastwood St SW16 ... 181 C4
Eatington Rd E10 ... 54 B4
Eaton Cl
Belgravia SW1 ... 258 A3
Stanmore HA7 ... 25 B6
Eaton Ct
Chislehurst BR7 ... 189 A4
Ealing W5 ... 87 D1
Edgware HA8 ... 26 C6
Southall UB1 ... 107 B6
Sutton SM2 ... 218 B2
6 Woodford E18 ... 37 A1
Eaton Dr
Brixton SW9 ... 138 D1
Kingston u T KT2 ... 176 C3
Eaton Gate
SW1 ... 115 A2 258 A4
Eaton Gdns RM9 ... 81 A1
Eaton Ho
Battersea SW11 ... 266 D1
Ealing W5 ... 87 D1
23 Limehouse E14 ... 119 B6
Eaton House Sch
SW1 ... 115 A2 258 A4
Eaton House The Manor
Sch SW4 ... 137 B1
Eaton La
SW1 ... 115 B3 258 D5
Eaton Lo SM2 ... 218 B2
Eaton Mans SW1 ... 258 A3
Eaton Mews N
SW1 ... 115 A3 258 B5
Eaton Mews S
SW1 ... 115 B3 258 C5
Eaton Mews W SW1. 258 B4
Eaton Park Rd N13 ... 16 D2
Eaton Pl
SW1 ... 115 A3 258 B5
Eaton Rd Enfield EN1 ... 5 C1
Hendon NW4 ... 46 C4
Isleworth TW3, TW7 .. 130 B1
Sidcup DA14 ... 168 D2
Sutton SM2 ... 218 B2
Eaton Rise Ealing W5 .. 87 D1
Wanstead E11 ... 55 C4
Eaton Row
SW1 ... 115 B3 258 C5
Eatons Mead E4 ... 19 C2
Eaton Sq
SW1 ... 115 A3 258 B5
Eaton Square Sch
SW1 ... 115 B2 258 C4
Eaton Terr
Belgravia
SW1 ... 115 A2 258 B4
Bow E3 ... 97 A4
Eaton Terr Mews
SW1 ... 258 A4
Eatonville Rd SW17 .. 158 D2
Eatonville Villas
SW17 ... 158 D2
Ebb Ct E16 ... 123 A6
Ebbisham Dr
SW8 ... 138 B6 270 C5
Ebbisham Rd KT4 ... 216 C6
Ebbsfleet Rd NW2 ... 69 A4
Ebdon Way SE3 ... 143 B2
Ebenezer Ho SE11 .. 261 C3
Ebenezer Mussel Ho 5
E2 ... 96 C5
Ebenezer St N1 ... 235 C2
Ebenezer Wlk CR4 ... 181 C2
Ebley Cl SE15 ... 139 D6
Ebner St SW18 ... 157 D6
Ebony Ct NW10 ... 67 D2
Ebony Ho
27 Bethnal Green
E2 ... 96 A4
10 West Hampstead
NW3 ... 69 D2
Ebor Cotts SW15 ... 155 C1
Ebor St E1, E2 ... 243 C6
Ebrington Rd HA3 ... 43 D3
Ebsworth St SE23 ... 162 D4
Eburne Rd N7 ... 72 A5
Ebury Bridge Rd
SW1 ... 115 A1 258 B1
Ebury Cl BR2 ... 226 A5
Ebury Mews
SW1 ... 115 B2 258 C4
Ebury Mews E SW1 . 258 C5
Ebury Mews SE27 ... 160 D1
Ebury Sq SW1 ... 258 B3

Ebury St
SW1 ... 115 B2 258 C4
Ecclesbourne Cl N13 .. 32 C5
Ecclesbourne Gdns
N13 ... 32 C5
Ecclesbourne Inf Sch
CR7 ... 205 A4
Ecclesbourne Jun Sch
CR7 ... 205 A4
Ecclesbourne Rd
Islington N1 ... 73 A1
Thornton Heath CR7 . 205 A4
Eccles Ct SE11 ... 260 D1
Eccleshill 3 BR2 ... 208 D5
Eccles Rd SW11 ... 136 D1
Eccleston Cl
Cockfosters EN4 ... 2 D1
Crofton BR6 ... 211 B1
Eccleston Cres RM6 ... 58 B2
Ecclestone Ct HA9 ... 66 A3
Ecclestone Mews
HA9 ... 66 A3
Ecclestone Pl HA9 ... 66 B3
Eccleston Ho 1
SW2 ... 160 C5
Eccleston Mews
SW1 ... 115 A3 258 B5
Eccleston Pl
SW1 ... 115 B2 258 C4
Eccleston Rd W13 ... 109 A5
Eccleston Sq Mews
SW1 ... 259 A3
Eccleston Sq
SW1 ... 115 B2 258 D3
Eccleston St
SW1 ... 115 B2 258 C4
Echelforde Dr
TW15 ... 170 C6
Echelford Prim Sch The
TW15 ... 170 D5
Echo Hts E4 ... 19 D3
Eckford St N1 ... 234 A4
Eckington Ho N15 ... 51 B3
Eckstein Rd SW11 ... 136 C1
Eclipse Ho N22 ... 32 B1
Eclipse Rd E13 ... 99 B2
Ector Rd SE6 ... 164 C2
Edam Ct 11 DA14 ... 168 A1
Edans Ct W12 ... 111 D4
Edbrooke Rd W9 ... 91 C3
Eddisbury Ho 7
SE26 ... 162 A1
Eddiscombe Rd
SW6 ... 135 B3
Eddison Ct N19 ... 72 A6
Eddy Cl RM7 ... 59 D3
Eddystone Rd SE4 ... 163 A6
Eddystone Twr SE8 ... 119 A1
Eddystone Wlk
TW19 ... 148 A4
Ede Cl TW4 ... 129 B2
Edenbridge Cl 20
SE16 ... 118 B1
Edenbridge Rd
Enfield EN1 ... 17 C5
Hackney E9 ... 74 D1
Eden Cl
Child's Hill NW3 ... 69 C6
Enfield EN3 ... 7 C5
Kensington W8 ... 255 B6
Wembley HA0 ... 87 D6
Edencourt W5 ... 88 B1
Edencourt Rd SW16 .. 181 B4
Eden Ct 3 N3 ... 29 B1
Edendale W3 ... 110 D6
Edenfield Gdns KT4 .. 215 D5
Eden Gr Islington N7 ... 72 B3
Walthamstow E17 ... 53 D4
Edenham High Sch
CR0 ... 207 B2
Edenham Way W10 ... 91 B2
Eden Ho
15 Battersea
SW11 ... 136 C2
Lisson Gr NW8 ... 237 A5
Edenhurst Ave SW6 .. 135 B2
Eden Lodge NW6 ... 68 D1
Eden Mews SW17 ... 158 A1
EDEN PARK ... 207 C5
Eden Park Ave BR3 ... 207 C4
Eden Park Sta BR3 . 207 C4
Eden Rd
Croydon CR0 ... 221 B4
Penge BR3 ... 185 A2
Walthamstow E17 ... 53 D4
West Norwood
SE27 ... 182 D5
Edensmuir Ct SE3 ... 143 A5
Edensor Gdns W4 ... 133 C5
Edensor Rd W4 ... 133 C5
Eden St KT1, KT2 ... 176 A1
Edenvale Cl CR4 ... 181 A3
Edenvale Rd CR4 ... 181 A3
Edenvale St SW6 ... 136 A3
Eden Way
Beckenham BR3 ... 207 C3
Bow E3 ... 97 B6
Eden Wlk 5 KT1 ... 176 A1
Ederline Ave SW16 ... 182 C1
Edgar Ct KT3 ... 199 C6
Edgar Ho
Homerton E9 ... 75 A3
South Lambeth SW8 . 270 A4
Wanstead E11 ... 55 A2
Edgar Kail Way
SE22 ... 139 C1
Edgarley Terr SW6 .. 264 A1
Edgar Rd Bromley E3 ... 97 D4
Dagenham RM6 ... 58 D2
Twickenham TW4 ... 151 B4
Yiewsley UB7 ... 104 A5
Edgar Wallace Cl 4
SE15 ... 139 C5
Edgbury Ct NW9 ... 45 A5
Edgcott Ho 2 W10 ... 90 C2
Edgeborough Way
BR1 ... 187 D2
Edge Bsns Ctr The
NW2 ... 68 B6
Edgebury BR7, SE9 ... 188 D6
Edgebury Prim Sch
BR7 ... 189 A6
Edgebury Wlk BR7 ... 167 A1
Edgecombe Ho
4 London SE5 ... 139 C3
Putney SW19 ... 157 A4
Edgecoombe Cl
KT2 ... 177 B3
Edgecoombe CR2 ... 222 C1
Edgecote Cl 7 W3 ... 111 A5
Edgecot Gr N15 ... 51 C4
Edgecumbe Ct 2
CR0 ... 206 A1
Edgefield Ave IG11 ... 79 D1
Edgefield Ct 3 IG11 ... 79 D1
Edge Hill Ave N3 ... 47 C5
Edge Hill Ct DA14 ... 189 D6
Edgehill Ct KT12 ... 194 C1
Edge Hill Ct SW19 ... 178 D3
Edgehill Gdns RM10 ... 81 C4
Edgehill Ho 4 SW9 .. 138 D3
Edgehill Rd
Ealing W13 ... 87 C2
Longlands BR7 ... 189 A6
Mitcham CR4 ... 181 B2
Edge Hill
Shooters Hill
SE18 ... 144 D6
Wimbledon SW19 ... 178 D3
Edgeley La SW4 ... 137 D2
Edgeley Rd SW4 ... 137 D2
Edgel St SW18 ... 135 D1
Edge Point Cl SE27 ... 182 D5
Edge St W8 .. 113 C5 245 B4
Edgewood Dr BR6 ... 227 D3
Edgewood Gn CR0 ... 206 D1
Edgeworth Ave NW4 .. 46 A4
Edgeworth Cl NW4 ... 46 A4
Edgeworth Cres
NW4 ... 46 A4
Edgeworth Ct 10 EN4 ... 2 C1
Edgeworth Ho NW8 . 229 A6
Edgeworth Rd
Barnet EN4 ... 2 C1
Eltham SE9 ... 143 D1
Edgington Rd SW16 .. 181 D4
Edgington Way
DA14 ... 190 D3
Edgson Ho SW1 ... 258 C2
EDGWARE ... 26 C6
Edgware Acad WC2. 240 B1
EDGWARE BURY ... 10 B3
Edgwarebury Ct HA8 .. 26 C5
Edgwarebury Gdns
HA8 ... 26 C5
Edgwarebury La
Edgware Bury HA8 ... 10 C2
Edgware HA8 ... 26 C5
Edgware Community
Hospl HA8 ... 26 D3
Edgware Ct HA8 ... 26 C4
Edgware Jun & Inf Schs
HA8 ... 26 C4
Edgware Rd Burnt Oak
Broadway HA8 ... 26 D3
Edgware Rd NW2 ... 68 C6
Edgware Rd High St
HA8 ... 26 C4
Edgware Rd W1, W2, NW1,
NW8 ... 92 C2 237 A3
Edgware Road Sta
(Bakerloo)
NW1 ... 92 C2 237 A3
Edgware Road Sta (Met,
Distr, Circle) NW1. 237 B3
Edgware Road The
Hyde NW9 ... 45 C5
Edgware Road West
Hendon Broadway
NW9 ... 46 A2
Edgware Sta HA8 ... 26 D4
Edgware Way (Watford
By-Pass) HA8 ... 27 A6
Edinburgh Cl
7 Bethnal Green
E2 ... 96 C5
Pinner HA5 ... 41 A2
Uxbridge UB10 ... 60 D4
Edinburgh Ct
1 Catford SE6 ... 164 D3
2 Kingston u T KT1 . 198 A6
Newham E13 ... 99 B5
10 Rotherhithe
SE16 ... 118 D5
West Barnes SM4 ... 200 D4
Edinburgh Dr UB10 ... 60 D4
Edinburgh Ho
3 Acton W3 ... 89 B1
Carshalton SM1 ... 218 B6
Hendon NW4 ... 46 C6
Maida Vale W9 ... 91 D4
Edinburgh Prim Sch
E17 ... 53 B4
Edinburgh Rd
Carshalton SM1 ... 218 B6
Edmonton N18 ... 34 A5
Hanwell W7 ... 108 D4
Newham E13 ... 99 B5
Walthamstow E17 ... 53 C4
Edington 20 NW5 ... 71 A2
Edington Rd
Abbey Wood SE2 ... 124 B3
Enfield EN3 ... 6 C3
Edison Bldg 7 E14 ... 119 C4
Edison Cl
Walthamstow E17 ... 53 C4
West Drayton UB7 ... 104 B4
Edison Ct SE10 ... 120 D3
Edison Dr
Southall UB1 ... 85 D1
Wembley HA9 ... 66 A6
Edison Gr SE18 ... 145 D5
Edison Ho
Walworth SE1 ... 262 C4
7 Wembley HA9 ... 67 A5
Edison Rd
Bexley DA16 ... 145 D4
Brimsdown EN3 ... 7 B3
Bromley BR2 ... 187 A1
Crouch End N8 ... 49 D3
Edis St NW1 ... 93 A6 231 B6
Editha Mans SW10 .. 266 A5
Edith Cavell Cl 2
N19 ... 50 A2
Edith Cavell Way
SE18 ... 144 A4
Edith Ct TW14 ... 149 B5
Edith Gdns KT5 ... 198 D2
Edith Gr
SW10 ... 136 A5 266 B4
Edith Ho 6 W6 ... 112 C1
Edithna St SW9 ... 138 A2
Edith Neville Cotts
NW1 ... 232 C2
Edith Neville Prim Sch
NW1 ... 93 D5 232 C3
Edith Pond Ct SE9 ... 166 D2
Edith Ramsay Ho 2
E1 ... 97 A2
Edith Rd
Dagenham RM6 ... 58 D2
South Norwood
SE25 ... 205 B4
Stratford New Town
E15 ... 76 B3
Upton Pk E6 ... 77 D1
West Kensington
W14 ... 113 A2 254 B3
Wimbledon SW19 ... 179 D4
Wood Green N11 ... 31 D3
Edith Row SW6 ... 265 D2
Edith St E2 ... 96 A5
Edith Summerskill Ho
SW6 ... 264 C4
Edith Terr
SW10 ... 136 A5 266 A4
Edith Villas
W14 ... 113 B1 254 C2
Edith Yd SW10 ... 266 B4
Edmansons' Cl N17 ... 33 D2
Edmeston Cl E9 ... 75 A2
Edmond Ct SE14 ... 140 C4
Edmonscote W13 ... 87 A2
EDMONTON ... 33 D6
Edmonton Ct 5
SE16 ... 118 C3
Edmonton Cty Lower
Sch N9 ... 17 C3
Edmonton Cty Upper
Sch EN1 ... 17 D4
Edmonton Green Sh Ctr
N9 ... 18 B2
Edmonton Green Sta
N9 ... 18 A2
Edmonton Wharf
N18 ... 34 D4
Edmund Gr TW13 ... 151 B2
Edmund Halley Way
SE10 ... 120 C4
Edmund Ho
Kennington SE17 ... 261 D1
New Cross Gate
SE14 ... 141 B4
Edmund Hurst Dr
E6 ... 100 D2
Edmund Rd
Mitcham CR4 ... 202 C6
Welling DA16 ... 146 A2
Edmundsbury Ct Est 16
SW9 ... 138 B1
Edmunds Cl UB4 ... 84 C2
Edmund St SE5 ... 139 B5
Edmunds Wlk N2 ... 48 C5
Edmund Waller Prim
Sch SE14 ... 140 D3
Ednam Ho SE15 ... 140 A6
Edna Rd SW20 ... 178 D1
Edna St
SW11 ... 136 C4 267 A1
Edred Ho E9 ... 75 A4
Edrich Ho SW4 ... 270 A1
Edric Ho SW1 ... 259 D4
Edrick Rd HA8 ... 27 A4
Edrick Wlk HA8 ... 27 A4
Edric Rd SE14 ... 140 D5
Edridge Cl WD23 ... 8 A6
Edridge Ho 9 SE27 .. 160 D1
Edridge Rd CR0 ... 221 B5
Edward Alleyn Ho
SE21 ... 161 C4
Edward Ave
Chingford E4 ... 35 D4
Morden SM4 ... 202 B4
Edward Betham CE
Prim Sch UB6 ... 86 A5
Edward Cl
Edmonton N9 ... 17 D4
Hampton TW12 ... 174 A5
Edward Ct
2 Ealing W5 ... 87 B3
Harrow HA1 ... 64 C6
2 Newham E16 ... 99 A2
Edward Dodd Ct N1. 235 D2
Edward Edward's Ho
SE1 ... 251 C3
Edwardes Pl W8 ... 254 D5
Edwardes Sq
W8 ... 113 B3 254 D5
Edward Friend Ho 6
N16 ... 73 C5
Edward Gr EN4 ... 14 B6
Edward Harvey Ct
DA17 ... 125 B1
Edward Ho
Paddington W2 ... 236 C5
Vauxhall SE11 ... 260 D2
Edward Kennedy Ho 18
W10 ... 91 A3
Edward Mann Cl 13
E1 ... 96 D1
Edward Mans 8
IG11 ... 79 D1
Edward Mews NW1 . 231 D3
Edward Pauling Ho
TW14 ... 149 D4
Edward Pauling Prim
Sch TW13 ... 149 C2
Edward Pinner Ct 5
KT6 ... 214 A6
Edward Pl SE8 ... 141 B6
Edward Rd
Bromley BR1 ... 187 C3
Chislehurst BR7 ... 188 D5
Croydon CR0 ... 205 C2
Dagenham RM6 ... 59 A3
Hampton TW12 ... 174 A5
Harrow HA2 ... 42 A6
Hatton TW14 ... 149 C6
New Barnet EN4 ... 14 B6
Northolt UB5 ... 84 C5
Penge SE20 ... 184 D4
Walthamstow E17 ... 52 D4
Edward Robinson Ho 3
SE14 ... 140 D5
Edward's Ave HA4 ... 62 C2
Edwards Cl KT4 ... 216 D6
Edward's Cotts 11
N1 ... 72 D1
Edwards Dr N11 ... 31 D3
Edwards Ho 7
TW10 ... 153 C1
Edward's La N16 ... 73 C6
Edwards Language Sch
W5 ... 110 A6
Edwards Mews
Islington N1 ... 72 C1
Marylebone
W1 ... 93 A1 238 A1
Edward Sq
Islington N1 ... 233 C5
1 Rotherhithe
SE16 ... 119 A5
Edwards Rd DA17 ... 125 C2
Edward St
New Cross SE14 ... 141 B5
10 Newham E16 ... 99 A3
Edward Temme Ave
E15 ... 76 D1
Edward Tyler Rd
SE12 ... 165 C2
Edward VII Mans
NW10 ... 90 D4
Edward Way TW15 ... 148 B2
Edward Wilson Prim
Sch W2 ... 91 D2
Edwina Ct SM1 ... 217 D4
Edwina Gdns IG4 ... 56 A4
Edwin Arnold Ct
DA15 ... 189 D6
Edwin Ave E6 ... 100 C5
Edwin Cl DA7 ... 147 B6
Edwin Ho SE15 ... 140 A5
Edwin Rd
Burnt Oak HA8 ... 27 B4
Twickenham TW1,
TW2 ... 152 C3
Edwin's Mead E9 ... 75 A4
Edwin St
Bethnal Green E1 ... 96 C3
Newham E16 ... 99 A2
Edwin Stray Ho
TW13 ... 151 C1
Edwin Ware Ct 4
HA5 ... 22 C1
Edwy Ho E9 ... 75 B4
Edwyn Cl EN5 ... 12 D5
Edwyn Ho SW18 ... 157 D5
Eel Pie Island*
TW1 ... 153 A3
Effie Pl SW6 ... 265 B3
Effie Rd
SW6 ... 135 C5 265 B3
Effingham Cl SM2 ... 217 D1
Effingham Ct SW19 .. 180 C3
Effingham Ho
37 Clapham SW8 ... 137 D3
9 Kingston u T KT2 . 176 D4
Effingham Lo 1
KT6 ... 198 A4
Effingham Rd
Hornsey N8 ... 50 C5
Lewisham SE12 ... 164 D6
Thames Ditton KT6,
KT7 ... 197 C2
Thornton Heath CR0 .. 204 B2
Effort St SW17 ... 180 C5
Effra Cl SW19 ... 179 D4
Effra Ct London SW2 .. 160 B6
South Norwood
SE19 ... 183 C3
Effra Mans SW2 ... 160 C6
Effra Par SW2 ... 160 C6
Effra Rd London SW2 .. 160 C6
Wimbledon SW19 ... 179 D4
Effra Road Ret Pk
SW2 ... 160 C6
EF International
Language Sch
SE1 ... 251 B3
Egan Way UB3 ... 105 C6
Egbert Ho E9 ... 75 A3
Egbert St
NW1 ... 93 A6 231 A6
Egbury Ho SW15 ... 155 D5
Egerton Cl HA5 ... 40 A5
Egerton Cres
SW3 ... 114 C2 257 B4
Egerton Ct
Leytonstone E11 ... 54 B2
5 Richmond TW10 .. 154 A6
Egerton Dr SE10 ... 141 D4
Egerton Gdns
Ealing W13 ... 87 B1
Hendon NW4 ... 46 B5
Ilford IG3 ... 79 D5
Knightsbridge
SW3 ... 114 C3 257 A5
Egerton Gdns Mews
SW3 ... 257 B5
Egerton Gdns NW10 ... 90 C6
Egerton Ho W4 ... 133 A6
Egerton Pl SW3 ... 257 B5
Egerton Rd
New Malden KT3 ... 199 D5
South Norwood
SE25 ... 205 C6
Stamford Hill N16 ... 51 D2
Twickenham TW2 ... 152 C4
Wembley HA0 ... 66 B1
Egerton Terr
SW3 ... 114 C3 257 B5
Egerton Way UB3 ... 126 D5
Eggardon Ct UB5 ... 64 A2
Egham Cl
Cheam SM3 ... 217 A6
Putney SW19 ... 157 A2
Egham Cres SM3 ... 217 A6
Egham Ct KT6 ... 197 D4
Egham Rd E13 ... 99 B2
Eglantine Rd SW18 ... 158 A6
Egleston Rd SM4 ... 20
Eglington Ct SE17 ... 13
Eglington Rd E4 ... 2
Eglinton Hill SE18 ... 14
Eglinton Prim Sch
SE18 ... 14
Eglinton Rd SE18 ... 14
Egliston Mews
SW15 ... 13
Egliston Rd SW15 ... 13
Egmont Ave KT6 ... 19
Egmont Rd
New Malden KT3 ... 199
Sutton SM2 ... 218
Tolworth KT6 ... 198
Walton-on-T KT12 ... 194
Egmont St SE14 ... 140
Egremont Ho SE13 ... 141
Egremont Rd SE27 ... 160
Egret Ho 11 SE16 ... 118
Egret Way UB4 ... 84
Eider Cl Hayes UB4 ... 84
Stratford E7 ... 76
Eider Ct 38 SE8 ... 14
Eighteenth Rd CR4 ... 204
Eighth Ave
Hayes UB3 ... 106
Ilford E12 ... 78
Eileen Ct BR7 ... 188
Eileen Rd SE25 ... 205
Eindhoven Cl SM5 ... 203
Einstein Ho HA9 ... 67
Eisenhower Dr E6 ... 100
Eisenhower Ho KT8 .. 175
Elaine Ct 13 NW3 ... 70
Elaine Gr NW5 ... 71
Elaine Ho N4 ... 50
Elam Cl SE5 ... 138
Elam St SE5 ... 138
Elan Ct E1 ... 96
Eland Pl CR0 ... 220
Eland Rd
Clapham SW11 ... 136
Croydon CR0 ... 220
Elba Pl SE17 .. 117 A2 262
Elberon Ave CR0 ... 203
Elbe St SW6 ... 136
Elborough Rd SE25 .. 206
Elborough St SW18 .. 157
Elbourne Trad Est
DA17 ... 125
Elbury Dr E16 ... 99
Elcho St
SW11 ... 136 C5 267
Elcot Ave SE15 ... 140
Elder Ave N8 ... 50
Elderberry Ct 2 EN2 ... 4
Elderberry Gr 10
SE27 ... 183
Elderberry Rd W5 ... 110
Elderberry Way E6 ... 100
Elder Cl Barnet N20 ... 13
Sidcup DA15 ... 167
Yiewsley UB7 ... 104
Elder Ct WD23 ... 8
Elderfield Ho 4
E14 ... 119
Elderfield Pl SW17 ... 181
Elderfield Rd E5 ... 74
Elderfield Wlk E11 ... 55
Elderflower Way E15 .. 76
Elder Gdns 9 SE27 .. 183
Elder Oak Cl SE20 ... 184
Elder Rd SE27 ... 183
Elderslie Cl BR3 ... 207
Elderslie Rd SE9 ... 166
Elder St E1 ... 95 D3 243
Elderton Rd SE26 ... 185
Eldertree Pl CR4 ... 181
Eldertree Way CR4 ... 181
Elder Wlk
Islington N1 ... 234
2 Lewisham SE13 .. 142
Elderwood Pl SE27 ... 183
Eldon Ave
Croydon CR0 ... 222
Heston TW5 ... 129
Eldon Ct NW6 ... 91
Eldon Gr NW3 ... 70
Eldon Ho SW9 ... 138
Eldon Jun & Inf Schs
N9 ... 18
Eldon Pk SE25 ... 206
Eldon Rd
Edmonton N9 ... 18
Kensington
W8 ... 113 D3 255
Tottenham N22 ... 32
Walthamstow E17 ... 53
Eldon St EC2 .. 95 B2 242
Eldonwall Est RM8 ... 59
Eldon Way NW10 ... 88
Eldred Rd IG11 ... 101
Eldrick Ct TW14 ... 149
Eldridge Cl TW14 ... 150

ge Ct
ondsey
6............ 118 A3
agenham RM10 ... 81 D2
or Cl
erhithe SE16 ... 118 D4
Tottenham N15 .. 51 D6
or Cres NW7 .... 28 D6
or Ct 13 E2...... 96 A6
or Gdns
et EN5 .... 12 D6
nham RM8........ 81 B6
or Gr
lake SW13 ..... 133 C2
idge UB10 .... 60 D5
or Ho
ammersmith
5............ 112 C1
entish Town
V5.............. 71 C3
erton SW19.... 179 D2
or Palmer Prim
NW5 .... 71 C4
or Rathbone Ho 1
.... 49 D2
or Rd
es Pk N11......... 32 A4
ney E8 .... 74 B1
ford E15......... 76 D2
or Smith Sch
.... 99 B5
or Smith Sch
st Beckton Site)
.... 99 C2
or St E3......... 97 C4
or Wlk 24
3............... 122 B2
ra Ave TW6 ..... 127 D2
ra Ct 6 NW2 ..... 68 C2
ric Ave SW9 .... 138 C1
ric Ho
Bow E3 .... 97 C4
thamstow E17 ..... 53 C5
ric La 2 SW9 ... 138 C1
ric Mans 1
.... 138 C1
ric Par
d IG3 .... 57 D1
iton KT6 .... 197 D3
dford E18 .... 37 A1
more Ct BR1 .... 210 A5
hant & Castle
vington
E1 ..... 116 D3 261 D5
ington SE1 ..... 261 D4
hant & Castle Sh
SE1 .... 117 A2 262 A4
hant & Castle Sta
beth
E1 ..... 116 D3 261 D5
vington
E17 ..... 117 A2 262 A4
hant La SE16 .... 118 C4
hant Rd
7 .... 117 A2 262 A4
Rd Ealing W13 ... 109 C4
es UB3 .... 105 B2
Rd N18 .... 34 D5
s Est N18 .... 34 D6
dale Rd SE24 .... 161 A6
Gr TW11 .... 174 D5
d Cl SE9 .... 143 C1
t Rd N5 .... 72 C4
da Cres SE6 ..... 185 C6
da Prim Sch
.... 185 C6
ow E1 .... 118 C6
ine Rd W7 .... 86 C2
l Cl BR6 .... 226 D3
r Ave Ealing W5 ... 110 A4
rnton Heath
W16 .... 204 A6
worth KT5, KT6 ... 198 D2
lesden NW10 ...... 67 B2
r Cl
khurst Hill IG9 .... 21 D2
tford SE8 .... 141 C5
ree WD6 .... 9 D4
enham UB10 .... 60 C6
wham E13 .... 99 C5
r Ct W14 .... 254 A5
r Ho Hayes UB4 ... 84 C2
eworth TW2 ...... 152 B5
alico SW1 .... 258 D1
thall UB1 .... 85 C1
th Hampstead
W6 .... 70 A1
r N8 .... 50 A6
r St SE16 .... 119 A3
n Ave
ford TW15 ...... 171 A4
mmersmith W12 ... 112 B3
rrow HA3 .... 25 B1
Elgin Ave continued
Westbourne Green
W9 .... 91 D3
Elgin Cl W12 .... 112 B4
Elgin Cres
Hatton TW6 .... 127 C3
Notting Hill
W11 ..... 113 A6 244 B6
Elgin Ct
6 Croydon CR0 .... 221 A4
Westbourne Green
W9 .... 91 D3
Elgin Ho Northolt UB5 .. 84 B5
8 Poplar E14 .... 97 D1
Elgin Mans W9 .... 91 D4
Elgin Mews N W9 ..... 91 D4
Elgin Mews S W9 ..... 91 D4
Elgin Mews W11 ...... 91 A1
Elgin Rd
Croydon CR0 .... 221 D6
Ilford IG3 .... 57 C2
Sutton SM1 .... 218 A5
Wallington SM6 ..... 219 C2
Wood Green N22 ...... 31 C1
Elgood Ave HA6 ...... 22 A3
Elgood Cl W11 .... 244 A3
Elgood Ho NW8 ...... 229 D3
Elham Cl BR1 .... 187 D3
Elham Ho 13 E5 ...... 74 B3
Elia Mews N1 .. 94 D5 234 C3
Elias Pl SW8 .... 138 C6
Elia St N1 ..... 94 D5 234 C3
Elibank Rd SE9 ...... 144 C1
Elim Est SE1 .... 263 A6
Elim St SE1 .... 263 A6
Elim Way E13 .... 98 D4
Eliot Bank SE23,
SE26 .... 162 B2
Eliot Bank Prim Sch
SE26 .... 162 B2
Eliot Cotts SE3 ...... 142 C3
Eliot Ct SW18 .... 157 D5
Eliot Dr HA2 .... 63 D6
Eliot Gdns SW15 ..... 134 A1
Eliot Hill SE13 .... 142 A3
Eliot Ho 10 TW10 .... 154 B5
Eliot Mews NW8 ...... 229 A3
Eliot Pk SE13 .... 142 A3
Eliot Pl SE3 .... 142 C3
Eliot Rd RM9 .... 80 D4
Eliot Vale SE3 .... 142 B3
Elis David Almshouses
CR0 .... 220 D4
Elizabethan Ct N3 .... 47 A6
Elizabeth Ave
Enfield EN2 .... 4 D2
Ilford IG1 .... 79 B6
Islington N1 .... 73 B1
Shoreditch
N1 .... 95 A6 235 B6
Elizabeth Barnes Ct 5
SW6 .... 135 D3
Elizabeth Blackwell Ho
N22 .... 32 C2
Elizabeth Blount Ct 4
E14 .... 97 A1
Elizabeth Cl
Cheam SM1 .... 217 B4
Paddington W9 ..... 236 B5
12 Poplar E14 .... 97 D1
Elizabeth Clyde Cl
N15 .... 51 C5
Elizabeth Cooper Lo
SW12 .... 159 A5
Elizabeth Cotts 5
TW9 .... 132 C4
Elizabeth Ct
Buckhurst Hill IG9 .... 21 B3
Chelsea SW10 ...... 266 D5
East Dulwich SE22 ... 140 A1
Kingston u T KT2 .... 176 A2
Marylebone NW8 .... 237 B6
South Croydon CR0 .. 221 C5
Sunbury TW16 ...... 194 C6
3 Teddington
TW11 .... 174 C5
Upper Tooting
SW17 .... 181 A5
West Barnes SM4 ... 201 A2
Westminster SW1 ... 259 D5
6 Woodford Green
E18 .... 37 A2
2 Woodford Green
IG8 .... 37 C3
10 Woolwich SE18 ... 122 B2
Elizabeth Finn Ho 1
W12 .... 112 A3
Elizabeth Fry Ho
UB3 .... 105 D2
Elizabeth Fry Pl
SE18 .... 144 A4
Elizabeth Garrett
Anderson Ho 9
DA17 .... 125 C3
Elizabeth Garrett
Anderson Hospl
NW1 .... 93 C3 239 B5
Elizabeth Garrett
Anderson Language
Coll N1 ..... 94 B5 233 D3
Elizabeth Gdns
East Acton W3 ...... 111 D5
Isleworth TW7 ...... 131 A1
Stanmore HA7 .... 25 C5
Sunbury TW16 ...... 194 C6
Elizabeth Ho
Cheam SM3 .... 217 A2
Friern Barnet N20 ..... 14 D1
15 Hammersmith
W6 .... 112 C1
Lambeth SE11 ...... 261 B3
Stanmore HA7 .... 26 A1
Wembley HA9 .... 66 B3
Elizabeth Ind Est
SE14 .... 140 D6
Elizabeth Kenny Ho
N1 .... 73 A2
Elizabeth Mews
28 Hackney E2 .... 96 A5
Maitland Pk NW3 ..... 70 D2
Elizabeth Pl N15 ...... 51 B5
Elizabeth Rd
Newham E6 .... 99 D6
South Tottenham N15 .. 51 C4
Elizabeth Ride N9 .... 18 B4
Elizabeth Selby Inf Sch
E2 .... 96 A4
Elizabeth Sq 13
SE16 .... 119 A6
Elizabeth St
SW1 .... 115 A2 258 B4
Elizabeth Terr SE9 ... 166 B5
Elizabeth Way
Feltham TW13 ...... 172 C6
South Norwood
SE19 .... 183 B3
Elkanette Mews N20 .. 14 A2
Elkington Point
SE11 .... 261 A3
Elkington Rd E13 ..... 99 B3
Elkstone Rd W10 ..... 91 B2
Ella Cl BR3 .... 185 C1
Ellacombe Ho 1
SW2 .... 160 C4
Ellaline Rd W6 .... 134 D6
Ella Mews NW3 .... 70 D4
Ellanby Cres N18 ..... 34 B5
Elland Ho 18 E14 ..... 97 B1
Elland Rd SE15 ...... 140 C1
Ellard Ct DA16 ...... 146 C2
Ella Rd N4, N8 .... 50 A2
Elle Ct N12 .... 29 D5
Ellement Cl HA5 ...... 40 D4
Ellena Ct N14 .... 16 A1
Ellenborough Ct N22 .. 32 D2
Ellenborough Ho 5
W12 .... 112 B6
Ellenborough Pl
SW15 .... 134 A1
Ellenborough Rd
Sidcup DA14 .... 191 A5
Tottenham N22 .... 33 A2
Ellen Cl BR1 .... 209 D6
Ellen Ct
6 Chingford E4 .... 20 A3
Lower Edmonton N9 ... 18 C2
Ellen Miller Ho 2
E17 .... 54 A4
Ellen St E1 .... 96 A1
Ellen Webb Dr HA3 .... 42 C6
Ellen Wilkinson Ho
12 Dagenham
RM10 .... 81 C5
7 Globe Town E2 ..... 96 D4
West Brompton SW6 264 D5
Ellen Wilkinson Prim
Sch E6 .... 100 A2
Ellen Wilkinson Sch for
Girls W3 .... 88 B1
Elleray Rd TW11 ..... 174 D4
Ellerby St SW6 ...... 134 D4
Ellerdale Cl 15 NW3 ... 70 A4
Ellerdale Rd NW3 ..... 70 A3
Ellerdale St SE13 .... 141 D2
Ellerdine Rd TW3 .... 130 B1
Ellerker Gdns TW10 .. 154 A5
Ellerman Ave TW2,
TW4 .... 151 B3
Ellerslie Ct 6 SM6 ... 219 B2
Ellerslie Gdns NW10 .. 90 A6
Ellerslie Ind Est
SW2 .... 160 A6
Ellerslie Rd W12 ..... 112 B5
Ellerton Ct W3 .... 110 D4
Ellerton Gdns RM9 .... 80 C1
Ellerton Lo N3 .... 29 C1
Ellerton Rd
Barnes SW13 .... 134 A4
Dagenham RM9 .... 80 C1
Surbiton KT6 .... 198 B1
Wandsworth SW17,
SW18 .... 158 B3
Wimbledon SW20 ... 178 A3
Ellery Cl 5 NW10 ..... 89 D5
Ellery Ho SE17 ...... 262 D3
Ellery Rd SE19 ...... 183 B3
Ellery St SE15 ...... 140 B3
Ellesborough Cl
WD19 .... 22 C5
Ellesmere Ave
Beckenham BR3 .... 185 D1
Edgware NW7 .... 11 B1
Ellesmere Cl
Leytonstone E11 ...... 54 D4
Ruislip HA4 .... 39 A2
Ellesmere Ct
Chiswick W4 .... 133 B6
Lewisham SE12 ..... 165 A3
Penge SE20 .... 184 B1
Ellesmere Gdns IG4 ... 56 A3
Ellesmere Gr EN5 ..... 13 B6
Ellesmere Rd Bow E3 .. 97 A5
Chiswick W4 .... 133 B6
Greenford UB6 .... 86 A3
Twickenham TW1 .... 153 C5
Willesden NW10 ...... 68 A3
Ellesmere St E14 ..... 97 D1
Ellies Mews TW15 ... 148 A2
Ellingfort Rd E8 ...... 74 B1
Ellingham Prim Sch
KT9 .... 213 D1
Ellingham Rd
Chessington KT9 .... 213 D2
Leyton E15 .... 76 B4
Shepherd's Bush
W12 .... 112 A4
Ellington Ct N14 ...... 15 D2
Ellington Ho SE1 .... 262 B5
Ellington Rd
Cranley Gdns N10 ..... 49 B5
Feltham TW13 ...... 171 D6
Hounslow TW3 ...... 129 D3
Ellington St N7 .... 72 C2
Elliot Cl Stratford E15 .. 76 C1
Wembley HA9 .... 66 C5
Woodford IG8 .... 37 D4
Elliot Ct 6 N15 .... 51 D5
Elliot Rd NW4 .... 46 B3
Elliott Ave HA4 .... 62 B6
Elliott Gdns TW17 ... 192 C5
Elliott Ho 3 CR7 .... 204 D5
Elliott Rd Acton W4 .. 111 C2
Brixton SW9 .... 138 D4
Bromley BR2 .... 209 D5
Camberwell SW9 .... 138 D4
Stanmore HA7 .... 25 A4
Thornton Heath CR7 . 204 D5
Elliott Sch SW15 .... 156 C5
Elliott's Pl N1 .... 234 D5
Elliott Sq NW3 .... 70 C1
Elliott's Row
SE11 ...... 116 D2 261 D4
Ellis Cl Burnt Oak HA8 .. 27 C4
New Eltham SE9 .... 167 A2
Willesden NW10 ...... 68 C2
Elliscombe Mount 11
SE7 .... 143 C6
Elliscombe Rd SE7 ... 143 C6
Ellis Ct W7 .... 86 D2
Ellisfield Dr SW15 ... 156 A4
Ellis Franklin Ct
NW8 .... 229 A4
Ellis Ho
Walthamstow E17 ..... 54 A4
Walworth SE17 ..... 262 C2
Ellison Gdns UB2 .... 107 B2
Ellison Ho 1 SE13 ... 142 A3
Ellison Rd
Barnes SW13 .... 133 D3
New Eltham DA15 ... 167 B3
Streatham SW16 .... 182 A3
Ellis Rd Mitcham CR4 .. 202 D3
Southall UB2 .... 108 A5
Ellis St SW1 .. 115 A2 258 A4
Elliston Ho 8 SE18 .. 122 C2
Ellora Rd SW16 ..... 181 D5
Ellswood Ct 18 KT6 .. 197 D2
Ellsworth St E2 .... 96 B4
Ellwood Ct 1 W9 ..... 91 D3
Elmar Ct SW6 .... 135 A3
Elmar Rd N15 .... 51 B5
Elm Ave Ealing W5 ... 110 B5
Ruislip HA4 .... 40 B2
Elm Bank Dr BR1 .... 187 D1
Elm Bank Gdns
SW13 .... 133 C3
Elm Bank Mans
SW13 .... 133 C3
Elmbank N14 .... 16 A4
Elmbank Way W7 ..... 86 B2
Elmbourne Dr DA17 .. 125 D2
Elmbourne Rd
SW17 .... 159 B1
Elmbridge Ave KT5 ... 199 A3
Elmbridge Cl HA4 ..... 40 A3
Elmbridge Dr HA4 .... 40 A3
Elmbridge Wlk E8 .... 74 A1
Elmbrook Cl TW16 ... 172 B2
Elmbrook Gdns SE9 .. 144 A1
Elmbrook Rd SM1 .... 217 B4
Elmbrook 3 E18 ...... 55 A6
Elm Cl
Buckhurst Hill IG9 .... 21 D2
Carshalton SM5 ..... 202 D1
Harrow HA2 .... 41 D3
Hayes UB3 .... 84 A1
Hendon NW4 .... 46 D4
South Croydon CR2 .. 221 C2
Tolworth KT5 .... 199 A2
Twickenham TW13,
TW2 .... 151 D2
Upper Holloway N19 ... 71 C6
Wanstead E11 .... 55 B3
West Barnes SW20 .. 200 C5
Elmcote HA5 .... 22 D1
Elmcourt Rd SE21,
SE27 .... 160 D2
Elm Court Sch SE27 161 A2
Elm Cres Ealing W5 .. 110 A4
Kingston u T KT2 .... 176 A2
Elmcroft Ave
Blackfen DA15 ..... 168 A5
Enfield N9 .... 18 B5
Golders Green NW11 .. 47 B2
Wanstead E11 .... 55 B5
Elmcroft Cl
Chessington KT9 .... 214 A5
Ealing W5 .... 87 D1
Feltham TW14 ...... 149 D5
Wanstead E11 .... 55 B5
Elmcroft Cres
Harrow HA2 .... 41 C6
Hendon NW11 .... 47 A2
Elmcroft Dr
Ashford TW15 ...... 170 C5
Chessington KT9 .... 214 A5
Elmcroft Gdns NW9 ... 44 C4
Elmcroft Highgate N6 .. 49 C2
Hornsey Vale N8 ..... 50 B4
Elmcroft St E5 .... 74 C4
Elmcroft Terr UB8 .... 82 C1
Elm Ct
5 Ashford TW16 .... 171 D3
Brixton SW9 .... 138 C4
Catford SE6 .... 163 D3
Chingford E4 .... 36 A4
4 Finchley N3 .... 29 C2
Lewisham SE13 ..... 142 B2
Mitcham CR4 .... 180 D1
42 Notting Hill W2 .... 91 C2
Strand EC4 .... 251 A6
Elmdale Rd N13 ...... 32 B5
Elmdene Cl BR3 .... 207 B4
Elmdene Rd SE18 ... 122 D1
Elmdene KT5 .... 199 A1
Elmdon Rd
Hatton TW6 .... 127 D2
Hounslow TW5 ..... 129 A3
Elm Dr Harrow HA2 ... 41 D3
Sunbury TW16 ...... 172 C1
Elmer Cl EN2 .... 4 B2
Elmer Ct HA1 .... 42 D3
Elmer Gdns
Edgware HA8 .... 26 D3
Isleworth TW7 ...... 130 B2
Elmer Ho NW1 ...... 237 A4
Elmer Rd SE6 .... 164 A4
Elmer's Dr TW11 .... 175 B4
ELMERS END 206 D6
Elmers End Rd BR3,
SE20 .... 206 C6
Elmers End Sta
BR3 .... 206 D5
Elmerside Rd BR3 ... 207 A5
Elmers Rd SE25 .... 206 A2
Elmfield Ave
London N8 .... 50 A4
Mitcham CR4 .... 181 A2
Teddington TW11 ... 174 D5
Elmfield Cl HA1 .... 64 C6
Elmfield Ct DA16 .... 146 B4
Elmfield Ho
6 Canonbury N5 ...... 73 A3
22 London N2 .... 30 B1
Paddington W9 .... 91 C3
Elmfield Mans 5
SW17 .... 159 A2
Elmfield Pk BR1 .... 209 A6
Elmfield Rd
Bromley BR1 .... 209 A6
Chingford E4 .... 20 B2
East Finchley N2 ..... 48 B6
Southall UB2 .... 107 A3
Upper Tooting SW17 .. 159 B2
Walthamstow E17 ..... 52 D3
Elmfield Way
Paddington W9 .... 91 C2
South Croydon CR2 .. 221 D1
Elm Friars Wlk NW1 ... 71 D1
Elmgate Ave TW13 ... 150 C1
Elmgate Ct HA8 .... 27 A5
Elmgate Gdns HA8 .... 27 B6
Elm Gdns
Claygate KT10 ..... 212 D2
East Finchley N2 ..... 48 A6
Enfield EN2 .... 5 B5
Mitcham CR4 .... 203 D5
Elm Gn W3 .... 89 C1
Elm Gr NW2 .... 68 D4
Elmgreen Cl 8 E15 ... 98 C6
Elm Gr Harrow HA2 ... 41 C2
Hornsey N8 .... 50 A3
Kingston u T KT2 .... 176 A2
Orpington BR6 ..... 211 D1
Elmgrove Cres HA1 ... 43 A4
Elmgrove Fst & Mid
Schs HA3 .... 43 A5
Elmgrove Gdns HA1 ... 43 A4
Elm Grove Par SM6 .. 219 A5
Elm Grove Rd SW13 .. 134 A3
Elmgrove Rd CR0 ... 206 B2
Elm Grove Rd W5 ... 110 A4
Elmgrove Rd HA1 ..... 42 D4
Elm Gr
Peckham SE15 ..... 140 A3
Sutton SM1 .... 217 D4
Wimbledon SW19 ... 179 A3
Woodford IG8 .... 36 D5
Yiewsley UB7 ...... 104 B6
Elm Hall Gdns E11 .... 55 B3
Elm Hatch HA5 .... 23 B3
Elm Ho
4 Cubitt Town
E14 .... 120 A4
2 Kingston u T KT2 .. 176 B3
Teddington TW11 ... 175 C3
Elmhurst Ave
London N2 .... 48 B6
Mitcham CR4 .... 181 B3
Elmhurst Cres N2 ..... 48 B5
Elmhurst Ct
Carshalton SM5 .... 218 B6
Croydon CR0 .... 221 B3
Elmhurst DA17 ..... 147 A6
Elmhurst Dr E18 ...... 37 A1
Elmhurst Lo 3 SM2 .. 218 A1
Elmhurst Mans
SW4 .... 137 D2
Elmhurst Prim Sch
E7 .... 77 B1
Elmhurst Rd
Chislehurst SE9 .... 166 A1
Enfield EN3 .... 6 C6
Tottenham N17 .... 33 D1
Upton E7 .... 77 B1
Elmhurst Sch CR2 ... 221 B3
Elmhurst St SW4 .... 137 D2
Elmhurst Villas
SE15 .... 140 C1
Elmington Cl DA5 ... 169 D5
Elmington Rd SE5 ... 139 B5
Elmira St SE13 ..... 141 D2
Elm La SE6 .... 163 B2
Elm Lawn Cl UB8 ..... 60 A1
Elmlea Dr UB3 .... 83 D2
Elm Lea Trad Est
N17 .... 34 B4
Elmlee Cl BR7 ...... 188 B4
Elmley Cl 12 E6 ..... 100 A2
Elmley St SE18 ..... 123 B2
Elm Lo SW6 .... 134 D4
Elmore Cl HA0 .... 88 A5
Elmore Ho SW9 ..... 138 D3
Elmore Rd Enfield EN3 .. 6 D5
Leyton E11 .... 76 B5
Elmore St N1 .... 73 B1
Elm Park Ave N15 .... 52 A3
Elm Park Ct HA5 ...... 40 C6
Elm Park Gdns
Chelsea
SW10 ..... 114 B1 256 C1
Hendon NW4 .... 46 D4
Elm Park Ho SW10 .. 256 C1
Elm Park La
SW3 .... 114 B1 256 C1
Elm Park Mans
SW10 .... 266 B6
Elm Park Rd
Chelsea
SW3 .... 136 B6 266 C6
Edmonton N21 .... 17 A4
Finchley N3 .... 29 B3
Pinner HA5 .... 40 D6
South Norwood
SE25 .... 205 D6
Walthamstow E10 ..... 53 A1
Elm Pk Stanmore HA7 .. 25 C5
Streatham SW2 ..... 160 B4
Elm Pl SW7 .. 114 B1 256 C2
Elm Quay SW8 ...... 269 C5
Elm Rd Barnet EN5 ..... 1 B1
Beckenham BR3 .... 185 B1
Chessington KT9 .... 214 A4
Claygate KT10 ..... 212 C2
East Bedfont TW14 .. 149 B4
Hackbridge SM6 .... 203 A1
Kingston u T KT2 .... 176 B2
Leyton E11 .... 76 B6
Mortlake SW14 ..... 133 A1
New Malden KT3 .... 199 B6
Sidcup DA14 .... 190 A6
South Norwood CR7 .. 205 B5

Elm Rd *continued*
Stoneleigh KT17 215 D2
Stratford E7 76 D2
Tottenham N22 32 D2
Walthamstow E17 54 A4
Wembley HA9 66 A3
Elm Rd W SM4 201 B2
Elm Row NW3 70 A5
Elms Ave
Hendon NW4 46 D4
Muswell Hill N10 49 B6
Elmscott Gdns N21 17 A5
Elmscott Rd BR1 186 D5
Elms Cotts 1 CR4 180 D1
Elms Cres SW4 159 D5
Elms Ct
Merton SW19 179 D3
Wembley HA0 65 A4
Elmsdale Rd E17 53 B5
Elms Gdns
Dagenham RM9 81 B4
Wembley HA0 65 A4
Elmshaw Rd SW15 156 A6
Elmside CR0 223 D2
Elmside Rd HA9 66 C5
Elms La HA0 65 A5
Elmsleigh Ave HA3 43 C5
Elmsleigh Ct SM1 217 D5
Elmsleigh Ho TW2 152 B2
Elmsleigh Rd TW2 152 B2
Elmslie Ct SE9 166 C5
Elmslie Point 2 E3 97 B2
Elms Mews W2 246 C6
Elms Park Ave HA0 65 A4
Elms Rd
Clapham Pk SW4 159 C6
Harrow HA3 24 C3
ELMSTEAD 188 A5
Elmstead Ave
Elmstead BR7 188 B5
Wembley HA9 66 B6
Elmstead Cl
Totteridge N20 13 C2
West Ewell KT19 215 C3
Elmstead Ct HA9 44 B1
Elmstead Gdns KT4 216 A5
Elmstead Glade
BR7 188 B4
Elmstead La BR7 188 B5
Elmstead Rd IG3 79 D6
Elmstead Woods Sta
BR7 188 A4
Elmsted Cres DA16 146 C6
Elms The
5 Ashford TW15 170 C5
Barnes SW13 133 D2
Claygate KT10 212 D1
Croydon CR0 205 A1
3 Harlesden NW10 89 C5
Kingsbury NW9 45 A3
Plashet E12 78 A2
Wallington SM6 219 C4
Elmstone Rd SW6 265 A2
Elm St WC1 94 B3 240 D5
Elmsway TW15 170 C5
Elmsworth Ave
TW3 129 D3
Elm Terr
Child's Hill NW2 69 C5
3 Eltham SE9 166 C5
Harrow HA3 24 B2
Elmton Ct NW8 236 C6
Elm Tree Ave KT10 196 C2
Elm Tree Cl
Ashford TW15 170 D5
Northolt UB5 85 B5
St John's Wood
NW8 92 B4 229 C2
Elm Tree Ct
5 Camberwell
SE5 139 A4
18 Charlton SE7 143 C6
Elmtree Ct HA4 40 A1
Elm Tree Ct NW8 229 C2
Elm Tree Rd
NW8 92 B4 229 C2
Elmtree Rd TW11 174 C5
Elm View Ct UB2 107 C2
Elm Way London N11 31 A4
North Cheam KT4 216 C5
West Ewell KT19 215 B3
Willesden NW10 67 C4
Elm Wlk
Child's Hill NW3 69 C6
Orpington BR6 226 B5
West Barnes SW20 200 D5
Elmwood Ave
Bowes Pk N13 32 A5
Feltham TW13 150 B1
Harrow HA3 43 B3
Elmwood Cl
Hackbridge SM6 219 B6
Stoneleigh KT17 216 A1
Elmwood Cres NW9 45 A5
Elmwood Ct
Battersea SW11 268 C2
Walthamstow E10 53 C1
Wembley HA0 65 A5
Elmwood Dr
Sidcup DA5 169 A4
Stoneleigh KT17 216 A1
Elmwood Gdns W7 86 C1
Elmwood Ho
Enfield EN2 4 D1
Feltham TW13 150 B1
Elmwood Inf Sch
CR0 204 D3
Elmwood Jun Sch
CR0 204 D2
Elm Wood Prim Sch
SE27 161 B1
Elmwood Rd
Chiswick W4 133 A6
Herne Hill SE24 161 B6
Mitcham CR4 202 D6
Thornton Heath CR0 204 D2
Elmworth Gr SE21 161 B2
Elnathan Mews W9 91 D3
Elphinstone Ct
SW16 182 A4
Elphinstone Rd E17 35 B1
Elphinstone St N5 72 D4
Elrington Rd
Dalston E8 74 A2
Woodford IG8 37 A5
Elsa Ct BR3 185 B2
Elsa Rd DA16 146 C3
Elsa St E1 97 A2
Elsdale Ho 14 E9 74 C2
Elsdale St E9 74 C1
Elsden Mews E2 96 C5
Elsden Rd N17 33 D2
Elsenham Rd E12 78 C3
Elsenham St SW18,
SW19 157 B2
Elsfield NW5 71 B3
Elsham Rd
Kensington
W14 113 A4 244 A1
Leyton E11 76 C4
Elsham Terr W14 244 A1
Elsiedene Rd N21 17 A4
Elsie Lane Ct W2 91 D2
Elsiemaud Rd SE4 163 B6
Elsie Rd SE22 139 D1
Elsinge Rd EN1 6 B6
Elsinore Ave TW19 148 A4
Elsinore Gdns NW2 69 A5
Elsinore Ho
12 Camberwell
SE5 139 A3
Islington N1 234 A5
7 Woolwich SE7 122 A2
Elsinore Rd SE23 163 A3
Elsinore Way TW9 132 D2
Elsley Ct HA9 66 D2
Elsley Prim Sch HA9 66 B2
Elsley Rd SW11 137 A2
Elsley Sch SW11 137 A2
Elspeth Rd
London SW11 136 D1
Wembley HA0 66 A3
Elsrick Ave SM4 201 C4
Elstan Way CR0 207 A2
Elstead Ct SM3 201 A1
Elstead Ho 9 SW2 160 B4
Elsted St
SE17 117 B2 262 D3
Elstow Cl Eltham SE9 166 B6
Ruislip HA4 40 D2
Elstow Gdns RM9 103 A6
Elstow Grange NW6 68 D1
Elstow Rd RM9 103 A6
ELSTREE 10 A5
Elstree Gdns
Abbey Wood
DA17 125 A2
Edmonton N9 18 B3
Ilford IG1 79 A3
Elstree Hill BR1 186 C3
Elstree Hill N WD6 9 D6
Elstree Hill S WD6 9 D4
Elstree Ho 3 HA7 25 C6
Elstree Pk WD6 11 B5
Elstree Rd
Bushey WD23 8 C4
Elstree WD6 9 A5
Elswick Rd SE13 141 D3
Elswick St SW6 136 A3
Elsworth Cl TW14 149 C3
Elsworthy Rd
NW3 92 C6 230 A6
Elsworthy Rise NW3 70 C1
Elsworthy Terr NW3 70 C1
Elsworthy KT7 196 C3
Elsynge Rd SW18 158 B6
Elsynge Road Mans
SW18 158 B6
ELTHAM 166 B6
Eltham CE Prim Sch
SE9 166 B6
Eltham Coll Jun Sch
SE9 165 D3
Eltham Coll SE9 165 D2
Eltham Green Rd
SE9 165 C6
Eltham Green Specialist
Sports Coll SE9 165 D5
Eltham High St SE9 166 B5
Eltham Hill SE9 166 A6
Eltham Hill Tech Coll
for Girls SE9 166 A5
Eltham Palace Rd
SE9 165 D5
Eltham Pal* SE9 166 A4
Eltham Park Gdns
SE9 144 C1
Eltham Rd SE9, SE12 165 B6
Eltham Sta SE9 166 B6
Elthiron Rd
SW6 135 C4 265 B1
Elthorne Ave W7 109 A4
Elthorne Ct
Feltham TW13 150 C3
Kingsbury NW9 45 B3
Elthorne Park High Sch
W7 108 D3
Elthorne Park Rd
W7 109 A4
Elthorne Rd
London NW9 45 B2
Upper Holloway N19 71 D6
Elthorne Way NW9 45 B3
Elthruda Rd SE13 164 B5
Eltisley Rd IG1 78 D4
Elton Ave Barnet EN5 13 B6
Wembley HA0 65 B3
Wembley UB6 64 D2
Elton Cl KT1 175 C3
Elton Ho 3 E3 97 B6
Elton Lo 4 W5 110 A6
Elton Pl N16 73 C3
Elton Rd KT2 176 C2
Elton St 11 N16 73 C3
Eltringham St
SW18 136 A1
Elvaston Ct EN5 12 C6
Elvaston Mews SW7 256 B6
Elvaston Pl
SW7 114 A3 256 B5
Elveden Ho 17 SW9 138 D1
Elveden Pl NW10 88 C5
Elveden Rd NW10 88 C5
Elvedon Rd TW13 149 D1
Elvendon Rd N13 32 A4
Elver Gdns 10 E2 96 A4
Elverson Rd SE8 141 D3
Elverson Rd Sta
SE8 141 D3
Elverton St
SW1 115 D2 259 C4
Elvin Ct NW9 45 A2
Elvington Gn BR2 208 D4
Elvington La NW9 27 C2
Elvin Ho 2 E9 74 C2
Elvino Rd SE26 185 A5
Elvis Rd NW2 68 C2
Elwill Way BR3 208 B5
Elwin St E2 96 A4
Elwood Ho N5 72 D5
Elwood St N4, N5 72 D5
Elworth Ho SW8 270 D3
Elwyn Gdns SE12 165 A4
Ely Cl SW20 177 D1
Ely Cotts SW8 270 C3
Ely Court Flats SW6 264 A1
Ely Ct Holborn EC1 241 B3
3 Maida Vale NW6 91 C5
Ely Gdns
Borehamwood
WD6 11 B6
Redbridge IG1 56 A2
Ely Ho Barnet EN4 2 C1
Northolt UB5 85 A6
22 Peckham SE15 140 A5
Elyne Rd N4 50 C3
Ely Pl EC1 94 C2 241 B3
Ely Rd Hatton TW6 127 D3
Hounslow TW4 128 C2
Leyton E10 54 A2
Thornton Heath CR0 205 B4
Elysian Ave BR5 211 D3
Elysium Gate 7
SW6 135 B3
Elysium Pl SW6 135 B3
Elysium St SW6 135 B3
Elystan Bsns Ctr
UB4 106 C6
Elystan Ct SW15 156 B6
Elystan Pl
SW3 114 D1 257 C2
Elystan St
SW3 114 C2 257 B3
Elystan Wlk N1 234 A5
Emanuel Ave W3 89 A1
Emanuel Ct Acton W3 89 B1
10 Leyton E10 53 D2
Emanuel Dr TW12 173 B5
Emanuel Sch SW11 158 C6
Embankment Gdns
SW3 136 D6 267 D6
Embankment Pier
WC2 116 A5 250 B4
Embankment Pl
WC2 250 B4
Embankment SW15 134 D3
Embankment Sta
WC2 116 A5 250 B4
Embankment The
TW1 153 A3
Embassy Ct
Ealing W5 110 B6
Kingston u T KT6 197 D4
Sidcup DA14 168 B1
St John's Wood NW8 229 D3
7 Wallington SM6 219 B2
8 Wanstead E18 55 A6
Welling DA16 146 B2
Wood Green N11 31 D4
Embassy Gdns BR3 185 B2
Embassy Ho 2 NW6 69 C1
Embassy Lo N3 29 B1
Emba St SE16 118 A4
Ember Cl BR5 211 A2
Embercourt Rd KT10, KT7,
KT8 196 C3
Ember Ct
2 Acton W12 111 C3
14 Hendon NW9 27 D1
Ember Farm Ave
KT8 196 B3
Ember Farm Way
KT8 196 B4
Ember Gdns KT10,
KT8 196 C2
Ember Ho 8 BR1 186 B5
Ember La KT10, KT8 196 B2
Emberson Ho 7 E17 54 A5
Emberton Ct EC1 234 C1
Emberton SE5 139 C6
Embleton Rd SE13 141 D1
Embleton Wlk
TW12 173 B5
Embry Cl HA7 25 A6
Embry Dr HA7 25 A4
Embry Way HA7 25 A6
Emden Cl UB7 104 C4
Emden St SW6 265 D2
Emerald Cl E16 100 A1
Emerald Ct N12 30 A6
Emerald Gdns RM8 59 C1
Emerald Rd NW10 89 B6
Emerald Sq UB2 106 D3
Emerald St
WC1 94 B2 240 C4
Emerson Apartments
N8 50 B6
Emerson Ct 8
SW19 179 A4
Emerson Gdns HA3 44 B3
Emerson Ho N16 73 C3
Emerson Rd IG1 56 C2
Emerson St
SE1 117 A5 252 A4
Emerton Cl DA6 147 A1
Emery Hill St SW1 259 B5
Emery St
SE1 116 C3 261 B6
Emilia Cl EN3 18 B6
Emily St 7 E16 98 D1
Emirates Stad (Arsenal
FC) N7 72 C4
Emlyn Gdns 3 W12 111 C3
Emlyn Rd W12 111 D3
Emmanual Ho SE18 123 B1
Emmanuel CE Prim Sch
NW6 69 C3
Emmanuel Ct 3 EN4 14 D3
Emmanuel Ho
Dulwich SE21 161 B1
Lambeth SE11 261 A3
Emmanuel Rd
Northwood HA6 22 A3
Streatham SW12 159 D3
Emma Rd E13 98 D5
Emma St E2 96 B5
Emmeline Ct KT12 194 C2
Emminster NW6 91 D6
Emmott Ave IG6 57 A4
Emmott Cl
London NW11 48 A3
Mile End E1 97 A3
Emperor's Gate
SW7 114 A2 256 A4
Empingham Ho 20
SE8 118 D2
Empire Ave N18 33 A4
Empire Ct HA9 66 D5
Empire Ho
Brompton SW3 257 A5
Edmonton N18 33 B4
Empire Par
Edmonton N18 33 B4
Wembley HA9 66 C5
Empire Rd UB6 65 C1
Empire Sq N19 72 A5
Empire Way HA9 66 C4
Empire Wharf E3 97 A6
Empire Wharf Rd
E14 120 B2
Empress Ave
Chingford E4 35 D3
Ilford IG1 78 C6
Wanstead E12 77 D6
Woodford IG8 36 D3
Empress Dr BR7 188 D4
Empress Mews 36
SE5 139 A3
Empress Par E4 35 C3
Empress Pl
SW5 113 C1 255 A1
Empress St SE17 139 A6
Empson St E3 97 D3
Emsworth Cl N9 18 C3
Emsworth St SW2 160 B2
Emu Rd SW8 137 B3
Enard Ho 28 E3 97 B5
Ena Rd SW16 204 A6
Enbrook St W10 91 A4
Enclave Ct EC1 241 D6
Endale Cl SM5 218 D6
Endeavour Way
Barking IG11 102 A5
Thornton Heath CR0 204 A2
Wimbledon SW19 179 D6
Endell St
WC2 94 A1 240 A1
Enderby St SE10 120 C1
Enderfield Ct BR7 188 C2
Enderley Cl HA3 24 C2
Enderley Ho SE19 183 D2
Enderley Rd HA3 24 C2
Endersby Rd EN5 12 C6
Endersleigh Gdns
NW4 46 A5
Endlebury Ct E4 20 B2
Endlebury Rd E4 20 A2
Endlesham Ct 2
SW12 159 A4
Endlesham Rd
SW12 159 A4
Endsleigh Gdns
Bloomsbury
WC1 93 D3 239 C6
Ilford IG1 56 D1
Kingston u T KT6 197 C3
Endsleigh Ind Est
UB2 107 B2
Endsleigh Mans 4
SW16 160 A1
Endsleigh Pl WC1 239 D6
Endsleigh Rd
Ealing W13 109 A6
Southall UB2 107 A2
Endsleigh St
WC1 93 D3 239 D6
Endway KT5 198 D2
Endwell Rd SE4 141 A3
Endymion Rd
Harringay N4 50 D2
Tulse Hill SW2 160 B5
Energen Cl NW10 67 C2
ENFIELD 6 B2
Enfield Chase Sta EN2 5 A2
Enfield Cloisters 7
N1 95 C4
Enfield Coll EN3 6 C2
Enfield Gram Sch EN2 5 B2
Enfield Gram Sch Lower
EN1 5 B3
ENFIELD HIGHWAY 6 C3
Enfield Ho 24 SW9 138 A3
ENFIELD LOCK 7 B6
Enfield Lock Sta EN3 7 A6
Enfield Rd
Brentford TW8 109 D1
De Beauvoir Town E8,
N1 73 C1
Enfield EN2 4 A2
Hatton TW6 127 C3
South Acton W3 110 D4
Enfield Ret Pk EN1 6 A2
Enfield Road Rdbt
TW6 127 C3
Enfield Sec Tuition Ctr
PRU N9 18 C3
ENFIELD TOWN 5 B1
Enfield Town Sta EN1 5 B2
ENFIELD WASH 6 D5
Enfield Wlk TW8 109 D1
Enford St W1 92 D2 237 C4
Engadine Cl CR0 221 D5
Engadine St SW18 157 C3
Engate St SE13 142 A1
Engel Pk NW7 28 C4
Engineer Cl SE18 144 C6
Engineers Way HA9 66 C4
England's La NW3 70 D2
England Way KT3 199 A5
Englefield BR1 188 A1
Englefield Cl
Enfield EN2
Orpington BR5 2
Thornton Heath CR0 2
Englefield Path
BR5 2
Englefield Rd N1
Englefield NW1 2
Engleheart Dr
TW14 1
Engleheart Rd SE6 1
Englewood Rd
SW12 1
English Gardening Sch
The SW3 136 D6 2
English Grounds
SE1 2
English Martyrs RC
Prim Sch
E1 95 D1 2
English St E3
Enid Stacy Ho 11
N19
Enid St SE16 117 D3 2
Enmore Ave SE25 2
Enmore Ct SW14 1
Enmore Gdns SW14 1
Enmore Rd
Croydon SE25 2
Putney SW15 1
Southall UB1
Ennerdale Ave HA3,
HA7
Ennerdale Cl
Cheam SM1 2
East Bedfont TW14 14
Ennerdale Ct E11 5
Ennerdale Dr NW9 4
Ennerdale Gdns HA9 4
Ennerdale Ho 3 N4 5
Ennerdale Rd
Erith DA7 14
Richmond TW9 13
Ennersdale Rd SE13 16
Ennis Ho 16 E14 9
Ennismore Ave
Chiswick W4 11
Greenford UB6 6
Ennismore Gdns
SW7 114 C3 25
Ennismore Gdns Mews
SW7 114 C3 25
Ennismore Gdns
KT7 19
Ennismore Mews
SW7 114 C3 25
Ennismore St
SW7 114 C3 25
Ennis Rd London N4 5
Shooters Hill SE18 14
Ennor Ct KT4 21
Ensbury Ho SW8 27
Ensign Cl TW19 14
Ensign Ct 12 E1 11
Ensign Dr N13 1
Ensign Ho 19 E14 11
Ensign St E1 11
Ensign Way
Stanwell TW19 14
2 Wallington SM6 22
Enslin Rd SE9 16
Ensor Mews SW7 25
Enstone Rd Enfield EN3
Ickenham UB10 6
Enterprise Cl CR0 20
Enterprise Ho IG11 10
Enterprise Ho E4 2
Enterprise Ho
36 Hackney E9 7
Walton-on-T KT12 19
Enterprise Row N15 5
Enterprise Way
College Pk NW10 9
Teddington TW11 17
Wandsworth SW18 13
Enterprise Works EN3
Enterprize Way SE8 11
Enthoven Ho SE18 12
Enton Pl TW3 12
Enversham Ct SE23 16
Epirus Mews SW6 26
Epirus Rd
SW6 135 B5 26
Epping Cl
Millwall E14 11
Romford RM7 5
Epping Forest* IG10 2
Epping Glade E4 2
Epping Ho 8 E5 7
Epping New Rd IG9 2
Epping Pl N1 7
Epping Way E4 1
Epple Rd
SW6 135 B4 26
Epsom Cl Erith DA7 14
Northolt UB5 6

n & Ewell High
KT19 ... 215 A3
n Ho SM1 ... 217 D4
n Rd
don CR0 ... 220 C4
l IG3 ... 57 D3
n E10 ... 54 A3
en SM3, SM4 ... 201 B2
n Sq TW6 ... 127 D3
in Ct N1 ... 234 D5
in Rd SE28 ... 124 B5
rth Rd TW7,
... 131 B5
rth St
... 95 B3 242 D5
y Sq 20 E2 ... 95 D4
nus St
... 115 D2 259 D3
wald St W12 ... 89 D1
s Dr SE28 ... 123 B4
y Dr BR3 ... 207 C1
y Ho SW7 ... 247 B1
y Pl NW6 ... 69 C1
Ct SW4 ... 270 B1
Gdns CR0 ... 223 D5
Ho London SE4 .. 141 B2
Wimbledon
V19 ... 179 A3
d Green N22 ... 32 C2
St W12 ... 112 A6
Clarke La IG11 .. 101 A4
Cl E7 ... 77 A4
son Cl SW18 ... 157 C6
Fletcher Ct 15
... 73 A1
Macdonald Ho
... 265 B1
Rd
enham RM6 ... 58 D2
est Gate E7 ... 77 A4
esden NW10 ... 67 D2
Shipman Terr 2
... 99 A3
on Ho
don SE13 ... 142 B1
nford Hill N16 ... 51 D1
St E3 ... 97 B3
Wilkins Ho 14
... 118 A1
ge Ho SE22 ... 139 D2
ge Rd W4 ... 111 B3
Cl Bromley BR1 ... 186 C3
rd IG3 ... 58 A3
Ct NW2 ... 68 C2
dale Ct 1 BR3 ... 185 C2
dale SE18 ... 145 B6
dale Terr SE18 ... 145 B6
H ... 147 D6
Rd
vedere DA17 ... 125 D1
n DA7 ... 147 D2
nger Rd SE14 ... 140 D3
mere Gdns
3 ... 109 A3
ne Cl TW4 ... 128 C3
ne Ho 3 N17 ... 33 D3
ne Rd
don SE13 ... 141 D1
th Tottenham N15 .. 51 D3
ne Side EN1 ... 18 A6
ngton Rd SE9 ... 167 A2
ld Ave E6 ... 100 A5
roft Way TW1 ... 152 D5
st Ave SE27 ... 182 D6
st Bevin Coll
17 ... 158 C2
st Cl BR3 ... 207 C4
st Cotts KT17 ... 215 D1
st Gdns W4 ... 132 D6
st Gr BR3 ... 207 B4
st Rd KT1 ... 176 D1
st Richards Twr
... 53 B3
st Simmonds Ho
4 ... 140 C3
st Sq KT1 ... 176 D1
st St E1 ... 96 D3
e Rd SW20 ... 178 C3
haw Pl SW15 ... 157 A6
Ho SE6 ... 163 D4
(Shaftesbury
ml)*
... 115 D6 249 C5
ngham Rd
15 ... 134 C2
dge Rd SW19 ... 179 C1
ngton Manor 6
5 ... 218 D5
ngton Rd W9 ... 91 B3
l Gdns Hayes UB4 .. 84 B3
st Barnes KT3 ... 200 A5
l St EC1 ... 95 A3 242 B5
ine Cl SM1 ... 218 C5
ine Cres N17 ... 52 B5
ine Hill NW11 ... 47 C4
ine Ho
Charlton SE7 ... 143 C6

Erskine Ho *continued*
Pimlico SW1 ... 259 A1
Erskine Rd
Carshalton SM1 ... 218 B5
Primrose Hill NW3 ... 70 D1
Walthamstow E17 ... 53 B5
Erwood Rd SE7 ... 122 A1
Esam Way SW16 ... 182 C5
Escot Rd TW16 ... 171 C3
Escott Gdns SE9 ... 188 A6
Escot Way EN5 ... 12 C6
Escreet Gr SE18 ... 122 C2
Escuan Lo N5 ... 73 A3
ESHER ... 212 A4
Esher Ave
Cheam SM3 ... 216 D5
Walton-on-T KT12 ... 194 A1
Esher CE Prim Sch
KT10 ... 212 A3
Esher Cl DA5 ... 169 A3
Esher Coll KT7 ... 196 C2
Esher Cres TW6 ... 127 D3
Esher Gdns SW19 ... 156 D2
Esher Ho 8 SW8 ... 137 D3
Esher Mews 4 CR4 .. 202 D6
Esher Park Ave
KT10 ... 212 A3
Esher Rd
East Molesey KT8 ... 196 B4
Ilford IG3 ... 79 C5
Esher Sta KT10 ... 212 B6
Eskdale Ave UB5 ... 85 B6
Eskdale Cl HA9 ... 65 D6
Eskdale EN1 ... 17 C6
Eskdale Rd DA7 ... 147 C4
Eskdale NW1 ... 232 A3
Esk Ho E3 ... 97 B3
Eskmont Ridge
SE19 ... 183 C3
Esk Rd E13 ... 99 B3
Esmar Cres NW9 ... 46 A2
Esme Ho SW15 ... 133 D1
Esmeralda Rd SE1 ... 118 A2
Esmond Ct Barnet EN5 .. 1 C1
Kensington W8 ... 255 D6
Esmond Gdns W4 ... 111 B2
Esmond Rd
Acton W4 ... 111 B3
Kilburn NW6 ... 91 B6
Esmond St SW15 ... 135 A1
Esparto St SW18 ... 157 D4
Espirit Ct E1 ... 243 C3
Espirit Ho 6 SW15 ... 157 A6
Essan Ho W13 ... 87 B2
Essence Ct HA9 ... 66 B6
Essenden Rd
Belvedere DA17 ... 125 C1
South Croydon CR2 .. 221 C1
Essendine Mans W9 ... 91 C4
Essendine Prim Sch
W9 ... 91 C4
Essendine Rd W9 ... 91 C4
Essex Ave TW7 ... 130 C2
Essex Cl Romford RM7 ... 59 D5
Ruislip HA4 ... 40 D1
Walthamstow E17 ... 53 A5
West Barnes SM4 ... 200 D2
Essex Ct
Barnes SW13 ... 133 D3
Hammersmith W6 ... 112 C3
Holborn EC4 ... 241 A1
South Norwood
SE19 ... 183 B4
Essex Gdns N4 ... 50 D3
Essex Gr SE19 ... 183 B4
Essex Ho 4 Acton W3 ... 88 C1
2 Poplar E14 ... 97 D1
Essex Lo 5 N10 ... 31 B1
Essex Mans E11 ... 54 B2
Essex Park Mews
W3 ... 111 C5
Essex Pk N3 ... 29 D4
Essex Place Sq 5
W4 ... 111 B2
Essex Pl W4 ... 111 A2
Essex Prim Sch E12 ... 78 A3
Essex Rd Acton W3 ... 111 A6
Barking IG11 ... 79 B1
Chingford E4 ... 20 C3
Chiswick W4 ... 111 B2
Enfield EN2 ... 5 B1
Ilford RM6 ... 58 C2
Islington N1 . 94 D6 234 D6
Leyton E10 ... 54 A3
Plashet E12 ... 78 A2
Romford RM7 ... 59 D5
Essex Rd S E11 ... 54 B2
Essex Rd
Walthamstow E17 ... 53 A3
Willesden NW10 ... 67 C1
Woodford E18 ... 37 B1
Essex Road Sta N1 ... 73 A1
Essex St
Forest Gate E7 ... 77 A3
Strand WC2 . 116 C6 251 A6
Essex Twr 4 SE20 ... 184 B2

Essex Villas
W8 ... 113 C4 245 A1
Essian St E1 ... 97 A2
Essington SW15 ... 157 A5
Essoldo Way HA8 ... 44 B6
Estate Way E10 ... 53 B1
Estcourt Rd
Croydon SE25 ... 206 B3
Fulham
SW6 ... 135 B5 264 C4
Estella Ave KT3 ... 200 B5
Estella Ho 15 W11 ... 112 D6
Estelle Rd NW3 ... 70 D4
Esterbrooke St SW1 . 259 C3
Este Rd SW11 ... 136 C2
Esther Cl N21 ... 16 C4
Esther Doe Lo N21 ... 16 C4
Esther Rd E11 ... 54 C2
Estoria Cl 22 SW2 ... 160 C4
Estreham Rd SW16 ... 181 D4
Estridge Cl TW3 ... 129 C1
Estuary Cl IG11 ... 102 B4
Eswyn Rd SW17 ... 180 D5
Etal Ho N1 ... 72 D1
Etchingham Ct N12 ... 30 A3
Etchingham Park Rd
N3 ... 29 D3
Etchingham Rd E15 ... 76 A4
Eternit Wlk SW6 ... 134 D4
Etfield Gr DA14 ... 190 B5
Ethelbert Cl BR1 ... 209 A6
Ethelbert Gdns IG2 ... 56 C4
Ethelbert Ho E9 ... 75 A4
Ethelbert Rd
Bromley BR1,
BR2 ... 209 A6
Wimbledon SW20 ... 178 D2
Ethelbert St SW12 ... 159 B3
Ethel Brooks Ho
SE18 ... 144 D6
Ethelburga St
SW11 ... 136 C4 267 B2
Ethelburga Twr
SW11 ... 267 B2
Ethel Cotts RM6 ... 58 D6
Etheldene Ave N10 ... 49 C5
Ethelden Rd W12 ... 112 B5
Ethel Rankin Ct 8
SW6 ... 135 B3
Ethel Rd
Ashford TW15 ... 170 A5
Newham E16 ... 99 B1
Ethel St SE17 ... 262 B3
Ethelworth Ct 4
SW2 ... 160 C3
Etheridge Rd NW2 ... 46 C2
Etherley Rd N15 ... 51 A4
Etherow St SE22 ... 162 A4
Etherstone Gn
SW16 ... 182 C6
Etherstone Rd
SW16 ... 182 C6
Ethnard Rd SE15 ... 140 B6
Ethronvi Rd DA7 ... 147 A2
Etienne Ho NW7 ... 28 C6
Etloe Ho E10 ... 53 C1
Etloe Rd E10 ... 75 C6
Eton Ave
East Barnet EN4 ... 14 C5
Finchley N12 ... 30 A3
Heston TW5 ... 129 C6
New Malden KT3 ... 199 B5
Primrose Hill NW3 ... 70 C1
Wembley HA0 ... 65 C4
Eton Cl SW18 ... 157 D4
Eton College Rd
NW3 ... 70 D2
Eton Ct
Hampstead NW3 ... 70 B1
Highgate N6 ... 49 B3
Wembley HA0 ... 65 C4
Eton Garages 11
NW3 ... 70 C2
Eton Gr
Lewisham SE13 ... 142 C2
Queensbury NW9 ... 44 C5
Eton Hall NW3 ... 70 D2
Eton Ho Hackney E9 ... 75 B2
Highbury N5 ... 72 D4
Eton Manor Ct E10 ... 75 C6
Eton Pl NW1 ... 71 A1
Eton Rd
Harlington UB3 ... 127 D5
Ilford IG1 ... 79 B4
Maitland Pk NW3 ... 70 D2
Eton Rise NW3 ... 70 D2
Eton St TW10 ... 154 A6
Eton Villas NW3 ... 70 D2
Etta St SE8 ... 141 A6
Ettrick Ho 8 E5 ... 74 B6
Ettrick St E14 ... 98 A1
Etwell Pl KT5 ... 198 B3
Euesden Cl N9 ... 18 B1
Eugene Cotter Ho
SE17 ... 262 D3
Eugenia Rd SE16 ... 118 C2
Eugenie Mews BR7 .. 188 D2

Eureka Rd 8 KT1 ... 176 C1
Euro Bsns Ctr 3 E15 .98 D6
Euro Cl NW10 ... 68 A2
Eurolink Bsns Ctr
SW2 ... 160 C6
Europa Pl EC1 ... 235 A1
Europe Rd SE18 ... 122 B3
Eustace Bldg SW8 .. 268 C5
Eustace Ho SE11 ... 260 C4
Eustace Pl SE18 ... 122 B2
Eustace Rd
Dagenham RM6 ... 58 D2
Newham E6 ... 100 A4
Walham Green
SW6 ... 135 C5 265 A4
Euston Ct 5 HA0 ... 66 A2
Euston Rd
Fitzrovia
NW1 ... 93 C3 239 B6
Thornton Heath CR0 . 204 C1
Euston Sq NW1 ... 232 C1
Euston Square Sta
WC1 ... 93 C3 239 B6
Euston Sta
NW1 ... 93 D4 232 C1
Euston St
NW1 ... 93 C4 232 B1
Euston Underpass
NW1 ... 239 A6
Evandale Rd SW9 ... 138 C3
Evangelist Rd NW5 ... 71 B4
Evans Cl E8 ... 73 D2
Evans Gr TW13 ... 151 C2
Evans Ho
34 Shepherd's Bush
W12 ... 112 B6
South Lambeth SW8 . 269 D3
Evans Rd SE6 ... 164 C2
Evanston Ave E4 ... 36 A3
Evanston Gdns IG4 ... 56 A3
Eva Rd RM6 ... 58 D2
Eve Ct CR4 ... 181 A1
Evelina Mans 9
SE5 ... 139 B5
Evelina Rd
London SE15 ... 140 C3
Penge SE20 ... 184 D3
Eveline Ct N10 ... 49 B4
Eveline Lowe Prim Sch
SE1 ... 118 A1
Eveline Rd CR4 ... 180 D2
Evelyn Ave
London NW9 ... 45 B5
Ruislip HA4 ... 39 D2
Evelyn Cl TW2 ... 151 D4
Evelyn Cres TW16 ... 171 D2
Evelyn Ct
Chislehurst SE9 ... 166 A2
Marylebone W1 ... 237 C1
Shacklewell E8 ... 74 A4
Shoreditch N1 ... 235 C3
Evelyn Denington Ct 2
N1 ... 72 D1
Evelyn Denington Rd
E6 ... 100 A3
Evelyn Dr HA5 ... 22 D3
Evelyn Fox Ct W10 ... 90 C2
Evelyn Gdns
Richmond TW9 ... 132 A1
South Kensington
SW7 ... 114 B1 256 C1
Evelyn Gr Ealing W5 ... 110 B5
Southall UB1 ... 85 B1
Evelyn Ho
Bedford Pk W12 ... 111 D4
3 Brixton SW2 ... 160 B6
Harrow HA1 ... 42 B4
18 Spitalfields E1 ... 96 A2
Evelyn Rd Acton W4 ... 111 B3
Cockfosters EN4 ... 2 D1
Ham TW10 ... 153 C1
Newham E16 ... 121 B5
Richmond TW9 ... 132 A2
Walthamstow E17 ... 54 A5
Wimbledon SW19 ... 179 D4
Evelyns Cl UB8 ... 82 C1
Evelyn St SE8 ... 119 A1
Evelyn Terr TW9 ... 132 A2
Evelyn Way
Sunbury TW16 ... 171 D2
Wallington SM6 ... 219 D4
Evelyn Wlk
N1 ... 95 B5 235 C3
Evelyn Yd W1 ... 239 C2
Evening Hill BR3 ... 186 A3
Evenlode Ho 5 SE2 ... 124 C4
Evenwood Cl SW15 .. 157 A6
Everard Ave BR2 ... 209 A1
Everard Ct N13 ... 16 B1
Everard Ho 33 E1 ... 96 A1
Everard Way HA9 ... 66 A5
Everatt Cl SW18 ... 157 B6
Everdale Ct N2 ... 48 C5
Eve Rd
Isleworth TW7 ... 131 A1
Leyton E11 ... 76 C4
Everdon Rd SW13 ... 134 A6

Eve Rd Tottenham N17 .. 51 C6
West Ham E15 ... 98 C5
Everest Ct
6 Chislehurst
SE9 ... 166 A2
South Norwood
SE19 ... 183 C2
Everest Pl E14 ... 98 A2
Everest Rd
Eltham SE9 ... 166 B6
Stanwell TW19 ... 148 A4
Everett Cl
Bushey WD23 ... 8 C3
Pinner HA5 ... 39 D6
Everett Ho
Islington N7 ... 72 C4
Walworth SE17 ... 262 C2
Everett Wlk DA17 ... 125 B1
Everglade Ho E17 ... 35 B1
Everglades
Beckenham BR2 ... 208 C6
Hounslow TW3 ... 130 A2
Everglade Strand
NW9 ... 27 D2
Evergreen Cl SE20 ... 184 C3
Evergreen Ct 6
SM2 ... 218 A2
Evergreen Sq 3 E8 ... 73 D1
Evergreen Way
UB3 ... 105 D6
Everilda St N1 ... 233 D5
Evering Rd E5, N16 ... 74 A5
Everington Rd N10 ... 30 D1
Everington St W6 ... 134 D6
Everitt Rd NW10 ... 89 B4
Everleigh St N4 ... 50 B1
Eversfield Ct SE12 ... 165 B2
Eversfield Gdns HA8,
NW7 ... 27 C3
Eversfield Rd TW9 ... 132 B3
Evershed Ho E1 ... 243 D2
Evershed Wlk W4 ... 111 B2
Eversholt Ct EN5 ... 14 A6
Eversholt St
NW1 ... 93 D4 232 C2
Evershot Rd N4 ... 50 B1
Eversleigh Ct N3 ... 29 C3
Eversleigh Rd
Clapham SW11 ... 137 A3
Finchley N3 ... 29 B3
New Barnet EN5 ... 14 A6
Newham E6 ... 99 D6
Eversley Ave HA9 ... 66 C6
Eversley Cl N21 ... 16 B5
Eversley Cres
Hounslow TW7 ... 130 B4
Ruislip HA4 ... 61 D6
Southgate N21 ... 16 C5
Eversley Ho 12 E2 ... 96 A4
Eversley Mount N21 ... 16 B5
Eversley Park Rd
N21 ... 16 B5
Eversley Pk SW19 ... 178 B5
Eversley Prim Sch
N21 ... 16 B5
Eversley Rd
Greenwich SE7 ... 143 B6
Kingston u T KT5 ... 198 B4
South Norwood
SE19 ... 183 B3
Eversley Way CR0 ... 223 C5
Everthorpe Rd SE15 ... 139 D2
Everton Bldgs NW1 ... 232 A1
Everton Ct HA0 ... 65 D4
Everton Dr HA7 ... 44 A6
Everton Rd CR0 ... 206 A1
Evesham Ave E17 ... 35 C1
Evesham Cl
Belmont SM2 ... 217 C1
Greenford UB6 ... 85 D5
Evesham Ct
2 Ealing W13 ... 109 A5
2 Richmond TW10 ... 154 B5
Evesham Gn SM4 ... 201 D3
Evesham Ho
1 Bethnal Green
E2 ... 96 C5
Pimlico SW1 ... 258 D2
St John's Wood NW8 229 A5
Evesham Rd
London N11 ... 31 D5
Morden SM4 ... 201 D3
Stratford E15 ... 76 D1
Evesham St W11 ... 112 D6
Evesham Way
Clapham SW11 ... 137 A2
Ilford IG5 ... 56 C6
Evesham Wlk
Brixton SW9 ... 138 C3
Camberwell SE5 ... 139 B3
Evry Rd DA14 ... 190 C4
Ewald Rd SW6 ... 135 B3
Ewanrigg Terr IG8 ... 37 C5
Ewart Gr N22 ... 32 C2
Ewart Pl 18 E3 ... 97 B5
Ewart Rd SE23 ... 162 D4
Ewe Cl N7 ... 72 A2

EWELL ... 215 C1
Ewell By-Pass KT17 .. 216 A1
EWELL COURT ... 215 C2
Ewell Court Ave
KT19 ... 215 C3
Ewell Park Gdns
KT17 ... 216 A1
Ewell Park Way
KT17 ... 216 A1
Ewell Rd
Cheam SM2, SM3 ... 216 D2
Surbiton KT6 ... 198 B2
Thames Ditton KT6,
KT7 ... 197 B2
Tolworth KT6 ... 198 D1
Ewelme Rd SE23 ... 162 C3
Ewen Cres SW2 ... 160 C4
Ewen Henderson Ct 10
SE14 ... 141 A5
Ewen Ho N1 ... 233 C5
Ewer St SE1 .. 117 A5 252 A3
Ewhurst Cl E1 ... 96 C2
Ewhurst Ct CR4 ... 202 B6
Ewhurst 19 SW15 ... 156 D5
Ewhurst Rd SE4 ... 163 B5
Exbury Ho Hackney E9 .. 74 C2
4 London SW9 ... 138 B1
Exbury Rd SE6 ... 163 C2
Excel Ct WC2 ... 249 D5
Excel Ex Ctr E16 ... 121 B6
Excelsior Cl KT1 ... 176 C1
Excelsior Gdns
SE13 ... 142 A3
Excelsior Ind Est
SE16 ... 140 C6
Exchange Apartments
4 BR2 ... 209 B5
Exchange Arc EC2 .. 243 B4
Exchange Cl N11 ... 15 A2
Exchange Ct WC2 ... 250 B5
Exchange Mans 2
NW11 ... 47 B2
Exchange Pl EC2 ... 243 A4
Exchange The IG1 ... 78 D6
Exchange Wlk HA5 ... 41 A2
Exeforde Ave TW15 .. 170 C6
Exeter Cl E6 ... 100 B1
Exeter Ct Kilburn NW6 .. 91 C5
Kingston u T KT6 ... 198 A4
Mitcham SW19 ... 180 C3
Exeter Gdns IG1 ... 56 B1
Exeter Ho
7 Barking IG11 ... 80 A1
Feltham TW13 ... 151 C2
Paddington W2 ... 236 A2
11 Peckham SE15 ... 140 A6
Putney SW15 ... 156 C5
Exeter Mans NW2 ... 69 A2
Exeter Mews
Fulham SW6 ... 265 A4
12 Hampstead NW6 ... 69 D2
Exeter Rd
Bexley DA16 ... 145 D3
Brondesbury NW2 ... 69 A2
Croydon CR0 ... 205 D2
Dagenham RM10 ... 81 D2
East Barnet N14 ... 15 B4
Enfield EN3 ... 6 D2
Harrow HA2 ... 63 A6
Hatton TW6 ... 127 C2
Lower Edmonton N9 ... 18 C2
Newham E16 ... 99 A2
Twickenham TW13 ... 151 B1
Walthamstow E17 ... 53 C4
Exeter St
WC2 ... 116 B6 250 C6
Exeter Way
Hatton TW6 ... 127 C3
2 New Cross SE14 .. 141 B5
Exford Ct SW11 ... 266 D2
Exford Gdns SE12 ... 165 B3
Exford Rd SE12 ... 165 B3
Exhibition Cl W12 ... 112 C6
Exhibition Rd
SW7 ... 114 B3 256 D6
Exit Rd N2 ... 30 B1
Exmoor Ho 25 E3 ... 97 A5
Exmoor St W10 ... 90 D2
Exmouth Ho
Clerkenwell EC1 ... 241 B6
6 Millwall E14 ... 119 D2
Exmouth Market
EC1 ... 94 C3 241 B6
Exmouth Mews
NW1 ... 232 B1
Exmouth Pl E8 ... 74 B1
Exmouth Rd
Bexley DA16 ... 146 C5
Hayes UB4 ... 83 C4
Ruislip HA4 ... 62 C5
Walthamstow E17 ... 53 B4
Exmouth St E1 ... 96 C1
Exning Rd E16 ... 98 D3
Exonbury NW8 ... 91 D6

Exon St
SE17 117 C2 263 A3
Explorer Ave TW19 148 A3
Explorers Ct 6 E14 120 B6
Express Dr IG3 58 B1
Express Wharf 10
E14 119 C4
Exton Cres NW10 67 A1
Exton Gdns RM8 80 C3
Exton Rd NW10 67 A1
Exton St SE1 116 C5 251 A3
Eyebright Cl 3 CR0 206 D1
Eyhurst Cl NW2 68 A6
Eylewood Rd SE27 183 A5
Eynella Rd SE21 161 D4
Eynham Rd W12 90 C1
Eynsford Cl BR5 211 A3
Eynsford Cres DA5 168 D3
Eynsford Ho
Borough The SE1 252 C2
12 Deptford SE15 140 C6
Walworth SE17 263 A3
Eynsford Rd IG3 79 C6
Eynsford Terr UB7 82 B1
Eynsham Dr SE2 124 B3
Eynswood Dr DA14 190 C5
Eyot Gdns W6 111 D1
Eyot Gn W4 111 D1
Eyre Ct NW8 229 C4
Eyre St Hill
EC1 94 C3 241 A5
Eysham Ct 12 EN5 13 D6
Eythorne Rd SW9 138 C4
Ezra St E2 95 D4

F

Faber Gdns NW4 46 A4
Fabian Rd
SW6 135 B5 264 D4
Fabian St E6 100 B3
Fabyc Ho TW9 132 C5
Factory La
Croydon CR0 220 D6
Tottenham N17 33 D1
Factory Rd E16 122 A5
Factory Yd W7 108 C5
Fagg's Rd TW14 150 A6
Fairacre
Hounslow TW7 130 B4
Kingston u T KT3 199 C6
Pinner HA5 40 A5
Fair Acres BR2 209 A4
Fairacres
Putney SW15 134 A1
Ruislip HA4 39 D2
Fairbairn Gn 1
SW9 138 D4
Fairbairn Hall E13 99 A3
Fairbank Ave BR6 226 D6
Fairbanks Rd N17 52 A6
Fairbourne Ho UB3 105 A3
Fairbourne Rd N17 51 C6
Fairbriar Residence
SW7 256 B4
Fairbridge Rd N19 71 D6
Fairbrook Cl N13 32 C5
Fairbrook Rd N13 32 C4
Fairburn Ct SW15 157 A6
Fairburn Ho
9 Stamford Hill
N16 51 C1
West Kensington
SW5 254 D1
Fairby Ho SE1 263 D4
Fairby Rd SE12 165 B6
Faircharm Trad Est
SE8 141 D5
Fairchild Cl 6
SW11 136 B3
Fairchild Ho
13 Hackney E9 74 C1
Pimlico SW1 259 B3
5 Shoreditch N1 95 C4
Fairchild Pl EC2 243 B5
Fairchild St EC2 243 B5
Fairclough Cl UB5 85 B3
Fairclough St E1 96 A1
Faircourt 14 NW3 70 D2
Faircroft
6 Forest Hill
SE26 184 C6
Stoke Newington N16 51 B1
FAIR CROSS 79 D3
Faircross Ave IG11 79 A6
Fair Cross IG11 79 C3
Faircross Par IG11 79 C3
Fairdale Gdns
Hayes UB3 106 A4
Putney SW15 134 B1
Fairdene Ct N7 72 A3
Fairey Ave UB3 105 D3
Fairfax Cl KT12 194 B1
Fairfax Gdns SE3 143 C4
Fairfax Ho
11 Brixton SW9 138 C3
5 Ealing W5 88 A4
6 Putney SW15 156 A6
Fairfax Mews
London N8 50 D5
Newham E16 121 B5
Putney SW15 134 C1
Fairfax Pl
Kensington W14 254 B5
South Hampstead
NW6 70 A1
Fairfax Rd Acton W4 111 C3
Hornsey N8 50 C5
South Hampstead
NW6 70 A1
Teddington TW11 175 B3
Fairfax Way N10 31 A3
Fairfield Ave
Edgware HA8 26 D3
Hendon NW4 46 B3
Ruislip HA4 39 A2
Twickenham TW2 151 D3
Fairfield NW1 232 A5
Fairfield Cl
Blackfen DA15 167 D5
Enfield EN3 7 A1
Mitcham SW19 180 C3
North Finchley N12 30 A6
West Ewell KT19 215 C3
Fairfield Cres HA8 26 D4
Fairfield Ct
Harlesden NW10 90 A6
1 London SW18 157 D6
Ruislip HA4 39 B1
8 Woodford IG8 37 A4
Fairfield Dr
Harrow HA2 42 A6
Wandsworth SW18 157 D6
Wembley UB6 87 C6
Fairfield E KT1 176 A1
Fairfield Gdns N8 50 A4
Fairfield Gr SE7 143 D6
Fairfield Ind Est
KT1 198 B6
Fairfield N KT1, KT2 176 A1
Fairfield N20 14 B4
Fairfield Path CR0 221 B5
Fairfield HA6 22 A1
Fairfield Pl KT1 198 A6
Fairfield Rd
Beckenham BR3 185 C1
Bexleyheath DA7 147 B3
Bow E3 97 C5
Edmonton N18 34 A6
Higham Hill E17 35 A1
Hornsey N8 50 A4
Ilford IG1 78 D2
Kingston u T KT1 176 A1
Petts Wood BR5 211 B3
Plaistow BR1 187 A3
Southall UB1 85 B1
South Croydon CR0 221 C5
Woodford IG8 37 A4
Yiewsley UB7 104 A6
Fairfields SE6 163 D4
Fairfields Cl NW9 45 A4
Fairfields Cres NW9 45 A4
Fairfield S KT1 176 B1
Fairfields Rd TW3 130 A2
Fairfield 4 E1 96 C2
Fairfield St SW18 157 D6
Fairfield Way
Barnet EN5 13 C6
West Ewell KT19 215 C3
Fairfield W KT1 176 A1
Fairfoot Rd E3 97 C3
Fairford Ave CR0 206 D4
Fairford Cl CR0 207 A4
Fairford Ct SM2 217 D1
Fairford SE6 163 C4
Fairford Gdns KT4 215 D5
Fairford Ho SE11 261 B3
Fairgreen EN4 2 D2
Fairgreen Ct EN4 2 D2
Fair Green Ct 1
CR4 202 D6
Fairgreen E EN4 2 D2
Fairgreen Rd CR7 204 D4
Fairhall Ct KT6 198 B2
Fairhaven Ave CR0 206 D3
Fairhaven Ct 7
CR2 221 A3
Fairhazel Gdns NW6 70 A1
Fairheathe SW15 156 D5
Fairholme Cl N3 47 A5
Fairholme Cres UB4 84 A3
Fairholme TW14 149 C4
Fairholme Gdns N3 47 A5
Fairholme Ho 4
KT3 199 C5
Fairholme Prim Sch
TW14 149 B3
Fairholme Rd
Ashford TW15 170 B5
Cheam SM1 217 B2
Fairholme Rd *continued*
Harrow HA1 42 D4
Ilford IG1 56 C2
Thornton Heath CR0 204 C2
West Kensington
W14 113 A1 254 B1
Fairholt Cl N16 51 C1
Fairholt Rd N16 51 B1
Fairholt St SW7 257 B6
Fairhurst 4 NW6 70 A2
Fairland Ho BR2 209 B5
Fairland Rd E15 76 D1
Fairlands Ave
Sutton SM1 217 C6
Thornton Heath CR7 204 C4
Woodford IG9 21 A2
Fairlands Ct 6 SE9 166 C5
Fairlawn Ave
Acton W4 111 A2
Bexley DA7 146 D3
East Finchley N2 48 C5
Fairlawn Cl
Claygate KT10 212 D2
Feltham TW13 173 B6
Kingston u T KT2 177 A4
Southgate N14 15 D5
Fairlawn Ct
3 Acton W4 111 A2
Charlton SE7 143 C5
Fairlawn Dr IG8 37 A3
Fairlawnes SM6 219 B3
Fairlawn Gdns UB1 107 B6
Fairlawn Gr W4 111 A2
Fairlawn Mans
SE14 140 D4
Fairlawn Pk SE26 185 A5
Fairlawn Prim Sch
(Annexe) SE23 162 C3
Fairlawn Prim Sch
SE23 162 C4
Fairlawn Rd SW19 179 B3
Fairlawns
4 Bowes Pk N11 32 A4
10 Chingford E4 20 A2
Fairlawn SE7 143 C6
Fairlawns Pinner HA5 22 D1
Putney SW15 156 D6
Sunbury TW16 194 A6
Twickenham TW1 153 C5
Fairlead Ho 6 E14 119 C3
Fair Lea Pl W5 87 C2
Fairlea Pl W5 87 D3
Fairleas 12 BR3 185 D1
Fairley Ct HA0 65 D3
Fairley House Sch
SW1 259 D2
Fairlie Ct
22 Bromley E3 97 D4
1 Tufnell Pk N7 71 D4
Fairlie Gdns SE23 162 C4
Fairlight Ave
Chingford E4 20 B2
Harlesden NW10 89 C5
Woodford IG8 37 A4
Fairlight Cl
Cheam KT4 216 C4
Chingford E4 20 B2
Fairlight Ct
Greenford UB6 86 B5
4 Harlesden NW10 89 C5
Fairlight TW12 173 D5
Fairlight Rd SW17 180 B6
Fairline Ct BR3 186 A1
Fairlop Ct E11 54 C1
Fairlop Pl NW8 229 D1
Fairlop Rd E11 54 B2
Fairmark Cl UB10 60 C2
Fairmead BR1 210 B5
Fairmead Cl
Bromley BR1 210 B5
Heston TW5 128 D5
Kingston u T KT3 199 B6
Fairmead Cres HA8 11 A1
Fairmead Ct
3 Chingford E4 20 C4
Oakleigh Pk N20 14 A4
Fairmead Gdns IG4 56 A4
Fairmead Ho E9 75 A4
Fairmead Rd
Lower Holloway N7,
N19 72 A5
Thornton Heath CR0 204 C2
Fairmeadside IG10 21 C6
Fairmead KT5, KT6 198 D1
Fairmile Ave SW16 181 D5
Fairmile Ho
St Paul's Cray
BR5 190 A1
Teddington TW11 175 A6
Fairmont Ave E14 120 B5
Fairmont Cl DA17 125 B1
Fairmont Ho 1 E3 97 C3
Fairmount Rd SW2 160 B5
Fairoak Cl BR5 210 D2
Fairoak Dr SE9 167 B6
Fairoaks Gr EN3 6 D6
Fairseat Cl WD23 8 C2
Fair St SE1 117 D4 253 C2
Fairstead Lo 4 IG8 37 A4
Fairstead Wlk N1 235 A6
Fair St TW3 130 A2
Fairthorn Rd SE7,
SE10 121 A1
Fairview Ave HA0 65 D2
Fairview Cl SE26 185 A5
Fair View Cl E17 35 A2
Fairview Cres HA2 41 C1
Fairview Ct
Ashford TW15 170 C5
Hendon NW4 28 D1
Kingston u T KT2 176 D2
Fairview Dr
Littleton TW17 192 B4
Orpington BR6 227 B4
Fairview Gdns IG8 37 B2
Fairview Ho 14 SW2 160 B4
Fairview Pl SW2 160 B4
Fairview Rd
Carshalton SM1,
SM5 218 C3
Enfield EN2 4 C4
South Tottenham N15 51 D3
Thornton Heath
SW16 182 B2
Fairview Way HA8 26 C6
Fairwall Ho 9 SE5 139 C4
Fairwater Ave DA16 146 A1
Fairwater Ho TW11 175 A6
Fairway Ave NW9 44 D6
Fairway DA6 169 A6
Fairway Cl
Croydon CR0 207 A4
Heston TW4 150 C6
Hounslow TW4 150 D6
North End NW11 48 A2
West Ewell KT19 215 A4
Fairway Ct
Edgware NW7 11 B1
12 Eltham SE9 166 C5
New Barnet EN5 13 D5
18 Rotherhithe
SE16 118 D4
Fairway Dr
Erith SE28 103 A1
Greenford UB6 63 D1
Fairway Est TW4 150 C6
Fairway Gdns
Ilford IG1 79 A3
West Wickham BR3 208 B3
Fairway BR5 211 B4
Fairway Prim Sch
NW7 11 B2
Fairways TW15 170 D4
Fairways Bsns Pk
E10 75 A6
Fairways
12 Chingford E4 20 A3
4 Hounslow TW7 130 C4
Stanmore HA7 26 A1
Teddington TW11 175 D3
Walthamstow E17 54 A5
Fairway The
Acton W3 89 C1
Bromley BR1, BR2 210 B4
East Molesey KT8 195 D6
Edgware NW7 11 B1
Edmonton N13 17 B1
Hillingdon UB10 82 B5
Kingston u T KT3 177 B2
New Barnet EN5 13 D5
Northolt UB5 64 A2
Ruislip HA4 62 D5
Southgate N14 15 C5
Wembley HA0 65 B6
Fairway
West Barnes
SW20 200 C6
Woodford IG8 37 C5
Fairweather Cl N15 51 C5
Fairweather Ct N13 32 B6
Fairweather Ho N7 72 A4
Fairweather Rd N16 52 A3
Fairwood Ct E11 54 B2
Fairwyn Rd SE26 185 A6
Faith Ct NW2 68 B2
Faithfull Ho N5 73 A3
Fakenham Cl
Hendon NW7 28 A3
5 Northolt UB5 63 C2
Fakruddin St E1 96 A3
Falcon Ave BR1 210 A5
Falconberg Ct W1 239 D2
Falconberg Mews
W1 239 D2
Falconbrook Prim Sch
SW11 136 B2
Falcon Cl
Chiswick W4 133 A6
Lambeth SE1 251 D4
Falcon Cres EN3 18 D6
Falcon Ct
3 Dulwich SE21 161 B2
Holborn EC4 241 A1
Islington N1 234 D3
Falcon Ct *continued*
New Barnet EN5 2 A1
Ruislip HA4 61 C6
6 Wanstead E18 55 B6
Falcon Dr TW19 148 A5
Falconer Ct N17 33 A3
Falconer Wlk 12 N7 72 B6
Falcon Gr SW11 136 C2
Falcon Ho
11 London SE15 139 D4
9 Merton SW19 179 D2
Falconhurst 4 KT6 198 A4
Falcon La SW11 136 C2
Falcon Lo
11 Paddington W9 91 C2
West Hampstead
NW3 69 D4
Falcon Pk Ind Est
NW10 67 C3
Falcon Point SE1 251 D5
Falcon Rd
Battersea SW11 136 C2
Enfield EN3 18 D6
Hampton TW12 173 B3
Falconry Ct KT1 198 A6
Falcon St E13 99 A3
Falcon Terr SW11 136 C2
Falcon Way
Feltham TW14 150 B6
Harrow HA3 44 A3
Hendon NW9 27 C1
Millwall E14 119 D2
Sunbury TW16 171 C1
Wanstead E11 55 A5
FALCONWOOD 145 C1
Falconwood Ave
DA16 145 C3
Falconwood Ct SE3 142 D3
Falconwood Par
DA16 145 D1
Falconwood Rd
CR0 223 C1
Falconwood Sta
SE9 145 B1
Falcourt Cl SM1 217 D3
Falkener Ct SW11 268 B1
Falkirk Ct 11 SE16 118 D5
Falkirk Gdns WD19 22 D5
Falkirk Ho W9 91 D4
Falkirk St N1 95 C5
Falkland Ave
Finchley N3 29 C3
Friern Barnet N11 31 B6
Falkland Ho
Catford SE6 186 A6
Kensington W8 255 C5
West Kensington
W14 254 C2
Falkland Park Ave
SE25 183 C1
Falkland Pl 2 NW5 71 C3
Falkland Rd
Barnet EN5 1 A3
Hornsey N8 50 C5
Kentish Town NW5 71 C3
Falkner House Sch
SW7 256 B2
Fallaize Ave IG1 78 D4
Falling La UB7 104 A6
Falloden Ct NW11 47 C5
Falloden Way NW11 47 C5
Fallodon Ho
6 London SW8 137 D3
Paddington W11 91 B2
Fallow Court Ave
N12 30 A4
Fallow Ct 20 SE16 118 A1
Fallowfield Ct HA7 9 A1
Fallowfield N4 72 B6
Fallowfields Dr N12 30 C4
Fallow Fields IG10 21 C4
Fallowfield HA7 9 A1
Fallows Cl N2 30 B1
Fallsbrook Rd
SW16 181 C4
Falman Cl N9 18 A3
Falmer Rd Enfield EN1 5 C1
Walthamstow E17 53 D6
West Green N15 51 B4
Falmouth Ave E4 36 C5
Falmouth Cl
London SE12 164 D6
Wood Green N22 32 B3
Falmouth Gdns IG4 55 D5
Falmouth Ho
Bayswater W2 247 A6
Kennington SE11 261 B2
15 Kingston u T KT2 175 D2
6 Pinner HA5 23 B3
Falmouth Rd
SE1 117 A3 262 B5
Falmouth St E15 76 B3
Falmouth Way E17 53 B4
Falstaff Ct SE11 261 C3
Falstaff Ho 18 N1 95 C5
Fambridge Cl SE26 185 B6
Fambridge Rd RM8 59 C1
Fane St W14 26
Fann St EC1 95 A3 24
Fanshawe Ave IG11 7
Fanshawe Cres RM9 8
Fanshawe Rd TW10 17
Fanshaw Ho 6 E17 5
Fanshaw St N1 9
Fantail Cl SE28 10
Fantail The BR6 22
Fanthorpe St SW15 13
Faraday Ave DA14 16
Faraday Cl N7 7
Faraday Ho
2 Balham SW12 15
4 Belvedere DA17 12
6 Gospel Oak NW5 7
5 Hampton TW12 17
Kensal Town W10 9
6 Poplar E14 11
Wembley HA9 6
Faraday Lo SE10 12
Faraday Pl KT8 19
Faraday Rd
Acton W3 11
East Molesey KT8 19
Kensal Town W10 9
Southall UB1 10
Stratford E15 7
Welling DA16 14
Wimbledon SW19 17
Faraday Way
Greenwich SE18 12
Thornton Heath CR0 20
Fareham Ho 13
SW15 15
Fareham Rd TW14 15
Fareham St W1 23
Farendon Ho 15
SM2 21
Farewell Pl CR4 18
Faringdon Ave BR2 21
Faringford Rd E15 7
Farjeon Ho NW6 7
Farjeon Rd SE3 14
Farleigh Ave BR2 20
Farleigh Ct CR2 22
Farleigh Ho 7 KT2 17
Farleigh Pl N16 7
Farleigh Rd N16 7
Farley Croft BR2 18
Farleycroft 1 CR0 20
Farley Ct
Kensington W14 25
Marylebone NW1 23
Farley Dr IG3 5
Farley Ho SE26 16
Farley Mews SE6 16
Farley Pl SE25 20
Farley Rd
Catford SE6 16
South Croydon CR2 22
Farlington Pl SW15 15
Farlow Rd SW15 13
Farlton Rd SW18 15
Farman Gr 2 UB5 8
Farman Terr HA3 4
Farm Ave
Child's Hill NW2 6
Harrow HA2, HA5 4
Streatham SW16 18
Wembley HA0 6
Farmborough Cl HA1 4
Farm Cl Barnet EN5 1
Buckhurst Hill IG9 2
Coney Hall BR4 22
Lower Halliford
TW17 19
Southall UB1 10
Sutton SM2 21
Uxbridge UB10 6
Walham Green SW6 26
Farmcote Rd SE12 16
Farm Cotts E17 5
Farm Ct NW4 4
Farmdale Rd
Greenwich SE10 12
Sutton SM5 21
Farm Dr CR0 22
Farm End E4 2
Farmer Ho 4 SE16 11
Farmer Rd E10 5
Farmers Rd SE5 13
Farmer St W8 24
Farmfield Rd BR1 18
Farm House Ct NW7 2
Farmhouse Rd
SW16 18
Farmilo Rd E17 5
Farmington Ave
SM1 21
Farm La
Croydon CR0 22
East Barnet N14 1
Farmlands Enfield EN2 4
Pinner HA5 4
Farmlands The UB5 6
Farmland Wlk BR7 18

Lane Trad Ctr
...... 135 C6 265 B5
.a
.... 135 C5 265 B4
eigh Ho SW9 ... 160 D6
eigh N14 .... 15 C4
Pl W8 .... 245 A4
Rd Edgware HA8 .. 27 A5
nton N21 .... 17 A3
en SM4 .... 201 D4
bridge NW10 .... 89 B6
n SM2 .... 218 B1
es Ditton KT10 . 195 C1
enham TW4 .... 151 A3
tead Ct 3
.... 219 B3
tead Rd
rd SE6 .... 185 D6
w HA3 .... 24 B1
St W1 .. 115 B6 248 C5
Vale DA5 .... 169 D5
View N3 .... 47 B6
Way IG9 .... 37 C6
way RM8 .... 80 C5
Way KT4 ...... 216 C5
Wlk NW11 ...... 47 C4
by Ho 2 W10 ... 91 B4
by Rd
ley BR1,
2 .... 186 C2
ooke SE9 ...... 143 C1
n Ave E17 .... 53 D6
n Hall 6
5 .... 182 A5
n Rd SW16 .... 182 A5
BOROUGH 227 B3
orough Ave
h Croydon
2 .... 223 A1
hamstow E17 ...... 53 A6
orough Cl HA9 .. 66 D6
orough Comm
on Mark BR2,
6 .... 226 B5
ngton BR6 .... 226 C4
orough Cres
ayes BR2 ...... 208 D1
h Croydon CR2 .. 223 A1
orough Ct 2
.... 227 A3
orough Hill
.... 227 C3
orough Ho 1
5 .... 156 A3
borough Prim Sch
.... 227 A3
orough Way
.... 227 B3
combe St SE16 .. 118 A4
dale Ave N13 ..... 17 A1
dale Cres UB6 ..... 86 A4
dale Ho 3 NW6 .. 91 D6
ell Mews SW5 .. 255 C2
ell Pl W3 .... 110 D6
ell Rd TW7 .... 130 B2
ell's Almshouses
.... 130 D3
field Ho 12
.... 160 B6
ham Cl N20 ...... 14 A4
ham Ct
Cheam SM3 ..... 217 A2
Southall UB1 ...... 86 A1
Stamford Hill N16 .. 51 C1
ham Gdns
20 .... 178 B1
ham Green Prim
IG3 .... 58 A3
ham Ho
ough The SE1 .... 252 A3
ylebone NW1 .... 237 B5
ham Pl SE1 .... 251 D3
ham Rd
ley DA16 .... 146 C3
rd IG3 .... 57 D2
ham Royal
.... 116 B1 260 D1
hurst Ho 7
1 .... 137 A3
ngham Ct
6 .... 181 D3
ngham Ho 9
.... 51 B2
ngham Rd N17 .... 34 A3
ley Ho 13 SW8 ... 137 D3
ley Rd
gford E4 .... 20 C4
th Norwood
25 .... 205 B5
sworth Ct SE10 .. 120 D3
sworth Ho 8
7 .... 182 D5
worth Ho 5
.... 120 B2
Cl BR1 .... 188 C1
e Rd W14 .... 112 D3

Farorna Wlk EN2 .... 4 C4
Farquhar Rd
Dulwich SE19 .... 183 D5
Wimbledon SW19 ... 157 C1
Farquharson Rd
CR0 .... 205 A1
Farrance Rd RM6 ..... 59 A2
Farrance St E14 ...... 97 C1
Farrans Ct HA3 .... 43 B2
Farrant Ave N22 ...... 32 D1
Farrant Cl BR6 .... 227 D1
Farrant Ho 15 SW11 .. 136 B2
Farrants Ct BR1 ...... 188 B1
Farr Ave IG11 .... 102 A5
Farrell Ho E1 .... 96 C1
Farren Rd SE23 ...... 163 A2
Farrer Ho SE8 .... 141 C5
Farrer Mews N8 .... 49 C5
Farrer Rd Harrow HA3 .. 44 A5
Hornsey N8 .... 49 D5
Farrer's Pl CR0 ...... 222 D4
Farrier Cl
Bromley BR1 .... 209 D6
Hillingdon UB8 .... 82 C1
Sunbury TW16 ...... 194 A5
Farrier Pl SM1 .... 217 D6
Farrier Rd UB5 .... 85 C5
Farriers Ct
Belmont SM2 .... 217 A1
Wimbledon SW19 .... 179 A3
Farriers Mews SE15 .. 140 C2
Farrier St NW1 .... 71 C1
Farriers Way WD6 .... 11 B6
Farrier Wlk
SW10 ...... 136 A6 266 A6
Farringdon La
EC1 .... 94 C3 241 B5
Farringdon Rd
EC1 .... 94 C3 241 B5
Farringdon Sta
EC1 .... 94 D2 241 C4
Farringdon St
EC4 .... 94 D1 241 C2
Farrington Pl BR7 .... 189 B3
Farrington & Stratford
House Sch BR7 .... 189 B3
Farrins Rents SE16 ... 119 A5
Farrow La SE14 ...... 140 C5
Farrow Pl SE16 ...... 119 A3
Farr Rd EN2 .... 5 B4
Farthingale Wlk E15 .. 76 B1
Farthing Alley 8
SE1 .... 118 A4
Farthing Ct 3 NW7 ... 29 A3
Farthing Fields 8
E1 .... 118 B5
Farthings Cl
Chingford E4 .... 20 C1
Pinner HA5 .... 40 B3
Farthing St BR6 ...... 226 B1
Farthings The 1
KT2 .... 176 C2
FARTHING STREET
.... 226 B1
Farwell Rd DA14 ..... 190 C6
Farwig La BR1 .... 187 A2
Fashion & Design Mus
The* SE1 .... 253 A2
Fashion Retail Acad The
W1 .... 239 C2
Fashion St E1 . 95 D2 243 D3
Fashoda Rd BR2 ..... 209 D5
Fassett Rd Dalston E8 .. 74 A2
Kingston u T KT1 .... 198 A5
Fassett Sq E8 .... 74 A2
Fauconberg Ct W4 ... 133 A6
Fauconberg Rd W4 .. 133 A6
Faulkner Cl 6 RM8 .... 58 D2
Faulkner Ho SW15 ... 134 C3
Faulkner's Alley EC1 241 C4
Faulkner St SE14 .... 140 C4
Fauna Cl
Dagenham RM6 .... 58 C3
Stanmore HA7 .... 25 D6
Faunce Ho 1 SE17 ... 138 D6
Faunce St
SE17 .... 116 D1 261 C1
Favart Rd
SW6 .... 135 C4 265 B2
Faversham Ave
Chingford E4 .... 20 D3
Enfield EN1 .... 17 B5
Faversham Ct SE6 ... 163 B3
Faversham Ho
Camden Town
NW1 .... 232 B5
Walworth SE17 ..... 263 A1
Faversham Rd
Beckenham BR3 .... 185 B1
Forest Hill SE6 ...... 163 B3
Morden SM4 .... 201 D3
F Ave SE18 .... 122 D3
Fawcett Cl
London SW11 ...... 136 B3
West Norwood
SW16 .... 182 C6
Fawcett Est E5 .... 52 A1

Fawcett Ho 25 SW9 .. 138 A3
Fawcett Rd
Croydon CR0 .... 221 A5
Willesden NW10 ...... 67 D1
Fawcett St
SW10 ...... 136 A6 266 A6
Fawcus Cl KT10 ..... 212 C2
Fawe Park Rd SW15 .. 135 B1
Fawe St E14 .... 97 D2
Fawkham Ho SE1 .... 263 D3
Fawley Ct SE27 ..... 160 D2
Fawley Lo 2 E14 .... 120 B2
Fawley Rd NW6 .... 69 D3
Fawnbrake Ave
SE24 .... 161 A6
Fawn Rd E13 .... 99 C5
Fawns Manor Cl
TW14 .... 149 A3
Fawns Manor Rd
TW14 .... 149 B3
Fawood Ave NW10 ..... 67 B1
Fayetville Ho 26 N19 .. 49 D2
Faygate Cres DA6 .... 169 C6
Faygate Ct CR2 ...... 220 D1
Faygate Rd SW2 ..... 160 B2
Fayland Ave SW16 ... 181 C5
Fazal Laj IG1 .... 79 A6
Fazerley Ct 49 W2 ..... 91 C2
Fearnley Cres TW12 .. 173 B4
Fearnley Ho SE5 .... 139 C3
Fearon St SE10 ..... 121 A1
Featherbed La CR0 ... 223 B1
Feathers Pl SE10 .... 142 B6
Featherstone Ave 4
SE23 .... 162 C2
Featherstone Ct
NW7 .... 28 A3
Featherstone High Sch
UB2 .... 107 A3
Featherstone Ho
UB4 .... 84 C2
Featherstone Ind Est
UB2 .... 107 A3
Featherstone Prim Sch
UB2 .... 106 C2
Featherstone Rd
Mill Hill NW7 .... 28 B4
Southall UB2 .... 107 A3
Featherstone St
EC1 .... 95 B3 242 C6
Featherstone Terr
UB2 .... 107 A3
Featley Rd SW9 ..... 138 D2
Federal Rd UB6 .... 87 C5
Federation Rd SE2 ... 124 C2
Fee Farm Rd KT10 ... 212 D1
Felbridge Ave HA7 .... 25 B2
Felbridge Cl SW16 ... 182 C6
Felbridge Ct
Croydon CR2 .... 221 A1
Feltham TW13 ...... 150 B3
Harlington UB3 ..... 127 B6
Felbridge Ho 21
SE22 .... 139 C2
Felbrigge Rd IG3 ...... 57 D1
Felday Rd SE13 ..... 163 D5
Felden Cl HA5 .... 23 A3
Felden St
SW6 .... 135 B4 264 C1
Feldman Cl N16 .... 52 A1
Feldspar Ct 6 EN3 ..... 7 A2
Felgate Mews 4
W6 .... 112 B2
Felhampton Rd SE9 .. 166 D1
Felhurst Cres RM10 ... 81 D4
Feline Ct 1 EN4 ...... 14 C5
Felix Ave N8 .... 50 A3
Felix Ct E17 .... 53 D4
Felix La TW17 .... 193 D3
Felix Manor BR7 ..... 189 C4
Felix Neubergh Ct
EN1 .... 5 C1
Felix Rd Ealing W13 ... 109 A6
Walton-on-T KT12 ... 194 A3
Felix St 19 E2 .... 96 B5
Felixstowe Ct E16 .... 122 D5
Felixstowe Rd
Abbey Wood SE2 .... 124 B3
College Pk NW10 ..... 90 B4
Edmonton N9 .... 34 A6
Tottenham N17 .... 51 D6
Fellbrigg Rd SE22 ... 161 D6
Fellbrigg St 21 E1 ..... 96 B3
Fellbrook TW10 ..... 153 B1
Fell Ho 11 N19 .... 71 C5
Fellmongers Yd 1
CR0 .... 221 A5
Fellowes Cl UB4 ...... 84 D3
Fellowes Ct UB3 ..... 127 B6
Fellowes Rd SM5 .... 218 C6
Fellows Ct E2 .... 95 D5
Fellows Rd NW3 ...... 70 C1
Fell Rd CR0 .... 221 A5
Fells Haugh 6 W3 ..... 89 A1
Felltram Way SE7 .... 121 A1
Fell Wlk HA8 .... 26 D2

Felmersham Cl 2
SW4 .... 137 D1
Felmingham Rd
SE20 .... 184 C1
Felnex Trad Est
SM6 .... 219 A6
Felpham Ct HA9 ...... 65 D4
Felsberg Rd SW2 .... 160 A4
Fels Cl RM10 .... 81 D5
Felsham Ho SW15 ... 134 D2
Felsham Mews
SW15 .... 134 D2
Felsham Rd SW15 ... 134 D2
Felspar Cl SE18 ..... 123 D1
Felstead Cl N13 .... 32 C5
Felstead Rd E11 ...... 55 A2
Felstead St E9 .... 75 B2
Felstead Wharf E14 .. 120 A1
Felsted Rd E16 .... 99 D1
FELTHAM 150 B2
Feltham Ave KT8 .... 196 C5
Felthambrook Ind Est
TW13 .... 150 B1
Felthambrook Way
TW13 .... 172 B6
Feltham Bsns Complex
TW13 .... 150 B2
Feltham Com Sch
TW13 .... 150 C2
Feltham Corporate Ctr
TW13 .... 150 B1
FELTHAMHILL 171 D5
Feltham Hill Jun & Inf
Schs TW13 .... 149 D1
Feltham Hill Rd
Ashford TW15 ...... 171 A4
Feltham TW13 ...... 172 C5
Feltham Rd
Ashford TW15 ...... 171 A6
Mitcham CR4 .... 181 A1
Feltham Sta TW13 ... 150 B3
Felton Cl BR5 .... 210 D3
Felton Gdns IG11 .... 101 C5
Felton Ho
Kidbrooke SE9 ...... 143 C1
Shoreditch N1 ...... 235 D5
Felton Lea DA14 ..... 189 D5
Felton Rd
Barking IG11 .... 101 C5
Ealing W13 .... 109 C4
Felton St N1 ... 95 B6 235 D5
Fenchurch Ave
EC3 .... 95 C1 243 A1
Fenchurch Bldgs
EC3 .... 243 B1
Fenchurch Pl EC3 ... 253 B6
Fenchurch St
EC3 .... 117 C6 253 B6
Fenchurch Street Sta
EC3 .... 117 C6 253 B6
Fen Ct EC3 .... 253 A6
Fendall Rd KT19 ..... 215 A3
Fendall St
SE1 .... 117 C3 263 B5
Fender Ct 5 SW4 .... 138 A3
Fendt Cl 8 E16 .... 98 D1
Fendyke Rd SE2,
DA17 .... 124 D3
Fenelon Pl
W14 .... 113 B2 254 D3
Fen Gr DA15 .... 167 D5
Fenham Rd SE15 .... 140 B5
Fenman Ct N17 .... 34 B2
Fenman Gdns IG3 .... 58 B1
Fenn Cl BR1 .... 187 A4
Fenn Ct HA1 .... 43 A4
Fennel Cl
Croydon CR0 .... 206 D1
Newham E16 .... 98 C3
Fennell St SE18 ..... 144 C6
Fenner Cl SE16 ..... 118 B2
Fenner Ho 25 E1 .... 118 B5
Fenner Sq 10 SW11 .. 136 B2
Fenn Ho TW7 .... 131 B4
Fenning Ct CR4 ..... 202 C5
Fenning St SE1 ..... 253 A2
Fenn St E9 .... 74 C3
Fenstanton Ave N12 ... 30 B5
Fenstanton 3 N4 ...... 50 B1
Fenstanton Prim Sch
SW2 .... 160 C3
Fen St E16 .... 120 D6
Fenswood Cl DA5 .... 169 C5
Fentiman Rd
SW8 .... 138 B5 270 C4
Fentiman Way HA2 .... 63 D6
Fenton Cl Dalston E8 ... 73 D2
Elmstead BR7 ...... 188 B5
South Lambeth SW9 .. 138 B3
Fenton Ct TW3 ...... 129 A5
Fenton Ho
Deptford SE14 ...... 141 A5
Heston TW5 .... 129 C6
Fenton House* NW3 ... 70 A5
Fenton Rd N17 .... 33 A3
Fenton's Ave E13 ..... 99 B5
Fentons SE3 .... 142 D5

Fenton St E1 .... 96 B1
Fenwick Cl 16 SE18 .. 144 C6
Fenwick Gr SE15 .... 140 A2
Fenwick Pl
Croydon CR2 .... 220 D1
Stockwell SW9 ..... 138 A2
Fenwick Rd SE15 ... 140 A2
Ferby Ct DA15 ...... 189 D6
Ferdinand Ho 1
NW1 .... 71 B1
Ferdinand Pl NW1 .... 71 A1
Ferdinand St NW1 .... 71 A1
Ferguson Ave KT5 ... 198 B4
Ferguson Cl BR2,
BR3 .... 208 B6
Ferguson Dr W3 ...... 89 B1
Ferguson Ho SE10 ... 142 A4
Ferguson's Cl E14 ... 119 C2
Fergus Rd N5 .... 72 D3
Fermain Ct E N1 ...... 95 C6
Fermain Ct N N1 ...... 95 C6
Fermain Ct W N1 ..... 95 C6
Ferme Park Rd N4,
N8 .... 50 B3
Fermor Rd SE23 ..... 163 A3
Fermoy Rd
Greenford UB6 .... 85 D3
West Kilburn W9 ...... 91 B3
Fern Ave CR4 .... 203 D5
Fernbank Ave
Walton-on-T
KT12 .... 195 A2
Wembley HA0 .... 64 D3
Fernbank IG9 .... 21 B3
Fernbank Mews
SW12 .... 159 C5
Fernbrook Cres
SE13 .... 164 C5
Fernbrook Dr HA2 .... 41 D2
Fernbrook Rd SE13 .. 164 C5
Ferncliff Rd E8 .... 74 A3
Fern Cl 3 N1 .... 95 C5
Ferncroft Ave
London N12 .... 30 D4
Ruislip HA4 .... 62 C6
West Hampstead
NW3 .... 69 C4
Fern Ct
Bexleyheath DA7 .... 147 C1
Chingford E4 .... 36 A4
New Cross Gate
SE14 .... 140 D3
Ferndale Ave
Hounslow TW4 ..... 129 A2
Walthamstow E17 ..... 54 B4
Ferndale BR1 .... 187 C1
Ferndale Cl DA7 .... 147 A4
Ferndale Ct 3 SE3 .. 142 D5
Ferndale Ho N16 ..... 51 B1
Ferndale Rd
Ashford TW15 ...... 170 A5
Brixton SW4, SW9 ... 138 B1
Croydon SE25 ...... 206 B4
Enfield EN3 .... 7 A6
Leyton E11 .... 76 D6
South Tottenham N15 .. 51 D4
Upton E7 .... 77 B1
Ferndale St E6 ...... 100 D1
Ferndale Way BR6 ... 227 B3
Fern Dene W13 ...... 87 B2
Ferndene NW9 .... 45 A4
Ferndene Rd SE24 ... 139 A1
Fernden Way RM7 .... 59 D3
Ferndown Ave BR6 ... 211 B1
Ferndown Cl
Pinner HA5 .... 23 A3
Sutton SM2 .... 218 B2
Ferndown Ct 6 UB1 ... 86 A1
Ferndown 5 KT6 .... 198 A4
Ferndown Lo 17
E14 .... 120 A3
Ferndown HA6 .... 22 A1
Ferndown Rd
Eltham SE9 .... 165 D4
South Oxhey WD19 .... 22 C6
Fernedown 7 E18 ..... 55 A6
Ferney Meade Way
TW7 .... 131 A3
Ferney Rd EN4 .... 15 A3
Fern Gr TW14 ...... 150 B4
Fernhall Dr IG4 ...... 55 D4
Fernhall N12 .... 30 C5
Fernham Rd CR7 .... 205 A6
Fernhead Rd W9 ...... 91 B4
Fernhead 12 SM1 ... 218 A4
Fernhill Ct
Chingford E17 .... 36 B1
Kingston u T KT2 .... 175 D5
Fernhill Gdns KT2 ... 176 A5
Fernhill Ho E5 .... 74 A6
Fern Hill Pl 3 BR6 .. 227 A3
Fern Hill Prim Sch
KT2 .... 176 A4
Fernhill St E16 ...... 122 B5
Fern Ho HA7 .... 24 D4
Fernholme Rd SE15 .. 162 D6
Fernhurst Gdns HA8 .. 26 C4

Fernhurst Rd
Ashford TW15 ...... 171 A6
Croydon CR0 .... 206 B1
Fulham
SW6 ...... 135 A4 264 B2
Fernie Ho SE22 ..... 139 D2
Fern La TW5 .... 107 B1
Fernlea Ho NW10 ..... 88 B4
Fernlea Rd
Balham SW12 ...... 159 B3
Mitcham CR4 .... 181 A2
Fernleigh Cl
Croydon CR0 .... 220 C4
West Kilburn W9 ...... 91 B4
Fernleigh Ct
Harrow HA2 .... 23 D1
Wembley HA9 .... 44 A1
Fernleigh Rd N21 ..... 16 D2
Fern Lo 13 SW16 .... 182 C5
Fernly Cl HA5 .... 40 A5
Fernsbury St WC1 .. 234 A1
Fernshaw Mans
SW10 .... 266 A5
Fernshaw Rd
SW10 ...... 136 A6 266 A5
Fernside Ave
Edgware NW7 .... 11 B1
Feltham TW13 ...... 172 B6
Fernside IG9 .... 21 B3
Fernside Ct NW4 ...... 28 D1
Fernside NW11 .... 47 C1
Fernside Rd SW12 ... 159 A4
Ferns Rd E15 .... 76 D2
Fern St E3 .... 97 C3
Fernthorpe Rd
SW16 .... 181 C4
Ferntower Rd N5 ..... 73 B3
Fernways IG1 .... 78 D4
Fern Wlk 18 SE16 ... 118 A1
Fernwood Ave
Streatham SW16 .... 181 D6
Wembley HA0 .... 65 C2
Fernwood Cl BR1 ... 187 C1
Fernwood Cres N20 ... 14 D1
Fernwood Ct N14 ..... 15 D3
Fernwood
Wandsworth
SW19 .... 157 B3
Wood Green N22 ..... 32 A3
Ferny Hill EN4 .... 3 A5
Ferranti Cl SE18 .... 121 D3
Ferraro Cl TW5 ..... 129 C6
Ferrers Ave
Wallington SM6 .... 219 D4
West Drayton UB7 ... 104 A4
Ferrers Rd SW16 ... 181 D5
Ferrestone Rd N8 ..... 50 B5
Ferrey Mews 19
SW9 .... 138 C3
Ferriby Cl N1 .... 72 C1
Ferrier Ind Est
SW18 .... 135 D1
Ferrier Point 6 E16 ... 99 A2
Ferrier St SW18 .... 135 D1
Ferring Cl HA2 .... 42 A1
Ferrings SE21 ...... 161 C1
Ferris Ave CR0 ..... 223 B5
Ferris Rd SE22 ..... 140 A1
Ferron Rd E5 .... 74 B5
Ferrour Ct N2 .... 48 B6
Ferrybridge Ho
SE11 .... 260 D5
Ferrydale Lo 4 NW4 ... 46 C5
Ferry Ho E5 .... 52 B1
Ferry Island Ret Pk
N17 .... 52 A6
Ferry La
Barnes SW13 ...... 133 D6
Brentford TW8 ..... 132 A6
Lower Halliford
TW17 .... 192 C1
Ferry Lane Ind Est
E17 .... 52 D5
Ferry Lane Prim Sch
N17 .... 52 B5
Ferry La
Richmond TW9 ..... 132 B6
Tottenham Hale N17 .. 52 B5
Ferrymead Ave UB6 ... 85 C5
Ferrymead Dr UB6 .... 85 C5
Ferrymead Gdns
UB6 .... 86 A5
Ferrymoor TW10 .... 153 B1
Ferry Quays Ctyd 13
TW8 .... 131 D6
Ferry Rd
Barnes SW13 ...... 134 A4
East Molesey KT8 ... 195 C6
Richmond TW11 .... 175 B5
Thames Ditton KT7 .. 197 B3
Twickenham TW1 ... 153 B3
Ferry Sq
1 Brentford
TW8 .... 132 A6

Ferry Sq continued
Lower Halliford TW17 ... 192 D2
Ferry St E14 ... 120 A1
Ferry Wks TW17 ... 192 C1
Festing Rd SW15 ... 134 D2
Festival Cl
Hillingdon UB10 ... 82 D6
Sidcup DA5 ... 168 D3
Festival Ct
Cheam SM1 ... 201 D1
5 Dalston E8 ... 73 D1
Festival Pier SE1 ... 116 B5 250 C4
Festival Pleasure Gdns SW11 ... 136 D5 267 C3
Festoon Way E16 ... 121 D6
Fetherston Ct RM6 ... 59 B3
Fetter La EC4 ... 94 C1 241 B2
Fettes Ho NW8 ... 229 D3
Fews Lodge RM6 ... 58 D5
Ffinch St SE8 ... 141 C5
Fidgeon Cl BR1 ... 210 C6
Field Cl Bromley BR1 ... 187 C1
Buckhurst Hill IG9 ... 21 C1
Chessington KT9 ... 213 C3
Chingford E4 ... 35 D4
Cranford TW4 ... 128 B4
East Molesey KT8 ... 195 D4
Harlington UB7 ... 127 A5
Ruislip HA4 ... 39 A1
Uxbridge UB10 ... 60 D6
Willesden NW2 ... 68 A6
Fieldcommon La KT12 ... 195 B1
Field Ct
Hampstead NW3 ... 70 A3
Holborn WC1 ... 240 D3
Lower Holloway N7 ... 72 A3
Wimbledon SW19 ... 157 C1
Field End Jun & Inf Schs HA4 ... 62 D6
Field End Rd HA5, HA4 ... 40 C1
Fieldend Rd SW16 ... 181 C2
Field End HA4 ... 62 C2
Fieldend TW11 ... 174 D6
Fielders Cl
2 Enfield EN1 ... 5 C1
Harrow HA2 ... 42 A1
Fieldfare Rd SE28 ... 124 C6
Fieldgate Mans 25 E1 ... 96 A2
Fieldgate St E1 ... 96 A2
Field Ho
4 Edmonton N9 ... 34 A6
Kensal Green NW10 ... 90 D4
8 Richmond TW10 ... 153 C1
Fieldhouse Cl E18 ... 37 B2
Fieldhouse Rd SW12 ... 159 C3
Fielding Ave TW2 ... 152 A1
Fielding Ho
Chiswick W4 ... 133 C6
6 Kilburn NW6 ... 91 C4
St John's Wood NW8 229 A6
Fielding Mews SW13 ... 134 B6
Fielding Prim Sch W13 ... 109 B3
Fielding Rd
Acton W4 ... 111 C3
Hammersmith W14 ... 112 D3
Fieldings The SE23 ... 162 C3
Fielding St SE17 ... 139 A6
Fielding Terr W5 ... 110 B6
Field La
Brentford TW8 ... 131 C5
Teddington TW11 ... 175 A5
Field Lo NW10 ... 67 D2
Field Mead NW9, NW7 ... 27 D3
Fieldpark Gdns CR0 ... 207 A1
Field Pl KT3 ... 199 D3
Field Point E7 ... 77 A4
Field Rd
Feltham TW14 ... 150 B5
Forest Gate E7 ... 77 A4
Fulham W6 ... 135 A6 264 A6
Tottenham N17 ... 51 C6
Fieldsend Rd SM3 ... 217 A3
Fields Est E8 ... 74 A1
Fieldside Cl BR6 ... 227 A4
Fieldside Rd BR1 ... 186 B5
Fields Park Cres RM6 ... 58 D4
Field St WC1 ... 233 C2
Fieldsway Ho N5 ... 72 C3
Field View Cl RM7 ... 59 C6
Fieldview Ct
2 Islington N5 ... 72 D3
London NW9 ... 44 C3
Field View TW13 ... 171 B6
Fieldview SW17, SW18 ... 158 B3
Fieldway Cres N5, N7 ... 72 C3
Fieldway RM8 ... 80 C4
Field Way
Greenford UB6 ... 85 D6
New Addington CR0 ... 223 D2
Fieldway BR5 ... 211 B3
Field Way HA4 ... 39 A1
Fieldway Sta CR0 ... 223 D1
Field Way NW10 ... 67 A1
Fieldwick Ho 14 E9 ... 74 D2
Fiennes Cl RM8 ... 58 C1
Fife Ct 5 W3 ... 88 C1
Fifehead Cl TW15 ... 170 A4
Fife Rd
Kingston u T KT2 ... 176 A1
Mortlake SW14 ... 155 A6
Newham E16 ... 99 A2
Tottenham N22 ... 32 D3
Fife Terr N1 ... 233 D4
Fifield Path SE23 ... 162 D1
Fifteenpenny Fields SE9 ... 166 C6
Fifth Ave Hayes UB3 ... 105 D5
Ilford E12 ... 78 B4
West Kilburn W10 ... 91 A4
Fifth Cross Rd TW2 ... 152 B2
Fifth Way HA9 ... 66 D4
Figge's Rd CR4 ... 181 A3
Filanco Ct W7 ... 108 D5
Filby Rd KT9 ... 214 B2
Filey Ave N16 ... 52 A1
Filey Cl SM2 ... 218 A1
Filey Ho SW18 ... 136 A1
Filey Waye HA4 ... 62 B6
Filigree Ct SE16 ... 119 B5
Fillebrook Ave EN1 ... 5 D3
Fillebrook Rd E11 ... 54 C1
Filmer Ho SW6 ... 264 B2
Filmer Mews SW6 ... 264 B2
Filmer Rd SW6 ... 135 B5 264 C3
Filston Rd DA8 ... 125 D1
Filton Cl NW9 ... 27 C1
Filton Ct 14 SE14 ... 140 C5
Finborough Rd
Upper Tooting SW17 ... 180 D4
West Brompton SW10 ... 135 D6 265 D6
Finchale Rd SE2 ... 124 A3
Fincham Cl UB10 ... 61 A5
Finch Ave SE27 ... 183 B6
Finch Cl Barnet EN5 ... 13 C6
Willesden NW10 ... 67 B2
Finch Ct DA14 ... 168 B1
Finchdean Ho SW15 ... 155 D4
Finch Dr TW14 ... 150 D4
Finch Gdns E4 ... 35 C5
Finch Ho 1 SE8 ... 141 D5
Finchingfield Ave IG8 ... 37 C3
Finch La EC2, EC3 ... 242 D1
FINCHLEY ... 29 D3
Finchley Cath High Sch N12 ... 13 D1
Finchley Central Sta N3 ... 29 C2
Finchley Ct N3 ... 29 D4
Finchley La NW4 ... 46 D5
Finchley Lo N12 ... 29 D5
Finchley Meml Hospl N12 ... 30 A3
Finchley Pk N12 ... 30 B6
Finchley Pl NW8 ... 229 C4
Finchley Rd
Hampstead NW3 ... 70 A2
London NW11 ... 47 B3
St John's Wood NW8 229 C4
Finchley Road & Frognal Sta NW3 ... 70 A3
Finchley Road Sta NW3 ... 70 A2
Finchley Way N3 ... 29 C3
Finch Lo 18 W9 ... 91 C2
Finch Mews 3 SE15 ... 139 D4
Finch's Ct 10 E14 ... 119 D6
Finden Rd E7 ... 77 C3
Findhorn Ave UB4 ... 84 B2
Findhorn St 8 E14 ... 98 A1
Findon Cl
Harrow HA2 ... 63 D5
Wandsworth SW18 ... 157 C5
Findon Rd
Edmonton N9 ... 18 B3
Shepherd's Bush W12 ... 112 A4
Fine Bush La HA4 ... 38 D3
Fineran Ct 16 SW11 ... 136 B1
Fingal St SE10 ... 120 D1
Fingest Ho NW8 ... 237 A6
Finians Cl UB10 ... 60 B1
Finland Rd SE4 ... 141 A2
Finland St SE16 ... 119 A3
Finlays Cl KT9 ... 214 C3
Finlay St SW6 ... 134 D4
Finley Ct 21 SE5 ... 139 A5
Finmere Ho 1 N4 ... 51 A2
Finnemore Ho N1 ... 235 A6
Finney La TW7 ... 131 A4
Finn Ho N1 ... 235 D2
Finnis St E2 ... 96 B3
Finnymore Rd RM9 ... 81 A1
FINSBURY ... 94 C4
Finsbury Ave EC2 ... 242 D3
Finsbury Cir EC2 ... 95 B2 242 D3
Finsbury Coll N4 ... 72 C6
Finsbury Cotts N22 ... 32 A3
Finsbury Ct EC2 ... 242 C4
Finsbury Ho N22 ... 32 A2
Finsbury Market EC2 ... 243 A4
Finsbury Mkt EC2 ... 243 A5
FINSBURY PARK ... 72 C6
Finsbury Park Ave N4 ... 51 A3
Finsbury Park Rd N4, N5 ... 72 D6
Finsbury Park Sta N4 ... 72 C6
Finsbury Pavement EC2 ... 95 B2 242 D4
Finsbury Rd N22 ... 32 B2
Finsbury Sq EC2 ... 95 B2 242 D4
Finsbury St EC2 ... 242 C4
Finsbury Way DA5 ... 169 B5
Finsen Rd SE5 ... 139 A2
Finstock Rd W10 ... 90 D1
Finton House Sch SW17 ... 158 D2
Finucane Ct TW9 ... 132 B2
Finucane Rise WD23 ... 8 A2
Finwhale Ho E14 ... 119 D3
Fiona Ct Enfield EN2 ... 4 D2
9 Kilburn NW6 ... 91 B5
Firbank Cl Enfield EN2 ... 5 A1
Newham E16 ... 99 D2
Firbank Rd SE15 ... 140 B3
Fir Cl KT12 ... 194 A2
Fircroft Gdns HA1 ... 64 C5
Fircroft N1 ... 94 D6 234 D6
Fircroft Prim Sch SW17 ... 158 D1
Fircroft Rd
Chessington KT9 ... 214 B4
Upper Tooting SW17 ... 158 D1
Fir Dene BR6 ... 226 C5
Firdene KT5 ... 199 A1
Fire Bell Alley KT6 ... 198 A3
Firebell Mews KT6 ... 198 A3
Fire Brigade Cotts HA5 ... 41 C5
Fire Brigade Pier SE1 ... 260 B4
Firecrest Dr NW3 ... 69 D5
Firefly Gdns E6 ... 100 A3
Firefly 7 NW9 ... 27 D1
Firemans Cotts N10 ... 49 A6
Fireman's Flats N22 ... 32 A2
Firepower (The Royal Artillery Mus)* SE18 ... 122 D3
Fire Station Alley EN5 ... 1 A3
Fire Station Flats TW7 ... 130 C3
Fire Station Mews 4 BR3 ... 185 D2
Firethorn Cl 4 HA8 ... 27 A6
Fir Gr KT3 ... 199 D3
Fir Grove Rd 25 SW9 ... 138 C3
Firhill Rd SE6 ... 163 C1
Fir Island NW7 ... 28 C5
Firle Ho 7 W10 ... 90 C2
Fir Lo SW15 ... 134 B1
Firmans Ct E17 ... 54 B5
Firmston Ho 9 SW14 ... 133 B2
Fir Rd Cheam SM3 ... 201 B1
Feltham TW13 ... 172 D5
Firs Ave
Fortis Green N10 ... 49 A5
Friern Barnet N11 ... 31 A4
Mortlake SW14 ... 133 A1
Firsby Ave CR0 ... 207 A1
Firsby Rd N16 ... 52 A1
Firs Cl Claygate KT10 ... 212 C2
Forest Hill SE23 ... 163 A4
Mitcham CR4 ... 181 B2
Muswell Hill N10 ... 49 A6
Firscroft N13 ... 17 A1
Firs Dr TW5 ... 128 B5
Firs Farm Prim Sch N13 ... 17 B1
Firs Ho N22 ... 32 C2
Firside Gr DA15 ... 167 D3
Firs La N21, N13 ... 17 A2
Firs Park Ave N21 ... 17 B3
Firs Park Gdns N21 ... 17 B3
First Ave Bexley DA7 ... 146 C5
Chadwell Heath RM6 ... 58 C4
Dagenham RM10 ... 103 D5
East Acton W3 ... 111 D5
East Molesey KT8 ... 195 C5
Edmonton N18 ... 34 C6
Enfield EN1 ... 17 D6
Hayes UB3 ... 105 D5
Hendon NW4 ... 46 C5
Manor Pk E12 ... 78 A3
Mortlake SW14 ... 133 C2
Newham E13 ... 99 A4
Walthamstow E17 ... 53 D4
Walton-on-T KT12 ... 194 B3
Wembley HA9 ... 65 D6
West Kilburn W10 ... 91 B3
First Cl KT8 ... 196 A6
First Cross Rd TW2 ... 152 C2
First Dr NW10 ... 67 A1
Firs The
Belmont SM2 ... 217 D1
Claygate KT10 ... 212 C2
Ealing W5 ... 87 D2
Forest Hill SE26 ... 184 C5
Oakleigh Pk N20 ... 14 B3
2 Penge SE26 ... 184 B5
Sidcup DA15 ... 167 D1
Upton Pk E6 ... 78 A1
Wimbledon SW20 ... 178 A3
Woodford IG8 ... 37 C3
First St SW3 ... 114 C2 257 B4
Firstway SW20 ... 178 C1
First Way HA9 ... 66 D4
Firs Wlk IG8 ... 37 A5
Firswood Ave KT19 ... 215 D3
Firth Gdns SW6 ... 135 A4 264 A1
Firtree Ave CR4 ... 181 A1
Fir Tree Ave UB7 ... 104 C3
Fir Tree Cl Ealing W5 ... 88 A1
Esher KT10 ... 212 A3
5 Orpington BR6 ... 227 D3
Streatham SW16 ... 181 C5
Worcester Pk KT19 ... 215 D4
Firtree Ct BR2 ... 208 D6
Fir Tree Gdns CR0 ... 223 C4
Fir Tree Gr SM5 ... 218 D1
Firtree Ho SE13 ... 164 B4
Fir Tree Ho 11 SE14 ... 140 C5
Firtree Lodge N21 ... 17 A2
Fir Tree Rd TW4 ... 129 A1
Fir Trees Cl SE16 ... 119 A5
Fir Tree Wlk EN1 ... 5 B2
Fir Wlk KT17, SM3 ... 216 D2
Fisher Cl
Croydon CR0 ... 205 D1
Holdbrook EN3 ... 7 C6
Southall UB6 ... 85 C4
Fisherdene KT10 ... 213 A1
Fisher Ho
Islington N1 ... 234 A5
9 Shadwell E1 ... 118 C6
2 Tufnell Pk N19 ... 71 C5
Fisherman Cl TW10 ... 175 C6
Fishermans Dr SE16 ... 118 D4
Fisherman's Wlk E14 ... 119 C5
Fishermans Wlk SE28 ... 123 C4
Fisher Rd HA3 ... 24 D1
Fishers Cl SW16 ... 159 D1
Fishers Ct
London SE14 ... 140 D4
6 Teddington TW11 ... 174 D5
Fisher's La W4 ... 111 B2
Fisher St
Holborn WC1 ... 240 C3
Newham E16 ... 99 A2
Fisherton St NW8 ... 92 B3 236 D6
Fisherton Street Est NW8 ... 92 B3 236 D5
Fishguard Way E16 ... 122 D5
Fishlock Ct 6 SW4 ... 138 A3
Fishponds Rd
Keston BR2 ... 225 D3
Upper Tooting SW17 ... 180 C6
Fish St Hill EC3 ... 252 D5
Fisk Cl TW16 ... 171 D4
Fiske Ct
Barking IG11 ... 101 B5
1 Merton SW19 ... 180 A3
Sutton SM2 ... 218 A1
Tottenham N17 ... 34 A2
Fitch Ct London SW2 ... 160 C6
8 Mitcham CR4 ... 181 A1
Fitzalan Rd
Church End N3 ... 47 B6
Claygate KT10 ... 212 C1
Fitzalan St SE11 ... 116 C2 261 A4
Fitzclarence Ho W11 ... 244 A2
Fitzgeorge Ave KT2, KT3 ... 177 B2
Fitz-George Ave W14 ... 254 A3
Fitzgerald Ave SW14 ... 133 C2
Fitzgerald Ct 1 E10 ... 53 D1
Fitzgerald Ho
15 Brixton SW9 ... 138 C3
Hayes UB3 ... 106 B5
14 Poplar E14 ... 97 D1
Fitzgerald Rd
Mortlake SW14 ... 133 B2
Thames Ditton KT7 ... 197 A3
Wanstead E11 ... 55 A4
Fitzhardinge Ho
Beckenham BR3 ... 185 D1
Marylebone W1 ... 238 A2
Fitzhardinge St W1 ... 238 A2
Fitzherbert Ho 11 TW10 ... 154 B5
Fitzhugh Gr SW18 ... 158 B5
Fitzjames Ave
Croydon CR0 ... 222 A6
West Kensington W14 ... 254 B3
Fitzjohn Ave EN5 ... 1 B1
Fitzjohn's Ave NW3 ... 70 B3
Fitzjohns Mans NW3 ... 70 A2
Fitzjohns Prim Sch NW3 ... 70 B3
Fitzmaurice Ho 17 SE16 ... 118 B2
Fitzmaurice Pl W1 ... 248 D4
Fitzneal St W12 ... 89 D1
FITZROVIA ... 93 C2
Fitzroy Cl N6 ... 48 D1
Fitzroy Cres W4 ... 133 B5
Fitzroy Ct London N6 ... 49 C3
Marylebone W1 ... 239 B5
Fitzroy Gdns SE19 ... 183 C3
Fitzroy Ho
Bermondsey SE1 ... 263 D2
12 Tower Hamlets E14 ... 97 B1
Fitzroy Lo N21 ... 16 D6
Fitzroy Mews W1 ... 239 A5
Fitzroy Pk N6 ... 48 D1
Fitzroy Rd NW1 ... 93 A6 231 A6
Fitzroy Sq W1 ... 239 A5
Fitzroy St W1 ... 93 C3 239 A5
Fitzroy Yd NW1 ... 231 A6
Fitzstephen Rd RM8 ... 80 C3
Fitzwarren Gdns N19 ... 49 C1
Fitzwilliam Ave TW9 ... 132 B3
Fitzwilliam Ho
4 Higham Hill E17 ... 35 A1
Richmond TW9 ... 131 D1
Fitzwilliam Hts 1 SE23 ... 162 C2
Fitzwilliam Mews E16 ... 121 A5
Fitzwilliam Rd SW4 ... 137 C2
Fitzwygram Cl TW12 ... 174 A5
Fiveacre Cl CR7 ... 204 C3
Five Acre NW9 ... 27 D1
Five Arch Bridge DA14 ... 191 A6
Five Arches Bsns Pk DA14 ... 190 D4
Five Elms Prim Sch RM8 ... 81 B5
Five Elms Rd
Dagenham RM9 ... 81 B5
Keston Mark BR2 ... 225 C5
Five Oaks Mews BR1 ... 165 A1
Fives Ct SE11 ... 261 C5
Fiveways SE9 ... 166 D2
Five Ways Cnr NW4 ... 28 A2
Fiveways CR0 ... 220 C4
Fiveways Rd SW9 ... 138 C3
Fiveways HA4 ... 39 B1
Flack Ct 15 E10 ... 53 D2
Fladbury Rd N15 ... 51 B3
Fladgate Rd E11 ... 54 C3
Flag Cl CR0 ... 206 D1
Flag Wlk HA5 ... 40 A3
Flambard Rd HA1, HA3 ... 43 A3
Flamborough Ho 12 SE15 ... 140 A4
Flamborough Rd HA4 ... 62 A5
Flamborough St E14 ... 97 A1
Flamingo Ct 2 SE8 ... 141 C5
Flamingo Gdns UB5 ... 85 A4
Flamstead Gdns RM9 ... 80 C1
Flamstead Rd RM9 ... 80 C1
Flamsted Ave HA9 ... 66 C2
Flamsteed Ct 15 SE13 ... 141 D4
Flamsteed Ho* SE10 ... 1
Flamsteed Rd SE7 ... 1
Flanchford Rd W12 ... 1
Flanders Cres SW17 ... 1
Flanders Ct E17 ...
Flanders Ho N16 ...
Flanders Mans 1 W4 ... 1
Flanders Rd
Acton W4 ... 1
Wallend E6 ... 1
Flanders Way E9 ...
Flandrian Cl EN3 ...
Flank St 9 E1 ... 1
Flansham Ho 2 E14 ...
Flash La EN2 ...
Flask Cotts 4 NW3 ...
Flask Wlk NW3 ...
Flatford Ho 2 SE6 ... 1
Flather Cl 12 SW16 ... 1
Flatiron Sq SE1 ... 2
Flatiron Yd SE1 ... 2
Flavell Mews SE10 ... 1
Flaxen Cl E4 ...
Flaxen Rd E4 ...
Flaxley Rd SM4 ... 20
Flaxman Ct
12 Belvedere DA17 ... 12
Soho W1 ... 23
Flaxman Ho
10 Chiswick W4 ... 1
Newington SE1 ... 26
Flaxman Rd SE5 ... 13
Flaxman Terr WC1 ... 93 D4 2
Flaxman Villas N2 ...
Flaxmore Ct
Erith DA7 ... 14
South Norwood CR7 ... 18
Flaxton Rd SE18 ... 14
Flecker Cl HA7 ... 2
Flecker Ho 6 SE5 ... 1
Fleece Dr N9 ... 3
Fleecefield Prim Sch N18 ... 3
Fleece Rd KT6 ... 19
Fleece Wlk N7 ...
Fleeming Cl E17 ...
Fleeming Rd E17 ...
Fleet Cl
East Molesey KT8 ... 19
Ruislip HA4 ... 3
Fleet Ct 1 W12 ... 1
Fleetfield WC1 ... 23
Fleet Ho
6 Brixton SW2 ... 16
4 Limehouse E14 ... 1
Fleet Pl EC4 ... 24
Fleet Prim Sch NW3 ... 7
Fleet Rd NW3 ... 7
Fleetside KT8 ... 19
Fleet Sq WC1 ... 23
Fleet St EC4 ... 94 C1 24
Fleet Street Hill 10 E1 ... 9
Fleet Terr SE6 ... 16
Fleetway WC1 ... 23
Fleetway West Bsns Pk UB6 ... 8
Fleetwood Cl
Chessington KT9 ... 2
Newham E16 ... 9
South Croydon CR0 ... 22
Fleetwood Ct
1 Newham E6 ... 10
Orpington BR6 ... 22
8 Stanwell TW19 ... 14
Fleet Wood 6 N16 ... 7
Fleetwood Rd
Kingston u T KT3 ... 19
Willesden NW10 ... 6
Fleetwood Sq KT3 ... 19
Fleetwood St N16 ... 7
Fleetwood Way WD19 ... 2
Fleming Cl 4 W9 ... 9
Fleming Ct
Croydon CR0 ... 22
Paddington W2 ... 23
Fleming Dr N21 ...
Fleming Ho
14 Bermondsey SE16 ... 11
Finsbury Pk N4 ... 5
5 Wembley HA9 ... 6
Fleming Mead CR4 ... 18
Fleming Rd
Camberwell SE17 ... 13
Southall UB1 ... 8
Fleming Way
Isleworth TW7 ... 13
Thamesmead SE28 ... 12
Fleming Wlk NW9 ... 2
Flemming Ave HA4 ... 6

ton Rd E10 ... 53 A1
er Bldgs WC2 ... 240 B1
er Cl E16 ... 122 D6
er Ct 9 NW5 ... 71 B4
er Ho 16 N16 ... 73 C4
er La E10 ... 54 A2
er Path 7
... 141 C5
er Rd W4 ... 111 A3
ers Cl BR2 ... 209 B5
er St 16 E1 ... 118 A6
ing Rd
ton SE7 ... 143 D6
r Clapton E5 ... 74 C5
n Rd N11 ... 32 A3
De Lis St E1 ... 243 C5
Gates 7
) ... 156 D4
ere Rd N17 ... 33 C2
ell Cl BR1 ... 186 C5
rs Ho 28 E1 ... 118 B5
Cl
reen Street Green
6 ... 227 D2
tratford E15 ... 76 D1
Ct CR0 ... 204 B3
Down Cl BR5 ... 190 A2
hill Cres SE3,
... 144 A3
n St
... 117 C1 263 B2
St SE17 ... 117 B2 262 D3
oft St WC2 ... 239 D1
n Ho 7 N1 ... 72 D1
haven Cl SE28 ... 124 A5
Mill Pl SW18 ... 157 D3
on St
ermondsey
16 ... 118 A4
ermondsey
16 ... 118 A4
en Rd SE5 ... 139 A4
La 5 TW1 ... 153 A3
St
... 136 C6 267 B6
Wlk
... 136 C6 267 B6
Cl E14 ... 97 D1
Gardens Prim Sch
... 112 B2
Gdns
nham RM6 ... 58 C3
ammersmith
5 ... 112 B2
St
... 116 A6 250 A6
St DA17 ... 125 B1
nce Ave
ld EN2 ... 5 A2
den SM4 ... 202 A4
nce Cl KT12 ... 194 B2
nce Ct
lew Barnet
5 ... 13 D6
hn's Wood W9 ... 229 B1
stead E11 ... 55 C5
Vimbledon
/19 ... 179 A4
nce Dr EN2 ... 5 A2
nce Elson Cl
... 78 C4
nce Gdns
wick W4 ... 133 A6
d RM6 ... 58 C2
nce Ho
ermondsey
16 ... 118 B1
rixton SW2 ... 160 B6
rooke SE18 ... 144 B4
ingston u T KT2 ... 176 B3
hepherd's Bush
1 ... 112 D6
Vandsworth
/18 ... 136 B1
nce Mans
am SW6 ... 264 C2
endon NW4 ... 46 B4
nce Nightingale
4 N1 ... 73 A2
nce Nightingale
* SE1 ... 250 D1
nce Rd
y Wood SE2 ... 124 C2
n W4 ... 111 B3
eckenham BR3 ... 185 A1
nley BR1 ... 187 A2
g W5 ... 110 A6
am TW13 ... 150 B3
bury Pk N4 ... 50 C2
ngston u T KT2 ... 176 B3
Cross Gate
4 ... 141 B4
hall UB2 ... 106 D3
pton Pk E6 ... 99 C6
on-on-T KT12 ... 194 B2
Ham E13 ... 99 A5
bledon SW19 ... 179 D4

Florence Root Ho 3
IG4 ... 56 B4
Florence St
Islington N1 ... 72 D1
London NW4 ... 46 C5
Newham E16 ... 98 D3
Florence Terr
Kingston u T
SW15 ... 155 C1
New Cross Gate
SE14 ... 141 B4
Florence Way
SW12 ... 158 D3
Florence White Ct
N9 ... 18 B1
Florentine Ho 3 IG1 ... 78 D6
Flores Ho 18 E1 ... 96 D2
Florey Sq N21 ... 16 B6
Florfield Rd E8 ... 74 B2
Florian Ave SM1 ... 218 B4
Florian SE5 ... 139 C4
Florian Rd SW15 ... 135 A1
Florida Cl WD23 ... 8 B2
Florida Ct BR2 ... 208 D5
Florida Rd CR7 ... 182 D2
Florida State Univ
WC1 ... 93 D2 239 D3
Florida St E2 ... 96 A4
Florin Ct
Bermondsey SE1 ... 253 C1
Edmonton N18 ... 33 C6
8 St George in t East
SE1 ... 118 A6
Floris Pl 7 SW4 ... 137 C2
Floriston Ave UB10 ... 61 A1
Floriston Cl HA7 ... 25 B2
Floriston Ct UB5 ... 63 D3
Floriston Gdns HA7 ... 25 B2
Florys Ct 7 SW19 ... 157 A3
Floss St SW15 ... 134 C3
Flower & Dean Wlk
E1 ... 243 D3
Flower La NW7 ... 27 D4
Flower Mews NW11 ... 47 A3
Flower Pot Cl N15 ... 51 D3
Flowers Cl NW2 ... 68 A5
Flowersmead SW17 ... 159 A2
Flowers Mews 1
N19 ... 71 C6
Flower Wlk The
SW7 ... 114 A4 246 B2
Floyd Rd SE7 ... 121 C1
Floyer Cl TW10 ... 154 B6
Fludyer St SE13 ... 142 C1
Flynn Ct 19 E14 ... 119 C6
Fogerty Cl EN3 ... 7 D6
Foley Cotts KT10 ... 212 D2
Foley Ct N12 ... 30 A5
Foley Ho 19 E1 ... 96 C1
Foley Mews KT10 ... 212 C2
Foley Rd KT10 ... 212 C1
Foley St W1 ... 93 C2 239 A3
Folgate St E1 ... 95 D2 243 C4
Foliot Ho N1 ... 233 C4
Foliot St W12 ... 89 D1
Folkestone Ct UB5 ... 63 D3
Folkestone Rd
Edmonton N18 ... 34 A6
Wallend E6 ... 100 C4
Walthamstow E17 ... 53 D5
Folkingham La 6
NW9 ... 27 C2
Folkington Cnr N12 ... 29 B5
Folland 6 NW9 ... 27 D1
Follett Ho SW10 ... 266 C4
Follett St E14 ... 98 A1
Folly La
Higham Hill E17 ... 35 A2
Walthamstow E4 ... 35 B3
Folly Wall E14 ... 120 A4
Fonda Ct 14 E14 ... 119 C6
Fontaine Ct
3 Beckenham
BR3 ... 185 B2
Southgate N14 ... 15 D2
Fontaine Rd SW16 ... 182 B3
Fontarabia Rd
SW11 ... 137 A1
Fontenelle SE5 ... 139 C4
Fontenoy Ho SE11 ... 261 C3
Fontenoy Rd SW12,
SW17 ... 159 C2
Fonteyne Gdns IG8 ... 37 D1
Fonthill Cl SE20 ... 184 A1
Fonthill Ct SE23 ... 162 C4
Fonthill Ho
Kensington W14 ... 254 B6
Pimlico SW1 ... 258 D2
Fonthill Mews N4 ... 72 B6
Fonthill Rd N4 ... 72 C6
Font Hills N2 ... 30 A1
Fontley Way SW15 ... 156 A4
Fontmell Cl TW15 ... 170 C5
Fontmell Pk TW15 ... 170 C5
Fontwell Cl
Harrow HA3 ... 24 C3
Northolt UB5 ... 63 C2

Fontwell Dr BR2 ... 210 C4
Football La HA1 ... 42 C1
Footpath The SW15 ... 156 A6
FOOTS CRAY ... 190 B4
Foots Cray High St
DA14 ... 190 D4
Foots Cray La DA14 ... 168 C3
Footscray Rd SE9 ... 166 D3
Forber Ho 25 E2 ... 96 C4
Forbes Cl NW2 ... 68 A5
Forbes Ct SE19 ... 183 C5
Forbes Ho 2 W4 ... 110 C1
Forbes St E1 ... 96 A1
Forbes Way HA4 ... 62 B6
Forburg Rd N16 ... 52 A1
Fordbridge Ct
TW15 ... 170 A4
Fordbridge Rd
TW15 ... 170 B5
Fordbridge Rdbt
TW15 ... 170 A4
Fordbridge Rd
Lower Halliford TW16,
TW17 ... 193 D3
Sunbury TW16 ... 194 A5
Ford Cl
Ashford TW15 ... 170 A4
12 Bow E3 ... 97 A5
Harrow HA1 ... 42 B2
Littleton TW17 ... 192 C4
Thornton Heath CR7 ... 204 D4
Fordcombe 18 NW5 ... 71 A2
Forde Ave BR1 ... 209 C6
Fordel Rd SE6 ... 164 B3
Ford End IG8 ... 37 B4
Fordham Cl EN4 ... 2 C2
Fordham Ho 11
SE14 ... 141 A5
Fordham 4 KT1 ... 176 C1
Fordham Rd EN4 ... 2 C2
Fordham St 18 E1 ... 96 A1
Ford Ho 2 EN5 ... 13 D6
Fordhook Ave W5 ... 110 C6
Ford Ho 2 SE18 ... 122 D1
Fordingley Rd W9 ... 91 B4
Fordington Ho 2
SE26 ... 162 B1
Fordington Rd N6 ... 48 D5
Fordmill Rd SE6 ... 163 C2
Ford Rd
Ashford TW15 ... 170 B6
Bow E3 ... 97 B5
Dagenham RM10 ... 81 C1
Ford's Gr N21 ... 17 A3
Fords Park Rd E16 ... 99 A1
Ford Sq E1 ... 96 B2
Ford St Bow E3 ... 97 A5
Canning Town E16 ... 98 D1
Fordwich Cl BR6 ... 211 D2
Fordwych Ct NW2 ... 69 A2
Fordwych Rd NW2 ... 69 A3
Fordyce Ho 3
SW16 ... 181 C6
Fordyce Rd SE13 ... 164 A6
Fordyke Rd RM8 ... 81 B6
Forecastle Ct E14 ... 119 C4
Foreign,
Commonwealth &
Home Offices
SW1 ... 250 A2
Foreland Ct NW4 ... 29 A2
Foreland Ho W11 ... 244 A6
Foreland St SE18 ... 123 B2
Foreshore SE8 ... 119 B2
Forest App
Chingford E4 ... 20 C4
Woodford IG8 ... 37 A3
Forest Ave E4 ... 20 C4
Fore St EC2 ... 95 A2 242 B3
Forest Bsns Pk E17 ... 52 D2
Forest Cl
Brondesbury NW6 ... 69 A1
Chislehurst BR7 ... 188 C2
Wanstead E11 ... 55 A4
Woodford IG8 ... 37 B6
Forest Croft SE23 ... 162 B2
Forest Ct Chingford E4 ... 20 D3
Leytonstone E11 ... 54 C5
14 Woodside Pk N12 ... 29 D6
Forestdale Ctr The
CR0 ... 223 B1
Forestdale N14 ... 31 D6
Forest Dene Ct 2
SM2 ... 218 A2
Forest Dr
Ashford TW16 ... 171 D3
Chingford IG8 ... 36 C3
Forest Dr E E11 ... 54 B3
Forest Dr
Keston Mark BR2 ... 226 A4
Wanstead E12 ... 77 D5
Forest Dr W E11 ... 54 B2
Forest Edge IG9 ... 21 D1
Fore St N18 ... 34 A6
Forester Rd SE15 ... 140 B2
Foresters Cl SM6 ... 219 D1

Foresters Cres DA7 ... 147 D1
Foresters Dr
Wallington SM6 ... 219 D1
Walthamstow E17 ... 54 B5
Foresters Homes The
DA7 ... 147 D1
Foresters Prim Sch
SM6 ... 219 D1
FOREST GATE ... 77 A3
Forest Gate Com Sch
E7 ... 77 A3
Forest Gate NW9 ... 45 C4
Forest Gate Sta E7 ... 77 A3
Forest Gdns N17 ... 33 D1
Forest Glade
Chingford E4 ... 36 C5
Leytonstone E11 ... 54 C3
Forest Gr E8 ... 73 D2
FOREST HILL ... 163 A3
Forest Hill Bsns Ctr
SE23 ... 162 C2
Forest Hill Ct 6
SE26 ... 162 B1
Forest Hill SE23 ... 162 C3
Forest Hill Ind Est
SE23 ... 162 C2
Forest Hill Rd SE22 ... 162 B5
Forest Hill Sec Sch
SE23 ... 162 D1
Forest Hill Sta SE23 ... 162 C2
Forest Ho 9 E4 ... 20 C4
Forestholme Cl
SE23 ... 162 C2
Forest Ho The SE23 ... 163 A3
Forest Hts IG9 ... 21 A2
Forest La E7, E15 ... 76 D3
Forest Lawns BR1 ... 187 C2
Forest Lea 8 E11 ... 54 D2
Forest Lo 1 SE23 ... 162 C1
Forest Mount Rd IG8 ... 36 B3
Fore St HA5 ... 40 A4
Forest Point E7 ... 77 B3
Forest Rd Dalston E8 ... 73 D2
Edmonton N9 ... 18 B3
Feltham TW13 ... 150 C1
Forest Gate E7 ... 77 A4
Leytonstone E11 ... 54 B2
Morden SM3, SM4 ... 201 C2
Richmond TW9 ... 132 C5
Romford RM7 ... 59 D6
Walthamstow E17 ... 53 C6
Woodford IG8 ... 21 A1
Fore Street Ave EC2 ... 242 C3
Forest Ridge
Beckenham BR3 ... 207 C6
Bromley BR2 ... 226 B4
Forest Rise E17 ... 54 B5
Forest Sch E17 ... 54 C5
Forest Side
Buckhurst Hill IG9 ... 21 C3
Chingford E4 ... 20 D3
Forest Gate E7 ... 77 B4
New Malden KT4 ... 199 D1
Forest St E7 ... 77 A3
Forest The E11 ... 54 C5
Forest Trad Est E17 ... 52 D6
Forest View Ave E10 ... 54 B4
Forest View
Chingford E4 ... 20 B4
Leytonstone E11 ... 54 D2
Forest View Rd
Chingford E17 ... 36 A2
Manor Pk E12 ... 78 A4
Forest Way
Orpington BR5 ... 211 D4
Sidcup DA15 ... 167 B4
9 Upper Holloway
N19 ... 71 C6
Woodford IG8 ... 37 B6
Forest Wlk N10 ... 31 B2
Forfar Rd
London
SW11 ... 137 A4 268 B2
Tottenham N22 ... 32 D2
Forge Cl
Harlington UB3 ... 127 B6
Hayes BR2 ... 209 A1
Forge Cotts W5 ... 109 D5
Forge Dr KT10 ... 213 A1
Forge La
Belmont SM3 ... 217 A1
Feltham TW13 ... 173 A5
Forge Lane Prim Sch
TW13 ... 173 A5
Forge La
Richmond TW10 ... 154 A3
Sunbury TW16 ... 194 A6
Forge Lo 2 TW7 ... 131 A2
Forge Mews
Addington CR0 ... 223 C3
Sunbury TW16 ... 194 A6
Forge Pl NW1 ... 71 A2
Forlong Path UB5 ... 63 A2
Forman Ct TW1 ... 152 D3
Forman Ho SE4 ... 140 D1
Forman Pl N16 ... 73 D4
Formby Ave HA3, HA7 ... 43 C6

Formby Ct 9 N7 ... 72 C3
Formosa Ho 1 E1 ... 97 A3
Formosa St W9 ... 91 D3
Formunt Cl E16 ... 98 D2
Forres Gdns NW11 ... 47 C3
Forrest Ct N7 ... 72 C2
Forrester Path
SE26 ... 184 C6
Forresters The HA5 ... 40 B3
Forrest Gdns SW16 ... 204 B6
Forrest Ho SW15 ... 134 C3
Forris Ave UB3 ... 105 D5
Forset Ct W1 ... 237 B2
Forset St W1 ... 92 C1 237 B2
Forstal Cl BR2 ... 209 A6
Forster Cl IG8 ... 36 B3
Forster Ho SE6 ... 164 B1
Forster Park Prim Sch
SE6 ... 164 C1
Forster Rd
Beckenham BR3 ... 207 A6
Streatham SW2 ... 160 A4
Thornton Heath CR0 ... 205 A2
Tottenham N17 ... 51 D6
Walthamstow E17 ... 53 A3
Forsters Cl RM6 ... 59 B3
Forsters Way UB4 ... 84 B1
Forston St N1 ... 95 A5 235 B4
Forsyte Cres SE19 ... 183 C2
Forsyte Ct KT2 ... 176 D2
Forsyth Ct
13 Dagenham
RM10 ... 81 D2
Harrow HA1 ... 42 B3
Kingston u T KT3 ... 177 C1
Forsythe Shades
BR3 ... 186 A2
Forsyth Gdns SE17 ... 138 D6
Forsyth Ho
14 Hackney E9 ... 74 C1
Pimlico SW1 ... 259 B3
Forsythia Cl IG1 ... 78 D3
Forsythia Ho SE4 ... 141 A2
Forsyth Pl EN1 ... 17 C6
Forterie Gdns IG3 ... 80 A4
Fortescue Ave
1 Hackney E8 ... 74 B1
Twickenham TW2 ... 152 A1
Fortescue Rd
Burnt Oak HA8 ... 27 B3
Mitcham SW19 ... 180 B3
Fortess Gr NW5 ... 71 C3
Fortess Rd NW5 ... 71 C4
Fortess Wlk NW5 ... 71 B3
Forthbridge Rd
SW11 ... 137 A1
Forth Ho 30 E3 ... 97 B5
Forties The 9 NW5 ... 71 C3
Fortior Ct N6 ... 49 C2
Fortis Cl E16 ... 99 C1
Fortis Ct N10 ... 49 A6
Fortis Gn N2, N10 ... 48 D6
FORTIS GREEN ... 48 D5
Fortis Green Ave N2 ... 48 D5
Fortis Green Cotts
N2 ... 48 D6
Fortismere Ave N10 ... 49 A6
Fortismere Sch N10 ... 30 D1
Fortismere Sch (South
Wing) N10 ... 49 A6
Fortnam Rd N19 ... 71 D6
Fortnums Acre HA7 ... 24 D4
Fort Rd
Bermondsey
SE1 ... 117 D2 263 D3
Northolt UB5 ... 63 C1
Fortrose Cl E14 ... 98 B1
Fortrose Gdns SW12,
SW2 ... 160 A3
Fort St Broadgate E1 ... 243 B3
Newham E16 ... 121 B5
Fortuna Cl N7 ... 72 B2
Fortune Ct
Barking IG11 ... 102 B5
6 Dalston E8 ... 73 D1
Fortune Gate Rd
NW10 ... 89 C6
Fortune Green Rd
NW6 ... 69 C4
Fortune Ho
Lambeth SE11 ... 261 A3
St Luke's EC1 ... 242 B5
Fortune La WD6 ... 9 D5
Fortunes Mead UB5 ... 63 A2
Fortune St
EC1 ... 95 A3 242 B5
Fortune Way NW10 ... 90 A4
Fortune Wlk 4
SE28 ... 123 B3
Forty Acre La E16 ... 99 A2
Forty Ave HA9 ... 66 B6
Forty Cl HA9 ... 66 B5
Forty Hall* EN2 ... 5 D6
FORTY HILL ... 5 D4
Forty Hill CE Prim Sch
EN2 ... 6 A6
Forty Hill EN2 ... 5 D5

Forty Hill Ho EN1 ... 5 D5
Forty La HA9 ... 66 D6
Forum Cl 7 E3 ... 97 C6
Forumside HA8 ... 26 C4
Forum The KT8 ... 195 D5
Forum Way HA8 ... 26 C4
Forval Cl CR4 ... 202 D4
Forward Bsns Ctr The
3 E16 ... 98 B3
Forward Dr HA3 ... 42 D5
Fosbrooke Ho SW8 ... 270 A3
Fosbury Ho 7 SW9 ... 138 B1
Fosbury Mews W2 ... 245 D5
Foscote Mews W9 ... 91 C2
Foscote Rd NW4 ... 46 B3
Foskett Ho 21 N2 ... 30 B1
Foskett Rd SW6 ... 135 B3
Foss Ave CR0, CR9 ... 220 C3
Fossdene Prim Sch
SE7 ... 121 B1
Fossdene Rd SE7 ... 121 B1
Fossdyke Cl UB4 ... 85 A2
Fosse Way W13 ... 87 A2
Fossil Rd SE13 ... 141 C2
Fossington Rd
DA17 ... 124 D2
Foss Rd SW17 ... 180 B6
Fossway RM8 ... 80 C6
Foster Ct
6 Camden Town
NW1 ... 71 C1
Canning Town E16 ... 120 D6
Hendon NW4 ... 46 C5
Foster Ho SE14 ... 141 B4
Foster La EC2 ... 95 A1 242 A2
Foster Rd Acton W3 ... 111 C6
Chiswick W4 ... 111 B1
Newham E13 ... 99 A3
Fosters Cl
Elmstead BR7 ... 188 B5
Woodford E18 ... 37 B2
Fosters Old Sch
DA16 ... 146 B3
Foster's Prim Sch
DA16 ... 146 C2
Foster St NW4 ... 46 C5
Foster Wlk NW4 ... 46 C5
Fothergill Cl E13 ... 99 A5
Fothergill Dr N21 ... 16 A6
Fotheringham Ct EN1 ... 5 D1
Fotheringham Rd EN1 ... 5 D1
Foubert's Pl W1 ... 239 A1
Foulden Rd N16 ... 73 D4
Foulden Terr N16 ... 73 D4
Foulis Terr
SW7 ... 114 B1 256 D2
Foulser Rd SW17 ... 159 A1
Foulsham Rd CR7 ... 205 B6
Foundary Ho 6 E14 ... 97 D2
Founder Cl 2 E6 ... 100 D1
Founders Cl UB5 ... 85 B4
Founders Ct EC2 ... 242 C2
Founders Gdns
SE19 ... 183 A3
Founders Ho SW1 ... 259 C2
Foundling Ct WC1 ... 240 A6
Foundling Mus The*
WC1 ... 94 A3 240 B6
Foundry Cl SE16 ... 119 A5
Foundry Mews NW1 ... 239 B6
Foundry Pl
Stepney E1 ... 96 C2
Wandsworth SW18 ... 157 D4
Fountain Cl UB8 ... 83 A2
Fountain Ct
Belgravia SW1 ... 258 C3
Blackfen DA15 ... 168 B5
New Malden KT3 ... 199 A5
5 Penge SE26 ... 184 C4
14 Shepherd's Bush
W11 ... 112 D4
Strand EC4 ... 251 A6
Fountain Dr
Dulwich SE19 ... 183 D6
Wallington SM5 ... 218 D1
Fountain Green Sq 34
SE16 ... 118 A4
Fountain Ho
33 Bermondsey
SE16 ... 118 A4
3 Brondesbury Pk
NW6 ... 69 A1
Mayfair W1 ... 248 A4
5 Mitcham SW19 ... 180 D1
Fountain Mews
1 Highbury N5 ... 73 A4
Maitland Pk NW3 ... 70 D2
Fountain Pl SW9 ... 138 C4
Fountain Rd
South Norwood
CR7 ... 183 A1
Upper Tooting SW17 ... 180 B6
Fountains Ave
TW13 ... 151 B1

Fountains Cl TW13 ... 151 B1
Fountains Cres N14 ... 16 A4
Fountains The
London N3 ... 29 D3
Loughton IG10 ... 21 D4
Fountayne Bsns Ctr
N15 ... 52 A5
Fountayne Rd
South Tottenham
N15 ... 52 A5
Stoke Newington N16 .. 74 A6
Fount St
SW8 ... 137 D5 269 D3
Fouracres EN3 ... 7 A4
Four Acres N12 ... 29 D6
Fourland Wlk HA8 ... 27 A4
Fournier St
E1 ... 95 D2 243 D4
Fourscore Mans E8 ... 74 A1
Four Seasons Cl E3 ... 97 C5
Four Seasons Cres
SM3 ... 217 B6
Four Square Ct
TW4 ... 151 C5
Fourth Ave
Hayes UB3 ... 105 D5
Ilford E12 ... 78 B4
West Kilburn W10 ... 91 A4
Fourth Cross Rd
TW2 ... 152 B2
Fourth Way
Wembley HA9 ... 66 D4
Wembley HA9 ... 67 A4
Four Tubs The WD23 ... 8 B4
Fourways 2 CR0 ... 221 D6
Four Wents The E4 ... 20 B2
Fovant Ct 5 SW8 ... 137 C3
Fowey Ave IG4 ... 55 D4
Fowey Cl E1 ... 118 B5
Fowey Ho SE11 ... 261 B2
Fowler Cl
London SW11 ... 136 B2
Sidcup DA14 ... 191 A5
Fowler Ho
5 Camberwell
SE5 ... 139 C3
Islington N1 . 94 D6 234 D6
South Lambeth SW8 . 269 D1
West Green N15 ... 51 B4
Fowler Rd
Forest Gate E7 ... 77 A4
Islington N1 . 94 D6 234 D6
Mitcham CR4 ... 181 A1
Fowler's Wlk W5 ... 87 D3
Fownes St SW11 ... 136 C2
Fox and Knot St EC1 241 D4
Foxberry Ct SE4 ... 141 B1
Foxberry Rd SE4 ... 141 A2
Foxborough Gdns
SE4 ... 163 C6
Foxbourne Rd
SW17 ... 159 A2
Foxbury Ave BR7 ... 189 B4
Foxbury Cl BR1 ... 187 B4
Foxbury Rd BR1 ... 187 B4
Fox Cl
Bethnal Green E1 ... 96 C3
Elstree WD6 ... 9 D5
Newham E16 ... 99 A2
Foxcombe Cl 11 E6 ... 99 D5
Foxcombe CR0 ... 223 D2
Foxcombe Rd 6
SW15 ... 156 A3
Foxcote SE5 ... 263 B1
Foxcroft N1 ... 233 D3
Foxcroft Rd SE18 ... 144 D4
Foxes Dale
Beckenham BR2 ... 208 B6
Blackheath Pk SE3 .. 143 A2
Foxfield NW1 ... 231 D5
Foxfield Prim Sch
SE18 ... 123 A1
Foxfield Rd BR6 ... 227 B6
Foxglove Cl
Bexley DA15 ... 168 A5
Edmonton N9 ... 18 C3
Southall UB1 ... 107 A6
Foxglove Ct 11 HA0 ... 88 A5
Foxglove Gdns E11 ... 55 C5
Foxglove La KT9 ... 214 C4
Foxglove Path SE28 .. 123 C5
Foxglove St W12 ... 111 D6
Foxglove Way SM6 ... 203 B1
Foxgrove Ave BR3 ... 185 D3
Foxgrove N14 ... 16 A1
Foxgrove Path WD19 .. 22 D5
Foxgrove Rd BR3 ... 186 A3
Fox Gr KT12 ... 194 B2
Foxham Rd N19 ... 71 D5
Fox Hill Gdns SE19 ... 183 D3
Fox Hill SE19 ... 183 D3
Foxhole Rd 2 SE9 ... 166 A6
Fox Hollow Cl 1
SE18 ... 123 C1
Fox Hollow Dr DA7 ... 146 D2
Fox Ho 2 SW11 ... 136 B1
Foxholt Gdns NW10 ... 67 A1
Foxhome Cl BR7 ... 188 C4
Fox Ho UB5 ... 85 A6
Fox House Rd DA17 .. 125 D1
Fox La Ealing W5 ... 88 A3
Keston BR2 ... 225 C3
Palmers Green N13 ... 16 B1
Foxlees HA0 ... 65 A4
Foxley Cl E8 ... 74 A3
Foxley Ct SM2 ... 218 A1
Foxley Ho 4 E3 ... 97 D4
Foxley Rd
Camberwell SW9 ... 138 D5
Thornton Heath CR7 . 204 D5
Foxley Sq 3 SW9 ... 138 D4
Foxmead Cl EN2 ... 4 B2
Foxmore St SW11 ... 267 C1
Fox Prim Sch
W8 ... 113 C5 245 A3
Fox Rd E16 ... 98 D2
Foxs Path CR4 ... 180 C1
Fox's Yd E2 ... 243 D6
Foxtail Ho TW3 ... 130 A4
Foxton Gr CR4 ... 180 B1
Foxton Ho E16 ... 122 C4
Foxton KT1 ... 198 C6
Foxwarren KT10 ... 212 D1
Foxwell Mews SE4 ... 141 A2
Foxwell St SE4 ... 141 A2
Foxwood Cl
Edgware NW7 ... 27 C6
Feltham TW13 ... 150 B1
Foxwood Green Cl
EN1 ... 17 C5
Foxwood Rd SE3 ... 142 D1
Foyle Rd
Greenwich SE3 ... 142 D6
Tottenham N17 ... 34 A2
Fradel Lo N16 ... 51 B1
Framfield Cl N12 ... 13 C1
Framfield Ct EN1 ... 17 C5
Framfield Rd
Ealing W7 ... 86 D1
Islington N5 ... 72 D3
Mitcham CR4 ... 181 A3
Framlingham Cl 2
E5 ... 74 C6
Framlingham Cres
SE9 ... 188 B6
Framlingham Ct 5
RM6 ... 58 B4
Frampton Cl SM2 ... 217 C1
Frampton Ct 3 W3 ... 111 A4
Frampton Ho NW8 .. 236 D5
Frampton NW1 ... 71 D1
Frampton Park Rd
E9 ... 74 C1
Frampton Rd TW4 ... 151 A6
Frampton St
NW8 ... 92 B3 236 D5
Francemary Rd SE4 .. 163 C6
Frances Ct
South Norwood
SE25 ... 183 D1
Walthamstow E17 ... 53 C3
Frances & Dick James
Ct 2 NW7 ... 29 A3
Frances Rd E4 ... 35 C4
Frances St SE18 ... 122 B2
Franche Court Rd
SW17 ... 158 A1
Francis Ave
Bexleyheath DA7 ... 147 C3
Feltham TW13 ... 150 A1
Ilford IG1 ... 79 B6
Francis Barber Cl
SW16 ... 182 B6
Franciscan Prim Sch
SW17 ... 181 A5
Franciscan Rd
SW17 ... 181 A6
Francis Chichester Way
SW11 ... 137 A4 268 B1
Francis Cl
6 Cubitt Town
E14 ... 120 B2
Littleton TW17 ... 192 C5
West Ewell KT19 ... 215 B4
Francis Ct
12 Deptford SE14 ... 140 D6
Ealing W5 ... 110 B6
Edgware NW7 ... 27 D5
Kingston u T KT5 ... 198 A5
Francis Gr SW19 ... 179 B4
Francis Ho NW10 ... 89 D6
Francis Holland Sch
Belgravia
SW1 ... 115 A2 258 B3
Marylebone
NW1 ... 92 D3 237 C6
Francis Ho
11 Shoreditch N1 ... 95 C6
Walham Green
SW10 ... 265 D4
Francis Rd
Fortis Green N2 ... 48 D5
Harrow HA1 ... 43 A4
Hounslow TW4 ... 128 D3
Ilford IG1 ... 79 B6
Leyton E10 ... 76 A6
Pinner HA5 ... 40 C4
Thornton Heath CR0 . 204 D2
Wallington SM6 ... 219 C2
Wembley UB6 ... 87 C6
Francis Snary Lo 11
SW18 ... 157 C6
Francis St Ilford IG1 ... 79 B6
Stratford E15 ... 76 C3
Westminster
SW1 ... 115 C2 259 B4
Francis Terrace Mews
16 N19 ... 71 C5
Francis Terr N19 ... 71 C5
Francis Wlk N1 ... 233 C6
Francklyn Gdns HA8 .. 10 C1
Franconia Rd SW4 ... 159 D6
Frank Bailey Wlk
E12 ... 78 C2
Frank Barnes Sch
NW3 ... 70 B1
Frank Beswick Ho
SW6 ... 264 D5
Frank Burton Cl 4
SE7 ... 121 B1
Frank Dixon Cl
SE21 ... 161 C3
Frank Dixon Way
SE21 ... 161 C3
Frankfurt Rd SE24 ... 161 A6
Frank Godley Ct
DA14 ... 190 B5
Frankham Ho 8
SE8 ... 141 C5
Frankham St SE8 ... 141 C5
Frank Ho SW8 ... 270 A4
Frankland Cl
Bermondsey SE16 ... 118 B2
Woodford IG8 ... 37 C5
Frankland Ho 4
SW12 ... 159 B4
Frankland Rd
Brompton
SW7 ... 114 B3 256 C5
Chingford E4 ... 35 C5
Franklin Bldg 5
E14 ... 119 C4
Franklin Cl
Greenwich SE13 ... 141 D4
Kingston u T KT1 ... 198 C6
Oakleigh Pk N20 ... 14 A4
West Norwood
SE27 ... 160 D1
Franklin Cres CR4 ... 203 C5
Franklin Ho
Beckenham BR2 ... 208 C6
New Cross SE4 ... 141 A3
26 Wapping E1 ... 118 B5
West Hendon NW9 ... 45 D2
Franklin Ind Est
SE20 ... 184 C2
Franklin Pas SE9 ... 144 A2
Franklin Pl SE13 ... 141 D4
Franklin Rd
Bexleyheath DA7 ... 147 A4
Penge SE20 ... 184 C3
Walton-on-T KT12 ... 194 A3
Franklins Mews HA2 .. 64 A6
Franklin Sq SW5 ... 254 D1
Franklin's Row
SW3 ... 114 D1 257 D2
Franklin St
13 Bromley E3 ... 97 D4
South Tottenham N15 .. 51 C3
Franklin Way CR0 ... 204 A2
Franklyn Rd
Walton-on-T KT12 ... 194 B3
Willesden NW10 ... 67 D2
Franks Ave KT3 ... 199 A5
Franks Ho TW7 ... 131 B1
Frank Slater Ho 4
IG3 ... 58 B1
Frank Soskice Ho
SW6 ... 264 D5
Frank St 5 E13 ... 99 A3
Frankswood Ave
Hillingdon UB7 ... 82 B1
Petts Wood BR2,
BR5 ... 211 A4
Frank Towell Ct
TW14 ... 150 A3
Frank Welch Ct HA5 ... 40 C5
Frank Whymark Ho 4
SE16 ... 118 C4
Franlaw Cres N13 ... 33 A6
Frans Ct HA4 ... 40 A1
Fransfield Gr SE26 ... 162 B1
Frans Hals Ct E14 ... 120 B3
Franshams WD23 ... 8 C2
Frant Cl SE20 ... 184 C3
Franthorne Way
SE6 ... 163 D1
Frant Rd CR7 ... 204 D4
Fraserburgh Ho 23
E3 ... 97 B5
Fraser Cl 3 E6 ... 100 A1
Fraser Ct
Battersea SW11 ... 267 A2
Heston TW3 ... 129 A5
Fraser Ho
Brentford TW8 ... 110 B1
40 Clapham SW8 ... 137 D3
3 Woolwich SE18 .. 122 C2
Fraser Rd
Edmonton N9 ... 18 B1
Walthamstow E17 ... 53 D3
Wembley UB6 ... 87 C6
Fraser Regnart Ct 12
NW5 ... 70 D3
Fraser St W4 ... 111 C1
Frating Cres IG8 ... 37 B4
Frazer Ave HA4 ... 62 C3
Frazier St
SE1 ... 116 C4 251 A1
Freame Ho N21 ... 17 B5
Frean St SE16 ... 118 A3
Frearson Ho WC1 ... 233 D2
Freda Corbett Cl 10
SE15 ... 140 A5
Frederica Rd E4 ... 20 B4
Frederica St 4 N7 ... 72 B1
Frederick Blg N1 ... 73 C2
Frederick Charrington
Ho 4 E1 ... 96 C3
Frederick Cl
Cheam SM1 ... 217 B3
Marylebone
W2 ... 114 D6 247 C6
Frederick Cres
Camberwell SW9 ... 138 D5
Enfield EN3 ... 6 C3
Frederick Ct SW6 ... 135 A2
Frederick Gdns
Cheam SM1 ... 217 B3
Thornton Heath CR0 . 204 D3
Frederick Ho
Ashford TW15 ... 170 A6
Southall UB1 ... 107 B6
Woolwich SE7 ... 122 A3
Frederick Pl SE18 ... 122 D1
Frederick Rd SM1 ... 217 B3
Frederick's Pl
City of London EC2 .. 242 C1
North Finchley N12 ... 30 A6
Frederick Sq 11
SE16 ... 119 A6
Frederick's Row EC1 234 C2
Frederick St
WC1 ... 94 B4 233 C1
Frederick Terr E8 ... 73 D1
Frederic Mews SW1. 248 A1
Frederic St E17 ... 53 A4
Fredora Ave UB4 ... 83 D3
Fred Styles Ho SE7 .. 143 C6
Fred Tibble Ct RM9 ... 81 A4
Fred Wigg Twr E11 ... 76 D6
Freedom Cl E17 ... 53 A5
Freedom St SW11 ... 136 D3
Freegrove Rd N7 ... 72 A3
Freehold Ind Ctr
TW4 ... 150 C6
Freeland Ct
Ealing W5 ... 110 B6
15 Sidcup DA14 ... 168 A1
Freeland Pk N3 ... 29 A1
Freeland Rd W5 ... 110 B6
Freelands Ave CR2 ... 222 D1
Freelands Gr BR1 ... 187 B2
Freelands Rd BR1 ... 187 B2
Freeling Ho NW8 ... 229 C6
Freeling St 7 N1 ... 72 B1
Freeman Cl
Northolt UB5 ... 63 A1
Upper Halliford
TW17 ... 193 C5
Freeman Ct SW16 ... 182 A1
Freeman Dr KT8 ... 195 B5
Freeman Ho 13
SW2 ... 160 A4
Freeman Rd SM4 ... 202 B4
Freemans La UB3 ... 105 C6
Freemantle Ave EN3 .. 18 D6
Freemantle St
SE17 ... 117 C1 263 A2
Freemason's Rd
CR0 ... 205 C1
Freemasons Rd E16 ... 99 B1
Freemens Hos 1
SW9 ... 138 B1
Freesia Cl BR6 ... 227 D3
Freethorpe Cl SE19 .. 183 C2
Freezeland Way
UB10 ... 60 D2
Freke Rd SW11 ... 137 A2
Fremantle Ho 14 E1 ... 96 B3
Fremantle Rd
Belvedere DA17 ... 125 C2
Ilford IG6 ... 57 A6
Fremont St E9 ... 96 C6
French Gdns KT12 ... 195 B1
French Pl E1 ... 243 B6
French St TW16 ... 172 C1
Frendsbury Rd SE4 ... 141 A1
Frensham Cl UB1 ... 85 B4
Frensham Ct
Canonbury N5 ... 73 A3
4 London NW9 ... 46 A5
Mitcham CR4 ... 202 B6
Frensham Dr
New Addington
CR0 ... 224 A1
Roehampton SW15 .. 156 A2
Frensham Ho 7
KT6 ... 198 A4
Frensham Rd SE9 ... 167 B2
Frensham St SE15 ... 140 A6
Frere St 6 SW11 ... 136 C3
Fresham Ho BR2 ... 208 D6
Freshfield Ave E8 ... 73 D1
Freshfield Cl SE13 ... 142 B1
Freshfield Dr N14 ... 15 B4
Freshfields CR0 ... 207 B1
Freshford St SW17,
SW18 ... 158 A1
Freshwater Cl
SW17 ... 181 A4
Freshwater Ct UB1 ... 85 C4
Freshwater Rd
Dagenham RM8 ... 59 A1
Streatham SW17 ... 181 A4
Freshwell Ave RM6 ... 58 C5
Fresh Wharf Est
IG11 ... 100 D6
Fresh Wharf Rd
IG11 ... 100 D5
Freshwood Cl BR3 ... 185 D2
Freston Gdns EN4 ... 15 A6
Freston Pk N3 ... 29 B1
Freston Rd W10,
W11 ... 112 D6
Freswick Ho 6 SE8 .. 119 A2
Freta Rd DA6 ... 169 B6
Freud Mus The*
NW3 ... 70 A2
Frewell Bldg EC1 ... 241 A4
Frewing Cl BR7 ... 188 C5
Frewin Rd SW18 ... 158 B3
Friar Mews SE27 ... 160 D1
Friar Rd UB4 ... 84 D3
Friars Ave
London N20 ... 30 C6
Roehampton SW15 .. 155 D1
Friars Cl Chingford E4 .. 20 A1
Ilford IG1 ... 57 B1
Lambeth SE1 ... 251 D3
16 Northolt UB5 ... 84 D4
Friars Ct
5 Wallington
SM6 ... 219 B4
Walthamstow E17 ... 35 B2
Friars Gate Cl IG8 ... 37 A6
Friars Gdns W3 ... 89 B1
Friars La TW9 ... 153 D6
Friars Mead E14 ... 120 A3
Friars Mews SE9 ... 166 C6
Friars Place La W3 ... 111 B6
Friars Prim Sch
SE1 ... 116 D4 251 D1
Friar's Rd E6 ... 99 D6
Friars Stile Pl 9
TW10 ... 154 A5
Friars Stile Rd
TW10 ... 154 A5
Friar St EC4 ... 241 D1
Friars Way W3 ... 89 B1
Friars Wlk
London N14 ... 15 B4
West Heath SE2 ... 124 D1
Friary Cl N12 ... 30 C5
Friary La IG8 ... 37 A6
Friary Park Ct 12 W3 .. 89 A1
Friary Rd Acton W3 ... 89 B1
London N12 ... 30 C6
Peckham SE15 ... 140 A5
Friary Way N12 ... 30 C6
Friday Grove Mews 11
SW12 ... 159 C4
FRIDAY HILL ... 20 C1
Friday Hill E4 ... 20 C1
Friday Hill E E4 ... 20 C1
Friday Hill W E4 ... 20 C2
Friday Rd CR4 ... 180 D3
Friday St
EC4 ... 117 A6 252 A6
Frideswide Pl NW5 ... 71 C3
Friendly Pl 16 SE13 ... 141 D4
Friendly St SE8 ... 141 C4
Friendly Street Mews
SE8 ... 141 C3
Friendship Way E15 ... 98 A6
Friendship Wlk UB5 ... 84 D4
Friends' Rd CR0 ... 221 B5
Friend St EC1 .. 94 D4 234 C2
FRIERN BARNET ... 31 A6
Friern Barnet La N20 .. 30 C6
Friern Barnet Rd
N11 ...
Friern Barnet Sch
N11 ...
Friern Bridge Ret Pk
N11 ...
Friern Ct N20 ...
Friern Mount Dr N20 ..
Friern Pk N12 ...
Friern Rd SE22 ... 1
Friern Watch Ave
N12 ...
Frigate Ho 7 E14 ... 1
Frigate Mews SE8 ... 1
Frimley Ave SM6 ... 2
Frimley Cl
New Addington
CR0 ... 2
Putney SW19 ... 1
Frimley Cres CR0 ... 2
Frimley Ct DA14 ... 1
Frimley Gdns CR4 ... 2
Frimley Ho CR4 ... 2
Frimley Rd
Chessington KT9 ... 2
Ilford IG3 ...
Frimley Way E1 ...
Frinstead Ho 1
W10 ... 1
Frinton Ct W13 ...
Frinton Dr IG8 ...
Frinton Mews IG2 ...
Frinton Rd
Newham E6 ...
Sidcup DA14 ... 1
South Tottenham N15 ..
Streatham SW17 ... 1
Friston St SW6 ... 1
Friswell Pl 1 DA6 ... 1
Fritham Cl KT3 ... 1
Frith Ct NW7 ...
Frith Ho
Bethnal Green E2 ...
Paddington NW8 ... 2
Frith La NW7 ...
Frith Manor Cotts
N12 ...
Frith Manor Prim Sch
N12 ...
Frith Rd
Croydon CR0 ... 2
Leyton E11 ...
Frith St W1 ... 93 D1 2
Frithville Ct 2 W12 .. 1
Frithville Gdns W12 .. 1
Frizlands La RM10 ...
Frobisher Cl HA5 ...
Frobisher Cres
TW19 ... 1
Frobisher Ct
Belmont SM2 ... 2
6 Forest Hill SE23 ... 1
1 Greenwich SE10 ... 1
Hendon NW9 ...
3 Shepherd's Bush
W12 ... 1
Frobisher Gdns
TW19 ... 1
Frobisher Ho
3 Ealing W5 ...
27 Wapping E1 ... 1
Frobisher Mews EN2 ..
Frobisher Pas E14 ... 1
Frobisher Pl SE14 ... 1
Frobisher Rd
London N8 ...
Newham E6 ... 1
Frobisher St SE10 ... 1
Froghall Cotts EN5 ...
Frogley Rd SE22 ... 1
Frogmore Ave UB4 ...
Frogmore Cl SM3 ... 2
Frogmore Ct UB2 ... 1
Frogmore Est NW10 ..
Frogmore Gdns
Cheam SM3 ... 2
Hayes UB4 ...
Frogmore Ind Est
Hayes UB3 ... 1
Highbury N5 ...
Frogmore SW18 ... 1
Frognal Ave
Harrow HA1 ...
Sidcup DA14 ... 1
Frognal Cl NW3 ...
Frognal Cnr BR7 ... 1
Frognal Ct NW3 ...
Frognal Gdns NW3 ...
Frognal La NW3 ...
Frognal NW3 ...
Frognal Par NW3 ...
Frognal Pl DA14 ... 1
Frognal Rise NW3 ...
Frognal Way NW3 ...
Froissart Rd SE9 ... 1
Frome Ho SE15 ... 1
Frome Rd N22 ...

ne St N1 95 A5 235 A4
mondes Rd SM3 217 A3
now's Cnr 14 111 A1
tenac NW10 68 B1
tier Works N17 33 C4
sbery Ct 23 EN3 7 C6
stic Wlk E1 243 D3
ide St SW8 137 B3
en Rd TW14 149 D4
att Rd N17 33 B3
Ct 5 E3 97 B4
ent Cl NW9 44 C3
ent Cres NW9 45 C3
ent Ctry Park HA3, 9, NW9 44 C2
ent Fields NW9 45 C3
ent Gr NW9 45 C3
ent Prim Sch /9 45 A2
ent Way HA9, /9 44 D2
Ho E6 77 C1
ng Pan Alley E1 243 C3
Rd
rlesden NW10 89 D6
ton Pk E6 77 D1
ton Ave CR0 222 A6
nsia St SE2 124 B1
beck Dr NW9 27 C2
beck Ho N7 72 B2
beck Way HA2 24 A1
bourne Rd E17 36 A1
bourne St E1 96 B2
bourn 9 KT1 176 C1
brook Rd N19 71 C4
cher Ct SE8 141 B6
cher Ho
Deptford SE8 119 B1
Shoreditch N1 95 C6
ord Mans 3 N19 72 A5
ord Rd KT19 215 B1
ord St SE16 118 B4
HAM 134 D3
ham Broadway Sh r SW6 265 B3
ham Broadway Sta /6 135 C5 265 B4
ham Broadway /6 135 C5 265 B3
ham Bsns Exchange /6 266 B1
ham Cl UB10 83 A3
ham Cross Sec Sch /6 135 A5 264 A3
ham Ct /6 135 C4 265 A2
ham High St /6 135 A3
ham Palace Rd SW6, 134 D6
ham Pal* SW6 135 A3
ham Park Gdns /6 135 B3
ham Park Rd /6 135 B3
ham Prep Sch
ham SW6 135 A3
ham /14 135 A6 264 B6
ham Prim Sch /6 135 C6 265 A5
am Rd
elsea SW10 136 A6 266 B6
ham W6 135 B4 264 D2
e Ho E5 74 B5
brooks Ave KT4 199 D1
er Cl
Bethnal Green 2 96 A3
shey WD23 8 B4
ington BR6 227 D3
er Rd RM8 80 C4
ers Ave KT6 214 B6
er's Ave IG8 36 D3
ers Ho 6 SW18 157 C6
er's Rd E18 36 D3
er St NW4 46 C5
ers Way N KT6 214 B5
ers Way S KT9 214 A5
er's Wood CR0 223 C3
er Terr IG1 79 B3
erton Ct TW11 175 A4
erton Rd
ydon CR0 205 D2
ndsworth SW18 158 A6
er Way UB3 105 D1
wood Prim Sch 57 A5
wood's Mews 235 D2
har Ct
Dulwich SE21 161 B2
Ealing W13 86 D3
biton KT5 198 B3

Fulmar Ho
12 Bermondsey SE16 118 D2
Marylebone NW8 237 B5
Fulmead St SW6 265 D1
Fulmer Cl TW12 173 A5
Fulmer Rd E16 99 D2
Fulmer Way W13 109 B3
Fulneck 1 E1 96 C2
Fulready Rd E10 54 B4
Fulstone Cl TW4 129 B1
Fulthorp Rd SE3 143 A3
Fulton Ct EN3 7 C5
Fulton Mews W2 246 A6
Fulton Rd HA9 66 C5
Fulwell Ct
Southall UB1 108 A6
Teddington TW11 174 C6
Fulwell Park Ave TW2 152 A2
Fulwell Rd TW11, TW12 174 B6
Fulwell Sta TW11 174 B6
Fulwood Ave HA0 88 B5
Fulwood Cl UB3 83 D1
Fulwood Ct
Harrow HA3 43 A3
Stanwell TW19 148 B5
Fulwood Gdns TW1 153 A5
Fulwood Pl WC1 240 D3
Fulwood Wlk SW19 157 A3
Furber St W6 112 B3
Furham Field HA5 23 C3
Furley Ho 7 SE15 140 A5
Furley Rd SE15 140 A5
Furlong Cl SM6 203 B1
Furlong Rd N7 72 C2
Furmage St SW18 157 D4
Furneaux Ave SE27 182 D5
Furness Ho SW1 258 C2
Furness Lo 4 SW14 132 D1
Furness Prim Sch The NW10 90 A5
Furness Rd
Harlesden NW10 90 A5
Harrow HA2 41 D1
Morden SM4 201 D3
Sands End SW6 135 D3
Furnival St EC4 94 C1 241 A2
Furrow La E9 74 C3
Furrows The KT12 194 C1
Fursby Ave N3 29 C4
Fursecroft W1 237 C2
Further Acre NW9 27 D1
Furtherfield Cl CR0 204 C3
Further Green Rd SE6 164 C3
Furze Cl WD19 22 C5
Furze Ct CR0 222 A6
FURZEDOWN 181 B6
Furzedown Dr SW17 181 B5
Furzedown Prim Sch SW17 181 A4
Furzedown Rd SW17 181 B5
Furzefield Cl BR7 188 D4
Furzefield Rd SE3 143 B5
Furzeground Way UB11 105 A5
Furzeham Rd UB7 104 A4
Furzehill Rd WD6 11 A6
Furze Inf Sch RM6 59 A3
Furzeland Ho 2 KT3 199 C2
Furze Rd CR7 205 A6
Furze St E3 97 C2
Furzewood TW16 172 A2
Fuschia Ct IG8 36 C4
Fuscia Ct TW13 149 D1
Fusion Ct SW15 155 C1
Futters Ct 1 NW10 89 C5
Fyfe Way BR1 187 A1
Fyfield Cl BR2, BR3 208 B5
Fyfield Ct E7 77 A2
Fyfield Ho RM9 80 B1
Fyfield N4 72 C6
Fyfield Rd
5 Brixton SW9 138 C2
Enfield EN1 5 C2
Walthamstow E17 54 B6
Woodford IG8 37 C3
Fynes St SW1 259 C4

G

Gable Cl HA5 23 C3
Gable Ct SE26 184 B6
Gable Ho 12 W4 111 C2
Gable Lo
Hadley Wood EN4 2 A5
5 North Finchley N12 30 A5
West Wickham BR4 208 A1

Gables Ave TW15 170 B5
Gables Cl
Camberwell SE5 139 C4
Lewisham SE12 165 A3
Gables The
Barking IG11 79 A2
Bromley BR1 187 B3
3 Clapham SW4 137 C2
Ealing W13 87 B1
Hampstead NW3 70 B6
Heston TW5 129 C6
Mitcham CR4 203 B6
Muswell Hill N10 49 A6
North Finchley N12 29 D5
Wembley HA9 66 B5
Gabriel Cl 1 TW13 173 A6
Gabriel Ho SE11 260 C4
Gabrielle Cl HA9 66 B5
Gabrielle Ct NW3 70 B2
Gabriel Mews NW2 69 B6
Gabriel St SE23 163 A4
Gabriel's Wharf SE1 251 A4
Gad Cl E13 99 B4
Gaddesden Ave HA9 66 B2
Gaddesden Ho EC1 235 D1
Gade Cl UB3 106 B5
Gadesden Rd KT19 215 A2
Gadsbury Cl NW9 45 D3
Gadsden Ho
6 Homerton E9 74 D2
8 Kensal Town W10 91 A3
Gadwall Cl E16 99 B1
Gadwall Way SE28 123 B4
Gagarin Ho SW11 136 B2
Gage Rd E16 98 C2
Gage St WC1 240 B4
Gainford Ho 18 E2 96 B4
Gainford St N1 94 C6 234 A6
Gainsboro Gdns UB6 64 C3
Gainsborough Ave E12 78 C3
Gainsborough Cl
Beckenham BR3 185 C3
Thames Ditton KT10 196 C1
Gainsborough Ct
11 Barnet EN5 1 D1
6 Bermondsey SE16 118 B1
Bromley BR2 209 C5
Dulwich SE21 161 C2
North Finchley N12 29 D5
Shepherd's Bush W12 112 C4
Gainsborough Gdns
Edgware HA8 26 C1
Golders Green NW11 47 B2
Hampstead NW3 70 B5
Isleworth TW7 152 B6
Gainsborough Ho
Dagenham RM8 80 B4
Enfield EN1 18 A6
Finsbury Pk N4 50 B1
3 Hampstead NW3 70 A4
5 Limehouse E14 119 A6
Westminster SW1 259 D3
Gainsborough Lodge HA1 42 C4
Gainsborough Mews 5 SE26 162 B1
Gainsborough Prim Sch
Hackney Wick E9 75 C2
Newham E15 98 C4
Gainsborough Rd
Bedford Pk W4 111 D2
Dagenham RM8 80 B5
Hayes UB4 83 B5
Leytonstone E11 54 C2
Newham E15 98 C4
New Malden KT3 199 B2
North Finchley N12 29 D5
Richmond TW9 132 B2
Gainsborough Sq DA6 146 D2
Gainsborough St 3 E9 75 B2
Gainsborough Studios N1 235 C5
Gainsborough Twr 7 UB5 84 D5
Gainsfield Ct 3 E11 76 C5
Gainsford Rd E17 53 B5
Gainsford St SE1 117 D4 253 D2
Gairloch Ho 2 NW1 71 D1
Gairloch Rd SE5 139 C3
Gaisford St NW5 71 C2
Gaitskell Ct SW11 136 C3
Gaitskell Ho
Camberwell SE17 139 B6
2 Newham E6 99 D6
3 Walthamstow E17 53 D6
Gaitskell Rd SE9 167 A3
Gaitskell Way SE1 252 A2
Galahad Rd
Edmonton N9 18 A1

Galahad Rd *continued*
Grove Pk BR1 187 A6
Galata Rd SW13 134 A5
Galatea Sq SE15 140 B2
Galaxy Bldg 6 E14 119 C2
Galaxy Ho EC2 242 D6
Galba Ct 1 TW8 131 D5
Galbraith St E14 120 A3
Galdana Ave EN5 2 A2
Galeborough Ave IG8 36 B3
Gale Cl
Hampton TW12 173 A4
Mitcham CR4 202 B6
Gale Ho
10 Brixton SW2 160 B6
Carshalton SM5 218 C3
Galena Ho
5 Hammersmith W6 112 B2
Plumstead Comm SE18 123 D1
Galena Rd W6 112 B2
Galen Pl WC1 240 B3
Galesbury Rd SW18 158 A5
Gales Gdns E2 96 B4
Gale St
Dagenham RM9 80 D1
Tower Hamlets E3 97 C2
Galgate Cl 4 SW19 157 A3
Gallants Farm Rd EN4 14 C3
Galleon Cl SE16 118 D4
Galleon Ho 8 E14 120 A2
Galleons Dr IG11 102 A4
Gallery Ct SW10 266 A5
Gallery Gdns UB5 84 D5
Gallery Rd SE21 161 B3
Galleywall Rd SE16 118 B2
Galleywall Road Trad Est 12 SE16 118 B2
Galleywood Ho 1 W10 90 C2
Galliard Cl N9 18 C5
Galliard Ct N9 18 A5
Gallia Rd N5 72 D3
Galliard Prim Sch N9 18 A4
Galliard Rd N9 18 A5
Gallica Ct SM1 201 D1
Gallions Cl IG11 102 A4
Gallions Mount Prim Sch SE18 123 D1
Gallions Prim Sch E6 100 D1
Gallions Rd E16 122 D6
Gallions Reach Shp Pk IG11 101 A2
Gallions Reach Sta E16 122 D6
Gallions View Rd SE28 123 C4
Gallon Cl SE7 121 C2
Gallop The
South Croydon CR2 222 B1
Sutton SM2 218 A1
Gallosson Rd SE18 123 C2
Galloway Rd W12 112 A5
Gallus Cl N21 16 B5
Gallus Sq SE3 143 B2
Galpin's Rd CR4, CR7 204 B5
Galsworthy Ave
Ilford RM6 58 B2
Tower Hamlets E14 97 A2
Galsworthy Cl SE28 124 B5
Galsworthy Cres SE3 143 C4
Galsworthy Ct W3 110 D3
Galsworthy Ho 4 W11 91 A1
Galsworthy Rd
Cricklewood NW2 69 A4
Kingston u T KT2 176 D2
Galton Ho SE18 144 B4
Galton St W10 91 A4
Galva Cl EN4 3 A1
Galvani Way CR0 204 B1
Galveston Ho 2 E1 97 A3
Galveston Rd SW15 157 B6
Galway Cl 28 SE16 118 B1
Galway Ho
Finsbury EC1 235 B1
7 Stepney E1 96 D2
Galway St EC1 95 A4 235 B1
Galy 5 NW9 27 D1
Gambetta St 3 SW8 137 B3
Gambia St SE1 116 D5 251 D3
Gambler Ho EC1 235 B1
Gambole Rd SW17 180 C6
Games Ho 6 SE7 143 C6
Games Rd EN4 2 D2
Gamlen Rd SW15 134 D1

Gamma Ct 9 CR0 205 B1
Gamuel Cl E17 53 C3
Gander Green Cres TW12 173 C2
Gander Green La KT4, SM1, SM3 217 B5
Gandhi Cl E17 53 C3
Gandolfi St 5 SE15 139 C6
Ganley Ct 19 SW11 136 B2
Gannet Ct 5 SE21 161 B2
Gannet Ho SE15 139 D4
Ganton St W1 239 B1
Ganton Wlk WD19 22 D6
GANTS HILL 56 C3
Gantshill Cres IG2 56 C4
Gants Hill IG2 56 C3
Gants Hill Sta IG2 56 C3
Gap Rd SW19 179 D5
Garage Rd W3 88 C1
Garand Ct 2 N7 72 B3
Garbett Ho 2 SE17 138 D6
Garbutt Pl W1 238 B3
Garden Ave
Bexleyheath DA7 147 C2
Mitcham CR4 181 B3
Garden City HA8 26 C4
Garden Cl
Ashford TW15 171 A4
Chingford E4 35 C5
Grove Pk SE12 165 B1
Hampton TW12 173 B5
Northolt UB5 85 A6
Roehampton SW15 156 B4
Ruislip HA4 61 D6
Wallington SM6 220 A3
Garden Cotts BR5 190 C1
Garden Ct
5 Belmont SM2 217 C1
10 Eltham SE9 166 C5
Hampton TW12 173 B5
North Finchley N12 29 D5
4 Richmond TW9 132 B4
12 South Acton W4 111 A3
South Croydon CR0 221 D5
4 Stanmore HA7 25 C5
St John's Wood NW8 229 C2
Strand EC4 251 A6
Wembley HA0 65 C5
Wimbledon SW20 178 D2
Gardeners Cl SE9 166 A1
Gardeners Rd CR0 204 D1
Garden Flats SW16 160 A1
Garden Ho
2 Finchley N2 30 B1
12 South Lambeth SW9 138 A3
Garden Hospl The NW4 46 C6
Gardenia Ct 1 BR3 185 C3
Gardenia Rd
Bromley BR1 210 C6
Enfield EN1 17 C5
Gardenia Way IG8 37 A5
Garden La
Bromley BR1 187 B4
Streatham SW2 160 B3
Garden Lodge Ct N2 48 B6
Garden Mews W2 245 B5
Garden Pl 28 E2 95 D6
Garden Prim Sch CR4 203 D6
Garden Rd
Bromley BR1 187 B4
Penge SE20 184 C2
Richmond TW9 132 C2
St John's Wood NW8 92 A4 229 B2
Walton-on-T KT12 194 B2
Garden Row SE1 116 D3 261 C6
Garden Royal 16 SW15 156 D5
Garden St E1 96 D2
Gardens The
Beckenham BR3 186 A2
East Bedfont TW14 149 B5
East Dulwich SE22 140 A1
Harrow HA1, HA2 42 A3
Pinner HA5 41 B3
Stamford Hill N16 51 D2
Garden Suburb Jun & Inf Schs NW11 47 B4
Garden Terr
Knightsbridge SW7 247 B1
Pimlico SW1 259 C2
Garden Way NW10 67 A2
Garden Wlk
Beckenham BR3 185 B2
Shoreditch EC2 95 C3 243 A6
Gardiner Ave NW2 68 C3
Gardiner Cl
Chislehurst BR5 190 C1
Dagenham RM8 80 D4
Enfield EN3 18 D5
Gardiner Ct NW10 89 B6

Gardiner Ho SW11 267 A2
Gardner Cl E11 55 B3
Gardner Ct
Highbury N5 73 A4
Hounslow TW3 129 C2
Tottenham N22 32 D1
Gardner Ho
Feltham TW13 151 B2
Southall UB1 106 D6
Gardner Ind Est SE26 185 B5
Gardner Pl TW14 150 B5
Gardner Rd E13 99 B3
Gardners Cl N11 15 A2
Gardners La EC4 252 A6
Gardnor Mans 14 NW3 70 A4
Gardnor Rd NW3 70 B4
Gard St EC1 234 D2
Garendon Gdns SM4 201 D2
Garendon Rd SM4 201 D2
Garenne Ct 10 E4 20 A3
Gareth Cl KT4 216 D6
Gareth Ct SW16 159 D1
Gareth Gr BR1 187 A6
Garfield Edmonton N9 18 B3
Enfield EN2 17 B6
Garfield Ho W2 237 C1
Garfield Mews 7 SW11 137 A2
Garfield Prim Sch
London N11 31 C5
Wimbledon SW19 180 A4
Garfield Rd
Chingford E4 20 B3
Clapham SW11 137 A2
Enfield EN3 6 C1
Newham E13 98 D3
3 Twickenham TW1 153 A3
Wimbledon SW19 180 A4
Garford St E14 119 C6
Garganey Ct NW10 67 B2
Garganey Wlk SE28 124 C6
Garibaldi St SE18 123 C2
Garland Ct 12 E14 119 C6
Garland Dr TW3 130 A3
Garland Ho
12 Kingston u T KT2 176 A2
Stoke Newington N16 73 B5
Garland Rd
Plumstead Comm SE18 145 B5
Stanmore HA7 26 A2
Garlands Ct CR0 221 B4
Garlands Ho NW8 91 D5
Garlands La HA1 42 D1
Garlands The HA1 42 D2
Garlick Hill EC4 117 A6 252 B6
Garlies Rd SE23 163 A1
Garlinge Ho 12 SW9 138 C4
Garlinge Rd NW2 69 B2
Garman Cl N18 33 B5
Garman Rd N17 34 C3
Garnault Mews EC1 234 B1
Garnault Pl EC1 234 B1
Garnault Rd EN1 5 D5
Garner Cl RM8 58 D1
Garner Rd E17 36 A2
Garner St E2 96 A5
Garnet Ct TW13 149 C1
Garnet Ho KT4 199 B1
Garnet Rd
South Norwood CR7 205 B5
Willesden NW10 67 C2
Garnet St E1 118 C6
Garnett Cl SE9 144 B2
Garnett Ho 5 NW3 70 D3
Garnett Rd NW3 70 D3
Garnett Way 3 E17 35 A2
Garnet Wlk 8 E6 100 A2
Garnham Cl 2 N16 73 D6
Garnham St 1 N16 73 D6
Garnies Cl SE15 139 D5
Garrad's Rd SW16 159 D1
Garrard Cl
Bexleyheath DA7 147 C2
Chislehurst BR7 188 D5
Garrard Ho BR2 209 C5
Garrard Wlk NW10 67 C2
Garratt Cl CR0 220 A4
Garratt Ho 8 N16 51 C1
Garratt La
Upper Tooting SW17, SW18 180 C6
Wandsworth SW18 157 D3
Garratt Park Sch SW18 158 A1
Garratt Rd HA8 26 C3

Garratts Rd WD23 8 A4
Garratt Terr SW17 180 C6
Garraway Ct SW13 134 C5
Garraway Ho SE21 161 D1
Garrett Cl W3 89 B2
Garrett Ho
8 Shepherd's Bush W12 90 B1
Teddington TW11 175 B4
Garrett St EC1 95 A3 242 B6
Garrick Ave NW11 47 A3
Garrick Cl Ealing W5 88 A3
1 Richmond TW9 153 D6
Wandsworth SW18 136 A1
Garrick Cres CR0 221 C6
Garrick Ct HA8 26 B6
Garrick Dr
Hendon NW4 28 C1
Plumstead SE18 123 B3
Garrick Gdns KT8 195 C6
Garrick Ho
Chiswick W4 133 C6
2 Kingston u T KT1 198 A5
Mayfair W1 248 C3
7 Streatham SW16 181 C5
Garrick Ind Ctr NW9 45 D4
Garrick Pk NW4 28 D1
Garrick Rd
Greenford UB6 85 D3
Richmond TW9 132 C3
West Hendon NW9 45 D3
Garrick's Ait KT8 174 A1
Garricks Ho KT1 175 D1
Garrick St WC2 116 A6 250 A6
Garrick's Villa TW12 174 A1
Garrick Way NW4 46 D5
Garrick Yd WC2 250 A6
Garrison Cl
Hounslow TW4 151 B6
Shooters Hill SE18 144 C5
Garrison La KT9 214 A1
Garrowsfield EN5 13 B6
Garsdale Cl N11 31 A4
Garsdale Terr SW5 254 D2
Garside Cl
Hampton TW12 173 D4
Plumstead SE28 123 B3
Garside Ct 5 N20 14 D2
Garsington Mews SE4 141 B2
Garson Ho W2 246 C6
Garston Ho 6 N1 72 D1
Garter Way SE16 118 D4
Garth Cl
Kingston u T KT2 176 B5
Ruislip HA4 40 D1
West Barnes SM4 200 D2
Garth Ct
Chiswick W4 133 B6
11 Harrow HA1 42 D3
Garth Dr N9 18 A2
Garth Ho NW2 69 B6
Garthland Dr EN5 12 C6
Garth Mews W5 88 A3
Garthorne Rd SE23 162 D4
Garth Rd
Child's Hill NW2 69 B6
8 Chiswick W4 111 B1
Kingston u T KT2 176 B5
West Barnes SM4 200 D2
Garth Road Ind Ctr The SM4 200 D1
Garthside TW10 176 A5
Garth The
Hampton TW12 173 D4
Harrow HA3 44 B3
North Finchley N12 29 D5
Garthway N12 30 C4
Gartmoor Gdns SW19 157 B3
Gartmore Rd IG3 79 D6
Garton Ho 6 N6 49 D2
Garton Pl SW18 158 A5
Gartons Cl EN3 6 C1
Gartons Way SW11 136 A2
Garvary Rd E16 99 B1
Garvens SE19 183 C5
Garway Rd W2 91 D1
Garwood Cl N17 34 B2
Garwood Lo N22 32 B3
Gascoigne Gdns IG8 36 C3
Gascoigne Pl 17 E2 95 D4
Gascoigne Prim Sch IG11 101 A6
Gascoigne Rd IG11 101 A5
Gascony Ave NW6 69 C1
Gascoyne Ho 2 E9 74 D1
Gascoyne Rd E9 74 D1
Gaselee St E14 120 A6
Gasholder Pl SE11 116 B1 260 D1
Gaskarth Rd
Balham SW12 159 B5
Burnt Oak HA8 27 A1
Gaskell Rd N6 48 D3
Gaskell St SW4 138 A3
Gaskin Ho N16 73 B5
Gaskin St N1 94 D6 234 C6
Gaspar Cl SW7 255 D4
Gaspar Mews SW5 255 D4
Gassiot Rd SW17 180 D6
Gassiot Way SM1 218 B5
Gasson Ho 24 SE14 140 D6
Gastein Rd W6 134 D6
Gastigny Ho EC1 235 B1
Gaston Bell Cl TW9 132 B2
Gaston Bridge Rd TW17 193 B3
Gaston Gate SW8 270 C2
Gaston Rd CR4 203 A6
Gaston Way TW17 193 B4
Gataker Ho 5 SE16 118 B3
Gataker St 6 SE16 118 B3
Gatcliff Cl SW1 258 B1
Gatcombe Ct BR3 185 C3
Gatcombe Ho 20 SE22 139 C2
Gatcombe Mews W5 110 B6
Gatcombe Rd
8 Newham E16 121 A5
Tufnell Pk N19 71 D5
Gatcombe Way EN4 2 D2
Gateacre Ct DA14 190 B6
Gate End HA6 22 A3
Gatefield Ct SE15 140 A2
Gateforth St NW8 237 A5
Gate Hill Ct W11 244 D4
Gatehill Rd HA6 22 A3
Gate Ho 4 KT6 198 A1
Gatehouse Cl KT2 177 A3
Gatehouse Sch E2 96 D5
Gatehouse Sq SE1 252 B4
Gateley Ho 6 SE4 140 D1
Gateley Rd SW9 138 B2
Gate Mews SW7 114 C4 247 B1
Gater Dr EN2 5 B4
Gatesborough St EC2 243 A6
Gates Ct SE17 262 A2
Gatesden WC1 233 B1
Gates Green Rd BR2, BR4 225 A4
Gateside Rd SW17 158 D1
Gates 4 NW9 27 D1
Gatestone Ct 10 SE19 183 C4
Gatestone Rd SE19 183 C4
Gate St WC2 94 B1 240 C2
Gateway Arc N1 234 C4
Gateway Bsns Ctr SE28 123 B3
Gateway Ho
Balham SW12 159 B5
4 Barking IG11 101 A6
3 Upper Tooting SW17 180 C4
Gateway Mews 4 E8 73 D3
Gateway Prim Sch NW8 92 B3 236 D6
Gateway Ret Pk E6 100 D3
Gateways Ct SM6 219 B3
Gateway SE17 139 A6
Gateways KT6 198 A4
Gateways The
Chelsea SW3 257 B3
Richmond TW9 131 D1
Gateway Trad Est NW10 89 D4
Gatfield Gr TW13 151 C2
Gatfield Ho TW13 151 C2
Gathorne Rd N22 32 C2
Gathorne St 19 E2 96 D5
Gatley Ave KT19 214 D3
Gatliff Rd SW1 115 B1 258 C1
Gatling Rd SE18, SE2 124 A1
Gatonby St SE15 139 D4
Gatting Cl HA8 27 A3
Gatting Way UB8 60 A2
Gatton Prim Sch SW17 180 C6
Gatton Rd SW17 180 C6
Gattons Way DA14 191 B6
Gatward Cl N21 16 D5
Gatward Gn N9 17 D2
Gatwick Ho 3 E14 97 B1
Gatwick Rd SW18 157 B4
Gauden Cl SW4 137 D2
Gauden Rd SW4 137 D2
Gaugin Ct 13 SE16 118 B1
Gauntlet Cl UB5 63 A1
Gauntlet 1 NW9 27 D1
Gauntlett Ct HA0 65 B3
Gauntlett Rd SM1 218 B3
Gaunt St SE1 262 A6
Gautrey Rd SE15 140 C3
Gautrey Sq 5 E6 100 B1
Gavel St SE17 262 D4
Gaven Ho N17 33 C1
Gaverick Mews 3 E14 119 C2
Gavestone Cres SE12 165 B4
Gavestone Rd SE12 165 B4
Gavestone Terr SE12 165 B4
Gaviller Pl 3 E5 74 B4
Gavina Cl SM4 202 C4
Gavin Ho 1 SE18 123 C2
Gawain Wlk N9 18 A1
Gawber St E2 96 C4
Gawsworth Cl E15 76 D3
Gawthorne Ave NW7 29 A5
Gawthorne Ct E3 97 C5
Gay Cl NW2 68 B3
Gaydon Ho W2 91 D2
Gaydon La NW9 27 C2
Gayfere Rd
Redbridge IG5 56 B6
Stoneleigh KT17 216 A3
Gayfere St SW1 116 A3 260 A5
Gayford Rd W12 111 D4
Gay Ho N16 73 C3
Gayhurst Ct 9 UB5 84 C4
Gayhurst Ho NW8 237 B6
Gayhurst Prim Sch E8 74 A1
Gayhurst Rd E8 74 A1
Gayhurst SE17 139 B6
Gaylor Rd UB5 63 B3
Gaymead NW8 91 D6
Gaynesford Rd
Forest Hill SE23 162 D2
Wallington SM5 218 D1
Gay Rd E15 98 B5
Gaysham Ave IG2 56 D4
Gaysham Hall IG5 56 D6
Gaysley Ho SE11 261 A3
Gay St SW15 134 D2
Gayton Cres NW3 70 B4
Gayton Ct
3 Harrow HA1 42 D3
New Malden KT3 199 D4
Gayton Ho E3 97 C3
Gayton Rd
Abbey Wood SE2 124 C3
Hampstead NW3 70 B4
Harrow HA1 43 A3
Gayville Rd SW11 158 D5
Gaywood Cl SW2 160 C3
Gaywood Rd E17 53 C6
Gaywood St SE1 261 D5
Gaza St SE17 116 D1 261 C1
Gaze Ho 11 E14 98 B1
Gean Ct 3 E11 76 B4
Gearies Inf Sch IG2 56 D4
Gearies Jun Sch IG2 56 D4
Geariesville Gdns IG6 56 D5
Gearing Cl SW17 181 A6
Geary Ho N7 72 B3
Geary Rd NW10 68 A3
Geary St N7 72 B3
GEC Est HA9 65 D6
Geddes Pl 3 DA6 147 C1
Gedeney Rd N17 33 A2
Gedge Ct CR4 202 C5
Gedling Ho SE22 139 D2
Gedling Pl SE1 263 D6
Geere Rd E15 98 D6
Gees Ct W1 238 B1
Gee St EC1 95 A3 242 A6
Geffrey's Ct SE9 166 A1
Geffrye Ct N1 95 C5
Geffrye Mus* E2 95 D5
Geffrye St E2 95 D5
Geldart Rd SE15 140 B5
Geldeston Rd E5 74 A6
Gellatly Rd SE14 140 D3
Gell Cl UB10 60 B5
Gemima Ct SM1 217 C3
Gemini Bsns Ctr E16 98 B3
Gemini Gr UB5 85 A4
Gemini Ho 11 E3 97 C6
Gemma Ct BR3 185 B1
General Gordon Pl SE18 122 D2
Generals Wlk The EN3 7 A6
General Wolfe Rd SE10 142 B4
Genesis Bsns Pk NW10 88 D5
Genesis Cl TW19 148 B3
Genesis Ho KT6 197 D1
Genesta Rd SE18 145 A6
Geneva Cl TW17 171 C1
Geneva Ct
Hendon NW9 45 D4
1 Putney SW15 156 D6
Geneva Ct *continued*
Stoke Newington N16 51 B1
Geneva Dr SW9 138 C1
Geneva Gdns RM6 59 A4
Geneva Rd
Kingston u T KT1 198 A5
Thornton Heath CR7 205 A4
Genever Cl E4 35 C5
Genista Rd N18 34 B5
Genoa Ave SW15 156 C6
Genoa Ho 18 E1 96 D3
Genoa Rd SE20 184 C2
Genotin Rd EN1 5 B2
Genotin Terr EN1 5 B2
Gentleman's Row EN2 5 A2
Gentry Gdns E13 99 A4
Geoffrey Chaucer Tech Coll SE1 117 B3 262 D5
Geoffrey Cl SE5 139 A3
Geoffrey Ct SE4 141 B2
Geoffrey Gdns E6 100 A5
Geoffrey Ho SE1 262 D6
Geoffrey Jones Ct NW10 90 A6
Geoffrey Rd SE4 141 B2
George Akass Ho 5 SE18 123 A1
George Beard Rd 11 SE8 119 B2
George Beare Lo 9 SW4 159 C6
George Belt Ho 8 E2 96 D4
George Carver Ho E7 77 A3
George Comberton Wlk 4 E12 78 C3
George Cres N10 31 A3
George Ct
Buckhurst Hill IG9 21 D2
St James WC2 250 B5
George Davies Lodge IG6 57 A4
George Downing Est N16 73 D6
George Eliot Ho SW1 259 B3
George Eliot Jun & Inf Schs NW8 92 B6 229 C6
George Elliot Ho SE17 262 A2
George Elliston Ho 13 SE1 118 A1
George Eyre Ho NW8 229 D3
George Gange Way HA3 42 D6
George Green's Sec Sch E14 120 A1
George Groves Rd SE20 184 A2
George Ho 8 SE26 184 B5
George Inn Yd SE1 252 C3
George La
Hayes BR2 209 B1
Lewisham SE13 164 A5
George Lansbury Ho
7 Bow E3 97 B4
3 Willesden NW10 67 C1
Wood Green N22 32 C2
George Lashwood Ct 12 SW9 138 B1
George La
Wanstead E18 55 B6
Woodford E18 37 A1
George Leybourne Ho 15 E1 118 A6
George Lindgren Ho SW6 264 D4
George Loveless Ho 4 E2 95 D4
George Lovell Dr EN3 7 C6
George Mathers Rd SE11 261 C4
George Mews NW1 232 A1
George Mitchell Sch E10 53 D1
George Parr Ho N21 16 D4
George Peabody Ct NW1 237 A4
George Rd
Chingford E4 35 C4
Kingston u T KT2 177 A3
New Malden KT3 199 D4
George Row SE16 118 A4
George's Mead WD6 10 A5
George Spicer Prim Sch EN1 5 D2
George Sq SW19 201 C6
George's Rd N7 72 B3
George's Sq SW6 264 D6
George St
Barking IG11 79 A1
6 Canning Town E16 98 D1
Ealing W7 108 C5
Hounslow TW3, TW5 129 B3
George St *continued*
Marylebone W1 92 D1 237 D2
George Street Sta CR0 221 A6
George St
Richmond TW10 153 D6
Southall UB2 107 A2
South Croydon CR0 221 B6
George Taylor Ct N9 18 B1
George Tingle Ho SE1 263 D6
George Tomlinson Prim Sch E11 54 C1
Georgetown Cl 4 SE19 183 C5
Georgette Pl SE10 142 A5
George Vale Ho 35 E2 96 A5
George V Ave HA2, HA5 41 C6
Georgeville Gdns IG6 56 D5
George V Way UB6 87 B6
George Walter Ho 11 SE16 118 C2
George Wyver Cl SW18 157 A4
George Yd
City of London EC3 242 D1
Mayfair W1 115 A6 248 B6
Georgiana St NW1 93 C6 232 B6
Georgian Cl
Hayes BR2 209 B1
Ickenham UB10 60 A4
Stanmore HA7 25 A3
Georgian Ct
Croydon CR0 205 B1
12 Hackney E9 96 C6
3 Hendon NW4 46 B4
Wembley HA9 66 D2
Georgian Ho HA0 65 A5
Georgian Lo HA5 40 B4
Georgian Village The E17 54 A6
Georgian Way HA1 64 B6
Georgia Rd
New Malden KT3 199 A5
South Norwood CR7 182 D2
Georgina Ct 5 TW1 153 C5
Georgina Gdns 10 E2 95 D4
Geraint Rd BR1 187 A6
Geraldine Ct 6 NW9 46 A5
Geraldine Rd
Brentford W4 132 C6
Wandsworth SW18 158 A6
Geraldine St SE11 261 C5
Gerald Mews SW1 258 B4
Gerald Rd
Belgravia SW1 115 A2 258 B4
Dagenham RM8 59 B1
Newham E16 98 D3
Gerard Ave TW4 151 C4
Gerard Ct NW2 68 D3
Gerard Rd
Barnes SW13 133 D4
Harrow HA1 43 A3
Gerards Cl SE16 118 C1
Gerboa Ct 6 E4 36 B5
Gerda Rd SE9 167 A2
Germander Way E15 98 C4
German Sch The TW10 153 D3
Gernigan Ho SW18 158 B5
Gernon Rd E3 97 A5
Geron Way NW2 68 C6
Gerrard Gdns HA5 40 A4
Gerrard Ho 5 SE14 140 D5
Gerrard Pl W1 249 D6
Gerrard Rd N1 94 D5 234 D4
Gerrards Cl N14 15 C6
Gerrard's Ct W5 109 D3
Gerrard St W1 115 D6 249 D6
Gerridge Ct SE1 261 B6
Gerridge St SE1 116 C3 261 B6
Gerry Raffles Sq E15 76 B2
Gertrude Rd DA17 125 C2
Gertrude St SW10 136 A6 266 B5
Gervase Cl HA9 67 A5
Gervase Rd HA8 27 B2
Gervase St SE15 140 B5
Getters Talmud Torah N16 51 B2
Ghent St SE6 163 C2
Ghent Way E8 73 D2
Giant Arches Rd SE24 161 A5
Giant Tree Hill WD23 8 B3
Gibbards Cott 1 IG11 79
Gibbfield Cl RM6 59
Gibbings Ho SE1 251
Gibbins Rd E15 76
Gibbon Ho NW8 236
Gibbon Rd Acton W3 111
Kingston u T KT2 176
Nunhead SE15 140
Gibbons Mews NW11 47
Gibbons Rd NW10 67
Gibbon's Rents SE1 253
Gibbon Wlk SW15 134
Gibbs Ave SE19 183
Gibbs Cl SE19 183
Gibbs Gn
Edgware HA8 27
West Kensington W14 113 B1 254
Gibbs Green Rd W14 113 B1 254
Gibbs Green Sch W14 113 B1 254
Gibbs Ho
6 Balham SW12 159
2 Bromley BR1 186
Gibbs Rd N18 34
Gibbs Sq SE19 183
Gibraltar Ho NW10 89
Gibraltar Wlk 28 E2 95
Gibson Bsns Ctr 10 N17 33
Gibson Cl
Bethnal Green E1 96
Chessington KT9 213
Isleworth TW7 130
Southgate N21 16
Gibson Ct
9 Friern Barnet N11 30
Hinchley Wood KT10 212
Gibson Gdns N16 73
Gibson Ho
South Croydon CR2 221
Sutton SM1 217
Gibson Rd
Dagenham RM8 58
Ickenham UB10 60
Lambeth SE11 260
Sutton SM1 217
Gibson's Hill SW16 182
Gibson Sq N1 94 C6 234
Gibson St SE10 120
Gideon Cl DA17 125
Gideon Mews W5 109
Gideon Rd SW11 137
Giesbach Rd N19 71
Giffard Rd N18 33
Giffen Square Mkt SE8 141
Giffin St SE8 141
Gifford Gdns W7 86
Gifford Ho
5 Clapham SW4 137
Greenwich SE10 120
Pimlico SW1 259
Gifford Prim Sch UB5 85
Gifford St N1 72
Gift La E15 98
Giggs Hill BR5 190
Giggs Hill Gdns KT7 197
Giggs Hill Rd KT7 197
Gilbert Cl
Kidbrooke SE18 144
1 Merton SW19 179
Gilbert Ct W5 88
Gilbert Gr HA8 27
Gilbert Ho
Barbican EC2 242
Deptford SE8 141
5 Globe Town E2 96
Pimlico SW1 258
South Lambeth SW8 270
5 Walthamstow E17 54
Gilbert Pl WC1 94 A2 240
Gilbert Rd
Belvedere DA17 125
Lambeth SE11 116 C2 261
Merton SW19 180
Pinner HA5 40
Plaistow BR1 187
Gilbert Scott Inf Com Sch CR2 223
Gilbert Scott Jun Com Sch CR2 223
Gilbert Sheldon Ho W2 236
Gilbertson Ho 11 E14 119
Gilbert St Enfield EN3 6
Hounslow TW3 130
Leyton E15 76

ert St *continued*
ylebone
/1 93 A1 238 B1
ey Cl UB10 60 D4
ey Rd SW17 180 C5
eys Yd NW1 71 A1
ourne Rd SE18 145 D6
Ho 5 E9 74 D2
Ave EN3 19 A6
Cres N16 52 A1
Ct NW7 28 A2
ea Cl HA5 23 C3
ea St W1 238 D3
en Cres NW5 71 A3
ersome St SE18 144 C6
ers Rd KT9 214 B2
Coppice SE19 183 D6
Ho
Bermondsey
E16 118 A3
ting Hill W11 91 C1
smead SE5 139 B4
id Cl UB8 82 D1
es Cres SE21 161 C5
es Pl SE21 161 C5
m Ho 9 SE16 118 C2
n Ct SE12 165 B1
n Gn WD23 8 A2
rds Mews 6
53 C5
rds Way E17 53 C5
Ave E16 99 A1
Ct SE18 123 A2
nder St E3 98 A3
spie Prim Sch
72 D5
spie Rd N4, N5 72 D5
tt Ave E6 100 A5
te Cnr TW7 131 A5
tt Ho N8 50 A6
tt Pl 27 E8 73 C3
tt Rd CR7 205 B5
tt St E8, N16 73 C3
oot NW1 232 A3
am Terr N17 34 A3
an Ho HA3 24 C4
an Park Rd SM3 201 B1
an St SE13 163 D6
es Ct
cup DA14 189 C6
thgate N21 16 B6
es St NW5 71 A3
ng Ct 5 NW3 70 C2
gham Ho SW1 259 A4
gham Mews
1 259 A4
gham Rd NW2 69 A5
gham Row
259 A4
gham St
1 115 C2 259 A4
gs Ct EN5 1 A1
son Wlk 19
6 118 A3
an Dr E15 98 D6
an Ho 24 E2 96 A5
ay Ho
lsea SW10 266 C5
Sutton SM1 218 B3
Ct 2 EN5 14 A6
t E14 119 B6
m Cl EN4 14 D3
ore Cl UB10 60 C5
ore Cres TW15 170 C4
ore Ct N11 30 D5
ore Ho SW4 136 D1
ore Rd SE13 142 B1
n Ave SW14 133 B1
n Cl
ham CR4 180 C1
dington W2 236 B4
n Cres
monton N18 33 D5
kenham TW2 151 D4
n Ho
Edmonton N9 18 A1
Malden KT3 199 C4
n Rd E5 75 A4
n Way UB3 127 B5
Ho W2 246 C6
nd Rd CR7 205 B5
ead Ho IG11 102 B5
ead Rd SW6 135 D3
on Rd
0 114 A1 256 B1
n Rd SE6 164 C1
our St
94 D1 241 D2
ell Cl E4 7 D1
ell Ct 7 E5 74 B4
eswyck Cl HA5 22 D2
Cnr W3 89 B2
Hill Sta SE19 183 C5
Hill SE19 183 C5
La SW15 134 B2
Moth IV*
) 142 A6

Gipsy Rd
Bexley DA16 146 D3
West Norwood SE27 183 B6
Gipsy Road Gdns
SE27 183 A6
Giralda Cl E16 99 D2
Giraud St E14 97 D1
Girdlers Rd W14 112 D2
Girdlestone Wlk N19 71 C6
Girdwood Rd SW18,
SW19 157 A4
Girling Ho 9 N1 95 C6
Girling Way TW14 128 A2
Gironde Rd
SW6 135 B5 264 D3
Girtin Ho
6 Belmont SM2 217 D1
4 Northolt UB5 84 D5
Girton Ave NW9 44 C6
Girton Cl UB5 64 A2
Girton Gdns CR0 223 C5
Girton Ho SW15 156 D5
Girton Rd
Forest Hill SE26 184 D5
Northolt UB5 64 A2
Girton Villas 6 W10 90 D1
Gisbourne Cl SM6 219 D5
Gisburn Ho 23 SE15 140 A5
Gisburn Mans N8 50 B5
Gisburn Rd N8 50 B5
Gissing Wlk N1 72 C1
Gittens Cl BR1 186 D6
Given-Wilson Wlk
E13 98 D5
Glacier Way HA0 87 D5
Gladbeck Way EN2 4 D1
Gladding Rd E12 77 D4
Gladebury Ct 2
SW19 179 B4
Glade Cl KT6 213 D6
Glade Gdns CR0 207 A2
Glade La UB2 107 D4
Gladeside Cl KT9 213 D1
Gladeside
Croydon CR0 206 D3
Southgate N21 16 B4
Gladesmore Com Sch
N15 52 A4
Gladesmore Rd N15 51 D3
Glades Sh Ctr The
BR1 187 A1
Gladeswood Rd
DA17 125 D2
Glade The
Bromley BR1 187 D1
Charlton SE7 143 C5
Croydon CR0 206 D3
Enfield EN2 4 C3
Hammersmith W12 112 B4
Southgate N21 16 B4
Stoneleigh KT17 216 A2
West Wickham BR4 223 D5
Woodford IG8 21 B1
Gladiator St SE23 163 A4
Glading Terr N16 73 D5
Gladioli Cl 6 TW12 173 C4
Gladsdale Dr HA5 40 B5
Gladsmuir Rd
Barnet EN5 1 A3
Upper Holloway N19 49 C1
Gladstone Ave
Feltham TW14 150 B5
Plashet E12 78 A1
Tottenham N22 32 D1
Twickenham TW2 152 B4
Gladstone Ct
12 Merton SW19 179 C3
Ruislip HA4 61 C6
Westminster SW1 259 D3
Willesden NW2 68 B3
Gladstone Gdns
TW3 130 A4
Gladstone Ho
6 Mitcham
SW19 180 D1
16 Poplar E14 97 C1
Gladstone Mews
3 Penge SE20 184 C3
Wood Green N22 32 C1
Gladstone Park Gdns
NW2 68 B5
Gladstone Park Sch
NW10 68 B3
Gladstone Par NW2 68 C5
Gladstone Pl KT8 196 C4
Gladstone Rd
Acton W4 111 B3
Buckhurst Hill IG9 21 C3
Farnborough BR6 227 A3
Kingston u T KT1 198 C6
Merton SW19 179 C3
Southall UB2 107 A4
Surbiton KT6 214 A6
Thornton Heath CR0 205 B2
Gladstone St SE1 261 C6
Gladstone Terr
SW8 137 B4 268 D2

Gladstone Way HA3 42 C6
Gladwell Rd
London N8 50 B3
Plaistow BR1 187 A4
Gladwin Ho NW1 232 B3
Gladwyn Rd SW15 134 D2
Gladys Dimson Ho
E7 76 D3
Gladys Rd NW6 69 C1
Glaisdale Sch SM2 217 B1
Glaisher St SE8 141 D6
Glamis Cres UB3 105 A3
Glamis Ct W3 110 D4
Glamis Est 3 E1 118 D6
Glamis Pl E1 118 C6
Glamis Rd E1 118 C6
Glamis Way UB5 64 A2
Glamorgan Cl CR4,
SW16 204 A6
Glamorgan Ct 4 W7 86 D2
Glamorgan Rd KT1 175 C3
Glandford Way RM6 58 B4
Glanfield Rd BR3 207 B5
Glanleam Rd HA7 25 D6
Glanville Ho 4
SW12 159 C4
Glanville Mews HA7 25 A5
Glanville Rd
Bromley BR2 209 B6
Clapham Pk SW2 160 A6
Glasbrook Ave TW2 151 B3
Glasbrook Rd SE9 165 D4
Glasbury Ho 5
SW9 138 B1
Glaserton Rd N16 51 C2
Glasford St SW17 180 D4
Glasfryn Ct HA2 64 B6
Glasgow Ho W9 91 D5
Glasgow Rd
Edmonton N18 34 B5
Newham E13 99 B5
Glasgow Terr
SW1 115 C1 259 A1
Glasier Ct 6 E15 76 C1
Glasse Cl W13 109 A6
Glasshill St
SE1 116 D4 251 D2
Glasshouse Cl UB8 82 D2
Glasshouse Fields
E1 118 D6
Glasshouse St
W1 115 C6 249 B5
Glasshouse The
SE13 142 A1
Glasshouse Wlk
SE11 116 B1 260 C2
Glasshouse Yd EC1 242 A5
Glasslyn Rd N8 49 D4
Glassmill La BR2 186 D1
Glass St 4 E2 96 B3
Glass Yd SE18 122 C3
Glastonbury Ave IG8 37 D4
Glastonbury Ct
12 Deptford SE14 140 C5
1 Ealing W13 109 A5
Glastonbury Ho
London SE12 164 D6
Pimlico SW1 258 C2
Glastonbury Pl 22 E1 96 C1
Glastonbury Rd
Edmonton N9 18 A3
Morden SM4 201 C2
Glastonbury St NW6 69 B3
Glaston Ct W5 109 D5
Glaucus St E3 97 D2
Glazbury Rd
W14 113 A1 254 B2
Glazebrook Cl SE21 161 B2
Glazebrook Rd
TW11 174 D3
Gleave Ct 7 N20 14 D2
Glebe Ave Enfield EN2 4 D2
Harrow HA3 44 A6
Mitcham CR4 180 C1
Ruislip HA4 62 B2
Uxbridge UB10 61 A4
Woodford IG8 37 A4
Glebe Cl
1 Chiswick W4 111 C1
Uxbridge UB10 61 A4
Glebe Cotts
Feltham TW13 151 C1
Sutton SM1 217 D4
Glebe Cres
Harrow HA3 44 A6
Hendon NW4 46 C5
Glebe Ct
15 Bromley E3 97 D4
Ealing W5 109 D5
Hanwell W7 108 B6
Lewisham SE3 142 C2
Mitcham CR4 202 D6
Palmers Green N13 16 C1
Ruislip HA4 39 B2
Stanmore HA7 25 C5
Glebe Fst & Mid Sch
HA3 44 A5

Glebe Gdns KT3 199 C2
Glebe Ho
8 Bermondsey
SE16 118 B3
Feltham TW13 151 C1
Glebe House Dr
BR2 209 B1
Glebe Ho 7 SE18 122 C2
Glebehyrst SE19 183 C6
Glebe La Barnet EN5 12 A5
Harrow HA3 44 A5
Glebeland Gdns
TW17 193 A3
Glebelands Ave
Ilford IG2 57 B2
Woodford E18 37 A1
Glebelands Cl
Camberwell SE5 139 C2
Finchley N2 30 B2
Glebelands
East Molesey KT8 195 D5
Leyton E10 75 D6
Mitcham CR4 202 C6
Glebelands Rd
TW14 150 A4
Glebe Path CR4 202 D6
Glebe Pl
SW3 136 C6 267 A6
Glebe Prim Sch
UB10 61 B4
Glebe Rd
Barnes SW13 134 A3
Belmont SM2 217 A1
Bromley BR1 187 A2
Dagenham RM10 81 D2
Dalston E8 73 D1
Finchley N3 30 A2
Hayes UB3 105 D5
Hornsey N8 50 B5
Stanmore HA7 25 C5
Wallington SM5 218 D2
Willesden NW10 68 A2
Glebe Sch BR4 224 B6
Glebe Side TW1 152 D5
Glebe Sq CR4 202 D6
Glebe St W4 111 C1
Glebe The
Chislehurst BR7 189 A2
Lewisham SE3 142 C2
New Malden KT4 199 D1
Streatham SW16 181 D6
West Drayton UB7 104 B2
Glebe Way
Feltham TW13 151 C1
West Wickham BR4 224 B6
Glebeway IG8 37 C5
Gledhow Gdns SW5 256 A3
Gledstanes Rd
W14 113 A1 254 B1
Gledwood Ave UB4 84 A2
Gledwood Cres UB4 83 D2
Gledwood Ct UB4 83 D2
Gledwood Dr UB4 83 D2
Gledwood Gdns UB4 84 A2
Gleed Ave WD23 8 B2
Gleeson Dr BR6 227 D4
Glegg Pl 3 SW15 134 D1
Glenaffric Ave E14 120 B2
Glen Albyn Rd
SW19 156 D2
Glenalla Rd HA4 39 D2
Glenalmond Ho
Ashford TW15 148 A1
2 Putney SW15 156 D5
Glenalmond Rd HA3 44 A5
Glenalvon Way 5
SE7 122 A2
Glena Mount SM1 218 A4
Glenarm Coll IG1 78 D6
Glenarm Rd E5 74 D4
Glen Ave TW15 170 C6
Glenavon Cl KT10 213 A1
Glenavon Ct KT4 216 B6
Glenavon Lo 5 E18 55 A6
Glenavon Rd E15 76 C1
Glenbarr Cl SE9 144 D2
Glenbow Rd BR1 186 C5
Glenbrook N EN2 4 B1
Glenbrook Prim Sch
SW4 159 D5
Glenbrook Rd NW6 69 C3
Glenbrook S EN2 4 B1
Glenbuck Ct 6 KT6 198 A3
Glenbuck Rd KT6 198 A3
Glenburnie Rd
SW17 158 D1
Glencairn Dr W5 87 C3
Glencairne Cl E16 99 D2
Glencairn Rd SW16 182 A3
Glen Cl TW17 192 C5
Glencoe Ave IG2 57 C2
Glencoe Dr RM10 81 C4
Glencoe Mans 6
SW9 138 C5
Glencoe Rd UB4 84 D3
Glencorse Gn WD19 22 D6
Glen Cres IG8 37 B4

Glencroft Ct SM1 217 C3
Glen Ct
6 Bromley BR1 186 D3
9 Penge SE20 184 B2
Sidcup DA14 190 A6
Glendale Ave
Edgware HA8 26 C6
Ilford RM6 58 C2
Wood Green N22 32 C3
Glendale Cl SE9 144 C2
Glendale Dr SW19 179 B5
Glendale Gdns HA9 44 A1
Glendale Mews
BR3 185 D2
Glendale Way SE28 124 C6
Glendall St SW9 138 B1
Glendarvon St
SW15 134 D2
Glendevon Cl HA8 10 D1
Glendish Rd N17 34 B2
Glendor Gdns NW7 27 B6
Glendower Gdns 10
SW14 133 B2
Glendower Pl SW7 256 C4
Glendower Prep Sch
SW7 114 B2 256 C4
Glendower Rd
Chingford E4 20 B3
Mortlake SW14 133 B2
Glendown Ho 2 E8 74 A3
Glendown Rd SE2 124 A1
Glendun Ct W3 111 C6
Glendun Rd W3 111 C6
Gleneagle Lo BR3 185 C2
Gleneagle Mews
SW16 181 D5
Gleneagle Rd SW16 181 D5
Gleneagles Cl
21 Bermondsey
SE16 118 B1
Crofton BR6 211 B1
South Oxhey WD19 22 D6
Gleneagles Ct 4
TW11 175 A5
Gleneagles W13 87 B2
Gleneagles Gn 1
BR6 211 B1
Gleneagles HA7 25 B4
Gleneagles Twr 2
UB1 86 A1
Gleneldon Mews
SW16 182 A6
Gleneldon Rd SW16 182 A6
Glenelg Rd SW2 160 A6
Glenesk Rd SE9 144 D1
Glenfarg Rd SE6 164 B3
Glenfield Cres HA4 39 B2
Glenfield Rd
Ashford TW15 171 A4
Ealing W13 109 B4
Streatham SW12 159 C3
Glenfield Terr W13 109 B5
Glenfinlas Way SE5 138 D5
Glenforth St SE10 120 D1
Glengall Ct SE23 163 A4
Glengall Gr E14 120 A3
Glengall Pass 2
NW6 91 C6
Glengall Rd
Bexley DA7 147 A2
Camberwell SE15 139 D6
Edgware HA8 10 D1
Kilburn NW6 91 B6
Woodford IG8 37 B4
Glengall Terr SE15 139 D6
Glengarnock Ave
E14 120 A2
Glengarry Rd SE22 161 D6
Glen Gdns CR0 220 C4
Glenham Dr IG2 56 D4
Glenhead Cl SE9 144 D2
Glenhill Cl N3 29 C1
Glen Ho 6 E16 122 C5
Glenhouse Rd SE9 166 C6
Glen Ho SM6 219 C4
Glenhurst Ave
Gospel Oak NW5 71 A4
Ruislip HA4 39 A1
Sidcup DA5 169 B3
Glenhurst 4 BR3 186 A2
Glenhurst Ct 1
SE19 183 D5
Glenhurst Rd
Brentford TW8 109 C1
North Finchley N12 30 B5
Glenhurst Rise
SE19 183 A3
Glenilla Rd NW3 70 C2
Glenister Ho UB3 106 B5
Glenister Park Rd
SW16 181 D3
Glenister Rd SE10 120 D1
Glenister St E16 122 C5
Glenkerry Ho 1 E14 98 A1
Glenlea Rd SE9 166 C6
Glenloch Ct 2 NW3 70 C2

Glenloch Rd
Enfield EN3 6 C3
Maitland Pk NW3 70 C3
Glenluce Rd SE3 143 A6
Glenlyon Rd SE9 166 C6
Glenmead IG9 21 C3
Glenmere Ave NW7 28 A4
Glen Mews E17 53 B4
Glenmill TW12 173 B5
Glenmore Ho 6
TW10 154 A5
Glenmore Lawns
W13 87 A1
Glenmore SW15 156 D5
Glenmore Rd
Bexley DA16 145 D4
Maitland Pk NW3 70 C2
Glenmore Way
IG11 102 A5
Glenmount Path 1
SE18 123 A1
Glennie Ct SE21 162 A3
Glennie Ho SE10 142 A4
Glennie Rd SE27,
SW16 160 C1
Glenny Rd IG11 79 A2
Glenorchy Cl UB4 85 A2
Glenpark Ct W13 109 A6
Glenparke Rd E7 77 B2
Glen Rd
Chessington KT9 214 A5
Newham E13 99 C3
Walthamstow E17 53 B4
Glenridding NW1 232 B3
Glen Rise IG8 37 B4
Glenrosa St SW6 136 A3
Glenrose Ct DA14 190 B5
Glenrose Ho 9
SM1 218 A4
Glenroy St W12 90 C1
Glensdale Rd SE4 141 B2
Glenshaw Mans 7
SW9 138 C5
Glenshiel Rd SE9 166 C6
Glentanner Way
SW17 158 B1
Glen Terr E14 120 A4
Glentham Gdns
SW13 134 B6
Glentham Rd SW13 134 B6
Glen The
Beckenham BR2 186 C1
Eastcote Village HA5 40 B4
Enfield EN2 4 D1
Locksbottom BR6 226 C5
Rayners La HA5 41 A2
Southall UB2 107 B1
South Croydon CR0 222 D5
Wembley HA9 65 D4
Glenthorne Ave
CR0 206 C1
Glenthorne Cl SM3 201 C1
Glenthorne Gdns
Cheam SM3 201 C1
Ilford IG6 56 D5
Glenthorne High Sch
SM3 201 C1
Glenthorne Mews
W6 112 B2
Glenthorne Rd
Friern Barnet N11 31 A5
Hammersmith W6 112 B2
Kingston u T KT1 198 B5
Walthamstow E17 53 A4
Glenthorpe SW15 134 A1
Glenthorpe Rd SM4 200 D4
Glenton Rd SE13 142 C1
Glentrammon Ave
BR6 227 D2
Glentrammon Cl
BR6 227 D3
Glentrammon Gdns
BR6 227 D2
Glentrammon Rd
BR6 227 D2
Glentworth Ct HA8 26 B5
Glentworth St
NW1 92 D3 237 D5
Glenure Rd SE9 166 C6
Glen View Rd BR1 187 D1
Glenview SE2 146 D6
Glenville Ave EN2 5 A5
Glenville Gr SE8 141 B5
Glenville Mews
SW18 157 C4
Glenville Rd KT2 176 C2
Glen Wlk TW7 152 B6
Glenwood Ave NW9 45 C1
Glenwood Cl HA1 42 D4
Glenwood Ct
7 Sidcup DA14 190 A6
6 Wanstead E18 55 A6
Glenwood Gdns IG2 56 C4
Glenwood Gr NW9 45 A1

Glenwood Ho 8 EN5..13 D6
Glenwood Rd
Edgware NW7........11 C1
Forest Hill SE6......163 C3
Harringay N15........50 D4
Hounslow TW3......130 B2
Stoneleigh KT17....216 A2
Glenwood Way CR0..206 D3
Glenworth Ave E14...120 B2
Gliddon Dr E5........74 B4
Gliddon Rd
W14........113 A1 254 A2
Glimpsing Gn DA18..125 A3
Glisson Rd UB10.......82 C5
Globe Ct SE18.......145 A6
Globe Pond Rd
SE16..................119 A5
Globe Prim Sch E2...96 C4
Globe Rd
Bethnal Green E1,
E2.....................96 C3
Stratford E15.........76 D3
Woodford IG8........37 C4
Globe St SE1 .117 B4 252 C1
Globe Terr 9 E2......96 C4
Globe Theatre The*
SE1...................252 A5
GLOBE TOWN........96 D4
Globe View EC4.....252 A6
Globe Yd W1.......238 C1
Glossop Ho TW7.....131 A1
Gloster Rd KT3......199 C5
Gloucester Ave
Camden Town
NW1.........93 A6 231 B6
Falconwood DA16...145 D1
Sidcup DA15.......167 C2
Gloucester Cir SE10..142 A5
Gloucester Cl
Thames Ditton
KT7.............197 A1
Willesden NW10......67 B1
Gloucester Cres
Camden Town
NW1.......93 B6 231 C6
Staines TW18......170 A4
Gloucester Ct
6 Acton W3...........88 C1
10 Belmont SM2.....217 C1
Borough The SE1....262 B6
City of London EC3..253 B5
Dulwich SE22.......162 A3
5 Ealing W7.........86 D2
Golders Green NW11..47 B2
Harrow HA1.........42 C6
Redbridge IG1........56 B2
Richmond TW9.......132 C5
8 Surbiton KT6.....197 D2
Gloucester Dr
Finsbury Pk N4.......72 D6
London NW11........47 C5
Gloucester Gate Mews
NW1..............231 C4
Gloucester Gate
NW1..............231 C4
Gloucester Gdns
Cockfosters EN4......15 A6
Golders Green NW11..47 B2
Paddington W2......236 A2
Redbridge IG1........56 A2
Sutton SM1........217 D6
Gloucester Gr HA8....27 B2
Gloucester Ho
Kilburn NW6..........91 C5
Richmond TW10.....154 C6
Gloucester Lo 9
CR0...............221 D6
Gloucester Mews
Paddington W2.....236 B1
Walthamstow E17.....53 C2
Gloucester Mews W
W2................236 B1
Gloucester Par
Bexley DA15.......168 A6
Hayes UB3.........105 A3
Gloucester Pk SW7..256 A4
Gloucester Pl Mews
W1.........92 D2 237 D3
Gloucester Pl
W1..........92 D2 237 D4
Gloucester Prim Sch
SE15.............139 C5
Gloucester Rd
Acton W3..........111 A4
Croydon CR0.......205 C2
Ealing W5.........109 C4
Edmonton N18........33 D5
Enfield EN2...........5 A5
Erith DA17.........125 B1
Feltham TW13......150 C3
Hampton TW12.....173 D3
Harrow HA1.........41 D4
Higham Hill E17......34 D1
Hounslow TW4.....129 A1
Gloucester Rd *continued*
Ilford E12...........78 B4
Kingston u T KT1,
KT2.............176 D1
Leyton E10...........53 C2
New Barnet EN5......14 A6
Richmond TW9......132 C5
South Kensington
SW7.....114 A2 256 A4
Teddington TW11....174 C5
Tottenham N17.......51 B6
Twickenham TW2....152 A3
Wanstead E11........55 C4
Gloucester Road Sta
SW7.......114 A2 256 A4
Gloucester Sq
6 Hackney E2........96 A6
Paddington
W2.......92 C1 237 A1
Gloucester St
SW1...........115 C1 259 A2
Gloucester Terr
W2..........92 A1 236 B1
Gloucester W14.....254 D3
Gloucester Way EC1..234 B1
Gloucester Wlk
W8.........113 C4 245 B2
Glover Cl SE2........124 C2
Glover Dr N18........34 C4
Glover Ho
London SE15........140 B1
2 South Hampstead
NW6................70 A1
Glover Rd HA5........40 D3
Glovers Gr HA4.......38 D2
Glovers Lo 24 TW10..153 D6
Glowhill Ct N12.......30 A3
Gloxinia Wlk TW12...173 C4
Glycena Rd SW11....136 D2
Glyn Ave EN4..........2 B1
Glyn Cl SE25.........183 C2
Glyn Ct Stanmore HA7..25 B4
West Norwood SE27..160 C1
Glyndale Grange
SM2..............217 D2
Glyndebourne Ct 5
UB5..................84 C4
Glyndebourne Pk
BR6................226 D6
Glynde Mews SW3...257 B5
Glynde Rd DA7......147 A2
Glynde Reach WC1..233 B1
Glynde St SE4.......163 B5
Glyndon Rd SE18....123 B2
Glyn Dr DA14........190 B6
Glynfield Rd NW10....67 C1
Glyn Mans W14.....254 B4
Glynne Rd N22........32 C1
Glyn Rd Clapton Pk E5..74 D4
Enfield EN3............6 C1
North Cheam KT4,
SM3..............216 D6
Glyn St SE11........260 C1
Glynwood Ct 7
SE23..............162 C2
Goater's Alley SW6..264 D3
Goat La EN1............5 D5
Goat Rd CR4.........202 D2
Goat Wharf TW8.....132 A6
Godalming Ave
SM6................220 B3
Godalming Rd E14....97 D2
Godbold Rd E15.......98 C4
Goddard Cl TW17....192 B6
Goddard Ct HA3.......25 A1
Goddard Ho SW19...156 D2
Goddard Pl N19.......71 C5
Goddard Rd BR3.....207 A5
Goddards Way IG1....57 B1
Goddarts Ho E17......53 C6
Godfrey Ave
Northolt UB5.........85 A6
Twickenham TW2.....152 B4
Godfrey Hill SE18....122 A2
Godfrey Ho EC1.....235 C1
Godfrey Rd SE18.....122 B2
Godfrey St
Chelsea
SW3.....114 C1 257 B2
Mill Meads E15.......98 A5
Godfrey Way TW4....151 B4
Goding St
SE11........116 A1 260 B1
Godley Rd SW18.....158 B3
Godliman St EC4....252 A6
Godman Rd SE15....140 B3
Godolphin Cl N13.....32 D4
Godolphin Ho
Primrose Hill NW3....70 C1
7 Streatham SW2..160 C3
Godolphin & Latymer
Sch W6............112 B2
Godolphin Pl W3....111 B6
Godolphin Rd W12...112 B4
Godson Rd CR0......220 C5
Godson St N1.......234 A4
Godstone Ct 1 N16...51 C1
Godstone Ho
Borough The SE1....262 D6
1 Kingston u T KT2..176 D4
Godstone Rd
Sutton SM1........218 A4
Twickenham TW1.....153 B5
Godstow Rd SE2.....124 C4
Godwin Cl
Shoreditch N1......235 B4
West Ewell KT19....215 A2
Godwin Ct NW1.....232 B4
Godwin Ho
2 Haggerston E2.....95 D5
Kidbrooke SE18......144 B4
Kilburn NW6..........91 D5
Godwin Jun Sch E7...77 B4
Godwin Prim Sch
RM9.................81 A1
Godwin Rd
Bromley BR1,
BR2.............209 C6
Forest Gate E7.......77 B4
Godwyn Ho 13 KT6...198 A3
Goffers Ho SE3......142 C3
Goffers Rd SE3,
SE13..............142 C3
Goffs Rd TW15.......171 B4
Goffton Ho 14 SW9...138 B3
Goidel Cl SM6.......219 D4
Golborne Gdns
5 Kensal Town
W10.................91 A3
West Kilburn W10.....91 B3
Golborne Mews 9
W10.................91 A2
Golborne Rd W10.....91 A2
Golda Cl EN5.........12 D5
Golda Ct N3..........29 B1
Goldbeaters Gr HA8...27 C3
Goldbeaters Prim Sch
HA8..................27 B2
Goldcliff Cl SM4.....201 C2
Goldcrest Cl
Newham E16.........99 D2
Woolwich SE28.....124 C6
Goldcrest Mews W5..87 D2
Goldcrest Way
Bushey WD23.........8 A3
New Addington CR0..224 B1
Golden Cres UB3.....105 D5
Golden Cross Mews 2
W11.................91 B1
Golden Ct
4 Barnet EN4.........2 C1
Ealing W7.........108 C6
Hounslow TW3......130 B3
10 Richmond TW9...153 D6
Golden Hinde The*
SE1...............252 C4
Golden Hind Pl 5
SE8................119 B2
Golden La
EC1.........95 A3 242 B5
Golden Manor W7...108 C6
Golden Mews SE20...184 C2
Golden Par 2 E17....54 A6
Golden Plover Cl
E16.................99 A1
Golden Sq
W1.........115 C6 249 B6
Golders Cl HA8.......26 D5
Golders Ct NW11.....47 B2
Golders Gdns NW11...47 B2
GOLDERS GREEN....47 B2
Golders Green Coll
NW11...............47 C1
Golders Green Cres
NW11...............47 C2
Golders Green Rd
NW11...............47 A2
Golders Green Sta
NW11...............47 C1
Golders Hill Sch
NW11...............47 C2
Goldersiea NW11.....47 C1
Golders Manor Dr
NW11...............47 A3
Golders Park Cl
NW11...............47 C1
Golders Rise NW4....46 D4
Golders Way NW11...47 B2
Golderton 2 NW4....46 C5
Goldfinch Rd SE28...123 B3
Goldhawk Ind Est The
W6................112 B3
Goldhawk Mews 2
W12...............112 B4
Goldhawk Rd W12...112 A3
Goldhawk Road Sta
W12...............112 C4
Goldhaze Cl IG8......37 D3
Gold Hill HA8.........27 B4
Goldhurst Terr NW6...70 A1
Goldie Ho N19........49 D2
Goldie Leigh Hospl
SE2...............146 C6
Golding Cl KT9......213 C2
Golding Ct 7 IG1.....78 C5
Golding St E1........96 A1
Goldington Cres
NW1..............232 C4
Goldington Ct NW1..232 C5
Goldington St
NW1.........93 D5 232 C4
Gold La HA8..........27 B4
Goldman Cl E2........96 A3
Goldmark Ho SE3....143 B2
Goldney Rd W9.......91 C3
Goldrill Dr N11.......15 A2
Goldsboro Rd
SW8.......137 D5 269 D3
Goldsborough Cres
E4...................20 A2
Goldsborough Ho
SW8...............269 D1
Goldsdown Cl EN3.....7 A3
Goldsdown Rd EN3.....7 A3
Goldsmid St 2
SE18..............123 C1
Goldsmith Ave
Acton W3..........111 B6
Dagenham RM7.......59 C2
Hyde The NW9........45 C3
Plashet E12..........78 A2
Goldsmith Cl HA2.....41 D1
Goldsmith Ct
Edgware HA8.........26 B6
St Giles WC1.......240 B2
Goldsmith Ho W3....111 B6
Goldsmith La NW9....45 A5
Goldsmith Rd
Acton W3..........111 B5
Friern Barnet N11.....30 D5
Higham Hill E17......34 D1
Leyton E10...........53 D1
Peckham SE15......140 A4
Goldsmiths Bldgs
W3................111 B5
Goldsmiths Cl W3...111 B5
Goldsmiths Coll, Univ of
London SE14......141 A4
Goldsmith's Ct N6....49 B3
Goldsmith's Pl 6
NW6................91 D6
Goldsmith's Row E2..96 A5
Goldsmith's Sq 17 E2 .96 A5
Goldsmith St EC2...242 B2
Goldthorpe NW1.....232 A5
Goldwell Ho SE22....139 C1
Goldwell Rd CR7.....204 B5
Goldwin Cl SE14.....140 C4
Goldwing Cl E16......99 A1
Golf Cl
South Norwood
SW16.............182 C2
Stanmore HA7........25 C3
Golf Club Dr KT2.....177 B3
Golfe Ho IG1.........79 B5
Golfe Rd IG1.........79 B5
Golfers View N12.....30 B6
Golf Rd Bromley BR1..210 C6
Ealing W5............88 B1
Golf Side Cl KT3.....177 C1
Golfside Cl N20.......14 C1
Golf Side TW2.......152 B1
Gollogly Terr 9
SE7................121 C1
Gomer Gdns TW11...175 A4
Gomer Pl TW11......175 A4
Gomm Rd SE16......118 C3
Gomshall Ave SM6...220 A3
Gondar Gdns NW6....69 B3
Gondar Mans NW6....69 B3
Gonson St SE8.......141 D6
Gonston Cl SW19....157 A2
Gonville Cres UB5....63 D2
Gonville Ct 6 EN4....14 D3
Gonville Ho 6
SW15..............156 D5
Gonville Prim Sch
CR7...............204 B4
Gonville Rd CR7.....204 B4
Gonville St SW6.....135 A2
Gooch Ho
Holborn EC1.......241 A4
Lower Clapton E5.....74 B5
Goodall Ho 10 SE4...140 D1
Goodall Rd E11.......76 A5
Goodbehere Ho 7
SE27..............183 A6
Gooden Ct HA1........64 C5
Goodenough Coll
WC1.........94 B3 240 C6
Goodenough Rd
SW19..............179 B3
Goodey Rd IG11......79 D1
Goodfaith Ho 18
E14...............119 D6
Goodge Pl W1.......239 B3
Goodge Street Sta
W1.........93 D2 239 C4
Goodge St
W1.........93 C2 239 B3
Goodhall Cl HA7......25 B4
Goodhall St NW10....89 D4
Good Hart Pl E14....119 A6
Goodhart Way BR4...208 C3
Goodhew Rd CR0....206 A3
Goodhope Ho 17
E14...............119 D6
Gooding Cl KT3......199 A4
Goodinge Cl N7.......72 A2
Goodinge Rd N7......72 A2
Gooding Ho 4 SE7...121 C1
Goodison Cl WD23.....8 A6
Goodland Ho 1
KT3...............199 C2
Goodman Cres
SW2...............159 D2
Goodman Rd E10......54 A2
Goodmans Ct HA0.....65 D4
Goodman's Stile 17
E1...................96 A1
Goodman's Yd E1,
EC3........117 D6 253 C6
GOODMAYES........58 B1
Goodmayes Ave IG3..58 A1
Goodmayes Hospl
IG3..................58 A4
Goodmayes La IG3....80 A5
Goodmayes Lodge
RM8.................80 A4
Goodmayes Prim Sch
IG3..................58 B1
Goodmayes Rd IG3...58 A1
Goodmayes Ret Pk
RM6.................58 B2
Goodmayes Sta IG3..58 A1
Goodrich Com Sch
SE22..............162 A5
Goodrich Ct 9 W10...90 D1
Goodrich Ho
20 Bethnal Green
E2..................96 C5
Stamford Hill N16.....51 C2
Goodrich Rd SE22....162 A5
Goodridge Ho E17....36 A3
Good Shepherd RC
Prim Sch
Catford BR1.......186 D6
New Addington CR0..223 D1
Good Shepherd RC
Prim Sch The
W12...............111 D4
Goodson Ho SM4....202 A2
Goodson Rd NW10....67 C1
Goodspeed Ho 20
E14...............119 D6
Goodsway
NW1.........94 A5 233 A4
Goodway Gdns E14...98 B1
Goodwill Ho 22 E14..119 D6
Goodwin Cl
Bermondsey
SE16.....117 D3 263 D5
Mitcham CR4.......202 B6
Goodwin Ct
East Barnet EN4......14 C5
Hornsey N8..........50 A6
2 Mitcham SW19...180 C3
Goodwin Dr DA14....168 D2
Goodwin Gdns CR0,
CR2...............220 D2
Goodwin Ho
Edmonton N9.........18 C3
2 Peckham SE15....140 B2
Goodwin Rd
Croydon CR0.......220 D3
Edmonton N9.........18 D3
Shepherd's Bush
W12...............112 A4
Goodwins Ct WC2...250 A6
Goodwin St N4.......72 C6
Goodwood Ave EN3....6 C6
Goodwood Cl
Morden SM4.......201 C5
11 Stanmore HA7.....25 C5
Goodwood Ct W1....238 D4
Goodwood Dr UB5....63 C2
Goodwood Ho
3 Acton Green
W4................111 A1
Penge SE26........184 B4
Goodwood Lo 1
SM6...............219 D5
Goodwood Mans 3
SW9...............138 C2
Goodwood Par BR3...207 A5
Goodwood Rd SE14...141 A5
Goodwyn Ave NW7....27 C5
Goodwyn Sch NW7....28 A5
Goodwyn's Vale N10..31 B2
Goodyear Ho 8 N2...30 B1
Goodyers Gdns NW4..46 D4
Goosander Ct 34
NW9.................27 D1
Goosander Way SE18,
SE28..............123 B3
Gooseacre La HA3....43 D4
Goose Green Cl
BR5...............19…
Goose Green Prim Sch
SE22..............13…
Goose Green Trad Est
SE22..............14…
Gooseley La E6.......10…
Goose Sq 8 E6........10…
Goossens Cl 1
SM1................21…
Gophir La EC4........25…
Gopsall St N1..95 B6 23…
Gordon Ave
Chingford E4..........3…
Isleworth TW1.......15…
Mortlake SW14.......13…
Stanmore HA7........2…
Gordonbrock Prim Sch
SE4................16…
Gordonbrock Rd
SE4................16…
Gordon Cl E17........5…
Gordon Cres
Croydon CR0.......20…
Hayes UB3..........10…
Gordon Ct
Edgware HA8.........2…
Hampton TW12......17…
5 Shepherd's Bush
W12..................9…
18 Wimbledon
SW20...............17…
Gordondale Rd SW18,
SW19...............15…
Gordon Dr TW17.....19…
Gordon Gdns HA8.....2…
Gordon Gr SE5........13…
Gordon Hill EN2.......
Gordon Hill Sta EN2...…
Gordon Ho
2 Ealing W5..........8…
Lee SE12.............16…
17 Shadwell E1.......11…
Gordon Hospl The
SW1.........115 D2 25…
Gordon House Rd
NW5..................7…
Gordon Inf Sch IG1...7…
Gordon Lo N16........5…
Gordon Mans
3 Barnet EN5.........
Marylebone WC1.....23…
Gordon Pl
W8..........113 C4 24…
Gordon Prim Sch
SE9.................14…
Gordon Rd
Ashford TW15.......14…
Avery Hill DA15.....16…
Barking IG11........10…
Beckenham BR3.....20…
Chingford E4..........2…
Chiswick W4........13…
Claygate KT10.......21…
Dagenham RM6........5…
Ealing W13..........10…
Edmonton N9..........1…
Enfield EN2...........
Finchley N3...........2…
Harrow HA3...........4…
Ilford IG1.............7…
Isleworth TW3.......13…
Kingston u T KT2.....17…
Leyton E15............7…
Peckham SE15........14…
Richmond TW9........13…
Shepperton TW17.....19…
Southall UB2........10…
Surbiton KT5.........19…
Wallington SM5.......21…
Wanstead E11..........5…
Woodford E18..........3…
Wood Green N11.......3…
Yiewsley UB7.........10…
Gordon Sq
WC1.........93 D3 23…
Gordon St
Bloomsbury
WC1.......93 D3 23…
Newham E13...........9…
Gordon Way
Barnet EN5...........
Bromley BR1.........18…
Gore Ct NW9...........4…
Gorefield Ho NW6.....9…
Gorefield Pl NW6.....9…
Gore Rd Hackney E9....9…
Merton SW20........17…
Goresbrook Rd
RM9..................1…
Gore St SW7..114 A3 25…
Gorham Ho 12 SW4..15…
Gorham Pl W11.......24…
Goring Gdns RM8.....8…
Goring Rd N11.........3…
Goring St EC3........24…
Goring Way UB6.......8…

leston Rd N15 51 B4
leston St
4 113 A2 254 B4
man Rd SE18 122 B2
ringe Park Ave
1 181 A3
ringe Park Prim Sch
1 181 A2
se Cl E16 99 A1
sefield Ho 6
1 119 C6
se Rd CR0 223 C5
se Rise SW17 181 A5
se Wlk UB7 82 A1
st Rd
ndon SW11 158 D5
rth Acton NW10 89 B3
such Pl 1 E2 95 D4
such St E2 95 D4
berton Rd SW12 159 A3
bury Hill KT9 214 A4
field Rd RM8 59 C1
field St
93 C2 239 A3
ford Gdns IG4 56 B4
ford Ho 25 E3 97 B5
hawk Gdns UB4 83 C5
ett Yd WC2 239 D2
ing Cl UB6 85 C4
ing Ho 2 E1 118 C6
ing Way SW9 138 C4
more Ct N9 18 B2
patric Home Ho
14 133 C2
patrick Rd N17 33 A2
PEL OAK 71 A4
pel Oak Prim Sch
/5 71 A4
pel Oak Sta NW5 71 A4
port Ho 9
15 156 A3
port Rd E17 53 B4
port Wlk N17 52 B5
sage Rd
lingdon UB10 60 B1
mstead SE18 123 B1
set St E2 96 A4
shill Rd BR7 188 C1
sington Cl BR7 188 D6
terwood St SE8 141 A6
tling Rd TW2 151 C3
ton Gdns CR7 204 C6
well Pl EC1 234 D1
well Rd
1 94 D4 234 D2
nic Ct
Camberwell
E5 139 A5
rlington UB3 127 B6
nic Rd TW2 152 B2
fried Mews NW5 71 C4
dhurst Ho 7
20 184 C3
dhurst Rd BR1 186 D5
gh Ho
ngton N1 234 D6
Kingston u T KT1 176 A1
gh Rd Enfield EN1 6 B3
atford E15 76 D4
gh Sq EC4 94 C1 241 B2
gh St
1 94 B3 240 D5
gh Wlk 14 E14 97 C1
ld Ct SE19 183 C5
lden Ho SW11 136 C3
lding Gdns CR7 183 A1
ldman Ho 33 E1 96 C3
ld Rd
t Bedfont
W14 149 C4
ckenham TW2 152 C3
ld's Gn UB8 104 D6
ld Terr 26 E8 74 B3
ston St
95 D1 243 C2
ton Rd E5 74 B4
rley Pl N15 51 C4
rley St N15 51 C4
rock Rd SE9 166 C6
an St E2 96 A6
er Ct 8 SW4 138 A3
ernment Row EN3 7 C6
ett Ave TW17 193 A4
er Cl E15 76 C1
an Ave
6 135 A4 264 A2
an Ho 22 E2 95 D4
an Lea 4 E18 55 A5
an Rd NW10 68 B2
er Cl SW4 159 C5
er Ct WC1 239 C6
er Ho
king IG11 79 A1
yes UB3 105 C6
per Tooting SW17 180 B4
er House Sch
9 67 A6

Gower Ho
12 Walthamstow
E17 53 D6
Walworth SE17 262 B2
Gower Mews WC1 239 D4
Gower Pl NW1,
WC1 93 D3 239 C6
Gower Rd
Hounslow TW7 130 D6
Upton E7 77 A2
Gower Sch The N7 72 A2
Gower St
WC1 93 D3 239 C5
Gower's Wlk E1 96 A1
Gowland Pl BR3 185 B1
Gowlett Rd SE15 140 A2
Gowlland Cl CR0 206 A2
Gowrie Rd SW11 137 A2
Graburn Way KT8 196 B6
Grace Ave DA7 147 B3
Grace Bsns Ctr CR4 202 D3
Gracechurch St EC2,
EC4 252 D6
Grace Cl
Burnt Oak HA8 27 A3
Mottingham SE9 165 D1
Grace Ct
5 Croydon CR0 220 D5
Twickenham TW2 152 C2
Gracedale Rd SW16 181 B5
Gracedyer Ho N22 32 A3
Gracefield Gdns
SW16 160 A1
Gracehill 2 E1 96 C2
Grace Ho
Kennington SE11 270 D6
Penge SE26 184 B5
Grace Jones Cl E8 74 A2
Grace Path 2 SE26 184 C6
Grace Pl E3 97 D4
Grace Rd CR0 205 A3
Graces Alley 14 SE1 118 A6
Grace's Mews SE5 139 C3
Graces Mews NW8 229 B3
Grace's Rd SE5 139 C3
Grace St E3 97 D4
Gradient The SE26 184 A6
Graeme Ct UB6 85 D4
Graeme Rd EN1 5 C3
Graemesdyke Ave
SW14 132 D1
Grafton Cl Ealing W13 87 A1
Twickenham TW4 151 B3
Worcester Pk KT4 215 C5
Grafton Cres NW1 71 B2
Grafton Ct
10 Dalston E8 74 A3
East Bedfont TW14 149 B3
Grafton Gdns
Dagenham RM8 81 A6
Harringay N4 51 A3
Grafton Ho
18 Bow E3 97 C4
12 Deptford SE8 119 B1
Grafton Jun & Inf Schs
RM8 81 B6
Grafton Mans SW4 137 C1
Grafton Mews W1 239 A5
Grafton Park Rd
KT4 215 C6
Grafton Pl
NW1 93 D4 232 D1
Grafton Prim Sch N7 72 A5
Grafton Rd
Acton W3 111 A6
Dagenham RM8 81 A6
Enfield EN2 4 B2
Gospel Oak NW5 71 A3
Harrow HA1 42 A4
Kingston u T KT3 199 C6
Thornton Heath CR0 204 C1
Worcester Pk KT4 215 C5
Grafton Sq SW4 137 C2
Grafton St
W1 115 B6 248 D5
Grafton Terr NW5 71 A3
Grafton Way
East Molesey KT8 195 B5
Marylebone W1 239 B5
Grafton Yd NW5 71 B2
Graham Ave
Ealing W13 109 B4
Mitcham CR4 181 A2
Graham Cl CR0 223 C6
Graham Ct
Bromley BR1 187 B3
5 Deptford SE14 140 D6
Northolt UB5 63 B3
GRAHAME PARK 27 C2
Grahame Park Way NW7,
NW9 27 D2
Grahame White Ho
HA3 43 D6
Graham Gdns KT6 198 A1
Graham Ho
5 Balham SW12 159 B4
6 Barnet EN5 1 D1

Graham Ho *continued*
Edmonton N9 18 C3
6 Tufnell Pk N19 71 D4
Woolwich SE18 144 D5
Graham Lo
Edgware HA8 26 B4
Hendon NW4 46 B3
Graham Mans
11 Barking IG11 80 A1
2 Hackney E8 74 B2
Graham Rd
Acton W4 111 B3
Bexleyheath DA6 147 C1
Dalston E8 74 A2
Hampton TW12 173 C6
Harringay N15 50 D6
Harrow HA3 42 C6
Hendon NW4 46 B3
Merton SW19 179 B3
Mitcham CR4 181 A2
Newham E13 99 A3
Graham St
N1 94 D5 234 D3
Graham Terr
SW1 115 A2 258 B3
Graham Twr W3 110 D3
Grainger Cl UB5 64 A3
Grainger Ct 22 SE5 139 A5
Grainger Rd
Isleworth TW7 130 D3
Tottenham N22 33 A2
Gramer Cl E11 76 B6
Grampian Cl
Harlington UB3 127 B5
Orpington BR6 211 D3
15 Sutton SM2 218 A1
Grampian Gdns NW2 47 A1
Grampians The 10
W14 112 D4
Gramsci Way SE6 163 D1
Granada St SW17 180 D5
Granard Ave SW15 156 B6
Granard Bsns Ctr
NW7 27 C4
Granard Ho 20 E9 74 D2
Granard Prim Sch
SW15 156 B5
Granard Rd SW11,
SW12 158 D4
Granary Cl N9 18 C4
Granary Ct 3 RM6 58 D2
Granary Mans SE28 123 A4
Granary Rd E1 96 B3
Granary Sq N1 72 C2
Granary St
NW1 93 D6 232 C5
Granary The SE8 141 C5
Granby Ho 13 SE18 122 B2
Granby Pl SE1 251 A1
Granby Rd
Eltham SE9 144 B2
Woolwich SE18 122 D3
Granby St
Bethnal Green E2 96 A3
Shoreditch E2 243 D6
Granby Terr
NW1 93 C5 232 A3
Grand Arc N12 30 A5
Grand Ave EC1 241 D4
Grand Ave E HA9 66 D3
Grand Ave N10 49 A5
Grand Avenue Prim Sch
KT5 199 A3
Grand Ave
Tolworth KT5 198 D3
Wembley HA9 66 C3
Grand Ct RM8 81 A5
Grand Depot Rd
SE18 122 C1
Grand Dr
Southall UB2 108 A4
West Barnes SM4,
SW20 200 C5
Granden Rd SW16 182 A1
Grandfield Ct W4 133 B6
Grandison Rd
London SW11 158 D6
North Cheam KT4 216 C5
Grand Junction Wharf
N1 235 A3
Grand Par London N4 50 D3
Mortlake SW14 133 A1
Tolworth KT6 198 C1
Wembley HA9 66 C6
Grand Union Cl W9 91 B2
Grand Union Cres E8 96 A6
Grand Union Ind Est
NW10 88 D5
Grand Union Way
UB2 107 C4
Grand Vitesse Ind Est
SE1 251 D3
Granfield St SW11 266 D1
Grange Ave
East Barnet EN4 14 D3
North Finchley N12 30 A5

Grange Ave *continued*
South Norwood
SE25 183 C1
Stanmore HA7 25 C1
Totteridge N20 13 A4
Twickenham TW2 152 C2
Woodford IG8 37 A3
Grange Cl
East Molesey KT8 195 D5
Edgware HA8 27 A5
Hayes UB3 83 C2
Heston TW5 129 B6
Grangecliffe Gdns
SE25 183 C1
Grange Cl
Sidcup DA15 168 A1
Woodford IG8 37 A3
Grangecourt Rd N16 51 C1
Grange Cres SE28 102 C1
Grange Ct
Belmont SM2 217 D1
4 Finchley N12 30 A4
Hackbridge SM6 219 B5
Harrow HA1 64 D5
Ilford IG6 57 A6
Littleton TW17 192 C5
Loughton IG10 21 D6
Northolt UB5 84 C5
Peckham SE15 139 D3
Pinner HA5 41 A6
Strand WC2 240 D1
Wembley HA0 65 C3
1 Willesden NW10 67 C4
Grange Dr BR7 188 B4
Grange Farm Cl HA2 64 A6
Grange Farm Est
TW17 193 C6
Grangefield NW1 72 A1
Grange Fst & Mid Schs
HA2 41 D1
Grange Gdns
London N14 15 D3
Pinner HA5 41 A5
South Norwood
SE25 183 C1
West Hampstead
NW3 69 D5
Grange Gr N1 73 A2
Grange Hill HA8 27 A5
Grangehill Pl SE9 144 B2
Grangehill Rd SE9 144 B1
Grange Hill SE25 183 C1
Grange Ho
6 Barking IG11 101 B6
Bermondsey SE1 263 C5
Willesden NW10 68 B1
Grange La SE21 161 D2
Grange Lo SW19 178 D4
Grange Mans KT17 215 D1
Grangemill 11 NW5 71 B4
Grangemill Rd SE6 163 C2
GRANGE MILLS 113 C3
Grange Mills SW12 159 C3
Grangemill Way
SE6 163 C2
GRANGE PARK 16 C6
Grange Park Ave
N21 17 A5
Grange Park Jun & Inf
Schs UB4 83 D3
Grange Park Pl
SW20 178 B3
Grange Park Prep Sch
N21 16 D5
Grange Park Prim Sch
N21 4 C1
Grange Park Rd
Leyton E10 53 D1
South Norwood CR7 205 B6
Grange Park Sta N21 16 D5
Grange Pk W5 110 A5
Grange Pl NW6 69 C1
Grange Prim Sch
Bermondsey
SE1 117 C3 263 A5
Ealing W5 109 D4
Newham E13 98 D4
Grange Rd
Barnes SW13 134 A4
Belmont SM2 217 C1
Bermondsey
SE1 117 D3 263 C5
Borehamwood WD6 10 B6
Burnt Oak HA8 27 B4
Chessington KT9 214 A4
Ealing W5 110 A5
East Molesey KT8 195 D5
Greenhill HA1 43 A4
Gunnersbury W4 110 D1
Hayes UB3 83 C1
Highgate N6 49 A3
Ilford IG1 79 A4
Kingston u T KT1 198 A6
Leyton E10 53 C1
Newham E13 98 D4
Orpington BR6 227 A6

Grange Rd *continued*
Roxeth HA2 64 B6
Southall UB1 107 A4
South Norwood SE19,
SE25 183 B1
Tottenham N17 34 A4
Walthamstow E17 53 A4
Willesden NW10 68 B2
Grange St N1 235 D5
Grange The
Bermondsey
SE1 117 D3 263 C5
Cockfosters EN4 2 D2
Croydon CR0 223 B6
Ealing W13 87 C2
7 Gunnersbury W4 110 D1
Hammersmith W12 112 B3
19 Maitland Pk NW3 70 D2
South Acton W3 110 D4
3 Walthamstow E17 53 A4
4 Wanstead E18 55 A6
Wembley HA0 66 C1
West Barnes KT3 200 A4
West Ewell KT19 215 B4
West Kensington
W14 113 B2 254 C3
Wimbledon SW19 178 D4
Grange Vale SM2 217 D1
Grange View Rd N20 14 A3
Grangeway Gdns
IG4 56 A4
Grangeway
London N12 29 D6
South Hampstead
NW6 69 C1
Grangeway The N21 16 D5
Grangeway IG8 37 C6
Grange Wlk
SE1 117 D3 263 C5
Grangewood Cl HA5 40 A4
Grangewood DA5 169 B3
Grangewood Ind Sch
E7 77 D1
Grangewood La
BR3 185 B4
Grangewood Sch
HA5 39 D4
Grangewood St E6 99 D6
Grange Yd
SE1 117 D3 263 C5
Granham Gdns N9 17 D2
Granite Apts E15 76 B2
Granite St SE18 123 D1
Granleigh Rd E11 76 C6
Grannary The 10
SE16 118 C4
Gransden Ave E8 74 B1
Gransden Ho 1
SE8 119 B1
Gransden Rd W12 111 D4
Grantbridge St
N1 94 D5 234 D4
Grantchester Cl HA1 64 D5
Grantchester 12
KT1 176 C1
Grant Cl London N14 15 C4
Shepperton TW17 192 D3
Tottenham N17 33 C1
Grant Ct
2 Chingford E4 20 A3
11 Hendon NW9 27 D1
Grantham Cl HA8 10 A1
Grantham Ct
Dagenham RM6 59 B2
Kingston u T KT2 175 D5
9 Rotherhithe
SE16 118 D4
Grantham Gdns RM6 59 B2
Grantham Gn WD6 11 A6
Grantham Ho
Ashford TW16 171 C3
12 Peckham SE15 140 A6
Grantham Pl W1 248 C3
Grantham Rd
Chiswick W4 133 C5
Little Ilford E12 78 C4
South Lambeth SW9 138 A3
Grant Ho
38 Clapham SW8 137 D3
Clerkenwell EC1 241 D4
Grantley Ho
2 Deptford SE14 140 D6
5 Putney SW19 156 D3
Grantley Pl KT10 212 A3
Grantley Rd TW4,
TW5 128 C3
Grantley St E1 96 D3
Grant Mus of Zoology &
Comparative
Anatomy*
WC1 93 D3 239 C5
Grantock Rd E17 36 B2
Granton Prim Sch
SW16 181 C3
Granton Rd Ilford IG3 58 A1
Sidcup DA14 190 C4
Streatham SW16 181 C2

Grant Pl 2 CR0 205 D1
Grant Rd
Battersea SW11 136 C2
Croydon CR0 205 D1
Harrow HA3 42 D6
Grants Cl NW7 28 D3
Grants Cotts KT10 212 B6
Grant St Islington N1 234 A4
Newham E13 99 A4
Grantully Rd W9 91 D4
Grant Way TW7 131 A6
Granville Ave
Feltham TW13 150 A2
Hounslow TW3,
TW4 151 C6
Lower Edmonton N9 18 C1
Granville Cl CR0 221 C6
Granville Ct
8 Deptford SE14 141 A5
Hornsey N4 50 B3
Shoreditch N1 235 D6
Granville Gdns
Ealing W5 110 B5
South Norwood
SW16 182 B3
Granville Gr SE13 142 A2
Granville Ho 18 E14 97 C1
Granville Ind Est
NW2 69 B6
Granville Mans 8
W12 112 C4
Granville Mews
DA14 190 A6
Granville Pk SE13 142 B2
Granville Pl
London N12 30 A3
Marylebone
W1 93 A1 238 A1
Pinner HA5 40 D6
Walham Green SW6 265 C3
Granville Point NW2 69 B6
Granville Rd
Bexley DA16 146 C2
Bowes Pk N13 32 B4
Child's Hill NW2 69 B6
Finchley N12 30 A3
Hayes UB3 105 D2
Hillingdon UB10 60 D2
Hornsey N4, N8 50 B3
Ilford IG1 78 D6
Kilburn NW6 91 C5
Merton SW19 179 C3
Sidcup DA14 190 B6
Tottenham N22 32 D2
Walthamstow E17 53 D3
Wandsworth SW18 157 B4
Woodford E18 37 B1
Granville Sq
3 Camberwell
SE15 139 C5
Finsbury
WC1 94 B4 233 D1
Granville St WC1 233 D1
Granwood Ct 5
TW7 130 C4
Grape St WC2 240 A2
Grapsome Cl KT9 213 C1
Grasdene Rd SE18 146 A5
Grasgarth Cl W3 111 A6
Grasmere Ave
Acton W3 111 B6
Kingston u T SW15 177 C6
Locksbottom BR6 226 D5
Merton SW19 201 C6
Ruislip HA4 39 A2
Twickenham TW3 151 D5
Wembley HA9 43 D1
Grasmere Cl TW14 149 D3
Grasmere Ct
Barnes SW13 134 A6
Bowes Pk N22 32 B4
Forest Hill SE26 184 A5
7 Sutton SM2 218 A2
Grasmere Gdns
Harrow HA3 25 A1
Locksbottom BR6 226 D5
Redbridge IG4 56 B4
Grasmere Ho 20 N16 73 B4
Grasmere NW1 231 D1
Grasmere Point 2
SE15 140 C5
Grasmere Prim Sch
N16 73 B4
Grasmere Rd
Bromley BR1 186 D3
Croydon SE25 206 B4
Locksbottom BR6 226 D5
Muswell Hill N10 31 B2
3 Newham E13 99 A5
Streatham SW16 182 B5
Tottenham N17 34 A4
Grasshaven Way
SE28 123 D5
Grassington Cl N11 31 A4

Grassington Rd DA14 190 A6
Grassmere Ct 6 EN1 17 C6
Grassmount SE23 162 B2
Grass Pk N3 29 B2
Grassway SM6 219 C4
Grasvenor Ave EN5 13 C5
Grasvenor Avenue Inf Sch EN5 13 C5
Grateley Ho 10 SW15 156 B3
Gratton Rd W14 113 A3 254 A5
Gratton Terr NW2 68 D5
Graveley Ave WD6 11 A6
Graveley Ho 7 SE8 119 A2
Graveley 18 KT1 176 C1
Gravel Hill
Bexley DA6 169 D6
Church End N3 29 B1
Gravel Hill Cl DA6 169 D5
Gravel Hill Prim Sch DA6 169 D6
Gravel Hill CR0, CR2 223 B1
Gravel Hill Sta CR0 223 A2
Gravel La E1 95 D1 243 C2
Gravel Rd
Keston Mark BR2 226 A6
Twickenham TW2 152 C3
Gravelwood Cl BR7 167 A1
Gravenel Gdns 5 SW17 180 C5
Graveney Gr SE20 184 C3
Graveney Rd SW17 180 C6
Graveney Sch SW17 181 B5
Gravesend Rd W12 112 A6
Graves Est DA16 146 B3
Gray Ave RM8 59 B1
Gray Ct 8 KT2 175 D6
Grayfriars Pas EC1 241 D2
Grayham Cres KT3 199 B5
Grayham Rd KT3 199 B5
Gray Ho SE17 262 B2
Grayland Cl BR1 187 D2
Grayland Ct WC1 233 C1
Grayling Cl E16 98 C3
Grayling Ct
Ealing W5 109 D5
Tottenham Hale N17 52 B5
Grayling Rd N16 73 B6
Grayling Sq E2 96 A4
Grays Cotts UB9 38 C1
Grays Court Hospl RM10 81 D1
Grayscroft Rd SW16 181 D3
Grays Farm Prim Sch BR5 190 B2
Grays Farm Production Village BR5 190 B2
Grays Farm Rd BR5 190 B2
Grayshott Ct 10 SM2 217 D1
Grayshott Rd SW11 137 A2
Gray's Inn Pl WC1 240 D3
Gray's Inn Rd WC1 94 B3 240 D6
Gray's Inn Sq WC1 94 C2 241 A4
Gray's Inn* WC1 94 B2 240 D4
Grays La TW15 170 D6
Grayson Ho EC1 235 B1
Gray's Rd UB10 60 A1
Gray St SE1 116 C4 251 B1
Grayswood Gdns SW20 178 B1
Grayswood Point 14 SW15 156 A3
Gray's Yd W1 238 B2
Graywood Ct N12 30 A3
Grazebrook Prim Sch N16 73 C6
Grazebrook Rd N16 73 B6
Grazeley Ct SE19 183 C5
Great Arthur Ho EC1 242 A5
Great Bell Alley EC2 242 C2
Great Benty UB7 104 A2
Great Brownings SE21 183 D6
Great Bushey Dr N20 13 D3
Great Cambridge Ind Est EN1 18 B6
Great Cambridge Junction N13, N18 33 B6
Great Cambridge Rd
Edmonton N9, N18 17 C3
Enfield EN1 6 A3
Great Castle St W1 239 A2
Great Central Ave HA4 62 C3
Great Central St NW1 92 D2 237 C4
Great Central Way NW10 67 B4
Great Chapel St W1 93 D1 239 C2
Great Chart St SW11 136 A1
Great Chertsey Rd
Chiswick SW14, W4 133 B4
Feltham TW13, TW2 151 C1
Great Church La W6 112 D1
Great College St SW1 116 A3 260 A6
Great Croft WC1 233 B1
Great Cross Ave SE3 142 C5
Great Cumberland Mews W1 237 C1
Great Cumberland Pl W1 92 D1 237 D1
Great Dover St SE1 117 B3 262 C6
Greatdown Rd W7 86 D2
Great Eastern Bldgs 10 E8 74 B2
Great Eastern Ent Ctr E14 119 D4
Great Eastern Pier E14 119 C1
Great Eastern Rd E15 76 B2
Great Eastern St EC2 95 C3 243 A6
Great Eastern Wharf SW11 267 B3
Great Elms Rd BR2 209 C5
Greatfield Ave E6 100 B3
Greatfield Cl
London SE4 141 C1
4 Tufnell Pk N19 71 C4
Great Field
Hendon NW9 27 D2
7 Kentish Town NW5 71 C3
Greatfields Dr UB8 82 C2
Greatfields Rd IG11 101 B5
Great Fleete Way IG11 102 C5
Great Galley Cl IG11 102 C4
Great Gatton Cl CR0 207 A2
Great George St SW1 116 A4 250 A1
Great Guildford Bsns Sq SE1 252 A3
Great Guildford St SE1 117 A5 252 A3
Great Hall The 1 E11 55 B5
Greatham Wlk 8 SW15 156 A3
Great Harry Dr SE9 166 C1
Great James St WC1 240 C4
Great Marlborough St W1 93 C1 239 A1
Great Maze Pond SE1 117 B4 252 D2
Great Newport St WC2 250 A6
Great North Rd
Barnet EN5 1 A2
East Finchley N2 48 C5
New Barnet EN5 13 D6
Great North Way (Barnet By-Pass) NW4 46 D6
Greatorex Ho 13 E1 96 A2
Greatorex St E1 96 A2
Great Ormond St Hospl for Children WC1 94 B3 240 C5
Great Ormond St WC1 94 B3 240 C5
Great Percy St WC1 94 C4 234 A2
Great Peter St SW1 115 D3 259 D5
Great Portland Street Sta W1 93 B3 238 D5
Great Portland St W1 93 B2 238 D4
Great Pulteney St W1 249 B6
Great Queen St WC2 94 A1 240 B2
Great Russell Mans WC1 240 A3
Great Russell St WC1 94 A2 240 A3
Great St Helen's EC3 243 A2
Great St Thomas Apostle EC4 252 B6
Great Scotland Yd SW1, WC2 116 A5 250 A4
Great Smith St SW1 115 D3 259 D6
Great South West Rd TW6, TW14, TW4 148 B6
Great South-West Rd TW5 128 B2
Great Spilmans SE22 161 C6
Greatstone Ho 10 SE20 184 C3
Great Strand NW9 27 D1
Great Suffolk St SE1 116 D5 251 D3
Great Sutton St EC1 94 D3 241 D5
Great Swan Alley EC2 242 C2
Great Thrift BR5 211 A5
Great Titchfield St W1 93 C2 239 A3
Great Tower St EC3 117 C6 253 A6
Great Trinity La EC4 252 B6
Great Turnstile WC2 240 D3
Great Western Ind Pk UB2 108 A4
Great Western Rd W2, W9 91 B2
Great West Ho TW8 131 C6
Great West Rd
Brentford TW7, TW8 131 B6
Chiswick W4, W6 133 B6
Heston TW5, TW7 129 B4
Hounslow TW5, TW7 130 B5
Great West Road Cedars Rd W4 133 A6
Great West Road Hogarth La W4 133 C6
Great West Trad Est TW8 131 B6
Great Winchester St EC2 95 B1 242 D2
Great Windmill St W1 115 D6 249 C6
Greatwood BR7 188 C3
Great Yd SE1 253 B2
Greaves Cl IG11 79 C1
Greaves Cotts 10 E14 97 A2
Greaves Ct N8 50 C5
Greaves Pl SW17 180 C6
Greaves Twr SW10 266 B4
Grebe Ave UB4 84 D1
Grebe Cl
Barking IG11 102 A3
Higham Hill E17 35 A3
Stratford E7 76 D3
Grebe Ct Cheam SM1 217 B3
18 Cubitt Town E14 120 A4
Grebe 3 NW9 27 D1
Grebe Terr 4 KT1 198 A6
Grecian Cres SE19 182 D4
Greek Ct W1 239 D1
Greek St W1 93 D1 239 D1
Greenacre Cl
Barnet EN5 1 B5
Northolt UB5 63 B3
Greenacre Ct E8 74 A3
Greenacre Gdns E17 54 A5
Greenacre Pl SM6 219 B6
Greenacres Ave UB10 60 C5
Greenacres
Bushey WD23 8 B2
Church End N3 29 A1
Greenacres Cl BR6 227 A4
Greenacres Dr HA7 25 B3
Greenacres SE9 166 C5
Green Acres UB4 84 B3
Greenacres Prim Sch SE9 166 C2
Greenacre Sq 26 SE16 118 D4
Green Acres
Sidcup DA14 189 D6
South Croydon CR0 221 D5
Greenacre Wlk N14 15 D1
Green Arbour Ct EC1 241 C2
Green Ave
Ealing W13 109 B3
Edgware NW7 27 C6
Greenaway Gdns NW3 69 D4
Greenaway Ho
Finsbury WC1 234 A1
St John's Wood NW8 229 A6
Greenaway Terr TW19 148 A3
Greenbank Ave HA0 65 A3
Greenbank Cl E4 20 A2
Greenbank Cres NW4 47 A5
Greenbank Lo 2 BR7 188 C2
Green Bank N12 29 D6
Greenbanks HA1 64 C4
Green Bank E1 118 B5
Greenbay Rd SE7 143 D5
Greenberry St NW8 230 A3
Greenbrook Ave EN4 2 A4
Green CE Prim Sch The N17 51 D6
Green CE Sch Holy Trinity (Inf Annexe) The N15 51 D5
Green Cl
Beckenham BR2 208 C6
Carshalton SM5 218 D6
Feltham TW13 173 A5
Kingsbury NW9 45 A3
North End NW11 48 A2
Greencoat Pl SW1 115 C2 259 B4
Greencoat Row SW1 259 B5
Green Court Ave CR0 222 B6
Greencourt Ave HA8 26 D2
Green Court Gdns CR0 222 B6
Greencourt Ho 25 E1 96 D3
Greencourt Rd BR5 211 C4
Greencroft Ave HA4 62 C6
Greencroft Cl E16 99 D2
Greencroft Gdns
Enfield EN1 5 C2
South Hampstead NW6 70 A1
Greencroft HA8 27 A5
Greencroft Rd TW5 129 B4
Green Ct
Ashford TW16 171 D4
2 Willesden NW10 67 C4
Greendale Cl SE22 161 C6
Greendale Ct CR2 221 A2
Green Dale SE22 161 C6
Greendale NW7 27 C6
Green Dragon Ct SE1 252 C3
Green Dragon Ho WC1 240 B2
Green Dragon La
Brentford TW8 110 B1
Southgate N21 16 D5
Green Dragon Prim Sch TW8 132 A6
Green Dragon Yd 24 E1 96 A2
Green Dr UB1 107 C5
Greene Ct 20 SE14 140 D6
Greene Ho SE1 262 C5
Green Elms IG6 57 A6
Green End
Chessington KT9 214 A4
Edmonton N21 16 D2
Greenend Rd W4 111 C4
Greener Ct 26 EN3 7 C6
Greener Ho 3 SW4 137 D2
Green Farm Cl BR6 227 D3
Greenfell Mans SE8 141 D6
Greenfield Ave KT5 198 D3
Greenfield Ct SE9 166 A1
Greenfield Dr
Bromley BR1 187 C1
Fortis Green N2 48 D5
Greenfield Gdns
Cricklewood NW2 69 A5
Crofton BR5 211 B2
Dagenham RM9 102 D6
Greenfield Ho 28 SW19 156 D3
Greenfield Rd
Dagenham RM9 102 C6
South Tottenham N15 51 C4
Whitechapel E1 96 A1
Greenfields Prim Sch WD19 22 C5
Greenfields UB1 85 C1
Greenfield Way HA2 41 D6
GREENFORD 86 A4
Greenford Ave
Ealing W7 86 C1
Southall UB1 107 B6
Greenford Gdns UB6 86 A4
Greenford High Sch UB6 85 C4
Greenford Rdbt UB6 86 B5
Greenford Rd
Greenford UB6 86 A3
Sudbury HA1, UB6 64 C3
Sutton SM1 217 D4
Greenford Sta UB6 86 B6
Greengate St E13 99 B4
Greengate UB6 65 B2
Green Gdns BR6 227 A3
Greenhalgh Wlk N2 48 A5
Greenham Cl SE1 251 A1
Greenham Cres E4 35 B4
Greenham Ho
5 Hackney E9 96 C6
Isleworth TW7 130 B2
Greenham Rd N10 31 A1
Greenhaven Dr SE28 102 B1
Greenheath Bsns Ctr 3 E2 96 B3
Green Hedges 8 TW1 153 C5
Greenheys Dr E18 54 D6
GREENHILL 42 D4
Greenhill IG9 21 C3
Greenhill Cts SE7 122 B1
Greenhill Gdns UB5 85 B5
Greenhill Gr E12 78 A4
Greenhill NW3 70 B4
Greenhill Par EN5 13 D6
Greenhill Pk
Harlesden NW10 89 C6
New Barnet EN5 13 D6
Greenhill Rd
Harlesden NW10 89 C6
Harrow HA1 42 C3
Greenhill's Rents EC1 241 C4
Greenhills Terr 18 N1 73 B2
Greenhill SM1 218 A6
Greenhill Terr
Northolt UB5 85 B5
Woolwich SE18 122 B1
Greenhill Way
Harrow HA1 42 C3
Wembley Pk HA9 66 D6
Greenhill HA9 66 D6
Green Hill SE18 122 B1
Greenhithe Cl DA15 167 C4
Green Ho TW7 130 D3
Greenholm Rd SE9 166 D6
Green Ho The 5 SW19 157 A3
Green Hundred Rd SE15 140 A6
Greenhurst Rd SE27 182 C5
Greening Ho SE13 142 B1
Greening St SE2 124 C2
Green La
Ashford TW16 171 D4
Chessington KT9 214 A1
Chislehurst SE9 166 D1
Dagenham RM8 81 B6
East Molesey KT8 195 D4
Edgware HA8 26 C5
Feltham TW13 173 A5
Hanwell W7 108 C4
Hendon NW4 46 D4
Hillingdon UB8 83 A2
Hounslow TW4 128 C1
Ilford IG1, IG3 79 C6
Morden SM4 201 D3
Greenland Cres UB2 106 D3
Greenland Ho
Bermondsey SE8 118 D1
4 Mile End E1 97 A3
Greenland Mews SE8 118 D1
Greenland Pl NW1 231 D6
Greenland Quay SE16 118 D2
Greenland Rd
Barnet EN5 12 C5
Camden Town NW1 93 C6 232 A6
Greenlands
Borehamwood WD6 11 B5
Chessington KT19 214 D3
Greenland St NW1 231 D6
Greenland Way CR0 203 D2
Green Lane Bsns Pk SE9 166 C2
Green Lane Cotts HA7 25 B6
Green Lane Gdns CR7 183 A1
Green Lane Mews SM4 201 D3
Green Lane Prim Sch KT4 200 B2
Green Lanes
London N4, N8, N15 50 D2
Palmers Green N13 16 C1
West Ewell KT19 215 C1
Green La
New Malden KT3 199 A4
New Malden KT4 200 A1
Penge SE20 184 D3
Shepperton TW17 193 A4
South Norwood CR7, SW16 182 C2
Stanmore HA7 25 B5
Greenlaw Ct W5 87 D1
Greenlaw Gdns KT3 199 D2
Greenlawn La TW8 109 D2
Greenlawns N12 29 D4
Green Lawns
Ruislip HA4 40
8 Woolwich SE18 122
Greenlaw St SE18 122
Green Leaf Ave SM6 219
Greenleaf Cl 8 SW2 160
Greenleaf Ct N20 14
Greenleafe Dr IG6 56
Greenleaf Prim Sch E17 53
Greenleaf Rd
5 Newham E6 99
Walthamstow E17 53
Greenleaf Way HA3 42
Greenlea Pk SW19 180
Green Leas TW16 171
Green Leas Cl TW16 171
Green Leas KT1 198
Greenleaves Ct TW15 170
Green Link Wlk TW9 132
Green Man Gdns W13 109
Green Man Intc E11 54
Green Man La
Ealing W13 109
Hatton TW14 128
Greenman St N1 95 A6 235
Greenmead Cl SE25 206
Greenmead Sch SW15 156
Green Moor Link N21 16
Greenmoor Rd EN3 6
Greenoak Pl EN4 2
Green Oaks UB2 106
Greenoak Way SW19 178
Greenock Rd
Mitcham SW16 181
11 South Acton W3 111
Greeno Cres TW17 192
Greenpark Ct HA0 65
Green Park Sta W1 115 C5 249
Green Park* SW1, W1 115 B4 248
Green Park Way UB6 86
Green Pond Cl E17 53
Green Pond Rd E17 53
Green Pt E15 76
Green Rd
East Barnet N14 15
Whetstone N20 14
Green Ride IG10, E4 21
Greenroof Way SE10 120
Green Sch (Girls) The TW7 131
Greens Ct W1 249
Green's Ct W11 244
Greens Ct HA9 65
Greens End SE18 122
Greenshank Cl E17 35
Greenshaw High Sch SM1 218
Greenshields Ind Est E16 121
Greenside Cl
Catford SE6 164
Whetstone N20 14
Greenside RM8 58
Greenside Prim Sch W12 112
Greenside Rd
Shepherd's Bush W12 112
Thornton Heath CR0 204
Greenside DA5 169
Greenslade Prim Sch SE18 145
Greenslade Rd IG11 79
Greensleeves Ho UB2 107
Greensleeves Manor SM2 21
Greenstead Ave IG8 37
Greenstead Cl IG8 37
Greenstead Gdns
Putney SW15 156
Woodford IG8 37
Green St Enfield EN3 6
Mayfair W1 115 A6 248
Newham E13 99
Greenstone Mews E11 55
GREEN STREET GREEN 227
Green Street Green Prim Sch BR6 227
Greenstreet Hill SE4 140

en St
unbury TW16 .... 172 A1
ton E7 .... 77 C1
eensward Ho
W6 .... 136 A3
een Terr EC1 .... 234 B1
een The Acton W3 .. 89 C1
uckhurst Hill IG9 .... 21 B3
hingford E4 .... 20 B3
aygate KT10 .... 212 D2
aling W5 .... 109 D6
dmonton N9 .... 18 A2
rith DA7 .... 147 C4
alconwood DA16 .... 145 C1
eltham TW13 .... 150 B2
rove Pk BR1 .... 165 A1
ackbridge SM6 .... 219 A6
ayes BR2 .... 209 A2
eston TW5 .... 129 C6
ngston u T KT3 .... 177 A1
erton SM4 .... 201 A5
almers Green N14 .... 15 D1
ichmond TW9 .... 131 D1
7 Richmond TW9 .... 153 D6
idcup DA14 .... 190 A5
outhall UB2 .... 107 B4
outhgate N21 .... 16 C4
t Paul's Cray BR5 .... 190 B3
tratford E15 .... 76 D2
utton SM1 .... 217 D5
ottenham N17 .... 33 A4
wickenham TW2 .... 152 C2
Jpper Halliford
TW17 .... 193 C5
Uxbridge UB10 .... 61 A6
Wallington SM5 .... 219 A4
Wanstead E11 .... 55 B3
Wembley HA0 .... 65 A6
Wimbledon SW19 .... 178 D5
Woodford IG8 .... 37 A5
een Vale
Bexley DA6 .... 168 D6
Ealing W5 .... 88 B1
eenvale Rd SE9 .... 144 C1
eenvale Sch SE23 163 A1
een Verges HA7 .... 25 D3
eenview Ave CR0 .. 207 A3
een View KT9 .... 214 B1
eenview Cl W3 .... 111 C5
eenview Ct
Ashford TW15 .... 170 B6
East Dulwich SE22 ... 140 A1
Oakleigh Pk N20 .... 14 A4
Wandsworth SW18 .. 158 C4
eenway Ave E17 .... 54 B5
een Way BR2 .... 210 A3
eenway BR7 .... 188 D5
eenway Cl
Finsbury Pk N4 .... 73 A6
Friern Barnet N11 .... 31 A4
Hendon NW9 .... 27 B1
2 South Tottenham
N15 .... 51 D5
Totteridge N20 .... 13 C2
eenway Ct
Hayes UB4 .... 84 B3
Ilford IG1 .... 56 D1
2 Newham E15 .... 98 C5
eenway RM8 .... 58 C1
een Way SE9 .... 165 D6
eenway Gdns
Croydon CR0 .... 223 B5
Greenford UB6 .... 85 D4
een Way Gdns
HA3 .... 24 C1
eenway Gdns NW9 .. 27 B1
eenway
Harrow HA3 .... 44 A4
Hayes UB4 .... 84 B3
Palmers Green N14 .... 16 A2
Pinner HA5 .... 22 B1
reenways
Beckenham BR3 .... 185 C1
5 Forest Hill SE26 .. 184 C6
Hinchley Wood KT10 . 212 C4
reenways The 1
TW1 .... 153 A5
reen Way TW16 .... 194 A5
reenway The
Harrow HA3 .... 24 C2
Hendon NW9 .... 27 B1
Hounslow TW4 .... 129 B1
Pinner HA5 .... 41 B3
Uxbridge UB8 .... 82 A5
West Ruislip UB10 .... 61 A6
reenway
Totteridge N20 .... 13 C2
Wallington SM6 .... 219 C4
West Barnes SW20 .. 200 C5
Woodford IG8 .... 37 C5
reenwell St W1 ... 238 D5
REENWICH 142 C6
reenwich Acad
SE10 .... 141 D4
reenwich Borough
Mus* SE18 .... 123 D1

Greenwich Bsns Ctr
SE10 .... 141 D5
Greenwich Bsns Pk
SE10 .... 141 D5
Greenwich Church St
SE10 .... 142 A6
Greenwich Coll
SE10 .... 142 A5
Greenwich Com Coll
Plumstead Ctr
SE18 .... 123 A2
Greenwich Cres E6 .. 100 A2
Greenwich Ct 11 E1 ... 96 B1
Greenwich High Rd
SE10 .... 141 D5
Greenwich Ho SE13 .. 164 B5
Greenwich Hts
SE18 .... 144 A5
Greenwich Ind Est
SE10 .... 141 D5
Greenwich London Coll
SE18 .... 122 D2
Greenwich Mkt 2
SE10 .... 142 A6
Greenwich Mkt
SE10 .... 142 A6
Greenwich Park*
SE10 .... 142 C5
Greenwich Park St
SE10 .... 142 B6
Greenwich Quay
SE8 .... 141 D6
Greenwich Sh Pk
SE7 .... 121 B2
Greenwich South St
SE10 .... 142 A4
Greenwich Sta
SE10 .... 141 D5
Greenwich View Pl
E14 .... 119 D3
Green Wlk
Bermondsey SE1 .... 263 A5
Hampton TW12 .... 173 B4
Hendon NW4 .... 46 D4
Ruislip HA4 .... 39 D1
Southall UB2 .... 107 C1
Green Wlk The E4 .... 20 B3
Greenwood Ave
Dagenham RM10 .... 81 D4
Enfield EN3 .... 7 A4
Greenwood Cl
Bushey WD23 .... 8 C3
Merton SM4 .... 201 A5
Orpington BR5 .... 211 C3
Sidcup DA15 .... 168 A2
Thames Ditton KT7 .. 197 A1
Greenwood Dr E4 .... 36 B5
Greenwood Gdns
N13 .... 16 D1
Greenwood Ho
Finsbury WC1 .... 234 A1
8 Nunhead SE4 .... 140 D1
Wood Green N22 .... 32 C2
Greenwood La
TW12 .... 173 D5
Green Wood NW5 .... 71 C3
Greenwood Mans 9
IG11 .... 80 A1
Greenwood Pk KT2 .. 177 C3
Greenwood Pl NW5 .... 71 B3
Greenwood Prim Sch
UB5 .... 64 A3
Greenwood 8
SW19 .... 156 D4
Greenwood Rd
Dalston E8 .... 74 A2
Hinchley Wood KT7 .. 213 A6
Isleworth TW7 .... 130 D2
Mitcham CR4 .... 203 D6
Thornton Heath CR0 . 205 A2
West Ham E13 .... 98 D5
Greenwoods The
HA2 .... 64 A5
Greenwood Terr
NW10 .... 89 B5
Greenwood 3 IG8 .... 37 A3
Green Wrythe Cres
SM5 .... 202 C1
Green Wrythe La
SM5 .... 202 C2
Green Wrythe Prim Sch
SM5 .... 202 B3
Green Yd WC1 .... 240 D6
Greer Rd HA3 .... 24 A2
Greet Ho SE1 .... 251 B1
Greet St SE1 .. 116 C5 251 B3
Greg Cl E10 .... 54 A3
Gregor Mews SE3 .... 143 A5
Gregory Cres SE9 .... 165 D4
Gregory Ho SE3 .... 143 B3
Gregory Pl W8 .... 245 C2
Gregory Rd
Dagenham RM6 .... 58 D5
Southall UB2 .... 107 C3
Greig City Acad N8 .... 50 A5
Greig Cl N8 .... 50 A4
Greig Ho 9 TW10 .... 153 C1

Greig Terr SE17 .... 138 D6
Grenaby Ave CR0 .... 205 B2
Grenaby Rd CR0 .... 205 B2
Grenada Ho 18 E14 .... 119 B6
Grenada Rd SE7 .... 143 C5
Grenade St E14 .... 119 B6
Grenadier St E16 .... 122 C5
Grena Gdns TW9 .... 132 B1
Grenard Cl SE15 .... 140 A5
Grena Rd TW10,
TW9 .... 132 B1
Grendon Gdns HA9 .... 66 C6
Grendon Ho
29 Hackney E9 .... 74 C1
Pentonville N1 .... 233 C3
Grendon St
NW8 .... 92 C3 237 A6
Grenfell Ct NW7 .... 28 B4
Grenfell Gdns
Harrow HA3 .... 44 A2
Ilford IG2 .... 57 D4
Grenfell Ho SE5 .... 139 A5
Grenfell Rd
Mitcham CR4,
SW17 .... 180 D4
Shepherd's Bush
W11 .... 112 D6
Grenfell Twr 5
W11 .... 112 D6
Grenfell Wlk 4
W11 .... 112 D6
Grengate Lodge 2
E13 .... 99 B4
Grenier Apartments 11
SE15 .... 140 B5
Grennell Cl SM1 .... 218 B6
Grennell Rd SM1 .... 218 A6
Grenoble Gdns N13 ... 32 C4
Grenville Cl
Church End N3 .... 29 B2
Tolworth KT5 .... 199 A1
Grenville Ct
3 Dulwich SE19 .... 183 D5
Ealing W13 .... 87 B2
Edgware HA8 .... 26 D6
Grenville Gdns IG8 ... 37 C3
Grenville Ho
28 Bow E3 .... 97 A5
4 Deptford SE8 .... 141 C6
Grenville Lo N6 .... 49 C2
Grenville Mans WC1 240 A6
Grenville Mews
Hampton TW12 .... 173 D5
South Kensington
SW7 .... 256 A3
Grenville Pl
Burnt Oak NW7 .... 27 B5
South Kensington
SW7 .... 114 A2 256 A4
Grenville Rd N19 .... 50 A1
Grenville St WC1 .... 240 B5
Gresham Almshouses
3 SW9 .... 138 B1
Gresham Ave N20 .... 30 D6
Gresham Cl Enfield EN2 . 5 A2
Sidcup DA5 .... 169 B5
Gresham Coll
EC1 .... 94 C2 241 B3
Gresham Ct TW3 .... 130 A4
Gresham Dr RM6 .... 58 B3
Gresham Gdns NW11 .. 47 A1
Gresham Ho
4 Teddington
TW11 .... 174 D5
3 Thames Ditton
KT7 .... 197 A2
West Barnes KT3 .... 200 B5
Gresham Lo E17 .... 53 D4
Gresham Pl 2 N19 .... 71 D6
Gresham Rd
Beckenham BR3 .... 185 A1
Brixton SW9 .... 138 C2
Canning Town E16 .... 99 B1
Croydon SE25 .... 206 A5
East Ham E6 .... 100 B5
Edgware HA8 .... 26 B4
Hampton TW12 .... 173 C4
Hillingdon UB10 .... 82 C5
Hounslow TW3,
TW5 .... 130 A4
Willesden NW10 .... 67 B3
Gresham St
EC2 .... 95 A1 242 B2
Gresham Way Est
SW19 .... 157 D1
Gresham Way
SW19 .... 157 C1
Gresley Cl London N15 . 51 B5
Walthamstow E17 .... 53 A3
Gresley Ho SW8 .... 269 D2
Gresley Rd N19 .... 49 C2
Gressenhall Rd
SW18 .... 157 B4
Gressenham Ct 7
HA7 .... 25 C6
Gresse St W1 .. 93 D1 239 C2
Gresswell Cl DA14 ... 168 A1

Greswell St SW6 .... 134 D4
Greta Ho SE3 .... 142 D6
Gretton Ho 2 E2 .... 96 C4
Gretton Rd N17 .... 33 D3
Greville Cl TW1 .... 153 B4
Greville Ct
Harrow HA1 .... 64 C4
3 Lower Clapton E5 ... 74 B5
Greville Hall NW6 .... 91 D5
Greville Ho
Harrow HA2 .... 42 B1
Knightsbridge SW1 .. 258 A6
Putney SW15 .... 134 D2
Greville Lo
5 Bayswater W2 .... 91 D1
16 London N12 .... 29 D6
Greville Mews 5
NW6 .... 91 D6
Greville Pl W9 .... 91 D5
Greville Rd
Kilburn NW6 .... 91 D5
Richmond TW10 .... 154 B5
Walthamstow E17 .... 54 A5
Greville St
EC1 .... 94 C2 241 B4
Grey Cl NW11 .... 48 A3
Grey Coat Hospital Sch
(St Michaels) The
SW1 .... 115 D2 259 C3
Grey Coat Hospital Sch
The SW1 ... 115 D3 259 C5
Greycoat Pl
SW1 .... 115 D3 259 C5
Greycoat St
SW1 .... 115 D3 259 C5
Greycot Rd BR3 .... 185 C5
Grey Court Sch
TW10 .... 153 C1
Grey Eagle St
E1 .... 95 D3 243 D5
Greyfell Cl HA7 .... 25 B5
Greyfriars 16 SE26 ... 162 A1
Greyfriars Ho SE3 .... 142 D6
Grey Ho 27 W12 .... 112 B6
Greyhound Ct WC2 .. 251 A6
Greyhound Hill NW4 .. 46 B6
Greyhound La
SW16 .... 181 D4
Greyhound Rd
College Pk NW10 .... 90 B4
Fulham W6 . 135 A6 264 A6
Sutton SM1 .... 218 A3
Tottenham N17 .... 51 C6
Greyhound Terr
SW16 .... 181 C2
Greyladies Gdns
SE10 .... 142 A3
Greys Park Cl BR2 .. 225 D3
Greystead Rd SE23 ... 162 C4
Greystoke Ave HA5 .... 41 C6
Greystoke Ct W5 .... 88 B3
Greystoke Dr HA4 .... 38 D3
Greystoke Gdns
Ealing W5 .... 88 B3
Enfield EN2 .... 3 D1
Greystoke Ho
Ealing W5 .... 88 A3
Peckham SE15 .... 140 A6
Greystoke Lo W5 .... 88 B3
Greystoke Park Terr
W5 .... 88 A4
Greystoke Pl EC4 ... 241 B2
Greystone Gdns HA3 .. 43 C3
Greystones TW2 .... 152 A2
Greyswood St SW16 .. 181 B4
Greytiles TW11 .... 174 D4
Grey Turner Ho W12 ... 90 A1
Grice Ct N1 .... 73 A2
Grierson Ho SW16 ... 181 C6
Grierson Rd
Forest Hill SE23 .... 162 D4
Forest Hill SE23 .... 163 A5
Griffin Cl NW10 .... 68 B3
Griffin Ct
8 Brentford
TW8 .... 132 A6
Chiswick W4 .... 111 D1
Griffin Ctr TW14 .... 150 B5
Griffin Ctr The KT1 . 175 D1
Griffin Ct W12 .... 112 B5
Griffin Gate SW15 .... 134 D2
Griffin Lo N12 .... 30 A6
Griffin Manor Way
SE28 .... 123 B3
Griffin Park (Brentford
FC) TW8 .... 131 D6
Griffin Rd
Plumstead SE18 .... 123 B1
Tottenham N17 .... 33 C1
Griffins Cl N21 .... 17 B4
Griffin Way
Sunbury TW16 .... 172 A1
Woolwich SE28 .... 123 C3
Griffith Cl RM8 .... 58 C1
Griffiths Cl KT4 .... 216 B6
Griffiths Ho 2
SE18 .... 144 D6

Griffiths Rd SW19 ... 179 D3
Griffon Ho 3 SW11 .. 136 C2
Griggs App IG1 .... 79 A6
Grigg's Pl SE1 .... 263 B5
Griggs Rd E10 .... 54 A3
Grilse Cl N9 .... 34 B6
Grimaldi Ho N1 .... 233 C4
Grimsby Gr E16 .... 122 D5
Grimsby St
8 Bethnal Green
E2 .... 96 A3
Shoreditch E2 .... 243 D6
Grimsdyke Fst & Mid
Sch HA5 .... 23 B4
Grimsdyke Rd HA5 .... 23 A3
Grimsel Path SE5 .... 138 D5
Grimshaw Cl N6 .... 49 A2
Grimston Rd SW6 .... 135 B3
Grimthorpe Ho EC1 . 241 C6
Grimwade Ave CR0 .. 222 A5
Grimwade Cl SE15 ... 140 C2
Grimwood Rd TW1 ... 152 D4
Grindall Cl CR0 .... 220 D4
Grindall Ho 26 E1 .... 96 B3
Grindal St SE1 .... 251 A1
Grindleford Ave N11 .. 15 A2
Grindley Gdns CR0 .. 205 D3
Grindley Ho 3 E3 .... 97 B2
Grinling Gibbons Prim
Sch SE8 .... 141 B6
Grinling Ho 6 SE18 .. 122 C2
Grinling Pl SE8 .... 141 C6
Grinstead Rd SE8 .... 119 A1
Grisedale NW1 .... 232 A2
Grittleton Ave HA9 .... 66 D2
Grittleton Rd W9 .... 91 C3
Grizedale Terr 8
SE23 .... 162 B2
Grogan Cl TW12 .... 173 B4
Groombridge Cl
DA16 .... 168 A6
Groombridge Ho 1
SE20 .... 184 D3
Groombridge Rd E9 ... 74 D1
Groom Cl BR2 .... 209 B5
Groom Cres SW18 ... 158 B4
Groome Ho SE11 .... 260 D3
Groomfield Cl
SW17 .... 181 A6
Groom Pl
SW1 .... 115 A3 258 B6
Grooms Dr HA5 .... 40 A4
Grosmont Rd SE18 ... 123 D1
Grosse Way SW15 .... 156 B5
Grosslea SM4 .... 202 B4
Grosvenor Ave
Canonbury N5 .... 73 A3
Harrow HA2 .... 41 D3
Hayes UB4 .... 83 D5
Mortlake SW14 .... 133 C2
Richmond TW10 .... 154 A6
Wallington SM5,
SM6 .... 219 A2
Grosvenor Bridge
SW1 .... 137 B6 268 D6
Grosvenor Cotts
SW1 .... 258 A4
Grosvenor Court Mans
W2 .... 237 C1
Grosvenor Cres
UB10 .... 82 D6
Grosvenor Cres Mews
SW1 .... 248 A1
Grosvenor Cres
Queensbury NW9 .... 44 C5
Westminster
SW1 .... 115 A4 248 B1
Grosvenor Ct
4 Acton W3 .... 110 C5
Brondesbury Pk NW6 .. 90 D6
3 Ealing W5 .... 110 A6
3 Edgware NW7 .... 27 B5
Gunnersbury W4 .... 110 D1
Leyton E10 .... 53 D1
Morden SM4 .... 201 C5
Oakwood N14 .... 15 C4
Penge SE19 .... 183 D4
22 Poplar E14 .... 97 B1
Putney SW15 .... 157 A6
1 Sutton SM2 .... 218 A2
Teddington TW11 .... 175 A4
3 Wanstead E11 .... 55 B4
2 Wimbledon
SW19 .... 179 A4
Grosvenor Gdns
Cricklewood NW2 .... 68 C3
Hornsey N10 .... 49 C6
Kingston u T KT2 .... 175 D4
Grosvenor Gdns Mews E
SW1 .... 258 D6
Grosvenor Gdns Mews
N SW1 .... 258 C5
Grosvenor Gdns Mews S
SW1 .... 258 D5
Grosvenor Gdns
Mortlake SW14 .... 133 C2
Newham E6 .... 99 D4

Grosvenor Gdns
continued
Southgate N14 .... 15 D6
Temple Fortune
NW11 .... 47 B4
Wallington SM6 .... 219 C1
Westminster
SW1 .... 115 B3 258 D5
Woodford IG8 .... 37 B4
Grosvenor Hill Ct
W1 .... 248 C6
Grosvenor Hill
Mayfair
W1 .... 115 B6 248 C6
Wimbledon SW19 .... 179 A4
Grosvenor Ho
5 Sutton SM1 .... 217 D3
Upper Clapton E5 .... 52 A1
Grosvenor Hts E4 .... 20 C4
Grosvenor Lo
London N20 .... 14 A1
4 Woodford E18 .... 36 D1
Grosvenor Par 1
W5 .... 110 C5
Grosvenor Park Rd
E17 .... 53 D4
Grosvenor Park
SE5 .... 139 A5
Grosvenor Pier SW1 269 C6
Grosvenor Pk SE5 .... 139 A6
Grosvenor Pl
SW1 .... 115 B4 248 C1
Grosvenor Rd
Acton Green W4 .... 111 A1
Bexley DA6 .... 169 A6
Brentford TW8 .... 131 D6
Croydon SE25 .... 206 A5
Dagenham RM8 .... 59 B1
Ealing W7 .... 109 A5
Edmonton N9 .... 18 B3
Erith DA17 .... 147 C6
Finchley N3 .... 29 C3
Hounslow TW3,
TW4 .... 129 B2
Ilford IG1 .... 79 A5
Leyton E10 .... 54 A1
Muswell Hill N10 .... 31 B2
Newham E6 .... 99 D6
Orpington BR6 .... 211 C3
Pimlico
SW1 .... 137 C6 269 B6
Richmond TW10 .... 154 A6
Southall UB2 .... 107 B3
Twickenham TW1 .... 153 A3
Upton E7 .... 77 B2
Wallington SM6 .... 219 B3
Wanstead E11 .... 55 B4
West Wickham BR4 .. 223 D6
Grosvenor Residences
1 W14 .... 112 D3
Grosvenor Rise E
E17 .... 53 D4
Grosvenor Sq
W1 .... 115 A6 248 B6
Grosvenor St
W1 .... 115 B6 248 C6
Grosvenor Terr SE5 .. 139 A6
Grosvenor The
NW11 .... 47 D2
Grosvenor Vale HA4 ... 61 D6
Grosvenor Way E5 .... 74 C6
Grosvernor Wharf Rd
E14 .... 120 B2
Grote's Bldgs SE3 .... 142 C3
Grote's Pl SE3 .... 142 C3
Groton Rd SW18 .... 157 D2
Grotto Ct SE1 .... 252 A2
Grotto Pas W1 .... 238 A4
Grotto Rd TW1 .... 152 D2
Grove Ave
Cheam SM1 .... 217 C2
Ealing W7 .... 86 C1
Finchley N3 .... 29 C3
Pinner HA5 .... 41 A5
Twickenham TW1 .... 152 D3
Wood Green N10 .... 31 C1
Grovebury Ct
Bexley DA6 .... 169 D6
Southgate N14 .... 15 D4
Grovebury Rd SE2 ... 124 B4
Grove Cl
East Barnet N14 .... 15 B4
Forest Hill SE23 .... 163 A3
Hayes BR2 .... 225 A6
Ickenham UB10 .... 60 C3
Kingston u T KT1 .... 198 B5
Grove Crescent Rd
E15 .... 76 B2
Grove Cres
Feltham TW13 .... 173 A6
Kingsbury NW9 .... 45 B5
Kingston u T KT1 .... 198 A6
Walton-on-T KT12 .... 194 B2
Woodford E18 .... 36 D1

Grove Ct Barnet EN5 1 B2
Camberwell SE5 139 C3
Clapham SW4 137 C2
Ealing W5 110 A5
East Molesey KT8 196 B4
3 Forest Hill SE26 185 A6
Hounslow TW3 129 C1
8 Kingston u T KT1 198 A6
New Malden KT3 199 C6
Penge SE20 184 B3
Seething Wells KT6 197 D4
South Kensington SW10 256 B1
St John's Wood NW8 229 C2
Grovedale Rd N19 71 D6
Grove Dwellings E1 96 C2
Grove End Gdns NW8 229 B3
Grove End NW5 71 B4
Grove End Ho NW8 229 C1
Grove End La KT10 196 B1
Grove End Rd NW8 92 B4 229 C1
Grove End E18 36 D1
Grove Farm Ct CR4 202 D4
Grovefield 1 N11 31 B6
Grove Footpath KT5 198 A5
Grove Gdns Enfield EN3 6 D5
Hendon NW4 46 A5
Lisson Gr NW8 92 C4 230 B1
Teddington TW11 175 A6
Grove Glade Shop Hall W13 109 A5
Grove Green Rd E11 76 B6
Grove Hall Ct Bow E3 97 C5
St John's Wood NW8 92 A4 229 B2
Grovehill Ct BR1 186 D4
Grove Hill HA1 42 C2
Grove Hill Rd
Camberwell SE5 139 C2
Harrow HA1 42 D2
Grove Hill E18 36 D1
Grove Ho
Blackheath SE3 142 D3
Chelsea SW3 267 B6
Hendon N3 46 D6
Grove House Rd N8 50 A5
Grove La
Camberwell SE5 139 C2
Hillingdon UB8 82 B3
Kingston u T KT1 198 A5
Groveland Ave SW16 182 B3
Groveland Ct EC4 242 B1
Groveland Rd BR3 207 B6
Grovelands Cl
Camberwell SE5 139 C3
Harrow HA2 63 D5
Grovelands Ct N14 15 D4
Grovelands KT8 195 C5
Grovelands Inf Sch KT12 194 B3
Grovelands KT1 197 D5
Grovelands Priory (Private Hospl) N14 16 A3
Grovelands Rd
Palmers Green N13 16 B1
South Tottenham N15 52 A3
St Paul's Cray BR5 190 A3
Groveland Way KT3 199 B4
Grove Lane Terr SE5 139 B3
Groveley Ho 7 N4 51 A2
Groveley Rd TW13, TW16 171 D5
Grove Lo
Clapham SW4 137 C1
Cranley Gdns N10 49 C5
Grove Mans
London SW4 136 D1
2 Shepherd's Bush W6 112 C4
3 Stamford Hill N16 52 A1
Grove Market Pl SE9 166 B5
Grove Mews W6 112 C3
Grove Mill CR4 202 C4
Grove Mill Pl SM5 219 A5
GROVE PARK W4 133 A4
SE9 165 B1
Grove Park Ave E4 35 D3
Grove Park Bridge W4 133 A5
Grove Park Gdns W4 133 A5
Grove Park Mews W4 133 A5
Grove Park Prim Sch W4 133 A6
Grove Park Rd
Chiswick W4 132 D5
Mottingham SE9, SE12 165 D2
South Tottenham N15 51 C5
Grove Park Sch NW9 45 A5
Grove Park Sta SE12 165 B1
Grove Park Terr W4 132 D6
Grove Pk
Camberwell SE5 139 C3
Kingsbury NW9 45 B5
Wanstead E11 55 B4
Grove Pl Acton W3 111 A5
Balham SW12 159 B5
Hampstead NW3 70 B5
Grove Prim Sch RM6 58 C4
Grover Ct SE13 141 D3
Grove Rd Acton W3 111 A5
Barnes SW13 133 D3
Belmont SM2 217 C2
Bow E3 97 A5
Brentford TW8 109 C1
Chingford E4 20 A1
Cockfosters EN4 2 C2
Dagenham RM6 58 C3
Ealing W5 109 D6
East Molesey KT8 196 B5
Edgware HA8 26 C4
8 Erith DA17 147 B6
Friern Barnet N11 31 B5
Hounslow TW3 129 C1
Kingston u T KT6 197 D4
Leytonstone E11 54 D2
Merton SW19 180 A3
Mitcham CR4 181 B1
North Finchley N12 30 B5
Pinner HA5 41 B4
Grove Rd Prim Sch TW3 129 C1
Grove Rd
Richmond TW10 154 B5
Shepperton TW17 193 A3
South Tottenham N15 51 C4
Spring Gr TW7 130 C4
Thornton Heath CR7 204 C5
Twickenham TW2 152 B1
Uxbridge UB8 60 A1
Walthamstow E17 53 D4
Grove Rd W EN3 6 C6
Grove Rd
Willesden NW2 68 C2
Woodford E18 36 D1
Grover Ho
4 London SW4 159 C6
Vauxhall SE11 260 D1
Groves Ho UB4 84 B4
Groveside Cl
Acton W3 88 C1
Carshalton SM5 218 C6
Groveside Ct SW11 136 B3
Groveside Rd E4 20 C1
Grove St
Deptford SE8 119 B1
Edmonton N18 33 D4
Grovestile Waye TW14 149 B4
Grove Terrace Mews NW5 71 B5
Grove Terr
Gospel Oak NW5 71 B4
Southall UB1 107 C6
Teddington TW11 175 A6
Grove The
Bexley DA6 146 D1
Dulwich SE21 162 A3
Ealing W5 110 A5
Edgware HA8 26 D6
Edmonton N13 32 C6
Enfield EN2 4 C3
Finchley N3 29 C3
Hendon NW11 47 A2
Highgate N6 49 A1
Hornsey N8 49 D4
Hounslow TW7 130 C4
Ickenham UB10 60 C3
Kingsbury NW9 45 B4
Sidcup DA14 191 A6
Southall UB6 86 A1
Stratford E15 76 C2
Stroud Green N4 50 B2
Teddington TW11 175 A6
1 Twickenham TW1 153 B5
Walton-on-T KT12 194 B2
West Wickham BR4 224 A6
Grove Vale
Chislehurst West BR7 188 C4
East Dulwich SE22 139 D1
Groveway
Dagenham RM8 80 D4
South Lambeth SW9 138 B4 270 D1
Grove Way
Thames Ditton KT10 196 A1
Wembley HA9 67 A3
Grovewood Ct 6 TW7 130 C4
Grovewood Ho NW2 69 B6
Grovewood 9 TW9 132 C4
Grummant Rd SE15 139 D4
Grundy St E14 97 D1
Gruneisen Rd N3 29 D3
Guardian Angels RC Prim Sch E3 97 A4
Guardian Ct SE12 164 C6
Guards Mus The* SW1 115 C4 249 B1
Gubyon Ave SE24 160 D6
Guerin Sq E3 97 B4
Guernsey Cl TW5 129 C5
Guernsey Gr SE24 161 A4
Guernsey Ho
10 Canonbury N1 73 A2
Enfield EN3 6 D5
Guernsey Rd
11 Canonbury N1 73 A2
Leytonstone E11 54 B1
Guibal Rd SE12 165 B3
Guildersfield Rd SW16 182 A3
Guildford Ave TW13 150 A2
Guildford Gr SE10 141 D4
Guildford Ho 23 SE5 139 A3
Guildford Rd
Chingford E17 36 A2
Ilford IG3 79 C6
Newham E6 100 B1
South Lambeth SW8 138 A4 270 B2
Thornton Heath CR0 205 B3
Guildford Way SM6 220 A3
Guildhall Bldgs EC2 242 C2
Guild Hall* EC2 95 A1 242 B2
Guildhall Ho EC2 242 C2
Guildhall Sch Music & Drama EC2 95 A2 242 B4
Guildhall Yd EC2 242 B2
Guildhouse St SW1 115 C2 259 A3
Guild Ho SW19 179 B4
Guildown Ave N12 29 D6
Guild Rd SE7 143 D6
Guildsway E17 35 B2
Guilford Ave KT5 198 B4
Guilford Pl WC1 240 C5
Guilford St WC1 94 A3 240 B5
Guilfoyle 2 NW9 27 D1
Guillemot Ct 28 SE8 141 B6
Guilsborough Cl NW10 67 C1
Guinness Cl
Hayes UB3 105 B3
Homerton E9 75 A1
Guinness Ct
Chelsea SW3 257 C3
6 Croydon CR0 221 D6
Finsbury EC1 235 B1
Primrose Hill NW8 230 B5
Whitechapel E1 243 D1
Guinness Sq SE1 263 A4
Guinness Trust Bldgs
Bermondsey SE1 253 A2
7 Bethnal Green E2 96 A5
Chelsea SW3 257 C3
Hammersmith W6 112 C1
Kennington SE11 261 C2
Guion Rd SW6 135 B3
Gujarat Ho 1 N16 73 C5
Gulland Cl WD23 8 A6
Gulland Wlk 21 N1 73 A2
Gullane Ho 24 E3 97 B5
Gull Cl SM6 220 A1
Gulliver Cl UB5 85 B6
Gulliver Ct CR2 220 D1
Gulliver Rd DA15 167 C2
Gulliver St SE16 119 B3
Gulston Wlk SW3 257 D3
Gumleigh Rd W5 109 C2
Gumley Gdns TW7 131 A2
Gumley House RC Convent Sch (Girls) TW7 131 A2
Gumping Rd BR5 227 A6
Gundulph Rd BR2 209 C6
Gunmakers La E3 97 A6
Gunnel Cl SE20 184 A6
Gunnell Cl SE25 206 A3
Gunnell Ct 3 CR4 180 C2
Gunnels Ct & Hastingwood Ct 6 IG9 21 C2
Gunner Dr 9 EN3 7 C6
Gunner La SE18 122 C1
GUNNERSBURY 110 D2
Gunnersbury Avenue (North Circular Rd) W3 110 C3
Gunnersbury Cl 8 W4 110 D1
Gunnersbury Cres W3 110 C4
Gunnersbury Ct 8 W3 110 D4
Gunnersbury Dr W5 110 B4
Gunnersbury Gdns W3 110 C4
Gunnersbury La W3 110 C4
Gunnersbury Manor W5 110 B5
Gunnersbury Mews 6 W4 110 D1
Gunnersbury Park W3 110 C3
Gunnersbury Park Mus* W3 110 C3
Gunnersbury RC Sch TW8 109 C1
Gunnersbury Sta W4 110 D1
Gunners Gr E4 20 A1
Gunners Rd SW18 158 B2
Gunnery Terr SE18 123 A3
Gunning St SE18 123 C2
Gunpowder Sq EC4 241 B2
Gun St E1 243 C3
Gunstor Rd N16 73 C4
Gunter Gr
Chelsea SW6 136 A5 266 A4
Hendon HA8 27 B2
Gunterstone Rd W14 113 A1 254 B2
Gunthorpe St E1 95 D1 243 D2
Gunton Rd
Streatham SW17 181 A4
Upper Clapton E5 74 B6
Gunwhale Cl SE16 118 D5
Gun Wharf
Old Ford E3 97 A6
Wapping E1 118 C5
Gurdon Ho 7 E14 97 C1
Gurdon Rd SE7 121 A1
Gurnell Gr W13 86 D3
Gurney Cl
Barking IG11 78 D2
Higham Hill E17 34 D2
Stratford E15 76 C3
Gurney Cres CR0 204 B1
Gurney Dr N2 48 A5
Gurney Ho
3 Bayswater W2 91 D1
14 Bethnal Green E2 96 A5
Hayes UB3 105 C2
Gurney Rd
London SW6 136 A2
Northolt UB5 84 C4
Stratford E15 76 C3
Wallington SM5 219 A4
Guru Nanak Sikh Prim & Sec Schs UB4 106 C5
Guthrie Ct SE1 251 B1
Guthrie St SW3 257 A2
Gutter La EC2 95 A1 242 A2
Guyatt Gdns CR4 181 A1
Guy Barnett Gr SE3 143 A2
Guy Rd SM6 219 D5
Guyscliff Rd SE13 164 A6
Guy's Hospl Sch SE1 117 B5 252 D3
Guy's Hospl SE1 117 B4 252 D2
Guy's Retreat IG9 21 C4
Guy St SE1 117 B4 252 D2
Gwalior Ho N14 15 C5
Gwalior Rd SW15 134 D2
Gwendolen Ave SW15 156 D6
Gwendolen Cl SW15 156 D6
Gwendolen Ho TW19 148 A3
Gwendoline Ave E13 99 B6
Gwendoline Ct TW15 170 A6
Gwendwr Rd W14 113 A1 254 B2
Gwent Ct 13 SE16 118 D5
Gwillim Cl DA15 168 A6
Gwilym Maries Ho 11 E2 96 B4
Gwydor Rd BR3 206 D6
Gwydyr Rd BR2 208 D6
Gwyn Cl SW6 136 A5 266 A3
Gwyn Jones Prim Sch E11 54 B2
Gwynne Ave CR0 206 D2
Gwynne Cl W4 133 D6
Gwynne Ho
Finsbury WC1 234 A1
6 Streatham SW2 160 B3
3 Wanstead E11 55 A4
Whitechapel E1 96 B2
Gwynne Pl WC1 233 D1
Gwynne Rd SW11 136 B3
Gye Ho 2 SW4 138 A1
Gylcote Cl SE5 139 B1
Gyles Pk HA7 25 C2
Gyllyngdune Gdns IG3 79 D5

H

Haarlem Rd 12 W14 112 D3
Haberdasher Pl 4 N1 95 C4
Haberdashers' Aske's Hatcham Coll SE4 141 A3
Haberdashers' Aske's Knights Acad BR1 187 A6
Haberdasher St N1 95 B4 235 D2
Haccombe Rd SW19 180 A4
HACKBRIDGE 219 B6
Hackbridge Park Gdns SM5 218 D6
Hackbridge Prim Sch SM5 203 A1
Hackbridge Rd SM5, SM6 219 A6
Hackbridge Sta SM6 219 B6
Hackford Rd SW9 138 B4 270 D2
Hackford Wlk SW9 138 C4
Hackforth Cl EN5 12 B6
Hackington Cres BR3 185 C4
HACKNEY 74 B2
Hackney Central Sta E8 74 B2
Hackney Cl WD6 11 B6
Hackney Coll (Poplar Ctr) E3 97 D3
Hackney Com Coll N1 95 C4
Hackney Downs Sta E8 74 B3
Hackney Free & Parochial CE Sec Sch E9 74 C2
Hackney Gr E8 74 B2
Hackney Hospl E9 75 A3
Hackney Rd E2 96 A5
Hackney Stadium Mkt* E15 75 C2
HACKNEY WICK 75 C2
Hackney Wick E9 75 B2
Hackney Wick Sta E9 75 C2
Hackworth Point 24 E3 97 D4
Hacon Sq 12 E8 74 B1
Hadar Cl N20 13 D3
Haddenham Ct SW17 180 B6
Hadden Rd SE28 123 C3
Hadden Way UB6 64 B2
Haddington Rd BR1 186 B6
Haddo Ho
Gospel Oak NW5 71 B4
Greenwich SE10 141 D6
Haddon Cl
Enfield EN1 18 A5
New Malden KT3 199 D4
Haddon Ct
East Acton W3 111 D6
Hendon NW4 46 C6
Haddon Gr DA15 168 A4
Haddon Rd SM1 217 D4
Haddo St SE10 142 A6
Haden Ct N4 72 C6
Hadfield Cl UB1 85 B4
Hadfield Ho
Edgware NW7 28 C6
37 Whitechapel E1 96 A1
Hadleigh Cl
17 Bethnal Green E1 96 C3
Merton SW20 179 B1
Hadleigh Ct 8 E4 20 C4
Hadleigh Ho 16 E1 96 C3
Hadleigh Lo 5 IG8 37 A4
Hadleigh Rd N9 18 B4
Hadleigh St E2 96 C4
Hadleigh Wlk 1 E6 100 A1
HADLEY 1 B2
Hadley Cl
Borehamwood WD6 10 B5
Southgate N21 16 C5
Hadley Ct
1 London N3 29
Stamford Hill N16 52
Hadley Gdns
Chiswick W4 11
Southall UB2 10
Hadley Gn EN5
Hadley Gn W EN5
Hadley Gr EN5
Hadley Green Rd EN5
Hadley Hall N21 16
Hadley Highstone EN5
Hadley Ho BR5 189
Hadley Hts EN5
Hadley Rd Barnet EN5
Belvedere DA17 125
Enfield EN2 4
Mitcham CR4 203
Hadley Ridge EN5
Hadley St NW1 71
Hadleyvale Ct EN5
Hadley View 9 EN5
Hadley Way N21 16
HADLEY WOOD 2
Hadley Wood Prim Sch EN4 2
Hadley Wood Rd
Barnet EN4 2
Barnet EN5
Hadley Wood Sta EN4 2
Hadlow Coll (Mottingham Ctr) SE12 165
Hadlow Coll Nature Reserve* SE12 165
Hadlow Ho SE17 263
Hadlow Pl SE19 184
Hadlow Rd
Bexley DA16 146
Sidcup DA14 190
Hadrian Cl
5 Old Ford E3 97
Stanwell TW19 148
Hadrian Ct Barnet EN5 1
11 Belmont SM2 217
Brockley SE4 141
Hadrian Est 33 E2 96
Hadrian's Ride EN1 17
Hadrian St SE10 120
Hadrian Way TW19 148
Hadstock Ho NW1 232
Hadyn Park Ct 13 W12 112
Hadyn Park Rd W12 112
Hafer Rd SW11 136
Hafton Rd SE6 164
Haggard Rd TW1 153
Hagger Ct E17 54
HAGGERSTON 95
Haggerston Rd E8 95
Haggerston Sch E2 95
Haggerston Studios 30 E8 95
Hague Prim Sch E2 96
Hague St 30 E2 96
Ha-Ha Rd SE7, SE18 144
Haig Ct BR7 188
Haig Ho 4 E2 96
Haig Pl SM4 201
Haig Rd E E13 99
Haig Rd
Hillingdon UB8 83
Stanmore HA7 25
Haig Rd W E13 99
Haigville Gdns IG6 56
Hailes Cl SW19 180
Haileybury Ave EN1 17
Hailey Rd DA18 125
Hailey Rd Bsns Pk DA18 125
Hailing Mews BR2 209
Hailsham Ave SW2 160
Hailsham Cl KT6 197
Hailsham Dr HA1 42
Hailsham Rd SW17 181
Hailsham Terr N18 33
Haimo Prim Sch SE9 165
Haimo Rd SE9 165
Hainault Bldgs E10 54
Hainault Bridge Par 5 IG1 78
Hainault Ct E17 54
Hainault Gore RM6 59
Hainault Rd
Dagenham RM6 59
Ilford RM6 58
Leytonstone E11 54
Hainault St Ilford IG1 78
New Eltham SE9 166
Haines Wlk SM4 201
Hainford Cl SE4 140
Haining Cl 3 W4 110
Hainthorpe Rd SE27 182
Hainton Cl E1 96

)erd Mews E5 74 B6
)utt Gdns RM9 81 B5
)utt St RM9 81 B4
:omb St N1 95 C6
:ot Ave DA6 169 D6
:roft Ct SM1 218 B4
:row St E1 96 B2
:yon Ho 3 EN1 17 C6
:yon Wharf 19
118 A5
dane Cl
ldbrook EN3 7 D5
iswell Hill N10 31 B3
dane Pl SW18 157 D3
dane Rd
lham
SW6 135 B6 264 D5
wham E6 100 A4
uthall UB1 86 A1
iamesmead SE28 124 D6
dan Rd E4 36 A4
don Rd SW18 157 B5
e Cl Chingford E4 20 A1
lgware HA8 27 A5
rpington BR6 227 A4
e Ct HA8 27 A5
e Dr NW7 27 B4
.E END 36 C4
e End Cl HA4 40 A3
e End Rd E17 36 B2
efield Rd N17 34 B2
e Gdns Acton W3 110 C5
ottenham Hale N17 52 A6
e Grove Gdns
W7 27 C5
le Ho Enfield EN3 6 D6
lestminster SW1 259 D2
e La NW7, HA8 27 B5
e Lo HA1 42 C2
e Rd Newham E6 100 A3
ottenham Hale N17 52 A6
es Ct 6 TW11 175 A5
es Ho 3 SW12 159 B4
esowen Rd SM4 201 D2
es Prior N1 233 C3
es St SE8 141 C5
le St E14 119 D6
lesworth Cl 3 E5 74 C6
lesworth Rd
E13 141 D2
le The Chingford E4 36 B3
ottenham Hale N17 52 A6
le Wlk W7 86 C2
ley Rd NW4 46 C3
lf Acre TW8 131 D6
lf Acre Mews
W8 131 D6
lf Acre Rd W7 108 C5
lfacre 14 HA7 25 C5
lf Acre 2 E18 55 A6
lf Moon Cres N1 233 D4
lf Moon Ct EC1 242 A3
lf Moon La SE24 161 A5
lfmoon Pas E1 243 D1
lf Moon St
/1 115 B5 248 D3
lford Cl HA8 26 D1
lford Ct KT9 214 A1
lford Ho 9
W15 156 D6
lford Rd
ckenham UB10 60 C3
eyton E10 54 B4
Richmond TW10 154 A6
West Brompton
SW6 135 C6 265 A5
lfway St DA15 167 C3
liburton Rd TW1,
W7 131 A1
liday Ho N1 73 B2
liday Wlk 4 N1 73 B2
lidon Cl E9 74 C3
lifax Cl TW11 174 C4
lifax 8 NW9 27 D1
lifax Rd Enfield EN2 5 B3
Greenford UB6 85 D6
lifax St SE26 162 B1
lifield Dr DA17 125 A3
ling Gr CR2 221 A1
ling Manor High Sch
CR2 220 D1
ling Park Gdns
CR2 220 D2
ling Park Rd
Croydon CR2 220 D3
South Croydon CR2 221 A2
ling Rd CR2 221 B2
liwell Ho 10 NW6 91 D6
lkett Ho 11 E2 96 C6
lkin Arc
SW1 114 D3 257 D6
lkin Mews SW1 258 A6
lkin Pl SW1 258 A6
lkin St
SW1 115 A4 248 B1
llam Cl BR7 188 B5
llam Ct W1 238 D4

Hallam Gdns HA5 23 A3
Hallam Ho
17 London SW9 138 C4
Pimlico SW1 259 B1
Hallam Mews W1 238 D4
Hallam Rd
Barnes SW13 134 B2
Harringay N15 50 D5
Hallam St W1 93 B2 238 D4
Hallane Ho SE27 183 A5
Hall Cl W5 88 A2
Hall Ct TW11 174 D5
Hall Dr Ealing W7 86 C1
Forest Hill SE26 184 C5
Halley Gdns SE13 142 B1
Halley Ho
16 Bethnal Green
E2 96 A5
8 Cubitt Town
SE10 120 D1
Halley Prim Sch E14 97 A2
Halley Rd E7, E12 77 D2
Halley St E14 97 A2
Hall Farm Cl HA7 25 B6
Hall Farm Dr TW2 152 B4
Hallfield Jun & Inf Schs
W2 91 D1
Hall Gate
NW8 92 A4 229 B2
Hallgate SE3 143 A2
Hall Gdns E4 35 B6
Halliards The KT12 194 A3
Halliday Ho 40 E1 96 A1
Halliday Sq UB2 108 B5
Halliford Cl TW17 193 C6
Halliford Rd
Sunbury TW16 194 A5
Upper Halliford TW16,
TW17 193 D5
Halliford Sch TW17 193 A2
Halliford St N1 73 B1
Hallingbury Ct 1
E17 53 D6
Halling Ho SE1 252 D1
Hallings Wharf Studios
2 E15 98 B6
Halliwell Ct 4 SE22 162 A6
Halliwell Rd SW2 160 B5
Halliwick Court Par 2
N12 30 D5
Halliwick Ct 1 N12 30 D5
Halliwick Ho N21 17 B5
Halliwick Rd N10 31 A2
Hall La
Chingford Hatch E4 35 B5
Harlington UB3 127 B5
Hendon NW4 28 A1
Hall Lane E4 35 A5
Hallmark Trad Ctr
HA9 67 A4
Hallmead Rd SM1 217 D5
Hall Oak Wlk NW6 69 B2
Hallowell Ave CR0 220 A4
Hallowell Cl CR4 203 A6
Hallowfield Way
CR4 202 C6
Hallows Gr TW16 171 D5
Hall Pl W2 92 B3 236 C5
Hall Rd
Dagenham RM6 58 D3
Isleworth TW7 152 B6
Leyton E15 76 B4
Newham E6 100 B6
St John's Wood
NW8 92 A4 229 B2
Halls Bsns Ctr UB3 106 A3
Hall Sch The NW3 70 B2
Hall Sch Wimbledon
SW15 156 A1
Hall Sch SW20 178 D2
Hallside Rd EN1 5 D5
Halls Terr UB10 82 D3
Hall St
Finsbury
EC1 94 D4 234 D2
North Finchley N12 30 A5
Hallsville Prim Sch
E16 99 A1
Hallsville Rd E16 98 D1
Hallswelle Par 1
NW11 47 B4
Hallswelle Rd NW11 47 B4
Hall The SE3 143 A2
Hall Twr W2 236 D4
Hall View SE9 165 D2
Hallywell Cres E6 100 B2
Halons Rd SE9 166 C4
Halpin Pl
SE17 117 B2 262 D3
Halsbrook Rd SE3 143 D2
Halsbury Cl HA7 25 B6
Halsbury Ct HA7 25 B6
Halsbury Ho 4 N7 72 B4
Halsbury Rd E UB5 64 A4
Halsbury Rd W12 112 B5
Halsbury Rd W UB5 63 D3
Halsend UB3 106 B5

Halsey St
SW3 114 D2 257 C4
Halsham Cres IG11 79 D3
Halsmere Rd SE5 138 D4
Halstead Cl 2 CR0 221 A5
Halstead Ct
Shoreditch N1 235 D3
Walthamstow E17 53 B2
Halstead Gdns N21 17 B3
Halstead Rd
Edmonton N21 17 B3
Enfield EN1 5 C1
Wanstead E11 55 B4
Halston Cl SW11 158 D5
Halstow 12 NW5 71 A2
Halstow Prim Sch
SE10 121 A1
Halstow Rd
Greenwich SE3,
SE10 121 A1
Kensal Green NW10 90 D4
Halsway UB3 106 A5
Halter Cl WD6 11 B6
Halton Cl N11 30 D4
Halton Cross St
N1 94 D6 234 D6
Haltone Ho 1 SW4 137 D3
Halton Ho 22 N1 72 D1
Halton Mans N1 72 D1
Halton Pl N1 235 A6
Halton Rd N1 94 D6 234 D6
Halt Robin La DA17 125 D2
Halt Robin Rd DA17 125 D2
Halyard Ho E14 120 A3
HAM 153 C1
Hamara Ghar 4 E13 99 C6
Hambalt Rd SW4 159 C6
Hamble Cl HA4 61 C6
Hamble Ct KT1 175 D3
Hambledon Chase
N4 50 A2
Hambledon Cl UB8 82 D3
Hambledon Ct
5 Ealing W5 110 A6
9 Wallington SM6 219 B2
Hambledon Gdns
SE25 205 D6
Hambledon Ho
2 Kingston u T
KT2 176 D4
Lower Clapton E5 74 B4
Hambledon Pl SE21 161 D3
Hambledon Rd
SW18 157 B4
Hambledon SE17 139 B6
Hambledown Rd
DA15 167 C4
Hamble St SW6 135 D2
Hambleton Cl KT4 216 C6
Hamble Wlk UB5 85 C5
Hambley Ho 5
SE16 118 B2
Hamblin Ho UB1 107 A6
Hambly Mans SW16 182 A4
Hamblyn Ct N16 51 D2
Hambridge Way
SW2 160 C4
Hambro Ave BR2 209 A1
Hambrook Ct 12
NW5 71 B4
Hambrook Rd SE25 206 B6
Hambro Rd SW16 181 D5
Hambrough Ho UB4 84 C2
Hambrough Prim Sch
UB1 107 B5
Hambrough Rd UB1 107 A5
Ham Cl TW10 153 C1
Ham Comm TW10 153 D1
Ham Croft Cl TW13 150 A1
Ham Ct 12 NW9 27 D1
Hamden Cres RM10 81 D5
Hamel Cl HA3 43 D5
Hamers Ho 19 SW2 160 C4
Hameway E6 100 C3
Ham Farm Rd KT2,
TW10 176 A6
Hamfrith Rd E15 76 D2
Ham Gate Ave
TW10 176 A6
Ham Ho* TW10 153 C2
Hamilton Ave
Cheam SM3 217 A6
Edmonton N9 18 A4
Ilford IG6 57 A4
Tolworth KT6, SM3 214 C6
Hamilton Cl
Ashford TW13 171 D5
Cockfosters EN4 2 D1
Rotherhithe SE16 119 A4
St John's Wood
NW8 92 B4 229 C1
Teddington TW11 175 B4
Tottenham N17 51 D6
Hamilton Cres
Edmonton N13 32 C6
Harrow HA2 63 B5
Hounslow TW3 151 D6

Hamilton Ct
9 Catford SE6 164 D3
Croydon CR0 206 A1
Ealing W5 110 B6
St John's Wood W9 229 A2
Hamilton Gdns
NW8 92 A4 229 B2
Hamilton Hall
NW8 92 A5 229 A3
Hamilton Ho
23 Bow E3 97 B4
Chiswick W4 133 C6
Kensington W8 245 C2
Oakleigh Pk N20 14 A4
1 Poplar E14 119 B6
Putney SW15 156 A6
10 Richmond TW9 132 C4
St John's Wood NW8 229 C2
Hamilton La N5 72 D4
Hamilton Lo 37 E1 96 C3
Hamilton Mews W1 248 C2
Hamilton Par TW13 172 A6
Hamilton Pk N5 72 D4
Hamilton Pk W N5 72 D4
Hamilton Pl
Mayfair
W1 115 A5 248 B3
Sunbury TW16 172 B3
Tottenham N17 33 D1
Hamilton Rd
Acton W4 111 C4
Barnet EN4 2 C1
Bexleyheath DA7 147 A3
Brentford TW8 131 D6
Ealing W5 110 A6
East Finchley N2 48 A6
Edmonton N9 18 A4
Feltham TW13 171 D6
Harrow HA1 42 C4
Hayes UB3 106 B6
Hendon NW11 47 A2
Higham Hill E17 35 A1
Ilford IG1 78 D4
Merton SW19 179 D3
Newham E15 98 C4
Sidcup DA15 190 A6
Southall UB1 107 B5
South Norwood CR7 205 B6
Twickenham TW2 152 C3
West Norwood SE27 183 B6
Willesden NW10 68 A3
Hamilton Road Ind Est
SE27 183 B6
Hamilton Road Mews 1
SW19 179 D3
Hamilton Sq
Bermondsey SE1 252 D2
Finchley N12 30 A4
Hamilton St SE8 141 C6
Hamilton Terr
NW8 92 A4 229 B2
Hamilton Way
Edmonton N13 32 D6
Finchley N3 29 C4
Hamlea Cl SE12 165 A6
Hamlet Cl SE13 142 C1
Hamlet Ct
14 Enfield EN1 17 C6
1 Hammersmith
W6 112 A2
Kennington SE11 261 C2
Hamlet Gdns W6 112 A2
Hamlet Ho SE9 166 C6
Hamlet Ind Est E9 75 C1
Hamleton Terr RM9 80 C1
Hamlet Rd SE19 184 A3
Hamlet Sq NW2 69 A5
Hamlets Way E3 97 B3
Hamlet The SE5 139 B2
Hamlet Way SE1 252 D2
Hamlin Cres HA5 40 C4
Hamlyn Cl HA8 10 A1
Hamlyn Gdns SE19 183 C3
Hamlyn Ho TW13 150 B3
Hammelton Ct 4
BR1 186 D2
Hammelton Gn 2
SW9 138 D4
Hammelton Rd BR1 187 A2
Hammers La NW7 28 A6
Hammersley Ho 8
SE14 140 C5
HAMMERSMITH 112 C2
Hammersmith Bridge
Rd W6, SW13 112 C1
Hammersmith
Broadway
Hammersmith
W6 112 C1
5 Hammersmith
W6 112 C2
Hammersmith Flyover
W6 112 C1
Hammersmith Gr
W6 112 C3

Hammersmith Hospl
W12 90 B1
Hammersmith Rd
Hammersmith
W6 112 D2
Kensington W14 254 B4
Hammersmith Sta
W6 112 C2
Hammersmith Terr 6
W6 112 A1
Hammet Cl UB4 84 D2
Hammett St EC3 253 C6
Hammond Ave CR4 181 B1
Hammond Cl
Barnet EN5 13 B6
Greenford UB6 64 B3
Hampton TW12 173 C2
Hammond Ct
1 Leyton E10 75 D6
1 Walthamstow E17 53 A4
Hammond Ho
10 Deptford SE14 140 C5
Millwall E14 119 D3
Hammond Lo 6 W9 91 C2
Hammond Rd
Enfield EN1 6 B3
Southall UB2 107 A3
Hammonds Cl RM8 80 C5
Hammonds Ho
TW19 148 B3
Hammond St NW5 71 C2
Hammond Way 2
SE28 124 B6
Hamonde Cl HA8 10 D2
Hamond Sq N1 95 C5
Ham Park Rd E15 76 D1
Hampden Ave BR3 185 A1
Hampden Cl NW1 232 D4
Hampden Ct
Harrow HA1 42 A5
10 Muswell Hill N10 31 A3
Hampden Gurney CE
Prim Sch
W1 92 C1 237 B2
Hampden Gurney St
W1 237 C1
Hampden La N17 34 A2
Hampden Rd
Beckenham BR3 185 A1
Harrow HA3 24 A1
Hornsey N8 50 C5
Kingston u T KT1 198 C6
Muswell Hill N10 31 A3
Tottenham N17 34 A2
Upper Holloway N19 71 D6
Hampden Sq N14 15 B3
Hampden Way N14 15 B2
Hampshire Cl N18 34 B5
Hampshire Ct
6 Barnes SW13 133 D3
Hendon NW4 46 D4
Hampshire Ho HA8 26 B3
Hampshire Hog La
3 Hammersmith
W6 112 B1
11 Hammersmith
W6 112 B2
Hampshire Rd N22 32 B3
Hampshire Sch The
SW7 114 C4 247 A1
Hampshire St NW5 71 D2
Hampson Way
SW8 138 B4 270 C2
HAMPSTEAD 70 A3
Hampstead Cl SE28 124 B5
Hampstead Coll of Fine
Arts & Humanities
NW3 70 C2
HAMPSTEAD GARDEN
SUBURB 47 D4
Hampstead Garden
Suburb Inst NW11 47 D4
Hampstead Gate
NW3 70 A3
Hampstead Gdns
NW11 47 C3
Hampstead Gn NW3 70 C3
Hampstead Gr NW3 70 A5
Hampstead Heath*
NW3 70 B6
Hampstead Heath Sta
NW3 70 C4
Hampstead High St
NW3 70 B4
Hampstead Hill Gdns
NW3 70 C4
Hampstead Hill Sch
NW3 70 C3
Hampstead Hts N2 48 A6
Hampstead La N6 48 C2
Hampstead Parochial
CE Prim Sch NW3 70 A4
Hampstead Rd
NW1 93 C4 232 A2
Hampstead Sch NW2 69 A4
Hampstead Sq 1
NW3 70 A5

Hampstead Sta NW3 70 A4
Hampstead Way
NW11 47 A3
Hampstead West 4
NW6 69 C2
Hampstead Wlk 1
E3 97 B6
HAMPTON 173 C1
Hampton Cl
Borehamwood
WD6 11 A6
Friern Barnet N11 31 B5
Kilburn NW6 91 C4
Wimbledon SW20 178 C3
Hampton Com Coll
TW12 173 C5
Hampton Court Ave
KT8 196 C3
Hampton Court Cres
KT8 196 B6
Hampton Court Landing
Stage KT8 196 C6
Hampton Court Pal*
KT8 196 D6
Hampton Court Par
KT8 196 C5
Hampton Court Rd KT1,
KT8 197 B6
Hampton Court Sta
KT8 196 C5
Hampton Court Way
KT10, KT7, KT8 196 C3
Hampton Ct
Hampton KT8 196 C6
1 Islington N1 72 D2
19 Rotherhithe
SE16 118 D5
Wood Green N22 31 C2
Hampton Farm Ind Est
TW13 151 A1
HAMPTON HILL 174 A5
Hampton Hill Bsns Pk
TW12 174 A5
Hampton Hill Jun Sch
TW12 174 A5
Hampton Ho DA7 147 D3
Hampton Inf Sch
TW12 173 C3
Hampton Jun Sch
TW12 173 C2
Hampton La TW13 173 A6
Hampton Rd E4 35 B5
Hampton Rd E
TW13 151 B1
Hampton Rd
Forest Gate E7 77 C3
Ilford IG1 79 A4
Leytonstone E11 54 B1
North Cheam KT4 216 B6
Teddington TW11,
TW12 174 C5
Thornton Heath CR0 205 A3
Twickenham TW2 152 B1
Hampton Rd W
TW13 151 A1
Hampton Rise HA3 44 A3
Hampton Road Ind Pk
CR0 205 A3
Hampton Sch TW12 173 C5
Hampton Sta TW12 173 C2
Hampton St
SE1 116 D2 261 D3
HAMPTON WICK 175 D3
Hampton Wick Inf Sch
TW11 175 D3
Hampton Wick Sta
KT1 175 C2
Ham Ridings TW10 176 B5
Ham Shades Cl 1
DA15 168 A1
Hamson Ct HA2 64 B6
Hamstead Gates 11
NW5 71 B2
Ham St TW10 153 C1
Ham The TW8 131 C5
Ham View CR0 207 A3
Ham Yd W1 249 C6
Hanameel St E16 121 B5
Hana Mews E5 74 B4
Hanbury Cl NW4 46 C6
Hanbury Ct HA1 42 D3
Hanbury Dr
2 Leyton E11 54 D2
Southgate N21 16 B6
Hanbury Ho
8 Bethnal Green
E1 96 A2
South Lambeth SW8 270 B5
Hanbury Mews N1 235 B5
Hanbury Rd
South Acton W3 110 D4
Tottenham N17 34 B1
Hanbury St
E1 95 D2 243 D4

Hancocke Ho 4 E17 . . 53 D6
Hancock Nunn Ho 1
NW3 . . . . 70 D1
Hancock Rd
Bromley E3 . . . . 98 A4
South Norwood
SE19 . . . . 183 B4
Handa Wlk 3 N1 . . . . . 73 A2
Handcroft Rd CR0 . . . 204 D1
Hand Ct WC1 . . . . 240 D3
Handel Cl HA8 . . . . 26 B4
Handel Ho TW2 . . . . . . 152 B5
Handel Mans
Barnes SW13 . . . . 134 C5
Bloomsbury WC1 . . . . 240 B6
Handel Par HA8 . . . . 26 C3
Handel Pl NW10 . . . . . . 67 B2
Handel St
WC1 . . . . 94 A3 240 B6
Handel Way HA8 . . . . . . 26 C3
Handen Rd SE12 . . . . . 164 D6
Handforth Rd
Brixton SW9 . . . . 138 C5
6 Ilford IG1 . . . . 78 D5
Handley Gr NW2 . . . . . . 68 D5
Handley Page Rd
SM6 . . . . 220 B1
Handley Rd E9 . . . . 96 C6
Handowe Cl NW4 . . . . . 46 A5
Handside Cl KT4 . . . . . 200 D1
Hands Wlk E16 . . . . 99 A1
Handsworth Ave E4 . . 36 B4
Handsworth Prim Sch
E4 . . . . 36 B4
Handsworth Rd N17 . . . 51 B6
Handtrough Way
IG11 . . . . 100 D5
Hanford Cl SW18 . . . . . 157 C3
Hanford Row SW19 . . 178 C4
Hanger Ct W5 . . . . 88 C3
Hanger Gn W5 . . . . 88 C3
Hanger Lane Sta W5 . . 88 A4
Hanger La (North
Circular Rd) W5 . . . . . 88 B2
Hanger Vale La W5 . . . . 88 B1
Hanger View Way
W3 . . . . 88 C2
Hangmans Cnr BR7 . . 188 D2
Hankey Pl
SE1 . . . . 117 B4 252 D1
Hankins La NW7 . . . . . . 11 C1
Hanley Ct N4 . . . . 50 B1
Hanley Gdns N4 . . . . . . 50 B1
Hanley Pl BR3 . . . . 185 C3
Hanley Rd N4, N19 . . . . 50 A1
Hanmer Wlk N7 . . . . 72 B6
Hannah Cl
Beckenham BR3 . . . . 208 A6
Wembley NW10 . . . . 67 A4
Hannah Ct
Palmers Green N13 . . . . 16 B2
5 Sutton SM1 . . . . . . 217 D2
Wimbledon SW19 . . . 178 D3
Hannah Mary Way 17
SE1 . . . . 118 A2
Hannah Mews SM6 . . . 219 C1
Hannay La N8 . . . . 49 D2
Hannay Wlk SW16 . . . 159 D2
Hannell Rd
SW6 . . . . 135 A5 264 B4
Hannen Ho SE5 . . . . . . 139 B2
Hannen Rd SE27 . . . . . 160 D1
Hannibal Rd
Stanwell TW19 . . . . . 148 A4
Stepney E1 . . . . 96 C2
Hannibal Way CR0 . . . 220 B2
Hanning Lo TW3 . . . . . 130 A1
Hannington Rd
SW4 . . . . 137 B2
Hanover Ave
Feltham TW13 . . . . . . 150 A2
Newham E16 . . . . 121 A5
Hanover Circ UB3 . . . . . 83 B1
Hanover Cl
Cheam SM3 . . . . 217 B4
Richmond TW9 . . . . . . 132 C5
Hanover Ct
Colindale NW9 . . . . 45 C6
Harrow HA1 . . . . 42 B2
1 Penge SE19 . . . . . . 184 A3
11 Pinner HA5 . . . . 23 B3
Shepherd's Bush
W12 . . . . 112 A5
Stamford Hill N16 . . . . . 51 D2
Hanover Dr BR7 . . . . . 189 A6
Hanover Gate Mans
NW1 . . . . 237 B6
Hanover Gdns SE11 . . 138 C6
Hanover Ho
1 New Barnet EN5 . . . . 2 A1
St John's Wood NW8 230 A3
Tolworth KT6 . . . . 198 C1
Hanover Lo N21 . . . . . . 16 D6
Hanover Mans 5
SW2 . . . . 160 C6
Hanover Mead NW11 . . 47 A3
Hanover Pk SE15 . . . . 140 A4
Hanover Pl
16 Bow E3 . . . . 97 B4
St Giles WC2 . . . . 240 B1
Hanover Prim Sch
N1 . . . . 95 A5 235 A4
Hanover Rd
Merton SW19 . . . . . . 180 A3
South Tottenham N15 . . 51 D5
Willesden NW10 . . . . . . 90 C6
Hanover Sq
W1 . . . . 93 B1 238 D1
Hanover St
Croydon CR0 . . . . 220 D5
Marylebone
W1 . . . . 93 B1 238 D1
Hanover Stps W2 . . . 237 B1
Hanover Terrace Mews
NW1 . . . . 92 C4 230 B1
Hanover Terr
Isleworth TW7 . . . . . . 131 A4
Lisson Gr
NW1 . . . . . . 92 D4 230 C1
Hanover Way DA6 . . . . 146 D2
Hanover West Ind Est
NW10 . . . . 89 B4
Hanover Yd N1 . . . . . . 235 A4
Hansard Mews
W14 . . . . 112 D4
Hansart Way EN2 . . . . . . 4 C4
Hanscomb Mews
SW4 . . . . 137 C1
Hans Cres
SW1 . . . . 114 D3 257 C6
Hanselin Cl HA7 . . . . . . 24 D5
Hansen Dr N21 . . . . 16 B6
Hanshaw Dr HA8 . . . . . . 27 B2
Hansler Ct 14 SW19 . . 157 A3
Hansler Gr KT8 . . . . . . 196 B5
Hansler Rd SE22 . . . . . 161 D6
Hansol Rd DA6 . . . . . . 169 A6
Hanson Cl
Balham SW12 . . . . 159 B4
Beckenham BR3 . . . . . 185 D4
Mortlake SW14 . . . . . . 133 A2
West Drayton UB7 . . . . 104 B3
Hanson Ct E17 . . . . 53 D3
Hanson Gdns UB1 . . . . 107 A4
Hanson Ho 2 E1 . . . . . 118 A6
Hanson St
W1 . . . . 93 C2 239 A4
Hans Pl SW1 . . 114 D3 257 C6
Hans Rd
SW3 . . . . 114 D3 257 C6
Hans St
SW1 . . . . 114 D3 257 D5
Hanway Ho 25 SW9 . . 138 C4
Hanway Pl W1 . . . . 239 C2
Hanway Rd W7 . . . . 86 C1
Hanway St W1 . . . . 239 C2
HANWELL 108 D5
Hanwell Sta W7 . . . . . 108 C6
HANWORTH 172 D6
Hanworth Ho SE5 . . . . 138 D5
Hanworth Rd
Ashford TW16 . . . . . . 172 A3
Feltham TW13 . . . . . . 150 B3
Hampton TW12 . . . . . 173 C5
Hounslow TW3,
TW4 . . . . 129 D1
Twickenham TW4 . . . . 151 B4
Hanworth Terr
TW3 . . . . 129 D1
Hanworth Trad Est
TW13 . . . . 151 A1
Hapgood Cl UB6 . . . . . . 64 B3
Harben Rd NW6 . . . . . . 70 A1
Harberson Rd
Balham SW12 . . . . 159 B3
West Ham E15 . . . . 98 D6
Harberton Rd N19 . . . . 49 C1
Harbet Rd
Highams Pk N18 . . . . . . 35 A4
Paddington
W2 . . . . 92 B2 236 D3
Harbex Cl DA5 . . . . 169 D4
Harbinger Prim Sch
E14 . . . . 119 D2
Harbinger Rd E14 . . . . 119 D2
Harbin Ho 5 SW2 . . . 160 C3
Harbledown Ho SE1 . 252 C1
Harbledown Rd
SW6 . . . . 265 A2
Harbord Cl SE5 . . . . . . 139 B3
Harbord Ho 5
SE16 . . . . 118 D2
Harbord St SW6 . . . . . 134 D4
Harborne Cl WD19 . . . . 22 C5
Harborough Ave
DA15 . . . . 167 D4
Harborough Rd
SW16 . . . . 182 B6
Harborough Sch N19 . 71 D6
Harbour Ave
SW10 . . . . 136 A4 266 B1
Harbour Exchange Sq
E14 . . . . 119 D4
Harbour Rd SE5 . . . . . 139 A2
Harbridge Ave
SW15 . . . . 156 A4
Harbury Rd SM5 . . . . . 218 C1
Harbut Rd SW11 . . . . . 136 B1
Harcombe Rd N16 . . . . 73 C5
Harcourt Ave
Edgware HA8 . . . . 11 A1
Little Ilford E12 . . . . 78 B3
Sidcup DA15 . . . . 168 C4
Wallington SM6 . . . . . 219 B4
Harcourt Cl TW7 . . . . . 131 A2
Harcourt Field SM6 . . 219 B4
Harcourt Ho
5 Chingford E4 . . . . . . 36 B5
27 Clapham SW8 . . . . 137 D3
Marylebone W1 . . . . . 238 C2
4 Willesden NW10 . . . . 68 C2
Harcourt Lo 2 SM6 . . 219 B4
Harcourt Rd
Bexley DA6 . . . . 147 A1
Brockley SE4 . . . . 141 B2
Bushey WD23 . . . . 8 A6
Merton SW19 . . . . 179 C3
Thornton Heath CR7 . 204 C3
Wallington SM6 . . . . . 219 B4
West Ham E15 . . . . 98 D5
Wood Green N22 . . . . . . 31 D2
Harcourt St
W1 . . . . 92 C2 237 B3
Harcourt Terr
SW10 . . . . 113 D1 255 D1
Hardcastle Cl SE25 . . . 206 A3
Hardcastle Ho
3 New Cross Gate
SE14 . . . . 141 A4
8 Peckham SE15 . . . . 140 A4
Hardcourts Cl BR4 . . . 223 D5
Hard Ct IG8 . . . . 37 C4
Hardel Rise SW2 . . . . . 160 D3
Hardel Wlk SE24,
SW2 . . . . 160 C4
Harden Ct 1 SE7 . . . . 122 A2
Harden Ho SE5 . . . . . . 139 C3
Harders Rd SE15 . . . . . 140 B3
Hardess St SE24 . . . . . 139 A2
Hardham Ho 5
SW2 . . . . 160 C5
Hardie Cl NW10 . . . . 67 B3
Harding Cl
Camberwell SE17 . . . 139 A6
South Croydon CR0 . . 221 D5
Harding Ct SE25 . . . . . 183 D1
Hardinge Cl UB8 . . . . . . 82 D1
Hardinge Cres SE18 . . 123 A3
Hardinge Rd
Edmonton N18 . . . . 33 C4
Willesden NW10 . . . . . . 90 C6
Hardinge St
Stepney E1 . . . . 96 C1
Woolwich SE18 . . . . . 122 D3
Harding Ho
Barnes SW13 . . . . 134 B6
Hayes UB3 . . . . 84 B1
14 Woolwich SE18 . . . 122 B2
Harding Pl SE23 . . . . . 163 A4
Harding Rd DA7 . . . . . . 147 B3
Hardings Cl KT2 . . . . . 176 B2
Hardings La SE20 . . . . 184 D4
Hardington 2 NW1 . . . . 71 A1
Hardman Rd
Greenwich SE7 . . . . . . 121 B1
Kingston u T KT2 . . . . 176 A1
Hardwick Cl 7 HA7 . . . . 25 C5
Hardwick Ct 8 E11 . . . . 55 A3
Hardwicke Ave
TW5 . . . . 129 C4
Hardwicke Ho 14 E3 . . . 97 D4
Hardwicke Mews
WC1 . . . . 233 D1
Hardwicke Rd
Acton W4 . . . . 111 B2
Bowes Pk N13 . . . . 32 A4
Richmond TW10 . . . . . 175 C6
Hardwicke St IG11 . . . 101 A6
Hardwick Gn W13 . . . . . 87 B2
Hardwick Ho
14 London SW8 . . . . . 137 D3
Marylebone NW8 . . . . 237 B6
Hardwick St
EC1 . . . . 94 C4 234 B1
Hardwick's Way
SW18 . . . . 157 C6
Hardwidge St SE1 . . . 253 A2
Hardy Ave
4 Newham E16 . . . . . 121 A5
Ruislip HA4 . . . . 62 B3
Hardy Cl Barnet EN5 . . . 13 A6
Pinner HA5 . . . . 40 D2
Rotherhithe SE16 . . . . 118 D4
Hardy Cotts 2 SE10 . . 142 B6
Hardy Ct
Greenwich SE3 . . . . . 142 D6
Hardy Ct *continued*
9 Wanstead E11 . . . . . 55 A5
Hardyng Ho 4 E17 . . . . 53 A5
Hardy Pas N22 . . . . 32 C1
Hardy Rd
Greenwich SE3 . . . . . 142 D6
Merton SW19 . . . . 179 D3
Walthamstow E4 . . . . . . 35 B4
Hardys Mews KT8 . . . . 196 C5
Hardy Way EN2 . . . . 4 C4
Hare and Billet Rd
SE3 . . . . 142 B3
Harebell Dr E6 . . . . . . 100 C2
Harecastle Cl UB4 . . . . 85 A3
Harecourt Rd N1 . . . . . 73 A2
Hare Ct EC4 . . . . 241 A1
Haredale Ho 24
SE16 . . . . 118 A4
Haredale Rd SE24 . . . . 139 A1
Haredon Cl SE23 . . . . . 162 D4
Harefield Cl EN2 . . . . 4 C4
Harefield Ct 4
SW19 . . . . 179 C3
Harefield KT10 . . . . . . 212 C5
Harefield Mews
SE4 . . . . 141 B2
Harefield Rd
Brockley SE4 . . . . 141 B2
Hornsey N8 . . . . 49 D4
Sidcup DA14 . . . . 168 D1
South Norwood
SW16 . . . . 182 B3
Uxbridge UB8 . . . . 60 A3
Hare La KT10 . . . . 212 C2
Hare Marsh E2 . . . . 96 A3
Harenc Sch Trust
DA14 . . . . 190 C5
Hare Pl EC4 . . . . 241 B1
Hare Row E2 . . . . 96 B5
Haresfield Rd RM10 . . . 81 C2
Harestone Ct CR2 . . . . 221 C2
Hare St SE18 . . . . 122 C3
Hare Wlk N1 . . . . 95 C5
Harewood Ave
Lisson Gr
NW1 . . . . . . 92 C3 237 B5
Northolt UB5 . . . . 63 B1
Harewood Cl UB5 . . . . . 63 B1
Harewood Ct HA3 . . . . . 24 C2
Harewood Pl W1 . . . . . 238 D1
Harewood Rd
Hounslow TW7 . . . . . 130 D4
Mitcham SW19 . . . . . 180 C4
South Croydon CR2 . . 221 C2
Harewood Row
NW1 . . . . 237 B4
Harewood Terr UB2 . . 107 B2
Harfield Gdns 1
SE5 . . . . 139 C2
Harfield Rd TW16 . . . . 172 D1
Harfleur Ct SE11 . . . . 261 C3
Harford Cl E4 . . . . 19 D4
Harford Ho
Camberwell SE5 . . . . 139 A6
Notting Hill W11 . . . . . . 91 B2
Harford Mews 6
N19 . . . . 71 D5
Harford Rd E4 . . . . 19 D4
Harford St E1 . . . . 97 A3
Harford Wlk N2 . . . . 48 B5
Hargood Cl HA3 . . . . . . 44 A3
Hargood Rd SE3 . . . . . 143 C4
Hargrave Mans 3
N19 . . . . 71 D6
Hargrave Park Prim Sch
N19 . . . . 71 C6
Hargrave Pk N19 . . . . . . 71 C6
Hargrave Pl N7 . . . . 71 D3
Hargrave Rd N19 . . . . . 71 C6
Hargraves Ho 14
W12 . . . . 112 B6
Hargwyne St SW9 . . . . 138 B2
Haringey Pk N8 . . . . . . 50 A3
Haringey Rd N8 . . . . . . 50 A5
Harington Terr N18 . . . 17 B1
Harkett Cl HA3 . . . . 24 D1
Harkett Ct HA3 . . . . 24 D1
Harkness Ct SM1 . . . . 201 D1
Harkness Ho 30 E1 . . . . 96 A1
Harland Ave
Sidcup DA15 . . . . 167 C2
South Croydon CR0 . . 222 A5
Harland Cl SW19 . . . . 201 D6
Harland Rd SE12 . . . . . 165 A3
Harlands Gr BR6 . . . . . 226 D4
Harlech Ct 1 SE23 . . . 162 C3
Harlech Gdns TW5 . . . 128 C5
Harlech Rd N14 . . . . 16 A1
Harlech Twr 5 W3 . . . 111 A4
Harlequin Ave TW8 . . . 131 A6
Harlequin Cl
Hayes UB4 . . . . 84 D2
Isleworth TW7 . . . . . . 152 C6
Harlequin Ct
Croydon CR2 . . . . 221 A1
Ealing W5 . . . . 109 C6
Willesden NW10 . . . . . . 67 B2
Harlequin Ho 1
DA18 . . . . 125 A3
Harlequin Rd TW11 . . 175 B3
Harlescott Rd SE15 . . 140 D1
HARLESDEN 89 D6
Harlesden Gdns
NW10 . . . . 89 D6
Harlesden Plaza 2
NW10 . . . . 89 D5
Harlesden Prim Sch
NW10 . . . . 89 C5
Harlesden Rd NW10 . . . 90 A6
Harlesden Sta NW10 . . 89 B5
Harleston Cl 4 E5 . . . . 74 C6
Harley BR7 . . . . 189 B2
Harley Cl HA0 . . . . 65 D2
Harley Cres HA1 . . . . . . 42 B5
Harley Ct Harrow HA1 . . 42 B5
Wanstead E11 . . . . 55 A2
Whetstone N20 . . . . 14 A1
Harleyford BR1 . . . . . . 187 C2
Harleyford Ct
Kennington SW8 . . . . 270 C6
Wembley HA0 . . . . 65 A4
Harleyford Manor 8
W3 . . . . 111 A5
Harleyford Rd
SE11 . . . . 138 B6 270 C6
Harleyford St SE11 . . . 138 C6
Harley Gdns
Orpington BR6 . . . . . . 227 C4
South Kensington
SW10 . . . . 114 A1 256 B1
Harley Gr E3 . . . . 97 B4
Harley Ho
Leytonstone E11 . . . . . . 54 B2
Marylebone NW1 . . . . 238 B5
Harley Pl W1 . . 93 B2 238 C3
Harley Rd
Hampstead NW3 . . . . . . 70 B1
Harlesden NW10 . . . . . . 89 C5
Harrow HA1 . . . . 42 B5
Harley St W1 . . 93 B2 238 C3
Harley Villas NW10 . . . . 89 C5
Harling Ct 3 SW11 . . 136 D3
Harlinger St SE18 . . . . 122 A3
HARLINGTON 127 A6
Harlington Cl UB7 . . . 127 A5
Harlington Cnr UB3 . . 127 B4
Harlington Com Sch
UB3 . . . . 105 B2
Harlington Rd DA7 . . . 147 A2
Harlington Rd E TW13,
TW14 . . . . 150 C3
Harlington Rd UB8 . . . . 82 C3
Harlington Rd W
TW14 . . . . 150 B5
Harlowe Ho 18 E8 . . . . . 95 D6
Harlow Mans 2
IG11 . . . . 78 D1
Harlow Rd N13 . . . . 17 B1
Harlyn Dr HA5 . . . . 40 B6
Harlyn Prim Sch HA5 . 40 B6
Harlynwood 19 SE5 . . 139 A5
Harman Ave IG8 . . . . . . 36 D4
Harman Cl
10 Bermondsey
SE1 . . . . 118 A1
Chingford E4 . . . . 36 B6
Cricklewood NW2 . . . . . 69 A5
Harman Dr
Blackfen DA15 . . . . . . 167 D5
Cricklewood NW2 . . . . . 69 A4
Harman Rd EN1 . . . . 17 D6
HARMONDSWORTH
. . . . 126 A6
Harmondsworth La
UB7 . . . . 126 B6
Harmondsworth Rd
UB7 . . . . 104 A2
Harmon Ho 7 SE8 . . . 119 B2
Harmony Cl NW11 . . . . 47 A4
Harmony Way
Bromley BR1 . . . . 187 A1
Hendon NW4 . . . . 46 C5
Harmood Gr NW1 . . . . . 71 B1
Harmood Ho 2 NW1 . . . 71 B1
Harmood St NW1 . . . . . 71 B1
Harmsworth St
SE17 . . . . 116 D1 261 C1
Harmsworth Way
N20 . . . . 13 C3
Harnage Ho TW8 . . . . 110 A1
Harness Rd SE28 . . . . 124 A4
Harney Ct SE14 . . . . . . 141 A4
Harold Ave
Erith DA17 . . . . 125 B1
Hayes UB3 . . . . 105 D3
Harold Ct
14 Rotherhithe
SE16 . . . . 118 D4
6 Teddington
TW11 . . . . 174 C5
Harold Est SE1 . . . . . . 263 B5
Harold Gibbons Ct 12
SE7 . . . . 143 C6
Harold Ho 16 E2 . . . . . . 96 D5
Harold Laski Ho EC1 23
Harold Maddison Ho
SE17 26
Harold Rd
Chingford E4 2
Hornsey N8 5
Leytonstone E11 5
Newham E13 . . . .
North Acton NW10 . . . .
South Norwood
SE19 18
South Tottenham N15 . . 5
Sutton SM1 21
Woodford IG8 3
Haroldstone Rd E17 . . . 5
Harold Wilson Ho
SW6 26
Haronton Ct E10 7
Harp Alley EC4 24
Harp Bsns Ctr The
NW2 6
Harpenden Rd
Wanstead E12 7
West Norwood SE27,
SW16 16
Harpenmead Point
NW2 6
Harper Cl N14 1
Harper Ho 3 SW9 . . . 13
Harper Mews SW17 . . 15
Harper Rd
Bermondsey
SE1 . . . . 117 A3 26
Newham E6 10
Harper's Yd N17 3
Harp Island Cl NW10 . . 6
Harp La EC3 25
Harpley Sq E1 9
Harpour Rd IG11 7
Harp Rd W7 8
Harpsden St SW11 . . . 26
Harpur Mews WC1 . . . 24
Harpur St
WC1 . . . . 94 B2 24
Harraden Rd SE3 14
Harrier Ave E11 5
Harrier Ct TW4 12
Harrier Ho 9 SW11 . . 13
Harrier Mews SE28 . . . 12
Harrier Rd NW9 2
Harriers Cl W5 11
Harrier Way E6 10
Harries Rd UB4 8
Harriet Cl E8 9
Harriet Gdns CR0 22
Harriet Ho
Walham Green
SW6 265
Walthamstow E17 53
Harriet St
SW1 . . . . 114 D4 247
Harriet Tubman Cl 21
SW2 160
Harriet Way WD23 8
Harriet Wlk
SW1 . . . . 114 D4 247
HARRINGAY 50
Harringay Gdns N8 . . . 50
Harringay Green Lanes
Sta N4 50
Harringay Rd N15 50
Harringay Sta N4 50
Harrington Cl
Wallington CR0 220
Willesden NW10 67
Harrington Ct
6 South Croydon
CR0 221
South Kensington
SW7 256
9 West Kilburn W9 . . . 91
Harrington Gdns
SW7 . . . . 114 A2 256
Harrington Hill E5 52
Harrington Hill Prim
Sch E5 52
Harrington Ho
2 Bromley BR1 187
Regent's Pk NW1 232
Upper Clapton E5 52
Westminster SW1 259
Harrington Rd
Croydon SE25 206
Leytonstone E11 54
South Kensington
SW7 . . . . . 114 B2 256
Harrington Road Sta
SE25 206
Harrington Sq
NW1 . . . . 93 C5 232
Harrington St
NW1 . . . . 93 C4 232
Harrington Way
SE18 121
Harriott Cl SE10 120
Harriott Ho 11 E1 96
Harris Acad CR4 203

ris City Tech Coll
19...183 D2
ris Cl Enfield EN2...4 D4
eston TW5...129 C4
ris Cotts 1 E15...98 D6
ris Ct HA9...66 B5
ris Girl's Acad
15...162 C6
ris Ho 11 Bow E3...97 C4
Brixton SW9...138 C2
ris Lo SE6...164 A3
rrison Cl N20...14 C3
rrison Ho SE17...262 C2
rrison Rd
agenham RM10...81 D2
tonebridge NW10...89 B6
rrisons Ct 1
14...140 D6
rrison's Rise CR0...220 D5
rrison St
/C1...94 A4 233 B1
rrison Way TW17...192 D4
rris Rd
agenham RM9...81 B3
rith DA7...147 B4
rris St
amberwell SE5...139 B5
Valthamstow E17...53 B2
rris Way TW16...171 C2
rrodian Sch The
W13...133 D5
rrogate Ct
2 Forest Hill
SE26...162 A1
9 New Southgate
N11...31 A4
rrold Ho 1 NW3...70 A1
rrold Rd RM8...80 B3
ARROW...42 B3
rrow Ave EN1...17 D5
rroway Rd SW11...136 B3
rrowby St
W1...92 C1 237 B2
rrow Cl KT9...213 D1
rrow Coll HA1...42 C2
rrow Coll (Harrow
Weald Campus)
HA3...24 C4
rrowdene Cl HA0...65 D4
rrowdene Ct
SW19...179 A5
rrowdene Gdns
TW11...175 A3
rrowdene Rd HA0...65 D4
rrow Dr N9...17 D3
rrowes Meade
HA8...10 C1
rrow Fields Gdns
HA1...64 C5
arrowgate Ho 22
E9...74 D2
arrowgate Rd E9...75 A1
arrow Gn E11...76 C5
arrow High Sch &
Sports Coll HA1...43 A3
arrow La E14...120 A6
arrow Lo SM2...218 B2
arrow Manor Way
SE2...124 C3
arrow Mus & Her Ctr*
HA2...42 A6
HARROW ON THE HILL
...42 C1
arrow-on-the-Hill Sta
HA1...42 C3
arrow Pk HA1...64 C6
arrow Pl E1...95 C1 243 B2
arrow Rd
Ashford TW15...148 C2
Barking IG11...101 C6
Carshalton SM5...218 C2
Ilford IG1...79 A4
Leyton E11...76 D5
Little Venice
W2...92 A2 236 B3
2 Newham E6...100 A6
Sudbury HA0...65 A4
Tokyngton HA9...66 C2
Wembley HA0...65 D3
Westbourne Green W2,
W9...91 C3
arrow Sch HA1...42 C1
arrow St NW1...237 A4
arrow View
Harrow HA1, HA2...42 B5
Hayes UB3...84 A1
Hillingdon UB10...83 A4
arrow View Rd W5...87 B3
arrow Way
Charlton TW17...171 A1
South Oxhey WD19...23 A6
ARROW WEALD...24 B2
arrow Weald Pk
HA3...24 B4
arrow & Wealdstone
Sta HA1...42 C5
arry Ct 18 NW9...46 A5
Harry Gosling Prim Sch
E1...96 A1
Harry Hinkins Ho
SE17...262 B1
Harry Lambourn Ho 10
SE15...140 B5
Harston Dr EN3...7 C5
Harston 15 KT1...176 C1
Hart Ct E12...78 C1
Harte Rd TW3...129 B3
Hartfield Ave
Borehamwood
WD6...10 C6
Northolt UB5...84 B5
Hartfield Cl WD6...10 C6
Hartfield Cres
Coney Hall BR4...225 A5
Merton SW19...179 B3
Hartfield Ct CR2...220 D1
Hartfield Gr SE20...184 C2
Hartfield Ho UB5...84 B5
Hartfield Rd
Chessington KT9...213 D3
Hayes BR4...225 A4
Merton SW19...179 C3
Hartfield Terr E3...97 C5
Hartford Ave HA3...43 B6
Hartford Rd
Old Bexley DA5...169 C5
West Ewell KT19...214 D2
Hart Gr W5...110 C5
Hart Grove Ct 3
W5...110 C5
Hartgrove Ct NW9...45 A5
Hart Gr UB1...85 C2
Hartham Cl
Isleworth TW7...131 A4
Lower Holloway N7...72 A3
Hartham Rd
Isleworth TW7...131 A4
Lower Holloway N7...72 A3
Tottenham N17...33 D1
Hart Ho Hayes UB4...83 B2
Streatham SW2...160 C3
Harting Rd SE9...166 A1
Hartington Cl
Farnborough BR6...227 A3
Harrow HA1...64 C4
Hartington Ct
Chiswick W4...132 D5
South Lambeth SW8...270 A2
Hartington Rd
Chiswick W4...133 A4
Ealing W13...109 B6
Newham E16...99 B1
Southall UB2...107 A3
South Lambeth
SW8...138 A5 270 A3
Twickenham TW1...153 B5
Walthamstow E17...53 A3
Hartismere Rd
SW6...135 B5 264 D4
Hartlake Rd E9...75 A2
Hartland Cl
Edgware HA8...10 C2
Enfield N21...17 A5
Hartland Ct 5 N11...30 D5
Hartland Dr
Edgware HA8...10 C2
Ruislip HA4...62 B4
Hartland NW1...232 B5
Hartland Rd
Camden Town NW1...71 B1
Cheam SM4...201 D2
Friern Barnet N11...30 D5
Hampton TW12...173 D6
Isleworth TW7...131 A2
Kilburn NW6...91 B6
Stratford E15...76 D1
Hartlands Cl DA5...169 B5
Hartlands The TW5...128 B6
Hartland Way
Croydon CR0...223 A6
Morden SM4...201 B2
Hartlepool Ct E16...122 D5
Hartley Ave
Edgware NW7...27 D5
Newham E6...100 A6
Hartley Cl
Bickley BR1...188 B1
Edgware NW7...27 D5
Hartley Ct Ealing W5...110 C5
5 Mitcham CR4...180 C2
Hartley Ho
Bermondsey SE1...263 D4
Finchley N3...29 D4
Putney SW15...156 A6
Hartley Prim Sch
E6...100 A6
Hartley Rd
Bexley DA16...146 C5
Leytonstone E11...54 D1
Thornton Heath CR0...205 A2
Hartley St E2...96 C4
Hart Lo EN5...1 A2
Hartmann Rd E16...122 A5
Hartmoor Mews EN3...6 D6
Hartnoll Ho 4 N7...72 C3
Hartnoll St N7...72 B3
Harton Cl BR1...187 D2
Harton Lodge 2
SE8...141 C4
Harton Rd N9...18 B2
Harton St SE8...141 C4
Hartopp Ct 20 N16...73 C5
Hartopp Point SW6...264 B4
Hartsbourne Ave
WD23...8 B2
Hartsbourne Cl WD23...8 B2
Hartsbourne Ct 5
UB1...86 A1
Hartsbourne Pk WD23...8 C2
Hartsbourne Prim Sch
WD23...8 B2
Hartsbourne Rd WD23...8 B2
Harts Gr IG8...37 A5
Hartshill Cl UB10...60 D2
Hartshorn Alley EC3...243 B1
Hartshorn Gdns E6...100 C3
Harts La IG11...78 D2
Hart's La SE14...141 A4
Hartslock Dr SE2...124 D4
Hartsmead Rd SE9...166 B2
Hart Sq SM4...201 C3
Hart St EC3...253 B6
Hartsway EN3...6 C1
Hartswood Gn WD23...8 B2
Hartswood Ho 10
SW2...160 A3
Hartswood Rd W12...111 D3
Hartsworth Cl E13...98 D5
Hartville Rd SE18...123 C2
Hartwell Cl SE22...140 A1
Hartwell Dr E4...36 A4
Hartwell Ho 2 SE7...121 B1
Hartwell St E8...73 D2
Harvard Ct
9 Eltham SE9...166 C5
West Hampstead
NW6...69 D3
Harvard Hill W4...132 D6
Harvard Ho
3 Camberwell
SE17...138 D6
Putney SW15...156 D5
Harvard Mans 18
SW11...136 B1
Harvard Rd
11 Acton Green
W4...111 A1
Gunnersbury W4...110 D1
Hounslow TW7...130 C4
Lewisham SE13...164 A6
Harvel Cres SE2...124 D1
Harvel Ct SE2...125 A1
Harvest Bank Rd
BR4...225 A5
Harvest Ct
Beckenham BR3...185 C3
Littleton TW17...192 C5
Harvesters Cl TW7...152 B6
Harvest La
Loughton IG10...21 D4
Thames Ditton KT7...197 A3
Harvest Rd TW13...150 A1
Harvey Ct
Battersea SW11...267 B2
Walthamstow E17...53 C4
Harvey Dr TW12...173 C2
Harvey Gdns
Greenwich SE7...121 C1
Leytonstone E11...54 D1
Harvey Ho
Barking IG11...79 A1
10 Bethnal Green E1...96 B3
Brentford TW8...110 A1
Dagenham RM6...58 D5
Hornsey N8...50 A6
Pimlico SW1...259 D1
Shoreditch N1...235 D5
Wembley Pk HA9...66 D6
Harvey Lo 8 W9...91 C2
Harvey Mews N8...50 B4
Harvey Point 7 E16...99 A2
Harvey Rd
15 Camberwell
SE5...139 B4
Hillingdon UB10...82 C5
Hornsey Vale N8...50 B4
Ilford IG1...78 D3
Leytonstone E11...54 D1
Ruislip UB5...62 C1
Twickenham TW4...151 B4
Walton-on-T KT12...194 A2
Harvey St N1...235 D5
Harvill Rd
Newyears Green
UB9...38 A2
Sidcup DA14...191 A5
Harvil Rd UB9, UB10...38 A2
Harvington Sch W5...87 D1
Harvington Wlk E8...74 A1
Harvist Rd NW6...91 A5
Harwell Cl HA4...39 B1
Harwood Ave
Bromley BR1...187 B1
Mitcham CR4...202 C6
Harwood Cl
London N12...30 C4
Wembley HA0...65 D4
Harwood Ct
Putney SW15...134 C1
Shoreditch N1...235 D5
Harwood Dr UB10...82 B6
Harwood Point
SE16...119 B4
Harwood Rd
SW6...135 D5 265 C3
Harwoods Yd N21...16 C4
Harwood Terr
SW6...135 D4 265 C2
Hascombe Ho 11
SW15...156 B3
Hascombe Terr 2
SE5...139 B3
Haselbury Rd N9...17 C1
Haseley End SE23...162 C4
Haselrigge Rd SW4...137 D1
Haseltine Prim Sch
SE26...185 B6
Haseltine Rd SE26...185 B6
Haselwood Dr EN2...4 D1
Haskard Rd RM9...80 D4
Hasker St
SW3...114 C2 257 B4
Haslam Ave SM3...201 A1
Haslam Cl
Islington N1...72 C1
Uxbridge UB10...61 A6
Haslam Ct N11...31 B6
Haslam Ho 12 N1...73 A1
Haslam St SE15...139 D4
Haslemere Ave
Barnet EN4...14 D3
Cranford TW5...128 C3
Ealing W13...109 A3
Hendon NW4...46 D3
Mitcham CR4, SW19...180 B1
Wandsworth SW18...157 D2
Haslemere Bsns Ctr
EN1...18 B6
Haslemere Cl
Hampton TW12...173 B5
Wallington SM6...220 A3
Haslemere Ct 5 N16...51 C1
Haslemere Gdns N3...47 B5
Haslemere & Heathrow
Est The TW4...128 B3
Haslemere Ind Est
Feltham TW14...150 A6
Wandsworth SW18...157 D2
Haslemere Prim Sch
CR4...180 B1
Haslemere Rd
Bexleyheath DA7...147 C3
Hornsey N8...50 A2
Ilford IG3...79 D6
Southgate N21...16 D3
Thornton Heath CR7...204 D4
Hasler Cl SE28...124 C6
Hasler Ct E12...78 A4
Haslett Rd TW17...171 C1
Hasluck Gdns EN5...14 A5
Hasmonean High Sch
(Boys) NW4...28 D1
Hasmonean High Sch
(Girls) NW7...28 A2
Hasmonean Prim Sch
NW4...46 D4
Hassard St E2...95 D5
Hassendean Rd SE3...143 B5
Hassett Rd E9...75 A2
Hassocks Cl SE23,
SE26...162 B1
Hassocks Rd SW16...181 D2
Hassock Wood BR2...225 D4
Hassop Rd NW2...68 D4
Hassop Wlk SE9...188 A6
Hasted Rd SE7...121 D1
Hasting Ct TW11...174 B5
Hastings Ave IG6...57 A5
Hastings Cl
New Barnet EN5...2 A1
17 Peckham SE15...140 A5
Wembley HA0...65 C4
Hastings Dr KT6...197 C3
Hastings Ho
Ealing W13...109 B6
Enfield EN3...6 C3
18 Shepherd's Bush
W12...112 B6
Hastings Hos WC1...233 A1
Hastings Ho
Tottenham N17...34 A2
6 Woolwich SE18...122 B2
Hastings Pl 1 CR0...205 D1
Hastings Rd
Croydon CR0...205 D1
Ealing W13...109 B6
Keston Mark BR2...226 A6
Tottenham N17...51 B6
Hastings Rd *continued*
Wood Green N11...31 D5
Hastings St
St Pancras
WC1...94 A4 233 A1
Woolwich SE18...123 A3
Hastingwood Ct
Newham E6...100 B5
Walthamstow E17...53 D4
Hastingwood Trad Est
N18...35 A4
Hastoe Cl UB4...85 A3
Hasty Cl CR4...181 A2
Hatcham Mews Bsns Ctr
SE14...140 D4
Hatcham Park Mews
SE14...140 D4
Hatcham Park Rd
SE14...140 D4
Hatcham Rd SE15...140 C6
Hatchard Rd N19...72 A6
Hatchcroft NW4...46 B6
HATCH END...23 A3
Hatch End High Sch
HA3...23 D2
Hatch End Sta HA5...23 C3
Hatchers Mews SE1...253 B1
Hatchett Rd TW14...149 A3
Hatchfield Ho 8
N15...51 C3
Hatch Gr RM6...59 A5
Hatch Ho
9 Muswell Hill
N10...31 A3
14 Richmond TW10...153 C1
Hatch La E4...20 C1
Hatch Pl KT2...176 B5
Hatch Rd SW16...182 A1
Hatch The EN3...6 D4
Hatchwoods IG8...36 D6
Hatcliffe Almshouses 8
SE10...120 C1
Hatcliffe Cl SE3...142 D2
Hatcliffe St SE10...120 D1
Hatfield Cl
Deptford SE14...140 D5
Ilford IG6...56 D6
Mitcham CR4...202 B5
Hatfield Ct
Greenwich SE3...143 A5
8 Northolt UB5...84 C4
Hatfield Ho
16 Kingston u T
KT6...198 A4
Leytonstone E11...54 D2
St Luke's EC1...242 A5
Hatfield Mead SM4...201 C4
Hatfield Mews RM9...81 A1
Hatfield Prim Sch
SM4...201 A3
Hatfield Rd
Acton W4...111 B4
Dagenham RM9...81 A1
10 Ealing W13, W7...109 A5
Stratford E15...76 C3
Hatfields
SE1...116 C5 251 B4
Hathaway Cl
Bromley BR2...210 B1
Ruislip HA4...61 D4
Stanmore HA7...25 A5
Hathaway Cres E12...78 C2
Hathaway Gdns
Ealing W13...87 A2
Ilford RM6...58 D4
Hathaway Ho 3 N1...95 C4
Hathaway Prim Sch
W13...86 D2
Hathaway Rd CR0...204 D2
Hatherleigh Cl
Barnet EN4...1 D4
Chessington KT9...213 D3
Edgware NW7...28 D3
Morden SM4...201 C5
Hatherleigh Ho
SM4...201 C5
Hatherleigh Rd HA4...62 A6
Hatherley Cres
DA14...168 A2
Hatherley Ct 6 W2...91 D1
Hatherley Gdns
London N8...50 A3
Newham E6...99 D4
Hatherley Gr W2...91 D1
Hatherley Ho 2 E17...53 C5
Hatherley Mews E17...53 C5
Hatherley Rd
Richmond TW9...132 B4
Sidcup DA14...168 A1
Walthamstow E17...53 C5
Hatherley St SW1...259 B3
Hathern Gdns SE9...188 C6
Hatherop Rd TW12...173 B3
Hathersage Ct N1...73 B3
Hathersley Ho 3
SW2...160 C4
Hathorne Cl 3
SE15...140 B3
Hathway Ho 3
SE15...140 C3
Hathway St 4 SE15...140 C3
Hatley Ave IG6...57 A5
Hatley Cl N11...30 D5
Hatley Rd N4, N7...72 B6
Hat & Mitre Ct EC1...241 D5
Hatstone Ct NW3...70 A3
Hatteraick St 6
SE16...118 C4
Hattersfield Cl
DA17...125 B2
HATTON...127 D1
Hatton Cl SE18...145 B5
Hatton Cross Rdbt
TW6...127 D2
Hatton Cross Sta
TW6...127 D1
Hatton Ct BR7...188 B3
Hatton Gdn
EC1...94 C2 241 B4
Hatton Gdns CR4...202 D4
Hatton Gn TW14...128 A1
Hatton Ho 17 E1...118 A6
Hatton Pl EC1...241 B4
Hatton Rd TW14,
TW6...149 C6
Hatton Rd N TW6...127 B4
Hatton Rd CR0...204 C1
Hatton Row NW8...236 D5
Hatton Sch IG8...55 D6
Hatton St NW8...236 D5
Hatton Wall
EC1...94 C2 241 B4
Haughmond 4 N12...29 D6
Haunch of Venison Yd
W1...238 C1
Hauteville Court Gdns
2 W6...111 D3
Havana Rd SW18,
SW19...157 C2
Havannah St E14...119 C4
Havant Rd E17...54 A6
Havelock Cl 13 W12...112 B6
Havelock Ct
8 Peckham SE15...140 B5
Southall UB2...107 B3
Havelock Hall 8
CR0...205 D1
Havelock Ho
4 Croydon CR0...205 D1
Forest Hill SE23...162 C3
Havelock Pl HA1...42 C3
Havelock Prim Sch
UB2...107 B3
Havelock Rd
Belvedere DA17...125 B2
Bromley BR2...209 C5
Croydon CR0...221 D6
Harrow HA3...42 C6
Southall UB2...107 C3
Tottenham N17...34 A1
Wimbledon SW19...180 A5
Havelock St
Ilford IG1...78 D6
Islington N1...94 A6 233 B6
Havelock Terr
SW8...137 B5 268 D3
Havelock Wlk SE23...162 C2
Haven Cl
Chislehurst SE9...166 B1
Hayes UB4...83 C3
Hinchley Wood KT10...212 C6
Sidcup DA14...190 C4
Wimbledon SW19...156 D1
Haven Ct
Beckenham BR3...186 A1
Hinchley Wood KT10...212 C6
Thornton Heath CR7...204 C6
Haven Gn W5...87 D1
Haven Green Ct W5...87 D1
Havenhurst Rise EN2...4 C3
Haven La W5...88 A1
Haven Lo
15 Enfield EN1...17 C6
Temple Fortune
NW11...47 B4
7 Woolwich SE18...122 D2
Haven Pl Ealing W5...109 D6
Hinchley Wood KT10...212 C6
Havenpool NW8...91 D6
Haven Rd TW15...148 D1
Haven St 18 NW1...71 B1
Haven The
Ashford TW16...172 A3
East Barnet N14...15 B5
Richmond TW9...132 C2
Havenwood HA9...66 D5
Havercourt 3 NW3...70 C2
Haverfield Gdns
TW9...132 C5
Haverfield Rd E3...97 A4

Haverford Way HA8 ... 26 B2
Havergal Villas N15 ... 50 D6
Haverhill Rd
Chingford E4 ... 20 A3
Streatham SW12 ... 159 C3
Havering Gdns RM6 ... 58 D4
Havering Ho N4 ... 51 A2
Havering 8 NW1 ... 71 B1
Havering St E1 ... 96 D1
Havering Way IG11 ... 102 B4
Haverley 15 SW20 ... 178 D3
Haversham Cl TW1 ... 153 D5
Haversham Ct UB6 ... 64 D2
Haversham Lo NW2 ... 68 D3
Haversham Pl N6 ... 70 D6
Haverstock Ct 2
BR5 ... 190 B1
Haverstock Hill NW3 ... 70 D2
Haverstock Rd NW5 ... 71 A3
Haverstock Sch NW1 ... 71 A2
Haverstock St
N1 ... 94 D5 234 D3
Haverthwaite Rd
BR6 ... 227 B5
Havilland Ct HA8 ... 26 B6
Havil St SE5 ... 139 C4
Havisham Ho 25
SE16 ... 118 A4
Havisham Pl SW16 ... 182 D3
Hawarden Gr SE24 ... 161 A4
Hawarden Hill NW2 ... 68 A5
Hawarden Rd E17 ... 52 D5
Hawberry Lo N7 ... 72 A2
Hawbridge Rd E11 ... 54 B1
Hawes Down Inf Sch
BR4 ... 208 B1
Hawes Down Jun Sch
BR4 ... 208 B1
Hawes La BR4 ... 224 C6
Hawes Rd
Bromley BR1 ... 187 B2
Edmonton N18 ... 34 B4
Hawes St N1 ... 72 D1
Haweswater Ho
TW1 ... 152 D6
Hawfinch 20 NW9 ... 27 D2
Hawgood St E3 ... 97 C2
Hawkdene E4 ... 20 A5
Hawke Ct UB4 ... 84 C3
Hawkedale Inf Sch
TW16 ... 193 D6
Hawke Ho 20 E1 ... 96 D3
Hawke Park Rd N22 ... 50 D6
Hawke Pl 29 SE16 ... 118 D4
Hawker Ct 10 KT2 ... 176 C3
Hawke Rd SE19 ... 183 C4
Hawker 28 NW9 ... 27 D2
Hawkesbury Rd
SW15 ... 156 B6
Hawkesfield Rd
SE23 ... 163 B2
Hawkesley Cl TW1 ... 175 A6
Hawkes Rd
Feltham TW14 ... 150 A4
Mitcham CR4 ... 180 D2
Hawkesworth Ho 5
SW4 ... 159 C5
Hawke Twr 4 SE14 ... 141 A6
Hawkewood Rd
TW16 ... 194 A6
Hawkfield Ct TW7 ... 130 C3
Hawk Ho 7 SW11 ... 136 C2
Hawkhurst Gdns
KT9 ... 214 A4
Hawkhurst Rd
SW16 ... 181 D2
Hawkhurst Way
New Malden KT3 ... 199 B4
West Wickham BR4 ... 223 D6
Hawkinge N17 ... 33 B1
Hawkins Cl
Burnt Oak NW7 ... 27 B5
Harrow HA1 ... 42 B2
Hawkins Ho
3 Deptford SE8 ... 141 C6
10 Richmond TW10 ... 153 C1
Hawkins Rd
Teddington TW11 ... 175 B4
Willesden NW10 ... 67 C1
Hawkins Way SE6 ... 185 C5
Hawkley Gdns SE27 ... 160 D2
Hawkridge Cl RM6 ... 58 C3
Hawkridge 19 NW5 ... 71 A2
Hawksbrook La
BR3 ... 208 A3
Hawkshaw Cl 28
SW2 ... 160 A4
Hawkshead Cl BR1 ... 186 C3
Hawkshead NW1 ... 232 A2
Hawkshead Rd
Acton W4 ... 111 C4
Willesden NW10 ... 67 D1
Hawkslade Rd SE15 ... 162 D6
Hawksley Rd N16 ... 73 C5
Hawks Mews 10
SE10 ... 142 A5
Hawksmoor Cl
2 Newham E6 ... 100 A1
Plumstead Comm
SE18 ... 123 C1
Hawksmoor Mews
E1 ... 118 B6
Hawksmoor Pl 2 E2 ... 96 A3
Hawksmoor Sch
SE28 ... 124 B6
Hawksmoor St 5
W6 ... 134 D6
Hawksmouth E4 ... 20 A4
Hawks Rd KT1 ... 176 B1
Hawkstone Rd SE16 ... 118 C2
Hawkwell Ct E4 ... 20 A1
Hawkwell Ho RM8 ... 81 C6
Hawkwell Wlk N1 ... 235 B6
Hawkwood Cres E4 ... 19 D5
Hawkwood La BR7 ... 189 A2
Hawkwood Mount 1
E5 ... 52 B1
Hawlands Dr HA5 ... 41 A2
Hawley Cl TW12 ... 173 B4
Hawley Cres NW1 ... 71 B1
Hawley Inf Sch NW1 ... 71 B1
Hawley Mews 4
NW1 ... 71 B1
Hawley Rd
3 Camden Town
NW1 ... 71 B1
London N18 ... 34 D5
Hawley St NW1 ... 71 B1
Hawley Way TW15 ... 170 D5
Haworth Ho 7
SW2 ... 160 C5
Hawstead Rd SE6 ... 163 D5
Hawsted IG9 ... 21 B4
Hawthorn Ave
Bowes Pk N13 ... 32 A5
Old Ford E3 ... 97 B6
South Norwood CR7 ... 182 D2
Hawthorn Cl
Cranford TW5 ... 128 B5
Hampton TW12 ... 173 C5
Petts Wood BR5 ... 211 B3
Hawthorn Cres
SW17 ... 181 A5
Hawthorn Ct
Littleton TW15 ... 171 A3
2 Pinner HA5 ... 22 C1
Putney SW15 ... 134 B2
Redbridge IG5 ... 56 B6
Hawthorn Ctr HA1 ... 43 A4
Hawthorn Ct
Richmond TW9 ... 132 D4
Sutton SM1 ... 217 C4
8 West Norwood
SW16 ... 182 C5
Hawthornden Cl N12 ... 30 C4
Hawthorndene Cl
BR2 ... 225 A6
Hawthorndene Rd
BR2 ... 225 A6
Hawthorn Dr
Coney Hall BR4 ... 224 C4
Harrow HA2 ... 41 C3
Hawthorne Ave
Harrow HA3 ... 43 A3
Mitcham CR4 ... 180 B1
Ruislip HA4 ... 40 B2
Wallington SM5 ... 219 A1
Hawthorne Cl
Bickley BR1 ... 210 B6
Kingsland N1 ... 73 C2
Sutton SM1 ... 218 A6
Hawthorne Cres
UB7 ... 104 B4
Hawthorne Ct
Chingford E4 ... 35 D4
Ealing W5 ... 110 A5
Pinner HA6 ... 22 A1
Hawthorne Gr NW9 ... 45 A2
Hawthorne Ho SW1 ... 259 B1
Hawthorne Mews
UB6 ... 86 A1
Hawthorne Rd
Bickley BR1 ... 210 B6
Edmonton N18 ... 33 D5
Walthamstow E17 ... 53 C6
Hawthorne Way N9 ... 17 D2
Hawthorn Farm Ave
UB5 ... 85 A6
Hawthorn Gdns W5 ... 109 D3
Hawthorn Gr
Edgware EN5 ... 11 D5
Enfield EN2 ... 5 B5
Penge SE20 ... 184 B2
Hawthorn Hatch
TW8 ... 131 B5
Hawthorn Ho SE14 ... 141 B4
Hawthorn Mews
NW7 ... 29 A2
Hawthorn Pl UB3 ... 105 D6
Hawthorn Rd
Bexleyheath DA6 ... 147 B1
Hawthorn Rd *continued*
Brentford TW8 ... 131 B5
Carshalton SM1 ... 218 C2
Feltham TW14 ... 150 A3
Hornsey N8 ... 50 A6
Wallington SM5,
SM6 ... 219 B1
Willesden NW10 ... 68 A1
Woodford IG9 ... 37 D6
Hawthorns The
2 Cheam SM2 ... 217 C2
Edgware NW7 ... 27 B4
Stoneleigh KT17 ... 216 A1
Hawthorns IG8 ... 21 A1
Hawthorn Terr
DA15 ... 167 D6
Hawthorn Way
TW17 ... 193 B5
Hawthorn Wlk W10 ... 91 A3
Hawtrey Ave UB5 ... 84 D5
Hawtrey Dr HA4 ... 40 A2
Hawtrey Rd NW3 ... 70 C1
Haxted Rd BR1 ... 187 B2
Haybridge Ho 1 E5 ... 74 C6
Hay Cl E15 ... 76 D1
Haycroft Gdns NW10 ... 90 B6
Haycroft Mans NW10 ... 90 A6
Haycroft Rd
London SW2 ... 160 A6
Surbiton KT6 ... 214 A6
Hay Currie St E14 ... 97 D1
Hayday Rd E16 ... 99 A2
Hayden Piper Ho
SW3 ... 267 C6
Hayden's Pl W11 ... 91 B1
Haydock Ave UB5 ... 63 C2
Haydock Gn UB5 ... 63 C2
Haydock Green Flats 2
UB5 ... 63 C2
Haydock Lo 2 SM6 ... 219 D5
Haydon Cl Enfield EN1 ... 17 C6
Kingsbury NW9 ... 45 A5
Haydon Ct NW9 ... 45 A5
Haydon Dr HA5 ... 40 A5
Haydon Ho W7 ... 108 D5
Haydon Park Rd
SW19 ... 179 D5
Haydon Rd RM8 ... 80 C6
Haydon Sch HA5 ... 39 D6
Haydon's Rd SW19 ... 180 A4
Haydons Road Sta
SW19 ... 180 A5
Haydon St E1,
EC3 ... 117 D6 253 C6
Haydon Way SW11 ... 136 B1
Haydon Wlk E1 ... 243 D1
HAYES UB3 ... 83 C1
BR2 ... 209 A2
Hayes Bridge Ret Pk
UB4 ... 106 D6
Hayes Chase BR4 ... 208 C3
Hayes Cl BR2 ... 225 A6
Hayes Cres
Cheam SM3 ... 216 D4
Temple Fortune
NW11 ... 47 B4
Hayes Ct
23 Camberwell
SE5 ... 139 A5
Streatham SW12 ... 160 A3
Wimbledon SW19 ... 179 A4
HAYES END ... 83 B3
Hayes End Cl UB4 ... 83 B2
Hayes End Dr UB4 ... 83 B3
Hayesend Ho SW17 ... 180 A6
Hayes End Rd UB4 ... 83 B3
Hayesford Park Dr
BR2 ... 208 D4
Hayes Gdn BR2 ... 209 A1
Hayes Gr SE15, SE22 ... 139 D1
Hayes & Harlington Sta
UB3 ... 105 D3
Hayes Hill Rd BR2 ... 208 D1
Hayes Hill BR2 ... 208 C1
Hayes La
Beckenham BR2,
BR3 ... 208 B5
Hayes BR2 ... 209 A4
Hayes Mead Rd
BR2 ... 208 C1
Hayes Park Sch UB4 ... 83 D3
Hayes Pl NW1 ... 237 B5
Hayes Prim Sch
BR2 ... 209 B1
Hayes Rd
Bromley BR2 ... 209 A5
Southall UB2 ... 106 B2
Hayes Sch BR2 ... 225 B6
Hayes Sta BR2 ... 208 D1
Hayes St BR2 ... 209 B1
HAYES TOWN ... 106 B5
Hayes Way BR3 ... 208 B5
Hayes Wood Ave
BR2 ... 209 B1
Hayfield Pas E1 ... 96 C3
Hayfield Yd 49 E1 ... 96 C3
Hayford Ct NW2 ... 68 D5
Haygarth Pl 2
SW19 ... 178 D5
Haygreen Cl KT2 ... 176 D4
Hay Hill W1 ... 115 B6 248 D5
Hayhurst N1 ... 234 D6
Hay La NW9 ... 45 B5
Hayland Cl NW9 ... 45 B5
Hay Lane Sch NW9 ... 45 A5
Hayles Bldgs SE11 ... 261 D4
Hayles St
SE11 ... 116 D2 261 C4
Haylett Gdns KT1 ... 197 D5
Hayley Ho DA17 ... 147 C6
Hayling Ave TW13 ... 150 A1
Hayling Cl 20 N16 ... 73 C3
Hayling Ct SM3 ... 216 C4
Haymaker Cl UB10 ... 60 B1
Hayman Cres UB4 ... 83 B5
Haymans Point SE11 ... 260 C2
Haymarket
SW1 ... 115 D6 249 C5
Haymeads Dr KT10 ... 212 A2
Haymer Gdns KT4 ... 216 A5
Haymerle Ho 6
SE15 ... 140 A5
Haymerle Rd SE15 ... 140 A6
Haymerle Sch SE15 ... 140 A6
Haymill Cl UB6 ... 86 D4
Haymills Ct W5 ... 88 B3
Hayne Ho W11 ... 244 A4
Hayne Rd BR3 ... 185 B2
Haynes Cl
Friern Barnet N11 ... 15 A1
Lewisham SE3 ... 142 C2
Tottenham N17 ... 34 B3
Haynes Dr N9 ... 18 B1
Haynes Ho 3 E9 ... 74 D2
Haynes La SE19 ... 183 C4
Haynes Rd HA0 ... 66 A1
Hayne St EC1 ... 94 D2 241 D4
Haynt Wlk SW20 ... 201 A6
Hay's Galleria* SE1 ... 253 A4
Hay's La SE1 ... 253 A4
Haysleigh Gdns
SE20 ... 184 A1
Haysleigh Ho SE20 ... 184 B1
Hay's Mews
W1 ... 115 B5 248 C4
Haystall Cl UB4 ... 83 C5
Hay St E2 ... 96 A6
Hayter Ct E11 ... 77 B6
Hayter Ho W12 ... 112 A6
Hayter Rd SW2 ... 160 B6
Haythorn Ho
SW11 ... 136 B4 266 D1
Hayton Cl 11 E8 ... 73 D2
Hayward Cl SW19 ... 179 D2
Hayward Ct
14 London SW4 ... 138 A3
Mitcham CR4 ... 180 B1
Hayward Gallery*
SE1 ... 116 B5 250 D4
Hayward Gdns
SW15 ... 156 C5
Hayward Ho
Islington N1 ... 234 A4
Lower Clapton E5 ... 74 B5
Hayward Rd
London N20 ... 14 A2
Thames Ditton KT7 ... 196 D1
Haywards Cl RM6 ... 58 C4
Haywards Pl EC1 ... 241 C6
Hayward's Pl EC1 ... 241 C6
Haywood Cl HA5 ... 22 D1
Haywood Ct N11 ... 31 D4
Haywood Lo 23 N7 ... 71 D3
Haywood Rd BR2 ... 209 D5
Haywood Rise BR6 ... 227 C3
Hazel Ave UB7 ... 104 C3
Hazelbank Rd SE6 ... 164 C2
Hazel Bank SE25 ... 183 C1
Hazelbank KT5 ... 199 A1
Hazelbourne Rd
SW12 ... 159 B5
Hazelbury Cl SW19 ... 179 C1
Hazelbury Gn N9 ... 17 C1
Hazelbury Inf Sch
N9 ... 17 C1
Hazelbury Jun Sch
N9 ... 17 C1
Hazelbury La N9 ... 17 C1
Hazel Cl
Brentford TW8 ... 131 B5
Croydon CR0 ... 206 D1
Edmonton N13 ... 17 B1
Hendon NW9 ... 27 D1
Mitcham CR4 ... 203 D5
Peckham SE15 ... 140 A3
Twickenham TW2 ... 152 A4
Upper Holloway N19 ... 71 C6
Hazelcroft Cl UB10 ... 60 B1
Hazelcroft HA5 ... 23 D4
Hazel Ct Ealing W5 ... 110 A6
8 Rotherhithe
SE16 ... 119 A5
9 West Norwood
SW16 ... 182 C5
Hazeldean Rd NW10 ... 67 B1
Hazeldene Dr HA5 ... 40 C6
Hazeldene Gdns
UB10 ... 83 A6
Hazeldene Rd
Bexley DA16 ... 146 C3
Ilford IG3 ... 80 B6
Hazeldon Rd SE4 ... 163 A6
Hazel Gdns HA8 ... 26 D6
Hazel Gr RM6 ... 59 A6
Hazelgreen Cl N21 ... 16 D3
Hazel Gr Enfield EN1 ... 18 A5
Feltham TW14 ... 150 A3
Forest Hill SE26 ... 184 D6
Orpington BR6 ... 226 D6
Wembley HA0 ... 88 A6
Hazel Ho London SE4 ... 141 B2
12 Maitland Pk NW3 ... 70 D2
Hazelhurst BR3 ... 186 B2
Hazelhurst Ct SE6 ... 186 A5
Hazelhurst Rd
SW17 ... 180 B6
Hazellville Rd N19 ... 49 D1
Hazel Mead EN5 ... 12 B6
Hazelmere Cl
Feltham TW14 ... 149 C5
Northolt UB5 ... 85 B5
Hazelmere Ct 10
SW2 ... 160 B3
Hazelmere Dr UB5 ... 85 B5
Hazelmere Rd
Kilburn NW6 ... 91 B6
Northolt UB5 ... 85 B5
Petts Wood BR5 ... 211 B5
Hazelmere Way
BR2 ... 209 A3
Hazelmere Wlk UB5 ... 85 B5
Hazel Rd
Kensal Green
NW10 ... 90 C4
Stratford E15 ... 76 C3
Hazeltree La UB5 ... 85 A4
Hazel Way
Bermondsey SE1 ... 263 C4
Walthamstow E4 ... 35 B4
Hazel Wlk BR2 ... 210 C3
Hazelwood Ave
SM4 ... 201 D5
Hazelwood Cl
Clapton Pk E5 ... 75 A5
Ealing W5 ... 110 A4
Harrow HA2 ... 41 D5
Hazelwood Cres N13 ... 32 C6
Hazelwood Ct
1 Edmonton N13 ... 32 C6
Surbiton KT6 ... 198 A3
1 Willesden NW10 ... 67 C5
Hazelwood Dr HA5 ... 22 B1
Hazelwood Ho
Beckenham BR2 ... 208 C6
Chingford E4 ... 20 B4
11 Deptford SE8 ... 119 A2
Edmonton N13 ... 32 D6
2 Sutton SM1 ... 218 A4
Hazelwood Jun & Inf
Schs N13 ... 32 C6
Hazelwood La N13 ... 32 C6
Hazelwood IG10 ... 21 D6
Hazelwood Lo BR4 ... 208 A2
Hazelwood Mans
SW6 ... 264 C2
Hazelwood Rd
Enfield EN1 ... 17 D5
Walthamstow E17 ... 53 A4
Hazlebury Rd SW6 ... 135 D3
Hazledean Rd CR0 ... 221 B6
Hazledene Rd W4 ... 133 A6
Hazlemere Gdns
KT4 ... 200 A1
Hazlemere 3 DA14 ... 190 A6
Hazlewell Rd SW15 ... 156 C6
Hazlewood Cres
W10 ... 91 A3
Hazlewood Twr W10 ... 91 B3
Hazlitt Cl TW13 ... 173 A6
Hazlitt Ct 4 SE28 ... 124 C5
Hazlitt Mews W14 ... 254 A5
Hazlitt Rd
W14 ... 113 A3 254 A5
Heacham Ave UB10 ... 61 A5
Headbourne Ho SE1 ... 262 D6
Headcorn 10 NW5 ... 71 A2
Headcorn Pl CR7 ... 204 B5
Headcorn Rd
Plaistow BR1 ... 187 A5
Thornton Heath CR7 ... 204 B5
Tottenham N17 ... 33 D3
Headfort Pl
SW1 ... 115 A4 248 B1
Headington Rd
SW18 ... 158 A2
Headlam Rd SW4 ... 159 D4
Headlam St E1 ... 96 B3
Headley App IG2 ... 56 D4
Headley Ave CR0,
SM6 ... 220 B3
Headley Cl KT19 ... 214 C2
Headley Ct SE26 ... 184
Headley Dr Ilford IG2 ... 56
New Addington CR0 ... 224
Headley Ho 5 BR5 ... 190
Heads Mews W11 ... 91
Headstart Montessori
Sch SW17 ... 180
Head St E1 ... 96
HEADSTONE ... 41
Headstone Dr HA1,
HA3 ... 42
Headstone Gdns HA2 ... 42
Headstone La
Harrow HA2, HA3 ... 23
Headstone HA2 ... 41
Headstone Lane Sta
HA3 ... 23
Headstone Rd HA1 ... 42
Headway Cl TW10 ... 175
Heald St SE8, SE14 ... 141
Healey Ho RM6 ... 59
Healey St NW1 ... 71
Healy Ct EN5 ... 12
Healy Dr 1 BR6 ... 227
Healy Ho
12 Kennington
SW9 ... 138
2 Tower Hamlets E3 ... 97
Heanor Ct 4 E5 ... 74
Hearne Rd W4 ... 132
Hearn Rise UB5 ... 84
Hearn's Bldgs SE17 ... 262
Hearnshaw St 1 E14 ... 97
Hearn St EC2 ... 95 C3 243
Hearnville Rd SW12 ... 159
Heart Hospl The
W1 ... 93 A2 238
Heart Raido W11 ... 112
Heart The KT12 ... 193
Heatham Pk TW2 ... 152
Heath Ave DA7 ... 146
Heathbourne Rd
WD23 ... 8
Heathbrook Prim Sch
SW4 ... 137
Heath Brow NW3 ... 70
Heath Bsns Ctr The
TW3 ... 130
Heath Cl
Croydon CR2 ... 220
Ealing W5 ... 88
Golders Green NW11 ... 47
Harlington UB3 ... 127
Heathcote Gr E4 ... 20
Heathcote Point 25
E9 ... 74
Heathcote Rd TW1 ... 153
Heathcote Sch E4 ... 20
Heathcote St
WC1 ... 94 B4 233
Heathcroft Ave
TW16 ... 171
Heathcroft W5 ... 88
Heathcroft Gdns E4 ... 36
Heathcroft NW11 ... 47
Heath Ct
Carshalton SM5 ... 218
Eltham SE9 ... 167
2 Hampstead NW3 ... 70
Leytonstone E11 ... 54
Stoke Newington N16 ... 51
Uxbridge UB8 ... 60
Heathdale Ave TW4 ... 129
Heathdene Dr DA17 ... 125
Heathdene N14 ... 15
Heathdene Rd
South Norwood
SW16 ... 182
Wallington SM5,
SM6 ... 219
Heath Dr SW20 ... 200
Heathedge SE23,
SE26 ... 162
Heath End Ct WD23 ... 8
Heatherbank
Chislehurst BR7 ... 188
Eltham SE9 ... 144
Heather Cl
Clapham SW8 ... 137
Hampton TW12 ... 173
Hillingdon UB8 ... 82
Hither Green SE13 ... 164
Isleworth TW7 ... 152
Newham E6 ... 100
Heather Ct
South Lambeth
SW4 ... 270
6 West Norwood
SW16 ... 182
Heatherdale Cl KT2 ... 176
Heatherdene Cl
London N12 ... 30
Mitcham CR4 ... 202
Heatherdene Ct
CR4 ... 202
Heatherdene Mans 2
TW1 ... 153

ner Dr EN2........4 D3
nerfold Way HA5,
..............39 D6
ner Gdns
nont SM2........217 C2
don NW11........47 A3
her Ho 11 E14.....98 A1
her La UB7.......82 A1
herlands TW16..172 A4
herley Ct N16.....74 A5
herley Dr IG5.....56 B6
herley Sch of Fine
SW10.........266 B3
her Lo N16........51 C1
her Park Dr HA0..66 C1
her Park Par
)..............66 B1
her Rd
lis Hill NW2.......67 D6
visham SE12.....165 A3
lthamstow E4.......35 B4
therset Cl KT10..212 A3
therset Gdns
16..............182 B3
herside Rd
cup DA14........168 C1
st Ewell KT19.....215 B1
thers The TW19..148 B4
ther Way HA7.....24 D4
ther Wlk
gware HA8........26 D5
ckenham TW4.....151 C4
st Kilburn W10.....91 A3
therwood Cl E12..77 C6
therwood Dr UB4.83 B5
thfield Ave
/18..............158 B4
thfield
ingford E4.........20 A1
islehurst BR7.....189 A4
thfield Cl
ston BR2.........225 C3
wham E16.........99 D2
thfield Ct
hford TW15......148 A1
Bow E3..........97 C5
Chiswick W4......111 B1
nge SE20........184 C3
lcup DA14.......190 B5
Sutton SM2......218 A2
andsworth SW18...158 B4
thfield Dr CR4...180 C2
thfielde N2......48 A4
thfield Gdns
ton Green W4.....111 A1
ackheath SE3.....142 C3
oydon CR0........221 B4
endon NW11.......46 D3
andsworth SW18...158 B5
thfield Ho SE3...142 C3
thfield Inf Sch
V2..............151 C3
thfield Jun Sch
V2..............151 C3
athfield La BR7...189 A4
athfield N TW1,
V2..............152 D4
athfield Park Dr
M6..............58 B4
athfield Pk NW2....68 C2
athfield Rd
exleyheath DA6.....147 B1
omley BR1........186 D3
oydon CR0........221 B4
eston BR2........225 D3
outh Acton W3.....110 D4
andsworth SW18...158 B5
athfield Rise HA4...39 A2
athfield Sch HA5...40 D2
athfield Sq SW18..158 B4
athfield S TW1,
V2..............152 D4
athfield Terr
hiswick W4........111 B1
umstead Comm
SE18............145 D6
athfield Vale
R2..............223 A1
athgate NW11......47 D3
athgate Pl NW3....70 D4
ath Gdns TW1.....152 D2
ath Gr
shford TW16......171 D3
enge SE20........184 C3
ath Ho
dcup DA15........189 D6
hornton Heath CR7..204 C4
xbridge UB10.......60 D4
ath Hurst Rd NW3..70 C4
ath La SE3........142 B3
athland Rd N16.....51 C1
athland Sch The
W4..............151 B5
athlands Cl
unbury TW16......172 A1
wickenham TW1....152 D3

Heathlands Ct
Hounslow TW4.....151 A6
Mitcham CR4.......203 A6
Heathlands Way
TW4..............151 A6
Heathlee Rd SE3.....142 D1
Heathley End BR7....189 A4
Heath Lo WD23........8 B3
Heath Mans
5 Hampstead
NW3.............70 A4
Putney SW15.......156 D5
Heathman's Rd
SW6........135 B4 264 D1
Heath Mead SW19...156 D1
Heathmere Prim Sch
SW15............156 A3
Heath Park Dr BR1...210 A6
Heath Park Gdns
NW3..............69 D5
Heath Park Ind Est
RM8..............59 A1
Heathpool Ct 8 E1....96 B3
Heath Rd
Clapham SW8.......137 B3
Dagenham RM6......59 A2
Harrow HA1.........42 A2
Hillingdon UB10......83 A3
Isleworth TW3,
TW7.............130 A1
South Norwood CR7..205 A6
Twickenham TW1.....152 D3
Heath Rise
Hayes BR2.........209 A3
Putney SW15.......156 D5
Heathrow Airport
London TW6.......126 D3
Heathrow Bvd UB7...126 B5
Heathrow Causeway Est
TW4..............128 B2
Heathrow International
Trad Est TW4......128 B2
Heathrow Prim Sch
UB7..............126 B6
Heathrow Terminal 4
Sta TW6..........149 A5
Heathrow Terminals 1,
2, 3 TW6.........126 D2
Heath Royal SW15....156 D5
Heath's Cl EN1........5 C3
Heathshott 8
TW10.............154 A5
Heathside Ave DA7...147 A3
Heath Side BR5......211 A2
Heathside Cl
Hinchley Wood
KT10............212 C5
Ilford IG2..........57 B4
Heathside
Hampstead NW3......70 B4
Hinchley Wood KT10..212 C5
Heathside Prep Sch
NW3..............70 A4
Heathside TW4.......151 B4
Heathstan Rd W12.....90 A1
Heath St NW3........70 A5
Heath Terr RM6.......58 D2
Heath The W7........108 C5
Heath View Cl N2.....48 A5
Heathview Ct SW19..156 D2
Heath View Dr SE2...146 D6
Heathview Gdns
SW15............156 C4
Heath View
Gospel Oak NW5......71 A4
London N2...........48 A5
Heathview Rd CR7...204 C5
Heath Villas
Hampstead NW3......70 B5
Plumstead Comm
SE18............123 D1
Heathville Rd N4,
N19..............50 A2
Heathwall St SW11...136 D2
Heathway CR0.......223 B5
Heathway Ct NW3.....69 C6
Heathway
Dagenham RM10......81 C2
Dagenham RM10.....103 C6
Greenwich SE3......143 A5
Heathway Ind Est
RM10..............81 D4
Heathway IG8........37 C5
Heathwood Ct
1 Hounslow
TW3.............129 D1
Streatham SW12.....159 C3
Heathwood Gdns
SE7..............122 A1
Heathwood Point 7
SE26.............162 D1
Heaton Cl E4.........20 A1
Heaton Ct 3 N20......14 D2
Heaton Ho
Chelsea SW10......266 B6
6 Peckham SE15....140 B3

Heaton Rd
London SE15.......140 B3
Mitcham CR4.......181 A3
Heaven Tree Cl N1....73 A3
Heaver Rd 24 SW11..136 B2
Heavers Farm Prim Sch
SE25.............205 D4
Heavitree Cl SE18....123 B1
Heavitree Ct E17.....35 D2
Heavitree Rd SE18....123 B1
Hebble Ho UB5........85 A6
Hebden Ct 24 E2......95 D6
Hebden Terr N17......33 C4
Hebdon Rd SW17.....158 C1
Hebe Ct SM1........218 A4
Heber Prim Sch
SE22.............161 D5
Heber Rd
Cricklewood NW2.....68 D4
East Dulwich SE22...161 D5
Hebron Rd W6.......112 B3
Hecham Cl E17.......35 A2
Heckfield Pl
SW6........135 C5 265 A3
Heckford Ho E14......97 D1
Heckford St E1......118 D6
Hector Ct
1 London SW9......138 C4
Putney SW15.......156 D6
Hector Ho 14 E2......96 B5
Hector 31 NW9........27 D2
Hector St SE18......123 C2
Heddington Gr N7.....72 B3
Heddon Cl TW7......131 A1
Heddon Court Ave
EN4...............14 D6
Heddon Court Par
EN4...............15 A6
Heddon Ct EN4.......15 A6
Heddon Rd EN4.......14 D6
Heddon St W1.......249 A6
Hedge Hill EN2........4 D4
Hedge La N13.........17 A1
Hedgeley IG4.........56 B5
Hedgemans Rd RM9...81 A1
Hedgemans Way
RM9...............81 A2
Hedgemoor Ct 1 E4...36 B5
Hedgerley Gdns UB6..86 A5
Hedgerow La EN5.....12 B6
Hedger's Gr E9.......75 A2
Hedger St SE11......261 C4
Hedge Wlk SE6......185 D6
Hedgewood Gdns
IG5...............56 C4
Hedgewood Specl Sch
UB4...............83 C4
Hedgley Mews
SE12.............164 D6
Hedgley St SE12.....164 D6
Hedingham Cl 6 N1...73 A1
Hedingham Ho 7
KT2..............176 A2
Hedingham Rd RM8...80 B3
Hedley Ct SW15.....156 D5
Hedley Ho E14......120 A3
Hedley Rd TW4......151 C4
Hedley Row N5, N16...73 B3
Hedsor Ho E2.......243 C6
Heenan Cl IG11.......79 A2
Heene Rd EN2.........5 B4
Heidegger Cres
SW13.............134 B5
Heigham Rd E6.......78 A1
Heighton Gdns CR0...220 D3
Heights Cl SW20.....178 B3
Heights The
Beckenham BR3.....186 A3
Greenwich SE7......121 C1
Hampstead NW3......70 A4
Northolt UB5........63 C3
Stroud Green N4.....50 C3
Heiron St SE17......138 D6
Helby Rd SW4.......159 D5
Heldar Ct SE1......252 D1
Helder Gr SE12.....164 D4
Helder St CR2......221 B2
Heldmann Cl TW7....130 B1
Helegan Cl BR6.....227 D4
Helena Cl EN4.........2 B5
Helena Ct W5.........87 D2
Helena Pl 3 E9.......96 C6
Helena Rd Ealing W5...87 D2
Newham E13.........99 A5
Walthamstow E17.....53 C4
Willesden NW10......68 B3
Helena Sq 12 SE16...119 A6
Helen Ave TW14.....150 B4
Helen Clare Ct EN2....4 D2
Helen Cl
East Finchley N2.....48 A6
East Molesey KT8....195 D5
Helen Ct N3..........47 A6
Helen Gladstone Ho
SE1..............251 C2
Helen Ho 9 E2.......96 B5

Helen Mackay Ho 10
E14...............98 B1
Helen Peele Cotts 10
SE16.............118 C3
Helenslea Ave NW11..47 C1
Helen's Pl E2.........96 C4
Helen St SE18.......122 D2
Helen Taylor Ho 5
SE16.............118 A2
Helford Cl HA4.......61 C6
Helgiford Gdns
TW16.............171 C3
Helios Rd CR4.......203 A1
Heliport Est The
SW11.............136 B3
Helix Ct 17 W11.....112 D5
Helix Gdns SW2......160 B5
Helix Ho TW7........131 B3
Helix Rd SW2........160 B5
Helix The SW19.....156 D2
Hellenic Coll of London
SW1........114 D3 257 C5
Hellen Way WD19.....22 D6
Hellings St E1......118 A5
Helme Cl SW19......179 B5
Helmet Row EC1.....242 B6
Helmore Rd IG11.....79 D1
Helmsdale Cl UB4....85 A3
Helmsdale Ho NW6....91 D5
Helmsdale Rd
SW16.............181 D2
Helmsley Pl E8.......74 B1
Helmsley St 7 E8.....74 B1
Helmsley 11 E18......55 A6
Helperby Rd NW10....67 C1
Helsby Ct NW8......236 C6
Helsinki Sq SE16....119 A3
Helston Cl HA5.......23 B3
Helston Ct N15.......51 C4
Helston Ho SE11.....261 B2
Helston NW1........232 B4
Helvetia St SE6.....163 B2
Helwys Ct E4.........36 A4
Hemans Est
SW8.......137 D5 269 D3
Hemans St
SW8.......137 D5 269 D3
Hemberton Rd SW9..138 A2
Hemery Rd UB6.......64 B3
Hemingford Cl N12....30 B5
Hemingford Rd
Cheam SM3.........216 C4
Islington N1..94 B6 233 D6
Heming Rd HA8........26 D3
Hemington Ave N11...30 D5
Hemlock Rd W12.....111 D6
Hemmen La UB3.......83 D1
Hemming Cl 6
TW12.............173 C2
Hemmings Cl DA14...168 B2
Hemmings Ct HA8.....27 A3
Hemmings Mead
KT19.............215 A2
Hemming St E1........96 A3
Hemmingway Cl
NW5...............71 A4
Hempstead Cl IG9....21 A2
Hempstead Rd E17....36 B1
Hemp Wlk SE17......262 D4
Hemsby Rd KT9......214 B2
Hemstal Rd NW6......69 C1
Hemswell Dr NW9.....27 C2
Hemsworth Ct N1.....95 C5
Hemsworth St N1.....95 C5
Hemus Pl SW3.......257 B1
Henchman St W12.....89 D1
Hendale Ave NW4.....46 B6
Hendale Ho 13 E5....74 B6
Henderson Cl NW10...67 A2
Henderson Ct
8 Deptford SE14....140 D6
Hampstead NW3......70 B3
Wandsworth SW18...158 C4
Woodside Pk N12.....29 D6
Henderson Dr
NW8.........92 B3 236 C6
Henderson Ho 7
RM10..............81 C5
Henderson Rd
Edmonton N9........18 B3
Forest Gate E7......77 C2
Hayes UB4...........84 A4
Thornton Heath CR0..205 B3
Wandsworth SW18...158 C4
Hendfield Ct 5
SM6..............219 B2
Hendham Rd SW17...158 D2
HENDON..............46 C3
Hendon Ave N3.......29 A2
Hendon Central NW4..46 B4
Hendon Central Sta
NW4...............46 B4
Hendon Hall Ct NW4..46 D6
Hendon Ho NW4......46 D4
Hendon La N3........29 B1
Hendon Lo NW4.......46 B6

Hendon Park Mans
NW4...............46 C4
Hendon Park Row
NW11..............47 B3
Hendon Pk Cotts
NW7...............11 D2
Hendon Prep Sch
NW4...............46 D6
Hendon Rd N9........18 A2
Hendon Sch NW4......46 D4
Hendon Sta NW4......46 A3
Hendon Terr TW15...171 B4
Hendon Way NW2,
NW4...............46 C3
Hendon Wood La
NW7...............12 A3
Hendre Ho SE1......263 B3
Hendren Cl UB6......64 B3
Hendre Rd
SE1.........117 C2 263 B3
Hendrick Ave SW12..158 D4
Heneage La EC3.....243 B1
Heneage Pl EC3.....243 B1
Heneage St
E1..........95 D2 243 D4
Henfield Cl
London N19..........49 C1
Old Bexley DA5.....169 C5
Henfield Rd SW19....179 B2
Hengelo Gdns CR4...202 B5
Hengist Rd
Eltham SE12........165 B4
Erith DA8..........147 D5
Hengist Way BR2,
BR3..............208 C5
Hengrave Rd SE23...162 D4
Hengrove Ct DA5....169 A3
Henley Ave SM3.....217 A5
Henley Cl
Greenford UB6.......86 A5
Hounslow TW7......130 D4
Rotherhithe SE16...118 C4
Henley Ct
Brondesbury NW2.....68 D2
Hendon NW4..........46 A6
Ilford IG1...........78 D4
Mitcham CR4........203 A6
Oakwood N14.........15 C4
Peckham SE15.......140 A2
Sidcup DA5.........169 B4
Henley Dr
Bermondsey
SE1.......117 D2 263 D4
Kingston u T KT2....177 D3
Henley Gdns
Dagenham RM6........59 A4
Pinner HA5...........40 B6
Henley Ho
London N12..........30 B5
Shoreditch E2.......243 D6
Henley Lo
South Norwood
SE25.............205 D5
Walthamstow E17.....53 B4
Henley Prior N1.....233 C3
Henley Rd
Edmonton N18........33 C6
Ilford IG1...........79 B4
Newham E16.........122 B4
Willesden NW10......90 C6
Henleys Cnr NW11....47 B5
Henleys Rdbt TW5...128 C3
Henley St SW11.....137 A3
Henley Way TW13....172 D5
Henlow Pl TW10.....153 D2
Hennel Cl SE23.....162 C1
Hennessy Rd N9......18 C2
Henniker Gdns E6...100 A4
Henniker Mews
SW3..............266 C6
Henniker Point E15...76 C3
Henniker Rd E15......76 B3
Henningham Rd N17...33 B2
Henning St
SW11.......136 C4 267 A1
Henrietta Barnett Sch
NW11..............47 D3
Henrietta Cl SE8....141 C6
Henrietta Ho
11 Hammersmith
W6...............112 C1
3 New Barnet EN5.....2 A1
3 South Tottenham
N15...............51 C3
Henrietta Mews
WC1..............240 B6
Henrietta Pl
W1..........93 B1 238 C2
Henrietta St
Strand
WC2.......116 A6 250 B6
Stratford New Town
E15...............76 A3
Henriques St E1......96 A1
Henry Addlington Cl
E6...............100 D2

Henry Cavendish Prim
Sch SW12.........159 C3
Henry Cl EN2..........5 C5
Henry Compton Sec Sch
SW6.........135 A4 264 A2
Henry Cooper Way
SE12.............187 D6
Henry Darlot Dr
NW7...............29 A5
Henry Dent Cl SE5...139 B2
Henry Dickens Ct
W11..............244 A4
Henry Doulton Dr
SW17.............181 B6
Henry Fawcett Prim Sch
SE11.............138 C6
Henry Green Prim Sch
RM8...............80 D6
Henry Hatch Ct
SM2..............218 A1
Henry Ho
Lambeth SE1.......251 B3
South Lambeth SW8..270 A4
St John's Wood NW8..230 A4
Henry Jackson Ho
SW15.............134 D2
Henry Jackson Rd
SW15.............134 D2
Henry Macaulay Ave 13
KT2..............175 D2
Henry Maynard Inf Sch
E17...............54 A4
Henry Maynard Jun Sch
E17...............54 A4
Henry Peters Dr
TW11.............174 C5
Henry Rd London N4...51 A1
New Barnet EN4......14 B6
Newham E6..........100 A5
Henry's Ave IG8......36 D5
Henryson Rd SE4....163 C6
Henry St BR1........187 B2
Henry Tate Mews
SW16.............182 C5
Henry Wise Ho SW1..259 B3
Hensford Gdns
SE26.............184 B6
Henshall Point 19 E3..97 D4
Henshall St N1.......73 B2
Henshawe Rd RM8.....80 D5
Henshaw St
SE17.......117 B2 262 C4
Hensley Point 28 E9...74 D2
Henslowe Rd SE22...162 A6
Henslow Ho 12
SE15.............140 A5
Henson Ave NW2......68 C3
Henson Cl BR6.......226 D6
Henson Ct 3 N5......73 A4
Henson Path HA3.....43 D6
Henson Pl UB5........84 C6
Henstridge Pl NW8..230 A5
Henty Cl
SW11.......136 C4 267 B2
Henty Wlk SW15.....156 B6
Henville Rd BR1.....187 B2
Henwick Prim Sch
SE9..............144 A2
Henwick Rd SE9.....144 A2
Hepburn Gdns BR2...208 D1
Hepburn Mews
SW11.............158 D6
Hepple Cl TW7......131 B3
Hepplestone Cl
SW15.............156 B5
Hepscott Rd E9.......75 C1
Hepworth Ct
Barking IG11.........80 A3
Cheam SM3..........201 C1
Chelsea SW1........258 C1
Islington N1.......234 C6
Hepworth Gdns IG11..80 A3
Hepworth Ho IG8......21 A1
Hepworth Rd SW16...182 A3
Hepworth Way
KT12.............193 D1
Heracles Cl SM6....220 A1
Heracles 30 NW9.....27 D2
Hera Ct 15 E14......119 C2
Herald Gdns SM6....219 B5
Heralds Pl SE11....261 C4
Herald St 5 E2.......96 B3
Herbal Hill EC1....241 B5
Herbert Chapman Ct
N5................72 D4
Herbert Cres SW1...257 D6
Herbert Ct 4 KT5....198 B3
Herbert Gdns
Chiswick W4........132 D6
Dagenham RM6........58 D2
Willesden Green
NW10..............90 B5
Herbert Ho E1.......243 C2

Herbert Mews 15 SW2 ... 160 C5
Herbert Morrison Ho SW6 ... 264 C5
Herbert Morrison Prim Sch SW8 ... 138 A5 270 A3
Herbert Pl
Hounslow TW3 ... 130 B3
Shooters Hill SE18 ... 144 D6
Herbert Rd
Bexleyheath DA7 ... 147 A3
Bromley BR2 ... 210 A4
Hendon NW9 ... 46 A3
Ilford IG3 ... 79 C6
Kingston u T KT1 ... 198 B6
Manor Pk E12 ... 78 A4
Merton SW19 ... 179 B3
Shooters Hill SE18 ... 144 D6
Southall UB1 ... 107 B5
South Tottenham N15 ... 51 D4
Walthamstow E17 ... 53 B2
Wood Green N11 ... 32 A3
Herbert St
Camden Town NW5 ... 71 A2
Newham E13 ... 99 A5
Herbrand Est WC1 ... 94 A3 240 A6
Herbrand St WC1 ... 94 A3 240 A6
Hercies Rd UB10 ... 60 C2
Hercules Ct 7 SE14 ... 141 A6
Hercules Pl N7 ... 72 A5
Hercules Rd SE1 ... 116 B3 260 D5
Hercules St N7 ... 72 A5
Hereford Ave EN4 ... 14 D3
Hereford Bldgs SW3 ... 266 D6
Hereford Ct
20 Belmont SM2 ... 217 C1
6 Croydon CR0 ... 205 D1
6 Ealing W7 ... 86 D2
Harrow HA1 ... 42 C6
Hereford Gdns
London SE13 ... 164 C6
Pinner HA5 ... 41 A4
Redbridge IG1 ... 56 A2
Twickenham TW2 ... 152 A3
Hereford Ho
7 Acton W3 ... 88 C1
5 Brixton SW2 ... 138 C1
28 Camberwell SE5 ... 139 A3
Edgware HA8 ... 26 B3
Knightsbridge SW3 ... 257 B6
Walham Green SW10 ... 265 D4
Hereford Mans 10 W2 ... 91 C1
Hereford Mews 11 W2 ... 91 C1
Hereford Pl SE14 ... 141 B5
Hereford Rd
Acton W3 ... 111 A6
Bayswater W2 ... 113 C6 245 B6
Ealing W5 ... 109 C3
Feltham TW13 ... 150 C3
Wanstead E11 ... 55 B4
Hereford Retreat 5 SE15 ... 140 A5
Hereford Sq SW7 ... 114 A2 256 B3
Hereford St E2 ... 96 A3
Hereford Way KT9 ... 213 D3
Herent Dr IG5 ... 56 B6
Hereward Gdns N13 ... 32 C5
Hereward House Sch NW3 ... 70 B2
Hereward Rd SW17 ... 180 D6
Herga Ct HA1 ... 64 C6
Herga Rd HA3 ... 42 D5
Heriot Ave E4 ... 19 C2
Heriot Rd NW4 ... 46 C4
Heriots Cl HA7 ... 25 A6
Heritage Cl
London SW9 ... 138 D2
Sunbury TW16 ... 172 A2
Heritage Ct SE8 ... 118 D1
Heritage Hill BR2 ... 225 C3
Heritage Ho
22 Putney SW19 ... 156 D3
3 Twickenham TW1 ... 153 A4
Heritage View HA1 ... 64 D5
Herlwyn Ave HA4 ... 61 C5
Herlwyn Gdns SW17 ... 180 D6
Herm Cl TW7 ... 130 A5
Hermes Cl 5 W9 ... 91 C3
Hermes Ct 4 SW9 ... 138 C4
Hermes Ho BR3 ... 185 A2
Hermes St N1 ... 234 A3
Hermes Way SM6 ... 219 D1
Hermes Wlk UB5 ... 85 C5
Herm Ho EN3 ... 6 D5
Hermiston Ave N8 ... 50 A4
Hermiston Ct
3 Hornsey N8 ... 50 A4
7 North Finchley N12 ... 30 B5
Hermitage Cl
1 Abbey Wood SE2 ... 124 C3
Claygate KT10 ... 213 A2
Enfield EN2 ... 4 D3
Littleton TW17 ... 192 C5
Snaresbrook E18 ... 54 D5
Hermitage Ct
2 Child's Hill NW2 ... 69 C5
Colney Hatch N11 ... 30 D4
3 Wanstead E18 ... 55 A5
14 Wapping E1 ... 118 A5
Hermitage Gdns
Child's Hill NW2 ... 69 C5
South Norwood SE19 ... 183 A3
Hermitage La
Child's Hill NW2 ... 69 C5
Croydon CR0 ... 206 A3
South Norwood SW16 ... 182 B3
Hermitage Prim Sch E1 ... 118 A5
Hermitage Rd
London N4, N15 ... 51 A3
South Norwood SE19 ... 183 B4
Hermitage Row 9 E8 ... 74 A3
Hermitage St W2 ... 236 C3
Hermitage The
Barnes SW13 ... 133 D4
Feltham TW13 ... 149 D1
Forest Hill SE23 ... 162 C3
Kingston u T KT1 ... 197 D5
Richmond TW10 ... 154 A6
Uxbridge UB8 ... 60 A2
Hermitage Villas SW6 ... 265 A6
Hermitage Wall E1 ... 118 A5
Hermitage Way HA7 ... 25 A2
Hermitage Wlk E18 ... 54 D5
Hermit Pl NW6 ... 91 D6
Hermit Rd E16 ... 98 D3
Hermit St EC1 ... 234 C2
Hermon Gr UB3 ... 106 A5
Hermon Hill E11 ... 55 A5
Herndon Rd SW18 ... 158 A6
Herne Cl Hayes UB3 ... 83 D1
Willesden NW10 ... 67 B3
Herne Ct WD23 ... 8 A4
HERNE HILL ... 161 A6
Herne Hill SE24 ... 139 A1
Herne Hill Ho SE24 ... 160 D5
Herne Hill Mans SE24 ... 161 A5
Herne Hill Rd SE24 ... 139 A1
Herne Hill Sch SE24 ... 161 A6
Herne Hill Stad SE24 ... 161 B5
Herne Hill Sta SE24 ... 160 D5
Herne Mews N18 ... 34 A6
Herne Pl SE24 ... 160 D6
Herne Rd KT6 ... 214 A6
Heron Cl
Buckhurst Hill IG9 ... 21 A3
Cheam SM1 ... 217 B3
Walthamstow E17 ... 35 B1
Willesden NW10 ... 67 C2
Heron Cres DA14 ... 189 C6
Heron Ct
Bromley BR2 ... 209 C5
16 Cubitt Town E14 ... 120 A3
7 Dulwich SE21 ... 161 B2
9 Forest Hill SE23 ... 162 C3
Ilford IG1 ... 78 D6
5 Kingston u T KT1 ... 198 A6
Merton SW20 ... 178 C1
Mitcham CR4 ... 180 C2
Ruislip HA4 ... 61 B6
Stanwell TW19 ... 148 A3
Herondale Ave SW18 ... 158 C3
Heron Dr N4 ... 73 A6
Herongate N1 ... 235 B6
Herongate Rd E12 ... 77 C6
Heron Hill DA17 ... 125 B2
Heron Ho
Battersea SW11 ... 267 B2
Ealing W13 ... 87 A3
Peckham SE15 ... 139 D4
Sidcup DA14 ... 168 B1
St John's Wood NW8 ... 230 A3
Teddington KT1 ... 175 C2
Heron Ind Est E15 ... 97 D5
Heron Mead EN3 ... 7 C5
Heron Mews IG1 ... 78 D6
Heron Pl
Marylebone W1 ... 238 B2
Heron Pl *continued*
Rotherhithe SE16 ... 119 A5
Heron Quays E14 ... 119 C5
Heron Quays Sta E14 ... 119 C5
Heron Rd
Croydon CR0 ... 221 C6
Herne Hill SE24 ... 139 A1
Isleworth TW1 ... 131 B1
Heronsforde W13 ... 87 C1
Heronsgate HA8 ... 26 C5
Heronsgate Prim Sch SE28 ... 123 B3
Heronslea Dr HA7 ... 26 A5
Heron's Lea N6 ... 48 D3
Herons Pl TW7 ... 131 B2
Heron Sq 27 TW10 ... 153 D6
Herons Rise EN4 ... 2 C1
Herons The E11 ... 54 D3
Heron Trad Est W3 ... 88 D2
Heron Way TW14 ... 128 A1
Heronway IG8 ... 37 C6
Herrick Ct 4 TW10 ... 175 D6
Herrick Ho
18 Camberwell SE5 ... 139 B5
17 Canonbury N16 ... 73 B4
Herrick Rd N5 ... 73 A5
Herrick St SW1 ... 115 D2 259 D3
Herries St W10 ... 91 A5
Herringham Rd SE7 ... 121 C3
Herrongate Cl EN1 ... 5 D3
Hersant Cl NW10 ... 90 A6
Herschell Rd SE23 ... 163 A4
Herschell's Mews SE5 ... 139 A2
Hersham Cl SW15 ... 156 A4
Hersham Rd KT12 ... 194 A1
Hershell Ct 1 SW14 ... 132 D1
Hertford Ave SW14 ... 133 C1
Hertford Cl EN4 ... 2 B2
Hertford Ct
16 London SW11 ... 136 C2
Newham E6 ... 100 B4
Palmers Green N13 ... 16 C1
Hertford Ho 5 UB5 ... 85 B3
Hertford Lo 10 SW19 ... 157 A3
Hertford Pl W1 ... 239 B5
Hertford Rd
Barking IG11 ... 78 D1
Barnet EN4 ... 2 A2
East Finchley N2 ... 48 C6
Edmonton N9 ... 18 B3
Enfield EN3 ... 6 C5
Hertford Rd High St EN3 ... 18 C6
Hertford Rd
Ilford IG2 ... 57 C3
Shoreditch N1 ... 95 C6
Hertford St W1 ... 115 B5 248 C3
Hertford Way CR4 ... 204 A5
Hertford Wlk 13 DA17 ... 125 C1
Hertmitage The 5 SE13 ... 142 A3
Hertslet Rd N7 ... 72 B5
Hertsmere Rd E14 ... 119 C6
Hertswood Ct 1 EN5 ... 1 A1
Hervey Cl N3 ... 29 C2
Hervey Park Rd E17 ... 53 A5
Hervey Rd SE3 ... 143 B4
Hesa Rd UB3 ... 106 A6
Hesewall Cl SW4 ... 137 C3
Hesketh Pl W11 ... 244 A5
Hesketh Rd E7 ... 77 A5
Heslop Ct 1 SW12 ... 159 A3
Heslop Rd SW12 ... 158 D3
Hesper Mews SW5 ... 113 D2 255 C3
Hesperus Cres E14 ... 119 D2
Hessel Rd W13 ... 109 B4
Hessel St E1 ... 96 B1
Hestercombe Ave SW6 ... 135 A4 264 B1
Hester Ct SW16 ... 181 C5
Hesterman Way CR0 ... 204 B1
Hester Rd
Battersea SW11 ... 136 C5 267 A3
Edmonton N18 ... 34 A5
Hester Terr TW9 ... 132 C2
Hestia Ho SE1 ... 253 A1
HESTON ... 129 B5
Heston Ave TW5 ... 129 A5
Heston Com Sch TW5 ... 129 C5
Heston Ctr The TW5 ... 106 C1
Heston Grange TW5 ... 129 B6
Heston Grange La TW5 ... 129 B6
Heston Ho
Gunnersbury W4 ... 110 D1
5 St Johns SE8 ... 141 C4
Heston Ind Mall TW5 ... 129 B5
Heston Inf Sch TW5 ... 129 C5
Heston Jun Sch TW5 ... 129 C5
Heston Phoenix Distribution Pk TW5 ... 128 C6
Heston Rd TW5 ... 129 C5
Heston St SE14 ... 141 C4
Hetherington Rd
Charlton TW17 ... 171 A1
Stockwell SW2, SW4 ... 138 A1
Hetherington Way UB10 ... 60 A4
Hethpool Ho W2 ... 236 C5
Hetley Gdns 1 SE19 ... 183 D3
Hetley Rd W12 ... 112 B4
Heton Gdns NW4 ... 46 A5
Hetty Rees Ct 6 N19 ... 50 A2
Hevelius Cl SE10 ... 120 D1
Hever Croft SE9 ... 188 C6
Heverfield Ct CR4 ... 180 D3
Hever Gdns BR1 ... 188 C1
Heverham Rd SE18 ... 123 C2
Hever Ho SE15 ... 140 D6
Heversham Ho SE15 ... 140 C6
Heversham Rd DA7 ... 147 C4
Hevingham Dr RM6 ... 58 C4
Heward Ct SE13 ... 142 A3
Hewens Rd UB4 ... 83 A3
Hewer Ho 6 SW4 ... 159 C6
Hewer St W10 ... 90 D2
Hewes Ho E17 ... 52 D5
Hewett Cl HA7 ... 25 B6
Hewett Ho
Putney SW15 ... 134 C3
7 Woolwich SE18 ... 122 D1
Hewett Rd RM8 ... 80 D4
Hewetts Quay 7 IG11 ... 101 A6
Hewett St EC2 ... 95 C3 243 B5
Hewish Rd N18 ... 33 C6
Hewison St E3 ... 97 B5
Hewitt Ave N22 ... 32 D1
Hewitt Cl CR0 ... 223 C5
Hewitt Ho 2 E4 ... 36 B5
Hewitt Rd N8 ... 50 D4
Hewlett Rd E3 ... 97 A5
Hewling Ho 1 N16 ... 73 C3
Hexagon Bsns Ctr UB4 ... 106 C6
Hexagon The N6 ... 48 D1
Hexal Rd SE6 ... 164 C1
Hexham Gdns TW7 ... 131 A5
Hexham Rd Barnet EN5 ... 1 D1
Cheam SM4 ... 201 D1
West Norwood SE27 ... 161 A2
Hexton Ct N4 ... 73 A6
Heybourne Rd N17 ... 34 B3
Heybridge Ave SW16 ... 182 B4
Heybridge Dr IG6 ... 57 B6
Heybridge 9 NW1 ... 71 B2
Heybridge Way E10 ... 53 B1
Heydon Ct BR4 ... 224 C6
Heydon Ho 3 SE14 ... 140 C4
Heyford Ave
Merton SW20 ... 201 B6
South Lambeth SW8 ... 138 A5 270 B4
Heyford Rd CR4 ... 180 C1
Heyford Terr SW8 ... 270 B4
Heygate St SE17 ... 117 A2 262 B4
Heylyn Sq E3 ... 97 B4
Heynes Rd RM8 ... 80 C4
Heysham Dr WD19 ... 22 D5
Heysham La NW3 ... 69 D5
Heysham Rd N15 ... 51 B3
Heythorp St SW18 ... 157 B2
Heythrop Dr UB10 ... 60 B4
Heyward Ct SM2 ... 217 C2
Heywood Ave NW9 ... 27 C2
Heywood Ct 2 HA7 ... 25 C5
Heywood Ho
11 Deptford SE14 ... 140 D6
6 Tulse Hill SW2 ... 160 C5
Heyworth Rd
Lower Clapton E5 ... 74 B4
Stratford E15 ... 76 D4
Hibbert Ho 13 E14 ... 119 C3
Hibbert Rd
Harrow HA3 ... 24 D1
Walthamstow E17 ... 53 B2
Hibbert St SW11 ... 136 B2
Hibernia Gdns TW3 ... 151 C6
Hibernia Point 9 SE2 ... 124 D4
Hibernia Rd TW3 ... 129 C1
Hibiscus Cl 6 HA8 ... 27 A6
Hibiscus Lo 5 E15 ... 76 C1
Hichisson Rd SE15 ... 162 C6
Hickes Ho 6 NW6 ... 70 B1
Hickey's Almshouses 7 TW9 ... 132 B1
Hickin Cl SE7 ... 121 D2
Hickin St 2 E14 ... 120 A3
Hickleton NW1 ... 232 B5
Hickling Ho 10 SE16 ... 118 B3
Hickling Rd IG1 ... 78 D3
Hickman Ave E4 ... 36 A4
Hickman Cl E16 ... 99 D2
Hickman Rd RM6 ... 58 C2
Hickmore Wlk SW4 ... 137 C2
Hickory Cl N9 ... 18 A4
Hicks Ave UB6 ... 86 C4
Hicks Cl SW11 ... 136 C2
Hicks Ct RM10 ... 81 D5
Hicks St SE8 ... 119 A1
Hidaburn Ct 7 SW16 ... 181 C6
Hidcote Gdns SW20 ... 200 B6
Hidcote Ho 11 SM2 ... 218 A1
Hide E6 ... 100 C1
Hide Pl SW1 ... 115 D2 259 C3
Hider Ct SE3 ... 143 C5
Hide Rd HA1 ... 42 B5
Hide Twr SW1 ... 259 C3
Hieover SE21 ... 161 A2
Higgins Ho 7 N1 ... 95 C6
Higginson Ho 2 NW3 ... 70 D1
Higgins Wlk TW12 ... 173 A4
Higgs Ind Est 5 SE24 ... 138 D2
High Acre EN2 ... 4 D2
Higham Ct 9 IG8 ... 37 A4
HIGHAM HILL ... 35 A2
Higham Hill Ho E17 ... 34 D2
Higham Hill Rd E17 ... 35 A1
Higham Ho E4 ... 35 C4
Higham Mews UB5 ... 85 B3
Higham Pl E17 ... 53 A6
Higham Rd
Tottenham N17 ... 51 B6
Woodford IG8 ... 37 A4
Highams Lodge Bsns Ctr E17 ... 52 D6
HIGHAMS PARK ... 36 A3
Highams Park Sch E4 ... 36 B4
Highams Park Sta E4 ... 36 B4
Higham Station Ave E4 ... 35 D4
Highams The E17 ... 36 A2
Higham St E17 ... 53 A6
High Ashton 11 KT2 ... 176 D3
Highbanks Cl DA16 ... 146 B5
Highbanks Rd HA5 ... 23 D4
Highbank Way N8 ... 50 C3
HIGH BARNET ... 1 B2
High Barnet Sta EN5 ... 1 C1
Highbarrow Rd CR0 ... 206 A1
High Beeches DA14 ... 191 A5
High Beech
South Croydon CR2 ... 221 C1
Southgate N21 ... 16 B5
High Birch Ct 7 EN4 ... 2 C1
Highbridge Ct 13 SE14 ... 140 C5
Highbridge Rd IG11 ... 100 D6
High Bridge Wharf SE10 ... 120 B1
Highbrook Rd SE3 ... 143 D2
High Broom Cres BR4 ... 207 D2
Highburty Mans 24 N1 ... 72 D1
HIGHBURY ... 72 D4
Highbury Ave CR7 ... 182 D1
Highbury Cl
New Malden KT3 ... 199 A4
West Wickham BR4 ... 223 D6
Highbury Cnr N5 ... 72 D2
Highbury Corner N5 ... 72 D2
Highbury Cres N5 ... 72 C3
Highbury Fields Sch N5 ... 72 D3
Highbury Gdns IG3 ... 79 C6
Highbury Grange N5 ... 73 A4
Highbury Gr N5 ... 72 D3
Highbury Grove Ct N5 ... 72 D2
Highbury Grove Sch N5 ... 73 A3
Highbury Hill N5 ... 72 D4
Highbury & Islington Sta N1 ... 72 D2
Highbury New Pk N5 ... 73 A4
Highbury Pk N5 ... 72 D4
Highbury Pl N5 ... 72 D3
Highbury Quadrant N5 ... 73 A5
Highbury Quadrant Prim Sch N5 ... 73 A4
Highbury Rd SW19 ... 17
Highbury Sq N14 ... 1
Highbury Station Rd N1 ... 7
Highbury Terrace Mews N5 ... 7
Highbury Terr N5 ... 7
High Cedar Dr SW20 ... 17
Highclears 6 IG9 ... 2
Highclere Rd KT3 ... 19
Highclere St SE26 ... 18
Highcliffe BR3 ... 18
Highcliffe Dr SW15 ... 15
Highcliffe W13 ... 8
Highcliffe Gdns IG4 ... 5
Highcombe Cl SE9 ... 16
Highcombe SE7 ... 14
High Coombe Pl KT2 ... 17
Highcroft Ave HA0 ... 8
Highcroft Gdns NW11 ... 4
Highcroft Highgate N6 ... 4
Hyde The NW9 ... 4
2 Kingston u T KT5 ... 19
Highcroft Point E17 ... 3
Highcroft Rd N19 ... 5
High Cross Ctr The N15 ... 5
High Cross Rd N17 ... 5
Highcross Way 4 SW15 ... 15
Highdaun Dr SW16 ... 20
High Dene EN2 ...
Highdown Rd SW15 ... 15
Highdown KT4 ... 21
High Dr KT2, KT3 ... 17
High Elms Ctry Pk* BR6 ... 22
High Elms Rd BR6 ... 22
High Elms IG8 ... 3
Highfield Ave
Erith DA8 ... 14
Greenford UB6 ... 6
Hendon NW11 ... 4
Kingsbury NW9 ... 4
Orpington BR6 ... 22
Pinner HA5 ... 4
Wembley HA9 ... 6
Highfield WD23 ... 8
Highfield Cl
Hither Green SE13 ... 16
Kingsbury NW9 ... 4
Long Ditton KT6 ... 19
Wood Green N22 ... 3
Highfield Ct
7 Barnet EN5 ... 1
Hendon NW11 ... 4
Mitcham CR4 ... 20
Southgate N14 ... 1
Wanstead E12 ... 7
Highfield Dr
Beckenham BR2 ... 20
Ickenham UB10 ... 6
West Ewell KT19 ... 21
West Wickham BR4 ... 22
Highfield Gdns NW11 ... 4
Highfield Hill SE19 ... 18
Highfield Ho N21 ... 1
Highfield Inf Sch BR2 ... 20
Highfield Jun Sch BR2 ... 20
Highfield Mews NW6 ... 6
Highfield Prim Sch
Edmonton N21 ... 1
Hillingdon UB10 ... 8
Highfield Rd
Acton W3 ... 8
Bexley DA6 ... 16
Bromley BR1 ... 21
Carshalton SM1 ... 21
Edmonton N21 ... 1
Feltham TW13 ... 15
Hendon NW11 ... 4
Hounslow TW7 ... 13
Orpington BR5, BR7 ... 21
St Paul's Cray BR5, BR7 ... 21
Tolworth KT5 ... 19
Upper Halliford TW16 ... 19
Walton-on-T KT12 ... 19
Highfield Sch SW18 ... 15
Highfields Gr N6 ... 4
Highfields SM1 ... 21
High Foleys KT10 ... 21
High Gables
Beckenham BR2 ... 18
Loughton IG10 ... 2
High Garth KT10 ... 21
HIGHGATE ... 4
Highgate Archway N6 ... 4

hgate Ave N6...49 B2
igate Ballet Sch
V11...47 D5
hgate Cemetery*
9...71 B6
hgate Cl N6...49 A2
h Gate Edge N2...48 C4
hgate High St N6...49 B1
hgate Hill N19...49 C1
hgate Ho 11
26...162 A1
hgate Hts N6...49 C3
hgate Prim Sch
...48 D3
hgate Private Hospl
...48 D3
hgate Rd NW5...71 B4
hgate Sch
ghgate N6...48 D2
ghgate N6...49 A2
hgate Spinney
...49 D3
hgate Sta N6...49 B3
hgate West Hill
...71 A6
hgate Wlk SE23...162 C2
hgate Wood Sec Sch
...49 C4
h Gr BR1...187 D2
hgrove Cl
ondon N11...31 A5
idmore BR7...188 A2
hgrove Ct BR3...185 C3
hgrove Ho HA4...40 A3
hgrove Mews
M5...218 D5
hgrove Point 2
W3...70 A4
hgrove Rd RM8...80 C4
hgrove Way HA4...40 A2
h Gr SE18...145 B4
h Hill Ferry 3 E5...52 B1
h Holborn Ho
C1...240 D3
h Holborn
C1...94 B2 240 C3
h La W7...86 B1
hland Ave W7...86 C1
hland Cotts SM6...219 C4
hland Croft BR3...185 D4
hland Ct E18...37 B2
hland Dr WD23...8 A4
hland Lo 3
E19...183 D3
hland Pk TW13...171 D6
hland Rd
exley DA6...147 C1
romley BR1...186 D2
nner HA6...22 A1
Vest Norwood SE19...183 C4
hlands Ave
cton W3...111 A6
outhgate N21...16 B6
hlands Cl
ornsey N4...50 A2
ounslow TW3...129 D4
hlands Ct SE19...183 C4
hlands Gdns IG1...56 B1
hlands Heath
W15...156 C4
hlands N20...14 B2
hlands Prim Sch
31...56 B1
hlands Rd EN5...13 C6
hlands Sch N21...4 C1
hlands The
arnet EN5...1 D1
dgware HA8...26 D1
hlawn Hall HA1...64 C5
hlea Cl NW9...27 C2
h Level Dr SE26...184 A6
hlever Rd W10...90 C2
h Limes 2 SE19...183 C4
h London 5 N6...49 D2
hmead Cres HA0...66 B1
hmead 9 N18...34 A5
h Mead HA1...42 D4
h Meadow Cl
A5...40 C5
h Meadow Cres
W9...45 B4
hmead SE18...145 D5
h Meads Rd E16...99 D1
h Mead BR4...224 C6
hmore Rd SE3...142 C5
h Mount
endon NW4...46 A3
1 Hornsey N4...50 A2
h Oaks EN2...4 B5
h Oaks Lo 9 E18...37 A1
h Park Ave TW9...132 C4
h Park Rd TW9...132 C4
h Par The SW16...160 A1
h Path SW19...180 A2
h Point
hislehurst SE9...166 D1
ighgate N6...49 A2
Highpoint EN5...14 A6
High Range SW20...178 C3
High Rd
Buckhurst Hill IG9,
IG10...21 C5
Bushey WD23...8 B3
Chadwell Heath RM6...58 C2
East Finchley N2...48 C6
Finchley N2, N12...30 A3
Friern Barnet N11...31 B5
Harrow HA3...24 C3
Ilford IG1...78 D6
Leyton E10...53 D3
Oakleigh Pk N20...14 A4
Seven Kings IG1, IG3...79 C6
South Tottenham N15,
N17...51 D5
Tottenham N17...33 D2
Wembley HA0, HA9...66 A3
Willesden NW10...68 A2
Woodford E18...37 A2
Wood Green N22...32 B3
High Ridge N10...31 B2
Highridge Pl EN2...4 B5
High Road Buckhurst
Hill 5 IG9...21 B2
High Road Eastcote
HA5...40 B4
High Road, Ickenham
UB10...61 A6
High Road Leyton
E10...75 D6
High Road Leytonstone
E11...76 C6
High Road Woodford
Gn IG8...37 A6
High St Mews
SW19...179 A5
High St N
Newham E6...100 A6
Plashet E12...78 A2
High St S E6...100 B4
High Sheldon N6...48 D3
Highshore Rd SE15...139 D3
Highshore Sch
SE15...139 D4
High Silver IG10...21 D6
High St Acton W3...110 D5
Barnet EN5...1 B1
Beckenham BR3...185 C1
Brentford TW8...132 A6
Bromley BR1...187 A1
Cheam SM1, KT17...217 A2
Claygate KT10...212 D2
Cranford TW5...128 B5
Croydon CR0...221 A5
Ealing W5...109 D6
East Molesey KT8...195 C5
Elstree WD6...9 D5
Farnborough BR6...227 A3
Feltham TW13...150 A2
Green Street Green
BR6...227 D2
Hampton TW12...174 A4
Harlington UB3...127 B6
Harrow on t H HA1...42 C1
Hornsey N8...50 B5
Hounslow TW3...129 D2
Ilford IG6...57 A6
Kingston u T KT1...175 D2
Kingston u T KT1...197 D6
Mill Hill NW7...28 B5
Newham E13...99 A5
New Malden KT3...199 C5
Highstone Ave E11...55 A3
Highstone Ct E11...54 D3
High St
Palmers Green
N14...15 D2
Penge SE20...184 D3
Pinner HA5...41 A6
High Street Collier's
Wood SW17, SW19...180 B4
High Street Harlesden
NW10...89 D5
High Street Harlington
TW6...127 B5
High Street Kensington
Sta W8...113 D4 245 C1
High St Ruislip HA4...39 C1
Shepperton TW17...193 A3
Sidcup DA14...190 A6
Southall UB1...107 B5
South Norwood CR7...205 B5
South Norwood
SE25...206 A5
Stratford Marsh E15...98 A6
Sutton SM1...217 D4
Sutton SM1, SM2...217 D3
Teddington TW11...175 A5
Thames Ditton KT7...197 A3
Twickenham TW2...152 A4
Wallington SM5...219 A4
Walthamstow E17...53 B5
Walton-on-T KT12...194 A1
Wanstead E11...55 A4
Wealdstone HA3...24 C1
High St *continued*
Wealdstone HA3...42 C6
Wembley HA9...66 B4
West Wickham BR4...207 D1
Wimbledon SW19...178 D5
Yiewsley UB7...104 A6
High The SW16...160 A1
High Timber St EC4...252 A6
High Tor Cl BR1...187 B3
High Tor View SE28...123 C5
High Trees
Cheam SM3...201 B2
Croydon CR0...207 A1
Hightrees Ct W7...108 C6
High Trees EN4...14 C6
Hightrees Ho SW12...159 A5
High Trees
Streatham SW2...160 C3
Uxbridge UB10...61 A6
Whetstone N20...14 A1
Highview Ave HA8...27 A6
High View Ave CR0,
SM6...220 B3
High View Cl
Loughton IG10...21 C6
South Norwood
SE19...183 D1
Highview N6...49 C3
High View Ct HA3...24 C3
Highview Ct
2 Loughton IG10...21 D6
2 Putney SW19...157 A3
Highview Gdns
Edgware HA8...27 A6
Hendon N3...47 A6
New Southgate N11...31 C5
Highview Ho
2 Buckhurst Hill
IG9...21 D1
1 Buckhurst Hill IG9...21 D1
High View Ho RM6...59 A5
Highview Hornsey N8...50 A2
Northolt UB5...85 A4
High View Par 1
IG4...56 B4
High View
6 Penge SE19...183 D3
Pinner HA5...40 C6
High View Prim Sch
London SW11...136 B1
Wallington SM6...220 A3
Highview Rd W13...87 A1
High View Rd N10...30 D2
Highview Rd DA14...190 B6
High View Rd
Snaresbrook E18...54 D6
South Norwood
SE19...183 B4
Highview SE18...144 D5
Highway Bsns Pk The 7
E1...118 D6
Highway The
Shadwell E1...118 C6
Stanmore HA7...25 A3
Highway Trad Ctr The
6 E1...118 D6
High Wigsell TW11...175 A5
Highwood Ave N12...30 A6
Highwood Cl
Dulwich SE22...162 A3
Orpington BR6...227 A6
Highwood Ct
Barnet EN5...13 C6
Whetstone N12...14 A1
Highwood Dr BR6...227 A6
Highwood Gdns IG5...56 B5
Highwood Gr NW7...27 B5
Highwood Hill NW7...11 D2
Highwood Rd N19...72 A5
Highwood IG8...36 D6
High Worple HA2...41 B1
Highworth Rd N11...31 D5
Highworth St NW1...237 B4
Hilary Ave CR4...203 A6
Hilary Cl Bexley DA8...147 D4
Walham Green SW6...265 C4
Hilary Ct N9...18 D3
Hilary Rd W12...111 D6
Hilbert Rd SM3...216 D5
Hilborough Cl
SW19...180 A3
Hilborough Ct 1 E8...95 D6
Hilborough Rd 1 E8...73 D1
Hilborough Way
BR6...227 B3
Hilda Lockert Wlk
SW9...138 D3
Hilda Rd Newham E16...98 C3
Upton Pk E6...77 D1
Hilda Terr 2 SW9...138 C3
Hilda Vale Cl BR6...226 D4
Hilda Vale Rd BR6...226 D4
Hildenborough Gdns
BR1...186 D4
Hildenborough Ho
BR3...185 B3
Hildenlea Pl BR2...186 C1
Hilditch Ho 7
TW10...154 B5
Hildred Ho SW1...258 C4
Hildreth St SW12...159 B3
Hildreth Street Mews 2
SW12...159 B3
Hildyard Rd SW6...265 B6
Hiley Rd NW10...90 C4
Hilfield La WD23...8 C6
Hilgrove Rd NW6...70 A1
Hiliary Gdns HA7...25 C1
Hillary Cres KT12...194 C1
Hillary Ct
3 Chislehurst
SE9...166 A2
13 Shepherd's Bush
W12...112 C4
Stanwell TW19...148 A3
Hillary Dr TW7...152 D6
Hillary Rd UB2...107 C3
Hillary Rise EN5...1 C1
Hillbeck Cl
Deptford SE15...140 C5
Deptford SE15...140 C6
Hillbeck Way UB6...86 B6
Hillborne Cl UB3...106 A1
Hillboro Ct
Leytonstone E11...54 B2
1 Woodford E18...36 D2
Hillborough Ct HA1...42 C2
Hillbrook Rd SW17...181 A6
Hillbrook Sch SW17...181 A6
Hill Brow BR1...187 D2
Hillbrow Ct KT10...212 A4
Hillbrow KT3...199 D6
Hillbrow Rd
Catford BR1...186 C4
Esher KT10...212 A4
Hillbrow 7 TW10...154 A5
Hill Bunker's DA17...125 C2
Hillbury Ave HA3...43 B4
Hillbury Rd SW17...159 B1
Hill Cl Barnet EN5...12 C6
Chislehurst BR7...188 D5
Dollis Hill NW2...68 B5
Hampstead Garden
Suburb NW11...47 C3
Harrow HA1...64 C5
Stanmore HA7...25 B6
Hillcote Ave SW16...182 C3
Hillcourt Ave N12...29 D4
Hillcourt N6...49 C3
Hillcourt Rd SE22...162 B5
Hill Cres Harrow HA1...43 A4
Kingston u T KT5...198 B4
North Cheam KT4...216 C6
Hillcrest Ave
Edgware HA8...26 D6
Pinner HA5...40 D5
Temple Fortune
NW11...47 B4
Hillcrest SE24...139 B1
Hillcrest Cl
Beckenham BR3...207 B3
Forest Hill SE26...184 A6
Hillcrest Ct
Brondesbury NW2...69 A3
8 Edgware HA8...26 D5
Lewisham SE6...164 B4
Sutton SM2...218 B2
Hill Crest DA15...168 B4
Hillcrest Gdns
Dollis Hill NW2...68 A5
Hendon N3...47 A5
Hinchley Wood
KT10...212 D5
Hillcrest N6...49 A2
Hillcrest Hts W5...88 A3
Hillcrest W11...244 C5
Hill Cres N20...13 D2
Hillcrest Rd
Acton W3...110 D5
Chingford E17...36 B1
Ealing W5...88 A2
Grove Pk BR1...187 A6
Loughton IG10...21 D5
Woodford E18...37 A1
Hillcrest N21...16 C4
Hillcrest View BR3...207 B3
Hillcroft Ave HA5...41 B3
Hillcroft Coll KT6...198 A3
Hillcroft Cres
Ealing W5...87 D1
Ruislip HA4...62 D5
Wembley HA9...66 B4
Hillcroft Rd E6...100 D2
Hillcroome Rd SM2...218 B2
Hillcross Ave SM4...201 A4
Hillcross Prim Sch
SM4...201 B5
Hill Ct Barnet EN4...2 C1
Ealing W5...88 B3
Hampstead NW3...70 C4
8 Norbiton KT2...176 D3
Northolt UB5...63 C3
Putney SW15...156 D6
14 Surbiton KT6...198 A4
Hill Ct *continued*
Wembley HA0...65 A4
9 Wimbledon
SW19...179 A4
Hilldale Rd SM1...217 B4
Hilldown Ct SW16...182 A3
Hilldown Rd
Hayes BR2...208 D1
South Norwood
SW16...182 B3
Hill Dr NW9...45 A1
Hilldrop Cres N7...71 D3
Hilldrop La N7...71 D3
Hilldrop Rd
Bromley BR1...187 B4
Kentish Town N7...71 D3
Hill Dr SW16...204 B6
Hill End
Orpington BR6...227 D6
Shooters Hill SE18...144 C4
Hillersdon Ave
Barnes SW13...134 A3
Edgware HA8...26 B5
Hillersdon Ho SW1...258 C2
Hillery Cl SE17...262 D3
Hill Farm Rd W10...90 D2
Hillfield Ave
Colindale NW9...45 C5
Hornsey N8...50 A5
Mitcham SM4...202 C4
Wembley HA0...66 B1
Hillfield Cl HA2...42 A5
Hillfield Ct NW3...70 C3
Hillfield Ho N5...73 A3
Hillfield La S WD23...8 D5
Hillfield Lo SW17...180 D5
Hillfield Mans NW3...70 C3
Hillfield Par SM4...202 B3
Hillfield Park Mews
N10...49 B5
Hillfield Pk
London N10...49 B5
Southgate N21...16 C2
Hillfield Rd
Hampton TW12...173 B2
West Hampstead
NW6...69 C3
Hillgate Pl
Balham SW12...159 B4
Kensington
W8...113 C5 245 A4
Hillgate St W8...245 A4
Hill Gate Wlk N6...49 C3
Hill Gr TW13...151 B2
Hill Ho Southall UB1...85 C1
Stanmore HA7...9 A1
Upper Clapton E5...52 B1
Hill House Ave HA7...24 D3
Hill House Cl N21...16 C4
Hill House Dr TW12...173 C2
Hill House Rd SW16...182 B5
Hill House Sch
SW1...114 D3 257 D5
Hill Ho SE28...123 C5
Hilliard Ct SM6...219 D2
Hilliard Ho 15 E1...118 B5
Hilliard's Ct E1...118 C5
Hillier Cl EN5...13 D5
Hillier Gdns CR0...220 C3
Hillier Ho 1 NW1...71 D1
Hillier Lo TW12...174 B5
Hillier Pl KT9...213 D2
Hillier Rd SW11...158 D5
Hilliers Ave UB8...82 C4
Hillier's La CR0, SM6...220 A5
HILLINGDON...82 D5
Hillingdon Ave
TW19...148 A3
Hillingdon Circus
UB10...60 D2
HILLINGDON HEATH
...82 D2
Hillingdon Hill UB10...82 B4
Hillingdon Hospl
UB8...82 B2
Hillingdon Manor Sch
UB8...82 D2
Hillingdon Par 6
UB10...82 D3
Hillingdon Prim Sch
UB10...82 D4
Hillingdon Rd UB10...82 A5
Hillingdon Sta UB10...60 D3
Hillingdon St SE17...138 D6
Hillington Gdns IG8...37 D1
Hill La HA4...39 A1
Hill Lo SW11...136 B1
Hillman Cl UB8...60 A3
Hillman Dr 12 NW10...90 C3
Hillman St E8...74 B2
Hillmarton Rd N7...72 A3
Hillmead Dr SW9...138 D1
Hill Mead Prim Sch
SW9...138 D1
Hillmont Rd KT10...212 C5
Hillmore Ct SE13...142 B2
Hillmore Gr SE26...185 A5
Hill Rd
Carshalton SM5...218 C2
Finchley N10...30 D2
Harrow HA1...43 A4
Mitcham CR4...181 B3
Pinner HA5...41 A3
St John's Wood
NW8...92 A5 229 B3
Sutton SM1...217 D3
Wembley HA0...65 B5
Hillreach SE7, SE18...122 B1
Hill Rise
East Finchley
NW11...47 D5
Enfield N9...18 B5
Forest Hill SE23...162 B3
Greenford UB6...86 A6
Hinchley Wood KT10...213 B6
Hillrise Mans N19...50 A2
Hillrise Rd N19...50 A2
Hill Rise
Richmond TW10...153 D6
Ruislip HA4...39 B1
Hillrise KT12...193 D2
Hillsboro Rd SE22...161 C6
Hillsborough Ct 13
NW6...91 D6
Hillsde 6 SM1...218 B3
Hillsgrove Cl DA16...146 C5
Hillsgrove Prim Sch
DA16...146 C5
Hillside Ave
London N11...30 D4
Wembley HA9...66 B4
Woodford IG8...37 C5
Hillside EN5...14 A6
Hillside Cl
Merton SM4...201 A5
St John's Wood NW8...91 D5
Woodford IG8...37 C5
Hillside Cres
Enfield EN2...5 B5
Harrow HA2...42 A1
Northwood HA6...22 A2
Hillside N8...49 D3
Hillside Ct
Hampstead NW3...69 D3
7 Kingston u T KT2...176 D3
Hillside Dr HA8...26 C5
Hillside Gdns
Chipping Barnet EN5...1 A1
Edgware HA8...26 B6
Friern Barnet N11...31 C4
Harrow HA3...44 A2
Highgate N6...49 B3
Northwood HA6...22 B2
Streatham SW2...160 C2
Wallington SM6...219 C1
Walthamstow E17...54 B6
Hillside Glen CR0...220 D4
Hillside SE10...142 B5
Hillside Gr
Hendon NW7...28 A3
Southgate N14...15 D4
Hillside Ho CR0...220 D4
Hillside Jun & Inf Schs
HA6...22 A3
Hillside NW9...45 B5
Hillside La BR2...224 D6
Hillside Mans EN5...1 B1
Hill Side EN5...14 A6
Hillside Rd
Beckenham BR2...208 D6
Belmont SM2...217 B1
Croydon CR0...220 D4
Ealing W5...88 A2
Northwood HA6, HA5...22 B3
Southall UB1...85 C3
South Tottenham N15...51 C3
Streatham SW2...160 C2
Surbiton KT5...198 C4
Hillside Rise HA6...22 A3
Hillside
Stonebridge NW10...89 B6
Wimbledon SW19...178 D4
Hillsleigh Rd
W14...113 B5 244 D4
Hillsley DA14...190 A6
Hills Mews 2 W5...110 A6
Hills Pl W1...239 A1
Hill's Rd IG9...21 B3
Hill St W1...115 B5 248 C4
Hillstone Ct 5 E3...97 D3
Hillstowe St E5...74 C5
Hill St TW10...153 D6
Hilltop Ave NW10...67 A1
Hill Top SM3...201 B2
Hilltop Ct
12 London SW18...136 B1
South Hampstead
NW8...70 A1
South Norwood
SE19...183 B2
Hill Top NW11...47 D5

Hilltop Gdns
Hendon NW4 ... 28 B1
Orpington BR6 ... 227 C6
Hilltop Ho 7 N6 ... 49 D2
Hilltop 7 E17 ... 53 D6
Hilltop Rd NW6 ... 69 C1
Hilltop Way HA7 ... 9 A1
Hillview Ave HA3 ... 44 A4
Hillview Cl
Pinner HA5 ... 23 B4
Wembley HA9 ... 66 B6
Hillview Cres
Orpington BR6 ... 211 D1
Redbridge IG1 ... 56 B3
Hillview Ct SE19 ... 183 C6
Hill View Dr
Bexley DA16 ... 145 C3
Woolwich SE28 ... 123 C5
Hillview Gdns
Harrow HA2 ... 41 C5
Hendon NW4 ... 46 D5
Hill View Gdns NW9 ... 45 B4
Hill View
Mitcham CR4 ... 204 A5
Primrose Hill NW1 ... 230 D6
Hillview Rd
Carshalton SM1 ... 218 B5
Chislehurst BR7 ... 188 D6
Hill View Rd KT10 ... 213 A1
Hillview Rd NW7 ... 28 D6
Hill View Rd BR6 ... 227 D6
Hillview Rd HA5 ... 23 B4
Hill View Rd TW1 ... 153 A5
Hillview SW20 ... 178 B3
Hillway Highgate N6 ... 71 A6
London NW9 ... 45 C1
Hill Wood Ho NW1 ... 232 C3
Hillworth 7 BR3 ... 185 D1
Hillworth Rd SW2 ... 160 C4
Hillyard Rd W7 ... 86 C2
Hillyard St SW9 ... 138 C4
Hillyfield Cl E9 ... 75 A3
Hillyfield E17 ... 35 A1
Hillyfield Prim Sch
E17 ... 53 A6
Hilly Fields Cres
SE4 ... 141 C2
Hilly Mead SW19 ... 179 A3
Hilsea Point 7
SW15 ... 156 B3
Hilsea St E5 ... 74 C4
Hilton Ave N12 ... 30 B5
Hilton Ho
4 Ealing W13 ... 87 C1
12 Finchley N2 ... 30 B1
Lower Holloway N7 ... 72 A4
9 Nunhead SE4 ... 140 D1
Hilversum Cres 10
SE22 ... 161 C6
Himley Rd SW17 ... 180 D4
Hinchlay Manor
KT10 ... 212 D5
Hinchley Cl KT10 ... 212 D5
Hinchley Dr KT10 ... 212 D5
Hinchley Way KT10 ... 213 A5
HINCHLEY WOOD ... 212 D6
Hinchley Wood Prim
Sch KT10 ... 213 A6
Hinchley Wood Sch &
Sixth Form Ctr
KT10 ... 213 A6
Hinchley Wood Sta
KT10 ... 212 D5
Hinckley Rd SE15 ... 140 A1
Hind Ct EC4 ... 241 B1
Hinde Mews W1 ... 238 B2
Hindes Rd HA1 ... 42 C4
Hinde St W1 ... 93 A1 238 B2
Hind Gr E14 ... 97 C1
Hindhead Cl UB8 ... 82 D2
Hindhead Gdns UB5 ... 85 A6
Hindhead Gn WD19 ... 22 C5
Hindhead Point 6
SW15 ... 156 B3
Hindhead Way SM6 ... 220 A3
Hind Ho
13 Deptford SE14 ... 140 D6
Islington N7 ... 72 C4
Hindhurst Ct NW9 ... 45 A5
Hindle Ho E8 ... 73 D3
Hindley Ho N7 ... 72 B5
Hindlip Ho SW8 ... 269 C1
Hindmans Rd SE22 ... 162 A6
Hindmans Way RM9 ... 103 B3
Hindmarsh Cl E1 ... 118 A6
Hindrey Rd E5 ... 74 B3
Hindsley's Pl SE23 ... 162 C2
Hines Ct HA1 ... 43 A4
Hinkler Rd HA3 ... 43 D6
Hinksey Path SE2 ... 124 D3
Hinstock NW6 ... 91 D6
Hinstock Rd SE18 ... 145 A5
Hinton Ave TW4 ... 128 D1
Hinton Cl SE9 ... 166 A3
Hinton Ct 3 E10 ... 75 D6
Hinton Rd
Brixton SE24 ... 138 D2
Edmonton N18 ... 33 C6
Wallington SM6 ... 219 C2
Hippisley Ct TW7 ... 130 D2
Hippodrome Mews
W11 ... 244 A5
Hippodrome Pl W11 ... 244 B5
Hirst Cres HA9 ... 66 A5
Hirst Ct SW1 ... 258 C1
Hispano Mews 17 EN3 ... 7 C6
Hitcham Rd E17 ... 53 B2
Hitchcock Cl TW17 ... 192 B6
Hitchin Sq E3 ... 97 A5
Hithe Gr 15 SE16 ... 118 C3
Hitherbroom Rd
UB3 ... 106 A6
Hither Farm Rd SE3 ... 143 C2
Hitherfield Prim Sch
SW16 ... 160 C2
Hitherfield Rd
Dagenham RM8 ... 81 A6
Streatham SW16,
SW27 ... 160 C1
HITHER GREEN ... 164 C5
Hither Green La
SE13 ... 164 B5
Hither Green Prim Sch
SE13 ... 164 B5
Hither Green Sta
SE13 ... 164 C5
Hitherlands SW12 ... 159 B2
Hitherwell Dr HA3 ... 24 B2
Hitherwood Ct
SE21 ... 183 D6
Hitherwood Dr
SE19 ... 183 D6
Hive Cl WD23 ... 8 B2
Hive Rd WD23 ... 8 C2
Hive Wood Ho E7 ... 77 A2
HM Prison Wormwood
Scrubs W12 ... 90 A1
HMS Belfast* SE1 ... 253 B4
Hoadly Rd SW16 ... 159 D2
Hobart Cl
East Barnet N20 ... 14 C2
Hayes UB4 ... 84 D3
Hobart Ct
Harrow HA1 ... 42 C2
Woodford IG8 ... 36 D6
Hobart Dr UB4 ... 84 D3
Hobart Gdns CR7 ... 205 B6
Hobart Ho 24 KT6 ... 198 A4
Hobart La UB4 ... 84 D3
Hobart Pl
Richmond TW10 ... 154 B4
Westminster
SW1 ... 115 B3 258 C6
Hobart Rd
Dagenham RM9 ... 80 D4
Hayes UB4 ... 84 D3
North Cheam KT4 ... 216 B5
Hobbayne Prim Sch
W7 ... 86 D1
Hobbayne Rd W7 ... 86 B1
Hobbes Wlk SW15 ... 156 B6
Hobb's Ct SE1 ... 253 D2
Hobbs Gn N2 ... 48 A6
Hobbs Mews IG3 ... 79 D6
Hobbs' Pl N1 ... 95 C6
Hobbs Rd 6 SE27 ... 183 A6
Hobby St EN3 ... 18 D6
Hobday St E14 ... 97 D1
Hobhouse Ct SW1 ... 249 D5
Hobill Wlk KT5 ... 198 B3
Hoblands End BR7 ... 189 C4
Hobsons Pl 7 E1 ... 96 A2
Hobury St
SW10 ... 136 B6 266 C5
Hockenden La BR5,
BR8 ... 191 D1
Hocker St 41 E2 ... 95 D4
Hockett Cl SE8 ... 119 B2
Hockington Ct 7
EN5 ... 13 D6
Hockley Ave E6 ... 100 A5
Hockley Ct 2 E18 ... 37 A2
Hockley Ho 4 E9 ... 74 C2
Hockley Mews IG11 ... 101 C5
Hockliffe Ho 5 W10 ... 90 C2
Hockney Ct 1 SE16 ... 118 B1
Hockworth Ho 7
N16 ... 51 C1
Hocroft Ave NW2 ... 69 B5
Hocroft Ct NW2 ... 69 B5
Hocroft Rd NW2 ... 69 B5
Hocroft Wlk NW2 ... 69 B5
Hodder Dr UB6 ... 86 D5
Hoddesdon Rd
DA17 ... 125 C1
Hodford Lo NW11 ... 69 C6
Hodford Rd NW11 ... 47 B1
Hodgkins Cl SE28 ... 124 D6
Hodgkins Mews HA7 ... 25 B5
Hodister Cl 26 SE5 ... 139 A5
Hodson Cl HA2 ... 63 B5
Hodson Pl EN3 ... 7 C5
Hoecroft Ct EN3 ... 6 C5
Hoe La EN1 ... 6 B5
Hoe St E17 ... 53 C4
Hoffman Gdns CR2 ... 222 B1
Hoffman Sq N1 ... 235 D2
Hofland Rd
W14 ... 113 A3 254 A6
Hogan Mews W2 ... 236 C4
Hogan Way E5 ... 74 A6
Hogarth Ave TW15 ... 171 A4
Hogarth Bsns Pk
W4 ... 133 C6
Hogarth Cl Ealing W5 ... 88 A2
Newham E16 ... 99 D2
Hogarth Cres
Mitcham SW19 ... 180 B2
Thornton Heath CR0 ... 205 A2
Hogarth Ct
8 Camden Town
NW1 ... 71 C1
City of London EC3 ... 253 B6
Dulwich SE19 ... 183 D6
Heston TW5 ... 129 A5
24 Whitechapel E1 ... 96 A1
Hogarth Gdns TW5 ... 129 C5
Hogarth Hill NW11 ... 47 B5
Hogarth Ho
Enfield EN1 ... 18 A6
12 Northolt UB5 ... 84 D5
1 Sutton SM1 ... 218 B3
Westminster SW1 ... 259 D3
6 West Norwood
SE27 ... 183 A6
Hogarth Ind Est
NW10 ... 90 A3
Hogarth La W4 ... 133 C6
Hogarth Pl SW5 ... 255 C3
Hogarth Rd
Barking RM8 ... 80 B3
Earl's Ct
SW5 ... 113 D2 255 C3
Edgware HA8 ... 26 C1
Hogarth Roundabout
W4 ... 133 C6
Hogarth's House*
W4 ... 133 C6
Hogarth Way TW12 ... 174 A2
Hogsmill Way KT19 ... 215 A4
Holbeach Cl 8 NW9 ... 27 C2
Holbeach Gdns
DA15 ... 167 D5
Holbeach Mews 1
SW12 ... 159 B3
Holbeach Prim Sch
SE6 ... 163 C4
Holbeach Rd SE6 ... 163 D4
Holbeck Row SE15 ... 140 A5
Holbein Ho
Chelsea SW1 ... 258 A2
10 Stanmore HA7 ... 25 C5
Holbein Mews
SW1 ... 115 A1 258 A2
Holbein Pl
SW1 ... 115 A2 258 A3
Holberry Ho 6
SE21 ... 183 C6
Holberton Gdns
NW10 ... 90 B4
HOLBORN ... 94 C2
Holborn Cir
EC1 ... 94 C2 241 B3
Holborn EC1 ... 94 C2 241 B3
Holborn Ho 1 W12 ... 90 B1
Holborn Pl WC1 ... 240 C3
Holborn Rd E13 ... 99 B3
Holborn Sta
WC1 ... 94 B2 240 C3
Holborn Viaduct
EC1 ... 94 D2 241 C3
Holborn Way CR4 ... 180 D1
Holbrook Cl
Enfield EN1 ... 6 A5
Highgate N19 ... 49 B1
Holbrook Ct W7 ... 108 C6
Holbrooke Ct N7 ... 72 A4
Holbrooke Pl 28
TW10 ... 153 D6
Holbrook Ho
Acton W3 ... 89 B2
Chislehurst BR7 ... 189 B2
5 Streatham SW2 ... 160 B3
Holbrook La BR7 ... 189 B3
Holbrook Rd E15 ... 98 D5
Holbrook Way BR2 ... 210 B4
Holburne Cl SE3 ... 143 C4
Holburne Gdns SE3 ... 143 D4
Holburne Rd SE3 ... 143 D4
Holcombe Hill NW7 ... 12 A1
Holcombe Ho SW9 ... 138 A2
Holcombe Pl SE4 ... 141 A2
Holcombe Rd
Ilford IG1 ... 56 C2
Tottenham Hale N17 ... 52 A6
1 Tottenham N17 ... 51 D6
Holcombe St W6 ... 112 B2
Holcote Cl DA17 ... 125 A3
Holcroft Ct W1 ... 239 A4
Holcroft Ho
Battersea SW11 ... 136 B2
Lewisham SE10 ... 142 A4
Holcroft Rd E9 ... 74 C1
Holden Ave
North Finchley N12 ... 29 D5
Welsh Harp NW9 ... 45 A1
Holdenby Rd SE4 ... 163 A6
Holden Cl RM8 ... 80 B5
Holden Ho
12 Deptford SE8 ... 141 C5
Islington N1 ... 235 A5
Holden Hts N12 ... 13 D1
Holdenhurst Ave
N12 ... 30 A3
Holden Lo N11 ... 31 C5
Holden Point E15 ... 76 B2
Holden Rd N12 ... 29 D6
Holden St SW11 ... 137 A3
Holdernesse Rd
Isleworth TW7 ... 131 A4
6 Upper Tooting
SW17 ... 159 A2
Holderness Ho SE5 ... 139 C2
Holderness Way
SE27 ... 182 D5
Holders Hill Ave
NW4 ... 46 D6
Holders Hill Cres
NW4 ... 28 D1
Holders Hill Dr NW4 ... 28 D1
Holders Hill Gdns
NW4 ... 29 A1
Holders Hill Par
NW7 ... 29 A2
Holders Hill Rd
Church End NW4,
NW7 ... 29 A2
Hendon NW4 ... 28 D1
Holdsworth Ho 5
SW2 ... 160 C4
Holford Ho
6 Bermondsey
SE16 ... 118 B2
Finsbury WC1 ... 233 D2
Holford Pl WC1 ... 233 D2
Holford Rd NW3 ... 70 A5
Holford St WC1 ... 234 A2
Holford Yd WC1 ... 234 A3
Holgate Ave SW11 ... 136 B2
Holgate Ct HA8 ... 26 B6
Holgate Gdns RM10 ... 81 C2
Holgate Rd RM10 ... 81 C3
Holgate St SE7 ... 121 D3
Holkham Ho 6 EN5 ... 1 A2
Hollam Ho N8 ... 50 B5
Holland Ave
Belmont SM2 ... 217 C1
Wimbledon SW20 ... 177 D2
Holland Cl
Coney Hall BR2 ... 224 D6
New Barnet EN5 ... 14 B4
Stanmore HA7 ... 25 B5
Holland Ct
Ashford TW15 ... 170 B4
Hendon NW7 ... 28 A4
6 Walthamstow E17 ... 54 A5
Holland Dr SE23 ... 163 A1
Holland Gdns
Brentford TW8 ... 132 A6
Kensington W14 ... 254 B6
Holland Gr SW9 ... 138 C5
Holland Ho E4 ... 36 A6
Holland House Sch
HA8 ... 26 D6
Holland Park Ave
Ilford IG3 ... 57 D4
Notting Hill
W11 ... 113 A5 244 B3
Holland Park Ct
W14 ... 244 B2
Holland Park Gdns
W14 ... 113 A4 244 A2
Holland Park Mews
W11 ... 113 B5 244 C3
Holland Park Rdbt
W12 ... 112 D4
Holland Park Rd
W14 ... 113 B3 254 D5
Holland Park Sch
W8 ... 113 B4 244 D2
Holland Park Sta
W11 ... 113 B5 244 C3
Holland Park
W11 ... 113 B5 244 C3
Holland Pas N1 ... 235 A6
Holland Pl W8 ... 245 C2
Holland Rd
Croydon SE25 ... 206 A4
Newham E15 ... 98 C4
Wallend E6 ... 78 C1
Wembley HA0 ... 65 D2
West Kensington
W14 ... 113 A3 254 B6
Willesden Green
NW10 ... 90 B5
Holland Rise Ho
SW9 ... 270 D3
Hollands The
Feltham TW13 ... 172 D6
New Malden KT4 ... 199 D1
Holland St
Kensington
W8 ... 113 C4 245 B2
Lambeth
SE1 ... 116 D5 251 D4
Holland Villas Rd
W14 ... 113 A4 244 A1
Holland Way BR2 ... 224 D6
Holland Wlk
Kensington
W14 ... 113 B4 244 D1
Stanmore HA7 ... 25 A5
Upper Holloway N19 ... 49 D1
Hollar Rd N16 ... 73 D5
Hollen St W1 ... 239 C2
Holles Cl TW12 ... 173 C5
Holles Ho 8 SW9 ... 138 C3
Holles St W1 ... 93 B1 238 D2
Holley Rd W3 ... 111 C4
Hollickwood Ave
N12 ... 30 D4
Hollickwood Prim Sch
N10 ... 31 B3
Holliday Sq 7
SW11 ... 136 B2
Hollidge Way RM10 ... 81 D1
Hollies Ave DA15 ... 167 D3
Hollies Cl
South Norwood
SW16 ... 182 C4
Twickenham TW1 ... 152 D2
Hollies End NW7 ... 28 B5
Hollies Rd W5 ... 109 C2
Hollies The
Harrow HA3 ... 43 A5
Oakleigh Pk N20 ... 14 B3
Upper Tooting
SW12 ... 159 C2
9 Wanstead E11 ... 55 A4
Wood Green N11 ... 31 D4
Hollies Way 1
SW12 ... 159 A4
Holligrave Rd BR1 ... 187 A2
Hollingbourne Ave
DA7 ... 147 B4
Hollingbourne Gdns
W13 ... 87 B2
Hollingbourne Rd
SE24 ... 161 A6
Hollingsworth Ct 7
KT6 ... 197 D2
Hollingsworth Rd
CR0 ... 222 B2
Hollington Cres
KT3 ... 199 D3
Hollington Ct BR7 ... 188 D4
Hollington Rd
Newham E6 ... 100 B4
Tottenham N17 ... 34 A1
Hollingworth Cl
KT8 ... 195 B5
Hollingworth Rd BR2,
BR5 ... 210 D2
Hollins Ho N7 ... 72 A4
Hollisfield WC1 ... 233 B1
Hollman Gdns
SW16 ... 182 D4
Holloway Cl UB7 ... 104 A1
Holloway La UB7 ... 104 B1
Holloway Rd
Leyton E11 ... 76 B5
Lower Holloway N7 ... 72 B4
Newham E6 ... 100 B4
Upper Holloway N19 ... 71 D6
Holloway Road Sta
N7 ... 72 B3
Holloway Sch N7 ... 71 D3
Holloway St TW3 ... 129 D2
Hollow Combe
SE20 ... 184 B6
Hollowfield Wlk UB5 ... 63 A2
Hollow The IG8 ... 36 D6
Holly Ave London N2 ... 47 D6
Stanmore HA7 ... 26 A1
Walton-on-T KT12 ... 194 D1
Hollybank Cl TW12 ... 173 C5
Holly Berry La 8
NW3 ... 70 A4
Hollybrake Cl BR7 ... 189 B3
Hollybush Cl
Harrow HA3 ... 24 C2
Wanstead E11 ... 55 A4
Hollybush Gdns E2 ... 96 B4
Hollybush Hill E11 ... 54 D3
Holly Bush Hill 4
NW3 ... 70 A4
Hollybush Ho 23 E2 ... 96 B4
Holly Bush La TW12 ... 173 C3
Hollybush Pl E2 ... 96 B4
Hollybush Rd KT2 ... 176 A4
Holly Bush Steps 6
NW3 ... 70 A4
Hollybush St E13 ... 99
Holly Bush Vale 10
NW3 ... 70
Holly Cl
Beckenham BR3 ... 208
Buckhurst Hill IG9 ... 21
Feltham TW13 ... 173
Wallington SM6 ... 219
Holly Cottage Mews
UB8 ... 82
Holly Cotts KT7 ... 197
Holly Cres
Beckenham BR3 ... 207
Chingford IG8 ... 36
Hollycroft Ave
Child's Hill NW3 ... 69
Wembley HA9 ... 66
Hollycroft Cl
Harmondsworth
UB7 ... 126
South Croydon CR2 ... 221
Hollycroft Gdns
UB7 ... 126
Holly Ct
16 Belmont SM2 ... 217
Catford SE6 ... 164
4 Sidcup DA14 ... 190
South Tottenham N15 ... 51
Hollydale Cl UB5 ... 63
Hollydale Dr BR2 ... 226
Hollydale Prim Sch
SE15 ... 140
Hollydale Rd SE15 ... 140
Hollydene
Bromley BR1 ... 186
Hither Green SE13 ... 164
5 Peckham SE15 ... 140
Hollydown Way E11 ... 76
Holly Dr E4 ... 19
Holly Farm Rd UB2 ... 107
Hollyfield Ave N11 ... 30
Hollyfield Rd KT5 ... 198
Hollyfield Sch & Sixth
Form Ctr The
KT6 ... 198
Holly Gdns UB7 ... 104
Holly Gr NW9 ... 45
Hollygrove WD23 ... 8
Hollygrove Cl TW3 ... 129
Holly Gr
Peckham SE15 ... 140
Pinner HA5 ... 23
Hollyhedge Ho SE3 ... 142
Holly Hedge Terr
SE13 ... 164
Holly Hill NW3 ... 70
Holly Hill Rd DA8,
DA17 ... 125
Holly Hill N21 ... 16
Holly Ho
Brentford TW8 ... 131
Ilford IG3 ... 58
Holly House Hospl
IG9 ... 21
Holly Lo SW20 ... 178
Holly Lodge Gdns
N6 ... 49
Holly Lodge SE13 ... 142
Holly Lodge Mans
N6 ... 71
Holly Lodge UB2 ... 107
Holly Lo Harrow HA1 ... 42
Kensington W8 ... 245
Southgate N21 ... 16
4 Wimbledon
SW19 ... 179
Hollymead SM5 ... 218
Holly Mews SW10 ... 256
Hollymount Cl 9
SE10 ... 142
Holly Mount NW3 ... 70
Hollymount Sch
SW20 ... 178
Holly Park Est N4 ... 50
Holly Park Gdns N3 ... 47
Holly Park Prim Sch
N11 ... 31
Holly Park Rd
Ealing W7 ... 108
Friern Barnet N11 ... 31
Holly Pk
East Finchley N3 ... 47
Hornsey N4 ... 50
Holly Pl NW3 ... 70
Holly Rd
6 Chiswick W4 ... 111
Hampton TW12 ... 174
Hounslow TW3 ... 129
Leytonstone E11 ... 54
Twickenham TW1 ... 153
Holly St E8 ... 73
Holly Terr N6 ... 49
Hollytree Cl SW19 ... 156
Holly Tree Ho SE4 ... 141
Holly Tree Lo EN2 ... 4
Hollyview Cl NW4 ... 46

y Village N6 ... 71 B6
y Way CR4 ... 203 D6
y Wlk Enfield EN2 ... 5 B2
mpstead NW3 ... 70 A4
ywood Ct W5 ... 110 B6
ywood Gdns UB4 .. 84 B1
ywood Lofts E1 . 243 C5
ywood Mews
'10 ... 266 A6
ywood Rd
elsea
SW10 .... 136 A6 266 A6
hams Pk E4 ... 35 A5
ywood Way IG8 ... 36 B4
nan Ho 2 E2 ... 96 D4
nan Hunt Ho
4 ... 254 A1
nan Rd
ndon SW11 ... 136 B3
st Ewell KT19 ... 215 A3
nbank Dr TW17 .. 193 C5
nbridge Gdns EN3 . 6 D1
nbrook Dr NW4 ... 46 D4
nbrook NW1 ... 232 B3
nbury Cl WD23 ... 8 C2
nbury Ct
tcham SW19 ... 180 C3
per Tooting
SW17 ... 158 D1
nbury Gdns
3 ... 105 D5
nbury Gr CR0 ... 223 B1
nbury Ho SW9 ... 160 D6
nbury Manor 9
14 ... 190 A6
nbury Pk BR7 ... 188 A3
nbury View 2
... 52 B1
nbush Ct NW4 ... 46 D4
nbush Rd SW15 .. 157 A5
ncote Gdns N5 ... 73 A3
ncroft Ho 10 E17 ... 53 D5
ncroft Way BR2 .. 210 B4
n Ct SE12 ... 165 B1
ndale Gdns NW4 .. 46 D4
ndale Rd
islehurst BR7 ... 189 A5
uth Hampstead
NW6 ... 69 C3
ndale Terr N15 ... 51 C3
ndene Ave
arrow HA2 ... 41 D6
endon NW7 ... 28 A4
rne Hill SE24 ... 161 A6
ndene Cl BR3 ... 186 A1
ndene Ct BR1 ... 210 A6
ndene N12 ... 29 D5
mead Rd
W6 ... 135 D5 265 D3
me Ct 12 TW7 ... 131 A2
mefield Ct 4
W3 ... 70 C2
mefield Ho W10 ... 91 A3
me Lacey Rd
12 ... 164 D5
meleigh Ct EN3 ... 6 C1
me Rd E6 ... 100 A6
mes Ave
ll Hill NW7 ... 29 A5
althamstow E17 ... 53 B6
mes Cl SE22 ... 140 A1
mes Ct
ingford E4 ... 20 B2
South Acton W4 .. 111 A3
South Lambeth
SW4 ... 138 A3
mesdale Ave
W14 ... 132 D1
mesdale Cl
25 ... 205 D6
mesdale Ho 12
W6 ... 91 C6
mesdale Rd
exley DA7 ... 146 D3
ghgate N6 ... 49 B2
chmond TW9 ... 132 B4
uth Norwood
SE25 ... 205 C5
ddington TW11 ... 175 C4
ornton Heath CR0 .. 205 B4
mesley Rd SE23 .. 163 A5
mes Pl SW10 ... 266 B6
mes Rd
ntish Town NW5 ... 71 B3
erton SW19 ... 180 A3
ickenham TW1 ... 152 D2
mes Terr SE1 ... 251 A2
meswood 1
12 ... 217 D1
meswood Ct 3
2 ... 32 C1
me Way HA7 ... 24 D4
mewood Gdns
V2 ... 160 B4
mewood Rd
uth Norwood
SE25 ... 205 C6

Holmewood Rd *continued*
Streatham SW2 ... 160 B4
Holmfield Ave NW4 ... 46 D4
Holmfield Ho E17 ... 54 B5
Holm Gr UB10 ... 60 C1
Holmhurst SE13 ... 164 B5
Holmhurst Rd DA17 .. 125 D1
Holmhurst SW19 ... 178 C3
Holmlea Ct CR0 ... 221 B4
Holmleigh Prim Sch
N16 ... 51 C1
Holmleigh Rd N16 ... 51 C1
Holm Oak Cl SW15 ... 157 B5
Holmoaks Ho BR3 ... 186 A1
Holmsbury Ho 6 N7 .. 71 D3
Holmsdale Ho
6 London N11 ... 31 B6
24 Poplar E14 ... 119 D6
Holmshaw Cl SE26 ... 185 A6
Holmside Ct SW12 ... 159 A5
Holmside Rd SW12 ... 159 A5
Holmsley Cl KT3 ... 199 D2
Holmsley Ho SW15 ... 155 D4
Holmstall Ave HA8 ... 27 A1
Holmstall Par HA8 ... 27 A1
Holm Wlk SE3 ... 143 A3
Holmwood Cl
Cheam SM2 ... 216 D1
Harrow HA2 ... 42 A6
Northolt UB5 ... 63 D2
Holmwood Ct
Kingston u T KT3 ... 199 B6
Sidcup DA14 ... 189 D5
3 Stamford Hill N16 .. 51 D2
Holmwood Gdns
London N3 ... 29 C1
Wallington SM6 ... 219 B2
Holmwood Gr NW7 ... 27 B5
Holmwood Mans
W3 ... 110 C5
Holmwood Rd
Chessington KT9 ... 214 A3
Ilford IG3 ... 79 C6
Holmwood 2 KT5 ... 198 B3
Holne Chase
London N2 ... 48 A3
Morden SM4 ... 201 C3
Holne Lo N6 ... 49 C3
Holness Rd E15 ... 76 D2
Holocaust Meml Gdn*
W2 ... 114 D4 247 D2
Holroyd Rd SW15 ... 156 C6
Holsgrove Ct W3 ... 111 C5
Holstein Way 6
DA18 ... 125 A3
Holst Mans SW13 ... 134 C5
Holstock Rd IG1 ... 79 A6
Holsworth Cl HA2 ... 42 A4
Holsworthy Ho 49 E3 .. 97 D4
Holsworthy Sq WC1 .. 240 D5
Holsworthy Way
KT9 ... 213 C3
Holt Cl London N10 ... 49 A5
Woolwich SE28 ... 124 C6
Holt Ct
Greenwich SE10 ... 142 A6
Stratford New Town
E15 ... 76 A3
Holt Ho SW2 ... 160 C5
Holtoake Ct 1 W5 ... 87 C3
Holtoake Ho 3 W5 ... 87 C3
Holton St E1 ... 96 D3
Holt Rd Newham E16 .. 122 A5
Wembley HA0 ... 65 C5
Holt The
Morden SM4 ... 201 C5
Wallington SM6 ... 219 C4
Holtwhite Ave EN2 ... 5 A3
Holtwhite's Hill EN2 ... 4 D4
Holwell Pl HA5 ... 41 A5
Holwood Park Ave BR2,
BR6 ... 226 B4
Holwood Pl 7 SW4 .. 137 D1
Holybourne Ave
SW15 ... 156 A4
Holy Cross Prep Sch
KT2 ... 177 A3
Holy Cross RC Prim Sch
SE6 ... 164 A3
Holy Cross RC Sch
SW6 ... 135 C4 265 A2
Holy Cross Sch The
KT3 ... 199 C4
Holy Family RC Coll
The
Walthamstow E17 ... 54 A5
Walthamstow E17 ... 54 A6
Holy Family RC Prim
Sch
Kidbrooke SE9 ... 143 C1
Poplar E14 ... 119 C6
Holy Ghost RC Prim Sch
SW12 ... 159 A4
Holyhead Cl Bow E3 ... 97 C4
3 Newham E6 ... 100 B2
Holyhead Ct KT1 ... 197 D5

Holy Innocents RC Prim
Sch BR6 ... 227 D5
Holyoake Ct SE16 ... 119 B4
Holyoake Wlk
Ealing W5 ... 87 C3
East Finchley N2 ... 48 A6
Holyoak Rd
SE11 ... 116 D2 261 D3
Holyport Rd SW6 ... 134 D5
Holyrood Ave HA2 ... 63 B4
Holyrood Gdns HA8 ... 26 D1
Holyrood Ho N4 ... 51 A1
Holyrood Mews 10
E16 ... 121 A5
Holyrood Rd EN5 ... 14 B5
Holyrood St
SE1 ... 117 C5 253 A3
Holy Trinity CE Jun Sch
SM6 ... 219 C4
Holy Trinity CE Prim
Sch
Belgravia
SW1 ... 115 A2 258 A4
Dalston E8 ... 73 D2
East Finchley N2 ... 48 B6
Forest Hill SE26 ... 162 C2
Hampstead NW3 ... 70 A2
Richmond TW10 ... 132 C1
Streatham SW2 ... 160 B4
Wimbledon SW19 ... 179 D4
Holy Trinity Coll Prep
Sch BR1 ... 187 C2
Holy Trinity Lamorbey
CE Prim Sch
DA15 ... 168 A3
Holy Trinity & Saint
Silas CE Prim Sch
NW1 ... 71 B1
Holywell Cl
35 Bermondsey
SE16 ... 118 B1
2 Greenwich SE3 ... 143 A6
Stanwell TW19 ... 148 A3
Holywell La EC2 ... 243 B6
Holywell Lo EN2 ... 4 B5
Holywell Row
EC2 ... 95 C3 243 A5
Holywell Way TW19 .. 148 A3
Homan Ct N12 ... 30 A6
Homan Ho 6 SW4 ... 159 D4
Homebush Ho E4 ... 19 D4
Homecedars Ho WD23 . 8 B3
Homecherry Ho 5
IG10 ... 21 D6
Home Cl
Carshalton SM5 ... 218 D6
Northolt UB5 ... 85 B4
Homecoppice Ho 1
BR1 ... 186 D3
Homecroft Rd
Forest Hill SE26 ... 184 C5
Tottenham N22 ... 33 A2
Homecross Ho 7
W4 ... 111 B2
Home Ct KT6 ... 197 D4
Homedale Ho SM1 ... 217 D4
Home Farm Cl
Thames Ditton
KT7 ... 196 D2
Upper Halliford
TW17 ... 193 C5
Home Farm Cotts
BR5 ... 190 D2
Homefarm Rd W7 ... 86 D1
Homefield Ave IG2 ... 57 C4
Home Field EN5 ... 13 B6
Homefield Cl
Hayes UB4 ... 84 D3
Willesden NW10 ... 67 A2
Homefield Ct NW4 ... 46 C5
Homefield Gdns
London N2 ... 48 B6
Mitcham CR4, SW19 .. 180 B1
Homefield Ho SE23 ... 162 D1
Homefield SM4 ... 201 C5
Homefield Pk SM1,
SM2 ... 217 D2
Homefield Pl 4
SW19 ... 178 D5
Homefield Prep Sch
SM1 ... 217 C3
Homefield Rd
Bromley BR1 ... 187 C2
Burnt Oak HA8 ... 27 B4
Chiswick W4 ... 111 D1
Walton-on-T KT12 ... 195 A2
Wembley HA0 ... 65 B4
Wimbledon SW19 ... 179 A4
Homefield St 14 N1 ... 95 C5
Homefirs Ho HA9 ... 66 B5
Homeheather Ho 5
IG4 ... 56 B4
Homelands Dr SE19 .. 183 C3
Home Lea BR6 ... 227 D3
Homeleigh Ct 8
SW16 ... 160 A1

Homeleigh Rd SE15 .. 162 D6
Homemead SW12 ... 159 B2
Homemead Rd
Bromley BR2 ... 210 B4
Wallington CR0 ... 203 C3
Home Mead HA7 ... 25 C2
Home Office SW1 ... 249 C1
Home Park Rd
SW19 ... 157 B1
Home Park Terr
KT1 ... 175 D1
Home Park Wlk
KT1 ... 197 D5
Home Rd SW11 ... 136 C3
Homer Dr E14 ... 119 C2
Homer Rd
Croydon CR0 ... 206 D3
Homerton E9 ... 75 A2
Homer Row W1 ... 237 B3
Homersham Rd
KT1 ... 176 D1
Homer St W1 .. 92 C2 237 B3
HOMERTON ... 74 D1
Homerton Coll of
Technology E9 ... 74 C3
Homerton Ct 2 EN4 ... 14 D3
Homerton Gr E9 ... 74 D3
Homerton High St
E9 ... 74 D3
Homerton Rd E9 ... 75 B3
Homerton Row E9 ... 74 C3
Homerton Sta E9 ... 74 D2
Homerton Terr E9 ... 74 C2
Homerton University
Hospl E9 ... 74 D3
Homesdale Cl E11 ... 55 A4
Homesdale Rd
Bromley BR1,
BR2 ... 209 C6
Orpington BR5 ... 211 C2
Homesfield NW11 ... 47 C4
Homes Of Rest (CE
Temperance Society)
IG1 ... 79 B5
Homestall Rd SE22 ... 162 C6
Homestead Ct EN5 ... 13 C6
Homestead Gdns
KT10 ... 212 C3
Homestead Paddock
N14 ... 15 B6
Homestead Pk NW2 ... 67 D5
Homestead Rd
Dagenham RM8 ... 81 B6
Fulham
SW6 ... 135 B5 264 D3
Homesteads The
BR3 ... 185 D4
Homestead The N11 ... 31 B6
Homewalk Ho 1
SE26 ... 184 C6
Homewaters Ave
TW16 ... 171 D2
Homewillow Cl N21 ... 16 D5
Homewood Cl
TW12 ... 173 B4
Homewood Cres
BR7 ... 189 C4
Homewood Gdns
SE25 ... 205 C4
Homewoods 2
SW12 ... 159 C4
Homildon Ho 10
SE26 ... 162 A1
Homington Ct KT2 ... 176 A3
Honduras St EC1 ... 242 A6
Honeybourne Rd
NW6 ... 69 D3
Honeybourne Way
BR5 ... 211 B1
Honeybrook Rd SW12,
SW4 ... 159 C4
Honey Cl RM10 ... 81 D2
Honeycroft Hill UB10 .. 60 A1
Honeyden Rd DA14 .. 191 A4
Honeyfield N4 ... 72 C6
Honey Hill UB10 ... 60 B1
Honey La EC2 ... 242 B1
Honey Lane Ho
SW10 ... 265 D6
Honeyman Cl NW6 ... 68 D1
Honeypot Bsns Ctr
HA7 ... 26 A2
Honeypot Cl NW9 ... 44 B5
Honeypot La HA3, HA7,
NW9 ... 44 B6
Honeysett Rd 3 N17 ... 33 D1
Honeysuckle Cl
UB1 ... 107 A6
Honeysuckle Ct
Ilford IG1 ... 78 D2
2 Lee SE12 ... 165 A4
6 Sutton SM2 ... 217 D2
Honeysuckle Gdns
CR0 ... 206 D1
Honeywell Jun & Inf
Schs SW11 ... 158 D5

Honeywell Rd
SW11 ... 158 D5
Honeywood Heritage
Ctr* SM5 ... 218 D4
Honeywood Ho 5
SE15 ... 140 A4
Honeywood Rd
Harlesden NW10 ... 89 D5
Isleworth TW7 ... 131 A1
Honeywood Wlk
SM5 ... 218 D4
Honister Cl HA7 ... 25 B2
Honister Gdns HA7 ... 25 B2
Honister Pl HA7 ... 25 B2
Honiton Gdns
Edgware NW7 ... 28 D3
1 Nunhead SE15 ... 140 C3
Honiton Ho 28 SE5 ... 139 A3
Honiton Rd
Bexley DA16 ... 145 D3
Kilburn NW6 ... 91 B5
Honley Rd SE6 ... 163 D4
Honnor Gdns TW7 ... 130 B3
HONOR OAK ... 162 C6
Honor Oak Park Sta
SE23 ... 162 D5
Honor Oak Pk SE23 .. 162 D5
Honor Oak Rd SE23 .. 162 C4
Honor Oak Rise
SE23 ... 162 C5
Honwell Ho 24 W2 ... 91 C2
Hood Ave
East Barnet N14 ... 15 B5
Mortlake SW14 ... 155 A6
Hood Cl CR0 ... 204 D1
Hoodcote Gdns N21 ... 16 D4
Hood Ct N7 ... 72 B5
Hood Ho 17 SE5 ... 139 B5
Hood Lo E11 ... 77 B6
Hood Rd SW20 ... 177 D3
HOOK ... 214 A4
Hooke Ct SE10 ... 142 A4
Hooke Ho 32 E3 ... 97 A5
Hooker's Rd E17 ... 52 D6
Hook Farm Rd BR2 ... 209 D4
Hookham Ct SW8 ... 269 C2
Hook Ho 9 SW27 ... 182 D5
Hooking Gn HA2 ... 41 D4
Hook La DA16 ... 146 A1
Hook Lane Prim Sch
DA16 ... 146 A2
Hook Rd KT19, KT17 .. 215 A1
Hook Rise N
Surbiton KT6 ... 214 A5
Tolworth KT6 ... 214 D6
Hook Rise South Ind Pk
KT6 ... 214 C5
Hook Rise South
KT6 ... 214 A5
Hook Rise S KT6,
KT9 ... 214 D6
Hooks Cl SE15 ... 140 B4
Hookstone Way IG8 ... 37 D3
Hook KT6 ... 214 A5
Hook The EN5 ... 14 B5
Hook Underpass
KT6 ... 214 A5
Hook Wlk HA8 ... 27 A4
Hooper Dr UB8 ... 82 D2
Hooper Ho 9 SW18 .. 157 B6
Hooper Rd E16 ... 99 A1
Hooper's Ct SW1 ... 247 C1
Hooper's Mews 4
W3 ... 111 A5
Hooper St E1 ... 96 A1
Hoop La NW11 ... 47 C2
Hoover Ho 5 SE6 ... 186 A6
Hope Cl
2 Brentford
TW8 ... 110 A1
Canonbury N1 ... 73 A2
Dagenham RM6 ... 58 D5
Grove Pk SE12 ... 165 B1
Sutton SM1 ... 218 A3
1 Woodford IG8 ... 37 C4
Hope Ct 1 SE1 ... 118 A1
Hopedale Rd SE7 ... 143 B6
Hopefield Ave NW6 ... 91 A5
Hopefield 3 W7 ... 108 D5
Hope Gdns 10 W3 ... 110 D4
Hope Pk BR1 ... 186 D3
Hopes Cl TW5 ... 129 C6
Hope St SW11 ... 136 B2
Hopetown St E1 ... 243 D3
Hopewell St SE5 ... 139 B5
Hop Gdns WC2 ... 250 A5
Hopgood St 5 W12 .. 112 C5
Hopkins Cl N10 ... 31 A3
Hopkins Ho 17 E14 ... 97 C1
Hopkins Mews E15 ... 98 D6
Hopkinson Ho 1
SW11 ... 137 A3
Hopkinson's Pl NW1 231 A6
Hopkins St
W1 ... 93 D1 239 C1
Hopley Ho W13 ... 109 B6
Hoppers Rd N21 ... 16 C2

Hoppett Rd E4 ... 20 C2
Hopping La N1 ... 72 D2
Hoppingwood Ave
KT3 ... 199 C6
Hoppner Rd UB4 ... 83 B5
Hop St SE10 ... 120 D2
Hopton Ct BR2 ... 209 A1
Hopton Gdns KT3 ... 200 A3
Hopton Ho 5 SW9 ... 138 D3
Hopton Par 2
SW16 ... 182 A5
Hopton Rd
Streatham SW16 ... 182 A5
Woolwich SE18 ... 122 D3
Hopton's Gdns SE1 . 251 D4
Hopton St
SE1 ... 116 D5 251 D4
Hoptree Cl N12 ... 29 D6
Hopwood Cl SW17 ... 158 A1
Hopwood Rd SE17 ... 139 B6
Hopwood Wlk E8 ... 74 A1
Horace Rd
Forest Gate E7 ... 77 B4
Ilford IG6 ... 57 A6
Kingston u T KT1 ... 198 B6
Horatio Ho
13 Haggerston E2 ... 95 D5
4 Merton SW19 ... 179 D3
Horatio Pl
9 Canary Wharf
E14 ... 120 A5
Merton SW19 ... 179 C2
Horatio St 11 E2 ... 95 D5
Horatius Way CR0 ... 220 B2
Horbury Cres
W11 ... 113 C6 245 A5
Horbury Lo TW12 ... 173 C3
Horbury Mews
W11 ... 113 B6 244 D5
Horder Rd
SW6 ... 135 A4 264 B1
Hordle Prom E 15
SE15 ... 139 D5
Hordle Prom N 4
SE15 ... 139 D5
Hordle Prom S 7
SE15 ... 139 D5
Horizon Bldg 22
E14 ... 119 C6
Horizon Sch N16 ... 73 C4
Horle Wlk SE5 ... 138 D3
Horley Cl DA6 ... 169 C6
Horley Rd SE9 ... 188 A6
Hormead Rd W9 ... 91 B3
Hornbeam Cl
Barking IG11 ... 102 B3
Buckhurst Hill IG9 ... 21 D1
Edgware NW7 ... 11 D1
Ilford IG1 ... 79 B3
Lambeth SE11 ... 261 A4
Northolt UB5 ... 63 B3
Hornbeam Cres
TW8 ... 131 B5
Hornbeam Gdns
KT3 ... 200 A3
Hornbeam Gr E4 ... 20 D1
Hornbeam Ho
1 Buckhurst Hill
IG9 ... 21 D1
2 Maitland Pk NW3 ... 70 D2
6 Penge SE20 ... 184 D3
6 Sidcup DA15 ... 168 A1
Hornbeam La E4 ... 20 C6
Hornbeam Rd
Buckhurst Hill IG9 ... 21 D1
Hayes UB4 ... 84 C2
Hornbeam Sq 8 E3 ... 97 B6
Hornbeams Rise N11 .. 31 A4
Hornbeam Terr
SM5 ... 202 C1
Hornbeam Way
BR2 ... 210 C3
Hornblower Cl 2
SE16 ... 119 A2
Hornbuckle Cl HA2 ... 64 B6
Hornby Cl NW3 ... 70 B1
Hornby Ho
6 Kennington
SE11 ... 138 C6
13 Richmond TW10 ... 153 C1
Horncastle Cl SE12 ... 165 A4
Horncastle Rd SE12 .. 165 A4
Hornchurch Cl KT2 .. 175 D6
Hornchurch N17 ... 33 B1
Horndean Cl 3
SW15 ... 156 A3
Horne Ho 4 SE18 ... 144 A4
Horner Ct E11 ... 76 B5
Horne Rd TW17 ... 192 C5
Horner Hos 18 N1 ... 95 C6
Horner La 3 CR4 ... 180 B1
Horne Way SW15 ... 134 C3
Hornfair Rd SE7 ... 143 D5
Horniman Dr SE23 ... 162 C4

Horniman Grange 7 SE23 ... 162 C3
Horniman Mus & Gdns* SE23 ... 162 B3
Horniman Sch SE23 ... 162 B3
Horning Cl SE9 ... 188 A6
Horn La Acton W3 ... 89 A1
Greenwich SE10 ... 121 A2
Woodford IG8 ... 37 A3
Horn Link Way SE10 ... 121 A2
Horn Park Cl SE12 ... 165 B6
Horn Park La SE12 ... 165 B5
Horn Park Prim Sch SE12 ... 165 B4
Hornsby House Sch SW12 ... 159 A3
Horns Croft IG11 ... 79 C1
Horns End Pl HA5 ... 40 C4
HORNSEY ... 50 A5
Hornsey Central Hospl N8 ... 49 D4
Hornsey La N6 ... 49 C2
Hornsey Lane Gdns N6 ... 49 C2
Hornsey Park Rd N8 ... 50 B6
Hornsey Rd N7, N19 ... 72 B6
Hornsey Rise Gdns N19 ... 50 A2
Hornsey Sch for Girls N8 ... 50 B4
Hornsey Sta N8 ... 50 B5
Hornsey St N7 ... 72 B3
HORNSEY VALE ... 50 B4
Hornshay St SE15 ... 140 C6
Horns Rd IG2, IG6 ... 57 A4
Hornton Ct W8 ... 245 B1
Hornton Pl W8 ... 245 B1
Hornton St W8 ... 113 C4 245 B2
Horrocks Ho SW15 ... 156 B6
Horsa Rd
Eltham SE12 ... 165 C4
Erith DA8 ... 147 D5
Horsebridge Cl RM9 ... 103 A6
Horsecroft Rd HA8 ... 27 B3
Horse & Dolphin Yd W1 ... 249 D6
Horse Fair KT1 ... 175 D1
Horseferry Pl SE10 ... 142 A6
Horseferry Rd Est SW1 ... 259 C5
Horseferry Rd
Limehouse E14 ... 119 A6
Westminster SW1 ... 115 D2 259 D4
Horse Guards Ave SW1 ... 116 A5 250 A3
Horse Guards Par* SW1 ... 115 D5 249 D3
Horse Guards Rd SW1 ... 115 D4 249 D2
Horse Leaze E6 ... 100 C1
Horsell Rd
Islington N5 ... 72 C3
St Paul's Cray BR5 ... 190 B2
Horselydown La SE1 ... 117 D5 253 C3
Horselydown Mans SE1 ... 253 C2
Horsemongers Mews SE1 ... 252 B1
Horsenden Ave UB6 ... 64 D3
Horsenden Cres UB6 ... 64 D3
Horsenden La N UB6 ... 64 D1
Horsenden La S UB6 ... 87 A6
Horsenden Prim Sch UB6 ... 64 C2
Horsendon Ho 11 N7 ... 71 D3
Horseshoe Cl
Cubitt Town E14 ... 120 A1
Dollis Hill NW2 ... 68 B6
Horse Shoe Cres UB5 ... 85 C5
Horseshoe Dr UB8 ... 82 C1
Horse Shoe Gn SM1 ... 217 D6
Horseshoe La
Barnet N20 ... 12 D3
Enfield EN2 ... 5 A2
Horse Yd N1 ... 234 D6
Horsfeld Gdns 1 SE9 ... 166 A6
Horsfeld Rd SE9 ... 165 D6
Horsfield Ho 18 N1 ... 73 A1
Horsford Rd SW2 ... 160 B6
Horsham Ave N12 ... 30 C5
Horsham Ct N17 ... 34 A2
Horsham Rd
Bexley DA6 ... 169 C6
East Bedfont TW14 ... 149 A5
Horsley Ct SW1 ... 259 D3
Horsley Dr
Kingston u T KT2 ... 175 D5
New Addington CR0 ... 224 A1
Horsley Ho 11 SE4 ... 140 D1
Horsley Rd
Bromley BR1 ... 187 B2
Chingford E4 ... 20 A2
Horsley St 3 SE17 ... 139 B6
Horsman Ho SE5 ... 139 A6
Horsman St SE5 ... 139 A6
Horsmonden Cl BR6 ... 211 D2
Horsmonden Rd SE4 ... 163 B5
Horston Ho N4 ... 51 A2
Hortensia Ho SW10 ... 266 A4
Hortensia Rd SW10 ... 136 A5 266 A4
Horticultural Pl 6 W4 ... 111 B1
Horton Ave NW2 ... 69 A4
Horton Bridge Rd UB7 ... 104 B5
Horton Cl UB7 ... 104 B5
Horton Ctry Pk KT19 ... 214 C1
Horton Ho
13 Deptford SE15 ... 140 C6
South Lambeth SW8 ... 270 C4
West Kensington W14 ... 254 A1
Horton Ind Pk UB7 ... 104 B5
Horton La KT19 ... 215 A1
Horton Par UB7 ... 104 A5
Horton Rd Hackney E8 ... 74 B2
Yiewsley UB7 ... 104 B5
Horton Road Ind Est UB7 ... 104 B5
Horton St SE13 ... 141 D2
Horton Way CR0 ... 206 D4
Hortus Rd
Chingford E4 ... 20 A2
Southall UB2 ... 107 B4
Horwood Ho
24 Bethnal Green E2 ... 96 B4
Marylebone NW8 ... 237 B6
Hosack Rd SW12, SW17 ... 159 A2
Hoser Ave SE12 ... 165 A2
Hosier La EC1 ... 94 D2 241 D3
Hoskins Cl UB3 ... 105 D1
Hoskin's Cl E16 ... 99 C1
Hoskins St SE10 ... 120 B1
Hospital Bridge Rdbt TW2 ... 151 D2
Hospital Bridge Rd TW2 ... 151 D3
Hospital of the Holy Trinity (Almshouses) 5 CR0 ... 221 A6
Hospital Rd TW3 ... 129 C2
Hospital Way SE13 ... 164 B4
Hospl for Tropical Diseases
Fitzrovia WC1 ... 93 C3 239 B5
Somers Town NW1 ... 232 D5
Hospl of St John & St Elizabeth NW8 ... 92 B5 229 C3
Hotham Cl KT8 ... 195 C6
Hotham Prim Sch SW15 ... 134 D1
Hotham Rd
Merton SW19 ... 180 A3
Putney SW15 ... 134 C2
Hotham Road Mews 12 SW19 ... 180 A3
Hotham St E15 ... 98 C6
Hothfield Pl SE16 ... 118 C3
Hotspur Ind Est N17 ... 34 B4
Hotspur Rd UB5 ... 85 C5
Hotspur St SE11 ... 116 C1 261 A2
Houblon Rd TW10 ... 154 A6
Houghton Cl
10 Dalston E8 ... 73 D2
Hampton TW12 ... 173 A4
Houghton Rd N15 ... 51 D5
Houghton Sq SW9 ... 138 A2
Houghton St WC2 ... 240 D1
Houlder Cres CR0 ... 220 D2
Houndsden Rd N21 ... 16 C5
Houndsditch EC3 ... 95 C1 243 B2
Houndsfield Prim Sch N9 ... 18 B4
Houndsfield Rd N9 ... 18 B4
HOUNSLOW ... 129 C3
Hounslow Ave TW3 ... 151 D6
Hounslow Bsns Pk TW3 ... 129 D1
Hounslow Central Sta TW3 ... 129 D2
Hounslow Ctr The TW3 ... 129 D2
Hounslow East Sta TW3 ... 130 A3
Hounslow Gdns TW3 ... 151 D6
Hounslow Heath Jun & Inf Schs TW4 ... 129 A2
Hounslow Heath Nature Reserve TW4 ... 151 A5
Hounslow Manor Sch TW3 ... 130 A2
Hounslow Rd
Feltham TW14 ... 150 B4
Hanworth TW13 ... 151 A2
Twickenham TW2, TW3 ... 152 A5
Hounslow Sta TW3 ... 151 D6
Hounslow Town Prim Sch TW3 ... 130 B2
HOUNSLOW WEST ... 128 D2
Hounslow West Sta TW3 ... 129 A3
Houseman Way 20 SE5 ... 139 B5
House of Detention* EC1 ... 94 C3 241 B6
Houses of Parliament* SW1 ... 116 A3 260 B6
Houston Ct 3 CR0 ... 205 C1
Houston Pl KT10 ... 196 C1
Houston Rd
Forest Hill SE23 ... 163 A1
Thames Ditton KT6 ... 197 B3
Houstoun Ct TW5 ... 129 B5
Hove Ave E17 ... 53 B4
Hoveden Rd NW2 ... 69 A3
Hove Gdns SM1 ... 201 D1
Hovenden Ho 6 SE21 ... 183 C6
Hoveton Rd SE28 ... 102 C1
Howard Ave DA5 ... 168 C4
Howard Bldg SW8 ... 268 C5
Howard Cl Acton W3 ... 88 D1
Ashford TW16 ... 171 D4
Brunswick Pk N11 ... 15 A2
Bushey WD23 ... 8 C4
Cricklewood NW2 ... 69 A4
Hampton TW12 ... 174 A4
Howard Ct
12 Barking IG11 ... 101 B6
Beckenham BR3 ... 186 A1
Lewisham SE10 ... 142 A4
Peckham SE15 ... 140 A2
Howard Ho
6 Brixton SW9 ... 138 C2
14 Deptford SE8 ... 141 B6
Fitzrovia W1 ... 238 D5
Penge SE20 ... 184 C2
6 Upper Clapton E5 ... 74 C6
Howard Mans E17 ... 53 D6
Howard Mews N5 ... 72 D4
Howard Prim Sch CR0 ... 221 A4
Howard Rd
Barking IG11 ... 101 B6
Canonbury N16 ... 73 B4
Cricklewood NW2 ... 68 D4
Croydon SE25 ... 206 A3
Ilford IG1 ... 78 D4
Isleworth TW7 ... 130 D2
Leyton E11 ... 76 C5
Newham E6 ... 100 B5
New Malden KT3 ... 199 D5
Penge SE20 ... 184 C2
Plaistow BR1 ... 187 A3
Southall UB1 ... 85 D1
South Tottenham N15 ... 51 C3
Surbiton KT5 ... 198 B3
Walthamstow E17 ... 53 D6
Howards Cl HA5 ... 22 B1
Howards Crest Cl BR3 ... 186 A1
Howard's La SW15 ... 134 C1
Howard's Rd E13 ... 99 A4
Howard St KT7 ... 197 B3
Howard Way EN5 ... 12 D6
Howard Wlk N2 ... 48 B5
Howarth Ct E15 ... 76 A3
Howarth Rd SE2 ... 124 A2
Howberry Cl HA8 ... 25 D4
Howberry Rd
South Norwood CR7 ... 183 B1
Stanmore HA7, H8 ... 25 D4
Howbury Rd SE15 ... 140 C2
Howcroft Cres N3 ... 29 C3
Howcroft Ho 3 E3 ... 97 B4
Howcroft La UB6 ... 86 B4
Howden Cl SE28 ... 124 D6
Howden Ct SE25 ... 183 D1
Howden Rd SE25 ... 183 D1
Howden St SE15 ... 140 A2
Howell Cl RM6 ... 58 D4
Howell Ct 2 E10 ... 53 D2
Howell Ho 5 N7 ... 71 D3
Howell Wlk SE1 ... 261 D3
Howe Lo TW1 ... 153 A4
Howerd Way SE18 ... 144 A4
Howes Cl N3 ... 47 C6
Howeth Ct 7 N11 ... 31 A4
Howfield Pl N17 ... 51 D6
Howgate Rd SW14 ... 133 B2
Howick Mans SE18 ... 122 A3
Howick Pl SW1 ... 115 C3 259 B5
Howie St SW11 ... 136 C5 267 A3
Howitt Cl
6 Maitland Pk NW3 ... 70 C2
Stoke Newington N16 ... 73 C4
Howitt Rd NW3 ... 70 C2
Howland Ho 9 SW16 ... 160 A1
Howland Mews E W1 ... 239 B4
Howland St W1 ... 93 C2 239 B4
Howland Way SE16 ... 119 A4
Howletts La HA4 ... 39 A3
Howletts Rd SE24 ... 161 A5
Howley Pl W2 ... 92 A2 236 B4
Howley Rd CR0 ... 221 A5
Howmic Ct 1 TW1 ... 153 C5
Howsman Rd SW13 ... 134 A6
Howson Rd SE4 ... 141 A1
Howson Terr TW10 ... 154 A5
How's St E2 ... 95 D5
Howton Pl WD23 ... 8 B3
HOXTON ... 95 C5
Hoxton Mkt 10 N1 ... 95 C4
Hoxton Point EC1 ... 95 C4
Hoxton Sq N1 ... 95 C4
Hoxton St N1 ... 95 C5
Hoylake Cres UB10 ... 60 D6
Hoylake Gdns
Mitcham CR4 ... 203 C6
Ruislip HA4 ... 40 B1
South Oxhey WD19 ... 22 D6
Hoylake Rd W3 ... 89 C1
Hoyland Cl 4 SE15 ... 140 B5
Hoyle Rd SW17 ... 180 C5
Hoy St E16 ... 98 D1
Hubbard Dr KT9 ... 213 D2
Hubbard Rd SE27 ... 183 A6
Hubbards Cl UB8 ... 82 D1
Hubbard St E15 ... 98 C6
Hub Buildings The 4 SW12 ... 159 B3
Huberd Ho SE1 ... 262 D6
Hubert Gr SW9 ... 138 A2
Hubert Ho NW8 ... 237 A5
Hubert Rd E6 ... 99 D4
Hucknall Ct NW8 ... 236 C6
Huddart St 6 E3 ... 97 B2
Huddleston Cl E2 ... 96 C5
Huddlestone Rd
Forest Gate E7 ... 76 D4
Willesden NW2 ... 68 B2
Huddleston Rd N7 ... 71 C4
Hudson Cl
Newham E15 ... 99 A6
15 Shepherd's Bush W12 ... 112 B6
Hudson Ct
Croydon SE25 ... 206 A5
1 Isle Of Dogs E14 ... 119 C1
4 Merton SW19 ... 179 D2
Hudson Ho
Chelsea SW10 ... 266 A4
5 Notting Hill W11 ... 91 A1
Hudson 27 NW9 ... 27 D2
Hudson Pl SE18 ... 123 A1
Hudson Rd
Erith DA7 ... 147 B4
Harlington UB7 ... 127 B6
Hudsons Ho N1 ... 235 D1
Hudson's Pl SW1 ... 115 C2 259 A4
Hudson Way N9 ... 18 C2
Huggin Ct EC4 ... 252 B6
Huggin Hill EC4 ... 252 B6
Huggins Ho 9 E3 ... 97 C4
Huggins Pl SW2 ... 160 B3
Hughan Rd E15 ... 76 B3
Hugh Astor Ct SE1 ... 261 D6
Hugh Clark Ho 13 W13 ... 109 A5
Hugh Dalton Ave SW6 ... 264 C5
Hughenden Ave HA3 ... 43 B4
Hughenden Gdns UB5 ... 84 C4
Hughenden Ho NW8 ... 237 A6
Hughenden Rd KT4 ... 200 A2
Hughendon EN5 ... 1 D1
Hughendon Terr E15 ... 76 A4
Hughes Cl N12 ... 30 A5
Hughes Ho
26 Bethnal Green E2 ... 96 C4
Camberwell SE5 ... 139 A4
Hughes Ho *continued*
15 Deptford SE8 ... 141 C6
Newington SE17 ... 261 D3
Hughes Mans E1 ... 96 A3
Hughes Rd
Ashford TW15 ... 171 A4
Hayes UB3 ... 106 B6
Hughes Terr 6 E16 ... 98 D2
Hughes Wlk CR0 ... 205 A2
Hugh Gaitskell Cl SW6 ... 264 C5
Hugh Gaitskell Ho
Stoke Newington N16 ... 73 D6
Willesden NW10 ... 67 D1
Hugh Herland KT1 ... 198 A6
Hugh Mews SW1 ... 258 D3
Hugh Morgan Ho 5 SW4 ... 137 D2
Hugh Myddelton Prim Sch EC1 ... 94 C4 234 B1
Hugh Platt Ho 20 E2 ... 96 B5
Hugh St SW1 ... 115 B2 258 D3
Hugo Ho SW1 ... 257 D6
Hugon Rd SW6 ... 135 D2
Hugo Rd N19 ... 71 C4
Huguenot Ct 9 E1 ... 96 A2
Huguenot Pl
London SW18 ... 158 A6
Spitalfields E1 ... 243 D4
Huguenot Sq SE15 ... 140 B2
Hullbridge Mews N1 ... 235 C6
Hull Cl SE16 ... 118 D5
Hull Ct SE5 ... 139 B3
Hull Pl E16 ... 123 A5
Hull St EC1 ... 235 A1
Hulme Pl SE1 ... 252 B1
Hulse Ave IG11 ... 79 C2
Humber Ct W7 ... 86 B1
Humber Dr W10 ... 90 D3
Humber Rd
Dollis Hill NW2 ... 68 B6
Greenwich SE3 ... 142 D6
Humberstone Rd E13 ... 99 C4
Humberton Cl E9 ... 75 A3
Humber Trad Est NW2 ... 68 B6
Humbolt Rd W6 ... 135 A6 264 A5
Hume Ct N1 ... 72 D1
Hume Ho 14 W11 ... 112 D5
Humes Ave W7 ... 108 D4
Hume Terr E16 ... 99 B1
Hume Way HA4 ... 40 A3
Humphrey Ct SW11 ... 266 D1
Humphrey St SE1 ... 117 D1 263 C2
Humphries Cl RM9 ... 81 B4
Humphry Ho 10 SW15 ... 156 D6
Hundred Acre NW9 ... 27 D1
Hungerdown E4 ... 20 A3
Hungerford Bridge WC2 ... 250 C4
Hungerford Ho SW1 ... 269 B6
Hungerford La WC2 ... 250 B4
Hungerford Prim Sch N7 ... 71 D2
Hungerford Rd
12 Camden Town N7 ... 71 D2
Lower Holloway N7 ... 72 A3
Hungerford St 21 E1 ... 96 B1
Hunsdon Cl RM9 ... 81 A2
Hunsdon Ho E5 ... 74 B5
Hunsdon Rd SE14 ... 140 D5
Hunslett St 20 E2 ... 96 C5
Hunstanton Ho NW1 ... 237 B4
Hunston Rd SM4 ... 201 D1
Hunt Cl W11 ... 112 D5
Hunt Ct London N14 ... 15 B4
10 Northolt UB5 ... 84 D5
Hunter Cl
Borehamwood WD6 ... 11 A6
Borough The SE1 ... 262 D5
Upper Tooting SW12 ... 159 A3
3 Wallington SM6 ... 220 A1
Huntercombe Roehampton Hospl The SW15 ... 156 A4
Huntercrombe Gdns WD19 ... 22 C5
Hunter Ct
8 London SE5 ... 139 B1
27 Streatham SW2 ... 160 C4
11 Wanstead E11 ... 55 A4
Hunter Ho
Bloomsbury WC1 ... 240 B6
Feltham TW14 ... 150 A3
Lambeth SE1 ... 251 D1
South Lambeth SW8 ... 269 D3
1 Tufnell Pk N19 ... 71 C5
Hunter Ho *continued*
West Brompton SW5. 2
Hunterian Mus* WC2 ... 94 B1 24
Hunter Lo 9 W9 ...
Hunter Rd
South Norwood CR7 ... 2
Wimbledon SW20 ... 1
Hunters Ct 5 TW9 ... 1
Hunter's Gr BR6 ... 2
Hunters Gr
Harrow HA3 ...
Hayes UB3 ... 1
Hunters Hall Prim Sch RM10 ...
Hunters Hall Rd RM10 ...
Hunters Hill HA4 ...
Hunters Lo
9 Edgware HA8 ... 2
10 Sidcup DA15 ... 1
Hunters Mdw SE19 ... 1
Hunters Rd
Chessington KT9 ... 2
Ilford IG1 ...
Hunters Sq RM10 ...
Hunters The 2 BR3 ... 1
Hunter St WC1 ... 94 A3 2
Hunters Way
Enfield EN2 ...
South Croydon CR0 ... 2
Hunter Wlk
Borehamwood WD6 ...
Newham E13 ...
Huntingdon Cl
Mitcham CR4, SW16 ... 2
Northolt UB5 ...
Huntingdon Ct
3 Barnet EN5 ...
Mortlake SW14 ... 1
Huntingdon Gdns
Chiswick W4 ... 1
North Cheam KT4 ... 2
Huntingdon Ho SW5 2
Huntingdon Rd
East Finchley N2 ...
Edmonton N9 ...
Huntingdon St
Canning Town E16 ...
Islington N1 ...
Huntingfield CR0 ... 2
Huntingfield Rd SW15 ... 1
Huntingford Ho SW15 ... 1
Hunting Gate Cl EN2 ...
Hunting Gate Dr KT9 ... 2
Hunting Gate Mews
Sutton SM1 ... 2
Twickenham TW2 ... 1
Huntings Farm IG1 ...
Huntings Rd RM10 ...
Huntington Ho NW2 ...
Huntley Cl TW19 ... 1
Huntley Ho 7 SE21 ... 1
Huntley St WC1 ... 93 D3 2
Huntley Way SW20 ... 1
Huntly Dr N3 ...
Huntly Rd SE25 ... 2
Hunton St E1 ...
Hunt Rd UB2 ... 1
Hunts Cl SE3 ... 1
Hunt's Ct WC2 ... 2
Huntshaw Ho 37 E3 ...
Hunt's La E15 ...
Huntsmans Cl TW13 ... 1
Huntsman St SE17 ... 2
Hunts Mead Cl BR7 ... 1
Hunts Mead EN3 ...
Huntsmoor Rd KT19 ... 2
Huntspill St SW17 ... 1
Hunts Slip Rd SE21 ... 1
Huntsworth Ct SE6 ... 1
Huntsworth Mews NW1 ... 92 D3 2
Huon Ct N20 ...
Hurdwick Ho NW1 ... 2
Hurdwick Pl NW1 ... 2
Hurleston Ho 11 SE8 ... 1
Hurley Cres SE16 ... 1
Hurley Ct 1 W5 ...
Hurley Ho
Lambeth SE11 ... 2
34 Shoreditch E2 ...
Hurley Lo SE22 ... 1
Hurley Rd UB6 ...
Hurlingham Bsns Pk SW6 ... 1
Hurlingham & Chelsea Sec Sch SW6 ... 1

ngham Court Mans
5...........135 C3
ngham Ct SW6..135 B2
ngham Gdns
6...........135 B2
ngham Rd
1 DA7........147 B5
ham SW6 ....135 B3
ngham Sch
15...........135 B1
ngham Sq
6............135 D2
ock Ho 1 N5.....72 D5
ock St N5 ....72 D5
stone Rd SE25 ..205 C4
Court Rd TW5 ..128 D3
Ct TW5 ....128 D3
on Cl 5 BR6 .....227 D2
n Rd SW17......159 A1
n Univ
1....... 94 A2 240 A4
en Cl SE3 ....142 C2
icane Rd SM6 ...220 B1
icane Trad Ctr
9..........28 A2
y Cl E15.........76 C1
ley Ct 11 KT6....197 D2
st Ave
ngford E4 ....19 C1
hgate N6 ....49 C3
stbourne KT10 ...212 D2
stbourne Cotts
5..........169 D4
stbourne Gdns
1............79 C2
tbourne Ho
15..........155 D5
stbourne Priors
2..........221 C2
stbourne Rd
23..........163 A3
st Cl
essington KT9 .... 214 C3
ngford E4 ....19 C1
mpstead Garden
Suburb NW11.......47 D3
ves BR2......... 208 D1
rtholt UB5 ....63 B3
stcombe IG9.......21 A2
stcourt Rd SM1 ..217 D6
st Ct
ckenham BR3 .... 185 C3
wham E6..........99 D2
uth Norwood
SE25......... 205 D5
odford IG8 ....37 B4
stdene Ave BR2 ..208 D1
stdene Gdns N15..51 C2
stfield BR2........209 A4
stfield Cres UB4...83 C2
stfield Rd KT8.....195 C6
st Gr KT12 ....193 D1
st Ho
Penge SE26 ......184 B5
ntonville N1...... 233 D3
est Heath SE2 .... 124 D1
st La
st Molesey KT8 ... 196 A6
st Heath SE2 .... 124 D1
st Lo London N8 ....49 D3
embley HA0 ....66 B1
stmead Ct HA8 ....26 D6
stmere Foundation
h for Boys
15 .... 168 C3
ST PARK 174 A1
st Park Prim Sch
8 .... 195 C6
st Pl Erith SE2.....146 D6
olwich SE2 ...... 124 C1
st Prim Sch
5 .... 168 D3
st Rd
ckhurst Hill IG9.....21 D3
oydon CR0 ....221 B3
st Molesey KT8,
KT12........... 195 C6
dcup DA5, DA15 ... 168 C3
uthgate N21........16 C3
althamstow E17 .....53 D6
alton-on-T
KT8&KT12 .... 194 D5
st Rise EN5 ....1 C2
st Springs DA5 ...169 A3
st St SE24........160 D5
st View Grange
2 ....220 D1
st View Rd CR2 ...221 C1
st Way CR2........221 C2
stway Wlk 2
1.............112 D6
stwood Ave
dcup DA5 .... 169 A3
anstead E18........55 B5
stwood Ct
ney Hatch N12 .....30 C4

Hurstwood Ct *continued*
Temple Fortune
NW11............47 B5
Hurstwood Dr BR1...210 B6
Hurstwood Rd NW11..47 B5
Hurtwood Rd KT12...195 B2
Husbourne Ho 8
SE8...............119 A2
Huson Cl NW3 ....70 C1
Hussain Cl HA1 ......64 D4
Hussars Cl TW4......129 A2
Husseywell Cres
BR2 ....209 A1
Hutching's St E14....119 C4
Hutching's Wharf 11
E14...............119 C4
Hutchings Wlk NW11..47 D5
Hutchins Cl E15 ......76 A1
Hutchins Ho 8
SW4...............159 D4
Hutchinson Ct RM6 ...58 D5
Hutchinson Ho 9
SE14..............140 C5
Hutchinson Terr HA9..65 D5
Hutchins Rd SE28....124 A5
Hutton Cl
Greenford UB6 ....64 B3
Woodford IG8 ....37 B4
Hutton Ct
1 Ealing W5.........87 C2
Edmonton N9.........18 C4
4 Finsbury Pk N4.....50 B1
Hutton Gdns HA3 .....24 A3
Hutton Gr N12 ....29 D5
Hutton Ho 19 E2 ......96 A4
Hutton La HA3 ....24 A3
Hutton Row 4 HA8 ....27 A3
Hutton St EC4 ...... 241 B1
Hutton Wlk HA3 ......24 A3
Huxbear St SE4 ......163 B6
Huxley Cl UB5 ....85 A6
Huxley Dr RM6........58 B2
Huxley Gdns NW10....88 B5
Huxley Ho
4 London SW9.......138 B3
Paddington NW8 .... 236 D5
West Heath SE2 .... 124 D1
Huxley Par N18 ....33 B5
Huxley Pl N13 ....16 D1
Huxley Rd
Edmonton N18........33 C6
Falconwood DA16 ... 145 D2
Leyton E10...........76 A6
Huxley Sayze N18.....33 B5
Huxley South N18.....33 B5
Huxley St W10........91 A4
Hyacinth Cl
3 Hampton
TW12........... 173 C4
Ilford IG1 ....78 D2
Hyacinth Ct 2 HA5 ...40 C6
Hyacinth Dr UB10.....60 A1
Hyacinth Rd SW15 ...156 A3
Hyde Cl
Ashford TW16 ...... 171 C4
Barnet EN5 ....1 B2
Newham E13 ....99 A5
Hyde Cres NW9 ....45 C4
Hyde Ct
Forest Hill SE23..... 163 A2
Hounslow TW4 ......151 B6
Kingsbury NW9 ....45 B2
Whetstone N20 ....14 B1
Hyde Estate Rd NW9 ..45 D4
Hyde Farm Mews
SW12..............159 D3
Hydefield Cl N21......17 B3
Hydefield Ct N9 ......17 C2
Hyde Ho
12 Ealing W13...... 109 A5
Hounslow TW3 ...... 130 A2
Hyde Ind Est The
NW9................45 D4
Hyde La
SW11.......136 C4 267 A2
Hyde Park Ave N21....17 B3
Hyde Park Cnr SW1 . 248 B2
Hyde Park Corner Sta
SW1....... 115 A4 248 B2
Hyde Park Cres
W2..........92 C1 237 A1
Hyde Park Gate Mews
SW7............. 246 B1
Hyde Park Gdns
Bayswater
W2...... 114 B6 246 D6
Edmonton N21.........17 A3
Hyde Park Gdns Mews
W2..........114 C6 247 A6
Hyde Park Mans
NW1.............. 237 A3
Hyde Park Pl W2 ... 247 B6
Hyde Park Square
Mews W2.......... 237 A1
Hyde Park Sq
W2..........92 C1 237 A1

Hyde Park St
W2............92 C1 237 A1
Hyde Park Twrs W2 . 246 A5
Hyde Park*
W2....... 114 D5 247 C3
Hyderabad Way E15...76 C1
Hyde Rd
Bexleyheath DA7.....147 B3
Richmond TW10......154 B6
Shoreditch N1 ....95 C6
Hyde Sch The NW9 ...45 D4
Hydeside Gdns N9 ....17 D2
Hyde's Pl 12 N1.......72 D1
Hyde St SE8 ....141 C6
Hyde Terr TW15,
TW16..............171 C4
HYDE THE 45 D4
Hydethorpe Ave N9 ...17 D2
Hydethorpe Rd
SW12..............159 C3
Hyde Vale SE10 ......142 A5
Hyde Way
Edmonton N9.........17 D2
Hayes UB3.......... 105 D2
Hyde Wlk SM4........201 C2
Hydon Ct N11.........30 D5
Hyh Ho E17...........35 D2
Hyland House Sch
E17.................36 B1
Hylands Rd E17.......36 B1
Hylda Ct NW5.........71 A5
Hylton St SE18.......123 D2
Hyndewood 14
SE23...............162 D1
Hyndman Ho
5 Dagenham
RM10..............81 C5
4 Tufnell Pk N19.....71 D4
Hyndman St SE15....140 B6
Hynton Rd RM8 ....80 C6
Hyperion Ho
27 Bow E3............97 A5
Streatham SW2......160 B4
Hyrstdene CR0.......220 D4
Hyrst The CR0 ....207 A1
Hyson Rd SE16.......118 B1
Hythe Ave DA7.......147 B5
Hythe Cl N18 ....34 A6
Hythe Ho 14 SE16 ....118 C4
Hythe Rd
College Pk NW10 .....90 A3
South Norwood CR7 ..183 B1
Hythe Road Ind Est
NW10...............90 A3
Hyver Hill NW7 ....11 B4

I

Ian Ct SE23 ....162 C2
Ian Hamilton Ho
NW1.............. 232 C2
Ian Mikardo Sch E3...97 D4
Ian Sq EN3 ....6 D4
Ibberton Ho
Kensington W14 .... 254 B5
South Lambeth SW8 . 270 C4
Ibbotson Ave E16 .....98 D1
Ibbott St 22 E1........96 C3
Iberia Ho 17 N19......49 D2
Iberian Ave CR0,
SM6...............220 A4
Ibex Ho E15 ....76 C3
Ibis Ct 16 SE8........141 B6
Ibis Ho E12...........78 B4
Ibis La W4...........133 A4
Ibis Way UB4 ....84 D1
Ibrox Ct 3 IG9.......21 C2
Ibsley Gdns SW15....156 A3
Ibsley Way EN4 ....2 C1
Ibstock Place Sch
SW15............. 155 C5
Icarus Ho 21 E3.......97 B4
Iceland Rd E3 ....97 C6
Iceland Wharf SE16 ..119 A2
Iceni Ct 23 Bow E3.....97 B6
Buckhurst Hill IG9.....21 B3
Ice Wharf NW1 ...... 233 B4
Ickburgh Est E5 ......74 B6
Ickburgh Rd E5........74 B5
Ickburgh Sch E5.......74 B5
ICKENHAM 60 C4
Ickenham Cl HA4 .....61 B6
Ickenham Rd HA4.....39 B1
Ickenham Sta UB10....61 A4
Ickleton Rd SE9.......188 A6
Icknield Dr IG2 ....56 D4
Ickworth Park Rd
E17.................53 A5
Icough Ct SE3 ....143 B5
Idaho Bldg 7 SE13...141 D4
Ida Rd N15 ....51 B5
Ida St E14............98 A1
Iden Cl BR2.........208 C6
Idlecombe Rd
SW17..............181 A4

Idmiston Rd
New Malden KT4.... 199 D2
Stratford E15.........76 D3
West Norwood SE21,
SE27............. 161 A2
Idmiston Sq KT4 .....199 D2
Idol La EC3 ...117 C6 253 A5
Idonia St SE8 ....141 C5
Iffley Ho 47 E2........95 D4
Iffley Rd W6..........112 B3
Ifield Ho SE17 ...... 263 B2
Ifield Rd
SW10...... 135 D6 265 D6
Ifor Evans Pl E1.......96 D3
Ightham Ho
Beckenham BR3 .....185 B3
Walworth SE17 ..... 263 A3
Ightham Rd DA8 .....147 C5
Ikon Ho 21 E1.........118 C6
Ikra Prim Sch N16....73 D4
Ilbert St W10 ....91 A4
Ilchester Gdns W2 .. 245 C6
Ilchester Mans W8.. 255 A6
Ilchester Pl
W14........113 B3 254 D6
Ilchester Rd RM8 .....80 C3
Ildersly Gr SE21......161 B2
Ilderton Prim Sch
SE16.............. 118 C1
Ilderton Rd SE15,
SE16...............140 C6
Ilex Cl TW16.........172 C1
Ilex Rd NW10 ....67 D2
Ilex Way SW16........182 C5
ILFORD 78 D6
Ilford Chambers 10
IG1.................78 D5
Ilford Hill IG1.........78 C5
Ilford Ho 14 N1 ....73 B2
Ilford Interchange
IG1.................78 C5
Ilford Jewish Prim Sch
IG6.................57 B6
Ilford La IG1..........78 D4
Ilford Prep Sch IG3...58 A1
Ilford Ret Pk IG1 .....79 A6
Ilford Sta IG1 ....78 D6
Ilford Ursuline High Sch
IG1.................78 D6
Ilfracombe Flats
SE1............... 252 B2
Ilfracombe Gdns
RM6................58 B2
Ilfracombe Rd BR1....164 D1
Iliffe St
SE17...... 116 D1 261 D2
Iliffe Yd
SE17...... 116 D1 261 D2
Ilkeston Ct 7 E5......74 D4
Ilkley Cl SE19........183 B4
Ilkley Ct N11..........31 A4
Ilkley Rd
Newham E16 ....99 C2
South Oxhey WD19 ....22 D5
Illingworth Cl CR4 ...202 B6
Illingworth Way EN1 ..17 C6
Ilmington Rd HA3.....43 D3
Ilminster Gdns
SW11..............136 C1
Ilsley Ct 8 SW8.......137 C3
Imber Cl
London N14 ....15 C4
Thames Ditton KT7 ...196 B1
Imber Court Trad Est
KT8................196 B3
Imber Cross KT7 .....196 D3
Imber Ct 4 SE9.......166 C5
Imber Gr KT10 ....196 B2
Imber Park Rd KT10..196 B1
Imber St N1 .... 235 C5
Immanuel Coll WD23 ..8 C4
Immanuel & St Andrew
CE Prim Sch
SW16.............. 182 A4
Impact Ct SE20 ......184 B1
Imperial Ave 5 N16...73 C4
Imperial Cl HA2.......41 C3
Imperial College Rd
SW7.........114 B3 256 C6
Imperial College London
SW7....... 114 B3 256 C6
Imperial Cres SW6...136 A3
Imperial Ct
Chislehurst BR7..... 188 D4
Harrow HA2 ....41 C2
St John's Wood NW8. 230 B4
Wembley HA9 ....66 C5
Whetstone N20 ....14 A1
Imperial Dr HA2 ......41 C3
Imperial Gdns CR4...203 B6
Imperial Ho
1 Bow E3...........97 A4
2 Poplar E14........119 B6
Strand WC2........ 240 C1
Imperial Mews 5 E6...99 D5
Imperial Pl BR7......188 C2

Imperial Rd
East Bedfont
TW14........... 149 C4
Walham Green SW6 . 265 D1
Wood Green N22.......32 A2
Imperial Sq SW6.... 265 D2
Imperial St E3........98 A4
Imperial Twrs 3
NW3...............70 A2
Imperial War Mus* SE1,
SE11 ...... 116 C3 261 B5
Imperial Way
Croydon CR0, CR9 ... 220 C2
Harrow HA3 ....44 A3
Longlands BR7...... 167 A1
Imperial Wharf Sta
SW10...... 136 A4 266 B1
Impington 19 KT1......176 C1
Imre Cl W12..........112 B5
Inca Dr SE9..........166 D4
Ince Terr 3 N15 ......50 D6
Inchmery Rd SE6 ....164 A3
Inchwood BR4, CR0...223 D4
Independant Jewish
Day Sch NW4 ....46 D4
Independence Ho 4
SW19..............180 B2
Independent Ind Est
UB7 .... 104 C5
Independent Pl E8....73 D3
Independents Rd
SE3................142 D2
Inderwick Rd N8......50 B4
Indescon Ct E14 .....119 D4
Indiana Bldg 7 SE8 ..141 C4
India St EC3 .... 243 C1
India Way W12 ......112 B6
Indigo Ct TW13 ......149 D1
Indigo Mews N16 .....73 B5
Indus Ct 16 SE15 ....139 D5
Indus Rd SE7 ....143 C5
Ingal Rd E13..........99 A3
Ingate Pl
SW8........137 B4 268 D1
Ingatestone Rd
Croydon SE25 ......206 B5
Wanstead E12........55 C1
Woodford IG8 ....37 B3
Ingelow Ho W8 .... 245 C2
Ingelow Rd SW8 .....137 B3
Ingersoll Rd
Enfield EN3 ....6 C5
Shepherd's Bush
W12..............112 B5
Ingestre Pl W1 ..... 239 B1
Ingestre Rd
Forest Gate E7 ....77 A4
Gospel Oak NW5......71 B4
Ingham Rd NW6 ......69 C4
Inglebert St
EC1 ....94 C4 234 A2
Ingleborough EN2 .....4 C3
Ingleborough St
SW9...............138 C3
Ingleby Ct N21........16 D3
Ingleby Dr HA1 ....64 B5
Ingleby Rd
Dagenham RM10......81 D2
Ilford IG1 ....56 D1
Lower Holloway N7....72 A5
Ingleby Way
Chislehurst West
BR7.............. 188 C5
Wallington SM6..... 219 D1
Ingle Cl HA5 ....41 B6
Ingledew Rd SE18....123 B1
Inglefield Sq 12 E1....118 B5
Ingle Ho 3 SW12.....159 D3
Inglehurst Gdns IG4 ..56 B4
Inglemere Ct CR4,
SW17..............180 D3
Inglemere Rd
Forest Hill SE23..... 162 D1
Mitcham CR4, SW17 . 180 D3
Inglesham Wlk E9 ....75 B2
Ingleside Cl BR3 .....185 C3
Ingleside Gr SE3.....142 D6
Inglethorpe Ho 6
E5.................74 A6
Inglethorpe St SW6 ..134 D4
Ingleton Ave DA16 ...168 A6
Ingleton Rd N18 ......34 A4
Ingleton St SW9 .....138 C3
Ingleway N12.........30 C4
Inglewood BR7 ......189 B4
Inglewood Cl E14.....119 C2
Inglewood Copse
BR1...............188 B1
Inglewood Ct 4
BR1...............186 D3
Inglewood Mans 11
NW6...............69 C3
Inglewood Rd NW6 ...69 C3
Inglis Ct W5.........110 B6
Inglis Ho 1 SW15.....156 C6
Inglis Rd
Croydon CR0 .... 205 D1

Inglis Rd *continued*
Ealing W5 ....110 B6
Inglis St SE5.........138 D4
Ingram Ave NW11.....48 A2
Ingram Cl
Lambeth SE11...... 260 D4
Stanmore HA7........25 C5
Ingram Ct EN1........17 D5
Ingram Ho
7 Harrow HA1.......42 D4
Old Ford E3 ....97 A6
Teddington KT8 ..... 175 C2
Ingram Lo 8 SW4 ....159 D5
Ingram Rd London N2 ..48 C5
South Norwood CR7 . 183 A2
Ingram Way UB6......86 B6
Ingrave Ho RM9 .....102 B6
Ingrave St SW11 .....136 C2
Ingrebourne Ct E4....19 D2
Ingrebourne Ho
2 Catford BR1.......186 B5
Lisson Gr NW8 ..... 236 D4
Ingress St 4 W4.....111 C1
Inigo Jones Rd SE7 ..144 A5
Inigo Pl WC2 .... 250 A6
Inkerman Rd NW5 ....71 B2
Inkerman Terr W8.... 255 B5
Inks Gn E4 ....36 A5
Inkster Ho 8 SW11 ..136 C2
Inkwell Cl N12........14 A1
Inman Rd
Harlesden NW10......89 C6
Wandsworth SW18 .. 158 A4
Inmans Row IG8......37 A6
Inner Circ
NW1........93 A4 231 A2
Inner Park Rd
SW19..............156 D2
Inner Ring E TW6 ....126 D2
Inner Ring W TW6 ...126 C2
Inner Temple* EC4... 251 A6
Inner Temple La
EC4 .... 241 A1
Innes Cl SW20 ....179 A1
Innes Gdns SW15 ....156 B5
Innes Lo SE23 ....162 D1
Innes Yd CR0 ....221 A5
Innisfree Ho NW2.....68 D2
Innis Ho SE17....... 263 A2
Inniskilling Rd E13....99 C5
Innova Bsns Pk EN3 ...7 B3
Innovation Cl HA0 ....88 A6
Inskip Cl E10 ....75 D6
Inskip Rd RM8.........58 D1
Insley Ho 18 E3 ....97 D4
Inst for Child Health
WC1........94 B3 240 C5
Institute Pl E8........74 B3
Instituto Espanol
Vicente Canada
Blanch W10.........91 A2
Inst of Neurology
Bloomsbury
WC1........94 A2 240 B4
St Pancras
WC1.......94 A3 240 B5
Int Coll of Accountancy
The SW17......... 158 D1
Integer Gdns E11 .....54 B2
Interchange The
Kentish Town NW5 ....71 B3
Thornton Heath CR0 . 204 D2
International Ave
TW5...............106 C1
International House
Language Sch
WC2..........94 A1 240 B2
International Sch of
London W3....... 110 C2
International Trad Est
UB2 ....106 B3
International Way
TW16...............171 C2
Inverary Pl SE18 .....145 B6
Inver Cl E5 ....74 C6
Inverclyde Gdns RM6..58 D5
Inver Ct
11 Bayswater W2 .....91 D1
4 Hammersmith
W6 .... 112 A3
Inveresk Gdns KT4 ..216 A5
Inverey Ho 2 N12.....29 D5
Inverforth Cl NW3 ....70 A6
Inverforth Ho NW3....70 A6
Inverforth Rd N11.....31 B5
Invergarry Ct 11 EN5 ..13 D6
Invergarry Ho NW6 ...91 D5
Inverine Rd SE7......121 B1
Invermead Cl W6 .....112 A2
Invermore Pl SE18 ...123 A2
Inverness Ave EN1 .....5 C4
Inverness Ct
8 Acton W3.........88 C1

Inverness Ct *continued*
10 Catford SE6 ..... 164 D3
Inverness Gdns W8 . 245 C3
Inverness Mews
Bayswater W2 ...... 245 D6
Newham E16 .... 122 D5
North Woolwich E16 . 123 A5
Inverness Pl W2 .... 245 D6
Inverness Rd
Edmonton N18 .... 34 B5
Hounslow TW3 ..... 129 C1
North Cheam KT4 ... 200 D1
Southall UB2 .... 107 A2
Inverness St NW1 ... 231 D6
Inverness Terr
W2 .... 113 D6 245 D6
Inverton Rd SE15 .... 140 D1
Invicta Cl
Chislehurst West
BR7 .... 188 C5
East Bedfont TW14 .. 149 D3
21 Tower Hamlets E3 .. 97 C2
Invicta Ct KT9 .... 214 B3
Invicta Ctr The
IG11 .... 102 A6
Invicta Gr UB5 .... 85 B4
Invicta Plaza SE1 ... 251 C4
Invicta Prim Sch
SE3 .... 143 A5
Invicta Rd SE3, SE7 ... 143 A6
Inville Rd
SE17 .... 117 B1 262 D1
Inwen Ct SE8 .... 119 A1
Inwood Ave TW3 ..... 130 A2
Inwood Bsns Pk
TW3 .... 129 D1
Inwood Cl CR0 .... 223 A6
Inwood Ct 12 NW1 .... 71 C1
Inwood Ho 19 SE22 ... 139 C2
Inwood Rd TW3 ...... 130 A1
Inworth St SW11 ..... 136 C3
Inworth Wlk N1 ...... 235 A6
Io Ctr Barking IG11 .. 101 D3
Woolwich SE18 ..... 123 A3
Iona Cl Catford SE6 ... 163 C4
Morden SM4 .... 201 D2
Ion Ct 8 E2 .... 96 A5
Ionian Bldg 19 E14 ... 119 A6
Ionian Ho 22 E1 .... 96 D3
Ipsden Bldgs SE1 .... 251 B2
Ipswich Ho SE4 ...... 162 D6
Ipswich Rd SW17 .... 181 A4
Irby Ho SW2 .... 160 C5
Ireland Cl E6 .... 100 B2
Ireland Pl N22 .... 32 A3
Ireland Yd EC4 ...... 241 D1
Irene Rd
Broom Hill BR6 ..... 211 D2
Parsons Green
SW6 ..... 135 C4 265 B1
Ireton Cl N10 .... 31 A3
Ireton Ho 22 SW9 .... 138 C3
Ireton St 12 E3 .... 97 C3
Iris Ave DA5 .... 169 A5
Iris Cl Croydon CR0 .... 206 D1
Newham E6 .... 100 A3
Surbiton KT6 .... 198 B2
Iris Cres DA7 .... 147 B6
Iris Ct Dagenham IG11 .. 80 B1
8 Peckham SE15 .... 140 B3
4 Pinner HA5 .... 40 C6
Iris Rd KT19 .... 214 D3
Iris Way E4 .... 35 B4
Iris Wlk 1 HA8 .... 27 A6
Irkdale Ave EN1 .... 5 D4
Iroko Ho 4 NW3 ...... 69 D2
Iron Bridge Cl
Southall UB2 .... 108 A5
Willesden NW10 ...... 67 C3
Iron Bridge Ho NW3 ... 70 D1
Iron Bridge Rd N
UB11 .... 104 C5
Iron Bridge Rd S
UB7 .... 104 C4
Irongate Ho EC3 .... 243 B2
Iron Mill Pl SW18 .... 157 D5
Iron Mill Rd SW18 .... 157 D5
Ironmonger La
EC2 .... 95 B1 242 C1
Ironmonger Pas
EC1 .... 235 B1
Ironmonger Row
EC1 .... 95 A4 235 B1
Ironmonger's Pl 22
E14 .... 119 C2
Ironside Cl SE16 ..... 118 D4
Ironside Ho E9 .... 75 A4
Ironworks 1 E3 .... 97 C6
Irvine Ave HA3 .... 43 B6
Irvine Cl N20 .... 14 C2
Irvine Ct
Marylebone W1 ..... 239 B5
Thornton Heath CR7 . 204 C3
Irvine Ho N7 .... 72 B2
Irvine Way BR6 ...... 211 D2
Irving Ave UB5 .... 84 D6
Irving Ct N22 .... 32 D2
Irving Gr SW9 .... 138 B3
Irving Ho SE17 .... 261 C1
Irving Mews N1 .... 73 A2
Irving Rd W14 .... 112 D3
Irving St WC2 .... 249 D5
Irwell Ct W7 .... 86 B1
Irwell Est 31 SE16 .... 118 C4
Irwin Ave SE18 ...... 145 C5
Irwin Cl UB10 .... 60 C5
Irwin Gdns NW10 ..... 90 B6
Isabel Hill Cl TW12 ... 173 C2
Isabella Cl N14 .... 15 C4
Isabella Ct 8 TW10 .. 154 B5
Isabella Dr BR6 ...... 227 A4
Isabella Ho
19 Hammersmith
W6 .... 112 C1
Kennington SE11 .... 261 C2
Isabella Pl KT2 ...... 176 B5
Isabella Rd E9 .... 74 C3
Isabella St SE1 ...... 251 C3
Isabel St SW9 .... 270 D2
Isambard Mews
E14 .... 120 A3
Isambard Pl SE16 .... 118 C5
Iseldon Ct N7 .... 72 A4
Isel Way 4 SE22 ..... 161 C6
Isham Rd SW16 ...... 182 A1
Isis Cl Putney SW15 ... 134 C1
Ruislip HA4 .... 39 A3
Isis Ct W4 .... 132 D5
Isis Ho
2 Edmonton N18 ..... 33 D4
Paddington NW8 .... 236 D5
Isis St SW18 .... 158 A2
Islamia Girls' High Sch
NW6 .... 91 A6
Islamia Prim Sch
NW6 .... 91 A6
Islamic Coll for
Advanced Studies
NW10 .... 68 B2
Island Centre Way 16
EN3 .... 7 C6
Island Farm Ave
KT8 .... 195 B4
Island Farm Rd KT8 .. 195 C4
Island Gardens Sta
E14 .... 120 A1
Island Ho Bromley E14 .. 98 A4
Morden SW19 ...... 202 A5
Island Rd
Deptford SE16 ...... 118 D2
Mitcham CR4 .... 180 D3
Island Row E14 .... 97 B1
Isla Rd SE18 .... 145 A6
Islay Gdns TW4 ...... 150 D6
Islay Wlk 17 N1 .... 73 A2
Isleden Ho N1 .... 235 A6
Isledon Rd N4, N7 ..... 72 C5
Islehurst Cl BR7 ..... 188 C2
ISLE OF DOGS 120 A2
ISLEWORTH 131 B2
Isleworth Bsns Complex
TW7 .... 130 D3
Isleworth Sta TW7 .. 130 D3
Isleworth & Syon Sch
for Boys TW7 ..... 130 C5
Isleworth Town Prim
Sch TW7 .... 131 A3
ISLINGTON 72 D2
Islington Arts & Media
Sch N4 .... 50 B1
Islington Bsns Ctr
N1 .... 235 B6
Islington Est
N1 .... 95 A6 235 A6
Islington Gn
N1 .... 94 D6 234 C5
Islington Green Sch
N1 .... 95 A6 235 A5
Islington High St
N1 .... 94 D5 234 C4
Islington Park Mews 1
N1 .... 72 D1
Islington Park St N1 .. 72 D1
Islington Sixth Form Ctr
N7 .... 72 C4
Islip Gdns
Burnt Oak HA8 .... 27 B3
Northolt UB5 .... 63 A1
Islip Manor Rd UB5 ... 63 A1
Islip St NW5 .... 71 C3
Ismailia Rd E7 .... 77 B1
Isobel Ho
10 Ashford TW16 ... 171 D3
Harrow HA1 .... 42 D4
Isokon Flats 3 NW3 .. 70 D3
Isom Cl E13 .... 99 B4
Issac Way SE1 ...... 252 B2
Italia Conti Acad of
Theatre Arts EC1 .. 242 A5
Ithell Ct HA0 .... 65 D3
Ivanhoe Dr HA3 .... 25 B1
Ivanhoe Ho
11 Balham SW12 .... 159 B4
31 Bow E3 .... 97 A5
Ivanhoe Rd
Hounslow TW4 ..... 128 D2
Peckham SE5 .... 139 D2
Ivatt Pl W14 .. 113 B1 254 D1
Ivatt Way N17 .... 50 D6
Iveagh Ave NW10 ..... 88 C5
Iveagh Cl
Ealing NW10 .... 88 C5
South Hackney E9 .... 96 D6
Iveagh Ct
4 Beckenham
BR3 .... 207 D6
Whitechapel EC3 .... 243 C1
Iveagh Ho
2 Brixton SW9 ...... 138 D3
Chelsea SW10 ...... 266 B4
Ivebury Ct 9 W10 .... 90 C1
Ivedon Rd DA16 ..... 146 C3
Ive Farm Cl E10 .... 75 C6
Ive Farm La E10 ...... 75 C6
Iveley Rd SW4 .... 137 C3
Iver Ct N1 .... 73 A2
Ivere Dr EN5 .... 13 D5
Iverhurst Cl DA6 ..... 168 D6
Iverna Ct W8 .... 255 B6
Iverna Gdns
Hatton TW14 .... 149 B6
Kensington
W8 ...... 113 C3 255 B6
Iverson Rd NW6 ...... 69 C2
Ivers Way CR0 ...... 223 D1
Ives Rd E16 .... 98 C2
Ives St SW3 .. 114 C2 257 B4
Ivestor Terr SE23 .... 162 C4
Ivimey St E2 .... 96 A4
Ivinghoe Cl EN1 .... 5 C4
Ivinghoe Ho 14 N7 .... 71 D3
Ivinghoe Rd
Barking RM8 .... 80 B3
Bushey WD23 .... 8 B4
Ivor Ct Hendon N3 .... 47 A6
Hornsey N8 .... 50 A3
Lisson Gr NW1 ..... 237 C6
Ivor Gr SE9 .... 166 D3
Ivor Ho DA14 .... 190 C5
Ivories The N1 .... 73 A1
Ivor Mayor Lo
SW12 .... 159 A5
Ivor Pl NW1 ... 92 D3 237 C5
Ivor St NW1 .... 71 C1
Ivory Ct TW13 .... 150 A3
Ivorydown BR1 ...... 187 A6
Ivory Ho
9 London SW11 .... 136 A2
St George in t East
E1 .... 253 D4
Ivory Sq 15 SW18 .... 136 A2
Ivybridge Cl
2 Twickenham
TW1 .... 153 A4
Uxbridge UB8 .... 82 A4
Ivybridge Ct 1 BR7 .. 188 C2
Ivybridge Ho 18
SE22 .... 139 C2
Ivybridge La WC2 ... 250 B5
Ivybridge Prim Sch
TW1 .... 152 D5
Ivybridge Ret Pk
TW7 .... 152 D6
Ivychurch Cl SE20 ... 184 C3
Ivy Church La SE1,
SE17 .... 263 C2
Ivy Cl Harrow HA2 ..... 63 B4
Pinner HA5 .... 40 C2
Sunbury TW16 ...... 172 C1
Ivy Cotts UB10 .... 82 C4
Ivy Cres W4 .... 111 A2
Ivy Ct
19 Bermondsey
SE16 .... 118 A1
Lewisham SE3 ..... 142 D1
Ivydale Prim Sch
SE15 .... 140 D1
Ivydale Rd
Carshalton SM5 ..... 218 D6
Nunhead SE15 ...... 140 D1
Ivyday Gr SW16 ..... 160 B1
Ivydene Cl SM1 ...... 218 A4
Ivydene KT12, KT8 ... 195 B4
Ivy Gdns London N8 ... 50 A3
Mitcham CR4 .... 203 D6
Ivy Ho Croydon CR0 ... 206 D1
6 Upper Clapton E5 ... 52 B1
Ivyhouse Rd RM9 ..... 81 A2
Ivy House Rd UB10 ... 60 D5
Ivy La TW4 .... 129 B1
Ivy Lo W8 .... 245 A4
Ivymount Rd SE27 ... 160 C1
Ivy Rd Brockley SE4 ... 141 C1
Cricklewood NW2 .... 68 C4
Hounslow TW3 ..... 129 D1
Newham E16 .... 99 A1
Southgate N14 .... 15 D4
Tolworth KT6 .... 198 C1
Ivy Rd *continued*
Upper Tooting
SW17 .... 180 C5
Walthamstow E17 .... 53 C3
Ivy St N1 .... 95 C5
Ivy Terr 3 IG2 .... 57 A3
Ivy Wlk RM9 .... 81 A2
Ixworth Pl
SW3 ...... 114 C2 257 A3
Izane Rd DA6 .... 147 B1

J

Jacaranda Cl KT3 .... 199 C6
Jacaranda Gr E8 ...... 73 D1
Jack Ashley Ct 5
NW9 .... 27 C2
Jackass La BR2 ...... 225 C2
Jack Barnett Way
N22 .... 32 B1
Jack Clow Rd E15 ..... 98 C5
Jack Cook Ho 9
IG11 .... 78 D1
Jack Cornwell St
E12 .... 78 C4
Jack Goodchild Way
KT3 .... 198 D6
Jack & Jill Sch
TW12 .... 173 C4
Jacklin Gn IG8 .... 37 A6
Jackman Ho 24 E1 ... 118 B5
Jackman Mews NW2 .. 67 C5
Jackman St E8 .... 96 B6
Jackson Cl
Hackney E9 .... 74 D1
Uxbridge UB10 ...... 60 A1
Jackson Ct
Forest Gate E7 ...... 77 B2
Wanstead E11 .... 55 B1
Jackson Ho
16 London SW11 .... 136 B2
13 New Southgate
N11 .... 31 C5
Jackson Rd
Barking IG11 .... 101 B6
Bromley BR2 .... 226 B6
East Barnet EN4 ..... 14 C5
Lower Holloway N7 ... 72 B4
Uxbridge UB10 ...... 60 A1
Jackson's La N6 ...... 49 B2
Jackson's Pl CR0 .... 205 C1
Jackson St SE18 ..... 144 C6
Jackson's Way CR0 .. 223 C5
Jackson Way UB2 .... 107 D4
Jack Taylor Sch
NW8 .... 92 A6 229 A6
Jack Tizard Sch
W12 .... 112 B5
Jack Walker Ct N5 .... 72 D4
Jacob Ct 24 EN3 .... 7 C6
Jacob Ho 14 DA18 ... 124 D4
Jacobin Lo N7 .... 72 A3
Jacob Mans 15 E1 .... 96 B1
Jacobs Cl RM10 .... 81 D4
Jacobs Ho E13 .... 99 C4
Jacobson Ct SW11 ... 267 B1
Jacobson Ho E1 ..... 243 C2
Jacob St SE1 .... 118 A4
Jacob's Well Mews
W1 .... 238 B2
Jacotts Ho W10 .... 90 C3
Jacqueline Cl UB5 .... 85 A6
Jacqueline Ho 8 E1 .. 96 D2
Jade Cl
Dagenham RM8 ...... 58 C1
Hendon NW2 .... 46 D2
Newham E16 .... 99 D1
Jaffe Rd IG1 .... 57 B1
Jaffray Rd BR2 ...... 209 D5
Jaggard Way SW12 .. 158 D4
Jagger Ho SW11 .... 267 C2
Jago Cl SE18 .... 145 A6
Jago Wlk SE5 .... 139 B5
Jamahirya Sch
SW3 ...... 136 C6 267 A6
Jamaica Rd
Bermondsey SE1 .... 253 D1
Bermondsey SE16 ... 118 B3
Thornton Heath CR7 . 204 D3
Jamaica St E1 .... 96 C2
James Allen's Girls' Sch
SE22 .... 161 C6
James Allens Pre-Prep
Sch SE21 .... 161 B5
James Anderson Ct 29
E2 .... 95 C5
James Ave
Cricklewood NW2 .... 68 C3
Dagenham RM8 ...... 59 B1
James Bedford Cl
HA5 .... 22 C1
James Boswell Cl 1
SW16 .... 182 C6
James Brine Ho 6
E2 .... 95 D4
James Campbell Ho 2
E2 .... 96 C5
James Cl
London NW11 .... 47 A3
8 Newham E13 ...... 99 A5
James Collins Cl W9 .. 91 B3
James Ct Chingford E4 . 20 B2
Finchley N12 .... 30 C3
Hendon NW9 .... 27 C1
Northolt UB5 .... 85 A5
3 Woodford E18 ..... 37 B1
James Dixon Prim Sch
SE20 .... 184 B3
James Docherty Ho 4
E2 .... 96 C5
James Dudson Ct
NW10 .... 67 A1
James Elliman Sch
SL2 ....
James Est CR4 ...... 180 D1
James Gdns N22 ...... 32 D3
James Hammett Ho 9
E2 .... 95 D5
James Ho Mile End E1 .. 97 A3
33 Rotherhithe
SE16 .... 118 D4
James Joyce Wlk 7
SE24 .... 138 D1
James La E10, E11 ..... 54 B3
James Lee Sq EN3 ..... 7 C5
**James Leicester Hall of
Residence** N7 .... 72 A2
James Lind Ho 6
SE8 .... 119 B2
James Middleton Ho 20
E2 .... 96 B4
James Newman Ct
SE9 .... 166 C1
Jameson Ct 6 E2 ..... 96 C5
Jameson Ho SE11 ... 260 C2
Jameson Lo N6 .... 49 C3
Jameson Pl 11 W3 ... 111 A4
Jameson St W8 ..... 245 B4
James Pl N17 .... 33 D2
James's Cotts TW9 .. 132 C5
James St
Barking IG11 .... 79 A1
Enfield EN1 .... 17 D6
James Stewart Ho
NW6 .... 69 B1
James St
Hounslow TW3 ..... 130 B2
Marylebone
W1 .... 93 A1 238 B1
James Stroud Ho
SE17 .... 262 B1
James St
WC2 ...... 116 A6 250 B6
Jamestown Rd
NW1 .... 93 B6 231 C6
Jamestown Way
E14 .... 120 B6
James Way WD19 ..... 22 D6
James Wolfe Prim Sch
SE10 .... 142 A5
Jamieson Ho TW4 ... 151 B5
Jamuna Cl E14 .... 97 A2
Jane Austen Hall 14
E16 .... 121 B5
Jane St E1 .... 96 B1
Janet Ct
4 Bexleyheath
DA7 .... 147 C1
Wood Green N22 ..... 32 B2
Janet St E14 .... 119 C3
Janeway Pl 2 SE16 .. 118 B4
Janeway St SE16 .... 118 A4
Janice Mews 3 IG1 ... 78 D5
Jansen Ho 5 SW15 ... 156 A6
Jansen Wlk SW11 ... 136 B1
Janson Cl
Stratford E15 .... 76 C3
Willesden NW10 ..... 67 C5
Janson Rd E15 .... 76 C3
Jansons Rd N15 .... 51 C6
Japan Cres N4 .... 50 B1
Japanese Sch The
W3 .... 110 C6
Japan Rd RM6 .... 58 D3
Jaquets Ct DA5 ..... 169 C2
Jardine Ho HA1 .... 42 C2
Jardine Rd E1 .... 118 D6
Jarman Ho
Bermondsey
SE16 .... 118 D2
16 Stepney E1 .... 96 C2
Jarrett Cl SW2 ...... 160 D3
Jarrow Cl SM4 ...... 201 D4
Jarrow Rd
Bermondsey
SE16 .... 118 C1
Dagenham RM6 ...... 58 C3
Tottenham Hale N17 ... 52 B5
Jarrow Way E9 .... 75 A4
Jarvis Cl
1 Barking IG11 ..... 101 B6
Barnet EN5 .... 12 D6
Jarvis Ho 3 SE15 ... 140 A4
Jarvis Rd
London SE22 13
South Croydon CR2 .. 22
Jasmine Cl Ilford IG1 ..
Orpington BR6 22
Southall UB1 10
Jasmine Ct
Lee SE12 16
11 Wallington SM6 ... 2
Wimbledon SW19 ... 17
Jasmine Gdns
Harrow HA2 6
West Wickham CR0 .. 22
Jasmine Gr SE20 18
Jasmine Sq 15 E3 ....
Jasmine Terr UB7 10
Jasmine Way KT7 19
Jasmin Ho SE4 1
Jasmin Lo 17 SE16 ... 1
Jasmin Rd KT19 21
Jasmin SE1 25
Jason Ct
2 London SW9 13
Marylebone W1 23
Jason Ho UB5 ....
Jason Wlk SE9 18
Jasper Cl EN3 ....
Jasper Ho KT4 19
Jasper Rd
Newham E16 9
Penge SE19 18
Jasper Wlk N1 23
Java Wharf SE1 25
Javelin Ct HA7 ....
Javelin Way UB5 8
Jawahar Bagh
SW16 18
Jaycroft EN2 ....
Jay Gdns BR7 18
Jay Ho SW15 13
Jay Mews
SW7 .... 114 A4 2
Jayson Ct 7 CR0 20
Jazzfern Terr HA0 6
Jean Batten Cl SM6 .. 22
Jean Darling Ho
SW10 26
Jean Ho 3 SW17 18
Jean Humbert Ho 2
SE27 18
Jean Pardies Ho 23
E1 9
Jebb Ave SW2 16
Jebb St E3 9
Jedburgh Rd E13 9
Jedburgh St SW11 ... 13
Jeddo Mews W12 11
Jeddo Rd W12 11
Jefferies Ho 13
NW10 6
Jefferson Bldg 3
E14 11
Jefferson Cl
Ealing W13 10
Ilford IG2 5
Jefferson Wlk 13
SE18 14
Jeffrey Row SE12 16
Jeffrey's Ct 2 SW4 .. 13
Jeffrey's Pl NW1 .....
Jeffreys Rd EN3 ......
Jeffrey's Rd SW4 13
Jeffrey's St NW1 7
Jeffs Cl TW12 17
Jeffs Rd SM1 21
Jeff Wooller Coll
WC1 .... 94 A2 24
Jefton Ct SM6 21
Jeger Ave E2 9
Jeken Rd SE9 14
Jelf Rd SW2 16
Jellicoe Ct E4 ....
Jellicoe Gdns HA7 ....
Jellicoe Ho
5 Bethnal Green
E2 9
Fitzrovia NW1 23
11 Putney SW15 15
Jellicoe Rd
4 Newham E13 ......
Tottenham N17 ......
Jemmett Cl KT2 17
Jemotts Ct 9 SE14 .. 14
Jem Paterson Ct
HA1 6
Jengar Cl SM1 21
Jenkins Ho SW8 26
Jenkins La IG11 10
Jenkinson Ho 12 E2 ... 9
Jenkins Rd E13 9
Jenner Ave W3 8
Jenner Cl DA14 19
Jenner Ct N21 ....
Jenner Ho
5 Belvedere
DA17 12
Greenwich SE3 14

er Pl SW13 134 B6
er Rd N16 73 D5
ett Rd CR0 220 C5
ifer Ho SE11 261 B3
ifer Rd BR1 164 D1
ngs Cl KT6 197 C2
ngs Ho SE10 120 B1
ngs Rd SE22 161 D5
y Hammond Cl
76 D5
y Hammond Prim
E11 76 C4
en Ho 10 E3 97 C3
on Way SE19 183 D3
on Ave DA7 147 A3
son Ct 17 SW4 138 A3
son Ho 6
7 138 D6
son Rd E7 77 C1
son St SE5 139 B4
tha Rd SW18 157 C5
o's La CR4 202 D5
an Pl SW6 265 A4
niah St 11 E14 97 D1
ny Bentham Ho 24
96 A4
ny's Gn N18 34 C6
yn St
115 C5 249 B4
ngham Ct
141 A4
ngham Rd
141 A4
ne Cres
3 92 C3 237 A6
ne Ct 2 N11 31 C5
ne Ho
ston u T KT1 175 D1
on Gr NW1 237 B4
ne Pl KT1 175 D1
ne St E1 95 D3 243 C5
ne Twr 5 W3 110 D4
ard St SE13 141 D2
old Lo SW15 134 C2
old St 24 N1 95 C5
ey Ave HA7 25 C1
ey Ct UB2 107 B3
ey Dr BR5 211 B3
ey Ho
Canonbury N1 73 A2
eld EN3 6 D5
ey Rd
onbury N1 73 A2
ng W7 109 A4
nslow TW5,
W7 130 B5
rd IG1 78 D4
onstone E11 54 B1
ham SW17 181 B4
ham E16 99 C1
ey St E2 96 B4
salem Pas EC1 241 C5
s Bay Ho 9 E14 98 B1
s Ct
Dagenham
M10 81 D2
Greenwich SE10 142 A4
ylebone W1 238 D1
ston Gdns
6 182 C4
nond Ave HA9 66 B2
nond Cl CR4 203 B6
nond Ct HA9 66 C2
nond Rd CR0 205 D2
nond Way HA7 26 A5
am Ave E5 52 B1
amine Rd W7 108 D5
el Ho
ancras WC1 233 A1
stminster SW1 259 D4
e Rd E10 54 A1
ca Rd SW18 158 A6
e Blythe La 4
50 A2
e Duffett Ho 11
139 A5
e's Cotts E17 53 A3
man Terr
7 192 C4
on Ho SE17 262 C3
op Ave UB2 107 B2
op Ct N1 234 D3
op Ho 9 W4 111 B2
op Pl CR4 202 C5
op Prim Sch
4 139 A1
op Sq E14 119 C5
ops Way CR0 203 C3
ops Wharf 4
3 131 C5
up Cl SE18 123 A2
en Ho 10 SE27 160 D1
ou Ho 16 N1 73 A2
ar Way UB5 85 A4
gton Way
2 165 B3
ns Ho 9 NW8 70 B1

Jewell Ho 3 SW12 159 C4
Jewel Rd E17 53 C6
Jewish Mus The*
Camden Town NW1 93 B6 231 D5
Finchley N3 29 D1
Jewry St EC3 95 D1 243 C1
Jews Row SW18 136 A1
Jews Wlk SE26 184 B6
Jeymer Ave NW2 68 C3
Jeymer Dr UB6 86 A6
Jeypore Rd SW18 158 A5
JFS Sch HA3 44 C3
Jillian Cl TW12 173 C3
Jim Bradley Cl 10 SE18 122 C2
Jim Griffiths Ho SW6 264 D5
Joan Cres SE9 165 D4
Joan Gdns RM8 81 A6
Joanna Ho 7 W6 112 C1
Joanne Ct EN1 17 C5
Joan Player Ho EN3 6 D6
Joan Rd RM8 81 A6
Joan St SE1 116 D5 251 C3
Joan Villas IG2 57 A2
Jocelin Ho N1 233 D5
Jocelyn Rd TW9 132 A2
Jocelyn St SE15 140 A4
Jockey's Fields WC1 94 B2 240 D4
Jodane Rd SE8 119 B2
Jodrell Cl TW7 131 A4
Jodrell Rd E3 75 B1
Joe Hunte Ct 2 SW27 182 D5
Joel St HA5, HA6 40 A5
Johanna Prim Sch SE1 116 C4 251 A1
Johanna St SE1 251 A1
John Adam St WC2 116 A6 250 B5
John Aird Ct W2 92 A2 236 B4
John Aldis Ho N22 32 B1
John Archer Way SW18 158 B5
John Ashby Cl SW2 160 A5
John Austin Cl KT2 176 B2
John Baird Ct SE26 184 D6
John Baird Ho 11 SE20 184 C3
John Ball Prim Sch SE3 142 C3
John Barker Ct NW6 69 A1
John Barker Ho IG1 79 B6
John Barnes Wlk E15 76 D2
John Barter Ho TW3 129 B3
John Betts' Ho W12 112 A3
John Betts Prim Sch W6 112 B3
John Bond Ho 2 E3 97 B5
John Bradshaw Rd N14 15 D3
John Brent Ho 8 SE8 118 D2
John Buck Ho NW10 89 D6
John Burns Dr IG11 79 C1
John Burns Prim Sch SW11 137 A3
Johnby Cl EN3 7 A6
John Campbell Rd 26 N16 73 C3
John Carpenter St EC4 251 C6
John Cartwright Ho 7 E2 96 B4
John Chilton Sch UB5 63 A1
John Clifford Ho N8 50 A3
John Clynes Ct SW15 134 B1
John Conwey Ho 23 SW2 160 C5
John Cornwell VC Ho 6 E12 78 C4
John Day Ho TW7 131 B2
John Dee Ho 3 SW14 133 B2
John Donne Prim Sch SE15 140 B4
John Drinkwater Cl E11 54 D2
John Dwight Ho SW6 135 D2
John Fearon Wlk 5 W10 91 A4
John Felton Rd 19 SE16 118 A4
John Fielden Ho 10 E2 96 B4
John Fisher St E1 118 A6
John F. Kennedy Specl Sch E15 98 B6

John Gooch Dr EN2 4 D4
John Harris Ho SE15 140 A2
John Harrison Way SE10 120 D3
John Hunt Ct 5 SE9 166 A2
John Islip St SW1 116 A2 260 A3
John Kaye Ct TW17 192 C4
John Keall Ho SW15 134 D2
John Keats Ho N22 32 B2
John Keats Lo EN2 5 B4
John Keble CE Prim Sch NW10 89 D6
John Kelly Tech Colls NW2 67 D5
John Kennedy Ct 1 N1 73 B2
John Kennedy Ho 1 SE16 118 D2
John Kennedy Lo 2 N1 73 B2
John King Ct 5 N19 71 D6
John Kirk Ho
22 Battersea SW11 136 B2
Beckenham BR3 207 A5
5 Streatham SW16 160 A1
John Knight Lo SW6 265 B4
John Lamb Ct HA3 24 C2
John Loughborough Sch N17 33 D1
John Lyon Sch The HA2 42 B1
John McDonald Ho 3 E14 120 A3
John McKenna Wlk 17 SE16 118 A3
John & Mary Sch NW5 71 D3
John Masefield Ho N15 51 B3
John Maurice Cl SE17 117 B2 262 C4
John Milton Prim Sch SW8 137 C5 269 A3
John Nettleford Ho 14 E2 96 B4
John Newton Ct DA16 146 B2
John Orwell Sports Ctr E1 118 B5
John Parker Cl RM10 81 D1
John Parker Sq 8 SW11 136 B2
John Parry Ct 28 N1 95 C5
John Paul II Sch SW19 156 D4
John Penn Ho SE8 141 B5
John Penn St SE13 141 D4
John Perrin Pl HA3 44 A2
John Perryn Prim Sch W3 89 C1
John Prince's St W1 238 D2
John Pritchard Ho 16 E1 96 A3
John Ratcliffe Ho 8 NW6 91 C4
John Rennie Wlk 1 E1 118 C5
John Roan Sch The SE3 142 C5
John Roll Way SE16 118 A3
John Ruskin Coll CR2 223 A1
John Ruskin Prim Sch SE5 139 A6
John Ruskin St SE5 139 A6
John's Ave NW4 46 C5
Johns Cl TW15 171 A6
John Scurr Ho 18 E14 97 A1
John Scurr Prim Sch E1 96 C3
John Silkin La SE8 118 D1
Johns La SM4 202 A4
John's Mews WC1 94 B3 240 D5
John Smith Ave SW6 135 B5 264 C4
John Smith Mews E14 120 B6
Johnson Cl E8 96 A6
Johnson Ct
Hendon NW4 46 A6
10 Wandsworth SW18 136 B1
Johnson Ho
Belgravia SW1 258 B3
23 Bethnal Green E2 96 A4
Somers Town NW1 232 B3
South Lambeth SW8 269 D3
Johnson Lo 12 W9 91 C2

Johnson Rd
Bromley Comm BR2 209 D4
Heston TW5 128 C5
Stonebridge NW10 89 B6
Thornton Heath CR0 205 B2
Johnson's Cl SM5 218 D5
Johnsons Ct EC4 241 B1
Johnsons Dr TW12 174 A2
Johnson's Ind Est UB3 106 A3
Johnson's Pl SW1 115 C1 259 A1
Johnson St
Southall UB2 106 D3
Stepney E1 96 C1
Johnsons Way NW10 88 D3
John Spencer Sq N1 72 D2
John's Pl E1 96 B1
John Stainer Com Prim Sch SE4 141 A2
John St
Croydon SE25 206 A5
Enfield EN1 17 D6
John's Terr CR0 205 C1
John St
Finsbury WC1 94 B3 240 D5
Hounslow TW3, TW5 129 A3
Johnston Cl SW9 270 D1
Johnstone Ho SE13 142 B2
Johnstone Rd E6 100 B4
Johnston Rd IG8 37 A5
Johnston Terr NW2 68 D5
John Strachey Ho SW6 264 D5
John Strype Ct E10 53 D1
John St E15 98 D6
John Trundle Ct EC2 242 A4
John Tucker Ho 3 E14 119 C3
John Walsh Twr E11 76 D6
John Wesley Ct 6 TW1 153 A3
John Wesley's House & Mus* EC1 242 D6
John Wheatley Ho
14 London N19 49 D2
West Brompton SW6 264 D5
John William Cl 12 KT2 175 D2
John Williams Cl SE14 140 D6
John Wilson St SE18 122 C2
John Wooley Cl SE13 142 C1
Joiners Arms Yd 1 SE5 139 B4
Joiners Ct 5 N20 14 D1
Joiner St SE1 252 D3
Joiners Yd N1 233 B3
Joint Rd N10 30 C2
Jolles Ho 9 E3 97 D4
Jollys La Harrow HA2 42 B1
Hayes UB4 84 D2
Jonathan Ct 9 W4 111 C2
Jonathan St SE11 116 B1 260 C2
Jones Ho
4 South Bromley E14 98 B1
Stamford Hill N16 51 C1
Jones Rd E13 99 B3
Jones St W1 248 C5
Jones Wlk 6 TW10 154 B5
Jonquil Gdns 5 TW12 173 C4
Jonson Cl Hayes UB4 84 A2
Mitcham CR4 203 B6
Jonson Ho
Borough The SE1 262 D5
16 Canonbury N16 73 B4
Jordan Cl HA2 63 B5
Jordan Ct SW15 134 D1
Jordan Hill N10 30 C2
Jordan Ho
12 London SE4 140 D1
Shoreditch N1 235 D5
Jordan Lo SW17 180 C5
Jordan Rd UB6 87 C6
Jordans Cl
Dagenham RM10 81 D4
Hounslow TW7 130 C4
Jordans Ho NW8 237 A5
Jordans Mews TW11 152 C2
Jo Richardson Comm Sch RM9 102 D6
Jo Richardson Com Sch RM9 80 C2
Joscoyne Ho 5 E1 96 B1
Josef Perrin Ho 1 SE27 183 B6
Joseph Ave W3 89 B1

Joseph Clarke Sch E4 36 B4
Joseph Conrad Ho SW1 259 B3
Joseph Ct N16 51 C2
Joseph Hardcastle Cl SE14 140 D5
Joseph Hood Prim Sch SW20 201 A6
Josephine Ave SW2 160 B6
Joseph Irwin Ho 11 E14 119 B6
Joseph Lancaster Prim Sch SE1 117 B3 262 C5
Joseph Lister Ct E7 77 A1
Joseph Lister Lo E11 55 B1
Joseph Powell Cl 1 SW12 159 C5
Joseph Priestley Ho 12 E2 96 B4
Joseph Ray Rd E11 76 C6
Joseph St E3 97 B3
Joseph Trotter Cl EC1 234 B1
Joshua Cl
Croydon CR2 220 D1
Muswell Hill N10 31 B3
Joshua St E14 98 A1
Joslings Cl W12 112 A6
Joslyn Cl EN3 7 C5
Josseline Ct 9 E3 97 A5
Joubert Mans SW3 257 B2
Joubert St SW11 136 D3
Jowett Ho 27 SW9 138 A3
Jowett St SE15 139 D5
Joyce Ave N18 33 D5
Joyce Butler Ho N22 32 B2
Joyce Dawson Way SE28 124 A6
Joyce Lattimore Ct N9 18 B1
Joyce Page Cl SE7 143 D6
Joy Ct NW2 68 D5
Joydon Dr RM6 58 B3
Joyner Ct UB1 107 B6
Joyners Cl RM9 81 B4
Joystone Ct 8 EN4 2 C1
Jubb Powell Ho N15 51 C3
Jubet Ho 9 N16 73 B4
Jubilee Ave
Chingford E4 36 A4
Romford RM7 59 D4
Twickenham TW2 152 A3
Jubilee Bldgs NW8 229 C4
Jubilee Cl
4 Harlesden NW10 89 D5
Kingsbury NW9 45 B3
Pinner HA5 22 C1
Romford RM7 59 D4
Teddington KT1 175 C2
Jubilee Cres
Cubitt Town E14 120 A3
Edmonton N9 18 A3
Jubilee Ct
Harrow HA3 44 A2
Hounslow TW3 129 D2
Islington N1 233 B6
Muswell Hill N10 49 A6
12 Sutton SM2 218 A2
Thornton Heath CR7 204 C5
Jubilee Dr HA4 63 A4
Jubilee Gdns UB1 85 C1
Jubilee Ho
3 Hampton TW12 173 C2
Lambeth SE11 261 B3
Jubilee Hts NW2 69 B2
Jubilee Lo HA7 25 A5
Jubilee Mans 10 E1 96 C1
Jubilee Mkt WC2 250 B6
Jubilee Park Ctry Pk BR2 210 C4
Jubilee Par IG8 37 C4
Jubilee Pl SW3 114 C1 257 B2
Jubilee Prim Sch
London SW2 160 C5
Stamford Hill N16 52 A1
Woolwich SE28 124 C6
Jubilee Rd
Cheam SM3 216 D1
Wembley UB6 87 B6
Jubilee St E1 96 C2
Jubilee The 2 SE10 141 D5
Jubilee Villas KT10 196 C1
Jubilee Way
East Bedfont TW14 150 A3
Merton SW19 179 D2
Sidcup DA14 168 A2
Tolworth KT4, KT9 214 D5
Jubilee Wks SW19 180 A1
Jubilee Wlk WD19 22 B6
Jubilee Yd SE1 253 C2
Judd St WC1 94 A4 233 A1

Jude St E16 98 D1
Judge Heath La UB3 83 B1
Judges' Wlk NW3 70 A5
Judge Wlk KT10 212 C2
Juer St SW11 136 C5 267 B3
Jules Thorn Ave EN1 6 A1
Julia Ct E17 53 D4
Julia Garfield Mews 4 E16 121 B5
Julia Gdns IG11 102 D5
Juliana Cl N2 48 A6
Julian Ave W3 110 D6
Julian Cl EN5 1 D2
Julian Ct SW13 133 D4
Julian Hill HA1 64 C6
Julian Ho SE21 183 C6
Julian Pl E14 119 D1
Julian's Prim Sch SW16 182 C6
Julian Taylor Path 7 SE23 162 B2
Julia St NW5 71 A3
Julien Rd W5 109 C3
Juliet Ho 11 N1 95 C5
Juliette Rd E13 99 A5
Julius Caesar Way HA7 9 D1
Julius Ct TW8 132 A5
Julius Ho 8 E14 98 B1
Julius Nyerere Cl N1 233 C5
Junction App
Battersea SW11 136 C2
Lewisham SE13 142 A2
Junction Mews W2 237 A2
Junction Pl W2 236 D2
Junction Rd
Ashford TW15 171 B5
Brentford TW8 109 D2
Croydon CR2 221 B3
Dartmouth Pk N19 71 C5
Junction Rd E RM6 59 A2
Junction Rd
Edmonton N9 18 A3
Harrow HA1 42 C3
Newham E13 99 B5
Tottenham Hale N17 52 A6
Junction Rd W RM6 59 A2
Junction Wembley Ret Pk The HA9 66 D4
Juniper Cl
Barnet EN5 12 D6
Chessington KT9 214 B3
Wembley HA9 66 C3
Juniper Cres NW1 71 A1
Juniper Ct
Dagenham RM6 58 C3
Harrow HA3 24 D2
Hounslow TW3 129 D1
Stoke Newington N16 73 B6
Thornton Heath CR0 204 C3
Juniper Dr SW18 136 A1
Juniper Gdns
Ashford TW16 171 D4
Streatham CR4 181 C2
Juniper Ho
12 Ealing W5 87 C2
6 Peckham SE14, SE15 140 C5
9 Richmond TW9 132 D4
Juniper La E6 100 A2
Juniper Rd IG1 78 D4
Juniper St 16 E1 118 C6
Juniper Way UB3 105 C6
Juno Ct 11 SW9 138 C5
Juno Ho 2 E3 97 C6
Juno Way Ind Est SE14 140 D6
Juno Way SE14 140 D6
Jupiter Ct
10 Brixton SW9 138 C5
8 Northolt UB5 84 D4
Jupiter Hts UB10 82 B6
Jupiter Way N7 72 B2
Jupp Rd E15 76 B1
Jupp Rd W E15 98 B6
Jura Ho SE16 119 A2
Jurston Ct SE1 251 B1
Justice Wlk SW3 267 A5
Justin Cl TW8 131 D5
Justin Ct 3 CR7 204 C4
Justines Pl E2 96 D4
Justin Plaza CR4 202 C5
Justin Rd E4 35 B4
Jute La EN3 7 A2
Jutland Cl N19 50 A1
Jutland Ho
4 London SE5 139 A3
10 Woolwich SE7 122 A2
Jutland Rd
Catford SE6 164 A4
Newham E13 99 A3
Jutsums Ave RM7 59 D3

Jutsums Ct RM7 ... 59 D3
Jutsums La RM7 ... 59 D2
Juxon Cl HA3 ... 23 D2
Juxon St
SE11 ... 116 B2 260 D4
JVC Bsns Pk NW2 ... 46 A1

K

Kaduna Cl HA5 ... 40 B4
Kaizen Prim Sch E13 . 99 B3
Kale Rd DA18 ... 125 A4
Kambala Rd SW11 ... 136 B2
Kangley Bridge Ctr
SE26 ... 185 B5
Kangley Bridge Rd
SE26 ... 185 B5
Kaplan Dr N21 ... 16 B6
Karachi Ho E15 ... 76 C2
Kara Way NW2 ... 68 D4
Karen Ct
Bromley BR1 ... 186 D2
2 Camberwell SE5 ... 139 C2
Forest Hill SE23 ... 163 A5
Karen Ho 7 N16 ... 73 B4
Karens Ct EN3 ... 6 D6
Karen Terr Ilford IG2 ... 57 B4
Leyton E11 ... 76 D6
Karenza Ct HA9 ... 43 C2
Kariba Cl N9 ... 18 C1
Karman Ct HA3 ... 42 C6
Karma Way HA2 ... 41 C1
Karoline Gdns UB6 ... 86 B5
Karyatis Ct EN1 ... 17 D6
Kashgar Rd SE18 ... 123 D2
Kashmir Rd SE7 ... 143 D5
Kasmin Ct NW10 ... 68 A1
Kassala Rd
SW11 ... 136 D4 267 D1
Katella Trad Est
IG11 ... 101 C4
Kates Cl EN5 ... 12 A6
Katharine Rd 1
TW1 ... 153 A3
Katharine St CR0 ... 221 A5
Katherine Cl 3
SE16 ... 118 D5
Katherine Ct
10 Forest Hill
SE23 ... 162 C3
Penge SE20 ... 184 C2
Katherine Gdns
SE9 ... 143 D1
Katherine Ho
15 Kensal Town
W10 ... 91 A3
6 South Croydon
CR0 ... 221 A5
South Norwood
SE19 ... 183 C4
Katherine Rd E6, E7 ... 77 C1
Katherine Sq W11 .. 244 A4
Kathleen Ave
Acton W3 ... 89 A2
Wembley HA0 ... 66 A1
Kathleen Ferrier Ct 4
N17 ... 33 D3
Kathleen Godfree Ct
SW19 ... 179 C5
Kathleen Moore Ct
BR4 ... 224 A6
Kathleen Rd SW11 ... 136 D2
Katrine Ct NW2 ... 68 C5
Kayemoor Rd SM2 ... 218 C2
Kay Rd SW9 ... 138 B3
Kays Ct EN3 ... 6 D1
Kay St
Bethnal Green E2 ... 96 A5
Welling DA16 ... 146 B4
Keadby Ho 2 UB5 ... 85 B4
Kean Ho 5 SE17 ... 138 D6
Kean St WC2 ... 94 B1 240 C1
Keates Est N16 ... 73 D6
Keatley Gn E4 ... 35 B4
Keats Ave E16 ... 121 B5
Keats Cl
Bermondsey SE1 ... 263 C3
Enfield EN3 ... 18 D6
Hampstead NW3 ... 70 C4
Hayes UB4 ... 84 A2
Mitcham SW19 ... 180 B4
Wanstead E11 ... 55 B4
Keats Ct HA0 ... 65 C5
Keats Gr NW3 ... 70 C4
Keats Ho
7 Beckenham
BR3 ... 185 D4
22 Bethnal Green E2 ... 96 C4
30 Camberwell SE5 .. 139 A5
Chelsea SW1 ... 269 B6
Harrow HA2 ... 64 C6
Keats House Mus*
NW3 ... 70 C4

Keats Par 3 N9 ... 18 A2
Keats Pl EC2 ... 242 C3
Keats Rd DA16 ... 145 D4
Keats Way
Croydon CR0 ... 206 C3
Southall UB6 ... 85 D2
West Drayton UB7 ... 104 B2
Kebbell Terr E7 ... 77 B3
Keble Cl
New Malden KT4 ... 199 D1
Northolt UB5 ... 64 A3
Keble Ct SW19 ... 179 C4
Keble Ho 4 SW15 ... 156 D5
Keble Pl SW13 ... 134 B6
Keble Prep Sch N21 .. 16 C4
Keble St SW17 ... 180 A6
Kechill Gdns BR2 ... 209 A2
Kedelston Ct E5 ... 75 A4
Kedeston Ct SM1 ... 201 D1
Kedge Ho 16 E14 ... 119 C3
Kedleston Dr BR5 ... 211 D4
Kedleston Wlk 21 E2 ... 96 B4
Kedyngton Ho 5
HA8 ... 27 A1
Keeble Cl SE18 ... 144 D6
Keedonwood Rd
BR1 ... 186 D5
Keel Cl Barking IG11 ... 102 C5
Rotherhithe SE16 ... 118 D5
Keel Ct 8 E14 ... 120 B6
Keeley Rd CR0 ... 221 A6
Keeley St
WC2 ... 94 B1 240 C1
Keeling Ct CR0 ... 220 D4
Keeling Ho 4 E2 ... 96 B5
Keeling Rd SE9 ... 165 D6
Keeling 2 TW11 ... 174 C5
Keelson Ho 9 E14 ... 119 C3
Keely Cl EN4 ... 14 C6
Keemor Cl SE18 ... 144 C5
Keens Cl SW16 ... 181 D5
Keen's Rd CR0 ... 221 A4
Keen's Yd N1 ... 72 D2
Keepers Ct 4 CR2 ... 221 A3
Keepers Mews
TW11 ... 175 C4
Keeper Wharf E1 ... 118 D6
Keepier Wharf 15
E1 ... 118 D6
Keep The
Forest Hill SE6 ... 163 C3
Kidbrooke SE3 ... 143 A3
Kingston u T KT2 ... 176 B3
Keeton's Rd SE16 ... 118 B3
Keevil Dr SW19 ... 157 A4
Keighley Cl N7 ... 72 A4
Keightley Dr SE9 ... 167 A3
Keilder Cl UB10 ... 82 C5
Keildon Rd SW11 ... 136 D1
Keir Hardie Est E5 ... 52 B1
Keir Hardie Ho
6 Belvedere
DA17 ... 125 C3
Fulham W6 ... 134 D6
15 Upper Holloway
N19 ... 49 D2
Willesden NW10 ... 67 D1
Keir Hardie Way
Barking IG11 ... 80 A1
Hayes UB4 ... 84 A4
Keir Hardy Prim Sch
E16 ... 99 A2
Keir The SW19 ... 178 C5
Keith Connor Cl 5
SW8 ... 137 B2
Keith Gr W12 ... 112 A5
Keith Ho NW6 ... 91 D5
Keith Park Rd UB10 ... 60 B1
Keith Rd
Barking IG11 ... 101 B5
Hayes UB3 ... 105 C3
Walthamstow E17 ... 35 B2
Keith Sutton Ho 3
SE9 ... 167 A2
Kelbrook Rd SE3 ... 144 A2
Kelby Ho N7 ... 72 B2
Kelceda Cl NW2 ... 68 A6
Kelf Gr UB3 ... 83 D1
Kelfield Ct 1 W10 ... 90 D1
Kelfield Gdns W10 ... 90 D1
Kelfield Mews W10 ... 90 D1
Kelham Ho 10 SE18 ... 144 D6
Kelland Cl 1 N8 ... 49 D4
Kelland Rd E13 ... 99 A3
Kellaway Rd SE3 ... 143 D3
Keller Cres E12 ... 77 D4
Kellerton Rd SE13 ... 164 C6
Kellett Ho N1 ... 235 D5
Kellett Rd SW2 ... 138 C1
Kelling Gdns CR0 ... 204 D2
Kellino St SW17 ... 180 D6
Kellner Rd SE28 ... 123 D3
Kellow Ho SE1 ... 252 C2
Kell St SE1 .. 116 D3 261 D6
Kelly Ave SE15 ... 139 D4

Kelly Cl
Upper Halliford
TW17 ... 171 C1
Willesden NW10 ... 67 B5
Kelly Ct 18 E14 ... 119 C6
Kelly Mews 4 W9 ... 91 B3
Kelly Rd NW7 ... 29 A4
Kelly St NW1 ... 71 B2
Kelly Way RM6 ... 59 A3
Kelman Cl SW4 ... 137 D3
Kelmore Gr SE22 ... 140 A1
Kelmscott Cl E17 ... 35 B2
Kelmscott Ct 2 HA7 .. 25 C6
Kelmscott 5 SE23 ... 162 D1
Kelmscott Gdns
W12 ... 112 A3
Kelmscott L Ctr E17 .. 53 B3
Kelmscott Rd SW11 .. 158 D6
Kelmscott Sch E17 ... 53 B3
Kelross Rd N5 ... 73 A4
Kelsall Cl SE3 ... 143 B3
Kelsall Mews TW9 ... 132 D4
Kelsey Gate 8 BR3 ... 185 D1
Kelsey La BR3 ... 207 C6
Kelsey Park Ave
BR3 ... 185 D1
Kelsey Park Man
BR3 ... 207 D6
Kelsey Park Rd BR3 .. 185 C1
Kelsey Park Sp Coll
BR3 ... 207 C6
Kelsey Rd BR5 ... 190 B1
Kelsey Sq BR3 ... 185 C1
Kelsey St E2 ... 96 A3
Kelsey Way BR3 ... 207 C6
Kelshall Ct N4 ... 73 A6
Kelso Ct SE20 ... 184 B3
Kelso Lo E18 ... 37 B1
Kelson Ho E14 ... 120 A3
Kelso Pl W8 . 113 D3 255 D6
Kelso Rd SM5 ... 202 A2
Kelvedon Cl KT2 ... 176 C4
Kelvedon Ct HA4 ... 62 C4
Kelvedon Ho SW8 ... 270 B2
Kelvedon Rd
SW6 ... 135 B5 264 D3
Kelvin Ave N13 ... 32 B4
Kelvinbrook KT8 ... 195 D6
Kelvin Cl KT19 ... 214 C2
Kelvin Cres HA3 ... 24 C3
Kelvin Ct
Chiswick W4 ... 133 A5
Harrow HA2 ... 42 A1
Isleworth TW7 ... 130 C3
Notting Hill W11 ... 245 A5
7 Penge SE20 ... 184 B2
8 Twickenham
TW1 ... 153 B5
Kelvin Dr TW1 ... 153 B5
Kelvin Gdns
Southall UB1 ... 85 C1
Thornton Heath CR0 . 204 A2
Kelvin Gr SE26 ... 162 B1
Kelvin Grove Prim Sch
SE26 ... 162 B1
Kelvin Gr KT6 ... 214 A5
Kelvington Cl CR0 ... 207 A2
Kelvington Rd SE15 .. 162 D6
Kelvin Ho 3 DA17 ... 125 C3
Kelvin Par BR6 ... 211 C1
Kelvin Rd Highbury N5 .. 73 A4
Welling DA16 ... 146 A2
Kelyway Ho 20 SW2 .. 160 C4
Kember St N1 ... 72 B1
Kemble Dr BR2 ... 226 A5
Kemble Ho
London SW9 ... 138 D2
Stanmore HA7 ... 24 D5
Kemble Rd
Croydon CR0 ... 220 D5
Forest Hill SE23 ... 162 D3
Tottenham N17 ... 34 A2
Kemble St
WC2 ... 94 B1 240 C1
Kemerton Rd
Beckenham BR3 ... 185 D1
Camberwell SE5 ... 139 A2
Croydon CR0 ... 205 D2
Kemey's St E9 ... 75 A3
Kemnal Rd BR7 ... 189 B5
Kemnal Tech Coll
DA14 ... 190 B3
Kemnal Warren
BR7 ... 189 B4
Kemp Ct SW8 ... 270 A3
Kempe Ho SE1 ... 262 D5
Kempe Rd NW6 ... 90 D5
Kemp Gdns CR0 ... 205 A3
Kemp Ho
Finsbury EC1 ... 235 C1
1 Globe Town E2 ... 96 D5
Wallend E6 ... 78 C2
Kempis Way 5
SE22 ... 161 C6
Kemplay Rd NW3 ... 70 B4
Kemp 28 NW9 ... 27 D2
Kemp Rd RM8 ... 58 D1

Kemps Ct NW2 ... 68 D5
Kemp's Ct W1 ... 239 C1
Kemps Dr E14 ... 119 C6
Kempsford Gdns
SW5 ... 113 C1 255 B1
Kempsford Rd
Lambeth SE11 ... 261 B3
Newington SE11 ... 261 C3
Kemps Gdns SE13 ... 164 A6
Kempshott Rd
SW16 ... 182 A3
Kempson Rd
SW6 ... 135 C5 265 B3
Kempthorne Rd
SE8 ... 119 B2
Kempton Ave
Northolt UB5 ... 63 C3
Sunbury TW16 ... 172 B2
Kempton Cl UB10 ... 61 A4
Kempton Ct
Stepney E1 ... 96 B2
Sunbury TW16 ... 172 B2
Kempton Ho 18 N1 ... 95 C6
Kempton Lo 3
SM6 ... 219 D5
Kempton Park Race
Course TW16 ... 172 C3
Kempton Park Sta
TW16 ... 172 B3
Kempton Rd E6 ... 100 B6
Kempton Wlk CR0 ... 207 A3
Kempt St SE18 ... 144 C6
Kemsing Cl
Coney Hall BR2 ... 224 D6
Sidcup DA5 ... 169 A4
South Norwood CR7 205 A5
Kemsing Ho SE1 ... 252 D1
Kemsing Rd SE10 ... 121 A1
Kemsley Ct
Ealing W13 ... 109 C5
St Paul's Cray BR5 ... 190 B2
Kemsley SE13 ... 163 D6
Kenbrook Ho
Kensington W14 ... 254 D5
8 Kentish Town
NW5 ... 71 C3
Kenbury Cl UB10 ... 60 C5
Kenbury Gdns 10
SE5 ... 139 A3
Kenbury Mans 18
SE5 ... 139 A3
Kenbury St SE5 ... 139 A3
Kenchester Cl
SW8 ... 138 A5 270 B3
Kencot Cl DA18 ... 125 B4
Kendal Ave Acton W3 .. 88 D2
Barking IG11 ... 101 C6
Edmonton N18 ... 33 B6
Kendal Cl
Camberwell SE5 ... 138 D5
East Bedfont TW14 ... 149 D3
Hayes UB4 ... 83 C5
Woodford IG8 ... 20 D2
Kendal Ct Acton W3 ... 88 C2
Brondesbury NW2 ... 69 A3
11 Chingford E4 ... 20 A3
Kendale Rd BR1 ... 186 C5
Kendal Gdns
Edmonton N18 ... 33 B6
Sutton SM1 ... 218 A6
Kendal Ho
Edgware HA8 ... 27 A6
Forest Hill SE23 ... 163 B3
32 Hackney E9 ... 74 C1
Islington N1 ... 233 D4
Penge SE20 ... 184 B1
Kendall Ave BR3 ... 185 A1
Kendall Ct
3 London SE22 ... 162 A6
Mitcham SW19 ... 180 B4
5 Penge SE19 ... 183 D3
Sidcup DA15 ... 168 A1
Kendall Ho SE12 ... 164 D4
Kendall Lo 5 BR1 ... 187 B2
Kendall Pl W1 ... 238 A3
Kendall Rd
Beckenham BR3 ... 185 A1
Isleworth TW7 ... 131 A3
Kidbrooke SE18 ... 144 A4
Kendalmere Cl N10 ... 31 B2
Kendal NW1 ... 231 D2
Kendal Par N18 ... 33 B6
Kendal Pl SW15 ... 157 B6
Kendal Rd NW10 ... 68 A4
Kendal Stps W2 ... 237 B1
Kendal St W2 .. 92 C1 237 B1
Kender Prim Sch
SE14 ... 140 C4
Kender St SE14 ... 140 C4
Kendoa Rd 1 SW4 ... 137 D1
Kendon Cl E11 ... 55 B4
Kendon Ho E15 ... 76 B1
Kendra Ct CR2 ... 220 D1
Kendra Hall Rd CR2 .. 220 D1
Kendrey Gdns TW2 ... 152 C4
Kendrick Ct 12
SE15 ... 140 B4

Kendrick Mews SW7 256 C3
Kendrick Pl SW7 ... 256 C3
Kenelm Cl HA1 ... 65 A5
Kenerne Dr EN5 ... 13 A6
Kenilford Rd SW12 ... 159 B4
Kenilworth Ave
Harrow HA2 ... 63 B4
Walthamstow E17 ... 53 C6
Wimbledon SW19 ... 179 C6
Kenilworth Cres EN1 ... 5 C4
Kenilworth Ct
7 Chingford E4 ... 20 A2
Fulham SW6 ... 135 A2
Twickenham TW2 ... 152 C2
Kenilworth Gdns
Hayes UB4 ... 83 D2
Ilford IG3 ... 79 D6
Southall UB1 ... 85 B4
South Oxhey WD19 ... 22 C5
Woolwich SE18 ... 144 D3
Kenilworth Ho HA7 ... 25 B3
Kenilworth Rd
Ashford TW15,
TW19 ... 148 A1
Bow E3 ... 97 A5
Ealing W5 ... 110 A5
Edgware HA8 ... 11 A1
Kilburn NW6 ... 91 B6
Orpington BR5 ... 211 A3
Penge SE20 ... 184 D2
Stoneleigh KT17 ... 216 A3
Kenilworth Terr 3
SM2 ... 217 C1
Kenley Ave NW9 ... 27 C2
Kenley Cl Barnet EN4 ... 2 C1
Sidcup DA5 ... 169 C4
St Paul's Cray BR7 ... 211 C6
Kenley Gdns CR7 ... 204 D5
Kenley Ho
5 Croydon CR0 ... 206 A1
6 St Paul's Cray
BR5 ... 190 B1
Kenley Rd
Kingston u T KT1,
KT3 ... 176 D1
Merton SW19 ... 201 C6
Twickenham TW1 ... 153 B5
Kenley N17 ... 33 B1
Kenley Wlk
Cheam SM3 ... 216 D4
Notting Hill W11 ... 244 A5
Kenlor Ct 6 HA8 ... 26 D5
Kenlor Rd SW17 ... 180 B5
Kenmare Ct 5 HA7 ... 25 C6
Kenmare Dr
Mitcham CR4 ... 180 D3
1 Tottenham N17 ... 33 D1
Kenmare Gdns N13 ... 33 A6
Kenmare Rd CR7 ... 204 C3
Kenmere Gdns HA0 ... 88 C6
Kenmere Rd DA16 ... 146 C3
Kenmont Gdns NW10 .. 90 B4
Kenmont Prim Sch
NW10 ... 90 B4
Kenmore Ave HA3 ... 43 A6
Kenmore Cl TW9 ... 132 C5
Kenmore Cres UB4 ... 83 D4
Kenmore Ct NW6 ... 69 C1
Kenmore Gdns HA8 ... 26 D1
Kenmore Park Fst &
Mid Schs HA3 ... 44 A6
Kenmore Rd HA3 ... 43 D5
Kenmure Mans W5 ... 87 C3
Kenmure Rd E8 ... 74 B3
Kenmure Yd E8 ... 74 B3
Kennacraig Cl 6
E16 ... 121 A5
Kennard Ho 12
SW11 ... 137 A3
Kennard Mans 6
N11 ... 30 D5
Kennard Rd
London N11 ... 30 D5
Stratford E15 ... 76 B1
Kennard St
9 London SW11 ... 137 A3
Newham E16 ... 122 B5
Kennedy Ave EN3 ... 18 C5
Kennedy Cl
Crofton BR5 ... 211 B1
1 Mitcham CR4 ... 181 A1
Newham E13 ... 99 A5
Pinner HA5 ... 23 B4
Kennedy Cox Ho 9
E16 ... 98 D2
Kennedy Ct
Ashford TW15 ... 171 A5
Bushey WD23 ... 8 B2
Kennedy Ho SE11 ... 260 C2
Kennedy Path W7 ... 86 D3
Kennedy Rd
Barking IG11 ... 101 C6
Ealing W7 ... 86 C2
Kennedy Wlk SE17 ... 262 D3
Kennet Cl SW11 ... 136 B1
Kennet Ct 47 W2 ... 91 C2
Kennet Dr UB4 ... 85 A2

Kenneth Ave IG1 ...
Kenneth Campbell Ho
NW8 ... 2
Kenneth Cres NW2 ...
Kenneth Ct SE11 ... 2
Kenneth Gdns HA7 ...
Kenneth More Rd 4
IG1 ...
Kennet Ho NW8 ... 2
Kenneth Rd RM6 ...
Kenneth Robbins Ho
N17 ...
Kenneth Younger Ho
SW6 ... 2
Kennet Rd
Isleworth TW7 ... 1
West Kilburn W9 ...
Kennet Sq CR4 ... 1
Kennet St E1 ... 1
Kennett Ho HA1 ...
Kennett Wharf La
EC4 ... 2
Kenninghall N18 ...
Kenninghall Rd
London N18 ...
Lower Clapton E5 ...
Kenning Ho 6 N1 ...
Kenning St 18 SE16 .. 1
Kennings Way
SE11 ... 116 C1 2
KENNINGTON ... 1
Kennington Ent Ctr
SE17 ... 2
Kennington La
SE11 ... 116 B1 2
Kennington Oval
SE11 ... 138 B6 2
Kennington Palace Ct
SE11 ... 2
Kennington Park Gdns
SE17 ... 1
Kennington Park Ho
SE11 ... 2
Kennington Park Pl
SE11 ... 1
Kennington Park Rd
SE11 ... 116 D1 2
Kennington Rd
SE11 ... 116 C2 2
Kennington Sta
SE17 ... 116 D1 2
Kennoldes SE21 ... 1
Kennyland Ct NW4 ...
Kenny Rd NW7 ...
Kenrick Pl W1 ... 2
KENSAL GREEN ...
Kensal Green Cemy (A
Souls)* NW10 ...
Kensal Green Sta
NW10 ...
Kensal Ho W10 ...
Kensal Rd W10 ...
KENSAL RISE ...
Kensal Rise Prim Sch
NW6 ...
Kensal Rise Sta
NW10 ...
KENSAL TOWN ...
KENSINGTON ... 1
Kensington Avenue
Prim Sch CR7 ... 1
Kensington Ave
Plashet E12 ...
South Norwood CR7 . 1
Kensington & Chelsea
Coll
Chelsea
SW10 ... 136 A5 2
Kensal Town W10 ...
Kensington Church Ct
W8 ... 2
Kensington Church St
W8 ... 113 C5 2
Kensington Church Wl
W8 ... 2
Kensington Cl N11 ...
Kensington Court Man
W8 ... 2
Kensington Court Mew
W8 ... 2
Kensington Court Pl
W8 ... 113 D3 2
Kensington Ct
2 Burnt Oak NW7 ...
Enfield EN2 ...
Kensington Ct Gdns
W8 ... 2
Kensington Ct
Hendon NW4 ...
Kensington
W8 ... 113 D4 2
Kensington Dr IG8 ...
Kensington Gardens*
W2 ... 114 A5 2
Kensington Gate
W8 ... 114 A3 2

ngton Gdns
ton u T KT1 197 D6
ridge IG1 56 B1
ngton Gdns Sq
91 D1
ngton Gore
114 B4 246 C1
ngton Hall Gdns
254 C2
ngton High St
113 C3 255 B6
ngton Ho 3
71 C3
ngton Hts
ow HA1 42 D3
ington W8 245 A3
ngton Lodge
85 C5
ngton Mall W8 245 B4
ngton Mans
255 B2
ngton Olympia Sta
113 A3 254 A6
ington Palace Gdns
113 D5 245 C4
ngton Pal*
113 D5 245 D3
ngton Park Gdns
113 B6 244 D5
ington Park Mews
91 B1
ington Park Rd
113 B6 244 D6
ington Pl
113 C5 245 A4
ington Prep Sch
135 B4 264 D2
ington Prim Sch
78 B2
ington Rd
sington
W7 114 A4 246 B1
tholt UB5 85 C5
sington Sports Ctr
244 A6
sington Sq
113 D4 245 C1
sington Terr
221 B1
sington Village
4 113 B2 254 D3
sington W W14 254 A4
sit Meml Coll N3 29 A1
sworth Ho EC1 235 D1
Ave
xley DA16 167 D6
genham RM9 103 C3
ing W13 87 B2
Cl
cham CR4,
W16 204 A5
bington BR6 227 C2
Ct Acton W3 88 B1
Haggerston E2 95 D5
ndon NW9 27 C1
Dr
ckfosters EN4 15 A6
ddington TW11 174 C5
tford Way UB5 85 A6
t Gate Way CR0 223 D3
t Gdns Ealing W13 87 B2
islip HA4 40 B3
t Ho
mberwell SE1 263 D1
Chiswick W4 111 C1
gware HA8 26 B3
arylebone W1 239 A2
mlico SW1 259 C1
chmond TW10 154 C6
t House La BR3 185 A5
t House Rd BR3 185 A4
t House Sta
3 185 A2
t House Station App
3 184 D2
tish Bldgs SE1 252 C3
tish Rd DA17 125 C2
NTISH TOWN 71 C3
tish Town CE Prim
ch NW5 71 C3
tish Town Rd
W1 71 B2
ntish Town Sta
W5 71 C3
ntish Town West Sta
W5 71 B2
ntish Way BR1,
2 209 B6
ntlea Rd SE28 123 C4
t Lo 9 SW19 156 D3
ntmere Ho SE15 140 C6
ntmere Rd SE18 123 C2
NTON 43 C3
nton Ave
arrow HA1 42 D2
outhall UB1 107 C6

Kenton Ave *continued*
Sunbury TW16 173 A1
Kenton Ct
2 Forest Hill SE26 185 A6
Harrow HA3 43 B3
3 Richmond TW10 153 D5
West Kensington W14 254 C5
Kenton Gdns HA3 43 C4
Kenton Grove Ho HA3 44 B4
Kenton Ho
20 Globe Town E1 96 C3
Highbury N5 72 C5
Kenton La
Harrow HA3 24 D3
Kenton HA3 43 C6
Kenton Park Ave HA3 43 D5
Kenton Park Cl HA3 43 C4
Kenton Park Cres HA3 43 D5
Kenton Park Mans HA3 43 C4
Kenton Park Par HA3 43 D4
Kenton Park Rd HA3 43 C5
Kenton Rd
Harrow HA3 43 C4
Homerton E9 74 D2
Kenton Sta HA3 43 B3
Kenton St WC1 240 A6
Kenton Way UB4 83 C4
Kent Pas NW1 237 C6
Kent Pk Ind Est SE15 140 B6
Kent Rd
Dagenham RM10 81 D3
East Molesey KT8 196 A5
Kingston u T KT1 197 D6
Richmond TW9 132 C5
South Acton W4 111 A3
Southgate N21 17 B4
West Wickham BR4 207 D1
Kent St Haggerston E2 95 D5
Newham E13 99 B4
Kent Terr NW1 92 C4 230 B1
Kent Twr SE20 184 B3
Kent View Gdns IG3 79 C6
Kent Way KT6 214 B6
Kentwell Cl SE4 141 A1
Kentwins N14 15 B6
Kentwode Gn SW13 134 A5
Kent Yard SW7 247 B1
Kenver Ave N12 30 B4
Kenward Rd SE9 165 D6
Kenway Rd SW5 113 D2 255 C3
Ken Way HA9 67 A5
Ken Wilson Ho 19 E2 96 A5
Kenwood Ave N14 15 D6
Kenwood Cl
North End NW3 48 B1
Sipson UB7 126 C6
Kenwood Ct NW9 45 A5
Kenwood Dr BR3 208 A6
Kenwood Gdns
Ilford IG2 56 C4
2 Wanstead E18 55 B6
Kenwood Ho
15 Brixton SW9 138 D1
Enfield EN1 17 C5
Kenwood Ho* NW3 48 C1
Kenwood Rd
Edmonton N9 18 A3
Highgate N6 48 D3
Kenworthy Rd E9 75 A2
Kenwrick Ho N1 233 D5
Kenwyn Dr NW2 67 D5
Kenwyn Rd
Clapham SW4 137 D1
Wimbledon SW20 178 C2
Kenya Rd SE7 143 D5
Kenyngton Dr TW16 172 A5
Kenyngton Manor Prim Sch TW16 172 A4
Kenyngton Pl HA3 43 C4
Kenyon Ho 31 SE5 139 A5
Kenyon St SW6 134 D4
Keogh Rd E15 76 D2
Kepler Ho 9 SE10 120 D1
Kepler Rd SW2, SW4 138 A1
Keppel Ho
Brompton SW3 257 A3
5 Deptford SE8 119 B1
Keppel Rd
Dagenham RM9 81 A4
Newham E6 100 B6
Keppel Row SE1 252 A3
Keppel St WC1 239 D4
Kerala Ct N17 33 D2
Kerbela St 3 E2 96 A3
Kerbey St E14 97 D1

Kerem Sch N2 48 B4
Kerfield Cres SE5 139 B4
Kerfield Pl SE5 139 B4
Kerridge Ct N1 73 C2
Kerrier Ho SW10 266 B3
Kerrington Ct 7 W12 112 C4
Kerrison Pl W5 109 D5
Kerrison Rd
Battersea SW11 136 C2
Ealing W5 109 D5
Mill Meads E15 98 B6
Kerrison Villas W5 109 D5
Kerry Ave HA7 25 D6
Kerry Cl Newham E16 99 B1
Palmers Green N13 16 B2
Kerry Ct HA7 25 D6
Kerry Ho 5 E1 96 C1
Kerry N7 72 A2
Kerry Path SE8 141 B6
Kerry Rd SE8 141 B6
Kerscott Ho 30 E3 97 D4
Kersey Gdns SE9 188 A6
Kersfield Ho SW15 156 D5
Kersfield Rd SW15 156 D5
Kershaw Cl SW18 158 B5
Kershaw Ho 7 SE27 160 D1
Kershaw Rd RM10 81 C5
Kersley Mews SW11 267 C1
Kersley Rd N16 73 C5
Kersley St SW11 136 D3
Kerstin Cl UB3 105 D6
Kerswell Cl N15 51 C4
Kerwick Cl 1 N7 72 B1
Keslake Mans NW10 90 D5
Keslake Rd NW6 90 D5
Kessock Cl N17 52 B4
Kestlake Rd DA5 168 C5
KESTON 225 D4
Keston Ave BR2 225 C3
Keston CE Prim Sch BR2 225 D3
Keston Cl
Bexley DA16 146 C5
Edmonton N18 17 B1
Keston Ct DA5 169 B4
Keston Gdns BR2 225 C4
Keston Ho SE17 263 B2
KESTON MARK 225 D6
Keston Mark BR2 226 A5
Keston Park Cl BR2 226 B5
Keston Rd
East Dulwich SE15 140 A2
Thornton Heath CR7 204 C3
West Green N17 51 B5
Kestrel Ave
East Ham E6 100 A2
Herne Hill SE24 161 A6
Kestrel Cl
Grahame Pk NW9 27 C1
Kingston u T KT2 175 D6
Neasden NW10 67 B3
Kestrel Ct
Higham Hill E17 34 D1
Ruislip HA4 61 B6
South Croydon CR2 221 A2
Wallington SM6 219 C3
Kestrel Ho
4 Battersea SW11 136 C2
Enfield EN3 19 A6
Finsbury EC1 235 A2
Kestrel Pl SE14 141 A6
Kestrel Way UB3 105 B4
Keswick Apartments 4 N17 51 D6
Keswick Ave
Kingston u T KT2, SW15 177 C5
Merton SW19 179 C1
Upper Halliford TW17 193 C6
Keswick Broadway 1 SW15 157 B6
Keswick Cl SM1 218 A4
Keswick Ct
13 Catford SE6 164 D3
2 East Dulwich SE22 162 A6
Keswick Dr EN3 6 C6
Keswick Gdns
Redbridge IG4 56 A5
Ruislip HA4 39 B3
Wembley HA9 66 A4
Keswick Ho 8 SE5 139 A4
Keswick Hts 9 SW15 157 A6
Keswick Lo E8 73 D2
Keswick Mews W5 110 A5
Keswick Rd
Bexleyheath DA7 147 C4
Broom Hill BR6 211 D1
Putney SW15 157 A6
Twickenham TW2 152 A5
West Wickham BR4 224 C6

Kettering Ct CR7 205 A5
Kettering Rd EN3 6 D6
Kettering St SW16 181 C4
Kett Gdns SW2 160 B6
Kettlebaston Rd E10 53 B1
Kettleby Ho SW9 138 D2
Kettlewell Cl N11 31 A4
Ketton Ho 11 W10 90 C3
Kevan Ct 6 E17 53 D5
Kevan Ho SE5 139 A5
Kevelioc Rd N17 33 A2
Kevin Cl TW4 128 D3
Kevington Cl BR5 211 D5
Kevington Dr BR5, BR7 211 D5
KEW 132 C6
Kew Bridge TW8 110 B1
Kew Bridge Ct 8 W4 110 C1
Kew Bridge Distribution Ctr TW8 110 B1
Kew Bridge Rd TW8 110 B1
Kew Bridge Sta TW8 110 B1
Kew Bridge Steam Mus* TW8 110 B1
Kew Coll TW9 132 C5
Kew Cres SM3 217 B5
Kew Ct KT2 176 A2
Kew Foot Rd TW9 132 A2
Kew Gardens Rd TW9 132 C4
Kew Gardens (Royal Botanic)* TW9 132 A4
Kew Gardens Sta TW9 132 C4
Kew Gn TW9 132 B6
Kew Green Prep Sch TW9 132 B6
Kew Green TW9 132 C6
Kew Lo 11 TW9 132 B4
Kew Montessori Sch TW9 132 C4
Kew Obsy* TW9 131 C2
Kew Pal* TW9 132 A5
Kew Pier TW9 132 C6
Kew Rd Finchley N2 30 C2
Richmond TW9, W4 132 B4
Kew Ret Pk TW9 132 D4
Kew Riverside Prim Sch TW9 132 D3
Key Cl E1 96 B3
Keyes Ct SE22 162 A6
Keyes Rd NW2 68 D3
Keyham Ho 31 W2 91 C2
Key Ho 9 SE11 138 C6
Keymer Rd SW2 160 B2
Keynes Cl N2 48 D6
Keynes Ct 9 SE28 124 B6
Keynsham Ave IG8 36 C6
Keynsham Gdns SE9 166 A6
Keynsham Ho 2 N4 51 A2
Keynsham Rd
Cheam SM4 201 D1
Eltham SE9 166 A6
Keynsham Wlk SM4 201 D1
Keyse Rd SE1 117 D3 263 C5
Keysham Ave TW5 128 A4
Keysham Ct HA9 66 A6
Keystone Cres N1 233 B3
Keywood Dr TW16 172 A4
Keyworth Cl E5 75 A4
Keyworth Pl SE1 261 D6
Keyworth Prim Sch SE17 116 D1 261 C2
Keyworth St SE1 116 D3 261 D6
Kezia St SE8 119 A1
Khalsa Ct N22 32 D2
Khama Rd SW17 180 C6
Khartoum Rd
Ilford IG1 78 D3
Newham E13 99 B4
Upper Tooting SW17 180 B6
Khyber Rd SW11 136 C3
Kibworth St SW8 138 B5 270 C3
KIDBROOKE 143 C3
Kidbrooke Gdns SE3 143 A4
Kidbrooke Gr SE3 143 B4
Kidbrooke Interchange SE3 143 C2
Kidbrooke La SE9 144 A1
Kidbrooke Park Cl SE3 143 B4
Kidbrooke Park Prim Sch SE3 143 C4
Kidbrooke Park Rd SE12, SE3 143 B2
Kidbrooke Sch SE3 143 D3
Kidbrooke Sta SE3 143 B2
Kidbrooke Way SE3 143 B3
Kiddens BR8 191 D1

Kidderminster Pl CR0 204 D1
Kidderminster Rd CR0 205 A2
Kidderpore Ave NW3 69 C4
Kidderpore Gdns NW3 69 C4
Kidd Ho RM9 81 B4
Kidd Pl SE7 122 A1
Kidlington Way NW9 27 C2
Kierbeck Bsns Complex E16 121 B4
Kiffen St EC2 242 D6
Kilberry Cl TW7 130 B4
Kilbrennan Ho 9 E14 98 A1
KILBURN 91 C6
Kilburn Bridge 14 NW6 91 C6
Kilburn Gate NW6 91 D5
Kilburn High Rd NW6 91 C6
Kilburn High Road Sta NW6 91 D6
Kilburn Ho 11 W9 91 B4
Kilburn La W10 91 A5
Kilburn Park Foundation Sch The NW6 91 B5
Kilburn Park Rd NW6 91 C4
Kilburn Park Sta NW6 91 C5
Kilburn Pl NW6 91 C6
Kilburn Priory NW6 91 D6
Kilburn Sq NW6 91 C6
Kilburn Sta NW2 69 B2
Kilburn Vale Est 13 NW6 91 C6
Kilburn Vale NW6 91 D6
Kilby Ct SE10 120 D3
Kildare Cl HA4 40 C1
Kildare Ct W2 91 C1
Kildare Gdns W2 91 C1
Kildare Rd E16 99 A2
Kildare Terr W2 91 C1
Kildare Wlk E14 97 C1
Kildoran Rd SW2 160 A6
Kildowan Rd IG3 58 A1
Kilgour Rd SE23 163 A5
Kilkie St SW6 136 A3
Killarney Rd SW18 158 A5
Killburns Mill Cl SM6 219 B6
Killearn Rd SE6 164 B3
Killester Gdns KT17, KT4 216 B4
Killick Ho SM1 217 D4
Killick St N1 94 B5 233 C3
Killieser Ave SW2 160 A2
Killigrew Ho TW16 171 C3
Killip Cl E16 98 D1
Killoran Ho 9 E14 120 A3
Killowen Ave UB5 64 A3
Killowen Rd E9 74 D2
Killyon Rd SW8 137 C3
Kilmaine Rd SW6 135 A5 264 B3
Kilmarnock Gdns RM8 80 C5
Kilmarnock Rd WD19 22 D6
Kilmarsh Rd W6 112 C2
Kilmartin Ave SW16 204 C6
Kilmartin Rd IG3 80 A6
Kilmington Rd SW13 134 A6
Kilmiston Ave TW17 193 A3
Kilmiston Ho TW17 193 A3
Kilmore Ho 17 E14 97 D1
Kilmorey Gdns TW1 131 B1
Kilmorey Rd TW1 131 B1
Kilmorie Prim Sch SE23 163 A2
Kilmorie Rd SE23 163 A2
Kilmuir Ho SW1 258 B3
Kiln Cl UB3 127 B6
Kiln Ct E14 119 B6
Kilner Ho 3 SE11 138 C6
Kilner St E14 97 C2
Kiln Mews SW17 180 B5
Kiln Pl NW5 71 A3
Kilnsey Ct 8 N11 31 A4
Kilnside KT10 213 A1
Kiloh Ct 1 SW11 136 C2
Kilpatrick Ct N16 51 D1
Kilpatrick Way UB4 85 A2
Kilpeck Ho 3 N4 51 A2
Kilravock Ho SE25 205 C6
Kilravock St W10 91 A4
Kilronan 5 W3 89 B1
Kilross Rd TW14 149 C3
Kilsby Wlk RM9 80 B2
Kilsha Rd KT12 194 C3
Kilvinton Dr EN2 5 B5

Kimbell Gdns SW6 135 A4 264 A1
Kimbell Pl SE9 143 C1
Kimber Ctr The SW18 157 C4
Kimber Ho 11 SE18 144 D6
Kimberley Ave
Ilford IG2 57 C2
Newham E6 100 A5
Nunhead SE15 140 C2
Kimberley Ct
Belvedere DA17 125 B2
Kilburn NW6 91 A6
Kimberley Dr DA14 168 D2
Kimberley Gate 3 BR1 186 D3
Kimberley Gdns
Enfield EN1 5 D2
Harringay N4 50 D4
Kimberley Ho 7 E14 120 A3
Kimberley Ind Est E17 35 B2
Kimberley Rd
Chingford E4 20 C3
Edmonton N18 34 B4
Kilburn NW6 91 A6
Leyton E11 76 B6
Newham E16 98 D3
Penge BR3 184 D1
Stockwell SW9 138 A2
Thornton Heath CR0 204 D3
Tottenham N17 34 A1
Walthamstow E17 35 B2
Kimberley Way E4 20 C3
Kimberley Wlk KT12 194 B2
Kimber Rd SW18 157 D4
Kimble Cres WD23 8 A4
Kimble Ho
Lisson Gr NW8 237 B6
1 Lower Holloway N7 72 A3
Kimble Rd SW17 180 B4
Kimbolton Cl SE12 164 D5
Kimbolton Row SW3 257 A3
Kimmeridge Gdns 3 SE9 188 A6
Kimmeridge Rd SE9 188 A6
Kimm Ho 16 E17 53 D6
Kimpton Ct 12 SE5 139 B4
Kimpton Ho SW15 156 A4
Kimpton Link Bsns Ctr SM3 217 B6
Kimpton Park Way SM3 217 B6
Kimpton Rd
Camberwell SE5 139 B4
Cheam SM3 217 B6
Kimpton Trade & Bsns Ctr SM3 217 B6
Kinburn St SE16 118 D4
Kincaid Rd SE15 140 B5
Kincardine Gdns W9 91 C3
Kinch Gr HA3, HA9 44 B2
Kincraig BR7 188 C2
Kindell Ho 4 SW14 133 B2
Kinder Cl SE28 124 D6
Kinder Ho N1 235 D4
Kindersley Ho 38 E1 96 A1
Kinder St 19 E1 96 B1
Kinderton Cl N14 15 C3
Kinefold Ho N7 72 A2
Kinfauns Rd
Ilford IG3 58 B1
Streatham SW2 160 C2
King Alfred Ave
Catford SE6 163 C1
Catford SE6 185 C6
King Alfred Sch NW11 47 D1
King Arthur Cl SE15 140 C5
King Athelstan Prim Sch KT1 198 B6
King Charles Cres KT5 198 B2
King Charles Ct 16 SE17 138 D6
King Charles Ho SW6 265 D4
King Charles' Rd KT5, KT6 198 B3
King Charles St SW1 116 A4 250 A2
King Charles Terr 11 E1 118 B6
King Charles Wlk 6 SW19 157 A3
King Ct 16 E10 53 D2
Kingcup Cl CR0 206 D1
King David La E1 118 C6
Kingdon Ho 8 E14 120 A3

Kingdon Rd NW6 ... 69 C2
Kingdown Cl W10 ... 90 D1
King Edward Dr KT6 ... 214 A5
King Edward Mans [12] E8 ... 96 B6
King Edward Mews SW13 ... 134 A4
King Edward Rd
Barnet EN5 ... 1 D1
Leytonstone E10 ... 54 A1
Walthamstow E17 ... 53 A6
King Edward's Gdns W3 ... 110 C5
King Edward's Gr TW11 ... 175 C4
King Edwards Mans SW6 ... 265 A3
King Edward's Rd
Barking IG11 ... 101 B5
Edmonton N9 ... 18 B4
Enfield EN3 ... 6 D1
Ruislip HA4 ... 39 B1
South Hackney E9 ... 96 C6
King Edward St EC1 ... 242 A2
King Edward The Third Mews [11] SE16 ... 118 B4
King Edward VII Hospl-Sister Agnes W1 ... 93 A2 238 B4
King Edward Wlk SE1 ... 116 C3 261 B6
King Fahad Acad The W5 ... 109 C2
King Fahed Acad W3 ... 111 D6
Kingfield Rd W5 ... 87 D3
Kingfield St E14 ... 120 A2
Kingfisher Ave E11 ... 55 B3
Kingfisher Cl
Harrow HA3 ... 24 D3
Woolwich SE28 ... 124 C6
Kingfisher Ct
[11] Battersea SW11 ... 136 C2
Cheam SM1 ... 217 B3
[17] Cubitt Town E14 ... 120 A4
East Molesey KT8 ... 196 C5
Enfield EN2 ... 4 B5
Hounslow TW3 ... 151 D6
Merton SW19 ... 179 B3
Putney SW19 ... 157 A2
Spring Gr TW3 ... 130 B3
Kingfisher Dr TW10 ... 175 B6
Kingfisher Ho
[16] Battersea SW18 ... 136 A2
Peckham SE15 ... 139 D4
West Kensington W14 ... 254 C6
Kingfisher Lo TW11 ... 175 A6
Kingfisher Mews SE13 ... 163 D6
Kingfisher Sq [19] SE8 ... 141 B6
Kingfisher St E6 ... 100 A2
Kingfisher Way
Croydon CR0 ... 206 D4
Neasden NW10 ... 67 B3
Kingfisher Wlk NW9 ... 27 C1
King Frederick IX Twr SE16 ... 119 B3
King Garth Mews SE23 ... 162 C2
King Gdns CR0 ... 220 D3
King George Ave
Ilford IG2 ... 57 B3
Newham E16 ... 99 D1
Walton-on-T KT12 ... 194 D1
King George Cl TW16 ... 171 C5
King George Hospl IG3 ... 58 A4
King George Sq TW10 ... 154 B5
King George's Trad Est KT9 ... 214 C4
King George St SE10 ... 142 A5
King George VI Ave CR4 ... 202 D5
King George V Sta E16 ... 122 C5
Kingham Cl
[3] Shepherd's Bush W11 ... 112 D4
Wandsworth SW18 ... 158 A4
Kingham Ind Est NW10 ... 89 B4
King Harolds Way DA7 ... 147 A5
King Henry Mews
Harrow HA2 ... 42 C1
[7] Orpington BR6 ... 227 D3
King Henry's Mews EN3 ... 7 C6
King Henry's Rd
Kingston u T KT1, KT3 ... 198 D6
Primrose Hill NW3 ... 70 C1
King Henry's Reach W6 ... 134 C6
King Henry St N16 ... 73 C3
King Henry's Wlk N1 ... 73 C2
King Henry's Yd [5] N16 ... 73 C3
King Henry Terr [10] E1 ... 118 B6
King Ho [5] W12 ... 90 B1
Kinghorn St EC1 ... 242 A3
King James St SE1 ... 116 D4 251 D1
King John Ct EC2 ... 243 B6
King John St E1 ... 96 D2
King John's Wlk SE9 ... 166 A5
Kinglake St SE17 ... 117 C1 263 B2
Kinglet Cl E7 ... 77 A2
Kingly Ct W1 ... 249 B6
Kingly St W1 ... 115 C6 249 A6
King & Queen Cl [4] SE9 ... 188 A6
King & Queen St SE17 ... 117 A1 262 B2
Kingsand Rd SE12 ... 165 A2
Kings Arbour UB2 ... 107 A1
King's Arms Ct E1 ... 96 A2
King's Arms Yd EC2 ... 242 C2
Kingsash Dr UB4 ... 85 A3
King's Ave TW16 ... 171 D4
Kings Ave BR1 ... 186 D4
King's Ave IG9 ... 21 D2
Kings Ave
Clapham Pk SW4 ... 160 A5
Dagenham RM6 ... 59 B3
Ealing W5 ... 87 D1
King's Ave TW3, TW5 ... 129 D4
Kings Ave
Muswell Hill N10 ... 49 A6
New Malden KT3 ... 199 D5
Kings Avenue Sch SW4 ... 160 A6
King's Ave
Southall UB1 ... 85 D1
Southgate N21 ... 16 D3
Kings Ave SM5 ... 218 D1
King's Ave IG8 ... 37 C5
King's Bench St SE1 ... 116 D4 251 D2
King's Bench Wlk EC4 ... 241 B1
Kingsbridge Ave W3 ... 110 B4
Kingsbridge Cres UB1 ... 85 B2
Kingsbridge Ct
Edmonton N21 ... 16 D2
Millwall E14 ... 119 C2
Kingsbridge Dr NW7 ... 28 D3
Kingsbridge Ho [10] SE20 ... 184 B2
Kingsbridge Ind Est IG11 ... 101 C4
Kingsbridge N16 ... 51 B1
Kingsbridge Rd
Barking IG11 ... 101 B5
North Kensington W10 ... 90 C1
Southall UB2 ... 107 B2
Walton-on-T KT12 ... 194 B2
West Barnes SM4 ... 200 D2
Kingsbridge Way UB4 ... 83 C4
KINGSBURY ... 45 B3
Kingsbury Green Prim Sch NW9 ... 44 D4
Kingsbury High Sch (Lower Sch) NW9 ... 45 A5
Kingsbury High Sch (Upper Sch) NW9 ... 44 D5
Kingsbury Hospl NW9 ... 44 C5
Kingsbury Rd
Kingsbury NW9 ... 44 D4
Kingsland N1 ... 73 C2
Kingsbury Sta NW9 ... 44 C4
Kingsbury Terr N1 ... 73 C2
Kingsbury Trad Est NW9 ... 45 B3
Kings Chase KT8 ... 196 A6
Kings Chase View EN2 ... 4 C3
Kingsclere Cl SW15 ... 156 A4
Kingsclere Ct
Colney Hatch N12 ... 30 C5
New Barnet EN5 ... 14 A6
Kingsclere Pl EN2 ... 5 A3
Kings Cl NW4 ... 46 D5
Kingscliffe Gdns SW19 ... 157 B3
King's Cl
Thames Ditton KT7 ... 197 A2
Walthamstow E10 ... 53 D2
Kings Cl KT12 ... 194 B1
King's Coll SE24 ... 161 B5
Kings College Ct NW3 ... 70 C1
King's College Hospl SE5 ... 139 B3
Kings College Rd
Primrose Hill NW3 ... 70 B1
Ruislip HA4 ... 39 D3
King's Coll London (Hampstead) NW3 ... 69 C4
King's Coll Sch SW19 ... 178 D4
King's Coll WC2 ... 116 B6 250 D6
King's Coll Univ SE1 ... 116 C5 251 A3
Kingscote NW11 ... 47 B1
Kingscote Rd
Bedford Pk W4 ... 111 B3
Croydon CR0 ... 206 B2
Kingston u T KT3 ... 199 B6
Kingscote St EC4 ... 251 C6
Kings Court Mews KT8 ... 196 B4
King's Court N SW3 ... 257 A1
Kingscourt Rd SW16 ... 160 A1
King's Court S SW3 ... 257 A1
King's Cres N4, N5 ... 73 A5
Kingscroft SW4 ... 160 A5
Kingscroft Rd NW2 ... 69 B2
KING'S CROSS ... 94 A5
King's Cross Bridge WC1 ... 233 B2
King's Cross Rd WC1 ... 94 B4 233 D1
King's Cross, St Pancras N1 ... 94 A4 233 A2
King's Cross Sta N1 ... 94 A5 233 B3
King's Cross (Thames Link) Sta WC1 ... 94 A4 233 B2
King's Cross WC1 ... 94 A4 233 B2
Kings Ct [6] N7 ... 72 B1
King's Ct BR3 ... 207 D6
Kings Ct
[2] Buckhurst Hill IG9 ... 21 D2
Chiswick W6 ... 112 A2
King's Ct [9] W5 ... 87 C2
Kings Ct
East Dulwich SE22 ... 140 A1
[16] Kingston u T KT2 ... 176 C3
Newham E13 ... 99 B6
Primrose Hill NW8 ... 230 C5
[10] Putney SW15 ... 156 A4
[3] Wallington SM6 ... 219 B2
Wembley Pk HA9 ... 66 D6
King's Ct SW19 ... 179 C4
Kingsdale Ct EN4 ... 2 D3
Kingsdale Gdns W11 ... 112 D5
Kingsdale Rd
Penge SE20 ... 184 D3
Plumstead Comm SE18 ... 145 D6
Kingsdale Sec Sch SE21 ... 161 C1
Kingsdown Ave
East Acton W3 ... 111 C6
West Ealing W13 ... 109 B4
Kingsdown Cl
[26] Deptford SE16 ... 118 B1
[8] Notting Hill W11 ... 91 A1
Kingsdown Ct SW11 ... 158 C5
Kingsdowne Rd KT6 ... 198 B2
Kingsdown Ho [1] E8 ... 74 A3
Kingsdown Rd
Cheam SM3 ... 217 A3
Leyton E11 ... 76 C5
[4] Upper Holloway N19 ... 72 A6
Kingsdown Way BR2 ... 209 A3
Kingsdown SW19 ... 178 D3
Kings Dr Edgware HA8 ... 26 B6
Surbiton KT5 ... 198 C3
King's Dr KT7 ... 197 B2
Kings Dr HA9 ... 66 D6
Kingsend Ct HA4 ... 39 C1
Kingsend HA4 ... 39 C1
Kings Farm Ave TW10 ... 132 C1
Kings Farm E17 ... 35 D2
Kingsfield Ave HA1, HA2 ... 42 A4
Kingsfield Ct HA1 ... 42 B2
Kingsfield Ho
Mottingham SE9 ... 165 D1
[7] Muswell Hill N10 ... 31 A3
[18] Stoke Newington N16 ... 73 C5
Kingsfield Rd HA1 ... 42 B2
Kingsford Com Sch E6 ... 100 B1
Kingsford St NW5 ... 70 D3
Kingsford Way E6 ... 100 B2
Kingsgate Ave N3 ... 47 C6
Kingsgate Bsns Ctr KT2 ... 176 A2
Kingsgate Cl
Erith DA7 ... 147 A4
Sidcup BR5 ... 190 C1
Kingsgate Est N1 ... 73 C2
Kingsgate Ho [29] SW9 ... 138 C4
Kingsgate Par SW1 ... 259 B5
Kingsgate Pl NW6 ... 69 C1
Kingsgate Prim Sch NW6 ... 69 C1
Kingsgate Rd
Hampstead NW6 ... 69 C1
Kingston u T KT2 ... 176 A2
Kingsgate HA9 ... 67 A5
Kings Gdns IG1 ... 57 B1
King's Gdns [6] NW6 ... 69 C1
Kings Grange HA4 ... 39 D1
Kingsground SE9 ... 166 A5
King's Gr
Peckham SE15 ... 140 B4
Peckham SE15 ... 140 B5
Kingshall Mews SE13 ... 142 A2
Kings Hall Rd BR3 ... 185 A2
Kings Head Hill E4 ... 19 D4
King's Head Yd SE1 ... 252 C3
King's Highway SE18 ... 145 D6
Kingshill Ave
Harrow HA3 ... 43 B5
Hayes UB4 ... 83 D4
New Malden KT4 ... 200 B2
Northolt UB5 ... 84 B4
Kingshill Cl UB4, UB5 ... 84 A4
Kingshill Ct [8] EN5 ... 1 A1
Kingshill Dr HA3 ... 43 B6
Kingshill SE17 ... 262 B4
Kingshold Rd E9 ... 74 C1
Kings Ho [19] E14 ... 119 B6
Kingsholm Gdns SE9 ... 144 A1
Kings Ho SW8 ... 270 B4
King's House Sch (Jun) TW10 ... 154 B6
King's House Sch TW10 ... 154 B6
Kingshurst Rd SE12 ... 165 A4
Kings Keep KT6 ... 198 A5
King's Keep [6] SW15 ... 156 D6
KINGSLAND ... 73 C2
Kingsland Gn [1] E8, N1 ... 73 C2
Kingsland High St E8 ... 73 D3
Kingsland NW8 ... 92 C6 230 B5
Kingsland Pas [2] E8 ... 73 C2
Kingsland Rd
Hoxton E2 ... 95 C5
Newham E13 ... 99 C4
Kingsland Sh Ctr [12] E8 ... 73 D2
King's La SM1 ... 218 B3
Kingslawn Cl SW15 ... 156 B6
Kingslee Ct [4] SM2 ... 217 D1
Kingsleigh Cl TW8 ... 131 D6
Kingsleigh Pl CR4 ... 202 D6
Kingsleigh Wlk BR2 ... 208 D5
Kingsley Ave
Ealing W13 ... 87 A1
Hounslow TW3 ... 130 A3
Southall UB1 ... 107 C6
Sutton SM1 ... 218 B4
Kingsley Cl
Dagenham RM10 ... 81 D4
East Finchley N2 ... 48 A4
Kingsley Ct
Bexley DA6 ... 147 C1
Edgware HA8 ... 10 D2
Snaresbrook E11 ... 54 D3
[1] Thamesmead SE28 ... 124 C5
Willesden NW2 ... 68 B2
Wood Green N22 ... 32 B3
Worcester Pk KT4 ... 215 D6
Kingsley Dr KT4 ... 215 D6
Kingsley Flats SE1 ... 263 B3
Kingsley Gdns E4 ... 35 C5
Kingsley Grange [1] E11 ... 55 A4
Kingsley High Sch HA3 ... 24 A3
Kingsley Ho
Chelsea SW3 ... 266 D5
[3] Clapham SW4 ... 137 D3
East Finchley NW11 ... 48 A3
[8] Kingston u T KT6 ... 198 A4
Kingsley Mews
Chislehurst West BR7 ... 188 D4
Dagenham RM9 ... 80 D4
[4] Ilford IG1 ... 78 D6
Kensington W8 ... 255 D5
[15] St George in t East E1 ... 118 B6
Kingsley Pl N6 ... 49 A2
Kingsley Prim Sch CR9 ... 204 C1
Kingsley Rd
Chingford E17 ... 36 A1
Edmonton N13 ... 32 D6
Harrow HA2 ... 64 A5
Hounslow TW3 ... 130 A3
Kilburn NW6 ... 91 B6
Orpington BR6 ... 227 D1
Pinner HA5 ... 41 B5
Thornton Heath CR0 ... 204 C1
Upton E7 ... 77 A1
Wimbledon SW19 ... 179 D5
Kingsley St SW11 ... 136 D2
Kingsley Way N2 ... 48 A4
Kingsley Wood Dr SE9 ... 166 B1
Kings Lo HA4 ... 39 C1
Kingslyn Cres SE19 ... 183 C2
Kings Mall Sh Ctr W6 ... 112 C2
Kingsman Par SE18 ... 122 B3
King's Mans SW3 ... 267 A5
Kingsman St SE18 ... 122 B2
Kingsmead Ave
Edmonton N9 ... 18 B3
Kingsbury NW9 ... 45 B2
Mitcham CR4 ... 203 C6
North Cheam KT4 ... 216 B5
Sunbury TW16 ... 172 C1
Tolworth KT6 ... 214 C6
Kingsmead EN5 ... 1 C1
Kingsmead Cl
Sidcup DA15 ... 168 A2
Teddington TW11 ... 175 B4
West Ewell KT19 ... 215 B1
Kingsmead Cotts BR2 ... 210 A1
Kingsmead Ct
Bromley BR1 ... 186 D3
Crouch End N6 ... 49 D2
Kingsmead Dr UB5 ... 63 B1
Kingsmead Ho E9 ... 75 A4
Kingsmead Lo
[9] Chingford E4 ... 20 A2
Sutton SM2 ... 218 B2
Kings Mead Pk KT10 ... 212 C1
Kingsmead Prim Sch E9 ... 75 A4
Kingsmead Rd SW2 ... 160 C2
Kingsmead TW10 ... 154 B5
Kingsmead Sch EN1 ... 6 A2
King's Mead Way E5, E9 ... 75 A4
Kingsmere SE6 ... 163 D3
Kingsmere Cl SW15 ... 134 D2
Kingsmere Ct NW9 ... 44 D1
Kingsmere Pk NW9 ... 45 A1
Kingsmere Pl N16 ... 51 B1
Kingsmere Rd SW19 ... 156 D2
Kingsmere BR7 ... 188 A2
King's Mews
[1] Clapham Pk SW4 ... 160 A6
Gray's Inn WC1 ... 94 B3 240 D5
Kingsmill Bsns Pk KT1 ... 198 B6
Kingsmill Gdns RM9 ... 81 B3
Kingsmill NW8 ... 92 B5 229 D4
Kingsmill Rd RM9 ... 81 B3
Kingsmill Terr NW8 ... 92 B5 229 D4
Kingsmount Ct SM1 ... 217 D4
Kingsnorth Ho [12] W10 ... 90 D1
Kingsnympton Pk KT2 ... 176 D4
Kings Oak Hospl (Private) The EN2 ... 4 C5
Kings Oak RM7 ... 59 C6
King's Orch SE9 ... 166 A5
King's Paddock TW12 ... 174 A2
King's Par [3] W12 ... 112 A3
Kingspark Bsns Ctr KT3 ... 199 A6
Kingspark Ct E18 ... 55 A6
King's Par NW10 ... 90 C6
King's Pas KT2 ... 1
King's Penny Ho [4] KT2 ... 1
Kings Pl
Acton Green W4 ... 11
Buckhurst Hill IG9 ... 2
Loughton IG10 ... 2
King's Pl SE1 ... 25
King Sq EC1 ... 95 A4 23
King's Quay SW10 ... 26
King's Rd
Barking IG11 ... 7
Chelsea SW3 ... 25
Chelsea SW10 ... 136 B6 26
Chingford E4 ... 2
Kings Rd W5 ... 8
King's Rd N18 ... 3
Kings Rd
Feltham TW13 ... 15
Harrow HA2 ... 6
King's Rd
Kingston u T KT2 ... 17
Leytonstone E11 ... 5
Long Ditton KT6 ... 19
Kings Rd CR4 ... 20
King's Rd
Mortlake SW14 ... 13
Newham E6 ... 9
Kings Rd
Orpington BR6 ... 22
Richmond TW10, TW9 ... 15
King's Rd
South Norwood SE25 ... 20
Teddington TW11, TW12 ... 17
Tottenham N17 ... 3
Twickenham TW1 ... 15
Kings Rd
Walton-on-T KT12 ... 19
West Drayton UB7 ... 10
Willesden NW10 ... 6
King's Rd SW19 ... 17
Kings Rd N22 ... 3
Kings Ride Gate TW10 ... 13
Kingsridge SW19 ... 15
Kings Road Bglws HA2 ... 6
King's Scholars' Pas SW1 ... 25
King St W3 ... 11
King Stairs Cl SE16 ... 11
King St N2 ... 4
King's Terr
Camden Town NW1 ... 93 C6 23
[10] Isleworth TW7 ... 13
King St W6 ... 11
Kingsthorpe Rd SE26 ... 184
King St Newham E13 ... 98
Newham E13 ... 99
Kingston Ave
Cheam SM3 ... 217
Feltham TW14 ... 149
Yiewsley UB7 ... 104
Kingston Bsns Ctr KT9 ... 214
Kingston By-Pass KT6, KT7, KT9 ... 213
Kingston By - Pass KT6 ... 214
Kingston Cl
Dagenham RM6 ... 59
Northolt UB5 ... 85
Teddington TW11 ... 175
Kingston Coll of F Ed KT1 ... 197
Kingston Coll of F Ed (M V Annex) KT2 ... 176
Kingston Cres BR3 ... 185
Kingston Ct HA3 ... 44
Kingston Gdns CR0 ... 220
Kingston Gram Sch KT2 ... 176
Kingston Hall Rd KT1 ... 197
Kingston Hill Ave RM6 ... 59
Kingston Hill KT2 ... 177
Kingston Hill Pl KT2, TW10 ... 177
Kingston Ho E SW7 ... 247
Kingston Ho [4] NW6 ... 69
Kingston Ho N SW7 ... 247
Kingston Hospl KT2 ... 176
Kingston Ho S SW7 ... 247
Kingston House Est KT6 ... 197
Kingston La
Teddington TW11 ... 175
Uxbridge UB8 ... 82
West Drayton UB7 ... 104
Kingston Lo [2] KT3 ... 199

ton Mus*
... 176 A1
ton Pl HA3 ... 24 D3
ton Rd
ord TW15 ... 170 A4
ord TW15 ... 170 B4
onton N9 ... 18 A2
KT17 ... 215 D1
d IG1 ... 79 A4
ston u T KT1,
3 ... 199 A5
ton SW19,
V20 ... 179 B1
Barnet EN4 ... 14 B6
ampton SW15,
V19 ... 156 B3
hall UB2 ... 107 B4
ington TW11 ... 175 B4
ston Sq SE19 ... 183 B5
ston Sta KT2 ... 176 A2
ston Univ Annex
... 176 B1
ston Univ
ston u T KT1 ... 198 A6
ston Vale KT2 ... 177 B5
ston Univ
hampton Vale
npus SW15 ... 155 D1
STON UPON
AMES ... 197 C6
STON VALE ... 177 B6
ston Vale
5 ... 155 C1
stown St
1 ... 93 A6 231 A6
Street Cloisters 8
... 112 B2
Street Coll
2 ... 112 C4
Street Par 7
... 153 A3
St
hmond TW9 ... 153 D6
thall UB2 ... 107 A3
James
W1 ... 115 C5 249 B4
and WC2 ... 250 A6
tenham N17 ... 33 D2
ckenham TW1 ... 153 A3
itechapel
C2 ... 95 A1 242 B1
s View Ct 1
20 ... 178 D3
swater Pl SW11 267 A3
sway Bsns Pk
12 ... 173 B2
sway Coll NW5 ... 71 B2
sway BR4 ... 224 D5
sway Cres HA2 ... 42 A5
s Way CR0 ... 220 B3
sway EN3 ... 18 B6
sway Est N18 ... 34 D4
s Way HA1 ... 42 C5
sway UB3 ... 83 A2
sway Mans
1 ... 240 C4
sway
rtlake SW14,
TW9 ... 132 D2
rth Finchley N12 ... 30 A4
tts Wood BR5 ... 211 B4
sway Pl EC1 ... 241 C6
sway Rd SM3 ... 217 A1
sway
anwell TW19 ... 148 A3
Giles WC2 .. 94 B1 240 C2
embley HA9 ... 66 A4
est Barnes KT3 ... 200 C4
oodford IG8 ... 37 C5
swear Ho 5
23 ... 162 C2
swear Rd
rtmouth Pk NW5 ... 71 B5
islip HA4 ... 62 A6
gs Well 25 NW3 ... 70 A4
gs Wlk Sh Mall
3 ... 114 D1 257 C2
swood Ave
eckenham BR2,
BR3 ... 208 C5
elvedere DA17 ... 125 B2
ampton TW12 ... 173 D4
ounslow TW3,
TW5 ... 129 B3
ensal Rise NW6 ... 91 A5
hornton Heath CR7 . 204 C4
gswood Cl
shford TW15 ... 171 B5
ofton BR6 ... 211 B2
ast Barnet N20 ... 14 A4
nfield EN1 ... 17 D6
ew Malden KT3 ... 199 D3
outh Lambeth SW8 . 270 B3
rbiton KT6 ... 198 A2
gswood Ct
hingford E4 ... 35 C5

Kingswood Ct *continued*
Hither Green SE13 ... 164 B5
Kings Wood Ct 4
NW6 ... 69 C1
Kingswood Ct 7
TW10 ... 154 B6
Kingswood Dr
Carshalton SM5 ... 202 D1
Dulwich SE19, SE21 .. 183 D6
Kingswood 31 E2 ... 96 C5
Kingswood Ho 3
KT2 ... 176 D4
Kingswood Mans 14
SM2 ... 217 C1
Kingswood Pk N3 ... 29 B1
Kingswood Pl SE13 .. 142 C1
Kingswood Prim Sch
SE27 ... 183 B5
Kingswood Rd
Beckenham BR2 ... 208 C6
Ilford IG3 ... 58 A2
Leytonstone E11 ... 54 C2
Merton SW19 ... 179 B2
Penge SE20 ... 184 C4
South Acton W4 ... 111 A3
Streatham SW2 ... 160 A4
Wembley HA9 ... 66 C5
Kingswood Terr
W4 ... 111 A3
Kingswood Way
SM6 ... 220 A3
Kingsworth Cl BR3 ... 207 A4
Kingsworthy Cl KT1 .. 198 B6
Kings Yd E15 ... 75 C2
Kingthorpe Rd NW10 .. 67 B1
Kingthorpe Terr 2
NW10 ... 67 B1
Kington Ho 18 NW6 ... 91 D6
Kingward Ho E1 ... 96 A2
Kingwell Rd EN4 ... 2 B5
Kingweston Cl NW2 ... 69 A5
King William IV Gdns
SE20 ... 184 C4
King William La 3
SE10 ... 120 C1
King William St
EC4 ... 117 B6 252 D6
King William Wlk
SE10 ... 142 A6
Kingwood Rd
SW6 ... 135 A5 264 A3
Kinlet Rd SE18 ... 145 A4
Kinloch Dr NW9 ... 45 C2
Kinloch St N7 ... 72 B5
Kinloss Ct NW3 ... 47 B5
Kinloss Gdns NW3 ... 47 B5
Kinloss Rd SM5 ... 202 A2
Kinnaird Ave
Bromley BR1 ... 186 D4
Chiswick W4 ... 133 A5
Kinnaird Cl BR1 ... 186 D4
Kinnear Ct 2 SW20 .. 178 D2
Kinnear Rd W12 ... 111 D4
Kinnerton Pl N SW1. 247 D1
Kinnerton Pl S SW1. 247 D1
Kinnerton St
SW1 ... 115 A4 248 A1
Kinnerton Yd SW1 .. 248 A1
Kinnoull Mans 10 E5 .. 74 B4
Kinnoul Rd
W6 ... 135 A6 264 A6
Kinross Ave KT4 ... 216 A6
Kinross Cl
Ashford TW16 ... 171 D5
Edgware HA8 ... 10 D2
Harrow HA3 ... 44 B4
Kinross Ct 1 SE6 ... 164 D2
Kinross Dr TW16 ... 171 D5
Kinross Ho N1 ... 233 C6
Kinross Terr E17 ... 35 B1
Kinsale Grange 10
SM2 ... 218 A2
Kinsale Rd SE15 ... 140 A2
Kinsella Gdns SW19 .. 178 B5
Kinsey Ho SE21 ... 183 C6
Kinsham Ho 5 E2 ... 96 A3
Kintore Way SE1 ... 263 C4
Kintyre Cl SW16 ... 204 B6
Kintyre Ct 17 SW2 ... 160 A4
Kintyre Ho 6 E14 ... 120 A5
Kinveachy Gdns
SE7 ... 122 A1
Kinver Ho N4 ... 51 B2
Kinver Rd SE26 ... 184 C6
Kipling Ct W7 ... 108 D6
Kipling Dr SW17 ... 180 B4
Kipling Ho 29 SE5 ... 139 A5
Kipling Pl HA7 ... 24 D4
Kipling Rd DA7 ... 147 A4
Kipling St
SE1 ... 117 B4 252 D2
Kipling Terr N9 ... 17 B2
Kipling Twr 3 W3 ... 111 A3
Kippington Dr SE9 ... 165 D3
Kirby Cl KT19 ... 215 D3
Kirby Est SE16 ... 118 B3
Kirby Gr SE1 .. 117 C4 253 A2

Kirby St EC1 ... 94 C2 241 B4
Kirby Way
Hillingdon UB8 ... 82 B3
Walton-on-T KT12 ... 194 C3
Kirchen Rd W13 ... 109 B6
Kirkby Cl N11 ... 31 A4
Kirkdale SE26 ... 162 B1
Kirkdale Rd E11 ... 54 C2
Kirkeby Bldg EC1 ... 241 A4
Kirkfield Cl W13 ... 109 B5
Kirkham Rd E6 ... 100 A1
Kirkham St SE18 ... 145 C6
Kirk Ho HA9 ... 66 A5
Kirkland Cl DA15 ... 167 C5
Kirkland Dr EN2 ... 5 A4
Kirkland Terr BR3 ... 185 C4
Kirkland Wlk 4 E8 ... 73 D2
Kirk La SE18 ... 145 A6
Kirkleas Rd KT6 ... 198 A1
Kirklees Rd
Dagenham RM8 ... 80 C3
Thornton Heath CR7 . 204 C4
Kirkley Ho N16 ... 51 C1
Kirkley Rd SW19 ... 179 C2
Kirkman Ho W1 ... 239 C3
Kirkman Pl W1 ... 239 C3
Kirkmichael Rd E14 ... 98 A1
Kirk Rd E17 ... 53 B3
Kirk Rise SM1 ... 217 D5
Kirkside Rd SE3 ... 143 A6
Kirkstall Ave N17 ... 51 B5
Kirkstall Gdns SW2 .. 160 A3
Kirkstall Ho SW1 ... 258 C2
Kirkstall Rd SW2 ... 160 A3
Kirkstead Ct E5 ... 75 A4
Kirksted Rd SM4 ... 201 D1
Kirkstone NW1 ... 232 A2
Kirkstone Way BR1 ... 186 C3
Kirkton Rd N15 ... 51 C5
Kirkwall Pl E2 ... 96 C4
Kirkwood Rd SE15 ... 140 B3
Kirn Rd W13 ... 109 B6
Kirrane Cl KT3 ... 199 D4
Kirtley Ho SW8 ... 269 B2
Kirtley Rd SE26 ... 185 A6
Kirtling St
SW8 ... 137 C5 269 A4
Kirton Cl W4 ... 111 B2
Kirton Gdns 23 E2 ... 95 D4
Kirton Rd E13 ... 99 C5
Kirton Wlk HA8 ... 27 A3
Kirwin Way SE5 ... 138 D5
Kisharon Day Sch
NW11 ... 47 B3
Kitcat Terr E3 ... 97 C4
Kitchener Rd
Dagenham RM10 ... 81 D2
East Finchley N2 ... 48 C6
South Norwood CR7 .. 205 B6
Tottenham N17 ... 51 C6
Upton E7 ... 77 B2
Walthamstow E17 ... 35 D2
Kite Ho 5 SW11 ... 136 C2
Kite Pl 9 E2 ... 96 A4
Kitley Gdns SE19 ... 183 D2
Kitson Rd
Barnes SW13 ... 134 A4
Camberwell SE5 ... 139 A5
Kittiwake Ct 26 SE8 ... 141 B6
Kittiwake Pl SM1 ... 217 B3
Kittiwake Rd UB5 ... 84 D4
Kittiwake Way UB4 ... 84 D2
Kitto Rd SE14 ... 140 D3
KITTS END ... 1 A5
Kitt's End Rd EN5 ... 1 A6
Kiver Rd N19 ... 72 A6
Klea Ave SW4 ... 159 C5
Kleffens Ct 2 SE3 ... 142 D5
Kleine Wharf 30 N1 ... 95 C6
Knaggs Ho 1 TW11 ... 174 C5
Knapdale Cl SE23 ... 162 B2
Knapmill Rd SE6 ... 163 D2
Knapmill Way SE6 ... 163 D2
Knapp Cl NW10 ... 67 C2
Knapp Rd
Ashford TW15 ... 170 B6
Bow E3 ... 97 C3
Knapton Mews
SW17 ... 181 A4
Knaresborough Dr
SW18 ... 157 D3
Knaresborough Ho 4
N4 ... 51 A2
Knaresborough Pl
SW5 ... 113 D2 255 C4
Knatchbull Rd
Brixton SE5 ... 138 D4
Stonebridge NW10 ... 89 B6
Knebworth Ave E17 ... 35 C2
Knebworth Ho
South Lambeth
SW8 ... 269 D1
2 Stoke Newington
N16 ... 73 C4
Walthamstow E17 ... 35 C2
Knebworth Rd 3
N16 ... 73 C4

Knee Hill Cres SE2 ... 124 C2
Knee Hill SE2 ... 124 C1
Kneller Gdns TW7 ... 152 B5
Kneller Ho 9 SW8 ... 137 D3
Kneller Rd
Brockley SE4 ... 141 A1
Isleworth TW2 ... 152 B5
New Malden KT3 ... 199 C2
Knevett Terr TW3 ... 129 C1
Knight Cl RM8 ... 80 C6
Knight Ct
1 Chingford E4 ... 20 A3
Stamford Hill N15 ... 51 C4
Knighten St E1 ... 118 B5
Knighthead Point 26
E14 ... 119 C4
Knight Ho
Walworth SE17 ... 263 A3
Worcester Pk KT4 ... 216 A6
Knightland Ho E5 ... 74 B6
Knightland Rd E5 ... 74 B6
Knightleas Ct NW2 ... 68 C2
Knightleys Ct E10 ... 53 A1
Knighton Cl
Croydon CR2 ... 220 D1
Woodford IG8 ... 37 B6
Knighton Dr IG8 ... 37 B6
Knighton Gn IG9 ... 21 B2
Knighton La IG9 ... 21 B2
Knighton Park Rd
SE26 ... 184 D5
Knighton Rd E7 ... 77 A4
Knightrider Ct EC4 .. 252 A6
Knightrider St EC4 .. 251 D6
Knights Arc SW1 ... 247 C1
Knight's Ave W5 ... 110 A4
KNIGHTSBRIDGE ... 114 C4
Knightsbridge Ct
SW1 ... 247 D1
Knightsbridge Gn
SW1 ... 247 C1
Knightsbridge Mews
BR7 ... 188 B3
Knightsbridge SW1,
SW7 ... 114 D4 247 C1
Knightsbridge Under
Sch SW7 ... 256 B3
Knights Cl
East Molesey KT8 ... 195 B4
Lower Clapton E9 ... 74 C3
Knights Ct WD23 ... 8 B3
Knight's Ct BR1 ... 164 D1
Knights Ct
11 Friern Barnet
N11 ... 30 D5
Kingston u T KT1 ... 198 A6
Penge BR3 ... 185 A2
Knightshayes Ho 8
NW4 ... 28 D1
Knight's Hill Sq
SE27 ... 182 D6
Knight's Hill SE19,
SE27 ... 182 D6
Knights Ho
Bermondsey SE1 ... 253 C2
South Lambeth SW8 . 270 B3
Knight's Ho SW10 ... 266 A4
Knights Ho SW5 ... 254 C2
Knight's Pk KT1 ... 198 A6
Knight's Pl TW2 ... 152 C3
Knights Rd
Newham E16 ... 121 A4
Stanmore HA7 ... 25 C6
Knight's Wlk SE11 ... 261 C3
Knightswood Cl HA8 ... 11 A2
Knightswood Ct N6 ... 49 D2
Knightswood Ho N12 . 30 A4
Knightwood Cres
KT3 ... 199 C3
Knivet Rd
SW6 ... 135 C6 265 A5
Knobs Hill Rd E15 ... 97 D6
Knockholt Rd SE9 ... 165 D6
Knole Cl CR0 ... 206 C3
Knole Ct UB5 ... 84 C4
Knole Gate DA15 ... 167 C1
Knole The SE9 ... 188 C6
Knoll Ct
Dulwich SE19 ... 183 D5
Orpington BR6 ... 227 D6
Knoll Dr N14 ... 15 A4
Knoll Ho NW8 ... 229 A4
Knoll Lo EN5 ... 14 A6
Knollmead Prim Sch
KT5 ... 215 A6
Knollmead KT4, KT5 .. 199 A1
Knoll Rd Bexley DA5 .. 169 C5
Sidcup DA14 ... 190 B6
Wandsworth SW18 ... 158 A6
Knoll Rise BR6 ... 211 D1
Knolls Cl KT4 ... 216 B5
Knoll The
Beckenham BR3 ... 185 D2
Ealing W13 ... 87 C2
Hayes BR2 ... 209 A1
Knolly's Cl SE27,
SW16 ... 160 C1

Knolly's Rd SE27,
SW16 ... 160 C1
Knot Ho SE1 ... 253 C3
Knottisford St E2 ... 96 C4
Knotts Green Mews
E10 ... 54 A3
Knotts Green Rd E10 .. 54 A3
Knowlden Ho 5 E1 ... 118 C6
Knowle Ave DA7 ... 147 B5
Knowle Cl SW9 ... 138 C2
Knowledge Point Sch
N7 ... 72 B2
Knowle Lo BR7 ... 188 B4
Knowle Rd
Bromley BR2 ... 226 A6
Twickenham TW2 ... 152 C3
Knowles Cl UB7 ... 104 A5
Knowles Ct 7 HA1 ... 42 D3
Knowles Hill Cres
SE13 ... 164 B6
Knowles Ho
Wandsworth
SW18 ... 157 D5
Willesden Green
NW10 ... 90 A6
Knowles Wlk SW4 ... 137 C2
Knowl Pk WD6 ... 10 A6
Knowlton Gn 1
BR2 ... 208 D4
Knowlton Ho 32
SW9 ... 138 C4
Knowl Way WD6 ... 10 B6
Knowsley Ave UB1 ... 107 D5
Knowsley Rd SW11 ... 136 D3
Knox Ct 16 SW4 ... 138 A3
Knox Ho SW15 ... 134 C3
Knox Rd E7 ... 77 A2
Knox St W1 ... 92 D2 237 C4
Knoyle Ho W14 ... 254 B6
Knoyle St SE14 ... 141 A6
Kobi Nazrul Prim Sch
E1 ... 96 A1
Koblenz Ho N8 ... 50 A6
Kohat Rd SW19 ... 179 D5
Korda Cl TW17 ... 192 B6
Kossuth St SE10 ... 120 C1
Kotree Way 16 SE1 ... 118 A2
Kramer Mews SW5 .. 255 C1
Kreedman Wlk 8 E8 .. 74 A3
Kreisel Wlk TW9 ... 132 B6
Kristina Ct 5 SM2 ... 217 C2
Kuala Gdns SW16 ... 182 B2
Kubrick Bsns Est E7 .. 77 B4
Kuhn Way E7 ... 77 A3
Kwesi Johnson Ct 4
N22 ... 32 C1
Kydbrook Cl BR5 ... 211 A2
Kyle Ho TW12 ... 174 A2
Kylemore Cl 3 E6 ... 99 D5
Kylemore Ct 4
W12 ... 112 A4
Kylemore Rd NW6 ... 69 C1
Kylestrome Ho SW1. 258 B3
Kymberley Rd HA1 ... 42 C3
Kynance Gdns HA7 ... 25 C2
Kynance Mews
SW7 ... 113 D3 255 D5
Kynance Pl SW7 ... 256 A5
Kynaston Ave CR7 ... 205 A4
Kynaston Cl HA3 ... 24 B3
Kynaston Cres CR7 ... 205 A4
Kynaston Ho 7
SW2 ... 160 B3
Kynaston Rd
Enfield EN2 ... 5 B4
Plaistow BR1 ... 187 A5
Stoke Newington N16 ... 73 C5
Thornton Heath CR7 . 205 A4
Kynaston Wood HA3 .. 24 B3
Kynersley Cl 1
SM5 ... 218 D5
Kynoch Rd N18 ... 34 D6
Kyrle Rd SW11 ... 159 A5
Kyverdale Rd N16 ... 51 D1

L

Laburnam Ct 12
SW16 ... 182 C5
Laburnham Cl HA0 ... 88 C6
Laburnham Ct
Child's Hill NW2 ... 69 B6
Sutton SM1 ... 217 C3
Laburnham Pl SE9 ... 166 C6
Laburnum Ave
Carshalton SM1 ... 218 C5
Edmonton N9 ... 17 D2
Tottenham N17 ... 33 B3
Yiewsley UB7 ... 104 B6
Laburnum Cl
Friern Barnet N11 ... 31 A4
5 Nunhead SE15 ... 140 C5
Walthamstow E4 ... 35 B4
Laburnum Cres
TW16 ... 172 B2

Laburnum Ct
26 Haggerston E2 ... 95 D6
Harrow HA1 ... 41 D3
5 Mitcham CR4 ... 181 A1
Stanmore HA7 ... 25 C6
Laburnum Gdns
Croydon CR0 ... 206 D1
Edmonton N21 ... 17 A2
Laburnum Gr
Edmonton N21 ... 17 A2
Hounslow TW3 ... 129 B1
Kingsbury NW9 ... 45 A2
Kingston u T KT3 ... 177 B1
Ruislip HA4 ... 39 B3
Southall UB1 ... 85 B3
Laburnum Ho
Dagenham RM10 ... 81 C6
New Cross SE4 ... 141 B3
6 Stoke Newington
N16 ... 73 B6
Laburnum JMI Sch
E2 ... 95 D6
Laburnum Lo 2 N3 ... 29 B1
Laburnum Rd
Hayes UB3 ... 105 D2
Merton SW19 ... 180 A3
Mitcham CR4 ... 181 A1
Laburnum St E2 ... 95 D6
Laburnums The E6 ... 100 A3
Laburnum Way
Southborough
BR2 ... 210 D2
Stanwell TW19 ... 148 B3
Lacebark Cl DA15 ... 167 D4
Lacewing Cl E13 ... 99 A4
Lacey Cl N9 ... 18 A2
Lacey Dr
Dagenham RM8 ... 80 C5
Edgware HA8 ... 26 B6
Hampton TW12 ... 173 B2
Lacey Ho 7 SE13 ... 142 A3
Lacine Ct 12 SE16 ... 118 D4
Lackington St EC2 .. 242 D4
Lackland Ho SE1 ... 263 D2
Lacland Ho SW10 ... 266 C4
Lacock Cl SW19 ... 180 A4
Lacock Ct 3 W13 ... 109 A5
Lacon Rd SE22 ... 140 A1
Lacrosse Way
SW16 ... 181 D2
Lacy Rd SW15 ... 134 D1
Ladas Rd SE27 ... 183 A5
Ladbroke Cres W11 ... 91 A1
Ladbroke Gdns
W11 ... 113 B6 244 C6
Ladbroke Gr
Kensal Town W10 ... 91 A2
Notting Hill
W11 ... 113 B6 244 C6
Ladbroke Grove Ho
W11 ... 244 C6
Ladbroke Grove Sta
W10 ... 91 A1
Ladbroke Ho E1 ... 243 D3
Ladbroke Mews
W11 ... 244 B3
Ladbroke Rd
Enfield EN1 ... 17 D5
Notting Hill
W11 ... 113 B5 244 C4
Ladbroke Sq
W11 ... 113 B6 244 D5
Ladbroke Terr
W11 ... 113 B5 244 D4
Ladbroke Wlk
W11 ... 113 B5 244 D4
Ladbrook Cl HA5 ... 41 B4
Ladbrooke Cres
DA14 ... 168 D1
Ladbrook Rd SE25 ... 205 B5
Ladderstile Ride KT2,
TW10 ... 176 D5
Ladderswood Way
N11 ... 31 C5
Ladlands SE22 ... 162 A4
Lady Alesford Ave
HA7 ... 25 B5
Lady Bankes Jun & Inf
Schs HA4 ... 62 A6
Lady Booth Rd 7
KT1 ... 176 A1
Ladybower Ct 6 E5 ... 74 D4
Ladycroft Gdns 6
BR6 ... 227 A3
Ladycroft Rd SE13 ... 141 D2
Ladycroft Way BR6 ... 227 A3
Ladycroft Wlk HA7 ... 25 D1
Lady Eleanor Holles Sch
The (Jun Girls)
TW12 ... 173 D5
Lady Eleanor Holles Sch
The (Senior Girls)
TW12 ... 173 D5

Lady Elizabeth Ho SW14..............133 A2
Ladyfern Ho 19 E3 ....97 C2
Lady Florence Ctyd 15 SE8..............141 C5
Ladygate La HA4......39 A3
Lady Hay KT4........215 D6
Lady Helen Seymour Ho 14 E13..............99 A5
Lady Margaret Prim Sch UB1..............85 B2
Lady Margaret Rd
Kentish Town NW5 ....71 C3
Southall UB1........85 B2
Lady Margaret Sch SW6....... 135 C4 265 A1
Lady Shaw Ct N13 ....16 B1
Ladysmith Ave
Ilford IG2 ....57 C2
Newham E6........ 100 A5
Ladysmith Cl NW7 ....28 A3
Ladysmith Rd
Edmonton N18........34 B5
Eltham SE9 .... 166 C5
Enfield EN1 ....5 D3
Harrow HA3.........24 C1
Newham E16........98 D4
Tottenham N17 ....34 A1
Lady Somerset Rd NW5..............71 B4
LADYWELL 163 C6
Ladywell Cl SE4........141 C1
Ladywell Ho 7 BR5..190 B1
Ladywell Hts SE4 ....163 B5
Ladywell Rd SE13....163 D6
Ladywell Sta SE13 .. 163 D6
Ladywell St 4 E15....98 D6
Ladywell Water Twr SE4..............163 C6
Ladywood Ave BR5...211 C4
Ladywood Rd KT6....214 C6
Lafitte Ho 22 N19 .....49 D2
Lafone Ave TW13 ....150 C2
Lafone Ho 11 SW2 ...160 A4
Lafone St SE1........117 D4 253 C2
Lagado Mews SE16 ..118 D5
Lagonda Ho 11 E3 ....97 C3
Lagonier Ho EC1..... 235 B1
Laidlaw Dr N21 ......16 B6
Laindon Ho 6 N16....51 D1
Laing Dean UB5 ......84 C6
Laing Ho SE5 ....139 A5
Laings Ave CR4 .....180 D1
Laings Cnr CR4 ......180 D2
Lainlock Pl TW3 .....129 D4
Lainson St SW18.....157 C4
Lairdale Cl SE21 .....161 A4
Laird Ho SE5 ....139 A5
Lairs Cl N7 ....72 A2
Lait Ho 3 BR3.......185 D2
Laitwood Rd SW12 ...159 B3
Lakanal 14 SE5 ......139 C4
Lake Ave BR1........187 A4
Lake Bsns Ctr N17....34 A3
Lake Cl
Dagenham RM8........80 D5
6 Wimbledon SW19..............179 B5
Lakedale Ct IG11 ....102 A3
Lakedale Rd SE18....123 C1
Lake Dr WD23 ....8 B2
Lake Farm Ctry Pk UB3 .... 105 C5
Lakefield Cl SE20 ....184 B3
Lakefield Rd N22 ......32 D1
Lake Gdns
Dagenham RM10.......81 C3
Hackbridge SM6 .....219 B5
Richmond TW10.......153 B2
Lakehall Gdns CR7...204 D4
Lakehall Rd CR7 .....204 D4
Lake Ho SE1......... 252 A1
Lake House Rd E11 ...77 A6
Lake Ho 4 SW27......182 D5
Lakehurst Rd KT19 ...215 C3
Lakeland Cl HA3 ....24 B4
Lakeman Ct CR7 .....183 A1
Lakenheath N14 ......15 D6
Laker Ct SW4........138 A3
Lake Rd Croydon CR0..223 B6
Dagenham RM6........58 D5
Wimbledon SW19 ....179 B5
Laker Pl SW15 ....157 A5
Lakeside Ave
Redbridge IG4........55 D5
Thamesmead SE28 .. 124 A5
Lakeside BR3........207 D6
Lakeside Cl
Ruislip HA4 ....39 B5
Sidcup DA15 .... 168 C6
South Norwood SE25.............. 184 A1

Lakeside Complex The SE2.............. 124 D5
Lakeside Cres EN4 ....14 D6
Lakeside Ct N4 ....51 A1
Lakeside WD6 ....10 C6
Lakeside Dr
Acton NW10 ....88 B4
Esher KT10 .... 212 A2
Keston Mark BR2 .. 226 A5
Lakeside Ealing W13 ...87 C1
Enfield EN2 ....3 D1
Finchley N3 ....29 D1
10 Kingston u T KT2 . 176 D3
Lakeside Lo NW4 .....47 A5
Lakeside Rd
Brook Green W14 ... 112 D3
Palmers Green N13....16 B1
Lakeside SM6........219 B4
Lakeside Way HA9 ....66 C4
Lakeside KT19 ....215 C2
Lakes Rd BR2........225 C3
Lakeswood Rd BR5...211 A3
Lake The WD23 ....8 B3
Lakeview Ct E4 ....36 B4
Lake View Ct SW1... 258 D6
Lakeview 23 E3 ......96 D5
Lake View HA8 ....26 B5
Lakeview Rd
Bexley DA16 ....146 B1
West Norwood SE27.............. 182 D5
Lake View Terr N18....33 D6
Lakis Cl NW3 ....70 A4
Laleham Ave NW7 .....11 B1
Laleham Ho E2 ..... 243 C6
Laleham Rd
Catford SE6........ 164 A4
Littleton TW17....... 192 C4
Lalor St SW6 ....135 A3
Lambarde Ave SE9...188 C6
Lambard Ho 4 SE10..............142 A5
Lamb Cl UB5 ....85 A4
Lamb Ct 16 E14 .....119 A6
Lamberhurst Ho 14 SE15..............140 C6
Lamberhurst Rd
Dagenham RM8.......59 B1
West Norwood SE27 . 182 C5
Lambert Ave TW9....132 D2
Lambert Ho
16 Brixton SW9..... 138 C3
19 Crouch End N19....49 D2
Lambert Lo TW8.....109 D1
Lambert Rd
Clapham Pk SW2.....160 B6
Newham E16.........99 B1
North Finchley N12 ....30 B5
Lambert's Pl CR0 ....205 B1
Lambert's Rd KT6....198 B4
Lambert St N1........72 C1
Lambert Way N12.....30 A5
Lambert Wlk HA9.....65 D5
LAMBETH 116 B4
Lambeth Acad SW4. 159 C6
Lambeth Coll (Brixton Ctr) SW2 ....160 B6
Lambeth Coll (Clapham Ctr) SW4 .... 159 C6
Lambeth Coll (Tower Bridge Ctr) SE1....... 117 C5 253 B3
Lambeth Coll (Vauxhall Ctr) SW8 .. 137 D4 269 C2
Lambeth Ct 8 SW18..............157 C6
Lambeth High St SE1........116 B2 260 C4
Lambeth Hill EC4 ... 252 A6
Lambeth Hospl SW9..............138 B2
Lambeth North Sta SE1....... 116 C3 261 A6
Lambeth Palace Rd SE1........116 B3 260 C6
Lambeth Pal* SE1 .... 116 B3 260 C5
Lambeth Pier SE1 .. 260 B5
Lambeth Prospect SE19..............183 B4
Lambeth Rd
Lambeth SE1...... 116 C3 261 B5
Thornton Heath CR0 . 204 D1
Lambeth Twrs SE11 . 261 A5
Lambeth Wlk SE11........116 B2 260 D4
Lambfold Ho N7 ......72 A2
Lamb Ho
28 Camberwell SE5.............. 139 A5
11 Camberwell SE5...139 B4
Greenwich SE10 .... 142 A6
Lamb La E8 ....74 B1
Lamble St NW5 ....71 A4
Lambley Rd RM9......80 B2
Lambolle Pl NW3 .....70 C2

Lambolle Rd NW3.....70 C2
Lambourn Cl
Hanwell W7........ 108 D4
9 Kentish Town NW5..............71 C4
Lambourne Ave SW19..............179 B6
Lambourne Ct 5 IG8..............37 C3
Lambourne Gdns
5 Barking IG11 ......79 D1
Chingford E4 ....19 C2
Enfield EN1 ....5 D3
Lambourne Gr
Deptford SE16...... 118 D1
Kingston u T KT1.... 176 D1
Lambourne Ho NW8 236 D4
Lambourne Pl SE3 ...143 B4
Lambourne Rd
Barking IG11.........79 D1
Ilford IG3 ....79 C6
Leytonstone E11 ......54 A2
Lambourn Ho BR1 ...188 A3
Lambourn Rd SW4 ...137 B2
Lambrook Ho 13 SE15..............140 A4
Lambrook Terr SW6.........135 A4 264 A2
Lamb's Bldgs EC1... 242 C5
Lamb's Cl N9 ....18 A2
Lamb's Conduit Pas WC1.............. 240 C4
Lamb's Conduit St WC1.........94 B3 240 C5
Lambscroft Ave SE9, SE12..............165 D1
Lambs Mdw IG8 ......37 D1
Lamb's Mews N1 ... 234 C5
Lamb's Pas EC1 ....95 B3 242 C5
Lamb St E1.....95 D2 243 C4
Lamb's Terr N9 ....17 B2
Lambs Wlk EN2........5 A3
Lambton Ct 2 N19....50 A1
Lambton Mews 4 N19 ....50 A1
Lambton Pl W11.... 244 D6
Lambton Rd
Finsbury Pk N19 ......50 A1
Wimbledon SW20 ... 178 C2
Lamb Wlk SE1...... 253 A1
Lamerock Rd BR1....186 D6
Lamerton Lo 10 TW9..............132 B4
Lamerton St 8 SE8..141 C6
Lamford Cl N17.......33 B3
Lamington St 3 W6..............112 B2
Lamlash St SE11.... 261 C4
Lamley Ho SE10......141 D5
Lammas Ave CR4 ....181 A1
Lammas Gn SE26 ....162 B1
Lammas Park Gdns W5..............109 C5
Lammas Park Rd W5..............109 D4
Lammas Rd
Homerton E9.........74 D1
Richmond TW10..... 175 C6
Walthamstow E10......53 A1
Lammas Sch The E10..............53 B1
Lammermoor Rd SW12..............159 B4
Lamont Rd Pas SW10.............. 266 C5
Lamont Rd SW10........136 B6 266 C5
Lamorbey Cl DA15 ...167 D2
Lamorna Cl E17.......36 A2
Lamorna Gr HA7......25 D1
Lampard Gr N16......51 D1
Lampern Sq 8 E2 ....96 A4
Lampeter Cl NW9.....45 C3
Lampeter Sq W6.... 264 A5
Lamplighter Cl 34 E1...96 C3
Lampmead Rd SE12 ..142 D1
Lamport Cl SE18.....122 B2
Lampson Ho 6 N19....71 C4
LAMPTON 129 D4
Lampton Ave TW5 ...129 D4
Lampton Ct TW5.....129 D4
Lampton House Cl SW19..............178 D6
Lampton Park Rd TW3..............129 D3
Lampton Rd TW3, TW5..............129 D3
Lampton Sch TW5.. 129 C4
Lanacre Ave NW9.....27 C2
Lanain Ct SE12 ......164 D4
Lanark Cl W5.........87 C2
Lanark Ct UB5 ....63 C3
Lanark Ho 12 SE1 ....118 A1
Lanark Mans
Paddington W9 ..... 236 B6

Lanark Mans *continued*
15 Shepherd's Bush W12.............. 112 C4
Lanark Mews NW8.. 229 B1
Lanark Pl W9.. 92 A3 236 B6
Lanark Rd W9..........92 A4 229 A1
Lanark Sq E14 ....119 D3
Lanata Wlk UB4.......84 D3
Lanbury Rd SE15.....140 D1
Lancashire Ct W1.... 248 D6
Lancaster Ave
Barking IG11....... 101 C6
Croydon CR4 ...... 204 A5
Hadley Wood EN4 ...... 2 B5
Wanstead E18........55 B5
West Norwood SE21, SE27.............. 161 A2
Wimbledon SW19 ... 178 D5
Lancaster Cl
Ashford TW15 ...... 170 A6
Beckenham BR2 .... 208 D5
10 De Beauvoir Town N1 ....73 C1
Grahame Pk NW9 .....27 D3
Kensington W2 ...... 245 C5
Kingston u T KT2 .... 175 D5
New Malden KT4.....200 B2
Stanwell TW19 ..... 148 A5
Tottenham N17 ....34 A3
Lancaster Cotts 1 TW10..............154 A5
Lancaster Ct
Bayswater W2...... 246 B6
1 Belmont SM2 ..... 217 C1
Parsons Green SW6 . 264 D3
Stanwell TW19 ..... 148 A3
Walton-on-T KT12 ....194 B2
West Norwood SE27.............. 160 D2
Lancaster Dr
Canary Wharf E14.............. 120 A5
Maitland Pk NW3 .....70 C2
Lancaster Gate Sta W2........ 114 B6 246 C6
Lancaster Gate W2..........114 A6 246 B6
Lancaster Gdns
Bromley BR1 .... 210 A4
Kingston u T KT2.... 175 D5
West Ealing W13.....109 B4
Wimbledon SW19 ... 179 A5
Lancaster Gr NW3 ....70 C2
Lancaster hall 14 E16..............121 A5
Lancaster Ho
Enfield EN2 ....5 B4
Putney SW15....... 134 C3
Stanmore HA7..........9 A1
Lancaster Ho SW1... 249 A2
Lancaster Ho SW18 ..157 D4
Lancasterian Prim Sch N17 ....33 D2
Lancaster Lo 2 W11..91 A1
Lancaster Mews
Bayswater W2...... 114 A6 246 B6
2 Richmond TW10.. 154 A5
3 Wandsworth SW18.............. 157 D6
Lancaster Pk TW10 ..154 A6
Lancaster Pl
Hounslow TW5 ..... 128 D3
Ilford IG1 ....79 A4
Strand WC2. 116 B6 250 C5
Twickenham TW1.... 153 A4
1 Wimbledon SW19.............. 178 D5
Lancaster Rd
Bowes Pk N11........31 D4
Dudden Hill NW10.....68 A3
Edmonton N18.........33 D5
Enfield EN2 ....5 B4
Finsbury Pk N4 ....50 C2
Harrow HA2 ....41 C4
Higham Hill E17........34 D1
Leytonstone E11 ......76 C6
New Barnet EN4 ......14 B6
Northolt UB5 ....64 A2
Notting Hill W11 ......91 A1
Southall UB1 .... 107 A6
South Norwood SE25.............. 206 A6
Upton E7 ....77 A1
Wimbledon SW19 ... 178 D5
Lancaster Road Ind Est 2 EN4..............14 B6
Lancaster Stables 10 NW3..............70 C2
Lancaster St SE1....... 116 D4 251 D1
Lancaster Terr W2.........114 B6 246 C6
Lancaster Wlk
Hayes UB3...........83 A1

Lancaster Wlk *continued*
Knightsbridge W2...... 114 A5 246 B4
Lancastrian Rd SM6..220 B1
Lancefield Ho SE15 ..140 B2
Lancefield St W10 .....91 B4
Lancell St N16.......73 C6
Lancelot Ave HA0.....65 D4
Lancelot Cres HA0.....65 D4
Lancelot Gdns EN4....15 A4
Lancelot Ho SM5 ....202 C1
Lancelot Pl SW7.......114 D4 247 C1
Lancelot Rd
Welling DA16....... 146 A2
Wembley HA0 ....65 D3
Lance Rd HA1 ....42 A2
Lancer Sq W8 ...... 245 C2
Lancey Cl SE7 ......122 A2
Lanchester Ct W2... 237 C1
Lanchester Rd N6.....48 D4
Lanchester Way SE14..............140 D4
Lancing Gdns N9 .....17 D3
Lancing Rd
Ealing W13 ....109 B6
Feltham TW13...... 149 D2
Ilford IG2 ....57 B2
Thornton Heath CR0 ..204 B2
Lancing St NW1 .... 232 C1
Lancresse Ct N1 ......95 C6
Landale Ct SE10 .....142 A4
Landale Ho 13 SE16 ..118 C3
Landau Ct 11 CR2 ....221 A3
Landcroft Rd SE22 ...161 D5
Landells Rd SE22 ....162 A5
Lander Ct EN5 ....14 A6
Landford Rd SW15 ...134 C2
Landgrove Rd SW19..............179 C5
Landin Ho 1 E14 .....97 C1
Landleys Field 21 N7..71 D3
Landmann Ho 16 SE16..............118 B2
Landmann Way SE14..............118 D1
Landmark Commercial Ctr N18..............33 C4
Landmark Hts E5 .....75 A4
Landon Pl SW1 ..... 257 C6
Landons Cl E14......120 A5
Landon Way TW15 ...170 D4
Landon Wlk 16 E14...119 D6
Landor Ct N16.........73 C3
Landor Ho 7 SE5 ....139 B5
Landor Rd SW9.......138 A2
Landor Wlk 11 W12 ...112 A4
Landra Gdns N21 .....16 D5
Landrake NW1...... 232 B5
Landridge Dr EN1...... 6 B5
Landridge Rd SW6....135 B3
Landrock Rd N8 ....50 B3
Landscape Rd IG8 ....37 B3
Landsdown Cl 6 EN5 .. 2 A1
Landseer Ave E12.....78 C3
Landseer Cl
Edgware HA8.........26 C1
Mitcham SW19 ......180 B2
Landseer Ct
Hayes UB4...........83 B5
10 Upper Holloway N19..............72 A6
Landseer Ho
Battersea SW11 .... 268 B1
16 Northolt UB5 ......84 D5
Paddington NW8..... 236 D6
Westminster SW1.... 259 D3
Landseer Rd
Cheam SM1........ 217 C2
Enfield EN1 ....18 A6
New Malden KT3.....199 B2
Upper Holloway N19...72 A6
Lands' End WD6 ....9 D5
Landstead Rd SE18...145 B5
Landulph Ho SE11 .. 261 B2
Landward Ct W1..... 237 B2
Lane Cl NW2 ....68 B5
Lane Ct SW11.......158 D4
Lane End DA7 ....147 D2
Lane Gdns
Bushey Heath WD23 ....8 C4
Claygate KT10...... 212 D1
Lane Mews E12.......78 B5
Lanercost Cl SW2....160 C2
Lanercost Gdns N14 ..16 A4
Lanercost Rd SW2 ...160 C2
Laneside Ave RM8 .... 59 B2
Laneside
Chislehurst BR7..... 189 A5
Edgware HA8.........27 A5
Lane The
Blackheath Pk SE3.............. 143 A2
St John's Wood NW8...... 92 A5 229 A3
Laneway SW15 ......156 B6
Laney Bldg EC1..... 241 A4

Lanfranc Ct HA1.......6
Lanfranc Rd E3.......9
Lanfrey Pl W14 25
Langbourn Ct E17.....5
Langbourne Ave N6...7
Langbourne Ho 7 SW2..............16
Langbourne Mans N6 7
Langbourne Pl E14 ..1
Langbourne Prim Sch SE21.............. 16
Langbourne Way KT10 2
Langbrook Rd SE3 ...14
Langcroft Cl SM5 2
Langdale Ave CR4....20
Langdale Cl
Camberwell SE17 ... 13
Dagenham RM8........5
Locksbottom BR6.... 22
Mortlake SW14 13
Langdale Cres DA7...14
Langdale Ct
3 Ealing W5.........8
9 Ilford IG1.........7
Ruislip HA4 6
Langdale Dr UB4......8
Langdale Gdns UB6 ...8
Langdale Ho SW1... 25
Langdale NW1...... 23
Langdale Par 8 CR4 20
Langdale Rd
Greenwich SE10 14
Thornton Heath CR7 . 20
Langdale St 25 E1.....9
Langdon Cres E6 10
Langdon Ct
Finsbury EC1....... 23
Harlesden NW10......8
Langdon Dr NW9 4
Langdon Ho 3 E14 ...9
Langdon Park Rd N6..4
Langdon Park Sec Sch E14..............9
Langdon Pk TW11....17
Langdon Pl SW14 13
Langdon Rd
Barking E6......... 10
Bromley BR2 20
Morden SM4 20
Langdon Sch E6.... 10
Langdons Ct UB2 10
Langdon Shaw DA14 18
Langdon Way 18 SE1..............11
Langdon Wlk SM4 ...20
Langford Cl
Shacklewell E8 74
7 South Tottenham N15..............51
St John's Wood NW8. 22
Langford Cres EN4.....2
Langford Ct NW8 ... 22
Langford Gn SE5.....13
Langford Ho 5 SE8 ..14
Langford Pl
Sidcup DA14 168
St John's Wood NW8.......92 A5 22
Langford Prim Sch SW6.............. 135
Langford Rd
Cockfosters EN4 2
4 Sands End SW6 .. 135
Woodford IG8........37
Langfords IG9.........2
Langham Cl 1 N15 ...50
Langham Ct
Hendon NW4.........46
Merton SW20 178
4 Putney SW15.... 156
Ruislip HA4 62
12 Twickenham TW1.............. 153
Langham Dr RM6 58
Langham Gdns
Burnt Oak HA8 27
Ealing W13 109
Richmond TW10..... 175
Southgate N21........16
Wembley HA0 65
Langham Ho SW4....159
Langham House Cl TW10..............175
Langham Ho 3 E11...55
Langham Mans SW5 255
Langham Park Pl BR2 208
Langham Pl
Chiswick W4 133
Fitzrovia W1 . 93 B2 238
Noel Pk N15 50
Langham Rd
Burnt Oak HA8 27

am Rd continued
ngton TW11.....175 B4
Green N15......51 A6
bledon SW20 ... 178 C2
am St
.........93 B2 238 D3
edge Cl N18....33 D4
edge La N18....33 D4
edge Lane Ind Est
.........33 D4
olm Cl SW12...159 D4
olme WD23......8 A3
orn Dr TW2....152 C4
orne Ct 10
..........70 B1
orne Ho 5
.........143 C6
orne Rd RM10 ..81 C1
Ho
h Lambeth
/8.........270 A3
well TW19 .....148 A3
ufnell Pk N19....71 C5
urst Ho 10
1..........137 A3
and Cres HA7...25 D1
and Dr HA5.....23 A3
and Gdns
don CR0........223 B6
t Hampstead
N3.............69 D3
and Ho 10 SE5..139 B5
er Tooting SW17..180 B5
and Mans NW3..69 D3
er Rd NW10.....90 C5
ey Ave
h Cheam KT4,
43.........216 D6
lip HA4........62 B6
biton KT6......198 A1
ey Cres
enham RM9.......80 D1
ware HA8........11 A1
ington UB3.....127 D5
stead E11.......55 C2
ley Ct
h Lambeth
V8..........270 A2
nd WC2........250 A6
Sutton SM2.....218 A2
ley Dr
h Acton W3.....110 D4
stead E11.......55 B2
ley Gdns
nley BR2.......209 C5
enham RM9.......80 D1
thborough BR5...210 D3
ley Gr KT3.....177 C1
ley Ho
Lower Clapton
5.............74 B3
Paddington W2....91 C2
ley La
3........138 A6 270 B6
ley Lawns SM2..218 B1
ley Manor BR3..208 A4
ley Mans SW8...270 B6
ley Park Rd SM1,
..........218 A1
ley Park Sch for
ys BR3........207 D3
ley Park Sch for
ls BR3........208 A3
ley Pk NW7......27 C4
ley Rd
kenham BR3....207 A5
worth TW7.....130 D3
ton SW19......179 C2
biton KT6.....198 A2
st Heath DA16...146 C6
ley Row EN5......1 B4
ley St
2........94 A1 240 A1
ley Way BR4....208 C2
mead Dr WD23....8 B3
mead Ho 34 E3...97 D4
mead St SE27...183 A6
more Ct DA6....146 D2
more Ho 39 E1...96 A1
port Ct KT12....194 C1
port Ho 1
9..........138 D3
ridge Mews
12..........173 B4
ridge 15 NW5....71 A2
royd Rd SW17...158 D2
side Ave SW15..134 A1
side Cres N14...15 D1
St E1...........96 C3
stone Way NW7..28 D3
ston Hughes Cl 5
4...........138 D1
thorn Ct EC2...242 D2
thorne Ct 3
..........186 A6
thorne Ho UB3..105 C2

Langthorne Hospl
E11...........76 B5
Langthorne Lo 30
SW2..........160 C4
Langthorne Rd E11...76 B5
Langthorne St SW6..134 D5
Langton Ave
Oakleigh Pk N20......14 B4
Wallend E6.........100 C4
Langton Cl
WC1.......94 B3 240 D6
Langton Ct SW15....157 B5
Langton Ho
Harrow HA2..........64 C6
Lambeth SE11.......260 D4
5 Streatham SW16..181 C6
Langton Pl SW18....157 C3
Langton Rd
Camberwell SW9....138 D5
Cricklewood NW2.....68 C5
East Molesey KT8...196 A5
Harrow Weald HA3....24 A3
Langton Rise SE22,
SE23..........162 B4
Langton St
SW10.......136 A6 266 B5
Langton Way
Greenwich SE3.....143 A5
South Croydon CR0..221 C4
Langtry Ho BR1.....187 B3
Langtry Pl SW6.....265 B6
Langtry Rd
Northolt UB5........84 D5
Paddington NW8......91 D6
Langtry Wlk
NW8........92 A6 229 A6
Langwood Chase
TW11..........175 C4
Langworth Dr UB4....84 B1
Langworthy HA5......23 C4
Lanherne Ho 7
SW19..........178 D3
Lanhill Rd W9........91 C3
Lanier Rd SE13......164 B5
Lanigan Dr TW3.....151 D6
Lankaster Gdns N2...30 B2
Lankers Dr HA2.......41 B3
Lankton Cl BR3.....186 A2
Lanner Ho 2 SW11..136 C2
Lannock Ct 2
SW17..........180 C4
Lannock Rd UB3.....105 D5
Lannoy Point SW6...264 B4
Lannoy Rd SE9......167 A3
Lanrick Rd E14.......98 C1
Lanridge Rd SE2....124 D3
Lansan Ct E11........76 D6
Lansbury Ave
Barking IG11........80 A1
Dagenham RM6........59 A4
Edmonton N18........33 C5
Feltham TW14.......150 B5
Lansbury Cl NW10....67 A3
Lansbury Ct 4
SE28..........124 B6
Lansbury Dr UB4.....83 D3
Lansbury Gdns 1
E14...........98 B1
Lansbury Ho 5
DA17..........125 B1
Lansbury Lawrence
Prim Sch E14.......97 D1
Lansbury Rd EN3......6 D4
Lansbury Way N18....33 C5
Lanscombe Wlk
SW8..........270 A3
Lansdell Ho 9 SW2..160 C5
Lansdell Rd CR4....181 A1
Lansdown Cl KT12...194 C1
Lansdowne Ave
Orpington BR6.....210 D1
West Heath DA7....146 D5
Lansdowne Cl
Tolworth KT5......214 D6
Twickenham TW1....152 D3
Wimbledon SW20....178 D3
Lansdowne Coll W2..245 C5
Lansdowne Copse 1
KT4...........216 A6
Lansdowne Cres
W11.......113 A6 244 B5
Lansdowne Ct
Redbridge IG5.......56 A6
2 Worcester Pk
KT4...........216 A6
Lansdowne Dr E8.....74 A1
Lansdowne Gdns
SW8.......138 A4 270 A2
Lansdowne Gr NW10..67 C4
Lansdowne Hill
SE27..........160 D1
Lansdowne Ho
19 Belmont SM2....217 D1
Enfield EN2..........4 C3
Notting Hill W11....244 C4
Lansdowne Int Coll Ltd
SW7...........256 B5

Lansdowne La SE7...121 D1
Lansdowne Mews
Greenwich SE7.....121 D1
Notting Hill W11....244 C4
Lansdowne Pl
Borough The SE1....262 D6
Penge SE19.........183 D3
Lansdowne Rd
Chingford E4........19 C2
Croydon CR0........205 B1
Finchley N3.........29 C3
Harrow HA1..........42 C2
Hayes UB8...........83 A1
Hounslow TW3.......129 D2
Ilford IG3..........57 D2
Leytonstone E11.....76 D6
Muswell Hill N10....31 C1
Notting Hill
W11.....113 A6 244 B5
Stanmore HA7........25 C4
Sundridge BR1......187 B3
Tottenham N17.......34 A2
Walthamstow E17.....53 C3
Wanstead E18........55 A6
West Ewell KT19....215 B1
Wimbledon SW19,
SW20..........178 C3
Lansdowne Rise
W11.......113 A6 244 B5
Lansdowne Row W1..248 D4
Lansdowne Sch
SW9...........138 B2
Lansdowne Terr
WC1...........240 B5
Lansdowne Way SW4,
SW8.......138 A4 270 B1
Lansdowne Wlk
W11.......113 B5 244 C4
Lansdowne Wood Cl 11
SE27..........160 D1
Lansdowne Workshops
SE7...........121 D1
Lansdown Ho 28
SE5...........139 A3
Lansdown Rd
Sidcup DA14.......168 B1
Upton E7............77 C1
Lansfield Ave N18....34 A6
Lanson Ho HA8........26 C4
Lantern Cl
Orpington BR6.....226 D4
Putney SW15.......134 A1
Wembley HA0.........65 D3
Lantern Ct
Southgate N14.......15 D3
4 Wimbledon
SW20..........178 D2
Lantern Ho
Millwall E14......119 C4
Woolwich SE18.....122 C1
Lanterns Ct E14....119 C3
Lanterns The N12....29 D4
Lantern Way UB7....104 B4
Lant Ho SE1........252 A1
Lantry Ct 1 W3.....110 D5
Lant St SE1...117 A4 252 B1
Lanvanor Rd SE15...140 C3
Lanyard Ho 4 SE8...119 B2
Lapford Cl W9........91 B3
Lapponum Wlk UB4....84 D2
Lapsang SE1........253 D3
Lapse Wood Wlk
SE22..........162 B3
Lapstone Gdns HA3...43 C3
Lapwing Ct
Grahame Pk NW9.....27 C1
Tolworth KT6......214 C5
Lapwing Terr E7......77 D3
Lapwing Twr 31
SE8...........141 B6
Lapwing Way UB4.....84 D1
Lapworth Ct W2.......91 D2
Lapworth 2 N11......31 B6
Lara Cl
Chessington KT9....214 A1
Lewisham SE13.....164 A5
Lara Lo SM1........217 C3
Larbert Rd SW16....181 C3
Larch Ave W3.......111 C5
Larch Cl
Balham SW12.......159 B2
Colney Hatch N11....31 A3
15 Deptford SE8....141 B6
Newham E13..........99 C3
10 Upper Holloway
N19............71 C6
Larch Cres
Hayes UB4...........84 D2
West Ewell KT19....214 D2
Larch Ct 41 W2.......91 C2
Larch Dene BR6.....226 C6
Larches Ave SW14...133 B1
Larches The
Edmonton N13........17 A1
Hillingdon UB10.....82 D5
Larchfield Ho 2 N5...73 A3
Larch Gn NW9........27 C2

Larch Gr DA15.......167 D3
Larch Ho Hayes UB4...84 C2
23 Rotherhithe
SE16..........118 C4
Larchmont HA4........39 B2
Larchmore Ct N19.....72 A6
Larch Rd
Cricklewood NW2.....68 C4
Leyton E10...........75 C6
Larch Tree Way
CR0...........223 C5
Larchvale Ct 20
SM2...........217 D1
Larch Way BR2......210 C2
Larchwood Rd SE9...166 D2
Larcombe Cl CR0....221 D4
Larcom St
SE17.......117 A2 262 B3
Larden Rd W3.......111 C4
La Retraite RC Girls Sch
SW12..........159 C4
Largewood Ave KT6..214 C6
Larissa St SE17....262 D3
Larix Ct NW10........90 A6
Larkbere Rd SE26....185 A6
Larken Cl WD23........8 A3
Larken Dr WD23........8 A3
Larkfield Ave HA3....43 B6
Larkfield Cl BR2....225 A6
Larkfield Rd
Longlands DA14....167 D1
Richmond TW9......132 A1
Larkhall La
SW4........138 A4 270 A1
Lark Hall Prim Sch
SW4...........137 D3
Larkhall Rise SW4...137 D3
Larkham Cl TW13....149 C1
Lark Row E2..........96 C6
Larksfield Gr EN1.....6 B4
Larks Gr IG11.........79 C1
Larkshall Bsns Ctr
E4.............20 B2
Larkshall Cres E4....36 A6
Larkshall Ct E4......36 A5
Larkshall Rd E4......36 B6
Larkspur Cl
Kingsbury NW9.......44 D4
4 Newham E6.......100 A2
Ruislip HA4..........39 A2
Tottenham N17........33 B3
Larkspur Ct SM6....219 B1
Larkspur Gr HA8......27 A6
Larkspur Way KT19..215 A3
Larkswood Ct E4.....36 B5
Larkswood Prim Sch
E4.............35 D6
Larkswood Rd E4.....35 D6
Larkswood Rise HA5..40 C5
Lark Way SM5.......202 C2
Larkway Cl NW9......45 B5
Larmenier & Sacred
Heart RC Prim Sch
W6............112 D2
Larnaca Ho SE1.....263 C6
Larnach Rd W6......134 D6
Larne Rd HA4.........39 D2
Larpent Ave SW15...156 C6
Larwood Cl UB6......64 B3
La Saint Union RC Sec
Sch NW5........71 A5
Lascelles Ave HA1...42 B2
Lascelles Cl E11.....76 B6
Lascelles Ho NW1...237 B5
Lascott's Rd N22.....32 B4
Laseron Ho 1 N15....51 D5
Lashford Ho HA8......27 A4
Lassa Rd SE9.......166 B6
Lassell St SE10....120 B1
Lasseter Pl SE3....142 D6
Latchett Rd E18......37 B2
Latchingdon Ct E17...52 D5
Latchmere Cl KT2,
TW10..........176 A5
Latchmere Jun & Inf
Schs KT2........176 B4
Latchmere La KT2,
TW10..........176 B5
Latchmere Rd
Battersea SW11....136 D3
Kingston u T KT2...176 B4
Latchmere St 5
SW11..........136 D3
Lateward Rd TW8....131 D6
Latham Cl
Newham E6.........100 A1
6 Twickenham
TW1...........153 A4
Latham Ct
3 Bowes Pk N11.....32 A4
7 Northolt UB5.....84 D4
Latham Ho
Stepney E1..........96 D1
18 Walthamstow E17..53 D6
Latham Rd
Bexleyheath DA6....169 C6
Twickenham TW1....152 D4

Latham's Way CR0...220 B6
Lathkill Cl EN1......18 A4
Lathkill Ct BR3.....185 B2
Lathom Jun Sch E6...78 A1
Lathom Rd E6.........78 B1
Lathwood Ho 6
SE26..........184 B5
Latimer Ave E6......100 B6
Latimer Cl
North Cheam KT4....216 B4
Pinner Green HA5.....22 C2
Latimer Gdns HA5....22 C2
Latimer Ho
11 Homerton E9.....74 D2
Notting Hill W11....244 D5
Latimer Ind Est 1
NW10...........90 C1
Latimer Pl W10.......90 C1
Latimer Rd Barnet EN5..1 D2
1 Croydon CR0.....220 D5
Forest Gate E7.......77 B4
North Kensington
W10............90 C1
South Tottenham N15..51 C3
Teddington TW11....174 D5
Wimbledon SW19....179 D4
Latimer Road Sta
W10...........112 D6
Latimer SE17.......263 A1
Latitude Ho NW1....231 C5
Latona Rd SE15.....140 A6
La Tourne Gdns
BR6...........227 A5
Lattimer Pl W4.....133 C6
Latton Cl KT12.....195 A2
Latvia Ct SE17.....262 B1
Latymer All Saints CE
Prim Sch N9........17 D2
Latymer Ct W6......112 D2
Latymer Rd N9........17 D3
Latymer Sch The N9..17 C2
Latymer Upper Sch
W6............112 A1
Latymer Way N9......17 C2
Laubin Cl TW1......131 B1
Lauder Cl UB5.......84 D5
Lauder Ct N14.......16 A4
Lauderdale Dr
TW10..........153 D1
Lauderdale Mans
W9.............91 D4
Lauderdale Rd W9....91 D4
Lauderdale Twr EC2..242 A4
Laud St Croydon CR0..221 A5
Vauxhall
SE11......116 B1 260 C2
Laughton Ho 11
SW2...........160 C5
Laughton Rd UB5.....84 D6
Launcelot Prim Sch
BR1...........187 A6
Launcelot Rd BR1,
SE12..........187 A6
Launcelot St SE1...251 A1
Launceston Ct CR7...204 C3
Launceston Gdns
UB6............65 C1
Launceston Pl
W8........114 A3 256 A5
Launceston Rd UB6...87 C6
Launch St E14......120 A3
Laundress La N16....74 A5
Laundry La 7 N1.....73 A1
Laundry Mews
SE23..........162 D4
Laundry Rd
W6........135 A6 264 A5
Launton Dr DA6.....146 D1
Laura Cl Enfield EN1..17 C6
Wanstead E11........55 C4
Laura Ct HA2.........24 A1
Lauradale Rd N2......48 D5
Laura Pl E5..........74 C4
Laurel Ave TW1.....152 D3
Laurel Bank Gdns 3
SW6...........135 B3
Laurel Bank Rd EN2....5 B4
Laurel Cl
Sidcup DA14.......168 A1
8 Upper Holloway
N19............71 C6
Upper Tooting
SW17..........180 C5
Laurel Cres CR0....223 C5
Laurel Ct Dalston E8..73 D1
2 Putney SW15....156 D6
9 Rotherhithe
SE16..........119 A5
South Norwood
SE25..........205 C4
8 Wembley HA0.....88 A5
Laurel Dr N21.......16 C4
Laurel Gdns
Bromley BR1.......210 A5
Chingford E4........19 D4
Ealing W7.........108 C5
Edgware NW7........11 B1

Laurel Gdns continued
Hounslow TW4.....129 A1
Laurel Gr
Forest Hill SE26....185 A6
Penge SE20........184 C3
Laurel Ho
Brentford W5......109 C2
9 Deptford SE8....141 B6
5 Hamstead NW3.....69 D2
Morden SM4........201 D4
Laurel La UB7.......104 A2
Laurel Manor SM2...218 A1
Laurel Mead Ct 8
E18............37 A2
Laurel Pk HA3........24 D3
Laurel Rd
Barnes SW13......134 A3
Teddington TW12...174 B5
Wimbledon SW20....178 B2
Laurels The
8 Belvedere
DA17..........125 C1
2 Buckhurst Hill IG9..21 C3
Bushey WD23..........8 C2
Finchley N3..........29 D4
Shortlands BR2....209 A5
9 Sundridge BR1...187 B2
Laurel St E8.........73 D2
Laurel View N12......13 D1
Laurel Way
Snaresbrook E18.....54 D5
Woodside Pk N20.....13 C1
Laurence Ct E10.....53 D2
Laurence Mews 12
W12...........112 A4
Laurence Pountney Hill
EC4...........252 C6
Laurence Pountney La
EC4...........252 D6
Laurie Gr SE14.....141 A4
Laurie Ho
Newington SE1.....261 D5
Notting Hill
W8........113 C5 245 A3
Laurie Rd W7.........86 C2
Laurier Rd
Croydon CR0.......205 D2
Dartmouth Pk NW5....71 B5
Laurimel Cl HA7......25 B4
Laurino Pl WD23.......8 A2
Lauriston Apartments
6 N17...........51 D6
Lauriston Ho 6 E9....74 D1
Lauriston Lo NW6....69 B2
Lauriston Rd
Homerton E9.........74 D1
Wimbledon SW19....178 D4
Lauriston Sch E9....96 D6
Lausanne Rd
Hornsey N8..........50 C5
St Johns SE15.....140 C4
Lavenham Ho E17.....35 D2
Lavell St N16........73 B4
Lavender Ave
Mitcham CR4.......180 D2
North Cheam KT4,
SM3...........216 C5
Welsh Harp NW9......45 A1
Lavender Cl
Bromley Comm
BR2...........210 A3
South Kensington
SW3...........266 D5
Wallington SM5.....219 B4
Lavender Ct
Colney Hatch N12....30 C4
East Molesey KT8...195 D6
Edgware HA8.........27 A5
Feltham TW14.......150 B5
South Lambeth SW4..270 B1
Sutton SM2........218 A1
Lavender Gdns
Clapham SW11.....136 D1
Enfield EN2..........4 D4
Stanmore HA3........24 C4
Lavender Gr
Dalston E8..........74 A1
Mitcham CR4.......180 C2
Lavender Hill
Clapham SW11.....137 A2
Enfield EN2..........4 D4
Lavender Ho
8 Richmond
TW9...........132 D4
14 Rotherhithe
SE16..........118 D5
Lavender Pl IG1......78 D3
Lavender Prim Sch
EN2.............5 C5
Lavender Rd
Battersea SW11....136 B2
Enfield EN2..........5 B4
Hillingdon UB8......82 B2
Rotherhithe SE16...119 A5

Lavender Rd *continued*
Sutton SM1 ... 218 B4
Thornton Heath CR0 ... 204 B3
Wallington SM5 ... 219 A4
West Ewell KT19 ... 214 D2
Lavender Rise UB7 ... 104 C4
Lavender St E15 ... 76 C2
Lavender Sweep SW11 ... 136 D1
Lavender Terr 12 SW11 ... 136 C2
Lavender Vale SM6 ... 219 D2
Lavender Way CR0 ... 206 D3
Lavender Wlk SW11 ... 136 D1
Lavendon Ho NW8 ... 237 B6
Lavengro Rd SE27 ... 161 A2
Lavenham Rd SW18 ... 157 C3
Lavernock Rd DA7 ... 147 C3
Lavers Rd N16 ... 73 C5
Laverstoke Gdns SW15 ... 156 A4
Laverton Mews SW5 255 D3
Laverton Pl SW5 ... 255 D3
Lavidge Rd SE9 ... 166 B2
Lavina Gr N1 ... 233 C4
Lavington Cl E9 ... 75 B2
Lavington Rd
Ealing W13 ... 109 B5
Wallington CR0 ... 220 B4
Lavington St SE1 ... 116 D5 251 D3
Lavinia Ct BR1 ... 186 C3
Lavisham Ho BR1 ... 187 B5
Lawdale Jun Sch E2 ... 96 A4
Lawdon Gdns CR0 ... 220 D4
Lawford Rd
Chiswick W4 ... 133 A5
De Beauvoir Town N1 ... 73 C1
Kentish Town NW5 ... 71 C2
Lawfords Wharf 18 NW1 ... 71 C1
Law Ho IG11 ... 102 A5
Lawless Ho 5 E14 ... 120 A6
Lawless St 12 E14 ... 119 D6
Lawley Ho 11 TW1 ... 153 D5
Lawley Rd N14 ... 15 B4
Lawley St E5 ... 74 C4
Lawman Ct 2 TW9 ... 132 B4
Lawn Cl Edmonton N9 ... 17 D4
Kingston u T KT3 ... 177 C1
Ruislip HA4 ... 61 D5
Sundridge BR1 ... 187 B3
Lawn Cres TW9 ... 132 C3
Lawn Farm Gr RM6 ... 59 A5
Lawnfield Ct NW6 ... 68 D1
Lawn Gdns W7 ... 108 C5
Lawn House Cl E14 ... 120 A4
Lawn La SW8 ... 138 B6 270 C6
Lawn Mans EN5 ... 1 B1
Lawn Rd
Beckenham BR3 ... 185 B3
Maitland Pk NW3 ... 70 D3
Lawns Ct HA9 ... 66 C6
Lawnside SE3 ... 142 D1
Lawns The
Belmont SM2 ... 217 A1
Blackheath SE3 ... 142 D2
Chingford E4 ... 35 C5
Harrow HA5 ... 23 D3
Sidcup DA14 ... 190 B6
South Norwood SE19 ... 183 B2
Stoke Newington N16 ... 73 C3
1 Wimbledon SW19 ... 179 B5
Lawn Terr SE3 ... 142 C2
Lawn The UB2 ... 107 C1
Lawn Vale HA5 ... 23 A1
Lawrence Ave
Edmonton N13 ... 32 D6
Higham Hill E17 ... 34 D2
Little Ilford E12 ... 78 C4
Mill Hill NW7 ... 27 D6
New Malden KT3 ... 199 C2
Stonebridge NW10 ... 89 B6
Lawrence Bldgs 1 N16 ... 73 D5
Lawrence Camp Cl N20 ... 14 B1
Lawrence Cl Bow E3 ... 97 C5
6 Shepherd's Bush W12 ... 112 B6
West Green N15 ... 51 C5
Lawrence Cres
Dagenham RM10 ... 81 D5
Edgware HA8 ... 26 C1
Lawrence Ct
Hornsey N10 ... 49 C6
Mill Hill NW7 ... 27 C5
4 South Acton W3 ... 111 A3
Stoke Newington N16 ... 73 D5
5 Woodford IG8 ... 37 C4

Lawrence Dr UB10 ... 61 A4
Lawrence Est TW4 ... 128 C1
Lawrence Gdns NW7 ... 11 D1
Lawrence Hall E13 ... 99 B3
Lawrence Hill E4 ... 19 C2
Lawrence Ho
Bowes Pk N22 ... 32 B4
20 Camden Town NW1 ... 71 B1
Westminster SW1 ... 259 D3
Lawrence La EC2 ... 242 B2
Lawrence Mans SW3 ... 267 A5
Lawrence Pl N1 ... 233 B6
Lawrence Rd
Coney Hall BR4 ... 225 A4
Ealing W5 ... 109 D2
Edmonton N18 ... 34 B6
Erith DA8 ... 147 D5
Hampton TW12 ... 173 B3
Hillingdon UB4 ... 83 A5
Hounslow TW4 ... 128 C1
Pinner HA5 ... 40 D4
Richmond TW10 ... 175 C6
South Norwood SE25 ... 205 D5
Tottenham N15 ... 51 C5
Upton Pk E6 ... 100 A6
West Ham E13 ... 99 B6
Lawrence St
Canning Town E16 ... 98 D2
Chelsea SW3 ... 136 C6 267 A5
Mill Hill NW7 ... 27 D6
Lawrence Trad Est SE10 ... 120 C2
Lawrence Univ SW7 256 B3
Lawrence Way NW10 ... 67 B5
Lawrence Weaver Cl SM4 ... 201 C3
Lawrence Yd N15 ... 51 C5
Lawrie Ct HA3 ... 24 D3
Lawrie Park Ave SE26 ... 184 B5
Lawrie Park Cres SE26 ... 184 B5
Lawrie Park Gdns SE26 ... 184 B5
Lawrie Park Rd SE26 ... 184 C5
Laws Cl SE25 ... 205 B5
Lawson Cl Ilford IG1 ... 79 B3
Newham E16 ... 99 C2
Wimbledon SW19 ... 156 D1
Lawson Ct
1 Finsbury Pk N4 ... 50 B1
13 Surbiton KT6 ... 197 D2
Lawson Gdns HA5 ... 40 B6
Lawson Ho
17 Shepherd's Bush W12 ... 112 B6
1 Woolwich SE18 ... 144 C6
Lawson Rd Enfield EN3 ... 6 C4
Southall UB1 ... 85 C3
Law St SE1 ... 117 B3 262 D6
Lawton Rd Barnet EN4 ... 2 B2
Bow E3 ... 97 A4
Leytonstone E10 ... 54 A1
Laxcon Cl NW10 ... 67 B3
Laxey Rd BR6 ... 227 D2
Laxfield Ct E8 ... 96 A6
Laxley Cl SE5 ... 138 D5
Laxmi Ct N3 ... 29 B2
Laxton Ct CR7 ... 205 A5
Laxton Path 1 SE4 ... 140 D1
Laxton Pl NW1 ... 238 D6
Layard Rd Enfield EN1 ... 5 D4
Rotherhithe SE16 ... 118 B2
South Norwood CR7 ... 183 B1
Layard Sq SE16 ... 118 B2
Laybourne Ho 18 E14 ... 119 C4
Laycock Prim Sch N1 ... 72 D2
Laycock St N1 ... 72 C2
Layer Gdns W3 ... 110 C6
Layfield Cl NW4 ... 46 B2
Layfield Cres NW4 ... 46 B2
Layfield Ho 1 SE10 ... 121 A1
Layfield Rd NW4 ... 46 B2
Laymarsh Cl DA17 ... 125 B3
Laymead Cl UB5 ... 63 A2
Laystall Ct EC1 ... 241 A5
Laystall St EC1 ... 241 A5
Layton Cres CR0 ... 220 D3
Layton Ct TW8 ... 109 D1
Layton Pl TW9 ... 132 C4
Layton Rd
Brentford TW8 ... 109 D1
Hounslow TW3 ... 129 D1
Layton's La TW16 ... 171 D1
Layzell Wlk SE9 ... 165 D3
Lazar Wlk 2 N7 ... 72 B6
Leabank Cl HA1 ... 64 C5
Leabank Sq E9 ... 75 C2
Leabank View N15 ... 52 A3
Leabourne Rd N16 ... 52 A2

LEA BRIDGE ... 74 D5
Lea Bridge Rd E10 ... 53 C2
Lea Cl TW2 ... 151 B4
Lea Cotts 10 CR4 ... 181 A1
Lea Cres HA4 ... 61 D4
Leacroft Ave SW12 ... 158 D4
Leacroft Cl
Southgate N21 ... 16 D2
3 Yiewsley UB7 ... 104 A6
Lea Ct
3 Bedford Pk W12 ... 111 C4
1 Chingford E4 ... 20 A2
3 Hillingdon UB10 ... 82 D3
2 Newham E13 ... 99 A4
Leadale Ave E4 ... 19 C2
Leadale Rd N16 ... 52 A3
Leadbeaters Cl 8 N11 ... 30 D5
Leadbetter Ct 12 NW10 ... 67 B1
Leadenhall Mkt EC3 ... 243 A1
Leadenhall Pl EC3 ... 243 A1
Leadenhall St EC3 ... 95 C1 243 A1
Leadenham Ct 15 E3 ... 97 C3
Leader Ave E12 ... 78 C3
Leadings The HA9 ... 67 A5
Leaf Cl KT7, KT8 ... 196 C4
Leaf Gr SE27 ... 182 C5
Leaf Ho Barnet EN5 ... 1 D1
9 Harrow HA1 ... 42 D4
Leafield Cl SW16 ... 182 D4
Leafield La DA14 ... 169 B1
Leafield Rd
Merton SW19, SW20 ... 201 B6
Sutton SM1 ... 217 C6
Leafy Gr BR2 ... 225 C3
Leafy Oak Rd SE12 ... 165 C1
Leafy Way CR0 ... 221 D6
Lea Gdns HA9 ... 66 B4
Leagrave St E5 ... 74 C5
Lea Hall Gdns E10 ... 53 C1
Lea Hall Rd E10 ... 53 C1
Lea Ho
2 Edmonton N9 ... 18 A1
Lisson Gr NW8 ... 237 A5
Leaholme Waye HA4 ... 39 A3
Lea Ho E5 ... 52 C1
Leahurst Rd SE13 ... 164 B6
Lea Int E9 ... 75 C3
Leake St
Lambeth SE1 ... 251 A1
South Bank SE1 ... 116 B4 250 D2
Lealand Rd N15 ... 51 D3
Leamington Ave
Bromley BR1 ... 187 C5
Farnborough BR6 ... 227 C4
Merton SM4 ... 201 B5
Walthamstow E17 ... 53 C4
Leamington Cl
Bromley BR1 ... 187 C5
Hounslow TW3 ... 152 A6
Plashet E12 ... 78 A3
Leamington Cres HA2 ... 63 B5
Leamington Ct
4 Forest Hill SE26 ... 162 A1
North Acton W3 ... 89 B2
Leamington Gdns IG3 ... 79 D6
Leamington Ho
Edgware HA8 ... 26 B5
4 Kensal Town W11 ... 91 B2
Leamington Pk W3 ... 89 B2
Leamington Pl UB4 ... 83 D3
Leamington Rd UB2 ... 106 D2
Leamington Rd Villas W11 ... 91 B2
Leamington Villas SE13 ... 164 C6
Leamore St W6 ... 112 C2
Leamouth Rd
Newham E6 ... 100 A2
South Bromley E14 ... 98 B1
Leander Ct
11 Edgware NW9 ... 27 C2
27 Hackney E9 ... 74 C1
St Johns SE8 ... 141 C4
5 Surbiton KT6 ... 197 D2
Leander Rd
Northolt UB5 ... 85 C5
Thornton Heath CR7 ... 204 B5
Tulse Hill SW2 ... 160 C5
Lea Park Trad Est E10 ... 53 B1
Lea Rd
2 Beckenham BR3 ... 185 C1
Enfield EN2 ... 5 B4
Southall UB2 ... 107 A2
Learner Dr HA2 ... 63 C6
Learoyd Gdns E6 ... 122 C6

Leary Ho SE11 ... 260 D1
Leas Cl KT9 ... 214 B1
Leas Dale SE9 ... 166 C1
Leas Gn BR7 ... 189 D4
Leaside Ave N10 ... 49 A5
Leaside Bsns Ctr EN3 ... 7 B3
Leaside Ct UB10 ... 82 D4
Leaside Ho 4 E5 ... 52 B1
Leaside Mans N10 ... 49 A6
Leaside Rd E5 ... 52 C1
Leasowes Rd E10 ... 53 C1
Lea Sq 22 E3 ... 97 B6
Leas The SE18 ... 144 D4
Leatherbottle Gn DA18 ... 125 B3
Leather Cl CR4 ... 181 A1
Leatherdale St
32 Bethnal Green E1 ... 96 C3
19 Globe Town E1 ... 96 D4
Leather Gdns E15 ... 98 C6
Leatherhead Cl N16 ... 51 D1
Leatherhead Rd KT9 ... 213 D1
Leather La EC1 ... 94 C2 241 B4
Leathermarket Ct SE1 ... 253 A1
Leathermarket St SE1 ... 117 C4 253 A1
Leather Rd SE16 ... 118 D2
Leathersellers Cl 5 EN5 ... 1 A2
Leathsale Rd HA2 ... 63 D5
Leathwaite Rd SW11 ... 158 D6
Leathwell Rd SE8 ... 141 D3
Lea Valley Prim Sch N17 ... 34 A3
Lea Valley Rd EN3 ... 19 B5
Lea Valley Technopark N17 ... 52 A6
Lea Valley Trad Est N18 ... 34 D5
Leaveland Cl BR3 ... 207 C5
Leaver Gdns UB6 ... 86 C5
Leavesden Rd HA7 ... 25 A4
Lea View Ho E5 ... 52 B1
Lebanon Ave TW13 ... 172 D5
Lebanon Ct 10 TW1 ... 153 B4
Lebanon Gdns SW18 ... 157 C5
Lebanon Park Mans TW1 ... 153 B4
Lebanon Pk TW1 ... 153 B4
Lebanon Rd
Croydon CR0 ... 205 C1
Wandsworth SW18 ... 157 C6
Lebanon Road Sta CR0 ... 221 C6
Lebrun Sq SE3 ... 143 B2
Lebus Ho NW8 ... 230 A3
Le Chateau CR0 ... 221 B5
Lechmere App IG8 ... 37 D1
Lechmere Ave IG8 ... 37 D1
Lechmere Rd NW2 ... 68 B2
Leckford Rd SW18 ... 158 A3
Leckhampton Pl 23 SW2 ... 160 C4
Leckwith Ave DA7 ... 147 A6
Lecky Ho NW2 ... 68 B4
Lecky St SW7 ... 114 B1 256 C2
Leclair Ho SE3 ... 143 B2
L'Ecole des Petits Sch SW6 ... 135 D3
Leconfield Ave SW13, SW15 ... 133 D2
Leconfield Ho SE5 ... 139 C2
Leconfield Rd N5 ... 73 B4
Lector Ct EC1 ... 241 B5
Leda Ave EN3 ... 6 D5
Leda Ct 9 SW9 ... 138 C5
Ledalle Ho NW2 ... 68 B5
Ledam Bldg EC1 ... 241 A4
Leda Rd SE18 ... 122 B3
Ledbury Ho 12 SE22 ... 139 C2
Ledbury Mews N W11 ... 91 C1
Ledbury Mews W W11 ... 245 A6
Ledbury Pl 10 CR0 ... 221 A4
Ledbury Rd
Croydon CR0 ... 221 B4
Kensington W11 ... 91 C1
Ledbury St SE15 ... 140 A5
Ledo Ho 1 N16 ... 73 B4
Ledrington Rd SE19 ... 184 A4
Ledway Dr HA9 ... 44 B2
LEE ... 164 D5
Lee Ave RM6 ... 59 A3
Leechcroft Ave DA15 ... 167 D6
Leechcroft Rd SM6 ... 219 A5
Lee Church St SE13 ... 142 C1
Lee Cl Higham Hill E17 ... 34 D2
New Barnet EN5 ... 2 A1

Lee Conservancy Rd E9 ... 75 B3
Leecroft Rd EN5 ... 1 A1
Lee Ct SE13 ... 142 B1
Leeds Ct
7 Carshalton SM5 ... 218 D5
Catford SE6 ... 163 D1
Clerkenwell EC1 ... 241 C6
Leeds Rd IG1 ... 57 B1
Leeds St N18 ... 34 A5
Leegate SE12 ... 164 D6
Lee Green SE12 ... 142 D1
Lee High Rd SE12, SE13 ... 142 C1
Lee Ho
3 Kentish Town N19 ... 71 D3
Wimbledon SW19 ... 179 D4
Leeke St WC1 ... 94 B4 233 C2
Leeland Mans 15 W13 ... 109 A5
Leeland Rd W13 ... 109 A5
Leeland Terr W13 ... 109 A5
Leeland Way NW10 ... 67 D4
Lee Manor Sch SE13 ... 164 C5
Lee Mews BR3 ... 207 A6
Lee Park Way N9, N18 ... 19 A1
Lee Pk SE3 ... 142 D2
Leerdam Dr E14 ... 120 A3
Lee Rd Enfield EN1 ... 18 A5
Lewisham SE3 ... 142 D1
Merton SW19 ... 179 D2
Mill Hill NW7 ... 28 D3
Wembley UB6 ... 87 C6
Lees Ct W1 ... 248 A6
Lees Ho SE17 ... 262 D1
Leeside EN5 ... 13 A5
Leeside Cres NW11 ... 47 C3
Leeside Ind Est N17 ... 34 B3
Leeside Rd N17 ... 34 B4
Leeside Trad Est N17 ... 34 C3
Leeside Works N17 ... 34 C3
Leeson Ho 7 TW1 ... 153 B4
Leeson Rd 12 SE24 ... 138 C1
Leesons Hill BR5, BR7 ... 211 D6
Leesons Way BR5 ... 189 D1
Lees Par UB10 ... 82 D3
Lees Pl W1 ... 115 A6 248 A6
Lees Rd UB8 ... 82 D3
Lee Sta SE12 ... 165 A5
Lee St E8 ... 95 D6
Lees The CR0 ... 223 B6
Leet Ct N16 ... 73 B4
Lee Terr SE3 ... 142 C2
Lee Valley Country Pk EN3 ... 7 C4
Lee Valley L Ctr N9 ... 19 A3
Lee Valley Riding Ctr E10 ... 52 D1
Lee Valley Sp Ctr E10 ... 75 D4
Leeve Ho 7 W9 ... 91 B4
Leeview Ct 7 E4 ... 20 A3
Lee View EN2 ... 4 D4
Leeward Ct 3 E1 ... 118 A5
Leeward Gdns SW19 ... 179 B5
Leeway Cl HA5 ... 23 B3
Leeway SE8 ... 119 B1
Leewood Cl SE12 ... 165 A5
Lefevre Wlk E3 ... 97 C6
Leffern Rd W12 ... 112 A4
Leff Ho 9 NW6 ... 69 A1
Lefroy Ho SE1 ... 252 A1
Lefroy Rd W12 ... 111 D4
Legard Rd N5 ... 72 D5
Legat Ct N4 ... 51 A4
Legatt Rd SE9 ... 165 D6
Leggatt Rd E15 ... 98 A5
Legge St SE13 ... 164 A6
Leghorn Rd
Plumstead SE18 ... 123 B1
Willesden Green NW10 ... 90 A5
Legion Cl N1 ... 72 C1
Legion Ct SM4 ... 201 C3
Legion Rd UB6 ... 86 A5
Legion Terr E3 ... 97 C6
Legion Way N12 ... 30 C3
Legrace Ave TW4, TW5 ... 128 D3
Leicester Ave CR4 ... 204 A5
Leicester Cl KT4 ... 216 C4
Leicester Ct
46 Paddington W2 ... 91 C2
St James WC2 ... 249 D6
5 Twickenham TW1 ... 153 D5
Leicester Gdns IG3 ... 57 C2
Leicester Ho
4 Brixton SW9 ... 138 D2
Carshalton SM5 ... 218 C5

Leicester Ho *continued*
5 Putney SW15 ... 15
2 Thames Ditton KT7 ... 19
Leicester Mews N2 ... 4
Leicester Pl WC2 ... 24
Leicester Rd
Barnet EN5 ...
Croydon CR0 ... 20
East Finchley N2 ... 4
Stonebridge NW10 ... 6
Wanstead E11 ... 5
Leicester Square Sta WC2 ... 115 D6 24
Leicester Sq* WC2 ... 115 D6 24
Leicester St WC2 ... 24
Leigham Ave SW16 ... 16
Leigham Cl
Streatham SW16 ... 18
9 Wallington SM6 ... 21
Leigham Court Rd SW16 ... 18
Leigham Dr TW7 ... 13
Leigham Hall Par 2 SW16 ... 16
Leigham Hall 3 SW16 ... 16
Leigham Vale SE27, SW16 SW2 ... 16
Leigh Ave IG4 ... 5
Leigh Cl KT3 ... 19
Leigh Close Ind Est KT3 ... 19
Leigh Cres CR0 ... 22
Leigh Ct Harrow HA2 ... 4
22 Tulse Hill SW2 ... 16
3 Woodford E18 ... 3
Leighfield Ho 5 N4 ... 5
Leigh Gdns NW10 ... 9
Leigh Ho
4 Kingston u T KT2 ... 17
9 Putney SW15 ... 15
Leigh Hunt Dr N14 ... 1
Leigh Orchard Cl SW16 ... 16
Leigh Pl
Feltham TW13 ... 15
Holborn EC1 ... 24
Welling DA16 ... 7
Leigh Rd Highbury N5 ... 7
Isleworth TW3 ... 13
Leytonstone E10 ... 5
Wallend E6 ... 7
Leigh St WC1 ... 94 A4 23
Leigh The KT2 ... 17
Leighton Ave
Little Ilford E12 ... 7
Pinner HA5 ... 4
Leighton Cl HA8 ... 2
Leighton Cres NW5 ... 7
Leighton Ct NW7 ... 2
Leighton Gdns
Thornton Heath CR0 ... 20
Willesden Green NW10 ... 9
Leighton Gr NW5 ... 7
Leighton Ho 7 KT6 ... 19
Leighton House (Art Gall & Mus)* W14 ... 25
Leighton Pl NW5 ... 7
Leighton Rd
Ealing W13 ... 10
Enfield EN1 ... 1
Harrow HA3 ... 2
Kentish Town NW5 ... 7
Leighton St CR0 ... 20
Leila Parnell Pl 14 SE7 ... 14
Leinster Ave SW14 ... 13
Leinster Gdns W2 ... 114 A6 24
Leinster Mews
7 Barnet EN5 ...
Bayswater W2 ... 24
Leinster Pl W2 ... 23
Leinster Rd N10 ... 4
Leinster Sq W2 ... 9
Leinster Terr W2 ... 24
Leisure Way N12 ... 3
Leitch Ho 8 NW8 ... 7
Leith Cl NW9 ... 4
Leithcote Gdns SW16 ... 18
Leithcote Path SW16 ... 16
Leith Hill BR5 ... 19
Leith Hill Gn BR5 ... 19
Leith Ho
7 Kentish Town N7 ... 7
13 Streatham SW2 ... 16
Leith Mans W9 ... 9
Leith Rd N22 ... 3

Towers 7
...217 D1
Yd 3 NW6 ...91 C6
Ave TW4,TW5 ...128 C3
a Cl E8 ...96 A6
Ho 3 UB5 ...84 D5
an St E1 ...96 A1
ark Cl HA7 ...25 C4
ay Ave SE12 ...165 B1
non Rd SE10 ...142 C6
na Ct E11 ...54 C2
na Rd E11 ...54 C2
oal Ho 28 E1 ...96 C2
on Gr TW14 ...150 A3
onwell Ct SE9 ...167 A6
onwell Dr SE9 ...167 A6
ford Cl N15 ...52 A4
ford Ct N4 ...73 A6
Cres N9 ...18 C2
Gardens Prim Sch
...112 C3
Gdns W6 ...112 C3
Kennedy Cl E4 ...36 A4
n Ct W13 ...109 C5
Clifton Ho 12
8 ...122 B2
al Terr 7 SW4 ...137 D2
lby Rd KT6 ...198 C1
Freeman Pl
6 ...264 C5
am Ho SE1 ...252 D1
am 11 NW5 ...71 A2
am Rd
h DA7 ...147 B6
isham SE12 ...142 D1
th Norwood CR7 ...183 B1
tton SM1 ...218 A3
ard Ave BR4 ...224 C6
ard Cl BR4 ...224 C6
ard Rd
mley BR2 ...210 B1
ydon CR0 ...205 A1
ge BR3 ...185 A4
on Rd NW2 ...68 C2
ox Gdns
ydon CR0 ...220 D4
ghtsbridge
W1 ...114 D3 257 C5
ox Gdns Mews
/1 ...257 C4
ox Gdns
dbridge IG1 ...56 B1
llesden NW10 ...67 D4
ox Ho
Belvedere
DA17 ...125 C3
Hackney E9 ...74 C2
Twickenham
TW1 ...153 D5
ox Rd
sbury Pk N4, N7 ...72 C6
lthamstow E17 ...53 C3
or Cl DA6 ...147 A1
sbury Way SE2 ...124 D3
s Rd E7 ...77 C1
thall Ho SW1 ...259 B1
thall Rd E8 ...74 A1
thorp Rd SE10 ...120 D2
tmead Rd BR1 ...164 D1
ton Rise TW9 ...132 A2
ton St SE18 ...123 B2
Williams Ct NW6 ...91 C5
Ct 4 TW8 ...131 D5
Cres SE6 ...185 D5
minster Rd SM4 ...202 A3
minster Wlk
4 ...202 A3
nard Ave SM4 ...202 A4
nard Ct
omsbury WC1 ...240 A6
rrow HA3 ...24 C3
nsington W8 ...255 A6
nard Day Ho 3
V5 ...71 B2
nard Ho 10 E17 ...54 A5
nard Pl 6 N16 ...73 C4
nard Rd
ingford E4 ...35 C4
monton N9 ...18 A1
rest Gate E7 ...77 A4
tcham CR4, SW16 ...181 C2
uthall UB2 ...106 D2
nard Robbins Path
SE28 ...124 B6
nard St
oadgate
EC2 ...95 B3 242 D6
wham E16 ...122 A5
nora Ho W9 ...236 A6
ntine Cl SE15 ...140 A5
pards Ct EC1 ...241 A4
pold Ave SW19 ...179 B5
pold Bldgs 14 E2 ...95 D4
pold Ct 12 SW19 ...179 B5
pold Mews E9 ...96 C6
pold Prim Sch
V10 ...67 D1

Leopold Rd
Ealing W5 ...110 B5
East Finchley N2 ...48 B6
Edmonton N18 ...34 B5
Walthamstow E17 ...53 C4
Willesden NW10 ...67 C1
Wimbledon SW19 ...179 B5
Leopold St E3 ...97 B2
Leopold Terr SW19 ...179 C5
Leopold Wlk SE11 ...260 C1
Leo St SE15 ...140 B5
Leo Yd EC1 ...241 D5
Leppoc Rd SW4 ...159 D6
Leroy St SE1 ...117 C2 263 A4
Lerry Cl W14 ...264 D6
Lerwick Ct 4 EN1 ...17 C6
Lerwick Ho SW18 ...136 A1
Lescombe Cl SE23 ...163 A1
Lescombe Rd SE23,
SE6 ...163 A1
Lesley Cl DA5 ...169 D4
Lesley Ct
8 Wallington
SM6 ...219 B4
Westminster SW1 ...259 C5
Leslie Gdns SM2 ...217 C1
Leslie Gr CR0 ...205 C1
Leslie Grove Pl CR0 ...205 C1
Leslie Park Rd CR0 ...205 C1
Leslie Prince Ct 8
SE5 ...139 B5
Leslie Rd
East Finchley N2 ...48 B6
Leyton E11 ...76 B4
Newham E16 ...99 B1
Leslie Smith Sq 7
SE18 ...144 C6
Lessar Ave SW4 ...159 C5
Lessar Ct SW4 ...159 C5
Lessingham Ave
Ilford IG5 ...56 C6
Upper Tooting
SW17 ...181 A6
Lessing St SE23 ...163 A4
Lessness Ave DA7 ...146 D5
LESSNESS HEATH ...125 D1
Lessness Heath Prim
Sch DA17 ...125 C1
Lessness Pk DA17 ...125 C1
Lessness Rd
Belvedere DA17 ...125 C1
Morden SM4 ...202 A4
Lester Ave E16 ...98 C3
Lester Ct 42 E3 ...97 D4
Lester Ho IG8 ...36 B3
Lestock Cl 2 SE25 ...206 A6
Lestock Ho SE3 ...143 D4
Lestor Ct TW7 ...130 D2
Leswin Pl N16 ...73 D5
Leswin Rd N16 ...73 D5
Letchford Gdns
NW10 ...90 A4
Letchford Mews
NW10 ...90 A4
Letchmore Ho 7
W10 ...90 C3
Letchworth Ave
TW14 ...149 D4
Letchworth Cl
Bromley BR2 ...209 A4
South Oxhey WD19 ...22 D5
Letchworth Dr BR2 ...209 A4
Letchworth St
SW17 ...180 D6
Lethaby Ho 15 SW4 ...138 B1
Lethbridge Cl SE13 ...142 A3
Letterstone Rd SW6 ...264 C3
Lettice St
SW6 ...135 B4 264 D1
Lett Rd E15 ...76 B1
Lettsom St SE5 ...139 C3
Lettsom Wlk 1 E13 ...99 A5
Leucha Rd E17 ...53 A4
Levana Cl SW19 ...157 A3
Levant Ho 17 E1 ...96 D3
Levehurst Ho SE27 ...183 A5
Levehurst Way SW4,
SW9 ...138 A3
Leven Cl WD19 ...22 D5
Levendale Rd SE23 ...163 B2
Leven Rd E14 ...98 B1
Leven Way UB3 ...83 C1
Lever Ct 15 E9 ...74 D2
Leverett St SW3 ...257 B4
Leverholme Gdns
SE9 ...188 C6
Leverington Pl N1 ...235 D1
Leverson St SW16 ...181 C4
Lever St EC1 ...95 A4 235 A1
Leverstock Ho SW3 ...257 B2
Leverton Pl NW5 ...71 C3
Leverton St NW5 ...71 C3
Levett Gdns IG3 ...80 A5
Levett Ho 8 SW16 ...181 C5
Levett Rd IG11 ...79 C2
Levine Gdns IG11 ...102 D5
Levison Way 2 N19 ...49 D1

Levita Ho NW1 ...232 D2
Levyne Ct EC1 ...241 A6
Lewes Cl UB5 ...63 C2
Lewes Ct 3 CR4 ...202 D6
Lewesdon Cl 13
SW19 ...156 D3
Lewes Ho
Bermondsey SE1 ...253 B2
Peckham SE15 ...140 A6
Lewes Rd
Bromley BR1 ...187 D1
Colney Hatch N12 ...30 C5
Leweston Pl N16 ...51 D2
Lewey Ho E3 ...97 B3
Lewgars Ave NW9 ...45 A3
Lewin Ct
4 Plumstead
SE18 ...123 C2
Streatham SW16 ...182 A4
Lewing Cl BR6 ...211 C1
Lewington Ct EN3 ...6 D6
Lewin Rd Bexley DA6 ...147 A1
Mortlake SW14 ...133 B2
Streatham SW16 ...181 D4
Lewin Terr TW14 ...149 B4
Lewis Ave E17 ...35 C2
Lewis Cl N14 ...15 C4
Lewis Cres NW10 ...67 B3
Lewis Ct 5 SE16 ...118 B1
Lewis Gdns N2 ...30 B1
Lewis Gr SE13 ...142 A2
LEWISHAM ...142 A1
Lewisham Bridge Prim
Sch SE13 ...141 D2
Lewisham Bsns Ctr
SE14 ...140 D6
Lewisham Coll SE4 ...141 C3
Lewisham Ct EN3 ...7 C5
Lewisham Ctr SE13 ...142 A2
Lewisham High St
SE13 ...163 D6
Lewisham Hill SE13 ...142 A3
Lewisham Hospl
SE13 ...163 D6
Lewisham Pk SE13 ...164 A5
Lewisham Rd SE13 ...142 A3
Lewisham Sta SE13 ...142 A2
Lewisham St SW1 ...249 D1
Lewisham Way SE4,
SE14 ...141 B4
Lewis Ho 2 E4 ...35 C5
Lewis King Ho BR1 ...187 B3
Lewis Pl E8 ...74 A3
Lewis Rd
Bexley DA16 ...146 C2
Mitcham CR4 ...180 C1
19 Richmond TW10 ...153 D6
Sidcup DA14 ...168 C1
Southall UB1 ...107 A4
Sutton SM1 ...217 D4
Lewis Silkin Ho 9
SE15 ...140 C6
Lewis Sports & L Ctr
SE19 ...183 D2
Lewis St NW1 ...71 B2
Lewiston Cl KT4 ...200 B2
Lewis Way RM10 ...81 D2
Lexden Dr RM6 ...58 B3
Lexden Rd Acton W3 ...110 D5
Mitcham CR4 ...203 D5
Lexdon Ct RM6 ...58 B3
Lexfield Ho N5 ...73 A4
Lexham Ct UB6 ...86 B6
Lexham Gardens Mews
W8 ...255 D5
Lexham Gdns
W8 ...113 D2 255 C4
Lexham Ho 9 IG11 ...101 B6
Lexham Mews
W8 ...113 C2 255 B4
Lexham Wlk W8 ...255 D5
Lexington Pl KT1 ...175 D2
Lexington St
W1 ...115 C6 249 B6
Lexton Gdns SW12 ...159 D3
Leyborne Ave W13 ...109 C4
Leyborne Pk TW9 ...132 C4
Leybourne Cl BR2 ...209 A3
Leybourne Ct 1
SE25 ...206 A6
Leybourne Ho 20
SE15 ...140 C6
Leybourne Rd
17 Camden Town
NW1 ...71 B1
Hillingdon UB10 ...83 A6
Leytonstone E11 ...54 D1
Queensbury NW9 ...44 C4
Leybourne St 5
NW1 ...71 B1
Leybridge Ct SE12 ...165 A6
Leyburn Cl E17 ...53 D5
Leyburn Gdns CR0 ...221 C6
Leyburn Gr N18 ...34 A4
Leyburn Ho SE18 ...144 A5
Leyburn Rd N18 ...34 B4
Leyden Mans 7 N19 ...50 A2

Leyden St E1 ...95 D2 243 C3
Leydon Cl SE16 ...118 D5
Leyes Rd E16 ...99 D1
Leyfield KT4 ...199 D1
Ley Ho SE1 ...252 A1
Leyland Ave EN3 ...7 A3
Leyland Ct 8 N11 ...31 B6
Leyland Gdns IG8 ...37 C5
Leyland Ho
6 Canary Wharf
E14 ...119 D6
12 Richmond TW10 ...153 C1
Leyland Rd SE12 ...165 A6
Leylands SW18 ...157 B5
Leylang Rd SE14 ...140 D5
Leys Cl Finchley N12 ...30 C3
Harrow HA1 ...42 B4
Leys Ct 9 SW9 ...138 C3
Leysdown Ho SE17 ...263 B2
Leysdown 9 NW5 ...71 A2
Leysdown Rd SE9 ...166 B2
Leysfield Rd W12 ...112 A4
Leys Gdns EN4 ...15 A6
Leyspring Rd E11 ...54 D1
Leys Rd E EN3 ...7 A4
Leys Rd W EN3 ...7 A4
Leys The
East Finchley N2 ...48 A5
Harrow HA3 ...44 B3
Ley St Ilford IG1 ...78 D6
Newbury Pk IG1, IG2 ...57 B1
Leyswood Dr IG2 ...57 C4
Leythe Rd W3 ...111 A4
LEYTON ...76 B5
Leyton Bsns Ctr E10 ...75 C6
Leyton Ct SE23 ...162 C3
Leyton Grange E10 ...53 C1
Leyton Green Rd E10 ...54 A3
Leyton Green Twrs
E10 ...54 A3
Leyton Ind Village
E10 ...52 D2
Leyton Link Est E10 ...53 A2
Leyton Midland Road
Sta E10 ...54 A1
Leyton Mills E10 ...76 A4
Leyton Park Rd E10 ...76 A5
Leyton Rd
Merton SW19 ...180 A3
Stratford E15 ...76 B2
Leyton Sixth Form Coll
E10 ...54 B3
Leyton Stadium (Leyton
Orient FC) E10 ...75 D5
Leyton Sta E11 ...76 A5
LEYTONSTONE ...54 D1
Leytonstone Bsns &
Spec Sch E11 ...54 C3
Leytonstone High Road
Sta E11 ...76 C6
Leytonstone Rd E15 ...76 C3
Leytonstone Sta E11 ...54 C1
Leyton Town Ctr E10 ...76 A5
Leywick St E15 ...98 C5
Lezayre Rd BR6 ...227 D2
Liardet St SE14 ...141 A6
Liberia Rd N5 ...72 D2
Libert Cl N18 ...33 D6
Liberty Ave SW19 ...180 B2
Liberty Ct IG11 ...102 C5
Liberty Ctr HA0 ...88 B6
Liberty Ho 11 E1 ...118 A6
Liberty Mews
Balham SW12 ...159 B5
Orpington BR6 ...227 D6
Liberty Sch CR4 ...180 C1
Liberty St
SW9 ...138 B4 270 D2
Libra Rd 7 Bow E3 ...97 B5
Newham E13 ...99 A5
Library Ct N17 ...51 D6
Library Mans 4
W12 ...112 C4
Library Par NW10 ...89 C6
Library Pl E1 ...118 B6
Library St
SE1 ...116 D4 251 D1
Libro Ct E4 ...35 C6
Lichen Ct IG6 ...56 D6
Lichfield Cl EN4 ...2 D2
Lichfield Ct
Kingston u T KT6 ...198 A4
Richmond TW9 ...132 A1
Lichfield Gdns TW10,
TW9 ...154 A6
Lichfield Gr N3 ...29 C1
Lichfield Ho 27 SE5 ...139 A3
Lichfield Rd
Dagenham RM8 ...80 C5
Edmonton N9 ...18 A2
Hounslow TW4 ...128 C2
Mile End E3 ...97 A4
Newham E6 ...99 D4
Northwood HA6 ...40 A6
Richmond TW9 ...132 B4
West Hampstead
NW2 ...69 A4

Lichfield Rd *continued*
Woodford IG8 ...36 C6
Lichfield Terr 1
TW9 ...154 A6
Lichlade Cl 7 BR6 ...227 D4
Lichport Ct N4 ...50 D1
Lickey Ho W14 ...264 D6
Lidbury Rd NW7 ...29 A4
Lidcote Gdns 22
SW9 ...138 B3
Liddall Way UB7 ...104 B5
Liddell Cl HA3 ...43 D6
Liddell Gdns NW10 ...90 C5
Liddell Rd NW6 ...69 C2
Lidding Rd HA3 ...43 D4
Liddington Rd E15 ...98 D6
Liddlesdale Ho E 6
KT2 ...176 D2
Liddlesdale Ho W 5
KT2 ...176 D2
Liddon Rd
Bromley BR1 ...209 D6
Newham E13 ...99 B4
Liden Cl E10, E17 ...53 B1
Lidfield Rd N16 ...73 B4
Lidgate Rd 22 SE15 ...139 D5
Lidiard Rd SW18 ...158 A2
Lidlington Pl NW1 ...232 B3
Lido Sq N17 ...33 B1
Lidyard Rd N19 ...49 C1
Liffey Ct Edmonton N9 ...18 C1
Willesden NW10 ...68 A1
Liffler Rd SE18 ...123 C1
Liffords Pl SW13 ...133 D3
Lifford St SW15 ...134 D1
Lightcliffe Rd N13 ...16 C1
Lighter Cl 16 SE16 ...119 A2
Lighterman Mews 15
E1 ...96 D1
Lighterman's Rd
E14 ...119 D4
Lighterman's Wlk
SW18 ...135 C1
Lightfoot Rd N8 ...50 A4
Light Horse Ct SW1 ...258 A1
Lightley Cl HA0 ...88 B6
Ligonier St E2 ...243 C6
Lilac Cl E4 ...35 B4
Lilac Ct
Colney Hatch N12 ...30 C4
3 Newham E13 ...99 C6
Teddington TW11 ...174 D6
Lilac Gdns
Croydon CR0 ...223 C5
Ealing W5 ...109 D3
Hayes UB3 ...83 C1
Lilac Ho SE4 ...141 B2
Lilac Pl
Vauxhall
SE11 ...116 B2 260 C3
Yiewsley UB7 ...104 B6
Lilac St W12 ...112 A6
Lilah Mews BR2 ...186 D1
Lilburne Gdns SE9 ...166 A6
Lilburne Rd SE9 ...166 A6
Lilburne Wlk NW10 ...67 A2
Lile Cres W7 ...86 C2
Lilestone Est NW8 ...236 D5
Lilestone Ho NW8 ...236 D6
Lilestone St
NW8 ...92 C3 237 A6
Lilford Ho 21 SE5 ...139 A3
Lilford Rd SE5 ...138 D3
Lilian Barker Cl
SE12 ...165 A6
Lilian Baylis Ho N1 ...73 A2
Lilian Baylis Tech Sch
SE11 ...116 B1 260 D1
Lilian Board Way
UB6 ...64 B3
Lilian Gdns IG8 ...37 B2
Lilian Rd SW16 ...181 C2
Lilian Rolfe Ho 5
SE27 ...183 B6
Lillechurch Rd RM8 ...80 C2
Lilleshall Rd SM4 ...202 B3
Lilley Cl E1 ...118 A5
Lillian Ave W3 ...110 C4
Lillian Cl 14 N16 ...73 C5
Lillian Rd SW13 ...134 B6
Lillie Ho N5 ...72 C3
Lillie Rd
SW6 ...135 B6 264 C5
Lillie Road Mans
SW6 ...264 B5
Lillieshall Rd SW4 ...137 C2
Lillie Yd
SW6 ...135 C6 265 A6
Lillington Ho N7 ...72 C4
Lilliput Ave UB5 ...85 B6
Lillywhite 21 NW9 ...27 D2
Lily Albon Ct RM9 ...81 B4
Lily Cl W14 ...112 D2
Lily Gdns HA0 ...87 C5
Lily Ho 7 HA9 ...66 A3
Lily Pl EC1 ...241 B4
Lily Rd E17 ...53 C3

Lilyville Rd
SW6 ...135 B4 264 C2
Limavady Ho 12
SE18 ...122 C2
Limborough Ho 5
E14 ...97 C2
Limbourne Ave RM8 ...59 B2
Limburg Rd SW11 ...136 C1
Lime Ave UB7 ...104 B6
Limeburner La
EC4 ...94 D1 241 C2
Lime Cl Bromley BR1 ...210 A5
Buckhurst Hill IG9 ...21 D2
Carshalton SM5 ...218 D6
Harrow HA3 ...25 A1
Pinner HA5 ...39 D6
Wapping E1 ...118 A5
Lime Cres TW16 ...172 C1
Limecroft Cl KT19 ...215 B1
Lime Ct
9 Harrow HA1 ...42 D3
Hendon NW4 ...28 C1
Kingston u T KT3 ...198 D6
9 Leyton E11 ...76 C6
Mitcham CR4 ...180 B1
Putney SW15 ...134 B2
Limedene Cl HA5 ...22 D2
Lime Gr Barnet N20 ...13 B3
Blackfen DA15 ...167 D5
Hayes UB3 ...105 B6
Kingston u T KT3 ...199 C6
Orpington BR6 ...226 D6
Ruislip HA4 ...40 B2
Shepherd's Bush
W12 ...112 C4
Twickenham TW1 ...153 A5
Walthamstow E4 ...35 B4
Limeharbour E14 ...119 D4
Lime Ho 7 TW9 ...132 D4
LIMEHOUSE ...119 A6
Limehouse Cswy
E14 ...119 B6
Lime House Ct 23
E14 ...97 B1
Limehouse Ct 5 E14 ...97 C1
Limehouse Cut 4
E14 ...97 D2
Limehouse Fields Est 14
E14 ...97 A2
Limehouse Link
(Tunnel) E14 ...119 B6
Limehouse Sta E14 ...97 A1
Lime Kiln Dr SE7 ...143 B6
Limekiln Pl SE19 ...183 D3
Limekiln Wharf 21
E14 ...119 B6
Limeleaf Ct HA8 ...27 A6
Lime Lo 3 TW16 ...171 D3
Limerick Cl SW12 ...159 C4
Limerick Ct 1
SW12 ...159 C4
Lime Row DA18 ...125 B3
Limerston St
SW10 ...136 A6 266 B5
Lime St Pas EC3 ...253 A6
Limes Ave
Barnes SW13 ...133 D3
Carshalton SM5 ...202 D1
Croydon CR0 ...220 C5
Edgware NW7 ...27 C4
Golders Green NW11 ...47 A2
North Finchley N12 ...30 A6
Penge SE20 ...184 B3
Limes Ave The N11 ...31 C5
Limes Ave E11 ...55 B5
Limes Cl
Ashford TW15 ...170 C5
3 Friern Barnet N11 ...31 C5
Limes Ct
Beckenham BR3 ...185 D1
Willesden NW6 ...68 D1
Limesdale Gdns HA8 ...27 A1
Limes Field Rd
SW14 ...133 C2
Limesford Rd SE15 ...140 D1
Limes Gdns SW18 ...157 C5
Limes Gr SE13 ...142 A1
Limes Rd
Beckenham BR3 ...185 D1
Thornton Heath CR0 ...205 B2
Limes Row BR6 ...226 D3
Limes The
Camberwell SE5 ...139 C2
3 Cheam SM2 ...217 C2
East Molesey KT8 ...195 D5
Kensington W2 ...245 B5
Keston Mark BR2 ...226 A6
Stanmore HA7 ...9 B2
Limestone Wlk 12
DA18 ...124 D4
Lime St
Walthamstow E17 ...53 A5
Whitechapel
EC3 ...95 C1 243 A1

Limes Wlk
Ealing W5 . . . . 109 D4
Nunhead SE15 . . . . . . 140 C1
Lime Terr W7 . . . . .108 C6
Lime Tree Ave KT10,
KT7 . . . . .196 C1
Limetree Cl SW2 . . . . .160 B3
Lime Tree Cl E11 . . . . . .55 C5
Lime Tree Ct
East Barnet EN4 . . . . . .14 C6
East Finchley N2 . . . . . .47 D6
Limetree Ct HA5 . . . . . .23 C3
Lime Tree Ct
14 Poplar E3 . . . . .97 C2
South Croydon CR2 . . 221 A2
Lime Tree Gr CR0 . . . .223 B5
Limetree Pl CR4 . . . . .181 B2
Lime Tree Rd TW5 . . . .129 D4
Lime Tree Wlk
Bushey WD23 . . . . .8 C2
Coney Hall BR4 . . . . . 224 D4
Enfield EN2 . . . . .5 A5
Limetree Wlk 2
SW17 . . . . .181 A5
Lime Wlk 11 E15 . . . . . .98 C6
Limewood Cl
Beckenham BR3 . . . . 208 A4
Ealing W13 . . . . .87 B1
Walthamstow E17 . . . . .53 B5
Limewood Ct IG4 . . . . .56 B4
Limpsfield Ave
Putney SW19 . . . . 156 D2
Thornton Heath CR7 . .204 B4
Limscott Ho 35 E3 . . . .97 D4
Linacre Cl SE15 . . . . . .140 B2
Linacre Ct W6 . . . . . . .112 D1
Linacre Rd NW2 . . . . . .68 B2
Linale Ho N1 . . . . 235 C3
Linberry Wlk 3
SE8 . . . . .119 B2
Linchmere Rd SE12 . .164 D4
Lincoln Ave
Osidge N14 . . . . .15 C2
Twickenham TW2 . . . . 152 A2
Wimbledon SW19 . . . 156 D1
Lincoln Cl
Croydon SE25 . . . . . . .206 B3
Greenford UB6 . . . . . . .86 A6
Harrow HA2 . . . . .41 B4
Lincoln Cres EN1 . . . . .17 D6
Lincoln Ct
Borehamwood
WD6 . . . . .11 B6
Enfield EN2 . . . . .5 B1
Grove Pk SE12 . . . . . . 165 C1
Hampton TW12 . . . . . .173 B5
Hendon NW4 . . . . .46 B5
2 Ilford IG2 . . . . .57 A3
Mitcham CR4 . . . . 204 A4
Redbridge IG1 . . . . .56 B2
5 South Croydon
CR2 . . . . 221 A3
Stoke Newington N16 . .51 B2
Lincoln Gdns IG1 . . . . .56 A2
Lincoln Green Rd
BR5 . . . . .211 D4
Lincoln Ho
Bloomsbury WC1 . . . . 240 D3
9 Dartmouth Pk
NW5 . . . . .71 C5
2 Islington N1 . . . . .73 A1
Knightsbridge SW1 . . 247 C1
10 Putney SW15 . . . 157 A6
Lincoln Lo 10 BR3 . . . .185 D1
Lincoln Mews NW6 . . . .91 B6
Lincoln Rd
Croydon SE25 . . . . . . .206 B6
East Finchley N2 . . . . . .48 C6
Enfield EN1, EN3 . . . . . . .18 B6
Harrow HA2, HA5 . . . . . .41 B4
Kingston u T KT3 . . . . 199 A6
Mitcham CR4 . . . . 204 A4
Newham E13 . . . . .99 B3
North Cheam KT4 . . . . .200 B1
Northwood HA6 . . . . . . .39 D6
Plashet E7 . . . . .77 D2
Sidcup DA14 . . . . .190 B5
Twickenham TW13 . . . .151 B1
Wembley HA0 . . . . .65 D2
Woodford E18 . . . . .37 A2
Lincoln's Inn Fields
WC2 . . . . 94 B1 240 D2
Lincoln's Inn*
WC2 . . . . 94 B1 240 D2
Lincoln St SW3 . . . . . 257 C3
Lincolns The NW7 . . . . . .11 D1
Lincoln St E11 . . . . .76 C6
Lincoln Terr 4
SM2 . . . . .217 C1
Lincoln Way
Charlton TW16 . . . . . . 171 C2
Enfield EN1 . . . . .18 B6
Lincombe Rd BR1 . . . . .164 D1
Linda Ct KT9 . . . . .213 D4
Lindal Cres EN2 . . . . .4 B1
Lindal Ct 1 E18 . . . . . .37 A2
Lindale SW19 . . . . .157 A2
Lindales The N17 . . . . .33 D4
Lindal Rd SE4 . . . . .163 B6
Lindbergh Rd SM6 . . .220 A1
Linden Ave Enfield EN1 . . 6 A4
Hounslow TW3 . . . . . . 151 D6
Kensal Rise NW10 . . . . .90 D5
Ruislip HA4 . . . . .40 A1
Thornton Heath CR7 . 204 D5
Wembley HA9 . . . . .66 B3
Linden Bridge Sch
KT4 . . . . 215 C5
Linden Cl Ruislip HA4 . .40 A1
Southgate N14 . . . . .15 C5
Stanmore HA7 . . . . .25 B5
Thames Ditton KT7 . . 197 A2
Linden Cotts 6
SW19 . . . . .179 A4
Linden Cres
Kingston u T KT1 . . . . .176 B1
Wembley UB6 . . . . .64 D2
Woodford IG8 . . . . .37 B4
Linden Ct
8 Battersea
SW18 . . . . .136 B1
1 Beckenham BR3 . . 207 D6
2 Bromley BR1 . . . . 186 D3
Edgware NW7 . . . . .27 B5
Penge SE20 . . . . .184 B3
1 Shepherd's Bush
W12 . . . . 112 C5
Sidcup DA14 . . . . 189 C6
11 Sutton SM2 . . . . . 218 A2
Lindenfield BR7 . . . . . .188 D1
Linden Gate SW20 . . . .200 C6
Linden Gdns
Chiswick W4 . . . . .111 B1
Enfield EN1 . . . . .6 A4
Notting Hill
W2 . . . . . . 113 C6 245 B5
Linden Gr
Kingston u T KT3 . . . . 199 C6
Nunhead SE15 . . . . . . 140 C2
Penge SE20 . . . . 184 C4
Teddington TW11 . . . . 174 D5
Linden Ho
Bromley BR1 . . . . .187 B3
10 Deptford SE8 . . . . .141 B6
Hampton TW12 . . . . . 173 D4
Walthamstow E17 . . . . . .35 B1
Linden Lawns HA9 . . . . 66 B4
Lindenlea Ct E17 . . . . .53 B5
Linden Lea N2 . . . . .48 A4
Linden Leas BR4 . . . . .224 B6
Linden Lodge Sch
SW19 . . . . 157 A3
Linden Lo N21 . . . . .16 B4
Linden Mans N6 . . . . . .49 B1
Linden Mews
Kensington W2 . . . . . 245 B5
Stoke Newington N1 . . .73 B3
Linden Pl CR4 . . . . . . .202 C5
Linden Rd
Brunswick Pk N11 . . . . .15 A2
Cranley Gdns N10 . . . . .49 B5
Hampton TW12 . . . . . 173 C2
Tottenham N15 . . . . .51 A5
Lindens The
Chiswick W4 . . . . 133 A4
New Addington CR0 . 224 A2
North Finchley N12 . . . .30 B5
5 Walthamstow E17 . .53 D5
Linden Way
Shepperton TW17 . . . 193 A4
Southgate N14 . . . . .15 C5
Lindeth Cl HA7 . . . . . . .25 B4
Lindfield Gdns NW3 . . .70 A3
Lindfield Hts NW3 . . . . .70 A3
Lindfield Rd
Croydon CR0 . . . . 205 D3
Ealing W5 . . . . .87 C3
Lindfield St E14 . . . . . . .97 C1
Lindford Christie
Stadium The W12 . . . .90 B2
Lindhill Cl EN3 . . . . .6 D3
Lindholme Ct 3
NW9 . . . . .27 C2
Lindisfarne Rd
Dagenham RM8 . . . . . . .80 C5
Wimbledon SW20 . . . 178 A3
Lindisfarne Way E9 . . .75 A4
Lindley Ct KT1 . . . . . . .175 C2
Lindley Ho
13 Peckham
SE15 . . . . 140 A5
9 Stepney E1 . . . . .96 C2
Lindley Pl TW9 . . . . . . .132 C4
Lindley Rd E10 . . . . .76 A6
Lindley St E1 . . . . .96 C2
Lindon Bennett Sch
TW13 . . . . 172 D5
Lindop Ho 8 E1 . . . . . .97 A3
Lindore Rd SW11 . . . . .136 D1
Lindores Rd SM5 . . . . .202 A1
Lindo St SE15 . . . . .140 C3
Lind Rd SM1 . . . . .218 A3
Lindrop St SW6 . . . . . .136 A3
Lindsay Cl KT9 . . . . . . .214 A1
Lindsay Ct
Battersea SW11 . . . . 266 D1
Sutton SM1 . . . . 217 C3
Lindsay Dr
Harrow HA3 . . . . .44 B4
Shepperton TW17 . . . .193 B3
Lindsay Ho 2 SE18 . .122 C2
Lindsay Rd
Hampton TW12 . . . . . 173 D6
North Cheam KT4 . . . .216 B6
Lindsay Sq
SW1 . . . . 115 D1 259 D2
Lindsell St 6 SE10 . . .142 A4
Lindsey Cl
Bickley BR1 . . . . 210 A6
Mitcham CR4, SW16 . 204 A5
Lindsey Ct N13 . . . . . . .16 C1
Lindsey Gdns TW14 . .149 B4
Lindsey Ho W5 . . . . . .109 D2
Lindsey Ho* SW10 . . . 266 D4
Lindsey Mews 18 N1 . . .73 A1
Lindsey Rd RM8 . . . . . . .80 C5
Lindsey St
EC1 . . . . .94 D2 241 D4
Lind St SE8 . . . . .141 D3
Lindum Rd TW11 . . . . .175 C3
Lindums The BR3 . . . .185 B4
Lindway SE27 . . . . .182 D5
Lindwood Cl 8 E6 . . .100 B2
Linear View HA9 . . . . . .66 D6
Linfield Cl NW4 . . . . . . .46 C5
Linfield WC1 . . . . 233 C1
Linford Ct 1 CR4 . . . .180 C2
Linford Ho 17 E2 . . . . . .96 A6
Linford Rd E17 . . . . .54 A6
Linford St
SW8 . . . . .137 C4 269 A1
Linford Street Bsns Est
SW8 . . . . 269 A2
Lingard Ho 11 E14 . . . .120 A3
Lingards Rd SE13 . . . . .142 A1
Lingey Cl DA15 . . . . . . .167 D2
Lingfield Ave KT1,
KT5 . . . . .198 B5
Lingfield Cl EN1 . . . . . .17 C5
Lingfield Cres SE9 . . . .145 B1
Lingfield Ct
Northolt UB5 . . . . .85 C5
Wimbledon SW19 . . . 178 D4
Lingfield Gdns N9 . . . . 18 B4
Lingfield Ho
5 Acton Green
W4 . . . . 111 A1
Lambeth SE1 . . . . 251 D1
Penge SE26 . . . . .184 B4
Lingfield Rd
North Cheam KT4 . . . 216 C5
Wimbledon SW19 . . . 178 D4
Lingham St SW9 . . . . .138 B3
Lingholm Way EN5 . . . .12 D6
Ling Rd E16 . . . . .99 A2
Lingrove Gdns IG9 . . . .21 B2
Ling's Coppice SE21 . .161 B2
Lingwell Rd SW17 . . . .158 C1
Lingwood DA7 . . . . . . .147 D3
Lingwood Gdns
TW7 . . . . .130 C5
Lingwood Rd E5 . . . . . . 52 A2
Linhope St
NW1 . . . . .92 D3 237 C5
Linkenholt Mans 3
W6 . . . . .111 D2
Linkfield KT8 . . . . .195 D6
Link Field BR2 . . . . . . .209 A3
Linkfield Rd TW7 . . . .130 D3
Link La SM6 . . . . .220 A2
Linklea Cl NW9 . . . . . . .27 C3
Link Prim Sch CR0 . . 220 A4
Link Rd
Dagenham RM9 . . . . . 103 D5
East Bedfont TW14 . . 149 D4
Friern Barnet N11 . . . . .31 A6
Hackbridge SM6 . . . . . 203 A1
Links Ave SM4 . . . . . . .201 C5
Linkscroft Ave
TW15 . . . . .170 D4
Links Ct N20 . . . . .14 B1
Links Dr N20 . . . . .13 D3
Link Sec Sch CR0 . . . 220 B4
Links Gdns SW16 . . . . .182 C3
Linkside Cl EN2 . . . . .4 C2
Linkside N12 . . . . .29 C4
Linkside Gdns EN2 . . . . .4 B2
Linkside KT3 . . . . .177 C1
Links Ind Est TW13 . . 151 A1
Links Prim Sch
SW17 . . . . 181 A4
Links Rd Acton W3 . . . . .88 C1
Ashford TW15 . . . . . . 170 A5
Mitcham SW16,
SW17 . . . . 181 A4
West Wickham BR4 . . 208 A1
Willesden NW2 . . . . . . .67 D6
Woodford IG8 . . . . .37 A5
Links Side EN2 . . . . .4 C2
Links The E17 . . . . .53 A5
Link St E9 . . . . .74 C3
Links View Cl HA7 . . . . .25 A4
Links View N3 . . . . .29 B3
Linksview N2 . . . . .48 D4
Links View Rd
Croydon CR0 . . . . 223 C5
Hampton TW12 . . . . . 174 A6
Links View SE18 . . . . . .144 D4
Links Way BR3 . . . . . . .207 C3
Linksway NW4 . . . . .28 D1
Links Way SW17 . . . . . .181 A4
Links Yd
10 Spitalfields E1 . . . . .96 A2
Spitalfields E1 . . . . . . 243 D4
Link The Acton W3 . . . . .88 D1
Chislehurst SE9 . . . . . 166 C1
Enfield EN3 . . . . .7 A4
Hendon NW2 . . . . .46 A1
Northolt UB5 . . . . .63 B3
Pinner HA5 . . . . .40 C2
Teddington TW11 . . . . 174 D4
Wembley HA0 . . . . .43 C1
Link Way BR2 . . . . .210 A2
Linkway
Dagenham RM8 . . . . . . .80 C4
Pinner HA5 . . . . .22 D2
Link Way TW10 . . . . . .153 B2
Linkway N4 . . . . .51 A2
Linkway The EN5 . . . . . .13 D5
Linkway SW20 . . . . . . .200 B5
Linkwood Wlk NW1 . . .71 D1
Linley Cres RM7 . . . . . .59 D6
Linley Ct
1 Dulwich SE21 . . . . 183 C6
Sutton SM1 . . . . 218 A4
Linley Rd N17 . . . . .33 C1
Linnell Cl NW11 . . . . . . .47 D3
Linnell Dr NW11 . . . . . .47 D3
Linnell Ho
Spitalfields E1 . . . . . . 243 C4
St John's Wood NW8 229 A6
Linnell Rd
Camberwell SE5 . . . . 139 C3
Edmonton N18 . . . . .34 A5
Linnet Cl Bushey WD23 . . 8 A3
Lower Edmonton N9 . . .18 D3
Woolwich SE28 . . . . . . 124 C6
Linnet Ct CR4 . . . . .180 C2
Linnet Mews SW12 . . .159 A4
Linnett Cl E4 . . . . .36 A6
Linom Rd SW4 . . . . . . .138 A1
Linscott Rd E5 . . . . .74 C4
Linsdell Rd IG11 . . . . .101 A6
Linsey St
Bermondsey
SE16 . . . . 118 A2
Bermondsey SE16 . . . 118 A3
Linslade Cl
Hounslow TW4 . . . . . 151 A6
Pinner HA5 . . . . .40 B6
Linslade Ho
10 Hackney E2 . . . . . . .96 A6
Marylebone NW8 . . . . 237 B6
Linstead St 1 NW6 . . .69 C1
Linstead Way SW18,
SW19 . . . . .157 A4
Linsted Ct SE9 . . . . . . .167 C5
Linster Gr WD6 . . . . . . .11 A6
Lintaine Cl W6 . . . . . . 264 B5
Linthorpe Ave HA0 . . . .65 C2
Linthorpe Rd
Cockfosters EN4 . . . . . . .2 C2
Stamford Hill N16 . . . . .51 C2
Linton Cl
Carshalton CR4 . . . . . 202 D2
2 Greenwich SE7 . . . . 121 C1
Welling DA16 . . . . .146 B4
Linton Gdns E6 . . . . . .100 A1
Linton Gr SE27 . . . . . . .183 A5
Linton Ho
Lower Holloway N7 . . . .72 B4
2 Tower Hamlets E3 . . .97 C2
Linton Mead Prim Sch
SE28 . . . . .124 B6
Linton Rd IG11 . . . . . . .79 A1
Lintons The
Barking IG11 . . . . .79 A1
Finchley N3 . . . . .29 B2
Linton St N1 . . . . 95 A6 235 B5
Linver Rd SW6 . . . . . . .135 C3
Linwood Cl SE5 . . . . . .139 D3
Linwood Cres EN1 . . . . . 6 A4
Linzee Rd N8 . . . . .50 A5
Lion Ave TW1 . . . . .152 D3
Lion Cl Ladywell SE4 . .163 C5
Littleton TW17 . . . . . . 192 A6
Lion Ct 12 NW9 . . . . . . .46 A5
Lion Ctr The TW13 . . 151 A1
Lionel Gdns SE9 . . . . .165 D6
Lionel Ho
Bowes Pk N22 . . . . .32 B4
5 Kensal Town W10 . . .91 A2
Lionel Mans 14
W14 . . . . .112 D3
Lionel Mews 13 W10 . . 91 A2
Lionel Rd SE9 . . . . . . .165 D6
Lionel Road N TW8 . .110 A2
Lionel Road Prim Sch
TW8 . . . . 110 A2
Lionel Road S TW8 . . .110 B1
Lion Gate Gdns
TW9 . . . . .132 B2
Lion Gate Mews
SW18 . . . . .157 C4
Lion House Sch
SW15 . . . . 134 D1
Lion Mills 36 E2 . . . . . . .96 A5
Lion Park Ave KT9 . . .214 C4
Lion Rd
Bexleyheath DA6 . . . . .147 B1
Edmonton N9 . . . . .18 A2
Newham E6 . . . . .100 B2
Thornton Heath CR0 . 205 A4
Twickenham TW1,
TW2 . . . . 152 D3
Lions Cl SE12 . . . . .165 D1
Lion Way TW8 . . . . . . .131 D5
Lion Wharf Rd TW7 . .131 B2
Lion Yd SW4 . . . . .137 D1
Liphook Cres SE23 . . .162 C4
Liphook Rd WD19 . . . . .22 D6
Lipton Cl SE28 . . . . . . .124 C6
Lipton Ct N14 . . . . .15 C4
Lipton Rd 9 E1 . . . . . . .96 D1
Lisa Lo 5 EN5 . . . . .13 D6
Lisbon Ave TW2 . . . . . .152 A2
Lisbon Cl E17 . . . . .35 B1
Lisburne Rd NW3 . . . . .70 D4
Lisford St SE15 . . . . . .139 D4
Lisgar Terr
W14 . . . . .113 B2 254 C4
Liskeard Cl BR7 . . . . . .189 A4
Liskeard Gdns SE3 . . .143 A4
Liskeard Ho SE11 . . . . 261 B2
Lisle Cl SW17 . . . . .181 B6
Lisle Ct NW2 . . . . .69 A5
Lisle St WC2 . 115 D6 249 D6
Lismirrane Ind Pk
WD6 . . . . .9 B5
Lismore Cir NW5 . . . . . .71 A3
Lismore Cl TW7 . . . . . .131 A3
Lismore Rd
South Croydon
CR2 . . . . 221 C2
Tottenham N17 . . . . . . .51 B6
Lismore 9 SW19 . . . . .179 B5
Lismore Wlk 4 N1 . . . .73 A2
Lissant Cl KT6 . . . . . . .197 D2
Lisselton Ho 3 NW4 . .46 D5
Lissenden Gdns NW5 . .71 A4
Lissenden Mans
NW5 . . . . .71 A4
Lisson Cotts NW1 . . . 237 B4
Lisson Gr NW1,
NW8 . . . . .92 C3 237 A6
LISSON GROVE 92 B3
Lisson Ho NW1 . . . . . 237 A4
Lisson St
NW1 . . . . .92 C2 237 A4
Lister Cl
Dagenham W3 . . . . .89 B2
Mitcham SW19 . . . . . 180 C2
Lister Com Sch E13 . . .99 B5
Lister Cotts WD6 . . . . . . .9 A6
Lister Ct Hendon NW9 . .27 C1
Stoke Newington N16 . .73 C6
Lister Gdns N18 . . . . . .33 A5
Lister Ho
Greenwich SE3 . . . . . 142 C6
Hayes UB3 . . . . 105 C2
Marylebone W1 . . . . . 238 C2
Spitalfields E1 . . . . .96 A2
Lister Hospl
SW1 . . . . 115 B1 258 C1
Lister Ho
6 Wembley HA9 . . . . .67 A5
West Heath SE2 . . . . . 124 D1
Lister Mews N7 . . . . . . .72 B4
Lister Rd E11 . . . . .54 D1
Lister Wlk SE28 . . . . . .124 D6
Liston Ho N21 . . . . .16 B6
Liston Rd
Clapham SW4 . . . . . . 137 C2
Tottenham N17 . . . . . . .34 A2
Liston Way 1 IG8 . . . . .37 C3
Listowel Cl 2 SW9 . . .138 C5
Listowel Rd RM10 . . . . .81 C5
Listria Lo N16 . . . . .73 D6
Listria Pk N16 . . . . .73 D6
Litcham Ho 23 E1 . . . . .96 D4
Litchfield Ave
Morden SM4 . . . . .201 B2
Stratford E15 . . . . .76 C2
Litchfield Ct E17 . . . . . .53 C3
Litchfield Gdns
NW10 . . . . .68 A2
Litchfield Rd SM1 . . . .218 A4
Litchfield St WC2 . . . 249 D6
Litchfield Way NW11 . .48 A4
Lithgow's Rd TW14,
TW6 . . . . .127 D1
Lithos Rd NW3 . . . . .70 A2
Little Acre BR3 207
Little Albany St
NW1 238
Little Argyll St W1 . . 239
Littleberry Ct NW7 . . . 28
Little Birches DA15 . .167
Little Boltons The
SW10 255
Little Bornes SE21 . . .183
Littlebourne 2
SE13 164
Little Britain EC1 . . . 242
Littlebrook Cl CR0 . . .206
Little Brownings
SE23 162
Littlebury Rd SW4 . . .137
Little Bury St N9 17
Little Bushey La WD23 . 8
Little Cedars N12 30
Little Chelsea Ho
SW10 266
Little Chester St
SW1 258
Little Cloisters SW1 . 260
Little College St
SW1 260
Little Combe Cl 13
SW15 156
Littlecombe SE7 143
Little Common HA7 9
Littlecote Cl SW19 . . .157
Littlecote Pl HA5 23
Little Cottage Pl
SE10 141
Littlecroft SE9 144
Little Ct Harrow HA1 . . .42
West Wickham BR4 . . 224
Littledale SE2 146
Little Deans Yd SW1 260
Little Dell Lo 8 N3 . . .29
Little Dimocks
SW12 159
Little Dorrit Ct SE1 . . 252
Little Ealing La W5 . .109
Little Ealing Prim Sch
W5 109
Little Edward St
NW1 231
Little Elms UB3 127
Little Essex St WC2 . 251
Little Ferry Rd TW1 . .153
Littlefield Cl
9 Kingston u T
KT1 176
Tufnell Pk N19 71
Littlefield Ct UB7 126
Littlefield Ho KT1 176
Littlefield Rd HA8 27
Little Friday Rd E4 20
Little Gearies IG6 56
Little George St
SW1 250
Little Gn TW9 131
Little Grange UB6 87
Little Green St NW5 . . .71
Littlegrove Ct 3 EN4 . .14
Littlegrove EN4 14
Little Halliards
KT12 194
LITTLE HEATH 58
Little Heath RM6 58
Little Heath Rd DA7 . .147
Littleheath Rd CR2 . . .222
Little Heath Sch RM6 . 58
Little Heath SE7 122
Little Holt 10 E11 55
LITTLE ILFORD 78
Little Ilford La E12 78
Little Ilford Sch E12 . . .78
Littlejohn Rd W7 86
Little Larkins EN5 13
Little London Cl UB8 . .82
Little Marlborough St
W1 239
Littlemead KT10 212
Littlemede SE9 166
Littlemoor Rd IG1 79
Littlemore Rd SE2 . . .124
Little Moss La HA5 23
Little Newport St
WC2 249
Little New St EC4 . . . 241
Little Oak Cl TW17 . . .192
Little Orchard Cl
HA5 23
Little Oxhey La
WD19 23
Little Park Dr TW13 . .151
Little Park Gdns EN2 . . . 5
Little Pluckett's Way
IG9 21
Little Portland St
W1 239
Little Potters WD23 8
Little Queens Rd
TW11 174
Little Rd UB3 105

Redlands BR1 .. 188 A1
rs Cl SW19 ..... 180 B2
Russell St
.... 240 A3
St James's St
.... 249 A3
St Leonards
4 .... 133 A2
Sanctuary
.... 250 A1
Smith St SW1 . 259 D6
Somerset St
.... 243 C1
LE STANMORE ... 26 B2
stone Cl BR3 .... 185 C4
Strand NW9 .... 27 D1
Thrift BR5 ..... 211 A5
Titchfield St
.... 239 A3
LETON 192 C6
ton Ave E4 ...... 20 D3
ton CE Inf Sch
7 .... 192 C6
LETON COMMON
.... 171 B3
ton Cres HA1 .... 64 D6
ton Ho TW15 ... 171 A3
ton La TW17,
18 .... 192 A4
ton Rd
row HA1 .... 64 D6
eton TW15,
W17 .... 171 A3
ton St SW18 .... 158 A2
Trinity La EC4 . 252 B6
Turnstile WC1 . 240 C3
LE VENICE 92 A2
Venice*
.... 92 A2 236 A4
Wood Cl BR5 ... 190 A2
wood Cl W13 ... 109 B3
wood SE13 ..... 164 A5
worth Ave
0 .... 212 B3
worth Common Rd
0 .... 212 B5
worth La KT10 . 212 B4
worth Pl KT10 . 212 B4
worth Rd KT10 . 212 C5
mere Ct [3] E8 ..... 95 D6
mere Rd E8 ...... 95 D6
pool Gr
7 .... 117 B1 262 C1
pool Ho N7 ...... 72 C2
pool Rd
ng W5 .... 109 D4
ngton N1 .... 234 B5
ngton N1, N7 ...... 72 C1
gston u T KT2 .... 176 C3
onstone E10 ...... 54 A3
wham E16 .... 98 C2
th Norwood CR7 . 205 A6
pool St
.... 95 C2 243 A3
pool Street Sta
.... 95 C2 243 A3
ey Cl
gston u T KT1 .... 198 B6
lwich SE28 ..... 123 A3
ey Mus* SE15 .... 140 B6
sey Pl SE15 ...... 140 A6
gstone Ct
net EN5 .... 1 A3
onstone E10 ...... 54 A3
well TW19 ..... 148 A3
gstone Ho [16]
.... 139 A5
gstone Lo
Paddington W9 ..... 91 C2
thamstow E17 ..... 35 C1
gstone Pl E14 ... 120 A1
gstone Prim Sch
.... 2 B2
gstone Rd
Battersea
W11 .... 136 B2
es Pk N13 .... 32 A5
worth TW3 ...... 130 A1
Meads E15 .... 98 A6
thall UB1 .... 106 D6
th Norwood CR7 .. 183 B1
thamstow E17 ..... 53 D3
Sch The SW2 . 160 A6
ia St W1 .... 239 B1
d St EC1 .. 95 A4 235 B1
n St SE3 .... 143 B5
lovery Ho [1]
.... 120 A4
lly Rd NW2 ..... 69 B6
ver Rd
oters Hill
E18 .... 144 C5
mbley HA9 .... 65 D4
hony Rd SM4 ... 202 B4
anor Rd NW2 .... 69 B6
ellyn Ct SE20 .... 184 C2
ellyn Ho [10] N19 .. 71 C5

Llewellyn St SE16 .... 118 A4
Lloyd Ave SW16 ...... 182 A2
Lloyd Baker St
WC1 .... 94 C4 234 A1
Lloyd Ct
Ladywell SE13 ...... 163 D6
Pinner HA5 .... 40 D4
[6] West Norwood
SE27 .... 160 D1
Lloyd Ho
[3] Beckenham
BR3 .... 185 D4
Bromley BR1 .... 187 B5
Stoke Newington N16 . 73 B5
Lloyd Mews EN3 .... 7 C5
Lloyd Park Ave CR0 .. 221 D4
Lloyd Park Ho E17 .... 53 C6
Lloyd Park Sta CR0 . 221 D4
Lloyd Rd
Dagenham RM9 .... 81 B1
Newham E6 .... 100 B6
North Cheam KT4,
SM3 .... 216 D5
Walthamstow E17 ..... 52 D5
Lloyd's Ave EC3 ..... 243 B1
Lloyd's Bldg*
EC3 .... 95 C1 243 A1
Lloyd's Pl SE3 .... 142 C3
Lloyd Sq WC1 .. 94 C4 234 A2
Lloyd's Row
EC1 .... 94 D4 234 C1
Lloyd St WC1 .. 94 C4 234 A2
Lloyds Way BR3 .... 207 B4
Lloyd Villas SE4 ...... 141 C3
Loampit Hill SE13 .... 141 D3
Loampit Vale SE13 ... 142 A2
Loanda Cl [17] E8 ...... 95 D6
Loats Rd SW2 .... 160 A5
Lobelia Cl [5] E6 ..... 100 A2
Locarno Cl [15] SW16 .. 181 C5
Locarno Rd
[6] Acton W3 .... 111 A5
Greenford UB6 .... 86 B3
Lochaber Rd SE13 ... 142 C1
Lochaline St W6 ...... 134 C6
Lochan Cl UB4 .... 85 A3
Lochbie [9] N4 .... 50 A2
Lochinvar St SW12 ... 159 B4
Lochleven Ho [9] N2 .... 30 B1
Lochmere Cl DA8 ..... 147 D6
Lochmore Ho SW1 .. 258 B3
Lochnagar St E14 ...... 98 A2
Lockbridge Ct [3] W9 .. 91 C2
Lock Chase SE3 .... 142 C2
Lock Cl UB2 .... 108 A4
Locke Ho
Nine Elms SW8 ..... 269 A2
Stamford Hill N16 ..... 51 D1
Lockesfield Pl E14 ... 119 D1
Lockesley Dr BR5 .... 211 D3
Lockesley Sq KT6 .... 197 D3
Locket Rd HA3 .... 24 D1
Lockfield Ave EN3 .... 7 B4
Lockgate Cl E9 .... 75 B3
Lockhart Cl
Barnsbury N7 .... 72 B2
Enfield EN3 .... 18 B6
Lockhart Lo [4] E4 ...... 20 C4
Lockhart St E3 .... 97 B3
Lockhurst St E5 .... 74 D4
Lockier Wlk HA9 .... 65 D5
Lockington Rd
SW8 .... 137 B4 268 D2
Lockmead Rd
Lewisham SE13 ..... 142 A2
South Tottenham N15 .. 52 A3
Lock Mews [9] NW1 ... 71 D2
Lock Rd TW10 .... 175 C6
LOCKSBOTTOM 226 D5
Lockside [17] E14 ...... 119 A6
Lock's La CR4 .... 181 A1
Locksley St E14 .... 97 B2
Locksmeade Rd
TW10 .... 175 C6
Lock View Ct [9]
E14 .... 119 A6
Lockwell Rd RM10 .... 81 C5
Lockwood Cl SE26 ... 184 D6
Lockwood Ct KT3 ..... 199 A5
Lockwood Ho [10]
SE11 .... 138 C6
Lockwood Ind Pk
N17 .... 52 B6
Lockwood Pl E4 .... 35 C4
Lockwood Sq SE16 .... 118 B3
Lockwood Way
Chessington KT9 ..... 214 C3
Higham Hill E17 .... 34 D1
Lockyer Cl EN3 .... 7 D5
Lockyer Est SE1 .... 252 D1
Lockyer Ho
[7] Greenwich
SE10 .... 120 D1
Putney SW15 .... 134 D2
South Lambeth SW8 . 270 A4
Lockyer St SE1 ..... 252 D1

Locomotive Dr
TW14 .... 150 A3
Locton Gn [4] E3 ...... 97 B6
Lodden Lo [13] SM2 ... 218 A1
Loddiges Ho [5] E9 .... 74 C1
Loddiges Rd E9 .... 74 C1
Loddon Ho NW8 .... 236 D5
Loder St SE15 .... 140 C5
Lodge Ave
Borehamwood
WD6 .... 10 B6
Croydon CR0 .... 220 C5
Dagenham RM8, RM9,
IG11 .... 80 B3
Harrow HA3 .... 44 A5
Mortlake SW14 ..... 133 C2
Lodge Cl
Edgware HA8 .... 26 C4
Edmonton N18 .... 33 A5
Hackbridge SM6 .... 203 A1
Isleworth TW7 .... 131 B4
Lodge Ct [3] HA0 ...... 66 A3
Lodge Dr N13 .... 32 C6
Lodge Gdns BR3 ..... 207 B4
Lodge Hill DA16 ..... 146 B5
Lodgehill Park Cl
HA2 .... 63 D6
Lodge Hill IG4 .... 56 A5
Lodge La Bexley DA5 .. 168 D5
New Addington CR0 . 223 D1
North Finchley N12 .... 30 A5
Lodge Mead Ct [5]
N3 .... 29 D3
Lodge Pl SM1 .... 217 D3
Lodge Rd
Bromley BR1 .... 187 C3
Hendon NW4 .... 46 C5
Lisson Gr
NW8 ...... 92 C4 230 A1
Sutton SM1 .... 217 D3
Thornton Heath CR0 . 204 D2
Wallington SM6 ...... 219 B3
Lodge The
[9] Chiswick W4 ..... 111 C3
[1] Sutton SM1 ..... 218 A4
Lodge Villas IG8 ...... 36 D4
Lodge Way
Charlton TW17 ...... 171 A1
Stanwell TW15 ..... 148 A2
Lodore Gdns NW9 .... 45 C4
Lodore Gn UB10 .... 60 A5
Lodore St E14 .... 98 A1
Lodsworth Ho SW11 268 A1
Lofthouse Pl KT9 .... 213 C2
Loftie St SE16 .... 118 A4
Lofting Ho [8] N1 ...... 72 C1
Lofting Rd N1 .... 72 C1
Lofts on the Park [24]
E9 .... 74 D2
Loftus Rd IG11 .... 79 A2
Loftus Rd (Queens Park
Rangers FC) W12 .. 112 B5
Loftus Rd W12 .... 112 B5
Logan Cl Enfield EN3 .... 6 D4
Hounslow TW4 ...... 129 B2
Logan Mews W8 .... 255 A4
Logan Pl W8 . 113 C2 255 A4
Logan Rd
Edmonton N9 .... 18 B2
Wembley HA9 .... 66 A6
Loggetts SE21 .... 161 C2
Logs Hill BR1, BR7 .... 188 A2
Logs Hill Cl BR7 ..... 188 A2
Lohmann Ho [5]
SE11 .... 138 C6
Lois Dr TW17 .... 192 D4
Lolesworth Cl E1 ... 243 D3
Lolland Ho [8] SE7 .... 122 A2
Lollard St
SE11 .... 116 C2 261 A3
Lollards Twr SE1 .... 260 C5
Loman St
SE1 .... 116 D4 251 D2
Lomas Cl CR0 .... 224 A1
Lomas St E1 .... 96 A2
Lombard Ave
Enfield EN3 .... 6 C4
Ilford IG3 .... 57 C1
Lombard Bsns Pk
Merton SW19 ...... 179 D1
Thornton Heath CR0 .. 204 B2
Lombard Ct
[14] Acton W3 .... 110 D5
City of London EC3 .. 252 D6
Lombard La EC4 .... 241 B1
Lombard Rd SW11 ... 136 B3
Lombard Rdbt CR0 ... 204 B2
Lombard Rd
Friern Barnet N11 ..... 31 B5
Merton SW19 ...... 179 D1
Lombard St
EC3 .... 95 B1 242 D1
Lombard Trad Est
SE7 .... 121 B2
Lombard Wall SE7 ... 121 B2
Lombardy Pl W2 .... 245 D5

Lombardy Ret Pk
UB3 .... 106 B6
Lomley Ho [10] SW2 ... 160 C5
Lomond Cl
Tottenham N15 .... 51 C4
Wembley HA0 .... 66 B1
Lomond Ct HA3 .... 42 D6
Lomond Gdns CR2 ... 223 A1
Lomond Gr SE5 ...... 139 B5
Lomond Ho [10] SE5 ... 139 B4
Loncroft Rd SE5 ..... 139 C6
Londesborough Ho [1]
N16 .... 73 C4
Londesborough Rd
N16 .... 73 C4
London Academy
HA8 .... 26 B6
London Acad of
Computing &
Electronics SW17 . 158 D1
London Aquarium*
SE1 .... 250 C1
London Bridge City Pier
SE1 .... 117 C5 253 A4
London Bridge EC4,
SE1 .... 117 B6 252 D5
London Bridge Hospl
SE1 .... 117 B5 252 D4
London Bridge Sta
SE1 .... 117 B5 252 D3
London Bridge St
SE1 .... 117 B5 252 D3
London Bridge Wlk
SE1 .... 252 D4
London Britannia Coll
N1 .... 95 B4 235 C2
London Business Sch
NW1 .... 92 D3 237 C6
London Butterfly Ho*
TW8 .... 131 B4
London Canal Mus*
N1 .... 94 A5 233 B4
London Central
Mosque*
NW8 .... 92 C4 230 B1
London Chest Hospl
E2 .... 96 C5
London City Airport
E16 .... 122 B5
London City Airport Sta
E16 .... 122 A5
London Clinic
NW1 .... 93 A3 238 B5
London Coll of
Advanced Studies
SE1 .... 252 C3
London Coll of Beauty
Therapy
W1 .... 93 C1 239 B1
London Coll of Bsns &
Computer Studies
SW4 .... 137 D1
London Coll of
Communication (Sch
of Printing &
Publishing)
SE11 ...... 116 D3 261 D5
London Coll of
Economics & Science
NW10 .... 89 A3
London Coll of Fashion
EC2 .... 95 C3 243 B6
London Coll of Fashion
(Mare St) E8 .... 74 B1
London Coll of
Fashion
Marylebone W1 ..... 238 D2
Marylebone W1 ..... 238 B1
Marylebone W1 ..... 238 C1
St Luke's EC1 . 95 A3 242 A5
London Coll of
International
Business Studies
WC1 .... 240 B3
London Ct [3] SW18 .. 157 C6
London Docklands
Visitor Ctr* E14 ... 120 A4
London Dungeon The*
SE1 .... 117 B5 252 D4
London Electronics Coll
SW5 .... 113 D1 255 C2
London Eye
(Millennium Wheel)*
SE1 .... 116 B4 250 C2
London Fields East Side
E8 .... 74 B1
London Fields Prim Sch
E8 .... 96 B6
London Fields Sta
E8 .... 74 B1
London Fields West
Side E8 .... 74 A1
London Fire Brigade
Mus* SE1 .... 252 A2
London Gas Mus The*
E3, E16 .... 98 B3

London Group Bsns Pk
NW2 .... 46 A1
London Ho
Edgware HA8 .... 26 A6
[13] Hammersmith
W6 .... 112 A2
London Ho TW9 ..... 132 B2
London Hospital Dental
Inst E1 .... 96 B2
London Ho NW8 .... 230 B4
London Independent
Hospl The E1 .... 96 D2
London Inst The
SW17 .... 181 B5
London Int Coll N7 ... 72 B5
London International
Film Sch
WC2 .... 94 A1 240 A1
London IT Coll IG2 ... 56 C3
London La
Bromley BR1 .... 186 D3
Hackney E8 .... 74 B1
London Metropolitan
Univ (Central Ho)
E1 .... 96 A1
London Metropolitan
Univ (Commercial Rd)
E1 .... 96 A1
London Metropolitan
Univ N7 .... 72 C3
London Metropolitan
Univ (Ladbrook Ho)
N5 .... 72 D3
London Metropolitan
Univ (Moorgate)
EC2 .... 95 B2 242 D3
London Metropolitan
Univ
Whitechapel
E1 .... 95 D1 243 C1
Whitechapel
E1 .... 95 D1 243 C2
Whitechapel
EC3 ...... 117 D6 253 C6
London Metropolitian
Univ (Spring Ho)
N7 .... 72 C2
London Mews W2 .. 236 D2
London Motorcycle
Mus* UB6 .... 86 A4
London Nautical Sch
The SE1 ... 116 C5 251 B4
London Oratory Sch The
SW6 .... 135 C5 265 B4
London Pavilion
SW1 .... 249 C5
London Peace Pagoda*
SW3 .... 267 D4
London Rd
Ashford TW15, TW18,
TW19, TW14 .... 148 B2
Brentford TW7, TW8 .. 131 B4
Bromley BR1 .... 186 D3
Carshalton CR4 ..... 203 A2
Enfield EN2 .... 5 B1
Forest Hill SE22,
SE23 .... 162 C3
Hackbridge SM6,
CR4 .... 219 B6
Harrow HA1 .... 64 C6
Hounslow TW3, TW7, TW1,
TW8 .... 130 B3
Kingston u T KT1,
KT2 .... 176 B1
Lambeth
SE1 ...... 116 D3 261 D6
Mitcham CR4 .... 180 D2
Morden SM4 .... 201 C5
Newham E13 .... 99 A5
Romford RM7, RM8 .... 59 C5
Stanmore HA7 .... 25 D6
Stoneleigh KT17, KT4,
SM3 .... 216 B3
Thornton Heath CR0, CR7,
SW16 .... 204 C3
Twickenham TW1 .... 153 A4
Wembley HA9 .... 66 A2
London Road Rdbt
TW1 .... 153 A5
London Sch of
Economics & Political
Science
WC2 .... 94 B1 240 D1
London Sch of Jewish
Studies NW4 .... 46 D5
London St EC3 ...... 253 B6
London Stile [5] W4 .. 110 C1
London Stock
Exchange*
EC2 .... 242 A2
London Stone Bsns Est
[15] SW11 .... 137 A3
London St W2 . 92 B1 236 C1
London Terr [1] E2 ..... 96 A5
London Tottenham Coll
N17 .... 33 D3

London Transport
Mus* WC2 .... 250 B6
London Wall Bldgs
EC2 .... 242 D3
London Wall
EC2 .... 95 B2 242 D3
London Wetland Ctr*
SW13 .... 134 B5
London Wetland Visitor
Ctr* SW13 .... 134 B4
London Wharf [4] E2 .. 96 B6
London Xtra Tuition
Coll N4 .... 72 D6
London Zoo*
NW1 .... 93 A5 231 A4
Lonesome Prim Sch
CR4 .... 181 B1
Lonesome Way CR4 .. 181 C2
Long Acre Ct W13 ..... 87 A2
Longacre Pl SM5 ..... 219 A2
Longacre Rd E17 ..... 36 B2
Long Acre
WC2 .... 94 A1 240 B1
Longbeach Rd
SW11 .... 136 D2
Longberrys NW2 ...... 69 B5
Longboat Row UB1 ... 85 B1
Longbridge Ho RM8 ... 80 B4
Longbridge Rd
Barking IG11 .... 79 C3
Dagenham RM8 .... 80 B4
Longbridge Way
SE13 .... 164 A6
Longbury Dr BR5 .... 190 B1
Longchamp Ct [13]
HA7 .... 25 C5
Longcliffe Ho SW18 .. 157 D6
Longcrofte Rd HA8 .... 25 D3
Longcroft SE9 .... 166 C1
Long Deacon Rd E4 ... 20 C3
LONG DITTON 197 C1
Long Ditton Inf Sch
KT6 .... 197 C1
Longdon Wood BR2 .. 226 A4
Longdown Rd SE6 ... 185 C6
Long Dr
Dagenham W3 .... 89 C1
Greenford UB6 .... 85 D6
Ruislip HA4 .... 62 D4
Long Elmes HA3 ...... 24 A2
Longfellow Rd
North Cheam KT4 .... 200 B1
Walthamstow E17 ..... 53 B3
Longfellow Way SE1 263 D3
Longfield Ave
Ealing W5 .... 109 C6
Enfield EN3 .... 6 C5
Hackbridge SM6 .... 203 A1
Hendon NW7 .... 28 A3
Walthamstow E17 ..... 53 A5
Wembley HA9 .... 44 A1
Longfield [3] BR1 ..... 186 D2
Longfield Cres SE23,
SE26 .... 162 C1
Longfield Ct [4] N2 .... 48 A6
Longfield Dr
Mitcham SW19 ..... 180 C2
Mortlake SW14 ..... 154 D6
Longfield Est SE1 ... 263 D3
Longfield Fst & Mid
Schs HA2 .... 41 C3
Longfield Ho
Ealing W5 .... 109 C6
Walthamstow E17 ..... 53 B4
Longfield IG10 .... 21 C6
Long Field NW9 ...... 27 D3
Longfield Rd W5 ...... 87 C1
Longfield St SW18 ... 157 C4
Longford Ave
Feltham TW14 ...... 149 D5
Southall UB1 .... 107 D6
Stanwell TW19 ..... 148 A3
Longford Cl
Feltham TW13 ...... 151 A1
Hampton TW12 ..... 173 C6
Hayes UB4 .... 106 D6
Longford Com Sch
TW14 .... 149 D4
Longford Ct
[1] Bedford Pk
W12 .... 111 C4
[2] Clapton Pk E5 ...... 74 D4
Hampton TW12 ..... 173 D4
[9] Hendon NW4 ...... 46 C5
Southall UB1 .... 107 C5
West Ewell KT19 .... 215 A4
Longford Gdns
Hayes UB4 .... 106 D6
Sutton SM1 .... 218 A6
Longford Ho
[1] Catford BR1 ...... 186 B5
Hampton TW12 ..... 173 C6
[7] Stepney E1 .... 96 C1

Longford Ind Est TW12 173 D4
Longford Rd TW2 151 D3
Longford St NW1 93 B3 238 D6
Longford Way TW19 148 A3
Longford Wlk 9 SW2 160 C4
Longhayes Ave RM6 58 D5
Longhayes Ct RM6 58 D5
Longheath Gdns CR0 206 C4
Longhedge Ho SE26 184 A6
Longhedge St SW11 137 A3
Longhill Rd SE6 164 B1
Long Ho SM5 218 C6
Longhook Gdns UB5 84 B4
Longhope Cl SE15 139 D6
Longhurst Ho 8 W9 91 B4
Longhurst Rd
Croydon CR0 206 B3
Lewisham SE13 164 C6
Long La
Bermondsey SE1 117 B4 252 D1
Croydon CR0 206 C3
East Finchley N2 48 B6
Erith DA7 147 B4
Finchley N3 29 D2
Hillingdon UB10 82 D6
Holborn EC1 94 D2 241 D4
Longland Ct
Bermondsey SE1 118 A1
Hackney E9 75 A3
Longland Dr N20 13 D2
LONGLANDS 167 B1
Longlands Ct
Higham Hill E17 35 A2
Mitcham CR4 181 A2
Notting Hill W11 244 D6
Sidcup DA15 167 D1
Longlands Park Cres DA15 167 C2
Longlands Prim Sch DA15 167 C1
Longlands Rd DA15 167 D1
Long La TW15,TW19 148 B3
Longleat Ct 3 DA6 147 A1
Longleat Ho SW1 259 C2
Longleat Rd EN1 17 C6
Longleat Way TW14 149 B4
Longleigh Ho 8 SE5 139 C4
Longleigh La SE2, DA7 146 C6
Longlents Ho 3 NW10 89 B6
Longley Ave HA0 88 B6
Longley Ho 5 N19 71 C4
Longley Rd
Harrow HA1 42 B5
Thornton Heath CR0 204 D2
Upper Tooting SW17 180 D4
Long Leys E4 36 A4
Longley St SE1 118 A2
Longley Way NW2 68 C5
Longman Ho
9 Globe Town E2 96 D5
10 Shoreditch E8 95 D6
Long Mark Rd 5 E16 99 D2
Longmarsh La SE28 123 C5
Longmead BR7 188 C1
Longmead Dr DA14 168 D2
Longmead Ho SE27 183 A5
Long Mead NW9 27 D2
Long Meadow Cl BR3, BR4 208 A2
Long Meadow 20 N7 71 D3
Longmeadow Rd DA15 167 C3
Longmead Prim Sch UB7 104 A2
Longmead Rd
Hayes UB3 105 D6
Thames Ditton KT7 196 D2
Upper Tooting SW17 180 D5
Longmoor Point 14 SW15 156 B3
Longmore Ave EN4, EN5 14 B5
Longmore St SW1 115 C2 259 A3
Longnor Rd E1 96 D4
Long Pond Rd SE3 142 C4
Long Rd SW4 137 C1
Longreach Ct IG11 101 B5
Long Reach Rd IG11 101 D3
Longridge Ho SE1 262 B5
Longridge La UB1 85 D1
Longridge Rd SW5 113 C2 255 B3
Long Ridges N2 49 A6
Longs Ct 2 TW9 132 B1
Long's Ct W1 249 D5
Longshaw Prim Sch E4 20 B1
Longshaw Rd E4 20 B1
Longshore SE8 119 B2
Longstaff Cres SW18 157 C4
Longstaff Rd SW18 157 C5
Long St E2 95 D4
Longstone Ave NW10 89 D6
Longstone Rd SW17 181 B5
Longthorne Ho 18 E3 97 B4
Longthornton Rd SW16 181 D1
Longthorpe Ct 9 W6 112 A2
Longton Ave SE26 184 A6
Longton Gr SE26 184 B6
Longville Rd SE11 261 D4
Longwalk Rd UB11 104 D5
Long Wlk
Bermondsey SE1 263 B6
Kingston u T KT3 199 A6
Shooters Hill SE18 144 D6
Longwood Bsns Pk TW16 193 D4
Longwood Dr SW15 156 A5
Longwood Gdns IG2, IG6, IG5 56 C6
Longwood Par IG6 56 D6
Longworth Cl SE28 102 D1
Long Yd WC1 94 B3 240 C5
Loning The Enfield EN3 6 C5
Hyde The NW9 45 D5
Lonsdale Ave
Newham E6 100 A3
Wembley HA9 66 A3
Lonsdale Cl
Edgware HA8 26 B5
Hillingdon UB8 83 A2
Mottingham SE12 165 D1
Newham E6 100 A3
Pinner HA5 23 A2
Lonsdale Cres IG2 56 D3
Lonsdale Dr EN2 16 A6
Lonsdale Dr N EN2 4 A1
Lonsdale Gdns CR7, SW16 204 B5
Lonsdale Ho
Fulham SW6 135 C2
6 Stoke Newington N4 51 A2
Lonsdale Mews
Notting Hill W11 91 B1
4 Richmond TW9 132 C4
Lonsdale Pl N1 72 C1
Lonsdale Rd
Barnes SW13 133 D5
Bexley DA7 147 B3
Chiswick W4 111 D2
Croydon SE25 206 B5
Kilburn NW6 91 B6
Leytonstone E11 54 D2
Notting Hill W11 91 B1
Southall UB2 106 D3
Lonsdale Sq
Islington N1 72 C1
Islington N1 234 B6
Loobert Rd N15 51 C6
Looe Gdns IG6 56 D6
Loop Rd BR7 189 A4
Lopen Rd N18 33 C6
Lopen Works N18 33 C6
Lopez Ho 6 SW9 138 A2
Lorac Ct 18 SM2 217 C1
Loraine Cl EN3 18 C6
Loraine Ct BR7 188 D5
Loraine Ho 1 SM5 219 B4
Loraine Rd
Chiswick W4 132 D6
Islington N7 72 B4
Lord Ave IG5 56 B6
Lord Chancellor Wlk KT2 177 A2
Lord David Pitt Ho 8 SE24 138 C1
Lordell Pl SW19 178 C4
Lorden Wlk 18 E2 96 A4
Lord Gdns IG5 56 B5
Lord Hills Rd W2 91 D2
Lord Holland La 5 SW9 138 C3
Lord Knyvetts Ct 3 TW19 148 A5
Lord Napier Pl W6 112 A1
Lord North St SW1 260 A5
Lord Roberts Mews SW6 265 C3
Lord Roberts Terr SE18 122 C1
Lords Cl
Feltham TW13 151 A2
West Norwood SE21 161 A2
Lord's Cricket Mus* NW8 92 B4 229 D1
Lords Ct 3 HA8 27 A3
Lordship Gr N16 73 B6
Lordship Ho 3 N16 73 B6
Lordship La SE22 161 D5
Lordship Lane Prim Sch N22 33 A2
Lordship La N22 33 B2
Lordship Park Mews N16 73 A6
Lordship Pk N16 73 B6
Lordship Pl SW3 267 A5
Lordship Rd
Northolt UB5 63 A1
Stoke Newington N16 73 B6
Lordship Terr N16 73 B6
Lord's Indoor Cricket Sch NW8 230 A2
Lord's (MCC & Middlesex Cty Cricket Ground)* NW8 92 B4 229 D2
Lordsmead Rd N17 33 C1
Lord St E16 122 A5
Lord's View NW8 229 D1
Lord Warwick St SE18 122 B3
Loreburn Ho 2 N7 72 B4
Lorenzo St N1, WC1 233 C2
Loretto Gdns HA3 44 A5
Lorian Cl N12 29 D6
Loring Rd
East Barnet N20 14 C2
Isleworth TW7 130 D3
Loris Rd W6 112 C3
Lorn Ct SW9 138 C3
Lorne Ave CR0 206 D2
Lorne Cl NW8 92 C4 230 B1
Lorne Ct Harrow HA1 42 C2
Putney SW15 156 D5
Lorne Gdns
Croydon CR0 206 D2
5 Hammersmith W11 112 D4
Wanstead E11 55 C5
Lorne Ho
Friern Barnet N11 31 B5
Hornsey N4 50 B2
7 Tower Hamlets E1 97 A2
Lorne Rd
Finsbury Pk N4 50 B1
Forest Gate E7 77 C4
Harrow HA3 24 D1
3 Richmond TW10 154 B6
Walthamstow E17 53 C4
Lorn Rd SW9 138 C3
Lorraine Ct
Beckenham BR3 186 A2
9 Belmont SM2 217 C1
10 Camden Town NW1 71 B1
Lorraine Pk HA3 24 C3
Lorrimore Rd SE17 138 D6
Lorrimore Sq SE17 138 D6
Lorton Ho 9 NW6 91 C6
Loseberry Rd KT10 212 B3
Lostock Ho 10 SW8 137 D3
Lothair Rd W5 109 D4
Lothair Rd N N4 50 D3
Lothair Rd S N4 50 D2
Lothbury EC2 95 B1 242 C2
Lothian Ave UB4 84 B2
Lothian Cl HA0 65 A5
Lothian Rd SW9 138 D4
Lothrop St W10 91 A4
Lots Rd SW10 136 A5 266 B3
Loubet St SW17 180 D4
Loudoun Ave IG6 56 D4
Loudoun Rd NW8 92 A6 229 B5
Loudwater Cl TW16 194 A5
Loudwater Rd TW16 194 A5
Loughborough Ct 7 SW9 138 D2
Loughborough Junction Sta SW9 138 D2
Loughborough Pk SW9 138 D1
Loughborough Prim Sch SW9 138 D3
Loughborough Rd SE5, SW9 138 D3
Loughborough St SE11 116 B1 260 D1
Lough Rd N7 72 B2
LOUGHTON 21 D5
Loughton Way IG9 21 D3
Louie Black Ho 4 SW19 179 A3
Louisa Cl E9 96 D6
Louisa Ct
Twickenham TW2 152 C2
Wood Green N11 31 D3
Louisa Gdns E1 96 D3
Louisa Ho SW15 133 D1
Louisa St E1 96 D3
Louis Ct 3 RM10 81 D2
Louise Bennett Cl 9 SE24 138 D1
Louise Ct
7 Bexley DA6 147 A1
4 Wanstead E11 55 B4
Wood Green N22 32 C2
Louise De Marillac Ho 26 E1 96 C2
Louise Graham Ho 5 IG11 101 B6
Louise Rd E15 76 C2
Louise White Ho 1 N19 49 D1
Louis Gdns BR7 188 B6
Louis Mews N10 31 B2
Louisville Rd SW17 159 A1
Lousada Lo N14 15 C5
Louvaine Rd SW11 136 B1
Lovage App E6 100 A2
Lovat Cl NW2 67 D5
Lovat La EC3 253 A5
Lovatt Cl HA8 26 D4
Lovatt Ct SW12 159 B3
Lovatt Dr HA4 39 D4
Lovat Wlk TW5 129 A5
Loveday Ho 2 SW2 160 C3
Loveday Rd W13 109 B5
Lovegrove St SE1 140 A6
Lovegrove Wlk E14 120 A5
Lovekyn Cl KT2 176 B1
Lovelace Ave BR2 210 C3
Lovelace Gdns
Barking IG11 80 A4
Surbiton KT6 197 D2
Lovelace Gn SE9 144 B2
Lovelace Ho 12 E8 95 D6
Lovelace Prim Sch KT9 213 C3
Lovelace Rd
East Barnet EN4 14 C4
Surbiton KT6 197 D2
West Norwood SE21 161 A3
Love La Cheam SM3 217 A2
City of London EC2 95 A1 242 B2
Croydon SE25 206 B6
Long Ditton KT6 213 D6
Mitcham CR4 202 C6
Morden SM4 201 D2
Loveland Mans 7 IG11 79 D1
Love La
Old Bexley DA5 169 C5
Pinner HA5 41 A6
Tottenham N17 33 D3
Lovel Ave DA16 146 A3
Love La SE18 122 D2
Lovelinch Cl SE15 140 C6
Lovell Ho Hackney E8 96 A6
4 Merton SW19 180 A2
Lovell Pl SE16 119 A3
Lovell Rd
Richmond TW10 153 C1
Southall UB1 85 D1
Loveridge Mews NW6 69 B2
Loveridge Rd NW6 69 B2
Lover's Wlk W1 115 A5 248 A3
Lovett Dr SM5 202 B2
Lovette Ho 4 E3 97 C4
Lovetts Pl SW18 135 D1
Lovett Way NW10 67 A3
Love Wlk SE5 139 B3
Lovibonds Ave
Hillingdon UB7 82 B1
Locksbottom BR6 226 D5
Lowbrook Rd IG1 78 D4
Lowdell Cl UB7 82 A1
Lowden Rd
Edmonton N9 18 B3
Herne Hill SE24 139 A1
Southall UB1 107 A6
Lowder Ho 6 E1 118 B5
Lowe Ave E16 99 A2
Lowell Ho 10 SE5 139 A5
Lowell St E14 97 A1
Lower Addiscombe Rd CR0 205 C1
Lower Addison Gdns W14 113 A4 244 A1
Lower Belgrave St SW1 115 B3 258 C5
Lower Boston Rd W7 108 C4
Lower Broad St RM10 103 C6
Lower Camden BR7 188 B2
Lower Church St CR0 220 D6
LOWER CLAPTON 74 C4
Lower Clapton Rd E5 74 C4
Lower Clarendon Wlk 9 W11 91 A1
Lower Comm S SW15 134 B2
Lower Coombe St CR0 221 A4
Lower Downs Rd SW20 178 D2
LOWER EDMONTON 18 B1
LOWER FELTHAM 149 D1
Lower Fosters NW4 46 C4
Lower George St 13 TW10 153 D6
Lower Gn W CR4 202 C6
Lower Gravel Rd BR2 210 B1
LOWER GREEN 195 C1
Lower Green Gdns KT4 200 A1
Lower Green Rd KT10 212 A6
Lower Grosvenor Pl SW1 115 B3 258 D6
Lower Grove Rd TW10 154 B6
LOWER HALLIFORD 193 C3
Lower Hall La E4 35 A6
Lower Hampton Rd TW12, TW16 172 D1
Lower Ham Rd KT2 175 D4
LOWER HOLLOWAY 72 A3
Lower James St W1 249 B6
Lower John St W1 249 B6
Lower Kenwood Ave EN2 16 A6
Lower Kings Rd KT2 176 A3
Lower Lea Crossing E14, E16 120 C6
Lower Maidstone Rd N11 31 C4
Lower Mall W6 112 B1
Lower Marsh La KT1, KT5 198 C5
Lower Marsh SE1 116 C4 251 A1
Lower Merton Rise NW3 70 C1
LOWER MORDEN 201 A2
Lower Morden La SM4 201 A3
Lower Mortlake Rd TW9 132 B2
Lower Park Rd
Belvedere DA17 125 C2
Friern Barnet N11 31 C5
4 Loughton IG10 21 D6
Lower Pk Acton W3 89 A3
5 Putney SW15 156 D6
LOWER PLACE 89 A5
Lower Place Bsns Ctr NW10 89 A5
Lower Queen's Rd IG9 21 D2
Lower Rd
Belvedere DA17 125 D3
Finchley N2 30 B2
Harrow HA2 42 B1
Rotherhithe SE16 118 C4
Sutton SM1 218 A4
Lower Richmond Rd
Mortlake SW14, TW9 132 D2
Putney SW15 134 C2
Lower Robert St WC2 250 B5
Lower Sand Hills KT6 197 C2
Lower Sloane St SW1 115 A1 258 A2
Lower Sq TW7 131 B2
Lower Strand NW9 27 D1
Lower Sunbury Rd TW12 173 C1
LOWER SYDENHAM 185 A6
Lower Sydenham Sta SE26 185 B5
Lower Teddington Rd KT1 175 D2
Lower Terr NW3 70 A5
Lower Thames St EC3 117 C6 253 A5
Lower Tub WD23 8 B4
Lowerwood Ct W11 91 A1
Lower Wood Rd KT10 213 B2
Lowestoft Cl 5 E5 74 C6
Lowestoft Mews E16 122 D4
Loweswater Cl HA9 65 D6
Loweswater Ho E3
Lowfield Rd
Dagenham W3
Hampstead NW6
Low Hall Cl E4
Low Hall La E17
Lowick Rd HA1
Lowland Gdns RM7
Lowlands Ct NW7
Lowlands NW3
Lowlands Rd
Harrow HA1
Pinner HA5
Lowman Rd N7
Lowndes Cl SW1 2
Lowndes Ct
Knightsbridge SW1 2
Marylebone W1 2
Lowndes Lo
Barnet EN5
SW1 2
Lowndes Pl
SW1 115 A3 2
Lowndes Sq
SW1 114 D4 2
Lowndes St
SW1 115 A3 2
Lownds Ct BR1 1
Lowood Ct SE19 1
Lowood Ho 12 E1 1
Lowood St E1 1
Lowry Cres CR4 1
Lowry Ct 3 SE16 1
Lowry Ho N17
Lowry Lo 1 HA0
Lowry Rd RM8
Lowther Cl WD6
Lowther Dr EN2
Lowther Hill SE23 1
Lowther Ho
Pimlico SW1 2
11 Shoreditch E8
Lowther Prim Sch SW13 1
Lowther Rd
Barnes SW13 1
Higham Hill E17
Islington N7
Kingston u T KT2 1
Stanmore HA7
Lowth Rd SE5 1
Lowton Lo E17
LOXFORD
Loxford Ave E6
Loxford Ho SW1 2
Loxford La IG1
Loxford Rd IG11
Loxford Sch of Science & Tech IG1
Loxham Rd E4
Loxham St WC1 2
Loxley Cl SE26 1
Loxley Hall E11
Loxley Ho HA9
Loxley Rd
Feltham TW12 1
Wandsworth SW18 1
Loxton Rd SE23 1
Loxwood Cl TW14 1
Loxwood Rd N17
Loyola Prep Sch IG9
LTC Coll London W1 2
Lubavitch House Sch (Jun Boys) E5
Lubbock Ct BR7 1
Lubbock Ho
21 Canary Wharf E14 1
Orpington BR6 2
Lubbock Rd BR7 1
Lubbock St SE14 1
Lucan Ho N1 2
Lucan Pl
SW3 114 C2 2
Lucan Rd EN5
Lucas Ave
Harrow HA2
Newham E13
Lucas Ct
Battersea SW11 2
Forest Hill SE26 1
Lucas Gdns N2
Lucas Ho
2 Clapham SW8 1
Walham Green SW10 2
Lucas Rd SE20 1
Lucas Sq NW11
Lucas St SE4, SE8 1
Lucas Vale Prim Sch SE8 1
Lucerne Cl N14
Lucerne Ct
5 Abbey Wood DA18 1

rne Ct continued
Beckenham BR3 ... 185 C3
rne Gr E17 ... 54 B5
rne Mews W8 ... 245 B4
rne Rd
hbury N5 ... 72 D4
ington BR6 ... 211 D1
th Norwood CR7 ... 205 A5
y Rd SE16 ... 118 A3
y Way SE16 ... 118 A2
e Ave TW15 ... 170 D4
en Rd
er Tooting
W17 ... 181 A6
ndsworth SW18 ... 157 D2
lle Ho SE26 ... 184 B4
know St SE18 ... 145 C5
orn Cl SE12 ... 164 D5
raft Ho 12 SW2 ... 160 A4
ons Ave IG9 ... 21 C3
Ashe Ho SE17 ... 261 D3
Brown Ho SE1 ... 252 B3
Cres W3 ... 89 A3
Gdns RM8 ... 81 A5
desdon Rd DA8 ... 147 C5
ord Cl
ydon CR0 ... 220 D4
ware NW9 ... 27 C1
gate Broadway
4 ... 241 D1
gate Cir
4 ... 94 D1 241 C1
gate Hill
4 ... 94 D1 241 D1
gate Ho EC4 ... 241 C1
gate Sq EC4 ... 241 D1
grove Ct EN4 ... 2 C1
grove Hall EN4 ... 2 C2
ham Cl SE28 ... 102 C1
ham NW5 ... 70 D3
Lo TW15 ... 148 A2
low Cl
omley BR2 ... 209 A6
rrow HA2 ... 63 B4
low Ct Acton W3 ... 111 A4
st Barnet EN4 ... 14 C6
low Rd Ealing W5 ... 87 C3
tham TW13 ... 172 A6
low St EC1 ... 242 A6
low Way N2 ... 48 A5
ovick Wlk SW15 ... 133 C1
well Ho W14 ... 254 B6
wick Mews
14 ... 141 A5
ield Rd SE2 ... 124 B3
man Rd SE12 ... 165 B1
ard Ho 2 W12 ... 112 B5
ard Rd SE15 ... 140 B4
g App E12 ... 78 C5
e Ho 32 E1 ... 96 B1
es Ct N3 ... 47 C6
e St EC2 ... 95 C3 243 A6
in Cres E4 ... 20 B1
in St E1 ... 96 C1
ingstone Cl BR5 ... 190 B3
ingstone Cres
5 ... 190 B3
ingstone Ho 21
15 ... 140 C6
ingstone La
13 ... 164 B5
ingstone Rd 3
17 ... 147 B6
ington Garth
rehamwood
WD6 ... 10 D6
omley BR1 ... 186 C3
chley N12 ... 29 B5
ington Rd
genham RM9 ... 81 A1
nge SE20 ... 184 A3
ot Gdns N19 ... 71 B6
worth Ave
ounslow TW5,
TW7 ... 130 A5
embley HA9 ... 43 C2
worth NW1 ... 71 D1
worth Cl HA2 ... 63 B5
worth Cres CR4 ... 180 C1
worth Ct N14 ... 16 A1
worth Dr HA5 ... 41 A2
worth Gdns HA2 ... 63 B6
worth Ho SW8 ... 270 C3
worth Rd
exley DA16 ... 145 D3
islehurst SE9 ... 166 A2
eckham SE15 ... 140 B3
worth SE17 ... 262 C2
worth Waye UB4 ... 84 B1
hen Rd HA9 ... 65 D6
niere Bldg The
... 77 D3
niere Ct 7
V17 ... 159 A2
hina Bldg 1 E14 ... 120 A5
nley Cl DA17 ... 125 C1
nley Ct WC2 ... 250 B5

Lumley Flats SW1 ... 258 A2
Lumley Gdns SM3 ... 217 A3
Lumley Ho KT3 ... 199 B1
Lumley Rd SM1,
SM3 ... 217 A3
Lumley St W1 ... 238 B1
Lumsdon NW8 ... 91 D6
Luna Ho 6 SE16 ... 118 A4
Lunan Ho 14 E3 ... 97 B5
Luna Rd CR7 ... 205 A6
Lundin Wlk WD19 ... 22 D6
Lund Point E15 ... 98 A6
Lundy Dr UB3 ... 105 C2
Lunham Rd SE19 ... 183 C4
Luntley Pl E1 ... 96 A2
Lupin Cl
Croydon CR0 ... 206 D1
Streatham SW2 ... 160 D2
Lupin Cres IG11 ... 78 D2
Lupino Ct SE11 ... 260 D4
Lupin Point SE1 ... 253 D1
Lupton Cl SE12 ... 187 B6
Lupton St NW5 ... 71 C4
Lupus Ct SE19 ... 183 B2
Lupus St
SW1 ... 115 C1 259 B1
Luralda Gdns E14 ... 120 B1
Lurgan Ave W6 ... 134 D6
Lurline Gdns
SW11 ... 137 A4 268 B2
Luscombe Ct BR2 ... 186 C1
Luscombe Ho SW18 ... 157 B6
Luscombe Way
SW8 ... 138 A5 270 A4
Lusher Ho SW15 ... 156 D5
Lushington Ho
KT12 ... 194 C3
Lushington Rd
Catford SE6 ... 185 D5
Willesden Green
NW10 ... 90 B5
Lushington Terr 11
E8 ... 74 A3
Lutea Ho SM2 ... 218 A1
Luther Cl HA8 ... 11 A2
Luther King Cl E17 ... 53 A3
Luther Mews 2
TW11 ... 174 D5
Luther Rd TW11 ... 174 D5
Luton Pl SE10 ... 142 A5
Luton Rd Newham E13 ... 99 A3
Sidcup DA14 ... 168 C1
Walthamstow E17 ... 53 B6
Luton St NW8 ... 92 B3 236 D5
Luttrell Ave SW15 ... 156 B6
Lutwyche Rd SE6 ... 163 B2
Lutyens Ho SW1 ... 259 A1
Luxborough Ho W1 ... 238 A4
Luxborough St
W1 ... 93 A2 238 A4
Luxborough Twr
W1 ... 238 A4
Luxembourg Mews 2
E15 ... 76 C3
Luxemburg Gdns
W6 ... 112 D2
Luxfield Rd SE9 ... 166 A3
Luxford St SE16 ... 118 D2
Luxmore St SE4 ... 141 B4
Luxor St SE5 ... 139 A2
Lyall Ave SE21 ... 183 D6
Lyall Mews
SW1 ... 115 A3 258 A5
Lyall Mews W SW1 ... 258 A5
Lyall St SW1 ... 115 A3 258 A5
Lyal Rd E3 ... 97 A5
Lyce e Francais Charles
de Gaulle (French
Univ Coll)
SW7 ... 114 B2 256 C4
Lycee The
SE11 ... 116 C1 261 B1
Lycett Ho 10 SW2 ... 160 A4
Lycett Pl 3 W12 ... 112 A4
Lychgate Ct 4 N12 ... 30 B5
Lychgate Manor HA1 ... 42 C2
Lych Gate Wlk UB3 ... 105 D6
Lyconby Gdns CR0 ... 207 A2
Lydd Cl DA14 ... 167 C1
Lydden Ct SE9 ... 167 C5
Lydden Gr SW18 ... 157 D4
Lydden Rd SW18 ... 157 D4
Lydd Rd DA7 ... 147 B5
Lydeard Rd E6 ... 78 B1
Lydford Cl 22 N16 ... 73 C3
Lydford NW1 ... 232 B5
Lydford Rd
Brondesbury NW2 ... 68 D2
Paddington W9 ... 91 B3
Tottenham N15 ... 51 B4
Lydgate Ho 8 N16 ... 73 C3
Lydhurst Ave SW2 ... 160 B2
Lydia Ct 2 N12 ... 30 A4
Lydia Lodge HA1 ... 64 C4
Lydney Cl
Camberwell SE15 ... 139 C5
Putney SW19 ... 157 A2

Lydon Rd SW4 ... 137 C2
Lydstep Rd BR7 ... 188 C6
Lydwell Ho 29 SW8 ... 137 D3
Lyford Rd SW18 ... 158 C3
Lyford St SE7 ... 122 A2
Lygoe Ho 18 N6 ... 49 D2
Lygoe Rd N2 ... 30 B2
Lygon Ho 2 E2 ... 96 A4
Lygon Pl SW1 ... 258 C5
Lyham Cl SW2 ... 160 A5
Lyham Rd SW2 ... 160 A5
Lyle Cl CR4 ... 203 A2
Lyle Ct SM4 ... 202 B3
Lyle Pk SW15 ... 156 D5
Lyly Ho SE1 ... 262 D5
Lyme Farm Rd SE12 ... 143 B1
Lyme Gr E9 ... 74 C1
Lyme Grove Ho 2
E9 ... 74 C1
Lymer Ave SE19 ... 183 D5
Lyme Rd DA16 ... 146 B4
Lymescote Gdns
SM1 ... 217 C6
Lyme St NW1 ... 93 C6 232 A6
Lyminge Cl DA14 ... 189 D6
Lyminge Gdns SW17,
SW18 ... 158 C3
Lymington Ave N22 ... 32 D1
Lymington Cl
Mitcham SW16 ... 181 D1
2 Newham E6 ... 100 B2
Lymington Ct SM1 ... 218 A5
Lymington Dr HA4 ... 61 B6
Lymington Gdns
KT19 ... 215 D3
Lymington Mans
NW6 ... 69 D2
Lymington Rd
Dagenham RM8 ... 58 D1
Hampstead NW6 ... 69 D2
Lyminster Cl UB4 ... 85 A2
Lympne N17 ... 33 B1
Lympstone Gdns
SE15 ... 140 A5
Lynbridge Gdns N13 ... 32 D6
Lynbrook Gr SE15 ... 139 C5
Lynchen Cl TW5 ... 128 B4
Lynch Wlk 2 SE8 ... 141 B6
Lyncott Cres SW4 ... 137 B1
Lyncourt SE3 ... 142 B3
Lyncroft Ave HA5 ... 41 A4
Lyncroft Gdns
Ealing W13 ... 109 C5
Hampstead NW6 ... 69 C3
Hounslow TW3 ... 152 A6
Lyncroft Mans 4
NW6 ... 69 C3
Lyndale Ave NW2 ... 69 B5
Lyndale Cl SE3 ... 142 D6
Lyndale NW2 ... 69 B5
Lyndean Ind Est
SE2 ... 124 C3
Lynde Ho
2 Clapham SW4 ... 137 D2
Walton-on-T KT12 ... 194 C3
Lynden Gate SW15 ... 156 B4
Lyndenhurst SE3 ... 142 D2
Lynden Hyrst CR0 ... 221 D6
Lyndhurst Ave
Colney Hatch N12 ... 30 D4
Edgware NW7 ... 27 C4
Mitcham SW16 ... 181 D1
Pinner HA5 ... 22 B2
Southall UB1 ... 107 D5
Sunbury TW16 ... 194 A6
Tolworth KT5 ... 198 D1
Twickenham TW2,
TW4 ... 151 C3
Lyndhurst BR7 ... 188 D4
Lyndhurst Cl
Bexleyheath DA7 ... 147 D2
Neasden NW10 ... 67 B5
Orpington BR6 ... 226 D4
South Croydon CR0 ... 221 D5
Lyndhurst Ct
8 Belmont SM2 ... 217 C1
11 Woodford E18 ... 37 A2
Lyndhurst Dr
Leytonstone E10 ... 54 A2
New Malden KT3 ... 199 D2
Lyndhurst Gdns
Barking IG11 ... 79 C2
Enfield EN1 ... 5 C1
Hampstead NW3 ... 70 B3
Hendon N3 ... 29 A2
Ilford IG2 ... 57 B3
Pinner HA5 ... 22 B2
Lyndhurst Gr SE5,
SE15 ... 139 D3
Lyndhurst Ho 2
SW15 ... 156 A4
Lyndhurst House Prep
Sch NW3 ... 70 B3
Lyndhurst Lo 3
E14 ... 120 B2
Lyndhurst Rd
Bexleyheath DA7 ... 147 D2

Lyndhurst Rd continued
Chingford E4 ... 36 A3
Edmonton N18 ... 34 A6
Greenford UB6 ... 85 D3
Hampstead NW3 ... 70 B3
Thornton Heath CR7 ... 204 C5
Tottenham N22 ... 32 C4
Lyndhurst Sch SE5 ... 139 B3
Lyndhurst Sq SE15 ... 139 D4
Lyndhurst Terr NW3 ... 70 B3
Lyndhurst Way
Belmont SM2 ... 217 C1
Camberwell SE15 ... 139 D3
Lyndon Ave
Bexley DA15 ... 167 D6
Hackbridge SM6 ... 219 A5
Pinner HA5 ... 23 A4
Lyndon Rd DA17 ... 125 C2
Lyndon Yd SW17 ... 179 D6
Lyndum Ct N22 ... 32 C2
Lyne Cres E17 ... 35 B2
Lyne Ct NW9 ... 45 B2
Lynegrove Ave
TW15 ... 171 A5
Lyneham Wlk
Hackney E5 ... 75 A3
Pinner HA5 ... 39 D6
Lynette Ave SW4 ... 159 C5
Lynfield Ct SE23 ... 162 D4
Lynford Cl
Barnet Gate EN5 ... 11 D6
Burnt Oak HA8 ... 27 A2
Lynford French Ho
SE17 ... 262 A2
Lynford Gdns
Edgware HA8 ... 10 D1
Ilford IG3 ... 79 D6
Lynford Terr N9 ... 17 D3
Lyngham Ct 10 N4 ... 50 A2
Lynhurst Cres UB10 ... 61 B1
Lynhurst Ct NW8 ... 229 C5
Lynhurst Rd UB10 ... 61 A1
Lynmere Rd DA16 ... 146 B3
Lyn Mews 12 E3 ... 97 B4
Lynmouth Ave
Enfield EN1 ... 17 D5
West Barnes SM4 ... 200 D2
Lynmouth Dr HA4 ... 62 B5
Lynmouth Gdns
Heston TW5 ... 128 D4
Wembley UB6 ... 65 B1
Lynmouth Rd
Fortis Green N2 ... 48 D5
Stamford Hill N16 ... 51 D1
Walthamstow E17 ... 53 A4
Wembley UB6 ... 87 B6
Lynn Cl
Ashford TW15 ... 171 B5
Harrow HA3 ... 24 B1
Lynn Ct SW16 ... 181 D5
Lynne Cl 7 BR6 ... 227 D2
Lynne Ct
Forest Hill SE23 ... 163 B4
Hampstead NW6 ... 69 D1
South Croydon CR2 ... 221 C4
Wimbledon SW20 ... 178 B2
Lynnett Ct E9 ... 75 A2
Lynnett Rd RM8 ... 58 D1
Lynne Way UB5 ... 84 D5
Lynne Wlk KT10 ... 212 A3
Lynn Ho SE15 ... 140 A6
Lynn Mews E11 ... 76 C6
Lynn Rd
Balham SW12 ... 159 B4
Ilford IG2 ... 57 B2
Leyton E11 ... 76 C5
Lynn St EN2 ... 5 B4
Lynsted Cl
Bexley DA6 ... 169 D6
Bromley BR1 ... 187 C1
Lynsted Ct 4 BR3 ... 185 A1
Lynsted Gdns SE9 ... 143 D2
Lynton Ave
Ealing W13 ... 87 A1
Hyde The NW9 ... 45 D5
North Finchley N12 ... 30 B6
Lynton Cl
Chessington KT9 ... 214 A4
Isleworth TW7 ... 130 D1
Willesden NW10 ... 67 D3
Lynton Cres IG2 ... 56 D3
Lynton Ct
Bowes Pk N13 ... 32 A5
9 Dagenham W3 ... 89 A1
Penge SE20 ... 184 B2
Sutton SM2 ... 218 A2
Lynton Est SE1 ... 118 A2
Lynton Gdns
Enfield EN1 ... 17 C4
Friern Barnet N11 ... 31 D4
Lynton Grange N2 ... 48 D6
Lynton Ho 16 W2 ... 91 D1
Lynton Lo N5 ... 72 D3
Lynton Mans SE1 ... 261 A6
Lynton Mead N20 ... 13 D2
Lynton Rd Acton W3 ... 110 D6
Bermondsey SE1 ... 117 D2

Lynton Rd continued
Chingford E4 ... 35 D5
Harrow HA2 ... 63 A6
Hornsey N8 ... 50 A4
New Malden KT3 ... 199 B4
Paddington NW6 ... 91 B5
Thornton Heath CR0 ... 204 C3
Lynton Terr 4 W3 ... 89 A1
Lynton KT7 ... 197 A2
Lynton Wlk UB4 ... 83 C4
Lynwood Cl
Harrow HA2 ... 63 A5
Woodford E18 ... 37 C2
Lynwood Ct TW15 ... 170 B5
Lynwood Dr KT4 ... 216 A6
Lynwood Gdns
Southall UB1 ... 85 B1
Wallington CR0 ... 220 B4
Lynwood Gr
Orpington BR6 ... 211 C1
Southgate N21 ... 16 C3
Lynwood Rd
Ealing W5 ... 88 A3
Thames Ditton KT7 ... 196 D1
Upper Tooting
SW17 ... 180 D6
Lynx Terr SW19 ... 157 C1
Lynx Way E16 ... 121 D6
Lyon Bsns Pk IG11 ... 101 C5
Lyon Ct HA4 ... 39 D1
Lyon Ho NW8 ... 237 A5
Lyon Meade HA7 ... 25 C2
Lyon Park Ave HA0 ... 66 B2
Lyon Park Jun & Inf
Schs HA0 ... 66 B1
Lyon Rd Harrow HA1 ... 42 D3
Merton SW19 ... 180 A2
Lyonsdown Ave EN5 ... 14 A5
Lyonsdown Ct EN5 ... 14 A6
Lyonsdown Rd EN5 ... 14 A6
Lyonsdown Sch EN5 ... 14 A6
Lyons Pl NW8 ... 92 B3 236 C5
Lyon St N1 ... 72 B1
Lyons Wlk W14 ... 254 A4
Lyon Way UB6 ... 86 C6
Lyoth Rd BR5 ... 227 A6
Lyric Dr UB6 ... 85 D3
Lyric Mews SE26 ... 184 C6
Lyric Rd SW13 ... 133 D4
Lysander Ct 8 EN5 ... 13 D6
Lysander Gdns KT5 ... 198 B3
Lysander Gr N19 ... 49 D1
Lysander Ho 10 E2 ... 96 B5
Lysander 20 NW9 ... 27 D2
Lysander Rd
Ruislip HA4 ... 61 B6
Wallington CR0 ... 220 B2
Lysander Way BR6 ... 227 A5
Lysia Ct SW6 ... 134 D5
Lysias Rd SW12 ... 159 B5
Lysia St SW6 ... 134 D5
Lysons Wlk SW15 ... 156 A6
Lytchet Rd BR1 ... 187 B3
Lytchet Way EN3 ... 6 C4
Lytchgate Cl CR2 ... 221 C1
Lytcott Dr KT8 ... 195 B6
Lytcott Gr SE22 ... 161 D6
Lytham Ave WD19 ... 22 D5
Lytham Cl SE28 ... 103 A1
Lytham Ct 5 UB1 ... 85 D1
Lytham Gr W5 ... 88 B4
Lytham St
SE17 ... 117 B1 262 C1
Lyttelton Cl NW3 ... 70 C1
Lyttelton Ct N2 ... 48 A4
Lyttelton Rd
Hampstead Garden
Suburb N2 ... 48 A4
Leyton E10 ... 76 A5
Lytten Ct 6 W12 ... 112 A4
Lyttleton Ct UB4 ... 84 C3
Lyttleton Ho 10 E9 ... 74 C1
Lyttleton Rd N8 ... 50 C6
Lytton Ave Enfield EN3 ... 7 A5
Southgate N13 ... 16 C2
Lytton Cl
Hampstead Garden
Suburb N2 ... 48 B4
Northolt UB5 ... 63 B1
Lytton Ct WC1 ... 240 B3
Lytton Gdns SM6 ... 219 D4
Lytton Gr SW15 ... 157 A5
Lytton Ho 3 TW12 ... 173 D4
Lytton Rd
Leytonstone E11 ... 54 C2
New Barnet EN5 ... 2 A1
Pinner HA5 ... 23 A3
Lytton Strachey Path 8
SE28 ... 124 B6
Lyveden Rd
Greenwich SE3 ... 143 B5
Mitcham SW17,
SW19 ... 180 D4

M

Mabbett Ho 2
SE18 ... 144 C6
Mabel Crout Ct SE9 ... 145 B1
Mabel Evetts Ct
UB3 ... 106 B6
Mabel Thornton Ho 12
N16 ... 73 B4
Maberley Cres SE19 ... 184 A3
Maberley Ct SE19 ... 184 A3
Maberley Rd SE19 ... 182 C2
Mabledon Pl NW1,
WC1 ... 232 D1
Mablethorpe Rd
SW6 ... 264 A3
Mabley St E9 ... 75 A3
Mablin Lo 3 IG9 ... 21 C3
McAdam Dr EN2 ... 4 D3
MacAllister Ho 8
SE18 ... 144 D6
Macaret Cl N20 ... 14 A4
MacArthur Cl E7 ... 77 A2
MacArthur Ho 4
SW2 ... 160 A4
Macartney Ho SE10 ... 142 B5
MacAulay Ave KT10 ... 212 C6
Macaulay CE Prim Sch
SW4 ... 137 B1
MacAulay Ct SW4 ... 137 B2
MacAulay Ho
2 Kensal Town
W10 ... 91 A2
10 Stoke Newington
N16 ... 73 C5
MacAulay Rd
Clapham SW4 ... 137 B2
Newham E6 ... 99 D5
MacAulay Sq SW4 ... 137 B1
MacAulay Way 2
SE28 ... 124 B5
McAuley Cl
Eltham SE9 ... 166 C6
Lambeth
SE1 ... 116 C3 261 A6
MacAuley Mews
SE13 ... 142 A3
McAusland Ho 5 E3 ... 97 B5
Macbean St SE18 ... 122 D3
Macbeth Ho 4 N1 ... 95 C5
Macbeth St W6 ... 112 B1
McBride Ho 6 E3 ... 97 B5
McCall Cl SW4 ... 138 A3
McCall Cres SE7 ... 122 A1
McCall Ho N7 ... 72 A4
Mccarthy Ct SW11 ... 267 B1
McCarthy Rd TW13 ... 172 D5
Macclesfield Rd
Croydon SE25 ... 206 C4
Shoreditch
EC1 ... 95 A4 235 A2
Macclesfield St W1 ... 249 D6
McClintock Pl EN3 ... 7 D6
McCoid Way SE1 ... 252 A1
McConnell Ho SW8 ... 269 C1
McCormick Ho 9
SW2 ... 160 C3
McCrone Mews 3
NW3 ... 70 B2
McCullum Rd E3 ... 97 B6
McDermott Cl
SW11 ... 136 C2
McDermott Rd
SE15 ... 140 A2
MacDonald Ave
RM10 ... 81 D5
MacDonald Ct TW3 ... 130 A1
McDonald Ho 1
KT2 ... 176 B3
MacDonald Ho 2
SW11 ... 137 A3
MacDonald Rd
Chingford E17 ... 36 A1
Dartmouth Pk N19 ... 71 C6
Forest Gate E7 ... 77 A4
Friern Barnet N11 ... 30 D5
McDonough Cl KT9 ... 214 A4
McDougall Ct TW9 ... 132 C3
Mcdougall Ho E2 ... 96 A4
McDowall Cl E16 ... 98 D2
McDowall Rd SE5 ... 139 A4
Macduff Rd
SW11 ... 137 A4 268 B2
Mace Cl E1 ... 118 B5
Mace Ho 2 E17 ... 53 D6
McEntee Ave E17 ... 35 A2
Mace St E2 ... 96 D5
McEwan Way E15 ... 98 B6
Macey Ho
Battersea SW11 ... 267 A1
10 Greenwich SE10 ... 142 A6
Macfarlane La TW7 ... 131 A6

Macfarlane Rd W12 112 C5
Macfarren Ho 7
W10 91 A4
MacFarren Pl NW1 238 B5
McGlashon Ho 15 E1 96 A3
McGrath Rd E15 76 D2
McGregor Ct 8 N1 95 C4
MacGregor Ho 2
SW12 159 D3
MacGregor Rd E16 99 C2
McGregor Rd W11 91 B2
Mcguffie Ct E17 53 B6
Machell Rd SE15 140 C2
McIndoe Ct N1 235 C6
McIntosh Cl SM6 220 A1
McIntosh Ho 14
SE16 118 C2
McIntyre Ct 19 SW4 138 A3
Mackay Ho 33 W12 112 B6
Mackay Rd SW4 137 B2
McKay Rd SW20 178 C4
McKellar Cl WD23 8 A2
McKenna Ho 3 E3 97 B5
Mackennal St
NW8 92 C5 230 B4
Mackenzie Cl 7
W12 112 B6
Mackenzie Ho
5 Dollis Hill NW2 68 A5
1 Hornsey N8 50 A5
Mackenzie Rd
Barnsbury N7 72 B2
Penge BR3 184 D1
Mackenzie Wlk E14 119 C5
McKerrell Rd SE15 140 A4
Mackeson Rd NW3 70 D4
Mackie Ho 18 SW2 160 C4
Mackie Rd SW2 160 C4
McKiernan Ct 2
SW11 136 C3
Mc Killop Way
DA14 190 C3
McKinlay Ct
Beckenham BR3 185 B1
Bexley DA16 146 C2
McKinnon Wood Ho 16
E2 96 A4
Mackintosh La E9 74 D3
Macklin Ho SE23 162 B2
Macklin St
WC2 94 A1 240 B2
Mackonochie Ho
EC1 241 A4
Mackrow Wlk 11
E14 120 A6
Macks Rd SE16 118 A2
Mackworth Ho NW1 232 A2
Mackworth St NW1 232 A2
Mac Laren Mews
SW15 134 C1
Maclean Rd SE23 163 A5
McLeod Ct SE21 162 A3
McLeod Ho 3 SE23 162 C2
McLeod Rd SE2 124 B2
MacLeod Rd N21 16 A6
McLeod's Mews
SW7 113 D2 255 D4
MacLeod St
SE17 117 A1 262 B1
Maclise Rd
W14 113 A3 254 A5
McManus Ho 3
SW11 136 B2
McMillan Ct 2 SE6 164 D3
Macmillan Ct HA2 41 C1
Macmillan Ho
Cricklewood NW4 68 B4
Lisson Gr NW8 230 B1
McMillan Ho SE4 141 A2
McMillan St SE8 141 C6
Macmillan Way
SW17 181 B6
Mcmorran Ho 4 N7 72 A4
McNair Rd UB2 107 D3
Macnamara Ho
SW10 266 C4
McNeil Rd SE5 139 C3
McNicol Dr NW10 89 A5
Macoma Rd SE18 145 B6
Macoma Terr SE18 145 B6
Maconochies Rd 9
E14 119 D1
Macquarie Way
E14 119 D2
McRae La CR4 202 D2
Macready Ho W1 237 B3
Macready Pl 2 N7 72 A4
Macroom Ho W9 91 B4
Macroom Rd W9 91 B4
Mac's Pl EC4 241 B2
Madame Tussaud's*
NW1 93 A3 238 A5
Mada Rd BR6 226 D5
Maddams St E3 97 D3
Madderfields Ct N11 31 D2
Maddison Cl
Finchley N2 30 A1
Teddington TW11 174 D4
Maddison Ct NW4 28 C1
Maddocks Cl DA14 191 A5
Maddocks Ho 3 E1 118 B6
Maddock Way SE17 138 D6
Maddox Ct 1 E4 20 B3
Maddox St W1 248 D6
Madeira Ave BR1 186 C3
Madeira Gr IG8 37 C4
Madeira Rd
Edmonton N13 16 D1
Leytonstone E11 54 C1
Mitcham CR4 202 D5
Streatham SW16 182 A5
Madeleine Cl RM6 58 C3
Madeley Ct W5 88 A1
Madeley Rd W5 88 A1
Madeline Gr IG1 79 B3
Madeline Rd SE20 184 A3
Madge Gill Way 4
E6 100 A6
Madge Hill W7 108 C6
Madinah Rd E8 74 A3
Madingley Ct TW1 153 C6
Madingley 11 KT1 176 C1
Madison Apartments
N11 31 D3
Madison Cres DA7 146 C5
Madison Ct 15 RM10 81 D2
Madison Gdns
Beckenham BR2 208 D6
Bexley DA7 146 C5
Madison Ho E3 98 A4
Madras Ho IG1 78 D4
Madras Pl N7 72 C2
Madras Rd IG1 78 D4
Madrid Rd SW13 134 A5
Madron St
SE17 117 C1 263 B2
Mafeking Ave
Brentford TW8 132 A6
Ilford IG2 57 B2
Newham E6 100 A5
Mafeking Rd
Enfield EN1 5 D2
Newham E16 98 D3
Tottenham N17 34 A1
Magdala Ave N19 71 C6
Magdala Rd
Isleworth TW7 131 A2
South Croydon CR2 221 B1
Magdalen Ct SE25 206 A4
Magdalene Cl 7
SE15 140 B3
Magdalene Gdns
E6 100 C3
Magdalene Ho 7
SW15 156 D5
Magdalene Rd
TW17 192 B6
Magdalen Pas E1 253 D6
Magdalen Rd SW18 158 B3
Magdalen St SE1 253 A3
Magee St SE11 138 C6
Magellan Ct 11
NW10 67 B1
Magellan Ho 16 E1 96 D3
Magellan Pl 25 E14 119 C2
Magna Ct UB6 86 B4
Magnaville Rd WD23 8 D4
Magnet Rd HA9 65 D6
Magnin Cl 5 E8 96 A6
Magnolia Cl
Kingston u T KT2 176 D4
Leyton E10 75 C6
Magnolia Ct
13 Belmont SM2 217 D1
Feltham TW14 150 A3
2 Finchley N12 29 D6
Forest Hill SE26 184 C5
Harrow HA3 44 B2
Hillingdon UB10 60 D2
Northolt UB5 85 A3
Richmond TW9 132 D4
Wallington SM6 219 B3
Wandsworth SW11 158 D5
Magnolia Gdns HA8 27 A6
Magnolia Ho 13 SE8 141 B6
Magnolia Lo E4 19 D1
Magnolia Pl
Clapham Pk SW4 160 A6
Ealing W5 87 D2
Magnolia Rd W4 132 D6
Magnolia Way KT19 215 A3
Magnolia Wharf
W4 132 D6
Magpie Cl
Edgware NW9 27 C1
Enfield EN1 6 A4
Forest Gate E7 76 D3
Magpie Hall Cl BR2 210 A3
Magpie Hall La BR2 210 B3
Magpie Hall Rd WD23 8 C2
Magpie Ho 7 E3 97 B6
Magpie Pl SE14 141 A6
Magri Wlk 22 E1 96 C2
Maguire Dr TW10 175 C6
Maguire St
SE1 117 D4 253 D2
Mahatma Gandhi Ind
Est 11 SE24 138 D1
Mahlon Ave HA4 62 B2
Mahogany Cl SE16 119 A5
Mahon Cl EN1 5 D4
Mahoney Ho SE14 141 B4
Maida Ave
Chingford E4 19 D4
Little Venice
W2 92 A3 236 B5
Maida Rd DA17 125 C3
MAIDA VALE 91 D4
Maida Vale Sta W9 91 D4
Maida Vale
W9 92 A4 229 A1
Maida Way E4 19 D4
Maiden Erlegh Ave
DA5 169 A3
Maiden La
Borough The
SE1 117 A5 252 B4
Camden Town NW1 71 D1
Strand WC2 116 A6 250 B6
Maiden Rd E15 76 C1
Maidenstone Hill
SE10 142 A4
Maids of Honour Row
4 TW9 153 D6
Maidstone Bldgs
SE1 252 C3
Maidstone Ct N11 31 D4
Maidstone Ho 4
E14 97 D1
Maidstone Rd
Friern Barnet N11 31 D4
Ruxley DA14 191 C3
Mail Coach Yd 23 E2 95 C4
Main Ave EN1 17 D6
Main Dr HA9 65 D5
Main Rd
Chislehurst BR5 190 C1
Sidcup DA14 167 C1
Mainridge Rd BR7,
SE9 188 C6
Main St TW13 172 D5
Mainwaring Ct 3
CR4 181 A1
Main Yd E9 75 C2
Mais Ho SE26 162 B2
Maismore St SE15 140 A6
Maison Alfort HA3 24 C2
Maisonettes The
SM1 217 B3
Maitland Cl
3 Greenwich
SE10 141 D5
Hounslow TW4 129 B2
Maitland Ct W2 246 C6
Maitland Ho
Chelsea SW1 269 A6
16 South Hackney E2 96 C5
MAITLAND PARK 70 D2
Maitland Park Rd
NW3 70 D2
Maitland Park Villas
NW3 70 D2
Maitland Pl E5 74 C4
Maitland Rd
Penge SE26 184 D4
Stratford E15 76 D2
Majendie Rd SE18 123 B1
Majestic Ct N4 50 D1
Majestic Way CR4 180 D1
Major Cl SW9 138 D2
Majorie Mews 6 E1 96 D1
Major Rd
22 Bermondsey
SE16 118 A3
Stratford New Town
E15 76 B3
Makepeace Ave N6 71 A6
Makepeace Mans N6 71 A6
Makepeace Rd
Northolt UB5 85 A6
Wanstead E11 55 A5
Makinen Ho 5 IG9 21 C3
Makins St SW3 257 B3
Malabar Ct 20 W12 112 B6
Malabar St E14 119 C4
Malam Ct SE11 261 A3
Malam Gdns 3 E14 119 D6
Malatia CR2 221 A2
Malay Ho 2 E1 118 C5
Malborough Ho 3
N20 14 D1
Malbrook Rd SW15 134 B1
Malbury Ct N22 32 A3
Malcolm Cl SE20 184 C3
Malcolm Cres NW4 46 A3
Malcolm Ct Ealing W5 88 B3
Hendon NW4 46 A3
Stanmore HA7 25 C5
Malcolm Ct *continued*
Stratford E7 76 D2
Malcolm Dr KT6 198 A1
Malcolm Ho 13 N1 95 C5
Malcolm Pl E2 96 C3
Malcolm Prim Sch
SE20 184 C3
Malcolm Rd
Bethnal Green E1 96 C3
Croydon SE25 206 A3
Ickenham UB10 60 B4
Penge SE20 184 C3
Wimbledon SW19 179 A4
Malcolmson Ho
SW1 259 D1
Malcolms Way N14 15 C6
Malcolm Way E11 55 A5
Malden Ave
Croydon SE25 206 B6
Northolt UB6 64 C2
Malden CE Prim Sch
KT4 199 C1
Malden Cres NW1 71 A2
Malden Ct
Stoke Newington
N4 51 A3
West Barnes KT3 200 B6
Malden Green Ave
KT4 200 A1
Malden Hill Gdns
KT3 199 D6
Malden Hill KT3 199 D6
Malden Junc KT3 199 D4
Malden Manor Prim Sch
KT3 199 C2
Malden Manor Sta
KT3 199 C2
Malden Pk KT3 199 D3
Malden Pl NW5 71 A3
Malden Rd
Camden Town
NW5 71 A2
Cheam KT4, SM3 216 D4
New Malden KT3,
KT4 199 D2
Malden Way (Kingston
By Pass) KT3, KT5 199 C4
Malden Way KT3 200 A5
Maldon Cl
Camberwell SE5 139 C2
Shoreditch N1 235 B6
Stratford New Town
E15 76 B3
Maldon Ct
Barking E6 100 C6
Wallington SM6 219 C3
Maldon Rd
Acton W3 111 A6
Edmonton N9 17 D1
Wallington SM6 219 B3
Maldon Wlk IG8 37 C4
Malet Pl WC1 239 C5
Malet St WC1 93 D2 239 D4
Maley Ave SE27 160 D2
Malford Ct E18 37 A1
Malford Gr E18 54 D6
Malfort Rd SE5 139 C2
Malham Cl N11 31 A4
Malham Rd SE23 162 D3
Malham Road Ind Est
SE23 162 D3
Malindi Ct N8 49 D4
Malins Cl EN5 12 C6
Malins Ct SW12 159 A5
Mallaig Ct HA8 10 D2
Mallams Mews 1
SW9 138 D2
Mallard Cl
1 Hackney E9 75 B2
Hanwell W7 108 C4
Kilburn NW6 91 C6
New Barnet EN5 14 B5
Twickenham TW4 151 C4
Mallard Ct
Chingford E4 20 B4
Ilford IG1 79 A6
Kingsbury NW9 45 A2
Little Ilford E12 78 B3
16 Richmond TW10 153 D5
Walthamstow E17 54 B6
Mallard Ho
8 Camberwell
SE15 139 D4
St John's Wood NW8 230 A3
Mallard Path 3
SE28 123 B3
Mallard Pl TW1 153 A1
Mallard Point 6 E3 97 C4
Mallards Rd
Barking IG11 102 A3
Woodford IG8 37 B3
Mallards E11 55 A2
Mallard Way NW9 45 A2
Mallard Wlk
Beckenham BR3 206 D4
Sidcup DA14 190 C4
Mall Ct W5 110 A6
Mallet Dr UB5 63 B3
Mallet Ho 11 SW15 156 A6
Mallet Rd SE13 164 B5
Malling Cl CR0 206 C3
Malling Gdns SM4 202 A3
Malling Ho 9 BR3 185 C3
Malling SE13 163 D6
Malling Way BR2 208 D2
Mallinson Ct 2 E11 76 C6
Mallinson Rd
Wallington SM6 219 D5
Wandsworth SW11 158 D6
Mallon Gdns E1 243 D3
Mallord St
SW3 136 B6 266 D6
Mallory Bldgs EC1 241 C5
Mallory Cl SE4 141 A1
Mallory Gdns EN4 15 A4
Mallory St
NW8 92 C3 237 B6
Mallow Cl CR0 206 D1
Mallow Ct
Colney Hatch N12 30 C4
Lewisham SE13 142 A3
Mallow Mead NW7 29 A3
Mallow St EC1 242 C6
Mallows The UB10 60 D5
Mall Rd W6 112 B1
Mall Studios 9 NW3 70 D3
Mall The
6 Bexley DA6 147 C1
Brentford TW8 131 D6
4 Bromley BR1 209 A6
Ealing W5 110 A6
Harrow HA3 44 B3
Kingston u T KT6 197 D4
Mortlake SW14 155 A6
Palmers Green N14 16 A1
Mall The (Prep Sch)
TW2 152 B1
Mall The
SW1 115 D5 249 C3
Malmains Cl BR3 208 B5
Malmains Way BR3 208 B5
Malmesbury Cl HA5 40 A5
Malmesbury 30 E2 96 C5
Malmesbury Prim Sch
Morden SM4 202 A3
Tower Hamlets E3 97 B4
Malmesbury Rd
Bow E3 97 B5
Morden SM4 202 A3
Newham E16 98 C2
Woodford E18 36 D2
Malmesbury Terr
E16 98 D2
Malmsey Ho SE11 260 D2
Malmsmead Ho E9 75 A3
Malorees Jun & Inf
Schs NW6 68 D1
Malory Cl BR3 185 A1
Malpas Dr HA5 40 D4
Malpas Rd
Dagenham RM9 80 D2
Hackney E8 74 B2
New Cross SE4 141 B3
Malta Rd E10 53 C2
Malta St EC1 241 D6
Maltby Dr EN1 6 B5
Maltby Rd KT9 214 C2
Maltby St
SE1 117 D3 263 C6
Maltham Terr N18 34 B4
Malthouse Dr
Chiswick W4 133 D6
Feltham TW13 172 D5
Malthouse Pas
SW13 133 C3
Malthus Path 7
SE28 124 C5
Malting Ho E14 119 B6
Maltings Cl SW13 133 C3
Maltings Lo W4 133 C5
Maltings W4 110 C1
Maltings Pl
Bermondsey SE1 253 B2
Parsons Green SW6 265 D1
Maltings The BR6 211 D1
Malting Way TW7 130 D2
Malt Mill SE1 253 C3
Malton Ho SE25 205 C5
Malton Mews
1 Notting Hill
W10 91 A1
Plumstead Comm
SE18 145 C6
Malton Rd W10 91 A1
Malton St SE18 145 C6
Maltravers St WC2 251 A6
Malt St SE1 140 A6
Malva Cl SW18 157 D6
Malvern Ave
Chingford E4 36 B3
Erith DA7 147 A5
Harrow HA2 63 B5
Malvern Cl
Bushey WD23
Ickenham UB10
Mitcham CR4 2
Notting Hill W10
Penge SE20 1
Surbiton KT6 1
Malvern Ct
Belmont SM2 2
5 East Barnet N20
15 Shepherd's Bush
W12 1
South Kensington
SW7 2
3 Surbiton KT6 1
Malvern Dr
Feltham TW13 1
Ilford IG3
Woodford IG8
Malvern Gdns
Cricklewood NW2
Harrow HA3
Malvern Ho
London N16
SE17 2
Malvern Lo N12
Malvern Mews NW6
Malvern Pl NW6
Malvern Rd
Dalston E8
Enfield EN3
Hampton TW12 1
Harlington UB3 1
Hornsey N8
Leytonstone E11
Maida Vale NW6
Newham E6 1
Surbiton KT6 1
Thornton Heath CR7 2
Tottenham Hale N17
Upper Holloway N19
Malvern Terr
Edmonton N9
Islington N1 2
Malvern Way W13
Malwood Rd SW12 1
Malyons Rd SE13 1
Malyons Terr SE13 1
Malyons The TW17 1
Managers St 8 E14 1
Manatee Pl SM6 2
Manaton Cl SE15 1
Manaton Cres UB1
Manbey Gr E15
Manbey Park Rd E15
Manbey Rd E15
Manbey St E15
Manbre Rd W6
Manbrough Ave E6 1
Manchester Ct E16
Manchester Dr W10
Manchester Gr E14 1
Manchester Ho
SE17 2
Manchester Mans
N19
Manchester Mews
W1 2
Manchester Rd
Cubitt Town E14 1
South Norwood CR7 2
Tottenham N15
Manchester Sq
W1 93 A1 2
Manchester St
W1 93 A2 2
Manchester Way
RM10
Manchuria Rd
SW11 1
Manciple St
SE1 117 B3 2
Mandalay Ho 6 N16
Mandalay Rd SW4 1
Mandarin Ct
6 Deptford SE8 1
Willesden NW10
Mandarin Way UB4
Mandela Cl
36 Shepherd's Bush
W12 1
Stonebridge NW10
Mandela Ho
Plumstead Comm
SE18 1
18 Spitalfields E2
Mandela Rd E16
Mandela St
Camden Town
NW1 93 C6 2
Kennington SW9 1
Mandela Way
SE1 117 C2 2
Manderville Ho SE1 2
Mandeville Cl
5 Greenwich
SE3 1

ndeville Cl *continued*
Merton SW19 179 A2
ndeville Ct
ampstead NW3 69 D3
ighams Pk E4 35 A6
ndeville Ctyd
W11 268 A1
ndeville Dr KT6 197 D1
ndeville Ho 8
W4 159 C6
ndeville Pl W1 238 B2
ndeville Prim Sch
5 74 D5
ndeville Rd
nfield EN3 7 A6
sleworth TW7 131 A3
ttleton TW17 192 C4
ortholt UB5 63 C1
sidge N14 15 C2
ndeville Sch UB5 63 B2
ndeville St E5 75 A5
ndrake Rd SW17 158 D1
ndrake Way 3
15 76 C1
ndrell Rd SW2 160 A6
nesty Ct N14 15 D4
nette St W1 239 D1
nfred Ct 7
W15 157 B6
nfred Rd SW15 157 B6
nger Rd N7 72 A2
ngold Way 4
A18 125 A3
nilla Ct RM6 58 B3
nilla St E14 119 C4
nister Rd SE2 124 A3
nitoba Ct 29
E16 118 C4
nitoba Gdns 6
R6 227 D2
nley Ct N16 73 D5
nley Ho SE11 261 A2
nley St NW1 231 A6
nly Dixon Dr EN3 7 A6
nn Cl 3 CR0 221 A5
nneby Prior N1 233 D3
nnering Ho 16
W2 160 B6
nning Ct 3 SE28 124 B5
nningford Cl EC1 234 C2
nning Gdns HA3 43 D2
nning Ho
3 Notting Hill
W11 91 A1
3 Walthamstow E17 54 A6
nning Pl TW10 154 B5
nning Rd
agenham RM10 81 C1
althamstow E17 53 A4
nningtree Cl
W19 157 A3
nningtree Rd HA4 62 B4
nningtree St 2
1 96 A1
nnin Rd RM6 58 B2
nnock Mews IG8 37 B2
nnock Rd N22 50 D6
nn's Cl TW7 152 D6
nns Rd HA8 26 C4
nny Shinwell Ho
W6 264 D5
noel Rd TW2 152 A2
nor Ave
ounslow TW4 128 D3
ew Cross SE4 141 B3
ortholt UB5 63 B1
norbrook SE12,
3 143 A1
nor Circus TW9 132 C2
nor Cl Barnet EN5 1 A1
dgware NW7 27 B5
igham Hill E17 35 A1
ingsbury NW9 44 D4
ew Malden KT4 199 C1
uislip HA4 39 D1
hamesmead SE28 102 C1
nor Cottages App
2 30 A1
nor Cotts N2 30 A1
nor Court Lo 12
8 37 A2
nor Court Rd
7 108 C6
nor Cres KT5 198 C3
nor Croft HA8 26 C4
nor Ct
1 Barking IG11 79 D1
1 Brixton SW2 160 B6
amberwell SE15 139 D4
hingford E4 20 C3
ortis Green N2 48 D4
iern Barnet N20 14 D1
unnersbury W3 110 C2
1 Hackbridge SM6 219 A5
arrow HA1 42 D3
ngston u T KT2 176 C2
sidge N14 15 D2

Manor Ct *continued*
Parsons Green SW6 265 D1
Streatham SW16 160 A1
Surbiton KT5 198 C3
8 Sutton SM1 218 A4
Twickenham TW2 152 A2
Walthamstow E10 53 D1
5 Wembley HA9 66 A3
Manordene Cl KT7 197 A1
Manordene Rd
SE28 102 D1
Manor Dr
East Barnet N14 15 B3
Edgware NW7 27 B5
Feltham TW13 172 D5
Friern Barnet N20 14 D1
Hinchley Wood KT10 213 A5
Manor Dr N KT3,
KT4 199 B2
Manor Dr
Sunbury TW16 172 A1
Surbiton KT5 198 C3
Manor Dr The KT4 199 D1
Manor Dr
Wembley HA9 66 B4
West Ewell KT19 215 C2
Manor Farm Ave
TW17 192 D3
Manor Farm Cl KT4 199 C1
Manor Farm Ct E6 100 B4
Manor Farm Dr E4 20 C1
Manor Farm Rd
Thornton Heath CR7,
SW16 182 C1
Wembley HA0 87 D5
Manorfield Cl 3 N19 71 C4
Manorfield Prim Sch
E14 97 D2
Manorfields Cl BR7 211 D6
Manor Gate UB5 63 A1
Manorgate Rd KT2 176 C2
Manor Gdns
8 Chiswick W4 111 C1
Clapham SW4 137 C3
Gunnersbury W3 110 C2
Hampton TW12 174 A3
Merton SW20 179 B1
Richmond TW10,
TW9 132 B1
Ruislip HA4 62 C3
South Croydon CR2 221 D2
Sunbury TW16 172 A1
Upper Holloway N7 72 A5
Manor Gr
Beckenham BR3 185 D1
Deptford SE15 140 C6
Richmond TW9 132 C2
Manor Gt SW15 157 A6
Manor Hall Ave NW4 28 D1
Manor Hall Dr NW4 28 D1
Manor Hall Gdns E10 53 C1
Manor Ho
Brentford TW8 109 C1
Manor Pk E12 77 D4
Osidge N14 15 D3
Paddington NW1 237 B4
Manor Ho The
Bexley DA5 169 D3
Chislehurst SE9 188 A5
Manor Ho TW2 152 C2
Manor House Ct
Lower Halliford
TW17 192 D2
Paddington W9 236 A5
Manor House Dr
NW6 68 D1
Manor House Est
HA7 25 B5
Manor House Gdns
E11 55 B3
Manor House Sta N4 50 D1
Manor House Way
TW7 131 B2
Manor Ho SM6 219 B3
Manor Jun & Inf Schs
IG11 79 D2
Manor La
Feltham TW13 150 A2
Harlington UB3 127 B6
Hither Green SE12 164 C5
Manor Lane Terr
SE13 164 C6
Manor La
Sunbury TW16 172 B1
Sutton SM1 218 A3
Manor Lo NW2 68 D2
Manor Mans
7 Hampstead
NW3 70 C2
Tufnell Pk N7 72 A5
Manor Mead Sch
TW17 192 D4
Manor Mews
New Cross SE4 141 B3
Paddington NW6 91 C5
Manor Mount SE23 162 C3

Manor Oak Mans
SE22 162 B5
Manor Par HA1 42 D3
MANOR PARK 78 A4
Manor Park Cl BR4 207 D1
Manor Park Cres
HA8 26 C4
Manor Park Dr HA2 41 D6
Manor Park Gdns
HA8 26 C4
Manor Park Par
SE13 142 B1
Manor Park Prim Sch
SM1 218 A3
Manor Park Rd
Chislehurst BR7 189 B2
Dagenham NW10 89 D6
East Finchley N2 48 B6
Manor Pk E12 77 D4
Sutton SM1 218 A3
West Wickham BR4 207 D1
Manor Park Sta E12 77 D4
Manor Par N16 73 D6
Manor Pk
Chislehurst BR7 189 B2
Lewisham SE13 164 C6
Richmond TW9 132 B1
Manor Pl
Chislehurst BR7 189 B1
East Bedfont TW14 150 A3
Mitcham CR4 203 C6
Newington
SE17 117 A1 262 A2
Sutton SM1 217 D4
Walton-on-T KT12 194 A2
Manor Prim Sch E15 98 C5
Manor Rd
Ashford TW15 170 C5
Barking IG11 79 D2
Barnet EN5 1 A1
Beckenham BR3 185 D1
Belmont SM2 217 B1
Bowes Pk N22 32 A4
Dagenham RM6 58 D3
Ealing W13 109 A6
East Molesey KT8 196 B5
Enfield EN2 5 B3
Harrow HA1 43 A3
Hayes UB3 84 A1
Higham Hill E17 35 A1
Loughton IG10 21 B5
Merton SW20 179 B1
Mitcham CR4 203 C6
Newham E15, E16 98 C4
Manor Rd N
Hinchley Wood
KT7 213 A6
Wallington SM5,
SM6 219 B4
Manor Rd
Old Bexley DA5 169 D3
Richmond TW10,
TW9 132 B1
Ruislip HA4 39 B1
Manor Rd S KT10 212 C4
Manor Rd
Sidcup DA15 168 A1
South Norwood
SE25 206 A6
Stamford Hill N16 51 C1
Teddington TW11 175 B5
Tottenham N17 34 B2
Twickenham TW2 152 B2
Wallington SM5,
SM6 219 B3
Walthamstow E10 53 C2
Walton-on-T KT12 193 D2
West Wickham BR4 223 D6
Manor Road Ho HA1 43 A3
Manor Sch NW10 90 C6
Manorside EN5 1 A1
Manorside Cl SE2 124 D2
Manorside Prim Sch
N3 30 A2
Manor Sq RM8 80 C6
Manor Street Est
SW3 267 B6
Manor The
Dulwich SE23 162 C4
Mayfair W1 248 C5
Manor Vale TW8 109 C1
Manor View N3 29 D1
Manor Way
Beckenham BR3 207 C6
Bromley BR2 210 A3
Chingford E4 36 B6
Colindale NW9 45 C5
Manorway EN1 17 C4
Manor Waye UB8 82 A6
Manor Way
Greenwich SE3 143 A1
Gunnersbury W3 110 C2
Harrow HA2 41 D5
Mitcham CR4 203 C6
New Malden KT4 199 D1
Orpington BR5 211 A5
Ruislip HA4 39 D1

Manor Way *continued*
Sidcup DA5 169 C3
Southall UB2 106 D2
South Croydon CR2 221 D2
Manor Way The
SM6 219 B4
Manorway IG8 37 C5
Manpreet Ct E12 78 B3
Manray Ct 2 N8 50 A4
Manresa Rd
SW3 114 C1 257 A1
Mansard Beeches
SW17 181 A5
Mansard Cl HA5 40 D6
Mansard Manor 4
SM2 218 A1
Manse Cl UB3 127 B6
Manse Ct DA14 190 C5
Mansel Ct SW11 267 B1
Mansel Gr E17 35 C2
Mansell Ho SW8 269 B2
Mansell Rd
Acton W3 111 B4
Southall UB6 85 D2
Mansell St E1 95 D1 243 D1
Mansel Rd SW19 179 B4
Manse Rd N16 73 D5
Mansergh Cl SE18 144 A5
Mansfield Ave
East Barnet EN4 15 A5
Ruislip HA4 40 B1
Tottenham N15 51 B5
Mansfield Cl N9 18 A5
Mansfield Ct 27 E2 95 D6
Mansfield Dr UB4 83 C3
Mansfield Hill E4 19 D3
Mansfield Ho SW15 156 D5
Mansfield Hts N2 48 D4
Mansfield Mews W1 238 C3
Mansfield Pl 28 NW3 70 A4
Mansfield Rd
Acton W3 88 D3
Chessington KT9 213 D3
Ilford IG1 78 C6
Maitland Pk NW3 70 D4
South Croydon CR2 221 B2
Walthamstow E17 53 B5
Wanstead E11 55 B3
Mansfield St
W1 93 B2 238 C3
Mansford St E2 96 A5
Manship Rd CR4 181 A2
Mansion Cl SW9 138 C4
Mansion Gdns NW3 69 D5
Mansion Ho* EC4 242 C1
Mansion House Pl EC3,
EC4 242 C1
Mansion House Sta
EC4 117 A6 252 B6
Mansion House St
EC2 242 C1
Mansions The NW6 69 B3
Manson Mews
SW7 114 B2 256 C3
Manson Pl
SW7 114 B2 256 C3
Manstead Gdns RM6 58 C2
Manston Ave UB2 107 C2
Manston NW1 71 C1
Manston Cl SE20 184 C2
Manstone Rd NW2 69 A3
Manston Gr KT2 175 D5
Manston Ho W14 254 B5
Manston N17 33 B1
Mantell Ho SW4 159 C6
Manthorpe Rd SE18 123 A1
Mantilla Rd SW17 181 A6
Mantle Rd SE4 141 A2
Mantlet Cl SW16 181 C3
Mantle Way E15 76 C1
Manton Ave W7 109 A4
Manton Cl UB3 105 C6
Manton Ho N16 73 B5
Manton Rd
Holdbrook EN3 7 C5
Plumstead SE2 124 A2
Mantua St 23 SW11 136 B2
Mantus Cl
Bethnal Green E1 96 C3
19 Stepney E1 96 C3
Mantus Rd E1 96 C3
Manus Way N20 14 A3
Manville Gdns
SW17 159 B1
Manville Rd SW17 159 B1
Manwood Rd SE4 163 B5
Manwood St E16 122 B5
Manygate La TW17 193 A3
Many Gates SW12 159 B2
Mapesbury Ct NW2 69 A3
Mapesbury Mews 1
NW9 46 A3
Mapesbury Rd NW2 69 A2
Mapeshill Pl NW2 68 C2
Mapes Ho 7 NW6 69 A1
Mape St E2 96 B3

Maple Ave
East Acton W3 111 C5
Harrow HA2 63 D6
Walthamstow E4 35 B4
Yiewsley UB7 104 B6
Maple Cl
Buckhurst Hill IG9 21 D1
Clapham Pk SW4 159 D5
Finchley N3 29 C4
Hampton TW12 173 B4
Hayes UB4 84 D4
Mitcham CR4 181 B2
Petts Wood BR5 211 B4
Ruislip HA4 40 B3
South Tottenham N16 52 A3
Maple Cres DA15 168 A5
Maplecroft Cl E6 100 A1
Maple Ct
Ashford TW15 171 B3
Catford SE6 163 D3
2 Croydon CR0 221 A4
7 Dagenham RM8 58 D2
Kingston u T KT3 199 B6
Newham E6 100 C2
6 Pinner HA5 22 C1
Sidcup DA14 190 B5
11 West Norwood
SW16 182 C5
8 Willesden NW2 68 D4
Mapledale Ave CR0 222 A5
Mapledene BR7 189 A5
Mapledene Est E8 74 A1
Mapledene Rd E8 74 A1
Mapledown Sch
NW2 46 C2
Mapledurham Ct 3
N13 32 C6
Maple Gdns
Grahame Pk HA8 27 C3
Stanwell TW19 148 A2
Maple Gr TW8 131 B5
Maple Gr Bsns Ctr
TW4 128 C1
Maple Gr Ealing W5 109 D3
Kingsbury NW9 45 A2
Southall UB1 85 B2
Maple Ho
2 Kingston u T
KT6 198 A4
11 Maitland Pk NW3 70 D2
5 New Cross SE8 141 B5
4 Richmond TW9 132 D4
Teddington KT1 175 C3
13 Walthamstow E17 53 D6
Maplehurst 2 BR2 186 C1
Maplehurst Cl KT1 198 A5
Maple Ind Est TW13 150 A1
Maple Inf Sch KT6 197 D4
Maple Leaf Dr
DA15 167 D3
Mapleleafe Gdns
IG6 56 D6
Maple Leaf Sq 27
SE16 118 D4
Maple Lo
Buckhurst Hill IG9 21 D3
Putney SW15 157 A5
Welsh Harp NW9 67 B6
Maple Mews
Paddington NW6 91 D5
Streatham SW16 182 B5
Maple Pl
Marylebone W1 239 B5
Tottenham N17 34 A3
Yiewsley UB7 104 B6
Maple Rd Hayes UB4 84 D4
Kingston u T KT6 197 D4
Leytonstone E11 54 C3
Penge SE20 184 C2
Maples Pl E1 96 B2
Maple St 5 E2 96 B5
Maplestead Rd
Dagenham RM9 102 B6
Streatham SW2 160 B4
Maple St W1 93 C3 239 B5
Maples The 4 KT1 175 C3
Maplethorpe Rd
CR7 204 D5
Mapleton Cl BR2 209 A3
Mapleton Cres
Enfield EN3 6 C5
Wandsworth SW18 157 D5
Mapleton Rd
Chingford E4 20 A1
Enfield EN1 6 B3
Wandsworth SW18 157 D5
Maple Tree Pl 7
SE3 144 A4
Maple Way TW13 150 B1
Maple Wlk W10 90 D3
Maplin Cl N21 16 B5
Maplin Ho 7 SE2 124 D4
Maplin Rd E16 99 B1
Maplin St E3 97 B4
Mapperley Cl 3 E11 55 A3
Mapperley Dr IG8 36 C3
Marabou Cl E12 78 A3

Marada Ho NW6 69 A1
Marais W4 133 A5
Maran Way DA18 124 D3
Marathon Way
SE28 123 D4
Marban Rd W9 91 B4
Marble Arch Sta
W1 92 D1 237 D1
Marble Arch*
W1 114 D6 247 D6
Marble Cl W3 110 D5
Marble Dr NW2 46 D2
Marbleford Ct 4 N6 49 D2
Marble Hill Cl TW1 153 B4
Marble Hill Gdns
TW1 153 B4
Marble Hill* TW1 153 C4
Marble Ho
Paddington W9 91 B3
Plumstead Comm
SE18 123 D1
Marble Quay SE1 118 A5
Marbrook Ct SE12 165 C1
Marcella Rd SW9 138 C3
Marcellina Way
BR6 227 D5
Marchant Ho 13
SW2 160 B6
Marchant Rd E11 76 B6
Marchant St SE14 141 A6
Marchbank Rd
W14 135 B6 264 D6
March Ct SW15 134 B1
Marchmont Ho 10
SW16 181 C5
Marchmont Rd
Richmond TW10 154 B6
Wallington SM6 219 C1
Marchmont St
WC1 94 A3 240 A6
March 23 NW9 27 D2
March Rd 7 TW1 153 A4
Marchside Cl TW5 128 D4
Marchwood Cl 9
SE5 139 C5
Marchwood Cres
W5 87 D1
Marcia Rd
SE1 117 C2 263 B3
Marcilly Rd SW18 158 B6
Marcol Ho W1 238 D2
Marcon Ct 23 E8 74 B3
Marconi Pl N11 31 B6
Marconi Rd E10 53 C1
Marconi Way UB1 85 D1
Marcon Pl E8 74 B3
Marco Rd W6 112 C3
Marcourt Lawns W5 88 A3
Marcus Ct
Brentford TW8 132 A5
Newham E15 98 C6
Marcus Garvey Mews
SE22 162 B6
Marcus Garvey Way 9
SE24 138 C1
Marcus Ho 14 SE15 139 D4
Marcus St
Wandsworth
SW18 157 D5
West Ham E15 98 D6
Marcus Terr SW18 157 D5
Mardale Ct NW7 28 A3
Mardale Dr NW9 45 B4
Mardell Rd CR0 206 D4
Marden Ave BR2 209 A3
Marden Cres CR0 204 B3
Marden Ho 6 E8 74 B3
Marden Rd
Thornton Heath
CR0 204 B3
Tottenham N17 33 C1
Marden Sq SE16 118 B3
Marder Rd W13 109 A4
Mardon HA5 23 B3
Mardyke Ho SE17 262 D4
Marechal Niel Ave
DA15 167 B1
Marechal Niel Par
DA15 167 B1
Maresby Ho E4 19 D2
Maresfield Gdns
NW3 70 A2
Maresfield CR0 221 C5
Mare St E8 74 B1
Marey Ct 10 CR2 221 A3
Marfleet Cl SM5 218 C6
Margaret Ave E4 19 D5
Margaret Bondfield Ave
IG11 80 A1
Margaret Bondfield
Ho
5 Bow E3 97 A5
22 Kentish Town N7 71 D3

Margaret Ct
Barnet EN4 . . . 2 B1
Marylebone W1 . . . 239 A2
Margaret Gardner Dr SE9 . . . 166 B2
Margaret Herbison Ho SW6 . . . 264 D5
Margaret Hill Ho 1 N8 . . . 50 A4
Margaret Ho
16 Hammersmith W6 . . . 112 C1
2 Sutton SM1 . . . 217 D5
Margaret Ingram Cl SW6 . . . 264 C5
Margaret Lockwood Cl KT5 . . . 198 B5
Margaret Mcmillan Ho 10 N19 . . . 49 D2
Margaret Rd
Barnet EN4 . . . 2 B1
Bexley DA5 . . . 168 D5
Stamford Hill N16 . . . 51 D1
Margarets Ct HA8 . . . 26 D5
Margaret's Ct E11 . . . 54 B2
Margaret St W1 . . . 93 C1 239 A2
Margaretta Terr SW3 . . . 136 C6 267 B6
Margaretting Rd E12 . . . 55 C1
Margaret Way IG4 . . . 56 A3
Margaret White Ho NW1 . . . 232 C2
Margate Rd SW2 . . . 160 A6
Margery Fry Ct N7 . . . 72 A5
Margery Park Rd E7 . . . 77 A2
Margery Rd RM8 . . . 80 D5
Margery St WC1 . . . 94 C4 234 A1
Margin Dr SW19 . . . 178 D6
Margravine Gdns
Hammersmith W6 . . . 112 D1
West Kensington W14 . . . 254 A2
Margravine Rd W6 . . . 135 A6 264 A6
Marham Gdns
Morden SM4 . . . 202 A3
Wandsworth SW17, SW18 . . . 158 C3
Mar Ho 4 SE7 . . . 143 C6
Maria Cl 13 SE1 . . . 118 A2
Maria Fidelis Convent Sch (Lower) NW1 . . . 93 C4 232 B1
Maria Fidelis Convent Sch (Upper) NW1 . . . 93 D4 232 C2
Marian Cl UB4 . . . 84 D3
Marian Ct Hackney E9 . . . 74 C3
1 Sutton SM1 . . . 217 D3
Marian Lo 5 SW20 . . . 178 D3
Marian Pl E2 . . . 96 B5
Marian Rd SW16 . . . 181 C2
Marian Sq E2 . . . 96 B5
Marian St 2 E2 . . . 96 B5
Marian Vian Prim Sch BR3 . . . 207 A4
Marian Way NW10 . . . 67 D1
Maria Terr E1 . . . 96 D3
Maria Theresa Cl KT3 . . . 199 B4
Maribor 13 SE10 . . . 142 A5
Maricas Ave HA3 . . . 24 B2
Marie Curie SE5 . . . 139 C4
Marie Lloyd Ct 13 SW9 . . . 138 B1
Marie Lloyd Gdns 1 N19 . . . 50 A2
Marie Lloyd Ho N1 . . . 235 C3
Marien Ct E4 . . . 36 B5
Marie Stopes Ct 3 N19 . . . 50 A2
Marigold Cl UB1 . . . 107 A6
Marigold Rd N17 . . . 34 C3
Marigold St SE16 . . . 118 B4
Marigold Way CR0 . . . 206 D1
Marilea Ct W5 . . . 109 D4
Marillic Ho NW7 . . . 28 C6
Marina App UB4 . . . 85 A2
Marina Ave KT3 . . . 200 B4
Marina Cl 1 BR2 . . . 209 A6
Marina Ct 12 Bow E3 . . . 97 C4
Greenford UB6 . . . 85 D5
Marina Dr DA16 . . . 145 C3
Marina Gdns RM7 . . . 59 D4
Marina Pl KT1 . . . 175 D2
Marina Point 4 E14 . . . 119 D3
Marina Way TW11 . . . 175 D3
Marine Dr
Barking IG11 . . . 102 B4
5 Woolwich SE18 . . . 122 B2
Marinefield Rd SW6 . . . 135 D3
Marinel Ho 28 SE5 . . . 139 A5
Mariner Gdns TW10 . . . 153 C1
Mariner Rd E12 . . . 78 C4
Mariners Mews E14 . . . 120 B2
Marine St SE16 . . . 118 A3
Marine Twr 28 SE8 . . . 141 B6
Marion Ave TW17 . . . 192 D4
Marion Ct 4 SW17 . . . 180 C5
Marion Gr IG8 . . . 36 C6
Marion Rd
Mill Hill NW7 . . . 28 A5
Thornton Heath CR0 . . . 205 B4
Marion Richardson Prim Sch E1 . . . 96 D1
Marischal Rd SE13 . . . 142 B2
Maritime Ho
5 Clapham SW4 . . . 137 C2
14 Woolwich SE18 . . . 122 D2
Maritime Ind Est SE7 . . . 121 B2
Maritime Quay 5 E14 . . . 119 C1
Maritime St E3 . . . 97 B3
Marius Mans 3 SW17 . . . 159 A2
Marius Rd SW17 . . . 159 A2
Marjorie Gr SW11 . . . 136 D1
Marjorie McClure Sch BR7 . . . 189 A2
Marjory Kinnon Sch TW14 . . . 149 C6
Markab Rd HA6 . . . 22 A5
Mark Ave E4 . . . 19 D5
Mark Cl
Bexleyheath DA7 . . . 147 A4
Keston Mark BR2 . . . 226 A4
Southall UB1 . . . 107 D5
Markeston Gn WD19 . . . 22 D6
Market Ctr The UB2 . . . 106 B2
Market Ct W1 . . . 239 A2
Market La
Burnt Oak HA8 . . . 27 A2
Shepherd's Bush W12 . . . 112 C4
Market Mews W1 . . . 115 B5 248 C3
Market Par
Croydon SE25 . . . 206 A5
1 Edmonton N9 . . . 18 A2
Feltham TW13 . . . 151 A2
Leyton E10 . . . 53 D3
Walthamstow E17 . . . 53 B6
Market Pavilion E10 . . . 75 C5
Market Pl
3 Acton W3 . . . 111 A5
1 Bermondsey SE16 . . . 118 B2
2 Bexleyheath DA6 . . . 147 C1
Brentford TW8 . . . 131 C5
East Finchley N2 . . . 48 C6
Enfield EN2 . . . 5 B2
Kingston u T KT1 . . . 175 D1
Marylebone W1 . . . 239 A2
Market Pl The NW11 . . . 47 D5
Market Rd
Barnsbury N7 . . . 72 A2
Richmond TW9 . . . 132 C2
Market Sq
Bromley BR1 . . . 187 A1
Poplar E14 . . . 97 D1
Market Sq The N9 . . . 18 B2
Market St E1 . . . 243 C4
Market Studios 14 W12 . . . 112 C4
Market St
Wallend E6 . . . 100 C5
Woolwich SE18 . . . 122 C2
Market The SM1, SM5 . . . 202 A1
Market Way
Poplar E14 . . . 97 D1
2 Wembley HA0 . . . 66 A3
Market Yd Mews SE1 . . . 263 A6
Markfield Beam Engine & Mus* N15 . . . 52 A4
Markfield Gdns E4 . . . 19 D4
Markfield Ho N15 . . . 52 A4
Markfield Rd N15 . . . 52 A4
Markham Ct NW4 . . . 46 C6
Markham Ho
1 Dagenham RM10 . . . 81 C5
9 Dulwich SE21 . . . 183 C6
Markham Pl SW3 . . . 257 C2
Markham Sq SW3 . . . 114 D1 257 C2
Markham St SW3 . . . 114 C1 257 B2
Mark Ho 3 E2 . . . 96 D5
Markhole Cl TW12 . . . 173 B3
Markhouse Ave E17 . . . 53 A3
Markhouse Pas E17 . . . 53 B3
Markhouse Rd E17 . . . 53 B3
Mark La EC3 . . . 117 C6 253 B6
Markland Ho W10 . . . 112 D6
Mark Lo 9 EN4 . . . 2 C1
Markmanor Ave E17 . . . 53 B2
Mark Mans W12 . . . 112 A4
Mark Rd N22 . . . 32 D1
Marksbury Ave TW9 . . . 132 C2
Marks Gate Jun & Inf Schs RM6 . . . 59 A6
Mark Sq EC2 . . . 243 A6
Mark St EC2 . . . 243 A6
Markstone Ho SE1 . . . 251 C1
Mark St E15 . . . 76 C1
Mark Wade Cl E12 . . . 55 D1
Markway The TW16 . . . 172 C1
Markwell Cl SE26 . . . 184 B6
Markyate Ho 6 W10 . . . 90 C3
Markyate Rd RM8 . . . 80 B3
Marland Ho SW1 . . . 257 D6
Marlands Rd IG5 . . . 56 B6
Marlang Ct BR3 . . . 186 B2
Marlborough Ave
Edgware HA8 . . . 10 D1
3 Hackney E8 . . . 96 A6
New Southgate N14 . . . 15 C1
Ruislip HA4 . . . 39 B3
Marlborough Cl
Broom Hill BR6 . . . 211 D3
Friern Barnet N20 . . . 14 D1
Mitcham SW19 . . . 180 C4
Newington SE17 . . . 261 D3
Marlborough Cres
Bedford Pk W4 . . . 111 C3
Harlington UB3 . . . 127 B5
Marlborough Ct
6 Beckenham BR3 . . . 185 C2
7 Bromley BR1 . . . 186 D3
7 Buckhurst Hill IG9 . . . 21 C2
Harrow HA1 . . . 42 B5
Kensington W8 . . . 255 A4
Marylebone W1 . . . 239 A1
Wallington SM6 . . . 219 C1
Marlborough Day Hospl NW8 . . . 92 A5 229 A4
Marlborough Dr IG5 . . . 56 A6
Marlborough Flats SW3 . . . 257 B4
Marlborough Fst & Mid Sch HA1 . . . 42 C5
Marlborough Gdns
Friern Barnet N20 . . . 14 D1
Surbiton KT6 . . . 197 D2
Marlborough Gr SE1 . . . 118 A1
Marlborough Hill
Harrow HA1 . . . 42 C5
St John's Wood NW8 . . . 92 A6 229 B5
Marlborough Ho
Marylebone NW1 . . . 238 D6
Richmond TW10 . . . 154 C6
Stoke Newington N4 . . . 51 A1
Marlborough Ho SW1 . . . 249 B3
Marlborough Ho SW19 . . . 156 D1
Marlborough La SE7 . . . 143 C5
Marlborough Lo
36 Stepney E1 . . . 96 C3
St John's Wood NW8 . . . 229 A3
Marlborough Mans 5 NW6 . . . 69 C3
Marlborough Mews 18 SW2 . . . 138 B1
Marlborough Par 1 UB10 . . . 82 D3
Marlborough Park Ave DA15 . . . 168 A3
Marlborough Pl NW8 . . . 92 A5 229 B4
Marlborough Prim Sch
Chelsea SW3 . . . 114 C2 257 B3
Isleworth TW7 . . . 131 A4
Marlborough 11 SW19 . . . 156 D3
Marlborough Rd
Acton Green W4 . . . 111 A1
Ashford TW15 . . . 170 A5
Bexley DA7 . . . 146 D2
Bowes Pk N22 . . . 32 B4
Brentford TW7 . . . 131 B5
Bromley BR2 . . . 209 C5
Chingford E4 . . . 35 D4
Dagenham RM8 . . . 80 C4
Ealing W5 . . . 109 D4
Edmonton N9 . . . 18 A3
Feltham TW13 . . . 150 D2
Hampton TW12 . . . 173 C4
Hillingdon UB10 . . . 82 D4
Leyton E15 . . . 76 C4
Mitcham SW19 . . . 180 C4
Richmond TW10 . . . 154 B5
Marlborough Rd *continued*
Romford RM7 . . . 59 D5
Southall UB2 . . . 106 C3
South Croydon CR2 . . . 221 A1
St James SW1 . . . 115 C5 249 B3
Sutton SM1 . . . 217 C6
Upper Holloway N19 . . . 72 A6
Upton E7 . . . 77 C1
Wanstead E18 . . . 55 A6
Woolwich SE18 . . . 123 A3
Marlborough Sch DA15 . . . 168 A4
Marlborough W9 . . . 229 A2
Marlborough St SW3 . . . 114 C2 257 B3
Marlborough Trad Est TW9 . . . 132 D4
Marlborough Yd N19 . . . 71 D6
Marlbury NW8 . . . 91 D6
Marler Rd SE23 . . . 163 B3
Marlesford Ct SM6 . . . 219 C4
Marlex Lo N3 . . . 29 D2
Marley Ave DA7 . . . 146 D6
Marley Cl
Harringay N15 . . . 50 D5
Southall UB6 . . . 85 C4
Marley Ho 14 W11 . . . 112 D6
Marley Wlk NW2 . . . 68 C3
Marl Field Cl KT4 . . . 200 A1
Marlfield Ct KT3 . . . 199 D2
Marlin Cl TW16 . . . 171 C4
Marlin Ct 5 DA14 . . . 190 A6
Marling Ct TW12 . . . 173 B4
Marlingdene Cl TW12 . . . 173 C4
Marlings Cl BR7 . . . 211 C5
Marlings Park Ave BR7 . . . 211 C6
Marlin Ho SW15 . . . 157 A6
Marlins Cl 3 SM1 . . . 218 A3
Marloes Cl HA0 . . . 65 D4
Marloes Rd W8 . . . 113 D3 255 C5
Marlow Cl SE20 . . . 206 B6
Marlow Cres TW1 . . . 152 D5
Marlow Ct
Colindale NW9 . . . 45 D6
1 Ealing W7 . . . 108 C5
6 Finchley N3 . . . 29 C2
Harrow HA1 . . . 42 A3
Osidge N14 . . . 15 C4
Willesden NW6 . . . 68 D1
Marlow Dr SM3 . . . 216 D5
Marlowe Bsns Ctr 2 SE14 . . . 141 A5
Marlowe Cl BR7 . . . 189 B4
Marlowe Ct
Chelsea SW3 . . . 257 B3
2 Dulwich SE19 . . . 183 D5
6 Kingston u T KT2 . . . 175 D6
Marlowe Gdns SE9 . . . 166 C5
Marlowe Ho
Kingston u T KT1 . . . 197 D5
15 Stoke Newington N16 . . . 73 C4
Marlowe Lo CR0 . . . 223 A6
Marlowe Rd E17 . . . 54 A5
Marlowe Sq CR4 . . . 203 C5
Marlowes The NW8 . . . 92 B6 229 C6
Marlowe Way CR0 . . . 220 A6
Marlow Gdns UB3 . . . 105 B3
Marlow Ho
Bermondsey SE1 . . . 263 C6
15 Kensington W2 . . . 91 D1
44 Spitalfields E2 . . . 95 D4
Teddington TW11 . . . 175 A6
Wallington CR0 . . . 220 A5
Marlow Rd
Newham E6 . . . 100 B4
Penge SE20 . . . 184 B1
Southall UB2 . . . 107 B3
Marlow Studio Workshops 43 E2 . . . 95 D4
Marlow Way SE16 . . . 118 D4
Marl Rd SW18 . . . 136 A1
Marlston NW1 . . . 231 D1
Marlton St SE10 . . . 120 D1
Marlwood Cl DA15 . . . 167 C2
Marmadon Rd SE18, SE2 . . . 123 D2
Marmara Apts 4 E16 . . . 121 A6
Marmion App E4 . . . 35 C6
Marmion Ave E4 . . . 35 B6
Marmion Cl E4 . . . 35 B6
Marmion Ho 13 SW12 . . . 159 B4
Marmion Mews 4 SW11 . . . 137 A2
Marmion Rd SW11 . . . 137 A1
Marmont Rd SE15 . . . 140 A5
Marmora Ho E1 . . . 97 A2
Marmora Rd SE22 . . . 162 C5
Marmot Rd TW4 . . . 128 D2
Marncrest Ct KT5 . . . 198 B4
Marne Ave
Friern Barnet N11 . . . 31 B6
Welling DA16 . . . 146 A2
Marnell Way TW4 . . . 128 D2
Marner Prim Sch E3 . . . 97 D3
Marne St W10 . . . 91 A4
Marney Rd SW11 . . . 137 A1
Marnfield Cres SW2 . . . 160 B3
Marnham Ave NW2 . . . 69 A4
Marnham Cres UB6 . . . 85 D5
Marnham Ct HA0 . . . 65 C3
Marnie Ct 11 E11 . . . 76 C6
Marnock Ho SE17 . . . 262 C2
Marnock Rd SE4 . . . 163 B6
Maroon St E14 . . . 97 A2
Maroons Way SE6 . . . 185 C5
Marqueen Twrs 1 SW16 . . . 182 B3
Marquess Rd N1 . . . 73 B2
Marquess Rd N N1 . . . 73 B2
Marquess Rd S 22 N1 . . . 73 A2
Marquis Cl HA0 . . . 66 B1
Marquis Ct
Barking IG11 . . . 79 C3
Finsbury Pk N4 . . . 50 B1
1 Kingston u T KT1 . . . 198 A5
Stanwell TW19 . . . 148 A3
Marquis Rd
Bowes Pk N22 . . . 32 B4
Finsbury Pk N4 . . . 50 C1
Kentish Town NW1 . . . 71 D2
Marrabon Cl DA15 . . . 168 A3
Marrick Cl SW15 . . . 134 A1
Marrick Ho 10 NW6 . . . 91 D6
Marrilyne Ave EN3 . . . 7 B5
Marriner Ct UB3 . . . 105 C6
Marriott Cl TW14 . . . 149 B5
Marriott Ho 8 SE6 . . . 186 A6
Marriott Rd
Finsbury Pk N4 . . . 50 B1
Muswell Hill N10 . . . 30 D2
Newham E15 . . . 98 C6
Marriotts Cl NW9 . . . 45 D3
Marryat Cl TW3 . . . 129 B1
Marryat Ct 12 W6 . . . 112 B2
Marryat Ho SW1 . . . 259 A1
Marryat Pl SW19 . . . 179 A6
Marryat Rd SW19 . . . 179 A6
Marryat Sq SW6 . . . 264 A2
Marryatt Ct W5 . . . 88 B1
Marsala Rd SE13 . . . 141 D1
Marsalis Ho 3 E3 . . . 97 C4
Marsden Rd
Camberwell SE15 . . . 139 D2
Edmonton N9 . . . 18 B2
Marsden St NW5 . . . 71 A2
Marsden Way 2 BR6 . . . 227 D4
Marshall Cl
Brunswick Pk N11 . . . 15 B1
Harrow HA1 . . . 42 B2
Hounslow TW4 . . . 151 B6
Wandsworth SW18 . . . 158 A5
Marshall Ct SW4 . . . 270 B1
Marshall Dr UB4 . . . 83 D2
Marshall Ho
5 New Malden KT3 . . . 199 C5
Paddington NW6 . . . 91 B5
Shoreditch N1 . . . 235 D4
Walworth SE17 . . . 262 C2
Marshall Path 10 SE28 . . . 124 B6
Marshall Rd
Leyton E10 . . . 75 D4
Tottenham N17 . . . 33 B2
Marshalls Gr SE18 . . . 122 A2
Marshall's Pl SE16 . . . 263 D5
Marshall's Rd SM1 . . . 217 D4
Marshall St W1 . . . 93 C1 239 B1
Marshalsea Rd SE1 . . . 117 A4 252 B2
Marsham Cl BR7 . . . 188 D5
Marsham Ct
19 Putney SW19 . . . 156 D3
Westminster SW1 . . . 259 D4
Marsham St SW1 . . . 115 D2 259 D4
Marsh Ave CR4 . . . 181 A1
Marshbrook Cl SE3 . . . 143 D2
Marsh Cl NW7 . . . 11 D1
Marsh Ct Dalston E8 . . . 74 A2
3 Merton SW19 . . . 180 A2
Marsh Dr NW9 . . . 45 D3
Marsh Farm Rd TW2 . . . 152 D3
Marshfield St E14 . . . 120 A3
Marsh Gate Bsns Ctr E15 . . . 98 A5
Marshgate Ctr The E15 . . . 97 D6
Marshgate La E15 . . . 75 D1
Marshgate Prim Sch TW10 . . . 15
Marsh Green Prim Sch RM10 . . . 10
Marsh Green Rd RM10 . . . 10
Marsh Hall HA9 . . . 6
Marsh Hill E9 . . . 7
Marsh Ho
Nine Elms SW8 . . . 26
Pimlico SW1 . . . 25
Marsh La
Edgware NW7 . . . 1
Leyton E10 . . . 75
Stanmore HA7 . . . 25
Tottenham N17 . . . 3
Marsh Point HA5 . . . 4
Marsh Rd Pinner HA5 . . . 4
Wembley HA0 . . . 87
Marshside Cl N9 . . . 1
Marsh St E14 . . . 11
Marsh Wall E14 . . . 11
Marshwood Ho 10 NW6 . . . 9
Marsland Cl SE17 . . . 26
Marsom Ho N1 . . . 23
Marston Ave
Chessington KT9 . . . 21
Dagenham RM10 . . . 8
Marston Cl
Dagenham RM10 . . . 8
South Hampstead NW6 . . . 7
Marston Ct
Barnet EN5 . . . 13
Sidcup DA14 . . . 189
Walton-on-T KT12 . . . 194
Marston Ho 23 SW9 . . . 13
Marston Rd TW11 . . . 17
Marston SE17 . . . 26
Marston Way SE19 . . . 18
Marsworth Ave HA5 . . . 2
Marsworth Cl UB4 . . . 8
Marsworth Ho 8 E2 . . . 9
Martaban Rd N16 . . . 7
Martello St E8 . . . 7
Martello Terr E8 . . . 7
Martell Rd SE21 . . . 16
Martel Pl E8 . . . 7
Marten Rd E17 . . . 3
Martens Ave DA7 . . . 14
Martham Cl SE28 . . . 12
Martha Rd E15 . . . 7
Martha's Bldgs EC1 . . . 24
Martha St E1 . . . 9
Marthorne Cres HA3 . . . 2
Martin Bowes Rd SE9 . . . 14
Martinbridge Trad Est EN1 . . . 1
Martin Cl
Lower Edmonton N9 . . . 1
Uxbridge UB10 . . . 8
Martin Cres CR0 . . . 20
Martin Ct
15 Cubitt Town E14 . . . 12
Lewisham SE12 . . . 16
Merton SW19 . . . 17
Southall UB2 . . . 10
Martindale Ave 2 E16 . . . 12
Martindale Ho 23 E14 . . . 11
Martindale SW14 . . . 15
Martindale Rd
Balham SW12 . . . 15
Hounslow TW4 . . . 12
Martin Dene DA6 . . . 16
Martin Dr UB5 . . . 6
Martineau Cl KT10 . . . 21
Martineau Dr TW1 . . . 13
Martineau Ho SW1 . . . 25
Martineau Mews N5 . . . 7
Martineau Rd N5 . . . 7
Martingale Cl TW16 . . . 19
Martingales Cl TW10 . . . 15
Martin Gdns RM8 . . . 8
Martin Gr SM4 . . . 20
Martin Ho
Newington SE1 . . . 26
7 New Malden KT3 . . . 19
South Lambeth SW8 . . . 27
Martini Dr EN3 . . .
Martin Jun & Inf Schs N2 . . . 3
Martin La EC4 . . . 25
Martin Rd RM8 . . . 8
Martin Rise DA6 . . . 16
Martins Cl BR4 . . . 22
Martins Mount EN5 . . .
Martins Pl SE28 . . . 12
Martin's Rd BR2 . . . 18
Martins The
Penge SE26 . . . 18

tins The *continued*
embley HA9 66 B5
tin St SE28 123 C5
tins Wlk
swell Hill N10 31 A2
oolwich SE28 123 C5
tin Way SW20,
4 201 B6
tlesham N17 33 C1
tlesham Wlk
W9 27 C2
tlet Gr 5 UB5 84 D4
tlett Ct WC2 240 B1
tlett Lo NW3 69 D4
tley Dr IG2 56 D4
tley Ho SW8 269 B2
tock Cl HA3 43 A5
tock Ct 10 SE15 140 B4
tock Gdns N11 31 A5
ton Cl SE6 163 C1
ton Rd 2 N16 73 C5
tyn Ct HA8 26 B6
tyn Ho SE2 146 D6
tynside 22 NW9 27 D2
vel Ho 5 SE5 139 B5
vell Ave UB4 84 A2
vels Cl SE12 165 B2
vels Lane Prim Sch
12 187 C6
vels La SE12 165 C1
ville Rd
V6 135 B5 264 C3
vin Ho 9 SE18 144 D6
vin St 3 E8 74 B2
well Cl BR4 224 D6
well Ct SE3 142 B3
wick Rd UB7 104 B4
wood Cl DA16 146 B2
wood Ct N3 29 D3
wood Dr NW7 28 D3
ry Adelaide Cl
ngston u T
SW15 155 C1
ngston u T SW15 177 C6
ry Adelaide Ho
2 236 D4
ry Ann Bldgs
8 141 C6
ryatt Ave HA2 63 D6
rybank SE18 122 B2
ry Cl HA7 44 B5
ry Datchelor Cl
5 139 B4
ry Dine Ct SW8 270 D3
ry Gn NW8 91 D6
rygold Ho TW3 130 A4
ry Ho
Hammersmith
W6 112 C1
Stockwell SW9 138 B3
ry James Ho 32
2 96 A5
ry Jones Ho 20
4 119 C6
ryland Ct KT1 176 D1
ryland Pk E15 76 C3
ryland Point E15 76 C2
ryland Prim Sch
15 76 C3
ryland Rd
addington W9 91 C3
outh Norwood CR7 182 D2
tratford New Town
E15 76 B3
ottenham N22 32 C4
rylands Ind Est
15 76 C3
ryland Sq E15 76 C3
rylands Rd W9 91 D3
ryland Sta E15 76 C2
ryland St E15 76 C3
ryland Way
W16 172 A1
ryland Wlk N1 235 A6
ry Lawrenson Pl 1
3 143 A5
RYLEBONE 93 B1
rylebone Ct 3
A0 66 A2
rylebone Flyover
W1 92 C2 237 A3
rylebone High St
1 93 A2 238 B4
rylebone La
1 93 A1 238 B2
rylebone Mews
1 238 C3
rylebone Pas W1 239 B2
rylebone Rd
W1 92 D2 237 D4
rylebone Sta
W1 92 D3 237 C5
rylebone St
1 93 A2 238 B3
rylee Way
E11 116 B2 260 D3
Mary Macarthur Ho
8 Belvedere
DA17 125 C3
11 Dagenham RM10 81 C5
15 Globe Town E2 96 D4
Mary McArthur Ho 12
N19 49 D2
Mary Macarthur Ho
W14 264 A6
Marymount
International Sch
KT2 177 A3
Maryon Gr SE7 122 A2
Maryon Mews NW3 70 C4
Maryon Rd SE7 122 A2
Mary Peters Dr UB6 64 B3
Mary Pl W11 113 A6 244 A5
Mary Rose Cl TW12 173 C2
Mary Rose Mall E6 100 B2
Maryrose Way N20 14 B3
Mary's Ct NW8 237 B6
Mary Seacole Villas 19
NW10 67 B1
Mary Secole Cl 21
E8 95 D6
Mary Smith Ct SW5 255 B3
Mary St 5 E16 98 D2
Mary's Terr TW1 153 A4
Mary St N1 95 A6 235 B5
Mary Tates Cotts
CR4 202 D5
Mary Terr NW1 232 A5
Maryville DA16 145 D3
Mary Way WD19 22 C6
Mary Wharrie Ho 4
NW3 70 D1
Marzena Ct TW2 152 A6
Masbro' Rd W14 112 D3
Mascalls Ct 13 SE7 143 C6
Mascalls Rd SE7 143 C6
Mascotte Rd 2
SW15 134 D1
Mascotts Cl NW2 68 B5
Masefield Ave
Borehamwood
WD6 10 D6
Southall UB1 107 C6
Stanmore HA7 24 D5
Masefield Cres N14 15 C5
Masefield Ct
New Barnet EN5 2 A1
Stoke Newington N5 73 B3
10 Surbiton KT6 197 D2
Masefield Gdns E6 100 C3
Masefield Ho 4
NW6 91 C4
Masefield La UB4 84 C3
Masefield Rd TW13 173 B6
Masefield View
BR6 227 A5
Masefield Way
TW19 148 B3
Masham Ho 13
DA18 124 D4
Mashie Rd W3 89 C1
Maskall Cl SW2 160 C3
Maskani Wlk SW16 181 C3
Maskell Rd SW17 158 A1
Maskelyne Cl
SW11 136 C4 267 B2
Mason Cl
Bermondsey
SE16 118 A1
Bexleyheath DA7 147 D2
Hampton TW12 173 B2
Newham E16 121 A6
Wimbledon SW20 178 D2
Mason Ct
4 Penge SE19 183 D3
Wembley HA9 66 C6
Mason Ho
15 Bermondsey
SE1 118 A2
8 Friern Barnet N11 31 C5
12 Hackney E9 74 C1
Mason Rd
Sutton SM1 217 D3
Woodford IG8 36 C6
Mason's Arms Mews
W1 248 D6
Mason's Ave
City of London EC2 242 C2
Croydon CR0 221 A5
Masons Ave HA3 42 D5
Masons Hill
Bromley BR2 209 B5
13 Woolwich SE18 122 D2
Masons Ho NW9 44 D4
Mason's Pl
Finsbury EC1 235 A2
Mitcham CR4 180 D2
Mason St
SE17 117 B2 262 D4
Mason's Yd
Finsbury EC1 234 D2
St James SW1 249 B4
Wimbledon SW19 178 D5
Massey Cl N11 31 B5
Massey Ct 6 E6 99 C6
Massie Rd E8 74 A2
Massingberd Way
SW17 181 B6
Massinger St SE1,
SE17 263 A3
Massingham St E1 96 D3
Masson Ave HA4 62 C2
Mast Ct 17 SE16 119 A2
Master Gunner's Pl 1
SE18 144 A4
Masterman Ho 1
SE5 139 B5
Masterman Rd E6 100 A4
Masters Cl SW16 181 C4
Masters Ct HA4 61 C6
Masters Dr SE16 118 B1
Masters Lo 24 E1 96 C1
Master's St 16 E1 96 D2
Mast House Terr
E14 119 C2
Mastin Ho SW18 157 C3
Mastmaker Rd E14 119 C4
Maswell Park Cres
TW3 152 A6
Maswell Park Rd
TW3 130 A1
Matara Mews SE17 262 A1
Matcham Rd E11 76 D5
Matching Ct 14 E3 97 C4
Matchless Dr SE18 144 C5
Matfield Cl BR2 209 A4
Matfield Rd DA17 147 C6
Matham Gr SE22 139 D1
Matham Rd KT8 196 B4
Mathart Ct E4 36 B4
Matheson Lang Ho
SE1 251 A1
Matheson Rd
W14 113 B2 254 C3
Mathews Ave E6 100 C5
Mathews Park Ave
E15 76 D2
Mathews Yd WC2 240 A1
Mathieson Ct SE1 251 D1
Mathieson Ho 10 E4 20 C4
Mathilda Marks-
Kennedy Jewish Prim
Sch NW7 27 B5
Mathison Ho SW10 266 A4
Matilda Cl SE19 183 B3
Matilda Ho E1 118 A5
Matilda St N1 94 B6 233 D6
Matlock Cl
Barnet EN5 12 D6
Herne Hill SE24 139 A1
Matlock Cres SM3 217 A4
Matlock Ct
7 Herne Hill SE5 139 B1
St John's Wood NW8 229 A4
Woodford IG8 36 D2
Matlock Gdns SM1,
SM3 217 A4
Matlock Pl SM1,
SM3 217 A4
Matlock Rd E10 54 A3
Matlock St E14 97 A1
Matlock Way KT3 177 B2
Maton Ho SW6 264 C4
Matson Ct IG8 36 C3
Matson Ho
9 Bermondsey
SE16 118 B3
16 Homerton E9 74 D2
Matthew Cl W10 90 D3
Matthew Ct
Mitcham CR4 203 D4
4 Walthamstow E17 54 A6
Matthew Parker St
SW1 249 D1
Matthews Ct N5 73 A4
Matthews Ho 8 E14 97 C2
Matthews Rd UB6 64 B3
Matthews St SW11 136 D3
Matthias Ct 12
TW10 154 A5
Matthias Ho 2 N16 73 C3
Matthias Rd N16 73 C3
Mattingly Way 3
SE15 139 D5
Mattison Rd N4 50 D3
Mattock La W5,
W13 109 C5
Maud Cashmore Way
SE18 122 B3
Maude Ho 3 E2 96 A5
Maude Rd
Camberwell SE5 139 C4
Walthamstow E17 53 A4
Maudesville Cotts
W7 108 C5
Maude Terr E17 53 A5
Maud Gdns
Barking IG11 101 D5
Newham E13 98 D5
Maudlins Gn E1 118 A5
Maud Rd Leyton E10 76 A5
Newham E13 98 D5
Maudslay Rd SE9 144 B2
Maudsley Ho TW8 110 A1
Maudsley Hospl The
SE5 139 B3
Maud St E16 98 D2
Maud Wilkes Cl 10
NW5 71 C3
Maugham Ct 5 W3 111 A3
Mauleverer Rd SW2 160 A6
Maultway Ct KT19 215 B3
Maundeby Wlk
NW10 67 C2
Maunder Rd 4 W7 108 D5
Maunsel St
SW1 115 D2 259 C4
Maureen Campbell Ct
TW17 192 D4
Maurer Ct 2 SE10 120 D3
Mauretania Bldg 11
E1 118 D6
Maurice Ave N22 32 D1
Maurice Browne Cl
NW7 28 D4
Maurice Ct
3 Brentford
TW8 131 D5
4 Mile End E1 97 A4
Wood Green N22 32 C2
Maurice Ho
Hither Green
SE12 164 D5
1 Stockwell SW9 138 B3
Maurice St W12 90 B1
Maurice Wlk NW11 48 A5
Maurier Cl UB5 84 C6
Mauritius Rd SE10 120 C2
Maury Rd N16 74 A5
Mauveine Gdns
TW3 129 C1
Mavelstone Cl BR1 188 A2
Mavelstone Rd BR1 188 A2
Maverton Rd E3 97 C6
Mavery Ct 5 BR1 186 D3
Mavis Ave KT19 215 C3
Mavis Cl KT19 215 C3
Mavis Ct 33 NW9 27 D1
Mavis Wlk 9 E6 100 A2
Mavor Ho N1 233 D5
Mawbey Ho SE1 263 D1
Mawbey Pl
SE1 117 D1 263 D1
Mawbey Rd SE1 263 D1
Mawbey St SW8 270 A3
Mawdley Ho SE1 251 B1
Mawney Cl RM7 59 D6
Mawney Rd RM7 59 D6
Mawson Cl SW20 179 A1
Mawson Ct N1 235 D5
Mawson Ho EC1 241 A4
Mawson La W4 133 D6
Maxden Ct SE15 140 A2
Maxey Gdns RM9 81 A4
Maxey Rd
Dagenham RM9 81 A4
Plumstead SE18 123 A2
Maxfield Cl N20 14 A4
Maxim Apartments 3
BR2 209 B5
Maxim Rd N21 16 C5
Maxted Pk HA1 42 C2
Maxted Rd SE15 139 D2
Maxwell Cl
Croydon CR0 204 A1
Hayes UB3 106 A6
Maxwell Ct SE21 162 A3
Maxwell Gdns BR6 227 D5
Maxwell Ho
Bowes Pk N22 32 B4
Chislehurst BR7 188 D3
12 Shooters Hill
SE18 144 D6
Maxwell Rd
Ashford TW15 171 A4
Fulham
SW6 135 D5 265 D3
Welling DA16 146 A2
West Drayton UB7 104 B2
Maxwelton Ave NW7 27 B5
Maxwelton Cl NW7 27 B5
Maya Angelou Ct E4 36 A6
Maya Cl SE15 140 B3
Mayall Cl EN3 7 C5
Mayall Rd SE24 160 D6
Maya Pl N11 31 D3
Maya Rd N2 48 A5
Maybank Ave
Wembley HA0 65 A3
Woodford E18 37 B1
Maybank Gdns HA5 40 A4
Maybank Rd E18 37 C2
May Bate Ave KT2 175 D2
Maybells Commercial
Est IG11 102 D5
Mayberry Pl KT5 198 B2
Maybourne Cl SE26 184 B5
Maybourne Grange
CR0 221 C6
Maybrook Ct E11 77 B6
Maybury Cl Enfield EN1 6 B5
Petts Wood BR5 210 D4
Maybury Ct
Beckenham BR3 185 B3
Croydon CR2 220 D3
Harrow HA1 42 B3
Marylebone W1 238 B3
Maybury Gdns NW10 68 B2
Maybury Mews N6 49 C2
Maybury Rd
Barking IG11 102 A5
Newham E13 99 C3
Maybury St SW17 180 C5
Maychurch Cl HA7 25 D3
May Cl KT9 214 B2
Maycroft
2 Hayes BR2 208 D1
Pinner HA5 22 B1
Maycross Ave SM4 201 C5
May Ct 2 SW19 180 A2
Mayday Gdns SE3 144 A3
Mayday Rd CR0, CR7 204 D3
Mayday University
Hospl CR7 204 D3
Maydeb Ct RM6 59 B3
Maydew Ho SE16 118 C2
Maydwell Ho 6 E14 97 C2
Mayerne Rd SE9 165 D6
Mayesbrook Rd
Barking IG11 101 D6
Dagenham RM8, IG3 80 B5
Mayesford Rd RM6 58 C2
Mayespark Prim Sch
IG3 80 A5
Mayes Rd N22 32 B1
Mayeswood Rd
SE12 187 C6
MAYFAIR 115 B6
Mayfair Ave
Bexley DA7 146 D4
Dagenham RM6 58 D3
Ilford IG1 56 C1
New Malden KT4 200 A1
Twickenham TW2 152 A4
Mayfair Cl
Beckenham BR3 185 D2
Surbiton KT6 198 A1
Mayfair Ct
2 Beckenham
BR3 185 D2
7 Croydon CR0 221 D6
Edgware HA8 26 B5
13 Wimbledon
SW19 179 A3
Mayfair Gdns
Tottenham N17 33 B4
Woodford IG8 37 A3
Mayfair Ho 11 SE1 118 A2
Mayfair Pl W1 248 D4
Mayfair Terr N14 15 D4
Mayfield Ave
Broom Hill BR6 211 D2
Chiswick W4 111 C2
Harrow HA3 43 B4
North Finchley N12 30 B6
Osidge N14 15 D2
West Ealing W13 109 B4
Woodford IG8 37 A4
Mayfield Cl
Ashford TW15 170 D4
Clapham Pk SW4 159 D6
Dalston E8 73 D2
Hillingdon UB10 82 D4
Long Ditton KT7 197 B1
Penge SE20 184 B2
Mayfield Cres
Enfield N9 18 B5
Thornton Heath CR7 204 B4
Mayfield Ct SM2 218 A1
Mayfield DA7 147 B2
Mayfield Dr HA5 41 B5
Mayfield Gdns
Ealing W7 86 C2
Hendon NW4 46 D3
Mayfield Ho
31 Bethnal Green
E2 96 B5
Stamford Hill N16 51 C2
Mayfield Mans
SW15 157 B6
Mayfield Prim Sch
W7 86 B1
Mayfield Rd
Acton W3 110 D6
Bedford Pk W12 111 C4
Bromley BR1 210 A4
Chingford E4 20 B2
Dagenham RM8 58 C1
Dalston E8 73 D1
Enfield EN3 6 D3
Higham Hill E17 35 A1
Hornsey Vale N8 50 B3
Merton SW19 179 B2
Newham E13 98 D3
Mayfield Rd *continued*
South Croydon CR2 221 B1
Sutton SM2 218 B2
Thornton Heath CR7 204 B4
Mayfield Sch & Coll
RM8 58 C1
Mayfields Cl HA9 66 C6
Mayfields HA9 66 C6
Mayfield Villas
DA14 190 C4
Mayflower Cl
Bermondsey
SE16 118 D2
Ruislip HA4 39 A3
Mayflower Ho 2
IG11 101 B6
Mayflower Lo
Hendon N3 47 B6
Muswell Hill N10 31 A2
Mayflower Prim Sch
E14 97 D1
Mayflower Rd SW9 138 A2
Mayflower St 1
SE16 118 C4
Mayfly Cl HA5 40 C2
Mayfly Gdns 12 UB5 84 D4
Mayford Cl
Balham SW12 158 D4
Penge BR3 206 D6
Mayford NW1 232 B4
Mayford Rd SW12 159 A4
May Gdns Elstree WD6 9 D5
Wembley HA0 87 C4
Maygood Ho N1 234 A4
Maygood St
N1 94 C5 234 A4
Maygrove Rd NW6 69 B2
Mayhew Cl E4 19 C1
Mayhew Ct 2 SE5 139 B1
Mayhill Rd
Barnet EN5 13 A5
Greenwich SE7 143 B6
Mayland Mans 4
IG11 78 D1
Maylands Dr DA14 168 D1
Maylands Ho SW3 257 B3
Maylands Rd WD19 22 C6
Maylie Ho 4 SE16 118 B4
Maynard Cl
Fulham
SW6 135 D5 265 D3
Tottenham N15 51 C4
Maynard Ct EN3 7 C5
Maynard Ho
Mile End E1 97 A4
Plumstead SE18 123 A2
Maynard Rd E17 54 A4
Maynards Quay E1 118 C6
Mayne Ct E8 74 A4
Maynooth Gdns
CR4 202 D2
Mayo Ct W13 109 B3
Mayo Ho 10 E1 96 C2
Mayola Rd E5 74 C4
Mayo Rd
Thornton Heath
CR0 205 B4
Walton-on-T KT12 194 A2
Willesden NW10 67 C2
Mayow Rd SE23,
SE26 184 D6
Mayplace Cl DA7 147 D2
Mayplace La SE18 144 D6
Mayplace Rd W
DA7 147 C1
Maypole Ct UB2 107 B4
May Rd Chingford E4 35 C4
Newham E13 99 A5
Twickenham TW2 152 C3
Mayroyd Ave KT6 214 C6
May's Buildings Mews
SE10 142 B5
May's Ct SE10 142 B5
Mays Ct WC2 250 A5
May's Hill Rd BR2 208 C6
Mays La EN5 12 C5
Maysoule Rd SW11 136 B1
Mays Rd TW11,
TW12 174 B5
Maystocks E18 55 C6
Mayston Mews 3
SE10 121 A1
May St W14 254 D1
May Terr IG1 78 D4
Maythorne Cotts
SE13 164 B5
Maytime Prep Sch
IG1 78 C5
Mayton St N7 72 B5
Maytree Cl HA8 11 A1
Maytree Ct
Mitcham CR4 203 A6
Northolt UB5 85 A4
May Tree Ho SE4 141 B2

Maytree La HA7 24 D3
Maytree Wlk SW2 160 C2
Mayville Prim Sch E11 76 C6
Mayville Rd
 Ilford IG1 78 D3
 Leyton E11 76 C6
Mayward Ho 7 SE5 139 C4
May Wlk E13 99 B5
Maywood Cl BR3 185 D3
May Wynne Ho E16 99 B1
Maze Hill Lodge 7 SE10 142 B6
Maze Hill SE10, SE3 142 C6
Maze Hill Sta SE10 142 C6
Mazenod Ave NW6 69 C1
Maze Rd TW9 132 C5
Mead Cl
 3 Camden Town NW1 71 A1
 Harrow HA3 24 B2
Mead Cres
 Carshalton SM1 218 C4
 Chingford E4 36 A6
Meadcroft Ho 4 KT3 199 C2
Meadcroft Rd SE17 138 D6
Mead Ct NW9 45 B4
Meade Cl W4 132 C6
Meader Ct SE14 140 D5
Meadfield HA8 10 D2
Meadfield Gn HA8 10 D2
Mead Field HA2 63 B5
Meadfoot Rd SW16 181 C2
Mead Gr RM6 58 D6
Mead House La UB4 83 B3
Mead Ho W11 244 C4
Meadhurst Pk TW16 171 C4
Mead Inf Sch The KT19 215 D4
Meadlands Dr TW10 153 D2
Meadlands Prim Sch TW10 175 C6
Mead Lo W4 111 B4
Meadow Ave CR0 206 D3
Meadowbank Cl SW6 134 C5
Meadowbank Gdns TW5 128 B4
Meadowbank
 Lewisham SE3 142 D2
 Primrose Hill NW3 70 D1
Meadow Bank 8 SW15 157 B6
Meadowbank Rd NW9 45 B2
Meadowbanks EN5 12 A6
Meadowbank
 Southgate N21 16 B5
 Surbiton KT5 198 B3
Meadowbrook Ct TW7 130 D2
Meadow Cl
 Barnet EN5 13 B5
 Bexley DA6 169 B6
 Catford SE6 185 C5
 Chingford E4 19 D3
 Chislehurst BR7 188 D5
 Enfield EN3 7 A5
 Hackney E9 75 B3
 Hinchley Wood KT10 212 D5
 Hounslow TW4 151 C5
 Northolt UB5 85 C5
 Richmond TW10 154 A3
 Ruislip HA4 39 D3
 Sutton SM1 218 A6
 West Barnes SW20 200 C5
Meadowcourt Rd SE3 142 D1
Meadow Croft BR1 210 B6
Meadowcroft 9 W4 110 C1
Meadowcroft Rd N13 16 C2
Meadow Dr
 Hendon NW4 28 C1
 Muswell Hill N10 49 B6
Meadowford Cl SE28 124 A6
Meadow Garth NW10 67 B2
Meadowgate Cl NW7 27 D5
Meadow Gate HA2 63 D5
Meadowgate Sch SE4 141 A2
Meadow Gdns HA8 27 A4
Meadow High Sch UB8 82 A2
Meadow Hill KT3 199 C3
Meadow La SE12 165 B1
Meadow Mews SW8 270 C5
Meadow Pl
 Chiswick W4 133 C5
 South Lambeth SW8 138 A5 270 B4
Meadow Rd
 Ashford TW15 171 B5
 Barking IG11 80 A1
 Beckenham BR2 186 C1
 Carshalton SM1 218 C3
 Claygate KT10 212 C2
 Dagenham RM9 81 B2
 Feltham TW13 151 A2
 Merton SW19 180 A3
 Pinner HA5 41 A5
 Southall UB1 107 B6
 South Lambeth SW8 138 B5 270 C4
Meadow Row SE1 262 A5
Meadows Cl E10 75 C6
Meadows Ct DA14 190 B4
Meadows End TW16 172 A2
Meadowside
 Eltham SE9 143 C1
 Twickenham TW1 153 D4
Meadow Stile CR0 221 A5
Meadowsweet Cl
 3 Newham E16 99 D2
 West Barnes KT3 200 C5
Meadow The BR7 189 A4
Meadow View
 Blackfen DA15 168 B4
 Harrow HA1 42 C1
Meadowview Rd SE6 185 C5
Meadow View Rd UB4 83 B3
Meadowview Rd DA5 169 B5
Meadow View Rd CR7 204 D4
Meadowview Rd KT19 215 C1
Meadowview TW17 193 A2
Meadow Waye TW5 129 A5
Meadow Way
 Kingsbury NW9 45 B4
 Locksbottom BR6 226 C5
 Ruislip HA4 40 B3
Meadow Way The HA3 24 C2
Meadow Way HA9 65 D4
Meadow Wlk
 Dagenham RM9 81 B2
 Hackbridge SM6 219 B5
 Wanstead E18 55 A5
 West Ewell KT17, KT19 215 D1
Meadow Wood Sch WD23 8 A6
Mead Plat NW10 67 A2
Mead Pl
 Croydon CR0 205 A1
 Hackney E9 74 C2
Mead Rd
 Chislehurst BR7 189 A4
 Edgware HA8 26 C4
 Richmond TW10 153 C1
Mead Road Inf Sch BR7 189 A4
Mead Row SE1 116 C3 261 A6
Meads Ct E15 76 D2
Meadside Cl BR3 185 A2
Meads La IG3 57 D2
Meads Rd Enfield EN3 7 A4
 Tottenham N22 32 D1
Meads The
 Cheam SM3 217 A5
 Edgware HA8 27 B4
 Hillingdon UB8 82 A3
Mead The
 Beckenham BR3 186 A2
 Ealing W13 87 B2
 Finchley N2 30 A1
 Ickenham UB10 60 C6
 Wallington SM6 219 D2
 West Wickham BR4 208 B1
Meadvale Rd
 Croydon CR0 206 A3
 Ealing W5 87 C3
Meadway
 Ashford TW15 170 C6
 Barnet EN5 1 C1
 Beckenham BR3 186 A2
Meadway Cl
 Barnet EN5 1 C1
 Hampstead Garden Suburb NW11 47 D3
 Pinner HA5 23 D4
Mead Way CR0 223 A6
Meadway Ct
 Dagenham RM8 81 B6
 Ealing W5 88 B2
 Hampstead Garden Suburb NW11 47 D3
Meadway Enfield EN3 6 D6
Meadway *continued*
 Esher KT10 212 A1
Meadway Gate NW11 47 C3
Meadway Gdns HA4 39 B3
Meadway NW11 47 D3
Mead Way BR2 209 A3
Meadway Ilford IG3 79 C4
 Palmers Green N14 16 A2
Mead Way HA4 39 B3
Meadway The
 Buckhurst Hill IG9 21 D3
 Lewisham SE3 142 B3
Meadway
 Tolworth KT5 199 A1
 Twickenham TW2 152 B3
 West Barnes SW20 200 C5
 Woodford IG8 37 C5
Meaford Way SE20 184 B3
Meakin Est SE1 263 A6
Meakin Ho N7 72 B3
Meanley Rd E12 78 A3
Meard St W1 239 C1
Meath Ho SE24 160 D5
Meath Rd Ilford IG1 79 A5
 Newham E15 98 D5
Meath St SW11 137 B4 268 C2
Mecklenburgh Pl WC1 240 C6
Mecklenburgh Sq WC1 94 B3 240 C6
Mecklenburgh St WC1 240 C6
Medburn St NW1 232 C4
Medcalf Rd EN3 7 B6
Medcroft Gdns SW14 133 A1
Medebourne Cl SE3 143 A2
Mede Ho BR1 187 B5
Medesenge Way N13 32 D4
Medfield St SW15 156 B4
Medhurst Cl 19 E3 97 A5
Median Rd E5 74 C3
Medina Ave KT10 212 C5
Medina Ct N7 72 C5
Medina Gr N7 72 C5
Medina Ho SE15 140 C1
Medina Rd N7 72 C5
Medland Cl CR4 203 A1
Medlar Cl 1 UB5 84 D5
Medlar Ho 3 DA15 168 A1
Medlar St SE5 139 A4
Medley Rd NW6 69 C2
Medora Rd SW2 160 B4
Medresco Ho NW3 70 B3
Medusa Rd SE6, SE13 163 D5
Medway Bldgs E3 97 A5
Medway Cl
 Croydon CR0 206 C3
 Ilford IG1 79 A3
Medway Ct
 South Norwood SE25 205 C4
 St Pancras WC1 233 A1
Medway Dr UB6 86 D5
Medway Gdns HA0 65 A4
Medway Ho
 Bermondsey SE1 252 D1
 6 Kingston u T KT2 175 D2
 Paddington NW8 237 A4
 Stoke Newington N16 73 B4
Medway Mews 35 E3 97 A5
Medway Par 1 UB6 86 D5
Medway Rd E3 97 A5
Medway St SW1 115 D3 259 D5
Medwin St SW4 138 B1
Meecham Ct 1 SW11 136 C3
Meerbrook Rd SE3 143 C2
Meers Ct SW20 178 C2
Meeson Rd E15 76 D1
Meeson St E5 75 A4
Meeting House Alley 7 E1 118 B5
Meeting House La SE15 140 B5
Mehetabel Rd E9 74 C3
Meister Cl IG1 57 B1
Melanda Cl BR7 188 B5
Melanie Cl DA7 147 A4
Melba Way SE13 141 D4
Melbourne Ave
 Bowes Pk N13 32 B4
 Ealing W13 109 A5
 Pinner HA2, HA5 41 D6
Melbourne Cl
 Broom Hill BR6 211 C2
 Ickenham UB10 60 C4
 Wallington SM6 219 C3
Melbourne Ct
 Hackney E5 75 A4
 Muswell Hill N10 31 B3
 Paddington W9 236 B6
 Penge SE20 184 A3
 Twickenham TW2 152 B3
Melbourne Gdns RM6 59 A4
Melbourne Gr SE22 139 D1
Melbourne Ho
 Hayes UB4 84 C3
 Kensington W8 245 A3
 South Norwood SE25 205 D5
Melbourne Mews
 Brixton SW9 138 C4
 Catford SE6 164 A4
Melbourne Pl WC2 240 D1
Melbourne Rd
 Ilford IG1 56 D1
 Leyton E10 53 D2
 Merton SW19 179 C2
 Newham E6 100 B5
 Teddington TW11 175 C4
 Wallington SM6 219 C3
 Walthamstow E17 53 A5
Melbourne Sq 21 SW9 138 C4
Melbourne Way EN1 17 D5
Melbray Mews 11 SW6 135 B3
Melbreak Ho 11 SE22 139 C2
Melbury Ave UB2 107 D3
Melbury Cl
 Claygate KT10 213 B2
 Elmstead BR7 188 B4
Melbury Ct W8 113 B3 254 D6
Melbury Dr SE5 139 C5
Melbury Gdns SW20 178 B2
Melbury Grange BR1 188 A2
Melbury Ho
 South Lambeth SW8 270 C4
 Twickenham TW2 152 B2
Melbury Rd
 Harrow HA3 44 B4
 Kensington W14 113 B3 254 D6
Melchester Ho 1 N19 71 D5
Melchester 5 W11 91 B1
Melcombe Ct NW1 237 C4
Melcombe Gdns HA3 44 B3
Melcombe Ho SW8 270 C3
Melcombe Pl NW1 237 C4
Melcombe Prim Sch W6 134 D6
Melcombe St NW1 92 D3 237 D5
Meldex Cl NW7 28 C4
Meldon Cl SW6 265 D2
Meldone Cl KT5 198 D3
Meldone KT3 199 B1
Meldrum Rd IG3 80 A6
Melfield Gdns SE6 186 A5
Melford Ave IG11 79 D2
Melford Cl KT9 214 B3
Melford Ct
 Bermondsey SE1 263 B6
 Dulwich SE22 162 A4
 Hackney E5 74 B5
 2 Sutton SM2 218 A1
Melford Rd
 Dulwich SE21, SE22 162 A3
 Ilford IG1 79 B6
 Leyton E11 76 C6
 Newham E6 100 B4
 Walthamstow E17 53 B5
Melfort Ave CR7 204 D6
Melfort Rd CR7 204 D6
Melgund Rd N5 72 C3
Melina Cl UB3 83 B2
Melina Ct
 Putney SW15 134 A2
 St John's Wood NW8 229 C1
Melina Pl NW8 92 B4 229 C1
Melina Rd W12 112 B4
Melior Ct N6 49 C3
Melior Pl SE1 253 A2
Melior St SE1 117 C4 253 A2
Meliot Rd SE6 164 B2
Melisa Ct N6 49 D2
Meller Cl SM6 220 A5
Melling Dr EN1 6 A4
Melling St SE18 145 C6
Mellington Ct 2 N16 74 A5
Mellis Ave TW9 132 D4
Mellish Cl IG11 101 D6
Mellish Ct KT6 198 A3
Mellish Flats E10 53 C2
Mellish Gdns IG8 37 A5
Mellish Ho 2 E1 96 B1
Mellish Ind Est SE18 121 D3
Mellish St E14 119 C3
Mellison Rd SW17 180 C5
Mellitus St W12 89 D1
Mellor Cl KT12 195 B2
Mellor Ct 2 SW19 180 A3
Mellor Ho 2 SE21 183 C6
Mellow La E UB4 83 A3
Mellow Lane Sch UB4 83 A3
Mellow La W UB10 83 A4
Mellows Rd
 Redbridge IG5 56 B6
 Wallington SM6 219 D3
Mells Cres SE9 188 B6
Mell St 6 SE10 120 C1
Melody La N5 73 A3
Melody Rd SW18 158 A6
Melon Pl W8 245 B2
Melon Rd Leyton E11 76 C5
 Peckham SE15 140 A4
Melrose Ave
 Borehamwood WD6 10 D6
 Cricklewood NW2 68 C3
 Greenford UB6 85 D5
 Mitcham CR4 181 B3
 Thornton Heath SW16 204 C6
 Tottenham N22 32 D2
 Twickenham TW2 151 D4
 Wimbledon SW19 157 C1
Melrose Cl
 Greenford UB6 85 D5
 Grove Pk SE12 165 B3
 Hayes UB4 84 A2
Melrose Cres BR6 227 B3
Melrose Ct
 5 Ealing W13 109 A5
 Wandsworth SW18 157 B5
Melrose Dr UB1 107 C5
Melrose Gdns
 Edgware HA8 26 D1
 Hammersmith W6 112 C3
 Kingston u T KT3 199 B6
Melrose Ho
 Maida Vale NW6 91 C4
 Pimlico SW1 258 D2
Melrose Rd
 1 Barnes SW13 133 D3
 Merton SW19 179 C2
 Pinner HA5 41 B5
 Wandsworth SW18 157 B5
Melrose Sch CR4 202 C6
Melrose Terr W6 112 C3
Melrose Tudor SM6 220 A3
Melsa Rd SM4 202 A3
Melthorne Dr HA4 62 C5
Melthorpe Gdns SE3 144 A4
Melton Cl HA4 40 C1
Melton Ct
 11 Croydon CR0 221 D6
 South Kensington SW7 256 D3
 Sutton SM2 218 A1
 1 Twickenham TW1 153 B4
Melton Ho E5 74 A6
Melton St NW1 93 D4 232 C1
Melville Ave
 Greenford UB6 64 D3
 South Croydon CR2 221 D3
 Wimbledon SW20 178 A3
Melville Cl UB10 61 B5
Melville Court Flats 8 W12 112 B4
Melville Ct
 4 Brentford W4 110 C1
 Rotherhithe SE8 119 A2
Melville Gdns N13 32 D5
Melville Ho
 Lewisham SE10 142 A4
 New Barnet EN5 14 B5
Melville Pl 4 N1 73 A1
Melville Rd
 Barnes SW13 134 A4
 Sidcup DA14 168 C2
 Stonebridge NW10 67 B1
 Walthamstow E17 53 B6
Melville Villas Rd W3 111 B5
Melvin Ct 11 TW9 132 C4
Melvin Rd SE20 184 C2
Melwood Ho 23 E1 96 B1
Melyn Cl N7 71 C4
Memel Ct EC1 242 A5
Memel St EC1 242 A5
Memess Path 4 SE18 144 C6
Memorial Ave E15 98 C4
Memorial Cl TW5 129 B6
Memorial Hospl SE18 144 C3
Memorial Hts IG2 57 B3
Menai Pl 2 E3 97 C5
Menard Ct EC1 235 B1
Mendham Ho SE1 263 A6
Mendip Cl
 Forest Hill SE26 18
 Harlington UB3 12
 North Cheam KT4 21
Mendip Ct
 12 Battersea SW11 13
 Deptford SE14 14
 1 East Barnet N20 1
Mendip Dr NW2, NW11 6
Mendip Ho HA3 4
Mendip Hos 12 E2 9
Mendip Ho 2 N4 5
Mendip Rd
 Battersea SW11 13
 Bushey WD23
 Ilford IG2 5
Mendora Rd SW6 135 B5 26
Menelik Rd NW2 6
Menin Wks CR4 18
Menlo Gdns SE19 18
Mennie Ho SE18 14
Mennis Ho SM5 21
Menon Dr N9
Menorah Foundation Sch HA8 2
Menorah Prim Sch NW11 4
Menotti St 6 E2 9
Menteath Ho 9 E14 9
Mentmore Cl HA3 4
Mentmore Terr E8 7
Mentone Ct SW8 27
Meon Ct TW7 13
Meon Rd W3 11
Meopham Rd CR4, SW16 18
Mepham Cres HA3 2
Mepham Gdns HA3 2
Mepham St SE1 116 C5 25
Mera Dr DA7 14
Merantun Way SW19 18
Merbury Cl
 Lewisham SE13 16
 Woolwich SE28 12
Merbury Rd SE28 12
Mercator Pl 4 E14 11
Mercator Rd SE13 14
Mercer Cl KT7 19
Merceron Ho 3 E2 9
Merceron St E1 9
Mercer Pl HA5 2
Mercers Cl SE10 12
Mercer's Cotts 8 E3 9
Mercers Mews N7 7
Mercers Pl W6 11
Mercers Rd N19 7
Mercer St WC2 94 A1 24
Merchant Ct E1 11
Merchants Cl SE25 20
Merchants Ho SE10 12
Merchants Lo 5 E17 5
Merchant St E3 9
Merchant Taylors' Almshouses SE13 14
Merchant Taylors Hall* EC3 24
Merchiston Rd SE6 16
Merchland Rd SE9 16
Merchon Ho N7 7
Mercia Gr SE13 14
Mercia Ho
 9 Camberwell SE5 13
 Charlton TW15 17
Mercie Ct SE22 16
Mercier Rd SW15 15
Mercury Ct
 8 Brixton SW9 13
 10 Millwall E14 11
Mercury Ctr TW14 15
Mercury Ho
 Brentford TW8 10
 6 Old Ford E3 9
Mercury 25 NW9 2
Mercury Rd TW8 10
Mercury Way SE14 14
Mercy Terr SE13 16
Merebank La CR0, SM6 22
Mere Cl
 Orpington BR6 22
 Putney SW15, SW19 15
Meredith Ave NW2 6
Meredith Cl HA5 2
Meredith Ho 17 N16 7
Meredith Mews SE4 14
Meredith St
 Finsbury EC1 23
 Newham E13 9
Meredith Twr W3 11
Meredyth Rd SW13 13

e End CR0 206 D2
e Rd TW17 192 D3
eside BR6 226 C6
eside Pk TW15 171 A6
tone Cl SE4 141 A1
eton Mans 6
141 C4
etune Ct SM4 201 B6
evale Cres SM4 202 A3
eway Industry
2 152 C4
eway Rd TW2 152 C3
ewood Cl BR1 188 C1
ewood Gdns
206 D2
eworth Cl BR2 208 D4
eworth Dr SE18 145 A5
eworth Ho 3
5 140 C6
ganser Ct 17
141 B6
ganser Gdns
8 123 B3
idan Ct SE13 142 B1
den Cl BR1 187 D3
den Ct SW3 257 A1
den Ho
Barnet EN5 1 A1
Hoxton N1 95 C6
idian Building*
0 142 B5
idian Ct
Bermondsey
E16 118 A4
Catford SE6 164 D3
ydon CR0 220 C4
idian Ho SE10 120 C2
idian Pl E14 120 A4
idian Prim Sch
0 142 B6
idian Rd SE7 143 D5
idian Sq E15 76 B1
idian Trad Est
7 121 B2
idian Way
field EN3 19 A5
wer Edmonton N9,
18 18 D1
idian Wlk N17 33 C4
field Rd SE9 143 C1
ino Cl E11 55 C5
ino Pl DA15 168 A6
ioneth Ct 7 W7 86 D2
ivale Rd
rrow HA1 42 A2
tney SW15 135 A1
lewood Dr BR7 188 B2
ley Ct NW9 45 A1
lin Cl
tcham CR4 202 C6
Northolt UB5 84 C4
uth Croydon CR0 221 C4
allington SM6 220 B2
lin Cres HA8 26 B2
lin Ct
ckenham BR2 208 D5
Ealing W7 86 D3
tcham CR4 180 C2
islip HA4 61 B6
anmore HA7 25 B5
ood Green N22 32 C2
ling Cl KT9 213 D3
lin Gdns BR1 165 A1
lin Gr BR3 207 C4
lin Ho
Chiswick W4 111 B1
field EN3 18 D6
est Hampstead
NW3 69 D4
lin 26 NW9 27 D2
lin Prim Sch
1 165 A1
lin Rd DA16 146 A1
lin Rd N DA16 146 A1
lin Rd E12 77 D6
lins Ave HA2 63 B5
lin Sch SW15 157 A6
lins Ct WC1 234 A1
lin St EC1 94 C4 234 A1
rmaid Ct
ermondsey
SE1 117 B4 252 C2
otherhithe SE16 119 B5
roud Green N4 50 C3
rmaid Ho 8 E14 120 A6
rmaid Twr 22
8 141 B6
roe Ct N16 73 C6
rredene St SW2 160 B5
rriam Ave 2 E9 75 B2
rriam Cl E4 36 A5
rrick Rd UB2 107 B3
rricks Ct 5
V14 132 D1
rrick Sq
1 117 B3 262 C6
rridale SE12 164 D6

Merridene N21 16 D5
Merrielands Cres
RM9 103 B5
Merrielands Ret Pk
RM9 103 B5
Merrilands Rd KT4 200 C1
Merrilees Rd DA15 167 C4
Merrilyn Cl KT10 213 A2
Merriman Rd SE3 143 C4
Merrington Rd SW6 265 B6
Merrion Ave HA7 25 D5
Merritt Gdns KT9 213 C2
Merritt Rd SE4 163 B6
Merrivale Ave IG4 55 D5
Merrivale
Camden Town
NW1 232 B5
Southgate N14 15 D6
Merrow Ct CR4 180 B1
Merrow St
SE17 117 B1 262 C1
Merrow Way CR0 224 A2
Merrow Wlk SE17 262 D2
Merrydown Way
BR7 188 B2
Merry Fiddlers RM8 81 B6
Merryfield Gdns HA7 25 C5
Merryfield Ho SE12 165 C1
Merryfield SE3 142 D3
Merryhill Cl E4 19 D4
Merry Hill Rd WD23 8 A3
Merryhills Ct N14 15 C6
Merryhills Dr EN2 4 A1
Merryhills Prim Sch
EN2 4 B1
Merryweather Ct
13 Dartmouth Pk
N19 71 C5
1 New Malden KT3 199 C4
Mersea Ho IG11 78 D2
Mersey Ct 10 KT2 175 D2
Mersey Ho 10 N7 72 C3
Mersey Rd E17 53 B6
Mersey Wlk UB5 85 C5
Mersham Dr NW9 44 D4
Mersham Pl
Penge SE20 184 B2
South Norwood CR7 183 B1
Mersham Rd CR7 183 B1
Merstone Ho SW18 157 D5
Merten Rd RM6 59 A2
Merthyr Terr SW13 134 B6
MERTON 179 C2
Merton Abbey Mills
SW19 180 A2
Merton Abbey Prim Sch
SW19 179 D2
Merton Ave
Chiswick W4 111 D2
Hillingdon UB10 60 D1
Northolt UB5 64 A3
Merton Coll SM4 201 B4
Merton Court Sch
DA14 190 C6
Merton Ct Barnet EN5 1 D1
Welling DA16 146 B3
Merton Gdns BR5 210 D4
Merton Hall Gdns
SW20 179 A2
Merton Hall Rd
SW19 179 A2
Merton High St
SW19 180 A3
Merton Ho SW18 157 C3
Merton Ind Pk
SW19 180 A2
Merton La N6 70 D6
Merton Lo
New Barnet EN5 14 A6
3 Streatham SW16 182 A5
Merton Mans SW20 178 D1
MERTON PARK 179 C1
Merton Park Par
SW19 179 B2
Merton Park Prim Sch
SW19 179 C1
Merton Park Sta
SW19 179 C2
Merton Pl 9 SW19 180 A3
Merton Rd
Barking IG11 79 D1
Croydon SE25 206 A4
Enfield EN2 5 B5
Harrow HA2 42 A1
Ilford IG3 57 D2
Leytonstone E17 54 A3
Merton SW19 179 D3
Wandsworth SW18 157 C4
Merton Rise NW3 70 C1
Merton Road Ind Est
SW18 157 C4
Merton Way
East Molesey KT8 196 A6
Hillingdon UB10 60 D1
Merttins Rd SE15 162 D6
Meru Cl NW5 71 A3
Mervan Rd SW2 138 C1

Mervyn Ave SE9 167 A2
Mervyn Ct SE18 145 C6
Mervyn Rd
Brentford W13 109 A3
Shepperton TW17 193 A2
Mervyn Stockwood Ho
1 SE9 167 A2
Messaline Ave W3 89 A1
Messent Rd SE9 165 D6
Messer Ct CR0 220 D4
Messeter Pl SE9 166 C5
Messina Ave NW6 69 C1
Messiter Ho N1 233 D5
Met Appts The
SE12 164 D6
Metcalfe Ho 28
SW8 137 D3
Metcalfe Wlk 2
TW13 173 A6
Metcalf Rd TW15 170 D5
Meteor St SW11 137 A1
Meteor Way SM6 220 A1
Metford Cres EN3 7 C5
Metherell Ho N21 17 B5
Metheringham Way
NW9 27 C2
Methley Ho 8 N7 72 B6
Methley St
SE11 116 C1 261 B1
Methodist Central
Hall*
SW1 115 D4 249 D1
Methuen Cl HA8 26 C3
Methuen Pk N10 49 B6
Methuen Rd
Belvedere DA17 125 D2
Bexleyheath DA6 147 B1
Edgware HA8 26 C3
Methwold Rd W10 90 D2
Metro Bsns Ctr The
SE26 185 B5
Metro Ctr UB4 106 C6
Metro Ho E7 77 B2
Metro Ind Ctr TW7 130 C3
Metropolis Apartments
5 SW12 159 B3
Metropolitan Benefit
Societies Almshouses
3 N1 73 C2
Metropolitan Bsns Ctr
9 N1 73 C1
Metropolitan Cl 23
E14 97 C2
Metropolitan Ctr The
UB6 85 D6
Metro Trad Ctr HA9 66 D4
Meudon Ct KT6 197 D4
Mews Pl IG8 37 A6
Mews St E1 118 A5
Mews The
Beckenham BR3 185 C2
Hampton TW12 174 A4
Hornsey N8 50 C5
Redbridge IG4 55 D4
Shoreditch N1 235 B6
Thornton Heath
SW16 182 B2
Tottenham N15 51 C5
5 Upper Holloway
N19 50 A1
Woolwich SE18 122 D1
Mexborough NW1 232 A5
Mexfield Rd SW15 157 B6
Meyer Gn EN1 6 A5
Meyer Ho 1 SW12 159 B4
Meymott St
SE1 116 D5 251 C3
Meynell Cres E9 74 D1
Meynell Gdns E9 74 D1
Meynell Rd E9 74 D1
Meyrick Ct CR7 204 C3
Meyrick Ho 8 E14 97 C2
Meyrick Rd
Battersea SW11 136 C2
Willesden NW10 68 A2
Miah Terr 10 E1 118 A5
Miall Wlk SE26 185 A6
Micawber Ave UB8 82 C3
Micawber Ct N1 235 B2
Micawber Ho 27
SE16 118 A4
Micawber St
N1 95 A4 235 B2
Michael Cliffe Ho
EC1 234 B1
Michael Faraday Ho
SE17 262 D1
Michael Faraday Sch
SE17 117 B1 262 D1
Michael Gaynor Cl
W7 108 D5
Michael Marshall Ho 2
SE9 167 A2
Michaelmas Cl
SW20 200 C6
Michael Rd
Leytonstone E11 54 D1

Michael Rd *continued*
Parsons Green
SW6 135 D4 265 D2
South Norwood
SE25 205 C6
Michaels Cl SE13 142 C1
Michael Sobell Sinai
Sch HA3 44 C3
Michaelson Ho 4
SE21 183 C6
Michael Tippet Sch
SE27 161 A2
Michael Tippett Sch
The SE11 116 C2 261 B3
Michelangelo Ct 14
SE16 118 B1
Micheldever Rd
SE12 164 D5
Michelham Gdns
TW1 152 D1
Michelle Ct
Acton W3 111 B6
North Finchley N12 30 A5
Michell Ho TW1 152 D3
Michels Almshouses 11
TW10 154 A6
Michelsdale Dr 3
TW9 132 A1
Michelson Ho SE11 260 D3
Michel's Row 2
TW9 132 A1
Michel Wlk SE18 122 D1
Michigan Ave E12 78 B4
Michigan Ho E14 119 C3
Michleham Down
N12 29 B6
Mickledore NW1 232 B3
Micklefield Ct CR0 204 D3
Mickleham Cl BR5 190 A1
Mickleham Gdns
SM3 217 A2
Mickleham Rd BR5 190 A1
Mickleham Way
CR0 224 B1
Micklethwaite Rd
SW6 135 C6 265 B5
Mickleton Ho 30 W2 91 C2
Midas Bsns Ctr RM10 81 D4
Midas Metro Ctr
SM4 200 D2
Midcroft HA4 39 C1
Middle Dene NW7 11 B1
Middlefielde W13 87 B2
Middlefield Gdns
IG2 56 D3
Middlefield
NW8 92 B6 229 C6
Middle Green Cl 3
KT5 198 B3
Middleham Gdns
N18 34 A4
Middleham Rd N18 34 A4
Middle La N8 50 A4
Middle Lane Mews
N8 50 A4
Middle La TW11 174 D4
Middle Mill KT5 198 B6
Middle Park Ave
SE9 165 D4
Middle Park Prim Sch
SE9 165 D4
Middle Rd
East Barnet EN4 14 C5
Finchley N10 30 C2
Harrow HA2 42 B1
Mitcham SW16 181 D1
12 Newham E13 99 A5
Middle Row Prim Sch
W10 91 A3
Middle Row W10 91 A3
Middlesborough Rd
N18 34 A4
Middlesex Bsns Ctr
UB2 107 B4
Middlesex Cl UB6 85 D3
Middlesex Coll of
Computing & Tech
HA0 66 A3
Middlesex Ct
5 Chiswick W4 111 D2
6 Harrow HA1 42 D4
Middlesex Cty Cricket
Sch N3 29 D1
Middlesex Ho
Marylebone W1 239 B4
4 Penge SE20 184 C3
Wembley HA0 87 D6
Middlesex Pas EC1 241 D3
Middlesex Pl 13 E9 74 C2
Middlesex Rd CR4 204 A4
Middlesex St
E1 95 D1 243 C2
Middlesex Univ (Cat
Hill) EN4 15 A6
Middlesex Univ (Enfield
Campus) EN3 18 C6

Middlesex Univ
(Hendon Campus)
NW4 46 B5
Middlesex Univ N17 33 D4
Middlesex Univ Trent
Park EN4 3 C3
Middle St
Croydon CR0 221 A5
Holborn EC1 242 A4
Middle Temple*
EC4 116 C6 251 A6
Middle Temple La
EC4 116 C6 251 A6
Middleton Ave
Chingford Green E4 19 B1
Greenford UB5 86 B5
Sidcup DA14 190 C5
Middleton Cl E4 19 B1
Middleton Ct
Bromley BR1 187 B3
New Barnet EN5 2 A1
Middleton Dr
Bermondsey
SE16 118 D4
Pinner HA5 40 A6
Middleton Gdns IG2 56 D3
Middleton Gr N7 72 A3
Middleton Ho
Dalston E8 73 D1
Newington SE1 262 C5
Middleton Mews N7 72 A3
Middleton Pl W1 239 A3
Middleton Rd
Carshalton CR4,
SM5 202 B2
Dalston E8 73 D1
Golders Green NW11 47 C2
Hayes UB3 83 B2
Middleton St E2 96 B4
Middleton Way
SE13 142 B1
Middle Way UB4 84 C3
Middleway NW11 47 D4
Middle Way SW16 181 D1
Middle Way The HA3 24 D1
Middlewich Ho 7
UB5 85 B3
Midfield Prim Sch
BR5 190 A3
Midfield Way BR5 190 B2
Midford Ho 1 NW4 46 D5
Midford Pl W1 239 B5
Midholm Cl NW11 47 D5
Midholm NW11 47 D5
Midholm Rd CR0 223 A6
Midholm HA9 44 C1
Midhope Ho WC1 233 B1
Midhope St WC1 233 B1
Midhurst Ave
Muswell Hill N10 49 A6
Thornton Heath CR0 204 C2
Midhurst Ct N8 50 A2
Midhurst Gdns UB10 61 A1
Midhurst Hill DA6 169 C6
Midhurst Ho 6 E14 97 B1
Midhurst Par N10 49 A6
Midhurst 1 SE26 184 C4
Midhurst Rd W13 109 A3
Midhurst Way E5 74 A4
Midland Mainline
Terminal
NW1 93 D5 232 D3
Midland Pl E14 120 A1
Midland Rd
Leytonstone E10 54 A2
St Pancras
NW1 94 A4 233 A2
Midland Terr
Cricklewood NW2 68 D5
Dagenham NW10 89 C3
Midlea Ho EN3 6 C4
Midleton Rd KT3 177 A1
Midlothian Ho NW2 68 B4
Midlothian Rd E3 97 B3
Midmoor Rd
Merton SW19 179 A2
Streatham SW12 159 C3
Midship Cl SE16 118 D5
Midship Point E14 119 C4
Midstrath Rd NW10 67 C4
Midsummer Apartments
7 SM2 217 C1
Midsummer Ave
TW4 129 B1
Midsummer Ct
Blackheath Pk
SE12 143 A1
Edgware HA8 10 D1
Harrow HA1 42 B4
Midway SM3 201 B2
Midway Ho EC1 234 D2
Midwinter Cl 3
DA16 146 A2
Midwood Cl NW2 68 B5
Mighell Ave IG4 55 D4
Milan Ct N11 31 D2
Milan Rd UB1 107 B4

Milborne Gr SW10 256 B1
Milborne Ho 11 E9 74 C2
Milborne St E9 74 C2
Milborough Cres
SE12 164 C5
Milbourne La KT10 212 A3
Milbourne Lodge Jun
Sch KT10 212 A2
Milbourne Lodge Sen
Sch KT10 212 B2
Milbrook Ct NW3 48 A1
Milbrook KT10 212 A2
Milburn Dr 1 UB7 104 A6
Milburn Ho SW20 178 B1
Milcote St SE1 251 D1
Mildenhall Rd E5 74 C5
Mildmay Ave N1 73 B2
Mildmay Ct N1 73 B3
Mildmay Gr N N1 73 B3
Mildmay Gr S N1 73 B3
Mildmay Ho 6
SW15 156 C6
Mildmay Mission Hospl
E2 95 D4
Mildmay Pk N1 73 B3
Mildmay Rd
Ilford IG1 78 D5
Stoke Newington N1 73 C3
Mildmay St N1 73 B2
Mildon Ho EN3 6 C3
Mildred Ave
Hayes UB3 105 B3
Northolt UB5 63 D3
Mildura Ct N8 50 B5
MILE END 97 A3
Mile End Pl E1 96 D3
Mile End Rd E1, E3 96 D3
Mile End Sta E3 97 B4
Mile End The E17 34 D2
Mile Rd
Hackbridge SM6 203 A1
Wallington CR0, CR4,
CR9 203 D1
Miles Bldgs NW1 237 A4
Miles Cl SE28 123 B5
Miles Coverdale Prim
Sch W12 112 C4
Miles Ct
Croydon CR0 220 D6
Stepney E1 96 B1
Miles Dr SE28 123 C5
Miles Ho 5 SE10 120 C1
Miles Lo Harrow HA1 42 B4
Stratford New Town
E15 76 B3
Milespit Hill NW7 28 C5
Miles Pl NW8 236 D4
Miles Rd Hornsey N8 50 A6
Mitcham CR4 202 C6
Miles St
SW8 138 A6 270 B5
Milestone Cl
Edmonton N9 18 A2
Sutton SM2 218 B1
Milestone Ct TW7 131 A4
Milestone Green
SW14 133 B1
Milestone Ho KT1 197 D5
Milestone Rd SE19 183 D4
Miles Way N20 14 C2
Milfoil St W12 112 A6
Milford Cl SE2 147 A6
Milford Ct
Southall UB1 107 C5
3 Stamford Hill N16 51 C1
Milford Gdns
Croydon CR0 206 D4
Edgware HA8 26 C3
Wembley HA0 65 D3
Milford Gr SM1 218 A4
Milford La
WC2 116 C6 251 A6
Milford Mews SW16 160 B1
Milford Rd
Ealing W13 109 B5
Southall UB1 107 C6
Milk St Bromley BR1 187 B4
City of London
EC2 95 A1 242 B2
Newham E16 122 D5
Milkwell Gdns IG8 37 B3
Milkwell Yd 7 SE5 139 A4
Milkwood Rd SE24 138 D1
Milk Yd E1 118 C6
Millais Ave E12 78 C3
Millais Cres KT19 215 C3
Millais Ct 9 UB5 84 D5
Millais Gdns HA8 26 C1
Millais Rd Enfield EN1 17 D6
Leyton E11 76 B4
New Malden KT3 199 C2
Millais Way KT19 215 A4
Milland Ho 11
SW15 156 A3

Millard Cl 21 N16 73 C3
Millard Terr RM10 81 C2
Millars Meadow Cl SE12 165 A6
Millbank Ho KT6 198 B2
Millbank Prim Sch SW1 115 D2 259 D3
Millbank SM6 219 D3
Millbank Way SE12 165 A6
Millbank SW1 116 A2 260 A3
Millbourne Rd TW13 173 A6
Mill Bridge EN5 13 B5
Millbrook Ave DA16 145 B1
Millbrooke Ct 7 SW15 157 A6
Millbrook Gdns RM6 59 A3
Millbrook Ho 4 SE15 140 A6
Millbrook Pl NW1 232 A4
Millbrook Rd
Brixton SW9 138 D2
Edmonton N9 18 B3
Millbrook 1 E18 55 A6
Mill Cl SM5 219 A6
Mill Cnr EN5 1 B4
Millcroft Ho SE6 185 D6
Mill Ct Hendon NW7 29 A2
Leyton E10 76 A5
14 Thamesmead SE28 124 B6
Millender Wlk SE16 118 C2
Millennium Bridge* SE1, EC4 252 A5
Millennium Bsns Ctr NW2 68 B6
Millennium City Acad W1 238 D3
Millennium Cl E16 99 B1
Millennium Dr E14 120 B2
Millennium Harbour E14 119 C4
Millennium Ho E17 52 D4
Millennium Pl 27 E2 96 B5
Millennium Prim Sch SE10 120 D3
Millennium Sq SE1 253 D2
Millennium Way SE10 120 C3
Miller Ave EN3 7 C5
Miller Cl
Bromley BR1 187 B5
Carshalton CR4 202 D2
Pinner HA5 22 C1
Miller Ct
Bexleyheath DA7 147 D2
8 Hendon NW9 46 A5
Miller Ho
Harringay N15 50 D5
9 Streatham SW2 160 A4
Miller Rd
Mitcham SW19 180 B4
Thornton Heath CR0 204 C1
Miller's Ave E8, N16 73 D3
Millers Cl NW7 28 A6
Miller's Ct 1 W4 111 D1
Millers Ct 3 HA0 88 A5
Millers Green Cl EN2 4 D2
Miller's House Visitor Ctr* 1 E3 98 A4
Millers Mead Ct SW19 180 B3
Miller's Terr 1 E8 73 D3
Miller St NW1 232 A4
Miller's Way W6 112 C4
Millers Wharf Ho E1 118 A5
Millers Yd N3 29 D3
Miller Wlk SE1 251 B3
Millet Rd UB6 85 D5
Mill Farm Ave TW16 171 C3
Millfarm Bsns Pk TW4 151 A4
Mill Farm Cl HA5 22 C1
Mill Farm Cres TW4 151 A3
Millfield Ave E17 35 B2
Millfield
Charlton TW16 171 B2
Finsbury Pk N4 72 C6
Kingston u T KT1 198 B6
Millfield La N6 70 D6
Millfield Pl N6 71 A6
Millfield Rd
Hendon HA8 27 A1
Twickenham TW4 151 B3
Millfields Com Sch E5 74 C4
Millfields Rd E5 74 C5
Mill Gdns SE26 162 B1
Mill Gn CR4 203 A2
Mill Green Bsns Pk CR4 203 A2
Mill Green Rd CR4 203 A2
Millgrove St 6 SW11 137 A3
Millharbour E14 119 D4
Millhaven Cl RM6 58 B3
MILL HILL 28 B5
Mill Hill SW13 134 A2
Mill Hill Broadway Sta NW7 27 C4
Mill Hill Circus NW7 27 D5
Mill Hill Cty High Sch NW7 11 C2
Mill Hill East Sta NW7 29 A3
Mill Hill Gr 11 W3 110 D5
Mill Hill Ind Est NW7 27 D4
Mill Hill Rd
Barnes SW13 134 A3
South Acton W3 110 D4
Mill Hill Sch NW7 28 B6
Mill Hill Terr 9 W3 110 D5
Mill Ho
4 Lewisham SE13 142 A2
Morden SM4 202 A5
Millhouse Pl SE27 182 D6
Mill Ho IG8 36 D5
Millicent Fawcett Ct N17 33 D2
Millicent Preston Ho 4 IG11 101 B6
Millicent Rd E10 53 B1
Milligan Ho SE23 163 B3
Milligan St E14 119 B6
Milliners Ho SW18 135 C1
Milling Rd HA8 27 B3
Millington Ho N16 73 B5
Millington Rd UB3 105 C3
Mill La
Brondesbury NW6 69 B3
Carshalton SM5 219 A5
Croydon CR0 220 C5
Dagenham RM6 59 A3
Mill Lane Trad Est CR0 220 B5
Mill La Sewardstone E4 7 D2
Woodford IG8 36 D5
Woolwich SE18 122 C1
Millman Ct
Bloomsbury WC1 240 C5
Greenwich SE3 143 B5
Millman Mews WC1 240 C5
Millman Pl WC1 240 D5
Millman St WC1 94 B3 240 C5
Millmark Gr SE14 141 A3
Millmarsh La EN3 7 B3
Millmead Bsns Ctr N17 52 B6
Millmead Ind Ctr N17 52 B6
Mill Mead Rd N17 52 B6
MILL MEADS 98 B5
Millner Ct SE4 141 B3
Mill Plat Ave TW7 131 A3
Mill Plat TW7 131 A3
Mill Pl
Chislehurst BR7 188 D2
Kingston u T KT1 198 B6
Limehouse E14 97 A1
Mill Pond Cl SW8 137 D5 269 D3
Millpond Est SE16 118 B4
Millpond Pl 2 SM6 219 A5
Mill Rd Ilford IG1 78 C5
Merton SW19 180 A3
Newham E16 121 B5
Twickenham TW2 152 A2
Mill Ridge HA8 26 C5
Mill River Trad Est EN3 7 A1
Mill Row N1 95 C6
Mills Cl UB10 82 C5
Mills Ct 9 Leyton E11 76 C5
Shoreditch EC2 95 C4
Mills Gr Hendon NW4 46 D6
1 South Bromley E14 98 A2
Mills Ho SW8 269 B2
Millshott Cl SW6 134 C4
Mills Ho E17 54 B6
Millside SM5 218 D6
Millside Pl TW7 131 B3
Millson Cl N20 14 B2
Mills Row W4 111 B2
Mill St
Bermondsey SE1 117 D4 253 D2
Kingston u T KT1 198 A6
Mayfair W1 249 A6
Millstream Cl N13 32 C5
Millstream Ho 14 SE16 118 B4
Millstream Rd SE1 117 D4 253 C1
Mill Trad Est The NW10 89 A4
Mill Vale BR2 186 D1
Mill View Cl KT17 215 D1
Mill View Gdns CR0 222 D5
MILLWALL 119 C3
Millwall Dock Rd E14 119 C3
Mill Way
Edgware NW7 27 C5
Feltham TW14 150 B6
Millway Gdns UB5 63 B2
Millwood Rd TW3, TW7 152 A6
Millwood St 10 W10 91 A2
Mill Yd E1 118 A6
Milman Cl HA5 40 D6
Milman Rd NW6 91 A5
Milman's Ho SW10 266 C5
Milman's St SW10 136 B6 266 C5
Milne Ct Enfield EN2 4 C3
4 Woodford E18 37 A2
Milne Field HA5 23 C3
Milne Gdns SE9 166 A6
Milne Ho 18 SE18 122 B2
Milner Bldg N16 73 B5
Milner Dr TW2 152 B4
Milner Ho
2 Battersea SW11 136 B2
Hayes UB4 84 B4
Milner Pl N1 94 C6 234 B6
Milner Rd
Dagenham RM8 80 C6
Kingston u T KT1 197 D6
Merton SW19 179 D2
Morden SM4 202 B4
Newham E15 98 C4
South Norwood CR7 205 B6
Milner Sq N1 72 D1
Milner St SW3 114 D2 257 C4
Milner Wlk SE9 167 B3
Milnthorpe Rd W4 133 B6
Milo Rd SE22 161 D5
Milrood Ho 5 E1 96 D2
Milroy Wlk SE1 251 C4
Milson Rd W14 113 A3 254 A6
Milsted Ho 23 E5 74 B3
Milton Ave
Barnet EN5 13 B6
Becontree NW10 89 B6
Carshalton SM1 218 C4
Crouch End N6 49 C2
Kingsbury NW9 45 A6
Plashet E6 78 A1
Thornton Heath CR0 205 B2
Milton Cl
Bermondsey SE1 117 D2 263 C3
Carshalton SM1 218 B5
Hampstead Garden Suburb N2 48 A3
Hayes UB4 84 A1
Milton Court Rd SE14 141 A6
Milton Cres IG2 57 A3
Milton Ct
Fulham SW6 135 A2
Ilford RM6 58 C2
Kingston u T KT2 176 A6
St Luke's EC2 242 C4
Twickenham TW2 152 C1
Uxbridge UB10 60 D5
9 Wandsworth SW18 157 C6
Milton Dr
Borehamwood WD6 10 D6
Littleton TW17 192 A5
Milton Gdns TW19 148 B3
Milton Gr
Friern Barnet N11 31 D5
Stoke Newington N16 73 C4
Milton Ho
12 Beckenham BR3 185 C3
19 Bethnal Green E2 96 C4
2 Camberwell SE5 139 B5
5 Kingston u T KT2 176 D4
Sutton SM1 217 C5
Milton House Mans E8 73 D4
Milton Lo
4 Sidcup DA14 190 A6
Southgate N21 16 D3
Twickenham TW1 152 D4
Milton Pk N6 49 C2
Milton Pl 3 N7 72 C3
Milton Rd Acton W3 111 B5
Belvedere DA17 125 C2
Bexley DA16 145 D4
Crouch End N6 49 C2
Ealing W7 108 D6
Hampton TW12 173 C3
Milton Rd *continued*
Harrow HA1 42 C5
1 Hendon NW9 46 A2
Mill Hill NW7 28 A5
Mitcham CR4 181 A3
Mortlake SW14 133 B2
Sutton SM1 217 C4
Thornton Heath CR0 205 B2
Tottenham N15 50 D6
Tulse Hill SE24 160 D6
Uxbridge UB10 60 D4
Wallington SM6 219 D2
Walthamstow E17 53 C5
Wimbledon SW19 180 A4
Milton St EC1, EC2 95 B2 242 C4
Milton Way UB7 104 B2
Milverton Dr UB10 61 A4
Milverton Gdns IG3 79 D6
Milverton Ho SE23 163 A1
Milverton NW5 71 A3
Milverton Rd NW6 68 C1
Milverton St SE11 116 C1 261 B1
Milverton Way SE9 188 C6
Milward St E1 96 B2
Milward Wlk 14 SE18 144 C6
Mimosa Ct
Colney Hatch N12 30 C4
South Lambeth SW4 270 B1
Mimosa Ho UB4 84 C2
Mimosa N15 51 B4
Mimosa Rd UB4 84 C2
Mimosa St SW6 135 B4 264 D1
Mina Rd SW19 179 C2
Minard Rd SE6 164 C3
Mina Rd SE17 117 C1 263 B2
Minchenden Cres N14 15 D1
Minchenden Ct N14 15 D2
Minchin Ho 10 E14 97 C1
Mincing La EC3 117 C6 253 A6
Minden Rd
Cheam SM3 217 B6
Penge SE20 184 B2
Minehead Ct HA2 63 C6
Minehead Rd
Harrow HA2 63 C5
Streatham SW16 182 B5
Mineral Cl EN5 12 C6
Mineral St SE18 123 C2
Minera Mews SW1 258 B4
Minerva Cl
Kennington SW9 138 C5
Sidcup DA14 189 C6
Minerva Rd
Becontree NW10 89 B4
Chingford E4 35 D3
Kingston u T KT1 176 B1
Minerva St E2 96 B5
Minerva Wlk EC1 241 D2
Minet Ave NW10 89 C5
Minet Ctry Pk UB2, UB3, UB4 106 C4
Minet Dr UB3 106 A5
Minet Gdns
Dagenham NW10 89 C5
Hayes UB3 106 B5
Minet Ho 20 E1 96 A1
Minet Jun & Inf Schs UB3 106 B5
Minet Rd SE5, SW9 138 D3
Minetta Ct 19 EN5 13 D6
Minford Gdns W14 112 D4
Mingard Wlk N7 72 B5
Ming St E14 119 C6
Minimax Cl TW14 150 A5
Ministry Way SE9 166 B2
Mink Ct TW4 128 C3
Minnie Bennett Ho SE3 143 C5
Minniedale KT5 198 B4
Minnow Wlk SE17 263 B3
Minories EC3 117 D6 253 C6
Minshaw Ct DA14 189 D6
Minshull Pl 23 BR3 185 C3
Minshull St SW8 269 C1
Minson Rd E9 96 D6
Minstead Gdns SW15 155 D4
Minstead Way KT3 199 C3
Minster Ave SM1 217 C6
Minster Ct EC3 253 B6
Minster Dr CR0 221 C4
Minster Gdns KT8 195 B5
Minsterley Ave TW16, TW17 193 C5
Minster Rd
Bromley BR1 187 B3
Brondesbury NW2 69 A3
Minster Wlk N8 50 A5
Minstrel Ct HA3 24 C1
Minstrel Gdns KT5 198 B5
Mint Bsns Pk 12 E16 99 A2
Mint Cl UB10 82 D4
Mintern Cl N13 16 D1
Minterne Ave UB2 107 C2
Minterne Rd HA3 44 B4
Minterne Waye UB4 84 C1
Mintern St N1 95 B5 235 D4
Minton Ho SE11 261 A4
Minton Mews 3 NW6 69 D2
Mint Rd SM5, SM6 219 B4
Mint St SE1 252 B2
Mint Wlk CR0 221 A5
Mirabel Rd SW6 135 B5 264 D4
Mirage Ctr The HA9 66 D4
Miranda Cl 19 E1 96 C2
Miranda Ct W3 88 B1
Miranda Ho
6 Belvedere DA17 125 C1
17 Hoxton N1 95 C5
Miranda Rd N19 49 C1
Mirfield Ct SE20 184 A1
Mirfield St SE7 121 D3
Miriam Ct DA14 190 B6
Miriam Rd SE18 123 C1
Mirravale Ct 11 IG9 21 C2
Mirravale Trad Est RM8 59 A2
Mirren Cl HA2 63 B5
Mirror Path SE12 165 C1
Misbourne Rd UB10 82 C6
Missenden Cl TW14 149 D3
Missenden Gdns SM4 202 A3
Missenden Ho NW8 237 A6
Missenden SE17 262 D1
Mission Gr E17 53 A4
Mission Grove Prim Sch E17 53 B5
Mission Pl SE15 140 A4
Mission Sq 13 TW8 132 A6
Mission The
13 Bermondsey SE16 118 B4
14 Poplar E14 97 B1
Missouri Ct HA5 40 C3
Misterton Ct SW11 266 D2
Mistletoe Cl CR0 206 D1
Mistley Thorn IG1 56 C2
Mistral Ct E4 19 D1
Mistral SE5 139 C4
Mistys Field KT12 194 C1
Mitali Pas 21 E1 96 A1
MITCHAM 202 D5
Mitcham Garden Village CR4 203 A4
Mitcham Ho 9 SE5 139 A4
Mitcham Ind Est CR4 181 A2
Mitcham Junction Sta CR4 203 A4
Mitcham La SW16 181 C5
Mitcham Pk CR4 202 C5
Mitcham Rd
Ilford IG3 57 D2
Newham E6 100 A4
Upper Tooting SW17 180 D5
Mitcham Sta CR4 202 C5
Mitchell Brook Prim Sch NW10 67 C2
Mitchellbrook Way NW10 67 B2
Mitchell Cl
Abbey Wood SE2 124 C2
Belvedere DA17 125 D3
Mitchell Ct SW14 133 C1
Mitchell Ho
Gunnersbury W4 110 D1
6 Islington N1 72 C1
31 Shepherd's Bush W12 112 B6
Mitchell 19 NW9 27 D2
Mitchell Rd
Edmonton N13 33 A5
Orpington BR6 227 D4
Mitchell's Pl SE21 161 C4
Mitchell St EC1 95 A3 242 B6
Mitchell Way
1 Bromley BR1 187 A2
Tokyngton NW10 67 A2
Mitchell Wlk E6 100 B2
Mitchison Rd N1 73 B2
Mitchley Rd N17 52 A6
Mitford Cl KT9 213 C2
Mitford Rd N19 72 A6
Mitre Bridge Ind Pk W10 90 B3
Mitre Cl
Shepperton TW17 193 B3
Sutton SM2 218 B1
Mitre Ct
Belvedere DA17 12
1 Ilford RM6 5
9 Woodford E18 3
Mitre Ho RM7 5
Mitre Rd
Lambeth SE1 116 C4 25
Newham E15 9
Mitre Sq EC3 24
Mitre St EC3 95 C1 24
Mitre The 9 E14 11
Mitre Way W10 9
Mizzen Ct E14 11
Moatbridge Sch SE9 16
Moat Cl BR6 22
Moat Cres N3 4
Moat Croft DA16 14
Moat Ct Eltham SE9 16
Sidcup DA15 16
Moat Dr Harrow HA1 4
5 Newham E13 9
Ruislip HA4 3
Moat Farm Rd UB5 6
Moatfield NW6 6
Moat Lodge The HA1 6
Moat Pl Acton W3 8
Stockwell SW9 13
Moat Sch The SW6 13
Moat Side Enfield EN3
Feltham TW13 17
Moat The KT3 17
Moberly Rd SW4 15
Mobey Ct SW4 27
Moby Dick RM6 5
Mocatta Ho 9 E1 9
Modbury Gdns NW5 7
Modder Pl SW15 13
Model Cotts SW14 13
Model Farm Cl SE9 16
Modling Ho 8 E2 9
Modoc Ho EN3 1
Moelwyn Hughes Ct N7 7
Moelyn Mews HA1 4
Moffat Ct
Upper Tooting SW17 18
Wimbledon SW19 17
Moffat Ho 24 SE5 13
Moffat Rd
Bowes Pk N13 3
South Norwood CR7 18
Upper Tooting SW17 180
Mogden La TW7 152
Mohammedi Pk Complex UB5 8
Mohawk Ho 33 E3 97
Mohmmad Khan Rd E11 54
Mohr Ct N22 3
Moidart Ct HA8 10
Moineau 18 NW9 27
Moira Cl N17 33
Moira Ct SW17 159
Moira Ho 13 SW9 138
Moira Rd SE9 144
Molasses Ho 1 SW11 136
Molasses Row 2 SW11 136
Mole Abbey Gdns KT8 195
Mole Ct
2 Bedford Pk W12 111
West Ewell KT19 215
Mole Ho NW8 236
Molember Ct KT7 196
Molember Rd KT8 196
Molescroft SE9 167
Molesey Ave KT12, KT8 195
Molesey Bsns Ctr KT8 195
Molesey Dr SM3 217
Molesey Ho E2 243
Molesey Hospl KT8 195
Molesey Park Ave KT8 195
Molesey Park Cl KT8 196
Molesey Park Rd KT8 196
Molesey Rd KT12 195
Molesford Rd SW6 265
Molesham Cl KT8 195
Molesham Way KT8 195
Molesworth Ho 9 SE17 138
Molesworth St SE13 142
Moliner Ct 4 BR3 185
Mollie Davis Ct SE19 183

llison Ave EN3 ... 7 B5
llison Dr SM6 ... 220 A1
llison Sq SM6 ... 219 D1
llison Way HA8 ... 26 C1
lly Huggins Cl
W12 ... 159 C4
lton Ho N1 ... 233 D5
lvic Ct BR3 ... 185 B1
lyneux Dr SW17 ... 181 B6
lyneux Ho W1 ... 237 B2
lyneux St
/1 ... 92 C2 237 B3
narch Cl
oney Hall BR4 ... 224 D4
ast Bedfont TW14 .. 149 C4
narch Ct
aling W5 ... 87 C2
ampstead Garden
Suburb N2 ... 48 A4
narch Dr E16 ... 99 D2
narch Mews
Valthamstow E17 ... 53 D3
Vest Norwood
SW16 ... 182 C5
narch Par CR4 ... 180 D1
narch Pl
uckhurst Hill IG9 ... 21 C2
utton SM1 ... 218 B3
narch Rd DA17 ... 125 C3
narchs Ct
1 Edgware NW7 ... 27 B5
Harrow HA2 ... 41 C2
narch's Way HA4 ... 39 C1
narch Way IG2 ... 57 B3
na Rd SE15 ... 140 C3
na St E16 ... 98 D2
nastery Gdns EN2 ... 5 B3
naveen Gdns
KT8 ... 195 D6
onck's Row SW18 .. 157 B5
onck St
SW1 ... 115 D3 259 D5
onckton Ct W14 ... 254 C6
onclar Rd SE5 ... 139 B1
oncorvo Cl
SW7 ... 114 C4 247 A1
oncrieff Cl 4 E6 ... 100 A1
oncrieff St SE15 ... 140 A3
ondial Way UB7 ... 127 A5
ondragon Ho SW8 270 B2
onega Prim Sch
E12 ... 77 D2
onega Rd E7, E12 ... 77 D2
onet Ct 15 SE16 ... 118 B1
oneyer Ho N1 ... 235 C2
onica Ct SW16 ... 181 D4
onica James Ho 12
DA14 ... 168 A1
onica Shaw Ct
NW1 ... 232 D3
onier Rd E3 ... 75 C1
onivea Rd BR3 ... 185 B3
onkbretton Ho E2 ... 96 A4
onk Ct W12 ... 112 A5
onk Dr E16 ... 121 A6
ONKEN HADLEY ... 1 A3
onken Hadley CE Prim
Sch EN4 ... 1 C4
onkfrith Ave N14 ... 15 B5
onkfrith Cl N14 ... 15 B4
onkfrith Prim Sch
N14 ... 15 A4
onkfrith Way N14 ... 15 B4
onkham's Ave IG8 ... 37 B5
onkham's Dr IG8 ... 37 B5
onkham's La IG8 ... 37 B6
onkleigh Rd SM4,
SW20 ... 201 A5
onkridge 3 N8 ... 49 D2
onks Ave
East Molesey KT8 ... 195 B4
New Barnet EN5 ... 14 A5
onks Cl
Abbey Wood SE2 ... 124 D2
Enfield EN2 ... 5 A3
Harrow HA2 ... 63 D6
Ruislip HA4 ... 62 D4
onks Cres KT12 ... 194 B1
onksdene Gdns
SM1 ... 217 D5
onks Dr W3 ... 88 C1
onksfield N4 ... 72 C6
ONKS ORCHARD .. 207 A3
onks Orchard Rd BR3,
CR0 ... 207 C2
onks Orchard Sch
CR0 ... 206 D4
onks Park Gdns
HA9 ... 66 D1
onks Pk HA9 ... 67 A2
onks Rd EN2 ... 5 A3
onk St SE18 ... 122 C2
onks Way
Beckenham BR3 ... 207 C3
Croydon BR5 ... 211 B1
Harmondsworth
UB7 ... 126 A6

Monks Way *continued*
Temple Fortune
NW11 ... 47 B5
Monkswell Ct N10 ... 31 A2
Monkswell Ho E2 ... 96 A4
Monkswood Gdns
Borehamwood
WD6 ... 11 B6
Ilford IG5 ... 56 C6
Monk Terr SE23 ... 163 B2
Monkton Ho
32 Bermondsey
SE16 ... 118 D4
22 Hackney E5 ... 74 B3
Monkton Rd DA16 ... 145 D3
Monkton St
SE11 ... 116 C2 261 B4
Monkville Ave NW11 .. 47 B5
Monkville Par 1
NW11 ... 47 B5
Monkwell Sq EC2 ... 242 B3
Monmouth Ave
Teddington KT1 ... 175 C3
Wanstead E18 ... 55 B6
Monmouth Cl
Bedford Pk W4 ... 111 B3
Bexley DA16 ... 146 A1
Mitcham CR4, SW16 . 204 A5
Monmouth Ct 9 W7 .. 86 D2
Monmouth Gr TW8 ... 110 A2
Monmouth Ho
5 Camden Town
NW5 ... 71 B2
Wandsworth SW18 .. 157 C5
Monmouth Pl W2 ... 91 D1
Monmouth Rd
Dagenham RM9 ... 81 B3
Hayes UB3 ... 105 D2
Lower Edmonton N9 ... 18 C2
Newham E6 ... 100 B4
Notting Hill W2 ... 91 C1
Monmouth St
WC2 ... 94 A1 240 A1
Monnery Rd N19 ... 71 C5
Monnow Rd SE1 ... 118 A2
Mono La TW13 ... 150 B2
Monoux Almshouses
E17 ... 53 D5
Monoux Gr E17 ... 35 C2
Monroe Cres EN1 ... 6 B4
Monroe Dr SW14 ... 154 D6
Monroe Ho
16 Crouch End N19 ... 49 D2
Lisson Gr NW8 ... 230 B1
Monro Gdns HA3 ... 24 C3
Monro Ho
16 Hampstead
NW3 ... 70 A4
Putney SW15 ... 156 B6
Monro Way E5 ... 74 A4
Monsal Ct E5 ... 75 A4
Monsell Ct 4 N4 ... 72 D5
Monsell Rd N4, N5 ... 72 D5
Monson Prim Sch
SE14 ... 140 D5
Monson Rd
Deptford SE14 ... 140 D5
Willesden Green
NW10 ... 90 B5
Mons Way BR2 ... 210 A3
Montacute Rd
Bushey WD23 ... 8 C4
Carshalton SM4 ... 202 B3
Forest Hill SE6 ... 163 B4
Montagu Cres N18 ... 34 B6
Montagu Ct W1 ... 237 D3
Montague Ave
Brockley SE4 ... 141 C1
Ealing W7 ... 108 D5
Montague Cl
Borough The SE1 ... 252 C4
Walton-on-T KT12 ... 194 A2
Montague Ct 16
DA14 ... 168 A1
Montague Fell HA0 ... 64 D4
Montague Gdns W3 .. 110 C6
Montague Pl
WC1 ... 93 D2 239 D4
Montague Rd
Ealing W13 ... 87 B1
Hanwell W7 ... 108 D4
Hornsey Vale N8 ... 50 B4
Hounslow TW3 ... 129 D2
Leytonstone E11 ... 76 D6
Merton SW19 ... 179 D3
Richmond TW10 ... 154 A5
Shacklewell E8 ... 74 A3
Southall UB2 ... 107 A2
Thornton Heath CR0 . 204 D1
Tottenham Hale N15 ... 52 A5
Uxbridge UB8 ... 60 A1
Montague Sq SE15 ... 140 C5
Montague St
Bloomsbury
WC1 ... 94 A2 240 A4
City of London EC1 .. 242 A3

Montague Terr 1
BR2 ... 209 A5
Montague Waye
UB2 ... 107 A3
Montague Works
HA0 ... 88 B5
Montagu Gdns
Edmonton N18 ... 34 B6
Wallington SM6 ... 219 C4
Montagu Ind Est N18 . 34 C6
Montagu Mans
W1 ... 92 D2 237 D3
Montagu Mews N
W1 ... 237 D3
Montagu Mews S
W1 ... 237 D2
Montagu Mews W
W1 ... 237 D2
Montagu Pl
W1 ... 92 D2 237 D3
Montagu Rd
Hendon NW4 ... 46 A3
Lower Edmonton N9,
N18 ... 18 C1
Montagu Row W1 ... 237 D3
Montagu Sq
W1 ... 92 D1 237 D2
Montagu St
W1 ... 92 D1 237 D2
Montaigne Cl SW1 .. 259 D3
Montalt Ho IG8 ... 36 D6
Montalt Rd IG8 ... 36 D5
Montana Bldg 4
SE13 ... 141 D4
Montana Gdns
Penge SE26 ... 185 B5
5 Sutton SM1 ... 218 A3
Montana Rd
Upper Tooting
SW17 ... 159 A1
Wimbledon SW20 ... 178 C2
Montbelle Prim Sch
SE9 ... 188 C6
Montbelle Rd SE9 ... 166 D1
Montcalm Cl
Hayes BR2 ... 209 A3
Yeading UB4 ... 84 B4
Montcalm Ho E14 ... 119 C3
Montcalm Rd SE7 ... 143 D5
Montclair Ct 21 N12 ... 29 D6
Montclare St
E2 ... 95 D3 243 C6
Monteagle Ave IG11 .. 79 A2
Monteagle Ct
Barking IG11 ... 79 A1
27 Hoxton N1 ... 95 C5
Monteagle Prim Sch
RM9 ... 102 B6
Monteagle Way
Nunhead SE15 ... 140 B2
Shacklewell E5 ... 74 A5
Montefiore Ct 2
N16 ... 51 D1
Montefiore St 2
SW8 ... 137 B3
Montego Cl 10 SW2 .. 138 C1
Montem Prim Sch
N7 ... 72 B5
Montem Rd
Forest Hill SE23 ... 163 B4
New Malden KT3 ... 199 C5
Montem St N4 ... 50 B1
Montenotte Rd N8 ... 49 C4
Monteray Studios
W10 ... 91 A5
Monterey Cl NW7 ... 27 C5
Montesole Ct 7 HA5 .. 22 C1
Montesquieu Terr 3
E16 ... 98 D1
Montford Pl
Kennington SE11 ... 138 C6
Kennington SE11 ... 261 A1
Montford Rd TW16 ... 194 A5
Montfort Ho
4 Bethnal Green
E2 ... 96 C4
Cubitt Town E14 ... 120 A3
Montfort Pl SW19 ... 156 D3
Montgolfier Wlk UB5 .. 85 A4
Montgomerie Ct 2
BR3 ... 185 C2
Montgomery Ave
KT10 ... 212 C6
Montgomery Cl
Blackfen DA15 ... 167 D5
Mitcham CR4 ... 204 A5
Montgomery Ct W4 .. 133 A6
Montgomery Gdns
SM2 ... 218 B1
Montgomery Ho 5
SW14 ... 133 B2
Montgomery Lo 38
E1 ... 96 C3
Montgomery Rd
Acton W4 ... 111 A2
Edgware HA8 ... 26 B4

Montholme Rd
SW11 ... 158 D5
Monthope Rd 17 E1 ... 96 A2
Montolieu Gdns
SW15 ... 156 B6
Montpelier Ave
Ealing W5 ... 87 C2
Sidcup DA5 ... 168 D4
Montpelier Cl UB10 ... 82 C6
Montpelier Ct
5 Beckenham
BR2 ... 208 D5
Ealing W5 ... 87 D2
Montpelier Gdns
Ilford RM6 ... 58 C2
Newham E6 ... 99 D4
Montpelier Gr NW5 ... 71 C3
Montpelier Mews
SW7 ... 257 B6
Montpelier Pl
Knightsbridge
SW7 ... 257 B6
21 Stepney E1 ... 96 C1
Montpelier Prim Sch
W5 ... 87 D2
Montpelier Rd
Ealing W5 ... 87 D2
Finchley N3 ... 30 A2
Peckham SE15 ... 140 B4
Sutton SM1 ... 218 A4
Montpelier Rise
Golders Green
NW11 ... 47 A2
Wembley HA9 ... 43 D1
Montpelier Row
Blackheath Vale
SE3 ... 142 D3
Twickenham TW1 ... 153 C4
Montpelier Sq
SW7 ... 114 C4 247 B1
Montpelier St
SW7 ... 114 C3 257 B6
Montpelier Terr
SW7 ... 247 B1
Montpelier Vale
SE3 ... 142 D3
Montpelier Way
NW11 ... 47 A2
Montpelier Wlk
SW7 ... 114 C3 257 B6
Montpellier Ct KT12 .. 194 B3
Montrave Rd SE20 ... 184 C3
Montreal Ho
Catford SE6 ... 163 D3
Hayes UB4 ... 84 B4
Montreal Pl WC2 ... 250 C6
Montreal Rd IG1 ... 57 A2
Montrell Rd SW2 ... 160 A3
Montrose Ave
Falconwood DA16 ... 145 C2
Hendon HA8 ... 27 B2
Kensal Rise NW6 ... 91 A5
Sidcup DA15 ... 168 A4
Twickenham TW2 ... 151 D4
Montrose Cl
Ashford TW15 ... 171 A5
Falconwood DA16 ... 145 D2
Woodford IG8 ... 37 A6
Montrose Cres
Finchley N12 ... 30 A4
1 Wembley HA0 ... 66 A2
Montrose Ct
2 Catford SE6 ... 164 D2
Hendon NW9 ... 27 A1
Knightsbridge
SW7 ... 114 B4 246 D1
Temple Fortune
NW11 ... 47 B5
Montrose Gdns
Mitcham CR4 ... 180 D1
Sutton SM1 ... 217 D6
Montrose Ho
Belgravia SW1 ... 248 B1
Millwall E14 ... 119 C3
Twickenham TW2 ... 151 D4
Montrose Pl
SW1 ... 115 A4 248 B1
Montrose Rd
East Bedfont
TW14 ... 149 B5
Harrow HA3 ... 24 D1
Montrose Villas 5
W6 ... 112 A1
Montrose Way
SE23 ... 162 D3
Montserrat Ave IG8 ... 36 B3
Montserrat Cl SE19 .. 183 B5
Montserrat Rd
SW15 ... 135 A1
Montway Hts SW19 .. 179 D3
Monument Gdns
SE13 ... 164 A6
Monument Sta
EC3 ... 117 B6 252 D6
Monument St
EC3 ... 117 B6 252 D6

Monument The*
EC3 ... 252 D6
Monument Way N17 .. 51 D6
Monza Bldg The E1 .. 118 C6
Monza St E1 ... 118 C6
Moodkee St SE16 ... 118 C3
Moody Rd SE15 ... 139 D4
Moody St E1 ... 96 D4
Moon Ct SE12 ... 143 A1
Moon Ho HA1 ... 42 D5
Moon La EN5 ... 1 B2
Moon St N1 ... 94 D6 234 C6
Moorcroft Ct 4 N3 ... 29 B1
Moorcroft HA8 ... 26 D2
Moorcroft Gdns
BR1 ... 210 A4
Moorcroft La UB8 ... 82 C2
Moorcroft Rd SW16 .. 160 A1
Moorcroft Sch UB8 .. 82 B1
Moorcroft Way HA5 ... 41 A4
Moordown SE18 ... 144 D4
Moore Cl
Mitcham CR4 ... 181 B1
Mortlake SW14 ... 133 A2
Wallington SM6 ... 220 A1
Moore Cres RM9 ... 102 B6
Moore Ct N1 ... 234 C5
Moorefield Rd N17 ... 33 D1
Moore Ho
16 Bethnal Green
E2 ... 96 C4
5 Greenwich SE10 .. 120 D1
Hornsey N8 ... 50 A5
7 Shadwell E1 ... 118 C6
Wandsworth SW17 ... 158 B1
1 West Norwood
SE27 ... 183 A6
Mooreland Rd BR1 ... 187 A2
Moore Park Ct SW6 . 265 D4
Moore Park Rd
SW6 ... 135 D5 265 C3
Moore Rd SE19 ... 183 A4
Moore St
SW3 ... 114 D2 257 C4
Moore Wlk E7 ... 77 A4
Moorey Cl 2 E15 ... 98 D6
Moorfield Ave W5 ... 87 D3
Moorfield Rd
Chessington KT9 ... 214 A3
Enfield EN3 ... 6 C4
Moorfields Ct 6
SW16 ... 181 C6
Moorfields
EC2 ... 95 B2 242 C3
Moorfields Eye Hospl
EC1 ... 95 B4 235 C1
Moorfields Highwalk
EC2 ... 242 C3
Moorgate EC2 . 95 B2 242 C3
Moorgate Pl EC2 ... 242 C2
Moorgate Sta
EC2 ... 95 B2 242 C3
Moorgreen Ho EC1 .. 234 C2
Moorhead Way SE3 .. 143 B2
Moorhouse 17 NW9 ... 27 D2
Moorhouse Rd
Harrow HA3 ... 43 D6
Notting Hill W2 ... 91 C1
Moorings Ho 3
TW8 ... 131 C5
Moorings The 5 E16 .. 99 C2
Moor La
Broadgate
EC2 ... 95 B2 242 C3
Chessington KT9 ... 214 A3
Moorland Cl TW4 ... 151 C4
Moorland Ct N21 ... 16 B5
Moorland Rd SW9 ... 138 D1
Moorlands Ave NW7 .. 28 B4
Moorlands
Chislehurst BR7 ... 188 D3
Northolt UB5 ... 85 A6
17 Wallington SM6 ... 219 B2
Moor Lane Jun Sch
KT9 ... 214 B3
Moormead Dr KT19 .. 215 C3
Moor Mead Rd
TW1 ... 153 A5
Moor Park Gdns
KT2 ... 177 C3
Moor Park Ho N21 ... 16 D4
Moor Pl EC2 ... 242 C3
Moorside Ct W13 ... 109 C5
Moorside Rd BR1 ... 186 D6
Moor St W1 ... 239 D1
Moortown Rd WD19 ... 22 C6
Moot Ct NW9 ... 44 C4
Morant Ho SW9 ... 138 B3
Morant Pl N22 ... 32 B2
Morant St E14 ... 119 C6
Mora Prim Sch NW2 .. 68 C4
Mora Rd NW2 ... 68 C4
Mora St EC1 ... 95 A4 235 B1
Morat St
SW9 ... 138 B4 270 D2
Moravian Cl SW3 ... 266 D5

Moravian Pl
SW10 ... 136 B6 266 D5
Moravian St 10 E2 ... 96 C4
Moray Ave UB3 ... 105 D5
Moray Cl HA8 ... 10 D2
Moray Ho
11 Kingston u T
KT6 ... 198 A4
9 Mile End E1 ... 97 A3
Moray Mews N4, N7 ... 72 B6
Moray Rd N4, N7 ... 72 B6
Mordaunt Gdns RM9 .. 81 A1
Mordaunt Ho
4 Becontree
NW10 ... 89 B6
34 Clapham SW8 ... 137 D3
Mordaunt Rd NW10 ... 89 B6
Mordaunt St SW9 ... 138 B2
MORDEN ... 201 D3
Morden Court Par
SM4 ... 201 D5
Morden Ct SM4 ... 201 D5
Morden Gdns
Greenford UB6 ... 64 D3
Mitcham CR4 ... 202 B5
Morden Hall SW19 ... 201 D6
Morden Hall Rd
SM4 ... 202 A5
Morden Hill SE13 ... 142 A3
Morden Ho
Morden SM4 ... 201 C5
19 Tulse Hill SW2 ... 160 C5
Morden La SE13 ... 142 A4
Morden Lo BR2 ... 186 B1
Morden Mount Prim
Sch SE13 ... 141 D3
MORDEN PARK ... 201 A3
Morden Park Sch
Sports Ctr SM4 ... 201 B4
Morden Prim Sch
SM4 ... 201 C4
Morden Rd
Dagenham RM6 ... 59 A2
Kidbrooke SE3 ... 143 A3
Merton SW19 ... 179 D1
Mitcham CR4, SM4 ... 202 B5
Morden Road Mews
SE3 ... 143 A3
Morden Road Sta
SW19 ... 179 D1
Morden South Sta
SM4 ... 201 C4
Morden Sta SW19 .. 201 D6
Morden St SE13 ... 141 D4
Morden Way SM3 ... 201 C2
Morden Wharf Rd
SE10 ... 120 C3
Mordern Ho NW1 ... 237 B5
Mordon Rd IG3 ... 57 D2
Mordred Rd SE6 ... 164 C2
Morecambe Cl 3 E1 .. 96 D2
Morecambe Gdns
HA7 ... 25 D6
Morecambe St
SE17 ... 117 A1 262 B2
Morecambe Terr
N18 ... 33 B6
More Cl
Canning Town E16 ... 98 D1
West Kensington
W14 ... 113 A2 254 A3
Morecoombe Cl
KT2 ... 176 D3
Morecroft TW2 ... 152 A2
Moredown Ho 3 E8 .. 74 A3
Moree Way N18 ... 34 A6
More House Sch
SW1 ... 114 D3 257 D5
Moreland Ct 3 NW2 .. 69 C5
Moreland Prim Sch
EC1 ... 94 D4 234 D1
Moreland St
EC1 ... 94 D4 234 D2
Moreland Way E4 ... 20 A1
Morella Rd SW11,
SW12 ... 158 D4
Morell Ho 5 SW9 ... 138 B3
Morello Ave UB8 ... 82 D2
Morello Ct HA9 ... 66 B5
Moremead Rd SE6 ... 185 C6
Morena St SE6 ... 163 D4
Moresby Ave KT5 ... 198 D2
Moresby Rd E5 ... 52 B1
Moresby Wlk 6
SW8 ... 137 B3
More's Gdn SW3 ... 266 D5
Moreton Ave TW7 ... 130 C4
Moreton Cl
Mill Hill NW7 ... 28 C4
Tottenham N15 ... 51 B3
Upper Clapton E5 ... 52 C1
Moreton Ho
Bermondsey SE16 ... 118 B3
Upper Tooting SW17 .. 180 B6

Moreton Pl
SW1........115 C1 259 B2
Moreton Rd
Croydon CR2........221 B3
North Cheam KT4....216 B6
Tottenham N15.......51 B3
Moreton St
SW1........115 D1 259 C2
Moreton Terr Mews N
SW1.............259 B2
Moreton Terr Mews S
SW1.............259 B2
Moreton Terr
SW1........115 C1 259 B2
Moreton Twr 3
W3...............110 D5
Morford Cl HA4.......40 B2
Morford Way HA4.....40 B2
Morgan Ave E17......54 B5
Morgan Cl RM10......81 C1
Morgan Ct
Ashford TW15......170 D5
5 Battersea SW11...136 B3
Carshalton SM5.....218 D4
Morgan Ho
Nine Elms SW8.....269 B2
Pimlico SW1.......259 B3
Morgan Rd
Islington N7.........72 C3
Notting Hill W10......91 B2
Plaistow BR1.......187 A3
Morgan's La UB3.....83 B2
Morgan St
Canning Town E16.....98 D2
Globe Town E3........96 D4
Morgan's Wlk SW11. 267 A3
Morgan Terr RM6.....58 C4
Moriah Jewish Day Sch
The HA5............41 A1
Moriatry Cl N7.......72 A4
Morie St SW18.......157 D6
Morieux Rd E10.......53 B1
Moring Rd SW17.....181 A6
Morkyns Wlk SE21...161 C1
Morland Ave CR0....205 C1
Morland Cl
Golders Green
NW11.............47 D1
Hampton TW12.......173 B5
Mitcham CR4.......202 C6
Morland Ct W12.....112 B4
Morland Est E8.......74 A1
Morland Gdns
Southall UB1.......107 D5
Stonebridge NW10....67 B1
Morland Ho
Kilburn NW6.........91 C6
Notting Hill W11......91 A1
Somers Town NW1..232 B3
Westminster SW1..260 A4
Morland Mews N1....72 C1
Morland Rd
Croydon CR0.......205 D2
Dagenham RM10......81 C1
Harrow HA3.........44 A5
Ilford IG1..........78 D6
Penge SE20........184 D4
Sutton SM1........218 A3
Walthamstow E17.....52 D4
Morley Ave
Chingford E4.........36 B3
Edmonton N18.......34 A6
Tottenham N22.......32 D1
Morley Cl BR6.......226 D6
Morley Coll
SE1........116 C3 261 B6
Morley Cres HA8......11 A2
Morley Cres E HA7....43 D6
Morley Cres HA4......62 C6
Morley Cres W HA7...43 C6
Morley Ct
Bromley BR3........186 B2
Chingford Hatch E4....35 B5
Lewisham SE13.....142 A1
Shortlands BR2.....208 D5
Morley Hill EN2........5 B5
Morley Ho
Stoke Newington
N16..............74 A6
Streatham SW2.....160 A4
W1...............238 D2
Morley Rd
Barking IG11........101 B6
Cheam SM3.........201 B1
Chislehurst BR7.....189 A2
Dagenham RM6........59 A4
Lewisham SE13.....142 A1
Leytonstone E10......54 A1
Newham E15.........98 D5
Twickenham TW1.....153 D5
Morley St
SE1........116 C4 251 B1
Morna Rd SE5.......139 A3
Morning La E9........74 C2
Morningside Prim Sch
E9..................74 C2
Morningside Rd
KT4...............216 C6
Mornington Ave
Bromley BR1.......209 D6
Ilford IG1..........56 C2
Mornington Avenue
Mans W14........254 C3
Mornington Ave
W14.........113 B2 254 C3
Mornington Cl IG8....37 A6
Mornington Cres
NW1.........93 C5 232 A4
Mornington Crescent
Sta NW1....93 C5 232 A4
Mornington Cres
TW5..............128 B4
Mornington Ct NW1. 232 A4
Mornington Gr E3....97 C4
Mornington Lo EN1...17 C6
Mornington Mews 2
SE5..............139 A4
Mornington Pl
4 New Cross
SE8.............141 B5
Regent's Pk NW1...232 A4
Mornington Rd
Ashford TW15......171 A5
Chingford E4.........20 B4
Greenford UB6.......85 D3
Leytonstone E11......54 D1
New Cross SE14,
SE8.............141 B5
Woodford IG8........36 D6
Mornington St
NW1.........93 B5 231 D4
Mornington Terr
NW1.........93 B5 231 D4
Mornington Wlk
TW10.............175 C6
Morocco St
SE1.........117 C4 253 A1
Morpeth Gr E9.......96 D6
Morpeth Rd E9.......96 D6
Morpeth Sec Sch E2..96 C4
Morpeth St E2........96 D4
Morpeth Terr
SW1........115 C2 259 A4
Morpeth Wlk N17.....34 B3
Morrab Gdns IG3.....79 D5
Morrel Cl EN5.........2 A2
Morrel Ct 11 E2.......96 A5
Morris Ave E12.......78 B3
Morris Blitz Ct 2
N16...............73 D4
Morris Cl
Croydon CR0.......207 A4
Orpington BR6......227 C5
Morris Ct
Chingford E4.........19 D1
Croydon CR0.......220 D4
3 Herne Hill SE5....139 B1
Morris Gdns SW18...157 C4
Morris Ho
17 Bethnal Green
E2................96 C4
Lisson Gr NW8.....237 A5
1 Stockwell SW4....138 A1
10 Tufnell Pk N19.....71 C4
Morrish Rd SW2.....160 A4
Morrison Ave
Chingford E4.........35 C4
Tottenham N17.......51 C6
Morrison Bldgs 5
E1.................96 A1
Morrison Ct
7 Barnet EN5.........1 A1
Finchley N12.........30 C3
Morrison Ho SW2....160 C3
Morrison Rd
Barking IG11.......103 A5
24 Brixton SW9......138 C3
Hayes UB4...........84 B4
Morrison St SW11...137 A2
Morrison Yd N17.....33 D1
Morris Pl N4.........72 C6
Morris Rd
Bow Comm E14.......97 D2
Dagenham RM8.......81 B6
Isleworth TW7......130 D2
Leyton E15..........76 C4
Morriss Ho
9 Bermondsey
SE16..............118 B4
5 Upper Clapton E5...74 B6
Morris St E1.........96 B1
Morris Stephany Ho 4
SE27..............182 D6
Morriston Cl WD19....22 C5
Morritt Ho 2 HA0....65 D3
Morse Cl E13.........99 A4
Morshead Mans W9...91 C4
Morshead Rd W9.....91 C4
Morson Rd EN3.......19 A5
Morston Gdns SE9...188 B6
Mortain Ho 9 SE16..118 B2
Morten Cl SW4......159 D5
Morteyne Rd N17.....33 B2
Mortgramit Sq
SE18..............122 C3
Mortham St E15......98 C6
Mortimer Cl
1 Child's Hill NW2....69 B5
Streatham SW16....159 D2
Mortimer Cres
Paddington NW6......91 D6
Worcester Pk KT4....215 B5
Mortimer Ct
St John's Wood
NW8..............229 B3
4 Whetstone N20.....14 A2
Mortimer Dr EN1.....17 C6
Mortimer Est NW6....91 D6
Mortimer Ho
6 Shepherd's Bush
W11..............112 D5
West Kensington
W14..............254 B3
Mortimer Lo 11
SW19..............157 A3
Mortimer Market
WC1...............239 B5
Mortimer Pl NW6.....91 D6
Mortimer Rd
De Beauvoir Town
N1..................73 C1
Ealing W13...........87 C1
Kensal Green NW10...90 C4
Mitcham CR4.......180 D2
Newham E6.........100 B4
Mortimer Sq W11....112 D6
Mortimer St
W1..........93 C2 239 B3
Mortimer Terr NW5...71 B4
MORTLAKE..........133 A2
Mortlake Cl CR0.....220 A5
Mortlake Dr CR4.....180 C2
Mortlake High St
SW14..............133 B2
Mortlake Ho 7 W4..111 A2
Mortlake Rd
Ilford IG1...........79 B4
Newham E16.........99 B1
Richmond SW14,
TW9..............132 C4
Mortlake Sta SW14. 133 A2
Mortlake Terr TW9...132 C5
Mortlock Cl SE15....140 B4
Mortlock Ct E12.....77 D4
Morton Cl
Hillingdon UB8.......82 B3
Stepney E1..........96 C1
Wallington SM6......220 B1
Morton Cres N14.....31 D6
Morton Ct UB5........64 A3
Morton Gdns SM6....219 C3
Morton Ho
Kennington SE17....138 D6
West Norwood SE27..183 B5
Morton Mews SW5..255 C3
Morton Pl SE1......261 A5
Morton Rd
Islington N1.........73 A1
Morden SM4........202 B4
Stratford E15........76 D1
Morton Way N14......31 D6
Morvale Cl DA17....125 B2
Morval Rd SW2......160 C6
Morven Rd SW17....158 D1
Morville Ho SW18....158 B5
Morville St E3........97 C5
Morwell St WC1.....239 D3
Moscow Pl W2.....245 C6
Moscow Rd
W2..........113 D6 245 C6
Mosedale NW1.....231 D1
Moseley Row SE10...120 D2
Moselle Ave N22......32 C1
Moselle Cl N8........50 B6
Moselle Ct N9........18 C1
Moselle Ho 2 N17....33 D3
Moselle Pl N17.......33 D3
Moselle Sch (main site)
N17................33 C1
Moselle Sch (Upper)
N17................51 A6
Moselle St N17.......33 D3
Mosque Tower 20 E1..96 A2
Mossborough Cl N12..29 D4
Mossbourne Com Acad
E8..................74 A3
Mossbury Rd SW11..136 C2
Moss Cl Pinner HA5....23 A1
Spitalfields E1........96 A2
Mossdown Cl DA17..125 C2
Mossford Ct IG6......56 D6
Mossford Gn IG6.....57 A6
Mossford St E3.......97 B3
Moss Gdns
Feltham TW13......150 A2
South Croydon CR2..222 D1
Moss Hall Cres N12...30 A4
Moss Hall Ct N12.....29 D4
Moss Hall Gr N12.....29 D4
Moss Hall Inf Sch
N12................29 D4
Moss Hall Jun Sch
N3.................29 D4
Mossington Gdns
SE16..............118 C2
Moss La HA5.........23 A1
Mosslea Rd
Bromley Comm
BR2.............209 D4
Orpington BR6......227 A5
Penge SE20........184 C4
Mossop St
SW3........114 C2 257 B4
Moss Rd RM10........81 C1
Mossville Gdns SM4..201 B5
Mosswell Ho 4 N10...31 A3
Moston Cl UB3.......105 D1
Mostyn Ave HA9......66 B3
Mostyn Gdns NW10...90 D5
Mostyn Gr E3.........97 C5
Mostyn Lo N5........73 A4
Mostyn Rd
Brixton SW9.......138 C4
Bushey WD23.........8 A6
Grahame Pk HA8......27 C3
Merton SW19.......179 B1
Mosul Way BR2......210 A3
Motcomb St
SW1........115 A3 258 A6
Moth Cl SM6........220 A1
Mothers Sq The 13
E5.................74 B4
Motley Ave EC2.....243 A6
Motley St SW8......137 C3
MOTSPUR PARK.....200 A3
Motspur Park Sta
KT3...............200 B4
Motspur Pk KT3.....200 A3
MOTTINGHAM.......165 D2
Mottingham Ct SE9..166 B3
Mottingham Gdns
SE9...............165 D3
Mottingham La SE9..165 C3
Mottingham Prim Sch
SE9...............166 B1
Mottingham Rd
Chislehurst SE9......166 B1
Ponders End N9......18 D4
Mottingham Sta
SE9...............166 B3
Mottisfont Rd SE2...124 B2
Moules Ct SE5.......139 A5
Moulins Rd E9........74 C1
Moulsford Ho
5 Lower Holloway
N7................72 A3
32 Paddington W2.....91 C2
Moulton Ave TW3,
TW5..............129 B3
Moundfield Rd N16...52 A3
Mound The SE9......166 C1
Mounsey Ho 13 W10..91 A4
Mountacre Cl SE26...183 D6
Mount Adon Pk SE21,
SE22..............162 A4
Mountague Pl 2
E14...............120 A6
Mountain Ho SE11...260 C2
Mountaire Ct NW9...45 B4
Mount Angelus Rd
SW15..............155 D4
Mount Ararat Rd
TW10..............154 A6
Mount Arlington 3
BR2...............186 C1
Mount Ash Rd SE26..162 B1
Mount Ave
Chingford E4........19 D1
Ealing W5...........87 D2
Southall UB1........85 C1
Mountbatten Cl
Plumstead Comm
SE18............145 C6
6 West Norwood
SE19............183 C5
Mountbatten Ct 8
IG9................21 D2
Mountbatten Gdns
BR3...............207 A5
Mountbatten Ho N6...49 A2
Mountbatten Mews
SW18..............158 A3
Mountbel Rd HA7.....25 A1
Mount Carmel 3 N7..72 B3
Mount Carmel RC Tech
Coll for Girls N19...49 D1
Mount Cl
Bromley BR1.......188 A2
Cockfosters EN4.......3 A1
Ealing W5...........87 C2
Mountcombe Cl
KT6...............198 A2
Mountcombe Ho
SW17..............180 B5
Mount Ct
6 Kingston u T
KT2.............176 D3
West Wickham BR4..224 C6
Mount Culver Ave
DA14..............190 D4
Mount Dr
Bexley DA6........169 A6
Harrow HA2, HA5.....41 B4
Welsh Harp HA9......67 A6
Mountearl Gdns SW16,
SW2...............160 B1
Mount Eaton Ct W5...87 C2
Mount Echo Ave E4...19 D3
Mount Echo Dr E4....19 D3
Mount Ephraim La
SW16..............159 D1
Mount Ephraim Rd
SW16..............159 D1
Mount Felix KT12....193 D1
Mountfield Cl SE6...164 B4
Mountfield Ct SE13..164 B5
Mountfield NW2......69 B6
Mountfield Rd
Ealing W5...........88 A1
East Finchley N3......47 C6
Wallend E6.........100 C4
Mountford Ho EN2......4 D1
Mount Ford St E1.....96 A1
Mountfort Cres N1....72 C1
Mountfort Terr 1
N1.................72 C1
Mount Gdns SE26....162 B1
Mount Gr HA8........27 B6
Mountgrove Rd N5....73 A5
Mounthurst Rd BR2..208 D2
Mountier Ct 12 E11...55 A4
Mountington Park Cl
HA3................43 D3
Mountjoy Cl SE2.....124 B4
Mountjoy Ho EC2....242 A3
Mount Lodge SW4...137 D1
Mount Lo N6.........49 C3
Mount Mews TW12...173 D2
Mount Mills EC1....234 D1
Mount Nod Rd SW16,
SW2...............160 B1
Mount Olive Ct W7...108 C4
Mount Par EN4.........2 C1
Mount Park Ave HA1..64 C6
Mount Park Cres W5..87 D1
Mount Park Rd
Ealing W5...........87 D1
Harrow HA1.........64 B5
Pinner HA5..........40 A4
Mount Pk SM5.......219 A1
Mount Pl 7 W3......110 D5
Mount Pleasant EN4...2 D1
Mount Pleasant Cotts
Osidge N14..........15 D4
Southall UB1.........85 C1
Mount Pleasant Cres
N4.................50 B2
Mount Pleasant
WC1..........94 C3 241 A5
Mount Pleasant Hill
E5.................74 C6
Mount Pleasant IG1..79 A3
Mount Pleasant La
E5.................52 B1
Mount Pleasant Pl
SE18..............123 B2
Mount Pleasant Rd
Ealing W5...........87 C3
Higham Hill E17......35 A1
Kingston u T KT3....199 A6
Lewisham SE13......164 A5
Tottenham N17.......33 C1
Willesden NW10......90 C6
Mount Pleasant HA4..62 D6
Mount Pleasant Villas
N4.................50 B2
Mount Pleasant
Wembley HA0........88 B6
West Norwood SE27..183 A6
Mount Prim Sch The
KT3...............199 A6
Mount Rd
Bexley DA6.........169 A6
Chessington KT9.....214 B3
Dagenham RM8.......59 B1
Dollis Hill NW2.......68 C5
East Barnet EN4......14 C6
Feltham TW13......151 A1
Hayes UB3..........106 A4
Hendon NW4..........46 A3
Kingston u T KT3....199 B6
Mitcham CR4.......180 C1
South Norwood
SE19..............183 B4
Wimbledon SW18,
SW19.............157 D2
Mount Row
W1..........115 B6 248 C5
Mount Sch NW7......28 C5
Mountside HA7.......25
Mounts Pond Rd SE3,
SE13...............142
Mount Sq The 3
NW3................70
Mount Stewart Ave
HA3.................43
Mount Stewart Jun &
Inf Schs HA3........43
Mount St
W1..........115 A6 248
Mount Terr E1........96
Mount The
Bexley DA6........169
Cheam SM1........217
Chislehurst BR7.....188
Finchley N2..........30
Hampstead NW3......70
Harrow HA1..........64
Kensington W8......245
Kingston u T KT3....199
North Cheam KT4....216
Northolt UB5.........63
6 South Croydon
CR2...............221
Upper Clapton E5.....74
Welsh Harp HA9......67
Whetstone N20.......14
Mount Tyndal NW3....48
Mount Vernon NW3...70
Mountview Cl NW11..48
Mountview Cotts
EN5.................11
Mountview Ct
Harringay N8.........50
3 Whetstone N20.....14
Mount View W5.......87
Mountview NW7......11
Mount View EN2.......4
Mountview HA6.......22
Mount View Rd
Chingford E4........20
Claygate KT10.......213
Hornsey Vale N4......50
Kingsbury NW9.......45
Mount View UB2.....106
Mountview 5
SW16..............160
Mount Villas SE27....160
Mountwood KT8......195
Mountwood Ho W5....87
Mourne Ho NW3......70
Movers La IG11......101
Movers Lane (Flyover)
IG11...............101
Mowat Ct KT4.......215
Mowatt Cl N19........49
Mowbray Ct
South Norwood
SE19.............183
Wood Green N22......32
Mowbray Gdns UB5...85
Mowbray Ho 5 N2....30
Mowbray Rd
Brondesbury NW6.....69
Edgware HA8.........26
New Barnet EN5......14
Richmond TW10.....153
South Norwood
SE19.............183
Mowlem Prim Sch
E2..................96
Mowlem St E2........96
Mowlem Trad Est
N17.................34
Mowll St SW9.......138
Moxon Cl E13........98
Moxon St Barnet EN5....1
Marylebone
W1.........93 A2 238
Moye Cl 10 E2........96
Moyers Rd E10.......54
Moylan Rd
W6..........135 A6 264
Moyle Ho SW1.......269
Moyne Ho 16 SW9....138
Moyne Pl NW10......88
Moynihan Dr N21.....16
Moys Cl CR0........204
Moyser Rd SW16.....181
Mozart St W10.......91
Mt Carmel RC Prim Sch
W5.................109 C3
Muchelney Rd SM4..202 A3
Mudchute Sta E14...119 D2
Mudie Ho 8 SW2....160 A4
Mudlarks Blvd 3
SE10...............120
Muggeridge Cl CR2..221
Muggeridge Rd
RM10................81 D4
Muirdown Ave
SW14...............133 B1
Muir Dr SW18.......158 C5
Muirfield Cl
23 Bermondsey
SE16...............118 B1

field Cl *continued*
th Oxhey WD19 22 C6
field Cres E14 119 D3
field Gn WD19 22 C6
field W3 89 C1
field Rd WD19 22 C6
head Quay
101 A5
kirk Rd SE6 164 A3
Rd E5 74 A5
St E16 122 A5
arton Ct BR7 189 B4
erry Ave TW19 148 A3
erry Bsns Ctr
6 118 D4
erry Cl Barnet EN4 2 B1
rlton SE7 143 D6
lsea SW3 266 D5
ngford E4 19 C2
t Dulwich SE22 162 A5
npstead NW3 70 B4
ndon NW4 46 C6
nsey N8 50 A4
tholt UB5 85 A5
eatham SW16 181 C6
erry Cres
ntford TW8 131 C5
st Drayton UB7 104 C4
erry Ct
king IG11 79 D1
xley DA16 145 D3
chley N2 48 C6
sbury EC1 234 D1
ngton N5 72 D3
Leyton E11 76 B4
Paddington W9 91 B4
Surbiton KT6 197 D2
ckenham TW1 152 D1
lesden NW10 67 B2
erry Ho
Bethnal Green
2 96 C4
Deptford SE8 141 B6
erry House Sch
e NW2 69 A3
berry La CR0 205 D1
berry Mews
w Cross SE14 141 B4
Wallington SM6 219 C2
berry Par UB7 104 C4
berry Pl
swick W6 112 A1
eenwich SE9 143 D1
berry Prim Sch
7 34 A1
berry Rd E8 73 D1
berry Sch for
rls
epney E1 96 B1
George in t East
E1 118 B6
berry St 7 E1 96 A1
berry Trees
V17 193 B2
berry Way
ord IG6 57 A5
oodford E18 37 B1
berry Wlk
V3 136 B6 266 D6
lgrave Chambers
12 217 D2
grave Hall SM2 217 D2
grave Ho 19
18 122 B2
grave Manor
12 217 D2
lgrave Prim Sch
18 122 C2
grave Rd
elmont SM2 217 C2
aling W5 87 D3
arrow HA1 65 A6
uth Croydon CR0 221 B5
est Kensington
W14 264 C6
illesden NW10 67 D4
oolwich SE18 122 C2
holland Cl CR4 181 B1
kern Rd N19 49 D1
llard Ho WC1 239 C4
llards Cl CR4 202 D1
llens Ho 7
W15 156 C6
llen Twr EC1 241 A5
ller Ho SE18 122 C1
ller Rd SW4 159 D5
llet Gdns 7 E2 96 A4
lletsfield WC1 233 B1
ll Ho 17 E3 97 B5
llins Path SW14 133 B2
llion Cl HA3 23 D2
llion Wlk WD19 22 D6
lready St NW8 237 A5
lti Way W3 111 C4
lton Ho E9 74 C1
lton Rd SW18 158 B4
lvaney Way SE1 252 D1

Mumford Rd SE24 160 D6
Muncaster Cl TW15 170 C6
Muncaster Rd
Ashford TW15 170 D5
Balham SW11 159 A6
Muncies Mews SE6 164 A2
Mundania Ct SE22 162 B5
Mundania Rd SE22 162 C5
Munday Ho SE1 262 C5
Munday Rd E16 121 A6
Munden Ho 5 E3 97 D4
Munden St
W14 113 A2 254 A4
Mundesley Cl WD19 22 C6
Mundford Rd E5 74 C6
Mundon Gdns IG1 57 B1
Mund St
W14 113 B1 254 D1
Mundy Ho 6 W10 91 A4
Mundy St N1 95 C4
Mungo-Park Cl WD23 8 A2
Munnery Way BR6 226 D6
Munning Ho 12 E16 121 B5
Munnings Gdns
TW7 152 B6
Munro Ho
Bermondsey SE1 252 D1
Lambeth SE1 251 A1
Munro Mews W10 91 A2
Munro Rd WD23 8 A6
Munslow Gdns SM1 218 B4
Munstead Ct 12
SM2 218 A1
Munster Ave TW4 151 A6
Munster Ct
Fulham SW6 135 B3
Teddington TW11 175 C4
Munster Gdns N13 33 A6
Munster Ho N17 33 D2
Munster Rd
Fulham
SW6 135 A5 264 B4
Teddington TW11 175 C4
Munster Residences
SW6 264 B2
Munster Sq
NW1 93 B3 238 D6
Munton Rd SE1,
SE17 117 A2 262 B4
Murchison Ave DA5 169 A3
Murchison Ho 1
W10 91 A2
Murchison Rd E10 76 A6
Murdoch Ho 4
SE16 118 C3
Murdock Cl E16 98 D1
Murdock St SE15 140 B6
Murfett Cl SW19 157 A2
Muriel Ct 18 E10 53 D2
Muriel St N1 94 B6 233 D6
Murillo Rd SE13 142 C1
Murley Ct N21 17 A4
Murphy Ho SE1 261 D6
Murphy St
SE1 116 C4 251 A1
Murray Ave
Bromley BR1 187 B1
Hounslow TW3 151 D6
Murray Cl SE28 123 C5
Murray Cres HA5 22 D2
Murray Ct
5 Harrow HA1 42 D3
Southall TW7 108 C3
Twickenham TW2 152 A2
Murray Grey Ho UB4 83 B2
Murray Gr N1 95 B5 235 C3
Murray Ho
1 North Finchley
N12 30 B5
20 Woolwich SE18 122 B2
Murray Mews NW1 71 D1
Murray Rd
Brentford W5 109 C2
Richmond TW10 153 C2
Wimbledon SW19 178 D4
Murray Sq E16 121 B6
Murray St NW1 71 D1
Murray Terr NW3 70 B4
Musard Rd
W6 135 A6 264 B6
Musbury St E1 96 C1
Muscal W6 264 A6
Muscatel Pl SE5 139 C4
Muschamp Prim Sch
SM5 218 C6
Muschamp Rd
Camberwell SE15 139 D2
Carshalton SM5 218 C6
Muscott Ho 15 E2 96 A6
Muscovy Ho DA18 125 A4
Muscovy St EC3 253 B6
Museum Ho 7 E2 96 C4
Museum in Docklands*
E14 119 C6
Museum Mans WC1 240 A3
Museum of Brands*
W11 91 B1

Museum of Domestic
Design &
Architecture*
EN4 15 A6
Museum St
WC1 94 A1 240 A2
Musgrave Cl EN4 2 A4
Musgrave Cres
SW6 135 C4 265 B2
Musgrave Ct SW11 267 A2
Musgrave Rd TW7 130 D4
Musgrove Ho 1 E9 74 D2
Musgrove Rd SE14 141 A4
Musical Mus The*
TW8 132 A6
Musjid Rd 7 SW11 136 B3
Muslim Coll The
W5 110 C6
Mus of Childhood
(V&A)* E2 96 C4
Mus of Culinary History
& Alimentation*
NW1 232 B4
Mus of Garden History*
SE1 260 C5
Mus of London*
EC2 95 A2 242 A3
Mus of Richmond*
TW10 153 D6
Mus of the Great
Eastern Rly* E16 122 C4
Mus of the Order of St
John* EC1 94 D3 241 C5
Musquash Way
TW4 128 C3
Muston Rd E5 74 B6
Mustow Pl 2 SW6 135 B3
Muswell Ave N10 31 B1
MUSWELL HILL 49 A6
Muswell Hill Broadway
N10 49 B6
Muswell Hill N10 49 C6
Muswell Hill Pl N10 49 B5
Muswell Hill Prim Sch
N10 49 B6
Muswell Hill Rd N10 49 A4
Muswell Mews N10 49 B6
Muswell Rd N10 31 B1
Mutrix Rd NW6 91 C6
Mutton Pl NW1 71 A2
Muybridge Rd KT3 177 A1
Myatt Garden Prim Sch
SE4 141 B3
Myatt Ho SE5 138 D3
Myatt Rd SW9 138 D4
Myatts Field Ct SE5 139 A4
Mycenae Rd SE3 143 A6
Mychell Ho 8
SW19 180 A3
Myddelton Ave EN1 5 C5
Myddelton Cl EN1 5 D4
Myddelton Gdns N21 17 A4
Myddelton Ho N8 50 A6
Myddelton Pas
EC1 94 C4 234 B2
Myddelton Pk N20 14 B2
Myddelton Rd N8 50 A5
Myddelton Sq
EC1 94 C4 234 B2
Myddelton St
EC1 94 C4 234 B1
Myddleton Ave N4 73 A6
Myddleton Ho 14 N2 30 B1
Myddleton Mews
N22 32 A3
Myddleton Rd N22 32 B3
Myers Ho 5 SE5 139 A5
Myers La SE14 140 D6
Myherin Ct SE23 163 B2
Mylis Cl SE26 184 B6
Mylius Cl SE14 140 C4
Mylne Cl W6 112 A1
Mylne Ho N21 17 B5
Mylne St EC1 234 A3
Mynterne Ct 16
SW19 156 D3
Myra St SE2 124 A2
Myrdle Ct 14 E1 96 A1
Myrdle St E1 96 A1
Myrna Cl SW19 180 C3
Myron Pl SE13 142 A2
Myrtle Alley SE18 122 C3
Myrtle Ave
Hatton TW14 149 C6
Ruislip HA4 40 B2
Myrtle Cl Barnet EN4 14 D3
Hillingdon UB8 82 B2
West Drayton UB7 104 B3
Myrtledene Rd SE2 124 A1
Myrtle Gdns W7 108 C5
Myrtle Gr Enfield EN2 5 B5
Kingston u T KT3 177 A1
Myrtle Ho SE14 140 D4
Myrtle Rd Acton W3 111 A5
Croydon CR0 223 C5
Edmonton N13 17 B1
Hampton TW12 174 A4

Myrtle Rd *continued*
Hounslow TW3 130 A3
Ilford IG1 78 D6
Newham E6 100 A6
Sutton SM1 218 A3
Walthamstow E17 53 A3
Myrtle Wlk 20 N1 95 C5
Mysore Rd SW11 136 D1
Myton Rd SE21 161 B1
Mytton Ho SW8 270 C3

N

N1 Shopping Ctr
N1 94 C5 234 B4
Nacton Ct 2 RM6 58 C4
Nadine St SE7 121 C1
Nadir Ct E11 55 A2
Naffenton Rise IG10 21 D6
Nagle Cl E17 36 B1
Nags Head Ct EC1 242 B5
Nag's Head La DA16 146 B2
Nags Head N7 72 B4
Nags Head Rd EN3 6 D1
Nags Head Sh Ctr The
N7 72 B4
Naima Jewish Prep Sch
NW6 91 D5
Nainby Ho SE11 261 A3
Nairn Ct
3 Wallington
SM6 219 C2
Wimbledon SW19 179 D4
Nairne Gr SE5, SE24 139 B1
Nairn Rd HA4 62 C2
Nairn St E14 98 A2
Naish Ct N1 233 B6
Naish Ho SW19 201 D6
Naldera Gdns SE3 143 A6
Nallhead Rd TW13 172 C5
Nalton Ho 4 NW6 70 A1
Namba Roy Cl
SW16 182 B6
Namton Dr CR7,
SW16 204 B5
Nan Clark's La NW7 11 D2
Nankin St E14 97 C1
Nansen Ct 1 E11 76 C6
Nansen Ho 8 NW10 67 B1
Nansen Rd SW11 137 A2
Nansen Village 5
N12 29 D6
Nant Ct NW2 69 B6
Nantes Cl SW18 136 A1
Nant Rd NW2 69 B6
Nant St E2 96 B4
Naomi Watts Ho 11
SW19 179 A3
Naoroji St WC1 234 A1
Napier Ave
Deptford E14 119 C1
Fulham SW6 135 B2
Napier Cl
New Cross SE14,
SE8 141 B5
West Drayton UB7 104 B3
West Kensington
W14 254 C6
Napier Ct
13 Croydon CR0 221 D6
Fulham SW6 135 B2
Grove Pk SE12 165 B1
Hayes UB4 84 C3
Shoreditch N1 235 C4
1 Surbiton KT6 197 D2
12 Wallington SM6 219 B2
Wembley HA0 65 D2
Napier Gr N1 95 A5 235 B4
Napier Ho
Eltham SE12 165 B1
Kennington SE17 138 D6
Napier Lo TW15 171 B4
Napier 15 NW9 27 D2
Napier Pl
W14 113 B3 254 C5
Napier Rd
Ashford TW15 171 B3
Belvedere DA17 125 B2
Bromley BR2 209 B5
College Pk NW10 90 B4
Croydon SE25 206 B5
Enfield EN3 18 D6
Isleworth TW7 131 A1
Kensington
W14 113 B3 254 C5
Leyton E11 76 C5
Newham E15 98 C5
South Croydon CR2 221 B1
Tottenham N17 51 C6
Wallend E6 100 C5
Wembley HA0 65 D2
Napier Terr N1 72 D1
Napier Wlk TW15 171 B3
Napoleon Rd
Hackney E5 74 B5
Twickenham TW1 153 B4

Napton Cl UB4 85 A3
Narbonne Ave SW4 159 C6
Narborough Cl UB10 61 A6
Narborough St
SW6 135 D3
Narcissus Rd NW6 69 C3
Nardini 12 NW9 27 D2
Naresby Fold HA7 25 C4
Narford Rd E5 74 A6
Narrow Boat Cl
SE28 123 B4
Narrow St
6 Acton W3 110 D5
Limehouse E14 119 A6
Narrow Way BR2 210 A3
Nascot St W12 90 C1
Naseby Cl
Hounslow TW7 130 C4
South Hampstead
NW6 70 A1
Naseby Ct DA14 189 D6
Naseby Rd
Dagenham RM10 81 C5
South Norwood
SE19 183 B4
NASH 225 A2
Nash Cl SM1 218 B5
Nash Ct HA3 43 B3
Nashe Ho SE1 262 C5
Nash Gn BR1 187 A4
Nash Ho
5 Millwall E14 119 C3
Pimlico SW1 258 D1
1 Walthamstow E17 53 D5
Nash La BR2 225 A2
Nash Rd
Brockley SE4 163 A6
Dagenham RM6 58 D5
Lower Edmonton N9 18 C2
Nash St NW1 231 D2
Nash Way HA3 43 B3
Nasmyth St W6 112 B3
Nassau Path 6
SE28 124 C5
Nassau Rd SW13 133 D4
Nassau St W1 239 A3
Nassington Rd NW3 70 D4
Natalie Cl TW14 149 B4
Natalie Mews TW2 152 B1
Natal Rd
Bowes Pk N11 32 A4
Ilford IG1 78 D4
South Norwood CR7 205 B6
Streatham SW16 181 D4
Nathan Ct N9 18 C4
Nathan Ho SE11 261 B3
Nathaniel Cl E1 243 D3
Nathaniel Ct E17 53 A3
Nathans Rd HA0 65 C6
Nathan Way SE28,
SE18 123 D3
National Army Mus*
SW3 136 D6 267 D6
National Fan Mus*
SE10 142 A5
National Film Theatre*
SE1 250 D4
National Gallery*
W1 115 D6 249 D5
National Hospl The
WC1 94 A3 240 B5
National Maritime
Mus* SE10 142 B6
National Physical
Laboratory TW11 174 C4
National Portrait
Gallery (Annexe)*
SW1 115 D5 249 D4
National Portrait
Gallery*
W1 115 D6 249 D5
National Theatre*
SE1 116 B5 250 D4
National Wks TW4 129 B2
Nation Way E4 20 A3
Natural History Mus*
SW7 114 B3 256 C5
Nat West Twr* EC2 243 A2
Nautilus Bldg The
EC1 234 B2
Naval Row E14 120 A6
Navarino Gr E8 74 A2
Navarino Mans E8 74 A2
Navarino Rd E8 74 A2
Navarre Rd E6 100 A5
Navarre St E2 243 C6
Navenby Wlk 13 E3 97 C3
Navestock Cl E4 20 A1
Navestock Cres IG8 37 C3
Navestock Ho IG11 102 B5
Navigation Ct E16 123 A6
Navigator Dr UB2 108 A4
Navy St SW4 137 D2
Naxos Bldg 9 E14 119 C4
Nayland Ho SE6 186 A6
Naylor Bldg W 4 E1 96 A1
Naylor Gr EN3 18 D6

Naylor Ho
23 Clapham SW8 137 D3
Walworth SE17 262 D2
5 West Kilburn W10 91 B4
Naylor Rd
Peckham SE15 140 B5
Whetstone N20 14 A2
Nayor Bldg E 6 E1 96 A1
Nazareth Cl SE15 140 B3
Nazrul St E2 95 D4
Neal Ave UB1 85 B3
Neal Cl HA6 22 A2
Nealden St SW9 138 B2
Neale Cl N2 48 A6
Neale Ct
Dagenham RM9 80 B2
Muswell Hill N10 31 B3
Neal St WC2 94 A1 240 A1
Neal's Yd WC2 240 A1
Near Acre NW9 27 D2
NEASDEN 67 B4
Neasden Cl NW10 67 C3
Neasden Junc NW10 67 C4
Neasden La
Church End NW10 67 C3
Neasden NW10 67 B5
Neasden La N NW10 67 C5
Neasden Sta NW10 67 C3
Neasham Rd RM8 80 B3
Neate St SE5 139 D6
Neath Gdns SM4 202 A3
Neathouse Pl SW1 259 A4
Neats Acre HA4 39 B2
Neatscourt Rd E16 99 D2
Nebraska Bldg 11
SE13 141 D4
Nebraska St
SE1 117 B4 252 C1
Neckinger Est SE16 263 D6
Neckinger
SE16 117 D3 263 D6
Neckinger St SE1 263 D6
Nectarine Way
SE13 141 D3
Nedahall Ct 4 NW11 47 B2
Needham Ct 20 EN3 7 C6
Needham Ho SE11 261 A3
Needham Rd W11 91 C1
Needham Terr NW2 68 D5
Needleman St SE16 118 D4
Needwood Ho N4 51 A1
Neela Cl UB10 60 D4
Neeld Cres
Hendon NW4 46 B4
Wembley HA9 66 C3
Neeld Ct HA9 66 C3
Neeld Par HA9 66 B3
Neil Cl TW15 171 A5
Neilson-Terry Ct 9
SW9 138 B1
Neil Wates Cres 17
SW2 160 C3
Nelgarde Rd SE6 163 C4
Nella Rd W6 134 D6
Nelldale Rd SE16 118 C2
Nellgrove Rd UB10 82 D3
Nell Gwynn Ave
TW17 193 B3
Nell Gwynn Ho SW3 257 B3
Nello James Gdns
SE27 183 B6
Nelson Cl
East Bedfont
TW14 149 D3
Hillingdon UB10 82 D4
2 Paddington NW6 91 C4
Thornton Heath CR0 204 D1
Walton-on-T KT12 194 B1
Nelson Ct
5 Carshalton
SM5 218 D5
Rotherhithe SE16 119 B5
Nelson Dock Pier
SE16 119 B5
Nelson Gdns
Bethnal Green E2 96 A4
Twickenham TW3,
TW4 151 C5
Nelson Grove Rd
SW19 180 A2
Nelson Ho 1 W5 88 A4
Nelson Hospl SW20 179 B1
Nelson La UB10 82 D4
Nelson Mandela Cl
N10 31 A1
Nelson Mandela Rd
SE3 143 C2
Nelson Pas EC1 235 B2
Nelson Pl N1 234 D3
Nelson Prim Sch
Twickenham TW2 151 D5
Wallend E6 100 C5
Nelson Rd
Ashford TW15 170 A5

Nelson Rd *continued*
Bromley BR2 . . . . 209 C5
Chingford E4 . . . . 35 D4
Edmonton N9. . . . . 18 B2
Enfield EN3 . . . . 18 D5
Erith DA17 . . . . 125 B1
Greenwich SE10 . . . . 142 A6
Harmondsworth
TW6 . . . . 126 B4
Harrow HA1 . . . . 42 C1
Hillingdon UB10. . . . . . 82 D4
Hornsey Vale N8 . . . . . . 50 B3
Merton SW19 . . . . . . 180 A3
New Malden KT3 . . . . . 199 B4
Sidcup DA14 . . . . 190 A6
Stanmore HA7 . . . . 25 C4
Tottenham N15 . . . . 51 C5
Twickenham TW2,
TW4 . . . . 151 C5
Wanstead E11. . . . . 55 B5
Nelson's Monument*
WC2. . . . . 250 A4
Nelson Sq
SE1. . . . . 116 D4 251 C2
Nelsons Row SW4 . . 137 D1
Nelson St Barking E6. . 100 C6
Canning Town E16 . . . 120 D6
Newham E6 . . . . 100 B5
Stepney E1 . . . . 96 B1
Nelsons Yd NW1 . . . . . . 232 A4
Nelson Terr N1 . . . . . 234 D3
Nelson Trad Est
SW19. . . . . 179 D2
Nemoure Rd W3. . . . . . 111 A6
Nene Gdns TW13 . . . . 151 B2
Nene Rd TW6, UB7. . . . 126 D4
Nene Road Rdbt
TW6. . . . . 126 D4
Nepaul Rd 17 SW11 . . 136 C2
Nepean St SW15 . . . . . 156 A4
Neptune Ct
Dagenham IG11 . . . . . 102 B4
13 Millwall E14 . . . . . 119 C2
Neptune Ho
2 Rotherhithe
SE16. . . . . 118 C3
14 Stoke Newington
N16. . . . . 73 C3
Neptune Rd
Harlington TW6 . . . . . 127 A4
Harrow HA1 . . . . 42 B3
Neptune St SE16. . . . . 118 C3
Nero Ct 6 TW8. . . . . . 131 D5
Nesbit Cl SE3. . . . . 142 C2
Nesbit Rd SE9 . . . . 143 D1
Nesbitt Ho DA6 . . . . . . 169 D6
Nesbitt Sq SE19. . . . . . 183 C3
Nesham Ho 14 N1. . . . . 95 C6
Nesham St E1 . . . . 118 A5
Ness St 9 SE16. . . . . . . 118 A3
Nesta Rd IG8 . . . . 36 D4
Nestle's Ave UB3. . . . . 105 D3
Nestor Ave N21. . . . . . . 16 D5
Nestor Ho 13 E2 . . . . . . 96 B5
Netheravon Rd
Chiswick W4 . . . . 111 D1
Ealing W7 . . . . 108 D5
Netheravon Rd S
W4. . . . . 111 D1
Netherbury Rd W5. . . 109 D3
Netherby Gdns EN2 . . . . 4 A1
Netherby Ho 23
SW8. . . . . 137 D3
Netherby Rd SE23. . . . 162 C4
Nether Cl N3 . . . . 29 C3
Nethercombe Ho 1
SE3. . . . . 143 A6
Nethercott Ho 27 E3 . . 97 D4
Nethercourt Ave N3. . . 29 C4
Netherfield Gdns
IG11. . . . . 79 B1
Netherfield Rd
Finchley N12 . . . . 29 D5
Upper Tooting
SW17 . . . . 159 A1
Netherford Rd SW4 . . 137 C3
Netherhall Gdns
NW3. . . . . 70 A3
Netherhall Way NW3. . 70 A3
Netherlands Rd EN5 . . 14 B5
Netherleigh Cl N6 . . . 49 B1
Nether St Finchley N3 . . 29 D4
North Finchley N12. . . . 30 A5
Netherton Gr
SW10. . . . . . 136 A6 266 B5
Netherton Ho 1 UB5. . 85 B4
Netherton Rd
Isleworth TW1. . . . . . 153 B6
Tottenham N15 . . . . . . 51 B3
Netherwood 24 N2. . . . 30 B1
Netherwood Rd
W14. . . . . 112 D4
Netherwood St NW6 . . 69 C2
Nethewode Ct
DA17 . . . . 125 D3
Netley Cl
Cheam SM3. . . . . 216 D3
New Addington CR0 . 224 A1
Netley Ct IG2. . . . . 57 B4
Netley Dr KT12. . . . . . . 195 B2
Netley Gdns SM4. . . . . 202 A2
Netley 13 SE5. . . . . 139 C4
Netley Prim Sch
NW1. . . . . 93 C4 232 A1
Netley Rd
Brentford TW8. . . . . . 132 A6
Cheam SM4 . . . . 202 A2
Ilford IG2 . . . . 57 B4
Walthamstow E17 . . . . . 53 B4
Netley St
NW1. . . . . 93 C4 232 A1
Nettlecombe NW1 . . . . 71 D1
Nettleden Ave HA9. . . . 66 C2
Nettleden Ho SW3 . . 257 B3
Nettlefold Pl SE27 . . . 160 D1
Nettlestead Cl 16
BR3 . . . . 185 C3
Nettleton Rd
Harlington TW6 . . . . . 126 D4
Ickenham UB10. . . . . . . 60 B4
New Cross Gate
SE14. . . . . 140 D4
Nettlewood Rd
SW16. . . . . 181 D3
Neuchatel Rd SE6. . . . 163 B2
Nevada Cl KT3. . . . . . . 199 A5
Nevada St SE10 . . . . . . 142 A6
Nevena Ct 3 SW2 . . . 160 C6
Nevern Mans SW5 . . 255 A2
Nevern Pl
SW5. . . . . . . 113 C2 255 B3
Nevern Rd SW5. . . . . 255 A3
Nevern Sq
SW5. . . . . . . 113 C2 255 B3
Nevil Ho 7 SW9 . . . . . 138 D3
Nevill Ct SW10. . . . . . 266 A4
Neville Ave KT3. . . . . . 177 B2
Neville Cl Acton W3. . . 111 A4
Hounslow TW3 . . . . . 129 D3
Leyton E11. . . . . 76 D5
Paddington NW6 . . . . . . 91 B5
Peckham SE15. . . . . . . 140 A4
Sidcup DA15 . . . . 189 D6
Somers Town NW1 . . 232 D3
Neville Ct 10 SW12. . . 159 C4
Neville Dr N2. . . . . 48 A3
Neville Gdns RM8. . . . . 80 D5
Neville Gill Cl SW18. . 157 D5
Neville Ho
Friern Barnet N11. . . . . 31 A6
5 Twickenham
TW1 . . . . 153 A4
Neville Pl N22 . . . . 32 B2
Neville Rd
Dagenham RM8. . . . . . . 80 D5
Ealing W5 . . . . 87 D3
Forest Gate E7 . . . . 77 B1
Kingston u T KT1. . . . 176 C1
Paddington NW6 . . . . . . 91 B5
Richmond TW10. . . . . . 153 C2
Thornton Heath CR0 . . 205 B2
Neville's Ct NW2. . . . . . 68 A5
Neville St
SW7. . . . . . . 114 B1 256 C2
Neville Terr SW7 . . . . 256 C2
Neville Wlk SM5 . . . . 202 C2
Nevill Rd N16. . . . . 73 C5
Nevin Dr E4 . . . . 19 D3
Nevin Ho UB3. . . . . 105 A3
Nevinson Cl SW18 . . . 158 B5
Nevis Rd SW17 . . . . . . 159 A2
Nevitt Ho N1 . . . . 235 D3
New Acres Rd SE28 . . 123 C5
NEW ADDINGTON . . . 224 B1
Newall Ho SE1. . . . . . . 262 B6
Newall Rd TW6 . . . . . . 127 A4
Newark Cres NW10 . . . 89 B4
Newark Ct KT12. . . . . . 194 C1
Newark Ho 3 SW9. . . 138 D3
Newark Knok E6. . . . . 100 C2
Newark Rd CR2. . . . . . . 221 B2
Newark St E1. . . . . 96 B2
Newark Way NW4. . . . . 46 A6
New Ash Cl N2 . . . . 48 B6
New Atlas Wharf
E14. . . . . 119 C3
New Barn Cl SM6 . . . . 220 B2
NEW BARNET 14 A6
New Barnet StaEN5 . . 14 B6
New Barns Ave CR4 . . 203 D5
New Barn St E13. . . . . . 99 B3
NEW BECKENHAM . . 185 A4
New Beckenham Sta
BR3 . . . . 185 B3
New Belmont Ho 4
SE23. . . . . 162 C3
New Bentham Ct 10
N1 . . . . 73 A1
Newbery Ho N1. . . . . . . 73 A1
Newbiggin Path
WD19. . . . . 22 C6
Newbold Cotts 4 E1. . 96 C1
Newbolt Ave SM3 . . . . 216 D3
Newbolt Ho SE17 . . . 262 C2
Newbolt Rd HA7 . . . . . . 24 D5
New Bond St
W1. . . . . 115 B6 248 D6
Newborough Gn
KT3 . . . . 199 B5
Newborough Ho
SW19. . . . . 180 B3
New Brent St NW4 . . . . 46 C4
Newbridge Ct SW17. . 180 A6
Newbridge Point 3
SE23. . . . . 162 D1
Newbridge SchRM6 . . 58 B4
New Bridge St
EC4 . . . . 94 D1 241 C1
New Broad St
EC2 . . . . 95 C2 243 A3
New Broadway
Ealing W5 . . . . 109 D6
7 Hillingdon UB10. . . . 82 D3
Teddington TW12. . . . 174 B5
New Bsns Ctr The
NW10. . . . . 89 D4
Newburgh Rd W3. . . . 111 A5
Newburgh St W1 . . . 239 B1
New Burlington Mews
W1. . . . . 249 A6
New Burlington Pl
W1. . . . . 249 A6
New Burlington St
W1. . . . . 249 A6
Newburn Ct N12 . . . . . . 30 A3
Newburn Ho SE11. . . 260 D2
Newburn St
SE11. . . . . . . 116 B1 260 D2
Newbury Ave EN3. . . . . . 7 B6
Newbury Cl UB5 . . . . . . 63 B2
Newbury Cotts 4
IG2. . . . . 57 A3
Newbury Ct
Hackney E5 . . . . 75 A3
Sidcup DA14 . . . . 189 D6
7 Wanstead E11 . . . . . 55 A5
Newbury Gdns
KT19 . . . . 215 D4
Newbury Ho
Barnet EN4 . . . . 2 B1
Brixton SW9 . . . . 138 D3
14 Kensington W2. . . . . 91 D1
Wood Green N22. . . . . . 32 A2
Newbury Mews NW5 . . 71 A2
NEWBURY PARK 57 B3
Newbury Park Prim Sch
IG2. . . . . 57 B3
Newbury Park Sta
IG2. . . . . 57 B3
Newbury Rd
Bromley BR2 . . . . 209 A6
Chingford E4 . . . . 36 A4
Harmondsworth
TW6 . . . . 126 B4
Ilford IG2 . . . . 57 C3
Newbury St EC1 . . . . 242 A4
Newbury Way UB5 . . . . 63 B2
New Butt La SE8 . . . . . 141 C5
Newby Cl EN1 . . . . 5 C3
Newby NW1 . . . . 232 A2
Newby Pl E14. . . . . 120 A6
Newby St SW8. . . . . . . 137 B2
New Caledonian Wharf
SE16. . . . . 119 B3
New Campden Ct 9
NW3. . . . . 70 A4
Newcastle Cl EC4 . . . 241 C2
Newcastle Ct EC4 . . . 252 B6
Newcastle Ho W1. . . . 238 A4
Newcastle Pl
W2. . . . . 92 B2 236 D4
Newcastle Row EC1. . 241 B5
New Cavendish St
W1. . . . . 93 B2 238 C3
New Change
EC4 . . . . 95 A1 242 A1
New Chapel Sq
TW13. . . . . 150 B3
New Charles St EC1. . 234 D2
NEW CHARLTON 121 C2
New Church Ct 3
SE19. . . . . 184 A3
New Church Rd
32 Camberwell
SE5. . . . . 139 A5
Camberwell SE5 . . . . 139 B6
New City Prim Sch
E13. . . . . 99 C4
New City Rd E13 . . . . . . 99 C4
New Cl
Feltham TW13 . . . . . . 173 A5
Morden SW19 . . . . . . 202 A6
New Colebrooke Ct
SM5 . . . . 219 A1
New College Ct 6
NW3. . . . . 70 A2
New College Mews 7
N1 . . . . 72 C1
New College Par 1
NW3. . . . . 70 B1
Newcombe Gdns
TW3. . . . . 129 B1
Newcombe Ho N5 . . . . 73 A3
Newcombe Pk
Edgware NW7. . . . . 27 C5
Wembley HA0 . . . . 88 B6
Newcombe Rise UB7. . 82 A1
Newcombe St W8. . . 245 B4
Newcome Gdns
SW16. . . . . 182 A6
Newcome Ho E5. . . . . . 74 B5
Newcomen Ho 5
NW5. . . . . 71 B4
Newcomen Rd
Battersea SW11 . . . . . 136 B2
Leyton E11. . . . . 76 D5
Newcomen St
SE1. . . . . 117 B4 252 C2
New Compton St
WC2. . . . . 94 A1 240 A1
New Concordia Wharf
SE1. . . . . 253 D2
Newcourt Ho 26 E2 . . . 96 B4
Newcourt St
NW8. . . . . 92 C5 230 A3
New Covent Garden
Flower Market
SW8. . . . . . . 138 A6 270 A5
New Covent Garden
Fruit & Vegetable Mkt
SW8. . . . . . . 137 D5 269 C3
New Crane Pl E1. . . . . 118 C5
New Crescent Yd 1
NW10. . . . . 89 D5
Newcroft Cl UB8. . . . . . 82 B2
Newcroft Ho 10
NW10. . . . . 67 B1
NEW CROSS 141 B4
NEW CROSS GATE . . 140 D4
New Cross Gate
SE14. . . . . 140 D4
New Cross Gate Sta
SE14. . . . . 141 A5
New Cross Hospl
SE14. . . . . 140 C5
New Cross Rd SE14 . . 141 A4
New Cross SE14 . . . . . 141 B5
New Cross StaSE14 . 141 B5
New Ct
City of London EC4 . . 241 A1
26 Hampstead NW3 . . . 70 A4
Northolt UB5. . . . . 63 D3
Stoke Newington N16 . . 51 B1
Newdales Cl N9 . . . . . . 18 A2
Newdene Ave UB5 . . . . 84 D5
New Den (Millwall FC)
TheSE16 . . . . 118 C1
Newdigate Ho
6 Kingston u T
KT2. . . . . 176 D4
5 Poplar E14 . . . . 97 B1
Newell St E14 . . . . 97 B1
NEW ELTHAM 167 A2
New Eltham Sta
SE9. . . . . 166 D3
New End NW3 . . . . 70 A5
New End Prim Sch
NW3. . . . . 70 A4
New End Sq NW3 . . . . . 70 B4
New England Est
IG11. . . . . 101 A5
Newent Cl
Camberwell SE15 . . . 139 C5
Carshalton SM5. . . . . 202 D1
New Farm Ave BR2. . . 209 A5
New Ferry App
SE18. . . . . 122 C3
New Fetter La
EC4 . . . . 94 C1 241 B2
Newfield Cl TW12. . . . 173 C2
Newfield Prim Sch
NW10. . . . . 67 D1
Newfield Rise NW2 . . . 68 B5
Newgale Gdns HA8 . . . 26 B2
New Garden Dr
UB7 . . . . 104 A4
Newgate Cl TW13 . . . . 151 A1
Newgate CR0. . . . . 205 A1
Newgate St
Chingford E4 . . . . 20 C1
Holborn EC1 . 94 D1 241 D2
New Globe Wlk SE1. . 252 A4
New Goulston St E1. . 243 C2
New Green Pl SE19 . . 183 C4
NEWHAM 98 D4
Newham Acad of Music
E6. . . . . 100 A6
Newham Coll of FE
E6. . . . . 100 B5
Newham Coll (Stratford
Campus) E15 . . . . 76 C1
Newham Ctr for Mental
Health E16. . . . . 99 D3
Newham General Hospl
E13. . . . . 99 C3
Newham Gn N22. . . . . . 32 C2
Newham Sch of Nursing
E3. . . . . 97 D3
Newham Sixth Form
Coll E13 . . . . 99 B3
Newham Sixth Form
Coll (Stratford Ctr)
E15. . . . . 76 B1
Newham's Row SE1. 253 B1
Newham Way
Beckton E6 . . . . 100 B3
Canning Town E13. . . . . 99 B2
Newhaven Cl UB3. . . . 105 D2
Newhaven Cres
TW15. . . . . 171 B5
Newhaven Gdns
SE9. . . . . 143 D1
Newhaven La 3 E16 . . 99 A2
Newhaven Rd SE25 . . 205 B4
New Heston Rd
TW5. . . . . 129 B5
New Horizons Ct
TW8. . . . . 131 A6
Newhouse Ave RM6 . . . 58 D6
Newhouse Cl KT3. . . . 199 C2
Newhouse 5 KT3. . . . 199 C2
Newhouse Wlk SM4. . 202 A2
Newick Cl DA5. . . . . . . 169 D5
Newick Rd E5 . . . . 74 C5
Newing Gn BR1. . . . . . 187 D3
NEWINGTON 116 D2
Newington Barrow Way
N7 . . . . 72 B5
Newington Butts SE1,
SE11. . . . . . . 116 D2 261 D3
Newington Cswy
SE1. . . . . 117 A3 262 A6
Newington Gn N16. . . . 73 B3
Newington Green Mans
N16 . . . . 73 B3
Newington Green Prim
SchN16 . . . . 73 B3
Newington Green Rd
N1 . . . . 73 B3
Newington Ind Est
SE17. . . . . 262 A3
New Inn Broadway
EC2 . . . . 243 B6
New Inn Ct The KT8 . . 196 B4
New Inn Sq EC2. . . . . 243 B6
New Inn St EC2 . . . . . 243 B6
New Inn Yd
EC2 . . . . 95 C3 243 B6
New James Ct SE15 . . 140 B2
New Jubilee Ct 1
IG8. . . . . 37 A3
New Kelvin Ave
TW11. . . . . 174 C4
New Kent Rd
SE1. . . . . 117 A2 262 B4
New King's Prim Sch
SW6. . . . . 135 B3
New King's Rd
SW6. . . . . . . 135 C4 265 B1
New King St SE8. . . . . 141 C6
Newland Cl HA5 . . . . . . 23 B4
Newland Ct
St Luke's EC1. . . . . . . 242 C6
Wembley HA9 . . . . 66 C6
Newland Dr EN1 . . . . 6 B4
Newland Gdns W13 . . 109 A4
Newland Ho
17 Deptford SE14 . . . 140 D6
Hornsey N8. . . . . 50 A6
Newland House Sch
Annex TW1 . . . . 174 D6
Newland House Sch
TW1. . . . . 174 D6
Newland Rd N8. . . . . . . 50 A6
Newlands Ave KT7 . . . 196 C1
Newlands Cl
Edgware HA8. . . . . 10 A1
Southall UB2 . . . . 107 A1
Wembley HA0 . . . . 65 C2
Newlands Croft
SE20. . . . . 184 D4
Newlands Ct
8 Eltham SE9. . . . . . 166 C5
6 Penge SE26 . . . . . . 184 C4
Streatham SW16 . . . . 182 A5
Newlands NW1 . . . . . . 232 A2
Newlands Pk SE26 . . . 184 D5
Newlands Pl EN5 . . . . . 12 D6
Newlands Quay E1. . . 118 C6
Newlands Rd
Thornton Heath
SW16. . . . . 182 A1
Woodford IG8 . . . . 20 D2
Newlands The
Thames Ditton
KT7. . . . . 196 C1
Wallington SM6. . . . . 219 D1
Newland St E16. . . . . . 122 B5
Newlands Way KT9. . . 213 C3
Newling Cl E6 . . . . 100 B1
New London St EC3 . 25
New Lydenburg
Commercial Est
SE7. 12
New Lydenburg St
SE7. 12
Newlyn Cl
Hillingdon UB8. 82
Orpington BR6. 227
Newlyn Gdns HA2. 4
Newlyn Ho
7 Pinner HA5. 23
7 Sutton SM1 218
Newlyn NW1 232
Newlyn Rd Barnet EN5 . .
Bexley DA16 145
Tottenham N17 33
NEW MALDEN 199
New Malden Sta
KT3 199
Newman Ct
3 Bromley BR1 187
8 Finchley N3 29
Newman Ho 11
TW10. 153
Newman Pas W1 239
Newman Rd
Bromley BR1 187
Hayes UB3. 106
Newham E13. 99
Thornton Heath CR0 . . 204
Walthamstow E17 52
Newman's Ct EC3. . . 242
Newman's Row WC2 240
Newman St
W1. . . . . 93 C2 239
Newman's Way EN4. . . . 2
Newman Terr 9
CR4 202
Newmarket Ave UB5 . . 63
Newmarket Gn SE9 . . 165
Newmarsh Rd SE28 . . 123
Newmill Ho E3 98
New Mill Rd BR5. 190
Newminster Rd
SM4 202
Newmount NW3 70
New Mount St E15 76
Newnes Path SW15 . . 134
Newnham Ave HA4. . . . 40
Newnham Cl
Loughton IG10. 21
Northolt UB5. 64
South Norwood CR7 . 183
Newnham Gdns UB5 . . 64
Newnham Ho
Catford SE6. 164
Loughton IG10. 21
9 Putney SW15. 156
Newnham Jun & Inf
Schs HA4. 40
Newnham Lo 10
DA17 125
Newnham Mews N22. . 32
Newnham Rd N22. 32
Newnhams Cl BR1 . . . 210
Newnham Terr SE1. . . 261
Newnham Way HA3 . . . 44
New North Com Sch
The N1 73
New North Pl EC2. . . 243
New North Rd
N1 . . . . 95 B6 235
New North Road Bridge
N1 235
New North St
WC1. . . . . 94 B2 240
Newnton Cl N4 51
New Oak Rd N2. 30
New Oxford St
WC1. . . . . 94 A1 240
New Palace Yd
SW1. . . . . 116 A4 250
New Par TW15. 170
New Park Ave N13 17
New Park Cl UB5 63
New Park Ct 26
SW2. 160
New Park Est N18. 34
New Park Ho N13. 32
New Park Par 14
SW2. 160
New Park Rd
Ashford TW15 171
Streatham SW2. 160
New Par UB7 104
New Place Sq SE16 . . 118
New Pl CR0. 223
New Plaistow Rd
E15. 98
New Pond Par HA4. . . . 62
Newport Ave
Blackwall E14 120
Newham E13. 99
Newport Cl EN3. 7
Newport Ct WC2. 249
Newport Ho 2 E3 97

port Lo 2 EN1 17 C6
port Mead
D19 22 D6
port Pl WC2 249 D6
port Rd
rnes SW13 134 A4
rmondsworth
TW6 126 C4
ayes UB4 83 B2
yton E10 76 B6
althamstow E17 53 A5
port Sch E10,
1 76 A6
port St
11 116 B2 260 D4
Priory Ct 9
V6 69 C1
Providence Wharf
4 120 B5
vquay Cres HA2 63 A6
vquay Ho SE11 261 A2
vquay Rd SE6 164 A2
Quebec St W1 237 D1
Rd
entford TW8 109 D1
arshalton CR4 203 A1
hingford E4 36 A6
agenham RM10 103 D5
ast Bedfont TW14 149 B5
ast Molesey KT8 195 C6
dmonton N9 18 B2
lstree WD6 9 D5
sher KT10 212 A4
eltham TW14 150 B3
inchley N10 30 C2
anworth TW13 173 A5
arlington TW6,
UB7 127 A5
arrow HA1 64 D4
endon NW7 29 A3
illingdon UB8 83 A2
ornsey N8 50 A4
ounslow TW3 129 D1
lford IG3 79 C6
ingston u T KT2 176 C3
ittleton TW17 192 D6
ichmond TW10 175 C6
tepney E1 96 B2
ottenham N22 33 A2
Welling DA16 146 B3
West Heath SE2 124 D1
ew River Cres N13 32 D6
ew River Ct N5 73 B4
ew River Sports &
Recreation Ctr
N22 32 D3
ew River Way N4 51 B2
ew Row
WC2 116 A6 250 A6
ew Rush Hall Sch
IG1 79 A6
ewry Rd TW1 153 A6
ew St Sq
EC4 94 C1 241 B2
ewsam Ave N15 51 B4
ew Scotland Yard*
SW1 115 D3 259 C6
ew Shepherd's Bush
Mkt* 6 W12 112 C4
ewsholme Dr N21 16 B6
EW SOUTHGATE 31 C6
ew Southgate Ind Est
10 N11 31 C5
ew Southgate Sta
N11 31 B5
ew Spitalfields Mkt
E10 75 C5
ew Spring Gdns Wlk
SE11 260 B1
ew Sq
East Bedfont
TW14 149 A3
St Giles WC2 94 B1 240 D2
ew Square Pas
WC2 241 A2
ewstead Ave BR6 227 C6
ewstead Cl N12 30 C4
ewstead Ct UB5 85 A4
ewstead Ho
Edmonton N9 17 D1
Islington N1 234 B4
ewstead Rd SE12 164 D4
ewstead Way
SW19 178 D6
ewstead Wlk SM5 202 A2
ewstead Wood Sch for
Girls BR6 227 B5
ew St EC2 95 C2 243 B3
ew Street Hill BR1 187 C5
ewton Ave
Acton W3 111 A4
Muswell Hill N10 31 B2
ewton Cl
Harrow HA2 63 C6
Walthamstow E17 53 A3
ewton Farm Fst & Mid
Sch HA2 63 B6

Newton Gr W4 111 C2
Newton Ho
22 Clapham SW8 137 D3
Paddington NW8 91 D6
1 Stepney E1 118 B6
10 Walthamstow E17 54 A6
Newton Ind Est RM6 58 D5
Newton Pl E14 119 C2
Newton Point 1 E16 98 D1
Newton Prep Sch
SW8 137 B4 268 D2
Newton Rd
Acton W3 111 A4
Cricklewood NW2 68 C5
Harrow HA3 24 C1
Isleworth TW7 130 D3
Kensington W2 91 D1
South Tottenham N15 52 A4
Stratford New Town
E15 76 B3
Welling DA16 146 A2
Wembley HA0 66 B1
Wimbledon SW19 179 A3
Newton St
WC2 94 A1 240 B2
Newton's Yd 14
SW18 157 C6
Newton Terr BR2 209 D3
Newton Way N18 33 A5
Newton Wlk HA8 26 D2
New Tower Bldgs 21
E1 118 B5
Newtown Ct
Battersea SW11 268 C1
Clapham SW4 159 B6
New Trinity Rd 1
N2 30 B1
New Union Cl E14 120 A3
New Union St EC2 242 C3
New Victoria Hospl
KT3 177 C2
New Wanstead E11 55 A3
New Way Rd NW9 45 C5
New Wharf Rd
N1 94 A5 233 B4
New Woodlands Sch
BR1 186 C6
NEWYEARS GREEN 38 B3
Newyears Green La
UB9 38 B3
New Zealand Ave
KT12 193 D1
Nexus Ct E11 54 C2
Niagara Ave W5 109 C2
Niagara Cl N1 235 B4
Niagara Ct 6 SE16 118 C3
Niagara Ho W5 109 C2
Nibthwaite Rd HA1 42 C4
Nicholas Cl UB6 85 D5
Nicholas Ct
Chiswick W4 133 C5
Golders Green NW11 47 C2
Lewisham SE12 165 A3
Newham E13 99 B4
Nicholas Gdns W5 109 D4
Nicholas Ho
Ealing W13 87 C1
Penge SE26 184 B4
2 Putney SW15 156 A6
Nicholas La EC2, EC4 252 D6
Nicholas Pas EC3 252 D6
Nicholas Rd
Bethnal Green E1 96 C3
Borehamwood WD6 10 B6
Dagenham RM8 81 B5
Wallington CR0 220 A4
Nicholas Stacey Ho 3
SE7 121 B1
Nicholay Rd N19 49 D1
Nichol Cl N14 15 D3
Nicholes Rd TW3 129 C1
Nichol La BR1 187 A3
Nicholl Ho N4 51 A1
Nicholls Almshouses
NW7 28 B5
Nicholls Ave UB8 82 C3
Nicholls Point E15 99 A6
Nicholl St E2 96 A6
Nichols Cl
Chessington KT9 213 C2
Finsbury Pk N4 50 C1
Nichols Ct E2 95 D5
Nichols Gn W5 88 A2
Nicholson Ct 9 N17 51 D6
Nicholson Ho SE17 262 C2
Nicholson Mews
KT1 198 A5
Nicholson Rd CR0 205 D1
Nicholson St SE1 251 C3
Nickelby Cl SE28 102 C1
Nickleby Cl UB8 82 D1
Nickleby Ho
18 Bermondsey
SE1 118 A4
7 Shepherd's Bush
W11 112 D5
Nickols Wlk SW18 135 D1

Nicola Cl Harrow HA3 24 B1
South Croydon CR2 221 A2
Nicola Terr DA7 147 A4
Nicol Cl 6 TW1 153 B5
Nicole Ho SE25 206 A6
Nicoll Ct
Dagenham NW10 89 C6
Muswell Hill N10 31 B3
Nicoll Pl NW4 46 B2
Nicoll Rd NW10 89 C6
Nicoll Way WD6 11 B6
Nicolson Dr WD23 8 A2
Nicolson 14 NW9 27 D2
Nicosia Rd SW18 158 C4
Niederwald Rd
SE26 185 A6
Nield Rd UB3 105 D4
Nigel Bldg EC1 241 A4
Nigel Cl UB5 85 A6
Nigel Ct N3 29 D3
Nigel Fisher Way
KT9 213 D1
Nigel Mews IG1 78 D4
Nigel Playfair Ave
W6 112 B1
Nigel Rd
Forest Gate E7 77 C3
Peckham SE15 140 A2
Nigeria Rd SE7 143 D5
Nighthawk 16 NW9 27 D2
Nightingale Ave
Chingford E4 36 C5
Harrow HA1 43 B1
Nightingale Cl
Carshalton SM5 219 A6
Chingford E4 36 C6
Chiswick W4 133 A6
Pinner HA5 40 C4
Nightingale Ct
14 Cubitt Town
E14 120 A3
Finsbury Pk N4 72 B6
1 Harrow HA1 42 D3
Penge SE19 183 D4
Sutton SM1 218 A3
1 Wanstead E11 55 B4
Nightingale Dr
KT19 214 D2
Nightingale Gr
SE13 164 B6
Nightingale Ho
Hayes UB3 105 D2
21 Hoxton E1 95 C6
4 North Kensington
W12 90 C1
7 St George in t East
E1 118 A5
Woolwich SE18 122 C1
Nightingale La
Balham SW11,
SW12 159 A5
Bromley BR1 187 D1
Hornsey N8 50 A6
Richmond TW10 154 A4
Wanstead E11 55 B4
Nightingale Lo
Edgware HA8 27 A4
5 Paddington W9 91 C2
Nightingale Mans 4
SW12 159 A5
Nightingale Mews
1 Bow E3 97 A5
Newington SE11 261 C4
8 Wanstead E11 55 B4
Nightingale Pl
Shooters Hill
SE18 144 D6
West Brompton
SW10 136 A6 266 B6
Nightingale Prim Sch
Shacklewell E5 74 A4
Wanstead E18 55 C5
Wood Green N22 32 B2
Woolwich SE18 122 D1
Nightingale Rd
Carshalton SM5 219 A6
Dagenham NW10 89 D5
Ealing W7 108 D5
East Molesey KT8 195 D4
Hackney E5 74 B5
Hampton TW12 173 C4
Orpington BR5 211 A3
Ponders End N9 18 C4
Walton-on-T KT12 194 B2
Wood Green N22 32 B3
Nightingale Sch
SW17 158 C2
Nightingale Sq
SW12 159 A4
Nightingales The
TW19 148 B3
Nightingale Vale
SE18 144 C6
Nightingale Way E6 100 A2
Nightingale Wlk SW18,
SW4 159 B5
Nile Cl N16 73 D5

Nile Ct N12 30 C4
Nile Dr N9 18 C2
Nile Ho N1 235 C2
Nile Path 6 SE18 144 C6
Nile Rd E13 99 C5
Nile St N1 95 B4 235 C2
Nile Terr SE1,
SE15 117 D1 263 D1
Nimegen Way 9
SE22 161 C6
Nimmo Dr WD23 8 B4
Nimrod Cl UB5 84 D4
Nimrod 12 NW9 27 C2
Nimrod Pas 4 N1 73 C2
Nimrod Rd SW16 181 B5
Nina Mackay Cl 10
E15 98 C6
Nine Acres Cl E12 78 A3
NINE ELMS 137 C5
Nine Elms Cl TW14 149 D3
Nine Elms La
SW8 137 D6 269 C5
Nineteenth Rd CR4 204 A5
Ninhams Wood BR6 226 C4
Ninth Ave UB3 106 A6
Nisbet Ho E9 74 D3
Nisbet 13 NW9 27 C2
Nisbett Wlk DA14 190 A6
Nita Ct SE12 165 A3
Nithdale Rd SE18 145 A5
Nithsdale Gr UB10 61 A5
Niton Cl EN5 12 D5
Niton Rd TW9 132 C2
Niton St SW6 134 D5
No 1 St SE18 122 D3
No 2 Willow Rd*
NW3 70 C4
Noam Prim Sch N12 29 D6
Nobel Dr TW6 127 C5
Nobel Ho 8 SE5 139 A3
Nobel Rd N18 34 C6
Noble Cnr TW5 129 C4
Noble Ct
Mitcham CR4 180 B1
Stepney E1 118 B6
Noblefield Hts N2 48 D4
Noble Ho 18 E1 118 A6
Noble St EC2 95 A1 242 A2
Noel Baker Ct 5 E11 76 C6
Noel Coward Ho
SW1 259 B3
Noel Ct TW4 129 B2
Noel Dene W5 109 C1
Noel Ho 3 NW3 70 B1
Noel 13 NW9 27 D2
NOEL PARK 32 D1
Noel Park Prim Sch
N22 32 C1
Noel Park Rd N22 32 C1
Noel Rd Acton W3 88 D1
Islington N1 94 D5 234 D4
Newham E6 100 A3
Noel Sq RM8 80 C4
Noel St W1 93 C1 239 B1
Noel Terr
Forest Hill SE23 162 C2
Sidcup DA14 190 B6
Noko NW10 90 D4
Nolan Way E5 74 A4
Noll Ho N7 72 B6
Nolton Pl HA8 26 B2
Nonsuch Ct SM3 217 A2
Nonsuch High Sch for
Girls SM3 216 D1
Nonsuch Ho 5
SW19 180 B2
Nonsuch Prim Sch
KT17 216 B3
Nook The SW19 180 A1
Noor Ul Islam Prim Sch
E10 76 A6
Nora Gdns NW4 46 D5
NORBITON 176 C1
Norbiton Ave KT1,
KT2 176 C1
Norbiton Common Rd
KT1, KT3 198 D6
Norbiton Hall KT2 176 B1
Norbiton Rd E14 97 B1
Norbiton Sta KT1 176 C2
Norbreck Gdns
NW10 88 B4
Norbreck Par NW10 88 B4
Norbroke St W12 111 D6
Norburn St W10 91 A2
NORBURY 182 C2
Norbury Ave
Isleworth TW3 130 B1
Thornton Heath CR7,
SW16 182 C1
Norbury Cl SW16 182 D2
Norbury Court Rd
SW16 182 A1
Norbury Cres SW16 182 C1
Norbury Cross
SW16 204 A6
Norbury Ct N12 30 A6

Norbury Gdns RM6 58 D4
Norbury Gr NW7 11 C1
Norbury Hill SW16 182 D3
Norbury Manor Bsns &
Enterprise Coll For
Girls CR7 182 C2
Norbury Manor Prim
Sch SW16 182 A2
Norbury Rd
Chingford E4 35 C5
Feltham TW13 149 D1
South Norwood CR7 205 A6
Norbury Rise SW16 204 A6
Norbury Sch HA1 42 C4
Norbury Sta SW16 182 B2
Norbury Trad Est
SW16 182 B1
Norcombe Gdns HA3 43 C4
Norcombe Ho 2
N19 71 D5
Norcott Cl UB4 84 C3
Norcott Rd N16 74 A5
Norcroft Gdns SE22 162 A4
Norcutt Rd TW2 152 C3
Norden Ho 25 E2 96 B4
Norden Point NW2 46 C1
Nore Ct NW10 68 A1
Norfolk Ave
Edmonton N13 32 D4
South Tottenham N15 51 D3
Norfolk Cl
Cockfosters EN4 3 A1
East Finchley N2 48 C6
Edmonton N13 32 D4
5 Twickenham
TW1 153 B5
Norfolk Cres
Paddington
W2 92 C1 237 B2
Sidcup DA15 167 C4
Norfolk Ct
5 Barnet EN5 1 A1
4 Ilford RM6 58 B4
Surbiton KT5 198 B3
Wembley HA0 65 C2
Norfolk Gdns DA7 147 B4
Norfolk Ho
13 Acton W3 88 C1
Beckenham BR2 208 D5
City of London EC4 252 A6
Edgware HA8 26 B3
Greenwich SE3 142 C6
11 Merton SW19 180 A3
Penge SE20 184 C2
4 Putney SW15 156 C4
Richmond TW10 154 C6
Shacklewell E8 73 D4
2 South Croydon
CR0 221 B6
3 Stanmore HA7 25 C5
St Johns SE8 141 C4
Norfolk House Rd
SW16 160 A1
Norfolk House Sch
N10 31 B1
Norfolk Ho SW1 259 D4
Norfolk Mans
Battersea SW11 267 D1
10 Wandsworth
SW18 157 C6
Norfolk Mews 12
W10 91 A2
Norfolk Pl
Paddington
W2 92 B1 236 D2
Welling DA16 146 A3
Norfolk Rd
Barking IG11 79 C1
Barnet EN5 1 C2
Claygate KT10 212 C3
Dagenham RM10 81 D3
Enfield EN3 18 B6
Feltham TW13 150 C3
Harrow HA1 41 D4
Higham Hill E17 34 D1
Ilford IG3 57 C2
Mitcham SW19 180 C4
Newham E6 100 B6
South Norwood CR7 205 A6
St John's Wood
NW8 92 B6 229 D5
Willesden NW10 67 C1
Norfolk Row SE1,
SE11 116 B2 260 C4
Norfolk Sq Mews
W2 236 D1
Norfolk Sq
W2 92 B1 236 D2
Norfolk St E7 77 A3
Norgrove St SW12 159 A4
Norhyrst Ave SE25 205 D6
Norland Ho 13 W11 112 D5
Norland Place Sch
W11 113 A5 244 A3
Norland Pl
W11 113 A5 244 B3
Norland Rd 16 W11 112 D5

Norlands Cres BR7 188 D2
Norland Sq
W11 113 A5 244 B3
Norley Vale SW15 156 A3
Norlington Rd E10,
E11 54 B1
Norlington Sch for Boys
E10 54 B1
Norman Ave
Feltham TW13 151 B2
Southall UB1 107 A6
Tottenham N22 33 A2
Twickenham TW1 153 C4
Norman Butler Ho 10
W10 91 A3
Normanby Cl SW15 157 B6
Normanby Rd NW10 67 D4
Norman Cl
Orpington BR6 227 A5
Tottenham N22 33 A2
Norman Cres
Heston TW5 128 D5
Pinner HA5 22 C2
Norman Ct
Dulwich SE22 162 A4
5 Finchley N3 29 C2
Finsbury Pk N4 50 C2
8 Hampton TW12 173 C2
Ilford IG2 57 B2
West Norwood
SW16 182 C5
Willesden NW10 68 A1
Woodford IG8 37 B5
Normand Croft Com
Sch W14 135 B6 264 D6
Normand Mews
W14 264 B6
Normand Rd
W14 135 B6 264 C6
Normandy Ave EN5 1 B1
Normandy Cl SE26 163 A1
Normandy Dr UB3 83 A1
Normandy Ho
8 Cubitt Town
E14 120 A4
4 Hendon NW4 28 D1
Normandy Rd SW9 138 C4
Normandy Terr E16 99 B1
Norman Gr E3 97 A5
Norman Ho
1 Cheam SM1 217 C2
Feltham TW13 151 B2
7 Leyton E11 76 C6
Lower Halliford
TW17 192 C2
South Lambeth SW8 270 A4
Normanhurst TW15 170 C5
Normanhurst Ave
DA7 146 D4
Normanhurst Dr
TW1 153 B6
Normanhurst Rd
St Paul's Cray
BR5 190 B1
Streatham SW2 160 B2
Walton-on-T KT12 194 D1
Normanhurst Sch E4 20 B4
Norman Par DA14 168 D2
Norman Rd
Ashford TW15 171 B4
Belvedere DA17 125 D3
Greenwich SE10 141 D5
Ilford IG1 78 D3
Leyton E11 76 C6
Merton SW19 180 A3
Newham E6 100 B3
South Tottenham N15 51 D4
Sutton SM1 217 C3
Thornton Heath CR7 204 D4
Normans Cl
Hillingdon UB8 82 A2
Willesden NW10 67 B2
Normansfield Ave KT1,
KT8 175 C3
Normanshire Dr E4 35 D6
Normans Mead
NW10 67 B2
Norman St
EC1 95 A4 235 B1
Normanton Ave SW18,
SW19 157 C2
Normanton Ct CR2 221 C3
Normanton Ho 6
SW4 159 C5
Normanton Pk E4 20 C2
Normanton Rd CR2 221 C2
Normanton St SE23 162 D2
Norman Way
Acton W3 88 D1
Palmers Green N14 16 A2
Normington Cl
SW16 182 C5
Norrice Lea N2 48 B4

Norris Ho
12 Hoxton N1 95 C6
15 South Hackney E9 96 C6
Norris 11 NW9 27 D2
Norris St SW1 249 C5
Norroy Rd SW15 134 D1
Norrys Cl EN4 2 D1
Norrys Rd EN4 2 D1
Norse Ho 13 SE5 139 A3
Norseman Cl 3 IG3 58 B1
Norseman Way UB6 85 D6
Norstead Pl SW15 156 A2
North Access Rd E17 52 D3
North Acre NW9 27 C2
NORTH ACTON 89 B4
North Acton Rd NW10 89 B4
North Acton Sta W3 89 B2
Northampton Gr N1 73 B3
Northampton Pk N1 73 B2
Northampton Rd
Croydon CR0 222 A6
Enfield EN3 7 A1
Finsbury EC1 94 C3 241 B6
Northampton Sq EC1 94 D4 234 C1
Northampton St N1 73 A1
Northanger Rd SW16 182 A4
North Audley St W1 115 A6 248 A6
North Ave Ealing W13 87 B2
Edmonton N18 34 A6
Harrow HA2 41 D3
Hayes UB3 106 A6
8 Richmond TW9 132 C4
Southall UB1 107 B6
Wallington SM5 219 A1
Northaw Ho 4 W10 90 C3
North Bank NW8 92 C4 230 A1
Northbank Rd E17 36 A1
North Beckton Prim Sch E6 100 B2
North Birkbeck Rd E11 76 B5
North Block 10 E1 118 C6
Northborough Rd SW16 182 A1
Northbourne BR2 209 A2
Northbourne Ho
21 Hackney E5 74 B3
Osidge N14 15 D4
Northbourne Rd SW4 159 D6
North Bridge House Sch NW3 70 A2
North Bridge House Senior Sch NW1 93 B6 231 C5
Northbrook CE Sch SE12 164 D6
Northbrook Rd
Barnet EN5 13 A5
Ilford IG1 78 C6
Lewisham SE13 164 C6
Thornton Heath CR0 205 B4
Wood Green N22 32 A3
Northburgh St EC1 94 D3 241 D6
Northbury Jun & Inf Schs IG11 79 A2
North Carriage Dr W2 114 C6 247 B6
NORTH CHEAM 216 C6
Northchurch Ho 19 E2 96 A6
Northchurch Rd
De Beauvoir Town N1 73 B1
Wembley HA9 66 C2
Northchurch SE17 262 D2
Northchurch Terr N1 73 C1
North Circular Rd
Edmonton N13 32 C5
Finchley N2 30 B2
Highams Pk E17 35 D2
Ilford IG1, E12 78 C4
Neasden NW2, NW10 67 C3
Temple Fortune N3, NW2, NW4 47 A4
Woodford E18 37 C1
North Cl Barnet EN5 12 C6
Bexley DA6 146 D1
Dagenham RM10 103 C6
East Bedfont TW14 149 B5
Northcliffe Cl KT4 215 C5
Northcliffe Dr N20 13 B3
North Cl SM4 201 A5
North Colonnade The E14 119 D5
North Common Rd
Ealing W5 110 A6

North Common Rd
continued
Uxbridge UB8 60 A3
Northcote Ave
Ealing W5 110 A6
Isleworth TW7 153 A6
Southall UB1 107 A6
Tolworth KT5 198 D2
Northcote Ho UB4 84 D2
Northcote Lodge Sch SW11 158 D5
Northcote 3 HA5 22 C1
Northcote Rd
Isleworth TW7 153 A6
Kingston u T KT3 199 B6
Sidcup DA14 189 C6
Thornton Heath CR0 205 B3
Walthamstow E17 53 A5
Wandsworth SW11 158 D6
Willesden NW10 67 C1
Northcott Ave N22 32 A2
North Countess Rd E17 35 B2
Northcourt W1 239 B4
NORTH CRAY 169 B1
North Cray Rd DA14 191 A5
North Cres
Finchley N3 29 B1
Marylebone WC1 239 C4
Newham E16 98 B3
Northcroft Ct 8 W12 112 A4
Northcroft Rd
Brentford W13 109 B3
West Ewell KT19 215 C1
North Crofts SE21 162 B3
North Cross Rd
East Dulwich SE22 162 A6
Ilford IG6 57 A5
North Ct SW1 260 A5
North Dene NW7 11 B1
Northdene Gdns N15 51 D3
North Dene TW5 129 D4
Northdown Cl HA4 61 D5
Northdown Gdns IG2 57 C4
Northdown Rd DA16 146 C3
Northdown St N1 94 B5 233 C3
North Dr
Beckenham BR3 207 D5
Hounslow TW3, TW7 130 A3
Orpington BR6 227 C4
Ruislip HA4 39 C2
Streatham SW16 181 C6
North Dulwich Sta SE21 161 B6
North Ealing Prim Sch W5 87 B3
North Ealing Sta W3 88 B1
NORTH END 70 A6
North End Ave NW3 70 A6
North End IG9 21 C4
North End Cres W14 113 B2 254 C3
North End CR0 221 A6
North End Ho W14 113 A2 254 B3
North End La BR6 226 D1
Northend Lodge 2 HA5 40 D6
North End NW3 70 A6
North End Par W14 254 B3
North End Rd
Golders Green NW11 47 D1
Wembley HA9 66 D5
West Kensington W14 113 B1 254 D1
North End Way NW3 70 A6
Northern Ave N9 17 D2
Northernhay Wlk SM4 201 A5
Northern Hts N8 49 D2
Northern Perimeter Rd TW6 127 C4
Northern Perimeter Rd (W) TW6 126 B4
Northern Rd E13 99 B5
Northern Relief Rd IG11 79 A2
Northern Star Ho N11 31 B5
Northesk Ho 6 E1 96 B3
North Eyot Gdns 5 W6 111 D1
Northey St E14 119 A6
NORTH FELTHAM 150 B6
North Feltham Trad Est TW14 128 B1
Northfield Ave
Pinner HA5 40 D5
West Ealing W13, W5 109 B4

Northfield Cl
Bromley BR1 188 A2
Hayes UB3 105 D3
Northfield Cres SM3 217 A4
Northfield Gdns RM9 81 B4
Northfield Hall N6 49 A2
Northfield Ho
2 Newham E13 99 C5
3 Peckham SE15 140 A6
Northfield Ind Est HA0 88 C6
Northfield IG10 21 D6
Northfield Par UB3 105 D3
Northfield Path RM9 81 B4
Northfield Pk UB3 105 D3
Northfield Rd
Cockfosters EN4 2 C2
Dagenham RM9 81 B4
Enfield EN3 18 B6
Heston TW5 128 D5
Plashet E6 78 B1
Stamford Hill N16 51 C2
West Ealing W13 109 B4
Northfields SW18 135 C1
Northfields Prospect SW18 135 C1
Northfields Rd W3 89 A2
Northfields Sta W5 109 C3
NORTH FINCHLEY 30 A6
Northfleet Ho SE1 252 C2
North Flower Wlk W2 114 B6 246 C5
Northgate Bsns Ctr EN1 6 B1
Northgate Ct 14 SW9 138 C2
Northgate Dr NW9 45 C3
North Gate NW8 92 C5 230 A3
North Gates N12 30 A2
North Gdns SW19 180 B3
North Glade The DA5 169 B3
North Gn NW9 27 C3
North Gower St NW1 93 C4 232 B1
North Greenwich Sta SE10 120 C4
North Gr Highgate N6 49 A2
Tottenham N15 51 B4
North Harringay Prim Sch N8 50 C5
NORTH HARROW 41 D2
North Harrow Sta HA2 41 D4
North Hill Ave N6 48 D3
North Hill Ct N6 49 A2
NORTH HILLINGDON 61 A2
North Hill N6 49 A3
North Ho 3 SE8 119 B1
NORTH HYDE 107 A1
North Hyde Gdns UB2, UB3 106 A3
North Hyde La UB2 107 A1
North Hyde Rd UB3 105 D3
Northiam N12 29 C6
Northiam St E9 96 B6
Northiam WC1 233 B1
Northington St WC1 94 B3 240 D5
NORTH KENSINGTON 90 D2
Northlands Ave BR6 227 C4
Northlands 4 BR1 187 C1
Northlands St SE5 139 A3
North La TW11 174 D4
Northleigh Ho 36 E3 97 D4
North Lo SW4 137 B1
North Lodge Cl SW15 156 D6
North Lo N22 31 D1
North London Bsns Pk N11 15 A1
North London Collegiate Sch The HA7, HA8 26 A5
North London Nuffield Hospl EN2 4 C3
North Lo EN5 14 A6
North Mall The N9 18 B2
North Mews WC1 94 B3 240 D5
North Middlesex University Hospl N18 33 C5
Northmoor 4 SE23 162 D1
North Mount N20 14 A2
Northolme Gdns HA8 26 C2
Northolme Rd N5 73 A4
Northolme Rise BR6 227 C6
Northolm HA8 27 B6
NORTHOLT 63 C1
Northolt Ave HA4 62 B3

Northolt Gdns UB6 64 D3
Northolt High Sch UB5 63 B2
Northolt Park Inf Sch UB5 63 D3
Northolt Park Sta HA2 63 D4
Northolt Rd HA2 64 A5
Northolt Sta UB5 63 C2
Northolt N17 33 C1
Northolt Trad Est UB5 63 D1
Northover BR1 164 D1
North Par
Chessington KT9 214 B3
Edgware HA8 26 C1
Southall UB1 85 C1
North Pas SW18 157 C6
North Pk SE9 166 C5
North Pl
Mitcham SW19 180 D3
Teddington TW11 174 D4
Northpoint BR1 187 A2
Northpoint Cl SM1 218 A5
Northpoint Sq 8 NW1 71 D2
North Point UB7 104 A5
North Pole La BR2 225 A2
North Pole Rd W10 90 C2
Northport St N1 235 D5
North Prim Sch UB1 107 B6
North Rd
Barnsbury N7 72 A2
Brentford TW8 132 A6
Bromley BR1 187 B2
Dagenham RM6 59 A4
Ealing W5 109 D3
East Bedfont TW14 149 B5
Edgware HA8 26 D2
Edmonton N9 18 B3
Erith DA17 125 D4
Finchley N2 30 C2
Hayes UB3 83 B2
Heston TW5 128 C6
Highgate N6 49 A2
Ilford IG3 79 C6
Plumstead SE18 123 C2
Richmond TW9 132 C3
Southall UB1 107 C6
Surbiton KT6 197 D3
West Drayton UB7 104 B3
1 West Wickham BR4 207 D1
Wimbledon SW19 180 A4
North Residence IG3 58 B4
North Ride W2 114 C6 247 A5
North Rise W2 237 B1
Northrop Rd TW6 127 C4
North Row W1 115 A6 248 A6
NORTH SHEEN 132 C3
North Sheen Sta TW10 132 C1
Northside Prim Sch N12 30 A5
Northside Rd BR1 187 A2
North Side Wandsworth Comm SW18 158 B6
Northspur Rd SM1 217 C5
North Sq Edmonton N9 18 B2
Hampstead Garden Suburb NW11 47 C4
North St Barking IG11 79 A1
Bexleyheath DA7 147 C1
Bromley BR1 187 A2
Carshalton SM5 218 D4
Clapham SW4 137 C2
Northstead Rd SW2 160 C2
North St Hendon NW4 46 C4
Isleworth TW7 131 A2
Newham E13 99 B5
North Tenter St E1 243 D1
North Terr SW3 257 A5
Northumberland Alley EC3 243 B1
Northumberland Ave
Enfield EN1 6 B4
Falconwood DA16 145 C2
Hounslow TW7 130 D4
Wanstead E12 55 C1
Westminster WC2 116 A5 250 A4
Northumberland Cl TW19 148 A5
Northumberland Cres TW14 149 C5
Northumberland Ct
3 Hounslow TW3 129 D1
South Croydon CR2 221 C3
Northumberland Gdns
Brentford TW7 131 A5
Bromley BR1 210 C5
Edmonton N9 17 D1

Northumberland Gdns
continued
Mitcham CR4 203 D4
Northumberland Gr N17 34 B3
Northumberland Heath Prim Sch DA8 147 D5
Northumberland Ho
Finchley N12 29 D4
Kentish Town NW5 71 C2
Northumberland Mans E5 74 C4
Northumberland Park Com Sch N17 34 A3
Northumberland Park Ind Est N17 34 B3
Northumberland Park Sports Ctr N17 34 A3
Northumberland Park Sta N17 34 B3
Northumberland Pk
Erith DA8 147 D5
Tottenham N17 34 A3
Northumberland Pl
Notting Hill W2 91 C1
20 Richmond TW10 153 D6
Northumberland Rd
Harrow HA2 41 C4
New Barnet EN5 14 A4
Newham E6 100 A1
Walthamstow E17 53 C2
Northumberland St WC2 250 A4
Northumbria Ct 10 TW9 132 A1
Northumbria St E14 97 C1
North Verbena Gdns 2 W6 112 A1
Northview Cres NW10 67 D4
Northview Dr IG8 37 D1
North View W5 87 C3
Northview 1 N7 72 A5
North View HA5 40 C2
Northview Prim Sch NW10 67 D4
North View Rd N8 49 D6
North View SW19 178 C5
North Villas NW1 71 D2
Northway Cir NW7 27 B6
Northway Cres NW7 27 C6
Northway Ct NW7 27 B6
North Way N11 31 C4
Northway NW11 47 D4
North Way N9 18 D2
Northway SM4 201 A5
North Way
Pinner HA5 40 D5
Queensbury NW9 44 D6
Northway Rd
Camberwell SE5 139 A2
Croydon CR0 205 D2
Northway Sch NW7 11 B1
Northways Par 2 NW3 70 B1
North Way UB10 60 A1
Northway SM6 219 C4
Northweald La KT2 175 D5
NORTH WEMBLEY 65 C6
North Wembley Sta HA0, HA9 65 D5
North Western Ave (Tylers Way) WD23 8 C6
North Western Ave (Watford By-Pass) WD6 9 B4
Northwest Pl N1 234 B4
North Wharf Rd W2 92 B2 236 C3
Northwick Ave HA3 43 B3
Northwick Circ HA3 43 C3
Northwick Cl
Harrow HA1 43 B1
Lisson Gr NW8 92 B3 236 C6
Northwick Ho NW8 236 B6
Northwick Park Hospl HA1 43 A2
Northwick Park Rd HA1 42 D3
Northwick Park Sta HA3 43 B2
Northwick Rd
South Oxhey WD19 22 C6
Wembley HA0 87 D6
Northwick Terr NW8 92 B3 236 C6
North Wlk
Bayswater W2 114 A6 246 A5
New Addington CR0 224 A3
Northwold Dr HA5 40 C6
Northwold Prim Sch E5 74 A6
Northwold Rd E5, N16 74 A6
NORTHWOOD 22 A3

Northwood Gdns
Greenford UB6 6
Ilford IG5 5
North Finchley N12 3
NORTHWOOD HILLS 2
Northwood Hills Cir HA6 2
Northwood Hills Sta HA6 2
North Wood Lo NW3 6
Northwood & Pinner Com Hospl HA6 22
Northwood Pl DA18 12
Northwood Prim Sch DA18 12
Northwood Rd
Forest Hill SE23 16
Highgate N6 4
South Norwood CR7 183
Wallington SM5 219
Northwood Sch HA6 22
Northwood Twr 1 E17 54
Northwood Way
Northwood HA6 22
1 West Norwood SE19 183
NORTH WOOLWICH 122
North Woolwich Rdbt E16 121
North Woolwich Rd E16 121
North Worple Way SW14 133
Norton Ave KT5 198
Norton Cl
Chingford E4 35
Enfield EN1 6
Norton Ct
Beckenham BR3 185
Ilford IG2 57
Norton Folgate E1 243
Norton Gdns SW16 182
Norton Ho
14 Globe Town E2 96
6 New Malden KT3 199
30 Stepney E1 96
16 Stockwell SW9 138
Norton Rd
Walthamstow E10 53
Wembley HA0 65
Norval Gn 1 SW9 138
Norval Rd HA0 43
Norvic Ho 5 SE5 139
Norway Gate SE16 119
Norway Pl E14 97
Norway St SE10 141
Norwegian Sch The SW20 178
Norwich Cres RM6 58
Norwich Ho 6 E14 97
Norwich Mews IG3 58
Norwich Pl 7 DA6 147
Norwich Rd
Forest Gate E7 77
Greenford UB6 85
Northwood HA6 39
South Norwood CR7 205
Norwich St EC4 94 C1 241
Norwich Wlk HA8 27
Norwood Ave HA0 88
Norwood Cl
Cricklewood NW2 69
Southall UB2 107
Twickenham TW2 152
Norwood Dr HA2 41
Norwood Gdns
Hayes UB4 84
Southall UB2 107
NORWOOD GREEN 107
Norwood Green Inf Sch UB2 107
Norwood Green Jun Sch UB2 107
Norwood Green Rd UB2 107
Norwood Heights Sh Ctr 18 SE19 183 C
Norwood High St SE27 183
Norwood Ho 25 E14 119
Norwood Hospl SE19 183
Norwood Junction Sta SE25 206
NORWOOD NEW TOWN 183
Norwood Park Rd SE27 183
Norwood Rd
Southall UB2 107 C
West Norwood SE24, SE27 160 D

wood Sch SE19 ... 183 A5
wood Terr UB2 ... 107 D2
ey St SE5 ... 139 B5
e Dame RC Girls
h SE1 ... 116 D3 261 D5
e Dame RC Prim
h SE18 ... 144 D6
on Rd SE25 ... 206 B5
ing Barn Rd
0 ... 90 D3
ingdale Sq W11 244 A4
ingham Ave E16 .. 99 C1
ingham Ct WC2. 240 A1
ingham Ho
Camberwell
E5 ... 139 A3
ke Newington N4 ... 51 A1
ingham Pl
... 93 A2 238 A4
ingham Rd
ydon CR2 ... 221 A3
worth TW7 ... 130 D3
tonstone E10 ... 54 A3
er Tooting
W17 ... 158 D3
ingham St W1 ... 238 A4
ingham Terr
1 ... 238 A5
TING HILL ... 113 B6
ing Hill & Ealing
gh Sch W13 ... 87 B2
ing Hill Gate Sta
1 ... 113 C5 245 A4
ing Hill Gate
... 113 C5 245 A4
ngwood Ho
... 244 A6
Bldg 1 E14 ... 119 C2
Ct E 3 E14 ... 120 A5
Ct W 2 E14 ... 120 A5
Mews SM4 ... 201 A2
r Cl BR6 ... 211 D2
Rd CR0 ... 205 A2
r Rd SE9 ... 167 A3
llo St
6 ... 135 C4 265 A2
ell Rd SW13 ... 134 A6
er Ct HA5 ... 41 B5
ER HILL ... 41 B6
er Hill High Sch
... 41 C5
er Hill HA5 ... 41 B5
a Rd SW17 ... 158 D1
a Way SE6 ... 164 C1
eus NW10 ... 89 A4
ng Cl SE13 ... 141 C2
eld Ct TW5 ... 129 B5
eld Lo 14 W9 ... 91 C2
nt Ct
atham SW16 ... 181 C6
Upper Holloway
19 ... 50 A1
ent Rd
bury Pk N19 ... 50 A1
th Norwood
25 ... 205 D6
nts Ct HA5 ... 23 A2
nt's Pk HA5 ... 23 B2
nt Terr
... 92 A5 229 B3
a Ct TW8 ... 131 D5
Ct EC2 ... 242 C2
aton Rd RM9 ... 81 A1
ham SW16 ... 181 D6
HEAD ... 140 C1
ead Cres SE15 ... 140 B2
ead Gn SE15 ... 140 B2
ead Gr SE15 ... 140 C2
ead La SE15 ... 140 B2
ead Sta SE15 .. 140 C3
ington Cl SE9 ... 166 A1
's Rd EN2 ... 5 A3
on Dr EN5 ... 12 C5
Cl HA8 ... 27 A2
ery Ave
eyheath DA7 ... 147 B2
don CR0 ... 222 D6
ley N3 ... 30 A1
ery Cl
m Hill BR6 ... 211 D2
don CR0 ... 222 D6
nham RM6 ... 58 D3
eld EN3 ... 6 D4
am TW14 ... 150 B4
Cross SE4 ... 141 B3
ey SW15 ... 134 D1
dford IG8 ... 37 B5
ery Ct
g W13 ... 87 A2
ottenham N17 ... 33 D3
ery Gdns
ehurst BR7 ... 188 D4
ld EN3 ... 6 D4
pton TW13 ... 173 B6
nslow TW4 ... 151 B6
ury TW16 ... 171 D1

Nursery La
Forest Gate E7 ... 77 A2
Hillingdon UB8 ... 82 A3
North Kensington
W10 ... 90 C2
Shoreditch E2 ... 95 D6
Nurserymans Rd N11 .. 15 A2
Nursery Rd
Finchley N2 ... 30 B2
Hackney E9 ... 74 C2
Loughton IG10 ... 21 C6
Merton SW19 ... 179 D1
Mitcham CR4 ... 202 C6
Osidge N14 ... 15 C4
Pinner HA5 ... 40 C6
South Norwood CR7 .. 205 B5
Stockwell SW9 ... 138 B1
Sunbury TW16 ... 171 D1
Sutton SM1 ... 218 A4
Wimbledon SW19 ... 179 A3
Nursery Row SE17 .. 262 C3
Nursery St N17 ... 33 D3
Nursery Walk Ct
NW4 ... 46 B6
Nursery Wlk NW4 ... 46 C6
Nurstead Rd DA8 ... 147 C5
Nutborn Ho SW19 ... 178 D4
Nutbourne St W10 ... 91 A4
Nutbrook St SE15 ... 140 A2
Nutbrowne Rd RM9 .. 103 B6
Nutchford EN1 ... 17 C5
Nutcroft Rd SE15 ... 140 B5
Nutfield Cl
Carshalton SM5 ... 218 C5
Edmonton N18 ... 34 A4
Nutfield Gdns
Ilford IG3 ... 80 A6
Northolt UB5 ... 84 C5
Nutfield Pl 1 CR7 ... 204 D5
Nutfield Rd
Dollis Hill NW2 ... 68 A5
East Dulwich SE22 ... 139 D1
Leyton E15 ... 76 A4
Thornton Heath CR7 . 204 D5
Nutfield Way BR6 ... 226 D6
Nutford Pl
W1 ... 92 D1 237 C2
Nuthatch Cl TW19 ... 148 B3
Nuthatch Gdns
SE28 ... 123 B4
Nuthurst Ave SW2 ... 160 B2
Nutkin Wlk UB8 ... 60 A1
Nutley Terr NW3 ... 70 B2
Nutmeg Cl E16 ... 98 C3
Nutmeg La E14 ... 98 B1
Nuttall St N1 ... 95 C5
Nutter La E11 ... 55 C4
Nutt Gr HA8 ... 9 D2
Nutt St SE15 ... 139 D5
Nutty La TW17 ... 193 A6
Nutwell St SW17 ... 180 C5
Nuxley Rd DA17 ... 125 C1
NW London Jewish Day
Sch NW6 ... 69 A1
Nyanza St SE18 ... 145 B6
Nye Bevan Est E5 ... 74 D5
Nye Bevan Ho SW6 .. 264 C4
Nye's Wharf SE1,
SE15 ... 140 A6
Nylands Ave TW9 ... 132 C3
Nymans Gdns SW20 .. 200 B6
Nynehead St SE14 ... 141 A5
Nyon Gr SE6 ... 163 B2
Nyton Cl N19 ... 50 A1

O

O2 Millennium Dome
The* SE10 ... 120 C5
Oak Apple Ct SE12 ... 165 A3
Oak Ave
Croydon CR0 ... 223 D6
Enfield EN2 ... 4 B5
Hampton TW12,
TW13 ... 173 A4
Heston TW5 ... 129 A5
Hornsey N8 ... 50 A5
Muswell Hill N10 ... 31 B3
Tottenham N17 ... 33 C3
Uxbridge UB10 ... 60 D6
West Drayton UB7 ... 104 C3
Oakbank Ave KT12 ... 195 B2
Oakbank Gr SE24 ... 139 A1
Oak Bank CR0 ... 224 A2
Oakbark Ho 10 TW8 .. 131 C5
Oakbrook 3 BR3 ... 185 D1
Oakbrook Cl BR1 ... 187 B6
Oakbury Rd SW6 ... 135 D3
Oak Cl
East Barnet N14 ... 15 B4
Sutton SM1 ... 218 A6
Oakcombe Cl KT3 ... 177 C2
Oak Cottage Cl 11
SE6 ... 164 D3
Oak Cotts W7 ... 108 C4
Oakcourt 17 SE15 ... 139 D5

Oak Cres E16 ... 98 C2
Oakcroft Bsns Ctr
KT9 ... 214 B4
Oakcroft Cl HA5 ... 22 B1
Oakcroft Ct SE3 ... 143 A4
Oakcroft Ho 3 KT3 .. 199 C2
Oakcroft Rd
Chessington KT9 ... 214 B4
Lewisham SE13 ... 142 B3
Oakcroft SE12 ... 165 B1
Oakcroft Villas KT9 ... 214 B4
Oak Ct Bickley BR1 ... 188 B1
Chingford E4 ... 35 D4
Oakdale Ave
Harrow HA3 ... 44 A4
Pinner HA6 ... 22 A1
Oakdale BR3 ... 186 A1
Oakdale Cl WD19 ... 22 C6
Oakdale Ct
Chingford E4 ... 36 A5
Upper Holloway N19 ... 72 A6
Oakdale N14 ... 15 B3
Oakdale Gdns E4 ... 36 A5
Oakdale Inf Sch E18 .. 37 B1
Oakdale Jun Sch E18 . 37 B1
Oakdale Lo NW4 ... 29 A2
Oakdale Rd
Leyton E11 ... 76 B6
Nunhead SE15 ... 140 C2
South Oxhey WD19 ... 22 C6
Streatham SW16 ... 182 A5
Tottenham N4 ... 51 B3
Upton E7 ... 77 B1
Woodford E18 ... 37 B1
Oakdale Way CR4 ... 203 A2
Oakdene Ave
Chislehurst West
BR7 ... 188 C5
Thames Ditton KT7 .. 197 A1
Oakdene Cl HA5 ... 23 B3
Oakdene Ct
Feltham TW12 ... 173 B6
1 Streatham SW16 . 182 A5
Oakdene Dr KT5 ... 199 A1
Oak Dene W13 ... 87 B2
Oakdene Ho
Enfield EN2 ... 4 D2
11 Stamford Hill N16 .. 51 C1
Oakdene Lo 3
SE20 ... 184 B3
Oakdene Mews
SM3 ... 201 B1
Oakdene 3 SE15 ... 140 B4
Oakdene Pk N3 ... 29 B3
Oakdene Rd
Hillingdon UB10 ... 82 D5
Orpington BR5 ... 211 D4
Oakdene 1 SE19 ... 183 C5
Oakden St
SE11 ... 116 C2 261 B4
Oake Ct SW15 ... 157 A6
Oakeford Ho W14 ... 254 B5
Oakend Ho 10 N4 ... 51 B2
Oaken Dr KT10 ... 212 D2
Oakenholt Ho 1
SE2 ... 124 D4
Oaken La KT10 ... 212 C3
Oakenshaw Cl KT6 ... 198 A2
Oakes Cl E6 ... 100 B1
Oakeshott Ave N6 ... 71 A6
Oakey La SE1 ... 261 A6
Oak Farm WD6 ... 11 A6
Oak Farm Jun & Inf
Schs UB10 ... 82 D6
Oakfield Ave HA3 ... 43 B6
Oakfield E4 ... 35 D5
Oakfield Cl
New Malden KT3 ... 199 D4
Ruislip HA4 ... 39 D3
Oakfield Ct
Clapham Pk SW4 ... 160 A5
2 Ealing W5 ... 110 C5
Finchley N3 ... 29 D2
Finsbury Pk N8 ... 50 A2
Hendon NW2 ... 46 D2
South Croydon CR2 .. 221 A2
Oakfield Gdns
Beckenham BR3 ... 207 C4
Carshalton SM5 ... 202 D1
Edmonton N18 ... 33 C6
Greenford UB6 ... 86 B4
3 West Norwood
SE19 ... 183 C5
Oakfield Ho 2 IG1 ... 78 D5
Oakfield La BR2 ... 225 C4
Oakfield Lo 8 IG1 ... 78 D5
Oakfield Prep Sch
SE21 ... 161 B3
Oakfield Rd
Ashford TW15 ... 170 D5
Croydon CR0 ... 205 A1
Finchley N3 ... 29 D2
Finsbury Pk N4 ... 50 C2
Higham Hill E17 ... 35 A1
Ilford IG1 ... 78 D5
Newham E6 ... 100 A6
Palmers Green N14 ... 16 A2

Oakfield Rd *continued*
Penge SE20 ... 184 B3
Wimbledon SW19 ... 156 D1
Oakfield Road Ind Est
11 SE20 ... 184 B3
Oakfields Rd NW11 ... 47 A3
Oakfield St
SW10 ... 136 A6 266 A6
Oakfields KT12 ... 194 A1
Oakford Rd NW5 ... 71 C4
Oak Gdns
Croydon CR0 ... 223 C6
Hendon HA8 ... 27 A1
Oak Grove Rd SE20 ... 184 C1
Oak Gr Ruislip HA4 ... 40 B1
Sunbury TW16 ... 172 B3
West Hampstead
NW2 ... 69 A4
West Wickham BR4 .. 208 A1
Oakhall Ct
Ashford TW16 ... 171 D5
Wanstead E11 ... 55 B3
Oakhall Dr TW16 ... 171 D5
Oak Hall Rd E11 ... 55 B3
Oakham Cl
Cockfosters EN4 ... 2 D2
Forest Hill SE6 ... 163 B2
Oakham Dr BR2 ... 208 D5
Oakham Ho 5 W10 ... 90 C3
Oakhampton Rd
NW7 ... 28 D3
Oakhill Ave
Pinner HA5 ... 23 A1
West Hampstead
NW3 ... 69 D4
Oak Hill IG8 ... 36 C3
Oakhill KT10 ... 213 A2
Oak Hill Cl IG8 ... 36 B3
Oakhill Coll N14 ... 15 A5
Oak Hill Cres
Chingford IG8 ... 36 C3
Surbiton KT6 ... 198 A2
Oak Hill Ct IG8 ... 36 C3
Oakhill Ct
Honor Oak SE23 ... 162 C5
Putney SW15 ... 157 B6
8 Surbiton KT6 ... 198 A3
Wimbledon SW19 ... 178 D3
Oak Hill Gdns E4 ... 36 C2
Oak Hill Gr KT6 ... 198 A3
Oakhill Ho BR5 ... 190 A2
Oak Hill Lo NW3 ... 69 D4
Oakhill Mans EN4 ... 14 C5
Oak Hill Park Mews
NW3 ... 70 A4
Oak Hill Pk NW3 ... 69 D4
Oakhill Pl SW15 ... 157 C6
Oakhill Prim Sch
IG8 ... 36 C4
Oakhill Rd
Beckenham BR3 ... 186 A1
Orpington BR6 ... 227 D6
Putney SW15 ... 157 B6
Oak Hill Rd KT6 ... 198 A3
Oakhill Rd
Sutton SM1 ... 218 A5
Thornton Heath
SW16 ... 182 B2
Oak Hill KT6 ... 198 A2
Oak Hill Way NW3 ... 70 A4
Oak Ho
13 Cubitt Town
E14 ... 120 A4
11 Finchley N2 ... 30 B1
8 Maitland Pk NW3 ... 70 D2
Penge SE20 ... 184 B1
2 Richmond TW9 ... 132 D4
13 Sidcup DA15 ... 168 A1
9 Stoke Newington
N16 ... 73 B6
Teddington TW11 ... 175 C4
Oakhouse Rd DA6 ... 169 C6
Oak Ho N22 ... 32 A3
Oakhurst Ave
East Barnet EN4 ... 14 C4
Erith DA7 ... 147 A5
Oakhurst Cl
Chislehurst BR7 ... 188 B2
Snaresbrook E17 ... 54 C5
4 Teddington
TW11 ... 174 C5
Oakhurst Ct E17 ... 54 C5
Oakhurst Gdns
Chingford E4 ... 20 D3
Erith DA7 ... 147 A5
Snaresbrook E11, E17 .. 54 C5
Oakhurst Gr SE22 ... 140 A1
Oakhurst Rd KT19 ... 215 B2
Oakington Ave
Harrow HA2 ... 41 C2
Hayes UB3 ... 105 B2
Wembley HA9 ... 66 B5
Oakington Cl TW16 .. 172 C1
Oakington Ct 1 EN2 ... 4 D3
Oakington Dr TW16 .. 172 C1
Oakington 14 KT1 ... 176 C1

Oakington Manor Dr
HA9 ... 66 C3
Oakington Manor Prim
Sch HA9 ... 66 D3
Oakington Rd W9 ... 91 C3
Oakington Way N8 ... 50 A2
Oak La Finchley N2 ... 30 B1
Friern Barnet N11 ... 31 D4
Isleworth TW7 ... 130 C1
Limehouse E14 ... 119 B6
Oakland Pl IG9 ... 21 A2
Oakland Rd E15 ... 76 C4
Oaklands Ave
Enfield N9 ... 18 B5
Hounslow TW7 ... 130 D6
Sidcup DA15 ... 167 D4
Thames Ditton KT10 .. 196 B1
Thornton Heath CR7 . 204 C5
West Wickham BR4 .. 223 D5
Oaklands BR7 ... 189 B4
Oaklands Cl
Bexley DA6 ... 169 B6
Chessington KT9 ... 213 C4
Orpington BR5 ... 211 C3
Oaklands CR0 ... 220 D3
Oaklands Ct
Beckenham BR3 ... 186 A1
Dagenham NW10 ... 89 C6
Orpington BR6 ... 227 A6
5 Shepherd's Bush
W12 ... 112 B5
Wembley HA0 ... 65 D3
Oaklands Dr TW2 ... 152 A4
Oaklands W13 ... 87 A2
Oaklands Gr W12 ... 112 A5
Oaklands Ho SE4 ... 141 B2
Oaklands Mews 1
NW2 ... 68 D4
Oaklands Park Ave
IG1 ... 79 A6
Oaklands Pas NW2 ... 68 D4
Oaklands Pl 8
SW4 ... 137 D1
Oaklands Prim Sch
W7 ... 108 D4
Oaklands Rd
Barnet N20 ... 13 B4
Bexley DA6 ... 169 B6
Bromley BR1 ... 186 C3
Cricklewood NW2 ... 68 D4
Ealing W7 ... 108 D4
Mortlake SW14 ... 133 B2
West Ealing W7,
W13 ... 109 A4
Oaklands Sch
Hounslow TW3 ... 130 B2
Loughton IG10 ... 21 D6
Oaklands Sec Sch E2 . 96 B4
Oaklands
Southgate N21 ... 16 B2
Twickenham TW2 ... 152 A4
Oaklands Way SM6 ... 219 D1
Oakland Way KT19 ... 215 C2
Oak La TW1 ... 153 A4
Oaklawn Ct HA7 ... 25 B4
Oak La IG8 ... 36 D6
Oakleafe Gdns IG6 ... 56 D6
Oaklea Pas KT1 ... 197 D6
Oakleigh Ave
East Barnet N20 ... 14 C3
Edgware HA8 ... 26 D2
Tolworth KT6 ... 214 D6
Oakleigh Cl N20 ... 14 D1
Oakleigh Cres N20 ... 14 C1
Oakleigh Ct
East Barnet EN4 ... 14 C5
Hendon HA8 ... 27 A1
7 Penge SE20 ... 184 B3
Southall UB1 ... 107 B5
Surbiton KT6 ... 214 B6
Oakleigh Gdns
Edgware HA8 ... 26 B5
Oakleigh Pk N20 ... 14 B3
Orpington BR6 ... 227 C4
Oakleigh Lodge IG3 ... 80 A5
Oakleigh Mews 2
N20 ... 14 A2
OAKLEIGH PARK ... 14 B3
Oakleigh Park Ave
BR7 ... 188 C2
Oakleigh Park Sta
EN4 ... 14 C4
Oakleigh Pk N N20 ... 14 B3
Oakleigh Pk S N20 ... 14 C3
Oakleigh Rd UB10 ... 61 A1
Oakleigh Rd N N20 ... 14 C2
Oakleigh Rd HA5 ... 23 B4
Oakleigh Rd S N11 ... 31 A6
Oakleigh Sch N20 ... 14 D1
Oakleigh Way
Mitcham CR4 ... 181 B2
1 Tolworth KT6 ... 198 D1
Oakley Ave
Barking IG11 ... 79 D1
Ealing W5 ... 110 C6
Wallington CR0 ... 220 A4

Oakley Cl
Chingford E4 ... 20 A1
Ealing W7 ... 108 C6
Hounslow TW7 ... 130 B4
7 Newham E6 ... 100 A1
Oakley Cres EC1 ... 234 D3
Oakley Ct
Carshalton CR4 ... 203 A2
Harlington UB7 ... 127 A5
Wembley HA0 ... 65 A4
Oakley Dr
Keston Mark BR2 ... 226 A5
Lewisham SE13 ... 164 B5
New Eltham SE9 ... 167 B3
Oakley Gdns
Chelsea
SW3 ... 136 C6 267 B6
Hornsey Vale N8 ... 50 B4
Oakley Ho
Chelsea SW1 ... 257 D4
Ealing W5 ... 110 C6
Oakley Pk DA5 ... 168 C4
Oakley Pl
SE1 ... 117 D1 263 C1
Oakley Rd
Croydon SE25 ... 206 B4
De Beauvoir Town N1 .. 73 B1
Harrow HA1 ... 42 C3
Keston Mark BR2 ... 226 A6
Oakley Sq
NW1 ... 93 C5 232 B4
Oakley St
SW3 ... 136 C6 267 A6
Oakley Wlk W6 ... 134 D6
Oak Lo 4 TW16 ... 171 D3
Oak Lodge Cl HA7 ... 25 C5
Oak Lodge Dr BR4 ... 207 D2
Oak Lodge Sch
Balham SW12 ... 159 A4
East Finchley N2 ... 48 A5
Oaklodge Way NW7 ... 27 D4
Oak Lodge 14 SE21 ... 161 B2
Oak Lo Southgate N21 .. 16 B5
10 Sutton SM1 ... 218 A4
Wanstead E11 ... 55 A2
6 Wembley HA0 ... 65 D3
Oakman Ho 29
SW19 ... 156 D3
Oakmead Ave BR2 ... 209 A3
Oakmead Ct HA7 ... 25 C6
Oakmeade HA5 ... 23 C4
Oakmead Gdns HA8 ... 27 B6
Oakmead HA1 ... 64 B5
Oakmead Pl CR4 ... 180 C2
Oakmead Rd
Balham SW12 ... 159 B3
Wallington CR0 ... 203 D3
Oakmere Rd SE2 ... 146 A6
Oakmont Pl 6 BR6 .. 211 B1
Oak Park Gdns
SW19 ... 156 D3
Oak Park Mews N16 .. 73 D5
Oak Rd Ealing W5 ... 109 D6
Kingston u T KT3 ... 177 B1
Oakridge Dr N2 ... 48 B6
Oakridge La BR1 ... 186 B5
Oakridge Rd BR1 ... 186 C6
Oak Rise IG9 ... 21 D1
Oak Row CR4 ... 181 C1
Oaks Ave
Feltham TW13 ... 151 A2
North Cheam KT4 ... 216 B4
West Norwood SE19 . 183 C5
Oaksford Ave SE26 ... 162 B1
Oaks Gr E4 ... 20 C2
Oakshade Rd BR1 ... 186 B6
Oakshaw Rd SW18 ... 157 D4
Oakshott Ct NW1 ... 232 C3
Oaks La Ilford IG2 ... 57 C5
South Croydon CR0 .. 222 C5
Oaks Park High Sch
IG2 ... 57 C4
Oaks Rd CR0 ... 222 C4
Oaks Sh Ctr The
W3 ... 111 A5
Oaks The
Brondesbury Pk
NW6 ... 68 D1
Chingford IG8 ... 36 C3
Enfield EN2 ... 4 D2
Finchley N12 ... 29 D6
Hayes UB4 ... 83 A5
Long Ditton KT6 ... 213 C5
Ruislip HA4 ... 39 C2
Southborough BR2 .. 210 C3
Wallington SM6 ... 219 C4
Willesden NW10 ... 68 B1
Wimbledon SW19 ... 179 A4
Woolwich SE18 ... 123 A1
Oaks Way
Surbiton KT6 ... 197 D1
Wallington SM5 ... 218 D1
Oakthorpe Ct N13 ... 33 A5

Oakthorpe Prim Sch
N13 .... 33 A5
Oakthorpe Rd N13 .... 32 C5
Oaktree Ave N13 .... 16 D1
Oak Tree Ave N2 .... 47 D6
Oak Tree Cl
Ealing W5 .... 87 C1
Stanmore HA7 .... 25 C3
Oak Tree Ct
Acton W3 .... 110 D6
8 Clapham Pk SW4 . 160 A6
Elstree WD6 .... 9 D5
Oak Tree Dell NW9 .... 45 B4
Oak Tree Dr N20 .... 13 D3
Oak Tree Gdns BR1 .... 187 B5
Oaktree Gr IG1 .... 79 B3
Oak Tree Ho W9 .... 91 D3
Oak Tree Rd
NW8 .... 92 C4 230 A1
Oaktree Sch EN4 .... 15 A5
Oaktrees Hostel HA8 .. 11 A2
Oakview Gdns N2 .... 48 B5
Oakview Gr CR0 .... 207 A1
Oakview Lo NW11 .... 47 B2
Oakview Rd SE6 .... 185 D5
Oak Village NW5 .... 71 A4
Oakway BR2 .... 186 B1
Oakway Cl DA5 .... 169 A5
Oak Way
Croydon CR0 .... 206 D3
East Acton W3 .... 111 C5
East Barnet N14 .... 15 B4
East Bedfont TW14 .. 149 C3
Oakways SE9 .... 166 D5
Oakway SW20 .... 200 C5
Oakwell Ho 24 SW8 .. 137 D4
Oak Wlk CR4 .... 203 A1
OAKWOOD 15 D6
Oakwood Ave
Beckenham BR2,
BR3 .... 186 A1
Bromley BR2 .... 209 B6
Mitcham CR4 .... 180 B1
Osidge N14 .... 15 D4
Southall UB1 .... 107 C6
Oakwood Cl
Chislehurst West
BR7 .... 188 C4
Lewisham SE13 .... 164 B5
Southgate N14 .... 15 C5
Oakwood Cres
Southgate N21 .... 16 B5
Wembley UB6 .... 65 B2
Oakwood Ct
Beckenham BR3 .... 186 A1
6 Chingford E4 .... 20 C4
Kensington
W14 .... 113 B3 254 C6
1 Newham E6 .... 100 A6
17 Sutton SM1 .... 218 A4
Oakwood Dr
Burnt Oak HA8 .... 27 A4
West Norwood SE19 . 183 C4
Oakwood Gdns
Ilford IG3 .... 79 D6
Orpington BR6 .... 227 A6
Sutton SM1 .... 217 C6
Oakwood La
W14 .... 113 B3 254 C6
Oakwood Park Rd
N14 .... 16 A5
Oakwood Pl CR0 .... 204 C3
Oakwood Rd
Hampstead Garden
Suburb NW11 .... 47 D4
Orpington BR6 .... 227 A6
Pinner HA5 .... 22 B1
Thornton Heath CR0 . 204 C3
Wimbledon SW20 ... 178 A2
Oakwood Sta N14 .... 15 C6
Oakwood View N14 .... 15 D4
Oakworth Rd W10 .... 90 D2
Oarsman Pl KT8 .... 196 C5
Oasis The 6 BR1 .... 187 C1
Oast Ct 8 E14 .... 119 B6
Oast Lo W4 .... 133 C5
Oates Cl BR2 .... 208 B6
Oatfield Ho 1 N15 .... 51 C3
Oatfield Rd BR6 .... 211 D1
Oat La EC2 .... 95 A1 242 B2
Oatland Rise E17 .... 35 A1
Oatlands Ct 3
SW19 .... 156 D3
Oatlands Dr KT13 .... 193 C1
Oatlands Rd EN3 .... 6 C4
Oatwell Ho SW3 .... 257 B3
Oban Cl E13 .... 99 C3
Oban Ct HA8 .... 10 D2
Oban Ho
5 Barking IG11 .... 101 B5
South Bromley E14 .... 98 B1
Oban Rd Newham E13 .. 99 C4
South Norwood
SE25 .... 205 B5
Oban St E14 .... 98 B1
Oberon Ho 5 N1 .... 95 C5
Oberon Way TW17 ... 192 A6
Oberstein Rd 15
SW11 .... 136 B1
Oborne Cl SE24 .... 160 D6
O'Brian Ho 10 E1 .... 96 D4
Observatory Gdns
W8 .... 245 B2
Observatory Mews
E14 .... 120 B2
Observatory Rd
SW14 .... 133 A1
Occupation La
Brentford W5 .... 109 D2
Shooters Hill SE18 ... 144 D4
Occupation Rd
Newington
SE17 .... 117 A1 262 A2
West Ealing W13 .... 109 B4
Ocean St E1 .... 96 D2
Ocean Wharf E14 .... 119 C4
Ochre Ct TW13 .... 149 D1
Ockbrook 3 E1 .... 96 C2
Ockendon Rd N1 .... 73 B2
Ockham Dr BR5 .... 190 A3
Ockley Ct
Sidcup DA14 .... 167 C1
Sutton SM1 .... 218 A4
Ockley Ho 8 KT2 .... 176 D4
Ockley Rd
Streatham SW16 .... 160 A1
Thornton Heath CR0 .. 204 B2
Octagon Arc EC2 .... 243 A3
Octagon The NW3 .... 69 C4
Octavia Cl CR4 .... 202 C4
Octavia Ho
Catford SE6 .... 163 D4
Kensal Town W10 .... 91 A3
Octavia Mews 1 W9 .. 91 B3
Octavia Rd TW7 .... 130 D2
Octavia St
SW11 .... 136 C4 267 B1
Octavia Way 12
SE28 .... 124 B6
Octavius St SE8 .... 141 C5
October Ct BR2 .... 208 D6
October Pl NW4 .... 46 D6
Odard Rd KT8 .... 195 C5
Odell Cl IG11 .... 79 D1
Odell Wlk SE13 .... 142 A2
Odeon Ct
Dagenham NW10 .... 89 C6
1 Newham E16 .... 99 A2
Odeon Par
Eltham SE9 .... 144 A1
Wembley UB6 .... 65 B2
Odeon The IG11 .... 79 B1
Odessa Inf Sch E7 .... 77 A3
Odessa Rd Leyton E7 .... 76 D4
Willesden Green
NW10 .... 90 A5
Odessa St SE16 .... 119 B3
Odette Ct N20 .... 14 A1
Odette Duval Ho 29
E1 .... 96 C2
Odette Ho 6 SE27 ... 183 B6
Odger St SW11 .... 136 D3
Odhams Wlk WC2 .... 240 B1
Odin Ho 6 SE5 .... 139 A3
O'Donnell Ct WC1 ... 240 B6
O'Driscoll Ho 4 W12 . 90 B1
Odyssey Bsns Pk
HA4 .... 62 B3
Offa's Mead E9 .... 75 A4
Offenbach Ho 12 E2 ... 96 D5
Offenham Rd BR7,
SE9 .... 188 B6
Offers Ct KT1 .... 198 B6
Offerton Rd SW4 .... 137 C2
Offham Ho SE17 .... 263 A3
Offham Slope N12 .... 29 B5
Offley Ho 10 E9 .... 74 D2
Offley Pl TW7 .... 130 B3
Offley Rd SW9 .... 138 C5
Offord Cl N17 .... 34 A4
Offord Rd N1 .... 72 B1
Offord St N1 .... 72 B1
Ogden Ho TW13 .... 173 A6
Ogilby St SE18 .... 122 B2
Ogilvie Ho 12 E1 .... 96 D1
Oglander Rd SE15 .... 139 D2
Ogle St W1 .... 93 C2 239 A4
Oglethorpe Rd RM10 .. 81 C5
O'Gorman Ho SW10 . 266 B4
O'Grady Ct 17 W13 .. 109 A5
O'Grady Ho 17 E17 .... 53 D6
Ohio Bldg 13 SE13 ... 141 D4
Ohio Rd E13 .... 98 D3
Oil Mill La W6 .... 112 A1
Okeburn Rd SW17 .... 181 A5
Okehampton Cl N12 .... 30 B5
Okehampton Cres
DA16 .... 146 C4
Okehampton Rd
NW10 .... 90 D6
Okeover Manor
SW4 .... 137 B1
Olaf Palme Ho
TW13 .... 150 B1
Olaf St W11 .... 112 D6
Old Bailey
EC4 .... 94 D1 241 D1
Old Barn Cl SM2 .... 217 A1
Old Barrack Yd SW1 . 248 A1
Old Barrowfield 7
E15 .... 98 C6
Old Bellgate Wharf
E14 .... 119 C3
Oldberry Rd HA8 .... 27 B4
Old Bethnal Green Rd
E2 .... 96 B4
OLD BEXLEY 169 D4
Old Bexley Bsns Pk
DA5 .... 169 D4
Old Bexley CE Prim Sch
DA5 .... 169 B3
Old Billingsgate Wlk
EC3 .... 253 A5
Old Bldgs WC2 .... 241 A2
Old Bond St
W1 .... 115 C6 249 A5
Oldborough Rd HA0 ... 65 C5
Old Brewery Mews
NW3 .... 70 B4
Old Bridge Cl UB5 .... 85 C5
Old Bridge St KT1 .... 175 D1
Old Broad St
EC2 .... 95 B1 242 D2
Old Bromley Rd
BR1 .... 186 B5
Old Brompton Rd SW5,
SW7 .... 114 A2 256 B3
Old Burlington St
W1 .... 115 C6 249 A5
Oldbury Ct E9 .... 75 A3
Oldbury Pl
W1 .... 93 A2 238 B4
Oldbury Rd EN1 .... 6 A3
Old Castle St
E1 .... 95 D1 243 D2
Old Cavendish St
W1 .... 238 C1
Old Change Ct EC4 .. 242 A1
Old Chapel Pl 2 N10 .. 49 B6
Old Charlton Rd
TW17 .... 193 A4
Old Chiswick Yd
W4 .... 133 C6
Old Church Ct N11 .... 31 B5
Old Church La
Ealing UB6 .... 87 A4
Stanmore HA7 .... 25 C4
Welsh Harp NW9 .... 67 B6
Old Church Path
KT10 .... 212 A4
Old Church Rd
Chingford E4 .... 19 C1
Stepney E1 .... 96 D1
Old Church St SW3 .. 256 D1
Old Claygate La
KT10 .... 213 A3
Old Clem Sq 12
SE18 .... 144 C6
Old College Ct
DA17 .... 125 D1
Old Compton St
W1 .... 93 D1 239 C1
Old Cote Dr TW5 .... 129 C6
Old Court Ho W8 ... 245 C1
Old Court (Mus &
Liby)* HA0 .... 65 C3
Old Court Pl
W8 .... 113 D4 245 C1
Old Covent Gdn*
WC2 .... 250 B6
Old Ctyd The BR1 .... 187 B2
Old Cty H* SE1 .... 250 C2
Old Dairy Mews
5 Balham SW12 ... 159 A3
4 Camden Town
NW5 .... 71 B2
Old Dairy Sq The
N21 .... 16 C4
Old Deer Park Gdns
TW9 .... 132 A2
Old Devonshire Rd
SW12 .... 159 B4
Old Dock Cl TW9 .... 132 C6
Old Dover Rd SE3 .... 143 B5
Oldegate Ho 1 E6 .... 99 D6
Old Farm Ave
Osidge N14 .... 15 C4
Sidcup DA15 .... 167 C2
Old Farm Cl TW4 .... 129 B1
Old Farm Ct UB2 .... 107 D2
Old Farm Rd E
DA15 .... 168 A2
Old Farm Rd
Hampton TW12 .... 173 C4
London N2 .... 30 B2
Old Farm Rd W
DA15 .... 167 D2
Oldfield Cl
Bromley BR1 .... 210 B5
Greenford UB6 .... 64 C2
Stanmore HA7 .... 25 A5
Oldfield Farm Gdns
UB6 .... 86 B6
Oldfield Gr SE16 .... 118 D2
Oldfield Ho
14 Chiswick W4 .... 111 C1
Streatham SW16 .... 181 B6
Oldfield House Unit
TW12 .... 173 B2
Oldfield La N UB6 .... 64 B1
Oldfield La S UB6 .... 86 A4
Oldfield Mews N6 .... 49 C2
Oldfield Prim Sch
UB6 .... 86 B5
Oldfield Rd
Bedford Pk W3,
W12 .... 111 D4
Bexleyheath DA7 .... 147 A3
Bromley BR1 .... 210 B5
Hampton TW12 .... 173 B2
Stoke Newington N16 .. 73 C5
Willesden NW10 .... 67 D1
Wimbledon SW19 ... 179 A4
Oldfields Cir UB5 .... 64 A2
Oldfields Rd SM1,
SM3 .... 217 C6
Oldfields Trad Est
SM1 .... 217 C5
Old Fire Station The
SE18 .... 144 D5
Old Fish St Hill EC4 . 252 A6
Old Fleet La EC4 .... 241 C2
Old Fold Cl EN5 .... 1 B4
Old Fold La EN5 .... 1 B4
OLD FORD 97 B6
Old Ford Ho CR0 .... 220 A5
Old Ford Prim Sch
E3 .... 97 B5
Old Ford Rd E2, E3 .... 96 D5
Old Ford Trad Ctr 18
E3 .... 97 C6
Old Forge Cl HA7 .... 25 A6
Old Forge Cres
TW17 .... 192 D3
Old Forge Mews
W12 .... 112 B4
Old Forge Rd
Enfield EN1 .... 5 D5
Upper Holloway N19 ... 71 D6
Old Forge Way
DA14 .... 190 B6
Old Gloucester St
WC1 .... 94 A2 240 B4
Old Hall Cl HA5 .... 23 A2
Old Hall Dr HA5 .... 23 A2
Oldham Ho 10 SE21 .. 183 C6
Oldham Terr W3 .... 111 A5
Old Hatch Manor
HA4 .... 40 A2
Old Hill
Chislehurst BR7 .... 188 C2
Orpington BR6 .... 227 C2
Oldhill St N16 .... 52 A1
Old Homesdale Rd
BR2 .... 209 C5
Old Hospital Cl SW12,
SW17 .... 158 D3
Old Ho The BR7 .... 189 B2
Old House Cl SW19 .. 179 A5
Old House Gdns 9
TW1 .... 153 C5
Old Howlett's La HA4 . 39 B3
Olding Ho 6 SW12 ... 159 C4
Old Jamaica Bsns Est 23
SE16 .... 118 A3
Old Jamaica Rd
SE16 .... 118 A3
Old James St SE15 ... 140 B2
Old Jewry
EC2 .... 95 B1 242 C1
Old Kenton La NW9 ... 44 D4
Old Kent Rd
Deptford SE1,
SE15 .... 140 B6
Walworth
SE1 .... 117 C1 263 B2
Old Kingston Rd
KT4 .... 215 A5
Old Laundry The 14
SW18 .... 136 B1
Old Lodge Pl 7
TW1 .... 153 B5
Old Lodge Way HA7 ... 25 A5
Old London Rd KT2 .. 176 A1
Old Maidstone Rd BR8,
DA14 .... 191 B3
OLD MALDEN 199 C1
Old Malden La KT4 ... 215 C6
Oldman Ct SE12 .... 165 B2
Old Manor Ct NW8 .. 229 B4
Old Manor Dr TW7 ... 152 A5
Old Manor House Mews
TW17 .... 192 C6
Old Manor Rd UB2 ... 106 D2
Old Manor Way BR7,
SE9 .... 188 B5
Old Manor Yd SW5 .. 255 C3
Old Market Ct SM1 ... 217 D4
Old Market Sq 11 E2 .. 95 D4
Old Marylebone Rd
NW1 .... 92 C2 237 B3
Oldmead Ho 8
RM10 .... 81 D2
Old Mill Ct E18 .... 55 C6
Old Mill Rd SE18 .... 145 B6
Old Mitre Ct EC4 .... 241 B1
Old Montague St E1 .. 96 A2
Old Nichol St
E2 .... 95 D3 243 C6
Old North St WC1 ... 240 C4
Old Nursery Pl
TW15 .... 170 D5
OLD OAK COMMON .. 89 D3
Old Oak Common La
NW10 .... 89 C3
Old Oak La NW10 .... 89 D4
Old Oak Prim Sch
W12 .... 89 D1
Old Oak Rd W3 .... 111 D6
Old Orchard Cl
Hadley Wood EN4 .... 2 B5
Hillingdon UB8 .... 82 C1
Old Orch TW16 .... 172 C1
Old Orch The NW3 .... 70 D4
Old Palace La TW9 ... 153 C6
Old Palace Prim Sch
E3 .... 97 D4
Old Palace Rd CR0 ... 221 A5
Old Palace Sch of John
Whitgift CR9 .... 220 D5
Old Palace Terr 8
TW9 .... 153 D6
Old Palace Yd 2
TW9 .... 153 D6
Old Paradise St
SE11 .... 116 B2 260 C4
Old Park Ave
Balham SW12 .... 159 A5
Enfield EN2 .... 5 A1
Old Park Gr EN2 .... 5 A1
Old Park Ho N13 .... 32 B6
Old Park La
W1 .... 115 B5 248 C3
Old Park Mews
TW5 .... 129 B5
Old Park Rd
Enfield EN2 .... 4 D2
Palmers Green N13 .... 32 B6
Plumstead Comm
SE2 .... 124 A1
Old Park Rd S EN2 .... 4 D1
Old Park Ridings
N21 .... 17 A6
Old Park View EN2 .... 4 D2
Old Perry St BR7 .... 189 C3
Old Post Office La
SE3 .... 143 B2
Old Pound Cl TW7 ... 131 A4
Old Priory UB9 .... 38 D2
Old Pye Street Est
SW1 .... 259 C5
Old Pye St SW1 .... 259 C6
Old Quebec St W1 .. 237 D1
Old Queen St
SW1 .... 115 D4 249 D1
Old Rd Enfield EN3 .... 6 C4
Lewisham SE13 .... 142 C1
Old Rectory Gdns
HA8 .... 26 C4
Old Redding HA3 .... 24 A6
Oldridge Rd SW12 ... 159 B4
Old Royal Free Pl
N1 .... 234 B5
Old Royal Free Sq
N1 .... 94 C6 234 B5
Old Ruislip Rd UB5 .... 84 C5
Old St Andrews Mans
NW9 .... 67 B6
Old School Cl
3 Beckenham
BR3 .... 185 A1
Merton SW19 .... 179 C1
Old School Cres E7 ... 77 A2
Old School Ct 8
N17 .... 51 D6
Old School Ho CR4 .. 202 C6
Old School Ho The
EN2 .... 4 D2
Old School Pl CR0 ... 220 C4
Old School Rd UB8 .... 82 B3
Old School Sq
12 Poplar E14 .... 97 C1
Thames Ditton KT7 .. 196 D3
Old School The
Bloomsbury WC1 .... 240 D4
Merton SW19 .... 179 C1
Old Seacoal La EC4 .. 241 C1
Old South Cl HA5 .... 22 D2
Old South Lambeth Rd
SW8 .... 138 A5 270 B4
Old Spitalfields Mkt
E1 .... 95 D2 2
Old Sq WC2 2
Old Stable Mews N5 ..
Old Station Rd UB3 .. 1
Old Station Yard The
E17 ....
Old St EC1 .... 95 B3 2
Oldstead Rd BR1 ....
Old St E13 ....
Old Street Sta
EC1 .... 95 B3 2
Old Studio Cl CR0 2
Old Sun Wharf E14 ..
Old Swan Wharf
SW11 2
Old Swan Yd SM5 2
Old Theatre Ct SE1 .. 2
Old Town
Clapham SW4 1
Croydon CR0 2
Old Tramyard SE18 ..
Old Twelve Cl W7 ..
Old Vicarage Sch
TW10 1
Old Vicarage The
CR4 2
Old Woolwich Rd
SE10 ....
Old York Rd SW18 1
Oleander Cl BR6 2
O'Leary Sq E1 ....
Oleastor Ct IG5 ....
Olga Prim Sch E3 ....
Olga St 20 E3 ....
Olinda Rd N16 ....
Oliphant St W10 ....
Olive Blythe Ho 14
W10 ....
Oliver Ave SE25 2
Oliver Bsns Pk NW10 .
Oliver Cl W4 1
Oliver Ct
Isleworth TW7 1
2 Penge SE26 1
Plumstead SE18 1
Olive Rd
Cricklewood NW2 ....
Ealing W5 1
3 Merton SW19 1
Newham E13 ....
Oliver Gdns E6 ....
Oliver Goldsmith
Prim Sch
Camberwell SE5 1
Kingsbury NW9 ....
Oliver Gr SE25 2
Oliver Ho
22 Bermondsey
SE16 ....
Notting Hill W11 2
South Lambeth SW8 . 2
Oliver House Prep Sc
SW4 ....
Oliver Mews SE15 ....
Oliver Rd
Kingston u T KT3 ....
Leyton E10 ....
Sutton SM1 2
Walthamstow E17 ....
Oliver's Yd EC1 2
Olive Tree Ho
7 Deptford SE15 ....
Stroud Green N4 ....
Olive Tree Sch The
SE13 1
Olivette St 1 SW15 ..
Olive Waite Ho NW6 .
Olivia Ct 1 EN5 ....
Ollard's Gr IG10 ....
Ollerton Gn E3 ....
Ollerton Rd N11 ....
Olley Cl SM6 ....
Ollgar Cl W12 ....
Olliffe St E14 ....
Olmar St SE1 ....
Olney Ho NW8 ....
Olney Rd SE17 ....
Olron Cres DA6 ....
Olven Rd SE18 ....
Olveston Wlk SM5 ..
Olwen Mews HA5 ....
Olyffe Ave DA16 ....
Olyffe Dr BR3 ....
Olympia Ex Ctr*
W14 .... 113 A3 2
Olympia Ind Est N22.
Olympian Ct 8 E14 ..
Olympia Way
W14 .... 113 A3 2
Olympia Yd W2 2
Olympic Ho 10 W10 ..
Olympic Ret Pk HA9 .
Olympic Way
Greenford UB6 ....
Wembley HA9 ....

ous Gr N22 32 C2
ous Sq E5 74 A5
Ave NW2 68 C4
Ct NW4 68 B4
ersley Ho N4 51 A2
ara St SE1 252 B3
ga Cl E14 119 D3
ga Ho SW10 266 B4
ga Pl N1 233 B3
ga St SE14 141 C4
ga Works E3 75 C1
aney Rd SE14 141 A4
ibus Bsns Ctr 72 A3
bus Way E17 35 C5
ne Rd SE15 139 D1
in Point 10 E1 118 A6
a Gate SE16 119 A3
ill Ho NW8 229 D3
ll Path 11
3 144 C6
ree Cl SE23 162 C5
r Cl RM6 58 C4
r Ho 15 N1 73 B2
r Rd
135 C6 265 B6
Rd E17 53 C2
ow Avenue Mans 10
0 154 A6
ow Ave TW10 154 A6
ow Cl
gford E4 20 B2
ing Hill W9 91 B4
nes Ditton KT7 196 C1
ow Cres BR7 188 D2
ow Ct SW10 256 B1
ow Dr DA14 168 D2
ow Gdns
sea
W7 114 B1 256 C2
ley Gdns N10 49 B4
thgate N21 16 C6
mes Ditton KT7 196 C1
lington SM6 219 C1
stead E18 55 C6
ow Ho 1 KT2 176 B2
ow Lo 28 SW2 160 C4
ow Mews E
256 C3
ow Mews W
256 C3
ow Par N14 15 B3
ow Rd
mond TW10 154 A5
rnton Heath CR0 204 C1
st Barnes KT3 200 A5
ow Sq
114 B2 256 D3
ow St EC1 241 B5
ow Way KT7 196 C1
rio St
116 D3 261 D6
rio Way E14 119 C6
Ct N11 31 D3
Ho KT4 199 B1
Mews 4 E15 76 D2
Cl E16 99 D1
Ct N11 31 D3
Ho KT4 199 B1
Mews 2 IG1 78 D6
St SE11 116 D1 261 C2
Air Theatre,
gent's Pk*
1 231 A1
nshaw Rd SE2 124 B2
nview SW17,
18 158 B2
a Ct 7 N19 71 D5
rating Theatre Mus
Herb Garret*
117 B5 252 D3
elia Gdns NW2 69 A5
r Terr SE15 140 A4
Ho NW8 230 B4
ssum Way TW4 128 C2
enheim Rd
3 142 A3
dan Apartments
6 69 C2
dans Rd NW3 70 D1
Studios E13 99 A5
ge Gr E11 76 C5
ge Hill Rd HA8 27 A3
ge Pl SE16 118 C3
gery Gallery The*
113 B4 244 C1
gery La SE9 166 B6
gery The TW10 153 C2
ge St
2 115 D6 249 D5
ge Yd WC2 239 D1
say Rd 25 N1 73 A2
ory La SW3 256 D2
ory RC Prim Sch
3 114 C1 257 A2
ory The*
7 114 C3 257 A5

Orbain Rd SW6 135 A5 264 B3
Orbel St SW11 136 C4 267 A1
Orb St SE17 117 B2 262 C3
Orchard Ave
Ashford TW15 171 A4
Carshalton CR4 203 A1
Croydon CR0 207 A1
East Finchley N3 47 C6
Erith DA17 147 B6
Hatton TW14 149 B6
Heston TW5 129 A5
Hinchley Wood KT7 213 A6
Kingston u T KT3 199 C6
Osidge N14 15 C4
Southall UB1 107 B5
Whetstone N20 14 B2
Orchard Bsns Ctr SE26 185 B5
Orchard Cl
Ashford TW15 171 A4
Bexleyheath DA7 147 A4
Bushey WD23 8 B3
Chingford E4 35 C6
Dollis Hill NW2 68 A5
Edgware HA8 26 A4
Honor Oak SE23 162 C5
Islington N1 73 A1
Kensal Town W10 91 A2
Northolt UB5 64 A2
Ruislip HA4 39 A2
Thames Ditton KT7 197 B2
Walton-on-T KT12 194 B2
Wanstead E11 55 B5
Wembley HA0 88 A6
West Barnes SW20 200 C5
West Ewell KT19 214 D2
Orchard Cotts
Chislehurst BR7 189 C4
Hayes UB3 105 C4
Orchard Cres
Edgware HA8 27 A5
Enfield EN1 5 D4
Orchard Ct
Barnes SW13 133 D2
Barnet EN5 1 D2
Croydon BR3 207 C1
Edgware HA8 26 B5
Hounslow TW7 130 B5
Marylebone W1 238 A2
New Malden KT4 200 A1
Penge SE26 184 D5
Southgate N14 15 C5
Wallington SM6 219 B3
Walthamstow E10 53 D1
1 Walton-on-T KT12 193 D1
Wood Green N22 32 A3
Orchard Dr
Blackheath Vale SE3 142 C3
Edgware HA8 26 B5
Upper Halliford TW17 193 C6
Orchard Gate
Colindale NW9 45 C5
Thames Ditton KT10 196 B1
Wembley UB6 65 B2
Orchard Gdns
Chessington KT9 214 A4
Sutton SM1 217 C3
Orchard Gn
Bromley BR1 187 C2
Orpington BR6 227 C6
Orchard Gr BR6 227 D6
Croydon CR0 207 A2
Edgware HA8 26 D2
Harrow HA3 44 B4
Orpington BR6 211 D1
Penge SE20 184 A3
Orchard Hill Coll SM6 219 B2
Orchard Hill SE13 141 D4
Orchard Ho
Camberwell SE5 139 A4
11 Rotherhithe SE16 118 C3
Shepherd's Bush W12 112 A5
Orchard Inf Sch The KT8 196 B5
Orchard Jun & Inf Sch The TW3 151 C6
Orchard La
Thames Ditton KT8 196 B3
Wimbledon SW20 178 B2
Woodford IG8 37 C6
Orchardleigh Ave EN3 6 C3
Orchard Lo N12 14 A1
Orchard Mead Ho NW11 69 C6
Orchardmede N21 17 B5
Orchard Mews N1 73 B1

Orchard Pl
Canning Town E14 120 C6
Tottenham N17 33 D3
Orchard Prim Sch E9 74 C1
Orchard Rd Barnet EN5 1 B1
Belvedere DA17 125 C2
Brentford TW8 131 C6
Bromley BR1 187 C2
Carshalton CR4 203 A1
Chessington KT9 214 A4
Dagenham RM10 103 C6
Enfield EN3 18 C6
Farnborough BR6 226 D3
Feltham TW14 150 A3
Hampton TW12 173 B3
Hayes UB3 106 A6
Highgate N6 49 B2
Hounslow TW4 151 C6
Isleworth TW1 153 B6
Kingston u T KT1 176 A1
Richmond TW9 132 C2
Sidcup DA14 189 C6
Sunbury TW16 172 B3
Sutton SM1 217 C4
Welling DA16 146 B2
Orchard Rise CR0 207 B1
Orchard Rise E DA15 167 D6
Orchard Rise
Kingston u T KT2 177 A2
Mortlake TW10 132 D1
Pinner HA5 39 D6
Orchard Rise W DA15 167 C6
Orchard Sch DA14 190 B5
Orchard School Sports Ctr SE20 184 A2
Orchardson Ho NW8 236 D5
Orchardson St NW8 92 B3 236 D5
Orchard Sq W14 254 C1
Orchard St
Marylebone W1 238 B2
Walthamstow E17 53 A5
Orchard Terr EN1 18 A5
Orchard The
Acton Green W4 111 B2
Ealing W5 87 D2
East Barnet N14 15 B6
Edgware HA8 26 C5
Enfield N21 17 B5
Ewell KT17 215 D1
Hampstead Garden Suburb NW11 47 C4
Hounslow TW3 130 A3
Lewisham SE3 142 B3
Totteridge N20 13 D3
Orchard Villas BR7 189 C4
Orchard Way
Ashford TW15 148 B2
Croydon BR3, CR0 207 A3
Enfield EN1 5 C2
Esher KT10 212 A2
Orchard Way Prim Sch CR0 207 A2
Orchard Way SM1 218 B4
Orchestra Ct HA8 26 D3
Orchid Cl
Chessington KT9 213 C1
1 Newham E6 100 A2
Southall UB1 85 A1
Orchid Ct
Catford BR1 164 B1
Harrow HA3 24 C2
Wembley HA9 66 A6
Orchid Gdns TW3 129 B1
Orchid Grange N14 15 C4
Orchid Lo N14 15 C4
Orchid Rd N14 15 C4
Orchid St W12 112 A6
Orde Hall St WC1 94 B2 240 C4
Orde Ho 10 N16 73 B4
Ordell Ct 36 E3 97 B5
Ordell Rd E3 97 B5
Orde 6 NW9 27 D2
Ordnance Cl TW13 150 A2
Ordnance Cres SE10 120 C4
Ordnance Hill NW8 92 B6 229 D5
Ordnance Mews NW8 229 D4
Ordnance Rd
Canning Town E16 98 D2
Enfield EN3 7 B6
Shooters Hill SE18 144 C6
Oregano Cl UB7 104 B6
Oregano Dr E14 98 B1
Oregon Ave E12 78 B4
Oregon Bldg 5 SE13 141 D4
Oregon Cl KT3 199 A5
Oregon Sq BR6 211 B1

Orestes Ct 9 E18 55 A6
Orestes Mews 1 NW6 69 C3
Orford Ct
Stanmore HA7 25 C4
Wallington SM6 219 C3
West Norwood SE27 160 D2
Orford Gdns TW1 152 D2
Orford Rd
Catford SE6 163 D1
Walthamstow E17 53 D4
Wanstead E18 55 B6
Organ Crossroads KT17 216 A1
Oriana Ct CR0 221 B1
Oriana Ho 3 E14 119 B6
Oriel Cl CR4 203 D6
Oriel Ct
6 Croydon CR0 205 B1
Hampstead NW3 70 A4
Oriel Dr SW13 134 C6
Oriel Gdns IG5 56 B6
Oriel Jun & Inf Sch TW13 151 A1
Oriel Rd Hackney E9 75 A2
Homerton E9 74 D2
Oriel Way UB5 63 D1
Oriental City NW9 45 B6
Oriental Rd E16 121 D5
Orient Ind Pk E10 75 C6
Orient St SE11 116 D2 261 C4
Orient Way
Lea Bridge E5 74 D5
Leyton E10 75 B6
Oriole Way SE28 124 B6
Orion Bsns Ctr SE14 118 D1
Orion Ct 10 HA8 26 D5
Orion Ctr The CR0 220 A6
Orion Ho 20 E1 96 B3
Orion Mews SM4 201 C5
Orion Point 5 E14 119 C2
Orion Prim Sch The NW9 27 D2
Orion Rd N11 31 A4
Orion Way HA6 22 A6
Orissa Rd SE18 123 C1
Orkney Ho N1 233 C6
Orkney St SW11 137 A3
Orlando Rd SW4 137 C2
Orleans Cl KT10 212 B6
Orleans Ct 9 TW1 153 B4
Orleans House Gallery* TW1 153 B3
Orleans Inf Sch TW1 153 B4
Orleans Park Sch TW1 153 B4
Orleans Rd
South Norwood SE19 183 B4
Twickenham TW1 153 C4
Orleston Mews N7 72 C2
Orleston Rd N7 72 C2
Orley Farm Rd HA1 64 C5
Orley Farm Sch HA1 64 B5
Orlop St SE10 120 C1
Ormanton Rd SE26 184 A6
Orme Ct Mews W2 245 D5
Orme Ct W2 113 D6 245 C5
Orme Ho 8 E8 95 D6
Orme La W2 113 D6 245 C5
Ormeley Rd SW12 159 B3
Orme Rd
Kingston u T KT1, KT3 176 D1
Sutton SM1 217 D2
Ormerod Gdns CR4 181 A2
Ormerod Ho 3 SW9 138 A2
Ormesby Cl SE28 124 D6
Ormesby Way HA3 44 B4
Orme Sq W2 245 C5
Ormiston Gr W12 112 B5
Ormiston Rd SE10 121 A1
Ormond Ave
Hampton TW12 173 D2
23 Richmond TW10 153 D6
Ormond Cl WC1 240 B4
Ormond Cres TW12 173 D2
Ormond Dr TW12 173 D3
Ormonde Ave BR6 227 A6
Ormonde Ct
Hendon NW4 46 D6
Putney SW15 134 C1
Ormonde Gate SW3 114 D1 257 D1
Ormonde Mans WC1 240 B4
Ormonde Pl SW1 258 B3
Ormonde Rd SW14 133 A2
Ormonde Rise IG9 21 C3
Ormonde Terr NW8 92 D6 230 C5
Ormond Ho 7 N16 73 B6
Ormond Mans WC1 240 C5

Ormond Mews WC1 240 B5
Ormond Rd
Finsbury Pk N4, N19 50 A1
Richmond TW10 153 D6
Ormond Yd SW1 249 B4
Ormrod Ct W11 91 B1
Ormsby SM2 217 D1
Ormsby Gdns UB6 86 A5
Ormsby Lo 7 W4 111 C3
Ormsby Pl N16 73 D5
Ormsby Point 6 SE18 122 D2
Ormsby St E2 95 D5
Ormside St SE15 140 C6
Ormskirk Rd WD19 22 D5
Ornan Rd NW3 70 C3
Orpen Ho SW5 255 B3
Orpen Wlk N16 73 C5
Orpheus Ho 25 N19 49 D2
Orpheus St SE5 139 B4
ORPINGTON 227 D6
Orpington Gdns N18 17 C1
Orpington Hospl BR6 227 D4
Orpington Mans N21 16 C3
Orpington Rd
Southgate N21 16 D3
St Paul's Cray BR7 211 C6
Orpington Sta BR6 227 C6
Orpwood Cl TW12 173 B4
Orsett Mews W2 92 A1 236 A2
Orsett St SE11 116 B1 260 D2
Orsett Terr
Bayswater W2 92 A1 236 A2
Woodford IG8 37 C3
Orsman Rd N1 95 C6
Orton Gr EN1 6 A4
Orton St E1 118 A5
Orville Rd SW11 136 B3
Orwell Cl UB3 105 C6
Orwell Ct Hackney E8 96 A6
Highbury N5 73 A4
Northolt UB5 85 A6
Orwell Ho W12 112 A6
Orwell Lo 2 E18 55 A5
Orwell Rd E13 99 C6
Osbaldeston Rd N16 52 A1
Osberton Rd SE12 165 A6
Osbert St SW1 259 C3
Osborn Cl E8 96 A6
Osborne Ave TW19 148 B3
Osborne Cl
Beckenham BR3 207 A5
Cockfosters EN4 2 D2
Feltham TW13 172 D5
Osborne Ct Ealing W5 88 A2
10 Surbiton KT6 198 A3
17 Walthamstow E10 53 D2
Osborne Gdns CR7 183 A1
Osborne Gr E17 53 B5
Osborne Mews E17 53 B5
Osborne Pl SM1 218 B3
Osborne Rd
Buckhurst Hill IG9 21 B3
Dagenham RM9 81 B3
Enfield EN3 7 A3
Erith DA17 147 B6
Finsbury Pk N4 50 C1
Forest Gate E7 77 B3
Hackney E9 75 B2
Hounslow TW3, TW4 129 B2
Kingston u T KT2 176 A3
Leyton E10 75 D6
Palmers Green N13 16 C1
South Acton W3 110 D4
Southall UB1 86 A1
South Norwood CR7 183 A1
Walton-on-T KT12 194 A1
Willesden NW2 68 B2
Osborne Sq RM9 81 B4
Osborne Terr 1 SW17 181 A5
Osborne Way KT9 214 B3
Osborn Gdns NW7 28 D3
Osborn La SE23 163 A4
Osborn St E1 95 D2 243 D4
Osborn Terr SE3 142 D1
Osbourne Ct HA2 41 D5
Osbourne Ho
Richmond TW10 154 C6
Twickenham TW2 152 A2
Oscar Faber Pl 8 N1 73 C1
Oscar St SE8 141 C3
Oseney Cres NW5 71 D2
Osgood Ave BR6 227 D3
Osgood Gdns 1 BR6 227 D3
OSIDGE 15 B2
Osidge Ct N14 15 B3
Osidge La N14 15 B3

Osidge Prim Sch N14 15 C3
Osier Cres N10 30 D2
Osier Ct E1 96 D3
Osier La SE10 120 D3
Osier Mews W4 133 D6
Osiers Ct 3 KT1 175 D2
Osiers Rd SW18 135 C1
Osier St E1 96 C3
Osier Way Leyton E10 75 D5
Mitcham CR4 202 D4
Oslac Rd SE6 185 D5
Oslo Ct
Mitcham SW19 180 B3
St John's Wood NW8 230 A3
Oslo Ho 2 SE5 139 A3
Oslo Sq SE16 119 A3
Osman Cl N15 51 B3
Osmani Prim Sch E1 96 A2
Osman Rd
Edmonton N9 18 A1
Hammersmith W6 112 C3
Osmington Ho SW8 270 D3
Osmond Cl HA2 64 A6
Osmond Gdns SM6 219 C3
Osmund St W12 89 D2
Osnaburgh St NW1 93 B3 238 D6
Osnaburgh Terr NW1 238 D6
Osney Ho 4 SE2 124 D4
Osney Wlk SM5 202 B3
Osprey Cl
Cheam SM1 217 B3
Higham Hill E17 35 A3
Keston Mark BR2 210 A1
Newham E6 100 A2
Wanstead E11 55 A5
West Drayton UB7 104 A4
Osprey Ct
7 Ealing W7 86 D3
Hampstead NW3 69 D3
Thornton Heath SW16 182 B1
Osprey Ho
Camberwell SE15 139 D4
Isleworth TW7 131 B2
3 Limehouse E14 119 A6
Walthamstow E4 35 B4
Osprey Mews EN3 18 B6
Osprey 7 NW9 27 D2
Ospringe Cl 6 SE20 184 C3
Ospringe Ct SE9 167 B5
Ospringe Ho SE1 251 B3
Ospringe Rd NW5 71 C4
Osram Ct W6 112 C3
Osram Rd HA9 65 D5
Osric Path 8 N1 95 C5
Ossian Mews N4 50 B2
Ossian Rd N4 50 B2
Ossie Garvin Rdbt UB4 106 C6
Ossington Bldgs W1 238 A3
Ossington Cl W2 245 B5
Ossington St W2 113 D6 245 C5
Ossory Rd SE1 140 A6
Ossulston St NW1 93 D5 232 D4
Ossultan Pl N2 48 A6
Ossulton Way N2 48 A5
Ostade Rd SW2 160 B4
Ostell Cres EN3 7 C5
Osten Mews SW7 113 D3 255 D5
OSTERLEY 130 B5
Osterley Ave TW7 130 B5
Osterley Cl BR5 190 A2
Osterley Cres TW7 130 D4
Osterley Ct
Hounslow TW7 130 B4
7 Northolt UB5 84 C4
Osterley Gdns
Southall UB2 108 A4
South Norwood CR7 183 A1
Osterley Ho 5 E14 97 D1
Osterley La
Isleworth TW7 108 C1
Southall UB2, TW7 107 D1
Osterley Lo 1 TW7 130 C4
Osterley Park* TW7 108 B1
Osterley Park Rd UB2 107 B3
Osterley Park View Rd W7 108 C4
Osterley Rd
Hounslow TW7 130 C4
Stoke Newington N16 73 C4
Osterley Sta TW7 130 B5
Osterley Views UB2 108 B4
Osterly Lodge UB2 107 B3
Oster Terr E17 52 D4

Ostlers Dr TW15 171 A5
Ostliffe Rd N13 33 A5
Oswald Bldg SW8 268 C5
Oswald Rd UB1 107 A5
Oswald's Mead E9 75 A4
Oswald St E5 74 D5
Oswald Terr NW2 68 C5
Osward Pl N9 18 B2
Osward Rd SW12, SW17 158 D2
Oswell Ho 9 E1 118 B5
Oswin St SE11 116 D2 261 D4
Oswyth Rd SE5 139 C3
Otford Cl Bexley DA5 169 D5
Bromley BR1 210 C6
Penge SE20 184 C2
Otford Cres SE4 163 B5
Otford Ho
Bermondsey SE1 252 D1
6 Deptford SE15 140 C6
Otha Ho 13 SW9 138 A3
Othello Cl SE11 261 C2
Otho Ct 5 TW8 131 D5
Otis St E3 98 A4
Otley App IG2 56 D3
Otley Ct N11 31 A4
Otley Dr IG2 56 D3
Otley Ho N5 72 D5
Otley Rd E16 99 C1
Otley Terr E5 74 D5
Ottawa Ho 4 HA4 40 C1
Ottaway Ct E5 74 A5
Ottaway St E5 74 A5
Otterbourne Rd
Chingford E4 20 B1
1 Croydon CR0 221 A6
Otterburn Gdns TW7 131 A5
Otterburn Ho 12 SE5 139 A5
Otterburn St SW17 180 D4
Otter Cl E15 98 A6
Otterden Cl BR6 227 C4
Otterden St SE6 185 C6
Otterfield Rd UB7 104 A6
Otter Rd UB6 86 A3
Ottershaw Ho BR5 190 B2
Otto Cl SE26 162 B1
Ottoman Ct W5 109 D2
Otto St SE17 138 D6
Otway Ct N4 50 B3
Otway Gdns WD23 8 C4
Oulton Cl Erith SE28 102 C1
Upper Clapton E5 74 C6
Oulton Cres IG11 79 D3
Oulton Rd N15 51 B4
Oulton Way WD19 23 B6
Oundle Ave WD23 8 A5
Our Lady Immaculate RC Prim Sch KT6 198 D1
Our Lady of Dolours RC Prim Sch W2 91 D2
Our Lady of Grace RC Inf Sch NW2 68 C6
Our Lady of Grace RC Jun Sch NW2 68 B5
Our Lady of Grace RC Prim Sch SE7 143 B6
Our Lady of Lourdes RC Prim Sch
Finchley N12 30 A2
Friern Barnet N11 31 C5
Lewisham SE13 142 B2
Our Lady of Lourdes RC Sch NW10 89 A6
Our Lady of Lourds RC Prim Sch E11 55 A3
Our Lady of Muswell Prim Sch N10 49 A6
Our Lady of Muswell RC Prim Sch N10 31 A1
Our Lady of the Rosary RC Prim Sch DA15 167 C5
Our Lady of the Visitation RC Prim Sch UB6 86 A3
Our Lady of Victories RC Prim Sch
Putney SW15 134 D1
South Kensington SW7 114 A2 256 B3
Our Lady Queen of Heaven RC Sch SW19 156 D4
Our Lady RC Prim Sch
Camden Town NW1 93 C6 232 B6
Poplar E14 97 B1

Our Lady & St John's RC Jun & Inf Sch TW8 109 C1
Our Lady & St Joseph RC Prim Sch N1 73 C2
Our Lady & St Philip Neri RC Prim Sch SE26 185 A6
Our Lady's Convent RC High Sch N15 51 C2
Ouseley Rd SW12 158 D3
Outer Circ NW8 92 D5 230 D3
Outgate Rd NW10 67 D1
Outram Pl N1 94 A6 233 B6
Outram Rd
Croydon CR0 221 D6
Muswell Hill N22 31 D2
Newham E6 100 A6
Outwich St EC3 243 B2
Outwood Ct CR2 221 A1
Outwood Ho 3 SW2 160 B4
Oval Ct Burnt Oak HA8 27 A3
8 Teddington TW11 174 D5
Oval Mans SE11 270 D6
Oval Pl SW8 138 B5 270 D4
Oval Prim Sch CR0 205 C1
Oval Rd
Camden Town NW1 93 B6 231 C6
Croydon CR0 205 C1
Oval Rd N RM10 103 D6
Oval Rd S RM10 103 D5
Oval Sta SE11 138 C6
Oval The Hackney E2 96 B5
Sidcup DA15 168 A4
Oval The (Surrey Cnty Crkt Gd) SE11 138 C6
Oval Way SE11 116 B1 260 D1
Overbrae BR3 185 C5
Overbrook Wlk HA8 26 C3
Overbury Ave BR3 208 A6
Overbury 1 BR3 208 A6
Overbury Ho 3 E5 74 D4
Overbury Rd N4, N15 51 B3
Overbury St E5 74 D4
Overcliff Rd SE13 141 C2
Overcourt Cl DA15 168 B5
Overdale Ave KT3 177 B1
Overdale Rd W5 109 C3
Overdown Rd SE6 185 D6
Overhill Rd SE21, SE22 162 A4
Overhill Way BR3 208 B4
Overlea Rd E5 52 A2
Overmead DA15 167 B4
Oversley Ho 17 W2 91 C2
Overstand Cl BR3 207 C4
Overstone Gdns CR0 207 B2
Overstone Ho 10 E14 97 C1
Overstone Rd W6 112 C2
Overstrand Mans SW11 268 A1
Overton Cl
Hounslow TW7 130 D4
Tokyngton NW10 67 A2
Overton Ct E11 55 A2
Overton Dr
Ilford RM6 58 C2
Wanstead E11 55 B2
Overton Grange Sch SM2 217 D1
Overton Ho SW15 155 D4
Overton Rd
Abbey Wood SE2 124 D3
Belmont SM2 217 C1
Brixton SW9 138 C3
Southgate N14 16 A6
Walthamstow E10 53 A1
Overton's Yd CR0 221 A5
Overy Ho SE1 251 C1
Ovesdon Ave HA2 41 B1
Ovett Cl SE19 183 C4
Ovex Cl E14 120 A4
Ovington Ct SW3 257 B5
Ovington Gdns SW3 257 B5
Ovington Mews SW3 257 B5
Ovington Sq SW3 114 C3 257 B5
Ovington St SW3 114 C2 257 B4
Owen Cl Hayes UB4 84 B4
Northolt UB5 63 A2
Thamesmead SE28 124 C5
Thornton Heath CR0 205 B3
Owen Ct UB4 84 B4
Owen Ho
Feltham TW14 150 A4
11 Tufnell Pk N19 71 C4
5 Twickenham TW1 153 B4
Owenite St SE2 124 B2

Owen Rd
Edmonton N13 33 A5
Hayes UB4 84 B4
Owen's Ct EC1 234 C2
Owens Mews 10 E11 76 C6
Owen's Row EC1 234 C2
Owen St EC1 234 C3
Owens Way SE23 163 A4
Owen Way NW10 67 A3
Owen Wlk 7 SE20 184 A3
Owgan Cl SE5 139 B5
Oxberry Ave SW6 135 A3
Oxbridge Ct 4 W4 110 D1
Oxendon St SW1, W1 115 D6 249 C5
Oxenford St SE15 139 D2
Oxenham Ho 13 SE8 141 C6
Oxenholme NW1 232 B3
Oxenpark Ave HA9 44 A2
Oxestalls Rd SE8 119 A1
Oxford Ave
Harlington TW6 127 D5
Hounslow TW5 107 C1
Merton SW20 179 A1
Southgate N14 15 C3
Oxford & Cambridge Mans NW1 237 B3
Oxford Circus Ave W1 239 A1
Oxford Circus Sta W1 93 C1 239 A1
Oxford Cir W1 93 C1 239 A1
Oxford Cl
Edmonton N9 18 B2
Littleton TW15, TW17 171 A3
Mitcham CR4 203 C6
Oxford Cres KT3 199 B3
Oxford Ct
10 Acton W3 88 C1
City of London EC4 252 C6
8 Ealing W7 86 D2
Gunnersbury W4 110 D1
17 Kingston u T KT6 198 A4
48 Paddington W2 91 C2
Sidcup DA14 189 D6
Oxford Dr
Bermondsey SE1 253 A3
Ruislip HA4 62 C6
Oxford Gardens Prim Sch W10 90 D1
Oxford Gate W6 112 D2
Oxford Gdns
Brentford W4 132 C6
Edmonton N21 17 A4
North Kensington W10 90 D1
Oakleigh Pk N20 14 B3
Oxford Ho N4 50 C1
Oxford Mews DA5 169 C4
Oxford Rd
Carshalton SM5 218 C3
Ealing W5 109 D6
Edmonton N9 18 B2
Enfield EN3 18 B6
Finsbury Pk N4 50 C1
Harrow HA1 42 A3
Ilford IG1 79 A3
Oxford Rd N W4 110 D1
Oxford Rd
Paddington NW6 91 C5
Putney SW15 135 A1
Sidcup DA14 190 B5
Oxford Rd S W4 110 D1
Oxford Rd
South Norwood SE19 183 B4
Stratford E15 76 B2
Teddington TW11, TW12 174 B5
Wallington SM6 219 C3
Wealdstone HA3 42 D6
Woodford IG8 37 D5
Oxford Sq W2 92 C1 237 B1
Oxford St W1 93 B1 238 D1
Oxford Way TW13 172 D6
Oxford Wlk UB1 107 B5
Oxgate Ct Par NW2 68 A6
Oxgate Ctr NW2 68 B6
Oxgate Ct NW2 68 A6
Oxgate Gdns NW2 68 B6
Oxgate La NW2 68 B6
Oxhawth Cres BR2 210 D3
Oxhey Dr S HA6 22 B5
Oxhey Dr WD19 22 B6
Oxhey La HA5 23 C5
Oxhey Ridge Cl HA6 22 B5
Oxhey Wood Prim Sch WD19 22 C6
Oxleas Cl DA16 145 B3
Oxleas E6 100 D1
Oxleay Rd HA2 41 C1
Oxleigh Cl KT3 199 C4
Oxley Cl SE1 118 A1
Oxleys Rd NW2 68 B5

Oxlip Cl 2 CR0 206 D1
Oxlow La RM10 81 C4
Oxonian St SE22 139 D1
Oxo Tower Wharf SE1 251 B5
Oxo Twr* SE1 251 B5
Oxted Cl CR4 202 B6
Oxted Ct N16 51 C1
Oxtoby Way SW16 181 D2
OYH Prim Sch NW4 46 D5
Oyster Catchers Cl E16 99 B1
Oyster Catcher Terr IG5 56 C6
Oyster Row E1 96 C1
Ozolins Way E16 99 A1

P

Pablo Neruda Cl 4 SE24 138 D1
Pace Pl E1 96 B1
Pacific Cl TW14 149 D3
Pacific Ho 15 E1 96 D3
Pacific Hts BR3 185 C3
Pacific Rd E16 99 A1
Pacific Wharf IG11 78 D1
Pacific Wharf SE16 118 D5
Packenham Ho
24 Crouch End N19 49 D2
21 Spitalfields E2 95 D4
Packham Ct KT4 216 C5
Packington Sq N1 95 A6 235 A6
Packington St N1 94 D6 234 D5
Packmores Rd SE9 167 B6
Padbury Cl TW14 149 B3
Padbury Ct E2 95 D4
Padbury Ho NW8 237 B6
Padbury SE17 263 B1
Padden Ct NW7 28 D3
Paddenswick Ct 2 W6 112 B3
Paddenswick Rd W6 112 A3
PADDINGTON 92 A2
Paddington Acad
Paddington W2 92 B2 236 C3
Paddington W9 91 C3
Paddington Cl UB4 84 D3
Paddington Com Hospl W9 91 C2
Paddington Ct
10 Ealing W7 86 D2
7 Wembley HA0 66 A2
Paddington Gn W2 92 B2 236 C4
Paddington Green Prim Sch NW8 92 B3 236 C5
Paddington Sta W2 92 B1 236 C2
Paddington St W1 238 A4
Paddock Cl
Forest Hill SE26 184 D6
Kidbrooke SE3 143 A3
New Malden KT4 199 C1
Northolt UB5 85 C5
Orpington BR6 226 D4
Paddock Ct SW20 200 C5
Paddock Gdns SE19 183 C4
Paddock Lo 13 EN1 17 C6
Paddock Rd
Bexley DA6 147 A1
Dollis Hill NW2 68 A6
Ruislip HA4 62 D5
Paddock Sch SW15 133 D1
Paddocks Cl HA2 63 D4
Paddocks Gn NW9 44 D1
Paddocks The
Addington CR0 223 C2
Cockfosters EN4 2 D2
Preston HA9 66 D6
Paddock The
Muswell Hill N10 49 B6
Uxbridge UB10 60 D4
Paddock Way
Chislehurst BR7 189 B3
11 Putney SW15 156 C4
Padfield Ct HA9 66 B5
Padfield Rd SE5 139 A2
Padley Cl KT9 214 B3
Padnall Ct RM6 58 D6
Padnall Rd RM6 58 D5
Padstone Ho 50 E3 97 D4
Padstow Cl BR6 227 D4
Padstow Ho 12 E14 119 B6
Padstow Rd EN2 4 D4
Padstow Wlk TW14 149 D3
Padua Rd SE20 184 C2
Pagden St SW8 268 D2
Pageant Ave NW9 27 C2
Pageant Cres SE16 119 B5

Pageantmaster Ct EC4 241 C1
Pageant Wlk CR0 221 C5
Page Cl
Dagenham RM9 81 A3
Hampton TW12 173 A4
Harrow HA3 44 B3
Page Cres CR0 220 D3
Page Ct NW7 28 A3
Page Green Rd N15 52 A4
Page Green Terr N15 51 D4
Page Heath La BR1 209 D6
Page Heath Villas BR1 209 D6
Page High N22 50 C6
Page Ho SE10 142 A6
Pagehurst Rd CR0 206 B2
Page Mdw NW7 28 A3
Page Rd TW14 149 B5
Page's Ct N10 31 A1
Page's Hill N10 31 A1
Page's La N10 31 A1
Page St Hendon NW7 28 A3
Westminster SW1 115 D2 259 D4
Page's Wlk SE1 117 C3 263 B5
Page's Yd W4 133 C6
Paget Ave SM1 218 B5
Paget Cl TW12 174 B6
Paget Ct UB7 104 A4
Paget Gdns BR7 188 D2
Paget Ho 15 E2 96 C5
Paget La TW7 130 C2
Paget Pl
Kingston u T KT2 177 A4
Thames Ditton KT7 196 D1
Paget Rd
Hillingdon UB10 83 A3
Ilford IG1 78 D4
Stoke Newington N16 51 B1
Paget Rise SE18 144 C5
Paget St EC1 234 C2
Paget Terr SE18 144 D6
Pagham Ho 6 W10 90 C3
Pagin Ho N15 51 C4
Pagitts Gr EN4 1 D4
Pagnell St SE14 141 B5
Pagoda Ave TW9 132 B2
Pagoda Gdns SE3 142 B3
Pagoda Gr SE27 161 A2
Paignton Rd
Ruislip HA4 62 A5
Tottenham N15 51 C3
Paine Ct SE3 142 D6
Paines Cl HA5 41 A6
Paine's La HA5 23 A1
Pain's Cl CR4 181 B1
Painsthorpe Rd 3 N16 73 C5
Painswick Ct 1 SE15 139 D5
Painters Mews SE16 118 A2
Painters Rd IG2, RM6 58 A6
Paisley Rd
Carshalton SM5 202 B1
Tottenham N22 32 D2
Paisley Terr SM5 202 B2
Pakeman Ho SE1 251 D2
Pakeman Prim Sch N7 72 B5
Pakeman St N7 72 B5
Pakenham Cl SW12 159 A3
Pakenham St WC1 94 B3 240 D6
Pakington Ho 22 SW9 138 A3
Palace Ave W8 113 D4 245 D2
Palace Court Gdns N10 49 C6
Palace Ct
Bromley BR1 187 B2
Eltham SE9 166 B5
Hampstead NW3 69 D3
Harrow HA3 44 A3
Kensington W2 113 D6 245 C5
South Norwood CR7 205 B5
Streatham SW2 160 C2
Palace Garden Mews W8 245 B4
Palace Gate
Hampton KT8 196 C6
Knightsbridge W8 114 A4 246 A1
Palace Gate Mews 4 N8 50 A5
Palace Gates Rd N22 31 D2
Palace Gdns IG9 21 D3
Palace Gdns Mews W8 113 D5 245 D3
Palace Gdns Sh Ctr EN2 5 B1

Palace Gn
Kensington W8 113 D5 24
New Addington CR0 22
Palace Gr
Bromley BR1 18
Penge SE19 18
Palace Mans W14 25
Palace Mews
Belgravia SW1 25
Fulham SW6 26
Walthamstow E17 5
Palace of Ind HA9 6
Palace Par E17 5
Palace Pl SW1 25
Palace Rd
Bromley BR1 18
East Molesey KT8 19
Hornsey N8 4
Kingston u T KT1 19
Penge SE19 18
Ruislip HA4 6
Streatham SE27, SW16, SW2 16
Wood Green N11 3
Palace Sq SE19 18
Palace St SW1 115 C3 25
Palace View
Bromley BR1 20
Croydon CR0 22
Grove Pk SE12 16
Palace View Rd E4 3
Palamos Rd E10 5
Palatine Ave N16 7
Palatine Rd N16 7
Palazzo Apartments 11 N1 7
Palemead Cl SW6 13
Palermo Rd NW10 9
Palestine Gr SW19 18
Palewell Cl BR5 19
Palewell Common Dr SW14 15
Palewell Pk SW14 13
Palfrey Pl SW8 138 B5 27
Palgrave Ave UB1 10
Palgrave Gdns NW1 92 C3 23
Palgrave Ho
7 Camberwell SE5 13
4 Maitland Pk NW3 7
Twickenham TW2 15
Palgrave Rd W12 11
Palissy St 35 E2 9
Palladino Ho 6 SW17 18
Pallant Ho SE1 26
Pallant Way BR6 22
Pallester Ct NW11 4
Pallet Way SE18 14
Palliser Ct W14 25
Palliser Ho
3 Greenwich SE10 14
21 Stepney E1 9
Palliser Rd W14 113 A1 25
Pallister Terr SW15 15
Pall Mall E SW1 115 D5 24
Pall Mall Pl SW1 24
Pall Mall SW1 115 D5 24
Palmar Cres DA7 14
Palmar Rd DA7 14
Palm Ave DA14 19
Palm Cl E10 7
Palm Ct
Beckenham BR3 20
18 Camberwell SE15 13
Stoke Newington N16 7
Wood Green N22 3
Palmeira Rd DA7 14
Palmer Ave KT4, SM3 21
Palmer Cl
Heston TW5 12
Northolt UB5 6
West Wickham BR4 22
Palmer Cres KT1 19
Palmer Gdns EN5 1
Palmer Ho
6 Deptford SE14 14
8 Kentish Town NW5 7
5 Tufnell Pk N19 7
Palmer Pl N7 7
Palmer Rd
Dagenham RM8 58
Newham E13 9
Palmer's Ct 11 N11 3
Palmers Gr KT8 19
PALMERS GREEN 1

's Green High
21 ... 16 C2
's Green Sta
... 32 B6
's La EN3 ... 6 C4
s Rd E2 ... 96 D5
's Rd N11 ... 31 C5
's Rd
ake SW14 ... 133 A2
on Heath
6 ... 182 B1
ston Cres
Pk N13 ... 32 B5
vich SE18 ... 145 A6
ston Ct
khurst Hill
... 21 C2
be Town E3 ... 96 D5
ston Ctr HA3 ... 42 D6
ston Ct
rbiton KT6 ... 197 D2
ton SM1 ... 218 A3
mstow E17 ... 53 B5
ston Gr [11]
... 179 C3
ston Ho
sea SW11 ... 268 B1
gton W8 ... 245 A3
ston Rd
Green W3 ... 111 A3
Pk N22 ... 32 B4
esbury NW6 ... 69 B1
urst Hill IG9 ... 21 C3
rough BR6 ... 227 A3
stead NW6 ... 69 C1
v HA3 ... 42 D6
low TW3 ... 130 A4
n SW19 ... 179 C3
ake SW14 ... 133 A1
SM1 ... 218 A3
on Heath CR0 ... 205 B4
enham TW2 ... 152 C5
E7 ... 77 B2
gton SM5 ... 219 A4
mstow E17 ... 53 B5
ston Way
... 268 D3
St SW1 ... 259 C6
r W5 ... 110 A3
ee Ct [5] N17 ... 33 D1
ee Ho [2]
... 140 D5
a Ct
ey N12 ... 29 D4
den NW10 ... 68 A1
Gdns HA5 ... 40 B4
Ho [14] E8 ... 95 D6
Ct [10] SM2 ... 217 D2
n Ct N4 ... 50 A2
Vay KT19 ... 215 B3
a Ho [6] E1 ... 96 D2
Ho SE18 ... 144 B4
s La EC2 ... 242 C1
s Rd
... 93 D5 232 D4
n Way [4]
... 71 D2
a Ct [4] KT6 ... 198 A3
a Rd NW6 ... 69 C2
d Mews IG2 ... 56 C3
d Rd SE2 ... 124 A3
ourne Ave
... 90 C2
ourne Ct
gh Pk N20 ... 14 A4
Tooting
7 ... 180 A6
ourne Dr HA7 ... 26 A5
ourne Ho [4]
... 72 A3
ourne NW1 ... 232 A1
d Pl UB1 ... 107 D6
ve EN5 ... 14 A6
rst Ave [8]
... 121 B5
rst Cl
otford SE14 ... 140 D5
rth TW7 ... 130 D2
rst Ho
nsington
0 ... 90 C1
ham SW16 ... 181 D5
rst Rd KT12 ... 194 C2
r Rd SW20 ... 178 B2
re Cl N5 ... 72 D4
re Ct [11] UB1 ... 86 A1
re Rd SE26 ... 162 B1
ma Ct N6 ... 49 C3
Gdns W12 ... 112 A6
r Dr NW10 ... 67 B3
s Cl N13 ... 32 D5
s The
BR1 ... 210 A6
WD23 ... 8 B3
A7 ... 147 B5
Fortune
1 ... 47 B4

Panton Cl CR0 ... 204 D1
Panton St SW1 ... 249 C5
Panyer Alley EC2 ... 242 A2
Papermill Cl SM5 ... 219 A4
Paper Mill Wharf
E14 ... 119 A6
Papillons Wlk SE3 ... 143 A2
Papworth Gdns N7 ... 72 B3
Papworth Way SW2 ... 160 C4
Parade Mans
[19] Camberwell
SE5 ... 139 A3
[2] Hendon NW4 ... 46 B4
Parade Mews SE27,
SW2 ... 160 D2
Parade The
Ashford TW16 ... 171 D3
Battersea
SW11 ... 136 D5 267 D4
Claygate KT10 ... 212 C2
Ilford IG2 ... 57 B3
Thornton Heath CR0 ... 204 A3
Thornton Heath CR7 ... 204 C6
Waddon CR0 ... 220 B3
Wembley UB6 ... 65 B3
Paradise Pas N7 ... 72 C3
Paradise Pl [15] SE7 ... 122 A2
Paradise Rd
Richmond TW10 ... 154 A6
South Lambeth SW4 ... 138 A3
Paradise Row E2 ... 96 B4
Paradise St SE16 ... 118 B4
Paradise Wlk
SW3 ... 136 D6 267 D6
Paragon Cl E16 ... 99 A1
Paragon Ct NW4 ... 29 A2
Paragon Gr KT5 ... 198 B3
Paragon Ho SE3 ... 142 D3
Paragon N8 ... 50 C5
Paragon Mews SE1 ... 262 D4
Paragon Pl
Blackheath Vale
SE3 ... 142 D3
Surbiton KT5 ... 198 B3
Paragon Rd E9 ... 74 C2
Paragon The
Kidbrooke SE3 ... 143 A3
Walworth SE17 ... 262 D4
Paramount Bldg
EC1 ... 241 C6
Paramount Ct WC1 ... 239 B5
Paramount Ho [10]
E11 ... 76 C5
Parbury Rd SE23 ... 163 A5
Parbury Rise KT9 ... 214 A2
Parchmore Rd CR7 ... 205 A6
Parchmore Way
CR7 ... 182 D1
Pardes House Gram
N3 ... 29 B1
Pardes House Prim
N3 ... 29 B1
Pardoner St
SE1 ... 117 B3 262 D6
Pardon St EC1 ... 241 D6
Parfett St E1 ... 96 A1
Parfew Ct [2] SE22 ... 162 B2
Parfitt Cl NW11 ... 48 A1
Parfrey St W6 ... 134 C6
Pargraves Ct HA9 ... 66 C6
Parham Dr IG2 ... 56 D4
Paris Gdn
SE1 ... 116 D5 251 C4
Parish CE Prim Sch
BR1 ... 187 A3
Parish Church CE Inf
Sch CR0 ... 220 D5
Parish Church CE Jun
Sch CR0 ... 220 D5
Parish Ct KT6 ... 198 A3
Parish Gate Dr
DA15 ... 167 C5
Parish La SE20 ... 184 D3
Paris Ho [12] E2 ... 96 B5
Parish Wharf [6]
SE7 ... 122 A2
Park App DA16 ... 146 B1
Park Ave Barking IG11 ... 79 A2
Bromley BR6 ... 226 C6
Edmonton N18 ... 34 A6
Enfield EN1 ... 17 C5
Park Ave E KT17 ... 216 A2
Park Ave Finchley N3 ... 29 D2
Golders Green NW11 ... 47 D1
Ilford IG1 ... 56 C1
Mitcham CR4 ... 181 B3
Mortlake SW14 ... 133 B1
Park Ave N
Dudden Hill NW10 ... 68 B3
Hornsey N8 ... 49 D5
Park Avenue Mews
CR4 ... 181 B3
Park Avenue Rd N17 ... 34 B3
Park Ave
Palmers Green
N13 ... 16 C1
Plaistow BR1 ... 187 A4

Park Ave *continued*
Ruislip HA4 ... 39 C3
Park Ave S N8 ... 49 D5
Park Ave
Southall UB1 ... 107 C5
Stratford E15 ... 76 C2
Twickenham TW3 ... 151 D5
Upper Halliford
TW17 ... 193 C6
Wallend E6 ... 100 C5
Wallington SM5 ... 219 A2
West Wickham BR4 ... 224 A6
Willesden NW2 ... 68 C2
Woodford IG8 ... 37 B5
Wood Green N22 ... 32 B2
Park Ave W KT17 ... 216 A2
Park Chase HA9 ... 66 B4
Park Cl Dollis Hill NW2 ... 68 B5
Ealing NW10 ... 88 B4
Hampton TW12 ... 174 A2
Harrow HA3 ... 24 C2
Isleworth TW3,
TW7 ... 152 A6
Kensington
W14 ... 113 B3 254 D6
Kingston u T KT2 ... 176 C2
Knightsbridge SW1 ... 247 C1
North Finchley N12 ... 30 B6
[13] South Hackney E9 ... 96 C6
Wallington SM5 ... 218 D2
Park Cotts [10] TW1 ... 153 B5
Park Crescent Mews E
W1 ... 238 D5
Park Crescent Mews W
W1 ... 238 C5
Park Cres Enfield EN2 ... 5 B1
Finchley N3 ... 30 A3
Harrow HA3 ... 24 C2
Regent's Pk
W1 ... 93 B3 238 C5
Twickenham TW2 ... 152 B3
Park Croft HA8 ... 27 A2
Parkcroft Rd SE12 ... 164 D4
Park Ct
Battersea SW11 ... 268 C2
[2] Beckenham BR3 ... 207 D6
[2] Chingford E4 ... 20 A2
Clapham Pk SW4 ... 159 D6
Dulwich SE21 ... 161 B1
[12] Hammersmith
W6 ... 112 A2
New Barnet EN5 ... 14 B4
New Malden KT3 ... 199 B5
North Finchley N12 ... 30 B5
Teddington KT1 ... 175 C2
Twickenham TW4 ... 151 D6
Upper Tooting
SW12 ... 159 A3
Wallington SM6 ... 220 A3
Walthamstow E17 ... 53 D4
Wembley HA9 ... 66 A3
Wood Green N11 ... 31 D3
Parkdale Cres KT4 ... 215 B5
Parkdale N11 ... 31 D4
Parkdale Rd SE18 ... 123 C1
Park Dr Acton W3 ... 110 C3
Enfield N21 ... 17 A5
Golders Green NW11 ... 47 D1
Harrow HA2 ... 41 C2
Mortlake SW14 ... 133 B1
Stanmore HA3 ... 24 C4
Woolwich SE7 ... 144 A6
Park Dwellings [7]
NW3 ... 70 D3
Park End
Bromley BR1 ... 186 D2
Hampstead NW3 ... 70 C4
Parker Cl
Newham E16 ... 122 A5
Wallington SM5 ... 218 D2
Parker Ct
Shoreditch N1 ... 235 B6
South Lambeth SW4 ... 270 A1
Wimbledon SW19 ... 179 A3
Parke Rd
Barnes SW13 ... 134 A4
Sunbury TW16 ... 194 A5
Parker Ho [4] SE18 ... 122 D1
Parker Mews WC2 ... 240 B2
Parker Rd CR0 ... 221 A4
Parkers Rd N10 ... 30 C2
Parker's Row SE1 ... 253 D1
Parkers Row [15]
SE16 ... 118 A4
Parker St
Newham E16 ... 122 A5
St Giles WC2 ... 94 A1 240 B2
Park Farm Cl
East Finchley N2 ... 48 A6
Pinner HA5 ... 40 B4
Park Farm Ct UB3 ... 105 C6
Park Farm Rd
Bromley BR1 ... 187 D2
Kingston u T KT2 ... 176 A3
Parkfield Ave
Feltham TW13 ... 150 A1
Harrow HA2 ... 24 A1

Parkfield Ave *continued*
Hillingdon UB10 ... 82 D4
Mortlake SW14 ... 133 C1
Northolt UB5 ... 84 D5
Parkfield Cl
Edgware HA8 ... 26 D4
Northolt UB5 ... 85 A5
Parkfield Cres
Feltham TW13 ... 150 A1
Harrow HA2 ... 24 A1
Ruislip HA4 ... 63 A5
Parkfield Ct SE14 ... 141 B4
Parkfield Dr UB5 ... 84 D5
Parkfield Gdns HA2 ... 41 D6
Parkfield Ho HA2 ... 23 D2
Parkfield [8] TW7 ... 130 C4
Parkfield Ind Est
SW11 ... 137 A3
Parkfield Par TW13 ... 150 A1
Parkfield Prim Sch
NW4 ... 46 B2
Parkfield Rd
Feltham TW13 ... 150 A1
Harrow HA2 ... 64 A5
New Cross SE14 ... 141 B4
Northolt UB5 ... 85 A5
Uxbridge UB10 ... 60 D6
Willesden NW10 ... 68 B1
Parkfields Ave
Welsh Harp NW9 ... 45 B1
Wimbledon SW20 ... 178 B1
Parkfields Cl SM5 ... 219 A4
Parkfields
Croydon CR0 ... 207 B1
Putney SW15 ... 134 C1
Parkfields Rd KT2 ... 176 B5
Parkfield St
N1 ... 94 C5 234 B4
Parkfield Way BR2 ... 210 B4
Park Flats N6 ... 48 C2
Parkgate Ave EN4 ... 2 A4
Parkgate Cl KT2 ... 176 D4
Parkgate Cres EN4 ... 2 A4
Park Gate Ct TW12 ... 174 A5
Park Gate Ealing W5 ... 87 D2
East Finchley N2 ... 48 B6
Parkgate Gdns
SW14 ... 155 B6
Parkgate House Sch
SW11 ... 137 A1
Parkgate SE3 ... 142 D2
Parkgate Mews N6 ... 49 C2
Parkgate Rd
Battersea
SW11 ... 136 C5 267 B3
Wallington SM5,
SM6 ... 219 B3
Park Gates HA2 ... 63 C4
Park Gate N21 ... 16 B4
Park Gdns
Kingston u T KT2 ... 176 B5
Queensbury NW9 ... 44 D6
Park Gr Bromley BR1 ... 187 B2
Edgware HA8 ... 26 B5
Newham E15 ... 99 A6
Park Grove Rd E11 ... 76 C6
Park Gr N11 ... 31 D3
Park Hall Rd
Dulwich SE21 ... 161 B1
East Finchley N2 ... 48 C5
Park Hall Road Trad Est
SE21 ... 161 B1
Park Hall SE10 ... 142 B5
Parkham Ct BR2 ... 186 C1
Parkham St
SW11 ... 136 C4 267 A1
Parkham Way N10 ... 31 C1
Park Heights Ct [21]
E14 ... 97 B1
Park High Sch HA7 ... 25 D1
Park Hill
Bromley BR1 ... 210 B5
Clapham Pk SW4 ... 159 D6
Park Hill Cl SM5 ... 218 C3
Park Hill Ct
Croydon CR0 ... 221 C6
Ealing W5 ... 87 D2
Upper Tooting
SW17 ... 158 D1
Park Hill Ealing W5 ... 87 D2
Forest Hill SE23 ... 162 C3
Parkhill Ho [1]
SW16 ... 182 C5
Parkhill Inf Sch IG5 ... 56 C6
Park Hill Inf Sch
CR0 ... 221 C5
Parkhill Jun Sch IG5 ... 56 C6
Park Hill Jun Sch
CR0 ... 221 C5
Park Hill IG10 ... 21 D6
Park Hill Rd BR2 ... 186 C1
Parkhill Rd
Chingford E4 ... 20 A4
Maitland Pk NW3 ... 70 D3
Old Bexley DA5 ... 169 B4
Sidcup DA15 ... 167 C1

Park Hill Rd
South Croydon
CR0 ... 221 C5
Wallington SM6 ... 219 B1
Park Hill TW10 ... 154 B5
Park Hill Rise CR0 ... 221 D5
Park Hill Sch KT2 ... 176 C3
Park Hill SM5 ... 218 D2
Park Hill Wlk [10]
NW3 ... 70 D3
Park Ho
[8] Camberwell
SE5 ... 139 B4
Finsbury Pk N4 ... 72 D6
Forest Hill SE26 ... 184 A5
[35] Hackney E9 ... 74 C1
Parkholme Rd E8 ... 74 A2
Park Ho
Richmond TW10 ... 154 A5
Sidcup DA14 ... 190 A5
Southgate N21 ... 16 B4
Park House Gdns
TW1 ... 153 C6
Parkhouse St SE5 ... 139 B5
Park Hts NW4 ... 46 B6
Parkhurst Ct N7 ... 72 A4
Parkhurst Gdns [2]
DA5 ... 169 C4
Parkhurst Rd
Bowes Pk N22 ... 32 B4
Friern Barnet N11 ... 31 A5
Little Ilford E12 ... 78 C4
Lower Holloway N7 ... 72 A4
Sidcup DA5 ... 169 C4
Sutton SM1 ... 218 B4
Tottenham N17 ... 34 A1
Walthamstow E17 ... 53 A5
Parkin Ho SE20 ... 184 D3
Parkinson Ct
Finsbury N1 ... 235 C1
Shoreditch EC1 ... 235 D2
Parkinson Ho [6] E9 ... 74 C1
Park La Cheam SM3 ... 217 A2
Cranford TW5 ... 128 A5
Dagenham RM6 ... 58 D3
Edmonton N9 ... 17 D1
Harrow HA2 ... 63 D5
Hayes UB4 ... 83 C3
Mayfair W1 ... 115 A6 248 A5
Mill Meads E15 ... 98 B6
Parkland Ct
Kensington W14 ... 244 A2
Stratford E15 ... 76 C3
Parkland Gdns [12]
SW19 ... 156 D3
Parkland Gr
Ashford TW15 ... 170 C6
Hounslow TW7 ... 130 D4
Parkland Mead BR1 ... 210 D6
Parkland Rd
Ashford TW15 ... 170 C6
Woodford IG8 ... 37 B3
Wood Green N22 ... 32 B1
Parklands WD23 ... 8 A5
Parklands Cl
Hadley Wood EN4 ... 2 B5
Ilford IG2 ... 57 A2
Mortlake SW14 ... 155 A6
Parklands Ct TW5 ... 128 D3
Parklands Dr N3 ... 47 A6
Parklands
East Dulwich
SE22 ... 162 B6
Highgate N6 ... 49 B2
Kingston u T KT5 ... 198 B4
Parklands Par TW5 ... 128 D3
Parklands Pl HA8 ... 26 B6
Parklands Rd SW16 ... 181 B5
Parklands Way KT4 ... 215 C6
Parklands [5] N20 ... 14 A2
Park Lane Cl N17 ... 34 A3
Park Lane Mans
CR0 ... 221 B5
Park Lane Prim Sch
HA9 ... 66 A4
PARK LANGLEY ... 208 B4
Park La
Richmond TW9 ... 131 D1
South Croydon CR0 ... 221 B5
Stanmore HA7 ... 9 A1
Teddington TW11 ... 174 D4
Tottenham N17 ... 34 A3
Wallington SM5,
SM6 ... 219 A3
Wembley HA9 ... 66 A4
Park Lawn CR7 ... 183 A1
Parklea Cl NW9 ... 27 C2
Park Lea Ct N16 ... 51 C2
Parkleigh Ct SW19 ... 179 D1
Parkleigh Rd SW19 ... 179 D1
Parkleys KT2,TW10 ... 175 D6
Park Lo [3] W5 ... 87 B3
Park Lofts [9] SW4 ... 160 A6
Park Lo N12 ... 30 A5
Park Lorne NW8 ... 230 B1

Park Lo
[11] South Hampstead
NW8 ... 70 B1
[10] Wapping E1 ... 118 B5
Willesden NW2 ... 68 C4
Park Mans
Battersea SW11 ... 267 C1
Bedford Pk W6 ... 111 D3
Forest Hill SE26 ... 162 C1
Fulham SW6 ... 264 B1
[5] Hendon NW4 ... 46 B4
Knightsbridge SW1 ... 247 C1
St John's Wood NW8 ... 230 A3
Vauxhall SW8 ... 270 B6
Park Mead DA15 ... 168 B5
Parkmead Gdns
NW7 ... 27 D4
Park Mead HA2 ... 63 D5
Parkmead SW15 ... 156 B5
Park Mews
Chislehurst BR7 ... 188 D4
Greenwich SE10 ... 120 D1
Kensal Rise W10 ... 91 A5
Stanwell TW19 ... 148 B4
Parkmore BR7 ... 188 D3
Parkmore Cl IG8 ... 37 A6
Park Nook Gdns EN2 ... 5 B6
Park Par Acton W3 ... 110 C3
Dagenham NW10 ... 89 D5
Hayes UB3 ... 83 C1
Kingsbury NW9 ... 45 B6
Park Place Dr W3 ... 110 C3
Park Place Ho [8]
SE10 ... 142 B6
Park Place Villas
W2 ... 236 B4
Park Pl
Canary Wharf
E14 ... 119 C5
Ealing W5 ... 109 D5
Gunnersbury W3 ... 110 C2
Hampton TW12 ... 174 A4
Shoreditch N1 ... 235 D6
St James
SW1 ... 115 C5 249 A4
Wembley HA9 ... 66 B4
Park Prim Sch E15 ... 76 D1
Park Rd
Ashford TW15 ... 170 D5
Beckenham BR3 ... 185 C3
Bromley BR1 ... 187 B2
Cheam SM3 ... 217 A2
Chipping Barnet EN5 ... 1 B1
Chislehurst BR7 ... 188 D4
Chiswick W4 ... 133 B6
Cockfosters EN4 ... 2 C1
Dagenham NW10 ... 89 C6
Park Rd E W3 ... 111 A4
Park Rd Ealing W7 ... 108 D6
East Finchley N2 ... 48 B6
East Molesey KT8 ... 196 A5
Edmonton N18 ... 34 A6
Park Rd E UB10 ... 82 A5
Park Rd
Feltham TW13 ... 172 D6
Hackbridge SM6 ... 219 B6
Hampton TW12 ... 174 A5
Hampton Wick KT1 ... 175 C2
Harringay N8, N15 ... 50 D5
Hayes UB4 ... 83 C2
Hendon NW4 ... 46 B3
Hornsey N8 ... 49 D4
Hounslow TW3,
TW7 ... 152 A6
Ilford IG1 ... 79 B5
Isleworth TW7 ... 131 B3
Kingsbury NW9 ... 45 B2
Kingston u T KT2,
TW10 ... 176 C3
Leyton E10 ... 53 C1
Lisson Gr NW1,
NW8 ... 92 C3 237 B6
Lower Halliford
TW17 ... 192 C1
Mitcham SW19 ... 180 C4
Park Rd N W4 ... 111 B1
Park Rd Newham E15 ... 99 A6
New Malden KT3 ... 199 B5
Park Rd N W3 ... 110 D4
Park Rd Osidge N14 ... 15 D4
Richmond TW10 ... 154 B5
South Norwood
SE25 ... 205 C5
Sunbury TW16 ... 172 B3
Teddington TW11 ... 174 D4
Twickenham TW1 ... 153 C5
Upton Pk E6 ... 99 C6
Uxbridge UB8 ... 60 A2
Wallington SM6 ... 219 B3
Walthamstow E17 ... 53 B4
Wanstead E12 ... 77 B6
Wembley HA0 ... 66 A2
Wood Green N11 ... 31 D3
Park Ridings N8 ... 50 C6

Park Rise
Forest Hill SE23 ... 163 A3
Harrow HA3 ... 24 C2
Park Rise Rd SE23 ... 163 A3
Park Road E 11 W3 ... 110 D4
Park Road Ho 3
KT2 ... 176 C3
Park Row SE10 ... 142 B6
PARK ROYAL ... 88 D4
Park Royal Bsns Ctr
NW10 ... 89 A3
Park Royal Metro Ctr
NW10 ... 88 D3
Park Royal Rd NW10,
W3 ... 89 A3
Park Royal Sta W5 ... 88 C3
Park Royal NW10 ... 88 D6
Park St James NW8 . 230 C5
Park Sch IG1 ... 56 D1
Park Sheen 3
SW14 ... 132 D1
Parkshot TW9 ... 132 A1
Parkside Ave
Bromley BR1 ... 210 A5
Wimbledon SW19 ... 178 D5
Parkside 1 BR3 ... 185 D1
Parkside Bsns Est
SE8 ... 141 A6
Parkside SM3 ... 217 A2
Park Side IG9 ... 21 B2
Parkside Cl SE20 ... 184 C3
Parkside Cres
Highbury N7 ... 72 C5
Tolworth KT5 ... 199 A3
Parkside Ct
Bowes Pk N22 ... 32 B4
2 Wanstead E11 ... 55 A3
Park Side NW2 ... 68 B4
Parkside Dr HA8 ... 10 C1
Parkside Ealing W5 ... 110 A6
East Acton W3 ... 111 C5
Parkside Est E9 ... 96 D6
Parkside N3 ... 29 D3
Parkside Gdns
East Barnet EN4 ... 15 A4
Wimbledon SW19 ... 178 D6
Parkside
Greenwich SE3 ... 142 D5
Hampton TW12 ... 174 A5
Hayes UB3 ... 105 C6
Hendon NW7 ... 28 A4
Parkside Lo DA17 ... 125 D1
Parkside Prep Sch
N17 ... 33 C2
Parkside (private)
Hospl SW19 ... 156 D1
Parkside Rd
Belvedere DA17 ... 125 D2
Hounslow TW3 ... 151 D6
Parkside DA14 ... 168 B2
Parkside St SW11 ... 268 A1
Parkside Terr N18 ... 33 B6
Parkside Way HA2 ... 42 A5
Parkside SW19 ... 178 D6
Park Sq E
NW1 ... 93 B3 238 D6
Park Square Mews
NW1 ... 238 C5
Park Sq W
NW1 ... 93 B3 238 C5
Park S SW11 ... 268 A1
Park St
Borough The
SE1 ... 117 A5 252 B4
Croydon CR0 ... 221 A6
Parkstead Rd SW15 ... 156 B6
Park St W1 ... 115 A6 248 A5
Parkstone Ave N18 ... 33 D5
Parkstone Rd
5 Peckham
SE15 ... 140 A3
Walthamstow E17 ... 54 A6
Park Stps W2 ... 247 B6
Park St TW11 ... 174 C4
Park Terr
Carshalton SM5 ... 218 C5
Enfield EN3 ... 7 A5
New Malden KT4 ... 200 A1
Park The Ealing W5 ... 109 D5
Forest Hill SE23 ... 162 C3
Golders Green NW11 ... 47 D1
Highgate N6 ... 49 A3
Sidcup DA14 ... 190 A5
Wallington SM5 ... 218 D3
Parkthorne Cl HA2 ... 41 D3
Parkthorne Dr HA2 ... 41 D3
Parkthorne Rd
SW12 ... 159 D4
Park Twrs W1 ... 248 C3
Park View Acad N15 ... 51 A5
Park View Cres N11 ... 31 B6
Park View Ct N12 ... 30 C6
Parkview Ct
Fulham SW6 ... 135 A3

Parkview Ct *continued*
Harrow HA3 ... 24 C3
Ilford IG2 ... 57 C3
Park View Ct NW9 ... 45 A5
Parkview Ct
Penge SE20 ... 184 B2
Twickenham TW1 ... 153 C4
Park View Ct SW18 ... 157 C5
Park View W3 ... 89 A2
Park View Dr CR4 ... 180 B1
Parkview UB6 ... 87 A4
Park View Gdns
Hendon NW4 ... 46 D4
Redbridge IG4 ... 56 B5
Wood Green N22 ... 32 C2
Park View N5 ... 73 A4
Park View Ho
Chingford E4 ... 35 C5
Hampton TW12 ... 174 A5
Streatham SE24 ... 160 D5
Park View KT3 ... 199 D6
Parkview Lo BR3 ... 207 D6
Park View Mans N4 ... 50 D2
Park View Mews 24
SW9 ... 138 B3
Park View
Morden SM4 ... 202 B4
Pinner HA5 ... 23 B2
Park View Rd DA16 ... 146 C2
Parkview Rd
Chislehurst SE9 ... 166 D2
Croydon CR0 ... 206 A1
Park View Rd
Ealing W5 ... 88 A2
Finchley N3 ... 29 D2
Hillingdon UB8 ... 82 C1
Pinner HA5 ... 22 B3
Southall UB1 ... 107 C5
Tottenham N17 ... 34 A1
Willesden NW10 ... 67 D4
Park View
Southgate N21 ... 16 B4
Wembley HA9 ... 66 D3
Willesden NW2 ... 68 C4
Yiewsley UB7 ... 104 A6
Park Village E
NW1 ... 93 B5 231 D3
Park Village W
NW1 ... 93 B5 231 C4
Park Villas RM6 ... 58 D3
Parkville Rd
SW6 ... 135 B5 264 C3
Park Vista Apartments
E13 ... 98 D4
Park Vista SE10 ... 142 B6
Park Walk Prim Sch
SW10 ... 136 B6 266 C5
Parkway
Abbey Wood
DA18 ... 125 A3
Camden Town
NW1 ... 93 B6 231 C5
Park Way Ct HA4 ... 39 D1
Park Way
East Molesey KT8 ... 195 D6
Edgware HA8 ... 26 D2
Enfield EN2 ... 4 C3
Feltham TW14 ... 150 B4
Friern Barnet N20 ... 30 D6
Gunnersbury W3 ... 110 C2
Parkway UB10 ... 60 D1
Parkway Ho SW14 ... 133 B1
Parkway Ilford IG3 ... 79 D5
Palmers Green N14 ... 16 A2
Parkway Prim Sch
DA18 ... 125 A3
Park Way Ruislip HA4 ... 40 A1
Temple Fortune
NW11 ... 47 A4
Parkway The
Cranford TW5 ... 128 B5
Hayes UB2, UB3, UB4,
TW5 ... 106 B3
Yeading UB4 ... 84 D2
Parkway Trad Est
TW5 ... 128 C6
Parkway
West Barnes
SW20 ... 200 D5
Woodford IG8 ... 37 C5
Park West Pl W1,
W2 ... 92 C1 237 B2
Park West
W2 ... 92 C1 237 B1
Park Wlk
Chelsea
SW10 ... 136 B6 266 C6
Highgate N6 ... 49 A2
Parkwood Ave KT10 ... 196 A1
Parkwood BR3 ... 185 C3
Parkwood Gr TW16 ... 194 A6
Parkwood Mews N6 ... 49 B3
Parkwood NW8 ... 230 C5
Parkwood Prim Sch
N4 ... 72 D6
Parkwood Rd
Hounslow TW7 ... 130 D4

Parkwood Rd *continued*
Old Bexley DA5 ... 169 B4
Wimbledon SW19 ... 179 B5
Parliament Ct NW3 ... 70 C4
Parliament Hill NW3 ... 70 C4
Parliament Hill Mans
NW5 ... 71 A4
Parliament Hill Sch
NW5 ... 71 A4
Parliament Mews
SW14 ... 133 A3
Parliament Sq*
SW1 ... 116 A4 250 A1
Parliament St
SW1 ... 116 A4 250 A2
Parliament View
Apartments SE11 .. 260 C4
Parma Cres SW11 ... 136 D1
Parminter Ind Est 24
E2 ... 96 B5
Parmiter St E2 ... 96 B5
Parmoor Ct EC1 ... 242 A6
Parnall Ho 11 SE19 ... 183 C6
Parnell Cl
Edgware HA8 ... 27 A6
Hammersmith W12 ... 112 B3
Parnell Ho WC1 ... 239 D2
Parnell Rd E3 ... 97 B6
Parnham Cl BR1 ... 210 D6
Parnham St E14 ... 97 A1
Parolles Rd N19 ... 49 C1
Paroma Rd DA17 ... 125 C3
Parr Cl N9 ... 34 B6
Parr Ct
Feltham TW13 ... 172 C6
Shoreditch N1 ... 235 C4
Parrington Ho 1
SW4 ... 159 D5
Parr Pl W4 ... 111 D2
Parr Rd Newham E6 ... 99 D6
Stanmore HA7 ... 26 A2
Parr's Pl TW12 ... 173 C3
Parr St N1 ... 95 B5 235 C4
Parry Ave E6 ... 100 B1
Parry Cl KT17 ... 216 A1
Parry Ho 32 E1 ... 118 B5
Parry Pl SE18 ... 122 D2
Parry Rd
South Norwood
SE25 ... 205 C6
West Kilburn W10 ... 91 A4
Parry St
SW8 ... 138 A6 270 B6
Parsifal Coll NW3 ... 69 C4
Parsifal Ho NW3 ... 69 C4
Parsifal Rd NW6 ... 69 C3
Parsley Gdns CR0 ... 206 D1
Parsloes Ave RM9 ... 81 A3
Parsloes Prim Sch
RM9 ... 81 B2
Parsonage Cl UB3 ... 83 D1
Parsonage Ct WD6 ... 11 A6
Parsonage Gdns EN2 ... 5 A3
Parsonage La
Enfield EN2 ... 5 B3
Sidcup DA14 ... 191 B6
Parsonage Manorway
DA17 ... 147 C6
Parsonage St E14 ... 120 A2
Parsons Cl SM1 ... 217 D5
Parsons Cres HA8 ... 10 C1
Parsons Gn
SW6 ... 135 C4 265 A1
PARSONS GREEN ... 135 C4
Parsons Green La
SW6 ... 135 C4 265 A2
Parsons Green Sta
SW6 ... 135 C4 265 A1
Parsons Hill SE18 ... 122 C3
Parsons Ho
Paddington W2 ... 236 C5
21 Streatham SW12 . 160 A4
Parsons Lo NW6 ... 69 D1
Parsons Mead KT8 ... 196 A6
Parson's Mead CR0 ... 204 D1
Parsons Rd
Edgware HA8 ... 10 C1
Newham E13 ... 99 C5
Parson St NW4 ... 46 C6
Parthenia Rd
SW6 ... 135 C4 265 B1
Partingdale La NW7 ... 28 D5
Partington Cl N19 ... 49 D1
Parton Lo 14 E8 ... 73 D2
Partridge Cl
Barnet EN5 ... 12 C5
Bushey WD23 ... 8 A3
1 Newham E16 ... 99 D2
Stanmore HA7 ... 26 A6
Partridge Ct EC1 ... 241 C6
Partridge Dr BR6 ... 227 A5
Partridge Gn SE9 ... 166 C1
Partridge Ho 22 E3 ... 97 B5
Partridge Rd
8 Hampton
TW12 ... 173 C4
Sidcup DA14 ... 189 C6

Partridge Sq 3 E6 ... 100 A2
Partridge Way N22 ... 32 A2
Pasadena Cl UB3 ... 106 B4
Pascall Ho SE17 ... 139 A6
Pascal St
SW8 ... 137 D5 269 D4
Pascoe Rd SE13 ... 164 B6
Pasley Cl SE17 ... 262 A1
Pasquier Rd E17 ... 53 A6
Passey Pl SE9 ... 166 B5
Passfield Dr E14 ... 97 D2
Passfield Ho SE18 ... 123 B2
Passfield Path 13
SE28 ... 124 B6
Passfields
Catford SE6 ... 164 A1
West Kensington
W14 ... 254 C1
Passing Alley EC1 ... 241 D5
Passingham Ho
TW5 ... 129 C6
Passmore Edwards Ho
N11 ... 31 D3
Passmore Gdns N11 ... 31 D4
Passmore Ho 12 N9 ... 18 A1
Passmore St
SW1 ... 115 A1 258 A2
Pasters Ct EN1 ... 17 D5
Pasteur Cl NW9 ... 27 C1
Pasteur Gdns N18 ... 33 A5
Paston Cl SM6 ... 219 C5
Paston Cres SE12 ... 165 B4
Pastor Ct N6 ... 49 C3
Pastor St SE1,
SE11 ... 116 D2 261 D4
Pasture Cl
Bushey WD23 ... 8 A4
Wembley HA0 ... 65 B5
Pasture Rd
Catford SE6 ... 164 D3
Dagenham RM9 ... 81 B3
Wembley HA0 ... 65 B5
Pastures Mead UB10 ... 60 C2
Pastures The N20 ... 13 B3
Patcham Terr SW8 ... 268 D2
Patch Cl UB10 ... 82 B6
Patching Way UB4 ... 85 A2
Pat Drew Ho BR1 ... 187 C2
Patent Ho E14 ... 97 D2
Paternoster La
EC4 ... 94 D1 241 D2
Paternoster Row EC2,
EC4 ... 95 A1 242 A1
Paternoster Sq
EC4 ... 94 D1 241 D2
Pater St W8 ... 113 C3 255 A5
Pates Manor Dr
TW14 ... 149 B4
Pathfield Rd SW16 ... 181 D4
Path The SW19 ... 179 D2
Pathway Ho SW17 ... 180 D4
Pathway Lo CR4 ... 180 D2
Patience Rd SW11 ... 136 C3
Patience Villas
SE13 ... 142 B2
Patio Cl SW4 ... 159 D5
Patmore Ho 9 N16 ... 73 C3
Patmore St
SW8 ... 137 C4 269 B2
Patmos Rd SW9 ... 138 D4
Paton Cl E3 ... 97 C4
Paton Ho 3 SW9 ... 138 B3
Paton St EC1 ... 235 A1
Patricia Ct
Chislehurst BR7 ... 189 B2
Woolwich DA16 ... 146 B5
Patrick Coman Ho
EC1 ... 234 C1
Patrick Connolly Gdns
41 E3 ... 97 D4
Patrick Rd E13 ... 99 C4
Patriot Sq E2 ... 96 B5
Patrol Pl SE6 ... 163 D5
Pat Shaw Ho 2 E1 ... 96 D3
Patshull Pl NW5 ... 71 C2
Patshull Rd NW5 ... 71 C2
Patson Cl E5 ... 74 D5
Pattenden Rd SE6 ... 163 B3
Patten Ho N4 ... 51 A1
Patten Rd SW18 ... 158 C4
Patterdale Cl BR1 ... 186 C4
Patterdale NW1 ... 231 D1
Patterdale Rd SE15 ... 140 C5
Patterson Ct SE19 ... 183 D4
Patterson Rd SE19 ... 183 D4
Pattina Wlk SE16 ... 119 A5
Pattinson Point 10
E16 ... 99 A2
Pattison Ho
Borough The SE1 ... 252 B2
1 Stepney E1 ... 96 D1
Pattison Rd NW2 ... 69 C5
Pattison Wlk SE18 ... 123 A1
Pat Williams Ho
SE27 ... 161 A1
Paul Byrne Ho 3 N2 ... 48 A6
Paul Cl E15 ... 76 C1

Paul Ct
7 Edmonton N18 ... 34 A6
Hendon N3 ... 29 A1
Paul Daisley Ct 2
NW6 ... 69 A1
Paulet Rd SE5 ... 138 D4
Paul Gdns CR0 ... 221 D6
Paulhan Rd HA3 ... 43 D5
Paul Ho 13 W10 ... 91 A3
Paulin Dr N21 ... 16 C4
Pauline Cres TW2 ... 152 A3
Pauline Ho 21 E1 ... 96 A2
Paulinus Cl BR5 ... 190 C1
Paul Julius Cl E14 ... 120 B6
Paul Robeson Cl E6 ... 100 C4
Paulson Ho 7 IG11 ... 78 D1
Paul St
Broadgate
EC2 ... 95 C3 243 A6
Newham E15 ... 98 C6
Paultons Ho SW3 ... 266 D6
Paultons Sq
SW3 ... 136 B6 266 D6
Paultons St
SW3 ... 136 B6 266 D5
Pauntley Ho 6 N19 ... 49 C1
Pauntley St 4 N19 ... 49 C1
Pavan Ct 29 E2 ... 96 C4
Paved Ct 9 TW9 ... 153 D6
Paveley Ct NW7 ... 28 D3
Paveley Dr
SW11 ... 136 C5 267 A3
Paveley Ho N1 ... 233 C3
Paveley St
NW8 ... 92 C3 237 B6
Pavement Mews 1
RM6 ... 58 D2
Pavement Sq CR0 ... 206 A1
Pavement The
Brentford W5 ... 110 A3
Clapham SW4 ... 137 C1
Leytonstone E11 ... 54 A1
11 West Norwood
SE27 ... 183 A6
Pavet Cl RM10 ... 81 D2
Pavilion Ct
Dagenham RM9 ... 103 A6
7 Hampstead NW3 ... 70 A4
Hampstead NW3 ... 70 B3
3 Paddington NW6 ... 91 C4
5 South Norwood
SW16 ... 182 B3
3 Wimbledon
SW19 ... 179 A3
Pavilion L Ctr The
BR1 ... 187 A1
Pavilion Lo HA2 ... 42 B1
Pavilion Mans 10
SW9 ... 138 B1
Pavilion Mews N3 ... 29 C1
Pavilion Rd
Knightsbridge
SW1 ... 114 D3 257 D5
Redbridge IG1 ... 56 B2
Pavilion Sq SW17 ... 158 D1
Pavilions The BR3 ... 185 C4
Pavilion St SW1 ... 257 D5
Pavilion Terr
Ilford IG2 ... 57 C4
8 North Kensington
W12 ... 90 C1
Pavilion Way
Burnt Oak HA8 ... 27 A3
Ruislip HA4 ... 62 C6
Pavillion Ct SW1 ... 268 C6
Pavitt Ct NW10 ... 68 A1
Pawleyne Cl SE20 ... 184 C3
Pawsey Cl E13 ... 99 A6
Pawson's Rd CR0 ... 205 A4
Paxford Rd HA0 ... 65 B6
Paxton Cl
Richmond TW9 ... 132 B3
Walton-on-T KT12 ... 194 C2
Paxton Ct
1 Forest Hill
SE26 ... 185 A6
Grove Pk SE9 ... 165 C1
Mitcham CR4 ... 180 D1
Paxton Ho SE17 ... 262 B2
Paxton Pl SE27 ... 183 C6
Paxton Prim Sch
SE19 ... 183 C4
Paxton Rd
Chiswick W4 ... 133 C6
Forest Hill SE23 ... 163 A1
Plaistow BR1 ... 187 A3
Tottenham N17 ... 34 A3
Paxton Terr SW1 ... 268 D6
Paymal Ho 33 E1 ... 96 C2
Payne Cl IG11 ... 79 D1
Payne Ho N1 ... 233 D5
Paynell Ct SE3 ... 142 C2
Payne Rd E3 ... 97 D5
Paynesfield Ave
SW14 ... 133 B2
Paynesfield Rd WD23 ... 8 D4
Payne St SE8 ... 141 B6

Paynes Wlk
W6 ... 135 A6
Payzes Gdns IG8 ...
Peabody Ave
SW1 ... 115 B1
Peabody Bldgs
6 Camberwell
SE5 ...
Walworth SE17 ...
Peabody Cl
Croydon CR0 ...
SW1 ...
Peabody Cotts N17 ...
Peabody Ct
9 Camberwell
SE5 ...
25 Enfield EN3 ...
St Luke's EC1 ...
Peabody Est
18 Bethnal Green
E2 ...
Borough The SE1 ...
Fulham
SW6 ... 135 B6
17 Hammersmith
W6 ...
Holborn EC1 ...
Lambeth SE1 ...
North Kensington
W10 ...
4 Ratcliff E1 ...
7 St George in t East
E1 ...
St Luke's EC1 ...
Strand WC2 ...
Streatham SE24 ...
Westminster SW1 ...
Peabody Hill SE21 ...
Peabody Sq SE1 ...
Peabody Twr EC1 ...
Peabody Yd N1 ...
Peace Cl
East Barnet N14 ...
Greenford UB6 ...
South Norwood
SE25 ...
Peace Ct 10 NW9 ...
Peace Gr HA9 ...
Peacehaven Ct 8
N10 ...
Peace St SE18 ...
Peach Ct E4 ...
Peaches Cl SM2 ...
Peaches Ct SM2 ...
Peach Gr E11 ...
Peach Rd
Feltham TW14 ...
London W10 ...
Peach Tree Ave UB7 ...
Peachum Rd SE3 ...
Peach Walk Mews 24
E3 ...
Peacock Ave TW14 ...
Peacock Cl
Dagenham RM8 ...
Walthamstow E4 ...
Peacock Ct EN1 ...
Peacock Ind Est N17 ...
Peacock St
SE17 ... 116 D2
Peacock Wlk E16 ...
Peacock Yd SE17 ...
Peaketon Ave IG4 ...
Peak Hill Ave SE26 ...
Peak Hill SE26 ...
Peak Hill Gdns
SE26 ...
Peak Ho N4 ...
Peak The SE26 ...
Peal Gdns W13 ...
Peall Rd Ind Est
CR0 ...
Peall Rd CR0 ...
Pear Ave TW17 ...
Pearce Cl 2 CR4 ...
Pearcefield Ave 5
SE23 ...
Pearce Ho
Camden Town N19 ...
7 Streatham SW2 ...
Westminster SW1 ...
Pear Cl
Kingsbury NW9 ...
New Cross Gate
SE14 ...
Pearcroft Rd E11 ...
Pear Ct 21 SE15 ...
Peardon St SW8 ...
Peareswood Gdns
HA7 ...
Pearfield Ho 1 N5 ...
Pearfield Rd SE23 ...
Pearl Cl Hendon NW2 ...
Newham E6 ...
Pearl Ct 18 NW9 ...
Pearl Rd E17 ...
Pearl St E1 ...

stones Ct
) 103 C6
nain Cl TW17 192 D4
nain Ho 9
142 A3
nan St
116 C4 251 B1
Pl SE1 251 A2
Rd E11 76 C5
croft Ct
135 D4 265 D1
croft Rd
135 D4 265 D1
se St 3 SE15 139 C6
son Cl Barnet EN5 1 D2
Camberwell SE5 139 A4
son Ct SM4 201 D4
son Ho SW15 134 C3
son's Ave SE8,
141 C4
son St E2 95 D5
son Way CR4 181 A2
Rd TW3 130 A2
Tree Ave UB7 82 B1
Tree Ave SW17 158 A1
Tree Cl
nley BR2 209 D4
ssington KT9 214 C3
ham CR4 180 C1
Shoreditch E2 95 D6
Tree Ct
orn EC1 241 B5
ey SW15 134 B1
dford IG8 37 B2
ree Gdns RM8 80 B4
Tree Ho
ckley SE4 141 B1
es UB8 83 A1
ree La E1 118 C6
Tree Rd TW15 171 A5
ree Rd EN1 5 C2
ree St
95 A3 242 A6
ree Way SE10 121 A2
y Ho 4 NW10 67 B1
y Pl E2 96 C4
ake Ct SM2 218 A1
Mead Terr E4 36 A6
ield Cl DA15 167 C1
orth Lo
Belmont SM2 217 D1
h Norwood
25 205 D5
orth Rd HA1 65 A6
armans Wood SE21,
162 A1
ett Sq 3 N5 72 D4
ford Pl SW9 138 C3
HAM 140 A4
ham Gr SE15 139 C5
ham High St
140 A4
ham Hill St
140 A5
ham Park Prim Sch
140 A5
ham Park Rd
140 A5
ham Rd SE5 139 C4
ham Rye
Dulwich
22 140 A1
ham SE15,
22 140 B1
ham Rye Sta
140 A3
water Ho 2
71 D2
water St NW5 71 C3
rs Wlk N7 72 A3
y Rd RM8 58 C1
y St E1 95 D3 243 D5
St E5 74 D4
orth Gdns 4
118 C2
les Ct UB1 86 A1
Cres SW19 178 D5
Centre
etropolitan Police
ning
ablishment)
45 D6
Cl Chingford E4 19 D2
onton N9 18 A1
Ct UB6 86 A4
Dr Colindale NW9 45 D6
bridge IG5 56 A6
Gr E2 96 C5
Pass W8 245 A3
Pl IG5 37 D1
Prec NW6 91 C5
Rd
borough BR6 227 A3
ow HA3 42 D6
mbley HA0, HA9 65 D5
dford E18 36 D2
St W8 113 C5 245 A3

Peel Way UB8 82 A2
Peel Yates Ho 13
SE7 122 A2
Peerglow Est EN3 18 C6
Peerless St
EC1 95 B4 235 C1
Pegamoid Rd N18 18 C1
Pegasus Cl N16 73 B4
Pegasus Ct
11 Acton W3 89 A1
Brentford TW8 110 B1
6 Buckhurst Hill IG9 21 D2
College Pk NW10 90 B4
Edmonton N21 17 A4
Harrow HA3 43 D4
Kingston u T KT1 197 D6
Sutton SM1 217 D6
Pegasus Ho 9 E1 96 D3
Pegasus Lo N21 17 A4
Pegasus Pl 2 SE11 138 C6
Pegasus Rd CR0,
CR9 220 C2
Pegasus Way N11 31 B4
Peggotty Way UB8 82 D1
Pegg Rd TW5 128 D5
Peggy Quirke Ct 2
HA0 66 A2
Pegley Gdns SE12 165 A2
Pegwell Ho 19 E5 74 B3
Pegwell St SE18 145 C5
Pekin St E14 97 C1
Pekoe SE1 253 D3
Peldon Ct TW10 154 B6
Pele Ct N17 33 B3
Pelham Ave IG11 101 D6
Pelham Cl SE5 139 C2
Pelham Cotts DA5 169 D3
Pelham Cres SW7 257 A3
Pelham Ct SW3 257 A3
Pelham Ho W14 254 C3
Pelham Pl
Chelsea SW7 257 A3
8 Ealing W7 86 D3
Pelham Prim Sch
Bexleyheath DA7 147 C2
Merton SW19 179 C3
Pelham Rd
Bexleyheath DA7 147 C2
Ilford IG1 79 B6
Merton SW19 179 C3
Penge BR3, SE20 184 C1
Tottenham N15 51 D5
Wanstead E18 55 B6
Wood Green N22 32 C1
Pelham St
SW7 114 B2 256 D4
Pelican Ho 8 SE8 119 B2
Pelican Pas 3 E1 96 C3
Pelier St SE17 139 A6
Pelinore Rd SE6 164 C2
Pella Ho SE11 260 D2
Pellant Rd
SW6 135 A5 264 B4
Pellatt Gr N22 32 C2
Pellatt Rd
East Dulwich
SE22 161 D6
Wembley HA9 66 A6
Pellerin Rd N16 73 C3
Pellew Ho 15 E1 96 B3
Pellings Cl BR2 208 C6
Pelling St E14 97 C1
Pellipar Cl N13 16 C1
Pellipar Gdns SE18 122 B1
Pellipar Rd SE18 122 B1
Pelly Ct 4 E17 54 A5
Pelly Rd E13 99 A5
Pelter St E2 95 D4
Pelton Ct CR2 221 A2
Pelton Rd SE10 120 C1
Pembar Ave E17 53 A6
Pemberley Chase
KT19 214 D3
Pemberley Cl KT19 214 D3
Pemberley Ho KT19 214 D3
Pember Rd NW10 90 D4
Pemberton Ct 18 E1 96 D4
Pemberton Gdns
Camden Town N19 71 C5
Dagenham RM6 59 A4
Pemberton Ho
SE26 184 A6
Pemberton Pl
Esher KT10 212 A5
2 Hackney E8 74 B1
Pemberton Rd
East Molesey KT8 196 A5
Harringay N4 50 D4
Pemberton Row
EC4 241 B2
Pemberton Terr N19 71 C5
Pembridge Ave
TW4 151 B3
Pembridge Cres
W11 113 C6 245 A6
Pembridge Gdns
W2 113 C6 245 A5

Pembridge Hall Sch
W2 113 C6 245 B5
Pembridge Mews
W11 113 C6 245 A6
Pembridge Pl
Notting Hill
W2 113 C6 245 B6
1 Wandsworth
SW15 157 C6
Pembridge Rd
W11 113 C6 245 A5
Pembridge Sq
W2 113 C6 245 B5
Pembridge Villas
W11 113 C6 245 A6
Pembroke Ave
Enfield EN1 6 B4
Harrow HA3 43 B6
Islington N1 94 A6 233 B6
Surbiton KT5 198 D4
Pembroke Bldgs
NW10 90 A4
Pembroke Cl SW1 248 B1
Pembroke Ct 11 W7 86 D2
Pembroke Gdns Cl
W8 255 A5
Pembroke Gdns
Dagenham RM10 81 D5
West Kensington
W8 113 B2 254 D4
Pembroke Hall NW4 46 C6
Pembroke Ho
Acton W3 111 A4
Chelsea SW1 258 A5
5 Clapham Pk SW2 160 A6
17 Kensington W2 91 D1
Putney SW15 156 A6
Upper Tooting SW17 180 B5
Pembroke Lo 2
SW16 160 B1
Pembroke Mews
8 Bow E3 97 A4
Bromley BR1 187 D1
Kensington W8 255 A5
Muswell Hill N10 31 A2
Pembroke Pl
Edgware HA8 26 C3
Isleworth TW7 130 C3
Kensington W8 255 A5
Pembroke Rd
Bromley BR1 187 D1
Edmonton N13 17 A1
Greenford UB6 85 D3
Hornsey N8 50 A5
Ilford IG3 57 D2
Kensington
W8 113 C2 255 A4
Mitcham CR4 181 A1
Muswell Hill N10 31 A3
Newham E6 100 B2
Ruislip HA4 39 D1
South Norwood
SE25 205 C5
South Tottenham N15 51 D4
Walthamstow E17 53 D4
Wembley HA9 65 D5
Pembroke Sq
W8 113 C3 255 A5
Pembroke St
N1 94 A6 233 B6
Pembroke Studios
W8 254 D5
Pembroke Terr
NW8 229 C5
Pembroke Villas
Kensington W8 255 A4
Richmond TW9 131 D1
Pembroke W14 254 D3
Pembroke Way UB3 105 A3
Pembroke Wlk W8 255 A4
Pembry Cl SW9 138 C4
Pembury Ave KT4 200 A2
Pembury Cl
Hackney E5 74 B3
Hayes BR2 208 D2
Pembury Cres DA14 169 A2
Pembury Ct UB3 127 B6
Pembury Ho
Camberwell SE5 139 C3
Keston Mark BR2 210 A1
Pembury Pl 15 E5, E8 74 B3
Pembury Rd
Croydon SE25 206 A5
Erith DA7 147 A6
Hackney E5 74 B3
Tottenham N17 33 D1
Pemdevon Rd CR0 204 C2
Pemell Cl 30 E1 96 C3
Pemell Ho 31 E1 96 C3
Pemerich Cl UB3 105 D1
Pempath Pl HA9 65 D6
Penair Lodge HA1 64 C5
Penally Pl N1 235 D6
Penang St E1 118 B5
Penard Rd UB2 107 D3
Penarth Ctr The
SE15 140 C6

Penarth Ct SM2 218 A1
Penarth St SE15 140 C6
Penates KT10 212 B4
Penberth Rd SE6 164 A3
Penbury Rd UB2 107 B1
Penceat Ct SE20 184 C1
Pencombe Mews
W11 244 D6
Pencraig Way SE15 140 B6
Pendall Cl EN4 2 C1
Penda Rd DA8 147 D5
Pendarves Rd
SW20 178 C2
Penda's Mead E9 75 A4
Pendell Ave UB3 127 D5
Pendennis Ho 15
SE8 119 A2
Pendennis Rd
Streatham SW16 182 A6
Tottenham N17 51 B6
Penderel Rd TW3 151 C6
Penderry Rise SE6 164 B2
Penderyn Way N7 71 D4
Pendlebury Ho 5
SE18 144 A4
Pendle Ho 18 SE26 162 A1
Pendle Rd SW16 181 B5
Pendlestone Rd E17 53 D4
Pendley Ho 18 E2 96 A6
Pendolino Way
NW10 66 D1
Pendragon Rd BR1 165 A1
Pendragon Sch
BR1 165 A1
Pendragon Wlk NW9 45 C3
Pendrell Ho WC2 239 D1
Pendrell Rd SE4 141 A3
Pendrell St SE18 145 B6
Pendula Dr UB4 84 D3
Penelope Ho 20
SW9 138 C4
Penerley Rd SE6 163 D3
Penfield Lo 7 W9 91 C2
Penfields Ho N7 72 A2
Penfold Cl CR0 220 C5
Penfold Ct 7 CR4 181 A1
Penfold Ho 14 SE18 144 D6
Penfold La DA5 168 D3
Penfold Pl
NW1 92 C2 237 A4
Penfold Rd N9 18 D3
Penfold St
NW8 92 B3 236 D5
Penford Gdns SE9 143 D2
Penford St SE5 138 D3
Pengarth Rd DA5 168 D5
PENGE 184 D4
Penge East Sta
SE20 184 C4
Penge La SE20 184 D3
Penge Rd
Newham E13 99 C6
South Norwood
SE25 206 A6
Penge West Sta
SE20 184 B4
Penhall Rd SE7 121 D2
Penhill Rd DA5 168 C4
Penhurst Mans SW6 264 C2
Penifather La UB6 86 B4
Peninsula Ct E14 119 D3
Peninsular Cl TW14 149 C5
Peninsular Park Rd
SE7 121 A2
Penistone Rd SW16 182 A3
Penketh Dr HA1 64 B5
Penmayne Ho SE11 261 B2
Penmon Rd SE2 124 A3
Pennack Rd SE15 139 D6
Penn Almshouses 1
SE10 142 A4
Pennant Mews
W8 113 D2 255 C4
Pennant Terr E17 35 B1
Pennard Mans 5
W12 112 C4
Pennard Rd W12 112 C4
Pennards The
TW16 194 C6
Penn Cl
Greenford UB6 85 D5
Harrow HA3 43 C5
Penn Ct NW9 45 B6
Pennefather Ho N1 73 B2
Pennells Ct TW5 129 C6
Penner Cl SW19 157 A2
Penners Gdns KT6 198 A2
Pennethorne Cl E9 96 C6
Pennethorne Ho
SW11 136 B2
Pennethorne Rd
SE15 140 B5
Penn Gdns BR7 188 D1
Penn Ho
7 Edmonton N9 18 A1
Lisson Gr NW8 237 A5
Pennine Dr NW2 68 D6

Pennine La NW2 69 A6
Pennine Mans NW2 69 A6
Pennine Par NW2 69 A6
Pennine Way UB7 127 B5
Pennington Cl 10
SE27 183 B6
Pennington Ct
4 Rotherhithe
SE16 119 A5
23 St George in t East
E1 118 A6
Pennington Dr N21 16 A6
Pennington Lo 18
KT5 198 A4
Pennington St E1 118 B6
Pennington Way
SE12 165 B2
Penniston Cl N17 33 A1
Penn La Bexley DA5 168 D5
Sidcup DA5 169 A5
Penn Rd N7 72 A4
Penn St N1 95 B6 235 D5
Penny Ct SW10 266 B6
Pennyfields E14 119 C6
Pennyford Ct NW8 236 C6
Penny La TW17 193 C2
Penny Mews SW12 159 B4
Pennymore Wlk W9 91 B3
Penny Rd NW10 88 D4
Pennyroyal Ave E6 100 C1
Penny Royal SM6 219 D2
Penpoll Rd E8 74 B2
Penpool La DA16 146 B2
Penray EN5 1 A2
Penrhyn Ave E17 35 C2
Penrhyn Cres
Mortlake SW14 133 A1
Walthamstow E17 35 C2
Penrhyn Gdns KT1 197 D5
Penrhyn Gr E17 35 C2
Penrhyn Rd KT1 198 A6
Penrith Cl
Beckenham BR3 185 D2
Putney SW15 157 A6
Penrith Pl SE27 160 D2
Penrith Rd
New Malden KT3 199 B5
South Norwood CR7 183 A1
Tottenham N15 51 B4
Penrith St SW16 181 C4
Penrose Gr
SE17 117 A1 262 A1
Penrose Ho
Camberwell SE17 262 A1
Southgate N21 16 B6
Penrose St
SE17 117 A1 262 A1
Penryn Ho SE11 261 C2
Penryn St
NW1 93 D5 232 C4
Penry St SE1 263 B3
Pensbury Pl SW8 137 C3
Pensbury St SW8 137 C3
Pensford Ave TW9 132 C3
Penshurst Ave
DA15 168 A5
Penshurst Ct
Croydon CR2 220 D1
1 Edgware HA8 26 D5
Penshurst Gdns HA8 26 D5
Penshurst Gn BR2 208 D4
Penshurst Ho 1
SE15 140 C6
Penshurst 2 NW5 71 A2
Penshurst Rd
Erith DA7 147 B4
Homerton E9 74 D1
Thornton Heath CR7 204 D4
Tottenham N17 33 D3
Penshurst Way SM2 217 C1
Penshurst Wlk 4
BR2 208 D4
Pensilver Cl EN4 2 C1
Penstemon Cl N3 29 C4
Pentavia Retail Pk
NW7 27 D3
Pentelow Gdns
TW14 150 A5
Pentire Rd E17 36 B2
Pentland Ave
Edgware HA8 10 D2
Littleton TW17 192 C4
Pentland Cl
Cricklewood NW11 69 A6
Lower Edmonton N9 18 C2
Pentland Gdns
SW18 158 A5
Pentland Ho
17 Camden Town
NW5 71 A2
7 Stamford Hill N16 51 D1
Pentland Pl UB5 85 A6
Pentland Rd
Bushey WD23 8 A5
1 Maida Vale NW6 91 C4
Pentlands BR3 186 A2
Pentlands Cl CR4 203 B6

Pentland St SW18 158 A5
Pentland Way UB10 61 A5
Pentlow St SW15 134 C2
Pentney Rd
5 Chingford E4 20 B3
Merton SW19,
SW20 179 A2
Streatham SW12 159 C3
Penton Gr N1 234 A3
Penton Ho
3 Abbey Wood
SE2 124 D4
Islington N1 234 A3
Sutton SM2 218 A1
Penton Pl
SE17 116 D1 261 D2
Penton Rise
WC1 94 B4 233 D2
Penton St N1 94 C5 234 A3
PENTONVILLE 94 B5
Pentonville Rd
N1 94 B5 233 C3
Pentrich Ave EN1 6 A5
Pentridge St SE15 139 D5
Pentyre Ave N18 33 B5
Penwerris Ave TW5,
TW7 130 A5
Penwerris Ct TW7 130 A5
Penwith Rd SW18 157 D2
Penwood Ct HA5 41 B5
Penwood Ho SW15 155 D5
Penwortham Ct 1
N22 32 C1
Penwortham Prim Sch
SW17 181 B4
Penwortham Rd
SW16 181 C4
Penylan Pl HA8 26 C3
Penywern Rd
SW5 113 C1 255 B2
Penzance Ho SE11 261 B2
Penzance Pl
W11 113 A5 244 B4
Penzance St
W11 113 A5 244 A4
Peony Ct IG8 36 C3
Peony Gdns W12 112 A6
Peperfield WC1 233 C1
Pepler Ho 17 W10 91 A3
Pepler Mews SE1 263 C1
Peploe Rd NW6 90 D5
Pepper Cl E6 100 B2
Peppercorn Cl CR7 183 B1
Peppermead Sq
SE13 163 C6
Peppermint Cl CR0 204 A2
Peppermint Pl 7
E11 76 C5
Pepper St
Borough The SE1 252 A2
Millwall E14 119 D3
Peppie Cl N16 73 C6
Pepsi Trocadero*
W1 249 C5
Pepys Cl UB10 60 D4
Pepys Cres
Barnet EN5 12 C6
2 Newham E16 121 A5
Pepys Ct SW20 178 C1
Pepys Ent Ctr 13
SE8 119 B2
Pepys Ho
14 Bethnal Green
E2 96 C4
Clapham Pk SW4 159 D6
Pepys Rd
New Cross Gate
SE14 140 D3
Wimbledon SW20 178 C2
Pepys Rise BR6 211 D1
Pepys St
EC3 117 C6 253 B6
Perak Ct KT5 199 A2
Peralte Terr CR4 204 A5
Perceval Ave NW3 70 C3
Perceval Ct UB5 63 C3
Percheron Cl TW7 130 D2
Percheron Ct 3
SW9 138 B2
Percheron Rd WD6 11 B5
Perch St E8 73 D4
Percival Ct N17 33 D3
Percival Gdns RM6 58 C3
Percival Ho 3 IG8 37 A6
Percival Rd Enfield EN1 5 D1
Feltham TW13 149 D2
Mortlake SW14 133 A1
Orpington BR6 226 D6
Percival St
EC1 94 D4 234 D1
Percival Way KT19 215 B4
Percy Ave TW15 170 C5
Percy Bilton Ct
TW5 129 D4

Percy Bryant Rd TW16 171 C3
Percy Bush Rd UB7 104 B3
Percy Cir WC1 94 B4 233 D2
Percy Ct 1 KT5 198 B3
Percy Gdns
Enfield EN3 18 D6
Hayes UB4 83 C4
5 Isleworth TW7 131 A2
New Malden KT4 199 C1
Percy Ho 4 SW16 181 C6
Percy Laurie Ho 6 SW15 134 D1
Percy Mews W1 239 C3
Percy Pas W1 239 C3
Percy Rd
Bexleyheath DA7 147 A3
Carshalton CR4 203 A2
Croydon SE25 206 A4
Edmonton N21 17 A4
Hampton TW12 173 C3
Ilford IG3 58 A2
Isleworth TW7 131 A1
Leytonstone E11 54 C2
Newham E16 98 C2
North Finchley N12 30 A5
Penge SE20 184 D2
Romford RM7 59 D6
Shepherd's Bush W12 112 A4
Twickenham TW2 152 A3
Percy St W1 93 D2 239 C3
Percy Terr BR1 210 D6
Percy Way TW2 152 A3
Peregrine Cl NW10 67 B3
Peregrine Ct
Bexley DA16 145 D4
Streatham SW16 182 B6
Peregrine Gdns CR0 223 A6
Peregrine Ho
6 Battersea SW11 136 C2
Finsbury EC1 234 D2
Peregrine Rd
Sunbury TW16 171 D1
Tottenham N17 33 B3
Peregrine Way SW19, SW20 178 C3
Performing Arts & Tech Sch SE25 205 B3
Perham Rd W14 113 A1 254 B1
Peridot St E6 100 A2
Perifield SE21 161 A3
Perimeade Rd UB6 87 C5
Period Wks E10 53 A1
Periton Rd SE9 143 D1
PERIVALE 87 B5
Perivale Gdns W13 87 B3
Perivale Grange UB6 87 A4
Perivale Ind Pk UB6 87 B5
Perivale La UB6 87 A4
Perivale Lo UB6 87 A4
Perivale New Bsns Ctr UB6 87 C5
Perivale Prim Sch UB6 87 C5
Perivale Sta UB6 87 A5
Perivale UB6 86 D5
Perkin Cl
Hounslow TW3 129 D1
Wembley HA0 65 B3
Perkins Ct TW15 170 B5
Perkins Ho 15 E14 97 B2
Perkins Rd IG2 57 B4
Perkins Rents SW1 259 C5
Perkins Sq SE1 252 B4
Perks Cl SE3 142 C2
Perley Ho 9 E3 97 B2
Perotti Ho SW6 135 D2
Perpins Rd SE9 167 C5
Perran Rd SE24, SW2 160 D2
Perren St NW5 71 B2
Perrers Rd W6 112 B2
Perrin Cl TW15 170 B5
Perrin Ct TW15 170 C6
Perring Est E3 97 C2
Perrin Grange HA9 66 B6
Perrin Rd HA0 65 B4
Perrins Ct HA3 44 B2
Perrin's Ct 20 NW3 70 A4
Perrin's La NW3 70 A4
Perrin's Wlk NW3 70 A4
Perronet Ho SE1 261 D5
Perry Ave W3 89 B1
Perry Cl UB8 82 D1
Perry Ct
6 Isle of Dogs E14 119 C1
2 Kingston u T KT2 176 A1
Sutton SM1 217 C3
Perry Ct continued
2 Tottenham N15 51 C3
Perryfield Way
Richmond TW10 153 B2
West Hendon NW9 45 D3
Perry Garth UB5 84 C6
Perry Gdns N9 17 C1
Perry Hall Prim Sch BR6 211 D3
Perry Hill SE6 163 B1
Perry Ho 24 SW2 160 A4
Perry How KT4 199 D1
Perryman Ho
Barking IG11 101 A6
Tottenham N17 34 B3
Perrymans Farm Rd IG2 57 B4
Perry Mead
Bushey WD23 8 A5
Enfield EN2 4 D3
Perrymead St SW6 135 D4 265 C1
Perrymount Prim Sch SE23 162 D2
Perryn Ct 1 TW1 153 A4
Perryn Ho W3 111 C6
Perryn Rd Acton W3 111 B6
1 Bermondsey SE16 118 B3
Perry Rise SE23 163 A1
Perry's Pl W1 239 C2
Perry St BR7 189 C4
Perry Street Gdns BR7 189 C4
Perry Vale SE23 162 D2
Perrywood Ho 17 E5 74 B3
Persant Rd SE6 164 C2
Perseverance Pl SW9 138 C5
Perseverance Works 17 E2 95 C4
Pershore Cl IG2 56 D4
Pershore Gr SM5 202 B3
Pershore Ho 11 W13 109 A5
Pert Cl N10 31 B4
Perth Ave Hayes UB4 84 C3
Kingsbury NW9 45 B2
Perth Cl Northolt UB5 63 C3
Wimbledon SW20 178 A1
Perth Ct 5 SE5 139 B1
Perth Ho 12 Acton W3 88 C1
Barnsbury N1 72 B1
Perth Rd
Barking IG11 101 B6
Beckenham BR3 186 A1
Finsbury Pk N4 50 C1
Ilford IG2 56 D3
Newham E13 99 B5
Tottenham N22 32 D2
Walthamstow E10 53 B1
Perth Terr IG2 57 A2
Perwell Ave HA2 41 B1
Perystreete SE23 162 C2
Petavel Rd TW11 174 C4
Petchey Acad The E8 73 D3
Peter Ave NW10 68 B1
Peter Best Ho 1 E1 96 B1
Peterboat Cl SE10 120 C2
Peterborough Ct EC4 241 B1
Peterborough Gdns IG1 56 A2
Peterborough Mews SW6 135 C3
Peterborough Prim Sch SW6 135 C3
Peterborough Rd
Carshalton SM5 202 C3
Fulham SW6 135 C2
Harrow HA1 42 D2
Leytonstone E10 54 B3
Peterborough Villas SW6 265 C2
Peter Bradley Ct RM9 81 B1
Peter Butler Ho 9 SE1 118 A4
Peterchurch Ho SE15 140 B6
Peter Fagan Ho UB3 105 C3
Petergate SW11 136 A1
Peterhead Ct 12 UB1 86 A1
Peter Heathfield Ho 4 E15 98 B6
Peter Hills Ho 6 SE16 118 A2
Peter Hills with St Mary's & St Paul's CE Prim Sch SE16 118 D5
Peter Ho SW8 270 A4
Peter James Bsns Ctr UB3 106 A4
Peter James Ent Ctr NW10 89 A4
Peter Kennedy Ct CR0 207 B3
Peterley Bsns Ctr 21 E2 96 B5
Peter Lyell Ct HA4 62 B6
Peters Cl
Bexley DA16 145 C3
Dagenham RM8 58 D1
Stanmore HA7 25 D4
Peter's Ct SW4 160 A5
Peters Ct 9 W2 91 D1
Petersfield Cl N18 33 A5
Petersfield Rd W3 111 A4
Petersfield Rise SW15 156 B3
PETERSHAM 154 A3
Petersham Cl
Richmond TW10 153 D2
Sutton SM1 217 C3
Petersham Dr BR5 190 A1
Petersham Gdns BR5 189 D1
Petersham Ho SW7 256 C4
Petersham La SW7 256 A6
Petersham Mews SW7 114 A3 256 B5
Petersham Pl SW7 114 A3 256 B6
Petersham Rd TW10 154 A3
Petersham Terr CR0 220 A5
Peter's La EC1 241 D4
Peter's Lo HA8 26 B4
Peter's Path SE26 184 B6
Peterstone Rd SE2 124 B4
Peterstow Cl SW19 157 A2
Peter St W1 115 D6 249 C6
Peterwood Pk CR9 220 B6
Peterwood Way CR0 220 B6
Petherton Ct
Brondesbury Pk NW10 90 D6
10 Harrow HA1 42 D3
Petherton Ho N4 51 A1
Petherton Rd N5 73 A3
Petiver Cl 28 E9 74 C1
Petley Rd W6 134 D5
Peto Pl NW1 238 D6
Peto St N E16 98 D1
Petrel Ct 8 SE21 161 B2
Petrie Cl NW2 69 A2
Petrie Ho 8 SE18 144 C6
Petrie Mus of Egyptian Archaeology* WC1 93 D3 239 C5
Petros Gdns 1 NW3 70 A2
Pettacre Cl SE28 123 A3
Petticoat Lane Mkt* EC2 95 D2 243 C3
Petticoat Sq E1 243 C2
Petticoat Twr E1 243 C2
Pettit's Pl RM10 81 C3
Pettit's Rd RM10 81 C3
Pettiward Cl SW15 134 C1
Pettman Cres SE18, SE28 123 B3
Pettsgrove Ave HA0 65 C3
Pett's Hill UB5 63 D3
Petts La TW17 192 C5
Pett St SE7 122 A2
PETTS WOOD 211 B5
Petts Wood Rd BR5 211 B4
Petts Wood Sta BR5 211 A4
Petty France SW1 115 D3 259 C6
Petty Wales EC3 253 B5
Petworth Cl UB5 63 B1
Petworth Gdns
Hillingdon UB10 83 A6
West Barnes SW20 200 B6
Petworth Ho 10 SE22 139 C2
Petworth Rd
Bexley DA6 169 C6
Colney Hatch N12 30 C5
Petworth St SW11 136 C4 267 B2
Petyt Pl SW3 136 C6 267 A5
Petyward SW3 114 C2 257 B3
Pevensey Ave
Enfield EN1 5 C3
Friern Barnet N11 31 D5
Pevensey Cl TW7 130 A5
Pevensey Ct
4 South Acton W3 110 D4
West Norwood SW16 160 C1
10 Woodford E18 37 A2
Pevensey Ho 5 E1 97 A2
Pevensey Rd
Feltham TW13 151 A3
Pevensey Rd continued
Forest Gate E7 77 A4
Upper Tooting SW17 180 B6
Peverel Ho RM10 81 C6
Peverel E6 100 C1
Peverett Cl N11 31 B5
Peveril Dr TW11 174 B5
Peveril Ho SE1 262 D5
Pewsey Cl E4 35 C5
Pewsham Ho N4 51 A1
Pewterers Ct N3 29 B2
Peyton Ho N11 31 A6
Peyton Pl SE10 142 A5
Pharamond NW2 68 D2
Pharaoh Cl CR4 202 D2
Pheasant Cl E16 99 B1
Phelps Ho SW15 134 D2
Phelp St SE17 139 B6
Phelps Way UB3 105 D2
Phene St SW3 136 C6 267 B6
Philadelphia Ct SW10 266 B3
Philbeach Gdns SW5 113 C1 255 A2
Phil Brown Pl 3 SW8 137 B2
Philchurch Pl 30 E1 96 A1
Philia Ho 4 NW1 71 C1
Philimore Cl SE18 123 C1
Philip Blairman Ho E1 243 C5
Philip Ct Enfield EN2 5 B4
Paddington W2 236 C4
Philip Gdns CR0 223 B6
Philip Ho
East Barnet N20 14 D2
12 Paddington NW6 91 D6
Philip La N15 51 C6
Philipot Almshouse SE9 166 B5
Philipot Path SE9 166 B5
Philippa Gdns SE9 165 D6
Philips Cl CR4 203 A1
Philip St E13 99 A3
Philip Turner Est 28 E9 74 C1
Philip Wlk SE15 140 A2
Phillimore Ct W8 245 B1
Phillimore Gardens Cl W8 113 C3 255 A6
Phillimore Gdns
Kensington W8 113 C4 245 A1
Willesden NW10 90 C6
Phillimore Pl W8 113 C4 245 A1
Phillimore Terr W8 255 B6
Phillimore Wlk W8 113 C3 255 B6
Phillip Ho E1 243 D3
Phillipp St N1 95 C6
Phillips Ct
Edgware HA8 26 C4
Hayes UB4 84 B4
Phillipson Ho 6 N12 29 D5
Philpot La EC3 253 A6
Philpot Sq SW6 135 D2
Philpot St E1 96 B1
Philson Mans 13 E1 96 B1
Phineas Pett Rd SE9 144 A2
Phipp's Bridge Rd CR4, SW19 202 B6
Phipps Bridge Sta CR4 202 B6
Phipps Hatch La EN2 5 A5
Phipps Ho
1 Greenwich SE7 121 B1
16 Shepherd's Bush W12 112 B6
Phipp St EC2 95 C3 243 A6
Phoebeth Rd SE4 163 C6
Phoenix Bsns Ctr 22 E3 97 C2
Phoenix Cl
18 Shoreditch E8 95 D6
Walthamstow E17 35 B1
West Wickham BR4 224 C6
Phoenix Ct
4 Brentford TW8 110 A1
Chingford E4 19 D1
Croydon SE25 206 A4
2 Deptford SE14 141 A6
Enfield EN3 6 C5
Feltham TW13 171 C6
Millwall E14 119 C2
8 New Barnet EN5 2 A1
Phoenix Ctr The 1 SM6 220 A1
Phoenix Dr BR2 225 D5
Phoenix High Sch W12 112 A6
Phoenix Ho
Chelsea SW1 258 A4
Kingston u T KT3 199 D6
Phoenix Ind Est HA1 42 D5
Phoenix Lodge Mans 1 W6 112 C2
Phoenix Pk NW2 68 A6
Phoenix Pl WC1 94 B3 240 D6
Phoenix Rd
Penge SE20 184 C4
Somers Town NW1 93 D4 232 C2
Phoenix Sch E3 97 B4
Phoenix Sch The NW3 70 A2
Phoenix St WC2 239 D1
Phoenix Trad Est UB6 87 D6
Phoenix Trad Pk TW8 109 D1
Phoenix Way TW5 128 D6
Phoenix Wharf Rd SE1 253 D1
Phyllis Ave KT3 200 B4
Phyllis Ho CR0 220 D4
Phyllis Hodges Ho NW1 93 D5 232 C3
Physic Pl SW3 136 D6 267 C6
Picador Ho 1 RM10 81 D2
Picardy Manorway DA17 125 D4
Picardy Rd DA17 125 C2
Picardy St DA17 125 C3
Piccadilly Arc SW1 249 A4
Piccadilly Circus Sta SW1 115 D6 249 C5
Piccadilly Cir* W1 115 D6 249 C5
Piccadilly Ct 5 N7 72 B2
Piccadilly Pl W1 249 B5
Piccadilly W1 115 C5 249 A4
Pickard Cl N14 15 D3
Pickard St EC1 234 D2
Pickering Ave E6 100 C4
Pickering Cl E9 74 D1
Pickering Ct N22 32 D2
Pickering Gdns
Croydon SE25 205 D3
Friern Barnet N11 31 A4
Pickering Ho
Brentford W5 109 C2
18 Kensington W2 91 D1
Stoke Newington N4 51 B2
4 Woolwich SE18 122 C2
Pickering Mews 9 W2 91 D1
Pickering Pl SW1 249 B3
Pickering St N1 234 D6
Pickets Cl WD23 8 C3
Pickets St SW12 159 B4
Pickett Croft HA7 25 D2
Pickett's Lock La N9 18 D2
Pickford Cl DA7 147 A3
Pickford La DA7 147 A3
Pickford Rd DA7 147 A2
Pickfords Wharf N1 235 A3
Pickhurst Gn BR2 208 D2
Pickhurst Inf Sch BR2 208 D3
Pickhurst Jun Sch BR2 208 D3
Pickhurst La BR2, BR3, BR4 208 C2
Pickhurst Mead BR2 208 D2
Pickhurst Pk BR2 208 D4
Pickhurst Rise BR4 208 B1
Pickwick Cl TW4 151 A6
Pickwick Ct SE9 166 B3
Pickwick Ho
21 Bermondsey SE16 118 A4
3 Shepherd's Bush W11 112 D5
Pickwick Mews N18 33 C5
Pickwick Pl HA1 42 C2
Pickwick Rd SE21 161 C4
Pickwick St SE1 252 A1
Pickwick Way BR7 189 A4
Pickworth Cl SW8 270 B3
Picton Ho 1 SW4 160 A4
Picton Pl
Marylebone W1 238 B1
Tolworth KT6 198 C1
Picton St SE5 139 B5
Picture Ho 6 SW16 160 A2
Pied Bull Ct WC1 240 B3
Pied Bull Yd WC1 240 B3
Piedmont Rd SE18 123 B1
Pield Heath Ave UB8 82 C3
Pield Heath House Sch UB8 82 A3
Pield Heath Rd UB8 82 B3
Pier Head E1 118 B5
Pierhead Wharf 37 E1
Pier Ho SW3
Piermont Pl BR1
Piermont Rd SE22
Pier Par 3 E16
Pierpoint Bldg 4 E14
Pier Rd
Feltham TW14
Newham E16
Pierrepoint Rd W3
Pierrepoint Row N1
Pierrepoint SE25
Pierson Ho 12 SE19
Pier St E14
Pier Terr SW18
Pier Way SE18
Pigeon Ct E4
Pigeon La TW12
Piggott Ho 2 E2
Pigott St E14
Pike Cl Bromley BR1
Hillingdon UB10
Pike Rd NW7
Pike's End HA5
Pikestone Cl UB4
Pikethorne 1 SE23
Pilgrimage St SE1 117 B4
Pilgrim Cl SM4
Pilgrim Hill SE27
Pilgrim Ho SE1
Pilgrims Cl UB5
Pilgrims Cloisters 10 SE5
Pilgrims Cl N13
Pilgrims Ct Enfield EN1
Greenwich SE3
Pilgrim's La NW3
Pilgrims Mews 12 E14
Pilgrim's Pl 6 NW3
Pilgrim's Rise EN4
Pilgrim St EC4
Pilgrims Way 5 E6
Pilgrims Way Prim Sch SE15
Pilgrim's Way CR2
Pilgrims Way
Upper Holloway N19
Wembley HA9
Pilkington Ct 1 NW9
Pilkington Rd
Orpington BR6
4 Peckham SE15
Pillions La UB4
Pilot Ind Ctr NW10
Pilsden Cl SW19
Piltdown Rd WD19
Pilton Est The CR0
Pilton Pl SE17
Pimento Ct W5
Pimlico Sta SW1 115 D1
PIMLICO
Pimlico Rd SW1 115 A1
Pimlico Sch SW1 115 C1
Pimlico Wlk 1 N1
Pinchbeck Rd BR6
Pinchin St E1
Pincombe Ho SE17
Pincott Pl SE4
Pincott Rd
8 Bexley DA6
Merton SW19
Pindar St EC2 95 C2
Pindock Mews W9
Pine Apple Ct SW1
Pine Ave
Stratford New Town E15
West Wickham BR4
Pine Cl
11 Dartmouth Pk N19
London E10
Osidge N14
3 Penge SE20
Stanmore HA7
Pine Coombe CR0
Pinecrest Gdns BR6
Pinecroft Cres EN5
Pinecroft
East Wickham DA16
Harrow HA3
Pine Ct UB5
Pinedene 2 SE15
Pinefield Cl E14
Pine Gdns Ruislip HA4
Surbiton KT5

ilade BR6 226 B4
ir
ury Pk N4,
9 72 B6
ridge N20 13 C3
oledon SW19 179 B5
Ho Bow E3 97 A6
otherhithe
16 118 C4
urst BR7 188 D4
urst Ct 6 W11 91 B1
urst HA7 25 A5
urst Wlk 4
211 B1
ands Cl 7 SE3 142 D5
.o SW15 157 A5
nartin Cl NW2 68 C5
l UB4 83 D3
Rd
swick Pk N11 15 A2
lewood NW2 68 D4
Ridge SM5 219 A1
Ct 11 SW19 156 D3
Rd BR1 188 A1
St EC1 94 C3 241 A6
The
ngate N14 15 C6
h Norwood
19 182 D4
ury TW16 194 A6
ton KT6 214 A5
ford IG8 21 A1
Tree Cl TW5 128 B4
Tree Ho SE14 140 D5
Tree Lo BR2 208 D5
Trees Dr UB10 60 A4
iew Ct 5 E4 20 A3
Wlk KT5 198 C3
wood Ave
ngdon UB8 82 B1
er HA5 23 D4
p DA15 167 C3
wood BR7 188 C4
wood Cl
ton BR6 211 B1
don CR0 223 A5
er HA5 23 D4
h Oxhey HA6 22 B5
wood Ct
ham Pk SW4 159 D5
eld EN2 4 D2
on SW19 179 D3
wood Dr BR6 227 C3
wood Gr W5 87 C1
wood Lo WD23 8 B3
wood Pl KT19 215 B4
wood Rd
nley BR2 209 A5
ham TW13 150 B1
t Heath SE2 146 D6
Wood TW16 172 A2
ld Rd SW16 182 A6
estone Cl UB7 126 A5
coat Cl TW13 150 B1
rton Ct KT2 176 D1
rton Pl SW16 181 D6
am Mans W4 110 C1
am Way (North
ular Rd) N12 31 A4
well Ave UB3 105 B2
well La UB3 105 B2
well Prim Sch
105 A2
y Gdns RM9 102 B6
ace Ho E14 120 A3
acle Hill DA7 147 D1
acle Hill N DA7 147 D1
acle Ho EC3 253 A5
acle The
enham RM6 59 A3
Kingsland N1 73 B2
ell Rd SE9 143 D1
ER 41 A6
er Ct
lington NW8 236 C6
er HA5 41 C5
er Gn HA5 22 C1
ER GREEN 22 C1
er Gr HA5 41 A4
er Hill HA5 22 B3
er Hill Rd HA5 22 C1
er Ho
Camberwell
5 139 A3
ner HA5 41 A6
er Park Ave HA2 24 A1
er Park Fst & Mid
s HA5 41 D6
er Park Gdns
24 A1
er Rd
ow HA1, HA2 42 A3
hwood HA6 22 A1
er HA2, HA5 41 C5
er Sta HA5 41 A5
er View HA1,
42 A4

PINNERWOOD PARK
22 C3
Pinner Wood Sch
HA5 22 C2
Pinn Way HA4 39 C2
Pintail Cl E6 100 A2
Pintail Ct 39 SE8 141 B6
Pintail Rd IG8 37 B3
Pintail Way UB4 84 D2
Pinter Ho 30 SW9 138 A3
Pinto Cl WD6 11 B5
Pinto Way SE3 143 B1
Pioneer Cl W12 90 B1
Pioneers Ind Pk
CR0 204 A1
Pioneer St SE15 140 A4
Pioneer Way W12 90 C1
Piper Cl N7 72 B3
Piper Rd KT1 198 C6
Pipers Gdns CR0 207 A2
Pipers Gn NW9 45 A4
Pipers Green La HA8 10 A1
Pipers Ho SE10 120 B1
Piper Way IG1 57 B1
Pipewell Rd SM5 202 C3
Pippenhall SE9 166 D5
Pippin Cl
Croydon CR0 207 B1
Dollis Hill NW2 68 B5
Pippin Ct 5 EN4 2 C1
Pippin Ho 17 W10 112 D6
Pippins Ct TW15 170 D4
Piquet Rd SE20 184 C1
Pirbright Cres CR0 224 A2
Pirbright Ho 11 KT2 176 D4
Pirbright Rd SW18 157 C3
Pirie St 6 E16 121 B5
Pitcairn Cl RM7 59 C5
Pitcairn Ct CR4 180 D3
Pitcairne Ct N21 16 B6
Pitcairn Ho 1 E9 74 C1
Pitcairn Rd CR4 180 D3
Pitchford St E15 76 C1
Pitfield Cres SE28 124 A5
Pitfield Ho N5 73 A3
Pitfield St N1 95 C5
Pitfield Way
Enfield EN3 6 C4
Tokyngton NW10 67 A2
Pitfold Cl SE12 165 B5
Pitfold Rd SE12 165 A4
Pit Ho NW10 67 B5
Pitlake CR0 220 D6
Pitman Ho
Southgate N21 16 B6
4 St Johns SE8 141 C4
Pitman St SE5 139 A5
Pitmaston Ho 2
SE13 142 A3
Pitsea Pl E1 96 D1
Pitsea St E1 96 D1
Pitshanger Ct 2 W5 87 C3
Pitshanger La W5 87 C3
Pitshanger Manor Mus
& Art Gallery*
W5 109 D5
Pitt Cres SW19 179 D6
Pitt Ho 4 SW11 136 B1
Pittman Gdns IG1 79 A3
Pitt Rd Harrow HA2 64 A6
Orpington BR6 227 A4
Thornton Heath CR0,
CR7 205 A4
Pitt's Head Mews
W1 248 B3
Pittsmead Ave BR2 209 A2
Pitt St W8 113 C4 245 B2
Pittville Gdns SE25 206 A6
Pixfield Ct BR2 186 D1
Pixham Ct 5 SW19 179 B5
Pixley St E14 97 B1
Pixton 14 NW9 27 C2
Pixton Way CR2 223 B1
Place Farm Ave BR5,
BR6 211 B1
Plains The 7 E4 20 C4
PLAISTOW E13 99 B4
BR1 187 A4
Plaistow Gr
Bromley BR1 187 B3
West Ham E15 98 D6
Plaistow Hospl E13 99 C5
Plaistow La BR1 187 C2
Plaistow Park Rd
E13 99 B5
Plaistow Prim Sch
E13 99 B5
Plaistow Rd E13, E15 98 D5
Plaistow Sta E13 98 D5
Plane St SE26 162 B1
Plane Tree Cres
TW13 150 B1
Planetree Ct W6 112 D2
Plane Tree Ho
Deptford SE8 141 A6
Greenwich SE7 121 D1

Plane Tree Wlk 4
SE19 183 C4
Plantagenet Cl
KT19 215 B4
Plantagenet Gdns
RM6 58 D2
Plantagenet Ho
SE18 122 B3
Plantagenet Pl RM6 58 D2
Plantagenet Rd EN5 2 A1
Plantain Gdns E11 76 B5
Plantain Pl SE1 252 C2
Plantation La EC3 253 A6
Plantation The SE3 143 A3
Plasel Ct E13 99 B6
PLASHET 78 A2
Plashet Gr E6 77 D1
Plashet Rd E13 77 B1
Plashet Sch E6 78 A1
Plassy Rd SE6 163 D4
Platehouse The 3
E14 119 D1
Platina St EC2 242 D6
Platinum Ct RM7 59 D6
Plato Pl 1 SW6 135 B3
Plato Rd SW2 138 A1
Platt Halls (a) 35
NW9 27 D1
Platt Halls (b) 37
NW9 27 D1
Platt Halls (c) 38
NW9 27 D1
Platt's Eyot TW12 173 C1
Platt's La NW3 69 C5
Platts Rd EN3 6 C4
Platt St NW1 232 C4
Plaxdale Ho SE17 263 A3
Plaxtol Cl BR1 187 C2
Plaxtol Rd DA8 147 C5
Plaxton Ct E11 76 D5
Playfair St W6 112 C1
Playfield Cres SE22 161 D6
Playfield Rd HA8 27 A1
Playford Rd
Finsbury Pk N4 72 B6
Finsbury Pk N4 72 C6
Playgreen Way SE6 185 C6
Playground Cl BR3 184 D1
Playhouse Yd EC4 241 C1
Plaza Bsns Ctr EN3 7 B3
Plaza Hts E10 76 A5
Plaza Sh Ctr
W1 93 C1 239 B2
Plaza Wlk NW9 45 A6
Pleasance Rd
Putney SW15 156 B6
St Paul's Cray BR5 190 B1
Pleasance The
SW15 134 B1
Pleasant Gr CR0 223 B5
Pleasant Pl N1 72 D1
Pleasant Row NW1 231 D5
Pleasant View BR6 227 A3
Pleasant View Pl
BR6 227 A3
Pleasant Way HA0 87 C5
Pleasaunce Ct SE9 144 B1
Plender Ct NW1 232 B5
Plender St
NW1 93 C6 232 B5
Pleshey Rd N7 71 D4
Plevna Cres N15 51 C3
Plevna Ho 1 N9 18 A1
Plevna Rd
Edmonton N9 18 B1
Hampton TW12 173 D2
Plevna St E14 120 A3
Pleydell Ave
Chiswick W6 111 D2
Penge SE19 183 D3
Pleydell Ct EC4 241 B1
Pleydell Gdns SE19 183 D4
Pleydell St EC4 241 B1
Plimsoll Cl E14 97 D1
Plimsoll Rd N4 72 D5
Plough Ct EC3 252 D6
Plough Farm Cl HA4 39 B3
Plough La SE22 161 D5
Plough Lane Cl CR0,
SM6 220 A3
Plough La
7 Teddington
TW11 175 A5
Wallington CR0,
SM6 220 A3
Wimbledon SW17,
SW19 180 A6
Ploughmans Cl NW1 232 C6
Ploughmans End
TW7 152 B6
Plough Mews 19
SW11 136 B1
Plough Pl EC4 241 B2
Plough Rd
Battersea SW11 136 B1
West Ewell KT19 215 B1
Plough St 16 E1 96 A1

Plough Terr SW11 136 B1
Plough Way SE16 119 A2
Plough Yd EC2 243 B5
Plover Ho 4 SW9 138 C5
Plover Way
Hayes UB4 84 D2
Rotherhithe SE16 119 A3
Plowman Cl N18 33 B5
Plowman Ho SW19 156 D2
Plowman Way RM8 58 C1
Plumbers Row E1 96 A1
Plumbridge St 7
SE10 142 A4
Plum Cl TW14 150 A3
Plumcroft Prim Sch
SE18 145 A6
Plume Ho SE10 141 D6
Plum Garth TW8 109 D2
Plum La SE18 145 A5
Plummer Ct SE13 163 D5
Plummer La CR4 180 D1
Plummer Rd SW4 159 D4
Plumpton Cl UB5 63 C2
Plumpton Ct SE23 163 A4
Plumpton Lo E5 74 D5
Plumpton Way SM5 218 C5
PLUMSTEAD 123 C2
PLUMSTEAD COMMON
145 D6
Plumstead Common Rd
SE18 145 A6
Plumstead High St SE18,
SE2 123 C2
Plumstead Manor/
Negus Sch SE18 145 B6
Plumstead Rd SE18,
SE28 123 A2
Plumstead Road
Covered Mkt
SE18 122 D2
Plumstead Sta SE18 123 B2
Plumtree Cl
Dagenham RM10 81 D2
Wallington SM6 219 D1
Plumtree Ct EC4 241 C2
Plymen Ho KT8 195 C4
Plymouth Ho
10 Barking IG11 80 A1
20 Lewisham SE10 141 D4
Plymouth Rd
Bromley BR1 187 B2
Newham E16 99 A2
Plymouth Wharf
E14 120 B2
Plympton Ave NW6 69 B1
Plympton Cl 8
DA17 125 A3
Plympton Pl NW1 237 A5
Plympton Rd NW6 69 B1
Plympton St NW8 237 A5
Plymstock Rd DA16 146 C5
Pocklington Cl NW9 27 C1
Pocklington Ct
SW15 156 A3
Pocklington Lo 6
W12 112 A3
Pocock Ave UB7 104 B3
Pocock St
SE1 116 D4 251 D2
Podmore Rd SW18 136 A1
Poets Cnr* SW1 260 A6
Poet's Rd N5 73 B3
Poets Way HA1 42 C5
Pointalls Cl N3 30 A1
Point Cl SE10 142 A4
Pointer Cl SE28 102 D1
Pointer Sch The
SE3 143 A5
Pointers Cl E14 119 D1
Point Hill SE10 142 A4
Point Ho SE10 142 A4
Point Pleasant
SW18 135 C1
Point Pl HA9 66 D1
Point Terr E7 77 B3
Point The HA4 62 A4
Point Wharf La
TW8 132 A5
Poland Ho 3 E15 98 B6
Poland St W1 93 C1 239 B1
Polaris Ct EN4 14 B6
Polebrook Rd SE3 143 C2
Polecroft La SE6 163 B2
Polehamptons The
TW12 174 A2
Pole Hill Rd
Chingford E4 20 A4
Hillingdon UB4 83 A4
Polesden Gdns
SW20 178 B1
Polesworth Ho 16
W2 91 C2
Polesworth Rd RM9 80 D1
Polish Inst & Sikorski
Mus* SW7 246 D1
Polish Univ Abroad
W6 112 A2

Polish War Meml
HA4 62 C2
Pollard Cl
Islington N7 72 B4
Newham E16 121 A6
Pollard Ct SM4 202 C4
Pollard Ho
Cheam KT4 216 C4
Islington N1 233 C3
Pollard Rd
East Barnet N20 14 C2
Morden SM4 202 B4
Pollard Row E2 96 A4
Pollards Cl IG10 21 C6
Pollards Cres SW16 204 A6
Pollards Hill E
SW16 204 B6
Pollards Hill N
SW16 204 B6
Pollards Hill S
SW16 204 B6
Pollards Hill W
SW16 204 B6
Pollard St E2 96 A4
Pollards Wood Rd
SW16 204 A6
Pollard Wlk DA14 190 C4
Pollen St W1 238 D1
Pollitt Dr
NW8 92 B3 236 D6
Pollock Ho W10 91 A3
Polperro Cl BR6 211 D3
Polperro Mans 3
NW6 69 C3
Polperro Mews
SE11 261 C4
Polsted Rd SE6 163 B4
Polsten Mews 2 EN3 7 C6
Polthorne Gr SE18 123 B2
Polworth Rd SW16 182 A5
Polygon Rd
NW1 93 D5 232 C3
Polygon The
1 Clapham SW4 137 C1
St John's Wood NW8 229 D6
Polytechnic St SE18 122 C2
Pomell Way E1 243 D2
Pomeroy Cl TW1 131 B1
Pomeroy Ct W11 91 A1
Pomeroy Ho 5 E2 96 D5
Pomeroy St SE14 140 C4
Pomfret Rd SE5 138 D2
Pomoja La N19 72 A6
Pomona Ho 10 SE8 119 A2
Pond Cl
Colney Hatch N12 30 C4
Kidbrooke SE3 143 A3
Pond Cottage La BR3,
BR4 207 C1
Pond Cotts SE21 161 C3
PONDERS END 18 D6
Ponders End Ind Est
EN3 19 A6
Ponders End Sta
EN3 19 A6
Ponder St 5 N7 72 B1
Pond Farm Est E5 74 C5
Pondfield End IG10 21 C4
Pondfield Ho
4 Islington N5 73 A3
West Norwood SE27 183 A5
Pondfield Rd
Dagenham RM10 81 D3
Locksbottom BR6 226 D5
West Wickham BR2 208 C1
Pond Gn HA4 61 C6
Pond Hill Gdns SM3 217 A2
Pond Ho
Chelsea SW3 257 A3
Stanmore HA7 25 B4
Pond Mead SE21 161 B5
Pond Path BR7 188 D4
Pond Pl
SW3 114 C2 257 A3
Pond Rd
Blackheath Vale
SE3 142 D3
Newham E15 98 C5
Pondside Cl UB3 127 B6
Pond Sq N6 49 A1
Pond St NW3 70 C3
Pond Way TW11 175 C4
Pondwood Rise
BR6 211 C2
Ponler St E1 96 B1
Ponsard Rd NW10 90 B4
Ponsford St E9 74 C2
Ponsonby Ho 13 E2 96 C5
Ponsonby Pl
SW1 115 D1 259 D2
Ponsonby Rd SW15 156 B4
Ponsonby Terr SW1 259 D2
Pontefract Ct UB5 63 D3
Pontefract Rd BR1 186 D5
Ponton Ho SW2 160 C3
Ponton Rd
SW8 137 D6 269 D5

Pontoon Dock Sta
E16 121 C5
Pont St Mews SW1 257 C5
Pont St SW1 114 D3 257 D5
Pontypool Pl SE1 251 C2
Pool Cl
Beckenham BR3 185 C5
East Molesey KT8 195 B4
Pool Ct SE6 163 C2
Poole Cl HA4 61 C6
Poole Court Rd
TW5 129 A3
Poole Ct
De Beauvoir Town
N1 73 C1
Hounslow TW5 129 A3
Poole Ho SE11 260 D5
Pool End Cl TW17 192 C4
Poole Rd
Homerton E9 74 D2
West Ewell KT19 215 B2
Pooles Bldgs EC1 241 A5
Pooles Ct IG3 80 A5
Pooles La SW10 266 A3
Pooles Park Prim Sch
N4 72 B6
Pooles Pk N4 72 C6
Poole St N1 95 B6 235 C5
Poole Way UB4 83 C4
Pooley Ho E1 96 D4
Pool Ho NW8 236 D4
Poolmans St SE16 118 D4
Pool Rd
East Molesey KT12,
KT8 195 B4
Harrow HA1 42 B2
Poolsford Rd NW9 45 C5
Poonah St E1 96 C1
Pope Cl
East Bedfont
TW14 149 D3
Mitcham SW17,
SW19 180 B4
Pope Ct 10 KT2 175 D6
Pope Ho
7 Bermondsey
SE16 118 B2
3 Camberwell SE5 139 B5
Pope John RC Prim Sch
W12 112 B6
Pope Rd BR2 209 D4
Pope's Ave TW2 152 C2
Popes Ct TW2 152 C2
Popes Dr N3 29 C2
Popes Gr CR0 223 B5
Pope's Gr TW1, TW2 152 D2
Pope's Head Alley
EC3 242 D1
Pope's La W5 110 A3
Pope's Rd SW9 138 C2
Pope Street Ct SE9 166 B3
Pope St SE1 253 B1
Popham Cl TW13 151 B1
Popham Ct N16 73 C5
Popham Gdns TW9 132 D2
Popham Rd
N1 95 A6 235 A6
Popham St
Islington N1 234 D6
Shoreditch
N1 95 A6 235 A6
Pop In Bsns Ctr HA9 66 D3
POPLAR 97 C1
Poplar Ave
Mitcham CR4 180 D2
Orpington BR6 226 D6
Southall UB2 107 D3
Yiewsley UB7 104 B6
Poplar Bath St 11
E14 119 D6
Poplar Bsns Pk E14 120 A6
Poplar Cl Hackney E9 75 B3
Pinner HA5 22 D2
Poplar Cres KT19 215 A2
Poplar Ct
Chingford E4 35 D4
Northolt UB5 84 C5
4 Streatham SW16 160 B1
13 Twickenham
TW1 153 C5
Wimbledon SW19 179 C5
Poplar Farm Cl
KT19 215 A2
Poplar Gdns KT3 177 B1
Poplar Gr
Friern Barnet N11 31 A4
Hammersmith W6 112 C4
Kingston u T KT3 199 B6
Wembley HA9 67 A5
Poplar High St E14 119 D6
Poplar Ho
Brockley SE4 141 B1
19 Rotherhithe
SE16 118 D4

Poplar Mews 4 W12 ... 112 C5
Poplar Mount DA17 ... 125 D2
Poplar Pl Hayes UB3 ... 106 A6
Kensington W2 ... 113 D6 245 D6
Woolwich SE28 ... 124 C6
Poplar Prim Sch SW19 ... 201 C6
Poplar Rd
Ashford TW15 ... 171 A5
Cheam SM3 ... 201 B1
Herne Hill SE24 ... 139 A1
Merton SW19 ... 179 C1
Poplar Rd S SW19 ... 201 C6
Poplars Cl HA4 ... 39 C1
Poplars Ho 14 E17 ... 53 D6
Poplars Rd E17 ... 53 D3
Poplar Sta E14 ... 119 D6
Poplars The
East Barnet N14 ... 15 B6
Kentish Town NW5 ... 71 C3
Poplar View HA9 ... 65 D6
Poplar Way
Feltham TW13 ... 150 B1
Ilford IG6 ... 57 A5
Poplar Wlk
Croydon CR0 ... 205 A1
Herne Hill SE24 ... 139 A1
Poppins Ct EC4 ... 241 C1
Poppleton Rd E11 ... 54 C3
Poppy Cl
Belvedere DA17 ... 125 D4
Hackbridge SM6 ... 203 A1
Northolt UB5 ... 63 B2
Poppy Ct HA3 ... 42 C6
Poppy La CR0 ... 206 C1
Porchester Ct W2 ... 91 D1
Porchester Gate W2 246 A5
Porchester Gdn Mews W2 ... 91 D1
Porchester Gdns W2 ... 113 D6 245 D6
Porchester Ho 3 E1 ... 96 B1
Porchester Mead BR3 ... 185 D4
Porchester Mews W2 ... 91 D1
Porchester Pl W2 ... 237 B1
Porchester Rd
Kensington W2 ... 91 D1
Kingston u T KT1 ... 176 D1
Porchester Sq W2 ... 91 D1
Porchester Terr N W2 ... 91 D1
Porchester Terr W2 ... 114 A6 246 A6
Porch Way N20 ... 14 D1
Porcupine Cl SE9 ... 166 A2
Porden Rd SW2 ... 138 B1
Porland Ct SE1 ... 262 C6
Porlock Ave HA1, HA2 ... 42 A1
Porlock Ho 5 SE26 ... 162 A1
Porlock Rd EN1 ... 17 D4
Porlock St SE1 ... 117 B4 252 D2
Porrington Cl BR7 ... 188 C2
Porson Ct SE13 ... 141 D2
Portal Cl
Hillingdon UB10 ... 60 B1
Ruislip HA4 ... 62 B4
West Norwood SE27 ... 160 C1
Portal Way W3 ... 89 B2
Portbury Cl 17 SE15 ... 140 A4
Portchester Cl SE24 ... 139 B1
Port Cres E13 ... 99 B3
Portcullis Lodge Rd EN1 ... 5 B2
Portelet Ct 1 N1 ... 95 C6
Portelet Rd E1 ... 96 D4
Porten Hos W14 ... 254 A5
Porten Rd W14 ... 254 A5
Porte 10 NW9 ... 27 D2
Porter Rd E6 ... 100 B1
Porters Ave RM8, RM9 ... 80 C3
Porter Sq N19 ... 50 A1
Porter St
Borough The SE1 ... 117 A5 252 B4
Marylebone W1 ... 237 D4
Porters & Walters Almshouses N22 ... 32 B3
Porters Way UB7 ... 104 B4
Porteus Rd W2 ... 236 B4
Portfleet Pl 34 N1 ... 95 C6
Portgate Cl W9 ... 91 B3
Porthallow Cl BR6 ... 227 D4
Porthcawe Rd SE26 ... 185 B6
Porthkerry Ave DA16 ... 146 A1
Port Ho 6 SW11 ... 136 A2
Port House The 6 E14 ... 119 D1
Portia Ct 12 IG11 ... 80 A1
Portia Way E3 ... 97 B3
Porticos The SW3 ... 266 C5
Portinscale Rd SW15 ... 157 B6
Portishead Ho 29 W2 ... 91 C2
Portland Ave
Blackfen DA15 ... 168 A5
New Malden KT3 ... 199 D2
Stamford Hill N16 ... 51 D2
Portland Cl
Dagenham RM6 ... 59 A4
New Malden KT4 ... 200 B2
Portland Commercial Est IG11 ... 102 C5
Portland Cotts
Feltham TW13 ... 173 A5
Wallington CR0 ... 203 D2
Portland Cres
1 Chislehurst SE9 ... 166 A2
Feltham TW13 ... 171 B6
Southall UB6 ... 86 A2
Stanmore HA7 ... 25 D1
Portland Cres W HA7 ... 43 D6
Portland Ct
7 De Beauvoir Town N1 ... 73 C1
1 Deptford SE14 ... 141 A6
1 Sutton SM2 ... 217 D2
Portland Dr EN2 ... 5 C5
Portland Gdns
Harringay N4 ... 50 D3
Ilford RM6 ... 58 D4
Portland Gr SW8 ... 138 B4 270 C2
Portland Hospl for Women & Children The W1 ... 238 D5
Portland Ho 19 SW2 ... 160 C3
Portland Mans SE25 ... 206 B4
Portland Mews W1 ... 239 B1
Portland Place Schs W1 ... 93 B2 238 D4
Portland Place Sch W1 ... 93 B2 238 D3
Portland Pl
Croydon SE25 ... 206 A5
Marylebone W1 ... 93 B2 238 D3
Portland Rd
Ashford TW15 ... 148 A1
Bromley BR1 ... 187 C5
Chislehurst SE9 ... 166 A2
Croydon SE25 ... 206 B4
Hayes UB4 ... 83 C4
Kingston u T KT1 ... 198 B6
Mitcham CR4 ... 180 C1
Notting Hill W11 ... 113 A5 244 B4
Notting Hill W11 ... 113 A6 244 A5
Southall UB2 ... 107 B3
Tottenham N15 ... 51 D5
Portland Rise N4 ... 51 A1
Portland Sq 4 E1 ... 118 B5
Portland St SE17 ... 117 B1 262 C1
Portland Terr
Edgware HA8 ... 26 C3
Richmond TW9 ... 131 D1
Portland Village W6 ... 112 C3
Portman Ave SW14 ... 133 B2
Portman Cl
Bexley DA7 ... 147 A2
Marylebone W1 ... 93 A1 238 A2
Portman Dr IG8 ... 37 D1
Portman Gate NW1 ... 237 B5
Portman Gdns
Hendon NW9 ... 27 B1
Hillingdon UB10 ... 60 C1
Portman Hall HA3 ... 24 B5
Portman Hts 1 NW3 ... 69 C5
Portman Lo N21 ... 16 D6
Portman Mews S W1 ... 238 A1
Portman Pl E2 ... 96 C4
Portman Rd KT1 ... 176 B1
Portman Sq W1 ... 93 A1 238 A2
Portman St W1 ... 93 A1 238 A1
Portman The NW11 ... 47 C2
Portman Twrs W1 ... 237 D2
Portmeadow Wlk SE2 ... 124 D4
Portmeers Cl E17 ... 53 C3
Portnall Rd W9 ... 91 B4
Portobello Ct Est W11 ... 91 B1
Portobello Ho 6 SW27 ... 182 D5
Portobello Mews W11 ... 245 A5
Portobello Rd W11 ... 113 B6 244 D6
Portobello Road Mkt* W10 ... 91 A2
Porton Ct KT6 ... 197 C3
Portpool La EC1 ... 94 C2 241 A4
Portree Cl N22 ... 32 B3
Portree St E14 ... 98 B1
Port Royal Pl 3 N16 ... 73 C3
Portrush Ct 9 UB1 ... 86 A1
Portsdown Ave NW11 ... 47 B3
Portsdown HA8 ... 26 C5
Portsdown Mews NW11 ... 47 B3
Portsea Hall W2 ... 237 B1
Portsea Ho 3 SW15 ... 156 B3
Portsea Mews W2 ... 237 B1
Portsea Pl W2 ... 237 B1
Portslade Rd SW8 ... 137 C3
Portsmouth Ave KT7 ... 197 A2
Portsmouth Rd
Esher KT10 ... 212 A5
Putney SW15 ... 156 C4
Thames Ditton KT6, KT7 ... 197 C3
Portsmouth St WC2 ... 240 D1
Portsoken St E1, EC3 253 C6
Portswood Pl SW15 ... 155 D5
Portugal Gdns TW2 ... 152 A2
Portugal St WC2 ... 94 B1 240 D1
Portway E15 ... 98 D6
Portway Gdns SE18 ... 143 D5
Portway Prim Sch E13 ... 98 D6
Poseidon Ct
Dagenham IG11 ... 102 B4
9 Millwall E14 ... 119 C2
Postern Gn EN2 ... 4 C2
Postern The EC2 ... 242 B3
Post La TW2 ... 152 B3
Postmasters Lodge HA5 ... 41 A2
Postmill Cl CR0 ... 222 D5
Post Office App E7 ... 77 B3
Post Office Way SW8 ... 137 D5 269 C4
Post Rd UB2 ... 107 D3
Postway Mews 1 IG1 ... 78 D5
Potier St SE1 ... 262 D5
Potter Cl CR4 ... 181 B1
Potteries The EN5 ... 13 C6
Potterill Ct TW11 ... 175 B3
Potterne Cl 5 SW19 ... 156 D4
Potters Cl
5 Camberwell SE15 ... 139 C5
Croydon CR0 ... 207 A1
Pottersfield EN1 ... 5 C1
Potters Fields SE1 ... 117 C5 253 B3
Potters Gr KT3 ... 199 A5
Potters Heights Cl HA5 ... 22 B3
Potter's La Barnet EN5 ... 1 C1
Streatham SW16 ... 181 D4
Potters Lo E14 ... 120 A1
Potters Mews 4 WD6 ... 9 D5
Potter's Rd EN5 ... 1 D1
Potters Rd SW6 ... 136 A3
Potter St HA5 ... 22 B2
Potter Street Hill HA5 ... 22 B3
Pottery La W11 ... 113 A5 244 B4
Pottery Rd TW8 ... 132 A6
Pottery St SE16 ... 118 B4
Pott St E2 ... 96 B4
Poulett Gdns TW1 ... 153 A3
Poulett Rd E6 ... 100 B5
Poullett Ho SW2 ... 160 D3
Poulters Wood BR2 ... 225 D3
Poulton Ave SM1 ... 218 B5
Poulton Cl E8 ... 74 B2
Poultry EC2 ... 95 B1 242 C1
Pound Cl
Long Ditton KT6 ... 197 C1
Orpington BR6 ... 227 B6
Pound Court Dr BR6 ... 227 B6
Pound Farm Cl KT10 ... 196 B1
Pound Green Ct 4 DA5 ... 169 C4
Pound La NW10 ... 68 A2
Pound Park Rd SE7 ... 121 D2
Pound Pl SE9 ... 166 C5
Pound St SM5 ... 218 D3
Pountney Rd SW11 ... 137 A2
Poverest Rd BR5 ... 211 D4
Povey Ho
Tulse Hill SW2 ... 160 C5
Walworth SE17 ... 263 A3
Powder Mill La TW2, TW4 ... 151 C3
Powell Cl
Chessington KT9 ... 213 D3
Edgware HA8 ... 26 B4
Wallington SM6 ... 220 A1
Powell Ct
Croydon CR2 ... 221 A4
19 Walthamstow E17 ... 53 D6
Powell Gdns RM10 ... 81 C4
Powell Ho 10 SW19 ... 179 A4
Powell Rd
Buckhurst Hill IG9 ... 21 C4
Hackney E5 ... 74 B5
Powell's Wlk W4 ... 133 D6
Powell Terr CR4 ... 204 A5
Powergate Bsns Pk NW10 ... 89 B4
Power Ho 13 TW9 ... 132 C4
Power Ho The W4 ... 111 D2
Power Rd W4 ... 110 C2
Powerscroft Rd
Lower Clapton E5 ... 74 C4
Sidcup DA14 ... 190 C4
Powers Ct TW1 ... 153 D4
Powis Ct Bushey WD23 ... 8 B3
Edgware HA8 ... 26 B6
Powis Gdns
Golders Green NW11 ... 47 B2
Notting Hill W11 ... 91 B1
Powis Ho WC2 ... 240 B2
Powis Mews W11 ... 91 B1
Powis Pl WC1 ... 94 A3 240 B5
Powis Rd E3 ... 97 D4
Powis Sq W11 ... 91 B1
Powis St SE18 ... 122 D2
Powis Terr W11 ... 91 B1
Powlesland Ct 21 E14 ... 97 A1
Powle Terr IG1 ... 79 B3
Powlett Ho NW1 ... 71 B2
Powlett Pl NW1 ... 71 B1
Pownall Gdns TW3 ... 129 D1
Pownall Rd
Hackney E8 ... 96 A6
Hounslow TW3 ... 129 D1
Pownsett Terr IG1 ... 79 A3
Powrie Ho 4 SW11 ... 136 B3
Powster Rd BR1 ... 187 B5
Powys Cl DA7 ... 146 D6
Powys Ct N11 ... 32 A5
Powys La
Bowes Pk N13 ... 32 A5
Palmers Green N14 ... 32 A6
Poynder Ct 3 N7 ... 72 A3
Poynder Lo TW7 ... 131 A4
Poynders Ct 9 SW4 ... 159 C5
Poynders Gdns SW12 ... 159 C4
Poynders Rd SW12, SW4 ... 159 D4
Poynings Rd N19 ... 71 C5
Poynings Way N12 ... 29 C5
Poyntell Cres BR7 ... 189 B2
Poynter Ct 11 UB5 ... 84 D5
Poynter Ho
Paddington NW8 ... 236 C6
10 Shepherd's Bush W11 ... 112 D5
Poynter Rd EN1 ... 18 A6
Poynton Rd N17 ... 34 A1
Poyntz Rd SW11 ... 136 D3
Poyser St E2 ... 96 B5
Praed Mews W2 ... 236 D2
Praed St W2 ... 92 B1 236 D2
Pragel St E13 ... 99 C5
Pragnell Rd SE12 ... 165 B2
Prague Pl SW2 ... 160 A6
Prah Rd N4 ... 72 C6
Prairie St SW8 ... 137 B3
Pratt Mews NW1 ... 232 A5
Pratt St NW1 ... 93 C6 232 A6
Pratt Wlk SE1, SE11 ... 116 B2 260 D4
Prayle Gr NW2 ... 46 D1
Preachers Ct EC1 ... 241 D5
Prebend Gdns W4, W6 ... 111 D2
Prebend Mans 4 W4 ... 111 D2
Prebend St N1 ... 95 A6 235 A6
Precinct Rd UB3 ... 106 A6
Precincts The SM4 ... 201 C3
Precinct The
Islington N1 ... 235 A5
Islington N5 ... 72 D3
Premier Corner NW6 ... 91 B5
Premier Ct EN3 ... 6 D5
Premier Ho 25 N1 ... 72 D1
Premier League Hall of Fame* SE1 ... 250 C2
Premier Lo N3 ... 29 C2
Premier Park Rd NW10 ... 88 D5
Premier Pk NW10 ... 88 D5
Premier Pl 17 E14 ... 119 C6
Prendergast Ho 7 SW4 ... 159 D4
Prendergast Rd SE3 ... 142 C2
Prendergast Sch SE4 ... 141 C1
Prentice Ct 2 SW19 ... 179 B5
Prentis Rd SW16 ... 181 D6
Prentiss Ct SE7 ... 121 D2
Presburg Rd KT3 ... 199 C4
Prescelly Pl HA8 ... 26 B2
Prescot St E1 ... 117 D6 253 D6
Prescott Ave BR5 ... 210 D3
Prescott Ho
Croydon CR0 ... 220 C5
13 Kennington SE17 ... 138 D6
Prescott Pl
Clapham SW4 ... 137 D1
Streatham SW16 ... 182 A3
Presentation Mews SW2 ... 160 B3
Preshaw Cres CR4 ... 202 C6
President Dr E1 ... 118 B5
President Ho EC1 ... 234 D1
President St EC1 ... 235 A2
Prespa Cl N9 ... 18 C2
Press Ho NW10 ... 67 B5
Press Rd NW10 ... 67 B5
Prestage Way 13 E14 ... 120 A6
Prestbury Rd E7 ... 77 C1
Prestbury Sq SE9 ... 188 B6
Prested Rd SW11 ... 136 C1
PRESTON ... 44 A1
Preston Ave E4 ... 36 B4
Preston Cl
Twickenham TW2 ... 152 C1
Walworth SE1 ... 263 A4
Preston Ct
5 New Barnet EN5 ... 2 A1
Northwood Hills HA6 ... 22 A1
Sidcup DA14 ... 189 D6
Walton-on-T KT12 ... 194 C1
Preston Dr
Bexley DA7 ... 146 D4
Wanstead E11 ... 55 C4
West Ewell KT19 ... 215 D2
Preston Gdns
Enfield EN3 ... 7 A6
Redbridge IG1 ... 56 A3
Willesden NW10 ... 67 C2
Preston Hill HA3 ... 44 B3
Preston Ho
Bermondsey SE1 ... 263 C6
3 Dagenham RM10 ... 81 C5
Walworth SE1 ... 263 A4
1 Woolwich SE18 ... 122 C2
Preston Manor High Sch HA9 ... 66 B6
Preston Park Prim Sch HA9 ... 43 D1
Preston Pl
Richmond TW10 ... 154 A6
Willesden NW2 ... 68 A2
Preston Rd
Leytonstone E11 ... 54 C3
Littleton TW17 ... 192 C4
South Norwood SE19 ... 182 D4
Wembley HA3, HA9 ... 66 A6
Wimbledon SW20 ... 177 D3
Preston Road Sta HA3 ... 44 A1
Prestons Rd BR2 ... 225 A6
Preston's Rd E14 ... 120 A5
Preston Waye HA3 ... 44 A1
Prestwich Terr SW4 ... 159 D6
Prestwick Cl UB2 ... 107 A1
Prestwick Ct
Southall UB1 ... 108 A6
Tottenham N17 ... 34 A3
Prestwick Rd WD19 ... 22 D6
Prestwood Ave HA3 ... 43 B5
Prestwood Cl
East Wickham SE18 ... 146 A6
Harrow HA3 ... 43 B5
Prestwood Gdns CR0 ... 205 A2
Prestwood Ho 3 SE16 ... 118 B3
Prestwood St N1 ... 235 B3
Pretoria Ave E17 ... 53 A5
Pretoria Cres E4 ... 20 A3
Pretoria Ho 3 HA4 ...
Pretoria Rd
Chingford E4 ...
Ilford IG1 ...
Leytonstone E11 ...
Pretoria Rd N N18 ...
Pretoria Rd
Newham E16 ...
Streatham SW16 ...
Tottenham N17 ...
Pretty Cnr HA6 ...
Prevost Rd N11 ...
Priam Ho 17 E2 ...
Price Cl Finchley NW7 ...
Upper Tooting SW17 ...
Price Ct HA1 ...
Price Ho N1 ...
Price Rd CR0 ...
Prices Ct SW11 ...
Price's St SE1 ...
Price's Yd N1 ...
Price Way TW12 ...
Prichard Ct
Battersea SW11 ...
Islington N7 ...
Pricklers Hill EN5 ...
Prickley Wood BR2 ...
Priddy's Yd 4 CR0 ...
Prideaux Ho WC1 ...
Prideaux Pl
Acton W3 ...
St Pancras WC1 ... 94 B4
Prideaux Rd SW9 ...
Pride Ct N1 ...
Pridham Rd CR7 ...
Priestfield Rd SE23 ...
Priestlands Park Rd DA15 ...
Priestley Cl N16 ...
Priestley Gdns RM6 ...
Priestley Ho
2 Camden Town NW5 ...
St Luke's EC1 ...
3 Wembley HA9 ...
Priestley Rd CR4 ...
Priestley Way
Hendon NW2 ...
Walthamstow E17 ...
Priestman Point 25 E3 ...
Priestmead Fst & Mid Schs HA3 ...
Priest Park Ave HA2 ...
Priests Bridge SW14 ...
Priest's Ct EC2 ...
Prima Rd SW9 ...
Primrose Ave
Enfield EN2 ...
Ilford RM6 ...
Primrose Cl
6 Bow E3 ...
Catford SE6 ...
Finchley N3 ...
Hackbridge SM6 ...
Harrow HA2 ...
Primrose Ct
2 Child's Hill NW2 ...
New Malden KT4 ...
Primrose Hill NW8 ...
11 Streatham SW12 ...
Primrose Gdns
Hampstead NW3 ...
Ruislip HA4 ...
PRIMROSE HILL ...
Primrose Hill Ct NW3 ...
Primrose Hill EC4 ...
Primrose Hill Rd
Primrose Hill NW1, NW3 ...
Primrose Hill NW1, NW3 ...
Primrose Hill Sch NW1 ... 93 A6
Primrose Hill Studios NW1 ...
Primrose Ho
7 Peckham SE15 ...
1 Richmond TW9 ...
Primrose La CR0 ...
Primrose Mans SW11 ...
Primrose Mews 9 NW1 ...
Primrose Pl TW7 ...
Primrose Rd
Walthamstow E10 ...
Woodford E18 ...
Primrose Sq E9 ...
Primrose St EC2 ... 95 C2

ose Way HA0....87 D5
ose Wlk
KT17.........215 D1
ew Cross Gate
4...........141 A5
la St W12.......90 A1
e Albert Ct
rose Hill NW8 .. 230 C5
ury TW16......171 C3
e Albert Rd
.........92 D6 230 C5
e Arthur Ct 18
................70 A4
e Arthur Mews 17
................70 A4
e Arthur Rd
................70 A3
e Charles Dr
................46 C2
e Charles Rd
...............142 D4
e Charles Way
...............219 B5
e Consort Dr
...............189 B2
e Consort Ho
...............260 B2
e Consort Rd
........114 B3 256 C6
edale Rd
........113 A5 244 B4
e Edward Mans
...............245 B6
e Edward Rd
................75 B2
e George Ave
................15 D6
e George Rd
................73 C4
e George's Ave
0...............178 C1
e Georges Rd
9...............180 B2
e Henry Rd
...............143 D5
e Imperial Rd
ehurst BR7.....188 D3
rooke SE18.......144 B4
e John Rd SE9..166 A6
elet St
.........95 D2 243 D4
e of Orange La 3
...............142 A5
e Of Wales Cl
................46 B5
e of Wales Dr
1.........137 A4 268 A2
e of Wales Mans
ersea SW11....268 B2
ham SW4........159 B6
e of Wales Pas
...............232 A1
e of Wales Prim
EN3...............7 B6
e of Wales Rd
kheath Vale
3.............142 D4
den Town NW5....71 A2
e Of Wales' Rd
...............218 B6
e Of Wales Rd
................99 C1
e Of Wales Terr
wick W4........111 C1
sington W8......245 D1
e Rd SE25.......205 C4
e Regent Ct 2
...............119 A5
e Regent La
................99 C3
e Regent Mews
...............232 A1
e Regent E16....99 C2
e Regent Rd
...............130 A2
e Regent Sta
...............121 C6
e Rupert Rd
...............144 B1
es Arc SW1....249 B4
es Ave
n W3..........110 C3
onton N13........32 C5
nley N3...........29 D2
well Hill N10......49 B6
ngton BR5.......211 C4
ensbury NW9......44 D5
e's Ave UB1......85 D1
es Ave
orth KT6........214 C6
ington SM5.......218 D1
dford IG8.........37 C6
d Green N22......31 D2
es Cir
.........94 A1 240 A2

Princes Cl
Edgware HA8.........26 C5
Finsbury Pk N4.......50 D1
Queensbury NW9.....44 C5
Sidcup DA14.......168 D1
Prince's Cl TW11,
TW12..............174 B6
Princes Coll WC1....240 A2
Princes Court Bsns Ctr
14 E1..............118 B6
Princes Ct
Brondesbury NW2.....69 A3
Hampstead NW3......70 B4
Kingston u T KT3....199 D6
Prince's Ct SE16.....119 B3
Princes Ct
Stepney E1.........118 B6
Wembley HA9........66 A3
Princes Dr HA1.......42 C6
Princes Gate Ct
SW7..............246 D1
Princes Gate Mews
SW7........114 B3 256 D6
Princes Gate
SW7........114 B4 246 D1
Prince's Gate
SW7........114 C4 247 A1
Princes Gdns
Acton W3............88 C2
Brompton
SW7.....114 B3 256 D6
Ealing W5...........87 C3
Princes Ho W11....245 A5
Princes La N10.......49 B6
Prince's Mews 1
W6................112 B1
Princes Mews TW3..129 C1
Prince's Mews
W2.........113 D6 245 C6
Princes Park Ave
Hayes UB3.........105 B6
Temple Fortune
NW11..............47 A4
Princes Park Circ
UB3...............105 B6
Princes Park Cl
UB3...............105 B6
Princes Park La
UB3...............105 B6
Princes Park Par
UB3...............105 B6
Princes Par NW11....47 A3
Prince's Plain BR2...210 A1
Princes Plain Prim Sch
BR2...............210 A2
Princes Pl
Notting Hill
W11.....113 A5 244 A4
St James SW1......249 B4
Princes Rd
Ashford TW15.......170 B5
Buckhurst Hill IG9.....21 C2
Ealing W13.........109 B5
Edmonton N18........34 C6
Feltham TW13.......149 D1
Ilford IG6............57 B5
Kew TW9............132 B4
Kingston u T KT2....176 C3
Prince's Rd SW14....133 B2
Princes Rd
Penge SE20.........184 D4
Richmond TW10......154 B6
Prince's Rd
Teddington TW11,
TW12..............174 B6
Wimbledon SW19...179 C4
Princes Rise SE13....142 A3
Princes Riverside Rd 7
SE16...............118 D5
Princessa Ct EN2.....17 B6
Princess Alexandra
School of Nursing
The E1.............96 B2
Princess Alice Ho 1
W10................90 C3
Princess Alice Way
SE28...............123 B4
Princess Ave HA9.....66 A6
Princess Beatrice Ho
SW10..............255 C1
Princess Cl SE28.....102 D1
Princess Cres N4.....72 D6
Princess Ct
Catford BR1........186 C4
3 Croydon CR0.....221 D6
Hampstead NW6......69 D1
Hounslow TW4......128 C2
Kensington W2.....245 D6
Marylebone W1.....237 C3
11 Wimbledon
SW19..............178 D3
Princess Frederica CE
Prim Sch NW10.....90 C5
Princess Grace Hospl
The W1.....93 A3 238 A5
Princess La HA4......39 C1

Princess Louise Cl
W2................236 D4
Princess Louise Hospl
W10................90 C2
Princess Mary Ho
SW1...............259 D3
Princess May Prim Sch
N16.................73 D4
Princess May Rd
N16.................73 C4
Princess Mews
Hampstead NW3......70 B2
Kingston u T KT1....198 B6
Princess Par RM10...103 C5
Princess Park Manor
N11.................31 A5
Princess Par BR6....226 C5
Prince's Sq
W2.........113 D6 245 C6
Princess Rd
Camden Town
NW1.......93 A6 231 B6
Paddington NW6......91 C5
Thornton Heath CR0..205 A3
Princess Royal
University Hospl
BR6...............226 C5
Princess St
Bexley DA7.........147 B2
Newington SE1.....261 D5
Princes St DA7......147 B1
Prince's St
EC2.........95 B1 242 C1
Princes St W1......238 D1
Prince's St TW10,
TW9...............154 A6
Princes St
Sutton SM1.........218 B4
Tottenham N17.......33 C4
Prince's Terr E13.....99 B6
Prince St SE8........141 B6
Princes Way
Acton W3...........110 C3
Buckhurst Hill IG9.....21 C2
Coney Hall BR4.....224 D5
Croydon CR0........220 B3
Putney SW15, SW19..157 A3
Ruislip HA4..........63 A4
Princes Yd W11......244 B3
Princethorpe Ho W2..91 D2
Princethorpe Rd
SE26...............184 D6
Princeton Ct SW15..134 D2
Princeton Mans
WC1...............240 C3
Princeton Mews 3
KT2...............176 C2
Princeton St
WC1.........94 B2 240 C4
Prince William Ct
TW15..............170 B5
Principal Cl N14......15 C3
Principal Sq E9.......74 D3
Pringle Gdns SW16..181 C6
Pringle Ho N21........16 B6
Printers Mews E3.....97 A6
Printer St EC4......241 B2
Printinghouse La
UB3...............105 C4
Printing House Yd 16
E2..................95 C4
Printon Ho 16 E3.....97 B2
Print Village Ind Est
SE15...............139 D3
Priolo Rd SE7........121 C1
Prior Ave SM2, SM5...218 C1
Prior Bolton St N1....72 D2
Prioress Ho 2 E3......97 D4
Prioress Rd SE27....160 D1
Prioress St SE1......262 D5
Prior Rd IG1..........78 C5
Priors Croft E17......35 B1
Priors Field UB5......63 A2
Priors Gdns HA4......62 C3
Priors Lo 4 TW10...154 A5
Priors Mead EN1.......5 C4
Prior St SE10........142 A5
Priors Wood KT10...212 D6
Prior Weston Prim
Sch
Broadgate
EC1.........95 B3 242 C6
St Luke's EC1..95 A3 242 B5
Priory Ave
Bedford Pk W4.....111 C3
Cheam SM3.........216 D4
Chingford E4.........19 C1
Hornsey N8..........49 D5
Petts Wood BR5.....211 B3
Walthamstow E17.....53 C4
Wembley HA0........64 D4
Priory CE Prim Sch
SW19..............179 D5
Priory Cl
Ashford TW16......172 A3
Barnet N20...........13 B4

Priory Cl *continued*
Beckenham BR3....207 A6
Chingford Green E4....19 B1
Chislehurst BR7......188 B2
East Barnet N14......15 B6
Finchley N3..........29 B2
Hampton TW12......173 B2
Hayes UB3..........106 B6
3 Merton SW19....179 D2
Ruislip HA4..........39 D1
Stanmore HA7.........8 D1
Wembley HA0.........64 D4
Woodford E18........37 A2
Priory Cres
Cheam SM3........216 D4
South Norwood
SE19..............183 A3
Wembley HA0........65 A5
Priory Ct Bushey WD23..8 A3
Cheam SM3........217 A4
City of London EC4..241 D1
Hampton TW12.....173 C3
Highgate N6.........49 B3
Homerton E9.........74 D3
Hounslow TW3.....129 D2
Ilford RM6...........58 B3
Newham E6..........99 D6
Nunhead SE15......140 C1
Roehampton SW15..133 D1
South Lambeth
SW8.....137 D4 269 D2
Walthamstow E17.....35 B1
4 Wembley HA0.....88 A5
Priory Dr
Stanmore HA7.........8 D1
West Heath SE2....124 D1
Priory Field Dr HA8...26 D6
Priory Gdns
Ashford TW15......171 B5
Barnes SW13......133 D2
6 Chiswick W4.....111 C2
Ealing W5...........88 A4
Hampton TW12......173 B2
Highgate N6.........49 B3
South Norwood
SE25..............205 D5
Wembley HA0........65 A4
Priory Gn N1........233 C4
Priory Grange N2.....48 D6
Priory Gr Barnet EN5...13 C6
South Lambeth
SW8.....138 A4 270 A1
Priory Hill HA0.......65 A4
Priory Ho
3 Charlton SE7....143 C6
Clerkenwell EC1....241 C6
Pimlico SW1.......259 C2
Spitalfields E1......243 C4
Priory Hospl Hayes
Grove The BR2....225 A6
Priory Hospl The
SW15..............133 D1
Priory House Ct
SE6...............163 D3
Priory Htss N1......233 D4
Priory La
East Molesey KT8...195 D5
Roehampton SW15..155 D6
Priory Leas SE9......166 A3
Priory Lo
7 Brentford W4.....110 C1
Coney Hall BR4.....224 C5
Ealing W5...........87 C1
Priory Mans
17 Maitland Pk
NW3................70 D2
South Kensington
SW10..............256 B1
Priory Park Rd
Kilburn NW6.........91 B6
Wembley HA0........65 A4
Priory Pk SE3........142 D2
Priory Rd
Barking IG11.........79 B1
Bedford Pk W4......111 B3
Cheam SM3........216 D4
Chessington KT9....214 A5
Hampstead NW6......69 D1
Hampton TW12.....173 C3
Hornsey N8..........49 D5
Hounslow TW3.....152 A6
Mitcham SW19......180 B3
Newham E6..........99 D5
Richmond TW9......132 C5
Thornton Heath CR0..204 C2
Priory Ret Pk SW19..180 B3
Priory Sch SE25.....205 D5
Priory St 16 E3.......97 D4
Priory Terr NW6......91 D6
Priory The
Croydon CR0........220 C5
Hornsey N8..........49 D5
21 Kingston u T KT6..198 A4
Lambeth SE1.......251 C1
Lewisham SE3......142 D1
Priory View WD23.....8 C4
Priory Villas N11......30 D5

Priory Way
Harmondsworth
UB7...............126 A6
Harrow HA2.........41 D5
Southall UB2.......106 D3
Priory Wlk
South Kensington
SW10....114 A1 256 B1
Sunbury TW16......172 A3
Priscilla Cl N15.......51 A4
Priscilla Ho 8
TW16..............171 D3
Pritchard Ho 38 E2....96 A5
Pritchard's Rd E2.....96 A5
Pritchett Cl 13 EN3.....7 C6
Priter Rd SE16.......118 A3
Priter Road Hostel 14
SE16...............118 A3
Private Rd EN1........17 C6
Probert Rd SW2.....160 C6
Probyn Ho SW1.....259 D4
Probyn Rd SW2......160 D2
Procter Ho 12 SE5...139 B5
Procter St
WC1.........94 B2 240 C3
Proctor Cl CR4.......181 A2
Proctor Ho 5 SE1....118 A1
Proctors Cl TW14....150 A3
Prodger 8 NW9.......27 D2
Progress Bsns Pk
CR9...............220 B6
Progress Way
Croydon CR0........220 B6
Enfield EN1..........18 A6
Wood Green N22......32 C2
Prologis Pk
Hounslow TW4.....128 C1
Wallington CR0.....203 D2
Prome Ho 3 N16......73 B4
Promenade Approach
Rd W4.............133 C5
Promenade Mans
HA8................26 C5
Promenade The
W4................133 C4
Pronto Trad Est UB4..83 C2
Prospect Cl
Belvedere DA17....125 C2
Forest Hill SE26.....184 B6
Hounslow TW5......129 B4
Ruislip HA4..........40 D2
Prospect Cotts
SW18..............135 C1
Prospect Cres TW2..152 A5
Prospect Hill E17.....53 D5
Prospect Ho
1 Dalston E8........73 D2
Islington N1........234 A3
3 Mitcham SW19....180 B2
Newington SE1.....261 D5
14 North Kensington
W10................90 D1
Prospect House Sch
SW15..............156 D4
Prospect Ho 9 E17....54 A6
Prospect Pl
Bromley BR2........209 B6
5 Child's Hill NW2....69 B5
2 Chiswick W4......111 B1
6 Deptford SE8......141 B6
East Finchley N2......48 B5
12 Hampstead NW3...70 A4
7 Lower Holloway
N7..................72 A4
Tottenham N17.......33 C3
Wapping E1........118 C5
Wimbledon SW20....178 B3
Prospect Quay
SW18..............135 C1
Prospect Rd
Barnet EN5...........1 D1
Child's Hill NW2......69 C5
Kingston u T KT6....197 C3
Woodford IG8........37 C5
Prospect Ring N2.....48 B6
Prospect St SE16....118 B4
Prospect Vale SE7,
SE18...............122 A2
Prospect Wharf E1...118 C6
Prospero Ho 7
DA17...............125 C1
Prospero Rd N19.....49 D1
Protea Cl E16.........98 D3
Protheroe Ho 11 N17..51 D6
Prothero Gdns NW4...46 B4
Prothero Ho 15
NW10...............67 B1
Prothero Rd
SW6........135 B5 264 C4
Proud Ho 16 E1.......96 B1
Prout Gr NW10.......67 D4
Prout Rd E5..........74 B5
Provence St N1......235 A4
Providence Ave HA2..41 C1
Providence Cl E9.....96 D6

Providence Ct
Harlington UB3......127 B5
Islington N1........234 C5
Mayfair W1.........248 B6
Providence La UB3...127 B5
Providence Pl N1...234 C5
Providence Rd UB7..104 B5
Providence Row Cl 30
E1..................96 B4
Providence Row N1..233 C3
Providence 1 SE16..118 A4
Providence Sq 36
SE1................118 A4
Providence Yd 1 E2..96 A4
Provident Ind Est
UB3................106 A4
Provincial Terr 2
SE20...............184 D3
Provost Ct NW3.......70 D2
Provost Rd NW3.......70 D1
Provost St N1..95 B4 235 C2
Prowse Ave WD23......8 A2
Prowse Pl NW1.......71 C1
Prudence La BR6....226 C4
Pruden Cl N14........15 C2
Prudent Pas EC2.....242 B1
Prusom's Island 8
E1.................118 C5
Prusom St E1........118 B5
Pryors The NW3.......70 B5
Public Record Office
TW9...............132 D5
Puccinia Ct TW19....148 A3
Pudding La EC3......252 D6
Pudding Mill La E15...97 D6
Pudding Mill Lane Sta
E15.................97 D6
Puddle Dock
EC4.......116 D6 251 D6
Puffin Cl
Barking IG11........102 B4
Beckenham BR3....206 D4
Puffin Ct 9 W13......86 D3
Puffin Terr IG5........56 C6
Puget Ct N12.........30 A5
Pugin Ct N1..........72 C1
Pulborough Rd
SW18..............157 B4
Pulborough Way
TW4...............128 C1
Pulford Rd N15.......51 B3
Pulham Ave N2.......48 B5
Pulham Ho SW8.....270 C3
Puller Rd EN5..........1 A3
Pulleyns Ave E6.....100 A4
Pullman Ct SW2.....160 B3
Pullman Gdns
SW15..............156 C5
Pullman Mews
SE12...............165 B1
Pullman Pl SE9......166 A6
Pulross Rd SW9......138 B2
Pulteney Cl
3 Isleworth
TW7...............131 A2
20 Old Ford E3.......97 B6
Pulteney Gdns 9
E18.................55 B6
Pulteney Rd E18......55 B6
Pulteney Terr
N1..........94 B6 233 D6
Pulton Ho SE4.......141 A1
Pulton Pl
SW6........135 C5 265 A3
Puma Ct E1..........243 C4
Puma Trade Pk CR4..202 B5
Pump Alley 8 TW8..131 D5
Pump Cl UB5.........85 C5
Pump Ct EC4........241 A1
Pump House Cl
Bromley BR2........186 D1
Rotherhithe SE16...118 C4
Pumphouse Educational
Mus The* SE16.....119 A5
Pumping Ho 3 E14..120 B6
Pumping Station Rd
W4................133 C6
Pump La
Deptford SE14......140 C5
Hayes UB3.........106 A4
Pump Pail N CR0....221 A5
Pump Pail S CR0....221 A5
Punchard Cres EN3....7 D5
Punderson's Gdns E2.96 B4
Puran Ho E13.........99 C5
Purbeck Ave KT3....199 D3
Purbeck Ct 2 N20.....14 C2
Purbeck Dr NW2......68 D6
Purbeck Ho SW8....270 C3
Purbrook Est SE1....253 B1
Purbrook Ho 2
SW15..............156 B3
Purbrook St SE1....263 B6

Purcell Cres SW6....135 A5 264 A4
Purcell Ho
Chelsea SW10....266 C5
Isleworth TW2....152 B5
Southall UB1....85 C1
Purcell Mews 2 NW10....67 C1
Purcell Rd UB6....85 D2
Purcells Ave HA8....26 C5
Purcell St N1....95 C5
Purchese St NW1....93 D5 232 D3
Purday Ho 4 W10....91 B4
Purdey Ct 3 KT4....200 A1
Purdon Ho 11 SE15....140 A4
Purdy St E3....97 D3
Purkis Cl UB3....105 A6
Purland Cl RM8....59 B1
Purland Rd SE28, SE18....123 D4
Purley Ave NW2....69 A6
Purley Oaks Prim Sch CR2....221 B1
Purley Pl N1....72 D1
Purley Rd
Edmonton N9....17 C1
South Croydon CR2....221 B1
Purley View Terr CR2....221 B1
Purley Way Cres CR0....204 B2
Purley Way
Croydon CR0, CR9....220 C3
Thornton Heath CR0....204 B1
Purneys Rd SE9....143 D1
Purrett Rd SE18....123 D1
Purser Ho 3 SW2....160 C5
Pursers Cross Rd SW6....135 B4 264 D2
Pursewardens Cl W13....109 C5
Pursley Rd NW7....28 B3
Purves Rd NW10....90 C5
Purvis Ho CR0....205 B2
Pusey Ho 20 E14....97 C1
Puteaux Ho 6 E2....96 D5
PUTNEY....156 C6
Putney Bridge App SW6....135 A2
Putney Bridge Rd SW15....135 B1
Putney Bridge Sta SW6....135 B2
Putney Comm SW15....134 C2
Putney Exchange Shopping Ctr SW15....134 D1
Putney Gdns RM6....58 B4
PUTNEY HEATH....156 C4
Putney Heath La SW15....156 D5
Putney Heath SW15....156 C5
Putney High Sch SW15....156 D6
Putney High St SW15....135 A1
Putney Hill SW15....156 D6
Putney Park Ave SW15....134 A1
Putney Park La SW15....156 B6
Putney Park Sch SW15....134 B1
Putney Pier SW15....135 A2
Putney School of Art & Design SW15....135 A1
Putney Sta SW15....135 A1
PUTNEY VALE....156 A1
Putney Wharf Twr SW15....135 A2
Pycombe Cnr N12....29 B6
Pycroft Way N9....34 A6
Pykewell Lo 13 E8....74 A3
Pylbrook Rd SM1....217 D5
Pylon Trad Est E16....98 B2
Pylon Way CR0....204 A1
Pym Cl EN4....14 B6
Pymers Mead SE21....161 A3
Pymmes Brook Dr EN4....2 C1
Pymmes Brook Ho 3 N10....31 A3
Pymmes Cl
Bowes Pk N13....32 B5
Tottenham N17....34 B2
Pymmes Gdns N N9....17 D1
Pymmes Gdns S N9....17 D1
Pymmes Green Rd N11....15 C1
Pymmes Mews N13....32 A5
Pymmes Rd N13....32 A5
Pynchester Cl UB10....60 C6
Pyne Rd KT6....198 C1
Pynfolds SE16....118 B4
Pynham Cl SE2....124 B3
Pynnacles Cl HA7....25 B5
Pynnersmead SE24....161 A6
Pyramid Ho N12....30 A6
Pyrford Ho 12 SW9....138 D1
Pyrland Rd
Richmond TW10....154 B5
Stoke Newington N5....73 B3
Pyrmont Gr SE27....160 D1
Pyrmont Rd W4....132 C6
Pytchley Cres SE19....183 A4
Pytchley Rd SE22....139 C2

Q

Quadrangle Cl SE1....263 A4
Quadrangle Ho The E15....76 C2
Quadrangle Lo SW19....179 C4
Quadrangle The
Chelsea SW10....266 B2
Fulham SW6....264 A3
Herne Hill SE24....161 A6
3 North Kensington W12....90 C1
Paddington W2....237 A2
Stanmore HA7....25 C3
Walthamstow E17....35 B1
Quadrant Arc W1....249 B5
Quadrant Bsns Ctr NW6....91 A6
Quadrant Cl NW4....46 B4
Quadrant Gr NW5....70 D3
Quadrant Ho E15....98 C4
Quadrant Rd
Richmond TW9....131 D1
Thornton Heath CR7....204 D5
Quadrant The
4 Kensal Green W10....90 D4
Richmond TW9....132 A1
Sutton SM2....218 A2
West Heath DA7....146 D5
Wimbledon SW20....179 A2
Quad Rd HA9....65 D5
Quaggy Wlk SE3....143 A1
Quainton Hall Sch HA1....42 C4
Quainton St NW10....67 B5
Quaker Ct EC1....242 B6
Quaker La UB2....107 C3
Quakers Course NW9....27 D2
Quaker's Pl E7....77 D3
Quaker St E1....95 D3 243 C5
Quakers Wlk N21....17 B5
Quality Ct WC2....241 A2
Quantock Cl UB3....127 B5
Quantock Ct
4 East Barnet N20....14 C2
Greenford UB6....64 C3
Quantock Dr KT4....216 C6
Quantock Gdns NW2....68 D6
Quantock Ho N16....51 D1
Quantock Mews 3 SE15....140 A3
Quarles Park Rd RM6....58 C3
Quarrendon St SW6....135 C3
Quarr Rd SM5....202 C3
Quarry Park Rd SM1....217 B2
Quarry Rd SW18....158 A5
Quarry Rise SM1....217 B2
Quarterdeck The E14....119 C4
Quartermain Ho SM4....202 A4
Quartermile La E10, E15....75 D4
Quayside Ct 6 SE16....118 D5
Quay West Ct TW11....175 B5
Quebec & Crown Wharves E14....97 B1
Quebec Ind Est SE16....119 A3
Quebec Mews W1....237 D1
Quebec Rd
Hayes UB4....84 C1
Ilford IG1....57 A2
Quebec Way SE16....119 A4
Quebec Wharf 22 E8....95 C6
Quedgeley Ct 3 SE15....139 D6
Queen Adelaide Ct SE20....184 C4
Queen Adelaide Rd SE20....184 C3
Queen Alexandra Mans WC1....233 A1
Queen Alexandra's Ct SW19....179 B5
Queen Anne Ave BR2....208 D6
Queen Anne Dr KT10....212 C1
Queen Anne Gate DA7....146 D2
Queen Anne Mews W1....238 D3
Queen Anne Rd E9....74 D2
Queen Annes Cl TW2....152 B1
Queen Anne's Gate SW1....115 D4 249 C1
Queen Anne's Gdns
Bedford Pk W4....111 C3
Ealing W5....110 A4
Enfield EN1....17 C5
Mitcham CR4....202 D6
Queen Anne's Gr
Bedford Pk W4....111 C3
Ealing W5....110 A4
Enfield EN1....17 C5
Queen Anne's Pl EN1....17 C5
Queen Anne St W1....93 B2 238 C3
Queen Anne Terr 9 E1....118 B6
Queenborough Gdns
Chislehurst BR7....189 B4
Ilford IG2....56 C5
Queen Caroline St W6....112 C1
Queen Charlottes & Chelsea Hospl W12....90 A1
Queen Ct WC1....240 B5
Queen Elizabeth Ct
Barnet EN5....1 B1
5 Kingsland N1....73 B2
Queen Elizabeth Gdns SM4....201 C5
Queen Elizabeth Hall & Purcell Room* SE1....250 D4
Queen Elizabeth Ho SW12....159 A4
Queen Elizabeth Hospl SE18....144 A5
Queen Elizabeth II Con Ctr SW1....249 D1
Queen Elizabeth II Jubilee Sch W9....91 B3
Queen Elizabeth II Pier SE10....120 D5
Queen Elizabeth Rd
Kingston u T KT2....176 B1
Walthamstow E17....53 A6
Queen Elizabeth's Cl N16....73 B6
Queen Elizabeth's Coll 15 SE10....142 A5
Queen Elizabeth's Dr N14....16 A3
Queen Elizabeth's Girls Sch EN5....1 B1
Queen Elizabeth's Hunting Lodge Mus* E4....20 D4
Queen Elizabeth St SE1....117 D4 253 C2
Queen Elizabeth's Wlk
Stoke Newington N16....73 B6
Wallington SM6....219 D4
Queen Elizabeth Wlk SW13....134 B4
Queenhithe EC4....252 B6
Queen Margaret Flats 22 E2....96 B4
Queen Margarets Ct N1....73 C3
Queen Margaret's Gr N1....73 C3
Queen Mary Ave SM4....200 D4
Queen Mary Cl KT9....214 C5
Queen Mary Ct TW19....148 A3
Queen Mary Rd
Charlton TW17....171 A1
South Norwood SE19....182 D4
Queen Mary's Ave SM5....218 D1
Queen Mary's Gdns* NW1....231 A1
Queen Mary's Hospl
Hampstead NW3....70 A5
Sidcup DA14....190 A4
Queen Mary's Univ Hospl SW15....156 A5
Queen Mary, Univ of London E1....97 A3
Queen of Denmark Ct SE16....119 B3
Queens Acre SM3....217 A1
Queen St Pl EC4....252 B6
Queens Ave TW13....172 C6
Queen's Ave N3....30 A2
Queens Ave N10....49 B6
Queen's Ave
Southall UB1....86 A1
Southgate N21....16 D3
Queens Ave
Stanmore HA7....25 C1
Whetstone N20....14 B2
Queen's Ave IG8....37 B5
Queensberry Ho 6 TW9....153 D6
Queensberry Mews W SW7....256 C4
Queensberry Pl
Chelsea SW7....114 B2 256 C4
Plashet E12....78 A3
Queensberry Way SW7....256 C4
Queensborough Ct N3....47 B5
Queensborough Mews W2....246 A6
Queensborough Pas W2....246 A6
Queensborough Terr W2....113 D6 245 D6
Queensbridge Ct 1 E2....95 D5
Queensbridge Inf Sch E8....73 D1
Queensbridge Pk TW7....152 C6
Queensbridge Rd
Dalston E8....73 D1
Shoreditch E2, E8....95 D6
QUEENSBURY....44 B6
Queensbury IG9....21 B3
Queensbury Circ Par HA3....44 A6
Queensbury Ct CR7....183 A1
Queensbury Rd
Kingsbury NW9....45 B2
Wembley HA0....88 B5
Queensbury Sta HA7, HA8....44 B6
Queensbury Station Par HA8....44 B6
Queensbury St N1....73 A1
Queen's CE Prim Sch The TW9....132 C5
Queen's Cir SW11....137 B5 268 C3
Queen's Cl HA8....26 C5
Queen's Club Gdns W14....135 A6 264 B6
Queen's Club The W14....113 A1 254 B1
Queen's Cl SM6....219 B3
Queen's Coll W1....93 B2 238 C3
Queenscourt HA9....66 A4
Queen's Cres NW5....71 A2
Queens Cres TW10....154 B6
Queenscroft Rd SE9....165 D5
Queen's Ct SW13....134 A2
Queens Ct SW11....268 C2
Queen's Ct BR3....185 C2
Queens Ct
Beckenham BR3....185 D3
Camberwell SE5....139 C3
Queen's Ct
Croydon CR2....221 A3
8 Ealing W5....87 C2
Hampstead Garden Suburb NW11....47 C4
Kensington W2....245 D5
1 Kingston u T KT2....176 C3
Queens Ct E10....53 C2
Queen's Ct E11....54 C2
Queens Ct 4 E14....119 B6
Queen's Ct 3 TW10....154 B5
Queens Ct
Sidcup DA14....190 A6
Stanmore HA7....25 B1
Queen's Ct NW8....229 C4
Queens Ct 8 NW11....47 B4
Queen's Ct CR7....204 C4
Queens Ct E17....53 C4
Queensdale Cres W11....112 D5
Queensdale W11....112 D5
Queensdale Pl W11....244 A3
Queensdale Rd
Notting Hill W11....112 D5
Notting Hill W11....113 A5 244 A3
Queensdale Wlk W11....244 A3
Queensdown Rd E5....74 B4
Queen's Dr Acton W3....88 C1
Queen's Dr *continued*
Finsbury Pk N4....72 D6
Queens Dr KT5....198 C3
Queen's Dr KT7....197 A3
Queens Dr E10....53 C2
Queen's Elm Par SW3....256 D2
Queen's Elm Sq SW3....256 D1
Queensferry Wlk N17....52 B5
Queensfield Ct SM3....216 C4
Queen's Gallery* SW1....115 B4 248 D1
Queensgate Ct N12....29 D5
Queens Gate Gdns BR7....189 B2
Queensgate Gdns SW15....134 B1
Queen's Gate Gdns SW7....114 A3 256 B5
Queensgate Ho 34 E3....97 B5
Queen's Gate Mews SW7....114 A3 256 B6
Queensgate Pl 10 NW6....69 C1
Queen's Gate Pl Mews SW7....114 A3 256 B5
Queen's Gate Pl SW7....114 A3 256 B5
Queens Gate IG4....56 B5
Queen's Gate Sch SW7....256 C4
Queen's Gate SW7....114 A3 256 B5
Queen's Gate Terr SW7....114 A3 256 B6
Queens Gate Villas E9....75 A1
Queen's Gdns
Bayswater W2....114 A6 246 A6
Ealing W5....87 C3
Heston TW5....129 A4
Queens Gdns NW4....46 C4
Queen's Gr NW8....92 B6 229 D5
Queen's Grove Rd E4....20 B3
Queen's Head Pas EC2....242 A2
Queen's Head St N1....94 D6 234 D5
Queen's Head Yd SE1....252 C3
Queens Ho 1 SE17....139 B6
Queen's Ho TW11....174 D4
Queen's House The* SE10....142 B6
Queens Keep 10 TW1....153 C5
Queens La
2 Ashford TW15....170 B6
Muswell Hill N10....49 B6
Queensland Ave
Edmonton N18....33 A4
Merton SW19....179 D2
Queensland Cl E17....35 B1
Queensland Ct N10....31 B3
Queensland Ho 2 E16....122 C5
Queensland Rd N7....72 C4
Queens Lo HA7....25 A5
Queens Manor Sch SW6....134 D5
Queen's Mans W6....112 D2
Queens Mans
Hampstead NW6....69 D3
Hendon NW4....46 B4
Queen's Mans N10....49 A6
Queensmead TW15....170 B5
Queens Mead HA8....26 B4
Queen's Mead Rd BR2....186 D1
Queensmead Sch HA4....62 D4
Queensmead NW8....92 B6 229 D6
Queensmere Cl SW19....156 D2
Queensmere Ct SW13....134 A6
Queensmere Rd SW19....156 D2
Queensmere 4 SM1....217 D3
Queens Mews 5 IG9....21 C2
Queen's Mews W2....113 D6 245 C6
Queensmill Rd SW6....134 D5
Queensmill Sch SW6....135 C3
Queen's Mkt E13....99 C6
Queens Parade Cl N11....30 D5
Queens Par W5....88 B1
Queen's Par 3 N11....30 D5
Queens Par 7 NW4....
Queens Park Com S
NW6....
Queens Park Ct 5 W10....
Queens Park Gdns TW13....
Queen's Park Prim S W10....
Queen's Park Sta NW6....
Queens Par 3 NW2....
Queen's Par N11....
Queen's Pas BR7....
Queen's Pl SM4....
Queen's Quay EC4....
Queen Sq WC1....94 A2
Queen's Rd
Barking IG11....
Beckenham BR3....
Bowes Pk N11....
Bromley BR1....
Buckhurst Hill IG9....
Chislehurst BR7....
Ealing W5....
Edmonton N9....
Enfield EN1....
Feltham TW13....
Finchley N3....
Hampton TW12....
Queens Rd UB3....
Queen's Rd
Hendon NW4....
Hounslow TW3....
Kingston u T KT2....
Leytonstone E11....
Mitcham CR4....
Queens Rd SM4....
Queen's Rd
Mortlake SW14....
New Cross Gate SE14, SE15....
Newham E13....
New Malden KT3....
Richmond KT2, TW10....
Richmond TW10....
Southall UB2....
Teddington TW11....
Thames Ditton KT7....
Thornton Heath CR0....
Queens Rd TW1....
Queen's Rd
Wallington SM6....
Walthamstow E17....
Welling DA16....
Queens Rd UB7....
Queen's Rd SW19....
Queen's Rd W E13....
Queens Reach KT8....
Queen's Ride SW13....
Queen's Rise TW10....
Queen's Road Sta SE15....
Queen's Row SE17....
Queen St
Bexleyheath DA7....
City of London EC4....117 A6
Croydon CR0....
Queens Terr Cotts W7....
Queens Terr HA3....
Queen's Terr TW7....
Queens Terr
Newham E13....
St John's Wood NW8....92 B5
Queensthorpe Rd SE26....
Queen St W1....115 B5
Queenstown Mews SW8....
Queenstown Rd SW8....137 B5
Queenstown Road Sta SW8....137 B4
Queen St N17....
Queensville Rd SW12, SW4....
Queens Walk Ho W5....
Queensway Bsns Ctr EN3....
Queensway
Coney Hall BR4....
Croydon CR0....
Enfield EN3....
Queens Way
Feltham TW13....
Hendon NW4....
Queensway
Kensington W2....113 D6
Orpington BR5....

nsway Sta
.... 113 D6 245 D5
nsway TW16 .... 172 B1
ns Well Ave
.... 30 C6
nswell Jun & Inf
s N20 .... 14 B2
ns Wlk
ord TW15 ...... 170 A6
gford E4 .... 20 B3
n's Wlk W5 ...... 87 C2
ns Wlk
row HA1 .... 42 C5
slip HA4 .... 62 C5
n's Wlk
.... 115 C5 249 A3
ns Wlk NW9 ..... 67 A6
nswood Ave
gford E17 .... 36 A2
pton TW12 ..... 173 D4
nslow TW3,
W5 .... 129 B3
rnton Heath CR7 . 204 C4
lington CR0,
M6 .... 219 D4
nswood Ct
Clapham Pk
W4 .... 160 A6
West Norwood
E27 .... 183 B6
nswood Gdns
.... 55 B1
nswood Pk N3 ... 29 A2
nswood Rd
kfen DA15 ...... 167 D5
est Hill SE23 ..... 163 A1
n's Wood Rd N6 . 49 B3
ns Yd E9 .... 75 C2
n's Yd W1 ...... 239 B5
n Victoria Ave
) 65 D1
n Victoria Meml*
1 .... 249 A2
n Victoria St
.... 117 A6 252 A6
n Victoria Terr 12
.... 118 B6
ch Ho 2 N19 ..... 71 D3
nerford Rd N7 .... 72 B3
don Ho 9 W10 .. 90 C3
nington Ct 5
5 .... 139 D6
nington Mans
6 .... 264 C2
nel Ho 7
12 .... 159 C4
tin Pl SE13 ..... 142 C2
tin Rd SE13 ..... 142 C2
nmore Cl BR1 ... 187 A4
nmore Rd
istow BR1 .... 187 A4
oud Green N4 ...... 50 C3
rin St SW6 ...... 136 A3
sted Ct 27 E8 ...... 74 B3
Mews NW6 ...... 91 C6
Rd NW6 .... 91 C6
k Rd W4 .... 111 C1
ks Rd SW19 ..... 179 D3
k St N1 ... 94 D5 234 D3
k Street Mews
.... 234 C3
kswood NW3 ...... 70 C1
t Nook BR2 ...... 225 D5
La SW15 ...... 134 D1
St Ealing W5 ...... 88 A5
hbury N4 .... 72 C5
St SE1 .... 252 A2
er St
hnal Green E2 ..... 96 A4
nstead Comm
E18 .... 123 D1
ing Ct 23 SE16 ... 118 D4
ce Ho TW13 ..... 150 A3
ce Rd SE13 ..... 141 D3
ta Dr EN5 .... 12 C6
tin Ave SW20 ..... 179 B2
tin Cl HA5 .... 40 B4
tin Ct W4 .... 133 A5
tin Kynaston Sch
8 .... 92 B6 229 C5
tock Ho 2
) 132 C4
ton Cl
kenham BR3 .... 208 A6
nford TW5 .... 128 B5
llington SM6 ...... 219 B4
ton Ho SW8 .... 270 A4
ton Rd KT7 ...... 197 A1
ton St SW18 ..... 158 A2
ey St 1 E14 ..... 120 B6
n Rd SE22 ...... 139 C2
wat-Ul-Islam Girls
E7 .... 77 B2

R

Rabbit Row W8 ..... 245 B4
Rabbits Rd E12 .... 78 A4
Rabbs Farm Prim Sch
UB7 .... 104 A6
Rabinal Ho EN3 .... 18 D6
Rabournmead Dr
UB5 .... 63 A3
Raby Rd KT3 .... 199 B5
Raby St E14 .... 97 A1
Raccoon Way TW4 ... 128 C3
Rachel Cl IG6 .... 57 B6
Rachel Ct SM2 .... 218 B1
Racine 15 SE5 .... 139 C4
Rackham Cl DA16 .... 146 B3
Rackham Mews
SW16 .... 181 C4
Racs Flats 9 SE1 .... 118 A2
Racton Rd
SW6 .... 135 C6 265 A5
Radbourne Ave W5 .. 109 C2
Radbourne Cl E5 ..... 74 D4
Radbourne Cres E17 .. 36 B1
Radbourne Ct HA3 .... 43 B3
Radbourne Rd
SW12 .... 159 D3
Radcliff Bldg EC1 ... 241 A4
Radcliffe Ave
Enfield EN2 .... 5 A4
Willesden Green
NW10 .... 90 A5
Radcliffe Coll
Marylebone
W1 .... 93 C1 239 A1
Soho W1 .... 93 D1 239 C2
Radcliffe Gdns SM5 .. 218 C1
Radcliffe Ho 10
SE16 .... 118 B2
Radcliffe Path 5
SW8 .... 137 B3
Radcliffe Rd
Bermondsey SE1 .... 263 B6
Harrow HA3 .... 25 A1
South Croydon CR0 .. 221 D5
Southgate N21 .... 16 D3
Radcliffe Sq SW15 ... 156 D5
Radcliffe Way UB5 ... 84 D4
Radcliff Mews
TW12 .... 174 A5
Radcot Point 2
SE23 .... 162 D1
Radcot St SE11 ..... 261 B1
Raddington Rd W10 ... 91 A2
Radfield Way DA15 ... 167 B4
Radford Ho
7 Bow Comm E14 .... 97 D2
Islington N7 .... 72 B3
Radford Rd SE13 ..... 164 A5
Radford Way IG11 ... 101 D4
Radipole Rd
SW6 .... 135 B4 264 C2
Radius Pk TW6 ...... 127 D1
Radland Rd E16 .... 99 A1
Radlet Ave SE23 ..... 162 B2
Radlett Cl E7 .... 76 D2
Radlett Pl
NW8 .... 92 C6 230 A6
Radley Ave IG3 .... 80 A4
Radley Cl TW14 ...... 149 D3
Radley Ct
4 Catford BR1 ..... 186 A6
25 Rotherhithe
SE16 .... 118 D4
Radley Gdns HA3 ..... 44 A5
Radley Ho
11 Abbey Wood
SE2 .... 124 D4
Marylebone NW1 .... 237 C6
Radley Lo 30 SW19 ... 156 D3
Radley Mews W8 ... 255 B5
Radley Rd N17 .... 33 C1
Radley's La E18 .... 37 A1
Radleys Mead RM10 ... 81 D2
Radley Sq E5 .... 74 C6
Radley Terr 1 E16 .... 98 D2
Radlix Rd E10 .... 53 C1
Radnor Ave
Bexley DA16 .... 168 B6
Harrow HA1 .... 42 C4
Radnor Cl
Chislehurst BR7 ..... 189 C4
Mitcham CR4 .... 204 A5
Radnor Cres
Redbridge IG4 .... 56 B4
Woolwich SE18 ...... 146 A5
Radnor Ct Ealing W7 ... 86 D1
6 Forest Hill SE23 .. 162 D1
Harrow HA3 .... 24 D2
Radnor Gdns
Enfield EN1 .... 5 C4
Twickenham TW1 .... 152 D2
Radnor Gr UB10 ...... 82 C5
Radnor Ho
East Molesey KT8 .... 196 B5
Radnor Ho *continued*
Thornton Heath
SW16 .... 182 B1
Radnor Lo W2 ...... 236 D1
Radnor Mews
W2 .... 92 B1 236 D1
Radnor Pl W2 . 92 C1 237 A1
Radnor Rd
Harrow HA1 .... 42 C4
Kensal Rise NW6 ...... 91 A6
Peckham SE15 ...... 140 A5
Twickenham TW1 .... 152 D2
Radnor St
EC1 .... 95 A4 235 B1
Radnor Terr
W14 .... 113 B2 254 C4
Radnor Way NW10 .... 88 D3
Radnor Wlk
Chelsea
SW3 ..... 114 D1 257 C1
Croydon CR0 .... 207 A3
21 Millwall E14 ..... 119 C2
Radstock Ave HA3 .... 43 B6
Radstock Cl N11 ...... 31 A4
Radstock St SW11 .. 267 A3
Radway Ho 38 W2 ..... 91 C2
Radwell Ho SW2 ..... 160 C6
Raebarn Ct 6
SW16 .... 160 A1
Raebarn Gdns EN5 .... 12 B6
Raeburn Ave KT5 .... 198 D3
Raeburn Cl
Hampstead Garden
Suburb NW11 .... 48 A3
Teddington KT1 ..... 175 D3
Raeburn Ho
5 Belmont SM2 .... 217 D1
6 Northolt UB5 ...... 84 D5
Raeburn Rd
Edgware HA8 .... 26 C2
Hayes UB4 .... 83 B5
Sidcup DA15 .... 167 C5
Raeburn St SW2 ..... 138 A1
Raffles Ct HA8 .... 26 B6
Raffles Ho NW4 .... 46 B5
Rafford Way BR1 .... 209 B6
RAF Mus* NW9 .... 28 A1
Ragged School Mus
The* E3 .... 97 A2
Raggleswood BR7 ... 188 C2
Raglan Cl TW4 .... 151 B6
Raglan Ct
Brixton SW9 .... 138 C2
Croydon CR0, CR2 ... 220 D3
Lee SE12 .... 165 A6
Wembley HA9 .... 66 C5
Raglan Jun & Inf Schs
EN1 .... 17 C4
Raglan Prim Sch
BR2 .... 209 D5
Raglan Rd
Belvedere DA17 ..... 125 B2
Bromley BR2 .... 209 C5
Enfield EN1 .... 17 D4
Walthamstow E17 ..... 54 B4
Woolwich SE18 ..... 123 A1
Raglan St NW5 .... 71 B2
Raglan Terr HA2 ...... 63 D4
Raglan Way UB5 ...... 64 A2
Ragley Cl W3 .... 111 A4
Ragwort Ct 1 SE26 .. 184 B5
Rahere Ho EC1 ..... 235 A2
Railey Mews NW5 ..... 71 C3
Railshead Rd TW1,
TW7 .... 131 B1
Railton Rd SE24 ..... 160 D6
Railway App
Bermondsey SE1 .... 252 D4
Harrow HA1, HA3 ..... 42 D5
Stroud Green N4 ...... 50 C3
11 Twickenham
TW1 .... 153 A4
Wallington SM6 ..... 219 B3
Railway Ave SE16 .... 118 C4
Railway Cotts
Hammersmith
W6 .... 112 C4
Ilford IG6 .... 57 B6
Railway Gr SE14 .... 141 B5
Railway Pl DA17 ..... 125 C3
Railway Rd TW11 .... 174 D6
Railway Rise SE22 ... 139 C1
Railway Side SW13 .. 133 C2
Railway St Ilford RM6 .. 58 C2
King's Cross N1 ..... 233 B3
Railway Terr
Chingford E17 .... 36 A2
Feltham TW13,
TW14 .... 150 A3
Ladywell SE13 ...... 163 D6
Rainborough Cl
NW10 .... 67 A2
Rainbow Ave E14 .... 119 D1
Rainbow Ct 3 SE14 .. 141 A6
Rainbow Ind Est
SW20 .... 178 B1
Rainbow Quay SE16 .. 119 A3
Rainbow Sch The
SW17 .... 158 A2
Rainbow St SE5 ...... 139 C5
Rainbow Works N15 .. 52 A4
Raine Gdns 4 IG8 .... 37 A6
Raines Ct N16 .... 73 D6
Raine's Foundation
Lower Sch E2 .... 96 B5
Raine's Foundation Sch
E2 .... 96 C5
Raine St E1 .... 118 B5
Rainford Ho 9 N7 .... 72 B6
Rainham Cl
Sidcup SE9 .... 167 C5
Wandsworth SW11 .. 158 C5
Rainham Ho NW1 .... 232 B5
Rainham Rd NW10 .... 90 C4
Rainham Rd N RM10 .. 81 D6
Rainham Rd S RM10 .. 81 D4
Rainhill Way E3 .... 97 C4
Rainsborough Ave
SE8 .... 119 A2
Rainsford Cl HA7 ..... 25 C5
Rainsford Ct NW10 .... 88 D5
Rainsford Ho 14
SW2 .... 160 B6
Rainsford Rd NW10 ... 88 D5
Rainsford St W2 .... 237 A2
Rainstar Est N18 ...... 34 C6
Rainton Rd SE7 ...... 121 A1
Rainville Rd W6 ..... 134 C6
Raisins Hill HA5 ...... 40 C6
Raith Ave N14 .... 15 D1
Raleigh Ave
Hayes UB4 .... 84 B2
Wallington SM6 ..... 219 D4
Raleigh Cl
Hendon NW4 .... 46 C4
Pinner HA5 .... 40 D2
Ruislip HA4 .... 61 D6
Raleigh Ct
Beckenham BR3 ..... 185 D2
4 Dulwich SE19 .... 183 D5
Ealing W13 .... 87 B2
7 Hammersmith
W12 .... 112 B4
2 Rotherhithe
SE16 .... 118 D5
Wallington SM6 ..... 219 B2
Raleigh Dr
East Barnet N20 ...... 14 C1
Esher KT10 .... 212 B3
Tolworth KT5 .... 199 A1
Raleigh Gdns
Mitcham CR4 .... 202 D6
Tulse Hill SW2 ...... 160 B5
Raleigh Ho
30 Clapham SW8 ... 137 D3
Isle of Dogs E14 .... 119 D4
1 Thames Ditton
KT7 .... 197 A2
Raleigh Mews
Islington N1 .... 234 D5
6 Orpington BR6 .... 227 D3
Raleigh Rd Enfield EN2 .. 5 B1
Feltham TW13 ...... 149 D2
Finchley N10 .... 30 C2
Hornsey N8 .... 50 C5
Penge SE20 .... 184 D3
Richmond TW9 ...... 132 B2
Southall UB2 .... 107 A1
Raleigh St N1 . 94 D6 234 D5
Raleigh Way
Feltham TW13 ...... 172 C5
Southgate N14 .... 16 A3
Ralph Ct 8 W2 .... 91 D1
Ralph Perring Ct
BR3 .... 207 C5
Ralston St SW3 ..... 257 C1
Ramac Ind Est SE7 .. 121 B1
Rama Cl SW16 .... 182 A3
Rama Ct HA1 .... 64 C6
Ramac Way SE7 ..... 121 B1
Rama La SE19 .... 183 D3
Ramar Ho 12 E1 ...... 96 A2
Rambler Cl SW16 .... 181 C6
Rambler Ct 11 NW9 ... 46 A5
Rame Cl SW17 .... 181 A5
Ramilles Cl SW2 ..... 160 A5
Ramillies Ho W1 .... 239 B1
Ramillies Pl
W1 .... 93 C1 239 A1
Ramillies Rd
Bedford Pk W4 ...... 111 B3
Blackfen DA15 ...... 168 B5
Edgware NW7 .... 11 C2
Ramillies St W1 .... 239 A1
Ramney Dr EN3 .... 7 A6
Rampart St E1 .... 96 B1
Ram Pas KT1 .... 175 D1
Rampayne St SW1 .. 259 C2
Rampton Cl E4 .... 19 C1
Ramsay Ho NW8 .... 230 A4
Ramsay Rd
Acton W3 .... 111 A4
Leyton E7 .... 76 D4
Ramscroft Cl N9 ...... 17 C4
Ramsdale Rd SW17 .. 181 A5
Ramsdean Ho 1
SW15 .... 156 B3
Ramsden Rd
Balham SW12 ...... 159 A4
Friern Barnet N11 ..... 30 D5
Ramsey Cl
Greenford UB6 .... 64 B3
West Hendon NW9 .... 45 D3
Ramsey Ct
Croydon CR0 .... 220 D6
Hornsey N8 .... 49 D4
Putney SW15 .... 156 C5
6 Upper Holloway
N19 .... 71 D6
Ramsey Ho
5 Battersea
SW11 .... 136 B1
14 Kennington SW9 .. 138 C5
7 Merton SW19 .... 179 D2
Ramsey Rd CR7 ..... 204 B3
Ramsey St E2 .... 96 A3
Ramsey Way N14 ..... 15 C4
Ramsfort Ho 4
SE16 .... 118 B2
Ramsgate Cl 10 E16 .. 121 B5
Ramsgate St E8 ...... 73 D2
Ramsgill App IG2 ..... 57 D5
Ramsgill Dr IG2 ...... 57 D5
Rams Gr RM6 .... 59 A5
Ram St SW18 .... 157 D6
Ramulis Dr UB4 .... 84 D3
Ramus Wood Ave
BR6 .... 227 C3
Rance Ho 12 SE7 .... 122 A2
Rancliffe Gdns SE9 .. 144 A1
Rancliffe Rd E6 ...... 100 A5
Randal Cremer JMI Sch
E2 .... 95 D5
Randall Ave NW2 ..... 67 D5
Randall Cl
SW11 ...... 136 C4 267 A2
Randall Ct NW7 .... 28 A3
Randall 9 NW9 .... 27 D2
Randall Pl SE10 ...... 142 A5
Randall Rd
SE11 ...... 116 B2 260 C3
Randall Row SE11 ... 260 C3
Randell's Rd
N1 .... 94 A6 233 B6
Randisbourne Gdns
SE6 .... 163 D1
Randle Rd TW10 ..... 175 C6
Randlesdown Rd
SE6 .... 163 D1
Randmore Ct 6
BR3 .... 185 C3
Randolf Ct
Paddington NW6 ...... 91 D5
St John's Wood NW8 229 A5
Randolph App E16 .... 99 C1
Randolph Ave
W9 .... 92 A4 229 A1
Randolph Cl KT2 .... 177 A5
Randolph Cres
W9 .... 92 A3 236 A6
Randolph Ct HA5 ..... 23 C3
Randolph Gdns NW6 .. 91 D5
Randolph Gr RM6 ..... 58 C4
Randolph Mews
W9 .... 92 A3 236 B5
Randolph Rd
Bromley BR2 .... 210 B1
Paddington
W9 .... 92 A3 236 B5
Southall UB1 .... 107 B4
Walthamstow E17 ..... 53 D4
Randolph St NW1 ..... 71 C1
Randon Cl HA2 .... 23 D1
Ranelagh Ave
Barnes SW13 ...... 134 A3
Fulham SW6 .... 135 B2
Ranelagh Cl HA8 ...... 26 C6
Ranelagh Ct HA8 ...... 26 C6
Ranelagh Dr
Edgware HA8 .... 26 C6
Twickenham TW1 .... 153 C6
Ranelagh Gardens Mans
SW6 .... 135 A2
Ranelagh Gardens (site
of Chelsea Flower
Show)*
SW1 ...... 115 A1 258 B1
Ranelagh Gdns
3 Bedford Pk
W6 .... 111 D3
Chiswick W4 .... 133 A5
Fulham SW6 .... 135 B2
Ilford IG1 .... 56 C1
Wanstead E11 .... 55 C4
Ranelagh Gr
SW1 .... 115 A1 258 B2
Ranelagh Ho SW3 ... 257 C2
Ranelagh Mans 4
SW6 .... 135 B3
Ranelagh Pl KT3 ..... 199 C4
Ranelagh Prim Sch
E15 .... 98 C5
Ranelagh Rd
Dagenham NW10 ..... 89 D5
Ealing W5 .... 109 D4
Leyton E11 .... 76 C4
Newham E15 .... 98 C5
Pimlico
SW1 ..... 115 C1 259 B1
Southall UB1 .... 106 D5
Tottenham N17 .... 51 C6
Wallend E6 .... 100 C5
Wembley HA0 .... 65 D2
Wood Green N22 ...... 32 B2
Ranfurly Rd SM1 ..... 217 C6
Rangdon St EC3 .... 243 C1
Rangefield Prim Sch
BR1 .... 186 C5
Rangefield Rd BR1 ... 186 D5
Rangemoor Rd N15 ... 51 D4
Ranger's House (The
Wernher
Collection)*
SE10 .... 142 B4
Ranger's Rd
Buckhurst Hill IG9,
IG10 .... 21 A4
Chingford E4 .... 20 D4
Rangers Sq SE10 ..... 142 B4
Range Villas TW17 ... 192 A2
Range Way TW17 .... 192 C2
Rangeworth Pl
DA15 .... 167 D1
Rangoon Ho 5 N16 ... 73 B4
Rankin Cl NW9 .... 45 C6
Rankine Ho SE1 ..... 262 A5
Ranleigh Gdns DA7 .. 147 B5
Ranmere St SW12 ... 159 B3
Ranmoor Cl HA1 ..... 42 B5
Ranmoor Gdns HA1 ... 42 C5
Ranmore Ave CR0 ... 221 D5
Ranmore Ct
Kingston u T KT6 .... 197 D4
3 Wimbledon
SW20 .... 178 D2
Rann Ho 1 SW14 .... 133 B2
Rannoch Cl HA8 ...... 10 D2
Rannoch Ct 9 KT6 ... 198 A4
Rannoch Rd W6 ..... 134 D6
Rannock Ave NW9 .... 45 C2
Ransford Ho 16
SE21 .... 183 C6
Ransomes Dock Bsns
Ctr SW11 .... 267 B3
Ransomes Mews
SW11 .... 267 B4
Ransom Rd 1 SE7 ... 121 C1
Ranston St NW1 .... 237 A4
Ranulf Rd NW2 .... 69 B4
Ranwell Cl 18 E3 ..... 97 B6
Ranwell Ho 17 E3 .... 97 B6
Ranworth Rd N9 ...... 18 C2
Ranyard Cl KT9 ..... 214 B5
Raphael Ct 9 SE16 .. 118 B1
Raphael Dr KT7 ..... 196 D2
Raphael St SW7 .... 247 C1
Rapide 15 NW9 ...... 27 C2
Rapley Ho 14 E2 ...... 96 A4
Rashleigh Ct 8
SW8 .... 137 B2
Rashleigh Ho WC1 .. 233 A1
Rasper Rd N20 .... 14 A2
Rastell Ave SW12 .... 159 D3
RATCLIFF 118 D6
Ratcliffe Cl SE12 .... 165 A4
Ratcliffe Cross St E1 .. 96 D1
Ratcliffe Ho 10 E14 ... 97 A1
Ratcliffe La 16 E14 ... 97 A1
Ratcliffe Orch 9
E1 .... 118 D6
Ratcliff Rd E7 .... 77 C3
Rathbone Ho
5 Canning Town
E16 .... 98 D1
Kilburn NW6 .... 91 C6
10 Wimbledon
SW19 .... 178 D3
Rathbone Mkt 3
E16 .... 98 D2
Rathbone Pl
W1 .... 93 D1 239 C2
Rathbone St
Canning Town E16 .... 98 D1
Fitzrovia W1 .. 93 C2 239 B3
Rathcoole Ave N8 ..... 50 B4
Rathcoole Gdns N8 ... 50 B4
Rathfern Prim Sch
SE6 .... 163 B3
Rathfern Rd SE6 .... 163 B3
Rathgar Ave W13 .... 109 C5
Rathgar Cl N3 .... 29 B1
Rathgar Rd SW9 ..... 138 D2
Rathmell Dr SW4 .... 159 D5
Rathmore Rd SE7 .... 121 B1

Ratier 16 NW9 27 C2
Rattray Ct 3 SE6 164 D2
Rattray Rd SW2 160 C6
Raul Rd SE15 140 A4
Raveley St NW5 71 C4
Raven Cl NW9 27 C1
Ravendale Rd TW16 171 D1
Ravenet Ct
Battersea SW11 268 C1
Clapham SW4 159 B6
Ravenet St SW11 137 B4 268 C1
Ravenfield Rd SW17 158 D1
Ravenhill Rd E13 99 C5
Raven Ho 10 SE16 118 D2
Ravenings Par IG3 58 A1
Ravenna Rd SW15 156 D6
Ravenor Ct UB6 85 D3
Ravenor Park Rd UB6 86 A4
Ravenor Prim Sch UB6 85 C4
Raven Rd E18 37 C1
Raven Row E1 96 B2
Ravensbourne Ave
Bromley BR2, BR3 186 C2
Catford BR2 186 B3
Stanwell TW19 148 A3
Ravensbourne Bsns Ctr BR2 225 D4
Ravensbourne Coll of Design & Communication BR7 188 B5
Ravensbourne Ct SE6 163 C4
Ravensbourne Gdns W13 87 B2
Ravensbourne Ho
10 Catford BR1 186 B5
Paddington NW8 237 A4
3 Twickenham TW1 153 C5
Ravensbourne Mans 9 SE8 141 C6
Ravensbourne Park Cres SE6 163 B4
Ravensbourne Pk SE6 163 C4
Ravensbourne Pl SE13 141 D3
Ravensbourne Rd
Bromley BR1, BR2 209 A6
Forest Hill SE23 163 B3
Twickenham TW1 153 C5
Ravensbourne Sch The BR2 209 B5
Ravensbourne Sta BR3 186 B3
Ravensbury Ave SM4 202 A4
Ravensbury Ct CR4 202 B5
Ravensbury Gr CR4 202 B5
Ravensbury La CR4 202 B5
Ravensbury Rd
Orpington BR5 211 D5
Wandsworth SW18 157 D2
Ravensbury Terr SW18 157 D2
Ravenscar Lo 14 SW19 178 D3
Ravenscar NW1 232 A5
Ravenscar Rd
Catford BR1 186 C6
Surbiton KT6 214 B6
Ravens Cl
Bromley BR2 186 D1
Enfield EN1 5 C3
Kingston u T KT6 197 D3
Ravenscourt Ave W6 112 A2
Ravenscourt Cl HA4 39 A2
Ravenscourt Gdns W6 112 A2
Ravenscourt Ho 13 W6 112 B2
Ravenscourt Park Mans 1 W6 112 B3
Ravenscourt Park Prep Sch W6 112 A2
Ravenscourt Park Sta W6 112 B2
Ravenscourt Pk W6 112 A2
Ravenscourt Pl W6 112 B2
Ravenscourt Rd
Hammersmith W6 112 B2
St Paul's Cray BR5 190 B1
Ravenscourt 1 N16 74 A5
Ravenscourt Sq W6 112 A3
Ravenscourt TW16 171 D2
Ravenscourt Theatre Sch W6 112 B2
Ravenscraig Rd N11 31 C6
Ravenscroft Ave
Golders Green NW11 47 B2
Wembley HA9 44 B2
Ravenscroft Cl 4 E16 99 A2
Ravenscroft Cres SE9 166 B1
Ravenscroft Ct NW11 47 B2
Ravenscroft Pk EN5 1 A1
Ravenscroft Point 26 E9 74 D2
Ravenscroft Prim Sch E16 99 A3
Ravenscroft Rd
Acton W4 111 A2
Newham E16 99 A2
Penge BR3 184 D1
Ravenscroft Sch a Tech Coll The N20 13 B4
Ravenscroft St E2 95 D4
Ravensdale Ave N12 30 B6
Ravensdale Commercial Est N16 52 A3
Ravensdale Gdns
Hounslow TW4 129 A2
South Norwood SE19 183 B3
Ravensdale Mans N8 50 A3
Ravensdale Rd
Hounslow TW4 129 A2
South Tottenham N16 51 D3
Ravensdon St SE11 116 C1 261 B1
Ravensfield Cl RM9 80 D4
Ravensfield Gdns KT19 215 C4
Ravenshaw St NW6 69 B3
Ravenshill BR7 188 D2
Ravens Ho KT1 175 D1
Ravenshurst Ave NW4 46 C5
Ravenside Cl N18 34 D5
Ravenside KT6 197 D4
Ravenside Ret Pk N18 34 D5
Ravenslea Rd SW11, SW12 158 D4
Ravensleigh Gdns BR1 187 B5
Ravensmead Rd BR2 186 B3
Ravensmede Way W4 111 D2
Ravensroost SE19 183 B2
Ravenstone Prim Sch SW12 159 A2
Ravenstone Rd
Hornsey N8 50 C6
West Hendon NW9 45 D3
Ravenstone SE17 117 C1 263 B1
Ravenstone St SW12 159 A3
Ravensview Ct KT6 197 D4
Ravens Way SE3, SE12 165 A6
Ravenswood Ave
Tolworth KT6 214 C6
West Wickham BR4 208 A1
Ravenswood N22 32 B4
Ravenswood Cres
Harrow HA2 63 B6
West Wickham BR4 208 A1
Ravenswood Gdns TW7 130 C4
Ravenswood Ind Est 5 E17 54 A5
Ravenswood Pk HA6 22 A4
Ravenswood Rd
Balham SW12 159 B4
Croydon CR0 220 D5
Walthamstow E17 54 A5
Ravens Wood Sch BR2 225 D5
Ravenswood DA5 169 A3
Ravensworth Ct SW6 265 A3
Ravensworth Rd
Chislehurst SE9 188 B6
College Pk NW10 90 B4
Raven Wharf SE1 253 C2
Ravey St EC2 95 C3 243 A6
Ravine Gr SE18 145 C6
Rav Pinter Cl N16 51 C2
Rawlings Cl
Beckenham BR3 208 A4
3 Orpington BR6 227 D3
Rawlings Cres HA9 66 D5
Rawlings St SW3 114 D2 257 C4
Rawlins Cl Hendon N3 47 A6
South Croydon CR2 223 B1
Rawlinson Ct NW2 46 C2
Rawlinson Ho SE13 142 B1
Rawlinson Point 8 E16 98 D2
Rawnsley Ave CR4 202 C4
Rawreth Wlk N1 235 B6
Rawson Ct SW11 268 B1
Rawson St SW11 137 B4 268 C1
Rawsthorne Cl E16 122 B5
Rawstone Wlk 5 E13 99 A5
Rawstorne Pl EC1 234 C2
Rawstorne St EC1 94 D4 234 C2
Raybell Ct TW7 130 D3
Rayburn Ct
1 Buckhurst Hill IG9 21 C3
West Kensington W14 254 A6
Ray Cl KT9 213 C2
Ray Ct Ealing W13 109 B5
Stanmore HA7 25 B5
Woodford IG8 37 D4
Raydean Rd EN5 13 D6
Raydons Gdns RM9 81 A3
Raydons Rd RM9 81 A3
Raydon St N19 71 B6
Rayfield Cl BR2 210 A3
Rayford Ave SE12 164 D4
Ray Gdns
Barking IG11 102 A5
Stanmore HA7 25 B5
Ray Ho
7 North Kensington W10 90 D1
Shoreditch N1 235 D5
Rayleas Cl SE18 144 D4
Rayleigh Ave TW11 174 C4
Rayleigh Cl N13 17 B1
Rayleigh Ct
2 Kingston u T KT1 176 B1
Tottenham N22 33 A2
Rayleigh Rd
Edmonton N13 17 B1
Merton SW19 179 B2
5 Newham E16 121 B5
Woodford IG8 37 C3
Rayleigh Rise CR2 221 C2
Ray Lodge Prim Sch IG8 37 D4
Ray Lodge Rd IG8 37 D4
Ray Massey Way 3 E6 100 A6
Raymead Ave CR7 204 C4
Raymede Twr W10 90 D2
Raymere Gdns SE18 145 C5
Raymond Ave
Brentford W13 109 A3
Woodford E18 36 D1
Raymond Bldgs WC1 240 D4
Raymond Cl SE26 184 C5
Raymond Ct N10 31 A3
Raymond Postgate Ct 5 SE28 124 B6
Raymond Rd
Beckenham BR3 207 A5
Ilford IG2 57 B2
Newham E13 99 C6
Wimbledon SW19 179 A4
Raymond Way KT10 213 A2
Raymouth Rd SE16 118 B2
Raynald Ho 15 SW16 160 A1
Rayne Ct
Bermondsey SE1 253 C2
Snaresbrook E18 54 D5
Rayne Ho
1 Balham SW12 159 A5
Paddington W9 91 D3
Rayner Ct 10 W12 112 C4
Rayners Cl HA0 65 D3
Rayners Cres UB5 84 B4
Rayners Gdns UB5 84 B4
Rayners La HA2 63 D6
RAYNERS LANE 41 B1
Rayners Lane Sta HA5 41 B2
Rayners La HA5 41 B3
Rayner's Rd SW15 157 A6
Rayner Twrs E10 53 C2
Raynes Ave E11 55 C2
Raynes Ct NW2 69 A4
Raynesfield SW20 200 C6
RAYNES PARK 200 C6
Raynes Park High Sch SW20 200 B6
Raynes Park Sta SW20 178 C1
Raynham Ave N18 34 A5
Raynham Ho 1 E1 96 D3
Raynham Prim Sch N18 34 A5
Raynham Rd
Edmonton N18 34 A5
Raynham Rd *continued*
Hammersmith W6 112 B2
Raynham Terr N18 34 A5
Raynham W2 237 A2
Raynor Cl UB1 107 B5
Raynor Pl N1 235 B6
Raynton Cl
Harrow HA2 41 A2
Hayes UB4 83 D3
Raynton Dr
Hayes UB4 83 C5
Hayes UB4 83 D3
Raynton Rd EN3 6 D6
Ray Rd KT8 195 D4
Rays Ave N18 34 C6
Rays Rd
Edmonton N18 34 C6
West Wickham BR4 208 A2
Ray St EC1 241 B5
Ray Wlk N7 72 B6
Raywood Cl UB7 127 A5
Reachview Cl 17 NW1 71 C1
Read Cl KT7 197 A2
Read Ct E17 53 D3
Reade Ct 6 W3 111 A3
Reade Wlk 5 NW10 67 C1
Read Ho
Friern Barnet N11 30 D6
4 Kennington SE11 138 C6
Reading Ho
Paddington W2 236 A1
Peckham SE15 140 A6
Reading La E8 74 B2
Reading Rd
Northolt UB5 64 A3
Sutton SM1 218 A3
Reading Way NW7 29 A5
Readman Ct 8 SE20 184 B2
Reads Cl IG1 78 D5
Reapers Cl NW1 232 C6
Reapers Way TW7 152 B6
Reardon Ho 5 E1 118 B5
Reardon Path 31 E1 118 B5
Reardon St E1 118 B5
Reaston St SE14 140 D5
Reay Prim Sch SW9 138 B5 270 D3
Rebecca Ct
3 Beckenham BR3 185 C2
Sidcup DA14 190 B6
Rebecca Ho 12 N12 29 D6
Reckitt Rd W4 111 C1
Record St SE16 140 C6
Recovery St SW17 180 C5
Recreation Rd
Bromley BR2 186 D1
Forest Hill SE26 184 D6
Southall UB2 107 A2
Recreation Way CR4, SW16 204 A6
Rector St N1 95 A6 235 A5
Rectory Bsns Ctr 5 DA14 190 B6
Rectory Cl
Chingford E4 19 C1
Finchley N3 29 B2
Littleton TW17 192 C6
Long Ditton KT6 197 C1
Sidcup DA14 190 B6
Stanmore HA7 25 B5
West Barnes SW20 200 C6
Rectory Cres E11 55 C3
Rectory Ct
Cranford TW5 128 C3
Feltham TW13 172 C6
Leyton E11 76 D5
Wallington SM6 219 C4
West Drayton UB7 104 A4
Woodford E18 36 D2
Rectory Field Cres SE7 143 C5
Rectory Gdns
Beckenham BR3 185 C2
6 Clapham SW4 137 C2
Hornsey N8 50 A5
Northolt UB5 85 B6
Rectory Gn BR3 185 B2
Rectory Gr
Clapham SW4 137 C2
Croydon CR0 220 D6
Hampton TW12, TW13 173 B6
Rectory La
Edgware HA8 26 C4
Long Ditton KT6 197 C1
Sidcup DA14 190 C6
Stanmore HA7 25 B5
Upper Tooting SW17 181 A5
Wallington SM6 219 C4
Rectory Orch SW19 179 A6
Rectory Paddock Sch BR5 190 C1
Rectory Park Ave UB5 85 B4
Rectory Pl SE18 122 C2
Rectory Rd
Barnes SW13 134 A3
Beckenham BR3 185 C2
Cranford TW5 128 C3
Dagenham RM10 81 D1
Hayes UB3 84 A1
Keston BR2 225 D1
Little Ilford E12 78 B3
1 London W3 111 A5
Shacklewell N16 73 D5
Southall UB2 107 B3
Sutton SM1 217 D5
Walthamstow E17 53 D5
Rectory Road Sta N16 73 D5
Rectory Sq E1 96 D2
Rectory Way UB10 60 D5
Reculver Ho 2 SE15 140 C6
Reculver Mews N18 34 A6
Reculver Rd SE16 118 D1
Red Anchor Cl SW3 267 A5
Redan Pl W2 91 D1
Redan St W14 112 D3
Redan Terr SE5 138 D3
Red Barracks Rd 4 SE18 122 B2
Redberry Gr SE23, SE26 162 C1
Redbourne Ave N3 29 C2
Redbourne Dr SE28 102 D1
Redbourne Ho
Finchley N3 29 C2
7 Poplar E14 97 B1
Redbourn Ho 10 W10 90 C3
REDBRIDGE 55 C3
Redbridge Coll RM6 58 B4
Redbridge Ct IG1 55 D3
Redbridge Ent Ctr IG1 79 A6
Redbridge Foyer IG1 79 A6
Redbridge Gdns SE5 139 C5
Redbridge La E IG4 56 A4
Redbridge La W E11 55 C3
Redbridge Prim Sch IG4 56 A4
Redbridge Rdbt IG4 55 D3
Redbridge Sta IG4 55 D3
Redburn St SW3 136 D6 267 C6
Redburn Trad Est EN3 18 D5
Redcar Cl UB5 63 D2
Redcar Ho SE26 184 B4
Redcar St SE5 139 A5
Redcastle Cl E1 118 C6
Red Cedars Rd BR6 211 C2
Redchurch St E2 95 D3 243 C6
Redcliffe Cl SW5 255 C1
Redcliffe Ct 2 E5 74 B5
Redcliffe Gdns
Chiswick W4 132 D5
Fulham SW10 135 D6 265 D6
Ilford IG1 56 C1
Redcliffe Mews SW10 255 D1
Redcliffe Pl SW10 266 A5
Redcliffe Rd SW10 136 A6 266 B6
Redcliffe Sch SW10 136 A6 266 A6
Redcliffe Sq SW10 113 D1 255 D1
Redcliffe St SW10 265 D6
Redclose Ave SM4 201 C4
Redclyffe Rd E6 99 C6
Redclyffe Terr 2 SM2 217 C1
Redclyf Ho 13 E1 96 C3
Redcroft 5 NW6 69 C2
Redcroft Rd UB1 86 A1
Red Cross Cotts SE1 252 B2
Redcross Way SE1 117 A5 252 B3
Redding Ho SE18 122 A3
Reddings Ave WD23 8 A6
Reddings Cl NW7 27 D6
Reddings The NW7 11 D1
Reddins Rd SE15 140 A6
Reddons Rd BR3 185 A3
Rede Pl W2 113 C6 245 B6
Redesdale Gdns TW7 131 A5
Redesdale St SW3 267 C6
Redfern Ave TW2, TW4 151 C4
Redfern Ho 6 E13 98 D6
Redfern Rd
Catford SE6 164 A4
Willesden NW10 67 C1
Redfield La SW5 113 D2
Redfield Mews SW5
Redfiff Est SE16
Redford Ave
Thornton Heath CR7
Wallington SM6
Redford Cl TW13
Redford Wlk N1
Redgate Dr BR2
Red Gates Sch CR9
Redgate Terr SW15
Redgrave Cl SE25
Redgrave Rd SW15
Red Hill BR7
Redhill Ct SW2
Redhill Dr HA8
Red Hill Prim Sch BR7
Redhill St NW1 93 B4
Red House* DA6
Red House La DA6
Red House Rd CR0
Red House Sq 20 N1
Redif Ho RM10
Redington Gdns NW3
Redington Ho N1
Redington Rd NW3
Redknap Ho TW10
Red La KT10
Redland Gdns KT8
Redlands Ct BR1
Redlands Prim Sch E1
Redlands Rd EN3
Redlands TW11
Redlands The 5 BR3
Redlands N15
Redlands Way SW2
Redleaf Cl DA17
Redleaves Ave TW15
Redlees Cl TW7
Red Leys UB8
Red Lion Bsns Ctr KT6
Red Lion Cl 9 SE17
Red Lion Ct
Holborn EC4
Hounslow TW3
Red Lion Hill N2
Red Lion La SE18
Red Lion Pl SE18
Red Lion Rd KT6
Red Lion Row SE17
Red Lion Sq WC1 94 B2
Red Lion St
Gray's Inn WC1 94 B2
Richmond TW10
Red Lion Yd W1
Red Lodge Rd BR3, BR4
Red Lo Ealing W5
West Wickham BR4
Redlynch Ct W14 113 A4
Redlynch Ho 27 SW9
Redman Bldg EC1
Redman Cl UB5
Redman Ho SE1
Redman's Rd E1
Redmayne Ho 15 SW9
Redmead La E1
Redmead Rd UB3
Redmill Ho 24 E1
Redmond Ho N1
Redmore Rd W6
Red Oak Cl BR6
Redo Ho 3 E12
Red Pl W1
Redpoll Way DA18
Red Post Hill SE21, SE24
Red Post Ho E6
Redriffe Rd E13
Redriff Prim Sch SE16
Redriff Rd SE16
Redroofs Cl BR3
Redrose Trad Ctr 1 EN4
Red Rover SW13
Redrup Ho 21 SE14
Redruth Cl N22
Redruth Gdns KT10
Redruth Ho SM2
Redruth Rd E9
Red Sq The N16

rt Cl
Cross Gate
4 141 A5
am E6 100 A2
n Rd N8 49 D5
rs Rd N22 32 C1
rs St E2 95 C4
ld Rd E5 74 D4
ay Dr TW2 152 A4
ng Path SE28 123 B4
ng Rd SM6 220 B1
ood Cl
w E3 97 C5
vell IG9 21 B2
gdon UB10 82 D5
e N14 15 D4
rhithe SE16 119 A5
p DA15 168 A3
Oxhey WD19 22 D6
ood Ct
lesbury NW6 69 A1
h End N19 49 D2
olt UB5 85 A4
urbiton KT6 197 D2
ood Est TW5 128 B6
ood Gdns E4 19 D5
ood Gr W5 109 B2
ood Mews
rd TW15 171 B3
apham SW4 137 B2
oods SW15 156 A3
ood Way EN5 12 D6
ood Wlk KT6 197 D1
Mews SW7 256 C4
Ave BR6 227 C5
Cl Lee SE12 165 A6
am E16 99 A2
Gdns RM10 81 D3
Rd RM10 81 D2
Way RM10 81 D2
am Cl N17 52 B5
am St SE15 140 A2
olm Villas N16 73 B4
Ho SW15 156 A5
Mans 6 E11 55 A3
Pl
am SW4 137 D1
er Halliford
/17 192 B1
Rd N17 33 D1
field Cl TW15 148 D1
field Rd
5 170 D6
s Pl NW1 71 C1
worth St
116 C2 261 B3
Ho E14 120 A3
glass Rd HA7 25 D6
Dr HA7 26 A6
Gdns CR0 205 D3
Ho 6 N17 33 D3
and Cl E12 78 C2
St N1 95 A6 235 B5
Farm Cl NW9 45 C3
es Ave NW9 45 B2
es Cnr CR0 220 D6
es Cnr Sta CR0 220 D6
es Ho
beth SE1 251 A1
air W1 248 A5
es Mews
115 A6 248 B5
es Rd Bromley E3 97 D3
ters Hill SE18 144 D6
ction Ho 9 E2 96 A3
ction The E16 122 D4
Apartments 1
209 B5
m Row N17 33 D1
m St SW11 136 D3
Cl Ealing W5 87 D2
lfields E1 96 A2
Cres SM6 219 B5
Ct
onton N18 33 D5
itcham CR4 202 D6
mbley HA0 65 D4
Dr N11 31 B5
Ho IG2 57 B3
La NW1 231 B5
Pl
ower Hamlets
97 B4
ham Green SW6 265 D3
Way HA3 44 A3
n Ho 1 N18 33 D4
n Way N1 95 C5
tta Ho TW11 175 A6
tta Point TW8 132 B6
Ct NW7 29 A2
ncy Cl Ealing W5 88 A1
pton TW12 173 B5
ncy Cres 3
28 D1
ncy Ct
ow E3 97 B5
eld EN1 17 B6

Regency Ct *continued*
4 Kingston u T KT5 198 B4
4 Penge SE19 184 A3
14 South Hackney E9 96 C6
Sutton SM1 217 D5
Wimbledon SW19 179 B3
7 Woodford E18 37 A1
Regency Dr HA4 39 C1
Regency Gdns KT12 194 C1
Regency Ho
Finchley N3 29 B1
Marylebone NW1 238 D6
Regency Lo
1 Buckhurst Hill IG9 21 D2
Harrow HA3 42 C6
South Hampstead NW3 70 B1
Regency Mews
Beckenham BR3 186 A2
Camberwell SW9 138 D5
Isleworth TW7 152 C6
1 Willesden NW10 68 A2
Regency Pl SW1 259 D4
Regency St
SW1 115 D2 259 D3
Regency Terr SW7 256 C2
Regency Way DA6 147 A2
Regency Wlk
Croydon CR0 207 B3
8 Richmond TW10 154 A6
Regeneration Rd SE16 118 D1
Regent Ave UB10 60 D1
Regent Bsns Ctr UB3 106 A4
Regent Cl
Cranford TW4 128 B4
Harrow HA3 44 A3
North Finchley N12 30 A5
Regent Ct
4 Finchley N3 29 D3
Lisson Gr NW8 230 A1
South Norwood SE19 182 D4
1 Stamford Hill N16 51 D2
Regent Gdns IG3 58 A2
Regent Ho W14 254 A4
Regent Pl
Croydon CR0 205 D1
St James W1 249 B6
Wimbledon SW19 180 A5
Regent Rd
Surbiton KT5 198 C4
Tulse Hill SE24 160 D6
Regents Ave N13 32 C5
Regents Bridge Gdns SW8 270 B4
Regents Canal Ho 19 E14 97 A1
Regents Cl Hayes UB4 83 C2
South Croydon CR2 221 C2
Regent's Coll NW1 93 A3 238 A6
Regents Ct
22 Beckenham BR3 185 C3
Bromley BR1 186 D3
Edgware HA8 26 A6
Hackney E8 96 A6
1 Kingston u T KT2 176 A2
Regent's Ct HA5 22 D1
Regents Dr BR2 225 D3
Regents Gate Ho 20 E14 119 A6
Regents Lo 9 SW2 160 B3
Regents Mews NW8 92 A5 229 B4
REGENT'S PARK 93 B4
Regent's Park Barracks NW1 231 D3
Regent's Park* NW1 93 A5 231 A3
Regent's Park Rd
Camden Town NW1 93 A6 231 A6
Hendon N3 47 B6
Primrose Hill NW3 71 A1
Regent's Park Sta NW1 93 B3 238 C5
Regent's Park Terr NW1 231 C6
Regents Plaza 2 NW6 91 D5
Regents Pl IG10 21 D4
Regent's Pl SE3 143 A3
Regent Sq
Belvedere DA17 125 D2
23 Bromley E3 97 D4
St Pancras WC1 94 A4 233 B1
Regent's Row E8 96 A6
Regent St
Brentford W4 110 C1
7 Kensal Green NW10 90 D4
Mayfair W1 115 C6 249 A6

Regents Wharf
3 Hackney E2 96 B6
Islington N1 233 C4
Regina Coeli RC Prim Sch CR2 220 D1
Regina Ct TW11 174 C5
Reginald Ct BR3 186 A2
Reginald Pl 6 SE8 141 C5
Reginald Rd
Deptford SE8 141 C5
Forest Gate E7 77 A2
Reginald Sorenson Ho E11 54 B2
Reginald Sq SE8 141 C5
Regina Point SE16 118 C3
Regina Rd
Ealing W13 109 A5
Finsbury Pk N4 50 B1
Southall UB2 107 A2
South Norwood SE25 206 A6
Regina Terr W13 109 B5
Regis Ct
East Bedfont TW14 149 B5
Hornsey N8 50 B5
Marylebone NW1 237 C4
Mitcham SW19 180 C2
Regis Pl 17 SW2 138 B1
Regis Rd NW5 71 B3
Regnart Bldgs NW1 232 B1
Regnolruf Ct KT12 194 A2
Reid Cl Hayes UB3 83 C1
Pinner HA5 40 A5
Reid Ct SW14 133 A3
Reidhaven Rd SE18 123 C2
Reigate Ave SM1 201 D1
Reigate Rd
Catford BR1 164 D1
Grove Pk BR1, SE12 165 A2
Ilford IG3 79 D6
Reigate Way SM6 220 A3
Reighton Rd E5 74 A6
Reizel Cl N16 51 D1
Relay Rd W12 112 C5
Relf Rd SE15 140 A2
Reliance Sq E2 243 B6
Relko Gdns SM1 218 B3
Relton Ct W3 110 C4
Relton Mews SW7 257 B6
Rembrandt Cl E14 120 B3
Rembrandt Ct
10 Bermondsey SE16 118 B1
Harrow HA3 43 A3
West Ewell KT19 215 D2
Rembrandt Rd
Edgware HA8 26 C1
Lewisham SE13 142 C1
Rembrant Cl SW1 258 A3
Remembrance Ave N2 47 D6
Remington Rd
Newham E6 100 A1
Tottenham N15 51 B3
Remington St N1 94 D5 234 D3
Remnant St WC2 240 C2
Remsted Ho 7 NW6 91 D6
Remus Rd E3 75 C1
Renaissance Ct SM1 202 A1
Renaissance Wlk 4 SE10 120 D3
Renbold Ho 5 SE10 142 A4
Rendlebury Ho 17 SE18 122 B2
Rendle Cl CR0 206 A4
Rendlesham Ho 3 E5, N16 74 A5
Rendlesham Rd
Enfield EN2 4 D4
Shacklewell E5 74 A5
Renforth St SE16 118 C4
Renfree Way TW17 192 C2
Renfrew Cl E6 122 C6
Renfrew Ct TW5 129 A3
Renfrew Ho
Paddington NW6 91 D5
Walthamstow E17 35 B1
Renfrew Rd
Hounslow TW5 129 A3
Kingston u T KT2 177 A3
Newington SE11 116 D2 261 C3
Renmuir St SW17 180 D4
Rennell Ho 18 E9 74 D2
Rennell St SE13 142 A2
Renness Rd E17 53 A6
Rennets Cl SE9 167 C6
Rennets Wood Ho SE9 167 B6
Rennets Wood Rd SE9 167 B6
Rennie Cotts 29 E1 96 C3

Rennie Ct
Holdbrook EN3 7 C5
Lambeth SE1 251 C4
Rennie Ho SE1 262 A5
Rennie St SE1 116 D5 251 C4
Renoir Ct 7 SE16 118 B1
Renovation The E16 122 D4
Renown Cl CR0 204 D1
Rensburg Rd E17 52 D3
Rensburg Villas E17 52 D4
Renshaw Cl 7 DA17 147 B6
Renshaw Cnr CR4 181 A2
Renshaw Ct SW19 179 A6
Renshaw Ho 11 SW27 182 D5
Renters Ave NW4 46 C3
Renton Cl SW2 160 B5
Renwick Rd IG11 102 B4
Repens Way UB4 84 D3
Rephidim St SE1 263 A5
Replingham Rd SW18 157 C3
Reporton Rd SW6 135 A5 264 B3
Repository Rd SE7, SE18 122 B1
Repton Ave
Hayes UB3 105 B2
Wembley HA0 65 C4
Repton Cl SM5 218 C3
Repton Ct
Beckenham BR3 185 D2
Southgate N21 16 C3
Repton Ho SW1 259 B3
Repton Rd
Harrow HA3 44 B5
Orpington BR6 227 D5
Repton St E14 97 A1
Reservoir Cl CR7 205 B5
Reservoir Rd
New Cross Gate SE4 141 A3
Ruislip HA4 39 B5
Southgate N14 15 C6
Reservoir Studios 14 E1 96 D1
Resham Cl UB2 106 C3
Resolution Way 14 SE8 141 C5
Resolution Wlk SE18 122 B3
Restell Cl SE3 142 C6
Restmor Way SM5, SM6 219 A6
Reston Pl SW7 246 A1
Restons Cres DA15, SE9 167 C5
Restoration Sq SW11 266 D1
Restormel Cl TW3 151 C6
Retcar Pl N19 71 B6
Retford St E2 95 C5
Retingham Way E4 19 D2
Retlas Ct HA1 42 B2
Retreat Cl HA3 43 C4
Retreat Cvn Site The IG9 21 A3
Retreat Ho 5 E9 74 C2
Retreat Pl E9 74 C2
Retreat Rd TW9 153 D6
Retreat The
Harrow HA2 41 C2
Kingsbury NW9 45 B4
Mortlake SW14 133 C2
North Cheam KT4 216 B6
South Norwood CR7 205 B5
Surbiton KT5 198 B3
Reunion Row E1 118 B6
Reveley Sq SE16 119 A4
Revell Rd
Cheam SM1 217 B2
Kingston u T KT1 176 D2
Revell Rise SE18 145 D6
Revelon Rd SE4 141 A2
Revelstoke Rd SW18, SW19 157 C2
Reventlow Rd SE9 167 A3
Reverdy Rd SE1 118 A2
Reverend Cl HA2 63 D5
Revesby Rd SM5 202 C3
Review Lo RM10 103 D5
Review Rd
Dagenham RM10 103 D6
Willesden NW2 67 D6
Rewell St SW6 136 A5 266 A3
Rewley Rd SM4 202 B3
Rew Lo 25 N2 30 B1
Rex Ave TW15 170 C5
Rex Ho TW13 151 A1
Rex Par 2 IG8 37 C4
Rex Pl W1 115 A5 248 B4
Reydon Ave E11 55 C3
Reygate Ct N4 51 A3

Reynard Cl
Brockley SE4 141 A2
Bromley BR1 210 C6
Reynard Dr SE19 183 D3
Reynard Mills Trad Est TW8 109 C1
Reynard Pl SE14 141 A6
Reynardson Rd N17 33 A3
Reynardson's Ct 10 N17 51 D6
Reynolah Gdns SE7 121 B1
Reynolds Ave
Chessington KT9 214 A1
Ilford RM6 58 C2
Little Ilford E12 78 C3
Reynolds Cl
Carshalton SM5 202 D1
Golders Green NW11 47 D2
Mitcham SW19 180 B2
Reynolds Ct
Ilford RM6 58 D6
Leyton E11 76 D5
Reynolds Dr HA8 44 B6
Reynolds Ho
Enfield EN1 18 A6
Finsbury Pk N4 50 A1
18 South Hackney E2 96 C5
St John's Wood NW8 229 D3
Westminster SW1 259 D3
Reynolds Pl
Greenwich SE3 143 B5
12 Richmond TW10 154 B5
Reynolds Rd
Acton Green W4 111 A3
Hayes UB4 84 C3
New Malden KT3 199 B2
Nunhead SE15 140 C1
Reynolds Way CR0 221 C4
Rheidol Mews N1 235 A4
Rheidol Terr N1 95 A6 235 A5
Rhein Ho N8 50 A6
Rheola Cl N17 33 D2
Rhoda St E2 95 D3 243 D6
Rhodes Avenue Prim Sch N22 31 C2
Rhodes Ave N22 31 C2
Rhodes Ho
Shepherd's Bush W12 112 B5
Shoreditch N1 235 C2
Rhodesia Rd
Leyton E11 76 B6
Stockwell SW9 138 A3
Rhodes-Moorhouse Ct SM4 201 C3
Rhodes St N7 72 B3
Rhodeswell Rd E14 97 B1
Rhodrons Ave KT9 214 A3
Rhondda Gr E3 97 B4
Rhyl Prim Sch NW5 71 A2
Rhyl Rd UB6 86 D5
Rhyl St NW5 71 A2
Rhys Ave N11 31 D3
Rialto Rd CR4 181 A1
Ribble Cl IG8 37 C4
Ribblesdale Ave
Friern Barnet N11 31 A4
Northolt UB5 63 D2
Ribblesdale Ho 11 NW6 91 C6
Ribblesdale Rd
Hornsey N8 50 B5
Streatham SW16 181 B5
Ribbon Dance Mews SE5 139 B4
Ribchester Ave UB6 86 D4
Ribston Cl BR2 210 B1
Ribstone Ho 12 E9 74 D2
Ricardo Path 5 SE28 124 C5
Ricardo St E14 97 D1
Ricards Lodge High Sch SW19 179 B5
Ricards Rd SW19 179 B5
Riccall Ct 2 NW9 27 C2
Riceyman Ho WC1 234 A1
Richard Alibon Prim Sch RM10 81 C3
Richard Anderson Ct 1 SE14 140 D5
Richard Atkins Prim Sch SW2 160 A4
Richard Burbidge Mans SW13 134 C6
Richard Burton Ct 4 IG9 21 C2
Richard Challoner Sch KT3 199 B2
Richard Cloudesley Sch EC1 95 A3 242 A5
Richard Cl SE18 122 A2
Richard Cobden Prim Sch NW1 93 C6 232 B5
Richard Ct
Ashford TW15 170 B5
1 Barnet EN5 1 A2

Richard Fell Ho 3 E12 78 C4
Richard Fox Ho N4 73 A5
Richard Ho 10 SE16 118 C2
Richard House Dr E16 100 A1
Richard Knight Ho SW6 265 B2
Richard Neale Ho 2 E1 118 B6
Richard Neve Ho 2 SE18 123 C2
Richards Cl
Bushey WD23 8 B4
Harlington UB3 127 B6
Harrow HA1 43 A4
Hillingdon UB10 82 C6
Richards Ct BR3 184 D2
Richard Sharples Ct 16 SM2 218 A1
Richardson Cl 19 E8 95 D6
Richardson Ct 20 SW4 138 A3
Richardson Gdns 12 RM10 81 D2
Richardson Ho
Isleworth TW7 130 D2
10 Poplar E14 97 C2
Richardson Rd E15 98 C5
Richardson's Mews W1 239 A5
Richards Pl E17 53 C6
Richard's Pl SW3 257 B4
Richard St 20 E1 96 B1
Richbell Pl WC1 240 C4
Richbell WC1 240 B4
Richborne Terr SW8 138 B5 270 D4
Richborough Ho
10 Deptford SE15 140 C6
14 Hackney E5 74 B4
Richborough Rd NW2 69 A4
Richbourne Ct W1 237 B2
Richens Cl TW3 130 B3
Riches Rd IG1 79 A6
Richfield Ct
4 Beckenham BR3 185 B2
Wembley HA0 66 A2
Richfield Rd WD23 8 A4
Richford Gate W6 112 C3
Richford Rd E15 98 D6
Richford St W6 112 C3
Richings Ho BR5 190 A2
Richland Ho 4 SE15 140 A4
Richlands Ave KT17 216 A4
Rich La SW5 255 C2
Richman Ho 10 SE8 119 B1
RICHMOND 131 C1
Richmond Adult Com Coll TW9 131 D1
Richmond Ave
Chingford E4 36 B5
Feltham TW14 149 C5
Hillingdon UB10 60 D2
Islington N1 94 B6 233 D6
Willesden NW10 68 C2
Wimbledon SW20 179 A2
Richmond Bldgs W1 239 C1
Richmond Bridge Mans 1 TW1 153 D5
Richmond Bridge TW1 153 D5
Richmond Circus TW9 132 A1
Richmond Cl
Borehamwood WD6 11 B6
Walthamstow E17 53 B3
Richmond Coll
Kensington W8 113 D3 255 D6
Richmond TW10 154 A4
Richmond Cres
Chingford E4 36 B5
Edmonton N9 18 A3
Islington N1 94 C6 234 A6
Richmond Ct
Bromley BR1 187 B3
12 Kingston u T KT2 176 C3
Knightsbridge SW1 247 D1
1 Loughton IG10 21 D6
Mitcham CR4 202 B6
4 New Southgate N11 31 A4
Wembley HA9 66 B6
Wimbledon SW20 178 B1
Richmond Dr TW17 193 B3
Richmond Gate TW10 154 B4

Richmond Gdns
Harrow HA3 ....24 D3
Hendon NW4........46 A4
Richmond Gn CR0 ...220 A5
Richmond Gr
Islington N1 ....72 D1
Surbiton KT5........198 B3
Richmond Healthcare Hamlet Hospl TW9.............. 132 A2
RICHMOND HILL 154 A5
Richmond Hill Ct 5 TW10.............154 A5
Richmond Hill TW10..............154 A5
Richmond Ho 12 SE26..............162 A1
Richmond Ho (Hampton Com Coll) TW12 ...173 B5
Richmond Ho
Regent's Pk NW1 ... 231 D3
Walworth SE17 ..... 262 C2
Richmond International Bsns Ctr 9 TW9 ...132 B1
Richmond Mans
Earl's Ct SW5 ...... 255 C2
Putney SW15....... 135 A2
13 Twickenham TW1............ 153 D5
Richmond Mews W1.............. 239 C1
Richmond Park* TW10............ 155 A3
Richmond Park Rd
Kingston u T KT2.... 176 A3
Mortlake SW14......133 B1
Richmond Pk IG10....21 D4
Richmond Pl SE18 ...123 A2
Richmond Rd
Bowes Pk N11........32 A4
Chingford E4..........20 B3
Dalston E8............74 A1
Ealing W5 .... 110 A4
Finchley N2...........30 A1
Forest Gate E7 ....77 B3
Ilford IG1 ....79 A5
Isleworth TW7....... 131 A2
Kingston u T KT2.... 176 A4
Leyton E11............76 B6
New Barnet EN5 ......14 A6
Thornton Heath CR7 . 204 D5
Tottenham N15 ....51 C3
Twickenham TW1.... 153 C4
Wallington CR0 ..... 220 A5
Wimbledon SW20 ....178 B2
Richmond Sta TW9 . 132 A1
Richmond St E13 .....99 A5
Richmond Terr SW1........116 A4 250 A2
Richmond upon Thames Coll TW2 .... 152 C4
Richmond Way
Hammersmith W12, W14 .... 112 D4
Wanstead E11........77 A6
Richmount Gdns SE3.................143 A2
Rich St E14...........119 B6
Rickard Cl
Hendon NW4.........46 A5
Streatham SW2...... 160 C3
Rickards Cl KT6...... 214 A6
Rickett St SW6...... 265 B6
Rickman Ho 23 E2 .....96 C3
Rickman St 24 E1 .....96 C3
Rickmansworth Rd HA5 ....22 C1
Rick Roberts Way E15...................98 B5
Rickthorne Rd 7 N19 ....72 A6
Rickyard Path SE9 ...144 A1
Riddell Ct SE1 ...... 263 C2
Riddell Lo EN2..........4 D3
Ridding La UB6 ....64 D3
Riddons Rd SE12.....187 C6
Rideout St SE18 .....122 B2
Rider Cl DA15........167 C5
Ride The
Brentford TW8...... 109 C1
Enfield EN3 ....6 D2
Ridgdale St E3 ....97 D5
Ridge Ave N21..........17 B4
Ridgebrook Rd SE3, SE9...................143 D2
Ridge Cl Hendon NW4 ..28 D1
Kingsbury NW9.......45 B5
Plumstead SE28 .....123 B4
Ridge Crest EN2 ....4 B4
Ridge Hill NW11 ......47 A1
Ridge Ho 4 KT2 .....176 D3
Ridgeleigh Ct 3 EN5....1 A2
Ridgemead Cl N13, N14 ....16 A2
Ridgemont Gdns HA8 ....27 A6
Ridgemount Ave CR0 ....222 D6
Ridgemount Cl 4 SE20...............184 B3
Ridgemount Gdns EN2 ....4 D3
Ridgeon Ct N22.......32 B4
Ridge Rd
Cheam SM3.........201 B1
Child's Hill NW2 ......69 B5
Edmonton N21.........17 B3
Hornsey Vale N8 ......50 B3
Mitcham CR4........181 B3
Ridges The E4 ....35 C6
Ridge Terr N21........17 A4
Ridge The Barnet EN5 .. 13 B6
Old Bexley DA5 ......169 B4
Orpington BR6.......227 B6
Surbiton KT5 .... 198 C4
Twickenham TW2.......152 B4
Ridgeview Cl EN5.....12 D5
Ridgeview Ct EN4.....15 C6
Ridgeview Rd N20 ....14 A1
Ridgeway Ave EN4 ....14 D5
Ridgeway Cres BR6 ..227 C5
Ridgeway Crescent Gdns BR6..........227 C5
Ridgeway Ct HA5 .....23 C3
Ridgeway Dr
Acton W3.......... 110 C3
Grove Pk BR1 ....187 B6
Ridgeway E DA15 ....167 D6
Ridge Way TW13.....151 A1
Ridgeway Gdns
Crouch End N6........49 C2
Redbridge IG4.........56 A4
Ridgeway BR2.........225 A6
Ridgeway Rd TW7 ...130 C4
Ridgeway Rd N TW7..............130 C5
Ridgeway 11 TW10...154 A5
Ridgeway The
Acton W3.......... 110 C3
Chingford E4 ....20 A3
Enfield EN2 ....4 B5
Finchley N3 ....29 D3
Friern Barnet N11.....30 D6
Golders Green NW11 ..47 B1
Kenton HA3...........43 C3
Kingsbury NW9........45 B5
Mill Hill NW7..........28 B6
North Harrow HA2 ....41 D3
Palmers Green N14....16 A2
Pinner HA2 ....41 B4
Ruislip HA4 ....40 A2
Stanmore HA7........25 C4
Wallington CR0 ......220 B5
Ridgeway KT12 ......193 D1
Ridgeway W DA15 ....167 C6
Ridge Way 7 SE19 ...183 C4
Ridgeway Wlk UB5.....63 A2
Ridgeway IG8 ....37 C6
Ridgewell Cl
Dagenham RM10.... 103 D6
Forest Hill SE26......185 B6
Shoreditch N1 .... 235 B6
Ridgmount Gdns WC1.........93 D2 239 C4
Ridgmount Pl WC1.. 239 C4
Ridgmount Rd SW18..............157 D6
Ridgmount St WC1.........93 D2 239 C4
Ridgway Ct SW19....178 D4
Ridgway Gdns SW19..................178 D3
Ridgway Pl SW19 ....179 A4
Ridgway Rd SW9.....138 D2
Ridgway The SM2....218 B1
Ridgway SW19, SW20...............178 D4
Ridgwell Rd E16 ......99 C2
Riding House St W1............93 C2 239 A3
Ridings Ave N21 ......17 A6
Ridings Cl N6..........49 C2
Ridings The
Ealing W5 ....88 B3
Oakleigh Pk EN4 .....14 B4
Sunbury TW16...... 172 A2
Surbiton KT5....... 198 C4
Riding The NW11 .....47 B2
Ridler Rd EN1 ....5 C5
Ridley Ave W13 ......109 B3
Ridley Cl IG11 ....79 D1
Ridley Ct
Orpington BR6...... 227 A4
Streatham SW16..... 182 A4
Ridley Ho 14 SW11 ...136 C2
Ridley Rd
Beckenham BR2 .... 208 D6
Dalston E8............73 D3
Forest Gate E7 ....77 C4
Ridley Rd *continued*
Merton SW19 ...... 179 D3
Welling DA16.......146 B4
Willesden Green NW10.............90 A5
Ridley Road Mkt E8 ..73 D3
Ridsdale Rd SE20....184 B2
Riefield Rd SE9......167 A6
Riesco Dr CR0.......222 C2
Riffel Rd NW2........68 C3
Rifle Ct SE11 ....138 C6
Rifle Pl W11.........112 D5
Rifle St E14...........97 D2
Riga Ho 12 E1 ....96 D2
Rigault Rd SW6......135 A3
Rigby Cl CR0........220 C5
Rigby Ho 2 N17......51 D6
Rigby La UB3........105 A4
Rigby Mews IG1......78 C6
Rigby Pl 8 EN3.........7 C6
Rigden St E14 ....97 D1
Rigeley Rd NW10 .....90 A4
Rigg App E10..........53 A1
Rigge Pl SW4.........137 D1
Rigg Ho 2 SW4......160 A4
Riggindale Rd SW16................181 D6
Rignold Ho 6 SE5 ...139 C3
Riley Ho 9 Bow E3 ....97 C3
Chelsea SW10...... 266 C5
1 Streatham SW4 .. 159 D4
Riley Rd
Bermondsey SE1...... 117 D3 263 C6
Enfield EN3 ....6 C5
Riley St SW10.......136 B5 266 C4
Rill Ho 16 SE5 ....139 C5
Rimini Ct SW12......158 D3
Rinaldo Rd SW12 ....159 B4
Ring Cl BR1 ....187 B3
Ringcroft St N7.......72 C3
Ringer's Rd BR1 .....209 A6
Ringford Ho SW18 ...157 B6
Ringford Rd SW18 ...157 C5
Ring Ho 15 E1 ....118 C6
Ringlet Cl E16 ....99 B2
Ringlewell Cl EN1...... 6 B3
Ringmer Ave SW6.........135 A4 264 B1
Ringmer Gdns 3 N19....................72 A6
Ringmer Ho 15 SE22...............139 C2
Ringmer Pl N21.......17 B6
Ringmer Way BR1....210 B4
Ringmore Rise SE23...............162 B4
Ring Rd W12 ....112 C5
Ringsfield Ho SE17.. 262 B1
Ringslade Rd N22..... 32 B1
Ringstead Bldgs SE6...................163 D4
Ringstead Ct SM1....218 B3
Ringstead Rd
Catford SE6........ 163 D4
Sutton SM1 ....218 B3
Ring Way N11 ....31 C4
Ringway UB2........107 A1
Ringwold Cl BR3.....185 A3
Ringwood Ave
Muswell Hill N2.......48 D6
Thornton Heath CR0 . 204 A2
Ringwood Cl HA5 .....40 C6
Ringwood Gdns
17 Millwall E14..... 119 C2
Roehampton SW15 .. 156 A3
Ringwood Rd E17..... 53 B3
Ringwood Way
Hampton TW12 ..... 173 C6
Southgate N21........16 D4
Ripley Cl
Bromley BR1 ....210 B4
New Addington CR0 . 224 A2
Ripley Ct 1 CR4 .....180 B1
Ripley Gdns
Mortlake SW14 ......133 B2
Sutton SM1 .... 218 A4
Ripley Ho
13 Kingston u T KT2.............. 176 D4
Mortlake SW14 ...... 133 C2
Nine Elms SW1 ..... 269 A6
5 Penge SE26 ....184 B5
Ripley Mews E11......54 C3
Ripley Rd
Belvedere DA17 .... 125 C2
Enfield EN2 ....5 A4
Hampton TW12 ..... 173 C3
Ilford IG3 ....79 D6
Newham E16..........99 C1
Riplington Ct SW15 ..156 B4
Ripon Cl UB5 ....63 C2
Ripon Ct 10 N11 ....31 A4
Ripon Gdns
Chessington KT9.... 213 D3
Redbridge IG1........56 A2
Ripon Rd
Edmonton N9.........18 B4
Shooters Hill SE18... 144 D6
Tottenham N17 ....51 B6
Ripon Way WD6 ....11 B6
Rippersley Rd DA16 ..146 A4
Ripple Ct 10 IG11 ....101 B6
Ripple Jun & Inf Schs IG11................79 C1
Ripple Rd
Barking IG11.........79 A1
Barking IG11....... 101 C6
Castle Green RM9... 102 A6
Rippleside Commercial Est IG11 .... 102 C5
Ripplevale Gr N1 .....72 B1
Rippolson Rd SE18...123 D1
Ripston Rd TW15 ....171 B5
Risborough Cl 4 N10 ....49 B6
Risborough Ct 5 N10 ....49 B6
Risborough Dr KT4...200 A2
Risborough Ho NW8 237 B6
Risborough SE17 ... 262 A4
Risborough St SE1... 251 D2
Risdon Ho 26 SE16 ....118 C4
Risdon St 27 SE16....118 C4
Risedale Rd DA7.....147 D2
Riseholme Ct E9......75 B2
Riseholme Ho 14 SE22................139 C2
Riseldine Rd SE23 ...163 A5
Rise The
Borehamwood WD6.............10 B6
Buckhurst Hill IG9.....21 D4
Chingford E4 ....20 C3
Edgware HA8.........26 D5
Edmonton N13........32 C6
Harrow HA2 ....24 A1
Hendon NW7..........27 D4
Hillingdon UB10.......82 B5
Neasden NW10........67 B5
Sidcup DA5 .... 168 C4
Wanstead E11.........55 A4
Wembley HA0, UB6....65 A3
Risinghill St N1..... 234 A4
Risingholme Cl HA3...24 C2
Risingholme Rd HA3 ..24 C1
Risings The E17.......54 B5
Rising Sun Ct EC1.... 241 D3
Risley Avenue Prim Sch N17 ....33 C2
Risley Ave N17 ....33 B2
Risley Ho 7 E9 ....74 D2
Rita Rd SW8 ..138 B5 270 C4
Ritches Rd N15 ....51 A4
Ritchie Ho
Crouch End N19.......49 D2
8 Rotherhithe SE16............ 118 C3
12 South Bromley E14...............98 B1
Ritchie Rd CR0 ......206 B3
Ritchie St N1 .. 94 C5 234 B4
Ritchings Ave E17.....53 A5
Ritherdon Rd SW17 ..159 B2
Ritson Ho N1....... 233 C5
Ritson Rd E8 ....74 A2
Ritter St SE18........144 C6
Ritz Par W5 ....88 B3
Rivaz Pl E9 ....74 C2
Riven Ct 10 W2 ....91 D1
Rivenhall Gdns E11, E18.....................54 D5
Riverains The SW11 . 266 C1
River Ave
Southgate N13.........16 D1
Thames Ditton KT7 .. 197 A2
Riverbank KT8........196 C5
River Bank N21........17 A4
Riverbank Rd BR1.....165 A1
River Bank KT7 ......196 D4
Riverbank Way TW8...................131 C6
River Barge Cl E14 ...120 A4
River Brent Bsns Pk W7 .... 108 C3
River Cl Ruislip HA4 ....39 D3
Southall UB2 .... 108 A4
Wanstead E11 ....55 C3
River Cotts BR5.......190 C1
Rivercourt Rd W6....112 B1
River Crane Way TW13................151 B2
River Ct
Kingston u T KT6 .... 197 D4
Lambeth SE1 .... 251 C5
Shepperton TW17 ... 193 A2
Wanstead E11 ....55 C3
Riverdale Cl IG11 ....102 B3
Riverdale Ct N21......17 B6
Riverdale Dr SW18 ...157 D3
Riverdale Gdns TW1...............153 C6
Riverdale Rd
Erith DA8.......... 125 D1
Feltham TW13 ....173 B6
Plumstead Comm SE18............ 123 D1
Sidcup DA5 ....169 B5
Twickenham TW1.... 153 C5
Riverdene HA8 ....11 A1
Riverdene Rd IG1.....78 D5
Riverfleet WC1 ..... 233 B2
Riverford Ho 28 W2 ...91 C2
River Front EN1........5 C2
River Gdns Bsns Ctr TW14..............128 B1
River Gdns
Carshalton SM5..... 219 A5
Feltham TW14 ....150 B6
River Grove Pk BR3 ..185 B2
Riverhead Cl E17 .....34 D1
River Ho
Barnes SW13 ...... 133 C3
1 Forest Hill SE26...162 B1
Riverholme KT8 .....196 C6
Riverhope Mans SE18..............122 A3
Riverine Lo HA7 ......25 A5
River La TW10 ....153 D3
Riverleigh Ct E4 ......35 A5
Rivermead Cl TW11..175 B5
Rivermead Ct
Ealing UB6...........87 A4
Fulham SW6 ....135 B2
Rivermead KT8 ......196 A6
Rivermead Ho
Hackney E9 ....75 A3
Sunbury TW16...... 194 C6
Rivermead KT6 ......197 D4
River Meads Ave TW13, TW2...................151 D1
River Mount KT12....193 D2
Rivernook Cl KT12 ...194 C4
River Park Gdns BR2...................186 B3
River Park Rd N22 ....32 B1
River Plate Ho EC2.. 242 D3
River Pl N1...........73 A1
River Rd
Barking IG11....... 101 D3
Buckhurst Hill IG9.....21 D3
River Reach TW11 ...175 C5
River Road Bsns Pk IG11............. 101 D4
Riversdale Gdns N22..32 C2
Riversdale Prim Sch SW18............ 157 C3
Riversdale Rd
Highbury N5 ....73 A5
Thames Ditton KT7 .. 197 A3
Riversdene N5.........73 A5
Riversfield Rd EN1 .....5 C2
Rivers Ho 11 TW8 ....110 C1
Riverside Apartments N13 ....32 B5
Riverside Ave KT8....196 B4
Riverside SW11..... 267 B4
Riverside Bsns Ctr SW18................ 157 D3
Riverside Bsns Pk SW19............. 180 A2
Riverside Cl
Chislehurst BR5..... 190 C1
Ealing W7 ....86 C3
Hackbridge SM6 .....219 B5
Kingston u T KT1.... 197 D5
Upper Clapton E5 .....74 C6
Riverside Ct
Chingford E4 ....19 D5
Lewisham SE12 ..... 142 D1
Nine Elms SW8 ..... 269 D6
Richmond TW11..... 175 C5
Riverside Dr
Chiswick W4 .... 133 C4
Mitcham CR4....... 202 C4
Richmond TW10......153 B1
Temple Fortune NW11.............47 A3
Riverside Est EN3.....19 A5
Riverside SE6........185 B6
Riverside Gdns
Enfield EN2 ....5 A3
Hammersmith W6 ....112 B1
Hendon N3 ....47 A6
Wembley HA0 ....88 A5
Riverside
Greenwich SE7 ......121 B3
Hendon NW4..........46 B2
Riverside Ho
Finchley N12 ....29 D6
14 Islington N1........73 A1
Morden SW19 ...... 202 A5
30 Richmond TW10.. 153 D6
Riverside Ind Est IG11............. 102 A4
Riverside Mans 4 E1..................118 C5
Riverside TW17......193 C2
Riverside Pl
New Southgate N11............
Stanwell TW19 .....
Riverside Prim Sch SE16.............
Riverside Rd
Mill Meads E15 .....
Sidcup DA14 ....
South Tottenham N15
Stanwell TW19 .....
Wandsworth SW17, SW19..........
Riverside
11 Rotherhithe SE16...........
St Pancras WC1.....
Sunbury TW16......
Riverside The KT8....
Riverside TW1......
Riverside Wlk
Isleworth TW7......
3 West Wickham BR4............
Riverside Works IG11..............
Riverside Workshops SE1..............
River St EC1 ... 94 C4
Riverstone Cl HA2 ...
Riverstone Ct KT2....
Riverston Sch SE12..
River Terr W6........
Riverton Cl W9 ......
Riverview CE Prim S KT19 ....
Riverview Ct 14 DA17 ....
River View EN2 ......
Riverview Gdns SW13...........
River View Gdns TW1.............
Riverview Gr W4.....
Riverview Hts SE18 ..
Riverview Lo NW9 ...
Riverview Pk SE6 ....
Riverview Rd
Chiswick W4 ....
West Ewell KT19.....
Riverview TW17 .....
River Way SE10......
Riverway N13........
River Way
Twickenham TW13, TW2............
West Ewell KT19....
River Wlk KT12 ......
Riverwood La BR7 ...
Rivet Ho SE1 ....
Rivington Ave IG8 ...
Rivington Cres NW7..
Rivington Ct
17 Dagenham RM10............
Willesden Green NW10..........
Rivington Pl EC2.....
Rivington St EC2.....
Rivington Wlk 4 E8 .
Rivulet Rd N17 ......
Rixon Ho SE18.......
Rixon St N7.........
Rixsen Rd E12 ....
Roach Rd E3 ....
Roads Pl N19........
Roan Ind Est CR4...
Roan St SE10........
Robart Ho 2 N12....
Robarts Cl HA5 ......
Robbins Hall EN3 ....
Robb Rd HA7 ....
Robert Adam St W1.
Roberta St E2 ....
Robert Bell Ho 2 SE16..............
Robert Blair Prim Sch N7 ....
Robert Browning Prim Sch SE17 .. 117 B1
Robert Burns Ho N17 ....
Robert Clack Lower S RM8.............
Robert Clack Upper S RM8.............
Robert Cl
Barking IG11........
Paddington W9 .....
Robert Dashwood Wa SE17.............
Robert Gentry Ho W14.............
Robert Gerard Ho 7 SE27.............
Robert Ho 12 HA1....

ert Jones Ho 3
6 118 A2
ert Keen Cl 18
5 140 A4
ert Lowe Cl
4 140 D5
erton Dr BR1 187 C2
ert Owen Ho
nam SW6 134 D4
Spitalfields E2 95 D4
ert Owen Lo 4
74 B4
ertsbridge Rd
202 B2
erts Cl
eam SM3 216 D1
/ Eltham SE9 167 B3
th Norwood CR7 205 B6
vsley UB7 104 A5
erts Ct
essington KT9 213 D3
ng W5 88 A1
ngton N1 234 D5
nge SE20 184 C2
esden NW10 67 C2
erts Ho
enham RM10 81 D1
rn Barnet N11 31 B5
Kidbrooke SE18 144 A4
West Norwood
E27 160 D1
erts Mews SW1 258 A5
ertson Ho
rooke SE18 144 B4
Lewisham SE10 142 A4
Upper Tooting
W17 180 C5
ertson Rd E15 98 A6
ertson St SW8 137 B3
erts Pl RM10 81 C2
ert's Pl EC1 241 B6
erts Rd
vedere DA17 125 C1
chley NW7 29 A4
hams Pk E17 35 D2
ert St
ydon CR0 221 A5
wham E16 122 D5
nstead SE18 123 B2
gent's Pk
W1 93 B4 231 D1
and WC2 250 B5
ert Sutton Ho 20
96 C1
eson St 7 E3 97 B2
na Cl DA6 146 D1
thwood HA6 22 A2
n Cl
ware NW7 11 C1
npton TW12 173 A5
n Cres E16 99 D2
n Ct
Cubitt Town
14 120 A3
lington SM6 219 C2
od Green N22 32 B3
n Gr
ntford TW8 131 C6
tmouth Pk N6 71 A6
row HA3 44 B3
n Hill Dr BR7 188 A4
n Ho NW8 230 A3
nhood Cl CR4 203 C6
n Hood Ct 2
217 D3
n Hood Dr HA3 24 D3
n Hood Gdns 12
120 A6
n Hood Inf Sch
217 C3
n Hood Jun Sch
217 D3
n Hood SW15 155 C1
n Hood La
ley DA6 169 A6
ckwall E14 120 A6
gston u T SW15 177 C6
nhood La CR4 203 C6
n Hood La SM1 217 D3
n Hood Prim Sch
15 177 C5
n Hood Way
ngston By Pass)
SW15, SW20 177 C5
n Hood Way
64 D2
nia Cl SE20 184 A2
nia Cres E10 75 D6
n La NW4 46 D6
nscroft Mews 18
) 141 D4
n's Ct
kenham BR3 186 B1
ham Pk SW4 160 A5
ns Ct
ve Pk SE12 165 C1
mond TW10 154 A5

Robins Ct *continued*
South Croydon CR2 221 C4
Robinsfield Inf Sch
NW8 92 C5 230 A4
Robins Gr BR4 225 A5
Robinson Cl
Enfield EN2 5 A2
11 Leyton E11 76 C5
Robinson Cres WD23 8 A3
Robinson Ct
5 Barnet EN4 14 D3
Islington N1 234 D6
4 Richmond TW9 132 B1
Thornton Heath CR0 204 D3
Robinson Ho
4 North Kensington
W10 90 D1
12 Tower Hamlets
E14 97 C2
Robinson Rd
Dagenham RM10 81 C4
Mitcham SW19 180 C4
South Hackney E2 96 C5
Robinson's Cl W13 87 A2
Robinson St SW3 267 C6
Robinwood Gr UB8 82 B3
Robinwood Pl
SW15 177 B6
Robsart St SW9 138 C3
Robson Ave NW10 68 A1
Robson Cl Enfield EN2 4 D3
Newham E6 100 A1
Robson Ct N12 30 A5
Robson Rd SE21,
SE27 161 A1
Roby Ho EC1 242 A6
Roch Ave HA8 26 B1
Rochdale Rd
Abbey Wood SE2 124 B2
Walthamstow E17 53 C2
Rochdale Way 4
SE8 141 C5
Rochdale 8 SE19 183 C4
Roche Ho 15 E14 119 B6
Rochelle Cl SW11 136 B1
Rochelle Ct
Beckenham BR3 185 D3
14 Stepney E1 96 C1
Rochelle St 31 E2 95 D4
Rochemont Wlk 2
E8 96 A6
Roche Rd SW16 182 B2
Roche Sch The
SW18 157 C6
Rochester Ave
Bromley BR1 187 B1
Feltham TW13 149 D2
Newham E13 99 C6
Rochester Cl
1 Blackfen DA15 168 B5
Enfield EN1 5 C4
Streatham SW16 182 A3
Rochester Ct
1 Bethnal Green
E2 96 B3
9 Camden Town
NW1 71 C1
Finchley N3 29 A1
Kingsbury NW9 45 B4
South Norwood
SE25 184 A1
Rochester Dr
Old Bexley DA5 169 C5
Pinner HA5 40 D4
Rochester Gdns
Redbridge IG1 56 B2
South Croydon CR0 221 C5
Rochester Ho
Bermondsey SE1 252 D1
18 Deptford SE15 140 C6
Rochester Mews
NW1 71 C1
Rochester Par
TW13 150 A1
Rochester Pl NW1 71 C1
Rochester Rd
Carshalton SM5 218 D4
Kentish Town NW1 71 C2
Northwood HA6 39 D6
Rochester Row
SW1 115 C2 259 B4
Rochester Sq NW1 71 C1
Rochester St SW1 259 C5
Rochester Terr NW1 71 C2
Rochester Way
Eltham SE9 144 C2
Kidbrooke SE3, SE9 143 D2
Rochester Wlk SE1 252 C4
Roche Wlk SM5 202 B3
Rochford Ave RM6 58 C4
Rochford Cl 2 E6 99 D5
Rochford N17 33 C1
Rochford Way CR0 204 A3
Rochford Wlk 3 E8 74 A1
Rochfort Ho 4 SE8 119 B1
Rock Ave 13 SW14 133 B2

Rockbourne Rd
SE23 162 D3
Rock Cl CR4 180 B1
Rockell's Pl SE22 162 B5
Rockfield Ho
Greenwich SE10 142 A6
2 Hendon NW4 46 D5
Rockford Ave UB6 87 B5
Rock Gdns RM10 81 D3
Rock Grove Way
SE16 118 A2
Rockhall Rd NW2 68 D4
Rockhampton Cl 4
SE27 182 C6
Rockhampton Rd
South Croydon
CR2 221 C2
West Norwood SE27,
SW16 182 C6
Rock Hill SE19 183 D6
Rockingham Cl
SW15 133 D1
Rockingham Ct 19
BR3 185 C3
Rockingham Gate
WD23 8 A5
Rockingham St
SE1 117 A3 262 A5
Rockland Rd SW15 135 A1
Rocklands Dr HA7 25 C1
Rocklands N3 29 B3
Rockley Ct 9 W14 112 D4
Rockley Rd W14 112 D4
Rockliffe Manor Prim
Sch SE18 145 D6
Rockmount Prim Sch
SE19 183 B4
Rockmount Rd
Plumstead Comm SE18,
SE2 123 D1
South Norwood
SE19 183 B4
Rocks La SW13 134 A2
Rock St N4 72 C6
Rockstraw Ho 5
NW3 70 D1
Rockware Ave UB6 86 C6
Rockware Bsns Ctr
UB6 86 B6
Rockways EN5 11 D5
Rockwell Gdns
SE19 183 C6
Rockwell Rd RM10 81 D3
Rockwood Ct N16 52 A2
Rocliffe St
N1 94 D5 234 D3
Rocombe Cres
SE23 162 C4
Rocque Ho SW6 264 C4
Rocque La SE3 142 D2
Rodborough Rd
NW11 47 C1
Rodd Est TW17 193 B4
Roden Gdns CR0 205 C3
Rodenhurst Ct SW4 159 D6
Rodenhurst Rd
SW4 159 D5
Roden St Ilford IG1 78 C5
Upper Holloway N7 72 B5
Roderick Ho 3
SE16 118 C2
Roderick Rd NW3 70 D4
Rodgers Cl WD6 9 D5
Rodgers Ho 4 SW4 159 D4
Rodin Ct N1 234 C5
Roding Ct 6 W12 111 C4
Roding Ho N1 234 A5
Roding Hospl IG4 55 D6
Roding La IG9 21 D3
Roding La N IG8 37 D1
Roding La S IG4 55 D5
Roding Lo IG1 55 D3
Roding Mews E1 118 A5
Roding Prim Sch
RM8 80 C3
Roding Rd
Hackney E5 75 A3
Newham E6 100 D2
Rodings Ct E4 36 B5
Rodings Row EN5 1 A1
Rodings The 4 IG8 37 C4
Roding Valley Sta
IG9 37 D6
Roding View IG9 21 D3
Rodmarton St
W1 92 D2 237 D3
Rodmell Cl UB4 85 A3
Rodmell Slope N12 29 B5
Rodmell WC1 233 B1
Rodmere St SE10 120 C1
Rodmill La SW2 160 A4
Rodney Cl
New Malden KT3 199 C4
Pinner HA5 41 A2
Thornton Heath CR0 204 D1
Walton-on-T KT12 194 C1
Rodney Ct NW8 236 B6

Rodney Gdns
Hayes BR4 225 A4
Pinner HA5 40 C4
Rodney Ho
4 Cubitt Town
E14 119 D2
Islington N1 233 D3
Notting Hill W11 245 A6
Rodney Pl
Merton SW19 180 A2
Newington
SE17 117 A2 262 B4
Walthamstow E17 35 B1
Rodney Rd
Mitcham CR4 202 C6
New Malden KT3 199 C4
Twickenham TW4 151 C4
Walton-on-T KT12 194 C1
Walworth
SE17 117 B2 262 C3
Wanstead E11 55 B5
Rodney St N1 94 B5 233 D3
Rodwall Pl HA8 26 C3
Rodway Rd
Bromley BR1 187 B2
Putney SW15 156 A4
Rodwell Cl 2 HA4 40 C1
Rodwell Rd SE22 161 D5
Roebourne Way
E16 122 C4
Roebuck Cl
Feltham TW13 172 B6
Tottenham N17 33 D4
Roebuck Ct
Chingford E4 36 A3
2 New Malden KT3 199 C4
Roebuck Hts IG10 21 C4
Roebuck La IG9 21 C3
Roebuck Rd KT9 214 C3
Roedean Ave EN3 6 C5
Roedean Cl EN3 6 C4
Roedean Cres
SW15 155 C6
Roe End NW9 45 A5
Roe Gn NW9 45 A4
Roe Green Jun & Inf
Schs NW9 44 D5
ROEHAMPTON 155 C4
Roehampton CE Prim
Sch SW15 156 B4
Roehampton Cl
SW15 134 A1
Roehampton Ct
SW13 134 A2
Roehampton Dr
BR7 189 A4
Roehampton Gate
SW15 155 C5
Roehampton High St
SW15 156 A4
Roehampton La
Putney SW15 156 A5
Roehampton SW15 156 B3
Roehampton Univ
(Digby Stuart Coll)
SW15 156 A6
Roehampton Univ
(Froebel Coll)
SW15 155 D5
Roehampton Univ
(Southlands Coll)
SW15 156 A6
Roehampton Univ
(Whitelands Coll)
SW15 156 A4
Roehampton Vale
SW15 155 D2
Roe La NW9 45 A5
Roe 5 NW9 27 D2
Roe Way SM6 220 A2
Roffey Ct 9 NW9 46 A5
Roffey St E14 120 A4
Rogate Ho E5 74 A5
Roger Ascham Prim Sch
E17 35 B2
Roger Dowley Ct 8
E2 96 C5
Roger's Almshouses 2
SW9 138 B1
Rogers Ct 16 E14 119 C6
Rogers Est 28 E2 96 C4
Rogers Gdns RM10 81 C3
Rogers Ho
9 Dagenham
RM10 81 C5
Westminster SW1 259 D4
Rogers Rd
Canning Town E16 98 D1
Dagenham RM10 81 C3
Upper Tooting
SW17 180 C6
Roger Stone Ct
NW10 67 B6
Roger St WC1 94 B3 240 D5
Rogers Wlk N12 13 D1
Rohan Pl 4 IG4 56 B4
Rojack Rd SE23 162 D3

Rokeby Gdns IG8 37 A2
Rokeby Ho
9 Balham SW12 159 B4
Bloomsbury WC1 240 C5
Rokeby Pl SW20 178 B3
Rokeby Rd SE4 141 B3
Rokeby Sch
Kingston u T KT2 177 A3
Stratford E15 76 B1
Rokeby St E15 98 C6
Rokeland Ho SE4 141 A1
Rokell Ho BR3 185 D5
Roker Park Ave
UB10 60 A4
Rokesby Cl DA16 145 B3
Rokesby Pl HA0 65 D3
Rokesly Ave N8 50 A4
Rokesly Jun & Inf Schs
N8 50 A4
Roland Ct SE19 183 D2
Roland Gdns
SW7 114 A1 256 B2
Roland Ho SW7 256 B2
Roland Mews 1 E1 96 D2
Roland Rd E17 54 B5
Roland Way
South Kensington
SW7 114 A1 256 B2
Walworth SE17 262 D1
Worcester Pk KT4 215 D6
Roles Gr RM6 59 A5
Rolfe Cl EN4 2 C1
Rolfe Ho N11 30 D6
Rolinsden Way BR2 225 D4
Rolland Ho W7 86 C2
Rollesby Rd KT19,
KT9 214 C2
Rollesby Way SE28 102 C1
Rolleston Ave BR5 210 D3
Rolleston Cl BR5 210 D2
Rolleston Rd CR2 221 B1
Roll Gdns IG2 56 C4
Rollins St SE15 140 C6
Rollit Cres TW3 151 C6
Rollit Ho N7 72 C3
Rollit St N7 72 C3
Rollo Ct SW11 268 C1
Rolls Bldgs EC4 241 B2
Rollscourt Ave
SE24 161 A6
Rolls Ct The E4 36 A5
Rolls Park Ave E4 35 D5
Rolls Park Rd E4 35 D5
Rolls Pas EC4 241 A2
Rolls Rd SE1 117 D1 263 D2
Rolt St SE8 141 A6
Rolvenden Gdns
BR1 187 D3
Rolvenden Pl N17 34 A2
Roman Cl
Feltham TW14 150 C6
South Acton W3 110 D4
Roman Ct 4 N7 72 B2
Romanfield Rd SW2 160 B4
Romanhurst Ave
BR2 208 C5
Romanhurst Gdns BR2,
BR3 208 C5
Roman Ind Est CR0 205 C2
Roman Lo 6 IG9 21 C3
Roman Rd
Chiswick W4 111 D2
Finchley N12 30 C2
Globe Town E2, E3 96 D5
Ilford IG1 78 D2
Muswell Hill N10 31 B3
Newham E6 100 A3
25 Old Ford E3 97 B6
Willesden NW2 68 C5
Roman Rise SE19 183 B4
Roman Road Prim Sch
E6 99 D3
Roman Sq SE28 124 A5
Roman Square Mkt 1
E3 97 B5
Roman Way
Barnsbury N7 72 B2
Croydon CR0 220 D6
4 Deptford SE15 140 C5
Enfield EN1 17 D6
Romany Gdns
Cheam SM3 201 C2
1 Higham Hill E17 35 A2
Romany Ho 8 N9 18 A1
Romany Prospect
SE19 183 B4
Romany Rise BR5 211 A1
Roma Rd E17 53 A6
Roma Read Cl
SW15 156 B4
Romayne Ho SW4 137 D2
Romberg Rd SW17 159 A1
Romborough Gdns
SE13 164 A6
Romborough Way
SE13 164 A6

Romeland Ct WD6 9 D5
Romeland WD6 9 D5
Romer Ho 9 SW2 160 B6
Romero Cl SW9 138 B2
Romero Sq SE9 143 C1
Romeyn Rd SW16 160 B1
ROMFORD 59 D4
Romford Ho 17 N1 73 B2
Romford Rd
Forest Gate E7,
E12 77 C3
Stratford E15 76 D2
Romford St E1 96 B2
Romilly Dr WD19 23 A6
Romilly Rd N4 72 D6
Romilly St W1 249 D6
Romily Ct SW6 135 A3
Rommany Ct SE27 183 B6
Rommany Rd SE27 183 B6
Romney Cl
Ashford TW15 171 A5
Chessington KT9 214 A4
7 Deptford SE14 140 C5
Harrow HA2 41 C2
North End NW11 48 A1
Tottenham N17 34 B2
Romney Ct
9 Hammersmith
W12 112 C4
9 Hampstead NW3 70 C2
15 Northolt UB5 84 D5
Romney Dr
Bromley BR1 187 D3
Harrow HA2 41 C2
Romney Gdns DA7 147 B4
Romney Ho
2 Blackwall E14 120 B6
Enfield EN1 18 A6
Sutton SM2 217 D2
Romney Mews W1 238 A4
Romney Par UB4 83 B5
Romney Rd
Greenwich SE10 142 B6
Hayes UB4 83 B5
New Malden KT3 199 B3
Romney Row NW2 68 D6
Romney St
SW1 116 A3 260 A5
Romola Rd SE24,
SW2 160 D3
Romsey Cl BR6 226 D4
Romsey Gdns RM9 102 D6
Romsey Rd
Dagenham RM9 102 D6
Ealing W13 109 A6
Romulus Ct 7 TW8 131 D5
Ronald Ave E15 98 C4
Ronald Cl BR3 207 B4
Ronald Ct EN5 1 D2
Ronald Ho
Eltham SE9 143 C1
4 Sutton SM1 218 B3
Ronald Ross Prim Sch
SW19 157 A4
Ronaldshay N4 50 C1
Ronalds Rd
Bromley BR1 187 A2
Islington N5 72 C3
Ronald St E1 96 C1
Ronaldstone Rd
DA15 167 C5
Rona Rd NW3 71 A4
Ronart St HA3 42 D6
Rona Wlk 20 N1 73 B2
Rondu Rd NW2 69 A3
Ronelean Rd KT6 214 B5
Ron Leighton Way
E6 100 A6
Ronnie La E12 78 C4
Ron Todd Cl RM10 103 C6
Ronver Lo E4 20 C1
Ronver Rd SE12 164 D3
Rood La EC3 117 C6 253 A6
Rookby Ct N21 16 D2
Rook Cl HA9 66 D5
Rookeries Cl TW13 150 C1
Rookery Cl NW9 45 D4
Rookery Cotts EN4 3 B2
Rookery Cres RM10 81 D1
Rookery Dr BR7 188 C2
Rookery La BR2 209 D3
Rookery Rd SW4 137 C1
Rookery Way NW9 45 D4
Rooke Way SE10 120 D1
Rookfield Ave N10 49 C5
Rookfield Cl N10 49 C5
Rook Lo IG1 55 D3
Rooks Heath High Sch
HA2 63 C5
Rooksmead Rd
TW16 172 A1
Rooks Terr UB7 104 A4
Rookstone Rd
SW17 180 D5

Rook Wlk E6 ... 100 A1
Rookwood Ave
Wallington SM6 ... 219 D4
West Barnes KT3 ... 200 A5
Rookwood Gdns E4 ... 20 D2
Rookwood Ho 2 IG11 ... 101 B5
Rookwood Rd N16 ... 52 A2
Roosevelt Ct 15 SW19 ... 157 A3
Rootes Dr W10 ... 90 D2
Ropemaker Rd SE16 ... 119 A3
Ropemaker's Fields 7 E14 ... 119 B6
Ropemaker St EC2 ... 95 B2 242 C4
Roper Ho 13 SE21 ... 183 C6
Roper La SE1 ... 117 C4 253 B1
Ropers Ave E4 ... 36 A5
Roper's Orch SW3 ... 267 A5
Roper St 1 SE9 ... 166 C5
Ropers Wlk 13 SE24 ... 160 C4
Roper Way CR4 ... 181 A1
Ropery Bsns Pk SE7 ... 121 C2
Ropery St E3 ... 97 B3
Rope St SE16 ... 119 A3
Ropewalk Gdns 18 E1 ... 96 A1
Rope Yard Rails SE18 ... 122 D3
Ropley St 6 E2 ... 96 A5
Rosa Alba Mews N5 ... 73 A4
Rosa Ave TW15 ... 170 C6
Rosa Freedman Ctr NW2 ... 46 C1
Rosalind Ct 6 IG11 ... 80 A1
Rosalind Ho 25 N1 ... 95 C5
Rosaline Rd SW6 ... 135 A5 264 B3
Rosaline Terr SW6 ... 264 B3
Rosamond St SE26 ... 162 B1
Rosamund Cl CR2 ... 221 B4
Rosamun St UB2 ... 107 A2
Rosa Parks Ho 8 SW9 ... 138 B3
Rosary Cl TW3, TW5 ... 129 A3
Rosary Ct 17 E1 ... 96 D2
Rosary Gdns
Ashford TW15 ... 170 D6
Bushey WD23 ... 8 C4
South Kensington SW7 ... 114 A2 256 B3
Rosary RC Inf Sch TW5 ... 129 C6
Rosary RC Jun Sch TW5 ... 129 C6
Rosary RC Prim Sch NW3 ... 70 C3
Rosaville Rd SW6 ... 135 B5 264 C3
Rosbury SW15 ... 157 A5
Roscastle Rd SE4 ... 163 A6
Roscoe St EC1 ... 95 A3 242 B5
Roscoff Cl HA8 ... 27 A2
Roscommon Ho 2 NW3 ... 70 B3
Roseacre Cl
Ealing W13 ... 87 B2
Littleton TW17 ... 192 C4
Roseacre Lo EN3 ... 6 C1
Roseacre Rd DA16 ... 146 B2
Rose Alley
Borough The SE1 ... 252 B4
Broadgate EC2 ... 243 B3
Rose Ave
Mitcham CR4 ... 180 D2
Morden SM4 ... 202 A4
Woodford E18 ... 37 B1
Rosebank Ave HA0 ... 64 D4
Rosebank Cl
Colney Hatch N12 ... 30 C5
Teddington TW11 ... 175 A4
Rosebank
2 Dagenham W3 ... 89 B1
Fulham SW6 ... 134 C5
Rosebank Gdns
Bow E3 ... 97 B5
1 Dagenham W3 ... 89 B1
Rosebank Gr E17 ... 53 B6
Rosebank SE20 ... 184 B3
Rosebank Rd
Hanwell W7 ... 108 C4
Walthamstow E17 ... 53 D3
Rosebank Villas E17 ... 53 C5
Rosebank Way W3 ... 89 B1
Rosebank Wlk
Camden Town NW1 ... 71 D1
14 Woolwich SE7 ... 122 A2
Rose Bates Dr NW9 ... 44 C5
Rosebay Ho 20 E3 ... 97 C2
Roseberry Gdns
Harringay N4 ... 50 D3
Orpington BR6 ... 227 C5
Roseberry Pl E8 ... 73 D2
Roseberry St SE16 ... 118 B2
Rosebery Ave
Finsbury EC1 ... 94 C4 234 B1
Harrow HA2 ... 63 B4
Kingston u T KT3 ... 199 D6
Plashet E12 ... 78 B2
Sidcup DA15 ... 167 C4
South Norwood CR7 ... 183 A1
Tottenham N17 ... 34 A1
Rosebery Cl SM4 ... 200 D3
Rosebery Ct
Chessington KT9 ... 214 B3
Holborn EC1 ... 241 A6
Mayfair W1 ... 248 C4
Rosebery Gdns
Ealing W13 ... 87 A1
Hornsey N8 ... 50 A4
Sutton SM1 ... 217 D4
Rosebery Ho 21 E2 ... 96 C5
Rosebery Ind Pk N17 ... 34 B1
Rosebery Mews N10 ... 31 C1
Rosebery Rd
Cheam SM1, SM2 ... 217 B2
Clapham Pk SW2 ... 160 A5
Isleworth TW3, TW7 ... 152 A6
Kingston u T KT1 ... 176 D1
Muswell Hill N10 ... 31 C1
Rosebery Sq
Holborn EC1 ... 241 A5
Kingston u T KT1 ... 176 D1
Rosebine Ave TW2 ... 152 B4
Rosebriars KT10 ... 212 A3
Rose Bruford Coll DA15 ... 168 B3
Rosebury Ct SW16 ... 182 B2
Rosebury Rd SW6 ... 135 D3
Rosebury Vale HA4 ... 62 A6
Rose Bush Ct NW3 ... 70 D3
Rose Cotts KT10 ... 212 B3
Rosecourt Rd CR0 ... 204 B3
Rosecroft Ave NW3 ... 69 C5
Rosecroft Gdns
Dollis Hill NW2 ... 68 A5
Twickenham TW2 ... 152 B3
Rosecroft Rd UB1 ... 85 C3
Rosecroft Wlk
Pinner HA5 ... 40 D4
Wembley HA0 ... 65 D3
Rosecroft N22 ... 32 B2
Rose & Crown Ct EC2 ... 242 A2
Rose & Crown Yd SW1 ... 249 B3
Rose Ct 7 Dalston E8 ... 73 D1
Harrow HA2 ... 64 A6
Ilford IG1 ... 78 D2
Islington N1 ... 234 C5
Muswell Hill N10 ... 31 B3
3 Pinner HA5 ... 40 C6
Spitalfields E1 ... 243 D3
7 Wembley HA0 ... 88 A5
10 Wimbledon SW19 ... 179 B5
Rosedale Ave UB3 ... 83 B2
Rosedale Cl
Abbey Wood SE2 ... 124 B3
Hanwell W7 ... 108 D4
Stanmore HA7 ... 25 B4
Rosedale Cnr BR7 ... 188 B2
Rosedale Coll UB3 ... 83 C1
Rosedale Ct N5 ... 72 D4
Rosedale Dr RM9 ... 80 B1
Rosedale Gdns RM9 ... 80 B1
Rosedale Ho N16 ... 51 B1
Rosedale Lo N14 ... 15 B4
Rose Dale BR6 ... 226 D6
Rosedale Pl CR0 ... 206 D2
Rosedale Rd
Dagenham RM9 ... 80 B1
Forest Gate E7 ... 77 C3
Richmond TW9 ... 132 A1
Stoneleigh KT17 ... 216 A3
Rosedale Terr W6 ... 112 B3
Rosedene Ave
Morden SM4 ... 201 C4
Southall UB6 ... 85 C4
Streatham SW16 ... 160 B1
Thornton Heath CR0 ... 204 A2
Rosedene Ct HA4 ... 39 C1
Rosedene Gdns IG2 ... 56 C5
Rosedene NW6 ... 90 D6
Rosedene Terr E10 ... 75 D6
Rosedew Rd W6 ... 134 D6
Rose End KT4 ... 200 D1
Rosefield Cl SM5 ... 218 C3
Rosefield Ct EN4 ... 2 D1
Rosefield Gdns E14 ... 119 C6
Roseford Ct 16 W12 ... 112 D4
Rose Garden Cl HA8 ... 26 A4
Rosegate Ho 32 E3 ... 97 B5
Rose Gdns
Ealing W5 ... 109 D3
Feltham TW13 ... 150 A2
Southall UB1 ... 85 C3
Rose Glen NW9 ... 45 B5
Rosehart Mews 8 W11 ... 91 C1
Rosehatch Ave RM6 ... 58 D6
Roseheath Rd TW4 ... 151 B6
ROSEHILL ... 202 A1
Rosehill Ave SM1, SM5 ... 202 A1
Rose Hill
Carshalton SM4, SM5 ... 202 A2
Cheam SM1 ... 201 D1
Rosehill KT10 ... 213 A2
Rosehill Ct SM4 ... 202 A2
Rosehill Gdns
Greenford UB6 ... 64 D3
Sutton SM1 ... 218 A6
Rosehill TW12 ... 173 C2
Rose Hill Park W SM1 ... 218 A6
Rosehill Rd SW18 ... 158 A6
Rose La RM6 ... 59 A5
Roseland Cl N17 ... 33 B3
Roseland Ho SW6 ... 135 A2
Rose Lawn WD23 ... 8 A3
Roseleigh Ave N5 ... 72 D4
Roseleigh Cl 15 TW1 ... 153 D5
Roselle Ct W5 ... 88 A1
Rosemary Ave
East Finchley NW2 ... 47 D5
East Molesey KT8 ... 195 C5
Edmonton N9 ... 18 B3
Enfield EN2 ... 5 C4
Finchley N3 ... 29 D1
Hounslow TW4 ... 128 D3
Rosemary Branch Bridge N1 ... 235 D6
Rosemary Cl
Hillingdon UB8 ... 82 C2
Thornton Heath CR0 ... 204 A3
Rosemary Cotts 4 SW19 ... 178 C3
Rosemary Ct 35 SE8 ... 141 B6
Rosemary Dr
Redbridge IG4 ... 55 D4
16 South Bromley E14 ... 98 B1
Rosemary Gdns
Chessington KT9 ... 214 A4
Dagenham RM8 ... 59 B1
Mortlake SW14 ... 133 A2
Rosemary Ho
Shoreditch N1 ... 235 D5
Willesden NW10 ... 90 B6
Rosemary La SW14 ... 133 A2
Rosemary Rd
Bexley DA16 ... 145 D4
Camberwell SE15 ... 139 D5
Wandsworth SW17 ... 158 A1
Rosemary St N1 ... 235 D6
Rosemary Works Sch N1 ... 95 B6 235 D5
Rosemead Ave
Feltham TW13 ... 149 D2
Mitcham CR4 ... 181 C1
Wembley HA9 ... 66 A3
Rosemead NW9 ... 46 A2
Rosemead Prep Sch SE27 ... 161 A2
Rose Mews N18 ... 34 B6
Rosemont Ave N12 ... 30 A4
Rosemont Mans 11 NW3 ... 69 D2
Rosemont Rd
Acton W3 ... 110 D6
Kingston u T KT3 ... 199 A6
Richmond TW10 ... 154 A5
South Hampstead NW3 ... 70 A2
Wembley HA0 ... 88 A6
Rosemoor Ho 14 W13 ... 109 A5
Rosemoor St SW3 ... 114 D2 257 C3
Rosemount Ct
2 Acton W3 ... 110 D5
South Norwood SE25 ... 205 C6
Rosemount Dr BR1 ... 210 B5
Rosemount Lo W3 ... 110 D6
Rosemount Point 10 SE23 ... 162 D1
Rosemount Rd W13 ... 87 A1
Rosemount Twrs 5 SM6 ... 219 C2
Rosenau Cres SW11 ... 267 C1
Rosenau Rd SW11 ... 136 D4 267 C2
Rosendale Prim Sch SE21 ... 161 A4
Rosendale Rd SE21, SE24 ... 161 A3
Roseneath Ave N21 ... 16 D3
Roseneath Pl 2 SW16 ... 182 B6
Roseneath Rd SW11 ... 159 A5
Roseneath Wlk EN1 ... 5 C1
Rosens Wlk HA8 ... 10 D1
Rosenthal Ho SE6 ... 163 D5
Rosenthal Rd SE6 ... 164 A5
Rosenthorpe Rd SE15 ... 162 D6
Roserton St E14 ... 120 A4
Rosery The CR0 ... 206 D3
Rose Sq SW7 ... 256 D2
Roses The IG8 ... 36 D3
Rose St Holborn EC4 ... 241 D2
Strand WC2 ... 116 A6 250 A6
Rosethorn Cl SW12 ... 159 D4
Rosetta Cl SW8 ... 270 B3
Rosetta Ct SE19 ... 183 C3
Rosetta Prim Sch E16 ... 99 B2
Rosetti Terr RM8 ... 80 B4
Roseveare Rd SE12 ... 187 C6
Roseville Ave TW3, TW4 ... 151 C6
Roseville Rd UB3 ... 106 A2
Roseville N21 ... 16 C3
Rosevine Rd SW20 ... 178 C2
Rosewall Ct SW19 ... 179 D5
Rose Way
Edgware HA8 ... 27 A6
Lee SE12 ... 165 A6
Roseway SE21 ... 161 B5
Rosewell Cl SE20 ... 184 B3
Rose Wlk
Surbiton KT5 ... 198 D4
West Wickham BR4 ... 224 B6
Rosewood Ave UB6 ... 65 A2
Rosewood Cl DA14 ... 168 C1
Rosewood Ct
Bromley BR1 ... 187 D2
Dagenham RM6 ... 58 C4
Kingston u T KT2 ... 176 C3
2 Leyton E11 ... 76 B4
Rosewood Dr TW17 ... 192 B4
Rosewood Gdns SE13 ... 142 A3
Rosewood Gr SM1 ... 218 A6
Rosewood Ho 9 NW3 ... 69 D2
Rosewood Sq W12 ... 90 A1
Rosher Cl E15 ... 76 B1
Roshni Ho SW17 ... 180 C4
Rosh Pinah Prim Sch
Edgware HA8 ... 10 D1
Edgware HA8 ... 26 C6
Rosina Ct SW17 ... 180 C5
Rosina St E9 ... 74 D2
Roskeen Ct 1 SW19 ... 178 C3
Roskell Rd SW15 ... 134 D2
Roskild Ct HA9 ... 66 B4
Roslin Ho 2 E1 ... 118 D6
Roslin Rd W3 ... 110 D3
Roslin Way BR1 ... 187 A5
Roslyn Cl CR4 ... 180 B1
Roslyn Rd N15 ... 51 C4
Rosmead Rd W11 ... 113 A6 244 B6
Rosoman Pl EC1 ... 241 B6
Rosoman St EC1 ... 234 B1
Rossal Ct 2 SE20 ... 184 B3
Rossall Cres NW10 ... 88 B4
Rossanne Ho N3 ... 29 D3
Ross Ave
Dagenham RM8 ... 59 B1
Finchley NW7 ... 29 A5
Ross Cl Harrow HA3 ... 24 A3
Hayes UB3 ... 105 B2
Northolt UB5 ... 64 B4
Ross Ct
Chislehurst BR7 ... 188 B3
Colindale NW9 ... 45 C6
Ealing W13 ... 87 B2
Edgware HA8 ... 10 D2
1 Hackney E5 ... 74 B4
4 Putney SW15 ... 156 D4
South Croydon CR2 ... 221 A2
Rossdale SM1 ... 218 C3
Rossdale Dr
Ponders End N9 ... 18 C5
Welsh Harp NW9 ... 45 A1
Rossdale Rd SW15 ... 134 C1
Rosse Gdns SE13 ... 164 B5
Rosse Mews SE3 ... 143 B4
Rossendale Cl EN2 ... 4 D6
Rossendale Ho 7 E5 ... 74 B6
Rossendale St E5 ... 74 B6
Rossendale Way NW1 ... 93 C6 232 B6
Rossendon Ct 1 SM6 ... 219 C2
Rossetti Ct WC1 ... 239 C4
Rossetti Gdns Mans SW3 ... 267 C6
Rossetti Ho SW1 ... 259 D3
Rossetti Mews NW8 ... 229 D5
Rossetti Rd SE16 ... 118 B1
Rossetti Studios SW3 ... 267 B6
Ross Ho
2 Kidbrooke SE18 ... 144 A4
Twickenham TW2 ... 151 D2
18 Wapping E1 ... 118 B5
Rossignol Gdns SM5 ... 219 A6
Rossindel Rd TW3 ... 151 C6
Rossington Cl EN1 ... 6 B5
Rossington St E5 ... 74 A6
Rossiter Fields EN5 ... 13 B5
Rossiter Rd SW12 ... 159 B3
Rossland Cl DA6 ... 169 D6
Rosslyn Ave
Barnes SW13 ... 133 D2
Chingford E4 ... 20 D2
Dagenham RM8 ... 59 C2
East Barnet EN4 ... 14 C5
Feltham TW14 ... 150 A5
Rosslyn Cl
Ashford TW16 ... 171 C4
Coney Hall BR4 ... 224 D5
Hayes UB3 ... 83 B2
Rosslyn Cres
Harrow HA1 ... 42 D5
Wembley HA9 ... 66 A4
Rosslyn Ct NW3 ... 70 C3
Rosslyn Hill NW3 ... 70 B3
Rosslyn Ho 8 TW9 ... 132 B4
Rosslyn Mans
8 Hampstead NW3 ... 70 A2
South Hampstead NW6 ... 70 A2
Rosslyn Mews 7 NW3 ... 70 B4
Rosslyn Park Mews NW3 ... 70 B3
Rosslyn Rd
Barking IG11 ... 79 B1
Twickenham TW1 ... 153 C5
Walthamstow E17 ... 54 A5
Rossmore Cl EN3 ... 6 D1
Rossmore Ct NW1 ... 237 C6
Rossmore Rd NW1 ... 92 C3 237 B6
Ross Par SM6 ... 219 B2
Ross Rd
South Norwood SE25 ... 205 C6
Twickenham TW2 ... 152 A3
Wallington SM6 ... 219 C3
Rossway Dr WD23 ... 8 B6
Ross Way SE9 ... 144 A2
Rosswood Gdns SM6 ... 219 C2
Rosswood Ho 13 SM6 ... 219 B2
Rosswood Lo CR0 ... 222 D6
Rostella Rd SW17 ... 180 B6
Rostrever Gdns UB3 ... 105 C5
Rostrevor Ave N15 ... 51 D3
Rostrevor Gdns UB2 ... 107 A1
Rostrevor Mans SW6 ... 264 C2
Rostrevor Mews SW6 ... 264 C1
Rostrevor Rd
Fulham SW6 ... 135 B4 264 C2
Wimbledon SW19 ... 179 C5
Rotary Ct KT8 ... 196 C6
Rotary Lo 12 SE27 ... 160 D1
Rotary St SE1 ... 261 D6
Rothay NW1 ... 231 D2
Rothbury Gdns TW7 ... 131 A5
Rothbury Rd E9 ... 75 C1
Rothbury Wlk N17 ... 34 A3
Rotheley Ho 39 E9 ... 74 C1
Rotherfield Ct
De Beauvoir Town N1 ... 73 B1
Shoreditch N1 ... 95 B6 235 C6
Rotherfield Prim Sch N1 ... 95 A6 235 B6
Rotherfield Rd
Enfield EN3 ... 6 D6
Wallington SM5 ... 219 A3
Rotherfield St
Islington N1 ... 73 A1
Shoreditch N1 ... 95 A6 235 B6
Rotherham Wlk SE1 ... 251 C3
Rotherhill Ave SW16 ... 181 D4
ROTHERHITHE ... 118 D3
Rotherhithe Bsns Est SE16 ... 1
Rotherhithe New Rd SE16 ... 1
Rotherhithe Old Rd SE16 ... 1
Rotherhithe Prim Sch SE16 ... 1
Rotherhithe Sta SE16 ... 1
Rotherhithe St SE16 ... 1
Rotherhithe Tunnel SE16 ... 1
Rother Ho SE15 ... 1
Rotherwick Hill W5 ...
Rotherwick Rd NW11 ...
Rotherwood Cl SW20 ... 1
Rotherwood Rd SW15 ... 1
Rothery St N1 ... 2
Rothesay Ave
Merton SW20 ... 1
Mortlake SW14, TW10 ... 1
Northolt UB6 ...
Rothesay Ct
4 Catford SE6 ... 1
Grove Pk SE12 ... 1
13 Kennington SE11 ... 1
Rothesay Rd SE25 ... 2
Rothley Ct NW8 ... 2
Rothsay Rd E7 ...
Rothsay St SE1 ... 117 C3 2
Rothsay Wlk 19 E14 ... 1
Rothschild Rd W4 ... 1
Rothschild St SE27 ... 1
Rothwell Ct
2 Bromley BR1 ... 1
4 Harrow HA1 ...
Rothwell Gdns RM9 ... 1
Rothwell Ho TW5 ... 1
Rothwell Rd RM9 ... 1
Rothwell St
10 Hampstead NW1 ...
Primrose Hill NW1 ... 2
Roth Wlk N7 ...
Rotten Row SW1 ... 114 D4 2
Rotterdam Dr E14 ... 1
Rouel Rd
Bermondsey SE16 ... 1
Bermondsey SE16 ... 1
Rougemont Ave SM4 ... 2
Roundabout Ho HA6 ...
Roundacre SW19 ... 1
Roundel Cl SE4 ... 1
Roundell Ho 14 SE21 ... 1
Rounders Ct 7 RM10 ...
Round Gr CR0 ... 2
Roundhay Cl SE23 ... 1
Roundhedge Way EN2 ...
Roundhill Dr EN2 ...
Round Hill SE23 ... 1
ROUNDSHAW ... 2
Roundshaw Ctr SM6 ... 2
Roundtable Rd BR1 ... 1
Roundtree Rd HA0 ...
Roundways HA4 ...
Roundway The
Claygate KT10 ... 2
Tottenham N17 ...
Roundwood Ave UB11 ... 1
Roundwood BR7 ... 1
Roundwood Cl HA4 ...
Roundwood Rd NW10 ...
Rounton Rd E3 ...
Rountree Ct 9 UB1 ...
Roupell Ho 7 KT2 ... 1
Roupell Rd SW2 ... 1
Roupell St SE1 ... 116 C5 2
Rousden St NW1 ...
Rouse Gdns SE21 ... 1
Routemaster Cl E13 ...
Routh Ct TW14 ...
Routh Rd SW18 ...
Routh St E6 ... 1
Rover Ho 26 N1 ...
Rowallan Ct 3 SE6 ... 1
Rowallan Rd SW6 ... 135 A5 2
Rowallen Par RM8 ...
Rowan Ave E4 ...
Rowan Cl Ealing W5 ...
Harrow HA7 ...
Ilford IG1 ...

an Cl *continued*
gston u T KT3 177 C1
eatham SW16 181 C2
mbley HA0 65 A5
an Cres SW16 181 C2
an Ct
Camberwell
E15 139 D5
est Hill SE26 184 C6
Kingston u T KT2 176 C3
wham E13 99 B5
ckenham TW4 151 D6
ndsworth SW11 158 D5
mbledon SW20 178 B1
an Dr NW9 46 A6
an Gdns CR0 221 D5
an Ho 9 Bow E3 97 B6
genham NW10 89 C3
st Bedfont TW14 149 B5
rd IG1 79 B3
Maitland Pk NW3 70 D2
cup DA14 167 D1
an N10 31 B1
an Pl UB3 105 D6
an Rd
ntford TW8 131 B5
ok Green W6 112 D2
7 147 A2
cham SW16 181 C1
st Drayton UB7 104 A2
ans The
ford TW16 171 D5
monton N13 17 A1
Sutton SM2 217 D2
an Terr W6 112 D2
antree Cl N21 17 B3
antree Rd
monton N21 17 B3
ield EN2 4 D3
an Way RM6 58 C6
an Wlk BR2 226 B5
Dartmouth Pk N19 71 C6
mpstead Garden
Suburb N2 48 A4
nsal Town W10 91 A3
New Barnet EN5 13 D6
anwood Ave
15 168 A3
anwood Mews
2 4 D3
ben Cl N20 13 D3
berry Cl SW6 134 C5
cross St
1 117 D1 263 D2
dell Rd UB5 85 C6
den Par E4 35 C4
den Park Gdns
35 C4
den Rd
kenham BR3 185 B2
ngford E4 35 D4
st Ewell KT19 215 A4
ditch La SW11 137 A3
don Ave NW10 68 B1
downs Rd RM9 81 B1
e Gdns IG11 102 A5
e Ho E9 74 C2
e La E9 74 C3
ena Cres SW11 136 C3
e Wlk HA2 63 C5
fant Rd SW12,
17 159 A2
hill Mans 11 E5 74 B4
hill Rd E5 74 B4
ington Cl W2 91 D2
land Ave HA3 43 C6
land Ct E16 98 D3
th Croydon CR0 221 C6
land Gr SE26 162 B1
land Hill
nshouses 7
15 170 C5
land Hill Ave
7 33 B4
land Hill Ho
251 C2
and Hill St NW3 70 C3
lands Ave HA5 23 D4
lands Cl
ndon NW7 28 A3
hgate N6 49 A3
lands Rd RM8 81 B6
and Way
ford TW15 171 B3
rton SW19 179 D2
ley Ave DA15 168 B4
ley Cl HA0 66 B1
ley Ct EN1 17 C6
ley Gdns N4 51 A2
ey Green Rd
12 A6
ley Ho SE8 141 C6
ey Ind Pk W3 110 D3
ley La EN5 11 D6
ley Rd N15 51 A4
ley Way NW8 229 A6
heys Pl UB7 104 A3

Rowlls Rd KT1 198 B6
Rowney Gdns RM9 80 C2
Rowney Rd RM9 80 B2
Rowntree Clifford Cl 7
E13 99 B4
Rowntree Cl NW6 69 C2
Rowntree Path 1
SE28 124 B5
Rowntree Rd TW2 152 C3
Rowse Cl E15 98 A6
Rowsham Ct HA1 64 C5
Rowsley Ave NW4 46 C6
Rowstock Gdns N7 71 D3
Rowstock 1 NW5 71 D2
Rowton Rd SE18 145 A5
Roxborough Ave
Harrow HA1 42 C2
Hounslow TW7 130 D5
Roxborough Pk HA1 42 C2
Roxborough Rd HA1 42 B3
Roxbourne Cl UB5 62 D2
Roxbourne Fst & Mid
Schs HA2 63 A6
Roxburgh Rd SE27 182 D5
Roxburn Way HA4 61 D5
Roxby Pl
SW6 135 C6 265 B6
ROXETH 64 A6
Roxeth Ct 6 TW15 170 C5
Roxeth Fst & Mid Sch
HA2 64 B6
Roxeth Green Ave
HA2 63 D6
Roxeth Gr HA2 63 D4
Roxeth Hill HA2 64 C6
Roxeth Manor Fst & Mid
Schs HA2 63 C5
Roxeth Mead Sch
HA2 64 B6
Roxford Cl TW17 193 C4
Roxford Ho 2 E3 97 D3
Roxley Rd SE13 163 D5
Roxton Gdns CR0 223 C3
Roxwell 10 NW1 71 B2
Roxwell Rd
Barking IG11 102 A5
Shepherd's Bush
W12 112 A4
Roxwell Trad Pk E10 53 A2
Roxwell Way IG8 37 C3
Roxy Ave RM6 58 C2
Royal Academy of
Dramatic Art*
WC1 93 D2 239 C4
Royal Acad of Arts*
W1 115 C6 249 A5
Royal Acad of Dance
SW11 266 D1
Royal Acad of Music
NW1 238 B5
Royal Albert Hall*
SW7 114 B4 246 C1
Royal Albert Sta
E16 122 A6
Royal Albert Way
E6 122 B6
Royal Arc W1 249 A5
Royal Armouries The*
E1 253 C5
Royal Avenue Ho
SW3 257 C2
Royal Ave
SW3 114 D1 257 C2
Worcester Pk KT4 215 C6
Royal Ballet Sch The
Hammersmith
W14 112 D1
St Giles WC2 94 A1 240 B1
Royal Ballet Sch (White
Lodge) The TW10 155 B3
Royal Brompton
Hospl
Chelsea
SW3 114 B1 256 C2
Chelsea
SW3 114 C1 257 A2
Royal Cir SE27 160 D1
Royal Cl
Deptford SE8 141 B6
Hillingdon UB7 82 B1
Ilford IG3 58 A2
Locksbottom BR6 226 D4
Putney SW19 156 D2
Stamford Hill N16 51 C1
Worcester Pk KT4 215 C6
Royal College of
Physicians Liby
NW1 93 B3 238 D6
Royal College St
NW1 93 C6 232 B6
Royal Coll of
Anaesthetists
WC1 240 C3
Royal Coll of Art
Sculpture Sch
SW11 136 C5 267 A3

Royal Coll of Art
SW7 114 B4 246 C1
Royal Coll of Midwives
W1 93 B2 238 C3
Royal Coll of Music
SW7 114 B3 256 C6
Royal Coll of
Obstetricians &
Gynaecologists
NW1 92 D3 237 C6
Royal Coll of
Ophthalmologists
NW1 238 A5
Royal Coll of
Paediatrics & Child
Health W1 238 D4
Royal Coll of
Pathologists
SW1 115 D5 249 C3
Royal Coll of Physicians
NW1 93 B3 238 D6
Royal Coll of
Radiologists W1 238 D4
Royal Coll of Science
SW7 114 B3 256 C6
Royal Coll of Speech
Language Therapists
SE1 252 C3
Royal Coll of Surgeons
WC2 94 B1 240 D2
Royal Connaught Apts
E16 121 D5
Royal Courts of Justice
WC2 94 C1 241 A1
Royal Crescent Mews
W11 112 D5
Royal Cres Ilford IG2 57 B3
Ruislip HA4 63 A5
Royal Crest Ho SM2 217 A1
Royal Cres
W11 113 A5 244 A3
Royal Ct
City of London EC3 242 D1
Enfield EN1 17 C5
9 Kingston u T KT2 176 D3
Mottingham SE9 166 B3
Rotherhithe SE16 119 B3
Ruislip HA4 40 A2
Royal Docks Com Sch
The E16 99 C1
Royal Docks Rd E6 100 D2
Royal Dr N11 31 A5
Royal Duchess Mews
SW12 159 B4
Royal Exchange Bldgs
EC3 242 D1
Royal Exchange*
EC3 242 D1
Royal Festival Hall*
SE1 116 B5 250 D3
Royal Free Hospl
NW3 70 C3
Royal Fusiliers Mus*
E1 253 C5
Royal Gdns W7 109 A3
Royal Geographical
Society SW7 246 D1
Royal Hill Ct 2
SE10 142 A5
Royal Hill SE10 142 A5
Royal Horticultural
Society (Lawrence
Hall & Conf Ctr)
SW1 259 C5
Royal Horticultural
Society (Lindley Hall)
SW1 259 C4
Royal Hospital (Army
Pensioners)*
SW1 115 A1 258 A1
Royal Hospital Rd
SW3 114 D1 257 D1
Royal Hospl and Home
SW15 157 A5
Royal La
Hillingdon UB7 82 B1
Hillingdon UB8 82 B3
Royal Langford
Apartments 3
NW6 91 D5
Royal London Est The
NW10 89 B5
Royal London Est
N17 34 B4
Royal London
Homeopathic Hospl
The WC1 94 A2 240 B4
Royal London Hospl
Archives & Mus*
E1 96 B2
Royal London Hospl
(Mile End) The E2 96 D4
Royal London Hospl (St
Clements) The E3 97 B4
Royal London Hospl
(Whitechapel) The
E1 96 B2

Royal Marsden Hospl
SW3 114 B1 256 D2
Royal Mews KT8 196 C6
Royal Mews The*
SW1 115 B3 258 D6
Royal Military Sch of
Music (Kneller Hall)
TW2 152 B5
Royal Mint Pl 6 E1 118 A6
Royal Mint St
E1 117 D6 253 D6
Royal National
Orthopaedic Hospl
Regent's Pk
W1 93 B3 238 D5
Stanmore HA7 9 C2
Royal National TNE
Hospl The
WC1 94 B4 233 C2
Royal Nat TN&E Hospl
The W5 87 C2
Royal Naval Pl SE14 141 B5
Royal Oak Ct
Dagenham RM8 80 C6
9 Shoreditch N1 95 C4
Royal Oak Mews 9
TW11 175 A5
Royal Oak Pl SE22 162 B5
Royal Oak Rd
Bexley DA6 147 C1
DA6 169 B6
5 Hackney E8 74 B2
Royal Oak Sta W2 91 D2
Royal Oak Yd SE1 253 A1
Royal Obsy The*
SE10 142 B5
Royal Opera Arc
SW1 249 C4
Royal Orchard Cl
SW18 157 A4
Royal Par
Blackheath Vale
SE3 142 D3
Chislehurst BR7 189 A3
11 Dagenham RM10 81 D2
Ealing W5 88 A4
Fulham SW6 264 A4
Royal Park Prim Sch
DA14 169 A1
Royal Par 12 TW9 132 C4
Royal Pl 11 SE10 142 A5
Royal Rd
Kennington SE17 138 D6
Newham E16 99 D1
Sidcup DA14 168 D1
Teddington TW11 174 B5
Royal Route HA9 66 B4
Royal Russell Sch
CR0 222 B3
Royal Sch Hampstead
The NW3 70 B4
Royal St SE1 116 B3 260 D6
Royal Tower Lo 3
SE1 118 A6
Royalty Ho W1 239 C1
Royalty Mews W1 239 C1
Royalty Studios W11 91 A1
Royal United Services
Mus* SW1 250 A3
Royal Veterinary Coll
NW1 93 D6 232 C5
Royal Victoria Pl 7
E16 121 B5
Royal Victoria Sq
E16 121 B6
Royal Victoria Sta
E16 121 A6
Royal Victor Pl E3 96 D5
Royal Wlk SM6 219 B5
Roycraft Ave IG11 101 D5
Roycroft Cl
Streatham SW2 160 C3
Woodford E18 37 B2
Roydene Rd SE18 123 C1
Roydon Cl 7 SW11 136 D3
Roy Gdns IG2 57 D4
Roy Gr TW12 173 D4
Royle Cres W13 87 A3
Roymount Ct TW2 152 C1
Roy Ridley Ho 6
SW4 137 D2
Roy Sq E14 119 A6
Royston Ave
Carshalton SM1 218 B5
Chingford E4 35 D5
Wallington SM6 219 D4
Royston Cl
Cranford TW5 128 B4
Walton-on-T KT12 194 A1
Royston Ct
Hinchley Wood
KT10 212 D6
New Cross SE4 141 B3
1 Newham E13 99 A6
Redbridge IG1 55 D3

Royston Ct *continued*
3 Richmond TW9 132 B4
Ruislip HA5 40 C2
Tolworth KT6 214 C6
Royston Gdns IG1 55 D3
Royston Gr HA5 23 C4
Royston Ho
Friern Barnet N11 31 A6
14 SE15 140 A6
Royston Lo SW19 180 A4
Royston Park Rd
HA5 23 C5
Royston Par IG1 55 D3
Royston Prim Sch
SE20 184 D2
Royston Rd
Penge SE20 184 D2
Richmond TW10 154 A6
Royston St 24 E2 96 C5
Roystons The KT5 198 D4
Rozel Ct 3 N1 95 C6
Rozelle Ct 1 CR7 204 C3
Rozel Rd SW4 137 C2
Rubastic Rd UB2 106 C3
Rubens Rd UB5 84 D5
Rubens St SE6 163 B2
Rubin Pl 14 EN3 7 C6
Ruby Ct TW13 149 D1
Ruby Rd E17 53 C6
Ruby St SE15 140 B6
Stonebridge NW10 67 A1
Ruby Triangle SE15 140 B6
Ruckholt Cl E10 75 D5
Ruckholt Rd E10 75 D5
Rucklidge Ave NW10 90 A5
Rudall Cres NW3 70 B4
Rudbeck Ho 11
SE15 140 A5
Ruddington Cl E5 75 A4
Ruddock Cl HA8 27 A3
Ruddstreet Cl SE18 123 A2
Rudge Ho 1 SE16 118 A3
Rudgwick Terr
NW8 92 C6 230 B5
Rudhall Ho 4 SW2 160 C5
Rudland Rd DA7 147 D2
Rudloe Rd SW12 159 C4
Rudolf Pl SW8 270 B5
Rudolph Ct SE22 162 B4
Rudolph Rd E13 98 D5
Paddington NW6 91 C5
Rudstone Ho 10 E3 97 D4
Rudyard Ct SE1 252 D1
Rudyard Gr NW7 27 A4
Ruegg Ho 5 SE18 144 C6
Ruffetts Cl CR2 222 B1
Ruffetts The CR2 222 B1
Ruffle Cl UB7 104 B4
Rufford Cl HA3 43 A3
Rufford St N1 94 A6 233 B6
Rufford Street Mews
N1 72 A1
Rufford Twr 5 W3 110 D5
Rufforth Ct 1 NW9 27 C2
Rufus Bsns Ctr
SW18 157 D2
Rufus Cl HA4 63 A5
Rufus Ho SE1 263 D6
Rufus St N1 95 C4
Rugby Ave
Edmonton N9 17 D3
Northolt UB6 64 B2
Wembley HA0 65 C4
Rugby Cl HA1 42 C5
Rugby Gdns RM9 80 C2
Rugby Mans W14 254 B4
Rugby Rd
Bedford Pk W4 111 C4
Dagenham RM9 80 C2
Queensbury NW9 44 D5
Twickenham TW1, TW2,
TW7 152 C5
Rugby St WC1 94 B3 240 C5
Rugg St E14 119 C6
Rugless Ho 2 E14 120 A4
Rugmere 4 NW1 71 A1
RUISLIP 39 B2
Ruislip Cl UB6 85 D3
RUISLIP COMMON 39 B4
Ruislip Ct HA4 61 D6
RUISLIP GARDENS 61 D5
Ruislip Gardens Prim
Sch HA4 61 D4
Ruislip Gardens Sta
HA4 62 A4
Ruislip Lido Rly*
HA4 39 B5
Ruislip Lido* HA4,
HA5 39 B5
RUISLIP MANOR 40 A1
Ruislip Manor Sta
HA4 40 A1
Ruislip Rd E
Ealing UB6, W7 86 D3
Greenford UB6 86 B3
Ruislip Rd UB6, UB5 85 C4
Ruislip Sta HA4 39 D1

Ruislip St SW17 180 D6
Rumball Ho 14 SE5 139 C5
Rumbold Rd
SW6 135 D5 265 D3
Rum Cl E1 118 C6
Rumford Ho SE1 262 A5
Rumsey Cl TW12 173 B4
Rumsey Rd SW9 138 B2
Runacres Ct SE17 262 A1
Runbury Circ NW9 67 B6
Runcorn Cl N17 52 B5
Runcorn Pl W11 244 A6
Rundell Cres NW4 46 B4
Rundell Twr SW8 270 C2
Runes Cl CR4 202 C5
Runnelfield HA1 64 C5
Running Horse Yd 12
TW8 132 A6
Runnymede Cl TW2 151 D4
Runnymede Cres
SW16 182 A2
Runnymede Ct
Roehampton
SW15 156 A3
1 Wallington SM6 219 B2
Runnymede Gdns
Greenford UB6 86 C5
Twickenham TW2 151 D4
Runnymede Ho
Hackney E9 75 A4
Richmond TW10 154 C6
Runnymede SW19 180 B2
Runnymede Rd
TW2 151 D5
Runway The HA4 62 C3
Rupack St 3 SE16 118 C4
Rupert Ave 6 HA9 66 A3
Rupert Ct W1 249 C6
Rupert Gdns SW9 138 D3
Rupert Ho SE11 261 B3
8 Upper Holloway
N19 71 D5
Rupert Rd
Bedford Pk W4 111 C3
Paddington NW6 91 B5
Upper Holloway N19 71 D6
Rupert St
W1 115 D6 249 C6
Rural Way SW16 181 B3
Rusbridge Cl E8 74 A3
Ruscoe Ho 12 SW27 182 D5
Ruscoe Rd E16 98 D1
Ruscombe Way
TW14 149 D4
Rusham Rd SW12 158 D4
Rushbrook Cres E17 35 B2
Rushbrook Ho 20
SW8 137 D3
Rushbrook Rd SE9 167 A2
Rushbury Ct 4
TW12 173 C2
Rushby Ct SW4 270 A1
Rush Common Mews 18
SW2 160 B4
Rushcroft Rd
Brixton SW2,
SW9 138 C1
Chingford E4 35 D3
Rush Croft Sch E4 35 D3
Rushcutters Ct 18
SE16 119 A2
Rushden Cl SE19 183 B3
Rushdene Ave EN4 14 C4
Rushdene Cl UB5 84 C5
Rushdene Cres UB5 84 C4
Rushdene Rd HA5 40 D3
Rushdene SE2 124 D3
Rushden Gdns
Ilford IG5 56 C6
Mill Hill NW7 28 C4
Rushen Wlk SM5 202 B1
Rushet Rd BR5 190 A1
Rushett Cl KT7 197 B1
Rushett Rd KT7 197 B2
Rushey Cl KT3 199 B5
Rushey Gn SE6 163 D4
Rushey Green Prim Sch
SE6 163 D3
Rushey Hill EN2 4 B1
Rushey Mead SE4 163 C6
Rushford Rd SE4 163 B5
Rush Green Rd RM7, RM8,
RM10 59 D1
Rushgrove Ave NW9 45 D5
Rushgrove Ct NW9 45 C4
Rushgrove St SE18 122 B2
Rush Hill Mews 3
SW11 137 A2
Rush Hill Rd SW11 137 A2
Rushlake Ho 3
SW11 137 A3
Rushley Cl BR2 226 A4
Rushman Villas
KT3 199 D5

Rushmead 5 E2 96 B4
Rushmead Cl CR0 221 D4
Rushmead TW10 153 B1
Rushmere Ct KT4 216 A6
Rushmere Ho 2 SW15 156 A3
Rushmere Pl SW19 178 D5
Rushmon Pl SM3 217 A2
Rushmoor Cl HA5 40 B5
Rushmore Cl BR1 210 A6
Rushmore Cres 9 E5 74 D4
Rushmore Ho
9 Kentish Town N7 71 D3
W14 254 B5
Rushmore Prim Sch E5 74 D4
Rushmore Rd
Clapton Pk E5 74 D4
Hackney E5 75 A4
Rusholme Ave RM10 81 C5
Rusholme Gr SE19 183 C5
Rusholme Rd SW15 157 A5
Rushout Ave HA3 43 B3
Rush The SW20 179 B2
Rushton Ho 26 SW8 137 D3
Rushton St N1 95 B5 235 D4
Rushworth St SE1 116 D4 251 D1
Rushy Meadow La SM5 218 C5
Rushy Meadow Prim Sch SM5 218 C5
Ruskin Ave DA16 146 A3
Feltham TW14 149 D5
Plashet E12 78 A2
Richmond TW9 132 C5
Ruskin Cl NW11 47 D3
Ruskin Ct
Herne Hill SE5 139 B2
SE9 166 B5
Southgate N21 16 B4
Ruskin Dr
North Cheam KT4 216 C6
Orpington BR6 227 C5
Welling DA16 146 A2
Ruskin Gdns
Ealing W5 87 D3
Harrow HA3 44 B5
Ruskin Gr DA16 146 A3
Ruskin Ho SW1 259 D3
Ruskin Par CR0 221 B3
Ruskin Park Ho SE5 139 B2
Ruskin Rd
Belvedere DA17 125 C2
Croydon CR0 220 D6
Isleworth TW7 130 D2
Southall UB1 107 A6
Tottenham N17 33 D2
Wallington SM5 219 A3
Ruskin Way SW19 180 B2
Ruskin Wlk BR2 210 B3
Edmonton N9 18 A2
Herne Hill SE24 161 A6
Rusland Ave BR6 227 B5
Rusland Hts HA1 42 C5
Rusland Park Rd HA1 42 C5
Rusper Cl
Cricklewood NW2 68 C5
Stanmore HA7 25 C6
Rusper Ct SW9 138 A3
Rusper Rd
Dagenham RM9 80 C2
Tottenham N17, N22 51 A6
Russel Cl BR3 208 A6
Russel Ct N14 15 D6
Russell Ave N22 32 D1
Russell Cl
Bexleyheath DA7 147 C1
Chiswick W4 133 D6
Greenwich SE7 143 C5
Ruislip HA4 62 C6
Stonebridge NW10 67 A1
Russell Ct
Battersea SW11 268 B1
Bloomsbury WC1 240 A5
Bromley BR1 186 D3
12 New Barnet EN5 2 A1
5 Peckham SE15 140 B3
St James SW1 249 B3
Streatham SW16 182 B5
Surbiton KT6 198 A2
Wallington SM6 219 C3
4 Walthamstow E10 53 D2
Wembley HA0 66 A1
Russell Gdns
East Barnet N20 14 C2
Ilford IG2 57 B2
Russell Gdns Mews W14 113 A3 254 A6
Russell Gdns
Richmond TW10 153 C2
Temple Fortune NW11 47 A3
W14 113 A3 254 A6
West Drayton UB7 104 C1
Russell Gr
33 Brixton SW9 138 C4
Edgware NW7 27 C6
Russell Ho
21 Poplar E14 97 C1
SW1 259 A2
Russell Kerr Cl W4 133 A5
Russell La N20 14 D2
Russell Lo
5 Chingford E4 20 A2
SE1 262 C6
Russell Mans WC1 240 B4
Russell Mead HA3 24 D2
Russell Par NW11 47 A3
Russell Pickering Ho 2 SW4 138 A2
Russell Pl
Hampstead NW3 70 C3
Rotherhithe SE16 119 A3
Russell Rd
Bowes Pk N13 32 B4
Buckhurst Hill IG9 21 C3
Chingford Hatch E4 35 B6
Crouch End N8 49 D3
East Barnet N20 14 C2
Enfield EN1 5 D5
Leyton E10 53 D3
Merton SW19 179 C3
Mitcham CR4 202 C6
Newham E16 99 B1
Northolt UB5 64 A3
Shepperton TW17 193 A2
Tottenham N15 51 C4
Twickenham TW1, TW2 152 D5
W14 113 A3 254 B5
Walthamstow E17 53 B6
Walton-on-T KT12 194 A3
West Hendon NW9 45 D3
Russell Sch The TW10 153 D3
Russell Square Ho WC1 240 A5
Russell Square Mans WC1 240 B4
Russell Square Sta WC1 94 A3 240 A5
Russell Sq WC1 94 A3 240 A5
Russell St WC2 116 A6 250 B6
Russell's Wharf 2 W9 91 B3
Russell Way SM1 217 D3
Russell Wlk 4 TW10 154 B5
Russet Ave TW16, TW17 193 C6
Russet Cl UB10 83 A3
Russet Cres N7 72 B3
Russet Ct
6 Barnet EN4 2 C1
Dollis Hill NW2 68 B5
Feltham TW13 149 C1
Russet Dr CR0 207 A1
Russet Ho TW3 129 B1
Russet House Sch EN1 6 B4
Russets Cl E4 36 B6
Russettings 1 HA5 23 B3
Russett Way SE13 141 D3
Russia Dock Rd SE16 119 A5
Russia La E2 96 C5
Russia Row EC2 242 B1
Russington Rd TW17 193 B3
Rusthall Ave W4 111 B3
Rusthall Cl CR0 206 C3
Rusthall Mans 3 W4 111 B2
Rustic Ave SW16 181 B3
Rustic Pl HA0 65 D4
Rustic Wlk E16 99 B1
Rustington Wlk SM4 201 B2
Ruston Ave KT5 198 D2
Ruston Gdns N14 15 A5
Ruston Mews W11 91 A1
Ruston Rd SE18 122 A3
Ruston St E3 97 B6
Rust Sq SE5 139 B5
Rutford Rd SW16 182 A5
Ruth Cl HA7 44 B5
Ruth Ct 16 E3 97 A5
Rutherford Cl
Hillingdon UB8 82 B3
Sutton SM2 218 B2
Rutherford Ct
Mitcham SW19 180 B3
Southgate N21 16 B6
Rutherford Ho
12 Bethnal Green E1 96 B3
Teddington TW11 174 D5
4 Wembley HA9 67 A5
Rutherford St SW1 115 D2 259 C4
Rutherford Twr 8 UB1 85 D1
Rutherford Way
Bushey WD23 8 C3
Wembley HA9 66 C4
Rutherglen Rd SE2 146 A6
Rutherwyke Cl KT17 216 A2
Ruth Ho W10 91 A3
Ruthin Cl NW9 45 C3
Ruthin Rd SE3 143 A6
Ruthven St E9 96 D6
Rutland Ave DA15 168 A4
Rutland Cl
Chessington KT9 214 B2
DA5 168 D3
Mitcham SW19 180 C3
Mortlake SW14 133 A2
Rutland Ct
15 Acton W3 88 C1
Chislehurst BR7 188 C2
Enfield EN3 18 B6
Herne Hill SE5 139 B1
Sidcup SE9 167 A2
SW7 247 B1
Twickenham TW2 152 C1
Rutland Dr
Morden SM4 201 C2
Richmond TW10 154 A3
Rutland Gate
Beckenham BR2 208 D5
Belvedere DA17 125 D1
Rutland Gate Mews SW7 247 A1
Rutland Gate SW7 114 C4 247 B1
Rutland Gdns
Dagenham RM8 80 C3
Ealing W13 87 A2
Rutland Gdns Mews SW7 247 B1
Rutland Gdns
South Croydon CR0 221 C4
Stoke Newington N4 51 A3
SW7 114 C4 247 B1
Rutland Gr W6 112 B1
Rutland Ho
Edgware HA8 26 B4
6 Northolt UB5 63 C2
2 Penge SE20 184 C2
10 Putney SW15 156 C4
Tolworth KT6 198 C1
W8 255 C5
15 Woolwich SE18 122 B2
Rutland Lo
Forest Hill SE6 163 B2
Teddington TW11 174 C5
Rutland Mews E SW7 257 B6
Rutland Mews S SW7 257 A6
Rutland Mews W SW7 257 A6
Rutland Park Gdns 1 NW2 68 C2
Rutland Park Mans 2 NW2 68 C2
Rutland Pk
Forest Hill SE6 163 B2
Willesden NW2 68 C2
Rutland Pl
Bushey WD23 8 B3
EC1 241 D4
Rutland Rd
Forest Gate E7 77 D1
Harrow HA1 42 A3
Hayes UB3 105 B2
Ilford IG1 78 D5
Mitcham SW19 180 C3
Southall UB1 85 C2
South Hackney E9 96 D6
Twickenham TW2 152 B2
Walthamstow E17 53 C3
Wanstead E11 55 B4
Rutland St SW7 257 B6
Rutland Studios NW10 90 A4
Rutland Wlk SE6 163 B2
Rutley Cl SE11 138 D6
Rutlish Rd SW19 179 C2
Rutlish Sch SW20 179 B1
Rutter Gdns CR4 202 B5
Rutters Cl UB7 104 C4
Rutt's Terr SE14 140 D4
Rutts The WD23 8 B3
Ruvigny Gdns SW15 134 D2
Ruvigny Mans SW15 134 D2
Ruxbury Ct TW15 148 A1
RUXLEY 191 A3
Ruxley Cl
Chessington KT19 214 D3
Sidcup DA14 191 A4
Ruxley Cnr DA14 191 A4
Ruxley Corner Ind Est DA14 190 D4
Ruxley Cres KT10 213 B1
Ruxley Ct KT19 215 A3
Ruxley Gdns TW17 193 A4
Ruxley La KT19 215 B3
Ruxley Mews KT19 214 D3
Ruxley Ridge KT10 213 A1
Ryall's Ct N20 14 D1
Ryan Cl Ruislip HA4 40 B1
SE9 143 C1
Ryan Ct SW16 182 A3
Ryan Dr TW8 131 A6
Ryan Ho 3 HA1 42 D4
Ryarsh Cres BR6 227 C4
Rycott Path SE22 162 A4
Rycroft Way N17 51 D6
Ryculff Sq SE3 142 D3
Rydal Cl NW4 29 A2
Rydal Cres UB6 87 C5
Rydal Ct Edgware HA8 26 B5
Wembley HA9 44 A2
Rydal Dr DA7 147 C4
West Wickham BR4 224 C6
Rydal Gdns
Kingsbury NW9 45 C4
Kingston u T SW15 177 C5
Twickenham TW2, TW3 151 D5
Wembley HA9 43 C1
Rydal Ho 25 SW8 137 D3
Rydal Lo N17 34 A3
Rydal Rd SW16 181 D6
Rydal Water NW1 232 A1
Rydal Way Enfield EN3 18 C5
Ruislip HA4 62 C4
Ryde Ho 1 NW6 91 C6
Rydens Ho SE9 165 C1
Rydens Rd KT12 194 D1
Ryde Pl TW1 153 D5
Ryder Cl BR1 187 B5
Ryder Ct Leyton E10 75 D6
SW1 249 B4
Ryder Dr SE16 118 B1
Ryder Ho
18 Bethnal Green E1 96 C3
5 Merton SW19 179 D2
Ryder's Terr NW8 92 A5 229 A4
Ryder St SW1 249 B4
Ryder Yd SW1 249 B4
Ryde Vale Rd SW12 159 C2
Rydon Mews SW19 178 C3
Rydons Cl SE9 144 A2
Rydon St N1 235 B6
Rydston Cl 2 N7 72 B1
Rye Cl DA5 169 D5
Ryecotes Mead SE21 161 C3
Ryecroft Ave TW2 151 D3
Ryecroft Cres EN5 12 B6
Ryecroft Rd BR5 211 B3
Lewisham SE13 164 A6
South Norwood SW16 182 C4
Ryecroft St SW6 135 D4 265 C1
Rye Ct BR3 185 B2
Ryedale Ct 7 TW12 173 C2
Ryedale SE22 162 B5
Ryefield Ave UB10 60 D1
Ryefield Cres HA5, HA6 22 A1
Ryefield Ct HA6 22 A1
Ryefield Path 7 SW15 156 A3
Ryefield Prim Sch UB10 83 B6
Ryefield Rd SE19 183 A4
Ryegates 2 SE15 140 B3
Ryehill Ct KT3 199 D2
Rye Hill Pk SE15 140 C1
Rye Ho 17 SE16 118 C4
Rye La SE15 140 A3
Ryeland Cl UB7 82 A1
Ryelands Cres SE12 165 C5
Ryelands Prim Sch SE25 206 B4
Rye Lane Mkt SE15 140 A3
Rye Oak Sch SE15 140 B2
Rye Rd SE15 140 D1
Rye The N14 15 C4
Rye Way HA8 26 B4
Rye Wlk SW15 156 D6
Ryfold Rd SW19 157 C1
Ryhope Rd N11 31 B6
Ryland Cl TW13 171 D6
Rylandes Rd NW2 68 A5
Ryland Ho 11 SW16 181 C5
Ryland Rd NW5 71 B2
Rylett Cres W12 111 D3
Rylett Rd W12 111 D3
Rylston Rd
Edmonton N13 17 B1
SW6 135 B6 264 C5
Rylton Ho KT12 194 A1
Rymer Rd CR0 205 C2
Rymer St SE24 160 D5
Rymill St E16 122 C5
Rysbrack St SW1 257 C6
Rythe Cl KT9 213 C1
Rythe Ct KT7 197 A2
Rythe Ho 7 BR1 186 B5
Rythe Rd KT10 212 C3

S

Saatchi Gallery Duke of York's HQ* SW3 114 D1 257 D2
Sabah Ct TW15 170 C6
Sabbarton St 9 E16 98 D1
Sabella Ct E3 97 B5
Sabine Rd SW11 137 A2
Sable Cl TW4 128 C2
Sable Ct 3 KT3 199 C4
Sable St N1 72 D1
Sach Rd E5 74 B6
Sacketts Ho 24 SW9 138 C4
Sackville Ave BR2 209 A1
Sackville Cl HA2 64 B5
Sackville Gdns IG1 56 B1
Sackville Ho
Hornsey N8 50 A5
10 Streatham SW16 160 A1
Sackville Rd SM2 217 C1
Sackville St W1 115 C6 249 B5
Sacred Heart High Sch W6 112 C2
Sacred Heart Jun Sch W6 112 D2
Sacred Heart Language Coll The HA3 24 C1
Sacred Heart Prim Sch, Battersea SW11 136 C3
Sacred Heart RC Prim Sch
East Barnet N20 14 C2
Islington N7 72 B3
Putney SW15 156 A6
Ruislip HA4 61 C6
Teddington TW11 175 B3
West Barnes KT3 200 A5
Sacred Heart RC Sec Sch SE5 139 A4
Saddlebrook Pk TW16 171 C3
Saddlers Cl
Barnet EN5 12 B6
Borehamwood WD6 11 B5
Pinner HA5 23 C5
Saddlers Mews SW8 270 B2
Teddington KT1 175 C2
Wembley HA0 64 D4
Saddlers Path WD6 11 B6
Saddlescombe Way N12 29 C5
Sadler Cl CR4 180 D1
Sadler Ho
17 Bromley E3 97 D4
EC1 234 C2
Sadlers Ho EN1 17 C6
Sadlers Ride KT8 174 A1
Saffron Ave E14 120 B6
Saffron Cl
Temple Fortune NW11 47 B3
Thornton Heath CR0 204 A3
Saffron Ct
East Bedfont TW14 149 A4
10 Kingsland N1 73 B2
Stratford E15 76 C3
Saffron Hill EC1 94 C2 241 B4
Saffron Ho 6 TW9 132 D4
Saffron St EC1 241 B4
Saffron Way KT6 197 D1
Saffron Wharf SE1 253 D2
Sage Cl 7 E6 100 B2
Sage Mews SE22 161 D6
Sage St E1 118 C6
Sage Way WC1 233 C1
Sage Yd KT6 198 B1
Sahara Ct UB1 107 A6
Saigasso Cl E16 99 D1
Sailacre Ho 10 SE10 120 D1
Sail Ct 10 E14 120 B6
Sailmakers Ct SW6 136 A2
Sail St SE11 116 B2 260 D4
Saimet 3 NW9 27 D2
Sainfoin Rd SW17 159 A2
Sainsbury Rd SE19 183 C5
St Agatha's Dr KT2 17
St Agatha's Gr SM5 20
St Agatha's RC Prim Sc
KT2 17
St Agnes Cl E9 9
St Agnes Pl SE11 13
St Agnes RC Prim Sch
E3 9
St Agnes RC Sch
NW2 6
St Aidans Ct IG11 10
St Aidan's Prim Sch
N4 5
St Aidan's RC Prim Sch
IG1 5
St Aidan's Rd
East Dulwich SE22 16
West Ealing W13 10
St Aiden's Ct W13 10
St Albans Ave
Bedford Pk W4 11
Feltham TW13 17
St Alban's Ave E6 10
St Alban's CE Prim Sch
EC1 94 C2 24
St Alban's Cl NW11 4
St Alban's Cres IG8 3
St Albans Cres N22 3
St Alban's Gdns
TW11 17
St Alban's Gr
Carshalton SM5 20
W8 113 D3 25
St Albans Ho 2
SW16 18
St Albans La NW11 4
St Albans Mans W8 25
St Alban's Pl
N1 94 D6 23
St Alban's RC Prim Sch
KT8 19
St Albans Rd
Barnet EN5
Cheam SM1 21
St Alban's Rd
Dagenham NW10 8
Dartmouth Pk NW5 7
St Albans Rd
Ilford IG3 5
Kingston u T KT2 17
St Alban's Rd IG8 3
St Alban's St SW1 24
St Albans Studios
W8 25
St Albans Terr W6 26
St Alban's Villas
NW5 7
St Alfege Pas SE10 14
St Alfege Rd SE7 14
St Alfege with St Peter CE Prim Sch
SE10 14
St Aloysius RC Coll
N19 4
St Aloysius RC Inf Sch
NW1 93 D4 23
St Aloysius RC Jun Sch
NW1 93 D5 23
St Alphage Ct NW9 4
St Alphage Gdn EC2 24
St Alphage Highwalk
EC2 24
St Alphage Wlk HA8 2
St Alphege Rd N9 1
St Alphonsus Rd
SW4 13
St Amunds Cl SE6 18
St Andrew & St Francis CE Prim Sch NW2 6
St Andrews Ave HA0 6
St Andrew's (Barnsbury CE Prim Sch
N1 94 B6 23
St Andrew's CE Prim Sch
Enfield EN1
Osidge N14 1
Stockwell SW9 13
St Andrew's CE Sch
N20 1
St Andrews Chambers
W1 23
St Andrews Cl 25
SE16 11
St Andrew's Cl NW2 6
St Andrews Cl SE28 10
St Andrew's Cl 2
TW7 13
St Andrews Cl KT7 19
St Andrew's Cl N12 3
St Andrews Cl
Ruislip HA4 6
Stanmore HA7 2
St Andrew's Cl
TW17 19

Andrews Cl
SW19 ... 179 D4
Andrew's Ct SM5 .. 218 C5
Andrews Ct W4 ... 133 A4
Andrew's Ct
2 Higham Hill E17 ... 35 A1
Kingston u T KT3 ... 199 D6
2 Wandsworth
SW18 ... 158 A2
Andrews Dr HA7 ... 25 C2
Andrew's Greek Sch
NW1 ... 71 C2
Andrew's Gr N16 ... 51 B1
Andrew's High Sch
CR0 ... 220 D4
Andrew's Hill
EC4 ... 94 D1 241 D1
Andrews Ho
11 Bermondsey
SE16 ... 118 B3
Bromley BR1 ... 187 B4
Andrew's Hospl
E3 ... 97 D3
Andrews Mans 9
E5 ... 74 B4
Andrew's Mans
W1 ... 238 A3
Andrews Mews
SE3 ... 143 A5
Andrew's Mews
N16 ... 51 C1
Andrews Mews 4
SW12 ... 159 D3
Andrew's Pl NW1. 238 D6
Andrews RC Prim
Sch SW16 ... 182 A5
Andrews Rd SM5 .. 218 C5
Andrew's Rd 3
CR0 ... 221 A4
Andrews Rd
DA14 ... 168 D1
Andrew's Rd
Dagenham W3 ... 89 C1
Enfield EN1 ... 5 B2
Hanwell W7 ... 108 C4
Andrews Rd E17 ... 35 A1
Andrew's Rd
Hillingdon UB10 ... 82 B6
Leytonstone E11 ... 54 C3
Newham E13 ... 99 B4
Andrews Rd N9 ... 18 C4
Andrew's Rd
Redbridge IG1 ... 56 B2
Surbiton KT6 ... 197 D3
Temple Fortune
NW11 ... 47 B3
Andrews Rd UB10 ... 60 B1
Andrew's Rd W14 264 B6
Andrews Rd NW9 ... 45 B1
Andrew's Rd NW2 .. 68 B2
Andrew's & St Mark's
CE Jun Sch KT6 ... 197 D4
Andrew's Sq
Notting Hill W11 ... 91 A1
Surbiton KT6 ... 197 D3
Andrew St EC4 ... 241 B3
Andrews Terr
WD19 ... 22 C5
Andrew's Twr
UB1 ... 108 A6
Andrews Way E3 ... 97 D3
Andrew's Wharf
SE1 ... 253 D2
Angela's Ursuline
Convent Sch E7 ... 77 B2
Anna Rd EN5 ... 12 D6
Anne RC Prim Sch
E1 ... 96 A3
Annes Catholic High
Sch for Girls (Upper)
N13 ... 32 C6
Anne's CE Prim Sch
SW18 ... 157 D6
Anne's Cl N6 ... 71 A5
Annes Cl WD19 ... 22 C6
Anne's Ct NW6 ... 91 A6
Annes Ct 8 SM2 .. 217 D2
Anne's Ct W1 ... 239 C1
Anne's Flats NW1 232 C2
Annes Gdns NW10 .. 88 B4
Anne's Pas E14 ... 97 B1
Anne's RC High Sch
for Girls EN2 ... 5 B1
Anne's RC Prim Sch
SE11 ... 138 B6 270 C6
Anne's Rd
Leyton E11 ... 76 B6
Wembley HA0 ... 65 D3
Anne's Row E14 ... 97 B1
Anne St E14 ... 97 B1
Anne's Trad Est 25
E14 ... 97 B1
Ann's IG11 ... 101 A6
Ann's CE Prim Sch
N15 ... 51 B4
Ann's Cres SW18 .. 158 A5
Ann's Ct NW4 ... 46 B6
St Ann's Ctr HA1 ... 42 C3
St Ann's Gdns NW5 ... 71 A2
St Ann's General Hospl
N4, N15 ... 51 A4
St Ann's Hill SW18 ... 158 A5
St Ann's Ho WC1 ... 234 A1
St Ann's La SW1 ... 259 D5
St Ann's Park Rd
SW18 ... 158 A5
St Ann's Rd 2 IG11 ... 101 A6
St Anns Rd SW13 ... 133 D4
St Ann's Rd
Edmonton N9 ... 17 D3
Harrow HA1 ... 42 C3
Shepherd's Bush
W11 ... 112 D6
Tottenham N15 ... 51 B4
St Ann's Sch
Ealing W7 ... 108 C5
Morden SM4 ... 201 D4
St Ann's St
SW1 ... 115 D3 259 D6
St Ann's Terr
NW8 ... 92 B5 229 D4
St Ann's Villas
W11 ... 113 A5 244 A3
St Ann's Way CR2 ... 220 D2
St Anselm RC Prim Sch
UB2 ... 107 B3
St Anselm's Ct
SW16 ... 182 A5
St Anselm's Pl W1 .. 248 C6
St Anselm's RC Prim
Sch
Harrow HA1 ... 42 C2
Upper Tooting
SW17 ... 159 A1
St Anselms Rd UB3 .. 105 D4
St Anthony's Ave IG8 .. 37 C3
St Anthony's Cl 8
E1 ... 118 A5
St Anthonys Cl
SW17 ... 158 C2
St Anthony's Ct
2 Balham SW12 ... 159 A5
Orpington BR6 ... 226 D6
Upper Tooting
SW17 ... 159 A2
St Anthony's Flats
NW1 ... 232 C3
St Anthony's Hospl
KT4 ... 200 D1
St Anthony's RC Prim
Sch
East Dulwich
SE22 ... 162 A5
Penge SE20 ... 184 B2
Upton E7 ... 77 B1
St Anthony's Way
TW14 ... 127 D1
St Antony's RC Prim Sch
IG8 ... 37 A6
St Antony's Rd E7 ... 77 B1
St Arvans Cl CR0 ... 221 C5
St Asaph Ct SE4 ... 140 D2
St Asaph Rd SE4 ... 140 D2
St Aubins Ct N1 ... 235 D6
St Aubyn's Ave
Hounslow TW3,
TW4 ... 151 C6
Wimbledon SW19 ... 179 B5
St Aubyns Cl BR6 ... 227 D5
St Aubyn's Ct SW19 .. 179 A4
St Aubyns Gdns
BR6 ... 227 D6
St Aubyns E18 ... 54 D5
St Aubyn's Rd SE19 .. 183 D4
St Aubyn's Sch IG8 ... 36 D3
St Audrey Ave DA7 ... 147 C3
St Augustine of
Canterbury CE Prim
Sch DA17 ... 125 B2
St Augustine's Ave
BR1, BR2 ... 210 A4
Ealing W5 ... 88 A4
South Croydon CR2 .. 221 A1
Wembley HA9 ... 66 A5
St Augustine's CE High
Sch NW6 ... 91 C5
St Augustine's CE Prim
Sch NW6 ... 91 D5
St Augustines Ct
BR3 ... 185 A1
St Augustine's Ct
E11 ... 54 D1
St Augustines Ct 4
EN5 ... 14 A6
St Augustine's Ho
NW1 ... 232 C2
Upper Tooting
SW17 ... 180 D6
St Augustine's RC
Prim Sch
Ilford IG2 ... 56 D4
W6 ... 135 A6 264 B5
St Augustine's Rd
Camden Town
NW1 ... 71 D1
DA17 ... 125 B2
St Augustines's RC Prim
Sch SE6 ... 186 A5
St Austell Cl HA8 ... 26 B1
St Austell Rd SE13 ... 142 B3
St Awdry's Rd IG11 ... 79 B1
St Barnabas CE Prim
Sch SW1 ... 115 A1 258 B2
St Barnabas Cl
Beckenham BR3 ... 186 A1
11 Dulwich Village
SE22 ... 161 C6
St Barnabas Ct HA3 ... 24 A2
St Barnabas' Gdns
KT8 ... 195 C4
St Barnabas Ho
CR4 ... 181 A3
St Barnabas Rd
Mitcham CR4 ... 181 A3
Sutton SM1 ... 218 B3
Walthamstow E17 ... 53 C3
Woodford IG8 ... 37 C3
St Barnabas & St
Philip's CE Prim Sch
W8 ... 113 C3 255 A5
St Barnabas St SW1. 258 B2
St Barnabas Terr E9 ... 74 D3
St Barnabas Villas
SW8 ... 138 A4 270 B2
St Bartholomew's CE
Prim Sch SE26 ... 184 C6
St Bartholomews CE
Prim Sch SE26 ... 162 C1
St Bartholomew's Cl
SE26 ... 184 C6
St Bartholomews Ct 6
E6 ... 100 A6
St Bartholomew's Hospl
EC1 ... 94 D2 241 D3
St Bartholomew's Rd
E6 ... 100 B5
St Bede's RC Inf Sch
SW12 ... 159 D3
St Bede's RC Prim Sch
RM6 ... 58 C4
St Benedict's Cl
SW17 ... 181 A5
St Benedict's Jun Sch
W5 ... 87 C2
St Benedict's Sch
W5 ... 87 D2
St Benets Cl SW17 ... 158 C2
St Benet's Gr SM5 ... 202 A2
St Benet's Pl EC3 ... 252 D6
St Bernadette RC Jun
Sch SW12 ... 159 C4
St Bernadette's Prim
Sch HA3 ... 44 B5
St Bernadette's RC Prim
Sch UB10 ... 82 D6
St Bernard Ho 6
E14 ... 120 A3
St Bernards Cl 8
SE27 ... 183 B6
St Bernards Ho 1
KT6 ... 214 A6
St Bernard's Rd E6 ... 99 D6
St Bernards CR0 ... 221 C5
St Blaise Ave BR1 ... 187 B1
St Bonaventure's RC
Sch E7 ... 77 A1
St Boniface RC Prim
Sch SW17 ... 180 D5
St Botolph St E1,
EC3 ... 95 D1 243 C2
St Brelades Ct N1 ... 235 D6
St Bride's Ave EC4 .. 241 C1
Edgware HA8 ... 26 B2
St Brides Cl DA18 ... 124 D4
St Bride's Pas EC4 .. 241 C1
St Bride St
EC4 ... 94 D1 241 C2
St Catherines Cl
Chessington KT9 ... 213 D2
Upper Tooting
SW17 ... 158 C2
St Catherines Ct
TW13 ... 150 A3
St Catherine's Ct 8
W4 ... 111 C3
St Catherine's Dr
SE14 ... 140 D3
St Catherines Farm Ct
HA4 ... 39 A3
St Catherines Mews
SW3 ... 257 C4
St Catherine's RC Sch
EN5 ... 1 C1
St Catherine's RC Sch
for Girls DA6 ... 169 D6
St Catherines Rd
Chingford E4 ... 19 C2
Ruislip HA4 ... 39 B3
St Catherine's Sch
TW1 ... 153 A2
St Catherines Twr 5
E10 ... 53 D2
St Cecilia's CE Sch
SW18 ... 157 B3
St Cecilia's Cl SM3 ... 201 A1
St Cecilia's RC Prim Sch
SM3 ... 216 D6
St Chads Cl KT6 ... 197 C2
St Chad's Gdns RM6 ... 59 A2
St Chad's Pl WC1 ... 233 C2
St Chad's RC Prim Sch
SE25 ... 205 C4
St Chad's Rd RM6 ... 59 A2
St Chad's St WC1 ... 233 B2
St Charles' Hospl
W10 ... 90 D2
St Charles Pl W10 ... 91 A2
St Charles RC Prim Sch
W10 ... 90 D2
St Charles RC Sixth
Form Coll W10 ... 90 D2
St Charles Sq W10 ... 90 D2
St Christina's Sch
NW8 ... 92 C5 230 B4
St Christopher's Cl
TW7 ... 130 C4
St Christophers Ct 15
N19 ... 71 C5
St Christophers Dr
UB3 ... 106 B6
St Christophers Gdns
CR7 ... 204 C6
St Christopher's Ho
NW1 ... 232 C3
St Christopher's Mews
SM6 ... 219 C3
St Christopher's Pl
W1 ... 238 B2
St Christopher's Sch
Beckenham BR3 ... 186 A1
Hampstead NW3 ... 70 B3
Wembley HA9 ... 66 B5
St Clair Dr KT4 ... 216 B4
St Clair Ho 17 E3 ... 97 B4
St Clair Rd E13 ... 99 B5
St Clair's Rd CR0 ... 221 C6
St Clare Bsns Pk
TW12 ... 174 A4
St Clare St EC3 ... 243 C1
St Clement Danes CE
Prim Sch
WC2 ... 94 B1 240 C1
St Clement & St James
CE Prim Sch
W11 ... 113 A5 244 A4
St Clements Ct N7 ... 72 B2
St Clement's Ct EC3. 252 D6
St Clements Ct
7 SE14 ... 140 D6
8 Shepherd's Bush
W11 ... 112 D6
St Clements Ho E1 .. 243 C3
Walton-on-T KT12 ... 194 A2
St Clement's Hts
SE26 ... 184 A6
St Clement's La
WC2 ... 240 D1
St Clements Mans 3
SW6 ... 134 D6
St Clements St N7 ... 72 C1
St Cloud Rd SE27 ... 183 B6
St Columba's Ct E15 .. 76 C4
St Columbas Ho 2
E17 ... 53 D5
St Columba's RC Boys
Sch DA6 ... 169 D6
St Columb's Ho 11
W10 ... 91 A2
St Crispins Cl NW3 ... 70 C4
St Crispin's Cl UB1 ... 85 B1
St Crispins Ct 1 UB1 .. 85 B1
St Cross St
EC1 ... 94 C2 241 B4
St Cuthberts Gdns 2
HA5 ... 23 B3
St Cuthberts Rd N13 .. 32 C4
St Cuthbert's Rd
NW2 ... 69 B2
St Cuthbert with St
Matthias Prim Sch
SW5 ... 113 D1 255 C2
St Cyprian's Greek
Orthodox Prim Sch
CR7 ... 183 A2
St Cyprian's St
SW17 ... 180 D6
St Davids Cl
27 Bermondsey
SE16 ... 118 B1
Wembley HA9 ... 67 A5
St David's Cl BR4 ... 207 D2
St David's Coll BR4. 207 D2
St David's Ct
Bromley BR1 ... 210 D6
8 Southall UB1 ... 86 A1
St David's Ct *continued*
1 Walthamstow E17 .. 54 A6
St Davids Ct 5 E11 ... 55 B4
St David's Dr HA8 ... 26 B2
St David's Pl NW4 ... 46 B2
St David's Sch
TW15 ... 148 B1
St David's Sq E14 ... 119 D1
St Denis Rd SE27 ... 183 B6
St Dionis Rd SW6 ... 135 B3
St Domingo Ho
SE18 ... 122 B3
St Dominic RC Prim Sch
NW5 ... 70 D3
St Dominics RC Prim
Sch E9 ... 75 A2
St Dominic's Sixth Form
Coll (RC) HA1 ... 64 C6
St Donatt's Rd SE14 .. 141 B4
St Dunstan's Alley
EC3 ... 253 A5
St Dunstan's Ave
W3 ... 111 B6
St Dunstan's CE Prim
Sch SM3 ... 217 A1
St Dunstans SM1 ... 217 B2
St Dunstans Cl UB3 .. 105 D2
St Dunstan's Coll
SE6 ... 163 C3
St Dunstan's Ct EC4. 241 B1
St Dunstan's Gdns
W3 ... 111 B6
St Dunstan's Hill
Cheam SM1, SM3 ... 217 A3
EC3 ... 253 A5
St Dunstan's La
Beckenham BR3 ... 208 A4
EC3 ... 253 A5
St Dunstan's Rd
Cranford TW5 ... 128 B3
Feltham TW13 ... 149 D1
Hammersmith W6 ... 112 D1
Hanwell W7 ... 108 C4
St Dunstans Rd E7 ... 77 C2
St Dunstan's Rd
SE25 ... 205 D5
St Edmund RC Sch
E14 ... 119 C2
St Edmunds Ave HA4 .. 39 B3
St Edmunds Cl
DA18 ... 124 D4
St Edmund's Cl NW8 230 C5
St Edmunds Cl
SW17 ... 158 C2
St Edmund's Ct NW8 230 C5
St Edmunds Dr HA7 ... 25 A2
St Edmund's La
TW2 ... 151 D4
St Edmund's RC Prim
Sch
Edmonton N9 ... 18 B3
Twickenham TW2 ... 151 D4
St Edmunds Rd N9 ... 18 A4
St Edmund's Rd IG1 .. 56 B3
St Edmund's Sq
SW13 ... 134 C6
St Edmund's Terr
NW8 ... 92 D6 230 C5
St Edward's CE Comp
Sch RM7 ... 59 C3
St Edward's Cl NW11 .. 47 C3
St Edwards Ct 3
E10 ... 54 A2
St Edward's Ct NW11 .. 47 C3
St Edwards RC Prim
Sch E6 ... 99 C6
St Edward's RC Prim
Sch NW1 ... 92 C3 237 B5
St Egberts Way E4 ... 20 A3
St Elizabeth Ct
North Finchley N12 ... 30 A6
9 Walthamstow E10 .. 53 D2
St Elizabeth RC Prim
Sch E2 ... 96 C5
St Elizabeth's RC Prim
Sch TW10 ... 154 B5
St Elmo Rd W12 ... 111 D4
St Elmos Rd SE16 ... 119 A4
St Elphege's RC Inf Sch
SM6 ... 220 A2
St Elphege's RC Jun Sch
SM6 ... 220 A2
SS Peter & Paul's RC
Prim Sch
Ilford IG1 ... 79 B5
Mitcham CR4 ... 202 D5
St Erkenwald Mews
IG11 ... 101 B6
St Erkenwald Rd
IG11 ... 101 B6
St Ermin's Hill SW1. 259 C6
St Ervan's Rd W10 ... 91 B2
St Eugene de Mazenod
Rc Prim Sch NW6 ... 69 C1
St Faith's CE Prim Sch
SW18 ... 158 A6
St Faith's Cl EN2 ... 5 A4
St Faith's Rd SE24 ... 160 D3
St Fillans Rd SE6 ... 164 A4
St Francesca Cabrini
Prim Sch SE23 ... 162 C5
St Francis Cl BR5 ... 211 C3
St Francis de Sales RC
Jun & Inf Sch N17 .. 33 D3
St Francis' Ho NW1. 232 C3
St Francis Lodge
HA0 ... 64 D5
St Francis of Assisi RC
Prim Sch W11 ... 112 D6
St Francis Pl SW12 ... 159 B5
St Francis RC Prim
Sch
SE15 ... 140 A5
Stratford E15 ... 76 C3
St Francis Rd SE22 ... 139 C1
St Francis Way IG1 ... 79 B4
St Francis Xavier Sixth
Form Coll SW12 ... 159 B5
St Frideswides Mews 5
E14 ... 98 A1
St Gabriel's CE Prim
Sch SW1 ... 115 C1 259 A1
St Gabriels Cl 3 E14 .. 97 D2
St Gabriel's Cl E11 ... 55 B1
St Gabriels Ct N11 ... 31 D3
St Gabriel's Rd NW2 .. 68 D3
St George Ho SW11. 268 B1
ST GEORGE IN THE
EAST ... 118 A6
St George's Ave
Ealing W5 ... 109 D4
Kingsbury NW9 ... 45 B5
Southall UB1 ... 107 B6
Tufnell Pk N7 ... 71 D4
Upton E7 ... 77 B1
St George's Battersea
CE Prim Sch
SW8 ... 137 C5 269 B3
St George's Bickley CE
Prim Sch BR1 ... 187 D1
St George's Bldgs
SE11 ... 261 D5
St George's Cath
NW1 ... 231 D2
St George's Cath RC Jun
& Inf Sch
SE1 ... 116 D3 261 C6
St George's CE Prim
Sch SE5 ... 139 C5
St George's Circ
SE1 ... 116 D3 261 C6
St Georges Cl SE28 .. 102 D1
St George's Cl NW11 .. 47 B3
St Georges Cl
Nine Elms SW8 ... 269 B2
Wembley HA0 ... 65 A5
St Georges Coll N7 ... 72 C5
St George's Ct SW3. 257 A4
St Georges Ct HA3 ... 43 A3
St George's Ct SW7. 256 A5
St Georges Ct E6 ... 100 B3
St George's Ct SE1 .. 261 C5
St Georges Ct
Penge SE20 ... 184 B2
Putney SW15 ... 135 B1
Walthamstow E17 ... 54 B4
St George's Dr
Ickenham UB10 ... 60 B6
South Oxhey WD19 ... 23 A6
SW1 ... 115 C1 259 A2
St George's Field
W2 ... 92 C1 237 B1
St George's Gdns
KT6 ... 214 D6
St George's Gr
SW17 ... 158 B1
St Georges Hanover Sq
Sch W1 ... 115 A6 248 B5
St George's Ho NW1 232 B3
St George's Hospl
SW17 ... 180 B5
St George's Ind Est
KT2 ... 175 D5
St Georges Ind Est
N22 ... 32 D3
St George's La EC3 .. 253 A6
St Georges Lo N10 ... 49 C5
St Georges Mews 11
NW1 ... 70 D1
St George's Mews
2 Rotherhithe
SE8 ... 119 B2
SE1 ... 261 B6
St Georges Pl N7 ... 71 D4
St George's RC Cath
SE1 ... 116 C3 261 B6
St George's RC Prim
Sch
Enfield EN2 ... 5 B3
Harrow HA1 ... 64 D5

St George's RC Sec Sch W9 91 D5
St Georges Rd W4 111 B4
St George's Rd BR3 185 D2
St Georges Rd BR1 210 B6
St Georges Rd Ctr RM9 81 B4
St Georges Rd RM9 81 A4
St George's Rd
Ealing W7 108 D5
Enfield EN1 5 D5
Feltham TW13 172 D6
Isleworth TW1 153 B6
2 Kingston u T KT2 176 C3
Leyton E10 76 A5
Mitcham CR4 203 B6
Newington SE1 116 D3 261 C5
Palmers Green N13 16 B2
St Georges Rd BR5 211 B3
St George's Rd
Redbridge IG1 56 B2
Richmond TW9 132 B2
Sidcup DA14 190 D4
Temple Fortune NW11 47 B3
Upton E7 77 B2
Wallington SM6 219 B3
St Georges Rd W BR1 188 A1
St George's Rd SW19 179 B4
St George's Residences 4 SW2 160 C6
St Georges's Ct EC4 241 C2
St Georges Sh & L Ctr HA1 42 C3
St Georges Sq 1 E14 119 A6
St George's Sq
Kingston u T KT3 199 C6
Rotherhithe SE8 119 B2
SW1 115 D1 259 C1
St George's Square Mews SW1 259 C1
St George's Sq E7 77 B1
St Georges Terr
Hampstead NW1 70 D1
NW1 230 D6
St George St W1 115 B6 248 D6
St George's Way SE15 139 C6
St George's Wlk CR0 221 A5
St George the Martyr CE Prim Sch WC1 94 B3 240 D5
St George Wharf SW8 270 A6
St Gerards Cl SW4 159 C6
St German's Pl SE3 143 A4
St German's Rd SE23 163 A3
St Gildas' RC Jun Sch N8 50 A2
ST GILES 94 A1
St Giles Ave
Dagenham RM10 81 D1
Uxbridge UB10 61 A4
St Giles Cir WC1 93 D1 239 D2
St Giles Cl BR6 227 B3
Dagenham RM10 81 D1
Heston TW3 129 A5
St Giles Coll WC1 94 A2 240 B4
St Giles Ct
Ealing W13 109 C5
WC2 240 A2
St Giles High St WC2 93 D1 239 D2
St Giles Ho 2 EN5 2 A1
St Giles Hospl SE5 139 C4
St Giles Ho SW16 160 A1
St Giles Pas WC2 239 D1
St Giles Rd SE5 139 C4
St Giles' Sch CR2 220 D2
St Giles Twr 3 SE5 139 C4
St Gilles Ho 18 E2 96 D5
St Gothard Rd SE21, SE27 183 B6
St Gregory Cl HA4 62 C4
St Gregory RC High Sch HA3 43 D4
St Gregory's RC Prim Sch W5 87 D2
St Helena Ho WC1 234 A1
St Helena Pier TW9 153 D6
St Helena Rd SE16 118 D2
St Helena St WC1 234 A1
St Helena Terr 31 TW9 153 D6
St Helens Coll UB10 60 C1
St Helen's Cres SW16 182 B2
St Helen's Gdns W10 90 D1
St Helen's Pl EC3 243 A2
St Helen's RC Inf Sch E17 54 A4
St Helen's RC Prim Sch E13 99 A3
St Helen's RC Sch SW9 138 C2
St Helens Rd 5 DA18 124 D4
St Helen's Rd
Ealing W13 109 C5
Redbridge IG1 56 B3
Thornton Heath SW16 182 B2
St Helens KT7 196 D2
ST HELIER 202 B2
St Helier Ave SM4 202 A3
St Helier Ct 4 N1 95 C6
St Helier Hospl SM5 202 A1
St Heliers Ave TW3, TW4 151 C6
St Helier's Rd E10 54 A3
St Helier Sta SM4 201 C3
St Hilary's Ct BR1 210 D6
St Hilda's Ave TW15 170 A5
St Hilda's Cl NW6 68 D1
St Hildas Cl SW17 158 C2
St Hilda's Rd SW13 134 B6
St Hildas Wharf E1 118 C5
St Hubert's Ho 2 E14 119 C3
St Hughes Cl SW17 158 C2
St Hugh's Rd SE20 184 B3
St Ignatius Coll EN1 6 B6
St Ignatius' RC Prim Sch N15 51 D3
St Ignatius RC Prim Sch TW16 172 A2
St Ives Ct NW2 69 A2
St Ivian Ct 3 N10 31 B1
ST JAMES 115 C5
St James Apartments 2 E17 53 A4
St James' Ave W13 109 A5
St James Ave
East Barnet N20 14 C1
Sutton SM1 217 C3
St James CE Jun Sch E7 77 A3
St James CE Prim Sch EN3 6 C3
St James' CE Prim Sch SE16 118 A3
St James Cl Barnet EN4 2 B1
East Barnet N20 14 C1
St James' Cl
New Malden KT3 199 D4
Ruislip HA4 62 C6
St James' Ct W4 111 B3
St James Ct
26 Bethnal Green E2 96 A4
10 Brentford W4 110 C1
1 Bromley BR2 187 A1
Forest Hill SE23 163 A3
St James' Ct 7 KT1 198 A6
St James Ct SE3 143 B4
St James' Ct SW1 259 B6
St James Ct
Thornton Heath CR0 204 D2
Wanstead E12 77 C6
St James Gate IG9 21 B3
St James Gdns IG6 58 B5
St James' Gdns HA0 66 A1
St James Ho N5 72 C3
St James Hts 3 SE18 123 A1
St James Independent Schs W14 113 A2 254 B4
St James Ind Mews 16 SE1 118 A1
St James Ind Sch for Boys TW1 153 A2
St James' Mans NW6 69 C1
St James Mews E14 120 A3
St James' RC High Sch NW9 27 D2
St James RC Prim Sch BR5 210 D4
St James Rd SM5 218 C5
St James' Rd
Edmonton N9 18 B2
Forest Gate E15 76 D3
St James Rd KT1 175 D1
St James' Rd
Mitcham CR4 181 A3
Surbiton KT6 197 D3
St James Rd SM1, SM2 217 C3
St James's App EC2 243 A5
St James's Ave
Beckenham BR3 207 A6
Hampton TW12 174 A5
South Hackney E2 96 C5
St James's CE Prim Sch N10 49 A5
St James School Flats 5 N7 72 C3
St James's Cl NW8 230 C5
St James's Cloisters 2 SE22 139 D1
St James's Cl
Upper Tooting SW17 158 D2
Woolwich SE18 123 A1
St James's Cotts 14 TW10 153 D6
St James's Cres SW9 138 C2
St James's Ct
8 Edmonton N18 34 A5
Harrow HA1 43 A3
St James's Dr
Balham SW12, SW17 158 D4
Upper Tooting SW17 158 D3
St James's Gdns W11 113 A5 244 A4
St James's Gr SW11 136 D3
St James's Hatcham CE Prim Sch SE14 141 A4
St James's La N10 49 B5
St James's SE14 141 A4
St James's Market SW1 249 C5
St James's Mews E17 53 A4
St James's Pal* SW1 115 C5 249 B3
St James's Park Sta SW1 115 D3 259 C6
St James's Pas EC3 243 B1
St James's Pk* SW1 249 C2
St James's Pk CR0 205 A2
St James's Pl SW1 115 C5 249 A3
St James's RC Prim Sch TW2 152 C1
St James's Rd
Bermondsey SE1, SE16 118 A2
Hampton TW12 173 D5
Peckham SE1 140 A6
Thornton Heath CR0 205 B2
St James's & St Michael's CE Prim Sch W2 114 A6 246 B6
St James's Sq SW1 115 C5 249 B4
St James's St SW1 115 C5 249 A4
Walthamstow E17 53 A4
St James's Terrace Mews NW8 230 C5
St James's Terr NW8 230 C6
2 Upper Tooting SW12 159 A3
St James St W6 112 C1
St James Street Sta E17 53 A4
St James The Great RC Prim Sch
Camberwell SE15 139 D4
South Norwood CR7 182 D1
St James Way DA14 191 A5
St James Wlk EC1 241 C6
St Jerome's Gr UB3 83 A1
St Joachim's RC Prim Sch E16 99 C1
St Joan of Arc RC Prim Sch N5 73 A4
St Joan's Rd N9 17 D2
St John Baptist CE Prim Sch BR1 186 A6
St John Evangelist RC Prim Sch N1 94 D5 234 C4
St John Fisher RC Fst & Mid Sch HA5 41 C5
St John Fisher RC Prim Sch
DA18 125 A3
Wembley UB6 87 C4
West Barnes SW20 200 D4
St John of Jerusalem CE Prim Sch E9 74 C1
ST JOHNS 141 C3
St John & St James CE Prim Sch
Edmonton N18 33 D5
Hackney E9 74 C3
St John's Angell Town CE Prim Sch SW9 138 C3
St John's Ave
Dagenham NW10 89 D6
Friern Barnet N11 30 D5
Putney SW15 156 D6
St John's CE First Sch HA7 25 A6
St John's CE JMI Sch N11 30 D6
St John's CE Prim Sch
Buckhurst Hill IG9 21 B3
Croydon CR0 222 D5
Enfield EN2 4 D6
Fulham SW6 135 A4 264 B2
Kingston u T KT1 198 A6
Penge SE20 184 C3
SE17 117 A2 262 B3
South Hackney E2 96 C5
Whetstone N20 14 A2
St John's CE Sch Stanmore HA7 25 A6
St John's Church Rd E9 74 C3
St Johns Cl N14 15 C5
St John's Cl SW6 265 A4
Wembley HA9 66 A3
St Johns Concert Hall* SW1 260 A5
St John's Cotts 2 SE20 184 C3
St John's Cres SW9 138 C2
St John's Ct IG9 21 B3
St Johns Ct 39 E1 118 B5
St John's Ct
Finsbury Pk N4 72 D6
Hammersmith W6 112 B2
2 Harrow HA1 42 D3
Saint John's Ct N5 72 D4
St John's Ct
Isleworth TW7 130 D3
Kingston u T KT1 198 A5
Lewisham SE13 142 A3
Leytonstone E11 54 D1
5 South Hampstead NW3 70 A2
St Johns Dr KT12 194 C1
St John's Dr SW18 157 D3
St John's Est SE1 253 C1
St John's Gdns W11 113 B6 244 C5
St John's Gr
3 Barnes SW13 133 D3
1 Richmond TW9 132 A1
Upper Holloway N19 71 C6
St John's Highbury Vale CE Prim Sch N5 72 D5
St John's Hill Gr SW11 136 B1
St John's Hill SW11 136 B1
St John's Ho 1 E14 120 A2
St Johns Ho
5 SE17 139 B6
Streatham SW16 182 A4
St John's La EC1 94 D2 241 D4
St John's Lodge 8 SE8 141 C4
St John's Mans E5 74 C3
St John's Par W13 109 B5
St John's Park Mans N19 71 C5
St John's Par 3 DA14 190 B6
St John's Path EC1 241 C5
St John's Pk SE3 143 A5
St John's Pl EC1 241 C5
St John's Prim Sch W13 109 A6
St John's RC Prim Sch SE16 119 A4
St John's Rd
Barking IG11 101 C6
Battersea SW11 136 C1
Canning Town E16 99 A1
Carshalton SM5 218 C5
Chingford E4 35 D6
Croydon CR0 220 D5
DA16 146 B2
East Ham E6 100 A6
East Molesey KT8 196 B5
Feltham TW13 173 B6
Harrow HA1 42 D3
St Johns Rd IG2 57 C2
St John's Rd TW7 130 D3
St Johns Rd KT3 199 A6
St John's Rd
Orpington BR5 211 C3
Penge SE20 184 C4
Richmond TW9 132 A1
Sidcup DA14 190 B6
Southall UB2 107 A3
Sutton SM1 217 D6
Teddington KT1 175 C1
St John's Rd *continued*
Temple Fortune NW11 47 B3
Tottenham N15 51 C3
Walthamstow E17 36 A1
Wembley HA9 66 A3
Wimbledon SW19 179 A4
St John's & St Clements CE Prim Sch SE15 140 A2
St John's Sch HA6 22 B4
St John's Sq EC1 94 D3 241 C5
St Johns Sta SE8 141 C3
St John St EC1 94 D3 241 C6
St John's Terr
Enfield EN2 5 B6
North Kensington W10 90 D3
SE18 145 B6
Upton E7 77 B2
St Johnstone Ho 17 N12 29 D6
St John's Upper Holloway CE Prim Sch N19 71 D6
St John's Vale SE8 141 C3
St John's Villas
4 Friern Barnet N11 30 D5
Upper Holloway N19 71 D6
W8 255 D5
St John's Way N19 49 D1
ST JOHN'S WOOD 92 B5
St John's Wood Ct NW8 229 D1
St John's Wood High St NW8 92 C5 230 A3
St John's Wood Park NW8 92 B6 229 C6
St John's Wood Pre-Prep Sch NW8 92 C4 230 A2
St John's Wood Rd NW8 92 B4 229 D1
St John's Wood Sta NW8 92 B5 229 C4
St John's Wood Terr NW8 92 C5 230 A4
St John the Baptist CE Jun Sch KT1 175 D3
St John the Baptist CE Prim Sch N1 95 B5 235 D3
St John the Divine CE Jun & Inf Sch SE5 138 D5
St John Vianney RC Prim Sch N8 50 D5
St Joseph RC Prim Sch W7 108 C5
St Joseph's Acad SE3 142 C2
St Josephs Cl BR6 227 D4
St Joseph's Cl W10 91 A2
St Joseph's Coll Mill Hill Missionaries NW7 27 D6
St Joseph's Convent Sch E11 55 A3
St Joseph's Ct E4 20 B4
St Josephs Ct
3 Dagenham NW10 89 D5
20 Walthamstow E10 53 D2
St Joseph's Dr UB1 107 B5
St Joseph's Flats NW1 232 C2
St Josephs Gr NW4 46 B5
St Joseph's Ho W6 112 D2
St Joseph's Hospice E9, E8 96 B6
St Joseph's RC Coll SW16 182 D4
St Joseph's RC Fst & Mid Sch HA3 25 A1
St Joseph's RC Inf & Jun Schs
Hendon NW4 46 B5
SE5 139 A5
St Joseph's RC Inf Sch
Leyton E10 75 C6
South Norwood SE19 183 A4
St Joseph's RC Jun & Inf Schs HA9 66 B3
St Joseph's RC Jun Sch
South Norwood SE19 183 A4
Walthamstow E10 53 D1
St Joseph's RC Prim Sch
Barking IG11 101 A6
St Joseph's RC Prim Sch *continued*
Bermondsey SE16 118
Bromley BR1 187
Chelsea SW3 114 D2 257
Dagenham RM9 81
Deptford SE8 141
Greenwich SE10 120
Kingston u T KT1 176
Paddington W9 92 A4 229
Rotherhithe SE16 118
St Giles WC2 94 A1 240
Upper Holloway N19 49
Wandsworth SW18 157
Willesden NW10 67
St Joseph's Rd N9 18
St Joseph's St SW8 268
St Joseph's Vale SE3 142
St Jude & St Paul's CE Prim Sch N1 73
St Jude's CE Prim Sch SE24 160
St Judes Ho 6 W10 91
St Jude's Prim Sch SE1 116 D3 261
St Jude's Rd E2 96
St Jude St N16 73
St Julian's Cl SW16 182
St Julian's Farm Rd SE27, SW16 182
St Julian's Rd NW6 91
St Katharine's Ho N1 234
St Katharine's Prec NW1 231
St Katharine's Way E1 117 D5 253
St Katherines Rd DA18 124
St Katherine's Row EC3 243
St Katherine's Wlk 1 W11 112
St Keverne Rd SE9 188
St Kilda Rd BR6 211
Ealing W13 109
St Kilda's Rd
Harrow HA1 42
Stamford Hill N16 51
St Kitts Terr SE19 183
St Laurence's Cl NW6 90
St Lawrence CE Jun Sch KT8 196
St Lawrence Cl HA8 26
St Lawrence Ct N1 235
St Lawrence Dr HA5 40
St Lawrence Ho SE1 263
St Lawrence RC Prim Sch TW13 150
St Lawrence St E14 120
St Lawrence Terr W10 91
St Lawrence Way SW9 138
St Leonard's Ave E4 36
St Leonards Ave HA3 43
St Leonard's CE Prim Sch SW16 181
St Leonards Cl 4 DA16 146
St Leonards Ct SW14 133
St Leonard's Ct N1 235
St Leonard's Gdns TW5 129
St Leonards Gdns IG1 79
St Leonard's Hospl N1 95
St Leonard's Rd
Becontree NW10 89
Claygate KT10 212
Croydon CR0 220
Ealing W13 109
Kingston u T KT6 197
St Leonards Rd SW14 133
St Leonard's Rd
South Bromley E14 98
Thames Ditton KT7 197
St Leonards Rise BR6 227
St Leonard's Sq
Camden Town NW5 71
Kingston u T KT6 197
St Leonard's St E3 97
St Leonard's Terr SW3 114 D1 257
St Leonard's Wlk SW16 182
St Loo Ave SW3 136 C6 267

Loo Ct SW3 267 C6
Louis Rd SE27 183 B6
Loy's Rd N17 51 D6
Lucia Dr E15 98 D6
Luke Prim Sch
16 98 D1
LUKE'S 95 A3
Luke's Ave
lapham SW4 137 D1
nfield EN2 5 B5
lford IG1 78 D3
Luke's CE Prim Sch
ubitt Town E14 120 B2
ingston u T KT2 176 B2
addington W9 91 B4
horeditch
EC1 95 A4 235 B1
Vest Norwood SE27 183 A5
Luke's Cl
roydon SE25 206 B3
t Luke's EC1 95 A3 242 B6
Luke's Ct W11 91 B1
Lukes Ct 6 E10 53 D2
Luke's Hospl
V1 93 C3 239 A5
Luke's Mews W11 91 B1
Luke's Path 1
G1 78 D3
Luke's RC Sixth Form
Coll DA14 189 D5
Luke's Rd
lotting Hill W11 91 B2
Jxbridge UB10 60 A1
Luke's Sq E16 98 D1
Luke's St SW3 257 B2
Luke's Woodside
Hospl N10 49 A5
Malo Ave N9 18 C1
Margaret
Clitherow RC Prim
Sch
Neasden NW10 67 B4
Voolwich SE28 124 B5
MARGARETS 153 A5
Margarets Ave
W15 170 D5
Margaret's Ave
M3 217 A5
Margarets Ave
A15 167 B1
Margaret's Ave
Harringay N8, N15 50 D5
Harrow HA2 64 A5
Margarets Ave
Hillingdon UB8 82 C3
Whetstone N20 14 A3
Margarets IG11 101 B6
Margarets Bsns Ctr
1 TW1 153 B5
Margaret's CE Prim
Sch
Barking IG11 79 A1
Voolwich SE18 123 A1
Margaret's Cres
W15 156 B6
Margaret's Ct
eyton E15 76 C4
Putney SW15 134 B1
E1 252 C3
9 Twickenham
TW1 153 B5
Margaret's Dr
W1 153 B6
Margaret's Gr
eyton E11 76 D5
E18 145 A6
wickenham TW1 153 A5
Margaret's La
V8 113 D3 255 C5
Margaret's Lee CE
Prim Sch SE13 142 C1
Margarets Lo
V3 110 D4
Margaret's Pass
E13 142 C2
Margaret's Path 4
E18 123 A1
Margaret's Rd
E4 141 B1
Margarets Rdbt
W1 153 B6
Margarets Rd HA8 26 D5
Margaret's Rd
anwell W7 108 C4
sleworth TW1 153 B6
ensal Green NW10 90 C4
Margarets Rd HA4 39 B3
Margaret's Rd
ottenham N17 51 C6
Vanstead E12 77 C6
Margaret's Sch
W3 69 D4
Margaret's Sta
W1 153 B5

St Margaret's Terr
SE18 123 A1
St Margaret St SW1 250 A1
St Margret's Ct N11 31 A6
St Mark's CE Acad
CR4 181 B1
St Mark's CE Prim
Sch
Bromley BR2 209 A6
Croydon SE25 206 A5
Kennington
SE11 138 B6 270 D6
St Mark's Cl
Barnet EN5 1 D2
Harrow HA1 43 B1
St Marks Cl 5 SE10 142 A5
St Mark's Cres
NW1 93 A6 231 B6
St Mark's Ct
Hanwell W7 108 C4
8 Walthamstow E10 53 D2
St Marks Gate E9 75 B1
St Mark's Gr
SW10 135 D5 265 D4
St Mark's Hill KT6 198 A3
St Mark's Ho 8 E17 54 A5
St Marks Ho 6
SE17 139 B6
St Mark's Hospl
EC1 94 D4 234 D2
St Mark's Hts 25
KT6 198 A4
St Marks Ind Est
E16 121 D5
St Mark's Mans 14
N4 72 B6
St Mark's Pl
Notting Hill W11 91 A1
Wimbledon SW19 179 B4
St Mark's Prim Sch
Hanwell W7 108 C4
Mitcham CR4 180 D1
Upper Holloway N19 72 A6
St Mark's RC Sch
TW3 129 C2
St Mark's Rd
Bromley BR2 209 B6
Croydon SE25 206 A5
Ealing W5 110 A5
Enfield EN1 17 D6
Hanwell W7 108 C4
Mitcham CR4 181 A1
St Marks Rd 15
NW10 90 D1
St Mark's Rd
North Kensington
W10 90 D2
Notting Hill W11 91 A1
Teddington TW11 175 B3
St Mark's Rise E8 73 D3
St Mark's Sq NW1 231 A5
St Mark St E1 95 D1 243 D1
St Martha's Convent
Jun Sch EN5 1 A1
St Martha's Senior Sch
EN4 1 C4
St Martin-in-the-Fields
High Sch for Girls
SW2 160 C3
St Martin of Porres RC
Prim Sch N11 31 C4
St Martin's Almshouses
NW1 232 A6
St Martin's App HA4 39 C2
St Martin's Ave E6 99 D5
St Martins Cl DA18 124 D4
St Martin's Cl
Enfield EN1 6 B4
NW1 232 A6
St Martins Cl WD19 22 C6
St Martins Ct N1 95 C6
St Martin's Ct WC2 250 A6
West Norwood
SE27 160 D2
St Martins La BR3 207 D4
St Martin's La
WC2 116 A6 250 A5
St Martin's Le Grand
EC1 242 A2
St Martin's Pl WC2 250 A5
St Martin's Rd
Edmonton N9 18 B2
Finchley N2 30 B2
Stockwell SW9 138 B3
St Martin's Sch NW7 27 B5
St Martin's St WC2 249 D5
St Martin's Way
SW17 158 A1
St Mary Abbots CE Prim
Sch W8 113 D4 245 C1
St Mary Abbot's Ct
W14 254 C5
St Mary Abbot's Pl
W8 254 D5
St Mary Abbots Terr
W14 254 D5

St Mary at Hill
EC3 117 C6 253 A5
St Mary Ave SM6 219 B5
St Mary Axe
EC3 95 C1 243 B2
St Marychurch St
SE16 118 C4
St Mary Graces Ct
E1 253 D5
St Marylebone CE Sch
The W1 93 A2 238 B4
St Mary le Bow
Church* EC2 242 B1
St Mary- le-Park Ct
SW11 267 B3
St Mary Magdalene
CE Prim Sch
Islington N7 72 C2
Paddington W2 91 D2
Peckham SE15 140 B3
Woolwich SE18 122 C2
St Mary Magdalen's
RC Prim Sch
Brockley SE4 141 A1
Mortlake SW14 133 B2
St Mary Magdelen's RC
Jun Sch NW2 68 B2
St Mary Newington Cl
SE17 263 B2
St Mary of the Angels
RC Prim Sch W2 91 C1
St Mary RC Prim Sch
W10 91 A3
St Mary Rd E17 53 D5
St Mary & St Joseph's
RC Sch DA14 189 D5
St Mary & St Michael
Prim Sch E1 96 C1
St Mary & St Pancras
CE Prim Sch
NW1 93 D5 232 C3
St Mary's App E12 78 B3
St Mary's Ave
Beckenham BR2 208 C6
Finchley N3 29 B1
St Marys Ave UB2 107 D2
St Mary's Ave
Teddington TW11 174 D4
Wanstead E11 55 B2
St Marys IG11 101 B6
St Mary's Bryanston
Square CE Sch
W1 92 D2 237 C4
St Mary's CE High Sch
(Lower & Upper)
NW4 46 C6
St Mary's CE High Sch
(Middle) NW4 46 C6
St Mary's CE Inf Sch
N8 50 B5
St Mary's CE Jun Sch
N8 50 A5
St Mary's CE Prim Sch
Chessington KT9 214 B2
East Barnet EN4 14 C5
Finchley N3 29 B3
St Mary's CE Prim Sch
(Inf) TW1 153 A4
St Mary's CE Prim Sch
N1 94 D6 234 D6
St Mary's CE Prim Sch
(Jun) TW1 153 B4
St Mary's CE Prim Sch
Long Ditton KT7 197 B1
Putney SW15 134 D2
Walthamstow E17 53 D5
Willesden NW10 67 C2
St Mary's Church Ho 11
E17 53 D5
St Mary's Cl BR5 190 B1
Chessington KT9 214 B1
Ewell KT17 215 D1
Sunbury TW16 194 A5
Tottenham N17 34 A2
St Mary's Coll TW1 152 D1
St Mary's Cottage Hospl
TW12 173 B2
St Mary's Cres
Hayes UB3 105 D6
Hendon NW4 46 B6
Hounslow TW7 130 C5
St Marys Ct SE2 124 D2
St Mary's Ct
Bedford Pk W6 111 D3
Ealing W5 109 D4
Finchley N12 30 A3
Kingston u T KT3 199 C6
Leytonstone E11 54 D1
St Marys Ct
Newham E6 100 B3
SE7 143 D5
St Mary's Ct SM6 219 C4
St Mary's Dr TW14 149 A4

St Mary's Est 2
SE16 118 C4
St Mary's Flats NW1 232 C2
St Mary's Gate W8 255 C5
St Mary's Gdns SE11 261 B4
St Mary's Gn 1 N2 48 A6
St Mary's Gr
Barnes SW13 134 B2
Chiswick W4 132 D6
Islington N1 72 D2
Richmond TW10,
TW9 132 B1
St Mary's Ho
Ealing W5 109 D3
N1 234 D6
St Mary's Hospl Medical
Sch W2 92 B1 236 D2
St Mary's Hospl
W2 92 B1 236 D2
St Mary's Kilburn CE
Prim Sch NW6 91 C6
St Mary's Lewisham CE
Prim Sch SE13 163 D6
St Mary's Lo E11 55 B3
St Mary's Mans
Dagenham NW10 89 C6
Paddington
W2 92 B2 236 C4
St Mary's Mews NW6 69 D1
St Mary's Path N1 234 D6
St Mary's Pl
Ealing W5 109 D4
Eltham SE9 166 C5
Kensington
W8 113 D3 255 C5
St Mary's RC High Sch
CR0 205 A1
St Mary's RC Inf Sch
Carshalton SM5 218 D4
Croydon CR0 205 B1
St Mary's RC Jun & Inf
Schs N15 51 B4
St Mary's RC Jun Sch
Croydon CR0 205 B1
Wallington SM5 218 D3
Walthamstow E17 54 A6
St Mary's RC Prim
Sch
Beckenham BR3 186 A3
Chingford E4 20 B3
Chiswick W4 133 C6
Clapham Pk SW4 159 C6
Clapham
SW8 137 B4 268 D2
Enfield EN3 6 D1
Hammersmith W14 112 D3
Isleworth TW7 131 A2
Merton SW19 179 C3
Paddington NW6 91 C5
SE9 166 C6
St Mary's Rd
Dagenham NW10 89 C6
Ealing W5 109 D5
East Barnet EN4 14 D4
East Molesey KT8 196 B4
Finchley N2 30 B2
Golders Green NW11 47 A2
Hayes UB3 105 D6
Hornsey N8 50 A5
St Marys Rd IG1 79 B6
St Mary's Rd
Leyton E10 76 A6
Long Ditton KT6 197 C1
Lower Edmonton N9 18 C3
Newham E13 99 B5
Nunhead SE15 140 C3
South Norwood
SE25 205 C6
Surbiton KT6 197 D3
Wimbledon SW19 179 B5
Worcester Pk KT4 215 C6
St Mary's & St John's CE
Prim Sch NW4 46 B4
St Mary's & St Peter's
CE Prim Sch
TW11 174 D5
St Mary's Sch
Hampstead NW3 70 B3
St Mary's Sq
Ealing W5 109 D4
W2 236 C4
St Mary's Stoke
Newington CE Prim
Sch N16 73 C6
St Mary's Terr W2 236 C4
St Mary St SE18 122 C2
St Mary's Twr EC1 242 B5
St Marys View HA3 43 C4
St Mary's Wlk
Hayes UB3 105 D6
SE11 261 B4
St Matthew's Ave
KT6 198 B1
St Matthew's CE Prim
Sch
Enfield EN3 18 C6
Surbiton KT6 198 A2

St Matthew's CE Prim
Sch *continued*
Wimbledon SW20 178 A2
Yiewsley UB7 104 A5
St Matthew's Ct 1
TW15 170 C5
St Matthews Ct
Muswell Hill N10 31 A1
SE1 262 A5
2 Stratford E15 76 D1
7 Walthamstow E10 53 D2
St Matthews Dr
BR1 210 B6
St Matthew's Ho 8
SE17 139 B6
St Matthew's Lo
NW1 232 B4
St Matthew's Rd
Clapham Pk SW2 160 B6
Ealing W5 110 A5
St Matthew's Row E2 96 A3
St Matthews Sch
Westminster
SW1 115 D3 259 D6
St Matthew St SW1 259 C5
St Matthias CE Prim
Sch E2 95 D3 243 D6
St Matthias Cl NW9 45 D4
St Matthias's CE Prim
Sch N16 73 C4
St Mauritius Ho
SE13 164 A6
St Maur Rd
SW6 135 B4 264 D1
St Mellion Cl SE28 102 D1
St Merryn Cl SE18 145 B5
St Merryn Ct BR3 185 C3
St Michael-at-Bowes
CE Jun Sch N13 32 C4
St Michael RC Prim Sch
TW15 170 C5
St Michael & St Martin
RC Prim Sch TW4 129 B2
St Michael's Alley
EC3 242 D1
St Michaels Ave N9 18 C4
St Michael's Ave HA9 66 C2
St Michael's CE Prim
Sch
Camden Town
NW1 93 C6 232 A6
Enfield EN2 5 A4
Forest Hill SE26 185 A6
Highgate N6 49 A2
Wandsworth SW18 157 B4
Wood Green N22 32 B2
St Michaels Cl BR1 210 A6
St Michael's Cl
Colney Hatch N12 30 C5
DA18 124 D4
Finchley N3 29 B1
St Michaels Cl
4 Newham E16 99 D2
Worcester Pk KT4 215 D6
St Michael's Cres
HA5 41 A3
St Michael's Ct N11 15 A1
St Michaels Ct 2
E14 98 A2
St Michael's Ct NW11 47 B2
St Michael's East
Wickham CE Prim
Sch DA16 146 C4
St Michael's Flats
NW1 232 C3
St Michael's Gdns
W10 91 A2
St Michaels Ho
SE26 185 B6
St Michael's Hospl
EN2 5 B4
St Michael's RC Gram
Sch N12 30 A5
St Michael's RC Prim
Sch E6 100 B5
St Michael's RC Sch
SE16 118 A4
St Michaels Rd
TW15 170 C5
St Michael's Rd
Cricklewood NW2 68 C4
Croydon CR0 205 A1
DA16 146 B2
Stockwell SW9 138 B3
Wallington SM6 219 C2
St Michael's Rise
DA16 146 B4
St Michael's St
W2 92 C1 237 A2
St Michael Steiner Sch
The SW18 157 C6
St Michael's Terr
N22 32 A2
St Mildred's Ct EC2 242 C1
St Mildreds Rd SE12,
SE6 164 D4

St Mirren Ct 8 EN5 14 A6
St Monica's RC Prim
Sch
Palmers Green
N14 16 A1
Shoreditch N1 95 C4
St Nicholas CE Prim
Sch TW17 192 D3
St Nicholas Cl WD6 9 D5
St Nicholas Ct E4 36 A4
St Nicholas Ctr 7
SM1 217 D3
St Nicholas Dr
TW17 192 C2
St Nicholas Elstree CE
Prim Sch WD6 9 D5
St Nicholas' Flats
NW1 232 C3
St Nicholas Glebe
SW17 181 A4
St Nicholas Ho SE8 141 C6
St Nicholas Mans
SW17 158 D2
St Nicholas Rd
Plumstead SE18 123 D2
Sutton SM1 217 D3
Thames Ditton KT7 196 D3
St Nicholas Sch NW9 67 A6
St Nicholas St SE8 141 C4
St Nicholas Way
SM1 217 D3
St Nicolas La BR7 188 A2
St Ninian's Ct N20 14 D1
St Norbert Gn SE4 141 A1
St Norbert Rd SE4 141 A1
St Olaf's Rd
SW6 135 A5 264 B3
St Olave's Ct EC2 242 C1
St Olaves Ct W2 245 C5
St Olave's Est SE1 253 B2
St Olave's Gdns
SE11 261 A4
St Olave's Mans
SE11 261 A4
St Olaves Prep Sch
SE9 166 D2
St Olave's Rd E6 100 C6
St Olave's Wlk
SW16 181 D1
St Olav's Sq 32
SE16 118 C4
St Osmund's RC Prim
Sch SW13 133 D4
St Oswald's Pl
SE11 116 B1 260 C1
St Oswald's Rd
SW16 182 D2
St Oswulf St SW1 259 D3
St Owen Ho SE1 263 B6
ST PANCRAS 94 A4
St Pancras Almshouses
13 NW5 70 D3
St Pancras Commercial
Ctr NW1 232 B6
St Pancras Ct
Finchley N2 30 B1
6 Wembley HA0 66 A2
St Pancras Hospl
NW1 93 D6 232 C5
St Pancras International
Sta WC1 94 A4 233 A2
St Pancras Way
NW1 93 D6 232 C6
St Patrick's Coll
W1 93 D1 239 C2
St Patricks Ct IG8 36 C3
St Patrick's RC Prim
Sch
Camden Town NW5 71 B3
Plumstead SE18 123 B2
Walthamstow E17 53 A5
St Paul's Acad SE2 146 A6
St Paul's & All Hallows
CE Jun & Inf Schs
N17 34 A3
St Paul's Ave
Harrow HA3 44 B5
Rotherhithe SE16 118 D5
Willesden NW2 68 C2
St Paul's Cath*
EC4 95 A1 242 A1
St Paul's Cath Sch
EC4 95 A1 242 A1
St Paul's CE Jun Sch
KT2 176 C3
St Pauls CE Prim Sch
TW8 131 D6
St Paul's CE Prim Sch
Chessington KT9 214 A4
Friern Barnet N11 31 B5
Hammersmith W6 112 C1

St Paul's CE Prim Sch *continued*
Hampstead NW3 70 D1
Mill Hill NW7 28 B6
SE17 117 A1 262 A2
Southgate N21 16 D4
St Paul's Church Yd EC4 95 A1 242 A1
St Paul's Cl
Ashford TW15 171 A5
Borehamwood WD6 11 A6
Carshalton SM5 202 C1
Chessington KT9 213 D4
St Pauls Cl W5 110 B4
St Paul's Cl SE7 121 D1
St Pauls Cl UB3 105 B1
St Paul's Cl TW3, TW4 129 A3
ST PAUL'S CRAY 190 A1
St Paul's Cray Rd BR7 189 B2
St Pauls Cres NW1 71 D1
St Paul's Ct
Clapham SW4 137 D1
Hounslow TW4 129 A2
6 Upper Holloway N19 72 A6
St Paul's Dr E15 76 B3
St Paul's Girls' Sch W6 112 D2
St Pauls Ho N17 34 A3
St Pauls Mews NW1 71 D1
St Paul's Pl N1 73 B2
St Paul's RC Coll TW16 172 A2
St Paul's RC Prim Sch
Thames Ditton KT7 196 C2
Wood Green N22 32 B1
St Pauls Rd IG11 101 A6
St Paul's Rd
Brentford TW8 131 D6
Canonbury N1 73 A2
St Pauls Rd TW9 132 B2
St Paul's Rd
South Norwood CR7 205 A6
Tottenham N17 34 A2
St Pauls Rise N13 32 D4
St Paul's Sch SW13 112 A1
St Paul's Sq BR2 187 A1
St Paul's Sta EC2 95 A1 242 A2
St Paul's Terr SE17 138 D6
St Paul St N1 235 B5
St Paul's Twr 14 E10 53 D2
St Pauls View WC1 234 A1
St Paul's Way Com Sch E3 97 C2
St Paul's Way
Finchley N3 29 D3
Tower Hamlets E3 97 C2
St Paul's Whitechapel CE Prim Sch E1 118 A6
St Paul's with St Michael's Prim Sch E8 96 A6
St Paul's Wood Hill BR5 189 D1
St Paul with St Luke CE Prim Sch E3 97 B2
St Peter Chanel RC Prim Sch DA14 190 C5
St Peter in Chains RC Inf Sch N8 50 A3
St Peter & Paul RC Prim Sch BR5 189 C1
St Peter & St Paul RC Prim Sch EC1 94 D3 241 D6
St Peter's Alley EC3 242 D1
St Peter's Ave
Edmonton N18 34 A6
37 Hackney E2 96 A5
St Peters Ave N12 30 C3
St Peter's Ave E17 54 C5
St Petersburgh Mews W2 245 C6
St Petersburgh Pl W2 113 D6 245 C5
St Peter's CE Prim Sch
Chiswick W6 112 A1
Paddington W9 91 C3
SE17 117 B1 262 C1
St Peter's Church Ct N1 234 D5
St Peter's Cl EN5 12 B6
St Peters Cl BR7 189 B3
St Peter's Cl
Bushey WD23 8 B3
Hackney E2 96 A5
St Peters Cl IG2 57 D5
St Peter's Cl HA4 62 D6
St Peters Cl SW17 158 C2
St Peters Ct KT8 195 C5
St Peter's Ct
Hendon NW4 46 C4
Lewisham SE12 164 D6
St Peters Ct
New Cross SE4 141 B3
28 Stepney E1 96 C3
St Peter's Eaton Square Prim Sch SW1 115 B3 258 D5
St Peter's Gdns SE27 160 C1
St Peter's Gr W6 112 A2
St Peter's Ho
4 SE17 139 B6
Stamford Hill N16 51 C2
St Peters Ho
Tottenham Hale N15 52 A5
WC1 233 B1
St Peters La BR5 190 A1
St Peter's London Docks CE Prim Sch E1 118 C5
St Peters Mews N4 50 D4
St Peter's Pl W9 91 D3
St Peter's Prim Sch CR2 221 C2
St Peter's RC Prim Sch
Dagenham RM9 103 B6
Woolwich SE18 122 D2
St Peter's Rd
Chiswick W6 112 A1
Croydon CR0 221 B4
East Molesey KT8 195 C5
Edmonton N9 18 B3
Isleworth TW1 153 B6
St Peters Rd KT1 176 C1
St Peter's Rd UB1 85 C2
St Peter's Sq
Chiswick W6 111 D1
Hackney E2 96 A5
St Peter's St
Croydon CR2 221 B3
Islington N1 94 D6 234 D5
St Peter's Street Mews N1 234 D4
St Peter's Terr SW6 264 B3
St Peter's Villas 5 W6 112 A2
St Peter's Way
De Beauvoir Town N1 73 C1
Ealing W5 87 D2
St Peters Way UB3 105 B1
St Peter's Wharf 8 W6 112 A1
St Philip Ho WC1 234 A1
St Philip's Ave KT4 216 B6
St Philips Gate KT4 216 B6
St Philip Sq 1 SW8 137 B3
St Philip's Rd
Dalston E8 74 A2
Surbiton KT6 197 D3
St Philip's Sch
Chessington KT9 213 D2
SW7 114 A2 256 B3
St Philip St SW8 137 B3
St Philip's Way N1 235 B5
St Philomena's Sch SM5 218 C3
St Quentin Ho SW18 158 B5
St Quentin Rd DA16 145 D2
St Quintin Ave W10 90 D2
St Quintin Gdns 21 W10 90 C2
St Quintin Rd E13 99 B5
St Raphaels Ho W13 109 C5
St Raphael's RC Prim Sch UB5 84 B5
St Raphael's Way NW10 67 A3
St Regis Cl N10 31 B1
St Regis Hts NW3 69 D5
St Richards Ct TW10 153 B1
St Richard's Ho NW1 232 C2
St Richard's with St Andrew's CE Prim Sch TW10 153 B1
St Robert Southwell RC Prim Sch NW9 45 A3
St Ronans Cl EN4 2 B5
St Ronans Cres IG8 37 A3
St Ronan's 2 N3 29 C2
St Rule St SW8 137 C3
St Savior's CE Inf Sch W5 109 D6
St Saviour's CE Prim Sch
Bow Comm E14 97 D2
Camberwell SE24 139 A2
St Saviour's CE Prim Sch *continued*
Paddington W9 91 D3
Walthamstow E17 53 B2
St Saviour's Coll SE27 183 B6
St Saviours Ct
Harrow HA1 42 C4
Muswell Hill N22 31 D1
St Saviours Ho 35 SE1 118 A4
St Saviours SW4 137 B1
St Saviour's RC Prim Sch SE13 142 A1
St Saviour's Rd
Clapham Pk SW2 160 B6
Thornton Heath CR0 205 A3
St Saviours & St Olaves CE Sch SE1 117 B3 262 D5
St Saviour's Wharf SE1 253 D2
St Scholastica's RC Prim Sch E5 74 A5
Saints Cl SE27 182 D6
Saints Dr E7 77 D3
St Silas Pl NW5 71 A2
St Simon's Ave SW15 156 C6
St Stephen's Ave
Ealing W13 87 B1
Shepherd's Bush W12 112 B4
Walthamstow E17 54 A4
St Stephen's CE Jun Sch TW1 153 B5
St Stephen's CE Prim Sch
Paddington W2 91 C2
Shepherd's Bush W12 112 C4
St Johns SE8 141 C3
SW8 138 B5 270 C4
St Stephen's Cl
Maitland Pk NW5 70 D3
NW8 230 B5
Southall UB1 85 C2
Walthamstow E17 53 D4
St Stephen's Cres
Notting Hill W2 91 C1
Thornton Heath CR7 204 C6
St Stephens Ct
Ealing W13 87 B1
Enfield EN1 17 C5
Hornsey Vale N8 50 B3
St Stephen's Gdns
Notting Hill W2 91 C1
4 Putney SW15 157 B6
Twickenham TW1 153 C5
St Stephen's Gr SE13 142 A2
St Stephens Ho 7 SE17 139 B6
St Stephen's Mews 34 W2 91 C2
St Stephens Par E6 77 C1
St Stephens Prim Sch E6 77 C1
St Stephen's RC Prim Sch DA16 146 A3
St Stephens Rd EN5 12 D6
St Stephen's Rd
Bow E3 97 B5
Ealing W13 87 C1
Enfield EN3 6 D6
Hounslow TW3, TW4 151 C6
St Stephens Rd E6 77 C1
St Stephen's Rd
Walthamstow E17 53 D4
Yiewsley UB7 104 A5
St Stephens Row EC4 242 C1
St Stephen's Terr SW8 270 C3
St Stephen's Wlk SW7 256 A4
St Swithin's La EC4 117 B6 252 C6
St Swithun's Rd SE13 164 B6
St Swithun Wells RC Prim Sch HA4 62 D5
St Teresa's RC Fst & Mid Sch HA3 24 A2
St Teresa's RC Prim Sch SM4 202 B3
St Teresa's RC Prim Sch The RM8 80 C4
St Theresa Ct E4 20 B4
St Theresa's RC Sch N3 47 D6
St Theresa's Rd TW14 127 D1
St Thomas a Beckett RC Prim Sch SE2 124 A3
St Thomas Becket RC Prim Sch SE25 206 A3
St Thomas' CE Prim Sch W10 91 A3
St Thomas' Cl KT6 198 B1
St Thomas Ct 10 NW1 71 C1
St Thomas' Ct HA5 23 A2
St Thomas Ct
Sidcup DA5 169 C4
11 Walthamstow E10 53 D2
St Thomas' Dr BR5 211 A1
Pinner HA5 23 A2
St Thomas Gdns IG1 79 A2
St Thomas Ho 2 E1 96 D1
St Thomas More Language Coll SW3 114 D2 257 C3
St Thomas More RC Comp Sch SE9 166 C5
St Thomas More RC Prim Sch
Bexley DA7 147 B3
SE9 144 A2
St Thomas More Sch N22 32 C3
St Thomas of Canterbury RC Prim Sch
Mitcham CR4 203 A6
SW6 135 B5 264 C4
St Thomas' Rd W4 133 A6
St Thomas Rd
Newham E16 99 A1
Osidge N14 15 D4
St Thomas's Gdns NW5 71 A2
St Thomas's Hospl Medical Sch SE1 116 B3 260 C5
St Thomas's Hospl SE1 116 B3 260 C6
St Thomas's Pl 20 E9 74 C1
St Thomas's Rd
Dagenham NW10 89 C6
Highbury N4, N5 72 C5
St Thomas's Sq E9 74 C1
St Thomas St SE1 117 B5 252 D3
St Thomas's Way SW6 135 B5 264 D4
St Thomas the Apostle Coll The SE15 140 C4
St Timothy's Mews 3 BR1 187 B2
St Ursula Gr HA5 41 A4
St Ursula Rd UB1 85 C1
St Ursula's Convent Sch SE10 142 B5
St Vincent Cl SE27 182 D5
St Vincent De Paul Ho 24 E1 96 C2
St Vincent De Paul RC Prim Sch SW1 115 C3 259 B6
St Vincent Ho SE1 263 C6
St Vincent Rd TW2 152 A5
St Vincent's Hospl HA5 39 D6
St Vincents La NW7 28 C6
St Vincent's RC Prim Sch
Acton W3 110 D6
Dagenham RM8 80 C6
Marylebone W1 93 A2 238 B3
St Vincents RC Prim Sch SE9 188 A6
St Vincent's RC Sch NW7 28 C5
St Vincent St W1 238 B3
St Wilfrid's Cl EN4 14 C6
St Wilfrid's Rd EN4 14 C6
St William of York RC Prim Sch SE23 163 A3
St Winefride's Ave E12 78 B3
St Winefride's RC Prim Sch E12 78 B3
St Winifred's RC Inf Sch SE12 164 C6
St Winifred's RC Jun Sch SE12 164 D4
St Winifred's Rd TW11 175 B4
Sakura Dr N22 31 D2
Sala Ho SE3 143 B1
Salamanca Pl SE1 260 C3
Salamanca St SE1, SE11 116 B2 260 C3
Salamander Cl KT2 175 C5
Salamander Quay KT1 175 D2
Salcombe Dr
Dagenham RM6 59 B3
Salcombe Dr *continued*
North Cheam SM4 200 D1
Salcombe Gdns
Clapham SW4 137 B1
Mill Hill NW7 28 C4
Salcombe Ho 6 SE23 162 C2
Salcombe Lo NW5 71 A4
Salcombe Pk IG10 21 D6
Salcombe Rd
Ashford TW15 148 A1
23 Stoke Newington N16 73 C3
Walthamstow E17 53 B2
Salcombe Sch N14 15 B4
Salcombe Villas 13 TW10 154 A6
Salcombe Way
Hayes UB4 83 C4
Ruislip HA4 62 A6
Salcot N4 72 B6
Salcott Rd
Wallington CR0 220 B4
Wandsworth SW11 158 D6
Salehurst Cl HA3 44 A4
Salehurst Rd SE4 163 B5
Salem Ho 15 E9 74 D2
Salem Pl CR0 221 A5
Salem Rd W2 113 D6 245 D6
Sale Pl W2 92 C1 237 A2
Salesian Coll SW11 136 C4 267 A1
Sale St E2 96 A3
Salford Ho 5 E14 120 A2
Salford Rd SW12, SW2 159 D3
Salhouse Cl SE28 102 C1
Salisbury Ave
Barking IG11 79 C1
Cheam SM1, SM2 217 B2
Hendon N3 47 B6
Salisbury Cl SE17 262 C4
Worcester Pk KT4 215 D5
Salisbury Ct
15 Bermondsey SE16 118 A3
Chiswick W4 111 C2
EC4 241 C1
Edgware HA8 26 B6
Enfield EN2 5 B1
Finchley N3 29 B1
Hackney E9 75 A3
Northolt UB5 63 D3
Salisbury Gdns
5 Buckhurst Hill IG9 21 D2
Wimbledon SW19 179 A3
Salisbury Hall Gdns E4 35 C4
Salisbury Ho
2 Islington N1 72 D2
Islington N1 234 C6
3 Poplar E14 97 D1
1 Ruislip HA4 40 C1
Stanmore HA7 25 A4
5 Wallington SM6 219 B3
Westminster SW1 259 D2
Wimbledon SW19 156 D1
Salisbury Lower Sch N9 18 C4
Salisbury Mans
Edmonton N9 18 A1
Harringay N4, N15 50 D4
Salisbury Mews
Bromley Comm BR2 210 A4
Fulham SW6 264 C3
Salisbury Pl
Camberwell SW9 138 D5
Marylebone W1 237 C4
Salisbury Prim Sch E12 78 A3
Salisbury Rd
Barnet EN5 1 A2
Bromley Comm BR2 210 A4
Chingford E4 19 C1
Croydon SE25 206 A3
Dagenham RM10 81 D2
East Bedfont TW6 149 A5
Enfield EN3 7 B6
Feltham TW13 150 C3
Forest Gate E7 77 A2
Harringay N4 50 D4
Harrow HA1 42 B4
Hounslow TW4 128 C2
Ilford IG3 79 C6
Kingston u T KT3 199 B6
Leyton E10 76 A6
Old Bexley DA5 169 C3
Pinner HA5 40 A5
Plashet E12 77 D3
Richmond TW9 132 A1
Southall UB2 107 A2
Tottenham N22 32 D1
Wallington SM5 218 D2
Walthamstow E17 54 A4
Salisbury Rd *continued*
West Ealing W13 109
Wimbledon SW19 179
Worcester Pk KT4 215
Salisbury Sq EC4 241
Salisbury St
10 Acton W3 111
NW8 237
Salisbury Terr SE15 140
Salisbury Upper Sch N9 18
Salisbury Wlk N19 71
Salix Cl TW16 172
Salix Ct N3 29
Salliesfield TW2 152
Sally Murray Cl E12 78
Salmen Rd E13 98
Salmond Cl HA7 25
Salmon La E14 97
Salmon Rd DA17 125
Salmons Brook Ho EN2 4
Salmons Rd
Chessington KT9 214
Edmonton N9 18
Salmon St
Kingsbury NW9 45
10 Poplar E14 97
Salomons Rd 2 E13 99
Salop Rd E17 52
Saltash Cl SM1 217
Saltash Rd DA16 146
Saltcoats Rd W4 111
Saltcroft Cl HA9 44
Saltdene N4 50
Salter Cl HA2 63
Salterford Rd SW17 181
Salter Ho 8 SW16 181
Saltern Ct IG11 102
Salter Rd SE16 119
Salters' Hall Ct EC4 252
Salter's Hill SE19 183
Salters Rd
North Kensington W10 90
Walthamstow E17 54
Salter St
College Pk NW10 90
11 Poplar E14 119
Salterton Rd N7 72
Salt Hill Cl UB8 60
Saltley Cl E6 100
Saltoun Rd SW2, SW9 138
Saltram Cl N15 51
Saltram Cres W9 91
Saltwell St E14 119
Saltwood Gr SE17 262
Saltwood Ho 19 SE15 140
Salusbury Prim Sch NW6 91
Salusbury Rd NW6 91
Salutation Rd SE10 120
Salvador SW17 180
Salvatorian RC Coll HA3 24
Salvia Gdns UB6 87
Salvin Rd SW15 134
Salway Cl IG8 37
Salway Ho E10 75
Salway Pl E15 76
Salway Rd E15 76
Salween Ho 2 N16 73
Samantha Cl E17 53
Samantha Ct E11 54
Samaritan Hospl for Women NW1 237
Sam Bartram Cl SE7 121
Sambrooke Ct EN1 17
Sambrook Ho 25 E1 96
Sambruck Mews SE6 163
Samels Ct W6 112
Samford Ho N1 234
Samford St NW8 237
Samira Cl E17 53
Sam Manners Ho 7 SE10 120
Sam March Ho 5 E14 98
Samos Rd SE20 184
Sampson Ave EN5 12
Sampson Cl DA17 125
Sampson Ct TW17 193
Sampson St E1 118
Samson Ct 5 DA17 125
Samson Ho SE18 123
Samson St E13 99
Samuel Cl SE14 140
Shoreditch E8 95
Woolwich SE18 122
Samuel Ct
Beckenham BR3 207
Shoreditch N1 95

nuel Gray Gdns
?2 ...175 D2
nuel Ho
5 Shoreditch E8 ...95 D6
3 West Norwood
SE27 ...182 D6
nuel Johnson Cl
N16 ...182 B6
nuel Jones Ind Est
1 SE15 ...139 C5
nuel Lewis Bldgs
1 ...72 C2
nuel Lewis Trust
wellings
3 Camberwell
SE5 ...139 A4
helsea SW3 ...257 A3
Valham Green
SW6 ...135 C5 265 B4
Vest Kensington
W14 ...254 B4
muel Lewis Trust Est
15 ...51 C3
muel Lo N3 ...29 B1
muel Rhodes Sch
1 ...94 C6 234 A6
muel Richardson Ho
V14 ...254 C3
muel's Cl 2 W6 ...112 C2
muel St SE15 ...139 D5
Voolwich SE18 ...122 B2
ncroft Cl NW2 ...68 B5
ncroft Ct SW11 ...267 B2
ncroft Ho SE11 ...260 D2
ncroft Rd HA3 ...25 A1
ncroft St
E11 ...116 B1 260 D2
nctuary Mews 15
8 ...73 D2
nctuary Rd TW19,
W6 ...148 C5
nctuary St SE1 ...252 B2
nctuary The
Morden SM4 ...201 C3
Sidcup DA5 ...168 D5
35 Wapping E1 ...118 B5
Westminster
SW1 ...115 D3 259 D6
ndale Cl N16 ...73 B5
ndall Cl W5 ...88 A3
ndall Ho 7 E3 ...97 A5
ndall Rd Ealing W5 ...88 A3
Kentish Town NW5 ...71 C2
ndal Rd
Edmonton N18 ...34 A5
New Malden KT3 ...199 C5
ndal St E15 ...98 C6
ndalwood Cl 11
E1 ...97 A3
ndalwood Dr HA4 ...39 A2
ndalwood Ho
DA15 ...167 D1
6 Hampstead NW3 ...69 D2
ndalwood Rd
TW13 ...150 B1
ndbach Pl SE18 ...123 A1
ndbourne Ave
SW19 ...179 D1
ndbourne
4 Kensington
W11 ...91 C1
14 Paddington NW8 ...91 D6
ndbourne Rd SE4 ...141 A3
ndbrook Cl NW7 ...27 B4
ndbrook Rd N16 ...73 C5
ndby Ct BR3 ...185 B2
ndby Gn SE9 ...144 A2
ndby Ho
11 Camberwell
SE5 ...139 C4
6 Kilburn NW6 ...91 C6
ndcroft Cl N13 ...32 D4
ndells Ave
Ashford TW15 ...171 A6
Ashford TW15 ...171 A6
ndell St SE1 ...251 A2
nderling Ct
20 SE8 ...141 B6
Woolwich SE28 ...124 C6
nders Cl TW12 ...174 A5
nders Ho
Streatham SW16 ...182 A4
WC1 ...234 A2
nders La NW7 ...28 C3
nderson Cl NW5 ...71 B4
nderson Ho 7
SE8 ...119 B1
nderson Sq BR1 ...210 C6
nderstead Ave
NW2 ...69 A6
nderstead Cl
SW12 ...159 C4
nderstead Rd
South Croydon
CR2 ...221 B1
Walthamstow E10 ...53 A1

Sanders Way 3 N19 ...49 D1
Sandfield Gdns CR7 ...204 D6
Sandfield Pl CR7 ...205 A6
Sandfield Rd CR7 ...204 D6
Sandfield WC1 ...233 B1
Sandford Ave N22 ...33 A2
Sandford Cl E6 ...100 B3
Sandford Ct
Barnet EN5 ...1 D2
Stamford Hill N16 ...51 C1
Sandford Rd
Bexley DA7 ...147 A2
BR2 ...209 A5
Newham E6 ...100 B4
Sandford Row SE17 ...262 D2
Sandford St SW6 ...265 D3
Sandgate Ho
14 Beckenham
BR3 ...185 C3
Ealing W5 ...87 C2
15 Hackney E5 ...74 B4
Sandgate La SW17,
SW18 ...158 C3
Sandgate Rd DA16 ...146 C5
Sandgate St SE15 ...140 B6
Sandgate Trad Est
SE15 ...140 B6
Sandham Ct SW4 ...270 B1
Sandham Point 10
SE18 ...122 D2
Sandhills Mdw
TW17 ...193 A2
Sandhills The SW10 ...266 B6
Sandhills CR0, SM6 ...219 D4
Sandhurst Ave
Harrow HA2 ...41 D3
Tolworth KT5 ...198 D2
Sandhurst Cl
Queensbury NW9 ...44 C6
South Croydon CR2 ...221 C1
Sandhurst Ct SW2 ...138 A1
Sandhurst Dr IG3 ...79 D4
Sandhurst Ho 12 E1 ...96 C2
Sandhurst Jun & Inf
Schs SE6 ...164 C3
Sandhurst Mkt SE6 ...164 A3
Sandhurst Rd
Bexley DA5 ...168 D6
Catford SE6 ...164 B3
DA15 ...168 A1
Ponders End N9 ...18 D5
Queensbury HA8,
NW9 ...44 C6
Sandhurst Way CR2 ...221 C1
Sandifer Dr NW2 ...68 D5
Sandiford Rd SM3 ...217 B6
Sandiland Cres BR2 ...224 D6
Sandilands Rd
SW6 ...135 D4 265 C1
Sandilands CR0 ...222 A5
Sandilands Sta CR0 ...221 D6
Sandison St SE15 ...140 A2
Sandland St WC1 ...240 D3
Sandling Rise SE9 ...166 C1
Sandlings Cl SE15 ...140 B3
Sandlings The
Tottenham N22 ...50 D6
5 Wood Green N22 ...32 C1
Sandmartin Way
CR4 ...203 A1
Sandmere Rd SW4 ...138 A1
Sandon Cl KT10 ...196 B1
Sandon Ct IG3 ...80 A5
Sandon Ho 5 SW2 ...160 A4
Sandow Commercial Est
UB3 ...105 D3
Sandow Cres UB3 ...105 D3
Sandown Ave KT10 ...212 A3
Sandown Cl TW5 ...128 A4
Sandown Ct 12 SM2 ...217 D1
Sandown Gate KT10 ...212 B5
Sandown Ho
2 Acton Green
W4 ...111 A1
Esher KT10 ...212 A4
Penge SE26 ...184 B4
Sandown Park
KT10 ...212 A6
Sandown Rd
Croydon SE25 ...206 B4
Esher KT10 ...212 A4
Sandown Way UB5 ...63 B3
Sandpiper Cl
Higham Hill E17 ...34 D3
Rotherhithe SE16 ...119 B4
Sandpiper Ct
13 Cubitt Town
E14 ...120 A3
1 SE8 ...141 C5
Sandpiper Rd SM1 ...217 B3
Sandpiper Terr IG5 ...56 D6
Sandpit Pl SE7 ...122 A1
Sandpit Rd BR1 ...186 C5
Sandpits Rd
Richmond TW10 ...153 D2
South Croydon CR0 ...222 D4

Sandra Cl
Hounslow TW3 ...151 D6
Tottenham N17 ...33 A2
Sandra Ho KT8 ...196 B4
Sandridge Cl
Hadley Wood EN4 ...2 C6
Harrow HA1 ...42 C5
Sandridge St 3 N19 ...71 C6
Sandringham Ave
SW20 ...179 A1
Sandringham Cl
Enfield EN1 ...5 C3
Ilford IG6 ...57 A6
1 Putney SW19 ...156 D3
Sandringham Cres
HA2 ...63 D6
Sandringham Ct
3 Beckenham
BR3 ...186 A2
Edgware HA8 ...26 D6
Hillingdon UB10 ...83 A3
Kingston u T KT2 ...176 A2
Marylebone W1 ...239 B1
Putney SW15 ...156 D5
18 Rotherhithe
SE16 ...118 D5
St John's Wood W9 ...229 B1
2 Twickenham
TW1 ...153 A3
Sandringham Dr
Ashford TW15 ...170 A6
DA16 ...145 C3
Sandringham Flats
WC2 ...249 D6
Sandringham Gdns
Cranford TW5 ...128 A4
East Molesey KT8 ...195 C5
Finchley N12 ...30 B4
Hornsey Vale N8 ...50 A3
Ilford IG6 ...57 A6
Sandringham Ho
Richmond TW10 ...154 C6
W14 ...254 A4
Sandringham Lo
BR6 ...226 C4
Sandringham Mews
TW12 ...173 B2
Sandringham Prim Sch
E7 ...77 C3
Sandringham Rd
Barking IG11 ...79 D2
BR1 ...187 A5
Dalston E8 ...73 D3
Forest Gate E7 ...77 C3
Golders Green NW11 ...47 A2
Leytonstone E10 ...54 B3
Northolt UB5 ...63 C1
Stanwell TW19,
TW6 ...148 A6
Thornton Heath CR0 ...205 A4
Tottenham N22 ...33 A1
Willesden NW2 ...68 B2
Worcester Pk KT4 ...216 A5
Sandrock Pl CR0 ...222 D4
Sandrock Rd SE13 ...141 C2
SANDS END ...136 A2
Sands End La
SW6 ...135 D4 265 D2
Sandstone La E16 ...121 B6
Sandstone Pl N19 ...71 B6
Sandstone Rd SE12 ...165 B2
Sandstone TW9 ...132 C5
Sandtoft Rd SE7 ...143 B6
Sandways 6 TW9 ...132 C4
Sandwell Cres 2
NW6 ...69 C2
Sandwell Mans 3
NW6 ...69 C2
Sandwich Ho
15 Rotherhithe
SE16 ...118 C4
WC1 ...233 A1
Sandwich St
WC1 ...94 A4 233 A1
Sandwick Cl NW7 ...28 A3
Sandy Bury BR6 ...227 B5
Sandycombe Ctr
TW9 ...132 C2
Sandycombe Rd
East Bedfont
TW14 ...150 A3
Richmond TW9 ...132 C3
Sandycoombe Rd
TW1 ...153 C5
Sandycroft SE2 ...146 A6
Sandy Dr TW14 ...149 C3
Sandy Hill Ave
SE18 ...122 D1
Sandy Hill La SE18 ...122 D2
Sandyhill Rd IG1 ...78 D4
Sandy Hill Rd SE18 ...122 D1
Sandy La
Belmont SM2 ...217 A1
BR5 ...190 D2
Eastbury HA6 ...22 A6
Harrow HA3 ...44 C3
Mitcham CR4 ...181 A2

Sandy Lane N SM6 ...219 D3
Sandy Lane S SM6 ...219 C1
Sandy La
Richmond TW10 ...153 D2
Teddington KT8,
TW11 ...175 B3
Walton-on-T KT12 ...194 C3
Sandy Lo N6 ...49 C2
Sandymount Ave
HA7 ...25 D5
Sandy Rd NW3 ...69 D6
Sandy Ridge BR7 ...188 C4
Sandy's Row E1 ...243 B3
Sandy Way
Croydon CR0 ...223 B5
Walton-on-T KT12 ...193 D1
Sanford La 3 N16 ...73 D6
Sanford St SE14,
SE8 ...141 A6
Sanford Terr N16 ...73 D5
Sanford Wlk SE14 ...141 A6
4 Stoke Newington
N16 ...73 D6
Sangam Cl UB2 ...107 A3
Sanger Ave KT9 ...214 B4
Sangley Rd
Catford SE6 ...164 A3
South Norwood
SE25 ...205 C5
Sangora Rd 17
SW11 ...136 B1
San Ho 29 E9 ...74 D2
Sankey Ho 22 E2 ...96 C5
Sansom Rd E11 ...76 D6
Sansom St
Camberwell SE5 ...139 B4
SE5 ...139 B5
Sans Wlk EC1 ...94 D3 241 C6
Santana SE18 ...144 D5
Santley Ho SE1 ...251 B1
Santley St SW4 ...138 B1
Santos Rd SW18 ...157 C6
Sapcote Trad Ctr
NW10 ...67 D2
Saperton Wlk SE11 ...260 D4
Saphora Cl BR6 ...227 B3
Sapperton Ct EC1 ...242 A6
Sapphire Cl
Dagenham RM8 ...58 C1
Newham E6 ...100 C1
Sapphire Ct 13 E1 ...118 A6
Sapphire Rd
Rotherhithe SE8 ...119 A2
Willesden NW10 ...67 A1
Saracen Cl CR0 ...205 B3
Saracen St E14 ...97 C1
Sarah Bonnell Sch
E15 ...76 C2
Sarah Ct UB5 ...85 B6
Sarah Ho
Roehampton
SW15 ...133 D1
8 Stepney E1 ...96 B1
Sarah Swift Ho SE1 ...252 D2
Sarah Turnbull Ho 2
SE18 ...122 B2
Sara Lane Ct 31 N1 ...95 C5
Saratoga Rd E5 ...74 C4
Sardeson Ho 13
SW27 ...182 D5
Sardinia Ho WC2 ...240 C1
Sardinia St WC2 ...240 C2
Sargents Hill N2 ...30 C2
Sarita Cl HA3 ...24 B1
Sarjant Path SW19 ...156 D2
Sark Cl TW5 ...129 C5
Sark Ho
9 Canonbury N1 ...73 A2
Enfield EN3 ...6 D5
Sark Twr SE28 ...123 A4
Sark Wlk E16 ...99 B1
Sarnersfield Ho
SE15 ...140 B6
Sarnes Ct 4 N11 ...31 B6
Sarnesfield Rd EN2 ...5 B2
Sarratt Ho 6 W10 ...90 C2
Sarre Rd NW2 ...69 B3
Sarsden Bldgs W1 ...238 B1
Sarsen Ave TW3 ...129 C3
Sarsfeld Rd SW12,
SW17 ...158 D3
Sarsfield Rd UB6 ...87 C5
Sartor Rd SE15 ...140 D1
Sarum Hall Sch NW3 ...70 C1
Sarum Ho W11 ...244 D5
Sarwan Ho 1 E7 ...77 C1
Sassoon Ho SE15 ...140 C3
Sassoon 4 NW9 ...27 D2
Satanita Cl E16 ...99 D1
Satchell Mead NW9 ...27 D2
Satchwell Rd 17 E2 ...96 A4
Satin Ct NW9 ...45 D5
Saturn Ho 4 E3 ...97 C6
Saul Ct 4 SE15 ...139 D6
Sauls Gn E11 ...76 C5
Saunders Cl
Ilford IG1 ...57 B1

Saunders Cl *continued*
14 Limehouse E14 ...119 B6
Saunders Ho 11
SW2 ...160 C3
Saunders Ness Rd
E14 ...120 B2
Saunders Rd
Hillingdon UB10 ...82 B6
Plumstead Comm
SE18 ...123 D1
Saunders St SE11 ...261 A4
Saunders Way SE28 ...124 B6
Saunderton Rd HA0 ...65 B3
Saunton Ave UB3 ...127 D5
Saunton Ct UB1 ...108 A6
Savage Gdns EC3 ...253 B6
Newham E6 ...100 B1
Savana N16 ...73 C6
Savannah Cl 9
SE15 ...139 D5
Savernake Ct HA7 ...25 B4
Savernake Ho N4 ...51 B2
Savernake Rd
Enfield N9 ...18 A5
Maitland Pk NW3 ...70 D4
Savery Dr KT6 ...197 C2
Savile Cl
New Malden KT3 ...199 C4
Thames Ditton KT7 ...197 A1
Savile Gdns CR0 ...221 D6
Savill Ct IG8 ...36 D4
Saville Cres TW15 ...171 B4
Saville Ho E16 ...122 D5
Saville Rd
Bedford Pk W4 ...111 B3
Dagenham RM6 ...59 B2
Newham E16 ...122 A5
Twickenham TW1 ...152 D3
Saville Row
Enfield EN3 ...6 D3
Hayes BR2 ...208 D1
W1 ...115 C6 249 A6
Savill Gdns SW20 ...200 A6
Savill Ho 2 SW4 ...159 D5
Savill Row IG8 ...36 D4
Savin Lo 7 SM2 ...218 A1
Savona Cl 16 SW19 ...178 D3
Savona Ct SW20 ...178 D2
Savona St
SW8 ...137 C5 269 A3
Savoy Ave UB3 ...105 C1
Savoy Circus W3 ...111 D6
Savoy Cl Edgware HA8 ...26 C5
Newham E15 ...98 C6
Savoy Ct
Earl's Ct SW5 ...255 B4
Strand WC2 ...250 B5
Savoy Hill WC2 ...250 C5
Savoy Mews SW9 ...138 A2
Savoy Par EN1 ...5 C2
Savoy Pier WC2 ...250 C5
Savoy Pl
WC2 ...116 B6 250 C5
Savoy Row WC2 ...250 C6
Savoy Stps WC2 ...250 C5
Savoy St
WC2 ...116 B6 250 C5
Savoy Way WC2 ...250 C5
Sawbill Cl UB4 ...84 D2
Sawkins Cl SW19 ...157 A2
Sawley Rd W12 ...112 A5
Sawmill Yd E3 ...97 A6
Sawtry Cl SM5 ...202 C2
Sawyer Cl N9 ...18 A2
Sawyer Ho 15 SE21 ...183 C6
Sawyer's Hill TW10 ...154 B4
Sawyers Lawn W13 ...87 A1
Sawyer St
SE1 ...117 A4 252 A2
Saxby Rd SW2 ...160 A4
Saxham Rd IG11 ...101 D5
Saxlingham Rd E4 ...20 B1
Saxon Ave TW13 ...151 B2
Saxon Bsns Ctr
SW19 ...180 A2
Saxonbury Ave
TW16 ...172 B1
Saxonbury Cl CR4 ...202 B6
Saxonbury Ct
16 Kentish Town
N7 ...71 D3
2 Lower Holloway
N7 ...72 A3
Saxonbury Gdns
KT6 ...197 C1
Saxon Cl
Hillingdon UB8 ...82 A2
Surbiton KT6 ...197 D3
Walthamstow E17 ...53 C2
Saxoncroft Ho
SW16 ...159 D1
Saxon Ct
Colney Hatch N12 ...30 C5
4 Edgware HA8 ...26 D5
Saxon Dr W3 ...88 D2
Saxonfield Cl SW2 ...160 B4
Saxon Gdns UB1 ...107 A6

Saxon Hall W2 ...245 C5
Saxon Ho
4 Clapham SW4 ...137 D1
Feltham TW13 ...151 B2
Saxon Prim Sch
TW17 ...192 C4
Saxon Rd
Ashford TW15 ...171 B4
Bow E3 ...97 B5
Bromley BR1 ...186 D3
Ilford IG1 ...78 D3
Kingston u T KT2 ...176 A2
Newham E6 ...100 B3
Southall UB1 ...107 A6
South Norwood
SE25 ...205 B4
Tottenham N22 ...32 D2
Wembley HA9 ...67 A5
Saxon Terr SE6 ...163 B2
Saxon Way N14 ...15 D5
Saxon Wlk DA14 ...190 C4
Saxony Par UB3 ...83 A2
Saxton Cl SE13 ...142 B2
Saxville Rd BR5 ...190 B1
Sayer Ho SE4 ...141 A1
Sayers Ho 4 N2 ...30 B1
Sayer's Wlk TW10 ...154 B4
Sayesbury La N18 ...34 A5
Sayes Court St SE8 ...141 B6
Sayes Ct SE8 ...141 B6
Sayline Ct CR0 ...221 B5
Scadbury Gdns BR5 ...190 A1
Scadbury Park Nature
Reserve* BR7 ...189 D4
Scads Hill Cl BR6 ...211 D3
Scafell NW1 ...232 A2
Scala St W1 ...239 B4
Scales Rd N17 ...52 A6
Scampston Mews 5
W10 ...90 D1
Scandrett St 38 E1 ...118 B5
Scarba Wlk N1 ...73 B2
Scarborough Rd
East Bedfont TW6 ...149 A5
Finsbury Pk N4 ...50 C1
Leytonstone E11 ...54 B1
Ponders End N9 ...18 C4
Scarborough St E1 ...243 D1
Scarbrook Rd CR0 ...221 A5
Scardale Ho 12 E5 ...74 B6
Scarle Rd HA0 ...65 D2
Scarlet Rd SE6 ...164 C1
Scarlette Manor Wlk 10
SE24 ...160 C4
Scarsbrook Ho 2
SW2 ...160 C5
Scarsbrook Rd SE3 ...143 D2
Scarsdale Pl W8 ...255 C6
Scarsdale Rd HA2 ...64 A5
Scarsdale Villas
W8 ...113 C3 255 B5
Scarth Rd SW13 ...133 D2
Scawen Cl SM5 ...219 A4
Scawen Rd SE8 ...119 A1
Scawfell St E2 ...95 D5
Scaynes Link N12 ...29 C6
Sceptre Ho 10 E1 ...96 C3
Sceptre Rd E2 ...96 C4
Schiller International
Univ SE1 ...116 C5 251 A3
Schofield Wlk SE3 ...143 A5
Sch of Pharmacy
WC1 ...94 A3 240 B6
Scholars Cl EN5 ...1 A1
Scholars Ct 5 N19 ...49 D1
Scholars Ho 6 E4 ...20 B3
Scholars Rd
Chingford E4 ...20 B3
Streatham SW12 ...159 C3
Scholefield Rd N19 ...71 D6
Scholey Ho SW11 ...136 C2
Schomberg Ho SW1 ...259 D4
Schonfeld Sq N16 ...51 B1
School App 21 E2 ...95 C4
Schoolbank Rd
SE10 ...120 D2
School Bell Cloisters 17
E3 ...97 A5
Schoolbell Mews 18
E3 ...97 A5
School Cotts
Bromley BR1 ...187 A3
Sidcup DA14 ...190 C5
School Flats SW8 ...270 A1
School Ho SE1 ...263 A4
Schoolhouse La E1 ...118 D6
School House La
TW11 ...175 C3
Schoolhouse Yd 9
SE18 ...122 D1
School La DA16 ...146 B2
Lower Halliford
TW17 ...192 D2
Pinner HA5 ...41 A5

School La *continued*
Surbiton KT6 198 B1
Teddington KT1 175 C2
School Pas
3 Kingston u T KT1 176 B1
Southall UB1 107 B6
School Rd
Ashford TW15 170 D4
Becontree NW10 89 B3
BR7 189 A3
Dagenham RM10 103 D6
East Molesey KT8 196 B5
Hampton TW12 174 A4
Hounslow TW3 130 A2
Ilford E12 78 B4
Littleton TW15 170 D3
Teddington KT1 175 C2
School Road Ave TW12 174 A4
School Sq SE10 120 D3
School Way RM8 80 C5
Schoolway N12 30 B4
School Wlk TW16 193 D6
Schooner Cl
Barking IG11 102 B4
Cubitt Town E14 120 B3
1 Rotherhithe SE16 118 D4
Schubert Rd
Elstree WD6 9 D5
Putney SW15 157 B6
Science Mus* SW7 114 B3 256 C5
Scilly Isles KT10 212 C6
Sclater St E1 243 D6
Scoles Cres SW2 160 C3
Scope Way KT1 198 A5
Scoresby St SE1 251 C3
Scoresdale SE19 183 C2
Scorton Ave UB6 87 A5
Scorton Ho 2 N1 95 C5
Scotch Comm W13 87 B2
Scotch Ho SW1 114 D4 247 C1
Scoter Cl IG8 37 B3
Scoter Ct 23 SE8 141 B6
Scot Gr HA5 22 D3
Scotia Bldg 10 E1 118 D6
Scotia Ct 3 SE16 118 C3
Scotia Rd 24 SW2 160 C4
Scotland Gn N17 33 D1
Scotland Green Rd EN3 18 D6
Scotland Green Rd N EN3 7 A1
Scotland Pl SW1 250 A3
Scotland Rd IG9 21 C3
Scotney Cl BR6 226 C4
Scotney Ho E9 74 C2
Scots Cl TW19 148 A3
Scotsdale Cl
Belmont SM3 217 A1
BR5 211 C5
Scotsdale Rd SE12 165 B6
Scotson Ho SE11 261 A3
Scotswood St EC1 94 C3 241 B6
Scotswood Wlk N17 34 A3
Scott Cl
Thornton Heath SW16 182 B2
West Drayton UB7 104 B2
West Ewell KT19 215 A3
Scott Ct Acton W4 111 B4
4 Clapham SW11 137 B3
17 Stoke Newington N16 73 C5
Scott Ellis Gdns NW8 92 B4 229 C1
Scottes La RM8 58 D1
Scott Farm Cl KT7 197 B1
Scott Gdns TW5 128 D5
Scott Ho
2 Barnsbury N7 72 B2
3 Edmonton N18 34 A5
4 Erith DA17 125 B1
Islington N1 235 C6
Lisson Gr NW8 237 A5
17 Millwall E14 119 C4
6 Newham E13 99 A5
Richmond TW10 153 C2
3 Stonebridge NW10 67 B1
Scott Lidgett Cres SE16 118 A4
Scott Rd HA8 26 D1
Scott's Ave
Ashford TW16 171 C3
Beckenham BR2 186 B1
Scotts Ct 6 W12 112 B4
Scotts Dr TW12 173 D3
Scotts Farm Rd KT19 215 A2
Scotts Ho DA16 146 C4
Scott's La BR2, BR3 186 B1
Scotts Park Prim Sch BR1 187 C2
Scotts Rd BR1 187 A3
Scott's Rd
Leytonstone E10 54 A1
Shepherd's Bush W12 112 B4
Scotts Rd UB2 106 D3
Scott's Sufferance Wharf SE1 253 D1
Scott St E1 96 B3
Scott's Way TW16 171 C3
Scott's Yd EC4 252 C6
Scott Trimmer Way TW3 129 A3
Scottwell Dr NW9 45 D4
Scott Wilkie Prim Sch E16 99 C1
Scoulding Ho 12 E14 119 C3
Scoulding Rd E16 99 A1
Scouler St E14 120 B6
Scout App NW10 67 C4
Scout La SW4 137 C2
Scout Way NW7 27 B6
Scovell Cres SE1 252 A1
Scovell Rd SE1 252 A1
Scratchwood Nature Trail* NW7 11 B4
Scrattons Terr IG11 103 A5
Scriven Ct 2 E8 95 D6
Scriven St E8 95 D6
Scrooby St SE6 163 D5
Scrope Bldg EC1 241 A4
Scrubs La NW10, W10, W12 90 B3
Scrutton Cl SW12 159 D4
Scrutton St EC2 95 C3 243 A5
Scudamore La NW9 45 A5
Scutari Rd SE22 162 C6
Scylla Cres TW6&TW14 148 D4
Scylla Rd
East Bedfont TW14, TW6 148 D5
Nunhead SE15 140 B2
Seabright St 27 E2 96 B4
Seabrook Dr BR4 224 C6
Seabrook Gdns RM7 59 C2
Seabrook Rd RM8 80 D5
Seacole Cl W3 89 B2
Seacole Ct N15 51 D4
Seacole Lo N21 16 B6
Seacon Twr 8 E14 119 C4
Seacourt Rd SE2 124 D4
Seacroft Gdns WD19 22 D6
Seafield Rd N11 31 D6
Seaford Cl HA4 61 B6
Seaford Ho 13 SE16 118 C4
Seaford Rd
Ealing W13 109 B5
Enfield EN1 5 C1
Tottenham N15 51 C4
Walthamstow E17 53 D6
Seaford St WC1 233 B1
Seaforth Ave KT3 200 B5
Seaforth Cres N5 73 A3
Seaforth Gdns
Southgate N21 16 C3
Woodford IG8 37 C5
Worcester Pk KT19 215 D3
Seaforth Lo 2 SW13 133 D3
Seaforth Pl SW1 259 B6
Seagrave Lo SW6 265 B6
Seagrave Rd SW6 135 C6 265 B6
Seagrove Cl E1 96 D2
Seagry Rd E11 55 B2
Seagull Cl IG11 102 A4
Seagull La E16 121 A6
Sealand Rd TW6 148 C5
Sealand Wlk UB5 85 A4
Seal Ho SE1 262 D6
Seal St E8 73 D4
Searle Ct 2 CR4 180 C2
Searle Pl N4 50 B1
Searles Cl SW11 136 C5 267 B3
Searles Dr E6 100 D2
Searles Rd SE1 262 D4
Searson Ho SE17 261 D3
Sears Ret Pk UB6 86 C6
Sears St SE5 139 B5
Seasalter Ho 10 SW9 138 C4
Seasprite Cl 10 UB5 84 D4
Seath Ho 4 SE26 184 B5
Seaton Ave IG3 79 D3
Seaton Cl
Isleworth TW2 152 B5
6 Newham E13 99 A3
Roehampton SW15 156 B4
Seaton Dr TW15 148 A2
Seaton Gdns HA4 62 A6
Seaton Point E5 74 A4
Seaton Rd
Bexley DA16 146 C5
Hayes UB3 105 B3
Mitcham CR4 180 C1
Twickenham TW2 152 A5
Wembley HA0 88 A5
Seaton Sq NW7 28 D3
Seaton St N18 34 A5
Seavington Ho 3 SE5 139 C2
Sebastian Ct 11 IG11 79 D1
Sebastian Ho 22 N1 95 C5
Sebastian St EC1 94 D4 234 D1
Sebastopol Rd N9 34 A6
Sebbon St N1 72 D1
Sebergham Gr NW7 28 A3
Sebert Rd E7 77 B4
Sebright Ho 22 E2 96 A5
Sebright Pas 29 E2 96 A5
Sebright Rd EN5 1 A2
Sebright Sch E2 96 A5
Secker Cres HA3 24 A2
Secker Ho SW9 138 D3
Secker St SE1 251 A3
Second Ave
Chadwell Heath RM6 58 C4
Dagenham RM10 103 D5
East Acton W3 111 D5
Edmonton N18 34 C6
Enfield EN1 17 D6
Hayes UB3 105 D5
Hendon NW4 46 D5
Kensal Town W10 91 A3
Manor Pk E12 78 A3
Mortlake SW14 133 C2
Newham E13 99 A4
Walthamstow E17 53 C4
Walton-on-T KT12 194 B3
Wembley HA9 65 D6
Second Cl KT8 196 A5
Second Cross Rd TW2 152 C2
Second Way HA9 66 D4
Secrett Ho 6 TW10 153 C1
Sedan Way SE17 117 C1 263 A2
Sedcombe Cl DA14 190 C6
Sedcote Rd EN3 18 D6
Sedding St SW1 258 A4
Seddon Ho EC2 242 A4
Seddon Rd SM4 202 B4
Seddon St WC1 94 B4 233 D1
Sedgebrook Rd SE3 143 D2
Sedgecombe Ave HA3 43 C4
Sedgefield Ct UB5 63 D3
Sedgeford Rd W12 111 D5
Sedgehill Rd SE6 185 D5
Sedgehill Sch SE6 185 D5
Sedgemere Ave N2 48 A6
Sedgemere Rd SE2 124 C3
Sedgemoor Dr RM10 81 C4
Sedge Rd N17 34 C3
Sedgeway SE6 164 D3
Sedgewick Ho SW19 156 D2
Sedgewood Cl BR2 208 D2
Sedgley Ho N4 72 B6
Sedgmoor Pl SE5 139 C5
Sedgwick Ave UB10 60 D1
Sedgwick Rd E10 76 A6
Sedgwick St E9 74 D3
Sedleigh Rd SW18 157 B5
Sedlescombe Rd SW6 135 C6 265 A6
Sedley Cl EN1 6 B5
Sedley Ct SE26 162 B2
Sedley Ho SE11 260 D2
Sedley Pl W1 238 C1
Sedum Cl NW9 44 D4
Seeley Dr SE21 183 C6
Seelig Ave NW9 46 A2
Seely Rd SW17 181 A4
Seething La EC3 117 C6 253 B6
SEETHING WELLS 197 D3
Seething Wells Halls of Residence KT6 197 C3
Seething Wells La KT6 197 C3
Sefton Ave
Edgware NW7 27 B5
Harrow HA3 24 B2
Sefton Cl BR5 211 D5
Sefton Ct TW5 129 D4
Sefton Lo 2 TW1 153 C5
Sefton Rd
Croydon CR0 206 A1
Orpington BR5 211 D5
Sefton St SW15 134 C2
Segal Cl SE23 163 A4
Sekforde St EC1 94 D3 241 C6
Sekhon Terr TW13 151 C1
Selan Gdns UB4 84 B2
Selbie Ave NW10 67 D3
Selborne Ave DA5 169 A3
Little Ilford E12 78 C4
Walthamstow E17 53 B5
Selborne Gdns
Hendon NW4 46 A5
Wembley UB6 87 A5
Selborne Ho SE1 252 C1
Selborne 2 SW11 137 A2
Selborne Prim Sch UB6 86 D5
Selborne Rd
1 Camberwell SE5 139 B3
Ilford IG1 78 C6
Kingston u T KT3 177 C1
Palmers Green N14 16 A1
Sidcup DA14 190 B6
South Croydon CR0 221 D5
Walthamstow E17 53 C4
Wood Green N22 32 B2
Selborne Wlk E17 53 B5
Selborne Wlk Sh Ctr E17 53 B5
Selbourne Ave KT6 214 C5
Selbridge Ct SW19 179 C4
Selby Chase HA4 62 B6
Selby Cl BR7 188 C4
Chessington KT9 214 A1
14 Newham E6 100 A2
Selby Ct TW2 152 B2
Selby Gdns UB1 85 C3
Selby Gn SM5 202 C2
Selby Ho 10 SW4 159 C5
Selby Rd
Ashford TW15 171 A4
Carshalton SM5 202 C2
Ealing W5 87 C3
Leyton E11 76 C5
Newham E13 99 B2
Penge SE20 184 A1
Tottenham N17 33 C4
Selby Sq 1 W10 91 A4
Selby St E1 96 A3
Selden Ho 2 SE15 140 C3
Selden Rd SE15 140 C3
Selden Wlk N7 72 B6
Seldon Ho
Nine Elms SW8 269 A3
Pimlico SW1 259 A1
Selena Ct N20 14 D1
SELHURST 205 B4
Selhurst Cl SW19 156 D3
Selhurst New Ct SE25 205 C3
Selhurst New Rd SE25 205 C3
Selhurst Park (Crystal Palace FC) SE25 205 C5
Selhurst Pl SE25 205 C3
Selhurst Rd
Edmonton N9 17 C1
South Norwood SE25 205 C4
Selhurst Sta SE25 205 C4
Selina Ho NW8 236 D6
Selinas La RM8 59 B2
Selkirk Ct N17 33 C1
Selkirk Ho N1 233 C6
4 Stoke Newington N16 73 C5
Selkirk Rd
Twickenham TW2 152 A3
Upper Tooting SW17 180 C6
Sellers Hall Cl N3 29 C3
Sellincourt Prim Sch SW17 180 C4
Sellincourt Rd SW17 180 C4
Sellindge Cl BR3 185 B3
Sellons Ave NW10 89 D6
Sellsby Ct N11 31 B5
Sellwood Dr EN5 12 D6
Selma Ho 7 W12 90 B1
Selman Ho 3 E9 75 A2
SELSDON 223 A1
Selsdon Ave CR2 221 B2
Selsdon Cl KT6 198 A4
Selsdon High Sch CR2 222 D1
Selsdon Park Rd CR0, CR2 223 B1
Selsdon Rd
Newham E13 99 C5
South Croydon CR2 221 B2
Wanstead E11 55 A2
West Norwood SE27 182 D6
Willesden NW2 67 D6
Selsdon Road Ind Est CR2 221 B2
Selsdon Way E14 119 D3
Selsea Pl N16 73 C3
Selsey Cres DA16 146 D4
Selsey St E14 97 C2
Selvage La NW7 27 B6
Selway Cl HA5 40 B6
Selway Ho SW8 270 B2
Selwood Ho
Chislehurst BR7 189 A4
1 Stoke Newington N4 51 B2
Selwood Pl SW7 114 B1 256 C2
Selwood Rd
Cheam SM3 201 B1
Chessington KT9 213 D4
Croydon CR0 206 B1
Selwood Terr SW7 256 C2
Selworthy Cl E11 55 A4
Selworthy Ho SW11 266 D2
Selworthy Rd SE6 163 B1
Selwyn Ave
Chingford E4 36 A4
Ilford IG3 57 D3
Richmond TW9 132 B2
Selwyn Cl TW4 129 A1
Selwyn Cres DA16 146 B1
Selwyn Ct
Edgware HA8 26 D3
Lewisham SE3 142 D2
8 Richmond TW10 154 B6
Walthamstow E17 53 C4
Wembley HA9 67 A5
Selwyn Ho 3 SW15 156 D5
Selwyn Inf Sch E4 36 A4
Selwyn Jun Sch E4 36 A4
Selwyn Prim Sch E13 99 A6
Selwyn Rd Bow E3 97 B5
Newham E13 99 B6
New Malden KT3 199 B4
Willesden NW10 67 C1
Semley Gate E9 75 B2
Semley Ho SW1 258 C3
Semley Pl SW1 115 B2 258 C3
Thornton Heath SW16 182 B1
Semley Rd SW16 182 A1
Senate St SE15 140 C3
Senators Lo 31 E3 97 A5
Senator Wlk 2 SE28 123 B3
Sencler Ho SE2 146 D6
Sendall Ct 13 SW11 136 B2
Seneca Rd CR7 205 A5
Senga Rd SM6 203 A1
Senhouse Rd SM3 216 D5
Senior St W2 91 D2
Senlac Rd SE12 165 B3
Sennen Rd EN1 17 D4
Sennen Wlk SE9 166 A1
Senrab St E1 96 D1
Sentinel Cl UB5 85 A3
Sentinel Ho NW4 46 C5
Sentinel Sq NW4 46 C5
September Ct UB1 107 D5
September Way HA7 25 B4
Sequoia Cl WD23 8 B3
Sequoia Gdns BR6 211 D2
Sequoia Pk HA5 23 D4
Seraph Ct EC1 95 A4 235 A2
Serbin Cl E10 54 A2
Serenaders Rd 20 SW9 138 C3
Sergeant Ind Est The SW18 157 D5
Serica Ct 14 SE10 142 A5
Serjeants' Inn EC4 241 B1
Serlby Ct W14 254 C6
Serle St WC2 94 B1 240 D2
Sermon La EC4 242 A1
Serpentine Ct 10 SE16 118 D4
Serpentine Gallery* W2 114 B4 246 D2
Serpentine Rd W2 114 D5 247 C3
Serpentine The* W2 114 C5 247 B3
Service Route No 1 E15 76 B1
Service Route No 2 1 E15 76 B1
Service Route No 3 2 E15 76 B1
Serviden Dr BR1 187 D2
Servite Ho
Beckenham BR3 185 B2
Bromley BR1 188 B1
East Barnet N14 15 B6
Lewisham SE13 141 D4
Penge SE26 184 C4
Worcester Pk KT4 215 D6
Servite RC Prim Sch SW10 136 A6 266 A6
Servius Ct 2 TW8 131 D5
Sessions Terr CR4 180
Setchell Rd SE1 117 D2 263
Setchell Way SE1 263
Seth St 25 SE16 118
Seton Ct 3 NW9 46
Seton Gdns RM9 80
Settle Point 11 E13 99
Settlers Ct 11 E14 120
Settles St E1 96
Settrington Rd SW6 135
Seven Acres
Carshalton SM5 218
Northwood HA6 22
Seven Dials WC2 94 A1 240
SEVEN KINGS 57
Seven Kings High Sch IG2 57
Seven Kings Rd IG3 79
Seven Kings Sta IG3 57
Seven Kings Way KT2 176
Seven Mills Prim Sch E14 119
Sevenoaks Rd BR6 227
Catford SE4 163
Sevenoaks Way BR5 190
Seven Sisters N15 51
Seven Sisters Prim Sch N15 51
Seven Sisters Rd
Finsbury Pk N4 72
Stoke Newington N4, N7, N15 51
Seven Sisters Sta N15 51
Seven Stars Cnr W12 112
Seven Stars Yd E1 243
Seventh Ave
Hayes UB3 106
Ilford E12 78
Seven Ways Par IG2 56
Severnake Cl E14 119
Severn Ave 2 W10 91
Severn Ct 11 KT2 175
Severn Dr Enfield EN1 6
Hinchley Wood KT10 213
Severn Way NW10 67
Severus Rd SW11 136
Seville Ho 11 E1 118
Seville Mews N1 73
Seville St SW1 247
Sevington Rd NW4 46
Sevington St W9 91
Seward Rd
Penge BR3 184
West Ealing W7 109
Seward St EC1 95 A4 235
SEWARDSTONEBURY 20
Sewardstone Gdns E4 19
Sewardstone Rd
Chingford E4 19
South Hackney E2 96
Sewdley St E5 74
Sewell Ho 7 N16 73
Sewell Rd SE2 124
Sewell St E13 99
Sextant Ave E14 120
Sexton Ct 7 E14 120
Sexton's Ho 5 SE13 142
Seychelle Ct BR3 185
Seymour Ave
Tottenham N17 34
West Barnes SM4 200
Seymour Cl
East Molesey KT8 196
Pinner HA5 23
Seymour Ct
Chingford E4 20
Dollis Hill NW2 68
Muswell Hill N10 31
Putney SW15 134
Southgate N21 16
Upper Clapton N16 52
Seymour Dr BR2 210
Seymour Gdns
Brockley SE4 141
Feltham TW13 172
Kingston u T KT5 198
Redbridge IG1 56
Ruislip HA4 40
Twickenham TW1 153
Seymour Ho
Bloomsbury WC1 240
1 Clapham SW8 137
Ruislip HA4 40
Somers Town NW1 232
Seymour Lo 14 KT1 175
Seymour Mews W1 238

eymour Pl
Croydon SE25 ....206 B5
Paddington
W1....... 92 D1 237 C2
eymour Rd
Acton W4..........111 A2
Carshalton CR4.......203 A2
Chingford E4.........19 D3
East Molesey KT8 ... 196 A4
Edmonton N9.........18 B2
Finchley N3..........29 D3
Hampton TW12 ..... 174 A5
Harringay N8.........50 D4
Newham E6..........99 D6
Teddington KT1 ..... 175 D2
Wallington SM5....... 219 A3
Walthamstow E10 .....53 B1
Wandsworth SW18 ...157 B5
Wimbledon SW19 ... 156 D1
eymour St
Paddington
W1....... 92 D1 237 D1
Woolwich SE18 ..... 123 A3
eymour Terr SE20...184 B2
eymour Villas
SE20.............184 A2
eymour Way TW16..171 C3
eymour Wlk
SW10.......136 A6 266 A6
eyssel St E14.......120 A2
haa Rd W3.........111 B6
habana Ct [3] W12 ..112 B5
hacklegate La
TW11...............174 C6
hackleton Cl SE23 ..162 B2
hackleton Ct
[3] Dulwich SE21.....161 B2
[2] Isle of Dogs E14 . 119 C1
[4] Shepherd's Bush
W12 ....112 B4
[7] Stanwell TW19... 148 A5
hackleton Ho
[5] Stonebridge
NW10............67 B1
[5] Wapping E1 ..... 118 C5
hackleton Lo
SW16..............181 D5
hackleton Rd UB1 ..107 B6
HACKLEWELL 73 D4
hacklewell Ho [3]
E8..................73 D4
hacklewell La E8 ....73 D3
hacklewell Prim Sch
E8..................73 D4
hacklewell Rd N16...73 D4
hacklewell Row E8 ..73 D4
hacklewell St [30] E2..95 D4
hadbolt Ave E4.......35 A5
hadbolt Cl KT4 .....215 D6
had Thames
SE1........ 117 D4 253 D2
HADWELL 118 C6
hadwell Ct UB5....... 85 B5
hadwell Dr UB5....... 85 B4
hadwell Gdns E1 ...118 C6
hadwell Pierhead
E1..................118 C6
hadwell Pl [1] E1....118 C6
hadwell Sta E1.......118 B6
hady Bush Cl WD23 ... 8 A4
haef Way TW11.......175 A3
haftesbury Ave
Enfield EN3...........6 D3
Feltham TW14 ...... 150 A5
Kenton HA3...........44 A3
New Barnet EN5 ....2 A1
Southall UB2 .... 107 C3
W1........ 115 D6 249 D6
West Harrow HA1,
HA2 ....42 A1
haftesbury Circ
HA2 ....42 A1
haftesbury Ct
Borough The SE1.... 262 C6
[1] Herne Hill SE5 ....139 B1
Ilford RM6...........58 C2
Newham E6......... 100 C1
haftesbury Ctr
NW10...............90 D3
haftesbury Ct
Shoreditch N1...... 235 C3
Streatham SW16.... 159 D1
[3] Thamesmead
SE28............ 124 C5
haftesbury Gdns
NW10...............89 C3
haftesbury High Sch
HA3 ....23 D2
haftesbury Ho
[11] Canning Town
E16...............98 D1
Croydon SE25 ...... 206 A3
[13] Stoke Newington
N16...............73 C5
Upper Tooting SW17 ..180 B6
W2................ 245 D6
Shaftesbury Lo [9]
E14................97 D1
Shaftesbury Mews
[2] Clapham Pk
SW4............ 159 C6
W8................255 B5
Shaftesbury Park
Chambers [1]
SW11..............137 A2
Shaftesbury Point
E13.................99 B5
Shaftesbury Prim Sch
E7..................77 C1
Shaftesbury Rd
Beckenham BR3 ......185 B1
Carshalton SM5...... 202 C2
Chingford E4 ....20 B3
Edmonton N18.........33 D4
Finsbury Pk N4, N19...50 A1
Leyton E10...........53 C1
Richmond TW9...... 132 A2
Upton E7 ....77 C1
Walthamstow E17 .....53 D3
Shaftesburys The
IG11...............101 A5
Shaftesbury St N1 .. 235 C3
Shaftesbury Waye
UB4 ....84 C1
Shaftesbury Way
TW2................152 B1
Shafteswood Ct
SW17..............158 D1
Shafto Mews SW1 .. 257 D5
Shafton Rd E9.......96 D6
Shaftsbury Park Prim
Sch SW11......... 137 A3
Shafts Ct EC3....... 243 A1
Shahjalal Ho [18] E2.....96 A5
Shakespeare Ave
[7] Becontree
NW10............89 B6
Feltham TW14 ...... 150 A5
Friern Barnet N11.....31 C5
Hayes UB4...........84 B2
Shakespeare Cl HA3 ..44 C2
Shakespeare Cres
E12.................78 B2
Shakespeare Ct EN5 ...1 D2
Shakespeare Dr HA3 ..44 B3
Shakespeare Gdns
N2 ....48 D5
Shakespeare Ho
[1] Erith DA17.......125 B1
[3] Hackney E9 ....74 C1
Osidge N14 ....15 D2
Shakespeare Rd
Acton W3.......... 111 A5
Brixton SE24 .... 138 D1
DA7 .... 147 A4
Ealing W7 .... 108 D6
Finchley N3 ....29 C2
Higham Hill E17.......34 D1
Mill Hill NW7.........28 A6
Shakespeare's Globe
Theatre (site of)*
SE1 .... 252 B4
Shakespeare Twr
EC2 .... 242 B4
Shakespeare Way
TW13...............172 C6
Shakspeare Mews [7]
N16 ....73 C4
Shakspeare Wlk N16 ..73 C4
Shalbourne Sq E9 ....75 B2
Shalcomb St
SW10........136 A6 266 B5
Shalden Ho SW15....155 D5
Shaldon Dr
Ruislip HA4 ....62 C5
West Barnes SM4 .... 201 A4
Shaldon Rd HA8 ......26 B1
Shalfleet Dr W10 ...112 D6
Shalford Cl BR6......227 A4
Shalford Ct N1 ..... 234 C4
Shalford Ho SE1 .... 262 D6
Shalford
Willesden Green
NW10.............90 A6
[3] Woodford IG8 .....37 C4
Shalimar Gdns W3...111 A6
Shalimar Lo W3 .....111 A6
Shalimar Rd W3 .....111 A6
Shallons Rd SE9.....188 D6
Shalstone Rd SW14,
TW9................132 D2
Shalston Villas KT5,
KT6 ....198 B3
Shamrock Ct E7 ......77 D3
Shamrock Ho
East Barnet N14 ......15 B4
Forest Hill SE26...... 184 A6
Shamrock Rd CR0.....204 B3
Shamrock St SW4....137 D2
Shamrock Way N14 ...15 B3
Shandon Ct SE4 .....141 A3
Shandon Rd SW4 ....159 C5
Shand St
SE1..........117 C4 253 B2
Shandy St E1 ....96 D3
Shane Ct EN2...........5 A3
Shan Ho WC1....... 240 C5
Shanklin Gdns WD19..22 C6
Shanklin Ho E17 ......35 B1
Shanklin Rd
Hornsey N8..........49 D4
Tottenham Hale N15 ...52 A5
Shannon Cl
Cricklewood NW2 .....68 D5
Southall UB2 .... 106 D1
Shannon Cnr Ret Pk
KT3 .... 200 A5
Shannon Cnr KT3 ....200 A5
Shannon Commercial
Ctr KT3........... 200 A5
Shannon Ct
Croydon CR0 .... 205 A1
[11] Peckham SE15 .... 139 D5
Stoke Newington N16 ..73 C5
Willesden NW10 ......68 A2
Shannon Gr SW9 ....138 B1
Shannon Pl
NW8.........92 C5 230 B4
Shannon Way BR3 ...185 D4
Shanti Ct SW18 ......157 C3
Shap Cres SM5 ......202 D1
Shapland Way N13....32 B5
Shapla Prim Sch
E1................. 118 A6
Shapwick Cl N11.....30 D5
Shardcroft Ave
SE24...............160 D6
Shardeloes Rd SE14..141 B3
Shard's Sq SE15 .....140 A6
Sharebourne Ho
SW2................160 C6
Sharland Cl CR7 .....204 C3
Sharman Ct DA14 ....190 A6
Sharman Ho [18] E14 ...98 A1
Sharnbrooke Cl
DA16 ....146 C2
Sharnbrook Ho W6 . 265 A6
Sharon Cl KT6 ....197 C1
Sharon Ct [1] N12 .....30 A4
Sharon Gdns E9 ......96 C6
Sharon Rd
Chiswick W4 ....111 B1
Enfield EN3 ....7 A3
Sharpe Cl W7 ....86 D2
Sharp Ho SW8.......137 B2
Sharples Hall St [8]
NW1.................70 D1
Sharpness Cl UB4.....85 A2
Sharpness Ct [2]
SE15................139 D5
Sharps La HA4.........39 B2
Sharratt St SE15 .....140 C6
Sharsted St
SE17........116 D1 261 C1
Sharvel La UB5 ....84 B6
Sharwood WC1 ..... 233 D3
Shaver's Pl SW1 .... 249 C5
Shaw Ave IG11 ......103 A5
Shawbrooke Rd
SE9.................143 D1
Shawbury Cl [9] NW9 ..27 C2
Shawbury Ct SE22 ...161 D6
Shawbury Rd SE22...161 D6
Shaw Cl Bushey WD23 ... 8 C2
Woolwich SE28 ....124 B5
Shaw Cotts SE23.....163 A1
Shaw Cres [6] E14.....97 A1
Shaw Ct
[8] Acton Green
W3............ 111 A3
[12] Battersea SW11..136 B2
Cheam SM4......... 202 A2
Upper Holloway N19...72 A6
Shaw Dr KT12 ....194 C2
Shawfield Ct UB7 ....104 A3
Shawfield Pk BR1.....187 D1
Shawfield St
SW3.........114 C1 257 B1
Shawford Ct [8]
SW15...............156 A4
Shawford Rd KT19 ...215 B2
Shaw Gdns IG11.....103 A5
Shaw Ho
[6] Erith DA17 ....125 B1
[5] Newham E16 ......122 C5
Shaw Path BR1 ......164 D1
Shaw Rd
Camberwell SE22 ... 139 C1
Catford BR1......... 164 D1
Enfield EN3 ....6 D4
Shaw Sq E17 ....35 A2
Shaws Wood Cotts
EN4 ....3 C3
Shaw Way SM6 .....220 A1
Shearing Dr SM4 ....202 A2
Shearling Way N7 ....72 A2
Shearman Rd SE3....142 D2
Shears Ct TW16......171 C3
Shearsmith Ho [19]
E1..................118 A6
Shears The TW16 ....171 C3
Shears Way TW16....171 C2
Shearwater Cl IG11..102 A4
Shearwater Ct [24]
SE8................141 B6
Shearwater Rd SM1..217 B3
Shearwater Way
UB4 ....84 D1
Sheaveshill Ave NW9..45 C5
Sheaveshill Ct NW9..45 C5
Sheaveshill Par NW9..45 C5
Sheba Ct N17.........34 A4
Sheba Pl E1 .... 243 D5
Sheen Common Dr SW14,
TW10..............154 C6
Sheen Court Rd
TW10..............132 C1
Sheen Ct TW10 ......132 C1
Sheendale Rd TW9...132 B1
Sheenewood SE26 ...184 B6
Sheen Gate Gdns
SW14..............133 A1
Sheengate Mans
SW14..............133 B1
Sheen Gr N1 .. 94 C6 234 A6
Sheen La SW14.......133 A1
Sheen Mount Prim Sch
SW14............. 154 D6
Sheen Pk TW10,
TW9................132 A1
Sheen Rd
Orpington BR5...... 211 D5
Richmond TW10,
TW9 ....132 B1
Sheen Way SM6 .....220 B3
Sheen Wood SW14...155 A6
Sheepcote Cl TW5 ...128 A5
Sheepcote La SW11..136 D3
Sheepcote Rd HA1 ....42 D3
Sheepcotes Rd RM6...59 A5
Sheephouse Way
KT3 ....199 C2
Sheep La E8..........96 B6
Sheep Walk Mews [7]
SW19...............179 A4
Sheepwalk TW17 ....192 B3
Sheerness Mews
E16.................122 D4
Sheerwater Rd E16 ...99 D2
Sheffield Ho [15]
SE15................139 D4
Sheffield Rd TW14,
TW6...............149 A6
Sheffield Sq [2] E3 ....97 B4
Sheffield St WC2.... 240 C1
Sheffield Terr
W8.........113 C5 245 B3
Sheffield Way TW14,
TW6...............149 B6
Shefton Rise HA6 .....22 A3
Shelbey Ct BR1 ......186 D2
Shelbourne Cl HA5.... 41 B6
Shelbourne Ho [20]
N19 ....49 D2
Shelbourne Rd N17 ....34 B2
Shelburne Ct SW15 ..156 D6
Shelburne Dr TW4 ...151 C5
Shelburne Ho [9]
SW16...............181 C5
Shelburne Rd N7 .....72 B4
Shelbury Cl DA14 ....168 A1
Shelbury Rd SE22....162 B6
Sheldon Ave N6 ......48 D3
Sheldon Cl
Penge SE20..........184 B2
SE12 ....165 B6
Sheldon Ct Barnet EN5 ..1 D1
SW8................ 270 A3
Sheldon Ho
Chingford E4 ....36 C4
[9] Homerton E9 ......74 D2
Teddington TW11..... 175 A4
Sheldon Pl E2 ....96 B5
Sheldon Rd
Cricklewood NW2 .....68 D4
DA7 ....147 B4
Dagenham RM9........81 A1
Edmonton N18.........33 C6
Sheldon Sq W2..... 236 B3
Sheldon St CR0.......221 A5
Sheldrake Cl E16 ....122 B5
Sheldrake Ho [15]
SE16...............118 D2
Sheldrake Pl
W8.........113 C4 245 A2
Sheldrick Cl CR4.....180 B1
Shelduck Cl E15 ......76 D3
Shelduck Ct [37] SE8 ..141 B6
Sheldwich Terr
BR2 ....210 A3
Shelford Ct [7] E5 .....52 B1
Shelford [20] KT1......176 C1
Shelford Pl N16.......73 B5
Shelford Rd EN5 ......12 C5
Shelford Rise SE19...183 D3
Shelgate Rd SW11 ...158 D6
Shell Cl BR2.........210 A3
Shell Ctr SE1....... 250 D3
Shellduck Cl NW9.... 27 C1
Shelley Ave
Greenford UB6 ....86 B4
Plashet E12..........78 A2
Shelley Cl BR6.......227 C5
Edgware HA8.........26 C6
Greenford UB6 ....86 B4
Hayes UB4...........84 A2
Peckham SE15........140 B3
Shelley Cres
Heston TW5........ 128 D4
Southall UB1 ....85 B1
Shelley Ct
Finsbury Pk N4 ....50 B1
[9] Kingston u T KT2 . 175 D6
SW3............... 267 D6
[13] Walthamstow E10 ..53 D2
[8] Wanstead E11 ......55 A5
Wembley HA0 ....65 C4
West Barnes KT3 ... 200 A4
Shelley Dr DA16 .....145 C4
Shelley Gdns HA0....65 C6
Shelley Ho
[21] Bethnal Green
E2...............96 C4
Chelsea SW1........ 269 A6
[9] Stoke Newington
N16...............73 C4
Walworth SE17 ..... 262 B2
Shelley N8 ....50 A6
Shelley Rd NW10.....89 B6
Shelley Way SW17 ...180 B4
Shellgrove Rd N16.....73 C3
Shellness Rd E5 ......74 B3
Shell Rd SE13........141 D2
Shellwood Rd
SW11...............136 D3
Shelly Lo EN2..........5 B4
Shelmerdine Cl E3....97 C2
Shelson Ave TW13 ...171 D6
Shelton Ct N21 ....16 C4
Shelton Rd SW19 ....179 C2
Shelton St
WC2.........94 A1 240 A1
Shene Bldg EC1..... 241 A4
Shene Sch SW14 .... 133 C1
Shenfield Ho [3]
SE18...............143 D5
Shenfield Rd IG8 .....37 B3
Shenfield St N1.......95 C5
Shenley Ave HA4......39 D1
Shenley Ho [3]
SW16...............182 B6
Shenley Rd
Camberwell SE5 .... 139 C4
Heston TW5........ 129 A4
Shenstone W13......109 C5
Shenstone Gdns IG2 ..57 D4
Shenstone Ho
SW16...............181 C5
Shepard Ho [18]
SW11...............136 B2
Sheperdess Pl N1... 235 B2
Shepherd Cl
Feltham TW13....... 173 A6
W1................ 248 A6
Shepherdess Wlk
N1 .... 95 A5 235 B3
Shepherd Ho
Barnsbury N7 ....72 A2
[10] Poplar E14........97 D1
Shepherd Mkt W1 .. 248 C3
SHEPHERD'S BUSH
..................112 B5
Shepherd's Bush
(Central Line) Sta
W12............. 112 D4
Shepherd's Bush Gn
W12...............112 C4
Shepherd's Bush
(Hamm & City) Sta
W12............. 112 C5
Shepherd's Bush Market
W12...............112 C4
Shepherd's Bush Pl
W12...............112 D4
Shepherd's Bush Rd
W6.................112 C3
Shepherds Cl RM6 ....58 D5
Shepherd's Cl N6 .....49 B3
Shepherds Cl
Orpington BR6...... 227 D5
Shepperton TW17 ... 192 D3
Stanmore HA7.........25 A5
Shepherds Ct
[8] Hammersmith
W12 .... 112 D4
[13] Harrow HA1.......42 D3
Shepherds Gn BR7....189 B3
Shepherd's Hill N6....49 C3
Shepherd's La E9......74 D2
Shepherds La SE28...123 C5
Shepherds Leas
SE9................145 B1
Shepherds Path UB5 ..63 A2
Shepherds Pl W1 ... 248 A6
Shepherd St
W1.........115 B5 248 C3
Shepherds Way
CR2 ....222 D1
Shepherds Wlk
Bushey WD23 ....8 B2
Dollis Hill NW2 ....68 A6
Shepherd's Wlk NW3 . 70 B4
Shepiston La UB3....105 A1
Shepley Cl SM5......219 A5
Shepley Ct SW16.....181 C6
Shepley Mews EN3.....7 C6
Sheppard Cl
Enfield EN1 ....6 B5
Kingston u T KT6..... 198 A5
Sheppard Dr SE16 ...118 B1
Sheppard Ho
[31] Hackney E2 ....96 A5
[8] Streatham SW2 .. 160 C3
Sheppard's Ct
Harrow HA1 ....42 C2
Wembley UB6 ....64 D2
Sheppard St E16......98 D3
SHEPPERTON 193 A3
Shepperton Bsns Park
TW17............. 193 A4
Shepperton Court Dr
TW17..............192 D4
Shepperton Ct
TW17..............192 D3
SHEPPERTON GREEN
..................192 D5
Shepperton Rd
Littleton TW17,
TW18 .... 192 A5
Orpington BR5...... 211 A3
Shoreditch
N1 ....95 B6 235 C6
Shepperton Sta
TW17............. 193 A4
Shepperton Studios
TW17..............192 B6
Sheppey Gdns RM9 ...80 C1
Sheppey Ho [16] E5 .....74 B4
Sheppey Rd RM9.....80 C1
Shepton Ct SW11 ... 266 D2
Shepton Hos [11] E2....96 C4
Sherard Ct N19 ....72 A5
Sherard Ho [24] E9 .....74 C1
Sherard Rd SE9.......166 A6
Sheraton Bsns Ctr
UB6 ....87 C5
Sheraton Cl WD6 .....10 B6
Sheraton Ho SW1... 268 D6
Sheraton Lo HA3.....42 C6
Sheraton St W1 .... 239 C1
Sheraton The [22]
KT6 ....198 A4
Sherborne Ave
Enfield EN3 ....6 C3
Southall UB2 .... 107 C2
Sherborne Cl UB4.....84 C1
Sherborne Cres
SM5................202 C2
Sherborne Ct SE20...184 C1
Sherborne Gdns
Ealing W13 ....87 B2
Queensbury NW9 .....44 C6
Sherborne Ho
Pimlico SW1 .... 258 D2
South Lambeth SW8 . 270 C3
Sherborne La EC4... 252 D6
Sherborne Rd BR5 ...211 D4
Cheam SM3........ 201 C1
Chessington KT9..... 214 A3
East Bedfont TW14 ...149 B3
Sherborne St
N1 ....95 B6 235 C6
Sherboro Rd [1] N15...51 D3
Sherbourne Ct
[1] Hampton
TW12........... 173 C2
[9] Sutton SM2 ..... 218 A2
SW5.............. 255 C4
Sherbourne Gdns
TW17..............193 C2
Sherbourne Pl HA7 ...25 A4
Sherbrooke Cl DA7...147 C1
Sherbrooke Ho [9]
E2..................96 C5
Sherbrooke Rd
SW6.........135 A5 264 B3
Sherbrooke Terr
SW6............... 264 B3
Sherbrooke Way
KT4 ....200 B2
Sherbrook Gdns N21..16 D4
Sherbrook Ho [2] N3 ...29 D3
Shere Cl KT9 ....213 D3
Sheredan Rd E4 .....36 C5
Shere Ho SE1....... 262 C6
Shere Lo [1] SW19....180 C3

Shere Rd IG2 56 C4
Sherfield Cl KT3 198 D5
Sherfield Gdns SW15 155 D5
Sheridan Bldgs WC2 240 B1
Sheridan Cl UB10 83 A3
Sheridan Cres BR7 188 D1
Sheridan Ct
Ealing W7 108 D6
Earl's Ct SW5 255 C3
Harrow HA1 42 B3
Hounslow TW4 151 A6
South Hampstead NW6 70 A1
South Lambeth SW9 270 D1
Sheridan Gdns HA3 43 D3
Sheridan Ho SE11 261 B3
7 Stoke Newington N16 73 C5
Sheridan Lo
Barnet EN5 1 D1
Bromley BR2 209 C5
East Barnet N14 15 B4
Sheridan N8 50 C5
Sheridan Mews E11 55 B3
Sheridan Pl
Barnes SW13 133 D2
Hampton TW12 174 A2
Harrow HA1 42 C2
Sheridan Rd
Belvedere DA17 125 C2
DA7 147 A2
Leyton E7 76 D5
Little Ilford E12 78 B3
Merton SW19 179 B2
Richmond TW10 153 C1
Sheridan St 34 E1 96 B1
Sheridan Terr UB5 63 D3
Sheridan Way 6 BR3 185 B2
Sheridan Wlk
Golders Green NW11 47 C3
Wallington SM5 218 D3
Sheringdale Prim Sch SW18 157 B3
Sheringham Ave
Feltham TW13 150 A1
Little Ilford E12 78 B3
Southgate N14 15 D5
Twickenham TW2 151 C3
Sheringham Ct 1 N3 29 C2
Sheringham Dr IG11 80 A3
Sheringham Ho NW1 237 B4
Sheringham Jun Sch E12 78 B4
Sheringham Mews 4 SW18 158 A2
Sheringham NW8 229 D6
Sheringham Rd
Islington N7 72 C2
Penge SE20 206 C6
Sheringham Twr UB1 107 D6
Sherington Ave HA5 23 C3
Sherington Prim Sch SE7 143 B6
Sherington Rd SE7 143 B6
Sheriton Ct SM1 217 C5
Sherland Rd TW1 152 D3
Sherleys Ct HA4 61 C6
Sherlies Ave BR6 227 C6
Sherlock Ct NW8 229 C6
Sherlock Holmes Mus* NW1 92 D3 237 D5
Sherlock Mews W1 238 A4
Sherman Gdns RM6 58 C3
Sherman Rd BR1 187 A2
Shernhall St E17 54 A5
Shernwood Ho 1 E18 55 A5
Sherrard Rd E7, E12 77 D2
Sherrards Way EN5 13 D5
Sherren Ho 35 E1 96 C3
Sherrick Green Rd NW10 68 B3
Sherriff Ct NW6 69 C2
Sherriff Rd NW6 69 C2
Sherringham Ave N17 34 A1
Sherrin Rd E10 75 D4
Sherrock Gdns NW4 46 A5
Sherry Mews IG11 79 B1
Sherston Ct
Finsbury WC1 234 A1
Newington SE1 261 D4
Sherwin Ho 1 SE11 138 C6
Sherwin Rd SE14 140 D4
Sherwood Ave
Greenford UB6 64 C3
Hayes UB4 84 B3
Sherwood Ave *continued*
Mitcham SW16 181 D2
Ruislip HA4 39 C3
Wanstead E18 55 B6
Sherwood
3 Barnet EN5 1 D1
Brondesbury NW6 69 A1
Sherwood Cl
Barnes SW13 134 B2
DA5 168 C5
Ealing W13 109 B5
Walthamstow E17 35 B1
Sherwood Ct
11 Battersea SW11 136 A2
Colney Hatch N12 30 C5
2 South Croydon CR2 221 A3
St Johns SE13 141 D3
Sutton SM1 217 C3
W1 237 C3
6 West Wickham BR4 207 D1
Sherwood Gdns
Barking IG11 79 B1
Bermondsey SE16 118 B1
Millwall E14 119 C2
Sherwood Hall 7 N2 48 A6
Sherwood Ho N4 51 A2
Sherwood KT6 213 D6
Sherwood Park Ave DA15 168 B5
Sherwood Park Prim Sch DA15 168 B5
Sherwood Park Rd
Mitcham CR4 203 D5
Sutton SM1 217 C3
Sherwood Park Sch SM6 219 D5
Sherwood Rd
Croydon CR0 206 B1
DA16 145 C2
Hampton TW12 174 A5
Harrow HA2 64 A6
Hendon NW4 46 C6
Ilford IG6 57 B5
Merton SW19 179 B3
Sherwood Sch The CR4 203 C5
Sherwood St W1 249 B6
Whetstone N20 14 B1
Sherwood Terr N20 14 B1
Sherwood Way BR4 224 A6
Shetland Cl WD6 11 B5
Shetland Rd Bow E3 97 B5
East Bedfont TW6 149 A5
Shield Dr TW8 131 A6
Shieldhall St SE2 124 C2
Shield Rd TW15 171 B6
Shifford Path SE23 162 D1
Shillaker Ct W3 111 D5
Shillibeer Ct N18 34 B5
Shillibeer Pl W1 237 B3
Shillingford Cl NW7 28 D3
Shillingford Ho 40 E3 97 D4
Shillingford St 23 N1 72 D1
Shilling Pl TW8 109 A5
Shillingstone Ho W14 254 B5
Shine Ho 3 N3 29 D3
Shinfield St W12 90 C1
Shinglewell Rd DA8 147 C5
Shinners Cl SE25 206 A4
Shipka Rd SW12 159 B3
Shiplake Ct SW17 180 B6
Shiplake Ho 45 E2 95 D4
Ship La SW14 133 A3
Shipley Ct SE20 184 A1
Shipley Ho 32 SW8 137 D3
Shipman Rd
Forest Hill SE23 162 D2
Newham E16 99 C1
Ship & Mermaid Row SE1 253 A2
Ship St SE8 141 C4
Ship Tavern Pas EC3 253 A6
Shipton Cl RM8 80 D5
Shipton Ho
7 Camden Town NW5 71 A2
14 Haggerston E2 95 D5
Shipton Rd UB8 60 B4
Shipton St E2 95 D4
Shipwright Rd SE16 119 A4
Shipwright Yd SE1 253 A3
Shirburn Cl SE23 162 C4
Shirbutt St E14 119 D6
Shirebrook Rd SE3 143 D2
Shire Ct DA18 124 D3
Ewell KT17 215 D1
Shirehall Cl NW4 46 D3
Shirehall Gdns NW4 46 D3
Shirehall La NW4 46 D3
Shirehall Pk NW4 46 D3
Shire Ho E11 76 D5
Shire Horse Way TW7 130 D2
Shire La BR6 227 B2
Shiremeade WD6 10 B6
Shire Mews TW2 152 A5
Shire Pl
12 Brentford TW8 131 C5
Wandsworth SW18 158 A4
Shires The TW10 176 A6
Shirland Mews W9 91 B4
Shirland Rd W9 91 C3
SHIRLEY 206 C1
Shirley Ave
Carshalton SM1 218 C4
Croydon CR0 206 D1
DA5 168 D3
Shirley Church Rd CR0 223 A5
Shirley Cl
Hounslow TW3 152 A6
Walthamstow E17 53 D4
Shirley Cres BR3 207 A5
Shirley Ct
8 Ealing W13 109 A5
Ilford IG2 57 B4
Kingsbury NW9 45 B4
2 South Norwood SW16 182 B3
Thornton Heath SW16 204 B6
Shirley Dr TW3 152 A6
Shirley Gdns
Barking IG11 79 C2
Ealing W7 108 D5
Shirley Gr
Clapham SW11 137 A2
Ponders End N9 18 D4
Shirley High Sch Performing Arts Coll CR0 222 D5
Shirley Hills Rd CR0 222 D3
Shirley Ho 13 SE5 139 B5
Shirley House Dr SE7 143 C5
Shirley Hts 6 DA6 147 A1
Shirley Lo 4 SE26 185 A6
SHIRLEY OAKS 207 A1
Shirley Oaks Hospl CR0 206 C2
Shirley Oaks Rd CR0 222 D6
Shirley Park Rd CR0 206 C1
Shirley Rd Acton W4 111 B4
Croydon CR0 206 B1
Enfield EN2 5 A2
Sidcup DA15 167 C1
Stratford E15 76 C1
Shirley St E16 98 D1
Shirley Way CR0 223 B5
Shirlock Rd NW3 70 D4
Shirwell Cl NW7 28 D3
Shobden Rd N17 33 B2
Shobroke Cl NW2 68 C5
Shoebury Rd E6 78 B1
Shoe La EC4 94 C1 241 B2
Shoelands Ct NW9 45 B6
Shona Ho E16 99 C2
Shooters Ave HA3 43 C5
SHOOTERS HILL 145 A4
Shooters Hill Rd
Blackheath Vale SE3, SE10 142 C4
SE18, SE3, SE7 143 D5
Shooters Hill SE18 144 C4
Shooters Rd EN2 4 D4
Shoot-Up Hill NW2 69 A2
Shopstop SW11 136 C1
Shore Bsns Ctr 31 E9 74 C1
Shore Cl
Feltham TW14 150 A4
Hampton TW12 173 A5
Shorediche Cl UB10 60 B5
SHOREDITCH 95 B5
Shoreditch Ct 2 E8 73 D1
Shoreditch High St E2 95 C3 243 B6
Shoreditch Ho N1 235 D1
Shore Gr TW13 151 C2
Shoreham Cl
Croydon CR0 206 C3
DA5 168 D3
Wandsworth SW18 157 D6
Shoreham Rd BR5 190 B1
Shoreham Rd (E) TW6 148 A6
Shoreham Rd (W) TW6 148 A6
Shoreham Way BR2 209 A3
Shore Ho SW8 137 B2
Shore Mews 30 E9 74 C1
Shore Pl E9 74 C1
Shore Point 2 IG9 21 B2
Shore Rd E9 74 C1
Shore Way 26 SW9 138 C3
Shorncliffe Rd SE1 117 D1 263 C2
Shorndean St SE6 164 A3
Shorne Cl 3 DA15 168 B5
Shornefield Cl BR1 210 C6
Shornells Way SE2 124 C1
Shorrolds Rd SW6 135 B5 264 D4
Shortcroft Mead Ct NW10 68 A3
Shortcroft Rd KT17 215 D1
Shortcrofts Rd RM9 81 B2
Shorter St EC3 117 D6 253 D6
Shortgate N12 29 B6
SHORTLANDS 208 C6
Shortlands W6 112 D2
Shortlands Cl DA17 125 B3
Edmonton N18 17 B1
Shortlands Gdns BR2 186 C1
Shortlands Gr BR2 208 B6
Shortlands UB3 127 B6
Shortlands Rd
Beckenham BR2, BR3 208 C6
Kingston u T KT2 176 B3
Walthamstow E10 53 D2
Shortlands Sta BR2 186 C1
Short La TW15, TW19 148 B3
Short Path SE18 144 D6
Short Rd
Chiswick W4 133 C6
Leyton E11 76 C6
Stanwell TW19 148 A5
Shorts Croft NW9 44 D5
Shorts Gdns WC2 94 A1 240 A1
Shorts Rd SM5 218 C3
Short St
7 Hendon NW4 46 C5
SE1 251 B2
Short Way N12 30 C4
Shortway SE9 144 A2
Short Way TW2 152 A4
Shotfield SM6 219 B2
Shott Cl SM1 218 A3
Shottendane Rd SW6 135 C4 265 A2
Shottery Cl SE9 166 A1
Shottfield Ave SW14 133 C1
Shottsford 1 W11 91 C1
Shoulder of Mutton Alley 10 E14 119 A6
Shouldham St W1 92 C2 237 B3
Showers Way UB3 106 A5
Shrapnel Cl SE18 144 A5
Shrapnel Rd SE9 144 B2
Shreveport Ho 23 N19 49 D2
Shrewsbury Ave
Harrow HA3 44 A5
Mortlake SW14 133 B1
Shrewsbury Cl KT6 214 A6
Shrewsbury Ho
Chelsea SW3 267 A5
Kennington SE11 270 D5
Shrewsbury House Sch KT6 214 A6
Shrewsbury La SE18 144 D4
Shrewsbury Mews 33 W2 91 C2
Shrewsbury Rd
Beckenham BR3 207 A6
Carshalton SM5 202 C2
Friern Barnet N11 31 D4
Harlington TW14, TW6 149 B5
Notting Hill W2 91 C1
Plashet E7 77 D2
Shrewsbury St W10 90 C3
Shrewsbury Wlk 9 TW7 131 A2
Shrewton Rd SW17 180 D3
Shri Swaminarayan Mandir* NW10 67 B2
Shroffold Rd BR1 164 D1
Shropshire Cl CR4 204 A5
Shropshire Ct W7 86 D1
Shropshire Ho WC1 239 B5
Shropshire Rd N22 32 B3
Shroton St NW1 92 C2 237 B4
Shrubberies The
Ilford IG2 57 D4
Woodford E18 37 A1
Shrubbery Cl N1 235 B5
Shrubbery Gdns N21 16 D4
Shrubbery Rd
Edmonton N9 18 A1
Southall UB1 107 C5
Shrubbery Rd *continued*
Streatham SW16 182 A6
Shrubbery The
2 Surbiton KT6 198 A1
7 Wanstead E11 55 B4
Shrub Ct 5 SM2 218 A2
Shrubland Gr KT4 216 C5
Shrubland Rd
Hackney E8 96 A6
Leyton E10 53 C2
Walthamstow E17 53 C4
Shrublands Ave CR0 223 C4
Shrublands Cl
Forest Hill SE26 162 C1
Whetstone N20 14 B2
Shrubsall Cl SE9 166 A3
Shrubs Ho SW1 259 D3
Shurland Ave EN4 14 B5
Shurland Gdns SE15 139 D5
Shurlock Dr BR6 227 A4
Shuters Sq W14 254 C1
Shuttle Cl DA15 167 D4
Shuttlemead DA5 169 B4
Shuttle St E1 96 A3
Shuttleworth Rd SW11 136 C3
Sibella Rd SW4 137 D3
Sibford Ct 5 CR4 202 D6
Sibley Cl Bexley DA6 169 A6
Bromley BR1 210 A4
Sibley Ct
Beckenham BR3 186 C1
Hillingdon UB8 83 A2
Sibley Gr E12 78 A1
Sibthorpe Rd SE12 165 C4
Sibthorp Rd 2 CR4 180 D1
Sibton Rd SM5 202 C2
Sicilian Ave WC1 240 B3
Sidbury St SW6 135 A4 264 A2
SIDCUP 190 A5
Sidcup By Pass Rd
Sidcup DA14 189 C6
St Paul's Cray BR5, BR7 190 B3
Sidcup Hill DA14 190 B5
Sidcup Hill Gdns DA14 190 C5
Sidcup Pl DA14 190 A5
Sidcup Rd SE9 166 A3
Sidcup Sta DA15 168 A2
Sidcup Tech Ctr DA14 190 D4
Siddeley Dr TW4 129 A3
Siddons Ct WC2 240 C1
Siddons Ho 8 NW3 70 D3
Siddons La NW1 92 D3 237 D5
Siddons Rd
Croydon CR0 220 D5
Forest Hill SE23 163 A2
Tottenham N17 34 A2
Side Rd E17 53 B4
Sidewood Rd SE9 167 B3
Sidford Ho SE1 260 D5
Sidford Pl SE1 116 B3 260 D5
Sidgwick Ho 26 SW9 138 A3
Sidi Ct 2 N15 50 D6
Sidings Mews N7 72 C4
Sidings The E11 54 A1
Sidlaw Ho N16 51 D1
Sidmouth Ave TW7 130 C3
Sidmouth Dr HA4 62 A5
Sidmouth Ho
18 Camberwell SE15 140 A5
Marylebone W1 237 B2
28 Streatham SW2 160 C4
Sidmouth Mews WC1 233 C1
Sidmouth Par NW2 68 C1
Sidmouth Rd
Bexley DA16 146 C5
Leyton E10 76 A5
Willesden NW2 68 C1
Sidmouth St WC1 94 B4 233 C1
Sidney Ave N13 32 B5
Sidney Boyd Ct NW6 69 C1
Sidney Elson Way E6 100 C5
Sidney Gdns TW8 131 D6
Sidney Godley (VC) Ho 31 E2 96 C4
Sidney Gr EC1 234 C3
Sidney Ho
4 Globe Town E2 96 D5
SE18 144 B4
Sidney Miller Ct 8 W3 110 D5
Sidney Rd
Beckenham BR3 185 A1
Croydon SE25 206 A4
Sidney Rd *continued*
Harrow HA2 42
Stockwell SW9 138
Twickenham TW1 153
Walton-on-T KT12 194
Wanstead E7 77
Wood Green N22 32
Sidney Sq E1 96
Sidney St E1 96
Sidworth St 6 E8 74
Siebert Rd SE3 143
Siedle Ho 9 SE18 144
Siege Ho 14 E1 96
Siemens Rd SE18 121
Sienna Ct TW13 149
Sienna SE28 123
Sierra Dr RM9 103
Sigdon Rd E8 74
Sigers The HA5 40
Signal Ho
9 London E8 74
SE1 252
Signmakers Yd NW1 231
Sigrist Sq 4 KT2 176
Silbury Ave CR4 180
Silbury Ho 9 SE26 162
Silbury St N1 235
Silchester Ct
Stanwell TW15 148
Thornton Heath CR7 204
Silchester Rd W10 90
Silecroft Rd DA7 147
Silesia Bldgs E8 74
Silex St SE1 116 D4 251
Silicone Bsns Ctr UB6 87
Silk Cl SE12 165
Silkfield Rd NW9 45
Silk Ho NW9 45
Silk Mills Path SE13 142
Silk Mills Sq E9 75
Silks Ct E11 54
Silk St EC2 95 A2 242
Silkstream Par HA8 27
Silkstream Rd HA8 27
Sillitoe Ho N1 235
Silsoe Ho NW1 231
Silsoe Rd N22 50
Silverbell Ct 1 N12 29
Silver Birch Ave E4 35
Silver Birch Cl
Forest Hill SE6 163
Friern Barnet N11 31
Ickenham UB10 60
SE28 124
Silver Birch Ct EN3 18
Silver Birch Gdns E6 100
Silverbirch Wlk 1 NW3 71
Silverburn Ho 4 SW9 138
Silver Cl HA3 24
Silvercliffe Gdns EN4 2
Silver Cl SE14 141
Silver Cres W4 110
Silver Ct N19 71
Silverdale Ave IG3 57
Silverdale Cl
Cheam SM1 217
1 Ealing W7 108
Northolt UB5 63
Silverdale Ct EC1 241
Silverdale Dr
Chislehurst SE9 166
Sunbury TW16 172
Silverdale EN2 4
Silverdale Factory Ctr UB3 106
Silverdale SE26 184
Silverdale Gdns UB3 106
Silverdale Ind Est UB3 106
Silverdale NW1 232
Silverdale Par IG3 57
Silverdale Rd
Bexleyheath DA7 147
Chingford E4 36
Hayes UB3 106
Petts Wood BR5 211
Silverhall St TW7 131
Silverholme Cl HA3 44
Silver Ind Est N17 33
Silver Jubilee Way TW4 128
Silverland St E16 122
Silver La BR4 224
Silverleigh Rd CR7 204
Silvermead 7 E18 37
Silvermere Rd SE6 163
Silver Pl W1 249
Silver Rd
Shepherd's Bush W12 112
St Johns SE13 141

vers 4 IG9 ... 21 C3
ver Spring Cl
N8 ... 147 D6
ver St
Edmonton N18 ... 33 C6
nfield EN1 ... 5 B2
verstone Ct 8
E1 ... 187 C1
verston Way HA7 ... 25 C4
ver Street Sta N18 . 33 D5
verthorne Lo EN1 ... 17 C6
verthorne Rd
W8 ... 137 B3
verthorn Gdns E4 .. 19 C2
verthorn 17 NW6 ... 91 D6
verton Lo SE19 ... 183 C3
verton Rd W6 ... 134 D6
VERTOWN ... 121 B4
vertown Way
E16 ... 121 A5
vertree La UB6 ... 86 B4
ver Way
Hillingdon UB10 ... 82 D5
Romford RM7 ... 59 D6
ver Wing Ind Est
CR0 ... 220 B2
ver Wlk SE16 ... 119 B5
verwood Cl BR3 ... 185 C3
vester Ho
7 Bethnal Green
E2 ... 96 C4
1 Notting Hill W11 ... 91 B1
Pinner HA5 ... 40 A5
3 Stepney E1 ... 96 B1
vester Rd SE22 ... 161 D6
vester St SE1 ... 252 C1
wex Ho E1 ... 243 C5
wood St SE16 ... 118 C1
mba Ct TW1 ... 152 D3
mla Ho SE1 ... 252 D1
mmil Rd KT10 ... 212 C3
mmonds Ct SW5 ... 255 C3
mmons Cl
Chessington KT9 ... 213 C2
East Barnet N20 ... 14 C3
mmons Dr RM8 ... 81 A5
mmons Gate
KT10 ... 212 A3
mmons Ho
20 Bethnal Green
E2 ... 96 A4
Finsbury Pk N7 ... 72 B6
mmons La E4 ... 20 B2
mmons Rd SE18 ... 122 D1
mmons' Way N20 ... 14 C2
mms Cl SM5 ... 218 C6
mms Ct SW6 ... 135 A2
mms Gdns N2 ... 30 A1
mms Rd SE1 ... 118 A2
mnel Rd SE12 ... 165 B4
mon Cl
W11 ... 113 B6 244 D6
mon Ct
Paddington W9 ... 91 C4
6 Woolwich SE28 ... 124 B5
monds Rd E10 ... 75 C6
mone Cl BR1 ... 187 D2
mon Lo 31 SW19 ... 156 D3
mon Marks Jewish
Prim Sch N16 ... 73 D6
mons Wlk E15 ... 76 B3
mpson Cl N21 ... 16 B6
mpson Dr W3 ... 89 B1
mpson Ho
Lisson Gr NW8 ... 230 A1
Vauxhall SE11 ... 260 C1
Wembley HA9 ... 65 D6
mpson Rd
Hounslow TW4 ... 151 B5
Richmond TW10 ... 175 C6
mpson's Rd BR2 ... 209 A6
Poplar E14 ... 119 D6
mpson St SW11 ... 136 C3
mpson Way KT6 ... 197 C3
m's Cotts KT10 ... 212 D2
ms Wlk SE3 ... 142 D1
nclair Ct
21 Beckenham
BR3 ... 185 C3
Canonbury N5 ... 73 A2
6 Croydon CR0 ... 221 D6
nclair Gdns W14 ... 112 D4
nclair Gr NW11 ... 46 D3
nclair Ho
Harrow HA7 ... 24 D4
3 South Norwood
SW16 ... 182 B3
1 Streatham SW12 . 159 D3
nclair Mans 13
W12 ... 112 D4
nclair Pl SE4 ... 163 C5
nclair Rd
Chingford Hatch E4 ... 35 B5
W14 ... 113 A3 254 A6
nclairs Ho 18 E3 ... 97 B5
nclare Cl EN1 ... 5 D4
ngapore Rd W13 ... 109 A5
Singer St EC2 ... 235 D1
Singlegate Prim Sch
SW19 ... 180 B3
Singleton Cl
Mitcham SW17 ... 180 D3
Thornton Heath CR0 . 205 A2
Singleton Rd RM9 ... 81 B3
Singleton Scarp N12 .. 29 C5
Sinnott Rd E17 ... 34 D2
Sion Ct TW1 ... 153 B3
Sion Ho SE13 ... 142 A1
Sion-Manning RC Sch
for Girls
Kensal Town W10 ... 91 A2
North Kensington
W10 ... 90 D2
Sion Rd TW1 ... 153 B3
Sippetts Ct IG1 ... 57 B1
SIPSON ... 126 C6
Sipson Cl UB7 ... 126 C6
Sipson La UB3, UB7 ... 126 D6
Sipson Rd
Harmondsworth
UB7 ... 126 C6
West Drayton UB7 ... 104 B2
West Drayton UB7 ... 104 C1
Sipson Way UB7 ... 126 C5
Sir Abraham Dawes
Cotts SW15 ... 135 A1
Sir Alexander Cl
W3 ... 111 D5
Sir Alexander Rd
W3 ... 111 D5
Sir Arthur Bliss Ct 4
SW19 ... 180 D1
Sir Cyril Black Way 2
SW19 ... 179 C3
Sirdar Rd
Mitcham CR4 ... 181 A4
Tottenham N22 ... 33 A1
W11 ... 113 A6 244 A5
Sir Francis Drake Prim
Sch SE8 ... 119 A1
Sir George Monoux
Sixth Form Coll
E17 ... 35 D1
Sir Henry Floyd Ct
HA7 ... 9 B2
Sirinham Point SW8 270 D5
Sirius Bldg 13 E1 ... 118 D6
Sir James Barrie Prim
Sch SW8 ... 137 C4 269 B1
Sir John Cass
Foundation &
Redcoat CE Sec Sch
E1 ... 96 D2
Sir John Cass's
Foundation Prim Sch
EC3 ... 95 C1 243 B1
Sir John Heron Prim
Sch E12 ... 78 B4
Sir John Kirk Cl 33
SE5 ... 139 A5
Sir John Lillie Prim Sch
SW6 ... 135 A6 264 B5
Sir Martin Bowes Ho 9
SE18 ... 122 C2
Sir Oswald Stoll
Foundation The
SW6 ... 265 C4
Sir Thomas Abney Sch
N16 ... 51 B1
Sir Thomas More Est
SW3 ... 136 B6 266 D5
Sirus Rd HA6 ... 22 A5
Sir William Burrough
Prim Sch E14 ... 97 A1
Sir William Powell's
Almshos SW6 ... 135 A2
Sise La EC4 ... 242 C1
Siskin Ho
Edmonton N9 ... 18 D3
14 Rotherhithe
SE16 ... 118 D2
Sisley Rd IG11 ... 101 D6
Sispara Gdns SW18 .. 157 B5
Sissinghurst Cl BR1 .. 186 C5
Sissinghurst Ho 17
SE15 ... 140 C6
Sissinghurst Rd
CR0 ... 206 A2
Sissulu Ct 8 E6 ... 99 C6
Sister Mabel's Way 15
SE15 ... 140 A5
Sisters Ave SW11 ... 136 D1
Sistova Rd SW12 ... 159 B3
Sisulu Pl SW9 ... 138 C2
Sitarey Ct 4 W12 ... 112 B5
Site of Changing of the
Guard* SW1 ... 249 A1
Sittingbourne Ave
EN1 ... 17 B5
Sitwell Gr HA7 ... 24 D5
Siverst Cl UB5 ... 63 D2
Sivill Ho 9 E2 ... 95 D4
Siviter Way RM10 ... 81 D1
Siward Rd
Bromley BR2 ... 209 C6
Tottenham N17 ... 33 B2
Wandsworth SW17 .. 158 A1
Six Bridges Ind Est 15
SE1 ... 118 A1
Sixpenny Ct IG11 ... 79 A2
Sixth Ave Hayes UB3 .. 105 D5
Ilford E12 ... 78 B4
West Kilburn W10 ... 91 A4
Sixth Cross Rd TW2 .. 152 A1
Skardu Rd NW2 ... 69 A3
Skeena Hill SW18,
SW19 ... 157 A4
Skeffington Rd E6 ... 100 B6
Skeffington St SE18 ... 123 A3
Skeggs Ho 5 E14 ... 120 A3
Skegness Ho 3 N7 ... 72 B1
Skelbrook St SW18 ... 158 A2
Skelgill Rd SW15 ... 135 B1
Skelley Rd E15 ... 76 D1
Skelton Cl 7 E8 ... 73 D2
Skelton Ho N16 ... 73 C3
Skelton Rd E7 ... 77 A2
Skelton's La E10 ... 53 D2
Skelwith Rd W6 ... 134 C6
Skenfrith Ho SE15 ... 140 B6
Skerne Rd KT2 ... 175 D2
Skerne Wlk KT2 ... 175 D2
Sketchley Gdns
SE16 ... 118 D1
Sketty Rd EN1 ... 5 D2
Skiers St E15 ... 98 C6
Skiffington Cl SW2 ... 160 C3
Skillen Lodge HA5 ... 22 D2
Skinner Ct E17 ... 53 C4
Skinner Pl SW1 ... 258 A3
Skinners Almshouses
N13 ... 16 C1
Skinners Company Sch
(Upper) N16 ... 51 D2
Skinner's Company's
Lower Sch E5 ... 52 B1
Skinners La EC4 ... 252 B6
Hounslow TW5 ... 129 D4
Skinner St
EC1 ... 94 C3 241 B6
Skipper Ct 6 IG11 ... 101 A6
Skipsea Ho SW18 ... 158 B5
Skipsey Ave E6 ... 100 B4
Skipton Cl N11 ... 31 A4
Skipton Dr UB3 ... 105 A3
Skipton Ho SE4 ... 141 A1
Skipwith Bldg EC1 .. 241 A4
Skipworth Rd E9 ... 96 C6
Skua Ct 33 SE8 ... 141 B6
Skyline Ct SE1 ... 263 C5
Skyline Plaza Bldg 19
E1 ... 96 A1
Skylines E14 ... 120 A4
Sky Peals Rd IG8 ... 36 B3
Sky Studios E16 ... 122 C4
Sladebrook Rd SE3 .. 143 D2
Slade Ct Barnet EN5 ... 1 D2
Brondesbury NW2 ... 69 A3
Muswell Hill N10 ... 31 B3
Sladedale Rd SE18 ... 123 C1
Slade Ho TW4 ... 151 B5
Sladen Pl 12 E5 ... 74 B4
Slades Cl EN2 ... 4 C2
Slades Dr BR7 ... 189 A6
Slades Gdns EN2 ... 4 C2
Slades Hill EN2 ... 4 C2
Slades Rise EN2 ... 4 C2
Slade The SE18 ... 145 C6
Slade Twr E10 ... 75 C6
Slade Way CR4 ... 181 A2
Slagrove Pl SE13 ... 163 D6
Slaidburn St
SW10 ... 136 A6 266 B5
Slaithwaite Rd
SE13 ... 142 A1
Slaney Ct NW10 ... 68 C1
Slaney Pl 1 N7 ... 72 C3
Slater Cl 18 SE18 ... 122 C2
Slatter 1 NW9 ... 27 D2
Slattery Rd TW13 ... 150 C3
Sleaford Ho 18 E3 ... 97 C3
Sleaford Ind Est
SW8 ... 137 C5 269 B3
Sleaford St
SW8 ... 137 C5 269 B3
Sleat Ho 11 E3 ... 97 B5
Sledmere Ct TW14 ... 149 C3
Slievemore Cl 8
SW4 ... 137 D2
Sligo Ho 8 E1 ... 96 D3
Slingsby Pl WC2 ... 250 A6
Slippers Pl SE16 ... 118 B3
Slipway Ho 1 E14 ... 119 D1
Sloane Avenue Mans
SW3 ... 257 C3
Sloane Ave
SW3 ... 114 C2 257 B3
Sloane Ct E SW3 ... 258 A2
Sloane Ct W SW3 ... 258 A2
Sloane Gate Mans
SW1 ... 258 A4
Sloane Gdns
Belgravia
SW1 ... 115 A2 258 A3
Orpington BR6 ... 227 A5
Sloane Ho 7 E9 ... 74 C1
Sloane Hospl BR3 ... 186 B2
Sloane Sq SW1 ... 257 D3
Sloane Square Sta
SW1 ... 115 A2 258 A3
Sloane St
SW1 ... 114 D3 257 D5
Sloane Terr Mans
SW1 ... 258 A4
Sloane Terr SW1 ... 258 A4
Sloane Wlk CR0 ... 207 B3
Sloan Ho RM10 ... 81 D1
Slocum Cl SE28 ... 124 C6
Slough La NW9 ... 45 A3
Sly St 17 E1 ... 96 B1
Smaldon Cl UB7 ... 104 C3
Smallberry Ave
TW7 ... 130 D3
Smallberry Green Prim
Sch The TW7 ... 131 A4
Smallbrook Mews
W2 ... 236 C1
Smallbugh Mans
HA0 ... 65 B4
Smalley Cl N16 ... 73 D5
Smallwood Prim Sch
SW17 ... 180 B6
Smallwood Rd
SW17 ... 180 B6
Smarden Cl DA17 ... 125 C1
Smarden Gr SE9 ... 188 B6
Smart's Pl
Edmonton N18 ... 34 A5
WC1, WC2 ... 240 B2
Smart St E2 ... 96 D4
Smeaton Cl KT9 ... 213 D2
Smeaton Ct SE1 ... 262 A5
Smeaton Rd
Holdbrook EN3 ... 7 C6
Wandsworth SW18 .. 157 C4
Smeaton St E1 ... 118 B5
Smedley St SW4 ... 137 D3
Smeed Rd E3 ... 75 C1
Smiles Pl SE13 ... 142 A3
Smith Cl SE16 ... 118 D5
Smithers Ho 3
SE20 ... 184 D3
Smithfield Mkt EC1 241 D3
Smithfield St
EC1 ... 94 D2 241 C3
Smithies Ct E15 ... 76 A3
Smithies Rd SE2 ... 124 B2
Smith's Ct W1 ... 249 C6
Smithson Rd N17 ... 33 B2
Smiths Point E13 ... 99 A6
Smith Sq
SW1 ... 116 A3 260 A5
Smith St
Surbiton KT5 ... 198 B3
SW3 ... 114 D1 257 C1
Smith's Yd SW18 ... 158 A2
Smith Terr
SW3 ... 114 D1 257 C1
Smithwood Cl
SW19 ... 157 A2
Smithy St E1 ... 96 C2
Smithy Street Sch
E1 ... 96 C2
Smock Wlk CR0 ... 205 A3
Smoothfield TW3 ... 129 C1
Smugglers Way
SW18 ... 135 D1
Smyrk's Rd
SE17 ... 117 C1 263 B1
Smyrna Mans 8
NW6 ... 69 C1
Smyrna Rd NW6 ... 69 C1
Smythe St E14 ... 119 D6
Snakes La E IG8 ... 37 C4
Snakes La EN4, N14 ... 3 C1
Snakes La W IG8 ... 37 B4
Snakey La TW13 ... 172 B6
SNARESBROOK ... 54 D6
Snaresbrook Coll
E18 ... 37 A1
Snaresbrook Dr HA7 .. 26 A6
Snaresbrook Hall 12
E18 ... 55 A6
Snaresbrook Ho E18 .. 54 D5
Snaresbrook Prim Sch
E18 ... 55 A5
Snaresbrook Rd E11 .. 54 D5
Snaresbrook Sta E11 . 55 A4
Snarsgate St W10 ... 90 C2
Sneath Ave NW11 ... 47 B2
Snell's Pk N18 ... 33 D4
Sneyd Rd NW2 ... 68 C4
Snowberry Cl E11 ... 76 B4
Snowbury Rd 6
SW6 ... 135 D3
Snow Ct 4 HA0 ... 65 D3
Snowden Ave UB10 ... 82 D5
Snowden St
EC2 ... 95 C3 243 A5
Snowdon Cres UB3 .. 105 A3
Snowdon Dr NW9 ... 45 C3
Snowdon Rd TW6 ... 149 A5
Snowdown Cl SE20 ... 184 D2
Snowdrop Cl 2
TW12 ... 173 C4
Snowe Ho SE27 ... 160 D1
Snow Hill EC1 . 94 D2 241 C3
Snowman Ho NW6 ... 91 D6
Snowsfields Prim Sch
SE1 ... 117 C4 253 A2
Snowsfields
SE1 ... 117 B4 252 D2
Snowshill Rd E12 ... 78 A3
Snowy Fielder Waye
TW7 ... 131 B3
Soames St SE15 ... 139 D2
Soames Wlk KT3 ... 177 C2
Soane Cl W5 ... 109 D4
Soane Ct 10 NW1 ... 71 C1
Soane Ho SE17 ... 262 D1
Soane Mus The*
WC2 ... 94 B1 240 C2
Soaphouse La TW8 .. 132 A5
Soham Rd EN3 ... 7 B6
SOHO ... 93 D1
Soho Mills SM6 ... 203 B1
Soho Parish CE Prim
Sch W1 ... 115 D6 249 C6
Soho Sq W1 ... 93 D1 239 C2
Soho St W1 ... 239 C2
Soho* W1 ... 93 D1 239 C2
Sojourner-Truth Cl 11
E8 ... 74 B2
Sola Ct 8 CR0 ... 205 B1
Solander Gdns
13 Shadwell E1 ... 118 C6
Stepney E1 ... 118 B6
Solar Ct N3 ... 29 D3
Soldene Ct N7 ... 72 B2
Solebay St E1 ... 97 A3
Solent Ct SW16 ... 182 B1
Solent Ho 6 E1 ... 97 A2
Solent Rd NW6 ... 69 C3
Solent Rise E13 ... 99 A4
Soley Mews WC1 ... 234 A2
Solidarity Ho 5
NW10 ... 68 C2
Solna Ave SW15 ... 156 C6
Solna Rd N21 ... 17 B4
Solomon Ave N9 ... 34 A6
Solomons Ct N12 ... 30 A3
Solomon's Pas SE15 . 140 B1
Solon New Rd SW4 .. 138 A1
Solon Rd SW2 ... 138 A1
Solway Cl TW4 ... 129 A2
Solway Ho 12 E1 ... 96 D3
Solway Rd
East Dulwich
SE22 ... 140 A1
Tottenham N22 ... 32 D2
Somaford Gr EN4 ... 14 B5
Somali Rd NW2 ... 69 B3
Somborne Ho 11
SW15 ... 156 A4
Sombrook Ho SE11 . 261 A3
Somerby Rd IG11 ... 79 B1
Somercoates Cl EN4 ... 2 C2
Somer Ct SW6 ... 265 A5
Somerfield Rd N4 ... 72 D6
Somerfield St SE16 .. 118 D1
Somerford Cl HA5 ... 40 A5
Somerford Grove Est
N16 ... 73 D4
Somerford Gr
Shacklewell N16 ... 73 D4
Tottenham N17 ... 34 A3
Somerford St E1 ... 96 B3
Somerford Way
SE16 ... 119 A4
Somerhill Ave DA15 .. 168 B4
Somerhill Rd DA16 ... 146 B3
Somerleyton Rd
SW9 ... 138 C1
Somersby Est SE20 ... 184 C3
Somersby Gdns IG4 ... 56 B4
Somers Cl NW1 ... 232 C4
Somers Cres W2 ... 237 A1
Somerset Ave
Chessington KT9 ... 213 D4
DA16 ... 145 D1
Wimbledon SW20 ... 178 B1
Somerset Cl
New Malden KT3 ... 199 C3
Tottenham N17 ... 33 B1
Woodford IG8 ... 37 A2
Somerset Ct
10 Buckhurst Hill
IG9 ... 21 C2
Ealing W7 ... 86 D1
2 Hampton TW12 .. 173 C2
Somerset Gdns
Highgate N6 ... 49 A2
St Johns SE13 ... 141 D3
Somerset Gdns *continued*
Teddington TW11 ... 174 C5
Thornton Heath
SW16 ... 204 B6
Tottenham N17 ... 33 C3
Somerset Hall N17 ... 33 C3
Somerset Ho
WC2 ... 116 B6 250 D6
Somerset Ho SW19 .. 157 A1
Somerset Lo
9 Brentford
TW8 ... 131 D6
5 New Barnet EN5 ... 14 A6
Putney SW15 ... 134 B1
Somerset Rd
Bedford Pk W4 ... 111 B3
Brentford TW8 ... 131 C6
Ealing W13 ... 109 C5
Edmonton N18 ... 33 D5
Harrow HA1 ... 42 A4
Hendon NW4 ... 46 C5
Holdbrook EN3 ... 7 C5
Kingston u T KT1 ... 176 B1
New Barnet EN5 ... 14 A6
Southall UB1 ... 85 C2
Teddington TW11 ... 174 C5
Tottenham N17 ... 51 D6
Walthamstow E17 ... 53 C3
Wimbledon SW19 ... 157 A1
Somerset Sq
W14 ... 113 B4 244 C1
Somerset Waye
TW5 ... 129 A5
Somersham Rd
DA7 ... 147 A3
Somers Pl SW2 ... 160 B4
Somers Rd
Tulse Hill SW2 ... 160 B5
Walthamstow E17 ... 53 B5
SOMERS TOWN ... 93 D4
Somers Town Est
NW1 ... 93 C5 232 B3
Somers Way WD23 ... 8 A4
Somerton Ave TW9 .. 132 D2
Somerton Rd
Cricklewood NW2 ... 69 A5
Nunhead SE15 ... 140 B1
Somertrees Ave
SE12 ... 165 B2
Somervell Rd HA2 ... 63 C3
Somerville Ave
SW13 ... 134 C6
Somerville Ct SW16 .. 181 D4
Somerville Ho 10
SW15 ... 156 D5
Somerville Point
SE16 ... 119 B4
Somerville Rd
Dagenham RM6 ... 58 C4
Penge SE20 ... 184 D3
Sonderburg Rd 13
N7 ... 72 B6
Sondes St SE17 ... 139 B6
Songhurst Cl CR0 ... 204 B3
Sonia Ct Edgware HA8 .. 26 B3
North Finchley N12 ... 30 A6
Sonia Gdns
Heston TW5 ... 129 C5
North Finchley N12 ... 30 A6
Willesden NW10 ... 67 D4
Sonning Ct CR0 ... 222 A6
Sonning Gdns
TW12 ... 173 A4
Sonning Ho 32 E2 ... 95 D4
Sonning Rd CR0 ... 206 A3
Soper Cl
Chingford Hatch E4 ... 35 B5
4 Forest Hill SE23 .. 162 D2
Soper Mews EN3 ... 7 C5
Sophia Cl N7 ... 72 B2
Sophia Ho
10 Hammersmith
W6 ... 112 C1
Tottenham N15 ... 51 D5
Sophia Rd
Newham E13 ... 99 B2
Walthamstow E10 ... 53 D1
Sophia Sq 14 SE16 ... 119 A6
Sopwith Ave KT9 ... 214 A3
Sopwith Cl KT2 ... 176 B5
Sopwith 2 NW9 ... 27 D2
Sopwith Rd TW5 ... 128 C5
Sopwith Way
Battersea
SW8 ... 137 B5 268 C4
Kingston u T KT2 ... 176 A2
Sorbus Ct EN2 ... 4 D3
Sorensen Ct 2 E10 ... 75 D6
Sorrel Cl SE28 ... 124 A5
Sorrel Gdns E6 ... 100 A2
Sorrel Ho TW3 ... 130 A4
Sorrel La 17 E14 ... 98 B1
Sorrell Cl
6 Brixton SW9 ... 138 C3

Sorrell Cl *continued*
SE14 ... 141 A5
Sorrento Rd SM1 ... 217 D5
Soseki Mus* SW4 ... 137 B2
Sotheby Rd N5 ... 73 A4
Sotheran Cl E8 ... 96 A6
Sotheron Pl SW6 ... 265 D3
Soudan Rd SW11 ... 136 D4 267 C1
Souldern Rd [10] W14 ... 112 D3
South Access Rd E17 .. 53 A3
South Acre NW9 ... 27 D1
Southacre Way HA5 ... 22 C2
SOUTH ACTON ... 110 D3
South Acton Sta W3, W4 ... 111 A3
South Africa Rd W12 ... 112 B6
SOUTHALL ... 107 A5
Southall Ct UB1 ... 107 B6
Southall Ent Ctr UB2 ... 107 C4
Southall La TW5 ... 106 B1
Southall Norwood Hospl UB2 ... 107 B3
Southall Pl SE1 ... 252 C1
Southall Sta UB1 ... 107 B4
Southall & West London Coll UB1 ... 107 A5
Southam Ho [9] W10 .. 91 A3
Southampton Bldgs WC2 ... 241 A3
Southampton Gdns CR4 ... 204 A4
Southampton Mews E16 ... 121 B5
Southampton Pl WC1 ... 240 B3
Southampton Rd
Maitland Pk NW5 ... 70 D3
Stanwell TW19, TW6 ... 148 B5
Southampton Row WC1 ... 94 A2 240 B4
Southampton St WC2 ... 250 B6
Southampton Way SE5 ... 139 C5
Southam St W10 ... 91 A3
South Audley St W1 ... 115 A5 248 B4
South Ave
Chingford E4 ... 20 A4
East Finchley NW11 ... 47 D5
South Avenue Gdns UB1 ... 107 B6
South Ave
Richmond TW9 ... 132 C3
Southall UB1 ... 107 B6
Wallington SM5 ... 219 A1
SOUTH BANK ... 116 B4
South Bank Bsns Ctr SW8 ... 137 D6 269 D5
Southbank International Sch NW3 ... 70 A2
Southbank International Sch (Westminster Campus) W1 ... 93 B2 238 C4
Southbank Int Sch W11 ... 113 C6 245 A5
South Bank Lo [2] KT6 ... 198 A3
South Bank KT6 ... 198 A3
South Bank Terr KT6 ... 198 A3
Southbank KT7 ... 197 B2
South Bank Univ
London SW8 ... 137 D4 269 D2
SE1 ... 116 D3 261 D6
SOUTH BEDDINGTON ... 219 C2
South Bermondsey Sta SE16 ... 118 C1
South Birkbeck Rd E11 ... 76 B5
South Black Lion La [7] W6 ... 112 A1
South Bldg SW1 ... 259 B6
South Block [20] E1 ... 118 C6
South Bolton Gdns SW10 ... 255 D2
SOUTHBOROUGH ... 197 D1 210 B3
Southborough Cl KT6 ... 197 D1
Southborough High Sch KT6 ... 214 A5
Southborough Ho SE17 ... 263 B2
Southborough La BR1, BR2 ... 210 B4
Southborough Prim Sch BR2 ... 210 C4
Southborough Rd
Bromley BR1, BR2 ... 210 A5
South Hackney E9 ... 96 D6
Surbiton KT6 ... 198 A1
Southborough Rd (The Lane) KT6 ... 198 A1
Southbourne Ave NW9 ... 27 B1
Southbourne Cl HA5 .. 41 A2
Southbourne Cres NW4 ... 47 A5
Southbourne Ct NW9 ... 27 A1
Southbourne Gdns
Ilford IG1 ... 79 A3
Ruislip HA4 ... 40 B1
SE12 ... 165 B6
Southbourne BR2 ... 209 A2
Southbridge Pl CR0 .. 221 A4
Southbridge Rd CR0 ... 221 A4
Southbridge Way UB2 ... 107 A4
SOUTH BROMLEY ... 98 B2
Southbrook Mews SE12 ... 164 D5
Southbrook Rd
Hither Green SE12 ... 164 D5
Thornton Heath SW16 ... 182 A2
South Building* SE10 ... 142 B5
Southbury Ave EN1 ... 6 A1
Southbury NW8 ... 229 B6
Southbury Prim Sch EN3 ... 6 C1
Southbury Rd
Enfield EN1 ... 5 D2
Enfield EN1, EN3 ... 6 B1
Southbury Sta EN3 ... 6 B1
South Camden Com Sch NW1 ... 93 D5 232 C4
South Carriage Dr SW1, SW7 ... 114 D4 247 C2
South Chelsea Coll SW9 ... 138 B1
Southchurch Ct
Bowes Pk N13 ... 32 B5
Newham E6 ... 100 B5
Southchurch Rd E6 .. 100 B5
South Cl Barnet EN5 ... 1 B2
DA6 ... 146 D1
Dagenham RM10 ... 103 C6
Highgate N6 ... 49 B3
Morden SM4 ... 201 C3
Pinner HA5 ... 41 B2
Twickenham TW2 ... 151 C1
West Drayton UB7 ... 104 C3
South Colonnade The E14 ... 119 D5
Southcombe St W14 254 A4
South Common Rd UB8 ... 60 A2
Southcote Ave
Feltham TW13 ... 150 A2
Tolworth KT5 ... 198 D2
Southcote Rd
Croydon SE25 ... 206 B3
Tufnell Pk N19 ... 71 C4
Walthamstow E17 ... 53 A4
Southcote Rise HA4 ... 39 B2
Southcott Ho
[31] Bromley E3 ... 97 D4
W9 ... 236 B5
South Countess Rd E17 ... 53 B6
South Cres
Newham E16 ... 98 B3
WC1 ... 239 C3
Southcroft Ave
DA16 ... 145 C2
West Wickham BR4 .. 224 A6
Southcroft SM1 ... 218 C3
Southcroft Rd BR6 ... 227 C5
Streatham SW17 ... 181 A4
South Cross Rd IG6 ... 57 A4
South Croxted Rd SE21 ... 183 B6
SOUTH CROYDON ... 221 B1
South Croydon Sta CR2 ... 221 B3
South Ct [17] SW15 ... 156 D5
Southdean Gdns SW19 ... 157 B2
Southdene Ct N11 ... 15 C1
South Dene NW7 ... 11 B1
Southdown Ave W7 .. 109 A3
Southdown Cres
Harrow HA2 ... 42 A1
Ilford IG2 ... 57 C4
Southdown Dr SW20 ... 178 D3
Southdown N7 ... 72 A2
Southdown Rd SW20 ... 178 D2
South Dr
Orpington BR6 ... 227 C3
Ruislip HA4 ... 39 C1
South Ealing Cemy W5 ... 109 D2
South Ealing Rd W5 ... 109 D3
South Ealing Sta W5 ... 109 D3
South Eastern Ave N9 ... 17 D1
South Eastern Univ N7 ... 72 B5
South Eaton Pl SW1 ... 115 A2 258 B4
South Eden Park Rd BR3 ... 207 D4
South Edwardes Sq W8 ... 255 A5
SOUTHEND ... 186 B6
South End Cl NW3 ... 70 C4
Southend Cl SE9 ... 166 D5
Southend Cres SE9 .. 166 D5
South End CR0 ... 221 A4
South End Gn NW3 ... 70 C4
Southend Ho SE9 ... 166 C4
Southend La SE6 ... 185 C6
Southend Rd BR3 ... 185 C2
South End Rd NW3 ... 70 C4
Southend Rd
Plashet E6 ... 78 B1
Woodford IG8 ... 37 D1
Southend Road (North Circular Rd) E17, E18 ... 36 C2
South End Row W8 ... 113 D3 255 D6
South End W8 ... 113 D3 255 D6
Southern Ave
East Bedfont TW14 ... 150 A3
South Norwood SE25 ... 205 D6
Southerngate Way SE14 ... 141 A5
Southern Gr E3 ... 97 B3
Southernhay IG10 ... 21 D6
Southern Perimeter Rd
Hatton TW14, TW6 ... 149 B6
West Bedfont TW19, TW6 ... 148 C5
Southern Rd
Fortis Green N2 ... 48 D5
Newham E13 ... 99 B5
Southern Road Prim Sch E13 ... 99 B5
Southern Row W10 ... 91 A3
Southern St N1 ... 233 C4
Southern Way
Greenwich SE10 ... 120 D3
Romford RM7 ... 59 C3
Southerton Rd W6 ... 112 C2
South Esk Rd E7 ... 77 C2
Southey Ho SE17 ... 262 B2
Southey Mews E16 ... 121 A5
Southey Rd
Brixton SW9 ... 138 C4
Merton SW19 ... 179 C3
Tottenham N15 ... 51 C4
Southey St SE20 ... 184 D3
Southfield EN5 ... 12 D5
Southfield Cl UB8 ... 82 C4
Southfield Cotts W7 ... 108 D4
Southfield Ct E11 ... 76 D5
Southfield Gdns TW1, TW2 ... 174 D6
Southfield Lo W4 ... 111 B4
Southfield Pk HA2 ... 41 D5
Southfield Prim Sch W4 ... 111 C4
Southfield Rd
Acton W4 ... 111 B4
Enfield EN3 ... 18 C5
St Paul's Cray BR7 .. 211 D6
SOUTHFIELDS ... 157 D3
Southfields Ave TW15 ... 170 D4
Southfields Com Coll SW18 ... 157 C3
Southfields Ct SM3 .. 217 C6
Southfields NW4 ... 46 B6
Southfields Rd SW18 ... 157 C5
Southfields Sta SW18 ... 157 B3
Southfields KT8 ... 196 C3
Southfleet Rd BR6 ... 227 C4
SOUTHGATE ... 16 B4
South Gate Ave TW13 ... 171 B6
Southgate Cir [3] N14 ... 15 D3
Southgate Coll N14 ... 15 D2
Southgate Ct N1 ... 73 B1
Southgate Gr N1 ... 73 B1
Southgate Ho [7] E17 .. 54 A6
Southgate Rd N1 ... 95 B6 235 D6
Southgate Sch EN4 ... 15 B6
Southgate Sta N14 ... 15 D3
Southgate Way N2 ... 30 C2
South Gdns
Mitcham SW19 ... 180 B3
Wembley HA9 ... 66 C6
South Gipsy Rd DA16 ... 146 D2
South Glade The DA5 ... 169 B3
South Gn NW9 ... 27 C2
South Greenford Sta UB6 ... 86 C4
South Gr N6 ... 49 A1
South Grove Ho N6 ... 49 A1
South Grove Prim Sch E17 ... 53 B3
South Gr
Tottenham N15 ... 51 B4
Walthamstow E17 ... 53 B4
SOUTH HACKNEY ... 96 C6
SOUTH HAMPSTEAD ... 70 A1
South Hampstead High Sch Jun Dept NW3 .. 70 A2
South Hampstead High Sch NW3 ... 70 B2
South Hampstead Sta NW8 ... 70 A1
South Harringay Jun & Inf Schs N4 ... 50 D4
SOUTH HARROW ... 63 D5
South Harrow Sta HA2 ... 64 A5
South Hill Ave HA1, HA2 ... 64 B5
South Hill BR7 ... 188 B4
South Hill Gr HA1 ... 64 C4
South Hill Pk Gdns NW3 ... 70 C4
South Hill Pk NW3 ... 70 C4
South Hill Rd BR2 ... 208 C5
Southholme Cl SE19 ... 183 C2
Southill La HA5 ... 40 B5
Southill Rd BR7 ... 188 B3
Southill St E14 ... 97 D1
South Island Pl SW9 ... 138 C5
SOUTH KENSINGTON ... 114 A1
South Kensington Sta SW7 ... 114 B2 256 D4
South Kensington Station Arc SW7 ... 256 D4
South Kenton Sta HA9 ... 43 C1
South La KT1 ... 197 D6
SOUTH LAMBETH ... 138 A4
South Lambeth Pl SW8 ... 270 B6
South Lambeth Rd SW8 ... 138 A5 270 B4
Southland Rd SE18 ... 145 D5
Southlands Ave BR6 ... 227 C3
Southlands Ct BR2 ... 209 D5
Southlands Dr SW19 ... 156 D2
Southlands Gr BR1 ... 210 A6
Southlands Rd BR1, BR2 ... 209 D5
Southland Way TW7 ... 152 B6
South La KT3 ... 199 B3
South La W KT3 ... 199 B5
South Lodge Ave CR4, CR7, SW16 ... 204 A5
South Lodge Cres EN2 ... 3 D1
South Lodge Dr N14 .. 15 D6
South London Montessori Sch SW11 ... 267 A1
South Lo
[6] New Barnet EN5 ... 13 D6
NW8 ... 229 C2
Twickenham TW2 ... 152 A5
South Mall The N9 ... 18 A1
South Mead NW9 ... 27 D2
Southmead Prim Sch SW19 ... 157 A3
Southmead Rd SW19 ... 157 A3
South Mead KT19 ... 215 D1
South Merton Sta SW20 ... 201 B6
South Molton La W1 ... 93 B1 238 C1
South Molton Rd E16 ... 99 A1
South Molton St W1 ... 93 B1 238 C1
Southmont Rd KT10 .. 212 C5
Southmoor Way E9 ... 75 B3
South Mount N20 ... 14 A2
SOUTH NORWOOD ... 205 C6
South Norwood Ctry Pk* SE25 ... 206 C5
South Norwood Hill SE19, SE25 ... 183 D1
South Norwood Prim Sch SE25 ... 206 A5
South Oak Rd SW16 .. 182 B6
Southold Rise SE9 ... 166 B1
Southolm St SW11 ... 137 B4 268 D1
South Ordnance Rd EN3 ... 7 C5
Southover BR1 ... 187 A5
Finchley N12 ... 29 C6
SOUTH OXHEY ... 22 B6
South Par W4 ... 111 B2
South Parade SW3 ... 114 B1 256 D2
South Par HA8 ... 26 C1
South Park Bsns Ctr IG3 ... 79 C6
South Park Cres
Catford SE6 ... 164 D3
Ilford IG1 ... 79 C5
South Park Ct [24] BR3 ... 185 C3
Southpark Ct SW19 .. 179 C4
South Park Dr IG3 ... 79 C4
South Park Gr KT3 ... 199 A5
South Park Hill Rd CR2 ... 221 B4
South Park Mews SW6 ... 135 D2
South Park Prim Sch IG3 ... 79 C5
South Park Rd
Ilford IG1 ... 79 B5
Wimbledon SW19 ... 179 D4
South Park Terr IG1 ... 79 C5
South Park Villas IG3 ... 79 C4
South Park Way HA4 .. 62 C3
South Par SM6 ... 219 C2
South Pl
Broadgate EC2 ... 95 B2 242 D3
Enfield EN3 ... 18 C6
South Pl Mews EC2 . 242 D3
South Pl KT5 ... 198 B2
Southport Rd SE18 ... 123 B2
South Quay Plaza E14 ... 119 D4
South Quay Sta E14 119 D4
South Rd
Brentford W5 ... 109 D2
Edgware HA8 ... 26 D2
Edmonton N9 ... 18 A3
Feltham TW13 ... 172 D5
Forest Hill SE23 ... 162 D2
Hampton TW12 ... 173 B4
Heston TW5 ... 128 D6
Mitcham SW19 ... 180 B4
Southall UB1 ... 107 B5
Twickenham TW2 ... 152 B1
West Drayton UB7 ... 104 C3
South Residence IG3 . 58 B4
South Ridge BR2 ... 209 C5
Southridge Pl SW20 ... 178 D3
South Rise Prim Sch SE18 ... 123 B1
South Rise W2 ... 247 B6
South Rise Way SE18 ... 123 B2
South Row SE3 ... 142 D3
SOUTH RUISLIP ... 62 D4
South Ruislip Sta HA4 ... 62 C3
Southsea Rd KT1 ... 198 A5
South Sea St SE16 ... 119 B3
Southside Comm SW19 ... 178 D4
Southside Ind Est SW8 ... 269 A2
Southside N7 ... 71 D4
South Side W6 ... 111 D3
Southside Quarter [4] SW11 ... 136 D3
Southside Sh Ctr SW18 ... 157 D5
Southspring DA15 ... 167 B4
South Sq
Hampstead Garden Suburb NW11 ... 47 D3
WC1 ... 241 A3
South St
Bromley BR1 ... 18
Enfield EN3 ... 1
Isleworth TW7 ... 13
Mayfair W1 . 115 A5 24
South Tenter St E1 ... 95 D1 24
South Terr
Muswell Hill N22 ... 3
Surbiton KT6 ... 19
SW7 ... 114 C2 25
South Thames Coll (Battersea Ctr) SW11 ... 136 D4 26
South Thames Coll (Putney Ctr) SW15 ... 15
South Thames Coll (Roehampton Ctr) SW15 ... 15
South Thames Coll (Tooting Ctr) SW17 ... 18
South Thames Coll (Wandsworth Ctr) SW18 ... 15
SOUTH TOTTENHAM ... 5
South Tottenham Sta N15 ... 5
South Vale HA1 ... 6
Southvale Rd SE3 ... 14
South Vale SE19 ... 18
Southview Ave NW10 ... 6
South View BR1 ... 18
South View Cl DA5 ... 16
Southview Cl SW17 .. 18
South View Cres IG2 .. 5
South View Ct
[8] Forest Hill SE23 ... 16
South Norwood SE19 ... 18
Southview Dr E18 ... 5
Southview Gdns SM6 ... 21
Southview Rd BR1 ... 18
South View Rd
Hornsey N8 ... 50
Pinner HA5 ... 22
South View SW19 ... 17
South Villas NW1 ... 71
Southville Cl
East Bedfont TW14 ... 14
West Ewell KT19 ... 215
Southville Cres TW14 ... 14
Southville Jun & Inf Schs TW14 ... 14
Southville SW8 ... 137 D4 26
Southville Rd
East Bedfont TW14 ... 14
Thames Ditton KT7 ... 19
SOUTHWARK ... 11
Southwark Bridge Rd SE1 ... 117 A5 25
Southwark Bridge SE1, EC4 ... 117 A6 25
Southwark Cath* SE1 ... 117 B5 25
Southwark Coll (Blackfriars Ctr) SE1 ... 251
Southwark Coll (Camberwell Ctr) SE5 ... 13
Southwark Coll (Grange Ctr) SE1 ... 26
Southwark Coll SE1 ... 116 D4 251
Southwark Coll (Surrey Docks Ctr) SE16 ... 11
Southwark Park Est [11] SE16 ... 11
Southwark Park Prim Sch SE16 ... 11
Southwark Park Rd SE16 ... 11
Southwark Pl BR1 ... 21
Southwark St SE1 ... 117 A5 25
Southwater Cl
Beckenham BR3 ... 18
[8] Poplar E14 ... 97
Southway Cl [9] W12 ... 11
South Way
Croydon CR0 ... 22
Friern Barnet N11 ... 31
Southway NW11 ... 47
South Way HA2 ... 41
Southway BR2 ... 20
South Way N9 ... 18

:hway
:teridge N20 ... 13 C2
allington SM6 ... 219 C4
th Way HA9 ... 66 C3
thway SW20 ... 200 D5
thwell Ave UB5 ... 63 C2
thwell Gdns
7 ... 256 A3
thwell Grove Rd
1 ... 76 C6
thwell Ho
Bermondsey
SE16 ... 118 B2
Stoke Newington
N16 ... 73 C3
thwell Rd
mberwell SE5 ... 139 A2
arrow HA3 ... 43 D3
ornton Heath CR0 ... 204 C3
th Western Rd
V1 ... 153 B5
thwest Rd E11 ... 54 B1
th Wharf Rd
2 ... 92 B1 236 D2
thwick Mews
2 ... 236 D2
thwick Pl W2 ... 237 A1
thwick St
2 ... 92 C1 237 A2
thwick Yd W2 ... 237 A1
JTH WIMBLEDON
... 179 D4
th Wimbledon Sta
V19 ... 179 D3
th Wlk
ney Hall BR4 ... 224 C5
ayes UB3 ... 83 B2
thwold Dr IG11 ... 80 A3
thwold Mans W9 ... 91 C4
thwold Prim Sch
... 74 B6
thwold Rd DA5 ... 169 D5
pper Clapton E5 ... 74 C6
thwood Ave
ghgate N6 ... 49 B2
ngston u T KT2,
KT3 ... 177 A2
thwood Cl BR1 ... 210 B5
orth Cheam KT4 ... 200 D1
thwood Ct EC1 ... 234 C1
ampstead Garden
Suburb NW11 ... 47 D4
thwood Dr KT5 ... 199 A1
th Woodford Sta
8 ... 37 B1
thwood Gdns
inchley Wood
KT10 ... 213 A5
ford IG2 ... 56 D5
thwood Hall N6 ... 49 B3
thwood Ho
ew Eltham SE9 ... 166 D2
otting Hill W11 ... 244 A6
thwood Hospl
Geriatric) N6 ... 49 A2
thwood Hts N6 ... 49 B2
thwood La N6 ... 49 A2
thwood Lawn Rd
6 ... 49 B2
thwood Mans N6 ... 49 B3
thwood Park N6 ... 49 A2
thwood Prim Sch
M9 ... 81 A4
thwood Rd SE9 ... 166 D2
Voolwich SE28 ... 124 B5
thwood Smith Ho 4
2 ... 96 B4
thwood Smith St
1 ... 234 C5
th Worple Ave
W14 ... 133 C2
thwyck Ho SW9 ... 138 C1
th Yd EC1 ... 242 C4
ereign Bsns Ctr
N3 ... 7 B2
vereign Cl
aling W5 ... 87 C2
uislip HA4 ... 39 C1
tepney E1 ... 118 B6
vereign Cres
E16 ... 119 A6
vereign Ct BR2 ... 210 B3
ast Molesey KT8 ... 195 B5
arlington UB7 ... 126 D5
3 Richmond TW9 ... 132 B1
3 Stepney E1 ... 118 B6
vereign Gr HA0 ... 65 D5
vereign Ho
shford TW15 ... 170 A6
3 Bethnal Green E1 ... 96 B3
hislehurst BR7 ... 189 B3
dgware NW7 ... 27 B6
3 Wimbledon
SW19 ... 179 A4
Voolwich SE18 ... 122 B3
vereign Mews
arnet EN4 ... 2 D2
Sovereign Mews
continued
6 Haggerston E2 ... 95 D5
Sovereign Pk NW10 ... 88 D3
Sovereign Pl HA1 ... 42 D4
Sovereign Rd IG11 ... 102 C4
Sovreign Ct HA6 ... 22 A2
Sowerby Cl SE9 ... 166 B6
Space Apartments
N22 ... 32 B3
Space Bsns Pk NW10 ... 88 D4
Spa Central 1
SW16 ... 182 A3
Space Waye TW14 ... 150 B6
Spa Cl SE19 ... 183 C2
Spa Ct
12 Bermondsey
SE16 ... 118 A3
Streatham SW16 ... 182 B6
Spafield St EC1 ... 241 A6
Spa Hill CR7, SE19 ... 183 B2
Spalding Cl HA8 ... 27 C3
Spalding Ct HA8 ... 26 B6
Spalding Ho SE4 ... 163 A6
Spalding Rd
Hendon NW4 ... 46 C3
Streatham SW17 ... 181 B5
Spanby Rd E3 ... 97 C3
Spangate SE3 ... 142 D2
Spaniards Cl NW11 ... 48 B1
Spaniards End NW3 ... 48 B1
Spaniards Rd NW3 ... 70 A6
Spanish Pl W1 ... 238 B2
Spanish Rd SW18 ... 158 A6
Spanswick Lo 2
N15 ... 50 D5
Spa Rd SE16 ... 117 D3 263 D5
Sparkbridge Rd HA1 ... 42 C5
Sparkes Cl BR2 ... 209 B5
Sparke Terr 2 E16 ... 98 D1
Sparkford Gdns N11 ... 31 A5
Sparkford Ho SW11 ... 266 D2
Sparks Cl Acton W3 ... 89 B1
Dagenham RM8 ... 80 D6
Hampton TW12 ... 173 A4
Sparrow Cl TW12 ... 173 A4
Sparrow Ct E4 ... 36 A4
Sparrow Dr BR5 ... 211 B1
Sparrow Farm Com Jun
Sch KT17 ... 216 B4
Sparrow Farm Dr
TW14 ... 150 D4
Sparrow Farm Inf Sch
TW14 ... 150 C4
Sparrow Farm Jun Sch
TW14 ... 150 C4
Sparrow Farm Rd KT17,
KT4 ... 216 B4
Sparrow Gn RM10 ... 81 D5
Sparrow's Farm L Ctr
SE9 ... 167 A4
Sparrows Herne
WD23 ... 8 A4
Sparrows La SE9 ... 167 A3
Sparrows Way WD23 ... 8 A4
Sparsholt Rd
Barking IG11 ... 101 C6
Finsbury Pk N19 ... 50 B1
Sparta St SE10 ... 142 A4
Spa Sch SE1 ... 118 A2
Spa View 6 SW16 ... 160 B1
Speakers' Corner*
W1 ... 114 D6 247 D6
Speaker's Ct 3 CR0 ... 205 B1
Speakman Ho SE4 ... 141 A2
Spearman St 8
SE18 ... 144 C6
Spear Mews
SW5 ... 113 C2 255 B3
Spearpoint Gdns IG2 ... 57 D5
Spears Rd N19 ... 50 A1
Speart La TW5 ... 129 A5
Spectacle Works
E13 ... 99 C4
Spectrum Ho NW5 ... 71 A4
Spectrum Twr 1
IG1 ... 79 A6
Spedan Cl NW3 ... 70 A5
Speechly Mews E8 ... 73 D3
Speed Ho EC2 ... 242 C4
Speedwell Ct 9 N12 ... 29 D6
Speedwell Ho 11
N12 ... 29 D6
Speedwell St 5
SE8 ... 141 C5
Speedy Pl WC1 ... 233 A1
Speer Rd KT7 ... 196 D3
Speirs Cl KT3 ... 199 D3
Spekehill SE9 ... 166 B1
Speke Rd CR7 ... 183 B1
Speldhurst Cl 2
BR2 ... 208 D4
Speldhurst Rd
Bedford Pk W4 ... 111 B3
Homerton E9 ... 74 D1
Spellbrook Wlk N1 ... 235 B6
Spelman Ho 15 E1 ... 96 A2
Spelman St E1 ... 96 A2
Spelthorne Coll
TW15 ... 170 B6
Spelthorne Gr
TW16 ... 171 D3
Spelthorne Inf Sch
TW15 ... 171 B4
Spelthorne Jun Sch
TW15 ... 171 B4
Spelthorne La TW15,
TW17 ... 171 A2
Spence Cl SE16 ... 119 B4
Spencer Ave
Bowes Pk N13 ... 32 B4
Hayes UB4 ... 84 A2
Spencer Cl BR6 ... 227 D6
Church End N3 ... 29 C1
Ealing NW10 ... 88 B4
Woodford IG8 ... 37 C5
Spencer Ct 5 BR6 ... 227 A3
6 Finchley N3 ... 29 D3
Wimbledon SW20 ... 178 B2
Spencer Dr N2 ... 48 A3
Spencer Gdns
SW14 ... 155 A6
Spencer Hill Rd
SW19 ... 179 A3
Spencer Hill SW19 ... 179 A3
Spencer Ho
31 Clapham SW8 ... 137 D3
Hendon NW4 ... 46 B4
24 Putney SW19 ... 156 D3
Spencer House Mus*
SW1 ... 115 C5 249 A3
Spencer Ho
Vale of Health NW3 ... 70 B5
Wimbledon SW19 ... 156 D1
Spencer Mews
Fulham W6 ... 264 A6
South Lambeth SW9 ... 270 C1
Spencer Park Ct
SW18 ... 158 B6
Spencer Pk
East Molesey KT8 ... 196 A4
Wandsworth SW18 ... 158 B6
Spencer Pl
16 Islington N1 ... 72 D1
SW1 ... 259 B5
Thornton Heath CR0 ... 205 B2
Spencer Rd
Acton W3 ... 111 A5
Bromley BR1 ... 186 D3
Carshalton CR4 ... 203 A2
Chingford E17 ... 36 A1
Chiswick W4 ... 133 A5
East Molesey KT8 ... 196 A4
Friern Barnet N11 ... 31 B6
Harrow HA3 ... 24 C1
Hornsey Vale N8 ... 50 B4
Hounslow TW3, TW5,
TW7 ... 130 A4
Ilford IG3 ... 57 D1
Mitcham CR4 ... 203 A6
Newham E6 ... 99 D6
South Croydon CR2 ... 221 C3
Tottenham N17 ... 34 A2
Twickenham TW2 ... 152 C2
Wandsworth SW18 ... 158 B6
Wembley HA0 ... 65 C6
Wimbledon SW20 ... 178 B2
Spencer Rise NW5 ... 71 B5
Spencer St
Finsbury
EC1 ... 94 D4 234 C1
Southall UB2 ... 106 D4
Spencer Wlk
23 Hampstead
NW3 ... 70 A4
Putney SW15 ... 134 D1
Spencer Yd SE3 ... 142 D3
Spenlow Ho 2
SE16 ... 118 A3
Spenser Ct 5
TW10 ... 175 D6
Spenser Gr N16 ... 73 C4
Spenser Mews SE21 ... 161 B3
Spenser Rd SE24 ... 160 D6
Spenser St SW1 ... 259 B6
Spens Ho WC1 ... 240 C5
Spensley Wlk N16 ... 73 B5
Speranza St SE18 ... 123 D1
Sperling Rd N17 ... 33 C1
Spert St E14 ... 119 A6
Speyside N14 ... 15 C5
Spey St E14 ... 98 A2
Spezia Rd NW10 ... 90 A5
Spice Ct
10 Battersea
SW11 ... 136 A2
2 St George in t East
E1 ... 118 A5
Spice Quay Htss
SE1 ... 253 D3
Spicer Cl
Brixton SE5, SW9 ... 138 D3
Walton-on-T KT12 ... 194 C3
Spicer Ct EN1 ... 5 C2
Spicer Ho E2 ... 96 A4
Spices Yd CR0 ... 221 A4
Spigurnell Rd N17 ... 33 B2
Spikes Bridge Rd
UB1 ... 107 A6
Spilsby Cl NW9 ... 27 C1
Spindle Cl SE18 ... 122 A3
Spindle Ho 8 DA15 ... 168 A1
Spindlewood Gdns
CR0 ... 221 C4
Spindrift Ave E14 ... 119 D2
Spinel Cl SE18 ... 123 D1
Spinnaker Cl IG11 ... 102 B4
Spinnaker Ct 2
KT1 ... 175 D2
Spinnaker Ho 21
E14 ... 119 C4
Spinnells Rd HA2 ... 41 B1
Spinney Cl
Beckenham BR3 ... 207 D5
New Malden KT3 ... 199 C4
Worcester Pk KT4 ... 215 D6
Yiewsley UB7 ... 104 A6
Spinney Dr TW14 ... 149 A4
Spinney Gdns
Dagenham RM9 ... 81 A3
Dulwich SE19 ... 183 D5
Spinney Oak BR1 ... 188 A1
Spinneys The BR1 ... 188 B1
Spinney The
Barnes SW13 ... 134 B6
Barnet EN5 ... 1 D3
Cheam SM3 ... 216 C4
DA14 ... 191 A5
Edgware HA7 ... 26 A6
Southgate N21 ... 16 C4
Streatham SW16 ... 159 D1
Sunbury TW16 ... 172 A2
Wembley HA0 ... 65 A5
Spire Ct 10 TW10 ... 154 A5
Spire Ho W2 ... 246 B6
Spires The EN5 ... 1 A2
Spirit Quay E1 ... 118 B5
SPITALFIELDS ... 95 D2
Spital Sq E1 ... 95 C2 243 B4
Spital St E1 ... 96 A2
Spital Yd E1 ... 243 B4
Spitfire Bsns Pk
CR0 ... 220 C2
Spitfire Est The
TW5 ... 106 C1
Spitfire Rd SM6 ... 220 A1
Spitfire Way TW5 ... 106 C1
Splendour Wlk
SE16 ... 118 C1
Spode Ho SE11 ... 261 A5
Spode Wlk NW3 ... 69 D3
Spondon Rd N15 ... 52 A5
Spoonbill Way UB4 ... 84 D2
Spooner Ho TW5 ... 129 C6
Spooner 8 NW9 ... 27 D3
Spooner Wlk SM6 ... 219 D3
Sporle Ct 6 SW11 ... 136 B2
Sportsbank St SE6 ... 164 A4
Spottons Gr N17 ... 33 A2
Spout Hill CR0 ... 223 C3
Spratt Hall Rd E11 ... 55 A3
Spray St SE18 ... 122 D2
Spreighton Rd KT8 ... 195 D5
Sprewell SW15 ... 157 A5
Spriggs Ho 14 N1 ... 72 D1
Sprimont Pl
SW3 ... 114 D1 257 C2
Springall St 9
SE15 ... 140 B5
Springalls Wharf 2
SE16 ... 118 A4
Springbank Rd
SE13 ... 164 C5
Springbank N21 ... 16 B5
Springbank Wlk
NW1 ... 71 D1
Springbourne Ct
BR3 ... 186 A2
Spring Bridge Rd
W5 ... 109 D6
Spring Cl Barnet EN5 ... 12 D6
Dagenham RM8 ... 58 D1
Springclose La SM3 ... 217 A2
Spring Cnr TW13 ... 149 D1
Spring Cott 10 W12 ... 112 A4
Spring Cotts KT6 ... 197 D4
Spring Court Rd EN2 ... 4 C5
Springcroft Ave N2 ... 48 D5
Spring Ct
Brondesbury NW2 ... 69 B2
Ealing W7 ... 108 B6
Edgware HA8 ... 26 B5
10 Wanstead E18 ... 55 B6
Springdale Rd N16 ... 73 B4
Spring Dr HA5 ... 40 A3
Springett Ho 15
SW2 ... 160 B6
Springfield Ave
Hampton TW12 ... 173 D4
Hornsey N10 ... 49 C6
Merton SW20 ... 201 B6
Springfield WD23 ... 8 B3
Springfield Cl
Finchley N12 ... 29 D5
Stanmore HA7 ... 9 A1
Springfield Com Prim
Sch N16 ... 52 A3
Springfield Ct
7 Dagenham W3 ... 89 A1
1 Friern Barnet N20 ... 14 D1
Hampstead NW3 ... 70 C1
2 Ilford IG1 ... 78 D3
9 Kingston u T KT1 ... 198 A6
Upper Clapton E5 ... 52 B1
Wallington SM6 ... 219 B3
Springfield Dr IG2 ... 57 A3
Springfield Gdns
BR1 ... 210 B5
Kingsbury NW9 ... 45 B4
Ruislip HA4 ... 40 B1
Upper Clapton E5 ... 52 B1
West Wickham BR4 ... 223 D6
Woodford IG8 ... 37 C3
Springfield Gr SE7 ... 143 C6
Sunbury TW16 ... 172 A2
Springfield Ho
Acton W3 ... 111 A5
1 Camberwell SE5 ... 139 C3
13 Dalston E8 ... 73 D2
Springfield Hospl
SW17 ... 158 C1
Springfield La NW6 ... 91 D6
Springfield Mount
NW9 ... 45 C4
Springfield Pl KT3 ... 199 A5
Springfield Prim Sch
TW16 ... 171 D1
Springfield Rd
Ashford TW15 ... 170 B5
Bexleyheath DA7 ... 147 D1
Bromley BR1 ... 210 B5
Chingford E4 ... 20 C4
Ealing W7 ... 108 C5
Friern Barnet N11 ... 31 C5
Harrow HA1 ... 42 C3
Hayes UB4 ... 106 C5
Kingston u T KT1 ... 198 A6
Newham E15 ... 98 C4
Penge SE26 ... 184 B5
Plashet E6 ... 78 B1
South Norwood CR7 ... 183 A2
St John's Wood
NW8 ... 92 A6 229 B5
8 Teddington
TW11 ... 175 A5
Tottenham Hale N15 ... 52 A5
Twickenham TW2 ... 151 C3
Wallington SM6 ... 219 B3
Walthamstow E17 ... 53 B3
Welling DA16 ... 146 B2
Wimbledon SW19 ... 179 B5
Springfield Rise
SE26 ... 162 B1
Springfields 16 EN5 ... 13 D6
Springfield
South Norwood
SE25 ... 206 A6
Upper Clapton E5 ... 52 B1
Springfield Wlk
3 BR6 ... 211 B1
Paddington NW6 ... 91 D6
Spring Gdns
East Molesey KT8 ... 196 A5
Islington N5 ... 73 A3
SW1 ... 116 A5 250 A4
Wallington SM6 ... 219 C3
Woodford IG8 ... 37 C3
Spring Gr
Brentford W4 ... 132 C6
Hampton TW12 ... 173 D2
Loughton IG10 ... 21 D5
Mitcham CR4 ... 181 A2
SPRING GROVE ... 130 C3
Spring Grove Cres TW3,
TW5 ... 130 A4
Spring Grove Prim Sch
TW7 ... 130 B3
Spring Grove Rd
Hounslow TW3, TW5,
TW7 ... 130 A4
Richmond TW10 ... 154 B6
Springhallow Sch
W13 ... 87 A1
Springhill Cl SE5 ... 139 B2
Spring Hill
Forest Hill SE26 ... 184 C6
Upper Clapton E5 ... 52 A2
Spring Ho
Merton SW19 ... 179 B2
WC1 ... 234 A1
Springhurst Cl CR0 ... 223 B4
Spring La SE25 ... 206 B3
Spring Lake HA7 ... 25 B6
Spring La
Muswell Hill N10 ... 49 A6
Upper Clapton E5 ... 52 B1
Spring Mews W1 ... 237 D4
SPRING PARK ... 223 B5
Spring Park Ave
CR0 ... 222 D6
Springpark Dr
Beckenham BR3 ... 208 A6
Stoke Newington N4 ... 51 A1
Spring Park Prim Sch
CR0 ... 223 C5
Spring Park Rd CR0 ... 222 D6
Spring Pl
Camden Town NW5 ... 71 B3
Church End N3 ... 29 C1
Springpond Rd RM9 ... 81 A3
Spring Rd TW13 ... 149 D1
Springrice Rd SE13 ... 164 B5
Spring Shaw Rd
BR5 ... 190 A2
Spring St W2 ... 92 B1 236 C1
Spring Terr TW10 ... 154 A6
Springtide Cl 10
SE15 ... 140 A4
Springvale Ave
TW8 ... 110 A1
Springvale Ct SE12 ... 143 A1
Spring Vale DA7 ... 147 D1
Springvale Terr 5
W14 ... 112 D3
Spring Villa Rd HA8 ... 26 C3
Springwater Cl
SE18 ... 144 C4
Springwater WC1 ... 240 C4
Springway HA1 ... 42 B2
Springwell Ave
NW10 ... 89 D6
Springwell Cl SW16 ... 182 B6
Springwell Ct TW5 ... 128 D3
Springwell Jun & Inf
Schs TW5 ... 129 A5
Springwell Rd
Heston TW5 ... 128 D4
West Norwood
SW16 ... 182 C5
Spring Wlk E1 ... 96 A2
Springwood Cl 8 E3 ... 97 C5
Springwood Cres
HA8 ... 11 A2
Springwood Ct CR2 ... 221 C4
Sprowston Mews E7 ... 77 A3
Sprowston Rd E7 ... 77 A3
Spruce Ct W5 ... 110 A3
Sprucedale Gdns
CR0 ... 222 D4
Spruce Hills Rd E17 ... 36 A1
Spruce Ho
2 Brentford
TW8 ... 131 C5
15 Rotherhithe
SE16 ... 118 D4
Spruce Pk BR2 ... 208 D5
Sprules Rd SE4 ... 141 A3
Spurfield KT8 ... 195 D6
Spurgeon Ave SE19 ... 183 B2
Spurgeon Rd SE19 ... 183 B3
Spurgeon's Coll
SE25 ... 183 C1
Spurgeon St
SE1 ... 117 B3 262 C6
Spur Ho 10 SW19 ... 179 D2
Spurling Rd
Dagenham RM9 ... 81 B2
East Dulwich SE22 ... 139 D1
Spur Rd
Brentford TW7 ... 131 B5
Edgware HA8 ... 26 A6
Feltham TW14 ... 128 B1
SE1 ... 116 C4 251 A2
Tottenham N15 ... 51 B5
Wallend IG11 ... 101 A4
Spurstowe Rd E8 ... 74 B2
Spurstowe Terr E8 ... 74 B3
Spurway Par 2 IG2 ... 56 B4
Square Rigger Row 7
SW11 ... 136 A2
Square The
Hammersmith
W6 ... 112 C1
Hayes UB11 ... 105 B5
Ilford IG1 ... 56 C2
Leyton E10 ... 76 A5
12 Richmond TW10 ... 153 D6
SW6 ... 265 A1
Wallington SM5 ... 219 A3
Woodford IG8 ... 37 A5
Squarey St SW17 ... 158 A1
Squire Ct 2 CR0 ... 205 C1
Squire Gdns NW8 ... 229 C1
Squire's Almshouses 7
E17 ... 53 D5
Squires Bridge Rd
KT17 ... 192 B5
Squires Ct
Finchley N3 ... 30 A2
SW4 ... 270 B1
Wimbledon SW19 ... 179 C6

Squires Ho 3 SE18 ..144 D6
Squires La N3 ....30 A2
Squire's Mount NW3 ..70 B5
Squire's Rd TW17.....192 C5
Squires The RM7......59 D3
Squires Wlk TW15 ....171 B3
Squires Wood Dr
BR7 ....188 B3
Squirrel Cl TW4......128 C2
Squirrel Mews W13 ..109 A6
Squirrels Cl
Hillingdon UB10.......60 C1
North Finchley N12 ....30 A6
Orpington BR6...... 211 C1
Squirrels Ct KT4 .....215 D6
Squirrels Gn KT4.....216 A6
Squirrel's La IG9 .....21 D1
Squirrels The
Bushey WD23 ....8 B5
Lewisham SE13.......142 B2
Pinner HA5 ....41 B6
Squirrels Trad Est
UB3 .... 105 D3
Squirries St E2 ....96 A4
Stable Cl
Kingston u T KT2.....176 B4
Northolt UB5.........85 C5
Stable Ct 4 SM6......219 A5
Stable Ho 9 SE16....118 C4
Stable Mews
Twickenham TW1.... 152 D3
West Norwood SE27. 183 A5
Stables End BR6 ......227 A5
Stables The IG9.......21 C4
Stables Way
SE11........116 C1 261 A2
Stable Way W10 ......90 C1
Stable Wlk N2.........30 B2
Stable Yd Rd
SW1........115 C4 249 B2
Staburn Ct HA8........27 A1
Stacey Ave N18.........34 C6
Stacey Cl E10..........54 B4
Stacey St Highbury N7..72 C5
Soho WC2 ... 93 D1 239 D1
Stack Ho SW1 ...... 258 B3
Stackhouse St SW1 . 257 C6
Stacy Path 13 SE5....139 C5
Staddon Cl BR3......207 A5
Stadium Bsns Ctr
HA9.................66 D5
Stadium Rd E NW2....46 C2
Stadium Rd
Hendon NW2.........46 C2
SE7, SE18 ....144 B6
Stadium Ret Pk HA9..66 C5
Stadium St
SW10.......136 A5 266 B3
Stadium Way HA9.....66 C4
Staffa Rd E10...........53 A1
Stafford Cl
Cheam SM3........ 217 A2
Maida Vale NW6......91 C4
Southgate N14........15 C6
Walthamstow E17.......53 B3
Stafford Cripps Ho
30 Bethnal Green
E2................96 C4
SW6............. 264 D5
Stafford Cross Bsns Pk
CR0 ....220 B3
Stafford Cross CR0...220 B3
Stafford Ct
Croydon CR0 .... 220 C4
Ealing W7 ....86 D1
Kensington W8 ...... 255 B6
South Lambeth SW8 . 270 A2
Stafford Gdns CR0 ...220 B3
Stafford Ho SE1 ..... 263 D2
Stafford Mans
13 Hammersmith
W14........... 112 D3
14 Stockwell SW4... 138 A1
SW11............. 267 C3
Stafford Morris Ho 9
E15.................98 C6
Stafford Pl
Richmond TW10......154 B4
SW1........ 115 C3 259 A6
Stafford Rd Bow E3.... 97 B5
Harrow HA3 ....24 A3
Kingston u T KT3.... 199 A6
Maida Vale NW6......91 C4
Plashet E7............77 D2
Ruislip HA4 ....61 D4
Sidcup DA14 .... 189 C6
Wallington CR0,
SM6 .... 220 A3
Staffordshire Ho N3 ..47 A6
Staffordshire St
Peckham SE15...... 140 A4
Peckham SE15.......140 B4
Stafford St W1 ..... 249 A4
Stafford Terr
W8.........113 C3 255 A6
Stag Cl HA8 ....27 A1
Stag Ct 16 SM6 ......219 B2
Stagg Hill EN4..........2 C6
Stag Hts 1 IG9........21 B2
Stag La Chigwell IG9 ...21 B2
Edgware HA8, NW9....45 A6
Stag Lane Fst & Mid
Schs HA8...........26 C1
Stag La SW15.........155 D2
Stags Ct KT7.........197 A2
Stagshaw Ho 17
SE22................139 C2
Stags Way TW7 ....130 D6
Stainbank Rd CR4....203 B6
Stainby Cl UB7.......104 A3
Stainby Rd N15.........51 D5
Staincliffe Ho 5
SM1................218 A4
Stainer Ho SE9 ......143 C1
Stainer St SE1 ...... 252 D3
Staines Ave SM3.....216 D6
Staines By-Pass
TW15..............170 A4
Staines Rd TW14.....149 B4
Staines Rd E TW12,
TW16..............172 C2
Staines Rd
Feltham TW14,
TW3 .... 150 C6
Hounslow TW3 ..... 129 C1
Ilford IG1 ....79 B4
Twickenham TW2.... 152 A1
Twickenham TW13,
TW2 .... 151 D1
Staines Rd W TW15 ..171 B3
Staines Wlk DA14....190 C4
Stainford Cl TW15 ...171 B5
Stainforth Rd
Ilford IG2 ....57 B2
Walthamstow E17 .....53 C5
Staining La EC2..... 242 B2
Stainmore Cl BR7....189 B2
Stainsbury St 25 E2 ...96 C5
Stainsby Rd E14 ......97 C1
Stainton Rd
Enfield EN3 ....6 C4
Lewisham SE13.......164 B4
Stalbridge Flats W1. 238 B1
Stalbridge Ho NW1 . 232 A3
Stalbridge St NW1 .. 237 B4
Stalham St SE16 .....118 B3
Stambourne Ho
SW8.............. 270 B2
Stambourne Way
Penge SE19........ 183 D3
West Wickham BR4.. 224 A5
Stamford Bridge
Stadium (Chelsea FC)
SW6....... 135 D5 265 C4
Stamford Brook Ave
W6.................111 D3
Stamford Brook Gdns
1 W6 ....111 D3
Stamford Brook Mans
2 W6 ....111 D2
Stamford Brook Rd
W6.................111 D3
Stamford Brook Sta
W6................ 111 D2
Stamford Cl
Harrow HA3 ....24 C3
2 London NW3 ....70 A5
Southall UB1 .... 107 C6
Tottenham Hale N15 ..52 A5
Stamford Cotts
SW10.............. 265 D4
Stamford Ct
Chiswick W6 .... 112 A2
Edgware HA8........26 B6
Stamford Dr BR2.....208 D5
Stamford Gdns RM9...80 C1
Stamford Gr E 1
N16 ....52 A1
Stamford Gr W 4
N16 ....52 A1
STAMFORD HILL 51 C1
Stamford Hill N16.....51 D1
Stamford Hill Mans 1
N16 ....51 D1
Stamford Hill Prim Sch
N15 ....51 B3
Stamford Hill Sta
N16 ....51 C2
Stamford Ho N15 ......52 A4
Stamford Hospl W6. 112 A2
Stamford Lo 2 N16...51 D2
Stamford Mans 2
N16 ....52 A1
Stamford Rd
Dagenham RM9.......80 C1
Kingsland N1.........73 C2
Newham E6........ 100 A6
South Tottenham N15 ..52 A4
Stamford St
SE1.........116 C5 251 B4
Stamp Pl E2..........95 D4
Stanard Cl N16 ....51 C2
Stanborough Cl
TW12..............173 B4
Stanborough Ho 4
E3..................97 D3
Stanborough Pas E8 ..73 D2
Stanborough Rd TW3,
TW7...............130 B2
Stanbridge Mans
SW15..............134 C2
Stanbridge Pl N21 ....16 D2
Stanbridge Rd
SW15..............134 C2
Stanbrook Ct W1 ... 249 A4
Stanbrook Rd SE2 ...124 B4
Stanburn Fst & Mid
Schs HA7...........25 C3
Stanbury Ct 16 NW3...70 D2
Stanbury Rd
Nunhead SE15...... 140 C3
Peckham SE15.......140 B3
Stancroft NW9........45 C4
Standale Gr HA4......39 A4
Standard Ind Est
E16.................122 B4
Standard Pl 13 EC2....95 C4
Standard Rd
Becontree NW10......89 B3
Belvedere DA17 .... 125 C1
DA6 .... 147 A1
Enfield EN3 ....7 A6
Hounslow TW4 ...... 129 A2
Standen Rd SW18....157 C4
Standfield Gdns
RM10................81 C2
Standfield Rd RM10...81 C3
Standish Ho
6 Chiswick W6..... 112 A2
SE9 ....143 B1
Standish Rd W6 .....112 A2
Standlake Point 1
SE23...............162 D1
Standor Ho 7 CR4...202 D6
Stane Cl SW19........179 D3
Stanedge Ct SW16 ...182 A5
Stane Gr SW4 ....138 A3
Stanesgate Ho 20
SE15...............140 A5
Stanetta Ct 3 RM6....58 B2
Stane Way SE18......144 A5
Stanfield Ho
8 Northolt UB5 ......84 D5
NW8 .... 236 D6
Stanfield Rd 14 E3 ...97 A5
Stanford Cl
Hampton TW12 ....173 B4
Romford RM7 ....59 D3
Ruislip HA4 ....39 A3
Stanford Ct
Friern Barnet N11.....31 A5
Kensington W8 ..... 255 D5
Walham Green SW6 . 265 D1
Stanford Ho IG11 ....102 B5
Stanford Pl
SE1.........117 C2 263 A3
Stanford Prim Sch
SW16.............. 181 D2
Stanford Rd
Friern Barnet N11.....30 D5
Thornton Heath
SW16........... 182 A1
W8........ 113 D3 255 D6
Stanford St SW1.... 259 C3
Stanford Way SW16 ..181 D1
Stangate Cres WD6 ...11 C6
Stangate Gdns HA7 ...25 B6
Stangate Lo N21.......16 B4
Stangate Mansi
TW1...............152 D1
Stangate SE1....... 260 D6
Stanger Rd SE25.....206 A5
Stanhope Ave
Harrow HA3 ....24 B2
Hayes BR2........ 209 A1
Hendon N3 ....47 B6
Stanhope Cl 28
SE16...............118 D4
Stanhope Ct N3.......29 B1
Stanhope Gate W1... 248 B4
Stanhope Gdns
Crouch End N6........49 C3
Dagenham RM8........81 B5
Edgware NW7 ....27 D5
Redbridge IG1.........56 B1
Stoke Newington N4 ...51 A3
SW7........ 114 A2 256 B4
Stanhope Gr BR3 ....207 B5
Stanhope Ho
Crouch End N6........49 C3
5 Friern Barnet N11 ...31 B6
4 Putney SW15.... 156 C6
SE8 ....141 B5
Stanhope Mews E
SW7........114 A2 256 B4
Stanhope Mews S
SW7............... 256 B3
Stanhope Mews W
SW7........114 A2 256 B4
Stanhope Park Rd
UB6 ....86 A3
Stanhope Par NW1.. 232 A2
Stanhope Pl W2 .... 237 C1
Stanhope Prim Sch
UB6 ....86 A3
Stanhope Rd
Barnet EN5 ....12 D5
Crouch End N6........49 C2
DA7 .... 147 A3
Dagenham RM8........81 B5
North Finchley N12 ....30 A5
Sidcup DA15 .... 190 A6
Southall UB6 ....86 A2
South Croydon CR0.. 221 C5
Wallington SM5..... 219 A1
Walthamstow E17 .....53 D4
Stanhope Row W1 .. 248 C3
Stanhope St
NW1.........93 C4 232 A1
Stanhope Terr
W2.........114 B6 246 D6
Stanier Cl SW5 ..... 254 D1
Stanlake Mews 7
W12................112 C5
Stanlake Rd W12 ....112 C5
Stanlake Villas 8
W12................112 C5
Stanley Ave
Barking IG11....... 101 D5
Beckenham BR2,
BR3............ 208 A6
Dagenham RM8.......59 B2
Greenford UB6 ....86 A6
Wembley HA0 ....66 A1
West Barnes KT3 ... 200 A4
Stanley Bldgs NW1.. 233 A3
Stanley Cl
Eltham SE9 .... 167 A3
SW8.............. 270 C5
Wembley HA0 ....66 A1
Stanley Cohen Ho
EC1 .... 242 A5
Stanley Cres
W11........113 B6 244 C6
Stanleycroft Cl
TW7...............130 C4
Stanley Ct
Belmont SM2....... 217 D1
11 Ealing W5.........87 C2
Wallington SM5..... 219 A1
Wimbledon SW19 ... 179 C4
Stanley Gardens Rd
TW11...............174 C5
Stanley Gdns
Bedford Pk W3 ..... 111 C4
Cricklewood NW2 .....68 C3
Mitcham CR4....... 181 A4
W11............. 244 C6
Wallington SM6..... 219 C2
Stanley Glynn Ct
BR7 ....188 C5
Stanley Gr
Clapham SW11 ..... 137 A3
Thornton Heath CR0 . 204 C3
Stanley Ho
35 Clapham SW8 ... 137 D3
Leytonstone E11 ......54 C3
Stanley Holloway Ct
E16..................99 A1
Stanley Ho
22 Poplar E14........97 C1
Wembley HA0 ....66 A1
Stanley Inf Sch
KT11 .... 174 C6
Stanley Jun Sch
KT11 .... 174 C6
Stanley Mans SW10 . 266 B6
Upper Tooting
SW17 .... 158 D2
Stanley Park Dr HA0 .. 88 B6
Stanley Park High Sch
SM5 .... 219 A2
Stanley Park Inf Sch
SM5 .... 218 D1
Stanley Park Jun Sch
SM5 .... 218 D1
Stanley Park Rd SM5,
SM6 ....219 A1
Stanley Rd
Acton Green W3 .... 111 A3
Ashford TW15 ...... 170 A5
Belmont SM2....... 217 D1
BR6 .... 211 D1
Bromley BR2 ...... 209 C5
Chingford E4 ....20 B3
East Finchley N2 ......48 B6
Edmonton N9.........17 D2
Enfield EN1 ....5 C2
Friern Barnet N11.....31 D5
Harringay N15.........50 D5
Harrow HA2 ....64 A6
2 Hendon NW9 ....46 A2
Ilford IG1 ....79 B6
Isleworth TW3...... 130 A1
Stanley Rd *continued*
Mill Meads E15 ....98 B6
Mitcham CR4....... 181 A3
Morden SM4 .... 201 C5
Mortlake SW14 ..... 132 D1
Muswell Hill N10.......31 B3
Northwood HA6........22 A2
Plashet E12...........78 A3
Sidcup DA14 ...... 168 A1
Southall UB1 .... 107 A6
Teddington TW11,
TW2 .... 174 C5
Thornton Heath CR0 . 204 C3
Twickenham TW2.....152 B1
Wallington SM5..... 219 A1
Walthamstow E10 .....53 D3
Wembley HA9 ....66 B2
Wimbledon SW19 ... 179 C4
Woodford E18 ....36 D2
Stanley St SE14, SE8 ..141 B5
Stanley Studios
SW10............. 266 B6
Stanley Tech High Sch
for Boys SE25..... 205 D6
Stanley Terr 8 N19 ...72 A6
Stanliff Ho 8 E14....119 C3
Stanmer St SW11 ....136 C3
STANMORE 25 A5
Stanmore Coll HA7 ...25 C4
Stanmore Gdns
Richmond TW9.......132 B2
Sutton SM1 .... 218 A5
Stanmore Hill HA7 ....25 A6
Stanmore Ho 21
SW8..............137 D3
Stanmore Lo HA7 .....25 B6
Stanmore Pl NW1... 231 D6
Stanmore Rd
Harringay N15........50 D5
Leytonstone E11 ......54 D1
Richmond TW9........132 B2
Stanmore Sta HA7....25 D6
Stanmore St
N1 .... 94 B6 233 C6
Stanmore Terr 3
BR3 ....185 C1
Stanmuir Lo NW9.....45 A4
Stannard Cotts 27 E1..96 C3
Stannard Ct SE6 .....163 D3
Stannard Mews E8....74 A2
Stannard Rd E8........74 A2
Stannary Pl SE11 ... 261 B1
Stannary St
SE11........116 C1 261 B1
Stannet Way SM6 ....219 C4
Stansbury Sq 3 W10..91 A4
Stansfeld Ho SE1 ... 263 D3
Stansfeld Rd E6 ......99 D1
Stansfield Rd
Cranford TW4,
TW5 ....128 B3
Stockwell SW9 ....138 B2
Stansgate Rd RM10 ...81 C5
Stanstead Cl BR2 ....208 D3
Stanstead Gr SE23 ...163 B3
Stanstead Ho E3......98 A3
Stanstead Manor
SM1 ....217 C2
Stanstead Rd
Forest Hill SE23,
SE6............. 163 A3
Wanstead E11........55 B4
Stansted Cres DA5 ...168 D3
Stansted Express
Terminal EC2 ..... 243 A4
Stansted Rd TW6 .....148 B5
Stanswood Gdns
SE5...............139 C5
Stanthorpe Cl
SW16..............182 A5
Stanthorpe Rd
SW16..............182 A5
Stanton Ave TW11 ...174 C4
Stanton Cl
Chessington
KT19........... 214 D3
North Cheam KT4 ... 200 D1
Stanton Ct 5 DA15 ...168 A1
Finchley N3 ....29 C2
Stoke Newington N16 ..51 B2
Stanton Ho 9 SE10 ..142 A6
Stanton Rd
Barnes SW13 ...... 133 D3
Thornton Heath CR0 . 205 A2
Wimbledon SW20 ... 178 D2
Stanton Sq SE26.....185 B6
Stanton Way SE26 ...185 B6
Stanway Ct 23 N1 ..... 95 C5
Stanway Gdns
Acton W3.......... 110 C5
Edgware HA8.........27 A5
Stanway St N1........95 C5
STANWELL 148 A3
Stanwell Fields CE Prim
Sch TW19......... 148 A4
Stanwell Rd
Ashford TW15 ...... 170 A6
Stanwell Rd *continued*
East Bedfont TW14, TW19
TW6 14
Stanwell TW15 14
Stanwick Rd
W14........113 B2 25
Stanworth Ct TW5 ...12
Stanworth St SE1... 25
Stanyhurst SE23 16
Stapenhill Rd HA0 6
Staplefield Cl
Pinner HA5 2
3 Streatham SW2.. 16
Stapleford Ave IG2....5
Stapleford Cl
Chingford E4.........2
Kingston u T KT1.... 19
Putney SW19....... 15
Stapleford Rd HA0 6
Stapleford N17 3
Stapleford Way
IG11...............10
Staplehurst Ct
SW11..............15
Staplehurst Ho 18 E5..7
Staplehurst Rd
Lewisham SE13..... 16
Sutton SM5 21
Staple Inn Bldgs
WC2.............. 24
Staple Inn WC2 24
Staples Cl SE16.......11
Staples Corner Bsns Pk
NW2................4
Staples Corner (East)
NW2................4
Staples Corner Ret Pk
NW2................4
Staples Corner (West)
NW2................4
Staple St
SE1.........117 B4 252
Stapleton Gdns
CR0 220
Stapleton Hall N4.....50
Stapleton Hall Rd N4..50
Stapleton Ho 19 E2 ...96
Stapleton Rd DA7....147
Orpington BR6...... 227
Upper Tooting
SW17 159
Stapley Rd DA17 125
Stapylton Rd EN5 1
Star Alley EC3 253
Star and Garter Hill
TW10...............154
Starboard Way E14 ..119
Starbuck Cl SE9 166
Star Cl EN3...........18
Starcross St
NW1.........93 C4 232
Star Ct UB10..........83
Stardome*NW1 238
Starfield Rd W12 112
Star & Garter Mans
SW15...............134
Star La E16............98
Starliner Ct N7 72
Starling Cl
Beckenham BR3 207
Buckhurst Hill IG9.....21
Pinner HA5 40
Starling Ct E13 99
Starling Ho NW8.... 230
Starling Wlk TW12...173
Starmans Cl RM9 103
Star Path UB5 85
Star Pl E1 118
Star Prim Sch E16....98
Star Rd
Hillingdon UB10.......83
Hounslow TW7 130
W14....... 113 B1 254
Star St W2 ....92 C1 237
Starts Cl BR6 226
Starts Hill Ave BR6...226
Starts Hill Rd BR6....226
Starveall Cl UB7 104
Star Works NW10.....90
Star Yd WC2...94 C1 241
State Farm Ave
BR6 227
Stateland Ct 10 N11...31
Staten Gdns TW1 152
Statham Ct N7........72
Statham Gr
Edmonton N18........33
Stoke Newington N16..73
Statham Ho SW8.... 269
Station App
Ashford TW15 170
Belmont SM2....... 217
Bexleyheath DA7.... 147
Chislehurst BR7..... 188
Dagenham NW10 89
Elmstead BR7 188
20 Finchley N12 29

n App *continued*
t Gate E7 77 B4
n Barnet N11 31 B5
m SW6 135 A2
ford UB6 64 B1
ton TW12 173 C2
BR2 209 A1
Town UB3 105 D3
ley Wood
.0 212 D5
ngston u T KT1,
2 176 C2
ham SE3 143 B2
ngham SE9 166 B3
Barnet EN5 2 A1
ew Malden KT4 200 A1
gton BR6 227 D6
e SE26 185 B5
r HA5 41 A6
mond TW9 132 C4
n Approach Rd
133 A5
n App
p HA4 39 D1
perton TW17 193 A4
outh Croydon
) 221 B6
n Ruislip HA4 62 B3
tham SW16 181 D5
ury TW16 172 A2
rbiton KT6 198 A3
amstow E17 53 C4
tead E11 55 A4
ng DA16 146 A3
bley HA0 65 B2
oodford E18 37 B1
ford IG8 37 B4
ford IG9 37 D6
ester Pk KT19 216 A3
sley UB7 104 A5
n Ave
rixton SW9 138 D2
ston u T KT3 199 C6
chmond TW9 132 C4
Ewell KT19 215 D1
n Bldgs
rd SE6 163 C4
on SW20 178 C1
n Blgs W5 110 B5
n Cl Finchley N3 29 C2
pton TW12 173 D2
n Cres
ord TW15 170 A6
nwich SE3 121 A1
nham N15 51 B5
bley HA0 65 B2
n Ct
ham CR4 202 C5
unhead SE15 140 C3
h Tottenham N15 51 D4
bley HA9 43 C1
ners Hall Ct
241 D1
n Estate Rd
4 150 B3
n Est BR3 206 D5
n Est 1 E18 37 B1
n Gdns W4 133 A5
n Gr HA0 66 A2
n Hill BR2 225 A6
n House Mews
34 A6
n Mans 9 N3 29 C2
n Mews Terr 4
121 A1
n Par Acton W3 88 C1
shford TW15 170 B6
ing IG11 79 A1
ont HA3 25 A1
fosters EN4 3 A1
lewood NW2 68 C2
nham RM10 81 C2
g W5 110 B5
are HA8 26 A3
ham TW14 150 B4
holt UB5 63 D4
sidge N14 15 D3
mond TW9 132 C4
ip HA4 61 B6
h Harrow HA2 63 D4
Upper Tooting
V12 159 A3
Vanstead E11 55 A4
dford IG9 37 D6
n Pas
Cross Gate
15 140 C4
dford E18 37 B1
n Pl N4 72 C6
n Rd
ord TW15 170 B6
ingside IG6 57 B6
es SW13 133 D3
enham BR2 186 C1
edere DA17 125 C3
eyheath DA7 147 A2
ley BR1 187 A2

Station Rd *continued*
Camden Town N19 71 C5
Carshalton SM5 218 D4
Chadwell Heath RM6 58 D2
Chessington KT9 214 A3
Chingford E4 20 B3
Church End N3 29 C1
Claygate KT10 212 C3
Croydon CR0 205 A1
Edgware HA8 26 C4
Edgware NW7 27 C4
Esher KT10 212 B6
Forest Gate E7 77 A4
Friern Barnet N11 31 B5
Greenhill HA1 42 D4
Hampton TW12 173 D2
Hampton Wick KT1 175 D2
Hanwell W7 108 C5
Harlesden NW10 89 D5
Hayes UB3 105 C2
Hendon NW4 46 A4
Hounslow TW3 129 D1
Ilford IG1 78 D5
Kingston u T KT2 176 C2
Lewisham SE13 142 A2
Leyton E10 76 A5
Manor Pk E12 78 A4
Merton SW19 180 A2
Station Rd N DA17 125 D3
Station Rd
New Barnet EN5 13 D6
North Harrow HA1,
HA2 41 D4
Orpington BR6 227 D6
Penge SE20 184 C4
Shepperton TW17 193 A4
Sidcup DA14, DA15 168 A1
Southgate N21 16 D3
South Norwood
SE25 205 D5
Sunbury TW16 172 A3
Teddington TW11 175 A4
Thames Ditton KT7 196 D2
Tottenham Hale N17 52 A6
Twickenham TW1 152 D4
Walthamstow E17 53 A4
West Acton W5 88 B1
West Barnes KT3 200 B4
West Drayton UB7 104 A4
West Wickham BR4 208 A1
Wood Green N22 32 B1
Station Rise SE27 160 D2
Station Sq BR5 211 A4
Station St
Newham E16 122 D5
Stratford E15 76 B1
Station Terr
Camberwell SE5 139 A4
Kensal Rise NW10 90 D5
Station View UB6 86 B6
Station Way
Cheam SM2, SM3 217 A1
Claygate KT10 212 C2
Woodford IG9 37 D6
Station Yd TW1 153 A4
Staton Ct 1 E10 53 D2
Staunton Ho SE17 263 A3
Staunton Rd KT2 176 B3
Staunton St SE8 141 B6
Staveley Cl
Hackney E9 74 C3
Lower Holloway N7 72 A4
New Cross Gate
SE15 140 C4
8 Peckham SE15 140 B4
Staveley Ct 4 E11 55 A4
Staveley Gdns W4 133 B4
Staveley Ho SE4 163 A6
Staveley NW1 232 A2
Staveley Rd
Ashford TW15 171 B4
Chiswick W4 133 B5
Stavers Ho 31 E3 97 B5
Staverton Rd NW2 68 C1
Stave Yard Rd SE16 119 A5
Stavordale Lo W14 254 D6
Stavordale Rd
Carshalton SM5 202 A2
Highbury N5 72 D4
Stayner's Rd E1 96 D3
Stayton Rd SM1 217 C5
Steadfast Rd KT1 175 D2
Steadman Ct EC1 242 B6
Steadman Ho 4
RM10 81 C5
Stead St
SE17 117 B2 262 C3
Steam Farm La
TW14 127 D1
Stean St E8 95 D6
Stebbing Ho 8
W11 112 D5
Stebbing Way IG11 102 A5
Stebondale St E14 120 A2
Stebon Prim Sch
E14 97 C2
Stedham Pl WC1 240 A2

Stedman Cl UB10 60 C5
Steedman St
SE17 117 A2 262 A3
Steeds Rd N10 30 D2
Steel App IG11 102 B5
Steele Rd
Acton Green W4 111 A3
Becontree NW10 89 A5
Isleworth TW7 131 A1
Leyton E11 76 C4
Tottenham N17 51 C6
Steele's Mews N
NW3 70 D2
Steele's Mews S
NW3 70 D2
Steele's Rd NW3 70 D2
Steele Wlk DA8 147 D5
Steel's La 23 E1 96 C1
Steen Way 7 SE22 161 C6
Steep Cl BR6 227 D2
Steep Hill
South Croydon
CR0 221 C4
Streatham SW16 159 D1
Steeple Cl
Fulham SW6 135 A3
Wimbledon SW19 179 A5
Steeple Ct
19 Bethnal Green
E1 96 B3
Wimbledon SW19 179 A5
Steeplestone Cl N18 33 A5
Steepleton Ct E11 54 A1
Steeple Wlk N1 235 B6
Steerforth St SW18 158 A2
Steering Cl N9 18 C3
Steers Mead CR4 180 D2
Steers Way SE16 119 A4
Steetley Ct 14 SM2 218 A1
Steinman Ct TW7 130 D2
Stelfax Ho WC1 233 D2
Stella Cl UB8 82 D2
Stella Rd SW17 180 D4
Stellar Ho 4 N17 33 D4
Stellman Cl E5 74 A5
Stembridge Rd
SE20 184 B1
Sten Cl 12 EN3 7 C6
Stephan Cl E8 96 A6
Stephen Cl BR6 227 D5
Stephen Ct 18
SW19 156 D3
Stephendale Rd
SW6 136 A3
Stephen Fox Ho 7
W4 111 C1
Stephen Hawking Sch
E14 97 A1
Stephen Mews W1 239 C3
Stephen Pl SW4 137 C2
Stephen Saunders Ct
SW11 158 C6
Stephens Ct
Brockley SE4 141 A2
E16 98 D3
Stephens Lo N12 14 A1
Stephenson Ct SM2 217 B1
Stephenson Ho
2 Gospel Oak
NW5 71 B4
6 Maitland Pk NW3 70 D3
Newington SE1 262 A6
West Heath SE2 124 D1
Stephenson Rd
Ealing W7 86 D1
Twickenham TW4 151 C4
Walthamstow E17 53 A4
Stephenson St
Dagenham NW10 89 D4
Newham E16 98 C2
Stephenson Way
NW1 93 C3 239 B6
Stephen's Rd E15 98 C6
Stephen St W1 239 C3
STEPNEY 96 D2
Stepney City E1 96 C2
Stepney Cswy E1 96 D1
Stepney Gn E1 96 D2
Stepney Greencoat CE
Prim Sch The E14 97 B1
Stepney Green Ct 4
E1 96 D2
Stepney Green Sch
E1 96 D2
Stepney Green Sta
E1 96 D3
Stepney High St E1 96 D2
Stepney Way
Mitcham CR4 181 A2
Stepney E1 96 C2
Sterling Ave HA8 26 B6
Sterling Cl NW10 68 A1
Sterling Gdns SE14 141 A6
Sterling Ho SE9 143 B1
Sterling Ind Est
RM10 81 D4
Sterling Pl W5 110 A2

Sterling Rd EN2 5 B5
Sterling St SW7 257 B6
**Sterling Way (North
Circular Rd)** N18 33 C5
Stern Cl IG11 102 C5
Sterndale Rd W14 112 D3
Sterne St W12 112 D4
Sternhall La SE15 140 A2
Sternhold Ave SW12,
SW2 159 D2
Sterry Cres RM10 81 C3
Sterry Dr
Thames Ditton
KT7 196 C3
Worcester Pk KT19 215 C4
Sterry Gdns RM10 81 C2
Sterry Rd
Barking IG11 101 D6
Dagenham RM10 81 C3
Sterry St SE1 252 C1
Steucers La SE23 163 A3
Stevanne Ct 1
DA17 125 C1
Steve Biko Ct W10 90 D3
Steve Biko La SE6 185 C6
Steve Biko Lodge 13
E13 99 A5
Steve Biko Rd N7 72 C5
Steve Biko Way
TW3 129 C2
Stevedale Rd DA16 146 C3
Stevedore St 3 E1 118 B5
Stevenage Rd
Fulham SW6 134 D4
Wallend E6 78 C2
Stevens Ave E9 74 C2
Stevens Cl
Beckenham BR3 185 C4
Hampton TW12 173 B4
Pinner HA5 40 C4
Stevens Ct BR3 185 C4
Stevens Gn WD23 8 A3
Stevens Ho KT1 175 D1
Stevens' La KT10 213 A2
Stevenson Cl EN5 14 B4
Stevenson Cres
SE16 118 B1
Stevenson Ho
1 Battersea
SW11 136 D3
6 Clapham Pk SW2 160 A6
NW8 229 A6
Wembley HA9 65 D6
Stevens Rd RM8 80 C5
Stevens St SE1 263 B6
Steventon Rd W12 111 D6
Stewards Holte Wlk 3
N11 31 B6
Stewart Ave TW17 192 C5
Stewart Cl BR7 188 D6
Hampton TW12 173 A4
Kingsbury NW9 45 A3
Stewart Fleming Prim
Sch SE20 206 C6
Stewart Headlam Prim
Sch E1 96 B3
Stewart Ho SE1 263 A5
Stanmore HA7 25 B5
Stewart Quay UB3 105 C4
Stewart Rainbird Ho 1
E12 78 C3
Stewart Rd E15 76 B4
Stewartsby Cl N18 33 A5
Stewart's Gr
SW3 114 C1 257 A2
Stewart's Rd
SW8 137 C4 269 A2
Stewart St E14 120 A4
Stew La EC4 252 A6
Steyne Ho
15 Acton W3 110 D5
11 Acton W3 111 A5
Steyne Rd W3 110 D5
Steyning Gr SE9 188 B6
Steynings Way N12 29 C5
Steyning Way TW4 128 C1
Steynton Ave DA5 168 D2
Stickland Rd DA17 125 C2
Stickleton Cl UB6 85 D4
Stifford Ho E1 96 C2
Stilecroft Gdns HA0 65 B5
Stile Hall Gdns W4 110 C1
Stile Hall Par 6
W4 110 C1
Stileman Ho 4 E3 97 B2
Stile Path TW16 194 A5
Stiles Cl BR2 210 B3
Erith DA8 125 D1
Stillingfleet Rd
SW13 134 A6
Stillington St
SW1 115 C2 259 B4
Stillness Jun & Inf Schs
SE23 163 A5
Stillness Rd SE23 163 B5
Stilwell Dr UB8 82 B3
Stilwell Rdbt UB8 104 D6

Stipularis Dr UB4 84 D3
Stirling Ave
Pinner HA5 41 A2
Upper Halliford
TW17 193 C6
Wallington SM6 220 A1
Stirling Cl
Sidcup DA14 189 D6
Streatham SW16 181 C2
Stirling Cnr EN5, WD6 11 B5
Stirling Ct
Clerkenwell EC1 241 C6
Ealing W13 109 B6
Strand WC2 240 C1
Stirling Gr TW3 130 A3
Stirling Ho 5 SE18 122 D1
Stirling Ind Ctr WD6 11 B6
Stirling Lo 7 EN5 14 A6
Stirling Mans NW6 70 A2
Stirling Rd
Harrow HA3 42 D6
Hayes UB3 106 B6
Newham E13 99 B5
South Acton W3 110 D3
Stanwell TW19,
TW6 148 B5
Stockwell SW9 138 A3
Tottenham N17 34 A2
Twickenham TW2 151 D4
Walthamstow E17 53 A6
Wood Green N22 32 D2
Stirling Ret Pk WD6 11 B5
Stirling Way
Borehamwood
WD6 11 B6
Thornton Heath CR0 204 A2
Stiven Cres HA2 63 B5
Stoatley Ho 10
SW15 156 A3
Stockbeck NW1 232 B3
Stockbridge Ho EN2 4 D3
Stockbury Rd CR0 206 C3
Stockdale Rd RM8 81 B6
Stockdove Way UB6 86 D4
Stocker Gdns RM9 80 C1
Stockfield Rd
Claygate KT10 212 C3
Streatham SW16 160 B1
Stockford Ave NW7 28 D3
Stockholm Ho E1 118 A6
Stockholm Rd SE16 118 C1
Stockholm Way 9
E1 118 A5
Stockhurst Cl SW15 134 D3
Stockingswater La
EN3 7 B2
Stockleigh Hall
NW8 230 B4
Stockley Acad UB8 82 B1
Stockley Cl UB7 104 D4
Stockley Ctry Pk
UB7 104 C6
Stockley Farm Rd
UB7 104 D3
Stockley Park Bsns Pk
UB11 105 A5
Stockley Rd UB7, UB8,
UB11 104 D4
Stock Orchard Cres
N7 72 B3
Stock Orchard St N7 72 B3
Stockport Rd SW16 181 D2
Stocks Ct 5 E1 96 D3
Stocksfield Rd E17 54 A6
Stocks Pl
Hillingdon UB10 82 C6
16 Limehouse E14 119 B6
Stock St E13 99 A5
Stockton Cl EN5 2 A1
Stockton Gdns
Edgware NW7 11 C1
Tottenham N17 33 A3
Stockton Ho 16 E2 96 B4
Harrow HA2 41 C1
Stockton Rd
Edmonton N18 34 B4
Tottenham N17 33 A3
STOCKWELL 138 A2
Stockwell Ave SW9 138 B2
Stockwell Cl BR1 187 B1
Stockwell Gdns
SW9 138 B4 270 C1
Stockwell Gn SW9 138 B3
Stockwell La SW9 138 B3
Stockwell Park Cres
SW9 138 B3
Stockwell Park Rd
SW9 138 B4 270 D1
Stockwell Park Sch
SW9 138 B4 270 C1
Stockwell Park Wlk
SW9 138 C2
Stockwell Prim Sch
SW9 138 B2
Stockwell Rd SW9 138 B3
Stockwell Sta SW4 138 A3
Stockwell St SE10 142 A6

Stockwell Terr SW9 270 C1
Stodart Rd SE20 184 C2
Stoddart Ho SW8 270 D5
Stodmarsh Ho 28
SW9 138 C4
Stofield Gdns SE9 165 D1
Stoford Cl SW19 157 A4
Stokenchurch St
SW6 135 D4 265 C1
STOKE NEWINGTON
73 C6
**Stoke Newington
Church St** N16 73 C6
Stoke Newington Comm
N16 73 D6
**Stoke Newington High
St** N16 73 D5
Stoke Newington Rd
N16 73 D4
Stoke Newington Sch
N16 73 B5
Stoke Newington Sta
N16 73 D6
Stoke Pl NW10 89 D4
Stoke Rd KT2 177 A3
Stokesby Rd KT9 214 B2
Stokes Ct N2 48 C5
Stokesley St W12 89 D1
Stokes Rd
Croydon CR0 206 D3
Newham E6 100 A3
Stokley Ct N8 50 A5
Stoll Cl NW2 68 C5
Stoms Path SE6 185 C5
Stonard Rd
Dagenham RM8 80 B4
Palmers Green N13 16 C1
Stondon Pk SE23 163 A5
Stondon Wlk 4 E6 99 D5
Stonebanks KT12 194 A2
Stone Bldgs
WC2 94 B2 240 D3
STONEBRIDGE 89 A6
Stonebridge Ct 9
NW10 67 B1
Stonebridge Ctr 6
NW10 89 B6
Stonebridge Ctr The
N15 52 A4
Stonebridge Park Sta
NW10 66 D1
Stonebridge Park
HA9 66 D1
Stonebridge Pk
NW10 67 B1
Stonebridge Rd N15 51 D4
Stonebridge Sch The
NW10 89 B6
Stonebridge Way
HA9 66 D2
Stonechat Sq 6 E6 100 A2
Stone Cl
Clapham SW4 137 C3
Dagenham RM8 81 B6
Yiewsley UB7 104 B5
Stonecot Cl SM3 201 A1
Stonecot Hill SM3 201 A1
Stone Cres TW14 149 D4
Stonecroft Way
CR0 204 A2
Stonecrop Cl NW9 45 B6
Stone Ct
Southgate N21 16 B6
4 Stratford E15 76 D1
Stonecutter St EC4 241 C2
Stonefield Cl DA7 147 C2
Ruislip HA4 63 A3
Stonefield N4 72 B6
Stonefield Mans N1 234 A5
Stonefield St
N1 94 C6 234 B6
Stonefield Way
Ruislip HA4 63 A3
SE7 143 D5
Stonegate 8 NW5 71 A2
Stone Gr HA8 26 B5
Stone Grove Ct HA8 26 B5
Stonegrove Gdns
HA8 26 A5
Stonegrove Ho HA8 26 B5
Stonehall Ave IG1 56 A3
Stone Hall Rd N21 16 C4
Stoneham Rd N11 31 C5
Stonehaven BR3 185 D1
Stonehill Bsns Pk
N18 34 D5
Stonehill Cl SW14 155 B6
Stonehill Ct E4 19 D4
Stonehill Rd
Brentford W4 110 C1
Mortlake SW14 155 B6
Stonehills Ct SE21 161 C1
Stonehill's Mans 3
SW16 160 A2

Stonehill Woods Pk DA14 .....191 D4
Stonehorse Rd EN3 ...18 C6
Stonehouse Ct EC2 . 243 B2
Stonehouse Ho 27 W2.....91 C2
Stonehouse NW1 ... 232 B5
Stone Lake Ind Pk SE7.....121 C2
Stone Lake Ret Pk SE7.....121 C2
STONELEIGH 216 A3
Stoneleigh Ave
Enfield EN1 .....6 B4
North Cheam KT17, KT4.....216 A5
Stoneleigh Broadway KT17 .....216 A3
Stoneleigh Cres KT19 .....215 D3
Stoneleigh Ct
Redbridge IG5.....56 A6
6 Tottenham N17 ....33 D1
Stoneleigh Fst Sch KT17 .....216 B4
Stoneleigh Lo 13 TW9.....132 B4
Stoneleigh Mews 15 E3.....97 A5
Stoneleigh Park Ave CR0 .....206 D3
Stoneleigh Park Rd KT19, KT4 .....216 A3
Stoneleigh Pl W11...112 D6
Stoneleigh Rd
Bromley BR1 ..... 210 D6
Carshalton SM5..... 202 C2
Redbridge IG5.....56 B6
Tottenham N17 .....33 D1
Stoneleigh Sta KT19 ..... 216 A3
Stoneleigh St W11...112 D6
Stoneleigh Terr N19...71 B6
Stonell's Rd SW11 ...158 D6
Stonemasons Cl N15..51 B5
Stonenest St N4 .....50 B1
Stone Park Ave BR3 .....207 D5
Stone Pl KT4 .....216 A6
Stone Rd BR2.....208 D4
Stones End St SE1 .. 252 A1
Stonewall E6.....100 C2
Stoneworth Ct SE25..206 A3
Stoney Alley SE18....144 C3
Stoneyard La E14 ....119 D6
Stoneycroft Cl SE12..164 D4
Stoney Deep TW11...175 A6
Stoneydown Ave E17..53 A5
Stoneydown Ho 2 E17.....53 A5
Stoneydown E17 .....53 A5
Stoneydown Park Sch E17.....53 A5
Stoneyfields Gdns HA8 .....27 A6
Stoneyfields La HA8...27 A6
Stoney La E1 ..... 243 B2
Penge SE19..... 183 D4
Stoney St SE1.....117 B5 252 C4
Stonhouse St SW4 ...137 D1
Stonor Rd W14.....113 B2 254 C3
Stonycroft Cl EN3.....7 A3
Stopes St SE15 .....139 D5
Stopford Rd
Newham E13.....99 A6
SE17 ..... 261 D1
Stopher Ho SE1..... 251 D1
Storace Ho 6 SW4...138 A1
Store Rd E16 .....122 C4
Storers Quay E14 .....120 B2
Store St
Bloomsbury WC1..... 93 D2 239 C4
Stratford New Town E15.....76 B3
Storey Ct NW8..... 229 C1
Storey Ho 23 E14.....119 D6
Storey Prim Sch E16..... 122 D5
Storey Rd
Highgate N6 .....48 D3
Walthamstow E17.....53 B5
Storey's Gate SW1..... 115 D4 249 D1
Storey St E16.....122 C4
Stories Rd SE5.....139 C2
Stork Rd E7 .....77 A2
Storksmead Rd HA8...27 C3
Storks Rd SE16 .....118 A3
Stormont House Sch E5.....74 B4
Stormont Rd
Clapham SW11 ..... 137 A1
Highgate N6 .....48 D2
Stormont Way KT9...213 C3
Stormount Dr UB3...105 A4
Storrington Rd CR0 ..205 D1
Storrington WC1..... 233 B1
Story St N1.....72 B1
Stotfold BR1.....188 A2
Stothard Ho 25 E1 .....96 C3
Stothard Pl E1..... 243 B4
Stothard St 12 E1 .....96 C3
Stott Cl SW18.....158 B5
Stoughton Ave SM3 ..217 A3
Stoughton Cl
Roehampton SW15 ..... 156 A3
SE11 ..... 260 D3
Stour Ave UB2.....107 C3
Stourbridge Ho 8 UB5 .....85 B3
Stour Cl BR2.....225 C4
Stourcliffe Cl W1 ... 237 C2
Stourcliffe St W1 ... 237 C1
Stour Ct UB1 ..... 86 B1
Stourhead Cl 6 SW19.....156 D4
Stourhead Gdns SW20.....200 A6
Stour Rd
Dagenham RM10.....81 C6
Hackney Wick E3.....75 C1
Stourton Ave TW13 ..173 B6
Stowage SE8 .....141 D6
Stow Cres E17.....35 A3
Stowe Cres HA4 .....39 A3
Stowe Gdns N9.....17 D3
Stowe Ho
Hampstead Garden Suburb NW11.....48 A3
11 Stoke Newington N16.....73 C5
Stowell Ho 2 N8 .....50 A5
Stowe Pl N15.....51 C6
Stowe Rd W12.....112 B4
Stowford Coll SM2.. 218 A1
Stowting Rd BR6.....227 C4
Stox Mead HA3 .....24 B2
Stracey Rd
Becontree NW10.....89 B6
Forest Gate E7 .....77 A4
Strachan Pl SW19, SW20.....178 C4
Stradbroke Gr
Buckhurst Hill IG9.....21 D3
Redbridge IG5.....56 C6
Stradbroke Rd N5.....73 A4
Stradbrook Cl HA2....63 B5
Stradella Rd SE24....161 A5
Straffan Lo 8 NW3 ...70 C2
Strafford Ho 9 SE8..119 B1
Strafford Rd
Acton W3..... 111 A4
Barnet EN5 .....1 A2
Hounslow TW3 .....129 B2
Twickenham TW1..... 153 A4
Strafford St E14 .....119 C4
Strahan Rd E3.....97 A4
Straightsmouth SE10.....142 A5
Straight The UB2.....107 A4
Strait Rd E6 .....122 B6
Straker's Rd SE15....140 B1
Strale Ho 17 N1.....95 C6
STRAND 116 B6
Strand Ct SE18.....123 D1
Strand Dr TW9.....132 D5
Strandfield Cl SE18 ..123 C1
Strand Ho SE28.....123 B5
Strand La WC2..... 250 D6
STRAND ON THE GREEN 132 C6
Strand-on-the-Green W4.....132 C6
Strand-on-the-Green Schs W4..... 132 C6
Strand Pl N18 .....33 C6
Strand
Strand WC2..... 116 B6 250 C6
Strand WC2..... 240 D1
Strang Ho N1..... 235 A5
Strangways Terr W14..... 254 C5
Stranraer Way
Barnsbury N1 .....72 A1
1 Stanwell TW6..... 148 A5
Strasburg Rd SW11.....137 B4 268 C1
Stratfield Ho SE12 ...165 A2
Stratfield Park Cl N21 .....16 D4
STRATFORD 76 A2
Stratford Ave UB10..... 82 B5
Stratford Bus Sta E15.....76 B1
Stratford Cir (Newham 6th Form Coll) E15..76 B2
Stratford Cl IG11 .....80 A1
Stratford Ct KT3 .....199 B5
Stratford Gr SW15 ...134 D1
Stratford House Ave BR1.....210 A6
Stratford International Sta E15.....76 A2
STRATFORD MARSH 97 D6
STRATFORD NEW TOWN 76 A3
Stratford Office Village The 1 E15.....76 C1
Stratford Pl W1..... 238 C1
Stratford Rd
Harlington TW6..... 149 A6
Hayes UB4.....84 B3
Hendon NW4.....46 D5
Newham E13.....99 A6
Southall UB2 ..... 107 A2
Thornton Heath CR7 . 204 D6
W8..... 113 C3 255 B5
Stratford Sch (Annexe) E7.....77 B2
Stratford Sch E7 .....77 A1
Stratford Sh Ctr E15..76 B1
Stratford Sta E15.....76 B1
Stratford Studios W8..... 255 C5
Stratford Villas NW1 ..71 D1
Stratford Workshops E15.....98 B6
Strathan Cl SW18.....157 A5
Strathaven Rd SE12 ..165 B5
Strathblaine Rd SW11.....136 B1
Strathbrook Rd SW16.....182 B3
Strathcona Rd HA9 ...65 D6
Strathdale SW16.....182 B5
Strathdon Dr SW17 ..158 B1
Strathearn Ave
Harlington UB3 ..... 127 D5
Twickenham TW2..... 152 A3
Strathearn Ho W2 .. 247 A6
Strathearn Pl W2.....114 C6 247 A6
Strathearn Rd
Sutton SM1 ..... 217 C3
Wimbledon SW19 ... 179 C6
Stratheden Par SE3...143 A5
Stratheden Rd SE3...143 A5
Strathfield Gdns IG11.....79 B2
Strathleven Rd SW2.....160 A6
Strathmore Ct NW8 . 230 A2
Strathmore Gdns
Edgware HA8.....26 D1
Finchley N3 .....29 D2
W8..... 245 B4
Strathmore Rd
Teddington TW11, TW2..... 174 C6
Thornton Heath CR0 ..205 B2
Wimbledon SW19 ... 157 C1
Strathmore Sch TW10..... 153 D2
Strathnairn St SE1 ...118 A2
Strathray Gdns NW3 ..70 C2
Strath Terr SW11.....136 C1
Strathville Rd SW18..157 D2
Strathyre Ave SW16 ..204 C6
Stratton Ave EN2 ..... 5 B6
Stratton Cl
DA7 .....147 A2
Edgware HA8.....26 B4
Heston TW5..... 129 C4
Merton SW19 ..... 179 C1
Walton-on-T KT12..... 194 C1
Stratton Ct
4 De Beauvoir Town N1 .....73 C1
10 Kingston u T KT6 . 198 A4
10 Pinner HA5.....23 B3
Strattondale St E14 ..120 A3
Stratton Dr IG11.....79 D2
Stratton Gdns UB1....85 C1
Stratton Ho HA8 .....26 B6
Stratton Lo 10 EN5.....1 D1
Stratton Rd
DA7 .....147 A2
Merton SW19 ..... 179 C1
Sunbury TW16..... 171 D1
Stratton St W1.....115 B5 248 D4
Strauss Rd W4.....111 B4
Strawberry Fields BR6 .....226 D3
STRAWBERRY HILL.....152 D1
Strawberry Hill Cl TW1.....152 D1
Strawberry Hill Rd TW1.....152 D1
Strawberry Hill Sta TW2..... 152 D1
Strawberry La SM5...219 A5
Strawberry Terr N10 ..30 D2
Strawberry Vale
Finchley N2 .....30 B2
Twickenham TW1..... 153 A1
Strayfield Rd EN2 .....4 D6
Streakes Field Rd NW2.....68 A6
Streamdale SE2 .....146 B6
Stream La HA8.....26 D5
Streamline Mews SE22.....162 A3
Streamside Cl BR2...209 A5
Edmonton N9.....17 D3
Stream Way DA17.....147 C6
Streatfeild Ave E6 ...100 B6
Streatfield Rd HA3, HA7 .....43 D6
STREATHAM 182 A4
Streatham & Clapham High Sch SW16 ... 159 D1
Streatham Cl SW16 ..160 A2
Streatham Common N SW16.....182 B5
Streatham Common S SW16.....182 B4
Streatham Common Sta SW16..... 181 D3
Streatham Ct SW16 ..160 A1
Streatham High Rd SW16, SW2 .....182 A5
STREATHAM HILL 160 A3
Streatham Hill & Clapham High Sch SW2.....160 B3
Streatham Hill Sta SW2..... 160 A2
Streatham Hill SW2 ..160 A3
STREATHAM PARK 181 C6
Streatham Pl SW2 ...160 A4
Streatham Rd CR4 .....181 A2
Streatham Sta SW16..... 181 D5
Streatham St WC1 .. 240 A2
STREATHAM VALE 181 D3
Streatham Vale SW16.....181 D3
Streathbourne Rd SW17.....159 A1
Streathem Wells Prim Sch SW2..... 160 C2
Streatleigh Par 4 SW16.....160 A2
Streatley Pl
27 Hampstead NW3.....70 A4
Hampstead NW3.....70 B4
Streatley Rd NW6.....69 B1
Streeters La SM6 ....219 D5
Streetfield Mews SE3.....143 A2
Streimer Rd E15 .....98 A5
Strelley Way W3.....111 C6
Stretford Ct 1 SW19.....179 A3
Stretton Lo W13 .....109 B6
Stretton Mans 16 SE8.....141 C6
Stretton Rd
Croydon CR0 ..... 205 C2
Richmond TW10..... 153 C2
Strickland Ct SE15.....140 A2
Strickland Ho 26 E2.....95 D4
Strickland Row SW18.....158 B4
Strickland St SE8 .....141 C4
Strickland Way 4 BR6.....227 D4
Stride Rd E13.....98 D5
Strimon Cl N9 .....18 C2
Stringer Hos 10 N1.....95 C6
Strode Cl N10 .....31 A3
Strode Ho 8 SW2....160 C3
Strode Rd
Forest Gate E7 .....77 A4
SW6..... 135 A5 264 A4
Tottenham N17 .....33 C1
Willesden NW10 .....68 A2
Strome Ho NW6 .....91 D5
Strone Rd E7, E12 .....77 D2
Strone Way UB4 .....85 A3
Strongbow Cres SE9.....166 B6
Strongbow Rd SE9...166 B6
Strongbridge Cl HA2..41 C1
Stronsa Rd W12 .....111 D4
Strood Ho
9 Penge SE20 ..... 184 C3
SE1 ..... 252 D1
Stroud Cres SW15....156 A1
Stroudes Cl KT4 .....199 D2
Stroud Field UB5 .....63 A2
Stroud Gate HA2.....63 D4
STROUD GREEN 50 C3
Stroud Green Gdns CR0 .....206 C2
Stroud Green Prim Sch N4 .....50 C1
Stroud Green Rd N4 ..50 C1
Stroud Green Way CR0 .....206 C3
Stroudley Ho SW8 .. 269 B2
Stroudley Wlk E3 .....97 D4
Stroud Rd
Croydon SE25 ..... 206 A3
Wimbledon SW19 ... 157 C1
Strouds Cl RM6.....58 B4
Stroud Way TW15.....171 A4
Strout's Pl 2 E2.....95 D4
Struan Ho 15 E11 .....55 A4
Strudwick Ct SW4 .. 270 B1
Strutton Ground SW1.....115 D3 259 C5
Strype St E1..... 243 C3
Stuart Ave
Ealing W5 .....110 B4
Harrow HA2 .....63 B5
Hayes BR2..... 209 A1
Hendon NW9.....46 A2
Walton-on-T KT12.....194 B1
Stuart Cl UB10.....60 C2
Stuart Cres
Croydon CR0 .....223 B5
Hayes UB3.....83 A1
Wood Green N22.....32 B2
Stuart Ct Chingford E4..20 D2
6 Croydon CR0 ..... 220 D5
2 Elstree WD6.....9 D5
Stuart Evans Cl DA16 .....146 C2
Stuart Gr TW11 .....174 C5
Stuart Ho
Hammersmith W6..... 112 C3
1 Homerton E9 .....74 D1
Queensbury NW9 .....44 C5
5 Stockwell SW4... 138 A1
W14..... 254 A4
Stuart Lo SE25.....183 C1
Stuart Mill Ho N1..... 233 C3
Stuart Pl CR4 .....180 D2
Stuart Rd Acton W3...111 A5
Barking IG11.....79 D1
DA16 .....146 B4
East Barnet EN4 .....14 D4
Harrow HA3 .....42 D6
Maida Vale NW6 .....91 C4
Nunhead SE15..... 140 C1
Richmond TW10.....153 B1
South Norwood CR7 . 205 A5
Wimbledon SW19 ... 157 C1
Stubbs Cl NW9 .....45 A4
Stubbs Dr SE16 .....118 B1
Stubbs Ho
Finsbury Pk N4 .....50 B1
1 Globe Town E2.....96 D4
Stubbs Mews RM8 .....80 B4
Stubbs Point E13 .....99 B3
Stubbs Way SW19.....180 B2
Stucley Pl 19 NW1 .....71 B1
Stucley Rd TW5, TW7.....130 A5
Studdridge St SW6...135 C3
Studd St N1 ...94 D6 234 C6
Studholme Ct NW3 ...69 C4
Studholme St SE15...140 B5
Studio Mews 5 NW4..46 C5
Studio Pl SW1..... 247 D1
Studios NW8 ..... 229 A4
Studios Rd TW17.....192 B6
Studios The
4 Clapham SW4 ... 137 C1
SW8..... 269 D1
Studland Cl DA15 .....167 D1
Studland Ho E14.....97 A1
Studland Rd
Ealing W7 .....86 C1
Forest Hill SE26..... 184 D5
Kingston u T KT2..... 176 A4
Studland SE17..... 262 C2
Studland St W6.....112 B2
Studley Ave E4 .....36 B3
Studley Cl E5.....75 A3
Studley Ct
13 Blackwall E14.....120 B6
DA14 .....190 B5
Redbridge IG4.....55 D3
Studley Dr IG4.....55 D3
Studley Grange Rd W7.....108 D4
Studley Rd
Dagenham RM9.....80 D1
South Lambeth SW4 . 138 A3
Upton E7 .....77 B2
Study Prep Sch The SW19..... 178 C5
Study Sch The KT3.. 199 C4
Stukeley Rd E7 .....77 B1
Stukeley St WC2.....94 A1 240 B2
Stumps Hill La BR3 ..1
Stunell Ho 23 SE14...1
Sturdee Ho 2 E2.....
Sturdy Ho 28 E3 .....
Sturdy Rd SE15 1
Sturge Ave E17 .....
Sturgeon Rd SE17.....117 A1 2
Sturges Field BR7....1
Sturgess Ave NW4 ....
Sturge St SE1.....117 A4 2
Sturmer Way N7.....
Sturminster Cl UB4 ...
Sturminster Ho SW8..... 2
Sturrock Cl N15 .....
Sturry St E14 .....
Sturt St N1..... 2
Stutfield St E1.....
Stuttle Ho 14 E1 .....
Styles Gdns SW9.....1
Styles Ho SE1..... 2
Styles Way BR3 2
Stylus Apartments 25 E1.....
Sudbourne Prim Sch SW2.....1
Sudbourne Rd SW2 ..1
Sudbrooke Rd SW12.....1
Sudbrook Gdns TW10.....1
Sudbrook La TW10...1
SUDBURY .....
Sudbury Ave HA0 .....
Sudbury Court Dr HA1 .....
Sudbury Court Rd HA1 .....
Sudbury Cres BR1 ...1
Wembley HA0 .....
Sudbury Croft HA0.....
Sudbury Ct
1 Ilford RM6.....
SW8..... 2
Sudbury Gdns CR0 ..2
Sudbury & Harrow Roa Sta HA0 .....
Sudbury Heights Ave UB6 .....
Sudbury Hill Cl HA0...
Sudbury Hill HA1 .....
Sudbury Hill Harrow S HA1 .....
Sudbury Hill Sta HA1 .
Sudbury Ho SW18....1
Sudbury E6.....1
Sudbury Prim Sch HA0 .....
Sudbury Rd IG11 .....
Sudbury Town Sta UB6 .....
Sudeley St N1 .....94 D5 2
Sudlow Rd SW18.....1
Sudrey St SE1 2
Suez Ave UB6.....
Suez Rd EN3.....
Suffield Ho SE17..... 2
Suffield Rd
Chingford E4 .....
Penge SE20..... 1
2 South Tottenham N15.....
Suffolk Cl WD6 .....
Suffolk Ct
3 Dagenham RM6 .....
Ilford IG3 .....
Walthamstow E17 .....
3 West Norwood SW16..... 1
Suffolk Ho
11 Acton W3.....
Beckenham BR2 2
8 Dartmouth Pk NW5.....
Edgware HA8.....
Penge SE20..... 1
4 South Croydon CR0..... 2
Suffolk La EC4..... 2
Suffolk Park Rd E17...
Suffolk Pl SW1 2
Suffolk Rd
Barking IG11.....
Barnes SW13 1
Dagenham RM10.....
Enfield EN3 .....
Harrow HA2 .....
Ilford IG3 .....
4 Newham E13 .....
Sidcup DA14 1
South Norwood SE25..... 2
Tottenham N15 .....
Willesden NW10 .....

k Rd *continued*
ester Pk KT4 ... 215 D6
ks Prim Sch
... 6 B3
k St
st Gate E7 ... 77 A4
... 115 D5 249 D4
House La E15 ... 98 A5
Loaf Wlk 6
... 96 C4
en Rd
am SW11 ... 137 A1
Ditton KT7 ... 197 B1
en Way IG11 ... 101 D5
Ho SE4 ... 141 A1
ave Gdns 11
... 112 C4
ave Rd W6 ... 112 C3
Rd SW2 ... 160 A4
n Ct SW6 ... 135 C3
n Ent Ctr
... 135 C2
an Prim Sch
... 135 C3
n Rd SW6 ... 135 C2
n Ho 11 E2 ... 96 D4
an Ave E16 ... 99 D2
an Cl
ersea SW11 ... 136 C2
es UB4 ... 84 C2
an Ct
roydon CR0 ... 206 A1
ford Hill N16 ... 51 D1
... 255 B4
an Ho
sea SW1 ... 268 D6
worth TW2 ... 152 B5
hall SE11 ... 260 D3
an Rd
... 116 C2 261 B4
ans Reach
2 ... 193 D2
an Way WD6 ... 9 C5
n Ho SE1 ... 118 A1
n Rd E11 ... 55 B5
n St Penge BR3 ... 184 D1
... 139 A5
al Ct E9 ... 76 B6
atra Rd NW6 ... 69 C2
urgh Rd SW12 ... 159 A5
ner Ave KT8 ... 196 C4
nercourt Rd E1 ... 96 C1
ner Crossing
... 196 C4
nerene Cl
6 ... 181 C3
nerfield Ave
ey Hatch N12 ... 30 C4
sal Rise NW6 ... 91 A5
nerfield 6
... 187 B2
nerfield Ho
... 80 D4
nerfield La
... 213 D6
nerfield Rd
ng W5 ... 87 B3
ghton IG10 ... 21 D5
nerfield St
2 ... 164 D4
ner Gdns KT8 ... 196 C4
ner Gr WD6 ... 9 D5
ner Hill
ehamwood
D6 ... 10 C6
... 188 C1
nerhill Cl BR6 ... 227 C5
nerhill Gr EN1 ... 17 C5
nerhill Rd N15 ... 51 B5
nerhill Villas
... 188 D2
nerhill Way
... 181 A2
ner Ho SE13 ... 142 B1
nerhouse Ave
... 129 A4
nerhouse Rd
... 73 C6
nerland Gdns
... 49 B6
nerland Grange
... 49 B6
nerlands Ave
... 111 A6
nerlands Lo
... 226 C4
nerlee Ave N2 ... 48 D5
nerlee Gdns N2 ... 48 D5
nerley St
8 ... 157 D2
ner Rd
Molesey KT8 ... 196 B4
mes Ditton KT7,
8 ... 196 D4
nersby Rd N6 ... 49 B3
ners Cl
nont SM2 ... 217 C1

Summers Cl *continued*
Wembley HA9 ... 44 D1
Summersell Ho
SE27 ... 183 B5
Summerside Prim Sch
N12 ... 30 B4
Summerskille Cl N9 ... 18 B2
Summers La N12 ... 30 B3
Summers Row N12 ... 30 C4
Summers St EC1 ... 241 A5
SUMMERSTOWN ... 158 A1
Summerstown
SW17 ... 180 A6
Summerton Way
SE28 ... 102 D1
Summer Trees
TW16 ... 172 B2
Summerville Gdns
SM1 ... 217 B2
Summerwood Rd TW1,
TW7 ... 152 D5
Summit Ave NW9 ... 45 B4
Summit Bsns Pk The
TW16 ... 172 A3
Summit Cl
Edgware HA8 ... 26 C3
Kingsbury NW9 ... 45 B5
Osidge N14 ... 15 C2
Summit Ct
5 Barnet EN5 ... 1 B2
Brondesbury NW2 ... 69 A3
Summit Dr IG8 ... 37 D1
Summit Est N16 ... 52 A2
Summit Rd
Northolt UB5 ... 63 C1
Walthamstow E17 ... 53 D5
Summit Way
Brunswick Pk N14 ... 15 B2
South Norwood
SE19 ... 183 C3
Sumner Ave SE15 ... 139 D4
Sumner Bldgs SE1 ... 252 A4
Sumner Cl BR6 ... 227 A4
Sumner Ct SW8 ... 270 A2
Sumner Gdns CR0 ... 204 C1
Sumner Ho 1 E3 ... 97 D2
Sumner Place Mews
SW7 ... 256 D3
Sumner Pl
SW7 ... 114 B2 256 D3
Sumner Rd
Harrow HA1 ... 42 A2
SE15 ... 139 D5
Sumner Rd S CR0 ... 204 C1
Sumner Rd CR0 ... 204 D1
Sumner St
SE1 ... 117 A5 252 A4
Sumpter Cl NW3 ... 70 A2
Sun Alley 6 TW9 ... 132 A1
Sun Alliance Ho
WC2 ... 241 A2
Sunbeam Cres W10 ... 90 C3
Sunbeam Rd NW10 ... 89 B3
SUNBURY ... 194 B6
Sunbury Ave
Edgware NW7 ... 27 B6
Mortlake SW14 ... 133 B1
Sunbury Cl KT12 ... 194 A3
SUNBURY COMMON
... 171 D3
Sunbury Court Island
TW16 ... 194 D6
Sunbury Court Mews
TW16 ... 172 D1
Sunbury Court Rd
TW16 ... 172 C1
Sunbury Cres TW13 ... 171 D6
Sunbury Cross
TW16 ... 172 A3
Sunbury Cross Ctr 5
TW16 ... 171 D3
Sunbury Ct 3 EN5 ... 1 A1
Sunbury Ct (Con Ctr)
TW16 ... 172 D1
Sunbury Ct 3 SE14 ... 140 D6
Sunbury TW16 ... 172 D1
Sunbury Gdns NW7 ... 27 B5
Sunbury Ho 38 E2 ... 95 D4
Sunbury Int Bsns Ctr
TW16 ... 171 C2
Sunbury La
Battersea
SW11 ... 136 B4 266 D2
Walton-on-T KT12 ... 194 A3
Sunbury Manor Sch
TW16 ... 171 D2
Sunbury Rd
Cheam SM3 ... 217 A5
Feltham TW13 ... 171 D6
Sunbury Sta TW16 ... 172 A2
Sunbury St SE18 ... 122 B3
Sunbury Way TW13 ... 172 C5
Sunbury Workshops 39
E2 ... 95 D4
Suncroft Pl SE26 ... 162 C1
Sun Ct EC3 ... 242 D1

Sunderland Ct
Dulwich SE22 ... 162 A4
12 Stanwell TW19 ... 148 A5
Sunderland Ho 26
W2 ... 91 C2
Sunderland Mount
SE23 ... 162 D2
Sunderland Point
E16 ... 123 A5
Sunderland Rd
Ealing W5 ... 109 D3
Forest Hill SE23 ... 162 D2
Sunderland Terr W2 ... 91 D1
Sunderland Way E12 ... 77 D6
Sundew Ave W12 ... 112 A6
Sundew Ct 9 HA0 ... 88 A5
Sundial Ave SE25 ... 205 D6
Sundial Ct KT5 ... 214 D6
Sundorne Rd SE7 ... 121 C1
Sundown Rd TW15 ... 171 A5
Sundra Wlk 26 E1 ... 96 D3
SUNDRIDGE ... 187 C4
Sundridge Ave
Bromley BR1,
BR7 ... 188 A3
DA16 ... 145 B2
Sundridge Ho
Bromley BR1 ... 187 B5
4 Homerton E9 ... 74 D1
Sundridge Par BR1 ... 187 B3
Sundridge Park Sta
BR1 ... 187 B3
Sundridge Rd CR0 ... 206 A1
Sunfields Pl SE3 ... 143 B5
Sun in the Sands
SE3 ... 143 B5
Sunken Rd CR0 ... 222 C3
Sunland Ave DA6 ... 147 A1
Sun La SE3 ... 143 B5
Sunleigh Ct HA0 ... 88 A6
Sunleigh Rd HA0 ... 88 A6
Sunley Gdns UB6 ... 87 A6
Sunley Ho E1 ... 243 D3
Sun Life Trad Est
TW14 ... 128 A2
Sunlight Cl SW19 ... 180 A4
Sunlight Sq 29 E2 ... 96 B4
Sunmead Rd TW16 ... 194 A6
Sunna Gdns TW16 ... 172 B1
Sunna Lo TW16 ... 171 D3
Sunniholme Ct CR2 ... 221 A3
Sunningdale Ave
Barking IG11 ... 79 B1
East Acton W3 ... 111 C6
Feltham TW13 ... 151 A2
Ruislip HA4 ... 40 C1
Sunningdale Cl
22 Bermondsey
SE16 ... 118 B1
Erith SE28 ... 103 A1
Newham E6 ... 100 B4
Stanmore HA7 ... 25 A3
3 Surbiton KT6 ... 214 A6
Sunningdale Ct
13 Kingston u T
KT2 ... 176 C3
13 Southall UB1 ... 86 A1
Sunningdale
Ealing W13 ... 87 B2
Friern Barnet N14 ... 31 D5
Sunningdale Gdns
Kingsbury NW9 ... 45 A4
W8 ... 255 B5
Sunningdale Lo HA8 ... 26 B5
Sunningdale Rd
BR1, BR2 ... 210 A4
Cheam SM1 ... 217 B4
Sunningfields Cres
NW4 ... 28 B1
Sunningfields Rd
NW4 ... 46 B6
Sunninghill Ct 9
W3 ... 111 A4
Sunninghill Gdns
IG2 ... 57 D4
Sunninghill Rd
SE13 ... 141 D3
Sunny Bank SE25 ... 206 A6
Sunny Cres NW10 ... 67 A1
Sunnycroft Rd
Hounslow TW3 ... 129 D3
Southall UB1 ... 85 C2
South Norwood
SE25 ... 206 A6
Sunnydale BR6 ... 226 C6
Sunnydale Gdns
NW7 ... 27 C4
Sunnydale Rd SE12 ... 165 B6
Sunnydene Ave
Chingford E4 ... 36 B5
Ruislip HA4 ... 62 A6
Sunnydene Gdns
HA0 ... 65 C2
Sunnydene St SE26 ... 185 A6
Sunnyfield NW7 ... 27 D6
Sunnyfields Prim Sch
NW4 ... 46 B6

Sunny Gardens Par
NW4 ... 28 B1
Sunny Gardens Rd
NW4 ... 46 C6
Sunnyhill Cl E5 ... 75 A4
Sunny Hill Ct NW4 ... 28 B1
Sunny Hill NW4 ... 46 B6
Sunnyhill Prim Sch
SW16 ... 182 B6
Sunnyhill Rd SW16 ... 182 A6
Sunnyhurst Cl SM1 ... 217 C5
Sunnymead Ave
CR4 ... 203 D6
Sunnymead Ct W5 ... 109 D6
Sunnymead Rd
Kingsbury NW9 ... 45 B2
Putney SW15 ... 156 B6
Sunnymede Ave
KT19 ... 215 C1
Sunnymede Dr IG6 ... 56 D5
Sunny Nook Gdns
CR2 ... 221 B2
Sunny Pl NW4 ... 46 C5
Sunny Rd The EN3 ... 6 D4
Sunnyside 4 NW2 ... 69 B5
Sunnyside Dr E4 ... 20 A4
Sunnyside Ho 3
NW2 ... 69 B5
Sunnyside Pl SW19 ... 179 A4
Sunnyside Rd
Crouch End N19 ... 49 D2
Ealing W5 ... 109 D5
Sunnyside Rd E N9 ... 18 A1
Sunnyside Rd IG1 ... 79 B5
Sunnyside Rd N N9 ... 18 A1
Sunnyside Rd S N9 ... 18 A1
Sunnyside Rd
Teddington TW11 ... 174 B6
Walthamstow E10 ... 53 C1
Sunnyside
Walton-on-T
KT12 ... 194 C4
Wimbledon SW19 ... 179 A4
Sunny View NW9 ... 45 B4
Sunny Way N12 ... 30 C3
Sun Pas 8 SE16 ... 118 A3
Sunray Ave BR2 ... 210 B3
Herne Hill SE5, SE24 ... 139 B1
Tolworth KT5 ... 214 D6
Sun Rd W14 ... 113 B1 254 C1
Sunrise Cl TW13 ... 151 B1
Sunrise View NW7 ... 27 D4
Sun St Pas
EC2 ... 95 C2 243 A3
Sunset Ave
Chingford E4 ... 19 D3
Woodford IG8 ... 36 D6
Sunset Ct 4 IG8 ... 37 C3
Sunset Gdns SE25 ... 183 D1
Sunset Ho HA3 ... 42 C6
Sunset Rd
Herne Hill SE5 ... 139 B1
SE28 ... 124 A5
Wimbledon SW19 ... 178 B5
Sunset View EN5 ... 1 A3
Sunshine Way CR4 ... 180 D1
Sun St EC2 ... 95 B2 242 D4
Sunwell Cl SE15 ... 140 B4
Superior Dr 4 BR6 ... 227 D2
Suraj Ho 6 N22 ... 32 C1
SURBITON ... 198 A2
Surbiton Boys Prep Sch
KT6 ... 198 A4
Surbiton Cres KT1,
KT6 ... 198 A5
Surbiton Ct KT6 ... 197 D3
Surbiton Hall Cl
KT1 ... 198 A5
Surbiton High Sch Jun
Girls Sch KT1 ... 198 A5
Surbiton High Sch
KT1 ... 198 A5
Surbiton Hill Pk
KT5 ... 198 C4
Surbiton Hill Rd
KT6 ... 198 A4
Surbiton Hospl KT6 ... 198 A3
Surbiton Par 11
KT6 ... 198 A3
Surbiton Rd KT1 ... 198 A5
Surbiton Sta KT6 ... 198 A3
Surcot Ho 2 SW4 ... 137 D3
Surlingham Cl SE28 ... 124 D6
Surma Cl E1 ... 96 A3
Surmans Cl RM9 ... 102 C6
Surrendale Pl W9 ... 91 C3
Surrey Canal Rd SE14,
SE16, SE8 ... 140 D6
Surrey Cl N3 ... 47 A6
Surrey Cres 1 W4 ... 110 C1
Surrey Ct 15 SM6 ... 219 B2
Surrey Gdns N4 ... 51 A3
Surrey Gr
Carshalton SM1 ... 218 B5
SE17 ... 263 A1
Surrey Ho
Edgware HA8 ... 26 B4

Surrey Ho *continued*
8 Rotherhithe
SE16 ... 118 D5
Surrey La
SW11 ... 136 C4 267 B1
Surrey Lo SW20 ... 178 C1
Surrey Mews SE27 ... 183 C6
Surrey Mount SE23 ... 162 B3
Surrey Quays Rd
SE16 ... 118 D4
Surrey Quays Sh Ctr
SE16 ... 118 D3
Surrey Quays Sta
SE16 ... 118 D2
Surrey Rd
Barking IG11 ... 79 C1
Dagenham RM10 ... 81 D3
Harrow HA1 ... 42 A4
Honor Oak SE15 ... 162 D6
West Wickham BR4 ... 207 D1
Surrey Row
SE1 ... 116 D4 251 D2
Surrey Sq
SE17 ... 117 C1 263 B2
Surrey Square Inf Sch
SE17 ... 117 C1 263 A2
Surrey Square Jun Sch
SE17 ... 117 C1 263 A2
Surrey St
Croydon CR0 ... 221 A5
4 Newham E13 ... 99 B4
WC2 ... 116 B6 250 D6
Surrey Terr SE17 ... 263 B2
Surrey Water Rd
SE16 ... 118 D5
Surrey Wharf SE1 ... 140 A6
Surridge Ct 15 SW9 ... 138 A3
Surridge Gdns SE19 ... 183 B4
Surr St N7 ... 72 A3
Sury Basin KT2 ... 176 A2
Susan Constant Ct 18
E14 ... 120 B6
Susan Lawrence Ho 4
E12 ... 78 C4
Susannah St E14 ... 98 A1
Susan Rd SE3 ... 143 B3
Susan Wood BR7 ... 188 C2
Sussex Ave TW7 ... 130 C2
Sussex Cl
New Malden KT3 ... 199 C5
Redbridge IG4 ... 56 B4
4 Twickenham
TW1 ... 153 B5
Upper Holloway N19 ... 72 A6
Sussex Cres UB5 ... 63 C2
Sussex Ct
4 Barnes SW13 ... 133 D3
Greenwich SE10 ... 142 A6
Mitcham CR4 ... 204 A4
Paddington W2 ... 236 C1
Sussex Gate N6 ... 48 D4
Sussex Gdns
Chessington KT9 ... 213 D2
Fortis Green N6 ... 48 D4
Harringay N4 ... 51 A4
Paddington
W2 ... 92 B1 236 D1
Sussex Ho
Edgware HA8 ... 26 B4
Hampstead NW3 ... 70 C2
Richmond TW9 ... 132 B3
Sussex House Sch
SW3 ... 114 D2 257 C4
Sussex Lo W2 ... 236 D1
Sussex Mans
South Kensington
SW7 ... 256 C3
Strand WC2 ... 250 B6
Sussex Mews E W2 ... 236 D1
Sussex Mews SE6 ... 163 C3
Sussex Mews W W2 ... 246 D6
Sussex Pl
22 Hammersmith
W6 ... 112 C1
Lisson Gr
NW1 ... 92 D3 237 C6
New Malden KT3 ... 199 C5
Paddington
W2 ... 92 B1 236 D1
Sussex Rd
Barking E6 ... 100 C6
Erith DA8 ... 147 D5
Harrow HA1 ... 42 A4
Mitcham CR4 ... 204 A4
New Malden KT3 ... 199 C5
Sidcup DA14 ... 190 B5
Southall UB2 ... 106 D3
South Croydon CR2 ... 221 B2
Uxbridge UB10 ... 61 A3
Wallington SM5 ... 218 D2
2 West Wickham
BR4 ... 207 D1
Sussex Ring N12 ... 29 C5
Sussex Sq
W2 ... 114 B6 246 D6
Sussex St
Newham E13 ... 99 B4

Sussex St *continued*
SW1 ... 258 D2
Sussex Way
Cockfosters EN4 ... 15 B6
Upper Holloway N7 ... 72 B5
Upper Holloway N7,
N19 ... 72 A6
Upper Holloway N19 ... 49 D1
Sutcliffe Cl NW11 ... 47 D4
Sutcliffe Ho UB3 ... 84 A1
Sutcliffe Rd
Bexley DA16 ... 146 C3
SE18 ... 145 C6
Sutherland Ave
Ealing W13 ... 87 B1
Falconwood DA16 ... 145 C1
Hayes UB3 ... 106 A2
Orpington BR5 ... 211 D4
Paddington
W9 ... 92 A3 236 A6
Sunbury TW16 ... 171 D1
Sutherland Cl EN5 ... 1 A1
Sutherland Ct
Kingsbury NW9 ... 44 D4
3 Paddington W9 ... 91 C3
Stoke Newington N16 ... 73 B5
Sutherland Dr
SW19 ... 180 B2
Sutherland Gdns
Mortlake SW14 ... 133 C2
North Cheam KT4 ... 200 B1
Sunbury TW16 ... 171 D1
Sutherland Gr
Putney SW18,
SW19 ... 157 B4
Teddington TW11 ... 174 C5
Sutherland Ho
Ealing W13 ... 109 A6
Kensington W8 ... 255 C5
Kidbrooke SE18 ... 144 B4
7 Putney SW15 ... 156 C4
Richmond TW10 ... 153 C2
9 South Hampstead
NW6 ... 70 A2
Sutherland Pl W2 ... 91 C1
Sutherland Rd
Belvedere DA17 ... 125 C3
Chiswick W4 ... 133 C6
Ealing W13 ... 87 A1
Edmonton N9 ... 18 B3
Enfield EN3 ... 18 D6
Southall UB1 ... 85 B1
Thornton Heath CR0 ... 204 C2
Tottenham N17 ... 34 A2
Walthamstow E17 ... 53 A6
Sutherland Row
SW1 ... 258 D2
Sutherland Sq
SE17 ... 117 A1 262 A1
Sutherland St
SW1 ... 115 B1 258 D2
Sutherland Wlk
SE17 ... 262 B1
Sutlej Rd SE7 ... 143 C5
Sutterton St N7 ... 72 B2
SUTTON ... 218 A2
Sutton Cl
Beckenham BR3 ... 185 D2
Pinner HA5 ... 40 A4
Sutton Coll of Liberal
Arts SM1 ... 217 D3
Sutton Common Rd
Cheam SM3 ... 201 C1
Sutton SM1, SM3 ... 217 D6
Sutton Common Sta
SM1 ... 217 D6
Sutton Courtenay Ho
SW17 ... 180 B6
Sutton Court Mans
W4 ... 133 A6
Sutton Court Rd
Chiswick W4 ... 133 A6
Hillingdon UB10 ... 82 D6
Newham E13 ... 99 C4
Sutton SM1 ... 218 A2
Sutton Cres EN5 ... 12 D6
Sutton Ct
Chiswick W4 ... 133 A6
Ealing W5 ... 110 A5
East Molesey KT8 ... 195 B4
8 Hackney E5 ... 74 B4
Penge SE19 ... 183 D3
Sutton SM2 ... 218 A2
Sutton Dene TW3 ... 129 D4
Sutton Est
SW3 ... 114 C1 257 B2
Sutton Est The 8
W10 ... 90 C2
Sutton Gdns
Barking IG11 ... 101 C5
Croydon CR0 ... 205 D4
Sutton Gn IG11 ... 101 C6
Sutton Gram Sch For
Boys SM1 ... 218 A3

Sutton Gr SM1 218 B3
Sutton Hall Rd TW5 129 C5
Sutton High Sch SM1 217 D2
Sutton Ho N21 16 B6
Sutton House* E9 74 C3
Sutton Hts SM2 218 B1
Sutton La EC1 241 D5
Hounslow TW3, TW4, TW5 129 B3
Sutton La N W4 111 A1
Sutton La S W4 133 A6
Sutton Park Rd SM1, SM2 217 D2
Sutton Par NW4 46 C5
Sutton Pl E9 74 C3
Sutton Rd
Barking IG11 101 C6
E13 98 D3
Heston TW5 129 C4
Higham Hill E17 34 D2
Muswell Hill N10 31 A2
Sutton Row W1 239 D2
Sutton Sq Hackney E9 74 C3
Hounslow TW5 129 B4
Sutton Sta SM2 218 A2
Sutton St E1 96 C1
Suttons Way EC1 242 B5
Sutton Way
Hounslow TW5 129 B4
North Kensington W10 90 C2
Sutton Wlk SE1 116 B5 250 D3
Swaby Rd SW17, SW18 158 A2
Swaffham Ct 1 RM6 58 C4
Swaffield Prim Sch SW18 158 A4
Swaffield Rd SW18 158 A4
Swain Cl SW16 181 B4
Swain Ho CR4 180 D3
Swain Rd CR7 205 A4
Swains Cl UB7 104 A4
Swain's La N6 71 B6
Swainson Ho N7 72 C4
Swainson Rd W3 111 D4
Swains Rd CR4, SW17 180 D3
Swain St NW8 92 C3 237 A6
Swakeleys Dr UB10 60 C3
Swakeleys Rdbt UB8, UB10 60 A4
Swakeleys Rd UB10 60 C5
Swakeleys Sch UB10 82 D5
Swaledale Cl N11 31 A4
Swallands Rd SE6 163 C1
Swallowbrook Bsns Ctr UB4 106 D5
Swallow Cl
Bushey WD23 8 A3
New Cross Gate SE14 140 D4
Swallow Ct
Chingford IG8 36 B3
Ilford IG2 56 D4
4 Paddington W9 91 C2
5 Ruislip HA4 40 C1
1 SE12 165 A4
Swallow Dr
Northolt UB5 85 C5
Willesden NW10 67 B2
Swallowfield NW1 231 D1
Swallowfield Rd SE7 121 B1
Swallowfield Way UB3 105 B4
Swallow Gdns SW16 181 D5
Swallow Ho
Hornsey N8 50 B6
NW8 230 A4
Swallow Pk KT6 214 B5
Swallow Pl
24 Poplar E14 97 B1
W1 238 D1
Swallows Ct 5 SE20 184 D3
Swallow St
Newham E6 100 A2
W1 115 C6 249 B5
Swaminarayan Sch The NW10 67 B2
Swanage Ct 5 N1 73 C1
Swanage Ho SW8 270 C3
Swanage Rd
Chingford E4 36 A3
Wandsworth SW18 158 A5
Swanage Waye UB4 84 C1
Swan And Pike Rd EN3 7 C5
Swan App E6 100 A2
Swanbourne Ho NW8 237 A6
Swanbourne SE17 262 A3
Swanbridge Rd DA7 147 C4
Swan Bsns Ctr 8 W4 111 B2
Swan Cl
Croydon CR0 205 C2
Feltham TW13 173 A6
Higham Hill E17 35 A3
Swan Ct Chelsea SW3 257 B1
Parsons Green SW6 265 A3
Poplar E14 97 B1
Swan Ctr SW17 158 A1
Swan Ct N20 14 A2
Swandon Way SW18 135 D1
Swan Dr NW9 27 C1
Swanfield St E2 95 D4
Swan Ho
De Beauvoir Town N1 73 B1
Enfield EN3 18 C6
Swan La EC4 117 B6 252 D5
Loughton IG10 21 C4
Swan Lane Pier EC4 117 B6 252 C5
Swan La N20 14 A1
Swanlea Sec Sch E1 96 B3
Swanley Ho SE17 263 B2
Swanley Rd DA16 146 C4
Swan Mead SE1 117 C3 263 A5
Swan Mews
Stockwell SW9 138 B3
SW6 265 A2
Swanmore Ct SW18 158 A5
Swann Ct 8 TW7 131 A2
Swanne Ho 12 SE10 142 A5
Swan Pas 5 E1 118 A6
Swan Pl SW13 133 D3
Swan Rd
Feltham TW13 173 A6
Greenwich SE18 121 D3
Rotherhithe SE16 118 C4
Southall UB1 85 D1
West Drayton UB7 104 A4
Swanscombe Ho
1 BR5 190 B1
11 Shepherd's Bush W11 112 D5
Swanscombe Point 7 E16 98 D2
Swanscombe Rd
5 Chiswick W4 111 C1
Shepherd's Bush W11 112 D5
Swansea Ct E16 122 D5
Swansea Rd
Enfield EN3 6 C1
Harlington TW14, TW6 149 B5
Swansland Gdns 2 E17 35 A2
Swan St TW7 131 B2
Swanston Ct TW1 152 D4
Swan St SE1 117 A4 252 B1
Swan The BR4 224 A6
Swanton Gdns SW19 156 D3
Swanton Rd DA8 147 D5
Swan Way EN3 6 D3
Swanwick Cl SW15 155 D4
Swan Wlk
Oatlands Pk TW17 193 C2
SW3 136 D6 267 C6
Swan Yd N1 72 D2
Swaton Rd E3 97 C3
Swaylands Rd DA17 147 C6
Swaythling Cl N18 34 B6
Swaythling Ho SW15 155 D5
Swedenborg Gdns E1 118 B6
Sweden Gate SE16 119 A2
Swedish Quays SE16 119 A3
Swedish Sch The SW13 134 A6
Sweeney Cres SE1 253 D1
Sweet Briar Gn N9 17 D1
Sweet Briar Gr N9 17 D1
Sweet Briar Wlk N18 33 D6
Sweetcroft La UB10 60 C1
Sweetmans Ave HA5 40 D6
Sweets Way N20 14 B2
Swell Ct E17 53 D3
Swetenham Wlk SE18 123 A1
Swete St E13 99 A5
Sweyn Pl SE3 143 A3
Swift Cl Harrow HA2 63 D6
Hayes UB3 83 D1
Higham Hill E17 35 A3
Thamesmead SE28 124 B6
Swift Ct SM2 217 D1
Swift Ctr CR0 220 B1
Swift Ho
16 Stepney E1 96 C1
15 Stoke Newington N16 73 C5
1 SW9 138 C5
8 Wanstead E18 55 B6
Swift Rd
Feltham TW13 173 A6
Southall UB2 107 B3
Swiftsden Way BR1 186 C4
Swift St SW6 135 B4 264 C2
Swinbrook Rd W10 91 A2
Swinburne Cres CR0 206 C3
Swinburne Ct 4 SE5 139 B1
Swinburne Ho 15 E2 96 C4
Swinburne Rd SW15 134 A1
Swinderby Rd HA0 66 A2
Swindon Cl IG3 57 C1
Swindon Rd TW6 149 A6
Swindon St W12 112 C5
Swinfield Cl TW13 173 A6
Swinford Gdns SW9 138 D2
Swingate La SE18 145 C5
Swingfield Ct BR2 209 D4
Swingfield Ho 4 E9 96 C6
Swinley Ho NW1 231 D2
Swinnerton St E9 75 A3
Swinson Ho 12 N11 31 C5
Swinton Cl HA9 44 D1
Swinton Ho 21 E2 96 A4
Swinton Pl WC1 233 C2
Swinton St WC1 94 B4 233 C2
Swires Shaw BR2 225 D4
Swiss Cottage NW3 70 B1
Swiss Cottage Sch
South Hampstead NW3 70 B1
St John's Wood NW8 92 B6 229 D6
Swiss Cottage Sta NW3 70 B1
Swiss Re Building* EC2 95 C1 243 B2
Swiss Terr 7 NW3 70 B1
Switch Ho 4 E14 120 B6
Swithland Gdns SE9 188 C6
Swyncombe Ave W5 109 B2
Swynford Gdns 7 NW4 46 A5
Sybil Elgar Sch UB2 107 B3
Sybil Mews N4 50 D3
Sybil Phoenix Cl SE8 118 D1
Sybil Thorndike Casson Ho SW5 255 B1
Sybil Thorndike Ho 12 N1 73 A2
Sybourn Inf Sch Annexe E10 53 A1
Sybourn Jun & Inf Schs E17 53 B2
Sybourn St E17 53 B2
Sycamore Ave
DA15 167 D5
Ealing W5 109 D3
East Finchley N3 47 D6
Hayes UB3 105 C6
Old Ford E3 97 B6
Sycamore Cl
Carshalton SM5 218 D4
Chislehurst SE9 166 A2
East Acton W3 111 C5
2 Edgware HA8 27 A6
Edmonton N9 34 A6
Feltham TW13 150 A1
New Barnet EN4 14 B5
Newham E16 98 C3
Northolt UB5 85 A6
South Croydon CR2 221 C3
Yiewsley UB7 104 B6
Sycamore Ct
4 Beckenham BR3 185 C2
Forest Gate E7 77 A2
3 Forest Hill SE26 184 C6
Golders Green NW11 47 A3
Hendon NW4 28 C1
Hillingdon UB8 82 C3
Hither Green SE12 164 D5
Hounslow TW4 129 A1
Kilburn NW6 91 C6
Surbiton KT6 198 A2
Tufnell Pk N19 71 D5
10 West Norwood SW16 182 C5
Sycamore Gdns
Hammersmith W6, W12 112 B3
Mitcham CR4 180 B1
Sycamore Gdns *continued*
Tottenham N15 51 D5
Sycamore Gr
Kingsbury NW9 45 A2
Kingston u T KT3 199 C6
Lewisham SE6 164 A5
Penge SE20 184 A2
Sycamore Hill N11 31 A4
Sycamore Ho
4 Buckhurst Hill IG9 21 D2
23 Finchley N2 30 B1
10 Maitland Pk NW3 70 D2
Penge SE20 184 D4
17 Rotherhithe SE16 118 D4
3 Shepherd's Bush W6 112 B4
2 Stoke Newington N16 73 B6
Teddington TW11 175 C3
Twickenham TW1 152 D2
Sycamore Lo 7 TW16 171 D3
Sycamore Lodge HA2 64 B6
Sycamore Lo SW15 134 B2
Sycamore Mews 4 SW4 137 C2
Sycamore Rd SW19, SW20 178 C4
Sycamore St EC1 242 A5
Sycamore Way TW11 175 C4
Sycamore Wlk
Ilford IG6 57 A5
1 Kensal Town W10 91 A3
Sydcote SE21 161 A3
Sydenham Ave
Penge SE26 184 B5
Southgate N21 16 B6
Sydenham High Sch SE26 162 B1
Sydenham High Sch GDST SE26 184 B5
Sydenham Hill SE21, SE22, SE23, SE26, SE19 162 A1
Sydenham Hill Sta SE21 161 D1
Sydenham Ho 16 KT6 197 D2
Sydenham Ind Est SE26 185 B5
Sydenham Park Mans 2 SE26 162 C1
Sydenham Park Rd SE23, SE26 162 C1
Sydenham Pk SE26 162 C1
Sydenham Rd
Forest Hill SE26 185 A6
Thornton Heath CR0 205 B2
Sydenham Rise SE23 162 B2
Sydenham Sta SE26 184 C6
Sydenham Station App 4 SE26 184 C6
Sydmons Ct SE23 162 C4
Sydner Mews N16 73 D4
Sydner Rd N16 73 D4
Sydney Chapman Way EN5 1 B3
Sydney Cl SW3 256 D3
Sydney Cotts KT10 212 D2
Sydney Cres TW15 170 D4
Sydney Ct Hayes UB4 84 C3
Surbiton KT6 214 A6
Sydney Gr NW4 46 C4
Sydney Ho
4 Chiswick W4 111 C2
Muswell Hill N10 31 B3
Sydney Mews SW3 256 D3
Sydney Pl SW7 257 A3
Sydney Rd
Abbey Wood SE2 124 D3
Bexley DA6 146 D1
Ealing W13 109 A4
East Bedfont TW14 150 A3
Enfield EN2 5 B1
Hornsey N8 50 C5
Muswell Hill N10 31 B3
Richmond TW10, TW9 132 A1
Sidcup DA14 189 C6
Sutton SM1 217 C4
Teddington TW11 174 D5
Wanstead E11 55 B3
West Barnes SW20 178 D1
Woodford IG8 37 A6
Sydney Russell Sch The RM9 80 D3
Sydney St SW3 114 C1 257 A2
Sydney Terr KT10 212 D2
Sylva Cotts 3 SE8 141 C4
Sylva Ct 3 SW15 156 D4
Sylvana Cl UB10 82 B6
Sylvan Ave
Church End N3 29 C1
Dagenham RM6 59 B3
Edgware NW7 27 D4
Wood Green N22 32 C3
Sylvan Ct
Finchley N12 29 D6
1 Kilburn NW6 91 D6
South Croydon CR2 221 A2
Sylvan Gdns KT6 197 D2
Sylvan Gr
Hampstead NW2 68 D4
SE15 140 B6
Sylvan Hill SE19 183 C2
Sylvan Ho N21 16 B6
Sylvan Rd Ilford IG1 79 A6
South Norwood SE19 183 D2
Upton E7 77 B2
Walthamstow E17 53 C4
Wanstead E11 55 A4
Sylvan Way
Coney Hall BR4 224 C4
Dagenham RM8 80 B5
Sylvan Wlk BR1 210 B6
Sylverdale Rd CR0 220 D5
Sylvester Ave BR7 188 B4
Sylvester Ct HA0 65 D3
Sylvester Ho 7 E8 74 B2
Sylvester Path 8 E8 74 B2
Sylvester Rd
Finchley N2 30 B1
Hackney E8 74 B2
Walthamstow E17 53 B2
Wembley HA0 65 C3
Sylvestrus Cl KT1 176 C1
Sylvia Ave HA5 23 B4
Sylvia Ct N1 235 C3
Wembley HA9 66 D1
Sylvia Gdns HA9 66 D1
Sylvia Lawla Ct N22 32 B1
Sylvia Pankhurst Ho
10 Dagenham RM10 81 C5
14 Globe Town E2 96 D4
Sylvia Young Theatre Sch NW1 237 B5
Symes Mews NW1 232 A4
Symington Ho SE1 262 C5
Symington Mews E9 74 D3
Symister Mews N1 95 C4
Symons St SW3 114 D2 257 D3
Symphony Cl HA8 26 D3
Symphony Mews 15 W10 91 A4
Syon Gate Way TW7, TW8 131 B5
Syon Ho & Pk* TW8 131 C4
Syon La
Brentford TW7, TW8 131 B5
Hounslow TW7 130 D6
Syon Lane Sta TW7 131 A5
Syon Lo 6 SE12 165 A4
Syon Park Cotts TW8 131 C4
Syon Park Gdns TW7 130 D5
Syon Park Sch TW7 131 B4
Syringa Ho SE4 141 B2

T

Tabard Ct 6 E14 98 A1
Tabard Ho SE1 262 D6
Teddington KT1 175 C2
Tabard St SE1 117 B3 262 C6
Tabernacle Ave 7 E13 99 A3
Tabernacle St EC2 95 B3 242 D6
Tableer Ave SW4 159 D6
Tabley Rd N7 72 A4
Tabor Ct 3 SM3 217 A2
Tabor Gdns SM2, SM3 217 B1
Tabor Gr SW19 179 B3
Tabor Rd W6 112 B3
Tachbrook Est SW1 115 D1 259 D1
Tachbrook Mews SW1 259 A4
Tachbrook Rd
East Bedfont TW14 149 D4
Southall UB2 106 D2
Tachbrook St SW1 115 C2 259 B3
Tack Mews SE4 141 C2
Tadbourne Ct 1 HA8 27 A3
Tadema Ho NW8 236 D5
Tadema Rd SW10 136 A5
Tadlow KT1
Tadmor Cl TW16
Tadmor St W12
Tadworth Ave KT3
Tadworth Ct 5 N11
Tadworth Ho SE1
Tadworth Rd NW2
Taeping St E14
Taffrail Ho 2 E14
Taffy's How CR4
Taft Way 14 E3
Taggs Ho KT1
Tailors Ct 9 SW16
Tailworth St 16 E1
Tait Ct 16 Old Ford E3
SW8
Tait Ho SE1
2 Tufnell Pk N19
Tait 7 NW9
Tait Rd CR0
Tait Rd Ind Est CR0
Takhar Mews SW11
Talacre Rd NW5
Talbot Ave N2
Talbot Cl N15
Talbot Cres NW4
Talbot Ct EC3
Neasden NW9
Talbot Gdns IG3
Talbot Grove Ho 10 W11
Talbot Ho
Highbury N7
Poplar E14
Talbot Pl SE3
Talbot Rd
Ashford TW15
Camberwell SE22
Dagenham RM9
Ealing W13
Forest Gate E7
Harrow HA3
Highgate N6
Isleworth TW1, TW7
Notting Hill W2
Notting Hill W11
Southall UB2
South Norwood CR7
Tottenham N15
Twickenham TW2
Wallend E6
Wallington SM5
Wembley HA0
Wood Green N22
Talbot Sq W2 92 B1
Talbot Wlk
Notting Hill W11
Willesden NW10
Talbot Yd SE1
Talcott Path 12 SW2
Talfourd Pl SE15
Talfourd Rd SE15
Talgarth Rd
Hammersmith W6
W14 113 A1
Talgarth Wlk NW9
Talia Ho E14
Talina Ctr SW6
Talisman Cl 2 IG3
Talisman Sq SE26
Talisman Way HA9
Tallack Cl HA3
Tallack Rd E10
Tall Elms Cl BR2
Talleyrand Ho SE5
Tallis Cl E16
Tallis Gr SE7
Tallis St EC4
Tallis View NW10
Tallow Rd TW8
Tall Trees SW16
Talma Gdns TW2
Talmage Cl SE23
Talman Gr HA7
Talma Rd SW2
Talmud Torah Chaim Meirim Sch N16
Talmud Torah Machzikei Hadass Sch E5
Talmud-Torah Yetev-Lev N16
Talwin St E3
Tamar Cl 20 E3
Tamar Ho
10 Cubitt Town E14
SE11
Tamarind Ct 8 W3
Tamarind Ho 4 SE15
Tamarind Yd 5 E1

sk Sq W12 111 D6
Sq IG8 37 B4
t SE7 122 A2
Way N17 52 A6
o 3 UB5 85 B4
Ho TW17 192 C2
Gdns KT4 215 C6
Ind Est
128 C1
Way TW4 128 C1
o SE6 163 C2
rth Ave IG8 36 C4
rth La CR4 203 B6
rth N7 72 A2
rth Pk CR4 203 B6
rth Pl 3
221 A6
rth Rd CR0 221 A6
rth St
135 C6 265 A5
d Rd N4 50 D3
Ctr SW19 180 B2
lge Ct SM2 217 D2
lge Dr BR6 211 B1
lge Pl 2
211 B1
d Ave NW2 67 D5
d Rd CR0 221 A4
Rd TW10 132 D2
berry Cl BR1 210 B5
Tree Cl N3 29 D1
wood Cl
don UB10 82 C3
Croydon CR0 222 C5
ore HA7 8 C2
wood Lo HA8 27 A4
wood Way
150 B1
Gr SW15 155 D4
Park Rd
173 B4
Ave TW17 192 D4
ere Gdns UB5 84 C5
ere Gr KT2 175 D5
ere N17 33 B1
ere Way NW9 27 C1
ere WC1 233 C1
st Ho 27
160 A4
st Wlk SE2 124 D3
ton Rd KT6 214 B6
ton St WC1 233 B1
ton Terr CR0 204 B3
ville Rd
182 A3
lge Rd NW2 68 B6
Ho
rton SW19 180 A2
253 B1
Point E13 99 A6
s Cl KT12 194 B3
s End La N18 33 C5
's Hill SE8 141 C4
s La IG6 57 A6
s Mews SE8 141 B4
St
g IG11 79 A2
117 C4 253 B1
s Yd 33 E2 96 B5
y Cl
nham BR3,
206 D4
ham RM10 81 D5
y Ho 22 E1 96 A2
gton Terr N5 72 C5
eld Rd SE26 184 D5
Cl N7 71 D3
ell St SE1 251 A1
Cl E6 100 C1
on Rd SW12 159 A3
e E16 98 D1
y Gr RM6 58 D6
th Gdns HA5 22 C1
d Ho 8 TW8 131 C5
d La DA5 169 C4
Rd NW3 70 D4
ry Cl SM2 217 D1
Ho 11 SE1 118 A4
Ct CR4 202 C5
Ho 36 E2 95 D4
NW3 70 B1
Rd N13 33 A6
St N1 95 A5 235 B3
field Rd
140 C2
g Cl 5 KT2 176 C3
E1 96 B3
St EN5 1 B2
4 BR3 185 D1
Ho 14 E1 96 D2
Ct HA0 65 D1
Rd SE22 161 C6
Wlk E1 118 C6
Cl TW14 149 C5
Ho W13 109 B5
Rdbt UB5 85 B6
d N17 34 A4

Tarleton Ct 2 N22 32 C1
Tarleton Gdns SE23 162 B3
Tarling Cl DA14 168 B1
Tarling Rd
Canning Town E16 98 D1
Finchley N2 30 A1
Tarling St E1 96 C1
Tarnbank EN2 16 A6
Tarnbrook Ct SW1 258 A3
Tarns The NW1 232 A2
Tarn St SE1 117 A3 262 A5
Tarnwood Pk SE9 166 B3
Tarplett Ho 22 SE14 140 D6
Tarquin Ho SE26 184 A6
Tarragon Cl SE14 141 A5
Tarragon Gr SE26 184 D4
Tarranbrae NW6 69 A1
Tarrant Ho E2 96 C4
Tarrant Pl W1 237 C3
Tarrantt Ho W14 254 A6
Tarriff Cres SE8 119 B2
Tarrington Cl SW16 159 D1
Tartan Ho 12 E14 98 A1
Tarver Rd
SE17 116 D1 261 D2
Tarves Way SE10 141 D5
Tash Pl N11 31 B5
Tasker Cl UB7 127 A5
Tasker Ho
3 Barking IG11 101 B5
17 Poplar E14 97 B2
Tasker Lo W8 245 A2
Tasker Rd NW3 70 D3
Tasman Ct
Ashford TW16 171 C3
9 Cubitt Town E14 119 D2
Tasman Ho 17 E1 118 B5
Tasmania Terr N18 33 A4
Tasman Rd SW9 138 A2
Tasman Wlk E16 99 D1
Tasso Rd
W6 135 A6 264 A6
Tasso Yd W6 264 A5
Tatam Rd NW10 67 B1
Tatchbury Ho SW15 155 D5
Tate Britain*
SW1 116 A2 260 A3
Tate Gdns WD23 8 C4
Tate Ho 13 E2 96 D5
Tate Modern*
EC4 116 D5 251 D4
Tate Rd Newham E16 122 B5
Sutton SM1 217 C3
Tatham Pl
NW8 92 B5 229 D4
Tatnell Rd SE23 163 A5
Tattersall Cl SE9 166 A6
Tatton Cres E5, N16 51 D2
Tatum St
SE17 117 B2 262 D3
Tauheed Cl N4 73 A6
Taunton Ave
Hounslow TW3 130 A3
Wimbledon SW20 178 B1
Taunton Cl SM3 201 C1
Taunton Dr Enfield EN2 4 C2
Finchley N2 30 A1
Taunton Ho W2 236 A1
Taunton Mews NW1 237 C5
Taunton Pl
NW1 92 D3 237 C6
Taunton Rd
Greenford UB6 85 D6
Lewisham SE12 164 D6
Taunton Way HA7 26 A1
Tavern Cl SM5 202 C2
Tavern Ct SE1 262 B5
Taverner Ho N16 73 B5
Taverners Cl W11 244 A3
Taverners Ct HA9 66 B6
Taverners Lo EN4 15 A6
Taverner Sq 4 N5 73 A4
Taverners Way E4 20 C3
Tavern La SW9 138 C3
Tavistock Ave
Mill Hill NW7 28 D3
Walthamstow E17 53 A6
Wembley UB6 87 A5
Tavistock Cl N16 73 C3
Tavistock Cres
Mitcham CR4 204 A5
Notting Hill W11 91 B2
Tavistock Ct
1 Croydon CR0 205 B1
WC1 239 D6
Tavistock Gdns IG3 79 C4
Tavistock Gr CR0 205 B2
Tavistock Ho 3 W11 91 B2
Tavistock Mews 3
W11 91 B1
Tavistock Pl
Bloomsbury
WC1 94 A3 240 A6
East Barnet N14 15 B5
Tavistock Rd
4 Beckenham
BR2 208 D5

Tavistock Rd *continued*
Carshalton SM5 202 B1
Croydon CR0 205 B1
DA16 146 C4
Dagenham NW10 89 D5
Edgware HA8 26 C2
Leyton E7 76 D4
Notting Hill W11 91 B2
Stratford E15 76 D2
Tottenham N4, N15 51 B3
Uxbridge UB10 61 A3
Wanstead E18 55 A6
Tavistock Sq
WC1 93 D3 239 D6
Tavistock St
WC2 116 A6 250 B6
Tavistock Terr N19 71 D5
Tavistock Twr SE16 119 A3
Tavistock Wlk SM5 202 B1
Taviton St
WC1 93 D3 239 C6
Tavy Bridge SE2 124 C4
Tavy Cl SE11 261 B2
Tawney Rd SE28 124 B6
Tawny Cl Ealing W13 109 B5
Feltham TW13 150 A1
Tawny Way SE16 118 D2
Tayben Ave TW2 152 C5
Taybridge Rd SW11 137 A1
Tayburn Cl E14 98 A1
Tayfield Cl UB10 61 A5
Tay Ho 10 E3 97 B5
Tayler Ct NW8 229 C6
Taylor Ave TW9 132 D3
Taylor Cl
Deptford SE8 141 B6
Hampton TW12 174 A5
Hounslow TW3 130 A4
3 Orpington BR6 227 D4
Tottenham N17 34 A3
Taylor Ct Ealing W13 109 C5
Penge SE20 184 C1
Stratford New Town
E15 76 A3
Taylor Ho
Carshalton SM5 218 C6
10 Streatham SW2 160 C3
Taylor Rd
Mitcham CR4 180 C3
Wallington SM6 219 B3
Taylor's Bldgs SE18 122 D2
Taylors Cl DA14 167 D1
Taylors Ct TW13 150 A2
Taylor's Gn W3 89 C1
Taylor's La Barnet EN5 1 B4
Forest Hill SE26 184 B6
Willesden NW10 67 C1
Taylorsmead NW7 28 A5
Taymount Grange 2
SE23 162 C2
Taymount Rise
SE23 162 C2
Tayport Cl N1 72 A1
Tayside Ct 6 SE5 139 B1
Tayside Dr HA8 10 D2
Taywood Rd UB5 85 B3
Teak Cl SE16 119 A5
Tealby Ct N7 72 B2
Teal Cl Enfield EN3 6 C6
Newham E16 99 D2
Teal Ct 30 SE8 141 B6
Wallington SM6 219 C3
Willesden NW10 67 B2
Teale St E2 96 A5
Tealing Dr KT19 215 B4
Teal Pl SM1 217 B3
Teal St 1 SE10 120 D3
Teasel Cl CR0 206 D1
Teasel Cres SE28 123 C5
Teasel Way E15 98 C4
Teather St 12 SE5 139 C5
Tebbs Ho 14 SW2 160 C4
Tebworth Rd N17 33 D3
Technology Pk NW9 45 C6
Teck Cl TW7 131 A3
Tedder Cl
Chessington KT9 213 C3
Hillingdon UB10 60 B1
Tedder 5 NW9 27 D3
Tedder Rd CR2 222 D1
TEDDINGTON 175 C5
Teddington Meml Hospl
TW11 174 C4
Teddington Park Rd
TW11 174 D6
Teddington Pk
TW11 174 D5
Teddington Sch
TW11 175 C4
Teddington Sta
TW11 175 A4
Ted Hennem Ho
RM10 81 D5
Tedman Ct SE13 142 A1
Ted Roberts Ho 25
E2 96 B5
Tedworth Gdns SW3 257 C1

Tedworth Sq
SW3 114 D1 257 C1
Tees Ave UB6 86 D5
Tees Ct W7 86 B1
Teesdale Ave TW7 131 A4
Teesdale Cl E2 96 B5
Teesdale Gdns
Isleworth TW7 131 A4
South Norwood
SE25 183 C1
Teesdale Rd E11 54 D2
Teesdale St E2 96 B5
Teesdale Yd 34 E2 96 B5
Teeswater Ct DA18 124 D3
Tee The W3 89 C1
Teevan Cl CR0 206 A2
Teevan Rd CR0 206 A2
Teign Mews SE9 166 A2
Teignmouth Cl
6 Clapham SW4 137 D1
Edgware HA8 26 B1
Teignmouth Gdns
UB6 87 A4
Teignmouth Par UB6 87 B5
Teignmouth Rd
Bexley DA16 146 C3
Brondesbury NW2 68 D2
Tejas Ct N3 47 A5
Tej Ct E7 77 D3
Telcote Way HA4 40 C2
Telegraph Hill NW3 69 D5
Telegraph La KT10 212 D3
Telegraph Mews
Ilford IG3 58 A1
Seven Kings IG3 57 D1
Telegraph Pl E14 119 D2
Telegraph Rd SW15 156 C4
Telegraph St EC2 242 C2
Telemann Sq SE3 143 B2
Telephone Pl SW6 264 D6
Telfer Cl 4 W3 111 A4
Telfer Ho
8 Dulwich SE21 183 C6
EC1 234 D1
Telferscot Prim Sch
SW12 159 D3
Telferscot Rd SW12 159 D3
Telford Avenue Mans 7
SW2 160 A3
Telford Ave SW12,
SW2 160 A3
Telford Cl
Penge SE19 183 D4
Walthamstow E17 53 A2
Telford Ct EN5 13 C6
Telford Dr KT12 194 C2
Telford Ho
2 Belvedere
DA17 125 C3
8 Kensal Town W10 91 A2
SE1 262 A6
Telford Parade Mans 8
SW2 160 A3
Telford Rd
3 Hendon NW9 46 A3
Kensal Town W10 91 A2
Telford Rd (North
Circular Rd) N11 31 C5
Telford Rd
Sidcup SE9 167 B2
Southall UB1 85 D1
Twickenham TW4 151 C4
Telford's Yd 21 SE1 118 A6
Telford Terr SW1 269 A6
Telford Way
Dagenham W3 89 C2
Hayes UB4 85 A2
Telham Rd E6 100 C5
Tell Gr SE22 139 D1
Tellson Ave SE18 144 A4
Telscombe Cl BR6 227 C6
Telscombe Ho SW11 268 A1
Temair Ho 1 SE10 142 A5
Temeraire Pl TW8 110 B1
Temeraire St SE16 118 C4
Tempelhof Ave NW2 46 C2
Temperley Rd
SW12 159 A4
Templar Ct RM7 59 D5
Templar Dr SE28 102 D1
Templar Ho
Hampstead NW2 69 B2
7 Upper Clapton E5 74 C6
Templar Pl TW12 173 C3
Templars Ave NW11 47 B3
Templars Cres N3 29 C1
Templars Dr HA3 24 B4
Templars Ho E15 75 D3
Templar St SE5 138 D3
Temple Ave
Croydon CR0 223 B5
Dagenham RM8 59 C1
EC4 116 C6 251 B6
Oakleigh Pk N20 14 B4
Temple Cl Finchley N3 29 B1
Leytonstone E11 54 C2
Woolwich SE18 123 A3

Templecombe Rd E9 96 C6
Templecombe Way
SM4 201 A4
Templecroft TW15 171 B4
Temple Ct Stepney E1 96 D2
SW8 270 A3
Templedene BR2 186 B1
Temple Dwellings 7
E2 96 B5
TEMPLE FORTUNE 47 A4
Temple Fortune Ct 9
NW11 47 B4
Temple Fortune Hill
NW11 47 C4
Temple Fortune Ho 3
NW11 47 B4
Temple Fortune La
NW11 47 C3
Temple Fortune Par 5
NW11 47 B4
Temple Gdns
Dagenham RM8 80 D5
Edmonton N21 16 D2
Temple Fortune
NW11 47 B3
Temple Gr Enfield EN2 4 D2
Golders Green NW11 47 C3
Temple Hall Ct E4 20 B2
Temple Ho
13 Battersea
SW11 136 C2
4 Tufnell Pk N7 71 C5
11 Walthamstow E17 53 D6
Temple La
EC4 94 C1 241 B1
Temple Lo EN5 14 B4
Templeman Rd W7 86 D2
Templemead Cl W3 89 C1
Temple Mead Cl HA7 25 B4
Templemead Ho E9 75 A4
Temple Mill La E10,
E15 76 A4
TEMPLE MILLS 75 D3
Temple Mills Rd E9 75 C4
Templemore DA14 190 B5
Temple Par EN5 14 B4
Temple Pk UB8 82 C4
Temple Pl
WC2 116 B6 250 D6
Temple Rd
Acton Green W4 111 A3
Cricklewood NW2 68 C5
Croydon CR0 221 B4
Ealing W5 109 D3
Hornsey N8 50 B5
Isleworth TW3 130 A1
Newham E6 100 A6
Richmond TW9 132 B2
Temple Sheen
SW14 155 A6
Temple Sheen Rd
SW14 133 A1
Temple Sta
WC2 116 C6 251 A6
Temple St E2 96 B5
Temple Terr N22 32 C1
Templeton Ave E4 35 D6
Templeton Cl
South Norwood
SE19 183 B2
25 Stoke Newington
N16 73 C3
Templeton Ct
Enfield EN3 6 C5
Walthamstow E10 53 D1
Templeton Pl
SW5 113 C2 255 B3
Templeton Rd N4,
N15 51 B3
Temple Way SM1 218 B5
Temple West Mews
SE11 261 C5
Templewood Ave
NW3 69 D5
Templewood W13 87 B2
Templewood Gdns
NW3 69 D5
Templewood Point
NW2 69 B6
Tempsford Cl EN2 5 A2
Tempsford Ct HA1 42 D3
Temsford Cl HA2 24 A1
Tenbury Cl E7 77 D3
Tenbury Ct SW12 159 D3
Tenby Ave HA3 25 B1
Tenby Cl
Dagenham RM6 59 A3
Tottenham N15 51 D5
Tenby Ct E17 53 A4
Tenby Gdns UB5 63 C2
Tenby Ho Hayes UB3 105 A3
Islington N7 72 C4
W2 236 A1
Tenby Rd DA16 146 D4
Dagenham RM6 59 A3
Edgware HA8 26 B1
Enfield EN3 6 C1

Tenby Rd *continued*
Walthamstow E17 53 A4
Tench St E1 118 B5
Tenda Rd SE16 118 B2
Tendring Ho SW2 160 C5
Tendring Way RM6 58 C4
Tenham Ave SW2 159 D2
Tenison Ct W1 249 A6
Tenison Way SE1 251 A3
Tenniel Cl W2 245 D6
Tennison Ave WD6 10 D6
Tennison Rd SE25 205 D4
Tennis St
SE1 117 B4 252 C2
Tenniswood Rd EN1 5 C4
Tennyson Ave
Kingsbury NW9 45 A6
Plashet E12 78 A1
Twickenham TW1 152 D3
Wanstead E11 55 A2
West Barnes KT3 200 B4
Tennyson Cl DA16 145 D4
Enfield EN3 18 D6
Feltham TW14 150 A5
Tennyson Ct 3
TW10 175 D6
Tennyson Ho
2 Erith DA17 125 B1
SE17 262 B2
Southall UB1 85 C1
Tennyson Rd
Ashford TW15 170 A5
Ealing W7 108 D6
Hounslow TW3 130 A3
Kilburn NW6 91 B6
Leyton E10 75 D6
Mill Hill NW7 28 A5
Penge SE20 184 D3
Stratford E15 76 C1
Walthamstow E17 53 B3
Wimbledon SW19 180 A4
Tennyson St SW8 137 B3
Tensing Ct TW19 148 A3
Tensing Ho N1 72 D2
Tensing Rd UB2 107 C3
Tentelow La UB2 107 D3
Tenterden Cl
Hendon NW4 46 D6
SE9 188 B6
Tenterden Dr NW4 46 D6
Tenterden Gdns
Croydon CR0 206 A2
Hendon NW4 46 D6
Tenterden Gr NW4 46 D6
Tenterden Ho SE17 263 B2
Tenterden Rd
Croydon CR0 206 A2
Dagenham RM8 81 B6
Tottenham N17 33 D3
Tenterden St W1 238 D1
Tenter Ground E1 243 C3
Tent Peg La BR5 211 A4
Tent St E1 96 B3
Tenzing Ct 4 SE9 166 A2
Tequila Wharf E14 97 A1
Terborch Way 6
SE22 161 C6
Tercelet Terr NW3 70 A4
Teredo St SE16 118 D3
Terence Ct 6 DA17 147 B6
Teresa Mews E17 53 C5
Teresa Wlk N10 49 B4
Terling Cl E11 76 D5
Terling Ho 9 W10 90 C2
Terling Rd RM8 81 C6
Terling Wlk N1 235 A6
Terminal Four Rdbt
TW6 149 A5
Terminus Pl SW1 258 D5
Tern Ho 9 SE15 139 D4
Terrace Gdns SW13 133 D3
Terrace Ho 2 N20 14 A1
Terrace La TW10 154 A5
Terrace Rd
Hackney E9 74 C1
Newham E13 99 B6
Walton-on-T KT12 194 B3
Terraces The 6
SW20 178 D3
Terrace The
Barnes SW13,
SW14 133 C3
Chingford E4 20 C1
Cranley Gdns N2 49 A5
EC4 241 B1
Kilburn NW6 91 C6
10 Rotherhithe SE8 119 B2
1 Woodford IG8 37 A4
Terrace Wlk RM9 81 A3
Terrall Apartments 7
N17 51 D6
Terrano Ho 1 TW9 132 D4
Terrapin Ct SW17 159 B1
Terrapin Rd SW17 159 B1

Terrapins KT6 197 D2
Terrick Rd N22 32 A2
Terrick St W12 90 B1
Terrilands HA5 41 B6
Territorial Ho SE11 261 B3
Terront Rd N15 51 A5
Terry Ct 8 SM6 219 C2
Terry Ho SW2 160 C3
Terry Lodge 2 CR7 204 C4
Tersha St TW9 132 B1
Tessa Sanderson Pl 6 SW8 137 B2
Tessa Sanderson Way UB6 64 B3
Testerton Wlk 3 W11 112 D6
Testwood Ct W7 108 C6
Tetcott Rd SW10 136 A5 266 A3
Tetherdown N10 49 A6
Tetherdown Prim Sch N10 49 A5
Tetty Way BR1, BR2 187 A1
Teversham La SW8 138 A4 270 B2
Teviot Cl DA16 146 B4
Teviot St E14 98 A2
Tewkesbury Ave
Forest Hill SE23 162 B4
Pinner HA5 41 A4
Tewkesbury Cl
Barnet EN4 2 B1
Tottenham N15 51 B3
Tewkesbury Ct N11 31 D4
Tewkesbury Gdns NW9 44 D6
Tewkesbury Rd
Carshalton SM5 202 B1
Ealing W13 109 A6
Tottenham N15 51 B3
Tewkesbury Terr N11 31 D4
Tewson Rd SE18 123 C1
Teyham Ct SW11 158 D5
Teynham Ave EN1 17 B5
Teynham Ct N12 30 A6
Teynham Gn BR2 209 A4
Teynham Ho SE9 167 B5
Teynton Terr N17 33 A2
Thackeray Ave N17 34 A1
Thackeray Cl
Hayes UB8 82 D1
Isleworth TW7 131 A3
Wimbledon SW19 178 D3
Thackeray Ct
Chelsea SW3 257 C2
Ealing W5 88 B1
West Kensington W14 254 A5
Thackeray Dr RM6 58 B2
Thackeray Ho
College Pk NW10 90 A4
WC1 240 A6
Thackeray Manor SM1 218 A3
Thackeray Mews E8 74 A2
Thackeray Rd
Clapham SW8 137 B3
Newham E6 99 D5
Thackeray's Almshouses SE6 163 D5
Thackeray St W8 255 D6
Thackery Lo TW14 149 B5
Thackrah Cl N2 30 A1
Thakeham Cl SE26 184 B5
Thalia Cl SE10 142 B6
Thame Rd SE16 118 D4
Thames Ave
Dagenham RM9 103 D3
Sands End SW10 136 A4 266 B2
Wembley UB6 86 D5
Thames Bank SW14 133 A3
Thamesbank Pl SE28 102 C1
Thames Barrier Visitor Ctr* SE18 121 D3
Thames Christian Coll SW11 136 B2
Thames Circ E14 119 C2
Thames Cl TW12 173 D1
Thames Cnr TW16 194 C6
Thames Cres W4 133 C5
Thames Ct Ealing W7 86 C1
Edmonton N9 18 C1
10 SE15 139 D5
West Molesey KT8 173 D1
THAMES DITTON 197 B2
Thames Ditton Fst Sch KT7 196 D3
Thames Ditton Island KT7 197 A3
Thames Ditton Jun Sch KT7 196 D2
Thames Ditton Sta KT7 196 D2
Thames Dr HA4 39 A3
Thames Eyot 8 TW1 153 A3
Thamesfield Ct TW17 193 A2
Thamesfield Ho TW17 193 A2
Thamesfield Mews TW17 193 A2
Thamesgate Cl TW10 175 B6
Thames Gateway Pk RM9 103 B4
Thames Haven KT6 197 D4
Thames Hts SE1 253 C2
Thameside Ctr TW8 132 B6
Thameside Ind Est E16 121 D4
Thameside Pl KT1 175 D2
Thameside TW11 175 D3
Thames Link Ho 7 TW9 132 A1
Thames Mdw KT12, TW17 193 C1
THAMESMEAD 124 A5
Thames Meadow KT8 195 C6
Thamesmead Sec Sch TW17 193 B3
Thamesmead Sh Ctr SE28 124 A6
Thames Mead KT12 194 A3
Thamesmere Dr SE28 124 A6
Thames Pl SW15 134 D2
Thamespoint TW11 175 D3
Thames Quay
Millwall E14 119 D4
SW10 266 B1
Thames Rd
Barking IG11 102 A4
Chiswick W4 132 D6
Newham E16 121 D5
Thames Reach
Fulham W6 134 C6
Woolwich SE28 123 C4
Thames Road Ind Est E16 121 D4
Thames Row TW9 132 B6
Thames Side
Teddington KT1 175 D2
Thames Ditton KT7 197 B3
Thames St
Hampton TW12 173 D1
Kingston u T KT1, KT2 175 D1
SE10 141 D6
Sunbury TW16 194 B6
Walton-on-T KT12 193 D2
Thamesvale Cl TW3 129 C3
Thames Valley Univ W5 109 D5
Thames View Ho TW12 194 A3
Thames View 2 IG1 79 A6
Thames View Inf Sch IG11 102 A5
Thames View Jun Sch IG11 101 D5
Thames View Lo IG11 101 C4
Thames Village W4 133 A4
Thames Wlk SW11 136 C5 267 A4
Thane Mans N7 72 B5
Thanescroft Gdns CR0 221 C5
Thanet Ct 14 W3 88 C1
Thanet Dr BR2 225 D5
Thanet Ho WC1 233 A1
1 West Norwood SE27 160 D1
Thanet Lo NW2 69 A2
Thanet Pl CR0 221 A4
Thanet Rd DA5 169 C4
Thanet St WC1 94 A4 233 A1
Thane Villas N7 72 B5
Thane Works N7 72 B5
Thanington Ct DA15 167 C5
Thant Cl E10 75 D5
Tharp Rd SM6 219 D3
Thatcham Ct N20 14 A4
Thatcham Gdns N20 14 A4
Thatcher Cl UB7 104 A4
Thatchers Way TW7 152 B6
Thatches Gr RM6 59 A5
Thavies Inn EC4 241 B2
Thaxted Ct N1 235 D3
Thaxted Ho
Bermondsey SE16 118 C2
Dagenham RM10 81 D1
Thaxted Lo 3 E18 55 B6
Thaxted Pl 9 SW20 178 D3
Thaxted Rd
Buckhurst Hill IG9 21 D4
SE9 167 A2
Thaxton Rd W14 135 B6 264 D6
Thayers Farm Rd BR3 185 A2
Thayer St W1 93 A1 238 B2
Theatre Sq E15 76 B2
Theatre St SW11 136 D2
Theberton St N1 94 D6 234 C6
Theed St SE1 116 C5 251 B3
Thelbridge Ho 28 E3 97 D4
Thelma Gdns SE3 144 A4
Thelma Gr TW11 175 A4
Theobald Cres HA3 24 A2
Theobald Rd
Croydon CR0 220 D6
Walthamstow E17 53 C2
Theobalds Ave N12 30 A6
Theobalds Ct N4 73 A6
Theobalds Park Rd EN2 4 D6
Theobald's Rd WC1 94 B2 240 C4
Theobald St SE1 262 C5
Theodora Way HA5 39 D6
Theodore Ct SE13 164 B5
Theodore Ho 1 SW15 156 A6
Theodore Rd SE13 164 B5
Therapia Lane Sta CR0 204 A2
Therapia La
Thornton Heath CR0 204 A2
Thornton Heath CR0 204 A3
Wallington CR0 203 D2
Therapia Rd SE22 162 C5
Theresa Rd W6 112 A2
Therfield Ct N4 73 A6
Thermopylae Gate E14 119 D2
Theseus Ho
2 South Bromley E14 98 B1
Theseus Wlk N1 234 D3
Thesiger Rd SE20 184 D3
Thessaly Ho SW8 269 A3
Thessaly Rd SW8 137 C4 269 B2
Thetford Cl N13 32 D4
Thetford Ct
3 Dulwich SE21 162 B2
New Malden KT3 199 C4
Thetford Gdns RM9 103 A6
Thetford Ho SE1 263 C6
Thetford Rd
Ashford TW15 148 A1
Dagenham RM9 80 D1
New Malden KT3 199 C4
Thetis Terr TW9 132 C6
Theydon Gr IG8 37 C4
Theydon Rd E5 74 C6
Theydon St E17 53 B2
Thicket Cres SM1 218 A4
Thicket Ct 14 SM1 218 A4
Thicket Gr
Dagenham RM9 80 C2
Penge SE20 184 A3
Thicket Rd
Penge SE20 184 B3
Sutton SM1 218 A4
Thicket The UB7 82 A1
Third Ave
Chadwell Heath RM6 58 C3
Dagenham RM10 103 D5
East Acton W3 111 D5
Enfield EN1 17 D6
Hayes UB3 105 D5
Little Ilford E12 78 B3
3 Newham E13 99 A4
Walthamstow E17 53 C4
Wembley HA9 65 D6
West Kilburn W10 91 A4
Third Cl KT8 196 A5
Third Cross Rd TW2 152 B2
Third Way HA9 66 D4
Thirleby Rd
Hendon HA8 27 B2
SW1 115 C3 259 B5
Thirlestane Ct N10 31 A1
Thirlestane Ho TW12 173 D6
Thirlmere Ave UB6 87 C4
Thirlmere Gdns HA9 43 D1
Thirlmere Ho
Isleworth TW1 152 D6
19 Stoke Newington N16 73 B4
Thirlmere NW1 231 D2
Thirlmere Rd
Muswell Hill N10 31 B2
Streatham SW16 181 D6
Thirlmere Rise BR1 186 D4
Thirsk Cl UB5 63 C2
Thirsk Rd
Clapham SW11 137 A1
Mitcham CR4 181 A3
South Norwood SE25 205 B5
Thistlebrook Ind Est SE2 124 C4
Thistlebrook SE2 124 C3
Thistlecroft Gdns HA7 25 D1
Thistle Ct N17 52 B5
Thistledene Ave HA2 63 A5
Thistledene KT7 196 C3
Thistledown Ct SE25 205 C6
Thistlefield Cl DA5 168 D3
Thistle Gr SW7 256 B1
Thistle Ho 10 E14 98 A1
Thistlemead BR7 188 D1
Thistlewaite Rd E5 74 B5
Thistlewood Cl 3 N7 72 B6
Thistleworth Cl TW7 130 B5
Thistley Cl N12 30 C4
Thistly Ct SE8 141 D6
Thomas a' Beckett Cl HA0 64 D4
Thomas Arnold Prim Sch RM9 81 B1
Thomas Baines Rd SW11 136 B2
Thomas Burt Ho 9 E2 96 B4
Thomas Buxton Jun & Inf Sch E1 96 A3
Thomas Cribb Mews E6 100 B1
Thomas Crowell Ct 29 N1 73 C3
Thomas Ct RM8 80 C6
Thomas Dean Rd SE26 185 B6
Thomas Dinwiddy Rd SE12 165 B2
Thomas Doyle St SE1 261 D6
Thomas Fairchild Com Sch N1 95 A5 235 B4
Thomas Gamuel Prim Sch E17 53 C3
Thomas Hardy Ho N22 32 B2
Thomas Hewlett Ho HA1 64 C4
Thomas Ho
9 Belmont SM2 217 D1
3 Hackney E9 74 C2
Thomas Hollywood Ho 3 E2 96 C5
Thomas Ho 4 SW4 138 A1
Thomas Jones Prim Sch W11 91 A1
Thomas' La SE6 163 C4
Thomas Lo E17 53 D4
Thomas Milner Ho 8 SE15 140 A5
Thomas More Bldg The HA4 39 C1
Thomas More Ho EC2 242 A3
Thomas More Sq E1 118 A6
Thomas More St E1 118 A5
Thomas More Way N2 48 A6
Thomas North Terr 4 E16 98 D2
Thomas Pl W8 255 C5
Thomas Pooley Ct KT6 198 A2
Thomas Rd E14 97 C2
Thomas Road Ind Est 2 E14 97 C1
Thomas Shearley Ct DA5 169 D4
Thomas's London Day Schs SW11 136 B4 266 D1
Thomas's Prep Sch Clapham SW11 158 D6
Thomas St SE18 122 D2
Thomas Tallis Sch SE3 143 B2
Thomas Wall Cl SM1 217 D3
Thomas Watson Cottage Homes The EN5 13 A6
Thompson Ave
Richmond TW9 132 C2
6 SE5 139 A5
Thompson Cl
Ilford IG1 79 A6
Morden SM3 201 C1
Thompson Ho
11 Kensal Town W10 91 A3
SE14 140 D6
Southall UB1 107 A6
Thompson Rd
Dagenham RM9 81 B5
Dulwich Village SE22 161 D5
Hounslow TW3 129 D1
Uxbridge UB10 60 A1
Thomson Cres CR0 204 C1
Thomson Ct 4 E8 74 A2
Thomson Ho
Pimlico SW1 259 D1
Walworth SE17 263 A3
Thomson Rd HA3 42 C6
Thorburn Ho SW1 248 A1
Thorburn Sq SE1 118 A2
Thorburn Way SW19 180 B2
Thoresby Ho N16 73 B5
Thoresby St N1 95 A4 235 B2
Thorkhill Gdns KT7 197 B1
Thorkhill Rd KT7 197 B2
Thornaby Gdns N18 34 B5
Thornaby Ho 15 E2 96 B4
Thorn Ave WD23 8 A3
Thornbill Ho 1 SE15 140 A5
Thornbridge Ct 10 EN5 13 D6
Thornbury Ave TW7 130 B5
Thornbury Cl
Edgware NW7 28 D3
Stoke Newington N16 73 C3
Thornbury Ct
Croydon CR2 221 B3
Hounslow TW7 130 C5
W11 245 A6
Thornbury Ho N6 49 C1
Thornbury Lo EN2 4 D2
Thornbury 3 NW4 46 C5
Thornbury Rd
Clapham Pk SW2 160 A5
Hounslow TW7 130 B4
Thornbury Sq N6 49 C1
Thornby Rd E5 74 C5
Thorn Cl BR2 210 C3
Thorncliffe Ct SW2 160 A5
Thorncliffe Rd
Clapham Pk SW2 160 A5
Southall UB2 107 B1
Thorn Cl UB5 85 B4
Thorncombe Rd SE22 161 C6
Thorncroft HA2 64 A5
Thorncroft Rd SM1 217 D4
Thorncroft St SW8 138 A5 270 A3
Thorndale BR7 188 B3
Thorndale Ho 10 N16 51 C1
Thorndean St SW18 158 A2
Thorndene Ave N11 15 A3
Thorndike Ave UB5 84 D6
Thorndike Cl SW10 136 A5 266 A4
Thorndike Ho SW1 259 C2
Thorndike Rd 21 N1 73 B2
Thorndike St SW1 115 D2 259 C3
Thorndon Cl BR5 189 D1
Thorndon Gdns KT19 215 C4
Thorndon Rd BR5 189 D1
Thorndyke Ct HA5 23 B3
Thorne Cl
Claygate KT10 213 A1
DA8 147 D6
Leyton E11 76 C4
Littleton TW15 171 A3
Newham E16 99 A1
Thorne Ho
34 Bethnal Green E2 96 C4
4 Cubitt Town E14 120 A3
Thorneloe Gdns CR0, CR9 220 D3
Thorne Pas 7 SW13 133 D3
Thorne Rd SW8 138 A5 270 B3
Thorne's Cl BR3 208 A6
Thorness Ct SW18 158 A5
Thorne St SW13, SW14 133 C2
Thornet Wood Rd BR1 210 C6
Thornewill Ho 8 E1 118 C6
Thorney Cres SW11 136 B5 266 D3
Thorneycroft Cl KT12
Thorneycroft Dr EN3
Thorneycroft Ho 11 W4
Thorney Ct W8
Thorney Hedge Rd W4
Thorney St SW1 116 A
Thornfield Ave NW7
Thornfield Ct NW7
Thornfield Ho 5 E14
Thornfield Par NW7
Thornfield Rd W12
Thornford Rd SE13
Thorngate Rd W9
Thorngrove Rd E13
Thornham Gr E15
Thorn Ham Ho SE1
Thornham St SE10
Thornhaugh St WC1
Thornhill Ave SE18
Surbiton KT6
Thornhill Bridge Wh N1
Thornhill Cres N1
Thornhill Ct N8
Thornhill Gdns
Barking IG11
Leyton E10
Thornhill Gr N1
Thornhill Ho
12 Chiswick W4
Islington N1
Thornhill Mews SW15
Thornhill Prim Sch N1
Thornhill Rd
Ickenham UB10
Islington N1 94 C6
Leyton E10
Surbiton KT6
Thornton Heath CR0
Thornhill Sq N1
Thornhill Way TW17
Thornicroft Ho 12 SW9
Thornlaw Rd SE27
Thornley Cl N17
Thornley Dr HA2
Thornley Pl 2 SE10
Thornsbeach Rd SE6
Thornsett Pl SE20
Thornsett Rd
Penge SE20
Wandsworth SW18
Thornsett Terr SE20
Thornton Ave
Chiswick W4
Streatham SW2
Thornton Heath CR0
West Drayton UB7
Thornton Cl UB7
Thornton Ct
Lower Holloway N7
West Barnes SW20
Thornton Dene BR3
Thornton Gdns SW12
Thornton Gr HA5
THORNTON HEATH
Thornton Heath Pon CR7
Thornton Heath Sta CR7
Thornton Hill SW19
Thornton Ho SE17
7 Wanstead E11
Thornton Lo
South Norwood CR7
8 Wimbledon SW19
Thornton Pl W1
Thornton Rd
Barnet EN5
Belvedere DA17
BR1
Carshalton SM5
Thornton Rd E SW19
Thornton Rd IG1
Thornton Rd Ind Est CR0
Thornton Rd
Leyton E11
Lower Edmonton N18
Mortlake SW14
Streatham SW12, SW2

ı Rd *continued*
Heath CR0,
.......204 B3
Ion SW19 ... 178 D3
ı Row CR7 ...204 C4
ı St SW9 ....138 C3
ı Way NW11 ..47 D4
e Ct W5......88 A2
e Prim Sch
.......121 D1
e Rd SE7....121 D1
e Gr CR4....180 B1
e St SE8 ....141 C4
ell Ct W7 ....108 C4
od Cl E18....37 B1
ood Gdns
.... 245 A2
ood Lo W8.. 245 A2
ood Rd
.......164 C6
roft Ct TW9..132 B3
od Gdns E15..76 C3
Ho SE1..... 252 A2
atham SW2.. 160 A4
Rd Ilford IG1..57 A1
reen N22......32 A3
ch Rd
..... 137 D5 269 D3
ank Rd
.......112 A5
Cl BR6.......227 C6
Hill SE26..... 184 D6
Hill W10 ....91 A1
Coombe Hospl
.......54 A6
Cres E17......35 B1
Ct Enfield EN2...4 D2
ooting
.... 180 C6
dale Gdns
.......56 D5
dale Rd N4....50 B1
Hall W5.......87 D2
Hall Prim Sch
.......36 B2
Hall Rd E17...36 A2
Ho N1...... 233 D5
Rd
IG11..........79 B1
rd E17.........36 A1
n u T KT2..... 176 A3
E7...........76 D4
n E6..........100 B6
am N15.......51 C3
wood Ave SE23,
.......162 B2
nd Ave UB10..61 A5
en Way 2
.......183 C5
ton Rd NW2...69 A5
n Rd E3.......97 A5
Almshouses
.......182 A5
Rd SW16......181 C5
St SE1....... 252 B3
er Cl 20 E8.....95 D6
St E1 ..95 D2 243 D3
Ho 2 SW9....138 B2
gold Ho 8
.......73 B2
needle St EC2,
.......95 B1 242 D1
ridges Bsns Ctr
.... 108 A4
ridges Prim Sch
.... 107 D3
olts La E2.....96 B3
olt St E14.....119 B6
orners DA7 ..147 D3
Cups Yd WC1.. 240 D3
Kings Yd W1 .. 248 C6
Meadows Mews
.......24 D2
Mill La E3......98 A4
Mills Studios
.......98 A4
Mun Ct EC2.... 242 B2
Oak La SE1.... 253 C2
Oaks Cl UB10...60 B5
ers Pl W11.... 244 A6
ood SE23,
.......162 D1
Rd KT9.......214 B2
Ho 2 SW9....138 B3
morten Rd
.......99 B1
norton Ave
.......95 B1 242 D2
norton St
.......95 B1 242 D2
ey Cl SE2 .....124 C3
ey Rd SM1.....217 D3
ey Way SM1...217 D3
Cl CR4.......181 B1
Gn HA2 ....41 C5
St SE17 ...... 262 A2
rer Rd RM9....103 B3

Thurbarn Rd SE6 ....185 D5
Thurbin Ho UB4 ......83 B2
Thurland Ho 3
SE16.......118 B2
Thurland Rd SE16....118 A3
Thurlby Cl HA1 ....43 A3
Thurlby Croft NW4....46 C6
Thurlby Rd
Wembley HA0 ....65 D2
West Norwood SE27 . 182 C6
Thurleigh Ave
SW12.......159 A5
Thurleigh Ct SW12...159 A5
Thurleigh Rd SW12 ..159 A5
Thurleston Ave
SM4.......201 A4
Thurlestone Ave
Colney Hatch N12.....30 D4
Ilford IG3.......79 D4
Thurlestone Cl
TW17.......193 A3
Thurlestone Ct 1
UB1.......85 D1
Thurlestone Par
TW17.......193 A3
Thurlestone Rd
SE27.......182 C6
Thurloe Cl SW7..... 257 A4
Thurloe Ct SW3..... 257 A3
Thurloe Place Mews
SW7....... 256 D4
Thurloe Pl
SW7.......114 B2 256 D4
Thurloe Sq
SW7.......114 C2 257 A4
Thurloe St
SW7.......114 B2 256 D4
Thurlow Cl E4........35 D4
Thurlow Ct 5 E11 ....55 A4
Thurlow Gdns HA0....65 D3
Thurlow Hill SE21....161 A2
Thurlow Ho 17
SW16.......160 A1
Thurlow Park Rd SE21,
SE24.......161 A2
Thurlow Rd
Hampstead NW3......70 B3
West Ealing W7..... 109 A4
Thurlow St
SE17.......117 C1 263 A1
Thurlow Terr NW5 ....71 A3
Thurlow Twrs SE27...160 C1
Thurlow Wlk SE17 .. 263 A1
Thurlston Rd HA4.....62 A5
Thurnby Ct TW2 .....152 C1
Thurnscoe NW1 .... 232 A5
Thursland Rd DA14 ..191 A5
Thursley Cres CR0 ...224 B1
Thursley Gdns
SW19.......156 D2
Thursley Ho
3 Kingston u T
KT2....... 176 D3
10 Streatham SW2 ..160 B4
Thursley Rd SE9 .....166 B1
Thurso Ho NW6.......91 D5
Thurso St SW17......180 B6
Thurstan Rd SW20 ...178 B3
Thurston Ho 4
BR3.......185 D4
Thurston Ind Est
SE13....... 141 D2
Thurston Rd
Southall UB1.........85 B1
St Johns SE8, SE13 .. 141 D3
Thurtle Rd E2 ....95 D5
Thurza Ct TW7.......130 D3
Thyer Cl BR6 ....227 A4
Thyme Cl SE3.........143 C2
Thyme Ct NW7.........29 A3
Thyra Gr N12..........29 D4
Tibbatt's Rd E3.......97 D3
Tibbenham Pl SE6 ...163 C2
Tibbenham Wlk E13 ..98 D5
Tibberton Sq N1.... 235 A6
Tibbets Cl SW19 ....156 D3
Tibbet's Corner
SW19.......156 D4
Tibbet's Ride SW19..156 D4
Tiber Cl 10 E3 ....97 C6
Tiber Gdns N1....... 233 B5
Ticehurst Cl BR5.....190 A3
Ticehurst Rd SE23 ...163 A2
Tickford Cl SE2 ......124 C4
Tickford Ho NW8 ... 230 A1
Tidal Basin Rd E16...120 D6
Tidbury Ct SW8...... 269 A3
Tideham Ho SE28 ....123 B5
Tidelock Ho SE28 ....123 B4
Tidemill Prim Sch
SE8....... 141 C5
Tidenham Gdns
CR0.......221 C5
Tideside Ct SE18.....122 A3
Tideslea Path SE28 ..123 B5
Tideslea Twr SE28....123 A4
Tideswell 10 NW5.....71 B4

Tideswell Rd
Croydon CR0 .... 223 C5
Putney SW15....... 134 C1
Tideway Cl TW10 ....175 C6
Tideway Ct 9 SE16 ..118 D5
Tideway Ho E14 .....119 C4
Tideway Ind Est
SW8....... 137 C6 269 B5
Tideway Wharf
SW13.......133 C3
Tideway Yd SW13 ....133 C3
Tidey St E3..........97 C2
Tidford Rd DA16 .....145 D3
Tidworth Ho 13
SE22.......139 C2
Tidworth Rd E3.......97 C3
Tiepigs La BR2, BR4 ..208 D1
Tierney Ct 4 CR0....221 D6
Tierney Rd SW2 .....160 A3
Tierney Terr SW2 ....160 A3
Tiffin Girls' Sch The
KT2....... 176 A4
Tiffin Sch KT2.......176 B1
Tiger Ho WC1 ...... 232 D1
Tiger La BR2 ....209 B5
Tiger Way E5.........74 B4
Tignel Ct W3 ....110 C4
Tigris Cl N9 ....18 C2
Tilbrook Rd SE3 .....143 C2
Tilbury Cl
14 Camberwell
SE15....... 139 D5
St Paul's Cray BR5 ...190 B1
Tilbury Ho 4 SE14...140 D6
Tilbury Rd
Leytonstone E10 ......54 A2
Newham E6.......100 B5
Tildesley Rd SW15 ...156 C5
Tile Farm Rd BR6 ....227 B5
Tilehurst NW1...... 231 D1
Tilehurst Point 2
SE2.......124 C4
Tilehurst Rd
Cheam SM3........ 217 A3
Wandsworth SW17,
SW18.......158 B3
Tile Kiln La
Edmonton N13........33 A5
Harefield UB9 ....38 D2
Upper Holloway N6....49 C1
Tileyard Rd N7 ....72 A1
Tilford Ave CR0 ......224 A1
Tilford Gdns SW19 ...156 D3
Tilford Ho 8 SW2....160 B4
Tilia Cl SM1 ....217 B3
Tilia Rd E5 ....74 B4
Tilia Wlk 21 SW9.....138 D1
Tiller Ho 28 N1 ....95 C6
Tiller Rd E14 ....119 C3
Tillet Sq SE16........119 A4
Tillett Cl NW10 ....67 A2
Tillet Way 6 E2 ......96 A4
Tilley Rd TW14.......150 A3
Tillingbourne Gdns
N3 .... 47 B6
Tillingbourne Way
N3 .... 47 B5
Tillingham Way N12 ..29 D6
Tilling Ho 1 SE15....140 B2
Tilling Rd NW2 ....46 C2
Tilling Way HA9.......65 D6
Tillman Ho 8 SW2....160 B3
Tillman St E1.........96 B1
Tilloch St 9 N1.......72 B1
Tillotson Ct SW8.... 269 D3
Tillotson Rd
Edmonton N9.........17 D2
Harrow HA3 ....23 D3
Ilford IG1 ....56 C2
Tilney Ct EC1 ...... 242 B6
Kingston u T KT6..... 197 D4
Woodford IG9 ....21 A2
Tilney Dr IG9.........21 A2
Tilney Gdns 12 N1 ....73 B2
Tilney Rd
Dagenham RM9.......81 B2
Southall UB2 .... 106 C2
Woodford IG9 ....21 A2
Tilney St W1 ...... 248 B4
Tilson Cl 2 SE15....139 C5
Tilson Gdns SW2,
SW4.......160 A4
Tilson Ho SW2.......160 A4
Tilson Rd N17 ....34 A2
Tilston Cl E11 ....76 D5
Tilton St SW6....... 264 B5
Tiltwood The W3 ....111 A6
Tilt Yard App SE9 ...166 B5
Timber Cl BR7........188 C1
Timbercroft La
SE18.......145 C5
Timbercroft Prim Sch
SE18....... 145 C5
Timbercroft KT19 ....215 C4
Timberdene NW4 .....28 D1
Timberland Cl 16
SE15.......140 A5

Timberland Rd E1 ....96 B1
Timber Mill Way
SW4.......137 D2
Timber Pond Rd
SE16.......118 D4
Timber St EC1 ..... 242 A6
Timberwharf Rd N16..52 A3
Time Sq E8.......73 D3
Times Sq SM1 ....217 D3
Timor Ct UB1........107 D5
Timothy Cl
Bexley DA6 .... 169 A6
1 Clapham Pk SW4 . 159 C6
Timothy Ho DA18 ....125 A4
Timsbury Wlk 5
SW15.......156 A3
Tina Ct
Forest Hill SE6.......163 B4
West Norwood
SW16....... 160 C1
Tindal St SW9 ....138 D4
Tinniswood Cl N5.....72 C3
Tinsley Cl SE25 ......206 B6
Tinsley Rd E1.........96 C2
Tintagel Cres SE22...139 D1
Tintagel Ct EC1 ..... 241 C6
Tintagel Dr HA7 ......25 D6
Tintagel Ho SE20 ....184 A3
Tintern Ave NW9.....44 D6
Tintern Cl
Putney SW15....... 157 A6
Wimbledon SW19 ... 180 A4
Tintern Ct W13 ......109 A6
Tintern Gdns N14.....16 A4
Tintern Ho
Belgravia SW1...... 258 C3
Regent's Pk NW1 ... 231 D3
Tintern Path NW9.....45 C3
Tintern Rd
Carshalton SM5......202 B1
Tottenham N22 ....33 A2
Tintern St SW4 ......138 A1
Tintern Way HA2......41 D1
Tinto Rd E16 ....99 A3
Tinwell Mews WD6 ...11 B6
Tinworth St
SE11.......116 A1 260 B2
Tippett Ct E6 ....100 B5
Tippetts Cl EN2 ....5 A4
Tipthorpe Rd SW11 ..137 A2
Tipton Dr CR0 ....221 C4
Tiptree Cl E4 ....20 A1
Tiptree Cres IG5.......56 C6
Tiptree Ct EN2.........5 B1
Tiptree Dr EN2.........5 B1
Tiptree 7 NW1 ....71 B1
Tiptree Rd HA4 ....62 B4
Tirlemont Rd CR2....221 A1
Tirrell Rd CR0 ....205 A3
Tisbury Ct W1 ...... 249 C6
Tisbury Rd SW16.....182 A1
Tisdall Pl
SE17.......117 B2 262 D3
Tissington Ct 4
SE16.......118 D2
Titan Bsns Est 3
SE8....... 141 C5
Titan Ct TW8 ....110 B1
Titchborne Row W2. 237 B1
Titchfield Rd
Carshalton SM5......202 B1
Enfield EN3 ....7 A6
Paddington
NW8...... 92 D6 230 C6
Titchfield Wlk SM5...202 B2
Titchwell Rd SW18...158 B3
Tite St SW3...136 D6 267 C6
Tithe Barn Cl KT2....176 B2
Tithe Barn Way UB5... 84 B5
Tithe Cl Hayes UB4 ....83 D2
Hendon NW7.......28 A2
Walton-on-T KT12 ....194 B3
Tithe Ct NW4 ....28 A2
Tithe Farm Ave HA2...63 C5
Tithe Farm Cl HA2 ....63 C5
Tithe Wlk NW7 ....28 A2
Titian Ave WD23 ....8 C4
Titley Cl E4.......35 C5
Titmus Cl UB8 ....83 A1
Titmuss Ave SE28 ....124 B6
Titmuss St W12......112 C4
Tivendale N8 ....50 A6
Tiverton Ave IG5......56 C6
Tiverton Cl CR0......205 D2
Tiverton Dr SE9......167 A3
Tiverton Prim Sch
N15.......51 B3
Tiverton Rd
Brondesbury Pk NW6,
NW10.......90 D6
Edgware HA8.........26 B1
Edmonton N18........33 C5
Hounslow TW3 ..... 130 A3
Ruislip HA4 ....62 A5
Tottenham N4, N15....51 B3
Wembley HA0 ....88 A5

Tiverton St
SE1.......117 A3 262 A6
Tiverton Way
Chessington KT9.... 213 D3
Edgware NW7.........28 D3
Tivoli Ct SE16........119 B5
Tivoli Gdns 11 SE7 ...122 A2
Tivoli Rd Hornsey N8...49 D4
Hounslow TW4 ...... 129 A1
West Norwood SE27 . 183 A5
Toad La TW4 ....129 B1
Tobago St 12 E14 ....119 C4
Tobin Cl NW3.........70 C1
Toby Ct N9 ....18 C4
Toby La E1 ....97 A3
Toby Way KT5, KT6 ...214 D6
Todber Ho W14..... 254 A6
Todd Ho 3 N2........30 B1
Todds Wlk N7 ....72 B6
Tokenhouse Yd EC2 . 242 C2
TOKYNGTON 66 D2
Tokyngton Ave HA9 ...66 C2
Toland Sq SW15 .....156 A6
Tolcairn Ct 2 DA17 ..125 C1
Tolcarne Dr HA5...... 40 B6
Tolchurch 2 W11......91 C1
Toldos Yakov Yosef sch
N16.......51 C1
Toley Ave HA3, HA9 ...44 A2
Tolhurst Dr 4 W10 ....91 A4
Tollbridge Cl W10.....91 A3
Tollesbury Gdns IG6 ...57 B6
Tollet St E1.......96 D3
Tollgate Dr
Dulwich SE21....... 161 C2
Hayes UB4......... 106 D6
Tollgate Ho 1 NW6 ...91 D5
Tollgate Prim Sch
Croydon CR0 .... 206 C3
Newham E13.......99 C3
Tollgate Rd E6.......100 A2
Tollhouse Way N19 ...71 C6
Tollington Ct N4 ......72 B6
Tollington Ho 4
N19.......72 A5
Tollington Pk N4......72 B6
Tollington Pl N4 ......72 B6
Tollington Rd N7 .....72 B4
Tollington Way N7 ....72 A5
Tolmers Sq
NW1.......93 C3 239 B6
Tolpaide Ho SE11 ... 261 A3
Tolpuddle Ave 1
E13.......99 C6
Tolpuddle St
N1 ....94 C5 234 A4
Tolsford Rd E5........74 B3
Tolson Ho 4 TW7....131 A2
Tolson Rd TW7 ......131 A2
Tolverne Rd SW20 ...178 C2
TOLWORTH 214 C6
Tolworth Broadway
KT6.......198 C1
Tolworth Cl KT6 .....198 D1
Tolworth Gdns RM6 ...58 D4
Tolworth Girls' Sch
KT6.......214 B5
Tolworth Hospl KT6. 214 C6
Tolworth Inf Sch
KT6.......198 B1
Tolworth Junc KT6...214 D6
Tolworth Jun Sch
KT6.......198 B1
Tolworth Par RM6.....59 A4
Tolworth Park Rd
KT6.......214 B6
Tolworth Rd KT6.....214 A6
Tolworth Rise N
KT5.......198 D1
Tolworth Rise S
KT5.......198 D1
Tolworth Sta KT5 ... 214 D6
Tolworth Underpass KT5,
KT6.......214 D6
Tomahawk Gdns 4
UB5.......84 D4
Tom Coombs Cl
SE9.......144 A1
Tom Cribb Rd SE18,
SE28.......123 B3
Tom Groves Cl E15....76 B3
Tom Hood Cl E15 .....76 B3
Tom Hood Sch E11 ...76 D5
Tom Jenkinson Rd 5
E16.......121 A5
Tomkyns Ho SE11... 261 A3
Tomline Ho SE1..... 252 A3
Tomlin's Gr E3........97 C4
Tomlinson Cl
5 Gunnersbury
W4....... 110 D1
Spitalfields E2 ....95 D4
Tomlins Orch IG11 ...101 A6
Tomlin's Terr E14 .....97 A1
Tomlins Wlk 4 N7....72 B6
Tom Mann Cl IG11 ...101 C6
Tom Nolan Cl E15.....98 C5

Tompion Ho EC1.... 241 D6
Tompion St EC1..... 234 D1
Tom Smith Cl SE10...142 C6
Tom Smith Ho 3
E17.......54 A4
Tomson Ho SE1..... 263 C6
Tom Williams Ho
SW6....... 264 C5
Tonbridge Cres HA3...44 A5
Tonbridge Hos WC1. 233 A1
Tonbridge Rd KT12,
KT8.......195 B5
Tonbridge St
WC1.......94 A4 233 A1
Toneborough 16
NW8.......91 D6
Tonfield Rd SM3 .....201 B1
Tonge Cl BR3........207 C4
Tonsley Hill SW18....157 D6
Tonsley Pl SW18 .....157 D6
Tonsley Rd SW18.....157 D6
Tonsley St SW18 .....157 D6
Tonstall Rd CR4......181 A1
Tony Law Ho SE12 ...165 A6
Tooke Cl HA5.........23 A2
Tookey Cl HA3 ....44 B2
Took's Ct EC4....... 241 A2
Tooley St
SE1.......117 C5 253 A3
Toorack Rd HA3 ......24 B1
Tooting Bec Gdns
SW16.......181 D6
Tooting Bec Lido
SW16....... 181 C6
Tooting Bec Rd
Furzedown SW17 ....181 B6
Streatham SW16.... 181 C5
Tooting Bec Sta
SW17....... 159 A1
Tooting Broadway Sta
SW17....... 180 C5
Tooting Broadway
SW17.......180 D5
TOOTING GRAVENEY
.......180 B5
Tooting Gr SW17.....180 C5
Tooting High St SW17,
SW19.......180 C5
Tooting Mkts SW17 . 180 D6
Tooting Sta SW17... 180 D4
Tootswood Rd BR2,
BR3.......208 C5
Topaz Ct TW13.......149 D1
Topaz Ho KT4........199 B1
Topaz Wlk NW2.......46 D2
Topcliffe Dr BR6.....227 B4
Topham Ho 8 SE10 ..142 A5
Topham Sq N17.......33 A2
Topham St EC1 ..... 241 A6
Top House Rise E4....20 A4
Topiary Sq TW9......132 B2
Topley St SE9........143 D1
Topmast Point 23
E14.......119 C4
Top Pk BR3.......208 C4
Topsfield Cl N8 ....49 C4
Topsfield Par N8......50 A3
Topsfield Rd N8 ......50 A4
Topsham Rd SW17 ...181 A6
Tora Ct 9 IG9 ....21 C2
Torbay Ct 13 NW1.....71 B1
Torbay Mans NW6 ....91 B6
Torbay Rd
Brondesbury NW6.....69 B1
Harrow HA2 ....63 A6
Torbay St 15 NW1 ....71 B1
Torbitt Way IG2.......57 D4
Torbridge Cl HA8......26 A3
Torbrook Cl DA5 .....169 A5
Torcross Dr SE23.....162 C2
Torcross Rd HA4......62 C5
Tor Ct W8 .... 245 B2
Torfell 5 E18.........36 D1
Tor Gdns
W8.......113 C4 245 A2
Tor Gr SE28.......123 C5
Tor Ho N6.......49 B3
Tormead Cl SM1 .....217 C2
Tormount Rd SE18 ...145 C6
Tornay Ho
Hackney E9 ....74 C1
N1 .... 233 C4
Toronto Ave E12 ......78 B4
Toronto Rd IG1 ....57 A1
Torquay Gdns IG4.....55 D5
Torquay Ho 1 SM6...219 D3
Torquay St W2........91 D2
Tor Rd DA16 ....146 C4
Torrence Ho 6 N19...71 C6
Torrens Ct SE5.......139 B2
Torrens Rd
Clapham Pk SW2.....160 B6
Stratford E15.........76 D2
Torrens Sq E15 ....76 D2

Way UB2 .....106 B3
t SW12 .....158 D3
:4 .... 252 A6
d
.....138 B5 270 D4
SE23 ....162 D2
on Ho W12 ...112 A5
IG1 ....57 C2
NW1 .... 232 B5
Ct TW7 .....130 D2
Wlk 11
..........132 A6
SE8 ....141 B6
Gdns N19 .....50 A1
Mews 10
...........175 A5
Rd
EN5 ....12 C6
Pk N4, N19 ...50 A1
e Ealing W5 ...110 B5
UB1 ....85 B1
y HA9 ....66 C2
IG2 ....57 B4
TW1 ....175 A6
Ho 17 E14 ....119 B6
St E14 ....119 B6
ve
chley N2 ......48 B6
EN1 ....17 D5
Church Rd
............134 B6
Church Sq
......117 A3 262 B6
l
ham SW4 ... 137 C1
w TW4 ..... 129 A1
Mark BR2 .. 210 A1
am SE13 ......142 B1
E11 ....76 C6
otts TW9 .....132 B2
res SW17 ....159 A2
t
gford E4 ......20 A2
ton N18 ....33 D4
SE9 .... 166 D5
y WC1 ...... 240 C6
Hill SE23 ..... 162 C1
wich SE7 ..... 121 D2
ton N1 ....95 C6
hithe SE16 ... 119 A4
ate N21 ....16 D3
on Heath
.... 205 C3
nham TW2 .... 152 C2
gton SM6 ..... 219 C1
den NW2 ....68 C3
edon SW19 .... 179 C4
Dr UB8 ....83 A1
Gdns E16 ......98 D2
ell SW2, SW9 ..138 B1
nstead E18 .....55 B6
Gn E1 ....96 C2
Gr 8 SE10 .....142 A4
Homes 14
............138 B1
Ho SE1 .... 262 B6
lthamstow E17 ..53 D6
Mews
SE20 ....184 B2
...............167 B5
worth SW18 ... 157 C3
Par TW3 ....129 D2
Pl
heath DA6 .....147 B1
London EC3 ... 253 C5
RC High Sch
er) IG8 ....37 A6
RC High Sch
er Sch) IG8 ....36 D6
RC High Sch
er) IG8 ....37 A6
Rd
inchley N2 ......48 B6
IG6 ....57 A6
ond TW9 ....132 B2
all UB1 .... 107 A5
worth SW17,
8 .... 158 C4
edon SW19 .... 179 C4
Green N22 ......32 A3
Green N22 ......32 B2
Rise SE24,
...............160 D4
St Mary's CE
Sch SW12 .... 159 A3
Sch
on CR0 .... 222 C6
ham RM10 ......81 C4
Sq
......117 C6 253 B6
St Enfield EN2 .... 5 A3
wham E16 ......99 A2
...... 117 B3 262 C6
Terr IG9 ....21 B4
Way
cton W3 ...... 111 D6
amstow E4 ......35 B4

Trio Pl SE1 ...117 A4 252 B1
Triscott Ho UB3 ....106 A5
Tristan Ct 34 SE8 .....141 B6
Tristan Sq SE3 ....142 C2
Tristram Cl E17 ....54 B6
Tristram Dr N9 ....18 A1
Tristram Rd BR1 ......186 D6
Triton Ct EC2 .... 242 D5
Woodford IG9 ....21 A2
Triton Ho 2 E14 .....119 D2
Triton Sq NW1 .... 239 A6
Tritton Ave CR0 ......220 A4
Tritton Ho N21 ....17 B5
Tritton Rd SE21,
SE27 ....161 B1
Triumph Cl UB7 ....127 A4
Triumph Ho IG11 .....102 A4
Triumph Rd E6 ....100 B1
Triumph Trad Est
N17 ....34 A4
Trocette Mans SE1 .. 263 B6
Trojan Ct
Brondesbury NW6 .....69 A1
9 Ealing W7 .... 109 A5
Trojan Ind Est NW10 ..67 D2
Trojan Way CR0 ......220 B5
Troon Cl
34 Bermondsey
SE16 ....118 B1
Erith SE28 .... 102 D1
Troon Ct UB1 ....108 A6
Troon Ho 9 E14 ....97 A1
Troon St E1 ....97 A1
Tropical Ct 2 W10 ....90 D4
Trosley Rd DA17 ......147 C6
Trossachs Rd SE22 ...161 C6
Trothy Rd SE1 ....118 A2
Trotman Ho 1
SE14 ....140 C4
Trott Rd N10 ....31 A3
Trott St
SW11 ....136 C4 267 A1
Trotwood Ho 3
SE16 ....118 B4
Troubridge Ct 12
W4 ....111 A1
Troughton Rd SE7 ....121 B1
Troutbeck NW1 ...... 231 D1
Troutbeck Rd SE14 ...141 A4
Trouville Rd SW4 ....159 C5
Trowbridge Rd E9 .....75 B2
Trower Ho 5 E9 ......75 A2
Trowlock Ave TW11 ..175 C4
Trowlock Island
TW11 ....175 D4
Trowlock Way
TW11 ....175 D4
Troy Ct W8 .... 255 A6
5 Woolwich SE18 .. 122 D2
Troyes Ho NW3 ....70 D3
Troy Rd SE19 ....183 B4
Troy Town Flats
SE15 ....140 A2
Troy Town SE15 ......140 A2
Trubshaw Rd UB2 .....107 D3
Trulock Ct N17 ....34 A3
Trulock Rd N17 ....34 A3
Truman Cl 2 HA8 ......27 A3
Truman's Rd 24 N16 ...73 C3
Trumpers Way W7 ...108 D3
Trumpeters Inn
TW9 ....153 C6
Trumpington Rd E7 ...76 D4
Trump St EC2 .... 242 B1
Trundlers Way WD23 ... 8 C3
Trundle St SE1 ...... 252 A2
Trundley's Rd SE8 ....118 D1
Trundleys Rd SE8 .....141 A6
Trundley's Terr SE8 ..118 D2
Truro Ct 2 N8 ....49 D4
Truro Gdns IG1 ....56 A2
Truro Ho
25 Paddington W2 .....91 C2
Pinner HA5 ....23 B2
Truro Rd
Walthamstow E17 .....53 B5
Wood Green N22 ....32 B3
Truro St NW5 ....71 A2
Truro Way UB4 ....83 C4
Truscott Ho 3 CR7 ...204 C3
Trusedale Rd E6 ......100 B1
Truslove Rd SE27 ....182 D5
Trussley Rd W6 ....112 C3
Trust Wlk SE21 ....160 D3
Tryfan Cl IG4 ....55 D4
Tryon Cres E9 ....96 C6
Tryon St
SW3 ....114 D1 257 C2
Trystings Cl KT10 ....213 A2
Tuam Rd SE18 ....145 B6
Tubbenden Cl BR6 ...227 C5
Tubbenden Dr BR6 ...227 B4
Tubbenden Jun & Inf
Schs BR6 ....227 B4
Tubbenden La BR6 ...227 C5
Tubbenden La S
BR6 ....227 B3

Tubbs Rd NW10 ....89 D5
Tudor Ave
Hampton TW12 .... 173 C3
North Cheam KT4 ....216 B4
Tudor Cl
Ashford TW15 .... 170 A6
BR7 ....188 B2
Cheam SM3 .... 217 A2
Chessington KT9 ...... 214 A3
Crouch End N6 ....49 C2
Hampstead NW3 ....70 C2
Hampton TW12 .... 174 A5
Hendon NW7 ....28 A4
Pinner HA5 ....40 A4
Tulse Hill SW2 ....160 B5
Wallington SM6 ...... 219 C1
Welsh Harp NW9 ....67 A6
Woodford IG8 ....37 B5
Tudor Coll WC1 ...... 233 A1
Tudor Court N HA9 ....66 C3
Tudor Court S HA9 ....66 C3
Tudor Cres EN2 .... 5 A4
Tudor Ct 2 Barnet EN5 .. 1 B1
3 Ealing W13 ....87 C1
Feltham TW13 .... 172 C6
Kingsland N1 ....73 C2
5 Rotherhithe
SE16 .... 118 D5
Sidcup DA14 .... 168 A1
South Acton W5 ...... 110 C4
4 Stanwell TW19 ... 148 A5
Teddington TW11 ..... 174 D4
Walthamstow E17 ......53 B2
Tudor Dr
Kingston u T KT2 ..... 176 A5
Walton-on-T KT12 ... 194 D1
West Barnes SM4 .... 201 A3
Tudor Ent Pk HA3 .....42 B6
Tudor Est NW10 ....88 D5
Tudor Gables NW7 ....27 D6
Tudor Gdns Acton W3 ..88 C1
Harrow HA3 ....24 B1
Mortlake SW14 .... 133 C2
Twickenham TW1 ..... 152 D3
Welsh Harp NW9 ....67 A6
West Wickham BR4 .. 224 A5
Tudor Gr E9 ....74 C1
Tudor Ho
Brook Green W14 ... 112 D2
Feltham TW13 .... 172 C6
34 Hackney E9 ....74 C1
Mitcham CR4 .... 181 A2
6 Muswell Hill N10 ....31 A3
Queensbury NW9 ....44 C5
Tolworth KT6 .... 198 C1
Tudor Lo 4 N12 ......29 D5
Tudor Mews
Walthamstow E17 ......53 B5
2 Willesden NW10 ....68 A2
Tudor Par
Dagenham RM6 ....58 D2
SE9 .... 144 A1
Tudor Pl SW19 ....180 C3
Tudor Prim Sch
Finchley N3 ....30 A2
Southall UB1 .... 107 A6
Tudor Rd
Ashford TW15 ....171 B4
Barking IG11 .... 101 D6
Barnet EN5 ....1 D2
Beckenham BR3 .... 208 A6
Chingford E4 ....35 D4
Croydon SE25 ....206 B4
Hackney E9 ....96 B6
Hampton TW12 .... 173 C3
Harrow HA3 ....24 B1
Hayes UB3 ....83 B1
Isleworth TW3 ....130 B1
Kingston u T KT2 ..... 176 C3
Newham E6 ....99 C6
Penge SE19 .... 183 D3
Pinner HA5 ....22 C1
Ponders End N9 ....18 C4
Southall UB1 .... 107 A6
Tudor Sq UB3 ....83 B2
Tudor St
EC4 ....116 C6 251 B6
Tudors The 2 BR3 ...185 D1
Tudor Way BR5 ....211 B3
Hillingdon UB10 ....60 C2
Osidge N14 ....15 D3
South Acton W3 ...... 110 C4
Tudor Well Cl HA7 ....25 B5
Tudor Wlk DA5 ....169 A5
Tudway Rd SE3, SE9 ..143 C1
Tufnell Ct 19 E3 ....97 B6
Tufnell Mans 7 N7 ...71 D4
TUFNELL PARK 71 D4
Tufnell Park Mans 2
N7 ....72 A5
Tufnell Park Prim Sch
N7 ....71 D4
Tufnell Park Rd N19,
N7 ....71 D4
Tufnell Park Sta N19 ..71 C4
Tufton Ct SW1 ...... 260 A5
Tufton Gdns KT8 .....173 D1

Tufton Rd E4 ....35 C6
Tufton St
SW1 ....116 A3 260 A5
Tugboat St SE28 ......123 C4
Tugela Rd CR0 ....205 B3
Tugela St SE6 ....163 B2
Tugmutton Cl BR6 ...226 D4
Tuke Sch SE15 ....140 B4
Tulip Cl Croydon CR0 ..206 D1
Hampton TW12 ....173 B4
5 Newham E6 ......100 B2
Southall UB2 .... 108 A4
Tulip Ct 1 HA5 ....40 C6
Tulip Gdns
Chingford E4 ....20 B1
Ilford IG1 ....78 D2
Tullis Ho 12 E9 ....74 C1
Tull St CR4 ....202 D2
Tulse Cl BR3 ....208 A6
TULSE HILL 160 D4
Tulse Hill Sta SE27 .. 160 D2
Tulse Hill
Tulse Hill SW2 ...... 160 C4
Tulse Hill SW27 ..... 160 D2
Tulse Ho SW2 ....160 C5
Tulsemere Rd SE21,
SE27 ....161 A2
Tumbling Bay KT12 ..194 A3
Tummons Gdns
SE25 ....183 C1
Tump Ho SE28 ....123 C5
Tunbridge Ct 1
SE26 ....162 A1
Tunbridge Ho EC1 .. 234 C2
Tuncombe Rd N18 ....33 C6
Tunis Rd W12 ....112 B5
Tunley Gn 12 E14 .....97 B2
Tunley Rd
Dagenham NW10 .....89 C6
Upper Tooting SW12,
SW17 .... 159 A2
Tunmarsh La E13 .....99 C4
Tunnan Leys E6 ....100 C1
Tunnel Avenue Trad Est
SE10 ....120 B4
Tunnel Gdns N11 .....31 C3
Tunnel Link Rd
TW6 ....148 C5
Tunnel Rd E TW6 ....126 D3
Tunnel Rd SE16 ....118 C4
Tunnel Rd W TW6 ....126 D4
Tunstall Cl BR6 ....227 C4
Tunstall Ct 14 TW9 ...132 B4
Tunstall Rd
Croydon CR0 .... 205 C1
Stockwell SW9 ....138 B1
Tunstall Wlk 10
TW8 ....132 A6
Tunstock Way DA17 ..125 A3
Tunworth Cl NW9 .....45 A3
Tunworth Cres
SW15 ....155 D5
Tun Yd SW8 ....137 B2
Tupelo Rd E10 ....75 D6
Tupman Ho 26 SE16 ..118 A4
Tuppy St SE28 ....123 A3
Turberville Ho 1
SW9 ....138 B2
Turenne Cl SW18 .....136 A1
Turin Rd N9 ....18 C4
Turin St E2 ....96 A4
Turkey Oak Cl SE19 ..183 C2
Turkey St EN1, EN3 ...... 6 C6
Turkey Street Sta EN3 . 6 C6
Turks Cl UB8 ....82 C4
Turk's Head Yd EC1 . 241 C4
Turks Row
SW3 .... 114 D1 257 D2
Turle Rd
Finsbury Pk N4 ....72 B6
Thornton Heath
SW16 .... 182 A1
Turlewray Cl N4 ....50 B1
Turley Cl E15 ....98 C6
Turnagain La EC4 ... 241 C2
Turnage Rd RM8 ....59 A1
Turnant Rd N17 ....33 A2
Turnberry Cl
24 Bermondsey
SE16 ....118 B1
Hendon NW4 ....28 D1
Turnberry Quay 1
E14 ....119 D3
Turnberry Way BR6 ..211 B1
Turnbull Ho N1 ...... 234 D6
Turnbury Cl SE28 ....102 D1
Turnchapel Mews 1
SW4 ....137 B2
Turner Ave
Mitcham CR4 .... 180 D2
Tottenham N15 ....51 C5
Twickenham TW2 .... 152 A1
Turner Cl
7 Brixton SW9 ...... 138 D4
Hampstead Garden
Suburb NW11 ....47 D3
Hillingdon UB4 ....83 A4

Turner Cl *continued*
Wembley HA0 ....65 D2
Turner Ct
9 Herne Hill SE5 .....139 B1
24 Rotherhithe
SE16 .... 118 C4
Turner Dr NW11 ....47 D3
Turner Ho
Finsbury Pk N4 ....50 B1
24 Millwall E14 ..... 119 C4
St John's Wood NW8 230 A4
Strand WC2 .... 250 B5
6 Twickenham
TW1 .... 153 D5
Westminster SW1 ... 259 D3
Turner Lo 10 SW19 ...156 D3
Turner Mews SM2 ...217 D1
Turner Pl SW11 ......158 C6
Turner Rd
Edgware HA8 ....26 B1
New Malden KT3 .....199 B2
Walthamstow E17 ......54 A6
Turners Cl N20 ....14 D1
Turners Ct Leyton E15 ..76 A4
New Barnet EN5 ....13 D5
Tottenham N15 ....51 B4
Turners Meadow Way
BR3 ....185 B2
Turner's Rd E3 ....97 B2
Turner St
Canning Town E16 .....98 D1
Stepney E1 ....96 B2
Turners Way CR0 ....220 C6
Turneville Rd
W14 ....135 B6 264 C6
Turney Prim & Sec
Specl Sch SE21 ... 161 A4
Turney Rd SE21 ....161 B4
Turnham Green Sta
W4 .... 111 C2
Turnham Green Terr
W4 ....111 C2
Turnham Ho SE4 ......141 A1
Turnham Prim Sch
SE4 .... 141 A1
Turnham Rd SE4 .....141 A1
Turnmill Ho 8
SW2 ....160 C6
Turnmill St
EC1 ....94 D2 241 C4
Turnour Ho 31 E1 ....96 B1
Turnpike Cl SE8 ....141 B5
Turnpike Ct DA6 ......146 D1
Turnpike Ho EC1 .... 234 D1
Turnpike La N8 ....50 C6
Turnpike Lane Sta
N15 ....50 D6
Turnpike La
Sutton SM1 .... 218 A3
Uxbridge UB10 ....82 A5
Turnpike Link CR0 ...221 C6
Turnpike Mews N8 ....50 C6
Turnpike Way TW7 ...131 A4
Turnpin La 3 SE10 ...142 A6
Turnstone Cl
Edgware NW9 ....27 C1
Newham E13 ....99 A4
Uxbridge UB10 ....60 D3
Turnstone Terr 11
W13 ....86 D3
Turpentine La
SW1 ....115 B1 258 D1
Turpin Cl 15 EN3 .... 7 C6
Turpington Cl BR2 ...210 A2
Turpington La BR2 ...210 A3
Turpin Ho SW11 .... 268 C2
Turpin Rd TW14 ....149 D5
Turpin Way
Upper Holloway
N19 ....49 D1
Wallington SM6 ......219 B1
Turquand St SE17 ... 262 B3
Turret Gr SW4 ....137 C2
Turret Ho KT2 ....176 A4
Turton Ho 5 SE18 ...144 D6
Turton Rd HA0 ....66 A3
Turville Ho NW8 .... 237 A6
Turville St E2 ...... 243 C6
Tuscan Ho 36 E2 ......96 C4
Tuscan Rd SE18 ....123 B1
Tuscany Ho E17 ....35 B1
Tuskar St SE10 ....120 C1
Tutorial Coll of West
London UB1 ....107 B5
Tuttlebee La IG9 ....21 A2
Tuttle Ho SW1 ...... 259 D1
Tweedale Ct E15 ....76 A3
Tweed Ct W7 ....86 C1
Tweeddale Gr UB10 ...61 A5
Tweeddale Prim Sch
SM5 ....202 B2
Tweeddale Rd SM5 ...202 B1
Tweed Ho E14 ....98 A3
Tweedmouth Rd E13 ..99 B5
Tweedy Cl EN1 ....17 D6
Tweedy Rd BR1 ....187 A2

Tweezer's Alley
WC2 .... 251 A6
Twelve Acre Ho 5
E12 ....78 C5
Twelvetrees Bsns Pk
E16 ....98 B3
Twelvetrees Cres E3 ..98 A3
Twentyman Cl IG8 ....37 A5
Twice Times
Montessori Sch
SW6 .... 135 C3
TWICKENHAM 152 D4
Twickenham Bridge
TW9 ....153 C6
Twickenham Cl CR0 ..220 B5
Twickenham Gdns
Harrow HA3 ....24 C3
Wembley UB6 ....65 A3
Twickenham Pl
KT7 ....212 D6
Twickenham Prep Sch
TW12 .... 174 A2
Twickenham Rd
Isleworth TW1,
TW7 .... 131 A2
Leyton E11 ....76 B6
Richmond TW1,
TW9 .... 131 C1
Teddington TW11 .... 175 A6
Twickenham TW13 ....151 B1
Twickenham Rugby
Football Union
Ground TW2 ...... 152 C5
Twickenham Sta
TW1 .... 153 A4
Twickenham Trad Ctr
TW1 .... 152 D5
Twig Folly Cl 21 E2 ...96 D5
Twilley St SW18 ......157 D4
Twine Cl IG11 ....102 B4
Twine Ct E1 ....118 C6
Twineham Gn N12 ....29 C6
Twining Ave TW2 ....152 B1
Twinn Rd NW7 ....29 A4
Twin Tumps Way
SE28 ....124 A6
Twisden Rd NW5 ....71 B4
Twiss Ho 6 SE18 ....122 D1
Twist Ho E10 ....75 D6
Two Bridges Ind Est
CR0 ....221 B2
Twybridge Way
NW10 ....67 A1
Twyford Abbey Rd
NW10 ....88 B4
Twyford Ave
Acton W3 .... 110 C6
Muswell Hill N2 ....48 D6
Twyford CE High Sch
W3 .... 110 D5
Twyford Cres W3 ....110 C5
Twyford Ct
Acton W3 .... 110 C6
Muswell Hill N10 ......49 A6
6 Wembley HA0 .....88 A5
Twyford Ho
Highbury N5 ....72 D5
6 Tottenham N15 ....51 C3
Twyford Par KT6 .....198 C1
Twyford Rd
Carshalton SM5 ......202 B1
Harrow HA2 ....41 D2
Ilford IG1 ....79 A3
Twyford St
N1 ....94 B6 233 C6
Twynholm Mans
SW6 .... 264 A4
Tyas Rd E16 ....98 D3
Tybenham Rd SW19 ..201 C6
Tyberry Rd EN3 .... 6 C2
Tyburn La HA1 ....42 D2
Tyburn Tree (site of)*
W2 .... 247 C6
Tyburn Way W1 ..... 247 D6
Tye La BR6 ....227 A3
Tyer's Est SE1 ...... 253 A2
Tyers Gate
SE1 ....117 C4 253 A1
Tyers Ho 1 SW16 ....181 C5
Tyers St
SE11 ....116 B1 260 C2
Tyers Terr
SE11 ....116 B1 260 D1
Tyeshurst Cl SE2 .....125 A1
Tylecroft Rd SW16 ...182 A1
Tylehurst Gdns IG1 ...79 A3
Tyler Cl Erith DA8 ....147 D5
Haggerston E2 ....95 D5
Tyler Ho SE3 ....142 B3
Tyler Rd UB2 ....107 D3
Tylers Ct
4 Walthamstow
E17 ....53 C5

Tylers Ct *continued*
5 Wembley HA0 .....88 A5
Tylers Gate HA3.......44 A3
Tylers Path SM5 .....218 D4
Tyler St
Greenwich SE10 .... 120 C1
SE10 .... 142 C6
Tylney Ave SE19......183 D5
Tylney Ho 10 E1.......96 B1
Tylney Rd BR1 ....187 D1
Forest Gate E7 ....77 C4
Tymperley Ct SW19 ..157 A3
Tynamara KT1 ....197 D5
Tynan Cl TW14........150 A3
Tyndale La N1 ....72 D1
Tyndale Mans N1 .....72 D1
Tyndale Terr 13 N1 ....72 D1
Tyndall Gdns E10 .....76 A6
Tyndall Rd DA16 .....145 D2
Leyton E10...........76 A6
Tyne Ct W7...........86 C1
Tyneham Cl 10
SW11..............137 A2
Tyneham Rd SW11 ...137 A2
Tyne Ho 8 KT2 ......175 D2
Tynemouth Cl E6 ....100 D1
Tynemouth Dr EN1..... 6 A5
Tynemouth Rd
Mitcham CR4....... 181 A3
Plumstead Comm
SE18.............. 123 C1
Tottenham N15 ....51 D5
Tynemouth St SW6...136 A3
Tynemouth Terr 9
N15 ....51 D5
Tyne St E1.......... 243 D2
Tynsdale Rd NW10 ....67 C2
Tynte Ct E9...........75 A3
Tynwald Ho 14
SE26...............162 A1
Type St E2............96 D5
Tyrawley Rd SW6 ... 265 C2
Tyrell Cl HA1 ....64 C4
Tyrell Ct SM5 ....218 D4
Tyrells Ct 3 SE15 ....140 B2
Tyrols Rd SE23.......162 D3
Tyrone Ct SW16......181 D5
Tyrone Rd E6.........100 B4
Tyron Way DA14 .....189 D5
Tyrrell Ave DA16 .....168 B6
Tyrrell Ho
Catford BR3........ 185 D5
SW1................ 269 B6
Tyrrell Rd SE22 ......140 A1
Tyrrell Sq CR4 ....180 C2
Tyrrel Way NW9.......46 A2
Tyrwhitt Rd SE4......141 C2
Tysoe Ave EN3 .... 7 B6
Tysoe St EC1........ 234 B1
Tyson Rd SE23 ....162 C4
Tyssen Com Prim Sch
N16 ....52 A1
Tyssen Pas N16........73 D5
Tyssen St Dalston E8 ...73 D2
Hoxton N1...........95 C5
Tysson Ho E9.........75 A1
Tytherton 23 E2.......96 C5
Tytherton Rd N19.....71 D5

U

Uamvar St E14........97 D2
Uckfield Gr CR4.......181 A2
Uckfield Rd EN3 .... 6 D6
Udall St SW1 .... 259 B3
Udimore Ho 11 W10...90 C2
Udney Park Rd
TW11..............175 A4
Uffington Rd
West Norwood
SE27............ 182 C6
Willesden Green
NW10...............90 B6
Ufford Cl HA3.........23 D3
Ufford Rd HA3 ....23 D3
Ufford St
SE1........116 C4 251 B2
Ufton Ct UB5 ....84 D4
Ufton Gr N1 ....73 B1
Ufton Rd N1...........73 C1
Uhura Sq 19 N16......73 C5
Ujima Ct
Finsbury Pk N19 ......50 A1
Streatham SW16.... 182 A6
Ujima Ho SW16.......182 A6
UK Coll of Bsns &
Computing IG2 .....56 C3
Uk Cotts UB3 ....105 B4
Ullathorne Rd
SW16..............181 C6
Ulleswater Rd N14 ....16 B1
Ullin St E14..........98 A2
Ullswater Cl
Bromley BR1 .... 186 C3
Hayes UB4...........83 C5
Kingston u T KT2,
SW15..............177 B6
Ullswater Cres
SW15..............177 B6
Ullswater Ct
Harrow HA2 ....41 C2
2 Woodford E18 .....37 A1
Ullswater Ho SE15 ...140 C6
Ullswater SW15......156 D5
Ullswater Rd
Barnes SW13 ...... 134 A5
West Norwood SE27,
SW16.......... 160 D2
Ulster Ct KT2 ....175 D4
Ulster Gdns N13 ....33 A6
Ulster Pl NW1 ...... 238 C5
Ulster Terr NW1..... 238 C6
Ulundi Rd SE3 ....142 C6
Ulva Rd SW15.........134 D1
Ulverscroft Rd SE22..162 A6
Ulverstone Rd SE27 ..160 D2
Ulverston Rd E17 .....36 B1
Ulysses Rd NW6 ......69 B3
Umberston St E1 ......96 B1
Umbria St SW15 .....156 A5
Umfreville Rd N4 ......50 D3
Umoja Ho N22.........32 B1
Una Ho 7 NW5 ....71 B2
Undercliff SE10.......142 A4
Undercliff Rd SE13...141 D2
UNDERHILL 13 C6
Underhill EN5 ....13 C6
Underhill Ct EN5.......13 C6
Underhill Ho 7 E14...97 C2
Underhill Jun & Inf
Schs EN5 ....13 A6
Underhill Pas NW1.. 231 D6
Underhill Rd SE21,
SE22..............162 B4
Underhill St NW1 ... 231 D5
Underne Ave N14 .....15 B2
Undershaft
EC3 ....95 C1 243 A1
Undershaw Rd BR1 ..164 D1
Underwood Ct 3
E10................53 D1
Underwood Ho
East Molesey KT8 ... 195 C4
Hammersmith W6....112 B3
Underwood CR0 .....224 A3
Underwood Rd
Bethnal Green E1 .....96 A3
Chingford E4 ....35 D5
Woodford IG8 ....37 D3
Underwood Row N1 235 B2
Underwood St
N1 ....95 A4 235 B2
Underwood The
SE9...............166 B2
Undine Rd E14........119 D2
Undine St SW17 .....180 D5
Uneeda Dr UB6 ....86 B6
Unicorn Bldg 14 E1 ..118 D6
Unicorn Prim Sch
BR3 .... 207 D4
Unicorn Sch TW9.....132 B4
Unicorn Works N17...34 C3
Union Cl E11 ....76 B4
Union Ct
45 Paddington W2.....91 C2
2 Richmond TW10.. 154 A6
South Lambeth SW4 . 138 A3
Union Dr E1...........97 A3
Union Gr SW8 ....137 D3
Union Mews 32
SW9...............138 A3
Union Pk 11 SE10 ....120 D1
Union Rd BR2 ....209 D4
Clapham SW8 ...... 137 D3
Friern Barnet N11.....31 D4
Northolt UB5 ....85 C5
Thornton Heath CR0 . 205 A2
Wembley HA0 ....66 A2
Union Sq N1... 95 A6 235 B5
Union St Barnet EN5 .... 1 A2
Kingston u T KT1.... 175 D1
Mill Meads E15 ....98 B6
SE1 .... 117 A5 252 A3
Union Terr HA2 ....41 C1
Union Wharf N1 .... 235 B4
Union Wlk E2..........95 C4
Union Yd W1 .... 238 D1
Unity Cl
West Norwood
SE19............ 183 A5
Willesden NW10 ....68 A2
Unity Mews NW1 ... 232 C4
Unity Rd EN3 .... 6 C6
Unity Terr HA2 ....63 D6
Unity Way SE18......121 D3
Univ Coll Jun Sch
NW3................70 A4
Univ Coll London
Bloomsbury
WC1...... 93 D3 239 C6
Bloomsbury
WC1........94 A3 240 B6
Univ Coll London
(Windeyer Inst)
W1..........93 C2 239 B4
Univ Coll London
(Wolfson Ho)
NW1........93 C4 232 B1
University Cl NW7 ....27 D3
University Coll Hospl
WC1.........93 C3 239 B6
University Coll Sch
NW3................70 A3
University Gdns
DA5 ....169 B4
University Mans
SW15..............134 D2
University Pl DA8 ....147 D5
University Rd SW19 ..180 B4
University St
WC1......... 93 C3 239 B5
University Way E16 ..122 D6
Univ of California
WC1........ 93 D2 239 D3
Univ of East London
RM8................80 A4
Univ of East London
(Duncan Ho) E15 ...98 B6
Univ of East London
(Holbrook Ctr)
E15.................98 D5
Univ of East London
Newham E16....... 122 C6
Stratford E15..........76 C2
Univ of Greenwich
Avery Hill Campus
Mansion Site SE9 . 167 A5
Univ of Greenwich
Avery Hill Campus
Southwood Site
SE9................167 B4
Univ of Greenwich
Rachel Mcmillan
Campus SE8 ...... 141 C6
Univ of Greenwich
Riverside Ho Annexe
SE18.............. 122 C3
Univ of Greenwich
SE10..............142 B6
Univ of London (King's
Coll Hall) SE5......139 B2
Univ of London Obsy
NW7.................27 D4
Univ of London (Queen
Mary & Westfield
Coll) E1 ....97 A3
Univ of London
WC1........ 93 D3 239 D5
Univ of Westminster
(Cavendish Campus)
W1......... 93 C2 239 A4
Univ of Westminster
(Harrow Campus)
HA1 ....43 A2
Univ of Westminster
(Marylebone Campus)
NW1......... 93 A2 238 A4
Univ of Westminster
NW1........ 93 C3 239 A6
Univ of Westminster
(Regent Campus,
Univ HQ)
W1......... 93 B1 238 D2
Univ of Westminster
(Regent Campus)
W1.......... 93 C2 239 A3
Uno Apartments 4
BR1 ....187 A2
Unwin Ave TW14.....149 B6
Unwin Cl SE15 ....140 A6
Unwin Rd
Isleworth TW7...... 130 C2
SW7........ 114 B3 256 D6
Upbrook Mews
W2......... 92 A1 236 B1
Upcerne Rd
SW10.......136 A5 266 B3
Upchurch Cl 8
SE20..............184 B3
Upcott Ho
33 Bromley E3........97 D4
4 Hackney E9 ....74 C1
Upcroft Ave HA8......27 A6
Updale Rd DA14 .....189 D6
Upfield Rd W7........86 D2
Upfield CR0 ....222 B5
Upgrove Manor Way 12
SE24..............160 C4
Uphall Prim Sch IG1..78 D3
Uphall Rd IG1 ....78 D3
Upham Park Rd W4..111 C2
Uphill Dr
Edgware NW7........27 C5
Uphill Dr *continued*
Kingsbury NW9.......45 A4
Uphill Gr NW7 ....27 C6
Uphill Rd NW7 ....27 C6
Upland Ct SE23 ......162 C2
Upland Prim Sch
DA7 ....147 B2
Upland Rd
Croydon CR2 ....221 B3
DA7 ....147 B2
East Dulwich SE22... 162 A5
8 Newham E13 ......99 A3
Sutton SM2 ....218 B1
Uplands Ave E17......34 D1
Uplands BR3 ....185 C1
Uplands Bsns Pk E17 .52 D6
Uplands Cl SW14 ....154 D6
Uplands Ct N21 ....16 C4
Uplands Park Rd EN2 .. 4 C3
Uplands Rd
East Barnet EN4 ......15 A3
Hornsey Vale N8 ......50 B4
Ilford RM6...........58 D6
Woodford IG8 ....37 D3
Uplands The HA4 .....40 A1
Uplands Way N21 .....16 C6
Uplands SE18........122 D1
Upnall Ho 16 SE15 ...140 C6
Upney Ct 2 IG11 .....79 D1
Upney La IG11........79 D1
Upney Sta IG11.......79 D1
Upnor Way SE17 .... 263 B2
Uppark Dr IG2........57 A3
Upper Abbey Rd
DA17 ....125 C2
Upper Addison Gdns
W14........113 A4 244 A2
Upper Bank St E14...119 D5
Upper Bardsey Wlk 7
N1 ....73 A2
Upper Belgrave St
SW1........115 A3 258 B6
Upper Berkeley St
W1..........92 D1 237 D1
Upper Beulah Hill
SE19...............183 C2
Upper Brighton Rd
KT6 ....198 A2
Upper Brockley Rd
SE4................141 B3
Upper Brook St
W1.........115 A6 248 A6
Upper Butts TW8 ....131 C6
Upper Caldy Wlk 18
N1 ....73 A2
Upper Camelford Wlk
14 W10 ....91 A1
Upper Cavendish Ave
N3 ....47 C6
Upper Cheyne Row
SW3.......136 C6 267 A6
UPPER CLAPTON 52 B1
Upper Clapton Rd E5..74 B6
Upper Clarendon Wlk
12 W11 ....91 A1
Upper Dengie Wlk
N1 .... 235 A6
UPPER EDMONTON ..34 B5
UPPER ELMERS END
..................207 B3
Upper Elmers End Rd
BR3 ....207 A4
Upper Farm Rd KT8 ..195 B5
Upper Fosters NW4 ....46 C5
Upper Gn W CR4.....180 D1
Upper Grosvenor St
W1.........115 A6 248 A5
Upper Grotto Rd
TW1...............152 D2
Upper Ground
SE1........116 C5 251 A4
Upper Grove Rd
DA17 ....147 B6
Upper Gr SE25.......205 D5
Upper Gulland Wlk 23
N1 ....73 A2
UPPER HALLIFORD
..................193 B5
Upper Halliford Rd
TW17..............193 C6
Upper Halliford Sta
TW16.............. 171 C1
Upper Hampstead Wlk
29 NW3 ....70 A4
Upper Ham Rd KT2,
TW10..............175 D6
Upper Handa Wlk 2
N1 ....73 A2
Upper Harley St
NW1.............. 238 B5
Upper Hawkwell Wlk
N1 .... 235 B6
UPPER HOLLOWAY ..71 D6
Upper Holloway Sta
N19 ....71 D6
Upper Holly Hill Rd
DA17 ....125 D1
Upper James St W1.. 249 B6
Upper John St W1 .. 249 B6
Upper Lismore Wlk 8
N1 ....73 A2
Upper Lodge Mews
TW12..............174 A4
Upper Mall W6 ......112 B1
Upper Marsh
SE1........116 B3 260 D6
Upper Montague St
W1..........92 D2 237 C3
Upper Mulgrave Rd
SM2...............217 A1
Upper North St E3,
E14.................97 C2
UPPER NORWOOD ..183 C3
Upper Park Rd
Belvedere DA17 .... 125 D2
BR1 .... 187 C2
Friern Barnet N11.....31 C5
Kingston u T KT2.... 176 C4
Maitland Pk NW3 .....70 D3
Upper Phillimore Gdns
W8.........113 C4 245 A1
Upper Pk IG10........21 D6
Upper Ramsey Wlk 19
N1 ....73 B2
Upper Rawreth Wlk
N1 .... 235 B6
Upper Rd Finchley N2 ...30 C2
Newham E13.........99 A4
Wallington SM6...... 219 D3
Upper Richmond Rd
SW15..............134 C1
Upper Richmond Rd W
TW10, SW14, SW15...133 A1
UPPER RUXLEY 191 C3
Upper St Martin's La
WC2.............. 250 A6
Upper Selsdon Rd
CR2 ....221 D1
Upper Sheridan Rd 3
DA17 ....125 C2
UPPER SHIRLEY 222 D4
Upper Shirley Rd
CR0 ....222 D5
Upper Sq TW7.......131 A2
Upper St N1 ...94 D6 234 C5
Upper Sunbury Rd
TW12..............173 C2
Upper Sutton La
TW5...............129 C4
UPPER SYDENHAM
..................184 A6
Upper Tachbrook St
SW1.............. 259 B4
Upper Talbot Wlk 7
W10................91 A1
Upper Teddington Rd
KT1, KT8 ....175 C2
Upper Terr NW3 ......70 A5
Upper Thames St
EC4 ....117 A6 252 B6
Upper Tollington Pk
N4 ....50 C1
Upperton Rd DA14 ...189 D5
Upperton Rd E E13....99 C4
Upperton Rd W E13...99 C4
UPPER TOOTING 158 D1
Upper Tooting Park
Mans 1 SW17......159 A2
Upper Tooting Pk
SW17..............158 D2
Upper Tooting Rd
SW17..............158 D1
Upper Town Rd UB6...85 D3
Upper Tulse Hill
SW2...............160 B3
Upper Vernon Rd
SM1 ....218 B3
UPPER WALTHAMSTOW
...................54 C6
Upper Walthamstow Rd
E17.................54 B6
Upper Wickham La
DA16 ....146 B4
Upper Wimpole St
W1..........93 A2 238 B4
Upper Woburn Pl NW1,
WC1.........93 D4 232 D1
Uppingham Ave HA7 ..25 C1
Upsdell Ave N13 ....32 C4
Upshire Ho E17.......35 B1
Upstall St SE5 ....138 D4
UPTON 77 B1
Upton Ave E7..........77 A1
Upton Cl
Cricklewood NW2 .....69 A5
Sidcup DA5 ....169 B5
Upton Cross E13.......99 A6
Upton Cross Prim Sch
E13.................99 B6
Upton Ct
Penge SE20........ 184 C3
Southall UB1 .... 107 D5
4 Wimbledon
SW19........... 178 D3
Upton Day Hospl
DA6 ...
Upton Dene SM2...
Upton Gdns HA3 ...
Upton Hts E7......
Upton La E7 ......
Upton Lodge Cl WD...
Upton Lo E7......
UPTON PARK ....
Upton Park Rd E7..
Upton Park Sta E13
Upton Prim Sch
DA5 ....
Upton Rd
Bexley DA6 ......
Edmonton N18......
Hounslow TW3 ....
SE18 ....
South Norwood CR7
Upton Rd S DA5....
Upton Villas 4 DA6
Upway N12........
Upwood Rd SE12...
Thornton Heath
SW16..........
Urban Mews N4 ....
Urlwin St SE5......
Urlwin Wlk SW9 ...
Urmston Dr SW19...
Urmston Ho 4 E14
Urquhart Ct BR3 ...
Ursula Lo DA14 ....
Ursula Mews N4...
Ursula St
SW11.......136 C...
Ursuline High Sch
SW20...........
Ursuline Prep Sch
SW19...........
Urswick Gdns RM9..
Urswick Rd
Dagenham RM9.....
Hackney E5, E9 .....
Usborne Mews SW8..
Usher Hall NW4....
Usher Rd E3.......
Usk Rd SW11 ......
Usk St E2 ....
Utah Bldg 3 SE13 ..
Utopia Ho 3 NW2 ..
Utopia Village
NW1........ 93 A...
Uvedale Rd
Dagenham RM10....
Enfield EN2 ....
Uverdale Rd
SW10.......136 A...
UXBRIDGE ....
Uxbridge Coll
Hayes UB3.........
Uxbridge UB8 .....
Uxbridge High Sch
UB8 ....
Uxbridge Rd
Acton W3, W5 .....
Ealing W13 ....
Feltham TW13......
Hampton TW12,
TW13...........
Hayes UB4.........
Hillingdon UB10, UB4
Kingston u T KT1,
KT6............
Shepherd's Bush
W12...........
Southall UB1, UB2, W5
W7 ....
Stanmore HA7......
Uxbridge Road (Harr...
Weald) HA3 ......
Uxbridge Road (Hatc...
End) HA5 ....
Uxbridge Road (Pinn...
HA5 ....
Uxbridge St
W8.........113 C5
Uxendon Cres HA3,
HA9 ....
Uxendon Hill HA9....
Uxendon Manor Pri...
Sch HA3...........

V

Vadnie Bish Ho NW5 .
Vaine Ho 4 E9 .....
Valance Ave E4 .....
Valan Leas BR2 .....
Vale Ave WD6.......
Vale Cl
Muswell Hill N2.....
Orpington BR6......
St John's Wood
W9 .... 92 A4
Twickenham TW1....
Vale Cres SW15.....

KT10...... 212 D1
A5 .... 41 A4
arnet EN5...... 1 D1
on W3...... 111 D5
s Wood
..... 92 A4 229 A1
HA0 .... 65 C5
N5 .... 13 C6
SE22 .... 139 D1
The W3 ..... 111 C5
n Sports Ctr
.... 65 B4
cton W3..... 111 B5
wington N4 ... 51 A2
/3 .... 88 C2
E23.......... 162 C2
Ave RM8 ..... 80 D6
Cir RM8 ...... 81 A5
House Mus*
.... 81 A6
Jun & Inf Schs
.... 80 D6
Wood Rd
.... 81 A5
Rd HA7 ...... 25 C6
o [1] SW2 .... 160 C3
Pl SW9 ..... 138 C1
e Ave DA5 ... 169 A3
e Ct
WD6 .... 9 D5
st Hill SE23 .. 162 D2
e Ho
ham Pk
.... 159 C5
Ford E3 .... 97 B6
e Pl
..... 116 D4 251 C2
e Rd
HA2 .... 64 A5
on E9 .... 74 D2
e Row SE1 .. 251 C1
es High Sch
.... 56 C3
es Rd IG1 ..... 56 D1
HEALTH 70 B5
Health NW3 ... 70 B5
BR1 .... 188 C1
e KT10 ...... 212 D1
n CR4 .... 203 D5
N KT6 .... 214 A6
S KT6 .... 214 A6
ewington
.... 51 A2
SM1 .... 217 D4
E7 .... 77 B2
ter Pk KT19,
.... 215 D5
Way E15 ..... 98 C4
Ct
SM2 .... 217 D1
WD23 .... 8 A4
e NW11 .... 47 B1
w N5 .... 72 D5
val N7 .... 72 A1
l TW12 ...... 173 C3
n The SW7 .. 256 A5
e Ct [2] EN5 ...... 1 D1
ood Rd BR1 ... 186 D5
r N4 .... 51 A3
e
d TW16 ...... 172 A4
wood NW11 .... 69 A6
n CR0 .... 222 D6
ton W3....... 111 C5
n TW14 ...... 150 B5
TW5 .... 129 A6
ll Hill N10 ..... 31 A2
HA4 .... 62 C4
ate N14 .... 16 A4
..... 136 B6 266 D6
ord IG8 .... 37 A3
Gr E13 .... 99 A5
Rd W3 .... 111 D4
Ct N10 .... 49 B5
Ho E9 .... 74 C2
St E8 .... 74 B2
Cl [13] UB5 ..... 84 D4
Ho
pitt Town
.... 120 A4
eenwich SE7 ... 121 C1
.... 266 D1
Way E6 ...... 100 B2
e Rd
l Green E1 ..... 96 A3
ll Hill N22 ...... 31 C1
n Rd E17 .... 54 A5
Ave N12 .... 30 B6
Charlton
ic FC) The
.... 121 C1
Cl HA5 .... 22 B1
Ct IG8 .... 37 B3
Dr NW9 .... 44 D3

Valleyfield Rd
SW16 .... 182 B5
Valley Fields Cres
EN2 .... 4 C3
Valley Gdns
Mitcham SW19 ...... 180 B3
Wembley HA0 .... 66 B1
Valley Gr SE7 .... 121 C1
Valley Ho
[4] Edmonton N9 ...... 18 A1
Upper Clapton E5 ..... 52 C1
Valleylink Est EN3 .... 19 A5
Valley Mews TW1 .... 153 A2
Valley Pl KT6 .... 198 A3
Valley Point Ind Est
CR0 .... 204 A2
Valley Prim Sch
BR2 .... 186 D1
Valley Prospect [3]
SE19 .... 183 C4
Valley Rd
Beckenham BR2 .... 186 C1
BR5 .... 190 B2
Streatham SW16 ..... 182 B6
Uxbridge UB10 .... 82 A5
Valley Side E4 .... 19 C3
Valleyside SE7 .... 121 D1
Valley Side Par E4 .... 19 C2
Valley View EN5 .... 13 A5
Valley Wlk CR0 .... 222 C6
Valliere Rd NW10 ..... 90 A4
Valliers Wood Rd
DA15 .... 167 C3
Vallis Way
Chessington KT9 .... 213 D4
Ealing W13 .... 87 A2
Val McKenzie Ave
N7 .... 72 C5
Valmar Rd SE5 .... 139 A4
Valmar Trad Est
SE5 .... 139 A4
Valnay St SW17 ...... 180 D5
Valognes Ave E17 ..... 35 A2
Valois Ho SE1 .... 263 C6
Valonia Gdns SW18 .. 157 B5
Vambery Rd SE18 .... 145 A6
Vanbern Ho NW5 ..... 71 A2
Vanborough Ct [4]
SM2 .... 218 A2
Vanbrough Cres UB5 .. 84 C6
Vanbrugh Cl [2] E16 ... 99 D2
Vanbrugh Ct SE11 .... 261 B3
Vanbrugh Dr KT12 ... 194 C3
Vanbrugh Fields
SE3 .... 142 D5
Vanbrugh Hill SE10,
SE3 .... 142 D6
Vanbrugh Ho [8] E9 ... 74 C1
Vanbrugh Mews
KT12 .... 194 C2
Vanbrugh Park Rd
SE3 .... 142 D5
Vanbrugh Park Rd W
SE3 .... 142 D5
Vanbrugh Pk SE3 .... 142 D5
Vanbrugh Rd W4 .... 111 B3
Vanbrugh Terr SE3 ... 142 D4
Vanburgh Cl BR6 ..... 211 C1
Vanburgh Ct [4] EN5 ..... 1 A1
Vanburgh Ho E1 .... 243 C4
Vancouver Rd
Edgware HA8 .... 26 D2
Forest Hill SE23 ..... 163 B2
Hayes UB4 .... 84 B3
Richmond TW10 ..... 175 C6
Vancover Ho [33] E1 ... 118 B5
Vanderbilt Rd
SW18 .... 158 A3
Vanderbilt Villas [1]
W12 .... 112 D4
Vanderville Gdns N2 .. 30 B1
Vandome Cl E16 ...... 99 B1
Vandon Ct SW1 ..... 259 B6
Vandon Pas SW1 .... 259 B6
Vandon St SW1 ..... 259 B6
Van Dyck Ave KT3 ... 199 B2
Vandyke Cl SW15 .... 156 D5
Vandyke Cross SE9 .. 166 A6
Vandy St EC2 .... 243 A5
Vane Cl
Hampstead NW3 ..... 70 B4
Harrow HA3 .... 44 B3
Vane Ho [18] N2 .... 30 B1
Vanessa Cl DA17 .... 125 C1
Vane St SW1 .... 259 B4
Vanfame Ct KT3 ..... 199 D6
Vange Ho [12] W10 ..... 90 C2
Van Gogh Cl [11]
TW7 .... 131 A2
Van Gogh Ct E14 .... 120 B3
Vanguard Bldg [6]
E14 .... 119 C4
Vanguard Cl
Newham E16 .... 99 B2
Thornton Heath CR0 . 204 D1
Vanguard Ho
[11] Hackney E8 .... 74 B1

Vanguard Ho *continued*
[7] Merton SW19 .... 180 A3
[6] Stanwell TW19 .... 148 A5
Vanguard St SE8 ..... 141 C4
Vanguard Trad Ctr
E15 .... 98 A6
Vanguard Way
Hatton TW6 .... 127 C3
Wallington SM6 ..... 220 A1
Van Lang Ho EN3 ..... 18 D6
Vanneck Sq SW15 .... 156 A6
Vanner Point [27] E9 ... 74 D2
Vanoc Gdns BR1 ..... 187 A6
Vansittart Rd E7 ...... 77 A4
Vansittart St [7]
SE14 .... 141 A5
Vanston Pl
SW6 .... 135 C5 265 B4
Vantage Ct
Harlington UB3 ..... 127 C5
[4] South Norwood
SW16 .... 182 B3
Vantage Mews [7]
E14 .... 120 A5
Vantage Pl W8 .... 255 B5
Vant Rd SW17 .... 180 D5
Vantrey Ho SE11 ..... 261 A3
Varcoe Rd SE16 ...... 118 C1
Vardens Rd SW11 .... 136 B1
Varden St E1 .... 96 B1
Vardon Cl W3 .... 89 B1
Vardon Ho SE10 ...... 142 A4
Vardy Ho HA7 .... 25 B5
Varey Ho E1 .... 97 A4
Varley Ho [5] NW6 ..... 91 C6
Varley Par NW9 .... 45 C5
Varley Rd E16 .... 99 B1
Varley Way CR4 ...... 180 B1
Varma Ct SE3 .... 143 A4
Varna Rd
Hampton TW12 ..... 173 D2
SW6 .... 135 B5 264 C3
Varndell St
NW1 .... 93 C4 232 A2
Varsity Dr TW1,
TW7 .... 152 D5
Varsity Row SW14 .... 133 A3
Vartry Rd N15 .... 51 C3
Vascroft Est NW10 .... 88 D3
Vassall Ho [3] E3 ...... 97 A4
Vassall Rd SW9 ...... 138 C5
Vat Ho SW8 .... 270 B4
Vauban Est SE16 ..... 263 D5
Vauban St
SE16 .... 117 D3 263 D5
Vaudeville Ct N4 ...... 72 C6
Vaughan Almshouses
TW15 .... 170 D5
Vaughan Ave
Chiswick W6 .... 111 D2
Hendon NW4 .... 46 A4
Vaughan Cl TW12 .... 173 A4
Vaughan Est [3] E2 .... 95 D4
Vaughan Fst & Mid Sch
HA1 .... 42 A3
Vaughan Gdns IG1 .... 56 B2
Vaughan Ho SE1 .... 251 C2
Vaughan Rd
Camberwell SE5 .... 139 A2
DA16 .... 145 D3
Harrow HA1 .... 42 B3
Stratford E15 .... 76 D2
Thames Ditton KT7 .. 197 B2
Vaughan St SE16 .... 119 B4
Vaughan Way E1 ..... 118 A5
Vaughan Williams Cl
SE8 .... 141 C5
VAUXHALL 116 A1
Vauxhall Bridge Rd
SW1 .... 115 C2 259 B3
Vauxhall Cross SE1,
SW8 .... 116 A1 260 B1
Vauxhall Gdns CR2 ... 221 A2
Vauxhall Gr
SW8 .... 138 B6 270 C6
Vauxhall Prim Sch
SE11 ...... 116 B1 260 D2
Vauxhall Sta
SE11 ...... 116 A1 260 B1
Vauxhall St
SE11 ...... 116 B1 260 D2
Vauxhall Wlk SE11 .. 260 C2
Vawdrey Cl E1 .... 96 C3
Vaynor Ho N7 .... 72 A4
Veals Mead CR4 ..... 180 C2
Vectis Ct SW18 ...... 157 D5
Vectis Gdns SW17 .... 181 B4
Vectis Rd SW17 ..... 181 B4
Veda Rd SE13 .... 141 C1
Vega Cres HA6 .... 22 A5
Vega Rd WD23 .... 8 A4
Veitch Cl TW14 ..... 149 D4
Veldene Way HA2 ..... 63 B5
Velde Way [1] SE22 ... 161 C6
Vellacott Ho [3] W12 ... 90 B1
Velletri Ho [17] E2 ...... 96 D5
Vellum Dr SM5 ...... 219 A5

Venables Cl RM10 ..... 81 D4
Venables St
NW8 .... 92 B2 236 D4
Vencourt Pl W6 ...... 112 A2
Venetian Rd SE5 ..... 139 A3
Venetia Rd
Ealing W5 .... 109 D4
Harringay N4 .... 50 D3
Venice Ct [14] SE5 ..... 139 A5
Venita Manor SE27 ... 182 C5
Venmead Ct [7]
DA17 .... 125 C2
Venner Rd SE26 ..... 184 C5
Venn Ho N1 .... 233 D5
Venn St SW4 .... 137 C1
Ventnor Ave HA7 ...... 25 B1
Ventnor Dr N20 .... 13 D2
Ventnor Gdns IG11 .... 79 C2
Ventnor Mans IG11 ... 79 C2
Ventnor Rd
Belmont SM2 .... 217 D1
SE14 .... 140 D5
Ventnor Terr N15 ..... 52 A5
Ventura Ho [12] SW2 ... 138 A1
Venture Cl DA5 ...... 169 A4
Venture Ct [3] SE12 ... 165 A4
Venue St E14 .... 98 A2
Venus Ho
[7] Millwall E14 ..... 119 C2
[8] Old Ford E3 .... 97 C6
Venus Mews CR4 .... 202 C6
Venus Rd SE18 ...... 122 B3
Vera Ave N21 .... 16 C6
Vera Ct
[1] Kensington W2 ..... 91 D1
Tottenham N22 .... 32 D2
Vera Lynn Cl [5] E7 .... 77 A4
Vera Rd
SW6 .... 135 A4 264 B2
Verbena Cl E16 .... 98 D3
Verbena Gdns [4]
W6 .... 112 A1
Verdant Ct [3] SE6 ... 164 C4
Verdant La SE6 ...... 164 C3
Verdayne Ave CR0 ... 222 D6
Verdi Cres W10 .... 91 A5
Verdun Rd
Barnes SW13 .... 134 A5
SE18 .... 146 A6
Vere Bank SW19 ..... 157 B3
Vereker Dr TW16 ..... 194 A6
Vereker Rd W14 ..... 254 B1
Vere St W1 .... 93 B1 238 C1
Verity Cl W11 .... 91 A1
Verity Ct N9 .... 18 D3
Verity Ho [20] E3 .... 97 B4
Vermeer Ct E14 ..... 120 B3
Vermillion Ct TW13 .. 149 D1
Vermont Cl EN2 .... 4 D1
Vermont Ho E17 ...... 35 B1
Vermont Rd
Sutton SM1 .... 217 D5
Wandsworth SW18 .. 157 D5
West Norwood SE19 . 183 C4
Verne Ct [9] W3 ...... 111 A3
Verneer Gdns SE15 .. 140 C1
Verney Gdns RM9 .... 81 A4
Verney Ho
Isleworth TW3 ...... 130 A1
Lisson Gr NW8 ..... 237 A6
South Kensington
SW10 .... 266 A6
Verney Rd
Bermondsey SE16 ... 118 B1
Dagenham RM9 ...... 81 A4
Verney St NW10 ...... 67 B5
Verney Way SE16 .... 118 B1
Vernham Rd SE18 ... 145 A6
Vernon Ave Ilford E12 .. 78 B4
West Barnes SW20 .. 178 D1
Woodford IG8 .... 37 B3
Vernon Cl
Stanwell TW19 ..... 148 A3
West Ewell KT19 .... 215 A2
Vernon Cres EN4 ..... 15 A5
Vernon Ct
Child's Hill NW2 ..... 69 B5
Ealing W5 .... 109 C6
Stanmore HA7 .... 25 B2
Vernon Dr HA7 .... 25 A2
Vernon Ho
Hyde The NW9 .... 45 D4
SE11 .... 260 D1
Vernon House Sch
NW10 .... 67 B3
Vernon Mews W14 .. 254 B3
Vernon Pl WC1 ..... 240 B3
Vernon Rd Bow E3 .... 97 B5
Feltham TW13 ...... 149 D2
Hornsey N8 .... 50 C6
Ilford IG3 .... 57 D1
Leytonstone E11 ..... 54 C1
Mortlake SW14 ..... 133 B2
Stratford E15 .... 76 C1
Sutton SM1 .... 218 B3
Walthamstow E17 .... 53 B4

Vernon Rise
Greenford UB6 .... 64 B3
WC1 .... 233 D2
Vernon Sq WC1 ..... 233 D2
Vernon St
W14 .... 113 A2 254 B3
Vernon Yd
W11 .... 113 B6 244 C6
Veroan Rd DA7 ...... 147 A3
Verona Ct
Chiswick W4 .... 111 C1
[10] SE14 .... 140 D6
Verona Dr KT6 ...... 214 A6
Verona Rd E7 .... 77 A1
Veronica Gdns CR4,
SW16 .... 181 C2
Veronica Ho
Brockley SE4 .... 141 B2
[46] Bromley E3 .... 97 D4
Veronica Rd SW17 ... 159 B2
Veronique Gdns IG6 .. 57 A4
Verran Rd SW12 ..... 159 B4
Versailles Rd SE20 ... 184 A3
Verulam Ave E17 ..... 53 B2
Verulam Bldgs WC1 . 240 D4
Verulam Ct
Hendon NW9 .... 46 A2
[4] Southall UB1 ...... 86 A1
Verulam Ho [1] W6 ... 112 C4
Verulam Rd UB6 ...... 85 C3
Verulam St
EC1 .... 94 C2 241 A4
Vervain Ho [2] SE15 ... 140 A5
Verwood Dr EN4 ...... 2 D2
Verwood Ho SW8 ... 270 D3
Verwood Lo [1] E14 ... 120 B2
Verwood Rd HA2 ...... 24 A1
Veryan Ct [3] N8 ...... 49 D4
Vesage Ct EC1 ...... 241 B3
Vesey Path [15] E14 .... 97 D1
Vespan Rd W12 ..... 112 A4
Vesta Ct SE1 .... 253 A1
Vesta Ho [9] E3 .... 97 C6
Vesta Rd SE4, SE14 .. 141 A3
Vestris Rd SE23 ..... 162 D2
Vestry House (Mus)*
E17 .... 53 D5
Vestry Mews [12]
SE5 .... 139 C4
Vestry Rd
Camberwell SE5 .... 139 C4
Walthamstow E17 .... 53 D5
Vestry St N1 .... 95 B4 235 C2
Vevey St SE23, SE6 ... 163 B2
Veysey Gdns RM10 ... 81 C5
Viaduct Pl [28] E2 ...... 96 B4
Viaduct Rd N2 .... 30 C1
Viaduct St E2 .... 96 B4
Viaduct The
Harrow HA2 .... 64 A5
Woodford E18 .... 37 B1
Vian St SE13 .... 141 D2
Vibart Gdns SW2 .... 160 B4
Vibart Wlk N1 ...... 233 B6
Vicarage Ave SE3 ... 143 A5
Vicarage Cl
New Malden KT4 .... 199 C1
Northolt UB5 .... 63 B1
Ruislip HA4 .... 39 B2
Vicarage Cres
SW11 ...... 136 B4 266 C1
Vicarage Ct
Beckenham BR3 .... 207 A6
East Bedfont TW14 .. 149 A4
Finchley N12 .... 29 D5
[7] Putney SW15 .... 156 A4
W8 .... 245 C2
Vicarage Dr
Barking IG11 .... 79 A1
Beckenham BR3 .... 185 C2
Mortlake SW14 ..... 155 B6
Vicarage Farm Ct
TW5 .... 129 B5
Vicarage Farm Rd TW3,
TW4, TW5 .... 129 A4
Vicarage Field Sh Ctr
The IG11 .... 79 A1
Vicarage Fields
KT12 .... 194 C3
Vicarage Gate
W8 .... 113 D5 245 C3
Vicarage Gdns
Mitcham CR4 ...... 202 C6
Mortlake SW14 ..... 155 B6
W8 .... 245 B3
Vicarage Gr SE5 .... 139 B4
Vicarage Ho [1] KT1 .. 176 B1
Vicarage La
Ilford IG1 .... 57 B1
Stratford E15 .... 76 D1
Wallend E6 .... 100 C4
Vicarage Mans N15 ... 51 A5
Vicarage Pk SE18 ... 123 A1
Vicarage Prim Sch
E6 .... 100 B4
Vicarage Rd
Ashford TW16 ...... 171 D4

Vicarage Rd *continued*
Croydon CR0 .... 220 C5
DA5 .... 169 D3
Dagenham RM10 ..... 81 D1
Hampton Wick KT1 .. 175 C2
Hendon NW4 .... 46 A3
Kingston u T KT1 .... 175 D1
Mortlake SW14 ..... 155 B6
Stratford E15 .... 76 D1
Sutton SM1 .... 217 D5
Teddington TW11 .... 175 A5
Tottenham N17 ...... 34 A2
Walthamstow E10 .... 53 D1
Woolwich SE18 ..... 123 A1
Vicarage The N8 ..... 50 B3
Vicarage Way
Harrow HA2 .... 41 C2
Neasden NW10 ...... 67 B5
Vicarage Wlk
SW11 ...... 136 B4 266 D2
Vicars Bridge Cl HA0 .. 88 A5
Vicar's Cl Enfield EN1 ... 5 C3
Newham E15 .... 99 A6
South Hackney E9 .... 96 C6
Vicar's Green Prim Sch
HA0 .... 87 C5
Vicars Hill SE13 ..... 141 D1
Vicar's Moor La N21 .. 16 D4
Vicars Oak Rd SE19 .. 183 C4
Vicar's Rd NW5 .... 71 A3
Vicar's Wlk RM8 ...... 80 B5
Viceroy Cl N2 .... 48 C6
Viceroy Ct
[5] Croydon CR0 ..... 205 B1
NW8 .... 230 B4
Viceroy Lo [6] KT6 ... 198 A4
Viceroy Par N2 .... 48 C6
Viceroy Rd
SW8 .... 138 A4 270 A2
Vic Johnson Ho [21]
E3 .... 97 B6
Vickers Cl SM6 ...... 220 B1
Vickers Ct [10] TW19 ... 148 A5
Vickery Ct EC1 ..... 242 B6
Vickery Ho [13] SW4 ... 138 A1
Vickery's Wharf [3]
E14 .... 97 C1
Victor Cazalet Ho
N1 .... 234 C6
Victor Gr HA0 .... 66 A1
Victor Ho [2] N20 ...... 14 D1
Victoria & Albert Mus*
SW7 .... 114 B3 256 D5
Victoria Arc SW1 ... 258 D5
Victoria Ave
Barnet EN4 .... 2 B1
East Molesey KT8 ... 195 D6
EC2 .... 243 B3
Finchley N3 .... 29 B2
Hackbridge SM5,
SM6 .... 219 A5
Hillingdon UB10 ...... 60 D1
Hounslow TW3,
TW4 .... 151 C6
Newham E6 .... 99 D6
Surbiton KT6 .... 197 D3
Wembley HA9 .... 66 D2
Victoria Bglws
DA14 .... 191 B3
Victoria Bldgs [13] E8 .. 96 B6
Victoria Bsns Ctr
DA16 .... 146 B3
Victoria Chambers
EC2 .... 243 A6
Victoria Cl Barnet EN4 .. 2 B1
East Molesey KT8 ... 195 C6
Harrow HA1 .... 42 D3
Hayes UB3 .... 83 B1
Victoria Coach Sta
SW1 .... 115 B2 258 C3
Victoria Coll WC2 ... 241 A2
Victoria Cotts
Ilford IG6 .... 57 A4
Muswell Hill N10 ..... 31 A1
[7] Richmond TW9 ... 132 C4
[3] Spitalfields E1 ..... 96 A2
Victoria Cres
Tottenham N15 ...... 51 C4
West Norwood SE19 . 183 C4
Victoria Ct
[5] Clapham Pk
SW4 .... 159 D5
[3] Penge SE26 ..... 184 C4
South Acton W3 .... 110 C4
[4] St George in t East
E1 .... 118 A6
[1] Wanstead E18 ..... 55 B6
Wembley HA9 .... 66 C2
Victoria Dock Rd
E16 .... 121 B6
Victoria Dr SW19 ... 156 D3
Victoria Emb
WC2 .... 116 C6 251 A5

Victoria Gdns
Heston TW5........ 129 A4
W11....... 113 C5 245 A4
Victoria Gr Mews
W2............... 245 C5
Victoria Gr
North Finchley N12....30 B5
W8........ 114 A3 256 A6
Victoria Hall 15 E16..121 A5
Victoria Ho
6 Clapham Pk
SW4........... 159 D5
Edgware HA8.........26 D4
2 Shepherd's Bush
W12........... 112 A4
SW1............. 258 C2
Victoria Ind Est W3...89 C2
Victoria Jun Sch
TW13...............150 B3
Victoria La Barnet EN5..1 B1
Hayes UB3..........105 B1
Victoria Lo 5
SW19..............178 C3
Victoria Mans
8 Islington N7.......72 C3
Willesden NW10......68 B1
Victoria Mews
Kilburn NW6.........91 C6
Wandsworth SW18..158 A3
Victoria Mills 1 E15..98 B6
Victorian Gr N16......73 C5
Victorian Hts 7
SW8...............137 B3
Victorian Rd N16.....73 D5
Victoria Park Ct 11
E9..................74 C1
Victoria Park Ind Ctr
E9..................75 B1
Victoria Park Lofts
E9..................96 D6
Victoria Park Rd E9...74 D1
Victoria Park Sq E2...96 C4
Victoria Pas NW8.... 236 C6
Victoria Place Sh Ctr
SW1...... 115 B2 258 D4
Victoria Pl 17 TW10..153 D6
Victoria Point 10 E13..99 A5
Victoria Rd
Barking IG11.........78 D2
Barnet EN4...........2 B1
Bexley DA6........ 147 C1
Bromley Comm BR2.. 209 D4
Buckhurst Hill IG9.....21 D2
Chingford E4.........20 C3
Chislehurst West
BR7............. 188 C5
Dagenham RM10......81 D3
Ealing W5...........87 B2
Edgware NW7.........27 D5
Edmonton N9.........17 D1
Feltham TW13.......150 B3
Finsbury Pk N4.......50 B1
Hendon NW4..........46 D5
Kensington
W8...... 114 A3 256 A6
Kilburn NW6.........91 B6
Kingston u T KT1.....176 B1
Leyton E11...........76 C4
Mitcham CR4........180 D3
Mortlake SW14......133 B2
Muswell Hill N22......31 D2
Newham E13..........99 A5
North Acton NW10....89 C3
Ruislip HA4..........62 B4
Sidcup DA15....... 168 A1
Southall UB2........107 B3
Surbiton KT6....... 197 D3
Sutton SM1.........218 B3
Teddington TW11.... 175 A4
Tottenham Hale N15....52 A5
Twickenham TW1.....153 B4
Walthamstow E17.....36 A1
Wanstead E18.........55 B6
Victoria Ret Pk HA4..62 D3
Victoria Rise SW4....137 B2
Victoria Sq SW1.... 258 D6
Victoria Sta
SW1...... 115 B2 258 D4
Victoria St
Erith DA17..........125 B1
Stratford E15.........76 C1
SW1...... 115 C3 259 B5
Victoria Terr
Dagenham NW10.....89 C3
Finsbury Pk N4.......50 C1
Harrow HA1.........42 C1
Victoria (Underground)
SW1...... 115 B3 258 D5
Victoria Villas TW9...132 B1
Victoria Way SE7....143 C6
Victoria Wharf E14...119 A6
Victoria Yd 28 E1.......96 A1
Victor Mills Cotts
BR8...............191 C3
Victor Rd
College Pk NW10.....90 B4
Harrow HA2.........42 A6
Penge SE20........ 184 D3
Teddington TW11.... 174 C6
Victors Dr TW12.....173 A4
Victor Seymour Inf Sch
SM5.............. 218 D4
Victors Way EN5.......1 B2
Victor Villas N9.......17 B1
Victory Ave SM4.....202 A4
Victory Bsns Ctr The
TW7.............. 130 D1
Victory Cl TW19......148 A3
Victory Ct IG11......102 B4
Victory Pl
6 Limehouse
E14........... 119 A6
SE17...... 117 B2 262 C4
West Norwood SE19.. 183 C4
Victory Rd
Merton SW19...... 180 A3
Wanstead E11........55 B5
Victory Road Mews 5
SW19..............180 A3
Victory Sch
SE17...... 117 A2 262 B4
Victory Way
Hounslow TW5..... 106 C1
Rotherhithe SE16... 119 A4
Victory Wlk SE8.......141 C4
Video Ct N4..........50 A2
Vidler Cl KT9........213 C2
Vienna Cl IG5........37 D1
View Cl Harrow HA1....42 B5
Highgate N6.........48 D2
View Cres N8.........49 D4
Viewfield Cl HA3......44 A2
Viewfield Rd DA5.....168 C3
Wandsworth SW18...157 B5
Viewland Rd SE18....123 D1
Viewpoint Ct 8 HA5..22 C1
Viewpoint Ealing W5..110 B6
3 Islington N5.......72 D3
Lewisham SE3...... 142 D2
View Point N20.......14 A4
View Rd N6...........48 D3
Viewside Lo N6.......49 C3
View The SE2........125 A1
Viga Rd N21..........16 C5
Vigilant Cl SE26......184 A6
Vignoles Rd RM7......59 C2
Vigo St W1....115 C6 249 A5
Vi & John Rubens Ho
IG2.................56 C3
Viking Cl 18 E3.......97 A5
Viking Ct
Hampton TW12..... 173 D2
New Barnet EN4......14 B6
Viking Gdns E6......100 A3
Viking Ho
3 Camberwell
SE5............ 139 A3
3 Woolwich SE7... 122 A2
Viking Pl E10..........53 B1
Viking Prim Sch UB5..84 D4
Viking Rd UB1.......107 A6
Villacourt Rd SE18...146 A6
Village Arc The 2
E4..................20 B3
Village Cl
Chingford E4.........36 A5
Hampstead NW3......70 B3
Village Ct
Blackheath SE3..... 142 C2
Walthamstow E17.....53 D4
Village Gate TW17...192 D4
Village Home The
IG6.................57 A6
Village Hts IG8.......36 D5
Village Inf Sch RM10..81 C1
Village Mount 19
NW3................70 A4
Village Park Cl EN1...17 C5
Village Rd Enfield EN1..17 C6
Hendon N3..........29 A1
Village Row SM2......217 C1
Village Sch The NW3..70 D2
Village The
Battersea SW11.... 136 D2
SE7............... 143 D6
Village Way
Ashford TW15...... 170 C6
Beckenham BR3.... 207 C6
Dulwich Village
SE21.............161 B5
Village Way E HA2....41 C2
Village Way
Ilford IG6...........57 A6
Pinner HA5..........41 B2
Willesden NW10......67 B4
Villa Rd SW9........138 C2
Villas On The Heath
NW3................70 A5
Villas Rd SE18.......123 A2
Villa St SE17..117 B1 262 D1
Villiers Ave
Kingston u T KT5.....198 B5
Twickenham TW2.....151 B3
Villiers Cl
Kingston u T KT5.....198 B5
Leyton E10...........75 C6
Villiers Ct
Oakleigh Pk N20......14 A4
SW11............. 267 B2
Villiers High Sch
UB1...............107 B5
Villiers Ho W5.......109 D6
Villiers Rd
Isleworth TW7...... 130 C3
Kingston u T KT1.....198 B6
Penge BR3......... 184 D1
Southall UB1........107 B5
Willesden NW2.......68 A2
Villiers St WC2..... 250 B4
Vincam Cl TW2......151 C4
Vince Ct N1........ 235 D1
Vincent Ave KT5.....215 A6
Vincent Cl
Avery Hill DA15..... 167 C3
Barnet EN5...........1 D2
Bromley BR2........209 B5
Harmondsworth
UB7............ 126 C6
Vincent Ct
Finsbury Pk N4.......50 A1
Hendon NW4.........46 D5
Marylebone W1...... 237 C2
Ruislip HA4..........62 B3
South Lambeth SW9.. 270 D1
Vincent Dr
Hillingdon UB10.......82 B6
Upper Halliford
TW17........... 193 C6
Vincent Gdns NW2....67 D5
Vincent Ho KT3.......199 D5
Vincent Mews 1 E3...97 C5
Vincent Rd
Acton Green W3.... 111 A3
Chingford E4.........36 B4
Croydon CR0....... 205 C2
Dagenham RM9.......81 A1
Hounslow West
TW4........... 128 D2
Kingston u T KT1.... 198 C6
Osterley TW7........130 B4
Tottenham N15.......51 A5
Wembley HA0........66 B1
Wood Green N22.....32 C1
Woolwich SE18..... 122 D2
Vincent Row TW12...174 A5
Vincents Cl SE16.....119 A4
Vincents Path UB5....63 A2
Vincent Sq
SW1....... 115 D2 259 C4
Wood Green N22......32 C1
Vincent St
Canning Town E16.....98 D2
Westminster
SW1..... 115 D2 259 D4
Vincent Terr
N1.............94 D5 234 D4
Vince St EC1....95 B4 235 D1
Vine Cl Surbiton KT5...198 B3
Sutton SM1........ 218 A5
West Drayton UB7... 104 C2
Vine Cotts
3 Ealing W7....... 108 C5
Southall UB2....... 107 D2
Vine Ct Harrow HA3....44 A3
Spitalfields E1........96 A2
Vinegar St E1........118 B5
Vinegar Yd SE1..... 253 A2
Vine Gdns IG1........79 A3
Vine Gr UB10.........60 C1
Vine Hill EC1....... 241 A5
Vine La
Hillingdon UB10.......82 B6
SE1....... 117 C5 253 B3
Uxbridge UB10.......60 B1
Vine Lo N12..........30 A4
Vine Pl Ealing W5....110 A5
Hounslow TW3...... 129 D1
Vine Rd
Barnes SW13...... 133 D2
BR6.............. 227 D2
East Molesey KT8.... 196 A5
Stratford E15.........76 D1
Vineries Bank NW7....28 B5
Vineries Cl
Dagenham RM9.......81 B2
Harmondsworth
UB7............ 126 C6
Vineries The
Enfield EN1...........5 C2
Southgate N14.......15 C5
Viners Cl KT12.......194 C3
Vine St Bridge EC1.. 241 B5
Vines Ave N3.........29 D2
Vine Sq W14........ 254 D1
Vines Sch The
SW11............. 137 A1
Vine St W1........ 249 B5
Vine St *continued*
Whitechapel
EC3....... 95 D1 243 C1
Vinewood Ct E17.....54 B4
Vineyard Ave NW7....29 A3
Vineyard Cl
Forest Hill SE6...... 163 C3
Kingston u T KT1.....198 B6
Vineyard Gr N3.......29 D2
Vineyard Hill Rd
SW19..............179 C6
Vineyard Path
SW14..............133 B2
Vineyard Rd TW13....150 A1
Vineyard Row KT1,
KT8...............175 C2
Vineyard Sch The
TW10............. 154 A5
Vineyards The
TW13..............150 A1
Vineyard Studios 3
E7..................77 C1
Vineyard The TW10...154 A6
Vineyard Wlk EC1... 241 A6
Viney Ct 9 SW4......159 D5
Vine Yd SE1........ 252 B2
Viney Rd SE13.......141 D2
Vining St SW2, SW9...138 C1
Vinlake Ave UB10.....60 C5
Vinson Ho N1........ 235 D3
Vinter Ct TW17......192 C4
Vintners Ct EC4..... 252 B6
Vintry Mews 3 E17...53 C5
Viola Ave
Feltham TW14...... 150 C5
SE2...............124 B1
Stanwell TW19..... 148 A3
Viola Ct HA8..........26 D3
Viola Sq W12........111 D6
Violet Ave Enfield EN2...5 B5
Hillingdon UB8........82 B2
Violet Cl Cheam SM3..201 A1
Hackbridge SM6..... 203 A1
Newham E16.........98 C3
32 SE8.............141 B6
Violet Ct 2 E15.......76 C1
Violet Gdns CR0.....220 D3
Violet Hill Ho NW8.. 229 A3
Violet Hill
NW8.........92 A5 229 A3
Violet La CR0........220 D3
Violet Rd Bromley E3....97 D3
Walthamstow E17.....53 C3
Woodford E18.........37 B1
Violet St E2..........96 B3
Violet Terr UB8.......82 C2
Violette Szabo Ho 4
SE27..............183 B6
VIP Trad Est SE7.... 121 C2
Virgil Pl W1........ 237 C3
Virgil St SE1..116 B3 260 D6
Virginia Cl KT3......199 A5
Virginia Ct
Ashford TW15...... 170 A6
7 Rotherhithe
SE16........... 118 D4
Virginia Ho
3 Blackwall E14.... 120 A6
Teddington TW11.... 175 A5
Virginia Prim Sch E2..95 D4
Virginia Rd
South Norwood
CR7............ 182 D2
10 Spitalfields E2.....95 D4
Virginia St E1.......118 A6
Virginia Wlk SW2....160 B5
Viridian Ct TW13.....149 D1
Viscount Cl N11......31 B5
Viscount Ct
9 Kensington
W11.............91 C1
1 Littleton TW15.... 171 A3
Viscount Dr E6......100 B2
Viscount Gr 3 UB5....84 D4
Viscount Point 6
SW19..............179 C3
Viscount Rd TW19....148 A3
Viscount St EC1..... 242 A4
Viscount Way TW6...127 C1
Vista Ave EN3..........6 D3
Vista Bldgs 19 E3.....97 B4
Vista Bldg The 14
SE18..............122 C2
Vista Dr IG4..........55 D4
Vista Ho 2 SW19....180 B2
Vista Hts SE23.......163 A4
Vista The Chingford E4..20 B4
SE9.............. 165 D4
Sidcup DA14....... 189 D5
Vista Way HA3........44 A3
Vitae Apartments 7
W6................112 A3
Vita Et Pax Sch N14..15 B6
Vittoria Ho N1...... 233 D5
Vittoria Prim Sch
N1......... 94 C5 234 A4
Viveash Cl UB3......105 D3
Vivian Ave
Hendon NW4.........46 B4
Wembley HA9........66 C2
Vivian Comma Cl 3
N4.................72 D5
Vivian Ct Finchley N12..29 D5
Paddington NW6......91 D5
Vivian Gdns HA9......66 C3
Vivian Ho N4..........51 B2
Vivian Mans 1 NW4..46 B4
Vivian Rd E3..........97 A5
Vivian Sq SE15.......140 B2
Vivian Way N2........48 B4
Vivien Cl KT9........214 A1
Vivienne Cl TW1.....153 D5
Voce Rd SE18........145 B5
Voewood Cl KT3......199 D3
Vogans Mill SE1.... 253 D2
Vogler Ho 3 E1......118 C6
Vogue Ct 8 BR1......187 B2
Vollasky Ho 5 E1.....96 A2
Volta Cl N9...........18 C1
Voltaire 2 SE5......139 D4
Voltaire Ct 13 SW11..137 A3
Voltaire Rd SW4.....137 D2
Voltaire 15 TW9......132 B4
Voltaire Way UB3....105 C6
Volt Ave NW10........89 C4
Volta Way CR0.......204 B1
Voluntary Pl E11......55 A3
Vora Ho HA0..........65 D2
Vorley Rd N19........71 C6
Voss Ct SW16........182 A4
Voss St E2...........96 A4
Voyager Bsns Est 10
SE16............. 118 A3
Voyagers Cl IG11....102 C1
Voysey Cl N3.........47 A6
Vulcan Cl E6........100 C1
Vulcan Gate EN2.......4 C3
Vulcan Rd SE4.......141 B3
Vulcan Sq E14.......119 C2
Vulcan Terr SE4......141 B3
Vulcan Way N7.......72 B2
Vyne Ho SM5.........218 D2
Vyner Ct E5..........74 A6
Vyner Rd W3........111 B6
Vyners Sch UB10......60 B4
Vyner St E2..........96 B6
Vyners Way UB10.....60 C3
Vyne The DA7........147 D2
Vyvyan Ho SE18......144 C4

W

Wadbrook St KT1....175 D1
Wadcroft Ct SE4......141 B2
Waddesdon Lo HA3...43 A3
Wadding St
SE17........117 B2 262 C3
Waddington Cl EN1....5 C1
Waddington Rd E15...76 B2
Waddington St E15...76 B2
Waddington Way
SE19..............183 B2
WADDON..........220 C4
Waddon Cl CR0......220 C5
Waddon Court Rd
CR0...............220 C5
Waddon Inf Sch
CR9.............. 220 C3
Waddon Marsh Sta
CR0.............. 220 C6
Waddon Marsh Way
CR0...............204 B1
Waddon New Rd
CR0...............220 D6
Waddon Park Ave
CR0...............220 C5
Waddon Rd CR0.....220 D5
Waddon Sta CR0.... 220 C4
Waddon Way CR0, CR2,
CR9...............220 D2
Wade Ct
Muswell Hill N10......31 B3
Wembley HA0........65 D5
Wade Ho
16 Bermondsey
SE1............. 118 A4
1 Enfield EN1.......17 C6
Wade's Gr N21........16 C4
Wade's Hill N21......16 C4
Wade's La TW11.....175 A5
Wadeson St E2.......96 B5
Wade's Pl E14.......119 D6
Wadeville Ave RM6....59 B2
Wadeville Cl DA17...125 C1
Wadham Ave E17.....35 D3
Wadham Cl TW17.....193 A2
Wadham Gdns
Greenford UB6.......64 B2
Primrose Hill
NW3...... 92 C6 230 A6
Wadham Ho N18......33 D5
Wadham Rd
Highams Pk E17.....35 D2
Wadham Rd *contin...*
Putney SW15......
Wadhurst Cl SE20...
Wadhurst Ct E6....
Wadhurst Rd W4...
Wadley Rd E11....
Wadsworth Bsns ...
UB6............
Wadsworth Cl
Enfield EN3......
Wembley UB6.....
Wadsworth Ct E10
Wadsworth Rd UB6
Wager St E3......
Waggoners Rdbt
TW5............
Waggon Mews N14
Waggon Rd EN4...
Waghorn Rd
Harrow HA3......
Newham E13......
Waghorn St SE15..
Wagner St SE15...
Wagon Rd EN4, EN5
Wagstaff Gdns RM9
Wagtail Cl NW9...
Wagtail Wlk BR3..
Waights Ct KT2...
Waikato Lo IG9...
Wainford Cl SW19..
Wainwright Gr TW...
Wainwright Ho 3
E1.............
Waite Davies Rd
SE12...........
Waitelands Ho KT3..
Waite St SE15....
Waithman St EC4..
Wakefield Ct 4
SE26...........
Wakefield Gdns
Redbridge IG1....
South Norwood
SE19..........
Wakefield Ho
Dulwich SE22.....
6 Peckham SE15..
Wakefield Mews
WC1............
Wakefield Rd
Friern Barnet N11..
20 Richmond TW10..
South Tottenham N1...
Wakefield St
Edmonton N18.....
Newham E6.......
St Pancras
WC1.............94 A...
Wakeford Cl SW4..
Wakehams Hill HA5
Wakeham St 9 N1..
Wakehurst Rd
SW11...........
Wakeling Ct E7....
Wakeling Ho 8
SE27...........
Wakeling La HA0...
Wakeling Rd W7...
Wakeling St 11 E14.
Wakelin Ho
Forest Hill SE23....
19 Islington N1....
Wakelin Rd E15....
Wakeman Ho HA8..
Wakeman Rd NW10
Wakemans Hill Ave
NW9............
Wakering Rd IG11..
Wakerley Cl 6 E6..
Wakley St
EC1.............94 D...
Walberswick St
SW8............
Walbrook Ct 32 N1..
Walbrook EC4.....
Walbrook Ho N9...
Walbrook 10 E18...
Walbrook Wharf
EC4............
Walburgh St E1....
Walcorde Ave SE17
Walcot Ct CR0....
Walcot Gdns SE11..
Walcot Ho 9 SE22..
Walcot Rd EN3....
Walcot Sq
SE11........116 C...
Walcott St SW1...
Waldair Ct E16....
Waldeck Gr SE27..
Waldeck Rd
Brentford W4.....
Ealing W13.......
Mortlake SW14....
Tottenham N15....
Waldeck Terr SW14

rave Ct
king IG11 ... 101 B6
dington
l ... 174 D5
rave Gdns
... 152 D1
rave Ho 5
... 156 C6
rave Pk
... 174 D6
rave Rd BR1 ... 210 B5
ham RM8 ... 80 C6
W5 ... 110 B6
ey N8 ... 50 C6
SE19 ... 183 D3
gton TW11 ... 174 D6
grave Sch
... 152 B1
rove CR0 ... 221 D5
nar Ave
W13 ... 109 C5
n SW6 ... 135 A3
nar Avenue Mans
... 264 A1
nar Rd SW19 ... 179 C5
Ave BR7 ... 188 B6
ton N13 ... 33 A6
Cl DA17 ... 125 B1
Ct SW8 ... 269 D2
Gdns CR7,
... 204 B5
Ho Barnet EN4 ... 2 C1
pham SW11 ... 137 A3
... 258 B3
Rd BR7 ... 188 B4
ham N17 ... 33 B2
shaw Rd
... 162 C3
St E1 ... 96 B1
Way NW7 ... 28 D4
Cl SW4 ... 159 C6
Ind Est BR1 ... 209 D6
Pl SW19 ... 180 C3
Rd BR1 ... 209 D6
e Pk NW10 ... 90 B4
f Cl CR2 ... 220 D1
m Cres SE23 ... 162 C3
m Park Rd
... 162 D3
m Pl 6
... 162 C3
st Way DA18 ... 125 B4
n Gdns BR2 ... 208 B6
n Ho 17 SW2 ... 160 B6
nhyrst CR0,
... 220 D4
n Mews SW3. 266 D6
n Rd
w HA1, HA2 ... 42 C1
sworth SW18 ... 158 A1
ns The CR0 ... 221 A4
n's Yd HA2 ... 64 B6
ock Rd SE28 ... 124 A6
n Cl HA7 ... 24 D4
nd Rd SE13 ... 142 A3
n Flats SE1 ... 263 A4
Ave SM5 ... 218 C3
Cl SE15 ... 140 B6
Farm Rd W3 ... 89 B2
n Acres SM6 ... 219 C2
St 1 E1 ... 97 A2
d Ave N20 ... 13 D4
d Ho N20 ... 14 A4
d Ho 28 E1 ... 96 B1
d Rd N16 ... 73 C4
Gdns RM9 ... 81 A1
n Ct 15 NW3 ... 70 D2
M GREEN ... 135 D5
n Green Arc
... 265 B4
n Gr
... 135 C5 265 A4
n Rise 1
... 179 A4
n Yd SW6 ... 265 A4
en Rd BR7 ... 188 C5
Cl Ealing W7 ... 108 C5
Bedfont TW14 ... 149 D4
Barnet N11 ... 31 C6
ton TW12 ... 173 B4
tead SE18 ... 123 A2
Ho NW1 ... 232 C3
Mews 9
... 160 C6
Prim Sch
... 15 D2
scroft Mead
... 161 A3
's Ct W1 ... 249 C6
's Lo 18 E14 ... 120 A4
's Pl SW15 ... 135 A1
shaw Ct 9
... 73 A1
The N2 ... 48 B6
he
rd TW16 ... 171 D3
ers Green N13 ... 16 C1

Walkynscroft 1
SE15 ... 140 B3
Wallace Cl SE28 ... 124 D6
Upper Halliford
TW17 ... 193 B5
Uxbridge UB10 ... 82 A5
Wallace Collection*
W1 ... 238 A2
Wallace Cres SM5 ... 218 D3
Wallace Ct
19 Enfield EN3 ... 7 C6
NW1 ... 237 B3
Wallace Ho N7 ... 72 B2
Wallace Lo N4 ... 50 C1
Wallace Rd N1, N5 ... 73 A2
Wallasey Cres UB10 ... 60 C5
Wallbrook Bsns Ctr
TW4 ... 128 B2
Wallbutton Rd SE4 ... 141 A3
Wallcote Ave NW2 ... 46 D1
Wall Ct N4 ... 50 B1
Walled Garden Cl
BR3 ... 207 D5
Walled Gdn The*
TW16 ... 194 B6
WALLEND ... 100 C6
Wall End Ct E6 ... 100 C6
Wall End Rd E6 ... 78 C1
Waller Dr HA6 ... 22 A2
Waller Rd SE14 ... 140 D3
Wallers Cl RM9 ... 103 B6
Wallett Ct 11 NW1 ... 71 C1
Wallflower St W12 ... 111 D6
Wallgrave Rd SW5 ... 255 C3
Wallingford Ave
W10 ... 90 D1
WALLINGTON ... 219 A2
Wallington Cl HA4 ... 39 A3
Wallington Ct 10
SM6 ... 219 B2
Wallington Cty Gram
Sch SM6 ... 219 B5
Wallington Green
SM6 ... 219 B4
Wallington Rd IG3 ... 57 D2
Wallington Sq 4
SM6 ... 219 C2
Wallington Sta SM6 ... 219 B2
Wallis Alley SE1 ... 252 B2
Wallis Cl SW11 ... 136 B2
Wallis Ho
5 New Cross Gate
SE14 ... 141 A4
Ruislip HA4 ... 39 A1
Ruislip HA4 ... 39 B1
Wallis Rd
Hackney Wick E9 ... 75 C2
Southall UB1 ... 85 D1
Wallorton Gdns
SW14 ... 133 B1
Wallside EC2 ... 242 B3
Wall St N1 ... 73 B2
Wallwood Rd E11 ... 54 B2
Wallwood St E14 ... 97 B2
Walmar Cl EN4 ... 2 B4
Walmer Cl BR6 ... 227 B4
Chingford E4 ... 19 D2
Walmer Gdns W13 ... 109 A4
Walmer Ho
8 North Kensington
W10 ... 90 D1
8 Penge SE20 ... 184 C3
Walmer Pl W1 ... 237 C4
Walmer Rd
North Kensington
W10 ... 90 C1
W11 ... 113 A6 244 A5
Walmer Terr SE18 ... 123 B2
Walmgate Rd UB6 ... 87 B6
Walmington Fold
N12 ... 29 C4
Walm La NW2 ... 68 C2
Walmsley Ho 1
SW16 ... 181 C6
Walney Wlk 6 N1 ... 73 A2
Walnut Ave UB7 ... 104 C3
Walnut Cl
Hayes UB3 ... 105 C6
Ilford IG6 ... 57 A5
SE8 ... 141 B6
Wallington SM5 ... 218 D3
Walnut Ct 2 E17 ... 54 A5
Walnut Gdns E15 ... 76 C3
Walnut Gr EN1 ... 17 B6
Walnut Ho 11 E3 ... 97 B6
Walnut Mews SM2 ... 218 A1
Walnut Rd E10 ... 75 D6
Walnut Tree Ave
CR4 ... 202 C6
Walnut Tree Cl
Barnes SW13 ... 133 D4
Chislehurst BR7 ... 189 A2
Walnut Tree Cotts
SW19 ... 179 A5
Walnut Tree Ho
SW10 ... 265 D6

Walnut Tree Rd
Brentford TW8 ... 132 A6
Charlton TW17 ... 171 A1
Dagenham RM8 ... 81 A6
Greenwich SE10 ... 120 C1
Heston TW5 ... 129 B6
Walnut Tree Walk Prim
Sch SE11 ... 116 C2 261 A4
Walnut Tree Wlk
SE11 ... 116 C2 261 A4
Walnut Way
Buckhurst Hill IG9 ... 21 D1
Ruislip HA4 ... 62 C2
Walpole Ave TW9 ... 132 B3
Walpole Cl
Pinner HA5 ... 23 C4
West Ealing W13 ... 109 C4
Walpole Cres 10
TW11 ... 174 D5
Walpole Ct
Ealing W5 ... 109 D5
7 Hammersmith
W14 ... 112 D3
South Hampstead
NW6 ... 70 A1
Twickenham TW2 ... 152 C2
2 Wallington SM6 ... 219 B3
Walpole Gdns
Acton Green W4 ... 111 A1
Twickenham TW2 ... 152 C1
Walpole Ho
Chislehurst BR7 ... 189 B2
East Molesey KT8 ... 195 C4
Walpole Lo W13 ... 109 C5
Walpole Mews NW8 ... 229 C5
Walpole Pl
9 Teddington
TW11 ... 174 D5
3 Woolwich SE18 ... 122 D2
Walpole Rd BR2 ... 209 D4
Mitcham SW19 ... 180 B4
South Croydon CR0 ... 221 B6
Surbiton KT6 ... 198 A3
Teddington TW11 ... 174 D5
Tottenham N17 ... 33 A1
Tottenham N17 ... 51 A6
Twickenham TW2 ... 152 C2
Upton E6 ... 77 C1
Walthamstow E17 ... 53 A5
Woodford E18 ... 36 D2
Walpole St
SW3 ... 114 D1 257 D2
Walrond Ave HA9 ... 66 A3
Walsham Cl SE28 ... 124 D6
Upper Clapton N16 ... 52 A1
Walsham Ho
New Cross Gate
SE14 ... 140 D3
SE17 ... 262 C2
Walsham Rd
Feltham TW14 ... 150 B4
New Cross Gate
SE14 ... 140 D3
Walsh Lodge HA4 ... 40 B3
Walsingham Gdns
KT19 ... 215 D3
Walsingham Ho
Chingford E4 ... 20 B4
Twickenham TW2 ... 152 B2
Walsingham Lo
SW13 ... 134 A4
Walsingham Mans
SW6 ... 265 D4
Walsingham NW8 ... 229 D6
Walsingham Pk
BR7 ... 189 B1
Walsingham Pl SW4,
SW11 ... 159 A5
Walsingham Rd
BR5 ... 190 B2
Ealing W13 ... 109 A5
Enfield EN2 ... 17 B6
Mitcham CR4 ... 202 D4
Shacklewell E5 ... 74 A5
Walsingham Wlk
DA17 ... 147 C6
Walter Besant Ho 20
E1 ... 96 D4
Walter Ct 3 W3 ... 89 A1
Walter Green Ho
SE15 ... 140 C4
Walter Ho SW10 ... 266 C4
Walter Hurford Par 5
E12 ... 78 C4
Walter Northcott Ho 2
NW6 ... 69 C3
Walter Rodney Cl
E12 ... 78 B2
Walter Savill Twr
E17 ... 53 C3
Walters Cl
Hayes UB3 ... 105 D4
SE17 ... 262 B3
Walters Ho
3 Camberwell
SE5 ... 139 C3
Islington N1 ... 234 D6

Walters Ho *continued*
10 Kennington SE17 ... 138 D6
Walter Sickert Hall
N1 ... 235 A3
Walters Rd EN3 ... 6 C1
Walter's Rd SE25 ... 205 C5
Walter St
Globe Town E2 ... 96 D4
2 Kingston u T KT2 ... 176 A2
Walters Way SE23 ... 162 D5
Walters Yd BR1 ... 187 A1
Walter Taylor Ct
SE4 ... 141 B1
Walter Terr E1 ... 96 D1
Walterton Rd W9 ... 91 C3
Walter Wlk HA8 ... 27 A4
Waltham Ave
Hayes UB3 ... 105 B3
Preston NW9 ... 44 C3
Waltham Ct
Chingford E17 ... 36 A2
Whetstone N20 ... 14 B1
Waltham Dr HA8 ... 44 C6
Waltham Forest Coll
E17 ... 35 D1
Waltham Gdns EN3 ... 6 C6
Waltham Green Ct
SW6 ... 265 C3
Waltham Ho NW8 ... 229 A6
10 Stockwell SW9 ... 138 B3
Waltham Park Way
E17 ... 35 C3
Waltham Pk E17 ... 35 C2
Waltham Rd
Carshalton SM5 ... 202 C1
Southall UB2 ... 107 A3
WALTHAMSTOW ... 53 D6
Walthamstow Acad
E17 ... 35 B2
Walthamstow Ave
E4 ... 35 C3
Walthamstow Ave
(North Circular Rd)
E4 ... 35 B4
Walthamstow Bsns Ctr
E17 ... 36 A1
Walthamstow Central
Sta E17 ... 53 C4
Walthamstow Mkt
E17 ... 53 C5
Walthamstow Queens
Road Sta E17 ... 53 C4
Walthamstow Sch for
Girls E17 ... 53 D5
Waltham Way E4 ... 19 C2
Waltheof Ave N17 ... 33 B2
Waltheof Gdns N17 ... 33 B2
Walton Ave
Cheam SM3 ... 217 B5
Harrow HA2 ... 63 B4
New Malden KT3 ... 199 D5
Wembley HA9 ... 66 D5
Walton Bridge Rd KT12,
TW17 ... 193 C2
Walton Cl
Dollis Hill NW2 ... 68 B6
Harrow HA1 ... 42 B5
Lea Bridge E5 ... 74 D5
SW8 ... 138 A5 270 B4
Walton Croft HA1 ... 64 C4
Walton Ct EN5 ... 14 A6
Walton Dr
Harrow HA1 ... 42 B5
Willesden NW10 ... 67 B2
Walton Gdns
Acton W3 ... 88 D2
Feltham TW13 ... 171 D6
Wembley HA9 ... 66 A6
Walton Gn CR0 ... 224 A1
Walton Ho E2 ... 243 D6
Ealing W5 ... 109 D2
1 Edmonton N9 ... 34 A6
1 Kingston u T KT2 ... 176 A3
Upper Holloway N7 ... 72 B5
10 Walthamstow E17 ... 53 D6
Wandsworth SW18 ... 157 C5
Walton La
Oatlands Pk KT13,
TW17 ... 193 B1
Shepperton TW17 ... 193 B2
Walton Oak Prim Sch
KT12 ... 194 C1
WALTON-ON-THAMES
... 194 C2
Walton Pl SW3 ... 257 C6
Walton Rd
East Molesey KT8,
KT12 ... 195 C5
Harrow HA1 ... 42 B5
Little Ilford E12 ... 78 C4
Newham E13 ... 99 C5
Sidcup DA14 ... 168 C1
Tottenham N15 ... 51 D5
Walton-on-T
KT12&KT8 ... 194 D4
Walton St Enfield EN2 ... 5 B4
SW3 ... 114 C3 257 B5

Walton Way
Acton W3 ... 88 D2
Mitcham CR4 ... 203 C5
Walt Whitman Cl 6
SE24 ... 138 D1
WALWORTH ... 117 B1
Walworth Pl
SE17 ... 117 A1 262 B1
Walworth Rd
SE17 ... 117 A1 262 B2
Walworth Sch
SE17 ... 117 C1 263 B1
Walwyn Ave BR1 ... 209 D6
Wanborough Dr
SW15 ... 156 B3
Wanderer Dr IG11 ... 102 C4
Wandle Bank
Mitcham SW19 ... 180 B3
Wallington CR0 ... 220 A5
Wandle Court Gdns
CR0 ... 220 A5
Wandle Ct
4 Bedford Pk
W12 ... 111 C4
Wallington CR0 ... 220 A5
West Ewell KT19 ... 215 A4
Wandle Ho
6 Catford BR1 ... 186 B5
NW8 ... 237 A4
Wandsworth SW18 ... 157 D4
Wandle Lodge SM6 ... 219 B6
Wandle Lo CR0 ... 220 A5
Wandle Pk Sta CR0 ... 220 C6
Wandle Rd
Croydon CR0 ... 221 A5
Hackbridge SM6 ... 219 B6
Morden SM4 ... 202 B4
Upper Tooting
SW17 ... 158 C2
Wallington CR0 ... 220 A5
Wandle Side
Hackbridge SM6 ... 219 B5
Wallington CR0 ... 220 B5
Wandle Tech Pk
CR4 ... 202 D2
Wandle Trad Est
CR4 ... 202 D2
Wandle Valley Sch
SM5 ... 202 C2
Wandle Way
Mitcham CR4 ... 202 D4
Wandsworth SW18 ... 157 D3
Wandon Rd
SW6 ... 135 D5 265 D3
WANDSWORTH ... 157 C5
Wandsworth Bridge Rd
SW6 ... 135 D4 265 C1
Wandsworth Common
Sta SW12 ... 158 D4
Wandsworth Common
West Side SW18 ... 158 A6
Wandsworth Gyratory
SW18 ... 157 D6
Wandsworth High St
SW18 ... 157 D6
Wandsworth Mus*
SW18 ... 157 D6
Wandsworth Plain
SW18 ... 157 D6
Wandsworth Rd
SW8 ... 138 A5 270 A3
Wandsworth Road Sta
SW4 ... 137 C3
Wandsworth Town Sta
SW18 ... 135 D1
Wangey Rd RM6 ... 58 D2
Wangford Ho 13
SW9 ... 138 D1
Wanless Rd SE24 ... 139 A2
Wanley Rd SE5 ... 139 B1
Wanlip Rd E13 ... 99 B3
Wansbeck Ct EN2 ... 4 D2
Wansbeck Rd E3, E9 ... 75 B1
Wansdown Pl
SW6 ... 135 D5 265 C4
Wansey St
SE17 ... 117 A2 262 B3
Wansford Rd IG8 ... 37 C2
WANSTEAD ... 55 C3
Wanstead Church Sch
E11 ... 55 A4
Wanstead Cl BR1 ... 187 C1
Wanstead High Sch
E11 ... 55 C3
Wanstead Hospl E11 ... 55 B5
Wanstead Hts 8 E11 ... 55 A4
Wanstead La IG1 ... 56 A3
Wanstead Park Ave
E12 ... 77 D6
Wanstead Park Rd
IG1 ... 56 A1
Wanstead Park Sta
E7 ... 77 B4
Wanstead Pl E11 ... 55 A4
Wanstead Rd BR1 ... 187 C1
Wanstead Sta E11 ... 55 B3
Wantage Rd SE12 ... 164 D6

Wantz Rd RM10 ... 81 D3
WAPPING ... 118 B5
Wapping Dock St 19
E1 ... 118 B5
Wapping High St
E1 ... 118 B5
Wapping La E1 ... 118 B5
Wapping Sta E1 ... 118 C5
Wapping Wall E1 ... 118 C5
Warbank La KT2 ... 177 D3
Warbeck Rd W12 ... 112 B4
Warberry Rd N22 ... 32 B1
Warboys App KT2 ... 176 D4
Warboys Cres E4 ... 36 A5
Warboys Rd KT2 ... 176 D4
Warburg Ho E2 ... 96 A4
Warburton Cl
6 Kingsland N1 ... 73 C2
Stanmore HA3 ... 24 B4
Warburton Ct
Peckham SE15 ... 140 A2
Ruislip HA4 ... 62 A6
Warburton Ho 5 E8 ... 96 B6
Warburton Rd
8 Hackney E8 ... 96 B6
Twickenham TW2 ... 151 D3
Warburton St 6 E8 ... 96 B6
Warburton Terr E17 ... 35 D1
Wardalls Ho 12 SE8 ... 141 B6
Ward Cl CR2 ... 221 C3
Wardell Cl NW7 ... 27 C3
Wardell Ct N2 ... 48 B6
Wardell Ho 7 SE10 ... 142 A6
Warden Ave HA2 ... 41 B1
Warden Rd NW5 ... 71 A2
Wardens Field Cl 2
BR6 ... 227 D2
Wardens Gr SE1 ... 252 A3
Wardle St E9 ... 74 D3
Wardley Lo E11 ... 54 D3
Wardley St SW18 ... 157 D4
Wardlow 8 NW5 ... 71 B4
Wardo Ave
SW6 ... 135 A4 264 A2
Wardour Mews W1 ... 239 B1
Wardour St
W1 ... 93 D1 239 C1
Ward Point SE11 ... 261 A3
Ward Rd
Camden Town N19 ... 71 C5
Mill Meads E15 ... 98 B6
Wardrew Ct 9 EN5 ... 14 A6
Wardrobe Pl EC4 ... 241 D1
Wardrobe Terr EC4 ... 251 D6
Wardrobe The 3
TW9 ... 153 D6
Wards Cotts TW19 ... 148 B4
Wards Rd IG2 ... 57 B2
Wards Wharf App
E16 ... 121 D4
Ware Ct Cheam SM1 ... 217 B4
Edgware HA8 ... 26 A6
Wareham Cl TW3 ... 129 D1
Wareham Ct 2 N1 ... 73 C1
Wareham Ho SW8 ... 270 C4
Warehouse W E16 ... 121 B6
Waremead Rd IG2 ... 56 D4
Ware Point Dr SE28 ... 123 B4
Warfield Rd
East Bedfont
TW14 ... 149 C4
Hampton TW12 ... 173 D2
Kensal Green NW10 ... 90 D4
Warfield Yd 6
NW10 ... 90 D4
Wargrave Ave N15 ... 51 D3
Wargrave Ho 16 E2 ... 95 D4
Wargrave Rd HA2 ... 64 A5
Warham Rd
Croydon CR2 ... 221 A3
Harringay N4 ... 50 D4
Harrow HA3 ... 24 D1
Warham St SE5 ... 138 D5
Waring Cl BR6 ... 227 D2
Waring Dr BR6 ... 227 D2
Waring Ho 25 E2 ... 96 A4
Waring Rd DA14 ... 190 C4
Waring St SE27 ... 183 A6
Warkworth Gdns
TW7 ... 131 A5
Warkworth Rd N17 ... 33 B3
Warland Rd SE18 ... 145 C5
Warley Ave
Dagenham RM8 ... 59 B2
Hayes UB4 ... 84 A1
Warley Cl E10 ... 53 B1
Warley Ho N1 ... 73 B2
Warley Rd Hayes UB4 ... 84 A2
Lower Edmonton N9 ... 18 C2
Woodford IG8 ... 37 B3
Warley St E2 ... 96 D4
Warlingham Rd
CR7 ... 204 D5
Warlock Rd W9 ... 91 C3

Warlow Cl 6 EN3 ... 7 C6
Warlters Cl N7 ... 72 A4
Warlters Rd N7 ... 72 A4
Warltersville Mans N19 ... 50 A2
Warltersville Rd N4, N8, N19 ... 50 A2
War Meml Homes W4 ... 133 B5
Warming Cl E5 ... 74 D5
Warmington Rd SE24 ... 161 A5
Warmington St 3 E13 ... 99 A3
Warminster Gdns SE25 ... 184 A1
Warminster Rd SE25 ... 184 A1
Warminster Sq SE25 ... 184 A1
Warminster Way CR4 ... 181 B1
Warmsworth NW1 ... 232 A6
Warmwell Ave NW9 ... 27 C2
Warndon St SE16 ... 118 C2
Warneford Rd HA3 ... 44 A6
Warneford St E9 ... 96 B6
Warne Pl 4 DA15 ... 168 B5
Warner Ave SM3 ... 217 A6
Warner Cl
Hampton TW12 ... 173 B5
Harlington UB3 ... 127 B5
Hendon NW9 ... 46 A2
Stratford E15 ... 76 C3
Warner Ct SM3 ... 217 A6
Warner Ho
1 Beckenham BR3 ... 185 D4
Harrow HA1 ... 42 B2
4 Homerton E9 ... 74 D2
Lewisham SE13 ... 141 D3
NW8 ... 229 A2
Warner Pl E2 ... 96 A4
Warner Rd
Bromley BR1 ... 186 D3
Camberwell SE5 ... 139 A4
Hornsey N8 ... 49 D5
Walthamstow E17 ... 53 A5
Warners Cl IG8 ... 37 A5
Warner St EC1 ... 94 C3 241 A5
Warner Yd EC1 ... 241 A5
Warnford Ho SW15 ... 155 C5
Warnford Ind Est UB3 ... 105 C4
Warnford Rd BR6 ... 227 D3
Warnham Court Rd SM5 ... 218 D1
Warnham Ho 6 SW2 ... 160 B4
Warnham Rd N12 ... 30 C5
Warnham WC1 ... 233 C1
Warple Mews W3 ... 111 C4
Warple Way W3, W12 ... 111 C4
Warren Ave
Bromley BR1 ... 186 C3
Leyton E11 ... 76 B5
Mortlake SW14, TW10 ... 132 D1
Orpington BR6 ... 227 D3
South Croydon CR2 ... 222 D1
Warren Cl DA6 ... 169 C6
Esher KT10 ... 212 A4
Hayes UB4 ... 84 C2
Ponders End N9 ... 18 D4
Wembley HA9 ... 65 D6
West Norwood SE21 ... 161 A4
Warren Comp Sch The RM6 ... 59 B4
Warren Cres N9 ... 17 D4
Warren Ct
17 Beckenham BR3 ... 185 C3
5 Croydon CR0 ... 205 C1
6 Ealing W5 ... 87 C2
Greenwich SE7 ... 143 C6
N1 ... 234 A4
Tottenham Hale N17 ... 52 A6
Warren Cutting KT2 ... 177 B3
Warrender Prim Sch HA4 ... 39 D2
Warrender Rd N19 ... 71 C4
Warrender Way HA4 ... 40 A2
Warren Dr UB6 ... 86 A3
Warren Dr N KT5, KT6 ... 198 D1
Warren Dr HA4 ... 40 D2
Warren Dr S KT5 ... 199 A1
Warren Dr The E11 ... 55 C2
Warren Farm Cotts RM6 ... 59 B5
Warren Fields HA7 ... 25 C6
Warren Gdns E15 ... 76 B3
Warren Hill IG10 ... 21 C6
Warren Ho 21 E3 ... 97 D4
Warren Jun Sch RM6 ... 59 B4
Warren La
Stanmore HA7 ... 9 A2
Woolwich SE18 ... 122 D3
Warren Mews W1 ... 239 A5
Warren Park Rd SM1 ... 218 C2
Warren Pk KT2 ... 177 A4
Warren Pond Rd E4 ... 20 D4
Warren Rd
Ashford TW15 ... 171 C3
Bexleyheath DA6 ... 169 C6
Bushey WD23 ... 8 B3
Chingford E4 ... 20 A2
Croydon CR0 ... 205 D1
Hayes BR2 ... 225 A6
Ickenham UB10 ... 60 B4
Ilford IG6 ... 57 B4
Isleworth TW2 ... 152 B5
Kingston u T KT2 ... 177 A4
Leyton E10 ... 76 A5
Mitcham SW19 ... 180 C4
Sidcup DA14 ... 168 C1
Wanstead E11 ... 55 C2
Willesden NW2 ... 67 D6
Warren Rise KT3 ... 177 B2
Warren Road Prim Sch BR6 ... 227 D4
Warrens Shawe La HA8 ... 10 D2
Warren Street Sta NW1 ... 93 C3 239 B6
Warren St W1 ... 93 C3 239 A5
Warren Terr RM6 ... 58 D5
Warren The
Hayes UB4 ... 84 A1
Heston TW5 ... 129 B5
Manor Pk E12 ... 78 A4
Worcester Pk KT19 ... 215 B5
Warren Way
Edgware HA8 ... 26 D1
Finchley NW7 ... 29 A4
Warren Wlk 1 SE7 ... 143 C6
Warren Wood Cl BR2 ... 225 A6
Warriner Dr N9 ... 18 A1
Warriner Gdns SW11 ... 137 A4 268 A1
Warrington Cres W9 ... 92 A3 236 A6
Warrington Ct
4 Croydon CR0 ... 220 D5
13 Merton SW19 ... 179 C3
Warrington Gdns W9 ... 236 A5
Warrington Rd
Croydon CR0 ... 220 D5
Dagenham RM8 ... 81 A6
Harrow HA1 ... 42 C4
22 Richmond TW10 ... 153 D6
Warrington Sq RM8 ... 80 D6
Warrior Cl SE28 ... 123 C5
Warrior Sq E12 ... 78 C4
Warsaw Cl HA4 ... 62 B2
Warspite Ho 3 E14 ... 119 D2
Warspite Rd SE18 ... 122 A3
Warton Rd E15 ... 98 A6
Warwall E6 ... 100 D1
Warwick Ave
Edgware HA8 ... 11 A1
Harrow HA2 ... 63 B4
Warwick Avenue Sta W9 ... 92 A3 236 A5
Warwick Ave W9 ... 92 A3 236 A5
Warwick Bldg SW8 ... 268 C5
Warwick Chambers W8 ... 255 A6
Warwick Cl
Bushey WD23 ... 8 C4
DA5 ... 169 B4
Hampton TW12 ... 174 A3
New Barnet EN4 ... 14 B6
Warwick Cres
Hayes UB4 ... 83 D3
Little Venice W2 ... 92 A2 236 A4
Warwick Ct
1 Beckenham BR2 ... 186 C1
Ealing W7 ... 86 D1
5 East Finchley N2 ... 48 A6
Friern Barnet N11 ... 31 D4
Harrow HA1 ... 42 C6
Merton SW19 ... 179 B2
13 New Barnet EN5 ... 13 D6
Northolt UB5 ... 63 C3
Surbiton KT6 ... 214 A6
3 Upper Clapton E5 ... 74 B6
WC1 ... 240 D3
Warwick Dene W5 ... 110 A5
Warwick Dr SW15 ... 134 B2
Warwick Gdns
Harringay N4 ... 51 A4
Warwick Gdns *continued*
Ilford IG1 ... 56 D1
Thames Ditton KT7 ... 196 D4
Thornton Heath CR7 ... 204 C5
W14 ... 113 B2 254 D4
Warwick Gr
Surbiton KT5 ... 198 B2
Upper Clapton E5 ... 52 B1
Warwick Ho
9 Acton W3 ... 88 C1
10 Brixton SW9 ... 138 C3
6 Kingston u T KT2 ... 176 A2
6 Putney SW15 ... 156 C4
Stoke Newington N4 ... 51 A1
Warwick House St SW1 ... 249 D4
Warwick Ho 5 SW19 ... 179 A3
Warwick La EC4 ... 94 D1 241 D1
Warwick Lo
Brondesbury NW2 ... 69 A3
Cheam SM1 ... 217 B4
Twickenham TW2 ... 151 D1
Warwick Mans SW5 ... 255 A4
Warwick Par HA7 ... 25 B1
Warwick Pas EC4 ... 241 D2
Warwick Pl
Ealing W5 ... 109 D4
Little Venice W9 ... 92 A2 236 A4
Warwick Pl N SW1 ... 259 A3
Warwick Rd
Ashford TW15 ... 170 A5
Barnet EN5 ... 1 D1
Bexley DA16 ... 146 C2
Chingford E4 ... 35 C5
Ealing W5 ... 110 A5
Edmonton N18 ... 33 D6
Enfield EN3 ... 7 B6
Friern Barnet N11 ... 31 D4
Hounslow TW4 ... 128 B2
Kingston u T KT3 ... 199 A6
Penge SE20 ... 206 B6
Plashet E12 ... 78 A3
Sidcup DA14 ... 190 B5
Southall UB2 ... 107 B3
Stratford E15 ... 76 D2
Sutton SM1 ... 218 A3
Teddington KT1 ... 175 C2
Thames Ditton KT7 ... 196 D4
Thornton Heath CR7 ... 204 C6
Twickenham TW2 ... 152 C3
Walthamstow E17 ... 35 B1
Wanstead E11 ... 55 B4
West Kensington W14, SW5 ... 113 B2 254 D4
Yiewsley UB7 ... 104 A5
Warwick Row SW1 ... 115 B3 258 D6
Warwick Sch for Boys E17 ... 54 A5
Warwickshire Path SE8 ... 141 B5
Warwick Sq EC4 ... 241 D2
Warwick Sq Mews SW1 ... 259 A3
Warwick Sq SW1 ... 115 C1 259 A2
Warwick St W1 ... 115 C6 249 B6
Warwick Terr
Leytonstone E17 ... 54 B4
SE18 ... 145 B6
Warwick W14 ... 113 B2 254 D3
Warwick Way SW1 ... 115 B2 258 D4
Warwick Yd EC1 ... 242 B5
Wasdale NW1 ... 231 D1
Washbourne Ct N9 ... 18 A2
Washbrook Ho SW2 ... 160 C5
Washington Ave E12 ... 78 B4
Washington Bldg 1 SE13 ... 141 D4
Washington Cl 45 E3 ... 97 D4
Washington Ct SW17 ... 180 D4
Washington Ho SW1 ... 247 C1
Walthamstow E17 ... 35 B1
Washington Rd
Barnes SW13 ... 134 A5
Kingston u T KT1 ... 176 C1
North Cheam KT4 ... 200 B1
Upton E6 ... 77 C1
2 Woodford E18 ... 36 D1
Wastdale Rd SE23 ... 162 D3
Watchfield Ct 7 W4 ... 111 A1
Watcombe Cotts TW9 ... 132 C6
Watcombe Rd SE25 ... 206 B4
Waterbank Rd SE6 ... 186 A6
Waterbeach Rd RM9 ... 80 C2
Water Brook La NW4 ... 46 C4
Watercress Pl N1 ... 73 C1
Waterdale Rd SE2 ... 146 A6
Waterden Cres E9 ... 75 C3
Waterden Rd E15 ... 75 C2
Waterer Ho 7 SE6 ... 186 A6
Waterer Rise SM6 ... 219 D2
Waterfall Cl N14 ... 15 C1
Waterfall Cotts SW19 ... 180 B4
Waterfall Rd
Mitcham SW19 ... 180 B4
New Southgate N11, N14 ... 15 C1
Waterfall Terr SW17 ... 180 C4
Waterfield Cl
Belvedere DA17 ... 125 C3
Woolwich SE28 ... 124 B5
Waterfield Gdns SE25 ... 205 C4
Waterford Ct 16 W13 ... 109 A5
Waterford Rd SW6 ... 135 D5 265 C3
Waterford Way NW10 ... 68 A3
Watergardens The KT2 ... 177 A4
Water Gardens The W2 ... 92 C1 237 B2
Watergardens The IG8 ... 37 A5
Watergate EC4 ... 251 C6
Watergate Ho 5 SE18 ... 122 C2
Watergate Sch SE6 ... 185 D5
Watergate St SE8 ... 141 C6
Watergate Wlk WC2 ... 250 B4
Water Gdns HA7 ... 25 B4
Waterglade Ctr The W5 ... 109 D6
Waterhall Ave E4 ... 36 C6
Waterhall Cl E17 ... 34 D2
Waterhead NW1 ... 232 A2
Waterhedge Mews EN1 ... 17 D6
Waterhouse Cl
Hammersmith W6 ... 112 D1
Hampstead NW3 ... 70 B3
Newham E16 ... 99 D2
Waterhouse Ct 7 TW11 ... 174 D5
Wateridge Cl E14 ... 119 C3
Wateringbury Cl BR5 ... 190 B1
Water La
16 Camden Town NW1 ... 71 B1
Edmonton N9 ... 18 B4
Ilford IG3 ... 79 D5
Water Lane Ho 29 TW10 ... 153 D6
Water La
Richmond TW10, TW9 ... 153 D6
SE14 ... 140 C5
Sidcup DA14 ... 169 B2
Stratford E15 ... 76 C2
Teddington KT1 ... 175 D2
Twickenham TW1 ... 153 A3
Water Lily Cl UB2 ... 108 A4
Waterloo Bridge SE1, WC2 ... 116 B6 250 D5
Waterloo Cl
East Bedfont TW14 ... 149 D3
Hackney E9 ... 74 C3
Waterloo Ct 4 HA0 ... 66 A2
Waterloo East Sta SE1 ... 116 C5 251 B3
Waterloo Gdns
26 Islington N1 ... 72 D1
South Hackney E2 ... 96 C5
Waterloo Int Sta SE1 ... 116 B4 250 D2
Waterloo Pier SE1 ... 250 C2
Waterloo Pl
Kew TW9 ... 132 C6
9 Richmond TW9 ... 132 A1
SW1 ... 115 D5 249 C4
Waterloo Rd
Dollis Hill NW2 ... 68 A6
Forest Gate E7 ... 76 D3
SE1 ... 116 C4 251 B2
Sutton SM1 ... 218 B3
Upton E6 ... 77 C1
Walthamstow E10 ... 53 C2
Waterloo Sta SE1 ... 116 C4 251 A2
Waterloo Terr N1 ... 72 D1
Waterlow Ct NW11 ... 47 D2
Waterlow Rd N19 ... 49 C1
Waterman Bldg 2 E14 ... 119 C4
Watermans Ct
12 Brentford TW8 ... 131 D6
Watermans Ct *continued*
2 Brentford TW8 ... 132 A6
Watermans Mews 1 W5 ... 110 A6
Waterman St SW15 ... 134 D2
Waterman Way E1 ... 118 B5
Watermark Ct RM6 ... 58 B3
Watermead TW14 ... 149 C3
Watermead Ho E9 ... 75 B3
Watermead La CR4 ... 202 D2
Watermeadow La SW6 ... 136 A3
Watermead Rd SE6 ... 186 A6
Watermead Way N17 ... 34 B1
Watermen's Sq 1 SE20 ... 184 C3
Water Mews SE15 ... 140 C1
Watermill Bsns Ctr EN3 ... 7 B3
Watermill Cl TW10 ... 153 C1
Watermill Ct SE13 ... 141 D2
Watermill La N18 ... 33 C5
Water Mill Way TW13 ... 151 C2
Watermill Way SW19 ... 180 A2
Watermint Quay N16 ... 52 A2
Water Rd HA0 ... 88 B6
Water's Edge SW6 ... 134 C4
Watersedge KT19 ... 215 A4
Watersfield Way HA8 ... 26 A3
Waters Gdns RM10 ... 81 C3
Watershipdown Ho 4 E11 ... 54 D2
Waterside Ave BR3 ... 207 D4
Waterside 11 BR3 ... 185 C2
Waterside Cl
Barking IG11 ... 80 A4
30 Bermondsey SE16 ... 118 A4
Northolt UB5 ... 85 B4
Old Ford E3 ... 97 B6
Surbiton KT6 ... 214 A6
Woolwich SE28 ... 123 D5
Waterside Ct
3 Hackbridge SM6 ... 219 A5
Lewisham SE13 ... 142 B1
Waterside Dr KT12 ... 194 B4
Waterside N1 ... 235 A3
Waterside Pl NW1 ... 231 B6
Waterside Point SW11 ... 267 B4
Waterside Rd UB2 ... 107 C3
Waterside Sch SE18 ... 123 B1
Waterside Trad Ctr W7 ... 108 C3
Waterside E17 ... 52 C3
Waterside Way SW17 ... 180 A5
Watersmeet Way SE28 ... 102 D1
Waterson St E2 ... 95 D4
Watersplash Cl KT1 ... 198 A6
Watersplash La
Hayes UB3 ... 106 A2
Southall TW5 ... 106 B1
Watersplash Rd TW17 ... 192 C5
Waters Pl SW15 ... 134 C3
Waters Rd
Catford SE6 ... 164 C1
Kingston u T KT1 ... 176 D1
Waters Sq KT1 ... 198 D6
Water St WC2 ... 251 A6
Water View Cl DA6 ... 168 D6
Waterview Ho 13 E14 ... 97 A2
Waterville Lo 6 N12 ... 30 A5
Waterways Bsns Ctr EN3 ... 7 C5
Waterworks Cnr E17 ... 36 C1
Waterworks La E5 ... 74 D6
Waterworks Rd SW2 ... 160 B5
Waterworks Yd 4 CR0 ... 221 A5
Watery La DA14 ... 190 B4
Hayes UB3 ... 105 B1
Merton SW19, SW20 ... 179 B1
Northolt UB5 ... 84 C5
Wates Way CR4 ... 202 D3
Wateville Rd N17 ... 33 A2
Watford Cl SW11 ... 267 B2
Watford Rd
Elstree WD6 ... 9 C5
Harrow HA1 ... 43 A1
Newham E16 ... 99 A2
Northwood HA6 ... 22 A4
Sudbury HA0, HA1 ... 65 B4
Watford Way (Barnet By-Pass) NW9 ... 27 D3
Watford Way NW4 ... 46 A5
Watkin Mews 18 EN3 ... 7 C6
Watkin Rd HA9 ... 66 D5
Watkins Ho
11 Cubitt Town E14 ...
Harrow HA1 ...
Watkinson Rd N7 ...
Watling Ave HA8 ...
Watling Ct EC4 ...
1 Elstree WD6 ...
Watling Gate NW9 ...
Watling Gdns NW2 ...
Watling Ho 10 SE18 ...
Watlings Cl CR0 ...
Watling St
Bexleyheath DA7 ...
4 Camberwell SE15 ...
City of London EC4 ... 95 A1
Watlington Gr SE26 ...
Watney Cotts SW14 ...
Watney Mkt* E1 ...
Watney Rd SW14 ...
Watneys Rd CR4 ...
Watney St E1 ...
Watson Ave
Cheam SM3 ...
Wallend E6 ...
Watson Cl
Mitcham SW19 ...
Stoke Newington N16 ...
Watson Ho 3 SW2 ...
Watsons Lo 4 RM10 ...
Watsons Mews W1 ...
Watsons Rd N22 ...
Watson's St SE8 ...
Watson St E13 ...
Wattisfield Rd E5 ...
Watts Cl N15 ...
Wattsdown Cl E13 ...
Watts Gr E3 ...
Watts Ho 6 W10 ...
Watt's La
Chislehurst BR7 ...
Teddington TW11 ...
Watts Rd KT7 ...
Watts St SE15 ...
Wapping E1 ...
Wat Tyler Ho N8 ...
Wat Tyler Rd SE10 ...
Wauthier Cl N13 ...
Wavel Ct
7 Streatham SW16 ...
7 Wapping E1 ...
Wavell Dr DA15 ...
Wavell Ho N6 ...
Wavel Mews
Hampstead NW6 ...
Hornsey N8 ...
Wavel Pl SE26 ...
Wavendon Ave W4 ...
Waveney Ave SE15 ...
Waveney Cl E1 ...
Waveney Ho SE15 ...
Waverley Ave
Chingford Hatch E4 ...
Sutton SM1 ...
Tolworth KT5 ...
Twickenham TW2, TW4 ...
Walthamstow E17 ...
Wembley HA9 ...
Waverley Cl BR2 ...
East Molesey KT8 ...
Hayes UB3 ...
Woodford E18 ...
Waverley Cres SE18 ...
Waverley Ct
5 Brondesbury NW6 ...
Enfield EN2 ...
North Finchley N12 ...
W1 ...
Waverley Gdns
Barking IG11 ...
Ealing NW10 ...
Ilford IG6 ...
Newham E6 ...
Northwood HA6 ...
Waverley Gr N3 ...
Waverley Ind Pk HA1
Waverley Pl
Finsbury Pk N4 ...
St John's Wood NW8 ... 92 B5
Waverley Rd
Croydon SE25 ...
Enfield EN2 ...
Finsbury Pk N8 ...
Harrow HA2 ...
Plumstead SE18 ...
Southall UB1 ...
Stoneleigh KT17, KT4 ...
Tottenham N17 ...
Walthamstow E17 ...
Woodford E18 ...

ey Sch EN3 ... 6 C1
ey Way SM5 ... 218 C2
Ct NW3 ... 70 D2
on Ho [2] E3 ... 97 B6
on Rd SW18 ... 158 A4
on St
... 115 B5 248 C4
ree Ct [9]
... 160 A3
ree Rd
ham SW2 ... 160 B3
ord E18 ... 37 A1
n NW5 ... 70 D3
Cres UB1 ... 85 C1
Ho UB4 ... 84 C2
Rd NW10 ... 89 B5
Way UB5 ... 85 B3
l Cl HA5 ... 22 D1
l La HA5 ... 22 D1
Point [1]
... 123 A3
ne Gr HA4 ... 39 A3
ve TW5 ... 128 A4
er Rd UB5 ... 85 A4
d Link SE9 ... 167 B5
d St SW11 ... 136 C3
d Ave E8 ... 74 A3
d Ho [12]
... 138 C3
ds Ct IG1 ... 79 B4
ds UB3 ... 83 B2
ds Mead
... 185 D2
Ho SE11 ... 261 A1
Pl
ley HA0 ... 65 D4
Norwood
... 160 D1
n Ct E8 ... 74 B2
Cl BR6 ... 227 D5
ete Ave CR0 ... 220 D5
ete Sq
rth Kensington
... 90 D1
epherd's Bush
... 112 D6
ete St SW18 ... 158 A2
le Ave WD23 ... 8 B5
le BR7 ... 189 B2
le Cl N14 ... 15 C5
le Commercial
511 ... 102 A5
le Ct
orth TW7 ... 130 C3
enham TW1 ... 153 C5
ley HA9 ... 66 C5
le Gdns RM10 ... 81 C3
le NW11 ... 47 A1
le Gr BR7,
... 188 B6
le Mews IG2 ... 56 C4
le
ake SW14 ... 155 A6
Addington CR0 ... 223 D2
Cl
ermondsey
6 ... 118 B1
... 226 A6
Fst & Mid Schs
... 24 D3
La HA3 ... 24 B2
Rd UB10 ... 82 C5
Rise HA3 ... 24 D2
Sq E5 ... 74 B6
DSTONE ... 42 D6
stone Rd
... 217 B6
The BR7 ... 188 B4
Way
UB4 ... 83 C4
ord RM7 ... 59 D3
wood Gdns
... 23 D4
Rd E4 ... 20 B1
Ct HA5 ... 41 A5
ale Ct EN5 ... 12 C6
ale Gdns EN2 ... 5 B4
ale Ho N4 ... 51 A2
ale Rd SE13 ... 142 B1
mouth Ho [1]
... 97 B2
Pl [13] E2 ... 96 B4
de Rd SE13 ... 141 D1
erbury Ho [3]
... 71 D5
erbury [6] W2 ... 91 C1
erill Ct SE25 ... 206 B3
erley Cl E3 ... 97 B2
ersfield Ct
... 166 B5
er Cl
ham E16 ... 122 D6
Croydon CR0 ... 221 D4
er Ct [2] E2 ... 96 B3
er Ho
thnal Green
... 96 A3

Weaver Ho *continued*
[1] Northolt UB5 ... 85 B3
Weavers Cl TW7 ... 130 C1
Weavers Ho [4] E11 ... 55 A3
Weaver's La
SE1 ... 117 C5 253 B3
Weaver St E1 ... 96 A3
Weavers Way
[6] Camden Town
NW1 ... 71 D1
NW1 ... 232 C6
Weaver Wlk SE27 ... 182 D6
Webb Cl NW10 ... 90 C3
Webb Ct [6] SE28 ... 124 B6
South Acton W3 ... 110 D4
Webber Cl WD6 ... 9 D5
Webber Ho [6] IG11 ... 78 D1
Webber Row
SE1 ... 116 D4 251 C1
Webber St
SE1 ... 116 D4 251 C1
Webb Est E5 ... 52 A2
Webb Gdns [1] E13 ... 99 A3
Webb Ho
[2] Dagenham
RM10 ... 81 C5
Feltham TW13 ... 151 A1
SW8 ... 269 D3
Webb Pl NW10 ... 89 D4
Webb Rd SE3 ... 142 D6
Webbscroft Rd RM10 ... 81 D4
Webbs Rd UB4 ... 84 B4
Webb's Rd SW11 ... 158 D6
Webb St SE1 ... 117 C3 263 A5
Webheath [6] NW6 ... 69 B1
Webley Ct [22] EN3 ... 7 C6
Webster Gdns W5 ... 109 D5
Webster Ho [16] N16 ... 73 C3
Webster Rd
Bermondsey
SE16 ... 118 A3
Leyton E11 ... 76 A5
Weddell Ho [23] E1 ... 96 D3
Wedderburn Rd
Barking IG11 ... 101 C6
Hampstead NW3 ... 70 B3
Wedgewood Ct
[1] Beckenham
BR2 ... 208 D5
DA5 ... 169 B4
Wedgewood Ho
SW1 ... 259 A1
Thames Ditton KT7 ... 196 D1
Wedgewood Mews
W1 ... 239 D1
Wedgewood Wlk
NW3 ... 69 D3
Wedgwood Ho
[17] Globe Town E2 ... 96 D4
SE11 ... 261 A5
Wedgwood Way
SE19 ... 183 A3
Wedlake St W10 ... 91 A3
Wedmore Gdns N19 ... 71 D6
Wedmore Rd UB6 ... 86 B4
Wedmore St N19 ... 71 D5
Weech Rd NW6 ... 69 C4
Weedington Rd NW5 ... 71 A3
Weedon Ho W12 ... 90 A1
Weekley Sq SW11 ... 136 B2
Weeks Ho TW10 ... 175 C6
Weigall Rd SE12,
SE3 ... 143 A1
Weighhouse St W1 ... 238 B1
Weighton Rd
Harrow HA3 ... 24 B2
Penge SE20 ... 184 B1
Weihurst Ct SM1 ... 218 C3
Weihurst Gdns SM1 ... 218 B3
Weimar St SW15 ... 135 A2
Weirdale Ave N20 ... 14 D2
Weir Hall Ave N18 ... 33 B4
Weir Hall Gdns N18 ... 33 B5
Weir Hall Rd N18 ... 33 B4
Weir Ho [8] SW12 ... 159 C4
Weir Rd Sidcup DA5 ... 169 D4
Streatham SW12 ... 159 C4
Walton-on-T KT12 ... 194 A3
Wimbledon SW18,
SW19 ... 157 D1
Weir's Pas NW1 ... 232 D2
Weiss Rd SW15 ... 134 D2
Welbeck Ave
Grove Pk BR1 ... 187 B6
Hayes UB4 ... 84 B3
Sidcup DA15 ... 168 A3
Welbeck Cl
New Malden KT3 ... 199 D4
North Finchley N12 ... 30 B5
Stoneleigh KT17 ... 216 A1
Welbeck Ct
Hayes UB4 ... 84 B3
W14 ... 254 C4
Welbeck Mans [10]
NW6 ... 69 C3
Welbeck Rd
Carshalton SM1 ... 218 B6

Welbeck Rd *continued*
Carshalton SM5 ... 202 C1
East Barnet EN4 ... 14 C5
Harrow HA2 ... 41 D1
Newham E6 ... 99 D4
Welbeck St
W1 ... 93 B1 238 C2
Welbeck Villas N21 ... 17 A3
Welbeck Way W1 ... 238 C2
Welbeck Wlk SM5 ... 202 B1
Welbourne Prim Sch
N17 ... 52 A6
Welbury Ct E8 ... 73 C1
Welby Ho N19 ... 49 D2
Welby St SE5 ... 138 D4
Welch Pl HA5 ... 22 C2
Welcome Ct E17 ... 53 C2
Weldon Cl HA4 ... 62 B2
Weldon Ct
Southgate N21 ... 16 B6
St Johns SE8 ... 141 C3
[7] Sutton SM1 ... 218 B3
Thornton Heath CR7 ... 204 D4
Weldon Dr KT8 ... 195 B5
Weld Pl N11 ... 31 B5
Welfare Rd E15 ... 76 C1
Welford Cl E5 ... 74 D5
Welford Ct
[12] Camden Town
NW1 ... 71 B1
[7] Clapham SW8 ... 137 C3
Welford Ho [4] UB5 ... 85 B3
Welford Pl SW19 ... 179 A6
Welham Rd SW16,
SW17 ... 181 B4
Welhouse Rd SM5 ... 202 C1
Wellacre Rd HA3 ... 43 B3
Wellan Cl DA15,
DA16 ... 168 B6
Welland Ct SE6 ... 163 B2
Welland Gdns UB6 ... 86 D5
Welland Ho SE15 ... 140 C1
Welland Mews E1 ... 118 A5
Wellands Cl BR1 ... 188 B1
Welland St SE10 ... 142 A6
Well App EN5 ... 12 C6
Wellbrook Rd BR6 ... 226 C4
Wellby Cl N9 ... 18 A3
Wellby Ct [1] E13 ... 99 C5
Wellclose Sq E1 ... 118 A6
Wellclose St [20] E1 ... 118 A6
Well Cl Ruislip HA4 ... 63 A5
Streatham SW16 ... 182 B6
Well Cottage Cl E11 ... 55 C2
Well Ct EC4 ... 242 B1
Wellday Ho [2] E9 ... 75 A2
Welldon Cres HA1 ... 42 C3
Welldon Ct
Harrow HA1 ... 42 C4
[1] West Dulwich
SE21 ... 161 B2
Welldon Park Fst Sch
HA2 ... 64 A4
Welldon Park Mid Sch
HA2 ... 64 A4
Weller Ho [23] SE16 ... 118 A4
Weller Mews [6]
BR2 ... 209 B5
Weller St SE1 ... 252 A2
Welles Ct [15] E14 ... 119 C6
Wellesley Ave W6 ... 112 B3
Wellesley Cl [8] SE7 ... 121 C1
Wellesley Court Rd [1]
CR0 ... 221 B6
Wellesley Cres TW2 ... 152 C1
Wellesley Ct
Cheam SM3 ... 201 A1
St John's Wood
W9 ... 92 A4 229 A2
Twickenham TW2 ... 152 C1
Wellesley Gr CR0 ... 221 B6
Wellesley Ho NW1 ... 232 C1
[12] Wimbledon
SW19 ... 179 A3
Wellesley Park Mews
EN2 ... 4 D3
Wellesley Pl
Camden Town
NW5 ... 71 A3
NW1 ... 232 C1
Wellesley Rd
Croydon CR0 ... 205 A1
Gospel Oak NW5 ... 71 A3
Gunnersbury W4 ... 110 D1
Harrow HA1 ... 42 C4
Ilford IG1 ... 57 A1
Sutton SM2 ... 218 A2
Twickenham TW2 ... 152 C1
Walthamstow E17 ... 53 C3
Wanstead E11 ... 55 A4
Wood Green N22 ... 32 C1
Wellesley Road Sta
CR0 ... 221 B6
Wellesley St E1 ... 96 D2
Wellesley Terr
N1 ... 95 A4 235 B2
Wellfield Ave N10 ... 49 B6

Wellfield Rd SW16 ... 182 B6
Wellfit St [6] SE24 ... 138 D2
Wellgarth Rd NW11 ... 47 D1
Wellgarth UB6 ... 65 B2
Well Gr N20 ... 14 B3
Wellgrove Sch N20 ... 14 B3
Well Hall Par SE9 ... 144 B1
Well Hall Pleasaunce*
SE9 ... 144 A1
Well Hall Rd SE9 ... 144 B1
Well Ho [11] N9 ... 18 A1
Wellhouse Rd BR3 ... 207 C5
Wellhurst Cl BR6 ... 227 D1
WELLING ... 146 B2
Wellingfield Ct [1]
DA16 ... 146 A2
Welling High St
DA16 ... 146 B2
Welling Sch DA16 ... 146 B4
Wellings Ho UB3 ... 106 B5
Welling Sta DA16 ... 146 A3
Wellington Arch*
SW1 ... 248 B2
Wellington Ave
Chingford E4 ... 19 D2
DA15 ... 168 A5
Edmonton N9 ... 18 B1
Hounslow TW3,
TW4 ... 151 C6
North Cheam KT4 ... 216 C5
Pinner HA5 ... 23 B2
South Tottenham N15 ... 52 A3
Wellington Bldgs
[15] Bow E3 ... 97 C4
SW1 ... 258 B1
Wellington Cl
Kensington W11 ... 91 C1
New Cross Gate
SE14 ... 140 D4
Walton-on-T KT12 ... 193 D1
Wellington Cres
KT3 ... 199 A6
Wellington Ct
Ashford TW15 ... 170 A6
Knightsbridge SW1 ... 247 C1
Stanwell TW19 ... 148 A4
St John's Wood NW8 ... 229 D3
Strand WC2 ... 250 A6
[5] Surbiton KT6 ... 198 A3
Teddington TW12 ... 174 B5
[4] Upper Tooting
SW17 ... 180 C4
Wandsworth SW18 ... 158 C6
Wellington Gdns
Greenwich SE7 ... 121 C1
Teddington TW12,
TW2 ... 174 B6
Wellington [1] NW9 ... 27 D3
Wellington Gr SE10 ... 142 B5
Wellington Ho
[4] Ealing W5 ... 88 A4
[18] Maitland Pk NW3 ... 70 D2
Northolt UB5 ... 63 C1
Wellington N8 ... 50 A5
Wellington Ho [6]
HA4 ... 40 C1
Wellington Hospl The
NW8 ... 92 B5 229 D3
Wellington Ho HA7 ... 9 A1
Wellington Mans
Shacklewell N16 ... 73 D4
[1] Walthamstow E10 ... 53 C1
Wellington Mews
East Dulwich
SE22 ... 140 A1
[3] Islington N7 ... 72 B2
SE7 ... 143 C6
Streatham SW16 ... 159 D1
Wellington Mus (Apsley
Ho)* SW1 ... 115 A4 248 B2
Wellington Par
DA15 ... 168 A6
Wellington Park Est
NW2 ... 68 A6
Wellington Pas [7]
E11 ... 55 A4
Wellington Pl
East Finchley N2 ... 48 C4
St John's Wood
NW8 ... 92 B4 229 D2
Wellington Prim Sch
Bow E3 ... 97 C4
Chingford E4 ... 19 D2
Hounslow TW3 ... 129 B3
Wellington Rd
Ashford TW15 ... 170 A5
Bexley DA5 ... 168 D6
Brentford W5 ... 109 C3
Bromley BR2 ... 209 C5
Enfield EN1 ... 17 C6
Erith DA17 ... 125 B1
Harrow HA3 ... 42 C6
Hatton TW14 ... 149 C6
Kensal Green NW10 ... 90 D4
Leyton E7 ... 76 D4
Newham E6 ... 100 B5

Wellington Rd N
TW4 ... 129 B2
Wellington Rd HA5 ... 23 B2
Wellington Rd S
TW4 ... 151 B6
Wellington Rd
St John's Wood
NW8 ... 92 B5 229 D3
Teddington TW12,
TW2 ... 174 B6
Thornton Heath CR0 ... 204 D2
Walthamstow E10 ... 53 A1
Walthamstow E17 ... 53 A5
Wanstead E11 ... 55 A4
Wimbledon SW19 ... 157 C2
Wellington Row E2 ... 96 A4
Wellington Sq
SW3 ... 114 D1 257 C2
Wellington St
[1] Barking IG11 ... 101 A6
WC2 ... 116 B6 250 C6
Woolwich SE18 ... 122 C2
Wellington Terr
Harrow HA1 ... 42 B1
[2] Wapping E1 ... 118 B5
Wellington Way E3 ... 97 C4
Welling Way DA16 ... 145 B2
Well La SW14 ... 155 A6
Wellmead IG3 ... 58 A2
Wellmeadow Rd
Brentford W7 ... 109 A2
Catford SE13, SE6 ... 164 C3
Wellow Wlk SM5 ... 202 B1
Well Rd Barnet EN5 ... 12 C6
Vale of Health NW3 ... 70 B5
Wells Cl
[2] Northolt UB5 ... 84 C4
South Croydon CR2 ... 221 C3
Wells Ct
[21] Hampstead
NW3 ... 70 A4
[4] Mitcham CR4 ... 180 C2
[1] Paddington NW6 ... 91 C5
Stoke Newington N1 ... 73 C3
Wells Dr NW9 ... 45 B1
Wells Gdns
Dagenham RM10 ... 81 D3
Redbridge IG1 ... 56 A2
Wells Ho
[4] Barking IG11 ... 80 A1
Ealing W5 ... 109 D6
Finsbury EC1 ... 234 C2
[12] Kensal Town W10 ... 91 A3
New Cross Gate SE4 ... 141 A3
Plaistow BR1 ... 187 B5
[9] Rotherhithe
SE16 ... 118 C3
Wells Ho The [2]
NW3 ... 70 B4
Wells House Rd
NW10 ... 89 C2
Wellside Gdns
SW14 ... 155 A6
Wells Mews W1 ... 239 B2
Wellsmoor Gdns
BR1 ... 210 C6
Wells Park Ct SE26 ... 184 B6
Wells Park Rd SE26 ... 184 B6
Wells Pl SW18 ... 158 A4
Wells Prim Sch IG8 ... 37 A6
Wellspring Cres HA9 ... 66 D5
Wells Rd BR1 ... 188 B1
Hammersmith W12 ... 112 C4
Wells Rise
NW8 ... 92 D6 230 C5
Wells Sq WC1 ... 233 D1
Wells St W1 ... 93 C1 239 B2
Wellstead Ave N9 ... 18 D4
Wellstead Rd E6 ... 100 C5
Wells Terr N4 ... 72 C6
Well St E9 ... 74 C1
Wells The N14 ... 15 D4
Well St E15 ... 76 C2
Wells Way
Brompton
SW7 ... 114 B3 256 C6
Camberwell SE5 ... 139 C6
Well Wlk NW3 ... 70 B5
Wellwood Ct SW15 ... 134 C1
Wellwood Rd IG3 ... 58 A2
Welmar Works
SW4 ... 137 D1
Welsby Ct W5 ... 87 C2
Welsford St SE1 ... 118 A2
Welsh Cl E13 ... 99 A4
WELSH HARP ... 45 C1
Welsh Harp Field
Centre NW9 ... 45 B1
Welsh Ho [14] E1 ... 118 B5
Welshpool Ho [22] E8 ... 96 A6
Welshpool St [1] E8 ... 96 B6
Welshside NW9 ... 45 C3
Welshside Wlk NW9 ... 45 C3
Welstead Ho [20] E1 ... 96 B1
Welstead Way W4 ... 111 D2
Weltje Rd W6 ... 112 A1
Welton Ct SE5 ... 139 C4

Welton Ho E1 ... 96 D2
Welton Rd SE18 ... 145 C5
Welwyn Ave TW14 ... 149 D5
Welwyn St E2 ... 96 C4
Welwyn Way UB4 ... 83 C3
WEMBLEY ... 65 D2
Wembley Arena HA9 ... 66 C4
Wembley Central Sta
HA9 ... 66 A3
Wembley Commercial
Ctr HA9 ... 65 D6
Wembley Conference
Ctr HA9 ... 66 C4
Wembley Exhibition
Halls HA9 ... 66 C4
Wembley High Tech
Coll HA0 ... 65 C5
Wembley Hill Rd
HA9 ... 66 B4
Wembley Hospl HA0 ... 65 D2
Wembley Mkt
[1] Wembley HA0 ... 66 A3
[1] Wembley Pk HA9 ... 66 C4
WEMBLEY PARK ... 66 C5
Wembley Park Bsns Ctr
HA9 ... 66 D5
Wembley Park Dr
HA9 ... 66 B5
Wembley Park Sta
HA9 ... 66 C5
Wembley Prim Sch
HA9 ... 66 A5
Wembley Rd TW12 ... 173 C2
Wembley Stadium Ind
Est
Wembley HA9 ... 66 C5
Wembley HA9 ... 66 D4
Wembley Stadium Sta
HA9 ... 66 B3
Wembley Stadium
HA9 ... 66 C3
Wembley Way HA9 ... 66 D2
Wembley HA0 ... 65 D2
Wemborough Rd
HA7 ... 25 C3
Wembury Mews N6 ... 49 C2
Wembury Rd N6 ... 49 B2
Wemyss Rd SE3 ... 142 D3
Wendela Ct HA1 ... 64 C6
Wendell Park Prim Sch
W12 ... 111 D4
Wendell Rd W12 ... 111 D4
Wenderholme CR2 ... 221 B3
Wendle Ct SW8 ... 270 A5
Wendling NW5 ... 70 D3
Wendling Rd SM1 ... 218 B6
Wendon Ct [13] SM6 ... 219 C2
Wendon St E3 ... 97 B6
Wendover Cl UB4 ... 85 A3
Wendover Ct
Acton W3 ... 88 D3
Becontree W3 ... 89 A3
Bromley BR2 ... 209 B6
[4] Child's Hill NW2 ... 69 C5
W1 ... 238 A3
Wendover Dr KT3 ... 199 D3
Wendover Ho
Bowes Pk N22 ... 32 B5
W1 ... 238 A3
Wendover Lo NW9 ... 45 D3
Wendover Rd
Blackheath SE9 ... 143 D2
Bromley BR1, BR2 ... 209 B6
Dagenham NW10 ... 89 D5
Wendover
SE17 ... 117 C1 263 A1
Wendover Way
Bexley DA16 ... 146 A1
Bushey WD23 ... 8 A5
Wendy Cl EN1 ... 17 D5
Wendy Ho [3] N12 ... 30 B5
Wendy Way HA0 ... 88 A6
Wengham Ho W12 ... 112 A6
Wenham Ho SW8 ... 269 A3
Wenlake Ho EC1 ... 242 A6
Wenlock Ct N1 ... 235 D3
Wenlock Gdns [13]
NW4 ... 46 A5
Wenlock Rd
Burnt Oak HA8 ... 27 A4
Shoreditch
N1 ... 95 A5 235 B3
Wenlock St
N1 ... 95 B5 235 C3
Wennington Rd E3 ... 96 D5
Wensdale Ho E5 ... 74 A6
Wensley Ave IG8 ... 37 A3
Wensley Cl
[6] Barnet N11 ... 31 A4
SE9 ... 166 B5
Wensleydale Gdns
TW12 ... 173 D3
Wensleydale Ho [8]
N4 ... 51 A2

Wensleydale Rd
TW12 .... 173 D3
Wensley Rd N18 .... 34 B4
Wentland Cl SE6 .... 164 B2
Wentland Rd SE6 .... 164 B2
Wentway Ct W13 .... 87 A3
Wentwood Ho 1 E5 ... 74 B6
Wentworth Ave
Borehamwood
WD6 .... 10 B6
Finchley N3 .... 29 C3
Wentworth Cl
Ashford TW15 .... 170 D6
Finchley N3 .... 29 D3
Hayes BR2 .... 225 A6
Long Ditton KT6 .... 213 D6
Morden SM4 .... 201 C2
Orpington BR6 .... 227 C3
Thamesmead SE28 .. 102 D1
Wentworth Cres
Hayes UB3 .... 105 B3
SE15 .... 140 A5
Wentworth Ct
Barnet EN5 .... 1 A2
7 Chingford E4 .... 36 B5
20 Kingston u T KT6 . 198 A4
Southall UB2 .... 106 C2
2 Surbiton KT6 .... 214 A6
Twickenham TW2 .... 152 C1
W6 .... 264 A5
Wandsworth SW18 .. 157 D5
Wentworth Dr HA5 .... 40 A4
Wentworth Dwellings
E1 .... 243 C2
Wentworth Gdns
N13 .... 16 D1
Wentworth Hall NW7 .. 28 C5
Wentworth Hill HA9 ... 44 B1
Wentworth Ho
Enfield EN1 .... 17 C5
4 Greenwich SE3 ... 143 A5
Wentworth Lo N3 .... 29 D3
Wentworth Mews E3 .. 97 B4
Wentworth Pk N3 .... 29 D3
Wentworth Pl HA7 .... 25 B4
Wentworth Rd
Manor Pk E12 .... 77 D4
Southall UB2 .... 106 D2
Temple Fortune
NW11 .... 47 B3
Thornton Heath CR0 . 204 C2
Wentworth St
E1 .... 95 D2 243 D3
Wentworth Tutorial Coll
NW11 .... 46 D3
Wentworth Way HA5 .. 41 A5
Wenvoe Ave DA7 .... 147 D3
Wepham Cl UB4 .... 84 D2
Wernbrook St SE18 .. 145 A6
Werndee Rd SE25 .... 206 A5
Werneth Hall Rd IG5 .. 56 C6
Werrington St
NW1 .... 93 C5 232 B3
Werter Rd SW15 .... 135 A1
Wesleyan Pl NW5 .... 71 B4
Wesley Ave
Becontree NW10 .... 89 B4
Hounslow TW3 .... 129 B3
Newham E16 .... 121 B5
Wesley Cl
Finsbury Pk N7 .... 72 B6
Harrow HA2 .... 64 A6
SE17 .... 261 D3
Wesley Ct W1 .... 238 B3
Wesley Ho SE24 .... 161 B5
Wesley Rd
Becontree NW10 .... 89 A6
Finchley N10 .... 30 C2
Hayes UB3 .... 84 A1
Leytonstone E10 .... 54 A2
Wesley Sq W11 .... 91 A1
Wesley St W1 .... 238 B3
Wessex Ave SW19 .... 201 C6
Wessex Cl
Hinchley Wood KT10,
KT7 .... 212 D6
Ilford IG3 .... 57 C3
Kingston u T KT1,
KT2 .... 176 D2
Wessex Ct
Putney SW15 .... 156 D6
5 Stanwell TW19 .... 148 A5
Wembley HA9 .... 66 B6
Wessex Dr HA5 .... 23 A3
Wessex Gardens Prim
Sch NW11 .... 47 A1
Wessex Gdns NW11 ... 47 A1
Wessex Ho SE1 .... 263 D1
4 Tufnell Pk N19 .... 71 D5
Wessex La UB6 .... 86 B5
Wessex St E2 .... 96 C4
Wessex Way NW11 .... 47 A1
Wesson Ho 3 CR0 ... 206 A1
West 12 Sh Ctr
W12 .... 112 D4
Westacott Cl N19 .... 49 D1
Westacott UB4 .... 83 C2
WEST ACTON 88 C1
West Acton Prim Sch
W3 .... 88 D1
West Acton Sta W3 ... 88 C1
West App BR5 .... 211 A4
West Arbour St E1 .... 96 D1
West Ave
East Finchley N2 .... 47 D6
Finchley N3 .... 29 C4
Hayes UB3 .... 105 D6
Hendon NW4 .... 46 D4
West Avenue Rd E17 .. 53 D5
West Ave Pinner HA5 ... 41 B2
Southall UB1 .... 107 B6
Wallington SM6 .... 220 A3
Walthamstow E17 .... 53 D4
West Bank
Barking IG11 .... 100 D6
Enfield EN2 .... 5 A3
Westbank Rd TW12 .. 174 A4
West Bank N16 .... 51 C2
WEST BARNES 200 C4
West Barnes La KT3,
SW20 .... 200 B5
WEST BEDFONT 148 B4
Westbeech Rd N22 .... 50 C6
Westbere Ct HA7 .... 25 D5
Westbere Dr HA7 .... 25 D5
Westbere Rd NW2 .... 69 A3
West Block 18 E1 .... 118 C6
Westbourne Ave
Cheam SM3 .... 217 A6
Dagenham W3 .... 89 B1
Westbourne Cl UB4 ... 84 C3
Westbourne Cres
W2 .... 246 C6
Westbourne Ct
Cheam SM3 .... 217 A6
W2 .... 236 A2
Westbourne Dr
SE23 .... 162 D2
Westbourne Gdns
W2 .... 91 D1
WESTBOURNE GREEN
.... 91 D3
Westbourne Gr Mews
7 W11 .... 91 C1
Westbourne Gr W2,
W11 .... 91 C1
Westbourne Gr Terr
W2 .... 91 D1
Westbourne Gr
W11 .... 113 B6 244 D6
Westbourne Ho
Heston TW5 .... 129 C6
SW1 .... 258 C2
8 Twickenham
TW1 .... 153 B4
Westbourne Par 4
UB10 .... 82 D3
Westbourne Park Rd
Notting Hill W2 .... 91 C1
Notting Hill W11 .... 91 B1
Westbourne Park Sta
W11 .... 91 B2
Westbourne Park Villas
W2 .... 91 D2
Westbourne Pl N9 .... 18 B1
Westbourne Prim Sch
SM1 .... 217 C5
Westbourne Rd
Barnsbury N7 .... 72 B2
Croydon CR0 .... 205 D3
DA7 .... 147 A5
Feltham TW13 .... 149 D1
Hillingdon UB8 .... 82 D3
Penge SE26 .... 184 D4
Westbourne St
W2 .... 114 B6 246 C6
Westbourne Terrace
Mews W2 .... 236 A2
Westbourne Terrace Rd
W2 .... 92 A2 236 A3
Westbourne Terr
W2 .... 92 A1 236 B2
Westbridge Cl W12 .. 112 A5
Westbridge Prim Sch
SW11 .... 267 A2
Westbridge Rd
SW11 .... 136 C4 267 A2
WEST BROMPTON .. 135 D6
West Brompton Sta
SW5 .... 113 C1 255 B1
Westbrook Ave
TW12 .... 173 B3
Westbrook Cl EN4 .... 2 B2
Westbrook Cres EN4 ... 2 B2
Westbrook Ct SE3 .... 143 B4
Westbrooke Cres
DA16 .... 146 C2
Westbrooke Rd
Bexley DA16 .... 146 C2
DA15 .... 167 B2
Westbrooke Sch
DA16 .... 146 D2
Westbrook Ho
5 Bethnal Green
E2 .... 96 C4
5 Clapham Pk SW4 . 159 C6
Westbrook Rd
Heston TW5 .... 129 B5
SE3 .... 143 B4
South Norwood CR7 .. 183 B1
Westbrook Sq EN4 .... 2 B2
West Brow BR7 .... 188 D5
Westbury Ave
Claygate KT10 .... 212 D2
Southall UB1 .... 85 C3
Tottenham N22 .... 32 D1
Wembley HA0 .... 66 A1
Westbury Cl
Ruislip HA4 .... 40 A2
Shepperton TW17 ... 192 D3
Westbury Ct
3 Barking IG11 .... 101 B6
Beckenham BR3 .... 185 D2
1 Buckhurst Hill IG9 .. 21 C2
Clapham SW4 .... 159 B5
11 New Barnet EN5 ... 14 A6
Tottenham N22 .... 33 A1
Westbury Gr N12 .... 29 C4
Westbury House Sch
KT3 .... 199 B4
Westbury Ho
1 Walthamstow
E17 .... 53 C5
6 Willesden NW10 ... 67 C1
Westbury La IG9 .... 21 C2
Westbury Lodge Cl
HA5 .... 40 D6
Westbury Pl 2
TW8 .... 131 D6
Westbury Rd
Barking IG11 .... 101 B6
Beckenham BR3 .... 207 A6
Bowes Pk N11 .... 32 A4
Bromley BR1 .... 187 D2
Buckhurst Hill IG9 .... 21 C3
Ealing W5 .... 88 A1
Feltham TW13 .... 150 D3
Finchley N12 .... 29 D5
Ilford IG1 .... 78 C6
New Malden KT3 .... 199 B4
Penge SE20 .... 184 D2
Thornton Heath CR0 .. 205 B3
Upton E7 .... 77 B2
Walthamstow E17 .... 53 C5
Wembley HA0 .... 66 A1
Westbury Terr E7 .... 77 B2
Westbush Ct 1
W12 .... 112 B4
West Carriage Dr
W2 .... 114 C5 247 A4
West Central St
WC1 .... 240 A2
West Chantry HA3 .... 23 D2
Westchester Ct NW4 .. 46 D6
Westchester Dr NW4 .. 46 D6
Westchester Ho W2. 237 C1
West Cl
Ashford TW15 .... 170 A6
Barnet EN5 .... 12 B6
Cockfosters EN4 .... 3 A1
Edmonton N9 .... 17 D1
Greenford UB6 .... 86 A5
Hampton TW12 .... 173 A4
Westcliff Ho 13 N1 .... 73 B2
West Cl HA9 .... 44 B1
Westcombe Ave
CR0 .... 204 B2
Westcombe Ct 1
SE3 .... 142 D5
Westcombe Dr EN5 ... 13 C6
Westcombe Hill SE3,
SE10 .... 143 A6
Westcombe Lodge Dr
UB4 .... 83 B2
Westcombe Park Rd
SE3 .... 142 D5
Westcombe Park Sta
SE3 .... 121 A1
West Common Rd
BR2 .... 225 B5
Westcoombe Ave
SW20 .... 177 D2
Westcote Rd SW16 ... 181 C5
Westcote Rise HA4 .... 39 A2
Westcott Cl BR1 .... 210 A4
2 South Tottenham
N15 .... 51 D3
Westcott Cres W7 .... 86 C2
Westcott Ho 1 E14 .. 119 D6
Westcott Rd SE17 .... 138 D6
West Cotts NW6 .... 69 C3
Westcroft Cl
Enfield EN3 .... 6 C5
West Hampstead
NW2 .... 69 A4
Westcroft Ct
3 Chiswick W6 .... 112 A2
Westcroft Ct *continued*
Kingsbury NW9 .... 44 D4
Westcroft Gdns
SM4 .... 201 B5
Westcroft Ho 2
SM5 .... 219 A4
Westcroft Rd SM5,
SM6 .... 219 A4
Westcroft Sq W6 .... 112 A2
Westcroft 1 SM5 .... 219 A4
Westcroft Way NW2 ... 69 A4
West Cromwell Rd
W14 .... 113 B1 254 D2
West Cross Ctr
TW8 .... 131 B6
West Cross Route W10,
W11 .... 112 D6
West Cross Way
TW8 .... 131 B6
West Croydon Sta
CR9 .... 205 A1
West Ct
Hounslow TW7 .... 130 A5
Sunbury TW16 .... 172 B1
Walthamstow E17 .... 53 D5
Wembley HA0 .... 65 C6
Westdale Rd SE18 .... 144 D6
Westdean Ave SE12 .. 165 C3
Westdean Cl SW18 ... 157 D5
Westdown Rd
Catford SE6 .... 163 C4
Leyton E15 .... 76 A4
WEST DRAYTON 104 B4
West Drayton Park Ave
UB7 .... 104 A3
West Drayton Prim Sch
UB7 .... 104 A4
West Drayton Rd
UB8 .... 82 D1
West Drayton Sta
UB7 .... 104 A5
West Drive Gdns
HA3 .... 24 B4
West Dr
Stanmore HA3 .... 24 B4
Streatham SW16 .... 181 C6
WEST DULWICH 161 A2
West Dulwich Sta
SE21 .... 161 B3
WEST EALING 109 B5
West Ealing Bsns Ctr
W13 .... 109 A6
West Ealing Sta
W13 .... 109 B6
West Eaton Pl Mews
SW1 .... 258 A4
West Eaton Pl SW1 .. 258 A4
West Ella Rd NW10 .... 67 C1
West End Ave
Leytonstone E10 .... 54 B4
Pinner HA5 .... 40 D5
West End Cl
Stonebridge NW10 .... 67 A1
Willesden NW10 .... 67 A1
West End Ct
Hampstead NW6 .... 69 D1
Pinner HA5 .... 40 D5
West End Gdns UB5 ... 84 C5
West End La
Hampstead NW6 .... 69 D2
Harlington UB7 .... 127 A5
Pinner HA5 .... 40 D5
West End Rd
Ruislip HA4, UB5 .... 62 A4
Ruislip UB5 .... 62 C1
Southall UB1 .... 107 A5
Westerdale Ct N5 .... 72 D4
Westerdale Rd 2
SE10 .... 121 A1
Westerfield Rd 1
N15 .... 51 D4
Westergate W5 .... 88 A2
Westergate Rd SE2 .. 147 A6
Westerham Ave N9 ... 17 C1
Westerham Dr
DA15 .... 168 C5
Westerham Ho SE1 . 262 D6
Westerham 18 KT6 .. 198 A4
Westerham Lo 10
BR3 .... 185 C3
Westerham NW1 .... 232 A5
Westerham Rd
Keston BR2 .... 225 D2
Walthamstow E10 .... 53 D2
Westerley Cres
SE26 .... 185 B5
Westerley Ct HA4 .... 62 B3
Western Ave
Dagenham W3 .... 89 B1
Hendon NW11 .... 46 D3
Hillingdon HA4, UB4, UB5,
UB10 .... 61 C1
Northolt UB5, UB6 .... 85 B6
Western Avenue Bsns
Pk W3 .... 88 D3
Western Ave
Ruislip UB8, UB9,
UB10 .... 60 B3
Wembley UB6 .... 87 C4
Western Beach Apts
E16 .... 121 A5
Western Ct
4 Dagenham W3 .... 89 B1
Finchley N3 .... 29 C4
3 Kilburn W9 .... 91 B5
Southall UB2 .... 107 A3
Western Dr TW17 .... 193 B3
Western Eye Hospl The
NW1 .... 92 D2 237 C4
Western Gateway
E16 .... 121 A6
Western Gdns W5 .... 110 C6
Western Ho 3 W9 .... 91 B3
Western Hts SM1 .... 217 C3
Western International
Market UB2 .... 106 B2
Western La SW12 .... 159 A4
Western Mews W9 .... 91 B3
Western Par EN5 .... 13 D6
Western Pl 19 SE16 .. 118 C4
Western Rd
Becontree NW10 .... 89 A3
Brixton SW9 .... 138 C2
Ealing W5 .... 109 D6
Fortis Green N2 .... 48 D5
Mitcham CR4, SW19 . 180 C1
Newham E13 .... 99 C5
Southall UB2 .... 106 D2
Sutton SM1 .... 217 C3
Walthamstow E17 .... 54 A4
Wood Green N22 .... 32 B1
Western Terr 3
W6 .... 112 A1
Western View UB3 .. 105 D4
Westernville Gdns
IG2 .... 57 A2
Western Way
New Barnet EN5 .... 13 D5
Plumstead SE28 .... 123 C4
Western Wharf 2
SE15 .... 140 A6
WEST EWELL 215 C1
West Ewell Inf Sch
KT19 .... 215 B3
West Farm Ct EN4 .... 2 D2
Westferry Cir E14 .... 119 C5
Westferry Rd E14 .... 119 C3
Westferry Sta E14 .. 119 C6
Westfield 1 BR6 .... 227 A3
Westfield Cl
Cheam SM1 .... 217 B4
Enfield EN3 .... 7 A2
Kingsbury NW9 .... 45 A6
SW10 .... 266 A3
Westfield Ct
1 Kensal Green
W10 .... 90 D4
Kingston u T KT6 .... 197 D4
Westfield Dr HA3 .... 43 D5
Westfield Gdns
Harrow HA3 .... 43 D5
Ilford RM6 .... 58 C3
Westfield Ho 6
SE16 .... 118 D2
Westfield La HA3 .... 43 D5
Westfield IG10 .... 21 C6
Westfield Pk HA5 .... 23 B3
Westfield Rd
Beckenham BR3 .... 185 B1
Cheam SM1 .... 217 B4
Croydon CR0 .... 220 D6
Dagenham RM9 .... 81 B4
Ealing W13 .... 109 A5
Edgware NW7 .... 11 C1
Kingston u T KT6 .... 197 D4
Mitcham CR4 .... 180 D1
Walton-on-T KT12 .... 195 A2
Westfields Ave
SW13 .... 133 C2
Westfields SW13 .... 133 D2
Westfields Rd W3 .... 88 D2
Westfield St SE18 .... 121 D3
Westfield Way
Mile End E1 .... 97 A3
Ruislip HA4 .... 61 D5
Westfield NW3 .... 69 C4
West Finchley Sta
N3 .... 29 D4
West Garden Pl W2 . 237 B1
Westgate Bsns Ctr
2 Kensal Town
W10 .... 91 A3
North Kensington
W10 .... 90 D3
Westgate Ct
6 Beckenham
BR3 .... 186 A2
15 Brixton SW9 .... 138 C2
Lewisham SE12 .... 165 A3
West Gate W5 .... 88 A4
Westgate Est TW14 . 148 D3
Westgate Rd
Beckenham BR3 ....
Croydon SE25 ....
Westgate St E8 ....
Westgate Terr
SW10 .... 135 D
West Gdns
Mitcham SW19 ....
Stepney E1 ....
Westglade Ct HA3 ....
WEST GREEN ....
West Green Pl UB6 ....
West Green Prim Sc
N15 ....
West Green Rd N15 ....
West Gr SE10 ....
Westgrove La SE10 ....
West Grove Prim Sc
N14 ....
West Gr IG8 ....
West Halkin St
SW1 .... 115 A3
West Hallowes SE9 ..
West Hall Rd TW9 ..
WEST HAM ....
West Ham Church P
Sch E15 ....
West Ham La E15 ..
WEST HAMPSTEAD
West Hampstead Me
NW6 ....
West Hampstead Sta
NW6 ....
West Hampstead
Thameslink Sta
NW6 ....
West Ham Sta E15 ..
West Harding St
EC4 ....
WEST HARROW ...
West Harrow Sta
HA1 ....
West Hatch Manor
HA4 ....
Westhaven SM1 ....
Westhay Gdns
SW14 ....
WEST HEATH ....
West Heath Ave
NW11 ....
West Heath Cl NW3 .
West Heath Ct NW11
West Heath Dr NW11
West Heath Gdns
NW3 ....
West Heath Rd
SE2, DA7 ....
West Hampstead
NW3 ....
WEST HENDON ....
WEST HILL ....
West Hill Ct N6 ....
Westhill Ct W11 ....
West Hill Hall HA2 ..
West Hill Harrow HA2
Highgate N6 ....
Westhill Pk
Dartmouth Pk N6 ....
Highgate N6 ....
West Hill Prim Sch
SW18 ....
West Hill SW15 ....
West Hill Rd SW18 ..
West Hill CR2 ....
West Hill Way N20 ..
West Hill HA9 ....
West Ho IG11 ....
Westholme BR6 ....
Westholme Gdns
HA4 ....
Westholm NW11 ....
Westhope Ho 29 E2 ..
West Ho 4 SE20 ....
Westhorne Ave SE9,
SE12 ....
Westhorpe Gdns
NW4 ....
Westhorpe Rd
SW15 ....
West Ho 9 SW12 ....
West House Cl
SW19 ....
Westhurst Dr BR7 ..
West India Ave E14 ..
West India Dock Rd
E14 ....
West India Ho 1
E14 ....
West India Quay Sta
E14 ....
WEST KENSINGTON
....
West Kensington Ct
W14 ....
West Kensington Ma
W14 ....

ensington Sta
..... 113 B1 254 C2
KILBURN 91 A4
ke Cl
UB4.......... 85 A3
rs Green N13....16 C1
ke Rd HA9 .....65 D6
ke 12 SE16 ....118 C2
nd Cl TW19 ...148 A5
nd Ct 9 UB5 ...84 D4
nd Dr
R4 ....224 D6
nd Ho 1
.............122 C5
nd Lo 1 BR1..187 C1
nd Pl N1....... 235 C2
nds Cl UB3....106 A2
nds Ct KT8....196 C5
nds Terr 3
.............159 C5
a SE16 ....118 B4
a Rd W7 ......109 A3
ea Sch N9 .....17 C1
igh Ave
.............156 C6
igh Ct
ey N12 ....29 D4
nstead E11 ......55 A4
igh Dr BR1....188 A2
igh Gdns
.............26 C1
inks HA0.........87 D4
nton Cl NW7....29 A4
odge Ave
.............110 C5
odge Ct W3...110 C5
odge Fst & Mid
HA5...........40 D5
odge Sch
.... 168 A1
ondon Acad
olt UB5.........63 A1
olt UB5..........85 A6
ondon Shooting
nds UB5 ....84 B5
Ct NW2........68 D2
Ho N9.........18 B3
acott Dr
.............149 D3
acott Ho
.... 236 D5
Hall W11 ..... 245 B4
ark Point 13
.............156 B3
ead Cnr SM5..218 C4
ead SW15.....156 B5
ead Rd SM1...218 B4
ead
HA4 ....62 C4
Ewell KT19...... 215 C2
eath Ho
.............68 A5
ere Dr NW7 .... 11 B1
ersea Cl 9
.............121 B5
ews SW1.... 259 A3
iddlesex Univ
TW7 .... 131 A3
ill Ct N4 ....73 A6
MINSTER 115 C4
inster Abbey
Sch
...... 115 D3 259 D6
inster Abbey*
...... 116 A3 260 A6
inster Acad
...... 92 C2 237 A4
inster Acad
of English)
.......93 C1 239 B2
inster Ave
.............182 D1
inster Boating
SW1.......... 269 C6
inster Bridge Rd
.......116 B4 250 C1
inster Bridge
W1....116 A4 250 B1
inster Cath Choir
SW1... 115 C2 259 B4
inster Cath RC
Sch
...... 115 D1 259 D2
inster Cath*
...... 115 C3 259 A5
inster City Hall
.... 259 B6
inster City Sch
.... 259 B6
inster Cl
Bedfont
4 .... 150 A3
gton TW11.... 175 A5
inster Coll of
puting HA9.....66 A3

Westminster Ct
22 Rotherhithe
SE16............ 118 D5
South Norwood CR7 . 183 A1
5 Wandsworth
SW18.......... 157 C6
Wanstead E11........ 55 B3
Westminster Dr N13 ..32 A5
Westminster Gdns
Barking IG11....... 101 C5
Chingford E4.........20 C3
SW1............... 260 A4
Westminster Ind Est
SE18............ 121 D3
Westminster Kingsway
Coll SW11 . 137 A4 268 B2
Westminster Kingsway
Coll (Regent's Park
Ctr) NW1 ... 93 C3 239 A6
Westminster Kingsway
Coll WC1 ....94 B4 233 C1
Westminster Pier
SW1.............. 250 B1
Westminster Rd
Carshalton SM1......218 B6
Ealing W7 .... 108 C5
Edmonton N9.........18 B3
Westminster Sch
SW1....... 116 A3 260 A6
Westminster Sta
SW1....... 116 A4 250 B1
Westminster Under Sch
SW1....... 115 D2 259 C3
Westmoat Cl BR3 ......186 A3
WEST MOLESEY 195 C5
Westmont Rd KT10...212 C6
Westmoor Gdns EN3 ... 6 D3
Westmoor Rd EN3 .... 6 D3
Westmoor St SE7 ....121 D3
Westmore Ct SW15 ...157 A6
Westmoreland Ave
DA16 ....145 C1
Westmoreland Dr
SM2...............217 D1
Westmoreland Ho
NW10................90 A4
Westmoreland Pl
5 Bromley BR1 .... 209 A6
Ealing W5 ....87 D2
Pimlico SW1 .... 258 D1
Westmoreland Rd
Barnes SW13 ...... 134 A4
Beckenham BR2,
BR3............ 208 D5
Bromley BR2 .... 209 A5
Camberwell SE17 ....139 B6
Queensbury NW9 .....44 B5
Westmoreland St
W1................ 238 B3
Westmoreland Terr
10 Penge SE20 ......184 B3
SW1....... 115 B1 258 D1
Westmorland Cl
3 Twickenham
TW1............153 B5
Wanstead E12........77 D6
Westmorland Ct
12 Surbiton KT6 .... 197 D2
Sutton SM1 .... 218 A5
Westmorland Rd
BR2 .... 209 A5
Harrow HA1 ....41 D4
Walthamstow E17 ......53 C3
Westmorland Way
CR4 ....203 D4
Westmount Ct W5 ....88 B2
Westmount Rd SE9...144 C1
WEST NORWOOD ...161 A1
West Norwood Sta
SE27.............. 160 D1
West Oak BR3 ....186 B2
Westoe Rd N9 ....18 B2
Weston Ave
East Molesey KT8 ....195 B5
Thames Ditton KT10,
KT7............. 196 C2
Westonbirt Ct 6
SE15...............139 D6
Weston Ct
Highbury N4 ....73 A5
3 Kingston u T KT1 . 198 A6
Oakleigh Pk N20 ......14 A4
Weston Dr HA7 ....25 B2
Weston Ed Ctr The
SE5............... 139 A3
West One Ho W1.... 239 A3
Westone Mans 6
IG11.................79 D1
West One Sh Ctr
W1.........93 B1 238 C1
Weston Gdns TW7 ....130 C4
Weston Gn
Dagenham RM9.......81 B4
Thames Ditton KT7 .. 196 C1
Weston Gr 1 BR1....186 D2
WESTON GREEN 196 D1

Weston Green Prep Sch
KT7 .... 196 C1
Weston Green Rd
KT7 ....196 C2
Weston Ho
6 Brondesbury
NW6..............69 A1
8 South Hackney E9 ..96 C6
Weston Lo KT7 ......196 D1
Weston Park Cl
KT7 ....196 C1
Weston Park Prim Sch
N8 ....50 B4
Weston Pk
Hornsey Vale N8 ......50 B3
Kingston u T KT1 ..... 176 A1
Thames Ditton KT10,
KT7............. 196 C1
Weston Rd
Acton Green W4 .... 111 A3
Bromley BR1 .... 186 D3
Dagenham RM9.......81 A4
Enfield EN2 ....5 B3
Thames Ditton KT7 .. 196 C1
Weston Rise N1,
WC1.........94 B4 233 D2
Weston St
SE1.........117 B4 252 D2
Weston Wlk 3 E8, E9.. 74 B1
Westover Hill NW3.....69 C6
Westover Rd SW18...158 A5
Westow Hill SE19 ....183 D4
Westow St SE19......183 C4
West Park Ave TW9 ..132 D4
West Park Cl
Heston TW5.........129 B6
Ilford RM6............58 D4
Westpark W5..........87 D1
West Park Rd
Richmond TW9...... 132 C4
Southall UB2 ....108 B5
West Parkside
Greenwich SE10 .... 120 D3
Greenwich SE10 .... 121 A2
West Pk SE9.........166 A3
West Plaza E14 ......119 D5
West Pl SW19........178 C5
Westpoint Apartments
N8 ....50 B5
Westpoint
Beckenham BR2 .....208 B6
Putney SW15........ 156 D5
West Point 2 SE1....118 A1
Westpoint Trad Est
W3..................88 D2
Westpole Ave EN4 ..... 3 B1
Westport Ct UB4 ......84 C3
Westport Rd E13 ......99 B3
Westport St E1 ....96 D1
West Poultry Ave
EC1 .... 241 C3
West Quarters W12 ....90 A1
West Quay Dr UB4 ....85 A2
West Ramp TW6 .....126 C4
West Rd
Chelsea
SW3..... 136 D6 267 D6
Clapham Pk SW4..... 159 D6
Dagenham RM6........59 A3
Ealing W5 ....88 A2
East Barnet EN4 ......15 A3
East Bedfont TW14 ...149 B4
Finchley N2 ....30 B2
Kingston u T KT2,
KT3............. 177 A2
Tottenham N17 ....34 B4
West Drayton UB7.....104 B3
West Ham E15........98 D6
West Ridge Gdns
UB6 ....86 A5
Westrow Dr IG11 .....80 A2
Westrow Gdns IG3 ....79 D5
Westrow SW15 ......156 C5
West Row W10 ....91 A3
WEST RUISLIP 61 B6
West Ruislip Ct HA4...61 B6
West Ruislip
Elementary Sch
UB10 ....61 A5
West Ruislip Sta HA4 .61 A6
West Sheen Vale
TW9...............132 B1
West Side Comm
SW19..............178 C5
Westside Ct 1 W9....91 C3
Westside
11 Hammersmith
W6............. 112 A2
Hendon NW4..........28 B1
Muswell Hill N2.......48 D6
West Silvertown Sta
E16............... 121 A5
West Smithfield
EC1 ....94 D2 241 D3
West Sq
SE11.......116 D3 261 C5

West St
30 Bethnal Green
E2.................96 B5
Bexleyheath DA7.....147 B2
Bromley BR1 .... 187 A1
Carshalton SM5...... 218 D4
Croydon CR0 .... 221 A4
Harrow HA1 ....42 C1
Leyton E11...........76 C5
West Street La SM5 ..218 D4
West Street Pl 1
CR0 ....221 A4
West St
Soho WC2 ... 93 D1 239 D1
Sutton SM1 .... 217 D3
Walthamstow E17 .....53 D4
West Surrey Est
TW15............. 171 A2
West Sutton Sta
SM1 .... 217 C4
West Temple Sheen
SW14..............154 D6
West Tenter St
E1...........95 D1 243 D1
West Terr DA15 ......167 C3
West Thames Coll
TW7.............. 130 C4
West Thamesmead Bsns
Pk SE28 .... 123 D3
West Thornton Prim
Sch CR0 ....204 B3
West Towers HA5 .....40 D3
West Twyford Prim Sch
NW10...............88 C5
Westvale Mews W3 ..111 C4
Westview Cl
North Kensington
W10...............90 C1
Willesden NW10 ......67 D3
Westview Cres N9 ....17 C4
Westview Ct
3 Elstree WD6........9 D5
1 Whetstone N20 ....14 A2
West View RM6 ....58 C4
Westview Dr IG8......37 D1
Westview W7..........86 C1
West View TW14 .....149 A4
West View Gdns WD6... 9 D5
Westville Rd
Shepherd's Bush
W12 .... 112 A4
Thames Ditton KT7 .. 197 A2
Westward Rd E4 ......35 B5
Westward Way HA3 ....44 A3
West Warwick Pl
SW1............... 259 A3
West Way BR5 ....211 B4
Burnt Oak HA8 ....27 A4
Westway Cl SW20....200 B6
West Way CR0 ....223 A5
Westway Ct UB5 ......85 C6
West Way N18 ....33 B6
Westway (Elevated Rd)
W10.................91 B2
West Way Gdns
CR0 ....222 D6
West Way TW5........129 B4
Westway Lo 35 W2...91 C2
West Way
Neasden NW10.......67 B5
Pinner HA5 ....40 D5
Ruislip HA4 ....39 D1
Westway W10, W12...112 A6
West Way TW17......193 B3
West Ways HA6 ....22 A1
Westways KT19.......215 D4
Westway SW20 ....200 C5
West Way BR4 ....208 C3
Westwell 4 NW5 .....71 A2
Westwell Rd SW16...182 A4
Westwell Road App
SW16..............182 A4
Westwick Gdns
Cranford TW4,
TW5............. 128 B3
Hammersmith W14 .. 112 D4
WEST WICKHAM ...224 C6
West Wickham Sta
BR3 .... 208 A2
Westwick 7 KT1.....176 C1
West Wimbledon Prim
Sch SW20..........200 B6
West Wlk
East Barnet EN4 ......15 A3
Hayes UB3.......... 106 A5
Westwood Ave
Harrow HA2 ....63 D4
South Norwood
SE19............ 183 A2
Westwood Bsns Ctr
NW10...............89 C3
Westwood Cl BR1....209 D6
Esher KT10 .... 212 A5
Ruislip HA4 ....38 D3
Westwood Coll
DA16 .... 145 C1

Westwood Ct
Enfield EN1 ....17 C5
3 Forest Hill SE23.. 162 C3
7 Wimbledon
SW19...........179 B5
Westwood Gdns
SW13..............133 D2
Westwood Hill SE26..184 B6
Westwood Ho
6 Shepherd's Bush
W12........... 112 C5
5 Stoke Newington
N4 ....51 B2
Westwood La DA16...145 D1
Westwood Language
College for Girls
SE19..............183 B3
Westwood Lo N12.....30 C5
Westwood Park Trad
Est W3 ....88 D3
Westwood Pk SE23...162 B4
Westwood Pl SE26 ...184 A6
Westwood Rd
Barnes SW13 ...... 133 D2
Ilford IG3 ....58 A2
Westwood Sch WD23 .. 8 B2
West Woodside
DA5 ....169 A3
Wetheral Ct SW17 ...180 B6
Wetheral Dr HA7......25 C1
Wetherby Cl UB5......63 D2
Wetherby Ct SE25....183 C1
Wetherby Gdns
SW5.......114 A2 256 A3
Wetherby Mans
SW5.............. 255 C2
Wetherby Mews
SW5.............. 255 D2
Wetherby Pl
SW7........114 A2 256 B3
Wetherby Rd EN2 ...... 5 A4
Wetherby Way KT9...214 A1
Wetherden St E17.....53 B2
Wetherell Rd E9 ......96 D6
Wetherill Rd N10 .....31 A2
Wevco Wharf SE15....140 B6
Wexford Ho 11 E1.....96 C2
Wexford Rd SW12....158 D4
Weybourne St
SW18..............158 A2
Weybridge Ct 19
SE16...............118 B1
Weybridge Ho N4.....51 A2
Weybridge Point 11
SW11..............136 D3
Weybridge Rd CR7...204 C5
Wey Ct KT19.........215 A4
Weydown Cl SW19...157 A3
Weyhill Ho 26 SE5....139 A3
Weyhill Rd 11 E1......96 A1
Wey Ho
6 Northolt UB5 ......85 B3
NW8 .... 236 D5
Weylands Cl KT12....195 B1
Weylond Rd RM8......81 B5
Weyman Rd SE3 .....143 C4
Weymarks The N17....33 B4
Weymouth Ave
Brentford W5........ 109 C3
Edgware NW7 ....27 C5
Weymouth Cl 1 E6 ..100 D1
Weymouth Ct
Belmont SM2........ 217 C1
5 Haggerston E2.....95 D5
15 Streatham SW2...160 B4
Weymouth Ho
Bromley BR2 .... 186 D1
Edgware HA8.........26 B4
Fitzrovia W1 .... 238 D4
South Lambeth SW8 . 270 C3
Weymouth Mews
W1..........93 B2 238 C4
Weymouth Rd UB4....83 C4
Weymouth St
W1..........93 B2 238 C4
Weymouth Terr E2 ....95 D5
Weymouth Wlk HA7...25 A4
Whadcoat St N4 ......72 C6
Whaddon Ho
10 Camberwell
SE5............. 139 C2
SW1............... 247 D1
Whalebone Ave RM6 .. 59 B3
Whalebone Gr RM6 ... 59 B3
Whalebone La E15....76 C1
Whalebone Lane N
RM6................59 A6
Whalebone Lane S RM6,
RM8................59 B2
Whales Yd E15........76 C1
Wharfdale Cl N11.....31 A4
Wharfdale Rd
N1 ....94 A5 233 B4
Wharfedale Ct 5 E5 ..74 D4
Wharfedale Gdns CR7,
SW16..............204 B6

Wharfedale St SW10 255 C1
Wharf La
19 Poplar E14........97 B1
Twickenham TW1..... 153 A3
Wharf Pl E2 ....96 B6
Wharf Rd Enfield EN3 ..19 A5
King's Cross
NW1....... 93 D6 232 D5
Shoreditch
N1 .... 95 A5 235 A3
Wharf Road
NW1.........94 A5 233 A4
Wharfside Rd E16.....98 C2
Wharfside HA0 ....88 A6
Wharf St E16 ....98 C2
Wharf View Ct 15
E14.................98 A1
Wharncliffe Dr UB1 ..108 B5
Wharncliffe Gdns
SE25...............183 C1
Wharncliffe Ho 3
SW15..............156 C6
Wharncliffe Rd
SE25...............183 C1
Wharton Cl NW10......67 C2
Wharton Ho SE1.... 263 C6
Wharton Rd BR1......187 B2
Wharton St
WC1.........94 B4 233 D1
Whateley Rd
East Dulwich
SE22............ 161 D6
Penge SE20 .... 184 D3
Whatley Ave SW20 ...201 A6
Whatman Ho 10 E14... 97 B1
Whatman Rd SE23 ...162 D4
Wheatcroft Ct SM1...201 D1
Wheatfields
Enfield EN3 ....7 A3
Newham E6......... 100 D1
Wheatfield Way
KT1 ....176 A1
Wheathill Ho SE20 ...184 B1
Wheathill Rd SE20 ...206 B6
Wheat Ho TW19 .....148 A3
Wheatland Ho 7
SE22...............139 C2
Wheatlands TW5 ....129 C6
Wheatlands Rd
SW17..............159 A1
Wheatley Cl NW4 .....28 A1
Wheatley Cres UB3 ..106 A6
Wheatley Gdns N9 ....17 C2
Wheatley Ho
Gospel Oak NW5......71 B4
3 Putney SW15..... 156 A4
Wheatley Mans 8
IG11................80 A1
Wheatley Rd TW7.....130 D2
Wheatley St W1 .... 238 B3
Wheat Sheaf Cl
E14................119 D2
Wheatsheaf Cl UB5 ...63 A3
Wheatsheaf La
Fulham SW6 .... 134 C5
SW8............... 270 B4
Wheatsheaf Par 7
BR4 ....207 D1
Wheatsheaf Terr
SW6............... 264 D3
Wheatstone Cl
SW19..............180 C2
Wheatstone Ho 7
W10.................91 A2
Wheatstone Rd W10 ..91 A2
Wheeler Ct 5
SW11..............136 B2
Wheeler Gdns N1.... 233 B6
Wheeler La E1...... 243 C4
Wheeler 2 NW9......27 D3
Wheeler Pl 2 BR2 ...209 B5
Wheelers Cross
IG11...............101 B5
Wheelers Dr HA4 .....39 A3
Wheeler's St SM1....217 C5
Wheelhouse The 4
E14................119 D1
Wheelock Cl DA8 ....147 D5
Wheelwright St N7 ...72 B1
Whelan Way SM6 ....219 D5
Wheldon Ct SE1 .... 253 C2
Wheler Ho E1 ...... 243 C5
Wheler St E1 ..95 D3 243 C5
Whellock Rd W4.....111 C3
Whernside Cl SE28...124 C6
WHETSTONE 14 A2
Whetstone Cl N20 ....14 B2
Whetstone Park
WC2.........94 B1 240 C2
Whetstone Rd SE3 ...143 D4
Whewell Rd N19......72 A6
Whichcote St SE1.... 251 A3
Whidborne Bldgs
WC1.............. 233 A1

Whidborne Cl SE8 141 C3
Whidborne St WC1 233 B1
Whimbrel Cl SE28 124 C6
Whimbrel Way UB4 84 D2
Whinchat Rd SE18, SE28 123 B3
Whinfell Cl SW16 181 D5
Whinyates Rd SE9 144 A2
Whippendell Cl BR5 190 B2
Whippendell Way BR5 190 B1
Whippingham Ho 22 E3 97 B4
Whipps Cross Ho E17 54 B4
Whipps Cross Hospl E10, E11 54 B3
Whipps Cross E17 54 B4
Whipps Cross Rd E11 54 C3
Whiskin St EC1 94 D4 234 C1
Whisperwood Cl HA3 24 C3
Whistler Gdns HA8 26 B1
Whistler Mews
Dagenham RM8 80 B3
23 SE15 139 D5
Whistlers Ave SW11 136 B5 266 D3
Whistler St N5 72 D3
Whistler Twr SW10 266 A3
Whistler Wlk SW10 266 B4
Whiston Ho 18 N1 72 D1
Whiston Rd E2 96 A6
Whitakers Lo EN2 5 B4
Whitbread Cl N17 34 A2
Whitbread Ctr EC1 242 C5
Whitbread Rd SE4 141 B1
Whitburn Rd SE13 142 A1
Whitby Ave NW10 88 D4
Whitby Ct
6 Lower Holloway N7 72 A4
3 New Southgate N11 31 A4
Whitby Gdns
Carshalton SM1 218 B6
Queensbury NW9 44 C6
Whitby Ho NW8 229 A5
Whitby Par HA4 62 C6
Whitby Rd
Carshalton SM1 218 B6
Harrow HA2 64 A5
Ruislip HA4 62 C6
Woolwich SE18 122 B2
Whitby St E1 243 C6
Whitcher Cl SE14 141 A6
Whitcher Pl NW1 71 C2
Whitchurch Ave HA8 26 B3
Whitchurch Cl HA8 26 B4
Whitchurch Ct SW17 180 B6
Whitchurch Fst & Mid Schs HA7 25 D3
Whitchurch Gdns HA8 26 B4
Whitchurch Ho
Catford SE6 164 A1
16 North Kensington W10 90 D1
Whitchurch La HA8 26 B3
Whitchurch Par HA8 26 C3
Whitchurch Rd W11 112 D6
Whitcomb Ct W1 249 D5
Whitcomb St WC2 115 D6 249 D5
Whitcome Mews TW9 132 D4
Whiteacre Mews SE11 261 B1
Whiteadder Way E14 119 D2
Whitear Wlk E15 76 B2
Whitebarn La RM10 103 C6
Whitebeam Ave BR2 210 C3
Whitebeam Cl SW9 270 D3
Whitebeam Ho 3 NW3 70 D2
White Bear Pl 1 NW3 70 B4
White Bear Yd EC1 241 A5
White Bridge Ave CR4 202 B6
White Bridge Cl TW14 149 D5
White Butts Rd HA4 62 D5
WHITECHAPEL 95 D1
Whitechapel High St E1 95 D1 243 D2
Whitechapel Mkt E1 96 A2
Whitechapel Rd E1 96 B2
Whitechapel Sta E1 96 B2
Whitechurch La 3 E1 96 A1
Whitechurch Pas 1 E1 96 A1
White City Cl W12 112 C6
White City Est W12 112 B6
White City W10 90 C1
White City Rd W12 112 C6
White City Sta W12 112 C6
Whitecliff Ho SW18 157 D5
White Conduit St N1 234 B4
Whitecote Rd UB1 86 A1
White Craig Cl HA5 23 C5
Whitecroft Cl BR3 208 B5
Whitecroft Way BR3 208 B5
Whitecross Pl EC2 242 D4
Whitecross St EC1 95 A3 242 B5
White Cube The, Art Gallery* N1 95 C4
Whitefield Ave NW2 46 C1
Whitefield Cl SW15 157 A5
Whitefield Sch
Chingford E17 36 A1
Hendon NW2 46 D2
Whitefoot La BR1 164 B1
Whitefoot Terr BR1 164 D1
Whitefriars Ave HA3 24 C1
Whitefriars Ct 9 N12 30 B5
Whitefriars Dr HA3 24 C1
Whitefriars Fst & Mid Sch HA3 24 C1
Whitefriars St EC4 94 C1 241 B1
Whitefriars Trad Est HA3 24 B1
White Gate Gdns HA3 24 D3
Whitegates 4 EN5 13 D6
White Gdns RM10 81 C2
Whitehall Cres KT9 213 D3
Whitehall Ct SW1 116 A5 250 B3
Whitehall Gdns
Acton W3 110 C5
Chingford E4 20 C3
Chiswick W4 132 D6
SW1 250 A3
Whitehall La IG9 21 A2
Whitehall Lo
Muswell Hill N10 49 A6
Woodford IG8 21 A1
Whitehall Mans 3 N19 49 C1
Whitehall Park Rd W4 132 D6
Whitehall Pk N19 49 C1
Whitehall Pl
Wallington SM5 219 B4
WC2, SW1 116 A5 250 A3
Whitehall Prim Sch E4 20 C2
Whitehall Rd
Bromley BR2 209 D5
Chingford E4 20 C2
Harrow HA1 42 C2
Thornton Heath CR7 204 C4
West Ealing W7 109 A4
Woodford IG8 21 A1
Whitehall St N17 33 D3
Whitehall SW1 250 A2
White Hart Ave SE28, SE18 123 D3
White Hart La SW13 133 C2
White Hart Lane Sec Sch N22 32 D3
White Hart Lane Sta N17 33 D3
White Hart Lane (Tottenham Hotspur FC) N17 34 A3
White Hart La NW10 67 D2
Whitehart Lo SW19 180 A4
White Hart Rdbt UB5 84 D5
White Hart Rd SE18 123 C2
White Hart St
Holborn EC4 241 D2
Kennington SE11 116 C1 261 B2
White Hart Terr N17 33 D3
White Hart Yd SE1 252 C3
Whitehaven Cl BR2 209 A5
Whitehaven Ct 5 DA6 147 A1
Whitehaven St NW8 237 A5
Whitehead Cl
Edmonton N18 33 B5
Wandsworth SW18 158 A4
Whitehead Ct
Muswell Hill N10 31 A2
Twickenham TW1 152 D4
Whitehead Ho 8 SW15 156 D6
Whitehead's Gr SW3 114 C2 257 B3
White Heart Ave UB8 83 A2
Whiteheath Ave HA4 39 A2
Whiteheath Inf Sch HA4 39 A3
Whiteheath Jun Sch HA4 39 A2
White Heron Mews TW11 174 D4
White Ho
2 Battersea SW11 136 B3
Lower Edmonton N9 18 C2
Whitehorn Ho 6 E1 118 C5
White Horse Hill BR7, SE9 188 C6
White Horse La E1 96 D2
Whitehorse La SE25 205 C5
Whitehorse Manor Inf Sch CR7 205 B5
Whitehorse Manor Jun Sch CR7 205 B5
Whitehorse Mews SE1 261 C6
White Horse Rd
Limehouse E1 97 A1
Newham E6 100 B4
Whitehorse Rd
South Norwood CR0, CR7 205 B3
Tower Hamlets E1 97 A2
White Horse St W1 115 B5 248 D3
White Horse Yd EC2 242 C2
White Ho 3 SW4 159 D4
White Ho The NW1 238 D6
Tottenham N17 51 C6
Upper Tooting SW17 180 D5
White House Ct
1 Beckenham BR3 186 A2
Osidge N14 15 D2
White House Dr HA7 25 C6
Whitehouse Est E10 54 A3
White House La EN2 5 A4
Whitehouse Way N14 15 B1
White Kennett St E1 243 B2
Whitelands Cres SW18 157 A4
Whitelands Ho SW3 257 D2
Whiteledges W13 87 C1
Whitelegg Rd E13 98 D5
Whiteley Ho 9 SW4 159 D4
Whiteley Rd SE19 183 B5
Whiteleys Ctr 10 W2 91 D1
Whiteleys Ho TW13 151 C1
Whiteleys Par 5 UB10 82 D3
Whiteleys Way TW13 151 C1
White Lion Ct EC3 243 A1
White Lion Hill EC4 116 D6 251 D6
White Lion St N1 94 C5 234 B3
Whitelock Ho 21 E9 74 D2
White Lodge Cl
Hampstead Garden Suburb N2 48 B3
Isleworth TW7 131 A3
Sutton SM2 218 A1
White Lodge Ct TW16 172 C2
White Lo
7 Ealing W5 87 C2
Golders Green NW11 47 B1
South Norwood SE19 182 D3
Whitely Ct TW13 151 B1
White Lyon Ct EC2 242 A4
Whiteness Ho 18 SW9 138 C4
White Oak Dr BR3 186 A1
White Oak Gdns DA15 167 D4
Whiteoak Ho SE19 183 A3
Whiteoaks La UB6 86 B5
White Orchards
Barnet N20 13 B3
Stanmore HA7 25 A5
White Post La E9 75 C2
White Post St SE14, SE15 140 C5
White Rd E15 76 C1
Whites Ave IG2 57 C3
Whites Dr BR2 208 D2
White's Grounds Est SE1 253 B2
White's Grounds SE1 117 C4 253 B2
White's Mdw BR1 210 C5
Whitespar DA14 189 D6
White's Row E1 95 D2 243 C3
White's Sq SW4 137 D1
Whitestile Rd TW8 109 D1
Whitestone La NW3 70 A5
Whitestone Wlk NW3 70 A5
White St UB1 106 D4
Whitethorn Ave UB7 104 B6
Whitethorn Gdns
Croydon CR0 222 B6
Enfield EN2 17 B6
Whitethorn Pl UB7 104 B5
Whitethorn St E3 97 C2
Whiteways NW4 46 D5
Whitewebbs Way BR5 189 D2
Whitfield Ct
3 Dulwich SE21 183 C6
Redbridge IG1 56 B2
SW4 270 A1
West Barnes SW20 178 D1
Whitfield Gdns W1 239 B4
Whitfield Ho NW8 237 A5
Whitfield Pl W1 239 B5
Whitfield Rd DA7 147 B5
Upton E6 77 C1
Whitfield St W1 93 C2 239 B4
Whitford Gdns CR4 202 D6
Whitgift Ave CR2 221 A3
Whitgift Ct CR2 221 A3
Whitgift Ctr CR0 221 A6
Whitgift Ho
Battersea SW11 267 A2
Croydon CR2 221 A3
Lambeth SE11 260 C4
Whitgift Sch CR2 221 A3
Whitgift St
Croydon CR0 221 A5
SE11 116 B2 260 C4
Whiting Ave IG11 78 D1
Whitings Hill Prim Sch EN5 12 C6
Whitings Rd EN5 12 C6
Whitings The IG2 57 C4
Whitings Way E6 100 C2
Whitington Ave EC3 243 A1
Whitland Rd SM5 202 B1
Whitley Cl TW19 148 A5
Whitley Ho SW1 269 B6
Whitley Rd N17 33 C1
Whitlock Dr SW19 157 A3
Whitman Ho 20 E2 96 C4
Whitman Rd E3 97 A3
Whitmead Cl CR2 221 C2
Whitmore Cl N11 31 B5
Whitmore Gdns NW10 90 C5
Whitmore High Sch HA1, HA2 42 A1
Whitmore Ho
Friern Barnet N11 30 D6
20 Hoxton E1 95 C6
Whitmore Prim Sch N1 95 B6 235 D5
Whitmore Rd
Beckenham BR3 207 B6
Harrow HA1 42 A2
Hoxton N1 95 C6
Whitnell Ct 7 SW15 156 D6
Whitnell Way SW15 156 D6
Whitney Ave IG4 55 D5
Whitney Ho 6 SE22 139 C2
Whitney Rd E10 53 D2
Whitney Wlk DA14 191 A4
Whitstable Cl
Beckenham BR3 185 B2
Ruislip HA4 61 C6
Whitstable Ho 11 W10 90 D1
Whitstable Pl 9 CR0 221 A4
Whitsters Ho SE1 253 C2
Whitstone La BR3 207 D4
Whittaker Ave TW10, TW9 153 D6
Whittaker Ct SW4 270 B1
Whittaker 8 NW9 27 D3
Whittaker Pl 28 TW10 153 D6
Whittaker Rd
Cheam SM3 217 B5
Forest Gate E6 77 D1
Whittaker St SW1 258 A3
Whittaker Way 19 SE1 118 A2
Whittam Ho SE27 183 A5
Whitta Rd E12 77 D4
Whittell Gdns SE26 162 C1
Whitten Lo N12 30 C6
Whittingham Com Prim Sch E17 35 A2
Whittingham Ct W4 133 C5
Whittingham 6 N17 34 B3
Whittingstall Mans SW6 264 D1
Whittingstall Rd SW6 135 B4 264 D1
Whittington Ave UB4 83 D2
Whittington Ct
Fortis Green N2 48 D4
Penge SE20 184 B1
Whittington Hospl The N19 71 C6
Whittington Mews N12 30 A6
Whittington Rd N22 32 A3
Whittington Way HA5 41 A4
Whittlebury Cl SM5 218 D1
Whittlebury Ho N4 51 A2
Whittle Cl
Southall UB1 85 D1
Walthamstow E17 53 A2
Whittle 4 NW9 27 D3
Whittle Rd
Heston TW5 128 C5
Southall UB2 107 D4
Whittlesea Cl HA3 24 A3
Whittlesea Path HA3 24 A2
Whittlesea Rd HA3 24 A2
Whittlesey St SE1 116 C5 251 B3
WHITTON 152 A4
Whitton Ave W UB5, UB6 64 B3
Whitton Cl UB6 65 B2
Whitton Dene TW3, TW7 152 B6
Whitton Dr UB6 65 A2
Whitton NW3 70 D1
Whitton Manor Rd TW7 152 A5
Whitton Rd
Hounslow TW3 151 D6
Twickenham TW1 153 A4
Whitton Road Rdbt TW1 152 D5
Whitton Sch TW2 151 D2
Whitton Sta TW2 152 A4
Whitton Waye TW2, TW3 151 C5
Whitton Wlk E3 97 C4
Whitwell Ho 11 E5 74 B6
Whitwell Rd E13 99 A4
Whitworth Cres 1 EN3 7 C6
Whitworth Ho SE1 262 B5
Whitworth Rd SE18 144 C5
South Norwood SE25 205 D5
Whitworth St SE10 120 C1
Whorlton Rd SE15 140 B2
Whychcote Point NW2 46 C2
Whymark Ave N22 50 D6
Whytecroft TW5 128 D5
Whyteville Ho E7 77 B2
Whyteville Rd E7 77 B2
Whytlaw Ho 10 E3 97 B2
Wickersley Rd SW11 137 A3
Wickers Oake SE19 183 D6
Wicker St 24 E1 96 B1
Wicket Rd UB6 87 A4
Wickets The TW15 170 A6
Wicket The CR0 223 C3
Wickfield Ho 32 SE16 118 A4
Wickford Ho 5 E1 96 C3
Wickford St E1 96 C3
Wickford Way E17 52 D5
Wickham Ave
Cheam KT4, SM3 216 C3
Croydon CR0 207 A1
Wickham Chase BR4 208 C2
Wickham Cl
Enfield EN3 6 C2
New Malden KT3 199 D4
Stepney E1 96 C2
Wickham Common Prim Sch BR4 225 A4
Wickham Court Rd BR4 224 A6
Wickham Court Sch BR4 224 B4
Wickham Cres BR4 224 A6
Wickham Ct DA16 145 C3
Wickham Gdns SE4 141 B2
Wickham Ho SW15 156 D5
Wickham La SE2 146 A6
Wickham Mews SE4 141 B3
Wickham Rd
Beckenham BR3 207 D6
Brockley SE4 141 B2
Wickham Rd *continued*
Chingford E4 ...
Croydon CR0 ...
Harrow HA3 ...
Wickham St
Bexley DA16 ...
Vauxhall SE11 116 B1
Welling DA16 ...
Wickham Way BR3 ...
Wick Ho 1 KT1 ...
Wick La Hackney E3 ...
Stratford Marsh E3 ...
Wickliffe Ave N3 ...
Wickliffe Gdns HA9 ...
Wicklow Ct SE26 ...
Wicklow Ho N16 ...
Wicklow St WC1 94 B4
Wick Rd Hackney E9 ...
Hackney E9 ...
Teddington TW11 ...
Wicks Cl SE12 ...
Wickstead Ho TW8 ...
Wicksteed Ho SE1 ...
Wickway Ct 7 SE15 ...
Wickwood St SE5 ...
Widdenham Rd N7 ...
Widdicombe Ave HA2 ...
Widdin St E15 ...
Widecombe Ct N2 ...
Widecombe Gdns IG4 ...
Widecombe Ho 32 SE5 ...
Widecombe Rd SE9 ...
Widecombe Way N2 ...
Widegate St E1 ...
Widenham Cl HA5 ...
Wide Way CR4 ...
Widewing Cl TW11 ...
Widford Ho N1 ...
Widford 8 NW1 ...
Widgeon Cl E16 ...
Widgeon Path SE28 ...
Widley Rd W9 ...
Widmer Ct TW5 ...
WIDMORE ...
Widmore Lodge Rd BR1 ...
Widmore Rd BR1 ...
Hillingdon UB8 ...
Widnes Ho 8 N7 ...
Wieland Rd HA6 ...
Wigan Ho E5 ...
Wigeon Way UB4 ...
Wiggins La TW10 ...
Wiggins Mead NW9 ...
Wigginton Ave HA9 ...
Wigham Ho IG11 ...
Wightman Rd N4, N8 ...
Wighton Mews TW7 ...
Wigley Rd TW13 ...
Wigmore Ct 4 W13 ...
Wigmore Hall* W1 ...
Wigmore Pl W1 93 B1
Wigmore Rd SM5 ...
Wigmore St W1 93 A1
Wigmore Wlk SM5 ...
Wigram Ct SW11 ...
Wigram Ho 7 E14 ...
Wigram Rd E11 ...
Wigram Sq E17 ...
Wigston Cl N18 ...
Wigston Rd E13 ...
Wigton Gdns HA7 ...
Wigton Pl SE11 ...
Wigton Rd E17 ...
Wilberforce Ct
Edgware HA8 ...
2 SE28 ...
Wilberforce Ho 4 SW11 ...
Wilberforce Mews 9 SW4 ...
Wilberforce Prim Sch W10 ...
Wilberforce Rd
Finsbury Pk N4 ...
Hendon NW9 ...
Highbury N4, N5 ...
Wilberforce Way SW19 ...
Wilbraham Ho SW8 ...
Wilbraham Pl SW1 ...
Wilbury Prim Sch N18 ...
Wilbury Way N18 ...
Wilby Mews W11 113 B5
Wilcox Cl SW8 ...

ox Gdns TW17 . . . 192 B6
ox Ho 5 E3 . . . . . . 97 B2
ox Pl SW1. . . . . . 259 B5
ox Rd
ton SM1 . . . . 217 D4
8. . . . . . . 138 A5 270 A4
dington TW11. . . . .174 B6
croft Gdns HA8. . . 25 D4
croft Manor
15. . . . . .156 C4
croft Rd SW15. . .156 C4
Ct WC2. . . 94 B1 240 C2
e Cl E8. . . . . 96 A6
e Pl
nonton N13. . . . . . . .32 D4
ndsworth SW18 . . .158 B4
er Cl HA4 . . . . 40 B1
e Rd DA8. . . . . . . .147 D5
erness Mews
4. . . . . .137 B1
erness Rd BR7 . .188 D3
erness The
t Molesey KT8 . . . 196 A4
mpton TW12 . . . . . 173 D6
erton Rd N16. . . . .51 C2
es Cotts SM3. . . .217 A2
fell Rd SE6. . . . . .163 D4
Goose Dr
4. . . . . .140 C4
Hatch NW11 . . . . . 47 C3
ing Ho 17 E9 . . . . .74 D2
Marsh Ct EN3. . . . . 7 A6
's Rents
. . . . .117 C3 263 A6
St WC2. . . 94 B1 240 C1
wood Cl SE12 . . .164 D4
wood Gr NW3 . . . . 48 A1
wood Rd NW11. . . 48 A2
wood Rise
11. . . . . .48 A1
wood Terr NW3. . . 48 A1
ord Cl EN2. . . . . 5 B2
ord Ho 3 SE18. . .122 D1
ord Rd CR0 . . . . . .205 A2
red Fienburgh Ho
. . . . .71 D4
red Owen Cl
19. . . . . .180 A4
red St
1. . . . . . . .115 C3 259 A6
rid Gdns W3. . . . . . .89 A2
es Rd 3 TW8. . . .132 A6
es St E1. . . 95 D2 243 D4
ie Ho SW1. . . . . . 259 D2
ins Cl
yes UB3. . . . . 105 D1
cham CR4. . . . . . . 180 C2
ins Ho SW1 . . . . 269 A6
inson Cl UB10 . . . . 83 A6
inson Ct SW17. . .180 B6
inson Gdns
7 . . . . .183 C2
inson Ho
eworth TW7. . . . . . 130 D2
. . . . 235 D3
ckenham TW2. . . . .152 B2
inson Rd E16. . . . . 99 C1
inson St
8. . . . . . . .138 B5 270 C3
inson Way W4. . .111 B4
in St NW5. . . . . 71 B2
s Gdns CR0. . . . . .207 A1
s Pl N1. . . . . 95 C5
an Rd N17 . . . . 33 C1
an Wall E16. . . . . 120 D6
ard St SW8 . . . . . . 137 B2
bury Ho 4 N7 . . . . 71 D3
cocks Cl KT9. . . . .214 A5
cott Rd W3 . . . . . . 110 D5
Crooks Gdns
. . . . .143 D1
enfield Rd NW10 . . 89 A5
enhall Ave EN5. . . . 14 A5
enhall Ct EN5 . . . . . 14 A5
enhall Dr UB3. . . .105 C6
enhall Rd SE18. . .122 D1
ersley Ave
ckfen DA15. . . . . . 167 D4
pington BR6. . . . . . .227 B5
ersley Cl DA15 . . .167 D3
LESDEN 67 D1
esden Community
spl The NW10 . . . . 68 A1
LESDEN GREEN . . 90 B6
esden Green Sta
2. . . . . .68 C2
esden Junction Sta
10. . . . . .89 D4
esden La NW2,
6. . . . . .68 D2
es Rd NW5. . . . . . . .71 B2
ett Cl BR5 . . . . . . .211 C3
Northolt UB5 . . . . . .84 C4
ett Ho
Newham E13 . . . . . . 99 A5
ckwell SW9 . . . . . 138 A2
ett Pl CR7 . . . . . . .204 C4

Willett Rd CR7. . . . . . .204 C4
Willett Way BR5 . . . . .211 C3
William Allen Ho
HA8 . . . . 26 B3
William Ash Cl RM9 . . . 80 B2
William Atkinson Ho
N17 . . . . 33 C3
William Banfield Ho 10
SW6. . . . . .135 B3
William Barefoot Dr
SE9. . . . . .166 C1
William Bellamy Jun & Inf Schs RM10 . . . . . .81 C6
William Blake Ho 2
SE15. . . . . .140 A3
William Bonney Est 10
SW4. . . . . .137 D1
William Booth Meml Training Coll SE5 . .139 B3
William Booth Rd
SE20. . . . . .184 A2
William Brown Ct
SE27. . . . . .160 D2
William Byrd Sch
UB3 . . . . 127 A6
William Carey Way
HA1 . . . . 42 C3
William Caslon Ho 23
E2. . . . . 96 B5
William Channing Ho 6
E2. . . . . 96 B4
William C Harvey Sch
N17 . . . . 33 B1
William Cl
26 Finchley N2 . . . . 30 B1
Lewisham SE13. . . . . 142 A2
Southall UB2 . . . . 108 A4
William Covell Cl EN2 . . 4 B5
William Ct
4 Belvedere
DA17 . . . . 125 C2
4 Ealing W5. . . . . 87 C2
Ilford IG6 . . . . 57 B5
William Davies Prim Sch E7 . . . . 77 D2
William Davis Prim Sch
E2. . . . . 96 A3
William Dromey Ct
NW6. . . . . 69 B1
William Dr HA7 . . . . 25 B5
William Dunbar Ho
NW6. . . . . 91 B5
William Dyce Mews 1
SW16. . . . . .181 D6
William Ellis Sch
NW5. . . . . 71 A5
William Ellis Way 16
SE16. . . . . .118 A3
William Evans Ho 9
SE8. . . . . .118 D2
William Ford CE Jun Sch RM10. . . . . .81 C1
William Gdns SW15 . . 156 B6
William Guy Gdns 47
E3. . . . . 97 D4
William Harvey Ho 1
SW19. . . . . .157 A3
William Ho N13. . . . . . . 32 D4
William Hogarth Prim Sch The W4. . . . . 111 C1
William Hunt Mans
SW13. . . . . .134 C6
William IV St
WC2. . . . . . . .116 A6 250 A5
William Margrie Cl 1
SE15. . . . . .140 A3
William Marsden Ho 2
SE27. . . . . .182 D6
William Mews
SW1. . . . . . . 114 D4 247 D1
William Morley Cl
E6. . . . . 99 D6
William Morris Acad
W6. . . . . 112 D1
William Morris Cl
E17. . . . . 53 B6
William Morris Gallery* E17 . . . . 53 C6
William Morris Ho
W6. . . . . 134 D6
William Morris Prim Sch CR4 . . . . 203 D6
William Morris Sch
E17. . . . . 35 A2
William Morris Way
SW6. . . . . .136 A3
William Patten Prim Sch N16. . . . . 73 D6
William Perkin Ct
UB6 . . . . 64 C2
William Pl 37 E3 . . . . . . 97 B5
William Rainbird Ho 9
N17 . . . . 33 D3
William Rathbone Ho 3
E2. . . . . 96 B4

William Rd
Regent's Pk
NW1. . . . . . 93 C4 232 A1
Sutton SM1 . . . . 218 A3
Wimbledon SW19 . . . 179 A3
William Rushbrooke Ho
4 SE16. . . . . 118 A2
Williams Ave E17 . . . . . 35 B2
William Saville Ho 2
NW6. . . . . 91 B5
William's Bldgs 1
E2. . . . . 96 C3
Williams Cl
SW6. . . . . . . .135 A5 264 B4
Williams Coll EC1. . . . 241 B3
Williams Dr TW3. . . . . 129 C1
Williams Gr
Kingston u T KT6. . . . 197 C3
Wood Green N22. . . . . . 32 C2
Williams Ho
10 Bow E3. . . . . 97 C4
9 Hackney E9 . . . . 96 B6
14 Streatham SW2 . . 160 C3
7 Tottenham N17 . . . . 33 D3
Willesden NW2. . . . . . . 68 C5
Williams La
Morden SM4 . . . . 202 A4
Mortlake SW14 . . . . . 133 A3
William Smith Ho 10
DA17 . . . . .125 C3
Williamson Cl SE10 . . 120 D1
Williamson Ct SE17 . 262 A1
Williamson Rd N4 . . . . 50 D3
Williamson St N7 . . . . . 72 A4
Williamson Way
NW7. . . . . 29 A4
William Sq 15 SE16. . . 119 A6
William's Rd W13. . . . 109 A5
Williams Rd UB2. . . . . 107 A2
William St
Barking IG11. . . . . 79 A1
Carshalton SM5. . . . . 218 D5
Williams Terr CR0. . . . 220 C2
William St
SW1. . . . . . . 114 D4 247 D1
Tottenham N17 . . . . . . 33 D3
Walthamstow E10. . . . . 53 D3
William Torbitt Prim Sch IG2 . . . . 57 D4
William Tyndale Prim Sch N1. . . . . 72 D1
William Wilberforce Ho
1 SE27 . . . . .182 D6
William Winter Ct 29
SW2. . . . . .160 C4
William Wood Ho 3
SE26. . . . . .162 C1
Willifield Way NW11 . . 47 C4
Willingale Cl IG8 . . . . . 37 C4
Willingdon Rd N22. . . . 32 D1
Willingham Cl 4
NW5. . . . . 71 C3
Willingham Terr
NW5. . . . . 71 C3
Willingham Way
KT1 . . . . .176 C1
Willington Ct E5. . . . . . 75 A5
Willington Prep Sch
SW19. . . . . .179 B5
Willington Rd SW9. . . 138 A2
Willis Ave SM2, SM5 . . 218 C2
Willis Ct CR7 . . . . 204 C3
Willis Ho
2 Ilford E12. . . . . 78 C5
8 Poplar E14 . . . . 119 D6
Willis Rd E15 . . . . 98 D5
Thornton Heath CR0 . 205 A2
Willis St E14. . . . . 97 D1
Willis Yd N14 . . . . 15 D4
Willows The CR0 . . . . 223 A6
Will Miles Ct 6
SW19. . . . . .180 A3
Willmore End SW19. . 179 D1
Willoughby Ave
CR0 . . . . .220 B4
Willoughby Gr N17. . . . 34 B3
Willoughby Ho EC2 . 242 C3
34 Wapping E1 . . . . . . 118 B5
Willoughby La N17. . . . 34 B3
Willoughby Mews
N17 . . . . 34 B3
Willoughby Park Rd
N17 . . . . 34 B3
Willoughby Rd
Hampstead NW3. . . . . . 70 B4
Hornsey N8 . . . . 50 C5
Kingston u T KT2. . . . . 176 B2
Twickenham TW1. . . . 153 D6
Willoughbys The
SW14. . . . . .133 C1
Willoughby St WC1 . 240 A3
Willoughby Way
SE7. . . . . 121 B2
Willow Ave
Barnes SW13 . . . . . . 133 D3
DA15 . . . . 168 A5
Yiewsley UB7. . . . . 104 B6

Willowbank SW6. . . . . 135 A2
Willowbank Rd
SE15. . . . . 139 D6
Willow Bank TW10 . . . 153 B1
Willowbay Cl EN5 . . . . . 12 D5
Willow Bridge Rd N1. . 73 A2
Willow Brook Prim Sch
E10. . . . . 53 C1
Willowbrook Rd
Southall UB2 . . . . 107 C3
Stanwell TW19 . . . . . 148 A2
Willow Bsns Pk
SE26. . . . . 162 C1
Willow Cl BR2 . . . . 210 B4
Brentford TW8. . . . . . 131 C6
Buckhurst Hill IG9. . . . . 21 D1
12 Catford SE6 . . . . . . 164 D3
Sidcup DA5 . . . . .169 B5
Willow Cotts
Carshalton CR4 . . . . . 202 D2
Feltham TW13 . . . . . . 151 A1
Richmond TW9. . . . . . 132 C6
Willowcourt Ave HA3. . 43 B4
Willowcroft SE3 . . . . . 142 D1
Willow Ct
Ashford TW16 . . . . . . 171 C3
5 Beckenham BR3. . . 185 C2
Brixton SW9 . . . . 138 C4
Chiswick W4 . . . . 133 C5
8 Dagenham RM8 . . . . 58 D2
EC2 . . . . 243 A6
Edgware HA8. . . . . 26 A6
6 Finchley N12 . . . . . . 29 D6
Harrow HA3 . . . . 24 D2
Headstone HA2. . . . . . . 24 A1
Ilford IG1 . . . . 79 A3
Islington N7 . . . . 72 B3
Kingston u T KT3. . . . . 198 D6
8 London E11 . . . . 76 C6
Mitcham CR4. . . . . . . 202 C5
40 Paddington W2. . . . . 91 C2
Willow Ctr The CR4 . .202 D3
Willow Ct
3 Streatham
SW16 . . . . .160 B1
Thornton Heath CR7 . . 205 B4
Willow Dean HA5 . . . . . 22 D1
Willow Dene WD23. . . . . 8 C4
Willowdene Cl TW2 . . 152 A4
Willowdene Ct N20 . . . 14 A4
Willowdene
Highgate N6 . . . . 48 D2
1 Peckham SE15 . . . . 140 B4
Willow Dene Sch
SE18. . . . . 145 C4
Willowdene 5
SE15. . . . . 140 B5
Willow Dr EN5. . . . . 1 A1
Willow End
Northwood HA6. . . . . . . 22 A4
Surbiton KT6 . . . . 198 A1
Totteridge N20 . . . . 13 C2
Willow Farm La
SW15. . . . . 134 B2
Willowfields Cl
SE18. . . . . 123 C1
Willowfield Sec Sch
E17. . . . . 52 D6
Willow Gdns
Heston TW5. . . . . 129 C4
Ruislip HA4 . . . . 61 D6
Willow Gn
Borehamwood
WD6. . . . . 11 B6
Grahame Pk NW9 . . . . . 27 C2
Willow Gr BR7 . . . . 188 D4
Newham E13. . . . . 99 A5
Ruislip HA4 . . . . 39 D1
Willow Hall NW3. . . . . . 70 B4
Willowhayne Dr
KT12 . . . . .194 B2
Willowhayne Gdns
KT4 . . . . .216 C4
Willow Ho TW14. . . . . .150 B6
Willow Ho
17 Finchley N2 . . . . 30 B1
9 Maitland Pk NW3. . . 70 D2
North Kensington
W10. . . . . 90 D3
Teddington TW11. . . . 175 C3
Willow La
Mitcham CR4. . . . . . . 202 D3
Woolwich SE18 . . . . . 122 C2
Willow Lo 6 TW16. . . .171 D3
Willow Lodge 10
SW8. . . . . 137 B2
Willow Lo
Fulham SW6 . . . . 134 D4
New Barnet EN5 . . . . . . 14 A6
Putney SW15. . . . . 134 B2
Willow Manor SM1. . . 217 B4
Willowmead Cl W5 . . . 87 D2
Willowmere
Esher KT10 . . . . 212 A4
Ladywell SE13. . . . . . 163 D6
Willow Mount CR0. . . . 221 C5

Willow Pl
SW1. . . . . . . .115 C2 259 B4
Willow Rd
Dagenham RM6. . . . . . . 59 A3
Ealing W5 . . . . 110 A4
Enfield EN1 . . . . 5 C3
Hampstead NW3. . . . . . 70 B4
New Malden KT3. . . . . 199 A5
Wallington SM6. . . . . .219 B1
Willows Ave SM4 . . . . 201 D4
Willows Cl HA5 . . . . 22 C1
Willows Ct 3 SW19 . .179 C3
Willows Sch The
UB4 . . . . 84 D3
Willow St
Broadgate
EC2. . . . . . . 95 C3 243 A6
Chingford E4 . . . . 20 B4
Willows Terr NW10. . . . 89 D5
Willows The
Beckenham BR3 . . . . 185 C2
Claygate KT10 . . . . . . 212 C2
Loughton IG10. . . . . 21 D6
Wallend E12 . . . . 78 C1
Whetstone N20 . . . . 14 A1
Willow Tree Cl
Hayes UB4. . . . . 84 C3
Northolt UB5 . . . . 63 A2
14 Old Ford E3 . . . . 97 B6
Willowtree Cl UB10 . . . 61 A5
Willow Tree Cl
SW18. . . . . .157 D3
Willow Tree Ct
DA14 . . . . 189 D5
5 Wembley HA0 . . . . . 65 D3
Willow Tree La UB4 . . . 84 C3
Willow Tree Prim Sch
UB5 . . . . 63 A2
Willowtree Way
SW16. . . . . .182 C2
Willow Tree Wlk
BR1 . . . . .187 B2
Willow Vale BR7 . . . . .188 D4
Shepherd's Bush
W12. . . . . 112 A5
Willow View SW19 . . . 180 B2
Willow Way
Finchley N3 . . . . 29 D3
Forest Hill SE26. . . . . 162 C1
9 Shepherd's Bush
W11. . . . . 112 D6
Sunbury TW16. . . . . . 194 A5
Twickenham TW2. . . . 151 D2
Wembley HA0 . . . . 65 A5
West Ewell KT19. . . . . 215 B2
Willow Wlk
Bermondsey
SE1. . . . . . 117 D2 263 C4
Cheam SM1, SM3 . . . . 217 B5
15 Finchley N2 . . . . 30 B1
Harringay N15. . . . . 50 D5
Locksbottom BR6. . . . 226 D5
Southgate N21. . . . . 16 B5
Walthamstow E17 . . . . . 53 B4
Willow Wood Cres
SE25. . . . . 205 C3
Willridge Ct E11 . . . . . . 54 B2
Willrose Cres SE2. . . . 124 B1
Willsbridge Ct 1
SE15. . . . . 139 D6
Wills Cres TW3 . . . . . . 151 D5
Wills Gr NW7 . . . . 28 B5
Will Thorne Pav The
E16. . . . . 100 A1
Wilman Gr E8 . . . . 74 A1
Wilmar Cl UB4. . . . . 83 B3
Wilmar Gdns BR4 . . . . 207 D1
Wilmcote Ho W2 . . . . . . 91 D2
Wilment Ct NW2. . . . . . 68 C5
Wilmer Cl KT2. . . . . . . 176 B5
Wilmer Cres KT2. . . . . 176 B5
Wilmer Gdns 22 N1 . . . 95 C6
Wilmer Ho 6 E3. . . . . . . 97 A5
Wilmer Lea Cl E15 . . . . 76 B1
Wilmer Pl N16. . . . . 73 D6
Wilmers Ct 5 NW10 . . 89 B6
Wilmer Way N14. . . . . . 31 D5
Wilmington Ave
W4. . . . . 133 B5
Wilmington Ct
SW16. . . . . .182 A3
Wilmington Gdns
IG11. . . . . 79 C1
Wilmington Sq
WC1. . . . . 94 C4 234 A1
Wilmington St WC1 . 234 A1
Wilmot Cl Finchley N2 . . 30 A1
SE15 . . . . 140 A5
Wilmot Ho 14 SM2 . . . 218 A2
Wilmot Pl
Camden Town
NW1. . . . . 71 C1
Ealing W7 . . . . 108 C5
Wilmot Rd Leyton E10. . 75 D6
Tottenham N17 . . . . 51 B6
Wallington SM5. . . . . 218 D3
Wilmot St E2. . . . . 96 B3

Wilmount St SE18. . . . 122 D2
Wilna Rd SW18 . . . . . . 158 A4
Wilnett Ct 4 RM6. . . . . . 58 B2
Wilnett Villas 5 RM6. . 58 B2
Wilsham St
W11. . . . . . . .113 A5 244 A4
Wilshaw Cl NW4 . . . . . . 46 A6
Wilshaw Ho 10 SE8. . . 141 C5
Wilshaw St SE14. . . . . 141 C4
Wilsmere Dr
Harrow HA3 . . . . 24 C3
Northolt UB5 . . . . 63 A3
Wilson Ave CR4. . . . . . 180 C2
Wilson Cl
Croydon CR2 . . . . 221 B3
Wembley HA9 . . . . 44 B2
Wilson Ct 9 SE28. . . . 123 A3
Wilson Dr HA9. . . . . 44 B2
Wilson Gdns HA1 . . . . . 42 A2
Wilson Gr SE16 . . . . . . 118 B4
Wilson Ho
33 Clapham SW8 . . . 137 D3
2 SE7. . . . . 143 C6
South Hampstead
NW6. . . . . 70 A1
Wilson Rd
Camberwell SE5 . . . . 139 C4
Chessington KT9 . . . . . 214 B2
Newham E6. . . . . 99 D4
Redbridge IG1. . . . . 56 B2
Wilson's Ave 4 N17. . . . 33 D1
Wilson's Pl E14. . . . . . . 97 B1
Wilson's Rd W6. . . . . . 112 D1
Wilson's Sch SM6 . . 220 A2
Wilson St
Broadgate
EC2. . . . . . . 95 B2 242 D4
Southgate N21. . . . . 16 C4
Walthamstow E17 . . . . . 54 A4
Wilstone Cl UB4 . . . . . . 85 A3
Wiltern Ct NW2. . . . . . . 69 A2
Wilthorne Gdns
RM10. . . . . 81 D1
Wilton Ave W4. . . . . . . 111 C1
Wilton Cres
Merton SW19 . . . . 179 B2
SW1. . . . . . . 115 A4 248 A1
Wilton Ct
3 Edgware HA8. . . . . . . 26 D5
Muswell Hill N10. . . . . . 31 A1
4 Richmond TW10. . . 154 A6
7 Stepney E1. . . . . 96 B1
7 Woodford IG8 . . . . . . 37 A4
Wilton Est E8. . . . . 74 A2
Wilton Gdns
East Molesey KT8 . . . 195 C6
Walton-on-T KT12 . . . 194 D1
Wilton Gr
Merton SW19 . . . . 179 B2
New Malden KT3. . . . 199 D3
Wilton Ho
8 Camberwell
SE22. . . . . 139 C2
Chislehurst BR7. . . . . . 189 B2
Ealing W13 . . . . 109 B6
Wilton Mews
SW1. . . . . . . .115 A3 258 B6
Wilton Par TW13. . . . . 150 B2
Wilton Pl
2 Beckenham
BR3. . . . . 208 A6
4 Harrow HA1. . . . . . . 42 D3
SW1. . . . . . . 115 A4 248 A1
Wilton Rd
Abbey Wood SE2 . . . . 124 C2
Cockfosters EN4 . . . . 2 D1
Hounslow TW4 . . . . . 128 D2
Mitcham SW19 . . . . . 180 C3
Muswell Hill N10. . . . . . 31 A1
Westminster
SW1. . . . . . 115 C2 259 A4
Wilton Row SW1. . . . . 248 A1
Wilton Sq N1 . . 95 B6 235 C6
Wilton St
SW1. . . . . . . .115 B3 258 C6
Wilton Terr SW1 . . . . 258 A6
Wilton Villas N1 . . . . 235 C5
Wilton Way E8. . . . . 74 A2
Wiltshire Cl
Edgware NW7. . . . . 27 D5
SW3. . . . . 257 C3
Wiltshire Ct
Barking IG11. . . . . 79 A2
2 Finsbury Pk N4. . . . . 50 B1
Wiltshire Gdns
Stoke Newington
N4 . . . . 51 A3
Twickenham TW2. . . . 152 A3
Wiltshire La
Pinner HA5 . . . . 40 A5
Ruislip HA4 . . . . 39 D6
Wiltshire Rd
Brixton SW9 . . . . 138 C2
Thornton Heath CR7 . 204 C6

Wiltshire Row N1 .... 95 B6 235 D5
Wilverley Cres KT3 ... 199 C3
Wimbart Rd SW2 .... 160 B4
WIMBLEDON 179 B4
Wimbledon Bridge SW19 .... 179 B4
Wimbledon Central SW19 .... 179 B4
Wimbledon Chase Prim Sch SW20 .... 179 A2
Wimbledon Chase Sta SW20 .... 179 A1
Wimbledon Cl 2 SW20 .... 178 D3
Wimbledon Coll SW19 .... 178 D3
Wimbledon Common Prep Sch SW19 ... 178 D3
Wimbledon Common* SW19 .... 178 B6
Wimbledon High Sch SW19 .... 179 A4
Wimbledon Hill Rd SW19 .... 179 B4
Wimbledon Lawn Tennis Mus* SW19 .... 157 A1
Wimbledon Park Ct SW19 .... 157 B3
Wimbledon Park Montessori Sch SW18 .... 157 C2
Wimbledon Park Prim Sch SW19 .... 157 D2
Wimbledon Park Rd SW18, SW19 .... 157 B3
Wimbledon Park Side SW19 .... 156 D3
Wimbledon Park Sta SW19 .... 157 C1
Wimbledon Rd SW17 .... 180 A6
Wimbledon Sch of Art Annexe SW19 ..... 179 C3
Wimbledon Sch of Art SW19 .... 179 A2
Wimbledon Stadium Bsns Ctr SW17 .... 157 D1
Wimbledon Stad SW17 .... 180 A6
Wimbledon Sta SW19 .... 179 B4
Wimbledon Windmill Mus* SW19 .... 156 C1
Wimbolt St E2 .... 96 A4
Wimborne Ave
Hayes UB4 .... 84 B1
Southall UB2 .... 107 C2
St Paul's Cray BR5, BR7 .... 211 D5
Wimborne Cl
Buckhurst Hill IG9 ..... 21 C2
Lewisham SE12 ..... 164 D6
North Cheam KT4 .... 200 C1
Wimborne Ct 1 UB5 .. 63 C2
Wimborne Dr
Pinner HA5 .... 41 A2
Queensbury NW9 ..... 44 C6
Wimborne Gdns W13 . 87 B2
Wimborne Ho
Canning Town E16 .... 120 D6
Croydon CR0 .... 206 C4
Marylebone NW1 .... 237 B5
South Lambeth SW8 . 270 D3
Upper Tooting SW12 .... 159 C1
Wimborne Rd
Edmonton N9 .... 18 A2
Tottenham N17 .... 33 C1
Wimborne 2 DA14 ... 190 B6
Wimborne Way BR3 .... 207 A5
Wimbourne Ct
Mitcham SW19 ...... 180 B3
N1 .... 235 C4
South Croydon CR2 .. 221 C2
Wimbourne St N1 .... 95 B5 235 C4
Wimbush Ho 3 N12 .. 29 D5
Wimpole Cl
Bromley BR2 .... 209 C5
1 Kingston u T KT1 . 176 C1
Wimpole Mews W1 .... 93 B2 238 C3
Wimpole St W1 .... 93 B1 238 C2
Wimshurst Cl CR0 ... 204 A1
Winans Wlk SW9 ..... 138 C3
Winant Ho 19 E14 .... 119 D6
Wincanton Cres UB5 .. 63 C3
Wincanton Ct 2 N11 .. 31 A4
Wincanton Gdns IG6 .. 56 D6
Wincanton Rd SW18 .... 157 B4
Winchcombe Rd SM5 .... 202 C1
Winchcomb Gdns SE9 .... 143 D2
Winchelsea Ave DA7 .... 147 B5
Winchelsea Cl SW15 .... 156 D6
Winchelsea Ho 16 SE16 .... 118 C4
Winchelsea Rd
Becontree NW10 ...... 89 B6
Forest Gate E7 .... 77 A4
Tottenham N17 .... 51 C6
Winchelsey Rise CR2 .... 221 D2
Winchendon Rd
Fulham SW6 ..... 135 B4 264 D2
Teddington TW11, TW12 .... 174 B6
Winchester Ave
Brondesbury NW6 ..... 69 A1
Heston TW5 .... 129 B6
Queensbury NW9 ..... 44 C6
Winchester Cl
Beckenham BR2 .... 208 D6
Enfield EN1 .... 17 C6
Kingston u T KT2 .... 176 D3
11 Newham E6 ...... 100 B1
SE17 .... 261 D3
Winchester Ct
15 Belvedere DA17 .... 125 C1
5 Higham Hill E17 .... 35 A2
Richmond TW9 .... 132 B2
W8 .... 245 C2
Winchester Dr HA5 ... 40 D4
Winchester Ho
5 Barking IG11 ...... 80 A1
Bayswater W2 .... 236 A1
Chelsea SW3 .... 266 D5
1 Greenwich SE18 .. 143 D5
24 Tower Hamlets E3 .. 97 B4
Twickenham TW1 .... 153 C4
Winchester Mews KT4 .... 216 D6
Winchester Pal* SE1 .... 252 C4
Winchester Pk BR2 .. 208 D6
Winchester Pl
6 Dalston E8 .... 73 D3
Highgate N6 .... 49 B1
Winchester Rd
Beckenham BR2 .... 208 D6
Bexley DA7 .... 146 D3
Chingford E4 .... 36 A3
Edmonton N9 .... 18 A3
Harlington UB3 ..... 127 C5
Harrow HA3 .... 44 A5
Highgate N6 .... 49 B1
Ilford IG1 .... 79 B5
Northwood HA6 .... 40 A6
South Hampstead NW3 .... 70 B1
St Margarets TW1 .... 153 B5
Twickenham TW13 .... 151 B1
Walton-on-T KT12 ... 194 A1
Winchester Sq SE1 .. 252 C4
Winchester St
Acton W3 .... 111 A4
SW1 .... 115 B1 258 D2
Winchester Wlk SE1 252 C4
Winchet Wlk CR0 .... 206 C3
Winchfield Cl HA3 .... 43 C3
Winchfield Ho SW15 .... 155 D5
Winchfield Rd SE26 .. 185 A5
Winch Ho
Isle of Dogs E14 .... 119 D3
SW10 .... 266 B4
Winchilsea Cres KT8 .... 174 A1
Winchilsea Ho NW8 . 229 D1
WINCHMORE HILL ... 16 D4
Winchmore Hill Rd N14, N21 .... 16 A4
Winchmore Hill Sta N21 .... 16 D4
Winchmore Sch N21 .. 17 A2
Winchmore Villas N21 .... 16 B4
Winchstone Cl TW17 .... 192 B5
Winckley Cl HA3 ...... 44 B4
Wincott St SE11 .... 116 C2 261 B3
Wincrofts Dr SE9 .... 145 B1
Windall Cl SE20 ...... 184 A2
Windborough Rd SM5 .... 219 A1
Windcott Ct HA3 ...... 43 C2
Windermere Ave
Golders Green N3 ..... 47 C6
Kensal Rise NW6 ...... 91 A6
Windermere Ave *continued*
Merton SW19 ...... 201 D6
Ruislip HA4 .... 40 D2
Wembley HA9 .... 43 C1
Windermere Cl BR6 .. 226 D5
East Bedfont TW14 .. 149 D3
Stanwell TW19 ..... 148 A2
Windermere Ct
Barnes SW13 ...... 133 D6
Barnet EN5 .... 1 D1
Carshalton SM5 ..... 219 A5
Wembley HA9 .... 43 C2
Windermere Gdns IG4 .... 56 A4
Windermere Gr HA9 .. 43 C1
Windermere Hall HA8 .... 26 B5
Windermere Ho
Isleworth TW1 ...... 152 D6
Tower Hamlets E3 ..... 97 B3
Windermere NW1 ... 231 D2
Windermere Point 3 SE15 .... 140 C5
Windermere 12 SW15 .... 156 D5
Windermere Rd
Brentford W5 .... 109 C3
Croydon CR0 .... 205 D1
Kingston u T SW15 .. 177 C5
Mitcham SW16 ..... 181 D1
Muswell Hill N10 ...... 31 B2
Southall UB1 .... 85 B2
Upper Holloway N19 ... 71 C6
West Wickham BR4 .. 224 C6
Windermere Way UB7 .... 104 B5
Winders Rd SW11 .... 136 C3
Windfield Cl SE26 .... 184 D6
Windham Rd TW9 .... 132 B2
Winding Way RM8 .... 80 C5
Windlass Pl SE8 ..... 119 A2
Windlesham Gr SW19 .... 156 D3
Windley Cl SE23 ..... 162 C2
Windmill Alley 7 W4 .... 111 C2
Windmill Ave UB2 .... 108 A4
Windmill Bridge Ho 1 CR0 .... 205 C1
Windmill Bsns Ctr UB2 .... 108 A5
Windmill Bsns Village TW16 .... 171 C2
Windmill Cl
Ashford TW16 ...... 171 C3
12 Bermondsey SE1 . 118 A2
Kingston u T KT6 .... 197 C2
4 Lewisham SE13 .. 142 A3
Windmill Ct
Brentford W5 .... 109 C2
Brondesbury NW2 ..... 69 A2
Bushey WD23 .... 8 B3
Windmill Dr BR2 ..... 225 C4
Clapham SW4 .... 159 B6
Cricklewood NW2 ..... 69 A5
Windmill Gdns
Brixton SW2 .... 160 B5
Enfield EN2 .... 4 C2
Windmill Gr CR0 .... 205 A3
Windmill Hill
Enfield EN2 .... 5 A2
1 Hampstead NW3 ... 70 A4
Hampstead NW3 ...... 70 A5
Ruislip HA4 .... 39 D1
Windmill Ho
4 Millwall E14 ..... 119 C2
SE1 .... 251 B3
Windmill La
Barnet Gate EN5 ...... 11 D5
Bushey WD23 .... 8 C3
Greenford UB6 .... 86 A2
Isleworth TW7, UB2, W7 .... 108 C2
Southall UB2 .... 108 A4
Stratford E15 .... 76 B2
Thames Ditton KT7 ... 197 B2
Windmill Lo TW16 ... 171 C2
Windmill Pas 10 W4 .... 111 C2
Windmill Pl UB1 ..... 108 A5
Windmill Rd
Brentford TW8, W5 .... 109 C1
Charlton TW16 ...... 171 C2
Chiswick W4 .... 111 C2
Edmonton N18 .... 33 B6
Hampton TW12 ..... 174 A5
Mitcham CR4 .... 203 C5
Roehampton SW19 ... 156 B1
Thornton Heath CR0 . 205 A2
Wandsworth SW18 ... 158 B5
Windmill Rd W TW16 .... 171 C1
Windmill Rise KT2 ... 176 D3
Windmill Row SE11 . 261 A1
Windmill St
Bloomsbury W1 .... 93 D2 239 C3
Bushey WD23 .... 8 C3
Windmill Terr TW17 .... 193 C2
Windmill Trad Est CR4 .... 203 C5
Windmill Way HA4 .... 39 D1
Windmill WC1 ...... 240 C4
Windmill Wlk SE1 ... 251 B2
Windmore Cl HA0 ..... 65 A3
Windrose Cl SE16 .... 118 D4
Windrush Cl
Battersea SW11 ..... 136 B1
Chiswick W4 .... 133 A5
Ickenham UB10 .... 60 B4
Windrush Ho NW8 .. 236 D4
Windrush KT3 .... 199 A5
Windrush La SE23 .... 162 D1
Windrush Prim Sch SE28 .... 124 B5
Windrush Rd NW10 ... 89 B6
Windsock Cl 1 SE16 .... 119 B2
Windsor Ave
Cheam SM3 .... 217 A5
East Molesey KT8 ... 195 C6
Edgware HA8 .... 10 D1
Higham Hill E17 ...... 35 A1
Hillingdon UB10 ...... 60 D1
Merton SW19 ...... 180 A2
New Malden KT3 .... 199 A4
Windsor Cl
Brentford TW8 ...... 131 B6
Chislehurst BR7 ..... 188 D5
Harrow HA2 .... 63 C5
Hendon N3 .... 29 A1
Pinner HA6 .... 22 A1
West Norwood SE27 . 183 A6
Windsor Cres
Harrow HA2 .... 63 C5
Wembley HA9 .... 66 D5
Windsor Ct
Battersea SW11 ..... 136 B3
Bayswater W2 ...... 245 C6
Bickley BR1 .... 210 A6
Bushey WD23 .... 8 A4
Chelsea SW3 .... 257 B2
2 Clapham SW4 ... 137 C1
Edgware HA8 .... 26 B3
Friern Barnet N11 .... 30 D5
Fulham SW6 .... 135 A2
Osidge N14 .... 15 C4
20 Rotherhithe SE16 .... 118 D5
Windsor Ctr The SE27 .... 183 A6
Windsor Ct
17 Sidcup DA14 .... 168 A1
South Norwood SE19 .... 183 C2
Sunbury TW16 ...... 172 A3
Temple Fortune NW11 .... 47 A3
Walthamstow E17 ..... 53 B6
4 Wandsworth SW18 .... 157 C6
West Hampstead NW3 .... 69 C4
5 West Wickham BR4 .... 207 D1
Windsor Dr EN4 ...... 14 D5
Windsor Gdns
Hayes UB3 .... 105 B3
Paddington W9 .... 91 C3
Wallington CR0 ..... 220 A5
Windsor Gr SE27 .... 183 A6
Windsor Hall 11 E16 .... 121 B5
Windsor Ho
4 Acton Green W4 .... 111 A1
Brondesbury NW2 ..... 69 A2
4 Globe Town E2 ..... 96 D4
2 Hendon NW4 ...... 28 D1
7 Northolt UB5 ...... 63 C2
Queensbury NW9 ..... 44 C5
Regent's Pk NW1 ... 231 D2
Shoreditch N1 ...... 235 B4
Stanmore HA7 .... 25 B5
Stoke Newington N4 ... 51 A1
Windsor Lo KT3 ..... 199 A4
Windsor Mews
Catford SE6 .... 164 A3
Forest Hill SE23 ..... 163 A3
Windsor Park Rd UB3 .... 127 D5
Windsor Pk SW19 .... 180 A2
Windsor Pl SW1 .... 259 B4
Windsor Rd
Ashford TW16 ...... 172 A4
Barnet EN5 .... 12 D5
Chingford E4 .... 35 D6
Cranford TW4, TW5 .. 128 C3
DA6 .... 147 A1
Dagenham RM8 .... 81 A5
Windsor Rd *continued*
Ealing W5 .... 110 A6
Forest Gate E7 .... 77 C3
Harrow HA3 .... 24 B2
Hendon N3 .... 29 A1
Ilford IG1 .... 79 A4
Kingston u T KT2 .... 176 A3
Leyton E10 .... 75 D6
Palmers Green N13 ... 16 C1
Richmond TW9 ...... 132 B3
Southall UB2 .... 107 B3
South Norwood CR7 . 182 D1
Teddington TW11 .... 174 B5
Tottenham N17 .... 34 A1
Upper Holloway N7 ... 72 A5
Wanstead E11 .... 77 A6
Willesden NW2 .... 68 B2
Worcester Pk KT4 ... 216 A6
Windsor St N1 .... 94 D6 234 D6
Windsor Terr N1 .... 95 A4 235 B2
Windsor Way W14 .... 113 A2 254 A4
Windsor Wharf E9 .... 75 B3
Windsor Wlk
Camberwell SE5 ..... 139 B3
Walton-on-T KT12 ... 194 D1
Windspoint Dr SE15 .. 140 B6
Windus Rd N16 .... 51 D1
Windus Wlk N16 ...... 51 D1
Windy Ridge BR1 .... 188 A2
Windy Ridge Cl SW19 .... 178 D5
Wine Cl E1 .... 118 C6
Wine Office Ct EC4 .. 241 B2
Winery La KT1 ...... 198 B6
Winey Cl KT9 .... 213 C1
Winfield Ho 3 SW11 .... 136 B3
Winford Ct 10 SE15 ... 140 A4
Winford Ho E3 .... 75 B1
Winford Par 6 UB1 ... 85 D1
Winforton St SE10 ... 142 A4
Winfrith Rd SW18 .... 158 A3
Wingate Cres CR0 ... 204 A3
Wingate Ho
26 Bromley E3 .... 97 D4
8 Stoke Newington N16 .... 73 B4
Wingate Rd
Hammersmith W6 .... 112 B3
Ilford IG1 .... 78 D3
Sidcup DA14 .... 190 C4
Wingate Trad Est 11 N17 .... 33 D3
Wingfield Ct
5 Blackwall E14 ..... 120 B6
Sidcup DA15 .... 167 D3
Wingfield Ho
Paddington NW6 ...... 91 D5
16 Spitalfields E2 ..... 95 D4
Wingfield Mews SE15 .... 140 A2
Wingfield Prim Sch SE3 .... 143 B2
Wingfield Rd
Kingston u T KT2 .... 176 C4
Leyton E15 .... 76 C4
Walthamstow E17 ..... 53 D4
Wingfield St SE15 ... 140 A2
Wingfield Way HA4 ... 62 B2
Wingford Rd SW2 .... 160 A5
Wingham Ho 3 SE26 .... 184 B5
Wingham 3 NW5 ...... 71 A2
Wingmore Rd SE24 .. 139 A2
Wingrad Ho 18 E1 .... 96 C2
Wingrave Rd W6 .... 134 C6
Wingrave SE17 ..... 262 C3
Wingreen 15 NW8 .... 91 D6
Wingrove Ho E4 ..... 19 D4
Wingrove Rd SE6 .... 164 C2
Wings Cl SM1 .... 217 C4
Winicotte Ho W2 .... 236 D4
Winifred Cl EN5 ...... 11 D5
Winifrede Paul Ho 7 NW5 .... 71 B4
Winifred Pl N12 ...... 30 A5
Winifred Rd
Dagenham RM8 .... 59 A1
Hampton TW12 ..... 173 C6
Merton SW19 ...... 179 C2
Winifred St E16 ..... 122 B5
Winifred Terr EN1 .... 17 D4
Winkfield Rd
Newham E13 .... 99 B5
Wood Green N22 ...... 32 C2
Winkley Ct
Cranley Gdns N10 ..... 49 B5
Harrow HA2 .... 63 C5
Winkley St 6 E2 ...... 96 B5
Winkworth Cotts 14 E1 .... 96 C3
Winlaton Rd BR1 .... 186 B6
Winmill Rd RM8 ...... 81 B5
Winn Bridge Cl IG8 ... 37 D2
Winn Common Rd SE18 145
Winnett St W1 249
Winningales Ct IG5 ... 56
Winnings Wlk UB5 63
Winnington Cl N2 48
Winnington Ho
19 Kensal Town W10 91
8 SE5 139
Winnington Rd
Enfield EN3 6
Hampstead Garden Suburb N2 48
Winnipeg Dr 3 BR6 227
Winnipeg Ho UB4 84
Winn Rd SE12 165
Winns Ave E17 53
Winns Mews N15 51
Winns Prim Sch The E17 35
Winns Terr E17 53
Winsbeach E17 36
Winscombe Cres W5 .. 87
Winscombe Ct W5 87
Winscombe St N19 71
Winscombe Way HA7 25
Winsford Rd SE6 163
Winsford Terr N18 33
Winsham Gr SW11 ... 159
Winsham Ho NW1 .. 232
Winslade Ho 4 E5 74
Winslade Rd SW2 160
Winslade Way SE6 ... 163
Winsland Mews W2 . 236
Winsland St W2 .... 92 B1 236
Winsley St W1 239
Winslow Cl
2 Neasden NW10 67
Pinner HA5 40
Winslow Gr E4 20
Winslow Rd W6 134
Winslow SE17 263
Winslow Way TW13 .. 151
Winsmoor Ct EN2 4
Winsor Prim Sch E6 100
Winsor Terr E6 100
Winstanley Rd SW11 136
Winston Ave NW9 45
Winston Cl
Harrow HA3 24
Romford RM7 59
Winston Ct 7 BR1 ... 187
Harrow HA3 23
Winston Ho WC1 239
Winston Rd N16 73
Winston Way IG1 79
Winston Wlk 2 W4 .. 111
Winter Ave E6 100
Winterberry Ct 22 N12 29
Winterborne Ave BR6 227
Winterbourne Ho W11 244
Winterbourne Inf Sch CR7 204
Winterbourne Jun Boys' Sch CR7 204
Winterbourne Jun Girls' Sch CR7 204
Winterbourne Rd
Dagenham RM8 80
Forest Hill SE6 163
Thornton Heath CR7 . 204
Winter Box Wlk TW10 154
Winterbrook Rd SE24 161
Winterburn Cl N11 31
Winterfold Cl SW19 .. 157
Wintergreen Cl 7 E6 100
Winterleys 7 NW6 91
Winter Lo 17 SE16 118
Winter's Ct E4 19
Winterslow Ho 20 SE5 139
Winters Rd KT7 197
Winterstoke Gdns NW7 28
Winterstoke Rd SE6 .. 163
Winterton Ct KT1 175
Winterton Ho 15 E1 ... 96
Winterton Pl SW10 .. 266
Winterwell Rd SW2 .. 160
Winthorpe Rd SW15 135
Winthrop Ho 10 W12 112
Winthrop St E1 96
Winthrop Wlk HA9 64

n Ave N11 31 C3
n Cl N9 18 D4
n Ct 15 KT6 197 D2
n Gdns HA8 26 B3
n Prim Sch
94 B5 233 C3
n Rd BR6 226 D4
n Way SW16 182 C5
ur Ho HA9 65 D6
l Ho 15 SE26 162 A1
Wood Cl
188 C4
each Rd CR0 205 B4
ech 5 N4 50 B1
en Ho SW8 270 D5
om Ct 7 TW7 131 A2
ons Cl RM7, RM9 59 D1
La NW7 28 A4
nan Ct 12
183 C5
nan Rd E10 75 C6
Rd E15 98 B6
on Rd SW17 158 D3
rt Rd SE3 143 D3
w Wlk N13 32 A4
Ho SW1 259 C2
Rd
am SW11 159 A6
aul's Cray BR5 190 B3
ria Cl BR6 226 D6
ria Cl
vare NW7 27 D4
d IG1 78 D3
ria Ho SE4 141 A2
ria Rd SE13 142 B1
w Ho 14 E2 96 A6
hurst La N6 49 A1
St E2 96 B4
wood Ho 10
138 C2
mbe Point 14
140 A4
m Ct Leyton E10 75 D5
r Tooting
/17 158 D1
m Ho 34 SE5 139 A3
m Rd
nham RM10 81 C3
g W13 109 B5
slow TW7 130 B4
e SE20 206 C6
rby Cl CR0 221 C4
rington Rd N5 72 C3
rs Cl KT9 213 C2
rs Mead NW9 27 D2
rs Pl EC1 242 B6
rston Way
166 C1
ngton Rd N2 30 C2
combe Rd
156 D4
Ho 4 E1 96 D3
La HA4 39 A4
Mead E4 20 B1
Cres CR0 224 A2
Ct
hall UB2 107 B2
240 A5
Gdns UB2 107 B2
Ho 2 SW2 160 B4
Ind Est UB2 107 B2
Point 8
156 B3
Rd N19 71 C6
ey Cl
nham UB10 60 B4
er HA5 23 B4
ey Path SE23 162 D1
nham Way E4 20 B1
n Ho KT3 199 B1
ring Cl KT2 175 D5
ring Ho 9
1 136 D3
rsham Rd BR1 186 D5
Ho KT2 198 B6
hoe Cl SE15 140 B2
hoe Ct TW4 129 B1
hoe Rd IG11 102 B5
ton Rd SE26 184 C5
n Ho SE9 143 C1
Prim Sch SW4 137 B1
d RM9 102 D6
La SW4 137 B1
rn Cl
ey WD23 8 A5
102 D1
bledon SW19 180 A4
rn Ct
Bermondsey
16 118 B1
don CR0 205 A1
A6 147 A1
mond TW9 132 B2
Woodford E18 37 A1
rn W13 87 B2
rn Pl
94 A3 240 A5

Woburn Rd
Carshalton SM5 202 C1
Croydon CR0 205 A1
Woburn Sq
WC1 93 D3 239 D5
Woburn Twr 14 UB5 84 D4
Woburn Wlk WC1 232 D1
Wodeham Gdns 1
E1 96 B2
Wodehouse Ave
SE15 139 D4
Wodehouse Ct 10
W3 111 A3
Woffington Cl KT1,
KT8 175 C2
Woking Cl SW15 133 D1
Wolcot Ho NW1 232 B3
Woldham Pl BR2 209 C5
Woldham Rd BR2 209 C5
Wolds Dr BR6 226 C4
Wolfe Cl Hayes BR2 209 A3
Yeading UB4 84 B4
Wolfe Cres
Greenwich SE7 121 D1
34 Rotherhithe
SE16 118 D4
Wolfe Ho 19 W12 112 B6
Wolferton Rd E12 78 B4
Wolffe Gdns 2 E15 76 D2
Wolf Fields Prim Sch
UB2 107 B2
Wolfington Rd
SE27 182 D6
Wolfram Cl SE13 164 C6
Wolfson Ct
4 Barnet EN4 14 D3
Golders Green NW11 47 A2
SE1 253 D2
Wolfson Hillel Prim Sch
N14 15 D5
Wolftencroft Cl
SW11 136 B2
Wollaston Cl SE1 262 A4
Wollotan Ho N1 234 B4
Wolmer Cl HA8 26 D6
Wolmer Gdns HA8 10 C1
Wolmer Rd HA8 26 D6
Wolseley Ave SW18,
SW19 157 C2
Wolseley Gdns W4 132 D6
Wolseley Rd
Acton W4 111 A2
Carshalton CR4 203 A2
Harrow HA3 42 C6
Hornsey N8 49 D4
Upton E7 77 B1
Wood Green N22 32 B2
Wolseley St
SE1 117 D4 253 D1
Wolsey Ave
Thames Ditton
KT7 196 D4
Wallend E6 100 C4
Walthamstow E17 53 B6
Wolsey Cl
Isleworth TW3 130 A1
Kingston u T KT2 176 D2
Southall UB2 108 A3
Wimbledon SW20 178 B3
Worcester Pk KT19,
KT4 216 A4
Wolsey Cres SM4 201 B2
Wolsey Ct
Bromley BR1 186 D3
SE9 166 B5
South Hampstead
NW6 70 A1
Wolsey Dr
Kingston u T KT2 176 A4
Walton-on-T KT12 194 D1
Wolsey Gr HA8 27 B3
Wolsey Ho
2 Hampton
TW12 173 D4
3 Kentish Town
NW5 71 D2
Wolsey Inf Sch CR0 224 A1
Wolsey Jun Sch
CR0 224 A1
Wolsey Mews
Kentish Town NW5 71 C2
Orpington BR6 227 D3
Wolsey Rd
Ashford TW15 170 B6
East Molesey KT8 196 B5
Enfield EN1 6 B3
Hampton TW12 174 A4
Stoke Newington N1 73 B3
Sunbury Comm
TW16 171 D4
Wolsey St E1 96 C2
Wolsey Way KT9 214 C3
Wolstenholme HA7 25 B5
Wolstonbury N12 29 C5
Wolvercote Rd SE2 124 D4
Wolverley St E2 96 B4
Wolverton Ave KT2 176 C2

Wolverton Gdns
Brook Green W6 112 D2
Ealing W5 110 B6
Wolverton Mans
W5 110 B5
Wolverton Rd HA7 25 B3
Wolverton SE17 263 A2
Wolverton Way N14 15 C6
Wolves La N22 32 C4
Womersley Rd N4,
N8 50 B3
Wonford Cl KT2,
KT3 177 C2
Wontner Cl 5 N1 73 A1
Wontner Rd SW12,
SW17 158 D2
Wooburn Cl UB8 82 D3
Wooburn Ct N14 15 D3
Woodall Cl
Chessington KT9 213 D2
15 Poplar E14 119 D6
Woodall Ho TW7 130 D2
Woodall Rd EN3 18 D5
Woodbank Rd BR1 164 D1
Woodbastwick Rd
SE26 185 A5
Woodberry Ave
Edmonton N21 16 D2
Harrow HA2 42 A5
Woodberry Cl
Ashford TW16 172 A4
Mill Hill NW7 28 D3
Woodberry Cres N10 49 B6
Woodberry Down Com
Prim Sch N4 51 A2
Woodberry Down N4 51 A2
Woodberry Gdns
N12 30 A4
Woodberry Gr
Finchley N12 30 A4
Stoke Newington N4 51 A2
Woodberry View N6 49 A3
Woodberry Way
Chingford E4 20 A4
Finchley N12 30 A4
Woodbine Cl TW2 152 B2
Woodbine Gr
Enfield EN2 5 B5
Penge SE20 184 B3
Woodbine La KT4 216 C5
Woodbine Pl E11 55 A3
Woodbine Rd DA15 167 C3
Woodbines Ave
KT1 197 D6
Woodbine Terr E9 74 C2
Woodborough Rd
SW15 134 B1
Woodbourne Ave
SW16 159 D1
Woodbourne Cl
SW16 160 A1
Woodbourne Dr
KT10 212 D2
Woodbourne Gdns
SM6 219 B1
Woodbridge Cl
4 Dollis Hill NW2 68 A5
10 Finsbury Pk N7 72 B6
Woodbridge Ct
Forest Gate E7 77 D3
Stoke Newington N16 73 B5
Woodbridge High Sch
IG8 37 B3
Woodbridge Ho E11 54 D1
Woodbridge Rd IG11 79 D3
Woodbridge St
EC1 94 D3 241 C6
Woodbrook Rd SE2 146 B6
Woodbrook Sch
BR3 185 B2
Woodburn Cl NW4 46 D4
Woodbury Cl
Croydon CR0 221 D6
Wanstead E11 55 B5
Woodbury Ct 1 W13 87 B3
Woodbury Gdns
Bromley SE12 187 B6
Eltham SE12 165 B1
Woodbury Ho 4
SE26 162 B1
Woodbury Park Rd
W13 87 B3
Woodbury Rd E17 53 D5
Woodbury St SW17 180 C5
Woodchester Sq W2 91 D2
Woodchurch Cl
DA14 167 B1
Woodchurch Dr
BR1 187 D3
Woodchurch Ho 15
SW9 138 C4
Woodchurch Rd
NW6 69 D1
Wood Cl
Bethnal Green E2 96 A3
Harrow HA1 42 B2
Kingsbury NW9 45 B2

Woodclyffe Dr BR7 188 C1
Woodcock Ct HA3 44 A2
Woodcock Dell Ave
HA3 43 D2
Woodcock Hill HA3 43 C3
Woodcock Ho 4
E14 97 C2
Woodcocks E16 99 D2
Woodcombe Cres
SE23 162 C3
Woodcote Ave
Mill Hill NW7 28 C4
Thornton Heath CR7 204 D5
Wallington SM6 219 B1
Woodcote Cl
Enfield N9 18 C5
Kingston u T KT2 176 B5
Woodcote Ct 14
SM6 219 B2
Woodcote Dr BR6 211 B2
Woodcote Ho 4
SE8 141 B6
Woodcote Mews
Loughton IG10 21 D4
Wallington SM6 219 B2
Woodcote Pl 1
SE27 182 D5
Woodcote Rd
Wallington SM6 219 C1
Wanstead E11 55 A2
Woodcott Ho 1
SW15 156 A4
Woodcroft Ave
Edgware NW7 27 C4
Stanmore HA7 25 A2
Woodcroft Cres
UB10 82 D6
Woodcroft Mews
SE8 119 A2
Woodcroft Prim Sch
HA8 27 C3
Woodcroft Rd CR7 204 D3
Woodcroft SE9 166 B1
South Croydon CR0 221 C5
Southgate N21 16 C3
17 Stanmore HA7 25 C5
Wembley UB6 65 A2
Wood Dene 6 SE15 140 B4
Wood Dr BR7 188 A4
Woodedge Cl E4 20 D3
WOOD END 83 D1
Wood End Ave HA2 64 A4
Wood End Cl UB5 64 B3
Woodend Gdns EN2 4 A1
Wood End Gdns UB5 64 A3
WOOD END GREEN 83 C2
Wood End Green Rd
UB3 83 C1
Wood End UB3 83 C1
Wood End Inf Sch
UB5 64 B3
Wood End Jun Sch
UB6 64 B3
Wood End La UB5 63 D3
Wood End Park Com
Sch UB3 105 A6
Woodend Rd E17 36 A1
Wood End Rd HA1,
UB5 64 B4
Woodend
South Norwood
SE19 183 A4
Sutton SM1 218 A6
Thames Ditton KT10 212 A6
Wood End Way UB5 64 A3
Wooder Gdns E7 77 A4
Wooderson Cl SE25 205 C5
Wooderson Ct 9
BR3 185 C2
Woodfall Ave EN5 13 B6
Woodfall Rd N4 72 C6
Woodfall St SW3 257 C1
Woodfarrs SE5 139 B1
Woodfield Ave
Colindale NW9 45 C5
Ealing W5 87 C3
Streatham SW16 159 D1
Wallington SM5 219 A1
Wembley HA0 65 C5
Woodfield Cl
1 Enfield EN1 5 C1
South Norwood
SE19 183 A3
Woodfield Cres W5 87 D3
Woodfield Ct SW16 159 D1
Woodfield Dr EN4 15 A3
Woodfield Gdns
KT3 199 D4
Woodfield Gr SW16 159 D1
Woodfield Ho
11 Forest Hill
SE23 162 D1
Hinchley Wood KT7 212 D6
New Malden KT3 199 D4
6 Upper Clapton E5 74 B6
Wood Green N11 31 D4
Wood Field NW3 70 D3

Woodfield Pl W9 91 B3
Woodfield Rd
Cranford TW4,
TW5 128 B3
Ealing W5 87 C3
Hinchley Wood KT10,
KT7 212 D6
Kensal Town W9 91 B2
Woodfield Rise WD23 8 B4
Woodfield Sch NW9 45 C1
Woodfields Ct SM1 218 A5
Woodfield SW16 182 B2
Woodfield Way N11 31 D3
WOODFORD 37 D5
Woodford Ave IG2, IG4,
IG5, IG8 56 B5
Woodford Bridge Rd
IG4 56 A5
Woodford Cres HA5 22 B1
Woodford Ct 15
W12 112 D4
Woodford Cty High Sch
IG8 36 D4
Woodforde Ct UB3 105 B1
WOODFORD GREEN 37 B3
Woodford Green Prep
Sch IG8 37 A4
Woodford Green Sch
IG8 36 D5
Woodford Ho
13 SE18 144 D6
5 Wanstead E18 55 A5
Woodford New Rd
Upper Walthamstow
E17 54 C6
Woodford E18 36 D3
Woodford Pl HA9 44 A1
Woodford Rd
Forest Gate E7 77 B4
Wanstead E18 55 A6
Woodford Sta IG8 37 B4
Woodford Trad Est
IG8 37 D1
WOODFORD WELLS 21 B1
Woodgate Ave KT9 213 D3
Woodgate Cres HA6 22 A4
Woodgate Dr SW16 181 D3
Woodgate Ho 12
KT6 198 A3
Woodger Rd W12 112 C4
Woodget Cl E6 100 A1
Woodglen SM4 202 C4
Woodgrange Ave
Ealing W5 110 C5
Enfield EN1 18 A5
Finchley N12 30 B4
Harrow HA3 43 D4
Woodgrange Cl HA3 43 D4
Woodgrange Ct 1
BR2 208 D1
Woodgrange Gdns
EN1 18 A5
Woodgrange Ho
W5 110 B5
Woodgrange Inf Sch
E7 77 B4
Woodgrange Mans
HA3 43 C4
Woodgrange Park Sta
E12 77 D3
Woodgrange Rd E7 77 A3
Woodgrange Terr
EN1 18 A5
WOOD GREEN 32 B2
Wood Green Sh City
N22 32 C1
Wood Green Sta N22 32 C1
Woodhall Ave
Dulwich SE21 161 D1
Pinner HA5 23 A2
Woodhall Dr
Dulwich SE21 161 D1
Pinner HA5 23 A2
Woodhall Gate HA5 22 D3
Woodhall Ho SW18 158 B5
Woodhall La WD19 23 A6
Woodhall NW1 232 A1
Woodhall Prim Sch
WD19 23 A6
Woodhall Rd HA5 22 D4
Woodham Ct E11 54 D5
Woodham Rd SE6 164 A1
Woodhatch Cl 16
E6 100 A2
Woodhaven Gdns
IG6 57 A5
Woodhayes BR7 188 D4
Woodhayes Rd SW19,
SW20 178 C4
Woodhead Dr BR6 227 C6
Woodheyes Rd
NW10 67 C3
Woodhill Cres HA3 43 D3
Woodhill Prim Sch
SE18 122 A2
Woodhill SE7, SE18 122 A2

Wood Ho
4 Clapham SW4 137 D3
6 Paddington NW6 91 B5
Woodhouse Ave UB6 86 D5
Woodhouse Cl
Hayes UB3 105 C3
Wembley UB6 86 D5
Woodhouse Eaves
HA6 22 A5
Woodhouse Gr E12 78 A2
Woodhouse Rd
Colney Hatch N12 30 C4
Leyton E11 76 D5
Woodhouse Sixth Form
Coll N12 30 B4
Woodhurst Ave
BR5 211 A3
Woodhurst Rd
Acton W3 111 A6
SE2 124 A2
Woodington Cl SE9 166 C5
Woodison St E3 97 A3
Woodknoll Dr BR7 188 B2
Wood La
Dagenham RM10 81 A5
Highgate N6 49 B3
Hounslow TW7 130 D5
Kingsbury NW9 45 B2
Woodland App UB6 65 A2
Woodland Cl
Kingsbury NW9 45 A3
Uxbridge UB10 60 D6
West Ewell KT19 215 C2
West Norwood SE19 183 C4
Woodford IG8 21 B1
Woodland Cres
18 Rotherhithe
SE16 118 D4
SE10 142 C6
Woodland Ct
Cheam SM1 217 C2
Temple Fortune NW4 47 A4
13 Wanstead E11 55 A4
Woodland Gdns
Cranley Gdns N10 49 B4
Isleworth TW7 130 C2
Woodland Gr SE10 120 C1
Woodland Hill SE19 183 C4
Woodland Hts SE3 142 C6
Woodland Mews
SW16 160 A1
Woodland Rd
Chingford E4 20 A3
Friern Barnet N11 31 B5
Penge SE19 183 D4
Thornton Heath CR7 204 C5
Woodland Rise
Cranley Gdns N10 49 B5
Wembley UB6 65 A2
WOODLANDS 130 C2
Woodlands Ave
Acton W3 110 D5
DA15 167 C3
Dagenham RM6 59 A2
Finchley N3 30 A2
Kingston u T KT3 177 B2
Ruislip HA4 40 D2
Wanstead E11 55 B1
Worcester Pk KT4 216 A6
Woodlands
Beckenham BR3 185 D3
Clapham SW4 137 B1
Woodlands Cl BR1 188 B1
Claygate KT10 212 D1
Temple Fortune
NW11 47 A4
Woodlands Ct
9 Bromley BR1 186 D2
Brondesbury Pk
NW10 90 D6
Dulwich SE22 162 B4
Southall UB1 107 C6
Woodlands Dr
Harrow HA7 24 D4
Sunbury TW16 172 C1
Woodlands N12 30 A4
Woodlands Fst & Mid
Sch HA8 26 B2
Woodlands Gdns
E17 54 C5
Woodlands Gr TW7 130 C3
Woodlands Gt
SW15 157 B6
Woodlands HA2 41 C5
Woodlands Jun & Inf
Schs IG1 79 B3
Woodlands Par
TW15 171 A4
Woodlands Park Rd
SE10 142 C6
Tottenham N15 51 A4
Woodlands Rd
Barnes SW13 133 D2
Bexleyheath DA7 147 A2

Woodlands Rd *continued*
Bickley BR1 188 B1
Enfield EN2 5 B4
Harrow HA1 42 D4
Ilford IG1 79 A5
Isleworth TW7 130 C3
Leyton E11 76 C6
Lower Edmonton N9 18 C3
Southall UB1 106 D5
Surbiton KT6 197 D2
Walthamstow E17 54 A6
Woodlands St SE13 164 B4
Woodlands NW11 47 A4
Woodlands The
East Barnet N14 15 B3
Harrow HA1 64 C6
Highbury N5 73 A4
12 Hornsey N8 50 A2
Isleworth TW7 130 D3
Lewisham SE13 164 B4
Mitcham CR4 203 A6
South Norwood SE19 183 A3
Stanmore HA7 25 B5
Thames Ditton KT10 212 A6
Woodland St 2 E8 73 D2
Woodlands E11 54 B2
Woodlands Way SW15 157 B6
Woodlands SW20 200 D5
Woodland Terr SE7 122 A2
Woodland Way
Abbey Wood SE2 124 D2
Croydon CR0 207 A1
Edgware NW7 27 D4
Merton SM4 201 B5
Mitcham CR4 181 A3
Petts Wood BR5 211 A4
Southgate N21 16 C2
Tolworth KT5 214 D6
West Wickham BR4 224 A5
Woodford IG8 21 B1
Woodland Wlk
Chessington KT19 214 C2
9 Greenwich SE10 120 C1
Hampstead NW3 70 C3
Wood Lane High Sch W12 90 B1
Wood La Ruislip HA4 61 C6
Shepherd's Bush W12 112 C6
Stanmore HA7 9 B2
Woodlawn Cl SW15 157 B6
Woodlawn Cres TW2 151 D2
Woodlawn Dr TW13 150 D2
Woodlawn Rd SW6 134 D4
Wood La IG8 36 D5
Woodlea Dr BR2 208 C4
Woodlea Lo EN1 17 C5
Woodlea Rd N16 73 C5
Woodleigh Ave N12 30 C4
Woodleigh Ct N22 32 B2
Woodleigh Gdns SW16 160 A1
Woodleigh
1 Kingston u T KT5 198 B4
3 Woodford E18 37 A2
Woodley Cl SW17 180 D3
Woodley La SM1, SM5 218 C5
Wood Lodge Gdns BR1 188 A3
Wood Lodge La BR4 224 A5
Woodlodge 4 SW19 179 B5
Woodman La E4 20 C6
Woodman Mews TW9 132 D4
Woodman Par 4 E16 122 C5
Woodmans Ct HA7 44 A6
Woodmans Gr NW10 67 D3
Woodmans Mews W12 90 B2
Woodmansterne Prim Sch SW16 181 D2
Woodmansterne Rd
Mitcham SW16 181 D2
Sutton SM5 218 C1
Woodman St E16 122 C5
Wood Mead N17 34 A4
Woodmere Ave CR0 206 D2
Woodmere Cl
11 Clapham SW11 137 A2
Croydon CR0 206 D2
Woodmere Ct N14 15 B4
Woodmere Gdns CR0 206 D2
Woodmere SE9 166 B3
Woodmere Way BR3 208 B4
Woodnook Rd SW16 181 B5
Woodpecker Cl
Bushey WD23 8 A3
Enfield N9 18 B5
Harrow HA3 24 D2
Woodpecker Ct TW2 151 D4
Woodpecker Ho E17 53 C6
Woodpecker Mews SE13 142 B1
Woodpecker Rd
6 SE14 141 A6
Woolwich SE28 124 C6
Wood Point 8 E16 99 A2
Woodquest Ave SE24 161 A6
Wood Rd
Littleton TW17 192 C5
Willesden NW10 67 A1
Wood Retreat SE18 145 B5
Wood Ride Barnet EN4 2 B4
Orpington BR5 211 C5
Woodridge Cl EN2 4 C4
Woodridge Prim Sch N12 13 C1
Woodridings Ave HA5 23 B2
Woodridings Cl HA5 23 B3
Woodridings Ct N22 31 D2
Woodriffe Rd E11 54 B2
Wood Rise HA5 40 A4
Woodrow Ave UB4 83 D3
Woodrow Cl UB6 65 B1
Woodrow Ct 3 N17 34 B3
Woodrow SE18 122 B2
Woodruff Ho 12 SW2 160 C5
Woodrush Cl 4 SE14 141 A5
Woodrush Way RM6 58 D5
Woodseer St E1 96 A2
Woodsford SE17 262 C1
Woodsford Sq W14 113 A4 244 B2
Woodshire Rd RM10 81 D5
Woods Ho SW8 269 A2
WOODSIDE 206 A4
Woodside Ave
Chislehurst BR7 189 A5
Croydon SE25 206 B4
Fortis Green N6 48 D5
North Finchley N12 30 A6
Thames Ditton KT10 196 C2
Wembley HA0 88 A6
Woodside IG9 21 C2
Woodside Cl
Ruislip HA4 39 B3
Stanmore HA7 25 B5
Tolworth KT5 199 A2
Wembley HA0 88 A6
Woodside Court Rd CR0 206 A2
Woodside Cres DA15 167 C1
Woodside Ct
Ealing W5 110 A5
Enfield EN2 4 D4
10 Finchley N12 29 D6
Palmers Green N13 16 C1
Wanstead E12 55 C1
Woodside End HA0 88 A6
Woodside Gdns
Chingford E4 35 D4
Tottenham N17 33 D1
Woodside Gn SE25 206 A3
Woodside Grange Rd N12 29 D6
Woodside Gr N12 14 A1
Woodside NW11 47 C4
Woodside Ho SW19 179 B4
Woodside Jun & Inf Sch CR0 206 A2
Woodside La DA5 168 D5
Whetstone N12 14 A1
Woodside N10 49 A6
WOODSIDE PARK 29 C6
Woodside Park Ave E17 54 B5
Woodside Park Int Sch N11 30 D5
Woodside Park Rd N12 30 A6
Woodside Pk SE25 206 B3
Woodside Pl HA0 88 A6
Woodside Rd BR1 210 A4
Coombe KT3 177 C1
Croydon SE25 206 B3
Kingston u T KT2 176 A3
Newham E13 99 C3
Northwood HA6 22 A3
Sidcup DA15 167 C1
Sutton SM1 218 A5
Woodford IG8 37 A6
Wood Green N22 32 C3
Woodside Sch
Belvedere DA17 125 D2
Walthamstow E17 54 A6
Woodside Sta SE25 206 B3
Woodside KT12 194 A1
Woodside Way
Croydon CR0 206 C3
Streatham CR4 181 C2
Woodside SW19 179 B5
Wood's Mews W1 115 A6 248 A6
Woodsome Rd NW5 71 B5
Wood's Pl SE1 263 B5
Woodspring Rd SW19 157 A2
Wood's Rd SE15 140 B4
Woodstar Ho 3 SE15 140 A5
Wood St Barnet EN5 1 A1
Carshalton CR4 203 A2
Chiswick W4 111 C1
City of London EC2 95 A1 242 B2
Custom Ho E16 121 B6
Woodstead Gr HA8 26 A4
Woods The
Eastbury HA6 22 A5
Uxbridge UB10 60 D4
Wood St
Kingston u T KT1 175 D1
Kingston u T KT2 176 A2
Woodstock Ave
Brentford W13 109 A3
Cheam SM3 201 B2
Golders Green NW11 47 A2
Isleworth TW7 153 A6
Southall UB1 85 B4
Woodstock Cl DA5 169 B3
Stanmore HA7 26 A1
Woodstock Cres N9 18 B5
Woodstock Ct
Kingston u T KT2 176 D1
Lee SE12 165 A5
Vauxhall SE11 260 D2
Woodstock Dr UB10 60 B4
Woodstock Gdns
Beckenham BR3 185 D3
Hayes UB4 83 D2
Ilford IG3 80 A6
Woodstock Grange W5 110 A5
Woodstock Gr W12 112 D4
Woodstock Ho
Hayes UB3 83 B2
2 Highbury N5 73 A4
Woodstock Lane N KT6 213 C6
Woodstock Lane S KT6, KT9, KT10 213 C4
Woodstock Mews W1 238 B3
Woodstock Rd
Bedford Pk W4 111 C3
Bushey WD23 8 D4
Chingford E17 36 B1
Finsbury Pk N4 50 C1
Golders Green NW11 47 B1
South Croydon CR0 221 B5
Upton E7 77 C1
Wallington SM5, SM6 219 A3
Wembley HA0 66 B1
Woodstock Rise SM3 201 B2
Woodstock Studios 17 W12 112 D4
Woodstock St W1 238 C1
Woodstock Terr E14 119 D6
Woodstock The SM3 201 B2
Woodstock Way CR4 181 C1
Woodstone Ave KT17, KT4 216 A3
Wood Street Sta E17 54 B5
Wood St E17 54 B5
Woodsyre SE26 183 D6
Woodthorpe Rd
Ashford TW15 170 A6
Putney SW15 134 B1
Woodtree Cl NW4 28 C1
Woodvale Ave SE25 183 D1
Wood Vale N10 49 C4
Woodvale Ct BR1 187 B1
South Norwood SE25 205 D6
Wood Vale SE22 162 B4
Woodvale Way NW11 68 D5
Woodvale Wlk SE27 183 A5
Woodview Ave E4 36 A6
Woodview Cl
Finsbury Pk N4 50 D2
Kingston u T SW15 177 B6
Orpington BR6 227 A6
Woodville Cl SE12 165 A6
Woodville Cl *continued*
Teddington TW11 175 A6
Woodville Ct
3 Lewisham SE10 142 A4
Southgate N14 15 C6
Woodville Gdns
Ealing W5 88 A1
Hendon NW11 46 D2
Ilford IG6 56 D5
Ruislip HA4 39 A2
Surbiton KT6 197 D2
Woodville Gr 2 DA16 146 A2
Woodville Ho SE1 263 C6
Sutton SM1 217 D4
Woodville Rd
Barnet EN5 1 D2
Ealing W5 87 D1
Golders Green NW11 47 A2
Leytonstone E11 54 D1
Morden SM4 201 C5
Paddington NW6 91 B5
Richmond TW10 153 C1
South Norwood CR7 205 B6
Stoke Newington N16 73 C3
Walthamstow E17 53 B5
Woodford E18 37 B1
Woodville SE3 143 B4
Woodville St 16 SE7 122 A2
Woodville The W5 87 D1
Woodward Ave NW4 46 A4
Woodward Cl KT10 212 D2
Woodwarde Rd SE22 161 C5
Woodward Gdns
Dagenham RM9 80 C1
Harrow HA7 24 D3
Woodward Rd RM9 80 C1
Wood Way BR6 226 C6
Woodway Cres HA1 43 A3
Woodwell St SW18 158 A6
Wood Wharf SE10 142 A6
Woodyard Cl NW5 71 A3
Woodyard La SE21 161 C4
Woodyates Rd SE12 165 B4
Woolacombe Rd SE3 143 C3
Woolacombe Way UB3 105 C2
Woolcombes Ct 4 SE16 118 D5
Woolden Ho 2 E4 20 C4
Wooler St SE17 117 B1 262 D2
Woolf Cl SE28 124 B5
Woolf Ct 7 W3 111 A3
Woolf Mews WC1 240 A6
Woollaston Rd N4 50 D3
Woolley Ho SW9 138 D2
Woollon Ho 1 E1 96 C1
Woolmead Ave NW9 46 A2
Woolmer Gdns N18 34 A5
Woolmer Ho 2 E5 74 B6
Woolmer Rd N18 34 A5
Woolmore Prim Sch E14 120 A6
Woolmore St E14 120 A6
Woolneigh St SW6 135 D3
Woolpack Ho 1 E9 74 C2
Wool Rd SW20 178 B4
Woolridge Way E9 74 C1
Woolstaplers Way SE16 118 A2
Woolston Cl E17 34 D1
Woolstone Ho 7 E2 96 A6
Woolstone Rd SE23 163 A2
Woolven Ho SE3 142 D6
WOOLWICH 122 D3
Woolwich Arsenal Sta SE18 122 D2
Woolwich Church St SE7, SE18 122 A3
Woolwich Comm SE18 144 C6
Woolwich Ct EN3 7 C5
Woolwich Dockyard Ind Est SE18 122 A3
Woolwich Dockyard Sta SE18 122 B2
Woolwich High St SE18 122 C3
Woolwich Manor Way E6 100 C1
Woolwich Manorway E16 122 D4
Woolwich Manor Way E16 122 D5
Woolwich New Rd SE18 122 D2
Woolwich Poly Sch for Boys SE28 124 A5
Woolwich Rd
Belvedere DA17 125 C1
DA7 147 C2
Erith SE2 125 B1
Woolwich Rd *continued*
Greenwich SE7, SE10 121 C2
Wooster Gdns E14 98 B1
Wooster Mews HA2 42 A6
Wooster Pl SE1 262 D4
Wootton KT10 212 A4
Wootton Gr N3 29 C2
Wootton Ho SE9 167 B5
Wootton St SE1 116 C5 251 B3
Worbeck Rd SE20 184 C1
Worcester Ave N17 34 A3
Worcester Cl
Croydon CR0 223 C6
Dollis Hill NW2 68 B5
Mitcham CR4 181 A1
Worcester Cres
Edgware NW7 11 C1
Woodford IG8 37 C6
Worcester Ct
Ashford TW15 170 D5
Ealing W7 86 D1
Finchley N12 29 D5
Harrow HA1 42 C6
44 Paddington W2 91 C2
12 Sutton SM2 217 D2
Walton-on-T KT12 194 C1
Worcester Pk KT4 215 C5
Worcester Dr
Ashford TW15 170 D5
Bedford Pk W4 111 C4
Worcester Gdns
Northolt UB6 64 B2
Redbridge IG1 56 A2
Wandsworth SW11 158 D6
Worcester Pk KT4 215 C5
Worcester Ho
Bayswater W2 236 A1
3 Islington N1 73 A1
Lambeth SE11 261 A5
9 Putney SW15 156 C4
Worcester Mews 2 NW6 69 D2
WORCESTER PARK 215 C4
Worcester Park Rd KT4 215 B5
Worcester Park Sta KT4 200 A1
Worcester Rd
Belmont SM2 217 D1
Higham Hill E17 34 D1
Ilford E12 78 B4
11 Wimbledon SW19 179 B5
Worcesters Ave EN1 6 A5
Worcesters Prim Sch EN1 5 D5
Wordsworth Ave
Greenford UB6 86 B5
Plashet E12 78 A1
Snaresbrook E18 54 D6
Wordsworth Ct
Harrow HA1 42 B2
New Barnet EN5 14 A6
Wordsworth Dr KT4, SM3 216 C4
Wordsworth Gdns WD6 10 C6
Wordsworth Ho
Maida Vale NW6 91 C4
15 SE18 144 C6
Wordsworth N8 50 C5
Wordsworth Par 1 N15 50 D5
Wordsworth Pl 11 NW5 70 D3
Wordsworth Rd
Bermondsey SE1 263 D3
Bexley DA16 145 C4
Hampton TW12, TW13 173 B6
Penge SE20 184 D3
Stoke Newington N16 73 C4
Wallington SM6 219 D2
Wordsworth Way UB7 104 B2
Wordsworth Wlk NW11 47 C5
Worfield St SW11 136 C5 267 B3
Worgan St
Rotherhithe SE16 118 D2
SE11 116 B1 260 C2
Working Men's Coll The NW1 93 C5 232 B4
Worland Rd E15 76 C1
World Bsns Ctr TW6 127 A4
WORLD'S END 4 C1
World's End La EN2 4 B1
Worlds End La BR6 227 D1
World's End Pas SW10 266 C4
World's End Pl SW10 266 B4
World Trade Ctr London E14 1
Worley Ct NW2
Worleys Dr BR6 2
Worlidge St W6 1
Worlingham Rd SE22 1
Wormholt Park Prim Sch W12 1
Wormholt Rd W12 1
Wormwood St EC2 2
Wornington Rd W10
Woronzow Rd NW8 92 C6 2
Worple Ave
Isleworth TW7 1
Wimbledon SW19 1
Worple Cl HA2
Worple Ct SW19 1
Worple Prim Sch TW7 1
Worple Rd
Isleworth TW7 1
Wimbledon SW19, SW20 1
Worple Road Mews SW19 1
Worple St SW14 1
Worple Way
Harrow HA2
Richmond TW10 1
Worship St EC2 95 C3 2
Worslade Rd SW17 1
Worsley Bridge Jun Sc BR3 1
Worsley Bridge Rd BR3, SE6 1
Worsley Ct N3
Worsley Grange BR7 1
Worsley Gr E5
Worsley Ho 9 SE23 1
Worsley Rd E11
Worsopp Dr SW4 1
Worth Cl BR6 2
Worthfield Cl KT19 2
Worth Gr SE17 2
Worthing Cl 5 E15
Worthing Rd TW5 1
Worthington Cl CR4 2
Worthington Ho
EC1 2
16 Streatham SW2 1
Worthington Rd KT6 1
Wortley Rd
Forest Gate E6
Thornton Heath CR0 2
Worton Ct TW7 1
Worton Gdns TW7 1
Worton Hall Ind Est TW7 1
Worton Rd TW7 1
Worton Way TW3, TW7 1
Wotton Ct 14 E14 1
Wotton Rd
Cricklewood NW2
18 SE8 1
Wouldham Rd E16
Wragby Rd E11
Wrampling Pl N9
Wrangthorne Wlk CR0 2
Wray Ave IG5
Wrayburn Ho 28 SE16 1
Wray Cres N4
Wray Ct N4
Wrayfield Rd SM3 2
Wray Ho 11 SW2 1
Wraysbury Cl TW4 1
Wrays Way UB4
Wrekin Rd SE18 1
Wren Ave
Cricklewood NW2
Southall UB2 1
Wren Cl E16
Lower Edmonton N9 1
Wren Cres WD23
Wren Ct
1 Barnet EN4
Croydon CR0 2
Wren Gdns RM9
Wren Ho 29 Bow E3
4 Hampton TW12 1
SW1 2
Wren Landing E14 1
Wrenn Ho SW13 1
Wren Path SE28 1
Wren Rd
Camberwell SE5 1
Dagenham RM9
Sidcup DA14 1
Wrens Ave TW15 1
Wren's Park Ho E5

n St WC1 . . 94 B3 240 D6
ntham Ave
10 . . 90 D5
nthorpe Rd
. . 186 C6
n View N6 . . 49 C1
nwood Way HA5 . . 40 B5
stlers Ct EC3 . . 243 A2
kham Rd E3 . . 97 C5
klemarsh Rd
. . 143 D4
glesworth St
4 . . 140 D5
ht Cl SE13 . . 142 B1
ht Gdns TW17 . . 192 C4
ht Ho SW15 . . 156 B6
hton Ct SM1 . . 217 B2
ht Rd TW5 . . 128 C5
hts Cl RM10 . . 81 D4
ht's Gn SW4 . . 137 D1
ht's La
. . 113 D3 255 C6
hts Pl NW10 . . 67 A2
ht's Rd E3 . . 97 B5
hts Rd SE25 . . 205 C6
ht's Row SM5 . . 219 B4
hts Wlk SW14 . . 133 B2
tle Ho 38 NW9 . . 27 D1
tham Ho
kenham BR3 . . 185 B3
. . 262 D6
tham Rd
net EN5 . . 1 A3
Camden Town
W1 . . 71 C1
6 . . 146 C4
ing W13 . . 109 C5
ttesley Rd SE18 . . 145 A6
lesden Green
W10 . . 90 A5
ughton Rd
11 . . 158 D5
ughton Terr
4 . . 46 B5
xall Rd RM9 . . 80 C2
xham Gdns N11 . . 31 D3
xham Rd SE28 . . 124 D6
xton Rd SE15 . . 140 C3
wr Cl UB8 . . 60 A3
wr Hill CR0 . . 221 B4
wr Pl N1 . . 234 C5
the Gn 2 SM5 . . 218 D5
the Green Rd
5 . . 218 D5
the La SM1, SM5,
4 . . 218 C5
THE THE . . 218 D6
fstan St W12 . . 89 D1
tt Cl Bushey WD23 . . 8 C4
tham TW13 . . 150 D3
yes UB4 . . 84 A2
therhithe SE16 . . 119 B4
tt Ct HA0 . . 66 A1
tt Dr SW13 . . 134 B5
tt Ho
ckheath Vale
SE3 . . 142 D3
V8 . . 236 D5
tt Park Mans 1
2 . . 160 A2
tt Park Rd SW2 . . 160 B2
tt Rd
rest Gate E7 . . 77 A2
ghbury N5 . . 73 A5
tt's La E17 . . 54 A6
ert St NW1 . . 239 A6
orne Ho NW10 . . 67 A1
orne Prim Sch
9 . . 166 D3
orne Way NW10 . . 67 A1
urn Ave EN5 . . 1 B2
he Gr CR2 . . 221 A1
herley Cl SE3 . . 142 D5
herley Cres EN5 . . 13 D5
hwood Ave
gware HA8 . . 25 D4
uth Norwood CR7 . 205 A6
hwood Cl
hford TW16 . . 172 A4
gware HA8 . . 25 D4
hwood End N6 . . 49 C2
hwood Gdns IG5 . . 56 C5
hwood Ho N4 . . 51 A2
hwood Way
19 . . 183 B4
clif Ct EC1 . . 234 C1
cliffe Cl DA16 . . 145 D4

Wycliffe Ho 13 N16 . . 73 C4
Wycliffe Rd
Battersea SW11 . . 137 A3
Wimbledon SW19 . . 179 D4
Wyclif St EC1 . . 234 C1
Wycombe Ct SE3 . . 143 A5
Wycombe Gdns
NW11 . . 69 C6
Wycombe Ho NW8 . . 237 A6
Wycombe Pl SW18 . . 158 A5
Wycombe Rd
Redbridge IG2 . . 56 B4
Tottenham N17 . . 34 A2
Wembley HA0 . . 88 C6
Wycombe Sq W8 . . 245 A3
Wydehurst Rd CR0 . . 206 B2
Wydell Cl SM4 . . 200 D3
Wydeville Manor Rd
SE12 . . 187 B6
Wye Cl
Ashford TW15 . . 170 D6
BR6 . . 211 D2
Ruislip HA4 . . 39 A3
Wye Ct W13 . . 87 B2
Wyemead Cres E4 . . 20 C2
Wyersdale Ho N4 . . 51 A2
Wye St SW11 . . 136 B3
Wyevale Cl HA5 . . 40 A6
Wyfold Ho 8 SE2 . . 124 D4
Wyfold Rd
SW6 . . 135 A5 264 A3
Wyke Cl TW7 . . 130 D6
Wyke Gdns W7 . . 109 A3
Wykeham Ave RM9 . . 80 C2
Wykeham Cl UB7 . . 126 C6
Wykeham Ct
Chislehurst BR7 . . 189 C4
Hendon NW4 . . 46 C4
Wykeham Gn RM9 . . 80 C2
Wykeham Hill HA9 . . 44 B1
Wykeham Ho SW19 . . 179 C2
Wykeham Prim Sch
NW10 . . 67 C5
Wykeham Rd
Harrow HA3 . . 43 B5
Hendon NW4 . . 46 C4
Wykeham Rise N20 . . 13 A3
Wykehurst Ho
SW17 . . 180 B5
Wyke Rd
Hackney Wick E3 . . 75 C1
Merton SW20 . . 178 C1
Wylchin Cl HA5 . . 39 D6
Wyldes Cl NW11 . . 48 A1
Wyldfield Gdns N9 . . 17 D2
Wyld Way HA9 . . 66 D2
Wyleu St SE23 . . 163 A4
Wylie Rd UB2 . . 107 C3
Wyllen Cl E1 . . 96 C3
Wylo Dr EN5 . . 12 A5
Wymering Mans 9
W9 . . 91 C4
Wymering Rd W9 . . 91 C4
Wymondham Ct
NW8 . . 229 D6
Wymond St SW15 . . 134 C2
Wynan Rd E14 . . 119 D1
Wynash Gdns SM5 . . 218 C3
Wynaud Ct N22 . . 32 B4
Wynbourne Ct SE20 . . 184 B1
Wyncham Ave DA15 . . 167 C3
Wynchgate
Harrow HA3 . . 24 C3
Southgate N14 . . 16 A4
Wyncroft Cl BR1 . . 210 B6
Wyndale Ave NW9 . . 44 C3
Wyndcliff Rd SE7 . . 143 B6
Wyndcroft Cl EN2 . . 4 D2
Wyndham Cl
Belmont SM2 . . 217 C1
Orpington BR6 . . 211 A1
Wyndham Cres
Camden Town N19 . . 71 C5
Hounslow TW4 . . 151 C5
Wyndham Ct
Brentford W7 . . 109 A2
1 Thornton Heath
CR0 . . 204 D3
Wyndham Deedes Ho 30
E2 . . 96 A5
Wyndham Ho SW1 . . 258 A3
Wyndham Lo TW7 . . 130 C4
Wyndham Mews W1 . . 237 C3
Wyndham Pl W1 . . 237 C3
Wyndham Rd
Barnet EN4 . . 14 D3
Brentford W13 . . 109 B3

Wyndham Rd *continued*
Forest Gate E6 . . 77 D1
Kingston u T KT2 . . 176 B3
SE5 . . 139 A5
Wyndhams Ct 4 E8 . . 73 D1
Wyndham St
W1 . . 92 D2 237 C4
Wyndham Yd W1 . . 237 C3
Wyndhurst Cl CR2 . . 220 D1
Wyneham Rd SE24 . . 161 B6
Wynell Rd SE23 . . 162 D1
Wynford Pl DA17 . . 147 C6
Wynford Rd
N1 . . 94 B5 233 D4
Wynford Way SE9 . . 166 B1
Wynlie Gdns HA5 . . 22 B1
Wynndale Rd E18 . . 37 B2
Wynne Ct 6 TW7 . . 131 A2
Wynne Ho SE14 . . 140 D4
Wynne Rd SW9 . . 138 C3
Wynn's Ave DA15 . . 168 A6
Wynnstay Gdns
W8 . . 113 C3 255 B6
Wynter Ho 20 SW9 . . 138 B3
Wynter St SW11 . . 136 A1
Wynton Gdns SE25 . . 205 D4
Wynton Pl W3 . . 88 D1
Wynyard Ho SE11 . . 260 D2
Wynyard Terr SE11 . . 260 D2
Wynyatt Ho EC1 . . 234 C2
Wynyatt St
EC1 . . 94 D4 234 C2
Wyre Gr Edgware HA8 . . 10 D1
Hayes UB3 . . 106 A2
Wyresdale Cres UB6 . . 86 D4
Wyteleaf Cl HA4 . . 39 A3
Wytham Ho NW8 . . 236 D5
Wythburn Ct W1 . . 237 C2
Wythburn Pl W1 . . 237 C2
Wythenshawe Rd
RM10 . . 81 C5
Wythens Wlk SE9 . . 166 D5
Wythes Cl BR1 . . 188 B1
Wythes Rd E16 . . 122 A5
Wythfield Rd SE9 . . 166 B5
Wyvenhoe Rd HA2 . . 64 A5
Wyvern Est The
KT3 . . 200 A5
Wyvil Prim Sch
SW8 . . 138 A5 270 B4
Wyvil Rd
SW8 . . 138 A5 270 A4
Wyvis St E14 . . 97 D2

X

Xavier Ho E17 . . 35 B1

Y

Yabsley St E14 . . 120 A5
Yaldam Ho SE1 . . 263 A3
Yalding Ho 20 E5 . . 74 B3
Yalding Rd SE16 . . 118 A2
Yale Cl TW4 . . 151 B6
Yale Ct NW6 . . 69 D3
Yarborough Rd 1
SW19 . . 180 B2
Yardley Cl E4 . . 19 D6
Yardley Ct SM3 . . 216 D4
Yardley La E4 . . 19 D6
Yardley Prim Sch E4 . . 20 A5
Yardley St WC1 . . 234 A1
Yard The N1 . . 233 B3
Yarlington Ct N11 . . 31 A5
Yarmouth Cres N17 . . 52 B4
Yarmouth Pl W1 . . 248 C3
Yarnfield Sq 15
SE15 . . 140 A4
Yarnton Way DA17,
DA18 . . 125 B3
Yarrow Cres E6 . . 100 A2
Yarrow Ho
12 Cubitt Town
E14 . . 120 A3
16 North Kensington
W10 . . 90 C2
Yateley St SE18 . . 121 D3
Yatesbury Ct E5 . . 75 A3
Yates Ct NW2 . . 68 D2
Yates Ho 22 E2 . . 96 A4
Yatton Ho 15 W10 . . 90 C2
YEADING . . 84 D3
Yeading Ave HA2 . . 41 A1
Yeading Ct UB4 . . 84 C3

Yeading Fork UB4 . . 84 C3
Yeading Gdns UB4 . . 84 B2
Yeading Ho UB4 . . 84 D2
Yeading Jun & Inf Schs
UB4 . . 84 C2
Yeading La
Hayes UB4 . . 84 B2
Northolt UB4, UB5 . . 84 C4
Yeadon Ho 14 W10 . . 90 C2
Yeames Cl W13 . . 87 A1
Yearby Ho W10 . . 90 C3
Yeate St N1 . . 73 B1
Yeatman Rd N6 . . 48 D3
Yeats Cl NW10 . . 67 C2
Yeend Cl KT8 . . 195 C5
Yeldham Ho W6 . . 112 D1
Yeldham Rd W6 . . 112 D1
Yellowhammer Ct
NW9 . . 27 C1
Yelverton Lo TW1 . . 153 C4
Yelverton Rd SW11 . . 136 B3
Ye Market CR0 . . 221 B3
Yenston Cl SM4 . . 201 C3
Yeoman Cl
Newham E16 . . 122 D6
West Norwood
SE27 . . 160 D1
Yeoman Ct
Heston TW5 . . 129 B5
8 Sutton SM1 . . 218 B3
Yeoman Dr TW19 . . 148 A3
Yeoman Rd UB5 . . 63 A1
Yeomans Acre HA4 . . 40 A3
Yeomans Mews
TW7 . . 152 B6
Yeoman's Row
SW3 . . 114 C3 257 B5
Yeoman St SE8 . . 119 A2
Yeomans Way EN3 . . 6 C3
Yeoman's Yd E1 . . 253 D6
Yeo St E3 . . 97 D2
Yeovil Cl BR6 . . 227 C6
Yeovil Ho
Finsbury Pk N7 . . 72 B6
North Kensington
W10 . . 90 C3
Yeovilton Pl KT2 . . 175 C5
Yerbury Prim Sch
N19 . . 71 D5
Yerbury Rd N19 . . 71 D5
Yeshivo Horomo
Tadmudical Coll
N16 . . 51 B1
Yesodey Hatorah Sch
N16 . . 51 D2
Yester Dr BR7 . . 188 A3
Yester Pk BR7 . . 188 B4
Yester Rd BR7 . . 188 B3
Yet Lev Ct E5 . . 52 A1
Yew Ave UB7 . . 104 A6
Yew Cl IG9 . . 21 D2
Yewdale Cl BR1 . . 186 C4
Yewfield Rd NW10 . . 67 D2
Yew Gr NW2 . . 68 D4
Yew Ho SE14 . . 141 B3
Yews The TW15 . . 170 D6
Yew Tree Ave N2 . . 47 D6
Yew Tree Cl DA16 . . 146 A4
Yewtree Cl HA2 . . 41 D5
Yew Tree Cl
3 Lewisham
SE13 . . 142 A2
New Malden KT4 . . 199 C1
Southgate N21 . . 16 C4
Yewtree Cl N22 . . 31 C2
Yew Tree Cotts
KT10 . . 212 B6
Yew Tree Ct
Elstree WD6 . . 9 D5
8 Stoke Newington
N16 . . 73 B6
8 Sutton SM2 . . 218 A1
4 Temple Fortune
NW11 . . 47 B4
Yew Tree Gdns RM6 . . 59 A4
Yew Tree Grange 2
W5 . . 109 C6
Yew Tree Ho
New Malden KT4 . . 199 C1
5 Surbiton KT6 . . 198 A1
Yew Tree Lo 10
SW16 . . 181 C6
Yewtree Rd BR3 . . 207 B6
Yew Tree Rd
East Acton W12 . . 111 D6
Hillingdon UB10 . . 82 B6
Yew Trees TW17 . . 192 B5

Yew Tree Wlk TW4 . . 151 B6
Yew Wlk HA1 . . 42 C1
YIEWSLEY . . 104 A6
Yiewsley Ct UB7 . . 104 A5
Yoakley Rd N16 . . 73 C6
Yoke Cl N7 . . 72 A2
Yolande Gdns SE9 . . 166 A6
Yonge Pk N4, N7 . . 72 C5
York Ave Ealing W7 . . 108 C5
Hayes UB3 . . 83 A1
Mortlake SW14 . . 155 A6
Sidcup DA15 . . 167 D2
Stanmore HA7 . . 25 B1
Walworth SE17 . . 262 B2
York Bldgs
WC2 . . 116 A6 250 B5
York Bridge
NW1 . . 93 A3 238 A6
York Cl
17 Camberwell
SE5 . . 139 A3
Ealing W7 . . 108 C5
Morden SM4 . . 201 D5
Newham E6 . . 100 B1
York Ct
Beckenham BR3 . . 186 B2
Kingston u T KT2 . . 175 D4
Palmers Green N13 . . 16 A1
Wallington SM6 . . 219 C3
York Gate NW1 . . 238 B5
Southgate N14 . . 16 A4
York Gr SE15 . . 140 C4
York Hill SE27,
SW16 . . 160 D1
York Ho Acton W3 . . 111 A6
Chelsea SW3 . . 257 D2
Chingford E4 . . 35 C6
Edgware HA8 . . 26 B4
Enfield EN2 . . 5 B4
Forest Hill SE26 . . 184 C5
1 Hendon NW4 . . 28 D1
1 Ilford IG1 . . 78 D6
Islington N5 . . 72 C3
Kensington W8 . . 245 C2
11 Kentish Town N7 . . 71 D2
Kew TW9 . . 132 C4
4 Kingston u T KT2 . . 176 B3
Lambeth
SE1 . . 116 B3 260 D5
Marylebone W1 . . 237 C4
Pentonville N1 . . 233 C3
Richmond TW10 . . 154 C6
South Norwood
SE25 . . 205 C5
York House Pl
W8 . . 113 D4 245 C2
York Ho 10 W3 . . 88 C1
Yorkland Ave DA16 . . 145 D1
Yorkley Ho 3 W10 . . 90 C3
York Mans
Battersea SW11 . . 268 B2
2 Hendon NW9 . . 46 A3
Marylebone W1 . . 238 A4
Walworth SE17 . . 262 B2
York Mews
Camden Town NW5 . . 71 B3
Ilford IG1 . . 78 C5
York Par
Brentford TW8 . . 109 D1
Hendon NW9 . . 46 A3
York Place Mans
NW1 . . 237 D4
York Pl
Battersea SW11 . . 136 B2
Ilford IG1 . . 78 C6
WC2 . . 250 B5
York Rd
Battersea SW11,
SW18 . . 136 B2
Belmont SM1, SM2 . . 217 C1
Brentford TW8 . . 109 D1
Chingford E4 . . 35 C5
Dagenham W3 . . 89 B1
Ealing W5 . . 109 C3
Edmonton N18 . . 34 B5
Forest Gate E7 . . 77 A2
Friern Barnet N11 . . 31 D4
Hounslow TW3 . . 129 D2
Ilford IG1 . . 78 C6
Kingston u T KT2 . . 176 B3
Leyton E10 . . 76 A5
New Barnet EN5 . . 14 B6
Pinner HA6 . . 22 A1
4 Richmond TW10 . . 154 B6
SE1 . . 116 B4 250 D2
Southgate N21 . . 17 B4
Teddington TW11 . . 174 C6

York Rd *coninued*
Thornton Heath CR0 . . 204 C2
Walthamstow E17 . . 52 D4
Wimbledon SW19 . . 180 A4
York Rise BR6 . . 227 C6
Dartmouth Pk NW5 . . 71 B5
York Road Bsns Ctr
SW11 . . 136 B3
York St Chambers
W1 . . 237 C4
Yorkshire Cl N16 . . 73 C5
Yorkshire Gdns N18 . . 34 B5
Yorkshire Grey SE9 . . 165 D6
Yorkshire Grey Pl 13
NW3 . . 70 A4
Yorkshire Grey Yd
WC1 . . 240 C3
Yorkshire Rd
Limehouse E14 . . 97 A1
Mitcham CR4 . . 204 A5
York Sq 12 E14 . . 97 A1
York St
Carshalton CR4 . . 203 A2
Paddington
W1 . . 92 D2 237 D4
Twickenham TW1 . . 153 A3
York Terr EN2 . . 5 A5
York Terr E
NW1 . . 93 A3 238 B5
York Terr W
NW1 . . 93 A3 238 A5
Yorkton St E2 . . 96 A5
York Way
Barnsbury N1, N7,
NW1 . . 72 A1
Chessington KT9 . . 214 A1
York Way Ct
Islington N1 . . 233 C5
Islington N1 . . 233 B5
York Way
Friern Barnet N20 . . 14 D1
N1 . . 233 B5
Twickenham TW13 . . 151 B1
Youngmans Cl EN2 . . 5 A4
Young Rd E16 . . 99 C1
Young's Bldgs EC1 . . 242 B6
Youngs Brewery Visitor
Ctr* SW18 . . 157 D6
Youngs Ct SW11 . . 268 B1
Youngs Rd IG2 . . 57 B4
Young St
W8 . . 113 D4 245 C1
Yoxall Ho 2 W10 . . 90 C3
Yoxford Ct 6 RM6 . . 58 B4
Yoxley App IG2 . . 57 A3
Yoxley Dr IG2 . . 57 A3
Yukon Rd SW12 . . 159 B4
Yunus Khan Cl E17 . . 53 C4

Z

Zambezie Dr N9 . . 18 C1
Zampa Rd SE16 . . 118 C1
Zander Ct E2 . . 96 A4
Zangwill Ho NW6 . . 91 B5
Zangwill Rd SE18,
SE3 . . 143 D4
Zealand Ave UB7 . . 126 A5
Zealand Ho
11 Camberwell
SE5 . . 139 A3
4 Woolwich SE7 . . 122 A2
Zealand Rd E3 . . 97 A5
Zenith Lo 7 N3 . . 29 D3
Zennor Rd SW12 . . 159 C3
Zenoria St SE22 . . 139 D1
Zermatt Rd CR7 . . 205 A5
Zetland Ho W8 . . 255 C6
Zetland St E14 . . 98 A2
Zeus Ho N1 . . 235 C1
Zion Ho 6 E1 . . 96 C1
Zion Pl CR7 . . 205 B5
Zion Rd CR7 . . 205 B5
Zircon Ct N11 . . 31 D3
ZK Pk CR0 . . 220 B5
Zoar St SE1 . . 117 A5 252 A4
Zodiac Ct CR0 . . 204 D1
Zodiac Ho 3 E3 . . 97 C3
Zoffany St N19 . . 71 D6

List of numbered locations

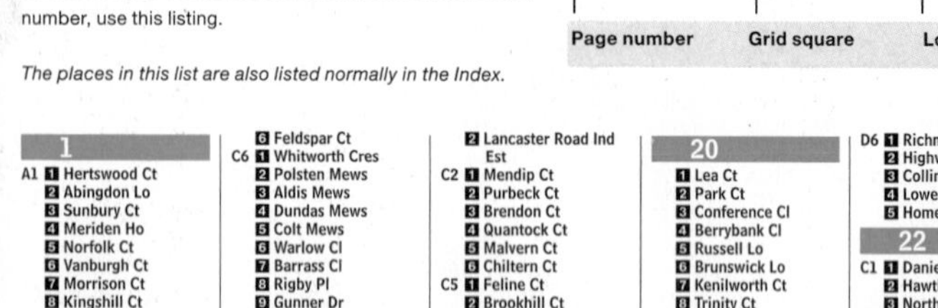

This atlas shows thousands more place names than any other London street atlas. In some busy areas it is impossible to fit the name of every place.

Where not all names will fit, some smaller places are shown by a number. If you wish to find out the name associated with a number, use this listing.

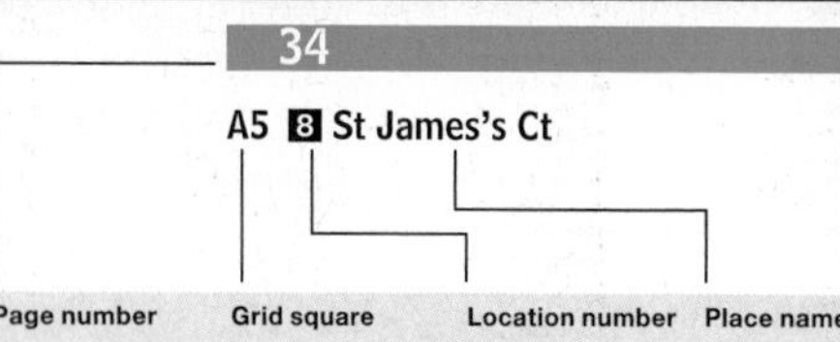

The places in this list are also listed normally in the Index.

1

A1 1 Hertswood Ct
2 Abingdon Lo
3 Sunbury Ct
4 Meriden Ho
5 Norfolk Ct
6 Vanburgh Ct
7 Morrison Ct
8 Kingshill Ct
9 Baronsmere Ct
10 Chartwell Ct
A2 1 Richard Ct
2 Alston Ct
3 Ridgeleigh Ct
4 Bartletts Cotts
5 Leathersellers Cl
6 Holkham Ho
7 Leinster Mews
B1 1 Olivia Ct
2 Tudor Ct
3 Gordon Mans
B2 1 Brake Shear Ho
2 Durham Ct
3 Huntingdon Ct
4 Cambridge Ct
5 Summit Ct
D1 1 Cranleigh Ct
2 Valeside Ct
3 Sherwood
4 Bradbury Ct
5 Chester Ho
6 Graham Ho
7 Highfield Ct
8 Amberley Ho
9 Hadley View
10 Stratton Lo
11 Gainsborough Ct
12 Christopher Ct
13 Bowmar Lo

2

A1 1 Hanover Ho
2 St Giles Ho
3 Henrietta Ho
4 Byron Ct
5 Preston Ct
6 Clivedon Ct
7 Battle House Mews
8 Phoenix Ct
9 Landsdown Cl
10 Comer Ho
11 Basil Ct
12 Russell Ct
13 Alice Cl
C1 1 Braeburn Ct
2 Bramley Ct
3 Cox Ct
4 Golden Ct
5 Pippin Ct
6 Russet Ct
7 High Birch Ct
8 Joystone Ct
9 Mark Lo
10 Edgeworth Ct

4

D3 1 Oakington Ct
2 Elderberry Ct
3 Blueberry Ct
4 Butterfield Ho

5

C1 1 Woodfield Cl
2 Fielders Cl

7

A2 1 Amethyest Ct
2 Bradmore Ct
3 Acer Ct
4 Cornell Ct
5 Durnsford Ct
6 Feldspar Ct
C6 1 Whitworth Cres
2 Polsten Mews
3 Aldis Mews
4 Dundas Mews
5 Colt Mews
6 Warlow Cl
7 Barrass Cl
8 Rigby Pl
9 Gunner Dr
10 Colgate Pl
11 Baddeley Cl
12 Sten Cl
13 Pritchett Cl
14 Rubin Pl
15 Turpin Cl
16 Island Centre Way
17 Hispano Mews
18 Watkin Mews
19 Wallace Ct
20 Needham Ct
21 Dryer Ct
22 Webley Ct
23 Frosbery Ct
24 Jacob Ct
25 Peabody Ct
26 Greener Ct
27 Bren Ct

9

D5 1 Watling Ct
2 Stuart Ct
3 Westview Ct
4 Potters Mews

13

D6 1 Rowan Wlk
2 Ford Ho
3 Glenwood Ho
4 Whitegates
5 Lisa Lo
6 South Lo
7 Hockington Ct
8 Lysander Ct
9 Ashwood Lo
10 Thornbridge Ct
11 Invergarry Ct
12 Eysham Ct
13 Warwick Ct
14 Chaucer Ct
15 Coleridge Ct
16 Springfields
17 Bure Ct
18 Florence Ct
19 Minetta Ct

14

A1 1 Belmont Ct
2 Terrace Ho
3 Croft Mews
4 Bluebell Ct
A2 1 Westview Ct
2 Oakleigh Mews
3 Mountview Ct
4 Mortimer Ct
5 Parklands
A6 1 Chiltern Ct
2 Gills Ct
3 Beaufort Ct
4 St Augustines Ct
5 Somerset Lo
6 Carlyle Lo
7 Stirling Lo
8 St Mirren Ct
9 Wardrew Ct
10 Apex Lo
11 Westbury Ct
B2 1 Davis Ct
2 Deerings Ct
3 Ashcroft Ct
B6 1 Redrose Trad Ctr
2 Lancaster Road Ind Est
C2 1 Mendip Ct
2 Purbeck Ct
3 Brendon Ct
4 Quantock Ct
5 Malvern Ct
6 Chiltern Ct
C5 1 Feline Ct
2 Brookhill Ct
3 Littlegrove Ct
4 Desmond Ho
D1 1 Springfield Ct
2 Victor Ho
3 Malborough Ho
4 Coopers Ct
5 Joiners Ct
D2 1 Bantock Ct
2 Burgess Ct
3 Heaton Ct
4 Bordley Ct
5 Garside Ct
6 Cranston Ct
7 Gleave Ct
D3 1 Wren Ct
2 Homerton Ct
3 Emmanuel Ct
4 Wolfson Ct
5 Robinson Ct
6 Gonville Ct

15

C6 1 Tregenna Cl
2 Catherine Ct
3 Conisbee Ct
4 Ashmead
D3 1 Dennis Par
2 Broadway The
3 Southgate Cir
4 Station Par
5 Bourneside
6 Bourneside Cres

17

C6 1 Wade Ho
2 Newport Lo
3 Halcyon Ho
4 Lerwick Ct
5 Anchor Ct
6 Grassmere Ct
7 Datchworth Ct
8 Trentham Lo
9 Austin Ct
10 Cedar Grange
11 Brookview Ct
12 Chestbrook Ct
13 Paddock Lo
14 Hamlet Ct
15 Haven Lo

18

A1 1 Plevna Ho
2 Lea Ho
3 Brook Ho
4 Valley Ho
5 Chiltern Ho
6 Blenheim Ho
7 Penn Ho
8 Romany Ho
9 Gilpin Ho
10 Anvil Ho
11 Well Ho
12 Passmore Ho
13 Durbin Ho
A2 1 Market Par
2 Beechwood Mews
3 Keats Par
4 Cedars Rd
5 Cross Keys Cl
6 Dorman Pl
7 Concourse The

20

1 Lea Ct
2 Park Ct
3 Conference Cl
4 Berrybank Cl
5 Russell Lo
6 Brunswick Lo
7 Kenilworth Ct
8 Trinity Ct
9 Kingsmead Lo
10 Fairlawns
A3 1 Knight Ct
2 Grant Ct
3 Chantry The
4 Bowyer Ct
5 Pineview Ct
6 Ellen Ct
7 Leeview Ct
8 Chelsea Ct
9 Bramley Ct
10 Garenne Ct
11 Kendal Ct
12 Fairways
13 Avon Ct
B3 1 Maddox Ct
2 Village Arc The
3 Cambridge Rd
4 Crown Bldgs
5 Pentney Rd
6 Scholars Ho
7 Cranworth Cres
C4 1 Connaught Ct
2 Woolden Ho
3 Fairmead Ct
4 Lockhart Lo
5 Cavendish Ct
6 Oakwood Ct
7 Plains The
8 Hadleigh Ct
9 Forest Ho
10 Mathieson Ho

21

B2 1 Stag Hts
2 Shore Point
3 Buckhurst Hill Ho
4 Beech Ave
5 High Road Buckhurst Hill
6 Highclears
C2 1 Westbury Ct
2 Palmerston Ct
3 Ibrox Ct
4 Richard Burton Ct
5 Queens Mews
6 Gunnels Ct & Hastingwood Ct
7 Marlborough Ct
8 Avenue The
9 Tora Ct
10 Somerset Ct
11 Mirravale Ct
C3 1 Rayburne Ct
2 Laurels The
3 Mablin Lo
4 Silvers
5 Makinen Ho
6 Roman Lo
D1 1 Highview Ho
1 Hornbeam Ho
2 Highview Ho
3 Bourne Ho
D2 1 Regency Lo
2 Kings Ct
3 Beech Ct
4 Sycamore Ho
5 Salisbury Gdns
6 Pegasus Ct
7 Buckhurst Ct
8 Mountbatten Ct
9 Atrium
D6 1 Richmond Ct
2 Highview Ct
3 Collins Ct
4 Lower Park Rd
5 Homecherry Ho

22

C1 1 Daniel Ho
2 Hawthorn Ct
3 Northcote
4 Edwin Ware Ct
5 Chalfont Wlk
6 Maple Ct
7 Montesole Ct
8 Viewpoint Ct

23

B3 1 Russettings
2 St Cuthberts Gdns
3 Cherry Croft Gdns
4 Claire Ct
5 Cornwall Ct
6 Falmouth Ho
7 Newlyn Ho
8 Chestnuts The
9 Dunford Ct
10 Stratton Ct
11 Hanover Ct

25

C5 1 Belgrave Gdns
2 Heywood Ct
3 Norfolk Ho
4 Garden Ct
5 Chatsworth Ct
6 Chartridge Ct
7 Hardwick Cl
8 Cheltenham Ct
9 Cargrey Ho
10 Holbein Ho
11 Goodwood Cl
12 Ascot Pl
13 Longchamp Ct
14 Halfacre
15 Burnham Ct
16 Dingle Ct
17 Woodcroft
18 Daneglen Ct
19 Buckingham Par
C6 1 Bickley Ct
2 Kelmscott Ct
3 Elstree Ho
4 Brompton Ct
5 Kenmare Ct
6 Burlington Park Ho
7 Gresenham Ct
8 Amora

26

D5 1 Penshurst Ct
2 Cranbourne Ct
3 Wilton Ct
4 Saxon Ct
5 Abbey Ct
6 Kenlor Ct
7 Daniel Ct
8 Hillcrest Ct
9 Hunters Lo
10 Orion Ct

27

A1 1 Colesworth Ho
2 Crokesley Ho
3 Curtlington Ho
4 Clare Ho
5 Kedyngton Ho
A3 1 Tadbourne Ct
2 Truman Cl
3 Lords Ct
4 Hutton Row
5 Compton Cl
6 Botham Cl
7 Bradman Row
A6 1 Iris Wlk
2 Sycamore Cl
3 Aster Ct
4 Firethorn Cl
5 Berberry Cl
6 Hibiscus Cl
B5 1 Monarchs Ct
2 Kensington Ct
3 Grosvenor Ct
4 Chasewood Ct
C2 1 Rufforth Ct
2 Riccall Ct
3 Lindholme Ct
4 Driffield Ct
5 Jack Ashley Ct
6 Folkingham La
7 Debden Cl
8 Holbeach Cl
9 Shawbury Cl
10 Daniel Ct
11 Leander Ct
12 Nimrod
13 Nisbet
14 Pixton
15 Rapide
16 Ratier
D1 1 Gauntlet
2 Guilfoyle
3 Grebe
4 Gates
5 Galy
6 Folland
7 Firefly
8 Halifax
9 Debussy
10 Crosbie
11 Grant Ct
12 Ham Ct
13 Deal Ct
14 Ember Ct
15 Canterbury Ct
16 Beaumont Ct
17 Cirrus
18 Defiant
19 Dessouter
20 Douglas
21 Cobham
22 Clayton
23 Camm
24 Bradon
25 Boarhound
26 Bodmin
27 Bleriot
28 Blackburn
29 Audax
30 Anson
31 Albatross
32 Arran Ct
33 Mavis Ct
34 Goosander Ct
35 Platt Halls (a)
36 Writtle Ho
37 Platt Halls (b)
38 Platt Halls (c)
D2 1 Slatter
2 Sopwith
3 Saimet
4 Sasson
5 Roe
6 Orde
7 Osprey
8 Prodger
9 Randall
10 Porte
11 Norris
12 Nardini
13 Noel
14 Nicolson
15 Napier
16 Nighthawk
17 Moorhouse

18 Moineau
19 Mitchell
20 Lysander
21 Lillywhite
22 Martynside
23 March
24 Kemp
25 Mercury
26 Merlin
27 Hudson
28 Hawker
29 Hawfinch
30 Heracles
31 Hector
32 Concourse The
1 Wellington
2 Wheeler
3 Whittaker
4 Whittle
5 Tedder
6 Cranwell Ct
7 Tait
8 Spooner

28

1 York Ho
2 Windsor Ho
3 Regency Cres
4 Normandy Ho
5 Allerton Ct
6 Beaulieu Ho
7 Dewlands Ct
8 Knightshayes Ho

29

2 Frances & Dick James Ct
3 Farthing Ct
4 Coniston Ct
1 Carlisle Lo
2 Laburnum Lo
3 Eden Ct
4 Moorcroft Ct
5 Clifford Lo
6 Acacia Lo
7 Cumberland Ct
8 Little Dell Lo
9 Cyprus Ct
10 Cyprus Ho
1 Sheringham Ct
2 St Ronan's
3 Crescent Rise
4 Elm Ct
5 Norman Ct
6 Marlow Ct
7 Dancastle Ct
8 Newman Ct
9 Station Mans
10 Alice Ct
1 Hadley Ct
2 Sherbrook Ho
3 Shine Ho
4 Regent Ct
5 Lodge Mead Ct
6 Spencer Ct
7 Zenith Lo
8 Burberry Ct
1 Silverbell Ct
2 Inverey Ho
3 Wimbush Ho
4 Tudor Lo
5 Duncan Ct
6 Phillipson Ho
1 Brookfield Ct
2 Magnolia Ct
3 Dunbar Ct
4 Haughmond
5 Nansen Village
6 Willow Ct
7 Birch Ct
8 Beechcroft Ct
9 Speedwell Ct
10 Woodside Ct
11 Speedwell Ho
12 Rebecca Ho
13 Ashbourne Ct
14 Forest Ct
15 Beecholme
16 Greville Lo
17 St Johnstone Ho
18 Ashbourne Cl
19 Clements Cl
20 Station App
21 Montclair Ct
22 Winterberry Ct
23 Caroline Ct

30

1 Sharon Ct
2 Lydia Ct
3 Beatrice Lo
4 Grange Ct
5 Blissland Ct
1 Archgate Bsns Ctr
2 Robart Ho
3 Danescroft
4 Cornelius Ct
5 Gable Lo
6 Waterville Lo
7 Chand Ho
B1 1 New Trinity Rd
2 Garden Ho
3 Todd Ho
4 Sayers Ho
5 Mowbray Ho
6 Bouchier Ho
7 Cleveland Ho
8 Goodyear Ho
9 Lochleven Ho
10 Berwick Ho
11 Oak Ho
12 Hilton Ho
13 East View Ho
14 Myddleton Ho
15 Willow Wlk
16 Craven Ho
17 Willow Ho
18 Vane Ho
19 Adelphi Ct
20 Annette White Lo
21 Foskett Ho
22 Elmfield Ho
23 Sycamore Ho
24 Netherwood
25 Rew Lo
26 William Cl
B5 1 Murray Ho
2 Damon Ho
3 Wendy Ho
4 Lychgate Ct
5 Clarence Ct
6 Carley Ct
7 Hermiston Ct
8 Cardrew Ct
9 Whitefriars Ct
D5 1 Halliwick Ct
2 Halliwick Court Par
3 Queen's Par
4 St John's Villas
5 Hartland Ct
6 Kennard Mans
7 Bensley Cl
8 Leadbeaters Cl
9 Gibson Ct
10 Burton Ct
11 Knights Ct
12 Constable Cl
13 Alderman Ct

31

A3 1 Campe Ho
2 Betstyle Ho
3 Pymmes Brook Ho
4 Mosswell Ho
5 Cavendish Ho
6 Tudor Ho
7 Kingsfield Ho
8 Peacehaven Ct
9 Hatch Ho
10 Hampden Ct
11 Crown Ct
A4 1 Cheddar Cl
2 Wincanton Ct
3 Whitby Ct
4 Richmond Ct
5 Tadworth Ct
6 Wensley Cl
7 Howeth Ct
8 Kilnsey Ct
9 Harrogate Ct
10 Ripon Ct
B1 1 Cedar Ct
2 Carisbrook
3 St Ivian Ct
4 Barrington Ct
5 Essex Lo
B6 1 Grovefield
2 Lapworth
3 Stewards Holte Wlk
4 Sarnes Ct
5 Stanhope Ho
6 Holmsdale Ho
7 Crosby Ct
8 Leyland Ct
9 Boundary Ct
10 Stateland Ct
C5 1 Barbara Martin Ho
2 Jerome Ct
3 Limes Cl
4 Arnos Grove Ct
5 Cedar Ct
6 Betspath Ho
7 Curtis Ho
8 Mason Ho
9 Danford Ho
10 New Southgate Ind Est
11 Palmer's Ct
12 Swinson Ho
13 Jackson Ho

32

A4 1 Brownlow Lo
2 Brownlow Ct
3 Latham Ct
4 Fairlawns
5 Beaumaris
C1 1 Penwortham Ct
2 Tarleton Ct
3 Holmeswood Ct
4 Kwesi Johnson Ct
5 Sandlings The
6 Suraj Ho
C6 1 Hazelwood Ct
2 Ashbourne Lo
3 Mapledurham Ct

33

D1 1 Kenmare Dr
2 Ashling Ho
3 Honeysett Rd
4 Wilson's Ave
5 Palm Tree Ct
6 Stoneleigh Ct
7 Brook St
D3 1 Charles Ho
2 Moselle Ho
3 Ermine Ho
4 Kathleen Ferrier Ct
5 Concord Ho
6 Rees Ho
7 Williams Ho
8 Nursery Ct
9 William Rainbird Ho
10 Gibson Bsns Ctr
11 Wingate Trad Est
D4 1 Regan Ho
2 Isis Ho
3 Boundary Ct
4 Stellar Ho
5 Cooperage Cl

34

A5 1 Angel Pl
2 Cross St
3 Scott Ho
4 Beck Ho
5 Booker Rd
6 Bridport Ho
7 Cordwain Ho
8 St James's Ct
9 Highmead
A6 1 Walton Ho
2 Alma Ho
3 Brompton Ho
4 Field Ho
5 Bradwell Mews
6 Angel Corner Par
7 Paul Ct
8 Cuthbert Rd
9 Brockenhurst Mews
B3 1 Kenneth Robbins Ho
2 Charles Bradlaugh Ho
3 Woodrow Ct
4 Cheviot
5 Corbridge
6 Whittingham
7 Eastwood Cl
8 Alnwick
9 Bamburgh
10 Bellingham
11 Briaris Cl

35

A1 1 Clayton Ct
2 St Andrew's Ct
3 Aranya Ct
4 Fitzwilliam Ho
A2 1 Romany Gdns
2 Swansland Gdns
3 Garnett Way
4 Claymore Ct
5 Winchester Ct
C5 1 Ainslie Ho
2 Lewis Ho

36

B5 1 Hedgemoor Ct
2 Hewitt Ho
3 Castle Ho
4 Bailey Ct
5 Harcourt Ho
6 Gerboa Ct
7 Wentworth Ct
D1 1 Chatham Rd
2 Washington Rd
3 Cherry Tree Ct
4 Grosvenor Lo
5 Torfell
D2 1 Hillboro Ct
2 Dorchester Ct

37

A1 1 Chiltons The
2 Ullswater Ct
3 Leigh Ct
4 Woburn Ct
5 Alveston Sq
6 Eaton Ct
7 Regency Ct
8 Cowley Ct
9 High Oaks Lo
A2 1 Lindal Ct
2 Hockley Ct
3 Woodleigh
4 Milne Ct
5 Cedar Ct
6 Elizabeth Ct
7 Silvermead
8 Laurel Mead Ct
9 Mitre Ct
10 Pevensey Ct
11 Lyndhurst Ct
12 Manor Court Lo
A3 1 New Jubilee Ct
2 Chartwell Ct
3 Greenwood
4 Clementine Wlk
A4 1 Terrace The
2 Broomhill Ct
3 Clifton Ct
4 Fairstead Lo
5 Hadleigh Lo
6 Broadmead Ct
7 Wilton Ct
8 Fairfield Ct
9 Higham Ct
10 Aston Ct
A6 1 Tree Tops
2 Cranfield Ct
3 Percival Ho
4 Raine Gdns
B1 1 Station Est
2 Station App
3 James Ct
C3 1 Liston Way
2 Elizabeth Ct
3 Coopersale Cl
4 Sunset Ct
5 Lambourne Ct
C4 1 Hope Cl
2 Rex Par
3 Shalford
4 Rodings The
5 Lawrence Ct
6 Cowan Lo

40

C1 1 Salisbury Ho
2 Rodwell Cl
3 Pretoria Ho
4 Ottawa Ho
5 Swallow Ct
6 Wellington Ho
7 Canberra Ho
C6 1 Tulip Ct
2 Hyacinth Ct
3 Rose Ct
4 Iris Ct
D6 1 Ashburton Ct
2 Northend Lodge

42

D3 1 Nightingale Ct
2 St John's Ct
3 Gayton Ct
4 Wilton Pl
5 Murray Ct
6 Cymbeline Ct
7 Knowles Ct
8 Charville Ct
9 Lime Ct
10 Petherton Ct
11 Garth Ct
12 Chalfont Ct
13 Shepherds Ct
D4 1 Crystal Ctr The
2 Blue Point Ct
3 Ryan Ho
4 Rothwell Ct
5 Bruce Ho
6 Middlesex Ct
7 Ingram Ho
8 Arless Ho
9 Leaf Ho
10 Becket Fold
11 Brandan Ho
12 Robert Ho

46

A2 1 Milton Rd
2 Stanley Rd
A3 1 Mapesbury Mews
2 York Mans
3 Telford Rd
A5 1 Pilkington Ct
2 Cousins Ct
3 Seton Ct
4 Frensham Ct
5 Chatton Ct
6 Geraldine Ct
7 Swynford Gdns
8 Miller Ct
9 Roffey Ct
10 Peace Ct
11 Rambler Ct
12 Lion Ct
13 Wenlock Gdns
14 Dogrose Ct
15 Harry Ct
16 Tribune Ct
17 Bonville Gdns
18 Pearl Ct
B4 1 Vivian Mans
2 Parade Mans
3 Georgian Ct
4 Florence Mans
5 Park Mans
6 Cheyne Cl
7 Queens Par
8 Central Mans
C5 1 Courtney Ho
2 Golderton
3 Thornbury
4 Ferrydale Lo
5 Studio Mews
6 Brampton La
7 Short St
8 Belle Vue Rd
9 Longford Ct
10 Ashwood Ho
D5 1 Midford Ho
2 Rockfield Ho
3 Lisselton Ho
4 Acrefield Ho

47

B2 1 Berkeley Ct
2 Exchange Mans
3 Beechcroft Ct
4 Nedahall Ct
B3 1 Charlton Lo
2 Clifton Gdns
B4 1 Hallswelle Par
2 Belmont Par
3 Temple Fortune Ho
4 Yew Tree Ct
5 Temple Fortune Par
6 Courtleigh
7 Arcade Ho
8 Queens Ct
9 Temple Fortune Ct
B5 1 Monkville Par
2 Ashbourne Par

48

A6 1 St Mary's Gn
2 Dunstan Cl
3 Paul Byrne Ho
4 Longfield Ct
5 Warwick Ct
6 Branksome Ct
7 Sherwood Hall

49

B6 1 Dorchester Ct
2 Old Chapel Pl
3 Athenaeum Pl
4 Risborough Cl
5 Risborough Ct
C1 1 Calvert Ct
2 Academy The
3 Whitehall Mans
4 Pauntley St
5 Archway Hts
6 Pauntley Ho
D1 1 Louise White Ho
2 Levison Way
3 Sanders Way
4 Birbeck Ho
5 Scholars Ct
D2 1 Eleanor Rathbone Ho
2 Christopher Lo
3 Monkridge
4 Marbleford Ct
5 High London
6 Garton Ho
7 Hilltop Ho
8 Caroline Martyn Ho
9 Arthur Henderson Ho
10 Margaret Mcmillan Ho
11 Enid Stacy Ho
12 Mary McArthur Ho
13 Bruce Glasier Ho
14 John Wheatley Ho
15 Keir Hardie Ho
16 Monroe Ho
17 Iberia Ho
18 Lygoe Ho
19 Lambert Ho
20 Shelbourne Ho
21 Arkansas Ho
22 Lafitte Ho
23 Shreveport Ho
24 Packenham Ho
25 Orpheus Ho
26 Fayetville Ho
27 Bayon Ho
D4 1 Kelland Cl
2 Truro Ct
3 Veryan Ct
4 Coulsdon Ct

50

A1 1 Beeches The
2 Lambton Ct
3 Nugent Ct
4 Lambton Mews
5 Mews The
A2 1 Marie Lloyd Gdns
2 Edith Cavell Cl
3 Marie Stopes Ct
4 Jessie Blythe La
5 Barbara Rudolph Ct
6 Hetty Rees Ct
7 Leyden Mans
8 Brambledown
9 Lochbie
10 Lyngham Ct
11 High Mount
12 Woodlands The
A4 1 Margaret Hill Ho
2 Manray Ct
3 Hermiston Ct
4 Carleton Ho
A5 1 Mackenzie Ho
2 Stowell Ho
3 Campsbourne Ho
4 Palace Gate Mews
B1 1 Lawson Ct
2 Wiltshire Ct
3 Fenstanton
4 Hutton Ct
5 Wisbech
D5 1 Wordsworth Par
2 Spanswick Lo
3 Barker Ho
D6 1 Langham Cl
2 Sidi Ct
3 Ince Terr

51

A2 1 Finmere Ho
2 Keynsham Ho
3 Kilpeck Ho
4 Knaresborough Ho
5 Leighfield Ho
6 Lonsdale Ho
7 Groveley Ho
8 Wensleydale Ho
9 Badminton Ct
B2 1 Selwood Ho
2 Mendip Ho
3 Ennerdale Ho
4 Delamere Ho
5 Westwood Ho
6 Bernwood Ho
7 Allerdale Ho
8 Chattenden Ho
9 Farningham Ho
10 Oakend Ho
C1 1 Godstone Ct
2 Farnham Ct
3 Milford Ct
4 Cranleigh Ct
5 Haslemere Ct
6 Belmont Ct
7 Hockworth Ho
8 Garratt Ho
9 Fairburn Ho
10 Thorndale Ho
11 Oakdene Ho
12 Briardale Ho
C3 1 Oatfield Ho
2 Perry Ct
3 Henrietta Ho
4 Bournes Ho
5 Chisley Rd
6 Twyford Ho
7 Langford Cl
8 Hatchfield Ho
D1 1 Stamford Hill Mans
2 Montefiore Ct
3 Berwyn Ho
4 Clent Ho
5 Chiltern Ho
6 Laindon Ho
7 Pentland Ho
D2 1 Regent Ct
2 Stamford Lo
3 Holmwood Ct
D3 1 Sherboro Rd
2 Westcott Cl
3 Cadoxton Ave
D4 1 Westerfield Rd
2 Suffield Rd
D5 1 Laseron Ho
2 Greenway Cl
3 Tottenham Gn E
4 Tottenham Gn E South Side
5 Deaconess Ct
6 Elliot Ct
7 Bushmead Cl
8 Beaufort Ho
9 Tynemouth Terr

51 D6
D6 1 Holcombe Rd
2 Rigby Ho
3 Chaplin Rd
4 Keswick Apartments
5 Ambleside Cl
6 Lauriston Apartments
7 Terrall Apartments
8 Old School Ct
9 Nicholson Ct
10 Reynardson's Ct
11 Protheroe Ho

52

A1 1 Stamford Gr E
2 Stamford Mans
3 Grove Mans
4 Stamford Gr W
B1 1 Hawkwood Mount
2 Holmbury View
3 High Hill Ferry
4 Leaside Ho
5 Courtlands
6 Ivy Ho
7 Shelford Ct

53

A4 1 Hammond Ct
2 St James Apartments
3 Grange The
A5 1 Bristol Park Rd
2 Stoneydown Ho
3 Callonfield
4 Hardyng Ho
C1 1 Wellington Mans
2 Clewer Ct
3 Cochrane Ct
C5 1 Westbury Ho
2 Hatherley Ho
3 Vintry Mews
4 Tylers Ct
5 Merchants Lo
6 Gillards Mews
7 Blacksmiths Ho
8 Central Par
D1 1 Fitzgerald Ct
2 Bechervaise Ct
3 Underwood Ct
D2 1 Staton Ct
2 Howell Ct
3 Atkinson Ct
4 Russell Ct
5 St Catherines Twr
6 St Lukes Ct
7 St Matthews Ct
8 St Mark's Ct
9 St Elizabeth Ct
10 Emanuel Ct
11 St Thomas Ct
12 Beaumont Ho
13 Shelley Ct
14 St Paul's Twr
15 Flack Ct
16 King Ct
17 Osborne Ct
18 Muriel Ct
19 All Saints Twr
20 St Josephs Ct
D5 1 Nash Ho
2 St Columbas Ho
3 Attlee Terr
4 Astins Ho
5 Lindens The
6 Kevan Ct
7 Squire's Almshouses
8 Berry Field Cl
9 Connaught Ct
10 Holmcroft Ho
11 St Mary's Church Ho
D6 1 Hallingbury Ct
2 Mace Ho
3 Gaitskell Ho
4 Hancocke Ho
5 Trinity Ho
6 Fanshaw Ho
7 Hilltop
8 Batten Ho
9 Bradwell Ho
10 Walton Ho
11 Temple Ho
12 Gower Ho
13 Maple Ho
14 Poplars Ho
15 Cedars Ho
16 Kimm Ho
17 O'Grady Ho
18 Latham Ho
19 Powell Ct
20 Crosbie Ho

54

A2 1 Ayerst Ct
2 Dare Ct
3 St Edwards Ct
A4 1 Collard's Almshouses
2 Ellen Miller Ho
3 Tom Smith Ho
A5 1 Northwood Twr
2 Walnut Ct
3 Albert Whicher Ho
4 Pelly Ct
5 Ravenswood Ind Est
6 Holland Ct
7 Emberson Ho
8 St Mark's Ho
9 Alfred Villas
10 Leonard Ho
11 Old Station Yard The
A6 1 St David's Ct
2 Golden Par
3 Chestnuts Ct
4 Matthew Ct
5 Gilbert Ho
6 Manning Ho
7 Southgate Ho
8 Boyden Ho
9 Prospect Ho
10 Newton Ho
D2 1 Buxton Ct
2 Hanbury Dr
3 Forest Lea
4 Watershipdown Ho

55

A3 1 Aldham Hall
2 Parkside Ct
3 Mapperley Cl
4 Weavers Ho
5 Cyna Ct
6 Reed Mans
7 Thornton Ho
8 Hardwick Ct
A4 1 Kingsley Grange
2 Station Par
3 Gwynne Ho
4 Staveley Ct
5 Thurlow Ct
6 Devon Ho
7 Wellington Pas
8 Wanstead Hts
9 Hollies The
10 Little Holt
11 Hunter Ct
12 Mountier Ct
13 Woodland Ct
14 Dudley Ct
15 Struan Ho
16 Westleigh Ct
A5 1 Shernwood Ho
2 Orwell Lo
3 Hermitage Ct
4 Gowan Lea
5 Woodford Ho
6 Eagle Ct
7 Newbury Ct
8 Shelley Ct
9 Hardy Ct
10 Dickens Ct
11 Byron Ct
A6 1 Millbrook
2 Half Acre
3 Elmbrook
4 Grange The
5 Glenavon Lo
6 Glenwood Ct
7 Ferndown
8 Embassy Ct
9 Orestes Ct
10 Walbrook
11 Helmsley
12 Snaresbrook Hall
B4 1 Nightingale Ct
2 Chelston Ct
3 Grosvenor Ct
4 Louise Ct
5 St Davids Ct
6 Cedar Ct
7 Shrubbery The
8 Nightingale Mews
B5 1 Great Hall The
2 Clock Ct
3 Langham Ho
B6 1 Victoria Ct
2 Kenwood Gdns
3 Thaxted Lo
4 Albert Rd
5 Albert Ho
6 Falcon Ct
7 Deborah Ct
8 Swift Ho
9 Pulteney Gdns
10 Spring Ct
11 Trinity Gdns

56

B4 1 High View Par
2 Spurway Par
3 Florence Root Ho
4 Rohan Pl
5 Homeheather Ho

57

A3 1 Catherine Ct
2 Lincoln Ct
3 Ivy Terr
4 Newbury Cotts

58

B1 1 Caledonian Cl
2 Talisman Cl
3 Norseman Cl
4 Frank Slater Ho
5 Brook's Mans
6 Brook's Par
B2 1 Mitre Ct
2 Coppins The
3 Stanetta Ct
4 Wilnett Ct
5 Wilnett Villas
B4 1 Sudbury Ct
2 Dunwich Ct
3 Cromer Terr
4 Norfolk Ct
5 Framlingham Ct
6 Yoxford Ct
C4 1 Swaffham Ct
2 Nacton Ct
3 Suffolk Ct
D2 1 Pavement Mews
2 Chadview Ct
3 Granary Ct
4 Bedwell Ct
5 Chapel La
6 Faulkner Cl
7 Maple Ct
8 Willow Ct
9 Cedar Terr

63

C2 1 Wimborne Ct
2 Haydock Green Flats
3 Brighton Dr
4 Blaydon Ct
5 Fakenham Cl
6 Rutland Ho
7 Windsor Ho

65

D3 1 Lowry Lo
2 Morritt Ho
3 Charles Goddard Ho
4 Snow Ct
5 Willow Tree Ct
6 Oak Lo

66

A2 1 Montrose Cres
2 Peggy Quirke Ct
3 Marylebone Ct
4 Waterloo Ct
5 Euston Ct
6 St Pancras Ct
7 Paddington Ct
8 Copland Mews
9 Coronet Par
10 Aylestone Ct
11 Charlotte Ct
A3 1 Wembley Mkt
2 Market Way
3 Lodge Ct
4 Central Sq
5 Manor Ct
6 Rupert Ave
7 Lily Ho
C4 1 Wembley Mkt

67

A5 1 Curie Ho
2 Darwin Ho
3 Priestley Ho
4 Rutherford Ho
5 Fleming Ho
6 Lister Ho
7 Edison Ho
B1 1 Biko Ho
2 Kingthorpe Terr
3 Scott Ho
4 Peary Ho
5 Shackleton Ho
6 Amundsen Ho
7 Brentfield Ho
8 Nansen Ho
9 Stonebridge Ct
10 Newcroft Ho
11 Magellan Ct
12 Leadbetter Ct
13 Jefferies Ho
14 Cowan Ct
15 Prothero Ho
16 Crawford St
17 Clark Ct
18 Diamond St
19 Mary Seacole Villas
C1 1 Beveridge Rd
2 Purcell Mews
3 George Lansbury Ho
4 Charles Hobson Ho
5 Reade Wlk
6 Westbury Ho
7 Bridge Ct
C4 1 Grange Ct
2 Green Ct
C5 1 Hazelwood Ct
2 Winslow Cl

68

A2 1 Regency Mews
2 Tudor Mews
3 Utopia Ho
4 Bell Flats
5 Angel Ct
A5 1 Bourne Ho
2 Carton Ho
3 Bidwell Ho
4 Woodbridge Cl
5 Mackenzie Ho
6 Banting Ho
C2 1 Rutland Park Gdns
2 Rutland Park Mans
3 Queens Par
4 Harcourt Ho
5 Solidarity Ho
6 Electra Ct
7 Cassandra Ct
8 Carlton Ct
D4 1 Oaklands Mews
2 Acer Ct
3 Maple Ct
4 Argyle Mans

69

A1 1 Christ Church Ct
2 Paul Daisley Ct
3 Fountain Ho
4 Kingston Ho
5 Waverley Ct
6 Weston Ho
7 Mapes Ho
8 Athelstan Gdns
9 Leff Ho
B1 1 Alma Birk Ho
2 Brooklands Ct
3 Brooklands Court Apartments
4 Cleveland Mans
5 Buckley Ct
6 Webheath
B5 1 Mortimer Cl
2 Primrose Ct
3 Sunnyside Ho
4 Sunnyside
5 Prospect Pl
C1 1 Linstead St
2 Embassy Ho
3 Acol Ct
4 Kings Wood Ct
5 Douglas Ct
6 King's Gdns
7 Carlton Mans
8 Smyrna Mans
9 New Priory Ct
10 Queensgate Pl
11 Brondesbury Mews
C2 1 Dene Mans
2 Sandwell Cres
3 Sandwell Mans
4 Hampstead West
5 Redcroft
C3 1 Orestes Mews
2 Walter Northcott Ho
3 Polperro Mans
4 Lyncroft Mans
5 Marlborough Mans
6 Alexandra Mans
7 Cumberland Mans
8 Cavendish Mans
9 Ambassador Ct
10 Welbeck Mans
11 Inglewood Mans
12 Dennington Park Mansions
C5 1 Portman Hts
2 Hermitage Ct
3 Moreland Ct
4 Wendover Ct
D2 1 Beswick Mews
2 Worcester Mews
3 Minton Mews
4 Doulton Mews
5 Laurel Ho
6 Sandalwood Ho
7 Iroko Ho
8 Banyan Ho
9 Rosewood Ho
10 Ebony Ho
11 Rosemont Mans
12 Exeter Mews

70

A1 1 Harrold Ho
2 Glover Ho
3 Byron Ct
4 Nalton Ho
A2 1 Petros Gdns
2 Heath Ct
3 Imperial Twrs
4 Fairhurst
5 St John's Ct
6 New College Ct
7 Chalford
8 Rosslyn Mans
9 Sutherland Ho
A4 1 Windmill Hill
2 Highgrove Point
3 Gainsborough Ho
4 Holly Bush Hill
5 Heath Mans
6 Holly Bush Steps
7 Pavilion Ct
8 Holly Berry La
9 New Campden Ct
10 Holly Bush Vale
11 Benham's Pl
12 Prospect Pl
13 Yorkshire Grey Pl
14 Gardnor Mans
15 Ellerdale Cl
16 Monro Ho
17 Prince Arthur Mews
18 Prince Arthur Ct
19 Village Mount
20 Perrin's Ct
21 Wells Ct
22 Bakers Pas
23 Spencer Wlk
24 Bird In Hand Yd
25 Kings Well
26 New Ct
27 Streatley Pl
28 Mansfield Pl
29 Upper Hampstead Wlk
A5 1 Hampstead Sq
2 Stamford Cl
3 Mount Sq The
B1 1 New College Par
2 Northways Par
3 Noel Ho
4 Campden Ho
5 Centre Hts
6 Hickes Ho
7 Swiss Terr
8 Leitch Ho
9 Jevons Ho
10 Langhorne Ct
11 Park Lo
12 Avenue Lo
B2 1 Belsize Park Mews
2 Baynes Mews
3 McCrone Mews
B3 1 Belsize Court Garages
2 Roscommon Ho
3 Akenside Ct
B4 1 White Bear Pl
2 Wells Ho The
3 Boades Mews
4 Flask Cotts
5 Coach House Yd
6 Pilgrim's Pl
7 Rosslyn Mews
C2 1 Banff Ho
2 Glenloch Ct
3 Havercourt
4 Holmefield Ct
5 Gilling Ct
6 Howitt Cl
7 Manor Mans
8 Straffan Lo
9 Romney Ct
10 Lancaster Stables
11 Eton Garages
D1 1 Hancock Nunn Ho
2 Higginson Ho
3 Duncan Ho
4 Mary Wharrie Ho
5 Rockstraw Ho
6 Cleaver Ho
7 Chamberlain St
8 Sharples Hall St
9 Primrose Mews
10 Rothwell St
11 St Georges Mews
D2 1 Alder Ho
2 Hornbeam Ho
3 Whitebeam Ho
4 Aspen Ho
5 Rowan Ho
6 Beech Ho
7 Chestnut Ho
8 Oak Ho
9 Willow Ho
10 Sycamore Ho
11 Maple Ho
12 Hazel Ho
13 Elaine Ct
14 Faircourt
15 Walham Ct
16 Stanbury Ct
17 Priory Mans
18 Wellington Ho
19 Grange The
D3 1 Cayford Ho
2 Du Maurier Ho
3 Isokon Flats
4 Palgrave Ho
5 Garnett Ho
6 Stephenson Ho
7 Park Dwellings
8 Siddons Ho
9 Mall Studios
10 Park Hill Wlk
11 Wordsworth Pl
12 Fraser Regnart Ct
13 St Pancras Almshouses

71

A1 1 Bridge Ho
2 Hardington
3 Mead Cl
4 Rugmere
5 Tottenhall
6 Beauvale
7 Broomfield
A2 1 Silverbirch Wlk
2 Penshurst
3 Wingham
4 Westwell
5 Chislet
6 Burmarsh
7 Shipton Ho
8 Stonegate
9 Leysdown
10 Headcorn
11 Lenham
12 Halstow
13 Fordcombe
14 Cannington
15 Langridge
16 Athlone Ho
17 Pentland Ho
18 Beckington
19 Hawkridge
20 Edington
B1 1 Ferdinand Ho
2 Harmood Ho
3 Hawley Rd
4 Hawley Mews
5 Leybourne St
6 Barling
7 Tiptree
8 Havering
9 Candida Ct
10 Lorraine Ct
11 Donnington Ct
12 Welford Ct
13 Torbay Ct
14 Bradfield Ct
15 Torbay St
16 Water La
17 Leybourne Rd
18 Haven St
19 Stucley Pl
20 Lawrence Ho
B2 1 Ashington
2 Priestley Ho
3 Leonard Day Ho
4 Old Dairy Mews
5 Monmouth Ho
6 Alpha Ct
7 Una Ho
8 Widford
9 Heybridge
10 Roxwell
11 Hamstead Gates
B4 1 Denyer Ho
2 Stephenson Ho
3 Trevithick Ho
4 Brunel Ho
5 Newcomen Ho
6 Faraday Ho
7 Winifrede Paul Ho
8 Wardlow
9 Fletcher Ct
10 Tideswell
11 Grangemill
12 Hambrook Ct
13 Calver
C1 1 Cherry Tree Ct
2 Chichester Ct
3 Durdans Ho
4 Philia Ho
5 Bernard Shaw Ct
6 Foster Ct
7 Bessemer Ct
8 Hogarth Ct
9 Rochester Ct
10 Soane Ct
11 Wallett Ct
12 Inwood Ct
13 Wrotham Rd
14 St Thomas Ct
15 Caulfield Ct
16 Bruges Pl
17 Reachview Cl
18 Lawfords Wharf
C3 1 Eleanor Ho

Falkland Pl
Kensington Ho
Willingham Cl
Kenbrook Ho
Aborfield
Great Field
Appleford
Forties The
Maud Wilkes Cl
Dunne Mews
Dowdeny Cl
Benson Ct
Tait Ho
Manorfield Cl
Greatfield Cl
Longley Ho
Lampson Ho
Davidson Ho
Palmer Ho
Lambourn Cl
10 Morris Ho
11 Owen Ho
Hunter Ho
Fisher Ho
Lang Ho
Temple Ho
Palmer Ho
Carlisle Ho
Durham Ho
Suffolk Ho
Lincoln Ho
10 Llewellyn Ho
11 Fell Ho
12 Aveling Ho
13 Merryweather Ct
14 Brennands Ct
15 St Christophers Ct
16 Francis Terrace Mews
1 Flowers Mews
2 Archway Cl
3 Sandridge St
4 Bovingdon Cl
5 Cavell Ct
6 Torrence Ho
7 Rowan Wlk
8 Laurel Cl
9 Forest Way
10 Larch Cl
11 Pine Cl
12 Alder Mews
13 Aspen Cl
1 Hillier Ho
2 Gairloch Ho
3 Cobham Mews
4 Bergholt Mews
5 Blakeney Cl
6 Weavers Way
7 Allensbury Pl
1 Rowstock
2 Peckwater Ho
3 Wolsey Ho
4 Pandian Way
5 Busby Mews
6 Caledonian Sq
7 Canal Bvd
8 Northpoint Sq
9 Lock Mews
10 Carters Cl
11 York Ho
12 Hungerford Rd
13 Cliff Road Studios
14 Cliff Ct
15 Camelot Ho
16 Church Studios
17 Camden Terr
1 Blake Ho
2 Quelch Ho
3 Lee Ho
4 Willbury Ho
5 Howell Ho
6 Holmsbury Ho
7 Leith Ho
8 Betchworth Ho
9 Rushmore Ho
10 Dugdale Ho
11 Horsendon Ho
12 Colley Ho
13 Coombe Ho
14 Ivinghoe Ho
15 Buckhurst Ho
16 Saxonbury Ct
17 Charlton Ct
18 Apollo Studios
19 Barn Cl
20 Long Meadow
21 Landleys Field
22 Margaret Bondfield Ho
23 Haywood Lo
1 Fairlie Ct
2 Trecastle Way
3 Dalmeny Avenue Est
4 Hyndman Ho
5 Carpenter Ho
6 Graham Ho
7 Tufnell Mans

D5 1 Melchester Ho
2 Norcombe Ho
3 Weatherbury Ho
4 Wessex Ho
5 Archway Bsns Ctr
6 Harford Mews
7 Opera Ct
8 Rupert Ho
9 All Saints Church
D6 1 Bowerman Ct
2 Gresham Pl
3 Hargrave Mans
4 Church Garth
5 John King Ct
6 Ramsey Ct

72

A3 1 Kimble Ho
2 Saxonbury Ct
3 Poynder Ct
4 Pangbourne Ho
5 Moulsford Ho
A4 1 Arcade The
2 Macready Pl
3 Cardwell Rd
4 Mcmorran Ho
5 Crayford Ho
6 Whitby Ct
7 Prospect Pl
A5 1 Northview
2 Tufnell Park Mans
3 Fulford Mans
4 Tollington Ho
A6 1 Bracey Mews
2 Christie Ct
3 Ringmer Gdns
4 Kingsdown Rd
5 Cottenham Ho
6 St Paul's Ct
7 Rickthorne Rd
8 Stanley Terr
9 Arundel Lo
10 Landseer Ct
B1 1 Kerwick Cl
2 Rydston Cl
3 Skegness Ho
4 Frederica St
5 Ponder St
6 Kings Ct
7 Freeling St
8 Coatbridge Ho
9 Tilloch St
B2 1 Burns Ho
2 Scott Ho
3 Wellington Mews
4 Roman Ct
5 Piccadilly Ct
B3 1 Culverin Ct
2 Garand Ct
3 Mount Carmel
B4 1 Buckmaster Ho
2 Loreburn Ho
3 Cairns Ho
4 Halsbury Ho
5 Chelmsford Ho
6 Cranworth Ho
B6 1 Berkeley Wlk
2 Lazar Wlk
3 Thistlewood Cl
4 Tomlins Wlk
5 Andover Ho
6 Barmouth Ho
7 Chard Ho
8 Methley Ho
9 Rainford Ho
10 Woodbridge Cl
11 Allerton Wlk
12 Falconer Wlk
13 Sonderburg Rd
14 St Mark's Mans
15 Athol Ct
C1 1 Mountfort Terr
2 Avon Ho
3 Buckland Ho
4 Dovey Lo
5 Carfree Cl
6 Mitchell Ho
7 New College Mews
8 Lofting Ho
9 Brooksby Ho
10 Cara Ho
C3 1 Slaney Pl
2 Eastwood Cl
3 Milton Pl
4 Hartnoll Ho
5 St James School Flats
6 Widnes Ho
7 Tranmere Ho
8 Victoria Mans
9 Formby Ct
10 Mersey Ho
11 Birkenhead Ho
12 Drayton Park Mews
C6 1 Brookfield
2 Churnfield
D1 1 Islington Park Mews
2 Evelyn Denington Ct
3 Bassingbourn Ho
4 Cadmore Ho
5 Adstock Ho
6 Garston Ho
7 Flitton Ho
8 Datchworth Ho
9 Battishill St
10 Almeida St
11 Edward's Cotts
12 Hyde's Pl
13 Tyndale Terr
14 Spriggs Ho
15 Barratt Ho
16 Spencer Pl
17 Chadston Ho
18 Whiston Ho
19 Wakelin Ho
20 Tressel Cl
21 Canonbury Ct
22 Halton Ho
23 Shillingford St
24 Highburty Mans
25 Premier Ho
26 Waterloo Gdns
D2 1 Hampton Ct
2 Salisbury Ho
D3 1 De Barowe Mews
2 Fieldview Ct
3 Viewpoint
4 Ashurst Lo
D4 1 Chestnuts The
2 Bowen Ct
3 Peckett Sq
D5 1 Hurlock Ho
2 Blackstock Ho
3 Vivian Comma Cl
4 Monsell Ct

73

A1 1 Astey's Row
2 Lincoln Ho
3 Worcester Ho
4 Melville Pl
5 Wontner Cl
6 Hedingham Cl
7 Laundry La
8 Base Apartments
9 Walkinshaw Ct
10 New Bentham Ct
11 Bentham Ct
12 Haslam Ho
13 Horsfield Ho
14 Riverside Ho
15 Eric Fletcher Ct
16 Annette Cres
17 Ashby Ho
18 Lindsey Mews
19 Cardigan Wlk
20 Red House Sq
A2 1 Crowline Wlk
2 Upper Handa Wlk
3 Handa Wlk
4 Lismore Wlk
5 Bardsey Wlk
6 Walney Wlk
7 Upper Bardsey Wlk
8 Upper Lismore Wlk
9 Sark Ho
10 Guernsey Ho
11 Guernsey Rd
12 Sybil Thorndike Ho
13 Clephane Rd
14 Florence Nightingale Ho
15 Jersey Ho
16 Jethou Ho
17 Islay Wlk
18 Upper Caldy Wlk
19 Caldy Wlk
20 Alderney Ho
21 Gulland Wlk
22 Marquess Rd S
23 Upper Gulland Wlk
24 Church Rd
25 Oransay Rd
A3 1 Pearfield Ho
2 Larchfield Ho
3 Beresford Terr
4 Pondfield Ho
5 Ashfield Ho
6 Elmfield Ho
A4 1 Fountain Mews
2 Woodstock Ho
3 Henson Ct
4 Taverner Sq
B1 1 Downham Ct
2 Trafalgar Point
B2 1 John Kennedy Ct
2 John Kennedy Lo
3 Ball's Pond Pl
4 Haliday Wlk
5 Queen Elizabeth Ct
6 Canonbury Hts
7 Pinnacle The
8 Threadgold Ho
9 Wakeham St
10 Saffron Ct
11 Callaby Terr
12 Tilney Gdns
13 Westcliff Ho
14 Ilford Ho
15 Ongar Ho
16 Greenhills Terr
17 Romford Ho
18 Bute Wlk
19 Upper Ramsey Wlk
20 Rona Wlk
21 Thorndike Rd
B4 1 Ledo Ho
2 Salween Ho
3 Prome Ho
4 Arakan Ho
5 Rangoon Ho
6 Mandalay Ho
7 Karen Ho
8 Wingate Ho
9 Jubet Ho
10 Orde Ho
11 Chindit Ho
12 Mabel Thornton Ho
13 Crawshay Ho
14 Avon Ho
15 Connaught Mans
16 Jonson Ho
17 Herrick Ho
18 Donne Ho
19 Thirlmere Ho
20 Grasmere Ho
B6 1 Chestnut Cl
2 Sycamore Ho
3 Lordship Ho
4 Clissold Ho
5 Beech Ho
6 Laburnum Ho
7 Ormond Ho
8 Yew Tree Ct
9 Oak Ho
C1 1 Dorchester Ct
2 Wareham Ct
3 Dorset Ct
4 Stratton Ct
5 Swanage Ct
6 Blandford Ct
7 Portland Ct
8 Oscar Faber Pl
9 Metropolitan Bsns Ctr
10 Lancaster Cl
11 Palazzo Apartments
C2 1 Kingsland Gn
2 Kingsland Pas
3 Metropolitan Benefit Societies Almshouses
4 Nimrod Pas
5 De Beauvoir Pl
6 Warburton Cl
7 Buckingham Mews
8 Aztec Ct
C3 1 Hewling Ho
2 Matthias Ho
3 Port Royal Pl
4 Cressington Cl
5 King Henry's Yd
6 Bronte Ho
7 Sewell Ho
8 Lydgate Ho
9 Patmore Ho
10 Congreve Ho
11 Elton St
12 Conrad Ho
13 Southwell Ho
14 Neptune Ho
15 Campion Ho
16 Webster Ho
17 Meredith Ho
18 Beckford Ho
19 Ashley Ct
20 Hayling Cl
21 Millard Cl
22 Lydford Cl
23 Salcombe Rd
24 Truman's Rd
25 Templeton Cl
26 John Campbell Rd
27 Gillett Pl
28 Bradbury St
29 Thomas Crowell Ct
C4 1 Londesborough Ho
2 Knebworth Ho
3 Knebworth Rd
4 Bransby Ct
5 Imperial Ave
6 Leonard Pl
7 Shakspeare Mews
8 Binyon Ho
9 Shelley Ho
10 Browning Ho
11 Burns Ho
12 Andrew Marvell Ho
13 Wycliffe Ho
14 Blake Ho
15 Marlowe Ho
16 Fletcher Ho
17 Chaucer Ct
C5 1 Gujarat Ho
2 Marton Rd
3 Painsthorpe Rd
4 Selkirk Ho
5 Defoe Ho
6 Edward Friend Ho
7 Sheridan Ho
8 Barrie Ho
9 Arnold Ho
10 MacAulay Ho
11 Stowe Ho
12 Carlyle Ho
13 Shaftesbury Ho
14 Lillian Cl
15 Swift Ho
16 Dryden Ho
17 Scott Ct
18 Kingsfield Ho
19 Uhura Sq
20 Hartopp Ct
D1 1 Hilborough Rd
2 Shoreditch Ct
3 Evergreen Sq
4 Wyndhams Ct
5 Festival Ct
6 Fortune Ct
7 Rose Ct
8 Ability Plaza
D2 1 Prospect Ho
2 Woodland St
3 Crosby Wlk
4 Kirkland Wlk
5 Bowness Cl
6 Carlisle Wlk
7 Skelton Cl
8 Camerton Cl
9 Buttermere Wlk
10 Houghton Cl
11 Hayton Cl
12 Kingsland Sh Ctr
13 Springfield Ho
14 Parton Lo
15 Sanctuary Mews
D3 1 Miller's Terr
2 Chow Sq
3 Drysdale Flats
4 Gateway Mews
5 Birkbeck Mews
6 Winchester Pl
D4 1 Coronation Ave
2 Morris Blitz Ct
3 Shacklewell Ho
4 Alexandra Ct
D5 1 Lawrence Bldgs
2 Cottage Wlk
3 Batley Pl
D6 1 Garnham St
2 Garnham Cl
3 Sanford La
4 Sanford Wlk
5 Abney Gdns
6 Fleet Wood

74

A1 1 Aldington Ct
2 Bayton Ct
3 Rochford Wlk
A2 3 Burdon Ct
4 Thomson Ct
5 Bruno Ct
A3 1 Kingsdown Ho
2 Glendown Ho
3 Moredown Ho
4 Blakeney Cl
5 Beeston Cl
6 Benabo Ct
7 David Devine Ho
8 Kreedman Wlk
9 Hermitage Row
10 Grafton Ct
11 Lushington Terr
12 Aspen Ct
13 Pykewell Lo
14 Albion Works Studios
A5 1 Ravenscourt
2 Mellington Ct
3 Rendlesham Ho
4 Carroll Ct
A6 1 Cazenove Mans
2 Chedworth Ho
3 Aldergrove Ho
4 Abbotstone Ho
5 Briggeford Cl
6 Inglethorpe Ho
7 Ashdown Ho
8 Epping Ho
9 Cypress Cl
B1 1 Fortescue Ave
2 Pemberton Pl
3 Weston Wlk
4 Bayford St Ind Ctr
5 Bayford St
6 Sidworth St
7 Helmsley St
8 Cyntra Pl
9 Signal Ho
10 All Nations Ho
11 Vanguard Ho
12 Hacon Sq
B2 1 Bohemia Pl
2 Graham Mans
3 Marvin St
4 Boscobel Ho
5 Royal Oak Rd
6 Colonnades The
7 Sylvester Ho
8 Sylvester Path
9 Doctor Spurstowe Almshouses
10 Great Eastern Bldgs
11 Sojourner-Truth Cl
B3 1 Birchington Ho
2 Bicknor Ho
3 Boxley Ho
4 Adisham Ho
5 Cranbrook Ho
6 Marden Ho
7 Broome Ho
8 Crandale Ho
9 Cheriton Ho
10 Ditton Ho
11 Langley Ho
12 Dymchurch Ho
13 Elham Ho
14 Davina Ho
15 Pembury Pl
16 Downs Ct
17 Perrywood Ho
18 Staplehurst Ho
19 Pegwell Ho
20 Yalding Ho
21 Northbourne Ho
22 Monkton Ho
23 Milsted Ho
24 Athlone Cl
25 Clarence Pl
26 Gould Terr
27 Quested Ct
28 Brett Pas
29 Marcon Ct
30 Appleton Ct
B4 1 Ross Ct
2 Downs La
3 Gaviller Pl
4 Robert Owen Lo
5 Apprentice Way
6 Arrowe Ct
7 Gilwell Ct
8 Sutton Ct
9 St Andrews Mans
10 Kinnoull Mans
11 Rowhill Mans
12 Sladen Pl
13 Mothers Sq The
14 Richborough Ho
15 Sandgate Ho
16 Sheppey Ho
B5 1 De Vere Ct
2 Redcliffe Ct
3 Greville Ct
4 Anthony Kendal Ho
B6 1 Wentwood Ho
2 Woolmer Ho
3 Warwick Ct
4 Winslade Ho
5 Morriss Ho
6 Woodfield Ho
7 Rossendale Ho
8 Ettrick Ho
9 Charnwood Ho
10 Boyne Ho
11 Whitwell Ho
12 Scardale Ho
13 Hendale Ho
14 Brampton Cl
15 Aveley Ct
16 Aldeburgh Cl
17 Dennington Cl
C1 1 Pitcairn Ho
2 Lyme Grove Ho
3 Shakespeare Ho
4 Upcott Ho
5 Loddiges Ho
6 Parkinson Ho
7 Sloane Ho
8 Vanbrugh Ho
9 Cambridge Pas
10 Lyttleton Ho
11 Victoria Park Ct
12 Tullis Ho
13 Fairchild Ho
14 Forsyth Ho
15 Tradescant Ho
16 Mason Ho
17 Capel Ho
18 Cordwainers Ct
19 Bridgeman Ho
20 St Thomas's Pl
21 Barclay Ho

74 C1
22 Clayton Ho
23 Danby Ho
24 Sherard Ho
25 Catesby Ho
26 Petiver Cl
27 Leander Ct
28 Philip Turner Est
29 Grendon Ho
30 Shore Mews
31 Shore Bsns Ctr
32 Kendal Ho
33 Classic Mans
34 Tudor Ho
35 Park Ho
36 Enterprise Ho
37 Alpine Gr
38 Clarendon Cl
39 Rotheley Ho
40 Bernie Grant Ho
C2 1 Woolpack Ho
2 Elvin Ho
3 Thomas Ho
4 Hockley Ho
5 Retreat Ho
6 Butfield Ho
7 Brooksbank Ho
8 Cresset Ho
9 Brooksbank St
10 Lennox Ho
11 Milborne Ho
12 Collent Ho
13 Middlesex Pl
14 Elsdale Ho
15 Devonshire Hall
16 Brent Ho
C6 1 Haybridge Ho
2 Framlingham Cl
3 Halesworth Cl
4 Harleston Cl
5 Lowestoft Cl
6 Howard Ho
7 Templar Ho
D1 1 Stuart Ho
2 Gascoyne Ho
3 Chelsfield Point
4 Sundridge Ho
5 Banbury Ho
6 Lauriston Ho
D2 1 Musgrove Ho
2 Cheyney Ho
3 Haynes Ho
4 Warner Ho
5 Gilby Ho
6 Gadsden Ho
7 Risley Ho
8 Baycliffe Ho
9 Sheldon Ho
10 Offley Ho
11 Latimer Ho
12 Ribstone Ho
13 Salem Ho
14 Fieldwick Ho
15 Lever Ct
16 Matson Ho
17 Wilding Ho
18 Rennell Ho
19 Dycer Ho
20 Granard Ho
21 Whitelock Ho
22 Harrowgate Ho
23 Cass Ho
24 Lofts on the Park
25 Heathcote Point
26 Ravenscroft Point
27 Vanner Point
28 Hensley Point
29 San Ho
D4 1 Cromford Path
2 Longford Ct
3 Overbury Ho
4 Heanor Ct
5 Wharfedale Ct
6 Ladybower Ct
7 Ilkeston Ct
8 Derby Ct
9 Rushmore Cres
10 Blackwell Cl
11 Belper Ct

75

A2 1 Chigwell Ct
2 Wellday Ho
3 Selman Ho
4 Vaine Ho
5 Trower Ho
B2 1 Mallard Cl
2 Merriam Ave
3 Gainsborough St
D6 1 Hammond Ct
2 Sorensen Ct
3 Hinton Ct

76

B1 1 Service Route No 2
2 Service Route No 3
B4 1 Mulberry Ct
2 Rosewood Ct
3 Gean Ct
4 Blackthorn Ct
5 Cypress Ct
C1 1 Stratford Office Village The
2 Violet Ct
3 Mandrake Way
4 Brimstone Ho
5 Hibiscus Lo
6 Glasier Ct
C3 1 Bordeaux Ho
2 Luxembourg Mews
3 Basle Ho
C5 1 Acacia Bsns Ctr
2 Brook Ct
3 Gainsfield Ct
4 Artesian Wlk
5 Doreen Capstan Ho
6 Apollo Pl
7 Peppermint Pl
8 Denmark St
9 Mills Ct
10 Paramount Ho
11 Robinson Cl
C6 1 Nansen Ct
2 Mallinson Ct
3 Barbara Ward Ct
4 Caradon Cl
5 Noel Baker Ct
6 Corigan Ct
7 Norman Ho
8 Willow Ct
9 Lime Ct
10 Owens Mews
11 Marnie Ct
12 Cotton Cl
D1 1 Flint Cl
2 St Matthews Ct
3 Ammonite Ho
4 Stone Ct
D2 1 Common The
2 Wolffe Gdns
3 College Pt
4 Onyx Mews
5 Candlelight Ct
6 Boltons The

77

A4 1 Bronte Cl
2 Anna Neagle Cl
3 Brownlow Rd
4 Carrington Gdns
5 Vera Lynn Cl
C1 1 Sarwan Ho
2 Bridgepoint Lofts
3 Vineyard Studios

78

C3 1 Stewart Rainbird Ho
2 Abraham Fisher Ho
3 Redo Ho
4 George Comberton Wlk
C4 1 Cardamom Ct
2 Annie Taylor Ho
3 Richard Fell Ho
4 Susan Lawrence Ho
5 Walter Hurford Par
6 John Cornwell VC Ho
7 Alfred Prior Ho
C5 1 Charlbury Ho
2 Willis Ho
3 Arthur Walls Ho
4 Blakesley Ho
5 Twelve Acre Ho
6 Beech Ct
7 Golding Ct
D1 1 Aveley Mans
2 Harlow Mans
3 Danbury Mans
4 Mayland Mans
5 Bowers Ho
6 Webber Ho
7 Paulson Ho
8 Collins Ho
9 Jack Cook Ho
D3 1 St Luke's Path
2 Springfield Ct
D5 1 Postway Mews
2 Oakfield Ho
3 Janice Mews
4 Kenneth More Rd
5 Clements Ct
6 Handforth Rd
7 Churchill Ct
8 Oakfield Lo
9 Langdale Ct
10 Ilford Chambers
D6 1 York Ho
2 Opal Mews
3 Florentine Ho
4 Kingsley Mews
5 Hainault Bridge Par

79

A6 1 Spectrum Twr
2 Thames View
3 City View
4 Centreway
5 Axon Pl
D1 1 Gibbards Cott
2 Upney Ct
3 Edgefield Ct
4 Manor Ct
5 Lambourne Gdns
6 Westone Mans
7 Loveland Mans
8 Edward Mans
9 Clarke Mans
10 Dawson Gdns
11 Sebastian Ct

80

A1 1 Bristol Ho
2 Canterbury Ho
3 Durham Ho
4 Wells Ho
5 Winchester Ho
6 Rosalind Ct
7 Exeter Ho
8 Wheatley Mans
9 Greenwood Mans
10 Plymouth Ho
11 Graham Mans
12 Portia Ct

81

C5 1 Markham Ho
2 Webb Ho
3 Preston Ho
4 Steadman Ho
5 Hyndman Ho
6 Clynes Ho
7 Henderson Ho
8 Blatchford Ho
9 Rogers Ho
10 Sylvia Pankhurst Ho
11 Mary Macarthur Ho
12 Ellen Wilkinson Ho
D2 1 Picador Ho
2 Centurion Lodge
3 Louis Ct
4 Watsons Lo
5 Carpenters Ct
6 Bell Ho
7 Rounders Ct
8 Oldmead Ho
9 Jervis Ct
10 Bartletts Ho
11 Royal Par
12 Richardson Gdns
13 Forsyth Ct
14 Eldridge Ct
15 Madison Ct
16 Bowery Ct
17 Rivington Ct

82

D3 1 Marlborough Par
2 Blenheim Par
3 Lea Ct
4 Westbourne Par
5 Whiteleys Par
6 Hillingdon Par
7 New Broadway

84

C4 1 Dilston Cl
2 Wells Cl
3 Willett Cl
4 Merlin Cl
5 Glyndebourne Ct
6 Albury Ct
7 Osterley Ct
8 Hatfield Ct
9 Gayhurst Ct
D4 1 Caravelle Gdns
2 Farman Gr
3 Viscount Gr
4 Tomahawk Gdns
5 Martlet Gr
6 Trident Gdns
7 Latham Ct
8 Jupiter Ct
9 Westland Ct
10 Seasprite Cl
11 Convair Wlk
12 Mayfly Gdns
13 Valiant Cl
14 Woburn Twr
15 Brett Cl
16 Friars Cl
D5 1 Medlar Cl
2 Cranberry Cl
3 Lely Ho
4 Girtin Ho
5 Cotman Ho
6 Raeburn Ho
7 Gainsborough Twr
8 Stanfield Ho
9 Millais Ct
10 Hunt Ct
11 Poynter Ct
12 Hogarth Ho
13 Constable Ho
14 Bonnington Ct
15 Romney Ct
16 Landseer Ho

85

B1 1 St Crispins Ct
B3 1 Weaver Ho
2 Caldon Ho
3 Ashby Ho
4 Welford Ho
5 Hertford Ho
6 Wey Ho
7 Middlewich Ho
8 Stourbridge Ho
B4 1 Netherton Ho
2 Keadby Ho
3 Tame Ho
4 Dorset Ct
D1 1 Thurlestone Ct
2 Disley Ct
3 Burgess Ct
4 Bayliss Cl
5 Lytham Ct
6 Winford Par
7 Brunel Pl
8 Rutherford Twr
9 Rountree Ct

86

A1 1 Farnham Ct
2 Gleneagles Twr
3 Birkdale Ct
4 Verulam Ct
5 Hartsbourne Ct
6 Ferndown Ct
7 Deal Ct
8 St David's Ct
9 Portrush Ct
10 Alnmouth Ct
11 Panmure Ct
12 Peterhead Ct
13 Sunningdale Ct
D2 1 Denbigh Ct
2 Devon Ct
3 Dorset Ct
4 Glamorgan Ct
5 Gloucester Ct
6 Hereford Ct
7 Merioneth Ct
8 Oxford Ct
9 Monmouth Ct
10 Paddington Ct
11 Pembroke Ct
12 Chadwick Cl
13 Cotts Cl
D3 1 Berkshire Ct
2 Buckingham Ct
3 Cardigan Ct
4 Carmarthen Ct
5 Cornwall Ct
6 Merlin Ct
7 Osprey Ct
8 Pelham Pl
9 Puffin Ct
10 Fulmar Ct
11 Turnstone Terr
D5 1 Medway Par
2 Brabstone Ho
3 Cotswold Ct

87

B3 1 Woodbury Ct
2 Edward Ct
3 Park Lo
C1 1 Hurley Ct
2 Amherst Gdns
3 Tudor Ct
4 Hilton Ho
C2 1 Hutton Ct
2 Cain Ct
3 Langdale Ct
4 William Ct
5 Castlebar Ct
6 Warren Ct
7 White Lo
8 Queen's Ct
9 King's Ct
10 Cheriton Cl
11 Stanley Ct
12 Juniper Ho
C3 1 Holtoake Ct
2 Pitshanger Ct
3 Holtoake Ho

88

A4 1 Nelson Ho
2 Gordon Ho
3 Frobisher Ho
4 Wellington Ho
5 Fairfax Ho
A5 1 Carlyon Mans
2 Ainslie Ct
3 Millers Ct
4 Priory Ct
5 Tylers Ct
6 Twyford Ct
7 Rose Ct
8 Laurel Ct
9 Sundew Ct
10 Campion Ct
11 Foxglove Ct
C1 1 Buckingham Ho
2 Chester Ct
3 Devon Ct
4 Essex Ho
5 Fife Ct
6 Gloucester Ct
7 Hereford Ho
8 Inverness Ct
9 Warwick Ho
10 York Ho
11 Suffolk Ho
12 Perth Ho
13 Norfolk Ho
14 Thanet Ct
15 Rutland Ct
16 Oxford Ct

89

A1 1 Avon Ct
2 Bromley Lo
3 Walter Ct
4 Lynton Terr
5 Acton Ho
6 Fells Haugh
7 Springfield Ct
8 Tamarind Ct
9 Lynton Ct
10 Aspen Ct
11 Pegasus Ct
12 Friary Park Ct
B1 1 Rosebank Gdns
2 Rosebank
3 Edinburgh Ho
4 Western Ct
5 Kilronan
B6 1 Carlyle Rd
2 Bernard Shaw Ho
3 Longlents Ho
4 Mordaunt Ho
5 Wilmers Ct
6 Stonebridge Ctr
7 Shakespeare Ave
C5 1 Futters Ct
2 Barrett Ct
3 Elms The
4 Fairlight Ct
D5 1 New Crescent Yd
2 Harlesden Plaza
3 St Josephs Ct
4 Jubilee Cl
5 Ellery Cl

90

B1 1 Holborn Ho
2 Clement Danes Ho
3 Vellacott Ho
4 O'Driscoll Ho
5 King Ho
6 Daley Ho
7 Selma Ho
8 Garrett Ho
C1 1 Latimer Ind Est
2 Pankhurst Ho
3 Quadrangle The
4 Nightingale Ho
5 Gordon Ct
6 Ducane Cl
7 Browning Ho
8 Pavilion Terr
9 Ivebury Ct
10 Olympic Ho
C2 1 Galleywood Ho
2 Edgcott Ho
3 Cuffley Ho
4 Addlestone Ho
5 Hockliffe Ho
6 Sarratt Ho
7 Firle Ho
8 Sutton Est The
9 Terling Ho
10 Danes Ho
11 Udimore Ho
12 Vange Ho
13 Binbrook Ho
14 Yeadon Ho
15 Yatton Ho
16 Yarrow Ho
17 Clement Ho
18 Danebury
19 Coronation Ct
20 Calderon Pl
21 St Quintin Gdns
C3 1 Princess Alice Ho
2 Yoxall Ho
3 Yorkley Ho
4 Northaw Ho
5 Oakham Ho
6 Markyate Ho
7 Letchmore Ho
8 Pagham Ho
9 Quendon Ho
10 Redbourn Ho
11 Ketton Ho
12 Hillman Dr
D1 1 Kelfield Ct
2 Downing Ho
3 Crosfield Ct
4 Robinson Ho
5 Scampston Mev
6 Girton Villas
7 Ray Ho
8 Walmer Ho
9 Goodrich Ct
10 Arthur Ct
11 Whitstable Ho
12 Kingsnorth Ho
13 Bridge Cl
14 Prospect Ho
15 St Marks Rd
16 Whitchurch Ho
17 Blechynden Ho
18 Waynflete Sq
19 Bramley Ho
20 Dixon Ho
D4 1 Westfield Ct
2 Tropical Ct
3 Chamberlayne M
4 Quadrant The
5 Queens Park Ct
6 Warfield Yd
7 Regent St
8 Cherrytree Ho
9 Artisan Mews
10 Artisan Quarter

91

A1 1 Malton Mews
2 Lancaster Lo
3 Manning Ho
4 Galsworthy Ho
5 Hudson Ho
6 Cambourne Mev
7 Upper Talbot Wl
8 Kingsdown Cl
9 Lower Clarendor
10 Talbot Grove Ho
11 Clarendon Wlk
12 Upper Clarendor
13 Camelford Wlk
14 Upper Camelforc
15 Camelford Ct
A2 1 Murchison Ho
2 MacAulay Ho
3 Chesterton Ho
4 Chiltern Ho
5 Lionel Ho
6 Watts Ho
7 Wheatstone Ho
8 Telford Ho
9 Golborne Mews
10 Millwood St
11 St Columb's Ho
12 Norfolk Mews
13 Lionel Mews
A3 1 Sycamore Wlk
2 Westgate Bsns C
3 Buspace Studios
4 Bosworth Ho
5 Golborne Gdns
6 Appleford Ho
7 Adair Twr
8 Gadsden Ho
9 Southam Ho
10 Norman Butler H
11 Thompson Ho
12 Wells Ho
13 Paul Ho
14 Olive Blythe Ho
15 Katherine Ho
16 Breakwell Ct
17 Pepler Ho
18 Edward Kennedy
19 Winnington Ho
A4 1 Selby Sq
2 Severn Ave
3 Stansbury Sq
4 Tolhurst Dr
5 John Fearon Wlk
6 Mundy Ho
7 Macfarren Ho
8 Bantock Ho
9 Banister Ho
10 Batten Ho
11 Croft Ho
12 Courtville Ho
13 Mounsey Ho
14 Bliss Mews
15 Symphony Mews
B1 1 Silvester Ho
2 Golden Cross Me
3 Tavistock Mews
4 Clydesdale Ho
5 Melchester
6 Pinehurst Ct
7 Denbigh Ho

1 Blagrove Rd
2 All Saints Ho
3 Tavistock Ho
4 Leamington Ho
1 Octavia Mews
2 Russell's Wharf
3 Western Ho
4 Kelly Mews
1 Boyce Ho
2 Farnaby Ho
3 Danby Ho
4 Purday Ho
5 Naylor Ho
6 St Judes Ho
7 Leeve Ho
8 Longhurst Ho
9 Harrington Ct
10 Mulberry Ct
11 Kilburn Ho
1 Claremont Ct
2 William Saville Ho
3 Western Ct
4 Bond Ho
5 Crone Ct
6 Wood Ho
7 Winterleys
8 Carlton Ho
9 Fiona Ct
1 Shottsford
2 Tolchurch
3 Casterbridge
4 Sandbourne
5 Anglebury
6 Weatherbury
7 Westbourne Gr Mews
8 Rosehart Mews
9 Viscount Ct
10 Hereford Mans
11 Hereford Mews
1 Ascot Ho
2 Ashgrove Ct
3 Lockbridge Ct
4 Swallow Ct
5 Nightingale Lo
6 Hammond Lo
7 Penfield Lo
8 Harvey Lo
9 Hunter Lo
10 Barnard Lo
11 Falcon Lo
12 Johnson Lo
13 Livingstone Lo
14 Nuffield Lo
15 Finch Lo
16 Polesworth Ho
17 Oversley Ho
18 Derrycombe Ho
19 Buckshead Ho
20 Combe Ho
21 Culham Ho
22 Dainton Ho
23 Devonport Ho
24 Honwell Ho
25 Truro Ho
26 Sunderland Ho
27 Stonehouse Ho
28 Riverford Ho
29 Portishead Ho
30 Mickleton Ho
31 Keyham Ho
32 Moulsford Ho
33 Shrewsbury Mews
34 St Stephen's Mews
35 Westway Lo
36 Langley Ho
37 Brindley Ho
38 Radway Ho
39 Astley Ho
40 Willow Ct
41 Larch Ct
42 Elm Ct
43 Beech Ct
44 Worcester Ct
45 Union Ct
46 Leicester Ct
47 Kennet Ct
48 Oxford Ct
49 Fazerley Ct
C3 1 Westside Ct
2 Byron Mews
3 Sutherland Ct
4 Fleming Cl
5 Hermes Cl
C4 1 Pentland Rd
2 Nelson Cl
3 Pavilion Ct
4 Masefield Ho
5 Austen Ho
6 Fielding Ho
7 Argo Bsns Ctr
8 John Ratcliffe Ho
9 Wymering Mans
C5 1 Wells Ct
2 Cambridge Ct
3 Ely Ct
4 Durham Ct
C6 1 Ryde Ho

2 Glengall Pass
3 Leith Yd
4 Daynor Ho
5 Varley Ho
6 Sandby Ho
7 Colas Mews
8 Bishopsdale Ho
9 Lorton Ho
10 Marshwood Ho
11 Ribblesdale Ho
12 Holmesdale Ho
13 Kilburn Vale Est
14 Kilburn Bridge
D1 1 Vera Ct
2 Alexander Mews
3 Gurney Ho
4 Burdett Mews
5 Greville Lo
6 Hatherley Ct
7 Bridge Field Ho
8 Ralph Ct
9 Peters Ct
9 Pickering Mews
10 Riven Ct
11 Inver Ct
12 Cervantes Ct
13 Bishops Ct
14 Newbury Ho
15 Marlow Ho
16 Lynton Ho
17 Pembroke Ho
18 Pickering Ho
19 Whiteleys Ctr
D3 1 Ellwood Ct
D5 1 Tollgate Ho
2 Regents Plaza
3 Royal Langford Apartments
D6 1 Sylvan Ct
2 Birchington Ct
3 Farndale Ho
4 Abbey Rd Motorist Ctr
5 Greville Mews
6 Goldsmith's Pl
7 Remsted Ho
8 Bradwell Ho
9 Cheshunt Ho
10 Haliwell Ho
11 Broadoak Ho
12 Philip Ho
13 Hillsborough Ct
14 Sandbourne
15 Wingreen
16 Toneborough
17 Silverthorn
18 Kington Ho
19 Marrick Ho

95

C4 1 Pimlico Wlk
2 Aske Ho
3 Hathaway Ho
4 Haberdasher Pl
5 Fairchild Ho
6 Burtt Ho
7 Enfield Cloisters
8 McGregor Ct
9 Royal Oak Ct
10 Hoxton Mkt
11 Bath Pl
12 Chapel Pl
13 Standard Pl
14 Cleeve Workshops
15 Cleeve Ho
16 Printing House Yd
17 Perseverance Works
18 Crooked Billet Yd
19 Drysdale Ho
20 Castlefrank Ho
21 School App
22 Basing House Yd
23 Mail Coach Yd
C5 1 Bracer Ho
2 Scorton Ho
3 Fern Cl
4 Macbeth Ho
5 Oberon Ho
6 Buckland Ct
7 Crondall Ct
8 Osric Path
9 Caliban Twr
10 Celia Ho
11 Juliet Ho
12 Bacchus Wlk
13 Malcolm Ho
14 Homefield St
15 Crondall Pl
16 Blanca Ho
17 Miranda Ho
18 Falstaff Ho
19 Charmian Ho
20 Myrtle Wlk
21 Arden Ho
22 Sebastian Ho
23 Stanway Ct
24 Jerrold St

25 Rosalind Ho
26 Cordelia Ho
27 Monteagle Ct
28 John Parry Ct
29 James Anderson Ct
30 Ben Jonson Ct
31 Sara Lane Ct
32 Walbrook Ct
C6 1 Portelet Ct
2 Trinity Ct
3 Rozel Ct
4 St Helier Ct
5 Corbiere Ho
6 Kenning Ho
7 Higgins Ho
8 Cavell Ho
9 Girling Ho
10 Fulcher Ho
11 Francis Ho
12 Norris Ho
13 Kempton Ho
14 Nesham Ho
15 Crossbow Ho
16 Catherine Ho
17 Strale Ho
18 Horner Hos
19 Stringer Hos
20 Whitmore Ho
21 Nightingale Ho
22 Wilmer Gdns
23 Arrow Ho
24 Archer Ho
25 Meriden Ho
26 Rover Ho
27 Bowyer Ho
28 Tiller Ho
29 Canalside Studios
30 Kleine Wharf
31 Benyon Wharf
32 Quebec Wharf
33 Belvedere Ct
34 Portfleet Pl
D4 1 Gorsuch Pl
2 Strout's Pl
3 Vaughan Est
4 George Loveless Ho
5 Baroness Rd
6 James Brine Ho
7 Arthur Wade Ho
8 Robert Owen Ho
9 Sivill Ho
10 Georgina Gdns
11 Old Market Sq
12 Cuff Point
13 Bakers Rents
14 Leopold Bldgs
15 Dunmore Point
16 Wingfield Ho
17 Gascoigne Pl
18 Mandela Ho
19 Virginia Rd
20 Briggs Ho
21 Packenham Ho
22 Gowan Ho
23 Kirton Gdns
24 Chambord Ho
25 Ducal St
26 Strickland Ho
27 Alliston Ho
28 Gibraltar Wlk
29 Equity Sq
30 Shacklewell St
31 Rochelle St
32 Sonning Ho
33 Culham Ho
34 Hurley Ho
35 Palissy St
36 Taplow Ho
37 Chertsey Ho
38 Sunbury Ho
39 Sunbury Workshops
40 Datchett Ho
41 Hocker St
42 Coll Sharp Ct
43 Marlow Studio Workshops
44 Marlow Ho
45 Shiplake Ho
46 Wargrave Ho
47 Iffley Ho
D5 1 Queensbridge Ct
2 Godwin Ho
3 Kent Ct
4 Brunswick Ho
5 Weymouth Ct
6 Sovereign Mews
7 Dunloe Ct
8 Cremer Bsns Ctr
9 James Hammett Ho
10 Allgood St
11 Horatio St
12 Cadell Ho
13 Horatio Ho
14 Shipton Ho
D6 1 Hilborough Ct
2 Scriven Ct
3 Livermere Ct

4 Angrave Ct
5 Angrave Pas
6 Benfleet Ct
7 Belford Ho
8 Orme Ho
9 Clemson Ho
10 Longman Ho
11 Lowther Ho
12 Lovelace Ho
13 Harlowe Ho
14 Pamela Ho
15 Samuel Ho
16 Acton Ho
17 Loanda Cl
18 Phoenix Cl
19 Richardson Cl
20 Thrasher Cl
21 Mary Secole Cl
22 Canal Path
23 Pear Tree Cl
24 Hebden Ct
25 Charlton Ct
26 Laburnum Ct
27 Mansfield Ct
28 Garden Pl
29 Amber Wharf
30 Haggerston Studios

96

A1 1 Whitechurch Pas
2 Manningtree St
3 Whitechurch La
4 Naylor Bldg W
5 Morrison Bldgs
6 Nayor Bldg E
7 Mulberry St
8 Albany Ct
9 Cornell Bldg
10 Dryden Bldg
11 Weyhill Rd
12 Colefax Bldg
13 Fordham St
14 Myrdle Ct
15 Buckle St
16 Plough St
17 Goodman's Stile
18 Ropewalk Gdns
19 Skyline Plaza Bldg
20 Minet Ho
21 Mitali Pas
22 Basil Ho
23 Bernhard Baron Ho
24 Hogarth Ct
25 Delafield Ho
26 Chandlery Ho
27 Berner Terr
28 Victoria Yd
29 Batson Ho
30 Harkness Ho
31 Drewett Ho
32 Dowler Ho
33 Everard Ho
34 Bicknell Ho
35 Danvers Ho
36 Philchurch Pl
37 Hadfield Ho
38 Kindersley Ho
39 Langmore Ho
40 Halliday Ho
A2 1 Arthur Deakin Ho
2 Albert Cotts
3 Victoria Cotts
4 Boden Ho
5 Vollasky Ho
6 Daplyn St
7 Hobsons Pl
8 Hanbury Ho
9 Huguenot Ct
10 Links Yd
11 Casson Ho
12 Ramar Ho
13 Greatorex Ho
14 Chicksand Ho
15 Spelman Ho
16 Tailworth St
17 Monthope Rd
18 Evelyn Ho
19 Bloomfield Ho
20 Davenant Ho
21 Pauline Ho
22 Tannery Ho
23 Don Gratton Ho
24 Green Dragon Yd
25 Fieldgate Mans
26 Mosque Tower
A3 1 Bentworth Ct
2 Hawksmoor Pl
3 Kerbela St
4 Fuller Cl
5 Kinsham Ho
6 Menotti St
7 Barwell Ho
8 Grimsby St
9 Reflection Ho
10 Fleet Street Hill
11 Bratley St
12 Weaver Ho

13 Cornerstone Ct
14 Stuttle Ho
15 McGlashon Ho
16 John Pritchard Ho
A4 1 Providence Yd
2 Lygon Ho
3 Brabner Ho
4 Delta St
5 Delta Point
6 Tillet Way
7 Mullet Gdns
8 Lampern Sq
9 Kite Pl
10 Elver Gdns
11 Cobden Ho
12 Eversley Ho
13 Lorden Wlk
14 Rapley Ho
15 Dence Ho
16 McKinnon Wood Ho
17 Satchwell Rd
18 Dickinson Ho
19 Hutton Ho
20 Simmons Ho
21 Swinton Ho
22 Yates Ho
23 Johnson Ho
24 Jeremy Bentham Ho
25 Waring Ho
26 St James Ct
27 Ebony Ho
28 Azure Ho
29 Westhope Ho
30 Hague St
A5 1 London Terr
2 Sturdee Ho
3 Maude Ho
4 Haig Ho
5 Jellicoe Ho
6 Ropley St
7 Guinness Trust Bldgs
8 Ion Ct
9 Columbia Rd
10 Moye Cl
11 Morrel Ct
12 Courtauld Ho
13 Drummond Ho
14 Gurney Ho
15 Atkinson Ho
16 Halley Ho
17 Goldsmith's Sq
18 Shahjalal Ho
19 Ken Wilson Ho
20 April Ct
21 Crofts Ho
22 Sebright Ho
23 Beechwood Ho
24 Gillman Ho
25 Cheverell Ho
26 Besford Ho
27 Dinmont Ho
28 Elizabeth Mews
29 Sebright Pas
30 Wyndham Deedes Ho
31 Sheppard Ho
32 Mary James Ho
33 Hadrian Est
34 Blythendale Ho
35 George Vale Ho
36 Lion Mills
37 St Peter's Ave
38 Pritchard Ho
A6 1 Broke Wlk
2 Rochemont Wlk
3 Marlborough Ave
4 Rivington Wlk
5 Magnin Cl
6 Gloucester Sq
7 Woolstone Ho
8 Marsworth Ho
9 Cheddington Ho
10 Linslade Ho
11 Cosgrove Ho
12 Blisworth Ho
13 Eleanor Ct
14 Wistow Ho
15 Muscott Ho
16 Boxmoor Ho
17 Linford Ho
18 Pendley Ho
19 Northchurch Ho
20 Debdale Ho
21 Broadway Market Mews
22 Welshpool Ho
23 Ada Ho
B1 1 Peter Best Ho
2 Mellish Ho
3 Porchester Ho
4 Dickson Ho
5 Joscoyne Ho
6 Silvester Ho
7 Wilton Ct
8 Sarah Ho
9 Bridgen Ho
10 Tylney Ho
11 Greenwich Ct

12 Damien Ct
13 Philson Mans
14 Siege Ho
15 Jacob Mans
16 Proud Ho
17 Sly St
18 Barnett St
19 Kinder St
20 Richard St
21 Hungerford St
22 Colstead Ho
23 Melwood Ho
24 Wicker St
25 Langdale St
26 Chapman Ho
27 Burwell Cl
28 Walford Ho
29 Welstead Ho
30 Norton Ho
31 Turnour Ho
32 Luke Ho
33 Dunch St
34 Sheridan St
35 Brinsley St
B2 1 Wodeham Gdns
2 Castlemaine St
3 Court St
B3 1 Rochester Ct
2 Weaver Ct
3 Greenheath Bsns Ctr
4 Glass St
5 Herald St
6 Northesk Ho
7 Codrington Ho
8 Heathpool Ct
9 Mocatta Ho
10 Harvey Ho
11 Blackwood Ho
12 Rutherford Ho
13 Bullen Ho
14 Fremantle Ho
15 Pellew Ho
16 Ashington Ho
17 Dinnington Ho
18 Bartholomew Sq
19 Steeple Ct
20 Orion Ho
21 Fellbrigg St
22 Eagle Ho
23 Sovereign Ho
24 Redmill Ho
25 Berry Ho
26 Grindall Ho
27 Collingwood Ho
B4 1 Charles Dickens Ho
2 Adrian Bolt Ho
3 William Rathbone Ho
4 Southwood Smith Ho
5 Rushmead
6 William Channing Ho
7 John Cartwright Ho
8 Charles Darwin Ho
9 Thomas Burt Ho
10 John Fielden Ho
11 Gwilym Maries Ho
12 Joseph Priestley Ho
13 Wear Pl
14 John Nettleford Ho
15 Thornaby Ho
16 Stockton Ho
17 Barnard Ho
18 Gainford Ho
19 Stapleton Ho
20 James Middleton Ho
21 Kedleston Wlk
22 Queen Margaret Flats
23 Hollybush Ho
24 Horwood Ho
25 Norden Ho
26 Newcourt Ho
27 Seabright St
28 Viaduct Pl
29 Sunlight Sq
30 Providence Row Cl
B5 1 Dinmont St
2 Marian St
3 Claredale Ho
4 Keeling Ho
5 Maple St
6 Winkley St
7 Temple Dwellings
8 Argos Ho
9 Helen Ho
10 Lysander Ho
11 Antenor Ho
12 Paris Ho
13 Nestor Ho
14 Hector Ho
15 Ajax Ho
16 Achilles Ho
17 Priam Ho
18 Peabody Est
19 Felix St

20 Cambridge Cres
21 Peterley Bsns Ctr
22 Beckwith Ho
23 Brookfield Ho
24 Parminter Ind Est
25 Ted Roberts Ho
26 Cambridge Ct
27 Millennium Pl
28 William Caslon Ho
29 Hugh Platt Ho
30 West St
31 Mayfield Ho
32 Apollo Ho
33 Tanners Yd
34 Teesdale Yd
B6 1 Welshpool St
2 Broadway Ho
3 Regents Wharf
4 London Wharf
5 Warburton Ho
6 Warburton St
7 Triangle Rd
8 Warburton Rd
9 Williams Ho
10 Booth Cl
11 Albert Cl
12 King Edward Mans
13 Victoria Bldgs
14 Andrews Wharf
C1 1 Woollon Ho
2 Dundalk Ho
3 Anne Goodman Ho
4 Newbold Cotts
5 Kerry Ho
6 Zion Ho
7 Longford Ho
8 Bromehead St
9 Athlone Ho
10 Jubilee Mans
11 Harriott Ho
12 Brayford Sq
13 Clearbrook Way
14 Rochelle Ct
15 Winterton Ho
16 Swift Ho
17 Brinsley Ho
18 Dean Ho
19 Foley Ho
20 Robert Sutton Ho
21 Montpelier Pl
22 Glastonbury Pl
23 Steel's La
24 Masters Lo
25 Stylus Apartments
26 Arta Ho
C2 1 Fulneck
2 Gracehill
3 Ockbrook
4 Fairfield
5 Dunstan Hos
6 Cressy Ct
7 Cressy Hos
8 Callahan Cotts
9 Lindley Ho
10 Mayo Ho
11 Wexford Ho
12 Sandhurst Ho
13 Addis Ho
14 Colverson Ho
15 Beckett Ho
16 Jarman Ho
17 Armsby Ho
18 Wingrad Ho
19 Miranda Cl
20 Drake Ho
21 Ashfield Yd
22 Magri Wlk
23 Jean Pardies Ho
24 St Vincent De Paul Ho
25 Sambrook Ho
26 Louise De Marillac Ho
27 Dagobert Ho
28 Le Moal Ho
29 Odette Duval Ho
30 Charles Auffray Ho
31 Boisseau Ho
32 Clichy Ho
33 Paymal Ho
C3 1 William's Bldgs
2 Donegal Ho
3 Pelican Pas
4 Frederick Charrington Ho
5 Wickford Ho
6 Braintree Ho
7 Doveton Ho
8 Doveton St
9 Cephas Ho
10 Sceptre Ho
11 Bancroft Ho
12 Stothard St
13 Redclyf Ho
14 Winkworth Cotts
15 Amiel St
16 Hadleigh Ho
17 Hadleigh Cl
18 Ryder Ho
19 Mantus Cl
20 Kenton Ho
21 Colebert Ho
22 Ibbott St
23 Rickman Ho
24 Rickman St
25 Stothard Ho
26 Barbanel Ho
27 Stannard Cotts
28 St Peters Ct
29 Rennie Cotts
30 Pemell Cl
31 Pemell Ho
32 Leatherdale St
33 Gouldman Ho
34 Lamplighter Cl
35 Sherren Ho
36 Marlborough Lo
37 Hamilton Lo
38 Montgomery Lo
39 Cleveland Gr
40 Cromwell Lo
41 Bardsey Pl
42 Charrington Ho
43 Hayfield Yd
44 Allport Mews
45 Colin Winter Ho
C4 1 Mulberry Ho
2 Gretton Ho
3 Merceron Ho
4 Montfort Ho
5 Westbrook Ho
6 Sugar Loaf Wlk
7 Museum Ho
8 Burnham Est
9 Globe Terr
10 Moravian St
11 Shepton Hos
12 Mendip Hos
13 Academy Ct
14 Pepys Ho
15 Swinburne Ho
16 Moore Ho
17 Morris Ho
18 Burns Ho
19 Milton Ho
20 Whitman Ho
21 Shelley Ho
22 Keats Ho
23 Dawson Ho
24 Bradbeer Ho
25 Forber Ho
26 Hughes Ho
27 Silvester Ho
28 Rogers Est
29 Pavan Ct
30 Stafford Cripps Ho
31 Sidney Godley (VC) Ho
32 Butler Ho
33 Butler St
34 Thorne Ho
35 Bevin Ho
36 Tuscan Ho
C5 1 Evesham Ho
2 James Campbell Ho
3 Thomas Hollywood Ho
4 James Docherty Ho
5 Ebenezer Mussel Ho
6 Jameson Ct
7 Edinburgh Cl
8 Roger Dowley Ct
9 Sherbrooke Ho
10 Calcraft Ho
11 Burrard Ho
12 Dundas Ho
13 Ponsonby Ho
14 Barnes Ho
15 Paget Ho
16 Maitland Ho
17 Chesil Ct
18 Reynolds Ho
19 Cleland Ho
20 Goodrich Ho
21 Rosebery Ho
22 Sankey Ho
23 Cyprus Pl
24 Royston St
25 Stainsbury St
26 Hunslett St
27 Baildon
28 Brockweir
29 Tytherton
30 Malmesbury
31 Kingswood
32 Colville Ho
C6 1 Halkett Ho
2 Christchurch Sq
3 Helena Pl
4 Swingfield Ho
5 Greenham Ho
6 Dinmore Ho
7 Anstey Ho
8 Weston Ho
9 Carbroke Ho
10 Bluebell Cl
11 Cherry Tree Cl
12 Georgian Ct
13 Park Cl
14 Regency Ct
15 Norris Ho
D1 1 Pattison Ho
2 St Thomas Ho
3 Arbour Ho
4 Bladen Ho
5 Antill Terr
6 Majorie Mews
7 Billing Ho
8 Dowson Ho
9 Lipton Rd
10 Chalkwell Ho
11 Corringham Ho
12 Ogilvie Ho
13 Edward Mann Cl
14 Reservoir Studios
15 Lighterman Mews
D2 1 Roland Mews
2 Beatrice Ho
3 Morecambe Cl
4 Stepney Green Ct
5 Milrood Ho
6 Panama Ho
7 Galway Ho
8 Jacqueline Ho
9 Crown Mews
10 Caspian Ho
11 Darien Ho
12 Riga Ho
13 Flores Ho
14 Taranto Ho
15 Aden Ho
16 Master's St
17 Rosary Ct
D3 1 Raynham Ho
2 Pat Shaw Ho
3 Colmar Cl
4 Withy Ho
5 Stocks Ct
6 Downey Ho
7 Bay Ct
8 Sligo Ho
9 Pegasus Ho
10 Barents Ho
11 Biscay Ho
12 Solway Ho
13 Bantry Ho
14 Aral Ho
15 Pacific Ho
16 Magellan Ho
17 Levant Ho
18 Adriatic Ho
19 Genoa Ho
20 Hawke Ho
21 Palliser Ho
22 Ionian Ho
23 Weddell Ho
24 Carlyle Mews
25 Greencourt Ho
26 Sundra Wlk
D4 1 Stubbs Ho
2 Holman Ho
3 Clynes Ho
4 Windsor Ho
5 Gilbert Ho
6 Chater Ho
7 Ellen Wilkinson Ho
8 George Belt Ho
9 Ayrton Gould Ho
10 O'Brian Ho
11 Sulkin Ho
12 Jenkinson Ho
13 Bullards Pl
14 Sylvia Pankhurst Ho
15 Mary Macarthur Ho
16 Trevelyan Ho
17 Wedgwood Ho
18 Pemberton Ct
19 Leatherdale St
20 Walter Besant Ho
21 Barber Beaumont Ho
22 Brancaster Ho
23 Litcham Ho
D5 1 Kemp Ho
2 Piggott Ho
3 Mark Ho
4 Sidney Ho
5 Pomeroy Ho
6 Puteaux Ho
7 Doric Ho
8 Modling Ho
9 Longman Ho
10 Ames Ho
11 Alzette Ho
12 Offenbach Ho
13 Tate Ho
14 Norton Ho
15 St Gilles Ho
16 Harold Ho
17 Velletri Ho
18 Bridge Wharf
19 Gathorne St
20 Bow Brook The
21 Twig Folly Cl
22 Palmerston Ct
23 Lakeview
24 Peach Walk Mews
25 Caesar Ct

97

A1 1 Hearnshaw St
2 Berry Cotts
3 Causton Cotts
4 Elizabeth Blount Ct
5 Carr St
6 Shaw Cres
7 Darnley Ho
8 Mercer's Cotts
9 Troon Ho
10 Ratcliffe Ho
11 Wakeling St
12 York Sq
13 Anglia Ho
14 Cambria Ho
15 Caledonia Ho
16 Ratcliffe La
17 Bekesbourne St
18 John Scurr Ho
19 Regents Canal Ho
20 Basin App
21 Powlesland Ct
A2 1 Waley St
2 Edith Ramsay Ho
3 Andaman Ho
4 Atlantic Ho
5 Pevensey Ho
6 Solent Ho
7 Lorne Ho
8 Cromarty Ho
9 Dakin Pl
10 Greaves Cotts
11 Donaghue Cotts
12 Ames Cotts
13 Waterview Ho
14 Limehouse Fields Est
A3 1 Formosa Ho
2 Galveston Ho
3 Arabian Ho
4 Greenland Ho
5 Coral Ho
6 Anson Ho
7 Cambay Ho
8 Lindop Ho
9 Moray Ho
10 Azov Ho
11 Sandalwood Cl
12 Broadford Ho
A4 1 Imperial Ho
2 Newport Ho
3 Vassall Ho
4 Maurice Ct
5 Creed Ct
6 Christopher France Ho
7 Beaumont Ct
8 Pembroke Mews
A5 1 Nightingale Mews
2 Bunsen Ho
3 Bunsen St
4 Beatrice Webb Ho
5 Margaret Bondfield Ho
6 Wilmer Ho
7 Sandall Ho
8 Butley Ct
9 Josseline Ct
10 Dalton Ho
11 Brine Ho
12 Ford Cl
13 Viking Cl
14 Stanfield Rd
15 Stoneleigh Mews
16 Ruth Ct
17 School Bell Cloisters
18 Schoolbell Mews
19 Medhurst Cl
20 Olga St
21 Conyer St
22 Diamond Ho
23 Daring Ho
24 Crane Ho
25 Exmoor Ho
26 Grenville Ho
27 Hyperion Ho
28 Sturdy Ho
29 Wren Ho
30 Ardent Ho
31 Senators Lo
32 Hooke Ho
33 Mohawk Ho
34 Ivanhoe Ho
35 Medway Mews
B1 1 Dora Ho
2 Flansham Ho
3 Gatwick Ho
4 Ashpark Ho
5 Newdigate Ho
6 Midhurst Ho
7 Redbourne Ho
8 Southwater Cl
9 Andersens Wharf
10 Whatman Ho
11 Butler Ho
12 Fitzroy Ho
13 Salmon St
14 Mission The
15 Aithan Ho
16 Britley Ho
17 Cheadle Ho
18 Elland Ho
19 Wharf La
20 Docklands Ct
21 Park Heights Ct
22 Grosvenor Ct
23 Lime House Ct
24 Swallow Pl
25 St Anne's Trad Est
B2 1 Wearmouth Ho
2 Elmslie Point
3 Grindley Ho
4 Stileman Ho
5 Wilcox Ho
6 Huddart St
7 Robeson St
8 Couzens Ho
9 Perley Ho
10 Whytlaw Ho
11 Booker Cl
12 Tunley Gn
13 Callingham Cl
14 Bowry Ho
15 Perkins Ho
16 Printon Ho
17 Tasker Ho
B4 1 Trellis Sq
2 Sheffield Sq
3 Howcroft Ho
4 Astra Ho
5 Frye Ct
6 Byas Ho
7 George Lansbury Ho
8 Regal Pl
9 Coborn Mews
10 Tredegar Mews
11 Cavendish Terr
12 Lyn Mews
13 Buttermere Ho
14 Coniston Ho
15 Tracy Ho
16 Hanover Pl
17 St Clair Ho
18 Longthorne Ho
19 Vista Bldgs
20 Verity Ho
21 Icarus Ho
22 Whippingham Ho
23 Hamilton Ho
24 Winchester Ho
B5 1 Roman Square Mkt
2 John Bond Ho
3 McKenna Ho
4 Dennis Ho
5 McAusland Ho
6 McBride Ho
7 Libra Rd
8 Dave Adams Ho
9 Regency Ct
10 Tay Ho
11 Sleat Ho
12 Brodick Ho
13 Ewart Pl
14 Lunan Ho
15 Cruden Ho
16 Anglo Rd
17 Mull Ho
18 Sinclairs Ho
19 Driftway Ho
20 Clayhall Ct
21 Berebinder Ho
22 Partridge Ho
23 Barford Ho
24 Gullane Ho
25 Gosford Ho
26 Dornoch Ho
27 Dunnet Ho
28 Enard Ho
29 Fraserburgh Ho
30 Forth Ho
31 Stavers Ho
32 Rosegate Ho
33 Crowngate Ho
34 Queensgate Ho
35 Towergate Ho
36 Ordell Ct
37 William Pl
B6 1 Hampstead Wlk
2 Waverton Ho
3 Elton Ho
4 Locton Gn
5 Birtwhistle Ho
6 Clare Ho
7 Magpie Ho
8 Hornbeam Sq
9 Rowan Ho
10 Barge La
11 Walnut Ho
12 Birdsfield La
13 Atkins Ct
14 Willow Tree Cl
15 Jasmine Sq
16 Tait Ct
17 Ranwell Ho
18 Ranwell Cl
19 Tufnell Ct
20 Pulteney Cl
21 Vic Johnson Ho
22 Lea Sq
23 Iceni Ct
24 Tamar Cl
25 Roman Rd
26 Valentine Ho
C1 1 Landin Ho
2 Thomas Road Ind
3 Vickery's Wharf
4 Abbotts Wharf
5 Limehouse Ct
6 Charlesworth Ho
7 Gurdon Ho
8 Trendell Ho
9 Menteath Ho
10 Minchin Ho
11 Donne Ho
12 Old School Sq
13 Anglesey Ho
14 Gough Wlk
15 Baring Ho
16 Gladstone Ho
17 Hopkins Ho
18 Granville Ho
19 Overstone Ho
20 Pusey Ho
21 Russell Ho
22 Stanley Ho
C2 1 Bredel Ho
2 Linton Ho
3 Matthews Ho
4 Woodcock Ho
5 Limborough Ho
6 Maydwell Ho
7 Underhill Ho
8 Meyrick Ho
9 Ambrose Ho
10 Richardson Ho
11 Carpenter Ho
12 Robinson Ho
13 Bellmaker Ct
14 Lime Tree Ct
15 Bracken Ho
16 Bramble Ho
17 Berberis Ho
18 Bilberry Ho
19 Ladyfern Ho
20 Rosebay Ho
21 Invicta Cl
22 Phoenix Bsns Ctr
23 Metropolitan Cl
24 Busbridge Ho
C3 1 Fairmont Ho
2 Healy Ho
3 Zodiac Ho
4 Buick Ho
5 Consul Ho
6 Bentley Ho
7 Cresta Ho
8 Daimler Ho
9 Riley Ho
10 Jensen Ho
11 Lagonda Ho
12 Ireton St
13 Navenby Wlk
14 Burwell Wlk
15 Leadenham Ct
16 Sleaford Ho
17 Bow Triangle Bsns Ctr
C4 1 Bow Ho
2 Denmark Pl
3 Marsalis Ho
4 Lovette Ho
5 Drapers Almhouses
6 Mallard Point
7 Creswick Wlk
8 Bevin Ho
9 Huggins Ho
10 Williams Ho
11 Harris Ho
12 Marina Ct
13 Electric Ho
14 Matching Ct
15 Wellington Bldgs
16 Grafton Ho
17 Berkeley Ho
18 Columbia Ho
C5 1 Vincent Mews
2 Menai Pl
3 Heathfield Ct
4 Redwood Cl
5 Acorn Ct
6 Primrose Cl
7 Briar Ct

Springwood Cl
Ironworks
Juno Ho
Chariot Cl
Saturn Ho
Hadrian Cl
Mercury Ho
Forum Cl
Venus Ho
Vesta Ho
Tiber Cl
Gemini Ho
Crown Close Bsns Ctr
Old Ford Trad Ctr
Colebrook Ho
Essex Ho
Salisbury Ho
Maidstone Ho
Osterley Ho
Norwich Ho
Clarissa Ho
Elgin Ho
Shaftesbury Lo
Shepherd Ho
Jeremiah St
Elizabeth Cl
Chilcot Cl
Fitzgerald Ho
Vesey Path
Ennis Ho
Kilmore Ho
Cygnet House N
Cygnet House S
Sumner Ho
David Hewitt Ho
St Gabriels Cl
Limehouse Cut
Colmans Wharf
Foundary Ho
Radford Ho
Broxbourne Ho
Roxford Ho
Biscott Ho
Stanborough Ho
Hillstone Ct
1 Bradley Ho
2 Prioress Ho
3 Alton Ho
4 Foxley Ho
5 Munden Ho
6 Canterbury Ho
7 Corbin Ho
8 Barton Ho
9 Jolles Ho
10 Rudstone Ho
11 Baxter Ho
12 Baker Ho
13 Insley Ho
14 Hardwicke Ho
15 Glebe Ct
16 Priory St
17 Sadler Ho
18 Ballinger Point
19 Henshall Point
20 Dorrington Point
21 Warren Ho
22 Fairlie Ct
23 Regent Sq
24 Hackworth Point
25 Priestman Point
26 Wingate Ho
27 Nethercott Ho
28 Thelbridge Ho
29 Bowden Ho
30 Kerscott Ho
31 Southcott Ho
32 Birchdown Ho
33 Upcott Ho
34 Langmead Ho
35 Limscott Ho
36 Northleigh Ho
37 Huntshaw Ho
38 Chagford Ho
39 Ashcombe Ho
40 Shillingford Ho
41 Patrick Connolly Gdns
42 Lester Ct
43 Franklin St
44 Taft Way
45 Washington Cl
46 Veronica Ho
47 William Guy Gdns
48 Denbury Ho
49 Holsworthy Ho
50 Padstone Ho

98

1 Glenkerry Ho
2 Carradale Ho
3 Langdon Ho
4 Balfron Twr
5 St Frideswides Mews
6 Tabard Ct
7 Delta Bldg
8 Findhorn St
9 Kilbrennan Ho
10 Thistle Ho
11 Heather Ho
12 Tartan Ho
13 Sharman Ho
14 Trident Ho
15 Wharf View Ct
A2 1 Mills Gr
2 St Michaels Ct
3 Duncan Ct
A4 1 Miller's House Visitor Ctr
B1 1 Lansbury Gdns
2 Theseus Ho
3 Adams Ho
4 Jones Ho
5 Sam March Ho
6 Arapiles Ho
7 Athenia Ho
8 Julius Ho
9 Jervis Bay Ho
10 Helen Mackay Ho
11 Gaze Ho
12 Ritchie Ho
13 Blairgowrie Ct
14 Circle Ho
15 Dunkeld Ho
16 Rosemary Dr
17 Sorrel La
18 East India Dock Road Tunnel
B3 1 Crescent Court Bsns Ctr
2 Ashmead Bsns Ctr
3 Forward Bsns Ctr The
B6 1 Victoria Mills
2 Hallings Wharf Studios
3 Poland Ho
4 Peter Heathfield Ho
5 Burford Rd
C5 1 Abbey Lane Commercial Est
2 Greenway Ct
C6 1 Barnby Sq
2 Barnby St
3 Brassett Point
4 David Lee Point
5 Worthing Cl
6 Bexhill Wlk
7 Old Barrowfield
8 Elmgreen Cl
9 Stafford Morris Ho
10 Nina Mackay Cl
11 Lime Wlk
D1 1 Newton Point
2 Sparke Terr
3 Montesquieu Terr
4 Crawford Point
5 Rathbone Ho
6 George St
7 Emily St
8 Fendt Cl
9 Sabbarton St
10 Briary Ct
11 Shaftesbury Ho
D2 1 Radley Terr
2 Bernard Cassidy St
3 Rathbone Mkt
4 Thomas North Terr
5 Mary St
6 Hughes Terr
7 Swanscombe Point
8 Rawlinson Point
9 Kennedy Cox Ho
10 Cooper St
D6 1 Harris Cotts
2 Moorey Cl
3 Euro Bsns Ctr
4 Ladywell St
5 Caistor Ho
6 Redfern Ho

99

A2 1 Odeon Ct
2 Edward Ct
3 Newhaven La
4 Ravenscroft Cl
5 Douglas Rd
6 Ferrier Point
7 Harvey Point
8 Wood Point
9 Trinity St
10 Pattinson Point
11 Clinch Ct
12 Mint Bsns Pk
A3 1 Webb Gdns
2 Eric Shipman Terr
3 Warmington St
4 Jellicoe Rd
5 Frank St
6 Seaton Cl
7 Tabernacle Ave
8 Upland Rd
9 Clove St
10 Edward St
A4 1 Bob Anker Cl
2 Lea Ct
3 Third Ave
4 Suffolk Rd
A5 1 Lettsom Wlk
2 Ashburton Terr
3 Grasmere Rd
4 Dimsdale Wlk
5 Rawstone Wlk
6 Scott Ho
7 Willett Ho
8 James Cl
9 Cordwainers Wlk
10 Victoria Point
11 Settle Point
12 Middle Rd
13 Steve Biko Lodge
14 Lady Helen Seymour Ho
A6 1 Royston Ct
B4 1 Barbers Alley
2 Grengate Lodge
3 Augurs La
4 Surrey St
5 Dongola Rd W
6 Bemersyde Point
7 Rowntree Clifford Cl
C2 1 Alliance Rd
2 Salomons Rd
3 Barnes Ct
4 Triangle Ct
5 Moorings The
C5 1 Wellby Ct
2 Northfield Ho
3 Bishop Wilfred Wood Ct
4 Castle Point
5 Moat Dr
C6 1 Tolpuddle Ave
2 Crown Mews
3 Lilac Ct
4 Hamara Ghar
5 Greenleaf Rd
6 Massey Ct
7 Florence Rd
8 Sissulu Ct
9 Austin Ct
D2 1 Partridge Cl
2 Vanbrugh Cl
3 Meadowsweet Cl
4 St Michaels Cl
5 Long Mark Rd
6 Congreve Wlk
D5 1 Foxcombe Cl
2 Rochford Cl
3 Kylemore Cl
4 Stondon Wlk
5 Imperial Mews
6 Dominica Cl
D6 1 Oldegate Ho
2 Gaitskell Ho
3 Cabot Way

100

A1 1 Hadleigh Wlk
2 Hawksmoor Cl
3 Fraser Cl
4 Moncrieff Cl
5 Burlington Cl
6 Dundonald Cl
7 Oakley Cl
8 Ashwell Cl
A2 1 Orchid Cl
2 Bellflower Cl
3 Partridge Sq
4 Larkspur Cl
5 Lobelia Cl
6 Stonechat Sq
7 Wintergreen Cl
8 Garnet Wlk
9 Mavis Wlk
10 Beacons Cl
11 Abbess Cl
12 Elmley Cl
13 Chetwood Wlk
14 Selby Cl
15 Denny Cl
16 Woodhatch Cl
A6 1 Oakwood Ct
2 Harrow Rd
3 Ray Massey Way
4 Madge Gill Way
5 Pilgrims Way
6 St Bartholomews Ct
B1 1 Bowers Wlk
2 Barton Cl
3 Clayton Cl
4 Dixon Cl
5 Gautrey Sq
6 Wakerley Cl
7 Canterbury Cl
8 Goose Sq
9 Coventry Cl
10 Butterfield Sq
11 Winchester Cl
B2 1 Fleetwood Ct
2 Lymington Cl
3 Holyhead Cl
4 Bondfield Rd
5 Tulip Cl
6 Ambrose Cl
7 Sage Cl
8 Lindwood Cl
D1 1 Weymouth Ct
2 Founder Cl
3 Admirals Ct

101

A6 1 Wellington St
2 St Ann's Rd
3 Cooke St
4 Gateway Ho
5 Ardleigh Ho
6 Skipper Ct
7 Hewetts Quay
B5 1 Anderson Ho
2 Rookwood Ho
3 Tasker Ho
4 Crispe Ho
5 Oban Ho
6 Earlsdown Ho
B6 1 Jarvis Cl
2 Mayflower Ho
3 Westbury Ct
4 Millicent Preston Ho
5 Louise Graham Ho
6 Grange Ho
7 Basing Ho
8 Barnes Ho
9 Lexham Ho
10 Ripple Ct
11 Waldegrave Ct
12 Howard Ct

104

A6 1 Milburn Dr
2 Cousins Cl
3 Leacroft Cl

108

C5 1 Marlow Ct
2 Andrewes Ct
3 Vine Cotts
4 Benjamin Ct
5 Broadway Bldgs
6 Clocktower Mews
7 Amberley Ho
8 Diamond Ct
D5 1 Silverdale Cl
2 Burdett Cl
3 Hopefield
4 Maunder Rd
5 Clare Ho

109

A5 1 Glastonbury Ct
2 Evesham Ct
3 Lacock Ct
4 Wigmore Ct
5 Melrose Ct
6 Brownlow Rd
7 Chignell Pl
8 Shirley Ct
9 Trojan Ct
10 Hatfield Rd
11 Pershore Ho
12 Hyde Ho
13 Hugh Clark Ho
14 Rosemoor Ho
15 Leeland Mans
16 Waterford Ct
17 O'Grady Ct
C6 1 Abbey Lo
2 Yew Tree Grange
3 Abinger Ct

110

A1 1 Burford Ho
2 Hope Cl
3 Centaur Ct
4 Phoenix Ct
A6 1 Watermans Mews
2 Hills Mews
3 Grosvenor Ct
4 Elton Lo
5 Hambledon Ct
C1 1 Surrey Cres
2 Forbes Ho
3 Haining Cl
4 Melville Ct
5 London Stile
6 Stile Hall Par
7 Priory Lo
8 Kew Bridge Ct
9 Meadowcroft
10 St James Ct
11 Rivers Ho
C5 1 Grosvenor Par
2 Oakfield Ct
3 Hart Grove Ct
4 Grosvenor Ct
D1 1 Churchdale Ct
2 Cromwell Cl
3 Cambridge Rd S
4 Oxbridge Ct
5 Tomlinson Cl
6 Gunnersbury Mews
7 Grange The
8 Gunnersbury Cl
9 Bellgrave Lo
D4 1 Cheltenham Pl
2 Beaumaris Twr
3 Arundel Ho
4 Pevensey Ct
5 Jerome Twr
6 Anstey Ct
7 Bennett Ct
8 Gunnersbury Ct
9 Barrington Ct
10 Hope Gdns
11 Park Road E
D5 1 Lantry Ct
2 Rosemount Ct
3 Moreton Twr
4 Acton Central Ind Est
5 Rufford Twr
6 Narrow St
7 Mount Pl
8 Sidney Miller Ct
9 Mill Hill Terr
10 Cheltenham Pl
11 Mill Hill Gr
12 Benjamin Ho
13 Arlington Ct
14 Lombard Ct
15 Steyne Ho

111

A1 1 Arlington Park Mans
2 Sandown Ho
3 Goodwood Ho
4 Windsor Ho
5 Lingfield Ho
6 Ascot Ho
7 Watchfield Ct
8 Belgrave Ct
9 Beverley Ct
10 Beaumont Ct
11 Harvard Rd
12 Troubridge Ct
13 Branden Lo
14 Fromow's Cnr
A2 1 Chiswick Green Studios
2 Bell Ind Est
3 Fairlawn Ct
4 Dukes Gate
5 Dewsbury Ct
6 Chiswick Terr
7 Mortlake Ho
A3 1 Blackmore Twr
2 Bollo Ct
3 Kipling Twr
4 Lawrence Ct
5 Maugham Ct
6 Reade Ct
7 Woolf Ct
8 Shaw Ct
9 Verne Ct
10 Wodehouse Ct
11 Greenock Rd
12 Garden Ct
13 Barons Gate
14 Cleveland Rd
15 Carver Cl
16 Chapter Cl
17 Beauchamp Cl
18 Holmes Ct
19 Copper Mews
A4 1 Belgrave Cl
2 Buckland Wlk
3 Frampton Ct
4 Telfer Cl
5 Harlech Twr
6 Corfe Twr
7 Barwick Ho
8 Charles Hocking Ho
9 Sunninghill Ct
10 Salisbury St
11 Jameson Pl
12 Castle Cl
A5 1 Rectory Rd
2 Derwentwater Mans
3 Market Pl
4 Hooper's Mews
5 Cromwell Pl
6 Locarno Rd
7 Edgecote Cl
8 Harleyford Manor
9 Coopers Ct
10 Avingdor Ct
11 Steyne Ho
B1 1 Chatsworth Lo
2 Prospect Pl
3 Townhall Ave
4 Devonhurst Pl
5 Heathfield Ct
6 Horticultural Pl
7 Merlin Ho
8 Garth Rd
9 Autumn Rise
B2 1 Disraeli Cl
2 Winston Wlk
3 Rusthall Mans
4 Bedford Park Mans
5 Essex Place Sq
6 Holly Rd
7 Homecross Ho
8 Swan Bsns Ctr
9 Jessop Ho
C1 1 Glebe Cl
2 Devonshire Mews
3 Binns Terr
4 Ingress St
5 Swanscombe Rd
6 Brackley Terr
7 Stephen Fox Ho
8 Manor Gdns
9 Coram Ho
10 Flaxman Ho
11 Thorneycroft Ho
12 Thornhill Ho
13 Kent Ho
14 Oldfield Ho
C2 1 Chestnut Ho
2 Bedford Ho
3 Bedford Cnr
4 Sydney Ho
5 Bedford Park Cnr
6 Priory Gdns
7 Windmill Alley
8 Castle Pl
9 Jonathan Ct
10 Windmill Pas
11 Chardin Rd
12 Gable Ho
C3 1 Fleet Ct
2 Ember Ct
3 Emlyn Gdns
4 Clone Ct
5 Brent Ct
6 Abbey Ct
7 Ormsby Lo
8 St Catherine's Ct
9 Lodge The
C4 1 Longford Ct
2 Mole Ct
3 Lea Ct
4 Wandle Ct
5 Beverley Ct
6 Roding Ct
7 Crane Ct
D1 1 Miller's Ct
2 British Grove Pas
3 British Grove S
4 Berestede Rd
5 North Eyot Gdns
D2 1 Flanders Mans
2 Stamford Brook Mans
3 Linkenholt Mans
4 Prebend Mans
5 Middlesex Ct
D3 1 Stamford Brook Gdns
2 Hauteville Court Gdns
3 Ranelagh Gdns

112

A1 1 Chisholm Ct
2 North Verbena Gdns
3 Western Terr
4 Verbena Gdns
5 Montrose Villas
6 Hammersmith Terr
7 South Black Lion La
8 St Peter's Wharf
A2 1 Hamlet Ct
2 Derwent Ct
3 Westcroft Ct
4 Black Lion Mews
5 St Peter's Villas
6 Standish Ho
7 Chambon Pl
8 Court Mans
9 Longthorpe Ct
10 Charlotte Ct
11 Westside
12 Park Ct
13 London Ho
A3 1 Elizabeth Finn Ho
2 Ashchurch Ct
3 King's Par
4 Inver Ct
5 Ariel Ct
6 Pocklington Lo
7 Vitae Apartments
A4 1 Becklow Gdns
2 Victoria Ho
3 Lycett Pl
4 Kylemore Ct
5 Alexandra Ct
6 Lytten Ct
7 Becklow Mews
8 Northcroft Ct
9 Bailey Ct
10 Spring Cott

112 A4
11 Landor Wlk
12 Laurence Mews
13 Hadyn Park Ct
14 Askew Mans
15 Malvern Ct
B1 1 Prince's Mews
2 Aspen Gdns
3 Hampshire Hog La
4 Blades Ct
B2 1 Albion Gdns
2 Flora Gdns
3 Lamington St
4 Felgate Mews
5 Galena Ho
6 Albion Mews
7 Albion Ct
8 King Street Cloisters
9 Dimes Pl
10 Clarence Ct
11 Hampshire Hog La
12 Marryat Ct
13 Ravenscourt Ho
B3 1 Ravenscourt Park Mans
2 Paddenswick Ct
3 Ashbridge Ct
B4 1 Westbush Ct
2 Goldhawk Mews
3 Sycamore Ho
4 Shackleton Ct
5 Drake Ct
6 Scotts Ct
7 Raleigh Ct
8 Melville Court Flats
9 Southway Cl
B5 1 Arlington Ho
2 Lugard Ho
3 Shabana Ct
4 Sitarey Ct
5 Oaklands Ct
6 Davenport Mews
B6 1 Abercrombie Ho
2 Bathurst Ho
3 Brisbane Ho
4 Bentinck Ho
5 Ellenborough Ho
6 Lawrence Cl
7 Mackenzie Cl
8 Carteret Ho
9 Calvert Ho
10 Winthrop Ho
11 Auckland Ho
12 Blaxland Ho
13 Havelock Cl
14 Hargraves Ho
15 Hudson Cl
16 Phipps Ho
17 Lawson Ho
18 Hastings Ho
19 Wolfe Ho
20 Malabar Ct
21 Commonwealth Ave
22 Charnock Ho
23 Canning Ho
24 Cornwallis Ho
25 Commonwealth Ave
26 Champlain Ho
27 Grey Ho
28 Durban Ho
29 Baird Ho
30 Campbell Ho
31 Mitchell Ho
32 Denham Ho
33 Mackay Ho
34 Evans Ho
35 Davis Ho
36 Mandela Cl
C1 1 Bridge Avenue Mans
2 Bridgeview
3 College Ct
4 Beatrice Ho
5 Amelia Ho
6 Edith Ho
7 Joanna Ho
8 Mary Ho
9 Adela Ho
10 Sophia Ho
11 Henrietta Ho
12 Charlotte Ho
13 Alexandra Ho
14 Bath Pl
15 Elizabeth Ho
16 Margaret Ho
17 Peabody Est
18 Eleanor Ho
19 Isabella Ho
20 Caroline Ho
21 Chancellors Wharf
22 Sussex Pl
C2 1 Phoenix Lodge Mans
2 Samuel's Cl
3 Broadway Arc
4 Brook Ho
5 Hammersmith Broadway
6 Broadway Ctr The
7 Cambridge Ct
8 Ashcroft Sq
C4 1 Verulam Ho
2 Grove Mans
3 Frobisher Ct
4 Library Mans
5 Pennard Mans
6 New Shepherd's Bush Mkt
7 Kerrington Ct
8 Granville Mans
9 Romney Ct
10 Rayner Ct
11 Sulgrave Gdns
12 Bamborough Gdns
13 Hillary Ct
14 Market Studios
15 Lanark Mans
C5 1 Linden Ct
2 Frithville Ct
3 Blomfield Mans
4 Poplar Mews
5 Hopgood St
6 Westwood Ho
7 Stanlake Mews
8 Stanlake Villas
9 Alexandra Mans
D3 1 Grosvenor Residences
2 Blythe Mews
3 Burnand Ho
4 Bradford Ho
5 Springvale Terr
6 Ceylon Rd
7 Walpole Ct
8 Bronte Ct
9 Boswell Ct
10 Souldern Rd
11 Brook Green Flats
12 Haarlem Rd
13 Stafford Mans
14 Lionel Mans
15 Barradell Ho
D4 1 Vanderbilt Villas
2 Bodington Ct
3 Kingham Cl
4 Clearwater Terr
5 Lorne Gdns
6 Cameret Ct
7 Bush Ct
8 Shepherds Ct
9 Rockley Ct
10 Grampians The
11 Charcroft Ct
12 Addison Park Mans
13 Sinclair Mans
14 Fountain Ct
15 Woodford Ct
16 Roseford Ct
17 Woodstock Studios
D5 1 St Katherine's Wlk
2 Dorrit Ho
3 Pickwick Ho
4 Dombey Ho
5 Caranday Villas
6 Mortimer Ho
7 Nickleby Ho
8 Stebbing Ho
9 Boxmoor Ho
10 Poynter Ho
11 Swanscombe Ho
12 Darnley Terr
13 Norland Ho
14 Hume Ho
15 Boundary Ho
16 Norland Rd
17 Helix Ct
D6 1 Frinstead Ho
2 Hurstway Wlk
3 Testerton Wlk
4 Grenfell Wlk
5 Grenfell Twr
6 Barandon Wlk
7 Treadgold Ho
8 St Clements Ct
9 Willow Way
10 Florence Ho
11 Dora Ho
12 Carton Ho
13 Agnes Ho
14 Marley Ho
15 Estella Ho
16 Waynflete Sq
17 Pippin Ho
18 Baseline Business Studios
118
A1 1 Hope Ct
2 West Point
3 Centre Point
4 East Point
5 Proctor Ho
6 Tovy Ho
7 Avondale Pavement
8 Brettinghurst
9 Colechurch Ho
10 Harman Cl
11 Avondale Ho
12 Lanark Ho
13 George Elliston Ho
14 Eric Wilkins Ho
15 Six Bridges Ind Est
16 St James Ind Mews
17 Winter Lo
18 Fern Wlk
19 Ivy Ct
20 Fallow Ct
21 Culloden Cl
22 Archers Lo
A2 1 Cadbury Way
2 Robert Bell Ho
3 Robert Jones Ho
4 William Rushbrooke Ho
5 Helen Taylor Ho
6 Peter Hills Ho
7 Charles Mackenzie Ho
8 Drappers Way
9 Racs Flats
10 Abbey Gdns
11 Mayfair Ho
12 Windmill Cl
13 Maria Cl
14 Townsend Ho
15 Mason Ho
16 Kotree Way
17 Hannah Mary Way
18 Langdon Way
19 Whittaker Way
A3 1 Rudge Ho
2 Spenlow Ho
3 Darnay Ho
4 Carton Ho
5 Giles Ho
6 Bowley Ho
7 Casby Ho
8 Sun Pas
9 Ness St
10 Voyager Bsns Est
11 Dockley Road Ind Est
12 Spa Ct
13 Discovery Bsns Pk
14 Priter Road Hostel
15 Salisbury Ct
16 William Ellis Way
17 John McKenna Wlk
18 Toussaint Wlk
19 Gillison Wlk
20 Bromfield Ct
21 Ben Smith Way
22 Major Rd
23 Old Jamaica Bsns Est
A4 1 Providence
2 Springalls Wharf
3 Flockton St
4 Meridian Ct
5 East La
6 Luna Ho
7 Axis Ct
8 Farthing Alley
9 Peter Butler Ho
10 Brownlow Ho
11 Tapley Ho
12 Copperfield Ho
13 Dombey Ho
14 Fleming Ho
15 Parkers Row
16 Wade Ho
17 Bardell Ho
18 Nickleby Ho
19 John Felton Rd
20 Flockton St
21 Pickwick Ho
22 Oliver Ho
23 Weller Ho
24 Haredale Ho
25 Havisham Ho
26 Tupman Ho
27 Micawber Ho
28 Wrayburn Ho
29 Dartle Ct
30 Waterside Cl
31 Burnaby Ct
32 Wickfield Ho
33 Fountain Ho
34 Fountain Green Sq
35 St Saviours Ho
36 Providence Sq
A5 1 Trade Winds Ct
2 Spice Ct
3 Leeward Ct
4 Bridgeport Pl
5 Tamarind Yd
6 Cape Yd
7 Nightingale Ho
8 St Anthony's Cl
9 Stockholm Way
10 Miah Terr
11 Seville Ho
12 Douthwaite Sq
13 Codling Cl
14 Hermitage Ct
15 Capital Wharf
16 Cinnabar Wharf East
17 Cinnabar Wharf Central
18 Cinnabar Wharf West
19 Halcyon Wharf
A6 1 Conant Mews
2 Hanson Ho
3 Royal Tower Lo
4 Victoria Ct
5 Swan Pas
6 Royal Mint Pl
7 Peabody Est
8 Florin Ct
9 Flank St
10 Onedin Point
11 Liberty Ho
12 Ensign Ct
13 Sapphire Ct
14 Graces Alley
15 George Leybourne Ho
16 Fletcher St
17 Hatton Ho
18 Noble Ho
19 Shearsmith Ho
20 Wellclose St
21 Telford's Yd
22 Breezer's Ct
23 Pennington Ct
B1 1 Hockney Ct
2 Toulouse Ct
3 Lowry Ct
4 Barry Ho
5 Lewis Ct
6 Gainsborough Ct
7 Renoir Ct
8 Blake Ct
9 Raphael Ct
10 Rembrandt Ct
11 Constable Ct
12 Da Vinci Ct
13 Gaugin Ct
14 Michelangelo Ct
15 Monet Ct
16 Weald Cl
17 Jasmin Lo
18 Birchmere Lo
19 Weybridge Ct
20 Florence Ho
21 Gleneagles Cl
22 Sunningdale Cl
23 Muirfield Cl
24 Turnberry Cl
25 St Andrews Cl
26 Kingsdown Cl
27 St Davids Cl
28 Galway Cl
29 Edenbridge Cl
30 Birkdale Cl
31 Tralee Ct
32 Woburn Ct
33 Belfry Cl
34 Troon Cl
35 Holywell Cl
B2 1 Market Pl
2 Trappes Ho
3 Thurland Ho
4 Ramsfort Ho
5 Hambley Ho
6 Holford Ho
7 Pope Ho
8 Southwell Ho
9 Mortain Ho
10 Radcliffe Ho
11 Southwark Park Est
12 Galleywall Road Trad Est
13 Trevithick Ho
14 Barlow Ho
15 Donkin Ho
16 Landmann Ho
17 Fitzmaurice Ho
18 Dodd Ho
B3 1 Perryn Rd
2 Chalfont Ho
3 Prestwood Ho
4 Farmer Ho
5 Gataker Ho
6 Gataker St
7 Cornick Ho
8 Glebe Ho
9 Matson Ho
10 Hickling Ho
11 St Andrews Ho
B4 1 Butterfield Cl
2 Janeway Pl
3 Trotwood Ho
4 Maylie Ho
5 Cranbourn Pas
6 Cranbourn Ho
7 Cherry Garden Ho
8 Burton Ho
9 Morriss Ho
10 Dixon's Alley
11 King Edward The Third Mews
12 Cathay St
13 Mission The
14 Millstream Ho
B5 1 China Ct
2 Wellington Terr
3 Stevedore St
4 Portland Sq
5 Reardon Ho
6 Lowder Ho
7 Meeting House Alley
8 Farthing Fields
9 Oswell Ho
10 Park Lo
11 Doughty Ct
12 Inglefield Sq
13 Chopin's Ct
14 Welsh Ho
15 Hilliard Ho
16 Clegg St
17 Tasman Ho
18 Ross Ho
19 Wapping Dock St
20 Bridewell Pl
21 New Tower Bldgs
22 Tower Bldgs
23 Chimney Ct
24 Jackman Ho
25 Fenner Ho
26 Franklin Ho
27 Frobisher Ho
28 Flinders Ho
29 Chancellor Ho
30 Beechey Ho
31 Reardon Path
32 Parry Ho
33 Vancover Ho
34 Willoughby Ho
35 Sanctuary The
36 Dundee Ct
37 Pierhead Wharf
38 Scandrett St
39 St Johns Ct
B6 1 Newton Ho
2 Richard Neale Ho
3 Maddocks Ho
4 Cornwall St
5 Brockmer Ho
6 Dellow Ho
7 Bewley Ho
8 Artichoke Hill
9 Queen Anne Terr
10 King Henry Terr
11 King Charles Terr
12 Queen Victoria Terr
13 Sovereign Ct
14 Princes Court Bsns Ctr
15 Kingsley Mews
C2 1 Damory Ho
2 Antony Ho
3 Roderick Ho
4 Pedworth Gdns
5 Banner Ct
6 Rotherhithe Bsns Est
7 Beamish Ho
8 Corbetts Pas
9 Gillam Ho
10 Richard Ho
11 George Walter Ho
12 Westlake
13 Adron Ho
14 McIntosh Ho
C3 1 Blick Ho
2 Neptune Ho
3 Scotia Ct
4 Murdoch Ho
5 Edmonton Ct
6 Niagara Ct
7 Columbia Point
8 Ritchie Ho
9 Wells Ho
10 Helen Peele Cotts
11 Orchard Ho
12 Dock Offices
13 Landale Ho
14 Courthope Ho
15 Hithe Gr
16 China Hall Mews
C4 1 Mayflower St
2 St Mary's Est
3 Rupack St
4 Frank Whymark Ho
5 Adams Gardens Est
6 Hatteraick St
7 East India Ct
8 Bombay Ct
9 Stable Ho
10 Grannary The
11 Riverside
12 Cumberland Wharf
13 Seaford Ho
14 Hythe Ho
15 Sandwich Ho
16 Winchelsea Ho
17 Rye Ho
18 Kenning St
19 Western Pl
20 Ainsty St
21 Pine Ho
22 Beech Ho
23 Larch Ho
24 Turner Ct
25 Seth St
26 Risdon Ho
27 Risdon St
28 Aylton Est
29 Manitoba Ct
30 Calgary Ct
31 Irwell Est
32 St Olav's Sq
33 City Bsns Ctr
C5 1 John Rennie Wl
2 Malay Ho
3 Wainwright Ho
4 Riverside Mans
5 Shackleton Ho
6 Whitehorn Ho
7 Wavel Ct
8 Prusom's Island
C6 1 Shadwell Pl
2 Gosling Ho
3 Vogler Ho
4 Donovan Ho
5 Knowlden Ho
6 Chamberlain Ho
7 Moore Ho
8 Thornewill Ho
9 Fisher Ho
10 All Saints Ct
11 Coburg Dwelling
12 Lowood Ho
13 Solander Gdns
14 Chancery Bldgs
15 Ring Ho
16 Juniper St
17 Gordon Ho
18 West Block
19 North Block
20 South Block
21 Ikon Ho
D2 1 John Kennedy Ho
2 Brydale Ho
3 Balman Ho
4 Tissington Ct
5 Harbord Ho
6 Westfield Ho
7 Albert Starr Ho
8 John Brent Ho
9 William Evans Ho
10 Raven Ho
11 Egret Ho
12 Fulmar Ho
13 Dunlin Ho
14 Siskin Ho
15 Sheldrake Ho
16 Buchanan Ct
17 Burrage Ct
18 Biddenham Ho
19 Ayston Ho
20 Empingham Ho
21 Deanshanger Ho
22 Codicote Ho
23 Buryfield Ct
D4 1 Schooner Cl
2 Dolphin Cl
3 Clipper Cl
4 Deauville Ct
5 Colette Ct
6 Coniston Ct
7 Virginia Ct
8 Derwent Ct
9 Grantham Ct
10 Serpentine Ct
11 Career Ct
12 Lacine Ct
13 Fairway Ct
14 Harold Ct
15 Spruce Ho
16 Cedar Ho
17 Sycamore Ho
18 Woodland Cres
19 Poplar Ho
20 Adelphi Ct
21 Basque Ct
22 Aberdale Ct
23 Quilting Ct
24 Chargrove Cl
25 Radley Ct
26 Greenacre Sq
27 Maple Leaf Sq
28 Stanhope Cl
29 Hawke Pl
30 Drake Cl
31 Brass Talley Alley
32 Monkton Ho
33 James Ho
34 Wolfe Cres
D5 1 Clarence Mews
2 Raleigh Ct
3 Katherine Cl
4 Woolcombes Ct

Tudor Ct
Quayside Ct
Princes Riverside Rd
Surrey Ho
Tideway Ct
Edinburgh Ct
Falkirk Ct
Byelands Cl
Gwent Ct
Lavender Ho
Abbotshade Rd
Bellamy's Ct
Blenheim Ct
Sandringham Ct
Hampton Ct
Windsor Ct
Balmoral Ct
Westminster Ct
Beatson Wlk
Barnardo Gdns
Roslin Ho
Glamis Est
Peabody Est
East Block
Highway Trad Ctr The
Highway Bsns Pk The
Cranford Cotts
Ratcliffe Orch
Scotia Bldg
Mauretania Bldg
Compania Bldg
Sirius Bldg
Unicorn Bldg
Keepier Wharf

119

Trafalgar Cl
Hornblower Cl
Cunard Wlk
Caronia Ct
Carinthia Ct
Freswick Ho
Graveley Ho
Husbourne Ho
Crofters Ct
Pomona Ho
Hazelwood Ho
Cannon Wharf Bsns Ctr
Bence Ho
Clement Ho
Pendennis Ho
Lighter Cl
Mast Ct
Rushcutters Ct
Boat Lifter Way
Edward Sq
Prince Regent Ct
Codrington Ct
Pennington Ct
Cherry Ct
Ash Ct
Beech Ct
Hazel Ct
Laurel Ct
St Georges Sq
Drake Ho
Osprey Ho
Fleet Ho
Gainsborough Ho
Victory Pl
Challenger Ho
Conrad Ho
Lock View Ct
Shoulder of Mutton Alley
Frederick Sq
Helena Sq
Elizabeth Sq
Sophia Sq
William Sq
Lamb Ct
Lockside
Adriatic Bldg
Ionian Bldg
Regents Gate Ho
Gransden Ho
Daubeney Twr
North Ho
Rochfort Ho
Keppel Ho
Camden Ho
Sanderson Ho
Berkeley Ho
Strafford Ho
Richman Ho
Hurleston Ho
Grafton Ho
Fulcher Ho
Citrus Ho
Windsock Cl
St George's Mews
Linberry Wlk
Lanyard Ho
Golden Hind Pl
James Lind Ho
Harmon Ho

8 Pelican Ho
9 Bembridge Ho
10 Terrace The
11 George Beard Rd
12 Colonnade The
13 Pepys Ent Ctr
B6 1 Hamilton Ho
2 Imperial Ho
3 Oriana Ho
4 Queens Ct
5 Brightlingsea Pl
6 Faraday Ho
7 Ropemaker's Fields
8 Oast Ct
9 Mitre The
10 Bate St
11 Joseph Irwin Ho
12 Padstow Ho
13 Bethlehem Ho
14 Saunders Cl
15 Roche Ho
16 Stocks Pl
17 Trinidad Ho
18 Grenada Ho
19 Kings Ho
20 Dunbar Wharf
21 Limekiln Wharf
22 Belgrave Ct
23 Eaton Ho
C1 1 Hudson Ct
2 Shackleton Ct
3 De Gama Pl
4 Mercator Pl
5 Maritime Quay
6 Perry Ct
7 Amundsen Ct
C2 1 Nova Bldg
2 Apollo Bldg
3 Gaverick Mews
4 Windmill Ho
5 Orion Point
6 Galaxy Bldg
7 Venus Ho
8 Olympian Ct
9 Poseidon Ct
10 Mercury Ct
11 Aphrodite Ct
12 Cyclops Mews
13 Neptune Ct
14 Artemis Ct
15 Hera Ct
16 Ares Ct
17 Ringwood Gdns
18 Dartmoor Wlk
19 Rothsay Wlk
20 Ashdown Wlk
21 Radnor Wlk
22 Ironmonger's Pl
23 Britannia Rd
24 Deptford Ferry Rd
25 Magellan Pl
26 Dockers Tanner Rd
C3 1 Bowsprit Point
2 St Hubert's Ho
3 John Tucker Ho
4 Broadway Wlk
5 Nash Ho
6 Fairlead Ho
7 Crosstrees Ho
8 Stanliff Ho
9 Keelson Ho
10 Clara Grant Ho
11 Gilbertson Ho
12 Scoulding Ho
13 Hibbert Ho
14 Cressall Ho
15 Alexander Ho
16 Kedge Ho
C4 1 Anchorage Point
2 Waterman Bldg
3 Jefferson Bldg
4 Pierpoint Bldg
5 Franklin Bldg
6 Vanguard Bldg
7 Edison Bldg
8 Seacon Twr
9 Naxos Bldg
10 Express Wharf
11 Hutching's Wharf
12 Tobago St
13 Bellamy Cl
14 Dowlen Ct
15 Cochrane Ho
16 Beatty Ho
17 Scott Ho
18 Laybourne Ho
19 Ensign Ho
20 Beaufort Ho
21 Spinnaker Ho
22 Bosun Cl
23 Topmast Point
24 Turner Ho
25 Constable Ho
26 Knighthead Point
C6 1 West India Ho
2 Berber Pl
3 Birchfield Ho

4 Elderfield Ho
5 Thornfield Ho
6 Gorsefield Ho
7 Arborfield Ho
8 Colborne Ho
9 East India Bldgs
10 Compass Point
11 Salter St
12 Garland Ct
13 Bogart Ct
14 Fonda Ct
15 Welles Ct
16 Rogers Ct
17 Premier Pl
18 Kelly Ct
19 Flynn Ct
20 Mary Jones Ho
21 Cannon Dr
22 Horizon Bldg
D1 1 Slipway Ho
2 Taffrail Ho
3 Platehouse The
4 Wheelhouse The
5 Chart House The
6 Port House The
7 Beacon Ho
8 Blasker Wlk
9 Maconochies Rd
D2 1 Brassey Ho
2 Triton Ho
3 Warspite Ho
4 Rodney Ho
5 Conway Ho
6 Exmouth Ho
7 Akbar Ho
8 Arethusa Ho
9 Tasman Ct
10 Cutty Sark Ho
D3 1 Turnberry Quay
2 Balmoral Ho
3 Aegon Ho
4 Marina Point
D6 1 Westcott Ho
2 Corry Ho
3 Malam Gdns
4 Blomfield Ho
5 Devitt Ho
6 Leyland Ho
7 Wigram Ho
8 Willis Ho
9 Balsam Ho
10 Finch's Ct
11 Poplar Bath St
12 Lawless St
13 Storey Ho
14 Abbot Ho
15 Woodall Cl
16 Landon Wlk
17 Goodhope Ho
18 Goodfaith Ho
19 Winant Ho
20 Goodspeed Ho
21 Lubbock Ho
22 Goodwill Ho
23 Martindale Ho
24 Holmsdale Ho
25 Norwood Ho
26 Constant Ho

120

A2 1 St John's Ho
2 Betty May Gray Ho
3 Castleton Ho
4 Urmston Ho
5 Salford Ho
6 Capstan Ho
7 Frigate Ho
8 Galleon Ho
9 Barons Lo
A3 1 Cardale St
2 Hickin St
3 John McDonald Ho
4 Thorne Ho
5 Skeggs Ho
6 St Bernard Ho
7 Kimberley Ho
8 Kingdon Ho
9 Killoran Ho
10 Alastor Ho
11 Lingard Ho
12 Yarrow Ho
13 Sandpiper Ct
14 Nightingale Ct
15 Robin Ct
16 Heron Ct
17 Ferndown Lo
18 Crosby Ho
A4 1 Llandovery Ho
2 Rugless Ho
3 Ash Ho
4 Elm Ho
5 Cedar Ho
6 Castalia Sq
7 Aspect Ho
8 Normandy Ho
9 Valiant Ho
10 Tamar Ho

11 Watkins Ho
12 Alice Shepherd Ho
13 Oak Ho
14 Ballin Ct
15 Martin Ct
16 Grebe Ct
17 Kingfisher Ct
18 Walkers Lo
19 Antilles Bay
A5 1 Lumina Bldg
2 Nova Ct W
3 Nova Ct E
4 Aurora Bldg
5 Arran Ho
6 Kintyre Ho
7 Vantage Mews
8 Managers St
9 Horatio Pl
10 Concordia Wharf
A6 1 Discovery Ho
2 Mountague Pl
3 Virginia Ho
4 Collins Ho
5 Lawless Ho
6 Carmichael Ho
7 Commodore Ho
8 Mermaid Ho
9 Bullivant St
10 Anderson Ho
11 Mackrow Wlk
12 Robin Hood Gdns
13 Prestage Way
B2 1 Verwood Lo
2 Fawley Lo
3 Lyndhurst Lo
4 Blyth Cl
5 Farnworth Ho
6 Francis Cl
B6 1 Quixley St
2 Romney Ho
3 Pumping Ho
4 Switch Ho
5 Wingfield Ct
6 Explorers Ct
7 Sexton Ct
8 Keel Ct
9 Bridge Ct
10 Sail Ct
11 Settlers Ct
12 Pilgrims Mews
13 Studley Ct
14 Wotton Ct
15 Cape Henry Ct
16 Bartholomew Ct
17 Adventurers Ct
18 Susan Constant Ct
19 Atlantic Ct
C1 1 Bellot Gdns
2 Thornley Pl
3 King William La
4 Bolton Ho
5 Miles Ho
6 Mell St
7 Sam Manners Ho
8 Hatcliffe Almshouses
9 Woodland Wlk
10 Earlswood Cl
D1 1 Baldrey Ho
2 Christie Ho
3 Dyson Ho
4 Cliffe Ho
5 Moore Ho
6 Collins Ho
7 Lockyer Ho
8 Halley Ho
9 Kepler Ho
10 Sailacre Ho
11 Union Pk
D3 1 Teal St
2 Maurer Ct
3 Mudlarks Blvd
4 Renaissance Wlk
5 Alamaro Lo

121

A1 1 Layfield Ho
2 Westerdale Rd
3 Mayston Mews
4 Station Mews Terr
A5 1 Capulet Mews
2 Pepys Cres
3 De Quincey Mews
4 Hardy Ave
5 Tom Jenkinson Rd
6 Kennacraig Cl
7 Charles Flemwell Mews
8 Gatcombe Rd
9 Badminton Mews
10 Holyrood Mews
11 Britannia Gate
12 Dalemain Mews
13 Bowes-Lyon Hall
14 Lancaster hall
15 Victoria Hall
A6 1 Clements Ave
2 Martindale Ave

3 Balearic Apts
4 Marmara Apts
5 Baltic Apts
6 Coral Apts
7 Aegean Apts
8 Capital East Apts
B1 1 Phipps Ho
2 Hartwell Ho
3 Nicholas Stacey Ho
4 Frank Burton Cl
B5 1 Beaulieu Ave
2 Charles Whincup Rd
3 Audley Dr
4 Julia Garfield Mews
5 Rayleigh Rd
6 Pirie St
7 Royal Victoria Pl
8 Pankhurst Ave
9 West Mersea Cl
10 Ramsgate Cl
11 Windsor Hall
12 Munning Ho
13 Drake Hall
14 Jane Austen Hall
15 Eastern Quay
C1 1 Ransom Rd
2 Linton Cl
3 Cedar Pl
4 Gooding Ho
5 Valiant Ho
6 Chaffey Ho
7 Benn Ho
8 Wellesley Cl
9 Gollogly Terr

122

A2 1 Harden Ct
2 Albion Ct
3 Viking Ho
4 Zealand Ho
5 Glenalvon Way
6 Parish Wharf
7 Elsinore Ho
8 Lolland Ho
9 Denmark Ho
10 Jutland Ho
11 Tivoli Gdns
12 Rance Ho
13 Peel Yates Ho
14 Rosebank Wlk
15 Paradise Pl
16 Woodville St
B2 1 Bowling Green Row
2 Sarah Turnbull Ho
3 Brewhouse Rd
4 Red Barracks Rd
5 Marine Dr
6 Hastings Ho
7 Centurion Ct
8 Cambridge Ho
9 Churchill Ct
10 Elizabeth Ct
11 Cambridge Barracks Rd
12 Len Clifton Ho
13 Granby Ho
14 Harding Ho
15 Rutland Ho
16 Townshend Ho
17 Rendlebury Ho
18 Milne Ho
19 Mulgrave Ho
20 Murray Ho
21 Chatham Ho
22 Biddulph Ho
23 Carew Ho
24 Eleanor Wlk
C2 1 Preston Ho
2 Lindsay Ho
3 Fraser Ho
4 Pickering Ho
5 Watergate Ho
6 Grinling Ho
7 Glebe Ho
8 Elliston Ho
9 Sir Martin Bowes Ho
10 Jim Bradley Cl
11 Bathway
12 Limavady Ho
13 Slater Cl
14 Vista Bldg The
C5 1 Westland Ho
2 Queensland Ho
3 Pier Par
4 Woodman Par
5 Shaw Ho
6 Glen Ho
7 Brocklebank Ho
D1 1 Branham Ho
2 Ford Ho
3 Wilford Ho
4 Parker Ho
5 Stirling Ho
6 Twiss Ho
7 Hewett Ho
8 De Haviland Dr
9 Schoolhouse Yd

D2 1 Beresford Sq
2 Central Ct
3 Walpole Pl
4 Anglesea Ave
5 Troy Ct
6 Ormsby Point
7 Haven Lo
8 Green Lawns
9 Eardley Point
10 Sandham Point
11 Bingham Point
12 Anglesea Mews
13 Masons Hill
14 Maritime Ho

123

A1 1 Glenmount Path
2 Claymill Ho
3 St James Hts
4 St Margaret's Path
5 George Akass Ho
A3 1 Wayatt Point
2 Albert Ho
3 Building 50
4 Building 49
5 Building 48
6 Building 47
7 Building 36
8 Blenheim Ho
9 Wilson Ct
B1 1 Bert Reilly Ho
B3 1 Apollo Way
2 Senator Wlk
3 Mallard Path
4 Fortune Wlk
C1 1 Fox Hollow Cl
2 Goldsmid St
C2 1 Gavin Ho
2 Richard Neve Ho
3 Bateson St
4 Lewin Ct

124

B5 1 Rowntree Path
2 MacAulay Way
3 Manning Ct
4 Chadwick Ct
5 Simon Ct
B6 1 Beveridge Ct
2 Hammond Way
3 Leonard Robbins Path
4 Lansbury Ct
5 Raymond Postgate Ct
6 Webb Ct
7 Curtis Way
8 Lytton Strachey Path
9 Keynes Ct
10 Marshall Path
11 Cross Ct
12 Octavia Way
13 Passfield Path
14 Mill Ct
15 Besant Ct
C3 1 Hermitage Cl
2 Chantry Cl
C4 1 Binsey Wlk
2 Tilehurst Point
3 Blewbury Ho
4 Coralline Wlk
5 Evenlode Ho
C5 1 Kingsley Ct
2 Wilberforce Ct
3 Shaftesbury Ct
4 Hazlitt Ct
5 Ricardo Path
6 Nassau Path
7 Malthus Path
8 Bright Ct
9 Cobden Ct
D4 1 Oakenholt Ho
2 Trewsbury Ho
3 Penton Ho
4 Osney Ho
5 St Helens Rd
6 Clewer Ho
7 Maplin Ho
8 Wyfold Ho
9 Hibernia Point
10 Duxford Ho
11 Radley Ho
12 Limestone Wlk
13 Masham Ho
14 Jacob Ho

125

A3 1 Harlequin Ho
2 Dexter Ho
3 Argali Ho
4 Mangold Way
5 Lucerne Ct
6 Holstein Way
7 Abbotswood Cl
8 Plympton Cl

125 A3

9 Benedict Cl
B1 1 Shakespeare Ho
2 Tennyson Ho
3 Dickens Ho
4 Scott Ho
5 Lansbury Ho
6 Shaw Ho
7 Chestnuts The
C1 1 Stevanne Ct
2 Tolcairn Ct
3 Chalfont Ct
4 Alonso Ho
5 Ariel Ct
6 Miranda Ho
7 Prospero Ho
8 Laurels The
9 Camden Ct
10 Newnham Lo
11 Court Lo
12 Flaxman Ct
13 Hertford Wlk
14 Riverview Ct
15 Winchester Ct
C2 1 Brushwood Lo
2 Bletchington Ct
3 Upper Sheridan Rd
4 William Ct
5 Samson Ct
6 Cowper Rd
7 Venmead Ct
C3 1 Cressingham Ct
2 Telford Ho
3 Kelvin Ho
4 Faraday Ho
5 Jenner Ho
6 Keir Hardie Ho
7 Lennox Ho
8 Mary Macarthur Ho
9 Elizabeth Garrett Anderson Ho
10 William Smith Ho
11 Baden Powell Ho
12 Baird Ho
13 Boyle Ho

129

D1 1 Heathwood Ct
2 Aldermead
3 Northumberland Ct

130

C4 1 Osterley Lo
2 St Andrew's Cl
3 Parkfield
4 Fairways
5 Granwood Ct
6 Grovewood Ct

131

A2 1 Brewery Mews Bsns Ctr
2 Forge Lo
3 Pulteney Cl
4 Tolson Ho
5 Percy Gdns
6 Wynne Ct
7 Wisdom Ct
8 Swann Ct
9 Shrewsbury Wlk
10 King's Terr
11 Van Gogh Cl
12 Holme Ct
C5 1 Canute Ho
2 Spruce Ho
3 Moorings Ho
4 Jessops Wharf
5 Corsell Ho
6 Barnes Qtr
7 Dorey Ho
8 Tanyard Ho
9 Booth Ho
10 Oakbark Ho
11 Bordeston Ct
12 Shire Pl
D5 1 Galba Ct
2 Servius Ct
3 Maurice Ct
4 Leo Ct
5 Otho Ct
6 Nero Ct
7 Romulus Ct
8 Pump Alley
D6 1 Brockshot Cl
2 Westbury Pl
3 Brook La N
4 Braemar Ct
5 Brook Ct
6 Clifden Ho
7 Cedar Ct
8 Cranbrook Ct
9 Somerset Lo
10 Alexandra Rd
11 Berkeley Ho
12 Watermans Ct
13 Ferry Quays Ctyd

132

A1 1 St John's Gr
2 Michel's Row
3 Michelsdale Dr
4 Blue Anchor Alley
5 Clarence St
6 Sun Alley
7 Thames Link Ho
8 Benns Wlk
9 Waterloo Pl
10 Northumbria Ct
A6 1 Ferry Sq
2 Watermans Ct
3 Wilkes Rd
4 Albany Par
5 Charlton Ho
6 Albany Ho
7 Alma Ho
8 Griffin Ct
9 Cressage Ho
10 Tunstall Wlk
11 Trimmer Wlk
12 Running Horse Yd
13 Mission Sq
14 Distillery Wlk
B1 1 Towers The
2 Longs Ct
3 Sovereign Ct
4 Robinson Ct
5 Calvert Ct
6 Bedford Ct
7 Hickey's Almshouses
8 Church Estate Almshouses
9 Richmond International Bsns Ctr
10 Abercorn Mews
B4 1 Primrose Ho
2 Lawman Ct
3 Royston Ct
4 Garden Ct
5 Capel Lo
6 Devonshire Ct
7 Celia Ct
8 Rosslyn Ho
9 Branstone Ct
10 Lamerton Lo
11 Kew Lo
12 Dunraven Ho
13 Stoneleigh Lo
14 Tunstall Ct
15 Voltaire
C4 1 Clarendon Ct
2 Quintock Ho
3 Broome Ct
4 Lonsdale Mews
5 Elizabeth Cotts
6 Sandways
7 Victoria Cotts
8 North Ave
9 Grovewood
10 Hamilton Ho
11 Melvin Ct
12 Royal Par
13 Power Ho
14 Station Ave
15 Blake Mews
D1 1 Hershell Ct
2 Deanhill Ct
3 Park Sheen
4 Furness Lo
5 Merricks Ct
D4 1 Terrano Ho
2 Oak Ho
3 Aura Ho
4 Maple Ho
5 Cedar Ho
6 Saffron Ho
7 Lime Ho
8 Lavender Ho
9 Juniper Ho

133

B2 1 Rann Ho
2 Craven Ho
3 John Dee Ho
4 Kindell Ho
5 Montgomery Ho
6 Avondale Ho
7 Addington Ct
8 Dovecote Gdns
9 Firmston Ho
10 Glendower Gdns
11 Chestnut Ave
12 Trehern Rd
13 Rock Ave
D3 1 Melrose Rd
2 Seaforth Lo
3 St John's Gr
4 Sussex Ct
5 Carmichael Ct
6 Hampshire Ct
7 Thorne Pas
8 Brunel Ct
9 Beverley Path

134

D1 1 Olivette St
2 Mascotte Rd
3 Glegg Pl
4 Crown Ct
5 Charlwood Terr
6 Percy Laurie Ho
D6 1 Cobb's Hall
2 Dorset Mans
3 St Clements Mans
4 Bothwell St
5 Hawksmoor St

135

B3 1 Plato Pl
2 Mustow Pl
3 Laurel Bank Gdns
4 Ranelagh Mans
5 Churchfield Mans
6 Bear Croft Ho
7 Elysium Gate
8 Ethel Rankin Ct
9 Arthur Henderson Ho
10 William Banfield Ho
11 Melbray Mews
D3 1 Brightwells
2 Broughton Road App
3 Bulow Ct
4 Langford Rd
5 Elizabeth Barnes Ct
6 Snowbury Rd

136

A2 1 Molasses Ho
2 Molasses Row
3 Cinnamon Row
4 Calico Ho
5 Calico Row
6 Port Ho
7 Square Rigger Row
8 Trade Twr
9 Ivory Ho
10 Spice Ct
11 Sherwood Ct
12 Mendip Ct
13 Chalmers Ho
14 Coral Row
15 Ivory Sq
16 Kingfisher Ho
B1 1 Burke Ho
2 Fox Ho
3 Buxton Ho
4 Pitt Ho
5 Ramsey Ho
6 Beverley Cl
7 Florence Ho
8 Linden Ct
9 Dorcas Ct
10 Johnson Ct
11 Agnes Ct
12 Hilltop Ct
13 Courtyard The
14 Old Laundry The
15 Oberstein Rd
16 Fineran Ct
17 Sangora Rd
18 Harvard Mans
19 Plough Mews
B2 1 Benham Cl
2 Milner Ho
3 McManus Ho
4 Wilberforce Ho
5 Wheeler Ct
6 Sporle Ct
7 Holliday Sq
8 John Parker Sq
9 Carmichael Cl
10 Fenner Sq
11 Clark Lawrence Ct
12 Shaw Ct
13 Sendall Ct
14 Livingstone Rd
15 Farrant Ho
16 Jackson Ho
17 Darien Ho
18 Shepard Ho
19 Ganley Ct
20 Arthur Newton Ho
21 Chesterton Ho
22 John Kirk Ho
23 Mantua St
24 Heaver Rd
25 Candlemakers
B3 1 Archer Ho
2 White Ho
3 Winfield Ho
4 Powrie Ho
5 Morgan Ct
6 Fairchild Cl
7 Musjid Rd
C2 1 Kiloh Ct
2 Lanner Ho
3 Griffon Ho
4 Kestrel Ho
5 Kite Ho
6 Peregrine Ho
7 Hawk Ho
8 Inkster Ho
9 Harrier Ho
10 Eagle Hts
11 Kingfisher Ct
12 Lavender Terr
13 Temple Ho
14 Ridley Ho
15 Eden Ho
16 Hertford Ct
17 Nepaul Rd
C3 1 Meecham Ct
2 McKiernan Ct
3 Banbury St
4 Colestown St
5 Crombie Mews
6 Frere St
D3 1 Stevenson Ho
2 Ambrose Mews
3 Harling Ct
4 Southside Quarter
5 Latchmere St
6 Dovedale Cotts
7 Roydon Cl
8 Castlemaine
9 Wittering Ho
10 Berry Ho
11 Weybridge Point

137

A2 1 Shaftesbury Park Chambers
2 Selborne
3 Rush Hill Mews
4 Marmion Mews
5 Crosland Pl
6 Craven Mews
7 Garfield Mews
8 Audley Cl
9 Basnett Rd
10 Tyneham Cl
11 Woodmere Cl
A3 1 Hopkinson Ho
2 MacDonald Ho
3 Rushlake Ho
4 Bishopstone Ho
5 Dresden Ho
6 Millgrove St
7 Farnhurst Ho
8 Walden Ho
9 Kennard St
10 Langhurst Ho
11 Atkinson Ho
12 Kennard Ho
13 Voltaire Ct
14 Barloch Ho
15 London Stone Bsns Est
B2 1 Turnchapel Mews
2 Redwood Mews
3 Phil Brown Pl
4 Bev Callender Cl
5 Keith Connor Cl
6 Tessa Sanderson Pl
7 Daley Thompson Way
8 Rashleigh Ct
9 Abberley Mews
10 Willow Lodge
11 Beaufoy Rd
B3 1 St Philip Sq
2 Montefiore St
3 Gambetta St
4 Scott Ct
5 Radcliffe Path
6 Moresby Wlk
7 Victorian Hts
C1 1 Polygon The
2 Windsor Ct
3 Trinity Cl
4 Studios The
5 Bourne Ho
C2 1 Clapham Manor Ct
2 Clarke Ho
3 Gables The
4 Sycamore Mews
5 Maritime Ho
6 Rectory Gdns
7 Floris Pl
C3 1 Seymour Ho
2 Lucas Ho
3 Durrington Twr
4 Amesbury Twr
5 Fovant Ct
6 Allington Ct
7 Welford Ct
8 Ilsley Ct
9 Blake Ct
10 Brooklands Ct
D1 1 Kendoa Rd
2 Felmersham Cl
3 Abbeville Mews
4 Saxon Ho
5 Gifford Ho
6 Teignmouth Cl
7 Holwood Pl
8 Oaklands Pl
9 Wilberforce Mews
10 William Bonney Est
D2 1 Chelsham Ho
2 Lynde Ho
3 Greener Ho
4 Towns Ho
5 Hugh Morgan Ho
6 Roy Ridley Ho
7 Lendal Terr
8 Slievemore Cl
9 Cadmus Cl
10 Clapham North Bsns Ctr
D3 1 Haltone Ho
2 Surcot Ho
3 Kingsley Ho
4 Wood Ho
5 Dalemain Ho
6 Fallodon Ho
7 Dartington Ho
8 Esher Ho
9 Kneller Ho
10 Lostock Ho
11 Croxteth Ho
12 Donnington Ho
13 Farnley Ho
14 Hardwick Ho
15 Bradfield Ho
16 Brocket Ho
17 Colchester Ho
18 Clive Ho
19 Chessington Ho
20 Rushbrook Ho
21 Stanmore Ho
22 Newton Ho
23 Netherby Ho
24 Oakwell Ho
25 Rydal Ho
26 Rushton Ho
27 Harcourt Ho
28 Metcalfe Ho
29 Lydwell Ho
30 Raleigh Ho
31 Spencer Ho
32 Shipley Ho
33 Naylor Ho
34 Mordaunt Ho
35 Stanley Ho
36 Alderley Ho
37 Effingham Ho
38 Grant Ho
39 Wilson Ho
40 Fraser Ho

138

A1 1 Morris Ho
2 Gye Ho
3 Clowes Ho
4 Thomas Ho
5 Stuart Ho
6 Storace Ho
7 Bedford Ho
8 Ascot Ct
9 Ascot Par
10 Ashmere Ho
11 Ashmere Gr
12 Ventura Ho
13 Vickery Ho
14 Stafford Mans
15 Beresford Ho
A2 1 Callingham Ho
2 Russell Pickering Ho
3 Ormerod Ho
4 Lopez Ho
5 Coachmaker Mews
A3 1 Barling Ct
2 Jeffrey's Ct
3 Brooks Ct
4 Dalmeny Ct
5 Fender Ct
6 Fishlock Ct
7 Bedser Ct
8 Gover Ct
9 Clarence Wlk
10 Barton Ct
11 Allom Ct
12 Garden Ho
13 Otha Ho
14 Hayward Ct
15 Surridge Ct
16 Knox Ct
17 Jephson Ct
18 Holmes Ct
19 McIntyre Ct
20 Richardson Ct
21 Cassell Ho
22 Pakington Ho
23 Bain Ho
24 Enfield Ho
25 Fawcett Ho
26 Sidgwick Ho
27 Jowett Ho
28 Beckett Ho
29 Arden Ho
30 Pinter Ho
31 Barrington Ct
32 Union Mews
B1 1 Freemens Hos
2 Roger's Almshou
3 Gresham Almsho
4 Exbury Ho
5 Glasbury Ho
6 Dalbury Ho
7 Fosbury Ho
8 Chalbury Ho
9 Neilson-Terry Ct
10 Pavilion Mans
11 Daisy Dormer Ct
12 George Lashwoo
13 Marie Lloyd Ct
14 Trinity Homes
15 Lethaby Ho
16 Edmundsbury Ct
17 Regis Pl
18 Marlborough Me
19 Alpha Ho
20 Beta Pl
21 Cedars Ho
B2 1 Turberville Ho
2 Thrayle Ho
3 Percheron Ct
4 Draymans Ct
B3 1 Maurice Ho
2 Thring Ho
3 Paton Ho
4 Huxley Ho
5 Morell Ho
6 Mary Ho
7 Beale Ho
8 Rosa Parks Ho
9 Birrell Ho
10 Waltham Ho
11 Burford Ho
12 Thornicroft Ho
13 Addington Ho
14 Goffton Ho
15 Redmayne Ho
16 Norton Ho
17 Aytoun Ct
18 Colwall Ho
19 Burrow Ho
20 Wynter Ho
21 Crowhurst Ho
22 Lidcote Gdns
23 Cumnor Cl
24 Park View Mews
C1 1 Electric Mans
2 Electric La
3 Connaught Mans
4 Clifton Mans
5 Hereford Ho
6 Chaplin Ho
7 Brixton Oval
8 Lord David Pitt H
9 Marcus Garvey V
10 Montego Cl
11 Bob Marley Way
12 Leeson Rd
C2 1 Buckmaster Cl
2 Albemarle Ho
3 Goodwood Mans
4 Angell Park Gdn
5 Fyfield Rd
6 Howard Ho
7 Harris Ho
8 Broadoak Ct
9 Burgate Ct
10 Witchwood Ho
11 Blacktree Mews
12 Chartham Ct
13 Chilham Ct
14 Northgate Ct
15 Westgate Ct
16 Dover Mans
C3 1 Norval Gn
2 Hilda Terr
3 Burton La
4 Church Gn
5 Lord Holland La
6 Sorrell Cl
7 Burton Rd
8 Holles Ho
9 Leys Ct
10 Warwick Ho
11 Fairfax Ho
12 Wayland Ho
13 Dudley Ho
14 Denchworth Ho
15 Fitzgerald Ho
16 Lambert Ho
17 Chute Ho
18 Bedwell Ho
19 Ferrey Mews
20 Serenaders Rd
21 Boatemah Wlk
22 Ireton Ho
23 Marston Ho
24 Morrison Rd
25 Fir Grove Rd
26 Shore Way
C4 1 Hector Ct
2 Jason Ct
3 Creon Ct
4 Hermes Ct
5 Argos Ct

admus Ct
ppollo Ct
lercury Ct
ounty Ho
easalter Ho
ownbarton Ho
arlinge Ho
loira Ho
vanley Ho
/oodchurch Ho
urlock Ho
allam Ho
/hiteness Ho
romstone Ho
enelope Ho
lelbourne Sq
loisters The
liffsend Ho
acketts Ho
anway Ho
rickworth Ho
edlynch Ho
todmarsh Ho
ingsgate Ho
hardin Ho
nnesley Ho
nowlton Ho
ussell Gr
amann Casey Ho
wift Ho
istowel Cl
eal Wlk
lover Ho
igburth Mans
lencoe Mans
lenshaw Mans
leveland Mans
eda Ct
upiter Ct
uno Ct
ealy Ho
shton Ho
amsey Ho
nnesley Ho
owley Rd
herwin Ho
egasus Pl
ilner Ho
ead Ho
ohmann Ho
lornby Ho
bel Ho
lythe Ho
ey Ho
ockwood Ho
lverstone Ho
lades Ho
othesay Ct
lahatma Gandhi Ind
st
ylan Rd
essemer Park Ind
st
ablo Neruda Cl
angston Hughes Cl
Valt Whitman Cl
ames Joyce Wlk
lice Walker Cl
ouise Bennett Cl
hadacre Ho
urwood Ho
yrford Ho
Vangford Ho
shford Ho
enwood Ho
loyne Ho
lveden Ho
arrara Cl
roughton Dr
ngela Davis Ind Est
ilia Wlk
ounty Ho
lallams Mews
mberley Ct
larper Ho
eicester Ho
tation Ave
Vellfit St
oughborough Ct
elinda Rd
iggs Ind Est
angport Ho
eagh Ho
lewark Ho
dgehill Ho
lopton Ho
shby Ho
levil Ho
airbairn Gn
ammelton Gn
oxley Sq
ilverburn Ho
utler Ho
alkeith Ho
urner Cl
athgate Ho
lack Roof Ho

D6 1 Faunce Ho
2 Garbett Ho
3 Harvard Ho
4 Doddington Pl
5 Kean Ho
6 Jephson Ho
7 Cornish Ho
8 Bateman Ho
9 Molesworth Ho
10 Walters Ho
11 Cruden Ho
12 Brawne Ho
13 Prescott Ho
14 Chalmer's Wlk
15 Copley Cl
16 King Charles Ct

139

A3 1 Bergen Ho
2 Oslo Ho
3 Viking Ho
4 Jutland Ho
5 Norvic Ho
6 Odin Ho
7 Baltic Ho
8 Nobel Ho
9 Mercia Ho
10 Kenbury Gdns
11 Zealand Ho
12 Elsinore Ho
13 Norse Ho
14 Denmark Mans
15 Dane Ho
16 Canterbury Cl
17 York Cl
18 Kenbury Mans
19 Parade Mans
20 Winterslow Ho
21 Lilford Ho
22 Bartholomew Ho
23 Guildford Ho
24 Boston Ho
25 Hereford Ho
26 Weyhill Ho
27 Lichfield Ho
28 Lansdown Ho
29 Honiton Ho
30 Pinner Ho
31 Baldock Ho
32 Widecombe Ho
33 Nottingham Ho
34 Witham Ho
35 Barnet Ho
36 Empress Mews
A4 1 Bertha Neubergh Ho
2 Mornington Mews
3 Badsworth Rd
4 Pearson Cl
5 Elm Tree Ct
6 Samuel Lewis Trust Dwellings
7 Milkwell Yd
8 Keswick Ho
9 Mitcham Ho
A5 1 Boundary Ho
2 Day Ho
3 Burgess Ho
4 Carlyle Ho
5 Myers Ho
6 Thompson Ave
7 Palgrave Ho
8 Winnington Ho
9 Brantwood Ho
10 Lowell Ho
11 Jessie Duffett Ho
12 Otterburn Ho
13 Crossmount Ho
14 Venice Ct
15 Bowyer St
16 Livingstone Ho
17 Gothic Ct
18 Coniston Ho
19 Harlynwood
20 Carey Ct
21 Finley Ct
22 Grainger Ct
23 Hayes Ct
24 Moffat Ho
25 Marinel Ho
26 Hodister Cl
27 Arnot Ho
28 Lamb Ho
29 Kipling Ho
30 Keats Ho
31 Kenyon Ho
32 New Church Rd
33 Sir John Kirk Cl
B1 1 Shaftesbury Ct
2 Mayhew Ct
3 Morris Ct
4 Swinburne Ct
5 Perth Ct
6 Tayside Ct
7 Matlock Ct
8 Hunter Ct
9 Turner Ct
B3 1 Selborne Rd

2 Hascombe Terr
B4 1 Joiners Arms Yd
2 Butterfly Wlk
3 Cuthill Wlk
4 Colonades The
5 Artichoke Mews
6 Peabody Bldgs
7 Brighton Ho
8 Park Ho
9 Peabody Ct
10 Lomond Ho
11 Lamb Ho
12 Kimpton Ct
13 Belham Wlk
14 Datchelor Pl
15 Harvey Rd
B5 1 Masterman Ho
2 Milton Ho
3 Pope Ho
4 Chester Ct
5 Marvel Ho
6 Flecker Ho
7 Landor Ho
8 Leslie Prince Ct
9 Evelina Mans
10 Langland Ho
11 Drinkwater Ho
12 Procter Ho
13 Shirley Ho
14 Drayton Ho
15 Bridges Ho
16 Cunningham Ho
17 Hood Ho
18 Herrick Ho
19 Dekker Ho
20 Houseman Way
21 Coleby Path
B6 1 Queens Ho
2 Arnside Ho
3 Horsley St
4 St Peter's Ho
5 St Johns Ho
6 St Marks Ho
7 St Stephens Ho
8 St Matthew's Ho
9 Red Lion Cl
10 Boyson Rd
11 Bradenham
C2 1 Harfield Gdns
2 Karen Ct
3 Seavington Ho
4 Appleshaw Ho
5 Birdsall Ho
6 Whitney Ho
7 Wheatland Ho
8 Wilton Ho
9 Walcot Ho
10 Whaddon Ho
11 Melbreak Ho
12 Ledbury Ho
13 Tidworth Ho
14 Riseholme Ho
15 Ringmer Ho
16 Petworth Ho
17 Stagshaw Ho
18 Ivybridge Ho
19 Inwood Ho
20 Gatcombe Ho
21 Felbridge Ho
22 Cowdray Ho
C3 1 Springfield Ho
2 Craston Ho
3 Walters Ho
4 Edgecombe Ho
5 Fowler Ho
6 Rignold Ho
7 Chatham Ho
C4 1 Barnwell Ho
2 Brunswick Villas
3 St Giles Twr
4 Bentley Ho
5 Dawson Ho
6 Dryden Ho
7 Mayward Ho
8 Longleigh Ho
9 Fairwall Ho
10 Bodeney Ho
11 Sandby Ho
12 Vestry Mews
13 Netley
14 Lakanal
15 Racine
C5 1 Tower Mill Rd
2 Tilson Cl
3 Granville Sq
4 Edgar Wallace Cl
5 Potters Cl
6 Dorton Cl
7 Samuel Jones Ind Est
8 Dibden Ho
9 Marchwood Cl
10 Pilgrims Cloisters
11 Beacon Ho
12 Teather St
13 Stacy Path
14 Rumball Ho
15 Ballow Cl

16 Rill Ho
C6 1 Downend Ct
2 Andoversford Ct
3 Pearse St
4 Watling St
5 Gandolfi St
D1 1 Dulwich Mews
2 St James's Cloisters
D4 1 Colbert
2 Voltaire
3 Finch Mews
4 Charles Coveney Rd
5 Bamber Rd
6 Crane St
7 Curlew Ho
8 Mallard Ho
9 Tern Ho
10 Crane Ho
11 Falcon Ho
12 Bryanston Ho
13 Basing Ct
14 Marcus Ho
15 Sheffield Ho
D5 1 Painswick Ct
2 Sharpness Ct
3 Mattingly Way
4 Hordle Prom N
5 Burcher Gale Gr
6 Calypso Cres
7 Hordle Prom S
8 Cinnamon Cl
9 Savannah Cl
10 Thames Ct
11 Shannon Ct
12 Amstel Ct
13 Danube Ct
14 Tilbury Cl
15 Hordle Prom E
16 Indus Ct
17 Oakcourt
18 Palm Ct
19 Rowan Ct
20 Blackthorn Ct
21 Pear Ct
22 Lidgate Rd
23 Whistler Mews
24 Boathouse Wlk
D6 1 Willsbridge Ct
2 Cam Ct
3 Quedgeley Ct
4 Saul Ct
5 Quenington Ct
6 Westonbirt Ct
7 Wickway Ct

140

A3 1 William Margrie Cl
2 William Blake Ho
3 Quantock Mews
4 Choumert Sq
5 Parkstone Rd
6 Atwell Rd
A4 1 Canal Head Public Sq
2 Angelina Ho
3 Jarvis Ho
4 Richland Ho
5 Honeywood Ho
6 Wakefield Ho
7 Primrose Ho
8 Hardcastle Ho
9 Dunstall Ho
10 Springtide Cl
11 Purdon Ho
12 Flamborough Ho
13 Lambrook Ho
14 Witcombe Point
15 Yarnfield Sq
16 Winford Ct
17 Portbury Cl
18 Robert Keen Cl
A5 1 Thornbill Ho
2 Vervain Ho
3 Woodstar Ho
4 Tamarind Ho
5 Hereford Retreat
6 Haymerle Ho
7 Furley Ho
8 Thomas Milner Ho
9 Applegarth Ho
10 Freda Corbett Cl
11 Rudbeck Ho
12 Henslow Ho
13 Lindley Ho
14 Collinson Ho
15 Sister Mabel's Way
16 Timberland Cl
17 Hastings Cl
18 Sidmouth Ho
19 Budleigh Ho
20 Stanesgate Ho
21 Breamore Ho
22 Ely Ho
23 Gisburn Ho
A6 1 Bowles Rd
2 Western Wharf
3 Northfield Ho
4 Millbrook Ho

5 Denstone Ho
6 Deerhurst Ho
7 Caversham Ho
8 Battle Ho
9 Cardiff Ho
10 Bridgnorth Ho
11 Exeter Ho
12 Grantham Ho
13 Aylesbury Ho
14 Royston Ho
B2 1 Tilling Ho
2 Goodwin Ho
3 Tyrells Ct
4 Citron Terr
5 Basswood Cl
6 Cheam St
B3 1 Walkynscroft
2 Ryegates
3 Hathorne Cl
4 Pilkington Rd
5 Russell Ct
6 Heaton Ho
7 Magdalene Cl
8 Iris Ct
B4 1 Willowdene
2 Pinedene
3 Oakdene
4 Beechdene
5 Hollydene
6 Wood Dene
7 Staveley Cl
8 Carnicot Ho
9 Martock Ct
10 Cherry Tree Ct
11 Kendrick Ct
B5 1 Tortington Ho
2 Credenhill Ho
3 Bromyard Ho
4 Hoyland Cl
5 Willowdene
6 Ashdene
7 Acorn Par
8 Havelock Ct
9 Springall St
10 Harry Lambourn Ho
11 Grenier Apartments
C3 1 Honiton Gdns
2 Selden Ho
3 Hathway Ho
4 Hathway St
5 Station Ct
C4 1 Trotman Ho
2 Boddington Ho
3 Heydon Ho
4 Boulter Ho
5 Astbury Bsns Pk
C5 1 Ambleside Point
2 Grasmere Point
3 Windermere Point
4 Roman Way
5 Laburnum Cl
6 Juniper Ho
7 Romney Cl
8 Hammersley Ho
9 Hutchinson Ho
10 Hammond Ho
11 Fir Tree Ho
12 Glastonbury Ct
13 Highbridge Ct
14 Filton Ct
15 Chiltern Ct
16 Cheviot Ct
C6 1 Penshurst Ho
2 Reculver Ho
3 Mereworth Ho
4 Camber Ho
5 Chiham Ho
6 Otford Ho
7 Olive Tree Ho
8 Aspen Ho
9 Lewis Silkin Ho
10 Richborough Ho
11 Dover Ho
12 Eynsford Ho
13 Horton Ho
14 Lamberhurst Ho
15 Canterbury Ind Pk
16 Upnall Ho
17 Sissinghurst Ho
18 Rochester Ho
19 Saltwood Ho
20 Leybourne Ho
21 Lullingstone Ho
D1 1 Laxton Path
2 Barlings Ho
3 Bayfield Ho
4 Coston Wlk
5 Coverham Ho
6 Gateley Ho
7 Dereham Ho
8 Greenwood Ho
9 Hilton Ho
10 Goodall Ho
11 Horsley Ho
12 Jordan Ho
D5 1 Richard Anderson Ct
2 Palm Tree Ho

3 Edward Robinson Ho
4 Antony Ho
5 Gerrard Ho
6 Palmer Ho
7 Pankhurst Cl
D6 1 Harrisons Ct
2 Grantley Ho
3 Sunbury Ct
4 Tilbury Ho
5 Graham Ct
6 Connell Ct
7 St Clements Ct
8 Henderson Ct
9 Jemotts Ct
10 Verona Ct
11 Heywood Ho
12 Francis Ct
13 Hind Ho
14 Donne Ho
15 Carew Ct
16 Burbage Ho
17 Newland Ho
18 Dobson Ho
19 Dalton Ho
20 Greene Ct
21 Redrup Ho
22 Tarplett Ho
23 Stunell Ho
24 Gasson Ho
25 Bryce Ho
26 Barnes Ho
27 Barkwith Ho
28 Bannister Ho
29 Apollo Ind Bsns Ctr

141

A4 1 Archer Ho
2 Browning Ho
3 Hardcastle Ho
4 Brooke Ho
5 Wallis Ho
A5 1 Batavia Ho
2 Marlowe Bsns Ctr
3 Batavia Mews
4 Woodrush Cl
5 Alexandra St
6 Primrose Wlk
7 Vansittart St
8 Granville Ct
9 Cottesbrook St
10 Ewen Henderson Ct
11 Fordham Ho
A6 1 Portland Ct
2 Phoenix Ct
3 Rainbow Ct
4 Hawke Twr
5 Chubworthy St
6 Woodpecker Rd
7 Hercules Ct
B5 1 Austin Ho
2 Exeter Way
3 Crossleigh Ct
4 Mornington Pl
5 Maple Ho
B6 1 Chester Ho
2 Lynch Wlk
3 Arlington Ho
4 Woodcote Ho
5 Cornbury Ho
6 Prospect Pl
7 Akintaro Ho
8 Mulberry Ho
9 Laurel Ho
10 Linden Ho
11 Ashford Ho
12 Wardalls Ho
13 Magnolia Ho
14 Howard Ho
15 Larch Cl
16 Ibis Ct
17 Merganser Ct
18 Wotton Rd
19 Kingfisher Sq
20 Sanderling Ct
21 Dolphin Twr
22 Mermaid Twr
23 Scoter Ct
24 Shearwater Ct
25 Brambling Ct
26 Kittiwake Ct
27 Diana Cl
28 Guillemot Ct
29 Marine Twr
30 Teal Ct
31 Lapwing Twr
32 Violet Cl
33 Skua Ct
34 Tristan Ct
35 Rosemary Ct
36 Cormorant Ct
37 Shelduck Ct
38 Eider Ct
39 Pintail Ct
C4 1 Admiralty Cl

2 Harton Lodge
3 Sylva Cotts
4 Pitman Ho
5 Heston Ho
6 Mereton Mans
7 Indiana Bldg
8 St John's Lodge
C5 1 Sandpiper Ct
2 Flamingo Ct
3 Titan Bsns Est
4 Rochdale Way
5 Speedwell St
6 Reginald Pl
7 Fletcher Path
8 Frankham Ho
9 Cremer Ho
10 Wilshaw Ho
11 Castell Ho
12 Holden Ho
13 Browne Ho
14 Resolution Way
15 Lady Florence Ctyd
16 Covell Ct
17 Albion Ho
C6 1 Dryfield Wlk
2 Blake Ho
3 Hawkins Ho
4 Grenville Ho
5 Langford Ho
6 Mandarin Ct
7 Bittern Ct
8 Lamerton St
9 Ravensbourne Mans
10 Armada St
11 Armada Ct
12 Benbow Ho
13 Oxenham Ho
14 Caravel Mews
15 Hughes Ho
16 Stretton Mans
D4 1 Washington Bldg
2 California Bldg
3 Utah Bldg
4 Montana Bldg
5 Oregon Bldg
6 Dakota bldg
7 Idaho Bldg
8 Atlanta Bldg
9 Colorado Bldg
10 Arizona Bldg
11 Nebraska Bldg
12 Alaska Bldg
13 Ohio Bldg
14 Charter Bldgs
15 Flamsteed Ct
16 Friendly Pl
17 Dover Ct
18 Robinscroft Mews
19 Doleman Ho
20 Plymouth Ho
D5 1 Finch Ho
2 Jubilee The
3 Maitland Cl
4 Ashburnham Retreat

142

A2 1 Bankside Ave
2 Elder Wlk
3 Yew Tree Cl
4 Mill Ho
A3 1 Ellison Ho
2 Pitmaston Ho
3 Aster Ho
4 Windmill Cl
5 Hertmitage The
6 Burnett Ho
7 Lacey Ho
8 Darwin Ho
9 Pearmain Ho
A4 1 Penn Almshouses
2 Jervis Ct
3 Woodville Ct
4 Darnall Ho
5 Renbold Ho
6 Lindsell St
7 Plumbridge St
8 Trinity Gr
9 Hollymount Cl
10 Cade Tyler Ho
11 Robertson Ho
A5 1 Temair Ho
2 Royal Hill Ct
3 Prince of Orange La
4 Lambard Ho
5 St Marks Cl
6 Ada Kennedy Ct
7 Arlington Pl
8 Topham Ho
9 Darnell Ho
10 Hawks Mews
11 Royal Pl
12 Swanne Ho
13 Maribor
14 Serica Ct
15 Queen Elizabeth's Coll
A6 1 Crescent Arc
2 Greenwich Mkt
3 Turnpin La
4 Durnford St
5 Sexton's Ho
6 Bardsley Hts
7 Wardell Ho
8 Clavell St
9 Stanton Ho
10 Macey Ho
11 Boreman Ho
12 Clipper Appts
B6 1 Frobisher Ct
2 Hardy Cotts
3 Palliser Ho
4 Bernard Angell Ho
5 Corvette Sq
6 Travers Ho
7 Maze Hill Lodge
8 Park Place Ho
D5 1 Westcombe Ct
2 Kleffens Ct
3 Ferndale Ct
4 Combe Mews
5 Mandeville Cl
7 Pinelands Cl

143

A5 1 Mary Lawrenson Pl
2 Bradbury Ct
3 Dunstable Ct
4 Wentworth Ho
A6 1 Nethercombe Ho
2 Holywell Cl
B6 1 Capella Ho
2 Collington Ho
C6 1 Warren Wlk
2 Wilson Ho
3 Priory Ho
4 Mar Ho
5 Langhorne Ho
6 Games Ho
7 Erskine Ho
8 Ducie Ho
9 Downe Ho
10 Bayeux Ho
11 Elliscombe Mount
12 Harold Gibbons Ct
13 Mascalls Ct
14 Leila Parnell Pl
15 East Mascalls
16 Birch Tree Ho
17 Cherry Tree Ct
18 Elm Tree Ct
19 Cedar Ct
D5 1 Winchester Ho
2 Brentwood Ho
3 Shenfield Ho
4 Chesterford Ho

144

A4 1 Master Gunner's Pl
2 Ross Ho
3 Dickson Ho
4 Horne Ho
5 Pendlebury Ho
6 Roberts Ho
7 Maple Tree Pl
C6 1 Lawson Ho
2 Mabbett Ho
3 Petrie Ho
4 Memess Path
5 Ruegg Ho
6 Nile Path
7 Leslie Smith Sq
8 Spearman St
9 Siedle Ho
10 Watling Ho
11 O'Neill Path
12 Old Clem Sq
13 Jefferson Wlk
14 Milward Wlk
15 Wordsworth Ho
16 Fenwick Cl
D6 1 Acworth Ho
2 Griffiths Ho
3 Squires Ho
4 Cowen Ho
5 Turton Ho
6 Alford Ho
7 Boxshall Ho
8 MacAllister Ho
9 Marvin Ho
10 Kelham Ho
11 Kimber Ho
12 Maxwell Ho
13 Woodford Ho
14 Penfold Ho

146

A2 1 Wellingfield Ct
2 Woodville Gr
3 Midwinter Cl
4 St Leonards Cl

147

A1 1 Woburn Ct
2 Arundel Ct
3 Longleat Ct
4 Upton Villas
5 Whitehaven Ct
6 Shirley Hts
7 Louise Ct
8 Bethany Ct
B6 1 Bevercote Wlk
3 Lullingstone Rd
4 Benjamin Ct
5 Charton Cl
6 Terence Ct
7 Renshaw Cl
8 Grove Rd
C1 1 Friswell Pl
2 Market Pl
3 Geddes Pl
4 Janet Ct
5 Broadway Sh Ctr
6 Mall The
7 Norwich Pl
8 Pincott Rd

148

A5 1 Stranraer Way
2 Deri Dene Cl
3 Lord Knyvetts Ct
4 Tudor Ct
5 Wessex Ct
6 Vanguard Ho
7 Shackleton Ct
8 Fleetwood Ct
9 Clifton Ct
10 Vickers Ct
11 Bristol Ct
12 Sunderland Ct

153

A3 1 Katharine Rd
2 Sandringham Ct
3 Garfield Rd
4 Arragon Rd
5 Flood La
6 John Wesley Ct
7 King Street Par
8 Thames Eyot
A4 1 Perryn Ct
2 Ivybridge Cl
3 Heritage Ho
4 Brook Ho
5 Neville Ho
6 Latham Cl
7 March Rd
8 Berkley Ct
9 Cole Court Lo
10 Cheltenham Ave
11 Railway App
A5 1 Greenways The
2 Cole Park View
B4 1 Melton Ct
2 Amyand Park Gdns
3 Crown Ct
4 Burrell Ho
5 Owen Ho
6 Brentford Ho
7 Leeson Ho
8 Westbourne Ho
9 Orleans Ct
10 Lebanon Ct
B5 1 Grove The
2 Cumberland Cl
3 Westmorland Cl
4 Sussex Cl
5 Norfolk Cl
6 Nicol Cl
7 Old Lodge Pl
8 Kelvin Ct
9 St Margaret's Ct
10 Park Cotts
11 St Margarets Bsns Ctr
12 Amyand Cotts
C1 1 Benson Ho
2 Bowes Lyon Ho
3 Cavendish Ho
4 Bentinck Ho
5 Clarke Ho
6 Secrett Ho
7 Edwards Ho
8 Field Ho
9 Greig Ho
10 Hawkins Ho
11 Newman Ho
12 Leyland Ho
13 Hornby Ho
14 Hatch Ho
C5 1 Howmic Ct
2 Sefton Lo
3 Ravensbourne Ho
4 Arlington Ct
5 Georgina Ct
6 Trevelyan Ho
7 Caradon Ct
8 Green Hedges
9 Old House Gdns
10 Queens Keep
11 Beresford Ct
12 Langham Ct
13 Poplar Ct
D5 1 Richmond Bridge Mans
2 Heatherdene Mans
3 Kenton Ct
4 Lennox Ho
5 Leicester Ct
6 Turner Ho
7 Blanchard Ho
8 Arosa Rd
9 Ashe Ho
10 Bevan Ct
11 Lawley Ho
12 Darling Ho
13 Richmond Mans
14 Beaulieu Cl
15 Roseleigh Cl
16 Mallard Ct
D6 1 Garrick Cl
2 Old Palace Yd
3 Wardrobe The
4 Maids of Honour Row
5 Hunters Ct
6 Queensberry Ho
7 Green The
8 Old Palace Terr
9 Paved Ct
10 Golden Ct
11 Brewers La
12 Square The
13 Lower George St
14 St James's Cotts
15 Church Wlk
16 Church Ct
17 Victoria Pl
18 Castle Yd
19 Lewis Rd
20 Wakefield Rd
21 Church Terr
22 Warrington Rd
23 Ormond Ave
24 Glovers Lo
25 Holbrooke Pl
26 Northumberland Pl
27 Heron Sq
28 Whittaker Pl
29 Water Lane Ho
30 Riverside Ho
31 St Helena Terr

154

A5 1 Lancaster Cotts
2 Lancaster Mews
3 Bromwich Ho
4 Priors Lo
5 Richmond Hill Ct
6 Glenmore Ho
7 Hillbrow
8 Heathshott
9 Friars Stile Pl
10 Spire Ct
11 Ridgeway
12 Matthias Ct
A6 1 Lichfield Terr
2 Union Ct
3 Carrington Lo
4 Wilton Ct
5 Egerton Ct
6 Beverley Lo
7 Bishop Duppa's Almshouses
8 Regency Wlk
9 Clear Water Ho
10 Onslow Avenue Mans
11 Michels Almshouses
12 Albany Pas
13 Salcombe Villas
B5 1 Chester Cl
2 Evesham Ct
3 Queen's Ct
4 Russell Wlk
5 Charlotte Sq
6 Jones Wlk
7 Hilditch Ho
8 Isabella Ct
9 Damer Ho
10 Eliot Ho
11 Fitzherbert Ho
12 Reynolds Pl
13 Chisholm Rd
B6 1 Alberta Ct
2 Beatrice Rd
3 Lorne Rd
4 York Rd
5 Connaught Rd
6 Albany Terr
7 Kingswood Ct
8 Selwyn Ct
9 Broadhurst Cl

156

A3 1 Farnborough Ho
2 Rushmere Ho
3 Horndean Cl
4 Highcross Way
5 Timsbury Wlk
6 Foxcombe Rd
7 Ryefield Path
8 Greatham Wlk
9 Gosport Ho
10 Stoatley Ho
11 Milland Ho
12 Clanfield Ho
13 Fareham Ho
14 Grayswood Point
A4 1 Woodcott Ho
2 Lyndhurst Ho
3 Wheatley Ho
4 Allbrook Ho
5 Bordon Wlk
6 Chilcombe Ho
7 Vicarage Ct
8 Shawford Ct
9 Eastleigh Wlk
10 Kings Ct
11 Somborne Ho
A6 1 Theodore Ho
2 Nicholas Ho
3 Bonner Ho
4 Downing Ho
5 Jansen Ho
6 Fairfax Ho
7 Devereux Ho
8 David Ho
9 Leigh Ho
10 Clipstone Ho
11 Mallet Ho
12 Arton Wilson Ho
B3 1 Ramsdean Ho
2 Purbrook Ho
3 Portsea Ho
4 Blendworth Point
5 Eashing Point
6 Hindhead Point
7 Hilsea Point
8 Witley Point
9 Buriton Ho
10 Grateley Ho
11 Hascombe Ho
12 Dunhill Point
13 Westmark Point
14 Longmoor Point
15 Cadnam Point
C4 1 Cumberland Ho
2 Devonshire Ho
3 Cornwall Ho
4 Norfolk Ho
5 Leicester Ho
6 Warwick Ho
7 Sutherland Ho
8 Carmarthen Ho
9 Worcester Ho
10 Rutland Ho
11 Paddock Way
C6 1 Inglis Ho
2 Ducie Ho
3 Wharncliffe Ho
4 Stanhope Ho
5 Waldegrave Ho
6 Mildmay Ho
7 Mullens Ho
D3 1 Sandringham Cl
2 Eastwick Ct
3 Oatlands Ct
4 Banning Ho
5 Grantley Ho
6 Caryl Ho
7 Duncombe Ho
8 Chilworth Ct
9 Kent Lo
10 Turner Lo
11 Marlborough
12 Parkland Gdns
13 Lewesdon Cl
14 Pines Ct
15 Ashtead Ct
16 Mynterne Ct
17 Arden
18 Stephen Ct
19 Marsham Ct
20 Doradus Ct
21 Acorns The
22 Heritage Ho
23 Conifer Ct
24 Spencer Ho
25 Chartwell
26 Blenheim
27 Chivelston
28 Greenfield Ho
29 Oakman Ho
30 Radley Lo
31 Simon Lo
32 Admirals Ct
D4 1 Brett Ho
2 Brett House Cl
3 Sylva Ct
4 Ross Ct
5 Potterne Cl
6 Stourhead Cl
7 Fleur Gates
8 Greenwood
D5 1 Balmoral Cl
2 Glenalmond
3 Selwyn Ho
4 Keble Ho
5 Bede Ho
6 Gonville Ho
7 Magdalene H
8 Armstrong H
9 Newnham Ho
10 Somerville H
11 Balliol Ho
12 Windermere
13 Little Combe
14 Classinghall
15 Chalford Ct
16 Garden Royal
17 South Ct
18 Anne Kerr Ct
19 Ewhurst
D6 1 Geneva Ct
2 Laurel Ct
3 Cambalt Ho
4 Langham Ct
5 Lower Pk
6 King's Keep
7 Whitnell Ct
8 Whitehead H
9 Halford Ho
10 Humphry Ho
11 Jellicoe Ho

157

A3 1 William Harv
2 Highview Ct
3 Cameron Ct
4 Galgate Cl
5 Green Ho The
6 King Charles
7 Florys Ct
8 Augustus Ct
9 Albert Ct
10 Hertford Lo
11 Mortimer Lo
12 Allenswood
13 Ambleside
14 Hansler Ct
15 Roosevelt Ct
A6 1 Claremont
2 Downside
3 Cavendish Cl
4 Ashcombe Ct
5 Carltons The
6 Espirit Ho
7 Millbrooke C
8 Coysh Ct
9 Keswick Hts
10 Lincoln Ho
11 Avon Ct
B6 1 Keswick Broa
2 Burlington M
3 Cambria Lo
4 St Stephen's
5 Atlantic Ho
6 Burton Lo
7 Manfred Ct
8 Meadow Bank
9 Hooper Ho
10 Aspire Bld
C6 1 Pembridge P
2 Adelaide Rd
3 London Ct
4 Windsor Ct
5 Westminster
6 Fullers Ho
7 Bridge Pk
8 Lambeth Ct
9 Milton Ct
10 Norfolk Mans
11 Francis Snary
12 Bush Cotts
13 Downbury M
14 Newton's Yd
D6 1 Fairfield Ct
2 Blackmore H
3 Lancaster M
4 Cricketers M
5 College Mews
6 Arndale Wlk

158

A2 1 Beemans Row
2 St Andrew's
3 Townsend M
4 Sheringham

159

1 Upper Tooting Mans
2 Cecil Mans
3 Marius Mans
4 Boulevard Th
5 Elmfield Man
6 Holdernesse
7 Lumiere Ct
A3 1 Heslop Ct

St James's Terr
Boundaries Mans
Station Par
Old Dairy Mews
Hollies Way
Endlesham Ct
Rayne Ho
St Anthony's Ct
Earlsthorpe Mews
Nightingale Mans
Holbeach Mews
Hildreth Street Mews
Coalbrook Mans
Hub Buildings The
Metropolis Apart-ments
Meyer Ho
Faraday Ho
Hales Ho
Frankland Ho
Graham Ho
Gibbs Ho
Dalton Ho
Ainslie Wlk
Rokeby Ho
Caistor Ho
Ivanhoe Ho
Catherine Baird Ct
Marmion Ho
Devonshire Ct
Blueprint Apartments
Limerick Ct
Homewoods
Jewell Ho
Glanville Ho
Dan Bryant Ho
Olding Ho
Quennel Ho
Weir Ho
West Ho
Neville Ct
Friday Grove Mews
Joseph Powell Cl
Cavendish Mans
Westlands Terr
Cubitt Ho
Hawkesworth Ho
Normanton Ho
Eastman Ho
Couchman Ho
Poynders Ct
Selby Ho
Valentine Ho
Gorham Ho
Deauville Mans
Deauville Ct
Timothy Cl
Shaftesbury Mews
Brook Ho
Grover Ho
Westbrook Ho
Hewer Ho
Batten Ho
Mandeville Ho
George Beare Lo
Sinclair Ho
MacGregor Ho
Ingle Ho
St Andrews Mews
Riley Ho
Bennett Ho
White Ho
Rodgers Ho
Dumphreys Ho
Homan Ho
Prendergast Ho
Hutchins Ho
Whiteley Ho
Tresidder Ho
Primrose Ct
Angus Ho
Currie Ho
Parrington Ho
Savill Ho
Blackwell Ho
Bruce Ho
Victoria Ct
Victoria Ho
Belvedere Ct
Ingram Lo
Viney Ct
Bloomsbury Ho
Belgravia Ho
Barnsbury Ho

160

De Montfort Ct
Leigham Hall Par
Leigham Hall
Endsleigh Mans
John Kirk Ho
Raebarn Ct
Wavel Ct
Homeleigh Ct
Howland Ho
Beauclerk Ho
Bertrand Ho
12 Drew Ho
13 Dowes Ho
14 Dunton Ho
15 Raynald Ho
16 Sackville Ho
17 Thurlow Ho
18 Astoria Mans
A2 1 Wyatt Park Mans
2 Broadlands Mans
3 Stonehill's Mans
4 Streatleigh Par
5 Dorchester Ct
6 Picture Ho
A3 1 Beaumont Ho
2 Christchurch Ho
3 Staplefield Cl
4 Chipstead Ho
5 Coulsdon Ho
6 Conway Ho
7 Telford Avenue Mans
8 Telford Parade Mans
9 Wavertree Ct
10 Hartswood Ho
11 Wray Ho
A4 1 Picton Ho
2 Rigg Ho
3 Watson Ho
4 MacArthur Ho
5 Sandon Ho
6 Thorold Ho
7 Pearce Ho
8 Mudie Ho
9 Miller Ho
10 Lycett Ho
11 Lafone Ho
12 Lucraft Ho
13 Freeman Ho
14 New Park Par
15 Argyll Ct
16 Dumbarton Ct
17 Kintyre Ct
18 Cotton Ho
19 Crossman Hos
20 Cameford Ct
21 Parsons Ho
22 Brindley Ho
23 Arkwright Ho
24 Perry Ho
25 Brunel Ho
26 New Park Ct
27 Tanhurst Ho
28 Hawkshaw Cl
A6 1 King's Mews
2 Clapham Court Terr
3 Clapham Ct
4 Clapham Park Terr
5 Pembroke Ho
6 Stevenson Ho
7 Queenswood Ct
8 Oak Tree Ct
9 Park Lofts
10 Ashby Mews
B1 1 Carisbrooke Ct
2 Pembroke Lo
3 Willow Ct
4 Poplar Ct
5 Mountview
6 Spa View
B3 1 Charlwood Ho
2 Earlswood Ho
3 Balcombe Ho
4 Claremont Cl
5 Holbrook Ho
6 Gwynne Ho
7 Kynaston Ho
8 Tillman Ho
9 Regents Lo
10 Hazelmere Ct
11 Dykes Ct
B4 1 Archbishop's Pl
2 Witley Ho
3 Outwood Ho
4 Dunsfold Ho
5 Deepdene Lo
6 Warnham Ho
7 Albury Lo
8 Tilford Ho
9 Elstead Ho
10 Thursley Ho
11 Brockham Ho
12 Capel Lo
13 Leith Ho
14 Fairview Ho
15 Weymouth Ct
16 Ascalon Ct
17 China Mews
18 Rush Common Mews
B6 1 Beatrice Ho
2 Florence Ho
3 Evelyn Ho
4 Diana Ho
5 Brixton Hill Ct
6 Austin Ho
7 Manor Ct
8 Camsey Ho
9 Romer Ho
10 Gale Ho
11 Byrne Ho
12 Farnfield Ho
13 Marchant Ho
14 Rainsford Ho
15 Springett Ho
16 Mannering Ho
17 Waldron Ho
C3 1 Valens Ho
2 Loveday Ho
3 Strode Ho
4 Ethelworth Ct
5 Harbin Ho
6 Brooks Ho
7 Godolphin Ho
8 Sheppard Ho
9 McCormick Ho
10 Taylor Ho
11 Saunders Ho
12 Talcott Path
13 Derrick Ho
14 Williams Ho
15 Baldwin Ho
16 Churston Cl
17 Neil Wates Cres
18 Burnell Ho
19 Portland Ho
C4 1 Ellacombe Ho
2 Booth Ho
3 Hathersley Ho
4 Brereton Ho
5 Holdsworth Ho
6 Dearmer Ho
7 Cherry Cl
8 Greenleaf Cl
9 Longford Wlk
10 Scarlette Manor Wlk
11 Chandlers Way
12 Upgrove Manor Way
13 Ropers Wlk
14 Tebbs Ho
15 Bell Ho
16 Worthington Ho
17 Courier Ho
18 Mackie Ho
19 Hamers Ho
20 Kelyway Ho
21 Harriet Tubman Cl
22 Estoria Cl
23 Leckhampton Pl
24 Scotia Rd
25 Charles Haller St
26 Sidmouth Ho
27 Hunter Ct
28 Onslow Lo
29 William Winter Ct
30 Langthorne Lo
C5 1 Eccleston Ho
2 Scarsbrook Ho
3 Purser Ho
4 Rudhall Ho
5 Hardham Ho
6 Heywood Ho
7 Haworth Ho
8 Birch Ho
9 Lansdell Ho
10 Lomley Ho
11 Laughton Ho
12 Woodruff Ho
13 Bascome St
14 Dudley Mews
15 Herbert Mews
16 Blades Lo
17 Dick Shepherd Ct
18 Charman Ho
19 Morden Ho
20 Bishop Ct
21 Blackburn Ct
22 Leigh Ct
23 John Conwey Ho
24 Bristowe Cl
C6 1 Crownstone Ct
2 Brockwell Ct
3 Nevena Ct
4 St George's Resi-dences
5 Hanover Mans
6 Fleet Ho
7 Langbourne Ho
8 Turnmill Ho
9 Walker Mews
10 Cossar Mews
11 Carter Ho
D1 1 Thanet Ho
2 Chapman Ho
3 Beaufoy Ho
4 Easton Ho
5 Roberts Ho
6 Lloyd Ct
7 Kershaw Ho
8 Wakeling Ho
9 Edridge Ho
10 Jeston Ho
11 Lansdowne Wood Cl
12 Rotary Lo

161

B2 1 Welldon Ct
2 Coppedhall
3 Shackleton Ct
4 Bullfinch Ct
5 Gannet Ct
6 Fulmar Ct
7 Heron Ct
8 Petrel Ct
9 Falcon Ct
10 Eagle Ct
11 Dunnock Ct
12 Dunlin Ct
13 Cormorant Ct
14 Oak Lodge
15 Corfe Lodge
C6 1 Velde Way
2 Delft Way
3 Arnhem Way
4 Isel Way
5 Kempis Way
6 Terborch Way
7 Steen Way
8 Deventer Cres
9 Nimegen Way
10 Hilversum Cres
11 St Barnabas Cl

162

A1 1 Tunbridge Ct
2 Harrogate Ct
3 Bath Ct
4 Leamington Ct
5 Porlock Ho
6 Cissbury Ho
7 Eddisbury Ho
8 Dundry Ho
9 Silbury Ho
10 Homildon Ho
11 Highgate Ho
12 Richmond Ho
13 Pendle Ho
14 Tynwald Ho
15 Wirrall Ho
16 Greyfriars
A6 1 Dorothy Charrington Ho
2 Keswick Ct
3 Kendall Ct
4 Halliwell Ct
B1 1 River Ho
2 Fordington Ho
3 Arbury Terr
4 Woodbury Ho
5 Gainsborough Mews
6 Forest Hill Ct
B2 1 Bromleigh Ct
2 Parfew Ct
3 Thetford Ct
4 Attleborough Ct
5 Dunton Ct
6 Frobisher Ct
7 Julian Taylor Path
8 Grizedale Terr
9 Worsley Ho
C1 1 Forest Lo
2 Sydenham Park Mans
3 William Wood Ho
C2 1 Fitzwilliam Hts
2 Taymount Grange
3 McLeod Ho
4 Featherstone Ave
5 Kingswear Ho
6 Salcombe Ho
7 Glynwood Ct
C3 1 Harlech Ct
2 Angela Ct
3 Westwood Ct
4 New Belmont Ho
5 Pearcefield Ave
6 Waldram Pl
7 Horniman Grange
8 South View Ct
9 Heron Ct
10 Katherine Ct
D1 1 Standlake Point
2 Radcot Point
3 Newbridge Point
4 Northmoor
5 Kelmscott
6 Radnor Ct
7 Heathwood Point
8 Ashleigh Point
9 Deepdene Point
10 Rosemount Point
11 Woodfield Ho
12 Clairville Point
13 Trevenna Ho
14 Hyndewood
D2 1 Pikethorne
2 Andrew Ct
3 Valentine Ct
4 Soper Cl

164

C4 1 Beaumont Terr
2 Littlebourne
3 Verdant Ct
D2 1 Kinross Ct
2 Montrose Ct
3 Rattray Ct
4 Rothesay Ct
D3 1 Edinburgh Ct
2 McMillan Ct
3 Rowallan Ct
4 Meridian Ct
5 Braemar Ct
6 Barrow Ct
7 Blair Ct
8 Darlington Ct
9 Hamilton Ct
10 Inverness Ct
11 Oak Cottage Cl
12 Willow Cl
13 Keswick Ct

165

A4 1 Swallow Ct
2 Honeysuckle Ct
3 Venture Ct
4 Cheriton Ct
5 Askham Lo
6 Syon Lo

166

A2 1 Portland Cres
2 Bourdillon Ct
3 Hillary Ct
4 Tenzing Ct
5 John Hunt Ct
6 Everest Ct
A6 1 Horsfeld Gdns
2 Foxhole Rd
C5 1 Roper St
2 Arcade The
3 Elm Terr
4 Imber Ct
5 Ashcroft Ct
6 Fairlands Ct
7 Brecon Ct
8 Newlands Ct
9 Harvard Ct
10 Garden Ct
11 Chiltern Ct
12 Fairway Ct

167

A2 1 Mervyn Stockwood Ho
2 Michael Marshall Ho
3 Keith Sutton Ho

168

A1 1 Ham Shades Cl
2 Aspen Ho
3 Medlar Ho
4 Cornel Ho
5 Stanton Ct
6 Hornbeam Ho
7 Beech Ho
8 Spindle Ho
10 Hunters Lo
11 Edam Ct
12 Monica James Ho
13 Oak Ho
14 Crescent Ct
15 Freeland Ct
16 Montague Ct
17 Windsor Ct
B5 1 Rochester Cl
2 Cobham Cl
3 Shorne Cl
4 Warne Pl

169

C4 1 Close The
2 Parkhurst Gdns
3 Chichester Ct
4 Pound Green Ct

170

B6 1 Station Par
2 Queens La
3 Copthorne Chase
4 Canterbury Ct
5 Church Par
C5 1 St Matthew's Ct
2 Dencliffe
3 Crest Ho
4 Bourne Ho
5 Elms The
6 Roxeth Ct
7 Rowland Hill Alm-shouses

171

A3 1 Viscount Ct
2 Blackthorne Ct
D3 1 Bishops Ct
2 Ash Lo
3 Lime Lo
4 Oak Lo
5 Elm Ct
6 Willow Lo
7 Sycamore Lo
8 Priscilla Ho
9 Sunbury Cross Ctr
10 Isobel Ho

173

A6 1 Gabriel Cl
2 Metcalfe Wlk
3 Dunmow Cl
4 Burgess Cl
5 Chamberlain Wlk
C2 1 Sherbourne Ct
2 Somerset Ct
3 Jubilee Ho
4 Rushbury Ct
5 Blenheim Ct
6 Hemming Cl
7 Ryedale Ct
8 Norman Ct
C4 1 Begonia Pl
2 Snowdrop Cl
3 Hyacinth Cl
4 Cyclamen Cl
5 Jonquil Gdns
6 Gladioli Cl
7 Daffodil Pl
8 Partridge Rd
D4 1 Acorn Cl
2 Wolsey Ho
3 Lytton Ho
4 Wren Ho
5 Faraday Ho

174

C5 1 Knaggs Ho
2 Keeling
3 Elizabeth Ct
4 Oakhurst Cl
5 Charles Ct
6 Harold Ct
D5 1 Waldegrave Ct
2 Luther Mews
3 Alice Mews
4 Gresham Ho
5 Traherne Lo
6 Fishers Ct
7 Waterhouse Ct
8 Oval Ct
9 Walpole Pl
10 Walpole Cres
11 Bychurch End

175

A5 1 Cherrywood Ct
2 Cambridge Ho
3 Cairngorm Cl
4 Gleneagles Ct
5 Christchurch Ave
6 Hales Ct
7 Plough La
8 Springfield Rd
9 Royal Oak Mews
10 Trinder Mews
C3 1 Belgravia Ho
2 Ash Ho
3 Crieff Ct
4 Maples The
D2 1 Wick Ho
2 Spinnaker Ct
3 Osiers Ct
4 Trent Ho
5 Arun Ho
6 Medway Ho
7 Avon Ho
8 Tyne Ho
9 Clyde Ho
10 Mersey Ct
11 Severn Ct
12 John William Cl
13 Henry Macaulay Ave
14 Seymour Lo
15 Falmouth Ho
16 Earlsfield Ho
D6 1 Byron Ct
2 Coleridge Ct
3 Tennyson Ct
4 Herrick Ct
5 Spenser Ct
6 Marlowe Ct
7 Brooke Ct
8 Gray Ct
9 Shelley Ct
10 Pope Ct
11 Dryden Ct

176

A1 1 Cleave's Almshos
2 Perry Ct
3 Drovers Ct
4 Gough Ho
5 Eden Wlk
6 Alderman Judge Mall
7 Lady Booth Rd
8 Caversham Ho
9 Littlefield Cl
10 Bentall Sh Ctr The

176 A1
11 Adams Wlk
12 Ceres Ct
A2 1 Regents Ct
2 Walter St
3 Canbury Bsns Pk
4 Sigrist Sq
5 Ashway Ctr
6 Warwick Ho
7 Hedingham Ho
8 Alexander Ho
9 Bramber Ho
10 Carisbrooke Ho
11 Dartmouth Ho
12 Garland Ho
A3 1 Walton Ho
2 Berkeley Cl
3 Canbury Ct
4 King's Penny Ho
B1 1 Vicarage Ho
2 Rayleigh Ct
3 School Pas
4 Chippenham
5 Camm Gdns
B2 1 Onslow Ho
2 Dowler Ct
B3 1 McDonald Ho
2 Elm Ho
3 Dale Ct
4 York Ho
5 Florence Ho
6 Florence Rd
7 Roupell Ho
8 Delft Ho
C1 1 Wimpole Cl
2 Burwell
3 Caldecote
4 Fordham
5 Connington
6 Chesterton Terr
7 Westwick
8 Eureka Rd
9 Fulbourn
10 Comberton
11 Madingley
12 Grantchester
13 Cambridge Grove Rd
14 Oakington
15 Harston
16 Graveley
17 Croxton
18 Brinkley
19 Impington
20 Shelford
21 Duxford
22 Cascadia Ho
C2 1 Farthings The
2 Brae Ct
3 Princeton Mews
4 Station App
C3 1 Queen's Ct
2 St George's Rd
3 Park Road Ho
4 Dagmar Rd
5 Tapping Cl
6 Arthur Rd
7 Borough Rd
8 Belvedere Ct
9 Braywick Ct
10 Dean Ct
11 Rowan Ct
12 Richmond Ct
13 Sunningdale Ct
14 Hawker Ct
15 Cromwell Ct
16 Kings Ct
D2 1 Trevallyn Lo
2 Chichester Ho
3 Beechcroft
4 Cedars The
5 Liddlesdale Ho W
6 Liddlesdale Ho E
7 Deerhurst
8 Brockworth
9 Alderton
D3 1 Bramley Ho
2 Abinger Ho
3 Thursley Ho
4 Ridge Ho
5 Clone The
6 Mount Ct
7 Hillside Ct
8 Hill Ct
9 Royal Ct
10 Lakeside
11 High Ashton
D4 1 Godstone Ho
2 Hambledon Ho
3 Kingswood Ho
4 Leigh Ho
5 Milton Ho
6 Newdigate Ho
7 Farleigh Ho
8 Ockley Ho
9 Effingham Ho
10 Dunsfold Ho
11 Pirbright Ho
12 Clandon Ho
13 Ripley Ho

178

C3 1 Roskeen Ct
2 Chimneys Ct
3 Aston Ct
4 Rosemary Cotts
5 Victoria Lo
D2 1 Beaufort Ho
2 Kinnear Ct
3 Ranmore Ct
4 Lantern Ct
5 Crescent Ho
D3 1 Kings View Ct
2 Wimbledon Cl
3 Beryl Harding Ho
4 Upton Ct
5 Marian Lo
6 Terraces The
7 Lanherne Ho
8 Cumberland Cl
9 Thaxted Pl
10 Rathbone Ho
11 Princess Ct
12 Claremont Lo
13 Downs Ct
14 Ravenscar Lo
15 Haverley
16 Savona Cl
17 Beaumont Ct
18 Gordon Ct
D5 1 Lancaster Pl
2 Haygarth Pl
3 Allington Cl
4 Homefield Pl

179

A3 1 Stretford Ct
2 Brunswick Ct
3 Pavilion Ct
4 Louie Black Ho
5 Warwick Ho
6 Erica Ho
7 Adyar Ct
8 Thornton Lo
9 Ash Ct
10 Broughton Ho
11 Naomi Watts Ho
12 Wellesley Ho
13 Mayfair Ct
A4 1 Walham Rise
2 Grosvenor Ct
3 Sovereign Ho
4 Holly Lo
5 Florence Ct
6 Linden Cotts
7 Sheep Walk Mews
8 Emerson Ct
9 Hill Ct
10 Powell Ho
B4 1 Aspen Lo
2 Gladebury Ct
3 Centre Court Sh Ctr
B5 1 Lawns The
2 Prentice Ct
3 Catherine Ct
4 Woodlodge
5 Pixham Ct
6 Lake Cl
7 Westwood Ct
8 Brambles The
9 Lismore
10 Rose Ct
11 Worcester Rd
12 Leopold Ct
C3 1 Ashbourne Terr
2 Sir Cyril Black Way
3 Willows Ct
4 Harefield Ct
5 Broadway Ho
6 Viscount Point
7 Carrington Ho
8 Cloisters Ho
9 Downing Ho
10 Bickley Ct
11 Palmerston Gr
12 Gladstone Ct
13 Warrington Ct
D2 1 Gilbert Cl
2 Becket Cl
3 Priory Cl
4 Hudson Ct
5 Ryder Ho
6 Eleanor Ho
7 Ramsey Ho
8 Colborne Ct
9 Falcon Ho
10 Spur Ho
D3 1 Hamilton Road Mews
2 Dowman Cl
3 Burleigh Lo
4 Horatio Ho

180

A2 1 Tanner Ho
2 May Ct
3 Marsh Ct
4 Lovell Ho
A3 1 Fiske Ct
2 Mellor Ct
3 Olive Rd
4 Allerton Ho
5 Victory Road Mews
6 Will Miles Ct
7 Vanguard Ho
8 Mychell Ho
9 Merton Pl
10 De Burgh Ho
11 Norfolk Ho
12 Hotham Road Mews
B1 1 Ripley Ct
2 Brooklands Ct
3 Horner La
B2 1 Yarborough Rd
2 Vista Ho
3 Prospect Ho
4 Independence Ho
5 Nonsuch Ho
6 Baron Ho
C2 1 Linford Ct
2 Searle Ct
3 Gunnell Ct
4 Wells Ct
5 Hartley Ct
C3 1 Shere Lo
2 Goodwin Ct
3 Cairn Ho
C4 1 Douglas Ct
2 Lannock Ct
3 Gateway Ho
4 Wellington Ct
C5 1 Robertson Ho
2 Dewar Ho
3 Jean Ho
4 Marion Ct
5 Gravenel Gdns
6 Palladino Ho
D1 1 Elms Cotts
2 Sibthorp Rd
3 Armfield Cotts
4 Sir Arthur Bliss Ct
5 Fountain Ho
6 Gladstone Ho
7 Chart Ho

181

A1 1 Kennedy Cl
2 Pearce Cl
3 Mainwaring Ct
4 Coningsby Ct
5 Laburnum Ct
6 Beaumont Ct
7 Penfold Ct
8 Fitch Ct
10 Lea Cotts
A5 1 Osborne Terr
2 Limetree Wlk
C5 1 Tyers Ho
2 Boothby Ho
3 Adams Ho
4 Burney Ho
5 Boswell Ho
6 Chesterfield Ho
7 Garrick Ho
8 Levett Ho
9 Shelburne Ho
10 Marchmont Ho
11 Ryland Ho
12 Flather Cl
13 Bank Bldgs
14 Carriage Pl
15 Locarno Cl
C6 1 Walmsley Ho
2 Chambers Ho
3 Fordyce Ho
4 Percy Ho
5 Langton Ho
6 Moorfields Ct
7 Hidaburn Ct
8 Salter Ho
9 Tailors Ct
10 Yew Tree Lo
D6 1 William Dyce Mews
2 Doctor Johnson Ho

182

A3 1 Spa Central
A5 1 Oakdene Ct
2 Hopton Par
3 Merton Lo
4 Bouverie Ct
5 Deerhurst
6 Farnan Hall
A6 1 Central Mans
2 Central Par
B3 1 Marqueen Twrs
2 Shirley Ct
3 Sinclair Ho
4 Vantage Ct
5 Pavilion Ct
B6 1 Ashleigh Ho
2 Roseneath Pl
3 Shenley Ho
4 Blytheswood Pl
C5 1 Parkhill Ho
2 Ash Ct
3 Alder Ct
4 Beech Ct
5 Acacia Ct
6 Blackthorn Ct
7 Cypress Ct
8 Hawthorn Ct
9 Hazel Ct
10 Sycamore Ct
11 Maple Ct
12 Laburnam Ct
13 Fern Lo
14 Colyton La
C6 1 James Boswell Cl
2 St Albans Ho
3 Suffolk Ct
4 Rockhampton Cl
5 Delphian Ct
6 Heather Ct
D5 1 Woodcote Pl
2 Joe Hunte Ct
3 Cork Tree Ho
4 Lake Ho
5 Cedars Ho
6 Portobello Ho
7 Cooper Ho
8 Farnsworth Ho
9 Hook Ho
10 Crest The
11 Renshaw Ho
12 Ruscoe Ho
13 Sardeson Ho
D6 1 William Wilberforce Ho
2 William Marsden Ho
3 Samuel Ho
4 Morris Stephany Ho
5 Church Ct

183

A6 1 Moore Ho
2 Chaucer Ho
3 Bushell Ho
4 Bligh Ho
5 Hobbs Rd
6 Hogarth Ho
7 Goodbehere Ho
8 Astley Ho
9 Elder Gdns
10 Elderberry Gr
11 Pavement The
12 Dunkirk St
B6 1 Josef Perrin Ho
2 Jean Humbert Ho
3 Charles Staunton Ho
4 Violette Szabo Ho
5 Lilian Rolfe Ho
6 Odette Ho
7 Robert Gerard Ho
8 St Bernards Cl
9 Champness Cl
10 Pennington Cl
11 Queenswood Ct
C4 1 Northwood Way
2 High Limes
3 Valley Prospect
4 Plane Tree Wlk
5 City Prospect
6 Bankside Way
7 Ridge Way
8 Rochdale
9 Barrington Wlk
10 Gatestone Ct
11 Childs La
12 Carberry Rd
13 Norwood Heights Sh Ctr
C5 1 Oakdene
2 Thorsden Way
3 Oakfield Gdns
4 Georgetown Cl
5 Bridgetown Cl
6 Mountbatten Cl
7 Brabourne Cl
8 Alexandra Wlk
9 Compton Ct
10 Battenburg Wlk
11 Burma Terr
12 Wiseman Ct
C6 1 Linley Ct
2 Mellor Ho
3 Whitfield Ct
4 Michaelson Ho
5 Holberry Ho
6 Hovenden Ho
7 Huntley Ho
8 Telfer Ho
9 Markham Ho
10 Oldham Ho
11 Parnall Ho
12 Pierson Ho
13 Roper Ho
14 Roundell Ho
15 Sawyer Ho
16 Ransford Ho
17 Carmichael Ho
18 Bonne Marche Terr Mews
D3 1 Hetley Gdns
2 Claybourne Mews
3 Highland Lo
4 Mason Ct
5 Kendall Ct
6 High View
D5 1 Glenhurst Ct
2 Marlowe Ct
3 Grenville Ct
4 Raleigh Ct
5 Beechwoods Ct
6 Burntwood View

184

A3 1 Hanover Ct
2 Brunswick Ct
3 New Church Ct
4 Regency Ct
7 Owen Wlk
8 Bargrove Cl
9 Beaver Cl
B2 1 Dorset Ho
2 Collingwood Cl
3 Chartwell Way
4 Essex Twr
5 Appletree Cl
6 Ditton Pl
7 Kelvin Ct
8 Readman Ct
9 Glen Ct
10 Kingsbridge Ho
11 Carlton Ct
12 Benhurst Ct
13 Carole Ho
14 Dover Ho
15 Bettswood Ct
B3 1 Avery Ct
2 Rossal Ct
3 Oakdene Lo
4 Ridgemount Cl
5 Blakewood Ct
6 Trenholme Cl
7 Oakleigh Ct
8 Upchurch Cl
9 Devon Ho
10 Westmoreland Terr
11 Oakfield Road Ind Est
B5 1 Ragwort Ct
2 Firs The
3 Wingham Ho
4 Seath Ho
5 Ripley Ho
6 Lathwood Ho
7 Hurst Ho
8 George Ho
9 Browne Ho
10 Beacon Ho
11 Bailey Ho
12 Agate Ho
C2 1 Challin St
2 Rutland Ho
3 Pine Cl
C3 1 Watermen's Sq
2 St John's Cotts
3 Gladstone Mews
4 Middlesex Ho
5 Bethesda Ct
6 Ospringe Cl
7 Goudhurst Ho
8 Walmer Ho
9 Strood Ho
10 Greatstone Ho
11 John Baird Ho
C4 1 Midhurst
2 Oliver Ct
3 Victoria Ct
4 Wakefield Ct
5 Fountain Ct
6 Newlands Ct
C6 1 Homewalk Ho
2 Grace Path
3 Sycamore Ct
4 Sydenham Station App
5 Greenways
6 Faircroft
D3 1 Groombridge Ho
2 Provincial Terr
3 Smithers Ho
4 West Ho
5 Swallows Ct
6 Hornbeam Ho
7 Blenheim Centre

185

A1 1 Clock House Ct
2 Blandford Ave
3 Old School Cl
4 Lynsted Ct
5 Florence Rd
A6 1 Paxton Ct
2 Kenton Ct
3 Grove Ct
4 Shirley Lo
B2 1 Ashton Ct
2 Coombe Ct
3 Fontaine Ct
4 Richfield Ct
5 Sheridan Way
C1 1 Christ Church R
2 Lea Rd
3 Stanmore Terr
C2 1 Erindale Ct
2 Montgomerie C
3 Rebecca Ct
4 Sycamore Ct
5 Willow Ct
6 Marlborough Ct
7 Bearsted Terr
8 Berwick Ct
9 Wooderson Ct
10 Beck River Pk
11 Waterside
C3 1 Gardenia Ct
2 Brackendale Ct
3 Daniel Ct
4 Moliner Ct
5 Chartwell Lo
6 Randmore Ct
7 Dover Ho
8 Lucerne Ct
9 Malling Ho
10 Westerham Lo
11 Brasted Lo
12 Milton Ho
13 Bradsole Ho
14 Sandgate Ho
15 Adelaide Ct
16 Nettlestead Cl
17 Warren Ct
18 Alton Ct
19 Rockingham Ct
20 Camellia Ct
21 Sinclair Ct
22 Regents Ct
23 Minshull Pl
24 South Park Ct
D1 1 Parkside
2 Tudors The
3 Oakbrook
4 Tara Ct
5 Redlands The
6 Cambria
7 Hillworth
8 Kelsey Gate
9 Burrells
10 Lincoln Lo
11 Courtlands
12 Fairleas
13 Ashdown Cl
14 Barons
D2 1 Clifton Ct
2 Mayfair Ct
3 Lait Ho
4 Fire Station Me
D4 1 Warner Ho
2 Clifford Ho
3 Lloyd Ho
4 Thurston Ho
5 Byron Ho
6 Blake Ho
7 Keats Ho

186

A2 1 White House Ct
2 Hunters The
3 Sandringham C
4 Glenhurst
5 Copperfields
6 Westgate Ct
A6 1 Dedham Ho
2 Flatford Ho
3 Langthorne Ct
4 Radley Ct
5 Hoover Ho
6 Brunner Ho
7 Waterer Ho
8 Marriott Ho
9 Bourbon Ho
B5 1 Longford Ho
2 Ingrebourne Ho
3 Brent Ho
4 Darent Ho
5 Beverley Ho
6 Wandle Ho
7 Rythe Ho
8 Ember Ho
9 Crane Ho
10 Ravensbourne H
C1 1 Warwick Ct
2 Maplehurst
3 Mount Arlingto
4 Arundel Ct
D2 1 Weston Gr
2 Gibbs Ho
3 Longfield
4 Hammelton Ct

acken Hill Cl
wnend Ct
eversh Ct
ameron Ho
oodlands Ct
ythwood Pk
omley Pk
omecoppice Ho
nden Ct
mberley Gate
glewood Ct
avery Ct
en Ct
arlborough Ct
awston Ct
endon Path

87

James Ct
itchell Way
arrington Ho
ewman Ct
no Apartments
omley Ho
ainton Cl
othwell Ct
Timothy's Mews
ndringham Lo
endall Lo
ummerfield
inston Ct
ogue Ct
aurels The
estland Lo
astland Ct
airsie Ct
orthlands
eechfield Cotts
asis The
romarty Ct
lverstone Ct

88

eaconsfield Par
ranley Par
immeridge Gdns
ing & Queen Cl
ybridge Ct
reenbank Lo

90

yril Lo
azlemere
ilton Lo
larlin Ct
onroy Ct
lenwood Ct
ulverton Ct
olmbury Manor
wanscombe Ho
averstock Ct
rrandene Ho
roomfield Ho
eadley Ho
enley Ho
adywell Ho
hudleigh
imborne
t John's Par
olly Ct
ectory Bsns Ctr

93

rchard Ct
ridge Ct

97

aleigh Ho
eicester Ho
resham Ho
apier Ct
arlington Ho
harminster Ct
lulberry Ct
eander Ct
linton Ho
ollingsworth Ct
loucester Ct
almerston Ct
edwood Ct
ursley Ct
estmorland Ct
awson Ct
lexander Ct
inton Ct
ydenham Ho
aroline Ct
llswood Ct
lasefield Ct

98

sh Tree Cl
hrubbery The
alvern Ct
ate Ho
ew Tree Ho
tation App

2 South Bank Lo
3 Bramshott Ct
4 Pandora Ct
5 Wellington Ct
6 Glenbuck Ct
7 Leighton Ho
8 Oakhill Ct
9 Downs View Lo
10 Osborne Ct
11 Surbiton Par
12 Woodgate Ho
13 Godwyn Ho
14 Ashby Ho
A4 1 Effingham Lo
2 Maple Ho
3 Channon Ct
4 Falconhurst
5 Ferndown
6 Viceroy Lo
7 Frensham Ho
8 Kingsley Ho
9 Rannoch Ct
10 Stratton Ct
11 Moray Ho
12 Dulverton Ct
13 Westerham
14 Hill Ct
15 Assheton-Bennett Ho
16 Hatfield Ho
17 Oxford Ct
18 Pennington Lo
19 Austin Ho
20 Wentworth Ct
21 Priory The
22 Sheraton The
23 Christopher Ct
24 Hobart Ho
25 St Mark's Hts
A5 1 Marquis Ct
2 Garrick Ho
A6 1 College Rdbt
2 Edinburgh Ct
3 Weston Ct
4 Grebe Terr
5 Heron Ct
6 Agar Ho
7 St James' Ct
8 Grove Ct
9 Springfield Ct
10 College Wlk
B3 1 Percy Ct
2 Holmwood
3 Middle Green Cl
4 Herbert Ct
B4 1 Woodleigh
2 Highcroft
3 Caernarvon Ct
4 Regency Ct
D1 1 Oakleigh Way
2 Chandler Ct

199

C2 1 Goodland Ho
2 Furzeland Ho
3 Oakcroft Ho
4 Meadcroft Ho
5 Newhouse
C4 1 Merryweather Ct
2 Roebuck Ct
3 Sable Ct
C5 1 Acacia Ho
2 Kingston Lo
3 Carrington Ct
4 Fairholme Ho
5 Marshall Ho
6 Norton Ho
7 Martin Ho

200

A1 1 Brookside Cres
2 Beverley Gdns
3 Purdey Ct
4 Avenue The
5 Briarwood Ct
6 Station App

202

D6 1 Fair Green Ct
2 Regal Ct
3 Lewes Ct
4 Esher Mews
5 Sibford Ct
6 Deseret Ho
7 Standor Ho
8 Langdale Par
9 Newman Terr

204

A2 1 Barcom Trad Est
2 Croydon Valley Trade Pk
C3 1 Rozelle Ct
2 Dunheved Ct
3 Truscott Ho
C4 1 Brigstock Par
2 Terry Lodge
3 Justin Ct

D3 1 Wyndham Ct
D5 1 Nutfield Pl
2 Braidwood Ho
3 Elliott Ho

205

B1 1 Tavistock Ct
2 Chartwell Cl
3 Speaker's Ct
4 Cumberland Ct
5 Viceroy Ct
6 Oriel Ct
7 Cherry Orchard Gdns
8 Sola Ct
9 Gamma Ct
C1 1 Windmill Bridge Ho
2 Squire Ct
3 Houston Ct
5 Warren Ct
D1 1 Hastings Pl
2 Grant Pl
3 Clive Ho
4 Havelock Ho
5 Bellmore Ct
6 Hereford Ct
7 Chequers Ct
8 Havelock Hall

206

A1 1 Farleycroft
2 Edgecumbe Ct
3 Wesson Ho
4 Sullivan Ct
5 Kenley Ho
6 Christopher Ct
7 Jayson Ct
A6 1 Leybourne Ct
2 Lestock Cl
3 Croftside The
D1 1 Cottongrass Cl
2 Oxlip Cl
3 Eyebright Cl

207

1 North Rd
2 Sussex Rd
3 Riverside Wlk
4 Christie Ho
5 Windsor Ct
6 Sherwood Ct
7 Wheatsheaf Par
D6 1 Linden Ct
2 Park Ct
3 Chilchester Ct
4 Iveagh Ct

208

A6 1 Overbury
2 Wilton Pl
D1 1 Woodgrange Ct
2 Maycroft
3 Farnborough Cres
D4 1 Knowlton Gn
2 Speldhurst Cl
3 Bidborough Cl
4 Penshurst Wlk
D5 1 Wedgewood Ct
2 Birches The
3 Eccleshill
4 Tavistock Rd
5 Montpelier Ct

209

A5 1 Montague Terr
2 Chatsworth Ho
A6 1 Marina Cl
2 Cheveney Wlk
3 Bromley Manor Mans
4 Mall The
5 Westmoreland Pl
B5 1 Reflex Apartments
2 Wheeler Pl
3 Maxim Apartments
4 Exchange Apartments
5 Axiom Apartments
6 Weller Mews

211

B1 1 Gleneagles Gn
2 Tandridge Pl
3 Springfield Wlk
4 Pinehurst Wlk
5 Cromer Pl
6 Oakmont Pl

214

A6 1 St Bernards Ho
2 Wentworth Ct
3 Sunningdale Cl
4 Arklow Mews
5 Edward Pinner Ct

216

1 Lansdowne Copse
2 Lansdowne Ct

217

A2 1 Cheam Court Flats
2 Farnham Ct
3 Tabor Ct
C1 1 Lancaster Ct
2 Redclyffe Terr
3 Kenilworth Terr
4 Lincoln Terr
5 Garden Ct
6 Ashwood Pk
7 Midsummer Apartments
8 Lyndhurst Ct
9 Lorraine Ct
10 Gloucester Ct
11 Banbury Ct
12 Camilla Ct
13 Lorac Ct
14 Kingswood Mans
15 Claremont Ho
16 Holly Ct
17 Castle Ho
18 Balmoral Ct
19 Davington Ct
20 Hereford Ct
C2 1 Norman Ho
2 Hawthorns The
3 Limes The
4 Alexa Ct
5 Kristina Ct
6 Beverley Ct
7 Chestnut Ct
D1 1 Holmeswood
2 Pebworth Lo
3 Addison Ct
4 Kingslee Ct
5 Raeburn Ho
6 Girtin Ho
7 Leith Towers
8 Courtlands
9 Thomas Ho
10 Grayshott Ct
11 Hadrian Ct
12 Sandown Ct
13 Magnolia Ct
14 Dunsfold Ct
15 Camberley Ct
16 Berrylands Ct
17 Brockham Ct
18 Alford Ct
19 Lansdowne Ho
20 Larchvale Ct
D2 1 Portland Ct
2 Durnston Ct
3 Barton Ct
4 Aplin Ct
5 Hannah Ct
6 Honeysuckle Ct
7 Rowans The
8 St Annes Ct
9 Bonnington Ho
10 Pamir Ct
11 Bradbourne Ct
12 Worcester Ct
D3 1 Marian Ct
2 Robin Hood Ct
3 Distin Ct
4 Queensmere
5 Grosvenor Ho
6 Cromer Mans
7 St Nicholas Ctr
D5 1 Dorothy Pettingel Ho
2 Margaret Ho

218

A1 1 Beauclere Ho
2 Melford Ct
3 Elmhurst Lo
4 Mansard Manor
5 Tranmere Ct
6 Beechcroft Lo
7 Savin Lo
8 Yew Tree Ct
9 Avondale Ct
10 Devonshire Ho
11 Hidcote Ho
12 Munstead Ct
13 Lodden Lo
14 Steetley Ct
15 Grampian Cl
16 Richard Sharples Ct
A2 1 Grosvenor Ct
2 Forest Dene Ct
3 Cedar Ct
4 Vanborough Ct
5 Shrub Ct
6 Evergreen Ct
7 Grasmere Ct
8 Heathfield Ct
9 Sherbourne Ct
10 Kinsale Grange
11 Linden Ct
12 Jubilee Ct
13 Langley Ct
14 Wilmot Ho
15 Farendon Ho

16 Alexander Ho
A3 1 Goossens Cl
2 Cliffe Wlk
3 Marlins Cl
4 Clowser Cl
5 Montana Gdns
6 Bournemouth Ct
7 Palmerston Ct
A4 1 Lodge The
2 Hazelwood Ho
3 Chesterton Ho
4 Clevedon Ho
5 Staincliffe Ho
6 Denewood Ho
7 Newlyn Ho
8 Manor Ct
9 Glenrose Ho
10 Oak Lo
11 Briar The
12 Fernhead
13 Branch Ho
14 Thicket Ct
15 Adam Ct
16 Arndell Ho
17 Oakwood Ct
B3 1 Hogarth Ho
2 Gillray Ho
3 Cramhurst Ho
4 Ronald Ho
5 Blythewood
6 Hillside
7 Weldon Ct
8 Yeoman Ct
D5 1 Kynersley Cl
2 Wrythe Gn
3 Bedford Villas
4 Chateau The
5 Nelson Ct
6 Errington Manor
7 Leeds Ct
8 Blair Ct

219

A4 1 Westcroft
2 Westcroft Ho
A5 1 Burnside Ct
2 Millpond Pl
3 Waterside Ct
4 Stable Ct
5 Manor Ct
B2 1 Runnymede Ct
2 Dolphin Ct
3 Kings Ct
4 Cheyne Ct
5 Hendfield Ct
6 Ellerslie Ct
7 Embassy Ct
8 Chandler Ct
9 Hambledon Ct
10 Wallington Ct
11 Jasmine Ct
12 Napier Ct
13 Rosswood Ho
14 Woodcote Ct
15 Surrey Ct
16 Stag Ct
17 Moorlands
B3 1 Cornelion Cotts
2 Walpole Ct
3 Farmstead Ct
4 Derby Ho
5 Salisbury Ho
6 Chatham Ho
B4 1 Loraine Ho
2 Harcourt Lo
3 Coniston Ct
4 Alcester Ct
5 Friars Ct
6 Campbell Ho
7 Brodie Ho
8 Lesley Ct
9 Birch Ct
10 Airborne Ho
C2 1 Rossendon Ct
2 Mulberry Mews
3 Nairn Ct
4 Wallington Sq
5 Rosemount Twrs
6 Connell Ho
7 Ashby Grange
8 Terry Ct
9 Leigham Cl
10 Clyde Works
11 Chandos Bsns Ctr
12 Beech Ho
13 Wendon Ct
D3 1 Torquay Ho
2 Ashburton Ho
D5 1 Goodwood Lo
2 Haydock Lo
3 Kempton Lo

220

A1 1 Phoenix Ctr The
2 Ensign Way
3 Hunter Cl
4 Cirrus Cl

D5 1 Latimer Rd
2 Cromwell Ho
3 Arundel Ct
4 Warrington Ct
5 Grace Ct
6 Stuart Ct
7 Bridge Par

221

A3 1 Trent Ct
2 Sherwood Ct
3 Archers Ct
4 Keepers Ct
5 Lincoln Ct
6 Mount The
7 Fairhaven Ct
8 Brockham Ct
9 Chelwood Ct
10 Marey Ct
11 Landau Ct
A4 1 West Street Pl
2 Maple Ct
3 St Andrew's Rd
4 Albury Ct
5 Chestnut Ct
6 Elgin Ct
7 Beechfield Ct
8 Barham Ct
9 Whitstable Pl
10 Ledbury Pl
A5 1 Fellmongers Yd
2 Halstead Cl
3 Mann Cl
4 Waterworks Yd
5 Chanderia Ct
6 Katherine Ho
A6 1 Otterbourne Rd
2 Charrington Rd
3 Tamworth Pl
4 Priddy's Yd
5 Hospital of the Holy Trinity (Almshouses)
B6 1 Wellesley Court Rd
2 Norfolk Ho
3 Station App
4 Suffolk Ho
5 Cherry Orchard Gdns
6 Harrington Ct
D6 1 Cheyne Ct
2 Fourways
3 Princess Ct
4 Tierney Ct
5 Sinclair Ct
6 Guinness Ct
7 Mayfair Ct
8 Bishopscourt
9 Gloucester Lo
10 Beverley Hyrst
11 Melton Ct
12 Cecil Ct
13 Napier Ct

227

A3 1 Westfield
2 Farnborough Ct
3 Fern Hill Pl
4 Churchill Ct
5 Spencer Ct
6 Ladycroft Gdns
7 Crabbs Croft Cl
8 Clifton Cl
D2 1 Brittenden Cl
2 Wardens Field Cl
3 Winnipeg Dr
4 Superior Dr
5 Huron Cl
6 Manitoba Gdns
7 Lynne Cl
8 Flint Cl
9 Bakers Mews
D3 1 Osgood Gdns
2 Amberley Cl
3 Rawlings Cl
4 Beblets Cl
5 Fir Tree Cl
6 Raleigh Mews
7 King Henry Mews
D4 1 Healy Dr
2 Marsden Way
3 Taylor Cl
4 Strickland Way
5 Dryland Ave
6 Adcot Wlk
7 Lichlade Cl

Hospitals

Hospitals with Accident and Emergency departments

- **Central Middlesex Hospital** 89 A4
  Acton Lane, Park Royal, London NW10 7NS
  020 8965 5733
- **Charing Cross Hospital** 112 D1
  Fulham Palace Road, London W6 8RF
  (A&E entrance off St Dunstan's Road)
  020 8846 1234
- **Chase Farm Hospital** 4 C5
  The Ridgeway, Enfield, Middlesex EN2 8JL
  020 8375 1010
- **Chelsea and Westminster Hospital** 136 A6 266 B5
  369 Fulham Road, London SW10 9NH
  020 8746 8080
- **Ealing Hospital** 108 B4
  Uxbridge Road, Southall, Middlesex UB1 3HW
  020 8967 5613
- **Hammersmith Hospital** 90 B1
  Du Cane Road, London W12 0HS
  020 8383 1111
- **Hillingdon Hospital** 82 B2
  Pield Heath Road, Uxbridge, Middlesex UB8 3NN
  01895 238282
- **Homerton University Hospital** 74 D3
  Homerton Row, E9 6SR
  020 8510 5555
- **King George Hospital** 58 A4
  Barley Lane, Goodmayes, Ilford, Essex IG3 8YB
  020 8983 8000
- **King's College Hospital** 139 B3
  Denmark Hill, (A&E in Ruskin Wing) SE5 9RS
  020 3299 9000
- **Kingston Hospital** 176 D2
  Galsworthy Road, Kingston-upon-Thames, Surrey KT2 7QB
  020 8546 7711
- **Lewisham Hospital** 163 D6
  High Street, Lewisham, London SE13 6JH
  020 8333 3000
- **Mayday University Hospital** 204 D3
  Mayday Road, Thornton Heath CR7 7YE
  020 8401 3000
- **Moorfields Eye Hospital (eyes only)** 95 B4 235 C1
  162 City Rd, London EC1V 2PO
  020 7253 3411
- **Newham General Hospital** 99 C3
  Glen Road, Plaistow, London E13 8SL
  020 7476 4000
- **North Middlesex University Hospital** 33 C5
  Sterling Way, Edmonton, London, N18 1QX
  020 8887 2000
- **Northwick Park Hospital** 43 A2
  Watford Road, Harrow, Middlesex HA1 3UJ
  020 8864 3232
- **Princess Royal University Hospital** 226 C5
  Farnborough Common, Orpington BR6 8ND
  01689 863000
- **Queen Elizabeth Hospital** 144 A5
  Stadium Rd, Woolwich SE18 4QH
  020 8836 6000
- **Queen Mary's Hospital** 190 A4
  Frognal Avenue, Sidcup,Kent DA14 6LT
  020 8302 2678
- **Royal Free Hospital** 70 C3
  Pond Street, London NW3 2QG
  020 7794 0500
- **Royal London Hospital (Whitechapel)** 96 B2
  Whitechapel Road, London E1 1BB
  020 7377 7000
- **St George's Hospital** 180 B5
  Blackshaw Road, London SW17 0QT
  020 8672 1255
- **St Helier Hospital** 202 A1
  Wrythe Lane, Carshalton, Surrey SM5 1AA
  020 8296 2000
- **St Mary's Hospital** 92 B1 236 D2
  Praed Street, Paddington W2 1NY
  (A&E entrance on South Wharf Rd)
  020 7886 6666
- **St Thomas' Hospital** 116 B3 260 C6
  Lambeth Palace Road, London SE1 7EH
  020 7188 7188
- **University College Hospital** 93 C3 239 B6
  235 Euston Rd, London NW1 2BU
  0845 155 5000
- **West Middlesex University Hospital** 131 A3
  Twickenham Road, Isleworth, Middlesex TW7 6AF
  020 8560 2121
- **Whipps Cross Hospital** 54 B3
  Whipps Cross Road, Leytonstone London E11 1NR
  020 8539 5522
- **Whittington Hospital** 71 C6
  Highgate Hill, London, N19 5NF
  020 7272 3070

- Acton Hospital W3 110 C4
- Ashford Hospital TW15 3AA 148 A2
- Athlone House (The Middlesex Hospital) N6 48 D1
- Atkinson Morley Hospital SW20 178 B3
- Barking Hospital IG11 79 D1
- Barnes Hospital SW14 133 C2
- Beckenham Hospital BR3 185 B1
- Bethlem Royal Hospital The BR3 207 C2
- Blackheath Hospital SE3 142 C2
- Bolingbroke Hospital The SW11 158 C6
- Bowden House Hospital (Private) HA1 64 C6
- British Home and Hospital for Incurables SW16 182 D5
- Bromley Hospital BR2 9AJ 209 B5
- Brompton Hospital SW3 114 B1 256 D2
- BUPA Bushey Hospital WD2 8 D3
- Carshalton, War Memorial Hospital SM5 218 D2
- Cassel Hospital TW10 175 D6
- Castlewood Day Hospital SE18 144 C4
- Central Middlesex Hospital NW10 7NS 89 A4
- Central Public Health Laboratory NW9 45 C6
- Chadwell Heath Hospital RM6 58 B4
- Charing Cross Hospital W6 8RF 112 D1
- Charter Nightingale Hospital The NW1 92 C2 237 B4
- Chase Farm Hospital EN2 8JL 4 C5
- Chelsea Hospital for Women SW3 114 C1 257 A2
- Chelsea and Westminster Hospital SW10 9NH 136 A6 266 B5
- Chingford Hospital E4 20 A1
- Chiswick Maternity Hospital W4 111 D1
- Clayponds Hospital and Day Treatment Ctr TW8 110 A2
- Clementine Churchill Hospital The HA1 64 D5
- Colindale Hospital NW9 45 C6
- Connaught Day Hospital E11 54 C3
- Coppetts Wood Hospital N10 30 D2
- Cromwell Hospital SW5 113 D2 255 C4
- Devonshire Hospital W1 93 A2 238 B4
- Dulwich Hospital SE22 139 C1
- Ealing Hospital UB1 3HW 108 B4
- East Ham Memorial Hospital E7 77 D1
- Eastman Dental Hospital WC1 94 B4 240 C6
- Edgware General Hospital HA8 26 D3
- Elizabeth Garrett Anderson and Obstetric Hospital WC1 93 C3 235 B5
- Farnborough Hospital BR6 226 C4
- Finchley Memorial Hospital N12 30 A3
- Fitzroy Nuffield Hospital W1 92 D1 237 C2
- Garden Hospital The NW4 46 C6
- Goldie Leigh Hospital SE2 146 C6
- Goodmayes Hospital IG3 58 A4
- Gordon Hospital The SW1 115 D2 259 C3
- Great Ormond St Hospital for Children WC1 94 B3 240 C5
- Grovelands Priory N14 16 A3
- Guy's Hospital SE1 117 B5 252 D2
- Hackney Hospital E9 75 A3
- Hamlet (Day) Hospital The TW9 132 A2
- Hammersmith Hospital W12 90 B1
- Harrow Hospital HA2 64 C6
- The Heart Hospital W1 93 B2 238 C3
- Hillingdon Hospital UB8 82 B2
- Homerton University Hospital E9 74 D3
- Hornsey Central Hospital N8 49 D4
- Hospital for Tropical Diseases WC1 232 C5
- Hospital of St John and St Elizabeth NW8 92 B5 229 C3
- Inverforth House Hospital NW3 70 A6
- Jewish Home and Hospital at Tottenham The N15 51 D5
- King George Hospital IG3 58 A4
- King's College Hospital SE5 139 B3
- Kings Oak Hospital (Private) The EN2 4 C5
- Kingsbury Hospital NW9 44 C5
- Kingston Hospital KT2 176 D2
- Langthorne Hospital E11 76 B5
- Lewisham Hospital SE13 163 D6
- Lister Hospital SW1 115 B1 258 C1
- London Bridge Hospital SE1 117 B5 252 D4
- London Chest Hospital E2 96 C5
- London Clinic NW1 93 A3 238 B5
- London Foot Hospital W1 93 C3 239 A5
- London Hospital (Mile End) The E2 96 D4
- London Hospital (St Clements) The E3 97 B4
- London Independent Hospital The E1 96 D2
- Maida Vale Psychiatric Hospital W9 92 A3 236 B6
- Manor House Hospital NW11 47 D1
- Marlborough Day Hospital NW8 92 A5 229 A4
- Maudsley Hospital The SE5 139 B3
- Mayday University Hospital CR7 204 D3
- Memorial Hospital SE18 144 C3
- Mildmay Mission Hospital E2 95 D4
- Molesey Hospital KT8 195 C4
- Moorfields Eye Hospital EC1 95 B4 235 C1
- Morland Road Day Hospital RM10 103 C6
- National Hospital for Neurology and Neurosurgery N2 48 C5
- National Hospital The WC1 94 A3 240 B5
- National Physical Laboratory TW11 174 C4
- Nelson Hospital SW20 179 B1
- New Cross Hospital SE14 140 C5
- New Victoria Hospital KT3 177 C2
- Newham General Hospital E13 99 C3
- Normansfield Hospital KT8 175 C3
- North London Nuffield Hospital EN2 4 C3
- North Middlesex University Hospital N18 33 C5
- Northwick Park Hospital HA1 43 A2
- Northwood Pinner and District Cottage Hospital HA6 22 A2
- Norwood Hospital SE19 183 B4
- Orpington Hospital BR6 227 D4
- Paddington Com Hospital W9 91 C2
- Penny Sangam Day Hospital UB2 107 B3
- Plaistow Hospital E13 99 C5
- Portland Hospital for Women and Children The W1 93 B3 238 D5
- Princess Grace Hospital The W1 93 A3 238 A5
- Princess Louise Hospital W10 90 C2
- Princess Royal University Hospital BR6 226 C5
- Priory Hospital The SW15 133 D1
- Putney Hospital SW15 134 C2
- Queen Charlotte's Hospital W12 90 B1
- Queen Elizabeth Hospital for Children The E2 96 A5
- Queen Elizabeth Hospital SE18 144 A5
- Queen Mary's Hospital DA14 6LT 190 A4
- Queen Mary's Hospital NW3 70 A5
- Queen Mary's University Hospital SW15 156 A5
- Queen's Hospital CR0 205 A3
- Roding Hospital IG4
- Royal Brompton and Nat Hea[rt] Hospital The SW3 114 C1 2
- Royal Ear Hospital WC1 93 C3 2
- Royal Free Hospital NW3
- Royal Hospital SW15
- Royal London Homeopathic Hospital The WC1 94 A2 2
- Royal London Hospital(Whitechapel) E1
- Royal Marsden Hospital SW3 114 B1 2
- Royal Masonic Hospital W6
- Royal National Orthopaedic Hospital HA7
- Royal National Orthopaedic Hospital W1 93 B3 2
- Royal Nat TN&E Hospital The W5
- Royal Nat TN&E Hospital The WC1 94 B4 2
- St Andrew's Hospital E3
- St Ann's General Hospital N4, N15
- St Anthony's Hospital KT4
- St Bartholomew's Hospital EC1 94 D2 2
- St Charles' Hospital W10
- St Christopher's Hospice SE26
- St George's Hospital SW17
- St Giles Hospital SE5
- St Helier Hospital SM5
- St Joseph's Hospice E9, E8
- St Leonard's Hospital N1
- St Luke's Hospital W1 93 C3 2
- St Luke's Woodside Hospital N10
- St Mark's Hospital EC1 94 D4 2
- St Mark's Hospital HA1
- St Mary's Cottage Hospital TW12
- St Mary's Hospital W2 92 B[1] D2
- St Michael's Hospital EN2
- St Pancras Hospital NW1 93 D6 2
- St Thomas's Hospital SE1 116 B3 2
- St Vincent's Hospital HA5
- Samaritan Hospital for Women NW1
- Shirley Oaks Hospital CR0
- Sloane Hospital BR3
- South Western Hospital SW9
- Southwood Hospital (Geriatric) N6
- Springfield Hospital SW17
- Stepney Day Hospital E1
- Surbiton Hospital KT6
- Teddington Memorial Hospital TW11
- Thorpe Coombe Hospital E17
- Tolworth Hospital KT6
- Travel Clinic, Hospital for Trop[ical] Diseases WC1 93 C3 2
- University College Hospital WC1 93 C3 2
- Upton Day Hospital DA6
- Wanstead Hospital E11
- Wellington Hospital (North) NW8 92 B5 2
- Wellington Hospital (South) NW8 92 B5 2
- Wembley Hospital HA0
- West Middlesex University Hospital TW7 6AF
- Western Hospital The NW1 92 D2 2
- Whipps Cross Hospital E11 1NR
- Whittington Hospital N19 5NF
- Willesden Community Hospit[al] The NW10
- Winifred House Hospital EN5

Places of interest

ıtral

t End

ılty Arch SW1 .... 249 D4
Market WC2 .... 250 B6
ıting House SW1 .... 250 A3
ı SW1 .... 250 B1
Library NW1 ...... 93 D4 232 D2
Mus WC1 .... 94 A2 240 A3
er W1 .... 93 C2 239 A4
gham Palace SW1 .115 C4 249 A1
t War Rooms SW1 .115 D4 249 D2
y Street W1 .... 93 C1 239 A1
ph SW1 .... 250 A2
ng of the Guard
of) SW1 .... 249 A1
own W1.......... 115 D6 249 D6
ce House SW1 ..... 115 C5 249 B3
tra's Needle WC2 ..116 B5 250 C5
uld Galleries WC2 .... 250 C6
Garden WC2 ...... 116 A6 250 B6
s House
VC1 .... 94 B3 240 D5
ng Street SW1 .....116 A4 250 A2
l 115 D6 249 C5
Park SW1,W1 ......115 B4 248 D2
Mus SW1 ....115 C4 249 B1
ust Memorial
en W2 ....114 D4 247 D2
Guards
e SW1............115 D5 249 D3
s of
ment SW1 ....116 A3 260 B6
Park W2 ....114 D5 247 C3
ter Square WC2 ....115 D6 249 D5
's Transport Mus WC2 .... 250 B6
Arch W1 ....114 D6 247 D6
dist Central
W1 ....115 D4 249 D1
al Gallery W1 ......115 D6 249 D5
al Portrait
ry W1............115 D6 249 D5
's Monument WC2 .... 250 A4
cotland Yard SW1 ..115 D3 259 C6
ment Square SW1 ..116 A4 250 A1
Trocadero W1 .... 249 C5
illy Circus W1 .....115 D6 249 C5
Victoria Memorial SW1 ... 249 A2
's Gallery SW1 .....115 B4 248 D1
Row SW1 ....114 D4 247 C2
Academy
s W1 115 C6 249 A5
Mews SW1 ....115 B3 258 D6
United Services
SW1 .... 250 A3
es's Palace SW1 ...115 C5 249 B3
es's Park SW1 .... 249 C2
ntine Gallery W2 ...114 B4 246 D2
W1............93 D1 239 C2
set House WC2 ....116 B6 250 D6
ers' Corner W1 .....114 D6 247 D6
ritain SW1 ....116 A2 260 A3
e Mus WC2 .... 250 B6
gar Square SW1 ...115 D5 249 D4
Tree (site of) W2 .... 247 C6
ce Collection W1 .... 238 A2
gton Arch SW1 .... 248 B2
gton Mus
ey House) SW1 .....115 A4 248 B2
inster Abbey SW1 ..116 A3 260 A6
inster
edral SW1 ....115 C3 259 A5

of England EC2............ 242 C1
an Arts and
erence Centre EC2 ... 95 A2 242 B4
al Criminal Court
Bailey) EC4.........94 D1 241 D2
n House EC3 ....117 C6 253 A5
Dr Johnson's House EC4 .... 241 B1
Gray's Inn WC1 .... 94 B2 240 D4
Guildhall EC2 .... 95 A1 242 B2
Inner Temple EC4 .... 251 A6
John Wesley's House &
Mus EC1 .... 242 D6
Lincoln's Inn WC2 .... 94 B1 240 D2
Lloyd's Building EC3 .... 95 C1 243 A1
Mansion House EC4 .... 242 C1
Merchant Taylors Hall EC2R 242 D1
Middle Temple EC4 ....116 C6 251 A6
Monument, The EC3 .... 252 D6
Mus of London EC2........ 95 A2 242 A3
Nat West Tower EC2 .... 243 A2
National Postal
Mus EC1 .... 95 A1 242 A2
Petticoat Lane Market EC2 95 D2 243 C3
Public Record Office
Mus EC4,WC2 .... 241 A2
Royal Exchange EC3 .... 242 D1
St Katharine Dock E1 ....117 D5 253 D4
St Mary le Bow Church EC2 ...... 242 B1
St Paul's Cathedral EC4 .... 95 A1 242 A1
Sir John Soane's
Mus WC2 .... 94 B1 240 C2
Spitalfields Market E1 ..... 95 D2 243 C4
Stock Exchange EC2 .... 241 D1
Tower Bridge E1,EC3,SE1 ...117 D5 253 C4
Tower of London EC3 .....117 D6 253 C5
Traitors Gate EC3 ....117 D5 253 C4
Ye Olde Cheshire Cheese EC4 .... 241 B2

Northern

Business Design Centre N1 94 C6 234 B5
Camden Market NW1 ...... 93 B6 231 D6
London Canal Mus N1 ..... 94 A5 233 B4
London Central
Mosque NW8............. 92 C4 230 B1
London Zoo NW1 .... 93 A5 231 A4
Lord's Cricket Ground NW8 92 B4 229 D2
Madame Tussaud's NW1 ... 93 A3 238 A5
Open Air Theatre, Regent's
Park NW1 .... 231 A1
Planetarium NW1 .... 93 A3 238 A5
Primrose Hill NW1.......... 92 D6 230 C6
Queen Mary's Gardens NW1 ..... 231 A1
Regent's Park NW1 .... 93 A4 231 A3
St George's Cathedral NW1 ...... 231 D2
Sherlock Holmes
Mus NW1 .... 92 D3 237 D5

Southern

Battersea Park SW11 .....137 A5 268 A3
Battersea Power
Station SW8 ....137 B6 268 D6
Brompton Oratory SW7 ...114 C3 257 A5
Bear Gardens
Mus SE1 ....117 A5 252 A4
Bermondsey Market SE1 ..117 C3 263 B8
Borough Market SE1 .... 252 C3
Design Mus SE1 ....117 D4 253 D2
Florence Nightingale
Mus SE1 .... 250 D1
Gabriel's Wharf SE1 .... 251 A4
George Inn SE1 .... 252 C3
Globe Theatre SE1 .... 252 A5
Hayward Gallery SE1 .....116 B5 250 D4
HMS Belfast SE1 .... 253 B4
Imperial War
Mus SE1 ....116 C3 261 B5
Lambeth Palace SE1 .....116 B3 260 C5
London Aquarium SE1 .... 250 C1
London Dungeon SE1 ....117 B5 252 D4
London Eye SE1 ....116 B4 250 C2
London Peace Pagoda SW11 .... 267 D4
Millennium Bridge SE1,EC4 ...... 252 A5
Mus of Garden History SE1 ...... 260 C5
National Film Theatre SE1 .... 250 D4
National Theatre SE1 .....116 B5 250 D4
Old County Hall SE1 .... 250 C2
Operating Theatre Mus and Herb
Garret SE1 ....117 B5 252 D3
Oxo Tower SE1 .... 251 B5
Royal Festival Hall SE1 ...116 B5 250 D3
Saatchi Gallery SE1 .... 250 C2
St George's RC
Cathedral SE1 ....116 C3 261 B6
Shakespeare's Globe Theatre
(site of) SE1 .... 252 B4
Southwark Cathedral SE1 117 B5 252 C4
Tate Modern SE1 ....116 D6 251 D4
Vinopolis SE1 ....117 B5 252 C4

Western

Albert Memorial SW7 ....114 B4 246 C1
Carlyle's House SW3............ 267 A5
Chelsea Barracks SW1 ...115 A1 258 B1
Chelsea Physic
Garden SW3 ....115 A1 267 C6
Commonwealth
Institute W8 ....113 C3 255 A6
Geological Mus SW7 .....114 B3 256 D5
Kensington Gardens W2 ..114 A5 246 B3
Kensington Palace W8 ...113 D5 245 D3
Leighton House W14 .... 254 D6
Lindsey House SW10 .... 266 D4
Little Venice W9 .... 92 A2 236 A4
National Army
Mus SW3 ....136 D6 267 D6
Natural History
Mus SW7 ....114 B3 256 C5
Ranelagh Gardens SW1 ..115 A1 258 B1
Royal Albert Hall SW7 ....114 B4 246 C1
Royal Hospital (Army
Pensioners) SW1 ....115 A1 258 A1
Science Mus SW7 ....114 B3 256 C5
Victoria and Albert
Mus SW7 ....114 B3 256 D5

East

Canary Wharf E14 ....119 D5
Docklands Mus E14 .... 119 D6
Epping Forest IG10 ....21 B6
Geffrye Mus E2 ....95 D5
London Docklands Visitor
Centre E14 ....120 A4
London Gas Mus E16 ....98 B3
Mus of Childhood (V&A) E2 ......96 C4
Museum of the Great Eastern
Railway E16 ....122 C4
Queen Elizabeth's Hunting
Lodge Mus E4 ....20 D4
Ragged School Mus E3 ....97 A2
Vestry House (Mus) E17 ....53 D5
Whitechapel Art Gallery E1 ....95 D1

North

Alexandra Palace N22 ....31 D1
Barnet Mus EN5 ....1 A1
Battle of Britain Mus NW9 ....27 D1
Bruce Castle Mus N17 ....33 C2
Church Farm House Mus NW4 ....46 B6
Coppetts Centre N12...............30 D3
Forty Hall EN2 ....5 D6
Freud Mus NW3 ....70 A2
Grange Mus of Community History
NW10 ....67 D4
Hampstead Heath NW3 ....70 B6
Harrow Mus and Heritage Centre
HA2 ....42 A6
Highgate Cemetery N19............71 B6
Kensal Green Cemetery
(All Souls) NW10 ....90 C4
Kenwood House NW3 ....48 C1
Old Court (Mus and Library) HA0 ..65 C3
RAF Mus NW9 ....28 A1
Ruislip Lido HA4,HA5 ....39 B5
Ruislip Lido Railway HA4 ....39 B5
White Cube N1 ....95 C4

South east

Blackheath SE3 ....142 C4
Brockwell Park SE24 ....160 D5
Cutty Sark SE10 ....142 A6
Docklands Heritage Mus SE16 ....119 B5
Dulwich Picture Gallery SE21 ....161 C4
Eltham Palace SE9 ....166 A4
Flamsteed House SE10 ....142 B5
Gipsy Moth IV SE10 ....142 A6
Greenwich Park SE10 ....142 C5
Horniman Mus and Gardens SE23 162 B3
Livesey Mus SE15 ....140 B6
Meridian Building SE10 ....142 B5
Millennium Dome SE10 ....120 C5
National Maritime Mus SE10 .....142 B6
Old Royal Observatory
Greenwich SE10 ....142 B5
Queen's House SE10 ....142 B6
Rotunda Mus SE18 ....122 B1
Scadbury Park Nature
Reserve BR7 ....189 D4
South Norwood Country
Park SE25 ....206 C5
Thames Barrier Visitor
Centre SE18 ....121 D3
Well Hall Pleasaunce SE9 ....144 A1

South west

Barnes Common SW13 ....134 A2
Clapham Common SW4 ....137 C1
Fulham Palace SW6 ....135 A3
Hampton Court Palace KT8 ......196 D6
Kingston Mus KT1 ....176 A1
Wandsworth Mus SW15 ....135 A1
Wetland Centre SW13 ....134 B5
Wimbledon Common SW19 ......178 B6
Wimbledon Lawn Tennis
Mus SW19 ....157 A1
Wimbledon Windmill Mus SW19 ..156 C1

West

Chiswick House W4 ....133 B6
Eel Pie Island TW1 ....153 A3
Gunnersbury Park Mus W3 ......110 C3
Ham House TW10 ....153 C2
Kew Bridge Steam Mus TW8 .....110 B1
Kew Gardens
(Royal Botanic Gardens) TW9 ...132 A4
Kew Observatory TW9 ....131 C2
Kew Palace TW9 ....132 A5
London Butterfly House TW8 .....131 B4
Marble Hill TW1 ....153 C4
Mus of Richmond TW10 ....153 D6
Musical Mus TW8 ....132 A6
Osterley Park TW7 ....108 B1
Pitshanger Manor Mus and
Art Gallery W5 ....109 D5
Portobello Road Market W10 .....91 A2
Richmond Park TW10 ....155 A3
Syon House TW8 ....131 C4
Walled Garden TW16 ....194 B6

Screen on Baker St
PADDINGTON STREET
BAKER STREET
MARYLEBONE
MARYLEBONE HIGH STREET
WEYMOUTH STREET
PORTLAND PLACE
GREAT PORTLAND STREET
HOWLAND ST
FITZROV
NEW CAVENDISH STREET
LANGHAM PLACE
MORTIMER STREET
PLACE
GEORGE ST
THAYER ST
Wigmore Hall
CAVENDISH SQUARE
CAVENDISH PLACE
REGENT ST
MANDEVILLE PL
PORTMAN SQUARE
WIGMORE STREET
JAMES ST
ORCHARD ST
PORTMAN ST
OUR ST
Niketown
Top Shop
HMV
OXFORD STREET
John Lewis
BHS
H&M
House of Fraser
Debenhams
Borders
Marks Spen
Laura Ashley
Oxford Circus
Palladium
Marks and Spencer
Selfridges
Bond Street
HMV
West One Shopping Centre
DAVIES STREET
NEW BOND STREET
REGENT STREET
Dickins & Jones
Liberty
Mothercare
Fenwick
Jaeger
Sotheby's
Hamleys
CONDUIT STREET
KNIGHTSBRIDGE
Curzon Minema
Burberry
Next
Knightsbridge
Harvey Nichols
BRUTON ST
Aquascu
BROMPTON ROAD
SLOANE STREET
MAYFAIR
BERKELEY SQUARE
Asprey and Garrard
Austin Reed
Cartier
Harrods
Gucci
Burlington Arcade
Waterstone
FITZMAURICE PL
BERKELEY ST
PICCADILLY
Hatchards
Chanel
Fortnum and Mason
ST. JAMES'S STREET
CHAMP PL
PONT STREET
CURZON STREET
Christi
Green Park
Curzon Mayfair
BROMPTON
GREEN PARK
Prada
CLIVEDEN PL
SLOANE SQUARE
Royal Court
Peter Jones
Sloane Square
WH Smith
KING'S ROAD
SLOANE ST
LOWER
CONSTITUTION HILL

Cinemas, theatres shopping streets

Empire	Cinema
Aldwych	Theatre
Purcell Room	Concert hall
Fortnum & Mason	Shop
	Shopping street
	– up-market
	– high street
	– books
	– electronics
	– furniture

Habitat
Heals
Drill Hall
The Pier
Goodge Street
GOODGE ST
TOTTENHAM COURT ROAD
STREET
MONTAGUE PL
SQUARE
SOUTHAMPTON ROW
BAYLEY ST
BEDFORD SQUARE
BLOOMSBURY ST
To Cochrane Theatre
BLOOMSBURY WAY
Odeon Tottenham Ct. Rd.
HOLBORN
Dominion
NEW OXFORD ST
Virgin
Forbidden Planet
Shaftesbury
The Plaza
STREET
Tottenham Court Road
Astoria
A. BORDE ST
ST. GILES HIGH ST
HIGH
New London
Books Etc
DRURY LANE
GT. QUEEN
KINGSWAY
WARDOUR STREET
Foyles
Curzon Phoenix
Odeon Covent Garden
ENDELL STREET
Peacock
Soho
Phoenix
Donmar Warehouse
CHARING CROSS ROAD
Blackwell's
UPPER ST. MONMOUTH ST
SOHO
Prince Edward
AVE
Cambridge
BOW ST
Fortune
Aldwych
ALDWYCH
New Ambassadors
Palace
ACRE
LONG
SHAFTESBURY
Curzon Soho
St Martin's
Covent Garden
Royal Opera House
Theatre Royal Drury Lane
Novello
STRAND
Arts Theatre
MARTIN'S LANE
Duchess
Queen's
Gielgud
Apollo
Warner Village West End
Leicester Square
Stanford's
Lyceum
STRAND
Lyric
The OTHER Cinema
Prince Charles
Noel Coward
Piccadilly
UGC Trocadero
UCI Empire
The Venue
Wyndham's
LANCASTER PL
Piccadilly Circus
Imax
Odeon Wardour St.
Odeon Leicester Square & Mezzanine
Vaudeville
Trocadero
Criterion
Duke of York's
Adelphi
Savoy
Prince of Wales
Coliseum
STRAND
Lillywhites
Odeon West End
ST. MARTIN'S LANE
Garrick
VICTORIA — EMBANKMENT
Odeon Haymarket
Odeon Panton St
ST. JAMES
WATERLOO BRIDGE
REGENT STREET
HAYMARKET
Comedy
Jermyn St
Mitsukoshi
Theatre Royal Haymarket
DUNCANNON ST
UGC Haymarket
Charing Cross
Her Majesty's
TRAFALGAR SQUARE
Charing Cross
New Players
Embankment
PALL MALL EAST
ST. JAMES
COCKSPUR ST
Playhouse
Queen Elizabeth Hall and Purcell Room
NORTHUMBERLAND AVENUE
Whitehall
MALL
Royal Festival Hall
ICA
Queen Elizabeth Hall and Purcell Room
National Film Theatre
Royal National Theatre
THE MALL
Royal Festival Hall
STAMFORD STREET
BFI London Imax
WATERLOO
SOUTH BANK
Waterloo East
St. James's Park Lake
JUBILEE GDNS
Waterloo
Young Vic
Waterloo International
Waterloo
WATERLOO
ROAD
THE CUT
ST JAMES'S PARK
YORK
Old Vic

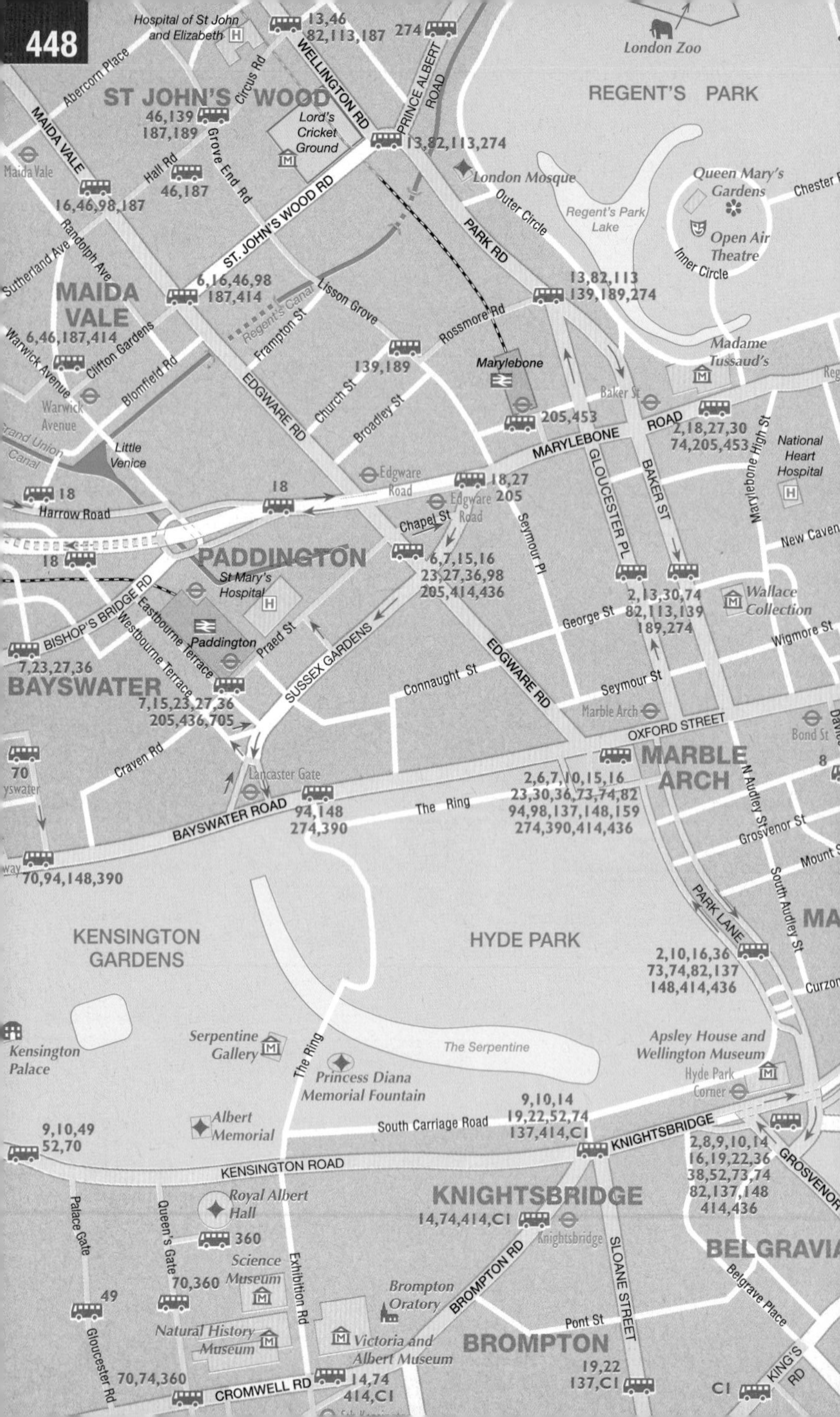
Hospital of St John and Elizabeth
13,46
82,113,187
274
London Zoo
REGENT'S PARK
Abercorn Place
Circus Rd
WELLINGTON RD
PRINCE ALBERT ROAD
ST JOHN'S WOOD
46,139
187,189
Lord's Cricket Ground
13,82,113,274
MAIDA VALE
Maida Vale
Hall Rd
Grove End Rd
46,187
London Mosque
Queen Mary's Gardens
Chester Rd
16,46,98,187
ST. JOHN'S WOOD RD
Outer Circle
Regent's Park Lake
Open Air Theatre
Randolph Ave
Sutherland Ave
PARK RD
Inner Circle
MAIDA VALE
6,16,46,98
187,414
Lisson Grove
13,82,113
139,189,274
Regent's Canal
Frampton St
Rossmore Rd
6,46,187,414
Clifton Gardens
Warwick Avenue
139,189
Madame Tussaud's
Blomfield Rd
Marylebone
Baker St
Warwick Avenue
Church St
Broadley St
205,453
ROAD
2,18,27,30
74,205,453
EDGWARE RD
MARYLEBONE
Grand Union Canal
Little Venice
GLOUCESTER PL
BAKER ST
Marylebone High St
National Heart Hospital
Edgware Road
18,27
205
18
18
Harrow Road
Edgware Road
Seymour Pl
Chapel St
New Cavendish
PADDINGTON
18
6,7,15,16
23,27,36,98
205,414,436
St Mary's Hospital
BISHOP'S BRIDGE RD
Eastbourne Terrace
Westbourne Terrace
Paddington
Praed St
George St
2,13,30,74
82,113,139
189,274
Wallace Collection
7,23,27,36
SUSSEX GARDENS
EDGWARE RD
Wigmore St
BAYSWATER
Connaught St
Seymour St
7,15,23,27,36
205,436,705
Marble Arch
OXFORD STREET
Bond St
Craven Rd
MARBLE ARCH
70
Lancaster Gate
2,6,7,10,15,16
23,30,36,73,74,82
94,98,137,148,159
274,390,414,436
N Audley St
8
BAYSWATER ROAD
94,148
274,390
The Ring
Grosvenor St
70,94,148,390
Mount St
PARK LANE
South Audley St
KENSINGTON GARDENS
HYDE PARK
2,10,16,36
73,74,82,137
148,414,436
Curzon St
Apsley House and Wellington Museum
Serpentine Gallery
The Serpentine
Kensington Palace
The Ring
Princess Diana Memorial Fountain
Hyde Park Corner
9,10,14
19,22,52,74
137,414,C1
Albert Memorial
South Carriage Road
9,10,49
52,70
KNIGHTSBRIDGE
2,8,9,10,14
16,19,22,36
38,52,73,74
82,137,148
414,436
GROSVENOR
KENSINGTON ROAD
KNIGHTSBRIDGE
Royal Albert Hall
14,74,414,C1
Knightsbridge
Palace Gate
Queen's Gate
360
BELGRAVIA
Science Museum
Exhibition Rd
70,360
Brompton Oratory
BROMPTON RD
SLOANE STREET
Belgrave Place
49
Pont St
Natural History Museum
Victoria and Albert Museum
BROMPTON
Gloucester Rd
70,74,360
19,22
137,C1
C1
KING'S RD
CROMWELL RD
14,74
414,C1

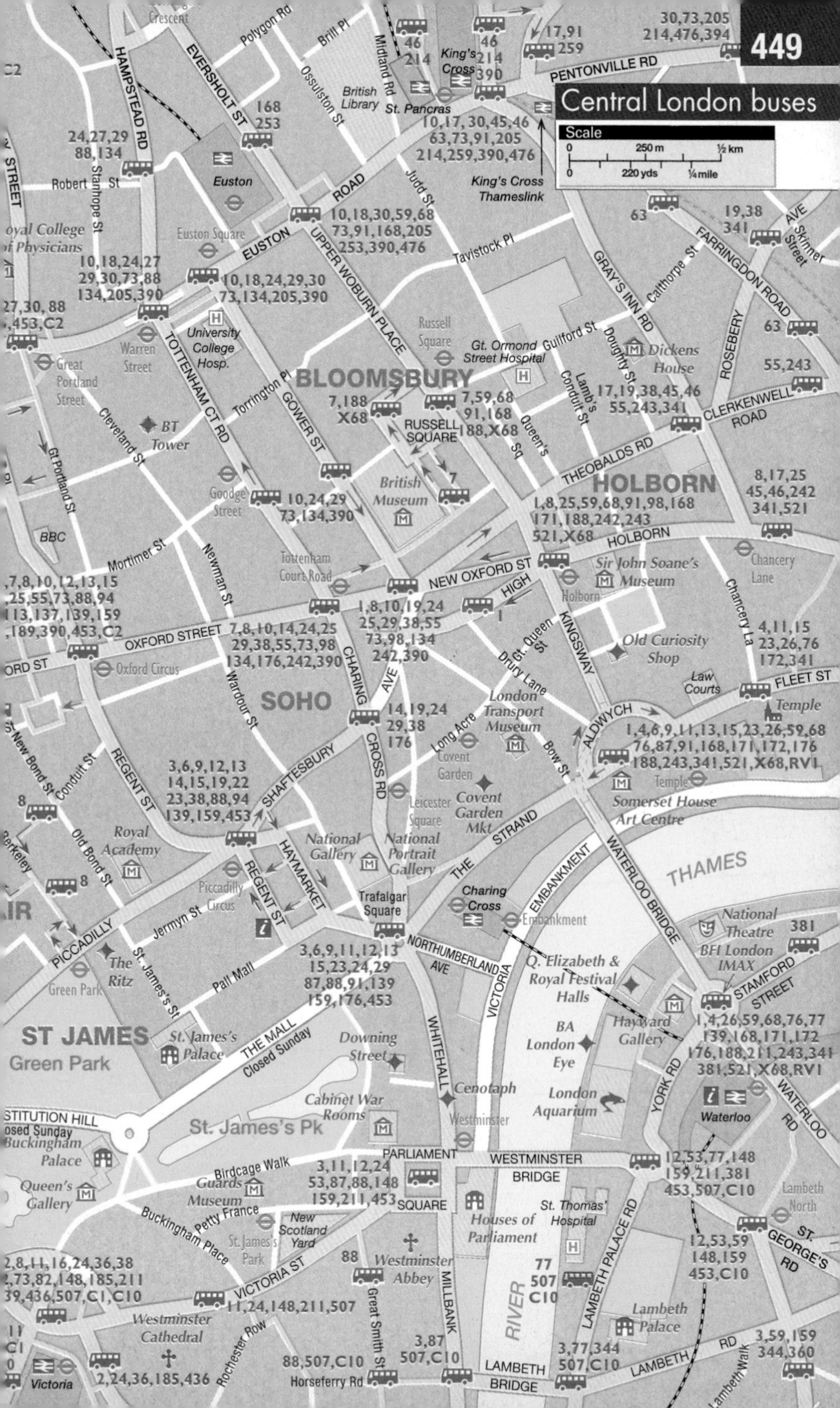
Central London buses
Scale
0
250 m
½ km
0
220 yds
¼ mile
Crescent
Polygon Rd
Brill Pl
Midland Rd
46
214
King's Cross
46
214
390
17,91
259
30,73,205
214,476,394
PENTONVILLE RD
HAMPSTEAD RD
EVERSHOLT ST
Ossulston St
British Library
St. Pancras
168
253
10,17,30,45,46
63,73,91,205
214,259,390,476
King's Cross Thameslink
24,27,29
88,134
Stanhope St
Robert St
STREET
Euston
Judd St
ROAD
10,18,30,59,68
73,91,168,205
253,390,476
63
19,38
341
AVE
Skinner Street
FARRINGDON ROAD
Royal College of Physicians
Euston Square
EUSTON
UPPER WOBURN PLACE
Tavistock Pl
GRAY'S INN RD
Calthorpe St
10,18,24,27
29,30,73,88
134,205,390
10,18,24,29,30
73,134,205,390
27,30,88
453,C2
University College Hosp.
Warren Street
TOTTENHAM CT RD
Russell Square
Gt. Ormond Street Hospital
Guilford St
Doughty St
Dickens House
ROSEBERY
63
Great Portland Street
55,243
BLOOMSBURY
Lamb's Conduit St
17,19,38,45,46
55,243,341
CLERKENWELL ROAD
Torrington Pl
GOWER ST
7,188
X68
7,59,68
91,168
188,X68
RUSSELL SQUARE
Queen's Sq
Cleveland St
BT Tower
Gt Portland St
THEOBALDS RD
HOLBORN
8,17,25
45,46,242
341,521
7
British Museum
Goodge Street
10,24,29
73,134,390
1,8,25,59,68,91,98,168
171,188,242,243
521,X68
HOLBORN
BBC
Mortimer St
Newman St
Tottenham Court Road
NEW OXFORD ST
Sir John Soane's Museum
Chancery Lane
Holborn
HIGH
7,8,10,12,13,15
25,55,73,88,94
113,137,139,159
189,390,453,C2
1,8,10,19,24
25,29,38,55
73,98,134
242,390
1
KINGSWAY
Chancery La
4,11,15
23,26,76
172,341
OXFORD STREET
7,8,10,14,24,25
29,38,55,73,98
134,176,242,390
Gt. Queen St
Old Curiosity Shop
ORD ST
Oxford Circus
CHARING
AVE
Drury Lane
Law Courts
FLEET ST
Wardour St
SOHO
London Transport Museum
Temple
14,19,24
29,38
176
ALDWYCH
1,4,6,9,11,13,15,23,26,59,68
76,87,91,168,171,172,176
188,243,341,521,X68,RV1
New Bond St
Conduit St
REGENT ST
SHAFTESBURY
CROSS RD
Long Acre
Covent Garden
Bow St
3,6,9,12,13
14,15,19,22
23,38,88,94
139,159,453
Temple
8
Covent Garden Mkt
Somerset House Art Centre
Leicester Square
Old Bond St
Royal Academy
National Gallery
National Portrait Gallery
THE STRAND
THAMES
Berkeley
HAYMARKET
WATERLOO BRIDGE
8
Piccadilly Circus
REGENT ST
EMBANKMENT
Charing Cross
IR
Jermyn St
Trafalgar Square
Embankment
National Theatre
381
PICCADILLY
The Ritz
St. James's St
NORTHUMBERLAND AVE
VICTORIA
Q. Elizabeth & Royal Festival Halls
BFI London IMAX
Green Park
Pall Mall
3,6,9,11,12,13
15,23,24,29
87,88,91,139
159,176,453
STAMFORD STREET
1,4,26,59,68,76,77
139,168,171,172
176,188,211,243,341
381,521,X68,RV1
ST JAMES
Green Park
St. James's Palace
THE MALL
Closed Sunday
Downing Street
WHITEHALL
BA London Eye
Hayward Gallery
YORK RD
Cenotaph
London Aquarium
Waterloo
WATERLOO RD
Cabinet War Rooms
STITUTION HILL
Closed Sunday
St. James's Pk
Westminster
Buckingham Palace
PARLIAMENT
WESTMINSTER BRIDGE
12,53,77,148
159,211,381
453,507,C10
Birdcage Walk
3,11,12,24
53,87,88,148
159,211,453
SQUARE
Lambeth North
Queen's Gallery
Guards Museum
Petty France
New Scotland Yard
Houses of Parliament
St. Thomas' Hospital
LAMBETH PALACE RD
ST. GEORGE'S RD
Buckingham Place
St. James's Park
Westminster Abbey
88
12,53,59
148,159
453,C10
2,8,11,16,24,36,38
73,82,148,185,211
39,436,507,C1,C10
VICTORIA ST
77
507
C10
11,24,148,211,507
Great Smith St
RIVER
Westminster Cathedral
Rochester Row
MILLBANK
Lambeth Palace
11
C1
10
3,87
507,C10
3,77,344
507,C10
3,59,159
344,360
Victoria
2,24,36,185,436
88,507,C10
Horseferry Rd
LAMBETH BRIDGE
LAMBETH RD
Lambeth Walk

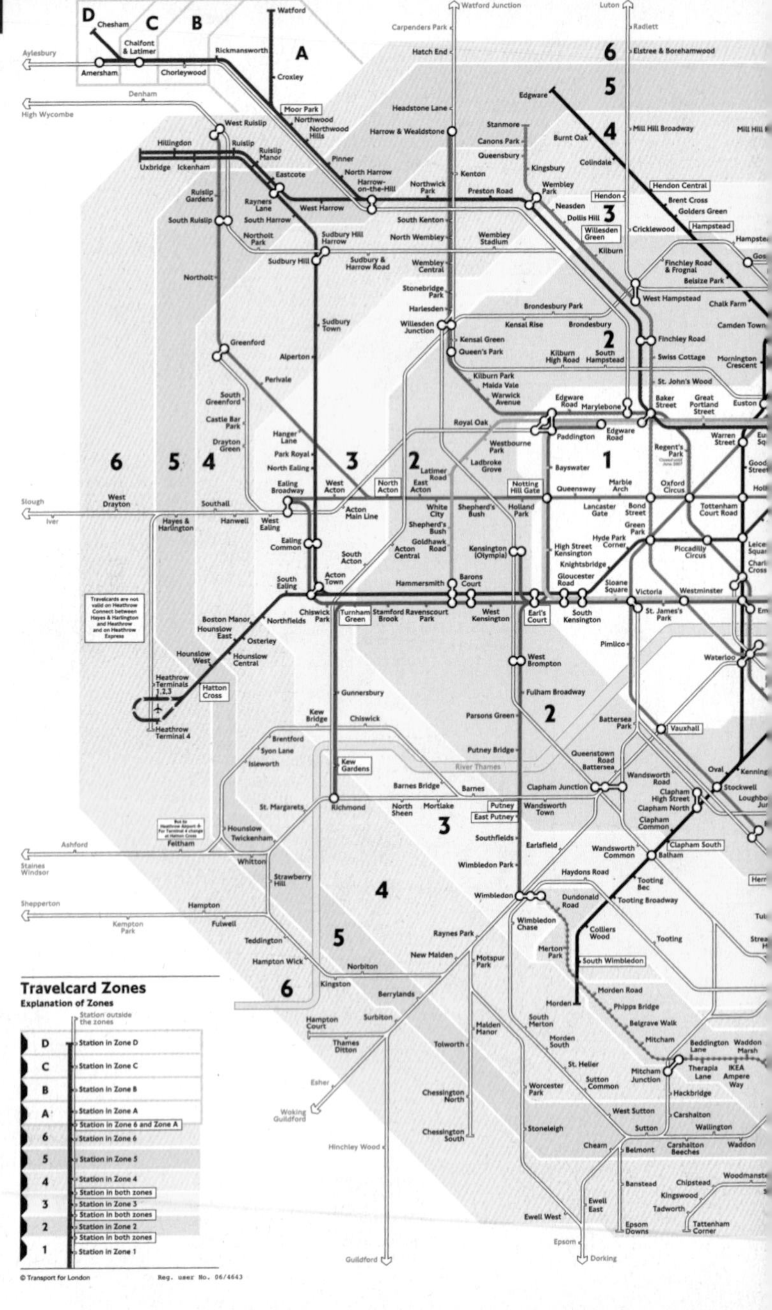

D
C
B
A
Chesham
Chalfont & Latimer
Amersham
Chorleywood
Rickmansworth
Watford
Croxley
Aylesbury
Denham
High Wycombe
Moor Park
Northwood
Northwood Hills
Pinner
North Harrow
Harrow-on-the-Hill
West Ruislip
Ruislip
Ruislip Manor
Hillingdon
Uxbridge
Ickenham
Eastcote
Ruislip Gardens
Rayners Lane
West Harrow
South Ruislip
South Harrow
Northolt Park
Sudbury Hill Harrow
Sudbury Hill
Sudbury & Harrow Road
Northolt
Greenford
Perivale
Alperton
Sudbury Town
South Greenford
Castle Bar Park
Drayton Green
Hanger Lane
Park Royal
North Ealing
Ealing Broadway
West Acton
North Acton
East Acton
Acton Main Line
West Ealing
Hanwell
Southall
West Drayton
Hayes & Harlington
Slough
Iver
Ealing Common
South Ealing
Acton Town
South Acton
Chiswick Park
Turnham Green
Stamford Brook
Ravenscourt Park
Northfields
Boston Manor
Hounslow East
Osterley
Hounslow West
Hounslow Central
Heathrow Terminals 1,2,3
Hatton Cross
Heathrow Terminal 4
Travelcards are not valid on Heathrow Connect between Hayes & Harlington and Heathrow and on Heathrow Express
Watford Junction
Carpenders Park
Hatch End
Headstone Lane
Harrow & Wealdstone
Kenton
Northwick Park
Preston Road
Wembley Park
South Kenton
North Wembley
Wembley Central
Wembley Stadium
Stonebridge Park
Harlesden
Willesden Junction
Kensal Green
Queen's Park
Kilburn Park
Maida Vale
Warwick Avenue
Royal Oak
Westbourne Park
Ladbroke Grove
Latimer Road
White City
Shepherd's Bush
Holland Park
Notting Hill Gate
Shepherd's Bush
Goldhawk Road
Acton Central
Kensington (Olympia)
Hammersmith
Barons Court
West Kensington
Earl's Court
Luton
Radlett
Elstree & Borehamwood
Edgware
Mill Hill Broadway
Mill Hill
Burnt Oak
Stanmore
Canons Park
Queensbury
Kingsbury
Colindale
Hendon Central
Hendon
Brent Cross
Golders Green
Neasden
Dollis Hill
Willesden Green
Cricklewood
Hampstead
Kilburn
Finchley Road & Frognal
Belsize Park
West Hampstead
Chalk Farm
Brondesbury Park
Kensal Rise
Brondesbury
Finchley Road
Camden Town
Swiss Cottage
Kilburn High Road
South Hampstead
Mornington Crescent
St. John's Wood
Edgware Road
Marylebone
Baker Street
Great Portland Street
Euston
Paddington
Edgware Road
Warren Street
Regent's Park
Bayswater
Queensway
Marble Arch
Oxford Circus
Tottenham Court Road
Lancaster Gate
Bond Street
Green Park
Hyde Park Corner
High Street Kensington
Knightsbridge
Piccadilly Circus
Gloucester Road
Sloane Square
Victoria
Westminster
South Kensington
St. James's Park
Pimlico
Waterloo
West Brompton
Fulham Broadway
Parsons Green
Putney Bridge
Battersea Park
Vauxhall
Queenstown Road Battersea
River Thames
Gunnersbury
Kew Bridge
Chiswick
Brentford
Syon Lane
Isleworth
Kew Gardens
Barnes Bridge
Barnes
Clapham Junction
Wandsworth Road
Clapham High Street
Clapham North
Clapham Common
Oval
Stockwell
St. Margarets
Richmond
North Sheen
Mortlake
Putney
East Putney
Wandsworth Town
Southfields
Earlsfield
Wandsworth Common
Clapham South
Balham
Wimbledon Park
Haydons Road
Tooting Bec
Tooting Broadway
Wimbledon
Dundonald Road
Wimbledon Chase
Colliers Wood
Tooting
Merton Park
South Wimbledon
Raynes Park
New Malden
Motspur Park
Morden
Morden Road
Phipps Bridge
Belgrave Walk
Mitcham
Mitcham Junction
Beddington Lane
Therapia Lane
Waddon Marsh
IKEA Ampere Way
Hackbridge
Carshalton
Wallington
West Sutton
Sutton
Sutton Common
St. Helier
Morden South
South Merton
Worcester Park
Malden Manor
Tolworth
Chessington North
Chessington South
Stoneleigh
Cheam
Belmont
Carshalton Beeches
Waddon
Banstead
Chipstead
Kingswood
Tadworth
Tattenham Corner
Epsom Downs
Ewell East
Ewell West
Epsom
Dorking
Guildford
Hinchley Wood
Esher
Woking Guildford
Hampton Court
Thames Ditton
Surbiton
Berrylands
Kingston
Norbiton
Hampton Wick
Teddington
Fulwell
Hampton
Kempton Park
Shepperton
Strawberry Hill
Whitton
Twickenham
Hounslow
Feltham
Ashford
Staines Windsor
Bus to Heathrow Airport & For Terminal 4 change at Hatton Cross
1
2
3
4
5
6
Travelcard Zones
Explanation of Zones
Station outside the zones
Station in Zone D
Station in Zone C
Station in Zone B
Station in Zone A
Station in Zone 6 and Zone A
Station in Zone 6
Station in Zone 5
Station in Zone 4
Station in both zones
Station in Zone 3
Station in both zones
Station in Zone 2
Station in both zones
Station in Zone 1
© Transport for London
Reg. user No. 06/4643

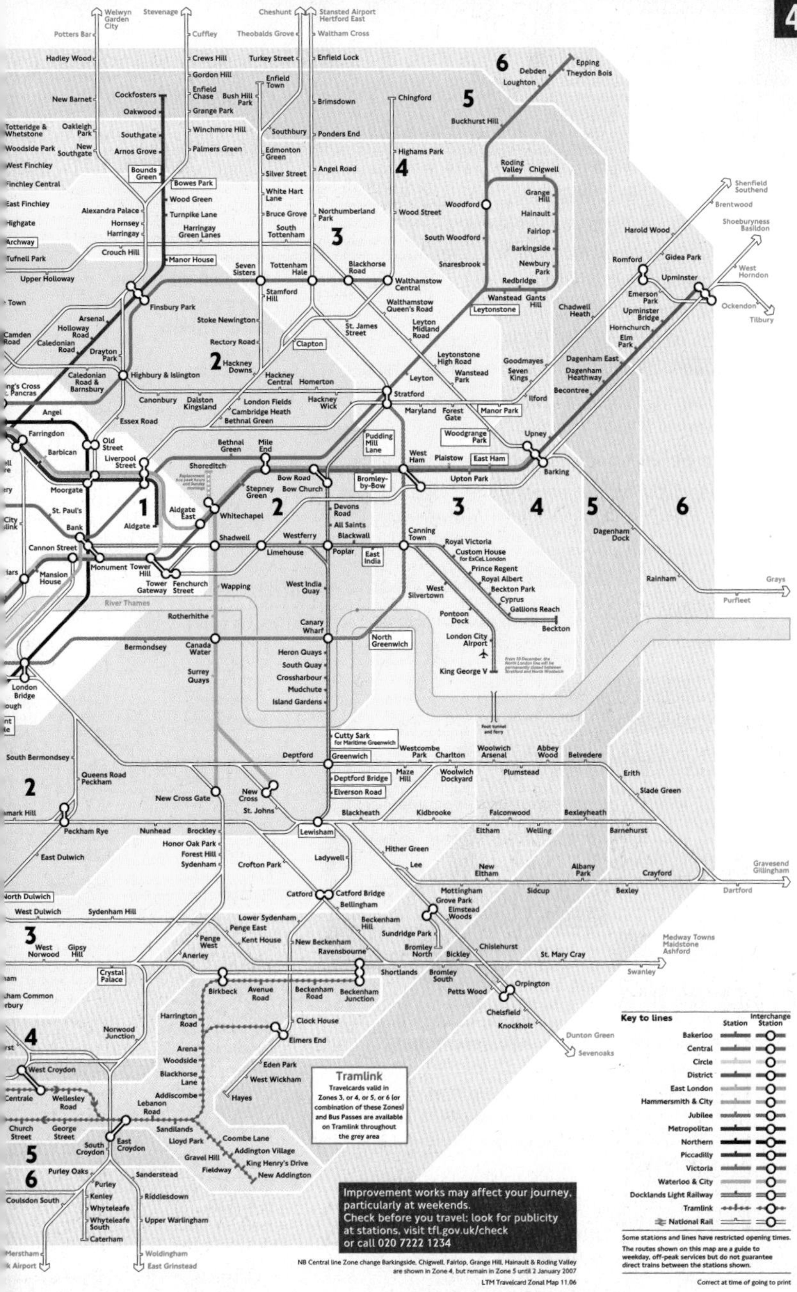

Tramlink

Travelcards valid in Zones 3, or 4, or 5, or 6 (or combination of these Zones) and Bus Passes are available on Tramlink throughout the grey area

Improvement works may affect your journey, particularly at weekends.
Check before you travel; look for publicity at stations, visit tfl.gov.uk/check or call 020 7222 1234

NB Central line Zone change Barkingside, Chigwell, Fairlop, Grange Hill, Hainault & Roding Valley are shown in Zone 4, but remain in Zone 5 until 2 January 2007

LTM Travelcard Zonal Map 11.06

Key to lines (Station / Interchange Station)

- Bakerloo
- Central
- Circle
- District
- East London
- Hammersmith & City
- Jubilee
- Metropolitan
- Northern
- Piccadilly
- Victoria
- Waterloo & City
- Docklands Light Railway
- Tramlink
- National Rail

Some stations and lines have restricted opening times.

The routes shown on this map are a guide to weekday, off-peak services but do not guarantee direct trains between the stations shown.

Correct at time of going to print

Website tfl.gov.uk

Transport for London

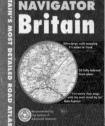